THE GUINNESS BOOK OF
ANSWERS

GUINNESS PUBLISHING

Senior Editor: Clive Carpenter
Editor: Tina Persaud
Systems support: Kathy Milligan
Design: David L. Roberts
Layout: Amanda Sedge
Cover design: Jon Lucas
Index: Marijka Skipp
Production Manager: Chris Lingard
Information Systems Manager: Alex Reid
Artwork, maps and diagrams: Ad Vantage Studios, Eddie
Botchway, Rhoda and Robert Burns, Pat Gibbon,
Peter Harper, The Maltings Partnership

9th Edition
First published 1993
Reprint 10 9 8 7 6 5 4 3 2 1 0

Published in Great Britain by Guinness Publishing Ltd,
33 London Road, Enfield, Middlesex

Printed and bound in Great Britain by the Bath Press, Bath

British Library Cataloguing in Publication Data
The Guinness Book of Answers
1. Miscellaneous facts
1. The Book of Answers
032.02

ISBN 0–85112–710–X

CONTRIBUTORS

Ronald Alley, formerly of the Tate Gallery, London
John Arblaster
Matthew Bennett, The Royal Military Academy Sandhurst
Ephraim Borowski, University of Glasgow
Antonia Boström,
Martin Caiger-Smith, The Photographer's Gallery, London
Clive Carpenter
Gill Carpenter
Kim Chesher
Dr Dominique Collon, The British Museum
Ian Crofton
John Cunningham
Robert Dearling
Beryl Dixon
Professor Ronald Draper, University of Aberdeen
Ben Dupré
Di Ellis, S.E.E.C
Geoff Endacott
Dr David Evans, University of Exeter
Dr Mark Evans, National Museum of Wales
Peta Evelyn, The Victoria and Albert Museum
Dr Trevor Ford, formerly of the University of Leicester
Dr Peter Forey, Natural History Museum
Dr D.P. Fowler, Jesus College, Oxford
Beatrice Frei
Tim Furniss
Dr Nigel Gauk-Roger
Professor Brian Gardiner, King's College, London
Professor Frank Glockling, University of Oxford
Dr Martin Godfrey, *GP* Magazine
Dr Janet Goodwyn, The Roehampton Institute, London
The late Dr Beverly Halstead
Dr Graham Handley, University of London
Richard Harding
Rosemary Harris, The Tate Gallery, London
Nigel Hawkes, of *The Times*
Dr Peter Hobson, Brunel the University of West London
Graham Holderness, The Roehampton Institute
Ingrid Holford
Robert Jameson
Ann Jones, The Tate Gallery
Dr Gareth Jones, University of Strathclyde
Colin Juneman
Dr Kim Knott, University of Leeds
Jeremy Lane, University of Sussex

Howard Loxton
Norris McWhirter
Anne Marshall
John Marshall
Peter Matthews
Carol Michaelson
Richard Milbank
Dr D.M.P. Mingos, Keble College, Oxford
Trevor Mostyn, Editor of *The Cambridge Encyclopedia of the Middle East and North Africa*
David J. Nash, University of Sheffield
Stewart Newport
Dr Chris Pass, University of Bradford
Tina Persaud
Dr John Pimlott, The Royal Military Academy Sandhurst
Rev. Will Pratt
Martin Redfern
Dr Jonathon Ree, Middlesex University
Aileen Reid
Alex Reid
Peter Reynolds, The Roehampton Institute, London
James Roberts
Samantha Roberts
Patrick Hickman Robertson
Dr Gillian Sales, King's College, London University
Denise Schulte
Andrew Scott, University College London
Dr Ian Shaw
Ian Sinclair
Dr Elizabeth Sirreyeh, University of Leeds
Dr Peter J. Smith, The Open University
Dr John Sommerville, MRCP, MRCGP
Lesley Stevenson
Brian Stone, The Open University
Michael J.H. Taylor
Mona Taylor
Dr David Thomas, University of Sheffield
Professor Anthony K. Thorlby, University of Sussex
Dr Francis Toase, The Royal Military Academy Sandhurst
Dr Loreto Todd, University of Leeds
E.C. Tupper
Michael Vickers, The Ashmolean Museum, Oxford
Dr John Walton, University College of Wales, Aberystwyth
David Wells
Dr Shearer West
Dr John Westwood
Alan Williams, University of Westminster
Conrad Wilson, *The Scotsman*
Andrew Wood

CONTENTS

VISUAL ARTS 376–399

THE PERFORMING ARTS 400–435

HISTORY 436–481

ECONOMY AND SOCIETY 482–511

THE INTERNATIONAL WORLD 512–681

SPACE AND TIME

THE NATURE OF THE UNIVERSE

COSMOLOGY

The *universe* is the sum total of all that exists, or has existed, both in space and time. *Cosmology* is the science of the cosmos or universe. Theoretical cosmology became possible in the 20th century when Albert Einstein's special (1905) and general (1915) theories (see Physical Sciences, Quantum Theory and Relativity) combined space and time into an indivisible four dimensional space-time continuum. However, theoretical views as to how the universe began are based on 20th-century advances in observational astronomy and high energy physics.

THE EXPANSION OF THE UNIVERSE

In 1868, the English astronomer Sir William Huggins (1824–1910) noted that the spectra of some stars were displaced towards the red end of the spectrum (*red-shifted*), but others were shifted towards the violet end (blue-shifted). This was interpreted as a Doppler effect, the change in the frequency of sound waves, light and electromagnetic radiation when the source and the observer become closer or more distant. This was first described in 1842 by the Austrian physicist Christian Doppler to explain why the noise from a moving vehicle appears to change pitch as it passes. The French physicist Armand Fizeau extended the principle to light waves in 1848.

Stars that are moving away from us are red-shifted; stars that are approaching us are blue-shifted. Red shift on a cosmological scale was discovered in 1912 by the American astronomer Vesto Melvin Slipher (1875–1969), who noted that nearly all nebulae – clouds of dust or gas – were highly red-shifted and only a few, including the Andromeda nebula, were blue-shifted. In 1924, the American astronomer Edwin Powell Hubble (1889–1953) was able to show that these nebulae were, in fact, galaxies in their own right.

Extensive measurements of galactic red-shifts (*z*) and magnitudes – and estimates of distance – led Hubble in 1929 to propose that the speed of recession of a galaxy (*v*) was related to its distance (*r*) by the relationship $v = z.c = H.r$, where c is the velocity of light and H is a constant known as the *Hubble Constant*. This formula is flawed when the red-shift exceeds 1 since it implies that v exceeds c but this problem was solved by modifying the formula to take into account Einstein's Special Relativity Doppler Formula:

$$z = \left[\frac{c + v}{c - v} \right]^{\frac{1}{2}} - 1$$

Hubble's Law states that the distance to a distant galaxy is in direct proportion to its observed velocity of recession. This indicates a uniformly expanding universe and implies that the age of the universe is in inverse proportion to c – the constant of proportionality – in the formula above. Current determinations of Hubble's Constant vary between 50 and 90 km/s/Mpc (kilometres per second per megaparsec). The median value of 70 km/s/Mpc agrees with the current estimated age of the universe of 14 000 million years, which has been calculated by *cosmochronology* (a measure of the relative abundance of radioactive nuclei used to determine the time scale for the nucleosynthesis of these nuclei).

The median value also accords with estimates of the ages of the stars in the oldest globular clusters.

THE BIG BANG THEORY

The realization that the universe was expanding, and also appeared to have a definable age, led to the suggestion that it may have initially existed as a point-like source or *singularity*. The theory of the expansion of the universe from a cataclysmic event known as the '*big bang*' was originally developed by the Russian mathematician and astronomer Aleksandr Friedmann (1888–1925) and the Belgian astronomer Georges LeMaître (1894–1966). The so-called 'standard model' – based upon their work – could not explain either the present large-scale uniformity of the universe or the smaller scale non-uniformity (i.e. the 'clumping' of matter into galaxies).

These problems were largely overcome by the introduction of the 'inflationary model' by Alan Guth in 1979 and the subsequent suggestion that all parts of the universe were in contact with each other during the initial critical period, but, when it was between 10^{-35} and 10^{-32} seconds old, it underwent a 10^{50} expansion. Subsequent, virtually linear, expansion has occurred until the universe has reached its present size. However, the sudden formation of the universe, which may have resulted from a quantum fluctuation, may only be explicable with the development of a quantum theory for gravity.

It is thought that the initial period lasted from 10^{-45} to 10^{-43} seconds (the *Planck Era*) when the temperature was 10^{32} K and the radius 10^{-54} cm. At the end of this time, gravity assumed its unique characteristics. After 10^{-35} seconds – when the temperature had dropped to 10^{27} K and the universe had expanded to 10^{-49} cm – the strong force may have separated from the electroweak force and triggered a 10^{50} expansion to a diameter of 10 cm (4 in). However, during the initial expansion period – which lasted until 10^{-32} seconds – the universe supercooled to 10^{22} K, causing the nucleation of matter (quarks and leptons, and an equal number of anti-particles), before returning to 10^{27} K. Particles and anti-particles began to annihilate each other to form photons of radiation. At the end of this period, all of the anti-particles had been destroyed and only one particle of matter per 1000 million present at the beginning remained. (The predominance of matter over anti-matter remains to be explained.)

Protons and neutrons began to form from quarks between 10^9 and 0.1 seconds as the temperature fell from 10^{14} K to 10^{10} K, and in the next 1000 seconds surviving neutrons combined with protons to form nuclei of the light elements deuterium, helium and lithium. Beyond this time, free neutrons spontaneously decayed and free protons (hydrogen nuclei) became dominant in the universe. After 100 000 years, the temperature had fallen to 4000 K, and ions and electrons combined together to form atoms. Proto-galaxies began to form when the temperature had fallen to 400 K. The formation of coherent galaxies is calculated to have begun 1000 million years after the big bang.

The 3 K MICROWAVE BACKGROUND

If the big bang model of the universe is correct, the universe should be filled with a uniform 'sea' of cosmic background radiation that was produced in the very early stages of the creation of the universe and cooled by its expansion. This cosmic background radiation was predicted by George Gamow (1904–68) in 1948 and discovered in the microwave region by Arno Penzias (1933–) and Robert W. Wilson (1936–) in 1965. Relating data for microwave radiation to an energy curve suggests a temperature of 2.74 K (-270.41 °C or -454.74 °F), which is virtually the temperature that would be expected if the universe had cooled from the primordial fireball proposed in the big bang theory.

The microwave background radiation appears to be *isotropic*; that is, it has the same physical properties in all directions. However, in April 1992 the COBE satellite detected differences in temperature of the order of parts per million. These have been interpreted as detection of the infinitesimal density fluctuations that caused local gravity instability in the expanding fireball and led to the formation of the proto-galaxies.

THE FUTURE OF THE UNIVERSE

Cosmological models developed by Friedmann (see above), H.P. Robison and A.G. Walker between 1922 and 1936 suggested that the universe could only have one of three endings.

The first suggestion was that there is insufficient matter in the universe to overcome the expansion. The universe was said to be 'open' and will therefore expand until all the hydrogen has been used up, after which the universe will become 'dead'.

The second possibility envisaged a 'closed' universe in which the amount of matter was sufficient to overcome the expansion of the universe and would eventually cause the universe to collapse back into the singularity from which it came. In this thesis, the possible creation of another universe from the singularity was suggested.

The third suggestion was that the universe is 'flat' – that is, the universe has just enough matter to overcome the expansion and will eventually reach a definite optimum size. However, such a universe will eventually die.

Which of these theories is correct will not be known until we are able to determine both the deceleration rate of the expansion of the universe and the exact amount of matter present in it.

THE EDGE OF THE OBSERVABLE UNIVERSE

Hubble's Law (see above) states that the speed of a galaxy is proportional to its distance and that when the speed becomes equal to the velocity of light the galaxy is no longer detectable. Such a galaxy is then said to be at the 'edge of the observable universe'. For a Hubble Constant of 70 km/s/Mpc, this is equivalent to a distance of 14 000 million light years. However, for a number of reasons, Hubble's Law breaks down at these large distances – for example, it does not take into account the fact that the universe is decelerating. Many models for assumed values of the deceleration parameter and density parameter would place the furthest galaxies well beyond the distance of 14 000 million light years obtained from Hubble's Law. This limit is in reality only the scale factor, or yardstick, by which the universe is measured. The true size of the universe is unknown because both the deceleration parameter and the density parameter are unknown.

DISTANCES WITHIN THE UNIVERSE

The time taken for light to travel to Earth from heavenly bodies may be used as a guide to the size of the universe. In the following list, the times given are surface to surface in the case of nearby objects.

Heavenly body from which light is travelling	*Time taken by light to travel from the heavenly body*
From the Moon (at mean distance)	1.26 sec
From the Sun (at mean distance)	8 min 17 sec
From Pluto (at mean distance)	5 hr 20 min
From the nearest star (Proxima Centauri)	4.22 years
From the centre of our Galaxy (present distance)	27 700 years
From the most distant star in our Galaxy (present distance)	62 700 years
From the nearest extra-galactic body (the Large Magellanic Cloud)	174 000 years
From the limit of naked eye vision (Andromeda galaxy)	2 309 000 years
From the most distant quasar known (QSO PC 1247 + 3406)	13 200 000 000 years
From the 'edge of the observable universe'	14 000 000 000 years

GALAXIES

A galaxy is a system of many thousands of millions of stars, together with interstellar gas and dust. The galaxies resulted from the accumulation of gas on the proto-galaxies that were formed by density fluctuations and gravity instabilities in the expanding primordial fireball. It is thought that they originally consisted only of those elements formed in the big bang (mainly hydrogen and helium). Most of the first stars formed were probably very large and are thought to have lasted for about one million years. Their destruction in supernova explosions led to the formation of the heavier elements in the form of cosmic dust. (Today, cosmic dust is thought to compose no more than 2% of all matter.)

The number of galaxies in the universe is estimated to be between 100 billion and a trillion (10^{11} to 10^{12}). Each galaxy contains about 100 billion stars. The total number of stars is calculated to be between 10^{22} and 10^{23}. Recent observations of the large-scale structure of the universe suggest that the galaxies may have been formed on the 'surfaces' of 'bubbles', each about 100 million light years in diameter. In the process, the centres of the bubbles became virtually devoid of matter.

THE CLASSIFICATION OF GALAXIES

In 1924, Hubble compared the magnitude changes of variable stars in our own galaxy (*Cepheid variables*) with similar stars in the Andromeda nebula. By so doing, he established that the distance to Andromeda is so great that it must be an independent galaxy. Having established the existence of other galaxies, Hubble formulated a classification of galaxies based upon their appearance. Hubble distinguished three types – elliptical, spiral and irregular galaxies.

Elliptical galaxies (E) appear as luminous elliptical discs with a smooth distribution of light. Their surface brightness decreases outward from the centre. Elliptical galaxies are further divided into types E0–7, according to their aspect in the sky. For example, E0 types are seen face on as circular discs, while E7 types are seen almost edge on.

Spiral galaxies are either normal (S), in which spiral shaped arms emerge directly from the nucleus, or barred (SB), in which the arms originate from a 'bar' that appears through the centre of the galaxy. Spiral galaxies are further divided into types a, b and c, depending on the extent of the 'unwinding' of the spiral arms and on the relative clarity of the arms and the nucleus. Lenticular (lens-shaped) galaxies (SO) appear to be intermediate between the elliptical and spiral types.

Irregular galaxies do not appear to have a definite structure. However, two types are distinguished – Irr I, which appears to be an extension of the spiral type Sc and includes the nearby Magellanic Clouds, and Irr II, which includes all galaxies that are peculiarly shaped.

COLD DARK MATTER

The dynamics of galaxies suggests that the mass of any galaxy, determined from the amount of light that it emits, is only about one-tenth of its true mass. This 'missing mass' – or more correctly 'missing light' – is called Cold Dark Matter. There is speculation whether Cold Dark Matter is an exotic form of matter unknown on Earth or ordinary matter (such as very cool stars) that are too dim to be detected by current astronomical instruments.

QUASARS

There is increasing evidence that the centres of regularly-shaped galaxies are powered by massive *black holes*. In our own galaxy there appears to be a two million solar mass black hole in the region of the radio point source Sagittarius A*.

The extremely active nuclei of distant galaxies are called *quasars* (short for quasi-stellar sources). These are characterized by being very luminous and by having extremely red-shifted spectra. The most luminous object in the sky – quasar HS 1946 + 7658 – is at least 1.5×10^{15} times more luminous than the Sun. Over 4500 quasars are now known. The most remote object currently known is quasar PC 1247 + 3406, which is at a distance of 13 200 million light years.

THE MILKY WAY GALAXY

Although only seen edge-on, our own Milky Way galaxy is considered to be a typical spiral galaxy. It is about 70 000 light years in diameter and is a member of the ellipsoidal so-called 'Local Group' of about 20 galaxies. The Local Group has a maximum extent of about six million light years. Its two dominant members are our own Milky Way galaxy and the Andromeda galaxy, which are at either end of its diameter. These two galaxies are approaching each other, with the stronger pull being exerted by the Andromeda galaxy. (Although these two galaxies will be closer within several thousand million years, they will not collide.)

The Local Group is part of the 'Local Supercluster', whose centre of gravity is close to the most prominent member of the group, the Virgo cluster. However, the centre of gravity is being drawn towards the even more massive Hydra-Centaurus supercluster, and both are being drawn towards a vast concentration of galaxies known as the 'Great Attractor'.

The Sun is located in the Orion spiral arm in the outer regions of the Milky Way. The Sun's present distance from the centre of the galaxy is 27 700 light years and its average distance from the centre is 29 700 light years. It will reach its minimum distance from the centre (*perigalacticon*) – a distance of 27 600 light years – in about 15 million years time. The orbital velocity of the Sun, and a large number of nearby stars, has been averaged to obtain the *local standard of rest*, which is 220 km/s (137 mi/sec). Based on this calculation, the orbital period of the Sun is 237 million years, but – probably because it is approaching perigalacticon – the Sun's actual motion is 17 km/s (11 mi/sec) faster than the local standard rest.

The principal galaxies, stars and constellations visible in the Northern sky and the Southern sky are shown on the star charts on p.12 and p.13 respectively.

STARS

Stars – of which our Sun is an example – are accretions of gas that radiate energy produced by nuclear-fusion reactions. They range in mass from about 0.06 to 100 solar masses, one solar mass being equivalent to the mass of the Sun. The properties of a star and the manner in which it evolves depend principally on its mass.

THE SKY AT NIGHT
THE NORTHERN HEMISPHERE

POPULAR NAMES OF CONSTELLATIONS
Aquarius the Water-carrier, **Aquila** the Eagle, **Aries** the Ram, **Auriga** the Charioteer or Waggoner,
Boötes the Herdsman, **Cancer** the Crab, **Capricorn** the Goat, **Centaurus** the Centaur, **Cygnus** the
Swan, **Gemini** the Twins (Castor and Pollux), **Leo** the Lion, **Libra** the Scales, **Lyra** the Lyre,
Orion the Hunter, **Pisces** the Fishes, **Sagittarius** the Archer, **Scorpio** the Scorpion, **Taurus** the Bull,
Ursa Major the Great Bear; also known as the Plough (UK) or the Big Dipper (USA), **Ursa Minor** the
Little Bear; also known as the Little Dipper (USA), **Virgo** the Virgin

THE SKY AT NIGHT
THE SOUTHERN HEMISPHERE

Pegasus
Triangle
Aries
Pisces
Cygnus
Aquarius
Pleiades
Taurus
Phoenix
Capricorn
Aquila
Eridanus
Lyra
Aldebaran
Orion
Sagittarius
Auriga
Southern
Triangle
Betelgeuse
Sirius
Southern
Cross
Scorpio
Gemini
Hercules
Castor
Milky Way
Centaurus
Libra
Pollux
Hydra
Cancer
Virgo
Arcturus
Boötes
Leo

POPULAR NAMES OF STARS
Pleiades the Seven Sisters, **Praesepe** (part of Cancer) the Beehive, **Sirius** the Dog Star

THE MAGNITUDE SCALE

Magnitude is a measure of stellar brightness. On the scale of magnitude, a first magnitude star is exactly 100 (or 2.511886[5]) times brighter than a sixth magnitude star. Therefore, the light of a star of any magnitude has a ratio of 2.511886 to that of a star of the next magnitude on the scale.

Nearby bodies that are exceptionally bright have a magnitude that is expressed as a negative quantity. The Sun – the brightest object in our sky – has a magnitude of -26.75, while the magnitudes of the Moon and Venus are respectively -12.74 and -4.40. At the other extreme, the faintest stars that can be seen on a clear night have a magnitude of $+6$. However, all of these values are the 'apparent magnitude' (m_V) as viewed from Earth. For purposes of comparison, the intrinsic brightness – the *absolute magnitude* – needs to known. The absolute magnitude is defined as the magnitude that a star would have if it were to be viewed at a distance of 10 parsecs (32.6 light years). On this basis, the Sun's absolute magnitude would be $+4.82$, or a four billionfold reduction in observed brightness. The absolute magnitude is related to the apparent magnitude and distance in parsecs (d) by means of the equation:

$$M_V = m_V + 5 - 5 \times \log(d)$$

STELLAR CLASSIFICATION

The colour of a star gives an indication of its temperature. Stars are classed according to their spectra in a sequence of decreasing temperature. Hot stars (known as type O) are blue, while cool stars (type M) are red. Stars closest to type O are called 'early'; those closest to type M are called 'late'. Each spectral type is sub-divided into ten grades, from 0 (early) to 9 (late). On this basis, the Sun is classified as a type G2 star. The types of star according to the *Henry Draper stellar classification* are:

Type O the hottest blue stars with surface temperatures between 25 000 and 40 000 °C (45 000 to 72 000 °F) and spectra dominated by ionized helium.

Type B hot blue stars with temperatures between 11 000 and 25 000 °C (20 000 and 45 000 °F) and spectra dominated by neutral helium.

Type A blue-white stars with temperatures between 7500 and 11 000 °C (13 500 and 20 000 °F) and spectra dominated by hydrogen, with some ionized metal lines present.

Type F white stars with temperatures between 6000 and 7500 °C (10 800 and 13 500 °F) and spectra dominated by neutral metal lines.

Type G yellow stars with temperatures between 5000 and 6000 °C (9000 and 10 800 °F) and spectra dominated by many metal lines.

Type K orange stars with temperatures between 3500 and 5000 °C (6300 and 9000 °F) and spectra dominated by neutral metal lines and some molecular bands.

Type M red stars with temperatures between 3000 and 3500 °C (5400 and 6300 °F) and spectra dominated by molecular bands.

This classification was introduced in 1920, but it was found to be inadequate as it assumes that all the stars in a particular class share identical characteristics. Therefore, in 1937, an extra dimension was added, based on stellar luminosity. This extra element classifies stars in groups ranging from type I (the 'supergiant' stars) to type VI (the 'sub-dwarfs'). Type V comprises dwarf stars, a certain size of star that is undergoing normal stellar evolution – this is known as a *main sequence* star). The full classification of the Sun – a yellow dwarf star type – is G2 V.

STELLAR EVOLUTION

Stars form from the gravitational contraction of a gas and dust cloud. A central core forms rapidly and

THE BRIGHTEST STARS

Rank	Name	Bayer designation	Visual magnitude Apparent	Absolute	Brightness on scale (Sun = 1)	Distance in light years
1	Sirius	α Canis Majoris	-1.46*	$+1.4$	24	8.7
2	Canopus[1]	α Carinae	-0.72	-8.5	220 000	1200
3	Rigel Kentaurus[1]	α Centauri	-0.27**	$+4.1$**	A 1.6 B 0.5	4.2
4	Arcturus	α Bootis	-0.04	-0.1	98	34
5	Vega	α Lyrae	$+0.03$	$+0.5$	56	26
6	Capella	α Aurigae	$+0.08$**	-0.6**	A 87 B 69	45
7	Rigel	ß Orionis	$+0.12$	-7.1	60 000	900
8	Procyon	α Canis Minoris	$+0.38$	$+2.7$	7.7	11.4
9	Achernar[1]	α Eridani	$+0.46$	-1.6	390	85
10	Betelgeuse	α Orionis	$+0.50$ v	-5.6 v, s	15 000	310
11	Hadar (Agena)[1]	ß Centauri	$+0.61$	-5.1	9900	460
12	Altair	α Aquilae	$+0.77$	$+2.3$	11	16
13	Aldebaran	α Tauri	$+0.85$ v	-0.8 v	180	68
14	Acrux	α Crucis	$+0.87$**	-4.3**	A 2900 B 1900	360
15	Antares	α Scorpii	$+0.96$ v	-4.7 v, s	6700	330
16	Spica	α Virginis	$+0.98$	-3.5	2200	260
17	Pollux	ß Geminorum	$+1.14$	$+1.0$	35	35
18	Fomalhaut	α Piscis Austrini	$+1.16$	$+2.0$	14	22
19	Deneb	α Cygni	$+1.25$	-7.5	88 000	1800
20	Mimosa	ß Crucis	$+1.25$	-5.0 s	8900	425
21	Regulus	α Leonis	$+1.35$	-0.7	170	85
22	Adhara	ε Canaris Majoris	$+1.50$	-4.4	5000	490

* The apparent visual magnitude of Sirius will reach a maximum of -1.67 by AD 61000. [1] Not visible from the British Isles. ** Combined magnitude for a double star system. v Average value for very variable magnitude. s Absolute magnitude estimated from spectroscopic data alone.

the remainder of the surrounding cloud falls on to the core to form a star. In the case of a star the size of the Sun, the whole process is thought to take less than one million years. The continuing gravitational collapse of the star is accompanied by an increase in temperature of the core, which eventually becomes hot enough and dense enough to initiate the nuclear fusion of hydrogen to helium. The vast amount of energy produced counteracts the gravitational collapse and the star achieves a state of equilibrium that can last up to 10 000 million years in the case of a star of the size of the Sun or perhaps only one million years in the case of a much more massive star.

Eventually a critical amount of hydrogen will have been used up and fusion reactions will stop in the helium-rich core. However, energy is still radiated from the surface, draining energy from the star. In an attempt to re-establish equilibrium, the core contracts, releasing gravitational energy. This results in fusion reactions in the hydrogen envelope that surrounds the core. The 'shell' of the star swells and, because of the reduced temperature, glows red rather than white, and the star becomes a *red giant*. The red giant stage lasts up to 100 million years in the case of a solar mass star such as the Sun, but for much less time in the case of a more massive star. During this stage, the core continues to contract and heat until it reaches a temperature at which the fusion of helium to carbon is triggered. Subsequent developments largely depend upon the mass of the star.

White dwarfs may eventually be formed from stars whose mass is similar to that of the Sun. In these stars, the temperatures are not high enough to trigger the fusion of carbon. The core continues to contract until prevented from doing so further when the electron fields surrounding the nuclei of the atoms becomes compressed. The surrounding envelope continues to expand and cool, and eventually separates from the core to form a transparent shell known as a *planetary nebula*, revealing the core as a small white star – a white dwarf. White dwarfs may be as small as the Earth but they possess a mass equivalent to that of the Sun. Therefore, the density of a white dwarf may be up to 100 000 times that of the Earth. White dwarfs continue to shine for several thousand million years, simply by using up the thermal energy that was stored up after the core collapsed. In time, however, they cool completely.

Neutron stars and pulsars may eventually be formed from stars of between eight and 50 solar masses. In these large stars, the contraction of the core leads to temperatures in excess of 1000 million °C (1800 million °F). This causes carbon and other elements to undergo fusion reactions until iron is formed and the core collapses. The outer layers of the envelope also collapse on to the core leading to the formation of very heavy elements. The energy involved is so great that the outer layers are blown back into space, leaving a very bright star known as a *supernova*. The ejection of this material is accompanied by radiation so intense that a supernova can briefly outshine a galaxy. The remaining core, which weighs 1–3 solar masses, is only 10–30 km (6–20 mi) in diameter. Its density is 10^{14} times that of the Earth. Such a density is possible because the electrons in the atoms collapse on to the nuclei and react with the protons to form neutrons. The whole star can be considered to be one gigantic nucleus and is known as a *neutron star*.

Some neutron stars – known as *pulsars* – spin. Their rotation can be detected as a pulse caused by an interaction between a star's emission of radiation

THE NEAREST STARS

Over the next 100 000 years the nearest approach to the Sun by any stars will be to within 2·84 light years by the binary system Alpha Centauri in AD 29700 (N.B. present distance 4·35 light years).

Name	Distance in light years	Visual magnitude Apparent	Visual magnitude Absolute	Brightness on scale Sun = 1
Proxima Centauri	4·22	11·05	15·49	0·000 056
Alpha Centauri	4·35	A −0·01 B 1·33	A 4·37 B 5·71	A 1·6 B 0·5
Barnard's Star	5·98	9·54	13·22	0·000 46
Wolf 359	7·75	13·53	16·65	0·000 019
Lalande 21185	8·22	7·50	10·49	0·0056
Luyten 726-8*	8·43	A 12·52 B 13·02	A 15·46 B 15·96	A 0·000 058 B 0·000 037
Sirius	8·65	A −1·46 B 8·68	A 1·42 B 11·56	A 24·0 B 0·0021
Ross 154	9·45	10·6	13·3	0·000 42
Ross 248	10·4	12·29	14·77	0·000 11
Epsilon Eridani	10·8	3·73	6·13	0·31
Ross 128	10·9	11·10	13·47	0·000 36
61 Cygni	11·1	A 5·22 B 6·03	A 7·56 B 8·37	A 0·084 B 0·040
Epsilon Indi	11·2	4·68	7·00	0·14
Luyten 789-6	11·2	A 12·7 B 13·4	A 15·0 B 15·7	A 0·000 089 B 0·000 047
Groombridge 34	11·2	A 8·08 B 11·06	A 10·39 B 13·37	A 0·0062 B 0·000 40
Procyon	11·4	A 0·38 B 10·7	A 2·65 B 13·0	A 7·7 B 0·000 56
Sigma 2398	11·6	A 8·90 B 9·69	A 11·15 B 11·94	A 0·0031 B 0·0015
Lacaille 9352	11·7	7·36	9·59	0·013
Giglas 51–15	11·7	14·81	17·03	0·000 014
Tau Ceti	11·8	3·50	5·71	0·46
Luyten's Star	12·3	9·82	11·94	0·0015
Luyten 725–32	12·5	12·04	14·12	0·000 20
Lacaille 8760	12·5	6·67	8·74	0·028
Kapteyn's Star	12·7	8·81	10·85	0·0041
Kruger 60	12·9	A 9·85 B 11·3	A 11·87 B 13·3	A 0·00016 B 0·00042

* The B star companion is known as UV Ceti.

and its magnetic field. Pulsars were first detected in 1967. A group of very fast rotating pulsars – known as *millisecond pulsars* – were discovered in 1982. The faster rotating pulsars are expected to be stable for several thousand million years. The spin rates of millisecond pulsars are so stable that it has been proposed that they could be used as 'stellar clocks'.

Black holes and quark stars may eventually be formed from stars in excess of 50 solar masses. In these very large stars, the collapse of the core is so extreme that the whole mass collapses into a single point or singularity. The intense gravitational field of such a star extends a 'sphere of influence' into space and prevents radiation (i.e. light) from escaping. In the case of a singularity of ten solar masses, the sphere of influence extends to a radius of 29.5 km (18.3 mi). Such a singularity would appear as a *black hole*, with a diameter of 59 km (37 mi).

Black holes can only be detected indirectly, by the X-rays given off when matter from a companion star is dragged into a black hole. Currently, the only black hole for which strong evidence exists is the central star of the binary system V404, which is 500 light years distant in the constellation Cygnus. This star appears to have a mass at least six times greater than the Sun and is therefore above the maximum value that has been calculated for a neutron star. Related to this inconsistency, there is increasing evidence that core collapse may have to overcome one further quantum barrier – the *quark barrier* – before a singularity can be formed. It is thought that the core collapses into a 'quark soup' of immense density, but, because detection methods are so indirect, it may not be possible to distinguish between these quark stars and black holes. It may be that only super-massive stars can collapse into black holes.

MULTIPLE AND VARIABLE STARS

At least 75% of all stars are members of a binary or multiple star system, in which physically related stars orbit one another under the influence of their mutual gravitational attraction. *Binary stars* consist of two stars each orbiting around their common centre of gravity. *Visual binaries* can be identified as two stars by means of a telescope. In the case of *astrometric binaries*, one star is revealed by telescope, but the peculiar motion of that star indicates that it is accompanied by an unseen companion. *Unresolved binaries* may be detected spectroscopically either as periodic oscillations in the lines of the spectra or as two superimposed spectra. They may also be detected by regular changes in the apparent brightness of the system when the stars periodically eclipse one another.

The variations observed in multiple star systems mimic true *variable stars*, which experience changes in brightness. In the case of young stars, such changes are irregular and may occur because these stars are still trying to achieve thermal equilibrium. In the case of old stars, irregular changes represent the final stages of the process of decay. *Pulsating stars* experience regular variations in brightness caused by the periodic expansion and contraction of their atmospheres. The Cepheid variables, examples of this type, undergo periodic changes in brightness that can be directly related to their absolute magnitudes. Based on this fact, observations of the pulsation periods are apparent magnitudes of similar stars in other galaxies can be used to estimate their absolute magnitudes and hence their distances.

THE SOLAR SYSTEM

THE AGE AND FORMATION OF THE SOLAR SYSTEM

Meteoric evidence suggests that the solar system is 4540 million years old. It is believed to have been formed in less than 25 million years from a globe of gas and dust that consisted mainly of hydrogen, but also included helium (about 25% of the total) and heavier elements (2%). During coalescence, the globe started to rotate and flatten. The central core rotated faster and therefore became denser than the outer regions.

In the outer regions, grains of dust and ice, and methane and ammonia, began to collide and coagulate into larger and larger bodies. It is thought that the initial larger bodies so formed were meteroids (see below), followed by small bodies known as planetismals and, finally, by protoplanets. The latter acquired large atmospheres from the reservoir of surrounding gases.

When the central core became dense enough and hot enough to trigger the fusion of hydrogen to helium, the resulting protostar – which was to become the Sun – emitted large amounts of matter and radiant energy in order to establish equilibrium. This emission blew away not only the remnants of the original globe of gas and dust, but also the primordial atmospheres of the inner planets. Most of the large atmospheres of the outer planets remained.

THE DEATH OF THE SOLAR SYSTEM

In about 5000 million years time the Sun will enter its red giant stage (see above). It will swell up to about 40 million km (25 million mi) in diameter and its luminosity will be so great that the inner planets will be roasted. The outer layers of the red giant's atmosphere will separate from the core to form a planetary nebula – a diffuse cloud of dust and gases. This separation will leave an exposed core that will contract to a white dwarf with about half of the mass of the present Sun and a diameter about one and half times that of the present planet Earth. The white dwarf star will continue shining for several thousand million years by using the thermal energy that was stored up in the collapse of the core, but eventually it will become a burnt out cinder.

THE SUN

Our nearest star, the Sun, is at a true distance of 1·00000102 astronomical units or 149 598 020 km (92 955 900 mi) from the Earth. The minimum distance between the Sun and the Earth – the *perihelion* – is 147 097 800 km (91 402 300 mi) – and the maximum distance – the *aphelion* – is 152 098 200 km (94 509 400 mi).

The Sun is classified as a 'yellow dwarf' star of spectral type G2 V. It has a diameter of 1 392 140 km (865 040 mi) – that is 109·13 times greater than that of the Earth – and a mass of $1·9889 \times 10^{27}$ tonnes ($1·9575 \times 10^{27}$ tons) – that is equivalent to 332 946·04 times the mass of the Earth.

The low density of the Sun, 1·408 g/cm^3, is consistent with its overall composition by mass of 73% hydrogen, 25% helium, and 2% of other elements. Its internal structure consists of a helium-rich core with a central temperature of 15 400 000 °C (27 720 032 °F). The core is surrounded by a radiative layer several hundred thousand kilometres thick, a convective layer several tens of thousands of kilometres thick – in which heat is transported by convection in the form of cells – and a 300 km (200 mi) outer layer – or *photosphere* – which represents the maximum depth of visibility within the Sun and reveals the convective layer cells as a patchwork of granules. The observed overall temperature of the photosphere is 5507 °C (9945 °F).

The Sun rotates at a rate of 25·38 days (27·28 days as viewed from Earth). This value is determined from observations of *sunspots*, which occur in this layer. The production of sunspots is due to magnetic anomalies. The darkness of the sunspots is actually a contrast effect since they are still very bright, but at a temperature about 2000 °C (3600 °F) less than the overall photosphere temperature.

The Sun's atmosphere consists of a *chromosphere*, which extends about 10 000 km (6000 mi) above the photosphere. It has a low density but a sufficiently high temperature that all elements are in an ionized state – its pinkish hue is due to the presence of ionized hydrogen. The outer atmosphere – or *corona* – appears as a white halo and is an extremely thin gas at very high temperature (1 000 000 °C/1 800 000 °F).

The most spectacular features – extending from the top of the chromosphere and into the corona – are huge jets of gas flung many thousands of kilometres into space and then looped back into the chromosphere by intense magnetic fields. The extremely high temperature of the corona continuously disperses the Sun's outer atmosphere into space in the form of a plasma of protons and electrons – the 'solar wind' – which permeates the whole of the solar system.

At the centre of the Sun, hydrogen undergoes nuclear fusion. In stars the size of the Sun this occurs mainly by direct proton–proton reaction, i.e. two protons react together to form a deuteron, a positron and a neutrino, then the deuteron reacts with another proton to form helium 3 and a photon, and the cycle is complete when two helium 3 nuclei react together to form helium 4 and two protons. The net result is that an extremely small amount of matter is converted to energy per cycle but the overall result for the Sun is that 4 million tonnes/ tons of matter is lost per second. However, the high temperature and luminosity of the Sun are not due directly to the nuclear reaction but to the energy generated by the extremely high internal gas pressures required to counteract the intense gravitational contraction pressure that acts on such a large mass. Acting alone, this source of energy could only supply the Sun's needs for several tens of millions of years, but this effect is extended to 10 000 million years since the nuclear fusion reaction replaces the energy lost through radiation.

THE TITIUS-BODE RULE

A theory by Titius of Wittenberg (Germany) in 1766 – publicized by Johan Bode in 1772 – suggested that the orbital distances adopted by the planets around the Sun may not be arbitrary. Titius noted that the simple series 4, 4 + (3 × 2^0), 4 + (3 × 2^1), 4 + (3 × 2^2) etc, when divided by ten, reproduced the orbital distances in astronomical units of the six known planets. The discovery of Uranus in 1781 also led to a satisfactory agreement.

The gap at 2·8 astronomical units (AU) was solved by the discovery of the asteroid Ceres in 1801 and the subsequent discovery of several thousand more asteroids orbiting between 2·3 and 3·3 AU. However, the total mass of the asteroids is only two-thousandths of the Earth's mass and therefore hardly planet size, but attempts to form a planet in this region may have been disrupted by nearby Jupiter when it may have been an even more massive protoplanet.

Beyond Uranus, the Titius-Bode prediction is that the next two planets would be at 38·8 and 77·2 AU respectively, but giant Neptune is actually at 30·1 AU and small Pluto at 39·5 AU. Whilst Pluto's orbit would appear to approximate to the Titius-Bode Rule, it is actually very eccentric and highly inclined and therefore the agreement is almost coincidental. However, the fact that the two planets do not obey the prediction has been interpreted as an indication of a catastrophe that may have befallen them during the early history of the solar system.

METEORITES

When a meteoroid – consisting of broken fragments originating from either comets or asteroids, and ranging in size from fine dust to bodies several km in diameter – becomes visible from Earth it is referred to as a meteor. When it penetrates to the Earth's surface it is known as a meteorite. Up to 150 meteorites – which may be either stony (aerolite) or metallic (siderite) – fall to the land surface of the Earth each year. A 'shooting star' is a tiny meteorite that burns up as it penetrates the atmosphere.

A meteorite shower is a 'swarm' of separate meteorites that arrive on the surface of the Earth at the same time. Such an occurrence is probably produced by the disintegration of a large meteorite at considerable altitude. Meteorite showers may contain many separate bodies – the record is held by an estimated 100 000 bodies falling at Pulutsk, Poland, in 1868.

Largest known meteorites

Location	Found	Weight
Hoba West[1] (Namibia)	1920	59 tonnes
Cape York[2] (Greenland)	1897	30.9 tonnes
Bacubirito (Mexico)	1863	27 tonnes
Mbosi (Tanzania)	1930	25 tonnes
Armanty (Mongolia)	not known	20 tonnes

[1] The meteorite found at Hoba West is a block 2.75 m (9 ft) long by 2.43 m (8 ft) broad.
[2] Known as the 'Tent' meteorite – and to the Eskimos as Abnighito – this is the largest meteorite exhibited in any museum. Discovered by the expedition of Commander (later Rear-Admiral) Peary on the west coast of Greenland, this meteorite is now displayed at the Hayden Planetarium in New York City, USA.

The largest of the 22 meteorites known to have fallen on the British Isles since 1653 fell at Barwell, Leicestershire, on 24 Dec 1965 and weighed at least 46.25 kg (102 lb). Its largest piece weighed 7.88 kg (17 lb 6 oz).

MEAN ELEMENTS OF THE PLANETARY ORBITS

Planet	Mean distance from Sun km	Mean distance from Sun miles	Orbital eccentricity	Orbital inclination	Sidereal period days	Mean orbital velocity km/s	Mean orbital velocity mps
Mercury	57 909 100	*35 983 000*	0·205631	7° 00′ 18″	87·9693	47·87	*29·75*
Venus	108 208 600	*67 237 700*	0·006775	3° 23′ 41″	224·7008	35·02	*21·76*
Earth	149 598 000	*92 955 900*	0·016711	– – –	365·2564	29·78	*18·51*
Mars	227 939 200	*141 634 800*	0·093395	1° 50′ 59″	686·9799	24·13	*14·99*
Jupiter	778 298 400	*483 612 200*	0·048485	1° 18′ 13″	4332·59	13·06	*8·12*
Saturn	1 429 394 000	*888 184 000*	0·055529	2° 29′ 21″	10759·2	9·66	*6·00*
Uranus	2 875 039 000	*1 786 466 000*	0·046298	0° 46′ 23″	30688·5	6·81	*4·23*
Neptune	4 504 450 000	*2 798 935 000*	0·008988	1° 46′ 14″	60182·3	5·44	*3·38*
Pluto	5 913 514 000	*3 674 490 000*	0·248576	17° 09′ 01″	90777·6	4·74	*2·94*

The minimum (perihelion) and maximum (aphelion) distances from the Sun can be calculated from the the mean distance (*a*) and eccentricity (*e*) through the formulae: Perihelion = *a*(1 − *e*) and Aphelion = *a*(1 + *e*).

The mean elements of the seven largest minor planets, or asteroids, are given under individual entries for Ceres, Pallas, Vesta, Hygeia, Davida, Interamnia, and Europa (see below).

PHYSICAL PARAMETERS OF THE PLANETS

Planet		Diameter km	Diameter miles	Equatorial sidereal rotation period d	h	m	s	Equatorial inclination	Mass* kg	Density g/cm³
Mercury		4 880	*3 032*	58	15	30	33·9	0°	3·302 × 10²³	5·428
Venus		12 103	*7 520*	R 243	00	26	38	177° 20′	4·869 × 10²⁴	5·245
Earth	Equ.	12 756	*7 926*		23	56	04·1	23° 26′	5·974 × 10²⁴	5·515
	Polar	12 714	*7 900*							
Mars	Equ.	6 794	*4 221*	1	00	37	22·7	25° 11′	6·419 × 10²³	3·934
	Polar	6 752	*4 196*							
Juniper	Equ.	142 984	*88 846*		9	50	30·0	3° 08′	1·899 × 10²⁷	1·325
	Polar	133 708	*83 082*							
Saturn	Equ.	120 536	*74 898*		10	39	22·1	26° 43′	5·685 × 10²⁶	0·685
	Polar	108 718	*67 560*							
Uranus	Equ.	51 118	*31 763*	R 17	14	24		97° 52′	8·683 × 10²⁵	1·271
	Polar	49 946	*31 035*							
Neptune	Equ.	49 532	*30 778*		16	07		30° 11′	1·024 × 10²⁶	1·638
	Polar	48 684	*30 251*							
Pluto		2 302	*1 430*	R 6	09	17	38	117° 35′	1·35 × 10²²	2·12

R = Retrograde motion.
* Mass excluding satellites.

The physical parameters of the seven largest minor planets, or asteroids, are given under individual entries for Ceres, Pallas, Vesta, Hygeia, Davida, Interamnia, and Europa – see below.

PHYSICAL PARAMETERS OF THE PLANETS ON THE SCALE EARTH = 1

Planet	Equatorial diameter	Volume	Mass excluding satellites	Surface gravity
Mercury	0·3825	0·0562	0·055 27	0·3769
Venus	0·9488	0·8569	0·815 00	0·9033
Earth	1·0000	1·0000	1·000 00*	1·0000
Mars	0·5326	0·1507	0·107 45	0·3795
Jupiter	11·209	1323·3	317·828	**
Saturn	9·449	766·3	95·161	**
Uranus	4·007	63·09	14·536	**
Neptune	3·883	57·74	17·148	**
Pluto	0·180	0·0059	0·0023	0·069

* The mass of the combined Earth–Moon system is 1·0123 Earth masses.
** Not comparable for the giant gas planets as they do not have a solid surface.

The equatorial diameters of the seven largest minor planets on the same scale are: Ceres 0.0712, Pallas 0.0378, Vesta 0.367, Hygeia 0.0359, Davida 0.0270, Interamnia 0.0261, and Europa 0.0245.

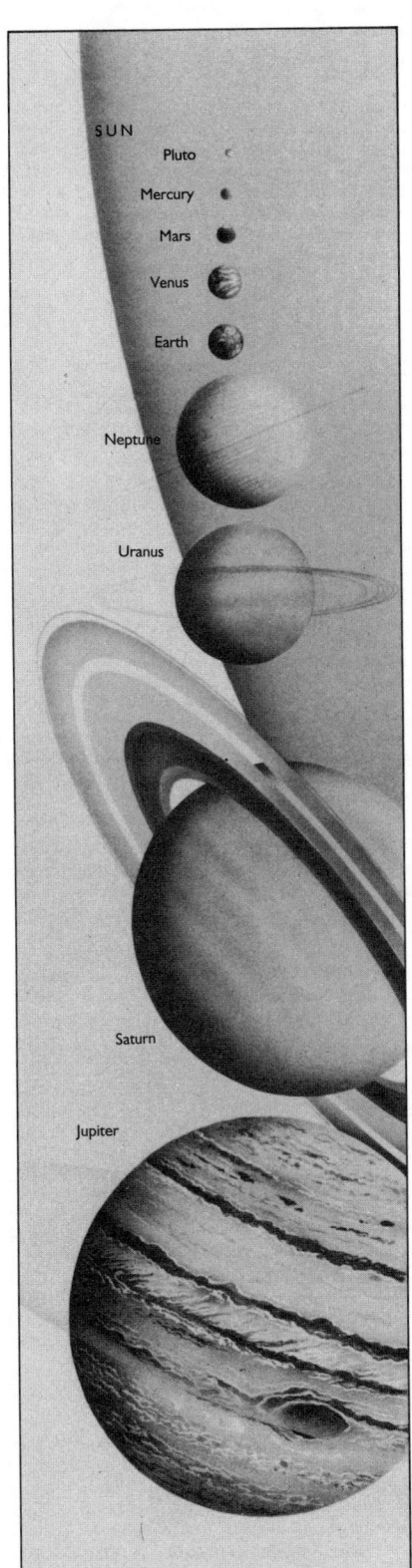

SUN
Pluto
Mercury
Mars
Venus
Earth
Neptune
Uranus
Saturn
Jupiter

THE INNER PLANETS

The four inner planets – Mercury, Venus, Earth and Mars – are small and rocky. Because the Earth is a member of the group of inner planets, they are often referred to as the *terrestrial planets*. However, they are four very different worlds.

MERCURY

Because of its proximity to the Sun, Mercury is difficult to see with the naked eye and only appears low in the west after sunset, or low in the east before sunrise. The first telescopic observation was made by the Polish astronomer Hevelius (1611–87), who saw that the planet has phases like the Moon.

Radar observations in the 1960s established that Mercury's rotational period is exactly two-thirds of the planet's orbital period. However, most of what we know about the planet derives from visits by the *Mariner 10* spacecraft in 1974 and 1975. Data returned by *Mariner 10* revealed that Mercury looks remarkably like the Moon, with similar craters and highlands, but it lacks the large frozen lava 'seas' or *maria*. The surface appears to be dominated by large basins representing epochs in the formation of the crust. The largest of these features is Caloris, which has a major diameter of 1340 km (830 mi) and appears to have six associated ring-like structures ranging in diameter from 630 km (390 mi) to 3700 km (2300 mi). The surface of Mercury is covered with a large number of impact craters, the largest of which is Boccaccio with a diameter of 160 km (100 mi). The deepest Mercurian crater is Ictinus, which is 4800 m (15 570 ft) from floor to rim.

Because the surface pressure is only one trillionth (10^{-12}) of that of Earth, Mercury has virtually no atmosphere. Therefore, temperatures on Mercury vary between 420 °C (790 °F) in the day and −180 °C (−290 °F) at night, with an average sunlit side temperature of 170 °C (340 °F). Because of the peculiar relationship between Mercury's rotation period and orbital period, a 'day' (sunrise to sunset) on the planet is equivalent to two Mercurian years or 176 Earth days.

Mercury has an iron-rich core – 3600 km (2200 mi) in diameter – containing 65% of the planet's mass. This accounts for the planet's extraordinarily high density compared with its size. A recent theory has associated Mercury's relatively thin surface layers with the same type of 'giant impact' that is thought to have formed the Moon (see below). However, in Mercury's case the debris could not be retained to form a satellite.

VENUS

Apart from the Moon, Venus is often the brightest object in the sky. However, like Mercury, Venus can only be seen with the naked eye in the morning or the evening. The planet has been the object of many space probes, starting with the *Mariner II* flyby in 1962. The most recent probe is the *Magellan* orbiter, which since 1990 has been carrying out precision radar mapping of the whole surface of Venus. There have also been a number of landings on the planet including the Soviet *Venera* series (1967–82) and *Vega 1* and *2* (1985), and the four US *Pioneer*Venus probes (1978).

Although similar in size to the Earth, Venus is an intensely hostile planet. Its atmosphere consists almost entirely of carbon dioxide at a pressure 94 times that of the Earth. Its average temperature of 464 °C (867 °F) – with little difference between the equator and the poles – is maintained by a runaway 'greenhouse effect' in which heat received from the Sun is trapped within the atmosphere. A thick planet-wide cloud cover between 50 and 75 km (30 and 45 mi) above the surface contains a high concentration of aerosol droplets of sulfuric acid – the source of the sulfur may be due to emanations from active volcanoes. The upper clouds sweep around the planet in about four to five days, which is equivalent to wind speeds of up to 360 km/h (220 mph).

Although the surface of Venus cannot be seen from the Earth, pictures sent back by the *Venera* probes 7, 9, 10, 13 and 14 indicate that the sunlight filtering through the clouds turns the grey rocks a pinkish-orange hue. Radar mapping indicates that the surface is essentially flat – with 80% of the surface being within 1 km (0.6 mi) of the planet's average radius – and covered by a vast network of faults and cracks. However, Venus has a number of notable highlands including Aphrodite Terra close to the equator, which is 9700 km (6000 mi) long and up to 3000 km (1900 mi) wide, and Ishtar Terra in the north, which is 2900 km (1800 mi) in diameter and contains the Maxwell Montes mountain chain, which rises up to 8 km (5 mi) above the surrounding plateau.

Although the rotation period of Venus is longer than its year, a Venusian 'day' (sunrise-to-sunrise) is equivalent to 116 Earth days.

EARTH

The Earth is the largest and densest of the four terrestrial planets. With an atmosphere containing 78% of nitrogen and 21% of oxygen at an average temperature of 15 °C (59 °F) and with two-thirds of its surface covered by ocean (with a mean depth of 3554 m / 11 660 ft), the Earth is the only planet in the solar system capable of initiating and sustaining life-forms. If the Sun maintains its present life cycle and does not experience a cataclysmic encounter with another star system, it is possible that the Earth may sustain life for at least another 4000 million years.

Detailed information on the Earth's interior, atmosphere and structure will be found in the chapter, Earth Sciences.

THE MOON

The Earth's only natural satellite has been investigated by many space probes, beginning with *Pioneer 4* in March 1959. The first pictures of the far side of the Moon were taken by *Luna 3* in October 1959. The first controlled landing on the Moon was made by *Surveyor 1* in May 1966, while the first manned landing was made in July 1969 (see Space Travel).

The Moon has an average diameter of 3475·1 km (2159·3 mi), making it larger than the planet Pluto. It has a mass of $7·343 \times 10^{19}$ tonnes ($7·232 \times 10^{19}$ tons) or 0·0123 Earth masses. The mean orbital distance is 384 399·1 km (238 854·5 mi), although the centre of gravity is displaced 1·8 km (1·1 mi) towards the Earth. The average minimum orbital distance – the *perigee* – is 363 295 km (225 741 mi) and the maximum orbital distance – the *apogee* – is 403 503 km (251 968 mi).

The Moon orbits the Earth in 27.321661 days (a *sidereal month*), with an average orbital velocity of 3683 km/h (2289 mph) and is in *synchronous rotation* –

i.e. it keeps the same face towards the Earth. Although only 59% of the Moon's surface is visible from Earth, extensive space-probe photography has now recorded the whole of the lunar surface. Surface features include craters, mountain ranges and broad plains – known as 'seas' or *maria* – that are filled with frozen lava. There is a marked absence of frozen lava lakes on the far side of the Moon. Although a few of the craters may be due to ancient volcanic activity, most are believed to be the result of multiple impacts by planetesmals early in the history of the solar system.

Because the Moon has no atmosphere, there is a wide variation in temperature between 117 °C (243 °F) at the equator at midday and – 163 °C (– 261 °F) after nightfall.

The Origins of the Moon A number of theories have been put forward to explain the origins of the Moon.

Certain rock and soil samples brought back from the Moon are the same age – 4500 million years – as the oldest rocks and meteorites found on Earth. This indicates that the Moon was formed early in the history of the solar system and must be taken into account in any theories of the Moon's origins. Three such theories promoted between 1950 and 1970 are now seen to suffer major defects.

The *fission theory* proposed that the Earth and Moon resulted from the fission of a single molten proto-planet, but it now appears that such a body would be too viscous to split apart in this manner.

The *co-accretion theory* suggested that the Earth and Moon were formed in a common orbit, but this appears to be unlikely as they have a different chemical composition (i.e. a large depletion of iron in the Moon compared to the Earth).

The *capture theory* suggested that the Moon was formed in a different place in the solar system and then captured by the Earth. The major objection to this theory is that, if capture had happened, the Moon would have had a highly elliptical orbit and could not have changed to its present circular orbit in the lifetime of the solar system.

A fourth theory – the *giant impact hypothesis* – is currently gaining acceptance. This suggests that during the violent early history of the solar system the newly formed Earth was struck by a Mars-sized planetesimal, which disrupted both the surface layers of the Earth and the planetesimal with such force that the debris was volatilized and flung into space by gas pressure. The gas remained in orbit just beyond the limit of instability (the *Roche limit*) – 18 500 km (11 500 mi) from the Earth's centre. Within 100 years this gas began to coalesce into a partly or fully molten Moon, which then began to recede from the Earth to its present orbit. Minor modifications suggest that there were several planetesimals in the impact rather than one, but the general outlines of the theory provide the most plausible explanation of the Moon's origin offered so far.

MARS

The outer of the four terrestrial planets has been investigated by a number of space probes, beginning with the flyby of *Mariner 4* in 1965. Much of what we know about Mars derives from *Mariner 9* – which orbited the planet in 1971 – and from the deployment of landing vehicles upon the planet by *Viking 1* and *2* in 1976.

Although, like Venus, Mars has an atmosphere composed almost entirely of carbon dioxide, its atmospheric pressure is only about one hundredth that of the Earth. The average temperature is −53 °C (−63 °F), that is 68 °C lower than the average temperature on Earth. The space probes reveal a complex surface consisting of flat deserts, craters, dormant volcanoes, mountain ranges and pole caps. A number of the volcanoes are of an immense size; for example, Olympus Mons, in the Tharsis region, which is 600 km (370 mi) in diameter and rises 26 km (16 mi) above the surrounding plain. There are also a number of large 'channels' such as Valles Marineris, which is 4000 km (2500 miles) long, up to 600 km (370 mi) wide, and 7 km (5 mi) deep. A covering of ash from ancient volcanoes has formed dark areas, such as Syrtis Major, which can be seen by telescope from Earth. Periodic sweeping of the ash on these plains changes the visible surface features. These changes were once interpreted as the growth and receding of vegetation, but it is now appears definite that there is no life on Mars. However, there are channels that appear to have been fashioned by water in the distant past, and water ice is still present under the frozen carbon dioxide pole caps.

SATELLITES OF MARS

The two extremely small, dark, irregularly shaped satellites of Mars – Phobos and Deimos – were discovered by Asaph Hall in August 1877. They appear to be composed of the same kind of material as the most common type of asteroids (see below) and, therefore, may be captured asteroids.

Phobos (Number I) *Discovered*: 1877. *Distance from Mars* 9378 km (5827 mi). *Diameter* 26 × 22 × 18 km (16 × 14 × 11 mi) – an average of 22 km (14 mi). The surface features of this highly irregularly shaped satellite are dominated by the crater Stickney, which has a diameter of 10 km (6 mi).

Deimos (Number II) *Discovered*: 1877. *Distance from Mars* 23 459 km (14 577 mi). *Diameter* 15 × 12 × 11 km (9 × 8 × 7 mi) – an average of 13 km (8 mi). The surface of this highly irregularly shaped satellite is pockmarked with numerous small craters filled with fine dust.

THE ASTEROIDS OR MINOR PLANETS

The Titus-Bode rule (see p.17) suggested that there was a gap in the series of known planets. The discovery of the minor planet Ceres in 1801 seemed to fill this gap. The discovery of a second minor planet at this distance in the following year appeared to confuse the issue, and by 1845 five such minor planets or asteroids were known. With the introduction of the photographic method of detection, the number of known asteroids leapt to 463 by 1900, to 1568 by 1950 and is now approaching 6000. Present estimates suggest that there are over 50 000 asteroids, mostly orbiting between Mars and Jupiter, although one group – the Atens – have average orbital distances less than that of the Earth. Other isolated asteroids have orbital extremes that extend beyond the mean distances of the outer giant planets.

Only one minor planet, Vesta (number 4), is visible to the naked eye, and only one, Gaspra (number 951), has been photographed close-up (by the *Galileo* spacecraft in 1991). The total mass of the asteroids is estimated to be only about one twenty-fifth of the mass of the Moon. The three largest minor planets –

Ceres, Pallas and Vesta – account for over half of this mass. Most asteroids are only a few metres in diameter. There are, however, seven asteroids with diameters in excess of 300 km (186 mi).

CERES

(Number 1). The largest minor planet, Ceres, was the first to be discovered – by the Italian Guiseppe Piazzi on 1 January 1801. Ceres has an equatorial diameter of 959 km (596 mi) and a polar diameter of 907 km (564 mi) – an average of 941 km (585 mi). Ceres is a little under half the size of the planet Pluto and has a diameter only a quarter of that of the Moon. It orbits at a mean distance of 414 million km (257.1 million mi) from the Sun in a period of 4.603 Earth years and has an orbital inclination of 10·60°. The surface composition of Ceres appears to be a special version of the *carbonaceous chrondites*, which are conglomerates of minerals – containing water and organic materials – that have been unaltered since the formation of the solar system. Carbonaceous chrondites are the most common material found on minor planets and also occur in meteorites.

PALLAS

(Number 2). Pallas was the second asteroid to be discovered – by the German Heinrich Olbers in 1802. It is an irregularly shaped body with equatorial diameters of 570 × 525 km (354 × 326 mi) and a polar diameter of 482 km (300 mi), giving an average of 524 km (326 mi). Pallas has a rotation period of 7.811 hours. It orbits at a mean distance of 414.8 million km (257.7 million mi) in a period of 4.616 years at a high orbital inclination angle of 34.80 degrees. The surface composition of Pallas appears to be unique and has not been identified.

VESTA

(Number 4). Vesta is the brightest of the minor planets and can sometimes just be seen with the naked eye. Like Pallas, it was discovered by Olbers in 1807. Vesta is irregularly shaped, with equatorial diameters of 566 × 531 km (352 × 330 mi) and a polar diameter of 467 km (290 mi), giving an average of 520 km (323 mi). It has a rotation period of 5.342 hours. Vesta orbits at a mean distance of 351.9 million km (218.7 million mi) in a period of 3.631 years at an orbital inclination of 7.14°. The surface composition of Vesta is thought to be unique to this asteroid and has not been unambiguously identified.

HYGEIA

(Number 10). Hygeia was discovered by A. de Gasparis in 1849. It has an average diameter of 457 km (284 mi) and a long rotation period of 27.659 hours. It orbits at a mean distance of 468.9 million km (291.3 million mi) in a period of 5.549 years at an orbital inclination of 3.84°. The surface of Hygeia appears to be covered with dust, but it is of the common carbonaceous chrondite type.

DAVIDA

(Number 511) Davida – which was discovered by R.S. Dugan in 1901 – is a very irregularly shaped minor planet with diameters of 417 × 333 × 292 km (259 × 207 × 181 mi), giving an average of 344 km (214 mi). It has a rotation period of 5.130 hours. Davida orbits at a mean distance of 475.0 million km (295.2 million mi) in a period of 5.659 years, with an orbital inclination of 15.93°. The surface composition of Davida is of the carbonaceous chrondite type.

INTERAMNIA

(Number 704). Interamnia was discovered by V. Cerulli in 1910. It has an average diameter of 333 km (207 mi) and a rotation period of 8.727 hours. Interamnia orbits at a mean distance of 458.0 million km (284.6 million mi) in a period of 5.327 years at an orbital angle of 17.30°. The surface composition of Interamnia appears to be a special version of the carbonaceous chrondite type.

EUROPA

(Number 52). Europa was discovered by H. Goldschmidt in 1858. It has an average diameter of 312 km (194 mi) and a rotation period of 5.631 hours. Europa orbits at a mean distance of 463.3 million km (287.9 million mi) in a period of 5.450 years at an orbital inclination of 7.46°. The surface composition of Europa is of the carbonaceous chrondite type.

NOTABLE ASTEROIDS

Nysa (Number 44). *Discovered:* 1857. *Diameter:* 70 km (43mi). Most asteroids are very dark. However, Nysa is one of a small number of very bright asteroids that reflect back nearly one half of the light that they receive from Sun.

Eros (Number 433). *Discovered:* 1898. *Average diameter:* 20 km (12 mi). An irregularly shaped asteroid whose orbit takes it far away from the main swarm of asteroids. In 1975 it came within 24 million km (15 million mi) of the Earth.

Hektor (Number 624). *Discovered:* 1907. *Dimensions:* about 440 km (273 mi) long, with cross-sectional diameters of 180 × 140 km (112 × 87 mi). Hektor is an extraordinary very dark, elongated asteroid It is dumbbell shaped and probably represents the crashing together of two or more regularly shaped asteroids. A member of the Trojan group of asteroids that is trapped in Jupiter's orbit.

Icarus (Number 1566). *Discovered:* 1949. *Diameter:* 900 m (2950 ft). Icarus has the shortest known rotation period of only 2.273 hours. It has a highly irregular orbit that takes it to halfway between Mercury and the Sun at perihelion.

Chiron (Number 2060). *Discovered:* 1977. *Diameter:* under 300 km (under 186 mi). One the remotest asteroids, Chiron orbits mainly between Saturn and Uranus. Observations have revealed a large, faint surrounding *coma* – luminous cloud – formed principally by the degassing of carbon dioxide from small areas of the asteroid's surface. This activity is characteristic of comets and has led to suggestions that Chiron is, in fact, the largest comet. However, Chiron does not show spectacular cometary behaviour.

Phaethon (Number 3200). *Discovered:* 1983. *Diameter:* 5 km (3 mi). Phaethon displays a large orbital eccentricity that brings it closer to the Sun than any other asteroid. It is only 21 million km (13 million mi) from the Sun at perihelion, when the surface temperature on the sunlit side rises to 450 °C (842 °F).

1991BA (temporary designation). *Discovered:* when it came within 170 000 km (105 600 mi) of the Earth on 18 January 1991. *Diameter:* 9 m (30 ft) – the smallest known asteroid. Its orbit brings it closer to Earth than any other asteroid.

Pholus (Number 5145). *Discovered:* 1992. The remotest object that appears to be an asteroid – however, see also 1992 QB₁, below. Its orbit reaches beyond the mean distance of Neptune to 4823 million km (2997 million mi) at aphelion.

THE OUTER PLANETS

The outer planets are very different from the inner planets. They are very much further away from the Sun and, with the exception of Pluto, they are much larger than the inner planets. Jupiter, Saturn, Uranus and Neptune are giant 'gas' planets with no discernible solid surfaces. The outermost planet, Pluto, has a solid surface but is tiny in comparison.

JUPITER

Jupiter is the largest planet in the solar system. When it is closest to the Earth, it is often the brightest object in the sky – apart from the Moon, Venus and Mars. Jupiter has been investigated by four space probes – *Pioneer 10* and *11* in 1973 and 1974 respectively, and *Voyager 1* and *2* in 1979. These probes led to the discovery of three new moons and Jupiter's ring system.

A model of the structure of Jupiter suggests that it has a rock-iron-ice core about 15 000 km (9000 mi) thick, weighing about 15 Earth masses. The core is surrounded by shell of metallic hydrogen, containing a small amount of helium, which extends up to 55 000 km (34 000 mi) from the centre of the planet. An outer envelope consists mainly of liquid molecular hydrogen. Jupiter has a gaseous hydrogen atmosphere, about 18% of which comprises helium and small quantities of compounds such as water, ammonia ices and ammonium hydrosulfide. These compounds impart the light and dark bands to the planet's atmosphere that can be observed by telescope from Earth.

The 'Great Red Spot' – which may have been observed as early as 1664 – appears to be a long-lived whirling storm in the planet's atmosphere. This 'Great Red Spot' may rise up to 8 km (5 mi) above the surrounding cloud. Its red colour may be due to the presence of phosphorus, derived from decomposition of the minor atmospheric constituent phosphine. The squashed appearance of Jupiter is entirely consistent with the rapid rotation of a gas sphere.

Jupiter radiates 67% more heat than it receives from the Sun. This is mainly due to dissipation of the primordial heat of the planet. A secondary source of heat is gravitational energy released as a result of the precipitation of helium in Jupiter's metallic core.

THE RINGS OF JUPITER

The ring system of Jupiter was discovered in March 1979. A bright central ring – 7000 km (4300 mi) in width and less than 30 km (20 mi) in thickness – has a maximum brightness at 126 100 km (78 400 mi) from the centre of Jupiter and an abrupt outer boundary at 129 130 km (80 240 mi) from the centre of the planet. A faint inner halo – 20 000 km (12 400 mi) in thickness – extends down to the top of the clouds that surround Jupiter. A very tenuous 'gossamer ring' extends out to 214 000 km (133 000 mi), beyond the main ring.

SATELLITES OF JUPITER

The 16 satellites, or moons, of Jupiter can be considered in four distinct clusters – four inner satellites, the four massive Galilean satellites, four satellites in a prograde orbit (orbiting in the same direction as Jupiter's rotation) at 163 Jupiter radii, and four satellites in a retrograde orbit at 314 Jupiter radii.

The Inner Satellites

Metis (Number XVI) *Discovered*: 1980. *Distance from Jupiter*: 127 960 km (79 520 mi). *Diameter*: 40 km (25 mi). Metis is embedded in the main ring of Jupiter.

Adrastea (Number XV) *Discovered*: 1980. *Distance from Jupiter*: 128 980 km (80 140 mi). *Diameter*: 26 × 20 × 16 km (16 × 12 × 10 mi), giving an average of 20 km (12 mi). Adrastea orbits just inside the edge of the main ring and may control it.

Amalthea (Number V) *Discovered*: 1892. *Distance from Jupiter*: 181 370 km (112 700 mi). *Diameter*: 262 × 146 × 134 km (163 × 91 × 83 mi), giving an average of 172 km (107 mi). The dark red colour of Amalthea's surface may be due to the capture of sulfur from the nearby volcanic satellite Io.

Thebe (Number XIV) *Discovered*: 1980. *Distance from Jupiter*: 221 890 km (137 880 mi). *Diameter*: 110 × 90 km (68 × 56 mi), giving an average of 100 km (62 mi).

The Galilean Satellites

The Galilean Satellites were named after Galileo Galilei (1564–1642), who independently observed them at the same time as Simon Marius (Simon Mayr; 1573–1624) in 1610. They have proved to be unique 'worlds', entirely different to Jupiter's other satellites.

Io (Number I). *Discovered*: 1610. *Distance from Jupiter*: 421 800 km (262 100 mi). *Diameter*: 3660 × 3637 × 3631 km (2274 × 2260 × 2256 mi), giving an average of 3643 km (2264 mi). Io is continuously subject to volcanic eruptions due to gravitational interactions with Jupiter. This has resulted in a vividly coloured surface that is covered with various forms of sulfur and its compounds.

Europa (Number II). *Discovered*: 1610. *Distance from Jupiter*: 671 000 km (417 000 mi). *Diameter*: 3130 km (1945 mi). Europa has a 'billiard ball' smooth surface that is covered with numerous thin dark lines. Its structure may comprise a 100 km (60 mi) thick water ice layer overlying a rocky core, but with an intermediate layer of liquid water.

Ganymede (Number III). *Discovered*: 1610. *Distance from Jupiter*: 1 070 400 km (665 100 mi). *Diameter*: 5268 km (3237 mi). The largest and heaviest satellite in the solar system, Ganymede has a mass 2·017 times greater than our own Moon. Its water ice surface has a strange darkened mottled appearance.

Callisto (Number IV). *Discovered*: 1610. *Distance from Jupiter*: 1 882 600 km (1 169 800 mi). *Diameter*: 4806 km (2986 mi). Callisto – the outermost Galilean satellite – has the most heavily cratered surface of any body in the solar system. It is dominated by two large multi-ringed basins – Valhalla, which shows ring structures up to 4000 km (2500 mi) in diameter, and Asgard, which shows ring structures up to 1600 km (1000 mi) in diameter.

The Outer Satellites

These small satellites – in two distinct orbits (see above) – may represent the disruption of two captured asteroids, a theory given strength by the fact that their surface composition appears to be similar to the carbonaceous chrodites found on asteroids.

Leda (Number XIII) *Discovered*: 1974. *Distance from Jupiter*: 11 094 000 km (6 893 000 mi). *Diameter*: 18 km (11 mi).

Himalia (Number VI) *Discovered*: 1904. *Distance from Jupiter*: 11 480 000 km (7 133 000 mi). *Diameter*: 156 km (97 mi).

Lysithea (Number X) *Discovered*: 1938. *Distance from Jupiter*: 11 720 000 km (7 282 000 mi). *Diameter*: 34 km (21 mi).

Elara (Number VII) *Discovered*: 1905. *Distance from Jupiter*: 11 737 000 km (7 293 000 mi). *Diameter*: 70 km (43 mi).

Ananke (Number XII) *Discovered*: 1951. *Distance from Jupiter*: 21 200 000 km (13 200 000 mi). *Diameter*: 25 km (16 mi).

Carme (Number XI) *Discovered*: 1938. *Distance from Jupiter*: 22 600 000 km (14 000 000 mi). *Diameter*: 40 km (25 mi).

Pasiphae (Number VIII) *Discovered*: 1908. *Distance from Jupiter*: 23 500 000 km (14 600 000 mi). *Diameter*: 56 km (35 mi).

Sinope (Number IX) *Discovered*: 1914. *Distance from Jupiter*: 23 700 000 km (14 700 000 mi). *Diameter*: 34 km (21 mi).

SATURN

The next planet out from the Sun is Saturn, with its magnificent system of rings. In 1610 Galileo became the first person to look at Saturn through a telescope. His low powered telescope did not reveal the rings distinctly, and Galileo thought he was looking at a 'triple planet'. It was not until 1659 that the Dutch physicist Christiaan Huygens (1629–95) realized Saturn's true nature. The planet has been investigated by three space probes – *Pioneer 11* in 1979 and *Voyager 1* and *2* in 1980 and 1981 respectively. These probes led to the discovery of three new satellites and the F and G rings.

Saturn is generally considered to be similar to Jupiter but on a smaller scale. Saturn has a similar rock–iron–ice core to Jupiter, but the metallic hydrogen layer is much smaller, extending only 26 000 km (16 000 mi) from the centre of the planet. It is also rich in helium but the outer molecular hydrogen envelope is depleted in this element because of the presence of an intermediate zone 3000 km (1900 mi) thick in which helium is precipitating out and falling into the metallic zone. The gravitational energy released from this 'precipitation' is the source of heat – Saturn radiates 76% more heat than it receives from the Sun.

THE RINGS OF SATURN

The distinct ring system surrounding Saturn's equator is composed of water ice or ice-covered material. Although the main ring system is 273 550 km (169 980 mi) in diameter, the overall thickness is only 10 m (33 ft), giving a total mass of only about 5×10^{-8} of that of Saturn. Although the main rings appear to consist of many thousands of individual ringlets, it is now thought that this is an optical effect caused by variations in reflectivity.

For details of the main features of the rings of Saturn, see the table on p.24.

SATELLITES OF SATURN

The 18 known satellites of Saturn appear to be either small misshapen water ice moons or medium-sized water ice satellites with rocky cores. The largest satellite, Titan, is big enough to have its own atmosphere.

Pan *Discovered*: 1990. *Distance from Saturn*: 133 580 km (83 000 mi). *Diameter*: 20 km (12 mi). Pan orbits at the centre of the 322 km (200 mi) wide Encke Gap in the A Ring.

THE RINGS OF SATURN

Feature	Distance from centre km	miles	Notes
Saturn radius	60 367	*37 510*	Radius at the 100 millibar level
D Ring inner edge	66 970	*41 610*	Tenuous dusty ring that may extend down to Saturn's surface
C Ring inner edge	74 510	*46 300*	The 270 km (168 mi) wide Maxwell Gap is located at
outer edge	92 030	*57 180*	87 500 km (54 400 mi)
B Ring inner edge	92 030	*57 180*	The eccentric Huygens Gap, which is 285–440 km
outer edge	117 520	*73 020*	(174–273 mi) wide, is located just beyond the edge of B Ring
Cassini Division			This 4650 km (2889 mi) wide gap contains many ringlet features, most notably the Huygens Ringlet, which is located 300 km (186 mi) from the edge of the B Ring. The suggestion that this gap contained two moons now appears to be incorrect
A Ring inner edge	122 170	*75 910*	The 322 km (200 mi) wide Encke Gap, centred at 133 585 km (83 006 mi), contains the satellite Pan.
outer edge	136 780	84 990	The 38 km (24 mi) wide Keeler Gap is located 270 km (168 mi) from the outer edge
F Ring centre	140 460	*87 280*	A multiple stranded eccentric ring varying in width from 30 to 500 km (19–311 mi), shepherded either side by the satellites Prometheus and Pandora
G Ring centre	170 100	*105 700*	This ring optically appears thin, although it is approximately 1000 km (600 mi) wide and possibly up to 1000 km thick
E Ring inner edge	181 000	*112 500*	Diffuse ring with maximum brightness near the orbit of
outer edge	483 000	*300 100*	the satellite Enceladus

Atlas (Number XV) *Discovered*: 1980. *Distance from Saturn*: 137 670 km (85 540 mi). *Diameter*: 37 × 34 × 27 km (23 × 21 × 17 mi), giving an average of 32 km (20 mi). Atlas controls the outer edge of the A Ring.

Prometheus (Number XVI) *Discovered*: 1980. *Distance from Saturn*: 139 380 km (86 610 mi). *Diameter*: 148 × 100 × 68 km (92 × 62 × 42 mi), giving an average of 100 km (62 mi). Prometheus is a highly irregularly shaped satellite, which controls the inner edge of the F Ring.

Pandora (Number XVII) *Discovered*: 1980. *Distance from Saturn*: 141 710 km (88 050 mi). *Diameter*: 110 × 88 × 62 km (68 × 55 × 39 mi), giving an average of 84 km (52 mi). Pandora is a highly irregularly shaped satellite, which – with Prometheus – controls the outer edge of the F Ring.

Epimetheus (Number XI) *Discovered*: 1980 (preliminary identification 1977). *Distance from Saturn*: 151 410 km (94 110 mi) – see below. *Diameter*: 138 × 110 × 110 km (86 × 68 × 68 mi), giving an average of 119 km (74 mi). Epimetheus is a highly irregularly shaped satellite with very low density. It may be made totally of porous water ice. Epimetheus interchanges orbit with Janus every four years with an average orbit for the two satellites of 151 450 km (94 110 mi).

Janus (Number X) *Discovered*: 1980 (preliminary identification 1966). *Distance from Saturn*: 151 460 km (94 110 mi) – see also Epimetheus, above. *Diameter*: 196 × 191 × 153 km (122 × 119 × 95 mi), giving an average of 179 km (111 mi). Janus is a highly irregularly shaped satellite with a very low density. It interchanges orbit with Epimetheus – see above.

Mimas (Number I) *Discovered*: 1789. *Distance from Saturn*: 185 530 km (115 280 mi). *Diameter*: 418 × 392 × 383 km (260 × 244 × 238 mi), giving an average of 398 km (247 mi). The surface features of Mimas are dominated by the 130 km (81 mi) diameter crater Herschel, with walls 5 km (3 mi) high and a central peak rising 6 km (4 mi) from the crater floor.

Enceladus (Number II) *Discovered*: 1789. *Distance from Saturn*: 238 030 km (147 900 mi). *Diameter*: 513 × 495 × 489 km (319 × 308 × 304 mi), giving an average of 499 km (310 mi). Enceladus is characterized by an extremely bright surface that reflects back all of the light it receives.

Tethys (Number III) *Discovered*: 1684. *Distance from Saturn*: 294 670 km (183 100 mi). *Diameter*: 1071 × 1056 × 1052 km (665 × 656 × 654 mi), giving an average of 1060 km (659 mi). Tethys is a large moon with an icy cratered surface, which is dominated by the 400 km (250 mi) diameter crater Odysseus and the huge valley Ithaca Chasma, which stretches at least two-thirds of the way around the satellite's circumference.

Telesto (Number XIII) *Discovered*: 1980. *Distance from Saturn*: 294 670 km (183 100 mi). *Diameter*: 30 × 25 × 15 km (19 × 16 × 9 mi), giving an average of 22 km (14 mi). Telesto – a highly irregularly shaped satellite – is trapped in the orbit of Tethys at a null gravity (Lagrangian) point in the Tethys-Saturn-Sun system.

Calypso (Number XIV) *Discovered*: 1980. *Distance from Saturn*: 294 670 km (183 100 mi). *Diameter*: 30 × 16 × 16 km (19 × 10 × 10 mi), giving an average of 19 km (12 mi). Like Telesto, Calypso is trapped at a Lagrangian point in the orbit of Tethys.

Dione (Number IV) *Discovered*: 1684. *Distance from Saturn*: 377 410 km (234 510 mi). *Diameter*: 1120 km (696 mi). Dione is a large icy satellite whose surface is pockmarked with craters, the largest of which – Aeneas – is 160 km (100 mi) in diameter.

Helene (Number XII) *Discovered*: 1980. *Distance from Saturn*: 377 410 km (234 510 mi). *Diameter*: 32 km (20 mi), but Helene is probably irregularly shaped. Helene accompanies Dione because it is trapped in a Lagrangian point in Dione's orbit (see above).

Rhea (Number V) *Discovered*: 1672. *Distance from Saturn*: 527 070 km (327 510 mi). *Diameter*: 1528 km (949 mi). Rhea is a large icy satellite, which is heavily cratered. Izanagi – the main crater – is 300 km (186 mi) in diameter.

Titan (Number VI) *Discovered*: 1655. *Distance from Saturn*: 1 221 860 km (759 230 mi). *Diameter*: 5150 km (3200 mi). After Ganymede, Titan is the second largest satellite in the solar system and is the only one to have an extensive atmosphere, which comprises mainly nitrogen with small amounts of methane and argon. The surface pressure is one and a half times that of Earth, but the surface is obscured from view by an orange haze that is the result of the formation of complex organic molecules in the upper atmosphere.

Hyperion (Number VII) *Discovered*: 1848. *Distance from Saturn*: 1 481 090 km (920 310 mi). *Diameter*: 360 × 280 × 225 km (224 × 174 × 140 mi), giving an average of 283 km (176 mi). Hyperion – a highly irregularly shaped satellite – is spinning chaotically with no fixed rotation period. It is possibly the remnant of a larger satellite (known as proto-Hyperion) that was struck by a stray comet.

Iapetus (Number VIII) *Discovered*: 1671. *Distance from Saturn*: 3 561 670 km (2 213 120 mi). *Diameter*: 1436 km (892 mi). Iapetus is a bright cratered icy satellite. About 40% of its surface – Cassini Regio – is covered by very dark dust, possibly the result of debris flung into Iapetus' orbit when proto-Hyperion (see above) was struck by a comet. The result is that one hemisphere of Iapetus reflects light efficiently while the other hemisphere appears dull.

Phoebe (Number IX) *Discovered*: 1898. *Distance from Saturn*: 12 954 000 km (8 049 000 mi). *Diameter*: 230 × 220 × 210 km (143 × 137 × 130 mi), giving an average of 220 mi (137 mi). Phoebe is a small dark remote satellite spining in 9.282 hours in a retrograde orbit (opposite to the sense of rotation of Saturn). Its surface composition appears to be identical to that of the most common type of asteroid and it is possible that Phoebe may be a captured asteroid.

URANUS

When the sky is very dark and very clear, Uranus can just be seen with the naked eye. The planet was discovered by William Herschel (1732–1822) in March 1781. Herschel was making a routine survey of the sky when he came across an object that did not look like a star. At first he thought he had found a comet, but subsequent calculation of the orbit showed it to be in remarkable agreement with the Titus-Bode Rule for planetary distances (see p. 17). The Uranian system was explored by the *Voyager 2* space probe in 1986. This led to the discovery of ten new moons and two new rings.

Because of its smaller size and higher density, the internal structure of Uranus may be different to that of Jupiter and Saturn. Models for Uranus suggest that the planet possesses a similar central rocky core, although it is surrounded by a 'sea' of water, methane and ammonia. The planet has an outer hydrogen atmosphere containing about 26% helium and a smaller amount of methane. (Methane gives Uranus its greenish colour.)

Unlike the other giant planets, Uranus does not radiate more heat than it receives from the Sun. (This may be because its various internal layers form a stable stratification.) The lack of energy radiation may also explain the bland appearance of the planet, which displays little evidence of clouds.

The large tilt of Uranus (98°) means that day and night on some parts of the planet may last up to 21 years, but the present sunlit 'south' pole – which points towards the Sun – and dark opposite pole show little difference in temperature. This suggests that there is a strong temperature equilibrium within the atmosphere of Uranus. The magnetic axis of Uranus is offset 7000 km (4300 mi) from the centre of the planet and is also inclined at an angle of 59° to the axis of rotation. This difference has been used to suggest that the large tilt of the equator may be due to a catastrophic collision between Uranus and one or more planetesimals early in its history.

THE RINGS OF URANUS

In 1977–78 it was discovered that Uranus had nine narrow rings orbiting the equator. Two further rings – a diffuse ring (1986 U2R) and a narrow ring (1986 U1R or Lambda) – were discovered by the *Voyager 2* imaging team in January 1986. The rings are very dark and probably rich in carbon, and the outermost ring, Epsilon, is shepherded by the satellites Cordelia and Ophelia.

THE RINGS OF URANUS

Feature	Distance from centre	
	km	miles
Uranus radius	25 559	15 882
1986 U2R inner edge	37 000	23 000
1986 U2R outer edge	39 500	24 500
6 centre	41 837	25 996
5 centre	42 235	26 244
4 centre	42 571	26 452
Alpha centre	44 718	27 786
Beta centre	45 661	28 372
Eta centre	47 176	29 314
Gamma centre	47 627	29 594
Delta centre	48 300	30 012
Lambda centre	50 024	31 083
Epsilon centre	51 149	31 783

With the exceptions of the very diffuse 1986 U2R ring and the dominant Epsilon ring, all the other rings are less than 12 km (7 miles) wide. The Epsilon ring width varies between 22 and 93 km (14 and 58 miles) and its orbit has the highest eccentricity at 0·00794.

SATELLITES OF URANUS

The five major satellites identified telescopically from Earth are all composed of water ice overlaying rocky cores. The ten small satellites orbiting inside the orbit of Miranda were discovered by the *Voyager 2* imaging team. They may have been formed by the fragmentation of a larger satellite 3500 million years ago. In 1992, scientists at the University of Colorado, USA, suggested that many additional small moons – 1–10 km (0.6–5.6 mi) in diameter – may orbit Uranus.

Cordelia (Number VI) *Discovered*: 1986. *Distance from Uranus*: 49 750 km (30 910 mi). *Diameter*: 26 km (16 mi). Cordelia and Ophelia act as shepherding satellites for the major ring (epsilon) of Uranus.

Ophelia (Number VII) *Discovered*: 1986. *Distance from Uranus*: 53 760 km (33 410 mi). *Diameter*: 32 km (20 mi). (See Cordelia, above.)

Bianca (Number VIII) *Discovered*: 1986. *Distance from Uranus*: 59 170 km (36 760 mi). *Diameter*: 44 km (27 mi).

Cressida (Number IX) *Discovered*: 1986. *Distance from Uranus*: 61 770 km (38 380 mi). *Diameter*: 66 km (41 mi).

Desdemona (Number X) *Discovered*: 1986. *Distance from Uranus*: 62 660 km (38 930 mi). *Diameter*: 58 km (36 mi).

Juliet (Number XI) *Discovered*: 1986. *Distance from Uranus*: 64 360 km (39 990 mi). *Diameter*: 84 km (52 mi).

Portia (Number XII) *Discovered*: 1986. *Distance from Uranus*: 66 100 km (41 070 mi). *Diameter*: 110 km (68 mi).

Rosalind (Number XIII) *Discovered*: 1986. *Distance from Uranus*: 69 930 km (43 450 mi). *Diameter*: 58 km (36 mi).

Belinda (Number XIV) *Discovered*: 1986. *Distance from Uranus*: 75 260 km (46 760 mi). *Diameter*: 68 km (42 mi).

Puck (Number XV) *Discovered*: 1985. *Distance from Uranus*: 86 000 km (53 440 mi). *Diameter*: 154 km (96 mi).

Miranda (Number V) *Discovered*: 1948. *Distance from Uranus*: 129 850 km (80 680 mi). *Diameter*: 481 × 468 × 466 km (299 × 291 × 290 mi), giving an average of 472 km (293 mi). Miranda – the smallest of the five outer satellites that are identifiable from Earth – has a most bizarre surface structure that is thought to be the result of being disrupted and reformed several times during its existence.

Ariel (Number I) *Discovered*: 1851. *Distance from Uranus*: 190 930 km (118 640 mi). *Diameter*: 1162 × 1156 × 1155 km (722 × 718 × 718 mi), giving an average of 1158 km (720 mi). The long grooves that cover the surface of Ariel may have resulted from the satellite being disrupted and reformed at least once.

Umbriel (Number II) *Discovered*: 1851. *Distance from Uranus*: 265 980 km (165 270 mi). *Diameter*: 1169 km (727 mi). The surface of Umbriel – which is much darker than the other major Uranian satellites – is pockmarked with craters.

Titania (Number III) *Discovered*: 1787. *Distance from Uranus*: 436 280 km (271 090 mi). *Diameter*: 1578 km (980 mi). Titania is densely pockmarked with craters and a few deep chasms, which may have been formed during the final solidification of the surface.

Oberon (Number IV) *Discovered*: 1787. *Distance from Uranus*: 583 430 km (362 530 mi). *Diameter*: 1523 km (946 mi). The main surface feature of Oberon is thought to be a crater several hundred km in diameter, but it was on the far side of the satellite during the *Voyager 2* encounter and only revealed itself as a central mountain peak rising 20 km (12 mi) above the surface of the planet.

NEPTUNE

Neptune is not visible to the naked eye, but can be observed by telecope. It was discovered in September 1846 by the German astronomers Johann Galle

(1812–1910) and Heinrich d'Arrest (1822–75), based on mathematical predictions by calculations by Urbain Le Verrier (1811–77) and John Couch Adams (1819–92). Le Verrier and Adams independently deduced that Uranus was being pulled by the gravity of another 'hidden' planet.

In 1989, the Neptune system was explored by the *Voyager 2* space probe, which led to the discovery of six new moons and confirmed the nature of Neptune's ring system. *Voyager* revealed what is – compared with Uranus – an extremely dynamic world with many discernible cloud features and wind speeds exceeding 2160 km/h (1340 mph) in the case of the equatorial easterlies and 1080 km/h (670 mph) in the case of the polar westerlies. A notable atmospheric feature is the 'Great Dark Spot', which is the smaller equivalent of the 'Great Red Spot' on Jupiter but still a larger feature than the planet Earth. This swirling storm rolls in a counterclockwise direction around the planet in 16 days.

Neptune owes its turbulent nature to the fact that the planet radiates back into space 161% more heat than it receives from the Sun. The reason for this amount of radiation is not known as the internal structure of Neptune is thought likely to be similar to that of docile Uranus. However, there may be some significance in the fact that the outer hydrogen atmosphere of Neptune contains more helium – 32% – than that of any of the other gas planets. Small amounts of methane in the atmosphere give Neptune its bluish appearance when observed from a distance.

Like Uranus, Neptune has a magnetic axis that is displaced from the axis of rotation – it is offset by 13 600 km (8500 mi) from the centre – that is, over one half of the planet's radius – and tilted at an angle of 47°. It is thought that this large difference may be the result of catastrophic events during the formation of the planet.

THE RINGS OF NEPTUNE

Although partial evidence for the existence of rings around Neptune was obtained prior to the *Voyager* observations, it was not until the space probe passed the planet that it was established that there are three distinct complete rings and a diffuse ring of material between 38 000 km (23 600 mi) and 59 000 km (36 700 mi) from the centre of the planet.

Galle Ring is a broad dusty ring about 1700 km (1060 mi) wide, centred at 41 900 km (26 000 mi) from the planet.

Leverrier Ring is a narrow dusty ring, 30 km (19 mi) wide, centred at 53 200 km (33 060 mi) from the planet.

Adams Ring is a narrow ring, 15 km (9 mi) wide, centred at 62 930 km (39 100 mi). The ring contains three dusty arcs – Liberté, Egalité and Fraternité – whose movements are controlled by the nearby satellite Galatea.

SATELLITES OF NEPTUNE

In 1989, the *Voyager 2* imaging team reported the discovery of six new satellites in addition to the two already known, but almost certainly one of these, Larissa, was detected in 1981. The five innermost satellites of Neptune are either close to or inside the *Roche Limit* of Neptune – the point at which the gravitational force of the planet should totally destroy such moons. It is thought that these inner moons may represent the break-up of larger bodies in the past. In 1992, scientists at the University of Colorado, USA, suggested that many additional small moons – 1–10 km (0.6–5.6 mi) in diameter – may orbit Neptune.

Naiad (Number III) *Discovered*: 1989. *Distance from Neptune*: 48 230 km (29 970 mi). *Diameter*: 58 km (36 mi).

Thalassa (Number IV) *Discovered*: 1989. *Distance from Neptune*: 50 070 km (31 110 mi). *Diameter*: 80 km (50 mi).

Despina (Number V) *Discovered*: 1989. *Distance from Neptune*: 52 530 km (32 640 mi). *Diameter*: 148 km (92 mi).

Galatea (Number VI) *Discovered*: 1989. *Distance from Neptune*: 61 950 km (38 490 mi). *Diameter*: 158 km (98 mi). Galatea controls the dust arcs in the Adams Ring.

Larissa (Number VII) *Discovered*: 1989 (probable preliminary identification 1981) *Distance from Neptune*: 73 550 km (45 700 mi). *Diameter*: 208 × 192 × 178 km (129 × 119 × 111 mi), giving an average of 192 km (119 mi).

Proteus (Number VIII) *Discovered*: 1989. *Distance from Neptune*: 117 650 km (73 100 mi). *Diameter*: 436 × 416 × 402 km (271 × 258 × 250 mi), giving an average of 416 km (258 mi). The most prominent feature on Proteus is the impact crater Bogle.

Triton (Number I) *Discovered*: 1846. *Distance from Neptune*: 354 760 km (220 440 mi). *Diameter*: 2705 km (1681 mi). The biggest of Neptune's satellites, Triton has a large orbital inclination (157°) and a retrograde orbit – opposite to the direction of rotation of Neptune. This suggests that Triton is a captured satellite that may have wreaked havoc in the early Neptunian system. *Voyager 2* showed the surface to be very colourful, with a 150–200 km (90–120 mi) thick water ice crust overlain by a brilliant coating of a mixture of nitrogen and methane ices. The slightly darkened reddish colour of the surface may be due to contamination with organic polymer materials. Triton's surface ices are at a temperature of $-235\,°C$ ($-391\,°F$), which is the coldest measured surface in the solar system. The surface has a strange mottled appearance known as a *cantaloupe* terrain because of its ressemblance to the fruit. Triton has a large bright polar cap in which vents or geysers eject nitrogen and dust 8 km (5 mi) up into the satellite's thin atmosphere.

Nereid (Number II) *Discovered*: 1948. *Distance from Neptune*: 5 513 410 km (3 425 870 mi). Diameter: 340 km (211 mi). The large eccentricity of its orbit suggests that this satellite may have been captured by Neptune's gravitational field.

PLUTO

The discovery of the outermost planet by Clyde Tombaugh (1906–) was announced on 13 March 1930, but little was known about the planet until after the discovery of its moon Charon on 22 June 1978.

The planet has a diameter only two-thirds of our own Moon and is a little over twice the size of the minor planet Ceres. Pluto appears to be the twin of Neptune's moon Triton, with a similar density and a similar surface covering consisting of a mixture of nitrogen and methane ices (together with carbon monoxide). The planet's thin atmosphere is probably predominantly nitrogen with small amounts of methane and carbon monoxide. Its surface temperature must be at least as low as that on Triton, $-235\,°C$ ($-391\,°F$).

A model of the interior of Pluto suggests a core of partially hydrated rock, surrounded by a water ice layer up to 320 km (200 mi) thick and an outer layer 10 km (6 mi) thick consisting mainly of methane ice. The orbit of Pluto is so eccentric that at perihelion it is closer to the Sun than Neptune is. This situation exists between 23 January 1979 and 15 March 1999. The two planets are locked in a resonance that prevents them from coming together.

1992 QB₁ Pluto may have lost its status as the outermost known body in the solar system on 14 September 1992 when the discovery of a 200 km (120 mi) diameter asteroid or comet – its status is still unknown – was announced. It was given the temporary designation 1992 QB₁. The mean distance of 1992 QB₁ from the Sun is greater than that of Pluto and could be as large as 8800 million km (5400 million mi).

SATELLITE OF PLUTO

Charon (Number I) *Discovered*: 1978. *Distance from Pluto*: 19 640 km (12 200 mi). *Diameter*: 1186 km (737 mi). Charon is large compared with its parent planet, having 9% of Pluto's mass – compared with the Moon, which has only 1.2% of the Earth's mass. It is in captive rotation with one face of Pluto and one face of Charon always opposite one another. Observations in 1992 indicate that Charon appears to consist mainly of water ice but with a small rocky core.

COMETS

Comets have long been known as apparitions in the sky and they have entered the folklore and literature of many societies. However, their structure is mundane – they consist mainly of a central nucleus that can be regarded as a 'dirty snowball'. On approaching the Sun, the ice in a comet starts to evaporate, producing a coma around the nucleus and a tail or tails behind. The tail is the streaming of ions and dust from the coma – the ions being repelled by sunlight and the dust by the solar wind. Thus, when moving away from the Sun, the tail of the comet leads.

Comets either orbit within the solar system or adopt parabolic orbits that sweep them outside the system. The source of comets is unknown. Jan Oort (1900–) suggested that there is a reservoir or 'cloud' of comets in the outer solar system as a residue from the original accretion disc from which the solar system was formed. A recent study suggests that there is an outer 'Oort Cloud', which has been described as a 'halo' of comets, orbiting between 20 000 and 50 000 astronomical units from the Sun. A denser inner concentration of comets, between 3000 and 20 000 astronomical units, is thought to contain about a million million (10^{12}) comets. It is suggested that periodic perturbations by giant interstellar molecular clouds, or close encounters with other stars, triggers the release of the comets into the inner solar system.

Halley's comet is the most famous and was named after Edmond Halley (1656–1742), who correctly predicted its return in 1758, 16 years after his death. In 1986 the space probe *Giotto* photographed the comet's nucleus and showed it to be an elongated, blackened iceball about 15 km (9 mi) long and 8 km (5 mi) in cross-section. Most comets are in very eccentric orbits with periods of several hundred years. Several new comets are discovered every year. The brightest comets tend to be those with very long periods and it is therefore impossible to predict when the next bright comet will appear.

MOONS

By the end of 1992, 61 satellites (moons) had been discovered in the solar system, orbiting the following planets: Earth (1), Mars (2), Jupiter (16), Saturn (18), Uranus (15), Neptune (8), and Pluto (1).

The average diameters of the largest moons are:

Moon	km	mi
1. Ganymede (Jupiter III)	5268	3273
2. Titan (Saturn VI)	5150	3200
3. Callisto (Jupiter IV)	4806	2986
4. Io (Jupiter I)	3643	2264
5. The Moon (Earth I)	3475	2159
6. Europa (Jupiter II)	3130	1945
7. Triton (Neptune I)	2705	1681
8. Titania (Uranus III)	1578	981
9. Rhea (Saturn V)	1528	949
10. Oberon (Uranus IV)	1523	946
11. Iapetus (Saturn VIII)	1436	892
12. Charon (Pluto I)	1186	737
13. Umbriel (Uranus II)	1169	727
14. Ariel (Uranus I)	1158	720
15. Dione (Saturn IV)	1120	696
16. Tethys (Saturn III)	1060	659

MILESTONES IN ASTRONOMY

1223 BC
The oldest known record of a total solar eclipse, found on a clay tablet in the ruins of Ugarit (Syria).

1059 BC
Possible sighting of Halley's comet by Chinese astronomers.

585 BC
Thales of Miletus correctly predicted the occurrence of a solar eclipse.

c. 500 BC
Pythagoras realized that the bright morning star and the bright evening star were the same body – Venus (originally named Aphrodite).

c. 440 BC
Philolaus suggested that the Earth is not the centre of the universe and that the Earth, Sun, Moon and the planets revolve around a central 'fire'. Meton of Athens correctly determined that the Sun and the Moon return to the same relative places in the sky every 19 years.

c. 350 BC
Chinese observers recorded the earliest known reference to a supernova. Aristotle surmised that the Earth is not flat. Eudoxus drew the first star map with a grid system for reference (longitude and latitude).

c. 300 BC
Chinese astronomers compiled star maps that were in use for several centuries.

c. 280 BC
Aristarchus asserted that the solar system is Sun-centred and estimated the distance to and the size of the Sun.

c. 240 BC
Eratosthenes of Cyrene calculated the circumference of the Earth from the angle of the Sun at Alexandria and Syene (Aswan), Egypt.

c. 150 BC
Hipparchus produced an accurate map of 1000 stars and divided them into classes of brightness.

130 BC
Hipparchus used a solar total eclipse and parallax to calculate the distance to and size of the Moon.

AD 140
Ptolemy assumed that the universe was Earth-centred. His mathematical model for the movements of the planets was in use for 14 centuries.

1054
Chinese astronomers observed a new very bright star in the constellation Taurus, the remnants of which are now observed as the Crab Nebula.

1252
The commencement of a 32-year task to produce a new set of planetary tables – the Alphonsine Tables – to replace those of Ptolemy.

1304
The artist Giotto painted the first realistic depiction of a comet.

1472
Johann Müller made the first accurate observations of the path of a comet across the sky.

1543
Copernicus established that the solar system is Sun-centred and not Earth-centred. This is usually considered to have been the beginning of modern astronomy.

1596
Tycho Brahe published his 'pre-telescope' star catalogue, the result of 20 years' observations.

1608
The invention of the telescope by Hans Lippershey in the Netherlands.

1609
Johannes Kepler published his first two laws of planetary motion – the third was published in 1619.

1610
Galileo Galilei and Simon Marius independently discovered the major moons of Jupiter using the newly invented telescope.

1631
The first observation of a transit of Mercury across the Sun by Gassendi. (The first observation of a transit of Venus was made eight years later by Horrocks and Crabtree.)

1638
The first identification of a variable star (Mira Ceti) by P. Holwarda.

1655
Christiaan Huygens discovered Titan, the major moon of Saturn, and correctly described Saturn's ring system.

1668
The first reflector telescope was built by Isaac Newton. (The principles of reflecting telescopes had been published five years earlier by James Gregory.)

1675
By observations of the Jupiter moon, Io, Ole Romer proved that light must have a definite velocity.

1687
The publication of Newton's mathematical theories of celestial mechanics. These explained the orbital motions of the planets and why the solar system is Sun-centred.

1705
Edmond Halley accurately predicted the return of Halley's comet in 1758.

1728
The discovery of the aberration of light by James Bradley.

1781
William Herschel discovered the planet Uranus. (He discovered the first four satellites of its moon system six years later.)

1801
Giuseppe Piazzi discovered the first and largest of the minor planets, Ceres.

1838
The first measurement of the distance of a star (61 Cygni) by Friedrich Bessel.

1846
Johann Galle discovered Neptune, working on the mathematical predictions of Urbain Le Verrier and John Couch Adams. The major Neptune moon, Triton, was discovered in the same year by William Lassel.

1862
The construction of the first great refractor telescopes.

1868
The discovery in the Sun's spectra independently by Norman Lockyer and Pierre Janssen of an element that had not been previously identified on Earth (helium).

1872
Henry Draper took the first photograph of the spectrum of a star (Vega).

1877
Asaph Hall discovered the two moons of Mars.

1897
A refracting telescope, 102 cm (40 in) in diameter, was built at the Yerkes Observatory, USA.

1915
Walter S. Adams' study of the binary companion to Sirius, Sirius B, led to the identification of white dwarf stars.

1919
Jean Perrin suggested that the Sun's energy could arise from the conversion of hydrogen into helium.

1923
Eleven years after his initial discovery, Vesto Slipher published his findings that most galaxies have their spectra shifted towards the red end of the spectrum (red-shifted) – a condition that was a requirement of an expanding universe.

1927
Abbé Georges Lemaître (and, independently, A. Friedmann) formulated the 'big bang' concept to try to explain the beginning of the universe.

1929
Edwin Hubble's measurement of the distances of nearby galaxies led to an understanding of the relationship between distance and red shift.

1930
Clyde Tombaugh discovered the outermost planet, Pluto, by systematic photography.

1932
The first detection of extra-terrestrial radio signals (from the Sagittarius constellation) by Karl Jansky.

1937
The first radio telescope was built in the USA.

1948
The completion of the 508 cm (200 in) Hale reflecting telescope at the Mount Palomar Observatory, USA.

1957
Eleanor and Geoffrey Burbidge, William A. Fowler, and Fred Hoyle introduced nucleocosmochronology as an independent method of estimating the age of the universe.

1961
Using radar, several separate research teams accurately determined the value of the astronomical unit.

1962
The existence of quasi-stellar radio sources or 'quasars' was established by Maarten Schmidt.

1964
The establishment by radar that the rotation period of Venus is very long (243 days) and retrograde.

1965
G.H. Pettengill and R.B. Dyce established that the rotation period of Mercury is exactly equal to two-thirds of its orbital period. Detection of the 3 K background radiation by Arno Penzias and Robert Wilson – considered as proof that the universe was once very hot.

1967
The detection of the pulsating radio source or 'pulsar' CP 1919 by Jocelyn Bell – considered as proof of the existence of neutron stars.

1973
First close-up views of Jupiter obtained by the *Pioneer 10* spacecraft.

1974
The first details of the surface features of Mercury were obtained from *Mariner 10* spacecraft.

1976
The world's largest reflecting telescope, 600 cm (236 in) in diameter, was completed at Mount Semirodriki, Caucasus, Russia.

1977
The discovery of the rings of Uranus. C. Kowal discovered the most distant asteroid, Chiron, orbiting between Saturn and Uranus.

1978
James W. Christy discovered Pluto's moon, Charon.

1979
Alan Guth proposed the 'inflationary' theory to explain the initial formation of the universe. The first visit to Saturn by a spacecraft, *Pioneer 11*.

1981
The *Voyager 1* and *2* observations of Saturn led to the discovery of 'shepherding' satellites that control the width of the F ring.

1983
The launch of IRAS – Infrared Astronomical Satellite – which gathers enormous amounts of data on the solar system and the universe as a whole.

1986
Voyager 2 discovered ten Uranian moons. Five space probes observed Halley's comet at close quarters.

1987
I. Shelton observed the nearest supernova for nearly four centuries (in the Large Magellanic Cloud).

1989
Voyager 2 encountered the Neptunian system and discovered six new moons.

1990
The Hubble Space Telescope was launched. *Magellan* began radar mapping of the planet Venus.

1992
Satellite *COBE* observed evidence for the beginning of galaxies. The first observation of an object in the solar system beyond the outermost planet, Pluto – see 1992 QB$_1$, p.27.

SPACE TRAVEL

1926 American scientist Robert Goddard fired the world's first liquid propellant rocket from Auburn, Massachusetts. It travelled 56 m (184 ft).

1931 Europe's first liquid fuelled rocket was fired by Joannes Winkler from Dessau, Germany.

1933 The first Soviet liquid propellant rocket, GIRD X, was fired to an altitude of 487 m (1598 ft).

1942 First successful launch of the German A-4, later called the V2, from Peenemünde, Germany. It travelled at 193 km (120 mi) and reached an altitude of 85 km (53 mi).

1945 Germany began test flights on its intercontinental ballistic missile prototype, A-10. It reached an altitude of 80 km (50 mi).

The US WAC Corporal flew 69 km (43 mi) from White Sands, New Mexico.

1946 First flight of the US-assembled V2, launched from White Sands, New Mexico. Mission 9 reached 161 km (100 mi) later that year.

1949 The US Bumper WAC, a two stage rocket comprising V2 and Corporal, reached space. The rocket launched from White Sands, New Mexico attained 393 km (244 mi) altitude.

Single-stage Russian rocket reached 109 km (68 mi) altitude.

First Viking research rocket launched from White Sands, New Mexico.

1950 Bumper 8 made the first launch from Cape Canaveral, Florida.

1954 Viking II reached an altitude of 254 km (158 mi)

USSR announced rocket flights of 386 km (240 mi).

1955 USA and USSR both announced plans to launch International Geophysical Year satellite.

1956 US Jupiter C reached 1094 km (680 mi) altitude.

1957 US Jupiter A reached 2414 km (1500 mi) altitude.

The nosecone from Jupiter C, flown 1931 km (1200 mi) down range from Cape Canaveral, Florida, is recovered in the Atlantic.

USSR launched first intercontinental ballistic missile which was later used to launch Sputnik 1, the first artificial Earth satellite.

SPACEFLIGHT

MANNED SPACEFLIGHTS (to 3 February 1993)

1 Vostok 1 (USSR 1)
12 Apr 1961
Yuri Gagarin
1 hr 48 min
Landed separately from craft.

2 Freedom 7 (USA 1)
5 May 1961
Alan Shepard
15 min 28 sec
Suborbital; splashdown.

3 Liberty Bell 7
(USA 2) 21 Jul 1961
Gus Grissom
15 min 37 sec
Spacecraft sank.

4 Vostok 2 (USSR 2)
6 Aug 1961
Gherman Titov
1 day 1 hr 18 min
At 25, youngest person ever in space.

5 Friendship 7
(USA 3) 20 Feb 1962
John Glenn
4 hr 55 min 23 sec
First American to orbit.

6 Aurora 7 (USA 4)
24 May 1962
Scott Carpenter
4 hr 56 min 5 sec
Landing overshoot of 250 miles.

7 Vostok 3 (USSR 3)
11 Aug 1962
Andrian Nikolyev
3 day 22 hr 22 min

8 Vostok 4 (USSR 4)
12 Aug 1962
Pavel Popovich
2 day 22 hr 56 min 57 sec
Came to within 6·4 km
(*4 miles*) of Vostok 3.

9 Sigma 7 (USA 5)
3 Oct 1962
Wally Schirra
9 hr 13 min 11 sec
Pacific splashdown.

10 Faith 7 (USA 6)
15 May 1963
Gordon Cooper
1 day 10 hr 19 min 49 sec
Final US one-man flight.

11 Vostok 5 (USSR 5)
14 Jun 1963
Valeri Bykovsky
4 day 23 hr 6 min
Solo flight record-holder.

12 Vostok 6 USSR 6
16 Jun 1963
Valentina Tereshkova
2 day 22 hr 50 min
First woman in space.

13 Voskhod 1 (USSR 7)
12 Oct 1964
Vladimir Komarov,
Konstantin Feoktistov,
Boris Yegerov
1 day 0 hr 17 min 3 sec
Riskiest flight, no spacesuits, no ejection seats, inside a 'Vostok'.

14 Voskhod 2 (USSR 8)
18 Mar 1965
Pavel Belyayev,
Alexei Leonov
1 day 2 hr 2 min 17 sec
Leonov makes first walk in space.

15 Gemini 3 (USA 7)
25 Mar 1965
Gus Grissom,
John Young
4 hr 52 min 51 sec
Grissom first man in space twice.

16 Gemini 4 (USA 8)
3 Jun 1965
James McDivitt,
Edward White
4 day 1 hr 56 min 12 sec
White walks in space.

17 Gemini 5 (USA 9)
21 Aug 1965
Gordon Cooper,
Charles Conrad
7 day 22 hr 55 min 14 sec
Breaks endurance record.

18 Gemini 7 (USA 10)
4 Dec 1965
Frank Borman,
James Lovell
13 day 18 hr 35 min 1 sec
Acted as rendezvous target; breaks endurance record.

19 Gemini 6 (USA 11)
15 Dec 1965
Wally Schirra,
Tom Stafford
1 day 1 hr 51 min 54 sec
First rendezvous in space.

20 Gemini 8 (USA 12)
16 Mar 1966
Neil Armstrong,
David Scott
10 hr 41 min 26 sec
Emergency landing after first space docking.

21 Gemini 9 (USA 13)
3 Jun 1966
Tom Stafford,
Eugene Cernan
3 day 20 min 50 sec
Rendezvous; spacewalk; bull's-eye splashdown.

22 Gemini 10 (USA 14)
18 Jul 1966
John Young,
Michael Collins
2 day 22 hr 46 min 39 sec
Docking; spacewalk; record altitude of 763 km (*474 miles*).

23 Gemini 11 (USA 15)
12 Sept 1966
Charles Conrad,
Richard Gordon
2 day 23 hr 17 min 8 sec
Docking; spacewalk;
altitude of 1368 km
(*850 miles*); automatic
landing.

24 Gemini 12 (USA 16)
11 Nov 1966
James Lovell,
Edwin Aldrin
3 day 22 hr 34 min 31 sec
Docking; record
spacewalk of over 2 hr.

Apollo 1 (USA)
27 Jan 1967
Gus Grissom, Edward
White, Roger Chaffee
Killed in spacecraft fire.

25 Soyuz 1 (USSR 9)
23 Apr 1967
Vladimir Komarov
1 day 2 hr 47 min 52 sec
Komarov killed when
parachute fails; intend-
ed to dock with Soyuz 2.

Soyuz 2 (USSR)
24 Apr 1967
Valeri Bykovsky, Alexei
Yeliseyev, Yevgeny
Khrunov
Flight cancelled; was to
have docked with Soyuz
1.

26 Apollo 7 (USA 17)
11 Oct 1968
Wally Schirra,
Donn Eisele,
Walt Cunningham
10 day 20 hr 9 min 3 sec
Earth orbit shakedown
of Command and Ser-
vice Module.

27 Soyuz 3 (USSR 10)
26 Oct 1968
Georgi Beregovoi
3 day 22 hr 50 min 45 sec
Failed to dock with
unmanned Soyuz 2.

USSR
Dec 1968
Zond Pavel Belyayev
Circumlunar flight
cancelled.

28 Apollo 8 (USA 18)
21 Dec 1968
Frank Borman, James
Lovell, William Anders
6 day 3 hr 42 sec
Ten lunar orbits over
Christmas.

29 Soyuz 4 (USSR 11)
14 Jan 1969
Vladimir Shatalov
2 day 23 hr 20 min 47 sec
Launched with one
man, returned with
three.

30 Soyuz 5 (USSR 12)
15 Jan 1969
Boris Volynov,
Alexei Yeleseyev,
Yevgeny Khrunov
3 day 0 hr 54 min 15 sec
Yeliseyev and Khrunov
spacewalk to Soyuz 4
after docking.

31 Apollo 9 (USA 19)
3 Mar 1969
James McDivitt,
David Scott,
Russell Schweickart
10 day 1 hr 54 sec
Test of Lunar Module
in Earth orbit;
spacewalk.

32 Apollo 10 (USA 20)
18 May 1969
Tom Stafford, John
Young, Eugene Cernan
8 day 3 min 23 sec
Lunar Module tested in
lunar orbit; came to 14·5
km (*9 miles*) of surface of
Moon.

33 Apollo 11 (USA 21)
17 Jul 1969
Neil Armstrong,
Michael Collins,
Edwin Aldrin
8 day 3 hr 18 min 35 sec
Armstrong and Aldrin
walk on Moon for over
2 hours.

34 Soyuz 6 (USSR 13)
11 Oct 1969
Georgi Shonin,
Valeri Kubasov
4 day 22 hr 42 min 47 sec
Welding tests.

35 Soyuz 7 (USSR 14)
12 Oct 1969
Anatoli Filipchenko,
Vladislav Volkov,
Viktor Gorbatko
4 day 22 hr 40 min 23 sec
Rendezvous to within
488 m (*1600 ft*) of Soyuz 8.

36 Soyuz 8 (USSR 15)
13 Oct 1969
Vladimir Shatalov,
Alexei Yeliseyev
4 day 22 hr 51 min 49 sec
Third flight in strange
troika mission by
Soviets.

37 Apollo 12 (USA 22)
14 Nov 1969
Charles Conrad,
Richard Gordon,
Alan Bean
10 day 4 hr 36 min 25 sec
Pinpoint landing near
Surveyor.

38 Apollo 13 (USA 23)
11 Apr 1970
James Lovell, Jack
Swigert, Fred Haise
5 day 22 hr 54 min 41 sec
Service module
exploded 55 hours into
mission; crew limped
home using Lunar
Module as lifeboat.

39 Soyuz 9 (USSR 16)
1 Jun 1970
Andiran Nikolyev,
Vitali Sevastyanov
17 day 16 hr 58 min 50 sec
Crew carried from craft
on stretchers suffering
acute stress of readap-
ting to gravity after
longest flight.

40 Apollo 14 (USA 24)
31 Jan 1971
Alan Shepard, Stuart
Roosa, Edgar Mitchell
9 day 2 min 57 sec
Shepard only Mercury
astronaut to walk on
Moon.

41 Soyuz 10 (USSR 17)
23 Apr 1971
Vladimir Shatalov,
Alexei Yeliseyev,
Nikolai Ruckavish-
nikov
1 day 23 hr 45 min 54 sec
Failed to enter Salyut 1
space station after soft
docking.

42 Soyuz 11 (USSR 18)
6 Jun 1971
Georgi Dobrovolsky,
Vladislav Volkov,
Viktor Patsayev
23 day 18 hr 21 min 43 sec
Crew died as craft
depressurized before
re-entry; not wearing
spacesuits.

43 Apollo 15 (USA 25)
26 Jul 1971
David Scott, Alfred
Worden, James Irwin
12 day 7 hr 11 min 53 sec
First lunar rover.

44 Apollo 16 (USA 26)
16 Apr 1972
John Young, Ken Mat-
tingly, Charles Duke

11 day 1 hr 51 min 5 sec
Space Shuttle approved
during mission; Mat-
tingly in lunar orbit
makes longest solo US
flight.

45 Apollo 17 (USA 27)
7 Dec 1972
Eugene Cernan, Ron
Evans, Jack Schmitt
12 day 13 hr 51 min 59 sec
Last manned expedition
to Moon this century.

46 Skylab 2 (USA 28)
25 May 1973
Charles Conrad, Joe
Kerwin, Paul Weitz
28 day 49 min 49 sec
Spacewalk to repair
severely disabled
Skylab 1 space station.

47 Skylab 3 (USA 29)
28 Jul 1973
Alan Bean, Owen Gar-
riott, Jack Lousma
59 day 11 hr 9 min 4 sec
Stranded in space tem-
porarily as Command
Module malfunctions.

48 Soyuz 12 (USSR 19)
27 Sept 1973
Vasili Lazarev,
Oleg Makarov
1 day 23 hr 15 min 32 sec
Test of space-station
ferry.

49 Skylab 4 (USA 30)
16 Nov 1973
Gerry Carr, Edward
Gibson, Bill Pogue
84 day 1 hr 15 min
31 sec
Longest US manned
spaceflight.

50 Soyuz 13 (USSR 20)
18 Dec 1973
Pyotr Klimuk,
Valetin Lebedev
7 day 20 hr 55 min
35 sec
Soviets and Ameri-
cans in space together
for first time, although
they don't meet.

51 Soyuz 14 (USSR 21)
3 Jul 1974
Pavel Popvich,
Yuri Artyukhin
15 day 17 hr 30 min
28 sec
First space spies, on
Salyut 3.

52 Soyuz 15 (USSR 22)
26 Aug 1974
Gennadi Serafanov,

Lev Demin
2 day 0 hr 12 min
11 sec
Failed to dock with
Salyut 3.

53 Soyuz 16 (USSR 23)
2 Dec 1974
Anatoli Filipchenko,
Nikolai Ruckavish-
nikov
5 day 22 hr 23 min
35 sec
Rehearsal for US–
USSR joint flight,
ASTP.

54 Soyuz 17 (USSR 24)
11 Jan 1975
Alexei Gubarev,
Georgi Grechko
29 day 13 hr 19 min
45 sec
Aboard Salyut 4.

55 Soyuz 18-1 (USSR 25)
5 Apr 1975
Vasili Lazarev,
Oleg Makarov
21 min 27 sec
Second stage failed;
flight aborted.

56 Soyuz 18 (USSR 26)
24 May 1975
Pyotr Klimuk,
Vitali Sevastyanov
62 day 23 hr 20 min 8 sec
Aboard Salyut 4.

57 Soyuz 19 (USSR 27)
15 Jul 1975
Alexei Leonov,
Valeri Kubasov
5 day 22 hr 30 min
51 sec
Docked with Apollo 18
in joint ASTP mission.

58 Apollo 18 (USA 31)
15 Jul 1975
Tom Stafford, Vance
Brand, Deke Slayton
9 day 1 hr 28 min
24 sec
Docked with Soyuz 19;
crew gassed during
landing, recovered.

59 Soyuz 21 (USSR 28)
6 Jul 1976
Boris Volynov,
Vitali Zholobov
49 day 6 hr 23 min
32 sec
Evacuated Salyut 5.
(Soyuz 20 was
unmanned.)

60 Soyuz 22 (USSR 29)
22 Sept 1976
Valeri Bykovsky,
Vladimir Aksyonov

7 day 21 hr 52 min
17 sec
Independent Earth
survey flight.

61 Soyuz 23 (USSR 30)
14 Oct 1976
Vyacheslav Zudov,
Valeri Rozhdestvensky
2 day 0 hr 6 min 35 sec
Failed to dock with
Salyut 5; splashed down
in lake.

62 Soyuz 24 (USSR 31)
7 Feb 1977
Viktor Gorbatko,
Yuri Glazkov
17 day 17 hr 25 min
50 sec
Aboard Salyut 5.

63 Soyuz 25 (USSR 32)
9 Oct 1977
Vladimir Kovalyonok,
Valeri Ryumin
2 day 0 hr 44 min
45 sec
Failed to dock with
Salyut 6.

64 Soyuz 26 (USSR 33)
10 Dec 1977
Yuri Romanenko,
Georgi Grechko
96 day 10 hr 0 min
7 sec
Aboard Salyut 6; broke
endurance record.

65 Soyuz 27 (USSR 34)
10 Jan 1978
Vladimir Dzhanibekov,
Oleg Makarov
5 day 22 hr 58 min
58 sec
Visitors to Salyut 6.

66 Soyuz 28 (USSR 35)
2 Mar 1978
Alexei Gubarev,
Vladimir Remek
7 day 22 hr 16 min
Remek was from
Czechoslovakia, first
non-American, non-
Soviet in space; visit
to Salyut 6.

67 Soyuz 29 (USSR 36)
15 Jun 1978
Vladimir Kovalyonok,
Alexander Ivanchenkov
139 day 14 hr 47 min
32 sec
Aboard Salyut 6; landed
in Soyuz 31.

68 Soyuz 30 (USSR 37)
27 Jun 1978
Pyotr Klimuk,
Miroslaw Hermas-
zewski

7 day 22 hr 2 min
59 sec
Visit to Salyut 6; Her-
maszewski from Poland.

69 Soyuz 31 (USSR 38)
26 Aug 1978
Valeri Bykovsky,
Sigmund Jahn
7 day 29 hr 49 min 4 sec
Visit to Salyut 6; Jahn
from East Germany;
landed in Soyuz 29.

70 Soyuz 32 (USSR 39)
25 Feb 1979
Vladimir Lyakhov,
Valeri Ryumin
175 day 0 hr 35 min
37 sec
Visit to Salyut 6; landed
in Soyuz 34, which was
launched unmanned.

71 Soyuz 33 (USSR 40)
10 Apr 1979
Nikolai Ruckavish-
nikov,
Georgi Ivanov
1 day 23 hr 1 min 6 sec
Failed to dock with
Salyut 6; Bulgarian
Ivanov only Inter-
cosmos visitor not to
reach space station.

72 Soyuz 35 (USSR 41)
9 Apr 1980
Leonid Popov,
Valeri Ryumin
184 day 20 hr 11 min
35 sec
Salyut 6 mission takes
Ryumin to 361 days'
space experience.

73 Soyuz 36 (USSR 42)
26 May 1980
Valeri Kubasov,
Bertalan Farkas
7 day 20 hr 45 min
44 sec
Visit to Salyut 6; Farkas
from Hungary; landed in
Soyuz 35.

74 Soyuz T2 (USSR 43)
5 Jun 1980
Yuri Malyshev,
Vladimir Aksyonov
3 day 22 hr 19 min
30 sec
Test of new Soyuz model
to Salyut 6. (Soyuz T1
was unmanned.)

75 Soyuz 37 (USSR 44)
23 Jul 1980
Viktor Gorbatko,
Pham Tuan
7 day 20 hr 42 min
Visit to Salyut 6; Tuan
from Vietnam; landed in
Soyuz 36.

76 Soyuz 38 (USSR 45)
18 Sept 1980
Yuri Romanenko,
Arnaldo Mendez
7 day 20 hr 43 min
24 sec
Visit to Salyut 6;
Mendez from Cuba.

77 Soyuz T3 (USSR 46)
27 Nov 1980
Leonid Kizim,
Oleg Makarov,
Gennadi Strekalov
12 day 19 hr 7 min
42 sec
Maintenance crew to
Salyut 5; first three-man
Soyuz since Soyuz 11
accident.

78 Soyuz T4 (USSR 47)
12 Mar 1981
Vladimir Kovalyonok,
Viktor Savinykh
74 day 17 hr 37 min
23 sec
Final Salyut 6 long-stay
crew; Savinykh 100th
person in space.

79 Soyuz 39 (USSR 48)
22 Mar 1981
Vladimir Dzhanib-
vekov, Jugderdemi-
dyin Gurragcha
7 day 20 hr 42 min
3 sec
Salyut 6 visit; Gur-
ragcha from Mongolia.

80 Columbia STS 1
(USA 32) 12 Apr 1981
John Young,
Bob Crippen
2 day 6 hr 20 min 52 sec
Maiden flight of Space
Shuttle.

81 Soyuz 40 (USSR 49)
15 May 1981
Leonid Popov,
Dumitru Prunariu
7 day 20 hr 41 min 52 sec
Final visiting crew to
Salyut 6; Prunariu from
Romania.

82 Columbia STS 2
(USA 33) 12 Nov 1981
Joe Engle, Dick Truly
2 day 6 hr 13 min
11 sec
First manned flight of
used vehicle.

83 Columbia STS 3
(USA 34) 22 Mar 1982
Jack Lousma,
Gordon Fullerton
8 day 0 hr 4 min 46 sec
Third test flight.

84 Soyuz T5 (USSR 50)
13 May 1982
Anatoli Berezevoi,
Valentin Lebedev
211 day 9 hr 4 min 32 sec
First, record-breaking,
visit to Salyut 7.

85 Soyuz T6 (USSR 51)
24 Jun 1982
Vladimir Dzhanibekov,
Alexander
Ivanchenkov,
Jean-Loup Chrétien
7 day 21 hr 50 min
52 sec
Visit to Salyut 7; Chrétien from France, first
W European in space.

86 Columbia STS 4
(USA 35) 27 Jun 1982
Ken Mattingly,
Hank Hartsfield
7 day 1 hr 9 min 31 sec
Military flight; final test
flight.

87 Soyuz T7 (USSR 52)
19 Aug 1982
Leonid Popov,
Alexander Serebrov,
Svetlana Savitskaya
7 day 21 hr 52 min
24 sec
Savitskaya second
woman in space after
20 years.

88 Columbia STS 5
(USA 36) 11 Nov 1982
Vance Brand, Robert
Overmyer, Joe Allen,
William Lenoir
5 day 2 hr 14 min 26 sec
First commercial
mission of Shuttle;
deployed two commu-
nications satellites;
first four-person flight.

89 Challenger STS 6
(USA 37) 4 Apr 1983
Paul Weitz, Karol
Bobko, Don Peterson,
Story Musgrave
5 day 0 hr 23 min
42 sec
Deployed TDRS 1;
limped into orbit after
upper stage failure; per-
formed spacewalk.

90 Soyuz T8 (USSR 53)
20 Apr 1983
Vladimir Titov,
Gennadi Strekalov,
Alexander Serebrov
2 day 0 hr 17 min
48 sec
Failed to dock with
Salyut 7; Serebrov
first person to fly
consecutive missions.

91 Challenger STS 7
(USA 38) 18 Jun 1983
Bob Crippen, Rick
Hauck, John Fabian,
Sally Ride,
Norman Thagard
6 day 2 hr 24 min
10 sec
Satellite deployment
mission is first by five
people; includes first US
woman in space.

92 Soyuz T9 (USSR 54)
27 Jun 1983
Vladimir Lyakhov,
Alexander Alexandrov
149 day 10 hr 46 min
Trouble with space
station, Salyut 7, halts
flight.

93 Challenger STS 8
(USA 39) 30 Aug 1983
Richard Truly, Dan
Brandenstein, Guoin
Bluford, Dale Gardner,
William Thornton
6 day 1 hr 8 min 40 sec
Night launch and
landing.

Soyuz T10-1 (USSR)
27 Sept 1983
Vladimir Titov,
Gennadi Strekalov
Launcher explodes on
pad; crew saved by
launch escape system.

94 Columbia STS 9
(USA 40) 28 Nov 1983
John Young, Brewster
Shaw, Owen Garriott,
Robert Parker,
Byron Lichtenberg,
Ulf Merbold
10 day 7 hr 47 min
23 sec
Flight of European
Spacelab 1; Merbold
from West Germany;
first six-up flight.

95 Challenger STS 41B
(USA 41) 3 Feb 1984
Vance Brand,
Robert Gibson,
Bruce McCandless,
Robert Stewart,
Ronald McNair
7 day 23 hr 15 min
54 sec
First independent
spacewalk using MMU
by McCandless; first
space mission to end at
launch site (Kennedy/
Canaveral).

96 Soyuz T10 (USSR 55)
8 Feb 1984
Leonid Kizim, Vladimir

Solovyov, Oleg Atkov
236 day 22 hr 49 min
Longest manned space
mission to date; Kizim
and Solovyov made
record six spacewalks.

97 Soyuz T11 (USSR 56)
3 Apr 1984
Yuri Malyshev,
Gennadi Strekalov,
Rakesh Sharma
7 day 21 hr 40 min
Visit to Salyut 7;
Sharma from India.

98 Challenger STS 41C
(USA 42) 6 Apr 1984
Bob Crippen,
Dick Scobee,
George Nelson,
Terry Hart,
James van Hoften
6 day 23 hr 40 min
5 sec
Repaired Solar Max;
with Soyuz T10 and T11
crews in space, 11 people
are up at once.

99 Soyuz T12 (USSR 57)
17 Jul 1984
Vladimir Dhzanibekov,
Svetlana Savitskaya,
Oleg Volk
11 day 19 hr 14 min
36 sec
Savitskaya becomes
first woman space-
walker, outside
Salyut 7.

100 Discovery STS 41D
(USA 43) 30 Aug 1984
Hank Hartsfield,
Michael Coats, Judy
Resnik, Steven Hawley,
Michael Mullane,
Charlie Walker
6 day 0 hr 56 min 4 sec
Launch pad abort in
June; three satellites
deployed; Walker first
industry-engineer
astronaut.

101 Challenger STS 41G
(USA 44) 5 Oct 1984
Bob Crippen, Jon
McBride, Sally Ride,
Kathy Sullivan,
David Leestma,
Marc Garneau,
Paul Scully Power.
8 day 5 hr 23 min 33 sec
First seven-up flight;
first carrying two
women; Ride first US
woman in space twice;
Sullivan first US woman
to spacewalk; Garneau
from Canada.

102 Discovery STS 51A
(USA 45) 8 Nov 1984
Rick Hauck, Dave
Walker, Joe Allen,
Dale Gardner,
Anna Fisher
7 day 23 hr 45 min
54 sec
Two spacewalks to
retrieve lost communic-
ations satellites and
return them to Earth.

103 Discovery STS 51C
(USA 46) 24 Jan 1985
Ken Mattingly, Loren
Shriver, Ellison
Onizuka, James Buchli,
Gary Payton
3 day 1 hr 33 min
13 sec
Military mission;
Payton first USAF
Manned Space Flight
Engineer.

104 Discovery STS 51D
(USA 47) 12 Apr 1985
Karol Bobko, Don Wil-
liams, Rhea Seddon, Jeff
Hoffman, David Griggs,
Charlie Walker, Jake
Garn
6 day 23 hr 55 min 23 sec
Deployed three commu-
nications satellites;
unscheduled EVA
(Extra-vehicular
activity) to attempt
repair of one; Senator
Jake Garn first pas-
senger observer in
space.

105 Challenger STS 51B
(USA 48) 29 Apr 1985
Bob Overmyer, Fred
Gregory, Don Lind,
William Thornton,
Norman Thagard,
Lodewijk van den
Berg, Taylor Wang
7 day 8 min 50 sec
Spacelab 3 research
mission.

106 Soyuz T13 (USSR 58)
6 Jun 1985
Vladimir Dzhanibekov,
Viktor Savinykh
112 day 3 hr 12 min
Complete overhaul of
Salyut 7 after systems
failures; Savinykh came
home in Soyuz T14 and
Georgi Grechko in
Soyuz T13.

107 Discovery STS 51G
(USA 49) 17 Jun 1985
Dan Brandenstein,
John Creighton,
Shannon Lucid, Steve

Nagel, John Fabian,
Patrick Baudry,
Abdul Aziz Al-Saud
7 day 1 hr 38 min 58 sec
Satellite deployment
and research mission;
first with three nations
represented, Baudry
from France (first non-
US, non-USSR nation to
make two flights),
Abdul Aziz Al-Saud, a
Prince from Saudi
Arabia.

108 Challenger STS 51F
(USA 50) 20 Jul 1985
Gordon Fullerton, Roy
Bridges, Karl Henize,
Anthony England,
Story Musgrave,
John-David Bartoe,
Loren Acton
7 day 22 hr 45 min 27 sec
Launch pad abort on
July 12; one engine
shutdown during
launch, causing abort-
to-orbit; Henize oldest
man in space at 58;
Spacelab 2 research
mission.

109 Discovery STS 51I
(USA 51) 27 Aug 1985
Joe Engle, Dick Covey,
William Fisher,
James van Hoften,
Mike Lounge
7 day 2 hr 14 min 42 sec
Three satellites
deployed; Leasat 3
captured, repaired and
redeployed.

110 Soyuz T14
(USSR 59) 17 Sept 1985
Vladimir Vasyutin,
Georgi Grechko,
Alexander Volkov
64 day 21 hr 52 min
Mission cut short after
Vasyutin becomes men-
tally disturbed;
Grechko returned in
Soyuz T13; Savinykh
stayed with Soyuz T14
and clocked up mission
time of 168 days.

111 Atlantis STS 51J
(USA 52) 3 Oct 1985
Karol Bobko, Ron
Grabe, Dale Hilmers,
Bob Stewart, William
Pailes
4 day 1 hr 45 min 30 sec
Military mission.

112 Challenger STS 61A
(USA 53) 30 Oct 1985
Hank Hartsfield, Steve
Nagel, Bonnie Dunbar,

Guion Gluford,
James Buchli,
Ernst Messerschmitt,
Reinhard Furrer,
Wubbo Ockels
7 day 44 min 51 sec
West German-funded
Spacelab D1 mission;
Messerschmitt and
Furrer from West Ger-
many; Ockels from Net-
herlands; first eight-up
mission.

113 Atlantis STS 61B
(USA 54) 27 Nov 1985
Brewster Shaw, Bryan
O'Connor, Mary
Cleave, Jerry Ross,
Sherwood Spring,
Rudolpho Neri Vela,
Charlie Walker
6 day 21 hr 4 min 50 sec
Neri Vela from Mexico;
Walker's third flight as
Shuttle payload special-
ist; Ross and Spring
assemble structures
during EVAs.

114 Columbia STS 61C
(USA 55) 12 Jan 1986
Robert Gibson, Charles
Bolden, Franklin
Chang-Diaz, George
Nelson, Steve Hawley,
Robert Cenker, Bill
Nelson
6 day 2 hr 4 min 9 sec
Much-delayed flight;
Bill Nelson, a
Congressman, second
'political' passenger.

Challenger STS 51L
(USA) 28 Jan 1986
Dick Scobee, Mike
Smith, Judith Resnik,
Ronald McNair,
Ellison Onizuka,
Christa McAuliffe,
Gregory Jarvis
73 sec
Disintegrated at
14 330 m (47 000 ft); crew
killed; first flight to
take off but not to
reach space; first
US in-flight fatalities.

115 Soyuz T15
(USSR 60) 13 Mar 1986
Leonid Kizim,
Vladimir Solovyov
125 day 0 hr 1 min
First mission to new
space station Mir 1; also
docked with Salyut 7;
Kizim clocks up over a
year in space
experience.

116 Soyuz TM2
(USSR 61) 5 Feb 1987
Yuro Romanenko,
Alexander Laveikin
326 day 11 hr 38 min
Record duration mis-
sion by Romanenko
aboard Mir 1. Landed in
Soyuz TM3 (Soyuz TM1
was unmanned). Lavei-
kin, 200th person in
space, returned after 174
days.

117 Soyuz TM3
(USSR 62) 22 Jul 1987
Alexander Viktorenko,
Alexander Alexandrov,
Muhammed Faris
7 day 23 hr 4 min 5 sec
Faris from Syria.
Alexandrov remains on
Mir for 160 days. Vik-
torenko and Faris land
in Soyuz TM2 with Lav-
eikin.

118 Soyuz TM4
(USSR 63) 21 Dec 1987
Vladimir Titov,
Musa Manarov,
Anatoli Levchenko
365 day 22 hr 39 min
Levchenko returns in
Soyuz TM3 with Roman-
enko and Alexandrov
after flight of 7 days.
Titov and Manarov
return in Soyuz TM6.

119 Soyuz TM5
(USSR 64) 7 Jun 1988
Anatoli Solovyov,
Viktor Savinykh,
Alexander Alexandrov
9 day 20 hr 10 min
Alexandrov second
Bulgarian in space.
Crew returns in Soyuz
TM4.

120 Soyuz TM6
(USSR 65) 31 Aug 1988
Vladimir Lyakhov,
Valeri Polyakov,
Abdol Mohmand
8 day 20 hr 27 min
Mohmand from Af-
ghanistan. Polyakov
remains on Mir. Lyak-
hov and Mohmand land
in Soyuz TM5 after
'stranded in space'
scare.

121 Discovery STS 26
(USA 56) 29 Sept 1988
Rick Hauck, Dick
Covey, Mike Lounge,
David Hilmers,
George Nelson
4 day 1 hr 0 min
America's return to

space 32 months after
Challenger disaster.
Nelson first American
to make successive
national spaceflights.

122 Soyuz TM7
(USSR 66) 26 Nov 1988
Alexander Volkov,
Sergei Krikalyov,
Jean-Loup Chrétien.
15 day 1 hr 10 min
Visit to Mir. First non-
US, non-USSR to make
two spaceflights and to
make a spacewalk.
Chrétien returned
after 25 days.

123 Atlantis STS 27
(USA 57) 2 Dec 1988
Robert Gibson, Guy
Gardner, Jerry Ross,
Mike Mullane,
William Shepherd
4 day 9 hr 6 min
Military mission to
deploy Lacrosse spy
satellite. With six
cosmonauts on Mir, 11
people are in space.

124 Discovery STS 29
(USA 58) 13 Mar 1989
Michael Coats, John
Blaha, James Buchli,
James Bagian, Robert
Springer
4 day 23 hr 39 min
Deployed TDRS satel-
lite. STS 28 delayed.

125 Atlantis STS 30
(USA 59) 4 May 1989
David Walker, Ron
Grabe, Norman
Thagard, Mary
Cleave, Mark Lee
4 day 0 hr 57 min
Deployed *Magellan* for
its journey to orbit the
planet Venus. First
deployment of a plan-
etary spacecraft from
a manned spacecraft.

126 Columbia STS 28
(USA 60) 8 Aug 1989
Brewster Shaw,
Richard Richards,
David Leestma,
James Adamson,
Mark Brown
5 day 1 hr 0 min
Military mission to
deploy KH-12 recon-
naissance satellite.

127 Soyuz TMB
(USSR 67) 6 Sept 1989
Alexander Viktorenko,
Alexander Serebrov
166 day 6 hr 58 min

Occupied Mir space station. First Soviet manned flight to operate commercial US experiments. First Soviet test of tethered MMU.

128 Atlantis STS 34 (USA 61) 18 Oct 1989 Donald Williams, Michael McCulley, Shannon Lucid, Franklin Chang-Diaz, Ellen Baker 4 day 23 hr 39 min Deployed Jupiter orbiter *Galileo*.

129 Discovery STS 33 (USA 64) 22 Nov 1989 Frederick Gregory, John Blaha, Story Musgrave, Manley Carter, Kathryn Thornton 5 day 0 hr 7 min Military mission to deploy Magnum elite spacecraft. First military manned spaceflight with civilian and female crew.

130 Columbia STS 32 (USA 63) 9 Jan 1990 Dan Brandenstein, James Wetherbee, Bonnie Dunbar, Marsha Ivin, Daivid Low 10 day 21 hr 0 min Retrieved LDEF from orbit.

131 Soyuz TM9 (USSR 68) 11 Feb 1990 Anatoli Solovyov, Alexander Balandin 179 day 2 hr 19 min Occupation of Mir space station. Included Soviet record 7 hr spacewalk

132 Atlantis STS 36 (USA 64) 28 Feb 1990 John Creighton, John Caspar, Mike Mullane, David Hilmers, Pierre Thuot 4 day 10 hr 18 min Military mission to deploy KH-12 reconnaissance satellite, which broke up in orbit later.

133 Discovery STS 31 (USA 65) 24 Apr 1990 Loren Shriver, Charles Bolden, Steven Hawley, Bruce McCandless, Kathryn Sullivan 5 day 1 hr 16 min Deployed Hubble Space

Telescope. Reached record 532 km Shuttle altitude.

134 Soyuz TM10 (USSR 69) 1 Aug 1990 Gennadi Manakov, Gennadi Strekalov 130 day 19 hr 36 min Occupation of Mir space station.

135 Discovery STS 41 (USA 66) 6 Oct 1990 Richard Richards, Robert Canbana, Thomas Akers, Bruce Melnick, William Shepherd 4 day 2 hr 10 min Deployed *Ulysses* solar polar orbiter.

136 Atlantis STS 38 (USA 67) 15 Nov 1990 Richard Covey, Frank Culbertson, Robert Springer, Carl Meade, Sam Gemar 4 day 21 hr 54 min Military mission.

137 Columbia STS 35 (USA 68) 2 Dec 1990 Vance Brand, Guy Gardner, Jeff Hoffman, Mike Lounge, Robert Parker, Ronald Parise, Samual Durrance 8 day 23 hr 5 min Launch of Astro-1 observatory.

138 Soyuz TM11 (USSR 70) 2 Dec 1990 Musa Manarov, Toyohiro Akiyama, Viktor Afanasyef. 175 day 1 hr 52 min New occupation of Mir space station with spacewalks. Akiyama – a Japanese journalist – returned to Earth with Soyuz TM10 after 7 days. With two people already aboard Mir, and STS 35 in orbit a record 12 people are in space at once.

139 Atlantis STS 37 (USA 69) 5 Apr 1991 Steven Nagel, Ken Cameron, Jay Apt, Linda Godwin, Jerry Ross 5 day 23 hr 33 min 44 sec Development of Gamma Ray Observatory and two spacewalks by Ross and Apt.

140 Discovery STS 39 (USA 70) 28 Apr 1991 Michael Coats, Blaine Hammond, Guion Bluford, Gregory Harbaugh, Richard Heib, Donald McMonagle, Charles Veach 8 day 7 hr 22 min 25 sec Star Wars research mission, first unclassified military flight, first with seven NASA astronauts.

141 Soyuz TM12 (USSR 71) 18 May 1991 Anatoli Artsebarski, Sergei Krikalyov, Helen Sharman 144 day 15 hr 22 min Sharman first Briton in space; returns in TM12. Krikalyov stays aboard Mir and returns after 311 days. Artsebarski and Krikalyov make six spacewalks in record 33 days.

142 Columbia STS 40 (USA 71) 5 Jun 1991 Bryan O'Connor, Sidney Gutierrez, James Bagian, Tamara Jernigan, Rhea Seddon, Drew Gaffney, Millie Hughes-Fulford 9 day 2 hr 14 min 20 sec Spacelab Life Sciences 1 mission. First mission with three women aboard.

143 Atlantis STS43 (USA 72) 2 Aug 1991 John Blaha, Michael Baker, James Adamson, David Low, Shannon Lucid 8 day 21 hr 21 min 25 sec Deployed TDRS satellite. Lucid first woman to make three flights and also oldest woman in space (48)

144 Discovery STS 48 (USA 73) 12 Sept 1991 John Creighton, Kenneth Reightler, Mark Brown, James Buchli, Sam Gemar 5 day 8 hr 27 min 51 sec Deployment of Upper Atmosphere Research satellite (UARS). Manoeuvred to avoid space debris.

145 Soyuz TM13 (USSR 72) 2 Oct 1991 Alexander Volkov,

Taktar Aubakirov, Franz Viebock 175 day 2 hr 52 min Aubakirov, first Kazakh and Viebock first Austrian in space, flying commercial missions. Both returned in TM12 after 7 day flight. Volkov remained on Mir.

146 Atlantis STS 44 (USA 74) 24 Nov 1991 Frederick Gregory, Terence Henricks, Story Musgrave, Mario Runco, James Voss, Thomas Hennen 6 day 22 hr 50 min 42 sec Deployed DSP early warning satellite and conducted reconnaissance mission, with first 'space spy' Hennen. Flight cut short.

147 Discovery STS 42 (USA 75) 22 Jan 1992 Ronald Grabe, Stephen Oswald, Norman Thagard, David Hilmers, William Readdy, Roberta Bondar, Ulf Merbold 8 day 1 hr 14 min 45 sec International Microgravity Laboratory mission. Bondar from Canada and Merbold from Germany. Thagard clocks up record 25-day Shuttle flight time on fourth mission.

148 Soyuz TM14 (Russia 1) 17 Mar 1992 Alexander Viktorenko, Alexander Kaleri, Klaus Dietrich Flade 145 day 14 hr 10 min New residents for Mir, while the German commercial passenger Flade returns in TM13 after 7-day mission.

149 Atlantis STS 45 (USA 76) 24 Mar 1992 Charles Bolden, Brian Duffy, Kathryn Sullivan, Michael Foale, David Leestma, Byron Lichtenberg, Dirk Frimout 8 day 22 hr 9 min 25 sec Atlas science mission. Frimout first Belgian in space.

150 Endeavour STS 49 (USA 77) 7 May 1992 Dan Brandenstein, Kevin Chilton, Rick

Heib, Bruce Melnick, Pierre Thuot, Kathryn Thornton, Tom Akers 8 day 21 hr 17 min 38 sec Retrieved Intelsat 6 and re-boosted it into geostationary orbit. Record-breaking 8 hr 29 min EVA by Thuot, Hieb and Akers, the third of four EVAs during the mission and the first by three crew.

151 Columbia STS 50 (USA 78) 25 Jun 1992 Richard Richards, Kenneth Bowersox, Bonnie Dunbar, Ellen Baker, Carl Meade, Lawrence De Lucas, Eugene Trinh 13 day 19 hr 30 min 4 sec Longest space shuttle mission and first to fly extended duration orbiter (EDO) cryogenic pallet. US Microgravity Laboratory mission 1.

152 Soyuz TM15 (Russia 2) 27 Jul 1992 Anatoli Solovyov, Sergei Avdeyev, Michel Tognini 188 day 21 hr 40 min New occupation of Mir. French visiting mission. Tognini returns in TM14 after 14-day flight.

153 Atlantis STS 46 (USA 79) 31 Jul 1992 Loren Shriver, Andrew Allen, Claude Nicollier, Marsha Ivins, Jeff Hoffman, Franklin-Chang Diaz, Franco Malerba 7 day 23 hr 15 min 5 sec Deployed Eureca and Tethered satellites. Nicollier first Swiss astronaut and first non-US NASA mission specialist. Malerba first Italian in space. Record five space nations being represented.

154 Endeavour STS 47 (USA 80) 12 Sept 1992 Robert Gibson, Curtis Brown, Mark Lee, Jay Apt, Jan Davis, Mae Jemison, Mamoru Mohri 7 day 22 hr 31 min 11 sec Japan's Spacelab J mission. Mohri second Japanese in space. Lee and Davis first married couple. Jemison first coloured female.

155 Columbia STS 52 (USA 81) 22 Oct 1992

James Wetherbee, Michael Baker, Charles Veach, William Shepherd, Tamara Jernigan, Steven MacLean 9 day 20 hr 56 min 13 sec Science research mission, also deployed Italian Lageos satellite.

156 Discovery STS 53 (USA 82) 2 Dec 1992 David Walker, Robert Cabana, Guion Bluford, James Voss, Michael Clifford 7 day 7 hr 19 min 17 sec Final Dept of Defense Shuttle mission.

157 Endeavour STS 54 (USA 83) 13 Jan 1993 John Casper, Donald McMonagle, Gregory Harbaugh, Mario Runco, Susan Helms 5 day 23 hr 38 min 17 sec Satellite deployment, science and EVA mission. Helms first female military officer in space.

158 Soyuz TM16 (Russia 3) 24 Jan 1993 Gennadi Manakov, Alexander Polishchuk Due to return July 1993 Crew rotation flight to Mir space station.

PLANNED FLIGHTS FOR 1993

February
Columbia STS 55 Steven Nagel, Terrence Henricks, Jerry Ross, Bernard Harris, Charles Precourt, Hans Schlegel, Ulrich Walter Spacelab D2 mission.

March
Discovery STS 56 Kenneth Cameron, Stephen Oswald, Kenneth Cockrell, Michael Foale, Ellen Ochoa Atlas 2 laboratory.

April
Endeavour STS 57 Ronald Grabe, Brian Duffy, David Low, Janice Voss, Nancy Sherlock, Jeff Wisoff Spacehab 1, Eureca retrieval.

July
Soyuz TM17 Vasily Tsibliyev, un-

named flight engineer, Jean-Paul Haignere New resident crew for Mir space station with French visiting mission.

August
Columbia STS 58 John Blaha, Richard Searfoss, Rhea Seddon, Shannon Lucid, David Wolf, William McArthur, Martin Fettman Spacelab Life Sciences 2.

November
Discovery STS 60 Charles Bolden, Kenneth Reightler, Franklin Chang-Diaz, Jan Davis,

Ronald Sega, Russian cosmonaut Spacehab 2, Wake Shield.

Soyuz TM18 New resident crew for Mir space station, to attempt 540-day mission.

December
Endeavour STS 61 Richard Covey, Kenneth Bowersox, Story Musgrave, Tom Akers, Jeff Hoffman, Kathryn Thornton Hubble Space Telescope servicing and repair to involve several EVAs.

NATIONAL MANNED SPACEFLIGHT TOTALS (to 3 February 1993)

Country	No. of flights	Day	Hr	Min	Sec
USSR	72	3835	8	16	44
Russia[1]	2	334	11	54	–
USA	83	674	6	0	25

Other nations which flew with the USSR/Russia and USA:

		Day	Hr	Min	Sec
France	4 (1 US/3 USSR)	53	12	33	44
Germany	5 (3 US/2 USSR)	41	4	33	3
Canada	3 (USA)	26	3	34	31
Japan	2 (1 US/1 USSR)	15	20	26	11
Bulgaria	2 (USSR)	11	19	11	6
Belgium	1 (USA)	8	22	9	25
Afghanistan	1 (USSR)	8	20	27	–
Switzerland	1 (USSR)	7	23	15	5
Italy	1 (USA)	7	23	15	5
Syria	1 (USSR)	7	23	4	5
Czecho-slovakia	1 (USSR)	7	22	16	–
Austria	1 (USSR)	7	22	13	–
Poland	1 (USSR)	7	22	2	59
India	1 (USSR)	7	21	40	–
UK	1 (USSR)	7	21	14	28
Hungary	1 (USSR)	7	20	45	44
Cuba	1 (USSR)	7	20	43	24
Mongolia	1 (USSR)	7	20	42	3
Vietnam	1 (USSR)	7	20	42	–
Romania	1 (USSR)	7	20	41	52
Saudi Arabia	1 (USA)	7	1	38	58
Holland	1 (USA)	7	0	44	51
Mexico	1 (USA)	6	21	4	50

[1] Russia became a separate independent state on 25 December 1991. The figures for Russia do not include figures from the Soyuz TM16 flight which is due to return in July 1993.

MOST EXPERIENCED SPACEWOMEN

Name (no. of flights)	Country	Day	Hr	Min	Sec
Bonnie Dunbar (3)	USA	31	17	15	33
Kathryn Sullivan (3)	USA	22	4	48	39
Shannon Lucid (3)	USA	20	22	39	41
Svetlana Savitskaya (2)	USSR	19	17	7	–
Tamara Jernigan (2)	USA	18	23	10	33
Marsha Ivins (2)	USA	18	20	15	43
Ellen Baker (2)	USA	18	19	9	28

MOST EXPERIENCED SPACEMEN

Name (no. of flights)	Country	Day	Hr	Min	Sec
Musa Manarov (2)	USSR	541	0	31	18
Sergei Krikalyov (2)	USSR	463	7	11	–
Yuri Romanenko (3)	USSR	430	18	21	30
Alexander Volkov (3)	USSR	391	11	54	–
Anatoli Solovyov (3)	USSR	377	20	9	–
Leonid Kizim (3)	USSR	374	17	57	42
Vladimir Titov (2)	USSR	367	22	56	48
Vladimir Solovyov (2)	USSR	361	22	50	–
Valeri Ryumin (3)	USSR	361	21	31	57
Vladimir Lyakhov (3	USSR	333	7	48	37
Alex Viktorenko (3)	USSR	319	20	12	5
Alex Alexandrov (2)	USSR	309	18	2	58

RECORDS IN MANNED SPACEFLIGHT

First in space: Yuri Gagarin (USSR) 12 April 1961.

First American in space: John Glenn 20 February 1962

First woman in space: Valentina Tereshkova (USSR) 16 June 1963.

First non-US, non-Soviet spaceman: Vladimir Remek (Czech) 2 March 1978.

First to walk in space: Alexei Leonov (USSR) 18 March 1965.

First military mission: Soyuz 14 (USSR) 3 July 1974.

First flight to the Moon: Apollo 8 (USA) 21 December 1968.

First landing on the Moon: Apollo 8 (USA) 16 July 1969.

First men on the Moon: Neil Armstrong and Buzz Aldrin (USA) 16 July 1969.

First military mission: Soyuz 14 (USSR) on 3 July 1974.

First mother in space: Anna Fisher (USA) 8 November 1984.

First passenger-observer: Jake Garn (USA) on 12 April 1985.

First rendezvous in space: Gemini 6 and 7 (USA) 16 December 1965.

First to fly solo in lunar orbit: John Young (USA) 18 May 1969.

First woman spacewalker: Svetlana Savitskaya (USSR) 17 July 1984.

First Briton in space: Helen Sharman 18 May 1991.

Oldest person in space: Vance Brand (USA) 59 years old on a spaceflight on 2 December 1990.

Youngest person in space: Gherman Stepanovich (USSR) 25 years old on a spaceflight on 6 Aug 1961.

Longest manned spaceflight: Vladimir Titov and Musa Manavov (USSR) spent 365 day 22 hr 39 min 47 sec on the Soyuz TM4 and Soyuz TM6 in 1987–88.

Greatest altitude: the crew of the Apollo 13 attained a distance of 400 187 km (248 655 mi) above the Earth's surface on 15 April 1970.

Greatest speed: the fastest speed at which humans have travelled is 39 897 km/h (24 791 mph) during the Apollo 10 mission on 26 May 1969.

Greatest fatalities: the largest number of fatalities in a single spaceflight was suffered aboard the American Challenger 51L on 28 January 1986 when seven crew (five men and two women) died.

MAJOR NATIONAL CIVILIAN SPACE AGENCIES

Canada The growing Canadian Space Agency is playing a major role in the USA's NASA Space Shuttle and Freedom space station programmes, providing remote manipulator systems.

China The Ministry of Astronautics manages the national space programme through several organizations. China launches its own applications satellites, using a range of boosters that are marketed commercially worldwide by the China Great Wall Industry Corporation.

Europe The European Space Agency is one of the world's leading space organizations, managing a diverse programme on behalf of members: Austria, Belgium, Denmark, Finland, France, Germany, Ireland, Italy, the Netherlands, Norway, Spain, Sweden, Switzerland and the UK. Current major programmes are the development of the Ariane 5 launcher; a manned space laboratory, Columbus, to be attached to the Freedom space station; and a series of environmental monitoring spacecraft.

France Centre National d'Etudes Spatiales (CNES) is Europe's busiest and largest national agency, organizing several manned flights to the Mir space station and planning to launch Europe's first military spy satellite, Helios.

Germany The German space agency is involved in manned spaceflights to the Russian Mir I and also aboard the US Space Shuttle. It has had to reduce its space budget owing to the costs of reunification.

India The Indian Space Research Organization (ISRO) has developed its own satellite launcher and has ambitious plans for an autonomous communications satellite system.

Italy The Italian Space Agency will be the first from Europe to play a role in the USA's Freedom space station, supplying a logistics module.

Japan The National Space Development Agency (NASDA) and Institute of Space and Astronautical Science manage a programme that includes a range of satellite launch vehicles, communications and science satellites and a module to be operated at the US Freedom space station.

Russia Since the break up of the USSR, the Russian Space Agency has emerged as the leading space organization in the CIS. It manages about 80% of the former Soviet programme which has, however, been hit by drastic budget cuts. The RSA is trying to offset this lack of funding by commercializing as much of its programme as possible.

UK The British National Space Centre may have a modest budget but has become the European leader in remote sensing and Earth observation work within the European Space Agency.

USA The National Aeronautics and Space Administration (NASA) is the world's leading space organization, managing major manned, science and applications programmes. It operates a Space Shuttle Fleet and plans to operate a permanently manned space station, Freedom in Orbit by the year 2000.

TIME

TIME SYSTEMS

Time forms the basis of many scientific laws, but time itself is very difficult to define. Time, like distance, separates objects and events, and for this reason can be regarded as the fourth dimension. However, time cannot be measured directly. We must make do with measuring the way in which the passage of time affects things.

The Earth's orbit is not circular but elliptical, so the Sun does not appear to move against the stars at a constant speed. Most everyday time systems are therefore based on a hypothetical 'mean Sun', which is taken to travel at a constant speed equal to the average speed of the actual Sun.

A *day* is the time taken for the Earth to turn once on its axis. A *sidereal day* is reckoned with reference to the stars and is the time taken between successive passes of the observer's meridian by the same star. (The *meridian* is an imaginary line from due north to due south running through a point directly above the observer.) One sidereal day is 23 hours 56 minutes 4 seconds. A *solar day* is calculated with respect to the mean Sun. The mean solar day is 24 hours long.

MEASURING TIME

The earliest device for measuring time was the *sundial*, which can be traced back to the Middle East c. 3500 BC. A sundial comprises a rod or plate called a *gnomon* that casts a shadow on a disc; where the shadow points indicates the position of the Sun and hence the time of day.

Mechanical clocks, driven by falling weights, appeared in the 14th century, and the first *mechanical watches*, driven by a coiled mainspring, in the 16th century. The first *pendulum clock* was invented by Christiaan Huygens (1629–95), a Dutch physicist, in the middle of the 17th century.

Pendulum clocks could not be used on board ships owing to the vessel's motion. In 1714 the British Longitude Board offered a prize for the development of a *marine chronometer*, as the ability to tell the time accurately is vital to navigation. The English clockmaker John Harrison (1693–1776) produced his first marine chronometer in 1735 after seven years' work on the problem.

The first *quartz clock*, operated by the vibrations of a quartz crystal when an electrical voltage is applied, appeared in 1929. The quartz clock is accurate to within one second in ten years. This was followed in 1948 by the *atomic clock*, which depends on the natural vibrations of atoms. The most accurate modern atomic clocks are accurate to one second in 1.7 million years.

A *year* is the time taken for the Earth to complete one orbit of the Sun. The Earth's true revolution period is 365 days 6 hours 9 minutes 10 seconds, and this is known as a *sidereal year*. However, the direction in which the Earth's axis points is changing due to an effect known as *precession*. The north celestial pole now lies near the star Polaris in the constellation Ursa Minor, thus Polaris is also known as the Pole

Star. By the year AD 14 000, the Earth's axis will point in a different direction and the bright star Vega in Lyra will be near the pole. This effect also means that the position of the Sun's apparent path across the sky is changing with respect to the stars. A *tropical year* compensates for the effects of precession and is 365 days 5 hours 48 minutes 45 seconds long. It is the tropical year that is used as the basis for developing a calendar.

The SI unit of time is the *second*, which was originally defined as $1/_{86\,400}$ of the mean solar day. However, as we have seen, the Earth is not a very good time-keeper, so scientists no longer use it to define the fundamental unit of time. The second is now defined as the duration of 9 192 631 770 periods of the radiation corresponding to the transition between the two hyperfine levels of the ground state of a caesium-133 atom.

Greenwich Mean Time (GMT) is the local time at Greenwich, England. The *Greenwich Meridian* is the line of 0° longtitude, which passes through Greenwich Observatory. The mean Sun crosses the Greenwich Meridian at midday GMT. Also known as *Universal Time* (UT), GMT is used as a standard reference time throughout the world. *Sidereal time* literally means 'star time'. It is reckoned with reference to the stars and not the Sun.

THE JULIAN AND GREGORIAN CALENDARS

By 46 BC the Roman calendar had become confused and in need of reform. On the advice of the Egyptian astronomer Sosigenes, Julius Caesar therefore introduced what became known as the Julian calendar. The year 46 BC – known as the 'Year of Confusion' – was lengthened to 445 days to bring it in line with the solar year.

Under the Julian calendar the solar year was calculated at 365 days and divided into 12 months. Each month contained 30 or 31 days except for February, which contained 28 days (or 29 days in a leap year). However, by 1582 an overestimation by Sosigenes of about 11 minutes a year had accumulated into a 10-day difference between the Julian calendar and the astronomical year. Pope Gregory XIII therefore ordered that 5 October 1582 should become 15 October, and that century years would only be leap years if divisible by 400 (i.e. 1600, 2000).

In error by 0.0005 days per year, the present Gregorian calendar will not need to be revised for many years.

SEASONS

The four seasons in the northern hemisphere are astronomically speaking:

Spring from the vernal equinox (about 21 March) to the summer solstice (21 or 22 June);

Summer from the summer solstice (21 or 22 June) to the autumnal equinox (about 21 September);

Autumn (or Fall in the USA) from the autumnal equinox (about 21 September) to the winter solstice (21 December or 22 December);

Winter from the winter solstice (21 or 22 December) to the vernal equinox (about 21 March).

In the southern hemisphere, of course, autumn corresponds to spring, winter to summer, spring to autumn and summer to winter.

The solstices (from Latin *sol*, sun; *sistere*, to stand still) are the two times in the year when the sun is farthest from the Equator and appears to be still. The equinoxes (from Latin *aequalis*, equal; *nox*, night) are the two times in the year when day and night are of equal length when the Sun crosses the equator.

The longest day has the longest interval between sunrise and sunset. It is the day on which the summer solstice falls and in the northern hemisphere occurs on 21 June, or more rarely on 22 June.

MONTHS OF THE YEAR

January	31 days; from the Roman republican calendar month Januarius, named after Janus, god of doorways and of beginnings.
February	28 days (29 in a leap year); from the Roman republican calendar month Februarius, named after Februa, the festival of purification held on the 15th.
March	31 days; from the Roman republican calendar month Martius, named after the god Mars.
April	30 days; from the Roman republican calendar month Aprilis. The Romans considered the month sacred to Venus and may have named it after her Greek equivalent Aphrodite. It may also have derived from the Latin *aperire*, 'to open', in reference to the spring blossoming.
May	31 days; from Roman republican calendar month Maius, probably named after the goddess Maia.
June	30 days; from the Roman republican calendar month Junius, probably named after the goddess Juno.
July	31 days; from the Roman republican calendar month Julius, named after Julius Caesar in 44 BC.
August	31 days; from the Roman republican calendar month Augustus named after the emperor Augustus in 8 BC.
September	30 days; seventh month of the early Roman republican calendar, from Latin *septem*, meaning 'seven'.
October	31 days; eighth month of the early Roman republican calendar, from the Latin *octo*, meaning 'eight'.
November	30 days; ninth month of the early Roman republican calendar, from the Latin *novem*, meaning 'nine'.
December	31 days; tenth month of the early Roman republican calendar, from Latin *decem*, meaning 'ten'.

LEAP YEAR

The use of leap years – years with an extra intercalary period – is common to most calendars. In the Gregorian calendar it is an extra day (29 February) that compensates for the quarter-day difference between a calendar year of 365 days and the astronomical year of 365.24219878 days. Every centennial year divisible by 400 and every other year divisible by four is a leap year.

The date when it will be necessary to suppress a further leap year, sometimes assumed to be AD 4000, AD 8000, etc., is not yet clearly definable, owing to minute variations in the Earth-Sun relationship.

The word 'leap' derives from the Old Norse *hlaupar*, indicating a leap in the sense of jump. The origin of the term probably derives from the observation that in a leap year any fixed-day festival falls on the next day of the week but one to that on which it fell in the preceding year, and not on the next day of the week as happens in common years.

THE PERPETUAL CALENDAR

There is a formula – which includes the table of values listed below – that works out the days of the week in any month in any year of the 20th century.

The method for working out the day of the week, using the table of values below, is as follows. Using 14 June 1947 as an example:

Add together

a) the date (14)	= 14
b) the value of the month (June)	= 4
c) the year	= 47
d) the leap years already experienced that century (divide the previous line by 4 and ignore the remainder; 47 divided by 4)	= 11
Total	**76**
Divide the total by 7	= 10
	remainder 6

The remainder is the value of the day of the week in the table below. 6 = Saturday, thus 14 June 1947 was a Saturday.

Month	Value
January	0 (Leap year 6)
February	3 (Leap year 2)
March	3
April	6
May	1
June	4
July	6
August	2
September	5
October	0
November	3
December	5

Day	Value
Monday	1
Tuesday	2
Wednesday	3
Thursday	4
Friday	5
Saturday	6
Sunday	0

THE NEW YEAR

In early medieval times Christian Europe regarded March 25 (Annunciation Day) as New Year's Day. Anglo-Saxon England, however, used December 25 to mark the year's beginning until William the Conqueror decreed that the year should begin on 1 January. England later fell into line with the rest of Christendom, recognizing the year's commencement as March 25. The introduction of the Gregorian Calendar in 1582 confirmed 1 January as New Year's Day.

The adoption of 1 January as New Year's Day in various European countries took place in the following years:

1522	Venice and some other Italian states;
1544	Catholic states and some Protestant states of Germany;
1556	Spain, Portugal, Catholic Netherlands;
1559	Denmark, Prussia, Sweden;
1564	France;
1583	Protestant Netherlands;
1600	Scotland;
1725	Russia;
1751	England.

DAYS OF THE WEEK

English name	Named after
Sunday	The Sun
Monday	The Moon
Tuesday	Tiw, the Anglo-Saxon counterpart of the Nordic god Tyr, son of Odin
Wednesday	Woden, the Ango-Saxon counterpart of Odin, the Nordic god of war
Thursday	Thor, the Nordic god of thunder, eldest son of Odin
Friday	Frigg, the Nordic goddess of love, wife of Odin
Saturday	Saturn, Roman god of agriculture and vegetation

THE JEWISH CALENDAR

It is thought that the Jewish Calendar, as used today, was popularly in use from the 9th century BCE. It is based on the biblical calculations that place the creation in 3761 BCE. The abbreviation BCE means Before the Common Era, while CE stands for Common Era; they correspond to BC and AD, respectively. The complicated rules of the Jewish Calendar with regard to festivals and fasts have resulted in a calendar scheme in which a Jewish year may be one of the following six types:

Minimal Common (353 days);
Regular Common (354 days);
Full Common (355 days);
Minimal Leap (383 days);
Regular Leap (384 days);
Full Leap (385 days).

MONTHS OF THE JEWISH CALENDAR

1. **Nisan**	30 days
2. **Iyar**	29 days
3. **Sivan**	30 days
4. **Tammuz**	29 days
5. **Ab**	30 days
6. **Elul**	29 days
7. **Tishri**	30 days
8. **Cheshvan (Marcheshvan)**	29/30 days*
9. **Kislev**	29/30 days*
10. **Tebet**	29 days
11. **Shebat**	30 days
12. **Adar**	29 days (30 in a leap year)
Ve-Adar †	29 days

* can have either 29 or 30 days depending on the year.

† a 13th month is intercalated into the calendar every 3rd, 6th, 8th, 11th, 14th, 17th and 19th year of a 19-year cycle. It contains all the religious observances that usually occur in Adar.

COMPARATIVE JEWISH CALENDAR 1993–1995

Sept 1993	1 2 3 4 5 6 7 8 9 10 11 12 13 14 15	16 17 18 19 20 21 22 23 24 25 26 27 28 29 30
Elul 5753	15 16 17 18 19 20 21 22 23 24 25 26 27 28 29	Tishri* 1 2 3 4 5 6 7 8 9 10 11 12 13 14 15

* Jewish New Year 5754

October	1 2 3 4 5 6 7 8 9 10 11 12 13 14 15	16 17 18 19 20 21 22 23 24 25 26 27 28 29 30 31
Tishri 5754	16 17 18 19 20 21 22 23 24 25 26 27 28 29 30	Cheshvan 1 2 3 4 5 6 7 8 9 10 11 12 13 14 15 16

November	1 2 3 4 5 6 7 8 9 10 11 12 13 14	15 16 17 18 19 20 21 22 23 24 25 26 27 28 29 30
Cheshvan	17 18 19 20 21 22 23 24 25 26 27 28 29 30	Kislev 1 2 3 4 5 6 7 8 9 10 11 12 13 14 15 16

December	1 2 3 4 5 6 7 8 9 10 11 12 13 14	15 16 17 18 19 20 21 22 23 24 25 26 27 28 29 30 31
Kislev	17 18 19 20 21 22 23 24 25 26 27 28 29 30	Tebet 1 2 3 4 5 6 7 8 9 10 11 12 13 14 15 16 17

Jan 1994	1 2 3 4 5 6 7 8 9 10 11 12	13 14 15 16 17 18 19 20 21 22 23 24 25 26 27 28 29 30 31
Tebet 5754	18 19 20 21 22 23 24 25 26 27 28 29	Shebat 1 2 3 4 5 6 7 8 9 10 11 12 13 14 15 16 17 18 19

February	1 2 3 4 5 6 7 8 9 10 11	12 13 14 15 16 17 18 19 20 21 22 23 24 25 26 27 28
Shebat	20 21 22 23 24 25 26 27 28 29 30 Adar	1 2 3 4 5 6 7 8 9 10 11 12 13 14 15 16 17

March	1 2 3 4 5 6 7 8 9 10 11 12	13 14 15 16 17 18 19 20 21 22 23 24 25 26 27 28 29 30 31
Adar	18 19 20 21 22 23 24 25 26 27 28 29	Nisan 1 2 3 4 5 6 7 8 9 10 11 12 13 14 15 16 17 18 19

April	1 2 3 4 5 6 7 8 9 10 11	12 13 14 15 16 17 18 19 20 21 22 23 24 25 26 27 28 29 30
Nisan	20 21 22 23 24 25 26 27 28 29 30	Iyar 1 2 3 4 5 6 7 8 9 10 11 12 13 14 15 16 17 18 19

May	1 2 3 4 5 6 7 8 9 10	11 12 13 14 15 16 17 18 19 20 21 22 23 24 25 26 27 28 29 30 31
Iyar	20 21 22 23 24 25 26 27 28 29	Sivan 1 2 3 4 5 6 7 8 9 10 11 12 13 14 15 16 17 18 19 20 21

June	1 2 3 4 5 6 7 8 9	10 11 12 13 14 15 16 17 18 19 20 21 22 23 24 25 26 27 28 29 30
Sivan	22 23 24 25 26 27 28 29 30	Tammuz 1 2 3 4 5 6 7 8 9 10 11 12 13 14 15 16 17 18 19 20 21

July	1 2 3 4 5 6 7 8	9 10 11 12 13 14 15 16 17 18 19 20 21 22 23 24 25 26 27 28 29 30 31
Tammuz	22 23 24 25 26 27 28 29	Ab 1 2 3 4 5 6 7 8 9 10 11 12 13 14 15 16 17 18 19 20 21 22 23

August	1 2 3 4 5 6 7	8 9 10 11 12 13 14 15 16 17 18 19 20 21 22 23 24 25 26 27 28 29 30 31
Ab	24 25 26 27 28 29 30	Elul 1 2 3 4 5 6 7 8 9 10 11 12 13 14 15 16 17 18 19 20 21 22 23 24

September	1 2 3 4 5	6 7 8 9 10 11 12 13 14 15 16 17 18 19 20 21 22 23 24 25 26 27 28 29 30
Elul	25 26 27 28 29	Tishri* 1 2 3 4 5 6 7 8 9 10 11 12 13 14 15 16 17 18 19 20 21 22 23 24 25

* Jewish New Year 5755

October	1 2 3 4 5	6 7 8 9 10 11 12 13 14 15 16 17 18 19 20 21 22 23 24 25 26 27 28 29 30 31
Tishri 5755	26 27 28 29 30	Cheshvan 1 2 3 4 5 6 7 8 9 10 11 12 13 14 15 16 17 18 19 20 21 22 23 24 25 26

November	1 2 3	4 5 6 7 8 9 10 11 12 13 14 15 16 17 18 19 20 21 22 23 24 25 26 27 28 29 30
Cheshvan	27 28 29	Kislev 1 2 3 4 5 6 7 8 9 10 11 12 13 14 15 16 17 18 19 20 21 22 23 24 25 26 27

December	1 2 3	4 5 6 7 8 9 10 11 12 13 14 15 16 17 18 19 20 21 22 23 24 25 26 27 28 29 30 31
Kislev	28 29 30	Tebet 1 2 3 4 5 6 7 8 9 10 11 12 13 14 15 16 17 18 19 20 21 22 23 24 25 26 27 28

Jan 1995	1	2 3 4 5 6 7 8 9 10 11 12 13 14 15 16 17 18 19 20 21 22 23 24 25 26 27 28 29 30 31
Tebet	29	Shebat 1 2 3 4 5 6 7 8 9 10 11 12 13 14 15 16 17 18 19 20 21 22 23 24 25 26 27 28 29 30

February	1 2 3 4 5 6 7 8 9 10 11 12 13 14 15 16 17 18 19 20 21 22 23 24 25 26 27 28
Adar	1 2 3 4 5 6 7 8 9 10 11 12 13 14 15 16 17 18 19 20 21 22 23 24 25 26 27 28

March	1 2	3 4 5 6 7 8 9 10 11 12 13 14 15 16 17 18 19 20 21 22 23 24 25 26 27 28 29 30 31
Adar	29 30	Ve-Adar 1 2 3 4 5 6 7 8 9 10 11 12 13 14 15 16 17 18 19 20 21 22 23 24 25 26 27 28 29

April	1 2 3 4 5 6 7 8 9 10 11 12 13 14 15 16 17 18 19 20 21 22 23 24 25 26 27 28 29 30
Nisan	1 2 3 4 5 6 7 8 9 10 11 12 13 14 15 16 17 18 19 20 21 22 23 24 25 26 27 28 29 30

| May | 1 2 3 4 5 6 7 8 9 10 11 12 13 14 15 16 17 18 19 20 21 22 23 24 25 26 27 28 29 | 30 31 |
| Iyar | 1 2 3 4 5 6 7 8 9 10 11 12 13 14 15 16 17 18 19 20 21 22 23 24 25 26 27 28 29 Sivan | 1 2 |

| June | 1 2 3 4 5 6 7 8 9 10 11 12 13 14 15 16 17 18 19 20 21 22 23 24 25 26 27 28 | 29 30 |
| Sivan | 3 4 5 6 7 8 9 10 11 12 13 14 15 16 17 18 19 20 21 22 23 24 25 26 27 28 29 30 Tammuz | 1 2 |

| July | 1 2 3 4 5 6 7 8 9 10 11 12 13 14 15 16 17 18 19 20 21 22 23 24 25 26 27 | 28 29 30 31 |
| Tammuz | 3 4 5 6 7 8 9 10 11 12 13 14 15 16 17 18 19 20 21 22 23 24 25 26 27 28 29 Ab | 1 2 3 4 |

| August | 1 2 3 4 5 6 7 8 9 10 11 12 13 14 15 16 17 18 19 20 21 22 23 24 25 26 | 27 28 29 30 31 |
| Ab | 5 6 7 8 9 10 11 12 13 14 15 16 17 18 19 20 21 22 23 24 25 26 27 28 29 30 Elul | 1 2 3 4 5 |

| September | 1 2 3 4 5 6 7 8 9 10 11 12 13 14 15 16 17 18 19 20 21 22 23 24 | 25 26 27 28 29 30 |
| Elul | 6 7 8 9 10 11 12 13 14 15 16 17 18 19 20 21 22 23 24 25 26 27 28 29 Tishri* | 1 2 3 4 5 6 |

* Jewish New Year 5756

THE ISLAMIC CALENDAR

The Islamic calendar is based on lunar years beginning with the year of the *Hejirah* (AD 622 of the Julian calendar), when Muhammad travelled from Mecca to Medina. It runs in cycles of 30 years, of which the 2nd, 5th, 7th, 10th, 13th, 16th, 18th, 21st, 24th, 26th and 29th are leap years. A year consists of 12 months containing alternately 30 days and 29 days, with the intercalation of one day at the end of the 12th month – Dhû'l Hijja – in a leap year. Common years have 354 days, leap years 355. The extra day is intercalated in order to reconcile the date of the first of the month with the date of the actual New Moon. Some Muslims register the first of the month on the evening that the crescent becomes visible.

Hejirah years are used principally in Iran, Turkey, Saudi Arabia and other states of the Arabian peninsula, Egypt, certain parts of India, and Malaysia.

MONTHS OF THE MUSLIM CALENDAR

1. Muharram	30 days
2. Safar	29 days
3. Rabîa I	30 days
4. Rabîa II	29 days
5. Jumâda I	30 days
6. Jumâda II	29 days
7. Rajab	30 days
8. Shaabân	29 days
9. Ramadan	30 days
10. Shawwâl	29 days
11. Dhû'l-Qa'da	30 days
12. Dhû'l Hijja	29 days (30 days in a leap year)

COMPARATIVE ISLAMIC CALENDAR 1993–1995

| Sept 1993 | 1 2 3 4 5 6 7 8 9 10 11 12 13 14 15 16 17 | 18 19 20 21 22 23 24 25 26 27 28 29 30 |
| Rabîa I 14 14 | 14 15 16 17 18 19 20 21 22 23 24 25 26 27 28 29 30 Rabîa II | 1 2 3 4 5 6 7 8 9 10 11 12 13 |

| October | 1 2 3 4 5 6 7 8 9 10 11 12 13 14 15 16 | 17 18 19 20 21 22 23 24 25 26 27 28 29 30 31 |
| Rabîa II | 14 15 16 17 18 19 20 21 22 23 24 25 26 27 28 29 Jumâda I | 1 2 3 4 5 6 7 8 9 10 11 12 13 14 15 |

| November | 1 2 3 4 5 6 7 8 9 10 11 12 13 14 15 | 16 17 18 19 20 21 22 23 24 25 26 27 28 29 30 |
| Jumâda I | 16 17 18 19 20 21 22 23 24 25 26 27 28 29 30 Jumâda II | 1 2 3 4 5 6 7 8 9 10 11 12 13 14 15 |

| December | 1 2 3 4 5 6 7 8 9 10 11 12 13 14 | 15 16 17 18 19 20 21 22 23 24 25 26 27 28 29 30 31 |
| Jumâda II | 16 17 18 19 20 21 22 23 24 25 26 27 28 29 Rajab | 1 2 3 4 5 6 7 8 9 10 11 12 13 14 15 16 17 |

| Jan 1994 | 1 2 3 4 5 6 7 8 9 10 11 12 13 | 14 15 16 17 18 19 20 21 22 23 24 25 26 27 28 29 30 31 |
| Rajab | 18 19 20 21 22 23 24 25 26 27 28 29 30 Shaabân | 1 2 3 4 5 6 7 8 9 10 11 12 13 14 15 16 17 18 |

| February | 1 2 3 4 5 6 7 8 9 10 11 | 12 13 14 15 16 17 18 19 20 21 22 23 24 25 26 27 28 |
| Shaabân | 19 20 21 22 23 24 25 26 27 28 29 Ramadan | 1 2 3 4 5 6 7 8 9 10 11 12 13 14 15 16 17 |

| March | 1 2 3 4 5 6 7 8 9 10 11 12 13 | 14 15 16 17 18 19 20 21 22 23 24 25 26 27 28 29 30 31 |
| Ramadan | 18 19 20 21 22 23 24 25 26 27 28 29 30 Shawwâl 1 2 3 4 5 6 7 8 9 10 11 12 13 14 15 16 17 18 |

| April | 1 2 3 4 5 6 7 8 9 10 11 | 12 13 14 15 16 17 18 19 20 21 22 23 24 25 26 27 28 29 30 |
| Shawwâl | 19 20 21 22 23 24 25 26 27 28 29 Dhû'l-Qa'da 1 2 3 4 5 6 7 8 9 10 11 12 13 14 15 16 17 18 19 |

| May | 1 2 3 4 5 6 7 8 9 10 11 | 12 13 14 15 16 17 18 19 20 21 22 23 24 25 26 27 28 29 30 31 |
| Dhû'l-Qa'da | 20 21 22 23 24 25 26 27 28 29 30 Dhû'l Hijja 1 2 3 4 5 6 7 8 9 10 11 12 13 14 15 16 17 18 19 20 |

| June | 1 2 3 4 5 6 7 8 9 | 10 11 12 13 14 15 16 17 18 19 20 21 22 23 24 25 26 27 28 29 30 |
| Dhû'l Hijja | 21 22 23 24 25 26 27 28 29 Muharram* 1 2 3 4 5 6 7 8 9 10 11 12 13 14 15 16 17 18 19 20 21 |

* Islamic New Year 1415

| July | 1 2 3 4 5 6 7 8 9 | 10 11 12 13 14 15 16 17 18 19 20 21 22 23 24 25 26 27 28 29 30 31 |
| Muharram | 22 23 24 25 26 27 28 29 30 Safar 1 2 3 4 5 6 7 8 9 10 11 12 13 14 15 16 17 18 19 20 21 22 |

| August | 1 2 3 4 5 6 7 | 8 9 10 11 12 13 14 15 16 17 18 19 20 21 22 23 24 25 26 27 28 29 30 31 |
| Safar | 23 24 25 26 27 28 29 Rabîa I 1 2 3 4 5 6 7 8 9 10 11 12 13 14 15 16 17 18 19 20 21 22 23 24 |

| September | 1 2 3 4 5 6 | 7 8 9 10 11 12 13 14 15 16 17 18 19 20 21 22 23 24 25 26 27 28 29 30 |
| Rabîa I | 25 26 27 28 29 30 Rabîa II 1 2 3 4 5 6 7 8 9 10 11 12 13 14 15 16 17 18 19 20 21 22 23 24 |

| October | 1 2 3 4 5 | 6 7 8 9 10 11 12 13 14 15 16 17 18 19 20 21 22 23 24 25 26 27 28 29 30 31 |
| Rabîa II | 25 26 27 28 29 Jumâda I 1 2 3 4 5 6 7 8 9 10 11 12 13 14 15 16 17 18 19 20 21 22 23 24 25 26 |

| November | 1 2 3 4 | 5 6 7 8 9 10 11 12 13 14 15 16 17 18 19 20 21 22 23 24 25 26 27 28 29 30 |
| Jumâda I | 27 28 29 30 Jumâda II 1 2 3 4 5 6 7 8 9 10 11 12 13 14 15 16 17 18 19 20 21 22 23 24 25 26 |

| December | 1 2 3 | 4 5 6 7 8 9 10 11 12 13 14 15 16 17 18 19 20 21 22 23 24 25 26 27 28 29 30 31 |
| Jumâda II | 27 28 29 Rajab 1 2 3 4 5 6 7 8 9 10 11 12 13 14 15 16 17 18 19 20 21 22 23 24 25 26 27 28 |

| Jan 1995 | 1 2 | 3 4 5 6 7 8 9 10 11 12 13 14 15 16 17 18 19 20 21 22 23 24 25 26 27 28 29 30 31 |
| Rajab | 29 30 Shaabân 1 2 3 4 5 6 7 8 9 10 11 12 13 14 15 16 17 18 19 20 21 22 23 24 25 26 27 28 29 |

| February | 1 2 3 4 5 6 7 8 9 10 11 12 13 14 15 16 17 18 19 20 21 22 23 24 25 26 27 28 |
| Ramadan | 1 2 3 4 5 6 7 8 9 10 11 12 13 14 15 16 17 18 19 20 21 22 23 24 25 26 27 28 |

| March | 1 2 | 3 4 5 6 7 8 9 10 11 12 13 14 15 16 17 18 19 20 21 22 23 24 25 26 27 28 29 30 31 |
| Ramadan | 29 30 Shawwâl 1 2 3 4 5 6 7 8 9 10 11 12 13 14 15 16 17 18 19 20 21 22 23 24 25 26 27 28 29 |

| April | 1 2 3 4 5 6 7 8 9 10 11 12 13 14 15 16 17 18 19 20 21 22 23 24 25 26 27 28 29 30 |
| Dhû'l-Qa'da | 1 2 3 4 5 6 7 8 9 10 11 12 13 14 15 16 17 18 19 20 21 22 23 24 25 26 27 28 29 30 |

| May | 1 2 3 4 5 6 7 8 9 10 11 12 13 14 15 16 17 18 19 20 21 22 23 24 25 26 27 28 29 30 | 31 |
| Dhû'l Hijja | 1 2 3 4 5 6 7 8 9 10 11 12 13 14 15 16 17 18 19 20 21 22 23 24 25 26 27 28 29 30 Muharram* 1 |

* Islamic New Year 1416

June   1 2 3 4 5 6 7 8 9 10 11 12 13 14 15 16 17 18 19 20 21 22 23 24 25 26 27 28 29   30
Muharram   2 3 4 5 6 7 8 9 10 11 12 13 14 15 16 17 18 19 20 21 22 23 24 25 26 27 28 29 30 Safar   1

July   1 2 3 4 5 6 7 8 9 10 11 12 13 14 15 16 17 18 19 20 21 22 23 24 25 26 27 28   29 30 31
Safar   2 3 4 5 6 7 8 9 10 11 12 13 14 15 16 17 18 19 20 21 22 23 24 25 26 27 28 29 Rabîa I 1 2 3

August   1 2 3 4 5 6 7 8 9 10 11 12 13 14 15 16 17 18 19 20 21 22 23 24 25 26 27   28 29 30 31
Rabîa I   4 5 6 7 8 9 10 11 12 13 14 15 16 17 18 19 20 21 22 23 24 25 26 27 28 29 30 Rabîa II 1 2 3 4

September   1 2 3 4 5 6 7 8 9 10 11 12 13 14 15 16 17 18 19 20 21 22 23 24 25   26 27 28 29 30
Rabîa II   5 6 7 8 9 10 11 12 13 14 15 16 17 18 19 20 21 22 23 24 25 26 27 28 29 Jumâda I 1 2 3 4 5

THE CHINESE CALENDAR

The ancient Chinese calendar is based on a lunar year and consists of 12 months of alternately 29 and 30 days, making 354 days in total. To keep the calendar in step with the solar year intercalary months are inserted. The months are numbered and sometimes given one of the 12 animal names that are usually attached to years and hours in the Chinese calendar (see Chinese Zodiac). The calendar was in use until the establishment of the republic (1911) when the Gregorian calendar was introduced, and was formally banned in 1930. The calendar is, however, still used unofficially in China, and the New Year festival remains a national holiday. It is also used in Tibet, Hong Kong, Singapore, and Malaysia.

The Chinese New Year begins at the first new moon after the Sun enters Aquarius, and therefore falls between 21 January and 19 February in the Gregorian calendar.

THE JAPANESE CALENDAR

The Japanese calendar has the same structure – in terms of years, months and weeks – as the Gregorian calendar. The difference lies in the numeration of the years as the Japanese chronology is based on a series of imperial epochs. As the Gregorian calendar calculates the years from one religious date, the Japanese calendar calculates each epoch from the accession of an emperor.

The four most recent epochs are based on the reigns of the last four emperors, who are referred to by their epoch names – their personal names are never used.

Epoch Meiji   13 Oct 1868–31 July 1912
(Emperor Mutsuhito)
Epoch Taisho   1 Aug 1912–25 Dec 1926
(Emperor Yoshihito)
Epoch Showa   26 Dec 1926–7 Jan 1989
(Emperor Hirohito)
Epoch Heisei   8 Jan 1989–
(Emperor Akihito)

The months are unnamed, simply numbered. The days of the week, however, do have names:

Nichiyobi	Sun-day (Sunday)
Getsuyobi	Moon-day (Monday)
Kayobi	Fire-day (Tuesday)
Suiyobi	Water-day (Wednesday)
Mokuyobi	Wood-day (Thursday)
Kinyobi	Metal-day (Friday)
Doyobi	Earth-day (Saturday)

INDIAN CALENDARS

The principal Indian calendars reckon their epochs from historical events such as the accession or death of a ruler or a religious founder.

The Vikrama era originated in northern India and is still used in western India. It dates from 23 February 57 BC in the Gregorian calendar.

The Saka era dates from 3 March AD 78 in the Gregorian calendar. It is based on the solar year – beginning with the spring equinox. The 365 days (366 in a leap year) are divided into 12 months. The first five months are of 31 days and the remaining seven of 30 – in a leap year the first six months are of 31 days and the last six of 30. In 1957 the Saka era was declared the national calendar of India, to run concurrently with the Gregorian calendar.

The Buddhist era dates from 543 BC, the believed date of Buddha's death (Nirvana), although many Buddhist sects adopt different dates for his death. The actual date of his death was 487 BC.

The Jain era dates from the death of the founder of the Jainist religion, Vardhamana, in 527 BC.

The Parsee (Zoroastrian) era dates from 16 June AD 632 in the Gregorian calendar.

THE COPTIC CALENDAR

The Coptic calendar – which is still used in areas of Egypt and Ethiopia – dates from 29 August AD 284 of the Gregorian calendar. The Coptic year is made up of 12 months of 30 days, followed by five complementary days. In a leap year – which immediately precedes the leap year of the Julian calendar – the last month is followed by six days.

THE ANCIENT GREEK CALENDAR

The chronology of Ancient Greece was based on cycles of four years – Olympiads – corresponding with the periodic Olympic Games held on the plain of Olympia in Elis. The intervening years were simply numbered, 1st, 2nd, etc., and each Olympiad was named after the victor of the Games. The first recorded Olympiad is Choroebus, 776 BC.

THE FRENCH REPUBLICAN CALENDAR

The French republican calendar was adopted in 1793, replacing the Gregorian calendar with a secular and more regular alternative. The year was divided into 12 months of 30 days with five (in leap years, six) supplementary days at the end of the year. Weeks were replaced by decades of ten days, which were named *primidi, duodi, tridi, quartidi, quintidi, sextidi, septidi, octidi, nonidi* and *décadi*. Each month comprised three decades. The era dated from 22 September 1792 of the Gregorian calendar. The republican calendar was abolished by Napoleon I on 1 January 1806.

The months of the calendar were:

Vendémiaire (meaning 'the month of the grape harvest'). Gregorian equivalent: 23 September to 22 October.

Brumaire (meaning 'the month of mist'). Gregorian equivalent: 23 October to 21 November.

Frimaire (meaning 'the month of frost'). Gregorian equivalent: 22 November to 21 December.

Nivôse (meaning 'the month of snow'). Gregorian equivalent: 22 December to 20 January.

Pluviôse (meaning 'the month of rain'). Gregorian equivalent: 21 January to 19 February.

Ventôse (meaning 'the month of wind'). Gregorian equivalent: 20 February to 21 March.

Germinal (meaning 'the month of buds'). Gregorian equivalent: 22 March to 20 April.

Floréal (meaning 'the month of flowers'). Gregorian equivalent: 21 April to 20 May.

Prairial (meaning 'the month of meadows'). Gregorian equivalent: 21 May to 19 June.

Messidor (meaning 'the month of harvest'). Gregorian equivalent: 20 June to 19 July.

Thermidor (meaning 'the month of heat'). Gregorian equivalent: 20 July to 18 August.

Fructidor (meaning 'the month of fruit'). Gregorian equivalent: 19 August to 22 September, including the supplementary days.

TIME ZONES

Until the last quarter of the 19th century the time kept was a local affair, or in smaller countries, based on the time kept in the capital city. But the spread of railways across the larger countries caused great confusion in time-keeping as timetables could not operate without standardization.

In 1880 Greenwich Mean Time (GMT) became the legal time in the British Isles and by 1884 international time zones had been established over much of the world.

The world is divided into 24 zones, or segments, each of 15° of longitude. Twelve zones are to the east of the Greenwich meridian (0°) and are therefore in advance of GMT. Twelve are to the west of the Greenwich meridian and are behind GMT. Each zone extends 7½° on either side of its central meridian.

The International Date Line runs down the 180° meridian – with some variations to include certain Pacific island nations entirely within one zone. Travelling eastward across the date line Sunday becomes Saturday; travelling westward across the date line Sunday becomes Monday.

Some large countries extend over several segments and are thus obliged to have several time zones.

THE USA

The 48 contiguous states of the USA are divided between the Eastern, Central, Mountain and Pacific time zones (respectively five, six, seven and eight hours behind GMT), while the addition of Alaska and Hawaii adds a further four time zones.

Eastern time is kept by: Connecticut, Florida (except far west), Georgia, Indiana, Kentucky (eastern part), Maine, Maryland, Massachusetts, Michigan, New Hampshire, New Jersey, New York State, North Carolina, Ohio, Pennsylvania, Rhode Island, South Carolina, Tennessee (eastern part), Vermont, Virginia, Washington DC and West Virginia.

Central time is kept in: Alabama, Arkansas, Florida (far west), Illinois, Iowa, Kansas (except far west), Kentucky (western part), Louisiana, Minnesota, Mississippi, Missouri, Nebraska (except far west), North Dakota (eastern part), Oklahoma, South Dakota (eastern part), Tennessee (western part), Texas (except far west) and Wisconsin.

Mountain time is kept in: Arizona, Colorado, Idaho (except far north), Kansas (far west), Montana, Nebraska (far west), New Mexico, North Dakota (western part), Oregon (far east), South Dakota (western part), Texas (far west), Utah and Wyoming.

Pacific time is kept in: California, Idaho (far north), Nevada, Oregon (except far east) and Washington State.

CANADA

Canada is divided the zones Atlantic, Eastern, Central, Mountain and Pacific (respectively four, five, six, seven and eight hours behind GMT).

Atlantic time is kept in: New Brunswick, Newfoundland, Nova Scotia, Prince Edward Island, Quebec (far east), and part of the Northwest Territories.

Canadian Eastern time is kept in: Ontario (except far west), Quebec (except far east), and part of the Northwest Territories.

Canadian Central time is kept in: Manitoba, Ontario (far west), Saskatchewan (far east), and part of the Northwest Territories.

Canadian Mountain time is kept in: Alberta, Saskatchewan (except far east), and part of the Northwest Territories.

Canadian Pacific time is kept in: British Columbia and Yukon.

AUSTRALIA

Australia has three zones (see map). However, owing to daylight saving schemes, for most of the year Australia has five time zones: Western Australia is eight hours ahead of GMT, South Australia is ten and a half hours, Northern Territory is nine and a half hours, Queensland is ten hours, and the rest of the country eleven hours ahead.

RUSSIA

Russia is divided into 11 time zones with all of European Russia four hours ahead of GMT. Crossing the border from Poland to the Kaliningrad enclave of Russia, watches are advanced by two hours.

EUROPE

Europe has three time zones: GMT, mid-European time (one hour in advance of GMT), and east European time (two hours in advance of GMT).

GMT in Europe is kept by: Iceland, Ireland, Portugal, and the UK.

Mid-European time is kept by: Albania, Andorra, Austria, Belgium, Bosnia, Croatia, Czech Republic, Denmark, France, Germany, Gibraltar, Hungary, Italy, Liechtenstein, Luxembourg, Macedonia (Skopje), Monaco, Netherlands, Norway, San Marino, Slovakia, Slovenia, Spain, Sweden, Switzerland, Vatican, and Yugoslavia (Serbia and Montenegro).

East European time is kept by: Belarus, Bulgaria, Cyprus, Estonia, Finland, Greece, Latvia, Lithuania, Moldova, Romania, and Ukraine.

A very few countries, or divisions of countries, do not adhere to the Greenwich system at all. Certain other countries, such as China, do not use a zoning system, and the whole nation – despite spanning more than one of the 24 segments – elects to keep the same time. Yet a third group – including Suriname, Iran, Afghanistan and India – use differences of half an hour.

SUMMER TIME

In 1916 legal time in the UK was advanced one hour ahead of GMT as a means of extending daylight in the evening. Between 1941 and 1945 and again in 1947, 'double summer time' was introduced in the UK. Since then Summer Time has been in force during most years, although between 1968 and 1971 British Standard Time – in which the legal time was one hour head of GMT throughout the year – was in force. British Summer Time is defined as 'the period beginning at two o'clock, GMT, in the morning of the day after the third Saturday in March or, if that day is Easter Day, the day after the second Saturday in March, and ending at two o'clock, GMT, in the morning of the day after the fourth Saturday in October'. This has been amended to bring the UK closer to the beginning and ending of daylight-saving time in neighbouring EC countries. In 1994 Summer Time begins on 27 March and ends on 23 October.

WATCHES AT SEA

A watch at sea is four hours, except the period between 4 p.m. and 8 p.m. which in the Royal Navy is divided into two short watches termed the first dog watch and the last dog watch. (The word 'dog' is here a corruption of 'dodge'.)

Midnight – 4 a.m.	Middle watch
4 a.m. – 8 a.m.	Morning watch
8 a.m. – noon	Forenoon watch
noon – 4 p.m.	Afternoon watch
4 p.m. – 6 p.m.	First dog watch
6 p.m. – 8 p.m.	Last/2nd dog watch
8 p.m. – midnight	First watch

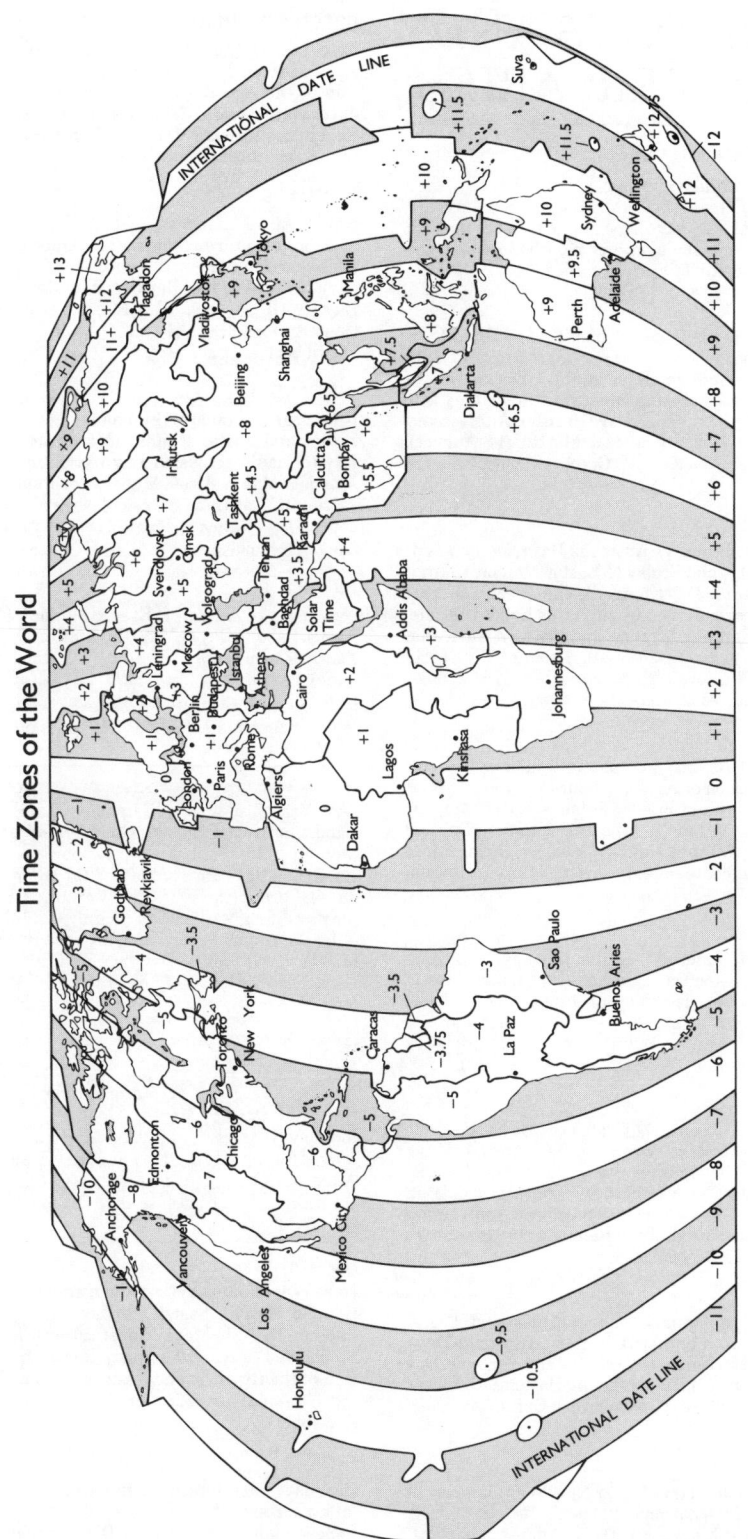

Time Zones of the World

HOLIDAYS AND ANNIVERSARIES

PUBLIC HOLIDAYS

The public holidays in major countries are listed below. The dates of some holidays – mainly those of a religious nature – vary from one year to the next. In such cases only the month or months in which the holiday normally falls are recorded.

ARGENTINA

New Year (1 January), Good Friday (March or April), Labour Day (1 May), Anniversary of 1810 Revolution (*National Day*; 25 May), Occupation of Islas Malvinas/Falkland Islands (10 June), Flag Day (20 June), Independence Day (10 July), Anniversary of Death of General de San Martín (17 August), Discovery of America (12 October), Christmas (25 December).

AUSTRALIA

New Year (1 January), Australia Day (*National Day*; 26 January), Good Friday to Easter Monday (March or April), Anzac Day (25 April), The Queen's Official Birthday (early June, although this holiday is celebrated in March in Victoria and Western Australia, and in May in Queensland), Labour Day (early October), Christmas (25–26 December; 25 December only in South Australia).

AUSTRIA

New Year (1 January), Epiphany (6 January), Easter Monday (March or April), Labour Day (1 May), Whit Monday (May or June), Corpus Christi (May or June), Assumption (15 August), *National Day* (26 October), All Saints' Day (1 November), Immaculate Conception (8 December), Christmas (25–26 December).

BELGIUM

New Year (1 January), Easter Monday (March or April), Ascension Day (April or May), Labour Day (1 May), Whit Monday (May or June), Independence Day (*National Day*; 21 July), Assumption (15 August), All Saints' Day (1 November), Armistice Day (11 November), Christmas (25 December).

BRAZIL

New Year (1 January), Tiradentes Day (21 April), Labour Day (1 May), Ascension Day (April or May), Corpus Christi (May or June), Independence Day (*National Day*; 7 September), Our Lady Aparecida (12 October), All Souls' Day (2 November), Anniversary of the Proclamation of the Republic (15 November), Christmas (25 December).

CANADA

New Year (1 January), Good Friday and Easter Monday (March or April), Victoria Day (mid-May), Canada Day (*National Day*; 1 July), Labour Day (early September), Thanksgiving Day (mid-October), Remembrance Day (11 November), Christmas (25–26 December).

CHINA

New Year (1 January), Lunar New Year (January or February), International Women's Day (8 March), Labour Day (1 May), Army Day (1 August), Teachers' Day (9 September), *National Days* (October 1–2).

CZECH REPUBLIC

New Year (1 January), Easter Monday (March or April), Labour Day (1 May), Liberation Day (8 May), Day of the Apostles St Cyril and St Methodius (5 July), Anniversary of the Proclamation of the Czech Republic (*National Day*; 28 October), Christmas (24–26 December).

DENMARK

New Year (1 January), Good Friday to Easter Monday (March or April), The Queen's Birthday (*National Day*; 19 April – not taken as public holiday), General Prayer Day (April or May), Ascension Day (April or May), Whit Monday (May or June), Constitution Day (5 June), Christmas (25–26 December).

FINLAND

New Year (1 January), Epiphany (6 January), Good Friday and Easter Monday (March or April), May Day (1 May), Ascension Day (April or May), Whit Monday (May or June), Midsummer Day (mid-June), All Saints' Day (in first week of November), Independence Day (*National Day*; 6 December), Christmas (25–26 December).

FRANCE

New Year (1 January), Easter Monday (March or April), Labour Day (1 May), Liberation Day (8 May), Ascension Day (April or May), Whit Monday (May or June), Bastille Day (*National Day*; 14 July), Assumption (15 August), All Saints' Day (1 November), Armistice Day (11 November), Christmas (25 December).

GERMANY

New Year (1 January), Epiphany (mainly Catholic Länder only; 6 January), Good Friday and Easter Monday (March or April), Labour Day (1 May), Ascension Day (April or May), Whit Monday (May or June), Corpus Christi (mainly Catholic Länder only; May or June), Assumption (mainly Catholic Länder only; 15 August), Day of Unity (*National Day*; 3 October), All Saints' Day (mainly Catholic Länder only; 1 November), Day of Prayer and Repentance (mid-November), Christmas (25–26 December).

GREECE

New Year (1 January), Epiphany (6 January), Clean Monday (February or March), Independence Day (*National Day*; 25 March), Good Friday to Easter Monday (Orthodox; March or April), Labour Day (1 May), Holy Spirit Day (May or June), Assumption (15 August), Ochi Day (Anniversary of Greek defiance to the Italian ultimatum of 1940; 28 October), Christmas (25–26 December).

HUNGARY

New Year (1 January), Anniversary of 1848 Revolution (15 March), Easter Monday (March or April), Labour Day (1 May), Constitution Day and St Stephen's Festival (20 August), Day of the Proclamation of the Republic and Anniversary of 1956 Uprising (*National Day*; 23 October), Christmas (25–26 December).

INDIA

(Holidays vary locally in India and not all of the following are observed throughout the country.) Pongal (January), Republic Day (*National Day*; 26 January), Maha Shrivratri (February), Holi

(March), Ram Navami (April), Mahabir Jayanti
(March or April), Good Friday (March or April), End
of Ramadan (March, April or May), Buddha Purnima
(May), Id-uz-Zuha, Feast of the Sacrifice (June, July
or August), Islamic New Year (July or August),
Janmashtami (August), Onam (August or Septem-
ber), Mahatma Gandhi's Birthday (2 October), Maha
Ashtami (October), Diwali (October), Durga Puja
(October or November), Guru Nanak Jayanti
(November), Christmas (25–26 December).

IRELAND
New Year (1 January), St Patrick's Day (*National
Day*; 17 March), Good Friday and Easter Monday
(March or April), June Bank Holiday Monday (early
June), August Bank Holiday Monday (early August),
October Bank Holiday Monday (late October),
Christmas (25–26 December).

ITALY
New Year (1 January), Epiphany (6 January), Easter
Monday (March or April), Liberation Day (25 April),
Labour Day (1 May), *National Day* (2 June – not
taken as a public holiday), Assumption (15 August),
All Saints' Day (1 November), National Unity Day (5
November), Immaculate Conception (8 December),
Christmas (25–26 December).

JAPAN
New Year (1 January), Coming of Age Day (15
January), National Foundation Day (11 February),
Vernal Equinox Day (21 March), Greenery Day (29
April), Constitution Memorial Day (3 May), Child-
ren's Day (5 May), Respect for the Aged Day (15
September), Autumnal Equinox Day (23 September),
Sports Day (10 October), Culture Day (3 November),
Labour Thanksgiving Day (23 November), The
Emperor's Birthday (*National Day*; 23 December).

MEXICO
New Year (1 January), Constitution Day (5 Feb-
ruary), Birthday of Benito Juárez (21 March), Good
Friday to Easter Monday (March or April), Labour
Day (1 May), Anniversary of the Battle of Puebla (5
May), President's Annual Message Day (1 Septem-
ber), Independence Day (*National Day*; 16 Septem-
ber), Discovery of America Day (12 October), All
Souls' Day (unofficial; 2 November), Anniversary of
the Revolution (20 November), Our Lady of
Guadeloupe (unofficial; 12 December), Christmas
(24–25 December).

NETHERLANDS
New Year (1 January), Good Friday and Easter
Monday (March or April), Queen's Day (*National
Day*; 30 April), National Liberation Day (5 May),
Ascension Day (April or May), Whit Monday (May or
June), Christmas (25–26 December).

NEW ZEALAND
New Year (1 January), Waitangi Day (*National Day*;
6 February), Good Friday to Easter Monday (March
or April), Anzac Day (25 April), The Queen's Official
Birthday (early June), Labour Day (late October),
Christmas (25–26 December).

NIGERIA
New Year (1 January), Good Friday to Easter
Monday (March or April), End of Ramadan (March,
April or May), Id al-Kabir (Feast of the Sacrifice;
June, July or August), Mouloud (Birthday of the
Prophet Muhammad; August, September or Octo-

ber), *National Day* (1 October), Christmas (25–26
December).

NORWAY
New Year (1 January), Maundy Thursday, Good
Friday and Easter Monday (March or April), May
Day (1 May), Ascension Day (April or May), Indepen-
dence Day (*National Day*; 17 May), Whit Monday
(May or June), Christmas (25–26 December).

PAKISTAN
Beginning of Ramadan (February, March or April),
Pakistan Day (*National Day*; 23 March), End of
Ramadan (March, April or May), Id al-Adha (July or
August), Islamic New Year (July or August), Inde-
pendence Day (*National Day*; 14 August), Ashoura
(June, July or August), Birthday of the Prophet
(August, September or October), Defence of Pakistan
Day (6 September), Anniversary of death of Quaid-i-
Azam (11 September), Allama Iqbal Day (9 Novem-
ber), Birthday of Quaid-i-Azam and Christmas (25
December). Good Friday and Easter Monday (March
or April), and Boxing Day (26 December) are optional
holidays for Christians only.

POLAND
New Year (1 January), Easter Monday (March or
April), Labour Day (1 May), *National Day* (3 May),
Victory Day (9 May), Corpus Christi (May or June),
Assumption (15 August), All Saints' Day (1 Novem-
ber), Anniversary of the Proclamation of the Polish
Republic (11 November), Christmas (25–26 Decem-
ber).

PORTUGAL
New Year (1 January), Carnival Day (February or
March), Good Friday (March or April), Liberty Day
(25 April), Labour Day (1 May), Corpus Christi (May
or June), Portugal Day (*National Day*; 10 June), St
Anthony's Day (Lisbon and south only; 13 June), St
John the Baptist's Day (Oporto and north only; 24
June), Assumption (15 August), Anniversary of the
Proclamation of the Republic (5 October), All Saints'
Day (1 November), Anniversary of the Restoration of
Independence (1 December), Immaculate Conception
(8 December), Christmas (25 December).

RUSSIA
New Year (1 January), Christmas (Orthodox; 7
January), International Women's Day (8 March),
May Day (1–2 May), Victory Day (9 May), Anniversary of the 1917 Revolution (7–8 November). (Public
holidays in Russia are under review. There is now no
official national day.)

SOUTH AFRICA
New Year (1 January), Good Friday to Easter
Monday (March or April), Ascension Day (April or
May), Workers' Day (1 May), Republic Day (*National
Day*; 31 May), Settlers' Day (5 September), Kruger
Day (10 October), Covenant Day (16 December),
Christmas (25–26 December).

SPAIN
New Year (1 January), Epiphany (6 January),
Maundy Thursday (not a public holiday in Catalo-
nia; March or April), Good Friday (March or April),
Easter Monday (Catalonia and Balearic Islands
only; March or April), St Joseph the Worker (1 May),
Corpus Christi (May or June), King Juan Carlos's
Saint's Day (24 June), St James (25 July), Assump-
tion (15 August), Day of the Hispanidad (*National*

Day – although not celebrated in Catalonia; 12 October), All Saints' Day (1 November), Constitution Day (6 December), Immaculate Conception (not a public holiday in Catalonia; 8 December), Christmas (25 December, plus 26 December in Catalonia and the Balearic Islands). (Additional local holidays are celebrated.)

SWEDEN

New Year (1 January), Epiphany (6 January), Good Friday and Easter Monday (March or April), May Day (1 May), Ascension Day (April or May), Whit Monday (May or June), Day of the Swedish Flag (*National Day* – although not celebrated as a public holiday; 6 June), Midsummer Day (24 or 25 June), All Saints' Day (1 November), Christmas (25–26 December).

SWITZERLAND

New Year (1–2 January), Good Friday and Easter Monday (March or April), Labour Day (not in all cantons; 1 May), Ascension Day (April or May), Whit Monday (May or June), *National Day* (not celebrated as a public holiday in all cantons; 1 August), Christmas (25–26 December). (Various additional holidays are celebrated in individual cantons or groups of cantons.)

TURKEY

New Year (1 January), End of Ramadan (March, April or May), National Sovereignty and Children's Day (23 April), Spring Day (1 May), Youth and Sports Day (19 May), Feast of the Sacrifice (June, July or August), Victory Day (30 August), Republic Day (*National Day*; 29 October).

UK

New Year (1 January; plus 2 January in Scotland only), St Patrick's Day (Northern Ireland only; 17 March), Good Friday (March or April), Easter Monday (March or April; not Scotland), May Day (early May; not Scotland), Liberation Day (Channel Islands only; 9 May), Spring Bank Holiday (late May in England, Wales and Northern Ireland; early May in Scotland); May Bank Holiday (Scotland only; late May), Anniversary of the Battle of the Boyne (Northern Ireland only; mid-July), Summer Bank Holiday (early August in Scotland; late August in England, Wales and Northern Ireland); Christmas (25–26 December).
NB In Scotland holidays which coincide with religious festivals are enjoyed in all areas and all industries. Other Bank holidays are often enjoyed only by banks and financial institutions. However, there are holidays specific to Scottish cities and regions (i.e. Glasgow and Edinburgh).

UKRAINE

New Year (1 January), Christmas (Orthodox; 7 January), May Day (1 May), Independence Day (*National Day*; 24 August), Referendum Day (1 December).

USA

New Year (1 January), Martin Luther King Day (mid-January), Washington-Lincoln Day (mid-February), Good Friday (March or April), Memorial Day (end of May), Independence Day (*National Day*; 4 July), Labor Day (early September), Columbus Day (12 October), Veterans' Day (11 November), Thanksgiving Day (end of November), Christmas (25 December).

NATIONAL DAYS

Afghanistan 18 August, Independence Day (international recognition of independence, 1919).

Albania 11 January, Proclamation of the Republic Day (1946).

Algeria 1 November, the anniversary of the beginning of the Revolution (1954).

Andorra 8 September, National Day, the festival of the coronation of the Virgin of Meritxell, the patron of Andorra.

Angola 11 November, Independence Day (1975).

Antigua and Barbuda 1 November, Independence Day (1981).

Argentina 25 May, the anniversary of the 1810 Revolution.

Armenia 23 September, Independence Day (1991).

Australia 26 January, Australia Day, the anniversary of the raising of the British flag at Port Jackson by Captain Cook (1788).

Austria 26 October, National Day, the anniversary of the referendum establishing perpetual neutrality (1955).

Azerbaijan 18 October, Independence Day (1991).

Bahamas 10 July, Independence Day (1973).

Bahrain 16 December, the anniversary of the accession of the Emir, Shaikh Isa (1961).

Bangladesh 16 December, National Day, the anniversary of the 1972 constitution.

Barbados 30 November, Independence Day (1966).

Belarus 25 August, Independence Day (1991).

Belgium 21 July, Independence Day, the anniversary of the presentation of the constitutional document of King Leopold I (1831).

Belize 21 September, Independence Day (1981).

Benin 30 November, National Day, the anniversary of the proclamation of the 1975 constitution.

Bhutan 17 December, National Day, the anniversary of the installation of the first king (1907).

Bolivia 6 August, Independence Day (1825).

Bosnia-Herzegovina does not have a recognized national day.

Botswana 30 September, Botswana Day, the anniversary of independence (1966).

Brazil 7 September, Independence Day, the anniversary of the proclamation of the independence of the Empire of Brazil by Dom Pedro I (1822).

Brunei 23 February, National Day, commemorates the anniversary of independent statehood, which was celebrated in Brunei on 23 February, 1984, although Brunei effectively became a fully sovereign state on 31 December 1983.

Bulgaria 3 March, National Day, the anniversary of the Treaty of San Stefano (1877), which established an autonomous principality of Bulgaria.

Burkina Faso 4 August, National Day, the anniversary of the eve of independence (1960).

Burundi 1 July, Independence Day (1962).

Cambodia 7 January (de facto), the anniversary of the fall of Phnom Penh to the forces of the (governing) State of Cambodia (1979).

Cameroon 20 May, Cameroon Day, the anniversary of the referendum that established the unitary state (1972).

Canada 1 July, Canada Day, the anniversary of the creation of the Confederation of Canada (1867).

Cape Verde 5 July, Independence Day (1975).

Central African Republic 1 December, National Day, the anniversary of the adoption of the name Central African Republic (1958).

Chad 11 August, Independence Day (1960).

Chile 18 September, National Day, the anniversary of the first proclamation of independence (1810).

China 1–2 October, National Days, the anniversary of the proclamation of the People's Republic of China (1949).

China (Taiwan) 10 October, Double Tenth Day, the anniversary of the end of Japanese occupation (1945).

Colombia 20 July, Independence Day (1819).

Comoros 6 July, Independence Day (1975).

Congo 15 August, Independence Day (1960).

Costa Rica 15 September, Independence Day (1821).

Côte d'Ivoire (Ivory Coast) 7 December, National Day, a combined celebration of the proclamation of the republic (4 December 1958) and independence (7 August 1960).

Croatia 30 June, National Day, commemorating the constitution of a sovereign state of Croatia (1991).

Cuba 1 January, Day of Liberation, the anniversary of the revolution led by Fidel Castro (1959).

Cyprus 1 October, Independence Day – although independence was achieved on 16 August 1960.

Czech Republic 28 October, the anniversary of the proclamation of the Czech Republic (1918).

Denmark 19 April, The Queen's Birthday – not taken as a public holiday.

Djibouti 27 June, Independence Day (1977).

Dominica 3 November, Independence Day (1978).

Dominican Republic 27 February, Independence Day (1844).

Ecuador 10 August, Independence (1830).

Egypt 23 July, National Day, the anniversary of the revolution of 1952.

El Salvador 15 September, Independence Day (1821).

Equatorial Guinea 5 March, Independence Day – independence was achieved on 12 October 1968.

Eritrea 24 May, Independence Day (1993).

Estonia 24 February, National Day, the anniversary of the proclamation of independence (1918).

Ethiopia 2 March, Battle of Adowa Day, the anniversary of the defeat of the Italians at Adowa (1896).

Fiji 10 October, Fiji Day, the anniversary of independence (1970).

Finland 6 December, Independence Day (1917).

France 14 July, National Day, the anniversary of the storming of the Bastille (1789).

Gabon 17 August, Independence Day (1960).

Gambia 18 February, Independence Day (1965).

Georgia 26 May, Independence Day, the anniversary of the proclamation of independence (1918).

Germany 3 October, Unity Day, the anniversary of the unification of the German Democratic Republic and the Federal Republic of Germany (1990).

Ghana 6 March, Independence Day (1957).

Greece 25 March, Independence Day, the anniver-

sary of the start of the rising against Turkey (1821).

Grenada 7 February, Independence Day (1974).

Guatemala 15 September, Independence Day (1821).

Guinea 2 October, Independence Day (1958).

Guinea-Bissau 24 September, Independence Day – although independence was achieved on 10 September, 1974.

Guyana 26 May, Independence Day (1966) and Republic Day, the anniversary of the proclamation of the republic (1970).

Haiti 1 January, Independence Day, the anniversary of the declaration of independence by Jean-Jacques Dessalines (1804).

Honduras 15 September, Independence Day (1821).

Hungary 23 October, National Day, the anniversary of the Hungarian Uprising (1956) and of the proclamation of the Republic of Hungary (1989).

Iceland 17 June, National Day, the anniversary of complete independence from Denmark (1944).

India 26 January, Republic Day, the anniversary of the declaration of the republic (1950).

Indonesia 17 August, National Day, the anniversary of the initial declaration of independence (1945).

Iran 11 February, National Day, the anniversary of the overthrow of the Shah (1979).

Iraq 14 July, Republic Day, the anniversary of the revolution that overthrew the monarchy (1958) and of the accession to power of the Arab Socialist Renaissance (Ba'ath) Party (1968).

Ireland 17 March, St Patrick's Day.

Israel 5 Iyyar (in Jewish calendar, see pp. 40–42), Independence Day (1948). (In the Gregorian calendar the Israeli declaration of independence took place on 14 May, 1948. The celebration of the anniversary occurs in April or May.)

Italy 2 June, National Day, the anniversary of the foundation of the republic (1946) – not taken as a public holiday.

Jamaica First Monday in August, Independence Day (6 August 1962).

Japan 23 December, The Emperor's Birthday.

Jordan 25 May, Independence Day, the anniversary of the coronation of King Abdullah (1946).

Kazakhstan 16 December, Independence Day (1991).

Kenya 12 December, Independence Day (1963).

Kiribati 12 July, Independence Day (1979).

Korea (North) 9 September, Independence Day, the anniversary of the foundation of the People's Democratic Republic of Korea (1948).

Korea (South) 15 August, Liberation Day, the anniversary of the end of Japanese occupation (1945).

Kuwait 25 February, National Day – the official anniversary of independence (1961), although Kuwait's independence was formally recognized on 19 June 1961.

Kyrgyzstan 31 August, Independence Day (1991).

Laos 2 December, National Day, the anniversary of the proclamation of the republic (1975).

Latvia 18 November, National Day, proclamation of the republic (1917).

Lebanon 22 November, Independence Day (1943).

Lesotho 4 October, Independence Day (1966).

Liberia 26 July, Independence Day (1847).
Libya 1 September, Revolution Day, the anniversary of the overthrow of the monarchy (1969).
Liechtenstein 15 August, the Assumption (see Christian Festivals) and the eve of the birthday of Prince Franz Joseph II (reigned 1938–89).
Lithuania 16 February, National Day, the anniversary of the declaration of independence (1918).
Luxembourg 23 June, National Day, the official birthday of the sovereign.
Macedonia 8 September, the anniversary of the vote to secede from Yugoslavia (1991).
Madagascar 26 June, Independence Day (1960).
Malawi 6 July, Republic Day, the anniversary of independence (1964) and of the proclamation of a republic (1966).
Malaysia 31 August, National Day, the anniversary of the independence of Malaya (1957).
The Maldives 26 July, Independence Day (1965).
Mali 22 September, National Day, the anniversary of the adoption of the name Mali (1960).
Malta 21 September, Independence Day (1964).
Marshall Islands 1 May, National Day, the anniversary of the present constitution of the Marshall Islands (1979).
Mauritania 28 November, National Day, the anniversary of the establishment of the republic (1958).
Mauritius 12 March, Independence Day (1968).
Mexico 16 September, Independence Day (1821).
Micronesia 10 May, National Day (Constitution Day), the anniversary of the present constitution of the Federated States of Micronesia (1979).
Moldova 27 August, Independence Day (1991).
Monaco 19 November, National Day, the feast of St Devote, patron saint of Monaco.
Mongolia 11 July, National Day, the anniversary of the recovery of independence (1921).
Morocco 3 March, the Festival of the Throne, the anniversary of the coronation of King Hassan II.
Mozambique 25 June, Independence Day (1975).
Myanmar (Burma) 4 January, Independence Day (1948).
Namibia 21 March, Independence Day (1990).
Nauru 31 January, Independence Day (1968).
Nepal 18 February, National Democracy Day, the birthday of King Tribhuvana (reigned 1911–55).
Netherlands 30 April, Queen's Day, the birthday of Queen Juliana (reigned 1948–80).
New Zealand 6 February, Waitangi Day, the anniversary of the signing of the Treaty of Waitangi between Britain and the Maori chiefs (1840).
Nicaragua 15 September, Independence Day (1821).
Niger 18 December, Republic Day, the anniversary of the proclamation of the republic (1958).
Nigeria 1 October, National Day, the anniversary of independence (1960) and the establishment of the republic (1963).
Norway 17 May, Independence Day, the anniversary of the adoption of the 1814 constitution.
Oman 18 November, National Day, associated with the birthday of the Sultan (19 November).
Pakistan 23 March, Pakistan Day, the anniversary of the adoption of the resolution by the Muslim

League to establish a Muslim state in the Indian subcontinent (1940) and of the proclamation of a republic (1956).
Panama 3 November, Independence Day (1903).
Papua New Guinea 16 September, Independence Day and Constitution Day (1975).
Paraguay 14–15 May, Independence Day (1811).
Peru 28–29 July, National Day, the anniversary of independence (1826).
The Philippines 12 June, Independence Day, the anniversary of the declaration of independence during the 1898 revolution.
Poland 3 May, National Day, the anniversary of the proclamation of the constitution of 1791.
Portugal 10 June, Portugal Day, the anniversary of the death of the 'national poet' Camoës (1580).
Qatar 3 September, National Day, in commemoration of independence (1 September 1971).
Romania 1 December, National Day, the anniversary of the reunion of Walachia, Moldavia and Transylvania (1918).
Russia has no official national day.
Rwanda 1 July, Independence Day (1962).
St Christopher and Nevis 19 September, Independence Day (1983).
St Lucia 22 February, Independence Day (1979).
St Vincent and the Grenadines 27 October, Independence Day (1979).
San Marino 3 September, National Day, the feast of St Marino, patron saint of the republic.
São Tomé e Príncipe 12 July, Independence Day (1975).
Saudi Arabia 23 September, the anniversary of the creation of the unified kingdom (1932) – not celebrated as a public holiday.
Senegal 4 April, National Day, the anniversary of the signature of the Accords of Paris (1960) that brought independence to Senegal on 20 August 1960.
Seychelles 29 June, Independence Day (1976).
Sierra Leone 27 April, Independence Day (1961).
Singapore 9 August, National Day, the anniversary of the declaration of independence (1965).
Slovakia 5 July, National Day, Day of the Apostles St Cyril and St Methodius.
Slovenia 25 June, National Day, the anniversary of the proclamation of sovereignty (1991).
Solomon Islands 7 July, Independence Day (1978).
Somalia 26 June, National Day, the anniversary of independence (1960).
South Africa 31 May, Republic Day, the anniversary of the declaration of the republic (1961).
Spain 12 October, the Day of the Hispanidad; honours Columbus' discovery of the Western hemisphere.
Sri Lanka 4 February, National Day, the anniversary of the attainment of independence as Ceylon (1948).
Sudan 1 January, Independence Day (1956).
Suriname 25 November, Independence Day (1975).
Swaziland 6 September, Independence Day (1968).
Sweden 6 June, the Day of the Swedish Flag – although not celebrated as a public holiday.
Switzerland 1 August, National Day, the anni-

versary of the alliance of the 'Forest Cantons' (1291). Not celebrated as a public holiday in all cantons.

Syria 16 November, National Day, the anniversary of the accession to power of President Assad (1970).

Tajikistan 9 September, Independence Day, (1991).

Tanzania 26 April, Union Day, the anniversary of the union of Tanganyika and Zanzibar (1964).

Thailand 5 December, The King's Birthday.

Togo 13 January, Liberation Day, the anniversary of the revolution of 1963.

Tonga 4 June, Independence Day (1970).

Trinidad and Tobago 31 August, Independence Day (1962).

Tunisia 20 March, Independence Day (1956).

Turkey 29 October, Republic Day, the anniversary of the election of Atatürk as the first president (1924).

Turkmenistan 27 October, Independence Day (1991).

Tuvalu 1 October, Independence Day (1978).

Uganda 9 October, Independence Day (1962).

United Arab Emirates 2 December, National Day, the anniversary of the establishment of the federation as an independent state (1971).

UK has no national day.

Ukraine 24 August, Independence Day (1991).

USA 4 July, Independence Day, the anniversary of the declaration of independence (1776).

Uruguay 25 August, Declaration of Independence Day (1825).

Uzbekistan 31 August, Independence Day (1991).

Vanuatu 30 July, Independence Day (1980).

Vatican City has no national day.

Venezuela 5 July, Independence Day (1811).

Vietnam 2 September, National Day, the anniversary of the original proclamation of independence (1945).

Western Samoa 1 January, Independence Day (1962).

Yemen 22 May, National Day, the anniversary of the reunification of Yemen (1990) – although not taken as a public holiday.

Yugoslavia (Serbia and Montenegro) 29–30 November, Republic Days, the anniversary of the establishment of the Partisan government (1943).

Zaïre 24 November, National Day, the anniversary of the establishment of the Second Republic (1965).

Zambia 24 October, Independence Day (1964).

Zimbabwe 18 April, Independence Day (1980).

OTHER NATIONAL DAYS

Apart from major religious holidays (see pp. 54–6), several other days are celebrated as public holidays in many countries. The most popular of these is **May Day** or **Labour Day**, which is observed as a holiday in honour of workers, usually on 1 May but in September or October in North America and Australasia. In the Hispanic world, a number of countries celebrate the discovery of the Americas by Columbus on 12 October (1492). Some Western countries continue to honour **Armistice Day** – also known as Veterans' or Remembrance Day – on 11 November, the day on which World War I ended in 1918.

CHRISTIAN FESTIVALS

(See also Saints' days)

Christian Sabbath is observed on Sunday, in accordance with the Fourth Commandment, which forbids work on the holy day.

Epiphany *6 January*. The Festival of the Epiphany commemorates the manifestation of the infant Christ to the Magi or 'wise men'. The festival was of great importance in the (Eastern) Orthodox Churches because it marked the proclamation, by the Patriarch of Alexandria, of the date of the next Easter. In western Europe, the Epiphany was a significant landmark in the Church and lay calendars, determining the dates of other festivals and activities later in the year, for example, ploughing in England began on the Monday of the first complete week after the Festival of the Epiphany. The festival is a public holiday in several European countries.

Shrove Tuesday *Any Tuesday between 3 February and 9 March*. Shrove Tuesday is the last day before the beginning of Lent – see Ash Wednesday, below. Shrovetide – the Sunday, Monday and Tuesday before Lent – were set aside as days for the confession of sins ('shrove' is the past tense of 'shrive', meaning 'to hear confession'). Shrove Tuesday was traditionally marked by festivities before the rigours of Lent and is commemorated by carnivals in, for example, Portugal, Brazil and parts of Germany. In England, Shrove Tuesday is also known as *Pancake Day*, the day on which fats that could not be consumed during Lent were used to make pancakes.

Ash Wednesday *Any Wednesday between 4 February and 10 March*. The first day of Lent, Ash Wednesday takes its name from the custom of scattering ashes on the heads of penitents (in its modern form, marking the forehead with ashes in the sign of the Cross).

Lent *February to March or March to April*. Lent is a period of 40 days beginning on Ash Wednesday and ending at midnight on Holy Saturday, the day before Easter Day. A reminder of the time spent by Christ in the wilderness, Lent is observed as a period of reflection, repentance and preparation for Easter. It used to be thought that the observance of Lent dated from the time of the first disciples, but it is now usually accepted that the practice probably began in the 4th century and may, originally, have been a fast of 40 hours. Lent begins on the following days between 1994 and 2000.

1994 16 February
1995 1 March
1996 21 February
1997 12 February
1998 25 February
1999 17 February
2000 8 March

Palm Sunday *Any Sunday between 15 March and 18 April*. Palm Sunday – the last Sunday of Lent – commemorates Christ's triumphal entry into Jerusalem when His way was lined by palm branches.

Maundy Thursday *Any Thursday between 19 March and 22 April*. Maundy Thursday – the last Thursday of Lent – takes its name from the Latin *dies mandati*, meaning 'the day of the mandate', referring to the mandate given by Christ to His disciples to love one another. It is marked in the Roman Catholic Church by the symbolic washing of feet by the priest, in commemoration of Christ washing the feet of the disciples. In England, Maundy money – specially minted coins – is distributed by the sovereign to as many elderly men and women as the sovereign's age.

Good Friday *Any Friday between 20 March and 23 April.* Good Friday is the commemoration of the Crucifixion. It is a public holiday in most Christian countries.

Holy Saturday *Any Saturday between 21 March and 24 April.* Holy Saturday – sometimes wrongly called 'Easter Saturday' – is the last day of Lent. Easter begins at the stroke of midnight at the end of Holy Saturday.

Easter Day *Any Sunday between 22 March and 25 April.* Easter Day is the celebration of the Resurrection of Christ. There is no historical basis for celebrating Easter in the spring as it is not known at what time of the year these events took place.

Easter is celebrated on the first Sunday after the Full Moon that happens on or following 21 March. If the Full Moon falls upon a Sunday, Easter is celebrated upon the following Sunday. The 'Moon' used in these calculations is not the celestial Moon but a hypothetical 'calendar Moon' whose cycles alternate in periods of 30 and 29 days. (Although the Orthodox Churches calculate Easter in the same manner as other Christian Churches, their festivities take place later because Eastern Christendom still uses the Julian calendar.) Easter falls on the following days between 1994 and 2000.

1994 3 April
1995 16 April
1996 7 April
1997 30 March
1998 12 April
1999 4 April
2000 23 April

The day following Easter Sunday is a public holiday in most Christian countries.

Ascension Day *Any Thursday between 30 April and 3 June.* Ascension Day – which falls 40 days after Easter Day – is when the Ascension of Christ into Heaven is celebrated. It is a public holiday in many Christian countries. Ascension Day falls on the following days between 1994 and 2000.

1994 12 May
1995 25 May
1996 16 May
1997 8 May
1998 21 May
1999 13 May
2000 1 June

Pentecost (Whit Sunday) *Any Sunday between 10 May and 13 June.* Pentecost – which falls seven weeks after Easter Day – commemorates the descent of the Holy Spirit upon the apostles. It marks the beginning of the activities of the Church on Earth. Its English name 'Whit' Sunday is said to come from 'White' Sunday in a reference to the white robes worn by the newly baptized. Whit Monday is a public holiday in many Christian countries. Pentecost falls on the following days between 1994 and 2000.

1994 22 May
1995 4 June
1996 26 May
1997 18 May
1998 31 May
1999 23 May
2000 11 June

Trinity Sunday *Any Sunday between 17 May and 20 June.* Trinity Sunday is a celebration of the Holy Trinity. In Churches of the Anglican Communion the remaining Sundays of the year are numbered 'after Trinity'.

Corpus Christi *Any Thursday between 21 May and 24 June.* Corpus Christi – celebrated on the Thursday following Trinity Sunday – is a major festival of the Roman Catholic Church held in devotion to the Eucharist. Corpus Christi is a public holiday in some Roman Catholic countries.

The Assumption *15 August.* The Feast of the Assumption of the Blessed Virgin Mary is a Roman Catholic and (Eastern) Orthodox festival commemorating the doctrine of the assumption of Mary – in both body and soul – into Heaven at the end of her earthly life. It is a public holiday in most Roman Catholic countries and in Greece.

All Saints' Day *1 November.* All Saints' Day – a public holiday in some Christian (mainly Roman Catholic) countries – is a celebration of the lives of all the saints of the Church, including those who are remembered on individual named saints' days.

All Souls' Day *2 November.* All Souls' Day – a public holiday in some Latin American countries – is a major Roman Catholic festival. It is a day of prayer for the souls of the departed now in Purgatory.

Advent Sunday *The Sunday nearest to 30 November, that is any Sunday between 27 November and 3 December.* Advent Sunday (Latin *adventus* meaning 'coming') is the beginning of the season of preparation for Christmas. There are usually three, and occasionally four, Sundays of Advent. Advent begins on the following days between 1993 and 2000.

1993 28 November
1994 27 November
1995 3 December
1996 1 December
1997 30 November
1998 29 November
1999 28 November
2000 3 December

Immaculate Conception *8 December.* The festival of the Immaculate Conception commemorates the (Roman Catholic) doctrine that Mary was conceived without sin. It is a public holiday in some Roman Catholic countries.

Christmas Eve *24 December.* The day before the celebration of Christmas. It is a public holiday in a few Christian countries.

Christmas Day *25 December.* The celebration of the birth of Christ to Mary at Bethlehem, probably in c. 4 BC. Christmas (literally 'Christ mass') has been celebrated by Christians from the earliest times. There is, however, no reason to assume that this historical event took place on 25 December. There is some evidence to suggest that Christ was born in September.

The early Church in the East celebrated both Christmas and the Epiphany on 6 January. In the West the Feast of the Nativity has been celebrated on 25 December since AD 336 in order to take the place of the pagan Sun festival held on or near the same date. By the end of the 4th century Christmas was celebrated on 25 December throughout Christendom, except in Armenia, which still commemorates 6 January. (Although the Orthodox Churches celebrate Christmas on 25 December, their festivities take place in January in the Gregorian calendar because Eastern Christendom still uses the Julian calendar.)

ORTHODOX FESTIVALS

Moveable Christian festivals in the Greek Orthodox
Church will occur on the following dates:

Beginning of Lent			
1994	March 14	1995	March 6
Holy Friday (Good Friday)			
1994	April 29	1995	April 21
Orthodox Easter			
1994	May 1	1995	April 23
Ascension			
1994	June 9	1995	June 1
Pentecost			
1994	June 19	1995	June 11
All Saints			
1994	June 26	1995	June 18

JEWISH FESTIVALS

Weekly festival Shabat (the sabbath) observed
on the seventh day of the week, Saturday, in commemoration of the day of rest taken by God after the
completion of the creation. It is the covenant
between God and the Jewish people. On the sabbath,
Jews are obliged to engage in worship and prayer at
home or in the synagogue and to avoid work.

Monthly festival Rosh Hodesh, the celebration
of the new moon.

Other festivals are celebrated according to the
Jewish calendar (see pp. 40–42). The equivalent date
in the Gregorian calendar varies from one year to
another. Jewish festivals commence on the evening
of the dates shown and last until sunset on the
following day.

15 Shebat – *Tu B'shevat* (Festival for New Trees). In
modern times this festival is associated with the
planting of trees in Israel.
13 Adar – *Taanit Ester* (Fast of Ester).
14 Adar – *Purim* (Festival of Lots). Purim commemorates the deliverance of Persian Jews from persecution in the 5th century BCE (see Jewish calendar).
14 Nisan – *Taanit Behorim* (Fast of the First-born).
27 Nisan – *Pesah* (Passover). The Passover commemorates the Israelites' servitude in Egypt and the
subsequent exodus from Egypt. It is called 'Passover'
because on the eve of the Jewish flight from Egypt
the last of the 10 plagues 'passed over' the homes of
the Israelites.
27 Nisan – *Yom Ha-Shoah* (Holocaust Day). A
modern commemoration of the victims of the Holocaust but not marked by a public holiday in Israel.
4 Iyar – *Yom H'zikharon* (Remembrance Day). A
modern commemoration but not marked by a public
holiday in Israel.
5 Iyar – *Yom Ha'Atzmaut* (Independence Day), an
Israeli public holiday.
18 Iyar – the 33rd Day of 'Counting the Omer'.
28 Iyar – *Yom Yerushalayim* (Jerusalem Day).
6–7 Sivan – *Shavuot* (the Festival of Weeks, or
Pentecost). This festival commemorates the revelation of the Torah (Law) at Sinai.
20 Sivan – the Fast of 20 Sivan.
17 Tammuz – the Fast of 17 Tammuz.
9 Ab – *Tisha B'Av* (the Fast of 9 Ab).
15 Ab – *Tu B'Av* (the Festival of 15 Ab).
1 Elul – Festival of 1 Elul.
1–2 Tishri – *Rosh Hashanah* (New Year). This festival celebrates the New Year of the Jewish Calendar

but also begins the Ten Days of Penitence that ends
on Yom Kippur (see below). These days are considered the Days of Judgement for all mankind.
Many rabbinic laws govern behaviour during this
time – they include the strict prohibition of work –
but celebrations are also enjoyed.
3 Tishri – *Tsom Gedaliah* (the Fast of Gedaliah).
10 Tishri – *Yom Kippur* (the Day of Atonement) is the
most solemn and holy day in the Jewish Calendar.
The festival is spent in prayer and fasting. Sins are
confessed in acts of reconciliation.
15 or 16–22 or 23 Tishri – *Sukkot* (the Festival of
Tabernacles). Commemorated in Israel by a series of
half-day public holidays, Sukkot is a remembrance of
the Israelites' wanderings after the Exodus. It is
named after the booths (*sukkot*, 'booth') that the
Israelites lived in during this time.
22 or 23 Tishri – *Shemini Atzeret* (the Eighth Day of
Conclusion). The final day of the Festival of Tabernacles is celebrated independently.
23 Tishri – *Simhat Torah* (Rejoicing in the Torah).
This festival is celebrated on the completion of the
cycle of readings from the Torah.
25 Kislev – 2 Tebet – *Hanukah* (the Festival of the
Dedication of the Temple, otherwise known as the
Festival of Lights). Celebrated for eight days, the
festival commemorates the revolt against the Seleucid ruler Antiochus IV Epiphanes and the rededi-
cation of the Temple in 164 BCE (see Jewish
calendar). The festival is characterized by songs,
candles, feasting and giving gifts to children.
10 Tebet – the Feast of 10 Tebet

ISLAMIC FESTIVALS

Many of the following festivals are public holidays in
Islamic countries. As these holidays are celebrated
according to the Islamic lunar calendar (see pp.
42–44), the equivalent date in the Gregorian calendar
varies from one year to another.

Weekly festival on Friday, the Day of Assembly.

Other festivals

1 Muharram	New Year's Day
1–10 Muharram	Muharram (New Year Festival)
12 Rabîa I	Eid Milad-un-Nabi (Festival of the Prophet's Birthday)
26 Rajab	Shab-i-Maraj (Festival of the Prophet's Night Journey and Ascension)
15 Shaabân	Night of Forgiveness
1–29/30 Ramadan	Ramadan; annual fast lasting a month observed by abstention from food, drink and sexual intercourse from dawn to dusk.
1 Shawwâl	Eid-ul-Fitr; Festival of Fast Breaking (end of Ramadan) celebrated by feasting and visiting graves.
9 Dhû'l Hijja	Day of Arafat
Dhû'l Hijja	Haj (Pilgrimage to Mecca)
10 Dhû'l Hijja	Eid-ul-Adha (Festival of Sacrifice, marking the end of the Pilgrimage to Mecca).

HINDU FESTIVALS

See also Hindu gods and goddesses.

January
Makar Sankranti, Winter solstice festival.
Pongal, harvest festival in southern India.

Kumbha Mela, festival held every 12 years; worshippers bathe in the waters at the confluence of the Ganges and Jumna rivers.

January–February

Vasanta Panchami, held in honour of goddess Saraswati.

Mahashivratri, 'Great Night of Shiva', celebrated by vigils, vows, fasting and worship of goddess Shiva.

February–March

Ramakrishna utsav (20 Feb), festival for Hindu saint Ramakrishna.

Holi, a boisterous festival characterized by the throwing of red powder and by bonfires (possible origins in the celebration of the god of sexual desire, Kama).

Shivrati, main festival in honour of Shiva; spent in meditation.

March–April

Ramanavami, celebrates the birth of Shi Rama observed in sanctity and fasting.

Hanuman Jayanti, in honour of the god Hanuman.

April–May

Baisakhi, New Year festival celebrated by giftgiving, feasting, praying and bathing in sacred waters.

May–June

Ganga Dussehra, in honour of goddess Ganga; devotees bathe in the sacred waters of the River Ganges.

June–July

Jagannatha (Ratha-yatra), celebrates Krishna as the Lord of the Universe.

July–August

Naga Panchami, celebrates the birth of serpents. Worshippers empty pots of milk over snakes from the temple of Shiva.

Raksha Bandhan, an old festival in which sisters give wrist decorations to their brothers to ward off evil spirits.

August–September

Ganesh Chaturthi, in honour of the elephant-headed god, Ganesh.

Janmashtani, celebrates the birth of Krishna.

September–October

Dussehra (Durja Puja), celebrates the goddess Durga during the period of Navratri ('Nine Nights').

Gandhi Jayanti (2 October), celebrates the birth of Mahatma Gandhi.

Diwali (October), a major festival honouring Laksmi, goddess of wealth. During this time merchants open fresh accounts. Festivities include visiting, exchanging gifts, decorating houses, feasting and wearing new clothes.

BUDDHIST FESTIVALS

Different festivals and, in some cases, different dates for the same festivals, are observed in the various countries where Buddhism is practised.

Uposatha Days are fortnightly meetings of the Buddhist monastic assembly – at times of full moon and new moon – to reaffirm the rules of discipline. These meetings exclude novices and laymen. The Uposatha Day is also the name given to the more modern weekly visit to a monastery by laymen.

Other festivals

New Year is celebrated in Burma/Myanmar (16–17 April), Sri Lanka (13 April), Thailand (between 13–16 April), Tibet (in February)

The Buddha's Birth, Enlightenment and Death is celebrated in Burma/Myanmar, Sri Lanka, and Thailand (as The Buddha's Cremation) in May or June, and in Tibet in May.

The Buddha's First Sermon is celebrated in June or July in Burma/Myanmar (in conjunction with the Beginnings of the Rains Retreat Festival), and in Sri Lanka and Tibet.

The Rains Retreat is celebrated in Thailand (between July and October.

Summer Retreat is celebrated in China between June and October.

The establishment of Buddhism in Sri Lanka is celebrated in Sri Lanka in June or July.

The Procession of the Month of Asala is celebrated in Sri Lanka in July or August.

Festival of Hungry Ghosts is celebrated in China in August.

The Buddha's Birth is celebrated in China in August.

Kuan-Yin is celebrated in China in August.

The Buddha's first visit to Sri Lanka is celebrated in Sri Lanka in September.

The Buddha's Descent from Tushita is celebrated in Tibet in October.

Kathina Ceremony is celebrated in Burma/Myanmar and Thailand in November.

Festival of Lights is celebrated in Sri Lanka and Thailand in November.

The Death of Tsongkhapa is celebrated in Tibet in November.

The Arrival of Sanghamitta is celebrated in Sri Lanka in December or January.

The Conjunction of Nine Evils and the Conjunction of the Ten Virtues is celebrated in Tibet in January.

Saints' Day is celebrated in Thailand in February.

SIKH FESTIVALS

The Sikh religion celebrates major festivals that coincide with some of the principal Hindu festivals. The main Sikh festivals are:

The Sikh New Year which is celebrated in April at the same time as the Hindu New Year, see above.

Diwali, the Festival of Lights, which is celebrated in November. This is basically the same festival that is observed by the Hindus, see above.

The Sikh Spring Harvest Festival which occurs during March.

JAIN FESTIVALS

Some of the principal Jain festivals are also celebrated at similar times to the major Hindu festivals, see above. Jain festivals do not however celebrate or honour any deity as the Jain religion shares with Buddhism a belief in no god.

During April, Jains celebrate the birthday of Mahavira, the aesthetic who founded the Jain religion in the 6th century BC.

The beginning of the Indian monsoon in July is the occasion of another major Jain religious festival.

Diwali – the Hindu Festival of Lights, which is celebrated in November – is a festival in the Jain calendar.

PARSI FESTIVALS

The principal religious festival in the Parsi calendar is the New Year (*No Ruz*) which is celebrated during March.

SHINTO FESTIVALS

Several major festivals are celebrated at Shinto temples in Japan during the year. The most important of these include:

Haru Matsuri, also known as *Toshigoi Matsuri* – the Spring Festival, which is traditionally the Prayer for a Good Harvest Festival in the religious calendar. In modern times, this festival has come to be associated with the civil Japanese public holiday, Vernal Equinox Day, which is observed on 21 March.

Aki Matsuri or *Niiname-sai* – the Autumn Festival, which is traditionally the Harvest Festival in the religious calendar. This holiday has come to be associated with the civil Japanese public holiday, Autumnal Equinox Day, which is observed on 23 September.

Rei-sai, which is an annual festival celebrated at each Shinto temple – not necessarily on the same day. The Annual Festival is the occasion of the temple's Divine Procession – *Shinko-sai* – when miniature shrines (*mikoshi*) are carried in procession throughout the area that is served by the temple in question.

The date of accession of the emperor is also of significance in Shinto belief. The present *Heisei* imperial epoch is dated from 8 January (Emperor Akihito succeeded to the throne on 8 January 1989).

WEDDING ANNIVERSARIES

A combination of traditional and commercial usage has resulted in the association of certain types of gift with specific wedding anniversaries.

	European usage	American usage
1st	cotton	gold jewellery
2nd	paper	garnet
3rd	leather	pearls
4th	fruit and flowers	blue topaz
5th	wooden	sapphire
6th	sugar	amethyst
7th	wool/copper	onyx
8th	bronze/pottery	tourmaline
9th	pottery/willow	lapis
10th	tin	diamond jewellery
11th	steel	turquoise
12th	silk/linen	jade
13th	lace	citrine
14th	ivory	opal
15th	crystal	ruby
20th	porcelain	emerald
25th	silver	silver jubilee
30th	pearl	pearl jubilee
35th	coral	emerald jubilee
40th	ruby	ruby jubilee
45th	sapphire	sapphire jubilee
50th	golden	golden jubilee
60th	diamond	diamond jubilee
70th	platinum	–

SIGNS OF THE ZODIAC

The zodiac – in astronomy – is an imaginary belt that extends 8° on either side of the annual path or *eliptic* of the Sun. The concept was devised in Mesopotamia c. 3000 BC. The orbits of the Moon and of the major planets of the solar system (except Pluto) lie entirely within the zodiac. It is divided into 12 equal areas – the *signs of the zodiac* – each of 30°. Each section is named after the constellation that at one time coincided with the sector. (A constellation is a group of stars that form an easily recognizable pattern, for example Ursa Major which is known in Britain as the Plough and in North America as the Big Dipper.) However, the signs of the zodiac no longer correspond to the constellations as proper allowance for leap days was not made in the original calculations and the constellations appear to have 'shifted' to the east.

In astrology the zodiac is a diagram depicting the zodiac belt with symbols representing each of the 12 sections of the zodiac. The zodiac – from the Greek *zoidiakos*, circle of animals – is used by astrologers to predict the future. Although the original periods during which the Sun appears to be in each of the constellations of the zodiac no longer apply, astrology nonetheless adheres to the original dates.

Astrology is the interpretation of the influence of planets and stars upon human lives. It is based upon the concept that if an event occurred while the planets were in a particular configuration, a similar event would be likely to happen when those planetary circumstances were repeated. Astrology originated in Mesopotamia and was developed in ancient Greece, before being absorbed into the Indian, Islamic and West European cultures. In ancient times astrology was regarded as a science. Although it has been condemned by various Christian councils, astrology retains great popularity through daily predictions in newspapers and specialist almanacs.

The signs of the zodiac are:

Aries (symbol: the Ram) The Sun is in the first sign of the zodiac from about March 21 to April 19.

Taurus (symbol: the Bull) The Sun is in Taurus from about April 20 to May 20.

Gemini (symbol: the Twins) The Sun is in Gemini from about May 21 to June 21.

Cancer (symbol: the Crab) The Sun is in Cancer from about June 22 to July 22.

Leo (symbol: the Lion) The Sun is in Leo from about July 23 to August 22.

Virgo (symbol: the Virgin) The Sun is in Virgo from about August 23 to September 22.

Libra (symbol: the Balance) The Sun is in Libra from about September 23 to October 23.

Scorpio (symbol: the Scorpion) The Sun is in Scorpio from about October 24 to November 21. (The second half of Scorpio is sometimes referred to as Ophiuchus – symbol: the Serpent-Bearer – by some European astrologers.)

Sagittarius (symbol: the Archer) The Sun is in Sagittarius from about November 22 to December 21.

Capricorn (symbol: the Goat) The Sun is in Capricorn from about December 22 to January 19.

Aquarius (symbol: the Water Carrier) The Sun is in Aquarius from about January 20 to February 18.

Pisces (symbol: the Fishes) The Sun is in Pisces from about February 19 to March 20.

EARTH SCIENCES
THE EARTH

THE EARTH'S STRUCTURE

There has been little penetration into the Earth's interior. The deepest mine (in South Africa) is only 3.8 km (2.4 mi) deep, and the deepest drilling (in Russia) is only 12.3 km (7.6 mi) deep – or 0.19% of the Earth's radius, which has an average value of 6371 km (3959 mi). The only other direct access to the internal nature of Earth is the study of lava flows from volcanic eruptions.

Unable to visit the Earth's deep interior or place instruments within it, scientists must explore in more subtle ways. One method is to measure natural phenomena, in particular the magnetic and gravitational fields, which are measured at the Earth's surface and from satellites. These observations are interpreted in terms of the planet's internal properties. A second approach is to study the Earth with non-material probes, the most important of which are the seismic waves emitted by earthquakes. As seismic waves pass through the Earth, they undergo sudden changes in direction and velocity at certain depths. These depths mark the major boundaries, or *discontinuities*, that divide the Earth into crust, mantle and core.

THE CRUST

The thin outermost layer of the Earth, the crust, has an average depth of 24 km (15 mi). The crust accounts for only 1.05 of the planet's volume and 0.5% of its mass. The sharp boundary between the crust and the mantle is called the *Mohorovičić discontinuity* (or *Moho* for short) after the Croatian seismologist Andrija Mohorovičić who discovered it in 1909.

There is a wide variation in the thickness of the crust and three main crustal types – continental, oceanic and transitional – have been identified. The *continental crust* averages between 30 and 50 km (19–31 mi) thick, although beneath the central valley of California, for example, the crust is only about 20 km (12 mi) thick, and beneath parts of major mountain ranges such as the Himalaya it can exceed 80 km (50 mi). By contrast, the *oceanic crust* is only 5 to 15 km (3–9 mi) thick and can be as little as 3 km (2 mi) under ocean fracture zones (see below). The *transitional zone* – of islands, island arcs and continental margins – averages 15 to 30 km (9–19 mi) in thickness.

The elements oxygen, silicon and aluminium dominate the crustal composition. The major mineral type – the feldspars – are alumino-silicates of the alkali and alkaline-earth metals. The second most common group – quartz – is silicon dioxide. The major rock types reflect this basic composition with differences mainly being due to small amounts of other minerals. By contrast, the oceanic crust is mainly basalt, which contains both feldspars and quartz, but has also notable amounts of olivine and pyroxene, which are magnesium iron silicates. The basalt is underlain by gabbro, which is a coarser grained rock of similar composition.

THE MANTLE

The mantle extends from the base of the crust to the core and is about 2865 km (1780 mi) thick. It occupies about 82.5% of the Earth's volume and 66.0% of its mass. The upper mantle is rich in olivine and pyroxenes, present in the rock type peridotite. Dis-continuities revealed by seismic data show several distinct layers in the mantle. The outermost – the *lithosphere* – is generally 50 to 100 km (31–62 mi) thick under the oceans and 100 to 200 km (62–124 mi) thick under the continents. The strong rigid lithosphere overlays a weak thick layer known as the *asthenosphere*. The athenosphere – which is 320 km (199 mi) thick – has an average temperature of about 1300° C (2372° F), which approaches the melting points of its constituent rocks. It is probable that *magma* – molten or semi-molten rock – is formed in this region.

A major discontinuity at a depth of 670 km (416 mi) from the surface separates the upper and lower mantles. Below this discontinuity there appears to be a change in mineral types brought about by the increasing pressure. There is also a 10% jump in density and a rise in temperature from about 1560° C (1840° F) to 1710° C (3110° F). The major mineral type in the lower mantle appears to be pyroxenes, especially magnesium silicate.

In the *D layer* – the lowest 200 km (124 mi) of the mantle – temperatures reach up to 2660° C (4820° F). It is thought that the D layer is richer in aluminium and calcium than the higher layers of the mantle.

THE CORE

The core extends from the base of the mantle to the Earth's centre and is 6964 km (4327 mi) in diameter. It accounts for only 16.3% of the Earth's volume but 33.5% of its mass. The discontinuity between the mantle and core is called the *core-mantle boundary* or, sometimes, the *Gutenberg discontinuity*, after its discoverer the German-American seismologist Beno Gutenberg. The core comprises two distinct parts – a liquid *outer core*, which is 2260 km (1404 mi) thick, and a solid *inner core*, which has a radius of 1222 km (759 mi).

The core is chemically distinct from the mantle and comprises about 89% iron and 6% nickel. The remaining 5% comprises a lighter element, which is possibly sulfur (sulphur) but the presence of oxygen and silicon cannot be ruled out. There is a 78% increase in density at the mantle-core boundary and a 700° C (1260° F) jump in temperature to about 3360° C (6080° F). There is a smooth increase in temperature to a maximum of about 4530° C (8190° F) at the centre of the core.

THE MAGNETIC FIELD

The Earth has a magnetic field, which is why a compass needle points approximately north at most places on the Earth's surface. The magnetic field has two parts. Most of it is that of a simple dipole; it is as if a giant bar magnet were placed at the centre of the Earth (although the magnet slopes at 11° to the Earth's axis of rotation). But a small proportion of it is much more complicated and changes very rapidly. This is why a compass needle points in a slightly different direction each year.

The rapid changing indicates that the magnetic field must be produced in a part of the Earth that is fluid, for no solid region could reorganize itself rapidly enough without shaking the planet to pieces. The only liquid zone inside the Earth is the outer core.

MASS AND DENSITY

The Earth, including its atmosphere, has a mass of $5 \cdot 974 \times 10^{21}$ tonnes (5 879 000 000 000 000 000 000 tons) – the average density is $5 \cdot 515$ times that of water.

The density of the Earth – in g/cm^3 – and the percentage mass of each layer (in terms of the total Earth mass) are given in the following table.

Layer	Density (g/cm^3)	% of mass
Ocean	1.020	0.03
Upper crust	2.600	0.27
Lower crust	2.900	0.23
Mantle	*	65.99
Outer core	11.238**	31.82
Inner core	12.980**	1.66

The Earth's atmosphere weighs $5 \cdot 24 \times 10^{15}$ tonnes (5 160 000 000 000 000 tons) or 0·000088 per cent of the total mass. The density of the Earth is being added to as the planet picks up cosmic dust, but estimates of this increase vary widely with 30 000 tonnes/tons a year being the upper limit.

* Mantle – the percentage of the mass is calculated as a remainder.
** Core –average density values have been obtained by integrating density-depth equations.

VOLUME

The volumes of the individual layers of the Earth are calculated using an average Earth radius (R_E) of 6371 km (3957 mi):

Layer	Outer radius	Inner radius	% of volume
Ocean	6371 km 3959 mi	6368 km 3957 mi	0.14
Crust	6368 km 3957 mi	6347 km 3944 mi	1.00
Mantle	6347 km 3944 mi	3482 km 2163 mi	82.53
Outer core	3482 km 2163 mi	1222 km 759 mi	15.62
Inner core	1222 km 759 mi		0.70

COMPOSITION

The overall composition of the Earth's crust, mantle and core in terms of major elements has been estimated as follows:

Oxide	%	O	Fe
SiO_2	48.0%	25.56%	–
MgO	34.3%	13.12%	–
FeO	7.9%	1.76%	6.14%
Al_2O_3	5.2%	2.45%	–
CaO	4.2%	1.20%	–
Others	0.4%	0.13%	*

* Assumes equal amounts of TiC_2 and Na_2O as the major remaining oxides.

This fits in with something else. The only conceivable way in which a magnetic field could be generated within the Earth is by the flow of very large electric currents, and electric currents need a conductor. The Earth's core is the most conductive zone in the whole Earth, because it consists largely of iron. The silicates of the mantle would simply not conduct well enough. An additional feature of the Earth's magnetic field is that it has reversed from north to south and back on numerous occasions over geological time. The evidence for this has come from examining the magnetic alignment of old rocks.

DIMENSIONS

The Earth is not a true sphere but an ellipsoid. Its equatorial diameter is 12 756·274 km (7 926·381 miles) and its polar diameter is 12 713·505 km (7 899·806 miles).

The Earth's equatorial circumference is 40 075·02 km (24 901·46 miles), and its polar meridianal circumference is 40 007·86 km (24 859·73 miles).

The volume of the Earth is 1 083 207 000 000 km^3 (259 875 300 000 cu. miles).

The Earth has a pear-shaped asymmetry with the north polar radius being 45 m (148 ft) longer than the south polar radius and there is also a slight ellipticity of the Equator since its long axis (about longitude 37°W) is 159 m (522 ft) greater than the short axis.

CONTINENTAL DRIFT

There is ever-increasing evidence that the Earth's land surface once comprised a single primeval land mass, now called Pangaea, and that this split during the Upper Cretaceous period (100 000 000 to 65 000 000 years ago) into two super-continents, the northern one called Laurasia and the southern one Gondwanaland (see map, p. 60). Throughout almost the whole of human history, most people have imagined the continents to be fixed in their present positions and the ocean floors to be the oldest and most primitive parts of the Earth. In the space of a few years during the early 1960s, however, both of these assumptions were overthrown in an intellectual revolution. It suddenly became possible to prove that the continents are drifting across the Earth's surface, that the ocean floors are spreading, and that none of the oceanic crust is more than about 200 million years old – less than 5% of the age of the Earth (4600 million years). The Earth's lithosphere – the rigid layer that comprises the crust and the uppermost mantle – is divided into 15 *plates* of various sizes. The plates 'float' on the partially molten layer – the asthenosphere – below, and it is because they are floating that they have the freedom to move horizontally. A few of the plates (for example, the Pacific) are almost completely oceanic, but most include both oceanic and continental lithosphere. There are no completely continental plates. The plate boundaries are the most tectonically active parts of the Earth – they are where most mountain building, earthquakes and volcanoes occur.

HOW CONTINENTAL DRIFT WAS PROVED

Many rocks contain minute magnetic particles,

CONTINENTAL DRIFT

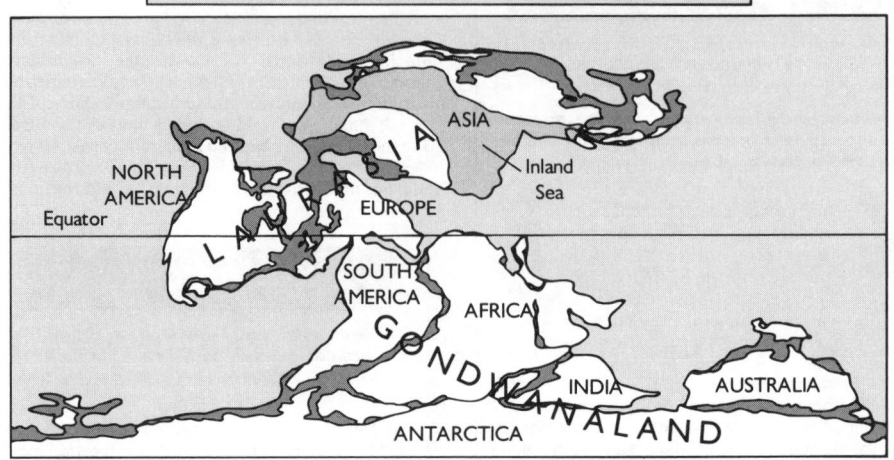

MID-CARBONIFEROUS PERIOD 355–300 million years ago

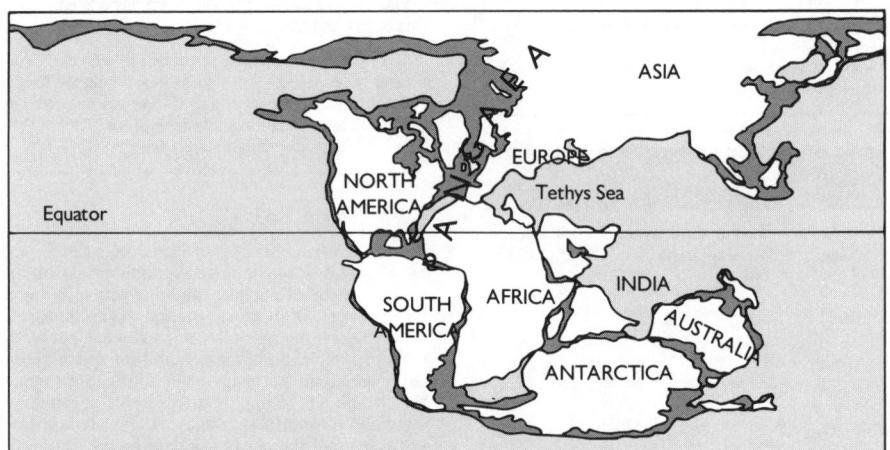

LATE TRIASSIC PERIOD 250–205 million years ago

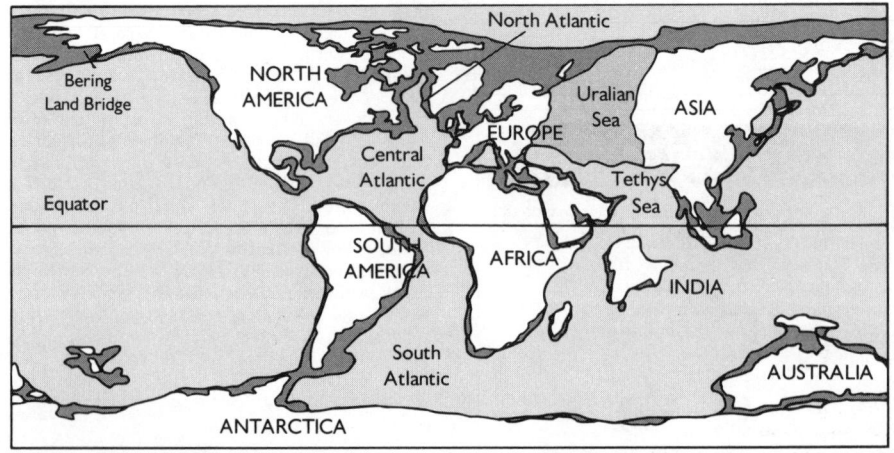

PALAEOCENE EPOCH 65–53 million years ago

usually oxides of iron and titanium. When a rock forms, these particles become magnetized in the direction of the Earth's magnetic field at the particular site. Using highly sensitive instruments, it is possible to measure this weak magnetism and from it determine the position of the north pole at the time the rock was formed. Scientists were surprised to discover that for rocks older than a few million years the north poles determined in this way did not lie at the present north pole, and that the older the rocks the greater was the discrepancy. They were even more surprised to find that rocks of the same age from different continents gave ancient north poles in quite different positions. There can only be one north pole at any given time, however, and that must lie close to the north end of the Earth's rotational axis. The only way of explaining the rock magnetic data, therefore, was to assume that the continents have drifted with respect to both the present north pole and each other.

THE CONTINENTS

The Earth's land surface comprises seven continents, each with their attendant islands. Europe, Africa and Asia, though politically distinct, physically form one land mass known as Afro-Eurasia, which covers 57.2 per cent of the Earth's land mass. Central America (which includes Mexico) is often included in North America (Canada, the USA and Greenland), with South America regarded as a separate continent. Europe includes all of Russia west of the Ural Mountains. Oceania embraces Australasia (Australia and New Zealand) and the non-Asian Pacific islands. The seventh continent is Antarctica.

ASIA

Area: 44 614 000 km^2 (17 226 000 sq mi).
Greatest extremity north to south*: 6435 km (4000 mi).
Greatest extremity east to west*: 7560 km (4700 mi).

Russia, which straddles the divide between Asia and Europe, does not recognize a dividing line between the two continents. However, a boundary running along the eastern foot of the Ural Mountains and following the boundary of Kazakhstan to the Caspian Sea is generally recognized internationally. The boundary between Asia and Europe in the Caucasus is disputed. Some authorities recognize the crest of the Caucasus Mountains between the Caspian and Black Seas as the dividing line, while others prefer a boundary following the valley of the River Manych to the estuary of the River Don. Howvever, the former Soviet republics of Armenia and Georgia – which are south of the crest of the Caucasus Mountains – regard themselves as European, and together with the island of Cyprus, which is physically an attendant island to Asia, they are sometimes regarded as part of Europe. In the East, the boundary between Asia and Oceania is also disputed. Western New Guinea – Irian Jaya – is politically part of Indonesia but is generally regarded as part of Oceania rather than part of Asia. The rest of Indonesia, the Philippines and Japan are regarded as part of Asia.

AFRICA

Area: 30 216 000 km^2 (11 667 000 sq mi).
Greatest extremity north to south*: 7080 km (4400 mi).
Greatest extremity east to west*: 6035 km (3750 mi).

The boundary between Africa and Asia is usually regarded as being the Suez Canal rather than the political boundary between Egypt and Israel. Africa includes a number of attendant islands, the largest of which are Madagascar, Mauritius, Réunion, Zanzibar and Bioko. The islands of Madeira, the Azores and the Canary Islands – although strictly attendant islands to Africa – are almost always included in Europe. The island of Socotra – which is politically part of Yemen – is almost always included in Asia although it is strictly an attendant island to Africa.

NORTH AMERICA

Area: 24 230 000 km^2 (9 355 000 sq mi).
Greatest extremity north to south*: 7885 km (5000 mi).
Greatest extremity east to west*: 6035 km (3750 mi).

North America includes Central America (up to the Panama–Colombia border) as well as Greenland, and the Caribbean islands of the Greater Antilles, the Leeward and Windward Islands. Hawaii is often included as part of North America because it is politically part of the USA, although it is physically part of Oceania.

SOUTH AMERICA

Area: 17 814 000 km^2 (6 878 000 sq mi).
Greatest extremity north to south*: 7240 km (4500 mi).
Greatest extremity east to west*: 5150 km (3200 mi).

South America includes the Caribbean islands of Trinidad and Tobago, the Venezuelan Lesser Antilles, and Aruba, Bonaire and Curaçao. The northern boundary of the continent is usually taken to be the political frontier between Panama and Colombia, rather than the Panama Canal. (Until the 20th century, what is now Panama was considered to be part of South America.)

ANTARCTICA

Area 14 245 000 km^2 (5 500 000 sq mi).
*Greatest extremity**: 4340 km (2700 km).

Antarctica includes a relatively small number of attendant islands.

EUROPE

Area: 10 505 000 km^2 (4 056 000 sq mi).
Greatest extremity north to south: 2900 km (1800 mi).
Greatest extremity east to west: 4000 km (2500 mi).

Europe excludes Asiatic Turkey, thus dividing the city of Istanbul between two continents. (The boundary between Europe and Asia is described above – see Asia.) The islands of Madeira, the Azores and the Canary Islands – although strictly attendant islands to Africa – are almost always included in Europe. The island of Cyprus – an attendant island to Asia – is often regarded as part of Europe.

OCEANIA

Area: 8 503 000 km^2 (3 283 000 sq mi).
*Greatest extremity** north to south*: 3000 km (1870 mi).
*Greatest extremity** east to west*: 3700 km (2300 mi).

Oceania comprises Australia, New Zealand and the entire island of New Guinea as well as the Melanesian, Micronesian and Polynesian islands. Hawaii – although physically part of Oceania – is often included in North America because it is politically part of the USA.

* excluding attendant islands.
** Australia.

GEOLOGY

THE FORMATION OF ROCKS

Rock can be one of three types – igneous, sedimentary or metamorphic. *Igneous rock* starts deep in the Earth as molten magma, which then forces its way up through the crust to cool and solidify. *Sedimentary rock* is mostly formed when rock of any type is weathered down into fine particles that are then re-deposited under water and later compressed. *Metamorphic rock* is igneous or sedimentary rock that has been subjected to high pressure and/or temperature, thereby changing its nature.

The Earth is perpetually recycling its rocks. Material brought to the surface is eroded, transported and ultimately returned to the Earth's interior, where it becomes available to begin the cycle all over again. This series of processes is known as the *rock cycle* or *geological cycle*. The energy to maintain it comes partly from the Sun (to fuel the erosion processes) and partly from the Earth's interior (to generate volcanic activity and uplift).

IGNEOUS ROCK

Magma – which comes to the Earth's surface via volcanic activity – comprises a mixture of oxides (compounds with oxygen) and silicates (compounds with silicon and oxygen). When it cools and solidifies, the oxides and silicates produce a complex mixture of mineral crystals. The nature and properties of the crystals in any particular igneous rock depend partly on the composition of the original magma and partly upon the physical conditions under which the magma crystallized. As compositions and conditions vary greatly, there are thousands of different igneous rock types.

Igneous rocks that form on the Earth's surface are known as *extrusive*. Those that form within the crust from magma that never reached the surface are known as *intrusive*. Intrusive rocks cool more slowly because, being surrounded by other rock rather than being open to the air, the heat cannot escape so readily. As a result, the crystals have longer to grow, and the mineral grains are larger (coarser).

Despite the many varieties of igneous rock, just six account for most of the igneous components of the crust. These are *granite, diorite* and *gabbro*, which are coarse-grained intrusive rocks, and *rhyolite, andesite* and *basalt*, which are fine-grained extrusive rocks.

SEDIMENTARY ROCKS

At least 75% of all sedimentary rock is known as *clastic sedimentary rock*, which means that it is derived from the erosion products of other rocks. All rocks, even those in the most massive of mountain ranges, are ultimately broken down into smaller and smaller fragments. When the particles become small enough they are then transported by water, wind or ice, usually ending up in the ocean. There they fall as sediment to the ocean floor where, under the pressure of subsequent deposits, they are compacted into hard rock. The most common sedimentary rock is *sandstone*.

The remaining 25% of sediment is either chemical or organic. Rivers dissolve minerals out of the rocks through which they pass, and the mineral solutions

end up in the oceans. When the oceans reach their saturation limit for the particular mineral concerned, the excess mineral is precipitated out chemically as solid particles, which fall to the ocean floor. The most common chemical sedimentary rock is *limestone* (calcium carbonate; $CaCO_3$). Not all limestone is precipitated chemically, however. Many ocean organisms extract calcium carbonate from water to build their shells, and when they die the shells sink to the ocean floor to form sediment in their own right. The most common organic sedimentary rock is again limestone, but there are other organisms that in a similar way generate silica (SiO_2) sediments.

Most sedimentary rocks are a mixture of clastic, chemical and organic, although one type usually predominates.

METAMORPHIC ROCK

When igneous or sedimentary rocks are subjected to high temperatures and pressures, especially in the presence of percolating fluids, their internal structures, and sometimes even their mineralogical compositions, may be changed. The processes involved are known collectively as *metamorphism*. The sort of temperatures and pressures required are, respectively, 300° C (572° F) and 100 megapascals (equivalent to almost 100 atmospheres).

The most extreme conditions in the Earth's crust occur at plate boundaries where continents collide. Most metamorphic rocks are thus generated in the roots of mountains. Depending upon temperature and pressure, there are various grades of metamorphism; but in the most intense (high-grade) metamorphism, rock structures, holes and even fossils are so completely obliterated that the original rock type can no longer be identified.

As a result of the realignment of minerals under pressure, many metamorphic rocks are layered, or banded. Sometimes the layering is visible; but even when it is not, it can often be detected by the way that the rock breaks. A common example is *slate*, which easily breaks into thin sheets along the layering.

Not all metamorphic rock is layered, however. Common examples of non-layered metamorphics are *marble*, formed by the metamorphism of limestone, and *quartzite*, which is derived from sandstone.

GEOCHRONOLOGY

The four eras into which geological time is usually divided are: the Cenozoic (Greek *kainos* 'new'), the most recent; the Mesozoic (Greek *mesos* 'middle'); the Palaeozoic (Greek *palaios* 'ancient'); and the Proterozoic (Greek *protos* 'first') or Precambrian. The Hadean and Archaen periods – usually regarded as divisions of the Proterozoic – are sometimes added before the Proterozoic as distinct eras (see p. 63).

In the 17th century, Archbishop Ussher dated the creation of the Earth as occurring in the year 4004 BC, while, in 1899, Lord Kelvin calculated that the Earth was some hundreds of millions of years old. At the beginning of the 20th century radioactive decay was used as a measurement of geochronology. In 1907 the American chemist and physicist B.B. Boltwood showed that a sample of pre-Cambrian rock dated from 1640 million years before the present (BP) measured by the uranium-lead method. Geological time now extends back about 4600 million years ago to the beginning of the Proterozoic era.

GEOLOGICAL TIMECHART

ERA	PERIOD	EPOCH	BEGAN MILLIONS OF YEARS AGO	GEOGRAPHY
C E N O Z O I C	QUATERNARY	HOLOCENE	0.01	Retreat of glaciers leaves continents, seas and landscapes in more or less their present forms.
		PLEISTOCENE	1.6	The thickest continental glaciers depressed the earth's crust to such an extent that large areas of northwestern Europe and North America are still rising at a considerable rate today (30 mm a year around Hudson Bay).
	TERTIARY	PLIOCENE	5.3	Time of marked, often rapid change. Uplift of the Isthmus of Panama results in the connection of North and South America.
		MIOCENE	23	Africa moves northwards into Eurasia. The Himalaya are raised as the Indian plate collides with Asia. The Red Sea opens and the Mediterranean has its origin.
		OLIGOCENE	34	The main phase of Alpine mountain-building begins, followed soon afterwards by East African and Red Sea rifting. South America separates from Antarctica.
		EOCENE	53	The Indian plate begins to collide with Eurasia (leading to the formation of the Himalaya in the Miocene). The Eurasian Basin opens as the final fragmentation of the Eurasian continent occurs. Pyrenean mountains form in the late Eocene. Australia separates from South America and Antarctica.
		PALAEOCENE	65	Iberia converges on Europe. The Atlantic and Pacific Oceans are linked through the straits of Panama.
M E S O Z O I C	CRETACEOUS		135	India separates from Antarctica, while Atlantic rifting brings about the separation of South America from Africa. Further opening of Atlantic and the separation of Greenland.
	JURASSIC		205	At the start of the Jurassic, rifting occurs between Gondwanaland and Laurasia, initially separating southern Europe from Africa and eventually tearing Pangaea in two. Central Atlantic opens.
	TRIASSIC		250	The start of the Mesozoic era sees all the major continents joined together. Consequently almost all of the earth's land surface is concentrated on one side of the globe, with the result that large areas lie far from the oceans and become very arid.
P A L A E O Z O I C	PERMIAN		300	Pangaea is formed and in the late Permian Siberia collides with northern Pangaea to form the Ural mountains.
	CARBONIFEROUS Divided in USA into Mississippian (early part) and Pennsylvanian (later part)		355	The major continents move closer and closer together, until, early in the next period, Laurasia collides with Gondwanaland to form the supercontinent Pangaea.
	DEVONIAN		410	The gap between Laurasia and Gondwanaland has narrowed, but ocean levels remain high.
	SILURIAN		438	Laurasia forms as Laurentia and Baltica become welded together. Ocean levels are high, probably from melting of the ice cap.
	ORDOVICIAN		510	Baltica moves from South Polar region towards the equator and closer to Laurentia. Meanwhile Gondwanaland moves towards the South Pole, and increased glaciation causes lowering of the sea level.
	CAMBRIAN		570	Near the end of the Precambrian most landmasses fused into a giant supercontinent, but by the late Cambrian Gondwanaland, Siberia and Laurentia are separate continents and more or less sit astride the equator.
	PRECAMBRIAN ERA		4600	North America, Greenland and Scotland united as Laurentia, equatorial in position. Gondwanaland in the southern hemisphere.

Modern dating methods, using the duration of radio-isotopic half-lives, include also the contrasts obtained from thorium-lead, potassium-argon, rubidium-strontium, rhenium-osmium, helium-uranium and, in the recent range of up to 40 000 years BP, carbon-14. Modern developments, using accelerator equipment, allow carbon-14 dating to extend back beyond 100 000 years. Other methods include thermoluminescence (used since 1968) and racemization of amino acids (used since 1972) – the latter method is dependent upon the rate of change from optically active to inactive forms over a long-term period of time.

FOSSILS

A fossil may be defined as an impression or remnant of a long-dead organism in a deposit of sedimentary rock. By studying rocks and the fossils preserved within them, scientists have been able to trace the momentous changes that the Earth has undergone since its formation. Sedimentary rocks are usually arranged in a succession of horizontal bands or *strata*, with the oldest strata lying at the bottom. Each band will often contain the fossilized remains of the plants and animals that died at the time at which the sediment was laid down. The strata of sedimentary rock are therefore like the pages of a book, each with a record of contemporary life etched upon it. Unfortunately, however, the record is far from complete. The process of sedimentation in any one place is invariably interrupted by periods in which new sediment is not laid down or existing sediment is eroded away. The succession of layers is further obscured by folding and faulting, and by mountain building.

However patchy the record may be, any interpretation of it depends on first establishing a chronology. Relative dating is usually achieved by correlating strata on the basis of their fossil content, since a specific assemblage of fossils will be characteristic of a stratum of a particular age. The discovery and study of fossils of extinct animals in the 18th and early 19th centuries began to stimulate evolutionary speculation.

FOSSILIZATION

In order for an organism to be preserved as a fossil, it must include hard parts capable of preservation and it must be covered rapidly after death to slow decomposition and safeguard it from destruction. The hard parts of some organisms are preserved unaltered – for example, the shells of clams. However, most fossilized remains are altered; for example, bones and shells may be *permineralized* – that is, they are made denser by the addition of calcium carbonate, iron and other minerals. Alternatively, the crystal structure of a shell may be *recrystallized*, althogh its outer appearance remains unaltered. *Replacement* of the hard parts of an organism is a common form of fossilization. This involves the dissolution of the existing hard structure and its replacement by another substance such as silica or hematite. Molds of organisms occur, in which the plant or animal itself has been destroyed and replaced by particles that eventually form sedimentary rock. Tracks of animals may be preserved as fossils in a similar manner.

MILESTONES IN THE FOSSIL RECORD

PreCambrian era   Many microfossils dating back 3.25 million years were perhaps produced by bacteria and by blue-green algae. Fossilized impressions of the first multicellular animals (coelenterates, annelids worms and arthropods) date back 590 million years.

Cambrian period   The fossil record of the start of the period is characterized by the emergence of many larger marine animals, including gastropods, trilobites, lamp shells, and graptolites. Nautiloids appeared at the end of the Cambrian period.

Ordovician period   Typical fossils include highly diversified trilobites, lamp shells, and tree-like graptolites, as well as new groups of gastropods, sea mats, the first sea urchins, the first ammonites and the first vertebrate remains – jawless fish.

Silurian period   Mass extinction at the end of the Ordovician period was followed by a rediversification of marine life. The fossil record includes the first true jawed fishes and the eurypterids (scorpion-like aquatic arthropods).

Devonian period   The fossil record shows a progressive colonization of the land by plants, including large vascular plants such as lycopods (club mosses as big as trees) and the first ferns. The first land animals included scorpions, wingless insects and the earliest tetrapod (a primitive amphibian).

Carboniferous period   Typical fossils include sharks and bony fish, and more diverse amphibians. The first conifers, the first reptiles and the earliest flying insects appeared. Graptolites became extinct.

Permian period   The fossil record includes more diverse conifers and reptiles. Trilobites became extinct.

Triassic period   Gymnosperm floras predominate in the fossil record, although ferns remained important. Many new groups emerged, including teleosts (the dominant fish group today), enormous marine reptiles such as ichthyosaurs and plesiosaurs, thecodonts (which evolved into flying reptiles), dinosaurs and the first mammals. The Triassic ended with the greatest mass extinction of all time, which eliminated many species of marine invertebrate.

Jurassic period   Floras include cycads, conifers and ginkgoes. Animals include marine and freshwater turtles, crocodiles, many types of dinosaur and the first undisputed bird (archaeopteryx).

Cretaceous period   The most spectacular vertebrates in the fossil record are the marine plesiosaurs, giant turtles and the newly-evolved mosasaurs. The end of the period saw widespread extinction, including ammonites, dinosaurs, ichthyosaurs and pterosaurs. Angiosperms (flowering plants) and the first grasses arose during the period.

Palaeocene epoch   Many mammalian groups – including the primates – made their appearance in the fossil record and modern families of flowering plants evolved.

Eocene epoch   Forests were of distinctly modern appearance. Typical mammalian fossils include artiodactyls, elephants, edentates, whales, rodents, carnivores and early higher primates. All bird orders appeared before the end of the epoch.

Oligocene epoch   The earliest monkeys appeared and the largest land mammal of all time – the rhinoceros-like titanotheres – became extinct.

Miocene epoch   The epoch was characterized by the spread of grasslands and the retreat of forests, and by the radiation of apes and horses.

Pliocene epoch   Although the plants were largely similar to today, distinct animals emerged, including mammoths and the first hominids.

MAJOR ROCKS AND ROCK TYPES

Other common rocks are recorded in the Geology Glossary.

Rock	Main constituents and formation
Andesite (igneous)	Formed from surface lava, volcanic plugs and dikes as well as volcanic ash and mud flows. Fine-grained rocks containing andesine (a feldspar) and pyroxene or biotite.
Basalt (igneous)	Formed by cooling of extrusive (i.e. on land surface or under water) lava flows. Contains about 50% silica and high quantities of feldspar, pyroxene and olivine minerals.
Breccia (sedimentary)	Formed from angular fragments of material – larger than 2 mm (0.08 in) across – from pre-existing rocks.
Chalk	Fine-grained white limestone (see below).
Clay (sedimentary)	Generic term for a wide range of sedimentary rocks formed of tiny clay mineral particles, organic and detrital materials (including quartz). Includes soils, clay shales, mudstones, glacial clays, etc.
Diorite (igneous)	Formed from the crystallization of magma or from a reaction between magma and a foreign rock. Medium- or coarse-grained containing about 66% feldspar.
Dolomoite (sedimentary)	Limestone (see below) that is formed when calcite is replaced after deposition by calcium magnesium carbonate – $CaMg(CO_3)_2$ – either through contact with sea water or by solution.
Gabbro (igneous)	Formed by cooling of intrusive molten rock. Medium- or coarse-grained with variable composition. Contains mainly feldspar and pyroxene.
Gneiss (metamorphic)	Formed from granite where the mineral content and structure has been changed through heating caused by intrusion of a new molten mass.
Granite (igneous)	Formed by slow cooling of intrusive molten material (i.e. within the Earth's body). Has large crystals – quartz, feldspars, mica.
Hornfels (metamorphic)	Fine-grained granular rock formed by thermal metamorphosis.
Limestone (sedimentary)	Pure forms are totally $CaCO_3$. Comprises the remains of microscopic organisms and always deposited in water. Fine-grained.
Marble (metamorphic)	Thermal changes to limestone result in the formation of marble, which is a granular crystalline rock.
Marl (sedimentary)	Generic term for a variety of fine-grained mudstones (see below). Calcareous and greensand types are common.
Mudstone (sedimentary)	Generic term for a variety of sedimentary rocks formed of tiny clay and silt particles. Characterized by a lack of lamination.
Nevadite	A rhyolite (see below) with large crystals in which the glassy components are so small that the rock is often mistaken for granite.
Obsidian	A black glassy rhyolite (see below).
Pitchstone	A glassy rhyolite (see below).
Pumice (igneous)	Formed from material thrown from a volcano. Contains a high proportion of air space.
Quartzite (metamorphic)	Formed from sandstone by recrystallization under high temperatures or by precipitation of silica. Solid quartz rock with no pores.
Rhyolite (igneous)	Formed from volcanic lava in which crystallization began prior to extrusion on the surface. Contains either large, single crystals or, when crystallization is rapid, forms a glassy microcrystalline matrix.
Sandstone (sedimentary)	Predominately quartz grains with other minor components. May preserve bedding structures from original deposition, e.g. dune bedding, ripples, etc.
Shale (sedimentary)	Formed by deposition of silt and clay particles in deep water. Contains clay minerals, quartz, feldspars, organic material and iron oxides. (See also clay, above.)
Silt	Unconsolidated aggregate of tiny sedimentary particles (see also siltstone, below).
Siltstone (sedimentary)	Consolidated tiny silt particles deposited by water. Typically occurs in thin layers. (See also silt, above.)
Slate (metamorphic)	Formed from sedimentary rocks that have been metamorphosed. Slates all show cleavage. New minerals may show up as marks or even crystals.

MAJOR METALLURGICAL MINERALS

Some minerals – for example iron and copper – occur in a number of ores; others are naturally occurring.

Mineral	Element	Abundance in crust parts per million)	Major uses include	Major deposits are worked in the following countries
Bauxite	Aluminium	81 000	Conductors, aircraft, ships, cars, foil	Australia, Guinea, Jamaica, Brazil, Russia
Cassiterite	Tin	1.5	Tin-plating, alloys (bronze and pewter)	Brazil, China, Malaysia, Indonesia, Bolivia
Chalconite, chalcopyrite, bornite, cuprite, etc.,	Copper	100	Conductors, alloys (brass, bronze), coinage, plumbing	Chile, USA, Russia, Canada, Zambia
Chromite	Chromium	under 700	Chromium-plating, stainless steel	South Africa, Russia, India, Albania, Turkey
Cinnabar	Mercury	under 1	Explosives, scientific instruments, dentistry	Russia, China, Spain, Algeria, Mexico
Galena	Lead	20	Batteries, roofing, radiological protection	Russia, Australia, USA, China, Canada
Garnierite, pentlandite	Nickel	under 80	Nickel-plating, steel alloys, gas-turbine engines, coinage	Russia, Canada, New Caledonia, Australia
Gold*	Gold	under 0.005	Source of value, jewellery, some electronic uses	South Africa, USA, Russia, Australia, Canada
Hematite, magnetite	Iron	50 000	Structures, machines cars, foil	Russia, Brazil, China, Australia, USA
Magnesite	Magnesium	25 000	Low-density alloys for aircraft, machinery, etc.	Russia, China, North Korea, Slovakia, Turkey
Pitchblende	Uranium	under 7	Nuclear power stations	Russia, Canada, Australia, USA, Namibia
Platinum*, sperrylite	Platinum	under 0.0005	Catalyst in chemical processes and in car exhausts	Russia, Finland, USA, Australia, Brazil
Silver*, sylvanite	Silver	under 1	Jewellery, silverware, photographic emulsions	Mexico, USA, Peru, Russia, Canada
Sphalerite	Zinc	under 80	Alloys (brass), galvanizing steel	Canada, Russia, Australia, China, Peru
Wolframite, scheelite	Tungsten	1.5	Lamp filaments, electronics, steel alloys, cutting tools	China, Russia, Mongolia, Austria, Portugal

* naturally occurring

The quantities of most metals in the crust are small – only iron, aluminium amd magnesium are really plentiful. We are able to extract them only because they are not evenly distributed but occur in local concentrations where mining is economically possible. There are far greater concentrations of some metals, such as iron and nickel, but for the moment they are beyond our reach.

The first metals to be used by humanity were those that occurred in their natural state and appeared in outcrops on the surface – gold, silver, iron (in the form of fallen meteorites) and copper. However, supplies of elemental iron and copper soon ran out, and during the the Bronze and Iron Ages it was discovered how to extract metals from their ores, in which they are chemically combined with other elements, most often oxygen and sulphur (sulfur).

WILL MINERALS RUN OUT?

Today, the consumption of all metals and minerals is rising fast. Will there be enough to go round? A number of studies carried out since the early 1960s have cast doubt on this. While iron and aluminium are abundant, there are many important metals – lead, zinc, tin, silver, platinum and mercury – the supplies of which seem less certain. In many cases, as one metal ore becomes scarcer, it can be replaced with another, or with plastic or composite material, but this is not always possible. For instance, there is, as yet, no substitute for silver in photographic emulsions or for platinum as an industrial catalyst.

At the same time it is important to remember that in mining we have only begun – quite literally – to scratch the surface. While many of the richest sources of metals have already been exhausted, higher prices and better technology make it feasible to extract metals economically from poorer ores and to tap less accessible deposits. Few mining engineers or geologists believe that there is any real danger of running out of important minerals in the immediate future.

GEMSTONES

Gemstones are minerals that possess a rarity and usually a hardness, colour or translucency which gives them strong aesthetic appeal. Hundreds of stones are mined as gems. The most important is diamond (a form of carbon) because its great hardness makes it important for tools in industry. The major source of diamonds is South Africa, where they are recovered from rock by deep mining. Where gemstones have been eroded from rocks by water, they may be found in gravel deposits. Sapphires and rubies, for instance, occur in such deposits in Sri Lanka. Diamond, emerald, ruby and sapphire used to be classified as 'precious stones' and the others listed here as 'semi-precious stones'. This distinction is generally no longer applied.

The principal gemstones are listed below in order of hardness on the Moh scale 1–10. Their chemical composition, colour and major sources are also given.

Diamond C; *Hardness:* 10.0; *Colour:* Clear (pure) often slight tinge of yellow, brown, red, black; *Major sources:* include South Africa, Namibia, Australia, Brazil, Russia. From Kimberlite pipes or alluvium.

Ruby (red corundum; Al2O3); *Hardness:* 9.0; *Colour:* red (owing to chromic oxide staining); *Major sources:* Brazil, Myanmar (Burma), Sri Lanka, Thailand, India, Australia. From pegmatite and metamorphic rocks.

Sapphire (blue corundum; Al_2O_3); *Hardness:* 9.0; *Colour:* blue (other colours of corundum may also be called sapphire; *Major sources:* Brazil, Myanmar (Burma), Sir Lanka, Thailand, India, Australia and USA. From pegmatite and metamorphic rocks.

Chrysoberyl (alexandrite; also known as cat's eye when brownish colour; $BeAl_2O_4$; *Hardness:* 8.5; *Colour:* green and yellow shades (transparent to translucent). *Major sources:* Brazil, Russia, Zimbabwe, Sri Lanka. From granitic rocks and pegmatite.

Topaz Al_2SiO_4; *Hardness:* 8.0; *Colour:* colourless, pale blue, pale yellow, greenish, rare pink. *Major sources:* Australia, Brazil, Russia, Sri Lanka, Namibia. In granitic pegmatites, rhyolites and quartz veins, and alluvial deposits.

Spinel $MgAl_2O_4$; *Hardness:*7.5–8.0; *Colour:* very variable, commonly red, translucent; *Major sources:* Myanmar (Burma), Sri Lanka, India, Thailand. Gem quality stones from alluvial gravels. Source is igneous rocks (e.g. gabbro) and some metamorphics.

Emerald (green beryl; $Be_3Al_2Si_6O_{18}$); *Colour:* green, transparent to translucent; *Major sources:* Russia, USA, Austria, Norway, Colombia, Zambia. Found in granites.

Aquamarine (blue-green beryl; $Be_3Al_2Si_6O_{18}$; *Hardness:* 7.5–8.0; *Colour:* pale blue-green transparent to translucent; *Major sources:* Brazil, Russia, UK (Northern Ireland).

Zircon $ZrSiO_4$; *Hardness:* 7.5; *Colour:* variable: light to reddish brown common – transparent forms best for gems; *Major sources:* widely distributed – best gemstone zircons found in pegmatites or concentrated in alluvial or beach gravels.

Tourmaline ; Na(or Mg, Fe, Li, Al, Mn)$_{3-}$ $Al_6(BO_3)_3Si_6O_{18}$; *Hardness:* 7.0; *Colour:* black, bluishblack – also reds and greens; *Major sources:* Brazil, Sri Lanka, USA, Russia.

Garnet group various silicates; *Hardness:*

6.5–7.0; *Colour:* varies according to composition, transparent to translucent; *Major sources:* widely distributed; metamorphic and igneous rocks.

Rose Quartz SiO_2; *Hardness:* 7.0; *Colour:* pink; *Major sources:* Brazil, Sri Lanka, USA, Russia.

Smoky quartz SiO_2; *Hardness:* 7.0; *Colour:* smoky brown, red, yellow; *Major sources:* UK (Scotland) Switzerland, USA, Russia, Brazil.

Rock Crystal (quartz; SiO_2); *Hardness:* 7.0; *Colour:* clear transparent; *Major sources:* widespread.

Amethyst SiO_2; *Hardness:* 7.0; *Colour:* purple; *Major sources:* Brazil, Sri Lanka, Germany, Madagascar, Uruguay, Russia.

Chrysoprase SiO_2; *Hardness:* 6.5–7.0; *Colour:* apple green; *Major sources:* USA, Germany.

Carnelian or **Cornelian** SiO_2; *Hardness:* 6.5–7.0; *Colour:* red, reddish brown; *Major sources:* widespread, including UK.

Agate SiO_2; *Hardness:* 6.5–7.0; *Colour:* striped, white-grey, blue; *Major sources:* Brazil, India, Germany, Namibia, Madagascar, UK (Scotland).

Onyx SiO_2; *Hardness:* 6.5–7.0; *Colour:* black and white stripes; *Major sources:* Brazil, India, Germany, Namibia, Madagascar, UK (Scotland).

Sardonyx SiO_2; *Hardness:* 6.5–7.0; *Colour:* redbrown and white stripes; *Major sources:* Brazil, India, Germany, Namibia, Madagascar, UK (Scotland).

Jasper SiO_2; *Hardness:* 6.5–7.0; brown, red, yellow; *Major sources:* Egypt, India.

Bloodstone SiO_2; *Hardness:* 6.5–7.0; *Colour:* red spots on dark green; *Major sources:* widespread.

Olivine (peridot; $(Mg, Fe)_2SiO_4$); *Hardness:* 6.5–7.0; *Colour:* green; *Major sources:* Australia, Brazil, Myanmar (Burma), Norway, USA.

Jadeite (Jade) $NaAlSi_2O_6$; *Hardness:* 6.5–7.0; *Colour:* green; *Major sources:* Myanmar (Burma), China, Canada, USA, New Zealand.

Moonstone $KAlSi_3O_8$; *Hardness:* 6.0–6.5; *Colour:* whitish blue with pearly sheen; *Major sources:* Brazil, Myanmar (Burma), Sri Lanka.

Opal $SiO_2.nH_2O$; *Hardness:* 5.5–6.5; *Colour:* milkywhite, sometimes black, body with rainbow streaks; *Major sources:* Australia, Mexico, Russia, Hungary.

Turquoise $CuAl_6(PO_4)_4(OH)_85H_2O$; *Hardness:* 5.5–6.0; *Colour:* sky blue, opaque; *Major sources:* Egypt, Iran, Turkey, USA.

Lapis Lazuli (Lazurite; $(NaCa)_8(Al, Si)_{12}O_{24}$ (S_1SO_4); *Hardness:* 5.0–5.5; *Colour:* azure blue, opaque; *Major sources:* Afghanistan, Chile, China (Tibet), Russia.

ORGANIC GEM MATERIAL

Amber $C_{40}H_{64}O_4$; *Hardness:* 2.0–2.5; *Colour:* yellow, honey; *Major sources:* Baltic coasts where producers include Lithuania, Poland, Sweden and Germany. Myanmar (Burma) is also a producer.

Coral $CaCo_3$; *Hardness:* varies, soft; *Colour:* various seas, including the Mediterranean Sea and the Indian and Pacific oceans. In the Mediterranean, Greece and Italy are producers of precious coral.

Pearl *Hardness:* varies, soft; *Colour:* Pearl grey, white; *Major sources:* various seas and rivers. Marine producers include Oman, UAE, Qatar, India, Sri Lanka and Mexico. Freshwater producers include Germany, China, and USA.

PHYSICAL GEOGRAPHY

THE OCEANS

The oceans cover a greater area of the Earth than does the land – 71% or almost three quarters of the Earth's surface. The three major oceans are the Pacific, Atlantic and Indian Oceans. The Pacific is the largest ocean, and covers more than a third of the surface of the Earth. The Arctic Ocean is smaller than the other three and is covered almost entirely by ice. Seas are smaller than the four oceans.

The depth of the oceans is very small compared with their area. The deepest part – in the Western Pacific – is only about 11 000 m (36 000 ft) deep. However this is greater than the height of the highest mountain on land, Mount Everest.

SEA WATER

Sea water has solid substances dissolved in it. Sodium and chlorine (which together in their solid form make up sodium chloride – common salt) are the most abundant of these, and together with magnesium, calcium and potassium they make up over 90% of the elements dissolved in sea water. Other elements are present only in very small amounts.

The saltiness, or salinity, of sea water depends on the amount of these substances dissolved in it. An average of about 3.5% of the volume of sea water consists of dissolved substances. High evaporation removes more of the pure water, leaving behind the dissolved substances, so the salinity is higher where evaporation is high, particularly if the sea water is also enclosed and cannot mix easily with the sea water in a larger ocean. This occurs, for example, in the Mediterranean and Red Seas. Low values of salinity occur in polar regions, particularly in the summer months when melting ice dilutes the sea water. Low salinity also occurs in seas such as the Baltic, which is linked to the Atlantic Ocean only by a narrow channel and which is fed by a larger number of freshwater rivers.

Most of the water on the Earth, about 94% of it, is in the oceans. More pure water is evaporated from the oceans than is returned as precipitation (rain, snow, etc) but the volume of water in the oceans remains the same because water is also returned to the oceans from the land by rivers.

WAVES

Sea water is rarely still: it is usually moving in waves, tides or currents. Waves are caused by wind blowing across the surface of the ocean. The height of a wave is determined by the wind speed, the time the wind has been blowing, and the distance the wave has travelled over the ocean. The highest wave ever recorded had a height of 34 m (116 ft), although usually they are much smaller. Waves play a very important role in the shaping of coastlines.

Water does not move along with the waves. Instead the water changes shape as a wave passes, moving in a roughly circular motion, rising towards a wave crest as it arrives and falling as it passes. This motion can be seen by watching a boat: the boat bobs up and down as the waves move past it but does not move along with the waves.

There is another type of wave in the ocean, which is not generated by the winds. These are *tsunami*. They are also popularly called *tidal waves*, but this name is quite wrong because they are not caused by tides. Tsunami are due to earthquakes or the eruption of undersea volcanoes, which move a large amount of water rapidly, disturbing the sea surface and creating waves that travel away from the area of the earthquake or volcano. Tsunami travel at very high speeds, around 750 km/h (470 mph). However, in the open ocean they cause little damage because their wave height is very low, usually less than 1 m (3¼ ft), but in shallow water they slow down and their height increases to 10 m (33 ft) or more, and they can cause extensive damage when they hit a shore.

TIDES

Tides are caused by the gravitational pull of the Moon and the Sun on the Earth, causing the level of the oceans to change. The pull is greatest on the side of the Earth facing the Moon, and this produces a high tide. The pull is weakest on the side away from the Moon, where the sea water rises away from the Moon, and this also gives a high tide.

The Sun is much further away than the Moon and although it is much larger its effect on tides is less than half that of the Moon. When both the Moon and the Sun are on the same or opposite sides of Earth, the pull is greatest, producing very high tides called *spring tides*. Weaker tides, called *neap tides*, occur when the Moon and the Sun form a right angle with the Earth, because the pulls of the two are in different directions. Spring tides occur every 14 days and neap tides half-way between each spring tide.

There are two high tides and two low tides every day in most parts of the Earth, but a few areas have only one high tide and one low tide, or a mixture, with one high tide being much higher than the other. The *tidal range* (the difference between the high and the low water levels) varies from place to place, from less than a metre (3¼ ft) in the Mediterranean Sea and Gulf of Mexico to 14.5 m (47½ ft) in the Bay of Fundy on the coast of Canada.

CURRENTS

The currents near the surface of the oceans, like waves, are driven by the winds. The wind drags the water along with the wind. Currents move much more slowly than the wind, with speeds of less than 8 km/h (5 mph). They do not flow exactly in the same direction as the wind, but are deflected to one side by the Earth's spin.

FEATURES OF THE SEA BED

The region of the sea bed closest to land is the *continental margin*, which is divided into the *continental shelf*, *slope* and (sometimes) the *continental rise*. The continental shelf is the shallowest – around 130 m (430 ft) deep – and is relatively flat. It is about 100 km (60 mi) wide. The sea water over continental shelves usually has abundant marine life and most fishing is done here. About a quarter of the world's supply of oil and gas comes from the rocks beneath the continental shelves.

OCEANIC RIDGES

These are vast, rugged, undersea mountain chains often, but not always, at the centre of oceans. On average they are some 1000 km (620 mi) wide and stand up to 3000 m (10 000 ft) above the adjacent ocean basins. They form a more or less linked system about 80 000 km (50 000 mi) long, and this system enters all the major oceans. Different parts of it have different names: in the centre and south Atlantic, for example, it is called the Mid-Atlantic Ridge; in the north Atlantic to the southwest of Iceland it is the Reykjañes Ridge; in the Pacific it is known as the East Pacific Rise. On average, ridge crests lie some 2500 m (8200 ft) below the ocean surface, but there are a few places, such as Iceland, where the rocks have risen above the water surface, forming an island.

Between the ocean ridges and the continental margins there are *abyssal plains*. These are very flat and featureless parts of the sea floor, around 4000 m (13 000 ft) deep. Abyssal plains are broken in some places by *seamounts*, underwater volcanoes that have erupted from the sea floor. Seamounts may rise above the sea surface to form islands, such as Hawaii.

The deepest parts of the oceans are the *ocean trenches*. These are on average about 100 km (62 mi) wide and 7000–8000 m (23 000–26 000 ft) deep, and may be thousands of kilometres long.

COASTS

On coastlines, new land can be created by the deposition of sediment, and existing land can be lost through marine erosion. What happens where on coasts depends on factors such as climate, coastal geology, the orientation of the coast to wind and waves, and human activities.

COASTAL FRONTIERS

COUNTRIES WITH THE LONGEST COASTLINES

Canada*	244 800 km (152 110 mi)
Russia**	103 000 km (64 000 mi)
Indonesia**	40 000 km (25 000 mi)
Australia*	36 735 km (22 826 mi)
Japan*	33 287 km (20 684 mi)
Norway*	21 347 km (13 264 mi)
USA*	19 924 km (12 380 mi)
China**	18 500 km (11 500 mi)

COUNTRIES WITH THE SHORTEST COASTLINES

Monaco	5.6 km (3.5 mi)
Nauru	19 km (12 mi)
Bosnia	20 km (13 mi)
Jordan	25 km (16 mi)
Slovenia	30 km (19 mi)
Zaïre	39 km (24 mi)
Iraq	45 km (28 mi)
Togo	50 km (31 mi)
Belgium	66 km (41 mi)

* including islands
** estimate; including islands

DEEP-SEA TRENCHES

Length (km)	Length (miles)	Name	Deepest point	Depth (m)	Depth (ft)
2250	1400	Mariana Trench,* W Pacific	Challenger Deep†	11 022	36 160
2575	1600	Tonga-Kermadec Trench,‡ S Pacific	Vityaz 11 (Tonga)	10 882	35 702
2250	1400	Kuril-Kamchatka Trench,* W Pacific		10 542	34 587
1325	825	Philippine Trench, W Pacific	Galathea Deep	10 497	34 439
		Idzu-Bonin Trench (sometimes included in the Japan Trench, see below)		9 810	32 196
800	500	Puerto Rico Trench, W Atlantic	Milwaukee Deep	9 220	30 249
320+	200+	New Hebrides Trench, S Pacific	North Trench	9 165	30 080
640	400	Solomon or New Britain Trench, S Pacific		9 140	29 988
560	350	Yap Trench,* W Pacific		8 527	27 976
1600	1000	Japan Trench,* W Pacific		8 412	27 591
965	600	South Sandwich Trench, S Atlantic	Meteor Deep	8 263	27 112
3200	2000	Aleutian Trench, N Pacific		8 100	26 574
3540	2200	Peru-Chile (Atacama) Trench E Pacific	Bartholomew Deep	8 064	26 454
		Palau Trench (sometimes included in the Yap Trench)		8 050	26 420
965	600	Romanche Trench, N-S Atlantic		7 864	25 800
2250	1400	Java (Sunda) Trench, Indian Ocean	Planet Deep	7 725	25 344
965	600	Cayman Trench, Caribbean		7 535	24 720
1040	650	Nansei Shotó (Ryukyu) Trench, W Pacific		7 505	24 630
240	150	Banda Trench, Banda Sea		7 360	24 155

* These four trenches are sometimes regarded as a single 7400 km (4600 mile) long system.
† In March 1959 the USSR research ship *Vityaz* claimed 11 022 m (36 198 ft), using echo-sounding only.
‡ Kermadec Trench is sometimes considered to be a separate feature. Depth 10 047 m (32 974 ft).

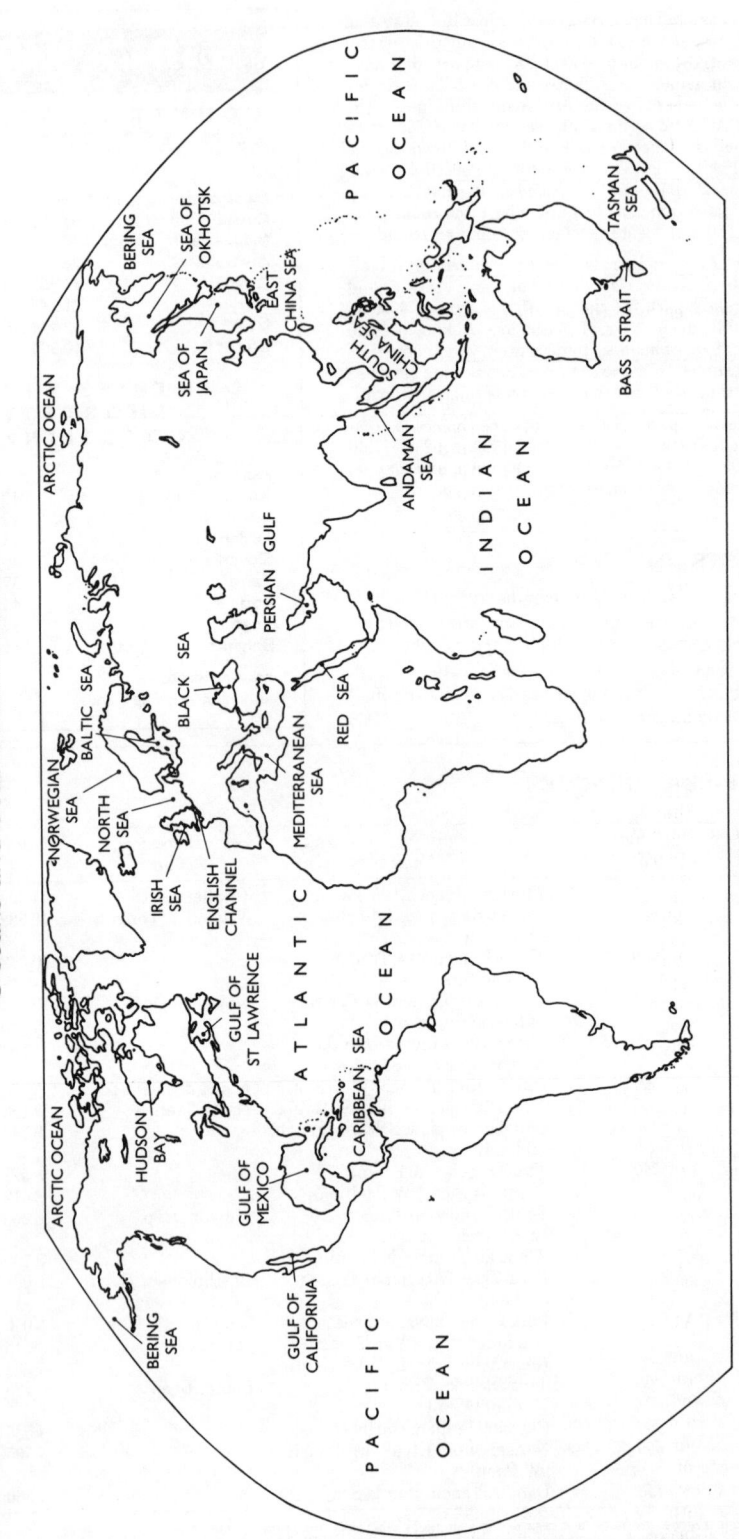

Oceans and Seas of the World

OCEANS

Ocean with adjacent seas	Area (millions km²)	Area (millions miles²)	Percentage of world area	Greatest depth (m)	Greatest depth (ft)	Greatest depth location	Average depth (m)	Average depth (ft)
Pacific	181·20	69·96	35·52	11 022	36 160	Mariana Trench	4188	13 740
Atlantic	106·48	41·11	20·88	9 460	31 037	Puerto Rico Trench	3736	12 257
Indian	74·06	28·59	14·52	7 542	24 744	Java Trench	3872	12 703
Total	361·74	139·66	70·92					

If the adjacent seas are detached and the Arctic regarded as an ocean, the oceanic areas are:

	Area (km²)	Area (m²)	Percentage of sea area
Pacific	166 240 000	64 190 000	46·0
Atlantic	86 560 000	33 420 000	23·9
Indian	73 430 000	28 350 000	20·3
Arctic	13 230 000	5 110 000	3·7
Other Seas	22 280 000	8 600 000	6·1

Ocean depths are zoned by oceanographers as *bathyl* (down to 2000 m or 6560 ft); *abyssal* (between 2000 m and 6000 m (6560 ft and 19 685 ft)) and *hadal* (below 6000 m (19 685 ft)).

SEAS

Principal seas	Average Area (km²)	Average Area (miles²)	depth (m)	depth (ft)
1. South China*	2 974 600	1 148 500	1200	4000
2. Caribbean Sea	2 753 000	1 063 000	2400	8000
3. Mediterranean Sea	2 503 000	966 750	1485	4875
4. Bering Sea	2 268 180	875 750	1400	4700
5. Gulf of Mexico	1 542 985	595 750	1500	5000
6. Sea of Okhotsk	1 527 570	589 800	840	2750
7. East China Sea	1 249 150	482 300	180	600
8. Hudson Bay	1 232 300	475 800	120	400
9. Sea of Japan	1 007 500	389 000	1370	4500
10. Andaman Sea	797 700	308 000	865	2850
11. North Sea	575 300	222 125	90	300
12. Black Sea	461 980	178 375	1100	3600
13. Red Sea	437 700	169 000	490	1610
14. Baltic Sea	422 160	163 000	55	190
15. Persian Gulf†	238 790	92 200	24	80
16. Gulf of St Lawrence	237 760	91 800	120	400
17. Gulf of California	162 000	62 530	810	2660
18. English Channel	89 900	34 700	54	177
19. Irish Sea	88 550	34 200	60	197
20. Bass Strait	75 000	28 950	70	230

* The Malayan Sea, which embraces the South China Sea and the Straits of Malacca (8 142 000 km²/3 144 000 miles²), is not now an entity accepted by the International Hydrographic Bureau.
† Also referred to as the Arabian Gulf or, popularly, 'the Gulf'.

MOUNTAINS

Mountains and mountain ranges are largely formed by the interaction of mountain-building processes (orogeny) and the subsequent erosional processes that tend to destroy them. The distribution of the world's major mountain ranges generally follows those belts of the Earth's landmasses where earthquakes and volcanoes are common. These phenomena are in turn caused by the collision of the moving plates that make up the Earth's lithosphere (see p. 54). Such collisions often result in the margin of one plate being forced upwards, and this process has resulted in the formation of many mountain ranges, although other processes may also play a part in mountain building.

The Earth's largest mountain ranges today – the Alps, Himalaya, Rockies and Andes – are all relatively young, resulting from plate collisions in the last 25 million years or so. Much older ranges include the Scottish Highlands, the Scandinavian mountains and the Appalachians in the USA, which are all around 300-400 million years old. The deeply eroded remnants of even older ranges – up to 3000 million years old – occur in many parts of Africa and Australia.

FOLDED MOUNTAINS

The world's largest and most complex continental mountain ranges are the result of the collision of tectonic plates. Mountains formed directly by plate collisions are known as *fold mountains*, because they are conspicuously folded, faulted and otherwise deformed by the hugh collision pressures. In some cases the collision is between landmasses. Thus India is pressing into the rest of Asia to form the Himalaya, and Africa is being forced into Europe, producing the Alps. In other cases the collision is between an oceanic plate and a continent. Thus the Pacific plate is spreading towards South America, forcing up the Andes. The Himalaya, the Alps and the Andes are still being formed, but some mountain ranges – for example, the Urals of Russia and the Appalachians of the USA – are the products of older, long-ceased plate collisions.

FAULT-BLOCK AND UPWARPED MOUNTAINS

Other types of mountain exist that have not been formed by plate collisions. In *fault-block mountains* a central block of the Earth's crust has sunk and the adjacent blocks have been forced upwards. Mountains of this type define the Basin and Range Province of the western USA (Nevada and parts of Utah, New Mexico, Arizona and California) and form the Sierra Nevada of California and the Teton Range of Wyoming.

In *upwarped mountains*, on the other hand, a central block has been forced upwards. Examples are the Black Hills of Dakota and the Adirondacks of New York.

VOLCANIC MOUNTAINS

Spectacular mountains may also be built by volcanic action. Mauna Loa in Hawaii, for example, is, at 10 203 m (33 476 ft), the world's highest mountain if measured from the Pacific Ocean floor, although less than half is above sea level. Much more important than such isolated volcanoes, however, are the oceanic ridges, the undersea mountain ranges along which the bulk of the Earth's volcanism takes place (see p. xx). Intense volcanism also occurs where oceanic and continental plates collide. The Andes, for example, owe not a little of their mass to volcanic activity.

WORLD'S HIGHEST MOUNTAINS

Key to Ranges: H = Himalaya   K = Karakoram.
Subsidiary peaks or tops in the same mountain massif are italicized.

Mountain	Height (m)	Height (ft)	Range	Date of First Ascent (if any)
1. Mount Everest*	8863	*29 078*	H	29 May 1953
Everest South Summit	*8750*	*28 707*	*H*	*26 May 1953*
2. K2 (Chogori)	8610	*28 250*	K	31 July 1954
3. Kangchenjunga	8598	*28 208*	H	25 May 1955
Yalung Kang (Kangchenjunga West)	*8502*	*27 894*	*H*	*14 May 1973*
Kangchenjunga South Peak	*8488*	*27 848*	*H*	*19 May 1978*
Kangchenjunga Middle Peak	*8475*	*27 806*	*H*	*22 May 1978*
4. Lhotse	8511	*27 923*	H	18 May 1956
Subsidiary Peak	*8410*	*27 591*	*H*	*unclimbed*
Lhotse Shar	*8383*	*27 504*	*H*	*12 May 1970*
5. Makalu I	8481	*27 824*	H	15 May 1955
Makalu South-East	*8010*	*26 280*	*H*	*unclimbed*
6. Dhaulagiri I	8167	*26 795*	H	13 May 1960
7. Manaslu I (Kutang I)	8156	*26 760*	H	9 May 1956
8. Cho Oyu	8153	*26 750*	H	19 Oct 1954
9. Nanga Parbat (Diamir)	8124	*26 660*	H	3 July 1953
10. Annapurna I	8091	*26 546*	H	3 June 1950
Annapurna East	*8010*	*26 280*	*H*	*29 Apr 1974*
11. Gasherbrum I (Hidden Peak)	8068	*26 470*	K	5 July 1958
12. Broad Peak I	8047	*26 400*	K	9 June 1957
Broad Peak Middle	*8016*	*26 300*	*K*	*28 July 1975*
Broad Peak Central	*8000*	*26 246*	*K*	*28 July 1975*
13. Shisham Pangma (Gosainthan)	8046	*26 398*	H	2 May 1964
14. Gasherbrum II	8034	*26 360*	K	7 July 1956

*known in Chinese as Qomolangma, in Nepalese as Sagarmatha and in Tibetan as Mi-ti gu-ti cha-pu long-na.

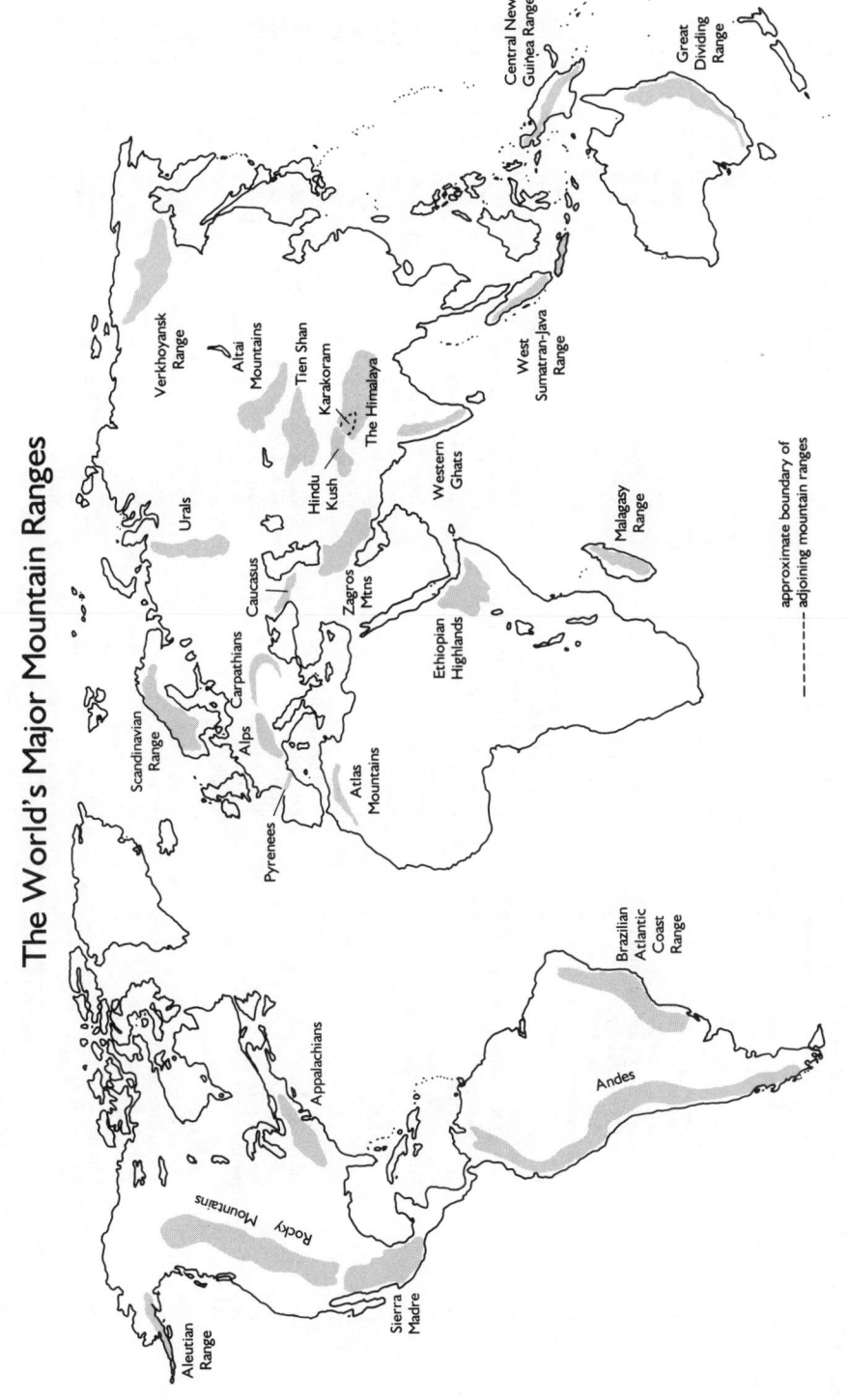

The World's Major Mountain Ranges

Central New Guinea Range
Great Dividing Range
Verkhoyansk Range
Altai Mountains
Tien Shan
Karakoram
The Himalaya
West Sumatran-Java Range
Urals
Hindu Kush
Western Ghats
Malagasy Range
Caucasus
Zagros Mtns
Carpathians
Ethiopian Highlands
Scandinavian Range
Alps
Atlas Mountains
Pyrenees
approximate boundary of
adjoining mountain ranges
Brazilian Atlantic Coast Range
Appalachians
Andes
Rocky Mountains
Sierra Madre
Aleutian Range

WORLD'S GREATEST MOUNTAIN RANGES

The greatest mountain system is the Himalaya–Karakoram–Hindu Kush–Pamir range with 104 peaks over 7315 m (24000 ft). The second greatest range is the Andes with 54 peaks over 6096 m (20000 ft).

Length (km)	Length (miles)	Name	Location	Culminating Peak	Height (m)	Height (ft)
7200	4500	Cordillera de Los Andes	W South America	Aconcagua	6960	22 834
4800	3000	Rocky Mountains	W North America	Mt Elbert (USA)	4400	14 433
3800	2400	Himalaya–Karakoram–Hindu Kush	S Central Asia	Mt Everest	8863	29 078
3600	2250	Great Dividing Range	E Australia	Kosciusko	2230	7 316
3500	2200	Trans-Antarctic Mts	Antarctica	Mt Vinson	5140	16 863
3000	1900	Brazilian Atlantic Coast Range	E Brazil	Pico de Bandeira	2890	9 482
2900	1800	West Sumatran-Javan Range	W Sumatra and Java	Kerintji	3805	12 484
2650	1650*	Aleutian Range	Alaska and NW Pacific	Shishaldin	2861	9 387
2250	1400	Tien Shan	Kyrgyzstan/China	Pik Pobeda	7439	24 406
2000	1250	Central New Guinea Range	Irian Jaya–Papua/N Guinea	Jayakusumu or Ngga Pulu†	5030	16 503
2000	1250	Altai Mountains	Russia/Mongolia	Gora Belukha	4505	14 783
2010	1250	Ural Mountains	Russia	Gora Narodnaya	1894	6 214
1930	1200	Kamchatka Mountains**	Russia	Klyuchevskaya Sopka	4850	15 910
1930	1200	Atlas Mountains	NW Africa	Jebel Toubkal	4165	13 665
1610	1000	Verkhoyanskiy Mountains	Russia	Gora Mas Khaya	2959	9 708
1610	1000	Western Ghats	W India	Anai Madi	2694	8 841
1530	950	Sierra Madre Oriental	Mexico	Citlaltépetl or Orizaba	5610	18 405
1530	950	Zagros Mountains	Iran	Zard Kuh	4547	14 921
1530	950	Scandinavian Range	Norway/Sweden	Galdhopiggen	2469	8 098
1450	900	Ethiopian Highlands	Ethiopia	Ras Dashan	4620	15 158
1450	900	Sierra Madre Occidental	Mexico	Nevado de Colima	4265	13 993
1370	850	Malagasy Range	Madagascar	Tsaratanana	2885	9 465
1290	800	Drakensberg	SE Africa	Thabana Ntlenyana (Lesotho)	3482	11 425
1290	800	Chersky Range	Russia	Gora Pobeda	3147	10 325
1200	750	Caucasus	Georgia/Rusia/Azerbaijan	El'brus, West Peak	5642	18 510
1130	700	Alaska Range	Alaska, USA	Mt McKinley, South Peak	6194	20 320
1130	700	Assam–Burma Range	Assam–W Burma	Hkakabo Razi	5881	19 296
1130	700	Cascade Range	Northwest USA–Canada	Mt Rainier	4392	14 410
1130	700	Central Borneo Range	Central Borneo	Kinabalu (Malaysia)	4101	13 455
1130	700	Appennines	Italy	Corno Grande	2931	9 617
1130	700	Appalachians	Eastern USA–Canada	Mt Mitchell	2037	6 684
1050	650	Alps	Central Europe	Mt Blanc (France)	4807	15 771

* Continuous mainland length (excluding islands) 720 km (450 miles).
** Comprises the Sredinnyy and Koryakskiy Krebets.
† Formerly known as Mount Sukarno and Cartensz Pyramide.

HIGHEST MOUNTAINS OF NORTH AND CENTRAL AMERICA

Mt McKinley (known to local Indians as Denali) is the only peak in excess of 6100 m (20 000 ft) in North and Central America. It was first climbed on 7 June 1913.

Name	Height (m)	Height (ft)	Country
1. Mt McKinley, South Peak	6194	20 320	Alaska, USA
2. Mt Logan	5951	19 524	Yukon, Canada
3. Citlaltépetl (Orizaba)	5610	18 405	Mexico
4. Mt St Elias	5489	18 008	Alaska, USA/Yukon, Canada
5. Popocatépetl	5452	17 887	Mexico
6. Mt Foraker	5304	17 400	Alaska, USA
7. Ixtaccihuatl	5286	17 342	Mexico
8. Mt Lucania	5227	17 150	Yukon, Canada
9. King Peak	5221	17 130	Alaska, USA
10. Mt Blackburn	5036	16 522	Alaska, USA
11. Mt Steele	5011	16 440	Alaska, USA
12. Mt Bona	5005	16 420	Alaska, USA

Note: Mt McKinley, North Peak, is 5934 m (*19 470 ft*).

HIGHEST MOUNTAINS OF SOUTH AMERICA

The mountains of the Andes are headed by Aconcagua at 6960 m (22 834 ft) – first climbed on 14 January 1897. Aconcagua is the highest mountain in the world outside the great ranges of Central Asia.

Name	Height (m)	Height (ft)	Country
1. Cerro Aconcagua	6960	22 834	Argentina
2. Ojos de Salado	6895	22 588	Argentina/Chile
3. Nevado de Pissis	6780	22 244	Argentina/Chile
4. Huascarán Sur	6768	22 205	Peru
5. Llullaillaco	6723	22 057	Argentina/Chile
6. Mercadario	6670	21 884	Argentina/Chile
7. Huascarán Norte	6655	21 834	Peru
8. Yerupajá	6634	21 765	Peru
9. Nevados de Tres Crucées	6620	21 720	Argentina/Chile
10. Coropuna	6613	21 696	Peru
11. Nevado Incahuasi	6601	21 657	Argentina/Chile
12. Tupungato	6550	21 490	Argentina/Chile
13. Sajama	6542	21 463	Bolivia
14. Nevado Gonzalez	6500	21 326	Argentina

HIGHEST MOUNTAINS OF AFRICA

All the peaks listed in Zaïre and Uganda are in the Ruwenzori Mountains.

Name	Height (m)	Height (ft)	Location
1. Kilimanjaro[1]	5894	19 340	Tanzania
Hans Meyer Peak, Mawenzi	5148	16 890	
Shira Peak	4005	13 139	
2. Mt Kenya (Batian)	5199	17 058	Kenya
3. Mt Ngaliema[2]	5118	16 763	Zaïre/Uganda
4. Duwoni[3]	4896	16 062	Uganda
5. Mount Baker (Edward Peak)	4843	15 889	Uganda
6. Mount Emin[4]	4798	15 741	Zaïre
7. Mount Gessi[5]	4715	15 470	Uganda
8. Sella Peak[6]	4626	15 179	Uganda
9. Ras Dashen (Rasdajan)	4620	15 158	Ethiopia
10. Humphreys Peak	4578	15 021	Uganda

[1] Uhuru Point (also called Kibo and formerly called Kaiser Wilhelm Spitze).
[2] Formerly called Mt Stanley and Margherita Peak.
[3] Formerly called Mt Speke and Vittorio Emanuele Peak.
[4] Formerly called Umberto Peak.
[5] Formerly called Iolanda Peak.
[6] Formerly called Mt Luigi di Savoia.

HIGHEST MOUNTAINS OF OCEANIA

Several of the mountains of West Irian (Indonesia) are known by more than one name. Some have changed their name since Dutch colonial days, and more than one mountain was (temporarily) renamed Sukarno or Peak Sukarno.

The two highest mountains in Polynesia are Mauna Kea – 4205 m (13 796 ft) – and Mauna Loa – 4170 m (13 680 ft). The former is an extinct volcano; the latter is an active volcano. Both are in Hawaii, which has been politically part of the USA since 21 Aug 1959.

The highest mountain in Australia is Mt Kosciusko – 2230 m (7316 ft) – in the Snowy Mountains, New South Wales.

The highest mountain in New Zealand is Mt Cook in Taranaki, North Island. Mt Cook – which is called Aorangi by the Maoris – is now 3754 m (12 315 ft) high. Before a major rock slide from the summit in December 1991, the mountain was 3764 m (12 349 ft).

Name	Height (m)	Height (ft)	Location
1. Jayakusumu or Ngga Pulu[1]	5030	*16 503*	West Irian
2. Daam	4922	*16 250*	West Irian
3. Jayakusumu Timur[2]	4840	*15 879*	West Irian
4. Trikora[3]	4730	*15 518*	West Irian
5. Enggea[4]	4717	*15 475*	West Irian
6. Mandala[5]	4640	*15 223*	West Irian
7. Mt Wilhelm	4509	*14 493*	Papua New Guinea

[1] Also known as Jaya. In Dutch colonial days, Jayakusumu was known as Carstensz Pyramid. For a time after Indonsian independence, the mountain was referred to as either Mount Sukarno or Peak Sukarno.
[2] Formerly known as Oost Carstensz.
[3] Formerly known as Wilhelmina. Following Indonesian independence the mountain was briefly known as Sukarno.
[4] Formerly known as Idenburg Top.
[5] Formerly known as Juliana.

HIGHEST MOUNTAINS OF ALPINE EUROPE

Subsidiary peaks or tops on the same massif have been omitted except in the case of Mont Blanc and Monte Rosa, where they have been indented in italic type.

Name	Height (m)	Height (ft)	Country	First Ascent
1. Mont Blanc	4807	*15 771*	France	1786
Monte Bianco di Courmayeur	4748	*15 577*	Italy[1]–France	1877
Le Mont Maudit	4465	*14 649*	Italy–France	1878
Picco Luigi Amedeo	4460	*14 632*	Italy	1878
Dôme du Goûter	4304	*14 120*	France	1784
2. Monte Rosa				
Dufourspitze	4634	*15 203*	Switzerland	1855
Nordend	4609	*15 121*	Swiss–Italian border	1861
Ostspitze	4596	*15 078*	Swiss–Italian border	1854
Zumstein Spitze	4563	*14 970*	Swiss–Italian border	1820
Signal Kuppe	4556	*14 947*	Swiss–Italian border	1842
3. Dom	4545	*14 911*	Switzerland	1858
4. Lyskamm (Liskamm)	4527	*14 853*	Swiss–Italian border	1861
5. Weisshorn	4506	*14 780*	Switzerland	1861
6. Täschhorn	4491	*14 733*	Switzerland	1862
7. Matterhorn	4476	*14 683*	Swiss–Italian border	1865
8. Dent Blanche	4357	*14 293*	Switzerland	1862
9. Nadelhorn	4327	*14 196*	Switzerland	1858
10. Grand Combin	4314	*14 153*	Switzerland	1859
11. Lenzspitze	4294	*14 087*	Switzerland	1870
12. Finsteraarhorn	4274	*14 021*	Switzerland	1829*

* Also reported climbed in 1812 but evidence lacking.

[1]The highest point in Italian territory is a shoulder of the main summit of Mont Blanc (Monte Bianco) through which a 4760 m (15 616 ft) contour passes. The highest top exclusively in Italian territory is Picco Luigi Amedeo (see above) to the south of the main Mont Blanc peak, which is itself exclusively in French territory.

HIGHEST MOUNTAINS OF CAUCASIA

The spine of the Caucasus Mountains forms the boundaries between Russia and Georgia, and Russia and Azerbaijan. The Caucasian spine includes the following peaks higher than Mont Blanc – 4807 m (15 771 ft).

Name	Height (m)	Height (ft)
1. Elbrus, West Peak	5642	18 510
Elbrus, East Peak	*5595*	*18 356*
2. Dykh Tau	5203	17 070
3. Shkhara	5201	17 063
4. Pik Shota Rustaveli	5190	17 028
5. Koshtantau	5144	16 876
6. Pik Pushkin	5100	16 732
7. Jangi Tau, West Peak	5051	16 572
Janga, East Peak	*5038*	*16 529*
8. Dzhangi Tau	5049	16 565
9. Kazbek	5047	16 558
10. Katyn Tau (Adish)	4985	16 355
11. Pik Rustaveli	4960	16 272
12. Mishirgi, West Peak	4922	16 148
Mishirgitau, East Peak	*4917*	*16 135*
13. Kunjum Mishirgi	4880	16 011
14. Gestola	4860	15 944
15. Tetnuld	4853	15 921

HIGHEST MOUNTAINS IN THE PYRENEES

The greater part of the boundary between Spain and France runs along the crest of the Pyrenees. The range contains the following peaks over 3200 m.

Name	Height (m)	Height (ft)
1. Pico de Aneto (Spain)	3407	11 178
2. Pico de Posets (Spain)	3375	11 073
3. Monte Perdido (Spain)	3352	10 997
4. Pico de la Maladeta (Spain)	3312	10 866
5. Pic de Vignemale (France/ Spain)	3298	10 820
6. Pic de Marboré (France)	3253	10 673

HIGHEST MOUNTAINS IN SCANDINAVIA

The Scandinavian peninsula consists mainly of uplands, including the following peaks over 2200 m.

Name	Height (m)	Height (ft)
1. Galdhoppigen (Norway)	2469	8098
2. Glittertind (Norway)	2468	8097
3. Skagastolstindane (Norway)	2405	7890
4. Snohetta (Norway)	2286	7500

HIGHEST MOUNTAINS IN THE CARPATHIANS

The great arc of the Carpathians stretches from the Danube near Bratislava, in Czechoslovakia, to central Romania. The range — which passes through Slovakia, southern Poland (as the Tatra Mountains) and the western Ukraine — contains the following peaks over 2400 m.

Name	Height (m)	Height (ft)
1. Gerlachovka (Slovakia)	2655	8711
2. Moldoveanu (Romania)	2544	8346
3. Negoiu (Romania)	2543	8343
4. Mindra (Romania)	2518	8261
5. Peleanga (Romania)	2511	8238
6. Rysy (Poland)	2499	8199

HIGHEST MOUNTAINS OF ANTARCTICA

The following mountains are the highest peaks surveyed in Antarctica. Large areas of Greater Antarctica remain unsurveyed, particularly the regions inland of Wilkes Land, Enderby Land and Queen Maud Land.

Name	Height (m)	Height (ft)
1. Mt Vinson	5140	16 863
2. Mt Tyree	4965	16 289
3. Mt Shinn*	4800	15 750
4. Mt Gardner	4690	15 387
5. Mt Epperley	4602	15 098
6. Mt Kirkpatrick	4511	14 799

* *volcanic*

LOWEST PEAKS

The lowest lying countries – in terms of the highest point above sea level – are as follows:

Maldives
an unnamed point 3 m (10 ft)
Marshall Islands
an unnamed point 6 m (20 ft)
Tuvalu
an unnamed point 6 m (20 ft)
Gambia
an unnamed point on the Senegalese border 43 m (141 ft)
Bahamas
Mount Alvernia on Cat Island 63 m (206 ft)
Nauru
an unnamed point on the central plateau 68 m (225 ft)
Qatar
Dukhan Heights 73 m (240 ft)
Kiribati
the highest point on Banaba Island 81 m (265 ft)
Bahrain
Jabal al-Dukhan 134 m (440 ft)
Monaco
Chemin de Révoirés 162 m (533 ft)
Denmark[1]
Yding Skovhoj 173 m (568 ft)
Singapore
Bukit Timah 177 m (581 ft)
Guinea-Bissau
an unnamed point on the Fouta Djallon plateau 180 m (591 ft)
Malta
an unnamed point 249 m (816 ft)
Lithuania
Juozapine 294 m (964 ft)

[1]'Metropolitan' Denmark – excluding the Faeroes and Greenland.

VOLCANOES

A volcano is a mountain, often conical in shape, which has been built up above an opening in the Earth's crust during violent and spectacular events called *eruptions*. When these occur, molten rock, or *magma*, wells up from deep below ground and is thrown out through the opening, frequently with other rock debris.

Few spectacles in nature are more awesome or more terrifying than volcanic eruptions. In the most violent ones, tremendous explosions inside the volcano hurl large rocks, cinders and great clouds of ash, steam and gas high into the sky from the *crater*, at the top. Streams of molten rock known as *lava*, and sometimes boiling mud, pour down the surrounding slopes destroying everything in their path.

Although above 800 volcanoes have been recorded as active in historic times, 500 to 350 million years ago there were very violent periods of volcanic activity. Many thousands of volcanoes erupted constantly, and many mountain ranges today consist of the remains of long dead volcanoes. Even now, thousands of volcanoes may be erupting unseen beneath the oceans. Many volcanoes soar to great heights amid the Earth's major mountain ranges. The highest is Aconcagua, a snow-clad peak 6960 m (22 834 ft) high in the Andes of Argentina.

Because Aconcagua no longer erupts, it is said to be *extinct*. Other volcanoes that have been quiet for a very long time but may erupt again are described as *dormant*. Volcanoes that are known to have erupted in historic times are referred to as *active*, and these are always dangerous. The highest volcano regarded as active is Ojos del Salado, which rises to a height of 6895 m (22 588 ft) on the frontier between Chile and Argentina. The mountain has recently produced vents emitting hot gases and steam known as *fumaroles*.

In modern times, scientists have been able to observe and record the dramatic birth and growth of new volcanoes. A famous example is Paricutín, Mexico, which began as a plume of smoke in a farmer's field in 1943 and by 1952 had grown more than 430 m (1400 ft). Another appeared 20 years later, when the volcanic island of Surtsey emerged from the sea off southern Iceland amid loud explosions and billowing clouds of ash and steam. The new island now occupies 2.5 km² (1 sq mi).

WHAT CAUSES VOLCANIC ERUPTIONS?

Volcanoes are like gigantic safety valves that release the tremendous pressures that build up inside the Earth. These pressures are affected by the constant movement of the plates that make up the surface crust (see p. 55). As a result of this movement, molten magma in the mantle is sometimes forced upward under pressure through any breaks it can find in the surface rocks. As it rises, gases dissolved in it are released by the fall in pressure, and the magma shoots out of the volcano in explosive eruptions.

THE EARTH'S VOLCANIC ZONES

Volcanoes are found where the Earth's crust is weakest, especially along the edges of the crustal plates and most notably in the 'Ring of Fire' around the Pacific Ocean plate. Large numbers of volcanoes, known as *abyssal volcanoes*, are also scattered over the ocean floors away from the plate margins. Here the crust is only about 5 km (3 mi) thick and is easily breached by molten magma rising from the mantle below. Localized hot spots in the mantle also cause the formation of volcanoes, such as those in the Hawaiian Islands and those found on land away from the plate margins.

SOME MAJOR VOLCANIC ERUPTIONS

Santoríni (Thera) *Height*: 584 m (1960 ft)
Location: Cyclades, Greece
Date: c. 1550 BC
A massive explosion virtually destroyed the island, and is thought by some to have contributed to the demise of Minoan civilization on nearby Crete. The disaster may also have given rise to the legend of the lost city of Atlantis.

Vesuvius *Height*: 1280 m (4198 ft)
Location: Bay of Naples, Italy
Date: AD 79
The towns of Pompeii, Herculaneum and Stabiae were completely buried, and thousands died. In 1631 3000 people were killed, since when there have been around 20 major eruptions, the last in 1944.

Unnamed *Height*: unknown
Location: North Island, New Zealand
Date: c. AD 130
Around 30 million tonnes (tons) of pumice were ejected, creating the vast caldera now filled by Lake Taupo. An area of c. 16 000 km² (6180 sq mi) was devastated – the most violent of all documented volcanic events.

Etna *Height*: 3311 m (10 855 ft)
Location: Sicily, Italy
Date: 1669
20 000 people were killed, and lava overran the west part of the city of Catania, 28 km (17 mi) from the summit.

Kelud *Height*: 1731 m (5679 ft)
Location: Java, Indonesia
Date: 1586
10 000 people killed. Another eruption in 1919 killed 5000 people.

Tambora *Height*: 2850 m (9350 ft)
Location: Jumbawa, Indonesia
Date: 1815
An estimated 150–180 km³ (36–43 cu mi) were blasted from the cone, which dropped in height from 4100 m (13 450 ft) to 2850 m (9350 ft) in minutes. About 90 000 people were killed in the explosion and subsequent giant wave, or died later of famine.

Krakatau *Height*: 813 m (2667 ft)
Location: Krakatau, Indonesia
Date: 1883
163 villages were wiped out and 36 380 people killed by the giant wave caused by this, the greatest volcanic explosion recorded – although possibly only one fifth of the Santoríni explosion. Rocks were thrown 55 km (34 mi) into the air, and dust fell 5330 km (3313 mi) away 10 days later. The explosion was heard over one thirteenth of the Earth's surface.

Mont Pelée *Height*: 1397 m (4582 ft)
Location: Martinique, West Indies
Date: 1902
Within three minutes a *nuée ardente* destroyed the town of St Pierre, killing all 26 000 inhabitants – except for one, a prisoner who survived in the thick-walled prison.

Mount St Helens *Height*: 2549 m (8360 ft)
Location: Washington State, USA
Date: 1980
66 people were presumed dead and 260 km² (100 sq mi) of forest destroyed. Smoke and ash rose to a height of 6000 m (20 000 ft), depositing ash 800 km (440 mi) away.

MAJOR VOLCANOES

Among the principal volcanoes active in recent times are:

Name	Height (m)	Height (ft)	Range or location	Country	Date of last notified eruption
Ojos del Salado	6895	22 588	Andes	Argentina/Chile	1981–steams
Llullaillaco	6723	22 057	Andes	Chile	1877
San Pedro	6199	20 325	Andes	Chile	1960
Guallatiri	6060	19 882	Andes	Chile	1960–subglacial
San José	5919	19 405	Andes	Chile	1931
Cotopaxi	5897	19 347	Andes	Ecuador	1975
El Misti	5862	19 220	Andes	Ecuador	1878
Tutupaca	5844	19 160	Andes	Ecuador	1902
Antisana	5793	18 995	Andes	Ecuador	1801–subglacial
Ubinas	5710	18 720	Andes	Peru	1969
Lascar	5641	18 507	Andes	Chile	1988–rumbles
Tupungatito	5640	18 504	Andes	Chile	1964
Orizaba	5610	18 405	Altiplano de Mexico	Mexico	1687
Isluga	5566	18 250	Andes	Chile	1960
Popocatépetl	5451	17 887	Altiplano de Mexico	Mexico	1920–steams
Ruiz	5435	17 820	Andes	Colombia	1985
Tolima	5249	17 210	Andes	Colombia	1943
Sangay	5230	17 159	Andes	Ecuador	1989–rumbles
Tungurahua	5048	16 550	Andes	Ecuador	1944
Guagua Pichincha	4880	16 000	Andes	Ecuador	1988–rumbles
Klyuchevsk Volcano	4850	15 913	Khrebet Mountains (Kamchatka Peninsula)	Russia	1992 plumes
Cumbal	4795	15 720	Andes	Colombia	1926
Purace	4590	15 059	Andes	Colombia	1977
Cerro Negro de Mayasquer	4499	14 750	Andes	Colombia	1936
Mt Rainier	4396	14 410	Cascade Range	USA	1882
Mt Shasta	4317	14 159	Cascade Range	USA	1855
El Galeras	4294	14 080	Andes	Colombia	1991 plumes
Doña Juana	4277	14 025	Andes	Colombia	1906
Tajumulco	4220	13 881	Sierra Madre	Guatemala	rumbles
Mauna Loa	4170	13 680	Hawaii	USA	1988–rumbles
Tacanáa	4078	13 379	Sierra Madre	Guatemala	rumbles
Mt Cameroon	4069	13 353	isolated mountain	Cameroon	1986
Erebus	3795	12 450	Ross Island	Antarctica	1990
Fujiyama	3776	12 388	Kanto	Japan	steams
Rindjani	3726	12 224	Lombok	Indonesia	1966
Pico de Teide	3716	12 192	Tenerife, Canary Is	Spain	1909
Semeru	3676	12 060	Java	Indonesia	rumbles
Nyiragongo	3470	11 385	Virunga	Zaïre	1982
Koryakskaya	3456	11 339	Kamchatka Peninsula	Russia	1957
Irazu	3452	11 325	Cordillera Central	Costa Rica	1991
Slamat	3428	11 247	Java	Indonesia	1988
Mt Spurr	3374	11 070	Alaska Range	USA	1992–steams
Mt Etna	3311	10 855	Sicily	Italy	1992

EUROPEAN VOLCANOES (ACTIVE IN HISTORICAL TIMES)

Name	Height (m)	Height (ft)		No. eruptions since 1700	Last eruption
Iceland (18 volcanoes)					
Eldeyjar	na	na	ephemeral island	4	1926
Trölladyngja	381	1250	central Iceland	0	1390
Hekla	1501	4920	southern Iceland	67	1980
Krakatindur	na	na	eruption from a fissure	2	1913
Surtsey	174	570	island	1	1967
Eyjafallajökull	1678	5500	subglacial eruption	1	1821
Katla	1449	4750	southern Iceland	6	1955
Laki	824	2700	southern Iceland	1	1783
Grimsvötn	na	na	subglacial erupton	33	1954
Öraefajökull	c.2356	c.6900	subglacial eruption	1	1727
Kverkfjöll	c.1861	c.6100	subglacial eruption	3	1729
Askja	1520	4983	central Iceland	2	1961
Sveinagja	946	3100	eruption from a fissure	1	1875
Myvatn	na	na	major lava flow from fissure	1	1729
Krafla	824	2700	northern Iceland	2	1984
Leirhafnarskörd	244	800	northern Iceland	1	1823
Mánáreyar			submarine	1	1867
Heimaey	na	na	Vestmann Islands	1	1973
Norway (1 volcano)					
Beerenberg	2546	8347	Jan Mayen Island	2	1970
Italy (7 volcanoes)					
Monte Nuovo	140	460	Flegrean Islands	1	1538
Vesuvius	1290	4230	Campania	Many	1944
Ischia	793	2600	Flegrean Islands	0	1301
Stromboli	932	3055	Eolian Islands	Many	1991
Vulcano	503	1650	Eolian Islands	6	1988– rumbles
Etna	3311	10 855	Sicily	Many	1992
Giulia Ferdinandeo			ephemeral island	3	1863
Mediterranean Sea (2 volcanoes)					
Pinne			submarine	2	1911
Foerstner			submarine	1	1891
Greece (1 volcano)					
Santoríni (Thera)	1316	4316	Santoríni, Cyclades	6	1950
Portugal – Azores (9 volcanoes)					
Faial	1049	3440	Faial Island	1	1958
Pico	2315	7713	Pico Island	3	1963
San Jorge Island	1060	3475		2	1964 ?
(unnamed) lat 38°30'N, long 27°25'W			submarine	2	1902
Santa Barbara	1029	3375	Terceira Island	2	1867
Castro Bank			submarine	1	1720
Sete Cidades	862	2825	San Miguel Island	4	1811
Agua de Pau	955	3130	San Miguel Island	0	1652
Furnas	810	2655	San Miguel Island	0	1630
Spain – Canaries (3 volcanoes)					
Caldera de Taburiente	1861	6100	La Palma	2	1971
Pico de Teide	3716	12 192	Tenerife	5	1909
Timanfaua	566	1855	Lanzarote	2	1824

The World's Longest Rivers and their Basins

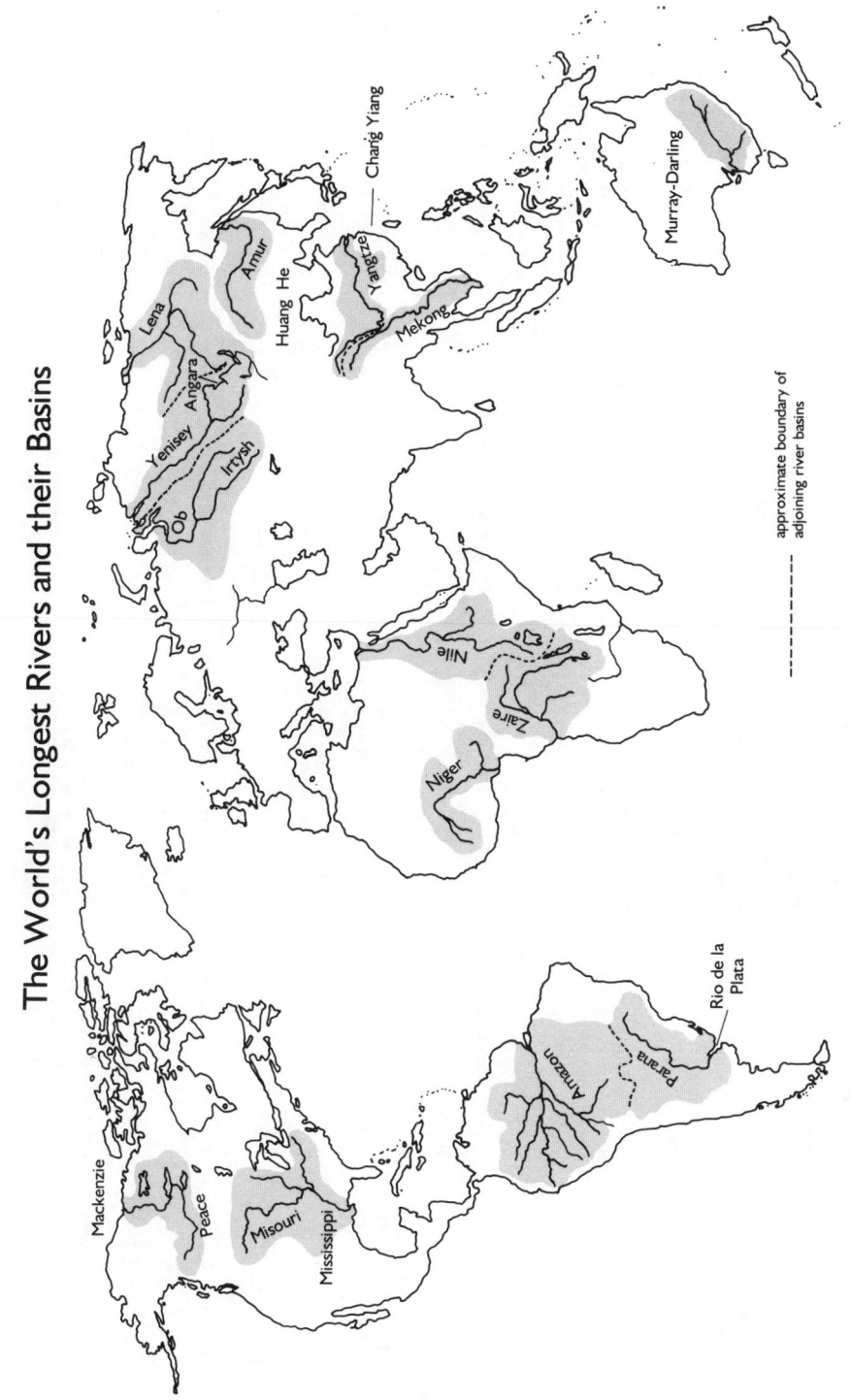

approximate boundary of
adjoining river basins

WORLD'S GREATEST RIVERS

Length (km)	(miles)	Name of Watercourse	Source	Course and Outflow	Basin Area (km²)	(miles²)	Mean Discharge Rate (m³/s)	(ft³/s)	Notes
1									
6670	4145	Nile (Bahr-el-Nil)–White Nile (Bahr el Jabel)–Albert Nile–Victoria Nile–Victoria Nyanza–Kagera–Luvironza	Burundi: Luvironza branch of the Kagera, a feeder of the Victoria Nyanza	Through Tanzania (Kagera), Uganda (Victoria Nile and Albert Nile), Sudan (White Nile), Egypt to eastern Mediterranean	3 350 000	1 293 000	3120	110 000	Navigable length to first cataract (Aswan 1545 km/960 miles). Egyptian Irrigation Dept. states length as 6700 km (4164 miles). Discharge 2600 m³/s (93 200 ft³/s) near Aswan. Delta is 23 960 km² (9250 miles²).
2									
6448	4007	Amazon (Amazonas)	Peru: Lago Villafro, head of the Apurimac branch of the Ucayali, which joins the Marañon to form the Amazonas	Through Colombia to Equatorial Brazil (Solimões) to South Atlantic (Canal do Sul)	7 050 000	2 722 000	180 000	6 350 000	Total of 15 000 tributaries, ten over 1600 km (1000 miles) including Madeira (3380 km 2100 miles). Navigable 3700 km (2300 miles) up stream. Delta extends 400 km (250 miles) inland.
3									
6300	3915	Yangtze (Chang Jiang)	Western China, Kunlun Shan Mts (as Tuotuo and Tongtian)	Begins W of Tuotuohe in Qinghai, through Yunnan Sichuan, Hubei, Anhui, Jiangsu, to Yellow Sea	1 960 000	756 000	21 800	770 000	Flood rate (1931) of 85 000 m³/s (3 000 000 ft³/s). Estuary 190 km (120 miles) long.
4									
6020	3741	Mississippi–Missouri–Jefferson–Beaverhead–Red Rock	Beaverhead County, southern Montana, USA	Through N. Dakota, S. Dakota, Nebraska–Iowa, Missouri–Kansas Illinois, Kentucky, Tennessee, Arkansas, Mississippi, Louisiana, South West Pass into Gulf of Mexico	3 224 000	1 245 000	18 400	650 000	Missouri is 3725 km (2315 miles) the Jefferson–Beaverhead–Red Rock is 349 km (217 miles). Lower Mississippi is 1884 km (1171 miles). Total Mississippi from Lake Itasca, Minn., is 3778 km (2348 miles) – longest river in one country. Delta is 36 000 km² (13 900 miles²).
5									
5540	3442	Yenisey–Angara–Selenga	Mongolia: Ideriin branch of Selenga (Selenge)	Through Buryatia (Russia) (Selenga feeder) into Ozero Baykal, thence via Angara to Yenisey confluence at Strelka to Kara Sea, northern Russia	2 580 000	996 000	19 000	670 000	Estuary 386 km (240 miles) long. Yenisey is 3540 km (2200 miles) long and has a basin of 2 050 000 km² (792 000 miles²). The length of the Angara is 1850 km (1150 miles).
6									
5464	3395	Hwang He (Yellow River)	China: W of Bayan, Qinghai Province	Through Gansu, Inner Mongolia, Henan, Shandong to Bo Hai (Gulf of Chile), Yellow Sea, North Pacific	979 000	378 000	2 800 to 22 650	100 000 to 800 000	Changed mouth by 400 km (250 miles) in 1852. Only last 40 km (25 miles) navigable.
7									
5409	3361	Ob'–Irtysh	Mongolia: Kara (Black) Irtysh via northern China (Xinjiang) feeder of Ozero Zaysan	Through Kazakhstan into Russia to Ob' confluence at Khanty Mansiysk, thence Ob' to Kara	2 978 000	1 150 000	15 600	550 000	Estuary (Obskaya Guba) is 725 km (450 miles) long. Ob' is 3679 km (2286 miles) long. Irtysh 2960 km

#	km	miles	River	Source	Course	Basin km²	Basin miles²	Flow	Flow (alt)	Notes
8	4880	*3032*	Río de la Plata–Paraná	Brazil: as Paranaíba. Flows south to eastern Paraguay border and into eastern Argentina	Emerges into confluence with River Uruguay to form Rio de la Plata, South Atlantic	4 145 000	*1 600 000*	27 500	*970 000*	After the 120 km (75 mile) long Delta estuary, the river shares the 340 km (210 mile) long estuary of the Uruguay called Rio de la Plata (River Plate).
9	4700	*2920*	Zaïre (Congo)	Zambia–Zaïre border, as Lualaba	Through Zaïre as Lualaba along to Zaïre (Congo) border to N.W. Angola mouth to S Atlantic	3 400 000	*1 314 000*	41 000	*1 450 000*	Navigable for 1730 km (1075 miles) from Kisangani to Kinshasa Estuary 96 km (60 miles) long.
10	4400	*2734*	Lena–Kirenga	Russia hinterland of W central shores of Ozero Baykal as Kirenga	Northwards through eastern Russia to Laptev Sea, Arctic Ocean	2 490 000	*960 000*	16 300	*575 000*	Lena Delta (45 000 km²/17 375 miles²) extends 177 km (110 miles) inland, frozen 15 Oct to 10 July. Second longest Russian river.
11	4350	*2702*	Mekong (Me Nam Kong)	Central Tibet (as Lants'ang), slopes of Dza-Nag-Lung-Mong, 5000 m (16 700 ft)	Flows into China, thence south to form Burma-Laotian and most of Thai-Laotian frontiers, thence through Cambodia to Vietnam into South China Sea	987 000	*381 000*	11 000	*388 000*	Max flood discharge 48 000 m³/s (1 700 000 ft³/s).
12	4345	*2700*	'Amur-Argun' (Heilongjiang)	Northern China in Khingan Ranges (as 'Argun')	North along Inner Mongolian–Russia and Manchuria–Russia border for 3743 km (2326 miles) to Tartar Strait, Sea of Okhotsk, North Pacific	2 038 000	*787 000*	12 400	*438 000*	Amur is 2824 km (1755 miles) long (711 600 basin and 388 000 flow); China Handbook claims total length to be 4670 km (2903 miles) of which only 925 km (575 miles) is exclusively in USSR territory.
13	4241	*2635*	Mackenzie–Peace	Tatlatui Lake, Skeena Mts, Rockies, British Columbia, Canada (as River Finlay)	Flows as Finlay for 400 km (250 miles) to confluence with Peace, 1690 km (1050 miles) to join Slave (415 km/258 miles) which feeds Great Slave Lake, from which flows Mackenzie (1733 km/1077 miles) to Beaufort Sea	1 841 000	*711 000*	11 300	*400 000*	Peace 1923 km (1195 miles).
14	4184	*2600*	Niger	Guinea: Loma Mts near Sierra Leone border	Flows through Mali, Niger and along Benin border into Nigeria and Atlantic	1 890 000	*730 000*	11 750	*415 000*	Delta extends 128 km (80 miles) inland and 200 km (130 miles) in coastal length.
15	3750	*2330*	Murray–Darling	Queensland, Australia: as the Condamine, a tributary of the Culgoa, which is a tributary of the Balonne-branch of the Darling	Balonne (intermittent flow) crosses into New South Wales to join Darling, which itself joins the Murray on the New South Wales–Victoria border and flows west into Lake Alexandrina, in South Australia	1 059 000	*408 000*	400	*14 000*	Darling c. 2740 km (1700 miles) Murray 2590 km (1609 miles) or 1870 km (1160 miles).

No.	km	miles	River	Source	Course					Notes
16	3540	*2200*	Zambezi (Zambeze)	Zambia: north-west extremity, as Zambezi	Flows after 72 km (45 miles) across eastern Angola for 354 km (220 miles) and back into Zimbabwe (as Zambezi), later forming border with eastern end of Caprivi strip of Namibia, thence over Victoria Falls (Mosi-Oatunya) into Kariba Lake. Thereafter into Mozambique and out into southern Indian Ocean	1 330 000	*514 000*	7 000	250 000	Navigable 610 km (380 miles) up to Quebrabasa Rapids and thereafter in stretches totalling another 1930 km (1200 miles).
17	3530	*2193*	Volga	Russia: in Valdai Hills NW of Moscow	Flows south and east in a great curve and empties in a delta into the north of the Caspian Sea	1 360 000	*525 000*	8 200	287 000	Delta exceeds 280 km (175 miles) inland and arguably 450 km (280 miles).
18	3380	*2100*	Madeira–Mamoré–Grande (Guapay)	Bolivia: rises on the Beni near Illimani	Flows north and east into Brazil to join Amazon at the Ilha Tupinambaram	Tributary of No. 2		15 000	530 000	World's longest tributary, navigable for 1070 km (663 miles).
19	3283	*2040*	Jurua	Peru: S of Puerto Portillo	Flows east and north into Brazil to join Amazon below Fonte Boa	Tributary of No. 2	—			World's second longest tributary. Navigable for 965 km (600 miles). Most pronounced meanders in Amazon Basin. Descends only 453 m (1486 ft) along its entire course.
20	3211	*1995*	Purus (formerly Coxiuara)	Peru: as the Alto Purus	Flows north and east into Brazil to join Amazon below Beruri	Tributary of No. 2	—			World's third longest tributary. Navigable for 2575 km (1600 miles). Pronounced meanders.
21	3185	*1979*	Yukon–Teslin	North-west British Columbia, Canada, as the Teslin	Flows north into Yukon Territory and into west Alaska, USA, and thence into Bering Sea	855 000	*330 0000*			Delta 136 km (85 miles) inland, navigable (shallow draft) for 2855 km (1775 miles)
22	3130	*1945*	St Lawrence	Head of St Louis River, Minn. USA	Flows into Lake Superior, thence Lakes Huron, Erie, Ontario to Gulf of St Lawrence and North Atlantic	1 378 000	*532 000*	10 200	360 000	Estuary 407 km (253 miles) long or 616 km (383 miles) to Anticosti Island. Discovered 1535 by Jacques Cartier.
23	3035	*1885*	Rio Grande (Rio Bravo del Norte)	South-western Colorado, USA; San Juan Mts	Flows south through New Mexico, USA, and along Texas-Mexico border into Gulf of Mexico, Atlantic Ocean	445 000	*172 000*	85	3 000	—
24	3019	*1876*	Syrdarya–Naryn	In Tien Shan Mountains of eastern Kyrgyzstan	Flows west through Kyrgyzstan then through Tajikistan, then north and west through	462 000	178 000	—		Known to the ancient Greeks as the Jaxartes.

		Name	Source	Course					Notes
25	*2989*	Nizhnaya Tunguska	In central Siberia, Russia	Flows east, then north and west to the Yenisey	471 000	*188 000*	–	–	Tributary of the Yenisey.
26	*2914*	São Francisco	Brazil: Serra da Canastra	Flows north and east into South Atlantic	700 000	*270 000*	–	–	Navigable 238 km (148 miles).
27	*2900*	Brahmaputra	South-western Tibet as Matsang (Tsangpo)	Flows east 1240 km (770 miles) south, then west through Assam, north-eastern India, joins Ganges (as Jamuna) to flow into Bay of Bengal, Indian Ocean	1 620 000	*626 000*	38 500	*1 360 000*	Joint delta with Ganges extends 360 km (225 miles) across and 330 km (205 miles) inland. Area 80 000 km² (30 800 mile²) the world's largest. Navigable 1290 km (800 miles).
28	*2880*	Indus	Tibet: as Sengge	Flows west through Kashmir, into Pakistan and out into northern Arabian Sea	1 166 000	*450 000*	5 500	*195 000*	Delta (area 8000 km²/3100 miles²) extends 120 km (75 miles) inland.
29	*2850*	Danube	South-western Germany: Black Forest as Breg and Brigach	Flows (as Donau) east into Austria, along Czech–Hungarian border as Dunaj into Hungary (440 km/273 miles) as Duna, to Yugoslavia as Dunav along Romania–Bulgaria border and through Romania as Dunarea to Romania–Ukraine border as Dunay, into the Black Sea	815 000	*315 000*	7 000	*250 000*	Delta extends 96 km (60 miles) inland. Flows in territory of 8 countries.
30	*2810*	Salween (Nu Chiang)	Tibet in Tanglha range	Flows (as Nu) east and south into western China, into eastern Burma and along Thailand border and out into Gulf of Martaban, Andaman Sea	325 000	*125 000*	–	–	–
31	*2800*	Tigris–Euphrates (Shatt al-Arab)	Eastern Turkey as Murat	Flows west joining the Fīrat, thence into Syria as Al Furāt and south and east into Iraq joining Tigris flowing into Persian Gulf at Iran–Iraq border as Shatt al-Arab	1 115 000	*430 000*	400 low 2 700 high	*50 000*	–
32=	*2740*	Tocantins	Brazil: near Brazilia as Paraná	Flows north to join Pará in the Estuary Báia de Marajó and the South Atlantic	905 000	*350 000*	10 000	*360 000*	Not properly regarded as an Amazon tributary. Estuary 440 km (275 miles) in length.
32=	*2740*	Orinoco	South-eastern Venezuela	Flows north and west to Colombia border, thence north and east to north-eastern Venezuela and the Atlantic	1 036 000	*400 000*	–	–	–

Length (km)	(miles)	Name of Watercourse	Source	Course and Outflow	Basin Area (km²)	(miles²)	Mean Discharge Rate (m³/s)	(ft³/s)	Notes
34= 2650	1650	Vilyuy	Evenky region of Central Siberia, Russia	Flows east and south to join tha Lena north of Yakutsk	491 000	190 000	–	–	Tributary of No. 10
34= 2650	1650	Xi Jiang (Si Kiang)	China: in Yünnan plateau as Nanp'an	Flows east as the Hungshui and later as the Hsün to emerge as the Hsi in the South China Sea, west of Hong Kong	602 000	232 300	–	–	Delta exceeds 145 km (90 miles) inland and includes the Pearl
36 2627	1632	Araguaia	In Mato Grosso, Brazil	Flows north and east to join the Tocantins			–	–	Tributary of No. 32
37 2600	1616	Kolyma	Russia: in Khrebet Suntarkhayata (as Kulu)	Flows north across Arctic Circle into eastern Siberian Sea	534 000	206 000	3 800	134 000	–
38= 2575	1600	Amu-Dar'ya (Oxus)	Wakhan, Afghanistan, on the border with Sinkiang China	Flows west to form Tajikistan–Afghan border as Pyandzh for 680 km (420 miles) and into Turkmenistan as Amu-Dar'ya. Flows north and west into Aral Sea	465 000	179 500	–	–	–
38= 2575	1600	Nelson–Saskatchewan	Canada: Bow Lake, British Colombia	Flows north and east through Saskatchewan and into Manitoba through Cedar Lake into Lake Winnipeg and out through northern feeder as Nelson to Hudson Bay	1 072 000	414 000	2 250	80 000	Saskatchewan 1940 km (1205 miles) in length
40 2540	1575	Ural	Russia: South-central Urals	Flows south and west into the Caspian Sea in Kazakhstan	220 000	84 900	–	–	–
41 2510	1553	Ganges (Ganga)	In the southern Himalaya (India)	Flows south and east to join the Brahmaputra to form Jamuna	976 000	377 000	–	–	–
42 2410	1500	Paraguay	Brazil: in the Mato Grosso as Paraguai	Flows south to touch first Bolivian then Paraguayan border, then across Paraguay to form border with Argentina. Joins the Paraná south of Humaitá	1 150 000	440 000	–	–	Tributary of No. 14

RIVERS AND LAKES

Rivers and lakes are the most important bodies of surface water on land masses. A river is a freshwater body confined in a channel which flows down a slope into another river, a lake or the sea, or sometimes into an inland desert. Small, narrow rivers may be called brooks, streams or creeks.

A lake is an inland body of water occupying a depression in the Earth's surface. Usually, lakes receive water from rivers, but sometimes only directly from springs. Lakes normally lose water into an outlet or river, but some, called *closed lakes*, have no outlet and lose water only by evaporation – for example, Lake Eyre in Australia and Great Salt Lake in Utah, USA.

WHERE DO RIVERS GET THEIR WATER FROM?

Rivers may receive their water from several sources, but all of these are indirectly or directly related to *precipitation* – a collective term for the fall of moisture onto the Earth's surface from the atmosphere. Rain falling on the ground may immediately run down slopes as *overland flow*, becoming concentrated and eventually forming a stream. This tends to occur when the ground surface is *impermeable* (i.e. water cannot pass through it, as is the case with some kinds of rock). It may also occur when the ground is already saturated with water, or when rainfall is very heavy.

Often, however, rivers receive their water from *springs*. This is because rainfall will commonly soak into the ground, to accumulate in the soil or to pass into permeable and porous rocks as *groundwater*. In *permeable* rock, water can pass right through the rock itself, whereas in *porous* rock there are holes and fissures through which water can pass. Springs occur where the top of the aquifer – a layer of rock containing water – intersects with the ground surface. Groundwater is important as a source for rivers in that it can supply water even when precipitation is not occurring, thereby constantly maintaining river flow.

A third source of water for rivers is the melting of solid precipitation (snow) or snow which has been turned to ice to form a glacier or ice sheet. This is particularly important in high-latitude and mountainous areas.

PERENNIAL, SEASONAL AND EPHEMERAL RIVERS

Rivers occur in all the world's major environments, even in polar areas and deserts. In temperate areas, such as Western Europe, northeastern USA and New Zealand, and in the wet tropics, enough precipitation tends to fall, fairly evenly throughout the year, to replenish groundwater constantly and therefore to allow rivers to flow all year round. These *perennial rivers* do, however, experience seasonal and day-to-day variations in the volume of water they carry (the *flow regime*), owing to seasonal fluctuations in precipitation and additional inputs from individual storms.

Some rivers may only flow seasonally, particularly in environments with Mediterranean-type climates, which have a very distinct wet, winter season and a dry summer. Rivers in glaciated areas may also have very seasonal flow regimes. *Glacial meltwater streams*, which receive their water directly from glaciers, usually only flow during the few months in the summer when the ice melts.

In dry desert climates, rivers may not flow for years on end, because of the infrequency of desert storms, and then only for a few days, or even hours. However, when storms do occur these *ephemeral rivers* may flow at great rates, because desert rainfall is often very heavy. This gives them considerable power and the ability to erode and transport large quantities of sediment.

Some deserts do possess perennial rivers. The Nile, for example, despite experiencing a distinctly seasonal flow regime, flows all year round through the Egyptian Desert; likewise, the Colorado River passes through desert areas of the southwestern USA. The reason that these and other rivers can successfully exist in deserts is that their *catchments* (source areas) lie in areas with wetter climates.

RIVER BASINS

Only some very short rivers are able to flow from a source to the sea without either being joined by others or becoming a *tributary* of a large river. Most rivers therefore form part of a *drainage network*, occupying a *drainage basin*. In fact, the whole of the Earth's land surface can be divided up into drainage basins, and these basins are separated by areas of relatively high ground called *watersheds*. Some drainage basins occupy only a few square kilometres, but others are enormous – the largest, the Amazon Basin, covers over 7 million sq km (2.7 million sq mi).

ARTIFICIAL LAKES

Artificial lakes – reservoirs – are either constructed as sources of water supply for an area and/or as sources to generate electricity by water-power.

LARGEST RESERVOIRS BY CAPACITY

Reservoir	Country	Capacity million m^3
Owen Falls (R. Nile)	Uganda	204.75
Bratskoye Res. (R. Angara)	Russia	169.20
Lake Nasser (R. Nile)	Egypt	169.00
Lake Kariba (R. Zambezi)	Zambia/ Zimbabwe	160.30
Lake Volta (R. Volta)	Ghana	148.00

LARGEST RESERVOIRS BY AREA

Reservoir	Country	Area km^2
Lake Volta (R. Volta)	Ghana	8482 (3275 sq mi)
Kuybyshev Res. (R. Volga)	Russia	2490 (961 sq mi)
Rybin Res. (R. Volga)	Russia	1768 (683 sq mi)

The World's Largest Lakes

1. Caspian Sea
(Russia, Kazakhstan,
Turkmenistan, Azerbaijan
and Iran)
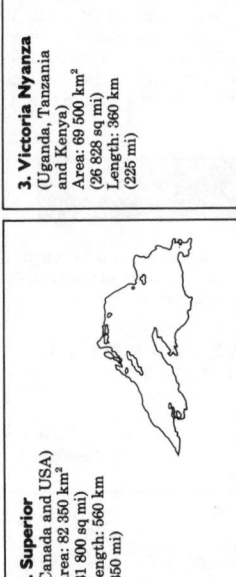
Area: 371 800 km²
(143 550 sq mi)
Length: 1225 km
(760 mi)

2. Superior
(Canada and USA)
Area: 82 350 km²
(31 800 sq mi)
Length: 560 km
(350 mi)
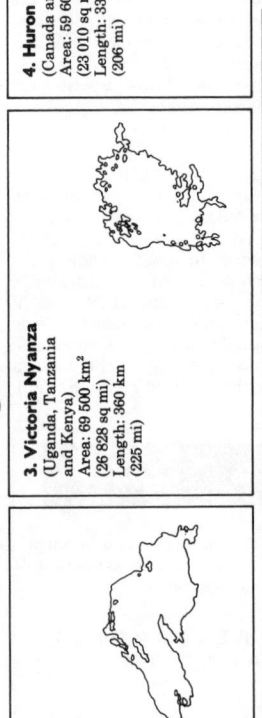

3. Victoria Nyanza
(Uganda, Tanzania
and Kenya)
Area: 69 500 km²
(26 828 sq mi)
Length: 360 km
(225 mi)

4. Huron
(Canada and USA)
Area: 59 600 km²
(23 010 sq mi)
Length: 330 km
(206 mi)

5. Michigan
(USA)
Area: 58 000 km²
(22 400 sq mi)
Length: 494 km
(307 mi)

**6. Aral Sea
(Aral 'skoye More)**
(Uzbekistan
and Kazakhstan)
Area: 40 000 km²
(15 444 sq mi)
Length: 350 km
(217 mi)
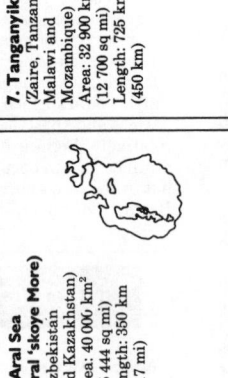

7. Tanganyika
(Zaire, Tanzania,
Malawi and
Mozambique)
Area: 32 900 km²
(12 700 sq mi)
Length: 725 km
(450 km)
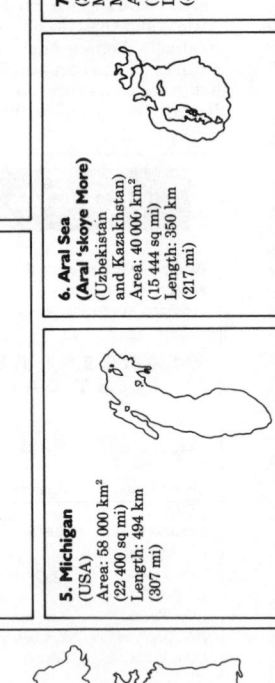

8. Great Bear
(Canada)
Area: 31 800 km²
(12 275 sq mi)
Length: 373 km
(232 mi)

9. Baikal
(Ozero Baykal)
(Russia)
Area: 30 500 km²
(11 780 sq mi)
Length: 620 km
(385 mi)

10. Malawi
(Malawi, Tanzania
and Mozambique)
Area: 29 600 km²
(11 430 sq mi)
Length: 580 km
(360 mi)

11. Great Slave
(Canada)
Area: 28 500 km²
(10 980 sq mi)
Length: 480 km
(298 mi)

12. Erie
(Canada and USA)
Area: 25 700 km²
(9 930 sq mi)
Length: 387 km
(241 mi)

13. Winnipeg
(Canada)
Area: 24 500 km²
(9464 sq mi)
Length: 428 km
(266 mi)

14. Ontario
(Canada and USA)
Area: 19 500 km²
(7520 sq mi)
Length: 310 km
(193 mi)

15. Ladoga
(Ozero Ladozhskoye)
(Russia)
Area: 17 700 km²
(6835 sq mi)
Length: 193 km
(120 mi)
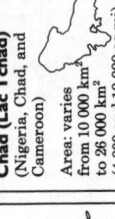

16. Balkhash (Ozero Balkhas) (Kazakh)
Area: 17 400 km²
(6720 sq mi)
Length: 482 km
(300 sq mi)

17. Onega
(Ozero Onezhskoye)
(Russia)
Area: 9600 km²
(3710 sq mi)
Length: 233 m
(145 ft)

18. Titicaca
(Lago Titicaca)
(Bolivia and Peru)
Area: 8300 km²
(3200 sq mi)
Length: 209 km
(130 mi)

19. Nicaragua
(Lago Nicaragua)
(Nicaragua)
Area: 8270 km²
(3190 sq mi)
Length: 160 km
(100 mi)

20. Athabasca
(Canada)
Area: 8100 km²
(3120 sq mi)
Length: 334 km
(208 mi)

Chad (Lac Tchad)
(Nigeria, Chad, and
Cameroon)
Area: varies
from 10 000 km²
to 26 000 km²
(4 000 and 10 000 mi²)
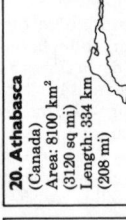

Eyre
maximum extent
(Australia)
Area: varies from
0 km² and 8900 km²
(3430 mi²)
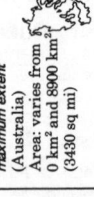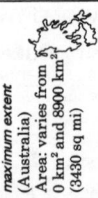

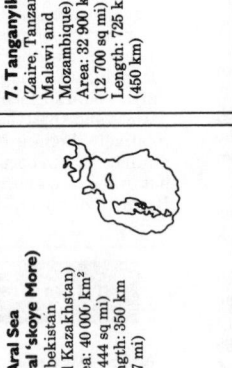
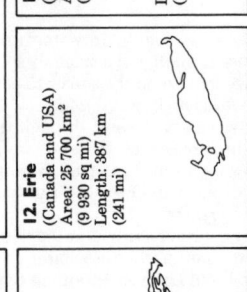
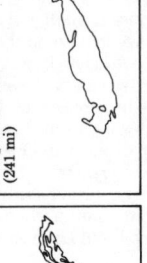
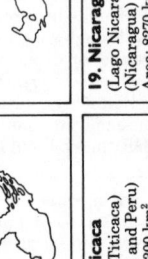
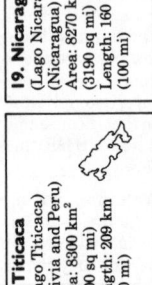
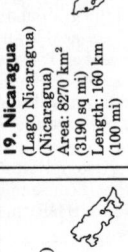
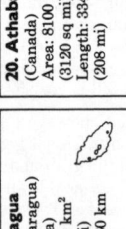

WATERFALLS

WORLD'S GREATEST WATERFALLS – BY HEIGHT

Name	Total Drop (m)	Total Drop (ft)	River	Location
1. Angel (highest fall – 2648 ft/807 m)*	979	*3212*	Cārrao, an upper tributary of the Caroni	Venezuela
2. Tugela (5 falls) (highest fall – 410 m/1350 ft)	947	*3110*	Tugela	Natal, S. Africa
3. Utigård (highest fall – 600 m/1970 ft)	800	*2625*	Jostedal Glacier	Nesdale, Norway
4. Mongefossen	774	*2540*	Monge	Mongebekk, Norway
5. Yosemite (Upper Yosemite – 435 m/1430 ft; Cascades in middle section – 205 m/675 ft; Lower Yosemite – 97 m/320 ft)	739	*2425*	Yosemite Creek, a tributary of the Merced	Yosemite Valley, Yosemite National Park, Cal., USA
6. Ø stre Mardøla Foss (highest fall – 296 m/974 ft)	656	*2154*	Mardals	Eikisdal, W. Norway
7. Tyssestrengane (highest fall – 289 m/948 ft)	646	*2120*	Tysso	Hardanger, Norway
8. Kukenaam (or Cuquenán)	610	*2000*	Arabopó, upper tributary of the Caroni	Venezuela
9. Sutherland (highest fall – 248 m/815 ft)	580	*1904*	Arthur	nr. Milford Sound, Otago, S. Island, New Zealand
10. Kile (or Kjellfossen) (highest fall – 149 m/490 ft)†	561	*1841*	Naerö Fjord feeder	nr. Gudvangen, Norway
11. Takkakaw (highest fall – 365 m/1200 ft)	502	*1650*	A tributary of the Yoho	Daly Glacier, British Columbia, Canada
12. Ribbon	491	*1612*	Ribbon Fall Stream	4·9 km (3 miles) west of Yosemite Falls, Yosemite National Park, Cal., USA
13. King George VI	487	*1600*	Utshi, upper tributary of the Mazaruni	Guyana
14. Roraima	457	*1500*	An upper tributary of the Mazaruni	Guyana

* There are other very high but seemingly unnamed waterfalls in this area.
† Some authorities would regard this as no more than a 'Bridal Veil' waterfall, i.e., of such low volume that the fall atomizes.

WORLD'S GREATEST WATERFALLS – BY VOLUME OF WATER

Name	Max. Height (m)	Max. Height (ft)	Mean Annual Flow m^3/s	Mean Annual Flow ft^3/s	Location
1. Buyoma (formerly Stanley) (7 cataracts)	60	*200*	17 000	*600 000*	Zaïre R., nr Kisangani, Zaïre
2. Guaíra (or Salto dos Sete Quedas) ('Seven Falls')	114	*374*	13 000*	*470 000*	Alto Parana R., Brazil/Paraguay
3. Khône	21	*70*	11 500	*410 000*	Mekong R., Laos
4. Niagara					
Horseshoe (Canadian)	48	*160*	5640	*199 300*	Niagara R., L. Erie to L. Ontario
American	50	*167*	360	*12 700*	Niagara R., L. Erie to L. Ontario
5. Paulo Afonso	58	*192*	2800	*100 000*	São Francisco R., Brazil
6. Urubu-punga	12	*40*	2700	*97 000*	Alto Parana R., Brazil
7. Cataratas del Iguazú (Quedas do Iguaçu)	93	*308*	1700	*61 660*	Iguazú R., Brazil/Argentina
8. Patos–Maribondo	35	*115*	1500	*53 000*	Rio Grande, Brazil
9. Victoria (Mosi-oa-tunya)					
Leaping Water	108	*355*	–	–	Zambezi R., Zambia
Main Fall	108	*355*	1100	*38 430*	Zambezi R., Zimbabwe
Rainbow Falls	108	*355*	–	–	Zambezi R., Zimbabwe
10. Churchill (formerly Grand)	75	*245*	35 000	*c. 9500*	Churchill R., Canada
11. Kaieteur (Köituök)	225	*741*	660	*23 400*	Potaro R., Guyana

* The peak flow has reached 50 000 m^3/s.

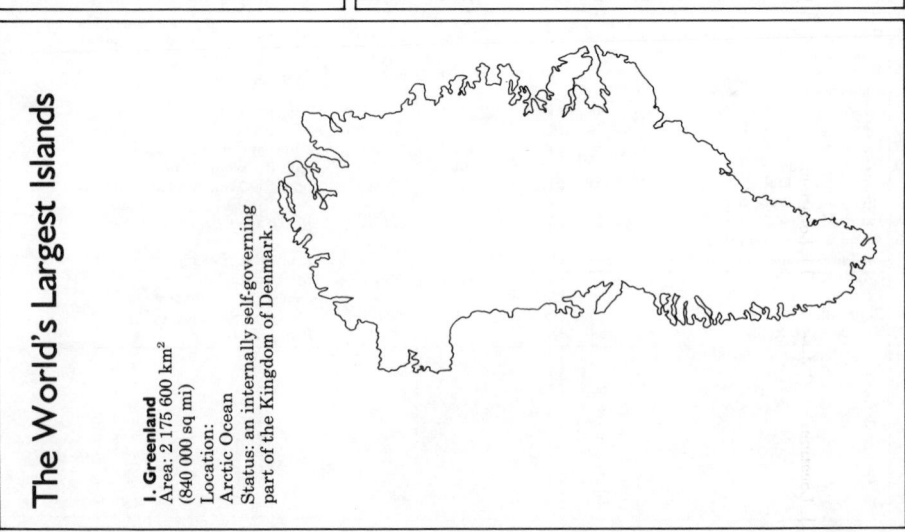

The World's Largest Islands

I. Greenland
Area: 2 175 600 km²
(840 000 sq mi)
Location:
Arctic Ocean
Status: an internally self-governing
part of the Kingdom of Denmark.

2. New Guinea
Area: 821 030 km²
(317 000 sq mi)
Location:
western Pacific

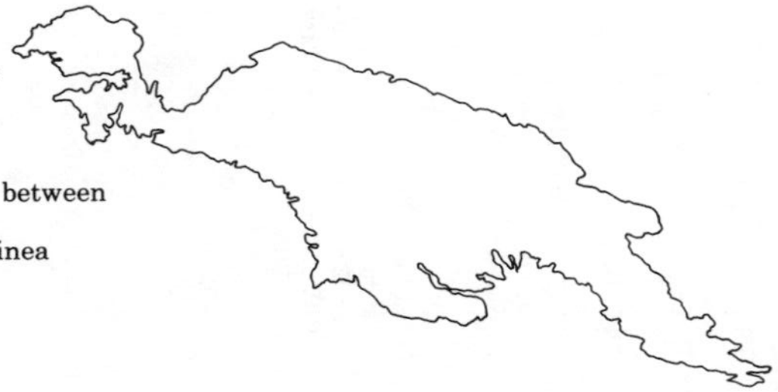

Status: divided between
Indonesia and
Papua New Guinea

3. Borneo
Area: 744 366 km²
(287 400 sq mi)
Location:
Indian Ocean

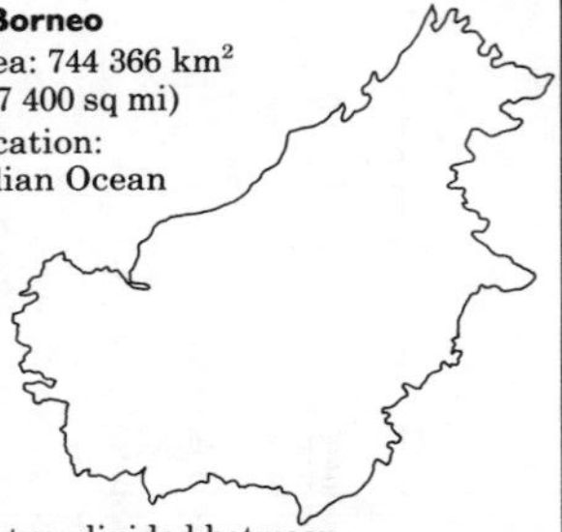

Status: divided between
Indonesia, Malaysia
and Brunei

4. Madagascar
Area: 587 041 km²
(226 658 sq mi)
Location:
Indian Ocean
Status: republic

5. Baffin Island
Area: 476 068 km²
(183 810 sq mi)
Location:
Arctic Ocean
Status: part of Nunavut
Territory, Canada

**6. Sumatra
(Sumatera)**
Area: 473 607 km²
(182 860 sq mi)
Location:
Indian Ocean
Status: part of
Indonesia

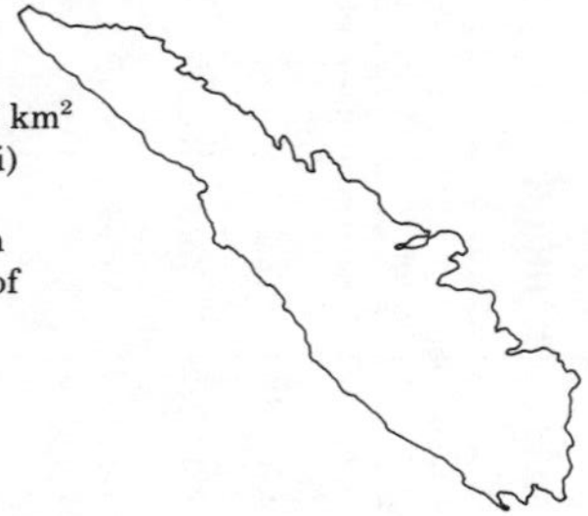

7. Honshu
Area: 230 448 km²
(88 976 sq mi)
Location:
NW Pacific
Status: part of Japan

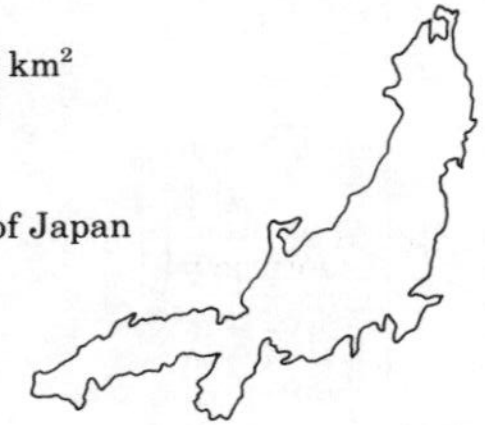

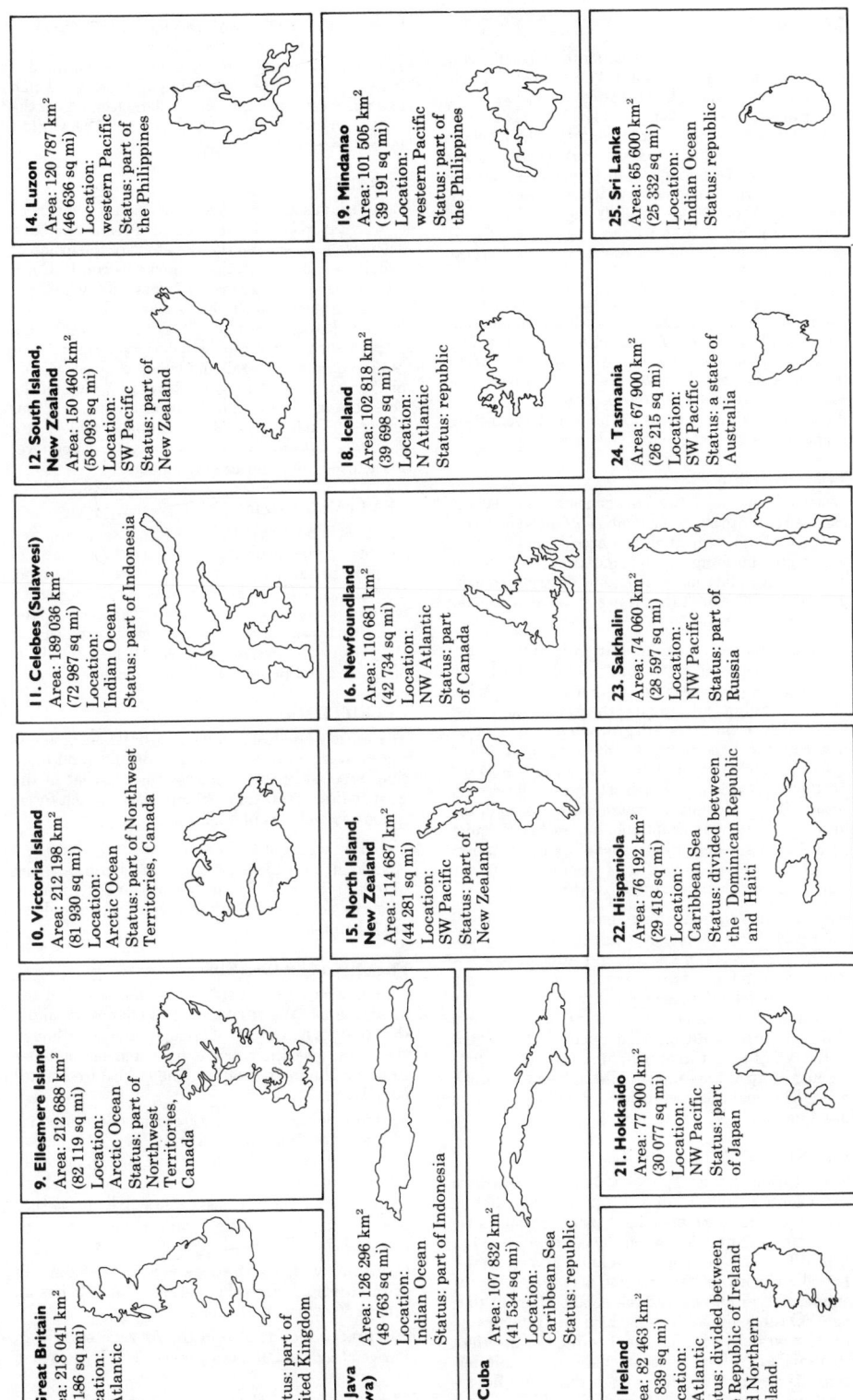

8. Great Britain
Area: 218 041 km²
(84 186 sq mi)
Location:
N Atlantic
Status: part of
United Kingdom

9. Ellesmere Island
Area: 212 688 km²
(82 119 sq mi)
Location:
Arctic Ocean
Status: part of
Northwest
Territories,
Canada

10. Victoria Island
Area: 212 198 km²
(81 930 sq mi)
Location:
Arctic Ocean
Status: part of Northwest
Territories, Canada

11. Celebes (Sulawesi)
Area: 189 036 km²
(72 987 sq mi)
Location:
Indian Ocean
Status: part of Indonesia

12. South Island, New Zealand
Area: 150 460 km²
(58 093 sq mi)
Location:
SW Pacific
Status: part of
New Zealand

13. Java (Jawa)
Area: 126 296 km²
(48 763 sq mi)
Location:
Indian Ocean
Status: part of Indonesia

14. Luzon
Area: 120 787 km²
(46 636 sq mi)
Location:
western Pacific
Status: part of
the Philippines

15. North Island, New Zealand
Area: 114 687 km²
(44 281 sq mi)
Location:
SW Pacific
Status: part of
New Zealand

16. Newfoundland
Area: 110 681 km²
(42 734 sq mi)
Location:
NW Atlantic
Status: part
of Canada

17. Cuba
Area: 107 832 km²
(41 534 sq mi)
Location:
Caribbean Sea
Status: republic

18. Iceland
Area: 102 818 km²
(39 698 sq mi)
Location:
N Atlantic
Status: republic

19. Mindanao
Area: 101 505 km²
(39 191 sq mi)
Location:
western Pacific
Status: part of
the Philippines

20. Ireland
Area: 82 463 km²
(31 839 sq mi)
Location:
N Atlantic
Status: divided between
the Republic of Ireland
and Northern
Ireland.

21. Hokkaido
Area: 77 900 km²
(30 077 sq mi)
Location:
NW Pacific
Status: part
of Japan

22. Hispaniola
Area: 76 192 km²
(29 418 sq mi)
Location:
Caribbean Sea
Status: divided between
the Dominican Republic
and Haiti

23. Sakhalin
Area: 74 060 km²
(28 597 sq mi)
Location:
NW Pacific
Status: part of
Russia

24. Tasmania
Area: 67 900 km²
(26 215 sq mi)
Location:
SW Pacific
Status: a state of
Australia

25. Sri Lanka
Area: 65 600 km²
(25 332 sq mi)
Location:
Indian Ocean
Status: republic

ISLANDS

An island is a body of land, smaller than a continent, that is completely surrounded by water. Islands occur in rivers, lakes, and the seas and oceans. They range in size from very small mud and sand islands of only a few square metres, to Greenland, which has an area of 2 175 600 km² (840 000 sq mi). There is some evidence that Greenland is in fact several islands overlaid by an icy cap without which it would have an area of 1 680 000 km² (650 000 sq mi). (Note that Australia is normally considered to be a continent rather than an island – see The World's Largest Islands, pp. 90–91.)

Islands, especially those in seas and oceans, have a range of origins. Islands can develop through constructional processes. They may also be formed by erosional processes that cause an area of land to become separated from the mainland. Rising sea levels can also lead to the development of islands, by drowning low-lying areas of land and separating higher areas from the main land mass.

VOLCANIC ISLANDS

When volcanic activity occurs beneath the oceans, it can lead to the growth of islands. This is often closely linked to the movement of the Earth's crustal plates, with island-building (e.g. Iceland) occurring both at constructive plate margins and at destructive margins. Volcanic islands (e.g. Hawaii) can also form far from any plate boundary.

Iceland, situated on the mid-Atlantic ridge, is the largest example of a volcanic island formed at a constructive plate margin. Iceland started forming about 20 million years ago – the age of the oldest rocks on the island. It is still growing in size today, as new material is periodically added, along a line of volcanic activity running from the southwest to the northeast of the island. Much of the volcanic activity responsible for Iceland's growth has not been in the form of spectacular eruptions, but rather as quiet extrusive fissure eruptions, involving the outpouring of large quantities of lava from cracks in the Earth's surface, giving rise to basaltic rocks.

Spectacular eruptions, have, however, also played their part. For example, in 1963, eruptions occurred off the south coast of Iceland. In the space of a few weeks, ash and lava built up on the sea floor and a new, small island named Surtsey was born. The newest island – created by vulcanism – is Pulau Batu Hairan ('Surprise Rock Island'), some 65 km (40 mi) to the NE of Kudat in Sabah, Malaysia. It was first sighted in April 1988 and doubled in height within a week. The island is presently 3.1 m (10 ft) high and has an area of 0.77 ha (1.9 acres).

ISLAND ARCHIPELAGOS

The collision of crustal plates at destructive margins can generate significant volcanic activity. If this occurs at the edge of a land mass it can cause mountain building, but when the collision zone lies beneath an ocean, island development can result. Islands which are born in this way do not occur singly, but in chains or archipelagos ('arcs') that parallel the plate boundary. This is well illustrated on the western side of the Pacific Ocean. Here thousands of islands – most of them volcanic but some formed by the folding up of the ocean floor – mark the western edge of the Pacific Plate. These islands start in the south at New Zealand, run north to the Tongan chain before heading west to New

Guinea, and north again through the Philippines, Japan, the Kurile island chain and finally the Aleutian Islands, which continue to the mainland of North America. The Indonesian archipelago, which extends westwards into the Indian Ocean from the island chains of the west Pacific, is the world's largest (see below).

CORAL ISLANDS

Coral islands and reefs are an important component of warm tropical and subtropical oceans and seas. They are formed from the skeletons of the group of primitive marine organisms known as corals. Coral islands develop where coral grows up towards the ocean surface from shallow submarine platforms – often volcanic cones. If the cone is totally submerged, then a coral atoll will develop – a circular or horseshoe-shaped coral ring which encloses a body of sea water called a lagoon. Upward growth of the coral ceases once sea level has been reached. Coral islands – such as the Maldives and Tuvalu – are therefore flat and low, unless a change in sea level has caused their elevation to change.

SEA LEVEL AND ISLANDS

Changes in sea level can cause new islands to appear or existing ones to disappear. During the last Ice Age eastern Britain was joined to mainland Europe, because sea levels were lower as much of the world's water was frozen in the ice caps and glaciers. As the ice melted, and the sea level rose, the North Sea and the Straits of Dover were re-established. By about 8500 years ago Britain was again an island.

ARCHIPELAGOS

The world's greatest archipelago, or island chain, is the crescent of some 3 700 main islands and more than 9300 islets that comprise the crescent of the East Indies – 5000 km (3500 mi) long – which forms Indonesia and part of Malaysia.

The archipelago of Micronesia – which includes the islands of the Federated States of Micronesia, the Marshall Islands, Palau, Tuvalu and Kiribati – comprises over 2000 main islands, of which only 90 are inhabited.

FRESHWATER ISLANDS

Islands also occur in freshwater lakes and in the estuarine mouths of rivers. Such islands are often the result of deposition of eroded material although they may owe their origin to a number of other causes including glaciation. The largest freshwater islands are:

Marajó which is a freshwater island in the mouth of the River Amazon, Pará state, Brazil. It has an area of 48 000 km² (18 500 sq mi) and is therefore larger than Switzerland.

Bananal in Tocantins state, Brazil, is the world's largest inland island (that is land surrounded by rivers). It has an area of 18 130 km² (7000 sq mi).

Caviana which is a freshwater island in the mouth of the River Amazon, Pará state, Brazil. It has an area of 5000 km² (1930 sq mi).

Gurupá which is also in the Amazon estuary in Pará state, Brazil. It has an area of 4864 km² (1878 sq mi).

Manitoulin in Lake Huron, Canada, is the largest island in a lake. It has an area of 2766 km² (1068 sq mi).

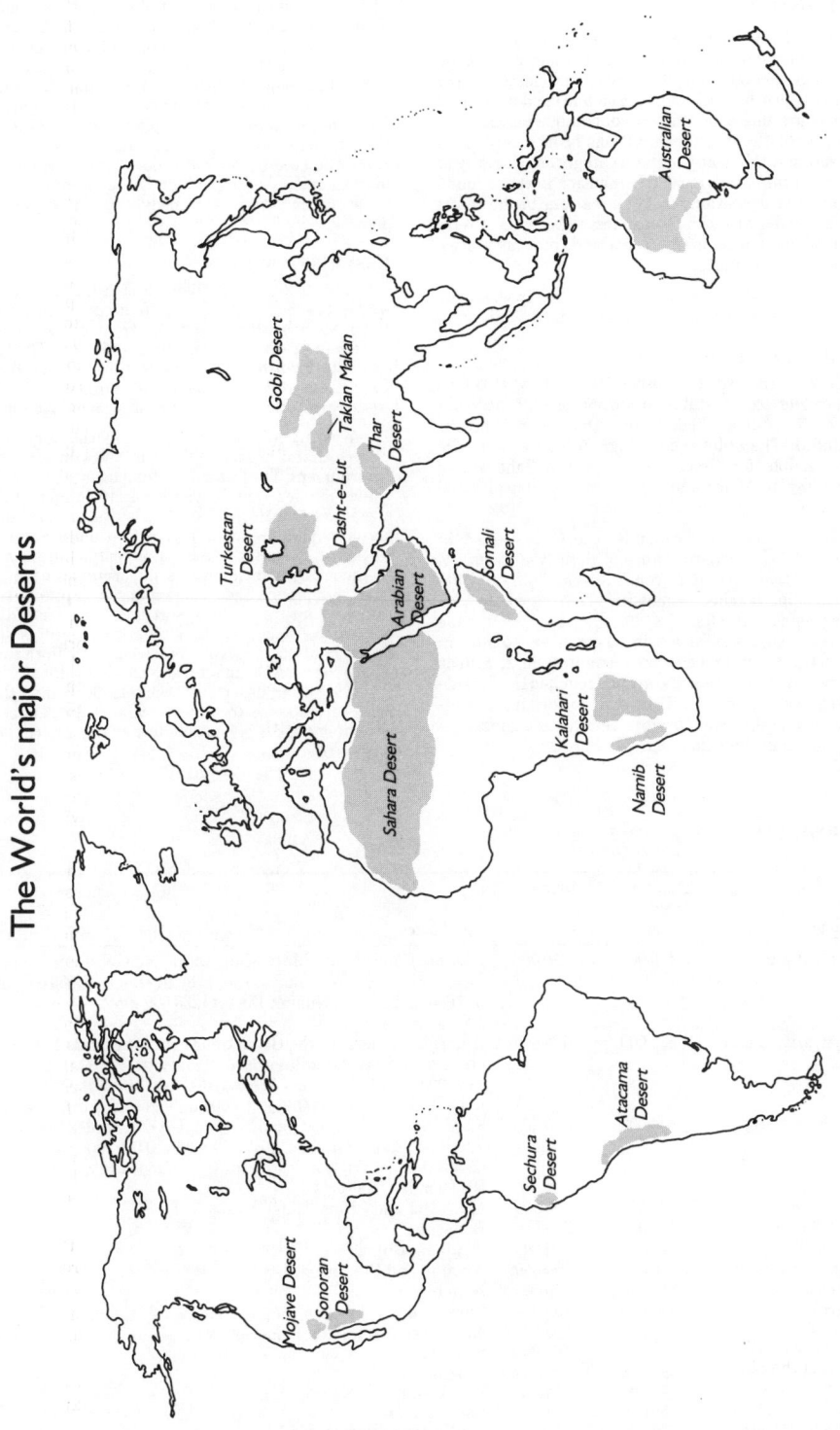

The World's major Deserts

DESERTS

Desert areas are defined in terms of aridity or the availability of water. Semi-arid areas receive on average 200–500 mm (8–20 in) of precipitation per annum, arid areas 25–200 mm (1–8 in) and hyper arid areas are those in which a continuous period of 12 months without any rainfall has been recorded. A desert may fall in any of these categories of aridity or may contain areas experiencing each of these conditions. The definitions and delineations of the desert areas listed are very approximate because deserts are advancing on many fronts and, in some places, are being reclaimed.

Globally, 13.3% of the world's land area is semi-arid, 13.7% is arid and 5.8% is hyper arid.

WHAT CAUSES DESERTS?

Many of the world's deserts coincide with areas characterized by stable atmospheric high pressure (see Climatology), conditions that do not favour rainfall. The sub-tropical high pressure belts are responsible for deserts such as the Sahara and Kalahari in Africa and the deserts of Australia and Arabia.

Other deserts – for example, the Gobi Desert in Central Asia – exist because of their *continentality*, that is, their distance from the sea. This prevents them being reached by moisture-bearing winds from the oceans. This effect may be enhanced by the shape of the landscape: for example, moist air coming in from the sea will precipitate on mountains as rain or snow, and by the time the air has reached the far side of the mountains it will be dry, so forming a *rain-shadow* desert. Such deserts occur, for example, to the north of the Himalaya.

The deserts of the west coast of southern Africa and South America – the Namib and Atacama Deserts – are affected by the presence of cold ocean currents running along the coast. These cool the air that they come into contact with, so preventing the evaporation of moisture from the ocean surface and the formation of rain. At some places in the Atacama Desert, no rain was recorded in the 400 years prior to 1971. The cold ocean water does, however, cause a high frequency of fog, which is the major source of moisture in these extremely dry or *hyper-arid* deserts.

DESERTIFICATION

When in 1949 the French explorer André Aubreville was in the Sahel of Africa, he discovered that the savannah grasslands and the tropical rain forest were being damaged by farming activities. The land was deteriorating, the trees were being cleared and the desert was advancing. He coined the word 'desertification' to describe what was happening.

There is an inbuilt assumption in the very word 'desert' that it has changed, that it was once a better environment. The Latin *desertus* means 'abandoned', which implies that it was formerly inhabited and adequately watered for agricultural or other activity. This, in turn, implies that deserts are the result of human activity and can somehow be reclaimed by planting wadis and around the fringes. Underlying such theories is a misconception about the very nature of the desert and the climate that created it. Most deserts are natural features. The desert landscape, its soils and what little flora there is are a perfect adaptation to that climate. By assuming that deserts are man-made rather than being a response to climate, we are in danger of assuming that it is possible to reclaim deserts on a large scale.

DESERTS

Name	Approx. area in km²	Approx. area in miles²	Territories
The Sahara	8 400 000	*3 250 000*	Algeria, Chad, Libya, Mali, Mauritania, Niger, Sudan, Tunisia, Egypt, Morocco, W. Sahara. Inc. Libyan Desert (1 550 000 km²/ 600 000 miles²) and Nubian Desert (260 000 km²/ 100 000 miles²))
Australian Desert	1 550 000	*600 000*	Australia. Embraces the Great Sandy (or Warburton) (420 000 km²/160 000 miles²), Great Victoria (325 000 km²/ 125 000 miles²), Simpson (Arunta) (310 000 km²/120 000 miles²), Gibson (220 000 km²/ 85 000 miles²) and Sturt Deserts
Arabian Desert	1 300 000	*500 000*	Saudi Arabia, Jordan, Oman, Yemen, UAE. Includes the Rub' al Khali or 'Empty Quarter' (647 500 km²/250 000 miles²), Syrian (325 000 km²/125 000 miles²) and An Nafud (129 500 km²/ 50 000 miles²) Deserts
The Gobi	1 040 000	*400 000*	Mongolia and China (Inner Mongolia)
Kalahari Desert	520 000	*200 000*	Botswana
Takla Makan	320 000	*125 000*	Xinjiang, China
Sonoran Desert	310 000	*120 000*	Arizona and California, USA and Mexico
Namib Desert	310 000	*120 000*	Namibia
Kara Kum*	270 000	*105 000*	Turkmenistan
Thar Desert	260 000	*100 000*	North-western India and Pakistan
Somali Desert	260 000	*100 000*	Somalia
Atacama Desert	180 000	*70 000*	Northern Chile
Kyzyl Kum*	180 000	*70 000*	Uzbekistan and Kazakhstan
Dasht-e Lut**	52 000	*20 000*	Eastern Iran
Mojave Desert	35 000	*13 500*	Southern California, USA
Desierto de Sechura	26 000	*10 000*	Northwest Peru

* Together known as the Turkestan Desert.
** Sometimes called Iranian Desert.

EARTHQUAKES

An earthquake is a sudden release of energy in the Earth's crust or upper mantle. As the planet's tectonic plates jostle against each other and become distorted, tremendous strain builds up – and from time to time the strain energy is discharged in zones where the rocks are weakest. The result is a sudden violent shock that can have highly destructive effects on the Earth's surface nearby.

The damaging effects of an earthquake are due to the vibrations (*seismic waves*) emitted by the shock. For a brief moment the waves shake the ground close to the earthquake, frequently producing permanent effects. Few people are ever killed or injured directly by an earthquake; death and injury are more likely to result from the collapse of buildings caused by the earthquake.

Whether or not there are people or buildings present, earthquakes may cause fissures to appear in the ground, produce changes in the level and tilt of the ground surface, divert rivers and streams, and trigger landslides and avalanches. Undersea earthquakes may also give rise to *tsunami* – huge amounts of sea water that can travel across the oceans for thousands of kilometres, causing devastation when they hit land.

WHERE EARTHQUAKES OCCUR

Most earthquakes take place along the boundaries of the tectonic plates – along oceanic ridges, transform faults and subduction zones – because this is where the plates interact most intensely, and hence where distortion and strain build-up are greatest. However, not all earthquakes occur along plate margins. In North America, for example, the most damaging earthquakes of historic times have taken place not in California, through which runs a transform fault (the San Andreas fault), but in South Carolina and Missouri, both of which are far from plate margins. The reasons for this are unclear, but earthquakes within the interiors of plates may be due to deep, still active faults remaining from a much earlier phase of plate tectonics. California is still America's most notorious seismic area, however, because it is there that earthquakes are most frequent.

The point at which an earthquake occurs is called the *focus*, or *hypocentre*. The point on the Earth's surface directly above the focus is called the *epicentre*. A world map of epicentres is largely a map of the Earth's plate boundaries.

All earthquake foci lie within about the upper 700 km (435 mi) of the Earth. Within this range, earthquakes are classified as *shallow* (focal depths of 0–70 km / 0–43 mi), *intermediate* (70–300 km / 43–186 mi), or *deep* (below 300 km / 186 mi). There are about three times as many intermediate earthquakes as there are deep ones, and about ten times as many shallow ones. It is the shallow shocks that produce most of the damage at the Earth's surface, for the obvious reason that they are closer to it. Collectively, the shallow earthquakes also release the most energy – about 75% of the total, compared to 3% for deep earthquakes.

MEASURING EARTHQUAKES

The size of an earthquake is specified by its magnitude, sometimes called the Richter magnitude after the American seismologist, Charles Richter, who devised the scale in the 1930s (see below). Magnitude is actually a measure of the size (*amplitude*) of the waves emitted by the earthquake. However, the magnitude scale is logarithmic. This means that each step up the scale represents a ten-fold increase in the amplitude of the emitted waves. Thus the waves from a magnitude-7 earthquake are 10 times bigger than those from a magnitude-6 shock, 100 times bigger than those from a magnitude-5 event, and so on.

Magnitude can also be regarded as a measure of the energy released by an earthquake, because energy is related to wave size. The relationship is such that each division on the magnitude scale represents an approximately thirty-fold difference in energy. Thus a magnitude-7 earthquake releases about 30 times more energy than a magnitude-6 shock and about 30 × 30 = 900 times more energy than a magnitude-5 event. This explains why most of the energy released by earthquakes comes from the very few big shocks that occur each year rather than from the million or so smaller earthquakes.

To specify the size of an earthquake in terms of its effects, an intensity scale is used. In the West (but not in Japan or the former Soviet republics, which use slightly different systems) this is usually the *Modified Mercalli Scale*

HISTORIC EARTHQUAKES

The six earthquakes in which the known loss of life has exceeded 100 000 have been:

Eastern Mediterranean In the eastern Mediterranean about 1 100 000 people were killed in an earthquake c. July 1201.

Shanxi Province, China On 2 February 1556, 830 000 were killed in an earthquake.

Calcutta, India On 11 October 1737, 300 000 died in an earthquake.

Tangshan, China An earthquake of 8.2 on the Richter Scale killed 242 000 at Tangshan on 27 July 1976. The original death toll of 655 237 was unaccountably reduced on 4 January 1977.

Gansu Province, China On 16 December 1920, 180 000 died in landslides accompanying an earthquake which registered 8·6 on the Richter Scale.

Kanto Plain, Japan An earthquake registering 8.3 on the Richter Scale killed 142 807 on the Kanto Plain, Honshu, Japan, on 1 September 1923. The material damage done in the Kanto Plain, which includes Tokyo, was estimated at £1 000 000 000.

The destructive effect of an earthquake depends not only on its size but also on the human population of the area affected, the nature of buildings and any other natural events that may be triggered. This is well indicated by the data below, which considers recent major earthquakes.

TWENTIETH-CENTURY EARTHQUAKES

Other notable earthquakes, with loss of life, during this century have included:

1906 (31 Jan): Colombian coast 8.6 on the Richter Scale.

1906 (18 Apr): San Francisco, USA 8.3 on the Richter Scale; 452 fatalities.

1908 (28 Dec): Messina, Italy 7.5 on the Richter Scale; 80 000 fatalities.

1915 (13 Jan): Avezzano, Italy 29 970 fatalities.

1920: Gansu, China (see above).

1923: Kanto Plain, Japan (see above).

1932 (26 Dec): Gansu Province, China 7.6 on the Richter Scale; 70 000 fatalities.

1935 (31 May): Quetta (which in 1935 was in India but is now in Pakistan). An earthquake registering 7.5 on the Richter Scale; 25 000 fatalities.

1939 (27 Dec): Erzincan, Turkey 7.9 on the Richter Scale; 30 000 fatalities.

1950 (15 Aug): Assam, India 8.6 on the Richter Scale; 1500 fatalities.

1952 (4 Nov): Kamchatka, Russia 8.5 on the Richter Scale.

1957 (9 Mar): Aleutian Islands, Alaska, USA 8.3 on the Richter Scale.

1960 (29 Feb): Agadir, Morocco 5.8 on the Richter Scale; 12 000 fatalities.

1960 (22 May): Lebu, Chile 8.3 on Richter Scale.

1964 (28 Mar): Anchorage, Alaska, USA 8.5 on the Richter Scale; 131 fatalities.

1970 (31 May): Northern Peru 7.7 on the Richter Scale; 66 800 fatalities.

1971 (9 Feb): Los Angeles, USA 6.5 on the Richter Scale; 64 fatalities.

1972 (23 Dec): Nicaragua 6.2 on the Richter Scale; 5000 fatalities.

1976 (4 Feb): Guatemala 7.5 on the Richter Scale; 22 700 fatalities.

1976: Tangshan, China (see above).

1977 (4 Mar): Bucharest, Romania 7.5 on the Richter Scale; 1541 fatalities.

1978 (16 Sep): Tabas, Northeast Iran 7.7 on the Richter Scale; 25 000 fatalities.

1980 (10 Oct): El Asnam, Algeria 7.5 on the Richter Scale; 2327 fatalities.

1980 (23 Nov): Potenza, Italy 6.8 on the Richter Scale; c. 3000 fatalities.

1982 (13 Dec): Yemen 6.0 on the Richter Scale; 2800 fatalities.

1983 (31 Mar): Papayan, Colombia 5.5 on the Richter Scale; 264 dead; 150 000 homeless.

1983 (26 May): North Honshu, Japan 7.7 on the Richter Scale; 58 deaths, mostly due to the effects of a tsunami.

1983 (30 Oct): Eastern Turkey 7.1 on the Richter Scale. Although there were 1233 fatalities, there was relatively little damage in this widely felt earthquake.

1985 (3 Mar): Algarroba, Chile 7.8 on the Richter Scale; 177 fatalities and 150 000 homeless.

1985 (19 Sep): Mexico City 8.1 on the Richter Scale; 20 000 fatalities. The effects of the first earthquake were compounded by a second on 20 September – 7.5 on the Richter Scale – which caused the collapse of damaged buildings. 31 000 homeless; 40 000 injured.

1987 (5 Mar): Northeast Ecuador 7.0 on the Richter Scale; 2000 fatalities in a series of earthquakes over 3 days. Although they largely affected areas of low population, 75 000 people were injured.

1988 (6 Nov): Southwest China 7.6 on the Richter Scale; over 1000 fatalities and 500 000 homeless.

1988 (7 Dec): Armenia 6.9 on the Richter Scale; 25 000 fatalities. Six large cities were devastated and 500 000 people were made homeless.

1989 (22 Jan): Tajikistan 5.3 on the Richter Scale; 574 deaths, all owing to the village of Sharora being blanketed in a mud-slide triggered by the earthquake.

1989 (17 Oct): San Francisco Bay, USA 7.1 on the Richter Scale; 67 deaths. There were relatively few deaths, probably owing to the strong building design in the major cities, but the old quarter of San Francisco was badly damaged, and the Oakland section of a raised highway collapsed. Billions of dollars' worth of damage was sustained.

1989 (29 Oct): Algiers, Algeria 6.0 on the Richter Scale; 24 deaths and 746 people injured.

1989 (27 Dec): Newcastle, NSW, Australia 5.5 on the Richter Scale; 40 deaths and over 120 people injured, partly resulting from a factory explosion. It was the first fatal earthquake in Australia, causing over Australian $50 million worth of damage.

1990 (27 Apr): Quinghai Province, China 6.9 on the Richter Scale; 115 fatalities, 160 injured and hundreds made homeless.

1990 (21 June): Roudbar, Northwest Iran 7.3 on the Richter; estimated 36 000 deaths in the heavily populated Caspian Sea coastal zone, with hundreds of towns and villages destroyed.

1990 (17 July): Luzon, Philippines 7.7 on the Richter Scale; over 1000 fatalities caused by an earthquake centred north of Manila.

1990 (6 Nov): Southern Iran 6.8 on the Richter Scale; 22 deaths and over 12 000 people made homeless.

1990 (13 Dec): Sicily, Italy 4.7 on the Richter Scale; 12 deaths and hundreds made homeless.

1991 (1 Feb): Northwest Frontier Province, Pakistan 6.7 on the Richter Scale; over 1000 casualties and thousands made homeless in the Pakistan/Afghanistan border area.

1991 (22 Apr): Costa Rica and Panama 7.5 on the Richter Scale; over 80 deaths and 800 injured.

1991 (29 Apr): Georgia 7.2 on the Richter Scale; over 100 fatalities.

1992 (14 Mar): Eastern Turkey 6.2 on the Richter Scale; over 1000 deaths with the devastation of the town of Erzinka.

1992 (28 Jun): Landers, California, USA 7.4 on the Richter Scale; 1 person killed and over 100 injured in the worst earthquake in California for 40 years.

1992 (12 Oct): Cairo, Egypt 5.9 on the Richter Scale; at least 540 deaths and 4000 injured. The fatalities were caused mainly by the collapse of poorly built tenement blocks. The worst casualties were sustained in the northeastern suburb of Heliopolis.

THE RICHTER SCALE

The Richter scale is the scale of measurement of earthquakes that we are most familiar with. It is a measurement of an earthquake's magnitude, and as such would mean little to the layman. However, it is possible to convert these readings to a scale of intensity.

Magnitude	Probable effects
1	Detectable only by instruments.
2	Barely detectable, even near the epicentre.
4·5	Detectable within 32 km (20 miles) of the epicentre; possible slight damage within a small area.
6	Moderately destructive.
7	A major earthquake.
8	A great earthquake.

THE MODIFIED MERCALLI SCALE

I Not felt except by a few people.

II Felt by a few people at rest. Delicately suspended objects swing.

III Felt noticeably indoors. Standing cars may rock.

IV Felt generally indoors. Sleeping people are woken. Cars rocked, windows rattle.

V Felt generally. Some plaster falls and dishes and windows are broken. Pendulum clocks stop.

VI Felt by all – many frightened. Chimneys and plaster damaged. Furniture moved and objects upset.

VII Everyone runs outdoors. Felt in moving cars. Moderate structural damage.

VIII General alarm. Weak structures badly damaged. Walls and furniture fall over. Water level changes in wells.

IX Panic. Weak structures totally destroyed, extensive damage to well-built structures, foundations and underground pipes. Ground fissured and cracked.

X Panic. Only strongest buildings survive. Ground badly cracked. Rails bent. Water slopped over river banks.

XI Panic. Few buildings survive. Broad fissures in ground. Fault scarps formed. Underground pipes out of service.

XII Total destruction. Waves seen in ground, and lines of sight and level are distorted. Objects thrown in the air.

BRITISH EARTHQUAKES

British earthquakes of an intensity sufficient to move the chair of the observer have been recorded on:

25 Apr	1180	Nottinghamshire
15 Apr	1185	Lincoln
1 June	1246	Canterbury, Kent
21 Dec	1246	Wells
19 Feb	1249	South Wales
11 Sept	1275	Somerset
21 May	1382	Canterbury, Kent
28 Dec	1480	Norfolk
26 Feb	1575	York to Bristol
6 Apr	1580	London (one fatality)
30 Apr	1736	Menstrie, Clackmannan
1 May	1736	Menstrie, Clackmannan
14 Nov	1769	Inverness (several killed)
18 Nov	1795	Derbyshire
13 Aug	1816	Inverness
23 Oct	1839	Comrie, Perth
30 July	1841	Comrie, Perth
6 Oct	1863	Hereford
22 Apr	1884	Colchester[1]
17 Dec	1896	Hereford
18 Sept	1901	Inverness
27 June	1906	Swansea
30 July	1926	Jersey
15 Aug	1926	Hereford
7 June	1931	Dogger Bank (5·6R)
11 Feb	1957	Midlands
26 Dec	1979	Longtown, Cumbria
19 July	1984	W. Britain & Ireland (5·5R)
2 Apr	1990	Shropshire (5·1R)

[1] At least three, possibly five, killed. Strongest ever in British Isles at 6 on the Richter scale.

GLACIATION

It has been estimated that over a tenth of the Earth's land surface – about 15 600 000 km^2 (6 020 000 sq mi) – is permanently covered with ice. Ice is in fact the world's biggest reservoir of fresh water, with over three quarters of the global total contained in ice sheets, ice caps and glaciers. These range in size from the huge Antarctic and Greenland ice sheets, to the small glaciers found in high-latitude and high-altitude mountain ranges.

Ice bodies develop where winter snowfall is able to accumulate and persist through the summer. Over time this snow is compressed into an ice body, and such ice bodies may grow to blanket the landscape as an *ice sheet* or *ice cap*. Alternatively, the ice body may grow to form a mass that flows down a slope – a *glacier* – often cutting a valley and eroding rock material that is eventually deposited at a lower altitude as the ice melts.

THE FORMATION OF ICE BODIES

Ice bodies develop mainly through the accumulation of snow, or sometimes by the freezing of rain as it hits an ice surface. Obviously, not all the snow that falls is turned into ice – during the northern-hemisphere winter over half the world's land surface and up to one third of the surfaces of the oceans may be blanketed by snow and ice. Most of this snow and ice is only temporary, as the Sun's warmth and energy are able to melt the cover during warm winter days or as winter passes into spring and summer.

In some places, however, the summer warmth is unable to melt all the snowfall of the previous winter. This may be because summer temperatures are rather low, or summer is very short, or because winter snowfall is very high. Where this occurs, snow lies all year round (this snow is sometimes called *firn* or *névé*) and becomes covered by the snow of the next winter. As this process continues from year to year, the snow that is buried becomes compressed and transformed into *glacier ice*.

Latitude and altitude both determine where permanent snow can accumulate. The level that separates permanent snow cover from places where the snow melts in the summer is called the *snowline* or *firnline*. The snowline increases in altitude towards the Equator: in polar regions it lies at sea level, in Norway at 1200–1500 m (4000–5000 ft) above sea level, and in the Alps at about 2700 m (9000 ft). Permanent snow and ice can even occur in the tropics close to the equator: in East Africa, for example, the snowline lies at about 4900 m (16 000 ft), so that glaciers are found on Mount Kenya, Kilimanjaro, and the Ruwenzori Mountains.

ICE SHEETS AND ICE CAPS

Ice sheets and ice caps are ice bodies that have grown into domes that blanket an area of land, submerging valleys, hills and mountains. Occasionally, 'islands' of land, called *nunataks*, protrude through the 'sea' of ice. Ice sheets are defined as having an area over 50 000 km^2 (19 000 sq mi); ice caps are smaller.

SEA ICE

There is no ice sheet over the North Pole because there is no land there – however, the Arctic Ocean is always frozen and, during the winter, Arctic *sea ice* covers about 12 million km^2 (4.6 million sq mi).

An area of sea ice that is joined to a coast is called an *ice shelf*. Ice shelves occur in the Arctic, joined to the coasts of northern Canada and Greenland, and in the Antarctic – notably the Ross Ice Shelf, which has an area greater than France. Ocean currents and seasonal melting can cause ice sheets to break up, creating areas of *pack ice* or smaller *ice floes*.

ICE MOVEMENTS

Ice bodies move and flow under the influence of gravity. The movement of frozen water is obviously much slower than when it is in its liquid form. Most glaciers flow at a velocity between 3 and 300 m (10 and 1000 ft) per year. Glaciers on steep slopes may move much faster, and the Quarayaq Glacier, which is supplied with ice from the Greenland Ice Sheet, averages 20–24 m (65–80 ft) per day. Many glaciers experience *surges* – which may last a few days or several years – when flow is extremely rapid, often equivalent to rates of up to 10 km (6 mi) a year.

GLACIERS AND LANDSCAPE

Glacier ice is a very powerful erosional agent, smoothing rock surfaces and cutting deep valleys. *Fjords* (for example, along the coasts of Norway and Alaska) are U-shaped glacial valleys that become submerged by the sea after the melting of the ice that produced them. U-shaped valleys are classically regarded as glacial features, but they can be formed by other processes – for example, by rivers in their middle and lower reaches.

A sliding glacier erodes by *plucking* blocks of rock from its bed and by *abrading* rock surfaces, i.e. breaking off small particles and rock fragments. The rock that is eroded is transported by the ice and deposited as the glacier travels down slope and melts. Glacial deposits can form distinct landforms such as *moraines* (ridges) and *drumlins* (small hills), or they may simply be deposited as *glacial till*, a blanket of sediment covering the landscape.

ICE AGES

Ice ages, more correctly called glacial periods, have been a major phenomenon of the last 2 millon years. Geological evidence, however, demonstrates that glacial periods have affected the Earth periodically over 2300 million years. It is not known why the Earth's atmosphere and surface change substantially, although it is generally thought that the causes of major ice ages relate to cyclic changes in the pattern and character of the Earth's orbit around the Sun.

Evidence for glacial periods comes from a range of sources, including studies of sediments accumulated in deep oceans and lake basins, and investigations of long cores of ice extracted from Antarctic and Greenland ice sheets. Ocean sediments are particularly valuable with their long, undisturbed sequences that can be dated using modern radiometric and palaeomagnetic methods.

It is thought that there have been between 15 and 22 glacials during the last 2 million years – they become harder to determine further back in time. At its height the most recent glacial period saw Canada and Scandinavia covered by great ice sheets. Ice caps centered on Highland Scotland, Snowdonia, the English Lake District and the Alps, with outlet and valley glaciers extending out over the lowlands.

RECENT GLACIAL PERIODS

The last six glacial periods (identified from ocean core evidence) have been dated as follows:

	began	ended
1.	72 000 years ago	10 000 years ago
2.	188 000 years ago	128 000 years ago
3.	280 000 years ago	244 000 years ago
4.	347 000 years ago	334 000 years ago
5.	475 000 years ago	421 000 years ago
6.	650 000 years ago	579 000 years ago

WORLD'S LONGEST GLACIERS

km	miles	
515	320	Lambert-Fisher Ice Passage, Antarctica
418	260	Novaya Zemlya, North Island, Russia
362	225	Arctic Institute Ice Passage, Victoria Land, E Antarctica
289	180	Nimrod–Lennox–King Ice Passage, E Antarctica
241	150	Denman Glacier, E Antarctica
225	140	Beardmore Glacier, E Antarctica
225	140	Recovery Glacier, W Antarctica
200	124	*Petermanns Gletscher, Knud Rasmussen Land, Greenland
193	120	Unnamed Glacier, SW Ross Ice Shelf, W Antarctica
185	115	Slessor Glacier, W Antarctica

* Petermanns Gletscher is the largest in the northern hemisphere: it extends 40 km (24.8 miles) out to sea.

The largest glacier in Europe is the Aletsch Glacier (Bernese Oberland, Switzerland), which is 35 km (22 miles) long.

The longest glacier in the Himalaya-Karakoram is the Hispar-Biafo Ice Passage, which is 122 km (76 mi) long.

GLACIATED AREAS OF THE WORLD

It is estimated that 15 600 000 km^2 (6 020 000 miles^2) or about 10·4 per cent of the world's land surface is permanently covered with ice.

Location	Extent km^2	miles^2
South polar regions	12 588 000	5 250 000
Antarctic icesheet	*12 535 000*	*4 839 000*
other Antarctic glaciers	*53 000*	*20 500*
North Polar Regions	2 070 000	799 000
Greenland ice sheet	*1 726 000*	*666 40095*
other Greenland glaciers	*76 200*	*29 400*
Canadian archipelago	*153 200*	*59 100*
Svalbard (Spitzbergen)	*58 000*	*22 400*
other Arctic islands	*55 700*	*21 500*
Asia	115 800	44 400
Alaska/Rockies	76 900	29 700
South America	26 500	10 200
Iceland	12 170	4 699
Alpine Europe	9 280	3 580
New Zealand	1015	391
Africa	12	5

CAVES

Caves are naturally occurring holes in the ground that can be penetrated by humans. They are often linked into complex systems of chambers and passageways, which can extend many kilometres in length, and penetrate deep into the Earth.

The entrances of many caves have provided shelter for both animals and humans in the past, and their accumulated remains can tell us much about extinct animal forms and the life of prehistoric man. Some caves are also noted for their animal life today: as well as numerous invertebrates, bats, birds, snakes and even crocodiles may make their homes in caves.

By far the majority of caves occur in limestone areas. This is because of the solubility of limestone in rainwater (H_2O) containing carbon dioxide (CO_2) in solution. This solution is carbonic acid (H_2CO_3), a weak acid that can attack limestone on its own, but its effects are much greater if it is augmented by acids from soil and vegetation. Not all limestones have caves as some, such as chalk, are mechanically weak and will not support cave roofs. Others have few caves owing to their high porosity, which allows the acidic water to pass through the whole rock mass without concentrating at any particular points.

Limestone landscapes with cave systems are known as *karst landscapes*, named after an area of Slovenia and Croatia. Karst landscapes are typified by a lack of surface streams, the presence of swallets (stream sinks) and collapse potholes, dry valleys (which once had streams now flowing underground), resurgences, and of bare rock pavements. These *limestone pavements* are intersected into areas known as *clints* by fissures about 50 cm (20 in) wide known as *grikes*, this process being caused by the etching out of joints and subsequent glacial smoothing.

Karst landscapes may also have numerous *dolines* (funnel-shaped hollows at joint intersections) and *poljes* (enclosed valleys with internal drainage through caves). Tropical karst is typified by towers and cones formed by intense downward erosion, with 'cockpits' separating cone-shaped hills.

Caves in rocks other than limestone include a variety of *sea caves* where erosion has etched out weaknesses in sea cliffs.

Lava caves occur in many basalt volcanic areas, such as Iceland, Hawaii, Kenya and Australia. They are generally tubes within lava flows where the molten material has flowed out from beneath the solidified crust. *Fissure caves* occur in a few hard-rock areas where fault zones have been widened by erosion.

Ice caves are of two sorts. First, there are *englacial tubes* through which streams of melt water run beneath glaciers. Though entirely in ice, they show many of the features of limestone caves, although rapid changes may take place owing to glacier movement. Second, there are caves in high mountain regions where the air within the cave rarely if ever rises above freezing point, so that water percolating in from the surface during the summer freezes into icicles, often very large, and sometimes joining into ice masses underground.

Depressions – see below – are sunken hollows in the surface of the ground. These may be caused by a number of natural processes including water erosion, glaciation, wind erosion, changes in sea level, and faulting.

WORLD'S DEEPEST CAVES

Name	Depth (m)	Depth (ft)
Réseau Jean Bernard, Haute-Savoie, France	1602	5256
Shakta Pantjukhina, Georgia	1508	4947
Sistema del Trave, Asturias, Spain	1441	4728
Aminakoateak, Navarre, Spain	1408	4630
Snezhnaya, Abkhazia, Georgia,	1370	4495
Sistema Huautla, Oaxaca, Mexico	1353	4439
Réseau de la Pierre-Saint-Martin, Pyrenees, France	1342	4403
Boj–Bulok, Tajikistan	1315	4313
Sisterna Cuicateca, Mexico	1243	4077
Réseau Rhododendrons-Gouffre Berger, Isère, France	1242	4072
V.V. Iljukhina, Georgia	1240	4068
Scwersystem, Salzburg, Austria	1219	3999
Gouffre Mirolda, Haute-Savoie France	1211	3973
Abisso Ulivifer, Apennines, Italy	1210	3969
Veliko Fbrego, Croatia	1198	3930
Complesso Fighiera Corchia, Tuscany, Italy	1190	3986
Sistema Aranonera, Aragon, Spain	1185	3888
Dachstein-Mammuthöhle, Upper Austria, Austria	1180	3871
Jubilaümsschacht, Salzburg, Austria	1173	3848
Sima 56 de Andara, Cantabrica, Spain	1169	3835
Anou Ifflis, Djurdjura, Tunisia	1159	3802
Gouffre de la Bordure de Tourugne, Pyrenees, France	1159	3802
Abisso Vive le Donne*, Alps, Italy	1156	3792
Sistema Badalona, Pyrenees, Spain	1149	3769
Pozu del Xiyo, Picos, Spain	1148	3765

* Current dye tracing tests indicate that this cave may be over 1800 m deep

WORLD'S LONGEST CAVE SYSTEMS

Name	Length (km)	Length (mi)
Mammoth Cave, Kentucky, USA	560	348
Optimisticeskaya, Ukraine	165	103
Hölloch, Schwyz, Switzerland	133	83
Jewel Cave, South Dakota, USA	127	79
Siebenhengste-Hohganthöhlen, Bern, Switzerland	110	68
Ozernaya, Ukraine	107	66
La Coume d'Hyouernède, Haute-Garonne, France	90	56
Ojo Guareña, Castile-Leon, Spain	89	55
Wind Cave, South Dakota, USA	82	51
Zoluska, Ukraine	82	51
Fisher Ridge Cave, Kentucky, USA	77	49
Gua Airjernih, Sarawak, Malaysia	75	47
Sistema Purificacion, Mexico	72	45

Friars Hole Cave, West Virginia, USA	69	*43*
Lechuguilla Cave, New Mexico, USA	67	*42*
Ease Gill, West Yorkshire, England, UK	66	*41*

WORLD'S LARGEST CAVE CHAMBERS

The following list gives the surface area of the floor of the largest known cave chambers.

Name	Area (m²)	Area (sq ft)
Sarawak Chamber*, Lubang Nasib Bagus, Gunung Mulu National Park, Sarawak, Malaysia	162 700	*1 751 287*
Torca del Carlista, Spain	76 600	*824 515*
Majlis al Jinn, Oman	58 000	*624 306*
Belize Chamber, Belize	50 000	*538 195*

* Sarawak Chamber is 700 m (2300 ft) in length, with an average width of 300 m (980 ft) and is nowhere less than 70 m (230 ft) high.

DEPRESSIONS

	Maximum depth below sea level	
World's deepest depressions	*(m)*	*(ft)*
Dead Sea, Jordan/Israel	395	*1296*
Turfan Depression, Xinjiang, China	153	*505*
Munkhafad el Qattâra (Qattâra Depression), Egypt	132	*436*
Poluostrov Mangyshlak, Kazakhstan	131	*433*
Danakil Depression, Ethiopia	116	*383*
Death Valley, California, USA	86	*282*
Salton Sink, California, USA	71	*235*
Zapadnyy Chink Ustyurta, Kazakhstan	70	*230*
Prikaspiyskaya Nizmennost', Russia/Kazakhstan	67	*220*
Ozera Sarykamysh, Uzbekistan/Turkmenistan	45	*148*
El Faiyûm, Egypt	44	*147*
Peninsula Valdiés Lago Enriquillo, Dominican Republic	40	*131*

Note: Immense areas of western Antarctica would be below sea level if stripped of their ice sheet. The deepest estimated crypto-depression is the bed rock on the Hollick–Kenyon plateau beneath the Marie Byrd Land ice cap (84° 37′ S 110° W) at – 2468 m (– 8100 ft).

The bed of Lake Baykal (Russia) is 1484 m (4872 ft) below sea level, and the bed of the Dead Sea (Israel/Jordan) is 792 m (2600 ft) below sea level.

The ground surface of large areas of Central Greenland under the overburden of ice up to 341 m (11 190 ft) thick are depressed to 365 m (1200 ft) below sea level.

The world's largest exposed depression is the Prikaspiyskaya Nizmennost', which includes the northern third of the Caspian Sea – which is itself 28 m (92 ft) below sea-level – and stretches up to 400 km (250 miles) inland.

The Qattâra Depression extends for 547 km (340 miles) and is up to 128 km (80 miles) wide.

WEATHER AND CLIMATE

Meteorology is the science of the atmosphere, from the Greek word '*meteorologica*', meaning 'matters of the atmosphere', and first used in a treatise by Aristotle.

Weather is the condition of the atmosphere at any one place and time, as described by air temperature and humidity, wind speed and direction, cloud amount and precipitation from cloud (drizzle, rain, snow, hail), together with atmospheric pressure, sunshine and visibility.

Climate is the normal weather condition for an area during a season or year. The climate of an area is obtained by averaging statistics of the various weather factors over a number of similar periods, monthly or seasonal, usually for periods of 30 years.

CONSTITUENTS OF AIR

Atmospheric air consists of gases in fixed proportion, and gases in variable quantities. The most important of the fixed proportion gases are:

Nitrogen which constitutes 78% of atmospheric air.

Oxygen which constitutes 21% of atmospheric air.

The most important of the variable gases are:

Ozone which occurs at high altitudes. It provides some protection against the ultraviolet rays from the sun.

Carbon dioxide which acts like glass in a greenhouse to retain heat in the lower atmosphere.

Water vapour acquired by evaporation from oceans, rivers, and even puddles. All fog, cloud and precipitation is produced from water vapour by condensation.

All these gases have weight and exert atmospheric pressure. This is measured in millibars (mb) where 1 mb = 100 newtons per m² = the pressure exerted by 0.75 mm of mercury.

WATER IN THE ATMOSPHERE

There is one basic supply of water in the world which is continually recycled. Water evaporates from oceans; vapour condenses again as dew, fog or cloud; rain or snow falls from clouds and percolates through soil back to the oceans, or is absorbed by plants and transpired as vapour from foliage.

The warmer the air, the more vapour it can hold, although there is a maximum capacity for every temperature. The path followed by an air mass determines its moisture content. Wind, which is moving air, is moist after a long sea track and relatively dry after a long land track.

Relative humidity is the actual vapour content of air, expressed as a percentage of the maximum possible at that temperture. If air is saturated its relative humidity (RH) is 100%, and the air temperature is called dew point. No more water can then be evaporated into air until air temperature rises above dew point, when its capacity for vapour also increases.

If air is not saturated, for instance has an RH of only 80%, then its temperature can only fall as far as dew point before some vapour has to be discarded as visible water drops. This is called *condensation*.

WEATHER

All wet weather phenomena are the result of air cooling to dew point or below. The higher the RH when such cooling begins, the quicker condensation will occur.

Air temperature falls when in contact with colder surfaces of land or sea, in which case dew, hoar frost or fog will result when dew point is reached.

Air also cools because of expansion when lifted into regions of lower atmospheric pressure. Air may have to rise over high ground, rise in thermal upcurrents, or be carried upwards on meeting air of different density. Cloud forms once air has cooled to dew point or below, and rain or snow may fall from cloud.

Therefore, topography has considerable effect upon weather. It is generally colder at the top of mountains, wetter on their windward side and drier on the leeward side because of rain lost over the top. In extreme cases, where the rain-bearing winds come mainly from one direction, the opposite side of a mountain range may develop into a rainshadow desert.

Air temperature rises when in contact with warming surfaces of land or sea. The Earth's chief heat source is the Sun, which is a radiant globe of gases that whirl in a vortex around an axis and transmits energy by electromagnetic waves of various wavelengths. The earth moves in an elliptical path around the Sun so that the distance between the two varies but is on average 150 million km (93 million miles).

Seasons exist because the Earth's axis is tilted at 66½° to the plane in which it travels around the Sun, and each hemisphere alternately leans towards or away from the Sun.

Day and night occur because the Earth rotates about its own axis once in 24 hours, so that everywhere alternately faces towards or away from the Sun.

Equinox means equality of day and night and happens when the Sun is vertical over the Equator on 21 March and 22 September.

Solstices are the two occasions occurring about 21 June and 21 December when the Earth's equator is furthest from the Sun, so that there is maximum and minimum daylight in the two hemispheres.

The Tropics of Cancer and Capricorn – 23° 27′ north and south of the Equator respectively – encompass the only regions of the Earth on which the Sun shines directly overhead at some time of the year.

All these different variations of the Sun's altitude over places on Earth means that air temperature is always higher at the Equator than at the Poles, always higher in summer than in winter, and mostly higher in the day than by night. However, temperature does not fall evenly from equatorial latitudes to polar regions, because of geographical complications. Sea temperature varies hardly at all from one day to another and only gradually over a whole season, so that the weather near the oceans is generally more equable and milder than inland. Inland, where soil responds well to the rise of the Sun, temperature can soar each day but fall equally rapidly under clear skies at night.

Air temperatures, either on the coast or inland, are often modified because of cloud cover.

CLOUD CLASSIFICATION

Clouds comprise water drops or ice crystals suspended in air. The water is condensed from air which rises into levels of lower atmospheric pressure, expands and cools to dew point. Air may be lifted in this manner over high ground, in thermals or at the convergence of air masses of different temperature, when cold air undercuts warm air. Water drops can remain liquid when supercooled to temperatures of −30 °C (−22 °F) but below this temperature an increasing number of water drops freeze to ice crystals. At temperatures lower than −40 °C (−40 °F), clouds consist of ice crystals alone. Water drops and crystals are transparent but take on shades between white and grey, depending upon how thick the clouds are and how light is bent on travelling through. Clouds may also be coloured when illuminated by the Sun.

Clouds are classified according to the height of their base above the ground and whether they are rounded (cumulus) or flat (stratus).

HIGH CLOUD

Cirrus, (Latin 'lock of hair'). Cirrus clouds contain ice crystals in air colder than −30° C (−22° F), and are usually higher than about 5000 m (16 500 ft). They are detached clouds forming delicate white filaments, or white, or mostly white, patches or narrow bands. They have a fibrous (hair-like) appearance or a silky sheen, or both. Cirrus are the highest of the standard cloud forms.

Cirrocumulus, rounded small clouds, rather than feathery or hair-like. They appear in the form of grains or ripples, and are often more or less regularly arranged.

Cirrostratus, a white veil of smooth fibrous ice crystal cloud, often seen making a halo around the Sun or Moon.

MEDIUM-LEVEL CLOUD

Medium-level clouds are composed of water drops, either warm or supercooled. Their bases can be anywhere between 2000 m (6500 ft) and 7000 m (23 000 ft).

Altocumulus are grey or white clouds having rounded shapes, sometimes touching.

Altostratus, a flat, thick sheet cloud, often obscuring the Sun and totally hiding it when about to rain or snow. Altostratus clouds are all shades of grey.

LOW CLOUD

Low cloud is defined as any which has its base at or below 2000 m (6500 ft).

Cumulus, detached clouds with sharp billowing upper contours which develop upwards in thermals. They vary in appearance from small fleeces to giant cauliflowers.

Cumulonimbus, the tallest of the cumulus clouds, they sometimes have an ice-crystal anvil-shaped top at the limit of convection. Cumulonimbus clouds give showers or rain, snow or hail, often with thunder and lightning.

Nimbostratus, flat, relatively shapeless clouds, often seen below altostratus clouds. These grey clouds – which often merge – give rain or snow.

Stratus, patches or sheets of shapeless low grey cloud, often thin enough to see the Sun through, especially when about to disperse. They often start as fog, and are later lifted by strengthening wind. Stratus clouds give drizzle and (in winter) snow grains.

Stratocumulus, patches of cloud, or whole sheets, with discernible rounded shapes. They are often formed by cumulus clouds spreading out under an inversion of temperature.

VEGETATION ZONES

Any attempt to define the world's vegetation regions is complicated by the fact that the *natural vegetation*, that is the vegetation as it was originally, has been greatly changed by human interference such as deforestation and agriculture. Elevation, slope, drainage, soil type, soil depth and climate all influence the vegetation distribution.

Climate is a major factor in determining the type and number of plants (and to a lesser extent animals) that can live in an area. Three main terrestrial ecosystems can be recognized: deserts, grasslands and forests. Precipitation is the element that determines which vegetation type will occur in an area. If the annual precipitation is less than 250 mm (10 in) then deserts usually occur. Grasslands can be found when precipitation is between 250 and 750 mm (10 and 30 in) per annum, while areas that receive more than 750 mm (30 in) rainfall a year are usually covered by forests.

The average temperature and the nature of the seasons in a region are important in that they can determine the type of desert, grassland or forest. Wherever the monthly average temperature exceeds 21 °C (70 °F) then hot deserts, savannah grasslands or tropical forests occur.

In the middle latitudes, the winter temperatures are low enough (one month or more below 5 °C/41 °F) to cause vegetation to become dormant. In autumn, growth stops, leaves are often shed and the plant survives the unfavourable winter months in a resting or dormant phase. In spring, when temperatures rise, new growth begins. In high latitudes, the winter conditions are such that between four and six months are dark and average temperature falls well below 0 °C (32 °F). The evergreen conifers can survive these conditions but growth is very slow and confined to the short, cool summers. In the highest latitudes, trees disappear and only small low-growing plants can survive the low temperatures.

CLIMATIC ZONES

Climate is merely average weather, and climatic patterns are complicated but logical results of meteorological and geographical factors. Temperature roughly follows the bands of latitude, warm near the Equator, cold in Polar regions, and often modified because of cloud cover created by the physical processes of the atmosphere. Low pressure generally breeds clouds and precipitation; high pressure areas have little or no cloud. There are four major pressure belts around the world.

Tropical low pressure, an area between 10° N and S of the Equator, where there is frequent and regular rain mainly from convection clouds. The large equatorial forests lie within this band.

Subtropical high pressure, an area approximately 10–40° N and S, where there is little cloud or rain. High pressure extends across to the interior of continents in middle latitudes during the winter, but

retreats into smaller cells over the relatively cold oceans during summer. The major hot deserts of the world lie within this subtropical belt.

Mid-latitude low pressure, an area of mainly low pressure in the mid latitudes 40–70° N or S, where there is frequent but irregular rain from depressions and convection clouds, interspersed with occasional spells of high pressure. The interiors of continents in this zone are very cold in winter (when there is high pressure) but hot in summer with some rain (low pressure). Regions bordering the oceans have a more equable climate, with much less fluctuation in temperature.

Polar high pressure, belts of mainly high pressure between the poles and 70° N and S, because the air is too cold to contain much water vapour.

The middle latitudes are called *temperate*, having cool summers and mild winters in maritime climates, and hot summers with cold winters in continental climates. There is very little change in temperature in equatorial regions because of season, but a great difference between winter and summer temperatures in polar regions.

The climatological statistics given in the table opposite enable you to confirm the differences in climate due to physical factors of geography and topography.

Rainfall increases when air is forced over high ground. Compare the precipitation figures of Bergen – which lies in the path of westerly moist air masses – and Stockholm in the rain shadow to the east of the Scandinavian Mountains.

Rainfall increases with proximity to the most frequent paths of depressions (areas of low pressure). Compare the precipitation totals of Dublin, often close to depression centres, with those of London which is usually more remote from centres of low pressure.

Rainfall is often markedly seasonal, when monsoon winds blow off cool sea on to warm land in summer, as at Darwin, Australia. Monsoon rain is particularly heavy over India and Pakistan when accentuated by the summer low pressure area over the Thar desert. Rainfall may also be seasonal because of the shift of the subtropical high-pressure belt. Beijing (Peking), China, for instance, has little rain in winter, but plenty in summer; Madrid, Spain, has little rain in summer, but experiences appreciably more in winter.

WEATHER MAPS

Weather forecasting is based upon upper-air data and surface weather observations made all over the world. The material is collected and retransmitted after processing, on an international telecommunications network organized by the World Meteorological Organization. Information is relayed in numerical code, with five or six numerals in each group, and each observation is plotted in symbol form on a map at the position it was made.

One of the items plotted on the map is atmospheric pressure. Forecasters draw in the isobars, which are lines joining places that have equal pressure, corrected to Mean Sea Level, at the same hour. These isobars form concentric patterns around low and high pressure centres and indicate the wind direction at 600 m (2000 ft) above ground, where it is deemed unaffected by the drag of surface friction.

AVERAGE RAINFALL IN SELECTED CITIES
(to the nearest 5 mm)

	J	F	M	A	M	J	J	A	S	O	N	D
In Europe												
Amsterdam	70	50	50	50	50	65	80	95	80	80	85	85
Athens	45	35	40	25	15	5	5	5	15	15	55	65
Bergen	190	145	140	110	100	115	140	180	235	245	205	195
Berlin	30	30	40	40	60	70	80	70	50	40	40	40
Bucharest	40	30	35	45	70	85	70	55	40	45	45	40
Budapest	40	40	35	45	60	75	60	55	40	40	65	50
Copenhagen	50	40	30	40	40	45	70	65	60	60	50	50
Dublin	70	50	50	45	60	55	60	75	75	70	70	80
Geneva	65	60	70	65	70	80	75	100	100	85	90	80
London	40	30	40	40	45	50	40	50	55	45	55	50
Madrid	40	40	45	45	40	30	10	10	30	50	50	45
Moscow	40	35	30	50	55	75	75	75	50	70	45	40
Paris	55	45	30	40	50	50	55	60	50	50	50	50
Prague	25	25	25	30	60	65	80	65	35	40	25	25
Rome	80	75	75	50	35	20	5	35	75	85	125	110
Stockholm	45	30	25	30	35	45	60	75	60	50	55	50
Vienna	40	45	45	45	70	65	85	70	40	55	55	45
Other Continents												
Bombay, India	5	0	5	5	15	520	710	440	300	90	20	0
Casablanca, Morocco	65	55	55	40	20	5	0	0	5	40	60	85
Dakar, Senegal	0	0	0	0	0	15	90	250	160	50	5	5
Darwin, Australia	385	310	250	95	15	5	<5	5	15	50	120	240
Douala, Cameroon	20	65	145	180	205	150	55	75	200	300	125	120
Jeddah, Saudi Arabia	30	0	0	0	0	0	0	0	0	0	40	10
New York, USA	85	80	105	90	90	85	95	130	100	8	90	85
Montreal, Canada	25	15	35	65	65	80	90	90	90	75	60	35
Peking, China	5	5	5	15	30	75	250	125	60	10	10	5
Tehran, Iran	40	25	30	25	15	0	5	0	0	5	25	25

AVERAGE TEMPERATURES IN SELECTED CITIES
(°C)

	J	F	M	A	M	J	J	A	S	O	N	D
In Europe												
Amsterdam	2	2	5	8	12	15	17	17	14	11	6	4
Athens	9	10	12	15	20	25	27	26	23	18	14	11
Bergen	1	1	3	6	10	13	14	14	12	9	4	2
Berlin	−1	1	4	8	13	17	18	17	14	8	4	1
Bucharest	−3	−1	5	11	16	20	22	22	18	11	5	0
Budapest	−1	2	6	12	16	20	21	21	17	11	6	2
Copenhagen	1	0	2	7	12	16	18	17	14	9	5	1
Dublin	5	5	6	8	11	14	15	15	13	10	7	4
Geneva	0	1	5	9	13	17	18	18	14	9	5	2
London	5	6	7	10	13	16	18	18	16	13	9	6
Madrid	5	7	10	13	16	21	24	24	20	15	9	6
Moscow	−9	−9	−4	4	12	17	18	17	11	4	−3	−8
Paris	3	4	7	10	14	17	19	18	16	11	7	4
Prague	1	2	3	8	13	16	19	17	14	8	3	1
Rome	8	9	11	14	17	22	24	24	21	17	13	9
Stockholm	−3	−3	−1	4	10	15	18	17	12	7	3	0
Vienna	−1	0	4	9	14	17	19	19	15	10	4	0
Other Continents												
Bombay, India	24	25	27	28	31	29	28	28	27	28	27	26
Casablanca, Morocco	12	13	15	16	18	20	22	23	22	19	16	13
Dakar, Senegal	21	20	21	22	23	26	27	27	27	27	26	23
Darwin, Australia	28	28	29	29	28	26	25	26	28	29	30	29
Douala, Cameroon	24	25	24	24	24	23	22	22	23	23	22	24
Jeddah, Saudi Arabia	23	25	27	29	30	32	33	31	30	28	27	25
New York, USA	0	0	5	11	16	22	25	24	20	15	8	2
Montreal, Canada	−10	−9	−3	6	13	18	21	20	15	9	2	−7
Peking, China	−5	−4	4	15	27	31	31	30	26	20	10	−5
Tehran, Iran	4	4	8	15	20	27	29	28	25	18	10	7

Wind blows parallel to the isobars so that low pressure is on the left hand when the wind is on the back, in the northern hemisphere (low pressure is on the right hand in the southern hemisphere). In other words, wind blows anticlockwise around low pressure areas (depressions, cyclones, hurricanes) in the northern hemisphere and clockwise around high pressure areas (anticyclones). Wind directions are reversed in the southern hemisphere. Wind speed is inversely proportional to the distance between the isobars (the stronger the wind, the closer the isobars) and can be measured by a specially graduated scale placed across the isobars.

From the other plotted data, forecasters can detect the boundaries between air masses having different temperature and humidity characteristics. A warm front is the surface boundary of approaching warm air with existing cool air. Warm air slides upwards over the cooler air ahead, to form sheet cloud several hundred kilometres ahead of the warm front, giving rain or snow in winter. A cold front is the surface boundary between vigorous cold which undercuts warmer air ahead, giving a line of huge shower clouds, often with torrential but short lived rain or snow. A cold front usually travels faster than a warm front, eventually catching up with it and lifting the warm air off the ground into the upper atmosphere. The fronts are then said to be occluded. The warm sector lies between the warm front and the cold front. Fronts are usually associated with low pressure circulations, as in the accompanying diagram.

On a black-on-white chart in the newspapers, a warm front is drawn as a thick line with semicircles on the side of advance; a cold front has triangles along the leading edge of the line; and an occlusion has both symbols. Diagrams of well defined fronts on weather charts (also called isobaric or pressure charts) show up clearly on satellite photographs as spiral or comma shaped cloud bands. Weather charts for the general public are broadcast on a regular basis, both on radio and TV. Most countries that border the oceans make special forecasts for shipping, dividing the sea areas into convenient sections. In the UK shipping bulletins, four times a day, each lasting five minutes, time is allotted for each particular area given in the chart shown on p. 105. Bulletins for UK land refer to the areas indicated on this map.

BEAUFORT SCALE

A scale of numbers, designated Force 0 to Force 12, was originally devised by Commander Francis Beaufort (1774–1857) (later Rear-Admiral Sir Francis Beaufort, KCB, FRS) in 1805. (Force numbers 13 to 17 were added in 1955 by the US Weather Bureau, but are not in international use since they are regarded as impractical.)

Force No.	Descriptive term	Wind speed km/h	mph	knots
0	Calm	0–1	0–1	0–1
1	Light air	1–5	1–3	1–3
2	Light breeze	6–11	4–7	4–6
3	Gentle breeze	12–19	8–12	7–10
4	Moderate breeze	20–29	13–18	11–16
5	Fresh breeze	30–39	19–24	17–21
6	Strong breeze	40–50	25–31	22–27
7	Near gale	51–61	32–38	28–33
8	Gale	62–74	39–46	34–40
9	Strong gale	75–87	47–54	41–47
10	Storm		55–63	48–55
11	Violent storm		64–73	56–63
12	Hurricane	119	74	64

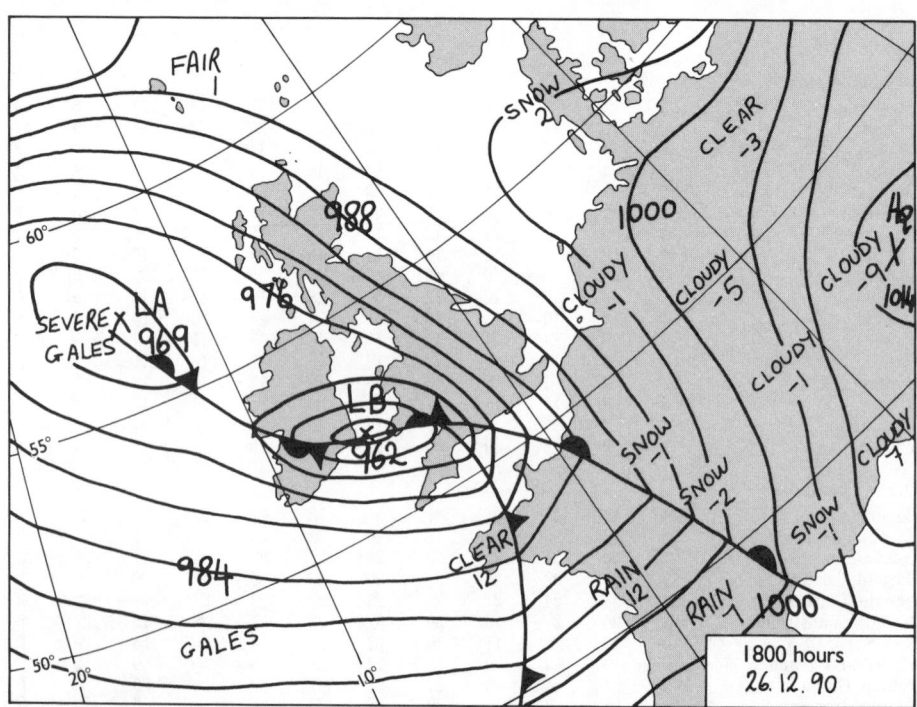

1800 hours
26.12.90

WEATHER REGIONS AND SEA AREAS

SOUTH-EAST ICELAND

FAEROES

FAIR ISLE

BAILEY

NORTH UTSIRE

SOUTH UTSIRE

VIKING

1 •

HEBRIDES

13 •

FORTIES

FISHER

CROMARTY

SCOTLAND

FORTH

GERMAN BIGHT

ROCKALL

MALIN

12 •

11 •

2 •

TYNE

DOGGER

NORTHERN IRELAND

NORTH-EAST ENGLAND

HUMBER

NORTH WEST ENGLAND

10 •

3 •

IRISH SEA

MIDLANDS

EAST ANGLIA

WALES

SOUTH-EAST ENGLAND

THAMES

4 •

SHANNON

9 •

LUNDY

CENTRAL SOUTHERN ENGLAND

DOVER

5 •

FASTNET

SOUTH-WEST ENGLAND

8 •

7 •

PORTLAND

6 •

WIGHT

PLYMOUTH

SOLE

BISCAY

FINISTERRE

Coastal stations include

1 Sumburgh
2 St. Abb's Head
3 Smith's Knoll (Automatic)
4 Dover
5 Royal Sovereign
6 Jersey
7 Channel Light Vessel (Automatic)
8 Land's End
9 Valentia
10 Ronaldsway
11 Malin Head
12 Tiree
13 Butt of Lewis

THE ENVIRONMENT

GLOBAL WARMING

THE GREENHOUSE EFFECT

The planet Earth is showing signs of gradually becoming warmer, a process known as the greenhouse effect. Scientists have discovered that the average temperature of the Earth's atmosphere has increased by 0.5 °C (0.9 °F) since accurate records began in about 1860. In absolute terms this is a very small increase, but the *rate* of temperature change – which is now faster than at any time in the past – is significant. This trend is called *global warming*.

The main reason for the greenhouse effect is a substantial increase in the so-called *greenhouse gases* such as carbon dioxide, methane, nitrous oxide, chlorofluorocarbons (CFCs) and, most recently, of benzine in the atmosphere. To understand how the greenhouse gases cause the rise in temperature we must understand the vertical structure of the atmosphere.

Each of the layers of the atmosphere has its own distinct chemical and physical properties. For example, in the troposphere the temperature cools rapidly. It is in the troposphere that most of our daily weather is formed and it is here too that most of the pollutants released into the atmosphere by human activities accumulate. The stratosphere is important as it is the layer in which atmospheric ozone is found.

The gaseous composition of the atmosphere allows approximately one half of the total energy from the Sun (solar radiation) to pass into the lower atmosphere, thus warming the planet. Eventually, the incoming energy – which has arrived as short-wave,

intensive radiation – is reflected back into space as long-wave dissipated energy. In this way the average temperature of the Earth remains relatively constant at $+14°C$. Greenhouse gases restrict the loss of the long-wave radiation and, as a result, the Earth's atmosphere is warming.

The atmosphere comprises a complex mixture of gases and water vapour.

Component gases of the lower atmosphere (by volume)

nitrogen 78.084%	*krypton* 0.00012%
oxygen 20.946%	*xenon* 0.00009%
argon 0.934%	*hydrogen* 0.00005%
carbon dioxide 0.033%	*nitrous oxide* 0.00005%
neon 0.00182%	*methane* 0.00002%
helium 0.00053%	

Since the beginning of the Industrial Revolution (from c. 1750), the composition of the atmosphere has been gradually changing. Most significantly, carbon dioxide has increased by 28%, from 265 parts per million (p.p.m.) in 1850 to 354 p.p.m. in 1989, and is predicted to rise to 600 p.p.m. by 2050. Carbon dioxide is currently responsible for 57% of the global warming trend, with 80% of the gas originating from the burning of fossil fuels (coal, petroleum, etc.).

Global carbon-dioxide emissions

The emission of carbon dioxide into the atmosphere by region/nation in 1989 was as follows:

World CO_2 production   21.863 billion tonnes

	billion tonnes	world total
North America	5.324	24.35%
US	4.869	22.27%
CIS & Eastern Europe	4.897	22.81%
Western Europe	2.619	11.97%
China	2.386	10.9%

Relative contributions to the greenhouse effect

It has been calculated that the relative contributions to the greenhouse effect in the 1980s were as follows:

carbon dioxide 50%
methane 18%
CFCs 14%
surface ozone 12%
nitrous oxide 6%

From about 1950, the chemical composition of the atmosphere has changed more rapidly. Industry has been responsible for the release of huge quantities of sulfur dioxide, hydrogen sulfide and nitrous oxides, all the result of burning fossil fuels. Agriculture has contributed large amounts of methane gas. Rice (paddy) fields contribute 115 million tonnes of methane every year, and 1.2 billion domesticated farm animals (particularly cattle), through the expulsion of intestinal gas, add a further 73 million tonnes. Methane comprises only 2 p.p.m. of the atmosphere, but its effectiveness as a greenhouse gas is about 30 times that of carbon dioxide, and its volume has increased by more than 400% over the last century.

The transportation systems of the world, especially aviation and motor vehicles, are responsible for the release of vast quantities of nitrous oxides, carbon dioxide, lead and benzine into the atmosphere. In the USA, all forms of transport consume 63% of all petroleum used each year. In Western Europe,

---

THE RIO DE JANEIRO CONFERENCE

In June, 1992 the United Nations Conference on Environment and Development (UNCED) met to examine the most critical environmental issues that the world would face in the next 25 years. A large number of conventions, declarations and action plans were presented. These can be summarized as follows:

1. Climate Change Convention.
2. Biological Diversity Convention.
3. Statement of Forest Principles.
4. The Rio Declaration.
5. Agenda 21.
6. Mechanisms for Financial Assistance for Developing Countries.
7. Establishment of a Sustainable Development Commission.

Probably the most important document was Agenda 21. This represents a major agreement for an action plan stretching well into the next century. It presents a strategy to hold and reverse the effects of environmental degradation and to promote environmentally sound and sustainable development in all countries. Although not legally binding, it reflects a global consensus and political commitment at the highest level on development and environmental cooperation.

this figure is 44%. In many countries, efforts are being made to increase the energy efficiency of transportation systems, and some progress has been made to reduce the reliance on the private motor car. In California, for example, legislation is being prepared to reduce the use of private cars by 1% per annum for the next 20 years.

THE EXTENT OF GLOBAL WARMING
The Intergovernmental Panel on Climate Change (IPCC) has concluded that based on a 'business-as-usual' scenario, (no change), mean global temperatures will rise by 0.3° C per decade. By 2030 an increase of more than 1° C will have occurred and by 2100 the increase will exceed 3° C.

The prediction of future planetary warming is a highly controversial subject. Some experts claim that the rise in average temperature is nothing more than a natural fluctuation in the long-term history of our planet. To support this view, they claim that the existence of the Ice Age which ended about 10 000 years ago is evidence of a cooling process, whereas the current increase in temperature is merely the reverse of this trend. However, most scientists now recognize the current rate of temperature increase to be beyond the normal range and ascribe the increase to human factors rather than to natural causes.

Supporters of the global-warming theory would argue that it has been the pollution produced by domestic, agricultural and industrial activities that has caused major changes to the atmosphere. They state that unless action is taken to reduce the release of the greenhouse gases then further warming of the atmosphere will occur.

To combat the threat of global warming an agreement, known as the Montreal Protocol, was reached by representatives of the main industrialized nations meeting in Montreal, Canada, in 1987. Under the terms of the Protocol, the use of CFCs was to be halved by 1998 and the use of halon – halogenated aliphatic hydrocarbons used in fire fighting – was to be at 1986 levels by 1992. However, by July 1990, scientific evidence had shown these targets to be insufficient to stem global warming, and an agreement was reached between the developing nations and the developed world to achieve a 50% reduction in the use of CFCs by 1995, an 85% cut by 1997 and a total ban in the developed world by 2000. The target for a total ban in the developing world is 2010. Halons will also be banned by 2000. Many nations wanted an even faster phasing out of these substances, but the USA, Japan and the (then) USSR claimed that it would be impossible to meet earlier targets. A fund of $240 million has been set up to help the economies of developing countries adapt to the ban on these substances.

THE IMPACT OF GLOBAL WARMING
It is thought that the impact of global warming on the planet would be unevenly distributed. The southern hemisphere, with its extensive oceans, would suffer less increase in temperature, as the seas would be able to absorb more heat than the land masses of the northern hemisphere. The Arctic region may become, on average, 8°C (13.4°F) warmer than at present by 2100. As a result, some of the polar ice sheet would melt, causing a rise in sea levels of 20–30 cm (8–12 in) by the middle of the 21st century, with predictions of a 60–100 cm (24–40 in) rise by 2100. This would threaten many low-lying areas with inundation, including the island nations of Kiribati, Tuvalu and the Maldives, as well as much of Bangladesh and parts of some important cities including New York, London, St Petersburg, Alexandria, Rotterdam and Venice.

CLIMATIC CHANGE
Profound climatic changes could also result. According to some meteorologists, the climatic belts of the northern hemisphere would be likely to move north, bringing a desert climate to the Mediterranean region and to California, Texas and Florida, and a Mediterranean-type climate to much of northwestern Europe. Storminess could also increase and rainfall totals could rise by as much as 15%, particularly in the high latitudes.

THE OZONE LAYER

The ozone layer is a naturally occurring zone found in the stratosphere, situated between 10–15 km (6–9 mi) above the Earth's surface. Ozone (O_3) is a natural component of the atmosphere. It is classified as a trace gas with a concentration of about 0.2 parts per billion (p.p.b.). A highly reactive and unstable gas, it is formed by the recombination of pairs of oxygen (O_2) atoms in the presence of intense solar radiation (mainly ultraviolet energy).

The most important function of the stratospheric ozone layer is to act as a shield against ultraviolet (UV) radiation from the Sun. In 1984, the British Antarctic Survey reported a thinning of the ozone layer over the South Pole. This depletion of ozone has been incorrectly called the *ozone hole*. It is not a hole – only a thinning of the ozone layer.

The depletion is caused by certain highly stable synthetic chemicals, which are the product of the petrochemical industry. These include chlorofluorocarbons (CFCs) used as propellants in aerosol spray cans, as refrigerant gases, solvent cleaners and in the manufacture of foam-blown plastics, and halons, used in fire-fighting equipment. These gases rise into the atmosphere, where they become partly decomposed into methyl chloroform and carbon tetrachloride. These gases become concentrated above the polar areas in the stratosphere and actively destroy the ozone molecules, thus allowing increased levels of ultraviolet light to reach the ground.

Exposure to UV light causes damage to crops, kills plankton and fish larvae, and can cause burning of the skin (sunburn) in humans. Severe sunburn produces temporary soreness, dehydration and sickness. In the longer term it can result in skin cancers, and is estimated to cause 100 000 additional eye cataracts worldwide. Epidemiologists in many hospitals in northern Europe have recorded a doubling in the incidence of skin cancers in recent years, while in Australia, doctors have claimed that a 1% decrease in the ozone layer results in a 3% increase in non-melanoma skin cancers in humans.

As a result of the Montreal Protocol (see above), CFCs and halons will be phased out by the year 2000, but so many CFCs already exist in the atmosphere that the concentration will continue to rise to 6 p.p.b. by 2000 before declining.

PHOTO-CHEMICAL SMOG
A second, and quite separate, environmental problem associated with ozone is the build-up of ground-level ozone to produce photo-chemical smog. This

hazard – first recorded in Los Angeles, California – now occurs worldwide in industrial cities. The amount of ground level ozone has doubled over Europe this century. A combination of oxides of nitrogen and volatile organic compounds in the presence of sunlight cause the formation of ground level ozone. These substances are almost entirely the result of human activity, for example motor-vehicle exhausts, and the chemical paint and ceramics industries.

The problem becomes most serious in summer, when stationary air masses allow the build-up of high concentrations of oxides of nitrogen and volatile organic compounds. The World Health Organization has set a safety limit of 120 p.p.b., though this figure is regularly exceeded and has reached a peak of 600 p.p.b. in California. (In Britain a maximum of 250 p.p.b. was reached in southern England in 1976.) Concentrations of 300 p.p.b. are sufficient to cause irritation to respiratory tissue and the eyes of humans, while even lower concentrations severely damage citrus fruits. It is estimated that agricultural output in Europe and North America is 5–10% lower than expected due to exposure to ozone.

The problem of oxides of nitrogen and volatile organic compounds is a serious one, but it is at present overshadowed by the international concern with the depletion of the ozone layer.

DROUGHT AND DESERTIFICATION

Nearly half the countries of the world face problems of drought. A drought occurs when an area of land does not receive enough water to sustain life at the existing levels. Droughts may be due to lower than normal amounts of precipitation, to higher evaporation as a result of warmer temperatures than normal, or to a combination of these two factors.

Drought years appear to occur in cycles. From records of the Nile floods over the last 2000 years, a cycle of varying length is apparent. In the well-known Biblical story, the pharaoh of Egypt dreamed of seven ears of grain, fat and healthy, followed by seven ears of shrivelled and thin grain. This symbolized a cycle of seven damp years followed by seven years of drought. In recent decades, the years between 1968–73 were drought years, from 1973 until 1979 adequate moisture occurred, while in 1980 another cycle of drought began.

Between 1982 and 1986 much of Africa was devastated by severe drought, which resulted in widespread human deprivation. Some 10 million people were forced to leave their homes in search of food and water. China, India and North America all suffered major droughts in the 1980s. In the summer of 1988 about 43% of the central states of the USA suffered a drought of intensity equal to that of the 'Dust Bowl' years 1926–34. The grain harvest in 1988 was 31% down on that of the previous year and financial losses reached $15 billion, making the drought the costliest natural disaster in US history.

The occurrence of major droughts appears to be linked to weather changes which affect up to 66% of the globe. Changes in atmospheric pressure-patterns combine at irregular intervals of between two and seven years to produce modifications to the flow of ocean currents in the southern hemisphere. The Pacific Ocean heats up between Papua New Guinea and Micronesia, resulting in the easterly flow of a powerful warm ocean current called El Niño ('the boy child'). It combines with other climatic changes over the southeastern Pacific to bring about the irregularity in ocean currents called the Southern Oscillation, which causes major weather disturbances lasting up to two years. On these occasions, serious droughts have occurred in India, Australia, Africa and Indonesia.

Prolonged drought in much of Western Europe in 1989–90 increased awareness of the need for proper water management. The options most frequently proposed are summarized below.

WATER MANAGEMENT APPROACHES

Input Approaches

Increase the usable supply by:

1. Building dams and creating lake reservoirs.
2. Diverting water from one region to another; draining swamps; and diverting rivers.
3. Tapping ground water.
4. Desalting seawater and purifying degraded water.
5. Towing icebergs from the Antarctic.
6. 'Controlling' the weather, for example by seeding clouds.

Control the pollution of existing supplies by preventing or limiting the addition of certain chemicals.

Redistribute population by:

1. Encouraging people to live in areas with adequate water.
2. Restricting population levels in areas with water problems (deserts or flood plains).

Decrease population growth.

Output Approaches

Decrease evaporation and plant transpiration.

Use better drainage for irrigated agriculture to minimize the salt build-up in soils.

Treat polluted waters before returning them to their sources.

Dispose of wastes by burial on land or sea or by injection into deep wells.

Reclaim waste water to allow multiple re-use.

Minimize wasteful and extravagant uses of water, and redesign industrial and other processes to use less water.

DESERTIFICATION

About 35% of the planet is classified as arid or semi-arid. True deserts – which have less than 250 mm (about 10 in) of rain a year – can be divided into cold deserts near the Earth's poles and hot deserts between about 20° and 30° latitude north and south of the Equator. Hot deserts cover about 20% of the land between the Tropics. Semi-arid areas receive up to 500 mm (about 20 in) a year.

ESTIMATE OF WORLD WATER REQUIREMENTS BY AD 2000

Human consumption of water has increased 35 times in the last 300 years. The rate of consumption is increasing by some 4–8% p.a. The figures in the following table are given in cubic kilometres.

Water Use	Total required	Amount returned as waste (%)	Amount required by 2000 (% increase)
Agricultural	2236	559 (25%)	2261 (19%)
Domestic	259	155 (60%)	
Industry	745	640 (86%)	1000 (34%)

Arid and semi-arid areas are increasing by about 6 million ha (over 23 000 sq mi) a year owing to a variety of reasons. Overgrazing by stock and the cultivation of poor soil are the principal causes. Poor water management (resulting in erosion, salinization and waterlogging), the cultivation of steeply sloping sites and changes in land use – particularly deforestation and strip mining – have also been important contributory factors. The process by which productive areas degenerate into land with up to 50% less productivity is called *desertification*, a term coined to describe the deterioration of land in the Sahel (see p. 94).

NATIONAL RIVERS AUTHORITY RIVER AND CANAL WATER CLASSIFICATION

Class		Current Potential Use
1A	Good	Water of high quality suitable for potable supply and with high amenity value
1B		Of lower quality than 1A but usable for substantially the same purposes
2	Fair	Waters suitable for potable supply after advanced treatment. Medium amenity quality
3	Poor	Waters polluted to an extent that fish are absent. Usable for low-grade industrial abstraction. Of considerable use if cleaned up
4	Bad	Grossly polluted waters which cause nuisance value

AVERAGE DAILY USE OF WATER IN THE UNITED STATES (litres)

Direct personal use		Indirect agricultural use		Indirect industrial use	
Shower (5 minutes)	100	One egg	150	Cooling water for electric power plants (per person per day)	2 700
Shaving/washing hands	14	One ear of corn	300		
Washing clothes	75	One loaf of bread	570		
Cooking	30	One kilo of flour	625	Sunday paper	1 060
Washing dishes	38	One kilo of beef	20 800	One kilo synthetic rubber	2 500
Toilet (4 flushes)	48			One kilo aluminium	8 340
House cleaning	30			One kilo steel	300
Sprinkling lawn (800 m²)	300			One litre petrol	7–25
				One motor car	380 000
Daily average: 635 litres		Daily average: 2 300 litres		Daily average: 4 000 litres	

Total daily average: 6 935 litres per person

COMMON DISEASES TRANSMITTED TO HUMANS THROUGH CONTAMINATED DRINKING WATER

Type of Organism	Disease	Effects
Bacteria	Typhoid fever	Diarrhoea, severe vomiting, enlarged spleen, inflamed intestine, often fatal if untreated
	Cholera	Diarrhoea, severe vomiting, dehydration; often fatal if untreated
	Bacterial dysentery	Diarrhoea; rarely fatal except in infants without proper treatment
	Enteritis	Severe stomach pain, nausea, vomiting; rarely fatal
Viruses	Infectious hepatitis	Fever, severe headache, loss of appetite, abdominal pain, jaundice, enlarged liver; rarely fatal but may cause permanent liver damage
	Polio	High fever, severe headache, sore throat, stiff neck, deep muscle pain, severe weakness, tremors, paralysis in legs, arms, and body; can be fatal
Parasitic protozoa	Amoebic dysentery	Severe diarrhoea, headache, abdominal pain, chills, fever, if not treated can cause liver abscess, bowel perforation, and death
	Giardia	Diarrhoea, abdominal cramps, flatulence, belching, fatigue
Parasitic worms	Schistosomiasis	Abdominal pain, skin rash, anaemia, chronic fatigue, and chronic general ill health

CHEMICAL CONTAMINANTS IN DRINKING WATER AND RELATED HEALTH HAZARDS

Contaminant	Effects
Inorganic Material	
Arsenic	Cancer of the liver, kidneys and blood, and nervous system damage
Cadmium	Kidney damage, anaemia, high blood pressure
Lead	Headaches, anaemia, nervous disorders, birth abnormalities, mental retardation especially in children
Mercury	Damage to central nervous system and kidneys
Nitrates	Respiratory problems particularly to the new born and chronically sick
Synthetic Organic Substances	
Benzine	Anaemia, leukemia, chromosome damage
Carbon tetrachloride	Cancer of the liver, kidney and lung. Damage to the central nervous system
Dionysian	Skin disorders, cancer and genetic malfunction
Ethylene	Cancer and male sterility
PCBs	Liver, kidney and lung damage

LAND POLLUTION

Since earliest times humans have been responsible for polluting the planet. As the population grew and industrial growth became greater, then so too did the amount and complexity of pollution.

Many old industrial areas bear the scars of extractive industries (coal mining, brick works, china clay quarries).

Land left standing without a present use as a result of past activity and which has been physically despoiled or disfigured is called *derelict land*. Often, in the past, lower standards of pollution control were exercised. Formal land-use planning was largely unknown in Europe and North America until 1945, and industrial land use was intermingled with residential and agricultural landscapes. As a result many degraded landscapes could be found, especially in old industrial areas.

Nowadays, derelict sites have become the focal point of rehabilitation projects in which wastes are made safe by burial or by detoxification, and the land reused for a totally new purpose. Governments of the developed world now recognize that the rehabilitation of polluted land areas requires a completely integrated approach. It involves preventing further pollution at source, minimizing the risk of harm to human health, applying the most appropriate and technologically advanced solutions to restoring degraded areas, and managing them by means of sustainable land-use policies.

The principle of *integrated pollution control*, in which air, water and land pollution become the total responsibility of one environmental management body, has been adopted in many developed countries.

WASTE DISPOSAL

A major problem facing developed countries throughout the world is the disposal of domestic and industrial rubbish. In the UK, industry produces about 100 million tonnes of waste each year, of which about 27 million tonnes are recycled and valued at over £2 billion. British domestic sources produce a further 20 million tonnes, of which only 1 million tonnes is recycled. Modern waste contains a high proportion of non-degradable products – plastics, metals and chemicals. These items can cause long-term contamination if disposed of incorrectly.

Packaging and packaging waste presents a special problem. In the EC, some 50 million tonnes of package waste was generated in 1991, of which only 19% was recycled. By 2002, EC regulations will ensure that 60% of packaging materials must be made from recycled materials, and 90% of all packaging waste must be recycled.

Traditionally, rubbish has been burned, dumped into disused quarries, or dumped at sea. None of these methods is wholly acceptable today. Burning can generate highly toxic gases, few old quarries remain to be filled in, and dumping at sea has created major pollution of bathing waters.

National and local authorities in many countries are encouraging the recycling of materials, the prevention of waste and the conservation of new resources. Waste minimization is being achieved by better design, longer design life and improved potential for re-use. The public is also becoming more educated in environmental issues.

WATER POLLUTION

Rivers and seas have been used for the dumping of wastes since earliest times. The constant flow of rivers and the tidal movements of seas have been used as a natural sink to disperse all forms of wastes.

Clean, fresh water is vital for the very survival of the human species. The assessment of water quality depends upon its intended use. Some of the main forms of pollution are:

1. Disease-carrying agents (bacteria, viruses, parasitic worms). These kill an estimated 25 000 people each day, mainly in the less developed countries.
2. Sediment and suspended matter (soil, silt and partially treated sewage).
3. Radioactive substances (from the nuclear power industry).
4. Organic chemicals (oil, plastics, pesticides, cleaning solvents, detergents).
5. Inorganic plant nutrients (nitrates and phosphates washed from agricultural land).
6. Waste heat (in the form of cooling water from power stations and industry).

RIVER POLLUTION

Rivers can normally dilute small amounts of pollution quickly and safely. When overloaded with pollutants, or when the volume of water is reduced during summer drought, dilution becomes impossible and pollution occurs.

In Britain, the National Rivers Authority is responsible for the prevention of water pollution. It uses a five-point classification scheme to monitor pollution (see the accompanying table). Even slightly polluted water is damaging for human health, especially so if consumed over a long time span (see the accompanying table).

Because of the health risk, most developed countries have comprehensive laws and regulations concerning water quality. Fines are imposed on persons or industries found guilty of polluting water courses. Much pollution occurs accidentally from leaching of nitrates, phosphates and pesticides from agricultural land, or from leaks in underground storage tanks (petrol and oil).

In less developed countries and in Eastern Europe most rivers are severely polluted. Over 66% of India's rivers are polluted and 90% of child deaths are attributable to water-borne disease. In Poland, almost 50% of the nation's water is unfit even for industrial use – 90% of Poland's river water is too polluted to drink and it has been forecast that by the year 2000 this figure will be 100%.

POLLUTION OF THE SEAS

The oceans receive not only pollution carried in by rivers, but also direct inputs of sewage, oil spills from tankers and offshore drilling platforms, and industrial waste deliberately dumped at sea. During the 1980s ocean dumping around the world amounted to more than 172 million tonnes of solid waste each year. About 80% of this was dredged materials, taken from rivers to maintain shipping channels. EC legislation will ban the dumping of this material into European waters by 1995.

About 20% of the solid waste dumped at sea is sewage sludge, a lethal mixture of toxic chemicals, infectious materials and settled solids from sewage treatment plants. In Britain, 16% of the sewage output is still discharged, untreated, to the sea. In Europe, as a whole, 28% of all sewage is still released in its untreated form to rivers and seas. Bathing beaches have become seriously contaminated and may be unsafe to use.

The EC 'Blue Flag' Campaign is awarded annually to beaches and ports that attain a high standard of environmental quality and also provide beach amenities, environmental education and information. New stricter standards were introduced in 1992 resulting in only 17 British beaches gaining the Blue Flag – compared to 35 in 1991. Water samples must contain fewer than 100 faecal coliforms/100 ml of water compared with the 2000 previously permitted.

An estimated 2 million sea birds and over 100 000 marine mammals die each year by poisoning or by becoming entangled in plastic netting.

Prevention of water pollution as well as cleaning up past pollution will be expensive. Britain will spend £13·7 billion between 1989 and 1992 on new sewage plants. The United Nations has calculated that it would cost $5 bn to provide treatment plants for Mediterranean sewage output. In the USA, greater use of technology is seen as the way to reduce water pollution. This method is called MACT (Maximum Available Control Technology). Many ecologists believe that reliance on this approach, the so-called 'technological fix', will become too expensive and has no guarantee of success. As an alternative, low cost treatment methods have been developed for use in developing countries. These include filtering sewage through marshes and land fill sites and, in Calcutta, settled sewage is used as a feedstock for fish (mainly carp) which can be used as a source of human food.

NUCLEAR DUMPING AT SEA

Between 1946 and 1982, 46 petabecquerels of dumped, packaged and liquid nuclear waste was dumped in more than 50 sites, mainly in the northern Atlantic and Pacific Oceans. Most waste came from civil and military power stations and reprocessing plants. In the 1980s, a moratorium on dumping nuclear wastes at sea was established by trade unions and by diplomatic concern.

AIR POLLUTION

Any particulate matter or gaseous material which accumulates in the atmosphere to such proportions that it causes harm to humans, other animals, vegetation, or damage to building materials can be described as an air pollutant. Nowadays, air pollution is primarily the result of human activity, but it is often overlooked that natural sources of air pollution can sometimes exceed the quantity of human-produced pollutants. In June 1991, Mount Pinatubo in the Philippines emitted about 18 million tonnes of SO_2 into the atmosphere, equivalent to all the SO_2 produced in the US in one year.

Pollutants from human activity have attracted notoriety because of their chemical complexity, their reactivity once released to the atmosphere and their interaction with all other living components of the biosphere.

Particulate matter (comprising smoke, soot, dust and liquid droplets) is normally considered to be the simpler form of air pollution as it can be removed from the atmosphere more easily than gaseous material. All particulate matter, even the finest aerosols, have a mass greater than air, and thus in still air will gravitate out of the atmosphere. Large particles, over 10 micrometers in size, normally fall out of the atmosphere within 5 or 6 hours of their release from source. The finest particles, smaller than 1 micrometer, can remain in the air for several months, or even years. They are also the most damaging as they can enter the lungs of animals and cause illness. Soot, rubber and tarmac particles are known to be carcinogenic to human lung tissue. Vegetation surfaces can become coated with fine dusts, thus reducing their ability to photosynthesize.

Gaseous pollution (comprising mainly SO_2, nitrogen dioxides and carbon dioxide) presents a major problem for modern societies and exacts enormous health and environmental costs. Gases are usually invisible but once released can be transported hundreds of kilometres and react with many other atmospheric components to produce secondary pollutants. It is these products rather than the primary pollutants that are usually responsible for vegetation damage and respiratory illness in humans.

So severe is the damage caused by air pollution that stringent legislation has been introduced by many governments, particularly in the developed world. Overall, urban air quality has improved during the 1980s, especially for the traditional pollutants such as sulfur dioxide (SO_2) which has fallen by up to 64% throughout Europe and North America. The UN estimated in 1987 that 70% of the world's population lived in cities where the level of suspended particles exceeded the World Health Organization guidelines, and 66% of the world's urban population are subjected to SO_2 levels above WHO guidelines.

New air pollutants are continually emerging, and for these emission-control measures must be found. For example, the increasing use of unleaded petrol, while resulting in a reduction of air-borne lead of up to 50%, has been accompanied by an increase in the amount of benzine added to petrol. The levels of benzine accumulating in the atmosphere have increased with an alarming rapidity, especially as it is a greater hazard to the atmosphere than CFCs.

ACID PRECIPITATION

Both 'wet' and 'dry' forms of acidic fallout can occur as a result of the combustion of large quantities of fossil fuels. Coal-fired power stations and other industrial processes emit sulfur dioxide and nitrogen oxides, which, when combined with atmospheric moisture, create *acid precipitation* (dilute sulfuric acid or nitric acid). Acid rain (or snow) is the main atmospheric fallout of industrial pollutants, although these may also occur as dry deposits (such as ash). Acid rain damages forests, plants and agriculture, raises the acid level in lakes and ground water, killing fish and other water-bound life, and contaminating drinking water.

Temperate forests have been seriously damaged by acid rain. The Black Forest in Germany has been steadily losing its trees through *Waldsterben* ('tree death'). The problem is also very acute in the north of Bohemia (Czech Republic). But Britain has the highest percentage of damaged trees in Europe – 67%. In Europe, it has been estimated that in 1987 the value of the timber harvest was reduced by 82 million cubic metres, worth $23 bn. In southern Norway 80% of the lakes are devoid of fish life, and Sweden has 20 000 acidified lakes. Acid rain upsets the fine

chemical balance in lakes that are home to numerous species of fish. Salmon, roach and trout are very sensitive to pH (i.e. acid) levels in their habitat. Even a slight dip in pH levels causes heavy metals such as aluminium, mercury, lead, zinc and cadmium to become more concentrated, decreasing the amount of oxygen the fish can absorb and eventually causing their death. The absence of large fish destabilizes the ecosystem and the effects are felt throughout the food chain. The ecosystem is seriously depleted, and only some smaller creatures, such as water beetles, seem able to survive.

Acid rain also causes damage to the soil. High levels of acid rain in the soil cause lead and other heavy metals to become concentrated and interrupt the life-cycles of microorganisms. The bacteria and fungi that help break down organic matter into nutrients are disturbed and soils can lose their ability to support forests or agriculture.

Not only ecosystems are damaged by acid precipitation. Corrosion of metal and rapid weathering of building materials has become a serious problem for the older buildings of Europe. Cathedrals and castles are suffering substantial damage. There is increasing evidence to suggest that acid aerosols may enter the respiratory system of human beings and animals, causing an intensification of respiratory illnesses such as bronchitis and asthma.

There are various methods of reducing the amount of pollutants reaching the atmosphere, such as lead-free petrol, catalytic converters attached to car exhausts (which destroy some of the harmful gases), and filter systems that reduce dangerous emissions from power stations and industry.

A CLASSIFICATION OF AIR POLLUTION TYPES

Particulate Matter		Gaseous Pollution	
Human derived	*Naturally derived*	*Human derived*	*Naturally derived*
smoke	volcanic dust	Gases from	Volcanic gases and
ash	smoke + ash	combustion	water vapour
grit	sea-salt particles	SO_2	
soot		CO_2	Gases from organic
dust		H_2S	decomposition
liquid droplets		NO_X	
(acid deposition)		HF	
particles of tarmac		PANs	
and rubber		CH_4	

COMPARISONS OF SOURCES OF SELECTED POLLUTANTS, EMISSIONS AND EXPOSURES

Pollutant	Major Emission Sources	Major Exposure Sources
Benzine	Industry; automobiles	Smoking
Tetrachloroethylene	Dry-cleaning shops	Dry-cleaned clothes
Chloroform	Sewage treatment plants	Showers
p-Dichlorobenzene	Chemical manufacturing	Air deodorizers
Particulates	Industry; automobiles; home heating	Smoking
Carbon monoxide	Automobiles	Driving; gas stoves
Nitrogen dioxide	Industry; automobiles	Gas stoves

DEFORESTATION

The tropical rain forests cover over 30 000 000 km² (12 000 000 sq mi), that is over 20% of the Earth's land surface. The vast sea of green leaves of these forests play a vital role in the climatic regime of the Earth. Chlorophylls in leaves drive the chemical reaction *photosynthesis* in which carbon dioxide enters the leaves through microscopic pores to be converted into sugar glucose. At the end of the reaction, oxygen is released by leaves. In this way the tropical rain forests provide much of the oxygen upon which we rely for life itself, and the destruction of considerable areas of these forests for logging and farming is of considerable concern.

In photsynthesis, quantities of carbon dioxide are used up. Thus, in a situation where plants and animals live together, the ratio is maintained in the existing levels of oxygen and carbon dioxide. This fine balance is in danger of being upset by the felling and burning of large areas of tropical forest. The imbalance caused through the increased emission of carbon dioxide that would result from the destruction of much of the rain forest through clearing and burning would gradually increase the amount of greenhouse gases in the atmosphere and could produce global warming.

An immense amount of water is held in the ecosystem of the tropical forests, which are both a result and a determinant of climate. The destruction of the forest not only increases erosion and the rate of runoff but also greatly reduces the humidity and, in turn, the precipitation of the area. Erosion is a major problem. Equatorial soils tend to be poor and lateritic. The forest cover affords them some protection, but, once cleared, the earth is exposed to severe erosion and leaching. The new farmland created by deforestation can support agriculture for only a couple of years. It is exhausted quickly and the topsoil is soon washed away. This is dramatically illustrated in Madagascar where the greater part of the tropical rain forest has been cleared for farming. Gullying has occurred within two or three years as deep-sided small valleys have been carved out and the soil has been eroded.

The rain forests are the 'lungs' of the planet. Once the rich and varied forests of the tropics covered virtually all of the Amazon Basin of South America, the West African coasts, the basin of the River Zaïre and its tributaries in central Africa, the islands of Indonesia and most of Malaysia and Papua New Guinea. Now, because of agricultural and other human pressure upon the land, vast swathes of equatorial forest have been cleared. Clearing and burning is destroying a resource that cannot be replaced. Between 1964 and 1984 some 13 100 000 km² (505 790 sq mi) of forest and woodland were destroyed worldwide – that is an area larger than Canada and Alaska combined. In some countries deforestation has been especially drastic. In Côte d'Ivoire, for example, 80% of the rain forest was destroyed between 1960 and 1990.

Brazil is gradually invading its great natural reserve, the Amazonian rain forest. In most years in the 1980s and early 1990s an area the size of Belgium was cleared and burned in the Amazon basin to create new pastures or farming land, or to allow for the construction of HEP dams. In Southeast Asia too there is much pressure on the rain forests, but Thailand, which has seen very considerable reduction of its forests, has banned logging altogether and both Indonesia nd the Philippines have enacted legal restrictions on the amount of timber that can be taken. Deforestation has been most evident in Malaysia where the extent of forest had decreased from nearly 320 000 km² (125 000 sq mi) in 1900 to 70 000 km² (27 000 sq mi) by 1992.

GLOSSARIES

CLIMATOLOGY AND METEOROLOGY GLOSSARY

adiabatic lapse rate   the rate at which air cools because of expansion when rising into regions of lower atmospheric pressure: 1° C per 100 m (5·4° F per 1000 ft) in clear air, less in cloud. Similar rates apply when air subsides into higher pressure and warms.

advection fog   fog that forms when air cools to dew point by travelling across a surface that is already colder, such as sea or snow.

air frost   air having a temperature of 0° C (32° F) or less.

air mass   a huge volume of air that has acquired temperature and humidity characteristics from its region of origin.

anabatic wind   an upslope wind created when air rises from a warming hillside and is replaced by cooler air from the valley.

anemometer   an instrument for measuring wind speed.

anticyclone   an area of high pressure, having a clockwise wind circulation in the northern hemisphere (anticlockwise in the southern).

aurora   spectacular displays of light, mostly seen in latitudes higher than 70°. Caused by electrical solar discharges, they sometimes appear like waving curtains.

atmospheric pressure   pressure due to the weight of the atmosphere. The pressure is less at higher altitudes than at sea level.

backing   a change of wind direction in an anticlockwise manner, e.g. from W back to SW.

ball lightning   a spherical glowing ball of electrically charged air.

banner cloud   a cloud that streams downwind from a mountain peak, formed in the rising eddy behind the peak.

barometer   an instrument for measuring atmospheric pressure.

barograph   a barometer connected to a pen and rotating drum, so as to make a trace of changing pressure on a chart.

Beaufort scale   numerals indicating the force and speed of the wind (see p. 104).

Berg wind   a hot, dry wind from the interior of South Africa, blowing down the mountains and offshore.

black ice a transparent film of ice, taking the colour of the surface (e.g. a road) on which it forms.

blizzard a strong wind carrying falling snow. It gives bad visibility and causes drifting.

blood rain rain coloured with dust particles carried on upper winds; in Europe often reddish-brown with dust from the Sahara.

blue moon the moon appears blue when excessive dust in the atmosphere (e.g. after a volcanic eruption) scatters more red light than blue.

Bora a cold, usually dry, NE wind blowing from the mountains in Slovenia, Croatia and NE Italy.

Brickfielder a very hot NE wind in SE Australia. It blows in summer, carrying dust and sand.

brockenspectre the magnified shadow of an observer cast on to cloud or fog from high ground.

buoyancy an air current is buoyant if it is warmer and therefore lighter than its surroundings.

Buys Ballot's law a convention used to locate areas of low pressure. When an observer has his back to the wind, low pressure is on the left hand in the northern hemisphere and on the right hand in the southern.

Buran a strong NE wind in Russia and Central Asia, most frequent in winter. Known as Purga when carrying snow.

calm conditions in which there is no perceptible movement of air.

cap cloud a cloud that sits above the summit of high ground, apparently stationary but in reality constantly forming on the windward edge and dispersing to leeward.

castellanus a cloud with a 'turretted' appearance, taller than it is wide. It often occurs at medium level, giving thunderstorms.

Celsius scale of temperature the temperature scale on which 0° C denotes freezing level and 100° C the boiling point of water. It is sometimes called Centigrade. See conversion tables p. 126.

Chinook a warm and dry wind that blows down the eastern side of the Rocky Mountains, USA.

climate a distinct pattern of weather found in a particular geographical zone (see p. 101).

cloud water drops or ice crytals held in suspension above the ground (see p. 101).

cloudburst a very heavy but shortlived downpour of rain.

col an area of light variable wind, between two anticyclones and two depressions.

condensation the change of state of water vapour (an invisible gas) into water drops.

conduction the transference of heat from one substance to another substance with which it is in contact. The transfer is always from the warmer surface to the colder.

contrail short for 'condensation trail'. A contrail is produced by an aircraft flying at heights above about 6000 m (20 000 ft). It may be persistent if the atmosphere is already moist.

convection the transmission of heat by movement of fluid particles, like air or water. Air which warms near the ground becomes less dense and rises, and cold air takes its place, to warm in turn.

convection rain rain that falls from convection (cumulus) clouds.

cyclone a (roughly circular) pressure pattern in which pressure is lower at the centre than on the periphery. Wind circulation around the centre is anticlockwise in the northern hemisphere and clockwise in the southern. The name 'cyclone' is more specifically used for intense storms in the Indian Ocean, Arabian Sea and Bay of Bengal. Cyclones in middle and high latitudes are called depressions or lows.

deepening a low-pressure circulation is said to deepen if the atmospheric pressure at its centre continues to fall.

depression a low-pressure circulation in middle or high latitudes. See cyclone.

deposition the change of vapour directly to ice crystals when air becomes saturated and dew point is below 0° C (32° F). Hoar frost results.

dew water drops condensed directly from air when the air temperature falls below a dew point that is warmer than 0° C (32° F).

dew point the temperature at which air becomes saturated, holding the maximum amount of vapour possible. Further cooling results in condensation.

desert an area in which rainfall is insufficient to support vegetation.

diffraction the bending of light rays around particles or water drops having the same diameter as the wavelength of light.

doldrums a belt of light variable winds near the Equator, outside the range of the trade winds. They give frequent rain storms and squalls.

drizzle precipitation consisting of very small water drops, less than 0·5 mm (0·02 in) diameter.

drought a long period of dry weather.

equatorial climate the tropical rainy climate experienced in a belt on and on either side of the Equator.

evaporation the change of state of water into invisible vapour.

eye of the storm the centre of a hurricane or cyclone. It is characterized by well-broken cloud, no rain, light wind, and wild seas.

false cirrus ice-crystal cloud at the top of a cumulonimbus cloud, which is drawn along by the wind into the shape of an anvil.

Fata Morgana a complicated mirage. It usually occurs over water, and is most frequently seen over the Strait of Messina, Italy.

Fahrenheit scale of temperature the scale of temperature in which 32° F denotes freezing level and 212° F the boiling point of water. See conversion tables p. 126.

filling a depression is said to fill when the pressure at its centre starts to rise.

flaschenblitz an unusual form of lightning that strikes upwards from the top of a cumulonimbus.

fog a layer of very small waterdrops forming upwards from the surface of the sea or ground and restricting visibility. See also advection fog, radiation fog.

fog bow a bow formed – in the same way as a rainbow – when the Sun shines on to smaller fog drops. The coloured rays overlap to form a white bow with only the faintest tinge of colour.

Föhn wind a dry, warm wind blowing down a mountain under certain conditions, and warming by compression on descent.

freezing rain rain which falls into air whose temperature is below freezing, and then freezes to ice. Also called glazed frost.

freezing the change of state of water into ice, starting at a temperature of 0° C (32° F).

front the surface boundary between air masses of different temperature and humidity, which confront each other from different directions.

frost see air frost, hoar frost.

funnel cloud a whirling, tapering cloud that descends from the main base of a storm cloud.

gale a wind in excess of force 7 on the Beaufort Scale.

geostrophic wind a wind that blows horizontally, because of pressure differences, parallel to the isobars and according to Buys Ballot's Law.

glaciation (in meteorology) the sudden change of supercooled water drops into ice crystals within a cloud.

glazed frost the coating of ice over subfreezing surfaces from freezing rain.

graupel soft, partly melted hail.

glory a ring of light, like a corona, seen around a brockenspectre.

greenhouse effect the accumulation of heat in a greenhouse because glass is more transparent to incoming solar radiation than it is to outgoing radiation from the surface beneath the glass. In the atmosphere, carbon dioxide and various other gases perform the same function as glass, trapping heat near the Earth. See p.106.

Gregale a strong NE wind blowing in the Mediterranean in the cooler months of the year.

gust a momentary increase in wind speed.

haboob any wind strong enough to raise sand into a sand storm, particularly in the Sudan.

hail ice pellets, created in strong vertical currents within cumulonimbus. Snow flakes or water drops are tossed up and down, alternately freezing and melting, until they are heavy enough to fall to the ground.

halo a ring of light around the Sun or Moon, caused by the refraction of light through ice-crystal cloud. A halo is reddish on the inside, bluish on the outside – the reverse order of corona colours.

Harmattan a dry and cool wind, blowing from the E or NE across NW Africa. It is often dust-laden and dry enough to wither vegetation.

hectopascal a unit of pressure – the equivalent to 1 millibar of pressure.

helm wind a strong, cold, often violent wind from the NE blowing down western slopes of Cumbria (England), mainly in late winter and spring.

high an area of high pressure or anticyclone. It brings fine weather in summer, but often frost or fog in winter. Winds blow clockwise in the northern hemisphere, anticlockwise in the southern.

hill fog low cloud covering high ground.

hoar frost the deposition of ice crystals directly out of the air when dew point is at or below 0° C (32° F) and the air is saturated with vapour.

humidity See relative humidity.

hurricane an intense low-pressure storm, affecting the West Indies and Gulf of Mexico. Similar storms in the Pacific are called typhoons. Circular winds around the centre follow Buys Ballot's Law and attain wind speeds in excess of 119 km/hr (64 knots or 74 mph).

hygrometer an instrument used for measuring the humidity of air.

inversion of temperature the conditions in which temperature increases with height in the atmosphere. This is a reverse of the normal situation in which temperature decreases with height.

isobar a line on a map joining places having equal atmospheric pressure (corrected to mean sea level) at a particular time.

isohyet a line on a map joining places having equal rainfall over a given period.

isotherm a line on a map joining places having equal temperature at the same time.

jet stream a strong but narrow belt of wind near the tropopause, blowing from west to east.

Karaburan a hot dusty NE wind in central Asia.

katabatic wind a downslope wind, created on otherwise calm nights with no cloud. The air nearest to the slope cools and flows downhill, to be replaced by warmer air from above the valley.

Khamsin a hot oppressive wind over Eygpt in early summer, often laden with desert sand.

knot a unit of speed used by sailors and aviators who have no fixed points of reference with which to measure distance against time. One knot denotes a speed of one nautical mile per hour – a nautical mile is the length of a minute of latitude, standardized as 1852 m (6080 ft).

land breeze a wind blowing during the night from cooling land onto warmer sea.

latent heat heat emitted, without a change in temperature, when vapour condenses to water drops or water freezes to ice.

lenticular cloud a cloud shaped like a lens.

leeward the side opposite from the direction of the wind; the sheltered side.

Levanter a moist E wind in the eastern Mediterranean. Often strong, it is most frequent from June to October.

lightning a discharge of an electric field within a cloud, usually cumulonimbus. It may occur within the cloud, from one cloud to another, or between the cloud and the ground.

low the circulation around a centre of low pressure. See cyclone.

lull a momentary fall in wind speed.

mackerel sky a sky featuring cirrocumulus or altocumulus, arranged as a regular pattern resembling the scales of a mackerel.

mare's tails wispy cirrus clouds.

mean sea-level pressure the atmospheric pressure corrected for the height of a barometer above sea level, by adding an imaginary column of air as high as the level at which the barometer is situated.

melting the change of state from ice to water.

microclimate a climate found in a very restricted area such as a valley, garden or even a room.

millibar an international unit by which atmospheric pressure is measured. Recently it was replaced by the hectopascal. 1 millibar (mb) = 1 hectopascal (hPa) where 1000 mb is the pressure exerted by 750·06 mm/29·53 in of mercury at 0° C.

mirage an optical illusion, caused by the bending of light when passing through adjacent layers of air that have different density. An inferior mirage is seen below the real object when light passes through very hot air, shimmering like water because of convection. A superior image is seen above the real object when light bends downwards through very cold dense air.

mist very small water drops suspended in air near the ground, reducing visibilty.

Mistral a cold dry NW or N wind, funnelling down the Rhône Valley before reaching the south coast of France.

monsoon a wind that changes direction markedly according to season, akin to a sea breeze – for example the seasonal winds of south Asia that blow from the SW in summer bringing heavy rainfall. The term 'monsoon' is also applied to the rainy season during which these winds blow.

nacreous clouds clouds having the appearance of mother-of-pearl. They form in the stratosphere, often in mountainous areas, and are seen after sunset.

noctilucent clouds wispy, bluish clouds, resembling cirrus, very high in the atmosphere – usually at an altitude of 80–85 km (50–55 miles). They are probably dust or ice particles.

occlusion the surface boundary between fresh cold air and modified cool air ahead. In effect, it is a cold front that has overtaken a warm front and lifted the warm air off the ground.

orographic rain rain that is caused entirely by forced lifting of moist air over high ground.

Pampero a very cold wind which blows over the Andes across from Argentina and Uruguay to the Atlantic.

parhelion a mock sun, sometimes called a sun dog, caused by refraction of light through ice crystals that have their axes aligned vertically. There may be two parhelia, one either side of the sun and at the same elevation as the sun.

precipitation a composite term that includes rain, drizzle, snow, sleet or hail, all of which fall from clouds.

permafrost that part of the soil which remains permanently frozen in cold climates.

pressure tendency the rate of change of atmospheric pressure. A rapid fall indicates deteriorating weather, a rapid rise indicates a temporary improvement, and a slow persistent rise a developing anticyclone.

prevailing wind the most frequent wind direction to affect a particular area.

Purga a strong NE wind in parts of Russia and Central Asia, often raising snow from the ground to give a blizzard.

radiation fog condensation within a layer of air near the ground that is cooling because of radiation heat loss from the Earth under clear skies. Light wind stirs saturated air into fog.

rain precipitation of water drops larger than 0·5 mm (0·02 in) in diameter.

rainbow a coloured arc of light in the sky, caused by refraction and internal reflection of light in raindrops. A rainbow can only be seen by an observer with his back to the Sun and facing distant rain. A primary rainbow has violet on the inside and red outside; a secondary rainbow, outside the primary, has colours in the reverse order.

rainfall the depth of all forms of precipitation for a given period as measured in a rain gauge.

rain shadow an area where rainfall is reduced because of protection by high ground from the prevailing, rain-bearing wind.

refraction the change of direction of light rays when passing through transparent media (water drops, ice crystals, air) that have different densities.

regelation the refreezing of water that has been temporarily melted because of pressure exerted on it.

relative humidity a measure of the actual vapour in air, as a percentage of the total amount that is required to saturate the air at that temperature.

ridge of high pressure isobars with exaggerated curvature extending from an anticyclone.

rime a crust of ice crystals that forms when supercooled water drops in fog make contact with solid objects whose temperature is less than 0° C (32° F). In calm air, rime builds up all around objects; in a light wind, mainly on the windward side.

Roaring Forties the region between latitudes 40° and 50° S where strong westerly winds prevail.

St Elmo's fire a discharge of static electricity from the masts of ships, wings of aircraft, etc, when the electrical field is strong. It is characterized by a bluish glow, often accompanied by a crackling noise.

scud shreds of low stratus below the main base of cloud. They appear to move very fast because they are so close to the ground.

sea breeze a daytime wind that blows from the sea to the shore, to replace air rising in thermals over the land.

sea fog an advection fog formed when warm air travels and condenses over colder sea.

secondary depression a depression that forms within the circulation of another depression, usually in a trough. It often develops at the expense of the original depression.

Seistan a strong N wind in summer in eastern Iran and Afghanistan, carrying dust and sand.

Shamal a hot, dry, dusty NW wind that blows in summer in Iraq and the Persian Gulf.

shower precipitation from a convection cloud, often heavy but usually short-lived.

Sirocco or **Scirocco** a hot dry S wind on the north coast of Africa, blowing from the Sahara.

sleet a mixture of snow and rain.

snow precipitation of ice crystals, latched together as feathery flakes.

smog (short for 'smoke-fog') fog that is heavily polluted.

Southerly Buster a sudden cold and strong S wind in southeast Australia.

squall a sudden strong wind, lasting only a few minutes. It often comes from a different direction from that which has just been experienced.

stable atmosphere the atmospheric condition in which a rising current of air soon becomes non-buoyant (i.e. colder than its surroundings) and ceases to rise. In such conditions, cumulus clouds remain small or do not form.

surface wind a wind that blows within 10 m (30 ft) of the surface of ground or sea.

sunshine the visible light received from the Sun.

sunshine recorder a glass sphere used to record hours of sunshine. It is mounted so as to focus the rays from the Sun and burn a trace upon a paper chart.

sun pillar a column of light, above or below the sun when it is low on the horizon, caused by reflection of light from the base of big storms. The intense vertical current at the centre is capable of much damage. See also funnel cloud.

trade winds are so named because as a belt of regular winds they were of benefit to sailing trading vessels. They blow on the equatorial side of the sub-tropical high-pressure belts, NE winds in the northern hemisphere, SE winds in the southern.

Tramontana a cool, dry N wind blowing across the Mediterranean coast of Spain.

tropopause the upper boundary of the troposphere.

tropical cyclone an intense low-pressure storm originating over tropical seas. It is called a hurricane in the Atlantic, and a typhoon in the Pacific.

trough of low pressure isobars with exaggerated curvature extending from a depression. It often brings cloud and rain.

turbulence the fluctuation of wind speed and direction. At ground level, turbulence is mainly due to surface friction.

typhoon the name given to a hurricane in the Pacific.

unstable atmosphere atmospheric conditions in which a rising current of air can remain buoyant (i.e. warmer than its surroundings) to great heights. It is characterized by the development of tall cumulonimbus.

veering a change of wind direction in a clockwise manner, e.g. from N to NE.

virga trails of precipitation falling from a cloud base but evaporating before reaching ground.

visibility the greatest distance at which an object can be seen with the naked eye.

warm front the surface boundary between a mass of warm air and cooler air ahead, over which the warm air slides.

waterspout a tornado that occurs over the sea, sucking up water from the sea.

wet-and-dry bulb thermometer a thermometer used for measuring relative humidity. Two identical thermometers are mounted alongside, one with its bulb wrapped in muslin kept moist by a wick dipping into water. Evaporation from the muslin uses up heat, so that the wet bulb thermometer reads lower than the dry, except when air is saturated and they read the same. Mathematical tables enable humidity and dew point to be obtained from the two readings.

whirlwind a local column of rotating and rising air, originating at ground level. They usually occur in hot weather when there is no cloud.

whiteout a visibility condition, in a snow storm or over extensive snow surfaces, where natural contours or landmarks are indistinguishable from each other or from cloud.

Williwaw a cold and strong downslope wind in Alaska.

wind air that is moving owing to pressure differences between places. Wind direction is desribed by the direction from which it blows, e.g. NW or 315° blows from the northwest towards the southeast.

wind vane a device for registering wind direction. The shorter arm, usually an arrow, points to the wind direction, while the broader fin blows downwind.

PHYSICAL GEOGRAPHY GLOSSARY

abyssal pertaining to the depths of the oceans.

affluent a tributary stream flowing into a larger stream or river.

aiguille (French, 'needle') a sharp point or pinnacle of rock.

alluvial fan a fan-shaped area of sediment deposited where the gradient of a stream or river is reduced and flow is slowed.

alluvium the fine sediment (sand, silt, clay) deposited by a river.

altitude height above sea level.

archipelago a group of islands.

arête a sharp ridge between two cirques.

artesian well a well that taps water held in a permeable layer of rock, sandwiched between two impermeable layers of rock in a basin. The rim of the permeable section of the basin is higher than the level of the well, so the water contained in the permeable layer pushes the water up out of the well.

atoll a ring of coral islands or coral reefs.

avalanche a mass of snow and/or ice that slides down a mountainside under its own weight.

bar shingle and sand deposited in a line or ridge across a bay or mouth of a river, or offshore, parallel to a beach.

barchan a crescent-shaped sand dune. Its shape is due to the effect of the wind from a constant direction.

bayou a swampy creek leading off a river, found in flat land.

bergschrund a gap between the upper edge of a glacier and the rock or ice wall in the back of a cirque. Also called a rimage.

bight a large bay.

bill a small peninsula.

bluff a vertical cliff, standing out prominently from the surrounding countryside.

bog an area of wet spongy ground consisting of waterlogged and partly decaying moss and other plants.

bore a tidal wave running up a river estuary.

boulder clay sediment consisting of a mix of clay

and boulders deposited by a glacier. Also called till.

bourne a stream that only flows intermittently.

bund (in the Indian subcontinent) an artificial embankment.

bush scrubland not cleared for cultivation.

butte a flat-topped hill, often with steep sides, formed in horizontal strata. A mesa is a large butte.

cairn a man-made heap of stones.

caldera a crater flanked by steep cliffs. It is usually formed when the top of a volcano has been eroded.

canal a man-made waterway, either for transport or irrigation.

canyon a river-cut gorge with steep sides, often of great depth.

cape a piece of land projecting into the sea.

cascade a small waterfall.

cataract a large waterfall.

cave an underground opening reached from the surface or from the sea.

cavern a cave.

chaparral dry scrubland, particularly in the southeastern USA.

chimney a wide vertical crack in a rock face.

cirque a rounded basin in a mountainside, formed by the action of a glacier. Also called a corrie or cwm.

cliff a steep face of rock.

col a pass or saddle between higher mountains.

coombe a short valley into the side of a hill.

confluence the point at which two rivers converge.

continent a single large landmass.

continental drift the movement of crustal plates on the molten rock that makes up the Earth's interior. See p. 55.

continental shelf the offshore seabed, down to a depth of 200 m (600 ft).

contour a line joining all points at the same height.

coral the exoskeleton of small marine animals of the same name, which live in colonies. When each animal dies the calcium-rich exoskeleton remains. As generation succeeds generation, masses of coral build up into reefs, atolls, etc.

coral reef a line of coral at or just below the surface of the sea.

cordillera parallel lines of mountains.

corrasion the mechanical erosion of rocks by the action of other rocks, gravel, etc., in a river or by wind-borne sand.

corrie a cirque.

corrosion the chemical erosion of rocks.

cove a small bay.

crater the hollow at the top of a volcanic cone, or the depression caused by the impact of a meteorite.

crevasse a vertical crack in a glacier or ice sheet.

cuesta a ridge or hill formed by sloping rock strata.

cwm a cirque.

dale an open valley, especially in northern England.

deep a marine valley or trench, considerably deeper than the surrounding seabed.

delta deposits of alluvium in a fan shape, formed where a river flows into the sea or a lake.

desert an area of arid and semi-arid climates where rainfall is low and moisture availability is scarce.

drowned valley a valley that has been submerged by a rise in sea level or by the land sinking.

drumlin a small hump-backed hill formed by the action of a glacier. Composed of boulder clay and sometimes with a rock core, swarms of drumlins are exposed as ice-sheets recede.

dune a wind-formed accumulation of sand.

dust bowl a dry region that has been badly managed agriculturally to such a degree that the topsoil has been removed by wind erosion.

dyke a vertical sheet of rock that cuts across the bedding or structural planes of the host rock.

earthquake a series of shock waves generated from a single point within the Earth's mantle or crust. See p. 90.

epicentre the point on the Earth's surface above the point at which the shock waves of an earthquake are generated.

Equator an imaginary circle around the Earth's circumference, midway between the poles.

equinox the time when the Sun appears vertically overhead at noon at the Equator – 21 March and 21 September.

erg a desert area composed of wind-blown sand and dunes.

erosion the removal or wearing away of the land surface by natural means.

estuary the mouth of a river, and the tidal stretch of that river immediately up-river of the mouth.

étang a shallow lake among coastal sand dunes.

fall line the line showing where a number of rivers leave an upland area for a lowland area, in each case passing over a waterfall or series of waterfalls.

fathom a unit of depth at sea: 1·83 m (6 ft).

fell bare hill or exposed upland area, especially in northern England.

fen marshy land in which peat is formed, especially in eastern England.

fjord a glaciated steep-sided valley that runs into the sea and is subsequently flooded. They are characterized by a great depth of water in the main body of the fjord, with a shallower bar across the mouth.

firth (known as a sea loch in Scotland) a narrow inlet in the sea coast; either an estuary or a fjord.

flood plain the plain on either side of a river formed by alluvial deposits left when the river floods and then recedes again.

fold a vertical bend in the rock strata, formed by compression within the Earth's crust.

forest a large area of land, extensively covered with trees.

frost hollow a hollow into which cold air sinks from the surrounding slopes. The hollow is therefore more liable to suffer frost than the surrounding land.

garrigue a form of scrub found in dry limestone areas around the Mediterranean.

geyser a hot spring of such depth that steam periodically forms, erupting from the mouth of the spring in a fountain of steam and hot water.

glacier a mass of ice, formed through the accumulation of snow and its transformation to ice under pressure. Glaciers slowly move down a valley towards the sea. See p. 98.

glen a long narrow steep-sided valley in Scotland.

gorge a deep, narrow, rugged valley with near-vertical walls.

grassland a large area where the rainfall is greater than that of a desert but not enough to support a forest.

great circle a circle on the Earth's surface whose centre is the Earth's centre, and hence the shortest route between two places follows the great circle on which both are situated.

gulf a large bay.

gully a narrow steep-sided channel formed by water erosion.

hammada a bare rocky desert.

hanging valley a glaciated valley entering a main valley part-way up the valley side.

headland an isolated cliff projecting into the sea.

hot spring a spring whose water is heated by hot volcanic rocks.

iceberg a massive lump of ice that has broken off the end of a glacier or ice sheet and floats in the sea or a lake.

ice floe a floating sheet of ice that has detached from an ice shelf.

ice sheet a great sheet of ice and snow covering a land mass.

ice shelf a mass of ice and snow floating on the sea.

inlet an opening into the sea or lake coast.

inselberg an isolated hill in a relatively flat area.

irrigation an artificial supply of water to a crop-producing area.

island a mass of land surrounded by water. It may occur in a river, a lake, a sea or an ocean.

islet a small island.

isthmus a narrow neck of land connecting two land masses.

jebel (in Arabic countries) a mountain range.

jungle a popular name for tropical rain forest.

karst a type of limestone scenery produced by water erosion of limestone rock. It is characterized by sinks, underground rivers and caves, and other erosion features. See p. 99.

kettle hole a hollow in the outwash plain of a glacier, formed where an ice block melts.

key or **cay** a small island or sandbank in the Caribbean.

knick point a point at which the slope of a river changes.

knoll a small rounded hill.

kyle (in Scotland) a channel of water or strait.

lagoon an expanse of water that has been separated from the sea by a narrow strip of land.

lake an expanse of water entirely surrounded by land.

landslide a mass of soil, mud and rock that slides down a mountainside or cliff-slope because of its own weight.

latitude a degree of latitude (°) is the angular distance of a point on the surface of the Earth, north or south of the Equator, taken from the centre of the Earth. A line of latitude is the line joining all points with the same degree of latitude, i.e. it is a circle with the axis of the Earth between the two poles at its centre. Compare longitude.

lava see Geology Glossary.

lava fountain a fountain of molten lava ejected from a volcano.

lava plateau a plateau formed from a flat sheet of volcanic rock.

levée a river-bank formed during flooding of the river. As the river water spreads out, alluvium is deposited, the greatest quantity being along the line of the river bank.

littoral that part of the seashore between high and low tide.

load solid material carried by a river, ranging from boulders to fine silt.

loch (in Scotland) an inlet of the sea, a fjord, or a lake.

longitude the angular distance between one of the Earth's meridians and the standard or Greenwich meridian.

longshore drift the movement of sand and shingle along the shore due to the action of the waves as they advance and retreat obliquely along the shore.

lough (in Ireland) an inlet of the sea, a fjord, or a lake.

lunar day the time between successive crossings of a meridian by the Moon – about 24 hours 50 minutes.

lunar month the time between two successive new Moons, i.e. the time the Moon takes to travel around the Earth once – 29½ days.

maelstrom a large whirlpool.

magnetic pole the point at which the Earth's magnetic flux is strongest. The magnetic poles do not coincide with the true poles. They also move slightly with time.

mangrove swamp a tropical coastal swamp characterized by the extensive growth of mangroves, whose long tangled roots drop from the trunks and branches of the mangroves, trapping sediment.

maquis a low scrub growing on rocky soil in the Mediterranean area.

marsh low-lying soft wet land.

massif a block of mountains that only breaks up into separate peaks towards the various summits.

meander a wide curve or loop in a river. These often link up in a series of meanders.

meridian half a great circle on the Earth's surface, finishing at each pole and cutting the Equator at right-angles, i.e. a line of longitude.

mesa a tableland with steep sides. Buttes are small mesas.

meteorite a solid lump of rock that enters the atmosphere from space and is large enough not to burn up in the atmosphere but to reach the Earth's surface.

midnight sun the appearance of the sun throughout the day and night. This occurs in latitudes close to the poles at times around the solstices.

monadnock an isolated hill or rock, left when the surrounding rock has been eroded more rapidly.

monsoon forest tropical forest found where a monsoon climate is prevalent. Because of the dry season between monsoons, it is not so dense as tropical equatorial forest.

moor an area of high rolling land covered in grass, heather and bracken, often with marshy areas.

moraine rock and other debris transported by a glacier. Terminal moraines are formed at the ends of glaciers; lateral moraines are formed at the sides of glaciers; median moraines are formed in the middle of glaciers where two glaciers meet and unite.

mountain a mass of high land projecting well above the level of the surrounding land.

muskeg (in northern Canada) a mossy swamp.

neap tide the small tidal difference between high and low tide, caused when the Sun and Moon are out of phase.

névé granular snow, formed as snow is gradually impacted. Eventually névé forms the ice of a glacier.

nunatak a mountain peak projecting through an ice sheet.

oasis an area in a desert in which water occurs, giving rise to fertile land and allowing cultivation.

ocean a very large area of seawater, divided off by or surrounding the continents.

outwash alluvium carried from the end of a glacier by the melting ice.

outwash plain a plain formed by the outwash of a glacier.

oxbow lake a lake formed when a river cuts off one of its meanders, leaving a crescent-shaped or horseshoe-shaped lake.

pack ice ice floes that have been forced together to form an almost continuous sheet.

pampas grasslands between the Andes and the Atlantic in South America.

pass a gap through a mountain range that is relatively easy to traverse.

pediment a sloping plain that leads up to a mountain range.

percolation the descent of water through porous rock.

permafrost ground that is always frozen solid.

piedmont pertaining to the foot of a mountain or mountain range.

plain an extensive area of flat or gently rolling land.

plateau an extensive area of flat or gently rolling land that is raised above the level of the surrounding land.

playa a lake in an area that experiences a dry climate. It is often dry seasonally or for many years and has a saline surface.

plug a vertical core of solidified lava at the centre of a volcanic cone.

polder (in the Netherlands) an area that has been reclaimed from the sea.

pole one end of the Earth's axis; it remains stationary while all other points on Earth rotate round the axis.

pothole a hole worn down through solid rock by the swirling action of water, or water and accompanying debris.

prairie flat or rolling plains, largely grasslands, that occupy the central areas of North America east of the Rockies.

profile the profile of a river is a cross-section of its total length, showing the various slopes and changes of slope.

promontory a headland.

puy (in France) an isolated cone of a long-extinct volcano.

quagmire soft wet ground that shakes when walked on. Known as a 'shoog-bog' in some parts of Scotland.

quicksand loose sand in a dense suspension in water. Although it may look solid, its properties are those of a liquid.

race a rapid marine current caused by the tides.

ravine a small steep-sided valley, usually caused by water erosion.

reef a line of rocks just below the surface of the sea.

reg an area of the desert consisting of gravel and small rocks, but no sand.

ria an inlet of the sea, formed from a submerged river valley.

rift a valley formed by the sinking of a section of land between two parallel faults.

river capture the process by which one river erodes a larger and larger valley, eventually cutting into the valley of another river and 'capturing' its waters.

river terrace flat land on either side of a river, left when a river erodes a channel well below the level of its flood plain.

roads or **roadstead** a large area of deepwater anchorage for ships, usually well protected from bad weather.

rognon (French, 'kidney') an isolated island of rock in a glacier.

run-off rainfall that pours over the ground surface and into streams and rivers.

salt dome a mass of salt that has been forced up through layers of rock until it lies relatively close to the Earth's surface.

salt lake a lake that has only a limited outlet or no outlet at all, occurring in an area experiencing a hot dry climate. As water evaporates, the concentration of salt in the water increases.

salt marsh an area of marsh that is flooded by seawater at high tides.

salt pan an area in which salt water has evaporated completely, leaving behind a deposit of salt.

sandbank a line or bank of sand just below the surface of the sea or of a river.

savanna or **savannah** an area of grassland with few trees, found to the north and south of the equatorial areas. There is a wet and a dry season each year, limiting the growth of trees.

scarp or **escarpment** a steep slope, often forming the steeper slope of a cuesta.

scree broken rocks at the foot of a rocky slope. They are broken off by the action of weathering and tumble down the slope. Also known as talus.

sea level the mean level between high and low tides.

sea loch sea fjord.

seif a linear sand dune with a sinuous crest.

serac a tower or band of very steep ice formed when the part of the glacier below it has fallen away.

shoal an area of sandbanks.

sidereal day the interval of time for a star to describe a circle around the pole star.

sierra a long mountain range, usually very jagged.

sill a slab of igneous rock, forced when molten between two layers of sedimentary rock and subsequently exposed by erosion.

snowfield a permanent mass of snow.

snowline the level above which snow is permanently present.

solar day the interval of time between successive appearances of the Sun in the meridian of any one place.

solstice the time when the Sun appears vertically overhead at its most northerly or southerly point – 21 June and 22 December.

sound a narrow inlet of the sea.

source the point at which a river begins – a spring, lake, etc.

spit a long narrow strip of shingle or sand, attached at one end to a land mass, projecting into the sea or across an estuary.

spring a flow of water up through the ground at a particular point. It can be permanent or intermittent.

spring tide the greatest tidal difference between high and low tide, caused when the Sun and Moon are in phase.

stack an isolated pillar of rock off the coast, caused by erosion.

steppes flat grasslands stretching from central Europe to eastern Russia and on into Central Asia.

strait a narrow stretch of sea connecting two large expanses of sea or ocean.

subtropical the region between the tropics and temperate regions.

swamp low marshland that is permanently wet.

swash a flow of water up a beach after a wave has broken.

taiga a vast belt of coniferous forests in the northern hemisphere, particularly Siberia.

talus another word for scree.

tarn a mountain lake, often occupying a cirque.

temperate the region experiencing cool summers and mild winters. It lies between subtropical regions and polar circles, excluding the continental and eastern coastal regions of the northern hemisphere.

tide the rise and fall of the surface of the sea, caused by the gravitational pull of the sun.

tombolo a bar joining an island to the mainland.

trench a long deep submarine valley.

tributary a river that flows into another river rather than into a lake or the sea.

Tropic of Cancer latitude 23°N. The position at which the Sun appears vertically overhead at midday on the 21 June solstice.

Tropic of Capricorn latitude 23°S. The position at which the Sun appears vertically overhead at midday on the 22 December solstice.

tropics the region between the Tropics of Cancer and Capricorn.

truncated spur a spur that has at some time been foreshortened by the action of a glacier.

tsunami a tidal wave caused by an earthquake under the sea's surface.

tundra the area in the northern hemisphere, north of the coniferous forest belt, characterized by the absence of trees. The ground is covered by mosses, lichens and a few other plants that can survive the long harsh winters and short cool summers.

undertow the undercurrent after a wave has broken on a beach.

volcanic ash particles of lava ejected by a vol-

cano and often falling over a wide area.

volcano a vent or fissure in the Earth's crust through which molten magma can force its way to the surface.

wadi a watercourse in the desert. It is usually dry but can contain water after the occasional rainstorms.

waterfall an abrupt fall of water in the course of a river. (See p. 89.)

water gap a gap in a ridge or line of hills, cut by a river.

watershed the dividing line, running along high land, between the tributaries feeding into two separate river systems.

water table the surface of a water-saturated part of the ground.

weir an artificial structure across a river, constructed to regulate flow.

well a hole dug from ground level to below the surface of the water table to gain access to water.

whirlpool a circular eddy of water, formed by the interaction of two or more currents.

year the time taken for the Earth to complete one revolution about the Sun.

zenith a point vertically above the ground.

GEOLOGY GLOSSARY

acid rock igneous rock with over 10% free quartz.

adobe a type of clay.

aeolian deposits particles carried and deposited by the wind.

alluvium sands and gravels carried by rivers and deposited along the course of the river.

amber a type of resin.

amorphous material having no regular arrangement.

anhedral having no crystalline structure.

anticline a fold system in the form of an arch.

aquifer a stratum of rock containing water.

arenaceous rocks sedimentary sandstones, deposited by wind or water.

argillaceous rocks sedimentary rocks deposited by water; usually marls, silts, shales, muds and clays.

ash fine material formed by volcanic explosions.

asphalt hydrocarbon, either solid or just fluid at normal temperatures.

asthenosphere a part of the Earth's mantle.

automorphic grains having a crystal structure.

ball clay reworked china clay.

banket a conglomerate of quartz.

basalt fine-grained basic igneous rock, sometimes with a glassy characteristic.

basic rock igneous rock containing little or no quartz.

batholith an intrusive mass of igneous rock.

bauxite an aluminium ore of aluminium oxide, out of which the easily leached ions have been removed.

bedding plane a surface parallel to the surface of deposition. Some rocks split along bedding planes; others have less obvious physical characteristics such as changes of particle size.

biolith rock of organic material, formed by organic processes.

bitumen a hydrocarbon mineral with a tarry texture, ranging from a viscous liquid to a solid.

black-band ironstone a sedimentary rock, formed principally from a form of coal and iron carbonate (siderite).

boghead coal coal formed from algal and fungal material.

bort anhedral diamonds in a granular mass.

boss a mass of igneous rock with steep contact surfaces with the surrounding rock.

boudinage the stretching of a rock layer to give a sausage-shaped structure.

boulder bed sedimentary rock consisting of boulders together with fine-grained material.

breccia a sedimentary rock consisting of angular material of more than 2 mm (0.08 in) diameter.

brown coal another name for lignite; a coal containing a low carbon content.

carbonate a large group of minerals, all having the carbonate group bond – CO_3 in common. They can be divided into sedimentary and non-sedimentary carbonates, limestone being the most common form of sedimentary carbonate.

carbonatite a magmatic rock consisting of calcium carbonate and occasionally other carbonates.

carstone a form of sandstone with a high proportion of limonite.

cassiterite tin oxide ore.

cataclasis the mechanical break-up of rock.

caulk barytes (barium sulphate).

celestite a strontium mineral found mainly in sedimentary rock.

ceylonite a spinel mineral.

chalcedony a silica-based mineral, found in many forms, some of which are semi-precious stones, e.g. agate, onyx, carnelian, jasper.

chalcocite copper sulfide ore.

chalcopyrite one of the principal copper ores.

chalk a fine-grained white limestone, calcium carbonate.

charnockite a granular rock, mainly consisting of quartz, feldspar and hypersthene.

chert a form of silica, found as bands and nodules in sedimentary rocks.

chiastolite a form of aluminium silicate.

china clay kaolin, formed by decomposition of feldspar in granite.

chlorite a green mineral consisting of talc units.

chondrites stony meteorites.

chromite a chromium ore, containing iron.

chrysocolla a copper ore mineral, copper silicate.

chrysoprase a green chalcedony.

chrysotile a form of asbestos.

cinnabar mercury sulfide, associated with volcanic activity.

citrine a yellow quartz.

clastic rock fragments of rock, transported to a site of deposition and built up into a conglomerate.

clay a sedimentary rock with a fine particle structure and a soft plastic texture when wet.

cleat jointing found in coal.

cleavage a flat plane of breakage, perhaps parallel to a crystal face.

cleavage plane the plane of fracture in a rock.

clint a ridge in a limestone rock surface.

coal stratified deposits of carbonaceous material, originally derived from decayed vegetable matter.

cobble a rock particle, between 125 mm (5 in) and 250 mm (10 in) in diameter.

columnar structure vertical columns or prisms, formed for example in lava and basalt, caused by the cooling of the rock.

competent the flow or flexion of a rock layer, in which it is not broken.

composite igneous bodies that have more than one material in them, e.g. due to intrusion.

concretion accumulations of sedimentary constituents in certain defined areas of rock, often around a nucleus.

conglomerate rounded pebbles cemented together in one mass.

convergence the metamorphosis of two dissimilar rocks so that they become similar.

corundum aluminium oxide, used as an abrasive and also found as gemstones, e.g. sapphire, ruby.

country rock the body of rock that encloses an intrusion by another rock, e.g. an igneous rock.

creep the gradual deformation of a rock by stress applied over a long time.

crystal a three-dimensional structure arising from the atomic structure of the substance. The symmetrical arrangement for a given substance means that the angles within the structure are constant for that substance.

culm Carboniferous rocks found in Devon and Cornwall (England).

cuprite copper oxide, an important copper ore.

deflation surface debris transported by the wind.

deformation any change in a bed or stratum after it has been formed.

dendritic branching into a many-fingered appearance.

denudation any process that results in a lowering of the land surface.

detritus particles of minerals and rocks formed by weathering and corrosion.

diamond a crystalline form of carbon. It has a cubic structure, distinguishing it from graphite.

diatomite the remains of unicellular organisms called diatoms. It is a highly-absorbent powdery material.

diorite a coarse-grained igneous rock consisting of feldspar plus ferromagnesium minerals.

dog-tooth spar calcite, crystallized into tooth-like forms.

dolerite an igneous rock similar to basalt.

dolomite calcium magnesium carbonate, or limestone with a substantial proportion of magnesium carbonate.

dyke a sheet of igneous rock that cuts across the bedding or structural planes of the host rock.

elaterite an elastic or rubbery form of bitumen.

elvan a dyke of granite.

emerald a green form of beryl.

emery fine granules of corundum and magnetite.

epidiorite a metamorphic granular rock derived from igneous rock and containing the minerals of diorite.

epidotes a group of rock-forming silicate minerals.

evaporite sediment left by the evaporation of salt water.

extrusive igneous rock that has flowed out at the Earth's surface.

fault a fracture plane in rock, along which displacement occurs.

feldspar silicate minerals, in which the silicon ions are in part replaced with aluminium ions. Calcium, sodium and potassium feldspars exist, as do the rare barium feldspars.

feldspathoid rock-forming silicates with sodium and/or potassium in the lattice structure. They never occur with quartz.

festoon bedding a type of cross-bedding.

fire clay argillaceous fossil soil found in some coal seams.

flint a type of chert.

flowage irreversible deformation, i.e. deforming a material beyond its elastic limit.

fluorite calcium fluoride, found as veins in rocks.

fold a flexing of a rock stratum.

fool's gold iron pyrites.

fossil the impression of an animal or plant, or its skeletal remains, buried by natural processes and then preserved.

fracture a break in a direction that is not a cleavage plane.

fuchsite a mica mineral containing chromium.

fulgurite a branching tube of fused silica, caused by lightning striking sandy soil.

gabbro a coarse-grained igneous rock, equivalent to basalt and dolerite. It contains feldspar, pyroxene and olivine as the major constituents.

galena lead sulfide, the most important lead ore.

gangue the material in which an ore deposit from the metal is not extracted.

gannister an arenaceous stratum found beneath coal seams.

gas cap a collection of gas above an oil deposit.

gems hard minerals, free from cleavages. Fragments are artificially cut and polished for decorative use.

garnet a semi-precious mineral with a wide range of colours, although red is the most commonly found.

geode a rock cavity containing crystals pointing inwards.

geosyncline an elongated basin, filled with sedimentary deposits. These deposits can then be deformed by orogenic forces.

gneiss banded coarse-grained rocks formed during metamorphosis.

granite a coarse-grained igneous rock, consisting essentially of quartz and feldspar and occurring as intrusive bodies in a variety of forms.

granule a rock particle of about 2–4 mm (0·08–0·16 in).

graphite a soft black form of carbon.

grike a cleft in a limestone pavement.

grit a rock in which the particle shape is angular.

gull a fissure which tapers downwards and is then filled with material from above.

gumbo a soil which, when wet, gives a sticky mud.

gypsum an evaporite calcium sulfate mineral found in clays and limestone.

hade a fault plane's angle to the vertical.

haematite an iron-oxide iron ore.

halite common salt, left as an evaporite.

hardness the mineral property propounded by Mohs. It measures the ability of one mineral to scratch another. Corundum – number 9 – can scratch topaz – number 8 – but not diamond – number 10.

10	Diamond	5	Apatite
9	Corundum	4	Fluorite
8	Topaz	3	Calcite
7	Quartz	2	Gypsum
6	Orthoclase	1	Talc

hard-pan strongly cemented material occurring below the surface of some sediments as a result of groundwater action.

hemicrystalline rocks containing both crystalline and glassy material.

hornfels a fine-grained granular rock formed by thermal metamorphosis.

hornstone a fine-grained volcanic ash.

horst an area thrown up between two parallel faults.

humus organic material in soil.

Iceland spar a variety of calcite.

igneous one of the three major divisions of rocks. Generally they are crystalline, although glassy forms can be found. They are either extrusive, i.e. produced on the Earth's surface as a result of volcanic action, or intrusive into other rocks, in which case they only appear on the Earth's surface if the surrounding rock is eroded.

impervious (a rock) not allowing the passage of water.

impregnation the in-filling of pores by mineral material, e.g. oil.

inclusion a portion of one material totally enclosed within another.

incretion a cylindrical hollow concretion.

inlier an area of older rock surrounded by younger rock.

interbedded (a layer of rock) situated between two other layers.

intermediate rock rock containing no more than 10% quartz plus a feldspar.

intrusion an igneous rock structure that has forced its way into pre-existing rock.

jade a gemstone of a hard compact aggregate.

jasper a red chert-like variety of chalcedony.

jet a homogeneous form of cannel coal or black lignite.

joint a fracture in a rock structure along which no movement can be observed.

kaolin the main constituent of china clay.

kieselguhr diatomite.

kimberlite a brecciated peridotite containing mica and other minerals.

kyanite an aluminium silicate.

labradorite a type of feldspar.

landscape marble a type of limestone that, when sliced at right angles to the bedding plane, reveals patterns reminiscent of a landscape scene.

laterite an iron-oxide ore, out of which the easily leached ions have been removed.

lava molten silicates that flow out of volcanoes. In

general they are basic, although acidic lava flows are known. Acidic lavas flow readily and tend to cover much larger areas, while basic lavas are more viscous.

leaching the removal of ions from a soil or rock by the through-flow of water.

lepidolite a type of mica.

lignite brown coal, low in carbon content.

limestone a group of sedimentary rocks consisting of carbonates, principally calcium carbonate. Calcite and dolomite are the most important limestone rocks.

limonite a group of iron oxides and hydroxides.

lithifaction the formation of a large rock from small fragments.

loam sand, silt and clay in equal proportions in a soil.

loess deposits of wind-blown fine particles.

lustre the ability of minerals to reflect light.

magma the molten fluid within the Earth's interior. Igneous rocks are formed from the magma, although various constituents of the magma will be lost during this process of consolidation.

magnesite magnesium carbonate.

magnetite an iron ore consisting of ferric oxide.

malachite a carbonate ore of copper.

marble metamorphosed limestone, usually with other compounds giving marble its recognizable appearance.

marl a mudstone with a high calcium content.

metamorphism the process of heating, pressure and chemical action that causes rocks to change from one form to another in the Earth's crust.

mica a large group of silica-based minerals, characterized by the fact that the crystal structure gives cleavage into flat flexible sheets.

migmatite a form of gneiss.

mobile belt a part of the Earth's crust in which metamorphosis, igneous activity and deformation occur.

monzonite coarse igneous rock with a high feldspar content.

mud wet clay soil in a near-liquid state.

mudstone a type of argillaceous rock, similar to shale, but without the property of splitting along bedding planes.

muscovite a type of mica.

natural gas gaseous hydrocarbons found together with oil deposits.

neck a volcanic plug.

nodule a rounded concretion.

obsidian a type of rhyolite with a black glassy sheen to it.

oceanite a type of basalt.

oil often called petroleum, oil is naturally occurring liquid hydrocarbon. It is invariably found in association with saline water and natural gas, and often with solid hydrocarbons.

oil shale a dark argillaceous rock. It does not contain liquid oil, but a solid organic material called kerogen, which gives oil on distillation.

olivine a group of silicates, containing ferrous iron and magnesium. They largely occur in igneous rocks.

onyx a type of banded chalcedony.

oolith a rounded lump of rock formed by accretion round a nucleus. Ooliths usually contain calcium minerals.

opal an amorphous type of silica, believed to have been derived from silica gel.

ore an aggregate of minerals from which a valued mineral is extracted.

orogeny the process or period of mountain building.

outlier a relatively small area of young rock, surrounded by older rock.

overburden soil found on top of a bed of useful mineral.

peat an early, earth-like form of coal. It is a dark-brown to black mass of partially decomposed vegetation.

pebble a rock fragment of 5–60 mm (0·2–2·3 in) diameter.

pedalfer leached soil in a region with high rainfall.

pegmatite a coarse-grained igneous rock, usually granitic. Very long crystals may be apparent.

peridot gem-quality olivine.

permeability the ability of water to percolate through a rock.

pervious rock rock through which water may pass via cracks, fissures, etc.

pitchblende uranium oxide ore.

plug the solidified lava and other material left in the neck of a volcano. Often the surrounding material is subsequently eroded away.

plutonic rock igneous material of a deep-seated origin, i.e. originating from the magma.

pudding stone a conglomerate.

pumice one of the pyroclastic rocks thrown out of a volcano. It contains a high proportion of air space.

pyrite iron sulfide.

pyroclastic rock a rock formed either by liquid lava thrown out of a volcano or solid lumps of surrounding rock broken up by volcanic action.

quartz a silica mineral with three different forms. Sand is the most common. Low quartz is a crystalline form, occurring in a variety of colours. At 573°C (1063°F) low quartz gives rise to high quartz, but its natural occurrence is rare.

red bed sedimentary rocks containing a high proportion of ferric minerals, giving them a reddish colour.

residual deposit minerals left when part of a rock is dissolved or leached away.

rhyolite a fine-grained or glassy volcanic rock, rich in quartz.

rock a mass of mineral material, usually consisting of more than one mineral type.

rock crystal a clear form of quartz.

ruby a red transparent form of corundum.

rudaceous rock sedimentary rock deposited as detritus by water or air, and divided into conglomerates and breccias.

rutile titanium oxide ore.

salt dome salt forced up through an overlying sediment as a dome. Under pressure salt behaves like a magma.

sand a type of quartz, formed of fine particles. It can also be taken to mean any fine particles of 0·0625–2 mm (0·0025–0·08 in).

sandstone arenaceous rocks, consisting of fine grains cemented together by a variety of minerals.

sapphire a blue transparent form of corundum.

schist a metamorphosed rock with the constituent minerals arranged in parallel.

scree fragments formed by the weathering of rocks.

sedimentary rock rock formed out of the material resulting from erosion and weathering, along with organic material. The principal sedimentary rocks are sandstone, limestone and shale. See p. 57.

shale a sedimentary rock composed of clay particles.

shingle gravel or pebbles found on beaches.

silica silicon dioxide, which can take a variety of forms, e.g. quartz, chalcedony, opal.

silicates the most prolific mineral group in the Earth's crust. They are based on a silicon-oxide structure, but a variety of other elements and ions can be substituted in this structure, particularly aluminium. The group includes the clays, the feldspars, the garnets, the micas, the silicas.

sill a sheet of igneous rock, lying along a bedding plane.

silt a type of argillaceous rock.

slate argillaceous rock that has been metamorphosed. The slates all show cleavage, and may have new minerals showing up as marks or even crystals.

soapstone any greasy rock, although usually applied to talc rocks.

soil the loose weathered material covering most of the Earth's land surface. It contains humus – a partially decomposed matter – which improves the fertility and water retention of the soil and so encourages plant growth.

spinels a group of minerals including magnetite and chromite.

stalactite calcium carbonate formed as a spike hanging down from the ceiling in a limestone cave.

stalagmite calcium carbonate formed as a spike standing up from the floor in a limestone cave.

stock an intrusive mass of igneous rock, smaller than a batholith.

streak a mineral's colour when in a powdered state, e.g. formed by scratching it.

subsoil partly weathered rock lying between the soil and the bedrock.

syenites a group of coarse-grained igneous rocks containing feldspars and feldspathoids.

talc magnesium silicate, the softest common mineral.

tar pit areas where asphalt or bitumen rises to the surface from an underground hydrocarbon source.

terra rossa red clayey soil formed as a result of carbonates being leached out of limestone.

topaz a clear semi-precious form of aluminium silicate.

tor piles of granite blocks, left by differential weathering of the rock around them.

touchstone a very hard fine-grained black form of basalt or chert.

tripoli a type of diatomite.

ultrabasic rock igneous ferromagnesian rock, with little or no feldspar, quartz or feldspathoid in it.

ultramarine a type of feldspathoid.

valley fill loose material filling or partly filling a valley.

vein a sheet of mineral that has intruded into a fissure or joint of a rock.

water table the upper limit of the groundwater saturation.

weathering the breaking down of stationary rocks by mechanical means, e.g. by the action of ice and the Sun, and by chemical means.

wind erosion the abrasive action of wind-driven particles of sand against stationary rocks.

wolframite a tungsten ore.

xenolith an inclusion of pre-existing rock in an igneous rock.

zeolites a group of silicates containing water of crystallization, and capable of reversible dehydration. They can act as powerful base exchangers.

zircon zirconium silicate.

MAPS AND MAPPING

Mapping was important to most early civilizations. From the ancient Greeks, the maps of Ptolemy – which were prepared during the second century AD – survive. His *Guide to Geography* included a collection of 27 maps that represented the then known parts of the globe. These maps were the basis of the revival of cartography, which reentered Europe via Muslim Spain in the 14th and 15th centuries. They were used by the great explorers da Gama, Columbus, Magellan, Drake, etc. By contrast, Roman mapping – which reverted to the concept of a flat Earth rather than a globe – is represented today by a single medieval copy of a Roman map.

The first modern atlases date from the 15th century. The greatest cartographer of the age of discovery was a Fleming, Gerardus Mercator, whose map of the continent of Europe was published in 1554. He devised a cylindrical projection – since known as Mercator – to represent the curved surface of the planet on a flat surface, the map. The use of precise scientific instruments, from the 18th century, and the systemmatic national surveys of major countries, since the early 19th century, have transformed cartography. Aerial photography (since 1945) and, more recently, mapping by satellite observation have revolutionized making maps. However, the basic problem of representing the curved surface of the Earth on a flat map remains a challenge.

The surface of the planet cannot be portrayed on a map without some modification of the shape of the land or the distances between places. The projection devised by Mercator to represent the round Earth on a flat map is still one of the most popular, although it does seriously distort the areas of countries furthest away from the Equator. We are all familiar with the Mercator world map on which Greenland appears as large as Africa, although Greenland is actually about 8% of the size of that continent. Many newer projections are now used, some of which emphasize a more realistic representation of the size of the land masses, while others concentrate upon a more accurate representation of distances.

CELSIUS AND FAHRENHEIT COMPARED

The two principal temperature scales are Celsius and Fahrenheit. Temperatures in a meteorological context are given in both in this and other chapters. The Celsius scale was devised in 1743 by J. P. Christen (1683–1755) but is referred to by its present name because of the erroneous belief that it was invented by the Swedish astronomer Anders Celsius (1701–44). The Fahrenheit scale is named after Gabriel Daniel Fahrenheit (1686–1736), a German physicist.

QUICK CONVERSION
To convert ° C to ° F, multiply the ° C reading by 9, divide by 5 and add 32.

To convert ° F to ° C, subtract 32 from the ° F reading and multiply by 5, divide by 9.

KELVIN SCALE
Scientists in a non-meteorological context most frequently employ the Kelvin Scale in which one degree kelvin (K) = 1/273·16 of the triple point of water (where ice, water and water vapour are in equilibrium).

TEMPERATURE COMPARISONS
The following tables compare points on the Celsius and Fahrenheit scales.

(1)	Absolute zero	=	− 273·15 °C	=	− 459·67 °F	=	0K
(2)	Zero Fahrenheit	=	− 17·8 °C	=	− 0·0 °F	=	255.35K
(3)	Freezing point of water	=	0·0 °C	=	32·0 °F	=	273.15K
(4)	Triple point of water	=	0.01 °C	=	32.02 °F	=	273.16K
(5)	Normal human blood temperature	=	36·9 °C	=	98·4 °F	=	310.05K
(6)	Boiling point of water (at standard pressure)	=	100·0 °C	=	212·0 °F	=	373.15K

− 40 °C = − 40 °F	1 °C = 34 °F	42 °C = 108 °F
− 39 °C = − 38 °F	2 °C = 36 °F	43 °C = 109 °F
− 38 °C = − 36 °F	3 °C = 37 °F	44 °C = 111 °F
− 37 °C = − 35 °F	4 °C = 39 °F	45 °C = 113 °F
− 36 °C = − 33 °F	5 °C = 41 °F	46 °C = 115 °F
− 35 °C = − 31 °F	6 °C = 43 °F	47 °C = 117 °F
− 34 °C = − 29 °F	7 °C = 45 °F	48 °C = 118 °F
− 33 °C = − 27 °F	8 °C = 46 °F	49 °C = 120 °F
− 32 °C = − 26 °F	9 °C = 48 °F	50 °C = 122 °F
− 31 °C = − 24 °F	10 °C = 50 °F	51 °C = 124 °F
− 30 °C = − 22 °F	11 °C = 52 °F	52 °C = 126 °F
− 29 °C = − 20 °F	12 °C = 54 °F	53 °C = 127 °F
− 28 °C = − 18 °F	13 °C = 55 °F	54 °C = 129 °F
− 27 °C = − 17 °F	14 °C = 57 °F	55 °C = 131 °F
− 26 °C = − 15 °F	15 °C = 59 °F	56 °C = 133 °F
− 25 °C = − 13 °F	16 °C = 61 °F	57 °C = 135 °F
− 24 °C = − 11 °F	17 °C = 63 °F	58 °C = 136 °F
− 23 °C = − 9 °F	18 °C = 64 °F	59 °C = 138 °F
− 22 °C = − 8 °F	19 °C = 66 °F	60 °C = 140 °F
− 21 °C = − 6 °F	20 °C = 68 °F	61 °C = 142 °F
− 20 °C = − 4 °F	21 °C = 70 °F	62 °C = 144 °F
− 19 °C = − 2 °F	22 °C = 72 °F	63 °C = 145 °F
− 18 °C = 0 °F	23 °C = 73 °F	64 °C = 147 °F
− 17 °C = 1 °F	24 °C = 75 °F	65 °C = 149 °F
− 16 °C = 3 °F	25 °C = 77 °F	66 °C = 151 °F
− 15 °C = 5 °F	26 °C = 79 °F	67 °C = 153 °F
− 14 °C = 7 °F	27 °C = 81 °F	68 °C = 154 °F
− 13 °C = 9 °F	28 °C = 82 °F	69 °C = 156 °F
− 12 °C = 10 °F	29 °C = 84 °F	70 °C = 158 °F
− 11 °C = 12 °F	30 °C = 86 °F	71 °C = 160 °F
− 10 °C = 14 °F	31 °C = 88 °F	72 °C = 162 °F
− 9 °C = 16 °F	32 °C = 90 °F	73 °C = 163 °F
− 8 °C = 18 °F	33 °C = 91 °F	74 °C = 165 °F
− 7 °C = 19 °F	34 °C = 93 °F	75 °C = 167 °F
− 6 °C = 21 °F	35 °C = 95 °F	76 °C = 169 °F
− 5 °C = 23 °F	36 °C = 97 °F	77 °C = 171 °F
− 4 °C = 25 °F	37 °C = 99 °F	78 °C = 172 °F
− 3 °C = 27 °F	38 °C = 100 °F	79 °C = 174 °F
− 2 °C = 28 °F	39 °C = 102 °F	80 °C = 176 °F
− 1 °C = 30 °F	40 °C = 104 °F	81 °C = 178 °F
0 °C = 32 °F	41 °C = 106 °F	82 °C = 180 °F

LIFE SCIENCES
THE LIVING WORLD

THE BEGINNING OF LIFE

Around every star in the universe – of which the Sun is but one – there is a zone, the *ecosphere*, where water could potentially exist as a liquid. Water is the prime requisite for life as we know it. If there is a body of sufficient mass in this zone (i.e. a planet), with sufficient gravitational force to hold onto water and a gaseous atmosphere, then the conditions for life may be present. The nature of the original conditions on the Earth can be worked out by considering our neighbouring planets, Venus and Mars, together with the gases that erupt from volcanoes. The major gases produced by volcanoes are carbon dioxide and water vapour – the main components of the oceans and the atmosphere. On Venus it is too hot for water to be liquid, on Mars too cold – but on the Earth it is just right. Simple compounds such as ammonia and methane are known to be able to combine with carbon dioxide and water if they are subjected to ultraviolet light (as emitted by the Sun) and if an electrical spark (such as might be provided by lightning) is passed through a mixture of these gases. From such reactions are formed simple *amino acids*. These are the building blocks of *proteins* – the essential components of living things.

PROTEIN

Proteins are chains of amino acids, and there is an almost infinite variety of forms that can be synthesized from the 20 different amino acids. They may be in the form of *enzymes*, which act as catalysts in various biochemical reactions, or they may take the form of structural materials.

DNA

One of the fundamental aspects of living things is their ability to replicate themselves and to pass on instructions for making new individuals from one generation to another. These instructions are contained in a special, complex molecule known as *deoxyribonucleic acid* or *DNA*, which is made up of various organic compounds. DNA has the capacity to replicate itself, and acts as a blueprint for making amino acids, and hence proteins.

VIRUSES

Viruses – which range in size from 0.000018 mm to 0.0006 mm – are very much in the grey area between living and non-living things, and are not usually ascribed their own kingdom. They consist of a single nucleic acid (DNA or RNA) surrounded by a layer of protein; sometimes there is a further layer. Viruses are completely dependent on living cells as vehicles in which to reproduce.

BACTERIA

Because viruses are parasitic upon more complex organisms, it is unlikely that they were the first forms of life, even though they are the simplest. The first evidence of life on Earth comes from minute globules preserved in rocks 3800 million years old, believed to be the fossils of primitive bacteria. Bacteria each consist of a single *cell* – the smallest biological unit able to function independently. The largest bacteria are only a few thousandths of a mm long. A typical bacterial cell consists of a cell wall within which is contained the *protoplasm* (a jelly-like substance) and strings of DNA. A single bacterium reproduces by splitting into two new cells, each one an exact copy of the original. This process can happen as often as once every 15 minutes.

The first bacteria were probably *heterotrophic*, i.e. they fed on the organic molecules in the early oceans. As the 'organic soup' was used up, new types of bacteria evolved, the *autotrophs*. Some autotrophs are capable of synthesizing their food from inorganic material, while others use light energy. About 2900 million years ago a new type of bacteria – known as *cyanobacteria* or *blue-green algae* – evolved. These bacteria had the ability to use light to photosynthesize. The waste product of photosynthesis is oxygen, and oxygen began to accumulate in the atmosphere and oceans. Whereas oxygen had previously been a poison for all living things, it was now exploited by new kinds of bacteria (described as *aerobic*) as a fuel for burning food to obtain energy. Like the most primitive bacteria, these bacteria were heterotrophic, and from them evolved all the higher animals. From the autotrophic bacteria evolved the plants, all of which use photosynthesis. In this way, animals and plants share a common ancestry.

PROTISTS

One of the most remarkable events in the history of life on Earth took place about 1500 million years ago. Suddenly the microscopic organisms – although still single-celled – became many times larger than the bacteria that preceded them. This event marked the origin of the protists, some of which are plant-like and others animal-like (the latter are known as *protozoans*). The largest protists are 1 mm long. The protists and all later, more advanced forms of life – fungi, plants and animals – are known as *eukaryotes* (meaning 'true kernel'). This is because the protoplasm in their cells is differentiated into *cytoplasm* and the *nucleus* (the 'kernel'). The nucleus is a separate part of the cell, surrounded by the cytoplasm, and contains the chromosomes, the structures into which the DNA is organized. In contrast to bacteria, the cells of protists also contain miniature organs, or *organelles*, which perform specialized tasks. One of the most important organelles is the *mitochondrion*, which contains enzymes that break up organic compounds to release energy.

LARGER ORGANISMS

The first sign of cells coming together to form large organisms is the sponges, a group of marine invertebrates that first evolved at least 570 million years ago. Sponges may grow up to 1 m (3¼ ft) across, and their structure is supported by a network of fibres or by skeletal spicules.

TAXONOMY

Taxonomy is concerned with the classification of living organisms into groups. Living organisms are named and ordered within a hierarchical classification based on various criteria such as similarity of structure or supposed evolutionary relationships. The Swedish naturalist Carolus Linnaeus (Carl von Linné; 1707–78) formulated rules for naming organisms in 1758. He recommended that every organism be given a generic name (e.g. *Homo* – man) with a species epithet (e.g. *H. sapiens* – 'wise' man). He further suggested that species should be grouped into successively more inclusive groupings, a system that is known as a taxonomic hierarchy. The most commonly used ranks are listed below, and – as can be seen – they are slightly different when applied to animals and plants. Often further ranks are created by adding the prefixes 'sub-' or 'super-'.

Animals	Plants
Kingdom	Kingdom
Phylum	Division
Class	Class
Order	Order
Family	Family
Genus	Genus
Species	Species

More than one system of classification exists, but most scientists believe that the diversity of life is best expressed in terms of five kingdoms: Monera, Protista, Fungi (or Myceteae), Plantae, and Animalia.

KINGDOM MONERA

This group of about 5000 species includes the bacteria, archae bacteria, cyanobacteria (blue-green algae) and mycoplasms. They are single-celled, sometimes in chains or filaments, and most are less than 0.001 mm in diameter. They vary in shape from almost spherical (coccus) to cone-shaped (vibrio) to rod-like (bacillus) to corkscrew-shaped (spirochaete). The genetic material floats free in the cytoplasm as a single loop of DNA (deoxyribonucleic acid). They reproduce asexually by simple binary fission and most survive in conditions of very low oxygen concentration.

About 14 phyla are usually recognized and, although they are structurally very similar, they show a great range of biochemistry. Fermenting bacteria are very important in the production of cheese and yoghurt. Chemoautotrophic bacteria – which manufacture food from simple chemicals – play a crucial role in recycling nitrites, sulfur and methane into compounds that other organisms can use. Both bacteria and cyanobacteria include forms that can fix atmospheric nitrogen and some use a primitive form of photosynthesis. Many pathogens, such as those causing salmonella, dysentry, cholera and anthrax, also belong to this group.

All other forms of life – fungi, protista, plants and animals – are formed of eukaryote cells: the DNA is organized into chromosomes contained within a nucleus inside the cell. There are organelles such as mitochondria and, in plants, chloroplasts, which carry out specific functions such as respiration and photosynthesis.

KINGDOM FUNGI (or MYCETEAE)

Fungi are plant-like organisms that have no chlorophyll, and hence cannot photosynthesize. The cell wall of fungi often contains chitin, and there are no motile cells at any stage of the life cycle. Fungi may be unicellular (e.g. yeasts) or, more usually, multicellular with a thread-like mycelium (made up of filaments called hyphae) and a distinct fruiting body. Many are parasites of plants and animals, while others are important in the process of decay and recycling. Excluding the slime moulds (usually considered as belonging to the Kingdom Protista; see below), and lichens (which are symbiotic associa-

tions of algae or cyanobacteria with a fungus), the true fungi fall into two divisions:

Division Mastigomycota a division of fungi that are either unicellular or have non-septate (unpartitioned) mycelia. Their spores are generally motile, dependent on water for their dispersal.

Division Amastigomycota a division of fungi that includes both unicellular and filamentous species. Reproduction is either sexual or asexual. There are four subdivisions:

Subdivision Zygomycotina includes simple fungi producing a resistant spore after sexual reproduction (e.g. *Mucor*, bread mould).

Subdivision Ascomycotina includes such fungi as yeasts, cup fungi and truffles. Following sexual reproduction they produce a characteristic sac (ascus) containing eight spores.

Subdivision Basidiomycotina includes mushrooms, toadstools and bracket fungi. Following sexual reproduction, the zygote produces many four-spore basidia, which are protected by fruiting bodies.

Subdivision Deuteromycotina includes fungi for which no reproductive stage is known. The best-known example is penicillin.

KINGDOM PROTISTA

This kingdom consists of organisms that may be unicellular or multicellular. If the organisms are multicellular, there is no organization of cells into organs, and many only reproduce asexually. A large number of taxonomists consider that this kingdom is 'artificial': it consists of organisms that cannot be easily fitted into other kingdoms. The kingdom comprises 27 phyla (or divisions), but little is known about many of them and in some cases the number of species is unknown. Phyla include:

Phylum Bacillariophyta a phylum of diatoms – small unicellular algae enclosed within a silica skeleton made of two interlocking halves. There are some 10 000 species, which are very common in both fresh and marine water. Some species can form poisonous blooms from time to time.

Phylum Chlorophyta better known as green algae. The phylum comprises approximately 7000 species of single-celled or multicellular organisms which usually live in freshwater, although some are seaweeds. These organisms are green because they contain chloroplasts and have cellulose cell walls, like true plants.

Phylum Sarcodina a phylum of unicellular organisms without chlorophyll. These organisms can move and feed by pushing out pseudopodia (e.g. amoebas). Some organisms, such as foraminifera, secrete a complicated shell of calcium carbonate.

Phylum Ciliophora a phylum of unicellular organisms covered with many tiny cilia that beat in a coordinated fashion to move the organism along. Paramecium is the best-known example.

Phylum Phaeophyta better known as brown seaweeds. There are about 1500 species which are common on rocky shores. Some are commercially important for yielding alginins, commonly used in the manufacture of ice creams and sweets.

Phylum Rhodophyta better known as red algae. The 4000 or so species of this phylum are multicellular and include many seaweeds. They contain special pigments in addition to chlorophyll and manufacture a special kind of starch. Some species yield agar, which is commercially important.

THE PLANT WORLD

KINGDOM PLANTAE

Plants are multicellular organisms composed of cells surrounded by a rigid cellulose wall. They contain chlorophyll *a* and *b*, amongst other pigments, and are capable of photosynthesis. Although many of the algae are multicellular (e.g seaweeds), and some can photosynthesize, they are more often ascribed to the Kingdom Protista, as they lack embryos and multicellular sex organs. In the true plants, the embryo, which is produced as a result of sexual reproduction, is surrounded by nutritive tissue. In the life cycle a *haploid generation* (containing one set of chromosomes) – called the gametophyte – alternates with a *diploid generation* (containing two sets of chromosomes) – the sporophyte. The most modern classification divides the plant kingdom into 10 divisions. The first 5 divisions listed produce spores as the units of dispersal, while the last 5 produce seeds. The spore-bearing plants are restricted by their need for damp conditions to reproduce.

DIVISION BRYOPHYTA

This division comprises the mosses, liverworts and hornworts. These plants have no roots or conducting tissue. In the life cycle, the gametophyte is the dominant phase.

All the other plant divisions have conducting tissue (xylem and phloem), roots, and leaves with a protective cuticle. In the life cycle, the sporophyte is the dominant generation; however, in the spore-bearing divisions the gametophyte plant is independent and in most cases is capable of photosynthesis.

DIVISION PSILOPHYTA

This minor division of herbaceous spore-bearing plants consists of the whisk ferns. There are two genera, found in tropical and warm temperate regions. Many are epiphytic (i.e. they grow on other plants without damaging them).

DIVISION LYCOPHYTA

This widespread and diverse division of spore-bearing plants consists of three major families: Isoetaceae (the quillworts), the Lycopodiaceae (Lycopods) and the Selaginellaceae (the last two both known as club mosses). The plants are generally small and herbaceous.

DIVISION SPHENOPHYTA

This division of spore-bearing plants now contains only a single genus, *Equisetum* (horsetails). However, in the Carboniferous period, giant horsetails and lycopods (see above) dominated the vast 'Coal measure' forests. Most horsetails today are small, and are distinguished by their hollow, segmented stems.

DIVISION PTERIDOPHYTA

This division, popularly known as the true ferns, is the most important group of spore-bearing plants today. True ferns often show complex pinnate leaves that carry spore-producing sacs. Ferns vary from giant tree ferns up to 25 m (82 ft) high, to filmy ferns with leaves only one cell thick.

In the seed-bearing plants the gametophyte is very reduced and develops within cones or flowers that produce the seed on the dominant sporophyte. These plants often show secondary growth and the development of bark. Four of the divisions of seed-bearing plants are sometimes grouped together as the gymnosperms – plants that bear naked seeds, usually in cones. In the fifth division, the flowering plants (Magnoliophyta), the developing seeds are protected within an ovary.

DIVISION CONIFEROPHYTA

The conifers comprise the dominant gymnosperm group, and includes pines, larches, spruces, firs,

---

POLLINATION IN FLOWERING PLANTS

In primitive plants, reproduction is a haphazard event, reliant upon water and wind to propagate the species. In contrast, the flowering plants use the flight of insects to improve the efficiency of their reproduction.

The coloured, scented petals of flowers attract insects. Once inside the bowl-shaped flower, the insect crawls around eating pollen and brushing it off the stamens and onto its body. The insect then visits the flower of another plant, where the pollen from the first plant is brushed onto the stigma, so fertilizing the second flower.

This achieves the all-important process of *cross-fertilization*, the process whereby genetic material from different plants is exchanged. This ensures the maintenance of vigour within the species, and allows it to produce variants that can colonize new localities. If the male and female organs in the flower reach maturity at different times, cross-fertilization – rather than self-fertilization – is assured.

Many amazing examples of special relationships between flowers and insects have developed. Many flowers produce a sugary fluid called *nectar*, which serves no other purpose than to attract the insects that feed on it. It is a 'reward' to the insects for helping in pollination, and it also appears to stop insects from eating the all-important pollen.

Many flowers, such as foxgloves, violets and rhododendrons, provide 'sign posts' to lead the insect into the flower. Some members of the orchid family have flowers that look like wasps or flies, and this deceives the appropriate insect into attempting to mate with the flower, so pollinating it.

Sometimes plant and insect become totally dependent on each other. The yucca plant of Central America can only be pollinated by the yucca moth. The moth lays its eggs only in the yucca flower and caterpillars can only eat the yucca plant. In this example the plant and the moth are totally dependent upon each other. Extinction of either species would spell doom for the other.

Douglas fir, western hemlock, cypresses, redwoods, yew and juniper. Conifers have waxy and often needle-shaped leaves, resinous wood, and male and female cones.

DIVISION CYCADOPHYTA

This gymnosperm group contains 11 genera of cycads, mostly in the tropics and sub-tropics. The cycads resemble small palms with short trunks, although some grow to over 10 m (33 ft).

DIVISION GINKGOPHYTA

This gymnosperm division has only one surviving species, *Ginkgo biloba* (the maidenhair tree), which is native to China. The ginkgo is a large, much-branched tree with fan-shaped leaves.

DIVISION GNETOPHYTA

This gymnosperm division contains only three living genera: *Gnetum* (tropical climbers and trees), *Ephedra* (drought-resistant shrubs), and the bizarre, desert-dwelling *Welwitschia* (one species), with its strap-like leaves. The flower-like organization of reproductive structures in gnetophytes suggests they may be the closest living relatives of the flowering plants.

DIVISION MAGNOLIOPHYTA

This division comprises the angiosperms or flowering plants. Flowers are thought by many scientists to have been derived from highly modified leaves. The male gametes (pollen) are produced in the anthers and the egg is enclosed within the ovary, to which is attached a style to receive the pollen. Anthers, ovaries and style are surrounded by petals and sepals to form the flower. The seed develops within the ovary, and the ovary wall often thickens to form a fruit. Many flowering plants show elaborate mechanisms of pollination and dispersal of the seeds.

The flowering plants are the most conspicuous plant group today. They comprise over 250 000 species,

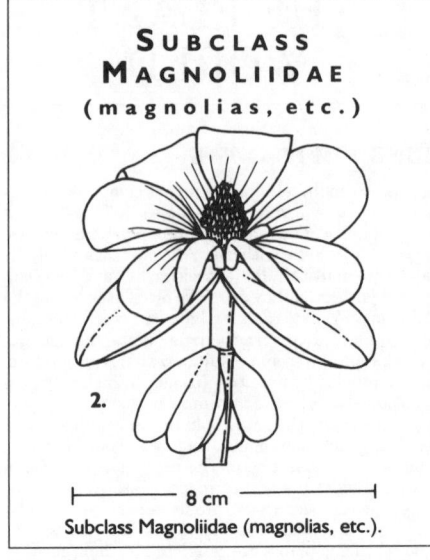

SUBCLASS MAGNOLIIDAE (magnolias, etc.)

2.

├────── 8 cm ──────┤

Subclass Magnoliidae (magnolias, etc.).

assigned to some 300 families contained within one of two classes, the Liliopsida (monocotyledons) and the Magnoliopsida (dicotyledons). All the subclasses are listed below, but only a selection of representative families are given for each, with representative plants in brackets.

Class Liliopsida The monocotyledons, comprising less than 30% of flowering-plant species. Distinguishing features include: a single seed leaf (cotyledon) in the embryo and young plant; parallel veins in leaves (which are usually long, narrow and pointed); floral organs in threes; and fibrous root systems. Most monocots are herbaceous; those that are trees (e.g. palms) lack wood and therefore cannot support a branching canopy. There are five subclasses:

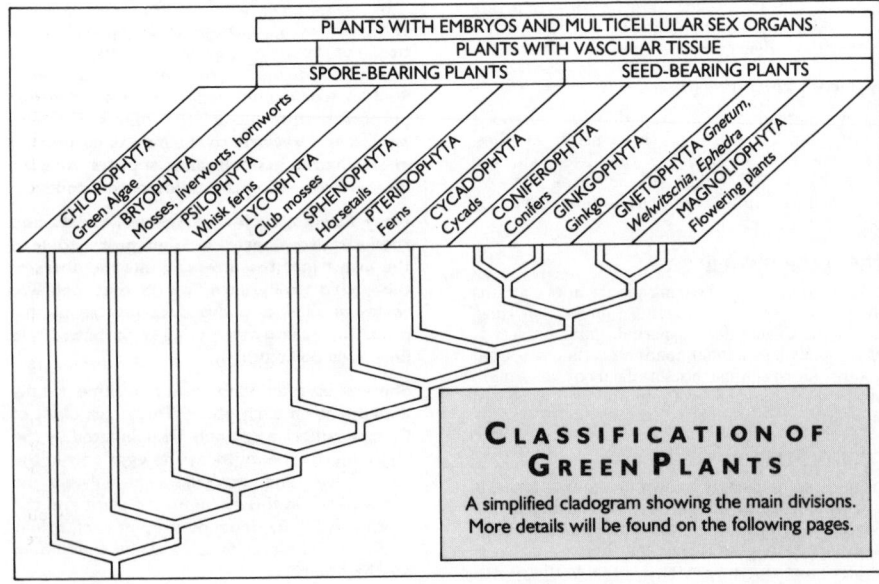

PLANTS WITH EMBRYOS AND MULTICELLULAR SEX ORGANS

PLANTS WITH VASCULAR TISSUE

SPORE-BEARING PLANTS — SEED-BEARING PLANTS

CHLOROPHYTA Green Algae / BRYOPHYTA Mosses, liverworts, hornworts / PSILOPHYTA Whisk ferns / LYCOPHYTA Club mosses / SPHENOPHYTA Horsetails / PTERIDOPHYTA Ferns / CYCADOPHYTA Cycads / CONIFEROPHYTA Conifers / GINKGOPHYTA Ginkgo / GNETOPHYTA *Gnetum, Welwitschia, Ephedra* / MAGNOLIOPHYTA Flowering plants

CLASSIFICATION OF GREEN PLANTS

A simplified cladogram showing the main divisions. More details will be found on the following pages.

Subclass Alismatidae: Alismataceae (water plantains), Potamogetonaceae (pondweed).

Subclass Arecidae: Arecaceae (formerly Palmae: palms).

Subclass Commelinidae: Commelinaceae (tradescantias), Bromeliaceae (bromeliads), Poaceae (formerly Graminae: grasses – including cereals – bamboo, reeds).

Subclass Zingiberidae: Zingiberaceae (gingers).

Subclass Liliidae: Liliaceae (lilies, tulips, bluebells), Alliaceae (onions, garlic), Amaryllidaceae (daffodils, snowdrops), Iridaceae (irises, crocuses, gladioli), Agavaceae (agaves), Asparagaceae (asparagus), Orchidaceae (orchids).

Class Magnoliopsida The dicotyledons, comprising over 70% of flowering-plant species. Distinguishing features include: two seed leaves (cotyledons); leaves with branching main veins connected by net-like venation; floral organs in fours or fives; and a persistent primary root system. Those that are trees are woody and can therefore support extensively branched canopies. There are six subclasses:

Subclass Magnoliidae: Magnoliaceae (magnolias), Lauraceae (laurels, bay, avocado), Nymphaeaceae (water lilies), Ranunculaceae (buttercups, clematis, delphiniums, anemones), Papaveraceae (poppies).

Subclass Hamamelidae: Hamamelidaceae (witch hazels), Platanaceae (plane trees, known as sycamores in the USA), Ulmaceae (elms), Urticaceae (nettles), Fagaceae (oaks, beeches), Betulaceae (birches, alders, hazels), Juglandaceae (walnuts).

Subclass Caryophyllidae: Caryophyllaceae (pinks), Chenopodiaceae (beets, spinach), Cactaceae (cacti), Polygonaceae (dock, knotgrass, buckwheat).

Subclass Dilleniidae: Paeoniaceae (peonies), Theaceae (camellias, tea plant), Violaceae (violets, pansies), Begoniaceae (begonias), Brassicaceae (formerly Cruciferae: cabbage, turnip, rape, mustard, wallflower), Salicaceae (willows, poplars, aspen), Ericaceae (heathers, rhododendrons, bilberry, cranberry), Primulaceae (primroses), Tiliaceae (lime trees), Euphorbiaceae (euphorbias, spurges).

Subclass Rosidae: Rosaceae (roses, strawberry, blackberry, raspberry, apple, cherry, plum, pear, hawthorn, rowan), Grossulariaceae (currants, gooseberries), Hydrangeaceae (hydrangeas), Saxifragaceae (saxifrages), Mimosaceae (acacias, mimosas), Fabaceae or Papilionaceae (formerly part of the Leguminosae, the legume family: peas, beans, soybean, peanut, clovers, vetches, gorse, brooms, lupins, lucerne), Myrtaceae (eucalyptuses), Rutaceae (citrus fruits: orange, grapefruit, lemon, lime), Hippocastanaceae (horse chestnut), Aceraceae (maples, sycamore), Geraniaceae (geraniums), Araliaceae (ivies, ginseng), Apiaceae (formerly Umbilliferae: carrot, parsley, coriander, caraway, hogweeds, hemlock, celery, parsnip, fennel, lovage), Aquifoliaceae (hollies), Vitaceae (grape vine, virginia creeper), Oleaceae (olive, ash).

Subclass Asteridae: Asteraceae (formerly Compositae: daisies, marigold, yarrow, chrysanthemum, thistles, dandelion, lettuce), Caprifoliaceae (honeysuckle, elder), Gentianaceae (gentians), Polemoniaceae (phloxes), Convolvulaceae (convolvulus, morning glory), Boraginaceae (borage, forget-me-not), Solanaceae (potato, tobacco, tomato, nightshades), Lamiaceae (formerly Labiatae: mints, deadnettles, basil, marjoram, thyme), Campanulaceae (bellflowers: campanulas, harebell).

PHOTOSYNTHESIS

The chemicals in plants that give them their green colour are the *chlorophylls*. The chlorophylls are particularly abundant in leaves, and are contained in *chloroplasts*, which are miniature organs within cells.

Chlorophyll strongly absorbs the blue and red regions of the light spectrum, and this ability is used to drive the most important single chemical reaction on Earth. This reaction, which maintains both plant and animal life, is photosynthesis.

In photosynthesis, carbon dioxide that has entered the plant from the air via the stomata (microscopic leaf pores) is transformed into the sugar glucose, and eventually sucrose and starch. This transformation is powered by the energy from sunlight absorbed by the chlorophylls. This is how the plant obtains the organic carbon needed for the synthesis of the materials of which it is composed.

As vegetation is the primary food of all animal food chains, it is by photosynthesis that almost all of the carbon enters the living world: hence it sustains life on Earth.

Overall, the chemical reaction of photosynthesis is: carbon dioxide + water + sunlight = glucose and oxygen. But this simple equation hides the complex chemical nature of photosynthesis, which comprises a set of reactions involved with the absorption of light (the *light reactions*) and a set that can take place in darkness (the *dark reactions*).

The essential feature of the light reactions is that the light energy absorbed by chlorophyll is used to split water molecules into hydrogen and oxygen. The oxygen ultimately released by plants is the source of all oxygen in the atmosphere of this planet

In the dark reactions carbon dioxide is converted into glucose by a complex cycle of chemical transformations, some of which use the hydrogen generated from water, and the chemical energy that has been produced from light energy.

Because in photosynthesis carbon dioxide is used up and oxygen given out as a waste product – the reverse of plant and animal respiration – the overall effect of plants and animals living together is to keep the levels of carbon dioxide and oxygen in the atmosphere more or less constant.

The felling and burning of vast areas of tropical forest, combined with industrial processes that produce vast quantities of carbon dioxide, may contribute to an imbalance in the atmosphere, and hece to the 'greenhouse effect'. (See The Environment – Deforestation, p. 113).

FRUITS

Common name	Scientific name	Geographical origin	Date first described or known
Apple	*Malus pumila*	Southwestern Asia	c. 450 BC
Apricot	*Prunus armeniaca*	Central and western China	BC (Piling and Dioscorides)
Avocado (pear)	*Persea americana*	Mexico and Central America	Early Spanish explorers, Clusius 1601
Banana	*Musa sapientum*	Southern Asia	Intro: Africa 1st century AD, Canary Is 15th century
Blackcurrants	*Ribes nigrum*	Northern Europe	First recorded in Britain in 17th-century herbals
Cherry	*Prunus avium*	Europe (near Dardanelles)	Prehistoric times
Coconut	*Cocus nucifera*	Pacific	Active planting since 12th century
Cranberry	*Oxycccus macrocarpus*	America	–
Custard apple	*Annona squamosa*	Peru and Ecuador	–
Date	*Phoenix dactylifera*	Unknown	Prehistoric times
Fig	*Ficus carica*	Syria westward to the Canary Is	c. 4000 BC (Egypt)
Gooseberry	*Ribes grossularia*	Europe	Fruiterer's bills from France (1276–92) of Edward I
Grape	*Vitis vinifera*	Around Caspian and Black Seas	c. 4000 BC
Grapefruit	*Citrus grandis*	Malay Archipelago and neighbouring islands	12th or 13th century
Kiwifruit	*Actinidia chinensis*	China	–
Lemon	*Citrus limon*	SE Asia	11th–13th centuries
Lime	*Citrus aurantifolia*	Northern Burma	11th–13th centuries
Lychee	*Litchi chinensis*	Southern China	–
Mandarin	*Citrus reticulata*	China	220 BC in China; Europe 1805
Mango	*Mangifera indica*	Southeastern Asia	c. 16th century; Cult. India 4th–5th century BC
Olive	*Olea europaea*	Syria to Greece	Prehistoric times
Orange	*Citrus sinensis*	China	2200 BC (Europe 15th century)
Papaya	*Carica papaya*	West Indian Islands or Mexican mainland	14th–15th centuries
Passion fruit	*Passiflora edulis*	South America	–
Peach	*Prunus persica*	China?	300 BC (Greece)
Pear	*Pyrus communis*	Western Asia	Prehistoric times
Persimmon	*Diospyros kaki*	China/Japan	Thousands of years
Pineapple	*Ananas comosus*	Guadeloupe	c. time of Columbus
Plum	*Prunus domestica*	Western Asia	Possibly AD 100
Pomegranate	*Punica granatum*	Iran	–
Quince	*Cydonia oblonga*	Northern Iran	BC
Raspberry	*Rubus idaeus*	Europe	Turner's Herbal of 1548
Redcurrants	*Ribes* species	Europe/Northern Asia	First description in German 17th-century herbals
Rhubarb	*Rheum rhaponticum*	Eastern Mediterranean lands and Asia Minor	2700 BC (China)
Strawberry	*Fragaria* species	Europe	Rome 200 BC
Ugli	*Citrus reticulata*	Jamaica	–
Water melon	*Citrullus laratus*	Central Africa	c. 2000 BC (Egypt)

VEGETABLES

Common name	Scientific name	Geographical origin	Date first described or known
Asparagus	*Asparagus officinalis*	Eastern Mediterranean	c. 200 BC
Aubergine	*Solanum melongena*	Asia	India 4000 years ago
Beetroot	*Beta vulgaris*	Mediterranean area	2nd century BC
Broad bean	*Vicia faba*	–	Widely cultivated in prehistoric times
Broccoli	*Brassica oleracea* (variety *Italica*)	Eastern Mediterranean	1st century AD
Brussels sprout	*Brassica oleracea* (variety *gemmifera*)	Northern Europe	1587 (northern Europe)
Cabbage	*Brassica oleracea* (variety *capitata*)	Eastern Mediterranean lands and Asia Minor	c. 600 BC
Carrot	*Daucus carota*	Afghanistan	c. 500 BC

Cauliflower	*Brassica oleracea* (variety *botrytis*)	Eastern Mediterranean	6th century BC
Celeriac	*Apium graveolens rapaceum*	Mediterranean	Wild plant first used by Greeks. By 17th century garden celery distinct from wild plant
Celery	*Apium graveolens*	Caucasus	c. 850 BC
Chicory	*Cichorium intybus*	Mediterranean	Ancient Greek or Rome
Chive	*Allium schoenoprasum*	Eastern Mediterranean	c. 100 BC
Courgette	*Cucurbita pepo*	Italy	–
Cucumber	*Cucumis sativus*	Northern India	2nd century BC (Egypt 1300 BC)
Egg plant	*Solanum melongena*	India, Assam, Burma	c. 450 AD (China)
Endive	*Cichorium endivia*	Eastern Mediterranean lands and Asia Minor	BC
Florence fennel	*Foeniculum vulgare dulce*	Italy	Brought to England in Stuart times
Garden pea	*Pisum sativum*	Central Asia	3000–2000 BC
Garlic	*Allium sativum*	Middle Asia	c. 900 BC (Homer)
Gherkin (W. Indian)	*Cucumis anguria*	Northern India	2nd century BC
Ginger	*Zingiber officinale*	SE Asia	Thousands of years old
Green beans	*Phaseolus vulgaris*	South America	Reached England by 1594
Globe artichoke	*Cynara scolymus*	Western and central Mediterranean	c. 500 BC
Jerusalem artichoke	*Helianthus tuberosus*	Canada	1616
Kale	*Brassica oleracea* (variety *acephala*)	Eastern Mediterranean lands and Asia Minor	c. 500 BC
Kohlrabi	*Brassica oleracea cauloraba*	Asia	Taken from Italy to Germany mid-16th century
Leek	*Allium porrum*	Middle Asia	c. 1000 BC
Lettuce	*Lactuca sativa*	Asia Minor, Iran, Turkistan	4500 BC (Egyptian tomb)
Mange tout	*Pisum sativum saccharatum*	Near East	17th century
Marrow	*Cucurbita pepo*	America?	16th–17th century (Mexican sites 7000–5500 BC)
Mushrooms	*Psalliota compestris*	Unknown	Mentioned in Ancient Rome and Greece
Musk melon	*Cucumis melo*	Iran	2900 BC (Egypt)
Okra	*Hibiscus esculentus*	Tropical Africa	Egypt 13th century
Olives	*Olea europaea*	Eastern Mediterranean	Found on coast of Syria and dated 4th millennium BC
Onion	*Allium cepa*	Middle Asia	c. 3000 BC (Egypt)
Parsley	*Petroselinum crispum*	Southern Europe	Used by Greeks and Romans
Parsnip	*Pastinaca sativa*	Caucasus	1st century BC
Peas	*Psium sativum*	The Near East	9570 BC Burma and Thailand
Pepper	*Capsicum frutescens*	Peru	Early burial sites, Peru; intro. Europe 1493
Potato	*Solanum tuberosum*	Southern Chile	c. 1530; intro. Ireland 1565
Pumpkin	*Cucurbita maxima*	Northern Andean Argentina	1591
Radish	*Raphanus sativus*	Western Asia, Egypt	c. 3000 BC
Red cabbage	*Brassica oleracea*	Mediterranean area and/or Asia Minor	England 14th century
Red kidney beans	*Phaseolus vulgaris*	Probably South America	–
Runner beans	*Phaseolus vulgaris*	Central America	c. 1500 (known from Mexican sites 7000–5000 BC)
Soybean	*Soja max*	China	c. 2850 BC
Spinach	*Spinacia oleracea*	Iran	AD 647 in Nepal
Spring onion	*Allium cepa*	Central Asia	Collected by 19th century botanists (reference to onions can be traced to 1st Egyptian dynasty 3200 BC)
Swede	*Brassica napobrassica*	Europe	1620
Sweet corn	*Zea mays*	Andes	Cult. early times in America; intro. Europe after 1492
Sweet potato	*Ipomoea batatas*	Tropical America	Prehistoric Peru
Tomato (technically a fruit)	*Lycopersicon esculentum*	Bolivia–Ecuador–Peru area	Italy c. 1550
Turnip	*Brassica rapa*	Greece	2000 BC
Water chestnuts	*Eleocharis dulcis*	Southern China	Neolithic times
Watercress	*Nasturtium officinale*	–	John Gerarde's Herball of 1597
White cabbage	*Brassica oleracea capita*	Mediterranean area and/or Asia Minor	Greek kales 600 BC. Germany 1150
Yams	*Discorea rotundra*	Africa	In England in 16th century

AGRICULTURAL CROPS

Apples About 25 species of the genus *Malus* are cultivated for their fruit. Thousands of varieties have been bred for cooking, for dessert (eating apples) or for brewing (cider). The apple originated in Southwest Asia and is known to have been cultivated c. 450 BC.

Bananas A fruit of the genus *Musa*, the banana is one of the world's major food crops. It is grown in the tropics, but its flavour and nutritional value is enjoyed all over the world. The cooking varieties, plantains, are starchy rather than sweet.

Barley An annual temperate grass of the genus *Hordeum*, especially *H. vulgare* and *H. distichum*. Widely grown, the grain is used in brewing and distilling, for making puddings and as animal feed. Barley probably originated in the Ethiopian highlands and was first cultivated in Egypt c. 5000 BC.

Cassava An edible tuberous plant *Manihot utilissima*, also known as manioc. It is cultivated throughout the tropical world; its tuberous roots producing cassava flour, breads, tapioca, an alcoholic drink and a laundry starch. Cassava was probably first cultivated by the Maya in Yucatán.

Cocoa beans Cocoa beans come from a tropical American tree *Theobroma cacao*. The beans are fermented and roasted to produce cocoa, chocolate and cocoa butter. The use of cocoa beans was first recognized by Pre-Columbian civilizations, and brought to Europe in the 16th century.

Coffee Coffee is a tropical evergreen shrub belonging to the genus *Coffea*. Its seeds, or beans, are roasted, ground and brewed with water to produce a beverage that is drunk by one third of the world's population. The two species, *Coffea arabica* and *Coffea robusta* are cultivated mostly in Latin America and Africa respectively. The earliest cultivated species, *Coffea arabica* was found in Arabia.

Cotton A number of subtropical shrubs, belonging to the genus *Gossypium*, are commonly referred to as cotton. Cotton fibres are grown to be made into a variety of fabrics. Members of the genus are native to most subtropical regions and the fibre has been used since early times.

Flax Flax (*Linum usitatissimum*) is a temperate plant grown for its fibre, from which linen is made, and for its seed (linseed, a source of oil). Flax fibres have been found in prehistoric settlements and in Ancient Egyptian tombs.

Maize Maize (*Zea mays*) is a tall annual grass grown for its grain, which is used for food, animal fodder and as a source of vegetable oil. In North America it is known as corn. Maize probably originated in Central America and was first cultivated in pre-colonial days in North, Central and South America.

Oats An annual temperate grass (*Avena sativa*), oats are widely grown. Its grain is mainly fed to livestock, but is also used in breakfast cereals and for biscuits. Oats originated as a weed in Western Europe and have been cultivated since early times.

Pears The pear is a temperate tree (*Pyrus communis*) related to the rose family. The second most important deciduous fruit tree, the pear is grown entirely for human consumption as a fruit or a drink (perry). Pears originated in western Asia and have been cultivated since early history.

Potatoes The potato (*Solanum tuberosum*) is a tuber-bearing plant grown for human and animal consumption. Native to the Andean region of South America, the potato has been cultivated since about AD 100 and was introduced to Europe by the Spanish in the 16th century and to England, reputedly, by Walter Raleigh.

Rapeseed A member of the mustard family, rapeseed or colza (*Brassica napus*) is grown for its seed from which an oil – used in cooking and as a fuel or a lubricant – is extracted. Colza is native to Europe.

Rice A tropical starchy cereal, rice (*Oryza sativa*) is grown almost entirely for human consumption. It is the staple crop of over one half of the world's population. The crop is produced under irrigation, and although it is largely confined to East, South and Southeast Asia, small quantities of rice have been grown in Europe since the Middle Ages. Rice is known to have been cultivated in India c. 3000 BC.

Rye Rye (*Secale cereale*) is an extensively grown temperate cereal. It is cultivated in areas in which the soil and the climate are not suitable for less hardy cereals. Rye is used to make flour and as a livestock feed. It is known to have been cultivated in Asia Minor about 6500 BC.

Soyabeans Soyabeans – known in North America as soybeans – is a subtropical legume (*Glycine soja*) grown for its beans, which are used for human consumption (for example, as a meat substitute or vegetable oil), for livestock feed, or as a source of oil for paints, fertilizers and adhesives. The plant has been cultivated in China since c. 3000 BC.

Sugar beet Sugar beet (*Beta vulgaris*) is, after sugar cane, the second most important source of sugar. A temperate crop, beet was grown for fodder long before being cultivated for sugar. Sugar was first extracted from beet in Germany in 1747.

Sugar cane Sugar cane is a thick perennial grass cultivated in tropical and subtropical regions. Its sweet sap is a major source of sugar and molasses, which, when fermented, produces rum. It is thought that sugar cane originated in New Guinea.

Tea Tea leaves come from the tea plant *Camellia sinensis*. The infusion of the leaves in boiling water produces a beverage that is drunk by half the world's population. Tea drinking is thought to originate in China, over two thousand years ago.

Tobacco The leaves of many species of *Nicotiana* are cured for smoking, snuff, and chewing. Wild tobacco (*Nicotiana rustica*) is the variety grown in southern and southeast Europe. Tobacco was widely cultivated in pre-colonial America.

Tomatoes The tomato (*Lycopersicon esculentum*) is a fruit that is part of the nightshade family. Subtropical in origin, it is grown entirely for human consumption. The tomato, which is native to the Peruvian-Ecuadorian Andes, was introduced to Italy via Mexico during the 16th century.

Wheat There are thousands of varieties of this temperate cereal, although the most widespread are *Triticum vulgare* (which is used for bread), *Triticum durum* (for pasta), and *Triticum compactum* (for making cakes and biscuits). The most important cereal, wheat is usually grown in preference to other cereals where conditions allow. Wheat was cultivated in the Euphrates Valley in Iraq about 7000 BC.

NATIONAL PARKS

Many countries have set aside areas for the conservation of the landscape and as a protected habitat for flora and fauna.

MAJOR NATIONAL PARKS IN AFRICA

Arusha (Tanzania) A region of mountains, swamps, forest and lakes. Area: 53 km^2 (137 sq mi). Fauna includes hippopotamus, elephants, various species of antelope and flamingos.

Etosha (Namibia) Semiarid plains around the Etosha Pan. Area: 22 270 km^2 (8598 sq mi). Fauna includes elephants, rhinoceros, lion, leopard, lynx, Burchell's zebra, and various species of antelope.

Gemsbok (Botswana) A region of desert, plains and grasslands in southeast Botswana. Area: 24 305 km^2 (9384 sq mi). Fauna includes eland, gemsbok, hartebeest, springbok, widebeest and kuku.

Hwange (Zimbabwe) Expanse of the Kalahari Desert, including Nyamandhlovu Pan. Area: 14 651 km^2 (5657 sq mi). Fauna includes black rhinoceros (for which it is a refuge), buffalo, brindled gnu, roan antelope, impala and sassaby.

Kafue (Zambia) A pleateau area including some of the Kalahari Desert in the South, and bordered by the Kafue river. Area: 22 400 km^2 (8650 sq mi). Fauna includes hippopotamus, black rhinoceros (for which the park is a refuge), crocodile, many species of antelope, and numerous birds.

Kruger (Transvaal, South Africa) An area of hills and plains. Area: 19 485 km^2 (7523 sq mi). Fauna includes white rhinoceros (for which the park is a refuge), African buffalo and red jackal.

Manovo-Gounda-Saint Floris (Central African Republic) Part of the upper basin of the Chari River. Area: 17 400 km^2 (6718 sq mi). Fauna includes buffalo, large antelope, many species of birds including egret.

Namib Desert/Naukluft (Namibia) The Park stretches from the Atlantic coast to the Namib Desert and the Naufkluft Mountains. Area: 23 400 km^2 (9035 sq mi). Fauna includes elephant, the desert golden mole, black-backed jackal, bat-eared fox, sand grouse, egret and lark.

Ngorongoro (Tanzania) Several extinct volcanic craters, some including lakes. Area: 3202 km^2 (8292 sq mi). Fauna includes a cross-section of wildlife typical of African savannah.

Serengeti (Tanzania) a large plain with hilly ranges and rocky kopjes. Area: 14 763 km^2 (5700 sq mi). Fauna includes elephant, black rhinoceros (for which the park is a refuge), lion, leopard, cheetah, hyena, buffalo, zebra, giraffe and various species of antelope.

Tsavo (Kenya) An area stretching from the semiarid plains in the southeast to the Chyulu Hills and the foothills of Mt Kilimanjaro in the West. Area: 20 821 km^2 (8039 sq mi). Fauna includes black rhinoceros (for which the park is a refuge), various species of antelope (lesser kudu, fringe-eared oryx, gerenuk, hartebeest), and numerous birds.

MAJOR NATIONAL PARKS OF ASIA

Angkor (Cambodia) Tropical forest surrounding the Angkor temple ruins. Area: 41 km^2 (107 sq mi). Primarily desinated to preserve the historic site.

Daisetsuzan (Japan) Part of the Ishikari vol-

canic mountain range in Hokkaido. Area: 2309 km^2 (892 sq mi). Fauna includes Asiatic black bear, northern pika, chipmunk, Japanese macaque, black woodpecker and three-toed woodpecker.

Fuji-Hakone-Izu (Japan) Comprises Mount Fuji, the Izu peninsula and the seven active volcanic islands of Izu. Area: 1232 km^2 (476 sq mi). Fauna includes skia deer, wild boar, Japanese macaque monkeys, Japanese dormouse, Japanese auk and many other birds.

Gir Lion (Gujarat, India) A hilly region on the Kathiawar Peninsula. Area: 1412 km^2 (545 sq mi). Fauna includes lion, leopard, hyena, antelope, deer, wild pig, sloth bear and monkey.

Khao Yai (Thailand) An area of mountains and plateaus in southwest Thailand. Area: 2168 km^2 (837 sq mi). Fauna includes elephant, tiger, wild boar, mongoose, civet, langur, gibbon and numerous birds (silver pheasant, red-billed blue magpie).

MAJOR NATIONAL PARKS IN EUROPE

Abruzzi (Italy) Part of the Apennine mountains. Area: 392 km^2 (151 sq mi). Fauna includes brown bear, chamois, golden eagle, lynx, polecat, wolf.

Bialowieski (Poland) and Belovezhskaya (Belarus) (contiguous) The best-preserved primeval lowland forest in Europe. Combined area: 358 km^2 (928 sq mi). Fauna includes European bison, tarpan, lynx, brown bear.

Cévennes (France) In the south of the Massif Central. Area: 844 km^2 (326 sq mi). Fauna includes genet, golden eagle, mountain sheep, wild boar.

Dartmoor (England, UK) Moorland in central Devon. Area: 945 km^2 (365 sq mi). Fauna includes fallow, red and roe deer, wild pony.

Gran Paradiso (Italy) In the Alps on the Piedmont-Valle d'Aosta border. Area: 700 km^2 (270 sq mi). Fauna includes chamois, golden eagle, otter, ibex, marten, ptarmigan, white grouse.

Hohe Tauern (Austria) In the eastern Alps – the park includes the Grossglockner. Area: 2589 km^2 (1000 sq mi). Fauna includes chamois, marmot.

Hortobágyi (Hungary) Steppe and marshes in central Hungary. Area: 520 km^2 (201 sq mi). Fauna includes many species of geese.

Lake District (England, UK) The mountains of Cumbria. Area: 2243 km^2 (866 sq mi). Fauna includes fell ponies, mountain sheep, red deer.

Pallas-Ounastunturi (Finland) On a plateau in Lapland. Area: 500 km^2 (193 sq mi). Fauna includes brown bear, crane, elk, lemming, reindeer, whooper swan.

Pembrokeshire Coast (Wales, UK) Coastal region of western Dyfed. Area: 583 km^2 (225 sq mi). Fauna includes many varieties of bird, including buzzard, chough, merlin and sea birds as well as grey seal, otter, polecat.

Pfälzerwald (Germany) The Palatinate plateau. Area: 1793 km^2 (692 sq mi). Fauna includes European bison, mountain sheep, mountain goat.

Rondane (Norway) A mountainous region on the borders of Hedmark and Oppland. Area: 572 km^2 (221 sq mi). Fauna includes brown bear, elk, golden eagle, lemming, lynx, reindeer, wolf.

Sarek (Sweden) A mountainous area in Lapland. Area: 1940 km^2 (749 sq mi). Fauna includes similar to Rondane, see above.

Skaftafell (Iceland) In the south of Iceland. Area: 500 km² (193 sq mi). Fauna includes bear, grey seal, many species of sea bird.

Snowdonia (Wales, UK) The mountainous area around Snowdon in Gwynedd. Area: 2171 km² (838 sq mi). Fauna includes otter, polecat, pine marten.

Vanoise (France) Along the Italian border in Savoy. Area: 528 km² (204 sq mi). Fauna includes chamois, golden eagle, otter, ibex, marten, ptarmigan, white grouse.

MAJOR NATIONAL PARKS IN NORTH AMERICA

Banff (Alberta, Canada) Mountainous terrain in the central Canadian Rockies. Area: 6641 km² (2564 sq mi). Fauna includes mule deer, caribou, elk, bear (grizzly and black) and golden eagle.

Carlsbad Caverns (New Mexico, USA) A system of 35 limestone caverns in the Guadelupe Mountains. Area: 73 km² (189 sq mi). Fauna includes bats and surface mammals.

Death Valley (California-Nevada, USA) A large low-lying desert, surrounded by mountains. Area: 8368 km² (3231 sq mi). Fauna includes desert bighorn sheep, cougar and fishes descended from fish of the Pleistocene Age. It is the lowest point in the Western Hemisphere.

Denali (Alaska, USA) A mountainous area on the northern flank of the Alaska Range, including North America's highest mountain, Mt McKinley. Area: 24 419 km² (9428 sq mi). Fauna includes moose, grizzly bear, Arctic ground squirrel, golden eagle.

Everglades (Florida, USA) A large flat area of swamps and islands, plus Florida Bay. Area: 5661 km² (2186 sq mi). Fauna includes manatee, saltwater crocodile, matamata and other turtles, cougar, ibis, bald eagle and kites.

Grand Canyon (Arizona, USA) Gorge of the Colorado River. Area: 4931 km² (1904 sq mi). Fauna includes 100 species of mammals, 100 varieties of birds and 25 kinds of reptiles and amphibians. The gorge's rocks represent a vast stretch of geological time.

Jasper (Alberta, Canada) Part of the eastern Canadian Rockies. Area: 10 878 km² (4200 sq mi). Fauna includes elk, moose, mountain caribou, cougar, osprey, golden eagle, and blue grouse.

Katmai (Alaska, USA) Area of dying volcanoes in the Aleutian Range. Area: 16 550 km² (6390 sq mi). Fauna includes the Alaskan brown bear (the largest land carnivore), caribou, moose, and many small mammals, birds and fish.

Lake Mead (Arizona-Nevada, USA) An area of canyons of the Colorado River. Area: 6057 km² (2309 sq mi). Fauna includes desert bighorn sheep, wild burro, cougar, bobcat and many small animals. The canyons contain fossils of prehistoric animals.

Redwood (California, USA) On the Pacific coast. Area: 442 km² (171 sq mi). Fauna includes Roosevelt elk, fox, squirrel, rabbit, salmon, trout, and numerous birds.

Rocky Mountain (Colorado, USA) A region in the Front Range of the Rocky Mountains. Area: 1068 km² (412 sq mi). Fauna includes bighorn sheep, elk, beaver, deer, cougar, golden eagle and hawks.

Wood Buffalo (Alberta-Northwest Territories, Canada) Area of open plains between Lake Athabasca and Great Slave Lake. Area: 44 800 km² (17 300 sq mi). Fauna includes bison (wood buffalo and plains buffalo), elk, moose, woodland caribou, bear (black and grizzly), lynx, whooping crane and grouse. The park is a refuge for bison and whooping cranes.

Yellowstone (Wyoming-Montana-Idaho, USA) Part of the Rocky Mountains. Area: 8984 km² (3469 sq mi). Fauna includes wapiti, bison and over 200 species of birds (trumpeter swan, tanager, Canada goose). The largest thermal area in the world, the park contains mud volcanoes, hot springs, sulfur pools and geysers.

Yosemite (California, USA) A region of canyons, gorges and peaks in the Sierra Nevada. It contains the highest waterfall in America, Yosemite Falls. Area: 3079 km² (1189 sq mi). Fauna includes bear, deer, ground squirrel, chipmunk, Steller's jay, Clark's nutcracker and mountain quail.

MAJOR NATIONAL PARKS IN OCEANIA

Fiordland (New Zealand) A rugged area on the southwestern coast of South Island. Area: 12 116 km² (4678 sq mi). Fauna includes seals and many birds (mountain parrot, bush hawk, kiwi), and land mammals introduced by man. The park is a refuge for the takahe and kakapo.

Kosciusko (New South Wales, Australia) An area of alpine peaks and plateaus in the Great Dividing Range. Area: 6297 km² (2431 sq mi). Fauna includes grey forester kangaroo, brush-tailed rock wallaby, wombats, marsupial and pouched mice, koala, local duck-billed platypus, and many birds (emu, currawongs).

Mount Aspiring (New Zealand) A mountainous region that includes the slopes of the Southern Alps on South Island. Area: 2873 km² (1109 sq mi). Fauna includes many varieties of birds (parakeets, owl parrot), red deer and opossum.

Uluru (Northern Territory, Australia) An area of rocky terrain, including Ayers Rock, the monolith cluster of Mt. Olga, and aboriginal rock paintings. Area: 1261 km² (487 sq mi). Fauna includes kangaroo, wallaby, euro, dingo, bandicoot rat, emu, and various snakes and lizards.

MAJOR NATIONAL PARKS IN SOUTH AMERICA

Amazonia (Brazil) Area of tropical rain forest along the Amazon river basin. Area: 10 000 km² (4000 sq mi). Fauna includes armadillo, capybara, tapir, great anteater, manatee, many species of monkey, and numerous species of bird (hummingbird, toucan, parrots and macaws).

Canaima (Venezuela) The large mountainous La Gran Sabana basin. Area: 30 000 km² (11 583 sq mi). Fauna includes jaguar, tiger cat, tapir, peccary, armadillo, agouti, capybara, opossums, spider monkeys, jacamars, harpy eagle and puffbirds.

Galápagos (Ecuador) Santa Cruz Island on the Galápagos archipelago. Area: 6790 km² (2621 sq mi). Fauna includes the giant tortoise, giant iguana, flamingo, pelican and Darwin's finches.

Manu (Peru) Comprises a rugged Andean area, part of the Amazon River system and tropical forest. Area: 15 328 km² (5918 sq mi). Fauna includes various birds and small mammals.

THE ANIMAL WORLD

KINGDOM ANIMALIA

One of the most important events in the evolution of life on Earth was the development of multicellular organisms – ranging from simple worms to complex insects and squids – from unicellular animal-like protists. Most groups of primitive multicellular invertebrates are found in very old fossil-bearing rocks, so it is clear that this major breakthrough occurred at least 600 million years ago.

The similarity in mineral composition of animal body fluids and sea water indicates that all groups of primitive animals arose in the sea. One of these groups (the echinoderms) is of particular interest in that they share a common ancestor with the chordates, from which all vertebrates – including man – evolved.

All animals are multicellular with some kind of interconnection – a nervous system – between the cells. Each cell is bounded by a simple flexible membrane, and, as they do not contain chloroplasts, all animals rely on an organic source of food. Sexual reproduction generally takes place between two different gametes, a motile sperm and non-motile egg.

Scientists group animals into approximately 28 phyla, although there is some disagreement as to whether certain small groups are distinct phyla.

SUBKINGDOM PARAZOA

The two phyla grouped in the subkingdom Parazoa comprise animals in which different cell types perform different functions – feeding, defence, reproduction, etc – although they are not grouped into tissues or organs. The sponges (Phylum Porifera) comprise some 5000 species inhabiting both fresh and marine waters.

SUBKINGDOM EUMETAZOA

All the remaining animals are grouped under the subkingdom Eumetazoa and assigned to either the division Radiata or the division Bilateralia. They are characterized by discrete tissues and organs which develop from early embryonic cell layers (ectoderm and endoderm).

DIVISION RADIATA

The animals in this division all show radial symmetry – the animal may be divided along more than one plane through the centre to give mirror-image halves. The body is organized as two layers of cells separated by a jelly-like middle layer, while the nervous system forms a diffuse net. The division comprises about 9600 species, assigned to two phyla. The phylum Cnidaria (Coelenterata) includes jellyfishes, sea anemones and the corals – animals possessing tentacles armed with stinging cells.

DIVISION BILATERALIA

The animals contained within this division may only be divided by one plane to yield mirror halves. They possess an extra embryonic cell layer – the mesoderm – which forms most of the body and in which, in most animals, there is a body cavity – the coelom – containing the digestive tract and other visceral organs.

SUBDIVISION ACOELOMATA

The members of the four phyla comprising this subdividion do not possess a coelom. The best known are members of the phylum Platyhelminthes, which includes the flatworms, the flukes (external and internal parasites) and the tapeworms (internal parasites). These have a recognizable head and a mouth that leads to a blind-ending gut with no anus.

SUBDIVISION PSEUDOCOELOMATA

The animals assigned to this subdivision possess a body cavity that is not developed as a true coelom. They are characterized by a through-gut with a mouth at one end and the anus at the other. Nine phyla are grouped within the subdivision, most of whose members are tiny inconspicuous animals living in sand and mud. The two most important phyla are the nematodes and the rotifers.

PHYLUM NEMATODA

The nematodes – or roundworms – comprise an extremely large group of at least 100 000 species (many undescribed). Unlike true worms they show no sign of segmentation of the body. Roundworms are found in nearly every terrestrial and aquatic environment. They include free-living forms as well as parasites, including hookworm and filaria (one of which causes elephantiasis).

PHYLUM ROTIFERA

Rotifers are minute wheel-like animals, so called because the beating of the crown of cilia resembles a spinning wheel. Most of the 2000 species live in fresh water.

SUBDIVISION COELOMATA

This vast subdivision includes all the remaining animals from earthworms to man. They are characterized by possession of a true coelom and nearly all have well-developed nervous and circulatory systems. The two types of coelomate animal are distinguished by a distinction based on early embryonic development. In members of the series Protostoma the hollow ball of cells, the blastula, which develops from the fertilized egg folds in on itself to form the gut and the resulting pore becomes the mouth. In the series Deuterostoma the first pore becomes the anus and the mouth develops later as a second opening.

SERIES PROTOSTOMA

In most systems of classification this series includes at least 11 phyla, some of which have very few members. Others are much more numerous – the molluscs and the arthropods are the two largest phyla in the animal kingdom. Phyla of the series Protostoma include:

PHYLUM ECTOPROCTA

The members of this phylum are sometimes called bryozoans or moss animals. There are about 5000 species which form colonies spreading over the surfaces of rocks and seaweeds. These tiny animals feed by means of tentacles.

PHYLUM ANNELIDA

The 9000 species of annelids (true worms) are characterized by an externally and internally segmented body, and a closed blood system (with discrete blood vessels). The phylum is divided into classes including:

Class Polychaeta the class containing the paddle (bristle) worms. These are mostly free-living marine animals with distinctive swimming appendages composed of many bristles on every segment. The mouth is equipped with jaws.

Class Oligochaeta the class including the familiar earthworms. In these annelids the bristles are inconspicuous.

Class Hirudinea the class containing the leeches, which are characterized by a sucker at either end. Some are free-living but many are blood-sucking parasites.

PHYLUM MOLLUSCA

This large and diverse group of animals comprises nearly 110 000 species. Most show no trace of segmentation. The body consists of a head, a foot and a hump usually covered by a shell (although sometimes the shell is contained within the body). There is an open circulation where the blood is simply pumped directly into a body cavity. There are seven classes of molluscs but only three are conspicuous in the modern world.

Class Gastropoda the class including snails, limpets and slugs. The body is coiled and is usually contained within a shell, which is reduced in slugs. There is a distinct head with eyes, and the mouth contains a rasp-like tongue – the extendable radula. The foot is particularly large.

Class Bivalvia (Lamellibranchiata) a class sometimes known as pelecypods. The body is enclosed completely within two shells covering either side of the body and hinged along one edge. The bivalves – most of which are marine – feed by filtering small particles out of a water stream that is passed over enlarged gills. Examples include clams, cockles and oysters.

Class Cephalopoda a class of molluscs in which the foot is developed into a series of tentacles. They include squids, cuttlefish and octupuses. The head is large with complex eyes, structurally very similar to our own. The shell is reduced and not externally obvious in most members of the class.

PHYLUM ARTHROPODA

The arthropods comprise by far the largest animal phylum. Over a million species have been described, most belonging to the class Insecta. Some scientists believe that another 10 million insects or more remain to be described. Arthropods have segmented bodies and segmented appendages, both encased in a chitinous exoskeleton. The rather rigid exoskeleton means that growth takes place in bursts between moults. As in molluscs, there is an open circulatory system. There are nine separate classes of arthropods including such diverse animals as centipedes, millipedes and horseshoe crabs as well as members of the three dominant classes.

Class Crustacea a class characterized by hard exoskeletons and segmented appendages. Nearly every segment of the body bears appendages that are modified for sensing (antennae), eating (mandibles etc.), walking and swimming, and respiration (gills). There are two pairs of antennae. The majority of crustaceans – such as waterfleas, crabs, ostracods and copepods – are aquatic but some are terrestrial (e.g. woodlice).

Class Insecta a mainly terrestrial group, although there are important aquatic insects and many have an aquatic larval stage. Insects have a distinct head, thorax and abdomen. There is a single pair of antennae, three pairs of legs, and usually one or two pairs of wings on the thorax. Most systems of classification assign the insects to about 25 orders that may be grouped in one of two subclasses. Insects represented in the subclass Heterometabola develop through successive stages (instars) of increasingly more 'adult' forms. Examples of this type include locusts and cockroaches (order Orthoptera).

Many insects go through a drastic metamorphosis in their development, changing from a larva (often grub-like) through a pupal stage to emerge in fully adult form (subclass Homometabola). Familiar examples are butterflies and moths (order Lepidoptera), flies (order Diptera), in which the hind pair of wings are modified as balancing organs, beetles (order Coleoptera) and bees, ants and wasps (Order Hymenoptera), which often show very complex social organizations.

Class Arachnida the class including the scorpions and spiders. The body is divided into two parts: the head and thorax form the front part carrying four pairs of legs; the abdomen forms the hind part and in spiders often carries spinnerets to spin webs.

SERIES DEUTEROSTOMA

These are animals in which the mouth develops as a secondary opening in early ontogeny. There are four phyla, but two – beardworms and arrow worms – are very small with about 150 species of uncommon animals in total. The two remaining phyla are the echinoderms and the very numerous and diverse chordates.

PHYLUM ECHINODERMATA

The echinoderms are exclusively marine animals characterized by five rows of tiny extensible tube feet that often protrude through a calcium carbonate skeleton. There are about 6000 species arranged in five classes of which the starfishes (class Asteroidea) and the sea urchins (class Echinoidea) are the most conspicuous.

PHYLUM CHORDATA

All chordates have a stiffening rod – the notochord – which provides a flexible support along the back. Above the notochord is a hollow nerve cord which, in most cases, is expanded as an elaborate brain. Chordates possess a true tail developed behind the anus. The phylum includes three rather small groups of small marine animals – subphylum Hemichordata (acorn worms), Subphylum Tunicata (sea squirts) and Subphylum Cephalochordata. The remaining subphylum Craniata is by far the largest, containing birds, fishes, reptiles and mammals.

SUBPHYLUM CRANIATA

The chordates assigned to this subphylum possess a recognizable brain, eyes and nose. They include several groups that are traditionally regarded as classes, although it has become apparent that at least two of these classes (the bony fishes and the reptiles) are not natural groups because some of their members are more closely related to members of other classes. However, the traditional classes are commonly retained as convenient groups.

ANIMAL KINGDOM

Subkingdom	Division	Subdivision	Series	Phylum	Subphylum	Class	Subclass	Representative species
Parazoa				Porifera				sponges
	Radiata			Cnidaria				sea anemones
		Acoelomata		Platyhelminthes				flatworms
		Pseudocoelomata		Nematoda Rotifera				roundworms wheel animalcules
		Coelomata		Ectoprocta				bryozoans
			Protostoma	Annelida		Polychaeta Oligochaeta Hirudinea		paddleworms earthworms leeches
				Mollusca		Gastropoda Bivalvia Cephalopoda		snails clams squids
Eumetazoa				Arthropoda		Crustacea Insecta Arachnida		crabs insects spiders
	Bilateralia			Echinodermata				sea urchins
			Deuterostoma	Chordata	Hemichordata Tunicata Cephalochordata			acorn worms sea squirts lancelets
					Craniata	Agiatha Chondrichthyes Osteichthyes Amphibia Reptilia Aves Mammalia		lampreys cartilaginous fishes bony fishes amphibians reptiles birds
							Marsupialia	marsupials
							Eutheria	placental mammals

Class Agnatha (Cyclostomata) the lampreys and hagfishes. These animals do not have true jaws – the mouth is circular and contains a rasping tongue.

Class Chondrichthyes a class of fishes possessing cartilaginous skeletons. The body is covered with tiny toothlike scales forming a shagreen. The 5000 species include sharks and rays.

Class Osteichthyes a class of bony fishes containing approximately 22 000 species. The internal skeleton is made of bone, and the body is covered with bony scales. Bony plates on the head include large opercula protecting the gills. The dominant group of bony fishes is the teleosts, which inhabit nearly every aquatic environment and include such fishes as herring, trout, perch and cod. There is considerable evidence to suggest that some of the bony fishes such as the coelacanth and the lungfishes are genealogically nearer to the tetrapods or land-dwelling vertebrates than to other fishes.

Class Amphibia a class of about 2000 members including frogs and toads. The amphibians are the most primitive of the land-dwelling vertebrates (tetrapods). Tetrapods are animals with pentadactyl limbs (hands and feet) and other adaptations for life on land, such as a stiff vertebral column to support the body and lungs to breathe air. Most amphibians have a smooth, moist skin used for gas exchange and must return to water or other moist places to lay their eggs.

Class Reptilia a class represented today by about 5000 species, including turtles, lizards, snakes, crocodiles and alligators. For 160 million years the dinosaurs, the most advanced reptiles of all time, dominated the world. Like fishes, the reptiles are not a natural group – some are more closely related to birds, while others are more closely related to mammals. Most reptiles are fully terrestrial and lay an egg with a leathery shell on land in which the embryo can develop to hatch as a miniature adult. The skin is dry and scaly. Reptiles maintain their body temperature by behaviour (sitting in the sun or hiding under rocks).

Class Aves one of the more obvious vertebrate classes, the 9000 species of birds are characterized by a covering of feathers. This is an adaptation both to flight and to the regulation of their body temperature by physiological means. The arm is developed as a wing. All birds lay hard-shelled eggs.

Class Mammalia the class characterized by body hair – which in many cases completely covers the body – and by the ability of the mother to nourish the young with milk produced by mammary glands. Mammals are able to regulate their body temperature internally. Other mammalian specializations include three separate bones within the middle ear (to permit acute hearing) and – in most cases – a complex dentition (incisors, canines, premolars and molars) which occurs as two generations of teeth. One group of mammals – the monotremes (the duck-billed platypus is the most famous example) – lays eggs, but the vast majority retain the egg within the body, where it develops.

Subclass Marsupialia (Metatheria) a group better known as marsupials. These animals bear their young at a very early stage of development and keep them in an external pouch containing the mammary glands until they are able to fend for themselves. The 260 or so species include wombats, opossums, kangaroos, the Tasmanian devil and the koala bear.

Subclass Eutheria a large group of placental mammals. The young of eutherians are retained by the mother and nourished through a placenta. There are some 3800 species of placentals traditionally divided between 19 orders. Different orders display a wide variety of tooth patterns reflecting specialized diets. The most significant orders are as follows:

Order Insectivora. Insectivores are generally small animals with long, low skulls and many teeth, which are not particularly specialized for any specific diet. Many scientists believe that the most primitive placentals must have been similar to these mammals. The order includes moles, shrews and hedgehogs.

Order Chiroptera. This order comprises the bats, the only mammals with the ability to fly. Bats achieve flight by flapping wings developed as a membrane stretched between four fingers and the hind limbs. Most navigate and capture food by a form of sonar known as echolocation.

Order Edentata. This order includes the anteaters, armadillos and sloths – mammals that show very reduced or absent dentition. The front teeth are absent and the tongue gathers food, often a diet of insects such as ants and termites.

Order Primates. This order includes the great apes (orang-utan, chimpanzees and the gorilla), monkeys, lemurs, tarsiers and man. The dentition is generalized because primates have a wide diet. In most cases, primates rely heavily on binocular vision – consequently the face is characteristically short and flat. Compared with other mammals few young are produced – often a single offspring – and the young are retained within the mother for a long time and are born at a very advanced stage. Primates are characterized by a long period of parental care.

Order Rodentia. The rodents form a very large order of small mammals with a distinctive dentition. The single pair of upper and lower incisors are chisel-like; they grow continually and the enamel is confined to the front surface. The canines and front premolars are absent, and the molars are specialized for grinding, with the upper teeth biting inside the lower teeth. Rodents give birth to large numbers of young at frequent intervals, and many also look after the young in nests. Examples include beavers, mice, squirrels, porcupines and marmots.

Order Lagomorpha. The lagomorphs include rabbits and hares. Their dentition is superficially like that of rodents, but there are two pairs of upper incisors and the cheek teeth are designed for cutting with the upper teeth biting the lower teeth. The hind legs are modified for jumping.

Order Cetacea. Cetaceans include whales and dolphins – large, fully aquatic mammals in which the hair is reduced and the limbs are developed as flippers. They also possess a horizontal tail fluke. Cetaceans have a high degree of social organization, including elaborate communication.

Order Carnivora. Carnivores are primarily flesh-eating mammals and their dentition has developed large stabbing canines with special meat-shearing cheek teeth (carnassials). Many members have acute vision and hearing. The order includes the cats, bears, racoons, stoats and dogs. The seals and walruses are sometimes included in this order or placed in the separate order Pinnipedia.

Order Proboscidea. A small order confined among living creatures to the elephants. They are characterized by cheek teeth that grow continuously and keep pace with the wear caused by continual grinding of vegetation.

Order Perissodactyla. Known as the odd-toed ungulates, the members of this order include tapirs, rhinoceroses and horses. They are characterized by cropping incisors coupled with grinding cheek teeth. In many members, the legs are long and there is a central axis to both the hand and foot; in horses and zebras this is exaggerated and results in a single toe being in contact with the ground.

Order Artiodactyla. The even-toed ungulates form a large group in which the third and fourth digits have been developed into a two-toed foot. Upper incisor teeth are rarely present; instead, there is a horny pad against which the lower incisors bite. The molar cheek teeth are high-crowned and used to grind vegetation. In most members, the stomach is four-chambered, allowing plant material to be broken down by bacterial action. Artiodactyls include pigs, hippopotamuses, camels, deer, giraffes, antelope, sheep and cattle.

THE CLASSIFICATION OF MAN

Rank		Distinguishing features
Kingdom	Animalia	nervous system
Subkingdom	Metazoa	multicellular
Phylum	Chordata	notochord (central nerve cord)
Subphylum	Vertebrata	backbone
Superdivision	Gnathostomata	jaws
Division	Osteichthyes	bone is the principal component of skeleton
Superclass	Tetrapoda	four limbs, the front pair being pentadactyl (five-digit)
Class	Mammalia	hair; sweat and milk glands
Subclass	Eutheria	placenta
Order	Primates	fingers with sensitive pads and nails
Family	Hominidae	upright posture, flat face, large brain; similar blood plasma protein
Genus	*Homo*	bipedal; manual dexterity
Species	*sapiens*	double-curved spine
Subspecies	*sapiens*	well-developed chin

VELOCITY OF ANIMAL MOVEMENT

The data on this topic are notoriously unreliable because of the many inherent difficulties of timing the movement of most animals – whether running, flying, or swimming – and because of the absence of any standardisation of the method of timing, of the distance over which the performance is measured, or of allowance for wind conditions.

The most that can be said is that a specimen of the species below has been time to have attained as a maximum the speed given.

kph	mph	Species
362	225	(a) Peregrine falcon (*Falco peregrinus*)
240+	150+	(b) Golden eagle (*Aquila chrysaetos*)
109	68	Sailfish (*Istiophorus platypterus*)
88·5+	55+	Pronghorn antelope (*Antilocapra americana*)
75·5	47	Grant's gazelle (*Gazella granti*)
75	46·61	Yellowfin tuna (*Thunnus albacares*)
72	45	Ostrich (*Struthio camelus*)
69·62	43·26	(c) Race horse (*Equus caballus*) (mounted)
67·14	41·72	(d) Greyhound (*Canis familiaris*)
64	40	(e) Eastern grey kangaroo (*Macropus giganteus*)
56–64	35–40	American free-tailed bat (*Tadarida brasiliensis*)
59·5	37	Blue wildebeeste (*Connochaetes taurinus*)
58	36	Dragonfly (*Austrophlebia costalis*)
55·5	34·5	Killer whale (*Orcinus orca*)
51·5	32	Giraffe (*Giraffa camelopardalis*)
45	28	Black rhinoceros (*Diceros bicornis*)
44·88	27·89	(f) Man (*Homo sapiens*)
44·4	27·6	Common dolphin (*Delphinus delphis*)
39	24·5	African elephant (*Loxodonta africana*)
32	20	Arabian camel (*Camelus dromedarius*)
c. 29	c. 18	Pacific leatherback turtle (*Dermochelys coriacea schlegeli*)
c. 27	c. 17	Gentoo penguin (*Pygosterlis papua*)
11·5	7·26	Honey-bee (*Apis mellifera*)
9·5	6	House rat (*Rattus rattus*)
7·24	4·5	Common flea (*Pulex irritans*) (jumping)
1·80	1·12	Centipede (*Scutiger coleoptrata*)
0·37	0·23	Giant tortoise
0·00062	0·00039	(g) Neptune crab (*Neptunus pelagines*)

(a) *45-deg angle of stoop in courtship display. Cannot exceed 100·5 kph (62·5 mph) in level flight.*
(b) *Vertical dive.*
(c) *Average over 402 m (440 yd).*
(d) *Average over 375 m (410 yd).*
(e) *Young mature females.*
(f) *Over 13·7 m (15 yd) (flying start)*
(g) *Travelled 163·3 km (101·5 miles) in 29 years.*

ENDANGERED SPECIES

Over 4500 species have been declared to be in danger. Threats to these animals include hunting, trapping, fishing, poison and pollution, the destruction of natural habitats and competition from introduced species. Endangered species are listed in the *Red Data Book* published by the International Union for the Conservation of Nature and Natural Resources. The numbers of endangered species vary from thousands to, in some cases, a handful of individuals. Over the last 300 years over 100 species of mammal and some 150 species of bird have disappeared.

armadillo Although some species of this South American mammal remain relatively common, the giant, three-banded, Burmeister's and pink fairy armadillos are in danger.

aye-aye Only about 20 individuals of this small Madagascan nocturnal primate – related to lemurs – remain in the wild.

bison Millions of the American bison (or buffalo) were slaughtered by Native North Americans and early settlers and hunters. Some 5000 survivors are largely confined to reserves.

Californian condor A member of the vulture family, the Californian condor may already be extinct in the wild.

European bison or wisent About 2000 European bison live in the Bialowieza Forest in Poland and Belarus, and in the Caucasus in Russia.

giant anteater Hunting by man and the disappearance of much of the habitat of this South American mammal have endangered the species.

giant panda The symbol of the Worldwide Fund for Nature, the giant panda lives only in the mountains of Sichuan in China. Unlike some endangered species, it has proved especially difficult to breed in captivity. Less than 700 individuals remain.

golden marmoset The Brazilian habitat of this small monkey is seriously under threat.

gorilla The loss of its habitat and illegal hunting have confined all three subspecies of gorilla to small pockets of African rain forest. Under 4000 of the Eastern lowland gorilla survive in Zaïre, while about 9000 of the Western lowland gorilla remain in Cameroon and the Central African Republic. The surviving 350 mountain gorillas are confined to the Ruwenzori Mountains on the borders of Uganda, Zaïre and Rwanda. The mountain gorillas of Rwanda received great publicity in the 1980s but, despite government protection, they remain endangered owing to the activities of poachers.

Grevy's zebra This zebra is endangered, in part because of the increasing aridity of its habitat in Ethiopia, Kenya and Somalia.

Indian lion Under 200 Indian lions remain, guarded in the Gir Forest National Park in Gujarat.

Japanese ibis Under a dozen of these wading birds are thought to have survived the destruction of their breeding grounds.

kakapo The kakapo or parrot owl of New Zealand has been hunted almost to extinction. It is thought that less than 10 individuals remain.

Komodo dragon Although the Komodo dragon, the largest living lizard, is protected by the Indonesian authorities, the activities of collectors have reduced the population to a dangerously low level.

lemur Some 14 species of these very small to medium primates lived in Madagascar earlier this century. Owing to drought and the deforestation, some of these species may already be extinct and the remainder are under threat.

mandrill The West African forest habitat of this monkey is rapidly being destroyed.

Mediterranean monk seal A European Community project aims to breed the monk seal in captivity and reintroduce it into the wild, where its numbers have been reduced to under 500 by hunting and pollution. Some countries have restrictions on fishing in the seal's breeding areas.

mountain zebra The mountain zebra is endangered because it has been pushed into more marginal areas of Namibia and South Africa by the pressure of agriculture on the land.

nene or Hawaiian goose The nene was rescued by Slimbridge Wildfowl and Wetlands Trust (Avon, UK) and successfully reintroduced to Hawaii, where some 500 nene now live in the wild.

Nile crocodile Seen as a threat by man, the Nile crocodile has become endangered owing to the activities of hunters.

orang-utan The destruction of the rain forest of Borneo and Sumatra has endangered this species.

Oriental white stork The drainage of marshes has been one of the principal threats to this Asian stork of which under 5000 remain.

oryx (Arabian) The Arabian oryx was hunted almost to extinction. The species is now protected and numbers have been increased in Jordan, Oman and Saudi Arabia by releasing animals bred in captivity.

Père David's deer This deer became extinct in the wild earlier this century and has been reintroduced to China from stock bred in zoos and parks in Europe.

pygmy chimpanzee The pygmy chimpanzee is threatened by the destruction of its habitat in Zaïre.

rhinoceros All species of rhinoceros are under threat, mainly because of the activities of poachers seeking its horns, which are regarded as an aphrodisiac in the Far East. The numbers vary: African black rhinoceros 3000; white rhinoceros (of East and South Africa) 3500; Indian rhinoceros 1700; Sumatran rhinoceros 700; Javan rhinoceros under 60.

Tasmanian wolf or thylacine The thylacine is thought to be extinct, but the recent claims of an expedition to have found its footprints have brought hopes that this marsupial may still be alive.

tiger Less than 4000 tigers survive. Of the four remaining subspecies – Indian, Sumatran, Javanese and Siberian – the latter is under the greatest threat.

three-toed sloth A slow-moving herbiverous animal, the three-toed sloth has been a victim of deforestation in South America.

whales Commercial whaling has placed a number of species under threat. The blue whale and the fin whale, in particular, have been hunted close to extinction.

white stork The white stork – which migrates from Europe and Asia to South Africa – is threatened by the drainage of marshes, by chemical pollution, the loss of nesting sites and by electricity transmission wires.

<table>
<tr><td>

MAJOR ZOOS

Amsterdam (Netherlands) Founded in 1836, the zoo exhibits nearly 1400 species and contains a famous animal behaviour laboratory.

Antwerp (Belgium) Antwerp Zoo houses over 1100 species, including important exhibits of black rhinoceros and Père David's deer. The zoo is famous for the innovative nature of its animal enclosures, especially in the reptile house.

Beijing/Peking (China) Beijing Zoo – established in 1906 – is known for its collection of rare Asian species, and its success in breeding the giant panda.

Berlin (Germany) One of the largest zoos in the world, Berlin Zoo was opened in 1841. The best known collections include the birds of prey, wild cattle and the aquarium.

Bronx Zoo (New York, USA) Founded in 1899, the Bronx Zoo includes several threatened species such as Père David's deer, the European bison and the okapi. Its other attractions include the collection of Asian mammals and birds.

Chicago (Brookfield) Opened in 1934, the Brook-field Zoo is known for its open-air, unbarred enclosures. It houses over 400 species of animal, especially those of the tropical rain forests.

Cologne (Germany) Cologne Zoo – which houses over 700 species – specializes in primates and is known for its aquarium.

Copenhagen (Denmark) The 2500 species in Copenhagen Zoo include a particularly comprehensive collection of birds. The zoo, founded in 1859, has bred a number of rare species, including the musk ox.

Frankfurt (Germany) Founded in 1858, the zoo exhibits over 600 species. This major collection is known for breeding endangered species, including the lowland gorilla, okapi and black rhinoceros.

London (UK) The Regent's Park Zoo (established 1828) has approaching 1000 species. London Zoo – which has the world's largest zoological library – has a separate collection of 250 species in spacious enclosures at Whipsnade in Bedfordshire.

Moscow (Russia) The Moscow Zoo, founded in 1864, houses a formidable collection of northern animals and exotic species. In total it contains over 3000 specimens of 550 species.

Paris (France) The Paris Zoo dates back to 1793. Its spacious natural enclosures include the famous Rocher, an artifical mountain for wild sheep. The zoo has about 300 species and is noted for breeding especially rare deer, wild horses and giraffes.

San Diego (USA) Founded in 1922, the San Diego Zoo is now the largest in the world. It uses barless mixed-species enclosures, with exotic plants providing the natural diet for some of the animals. Among the 800 species, koalas and pygmy chimpanzees have successfully bred.

Metro Toronto Zoo (Canada) Opened in 1974, Metro Toronto Zoo is one of the largest zoos in the world. The 280 species of animal are grouped by continent in mixed-species enclosures. Indigenous plants are used to create natural settings.

</td></tr>
</table>

PREHISTORIC ANIMALS

DINOSAURS

The dinosaurs, the most advanced reptiles of all time, dominated the Earth for 140 millon years – compared with the 2 million years that man has been on the planet. Unlike living reptiles – which either crawl or walk with their limbs extended out to their sides – dinosaurs walked with their limbs directly under their bodies, just like modern mammals and birds. However, like modern reptiles, most dinosaurs were probably cold-blooded. Many dinosaurs were of gigantic size, some weighing up to 100 tonnes. Nearly 1000 species have been identified, and although the word 'dinosaur' is from the Greek for 'terrible lizard', there were herbivores as well as carnivores.

The ancestors of the dinosaurs are found among the early *thecodonts* ('socket teeth') that lived in the early Triassic period 235 million years ago. Primitive thecodonts resembled modern crocodiles (which also evolved from them). They developed thick, flattened muscular tails for swimming, and longer and more powerful hind limbs to provide the initial thrust for lurching at their prey. When they emerged onto dry land, the first dinosaurs lifted their smaller forelimbs and ran on their hind limbs as bipeds, with the heavy muscular tail acting as a counterbalance. There were two orders of dinosaur, the Saurischia ('lizard-hipped') – and the ('bird-hipped') Ornithischia. *Saurischians* – whose pelvic girdle was like that of modern lizards – included exclusively two-legged carnivores such as *Tyrannosaurus* and enormous four-legged, predominately plant-eating semi-aquatic sauropods such as *Diplodocus*. *Ornithischians* – whose pelvic girdle was like that of birds – included ankylosaurs, ceratopsians, hadrosaurs, stegosaurs, and *Iguanodon*. Species included:

ankylosaurus ('fused lizard'), a dinosaur whose body was covered in a thick armour of fused bony plates.

apatosaurus the original brontosaur; weighed 30 tonnes. It lived for 120 years, equally at home swimming in lakes and walking on land.

baryonyx ('heavy claw'), named 'Claws' after the massive claw on its hand, thought to have been for disembowelling dinosaurs or catching fish.

brachiosaurus ('arm lizard'), 12 m (39 ft) tall and 23 m (75 ft) long; a dinosaur that weighed 80 tonnes and had long front legs.

compsognathus a chicken-sized dinosaur that fed on lizards. It was related to birds.

deinonychus ('terrible claw'), 3 m (10 ft) long; a leaping dinosaur with a sickle-like claw on its hind feet for killing prey.

diplodocus total length 23 m (75 ft); a brontosaur with the longest known tail of all dinosaurs – 11 m (36 ft) long.

gallimimus ('chicken-mimic'), 4 m (13 ft) long; an ostrich-like dinosaur, with a large beak and no teeth.

iguanodon ('iguana tooth'), a plant-eating dinosaur with a pronounced bony spike on its 'thumb'.

kentrosaurus ('centre lizard'), a dinosaur with long sharp spikes running along the back and the tail.

maiasaurus ('mother lizard'), a duck-billed dinosaur which built nests and cared for its young in 'dinosaur nurseries'.

mamenchisaurus total length 23 m (75 ft); a

brontosaur with the longest known neck of all dinosaurs – 11 m (36 ft).

megalosaurus ('giant lizard'), 9 m (30 ft) long; a flesh-eater, the first dinosaur ever discovered.

mussaurus ('mouse lizard'), 200 mm (8 in) long; the smallest known relative of the brontosaurs.

pachycephalosaurus ('thick-head lizard'), a bone-headed dinosaur with a distinctive massive bony thickening on the top of head forming a 'battering ram'.

parasaurolophus ('near ridged lizard'), a duckbilled dinosaur with a 2 m (7 m) long hollow crest – containing nasal passages – projecting behind its head.

plateosaurus ('flat lizard'), 6 m (20 m) long; a plant-eating ancestor of the brontosaurs. It had a strong claw on each hand and small serrated teeth.

polacanthus ('many spines'), 4 m (13 ft) long; a dinosaur with a large square bony 'blanket' over its hips and triangular plates along its back and tail.

protoceratops ('first horned'), 2 m (7 ft) long; the ancestor of triceratops. It possessed a similar bony frill over the neck but had no horns.

pterodactyl a flying reptile, whose membranous wings had spans of up to 11–12 m (36–39 ft).

saltasaurus ('lizard from Salta, Argentina'), a brontosaur with bony plates – each 12 cm (5 in) in diameter – embedded in the skin.

seismosaurus ('earthquake lizard'), 33 m (108 ft) long; probably the largest land animal that has ever lived.

shantungosaurus ('Shantung lizard'), 12 m (39 ft) long; the largest of the duck-billed dinosaurs.

stegosaurus ('roof lizard'), 9 m (30 ft) long, a dinosaur with two pairs of spikes on its tail, and a row of large triangular plates – 1 m high – running along its back.

supersaurus 15 m (49 ft) tall and 30 m (98 ft) long; a large dinosaur that may have weighed up to 100 tonnes.

torosaurus ('bull lizard'), a dinosaur with a bony frill extending over its shoulders. Its skull – 2.6 m (8.5 ft) long – was the largest known of any land animal.

triceratops ('three horned'), 9 m (30 ft) long; a dinosaur with a bony frill over its neck and three long horns on its forehead.

tyrannosaurus ('tyrant lizard'), 12 m (39 ft) long; a slow moving flesh-eating scavenger with relatively small two-fingered hands.

BIRDS

Birds share a common ancestry with reptiles. The first bird – archaeopteryx – had many characteristics in common with dinosaurs.

aepyornis a giant ostrich-like bird – the largest ever known. Its remains found in Mauritius gave rise to the 'Roc' of Sinbad and its fossilized eggs – the largest known eggs – were used to hold sailors' rum.

archaeopteryx (meaning 'ancient wing') the first bird, it appeared about 175 million years ago. In many respects it was indistinguishable from small carniverous dinosaurs, but the fact that it was covered in perfect feathers indicates that it was warm-blooded and that it could fly. It had a long bony tail and teeth in its jaws.

diatryma a tall – 2 m (7 ft) – flightless bird. This flesh-eater lived at the beginning of the age of mammals, 60 million years ago.

gigantornis a bird – with an 8 m (26 ft) wingspan – dating from c. 50 million years old.

hesperornis ('western bird'), a flightless diving bird with teeth.

ichthyornis ('fish bird'), a tern-like bird with teeth in its jaws.

MAMMALS

The first reptiles that conquered the land about 295 million years ago were the mammal-like reptiles or paramammals. From detailed study of their skulls, it is presumed that the mammals orginated from them. The first true mammals appeared during the later Triassic period about 220 million years ago.

arsinoitherium a rhinoceros-like animal with horns side by side on its snout; c. 35 million years old.

basilosaurus a 20 m (66 ft) long small-headed whale with the appearance of a 'sea serpent'. It lived c. 50 million years ago.

brontotherium a large rhinoceros-like animal, 2.5 m (8 ft) at the shoulder. It had double-curved horns at the tip of the snout, and lived c. 30 million years ago.

coelodonta a thick-haired woolly rhinoceros, which lived during the last Ice Age.

diprotodon a giant rhinoceros-sized wombat; 4 m (13 ft) long.

enteledon a giant pig-like animal; 2 m (7 ft) long. With bony projections on its lower jaws and sides of its skull, it has been called the ugliest mammal ever.

glyptodon a heavily armoured relative of the armadillo – 3.3 m (11 ft) long and 1.5 m (5 ft) high.

icaronycteris first known insect-eating bat; c. 50 million years old.

indricotherium a giant hornless rhinoceros, weighing 30 tonnes, and standing 5.5 m (18 ft) at the shoulder; c. 30 million years old.

kuehneotherium , the first true mammal, about the size of a shrew, dating from 220 million years ago.

mammuthus the woolly mammoth, a thick-haired elephant with spirally curved tusks inha-biting the tundra during the last Ice Age.

megaloceros a giant deer whose antlers had a 3.7 m (12 ft) span and weighed 45 kg (99 lb). It lived during the last Ice Age.

megatherium a giant ground sloth – 5.5 m (18 ft) tall – with huge clawed feet.

pakicetus the first toothed whale, c. 53 million years old. It had four paddle-like legs.

procoptodon a giant short-faced kangaroo stand-ing 3 m (10 ft) tall.

propalaeotherium a 40 cm (16 in) high four-toed horse; c. 50 million years old.

purgatorius named after Purgatory Hill, Mon-tana, USA, where remains of this first primate were found alongside dinosaur remains.

smilodon a sabre-tooth cat with long stabbing canine teeth.

thoatherium a one-toed horse-like litoptern, not related to true horses.

thylacoleo a marsupial lion with incisor 'stab-bing' teeth at front of jaws.

thylacosmilus a pouched (marsupial) sabre-tooth cat, unrelated to true sabre-tooths; c. 15 million years old.

DOMESTICATED ANIMALS

Wild species have been harnessed by human beings for their own uses, principally agriculture. Breeds have been developed by artificial selection.

PRINCIPAL BREEDS OF CATTLE

Most breeds of domestic cattle are descended from the wild aurochs, massive horned artiodactyls that once roamed over Europe and Asia, but had been driven to extinction by 1627. The majority of modern breeds of cattle evolved during the 18th century when 'livestock improvers' selected stock with desired characteristics for breeding purposes.

BEEF CATTLE

The following breeds are popular in Britain and in continental western Europe.

Aberdeen Angus black hornless cattle developed as a breed in northeast Scotland at the end of the 18th century.

Blonde d'Aquitaine a popular white breed of beef cattle from southwest France.

Blue Grey a popular cross between Galloway cows and white Shorthorn bulls.

Charolais the large white Charolais was developed in the 18th and 19th centuries as a draught animal from a cross between local French cattle and the white Shorthorn.

Chianina probably the largest and heaviest cattle in common use, this white Italian breed was developed originally for draught.

Devon (or North Devon) an ancient breed, it is descended from the red cattle common in western England since the Middle Ages.

Galloway the thick-coated black Galloway is an ancient breed from southwest Scotland. The Belted Galloway is similar except that it has a 'belt' of white hair around the middle of its body.

Hereford the red Hereford, descended from ancient Welsh cattle, is easily recognized by its distinctive white 'mask'. It is often crossed with the Friesian or the Aberdeen Angus.

Highland the traditional Scottish large-horned breed has a long coat which can vary between yellow and dark red.

Limousin a red and white breed from the Massif Central of France; similar to the Hereford but larger, it lacks the Hereford's distinctive mask.

Lincoln Red a red breed whose colour can recess to black, the Lincoln Red was developed by crossing the old Lincolnshire breed with the Shorthorn.

Luing a modern red Scottish breed developed by crossing the Beef Shorthorn and Highland cattle.

Maine-Anjou a red and white breed from northwest France. Originally a dual-purpose breed, but in Britain it tends to be kept largely for beef.

Shorthorn (or Beef Shorthorn) a breed of red, roan or white horned cattle developed by the Colling brothers of County Durham at the end of the 18th century. The Shorthorn is popular in virtually all cattle-raising areas of the world and is known in North America as the Durham.

Sussex a red horned breed from the Weald of Kent and Sussex, believed to be descended from the old Celtic cattle of Britain.

DUAL-PURPOSE BREEDS OF CATTLE

The following breeds are commonly kept in Britain and in continental western Europe for both milk and beef.

Dexter the smallest of British breeds, the red or black Dexter originated in southwest Ireland. It is thought to be the closest surviving relative of the domesticated cattle of Bronze Age Britain.

Meuse-Rhine-IJssel popularly known in the UK as the MRI, this Dutch breed is widespread in Europe and increasing in popularity in the UK.

Red Poll a widely distributed breed originating in East Anglia. It is sometimes crossed with the Danish Red.

Shorthorn (Dairy) this dark red breed has lost favour in Britain to breeds that mature more quickly.

Simmental a golden red Swiss breed, developed in continental Europe mainly for beef.

South Devon a horned red breed, the largest of any British breed.

Welsh Black an uncommon breed developed from traditional Welsh varieties.

DAIRY CATTLE

The following breeds of cattle are among those more commonly kept for dairying in Britain and western continental Europe.

Ayrshire a hardy heavy breed, the red and white Ayrshire originated in southwest Scotland.

Danish Red a popular European breed from which the red British Dane has been developed.

Friesian (or Holstein-Friesian) one of the most popular breeds of cattle in the world, the Friesian is easily recognizable by its distinctive black and white markings. Originating in the Netherlands and Friesland, the Friesian was first imported into Britain in the 1890s and now outnumbers all other dairy breeds.

Guernsey the Guernsey originated in isolation on the Channel Island of the same name. It is similar in appearance to the Jersey but is larger and more yellow in colour.

Jersey the Jersey is of similar Channel Island origin to the Guernsey. This small fawn-coloured breed has distinctive black eyelashes.

Kerry a black breed, native to southwest Ireland.

PRINCIPAL BREEDS OF SHEEP

Evidence suggests that sheep are descended from a wild species similar to the mouflon and were domesticated about 10 500 years ago in the eastern Mediterranean. With selective breeding the characteristic thick woolly coat was developed. There is a greater variety of breeds of sheep than of cattle in Britain. Some 40 breeds have been developed, suitable for almost every type of rural environment from mountains to chalk downland to marshes.

LONGWOOL BREEDS

The following longwool breeds are popular in Britain and western continental Europe. These breeds are all large, with heavy fleeces and (except for the Masham) white faces. Most longwools are kept primarily for their wool, although the Romney Marsh is kept mainly for its meat.

Border Leicester developed from the Leicester in the 19th century, it is smaller and lighter than its progenitor.

Cotswold a traditional breed, from the Cotswold Hills of Oxfordshire and Gloucestershire. It is kept for meat and wool.

Devon Longwool smaller than but similar in appearance to the South Devon.

Leicester developed from a traditional Leicestershire breed in the 18th century, the Leicester has been used to improve or develop virtually all the other British longwool breeds.

Lincoln the largest of the British sheep. It has wool of great length.

Masham a popular cross between the Wensleydale and blackfaced mountain ewes. It has a curly fleece and a black and white face.

Merino one of the most widespread breeds in the world, the Merino and the many varieties developed from it are popular in Australia and North America. The Merino has been bred in Spain for its fine wool since the 12th century.

Merino Romney a cross which is popular in Australia.

Rambouillet the largest of the European fine wool sheep, the Rambouillet was developed from the Merino in France at the end of the 18th century. The breed is widespread in the USA.

Romney Halfbred a cross between the Romney Marsh and the Cheviot which has been developed for fat lamb production.

Romney Marsh (or Kent) the smallest of the British longwools, the Romney Marsh was bred for mutton rather than for wool.

Roscommon the only significant breed of sheep native to Ireland, the Roscommon has lost favour to larger breeds.

South Devon a large hardy breed, popular in the West Country of England.

Wensleydale originating in Yorkshire, the Wensleydale is known for the fine quality of its wool.

THE DOWN BREEDS

Smaller than the longwools, the Down breeds have short wool, dark faces and wide hindquarters. The Down breeds originated in the chalk downlands of southern England and have been introduced successfully to North America, Australia and New Zealand. They are kept for both wool and meat.

Dorset Down a breed with the appearance of a smaller version of the Hampshire.

Hampshire a large hardy breed with medium wool and dark legs. It was developed by crossing the traditional Berkshire Knot and Wiltshire Horned breeds with the Southdown. It is one of the most popular meat producers in the USA.

Oxford (or Oxford Down) a large sheep developed as a cross between the Hampshire and the Cotswold.

Shropshire a cross between the Southdown and ancient breeds in the English Midlands. The Shropshire is rare in Britain although popular in the USA.

Suffolk a large breed known for its fine mutton,

the Suffolk is a cross between the Southdown and the Norfolk, which is now extinct.

Southdown a sheep with a rounded body known for the quality of its meat. It was the earliest of the Down breeds to be improved and has been used to produce or to improve all the other Down breeds.

OTHER SHORTWOOL BREEDS

The shortwool breeds listed below were developed independently from the Down breeds. These sheep are kept for meat rather than for wool.

Devon closewool a shortwool sheep easily recognized by its distinctive speckled face.

Dorset Horn a medium-sized horned breed, the Dorset is widely kept in the UK, North America and Australia.

Ile-de-France one of the most popular European breeds, the Ile-de-France is an important mutton producer.

Kerry Hill a Welsh sheep resembling the Devon closewool, but with slightly longer wool and a smaller body.

Ryeland a breed similar to the Kerry Hill, but uncommon outside the Welsh Marches, where it originated.

Wiltshire Horned (or Western Horned) a traditional breed with a white face and horns.

MOUNTAIN BREEDS

The following horned, blackfaced British breeds were all developed for difficult mountainous areas. They are therefore hardy and strong-wooled.

Cheviot a widespread medium-sized breed with a white face and very little wool on the head. It originated in the Scottish Borders and is commonly crossed with the Border Leicester.

Clun Forest a popular breed in the Welsh Marches, the Clun Forest was developed from the Scottish Blackface.

Dartmoor a large coarse-wooled breed that originated in Devon.

Exmoor Horned (or Porlock) a small hardy breed, largely confined to southwest England.

Herdwick the hardiest of all the English breeds, the coarse-wooled Herdwick was developed in the Lake District.

The Lonk a sturdy breed native to the southern Pennines and the Peak District of England.

Scottish Blackface known for the strength of its wool, this breed from the Highlands of Scotland may vary in size according to its surroundings and parentage.

Swaledale a coarse-wooled sheep originating in Yorkshire.

Welsh Mountain the smallest common British breed, the Welsh Mountain sheep is coarse-wooled and very hardy.

NEW BREEDS

A number of new breeds have been developed since the 1950s, crossing British and European sheep. Of these the best known are the Cobb 101 (a cross between the Finnish Landrace and the Suffolk) and the Colbred (a cross between the Border Leicester, Clun Forest, Dorset Horn and East Friesland).

PRINCIPAL BREEDS OF PIGS

Domestic pigs fall into three types: the pork type (whose carcasses average about 45 kilos / 100 lb), the bacon type (whose carcasses average about 70 kilos / 150 lb), and the larger 'lard' type (whose carcasses average at least 100 kilos / 220 lb).

China has by far the largest population of pigs in the world but the scientific of breeding of pigs has been concentrated in western Europe and the USA. The most popular breeds outside China are the Yorkshire Large White (often known in Europe as the Large White), the Landrace and the Berkshire, and many of the American breeds listed below have these in their ancestry. The three Chinese breeds listed are among the most populous in the world.

Beltsville two US breeds (one black, one red) that are raised for meat.

Berkshire a medium-sized mainly black breed, popular throughout the English-speaking world and in Japan and Latin America. It is kept for both pork and bacon.

Chester White a large 'lard' type bred in the USA. White with a pinkish skin, the docile Chester White is very prolific.

Duroc a 'red' pig characterized by its drooping ears. Widespread in the Americas and continental Europe, the Duroc is a 'lard' type.

Hampshire an American meat breed. It has a long black body.

Jia Xing a large prolific Chinese 'lard' breed.

Jin Hua a Chinese breed of similar characteristics to the above.

Landrace a Danish breed that has spread throughout Europe. This white very long-bodied breed is kept for bacon.

Large White the most popular breed of pig in the world. Bred in northern England in the 18th century, this prolific breed now has a worldwide distribution. It is kept for pork and bacon.

Maryland a medium-sized black and white US breed that is kept for meat. It is a cross between the Berkshire and the Landrace.

Mei Shan a large prolific Chinese breed.

Minnesota three US meat breeds of various colours.

Piétrain a Belgian black and white breed that is widespread in western Europe.

Tamworth a traditional English breed that is characterized by its many colours, including black and red. A large pig it is found throughout the English-speaking world where it is used for cross-breeding with various bacon breeds.

Yorkshire Large White see Large White.

COLLECTIVE NOUNS

Angel fish	Host
Animals	Menagerie, Tribe
Antelope	Herd, Troop
Ants	Army, Column, State, Swarm
Apes	Shrewdness
Asses	Herd, Pace
Baboons	Troop
Badger	Cete, Colony
Barracuda	Battery
Bass	Fleet
Bears	Sloth
Beavers	Colony
Bees	Cluster, Erst, Hive, Swarm
Birds	Congregation, Dissimulation (young), Flight, Flock, Volery, Volley
Bison	Herd
Bitterns	Sedge, Siege
Bloodhounds	Sute
Boars	Herd, Singular, Sounder
Budgerigars	Chatter
Buffalo	Herd
Bustard	Flock
Camels	Caravan, Flock
Capercaillie	Tok
Caterpillars	Army
Cats	Chowder, Clowder, Cluster
Cats, wild	Dout
Cattle	Drove, Herd
Chamois	Herd
Chickens	Brood, Clutch, Peep
Choughs	Chattering
Clams	Bed
Cockles	Bed
Colts	Race, Rag, Rake
Coots	Covert, Raft
Cormorants	Flight
Cranes	Herd, Siege
Crows	Clan, Hover, Murder
Curlews	Herd
Deer	Herd, Leash
Dogfish	Brood, Troop
Dogs	Cowardice, Kennel, Pack
Dogs (hunting)	Cry
Dolphins	Pod, School
Donkeys	Herd, Drove
Dottrel	Trip
Doves	Dole, Flight, Prettying
Ducklings in nest	Clutch
Ducklings off nest	Clutch
Ducks (diving)	Dopping, Dropping
Ducks (flying)	Flush, Plump, Team
Ducks (on land)	Flight, Flock, Leash, Mob Sail
Ducks (on water)	Badeling, Paddling, Sail
Eagles	Convocation
Eels	Swarm
Elephants	Herd
Elk (Europe)	Gang
Falcons	Cast
Ferrets	Business, Cast, Fesynes
Finches	Charm, Flight
Fish	Haul, Run, School, Shoal
Flamingos	Flurry, Regiment, Skein
Flies	Business, Cloud, Scraw, Swarm
Foxes	Earth, Lead, Skulk
Foxhounds	Pack
Frogs	Army, Colony
Geese (flying)	Flock, Gaggle, Skein
Geese (on land)	Gaggle
Geese (on water)	Gaggle, Plump
Giraffes	Corps, Herd, Troop
Gnats	Cloud, Horde, Swarm
Goats	Flock, Herd, Tribe, Trippe
Goldfinch	Charm, Chattering, Chirp, Drum
Goldfish	Troubling
Goshawks	Flight
Grasshoppers	Cloud

Greyhounds	Brace, Leash, Pack
Grouse	Brood, Covey, Pack
Guillemots	Bazaar
Gulls	Colony
Hares	Down, Drove, Husk, Lie, Trip
Hart	Herd, Stud
Hawks	Cast
Hedgehogs	Array
Hens	Brood, Flock
Heron	Scattering, Sedge, Siege
Herring	Army, Gleam, Shoal
Hippopotamuses	Herd, School
Hogs	Herd, Drove, Sounder
Horses	Harass, Herd, Stable, Stud, Troop
Horses (race)	Stable, String
Hounds	Brace, Couple, Cry, Mute, Pack, Stable
Ibis	Crowd
Insects	Swarm
Jays	Band, Party
Jellyfish	Brood, Smuck
Kangaroos	Herd, Mob, Troop
Kittens	Brood, Kindle, Litter
Lapwings	Deceit, Desert
Larks	Exultation
Lemurs	Troop
Leopards	Leap
Lice	Flock
Lions	Flock, Pride, Sawt, Souse, Troop
Locusts	Cloud, Horde, Plague, Swarm
Mackerel	School, Shoal
Magpies	Tiding, Tittering
Mallards (on land)	Bord, Flock, Flush, Suite, Sute
Mallards (on water)	Sord
Mares	Flock, Stud
Martens	Raches, Richesse
Mice	Nest
Minnows	Shoal, Steam, Swarm
Moles	Company, Labour, Movement, Mumble
Monkeys	Troop
Moose	Gang, Herd
Mules	Barren, Cartload, Pack, Span
Mussels	Bed
Nightingale	Match, Puddling, Watch
Ostrich	Flock, Troop
Otters	Bevy, Family
Owls	Parliament, Stare
Oxbirds	Fling
Oxen (domestic)	Drove, Rake, Team, Yoke
Oxen (wild)	Drove, Herd
Oyster	Bed
Parrots	Flock
Partridges	Covey
Passenger pigeons	Roost
Peacocks	Muster
Peafowl	Muster, Ostentation, Pride
Penguins	Colony, Rookery
Perch	Pack, Shoal
Pheasants	Brook, Ostentation, Pride, Nye
Pigeons	Flight, Flock
Piglets	Farrow
Pigs	Litter, Herd, Sounder
Pilchards	Shoal
Plover	Congregation, Flight, Stand, Wing

Polecats	Chine
Ponies	Herd
Porpoises	Gam, Pod, School
Poultry	Flock
Poultry (domestic)	Run
Ptarmigan	Covey
Pups	Litter
Quail	Bevy, Covey
Rabbits	Bury, Colony, Nest, Warren
Raccoons	Nursery
Racehorses	Field, String
Rats	Colony
Ravens	Unkindness
Redwings	Crowd
Rhinoceros	Crash
Roach	Shoal
Roe deer	Bevy
Rooks	Building, Clamour, Parliament
Ruffs	Hill
Sandpipers	Fling
Sardines	Family
Seals, elephant	Rookery, Team, Troop
Seals	Harem, Herd, Pod, Rookery
Sheep	Down, Drove, Flock, Hurtle, Trip
Sheldrakes	Dapping, Dropping
Smelt	Quantity
Snakes	Den, Pit
Snakes (young)	Bed
Snipe	Walk, Whisper, Wish, Wisp
Spaniels	Couple
Sparrows	Host, Surration, Quarrel
Spiders	Cluster, Clutter
Squirrels	Drey
Starlings	Chattering, Crowd, Murmuration
Sticklebacks	Shoal
Stoats	Pack
Storks	Herd, Mustering
Swallows	Flight
Swans	Bank, Bevy, Game, Herd, Squadron, Teeme, Wedge, Whiteness
Swifts	Flock
Swine	Doyet, Dryft
Swine (wild)	Sounder
Teal (on land)	Bunch, Coil, Knab, Raft
Teal (on water, rising from water)	Spring
Thrush	Mutation
Tigers	Ambush
Toads	Knab, Knot
Trout	Hover
Turkeys	Dule, Raffle, Rafter
Turtles	Bale, Dole
Turtle Doves	Pitying
Vipers	Den, Nest
Walrus	Herd, Pod
Wasps	Herd, Nest, Pladge
Weasels	Pack, Pop
Whales	Colony, Gam, Herd, Pod, School
Whiting	Pod
Widgeon	Coil, Company, Flight, Knob
Wildfowl	Plump, Sord, Sute, Trip
Wolves	Pack, Rout
Woodcocks	Covey, Fall, Flight, Plump
Woodpeckers	Descent
Wrens	Herd
Zebras	Herd

THE SKELETON

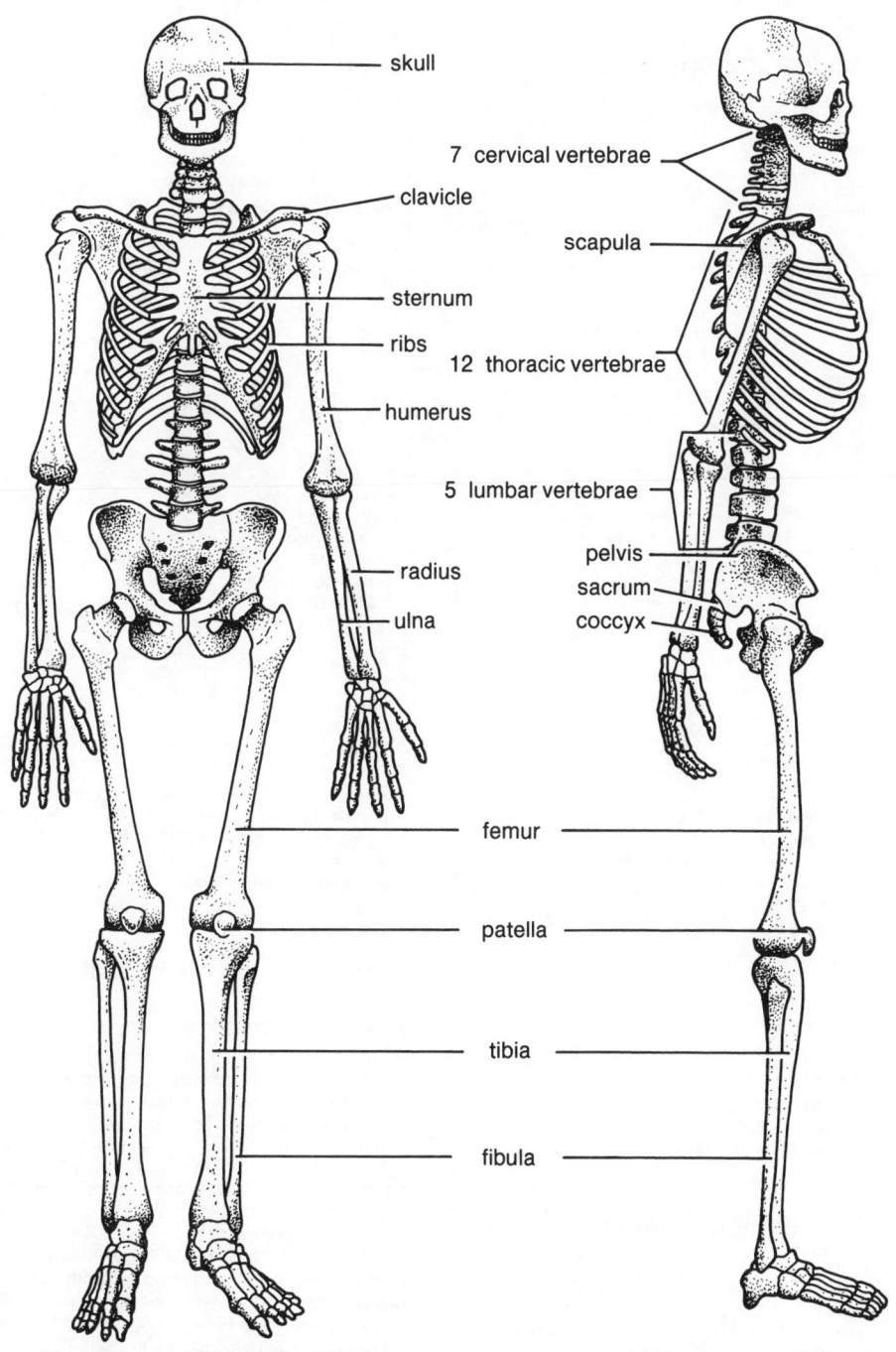

skull

7 cervical vertebrae

clavicle

scapula

sternum

ribs

12 thoracic vertebrae

humerus

5 lumbar vertebrae

radius

pelvis

sacrum

coccyx

ulna

femur

patella

tibia

fibula

HUMAN ANATOMY AND PHYSIOLOGY

THE HUMAN BODY

BONES IN THE HUMAN BODY

Skull	Number
occipital	1
parietal – 1 pair	2
sphenoid	1
ethmoid	1
inferior nasal conchae – 1 pair	2
frontal – 1 pair, fused	1
nasal – 1 pair	2
lacrimal – 1 pair	2
temporal – 1 pair	2
macilla – 1 pair	2
zygomatic – 1 pair	2
vomer	1
palatine – 1 pair	2
mandible – 1 pair, fused	1
	22

Ears	
malleus	2
incus	2
stapes	2
	6

Vertebrae cervical	7
thoracic	12
lumbar	5
sacral – 5 vertebrae fuse together to form the sacrum	1
coccyx – lowermost element of the back bone (vestigial human tail)	1
	26

Vertebral ribs	
ribs, 'true' – 7 pairs	14
ribs, 'false' – 5 pairs, of which 2 pairs are floating	10
	24

Sternum (breast bone)	
manubrium	1
sternebrae	1
xiphisternum	1
	3

(in the throat)	1

Pectoral girdle	
clavicle – 1 pair	2
scapula (including coracoid) – 1 pair	2
	4

Upper extremity (each arm)	
humerus	1
radius	1
ulna	1
carpus:	
scaphoid	1
lunate	1
triquetral	1
pisiform	1
trapezium	1
trapezoid	1
capitate	1
hamate	1
metacarpals	5
phalanges:	
first digit (thumb)	2
second digit	3
third digit	3
fourth digit	3
fifth digit	3
	30

Pelvic girdle	
ilium, ischium and pubis (combined) – 1 pair of hip bones (innominate)	2

Lower extremity (each leg)	
femur	1
tibia	1
fibula	1
tarsus:	
talus	1
calcaneus	1
navicular	1
cuneiform, medial	1
cuneiform, intermediate	1
cuneiform, lateral	1
cuboid	1
metatarsals	5
phalanges:	
first digit (big toe)	2
second digit	3
third digit	3
fourth digit	3
fifth digit	3
	29

Total	
Skull	**22**
The ears	**6**
Vertebrae	**26**
Vertebral ribs	**24**
Sternum	**3**
Throat	**1**
Pectoral girdle	**4**
Upper extremity (arms): 2 × 30	**60**
Hip bones	**2**
Lower extremity (legs): 2 × 29	**58**
	206

ORGANS OF THE HUMAN BODY

ALIMENTARY (DIGESTIVE) SYSTEM

Food passes from the mouth and oesophagus – a 23 cm (9 in) muscular tube from the throat – to the stomach, which acts as a collecting bag and begins the process of digestion by a churning action, and by secreting hydrochloric acid and other juices (*pepsin*). Food then passes to the small intestine (small bowel) comprising the *duodenum, jejunum* and *ileum*. The duodenum is 25 cm (10 in) long, the jejunum 2.5 m (8 ft), and the ileum 4 m (13 ft) long. The liver (by means of the gall bladder) and the pancreas also secrete digestive juices into the duodenum. Both digestion and absorption of nutrients take place in the small intestine before food reaches the large intestine (colon), which is 1.5 m (5 ft) long. In the colon, body fluids are reabsorbed. Waste matter is excreted through the rectum.

THE LIVER

A vital organ – weighing about 2 kg (4 lb) – the liver has four functions:

1. The production of bile to emulsify fat in the bowel and so allow its absorption.
2. The reception of all the products of food absorption. The liver controls the storage and release of these products as energy sources. Carbohydrates are stored as glycogen, and the liver, using insulin from the pancreas, controls the body's sugar level.
3. The purification of blood by removing toxins and worn-out red cells.
4. The production of proteins for blood clotting.

CIRCULATION AND RESPIRATORY SYSTEM

The ribs enclose the thoracic cavity, within which lie the heart and the two lungs. The heart weighs 250–300 g (9–11 oz) and is approximately the size of a clenched fist. It is a muscular pump, which squeezes blood out through the arteries with each beat. The arteries carry blood away from the heart through a series of branching and progressively smaller blood vessels (capillaries), which then join together again to form the veins, which return blood to the heart. The heart is divided into four compartments or chambers (*atria* and *ventricles*). The right atrium collects blood from the veins and passes it to the right ventricle, which then pumps the blood to the lungs. In the capillaries of the lungs the process of breathing (respiration) replaces the blood's oxygen content, before the blood returns to the left side of the heart. It collects in the left atrium, then passes through the mitral valve to the left ventricle (the largest chamber of the heart), which pumps it out to the rest of the body via the aortic valve and *aorta* – the largest blood vessel of the body.

At a rate of 70 heart beats per minute the heart pumps approximately 5 litres (9 pt) of blood per minute, but it can pump 20 litres (35 pt) per minute during vigorous exercise, when the heart rate increases to about 150 per minute. The average total lung volume is about 5 litres, but normal breathing only draws about 1–2 litres (4–5 pt) of air in and out with each breath. The oxygen in the air is passed into the bloodstream in exchange for carbon dioxide, which is exhaled.

URINARY SYSTEM

The two kidneys lie behind the abdominal organs, below the ribs on either side of the spine. They measure about 15 cm (6 in) in length, and each weighs 150 g (5 oz). The kidneys purify the blood in a complex system of microscopic syphons (*glomeruli* and *nephrons*), producing urine, which is then passed through drainage tubes (*ureters*) to the bladder, where urine is stored before excretion through the urethra.

BLOOD AND LYMPHATIC SYSTEM

The average blood volume is 5.5 litres (10 pt), consisting of 55 per cent plasma and 45 per cent blood cells of three types. Red blood cells (*erythrocytes*) – which are biconcave discs containing the chemical *haemoglobin* – carry oxygen. There are approximately 5 million red cells per mm^3 of blood, each with a lifespan of about 120 days. The white cells (*leucocytes*) are fewer in number (8000 per mm^3) and act to combat infection. The third type of cell – platelets – helps in the normal process of blood clotting.

ENDOCRINE ORGANS

The chemicals that these glands secrete directly into the bloodstream are hormones that regulate many aspects of the body's performance.

Pituitary gland a gland situated at the base of the brain, producing hormones that control the other endocrine glands: a hormone that regulates growth; a hormone that causes the uterus to contract during childbirth; a hormone that causes the mammary glands (breasts) to produce milk; and a hormone that regulates the concentration of the urine.

Thyroid gland a gland situated in front of the windpipe. Thyroid hormone controls the rate of chemical reactions in body cells (the metabolic rate).

Parathyroid glands four glands that are embedded within the thyroid. They control calcium levels in the body.

Pancreas a gland secreting the hormone insulin, which regulates glucose levels in the body. A deficiency of insulin causes diabetes mellitus.

Adrenal glands glands that produce adrenalin, which prepares the body for stress ('fight or flight') by increasing heart rate and blood pressure. They also produce cortisone, which has a variety of metabolic effects.

Ovaries produce the female sexual hormones *oestrogen* and *progesterone*, and release one egg (*ovum*) per month during the woman's reproductive life.

Testes two glands that produce sperms and the male hormone *testosterone*.

SKIN

The skin can also be classed as an organ. It accounts for 16 per cent of the body's weight, and has an average surface area of 18 000 cm^2 (2800 in^2). Among its functions is the control of heat loss.

BRAIN AND NERVOUS SYSTEM

The human brain – which on average weighs about 1.4 kg (3 lb) – contains 10 000 million nerve cells, each of which has a potential 25 000 interconnections with other cells. The brain relays and receives electrical impulses through the senses, and through the nerves and spinal cord. There are 12 pairs of cranial nerves supplying the face and head. Nerves in other areas of the body can be classified as motor (which supply movement), sensory (which recognize touch, pain and temperature, and sense body position), and autonomic (which regulate the internal body activities that we are not normally aware of, e.g. bowel activity, breathing, heart rate, etc.).

HUMAN DENTITION

Man has two sets of teeth during his lifetime. The 20 primary teeth are acquired between the ages of six months and two years. They are lost from about the age of six onwards when the permanent teeth begin to appear. There are 32 permanent teeth in all:

Eight incisors the central (front) teeth, four upper and four lower, which have a cutting function.

Four canine teeth the pointed fang-like teeth on either side of the incisors.

Eight pre-molars two in each quadrant of the mouth; each has two cusps.

12 molars three in each quadrant of the mouth; the upper molars have four cusps, and the lower molars five cusps, to allow efficient grinding of food. The furthest back molar in each gum is the wisdom tooth, usually appearing at the age of 18–20 or later.

MEDICINE

MILESTONES IN MEDICINE

9000 BC Early physicians and wound-healers of the New Stone Age develop the first recorded operation – trephination. A flint knife or scraper was used to cut out a circular piece of bone from the skull. It was probably carried out on people with nervous or mental conditions in order to release the demon that was thought to cause the problem.

5000–2000 BC The Sumerians – and later the Assyrians and Babylonians – develop the first concepts of systematic medical thought. Medicine was essentially magic, and it was believed that blood was the carrier of every vital function, and the liver was the seat of all life processes.

The Sumerians were also the first to use 'drugs', made from parts of the lotus, olive, myrtle, garlic, animal parts and even excrement. They were formed into pills, powders, enemas and so on. Bronze tools were also developed for the practice of surgery.

1900 BC The code of Hammurabi in Mesopotamia – the world's first legal code – laid down for the first time a system of payments and penalties for surgeons doing operations.

1570 BC The Ancient Egyptian Ebers Papyrus describes a series of recipes for treating diseases of the internal organs. The Egyptian physicians used an astonishing variety of drugs, but magic and religion were still used to treat most ailments.

800–300 BC The Ancient Greeks develop ideas of scientific medicine and discover the basic elements of anatomy, physiology and pathology.

The Greeks, however, develop the erroneous theory of the four humours, which stated that everything was made from combinations of the four *elements*: earth, air, fire and water. They thought that in the body the elements blend to form four *humours*: blood (hot and wet), yellow bile (hot and dry); black bile (dry and cold) and phlegm (cold and wet). Good mental and physical health were supposed to depend on the correct balance of the humours.

600 BC Founding of first true medical schools at Cos and Cnidos.

460–370 BC Hippocrates of Cos, the father of medicine, develops the *Hippocratic Corpus*, a body of medical thought that was taught to all physicians down the centuries. His code of ethics – the Hippocratic Oath – is traditionally sworn by those entering the apprenticeship of medicine.

384–322 BC Aristotle codifies science. He describes for the first time organs such as the uterus and stomach. Aristotle also had a vast influence on medical thought and for the next 2000 years Aristotelian philosophy ruled the course of medical thinking.

50 AD The first hospitals (*valetudinaria*) are founded by the Romans, principally for the care of injured soldiers. These later form the basis for the medieval hospital system.

129–99 AD Galen of Pergamum (130–201) carries out dissections of animals (but not humans) and produces many influential texts on medicine based upon the earlier works of Hippocrates and Aristotle. His writings, though containing many errors, provided the theoretical basis for medical practice for the next 1000 years.

200–1500 The fall of the Roman Empire and subsequent 'Dark Ages' lead to a decline in the practice of medicine in the West. Greek learning was preserved and developed by Arab scholars such as Razes (860–932) and Avicenna (980–1036).

1542 Publication of *De Humani Corporis Fabrica* by the Flemish anatomist Andreas Vesalius (1514–64). It shows the inadequacies of Galen and is the first accurate anatomy book, based on the dissection of human corpses. It lays the foundation for modern anatomy. The advent of printing meant that the book was distributed around Europe and led to great improvements in surgical techniques.

1545 Ambroise Paré (1510–90), a French surgeon discovers that gunshot wounds were not poisonous and so did not require boiling oil – cauterization – to treat them or to stop bleeding after amputation; ligatures would suffice.

1546 Girolamo Fracastoro (1484–1553) from Verona, Italy, introduces the idea that disease is spread by minute germs, invisible to the human eye. His theory is not proved until the 19th century.

1530–36 Philippus Aureolus Paracelsus (1493–1541), a Swiss physician introduces the use of chemicals into medicine, pioneering the use of mercury and laundanum.

1615 The Englishman, William Harvey (1578–1657) discovers that blood circulates in one direction around the body.

1632–1723 Anton van Leeuwenhoek, a Dutchman, uses an early microscope to examine the tissues of blood cells and spermatozoans. He described bacteria for the first time in 1683.

1708–77 The Swiss Albrecht von Haller pioneers the science of neurology, discovering the actions of the nervous system.

1715 Giovanni Morgagni (1682–1771) begins his work into pathological anatomy. He argued that disease was localized in specific parts of the body.

1796 Edward Jenner (1742–1823) performs the world's first vaccination. He discovers that inoculation with the cowpox virus gives immunity to smallpox. His discovery, although initially resisted, led to immunization against various other diseases.

1817 René Laennec (1781–1826) invents the stethoscope.

1833 The American army surgeon, William Beaumont (1785–1853) demonstrates the actions of the stomach by studying a man who, having been shot in the stomach, had a permanent fistula through which he could observe its functions.

1846 The American William Morton (1819–68) uses anaesthesia (ether) for the first time. He removes a tooth.

1850–80 The Frenchman Louis Pasteur (1822–95) and the German Robert Koch (1843–1910) found the science of microbiology. They discover that diseases such as anthrax, rabies and tuberculosis are caused by microscopic organisms called bacteria.

1854 The Englishwoman Florence Nightingale (1820–1910), arrives at Scutari, Constantinople (Istanbul) during the Crimean War. Her caring administrations to the 10 000 wounded soliders led to a reform of nursing.

1865 Louis Pasteur (see above) discovers a method of preserving perishable food stuffs (pasteurization) that contributed immeasurably to public health.

1865 The Englishman Joseph Lister (1827–1912) introduces antisepsis, the destruction of bacteria, using a carbolic acid spray to sterilize his operating theatre.

1879 Ivan Pavlov (1849–193) discovers the conditioned reflex using experiments in dogs.

1893 The Austrian Sigmund Freud (1856–1939) publishes his landmark paper *On the Psychical Mechanism of Hysterical Phenomenon*, pioneering, with Carl Gustav Jung (1875–1961), psychoanalysis.

1895 The German physicist Wilhelm Konrad Rontgen (1845–1923) discovers X-rays.

1896 The Italian Riva Rocci (1863–1936) invents the mercury sphygmomanometer, now used worldwide to measure blood pressure.

1899 Aspirin introduced to the market by Farbenfabriken Bayer, a German pharmaceutical company.

1900 Jules Bordet (1870–1961) discovers antibodies.

1921 Insulin isolated and used for the treatment of diabetes by Sir Frederick Banting (1891–1941) and Charles Best (1899–1978).

First attempts at microsurgery.

1928 Penicillin is discovered by Scotsman, Sir Alexander Fleming (1881–1955). The new drug was an extract from a mould, *Penicillin rubrum* which he found growing among some dying bacterial colonies. His discovery leads to the development of antibiotics.

Cervical smear test invented by the Greek American George Papanicolaou (1883–1962).

1935 First lobotomy performed.

1945 Kidney dialysis machine invented by Willem Kolff (1911–) of the Netherlands.

1951 Double helix structure of DNA discovered by American James D. Watson (1928–) and Englishman Francis Crick (1916–). The discovery laid the foundations for modern molecular biology.

Introduction of oral contraceptive drugs.

1954 First successful kidney transplant.

1955 Open heart surgery first performed.

1967 South African surgeon Christiaan Barnard (1922–) carries out first heart transplant. His patient, Louis Washkansky died of pneumonia 18 days later.

Amniocentesis for studying a foetus in the womb first established.

1970 CAT-Scan (computerized axial tomography) invented.

1978 In-vitro fertilization produces first 'test' tube baby, Louise Joy Brown.

1981 First clinical description of AIDS.

1984 First successful gene therapy performed on animals.

1988 Scanning tunneling microscope produces first clear images of molecule structure.

MODERN DRUGS

The 20th century has seen the development of vast numbers of potent drugs. Milestones in therapeutic advances between 1900 and the 1960s have included:

1917 Oxygen first used therapeutically.

1921 Insulin (used to treat diabetes) isolated by Frederick Banting and C.H. Best in Toronto, Canada.

1929 Progesterone and testosterone isolated.

1935 Tubocurarine – a muscle-relaxing drug – isolated by Harold King.

1937 The first antibiotics – sulphonamides – introduced. Sulphapyridine (May and Baker 693) was the most widely used of the early antibiotics, the first effective treatments for infection.

1938 Phenytoin – an anticonvulsant used to treat epilepsy – introduced.

1939 DDT (dichloro-diphenyl-trichloroethane) developed by the Swiss chemist Dr Paul Muller. A powerful insecticide, DDT vastly lowered the incidence of malaria by killing malaria-carrying mosquitoes.

1940 Penicillin first used therapeutically by Sir Howard Florey and E.B. Chain. (In 1928 the Scottish bacteriologist Sir Alexander Fleming had discovered that penicillin would inhibit bacterial growth.)

1943 Streptomycin introduced – the first antibiotic effective against tuberculosis.

1948 Imipramine – an anti-depressant – introduced.

1949 Cortisone – one of a number of steroid hormones secreted by the adrenal gland – first used therapeutically in 1949 to reduce inflammation in rheumatoid arthritis.

1951 Halothane – a safer anaesthetic gas – introduced.

1954 Methyldopa and Reserpine – the first effective treatments for high blood pressure – introduced.

1955 Oral contraceptives introduced. The first field studies of a pill that could prevent ovulation were conducted in Puerto Rico.

Early 1960s Chlordiazepoxide (Librium) and diazepan (Valium) introduced – tranquillizers for the treatment of tension and anxiety.

In the last few decades drugs have been discovered and developed to treat every body system and many diverse features within each system. Mentioned below are some of the most commonly prescribed drugs (except antibiotics and contraceptives), classified according to their use. Drugs are in general listed below under their 'generic names' rather than the trade names.

CARDIOVASCULAR SYSTEM

Beta-blockers are used to slow heart rate, reduce high blood pressure and reduce anginal pain, particularly precipitated by exercise.

Calcium antagonists relax the muscle layer in the walls of blood vessels, and are used to treat high blood pressure. angina, and in some disorders of heart rhythm.

Ace inhibitors are used in the treatment of high blood pressure, and recently also for cardiac failure. They act on the angiotensin-converting enzyme – ACE – within the kidney to modify levels of a chemical that controls blood pressure by constricting blood vessels.

Nitrates are derived from the explosive agent nitroglycerine. They are used to dilate blood vessels and so ease anginal pain.

Digoxin is widely used to treat atrial fibrillation (a rapid and irregular heart rhythm) and cardiac failure.

Diuretics ('water tablets') stimulate urinary production. They are used to treat cardiac failure by removing excess fluid from the lungs, to reduce congestion in the liver, and to reduce fluid retention in the legs. Some diuretics can also be used to treat high blood pressure.

RESPIRATORY SYSTEM

Beta$_2$ agonists relax the muscle in the walls of the bronchial tubes, and thus relieve the spasm occurring in these airways in asthma. At first they were mainly given orally, but in recent years they have usually been administered by inhalation.

Sodium cromoglycate is administered by inhalation to treat asthma caused by allergy (mainly asthma in childhood). It does so by blocking the release of histamine from the mast cells and thus reducing inflammation in the bronchial tubes.

Inhaled steroids can be used in very low dosage to treat asthma. The steroid reduces the sensitivity of the bronchial tubes, but it is not absorbed into the rest of the body.

GASTROINTESTINAL SYSTEM

Antacids include a large number of preparations all of which are alkaline, can neutralize gastric acids, and thus reduce indigestion.

H$_2$ antagonists block the nerve endings in the stomach responsible for the secretion of gastric acid. These drugs have proved a very effective treatment for duodenal ulcers.

MAJOR COMMUNICABLE DISEASES

TRANSMISSION OF DISEASES

An infectious disease is one in which one living organism inhabits and multiplies on or within another, harming it in the process, either by the production of toxic substances or by damaging, digesting or destroying part or all of its cellular structure. Such harmful organisms are mostly microscopic – viruses, bacteria and protozoans – but also include various kinds of fungus, worms and arthropods.

Infections can be transmitted in the following ways:

Airborne transmission infection through infected droplets in the air from the nose, throat/lungs or saliva, or from dust particles from fallen skin.

Contamination infection through food or water supplies containing infected material such as faeces or urine.

Direct contact (contagion) infection from close contact with an infected person.

Sexual transmission infection through vaginal or anal intercourse, or oral sex. The use of condoms may reduce the risk of infection.

Blood-borne transmission infection through the injection of contaminated blood or blood products, or by improperly sterilized instruments. Blood-borne transmission is most common among haemophiliacs and intravenous drug users, and is occasionally the result of tattooing or acupuncture.

Animal-borne transmission infection through the injection of contaminated saliva; e.g. malaria (carried by the mosquito) and bubonic plague (transmitted by flea bites).

AIDS

Aids – acquired immune deficiency syndrome – was first identified in Los Angeles, USA, in 1981. The virus responsible for causing AIDS was isolated in 1983 and is now known as HIV (human immunodeficiency virus). The disease is spreading rapidly throughout the Western world, and has reached epidemic proportions in the countries of eastern and central Africa.

The virus attacks one particular type of white blood cell in the body (the helper/inducer lymphocytes) and this causes immunosuppression (reduced ability to combat infection). It may also attack the nervous system and cause dementia. Acute infection with HIV after exposure leads to the production of antibodies (sero-conversion). These antibodies are detected by blood tests which become positive on average within three months of the virus being acquired, but may take up to 12 months or longer to appear. In some cases there may be no symptoms during the period of sero-conversion; in other cases a transient flu-like illness with gland swelling and muscle aches may occur.

Not all patients who sero-convert go on to experience chronic infection. In those patients who do, the infection may be without symptoms, or may give rise to illnesses of varying degrees of severity – known as PGL, ARC or AIDS itself. Current knowledge suggests that between 10 and 30 per cent of HIV-antibody-positive patients progress to AIDS within five years.

PGL – persistent generalized lymphodenopathy – is the mildest illness caused by HIV infection. It is characterized by the swelling of lymph glands at various sites of the body, but there are no other symptoms. Many patients with PGL remain well for several years.

ARC – AIDS-related complex – is the second stage of the disease, during which there is some impairment of the immune system as well as lymph gland enlargement. Symptoms may include episodes of fever, weight loss, night sweats, diarrhoea, coughing, skin rashes and profound fatigue. Blood tests may show reduced numbers of white blood cells, anaemia, or changes in blood proteins. ARC is usually only diagnosed if such symptoms or blood-test abnormalities persist over a three-month period.

AIDS itself is diagnosed once certain specific infections or types of tumour begin to appear. The most common infection is an unusual form of pneumonia (*Pneumocystis carinii*); the most common tumour is Kaposi's sarcoma – a form of skin cancer that may spread to the internal organs. The course of the disease usually involves increasingly serious episodes of infection and it is often fatal within two years. Approximately 30 per cent of subjects suffer dementia by the later stages of their disease. Recent advances in treatment have included better treatments for the episodes of infection, and the development of a drug known as AZT, which shows promise in modifying the disease itself.

Most estimates of the numbers of people in Britain who are HIV-antibody positive are in excess of 100 000. Although about 80 per cent of the carriers of the virus are homosexual men, the AIDS virus is spreading more rapidly among heterosexuals. In 1992 the United Nations World Health Organization (WHO) announced that the number of persons infected by HIV worldwide was between 10 000 000 and 12 000 000, an increase of 1 000 000 cases since the beginning of 1991. WHO predicted that by the year 2000 the number of people who were HIV positive would be in excess of 40 000 000. In Europe and North America AIDS is at present more common in homosexual men and intravenous drug users, but in Africa heterosexual infection is much more frequent.

The only ways of acquiring HIV infection or AIDS are:
1. by having oral sex or sexual intercourse with someone who carries the virus, particularly if this is anal intercourse;
2. by sharing needles or other instruments contaminated with the blood of someone carrying the virus;
3. by receiving blood or blood products from someone with the virus (in the past some haemophiliacs have acquired the AIDS virus from treatment with blood products, but all blood products and blood transfusions in countries of the developed world are now thoroughly tested before use);
4. mothers who have the virus may pass it on to their babies.

ANTHRAX

Anthrax is a form of blood poisoning in cattle, sheep and horses that is normally fatal. It can upon rare occasions be passed to vets or butchers disposing of infected carcases or to those handling infected animal hides, wool or bone meal. The initial lesion is usually on the hand – a painful swollen boil with a black crust and surrounding redness. If untreated, blood poisoning (septicaemia) may result. It can be cured by penicillin, and a vaccine exists for those in high-risk occupations.

CHICKENPOX (VARICELLA)

Chickenpox is caused by the same virus as shingles (*Herpes zoster*). It is a mild disease, common in childhood and infectious from four days before the rash appears until seven days after the rash appears. The incubation period is usually 14 days. The rash – which may be preceded by mild headache or fever – begins as red spots, which over a few hours become raised and topped by a clear blister. Over two to three days these small blisters become opalescent and then scab over, with several crops of blisters appearing over a perod of five to seven days. The rash can occur on any part of the body – including the mouth and scalp – but tends to be most profuse on the trunk. No specific treatment is needed, except to relieve itch and prevent scratching with dirty finger nails. Complications are rare and there is no vaccine.

CHOLERA

Cholera is an acute infection of the intestine that causes profuse watery diarrhoea, vomiting and dehydration. It is caused by consuming water or food contaminated by the bacterium *Vibrio comma*, which is found in faeces. In 1854 the Englishman John Snow proved that cholera is transmitted in contaminated water when he stopped an epidemic by removing the pump handle from a well that he suspected was the source of infection. The last epidemic in Britain was in Cleethorpes in 1879. Today the disease is largely restricted to the tropics. Prevention is achieved by the availability of a clean water supply. Vaccination – two injections at an interval of two to four months – is effective for six to nine months, after which booster doses are needed.

COMMON COLD (CORYZAL)

At least 40 different viruses – either airborne or transmitted by direct contact – can cause sneezing, coughing, sore throat, running eyes and nose, headache and mild fever. Aspirin may help reduce the symptoms.

DIPHTHERIA

Diphtheria is an infection of the pharynx caused by airborne bacteria. The symptoms are an initial sore throat, obstructed breathing and inflammation of the heart. The condition is complicated by the formation of a membrane of dead tissue that can totally obstruct the airway and necessitate a tracheotomy – a surgical opening in the neck over the windpipe to allow breathing. Immunization programmes have eradicated diphtheria in the UK, where as recently as 1941 the disease caused 1622 deaths. Immunization is achieved by a series of three injections in infancy – combined with injections against tetanus and, usually, whooping cough – and booster doses at school age.

DYSENTERY

Two types of dysentery occur – *bacillary dysentery*, which is caused by the bacterium *Shigella*, and *amoebic dysentery*, caused by the amoeba *Entamoeba hystolytica*. Both types cause profuse diarrhoea (often containing blood), abdominal pain, weight loss and dehydration. Complications include liver abscesses. Amoebic dysentery is confined to the tropics. Bacillary dysentery occurs worldwide as a result of contamination of food by faecal bacteria, usually carried by water. The disease can be mild, but even after complete recovery the organism can still be excreted for several weeks. Prevention is through high standards of hygiene and the provision of a clean water supply. No immunization exists.

FOOD POISONING (GASTROENTERITIS)

Most short-lasting cases of sickness or diarrhoea are due to *viral gastroenteritis*. The commonest cause is human rotavirus, to which children under the age of three are particularly susceptible. The treatment is to stop all solid-food intake, and to concentrate instead on fluid intake to prevent dehydration. In babies, feeds of boiled water are given instead of milk. Breast-fed babies are less likely to get gastroenteritis.

Bacterial gastroenteritis may be caused by a number of bacteria, including *Salmonella*, *Listeria* and, more rarely, *Clostridium botulinum* (which causes the often fatal disease called *botulism*). Raw meat, poultry or eggs can be contaminated by the *Salmonella* bacterium, which is able to survive deep freezing. If thawing is not complete, or if the cooking time or temperature is inadequate, the cooked food remains infected. Symptoms of diarrhoea, fever and vomiting usually begin 12 to 48 hours after the food has been consumed. If complications such as septicaemia (blood poisoning) occur, the patient is treated with antibiotics. Without treatment, an infected person may become a carrier, although showing no symptoms.

Other forms of food poisoning are due to the release of a toxic chemical from the contaminating organism, rather than infection by the organism itself. Such infection usually begins within one to six hours of ingestion. Examples include *staphylococcal toxin* (often from infected cream, sometimes from meat or poultry) and the toxin of *Bacillus cereus* (from fried rice). All forms of gastroenteritis may be prevented by high standards of hygiene in food preparation and by the provision of a clean water supply.

GERMAN MEASLES (RUBELLA)

The first symptoms of German measles – a headache and sore throat – are followed by mild fever, a pink blotchy rash (first on the face, then on the body) and swelling of the lymph glands at the back of the neck. Cases are mildly infectious from five days before until five days after the rash appears. The incubation period is usually 17 to 18 days. There may be transient joint soreness, particularly in adults, but serious complications are very rare. However, German measles in a woman in the first three months of pregnancy can cause foetal damage – in the first month the risk of congenital abnormalities of eyes, ears or heart is 50 per cent. This falls to about four per cent by the fourth month.

Transmission is by direct contact with an infected person. In the UK immunization programmes were until recently aimed mainly at teenage girls. However, vaccination is now usual from the age of 14 months since the introduction in 1988 of the measles, mumps and rubella vaccine, which has been used for some years in North America.

GLANDULAR FEVER

Glandular fever – or infectious mononucleosis – is caused by the Epstein-Barr virus. Transmission is by direct contact and, because it mainly affects young adults (aged 15 to 25), a popular theory was that it was contracted by kissing. The initial symptom is a particularly sore throat, often producing a thick white coating over the area of the tonsils. Other characteristics include fever and enlargement of the lymph glands of the neck and sometimes also of the liver and spleen. This enlargement can last ten or more days and is often followed by a period of severe fatigue and mild depression before complete recovery. No treatment other than rest is available. Diagnosis can be confirmed by blood tests. No immunization is available.

GONORRHEA

Gonorrhea is a sexually transmitted (venereal) disease caused by the bacterium *Neisseria gonorrhoea*. It has an average incubation period of four days. In men it almost always causes a purulent discharge at the tip of the penis. Complications include infection of the epididymis (the tube behind the testicle) and of the prostate gland, or, in later stages, a narrowing of the urethra (urine tube). One half of the women infected by the disease may initially have no symptoms; others may suffer vaginal discharge, urinary symptoms and/or abdominal pain. The pain is due to infection spreading to the pelvic organs, including the Fallopian tubes, which may become scarred and blocked, sometimes leading to infertility. Penicillin is usually an effective cure. No immunization exists.

HEPATITIS

Hepatitis is inflammation of the liver, usually caused by a virus. It can also be caused by excessive alcohol or drug consumption. Viral hepatitis is classified as A, B, and Non A, Non B. There is no effective antiviral drug.

Hepatitis A – also called infectious hepatitis – is transmitted by close contact or faecal contamination of food or water. Following an incubation period of two to six weeks, initial symptoms include fever, nausea, weakness, discomfort and tenderness over the liver area. After about the first four days of the illness, jaundice (yellow skin) develops and the patient passes dark urine and pale faeces. Jaundice lasts one or two weeks and then appetite returns. A complete recovery is usual. An injection of human immunoglobulin gives temporary protection to travellers to those areas of the Third World where the disease is endemic.

Hepatitis B – also called serum hepatitis – is blood borne, usually transmitted by sharing contaminated needles or through sexual contact. The incubation period varies between one and five months. Symptoms identical to Hepatitis A may develop, but a high percentage of cases are 'sub-clinical', i.e. the illness is mild without evidence of jaundice. In about 19 out of 20 cases the patient becomes free of the virus within four to six months. One case in 20 becomes a chronic carrier, liable to pass on infection by blood or sexual contact, and liable to develop liver complications such as cirrhosis. Only 1 in 1000 cases dies of acute hepatitis. Immunization by a series of three injections is now available for those at high risk, e.g. nurses, doctors and dentists.

HERPES SIMPLEX

There are two common types of herpes simplex, a viral infection transmitted by direct contact.

The most common lesion produced by *Type I* of this virus is the 'cold sore' – a small crop of painful blisters that usually develop around the lips or nose and last for several days before fading. The virus may then be latent and flare up again in response to such events as another infection, trauma, emotional upset or exposure to sunlight. Other infections include blisters of the fingers (whitlow), ulceration of the cornea of the eye, and, rarely, a serious encephalitis (brain infection) to which infants are vulnerable. Those suffering from 'cold sores' should therefore avoid close contact with infants.

A variety of *Type II* of this virus causes genital herpes, a painful recurrent blistering eruption of the genitalia similar in appearance to a 'cold sore' but transmitted through sexual contact. Treatment with idoxuridine limits attacks, but does not prevent recurrence. No immunization exists.

HERPES ZOSTER

see Chickenpox and Shingles.

INFLUENZA

Influenza is an airborne viral infection. Symptoms include fever, muscle pain, sore throat, coughing, loss of appetite and general weakness. Complications include viral pneumonia, which can lead to a rapidly progressive pneumonia owing to further bacterial infection by staphylococci. Influenza may be fatal in elderly people. Pandemics can occur, such as in April–November 1918, when 21.6 million people are estimated to have died. Various types of influenza virus exist, and the virus has the capacity to change through time. Immunity from previous exposure or from vaccination is therefore never complete, and second or further attacks in the one individual can occur.

LEGIONNAIRE'S DISEASE

Legionnaire's disease is an uncommon form of pneumonia identified in 1976 and caused by the bacterium *Legionella pneumophilia*. It is transmitted airborne in water droplets from contaminated supplies, often through air-conditioning systems or showers. Symptoms include fever, coughing, chest pain and breathlessness, and the disease is sometimes fatal.

LEPROSY

Leprosy is a chronic inflammatory disease caused by the bacterium *Mycobacterium leprae*, which is transmitted by prolonged or close contact. The characteristics are very variable. Mild cases may show only a small area of altered skin pigmentation, which may heal spontaneously. Other cases progress to a thickening of superficial nerves, areas of skin without feeling, and muscle paralysis. In extreme forms there is distortion of the skin by nodule formation, thickening, fissuring and ulceration, resulting in the deformity and disfigurement that are traditionally feared. Control with sulphone drugs is possible, and some use has been made of plastic surgery.

MALARIA

Malaria is caused by a protozoa of one of four types – *Plasmodium ovale*, *P. malaria*, *P. vivax* and *P. falciparum* – and is transmitted to the bloodstream of man by the female anopheles mosquito. This mode of transmission was first proved in 1895 by the English bacteriologist Sir Ronald Ross, who discovered the protozoa in the gastrointestinal tract of the mosquito. Infection results in the destruction of red blood cells, causing intermittent fever and anaemia. The incubation period and the severity of the disease depends on the infecting species. *P. falciparum* – the most dangerous infection – causes malignant tertian malaria, in which the brain can be affected, and fits or coma – and even sudden death – may occur.

Every year in the tropics more than one million people still die of malaria and two million new cases appear, despite worldwide efforts to control the disease. All efforts at controlling malaria focus on the mosquito – the carrier – and include the destruction of the mosquito's breeding grounds, treating water with chemicals to destroy mosquito larvae, and the use of insecticides to kill adult mosquitoes. Drugs can be used to treat infected people, and measures – such as the use of nets, repellents and suitable clothing – can be taken to prevent the mosquito biting. Throughout the 1950s and 1960s the World Health Organization had considerable success in malaria eradication, particularly in the USA and Europe. The programme also led to a 500-fold decrease in malaria in India. Unfortunately resistance of mosquitoes to DDT then developed, and in many areas in the 1970s eradication began to falter.

The drugs used to prevent malaria are becoming more complex because in certain areas of the world malaria has become resistant to drugs that were previously effective. Whatever drug is used must be started one week before travel into the endemic area and should be continued for four to six weeks after leaving the area. In North Africa and the Middle East chloroquine taken once per week or proguanil taken daily are the usual preventative. For the Indian sub-continent, China, Africa and South America both drugs are advised in combination. For some parts of Southeast Asia pyrimethamine and chloroquine are advised.

MEASLES (RUBEOLA)

Measles is a viral airborne infection. An incubation period of between 8 and 14 days precedes the onset of fever and catarrhal symptoms, which last for three days before the rash appears. The rash is red and blotchy, usually starting behind the ears and spreading to the face and trunk. The inside of the cheeks may be red and Koplik's spots (little white spots – like grains of salt – in the area behind the lower back teeth) confirm the diagnosis. Other characteristics include running eyes and nose. The rash fades after three or four days. Cases are highly infectious from the onset of the fever and the catarrhal phase until the rash fades. Bacterial infections of the ears, sinuses and chest are the most immediate complications. A rare but serious progressive brain disease known as subacute sclerosing panencephalitis can occur four or more years after infection.

Immunization is recommended from the age of 14 months and, since October 1988 in the UK, is combined with a vaccine for mumps and rubella (German measles). The intensive use of this vaccine has made measles an extremely rare condition in North America in recent years.

MENINGITIS

Meningitis is a viral or bacterial infection causing inflammation of membranes surrounding the brain.

Bacterial meningitis can be caused by a number of organisms – the most common are mengingococcal meningitis, pneumococcal meningitis and haemophilus meningitis. *E. coli* meningitis occurs mainly in new-born infants. The symptoms of bacterial meningitis are fever, severe headache, neck stiffness, intolerance of bright lights and vomiting. The speed of onset depends on the infecting organism – tubercular meningitis has a gradual onset. Meningococcal meningitis is particularly rapid and can cause sudden collapse and the rapid appearance of a rash looking like small bruises or blood blisters. Antibiotic therapy must be started with the utmost urgency.

Viral meningitis can be caused by a great number of viruses. The symptoms are similar but less severe than those of bacterial meningitis. Spontaneous recovery can be expected without specific treatment.

MUMPS

Mumps is caused by an airborne paramyxovirus. Its incubation period is usually 21 days. Initial symptoms are three to five days of mild fever and vague malaise followed by tender swelling of the parotid glands (the salivary glands on the side of the face, in front of and below the ears). Usually both sides are affected, but one side may become swollen one or two days before the other. The swelling lasts several days, and cases are infectious for one week before the swelling and until the swelling subsides. Possible complications include inflammation of the testicles (orchitis) in adult males, inflammation of the pancreas, and a mild viral meningitis. In North America, Britain and some European countries, immunization is available by means of a single injection combined with vaccination against measles and rubella (German measles).

MYALGIC ENCEPHALOMYELITIS (ME)

Myalgic encephalomyelitis is a condition probably developing as a sequel to various viral infections, most notably to Coxsackie virus infection. The symptoms are diverse, but include muscle fatigue and muscle pain provoked by minimal exercise and relieved or prevented by adequate rest. The condition is similar to the fatigue encountered after glandular fever, but may last for months – or even years. The condition is also known as post-viral syndrome and Royal Free disease, so called because of an apparent epidemic in the Royal Free Hospital, London, in the 1950s. No treatment is available.

PLAGUE

Plague is a disease of rodents that can be transmitted to man by flea bites or by airborne infection. It is caused by the bacterium *Yersinia pestis*. Symptoms include fever, weakness, delirium and painful buboes (swelling of lymph nodes). The condition is often fatal. During the 14th century – when the condition was known as the Black Death – one quarter of the population of Europe died because of plague. The Great Plague of London (1664–65) caused the death of one person in seven in the city.

PNEUMONIA

Pneumonia is a bacterial or viral infection transmitted by direct contact or by airborne infection. The principal characteristic is the inflammation of one or both lungs, in which the air sacs become filled with liquid. This causes pain and difficulty in breathing. Pneumonia can be fatal, particularly in the elderly.

POLIOMYELITIS

Polio is a viral infection of the nervous system transmitted by direct contact. It is no longer endemic in Britain, where as recently as 1948 polio caused 241 deaths in England and Wales. The majority of cases are characterized by mild fever, headache, stiffness of the neck and gastrointestinal symptoms lasting only a few days. However, other cases develop meningitis or paralysis of muscles. Paralysis may affect the breathing muscles – causing respiratory failure – or the limb muscles – resulting in permanent muscle thinning and weakness. Polio has been eradicated by immunization in the majority of developed countries. The oral vaccine Sabin is given from infancy with later booster doses. The earlier Salk vaccine was given by injection.

RABIES

Rabies is an acute viral infection endemic in warm-blooded animals in Africa and Eurasia as far west as central France. Ordinarily fatal in man, it is transmitted in the saliva of warm-blooded animals through broken skin as a result of a bite (e.g. from dogs, foxes, bats). The symptoms include spasm of the throat muscles when swallowing is attempted, aversion to water (hence the alternative name 'hydrophobia'), maniacal behaviour, and finally involvement of other muscles to cause paralysis and death. Vaccine is available for those in high-risk occupations. The last case contracted by man in the UK was in 1922.

RHEUMATIC FEVER

Rheumatic fever is caused by streptococcal bacteria and can, like scarlet fever, occur as a sequel to tonsillitis. The symptoms are fever and an arthritis that seems to move from one joint to another, causing swelling and pain. Rheumatic fever may cause damage to the heart valves, damage which only becomes apparent in later years. Occasionally it can cause chorea (St Vitus's dance), a type of involuntary movement. The disease can recur, but is today very much less common than 50 years ago. No immunization exists.

RUBELLA

See German measles.

SCARLET FEVER (SCARLATINA)

Scarlet fever is a throat infection caused by an airborne bacterium *Streptococcus pyogenus*. Symptoms include fever and a sore throat, complicated by the appearance of a uniform pink blush of the skin, which on close inspection appears as many fine red points. The cheeks are usually flushed and the area round the lips is white (circumoral pallor). The tongue has a strawberry-like colour. About a week after the rash appears there is often peeling of the skin, especially on the hands and feet. The condition is sometimes accompanied by ear and kidney infections. The incubation period is between two and five days and cases are infectious for up to ten days unless treated with penicillin. In recent years this disease seems to have become much milder in developed countries, in part because of the use of antibiotics and in part because of improved social conditions. Complications are now accordingly rare.

SCHISTOSOMIASIS (BILHARZIA)

Bilharzia is a tropical disease caused by infestation of the body with larvae of the parasitic flatworm *Schistosoma*. Eggs excreted in the faeces or urine of infected people undergo part of the larval development in freshwater snails. Larvae released by the snails penetrate the skin of people bathing in infected water and colonize blood vessels in the intestine. Symptoms include diarrhoea, and an enlargement of the spleen and liver. The condition can be fatal.

SHINGLES (HERPES ZOSTER)

Shingles is caused by a reactivation of the *Herpes zoster* virus which causes chickenpox. The virus may be present and dormant in the nerve root for years before reactivation. This painful condition is therefore not truly infectious, but it is possible to pass it on as chickenpox by close physical contact. Symptoms include groups of small blisters on a red base that appear in the skin area supplied by a particular nerve root, for example in a narrow band round one side of the chest or abdomen. The groups of blisters commonly occur in a band on one side of the face, or on one limb. Pain may precede the rash by two to three days, and may endure at the site for an average of six weeks. Sensitivity (post-herpetic neuralgia) may last for months.

SMALLPOX

The World Health Organization has declared the world free of smallpox from 1 January 1980. Vaccination is only needed for certain research scientists.

SYPHILIS

Syphilis is a sexually transmitted (venereal) disease caused by the bacterium *Treponema pallidum*. The disease has three stages. The primary stage begins after an incubation phase of (usually) two to four weeks and is characterized by a firm ulcer on the site of infection, usually the genitalia, accompanied by swelling in the nearest lymph glands (e.g. the groin). The secondary stage – six weeks later – has varying characteristics, including skin rashes, mouth ulcers, glandular swelling, and fever with muscle aches. The tertiary stage follows after a long dormant period (up to 25 years) and can affect any organ of the body but particularly the brain and nerves, possibly causing insanity, blindness and loss of balance. Syphilis may also cause localized swellings (gumma) in the skin, bones or heart. Diagnosis is by blood tests, and treatment by penicillin.

TETANUS (LOCKJAW)

The bacterium *Clostridium tetani* is widespread in nature, commonly occurring in the topsoil. Tetanus spores can gain access to the body through cuts, resulting in intense muscle spasm ('lockjaw'). Prevention is by immunization with tetanus toxoid, given as three doses in infancy with booster doses at school age and then every five years. If immunity has waned the initial three doses are repeated.

THRUSH

Thrush is a fungal disease caused by the fungus *Candida albicans*, which lives in the alimentary canal and the vagina. Thrush arises when the growth of fungus increases, in some cases following a course of broad-spectrum antibiotics. It can be passed to a baby at birth. Thrush is characterized by white patches in the mouth (particularly in infants) and by irritation of the vagina.

TUBERCULOSIS (TB)

Tuberculosis is caused by the bacterium *Mycobacterium tuberculosis*, first discovered in 1882 by the German scientist Robert Koch (1843–1910). Evidence of this disease has been found in an Egyptian mummy from the 10th century BC. The mortality rate in England and Wales in the 1850s was 60 000 per year, both adults and children dying of what was known as 'consumption'. Two strains of organism exist – human and bovine. The main source of bovine tuberculosis was infected milk, but this has been eliminated in the developed world by pasteurization. The source of the human strain is the respiratory tract of an 'open' case of pulmonary tuberculosis, i.e. the organism is coughed up or breathed out by the sufferer.

The initial infection is in the lungs and the lymph glands in the middle of the chest cavity. In the majority of cases there are no symptoms and the infection heals without treatment, but may leave a scar on the lung. During this primary infection the body develops an immunity that can be detected by means of the Mantoux test. In this test a tiny amount of dead tubercle is injected just under the skin surface and if immunity is present a raised red lump develops. In a minority of primary infections, insufficient immunity develops and the infection spreads either all through the lungs (consumption or miliary pulmonary tuberculosis) or to other organs, leading to meningitis or kidney or bone infection. In cases where the primary illness has disappeared, the infection can flare up again years later, particularly if there is undernourishment or general debility. This is known as chronic tuberculosis and most commonly affects the lungs, but can affect any organ.

Modern drug treatment is very effective for all forms of the disease, but 'open' cases are still kept in isolation until their sputum becomes free of the infecting organism. Immunization is achieved by BCG (*Bacille Calmette-Guérin*), a live attenuated vaccine (i.e. a very mild form of TB) first used in 1906. It is given by injection into the skin and results in a small ulcer that heals after several weeks, leaving a scar.

TYPHOID

Typhoid is an infection of the digestive system caused by the bacterium *Salmonella typhi*, transmitted to the body by faecally contaminated food or water. Symptoms begin with fever and progress to a rash and profuse diarrhoea with blood loss. Untreated, the mortality rate is 10 to 15 per cent; the remainder of cases recover after about three weeks, although some three per cent become chronic carriers without symptoms. The last major epidemic in the UK was in Aberdeen in 1964, when 414 cases occurred. Immunization is achieved with two injections at an interval of one month, and immunity lasts for five years.

TYPHUS

Typhus is the name given to a group of closely related acute infectious diseases caused by *Rickettsia* parasites, which are transmitted by lice, fleas or ticks. Typhus is characterized by severe headaches, rash, high fever and delirium, and can be fatal. Typhus has been eliminated from the developed world but remains a threat to undernourished people living in unhygienic conditions in developing countries.

VARICELLA

See Chickenpox.

WHOOPING COUGH (PERTUSSIS)

Whooping cough is an acute respiratory infection caused by the bacterium *Bordetella pertussis*. It is transmitted by direct contact or by airborne infection. In developing countries, where poor nutrition exists, whooping cough has a considerable death rate. It can affect any age group, but is most common in children and is most severe in young babies. The illness begins with what seems to be an ordinary cold, but, instead of improving after a few days, the cough becomes progressively worse and is most severe at night. There are spasms of coughing, with one cough after another, until the child is forced to take in breath rapidly with a loud whooping sound. During an attack the child becomes red (or even blue) in the face, with streaming eyes. A severe coughing spasm usually ends with a bout of vomiting. These symptoms may persist for several weeks before easing, but often a cough at night may persist for several months after the infection. Complications include middle ear infection, pneumonia, and encephalitis (brain infection).

The incubation period is seven to ten days. The disease is highly infectious from seven days after exposure to three weeks after the symptoms develop. Before the introduction of vaccine in 1957 there were on average some 100 000 cases per year in the UK. By 1973, when vaccine acceptance was 80 per cent, cases had fallen to 2400. In the mid-1970s levels of vaccination fell to about 30 per cent and major epidemics followed in 1977, 1979, 1981 and 1983. Mortality from whooping cough in the UK in the 1970s remained about 1 per 1000 notified cases, with a higher death rate for infants under one year. Three vaccinations are usually given in combination with diphtheria and tetanus vaccine. Complications of vaccination are very rare, and are considerably less likely than a child dying of the disease.

NON-INFECTIOUS DISEASES

Diseases that are not transmitted have – in the developed world – replaced infections as the primary health problem. Infectious diseases such as smallpox, tuberculosis and diphtheria have been ousted from their positions as major killers by cancer, heart disease and strokes.

While factors such as an inappropriate diet, lack of exercise, excessive intake of alcohol and tobacco smoking have to take the blame for many of the diseases that afflict people today, they are not the only culprits. The genes that each of us inherits from our parents may also put us at risk from developing heart disease, schizophrenia, rheumatoid arthritis or certain types of cancer. More than 4000 genetic diseases result from the inheritance of a mutant gene.

MAJOR GENETIC DISEASES AND DISORDERS

Cystic fibrosis a hereditary mutation resulting in abnormally thick mucous secretions in the lungs and intestine. Treatment for digestive problems and lung infections can help to prolong the lives of people with cystic fibrosis, many of whom survive into their mid-twenties.

Diabetes mellitus a common and – as yet – incurable metabolic disease. In many cases the disease is genetically determined but it can also be precipitated by certain viral infections, toxins, chronic disease or pregnancy (usually temporary). In all cases, the primary defect is an absolute or relative deficiency of pancreatic insulin. Insulin deficiency results in profound metabolic derangements, the most common of which is hyperglycaemia (blood glucose levels above the normal range of 50 to 120 mg per 100 millilitres).

As blood sugar rises, glucose appears in the urine, carrying water with it and giving rise to the increased urine output and thirst that characterizes the disorder. Fat metabolism may also be enhanced leading to the accumulation of acidic by-products which, if unchecked, can result in coma or death. Diabetics can become susceptible to degenerative complications involving the nerves, eyes, kidneys and blood vessels, and it is these secondary problems that make diabetes such a devastating disease. Many diabetics are treated by dietary restrictions and the use of drugs, but some are dependent upon daily administration of insulin to control their symptoms.

Down's syndrome a chromosomal abnormality in which the affected child has an extra copy of chromosome number 21. The condition is characterized by a flat face and nose, a vertical fold of skin at the inner edge of the eye, short fingers, and mental retardation. Formerly known as mongolism, the syndrome is named after the English physician John Langdon-Down (1828–96).

Huntington's chorea a particularly distressing hereditary disease, affecting one person in 20 000. Dementia (a disorder of the mental processes) and uncontrolled movements occur, but the symptoms fail to become apparent until the affected person has reached middle age. By this time, he or she has often had children who risk suffering the same fate.

Sickle-cell disease a hereditary blood disease that mainly affects people with malarial immunity – usually people from Africa and their descendants – although it was common in malarial parts of Europe. Large numbers of red blood cells in sufferers become sickle-shaped and can cause obstructions in the blood vessels, with possible damage to organs such as the kidneys and the brain. No satisfactory treatment has yet been developed.

Thalassaemia a hereditary disease caused by a haemoglobin deficiency. Affected red blood cells cannot function normally, resulting in anaemia, enlargement of the spleen, and bone-marrow disorders. Thalassaemia – which is common in Mediterranean countries, Asia and Africa – can be treated by repeated blood transfusions.

MAJOR ENVIRONMENTAL DISEASES

Environmental hazards such as radiation and pollutants account for some types of disease. People normally encounter only small doses of radiation, from diagnostic X-rays or perhaps as a treatment for cancer. In addition, everyone is exposed to low background levels of natural radiation from the Sun and from some types of rock. However, excessive doses of radiation may follow accidents, for example at nuclear reactors.

Chemical hazards are probably more often encountered at work than at home. The list of industrial diseases is long and includes poisoning by lead, mercury and other heavy metals.

Asbestosis an industrial disease caused by inhaling fibres of asbestos. The lungs become fibrous and the affected person not only experiences increasing breathlessness, with failure of the heart and lungs, but also has an increased risk of developing lung cancer.

Lead poisoning a debilitating condition resulting from an accumulation of lead in the body, usually from water pipes or lead-based paint. Symptoms are variable and include digestive problems, irritability, severe abdominal pain, constipation, anaemia and paralysis. The illness can be acute in children, and may result in brain damage, blindness, deafness and death.

Radiation sickness a disease caused by high exposures of radiation. It is characterized by loss of cells from the bone marrow and the lining of the stomach. The person loses appetite and suffers diarrhoea, sickness, chills, fever and extreme tiredness. Death may follow because of the damage to the bowel and bone marrow, the latter resulting in loss of resistance to infection and severe anaemia. Long-term sufferers are at risk of developing cancers.

CANCER

Cancer occurs when cells grow out of control. A single cell can accumulate changes in its genes that allow it to replicate in an uncontrolled way. Such a cell can give rise to a tumour, which may manifest itself as a palpable lump or mass. Once cells become cancerous they lose the function that they once had; they simply reproduce themselves indefinitely.

A tumour is said to be *benign* if it remains localized in the place where it originated. Nevertheless, benign tumours can be life-threatening if they jeopardize normal structures, e.g. benign tumours of the brain. *Malignant* tumours have the capacity to spread around the body. Individual cells, or groups of cells, can detach themselves from the primary tumour, migrate via the blood or the lymph and become deposited on other organs. There they form secondary tumours.

In many cases the cause of the cancer is unknown. Treatment for cancer varies according to the type of tumour, the site of the primary tumour, and the extent of the spread of cancerous cells. Chemotherapy – drug therapy – can produce long remissions in some forms of cancer, but side effects occur as normal cells are damaged and white blood cells become depleted. Radiation therapy uses ionizing radiation – including X-rays and gamma rays – to destroy cancer cells. Surgery is used to remove malignant growths but is only effective if cancer cells have not migrated into other parts of the body.

Carcinoma a cancer of the skin (*melanoma*) or of the inner tissues that cover the internal cavity structures of the breast, the respiratory tracts (including lung cancer), the gastro-intestinal tract (including cancers of the stomach, colon and rectum), the endocrine glands and the genitourinary tract (including cancers of the prostate, testes, fallo-

HOSPITALS

The following countries have the smallest number of inhabitants per hospital bed:

Country	Number of inhabitants for every hospital bed
Nauru	34
Monaco	56
Sweden	57
Iceland	61
Norway	64
Australia	66
North Korea	74
Luxembourg	77
Italy	79
Japan	84
Finland	85
Netherlands	86
Austria	96
Germany	96
France	100
United Kingdom	175

pian tubes, ovaries, bladder and kidneys).

Leukaemia a cancer of the blood-forming tissues, related to sarcoma.

Lymphoma a cancer of the lymphoid cells; either Hodgkin's disease or non-Hodgkin's disease.

Sarcoma a cancer of the connective tissues, including bones, muscles, blood vessels and fibrous tissues.

HEART DISEASES

Heart disease is the leading cause of death in developed countries. Diseases of the heart may be genetic or caused by infection or environmental factors. There are four principal types:

Congenital cardiovascular disease a heart disease affecting one person in 200. The most common conditions include abnormalities of valves, narrowing of the aorta, shunt lesions (a malformation that allows oxygen-rich blood to be pumped back to the lungs) or the tetralogy of Fallot (a defect that commonly causes 'blue babies'). Some of these conditions may be hereditary, but often the reason for a defect is unknown. In many cases surgery to correct such defects is possible.

Coronary heart disease is the most common heart disease in developed countries and the most common cause of sudden death. The coronary arteries supply blood to the heart muscle. If the lining of these arteries becomes gradually thickened by fatty tissue (atheroma), the blood supply decreases. This causes episodes of chest pain (angina) often brought on by exercise. If a blood clot then develops at one such thickened area (coronary thrombosis), the artery becomes completely blocked causing a heart attack (myocardial infarction) or even sudden death. The main factors which put an individual at risk of coronary disease are cigarette smoking, high blood pressure and high levels of cholesterol in the blood. Other risk factors include obesity, lack of exercise, diabetes, stress and genetic factors such as a family history of coronary disease. Many drug treatments

are now available and surgery can bypass a narrowed artery.

Hypertensive heart disease a condition resulting from prolonged, untreated high blood pressure (hypertension). The high pressure within the arteries forces the heart to pump against a greater resistance. This strain initially causes an increase in the thickness of the heart muscle, and then an enlargement of the heart itself. If left untreated, the heart becomes unable to cope and heart failure results.

Rheumatic heart disease is becoming less common in developed countries, but remains a major problem in the Third World. It is a delayed complication of rheumatic fever which has usually occurred in childhood. Over the years, scarring of the heart valves causes increased narrowing of the valve (sterosis), or failure of the valve to close completely, thus allowing a back-flow of blood in the wrong direction (regurgitation or incompetence). By middle age breathlessness or heart failure may result. Surgical splitting of the valve (valvotomy) or valve replacement can be dramatically beneficial.

ALLERGIES

An allergy is a hypersensitivity or an abnormal response in the body to contact with a particular substance. The term was first used in 1906 by the German paediatrician Baron Clemens von Pirquet to describe an abnormal reaction to tuberculin. The reaction may provoke illnesses such as asthma, or may be mild, producing slight discomfort and inconvenience. Many individuals have only one specific allergy (for example to a particular food or drug), but some have an inherited susceptibility to allergy in general (atopy). Examples of allergy include:

Hay fever (allergic rhinitis) is a seasonal allergy characterized by sneezing, nasal congestion and itching of the eyes, and is caused by sensitivity to pollen from grass or trees in the spring and summer months.

Hives (urticaria) an intensely itchy skin reaction characterized by raised smooth red or pale weals. In severe cases there may be swelling of the lips or the skin around the eyes. The causal allergy may be to food (e.g. fish, eggs, berries), to drugs (e.g. penicillin), or to contact with chemicals, feathers or fur. Allergy to drugs may also take the form of a red blotchy rash rather like measles.

Asthma is a respiratory disorder characterized by wheezing owing to narrowing of the airways (bronchi), partly because of spasm in the muscle of the bronchi, and partly because of swelling and congestion of the lining (mucosa) of the bronchi. Childhood asthma, unlike asthma in later life, often occurs in those who are atopic (prone to allergy), and allergy to such things as house dust, feathers, pollen, and animal fur or hair can trigger asthma attacks. There is often a family history of allergy; boys are more often affected than girls, and childhood asthma may disappear at puberty. Attacks can also be triggered by infections, by irritants such as cold air or cigarette smoke, or by stress. Many drug treatments are now available, many in the form of inhalers.

ARTHRITIS

Arthritis is a term applied to a variety of conditions which cause pain in the joints. There are two main categories.

Osteoarthritis is the most common form of arthritis. It is a degeneration caused by 'wear and tear'. The cartilage covering the bone ends becomes eroded and this eventually leads to roughening and swelling of the bone itself, especially at the edges of the joint. Surgery to replace hip and knee joints which have been badly affected by osteoarthritis is now commonly performed.

Inflammatory arthritis takes many different forms but is in general due to inflammation of the tissues lining the joints (synovium). The milder forms are popularly known as *rheumatism*; more severe forms can be due to rheumatoid arthritis, gout, or bacterial infection. In rheumatoid arthritis the body's immune system starts to react against its own synovial tissue, damaging it, and in the process causing pain, stiffness and swelling of the joints. Any joint may be affected, but the fingers are often an obvious site. In its severe forms, progressive deformity of joints occurs. In gout, tiny crystals of the chemical uric acid are deposited within the joint (characteristically the joint at the base of the big toe) causing intense pain and tenderness. Bacterial infection causing arthritis is uncommon and results from an open wound, or spread of infection from another area in the body (e.g. pneumonia or venereal disease).

PHYSICIANS

The following countries have the smallest number of inhabitants for every physician:

Country	Number of inhabitants per physician
Czech Republic	280
Spain	290
Italy	329
Norway	319
Belgium	331
Austria	347
Sweden	358
Luxembourg	363
Bulgaria	364
Denmark	380
France	382
Iceland	382
Finland	423
USA	457
Netherlands	468
Australia	470
UK	603

MEDICAL AND SURGICAL SPECIALITIES

In most hospitals there are departments dealing with different specialities – for example, departments of neurology or paediatrics. The most important medical specialities include:

anaesthetics the study of the loss of sensation (especially pain) or consciousness by drugs: in *general anaesthetics* consciousness is lost; in *local anaesthetics* the loss of sensation applies only to a specific part of the body.

anatomy the study of the structure of the body.

audiology the assessment of hearing.

aurology the study and treatment of diseases of the ear.

bacteriology the study and treatment of bacterial (and usually also viral) infections.

bioengineering the study of the mechanical workings of the body, particularly with reference to artificial limbs and powered appliances that the body can use.

biophysics the study of electrical impulses in the body; this may be applied to an assessment of muscle disease.

cardiology the study and treatment of heart disease.

chemotherapy the treatment of diseases by drugs.

community medicine the prevention of the spread of disease and the increase of physical and mental well-being within the community.

cryosurgery the use of freezing techniques in surgery.

cytogenetics the study of chromosomes and their correlation with heredity.

cytology (medical) the microscopic study of body cells.

dentistry the treatment and extraction of teeth.

dermatology the study and treatment of skin diseases.

diabetics the study and treatment of diabetes.

embryology the study of the growth of the baby from the moment of conception to about the 20th week of pregnancy.

endocrinology the study and treatment of diseases of the glands that produce hormones.

ENT otorhinolaryngology (see below).

entomology (medical) the study of insects and moths with particular reference to the transmission of disease.

epidemiology the study of the occurrence, transmission and control of epidemics.

forensic medicine the study of injury and disease caused by criminal activity and the detection of crime by medical knowledge.

gastroenterology the study and treatment of diseases of the stomach and intestines.

genetics the study of inherited characteristics, disease and malformations.

genito-urinary medicine the study of diseases of the sexual and urine-producing organs.

geriatrics the study and treatment of the diseases and condition of elderly people.

gerontology the study of diseases of elderly people and in particular the study of the ageing process.

gynaecology the study and treatment of diseases of women, in particular the diseases of the genito-urinary tract.

haematology the study and treatment of blood diseases.

histochemistry the study of the chemical environment of the body cells.

histopathology the microscopic study of cells.

immunology the study of the immunity of the body to disease and other harmful outside influences.

laryngology the study and treatment of throat diseases.

metabolic diseases diseases of the interior workings of the body, e.g. disorders of calcium absorption, thyroid disease, or adrenal gland disease.

microbiology (medical) the study of the workings of cells.

nephrology the study and treatment of kidney disease.

neurology the study and treatment of a wide range of diseases of the brain and/or the nervous system.

neurosurgery operations on the brain or nervous system.

nuclear medicine the treatment of diseases with radioactive substances.

obstetrics the care of pregnant women and the delivery of children.

oncology the study and treatment of cancer.

ophthalmic optics (optometry) the assessment of visual disorders, the examination of eyes, and the provision of corrective treatment in the form of visual aids, e.g. spectacles or contact lenses.

optics, dispensing the dispensing of spectacles or contact lenses (cf. ophthalmic optics).

orthodontology the branch of dentistry concerned with the prevention and correction of irregularities in teeth.

orthopaedics the study and treatment of fractures and bone diseases.

orthoptics the correction of defective vision, e.g. the treatment of squints of the eye.

orthotics the provision of artificial and mechanical aids, e.g. braces to assist weakened limbs.

otology the study and treatment of diseases of the ear.

otorhinolaryngology the study and treatment of diseases of the ear, nose and throat; also known as ENT.

paediatrics the study and treatment of the diseases of children.

parasitology (medical) the study and treatment of infections of the body caused by worms, insects and other parasites.

pathology the branch of medicine concerned with the cause, origin and nature of disease.

pharmacology the use of drugs in relation to medicine.

physical medicine the treatment of injuries by exercise or electrical treatments, or the preparation of the body for surgery by similar means (see physiotherapy.)

physiology the study and understanding of the normal workings of the body.

physiotherapy the practice of physical medicine (see above).

plastic surgery the reconstruction or alteration of damaged or abnormal parts of the body by surgery.

proctology the study and treatment of diseases of the rectum.

prosthetics the making of artificial limbs and related appliances.

psychiatry the study and treatment of mental disorders.

psychoanalysis the investigation of the formation of mental illness by long-term repeated discussion between the patient and a psychoanalyst.

psychology the study of the mind, with particular reference to the measurement of intellectual activity.

psychotherapy the treatment of mental disorders by psychological methods, rather than by drugs or other physical treatments.

radiobiology the treatment or investigation of disease using radioactive substances.

radiography the taking of X-rays.

radiology the study of X-rays.

radiotherapy the treatment of diseases using X-rays.

renal diseases diseases of the kidney or urinary tract.

rheumatology the study and treatment of diseases of muscles and joints.

rhinology the study and treatment of diseases of the nose.

therapeutics curative medicine; the healing of physical and/or mental disorders.

thoracic surgery surgery on the chest or heart.

toxicology the study of poisons, their effects and antidotes.

urology the study and treatment of diseases of the kidney and the urinary tract.

vascular disease diseases of the blood vessels.

venereology the study and treatment of sexually transmitted diseases.

virology the study and treatment of virus diseases.

SCHOOLS OF PSYCHOLOGY

Adlerian psychology see individual psychology.

analytical psychology a branch of psychology developed by Jung as a result of disagreements with Freud. See Jungian theory.

behavioural psychology a school of psychology largely based on the work of B.F. Skinner (see below). Its central tenet is that human behaviour can be modified by reinforcement, i.e. the provision of a 'reward' – either physical or social – or the avoidance of punishment. It assumes that the symptom is the illness and that the patient can be 'cured' by deconditioning and reconditioning.

body-centred psychology a loose grouping of therapies and ideas – rather than a school of psychology – in which work on the physical body results in an alteration in the personality or the image of self. It includes such diverse philosophies and therapies as yoga, the Alexander technique and rolfing (see Complementary medicine) and T'ai Chi.

clinical psychology a practically based area of psychology in which research findings and methods are applied to human behaviour, both normal and abnormal. It is a broadly based discipline, encompassing experimental psychology, social psychology, environmental psychology, and ethology.

developmental psychobiology the study of biological processes and systems that affect the development of behaviour. In particular, interest focuses on the behavioural characteristics enabling species to cope with environmental challenges, and the behaviour and development of the young as they relate to their environment.

ego psychology a branch of psychoanalytical theory that has developed from Freud's book *The Ego and the Id*. It is now associated with Freud's daughter, Anna Freud (see below), who developed the thinking in *The Ego and the Mechanisms of Defence*. Ego psychology concentrates on the manner in which the individual develops and acquires functions that enable him to control his impulses and his environment and to act independently.

existential analysis an area of psychology heavily influenced by existential philosophers such as Sartre and Heidegger (see Philosophy). Essentially it lays emphasis on the here and now, expecting the patient to take responsibility for his actions through which his life will take on meaning. There is little emphasis on the unconscious mental processes dwelt on by other schools of psychology.

Freudian psychoanalysis the classical psychoanalysis that can be traced back directly to teachings and writings of Freud (see below), particularly to his *An Outline of Psychoanalysis*.

humanistic psychology a branch of psychology in which the self-image of the patient (client) is paramount. The therapist is honest with the patient, but does not seek to change the patient by any approval or disapproval. This school was developed by the American psychologist Carl Ransom Rogers.

individual psychology a branch of psychoanalysis founded by Adler (see below), who regarded the individual as responsible for his own actions and able to work towards his own goals.

Jungian theory a branch of psychology contained within the ideas of Carl Gustav Jung (see below) and covering a very wide spectrum of psychology.

Kleinian theory a branch of psychology contained in the ideas of Klein (see below), who laid emphasis on the first year of a child's life as being a time rich in fantasy and a time during which the origins of neurosis occur.

learning theory a group of psychological theories that aim to explain individual behaviour and personality arising as a result of learned reactions and responses to the environment. This is in contrast to psychoanalysis, which sees behaviour and personality arising as a result of developmental processes.

neo-Freudian theory a variety of psychological thought united by the common thread that those who formulated its ideas initially espoused Freud's ideas on psychoanalysis, but subsequently broke away from, or modified, or added to, Freud's thinking. In general neo-Freudian theory emphasizes the social needs of individuals to a greater extent than Freud did.

neurolinguistics a combination of psychology, linguistics and neurology that looks at the acquisition of language, its production and processing, and its disruption or disturbances, especially those disturbances related to organic brain disease.

neuropsychiatry the study of organic brain disorders and the effects they have on behaviour and personality.

phenomenology literally, the study of phenomena, i.e. of the experiences that we have and the effect they have on personality and behaviour.

psychiatry the treatment and study of mental, emotional, personality and behavioural disorders.

psychoanalysis a method of treating mental illness, originated by Sigmund Freud. Psychoanalysis aims to bring to the surface those fears and conflicts between instinct and conscience that have been pushed into the unconscious.

psychology the study of the mind, of behaviour and of thinking.

psychopathology the study of the abnormal workings of the mind and of abnormal behaviour.

psychosynthesis a branch of psychological thinking that aims to bring together those elements of personality that are at odds with each other.

psychotherapy the treatment of mental disturbance, personality problems, behavioural difficulties, etc., by psychological means. Invariably a strong link is forged between the therapist and the patient, who often meet on a one-to-one basis.

radical therapy a relatively recent movement in psychology that calls into question society's definitions of such words as 'sane' and 'insane'. In radical therapy, 'insanity' – if there is such a thing – is seen as a social problem needing social solutions. Radical therapy – which undermines the medical model of psychology – was developed by R.D. Laing, and derives much from existentialism and humanism (see Philosophy).

social psychiatry the examination of mental disorder as a part of society. Both the social causes of such disorders and the social methods of prevention are looked at.

MAJOR PSYCHOLOGISTS

Alfred Alder (1870–1937), Austrian psychiatrist who coined the term inferiority feeling (later inaccurately called the inferiority complex). He developed a system of individual and supportive psychotherapy to help those emotionally crippled by feelings of inferiority.

Sigmund Freud (1856–1939), Austrian psychiatrist and originator of psychoanalysis. (See Ego psychology, Freudian analysis, and psychoanalysis above.)

Karen Horney (1885–1956), German-born American neo-Freudian psychologist who concentrated on the experience of childhood as the basis for neurosis, postulating that such neuroses can be avoided by good child care.

Carl Gustav Jung (1875–1961), Swiss psychologist – initially associated with Sigmund Freud in the development of psychoanalysis – who subsequently developed his own ideas. One of his most important contributions was to develop a 16-category typology of character, e.g. introversion, extraversion, thinking, feeling, etc.

Melanie Klein (1875–1961), Austrian-born British psychologist whose theories were in general within the mainstream of Freudian psychoanalysis, although there were important departures in child psychiatry. See Kleinian theory above.

Henry Stack Sullivan (1892–1949), American neo-Freudian psychiatrist whose ideas on personality were based on his observations of the patterns existing in social and interpersonal relations, and the development of personality within these patterns.

Anna Freud (1895–1952), Austrian-born British founder of child psychoanalysis. See Ego psychology above.

Erich Fromm (1900–80), German-born American neo-Freudian psychologist who was influenced by existential philosophy. He came to emphasize the part that society as a whole – its structures, expectations, etc. – has to play in determining the way in which an individual copes with basic human needs.

Jacques Lacan (1901–81), French psychoanalyst who introduced elements of structuralism and linguistics into psychoanalysis and psychology.

B(urrhus) F(rederic) Skinner (1904–), American psychologist whose work was the basis of behavioural psychology.

R(onald) D(avid) Laing (1927–), Scottish psychiatrist responsible for much pioneering work in the area of radical therapy and for bringing a more humanistic approach to psychology.

PSYCHIATRIC CONDITIONS

affective disorder a psychosis in which disturbances of mood occur.

alienation a state of feeling in which the patient feels set apart from or removed from either himself or others.

anxiety an irrational fear, often in response to an unrecognized stimulus.

autism a childhood disorder, often persisting into adulthood, in which the patient appears to be cut off from his environment; the senses function normally, but there appears to be little perception.

behaviour disorders a group of conditions in which the behaviour of the patient is unacceptable to society.

catatonia a schizophrenic condition in which the patient suffers periods of excitement and/or stupor, during which he seems out of touch with his environment.

conversion hysteria a psychoneurosis in which the patient's symptoms are physical complaints, i.e. the symptoms are physical in their expression but psychoneurotic in their origin.

delusion a fixed idea, held by a patient, that is at variance with the beliefs and ideas held by normal people.

dementia a physical deterioration in the brain, resulting in mental deterioration and disorder.

depersonalization a feeling of unreality.

depression a disorder of mood in which the patient suffers from low spirits (the traditional 'melancholy'), an impairment of some mental processes, and often a lack of sleep and appetite.

disassociation the existence of two or more mental processes that lack any connection.

engulfment an extreme form of anxiety in which all relationships with others are seen as threatening.

exhibitionism a compulsive behaviour pattern, usually taken to mean the sexual perversion, invariably on the part of the male, in which the sex organs are exposed to a female.

extraversion an outgoing behaviour pattern. This is a component, to a greater or lesser extent, of most people's behaviour; it only becomes a problem when taken to extremes. Compare introversion.

fixation an attachment to a concept, object or person, usually appropriate to an earlier stage of development.

fugue a period of seemingly automatic behaviour which the subject subsequently cannot remember.

hallucination a sensation with no physical origin. Hallucinations can occur as a result of physical illness, or they can be psychotic, usually associated with schizophrenia.

hebephrenia a form of schizophrenia in which the sufferer neglects his person and appears withdrawn, often with unusual mannerisms.

hypochondriasis an imagined belief on the patient's part that he is ill, often with an incurable complaint.

hysteria a form of neurosis, involving anxiety and physical symptoms, usually associated with a part of the body about which the patient is concerned, although there is an absence of any physical foundation for these symptoms.

implosion the fear of being destroyed by reality.

inferiority complex a feeling of inadequacy.

inhibition the suppression of a function by the operation of another function.

introversion an introspective behaviour pattern. This is a component, to a greater or lesser extent, of most people's behaviour; it only becomes a problem when taken to extremes.

involutional melancholia a severe depression occurring at the time of the menopause.

mania a psychosis in which elation, excitement, insomnia and sometimes exhaustion eventually lead to rapid and aimless thought.

manic depressive psychosis a psychosis in which a cycle of depression and elation repeats itself. The patient is seemingly unable to control the cycle.

neurosis a mental disorder of the personality in which there is no organic damage to the nervous system. Someone suffering from a neurosis is aware that something is wrong. Compare psychosis.

obsessional neurosis a neurosis characterized by obsessions, i.e. ideas that constantly impose themselves on the patient's thinking. The resulting behaviour is repetitive, even ritualistic.

paranoia a psychosis in which the patient suffers from delusions of persecution, often organized into a complex and coherent system that controls the patient's life.

phobia an unrealistic and excessive fear of an object or situation; a form of anxiety.

psychomotor acceleration the speeding up of thoughts and actions that occurs in mania.

psychomotor retardation the slowing down of thoughts and actions that occurs in depression.

psychopathy an antisocial, irresponsible aggressive behaviour pattern that is often impulsive.

psychosis a mental disorder that leaves the patient out of touch with reality; he is unaware of his disorder. Psychoses can either be organic, in which case disease of the brain can be shown, or functional, in which no damage to the brain can be observed.

psychosomatic illness the physiological symptoms and disturbances of function caused by the patient's personality and psychological disturbances.

regression a behaviour pattern more appropriate to an earlier stage of life, often sparked off by stress.

schizophrenia a functional psychosis characterized by disturbances of thinking, motivation and mood, coupled with hallucinations and delusions.

traumatic neurosis a neurosis that develops shortly after an unexpected and traumatic experience. The neurosis involves the periodic reliving of the traumatic experience.

PHOBIAS

A phobia is an intense and irrational fear of an object, a situation or an organism. Terms have been coined for a wide range of phobias, including the following:

ANIMAL AND PLANT PHOBIAS

animals	zoophobia
bacteria	bacteriophobia, microphobia
bees	apiphobia, melissophobia
birds	ornithophobia
cats	ailurophobia, gatophobia
chickens	alektorophobia
dogs	cynophobia
feathers	pteronophobia
fish	ichthyophobia
flowers	anthophobia
fur	doraphobia
horses	hippophobia
insects	entomophobia
leaves	phyllophobia
lice	pediculophobia
mice	musophobia
microbes	bacilliphobia
parasites	parasitophobia
reptiles	batrachophobia
snakes	ophidiophobia, ophiophobia
spiders	arachnophobia
trees	dendrophobia
wasps	spheksophobia
worms	helminthophobia

ENVIRONMENTAL PHOBIAS

auroral lights	auroraphobia
clouds	nephophobia
dampness, moisture	hygrophobia
flood	antlophobia
fog	homichlophobia
ice, frost	cryophobia
lakes	limnophobia
lightning	astraphobia
meteors	meteorophobia
precipices	cremnophobia
rain	ombrophobia
rivers	potamophobia
sea	thalassophobia
snow	chionophobia
stars	siderophobia
sun	heliophobia
thunder	brontophobia, keraunophobia
water	hydrophobia
wind	ancraophobia

FOOD AND DRINK PHOBIAS

drink, alcohol	potophobia
drinking	dipsophobia
eating	phagophobia
food	sitophobia
meat	carnophobia

HEALTH AND ANATOMICAL PHOBIAS

beards	pogonophobia
blood	haematophobia
cancer	cancerophobia, carcinophobia
childbirth	tocophobia
cholera	cholerophobia
death, corpse	necrophobia, thanatophobia
deformity	dysmorphophobia
disease	nosophobia, pathophobia
drugs	pharmacophobia
eyes	ommatophobia
faeces	coprophobia
germs	spermophobia
hair	chaetophobia
heart conditions	cardiophobia
heredity	patroiophobia
illness	nosemaphobia
infection	mysophobia
inoculations, injections	trypanophobia
insanity	lyssophobia, maniaphobia
knees	genuphobia
leprosy	leprophobia
mind	psychophobia
physical love	erotophobia
poison	toxiphobia
pregnancy	maieusiophobia
semen	spermatophobia
sex	genophobia
sexual intercourse	coitophobia
skin	dermatophobia
skin disease	dermatosiophobia
soiling	rypophobia
surgical operations	ergasiophobia
syphilis	syphilophobia
teeth	odontophobia
tuberculosis	phthisiophobia
venereal disease	cypridophobia
vomiting	emetophobia
wounds, injury	traumatophobia

INANIMATE OBJECT PHOBIAS

books	bibliophobia
crystals, glass	crystallophobia
glass	nelophobia
machinery	mechanophobia
metals	metallophobia
mirrors	eisoptrophobia
missiles	ballistophobia
money	chrometophobia
needles	belonophobia
pins	enetephobia
points	aichurophobia
slime	blennophobia, myxophobia
string	linonophobia

MISCELLANEOUS PHOBIAS

certain names	onomatophobia
darkness	nyctophobia
dawn	eosophobia
daylight	phengophobia
depth	bathophobia
dirt	mysophobia
disorder	ataxiophobia
draughts	anemophobia
dreams	oneirophobia
duration	chronophobia
dust	amathophobia, koniphobia
electricity	electrophobia
everything	pantophobia
failure	kakorraphiaphobia

fall of man-made satellites	keraunothnetophobia
fears	phobophobia
fire	pyrophobia
flashes	selaphobia
flogging	mastigophobia
freedom	eleutherophobia
ghosts	phasmophobia
graves	taphophobia
gravity	barophobia
ideas	ideophobia
imperfection	atelophobia
jealousy	zelophobia
justice	dikephobia
marriage	gamophobia
monsters, monstrosities	teratophobia
music	musicophobia
names	nomatophobia
narrowness	anginaphobia
neglect of duty	paralipophobia
new things	neophobia
night, darkness	achluophobia
novelty	cainophobia
nudity	gymnophobia
number 13	triskaidekaphobia, terdekaphobia
one thing	monophobia
poverty	peniaphobia
punishment	poinephobia
responsibility	hypegiaphobia
ridicule	katagelophobia
ruin	atephobia
rust	iophobia
shock	hormephobia
stealing	kleptophobia
stillness	eremophobia
strong light	photophobia
void	kenophobia
weakness	asthenophobia
words	logophobia
work	ergophobia
writing	graphophobia

PHOBIAS CONCERNING GROUPS

black people	negrophobia
children	paediphobia
human beings	anthropophobia
men	androphobia
robbers	harpaxophobia
women	gynophobia
young girls	parthenophobia

PHOBIAS CONCERNING RELIGION

churches	ecclesiaphobia
demons	demonophobia
God	theophobia
heaven	ouranophobia
hell	hadephobia, stygiophobia
sacred things	hierophobia
Satan	Satanophobia
sinning	peccatophobia

SENSORY PHOBIAS

being cold	frigophobia
being dirty	automysophobia
being scratched	amychophobia
being touched	haphephobia
blushing	ereuthophobia, eyrythrophobia
cold	cheimatophobia

colour	chromatophobia, chromophobia, psychrophobia
fatigue	kopophobia, ponophobia
heat	thermophobia
itching	acarophobia, scabiophobia
noise	phonophobia
odours	osmophobia
odours (body)	osphresiophobia
pain	algophobia, odynophobia
pleasure	hedonophobia
sleep	hypnophobia
smell	olfactophobia
smothering, choking	pnigerophobia
sound	akousticophobia
speaking	halophobia
speaking aloud	phonophobia
speech	lalophobia
sourness	acerophobia
stings	cnidophobia
stooping	kyphophobia
taste	geumatophobia
thinking	phronemophobia
touch	haptophobia
touching	haphephobia, thixophobia
trembling	tremophobia

SITUATION PHOBIAS

being alone	monophobia, autophobia
being beaten	rhabdophobia
being bound	merinthophobia
being buried alive	taphophobia
being looked at	scopophobia
crowds	demophobia, ochlophobia
enclosed spaces	claustrophobia
going to bed	clinophobia
heights	acrophobia, altophobia
high places	hypsophobia
home	domatophobia, oikophobia
home surroundings	ecophobia
infinity	apeirophobia
passing high objects	batophobia
places	topophobia
open spaces	agoraphobia
school	scholionophobia
shadows	sciophobia
sitting idle	thaasophobia
standing	stasophobia
standing upright	stasiphobia
solitude	eremitophobia, eremophobia

TRAVEL PHOBIAS

crossing a bridge	gephyrophobia
crossing streets	dromophobia
flying, the air	aerophobia
motion	kinesophobia, kinetophobia
sea swell	cymophobia
speed	tachophobia
travel	hodophobia
travelling by train	siderodromophobia
vehicles	amaxophobia, ochophobia
walking	basiphobia

NOBEL PRIZEWINNERS IN PHYSIOLOGY OR MEDICINE

The Nobel Prize for achievement in physiology or medicine is awarded annually under the terms of the will of Alfred Nobel by the Royal Caroline Medico-Chirurgical Institute in Stockholm (Sweden).

1901 Emil von Behring, German: serum therapy
1902 Sir Ronald Ross, English: discovery of how malaria enters an organism
1903 Niels R. Finsen, Danish: light radiation treatment of skin diseases
1904 Ivan Pavlov, Russian: physiology of digestion
1905 Robert Koch, German: tuberculosis research
1906 Camillo Golgi, Italian, and S. Ramón y Cajal, Spanish: structure of nervous system
1907 Alphonse Laveran, French: discovery of the role of protozoa in diseases
1908 Paul Ehrlich, German, and Ilya Mechnikov, Russian: immunity systems research
1909 Emil Kocher, Swiss: physiology, pathology and surgery of thyroid gland
1910 Albrecht Kossel, German: cellular chemistry research
1911 Allvar Gullstrand, Swedish: dioptics of the eye
1912 Alexis Carrel, French: vascular suture and transplantation of organs
1913 Charles Richet, French: anaphylaxis research
1914 Robert Bárány, Austrian: vestibular apparatus of the inner ear
1915–18 No awards
1919 Jules Bordet, Belgian: immunity system
1920 August Krogh, Danish: discovery of the capillary motor-regulating mechanism
1921 No award
1922 Archibald Hill, English: heat production in muscles; and Otto Meyerhof, German: metabolism of lactic acid in muscles
1923 Sir Frederick Banting, Canadian, and J.J.R. Macleod, Scottish: discovery of insulin
1924 Willem Einthoven, Dutch: discovery of electrocardiogram mechanism
1925 No award
1926 Johannes Fibiger, Danish: cancer research
1927 J. Wagner von Jauregg, Austrian: malaria inoculation in dementia paralytica
1928 Charles Nicolle, French: typhus research
1929 Christiaan Eijkman, Dutch: discovery of antineuritic vitamin; and Sir Frederick Hopkins, English: discovery of growth stimulating vitamins
1930 Karl Landsteiner, American (naturalized): grouping of human blood
1931 Otto Warburg, German: discovery of the nature and action of a respiratory enzyme
1932 Edgar D. Adrian (Lord Adrian) and Sir Charles Sherrington, English: the function of neurons
1933 Thomas Hunt Morgan, American: the role of chromosomes in transmission of heredity
1934 George R. Minot, William P. Murphy and George H. Whipple, American: liver therapy to treat anaemia
1935 Hans Spemann, German: organization in embryos
1936 Sir Henry Dale, English, and Otto Loewi, German: chemical transmission of nerve impulses
1937 Albert Szent-Györgyi, Hungarian: biological combustion

1938 Corneille Heymans, Belgian: role of sinus and aortic mechanisms in respiration regulation
1939 Gerhard Domagk, German (declined – Hitler refused to allow Germans to accept Nobel Prizes): antibacterial effect of prontosil
1940–1942 No awards
1943 Henrik Dam, Danish: discovery of Vitamin K; and Edward A. Doisy, American: discovery of chemical nature of vitamin K
1944 Joseph Erlanger, and Herbert S. Gasser, American: differentiated functions of nerve fibres
1945 Sir Alexander Fleming, Scottish, Ernst Boris Chain, British (naturalized), and Howard Florey (Lord Florey), Australian: discovery of penicillin and its curative value
1946 Hermann J. Muller, American: production of mutations by X-ray irradiation
1947 Carl F. Cori and Gerty Cori, American (naturalized): discovery of catalytic conversion of glycogen; and Bernardo Houssay, Argentinian: pituitary hormone function in sugar metabolism
1948 Paul Müller, Swiss: properties of DDT
1949 Walter Rudolf Hess, Swiss: discovery of function of the midbrain; and António Egas Moniz, Portuguese: therapeutic value of leucotomy in psychoses
1950 Philip S. Hench and Edward Kendall, American, and Tadeusz Reichstein, Swiss: adrenal cortex hormones research
1951 Max Theiler, South African: yellow fever research
1952 Selman A. Waksman, American (naturalized): discovery of streptomycin
1953 Fritz A. Lipman, American (naturalized), and Sir Hans Krebs, British (naturalized): discovery of coenzyme, a citric acid cycle in metabolism of carbohydrates
1954 John F. Enders, Thomes H. Weller and Frederick Robbins, American: tissue culture of poliomyelitis viruses
1955 Axel Hugo Theorell, Swedish: nature and mode of action of oxidation enzymes
1956 Werner Forssmann, German, Dickinson Richards, American, and André F. Cournand, American (naturalized): heart catheterization and circulatory changes
1957 Daniel Bovet, Italian (naturalized): production of synthetic curare
1958 George W. Beadle and Edward L. Tatum, American: genetic regulation of chemical processes; and Joshua Lederberg, American: genetic recombination
1959 Severo Ochoa, American (naturalized), and Arthur Kornberg, American: production of artificial nucleic acids
1960 Sir MacFarlane Burnet, Australian, and Sir Peter B. Medawar, English: research into acquired immunity in tissue transplants
1961 Georg von Békésy, American (naturalized): functions of the inner ear
1962 Francis Crick, English, James D. Watson American, and Maurice Wilkins, English: molecular structure of DNA
1963 Sir John Eccles, Australian, Sir Alan Lloyd Hodgkin, English, and Sir Andrew Huxley, English: transmission of nerve impulses along a nerve fibre
1964 Konrad Bloch, American (naturalized), and Feodor Lynen, German: research into cholesterol and fatty acid metabolism

1965 François Jacob, Jacques Monod and André Lwoff, French: research into regulatory activities of body cells

1966 Charles B. Huggins, American (naturalized), and Francis Peyton Rous, American: cancer research

1967 Haldan Keffer Hartline and George Wald, American, and Ragner A. Granit, Swedish: chemical and physiological visual processes in the eye

1968 Robert W. Holley, American, H. Gobind Khorana, American (naturalized), and Marshall W. Nirenberg, American: research into deciphering the genetic code

1969 Max Delbrück, American (naturalized), Alfred D. Hershey, American, and Salvador E. Luria, American (naturalized): research into viruses and viral diseases

1970 Julius Axelrod, American, Sir Bernard Katz, British (naturalized), and Ulf von Euler, Swedish: chemistry of nerve transmission

1971 Earl W. Sutherland, American: the action of hormones

1972 Gerald M. Edelman, American, and Rodney Porter, English: research into the chemical structure of antibodies

1973 Karl von Frisch and Konrad Lorenz, Austrian, and Nikolaas Tinbergen, Dutch: animal behaviour patterns

1974 Albert Claude, American (naturalized), Christian R. de Duve, Belgian, and George E. Palade, American (naturalized): structural and functional organization of cells

1975 Renato Dulbecco, American (naturalized), Howard M. Temin and David Baltimore, American: interactions between tumour viruses and the genetic material of the cell

1976 Baruch S. Blumberg and Daniel Carleton Gajdusek, American: the origin and spread of infectious diseases

1977 Rosalyn S. Yalow, Roger Guillemin and Andrew Schally, American: development of radioimmunoassay and research on pituitary hormones

1978 Werner Arber, Swiss, Daniel Nathans and Hamilton O. Smith, American: discovery and application of enzymes that fragment DNA

1979 Allan M. Cormack, American (naturalized), and Sir Godfrey N. Hounsfield, English: development of computerized axial tomography scanning

1980 Baruj Benacerraf, American (naturalized), George D. Snell, American and Jean Dausset, French: genetic control of the immune response to foreign substances

1981 Roger W. Sperry, American: functions of the celebral hemispheres; and Torsten N. Wiesel, Swedish, and David H. Hubel, American (naturalized): visual information processing by the brain

1982 Sune K. Bergström and Bengt I. Samuelsson, Swedish, and Sir John R. Vane, English: biochemistry and physiology of prostaglandins

1983 Barbara McClintock, American: discovery of mobile plant genes which affect heredity

1984 Niels K. Jerne, British/Danish, Georges J. F. Köhler, German, and César Milstein, Argentinian: technique for producing monoclonal antibodies

1985 Michael S. Brown and Joseph L. Goldstein, American: discovery of cell receptors involved in cholesterol metabolism

1986 Stanley Cohen, American, and Rita Levi-Montalcini, Italian: discovery of chemical agents that help regulate cell growth

1987 Tonegawa Susumu, Japanese: research into genetic aspects of antibodies

1988 Sir James W. Black, Scottish, Gertrude B. Ellison and George H. Hitchings, American: development of new classes of drugs

1989 Harold Varmus and Michael Bishop, American: cancer research

1990 Joseph Murray and E. Donnall Thomas, American: transplant surgery.

1991 Erwin Neher and Bert Sakmann, German: cell biology, particularly the understanding of disease mechanisms

1992 Edmond Fischer and Edwin Krebs, American: discovery (in the 1950s) of a cellular regulatory mechanism used to control a variety of metabolic processes.

CAUSES OF DEATH

The principal causes of death in developing countries and industrial countries vary greatly. Athough the main reason for this difference is the lack of resources for health care in developing states other factors are also involved. For example, certain diseases are endemic in tropical latitudes.

In the industrialized countries of the Western world the principal causes of death are, on average, as follows:

Heart and circulatory diseases	*33%*
Cancer	*19%*
Strokes	*13%*
Accidental death (car and air accidents, murder, etc.)	*5%*
Respiratory diseases (influenza, pneumonia and bronchitis)	*3%*

The next most common causes of death in the developed world – although not in order – are suicide, congenital defects, cirrhosis of the liver, AIDS and diabetes.

In the UK, the principal causes of death are heart and circulatory diseases including strokes (46%), cancer (25%), respiratory diseases (11%), digestive diseases (including stomach and duodenal ulcers, cirrhosis of the liver and appendicitis) (3%), and accidental disease (2%).

In developing countries the principal cause of death is diarrheic illness (including colitis and gastroenteritis). Children are particularly prone in this respect. The second most common cause of death in developing countries is influenza and pneumonia, especially among the elderly. This is followed, in order, by accidental death (including murder, death in natural disasters and war casualties) and cancer.

In some countries, for example Zambia and Uganda, AIDS is one of the principal causes of death. Other common causes of death in the developing world include heart disease, strokes, measles, tuberculosis, congenital defects, whooping cough, malaria and meningitis.

COMPLEMENTARY MEDICINE

Complementary medicine encompasses all the forms of healing that lie outside the sort of medicine people normally receive from a GP or hospital. It includes a wide variety of different therapies used by millions of people worldwide to treat every ill imaginable. That they appear to work in some cases is beyond doubt. How they work, however, is still to a large extent a mystery. Medical science has made great advances and has long seemed to promise a 'pill for every ill'. Virtually every drug, however, has been shown to have some side effects and many patients have become dissatisfied with the inability of orthodox treatments to cure certain conditions – particularly chronic diseases such as arthritis. The common feature that seems to run through every one of the alternative treatments is the importance placed on the whole person, not just on specific symptoms – this is known as the *holistic* approach.

ALTERNATIVE MEDICINE

The terms 'alternative medicine' and 'complementary medicine' are both used. Alternative' is perceived to imply that the treatment is an alternative to conventional medicine; 'complementary' is perceived to imply that the treatment is received to complement conventional medicine. The most common forms of complementary medicine are:

HERBALISM

Herbalism is an ancient form of medicine. From the dawn of humanity, people have been using plants to cure their illnesses. From the Middle Ages, herbals – manuals listing the names of plants and what they could be used for – were widely used. In the 17th century Nicholas Culpeper (1616–54) combined herbalism with astrology in his *Herbal*. Herbalists today use the roots, leaves, stems, flowers and seeds of plants to produce medicines. A large number of orthodox modern medicines are also derived from plants – the heart drug *digoxin* is produced from the foxglove, and the group of painkillers known as *opiates* are derived from the opium poppy. Once a diagnosis has been made, the herbalist will dilute a concentrated extract of a certain herb in water or mix it into a paste to form a cream or ointment. Conditions such as arthritis, colds and coughs, skin problems, digestive disorders and minor injuries are regarded as the most likely to benefit from herbalism.

HOMOEOPATHY

Homoeopathy was invented by a German doctor, Samuel Hahnemann (1755–1843). He reasoned that since many of the symptoms people suffer during illness – fever or pain, for example – are actually visible signs of the body's own defences working against the disease, it would make sense to try to boost these defences. He based his therapy on the principle that 'like cures like', giving patients tiny quantities of substances known to produce exactly these symptoms in healthy people. One homoeopathic remedy for fever, for instance, is sulphur, which produces a feeling of heat and promotes sweating if taken by mouth in larger doses. Homoeopathy offers remedies for virtually every medical complaint, but it is less frequently used in acute or life-threatening illness. Homoeopathic remedies are prescribed by some GPs as well as by homoeopaths.

In order to produce the tiny quantities that are needed for homoeopathic remedies, the active substance must be diluted. This process is known as *potentizing*. The active substance is diluted in proportions of 1 to 10, usually in distilled water, and this dilution is carried out six or more times in succession – the homoeopathic 'potency 6' is one million times diluted. Theoretically, with sufficient dilution, there can be none of the active substance left. So how is it that these remedies can still work? The secret is claimed to lie in the rapid shaking or *succussion* that must be performed after each dilution. If the succussion is not carried out, the remedy is ineffective. The explanation for this phenomenon is best given by comparing each molecule of the homoeopathic remedy, suspended in the dilution, to a person walking across a snow-field. Once the person has passed by, nothing physical remains, and only the footprints are left in the snow. Although there are few if any molecules of the active ingredient left, its 'footprints', thought to be produced by succussion, remain to do their work in the body.

AROMATHERAPY

Aromatherapy is principally a massage technique in which essential oils derived from herbs, flowers and spices are rubbed into the skin and eventually inhaled. The natural fragrances these oils produce are said to be particularly effective for psychological complaints such as anxiety or depression, but are used to treat a range of conditions including skin disorders and burns.

ACUPUNCTURE

Acupuncture originated in China over 5000 years ago. The technique uses fine needles inserted at specific points on the body in order to restore the balance of an inner 'life force' known as *chi* energy and believed to flow along a number of *meridians* or channels in the body. Each of the 12 main meridians is believed to have its own pulse – six in each wrist – and the acupuncturist checks these carefully in order to decide which points to stimulate. The technique has been shown to be remarkably successful at stopping pain, and in China major operations have been carried out using only acupuncture for pain relief. Scientists have discovered that the needles appear to make the body produce its own natural painkillers, *endorphins*. Acupuncture is also claimed to be effective in treating a wide range of diseases, including respiratory, digestive, bone and muscle disorders.

REFLEXOLOGY

Like acupuncture, reflexology is based on the idea that the body contains channels of 'life force'. Reflexologists believe that this force exists in 10 'zones' of energy that each begin in the toes and end in the fingers. By touching and feeling the toes and feet, reflexologists claim to be able to feel blocks in these channels of energy (they say these feel like crystals below the skin surface), and by manipulating and massaging the foot in a specific way they try to move the blockage, thus curing the illness. Like acupuncture, reflexology is used to treat most conditions.

OSTEOPATHY

Osteopathy is a manipulative technique founded by the American doctor Andrew Taylor Still (1828–1917). Joints are pushed and occasionally pulled so as to restore them to their natural positions, thus relieving tensions on surrounding muscles, tendons and ligaments. Osteopaths tend to concentrate their work on the spine since this contains the spinal chord and all the nerves that control the body. Back pain is the disorder most commonly treated by an osteopath.

CHIROPRACTIC

Chiropractic was founded by the American osteopath D.D. Palmer. The central philosophy of chiropractic is that malalignments or 'subluxations' of the bones in the spine cause disturbances of the nervous and vascular systems leading to disease not only in the bones and muscles themselves, but in any organ of the body. Chiropractitioners work with the help of X-rays to discover where the malalignments are and to identify 'intersegmental dysrelationships'. They then manipulate the bones use short, but very forceful, thrusts to the 'subfluxed' joint, thus relieving the root cause of the problem. However, chiropractic should not be used in any case of bone malignancy or where the spinal chord is compressed. The rapid, forceful thrusts can lead to fracture and paralysis in these cases. Unlike osteopathy, which is often regarded as complementary to orthodox medicine, chiropractors regard their philosophy as a completely alternative system of medicine.

THE ALEXANDER TECHNIQUE

The Alexander technique is a method of producing postural changes, which are claimed to relieve a number of physical disorders. The technique was developed in the 19th century by an Australian actor, Matthias Alexander (1869–1955). He realized that the position of his head and neck were the cause of his frequent loss of voice during performances, and found that by altering his posture he could cure himself. During a series of lessons – 12 or more – the person 'relearns' how to use the body, breaking harmful postural habits. The technique is claimed to be beneficial for everyone, but in particular for those who have suffered long spells of general ill health – lethargy and poor sleeping, for example.

BIOFEEDBACK

Biofeedback is used to help people learn to control physical phenomena governed by the autonomic nervous system, such as blood pressure, heartbeat and temperature. Electrodes placed on the body pick up electrical impulses produced by physical changes. The impulses are transformed by the biofeedback machine into an electronic sound, or shown by the rise and fall of a needle on a dial. The person concentrates on changing the tone of the sound or on causing the needle to move and in doing so learns, for instance, to lower blood pressure or slow down the heartbeat.

IRIDOLOGY

Iridology is the study of the iris as a tool for diagnosing illness. It is used by a range of alternative therapists including osteopaths, acupunturists, herbalists and homeopaths. The left side of the body is reflected in the left eye and vice versa. The head is revealed at the top, the feet at the bottom of the eye.

There are three zones: the inner zone represents the functions of digestion and absorption; the middle zone transport utilization and elimination by the kidneys; and the outer zone, structure, skeleton and skin.

OTHER ALTERNATIVE THERAPIES

Other alternative therapies include:

Anthroposophical medicine Formulated by the Austrian scientist Rudolph Steiner (1861–1925), anthroposophy is based on the premise that the human intellect can contact spirit worlds. Anthroposophical medicine is not, strictly speaking, a therapy but rather an attitude to health. Using homeopathic remedies, it stresses the need for a doctor to attain a spiritual understanding of both the patient and the plants used in treatment.

Applied kinesiology (or touch for healing) is a therapy that is often used in conjunction with chiropractic. Its practitioners use a system of 'muscle testing' to identify weaknesses in individual organs of the body and in muscles. The aim is to balance these weak elements by touch.

Bach flower remedies Dr Edward Bach (1880–1936) used plants to impregnate spring water and dew to produce 38 flower herbal remedies. These are used by practitioners in the treatment of conditions such as anxiety and depression.

Biochemics The German chemist Dr W.H. Schuessler recognized 12 inorganic salts and oxides in the human body. He maintained that – for the body to be healthy – these salts and oxides should be kept in a natural balance. By using homeopathic methods, practitioners of biochemics seek to redress any imbalance in these – and in any of an addition 30 trace elements since identified.

Colour therapy Colour therapists use different colours – in the form of light – as a treatment for various conditions, including stress. They claim that specific energies possessed by each colour have a restorative effect upon patients.

Hydrotherapy Water is used in a number of therapies, for example to stimulate circulation or in colonic irrigation. Various elimination treatments – including sweating, mineral waters, etc. – are also employed.

Megavitimin therapy Megavitimin therapy – or orthomolecular medicine – is treatment by large measured doses of Vitamin C. This therapy was developed by the chemistry Nobel Prize winner Dr Linus Pauling in the 1960s and 1970s. It now embraces treatment with other vitamins.

Naturopathy Naturopaths treat themselves using the healing forces that they claim are present within them.

Rolfing is a system of deep massage developed by Dr Ida Rolf in the 1920s and 1930s to break down connective tissues that have become thickened.

Shiatsu is a Japanese system of deep massage used to stimulate acupuncture points (see above). Claimed to be a preventative as well as a cure, Shiatsu is widely practised within Japanese families. When a practitioner treats him- or herself, the therapy is referred to as *Do-in*.

NUTRITION

Nutrition as a science is said to have founded by the chemist Antoine Lavoisier (1743–94) towards the end of the 18th century. It is the study of all the processes of growth, maintenance and repair of the living body that are dependent upon the digestion of food. The term 'food' is used to cover any solid or liquid matter that provides materials that can be used for growth, repair, energy, maintenance or protection.

The term 'nutrient' refers to the components of foods that can perform these functions. All nutrients are present in the correct proportions in the diets of healthy people. A lack of the necessary minimum amount of any nutrient leads to a state of malnutrition. A general deficiency of all nutrients produces undernutrition or, in extreme cases, starvation.

OTHER ESSENTIAL NUTRIENTS

Although not strictly nutrients water and fibre are essential for a healthy diet. Water is essential to life. It helps digestion and the elimination of waste products, and lubricates all the body joints and tissues.

Fibre – non starch polysaccharide (NSP) – together with water increases the bulk of food and so aids digestion of food and the elimination of waste products. Minerals are essential to a number of body processes.

Calcium works with phosphorus to give teeth and bones their hardness and strength. It helps blood to clot after an injury, and ensures muscles and nerves work properly. Calcium is found in milk, cheese, bread, green vegetables, pulses and canned fish.

Sodium, Potassium and Chloride help to maintain the correct salt concentration of body fluids. The minerals are found in milk, meat, vegetables, cheese, fruit, fish, nuts and table salt.

NUTRIENTS

Nutrient	Function	Sources of nutrient	Result of excess/deficiency
Protein	Growth; repairs and replaces damaged cells; energy	Meat, fish, eggs, cheese, milk, peas, beans, bread, rice, wheat, maize, nuts	Excess animal protein leads to too much saturated fat. Severe deficiency leads to kwashiorkor
Fat (Saturated, monounsaturated, polyunsaturated)	Energy store, body insulation, forms part of cell membranes	Saturated: butter, margarine, lard, cream, cheese. Polyunsaturated: sunflower and corn oil, fish, soft margarine	Correlation between heart disease and high fat intake. Too little fat means deficiency of fatty acids and fat soluble vitamins
Carbohydrates	Quick energy store; often source of dietary fibre	Sugar, sweets, cakes, jams, cereal, bread, biscuits, potatoes, pasta, some fruit, vegetables	Excess sugar causes obesity, dental caries and contributes towards diabetes. A deficiency can result in a diet too high in fat, and lacking in dietary fibre.
Vitamin A	Essential for growth; vision in poor light; the body's immune system	Dairy products, fish-liver oils, egg yolks, carrots and green vegetables	Deficiency causes stunted growth, night blindness, and susceptibility to infection
Vitamin B group*	Important for metabolism, growth, and healthy nerves, muscles and blood	Meat, yeast, wholemeal bread, cereals, pulses, milk, eggs, fish	Deficiency of vitamin B can cause beriberi, pellagra, skin problems, anaemia
Vitamin C	Helps absorb iron, keeps skin healthy, helps form blood cells, helps form body tissue	Citrus fruit (oranges, lemons), potatoes, cabbage, peppers, peas, tomatoes, apples	Deficiency causes scurvy (weakened capillaries, internal haemorrhaging, anaemia, general debility)
Vitamin D	Helps form healthy bones and teeth; helps body absorb calcium and phosphorus	Produced within body when exposed to sunlight. Also available in cream, margarine, butter, milk, cheese, egg yolk, vegetable oils	Deficiency causes rickets (in children), softening of bones (in adults)
Vitamin E	The actual function of vitamin unknown, thought to help in reproduction	Vegetable oils, cream, butter, cheese, egg yolk	Unknown
Vitamin K	Essential to blood clotting	Spinach, caulifower, cabbage, peas, cereal	Deficiency causes lengthy blood clotting

*B₁ Thiamine; Folic Acid; B₂ Riboflavin; B₃ Niacin; B₆ Pyridoxine); B₁₂ (Cyanocobalamin)

Iodine is essential for the formation of thyroid gland hormones, which help to control the chemical processes in the body. Iodine is present in water, green vegetables and fish.

Phosphorus works with calcium to give teeth and bones their strength and hardness. It also helps liberate energy from food. It is present in yeast extracts, cheese, eggs, wholemeal bread, fish, nuts and meat.

Iron is used for transporting oxygen in red blood cells. It is present in meat, kidney, liver, heart, treacle, bread, chocolate and cocoa.

Magnesium helps in the formation of healthy bones. It aids the maintenance of healthy muscles and nerves. It is present in tea, nuts, spices, cereals and wholegrain breads.

Zinc is involved in producing several enzymes. Zinc also forms part of the structure of cell membranes.

Copper helps in the production of various enzymes. It is present in liver, fish and green vegetables.

Selenium is involved in the production of various enzymes. It is present in cereals and meat.

Fluoride helps in the formation of healthy teeth and bones. It is present in drinking water, tea and fish.

A BALANCED DIET

An individual's personal dietary requirements depend on many factors such as age, sex and size. It is impossible to know how much of a particular nutrient an individual requires without doing complicated biochemical tests. It is possible, however, to estimate the amount of each nutrient needed by virtually everybody in the population. These 'Recommended Daily amounts' are defined for different ages and different states – for example requirements are greater in pregnancy.

A person's energy requirements also depend on their level of activity. Any excess energy taken in is stored in the form of fat. It is therefore important to ensure that the energy taken in is not greater than the amount expended.

The proportion of energy derived from fat, carbohydrate and protein is important, and current dietary guidelines suggest that no more than 35% of energy should come from fat, 10% from protein and 50% from carbohydrates. A diet high in fat, particularly 'saturated fat' (as found in red meat and dairy products), has been linked to the development of coronary heart disease. Most people would benefit from reducing their total fat intake, particularly if it contains a lot of saturated fatty acids.

To ensure the right balance of nutrients in a diet it is important to base one's eating on a wide range of foods. This should also ensure that adequate amounts of vitamins and minerals are consumed.

HIDDEN SUGARS

In the UK, the average person eats approximately 38 kgs (84 lbs) of sugar a year, plus more in the form of glucose and honey. Much of that sugar is hidden in foods, so it is not always obvious how much is being eaten. The sugar content of some common foods are given below.

	Sugar content as %	Approx. sugar content (tsp)
Small tube boiled sweets	98	10
Drinking chocolate (3 tsp)	75	2½
Jam (1 tbp)	68	3
Milk chocolate (50 gms)	45	6
Dried tomato soup (1 pkt)	40	8
Instant custard (1 pkt)	38	6¾
Chocolate biscuit (1)	33	2
Slice of chocolate cake (med)	26	2
Sweet pickle (3 tsp)	25	¾
Slice lemon meringue pie (med)	22	3
Carton fruit yoghurt (small)	15	4½
Ice cream (small brick)	15	2
Salad cream	13	½
Dried chicken soup	10	2
Can of cola	10	7
Cornflakes (6 tbp)	8	¼
Peanut butter (1 tbp)	3	1

FIBRE CONTENT IN SELECTED FOODS

Food	gms of fibre per 100 gms
All Bran	27.0
Wheat bran	44.0
Lentils	12.0
Figs	19.0
White flour	4.0
Wholemeal flour	10.0
Butter beans	22.0
Cornflakes	11.0
Sponge cake	1.0
Bread: granary	7.0
wholemeal	9.0
white	4.0
Prunes	16.0
Peanuts	8.0
Chickpeas	15.0
Spaghetti	6.0
Oatmeal	8.0
Apples	2.0
Lettuce	1.5

AVERAGE DAILY ENERGY REQUIREMENTS (Kcal/kJoule)

	Heavy activity		Moderate activity		Light activity	
	Kcal	kJoule	Kcal	kJoule	Kcal	kJoule
Men	2730	11 430	2314	9688	2015	8436
Women	2912	12 192	2624	10 986	2496	10 450

FAT CONTENT IN SELECTED FOODS

Food	gms fat per 100 gms
Almonds	54.0
Bacon	29.0
Baked Beans	0.5
Beef	20.0
Bread: white	1.7
brown	2.2
Butter	82.0
Cod	0.7
Cheddar cheese	34.0
Chicken	4.0
Chocolate biscuit	27.0
Cottage cheese	0.5
Cream, double	48.0
Flavoured yoghurt	1.0
Lamb	36.0
Mackerel	16.0
Mars bar	19.0
Mayonnaise	79.0
Milk: whole	3.8
skimmed	0.1
Potatoes	0.0
Pork	30.0
Salad cream	27.0

ADDITIVES

Additives are artificial or natural chemicals that are added to food to prolong their shelf life, alter colour, enhance flavour and improve nutritional value. Acceptable, established additives are now classified as 'Generally Regarded as Safe' (GRAS); new ones must undergo years of testing to ensure freedom from harmful effects. The EC assesses additives and grants permitted ones *E numbers*, which must appear on food labels. Many of these E-number additives are natural (or identical to natural) substances, such as Vitamin C (ascorbic acid, an anti-oxidant and acidulant). Others are artificial, such as tartrazine, a yellow-orange dye currently implicated in food allergies. The categories of additives include:

Acidulants add or control acidity or sourness.

Anticaking agents stop powdered products from coagulating into lumps.

Antioxidants prevent fatty foods from going rancid by retarding their natural oxidation.

Bleaching agents whiten flours.

Clarifying agents – the most common of which is gelatin – are used in vinegars and fruit juices.

Colourings enhance the appearance of foods.

Emulsifiers alter the texture and consistency of food, and stop the ingredients from separating out. **Stabilizers** do the same thing.

Enhancers heighten smell and flavour. Monosodium glutamate (MSG) is a flavour enhancer.

Firming agents restore the shape and texture of vegetables damaged during processing.

Flavours alter or intensify taste. They may be artificial or natural and include artificial sweetners.

Leavening agents lighten the texture of baked food. They include sodium bicarbonate but not yeast.

Preservatives, by controlling the growth of bacteria and fungi, slow down the rate of spoilage.

E NUMBERS: COMMON ADDITIVES

Antioxidants

	Name	Use
E310	propyl gallate	vegetable oils, chewing gum
E311	octyl gallate	
E312	dodecyl gallate	
E320	butylated hydroxynisole (BHA)	beef stock cubes; cheese spread
E321	butylated hydroxytoluene (BHT)	chewing gum

Colouring agents

E102	tartrazine	soft drinks
E104	quinoline yellow	
E110	sunset yellow	biscuits
E120	cochineal	alcholic drinks
E122	carmoisine	jams and preserves
E123	amaranth	
E124	ponceau 4R	desert mixes
E127	erythrosine	glacé cherries
E131	patent blue V	
E132	indigo carmine	
E142	green S	pastilles
E150	caramel	beers, soft drinks, sauces, gravy browning
E151		
E160(b)	annatto; bixin; norbixin	crisps
E180	pigment rubine (lithol rubine BK)	

Emulsifiers and stabilizers

E407	carageenan	jelly mixes; milk shakes
E413	tragacanth	sald dressings; processed cheese

Preservatives

E210	benzoic acid
E211*	sodium benzoate
E212*	potassium benzoate
E213*	calcium benzoate
E214*	ethyl para-hydroxy-benzoate
E215*	sodium ethyl para-hydroxy-benzoate
E216*	propyl para-hydroxy-benzoate
E217*	sodium propyl para-hydroxy-benzoate
E218*	methyl para-hydroxy-benzoate
E220	sulphur dioxide
E221†	sodium sulphate
E222†	sodium bisulphite
E223†	sodium metabisulphite
E224†	potassium metabisulphite
E226†	calcium sulphite
E227†	calcium bisulphite
E249‡	potassium nitrite
E250‡	sodium nitrite
E251‡	sodium nitrite
E252‡	potassium nitrate

* beer, jam, salad cream, soft drinks, fruit pulp, fruit pie filling, marinated herring and mackerel.

† dried fruit, dehydrated vegetables, fruit juices, syrups, sausages, fruit-based dairy desserts, cider, beer, wine.

‡ bacon, ham, cured meats, corned beef, some cheeses.

FOOD PRESERVATION

Food preservation is the treatment of food to enable it to maintain its quality and prevent it from deteriorating. Many food stuffs are seasonal, although fruits and vegetables that were traditionally only available after their harvest are now generally available all year round as imports from abroad. Bacterial growth may be prevented by canning, drying, deep-freezing, salting, pickling and irradiation. There are, however, time limits beyond which food should not be used. Many products carry a 'best before' date after which they become unpleasant and then unsafe to consume. *The following lists are a guide to the time beyond which a food product is no longer at its best and, in many cases, unsafe.*

PACKET FOODS

biscuits (plain)   keep for five months unopened, 10 days opened.

biscuits (with 'cream' fillings)   three months unopened; seven days opened.

coffee (beans)   nine months unopened, seven days opened.

coffee (ground)   up to 18 months unopened, seven days opened.

custard powder   nine months.

dried beans   nine months – they will last for much longer but are past their best by nine months.

dried fruit (most)   nine months unopened, six months opened.

flour (plain)   13 months.

flour (self-raising)   10 months.

flour (wholemeal)   up to six months.

muesli   up to six months.

pasta   nine months.

porridge oats   up to a year.

rice   nine months.

sugar   up to 18 months.

tea   up to 18 months unopened, one month opened.

FOOD IN BOTTLES AND JARS

coffee (instant)   up to 18 months unopened, one month opened.

honey   up to two years unopened, several days opened.

jam   up to two years unopened, several days opened.

lemonade   up to a year unopened, two days opened.

meat and fish pastes   up to six months unopened, several days opened.

FOOD IN A REFRIGERATOR

bacon (loose)   10 days.

bacon (vacuum packed)   two weeks.

beef and veal   up to five days.

butter   two months.

cheese (hard)   three weeks (unopened), one week opened.

cheese (soft)   up to five days.

eggs   one month.

fish   two days.

ham   two days.

lamb   up to five days.

milk   three days.

mince (any variety)   one day.

pork (cooked)   two days.

pork (uncooked)   one day.

poultry (uncooked)   one day.

TINNED FOOD

fish   two years.

fruit (except prunes and rhubarb)   18 months.

meat   five years – although pasteurized meat in tins weighing over 1 kilo (2 lb 2 oz) keep for only less than one year and should be stored in the refrigerator.

potatoes   18 months.

prunes and rhubarb   one year.

vegetables   two years.

FOOD IN A FREEZER

bacon rashers (vacuum packed)   six months.

bacon joints (vacuum packed)   three months.

beef joints and cuts   one year.

bread   about five months.

cakes (decorated or filled)   three months.

cakes (dry)   up to nine months.

casseroles (cooked)   three months.

chicken   up to one year – freeze giblets for no longer than three months.

chipped potatoes (raw)   up to six months.

cream (whipped or whipping)   one month – other creams will not freeze without separating.

egg whites   one year.

egg yolks   six months – will only keep if one pinch of salt per egg is added.

fish (herring, mackerel and salmon)   up to three months.

fish (white)   five months.

fruit (cooked or in sugar)   up to one year.

fruit (plain)   nine months.

fruit juice   five months.

fruit pies (cooked)   up to four months.

game   about six months.

ice cream   up to two months.

meat pies (cooked)   about three months.

mince   up to three months.

pastry (uncooked)   nine months.

pâté   one month.

pork joints and cuts   nine months.

sandwiches   one month.

sausages   three months.

veal   nine months.

vegetables (blanched)   about nine months.

venison   no longer than eight months.

The limits given above are a guide to the average keeping times and assume that the product is fresh and in perfect condition, and that it is stored in ideal conditions. Any 'best before' date on the product should be used rather than those listed here. If you are in any doubt about the freshness or safety of a product do not use it.

GLOSSARIES

NUTRITION OR FOOD SCIENCE GLOSSARY

additives artificial or natural chemicals that are added to food to prolong shelf life, alter colour, enhance flavour or improve nutritional value.

anaemia a condition in which the haemoglobin concentration in the blood falls below a healthy level.

balanced diet a diet that provides the adequate amount of food energy, optimum proportions of protein, starch and fat, sufficient dietary fibre, adequate amounts of minerals, trace metals, vitamins and essential fatty acids.

basal metabolic rate (BMR) the rate at which energy is used to maintain body processes and body temperature when the body is in repose.

beriberi a disease – endemic in Southeast Asia – that is caused by lack of vitamin B_1 (thiamine). It is characterized by fatigue, loss of memory, irritability, insomnia, confusion and paralysis. (The name is derived from the Sinhalese word for 'weakness'.)

Calorie a unit of energy. One Calorie (also referred to as a kilogram calorie, kilocalorie or large calorie; 1000 calories) equals 4.1868 kilojoules (kJ). The modern unit of energy is the joule (qv).

carbohydrate a compound containing carbon, hydrogen and oxygen. Carbohydrates – which form an important part of the diet – mainly contribute energy. They include sugars, starches and celluloses, and are chemically classified into three types – monosaccharides, disaccharides and polysaccharides.

cholesterol a steroid found in animal fats.

digestion the conversion of available nutrients in foodstuffs into a form that can be easily absorbed by the body.

disaccharide a common sugar (qv).

enzyme a protein catalyst.

fats naturally occurring substances consisting mainly of glycerides and fatty acids.

food substances taken into an organism that play a part in maintaining and regulating its life, growth, repair and reproduction.

glycogen a polysaccharide built up from glucose units. The form in which carbohydrate is stored in the muscles and liver of animals and humans.

joule a unit of energy. Work done by a force of one newton acting through a distance of one metre.

kwashiorkor a protein-deficiency disease that is found mainly in countries of the developing world. It is characterized by retarded growth and development, a protuberant abdomen, muscle wasting and fluid retention.

malnutrition a disturbance of the form or function of an organism resulting from a deficiency or excess of one or more nutrients.

marasmus a protein-deficiency disease that is found mainly in the countries of the developing world. It is characterized by emaciation, weakness and irritability. If untreated it can cause retardation of growth and mental development in children.

mastication the process of chewing food.

metabolism the chemical changes that take place in a living organism.

minerals inorganic substances that are necessary for the body. They are obtained from foods, usually in the form of salts.

monosaccharide a common sugar (qv).

nutrients components of foodstuffs that can be used by living organisms for the processes of life and growth.

obesity a condition in which excess amounts of fat accumulates in the body.

osteomalacia a disease suffered by adults. It is caused by a deficiency of vitamin D and is characterized by bone softening.

polyunsaturated animal or vegetable fats consisting of long carbon chains with many double bonds. Polyunsaturated compounds do not contain cholesterol.

protein complex compounds built up from some thousands of amino acid units.

rickets a disease suffered by children. It is caused by a deficiency of vitamin D and is characterized by softened bones that cause bowed legs and curvature of the spine.

saturated animal or vegetable fats containing a high proportion of fatty acids with single bonds.

scurvy a disease caused by a lack of vitamin C. It is characterized by poor healing of wounds, spontaneous bleeding in gums, skin joints and muscles.

sugar a simple crystalline carbohydrate that dissolves in water. The most common sugars are monosaccharides and disaccharides.

tissue a collection of similar cells having the same function.

vegetable a plant (or part of a plant) used as a foodstuff.

vitamin an organic substance essential for the body's metabolism in minute amounts in the diet. Vitamins often act as co-enzymes.

BOTANY GLOSSARY

abscission the shedding of a leaf, fruit, flower, etc., by a plant.

absorption the taking up of water, solutes and other substances by both active and passive mechanisms. Also, the taking up of radiant energy (from the sun) by pigments in plants.

achene a simple one-seeded indehiscent dry fruit.

active transport the transport of substances across a membrane – e.g. cell membrane – against a concentration gradient.

ADP adenine diphosphate. The conversion of ADP to ATP is of central importance in the storage of light energy absorbed during photosynthesis.

adventitious organs organs that arise in unexpected sites, e.g. leaves that grow roots.

aerial root a root that appears above soil level, usually hanging down in moist air.

aerobe an organism that can live only in the presence of oxygen.

aerobic respiration respiration involving the oxidation of organic substrates and the associated absorption of free oxygen.

alcoholic fermentation anaerobic respiration in which glucose is broken down to form ethanol and carbon dioxide. The process is carried out by yeasts.

algae a diverse group of simple plants – largely aquatic and unicellular.

alpine a regional community of plants found in high mountainous regions and on high plateaux.

alternation of generations the occurrence of an asexual and a sexual reproductive form during the life cycle of a plant.

amino acid an organic compound containing one or more amino groups. About 20 commonly occur as the basic 'building blocks' of proteins.

anaerobe an organism that can live in the absence of free oxygen.

anaerobic respiration a number of processes by which chemical energy is obtained from various substrates without the use of free oxygen.

androdioecious male and hermaphrodite flowers occurring on separate plants.

androecium the male component of a flower, consisting of several stamens.

andromonoecius male and hermaphrodite flowers carried on the same plant.

anemophily pollination by wind.

angiosperms the flowering plants.

annual any plant that germinates from seed, grows, flowers, produces seeds and then dies, all within a single year.

annual ring the ring of new wood added to the existing core of wood on a tree in a single year.

anther the tip of the stamen that produces the pollen grains.

antheridium the male sex organ in lower plants.

aphids insects that feed by sucking plant juices.

apomixis asexual reproduction.

arboretum an area in which woody plants are grown.

asexual reproduction the formation of new individuals from the parent plant without the fusion of gametes.

ATP adenosine triphosphate, a nucleotide occurring in all plants. It has one more phosphate grouping than ADP and it is the addition of this grouping that acts as an energy store.

auricle a small projection from the base of a leaf or petal.

auxin a variety of plant growth hormones that promote the elongation of shoots and roots.

axil the upper angle formed where the leaf or a similar organ joins the stem.

backcross a hybrid between an individual plant and one of its parents. Backcrossing is used to introduce desirable genes into a cultivated variety of a plant.

bacteria microscopic unicellular plants with cell nuclear material not separated from the rest of the cell contents by a nuclear membrane.

bark the protective layer of dead cells outside the vascular cambium in the stems and roots showing secondary growth.

benthos any plant living on the seabed or a lake bed.

berry any many-seeded fleshy indehiscent fruit.

biennial any plant that takes two years to complete its life cycle, growing vegetatively in the first year, then flowering, seeding and dying in the second year.

binomial nomenclature the system of naming plants using a generic name and a specific epithet. The system was developed by Linnaeus.

biochemistry the study and use of metabolism and metabolic chemicals.

biological control the control of pests by making use of their natural predators.

blight a plant disease in which leaf damage is sudden and acute.

bloom (algae) a noticeable increase in the numbers of a species in the plankton.

bolting the premature production of flowers and seeds.

bract a small leaflike structure that subtends a flower or inflorescence.

bracteole a small bract, typically on a flower stalk.

bud a short axis bearing a densely packed series of leaf or flower primordia produced by an apical meristem.

budding asexual reproduction in which a new individual is produced by an outgrowth of the parent.

bulb a fleshy underground modified shoot, made up of swollen scale leaves or leaf bases. It is a perennating organ, allowing the plant to survive for many years.

bulbil a small bulb found on an aerial bud. It functions as a means of vegetative propagation.

callus parenchymatous cells formed at the site of a wound.

calyx the sepals; the outer whorl of the perianth.

cambium a meristem that occurs parallel to the long axis of an organ. It is responsible for secondary growth.

canker a plant disease in which there is an area of necrosis which becomes surrounded by layers of callus tissue.

capillary action the process in which the effect of surface tension on a liquid in a fine tube causes that liquid to rise. The supply of water throughout a plant is largely the result of capillary action.

carbohydrates any of a large variety of organic compounds containing carbon, hydrogen and oxygen. They are energy storage molecules and form structural components.

carbon dioxide an incombustible gas that is converted to carbohydrates in plants by photosynthesis.

carpel the female reproductive organs of plants. They consist of the ovary, style and stigma, and carry and enclose the ovules in flowering plants.

catkin a hanging unisexual inflorescence, designed for wind pollination.

cellulose a carbohydrate consisting solely of glucose units. It is present in plant cell walls as highly organized microfibrils.

chlorophyll the main class of photosynthetic pigment. They absorb red and blue light and reflect green light; hence the characteristic green colour of photosynthetic plants.

chloroplast a green plastid in plant cells. It contains photosynthetic pigment molecules.

chlorosis a disorder in plants in which the chlorophyll levels drop, producing a yellow or pale unhealthy plant.

ciliate any part of the plant fringed with hairs.

circadian rhythm a cycle in which physiological responses occur at 24-hourly intervals, e.g. opening and closing of stomata, change in position of leaves.

cladode a stem structure resembling a leaf, usually produced as an adaptation to dry conditions.

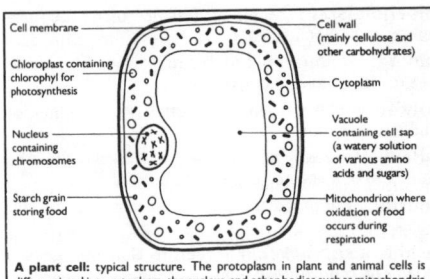

A plant cell: typical structure. The protoplasm in plant and animal cells is differentiated into cytoplasm, the nucleus, and other bodies such as mitochondria and chloroplasts.

Labels in diagram:
Cell membrane
Chloroplast containing chlorophyl for photosynthesis
Nucleus containing chromosomes
Starch grain storing food
Cell wall (mainly cellulose and other carbohydrates)
Cytoplasm
Vacuole containing cell sap (a watery solution of various amino acids and sugars)
Mitochondrion where oxidation of food occurs during respiration

The leaves will be reduced when a plant bears cladodes.

cleistogamy the self-pollination of flowers which do not open to reveal the reproductive organs, thus preventing cross-pollination.

climacteric the rise in respiration rate in some fruits during ripening.

club root a fungal disease in which roots become swollen and malformed, causing wilting, yellowing and stunting.

coenocarpium fruit that includes ovaries, floral parts and receptacles of a number of flowers on a fleshy axis.

collenchyma long cells with thickened but non-lignified primary cell walls; a supporting tissue.

contractile root a specialized thickened root that pulls a rhizome, bulb, corm, etc., down into the soil.

coppicing cutting trees back to ground level every 10–15 years. New shoots from the base are therefore encouraged and can be harvested when the coppice is next cut back.

cordate heart-shaped, e.g. leaves.

corm a short swollen underground stem, acting as an organ of perennation and vegetative propagation.

corolla the petals.

corolla tube the fusion of the edges of the petals.

corona a crown-like leafy outgrowth of a corolla tube.

corymb a flat-topped cluster of flowers on lateral stalks of different lengths.

cotyledon the first leaf or leaves of the embryo in seed plants. In non-endosperm seeds they are used as food storage organs.

cross-pollination pollination in which pollen from one individual is transferred to the stigma of another individual.

cultivar a variety or strain of plant produced artificially and not found in the natural population.

cuticle a layer of cutin on the surface of aerial parts of a plant, broken only by stomata and lenticels. It acts to conserve water.

cutin a waterproof substance that forms the waxy cuticle.

cutting a common form of artificial propagation whereby a portion of a living plant is detached and grown in soil or culture medium.

cymose an inflorescence in which apical tissues of the main and lateral stems differentiate into flowers.

cryptophyte any plant with perennating buds below ground or water.

damping off a disease of seedlings in which they

rot at soil level and then die. The condition is caused by crowded conditions and cold wet soil.

dark reactions part of the photosynthetic process that is not light dependent. Stored energy in ATP is used to convert carbon dioxide to carbohydrate.

deciduous woody perennial trees that shed their leaves before the winter or dry season.

decumbent a stem that lies along the ground.

deficiency disease a disease caused by the lack of an essential nutrient, especially minerals.

definite growth the maximum size beyond which the plant can grow no more.

dehiscence the bursting open of certain plant organs at maturity – especially reproductive structures – to release their contents.

denitrification the loss of nitrate from the soil owing to the action of denitrifying bacteria.

dentate a leaf margin that is toothed.

dichogamy anthers and stima maturing at different times on the same plant, thus reducing the chance of self-fertilization.

dicliny the male and female reproductive parts in different flowers.

dicotyledons those angiosperms with embryos with two cotyledons. The group includes hardwood trees, shrubs and many herbaceous plants.

diffusion the movement of ions or molecules in solution down a concentration gradient. It is involved in, for example, transpiration and the uptake of carbon dioxide.

dioecious the male and female reproductive organs on different individuals, making cross-fertilization necessary and ensuring genetic variation.

DNA the abbreviation for deoxyribonucleic acid, the chemical constituent of genes. It determines the inherited characteristics of a plant.

dormancy an inactive phase of seeds, spores and buds, often in order to survive adverse conditions.

double fertilization the process – in most flowering plants – where two male gametes participate in fertilization. One fuses with the female gamete to give the zygote which grows into the embryo, while the other fuses with the polar nuclei or definitive nucleus to give the endosperm.

double flower a flower with more than the usual number of petals.

drupe any fleshy indehiscent fruit with seed or seeds surrounded by woody tissue.

embryo a young plant after fertilization has taken place.

endocarp the innermost layer of the pericarp of an angiosperm fruit, outside the seeds. It can sometimes be woody.

endosperm the storage tissue in seeds of angiosperms.

entomophily pollination by insects.

enzyme a large protein molecule that can catalyse specific biochemical reactions.

epicalyx a calyx-like extra ring of floral appendages below the calyx, resembling a ring of sepals.

epicotyl the apical end of the axis of an embryo, immediately above the cotyledon or cotyledons. It grows into the stem.

epidermis the outer layer of cells of a plant.

epigeal the germination of the seed in which the cotyledons are raised above the surface of the ground by elongation of the hypocotl, thus forming the first leaves.

epigyny the floral parts found above the ovary.

epiphyte any plant with no roots in the soil. It is usually supported by another plant, and gets its nutrients from the air, rain and organic material on the surface of the other plant.

etiolation a disorder where plants become pale and elongated when they are grown in insufficient light and grow towards what light there is.

eukaryotic organisms with cells that have nuclei.

evergreen woody perennial plants that keep their leaves throughout the year, shedding and replacing leaves on a continuous basis.

exocarp the outermost layer of an angiosperm fruit, usually forming a skin.

F_1 generation the first filial generation obtained in breeding experiments.

F_2 generation the second filial generation, obtained by crossing the F_1 generation.

F_1 hybrid the first filial generation produced by crossing two selected parental pure lines. They do not breed true.

fermentation the anaerobic respiration of glucose and other organic substrates to obtain energy.

floral diagram a representation of flower structure. The whorls of floral parts are shown as a series of concentric circles.

floral formula the use of symbols, numbers and letters to record floral structure.

floret a small flower.

flower the sexual reproductive unit of angiosperms, consisting of perianth, androecium and gynoecium, all arising from the receptacle.

forest a plant community in which the dominant species are trees.

fragmentation asexual reproduction in which the parent splits into two or more pieces which develop into new individuals.

frond a large leaf or leaflike structure.

fruit the ripened ovary of a flower, plus any accessory parts associated with it.

fungi saprophytic, parasitic and symbiotic eukaryotic organisms, lacking chlorophyll, whose plant body is typically a mycelium.

gall an abnormal swelling or outgrowth on a plant caused by an attack by a parasite.

gamete a cell or nucleus that can undergo sexual fusion with another gamete to form a zygote, which in turn develops into a new individual.

gametophyte the generation in the life cycle of a plant that produces the gametes.

gamopetalous petals fused along their margins forming a corolla tube.

gamosepalous sepals that are fused to form a tubular calyx.

garigue scrub woodland on limestone areas with low rainfall and thin soils.

gemma a multicellular structure for vegetative reproduction found on some mosses and liverworts.

gene a unit of inheritance formed from DNA.

genotype the genetic make-up of an organism, as opposed to its physical appearance.

genus a group of obviously homologous species.

germination the changes undergone by a reproductive body, e.g. zygote, spore, pollen, grain, seed, before and during the first signs of growth.

glabrous a plant surface that has no hairs.

glaucous plant surfaces with a waxy blue-grey bloom.

gley a waterlogged soil lacking in oxygen.

glume bracts subtending each spikelet in the flowers of grasses.

grafting an artificial means of propagation by which a segment of the plant to be propagated is attached to another plant so that their vascular tissues combine.

grassland a plant community in which grasses are the dominant group.

green manure a fast-growing crop grown at the end of the season and then ploughed or dug in, thus increasing the amount of organic matter in the soil.

growth ring secondary xylem produced in a growing period in the stems and roots of many plants. When the stem or root is sliced across this ring is visible.

guard cells a pair of bow-shaped cells surrounding each stomatal pore and forming the stoma. The opening of the stoma is controlled by changes in the turgidity of the guard cells.

guttation the exudation of water in liquid form from plants.

gymnosperm any vascular plant with naked seeds borne on a sporophyll and not in an ovary.

gynandrous (flowers) stamens and styles united in a single structure.

gynodioecious plants that bear female and hermaphrodite flowers on separate individuals.

gynoecium the female part of the angiosperm flower, consisting of one or more carpels.

gynomonoecious plants that bear female and hermaphrodite flowers on the same individual.

halophyte any plant that can live in soil with a high salt concentration.

hardening the gradual exposure of plants to lower temperatures in order to increase the resistance to frost, prior to planting out.

hard seed a seed with a hard coat that is impervious to water.

hastate a leaf shaped like a three-lobed spear.

haustorium an organ produced by a parasite to absorb nutrients from the host plant.

heartwood the central part of secondary xylem in some woody plants. It is derived from the sapwood that has deteriorated with age.

helophyte any marsh plant with perennating buds in the mud at the bottom of the lake.

hemicellulose a carbohydrate found in plant cell walls, often in association with cellulose. Unlike cellulose, it can be broken down by enzymes and thus used as a nutrient reserve.

hemicryptophyte any plant with perennating buds just below the soil surface.

herbaceous perennial any plant that lives for many years, surviving each winter as an underground storage or perennating organ, the leaves and flowers dying back.

herbarium dried pressed plants kept in a collection.

herbicide any chemical that kills plants.

hermaphrodite any plant bearing both male and female reproductive parts in the same flower.

hesperidium any berry with a leathery epicarp, e.g. citrus fruit.

heteroblastic development the progressive development in the form and size of successive organs such as leaves.

heterophylly the condition of having two or more leaf types differing in morphology and function.

heterostyly the condition of having two or more different arrangements of the reproductive parts in the flowers of a single species.

hilium a scar on the seed coat at the point of abscission.

hip a type of pseudocarp fruit.

homogamy the maturation of anthers and stigmas at the same time.

honey guide dots or lines on petals that guide pollinating insects to the nectaries.

humus a soft moist organic matter in the soil, derived from rotting plant and animal matter.

hybrid an individual plant produced by genetically distinct parents.

hybrid sterility the inability of some hybrids to produce gametes.

hydrophily pollination by water transport of pollen grains.

hydrophyte any plant that is adapted to living in water or in waterlogged conditions.

hydroponics the growth of plants, for example in sand, to which nutrients are added in a liquid fertilizer.

hypha a branched filament of fungi.

hypocotl that part of the stem between the cotyledons and the radicle in the embryo.

hypogeal seed germination in which the cotyledons remain below ground owing to a lack of growth of the hypocotl.

hypogyny the floral parts inserted below the ovary.

indefinite growth unlimited growth, i.e. the plant or parts of the plant continue to grow throughout their lives.

indehiscent a fruit or fruiting body that does not open to disperse its seeds.

inflorescence a group of flowers carried on the same stalk.

insectivorous plant a plant that can obtain its nutrients by digesting insects and other tiny animals, in addition to photosynthesizing.

integument a protective envelope around the ovule of seed plants. Most gymnosperms have one integument, while most angiosperms have two.

keel the pair of fused lower petals in pea flowers.

key a list of characteristics enabling rapid identification of species.

kingdom one of the five major divisions into which all living organisms are classified.

labellum the distinct lower three petals of an orchid.

lamina the flattened bladelike section of a leaf.

lanceolate (leaves) narrow; tapering at both ends.

layering plant propagation in which runners or stolons are pegged down to the ground encouraging roots to form at that point.

leaching the washing out of minerals and other nutrients from the soil.

leaf the principal photosynthetic organ of green plants. It is formed as a lateral outgrowth from the stem, and consists of the lamina, petiole and leaf base.

leaf base the point of attachment of a leaf to the stem.

leaf spot a disease involving spots of dead tissue on the leaves.

legume a dry dehiscent fruit containing one or more seeds. It is also a general name for the plants in the family Leguminosae (the pea family).

lemma the lower of a pair of bracts beneath each flower in a grass.

lenticel a small pore containing loose cells in the periderm of plants. Gaseous exchange takes place through the lenticel.

lichen plants composed of a fungus and algae in symbiotic relationships. The lichen is distinct from either of its constituents.

life cycle the various stages an organism passes through, from fertilized egg in one generation to fertilized egg in the next generation.

light reactions those reactions in the photosynthetic chain that are dependent on light.

lignin a carbohydrate polymer making up about a quarter of the wood of a tree.

liming the addition of lime to the soil to decrease the acidity of the soil and to improve the soil structure.

linear (leaves) flat and parallel-sided leaves.

lipid water-insoluble fatty acids, consisting of carbon, hydrogen and oxygen plus some other elements. Their functions vary, but they include storage, and have structural functions.

lipoprotein an association of lipid and protein usually found in plant cell membranes.

lithophyte any plant that grows on rocky ground.

macronutrient a chemical element required by a plant in relatively large amounts.

maquis a stunted woodland in semi-arid areas that have been deforested.

meadow a moist grassland maintained by mowing.

meristem a part of a plant containing actively- or potentially actively-dividing cells.

mesocarp the middle layer of the pericarp of an angiosperm fruit – absent in some species.

mesophyte any plant with no adaptations to environmental extremes.

microflora small plants found in a given area.

micronutrient a chemical element required in small quantities, i.e. a trace element.

midrib the vein running down the middle of a leaf.

mildew a fungal disease of plants in which the fungus is seen on the plant surface.

monadelphous stamen filaments fused to form a tube.

monochasium a cymose inflorescence in which only one axillary bud develops into a lateral branch at each node.

monocotyledons angiosperms possessing one cotyledon in the embryo. The group includes palms, grasses, orchids, lilies.

monoecious female and male reproductive parts in separate floral structures on the same plant.

monopodial branching the condition in which secondary shoots or branches arise behind the main growing tip and remain subsidiary to the main stem.

morphology that branch of biology concerned with the form and structure of organisms.

mould a fungus that produces a velvety growth on the surface of its host.

multiple fruit fleshy fruit incorporating the ovaries of many flowers and derived from a complete inflorescence.

mycelium a loose mass of branching and inter-woven fungal hyphae.

mycorrhiza the symbiotic relationship between a fungus and the roots of a plant.

nastic movement a plant response caused by an external stimulus. The stimulus acts merely as a trigger, and does not control the plant's response.

necrosis the death of part of a plant while the rest of the plant continues to live.

nectaries the glands at the base of a flower that secrete nectar in order to attract insect pollinators.

node the point on the plant stem at which one or more leaves develop.

offset a type of runner; a short shoot that develops from an axillary bud near the base of the stem and goes on to form a daughter plant.

ontogeny the changes that occur during the life cycle of an organism.

opposite (leaves) pairs of leaves arising at each node.

ornithophily pollination by birds.

osmosis the passage of certain molecules in a solution, down a concentration gradient and across a semipermeable membrane that prevents the passage of other molecules. In plants it is usually water molecules that pass across the membrane, equalizing solute concentrations on either side of the membrane.

ovary the swollen basal part of the carpel in angiosperms containing the ovule or ovules.

ovule the female gamete and its protective and nutritional tissues. It develops into the seed after fertilization.

palea the upper bract of the pair found beneath each floret in a grass inflorescence.

panicle an inflorescence in which the flowers are formed on stalks arising spirally or alternately from the main stem.

pappus a modified calyx consisting of a fine ring of hairs or teeth that persists after fertilization, aiding wind dispersal of the seeds.

parasitism the relationship between two organisms in which one is wholly dependent on the other for food, shelter, etc.

parenchyma unspecialized tissue in a plant, often forming a ground tissue in which other tissues are located.

parthenocarpy the production of a fruit without the process of fertilization.

pasture moist grassland maintained by grazing.

peat partially decomposed plant material, built up in poorly-drained areas.

pedicel a stalk attaching flowers to the main stem of the inflorescence.

pepo any berry with a hard exterior.

perennate any plant that is able to live from one growing season to another, usually with a period of reduced activity between seasons.

perennial any plant that lives for many years.

perianth the protective structure encircling the reproductive parts, consisting of the calyx and corolla or a ring of petals.

pericarp the wall of the fruit, derived from the ovary wall.

periderm the protective secondary tissue replacing the epidermis as the outer cellular layer of stems and roots.

perigyny floral parts inserted on the receptacle at about the same level as the ovary.

permanent wilting point the point at which the amount of water in the soil is so low that a plant wilts and will not recover unless water is added to the soil.

petal a unit of the corolla, thought to be a modified leaf.

petiole the stalk that attaches the leaf lamina to the stem.

phanerophyte any plant with perennating buds on upright stems well above soil level.

phellem the compact protective tissue replacing the epidermis as the outer layer in plants with secondary growth.

phloem the vascular tissue in plants responsible for translocation of nutrients.

photic zone the surface waters of lakes and seas, in which light penetrates and which is inhabited by plankton.

photoperiodism the alternation of day and night, controlling the physiological mechanisms of many plants.

photorespiration respiration that occurs in plants in the light.

photosynthesis a series of reactions in green plants in which light energy from the sun is used to drive reactions which convert carbon dioxide and water to carbohydrates and thence to other materials.

phycobiont an algal partner in a lichen.

phyllode a flattened petiole which performs the functions of a leaf.

phyllody the transformation of parts of a flower into leaflike structures.

pileus the cap of a mushroom or toadstool.

piliferous layer the absorbent part of the root epidermis. It is covered with root hairs.

pinna a first-order leaflet in a compound leaf.

pinnule a second-order leaflet in a compound leaf, i.e. each pinna is divided into a number of pinnules.

pistil a single carpel or group of carpels.

pith an area of parenchyma in the centre of many plant stems.

plankton microorganisms that float in surface waters of seas and lakes.

plumule an embryonic shoot derived from the epicotyl.

pollard to prune back a tree to the main trunk.

pollen the microspores, containing the male gamete, released in large numbers as a fine powder by gymnosperms and angiosperms.

pollen sac the chambers on the anther in which pollen is formed.

pollination the transfer of pollen from the male to the female parts in seed plants, i.e. from the anthers to the stigma.

pome a fleshy pseudocarp in which tissues develop from the receptacle and enclose the true fruit.

prickle a short pointed outgrowth from the epidermis.

primary growth the increase in size as a result of cell division at apical meristems.

procumbent any plant that trails loosely along the ground.

prokaryotic organisms in which the nuclear-material is not separated from the rest of the cell contents.

proteins large molecules consisting of carbon, hydrogen, nitrogen, oxygen and other elements. Plant proteins can largely be grouped as enzymes or structural and contractile proteins.

pruning cutting back some or all of the branches of woody plants, usually to promote growth in selected areas of the plant.

pseudocarp any fruit consisting of tissues other than those derived from the gynoecium.

raceme an inflorescence in which flowers are formed on individual pedicels on the main axis.

radicle an embryonic root, normally the first organ to emerge on germination.

receptacle the area at the end of the main axis of the flower, to which the floral parts are attached.

respiration the breakdown of food substances, utilizing molecular oxygen, in order to release energy.

rhizome an underground stem that acts as a means of vegetative propagation.

root a section of a plant – usually underground – that is involved with fixing the plant in position and absorbing water and nutrients. It can be used as a food storage organ.

root hair a projection from a single cell in the root epidermis. Root hairs increase the surface area for absorption.

root nodule a lumpy growth that develops on the roots of leguminous plants as a result of symbiotic infections involved with nitrogen fixation.

rosette plant any plant with leaves radiating outwards on the surface of the soil.

runner a creeping stem arising from an axillary bud, giving rise to new plants at the nodes.

rusts fungal infections causing dark rust-coloured spots on the leaves or stem.

samara an achene with the pericarp extended into a wing.

sap a liquid containing mineral salts and sugars dissolved in water, found in xylem and phloem-vessels.

saprophyte any plant that feeds on dead and decaying organic material.

sapwood the outer functional part of the secondary xylem.

scape a leafless stem of a solitary flower or inflorescence.

schizocarp a dry fruit formed from two or more one-seeded carpels that divide into one-seeded units when mature.

scion a shoot or bud cut from one plant and grafted or budded on to another.

sclerenchyma a strengthening tissue composed of dead cells.

seaweed a group of large algae found in the littoral zone and floating freely in the sea.

secondary growth the increase in diameter of a plant organ as a result of cell division in the cambium.

seed the structure that develops from the fertilized ovule in seed plants. It usually contains the embryo and a food store.

seedling a young plant.

self-incompatability the inability of gametes from the same plant to fertilize each other or form a viable embryo.

self-pollination the transfer of pollen to the stigma of the same flower or flowers on the same plant.

seminal roots roots growing from the base of the stem and taking over from the radicle during early seedling growth.

sepal an individual unit of the calyx, usually green. They may be of a different colour and take over the function of petals.

sessile unstalked.

shade plant any plant that is able to flourish in conditions of low light.

silicula a broad dry dehiscent fruit developed from the fusion of two carpels.

siliqua a structure similar to a silicula, but longer in size.

smut a fungal disease in which a black spore mass appears on the host.

soil the surface layer of the Earth's crust, consisting of water, air, living organisms, dead and decaying organisms and mineral particles.

species in the classification of plants, a single breeding group differentiated from other breeding groups by marked characteristics.

spine a modified leaf or part of a leaf, forming a pointed structure.

spore a simple asexual unicellular reproductive unit.

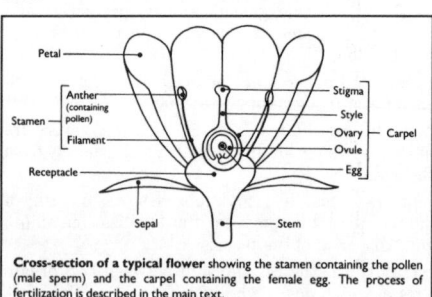

Cross-section of a typical flower showing the stamen containing the pollen (male sperm) and the carpel containing the female egg. The process of fertilization is described in the main text.

stamen the male reproductive organ in flowering plants. Together the stamens make up the androecium and produce the pollen on the anthers.

starch the most common and important food reserve carbohydrate in plants.

stele the vascular cylinder responsible for transport of water and solutes in the stems and roots of vascular plants.

stem that part of the plant above ground that carries the leaves, buds and reproductive parts.

stigma the tip of the carpel that receives the pollen

at the time of pollination and on which the pollen germinates.

stock a plant on to which shoots or buds are grafted.

stolon a long branch that bends over and touches the ground, at which point a new plant may develop.

stoma a pore in the epidermis of the aerial parts of a plant, especially the leaves, through which gaseous exchange occurs.

style that portion of the carpel between the ovary and stigma.

substrate molecules upon which enzymes act.

succulent a plant that conserves water by storing it in a swollen stem or leaves.

sucker a shoot that develops from the roots and forms its own root system.

swamp vegetation found in stagnant or slow-flowing water.

symbiosis an intimate relationship between two (or more) organisms, in which both benefit.

sympodial branching the process where the apical bud dies at the end of one season and growth continues in the next season from the lateral bud immediately below.

syncarpous a gynoecium with fused carpels.

syngenesious an androecium with fused anthers.

taproot a large tough vertical primary root, often penetrating deep into the soil. It can sometimes be a specialized food store.

taxis a directional movement of a whole plant in response to external stimuli.

tendril a modified inflorescence, branch or leaf of a climbing plant that can coil around objects to support the plant.

testa the protective outer covering of a seed.

thallus a plant body undifferentiated into leaves, stem and roots.

thorn a modified reduced branch forming a pointed woody structure. It has a vascular structure within it.

tiller a shoot that grows from the base of the stem when the main stem has been cut back, as in coppicing.

toadstool the inedible fruiting body of fungi.

transpiration the loss of water by evaporation from a plant's surfaces, especially through the stoma. This water loss sucks up water through the rest of the plant, from the roots upwards.

trifoliate a compound leaf with three leaflets.

trimerous an arrangement, especially in mono-cotyledons, in which the floral parts in each whorl are inserted in threes or multiples of three.

tropism the directional growth of a plant in response to an external stimulus. It can be positive or negative.

tuber the swollen underground part of a stem or root, used for food storage. It lasts for only one year.

turgor the pressure of cell contents on cell walls, swelling them out as the cell takes in water by osmosis. Turgidity is the main effect that keeps non-woody plants erect.

umbel an inflorescence in which flowers are borne on undivided stalks that arise from the main stem. The arrangement of these stalks is such that the flowers form a flat-topped plate or umbrella.

variegation streaks of different colouring in a plant organ, especially leaves and petals.

vascular bundle a strand of primary vascular tissue, consisting largely of xylem and phloem.

vegetative reproduction asexual reproduction in which specialized multicellular organs are formed and detached from the parent, generating new individuals.

vein a vascular bundle in a leaf.

venation the pattern of veins in a leaf.

vernalization the promotion of flowering by exposing young plants to cold.

vernation a pattern of rolling and folding of leaves in a bud.

vivipary young plants forming at the axils of flowers, or the germination of seeds on the parent plant before release.

weed any plant growing where it is not wanted.

wilt any plant disease causing inadequate water supply and thus wilting.

witches' broom a disorder characterized by a mass of twigs grown in response to an infection.

xylem the vascular tissue responsible for transporting water and solutes from the roots up to the leaves and other aerial parts. It constitutes the woody tissues.

zygote the product of the fusion of two gametes, before it undergoes subsequent cell division.

MEDICAL GLOSSARY

abdomen the space enclosing the digestive tract and organs, in addition to various other organs. The upper limit of the abdomen is the diaphragm; the lower limit is the pelvis.

abortion the termination of a pregnancy before the foetus can survive outside the uterus.

abscess a local infection causing inflammation and the production of pus.

accommodation the action of focusing the eye, caused by altering the thickness of a lens.

acetylsalicylic acid better known as aspirin. It relieves pain, lowers a raised temperature and reduces inflammation.

Achilles tendon the tendon in the heel, linking the muscles in the calf to the heel bone.

achondroplasia a form of dwarfism, caused by defective development of the bones of the skull and limbs.

acne an overproduction of grease by the sebaceous glands. The openings of the glands become blocked and act as foci of infection.

acromegaly an excess of growth hormone, resulting in – among other symptoms – enlargement of the hands and feet.

ACTH the usual name for adrenocorticotrophic hormone. It is produced by the pituitary gland and acts upon the adrenals.

acute the adjective used to describe a disease of rapid onset and short duration.

addiction a craving for a drug, resulting in tolerance of the drug and eventually physical dependence on it.

adenoid a lymph tissue at the back of the nose.

ADH the usual name for antidiuretic hormone. It is produced by the pituitary and affects the kidneys.

adrenalin a hormone produced by the adrenal

glands. It stimulates the heart, circulatory system and respiratory system, and inhibits digestion.

adrenals the adrenal glands. The adrenals are endocrine glands attached to the upper part of each kidney. They produce adrenalin (see above), cortisol (which affects the storage of glucose) and aldosterone (which affects the kidneys).

afterbirth the placenta.

AIDS Acquired Immune Deficiency Syndrome, a disease transmitted sexually or by exchange of blood or other body fluids.

aldosterone a hormone produced by the adrenals. It affects the kidneys, regulating the excretion of salt.

alimentary canal the mouth, oesophagus, stomach and intestines.

alveolus the air sac in the lungs where oxygen and carbon dioxide are exchanged between the air and the blood.

amenorrhoea the lack of menstrual periods.

amniocentesis taking a sample of the amniotic fluid from around the foetus in a pregnant woman. Analysis of the sample gives many indications as to the state of the foetus.

amnion the bag of membranes containing the foetus and amniotic fluid during pregnancy.

anaemia a lack of haemoglobin in the blood. This may be due to loss of blood or to defective production of haemoglobin. As haemoglobin carries oxygen in the bloodstream, anaemia gives rise to symptoms of tiredness and malaise.

anaesthetic a drug that removes sensation in a particular area or throughout the body.

analgesic a drug used to relieve pain.

anastomosis an operation joining two cut tubes, e.g. two lengths of intestine from which a diseased section has been removed.

aneurysm a bulge in an artery wall, caused by an area of weakness.

angina pain in the chest caused by insufficient supply of blood (and therefore oxygen) to the heart muscle. It is due to diseased coronary arteries.

ankylosis a loss of movement in a joint, usually caused by arthritis.

anorexia a neurosis involving loss of appetite and rejection of food.

antibiotic a naturally occurring or synthetic drug that kills bacteria. Antibiotics are used to treat bacterial infections.

antibody a chemical produced by the body's immune system in order to neutralize a specific harmful chemical or substance.

anticoagulant a drug that prevents blood from clotting.

antigen a chemical against which an antibody is formed and which the antibody 'attacks'.

antiserum serum extracted from the blood of an animal that is immune to a specific microorganism, e.g. hepatitis.

antitoxin an antibody that neutralizes a specific toxin or antigen.

arrhythmia an alteration in the natural rhythm of the heart.

arteriosclerosis a loss of elasticity in the arteries.

artery the blood vessels carrying oxygenated blood away from the heart.

arthritis an inflammation of a joint, giving pain and restricted movement.

aspirin see acetylsalicylic acid.

asthma a contraction of the air tubes in the lungs, caused by infection, allergy or stress. It results in very difficult breathing.

athlete's foot a fungal infection of the skin between the toes.

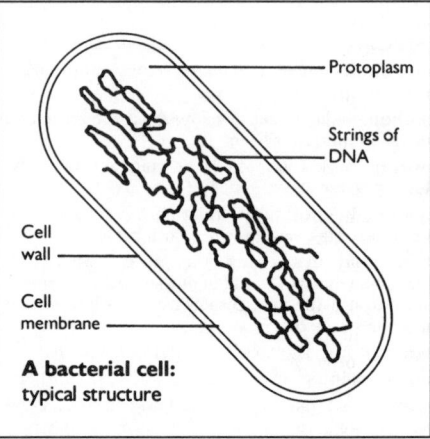

Protoplasm

Strings of DNA

Cell wall

Cell membrane

A bacterial cell: typical structure

bacteria microorganisms – capable of being seen with a light microscope – that live off living, dead or inorganic material.

barbiturates a group of drugs used as sedatives, as anaesthetics and to promote sleep. They are potentially addictive drugs.

bedsore the common name for decubitus ulcer. Pressure of skin and tissue against bone is caused by prolonged time spent in bed. The blood supply to the area is reduced and eventually a slow-healing ulcer is formed.

benign the adjective used to decsribe a mild, usually self-limiting, form of a disease.

bile a secretion of the liver, formed by the breakdown of haemoglobin. It helps in the digestion of fats in the small intestine.

biopsy the removal of a piece of living tissue for examination.

bladder the muscular bag into which urine drains from the kidneys, before being passed out via the urethra.

blood pressure the pressure in the arteries, caused by the pumping action of the heart. It fluctuates with the heartbeat.

breech delivery the delivery of a baby at birth bottom first (instead of head first).

bronchitis an inflammation of the airways in the lungs, i.e. the bronchi and the bronchioles. The condition is often caused by infection. Overproduction of mucus is a common symptom.

bruise a bump or knock causing bleeding into the skin and surface tissues. As the blood decomposes, it gives the characteristic colours – blue and black – of a bruise.

calcitonin a hormone produced by the thyroid. It lowers the concentration of calcium in the blood.

callus a hard area of skin, formed as a result of pressure or friction.

cancer an uncontrolled cell growth, in which the body's usual checks and controls are absent for some reason.

capillary a blood vessel of one cell diameter. Capillaries form a network within the tissues and act as a link between the arteries and veins.

carcinogen a substance or drug with the potential of causing cancer.

cardiac pertaining to the heart.

cataract an opaque area that develops on the lens of the eye.

cautery a small burn – caused electrically or by use of a laser – used to seal small cut blood vessels.

cerebrospinal fluid the fluid, derived from blood, which surrounds, and is found within cavities of, the brain and spinal cord.

cervical either pertaining to the cervix of the womb or pertaining to the neck of the womb.

chemotherapy the treatment of a disease with chemicals.

cholesterol a fatty chemical, found throughout the body. When deposited in the blood vessels, it can cause blockages.

chorea uncontrolled jerky muscular contractions.

chromosome that part of a cell which contains genetic material.

chronic the adjective used to describe a disease of slow onset and long duration.

cirrhosis a disease of the liver caused by scarring. The scar tissue is hard and fibrous and eventually is liable to affect the whole liver.

clavicle the collarbone.

cold an infection – initially viral – of the mucous membranes of the nose and throat.

cold sore an infection with the herpes virus around the mouth, causing raised blisters.

colitis an inflammation of the colon or large intestine caused by infection. (The cause of ulcerative colitis is unknown.)

colon the large intestine, from the ileum to the rectum.

congenital relating to a nonhereditary condition, abnormality or disease present at birth.

conjunctivitis an inflammation of the conjunctiva of the eye, usually caused by viral or bacterial infection.

consumption traditionally an alternative name for tuberculosis.

corn a form of callus on the foot.

coronary arteries the arteries providing the blood supply to the heart muscle.

costal pertaining to the ribs.

cramp a spasm of a muscle or group of muscles.

Crohn's disease an inflammation of the final section of the small intestine (the ileum). The cause is unknown.

cystitis an inflammation of the bladder, usually due to a bacterial infection.

dandruff a condition in which flakes of skin are shed from the scalp.

diabetes in full, diabetes mellitus. A disease caused by a deficiency of – or an inability to make proper use of – insulin formed in the pancreas.

diagnosis the identification of a disease from various signs and symptoms.

dialysis the removal of harmful waste products from the blood by an osmotic process in an artificial kidney.

diaphragm the domed sheet of muscle separating the thoracic cavity from the abdominal cavity.

dilatation a process of widening, either by means of one of the body's reflexes or by mechanical means.

disc a cartilaginous pad between each vertebra, acting as a shock absorber and imparting flexibility to the spinal column as a whole.

diuretic a drug used to increase the flow of urine.

drug a chemical given to help relieve the symptoms of a disease or to modify any of the body's natural processes.

duodenum the first section of the small intestine, between the stomach and the jejunum.

dysmenorrhoea painful menstrual periods.

dyspnoea difficulty in breathing.

ECG an electrocardiogram – a measurement of the electrical changes in the heart muscle.

ECT electroconvulsive therapy. The application of an electric shock to the scalp, used to treat certain mental illnesses, especially depression.

ectopic pregnancy a pregnancy in an abnormal position, e.g. in the Fallopian tube.

eczema an inflammatory condition of the skin, often caused by an allergy.

EEG an electroencephalogram – a measurement of electrical changes in the brain.

embolism the blockage of an artery by an air bubble or, more commonly, a blood clot.

emetic a drug given to induce vomiting.

emphysema damage to the lungs where the tiny air sacs at the ends of the airways break down, leading to breathlessness.

encephalitis a viral infection of the brain.

endemic a disease that is always present in a given area.

endocrine gland a ductless gland that releases secretions (hormones) into the bloodstream, rather than into a duct for local use.

endoscopy the examination of internal organs using a tube lit from the inside; fibre-optics are invariably used now.

enteritis an inflammation of the intestine, usually caused by infection.

epilepsy a nervous disorder characterized by convulsive attacks or fits. The cause is unknown.

erythrocyte a red blood cell.

Eustachian tube a passage leading from the back of the nose to the middle ear.

expectorant a drug that loosens mucus in the respiratory tract, particularly the lungs, and aids coughing.

faeces the waste residue of food, dead and live bacteria, and water, expelled from the rectum.

farmer's lung an allergic response to fungi found in hay, straw, etc.

fibrin a protein produced in the blood during the clotting process. It forms the matrix within which the clot forms.

fibroid a lumpy benign tumour of the uterus.

fistula a passage between two parts of the body, either as a result of a wound, e.g. a stab wound, or as a result of a deliberate operation.

foetus an unborn baby, more advanced than an embryo in that it is recognizably human.

forearm the part of the arm between the elbow and the wrist.

fracture a broken bone, either completely or partially broken.

frostbite damage to the skin and deeper tissues caused by the formation of ice crystals.

fungi very simple plant forms with a parasitic or saprophytic lifestyle. Some forms cause infections, usually of the skin but sometimes internally.

gall bladder the sac under the lower side of the liver that acts as a storage organ for bile.

gall stone a solid crystalline lump precipitated from the bile in the gall bladder.

gamma globulin blood proteins responsible for immunity to specific diseases. They can be separated and given to non-immune patients, thus conferring short-term immunity.

gangrene the death and bacterial decay of tissue.

gastric pertaining to the stomach.

gastric ulcer a stomach ulcer.

gastritis an inflammation of the stomach lining.

gastroenteritis an inflammation of the stomach and intestine.

gingivitis an inflammation of the gums, caused by infection.

glaucoma a disease of the eye in which high pressure within the eyeball resulting in defects in vision.

goitre a swelling of the thyroid gland.

gout the formation of uric acid crystals around joints.

gullet the oesophagus.

haemoglobin the complex protein molecule that gives red blood cells their colour. It transports oxygen in the bloodstream.

haemolysis the breakdown of red blood cells.

haemophilia an inherited disease characterized by an inability of the blood to form clots.

haemorrhage bleeding.

halothane an anaesthetic gas.

hamstring muscles the muscles at the back of the thigh that flex the knee.

hay fever an allergy to pollen, particularly grass pollens. It causes acute irritation to the mucous membranes of the nose and to the conjunctiva of the eye.

hemiplegia a paralysis of one half of the body caused by damage or disease in the opposite half of the brain.

hepatic pertaining to the liver.

hepatitis an inflammation of the liver, usually viral.

hernia a rupture, or protrusion of an organ from one body compartment into another compartment.

herpes a group of inflammatory diseases of the skin. *Herpes simplex* causes cold sores and venereal herpes; the other group, *Herpes zoster*, causes shingles.

hiatus hernia the protrusion of a section of the stomach through the oesophageal opening in the diaphragm.

Hodgkin's disease a form of cancer of the lymph tissues, resulting in lowered resistance to infections.

hormone a chemical, released directly into the bloodstream by one organ (an endocrine gland) in order to regulate other organs or body functions.

hypertension raised blood pressure.

hyperthermia high body temperature.

hypochondria a preoccupation with or anxiety about one's health.

hypoglycaemia a condition characterized by too low a level of glucose in the blood.

hypothermia a condition characterized by a considerably lowered body temperature.

iatrogenic a disease or condition produced as a result of treatment given for another disease or condition.

ileum the latter section of the small intestine, leading into the large intestine.

ilium the haunch bone; part of the pelvis.

immunity the natural or acquired resistance of a body to invading, i.e. 'foreign', chemicals. The immune system can deal with 'invaders' larger than chemicals, e.g. microorganisms, transplants, but this is because it reacts to chemicals on the surface of the microorganism or transplant.

immunization the production of immunity to a specific disease.

incontinence the inability to control the emptying of the bladder or bowels.

incubation period the time it takes between infection by a disease-carrying microorganism and the production of symptoms of the disease.

infarct an area of dead tissue resulting from a blocked blood vessel.

infection the entry of microorganisms into the body, their subsequent multiplication and the production of disease symptoms.

inflammation heat, redness, pain and swelling produced as defensive reaction by the body to infection or damage.

inoculation a form of immunization in which a live harmless variant of the disease-causing microorganism is used to infect the body, producing immunity to both the harmless and harmful microorganisms.

insulin a hormone produced in the pancreas which regulates the metabolism of sugars by controlling the uptake of glucose from the blood by the body's cells.

intercostal muscles the muscles between the ribs.

ischaemia a lack of blood to part of the body.

islets of Langerhans the groups of cells in the pancreas responsible for the production of insulin.

IUD a intrauterine device, a form of contraception. A coil or loop implanted in the uterus prevents a fertilized ovum from embedding in the uterus wall and developing into an embryo.

jaundice a disease characterized by yellowing of skin. It is caused by a build-up of bile pigments in the blood.

jejunum the middle section of the small intestine, between the duodenum and the ileum.

jugular pertaining to the neck.

lacrimal pertaining to tears, e.g. the lacrimal gland above the eye.

laparotomy an incision in the abdominal wall, usually for purposes of examination.

large intestine the latter part of the intestine,

between the small intestine and the rectum.

larynx the voice box, at the front of the throat.

lesion an injury, wound or harmful disturbance to an organ or tissue.

leucocyte a white blood cell.

leukaemia a form of cancer characterized by over-production of underdeveloped – and therefore useless – white blood cells.

lice insects which infest the hair of the body. Their eggs are called nits.

ligament a fibrous band of tissue holding two bones together at a joint.

linctus a syrupy medicine given to soothe coughing.

lumbar pertaining to the lower back.

lymph a fluid from the blood which leaks out of the capillaries, bathes the tissues and returns to the blood system via the lymphatic system.

lymphatic system a network of vessels and glands which collect and filter the lymph before returning it to the blood system.

malignant the adjective used to describe a severe, often fatal, form of a disease.

malnutrition a deficiency in the quality or quantity of food.

meconium a fluid consisting largely of mucus and bile, passed out of an infant's bowels soon after birth.

menarche the appearance of menstruation at puberty.

meninges the membranes enclosing the brain and spinal cord.

meningitis an inflammation of the meninges caused by viral or bacterial infection.

menopause the disappearance of menstruation, usually between the ages of about 40 and 50.

menorrhagia heavy bleeding during menstruation.

metabolism the sum total of the chemical reactions in the body by which nutrients are converted to energy, tissues are renewed, replaced and regenerated and waste products are broken down.

microorganism any organism too small to be seen with the naked eye. In medicine, usually taken to mean viruses, bacteria and some fungi and protozoans.

migraine an acute form of headache, perhaps allergic in origin, sometimes causing nausea and visual disturbances.

miscarriage an accidental abortion.

multiple sclerosis a chronic disease in which areas of the central nervous system degenerate. A variety of symptoms can be involved, depending on the areas of degeneration. These symptoms can appear and disappear at random.

myasthenia gravis a progressive form of muscle disease in which voluntary muscles become weaker.

myocardial pertaining to the heart muscle.

narcolepsy a disease characterized by periods of uncontrollable sleepiness.

narcotic a drug producing dulling or loss of consciousness.

nausea the urge to vomit.

neonatal pertaining to newborn babies.

nephritis an inflammation of the kidney, caused by infection, chemical poisoning or other reasons.

neuralgia an acute pain originating in a nerve.

neuritis an inflammation of a nerve.

nit the egg of a louse, found firmly attached to a hair or to fibres of clothing.

nystagmus a reflex rapid movement of the eyes, designed to keep moving objects in view.

obesity an excess of body fat.

oedema an excess of fluid in the tissues, either generally or locally, causing swelling.

oesophagus the section of the digestive tract between the pharynx and the stomach.

organ a distinct structure in the body designed to perform a particular function.

osteoarthritis the destruction of the cartilaginous surfaces that allow bones to move over each other.

osteoporosis a weakening of the bones in old age caused by a reduction in the calcium content of the bones.

oxytocin a hormone produced by the pituitary gland. It stimulates contractions of the uterus during labour.

palate the roof of the mouth. The hard palate is at the front, the soft palate at the back.

pancreas a gland at the back of the abdomen. It secretes digestive juices into the small intestine, and also acts as an endocrine gland, producing insulin from the islets of Langerhans.

pandemic a widespread epidemic.

paracetamol an analgesic.

paraplegia a paralysis of the lower half of the body.

parathyroids a group of small endocrine glands associated with the thyroid gland. They produce parathormone, which controls the level of calcium in the blood.

Parkinson's disease a form of paralysis in which the muscles become stiff, movement awkward, and a rhythmic twitching affects the muscles locally or generally.

patella the kneecap.

pectoral pertaining to the chest.

pelvis the ring of bone which forms the base of the abdominal cavity and which forms the hip joint on each side.

peptic ulcer an ulcer of the stomach or duodenum.

pericarditis an inflammation of the pericardium or fibrous sheath surrounding the heart.

perinatal pertaining to the period shortly before, during and shortly after birth.

peristalsis the rhythmic contractions producing flow along the digestive tract.

peritoneum the membrane lining the abdominal cavity.

peritonitis an inflammation of the peritoneum.

pharynx the part of the throat, from the back of the nose to the opening of the oesophagus, concerned with both breathing and swallowing.

phlebitis an inflammation of a vein, usually caused by a blockage of the vein by a clot.

phlegm mucus.

phrenic pertaining to the diaphragm.

piles haemorrhoids; distended varicose veins just inside the anus.

pituitary an endocrine gland on the underside of the brain. It produces a number of hormones: ACTH, which controls the adrenal glands; thyrotrophic hormone which controls the thyroid gland; gonadotrophic hormones, which control the ovaries and testes; growth hormone, controlling growth; prolactin, controlling milk production in the breasts; oxytocin, controlling contraction of the uterus during labour; and ADH, controlling loss of water from the body in the urine.

plasma the fluid component of blood.

platelet a small particle found in blood. Platelets are involved in the clotting mechanism.

pleura a double membrane surrounding the lungs.

pleurisy an inflammation of the pleura, usually caused by infection.

pneumonia an inflammation of the lungs, caused by infection. It affects the alveoli or air pockets at the ends of the airways.

pneumothorax a condition characterized by air between the lungs and chest wall, impairing breathing.

polycythaemia the opposite of anaemia; an excess of red blood cells.

polyp a tumour, usually benign, growing from a mucous membrane and attached to the membrane by a stalk.

poultice a hot dressing applied to inflamed surface areas.

prickly heat a blockage of sweat glands resulting in the production of tiny blisters and an irritating rash.

progesterone a hormone produced in the ovaries. It acts on the uterus to prepare to receive fertilized ovum.

prognosis a forecast of the course a disease will take.

prolactin a hormone produced by the pituitary that stimulates the breasts to secrete milk.

prolapse the displacement of an organ from its normal position.

prophylaxis the prevention of disease.

prostate gland a gland found only in males. It secretes part of the seminal fluid into the urethra.

prosthesis an artificial replacement for part of the body.

psoriasis scaly red blotches formed on the skin. The complaint tends to come and go, for unknown reasons.

puerperal pertaining to childbirth.

pulmonary pertaining to the lungs.

pus dead cells, dead white blood cells, dead bacteria and tissue fluid.

pyloric stenosis a constriction of the outlet from the stomach to the duodenum.

rabies a disease of certain carnivores, transmitted to humans via an animal bite. Symptoms include fever, delirium, muscle spasms and paralysis. Spasm of the throat muscles causes the inability to drink or hydrophobia.

rectum the last section of the digestive tract, between the large intestine and anus.

referred pain a pain occurring in a different part of the body from the site of injury or trauma.

reflex an automatic response to a stimulus.

remission a temporary subsidence of the symptoms of a disease.

renal pertaining to the kidneys.

rheumatic fever an acute disease – generally of children and adolescents – involving raised temperature and inflammation of various parts of the body at different times, including the joints and the valves and lining of the heart.

rheumatism pain or inflammation of the joints or muscles.

rheumatoid arthritis the formation of inflamed knots of fibrous tissue, usually around joints.

rickets faulty bone growth caused by a deficiency of vitamin D.

rodent ulcer a type of skin cancer in which a hard lump appears on the face. The centre of the lump subsequently breaks down to form an ulcer.

sciatica a pain in the region of the sciatic nerve at the back of the thigh, calf and foot.

sclerosis a thickening or hardening of a particular tissue.

scoliosis the curvature of the spine sideways.

sebum the greasy material formed by the sebaceous glands of the skin.

sedative a drug that calms or renders someone sleepy.

senility the mental, or physical, deterioration of organs – especially the brain – in old age.

sepsis an infection of tissues, causing damage.

septicaemia the spread of an infection into the blood, which carries the infecting agent throughout the body.

serum a straw-coloured fluid that separates from the blood as it clots.

shingles another name for *Herpes zoster*; a viral infection of nerves, causing painful blisters on the skin in the area that the infected nerve serves.

shock a sudden drop in blood pressure causing failure of the blood circulation system.

sign any indication of a disease observed by the doctor, nurse, etc.

sinew a tendon or ligament.

sinus a hollow cavity opening off a passageway, e.g. the nasal sinuses opening off the nose. It can also mean merely a bulge in a tube.

sinusitis an inflammation of the mucous membrane of the nasal sinuses.

spasm an uncontrolled contraction of a muscle or group of muscles.

spastic paralysis the loss or limitation of controlled movement in various muscles, caused by disease of the nervous system.

sphincter a ring of muscle around an opening to a hollow or tubular organ.

spina bifida a congenital disease in which the vertebrae do not close over the spinal column, allowing the meninges to protrude.

spleen an organ at the top of the abdominal cavity, responsible for white blood cell production, breakdown of red blood cells and some control of immunity.

spondylitis an inflammation of the vertebrae, often with loss of mobility.

sputum mucus.

squint a poor alignment of the eyes; they either turn inwards (convergent squint) or outwards (divergent squint).

stenosis a constriction or narrowing of a tube, e.g. part of the digestive tract.

stroke an interruption of blood supply to part of the brain.

subcutaneous beneath the skin.

suture the surgical stitching used to close a wound or incision.

symptom any indication of a disease observed by the patient.

syndrome a group of symptoms that frequently occur together, although they may not always be caused by the same disease.

systemic pertaining to the body as a whole.

temperature the 'normal' body temperature is between 36°C and 37·5°C (97–99.5 °F) when taken in the mouth. However, it will vary between these limits during the day and, for women, during their menstrual cycle.

tendon a fibre joining muscle to bone.

tetanus an infection of a wound with the bacterium *Clostridium tetani*. The bacteria produces a poison which causes the characteristic muscle spasms.

thorax the space enclosing the heart, lungs and oesophagus. It is bounded by the rib-cage and the diaphragm.

thrombosis a partial or complete blockage of a blood vessel by a blood clot.

thrombus a blood clot formed on the inside surface of a blood vessel.

thrush an infection by fungus of a mucous membrane, usually of the mouth or vagina.

thyroid an endocrine gland in the neck. It produces thyroxine, which controls energy production in the tissues; and calcitonin, which controls the calcium levels in the blood.

tissue a collection of cells, usually of the same type, specialized to perform a particular function.

tolerance the need to administer larger and larger doses of a drug over time, as the body gets used to it.

tomography an X-ray examination in which a 'slice' of the body is looked at.

tonsil a lymph tissue at the back of the mouth.

topical pertaining to the surface of the body.

tourniquet a constricting strap or band applied to a limb to stop arterial bleeding.

toxaemia poisoning of the blood by toxins from infecting bacteria.

toxin a poisonous substance, usually produced by bacteria.

toxoid a toxin that has been chemically modified to render it harmless. It is still able to produce an immune response when used to immunize against the original toxin.

trachea the windpipe. A tube strengthened with cartilage that runs between the larynx and the bronchi that pass into the lungs.

tranquillizer a drug used to calm the mood without inducing sleepiness.

transfusion a transfer of blood from a healthy to an ill person.

transplantation the transfer of a healthy organ to a patient to replace a diseased organ.

trauma physical damage to tissue, e.g. a wound.

tropical ulcer an ulceration of the skin, usually on the leg, commonly found in the tropics. It is very slow to heal.

tubal pregnancy a form of ectopic pregnancy occurring in the Fallopian tubes.

tumour a group of cells that starts to divide without the usual checks and controls imposed by the body. It may be malignant or benign.

ulcer a breakdown of the skin or mucous membrane that heals very slowly or not at all.

ultrasound sound waves at a frequency well above the range of human hearing, used to provide an image of internal structures.

ureter the tube leading from the kidney to the bladder.

urethra the tube leading from the bladder to the exterior.

uvula the soft projection hanging down at the back of the mouth.

vaccination the use of dead or a harmless form of a microorganism to produce artificial immunity to the harmful form of the microorganism.

vaccine the dead or harmless microorganisms used in a vaccination.

varicose veins swollen veins, usually in the legs, caused by the collapse of the valves in the veins allowing backflow of blood.

vascular pertaining to blood vessels.

vein a blood vessel returning blood from the tissues to the heart. Apart from the vein carrying blood from the lungs to the heart, all veins carry deoxygenated blood.

venereal disease a sexually transmitted disease.

vertigo a form of dizziness in which the subject feels the surroundings are spinning round.

viruses microorganisms, smaller than bacteria

VIRUS REPRODUCTION

1 Virus approaches cell

2 Virus attaches to cell and injects its DNA into it

3 Cell is made to replicate virus's DNA

4 New viruses are formed inside cell

5 The cell bursts and the new viruses are spread out

Viruses, the most basic forms of life, simply consist of a protein coat protecting a strand of DNA. They can only reproduce inside the living cells of other organisms, and the cells are destroyed in the process. This is why viruses cause diseases.

and incapable of being seen with a light microscope. They can only reproduce inside living cells.

vitamins chemicals found in foodstuffs or synthesized by the body. They are not nutrients, but are essential for the normal functioning of growth, repair and reproduction.

wart a small tumour of the outer layer of the skin caused by a virus.

ZOOLOGY GLOSSARY

abdomen the rear section of an arthropod, often divided into segments. Alternatively, in vertebrates, the body cavity in which the principal digestive organs are found.

abomasum the fourth chamber of a ruminant's stomach.

accommodation the adjustments to the eye by which an object is brought into focus.

acetyl choline a neurotransmitter chemical found in the nervous systems of both vertebrates and invertebrates.

acoelomate an animal lacking any form of coelom.

adipose tissue a fatty tissue occurring under the skin in mammals.

adrenalin a hormone secreted in many groups of higher animals. It is said to prepare the body for 'fight and flight'. Adrenalin is also found in the nervous system acting as a neurotransmitter.

afferent a nerve that passes information back to the central nervous system, i.e. a sensory nerve.

aggression animal behaviour designed to frighten off another animal, usually of the same species, from a designated territory.

agonistic behaviour behaviour associated with aggression, but actually involving little violence.

air sac the extension of a bird's respiratory system into other parts of the body. Expansion and contraction of these sacs, with movement of the body, speed up the movement of air in and out of the bird's lungs. The air sacs also help diminish a bird's weight.

albinism an absence of pigments in the hair, skin and eyes.

alimentary canal the tube down which food passes, and in which it is broken down and digested.

alveolus an air sac at the end of a bronchiole in the lungs of reptiles and mammals. It is in the alveoli that gas exchange occurs between the air and the blood.

amino acid the constituent molecular 'building brick' of proteins.

amnion the membrane containing the embryo and the fluid in which it is bathed.

amphibia animals that can live both in water and on land. They represent the first group of animals to develop two pairs of pentadactyl limbs.

antenna a jointed appendage found on the heads of many arthropods. It is usually sensory.

anticoagulant a chemical that prevents blood from clotting.

anus the final opening of the alimentary tract.

aorta the large blood vessel that carries blood from the heart to the body. It is found in the higher four-limbed animals.

arteriole a small artery linking an artery to the capillaries.

artery a blood vessel taking blood away from the heart.

arthropod an invertebrate having an exoskeleton made of chitin, jointed limbs and a segmented body, e.g. arachnids, insects, crustaceans and centipedes.

articulation the movement of one part of a skeleton over another, often at a joint.

asexual reproduction a form of reproduction by budding that occurs only in the lower animals, e.g. the protozoa.

assimilation the incorporation of the simple molecules resulting from digestion into more complex molecules.

atlas vertebra the first vertebra; it allows free movement of the head.

autonomic nervous system the vertebrate nervous system concerned with controlling bodily functions. It consists of the sympathetic and parasympathetic nervous system.

axis vertebra the second vertebra; its articulation with the atlas vertebra allows rotational movement of the head.

barb a hair-like structure attached to the shaft of a feather.

barbule one of the 'teeth' on the barb of a feather. The barbules interlock, linking the barbs together.

bilateral symmetry the arrangement of the body and organs of an animal in only one plane of symmetry.

bile a secretion of the liver in vertebrates. It is formed from the breakdown of blood cells, and helps in digestion of fats.

bivalves a group of molluscs in which the body is enclosed within a shell consisting of two hinged halves, or valves, e.g. clams, cockles, oysters and mussels.

bladder a fluid- or gas-filled sac, often taken to mean the muscular sac into which urine drains from the kidneys.

blastula the early stage in the development of an animal embryo after fertilization.

blood the fluid that occupies the vascular system. It carries respiratory gases, digestive and excretory products and other biochemicals.

blubber a thick layer of subcutaneous fat found in many marine mammals.

bone a form of tissue, rich in calcium, that forms the endoskeleton of the higher vertebrates.

brain the forward section of the nervous system. In invertebrates it consists of ganglia; in vertebrates it consists of an enlarged part of the neural tube.

bronchiole a tube leading to the alveoli in the lungs.

bronchus one of two tubes, each tube leading to one of the lungs in vertebrates.

buccal cavity the mouth cavity.

caecum an outgrowth of the alimentary canal.

canine tooth a pointed tooth found in mammals. It is used for gripping and tearing, and is prominent in carnivores.

capillaries fine blood vessels forming a network in vertebrate tissues. They carry respiratory gases, nutrients and waste products to and from the tissues.

carapace the shell of some crustaceans, e.g. crabs, and of some reptiles, e.g. tortoise.

carnassial teeth the modified molar and premolar teeth in many carnivores. They have sharp cutting edges for dealing with meat, bones, ligaments, etc.

carnivore a meat-eating animal.

carpals bones found in the pentadactyl limb of the higher vertebrates.

cartilage a tough slippery flexible tissue, found in all vertebrates. It has skeletal functions, and some of the lower vertebrates have skeletons consisting entirely of cartilage.

central nervous system that part of the nervous system which coordinates the activities of the other parts of the nervous system. It ranges in complexity from a simple series of paired ganglia to the brain and spinal cord of vertebrates.

cephalopod a marine mollusc with well-developed head and eyes and sucker-bearing tentacles, e.g. octopuses, squids and cuttlefish.

chaeta a stiff bristle found on the body segments of worms.

chela pincers found in arthropods.

chitin the polymeric chemical that comprises the exoskeleton of arthropods.

chordates animals which have a notochord, either in the embryo or adult form.

chromatophore a cell containing pigment that is involved in colour changes.

chrysalis the pupal form of butterflies and moths.

cilium (plural **cilia**) a very fine hair, capable of independent movement. Unlike flagella, cilia are usually found in groups. They can only beat in one direction, and usually move in synchrony.

class in taxonomy, a primary grouping or classification into which a phylum or division is divided, e.g. Amphibia, Reptilia and Mammalia are three classes of phylum Chordata.

clitellum the 'saddle' of earthworms, involved in copulation.

cloaca the chamber into which the alimentary canal, the kidneys and the reproductive organs open.

coccyx a fused group of vertebrae at the base of the spine in tailless primates.

cocoon a protective covering around the eggs or larvae of many invertebrates.

coelenteron the body cavity in lower animals that functions as a digestive cavity. There is one opening, and the cavity itself is lined with two layers of cells.

coelom a body cavity in higher animals.

compound eye the simple eye found in crustaceans and insects. It is formed from hundreds of single light receptors, which build up a compound image.

cone a light-sensitive cell in the eyes of vertebrates. It detects colour and detail.

cranium the skull of vertebrates.

crop a section of the alimentary canal capable of being distended in order to store food.

crustacean a (mainly) aquatic arthropod protected by a shell-like cover, e.g. crab, lobster, shrimp, woodlice, barnacles and water flea.

deciduous teeth the first set of teeth in mammals. These are shed to make way for the adult teeth.

defaecation the discharge of waste from the body through the anus.

demersal inhabiting the sea or lake floor.

dental formula an expression of the arrangement of teeth in mammals. It indicates the number of incisors, canines, premolars and molars in one side of the upper and lower jaw.

dentine the main bulk of a tooth. It is served by blood vessels and covered with enamel.

diaphragm the dome of muscle separating the thoracic and abdominal cavities in mammals.

diastole the phase of the heart beat in which the heart muscle is relaxed.

digestion the breakdown of foodstuffs into simple molecules that can be absorbed and used by the organism.

digit a finger or toe of the vertebrate pentadactyl limb.

dorsal the surface of an animal nearest to the notochord or spinal cord.

ear a vertebrate organ, primarily of balance but subsequently adapted as an organ of hearing.

ecdysis moulting. The shedding of the exoskeleton in arthropods to allow for growth, or the shedding of the outer layer of skin in reptiles.

efferent a nerve that passes information from the central nervous system out to the tissues and organs of the body.

egg a structure containing the ovum and in which the embryo develops. It contains yolk, which nourishes the embryo during its development, and a number of membranes enclosing the contents, including an outer protective membrane, sometimes calcareous.

embryo the structure that develops from the zygote prior to birth or hatching.

enamel hard white material that encases the exposed surface of a mammalian tooth.

endocrine gland a type of gland found in vertebrates and some invertebrates, in which the secretion passes into the bloodstream and thus to the organ or organs on which it acts.

endoskeleton a rigid and often articulated structure that lies within the body tissues. It provides support and shape, and often sites of attachment for muscles.

epiglottis a cartilaginous flap that closes off the windpipe of mammals during the swallowing reflex.

excretion the elimination of waste chemicals from the body. This is not the same as defaecation.

exocrine gland a gland, found in vertebrates, in which the secretion is carried down a duct to the site of activity.

exoskeleton a rigid articulated structure that lies outside the body tissues. It provides protection, support and often sites of attachment for muscles.

faeces the remains of undigested food, bile, dead cells and bacteria, expelled through the anus.

fat body in amphibians, the fat body consists solely of fat, and provides them with food reserves during hibernation. In insects, it consists of fat, protein and other reserves, and provides nourishment during metamorphosis as well as during hibernation.

feathers light, flat epidermal structures that form the plumage of birds. There are three types of feather: contour feathers have barbs and barbules that lock together (these are the feathers on the wings and tail associated with flight); down feathers and filoplumes are fluffy feathers more important for heat retention.

fibrin a protein that forms a fibrous matrix as the basis of a blood clot.

filoplume hairlike feathers scattered over the

surface of a bird. They are important in heat retention.

fin a firm appendage forming an organ of balance or locomotion on fishes and other aquatic animals. The lateral fins of fishes are based on the pentadactyl limb, the two pectoral fins corresponding to fore limbs, the pelvic fins to the hind limbs. These, and the median and anal fin, are used for steering and balance. The caudal fin on the tail is used for propulsion.

flagellum a hairlike filament found on a cell surface. Its movement causes the cell, or the fluid around it, to move.

follicle a small sac or cavity.

gall bladder the storage organ for bile produced in the liver.

gamete a reproductive cell that can undergo fertilization.

ganglion a mass of nervous tissue, rich in nerve cell bodies. In invertebrates, ganglia form the central nervous system.

gestation the time between conception, i.e. fertilization, and birth.

gill the respiratory organ in marine and freshwater animals. Each gill has a rich blood supply, promoting gas exchange between the blood and the surrounding water.

gizzard part of the alimentary canal designed to break up hard foods.

gland an organ that secretes a specific chemical or group of chemicals, either into the bloodstream or into a specific site of activity.

glottis the opening of the larynx into the pharynx.

glycogen a storage compound in animals. It is a polymer of glucose.

gonad an organ which produces ova or sperm.

grey matter the region of the vertebrate brain that contains nerve cell bodies and synapses.

gut the alimentary canal.

haem the basis of many respiratory pigments, e.g. haemoglobin, as it can combine reversibly with oxygen.

haemocoel the body cavity containing the blood in arthropods and crustaceans.

hair cornified threads produced by follicles in the skin of mammals. The colour is due to melanin pigment. The function of hair is largely heat retention.

hallux a vestigial digit on the inside of the rear limbs of most higher terrestrial vertebrates.

haltere a modified wing of flies that provides information on stability in flight.

haw the nictitating membrane found in reptiles, birds and some domestic animals – e.g. horse and cat – that can be drawn upwards across the eye.

heart an organ found in all vertebrates and many invertebrates that drives blood around the body unidirectionally.

herbivore a plant-eating animal.

heterocercal any fish whose vertebral column extends into the tail fin. It is upturned, giving the fin a larger dorsal lobe than ventral lobe.

hibernation a period of time during winter when an animal becomes inactive and the basal metabolic rate drops, thus conserving energy.

hominid a primate in the family *Hominidae*, including early and modern man.

homiothermy the maintenance of the body temperature at a relatively constant level – this is often referred to as being 'warm-blooded'.

homocercal any fish whose tail fin does not contain the vertebral column, but is supported with fin rays.

hormone a chemical secreted by endocrine glands. Carried by the bloodstream, each hormone has a specific and often regulatory effect upon a particular organ.

ileum a section of the small intestine in mammals, immediately before the colon.

imago the sexually mature adult form of an insect.

implantation the attachment of a vertebrate fertilized ovum to the wall of the uterus.

impulse the passage of an electric current along a nerve fibre.

incisor the front teeth of mammals. They are sharp and are used for biting and gnawing of food.

instar the form adopted by an insect between moults.

insulin an important animal hormone responsible for the control of glucose levels in the blood.

intestine that part of alimentary canal in which food is digested and absorbed.

invertebrate an animal lacking a backbone or spinal column or notochord, e.g. molluscs, worms, jellyfish, coral.

iris a ring of pigmented tissue which lies over the lens of the eye in invertebrates and cephalopods. The diaphragm that controls the size of the pupil.

joint a point of contact between two body elements in invertebrates or between two bony or cartilaginous elements in vertebrates.

keel the large blade or projection from the sternum of bats and birds. It provides the surface area for the attachment of the flight muscles.

keratin the structural protein found in horn, claws, beaks, nails, hair, etc., and in the outer cells of the epidermis of vertebrates.

kidney one of two excretory organs found in vertebrates.

labrum the upper 'lip' in insects that helps in feeding.

lactation milk production. One of the chief characteristics of mammals.

lacteal lymph vessels in vertebrates, involved in the absorption of digested fats in the intestine.

larva a form taken by many animals between hatching from the egg and metamorphosing into the adult, e.g. caterpillars, tadpole.

larynx the area of the throat that controls the swallowing reflex and that contains the vocal cords.

lateral line a system of receptors for the detection of vibration (sound) and movement, arranged in a line down each side of fish and some amphibians.

lens the transparent body in the eye designed to focus light on to the retina in vertebrates.

ligament a band of fibre holding two bones together at a vertebrate joint.

liver the largest internal organ found in vertebrates. It is responsible for the major metabolic functions.

lung a respiratory organ found in vertebrates.

lung book a respiratory organ found in some insects.

lymphatic system a system of tubes containing lymph, found in vertebrates. It collects tissue fluid and returns it to the blood system, transports digested fats, and is involved in the immune system. Flow in the lymphatic system is effected by lymph hearts in some vertebrates, and by muscular and respiratory movements in mammals.

mammals a group of vertebrates characterized by being homiothermic, having hair on the skin, giving birth to well-developed young which have been nourished within the womb by a placenta and which are subsequently suckled at the mammary glands.

mammary gland a milk-producing gland found in all female mammals.

mandible the lower jaw in invertebrates.

mantles folds of skin in molluscs which secrete the shell, if present, and protect the gills.

marsupium a pouch possessed by female marsupials. The mammary glands are found within the pouch, and the young finish their development there after birth.

maxilla either a feeding appendage found in arthropods, or the upper jawbone of vertebrates.

meatus the passage leading from the outer ear to the eardrum.

median eye a third eye in the top of the head found in many invertebrates. It is formed from an outgrowth of the brain, and is represented vestigially in vertebrates by the pineal body.

medulla the central part of an organ.

melanin a pigment found in skin, hair, etc.

meninges the membranes surrounding the central nervous system of vertebrates and the spaces within it.

metacarpals bones found in the pentadactyl limb of the higher vertebrates.

metameric segmentation the division of the body into a number of similar segments along its length.

metamorphosis the change from the larval to the adult stage of an animal – a process found in insects and amphibians.

metatarsals bones found in the vertebrate pentadactyl limb. They are greatly elongated in running animals.

migration the movement of whole populations of animal species between two regions, often at roughly the same time each year.

mimicry the ability of one animal to resemble another, usually for protection.

mitral valve the heart valve of the higher vertebrates.

molar a chewing tooth occurring at the rear of the jaw in animals.

mucous membrane a surface membrane that secretes mucus.

mucus a slimy protective secretion that does not dissolve in water.

muscle a contractile tissue that produces movement in invertebrates and vertebrates.

myelin sheath a membranous sheath around nerve fibres.

nasal cavity the cavity in the head of vertebrates containing the organs of smell.

nephridium an excretory organ in invertebrates.

nerve fibre the long thin unbranched section of a nerve cell that transmits the nerve messages over long distances within the body.

nerve net a simple form of nervous system found in the invertebrates.

neurone the chief nerve cell in the nervous system. It consists of a cell body, a number of finger-like dendrites which link up with other nerve cells, and one or more nerve fibres or axons which transport impulses over relatively long distances.

nidiculous any bird that hatches in an undeveloped state and is unable to fend for itself.

nidifugous any bird that hatches in a well-developed state and is soon able to fend for itself.

notochord a form of primitive cartilaginous spinal column. It is found in adult forms of the lower vertebrates, and in embryonic forms of the higher vertebrates.

nymph an immature form of some insects, in which the wings and reproductive organs are not fully developed.

ocellus a simple form of eye, consisting of a collection of light-sensitive cells, found in some invertebrates, especially insects. It is not capable of forming an image.

oesophagus the gullet – the tube by which food passes from the mouth to the digestive tract.

oestrous cycle the reproductive cycle of female mammals.

oestrus the period of the oestrous cycle when the female mammal is 'on heat', i.e. copulation can occur.

olfactory organs organs of smell.

omasum the third chamber of a ruminant's stomach.

ommatidium a single unit in the compound eye of arthropods.

omnivore any animal that eats both plants and animals.

operculum the muscular flap covering the gills in bony fish.

optic chiasma the point at which the optic nerves cross over between the vertebrate eyes and brain.

optic nerve the nerve connecting the vertebrate eye with the brain.

orbit the socket of the vertebrate skull in which the eye lies.

order in taxonomy, a group into which a class is divided, e.g. Carnivora, Primates and Rodentia are three orders of the class Mammalia.

ossification the process by which bone is formed from cartilaginous or other tissue.

ovary the reproductive organ of female animals, producing ova and female sex hormones.

oviparous any female animal that lays eggs within which the embryo develops.

ovoviviparous any female animal in which the fertilized ova develop within the body but not receive nourishment from it (e.g. certain reptiles, fish, etc).

ovulation the release of an ovum from the ovary.

ovum (plural **ova**) an unfertilized non-motile female gamete.

pacemaker a group of cells that provides a rhythmic series of electrical impulses that drives an organ – most commonly applied to the cells in the vertebrate heart that are responsible for providing the electrical impulses for the heartbeat.

palate the roof of the mouth in vertebrates.

palp a head or mouth appendage found in many vertebrates.

parasympathetic nervous system part of the autonomic nervous system in vertebrates.

parturition the passage of the foetus out of the female's body at the end of pregnancy in mammals.

pecking order the social hierarchy found in many animals that live in groups.

pectoral fins the forward pair of lateral fins found in fishes.

pectoral girdle the ring of bones in vertebrates to which the fore limbs articulate.

pelagic any animal inhabiting the open waters of the sea or a lake.

pelvic fins the rear pair of lateral fins in fishes.

pelvic girdle the ring of bones in vertebrates to which the hind limbs articulate.

pentadactyl limb the characteristic limb of the vertebrates, with five digits or 'fingers'.

peripheral nervous system those parts of the nervous system not included in the central nervous system.

peristalsis the waves of contraction that pass down tubular organs, particularly the digestive tract.

phalange one of the types of bones of the pentadactyl limb.

pheromone a chemical produced by one animal, designed to elicit a response in another animal of the same species.

phylum the second taxonomic grouping after kingdom and before class.

pineal body a downgrowth of the vertebrate brain with endocrine functions. In some lower vertebrates it functions as the median eye.

pinna the outermost part of the outer ear in some mammals.

pituitary gland the major endocrine gland in vertebrates, occurring as downgrowth of the brain. It produces a wide range of hormones, many of them controlling other endocrine glands.

placenta the series of membranes within the uterus of viviparous animals that nourishes the developing foetus. It allows a close association of the foetal and maternal blood systems.

pleural membranes the membranes enclosing the mammalian lungs.

plexus a network of nerve cells.

poikilothermy the inability to regulate the body temperature, which therefore assumes that of the surroundings.

pollex the inner digit on the forelimbs of the higher vertebrates. It is often vestigial, or may be adapted for a variety of purposes.

polymer a naturally occurring or synthetic compound, e.g. starch.

polyp a non-motile form of those coelenterates that have the medusoid motile form.

premolar the grinding and chewing teeth occurring between the canines and molars in the jaws of mammals.

pupa a non-feeding form of an insect in which metamorphosis from a larva to an adult occurs.

pupil the opening in the iris of the eye of vertebrates and some invertebrates, through which light enters the eye.

rachis the shaft of a feather.

radial symmetry the form of symmetry found in sedentary animals, e.g. the coelenterates, in which the body is symmetrical about a number of planes passing through a central axis.

radula a strip on the tongue of molluscs that carries teeth to rasp food off rocks, etc. As the teeth are worn away they are replaced.

reflex an automatic response to a stimulus.

regeneration the regrowth or replacement of tissues and body parts lost owing to injury. Extensive regeneration is possible in many invertebrates, but regeneration is much more limited in the vertebrates.

retina a layer of sensory cells in the eyes of vertebrates and some molluscs.

rod a light-sensitive cell in the retina of vertebrate eyes.

rumen the first chamber in the stomach of ruminants.

ruminants a group of higher mammals, including cattle and sheep, in which the digestive system allows food to be swallowed and then digested later.

saliva a secretion of mucus and enzymes which moistens the food and starts off the process of digestion.

scolex the head of a tapeworm, which anchors it to the intestinal wall of the host.

sebum a greasy material produced by the sebaceous glands in the skin of mammals. It greases the hair and protects the skin.

sessile any animal which lives attached to a fixed surface or to another animal.

sibling one of a number of offspring of the same two parents.

sinus any body cavity or recess.

smooth muscle a vertebrate muscle tissue, under involuntary control, usually found around hollow organs. It can produce long-term contractions.

sperm the motile male gamete formed in the testes of male animals.

sphincter a ring of muscle around the opening to a hollow organ.

spinal cord that part of the central nervous system in vertebrates enclosed within the spinal column.

spinneret the openings on the abdomen of a spider out of which silk is produced to make webs, tie up prey, spin cocoons, etc.

spiracle a gill slit in fish, or the opening of the tracheae in insects.

striated muscle a vertebrate muscle – with a striped appearance – under voluntary control. Important in locomotion, it produces rapid powerful contractions.

stridulation the production of sound by insects, usually by rubbing body parts together.

succus entericus digestive secretions of the walls of the small intestine in vertebrates.

swim bladder an air bladder found in many fish. It is used in maintaining depth when swimming.

sympathetic nervous system part of the vertebrate autonomic nervous system.

synapse the point of contact between nerve cells at which the nerve impulse passes from one cell to another.

systole the phase of the heart beat in which the

heart muscle is contracted.

tarsals bones in the rear pentadactyl limbs of vertebrates.

telson the tail appendage found in some arthropods.

tendon a fibrous band connecting a muscle to a bone.

testis the male reproductive organ that produces sperms and male sex hormones.

tetrapod any vertebrate having four limbs.

thorax the middle section of arthropods, particularly of insects. In vertebrates, the thorax is the body cavity containing the heart and lungs.

tone the state of partial contraction of a muscle which maintains body posture.

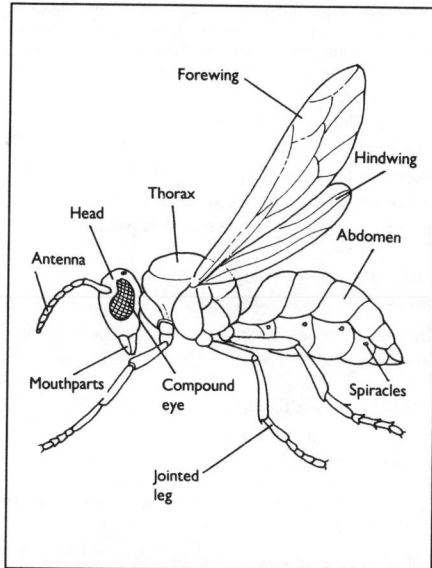

ventral the surface of an animal furthest away from the notochord or spinal column.

venule a small blood vessel linking a vein to the capillary network.

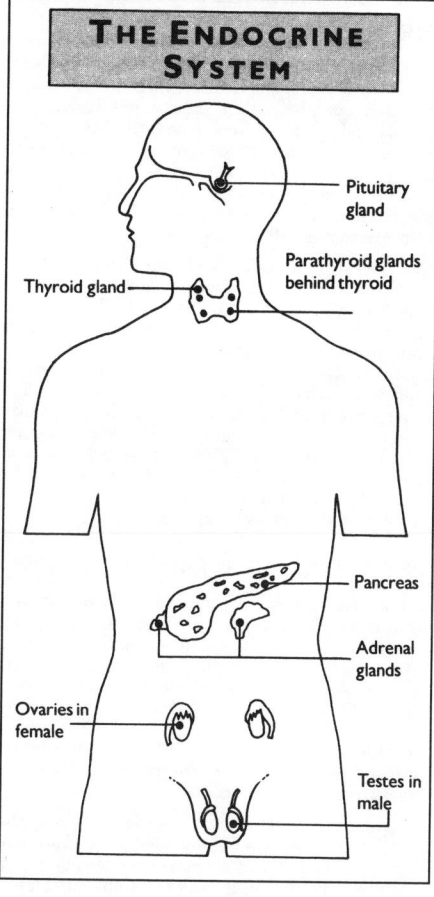

THE ENDOCRINE SYSTEM

trachea in arthropods, the tracheae are tubes that take air to the tissues. In vertebrates, the trachea is the windpipe, taking air from the larynx to the lungs.

umbilical cord the connection between the embryo and the placenta in pregnant mammals.

ungulates a group of mammals that graze, that have hooves and that walk on the tips of elongated and adapted pentadactyl limbs.

urea the waste product of mammals and many other animals.

uric acid the waste product of birds and some other animals.

urine liquid produced in the kidney, containing waste products such as urea or uric acid.

uterus the womb in mammals.

vascular system the fluid-filled spaces in the body, e.g. the blood vascular system.

vasoconstriction a constriction of a blood vessel.

vasodilatation an increase in the diameter of a blood vessel.

vein a blood vessel that carries blood from the tissues to the heart.

venation the arrangement of veins in an insect's wing.

vertebra a separate bone of the vertebral column.

vertebral column bones or cartilage in close apposition, running in a line from the skull to the tail of vertebrates and enclosing the spinal cord.

vertebrate any animal having a backbone or vertebral column or notochord, e.g. fishes, amphibians, reptiles, birds, mammals.

villus a projection from a body surface – usually designed to increase the surface area of a tissue.

viviparous any animal in which embryos develop within and are nourished by the mother.

vocal cords elastic fibres in the larynx that produce sounds in vertebrates.

white matter the region of the vertebrate central nervous system consisting of nerve cell fibres.

yolk the nutrient store in eggs.

zoology the study of animals and their behaviour, including their classification, structure, physiology and history.

zoonosis any disease or infection that can be passed on from man to animals.

THE PHYSICAL SCIENCES
WEIGHTS AND MEASURES

MEASUREMENT

Measurement – in terms of length, weight or capacity – involves *comparison*. The measurement of any physical quantity entails comparing it with an agreed and clearly defined *standard*. The result is expressed in terms of agreed *units*. Each measurement is expressed in terms of the appropriate unit preceded by a number which is the *ratio* of the measured quantity of that unit. The science of measurement is called *metrology*.

Crude measurements probably date back to prehistory. The first – units of weight and length – were based upon parts of the human body. The average pace of a man was a common unit in many ancient civilizations. The length of the human thumb was another widely used measure – in England, it was the precursor of the inch. The length of ploughs and of other agricultural implements were also frequently used as early units of measurement. As civilization and trade developed the need for standardization grew. Units were fixed by local tradition or by national rulers, and many different (though sometimes related) systems developed.

THE METRIC SYSTEM

The metric system was adopted in Revolutionary France in 1799 to replace the existing traditional illogical units. It was based upon a natural physical unit to ensure that it should be unchanging. The unit selected was 1/10 000 000 of a quadrant of a great circle of the Earth, measured around the poles of the meridian that passed through Paris. This unit – equivalent to 39.37003 inches in the British Imperial system – was called the metre (from Greek *metron*, 'measure').

Several other metric units are derived from the metre. The gram – the unit of weight – is one cubic centimetre of water at its maximum density, while the litre – the unit of capacity – is one cubic decimetre. Prefixes – from Danish, Latin and Greek – are used for multiples of ten from *atto* ($\times 10^{-18}$) to *exa* ($\times 10^{18}$) – see below.

In 1875 an international conference established the International Bureau of Weights and Measures and founded a permanent laboratory at Sèvres, near Paris, where international standards of the metric units are kept and metrological research is undertaken. The prototype metre was an archive standard rather than an actual measurement upon the ground. In 1983 the metre was redefined as the length of the path travelled by light in vacuum during a time interval of 1/299 792 458 of a second.

The metric system is centred on a small number of *base units*. These relate to the fundamental standards of length, mass and time, together with a few others to extend the system to a wider range of physical measurements, e.g. to electrical and optical quantities. There are also two geometrical units that are sometimes referred to as *supplementary units*. These few base units can be combined to form a large number of *derived units*. For example, units of area, velocity and acceleration are formed from units of length and time. Thus very many different kinds of measurement can be made and recorded employing very few base units.

SI UNITS

A number of systems of units based upon the metric system have been in use. Initially the *cgs system* – based upon the centimetre for length, the gram for mass and the second for time – was widespread. It has, however, largely been replaced by the *mks system* in which the fundamental units are the metre for length, the kilogram for mass and the second for time. The mks system is central to the *Système International d'Unités*, which was adopted by the 11th General Conference on Weights and Measures in 1960. The SI units are now employed for all scientific and most technical purposes, and are in general use for most other purposes in the majority of countries. The SI base units are:

metre the unit of length;

kilogram the unit of mass;

second the unit of time;

ampere the unit of electric current;

kelvin degree of temperature measured on the Kelvin scale;

candela the unit of luminous intensity;

mole the unit of substance.

Details of these and supplementary and derived SI units are given in the tables below.

OTHER SYSTEMS

The most widely used remaining systems of units are the related (British) Imperial System and the US Customary Units. Although the names of most of the units of both systems are the same, the sizes of some of the units differ.

IMPERIAL SYSTEM

The two basic units are the yard (the unit of length) and the pound (the unit of mass). Subdivisions and multiples of these units are traditional in origin and do not follow the logical tenfold stages of the metric system.

The Imperial System is complicated by the existence of three different systems of measurement of weight. The *avoirdupois system* is the most widely used. The *troy system* is used to measure precious metals, while the *apothecaries' system* uses the same units as the troy system but with certain differences of name.

The use of the metric system was legalized in the United Kingdom in 1897. The intention to switch to the metric system 'within ten years' was declared on 24 May 1965 by the President of the Board of Trade, although on 23 March 1976 the Government decided not to proceed with the second reading of the Weights and Measures (Metrication) Act. However, since 1965 the metric system has replaced the Imperial System for many purposes, although loose fruit and vegetables continue to be sold by the pound, the pint and the dram will remain as the unit of capacity for alcohol, and the mile will not be replaced as the standard unit of length over long distances.

US CUSTOMARY UNITS

Some units of the Imperial system have fallen into disuse in North America. The yard, for example, is only encountered in sport. The differences between

English and American units make conversion difficult; for example, a ton in Britain is a unit of mass equivalent to 2240 pounds (or 1016.046 909 kg), while a ton in the USA and Canada is equivalent to 2000 pounds (or 907.184 kg). There are also considerable differences between the English and American gallon, and the English and American bushel.

METRIC UNITS

UNITS OF LENGTH

10 ångström	=	1 nanometre
1000 nanometres	=	1 micrometre
1000 micrometres	=	1 millimetre
10 millimetres	=	1 centimetre
10 centimetres	=	1 decimetre
1000 millimetres	=	1 metre
100 centimetres	=	1 metre
10 decimetres	=	1 metre
10 metres	=	1 dekametre
10 dekametres	=	1 hectometre
10 hectometres	=	1 kilometre
1000 metres	=	1 kilometre
1000 kilometres	=	1 megametre

Nautical

1852 metres	=	1 int. nautical mile

UNITS OF AREA

100 sq millimetres	=	1 sq centimetre
100 sq centimetres	=	1 sq decimetre
100 sq decimetres	=	1 sq metre
100 sq metres	=	1 are
100 ares	=	1 hectare
1000 sq metres	=	1 hectare
100 hectares	=	1 sq kilometre

UNITS OF WEIGHT (MASS)

1000 milligrams	=	1 gram
10 grams	=	1 dekagram
10 dekagrams	=	1 hectogram
10 hectograms	=	1 kilogram
100 kilograms	=	1 quintal
1000 kilograms	=	1 tonne

UNITS OF VOLUME

1000 cu millimetres	=	1 cu centimetre
1000 cu centimetres	=	1 cu decimetre
1000 cu decimetres	=	1 cu metre
1000 cu metres	=	1 cu dekametre

UNITS OF CAPACITY

10 millilitres	=	1 centilitre
10 centilitres	=	1 decilitre
10 decilitres	=	1 litre
1000 millilitres	=	1 litre
1 litre	=	1 cu decimetre
10 litres	=	1 dekalitre
10 dekalitres	=	1 hectolitre
10 hectolitres	=	1 kilolitre
1 kilolitre	=	1 cu metre

THE SI UNITS

BASE UNITS

Quantity	Unit	Symbol	Definition
length	metre	m	the length of a path travelled by light in a vacuum during a time interval of 1/299 792 458 of a second.
mass	kilogram	kg	the mass of the international prototype of the kilogram, which is in the custody of the Bureau International des Poids et Mésures (BIPM) at Sèvres near Paris, France.
time	second	s	the duration of 9 192 631 770 periods of the radiation corresponding to the transition between the two hyperfine levels of the ground state of the caesium-133 atom.
electric current	ampere	A	that constant current which, if maintained in two straight parallel conductors of infinite length of negligible circular cross-section, and placed 1 metre apart in a vacuum, would produce between these conductors a force equal to 2×10^{-7} newtons per metre of length.
thermodynamic temperature	kelvin	K	the fraction 1/273·15 of the thermodynamic temperature of the triple point of water. The triple point of water is the point where water, ice and water vapour are in equilibrium.
luminous intensity	candela	cd	the luminous intensity, in a given direction, of a source that emits monochromatic radiation of frequency 540×10^{12} Hz and has a radiant intensity in that direction of (1/683) watts per steradian.
amount of substance	mole	mol	the amount of substance of a system that contains as many elementary entities as there are atoms in 0·012 kilogram of carbon-12.

SUPPLEMENTARY UNITS

plane angle	radian	rad	the plane angle between two radii of a circle that cut off on the circumference an arc equal in length to the radius.
solid angle	steradian	sr	the solid angle that, having its vertex in the centre of a sphere, cuts off an area of the surface of the sphere equal to that of a square having sides of length equal to the radius of the sphere.

DERIVED UNITS

Quantity	Unit	Symbol	Other SI units
area	square metre	m^2	–
volume	cubic metre	m^3	–
velocity	metre per second	$m \cdot s^{-1}$	–
angular velocity	radian per second	$rad\ s^{-1}$	–
acceleration	metre per second squared	$m \cdot s^{-2}$	–
angular acceleration	radian per second squared	$rad\ s^{-2}$	–
frequency	hertz	Hz	s^{-1}
density	kilogram per cubic metre	$kg \cdot m^{-3}$	–
momentum	kilogram metre per second	$kg \cdot m \cdot s^{-1}$	–
angular momentum	kilogram metre squared per sec.	$kg \cdot m^2 \cdot s^{-1}$	–
moment of inertia	kilogram metre squared	$kg \cdot m^2$	–
force	newton	N	$kg \cdot m \cdot s^{-2}$
pressure, stress	pascal	Pa	$N \cdot m^{-2} = kg \cdot m^{-1} \cdot s^{-2}$
work, energy, quantity of heat	joule	J	$N \cdot m = kg \cdot m^2 \cdot s^{-2}$
power	watt	W	$J \cdot s^{-1} = kg \cdot m^2 \cdot s^{-3}$
surface tension	newton per metre	$N \cdot m^{-1}$	$kg \cdot s^{-2}$
dynamic viscosity	newton second per metre squared	$N \cdot s \cdot m^{-2}$	$kg \cdot m^{-1} \cdot s^{-1}$
kinematic viscosity	metre squared per second	$m^2 \cdot s^{-1}$	
temperature	degree Celsius	°C	–
thermal coefficient of linear expansion	per degree Celsius, or per kelvin	$°C^{-1}, K^{-1}$	–
thermal conductivity	watt per metre degree C	$W \cdot m^{-1} \cdot °C^{-1}$	$kg \cdot m \cdot s^{-3} \cdot °C^{-1}$
heat capacity	joule per kelvin	$J \cdot K^{-1}$	$kg \cdot m^2 \cdot s^{-2} \cdot K^{-1}$
specific heat capacity	joule per kilogram kelvin	$J \cdot kg^{-1} \cdot K^{-1}$	$m^2 \cdot s^{-2} \cdot K^{-1}$
specific latent heat	joule per kilogram	$J\ kg^{-1}$	$m^2 \cdot s^{-2}$
electric charge	coulomb	C	$A \cdot s$
electromotive force, potential difference	volt	V	$W \cdot A^{-1} = kg \cdot m^2 \cdot s^{-3} \cdot A^{-1}$
electric resistance	ohm	Ω	$V \cdot A^{-1} = kg \cdot m^2 \cdot s^{-3} \cdot A^{-2}$
electric conductance	siemens	S	$A \cdot V^{-1} = kg^{-1} \cdot m^{-2} \cdot s^3 \cdot A^2$
electric capacitance	farad	F	$A \cdot s \cdot V^{-1} = kg^{-1} \cdot m^{-2} \cdot s^4 \cdot A^2$
inductance	henry	H	$V \cdot s \cdot A^{-1} = kg \cdot m^2 \cdot s^{-2} \cdot A^{-2}$
magnetic flux	weber	Wb	$V \cdot s = kg \cdot m^2 \cdot s^{-2} \cdot A^{-1}$
magnetic flux density	tesla	T	$Wb \cdot m^{-2} = kg \cdot s^{-2} \cdot A^{-1}$
magnetomotive force	ampere	A	–
luminous flux	lumen	lm	$cd \cdot sr$
illumination	lux	lx	$lm \cdot m^{-2} = cd \cdot sr \cdot m^{-2}$
radiation activity	becquerel	Bq	s^{-1}
radiation absorbed dose	gray	Gy	$J \cdot kg^{-1} = m^2 \cdot s^{-2}$

MULTIPLES AND SUBMULTIPLES

In the metric system the following decimal multiples and sub-multiples are used:

Prefix	Symbol	Value	Factor
yocto- (Latin *octo* = eight)	y	septillionth	$\times 10^{-24}$
zepto- (Latin *septo* = seven)	z	sextillionth	$\times 10^{-21}$
atto- (Danish *atten* = eighteen)	a	quintillionth	$\times 10^{-18}$
femto- (Danish *femtem* = fifteen)	f	quadrillionth	$\times 10^{-15}$
pico- (L. *pico* = minuscule)	p	trillionth	$\times 10^{-12}$
nano- (L. *nanus* = dwarf)	n	thousand millionth part or billionth[1]	$\times 10^{-9}$
micro- (Gk. *mikros* = small)	*m*	millionth part	$\times 10^{-6}$
milli- (L. *mille* = thousand)	m	thousandth part	$\times 10^{-3}$
centi- (L. *centum* = hundred)	c	hundredth part	$\times 10^{-2}$
deci- (L. *decimus* = tenth)	d	tenth part	$\times 10^{-1}$
deka- (Gk. *deka* = ten)	da	tenfold	$\times 10$
hecto- (Gk. *hekaton* = hundred)	h	hundredfold	$\times 10^2$
kilo- (Gk. *chilioi* = thousand)	k	thousandfold	$\times 10^3$
mega- (Gk. *megas* = large)	M	millionfold	$\times 10^6$
giga- (Gk. *gigas* = mighty)	G	thousand millionfold or billionfold	$\times 10^9$
tera- (Gk. *teras* = monster)	T	trillion	$\times 10^{12}$
peta- (Gk. *penta* = five)	P	quadrillion	$\times 10^{15}$
exa- (Gk. *hexa* = six)	E	quintillion	$\times 10^{18}$
zetta- (Latin *septo* = seven)	Z	sextillion	$\times 10^{-21}$
yotta- (Latin *octo* = eight)	Y	septillion	$\times 10^{-24}$

[1] In the UK and Germany it has been customary to advance by increments of one million, and in France and the USA in increments of a thousand. Thus in the UK, one billion was originally defined as one million million; a billion is now increasingly used in the sense of one thousand million in the UK.

THE IMPERIAL SYSTEM

DEFINITION OF UNITS
defined by the Weights and Measures Act, 1963.

yard (yd)   is equal to 0·9144 metre.

pound (lb)   is equal to 0·45359237 kilogram.

gallon (gal)   is the space occupied by 10 pounds weight of distilled water of density 0·998859 gram per millilitre weighed in air of density 0·001217 gram per millilitre against weights of density 8·136 gram per millilitre.

OTHER BASIC UNITS OF LENGTH EMPLOYED

animal stature   the hand = 4 in. *NB* – a horse of, for example, 14 hands 3 in. to the withers is often written 14·3 hands.

surveying   the link = 7·92 in or one hundredth part of a chain.

approximate   the span = 9 in (from the span of the hand).

biblical   the cubit = 18 in.

approximate   the pace = 30 in. (from the stride).

nautical   the cable = 120 fathoms or 240 yd. the fathom = 6 feet.

navigation   the UK nautical mile = 6080 ft (1 second of arc at the Equator).

navigation   the International nautical mile (adopted also by the USA on 1 July 1954) = 6076·1 ft (0·99936 of a UK nautical mile).

METRIC AND IMPERIAL CONVERSIONS

(* = exact)

Column One	Equivalent	Column Two	To convert Col.2 to Col.1 multiply by	To convert Col.1 to Col.2 multiply by
Length				
inch (in)	–	centimetre (cm)	0·393 700 78	2·54*
foot (ft)	12 in	metre	3·280 840	0·3048*
yard (yd)	3 ft	metre	1·093 61	0·9144*
mile	1760 yd	kilometre (km)	0·621 371 1	1·609 344*
fathom	6 ft	metre	0·546 80	1·8288*
chain	22 yd	metre	0·049 70	20·1168*
UK nautical mile	6080 ft	kilometre	0·539 611 8	1·853 184*
International nautical mile	6076·1 ft	kilometre	0·539 956 8	1·852*
ångström unit (Å)	10^{-10} m	nanometre	10	10^{-1}
Area				
square inch	–	square centimetre	0·155 00	6·4516*
square foot	144 sq in	square metre	10·763 9	0·092 903*
square yard	9 sq ft	square metre	1·195 99	0·836 127*
acre	4840 sq yd	hectare (ha) (10^4 m^2)	2·471 05	0·404 686*
square mile	640 acres	square kilometre	0·386 10	2·589 988*
Volume				
cubic inch	–	cubic centimetre	0·061 024	16·387 1*
cubic foot	1728 cu in	cubic metre	35·314 67	0·028 317*
cubic yard	27 cu ft	cubic metre	1·307 95	0·764 555*
Capacity				
litre	100 centilitres	cubic centimetre or millilitre	0·001*	1000*
pint	4 gills	litre	1·759 753	0·568 261
UK gallon	8 pints or 277·4 in^3	litre	0·219 969	4·546 092
barrel (for beer)	36 gallons	hectolitre	0·611 026	1·636 59
US gallon	0·832675 UK gallons	litre or dm^3	0·264 172	3·785 412
US barrel (for petroleum)	42 US gallons	hectolitre	0·628 998	1·589 83
fluid ounce	0·05 pint	millilitre	0·035 195	28·413 074
Velocity				
feet per second (ft/s)	–	metres per second	3·280 840	0·3048
miles per hour (mph)	–	kilometres per hour	0·621 371	1·609 344
UK knot (1·00064 Int knots)	nautical mile/hour	kilometres per hour	0·539 611 8	1·853 184
Acceleration				
foot per second per second (ft/s^2)	–	metres per second per second (m s^{-2})	3·280 840	0·3048*
Mass				
grain (gr)	1/480th of an oz troy	milligram (mg)	0·015 432 4	64·798 91
dram (dr)	27·3438 gr	gram	0·564 383	1·771 85
ounce (avoirdupois)	16 drams	gram	0·035 274 0	28·349 523 125
pound (avoirdupois)	16 ounces	kilogram	2·204 62*	0·453 592 37*
stone	14 pounds	kilogram	0·157 473 04	6·350 293 18*
quarter	28 pounds	kilogram	0·078 737 5	12·700 586 36*
hundredweight (cwt)	112 pounds	kilogram	0·019 684 1	50·802 345 44*
ton (long)	2240 pounds	tonne (= 1000 kg)	0·984 206 5	1·016 046 908 8

Note: A pound troy consists of 12 ounces troy each of 480 grains

Density

pounds per cubic inch	–	grams per cubic centimetre	0·036 127 2	27·6799
pounds per cubic foot	–	kilograms per cubic metre	0·062 428 0	16·0185

Force

dyne (dyn)	10^{-5} newton	newton	10^5	10^{-5}
poundal (pdl)	–	newton	7·233 01	0·138 255
pound-force (lbf)	–	newton	0·224 809	4·448 22
tons-force	–	kilonewton (kN)	0·100 361	9·964 02
kilogram-force (kgf) (or kilopond)	–	newton	0·101 972	9·806 65

Energy (Work, Heat)

erg	10^{-7} joule	joule	10^7	10^{-7}
horse-power (hp) (550 ft/lbf/s)	–	kilowatt (kW)	1·341 02	0·745 700
therm	–	mega joule (MJ)	0·009 478 17	105·506
kilowatt hour (kWh)	–	mega Joule (MJ)	0·277 778	3·6
calorie (international)	–	joule	0·238 846*	4·1868*
British thermal unit (Btu)	–	kilo-joule (kJ)	0·947 817	1·055 06

Pressure, Stress

millibar (mbar or mb)	1000 dynes/cm^2	Pa	0·01*	100*
standard atmosphere (atm)	760 torrs	kPa	0·009 869 2	101·325
pounds per square inch (psi)	–	Pa	0·000 145 038	6894·76
pounds per square inch (psi)	–	kilogram-force per cm^2	14·223 3	0·070 307 0

IMPERIAL UNITS

UNITS OF LENGTH

12 inches	=	1 foot
3 feet	=	1 yard
5½ yards	=	1 rod, pole or perch
4 rods	=	1 chain
10 chains	=	1 furlong
5280 feet	=	1 mile
1760 yards	=	1 mile
8 furlongs	=	1 mile

Nautical

6 feet	=	1 fathom
100 fathoms	=	1 cable length
6080 feet	=	1 nautical mile

UNITS OF AREA

144 sq inches	=	1 sq foot
9 sq feet	=	1 sq yard
304¼ sq yards	=	1 sq rod, pole or perch
40 sq rods	=	1 rood
4 roods	=	1 acre
4840 sq yards	=	1 acre
640 acres	=	1 sq mile

UNITS OF WEIGHT

avoirdupois

437½ grains	=	1 ounce
16 drams	=	1 ounce
16 ounces	=	1 pound
14 pounds	=	1 stone
28 pounds	=	1 quarter
4 quarters	=	1 hundredweight
20 hundredweights	=	1 ton

UNITS OF VOLUME

1728 cu inches	=	1 cu foot
27 cu feet	=	1 cu yard
5·8 cu feet	=	1 bulk barrel

Shipping

1 register ton	=	100 cubic feet

UNITS OF CAPACITY

8 fluid drahms	=	1 fluid ounce
5 fluid ounces	=	1 gill
4 gills	=	1 pint
2 pints	=	1 quart
4 quarts	=	1 gallon
2 gallons	=	1 peck
4 pecks	=	1 bushel
8 bushels	=	1 quarter
36 gallons	=	1 bulk barrel

MISCELLANEOUS UNITS

WATER

1 litre	weighs 1 kilogram
1 cubic metre	weighs 1 tonne
1 UK gallon	weighs 10·022 lb
1 UK gallon salt water	weighs 10·3 lb

SPEED

1 knot	=	1 nautical mph

BEER, WINES AND SPIRITS

Proof spirit contains 57·03% pure alcohol by volume (at 50 °F).

Proof strength in degrees = % of alcohol by volume (at 50 °F) multiplied by 1·7535.

Beer

nip	=	¼ pint
small	=	½ pint
large	=	1 pint
flagon	=	1 quart
anker	=	10 gallons
tun	=	216 gallons

Wines and spirits

tot (whisky)	=	⅙, ⅕, ¼, or ⅓ gill
noggin	=	1 gill
bottle	=	1⅓ pints

Champagne

2 bottles	=	1 magnum
4 bottles	=	1 jeroboam

20 bottles	=	1 nebuchadnezzar

TYPE SIZES

Depth

72¼ points (approx)	=	1 inch
1 didot point	=	0·376 mm

Width

1 pica em	=	12 points

BOOK SIZES

Crown Quarto	=	246 × 189 mm
		7½ × 10 in
Crown Octavo	=	186 × 123 mm
		5 × 7½ in
Demy Quarto	=	276 × 219 mm
		8¾ × 11¼ in
Demy Octavo	=	216 × 138 mm
		5⅝ × 8¾ in
Royal Quarto	=	312 × 237 mm
		10 × 12½ in
Royal Octavo	=	234 × 156 mm
		6¼ × 10 in
A4	=	297 × 210 mm
		8¾ × 11¼ in
A5	=	210 × 148 mm
		5¾ × 9 in

CROPS

UK (imperial) bushel of wheat	=	60 lb
barley	=	50 lb
oats	=	39 lb
rye	=	56 lb
rice	=	45 lb
maize	=	56 lb
linseed	=	52 lb
potatoes	=	60 lb
US bushel: as above except		
barley	=	48 lb
linseed	=	56 lb
oats	=	32 lb
bale (cotton):		
US (net)	=	480 lb
Indian	=	392 lb

UNITS OF ENERGY

1000 British thermal units (Btu)	=	0·293 kW h
100 000 Btu	=	1 therm
1 UK horsepower	=	0·7457 kilowatt

PAPER SIZES

Large post	=	419·1 × 533·4 mm
		16½ × 21 in
Demy	=	444·5 × 571·5 mm
		17½ × 22½ in
Medium	=	457·2 × 584·2 mm
		18 × 23 in
Royal	=	508 × 635 mm
		20 × 25 in
Double crown	=	508 × 762 mm
		20 × 30 in
'A' Series (metric sizes)		
A0	=	841 × 1189 mm
		33⅛ × 46¾ in
A1	=	594 × 841 mm
		23⅜ × 33⅛ in
A2	=	420 × 594 mm
		16½ × 23⅜ in
A3	=	297 × 420 mm

		11¾ × 16½ in
A4	=	210 × 297 mm
		8¼ × 11¾ in
A5	=	148 × 210 mm
		5⅞ × 8¼ in

PETROLEUM

1 barrel	=	42 US gallons
	=	34·97 UK gallons
	=	0·159 cubic metre

PRECIOUS METALS

24 carat implies pure metal

1 metric carat	=	200 milligrams
1 troy (fine) ounce	=	480 grains

PAPER QUANTITIES

In the UK, paper is traditionally bought in the following measures:

Writing paper

480 sheets = 1 ream; 24 sheets = 1 quire; 20 quires = 1 ream

Printing paper

516 sheets = 1 ream; 2 reams = 1 bundle; 5 bundles = 1 bale

INTERNATIONAL CLOTHING SIZES

The tables below should be used as approximate guides as actual sizes may vary according to manufacturers. *It is wise to check all measurements in centimetres.*

Ladies' coats and jackets

UK	8/	10/	12/		14/	16/	18/
	30	32	34		36	38	40
USA	6	8	10		12	14	16
Germany/ Netherlands	34	36	38		40	42	44
Italy/ Scandinavia	36	38	40		42	44	46
Spain	40	42	44		46	48	50
France/ Belgium	38/	40/	42/		44/	46/	48/
Japan	7	9	11		13	15	17

Men's suits and overcoats use the same sizes (46 to 56) in the above countries (except Japan).

Men's shirts

EC	36	37	38		39	40	41
UK/ USA	14	14½	15		15½	16	16½

Ladies' shoes

UK	3	4	5		6	7
USA	6½	7½	8½		9½	10½
EC	36	37	38		39	40
Japan	22	23	24		25	25½

Men's shoes

UK	6	7	8		9	10
USA	6½	7½	8½		9½	10½
Europe except Scandinavia	39	40	41		42	43
Scandinavia	40	41	42		43	44

PHYSICS

MOTION AND FORCE

Physics is the study of the basic laws that govern matter. *Mechanics* is the branch of physics that describes the movement or motion of objects, ranging in scale from a planet to the smallest particle within an atom. Sir Isaac Newton developed a theory of mechanics that has proved highly successful in describing most types of motion, and his work has been acclaimed as one of the greatest advances in the history of science. The Newtonian approach, although valid for velocities and dimensions within normal experience, has shown to fail for velocities approaching the speed of light and for dimensions on a subatomic scale. Newton's discoveries are therefore considered to be a special case within a more general theory.

MOTION

When a body is in *motion* it can be thought of as moving in space and time. If a body moves from one position to another, the straight line joining its starting point to its finishing point is its *displacement*. This has both magnitude and direction, and is therefore said to be a *vector quantity*. The motion is *linear*. The rate at which a body moves, in a straight line or *rectilinearly*, is its *velocity*. Again, this has magnitude and direction and is a vector quantity. In contrast, the *speed*, which has magnitude, but is not considered to be in any particular direction, is a *scalar quantity*. The *average velocity* of the body during this rectilinear motion is defined by the total time taken. Its dimensions are therefore length divided by time, and are given in metres per second ($m\ s^{-1}$). The *instantaneous velocity* (the velocity at any instant) at any point is the rate of change of displacement at that point.

If the body moves with a changing velocity, then the rate of change of the velocity is an *acceleration*. This is defined as the change in velocity in a given time interval. Its dimensions are velocity divided by time, and are given in metres per second per second ($m\ s^{-2}$). When a body moves with uniform acceleration (uniformly accelerated motion), the displacement, velocity and acceleration are related. These relationships are described in the *kinematic equations*, sometimes called the *laws of uniformly accelerated motion*. *Kinematics* is the study of bodies in motion, ignoring masses and forces.

The Italian physicist and astronomer Galileo Galilei (1564–1642) investigated the motion of objects falling freely in air. He believed that all objects falling freely towards the Earth have the same downward acceleration. This is called the *acceleration due to gravity* or the *gravitational acceleration*. Near the surface of the Earth it is $9.80\ m\ s^{-2}$, but there are small variations in its value depending upon latitude and elevation. When real motion is considered, both the magnitude and the direction of the velocity have to be investigated. A golf ball, hit upwards, will return to ground. During flight its velocity will change in both magnitude and direction. In this case, instead of average velocity, the *instantaneous velocities* have to be evaluated.

CIRCULAR MOTION

If a body moves in a circular path at constant speed its direction of motion (and therefore its velocity) will be changing continuously. Since the velocity is changing, the body must have acceleration, which is also changing continuously. Thus the laws of uniformly accelerated motion do not apply. The acceleration of a body moving in a circular path is called the *centripetal* ('centre-seeking') *acceleration*. This is directed inwards, towards the centre of the circle.

NEWTON'S LAWS OF MOTION

Newton's laws of motion state relationships between the acceleration of a body and the forces acting on it. A *force* is something that causes a change in the acceleration of an object.

Newton's first law: *A body will remain at rest or travelling in a straight line at constant speed unless it is acted upon by an external force.*

The force has to be an external one – in general, a body does not exert a force upon itself. The tendency of a body to remain at rest or moving with constant velocity is called the *inertia* of the body. The inertia is related to the *mass*, which is the amount of substance in the body. The unit of mass is the *kilogram* (kg).

Newton's second law: *The resultant force exerted on a body is directly proportional to the acceleration produced by the force.*

$$F = ma$$
$$F = mv_2 - mv_1$$

where F is the force exerted
  m is the mass of the body
  a is the acceleration
  v_1 is the initial velocity
  v_2 is the final velocity

The unit of force is the *newton* (N), which is defined as the force that, acting on a body of mass 1 kg, produces an acceleration on $1\ m\ s^{-2}$. The mass of a body is often confused with its weight. Mass is the amount of matter in the body, whereas the *weight* is the gravitational force acting on the body, and varies with location. Thus a body will have the same mass on the Moon as on Earth, but its weight on the Moon will be less than on Earth because the gravitational force on the Moon is approximately one sixth of that on Earth. Newton expressed his second law by stating that the force acting on a body is equal to the rate of change in its 'quantity of motion', which is now called *momentum*. The momentum of a body is defined as the product of its mass and velocity.

Newton's third law: *To every action there is an equal and opposite reaction.*

This law states that a single isolated force cannot exist on its own: there is always a resulting 'mirror-image' force. This means that, because any two masses exert on each other a mutual gravitational attraction, the Earth is always attracted towards a ball as much as the ball is attracted towards the Earth. Because of the huge difference in their sizes, however, the observable result is the downward acceleration of the ball. The *principle of the conservation of momentum* follows from this third law. This states that, when two bodies interact, the total momentum before impact is the same as the total momentum after impact. Thus the total of the components of the momentum in any direction before and after the interaction are equal.

GRAVITATION

Gravitational force is one of the four fundamental forces that occur in nature. The others are the electromagnetic force, the strong nuclear force, and the weak nuclear force. The electromagnetic and weak forces have recently been shown to be a part of an electro-weak force. Gravitational force is the mutual force of attraction between masses. The gravitational force is much weaker than the other forces mentioned above. However, this long-range force should not be thought of as a weak force. An object resting on a table is acted on by the gravitational force of the whole Earth – a significant force. The almost equal force exerted by the table is the result of short-range forces exerted by molecules on its surface.

NEWTON'S LAW OF GRAVITATION

Newton's law of gravitation states:

Every particle in the universe attracts every other particle with a force that is directly proportional to the product of their masses and inversely proportional to the square of the distance between them.

$F = G$ multiplied by $m_1 m_2$ divided by x^2

where F is the force
G is the gravitational constant
$m_1 m_2$ are the masses
x is the distance between the particles

Newton's law of gravitation was first described in his *Philosophiae Naturalis Principia Mathematica* ('The Mathematical Principles of Natural Philosophy'), which he wrote in 1687. Newton used the notion of a *particle*, by which he meant a body so small that its dimensions are negligible compared to other distances. The law is an 'inverse-square law', since the magnitude of the force is inversely proportional to the square of the distance between two masses.

FORCES OF NATURE

Force	Range	Quanta	Mass (GeV)	Spin	Notes
gravity	very long	graviton	0 ?	2	acts on all matter, weak within the atom
weak	less than 10^{-16} cm	charged $W^{\pm}$	80.5	1	acts on all the basic particles, leptons and quarks, involved in radioactive processes
		neutral Z^0	91.1	1	
electromagnetic	very long	photon (γ)	0	1	acts on all charged particles; provides the basis to the reactions of chemistry and hence biology
strong	less than 10^{-13} cm	Gluon (g)	0 ?	1	acts on the quarks allowing them free movement within the hadrons, i.e. the mesons and baryons, but confines them within these particles

THE FUNDAMENTAL PHYSICAL CONSTANTS

Quantity	Symbol	Value	Units
General Constants	speed of light in vacuo	c	$2\cdot99792458 \times 10^8$	$\text{m}\cdot\text{s}^{-1}$
	elementary charge	e	$1\cdot60217733(49) \times 10^{-19}$	C
	Planck constant	h	$6\cdot6260755(40) \times 10^{-34}$	J·s
	gravitational constant	G	$6\cdot67259(85) \times 10^{-11}$	$\text{m}^3\cdot\text{s}^{-2}\cdot\text{kg}^{-1}$
Matter in Bulk	Avogadro constant	N_A	$6\cdot0221367(36) \times 10^{23}$	mol^{-1}
	atomic mass constant	m_u	$1\cdot6605402(10) \times 10^{-27}$	kg
			$9\cdot3149432(28) \times 10^2$	MeV
	Faraday constant	$F = N_A e$	$9\cdot6485309(29) \times 10^4$	$\text{C}\cdot\text{mol}^{-1}$
	molar gas constant	R	$8\cdot314510(70)$	$\text{J}\cdot\text{mol}^{-1}\cdot\text{K}^{-1}$
			$8\cdot205783(70) \times 10^{-5}$	$\text{m}^3\cdot\text{atm}\cdot\text{mol}^{-1}\cdot\text{K}^{-1}$
	molar volume of ideal gas (at 273·15K and 1 atm)	V_m	$2\cdot241410(19) \times 10^{-2}$	$\text{m}^3\cdot\text{mol}^{-1}$
	Boltzmann constant	$k = R/N_A$	$1\cdot380658(12) \times 10^{-23}$	$\text{J}\cdot\text{K}^{-1}$
Electron	electron rest mass	m_e	$9\cdot1093897(54) \times 10^{-31}$	kg
			$0\cdot51099906(15)$	MeV
	electron specific charge	e/m_e	$1\cdot75881962(53) \times 10^{11}$	$\text{C}\cdot\text{kg}^{-1}$
Proton	proton rest mass	m_p	$1\cdot6726231(10) \times 10^{-27}$	kg
			$9\cdot3827231(28) \times 10^2$	MeV
Neutron	neutron rest mass	m_n	$1\cdot6749286(10) \times 10^{-27}$	kg
			$9\cdot3956563(28) \times 10^2$	MeV
Energy Conversion	million electron volt unit	MeV	$1\cdot78266270(54) \times 10^{-30}$	kg
			$1\cdot60217733(49) \times 10^{-13}$	J

The constants (see p. 203) are called 'fundamental' since they are used universally throughout all branches of science. Increasing experimental accuracy as well as advances in theory require a complete revision of the constants during each decade, the last revision being carried out in 1986. In the values recorded in the accompanying table the figures in brackets following the last digits are estimated uncertainties of those digits. Note that the speed of light is now exactly defined.

WAVE THEORY

Water waves are a phenomenon that can be seen, and the effects of sound waves are sensed directly by the ear. Some of the waves in the electromagnetic spectrum (see below) can also be sensed by the body: light waves by the eye, and the heating effect of infrared by the skin. There are other electromagnetic waves, however, that cannot be experienced directly through any of the human senses, and even infrared can generally only be observed using specialized detectors.

Wave phenomena are found in all areas of physics, and similar mathematical equations are used in each application. Some of the general principles of wave motions are explored here.

WAVE TYPES AND CHARACTERISTICS

A *travelling wave* is a disturbance that moves or *propagates* from one point to another. *Mechanical waves* are travelling waves that propagate through a material – as, for example, happens when a metal rod is tapped at one end with a hammer. An initial disturbance at a particular place in a material will cause a force to be exerted on adjacent parts of the material. An *elastic force* then acts to restore the material to its equilibrium position. In so doing, it compresses the adjacent particles and so the disturbance moves outward from the source. In attempting to return to their original positions, the particles overshoot, so that at a particular point a *rarefaction* (or stretching) follows a *compression* (or squeezing). The passage of the wave is observed as variations in the pressure about the equilibrium position or by the speed of oscillations. This change is described as *oscillatory* (like a pendulum) or *periodic*.

There are two main types of periodic oscillation – *tranverse* or *longitudinal*.

Transverse waves In transverse waves the vibrations are perpendicular to the direction of travel.

Longitudinal waves In longitudinal waves the vibrations are parallel to the direction of travel.

Sound waves Sound waves are alternate compressions and rarefactions of whatever material through which they are travelling, and the waves are longitudinal.

Water waves Water waves may be produced by the wind or some other disturbance. The particles move in vertical circles so there are both transverse and longitudinal displacements. The motion causes the familiar wave profile with narrow peaks and broad troughs.

Wave motions transfer energy – for example, sound waves, seismic waves and water waves transfer mechanical energy. However, energy is lost as the *amplitude* – the maximum displacement from the equilibrium position – diminishes, and the wave is said to be *attenuated*. There are two distinct processes – *spreading* and *absorption*. In many cases there is little or no absorption – electromagnetic radiation from the Sun travels through space without any absorption at all, but planets that are more distant than the Earth receive less radiation because it is spreading over a larger area and so the *intensity* (the ratio of power to area) decreases according to an inverse-square law.

The same applies to sound in the atmosphere. In some cases, however, energy is absorbed in a medium, as, for example, when light enters and exposes a photographic film, or when X-rays enter flesh. For homogeneous radiation, absorption is *exponential*; for example, if half the radiation goes through 1 mm of absorber, a quarter would go through 2 mm and an eighth through 3 mm.

The *frequency* (*f*) of the wave motion is defined as the number of complete oscillations or cycles per second. The unit of frequency is the *hertz* (Hz), named after the German physicist Heinrich Rudolf Hertz: 1 hertz = 1 cycle per second. The *wavelength* is the distance between two successive peaks or troughs in the wave. The *speed of propagation* of the compressions, or *phase speed* of the wave, is equal to the product of frequency and the wavelength.

Waves originating from a point source will propagate outwards, in all directions, forming *wavefronts*; these wavefronts will be circular or spherical if propagating through a homogeneous medium.

REFLECTION AND REFRACTION

If a wave travels from one medium to another, the direction of propagation is changed or 'bent'; the wave is said to be *refracted*. The wave will travel in the first medium with velocity v_1, and will come upon the surface of the second medium with the angle of incidence *i*. The wave will then be refracted – *r* representing the angle of refraction. The new velocity – v_2 – will be less than velocity v_1 if the second medium is more dense than the first medium, but greater than v_1 if the second medium is less dense. The velocities are related by:
$v_1/v_2 = \sin i/\sin r$. The ratio sin *i*/*sin* r is a constant. This relationship was formulated by the Dutch astronomer Willebrord Snell (1591–1626) and is known as *Snell's Law*.

INTERFERENCE

If several waves are travelling through a medium, the resultant at any point and time is the vector sum of the amplitudes of the individual waves. This is known as the *superposition principle*. Two or more waves combining together in this way exhibit the phenomenon of *interference*. If the resultant wave amplitude is greater than those of the individual waves then *constructive interference* is taking place; if it is less, *destructive interference* occurs. If two sound waves of slightly different frequencies and equal amplitudes are played together then the resulting sound has what is called *varying amplitude*.

AMPLITUDE AND FREQUENCY MODULATION

Radio waves can be used to carry sound waves by superimposing the pattern of the sound waves onto the radio wave. This is called *modulation*, and is one of the basic forms of radio transmission. There are two ways of modulating radio waves. In *amplitude modulation* (AM) the amplitude of the radio *carrier wave* is made to vary with the amplitude of the sound signal. For *frequency modulation* (FM) the frequency of the carrier wave is made to vary so that the variations are in step with the changes in amplitude of the sound signal.

STANDING OR STATIONARY WAVES

These are the result of confining waves in a specific region. When a travelling wave, such as a wave propagating along a guitar string towards the bridge, reaches the support, the string must be almost at rest. A force is exerted on the support that then reacts by setting up a reflected wave travelling back along the string. This wave has the same frequency and wavelength as the source wave. At certain frequencies the two waves, travelling in opposite directions, interfere to produce a stationary- or standing-wave pattern. Each pattern or mode of vibration corresponds to a particular frequency.

DIFFRACTION

Waves will usually proceed in a straight line through a uniform medium. However, when they pass through a slit with width comparable to their wavelength, they spread out, i.e. they are diffracted. Thus waves are able to bend round corners.

Huygens' principle was proposed in 1676 by the Dutch physicist Christiaan Huygens (1629–95) to explain the laws of reflection and refraction. He postulated that light was a wave motion. Each point on a wavefront becomes a new or secondary source. Diffraction describes the interference effects observed between light derived from a continuous portion of a wavefront.

STATICS, FRICTION AND ELASTICITY

In addition to the fundamental forces (described above), other forces such as frictional, elastic and viscous forces may be encountered. Because of their different natures, solids and fluids appear in some ways to react differently to similar applied forces.

Solids: When forces are applied to solids they tend to resist. Friction inhibits displacement, but is overcome after a certain limit. Bodies may be deformed by tensions.

Fluids: Fluids, although lacking definite shape, are held together by internal forces. They exert pressure on the walls of the containing vessel. Fluids – by definition – have a tendency to flow; this may be greater in some substances than in others and is governed by the viscosity of the fluid.

STATIC EQUILIBRIUM

Newton's first law (see above), stated for a single particle, can also apply to real bodies that have definite sizes and shapes and consist of many particles. Such a body may be in *equilibrium*, which means it is at rest or moving with constant velocity in a straight line. This means that it is acted on by *zero net force*, and that it has no tendency to rotate.

A body is acted on by zero force if the total or resultant of all the forces acting on it is zero – i.e. all the forces cancel each other out. If a body is at rest it is in *static equilibrium*. Studies of such conditions are important in the design of bridges, dams and buildings.

FORCES INVOLVED IN ROTATION

Torque (or *moment of a force*) measures the tendency of a force to cause the body to rotate. In this case the force causes *angular acceleration*, which is the *rate of change of angular momentum* of the body. Torque is defined as the product of the force acting on a body and the perpendicular distance from the axis of the rotation of the body to the line of action of the force. Torque has units of force × distance, usually expressed as *newton metres* (N m).

Torque: *Torque or moment of a force = force × perpendicular distance = Fd.*

Torque is increased if either the force or the perpendicular distance is increased. If a wedge is used to keep open a door, it has maximum effect if it is placed on the floor as far from the hinge as possible.

When a body is acted upon by two equal and opposite forces, not in the same line, then the result is a *couple*, which has a constant turning moment about any axis perpendicular to the plane in which they act. When the total or net torque on a body is zero about any axis, the body is in *equilibrium*. A body is in stable equilibrium if a small linear displacement causes a force to act on the body to return it to its previous position, or an angular displacement causes a couple to act to bring it back to its previous position, called the *equilibrium position*.

CENTRE OF MASS

The *centre of mass* of a body is a point, normally within the body, such that the net resultant force produces an acceleration at this point, as though all the mass of the body were concentrated there. For bodies of certain shapes this point may lie outside the object.

If a uniform gravitational field is present, the centre of gravity coincides with the centre of mass. Thus all the weight can be considered to act at this single point. The stability of an object is helped by keeping the centre of gravity as low as possible, thus a racing car is low-slung to improve stability.

FRICTION

Sliding friction occurs when a solid body slides on a rough surface. Its progress is hindered by an interaction of the surface of the solid with the surface it is moving on. This is called *kinetic frictional force*.

Another type of friction is called *static friction*. Before the object moves, the resultant force acting on it must be zero. The frictional force acting between the object and the surface on which it rests cannot exceed its limiting value. Thus, when the other forces acting on the object, against friction, exceed this value the object is caused to accelerate. The limiting or maximum value of the frictional force occurs when the stationary object acted on by the resultant force is just about to slip.

Both these types of friction involve interaction with a solid surface. The frictional forces depend on the two contacting surfaces and in particular on the presence of any surface contaminants. The friction between metal surfaces is largely due to adhesion, shearing and deformation within and around the regions of real contact. Energy is dissipated in friction and appears as internal energy, which can be observed as heat – thus car brakes heat up when used to slow a vehicle. The results of friction may be reduced by the use of lubricants between the surfaces in contact. This is one of the functions of the oil used in car engines.

A further type of friction is *rolling friction*, which occurs when a wheel rolls. Energy is dissipated through the system, because of imperfect elasticity (see below). This effect does not depend upon surfaces and is unaffected by lubrication.

ELASTICITY

Elasticity deals with deformations that disappear when the external applied forces are removed. Most bodies may be deformed by the action of external forces and behave elastically for small deformations.

Strain is a measure of the amount of deformation. *Stress* is a quantity proportional to the force causing the deformation. Its value at any point is given by the magnitude of the force acting at that point divided by the area over which it acts.

It is found that for small stresses the stress is proportional to the strain. The constant of proportionality is called the *elastic modulus* and it varies according to the material and the type of deformation.

Young's modulus refers to changes in the length of a material under the action of an applied force.

The shear modulus relates to another type of deformation – that of planes in a solid sliding past each other.

The bulk modulus characterizes the behaviour of a substance subject to a uniform volume comparison.

HOOKE'S LAW

A special example of deformation is the extension or elongation of a spring by an applied force. *Hooke's law*, formulated by the English scientist Robert Hooke (1635–1703), states that, for small forces, the extension is proportional to the applied force. Thus a spring balance will have a uniform scale for the measurement of various weights.

In scientific terms, steel spring – which returns to its initial state readily – is almost *perfectly elastic*. In contrast, a soft rubber ball dropped on hard ground bounces to only about half its initial height, demonstrating *imperfect elasticity*.

VISCOSITY

Some bodies behave elastically for low values of stress, but above a critical level they behave in a perfectly viscous manner and 'flow' like thick treacle, with irreversible deformation. This is called *plastic flow*.

Viscosity relates to the internal friction in the flow of a fluid – how adjacent layers in the fluid exert retarding forces on each other. This arises from cohesion of the molecules in the fluid. In a solid, the deformation of adjacent layers is usually elastic. In a fluid, however, there is no permanent resistance to change of shape; the layers can slide past each other, with continuous displacement of these layers.

Fluids are described as *newtonian* if they obey Newton's law that the ratio of the applied stress to the rate of shearing has a constant value. This is not true for many substances. Some paints, for example, do not have constant values for the coefficient of viscosity; as the paint is stirred it flows more easily and the coefficient is diminished. Molten lava is another non-newtonian fluid.

If adjacent layers flow smoothly past each other the steady flow is described as *laminar flow*. If the flow velocity is increased the flow may become disordered with irregular and random motions called *turbulence*. Smoke rising from a cigarette starts with smooth laminar flow but soon breaks into turbulent flow with the formation of eddies. *Reynold's number* is used to predict the onset of turbulence. It is defined as:

Re = (speed × density × dimension) divided by viscosity

or, alternatively, as the ratio is the inertial force to the viscous force:

Re = inertial force divided by the viscous force

This is a pure ratio as it has no units. It is a characteristic of the system and the dimension may be the diameter of a pipe or the radius of a ballbearing. Viscosity is relevant for small values of Reynold's number. Above a certain value, turbulence is likely to break out. Thus, for the fall of a very small raindrop, resistance is viscous and is proportional to the product of the density of air, the radius of the raindrop and its speed. For a large raindrop, the resistance is proportional to the product of the density of air, the square of the radius of the raindrop and the square of its speed.

FLUIDS AT REST

Pressure is defined as the perpendicular or normal force per unit area of a plane surface of a fluid, and its unit is the *pascal* (Pa), equivalent to 1 newton per square metre (N m²). At all points in the fluid the depth of pressure is the same. The pressure depends only on depth in an enclosed fluid, and is independent of cross-sectional area.

Atmospheric pressure may be measured using a barometer. At sea level, it is equivalent to the weight of a column of mercury about 0.76 m high, which is about 1.01×10^5 Pa. It varies by up to about 5%, depending on the weather systems passing overhead.

ARCHIMEDES' PRINCIPLE

The *buoyancy force* was described by the Greek mathematician and physicist Archimedes (287–212 BC). *Archimedes' principle* states that an object placed in a fluid is buoyed up by a force equal to the weight of fluid displaced by the body.

A body with density greater than that of the fluid will sink, because the fluid it displaces weighs less than it does itself. A body with density less than that of the fluid will float.

mass divided by volume = density

A submarine varies its density by flooding ballast tanks with sea water or emptying them; this enables it to dive or rise to the surface.

SURFACE TENSION

Surface tension occurs at an interface between a liquid and either a gas or a solid. Molecules in a liquid exert forces on other molecules. At the surface there is asymmetry in these forces, resulting in surface tension. Thus falling rainwater coalesces into spherical drops.

THERMODYNAMICS

Thermodynamics is the study of heat and temperature. *Heat* is a form of energy, and the *temperature* of a substance is a measure of its internal energy. One fundamental principle in the study of thermodynamics is the *conservation of energy*. This theory was developed in the late 19th century by about a dozen scientists, including James Joule (1818–89), a brewery-owner from the north of England, and Baron Herman von Helmholtz (1821–94), a German physiologist. Although there seemed to be plenty of evidence in the world that energy was not conserved, this important principle was eventually established.

Much of the energy that seems to be lost in typical interactions – such as a box sliding across a floor – is converted into internal energy: in the case of the sliding box, this is the kinetic energy (see below) gained by the atoms and molecules within the box and the floor as they interact and are pulled from their equilibrium positions. The name given to the energy in the form of hidden motion of atoms and molecules is *thermal energy*. Strictly speaking, heat is transferred between two bodies as a result of a change in temperature, although the term 'heat' is commonly used for the thermal energy as well. Processes that turn kinetic energy, which is the organized energy of a moving body, into thermal energy, which is the disorganized energy due to the motion of atoms, include friction and viscosity.

WORK AND ENERGY

When a force (see above) acts on a body, causing acceleration in the direction of the force, *work* is done. The work done on a body by a constant force is defined as the product of the magnitude of the force and the consequent displacement of the body in the direction of the force.

The units used to measure work are *joules* (sometimes referred to as *newton metres*). A joule (J) is defined as the work done on a body when it is displaced 1 metre as the result of the action of a force of 1 newton acting in the direction of motion.

$1 \text{ J} = 1 \text{ N m}$

Energy is the capacity of a body to do work. The total energy stored in a *closed system* – one in which no external forces are experienced – remains constant, however it may be transformed. This is the principle of *conservation of energy*. It may take the form of:

mechanical energy (kinetic or potential; see below);
electrical energy;
chemical energy; or
heat energy.

There are other forms of energy including;
gravitational energy;
magnetism;
the energy of electromagnetic radiation; and
the energy of matter.

KINETIC ENERGY

The *kinetic energy* of a body is the energy it has because it is moving. Kinetic energy is equal to half the product of the mass and the square of the velocity – thus the kinetic energy of a body mass m moving at velocity v is $\frac{1}{2}mv^2$.

POTENTIAL ENERGY

As well as kinetic energy, which is energy of motion, a body can have *potential energy*. In contrast to the kinetic energy, which is dependent upon velocity, potential energy is dependent upon position.

The gravitational potential energy of a body of mass m at a height h above the ground is mgh, where g is the acceleration due to gravity.

This gravitational potential energy is equal to the work that the Earth's gravitational field will do on

the body as it moves to ground level. Potential energy can be converted into kinetic energy or it can be used to do work. It acts as a store of energy. If a body moves upward against the gravitational force, work is done on it and there is an increase in gravitational potential energy.

TEMPERATURE

Temperature is a measure of the internal energy or 'hotness' of a body, not the heat of the body. Thermometers are used to measure temperature. They may be based on:

the change in *volume* of a liquid (as in a mercury thermometer);
the change in *length* of a strip of metal (as used in many thermometers); or
the change in *electrical resistance* of a conductor.

Other parameters may also be involved in measuring temperature.

The *thermodynamic temperature scale* – also known as the *kelvin scale* or the *ideal gas scale* – is based on a unit called the *kelvin* (K); the scale is used in both practical and theoretical physics. An *ideal gas* is one that would obey all the gas laws (see below) perfectly. In fact no gas is ideal, but most behave sufficiently closely that the gas laws can be used in calculations. At ordinary temperatures and pressures, dry air can be considered as a very good approximation to an ideal gas.

GAS LAWS

The *ideal gas law* combines *Boyle's law* with *Charles's law*. It states that gas at low pressure (p_1) multiplied by high volume (V_1) divided by low temperature (T_1) = higher pressure (p_2) multiplied by decreased volume (V_2) divided by higher temperature (T_2).

On the Kelvin scale the freezing point of water is 273.15 K (0 °C or 32 °F) and its boiling point is 373.15 K (100 °C or 212 °F): one degree kelvin is equal in magnitude to one degree on the Celsius scale. The temperature of 0 (zero) K is known as *absolute zero*. At absolute zero (-273.15°C), for an ideal gas, the volume would be infinitely large and the pressure zero.

HEAT AND INTERNAL ENERGY

The molecular energy (kinetic and potential) within a body is called *internal energy*. When this energy is transferred from a place of high energy to one of lower energy, it is described as a flow of heat.

If two bodies of different temperatures are placed in thermal contact with each other, after a time they are found both to be at the same temperature. Energy is transferred from the warmer to the colder body, until both are at a new *equilibrium temperature*. Heat is a form of energy, and heat flow is a transfer of energy resulting from differences in temperature.

The unit of internal energy and heat is the *joule*, as defined above. Units used previously include the *calorie*, which is equivalent to 4.2 joules and is defined as the heat required to raise the temperature of 1 gram of water from 14.5 °C to 15.5 °C. (The unit used by nutritionists is referred to as the calorie but is actually the *kilocalorie*, which is equal to 1000 calories, and is equivalent to 4200 joules.)

THE KINETIC THEORY OF GASES

The kinetic theory of gases takes Newton's laws (see above) and applies them statistically to a group of molecules. It treats a gas as if it were made up of extremely small – dimensionless – particles, all in constant random movement. It is based on an ideal gas.

One conclusion is that the pressure and volume of such a gas are related to the average kinetic energy for each molecule. The kinetic theory explains that pressure in a gas is due to the impact of the molecules on the containing walls around the gas.

The temperature of an ideal gas is a measure of the average molecular kinetic energies. At a higher temperature the mean speed of the molecules is increased. For air at room temperature and atmospheric pressures the mean speed is about 500 m s^{-1} (about 1800 km/h or 1100 mph, the velocity of a rifle bullet).

The internal energy of a gas is associated with the motion of its molecules and their potential energy. For a gas that is more complex than one with monatomic molecules, account has to be taken of energies associated with the rotation and vibration of its molecules, as well as their speed.

A *thermally isolated system* is one that neither receives nor transmits transfer of heat, although the temperature within the system may vary. Such a system is called *adiabatic.* One in which the temperature remains constant is an *isothermic* system.

If mechanical or electrical work is performed on a thermally isolated system, its internal energy increases. James Joule observed the effects of doing measured amounts of work on insulated bodies (thermally isolated systems). He discovered an equivalence relation between the amount of work done *(W)* and the heat gained *(Q)*:

$$W = JQ$$

The constant *J* was described by Joule as the *mechanical equivalent of heat.*

LAWS OF THERMODYNAMICS

The first law of thermodynamics is a development of the law of conservation of energy, which states that in any interaction, energy is neither created nor destroyed. If, during an interaction, a quantity of heat (*Q*) is absorbed by a body, it is equal to the sum of the increase in internal energy *U* of the body and any external work *W* done by the body:

$$Q = U + W$$

The increase in internal energy will be made up of an increase in the kinetic energy of the molecules in the body and an increase in their potential energy, since work will have been done against intermolecular forces as the body expands.

The change in internal energy of a body thus depends only on its initial and final states. The change may be the result of an increase in energy in any form – thermal, mechanical, gravitational, etc. Another statement of this law is that it is possible to convert work totally into heat.

The second law of thermodynamics states that the converse is not true. There are several ways in which the second law may be stated but, essentially, it means that heat cannot itself flow from a cold object to a hot object. Thus the law shows that certain processes may only operate in one direction.

ENTROPY

Entropy is a parameter used in statistical mechanics to describe the disorder or *chaos* of a system. A highly disordered state is one in which molecules move haphazardly in all directions, with many different velocities. An alternative form of the second law of thermodynamics is that the entropy of the universe never decreases. It follows from this analysis that the universe is moving through increasing disorder towards thermal equilibrium. Therefore the universe cannot have existed for ever, otherwise it would have reached this equilibrium state already.

LATENT HEAT

When heat flows between a body and its surroundings there is usually a change in the temperature of the body, as well as changes in internal energies. This is not so when a change of form occurs, as from solid to liquid or from liquid to gas. This is called a *phase change* and involves a change in the internal energy of the body only.

The amount of heat needed to make the change of phase is called the *hidden* or *latent heat.* To change water at 100 °C to water vapour requires nearly seven times as much heat (*latent heat of vaporization*) as to change ice to water (*latent heat of fusion*). This varies for water at different temperatures – more heat is required to change it to water vapour at 80 °C, less at 110 °C. In each case the attractive forces binding the water molecules together must be loosened or broken. The transfer of water vapour through the Earth's atmosphere towards the poles from equatorial regions is an effective way of transferring energy. When water turns into water vapour the latent heat of vaporization is absorbed and the atmosphere cools; when the vapour turns to rain and is deposited, the latent heat is given out to the atmosphere. A similar cycle takes place in a heat pump or refrigerator.

HEAT TRANSFER

Heat conduction occurs when kinetic and molecular energy is passed from one molecule to another. Metals are good conductors of heat because of electrons that transport energy through the material. Air is a poor conductor in comparison. Thus a string vest keeps its wearer warm by trapping air and so preventing the conduction of heat outwards from the body.

Heat convection results from the motion of the heated substance. Warm air is less dense than cold air and so, according to Archimedes' principle, rises. Convection is the main mechanism for mixing the atmosphere and diluting pollutants emitted into the air.

Radiation is the third process for heat transfer. All bodies radiate energy in the form of electromagnetic waves. This radiation may pass across a vacuum, and thus the Earth receives energy radiated from the Sun. A body remains at a constant temperature when it both radiates and receives energy at the same rate. This principle is used in the construction of the Thermos flask.

QUANTUM THEORY AND RELATIVITY

Three of the most important theories of the 20th century are the quantum theory and the theories of special and general relativity. When special relativity is combined with the full quantum theory and with electromagnetism, almost all of the physical world is described by it. The most important application is in the theory of subatomic particles. General relativity is as yet not fully combined with quantum theory and is a theory of gravity and cosmology.

The physical world is not as simple as the theories of Newton supposed, although such views are appropriate simplifications for large objects moving relatively slowly with respect to the observer. *Quantum mechanics* is the only correct description of effects on an atomic scale, and special relativity must be used when speeds approaching the speed of light, with respect to the observer, are involved.

THE DEVELOPMENT OF QUANTUM THEORY

At the very beginning of the 20th century scientists such as the German physicist Max Planck (1858–1947) discovered that the theories of classical physics were not sufficient to explain certain phenomena on the subatomic scale, particularly in the field of electromagnetic radiation and the study of light waves. Their work resulted in the development of the quantum theory, which states that *nothing can be measured or observed without disturbing it*: the observer can affect the outcome of the effect being measured.

The Scottish physicist James Clerk Maxwell (1831–79) had developed a theory about the electromagnetic-wave nature of light, and this was crucial to the development of quantum theory. Maxwell showed that at any point on a beam of light there is a magnetic field and an electric field that are perpendicular to each other and to the direction of the light beam. The fields oscillate millions of times every second, forming a wave pattern.

PHOTONS

If light is directed onto a piece of metal in a vacuum, electrons are knocked from the surface of the metal. This is the *photoelectric effect*. For light of a given wavelength, the number of electrons emitted per second increases with the intensity of the light, although the energies of the electrons are independent of the wavelength.

This discovery led the German physicist Albert Einstein (1879–1955) to deduce that the energy in a light beam exists in small discrete packets called *photons* or *quanta*. These can be detected in experiments in which light is allowed to fall on a detector, usually photographic film. This has led to the theory of the *dual nature of light*, which behaves as a wave during interference experiments but as a stream of particles during the photoelectric effect. Further work on this phenomenon has led to the acceptance of *wave-particle duality*, which is a fundamental principle in quantum physics. The way a system is described depends upon the apparatus with which it is interacting: light behaves as a wave when it passes through slits in an interference experiment, but as a stream of particles when it hits a detector.

UNCERTAINTY

Werner Karl Heisenberg (1901–76), a German physicist, interpreted wave-particle duality differently. He proposed that when a beam of light is directed at a screen with two slits, the interference pattern formed exists only if we do not know which slit the photon passed through. If we make an additional measurement and determine which slit was traversed, we destroy the interference pattern. Heisenberg showed that it was impossible to measure position and momentum simultaneously with infinite accuracy; he expressed his findings in the *uncertainty principle* named after him. This changed the thinking

about the precision with which simultaneous measurements of two physical quantities can be made.

PARTICLES

Matter is made up of vast numbers of very small particles. The behaviour of these particles cannot be described by the theories of classical physics, since there is no equivalence to subatomic particles in everyday mechanics. Thus it is not helpful to discuss the behaviour of electrons in atoms in terms of tiny 'planets' orbiting a 'sun'.

Louis Victor de Broglie (1892–1987), the French physicist, suggested that if light waves can behave like particles, then particles might in certain circumstances behave like waves. Later experiments confirmed that under appropriate conditions particles can exhibit wave phenomena.

ATOMIC ENERGY LEVELS

Quantum systems are described by a mathematical equation known as the *Schrödinger equation* after the Austrian physicist Erwin Schrödinger (1887–1961), who first formulated it. In situations such as where a negatively charged electron is bound to the positively charged nucleus of an atom, the Schrödinger equation has solutions for only *discrete* or *quantized* allowed values of the energy of the electron. The energy of an electron in an atom cannot take a lower value than the least of the allowed values – the *ground state* – so the electron cannot fall into the nucleus.

If an atom, through the interaction of forces on it, is excited into an allowed state of energy that is higher than the ground state, it can emit a photon and jump into the ground state. The energy of the photon is equal to the difference in energy levels of the two states. The energy of the photon is related to the wavelength of the light wave associated with it – thus light can be emitted by atoms only at particular wavelengths.

QUANTUM MECHANICS

Quantum mechanics is the study of the observable behaviour of particles. This includes electromagnetic radiation in all its details. In particular, it is the only appropriate theory for describing the effects that occur on an atomic scale.

Quantum mechanics deals exclusively with what can be observed, and does not attempt to describe what is happening in between measurements. This is not true of classical theories, which are essentially complete descriptions of what is occurring whether or not attempts are made to measure it.

In quantum mechanics the experimenter is directly included in the theory. Quantum mechanics predicts all the possible results of making a measurement, but it does not say which one will occur when an experiment is actually carried out. All that can be known is the probability of something being seen. In some experiments one event is very much more likely than any other, therefore most of the time this is what will be found, but sometimes one of the less probable events will occur. It is impossible to predict which will occur; the only way to find out is by making the appropriate measurement.

For example in an isotope of the element americium, 19% of the nuclei decay purely by alpha-particle emission and 81% decay by alpha emission followed by photon emission. For any individual americium nucleus it is not possible to say which decay will occur, only what will be observed on average.

In some experiments the same event can occur in different ways. What is measured depends on whether it is known which of the possible paths was taken. Thus any additional knowledge, which can only be gained by making an additional measurement, changes the outcome of the first experiment.

SPECIAL RELATIVITY

Inertial frames Physical laws such a Newton's laws of mechanics are stated with respect to some *frame of reference* that allows physical quantities such as velocity and acceleration to be defined. A frame of reference is called *inertial* if it is unaccelerated and it does not contain a gravitational field.

Einstein's relativity principle In 1905 Einstein stated that all inertial frames are equally good for carrying out experiments. This assumption, coupled with the evidence that the speed of light is the same in all frames, led Einstein to develop the theory of special relativity. This theory has been extensively tested using particle accelerators, where electrons or protons travel at speeds within a fraction of 1% of the speed of light. The masses of such particles measured by an observer in the laboratory in which the particles are travelling are higher than the masses measured by an observer at rest with respect to the particles.

Time The classical view of time is that if two events take place simultaneously with reference to one frame then they must also occur simultaneously within another frame. In terms of special relativity, however, two events that occur simultaneously in one frame may not be seen as simultaneous in another frame moving relative to the first. The sequence of cause and effect in related events is not, however, affected. Light plays a special role in synchronizing clocks in different frames because it has the same speed in all frames. In the classical view all observers have the same time scale, whereas in special relativity every inertial observer requires an individual time scale.

Space-time An important feature of special relativity is that time and space have to be considered as unified and not as two separate things. This means that time is related to the frame of reference in which it is being measured. This is a different view of space to that of Newton.

Length contraction The equations of special relativity lead to the very simple prediction that the length of a moving body in the direction of its motion measured in another frame is reduced by a factor dependent on its velocity with respect to the observer. What this means is that a car travelling very fast on a motorway would be measured by a stationary observer to be slightly shorter and heavier than usual, although the driver would not determine any difference. The length of a body is greatest when it is measured in a frame travelling *with* the body; as the speed of the body *relative to* the frame of reference approaches the speed of light the measured length approaches zero.

Time dilation A similar effect happens to moving clocks (which can be any regularly occurring phenomenon, such as the vibration of atoms – the basis of atomic clocks – or the decay of particles). A clock moving with a uniform velocity in one frame is measured as running slow in another frame. Its fastest rate is in its own frame, and at speeds – relative to the observer – approaching the speed of light the clock rate approaches zero.

Paradox of reality? Both of the above effects of length and time contraction have been the inspiration of numerous 'paradoxes' (and some science-fiction writing), and have been criticized on such grounds. But this simply goes to show that our 'common-sense' view of the world is rooted in frames that travel with respect to the observer at tiny speeds compared to that of light, and is just as inappropriate in describing these phenomena as it is in describing the quantum effects of the atomic world. Time dilation has been measured experimentally both with decaying particles and with actual macroscopic clocks. In all cases the effects predicted by special relativity were encountered.

GENERAL RELATIVITY

This is an extension of the theory of special relativity to include gravitational fields and accelerating reference frames. Gravitational fields arise because of the distortions of space-time in the vicinity of large masses, and space-time is no longer thought of as having an existence independent of the mass in the universe. Rather, space-time, mass and gravity are interdependent.

ACOUSTICS

The range of frequencies for which sound waves are audible to humans is from 20 to 20 000 Hz (i.e. vibrations or cycles per second) – the higher the frequency, the higher the pitch. In music, the A above middle C is internationally standardized at 440 Hz. For orchestral instruments, the frequencies range between 6272 Hz achieved on a handbell, and 16.4 Hz on a sub-contrabass clarinet.

Frequencies that are lower than the human audible range are referred to as *infrasonic*, and those above as *ultrasonic*. Many mammals such as dolphins and bats have sensitive hearing in the ultrasonic range, and they use high-pitched squeaks for echolocation. Large animals such as whales and elephants use frequencies in the infrasonic range to communicate over long distances.

THE VELOCITY OF SOUND

Sound shares the general characteristics of other wave forms. Sound waves are longitudinal compressions (squeezings) and rarefactions (stretchings) of the medium through which they are travelling, and are produced by a vibrating object.

If a sound wave is travelling in any medium then the pressure variations formed along its path cause strains as a result of the applied stresses. The velocity of the sound is given by the square root of the appropriate elastic modulus divided by the density.

The velocity of sound – as with the velocity of other types of wave – differs in different media. In still air at 0 °C, the velocity of sound is about 331 m s^{-1} (1191.6 km/h, or 740 mph). If the air temperature rises by 1 °C, then the velocity of sound increases by about 0.6 m s^{-1}. The velocity of sound in a metal such as steel is about 5060 m s^{-1}. Sometimes, in a Western film, someone will put an ear to a railway line to listen for an oncoming train. This works because the sound wave travels much faster through the steel track than through the air.

The fact that the velocity of sound varies in different media is one reason why seismic techniques can be used to probe layers of rock or minerals underground. Similarly ultrasonic scanning can be used in medicine – for example, in the imaging of a baby in its mother's womb. In each case variations in materials are shown up through variations in the time it takes sound waves to travel to the detector.

REFRACTION OF SOUND

At night the air near the ground is often colder than the air higher up, as the Earth cools after sunset. Thus a sound wave moving upward will be slowly bent back towards the horizontal as it meets warmer layers of air. Eventually it will be reflected back downwards. Under these circumstances sound can be heard over long distances. This phenomenon is explained by Snell's law of refraction (see below); layers of air at different temperatures act as different media through which sound travels at different velocities.

CHARACTERISTICS OF NOTES

There are three main characteristics of the notes played by musical instruments. *Loudness* would seem to be the most simple, but it is complicated by the non-linear response of the ear. At 100 Hz and 10 000 Hz the hearing threshold is about 40 db compared to the 0 db at 2500–4000 Hz. Thus the concept of loudness is not dependent just on the energy reaching the ear, but also on frequency.

Pitch is closely related to frequency. If the frequency of vibration is doubled the pitch rises by one octave. In general, the higher the frequency the higher the pitch.

Sounds created by musical instruments are not simple waveforms, but are the result of several waves combining. This complexity results in *tone quality* or *timbre* of a note played by a particular musical instrument. Even a 'pure' note may contain many waves of different frequencies. These frequencies are *harmonics* or *multiples* of the fundamental or lowest frequency, which has 2 nodes and 1 antinode, and is called the *first harmonic*. The second harmonic has 3 nodes and 2 antinodes. The wavelength is halved and the frequency is doubled. The *third harmonic* has 4 nodes and 3 antinodes. The wavelength is one third of the original wavelength, and the frequency has tripled. Different instruments emphasize different harmonics. Musical synthesizers are able to mimic instruments by mixing the appropriate harmonics electronically at various amplitudes.

OPTICS

Optics is the branch of physics that deals with the high-frequency electromagnetic waves that we call light. Optics is concerned with the way in which light propagates from sources to detectors via intermediate lenses, mirrors and other modifying elements. The electromagnetic spectrum includes a wide range of waves in addition to light, light being that small part of the spectrum that can be detected by the human eye.

This region, with wavelengths from 700 nanometres (nm; $1 \text{ nm} = 10^{-9} \text{ m}$) in the red region to 400 nm in violet (see the prism, below), is extended for practical optical systems into the ultraviolet and the mid-infrared regions. For many purposes light can be treated as a classical wave phenomenon (see above), but some effects can only be described by using the full quantum theory (see p. 208.

A *beam* of light may be considered to be made up of many *rays*, all travelling outwards from the source. This approach is used in ray diagrams. In geometric simplifications, rays of light are drawn as straight lines. The wavelength and amplitude of light waves are very short compared to the other dimensions of the systems. The basic concept is very simple: light travels in straight lines unless it is reflected by a mirror or refracted by a lens or prism (see below).

A point source of light emits rays in all directions. For an isolated point source in a vacuum the geometric wavefront will be a sphere. The variation of the speed of light in different materials must be taken into account – the speed of light (as of other electromagnetic waves) in a vacuum is $3 \times 10^8 \text{ m s}^{-1}$ (300 000 km or 186 000 miles per second), but it travels more slowly through other media. Light waves have transverse magnetic and electric fields.

REFLECTION AND REFRACTION

Light is reflected and refracted (i.e. bent) in the same way as other waves. In the case of a single-colour beam of light falling or *incident upon* a transparent material such as a block of glass, angle i is said to be the angle of *incidence* of the beam. Part of the beam is reflected at an angle t, the angle of *reflection*; and part is transmitted according to the law of refraction, and r is the angle of *refraction*.

Snell's law of refraction can be stated as:

$$n_1 \sin i = n_2 \sin r$$

where n_1 and n_2 are the refractive indices of the materials.

Basically, the *refractive index* of a material determines how much it will refract light.

The refractive index of a material is often expressed relative to another material. If no other material is quoted, the refractive index is assumed to be relative to air. The refractive index of a medium can also be derived as the ratio of the speed of light in a vacuum to the speed of light in the medium. The refractive index for a typical optical glass is 1.6, whereas the refractive index of diamond is about 2.4 in visible light.

THE PRISM

The refractive index of optical glasses is not constant for light of all frequencies. It is greater at the violet end and less at the red end of the spectrum. This means that a beam of light containing a mixture of different frequencies, for example sunlight, will leave a prism with the different frequencies bent by different amounts.

A *prism* is a block of glass with a triangular cross-section; it is used to deviate a beam of light by refraction. A beam of white light will be split into its component monochromatic coloured lights – from red to violet – which will form the familiar rainbow effect. Any light can be split up in this way; the display of separated wavelengths is called the *spectrum* of the original beam.

The effect of prisms on light has been well known for many centuries. Newton used this effect, called *dispersion*, to produce and study the spectrum of sunlight. Under the right conditions dispersion occurring in spherical raindrops in the atmosphere produces a rainbow.

TOTAL INTERNAL REFLECTION

When light travels from one medium to another, less dense medium it is *deviated* or turned away from the *normal* – perpendicular to the interface at the point of incidence. This means the angle of refraction (*r*) is greater than the angle of incidence (*i*). When the angle of refraction is less than 90°, some of the incident light will be refracted and some will be reflected. If the angle of incidence increases, the angle of refraction will increase more. It is possible to increase the angle of incidence to such a value that eventually the refracted ray disappears and all the light is reflected. This is known as *total internal reflection*.

THE LENS

A lens is a piece of transparent material made in a simple geometric shape. Usually at least one surface is spherical, and often both are. Under appropriate conditions a lens will produce an image of an object by refraction of light. It does this by bending rays of light from the object.

Some rays are refracted more than others, depending how they arrive at the surface of the lens. The lens affects the velocity of the rays, since light travels more slowly in a dense medium such as the lens than in a less dense medium such as air. In this way, the expanding geometric wavefront that is generated by the object is changed into a wavefront which, for a *convex* or *converging lens*, converges to a point behind the lens. If the object is located a long way from the lens (strictly an *infinite* distance, but a star is an excellent approximation for practical purposes) this point is known as the *rear focal point* or *principal focus* of the lens.

A lens has two principal foci – one on each side. The distance between the optical centre of the lens and the principal focus is the *focal length (f)*. If a point source of light is placed at the principal focus of the convex lens, the rays of light will be refracted to form a parallel beam.

MIRRORS

Mirrors are reflecting optical elements. Plane mirrors are used to deviate light beams without dispersion or to reverse or invert images. Curved mirrors, which usually have spherical or parabolic surfaces, can form images, and are often used in illumination systems such as car headlamps.

Mirrors can be coated with metals such as aluminium or silver, which have high reflectance for visible light (or gold for the infrared). Alternatively, they may be coated with many thin layers of non-metallic materials for very high reflectances over a more restricted range of frequencies. A freshly coated aluminium mirror will reflect about 90% of visible light. Special mirrors, such as those used in lasers, can reflect over 99.7% of the light at one frequency.

THE MICROSCOPE AND THE TELESCOPE

The *microscope* is a device for making very small objects visible. It was probably invented by a Dutch spectacle-maker, Zacharias Janssen (1580–1638), in 1609. Essentially, it is an elaboration of the simple magnifying glass. The *objective* – a lens with short focal length – is used to form a highly magnified image of a small object placed close to its focal point. This can be viewed directly, by means of another lens called the *eyepiece*. It can also be recorded directly on film or viewed via a video camera.

The *telescope* is used to form an enlarged image of an infinitely distant object, and the enlarged image is viewed by the observer by means of an eyepiece. The term 'infinite' is used relatively in this context: compared with the length of the telescope, the distance of the object can be considered as infinite. Telescopes are often made with reflecting mirrors instead of glass lenses, as large lenses sag under their own weight, thereby introducing distortions into the image. The primary mirror is often a large concave paraboloid.

FIBRE OPTICS

Light can be transmitted over great distances by the use of flexible glass fibres. These fibres are usually each less than 1 mm (1/25 in) in diameter, and can be used singly or in bunches. Each fibre consists of a small core surrounded by a layer of 'cladding' glass with a slightly lower refractive index. Certain rays experience total internal reflection (see above), and this, coupled with the very low absorption of modern silica glasses, allows light to travel very long distances with little reduction in intensity. Fibre optics provide the basis of endoscopy, a medical diagnostic technique, and are also used extensively in telecommunications, as light in a fibre optic cable can carry more digital (on or off) signals with less loss of intensity than a copper wire carrying electrical digital signals.

LASERS

The term 'laser' is derived from the technical name for the process – Light Amplification by Stimulated Emission of Radiation. *Stimulated emisson* is the emission of a photon – a particle of light.

When an amplifying material, such as gas, crystal or liquid, is placed between appropriate mirrors, photons from a light beam repeatedly pass through it stimulating more photons and thus increasing their number with each pass. The additional photons all have the same frequency, phase and direction. One of the mirrors is made so that a small amount of light passes through it; this is the external laser beam, which can be continuous or pulsed. This beam can be focused onto very small areas and the intensity – the ratio of power to area – can be very great, enabling some lasers to burn through thick metal plates. Lasers have a wide variety of uses, for example in surveying, communications and eye surgery.

ATOMS

Of the fundamental forces that are important in the natural world, the gravitational force is the dominant long-range force when the motion of planets and other celestial bodies is considered. When the smallest entities are investigated, the other fundamental forces – the electromagnetic force, the *strong force* (which holds together the atomic nucleus) and the *weak force* (which is involved in nuclear decay) – become important.

The word *atom* is derived from an ancient Greek word for a particle of matter so small it cannot be split up. In his atomic theory of 1803, the British chemist John Dalton (1766–1844) defined the atom as the smallest particle of an element that retained its chemical properties. Various phenomena could be explained using this hypothesis – which still holds good today.

ATOMIC STRUCTURE

However, no physical description of the atom was

available until after the discovery of the *electron* in 1897 by the British physicist J.J. Thompson (1856–1940). The nuclear atom was proposed by the English physicist Ernest Rutherford (1871–1937) in 1911. His model consists of a small but dense central *nucleus*, which is positively charged, orbited by negatively charged electrons. The nucleus contains over 99.9% of the mass of the atom, but its diameter is of the order of 10^{-15} m – compared to the much larger size (about 10^{-10} m) of the atom.

The electron was first recognized by its behaviour as a particle. In 1923 a *wave-particle duality* for atomic particles – analogous to the concept of the wave-particle duality of light proposed by the French physicist Louis Victor de Broglie (1892–1987) – was put forward. The wavelength of a particle would be equal to the Planck constant divided by its momentum.

As the wavelength is dependent on momentum it can take any value. For an electron the wavelength can be of the order of the atomic diameter. This led to the development of the *electron microscope*. At suitable energy levels the wavelength of electrons and neutrons can be equivalent to the atomic spacing in solids. Thus a crystal can be used as a *diffraction grating* (as for X-rays). This has led to a better understanding of the way in which the electrons orbit the atomic nucleus.

The Danish physicist Niels Bohr (1885–1962) had suggested that electrons were allowed to move in circular orbits or *shells* around the nucleus, but that only certain orbits were *allowable*. This theory was able to explain many of the features of the spectrum of light emitted by excited hydrogen atoms. The wavelengths of the spectral lines are related to the energy levels of the allowed orbits. The wave theory of the electron provided a reason for the allowed orbits. These would be those whose circumference was a multiple of the electron's wavelength.

When Rutherford showed experimentally that an atom must consist of a small nucleus surrounded by electrons, there was a fundamental problem. To avoid collapsing into the nucleus, the electrons would have to move in orbits – as Bohr had proposed. This means that they must have continuous acceleration towards the nucleus. But, according to the electromagnetic theory, an accelerated charge must radiate energy, so no permanent orbit could exist. Bohr therefore argued that energy could not be lost continuously but only in quanta (discrete amounts) equivalent to the difference in energies between allowed orbits. Thus light would be emitted when an electron jumps from one allowed level to another of lower energy.

NUCLEAR STRUCTURE

With the exception of the hydrogen atom, which only contains one proton, atomic nuclei contain a mixture of protons and neutrons, collectively known as *nucleons*. The *proton* carries a positive charge, equal in magnitude to that of the negatively charged electron. The *neutron* is of similar size but is electrically neutral. Each has a mass about 1836 times that of the electron (which has a rest mass of 9.11×10^{-31} kg). The protons and neutrons in the atomic nucleus are held tightly together by the *strong nuclear force*, which overcomes the much weaker electromagnetic force of repulsion between positively charged protons.

The mass of a nucleus is always less than the sum of the masses of its constituent nucleons. This is explained using the relationship derived by Einstein. If the nucleus is to be separated into protons and neutrons then the strong nuclear force needs to be overcome and energy has to be supplied to the nucleus – from an external source – to break it up. This energy is called the *binding energy* and is related to the *mass defect* (the difference between the masses of the nucleus and its component parts). Those nuclei with large binding energies per nucleon are most stable; these have about 50–75 nucleons in the nucleus.

NUCLEAR POWER – FISSION AND FUSION

Nuclear power comes from either of two processes – *fission* and *fusion*, which are both forms of *nuclear reaction*. In the fission process a large nucleus, such as uranium-235 (^{235}U), splits to form two smaller nuclei that have greater binding energies than the original uranium. Thus energy is given out in the process. Fission is used in nuclear reactors and in atomic weapons. There are other isotopes in addition to uranium-235, such as plutonium-239, that give rise to fission.

In the fusion process, two light nuclei fuse together to form two particles, one larger and one smaller than the original nuclei. Usually one of them is sufficiently strongly bound to give a great release of energy. The fusion of hydrogen to form helium is a power source in stars such as the Sun, although the solar fusion process differs in detail from the simpler process described. Nuclear fusion is the basis of the hydrogen bomb, and research is continuing into the possible use of fusion in power generation.

RADIOACTIVITY

Radiation – either as a spontaneous emission of particles or as an electromagnetic wave – may occur from certain substances. This is *radioactivity*. The three types of radiation are from:

alpha decay,
beta decay, and
gamma decay.

Alpha (α) decay produces nuclei of helium that each contain two neutrons and two protons. They are called *alpha-particles* and are formed in spontaneous decay of the parent nucleus. Thus uranium-238 decays to thorium-234 with emission of an alpha-particle.

Beta (β) decay In beta decay the emitted particles are either electrons or *positrons* (identical to the electron but with a positive charge). The parent nucleus retains the same number of nucleons but its charge varies by plus or minus 1. In these processes another kind of particle – either a *neutrino* or *antineutrino* – is produced. The neutrino has no charge (the word means 'little neutral one') and a mass that – if it could be measured at rest – would probably be zero. The *relativistic mass* can, however, be significant, as the speed – with respect to any observer – is that of electromagnetic radiation.

Gamma (λ) decay In gamma decay high-energy photons may be produced in a process of radioactive decay if the resultant nucleus jumps from an excited energy state to a lower energy state.

The rate at which radioactive decay takes place depends only on the number of radioactive nuclei that are present. Thus the *half-life*, or the time taken for half a given number of radioactive nuclei to decay, is characteristic for that type of nucleus. The isotope carbon-14 has a half-life of 5730 years, and measurement of its decay is used in carbon-dating of organic material. Decay can result in a series of new elements being produced, each of which may in its turn decay until a stable state is achieved.

NUCLEAR PARTICLES

Over 200 elementary particles are now known. They may be divided into two types: *hadrons* and *leptons*.

Hadrons (from the Greek for 'bulky') are heavy particles that are affected by the strong force.

Leptons (from the Greek for 'small') are generally light particles, such as electrons and neutrinos (see above), that are not subject to the strong force.

A further very important distinction is that between *fermions* (Fermi-Dirac particles) and *bosons* (Bose-Einstein particles). Fermions have a permanent existence, whereas bosons can be produced and destroyed freely, provided the laws of conservation of charge and of mechanics are obeyed. Leptons are fermions.

Every type of particle is thought to have a companion *antiparticle*, that is, a particle with the same mass but opposite in some other characteristic such as charge. Thus the positron with positive charge is the antiparticle of the negatively charged electron. Some particles such as the photon may be their own antiparticles.

Whilst the leptons are thought to be fundamental particles, the hadrons are thought to be made up of *quarks* (a word borrowed from James Joyce's novel *Finnegans Wake*). Quarks may have fractional electrical charge. It is probable that free quarks do not exist.

If three quarks combine, the resulting hadron is called a *baryon*; if a quark and an antiquark combine the result is called a *meson*. A meson is a boson; it is a short-lived particle that jumps between protons and neutrons, thus holding them together. In the same way that Mendeleyev's table of chemical elements predicted new elements such as gallium and germanium that were subsequently discovered, so a pattern of hadrons may be drawn up based on combinations of different types of quark. This pattern is called the *eight-fold way* – a term borrowed from Buddhism. It predicted the existence of the omega-particle (Ω-particle), the discovery of which in 1963 helped to validate the theory.

There are believed to be six types or *flavours* of quark – up, down, charmed, strange, top and bottom. Evidence for the existence of all except the top quark is now available.

Quarks carry electrical charge and another type of charge called *colour*. The force associated with the colour charge binds the quarks together and is thought to be the source of the strong force binding the hadrons together. Thus the colour force is the more fundamental force. The weak force is associated with the radioactive beta-decay of some nuclei. It has been shown – in the theory of the *electroweak* force – that the electromagnetic and weak forces are linked. This theory predicted the existence of the W and Z° particles, which were discovered at the CERN nuclear accelerator at Geneva during 1982–83.

NUCLEAR ACCELERATORS

Accelerators are large machines that accelerate particle beams to very high speeds, so enabling research into particle physics. Electric fields are used to accelerate the particles, either in a straight line (*linear accelerator*) or in a circle (*cyclotron*, *synchrotron* or *synchrocyclotron*). Powerful magnetic fields are used to guide the beams. Energy levels of the particles may be as high as several hundred giga electronvolts. An electronvolt (eV) is the increase in energy of an electron when it undergoes a rise in potential of 1 volt: $1 \text{ eV} = 1.6 \times 10^{-19}$ joules (J). Nuclear accelerators have provided experimental evidence for the existence of numerous subatomic particles predicted in theory.

ELECTROMAGNETISM

Electromagnetism is the study of effects caused by stationary and moving electric charges. Electricity and magnetism were originally observed separately, but in the 19th century, scientists began to investigate their interaction. This work resulted in a theory that electricity and magnetism were both manifestations of a single force, the electromagnetic force.

The electromagnetic force is one of the fundamental forces of nature, the others being gravitational force and the strong and weak nuclear forces. Recently the electromagnetic and weak forces have been shown to be manifestations of an electro-weak force. Magnetism has been known about since ancient times, but it was not until the late 18th century that the electric force was identified – by the French physicist Charles Augustin Coulomb (1736–1806).

MAGNETISM

Metallic ores with magnetic properties were being used around 500 BC as compasses. It is now known that the Earth itself has magnetic properties. Investigation of the properties of magnetic materials led to the concept of *magnetic fields*, showing the force one magnet exerts on another. These lines of force can be demonstrated by means of small plotting compasses or iron filings. An important feature of a magnet is that it has two poles, one of which is attracted to the Earth's magnetic north pole, while the other is attracted to the south pole. Conventionally, the north-seeking end of a magnet is called its *north pole*, and the other is the *south pole*. Magnets are identified by the fact that unlike or opposite poles (i.e. north and south) attract each other, while like poles (north and north, or south and south) repel each other.

Magnetic effects are now known to be caused by moving electric charges. Atomic electrons are in motion, and thus all atoms exhibit magnetic fields.

STATIC ELECTRIC CHARGES

In dry weather, a woollen sweater being pulled off over the hair of the wearer may crackle; sparks may even be seen. This is caused by an *electric charge*, which is the result of electrons being pulled from one surface to the other. Objects can gain an electric charge by being rubbed against another material.

Experiment has shown that there are two types of charge. These are now associated with the negative and positive charges on electrons and protons respectively. Similar electric charges (i.e. two positives, or two negatives) repel each other and unlike charges (i.e. a positive and a negative) attract. (Note that the terms 'positive' and 'negative' are merely conventions for opposite properties.) No smaller charge than that of the electron has been detected.

The force of repulsion or attraction is known as the *electric force*. It is described by *Coulomb's law*, an inverse-square law similar to the law for the gravitational force (see above). Coulomb's law states that the attractive or repulsive force (F) between two point (or spherically symmetrical) charges is given by:

$$F = k \frac{Q_1 Q_2}{r^2}$$

where k is a constant, Q_1 and Q_2 are the magnitudes of the charges, and r is the distance between them. The force acts along the direction of r. The unit of charge is called a *coulomb* (C) and is the quantity of electric charge carried past a given point in 1 second by a current of 1 ampere (see below).

ELECTRIC FIELD

Arrows can be plotted to show the magnitude and direction of the magnetic force that acts at points around a magnet, or the electric force that acts on a unit charge at each point. In the latter case, such a map would show the distribution of the electric field intensity. It is measured in terms of a force per unit charge, or newtons per coulomb.

In the same way that a mass may have gravitational potential energy because of its position, so a charge can have *electrical potential energy*. This potential per unit charge is measured in *volts* (V), named after the Italian physicist Alessandro Volta (1745–1827). The volt may be defined as follows: if one joule is required to move 1 coulomb of electric charge between two points, then the *potential difference* between the points is 1 joule per coulomb = 1 volt.

The electrical potential may vary with distance. This change may be measured in volts per metre (V m^{-1}). The Earth's surface is negatively charged with an average electric field over the whole of its surface of about 120 V m^{-1}. In the presence of thunderclouds or where the air is highly polluted the field may be much greater. This field is maintained partially by thunderstorms, which transfer negative charge to the Earth. Dry air can only allow an electric field of 3×10^6 V m^{-1} to build up before there is a sudden breakdown – a lightning flash. If water droplets are present, then the value is lower, perhaps 1×10^6 V m^{-1}.

ELECTRIC CURRENT, CONDUCTORS AND INSULATORS

Electric current consists of a flow of electrons, usually through a material but also through a vacuum, as in a cathode-ray tube in a TV set. Current flows when there is a *potential difference* or *voltage* (see above) between two ends of a conductor (see below). Conventional current flows from the positive terminal to the negative terminal. However, electron flow is in fact from negative to positive.

For measurement purposes, an electric current is defined as the rate of flow of charge. The unit of electric current is the *ampere* (A), often abbreviated to amp:

1 ampere = 1 coulomb per second.

The ampere is named after the French physicist André Marie Ampère (1775–1836), who pioneered work on electricity and magnetism.

A material that will allow an electric current to flow through it is a *conductor*. The best conductors are metals. A material that will not allow an electric current to flow is an *insulator*. Effective insulators include rubber, plastic and porcelain.

ELECTROMAGNETIC FIELDS

In 1820 the Danish physicist Hans Christiaan Oersted (1777–1851) discovered that a copper wire bearing an electric current caused a pivoted magnetic needle to be deflected until it was tangential to a circle drawn around the wire. This was the first connection to be established between the electrical and magnetic forces. Oersted's work was developed by the French scientists Jean-Baptiste Biot (1774–1862) and Félix Savart (1791–1841), who showed that the field strength of a current flowing in a straight wire varied with the distance from the wire. Biot and Savart were able to find a law relating the current in a small part of the conductor to the magnetic field. Ampère, at about the same time, found a more fundamental relationship between the current in a wire and the magnetic field about it.

We now believe that the Earth's magnetic field is generated by the motion of charged particles in the liquid iron part of the core. This is known as the *dynamo theory*.

From Newton's third law (see above) and Oersted's observation it might be expected that a magnetic field can exert a force on a moving charge. This is observed if a magnet is brought up close to a cathode-ray tube in a TV set. The beam of electrons moving from the cathode to the screen is deflected. The force acts in a direction perpendicular to both the magnetic field and the direction of electron flow. If the magnetic field is perpendicular to the direction of the electrons, then the force has its maximum value. This is the second way in which the electric and magnetic properties are linked.

ELECTROMAGNETIC INDUCTION

The next advance came in 1831, when the English physicist Michael Faraday (1791–1867) found that an electric current could be induced in a wire by another, changing current in a second wire. Faraday published his findings before the American physicist Joseph Henry (1797–1878), who had first made the same discovery. Faraday showed that the magnetic field at the wire had to be changing for an electric current to be produced. This may be done by changing the current in a second wire, by moving a magnet relative to the wire, or by moving the wire relative to a magnet. This last technique is that employed in a dynamo generator, which maintains an electric current when it is driven mechanically. An electric motor uses the reverse process, being driven by electricity to provide a mechanical result.

MAXWELL'S THEORY

The work of the Scottish physicist James Clerk Maxwell (1831–79) on electromagnetism is of immense importance for physics. It united the separate concepts of electricity and magnetism in terms of a new *electromagnetic force*. Maxwell extended the ideas of Ampère, when, in 1864, he proposed that a magnetic field could also be caused by a changing electric field. Thus, when either an electric or magnetic field is changing, a field of the other type is induced. Maxwell predicted that electrical oscillations would generate electromagnetic waves, and he derived a formula giving the speed in terms of electric and magnetic quantities. When these quantities were measured he calculated the speed and found that it was equal to the speed of light in a vacuum. This suggested that light might be electromagnetic in nature – a theory that was later confirmed in various ways. Thus, when an electric current in a wire changes, electromagnetic waves are generated, which will be propagated with a velocity equal to that of light.

The electric and magnetic field components in electromagnetic waves are perpendicular to each other and to the direction of propagation. The existence of electromagnetic waves was demonstrated experimentally in 1887 by the German physicist Heinrich Rudolf Hertz (1857–94) – who also gave his name to the unit of frequency. In his laboratory, Hertz transmitted and detected electromagnetic waves, and he was able to verify that their velocity was close to the speed of light.

THE ELECTROMAGNETIC SPECTRUM

Prior to Maxwell's discoveries it had been known that light was a wave motion, although the type of wave motion had not been identified. Maxwell was able to show that the oscillations were of the electric and magnetic field. Hertz's waves had a wavelength of about 60 cm; thus they were of much longer wavelength than light waves.

Nowadays we recognize a spectrum of electromagnetic radiation that extends from about 10^{-15} m to 10^9 m. It is subdivided into smaller, sometimes overlapping, ranges. The extension of astronomical observations from visible to other electromagnetic wavelengths has revolutionized our knowledge of the universe.

Radio waves have a large range of wavelengths – from a few millimetres up to several kilometres.

Microwaves are radio waves with shorter wavelengths, between 1 mm and 30 cm. They are used in radar and microwave ovens.

Infrared waves of different wavelengths are radiated by bodies at different temperatures. (Bodies at higher temperatures radiate either visible or ultraviolent waves.) The Earth and its atmosphere, at a mean temperature of 250 K (-23 °C or -9.4 °F) radiates infrared waves with wavelengths centred at about 10 micrometres (μ m) or 10^{-5} (1 μ m = 10^{-6} m).

Visible waves have wavelengths of 400–700 nanometres (nm; 1 nm = 10^{-9} m). The peak of the solar radiation (temperatures of about 6000 K/6270 °C/11 323 °F) is at a wavelength of about 550 nm, where the human eye is at its most sensitive.

Ultraviolet waves have wavelengths from about 380 nm down to 60 nm. The radiation from hotter stars (above 25 000 K/25 000 °C/45 000 °F) is shifted towards the violet and ultraviolet parts of the spectrum.

X-rays have wavelengths from about 10 nm down to 10^{-4} nm.

Gamma rays have wavelengths less than 10^{-11} m. They are emitted by certain radioactive nuclei and in the course of some nuclear reactions.

Note that the *cosmic rays* continually bombarding the Earth from outer space are not electromagnetic waves, but high-speed protons and x-particles (i.e. nuclei of hydrogen and helium atoms) together with some heavier nuclei.

ELECTRICITY IN ACTION

There have been several key advances in the application of electricity towards developing our civilization. The first two were the dynamo and the electric motor. The dynamo provided a way of producing electricity in large quantities, and the electric motor provided a way of converting electric current into mechanical work.

The evolution of electromagnetic theory (see above) provided the basis for the modern communications industry through radio and television, while the miniaturization of electronic components using semiconductor materials enabled powerful computers to be built for control purposes and to handle large amounts of information.

BATTERIES AND CELLS

Electric current is the flow of electrons through a conductor. The first source of a steady electric current was demonstrated by the Italian physicist Alessandro Volta (1745–1827) in 1800. His original *voltaic pile* used chemical energy to produce an electric current. The pile consisted of a series of pairs of metal plates (one of silver and one of zinc) piled on top of each other, each pair sandwiching a piece of cloth soaked in a dilute acid solution.

The same principle is still used today. The plates are called *electrodes* and must be made of dissimilar metals. Alternatively, one may be made of carbon. The positive electrode – the one from which electrons flow inside the cell – is called the *anode*. The negative electrode is the *cathode*. The acid solution is called the *electrolyte* and in a dry cell is absorbed into a paste.

A single cell can normally produce only a small voltage, but a number of them connected in a series (positive to negative) will give a higher voltage. A series of cells connected in this way is called a *battery*. Some batteries, known as *accumulators*, are designed so that they can be 'recharged' by the passage of an electric current back through them. Similar principles as those used in cells are used in electrolysis and electroplating.

CIRCUITRY

A circuit is a complete conductive path between positive and negative terminals; conventionally current flows from positive to negative, although the direction of electron flow is actually from negative to positive. When electrical components such as bulbs and switches are joined end to end the arrangement is a *series* connection. When they are connected side by side, this is called *parallel* connection.

RESISTANCE

When an electric current passes through a conductor there is a force that acts to reduce or *resist* the flow. This is called the *resistance* and is dependent upon the nature of the conductor and its dimensions. The unit of resistance is the *ohm* (Ω), named after the German physicist Georg Simon Ohm (1787–1854). He discovered a relationship between the current (I), voltage (V) and resistance (R) in a conductor:

$$V = IR.$$

This is known as Ohm's law.

POWER

Power is the rate at which a body or system does work. The power in an electric conductor is measured in *watts* (W), named after the British engineer James Watt (1736–1819). One watt is one joule per second, or the energy used per second by a current of one amp flowing between two points with a potential difference of one volt.

In an electric conductor, the power (W) is the product of the current (I) and the voltage (V).

LIGHTING, HEATING AND FUSES

A light bulb consists of a glass envelope containing an inert ('noble') gas, usually argon, at low pressure. The bulb has two electrodes connected internally by a *filament* – a fine coiled tungsten wire of high resistance. The passage of a suitable electric current through the filament will raise its temperature sufficiently to make it glow white hot (2500 °C / 4500 °F). The inert gas prevents the filament from evaporating. The efficiency of filament lamps is low. *Gas discharge lamps* are much more efficient. They consist of a glass tube with electrodes sealed into each end. The tube is filled with a gas such as neon, sodium or mercury vapour, which can be *excited* to emit light by the application of a high voltage to the electrodes.

When electrons pass through a wire they cause the atoms in it to vibrate and generate heat – the greater the resistance, the greater the heat generated. This effect is used in electric heating devices. An electric radiant heater glows red hot. The temperature reached by using a special tough resistance wire is 900 °C (1650 °F). The connecting wires are of low resistance and stay cool.

If a small resistance consisting of wire with a low melting point is connected in a circuit the amount of current that can flow will be limited by that resistance. If too much current flows the resistance will overheat and melt, breaking the circuit. This resistance is called a *fuse* and can be used as a device to protect circuits from current overload.

ALTERNATING CURRENT AND DIRECT CURRENT

There are two types of current electricity. The type produced by a battery is *direct current* (DC), in which there is a constant flow of electrons in one direction. The type used in most electrical appliances is *alternating current* (AC), in which the direction of flow of electrons alternates. The frequency of alternating current can vary over an enormous range. The electric mains operate at 50 Hz (cycles per second) in the UK and Europe, and at 60 Hz in the USA. Most of today's electricity is produced by AC generators. These were developed following Faraday's discovery of the induction of a current in a circuit as a result of a changing magnetic field.

GENERATORS AND MOTORS

A *dynamo* is an electrical current generator, consisting of a coil that is rotated in a magnetic field by some external means. The source of the rotation may be a turbine in which blades are moved by the passage through them of water, as in a hydroelectric plant, or steam, produced from a boiler heated by nuclear fission or by burning fossil fuels. Wind turbines spin as a result of the passage of air through the large rotors. Different types of generator produce either AC or DC current, while *alternators* (used to charge car batteries) produce AC current that is then rectified to DC current using semiconductor diodes.

An *electric motor* is a similar device to a generator, but works in reverse. An electric current is applied to the coil windings, causing rotation of the *armature*, which consists of a shaft on which are mounted electromagnet windings.

CONDUCTORS AND SEMICONDUCTORS

A metal consists of an array of positive ions in a 'sea' of free electrons. The electrons move randomly with mean speeds of around 10^6 m s^{-1}. When a potential difference is applied across a metal a small drift velocity is added. The metal atoms are thought to give up one or more electrons, which can then migrate freely through the material. These electrons move in a zigzag manner along a conductor. As a result their typical velocity, called the *drift velocity*, is small, in the order of 10^{-4} m s^{-1}. Thus it would take more than an hour to move one metre. Note that the electric signals that drive the electrons travel with a speed in the order of 10^8 m s^{-1} in some circuits.

This classical picture of electron conduction explains some but not all conduction phenomena. For these a quantum mechanical model is required (see p. 209). This model explains the basis of semiconductors, which now play such an important part in electronics.

Metals are good conductors of electricity because there are always many unoccupied quantum states into which electrons can move. Non-metallic solids and liquids have nearly all their quantum states occupied by electrons, so it is difficult to produce large currents. If the numbers of unoccupied states and of electrons free to move into them are small the material is an *insulator*. If there are more free electrons and unoccupied states the substance is called a *semiconductor*.

Semiconductors have a charge-carrier density that lies between those of conductors and insulators. Two metal-like elements, silicon and germanium, are the two semiconductors used most frequently. These may be 'doped' with an impurity to modify their conduction behaviour – *n-type* doping increases the number of free electrons, *p-type* increases the number of unoccupied states. If the doping results in the charge carriers being negative electrons, then the result is an *n-type semiconductor*. If electron deficiencies or holes are the charge carriers, then the result is a *p-type semiconductor*.

Most semiconductor devices are made from materials that are partly p-type and partly n-type. The boundary between them is known as a *p-n junction*. Such a device, called a *semiconductor diode*, will act as a *rectifier*, a device used to convert alternating current to direct current.

TRANSISTORS

A transistor consists of semiconductor material in n-p-n or p-n-p form. The middle part is the *base* and the ends are the *emitter* and *collector*. An *integrated circuit* consists of many transistors, rectifiers or other components embedded in a chip of silicon.

SUPERCONDUCTIVITY

Superconductivity was discovered by the Dutch physicist Kamerlingh Onnes (1853–1926) in 1911. Below a certain critical temperature, various metals show zero resistance to current flow. Once a current is started in a closed circuit, it keeps flowing as long as the circuit is kept cold. The critical temperature for aluminium is 1.19 K (–272 °C / –457 °F), and similar values hold for other metals. Some alloys have higher critical temperatures. Up to 1986 the highest transition temperature known was about 25 K (–248 °C / –414 °F). More recently a new class of copper oxide and other materials have shown superconductivity up to at least 125 K (–148 °C / –234 °F). These developments promise enormous savings in energy.

SOLAR CELLS

The *photovoltaic effect* occurs when light is absorbed by a p-n or n-p junction. Electrons are liberated at the junction by an incident photon and diffuse through the n-type region. The hole drifts through the p-type layer until it recombines with an electron flowing round the external circuit.

The first practical photovoltaic device – called a solar cell – was made in 1954. In essence a solar cell is a light-emitting diode acting in reverse – it converts light into electric current, which is the basis of solar power.

Direct solar energy is one of the simplest sources of power. Building designs, old and new, take advantage of it for heating and lighting. Today, more active designs are becoming widespread. Each square metre (11¾ sq ft) of a solar collector in northern Europe receives roughly 1000 kilowatt-hours of solar energy in the course of a year, and can use about half of this to heat water. A similar collector in California receives twice as much energy as this.

Solar (or photovoltaic cells), which use the Sun's radiation to generate energy, are also becoming cheaper and more efficient. Earlier cells, made from large slices of crystalline silicon, were very expensive, but new materials, such as amorphous silicon and gallium arsenide, are bringing the price down towards the goal of about one dollar per watt. The latest experimental solar cells are able to convert about a third of the energy in sunlight to electricity. Solar cells are already proving the best option for producing electricity reliably in remote locations.

MILESTONES IN PHYSICS

Physics is very much concerned with fundamental particles – the building blocks out of which the Universe is constructed – and the forces which bind and regulate them. Many theories have been proposed from time to time to provide a better understanding of the vast number of facts and observations which have accumulated. The main development of physics is essentially a series of unifications of these theories.

c. 600 BC   Thales of Miletus (?624–546 BC), Greek philosopher, observed the effects of an electrostatic force when amber attracted light objects.

400 BC   Democritus (c. 460–370 BC), Greek philosopher, asserted that all matter was composed of minute, indivisable particles – *atoma* – and that physical phenomena may be explained by the way these move and combine.

c. 290 BC   Archimedes (c. 290–212 BC), Greek mathematician and physicist, established the principles of the lever and of the centre of gravity and made important contributions to hydrostatics. In his work he demonstrated the application of mathematics to physical experience.

c. 100 BC   Hero of Alexandria (c. 100 BC) discovered the laws of reflection of light. He is also credited with the invention of the syphon.

AD 120   Claudius Ptolemy (AD c. 100–178), Greek mathematician and astronomer, published the results of his experiments with the refraction of light in his *Optica*.

1266   Roger Bacon (?1220–94), English philosopher and scientist, published his *Opus Majus*, part of his compendium in which he described his work on the laws of reflection and refraction. Bacon – a Franciscan monk – was the first to use glass lenses to correct visual defects of the eye. In all his work, he stressed the importance of experiment in scientific method.

1490   Leonardo da Vinci (1452–1519) observed the effects of surface tension on the behaviour of liquids in fine-bore tubes.

1600   William Gilbert (1540–1603), English physicist and physician to Elizabeth I, published his *De magnete*. This described the Earth's magnetic field and important concepts in terrestrial magnetism.

1604   Johann Kepler (1571–1630), German astronomer, described the essential optical structure of the human eye.

1608   Hans Lippershey (c. 1570–c. 1619), Dutch optician, is said to have invented the first practical reflecting telescope.

1609   Galileo Galilei (1564–1642), Italian mathematician, astronomer and physicist, constructed an astronomical telescope with a concave eyepiece – the *Galilean telescope*. This enabled him to observe the lunar surface.

Galileo also discovered the period of swing of a simple pendulum deepened on its length – a lamp swinging in Pisa cathedral is said to have stimulated his researches.

1611   Santorio Santorio (1561–1636), Italian physician, added a scale to the rudimentary thermoscope of Galileo – a device for simply indicating changes in temperature without measuring them. He thus produced one of the first thermometers and calibrated it with melting ice and with the heat of a candle.

1622   Willebrord Snell (1591–1626), Dutch physicist, formulated the law of refraction of light bearing his name: at the boundary of transparent media the ratio of the sine of the angle of refraction to the sine of the angle of incidence is constant.

1631   Paul Vernier (1580–1637), French mathematician, invented the scale, bearing his name, which enables small, very accurate, fractional readings of length to be made in scientific instruments.

1644   Evangelista Torricelli (1608–1647), Italian physicist, demonstrated the much-debated existance of a vacuum and also discovered the principle of the mercury thermometer.

1657   Otto van Guericke (1602–86), German physicist, following on the work of Torricelli and others, invented the vacuum pump. He used this in his celebrated experiment at Magdeburg, Germany, to evacuate the air from two copper hemispheres joined together. Two teams of horses, attached to each other, failed to separate them and so graphically demonstrated the pressure of the atmosphere.

1660   Hon Robert Boyle (1627–91), Irish scientist, published his *New experiments phsyio-mechanical, touching the spring of the air and its effects*. A later edition of this contained the well-known law named after him: at constant temperature, the volume of a gas is inversely proportional to the presure.

1672   Sir Isaac Newton (1642–1703), English physicist and mathematician, presented a reflecting telescope to the Royal Society. This had a magnifying power of 38 diameters.

1678   Robert Hooke (1635–1703), English physicist, formulated the law named after him: within the elastic limit, the extension of spring is directly proportional to the force producing it.

1684 Newton started writing his masterpiece, *Philosophiae naturalis principia mathematica*, published in 1687. It stated his three fundamental laws of motion, introduced the term 'gravitation' and expounded the universal law of gravitation: every particle in the universe attracts every other particle with a force proportional in magnitude to the product of the masses of the particles and inversely proportional to the square of the distance between them. Newton also supplied the mathematical equipment for dealing with these concepts in the form of calculus which he discovered independently of the German mathematician Gottfried Wilhelm Leibniz (1646–1716).

1687 Newton produced the great unifying theory of gravitation which linked the falling apple with the force which keeps the stars and planets in their courses. This made available for further scientific investigation one of the basic universal forces of nature, the force of gravity.

1690 Christiaan Huygens (1629–95), Dutch physicist, published his *Traité de la lumière* in which he formulated a wave theory of light. This was in contradistinction to Newton's view that light consisted of particles or corpuscals.

1698 Newton derived a formula for calculating the velocity of sound in air based on the atmospheric pressure and its density.

1704 Newton's *Optics* was published. In this he argued that light is corpuscular in nature and that white light is a complex mixture of colours.

1714 Daniel Gabriel Fahrenheit (1686–1736), German physicist, invented the mercury thermometer and temperature scale which took 32° as the freezing point of melting ice and 96° as the temperature of blood heat. The Fahrenheit scale now takes 212° as the temperature of steam to be the upper fixed point.

1742 Anders Celsius (1701–44), Swedish astronomer, produced the Celsius scale of temperature. This takes 0° and 100°, the temperatures of melting ice and of steam, for the lower and upper fixed points respectively. (The Celsius scale was until recent years commonly referred to as the Centigrade scale in the UK.)

1752 Benjamin Franklin (1706–90), American statesman and scientist, conducted his famous experiment in which he flew a kite in a thunderstorm and thus showed the identity of lightning and the electric sparks of the laboratory. Following from this he invented the lightning conductor.

1785 Charles Augustin de Coulomb (1736–1806), French physicist, designer of the torsion balance, enunciated the law named after him: the force between two electrically charged bodies is proportional to the product of the charges on them and inversely proportional to the square of the distance between them.

1798 Henry Cavendish (1731–1810), English physicist and chemist, published the result of his difficult and exacting experiments to determine the mean density of the Earth. He obtained a better value than 1% of the value accepted today.

1798 Pierre-Simon Laplace (1749–1827), French mathematician and physicist, published the first of the five volumes of his *Traité de mécanique céleste* describing the solar system in terms of Newtonian gravitation. It thus represents a peak in mechanistic thinking in which the universe is regarded as an enormous deterministic machine.

1798 Count Rumford, Benjamin Thompson (1753–1814), Anglo-American physicist, concluded that heat was a form of energy – as a result of the work on boring cannon barrels that he was superintending. This marked the end of the old *caloric* theory in which heat was regarded as 'mysterious' fluid and it paved the way for the later work of John Prescott Joule (1818–89), English physicist, who determined the mechanical equivalent of heat to be 4.18 x10^7 erg per calorie. The unit of energy, the joule, is named after him.

1799 The standard metre length was adopted in France.

1800 Alessandro Volta (1745–1827), Italian physicist, published an account of his invention the voltaic pile. This, the first battery, was made of a succession of 'cups' of zinc and copper alternately.

1801 Thomas Young (1773–1829), English physicist, demonstrated the interference and diffraction of light waves and showed how the wave theory of light could explain the phenomena of reflection and refraction.

1817 Augustin Jean Fresnel (1788–1827), French physicist, explained the polarization of light, a property first dioscovered by Etienne Louis Malus (1775–1812) in 1808.

1820 Hans Christian Oersted (1777–1851) of Denmark discovered that the flow of electric current in a conductor would cause a nearby compass needle to be deflected (see p. 207).

1820 André Marie Ampère (1775–1836), French physicist, having seen Oersted's demonstrations, went on to develop more detailed, quantitative results in electromagnetism.

1821 Michael Faraday (1791–1867), English physicist, demonstrated the principle of the electric motor in a celebrated experiment in which a current-carrying conductor rotated around a permanent magnet. **1824** Nicholas Léonard Sadi Carnot (17 96–1832), French physicist, published *Réflexions sur la puissance motrice de feu* in which he explored the theoretical efficiency of the steam engine. He thus laid the foundations of thermodynamics and his work formed the basis for both the first and second laws of thermodynamics.

1827 George Simon Ohm (1787–1854), German physicist, published *Die galvanische Kette, mathematisch bearbeitet* (The galvanic circuit, treated mathematically), which stated the law named after him: the potential difference in an electric circuit is equal to the product of the current flowing and the resistance. The latter quantity is measured in units named after him, the ohm.

1831 Faraday published the principle of magnetic induction which led to the invention of the dynamo. He showed that a change in the magnetic field surrounding a conductor could cause a flow of electrical current.

1842 Christian J. Doppler (1803–53), Austrian physicist, stated the effect named after him. This relates the perceived change in wavelength caused by the relative motion of source and observer.

1848 Kelvin, using an electric thermometer, determined the temperature of absolute zero as -273 °C.

1849 Armand-Hippolyte-Louis Fizeau (1819–96), French physicist, measured the velocity of light by terrestrial methods, obtaining reasonably accurate values.

1850 Rudolf Julius Clausius (1822–88), German physicist, and Lord Kelvin, William Thomson (1824–1907), Scottish physicist, each formally expounded the second law of thermodynamics.

1865 The unification between magnetism and electricity was brought to full flower by the Scottish physicist James Clerk Maxwell (1831–79) in his great electromagnetic theory, which described every known kind of magnetic and electric behaviour.

1879 Sir William Crookes (1832–1919), English physicist and chemist, devised a tube – now named after him – which revealed the presence of cathode rays. These rays were subsequently shown by Thomson to be streams of electrons.

1887 Heinrich Hertz (1857–94), the German physicist, performed a classic experiment in which electromagnetic waves were produced and transmitted across the laboratory. This laid the foundation for radio transmission and provided ample vindication for Maxwell's theory.

Albert Abraham Michelson (1852–1931), American physicist, and Edward Williams Morley (1838–1923), American chemist, conducted heir classic experiment in which they measured the velocity of light in mutually perpendicular directions in an attempt to detect the Earth's supposed motion through the aether. No difference in velocity was discerned and this null result was a cornerstone in Einstein's special theory of relativity in 1905.

1892 Jules Henri Poincaré (1854–1912), French mathematician and philosopher, published the first of three volumes *Lesxméthodes nouvelles de la mévcanique céleste* which summarized his mathematical approach to astronomy and in particular the 'three-body' problem. It was from this work that the first notions of chaos theory, now so important in contemporary scientific thinking, may be traced.

1895 X-rays were discovered by Wilhelm von Röntgen (1845–1923), a German physicist. When experimenting with the passage of electrical dischares through gases, he noticed that fluorescent material near his apparatus glowed.

1896 Henri Becquerel (1852–1908), French physicist, discovered that uranium salts, even in the dark, emit a radiation similar to Röntgen's X-rays and would fog a photographic plate. This was later called radioactivity.

1897 Joseph John Thomson (1865–1940), English physicist, discovered the first of the fundamental particles, the electron, which is the basic unit of negative electricity.

1898 Marie Curie (1867–1934), Polish chemist, working with her French husband, Pierre (1859–1906), announced the existence of two new chemical elements which powerfully emit radiation. She gave the name radioactivity to this active phenomena.

The New Zealand-born physicist Ernest Rutherford (1871–1937) and the English chemist Frederick Soddy (1877–1956) formulated a theory of radioactivity that forms the basis of our present understanding of the phenomenon. Three types of radioactivity were identified, *a*-rays, ß-rays and λ-rays.

1900 The quantum theory was proposed by the German physicist Max Planck (1858–1947). This arose out of yet another problem that had been insoluble up to that time. Calculations showed that the energy emitted from a hot body should be, at very short wavelengths, practically infinite: this was clearly not so. The calculations were satisfactory for radiation of longer wavelengths in that they agreed

with the experiment. To resolve this difficulty, Planck made the very novel suggestion that energy was radiated from the body, not in a continuous flow of waves as it had been supposed up to then, but rather in distinct individual bundles. He called a bundle of energy a quantum.

1905 Albert Einstein (1879–1955) published his theory of the photoelectric effect. Einstein followed Planck's ideas and could see that the incident light must consist of a stream of quanta, that is, bundles of light, which came to be known as photons. A photon striking a metal surface is absorbed by an electron in it, the electron having more energy as a result. This causes it to jump from the surface, and since photons have greater energy at shorter wavelengths, so shorter wavelength light causes the emission of higher energy electrons. And, of course, the greater the intensity of the light the more quanta will be striking the surface and so more electrons will be emitted. Thus, the idea of the quantum enabled Einstein to account for the phenomena of the photoelectric effect. This was an early triumph for the new quantum theory, which was to prove fundamental in the subsequent development in physics.

1905 This year also saw the publication of Einstein's *Special (or Restricted) Theory of Relativity*. It had been said that as a child he had wondered what would happen if it were possible to travel fast enough to catch a ray of light and that this led him some years later to formulate his celebrated theory. This theory arises from an apparent contradiction between two basic postulates.

1. The velocity of light in a vacuum is a constant for all observers regardless of their state of motion relative to the light source.

2. The special principle of relativity which states that the laws of physics are the same for all observers in uniform motion relative to each other.

Imagine a train travelling with a uniform velocity v relative to the railway embankment and a ray of light transmitted with velocity c along the embankment parallel, and in the direction of the train. For an observer in the train the velocity of the light should appear to be $c–v$: obviously less than c. But this violates the special principle of relativity above: the velocity of light must be the same for an observer on the embankment and an observer on the train. The reconciliation of these two apparently contradictory conclusions is the basis for the special theory and is achieved by surrendering the concepts of absolute time, absolute distance and of the absolute significance of simultaneity. Relative theory thus confirms an important unification in physics between two of its very basic concepts: mass and energy, with the former being a congealed form of the latter with a transmission constant being the speed of light (c) squared: $E = mc^2$.

1911 Ernest Rutherford proposed a model of the atom that is the basis of our ideas of atomic structure to this day. He had from the first recognized the value of the fast-moving a-particles emitted naturally from radioactive materials as probes for discovering the nature of the atom. He arranged for a-particles to bombard a thin gold foil and found that while many passed straight through, a few were deflected at comparatively large angles, some even 'bouncing' back towards the source. He concluded from this that the mass of the atom was concentrated at its centre in a minute nucleus consisting of positively charged particles called protons. Around the nucleus and at a relatively large distance from it revolved the negatively charged electrons. The combined negative charges of the electrons exactly balanced the total positive charge of the nucleus. This important model of the atom suffered from a number of defects. One of these was that from Maxwell's electromagnetic theory the atom should produce light of all wavelengths, whereas, in fact, atoms of each element emit light consisting of a number of definite wavelengths – a spectrum – which can be measured with great accuracy. This spectrum for each element is unique.

1913 The difficulties of the Rutherford atom were overcome by the Danish physicist Niels Henrik David Bohr (1885–1962), who proposed that electrons were permitted only in certain orbits but could jump from one permitted orbit to another. In so jumping the electron would gain or lose energy in the form of photons. In this way the spectrum of light emitted, or absorbed, by an atom would relate to its individual structure. The theoretical basis to Bohr's work was confirmed by Einstein in 1917 and the Bohr theory went on successfully to explain other atomic phenomena. However, after many outstanding successes over a number of years, an increasing number of small but important discrepancies appeared with which the Bohr theory could not cope.

1919 Rutherford performed the first artificial nuclear disintegration when he bombarded nitrogen atoms with a-particles from radon-C. He demonstrated that protons were emitted as a result of the disintegration and this confirmed that the proton was, indeed, a nuclear particle.

1924 Louis-Victor de Broglie (1892–1976), French physicist, postulated that the dual wave-particle nature of light might be shown by other particles and particularly by electrons.

Electron waves were demonstrated experimentally in 1927 by the Americans C. J. Davisson (1881–1958) and L. H. Germer (1896–1971). Subsequently, de Broglie's idea of matter waves was extended to other particles – protons, neutrons, etc. All matter has an associated wave character, but for the larger bodies of classical mechanics, the wavelengths are too small for their effects to be detectable.

1926 Erwin Schrödinger (1887–1961), Austrian-born physicist, took up the idea of de Broglie waves and applied them to the Bohr atom. The solutions to the resulting wave equation gave the allowed orbits or energy levels more accurately than the quantized orbits in the Bohr atom. Max Born (1882–1970), German physicist, interpreted these solutions in terms of probability, i.e. they gave the probability of finding an electron in a given volume of space within the atom.

1927 The German physicist Werner Karl Heisenberg (1901–76) formulated his Uncertainty Principle. This states that there is a definite limit to the accuracy with which certain pairs of measurements can be made. The more accurately one quantity is known, the less accurate is our knowledge of the other. Position and momentum is an example of such a pair of measurements. The more exactly we know the position of, say, an electron, the less will we know about its momentum. The uncertainty principle provides the main reason why the classical mechanics of Newton do not apply to atomic and subatomic phenomena.

1928 P.A.M. Dirac (1902–84), an English physicist and mathematician, introduced a theory of the electron that successfully brought together the ideas of quantum mechanics thus far developed with those of relativity. As a result of this, the important concept of electron spin previously advanced by Bohr became theoretically justified.

Dirac's equations revealed a negative quantity that led to the prediction of the existence of the antielectron, a particle identical to the electron, of the same mass but of opposite electric charge. This major idea, that there could exist *antimatter* in the universe composed of antiparticles, arises from Dirac's bold prediction.

1932 Ernest Orlando Lawrence (1901–58), American physicist, developed the *cyclotron*. This was one of the first machines constructed for artificially accelerating charged particles to high velocities for research.

1932 Carl David Anderson (1905–), American physicist, announced the discovery of the antielectron predicted a few years previously by Dirac. This was the first particle of antimatter to be discovered and he named it the *positron*.

Sir John Douglas Cockcroft (1897–1967), English physicist, and Ernest Thomas Sinton Walton (1903–), Irish physicist, were the first to produce a nuclear reaction with artificially accelerated particles. They used a voltage multiplier to accelerate protons to 710 keV which reacted with lithium nuclei.

James Chadwick (1891–1974), English physicist, discovered the *neutron*, a constituent of the atomic nucleus of zero charge and only slightly heavier than the proton.

1933 Wolfgang Pauli (1900–58), Austrian physicist, postulated the existence of the *neutrino*, a neutral particle of negligible mass in order to explain the fact that in β-emission in radioactivity there was a rather greater loss of energy than could be otherwise explained.

1934 Hideki Yukawa (1907–81), Japanese physicist, sought to explain the forces that held the particles in the nucleus together – the *strong force* – and called the force-carrying particles in this case *mesons*. The meson predicted by Yukawa, the *pi meson* or *pion*, was discovered by Cecil F. Powell (1903–69) of Bristol University in 1947.

1938 Nuclear fission was discovered by Otto Hahn (1879–1968) and Fritz Strassman (1902–) by bombarding uranium with neutrons, when trying to produce transuranic elements. They succeeded in producing elements lighter than uranium. Enrico Fermi (1901–54) suggested that the neutrons released in fission could themselves induce further fission and that it should be possible to sustain a chain reaction.

1942 The first nuclear reactor, set up by Fermi in the University of Chicago, became critical.

1953 Murray Gell-Mann (1929–), American physicist, introduced a concept he called **strangeness**, a quality akin in some ways to electric charge, which helped to account for the increased lifetimes of the strange particles. Aided by this idea, it was found that particles could be fitted into patterns according to the amount of strangeness they possessed.

1954 In June 1954 the world's first nuclear-powered generator produced electricity (5MW) at Obnisk near Moscow, and in August 1956 the first large-scale (50MW) nuclear power generating station, Calder Hall, Cumberland (Cumbria), started up.

1953 Gell-Mann proposed the idea that hadrons – complex particles – were composed of more basic particles called 'quarks'.

THE PARTICLES OF PHYSICS – LEPTONS AND QUARKS

Generation	Name	Electric Charge	Mass (MeV)	Quark Flavour	Electric Charge	Mass (MeV)*	Strangeness	Charm	Bottomness	Topness
First Family	electron	-1	0.511	d (down)	$-\frac{1}{3}$	350	0	0	0	0
	electron neutrino	0	0?	u (up)	$+\frac{2}{3}$	350	0	0	0	0
Second Family	muon	-1	105.658	s (strange)	$-\frac{1}{3}$	500	-1	0	0	0
	muon neutrino	0	0?	c (charm)	$+\frac{2}{3}$	1500	0	+1	0	0
Third Family	tau	-1	1784.1	b (bottom)	$-\frac{1}{3}$	5000	0	0	-1	0
	tau neutrino	0	0?	t (top)	$+\frac{2}{3}$	50 000	0	0	0	+1

* Because of the strong colour force, the masses of quarks depend on the distance over which they are measured. The approximate values given in the table are those that appear to be the sum of masses of the hadrons (the 'long distance' masses) while the 'short distance' or Lagrangian masses are those that are required by the theory of quantum chromodynamics, i.e. for the u, d, s, and c quarks. These are approximately 6, 10, 200 and 1300 MeV respectively, whilst the masses of the bottom and top quarks are too approximately known to distinguish between the long and short distance masses.

1965 It was realized that quarks with exactly the same quantum numbers cannot exist together and therefore must possess an extra degree of freedom known as 'colour', a concept introduced by M. Y. an and Y. Nambu.

1967–70 Following original concepts developed by C.N. Yang (1922–) and R. Mills (1924–) in 1954 and J. Schwinger (1918–) in 1957, the standard model to describe electro-weak interactions was introduced by S. Weinberg (1933–) and A. Salam (1926–) in 1967–68 and generalized by S.L. Glashow (1932–) in 1970. In this model both weak and electromagnetic interactions are described in a unified theory which requires the existence not only of the massless photon but also of very massive intermediate particles which are both charged (the W±) and neutral (the Z^0).

1974 A heavy meson was discovered with a lifetime that was much longer than would be expected at this mass level. Such a phenomena is usually explained in terms of the existence of a unique quantum number. The particle was named 'psi' or 'J'.

1977 The unexpected discovery in 1975 of a heavy lepton (the 'tau') led immediately to the suggestion of the existence of a tau neutrino and of two very heavy quarks in order to preserve quark-lepton symmetry. The new quarks were given the names 'bottom' and 'top' (the alternative names 'beauty' and 'truth' now appear to have been dropped). The discovery in November 1977 of two very heavy mesons with masses close to 10 000 MeV but with very long lifetimes similar to those of the psi mesons was considered as confirmation of the existence of the bottom quark, although the mesons consisted of bottom quarks and their anti-quarks and therefore showed zero net bottom.

1983 The existence of both the W± in January 1983 and the Z^0 in August 1983 were established at *Centre Européen de la Recherche Nucléaire* (CERN), Geneva, Switzerland (see 1967–70 above).

1986 Experiments in January led to a revolution in the development of superconductive materials. Superconductivity is defined as 'a complete lack of electrical resistance' and was discovered by H. Kamerlingh Onnes (1853–1926) in 1911. Over the next 75 years it was considered to be a very low-temperature effect with the maximum superconducting temperature attained being 23 K (– 250 °C), so the technique was extremely limited in use. However, in experiments by K. A. Muller and J. G. Bednorz of IBM, Zurich, in 1986, superconductivity was observed at 35 K (– 238 °C) in a mixed oxide of barium, lanthanum, and copper. In 1987 two groups in the USA and China independently reported attaining superconductive temperatures of about 90 K (– 183 °C) in a mixed oxide of yttrium, barium, and copper. Research continues and the current record holder is 125 K (– 148 °C) for a mixed oxide of thallium, barium, calcium, and copper. Such temperatures are within the range of liquid nitrogen and will dramatically reduce the cost of using superconductivity in engineering applications.

1991 A number of particles that are important in the theories of modern physics remain to be discovered: these include the tau neutrino, the top quark, and the Higgs boson (a particle suggested by Peter Higgs of the University of Edinburgh in order to explain the manifestly different behaviour of the electromagnetic and weak interaction mechanisms).

NOBEL PRIZEWINNERS IN PHYSICS

1901 Wilhelm Röntgen, German. Discovered X-rays

1902 Hendrik Antoon Lorentz, Netherlands and Pieter Zeeman, Netherlands. Investigated the influences of magnetism on radiation

1903 Antoine-Henri Becquerel, French. Discovered spontaneous radioactivity.
Pierre Curie, French and Marie Curie, French (naturalized citizen). Investigated radiation phenomena (inspired by Becquerel's discovery)

1904 Lord Rayleigh, English. Discovered argon, an unreactive gas in the atmosphere

1905 Philipp Lenard, German. Research on cathode rays

1906 Sir J. J. Thomson, English. Investigated electrical conductivity of gases

1907 A. A. Michelson, USA (German-born). Established the speed of light as a constant, and other spectroscopic and metrological investigations

1908 Gabriel Lippmann, French. Photographic reproduction of colours

1909 Guglielmo Marconi, Italian and Karl Braun, German. Developed wireless telegraphy

1910 J. van der Waals, Dutch. Investigated the relationships between the states of gases and liquids

1911 Wilhelm Wien, German. Investigated the laws governing heat radiation

1912 Nils Gustav Dalén, Swedish. Invented automatic regulators for lighting buoys and beacons

1913 H. Kamerlingh Onnes, Dutch. Studied properties of matter at low temperatures; produces liquid helium

1914 Max von Laue, German. Achieved diffraction of X-rays using crystals

1915 Sir William Bragg, English and Sir Lawrence Bragg, English. Analysed crystal structure using X-rays

1916 No award

1917 Charles Barkla, English. Discovered characteristics of X-radiation of elements

1918 Max Plank, German. Formulated the first quantum theory

1919 Johannes Stark, German. Discovered the Doppler effect in positive ion rays and the division of spectral lines when the source of light is subjected to strong electric force fields

1920 Charles Guillaume, Swiss. Discovered anomalies in alloys

1921 Albert Einstein, German-American Elucidated theories fundamental to theoretical physics

1922 Niels Bohr, Danish. Investigated atomic structure and radiation

1923 Robert Millikan, USA. Worked on elementary electric charge and the photoelectric effect

1924 Karl Siegbahn, Swedish. Worked on X-ray spectroscopy

1925 James Franck, German and Gustav Hertz, German. Defined the laws governing the impact of an electron upon an atom

1926 Jean-Baptiste Perrin, French. Worked on the discontinuous structure of matter

1927 Arthur Holly Compton, USA. Discovered wavelength change in diffused X-rays
Charles Wilson, Scottish. Invented the Cloud Chamber; made visible the paths of electrically charged particles

1928 Sir Owen Richardson, English. Discovered Richardson's Law; concerns the electron emissions by hot metals

1929 Louis de Broglie, French. Discovered the wave nature of electrons

1930 Sir C. Raman, Indian. Worked on light diffusion; discovered the Raman effect

1931 No award

1932 Werner Heisenberg, German. Formulated the indeterminacy principle of quantum mechanics

1933 P.A.M Dirac, British and Erwin Schrödinger, Austrian. Introduced wave-equations in quantum mechanics

1934 No award

1935 Sir James Chadwick, English. Discovered the neutron

1936 Victor Hess, Austria. Discovered cosmic radiation

1937 Clinton Davisson, USA and Sir George Thomson, English. Demonstrated the interference phenomenon in crystals irradiated by electrons

1938 Enrico Fermi, Italian. Discovered radioactive elements produced by neutron irradiation

1939 Ernest Lawrence, USA. Invention of the cyclotron

1940 −1942 No awards

1943 Otto Stern, USA (naturalized citizen). Discovered the magentic moment of the proton

1944 Isoder Rabi, USA (naturalized citizen). Resonance method for observing the magnetic properties of atomic nuclei

1945 Wolfgang Pauli, Austria. Discovered the exclusion principle

1946 Percy Bridgman, USA. Made discoveries in high-pressure physics

1947 Sir Edward Appleton, English. Discovered the Appleton Layer in the upper atmosphere

1948 Patrick Blackett, English. Made discoveries in nuclear physics and cosmic radiation

1949 Hudeki Yukawa, Japan. Predicted the existence of mesons

1950 Cecil Powell, English. Photographic method of studying nuclear processes; discoveries about mesons

1951 Sir John Cockcroft, English and Ernest Walton, Irish. Pioneered the use of accelerated particles to study atomic nuclei

1952 Felix Bloch, USA (naturalized citizen) and Edward Purcell, USA. Discovered nuclear magnetic resonance in solids

1953 Frits Zernike, Dutch. Phase-contrast microscopy method

1954 Max Born, British (German-born). Statistical studies on wave functions
Walther Bothe, German. Invention of coincidence method

1955 Willis Lamb, Jr., USA. Discoveries in the hydrogen spectrum
Polykarp Kusch, USA (naturalized citizen). Measured the magnetic moment of the electron

1956 William Shockley, USA, John Bardeen, USA and Walther Brattain, USA. Investigated semi-conductors and discovered the transistor effect

1957 Tsung-Dao Lee, Chinese and Chen Ning Yang, Chinese. Discovered violations of the principle of parity

1958 Pavel A. Cherenkov, Russian, Ilya M. Frank, Russian and Igor Y. Tamm, Russian. Investigated the effects produced by high-energy particles; the Cherenkov effect

1959 Emilio Segrè, USA (naturalized citizen) and Owen Chamberlain, USA. Confirmed the existence of the antiproton

1960 Donald Glasser, USA. Developed the bubble chamber; the device that enables the tracks of ionizing particles to be photographed

1961 Robert Hofstadter, USA. Determined shape and size of atomic nucleons
Rudolf Mössbauer, German. Discovered the Mössbauer effect; the emission of gamma rays from certain crystal substances

1962 Lev D. Landau, Russian. Contributed to the understanding of condensed states of matter

1963 J. H. D. Jensen, German and Maria Goeppert Mayer, USA (naturalized citizen). Developed shell model theory of the structure of atomic nuclei
Eugene Paul Wigner, USA (naturalized citizen). Principles governing interaction of protons and neutrons in the nucleus

1964 Charles H. Townes, USA, Nikolay G. Basov, Russian and Aleksandr M. Prokhorov, Russian. Quantum electronics leading to construction of instruments based on maser-laser principles

1965 Julian S. Schwinger, USA, Richard P. Feynman, USA, Tomonaga Shin'ichiro, Japan. Basic principles of quantum electrodynamics

1966 Alfred Kastler, French. Optical methods for studying Hertzian resonances in atoms

1967 Hans A. Bethe, USA (naturalized citizen). Discoveries concerning the energy production of stars

1968 Luis W. Alvarez, USA. Discovered resonance states as part of work with elementary particles

1969 Murray Gell-Mann, USA. Classification of elementary particles and their interactions

1970 Hannes Alfvén, Swedish and Louis Néel, French. Magneto-hydrodynamics and antiferromagnetism and ferrimagnetism

1971 Dennis Gabor, British (Hungarian-born). Invented holography

1972 John Bardeen, USA, Leon N. Cooper, USA and John R. Schrieffer, USA. Developed the theory of superconductivity

1973 Leo Esaki, Japan, Ivar Giaever, USA (naturalized citizen) and Brian Josephson, Welsh. Tunnelling in semiconductors and superconductors

1974 Sir Martin Ryle, English and Antony Hewish, English. Radio astronomy

1975 Aage Bohr, Danish, Ben R. Mottelson, Danish (naturalized citizen) and L. James Rainwater, USA. Understanding of the atomic nucleus that paved the way for nuclear fusion

1976 Burton Richter, USA and Samuel C. C. Ting, USA. Discovered new class of elementary particles (psi, or J)

1977 Philip W. Anderson, USA, Sir Neville Mott, British, and John H. Van Vleck, USA. Contributed to understanding the behaviour of electrons in magnetic, non-crystalline solids

1978 Pyotr L. Kapitsa, Russian. Invented the helium liquefier, and applications
Arno A. Penzias, USA (naturalized citizen) and Robert W. Wilson, USA. Discovered cosmic microwave background radiation (support for big-bang theory)

1979 Sheldon Glashow, USA, Abdus Salam, Pakistani, and Steven Weinberg, USA. Established analogy between electromagnetism and the 'weak' interactions of subatomic particles

1980 James W. Cronin, USA and Val L. Fitch, USA. Simultaneous violation of both charge-conjugation and parity-inversion

1981 Kai M. Siegbahn, Swedish, Nicolaas Bloembergen, USA (naturalized citizen). Electron spectroscopy for chemical analysis
Arthur L. Schalow, USA. Applications of lasers in spectroscopy

1982 Kenneth G. Wilson, USA. Analysis of continuous phase transitions

1983 Subrahmanyan Chandrasekhar, USA and William A. Fowler, USA. Contributed to understanding the evolution and devolution of stars

1984 Carlo Rubbia, Italian and Simon van der Meer, Dutch. Discovered subatomic particles (W;Z), supporting the electro-weak theory

1985 Klaus von Klitzing, German. Discovered the Hall effect, permitting exact measurements of electrical resistance

1986 Ernst Ruska, German, Gerd Binnig, German and Heinrich Rohrer, Swiss. Developed special electron microscopes

1987 J. Georg Bednorz, German and K. Alex Müller, Swiss. Discovered new superconducting materials

1988 Lwon Lederman, USA, Melvin Schwartz, USA and Jack Steinberger, USA. Researched subatomic particles

1989 Norman Harvey, USA. Developed the separated field method
Hans Dehmelt, USA, and Wolfgang Paul, German. Developed and exploited the ion trap

1990 Richard E. Taylor, Canadian, Jerome Friedman, USA, and Henry Kendall, USA. Proved the existence of the quark

1991 Pierre-Gilles de Gennes, France. Studies in changes in liquid crystals

1992 George Charpak, France (naturalized citizen). Devised an electronic detector that reads trajectories of sub-atomic particles.

THE KINEMATIC EQUATIONS

For a body moving in a straight line with uniformly accelerated motion:

1. $v = u + at$

2. $s = ut + \frac{1}{2}at^2$

3. $v^2 = u^2 + 2as$

4. $s = \frac{1}{2}t(u + v)$

where s = displacement;
t = time;
u = initial or starting velocity;
v = velocity after time t;
a = acceleration

THE FORCES OF NATURE

The four basic forces that exist in nature are firmly established – gravity, the weak force, the electromagnetic force, and the strong force. They are listed in the table on p. 203 in ascending order of strength.

The forces all involve the exchange of force-carrying particles or 'quanta', which are known as *bosons* since they have integral spin, i.e. 0, 1 or 2.

The strong force is explained by the theory known as *quantum chromodynamics*, which requires the existence of eight gluons, six carrying the colour charge and two that are colour neutral.

The weak and electromagnetic forces have been successfully described in terms of a single 'electroweak' theory, while efforts continue to produce a unified theory of all four forces.

CHEMISTRY

Alchemy, from which chemistry derives its name, probably originated in Khimi, 'the land of black earth', in Egypt, where – 4000 years ago – it was discovered that heat could isolate metals and glasses in minerals. Alchemy spread throughout the Arab world and Asia. An aim of alchemy was the transmutation of metals: alchemists strove for a 'philosopher's stone' that could convert 'base' metals such as iron and lead into the 'noble' metal gold. They thought that the philosopher's stone would also be the 'elixir' of immortality. Much experimentation followed, leading to the development of techniques that formed the basis of modern chemistry.

THE AIMS OF MODERN CHEMISTRY

In modern chemistry, the philosopher's stone has been replaced by a fundamental belief in the importance of understanding the physical laws that govern the behaviour of atoms and molecules. Such an understanding has resulted in the development of methods for converting cheaply available and naturally occurring minerals, gases and oils into substances that have high commercial or social value. The discovery that iron could be made into steel by chemical means played a major part in the Industrial Revolution. In the 20th century, spectacular increases in the yields of cereals from an acre of farmland can be traced to the discovery in Germany in 1908 that nitrogen from air could be converted into ammonia fertilizers. Similarly, the greater understanding of the structures and reactions of carbon-based (organic) compounds has resulted in products such as medicines and synthetic fibres that affect all our lives.

ELEMENTS AND MOLECULES

The structure of atoms serves as a convenient starting point for discussing chemical phenomena. In chemical processes, the nuclei of atoms remain unchanged – shattering at once the alchemist's dream of transmuting elements. The great variety of known chemical compounds results from the different ways in which the electrons of atoms are able to interact either with atoms of the same kind or with atoms of a different kind. In an *element*, all the atoms are of the same kind, but the varying strengths of the interactions between the electrons in different types of atom means that elements have very different properties. For example, helium melts at $-272\,°C\,(-458\,°F)$, whereas carbon in the form of diamond has a melting point of $3500\,°C\,(6332\,°F)$. This ability of electrons to interact between atoms is known as *chemical bonding*. The elements nitrogen, oxygen, fluorine and chlorine form strong bonds, with two identical atoms linked together. They therefore exist at room temperature as gases, with pairs of linked atoms moving chaotically in space. Two or more atoms linked in this fashion are described as *molecules*, and a shorthand notation is used to describe their chemical identity. The atomic symbol for the element is used in conjunction with the number of atoms present to define the *chemical formula* of the molecule. The elements described above are therefore designated, respectively, by the formulae N_2, O_2, F_2 and Cl_2.

Other familiar elements, such as sulfur and phosphorus, form additional bonds to like atoms, and their formulae reflect this fact. Thus sulfur forms a ring of eight atoms and is described by the formula S_8. As the number of atoms in the fundamental unit increases, the element is no longer a gas but becomes a solid with a low melting point; thus sulfur can be extracted from the Earth as a molten fluid. Most elements do not form discrete molecular entities such as those described above, but have structures that are held together by chemical bonds in all directions. Most of the 109 known elements are metals, such as iron and copper, and have *infinite structures* of this kind. Such elements can no longer be given distinct molecular formulae and are therefore represented by the element symbol alone; thus iron, for example, is represented simply as Fe.

CHEMICAL COMPOUNDS

In *chemical compounds*, the atoms of more than one element come together to form either molecules or infinite structures. They are described by formulae similar to those given above for elements. For example, water has a finite structure based on one oxygen atom chemically bonded to two hydrogen atoms and is denoted by the formula H_2O. Common salt (sodium chloride; NaCl) has sodium (Na) and chlorine (Cl) atoms linked together in an infinite three-dimensional lattice.

In a pure chemical compound, all the molecules have the same ratio of different atoms and behave in an identical chemical fashion. Thus a pure sample of water, for example, behaves identically to any other pure sample, however different their origins may be. Furthermore, the same ratios of atoms are retained irrespective of whether the compound is a solid, a liquid or a gas. For example, ice, water and water vapour all have molecules with the constitution H_2O. The transformation of ice into water and then into water vapour by heating is not a chemical reaction because the identities of the molecules do not change.

From the 109 chemical elements now known, more than 2 million chemical compounds have been made during the last 100 years. The chemist views chemistry as a set of molecular building blocks, constructing more and more complex and diverse molecular structures, the variety of which is limited only by his or her imagination. It is important to emphasize that the properties of a chemical compound are unique and not a sum of the properties of the individual elements from which it is made. For example, common salt does not have any properties remotely like those of metallic sodium, which catches fire on contact with water, or chlorine, which is a harmful yellow-green gas. Although all compounds are unique, they can be classified into broad families based on common chemical properties. Acids, bases, salts, and oxidizing and reducing agents are examples of such families. Classifications reflecting the atoms present are also useful for cataloguing purposes: for example, hydrides, chlorides and oxides indicate compounds containing hydrogen, chlorine and oxygen respectively. Another particularly important classification is that of organic compounds, which contain carbon and are not only important for life processes but make up many modern industrial chemicals such as plastics, paints and artificial fibres.

MIXTURES

When elements or compounds are mixed together but not chemically bonded, they form a *chemical mixture*. A mixture can be of two solids (e.g. salt and sand), two liquids, two gases or permutations of these. A mixture can be separated into its pure chemical constituents by either chemical or physical means. For example, adding water to the sand-salt mixture dissolves the salt, leaving the sand in a pure state. The salt and water is itself a mixture described as a *solution*, from which the pure salt can be obtained by boiling off the water.

The modern-day chemist has many other techniques for separating mixtures, such as distillation, chromatography, crystallization and electrolysis. The petrochemical industry is a prime example of how this technology can be used to convert natural gas and crude oil into a range of useful commercial and domestic products.

ELEMENTS

The world we see around us is made up of a limited number of chemical elements. In the Earth's crust, there are 82 stable elements and a few unstable (radioactive) ones. Among the stable elements, there are some, such as oxygen and silicon, that are very abundant, while others – the metals ruthenium and rhodium, for example – are extremely rare. Indeed, 98% of the Earth's crust is made up of just eight elements – in order of decreasing abundance, oxygen, silicon, aluminium, iron, calcium, sodium, magnesium and potassium.

THE PERIODIC TABLE

Each element is associated with a unique number, called its *atomic number*. This represents the number of protons – positively charged particles – in the nucleus of each atom of the element. Hydrogen has one proton, so it is the first and lightest of the elements and is placed first in the Periodic Table. Helium has two protons, and is thus the second lightest element and is placed second in the Table; and so we continue through each of the elements, establishing their order in the Table according to their atomic numbers.

The atomic number of bismuth is 83, and this number of protons represents the upper limit for a stable nucleus. Beyond 83, all elements are unstable, although their radioactive decay may be so slow that some of them, such a thorium and uranium, are found in large natural deposits.

The largest atomic number so far observed is 109, but only a few atoms of this element have been made artificially, so little is known about it. Its name is unnilennium, meaning 'one-zero-nine'.

THE HISTORY OF THE PERIODIC TABLE

The discovery of the Periodic Table was made possible by an Italian chemist, Stanislao Cannizzaro (1826–1910), who in 1858 published a list of fixed atomic weights (now known as standard atomic weights) for the 60 elements that were then known. By arranging the elements in order of increasing atomic weight, a curious repetition of chemical properties at regular intervals was revealed. This was noticed in 1864 by the English chemist John Newlands (1838–98), but his 'law of octaves' brought him nothing but ridicule.

It was left to the Russian chemist Dmitri Mendeleyev (1834–1907) to make essentially the same discovery five years later. What Mendeleyev did, however, was so much more impressive that he is rightly credited as the true discoverer of the Periodic Table.

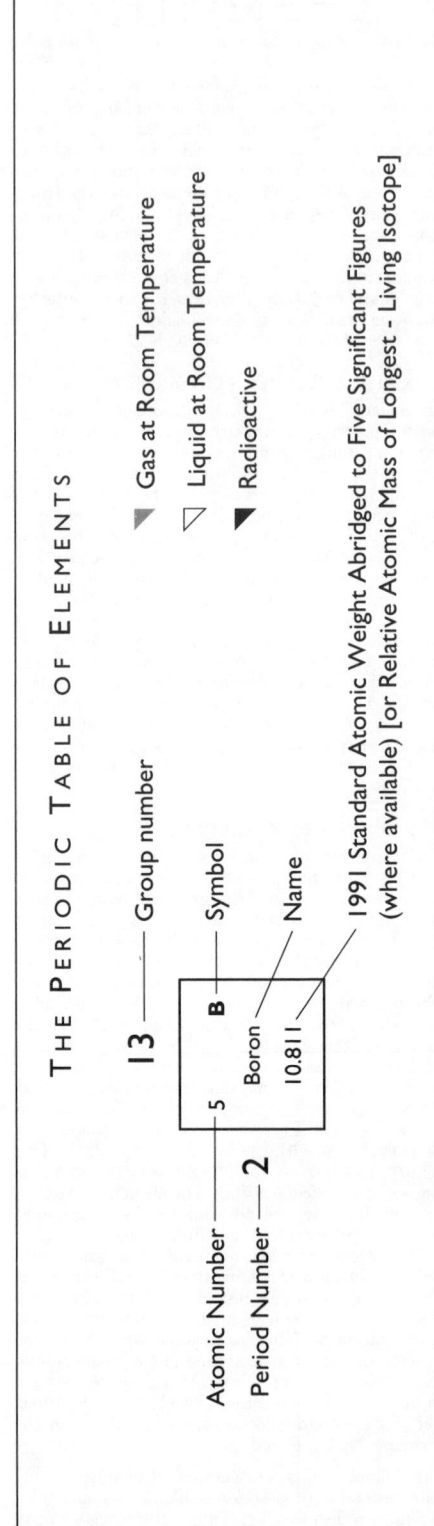

Periodic Table of the Elements

Group	1	2	3	4	5	6	7	8	9	10	11	12	13	14	15	16	17	18
Period 1	1 **H** Hydrogen 1.0079																	2 **He** Helium 4.0026
Period 2	3 **Li** Lithium 6.941	4 **Be** Beryllium 9.0122											5 **B** Boron 10.811	6 **C** Carbon 12.011	7 **N** Nitrogen 14.007	8 **O** Oxygen 15.999	9 **F** Fluorine 18.998	10 **Ne** Neon 20.180
Period 3	11 **Na** Sodium 22.990	12 **Mg** Magnesium 24.305											13 **Al** Aluminium 26.982	14 **Si** Silicon 28.086	15 **P** Phosphorus 30.974	16 **S** Sulfur 32.066	17 **Cl** Chlorine 35.453	18 **Ar** Argon 39.948
Period 4	19 **K** Potassium 39.098	20 **Ca** Calcium 40.078	21 **Sc** Scandium 44.956	22 **Ti** Titanium 47.88	23 **V** Vanadium 50.942	24 **Cr** Chromium 51.996	25 **Mn** Manganese 54.938	26 **Fe** Iron 55.847	27 **Co** Cobalt 58.933	28 **Ni** Nickel 58.693	29 **Cu** Copper 63.546	30 **Zn** Zinc 65.39	31 **Ga** Gallium 69.723	32 **Ge** Germanium 72.61	33 **As** Arsenic 74.922	34 **Se** Selenium 78.96	35 **Br** Bromine 79.904	36 **Kr** Krypton 83.80
Period 5	37 **Rb** Rubidium 85.468	38 **Sr** Strontium 87.62	39 **Y** Yttrium 88.906	40 **Zr** Zirconium 91.224	41 **Nb** Niobium 92.906	42 **Mo** Molybdenum 95.94	43 **Tc** Technetium [97.907]	44 **Ru** Ruthenium 101.07	45 **Rh** Rhodium 102.91	46 **Pd** Palladium 106.42	47 **Ag** Silver 107.87	48 **Cd** Cadmium 112.41	49 **In** Indium 114.82	50 **Sn** Tin 118.71	51 **Sb** Antimony 121.76	52 **Te** Tellurium 127.60	53 **I** Iodine 126.90	54 **Xe** Xenon 131.29
Period 6	55 **Cs** Caesium 132.91	56 **Ba** Barium 137.33	57 – 71 LANTHANIDES	72 **Hf** Hafnium 178.49	73 **Ta** Tantalum 180.95	74 **W** Tungsten 183.84	75 **Re** Rhenium 186.21	76 **Os** Osmium 190.23	77 **Ir** Iridium 192.22	78 **Pt** Platinum 195.08	79 **Au** Gold 196.97	80 **Hg** Mercury 200.59	81 **Tl** Thallium 204.38	82 **Pb** Lead 207.2	83 **Bi** Bismuth 208.98	84 **Po** Polonium [208.98]	85 **At** Astatine [209.99]	86 **Rn** Radon [222.02]
Period 7	87 **Fr** Francium [223.02]	88 **Ra** Radium [226.03]	89 – 103 ACTINIDES	104 **Unq** Unnilquadium [261.11]	105 **Unp** Unnilpentium [262.11]	106 **Unh** Unnilhexium [263.12]	107 **Uns** Unnilseptium [262.12]	108 **Uno** Unniloctium [265.13]	109 **Une** Unnilennium [266.14]									

Lanthanides

57 **La** Lanthanum 138.91	58 **Ce** Cerium 140.12	59 **Pr** Praseodymium 140.91	60 **Nd** Neodymium 144.24	61 **Pm** Promethium [144.91]	62 **Sm** Samarium 150.36	63 **Eu** Europium 151.96	64 **Gd** Gadolinium 157.25	65 **Tb** Terbium 158.93	66 **Dy** Dysprosium 162.50	67 **Ho** Holmium 164.93	68 **Er** Erbium 167.26	69 **Tm** Thulium 168.93	70 **Yb** Ytterbium 173.04	71 **Lu** Lutetium 174.97

Actinides

89 **Ac** Actinium [227.03]	90 **Th** Thorium 232.04	91 **Pa** Protactinium 231.04	92 **U** Uranium 238.03	93 **Np** Neptunium [237.05]	94 **Pu** Plutonium [244.06]	95 **Am** Americium [243.06]	96 **Cm** Curium [247.07]	97 **Bk** Berkelium [247.07]	98 **Cf** Californium [251.08]	99 **Es** Einsteinium [252.08]	100 **Fm** Fermium [257.10]	101 **Md** Mendelevium [258.10]	102 **No** Nobelium [259.10]	103 **Lr** Lawrencium [262.11]

Mendeleyev's genius lay in the fact that he recognized that there was an underlying order to the Periodic Table – he did not design the Periodic Table, he *discovered* it. If he was right, he knew that there should be places in his table for new elements. He was so confident in his discovery that he predicted the properties of these missing elements – and his predictions were subsequently shown to be accurate.

However, there were so-called 'rare earth' elements that simply could not be fitted in to the table, whilst tellurium had a higher atomic weight than iodine, the next higher element in the table, whereas the reverse should have occurred. These problems were solved in 1913 by the English physicist Henry Moseley (1887–1915) who showed that the fundamental number for an element is the number of positive charges in the nucleus – its atomic number. It was then quickly established that not only did tellurium have a lower atomic number than iodine – the atomic weight abnormality was later shown to be due to an isotopic effect – but also that there were actually only 15 true rare earth elements – now known as *lanthanides*. One of the lanthanides (element 61) was missing. It was eventually produced artificially in 1945.

STRUCTURE OF THE PERIODIC TABLE

The periodic table is no longer arranged according to atomic weight but according to atomic number, which is the number of positively-charged electrons arranged in orbits or 'shells' around the nucleus. Electrons can be thought of as moving around the nucleus in certain fixed orbits or 'shells', the electrons in a particular shell being associated with a particular energy level. With regard to an atom's chemical behaviour, it is the electrons in the outer shell that are most important. The major energy levels are numbered 1, 2, 3, etc., counting outwards from the nucleus. This number is called the *principal quantum number*, and is given the symbol n. Each energy level can hold only a certain number of electrons; the further out it is, the more it can accommodate. The maximum capacity of each shell is $2n^2$.

The *inert gases* helium to radon have completely filled shells are are chemically inert. The *alkali metals* lithium to francium have one extra electron above a closed shell and chemically very active since they can easily donate the extra electron in chemical reactions. Similarly the *halogen elements* flourine to astatine – which have one less electron than a closed shell – are also chemically very active as they can easily absorb an electron in chemical reactions. The elements are therefore arranged across the periodic table in *group number* coresponding approximately to the filling of the shells, ranging from Group 1 - the alkali metals – to Group 18, the inert gases.

The filling of the principal quantum shells leads to a repeat of sub-shell filling and, therefore, a repeat of physical and chemical properties. The elements are therefore arranged in tiers or *Periodic Number* corresponding to the filled shells, with Period 1 comprising hydrogen and helium, Period 2 being lithium to neon, Period 3 comprising sodium to argon and so on.

The *lanthanides* and *actinides* are a special case since they represent mainly a filling of inner rather than outer shells with increasing atomic number. The fact that they have to be included in separate tables indicates a minor defect in the way the

periodic table is presented. Hydrogen is also a special case. It has only one electron and could therefore be presented with the alkalis – but it is definitely not an alkali metal. Hydrogen also has one less electron than a filled shell and therefore could be included with the halogens – but it is definitely not related to these elements. It is therefore usual to place hydrogen separate and above the main table either above Group 1 or above Group 17.

The development of the periodic table was undoubtedly instrumental in the development of the atomic theory and the periodic trends shown by the elements in both physical and chemical properties can be used to estimate values which will probably never be obtained in coherent form, for example the highly radioactive alkali metal francium, the halogen astatine and the later actinide elements.

CHEMICAL BONDS

Although there are only 109 known elements, there are millions of chemical substances found in nature or made artificially. These substances are not simply mixtures of two or more elements: they are specifically determined chemical compounds, formed by combining two or more elements together in a chemical reaction. The chemical 'glue' that holds these compounds together is known as *chemical bonding*.

The properties of compounds vary very widely. Some are highly reactive, others inert; some are solids with high melting points, others are gases. Furthermore, the properties of a compound are generally very different from those of its constituent elements. To understand how and why these differences arise, we need to understand the different types of chemical bond.

IONIC BONDING

The atoms of the element neon have a full outer shell of electrons, with the electron configuration 2.8. This arrangement is very stable and neon is not known to form chemical bonds with any other element. An atom of the element sodium (Na) has one more electron than neon (configuration 2.8.1), while an atom of the element fluorine (F) has one electron less (configuration 2.7). If an electron is transferred from a sodium atom to a fluorine atom, two species are produced with the same stable electron configuration as neon. Unlike neon, however, the species are charged and are known as *ions*. The sodium atom, having lost a (negative) electron, has a net positive charge and is known as a *cation* (written Na^+), while the fluorine atom, having gained an electron, has a net negative charge and is called a fluoride *anion* (written F^-).

When oppositely charged ions such as Na^+ and F^- are brought together, there is a strong attraction between them; a large amount of energy is released – the same amount of energy as would have to be supplied in order to separate the ions again. This force of attraction is called an *ionic* (or *electrovalent*) *bond*. The energy released more than compensates for the energy input required to transfer the electron from the sodium atom to the fluorine atom. Overall there is a net release of energy and a solid crystalline compound – sodium fluoride (NaF) – is formed.

Atoms that have two more electrons than the nearest noble gas (such as magnesium, configuration 2.8.2) or two less (such as oxygen, 2.6) also form ions having the noble-gas configuration by transfer of

THE 109 ELEMENTS (see also notes p. 234)

Atomic Number	Symbol	Element Name	Derived From	Discoverers	Year	Atomic Weight (Note 3)	Density At 20°C (Unless Otherwise Stated) (g/cm³) (Note 4)	Melting Point (°C)	Boiling Point (°C)	Number Of Nuclides
1	H	Hydrogen	Greek 'hydro genes' = water producer	H. Cavendish (UK)	1766	1·007 94	0·0871 (solid at mp) / 0·000 089 89 (gas at 0°C)	−259·198	−252·762	3
2	He	Helium	Greek 'helios' = sun	J. N. Lockyer (UK) and P. J. C. Janssen (France)	1868	4·002 602	0·190 8 (solid at mp) / 0·000 178 5 (gas at 0°C)	−272·375 at 24·985 atm (Note 5)	−268·928	8
3	Li	Lithium	Greek 'lithos' = stone	J. A. Arfwedson (Sweden)	1817	6·941	0·5334	180·54	1339	8
4	Be	Beryllium	Greek 'beryllion' = beryl	N. L. Vauquelin (France)	1798	9·012 182	1·846	1287	2471	9
5	B	Boron	Persian 'burah' = borax	L. J. Gay Lussac and L. J. Thenard (France) and H. Davy (UK)	1808	10·811	2·333 (b Rhombahedral)	2130	3910	13
6	C	Carbon	Latin 'carbo' = charcoal	Prehistoric	/;ED;/	12·011	2·266 (Graphite) / 3·515 (Diamond)	3530 (Note 6)	3870 (Note 6)	15
7	N	Nitrogen	Greek 'nitron genes' = saltpetre producer	D. Rutherford (UK)	1772	14·006 74	0·9426 (solid at mp) / 0·001 250 (gas at 0°C)	−210·000	−195·798	13
8	O	Oxygen	Greek 'oxys genes' = acid producer	C. W. Scheele (Sweden) and J. Priestley (UK)	1772–1774	15·9994	1·359 (solid at mp) / 0·001 429 (gas at 0°C)	−218·792	−182·954	15
9	F	Fluorine	Latin 'fluo' = flow	H. Moissan (France)	1886	18·998 403	1·780 (solid at mp) / 0·001 696 (gas at 0°C)	−219·673	−188·191	14
10	Ne	Neon	Greek 'neos' = new	W. Ramsay and M. W. Travers (UK)	1898	20·179 7	1·434 (solid at mp) / 0·000 899 9 (gas at 0°C)	−248·594	−246·053	17
11	Na	Sodium	English 'soda'	H. Davy (UK)	1807	22·989 768	0·9688	97·82	882	17
12	Mg	Magnesium	Magnesia, a district of Thessaly	H. Davy (UK)	1808	24·3050	1·737	650	1095	17
13	Al	Aluminium	Latin 'alumen' = alum	H. C. Oerstedt (Denmark) and F. Wöhler (Germany)	1825–1827	26·981 539	2·699	660·323	2516	18
14	Si	Silicon	Latin 'silex' = flint	J. J. Berzelius (Sweden)	1824	28·0855	2·329	1414	3190	21
15	P	Phosphorus	Greek 'phosphorus' = light bringing	H. Brand (Germany)	1669	30·973 762	1·825 (White) / 2·361 (Violet) / 2·708 (Black)	44·13 / 597 at 45 atm / 606 at 48 atm	277 / 431 sublimes / 453 sublimes	21
16	S	Sulfur (Note 1)	Sanskrit 'solvere'; Latin 'sulfurum'	Prehistoric	/;ED;/	32·066	2·070 (Rhombic)	115·18	444·614	22
17	Cl	Chlorine	Greek 'chloros' = green	C. W. Scheele (Sweden)	1774	35·4527	2·038 (solid at mp) / 0·003 214 (gas at 0°C)	−100·97	−33·97	20
18	Ar	Argon	Greek 'argos' = inactive	W. Ramsay and Lord Rayleigh (UK)	1894	39·948	1·622 (solid at mp) / 0·001 784 (gas at 0°C)	−189·344	−185·848	20
19	K	Potassium (Kalium)	English 'potash'	H. Davy (UK)	1807	39·0983	0·8591	63·58	758	20
20	Ca	Calcium	Latin 'calx' = lime	H. Davy (UK)	1808	40·078	1·526	842	1495	19

Atomic Number	Symbol	Element Name	Derived From	Discoverers	Year	Atomic Weight (Note 3)	Density At 20°C (Unless Otherwise Stated) (g/cm³)(Note 4)	Melting Point (°C)	Boiling Point (°C)	Number Of Nuclides
21	Sc	Scandium	Scandinavia	L. F. Nilson (Sweden)	1879	44·955 910	2·989	1541	2830	16
22	Ti	Titanium	Latin 'Titanes' = sons of the earth	M. H. Klaproth (Germany)	1795	47·88	4·504	1672	3360	20
23	V	Vanadium	Vanadis, a name given to Freyja, the Norse goddess of beauty and youth	N. G. Sefström (Sweden)	1830	50·9415	6·099	1928	3410	19
24	Cr	Chromium	Greek 'chromos' = colour	N. L. Vauquelin (France)	1798	51·9961	7·193	1860	2680	21
25	Mn	Manganese	Latin 'magnes' = magnet	J. G. Gahn (Sweden)	1774	54·938 05	7·472	1246	2051	21
26	Fe	Iron (Ferrum)	Anglo-Saxon 'iren'	Earliest smelting	c. 4000 BC	55·847	7·874	1538	2840	22
27	Co	Cobalt	German 'kobold' = goblin	G. Brandt (Sweden)	1737	58·933 20	8·834	1495	2940	22
28	Ni	Nickel	German abbreviation of 'Kupfernickel' (devil's 'copper') or niccolite	A. F. Cronstedt (Sweden)	1751	58·6934	8·905	1455	2890	24
29	Cu	Copper (Cuprum)	Cyprus	Prehistoric (earliest known use)	c. 8000 BC	63·546	8·934	1084·62	2570	25
30	Zn	Zinc	German 'zink'	A. S. Marggraf (Germany)	1746	65·39	7·140	419·527	908	25
31	Ga	Gallium	Latin 'Gallia' = France	L. de Boisbaudran (France)	1875	69·723	5·912	29·765	2203	24
32	Ge	Germanium	Latin 'Germania' = Germany	C. A. Winkler (Germany)	1886	72·61	5·327	938·2	2770	25
33	As	Arsenic	Latin 'arsenicum'	Albertus Magnus (Germany)	c. 1220	74·921 59	5·781	817 at 38 atm	603 sublimes	23
34	Se	Selenium	Greek 'selene' = moon	J. J. Berzelius (Sweden)	1818	78·96	4·810 (Trigonal)	221·14	685	23
35	Br	Bromine	Greek 'bromos' = stench	A. J. Balard (France)	1826	79·904	3·937 (solid at mp) 3·119 (liquid at 20°C)	−7·25	59·74	26
36	Kr	Krypton	Greek 'kryptos' = hidden	W. Ramsay and M. W. Travers (GB)	1898	83·80	2·801 (solid at mp) 0·003 749 (gas at 0°C)	−157·374	−153·340	25
37	Rb	Rubidium	Latin 'rubidus' = red	R. W. Bunsen and G. R. Kirchhoff (Germany)	1861	85·4678	1·534	39·29	687	28
38	Sr	Strontium	Strontian, a village in Highland region, Scotland	W. Cruikshank (UK)	1787	87·62	2·582	769	1388	28
39	Y	Yttrium	Ytterby, in Sweden	J. Gadolin (Finland)	1794	88·905 85	4·468	1522	3300	24
40	Zr	Zirconium	Persian 'zargun' = gold coloured	M. H. Klaproth (Germany)	1789	91·224	6·506	1854	4360	24
41	Nb	Niobium	Latin 'Niobe' daughter of Tantalus	C. Hatchett (UK)	1801	92·906 38	8·595	2472	4860	25
42	Mo	Molybdenum	Greek 'molybdos' = lead	P. J. Hjelm (Sweden)	1781	95·94	10·22	2623	4710	24
43	Tc	Technetium	Greek 'technetos' = artificial	C. Perrier (France) and E. Segré (Italy/USA)	1937	(97·9072)	11·40	2180	4860	23
44	Ru	Ruthenium	Ruthenia (in Ukraine)	K. K. Klaus (Estonia)	1844	101·07	12·37	2333	4310	25

Atomic Number	Symbol	Element Name	Derived From	Discoverers	Year	Atomic Weight (Note 3)	Density At 20°C (Unless Otherwise Stated) (g/cm³) (Note 4)	Melting Point (°C)	Boiling Point (°C)	Number Of Nuclides
45	Rh	Rhodium	Greek 'rhodon' = rose	W. H. Wollaston (UK)	1804	102·905 50	12·42	1962	3700	24
46	Pd	Palladium	The asteroid Pallas (discovered 1802)	W. H. Wollaston (UK)	1803	106·42	12·01	1554·7	2970	27
47	Ag	Silver (Argentum)	Anglo-Saxon 'seolfor'	Prehistoric (earliest silversmithery)	c. 4000 BC	107·8682	10·50	961·78	2167	29
48	Cd	Cadmium	Greek 'kadmeia' = calamine	F. Stromeyer (Germany)	1817	112·411	8·648	321·068	768	33
49	In	Indium	indigo spectrum	F. Reich and H. T. Richter (Germany)	1863	114·818	7·289	156·599	2019	32
50	Sn	Tin (Stannum)	Anglo-Saxon 'tin'	Prehistoric (intentionally alloyed with copper to make bronze)	c. 3500 BC	118·710	7·288	231·928	2590	33
51	Sb	Antimony (Stibium)	Lower latin 'antimonium'	Near historic	c. 1000 BC	121·757	6·693	630·636	1635	29
52	Te	Tellurium	Latin 'tellus' = earth	F. J. Muller (Baron von Reichenstein) (Austria)	1783	127·60	6·237	449·81	989	33
53	I	Iodine	Greek 'iodes' = violet	B. Courtois (France)	1811	126·904 47	4·947	113·6	185·1	33
54	Xe	Xenon	Greek 'xenos' = stranger	W. Ramsay and M. W. Travers (UK)	1898	131·29	3·410 (solid at mp) 0·005897 (gas at 0°C)	-111·774	-108·083	36
55	Cs	Caesium	Latin 'caesius' = bluish-grey	R. W. von Bunsen and G. R. Kirchoff (Germany)	1860	132·905 43	1·896	28·46	668	36
56	Ba	Barium	Greek 'barys' = heavy	H. Davy (UK)	1808	137·327	3·595	729	1740	31
57	La	Lanthanum	Greek 'lanthano' = conceal	C. G. Mosander (Sweden)	1839	138·9055	6·145	921	3410	30
58	Ce	Cerium	The asteroid Ceres (discovered 1801)	J. J. Berzelius and W. Hisinger (Sweden) and M. H. Klaproth (Germany)	1803	140·115	6·688 (beta) 6·770 (gamma)	799	3470	30
59	Pr	Praseodymium	Greek 'prasios didymos' = green twin	C. Auer von Welsbach (Austria)	1885	140·907 65	6·772	934	3480	29
60	Nd	Neodymium	Greek 'neos didymos' = new twin	C. Auer von Welsbach (Austria)	1885	144·24	7·006	1021	3020	30
61	Pm	Promethium	Greek demi-god 'Prometheus' – the fire stealer	J. Marinsky, L. E. Glendenin, and C. D. Coryell (USA)	1945	(144·9127)	7·141	1042	3000	28
62	Sm	Samarium	The mineral Samarskite (named after Col. M. Samarski, a Russian engineer)	L. de Boisbaudran (France)	1879	150·36	7·517	1077	1794	30
63	Eu	Europium	Europe	E. A. Demarçay (France)	1901	151·965	5·243	822	1556	29
64	Gd	Gadolinium	Johan Gadolin (1760–1852)	J. C. G. de Marignac (Switzerland)	1880	157·25	7·899	1313	3270	27
65	Tb	Terbium	Ytterby, in Sweden	C. G. Mosander (Sweden)	1843	158·925 34	8·228	1356	3230	26
66	Dy	Dysprosium	Greek 'dysprositos' = hard to get at	L. de Boisbaudran (France)	1886	162·50	8·549	1412	2570	29
67	Ho	Holmium	Holmia, a Latinized form of Stockholm	J. L. Soret (France) and P. T. Cleve (Sweden)	1878–1879	164·930 32	8·794	1474	2700	29
68	Er	Erbium	Ytterby, in Sweden	C. G. Mosander (Sweden)	1843	167·26	9·064	1529	2810	29

Atomic Number	Symbol	Element Name	Derived From	Discoverers	Year	Atomic Weight (Note 3)	Density At 20°C (Unless Otherwise Stated) (g/cm³) (Note 4)	Melting Point (°C)	Boiling Point (°C)	Number Of Nuclides
69	Tm	Thulium	Latin and Greek 'Thule' = Northland	P. T. Cleve (Sweden)	1879	168·934 21	9·319	1545	1950	31
70	Yb	Ytterbium	Ytterby, in Sweden	J. C. G. de Marignac (France)	1878	173·04	6·967	817	1227	30
71	Lu	Lutetium	Lutetia, Roman name for the city of Paris	G. Urbain (France)	1907	174·967	9·839	1665	3400	35
72	Hf	Hafnium	Hafnia = Copenhagen	D. Coster (Netherlands) and G. C. de Hevesy (Hungary/Sweden)	1923	178·49	13·28	2230	4700	31
73	Ta	Tantalum	'Tantalus' – a mythical Greek king	A. G. Ekeberg (Sweden)	1802	180·9479	16·67	3020	5490	31
74	W	Tungsten (Wolfram)	Swedish 'tung sten' = heavy stone	J. J. de Elhuyar and F. de Elhuyar (Spain)	1783	183·84	19·26	3420	5860	33
75	Re	Rhenium	Latin 'Rhenus' = the river Rhine	W. Noddack, Fr. I. Tacke and O. Berg (Germany)	1925	186·207	21·01	3185	5610	33
76	Os	Osmium	Greek 'osme' = odour	S. Tennant (UK)	1804	190·23	22·59	3127	5020	35
77	Ir	Iridium	Latin 'iris' = a rainbow	S. Tennant (UK)	1804	192·22	22·56	2446	4730	33
78	Pt	Platinum	Spanish 'platina' = small silver	A. de Ulloa (Spain)	1748	195·08	21·45	1768·1	3870	35
79	Au	Gold (Aurum)	Anglo-Saxon 'gold'	Prehistoric	;ED/	196·966 54	19·29	1064·18	2870	32
80	Hg	Mercury (Hydrargyrum)	'Hermes' (Latin 'Mercurius'), the divine patron of the occult sciences	Near historic	c. 1600 BC	200·59	14·17 (solid at mp) / 13·55 (liquid at 20°C)	;SC mi;/38·829	356·661	33
81	Tl	Thallium	Greek 'thallos' = a budding twig	W. Crookes (UK)	1861	204·3833	11·87	303	1468	29
82	Pb	Lead (Plumbum)	Anglo-Saxon 'lead'	Prehistoric	;ED/	207·2	11·35	327·462	1748	34
83	Bi	Bismuth	German 'weissmuth' = white matter	C. F. Geoffroy (France)	1753	208·980 37	9·807	271·402	1566	30
84	Po	Polonium	Poland	Mme. M. S. Curie (Poland/France)	1898	(208·9824)	9·155	254	948	27
85	At	Astatine	Greek 'astos' = unstable	D. R. Corson and K. R. Mackenzie (USA) and E. Segré (Italy/USA)	1940	(209·9871)	7·0	302	377	28
86	Rn	Radon	Latin 'radius' = ray	F. E. Dorn (Germany)	1900	(222·0176)	4·7 (solid at mp) / 0·010 04 (gas at 0°C)	;SC mi;/64·9	;SC mi;/61·2	31
87	Fr	Francium	France	Mlle. M. Perey (France)	1939	(223·0197)	2·8	23	650	31
88	Ra	Radium	Latin 'radius' = ray	P. Curie (France), Mme. M. S. Curie (Poland/France), and M. G. Bemont (France)	1898	(226·0254)	5·50	707	1530	28
89	Ac	Actinium	Greek 'aktinos', genetive of 'aktis' = a ray	A. Debierne (France)	1899	(227·0278)	10·04	1230	3600	26
90	Th	Thorium	'Thor', the Norse god of thunder	J. J. Berzelius (Sweden)	1829	232·0381	11·72	1760	4660	25
91	Pa	Protactinium	Greek 'protos' = first, plus actinium	O. Hahn (Germany) and Fr. L. Meitner (Austria); F. Soddy and J. A. Cranston (UK)	1917	231·03588	15·41	1570	4490	24
92	U	Uranium	The planet Uranus (discovered 1781)	M. H. Klaproth (Germany)	1789	238·0289	19·05	1134	4160	20

Atomic Number	Symbol	Element Name	Derived From	Discoverers	Year	Atomic Weight (Note 3)	Density At 20°C (Unless Otherwise Stated) (g/cm³) (Note 4)	Melting Point (°C)	Boiling Point (°C)	Number Of Nuclides
93	Np	Neptunium	The planet Neptune	E. M. McMillan and P. H. Abelson (USA)	1940	(237·0482)	20·47	637	4090	18
94	Pu	Plutonium	The planet Pluto	G. T. Seaborg, E. M. McMillan, J. W. Kennedy and A. C. Wahl (USA)	1940–1941	(244·0642)	20·26	640	3270	17
95	Am	Americium	America	G. T. Seaborg, R. A. James, L. O. Morgan and A. Ghiorso (USA)	1944–1945	(243·0614)	13·76	1176	2023	13
96	Cm	Curium	Pierre Curie (1859–1906) (France) and Marie Curie (1867–1934) (Poland/France)	G. T. Seaborg, R. A. James and A. Ghiorso (USA)	1944	(247·0703)	13·68	1340	3180	14
97	Bk	Berkelium	Berkeley, a town in California, USA	S. G. Thompson, A. Ghiorso and G. T. Seaborg (USA)	1949	(247·0703)	14·65	1050	2710	11
98	Cf	Californium	California	S. G. Thompson, K. Street Jr., A. Ghiorso and G. T. Seaborg (USA)	1950	(251·0796)	15·20	900	1612	18
99	Es	Einsteinium	Dr Albert Einstein (1879–1955) (USA, b. Germany)	A. Ghiorso et al (USA)	1952	(252·0829)	9·05	860	996	14
100	Fm	Fermium	Dr Enrico Fermi (1901–1954) (Italy)	A. Ghiorso et al (USA)	1953	(257·0951)	9·42	852	1077	18
101	Md	Mendelevium	Dmitriy I. Mendeleyev (1834–1907) (Russia)	A. Ghiorso, B. G. Harvey, G. R. Choppin, S. G. Thompson and G. T. Seaborg (USA)	1955	(258·0986)	—	—	—	13
102	No	Nobelium	Alfred B. Nobel (1833–1896) (Sweden)	(Note 2)	1958	(259·1009)	—	—	—	11
103	Lr	Lawrencium	Dr Ernest O. Lawrence (1901–1958) (USA)	(Note 2)	1961	(262·11)	—	—	—	10
104	Unq	Unnilquadium *	Un-nil-quad (1-0-4)	A. Ghiorso, M. Nurmia, J. Harris, K. Eskola and P. Eskola (USA/Finland)	1969	(261·1087)	—	—	—	10
105	Unp	Unnilpentium *	Un-nil-pent (1-0-5)	A. Ghiorso, M. Nurmia, K. Eskola, J. Harris and P. Eskola (USA/Finland)	1970	(262·1138)	—	—	—	8
106	Unh	Unnilhexium *	Un-nil-hex (1-0-6)	A. Ghiorso et al (USA)	1974	(263·1182)	—	—	—	4
107	Uns	Unnilseptium *	Un-nil-sept (1-0-7)	G. Münzenberg (Germany)	1981	(262·1229)	—	—	—	2
108	Uno	Unniloctium *	Un-nil-oct (1-0-8)	G. Münzenberg (Germany)	1984	(265·1302)	—	—	—	2
109	Une	Unnilennium *	Un-nil-enn (1-0-9)	G. Münzenberg (Germany)	1982	(266·1376)	—	—	—	1

See notes on p.234.

electrons – in this case Mg^{2+} and O^{2-}. The ionic compound magnesium oxide (MgO) has the same arrangement of ions as NaF, but since the ions in MgO have a greater charge, there is a stronger force between them. Thus more energy must be supplied to overcome this force of attraction, and the melting point of MgO is higher than that of NaF. Although the ions are fixed in position in the solid crystal, they become free to move when the solid is melted. As a liquid, therefore, the compound becomes electrolytic and is able to conduct electricity.

Many other more complex ionic structures are known. The formula of any ionic compound can be worked out by balancing the charges of its ions. For example, Mg^{2+} and F^- form MgF_2, while Na^+ and O^{2-} form Na_2O.

COVALENT BONDING

If we bring together two fluorine atoms, each with seven outer electrons (one less than neon), the formation of two ions with the noble-gas configuration is not possible by transfer of electrons. If, however, they share a pair of electrons – one from each atom – then both effectively achieve the noble-gas configuration and a stable molecule results.

There is a force of attraction between the shared pair of electrons and both positive nuclei, and this is what is known as a *covalent bond*. The stronger the attraction of the nuclei for the shared pair, the stronger the bond.

An atom of oxygen, having two electrons less than neon, must form two covalent bonds to attain a share in eight electrons. For example, a molecule of water (H_2O), consisting of two hydrogen atoms (H) and one oxygen atom (O), has two covalent O–H bonds. Another way for oxygen to achieve the stable noble-gas configuration is to form two bonds to the same atom. Thus two oxygen atoms bond covalently to one another by sharing two pairs of electrons. This is known as a *double bond*.

Like oxygen, sulfur (S) has six outer electrons and again needs to form two bonds to attain a share in eight electrons. There are two ways in which sulfur atoms join together – either in rings of eight atoms (S_8) or in long chains of many atoms bonded together. The different forms in which elemental sulfur exist are known as *allotropes*; other elements found in allotropic forms include carbon (graphite and diamond; see below) and oxygen (oxygen and ozone).

Atoms of nitrogen (N), containing five outer electrons, need to form three covalent bonds to attain a share in eight electrons. This may be done, for example, by forming one bond to each of three hydrogen atoms, to give ammonia (NH_3; see p. 226). Another possibility is to form all three bonds to a second nitrogen atom, which produces a nitrogen molecule (N_2; see p. 226), containing a *triple covalent bond*.

The carbon atom (C), which has four outer electrons, needs to form four bonds to attain the noble-gas configuration. Thus a carbon atom forms one bond to each of four hydrogen atoms to give methane (CH_4). Although carbon is not known to form a quadruple bond to another carbon atom, some other elements, such as the heavy metal rhenium, do form such quadruple bonds.

GIANT MOLECULES

Although two carbon atoms do not form a quadruple bond to one another, carbon atoms can combine to form a giant crystal lattice in which each atom is bonded to four others by single covalent bonds. This is the structure of diamond, one of the allotropes of elemental carbon. Many other elements and compounds exist as giant covalent crystal lattices, including quartz, which is a form of silicon dioxide (SiO_2). Crystals of these substances contain many millions of atoms held together by strong covalent bonds, so that a large amount of energy is needed to break them. Thus these substances all have high melting points and are hard solids.

INTERMOLECULAR FORCES

As we have seen, two neon atoms do not form covalent bonds with one another because of their full outer shells of electrons. There are, however, weak forces of attraction between two neon atoms. We know this because, when neon gas is compressed or cooled, it eventually turns into a liquid in which the atoms are weakly attracted to one another. These weak forces are called *van der Waals forces* and their strength depends on the size of the molecule.

Bromine (Br_2) is made up of large covalently bonded molecules that have much stronger van der Waals forces between them than exist between atoms of neon. Thus at room temperature bromine exists as a mixture of liquid and vapour. However, the forces *between* the bromine molecules are much weaker than covalent bonds, so that – while it is easy to separate the bromine molecules from one another and vaporize the liquid – it requires much more energy to separate the bromine atoms by breaking the covalent bond between them.

HYDROGEN BONDS

Some small molecules have much higher melting and boiling points than would be expected on the basis of their size. One such example is water (H_2O), which has about the same mass as a neon atom but has a much higher melting point. There must therefore be unusually strong intermolecular forces between the water molecules. Although the oxygen and hydrogen atoms share a pair of electrons in a covalent bond, the oxygen atom exerts a stronger 'pull' on these electrons and so becomes electron-rich, leaving the hydrogen atom electron-poor. As a result, there is a force of attraction between hydrogen and oxygen atoms on neighbouring molecules. This is known as *hydrogen bonding*.

As well as accounting for the surprisingly high melting point of water, hydrogen bonding is responsible for the rigid open structure of ice crystals, and is very important in influencing the structures and properties of biological molecules. Although hydrogen bonds are stronger than van der Waals forces, they are still much weaker than covalent bonds.

CHEMICAL REACTIONS

Chemical reactions are the means by which new substances are formed from old ones. Among the chemical reactions occurring everywhere around us are the changes that take place when fuels are burnt, the industrial methods by which metals are extracted from their ores, and the processes controlling life itself.

During a chemical reaction, the atomic constituents of the substances that react together (the *reactants*) are rearranged to produce different substances (the *products*). Thus, for example, in the reaction of potassium (K) with water (H_2O), potassium hydroxide (KOH) and hydrogen gas (H_2) are formed. This information can be represented as a chemical equation. By convention the reactants appear on the left-hand side and the products on the right. Letters may also be added after each chemical species to indicate its physical state – s means 'solid', l 'liquid', aq 'aqueous' (solution) and g 'gas'.

$$2K(s) + 2H_2O(l) \rightarrow 2KOH(aq) + H_2(g)$$

An essential characteristic of chemical reactions is that there is an exchange of energy between the reacting system and the surroundings. So much heat is liberated during the reaction of potassium and water that the highly flammable hydrogen gas frequently ignites above the molten metal.

STOICHIOMETRY

According to the *law of constant composition*, matter cannot be created or destroyed during a chemical reaction. Thus in the reaction described above, the number of atoms of potassium, hydrogen and oxygen (calculated by multiplying each element in the equation by the numbers placed before the chemical formula) is the same before and after the reaction, and the equation is said to be balanced. The numerical proportions in which substances combine to form the products of a chemical reaction is described as the reaction *stoichiometry*.

A balanced equation is thus a quantitative statement about the chemical reaction concerned. Such an equation (in conjunction with the mole concept; see below) enables us to predict how much product will be formed from a given mass of reactants.

THE MOLE CONCEPT

A *mole* is a measure of the amount of substance, based on the atomic theory of matter. A mole is defined as *the number of carbon atoms in 12 grams of the isotope carbon-12* and has the colossal value of 6.022×10^{23}. Every chemical compound has a fixed *relative molecular mass* or RMM (determined by the relative atomic masses of its constituent elements); so that molecular quantities (the number of moles) of any substance can be found using simple arithmetic.

REACTIONS OF ACIDS AND BASES

Acids may be defined as substances that tend to donate protons – ionized hydrogen atoms – to other molecules. For example, gaseous hydrogen chloride dissolves in water to form hydrochloric acid, by donating a proton to the water molecule. The products of the reaction are ions – electrically charged species. Many non-metal oxides form acids when dissolved in water; for example, sulfur trioxide gas (SO_3) dissolves in water to form sulfuric acid (H_2SO_4) – the reaction that occurs in the formation of acid rain.

By contrast, *bases* are defined as proton acceptors, capable of accepting protons from hydronium ions present in solution. Examples of bases include sodium and potassium hydroxides (NaOH and KOH), which generate aqueous hydroxide ions in solution. Many metal oxides are also basic, such as calcium oxide (CaO; lime). Aqueous solutions of bases are known as *alkalis*.

Acids and bases can be detected by their effects on a class of natural dyes called *indicators*. The best-known indicator is *litmus*, a dye derived from lichen, which is turned red by acids and blue by bases.

Acids and bases react together to form compounds known as *salts*, which are neither acidic nor basic. For example, sodium hydroxide reacts with hydrochloric acid to form sodium chloride.

The end-points of such *neutralization reactions* can be determined visually by the choice of an appropriate indicator, which changes colour when acid and base are exactly neutralized, i.e. when they have completely reacted. Neutralizations are of great importance in quantitative chemical analysis.

PRECIPITATION REACTIONS

Ionic compounds that dissolve water produce *electrolyte* solutions. These consist of ions moving randomly throughout the solution; for example, sodium chloride in aqueous solution contains sodium and chloride ions. These ions are responsible for the electrical conductivity of electrolytes (see below).

Silver nitrate is another ionic solid that dissolves readily in water, producing a colourless solution of aqueous silver and nitrate ions. If solutions of silver nitrate and sodium chloride are mixed, a white turbidity (cloudiness) forms instantly. This is due to the *precipitation* of fine particles of highly insoluble silver chloride. The precipitate gradually accumulates at the bottom of the vessel, leaving colourless sodium nitrate in solution. The reaction is one in which ions are exchanged between partners. It is possible to predict the outcome of precipitation reactions from a knowledge of the solubilities of the various species involved.

OXIDATION AND REDUCTION

Magnesium metal (Mg) burns with an incandescent white flame in air because of a vigorous reaction with oxygen, forming magnesium oxide:

$$2Mg(s) + O_2(g) \rightarrow 2MgO(s)$$

This is an example of the class of reactions known as *oxidations*, which include all combustion processes such as those occurring when fuels burn in air, as well as the reactions that cause metals to corrode in air.

The transfer of electrons between chemical species is a common process in many chemical reactions, so the term oxidation has come to possess a wider meaning than that implying solely the addition of oxygen atoms to an element or compound. As in the case of magnesium oxide above, oxidation means the loss of electrons by a compound. The opposite process – *reduction* – implies a gain of electrons. In the equation above, magnesium is said to be oxidized, while oxygen is reduced. The overall reaction is described as a *redox* process. Many metals are extracted from their ores by reduction reactions.

ELECTROLYSIS

If an electric current is passed through an electrolyte such as an aqueous solution of copper (II) chloride, a redox process known as *electrolysis* occurs. Positively charged Cu^2 ions are attracted to the negative electrode – the cathode – where they take up two electrons each and are thereby reduced to copper metal, which is deposited on the cathode. At the same time, the negatively charged Cl ions are attracted to the positive electrode – the anode – where they give up their extra electrons (i.e. are oxidized) to form chlorine gas. Electrolysis is the basis of *electroplating*, in which a thin layer of metal, such as copper, tin, chromium or silver, is applied as a protective or decorative finish on cheaper and less durable materials.

REACTION EQUILIBRIA

The reactions described so far have gone to completion, i.e. a fixed quantity of reactants is converted into a fixed quantity of products. However, in general such a state of affairs is more the exception than the rule. The end of a reaction occurs when there is no further change in the amount of products formed or reactants destroyed: this is the point at which the reaction is said to have reached *equilibrium*. At equilibrium, there may be appreciable amounts of reactants still present. For example, when acetic acid is dissolved in water, it forms a *weak acid*, because at equilibrium there is only a low concentration of hydronium ions.

The position of equilibrium in a chemical reaction (whether it favours reactants or products) depends in a detailed way on the thermodynamic properties of all the species involved.

RATES OF CHEMICAL REACTIONS

Very often it is important to know not only where the position of a chemical equilibrium lies but how fast it is reached. A graphic example is provided by a mixture of hydrogen gas and oxygen gas at room temperature. If undisturbed, the mixture does not react, but if a spark is passed through the gases, there is a violent explosion leading to the formation of water. Thus temperature is seen to exert a strong influence on the rate at which a reaction proceeds – the higher the temperature, the faster the reaction.

On the other hand, the same reaction can be made to proceed smoothly at room temperature by the addition of finely divided platinum metal, which acts as a catalyst. A *catalyst* is a substance that is not chemically transformed during a reaction but whose presence serves to accelerate its rate. Catalysts play an extremely important role in many industrial processes, where they allow reactions to be carried out under conditions that would otherwise have to be much more severe.

Another factor influencing the rate of reaction is the intrinsic reactivity – i.e. willingness to undergo chemical reaction – of the chemical species involved.

SMALL MOLECULES

Although the Earth's atmosphere consists almost entirely of two gases – nitrogen and oxygen – a number of other gases are present at low concentration, together with varying amounts of water vapour. With the exception of the noble gases, most other components of air form part of natural cycles, each remaining in the atmosphere only for a limited time. Not only are these gases of major importance in relation to industrial processes that dominate economies throughout the world, but cyclical processes involving water, oxygen, carbon dioxide and nitrogen – together with solar radiation – are essential to plant and animal life.

Current interest in various atmospheric gases centres on the possible global effects of changes in their atmospheric concentration due to human activities. Increase in carbon dioxide may upset the heat balance at the Earth's surface, while the use of chlorofluorocarbons (CFCs) might result in depletion of the ozone layer, thereby allowing destructive high-energy solar radiation to reach the Earth's surface.

Although these small molecules are simple in the sense that they are composed of few atoms, their structures and – for those with three or more atoms – their shapes vary. In most cases, their atoms are held together in the molecule by two, four or six electrons, resulting in single, double or triple covalent bonds.

HYDROGEN

Hydrogen (H_2) is the simplest of all stable molecules,

consisting of two protons and two electrons. It is a colourless, odourless gas and is lighter than air. Most hydrogen is used on the site where it is produced, but it is also transported as compressed gas in steel cylinders and in liquid form at very low temperature.

WATER

The total amount of water (H_2O) on Earth is fixed, and most is recycled and re-used. The largest reservoirs are the oceans and open seas, followed by glaciers, ice caps and ground water. Very little is actually contained within living organisms, although water is a major constituent of most life forms.

Water is one of the most remarkable of all small molecules. On the basis of its molecular weight (18), it should be a gas; its high boiling point (100 °C / 212 °F) is due to the interaction of water molecules with each other (hydrogen bonding), which effectively increases its molecular weight. Water is also unusual in that – as ice – it is less dense than the liquid at the same temperature.

CARBON DIOXIDE AND OXYGEN

Carbon dioxide (CO_2) is a colourless gas with a slight odour and an acid taste. It is available as gas, as liquid and as the white solid known as 'dry ice'. Its cycle in nature is tied to that of oxygen, the relative levels of the two gases in the atmosphere (apart from human activity) being regulated by the photosynthetic activity of plants. It is produced on a vast scale, mostly as a by-product of other processes.

With the ever-increasing input of carbon dioxide to the atmosphere, due largely to the burning of fossil fuels and forests and the manufacture of cement, the natural 'sinks' for carbon dioxide – chiefly photosynthesis and transfer to the oceans – can no longer keep pace with the total input. If this imbalance continues, it is thought that levels will be reached where the infrared-absorbing properties of carbon dioxide will result in a progressive warming of the Earth's atmosphere, accompanied by melting of the polar ice and flooding of what is now dry land – the so-called *greenhouse effect* (see also The Environment). This is perhaps too extreme and pessimistic a view: in the past there have been many warm interglacial periods due to factors not ascribable to human activity.

Oxygen (O_2) is a highly reactive colourless, odourless and tasteless gas. At low temperature, it condenses to a pale blue liquid, slightly denser than water. Oxygen supports burning, causes rusting and is vital to both plant and animal respiration.

OZONE

Ozone (O_3) is a highly toxic, unstable, colourless gas. Its primary importance stems from its formation in the stratosphere. In this layer of the atmosphere, temperature increases with height, principally because of the reaction of high-energy ultraviolet solar radiation with oxygen.

Ozone in the stratosphere functions as a very effective filter for high-energy ultraviolet solar radiation. Radiation in this energy range is sufficiently high to break bonds between carbon and other atoms, making it lethal to all forms of life. It is currently thought that the introduction of CFCs (used in sprays and refrigerators) and the related 'halons' (used in fire extinguishers) may contribute

to the partial or even total destruction of the ozone layer. These classes of compounds are highly volatile, chemically very stable and essentially insoluble in water, so that they are not washed out of the atmosphere by rain. When, by normal convection, they reach the stratosphere, they react destructively with ozone.

CARBON DIOXIDE

Carbon monoxide (CO) is a colourless, odourless, toxic gas. The input to the atmosphere due to human activity is about 360 million tonnes (tons) per year, mostly from the incomplete combustion of fossil fuels. The natural input is some 10 times this figure and results from the partial oxidation of biologically produced methane. The background level of 0.1 parts per million (ppm) can rise to 20 ppm at a busy road intersection, and a five-minute cigarette gives an intake of 400 ppm.

Since the atmospheric level of carbon monoxide is not rising significantly, there must be effective sink processes, one being its oxidation in air to carbon dioxide. In addition, there are soil microorganisms that utilize carbon monoxide in photosynthesis.

NITROGEN

Nitrogen (N_2) is a colourless, odourless gas. Although very stable and chemically unreactive, it cycles both naturally and as a result of its use in the chemical industry. The natural cycle results from the ability of some types of bacteria and blue-green algae (in the presence of sunlight) to 'fix' nitrogen – i.e. to convert it into inorganic nitrogen compounds (ammonium and nitrate salts) that can be assimilated by plants. Since 1913 human activity has increasingly contributed to the cycling of nitrogen, because of the catalytic conversion of nitrogen into ammonia (used mainly in nitrate fertilizers, see below), which ultimately reverts to nitrogen gas.

OXIDES OF NITROGEN

The presence of nitric oxide (NO) and nitrogen dioxide (NO_2) at high levels in the atmosphere is closely connected with the internal-combustion engine. At the high temperature reached when petroleum and air ignite, nitrogen and oxygen combine to form nitric oxide, which slowly reacts with more oxygen to form nitrogen dioxide. Most internal-combustion engines also produce some unburnt or partially burnt fuel: in the presence of sunlight, this reacts with nitrogen dioxide by a sequence of fast reactions, forming organic peroxides, which are the harmful constituents of photochemical smog (smoke plus fog).

AMMONIA

Ammonia (NH_3) is a colourless gas with a penetrating odour, and is less dense than air. It is highly soluble in water, giving an alkaline solution. World production is of the order of 100 million tonnes (tons) a year, most of which is converted into fertilizers (80%), plastics (9%) and explosives (4%).

OXIDES OF SULFUR

Both sulfur dioxide (SO_2) and sulfur trioxide (SO_3) are pungent-smelling acidic gases, which are produced by volcanic action and – to the extent of some 150 million tonnes (tons) a year – by the burning of fossil fuels and smelting operations.

The level of sulfur dioxide in unpolluted air is 0.002 parts per million (ppm), but in the 1952 London smog the levels rose to 1.54 ppm, accompanied by a dramatic increase in the death rate. In the atmosphere, sulfur dioxide is slowly oxidized to sulfur trioxide, water droplets and particulate matter in the air. Ultimately the latter is deposited as dilute sulfuric acid – *acid rain*.

METALS

Metals are usually defined by their physical properties, such as strength, hardness, lustre, conduction of heat and electricity, malleability and high melting point. They can also be characterized chemically as elements that dissolve (or whose oxides dissolve) in acids, usually to form positively charged ions (cations). By either definition, more than three quarters of the known elements can be classified as metals. They occupy all but the top right-hand corner of the Periodic Table (see p. 227), the remainder being non-metals. A few elements on the borderline, such as germanium, arsenic and antimony, have some of the properties of metals and are often classed as *metalloids*.

Given such a large number of metals, it is not surprising that some of them have rather untypical properties. For instance, mercury is a liquid at room temperature, and – with the exception of lithium – all the alkali metals melt below 100 °C (212 °F). The alkali metals are also quite soft – they can easily be cut with a knife – and extremely reactive – rubidium and caesium cannot be handled in air and may react explosively with water.

OCCURRENCE

Most metals occur naturally as oxides, while some – mostly the heavier ones, such as mercury and lead – occur as sulfides. Only a few – the noble and coinage metals – are found in the metallic state, being chemically the most inert metals.

A few metals do not occur naturally at all, because they are radioactive and have decayed away. Technetium and all the elements with higher atomic numbers than plutonium are made by the 'modern alchemy' of nuclear reactors or accelerators, while promethium is found only in minute amounts as a product of the spontaneous fission of uranium. The very heaviest elements have been obtained only a few atoms at a time, and are intensely radioactive.

THE DISCOVERY AND EXTRACTION OF METALS

Artificial elements have of course been known only in modern times, since the 1940s or later. The discovery of most other metals was also comparatively recent: with the exception of zinc, platinum and the handful of metals known to the Ancients, all metals have been discovered since 1735. The only metals known in antiquity were copper, silver, gold, iron, tin, mercury and lead. Of these, it was not the most abundant – iron – that was discovered first: the Bronze Age came before the Iron Age. The reason for this is that it is easier to extract the metals used in bronze – copper and tin – from their minerals than it is to extract iron from its ores. The discovery of copper is thought to have been accidental: pieces of the metal ore used in fireplaces came into contact with the hot charcoal, so releasing the metal. Essentially the same process under controlled conditions (*smelting*) is used in modern blast furnaces. Any of the metals from manganese (Mn) to zinc (Zn) in the Periodic Table can be obtained by roasting their

oxides with coke at temperatures of up to about 1600° C (2912° F). (See Technology.)

The ores of the lighter, more reactive metals cannot be reduced by carbon at practical temperatures, because their atoms are more strongly bonded in the ore. These metals are usually obtained by electrolysis or by the reaction of their compounds with an even more reactive metal. For instance, the reduction of aluminium oxide with carbon requires a temperature in excess of 2000° C (3632° F); so electrolysis of a melt of aluminium oxide in a mixture of cryolite (a double fluoride of aluminium and sodium) and calcium fluoride at about 950° C(1742° F) is used. On the other hand, titanium is obtained by converting its oxide into the chloride, which is then reduced with elemental sodium or magnesium.

CONDUCTIVITY

The conduction of heat and electricty that characterizes metals is due to their unique type of bonding. The solid metals behave as if they were composed of arrays of positively charged ions, with electrons free to move throughout the crystalline structure of the metal. This results in high electrical conductivity. The conduction of heat can also be seen in terms of the motion of electrons, which becomes faster as temperature rises. Since the electrons are mobile, the heat can be conducted readily through the solid.

The majority of metals are good conductors of electricity, but germanium and tin (in the form stable below 19°C/64°F) are semiconductors.

MECHANICAL STRENGTH

Many metals are used because of their strength. However, most pure metals are actually quite soft. In order to obtain a tough hard metal, something else has to be added. For instance, the earliest useful metal was not copper but bronze, which is copper alloyed with tin. Similarly, iron is never used in the pure state but as some form of steel.

The softness of a pure metal results from a lack of perfection in the crystal framework formed by its atoms. Even when the most rigorous conditions are employed, it is impossible to grow any material in perfect crystalline form. There will always be some atoms in the wrong place or missing from their proper place. When solidification occurs fairly rapidly, as when a molten metal is cooled in a mould, even more defects occur. Under bending or shearing, such defects can move and allow the metal to change shape easily. When the foreign atoms of an alloying element are present, they usually have a different size from those of the host and cannot easily fit into the crystal lattice. They therefore tend to site themselves where the lattice is irregular, i.e. where the defects are. The effect of this is preevnt the defects from moving, and so to increase the rigidity of the metal.

ORGANIC CHEMISTRY

The molecular basis for life processes, which have evolved with such remarkable elegance around carbon as the key element, is beginning to be understood, thanks to the combined triumphs of biological, chemical and physical scientists during the last hundred years.

Although the chemist can now make synthetically almost any chemical compound that nature produces, the challenge remains to achieve this objective routinely with the efficiency and precision that characterizes the chemistry of living systems.

There is something very special about the chemistry of carbon that has singled it out as the atomic building block from which all naturally occurring compounds in living systems are constructed. The subject that deals with this important area of science, nestling between biology and physics, has become so vast and significant that it has earned recognition as a separate field of scientific investigation. As it was originally thought that such carbon-based compounds could be obtained only from natural sources, this field of study became known as *organic chemistry*.

THE CARBON ATOM

Carbon's unique feature is the readiness with which it forms bonds both with other carbon atoms and with atoms of other elements. Having four electrons in its outer shell, a carbon atom requires four electrons to attain a stable noble-gas configuration. It therefore forms four covalent bonds with other atoms, each of which donates a single electron to each bond. In this way the electronic requirements are satisfied, and a three-dimensional 'tetracovalent' environment is built up around the carbon atom.

Carbon bonds are found both in pure forms of carbon (graphite and diamond) and in association with other atoms in a vast array of compounds. Compounds consisting of just carbon and hydrogen – *hydrocarbons* – are extremely important, notably as the principal constituents of fossil fuels. In addition carbon readily bonds with many other atoms, including oxygen, nitrogen, sulfur, phosphorus and the halogens, such as chlorine and bromine.

FUNCTIONAL GROUPS

Carbon combines with itself and other atoms to produce open-chain (*acyclic*) and ring (*cyclic*) skeletons, into which are built highly characteristic arrangements of atoms, known as *functional groups*. The diverse but predictable chemical behaviour of the different functional groups is a consequence of their ability either to attract or to repel electrons compared with the rest of the carbon skeleton. The overall effect of the resulting charge distribution is to create a molecule in which some regions are slightly negatively charged (*nucleophilic*), and others slightly positively charged (*electrophilic*).

Most organic reactions involve the electrophilic and nucleophilic centres of different molecules coming together as a prelude to the formation of new covalent bonds.

AMINO ACIDS

Amino acids, from which proteins are synthesized in living organisms, are characterized by their possession of two functional groups – a carboxylic-acid group (CO_2H) and an amino group (NH_2). Different amino acids, often with very different properties, are distinguished by the identity of a third group – a methyl group (CH_3) in the case of alanine.

Alanine is one of the 20 naturally occurring amino acids. A detailed examination of its structure reveals another feature of paramount importance to the modern chemist. The four groups bonded to the central carbon atom are arranged in such a way as to define a tetrahedron in three dimensions. This spatial arrangement (or *configuration*) can exist in two

different forms, one the non-superimposable mirror image of the other. They differ as our right hand does to our left, so the central carbon atom is said to be *chiral* (from the Greek for 'hand') or asymmetric. The two different forms are known as *enantiomers*.

Molecular recognition – based upon chirality – is prevalent in the chemistry of the molecules of life. Nucleic acids (DNA and RNA), polysaccharides (large natural sugar molecules) and proteins, especially enzymes, all discriminate between enantiomers in their respective modes of action.

NOBEL PRIZEWINNERS IN CHEMISTRY

1901 Jacobus van't Hoff, Dutch. Laws of chemical dynamics and osmotic pressure
1902 Emil Fischer, German. Work on sugar and purine syntheses
1903 Svante Arrhenius, Swedish. Theory of electrolytic dissociation
1904 Sir William Ramsay, Scottish. Discovery and periodic system classification of inert gas elements
1905 Adolf von Baeyer, German. Work on organic dyes and hydroaromatic compounds
1906 Henri Moissan, French. The Moissan furnace; and isolation of fluorine
1907 Eduard Buchner, German. Discovery of non-cellular fermentation
1908 Lord Ernest Rutherford, British. Atomic structure and the chemistry of radioactive substance
1909 Wilhelm Ostwald, German. Pioneered catalysis, chemical equilibrium and reaction velocity work
1910 Otto Wallach, German. Pioneer work on alicyclic combinations
1911 Marie Curie, French (naturalized citizen). Discovery of radium and polonium; isolation of radium
1912 Victor Grignard, French. Grignard reagents
       Paul Sabatier, French. Method of hydrogenating compounds
1913 Alfred Werner, Swiss (naturalized citizen). Work on the linkage of atoms in molecules
1914 Theodore Richards, USA. Precise determination of atomic weights of many elements
1915 Richard Willstätter, German. Pioneered research on plant pigments, especially chlorophyll
1916 No award
1917 No award
1918 Fritz Haber, German. Synthesis of ammonia
1919 No award
1920 Walther Nernst, German. Work in thermochemistry
1921 Frederick Soddy, English. Studied radioactive materials; occurrence and nature of isotopes
1922 Francis Aston, English. Work on mass spectrography; whole number rule
1923 Fritz Pregl, Austrian. Method of microanalysis of organic substances
1924 No award
1925 Richard Zsigmondy, German. Elucidation of the heterogeneous nature of colloidal solutions
1926 Theodor Svedberg, Swedish. Work on disperse systems
1927 Heinrich Wieland, German. Research into the constitution of bile acids

1928 Adolf Windaus, German. Constitution of sterols and their connection with vitamins

1929 Sir Arthur Harden, English, and H. von Euler-Chelpin, Swedish (naturalized citizen). Studied sugar fermentation and the enzymes involved in the process

1930 Hans Fischer, German. Chlorophyll research, and discovery of haemoglobin in the blood

1931 Karl Bosch, German, and Friedrich Bergius, German. Invention and development of high-pressure methods

1932 Irving Langmuir, USA. Furthered understanding of surface chemistry

1933 No award

1934 Harold Urey, USA. Discovered heavy hydrogen

1935 Frédéric Joliot-Curie, French, and Irène Joliot-Curie, French. Synthesis of new radioactive elements

1936 Peter Debye, Dutch. Work on dipole moments and the diffraction of X-rays and electrons in gases

1937 Sir Walter Haworth, English. Carbohydrate and vitamin C research
Paul Karrer, Swiss. Carotenoid, flavin, and vitamin research

1938 Richard Kuhn, German. Carotenoid and vitamin research (award declined as Hitler forbade Germans to accept Nobel prizes)

1939 Adolf Butenandt, German. Work on sex hormones (award declined as Hitler forbade Germans to accept Nobel prizes)

1940–1942 No awards made

1943 George von Hevesy, Hungarian. Use of isotopes as tracers in research

1944 Otto Hahn, German. Discovery of the fusion of heavy nuclei

1945 Arturri Virtanen, Finnish. Invention of fodder preservation method

1946 James Sumner, USA. Discovery of enzyme crystallization
John Northrop, USA, and Wendell Stanley, USA. Preparation of pure enzymes and virus proteins

1947 Sir Robert Robinson, English. Research on alkaloids and plant biology

1948 Arne Tiselius, Swedish. Electrophoretic and adsorption analysis research; serum proteins

1949 William Giauque, USA. Behaviour of substances at very low temperatures

1950 Otto Diels, German, and Kurt Alder, German. Discovery and development of diene synthesis

1951 Edwin McMillan, USA, and Glenn Seaborg, USA. Discovery of and research on transuranium elements

1952 Archer Martin, English and Richard Synge, English. Development of partition chromatography

1953 Hermann Staudinger, German. Work on macromolecules

1954 Linus Pauling, USA. Studied the nature of the chemical bond

1955 Vincent Du Vigneaud, USA. First to synthesize a polypeptide hormone

1956 Nikolay Semyonov, Russian, and Sir Cyril Hinshelwood, English. Work on the kinetics of chemical reactions

1957 Sir Alexander Todd, Scottish. Work on nucleotides and nucleotide coenzymes

1958 Frederick Sanger, English. Determined the structure of the insulin molecule

1959 Jaroslav Heyrovsky, Czechoslovakian. Discovered and developed polarography

1960 Willard Libby, USA. Developed radio-carbon dating

1961 Melvin Calvin, USA. Studied the chemical stages that occur in photosynthesis

1962 John C. Kendrew, British, and Max F. Perutz, British (Austrian-born). Determined the structure of haemoproteins

1963 Giulio Natta, Italian, and Karl Ziegler, German. Structure and synthesis of plastics polymers

1964 Dorothy M. C. Hodgkin, English. Determined the structure of compounds essential in combating pernicious anaemia

1965 Robert B. Woodward, USA. Synthesized sterols, chlorophyll, etc. (previously produced only by living things)

1966 Robert S. Mulliken, USA. Investigated chemical bonds and electronic structure of molecules

1967 Manfred Eigen, German, Ronald G. W. Norrish, English, and George Porter, English. Studied extremely fast chemical reactions

1968 Lars Onsager, USA (naturalized citizen). Theory of the thermodynamics of irreversible processes

1969 Derek H. R. Barton, British, and Odd Hasell, Norwegian. Determined the actual 3-dimensional shape of certain organic compounds

1970 Luis F. Leloir, Argentinian (naturalized citizen). Discovered sugar nucleotides and their role in carbohydrate biosynthesis

1971 Gerhard Herzberg, Canadian. Researched the structure of molecules

1972 Christian B. Anfinsen, USA, Stanford Moore, USA, and William H. Stein, USA. Contributed to the fundamentals of enzyme chemistry

1973 Ernst Fischer, German, and Geoffrey Wilkinson, British. Organometallic chemistry

1974 Paul J. Flory, USA. Studied long-chain molecules

1975 J. W. Cornforth, British, and Vladimir Prelog, Swiss. Worked on stereochemistry

1976 William N. Lipscomb, USA. Structure of boranes

1977 Ilya Prigogine, Belgian. Advanced thermodynamics

1978 Peter D. Mitchell, British. Theory of energy transfer processes in biological systems

1979 Herbert C. Brown, USA (naturalized citizen) and Georg Wittig, German. Introduced boron and phosphorus compounds in the synthesis of organic compounds

1980 Paul Berg, USA. First preparation of a hybrid DNA.
Walter Gilbert, USA, and Frederick Sanger, English. Chemical and biological analysis of the structure of DNA

1981 Fukui Kenichi, Japanese, and Roald Hoffmann, USA (naturalized citizen). Orbital symmetry interpretation of chemical reactions

1982 Aaron Klug, British (naturalized citizen). Determined the structure of some biologically active substances

1983 Henry Taube, Canadian. Studied electron transfer reactions

1984 Bruce Merrifield, USA. Formulated method of polypeptide synthesis

1985 Herbert A. Hauptman, USA, and Jerome

Karle, USA. Developed means of mapping the chemical structure of small molecules

1986 Dudley R. Herschbach, USA, Yuan T. Lee, USA, and John C. Polanyi, Canadian. Introduced methods for analysing basic chemical reactions

1987 Donald J. Cram, USA, Charles J. Pedersen and Jean-Marie Lehn, French. Developed molecules that could link with other molecules

1988 Johann Deisenhofer, German, Robert Huber, German, and Hartmut Michel, German. Studied the structure of the proteins

needed in photosynthesis

1989 Tom Cech, USA, and Sidney Altman, USA. Established that RNA catalyses biochemical reactions

1990 Elias Corey, USA. Worked on synthesizing chemical compounds based on natural substances

1991 Richard R. Ernst, Swiss. For refining the technology of nuclear magnetice resonance imaging (NMR and MRI)

1992 Rudolph A. Marcus, USA. For mathematical analysis of the cause and effect of electrons jumping from one molecule to another

ELEMENTARY FACTS

Of the 109 elements – see pp. 226–34 – 94 exist naturally and a further 15 transuranic elements (numbers 95 to 109) have been produced artificially.

At room temperatures, these elements consist of 2 liquids, 11 gases and 96 solids (based on the firm assumption that elements 101 to 109 would prove to be solids if they could be obtained at more than a few atoms at a time). On this basis 88 elements can be considered metallic.

Most common element
The commonest element in the Universe is hydrogen (H), which comprises over 90% of the Universe and 70.68% of the Solar System.

Oxygen is thought to be the commonest element in the Earth's crust, accounting for 46.4% of its total weight. However, if the iron-rich theory of the core is correct then iron (Fe) is the commonest element in the Earth, accounting for 34%.

The commonest element in the Earth's atmosphere is nitrogen (N), which is present at 78.08 per cent by volume – 75.52 per cent by mass.

Rarest (natural) element
The rarest naturally occurring element in the Earth's crust is astatine (At). Only 0.16 gm (0.0056 oz) of this element is present in the Earth's crust.

The least abundant element in the Earth's atmosphere is the radioactive gas radon (Rn), with a volume of 6×10^{-18} parts per million (ppm). This is only 2.4 kg (5.3 lb) overall, but concentrated amounts of this radioactive gas in certain granitic areas have been blamed for a number of cancer deaths.

Newest element
Only three atoms of element 108 – provisional name unniloctium (Uno); proposed name hassium (Hs) – have been discovered – by G. Münzenberg et al at the Gesellschaft für Schwerionenforschung, Darmstadt, Germany in April 1984.

Most dense element
The densest solid at room temperature is osmium (Os), at 22.59 g/cm^3 (0.8161 lb/in^3).

The least dense element at room temperature is the metal lithium (Li) at 0.5334 g/cm^3 (0.01927 lb/in^3), although the density of solid hydrogen at its melting point of -259.192 °C (-434.546 °F) is only 0.0871 g/cm^3 (0.00315 lb/in^3).

At normal temperature and pressure, the lightest gas is hydrogen (H) at 0.00008989 g/cm^3 (0.005612 lb/ft^3) and the densest gas is radon at 0.01005 g/cm^3 (0.6274 lb/ft^3).

THE NOBEL PRIZES

The six Nobel Prizes (five before the addition of a prize for economic science in 1969) are awarded annually from a fund established under the terms of the will of Alfred Bernhard Nobel (1833–96), a Swedish chemist, industrialist and engineer who made his fortune through his invention of dynamite. His interest in science and literature – and his pacifism – determined the fields in which the first five prizes were established: physics, chemistry, medicine and physiology, literature and peace.

Alfred Nobel stipulated certain organizations in Sweden and Norway as the awarding bodies for specific prizes:

Chemistry – the Royal Swedish Academy of Sciences, Stockholm, Sweden;

Literature – the Swedish Academy, Stockholm;

Medicine and Physiology – the Royal Caroline Medico-Chirurgical Institute, Stockholm, Sweden;

Peace – the Norwegian Nobel Committee, which is appointed by the Norwegian Parliament, the Storting.

Physics – the Royal Swedish Academy of Sciences, Stockholm;

Economic Science – the sixth Nobel Prize – was established by the Royal Bank of Sweden in 1968 and first awarded in the following year. The awarding body for this additional prize is the Royal Swedish Academy of Sciences, Stockholm.

Nobel's will established the Nobel Foundation as the legal owner and administrator of the prizes. The Foundation is, however, not a participant in the deliberations concerning the annual award of the prizes.

Prizes are awarded to one, two or three persons or (in the case of the Peace Prize) to an organization. Awards are withheld when no worthy candidate can be found – as is sometimes the case with the Peace Prize – or the international situation is such that the gathering of relevant information by the Swedish and Norwegian awarding bodies is not possible – as was the case during the two World Wars. Two prizes may be awarded in a single field in one year if the prize has been withheld in a previous year. An individual may be awarded a prize upon more than one occasion.

The awarding bodies invite nominations from suitable international bodies and individuals. (Self-nomination is not allowed.) Nominations must be received by the six Nobel committees by 1 February in the year in which the award is to be made. The secret deliberations of the committees last from February until the following autumn. Each Nobel committee must have reached its verdict by 15 November. Prizes are awarded on 10 December – the anniversary of the death of Nobel – at a ceremony in Stockholm; the Peace Prize is awarded in Oslo.

MATHEMATICS

of arithmetic, so that both generality and rigour were advanced.

MATHEMATICS AND EMOTION

To the amazement of those who don't like mathematics, mathematicians actually find mathematics enjoyable! They also find a sense of form and beauty an aid when they are doing mathematics.

G. H. Hardy claimed that many popular puzzles are really bits of mathematics in disguise and that everyone enjoys getting a 'kick' out of solving them.

Serge Lang was asked, 'Why do you do this kind of work?' 'Because it gives me chills in the spine.'

Roger Penrose writes that 'It is a mysterious thing how something which looks attractive may have a better chance of being true than something which looks ugly.'

HIGHEST NUMBERS

The highest lexicographically accepted named number in the system of successive powers of ten is the centillion, first recorded in 1852. It is the hundredth power of one million, or 1 followed by 600 noughts.

The number 10^{100} is designated a googol. The term was suggested by the nine-year old nephew of the American mathematician Dr Edward Kasner. Ten raised to the power of a googol is described as a googolplex.

The highest named number outside the decimal notation is the Buddhist *asankhyeya*, which is equivalent to 10^{140} and is mentioned in Jain works of c. 100 BC.

The highest number ever used in a mathematical proof is a bounding value published in 1977 and known as *Graham's number*. It concerns bi-chromatic hypercubes and is inexpressible without the special 'arrow' notation devised by Knuth in 1976 and then extended to 64 layers.

Many people think of mathematics in terms of rules to be learned in order to manipulate symbols or study numbers or shapes in the abstract for their own sake. Mathematical theory does develop in the abstract; it need have no dependence on anything outside itself. The truth of the theory is measured by logic rather than experiment. However, one of its most valuable uses is in describing or modelling processes in the real world, and thus there is constant interaction between pure mathematics and applied mathematics.

Mathematics may be considered as the very general study of the structure of systems. Since the study is unrelated to the physical world, rigorous formal proofs are sought, rather than experimental verifications. Theory is presented in terms of a small number of given truths (known as *axioms*) from which the entire theory can be inferred.

Thus, the aims are for generality in approach and rigour in proof, aims that explain the traditional concern of mathematicians for the unification of seemingly different branches of mathematics. As an example, René Descartes showed that geometrical figures could be described in terms of algebra, enabling geometric proofs to be established in terms

APPLIED MATHEMATICS AND MODELLING

There is no sharp boundary between the study of mathematical systems in the abstract (the field of *pure mathematics)* and the study of such systems to make inferences about certain physical systems that are described by the mathematical theory (the field of *applied mathematics)*. In principle, any branch of mathematics may turn out to describe some physical, economic, biological, medical, or other system. *Modelling* a physical system consists of seeking a formal mathematical theory that conforms with the properties of the physical system. Often, as for example in computer simulations of space travel, the mathematical theories are very large and complex, but sometimes the model can be quite simple. Sometimes, known mathematics can describe and predict the behaviour of the system; at other times, the modelling can give rise to completely new branches of mathematics.

Applied mathematics encompasses many specialized fields in which the relationships between the experimental findings and the mathematical theories are well established. Although the subject can include the application of statistical theory to such areas as sociology, the term is usually restricted to the application of the methods of advanced calculus, linear algebra and other branches of advanced mathematics to physical and technological processes.

NOTABLE MATHEMATICIANS

Pythagoras (c. 582–500 BC), Greek philosopher. Born in Samos, he founded a religious community at Croton in southern Italy. The Pythagorean brotherhood saw mystical significance in the idea of number. He is popularly remembered today for Pythagoras' theorem.

Euclid (c. 3rd century BC), Greek mathematician. Euclid devised the first axiomatic treatment of geometry and studied irrational numbers. Until recent times, most elementary geometry textbooks were little more than versions of Euclid's great book *The Elements*.

Archimedes (c. 287–212 BC), Greek mathematician, philosopher and engineer, born in Syracuse, Sicily. His extensions of the work of Euclid especially concerned the surface and volume of the sphere and the study of other solid shapes. His methods anticipated the fundamentals of integral calculus.

al Khwarizmi (Muhammad ibn Musa al Khwarizmi; c. 825), Iraqi mathematician who described the Hindu system of counting. His book on algebra was influential in Europe when translated into Latin in the 12th century. The name of his treatise on algebra, *Hisab al-jabr w'al-muqabalah*, or 'the science of reduction and cancellation', gave us our word 'algebra', and the modern term 'algorithm' is derived from his name.

Leonardo Pisano or **Fibonacci** (c. 1175–c. 1250), Italian mathematician. Leonardo is famous for *Liber Abaci*, an account of elementary arithmetic and algebra that popularized the Hindu system of counting in Europe. It contains the problem of the breeding rabbits, which gives rise to the famous *Fibonacci sequence*, 1, 1, 2, 3, 5, 8, 13... in which each number is the sum of the previous two. This sequence has many uses, including the design of efficient computer sorts.

Girard Desargues (1591–1661), French engineer, architect and geometrician who invented modern projective geometry. Desargues was the author of *Brouillon Project*, one of the most neglected works in the history of mathematics, lost and only rediscovered in 1845. He is remembered for *Desargues' theorem* on pairs of triangles in perspective.

René Descartes (1596–1650), French philosopher, mathematician and military scientist. Descartes sought an axiomatic treatment of all knowledge, and is known for his doctrine that all knowledge can be derived from the one certainty: *Cogito ergo sum* ('I think therefore I am'). His greatest contribution to mathematics was the creation of analytical geometry, which allows geometrical problems to be solved by algebra, and algebraic ideas to be expressed in geometrical imagery. This great invention appeared as the final Appendix to his *Discourses on Method*; the other Appendices dealt with optics and meteorological phenomena, including the rainbow.

Pierre de Fermat (1601–65), French lawyer who studied mathematics as a hobby. He contributed to the development of calculus, analytic geometry, and the study of probability (with Pascal). Fermat is regarded as the creator of the modern theory of numbers. He is most famous for his last theorem, which he claimed to have solved, without recording his proof. In 1908 a prize of 100 000 German marks was offered for a correct proof but the theorem remains unsolved to this day.

Blaise Pascal (1623–62), French mathematician who discovered what became known as *Pascal's theorem* at the age of 16, when he was writing a book on conic sections. At the age of 19, to aid his father's statistical work, he invented the first calculating machine, which performed addition and subtraction. He also investigated what became known as *Pascal's triangle*, and helped to develop the theory of probability, before abandoning mathematics and turning to theology.

Kowa Seki (1642–1708), Japanese mathematician who invented a form of calculus, and who used determinants before Leibniz. Seki suggested that an equation of the nth degree has in general n roots. He also gave 355/113 as an approximation to π, used positive and negative numbers and algebraic quantities, and studied magic squares.

Sir Isaac Newton (1643–1727), English mathematician, astronomer and physicist (see also p. 194). Newton came to be recognized as the most influential scientist of all time. He developed differential calculus and his treatments of gravity and motion form the basis of much applied mathematics.

Gottfried Wilhelm Leibniz (1646–1716), German mathematician, philosopher, logician, linguist, lawyer and diplomat. Leibniz and Newton invented calculus independently, although Leibniz's notation was superior. He was the first, in 1671, to build a calculating machine that could multiply. He was the first European mathematician to consider determinants, unaware that Kowa Seki had studied them a decade earlier. Leibniz also studied binary numbers and found mystical significance in the creation of all numbers out of nothing and unity.

Leonhard Euler (1707–83), Swiss-born mathematician, who worked mainly in Berlin and St Petersburg. He was particularly famed for being able to perform complex calculations in his head, and so was able to go on working after he went blind. He worked in almost all branches of mathematics and made particular contributions to analytical geometry, trigonometry and calculus, and thus to the unification of mathematics. Euler was responsible for much of modern mathematical notation.

Carl Friedrich Gauss (1777–1855), German mathematician who developed the theory of complex numbers (see p. 241). He was director of the astronomical observatory at Göttingen and conducted a survey, based on trigonometric techniques, of the kingdom of Hanover. He published works in many fields, including the application of mathematics to electrostatics and electrodynamics.

Baron Augustin-Louis Cauchy (1789–1857), French mathematician and physicist who developed the modern treatment of calculus and the theory of functions. He introduced rigour to much of mathematics. As an engineer he contributed to Napoleon's preparations to invade Britain, and he twice gave up academic posts to serve the exiled Charles X.

János Bolyai (1802–60), Hungarian mathematician who – despite being warned by his father against the attempt – investigated Euclid's parallel postulate. Bolyai eventually developed a non-Euclidean geometry, only to discover to his horror that Gauss had anticipated his work.

George Boole (1815–64), English mathematician. Despite being largely self-taught, Boole became Professor of Mathematics at University College, Cork. He laid the foundations of Boolean algebra, which was fundamental to the development of the digital electronic computer.

George Cantor (1845–1918), Russian-born mathematician who spent most of his life in Germany. His most important work was on finite and infinite sets. He was greatly interested in theology and philosophy.

Felix Christian Klein (1849–1925), German mathematician who introduced a programme for the classification of geometry in terms of group theory. His interest in *topology* (the study of geometric figures that are subjected to deformations) produced the first description of what became known as a *Klein bottle*, which has a continuous one-sided surface.

David Hilbert (1862–1943), German mathematician. In 1901, Hilbert listed 23 major unsolved problems in mathematics, many of which still remain unsolved. His work contributed to the rigour and unity of modern mathematics and to the development of the theory of *computability*.

(Jules) Henri Poincaré (1854–1912), French mathematician who is often said to have been the last mathematician to have a grasp of all the known branches of the subject. Poincaré worked on the theory of functions, differential equations, topology, celestial mechanics, mathematical physics, number theory, and non-Euclidean geometry, as well as writing on the philosophy of science and mathematics, and publishing many popular essays.

Hermann Minkowski (1864–1909), Lithuanian-born German mathematician who won the *Grand Prix des Sciences Mathématiques* of the Paris Academy of Sciences at the age of 18. (Minkowski had previously abandoned his claims to a university prize in favour of a needy colleague.) He contributed to geometry and to the theories of numbers and of relativity. Einstein said that without Minkowski's contribution, the general theory of relativity would not have been possible.

Lord Bertrand Russell (1872–1970), English philosopher and mathematician. Russell did much of the basic work on mathematical logic and the foundations of mathematics. He found the paradox, now named after him, in the theory of sets proposed by the German logician Gottlob Frege (1848–1925), and went on to develop the whole of arithmetic in terms of pure logic. He was jailed for his pacifist activities in World War 1. In 1950, he was awarded the Nobel Prize for Literature.

Emmy Noether (Amalie Noether; 1882–1935), German mathematician who was described as 'the most creative abstract algebraist of modern times'. Initially, she had difficulty in obtaining a lectureship because she was a woman. In 1933 Noether was dismissed from her post by the Nazis because she was Jewish, and went to the USA where she lectured until her death.

Srinivasa Aaiyangar Ramanujan (1887–1920), Indian mathematician. At the age of 16, Ramanujan devoted his life to mathematics after reading a book summarizing European mathematics. He had an astonishing intuition for the correct results, although many were not proved until later. He was discovered by the English mathematician G.H. Hardy, with whom he later collaborated at Cambridge.

Kurt Gödel (1906–78), Austrian-born American mathematician. Gödel stunned mathematicians in the 1930s by showing that Hilbert's dream of a general method of proving any mathematical theorem could not be realized.

Alan Turing (1912–54), English mathematician who pioneered computer theory. Turing discovered that it is impossible in general to predict if or when the Turing machine – a universal automatic machine capable of mathematical problem-solving which he designed – would stop.

John Horton Conway (1938–), English mathematician who is famous for his serious studies of mathematical recreations. Conway developed the 'Game of Life', in which an object is made up of a number of squares of an infinite chessboard. The object grows, decays and 'dies' according to very simple rules. The 'Game' can be used to simulate a general-purpose computer.

SOME MILESTONES IN GEOMETRY AND TRIGONOMETRY

From c. 3000 BC	Babylonians made early developments in geometry and measurement.
6th century BC	Pythagoras' theorem.
4th century BC	Eudoxus' geometry of irrational numbers.
330 BC	Euclid's *Elements* published.
3rd century BC	Archimedes described the relationship between the surface and volume of a sphere. Apollonius of Rhodes described conic sections.
2nd century BC	Menelaus and Ptolemy developed spherical triangles for astronomy.
AD 1637	Descartes developed analytical geometry.
1639	Desargues' Theorem.
1640	Pascal's Theorem – with Desargues' Theorem, the beginning of projective geometry.
1822	Poncelet's work on projective geometry – the principle of duality and imaginary points.
1825–32	Bolyai and Lobachevsky developed non-Euclidean geometry.
1844–61	Grassman developed the theory of n-dimensions.
1847	von Staudt's axioms – the development of planes in projective geometry.
1851	Foucault's pendulum
1854	Riemann's inaugural lecture at Göttingen gave a comprehensive view of geometry.
1867	Helmholtz investigated the properties of non-Euclidean space.
late 19th century	Dedekind and Cantor supplemented the geometrical method of analysis.
1902	Hilbert's *Foundations of Geometry*.
1911	Brouwer developed topology.
20th century	The development of transformation geometry.

TRIGONOMETRY

A simple example of a mathematical model is the representation of a portion of the Earth's surface by a set of interlocking triangles, from the measurement of which maps may be constructed. The triangulation model uses the rules of geometry and trigonometry to derive angles and distances that cannot be measured directly.

Geometry establishes that two triangles each have angles of the same sizes if, and only if, corresponding pairs of sides are in the same proportions.

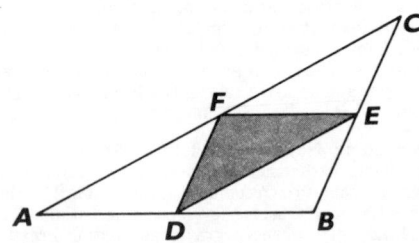

Here D, E and F are the centre-points of sides AB, BC and CA respectively. So, DE is half the length of AC, EF is half the length of AB, and FD is half the length of BC. Thus, the shaded triangle, DEF, is *similar* to the large triangle, and the angles at D, E and F are, respectively, equal to those at C, A and B. Furthermore, the triangles ADF, FEC, DBE and EFD are all *congruent*, i.e. identical in shape and size, and are thus all similar to triangle ABC.

A right-angled triangle is a triangle where one of the angles is 90°. *Pythagoras' theorem* (see p. 252) states that, in a right-angled triangle, the square of the length of the *hypotenuse* (the side opposite the right angle) equals the sum of the squares of the lengths of the other two sides. So, in the triangle shown, below, $AC^2 = AB^2 + BC^2$.

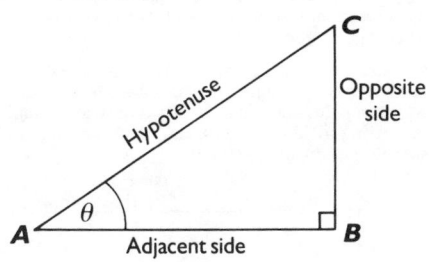

Trigonometry relies on the recognition that in a right-angled triangle the ratio of the lengths of pairs of sides depends only on the sizes of the two acute angles (i.e. angles less than 90°) of the triangle.

These ratios are given names. For example, the *sine* of an angle is the ratio of the side opposite the given angle to the hypotenuse. The Greek letters θ *(theta)* and φ *(phi)* are usually used to denote the angles; thus in the triangle shown we say that the sine of θ, usually written sin θ, is BC/AC. Similarly, since the *cosine* (cos) of the angle is the ratio of the side adjacent to the given angle to the hypotenuse, cos θ is AB/AC. The third basic ratio is the *tangent* (tan), which is the ratio of the opposite to the adjacent side, BC/AB in the example; it is easy to see that tan θ must always equal sin θ / cos θ. Pythagoras' theorem can be used to establish some very useful values for sin, cos and tan.

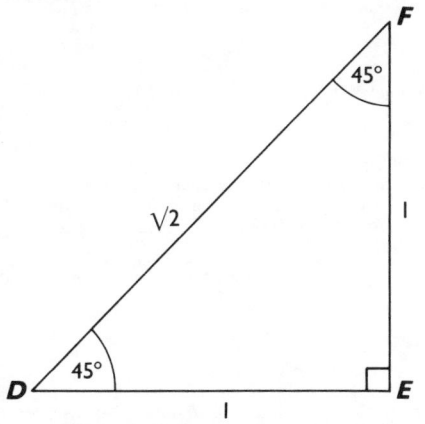

In triangle DEF, DE = EF = 1, so the angles at D and F are equal, that is they are each 45° (the internal angles of a triangle add up to 180°). Using Pythagoras' theorem, $DF^2 = 1^2 + 1^2 = 2$, so DF = √2. We can therefore conclude:

$$\sin 45° = \frac{1}{\sqrt{2}};$$

$$\cos 45° = \frac{1}{\sqrt{2}};$$

$$\tan 45° = 1$$

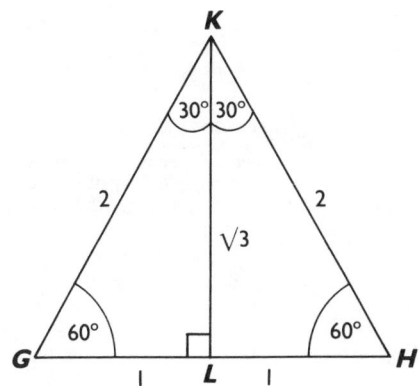

In triangle GHK, GH = HK = KG = 2, so the angles at G, H and K are equal, that is they are each 60°. Using Pythagoras' theorem, $KL^2 + 1^2 = 2^2$, so KL = √3. We therefore have:

$$\sin 60° = \frac{1}{2}\sqrt{3} = \cos 30°$$

$$\cos 60° = 1/2 = \sin 30°$$

$$\tan 60° = \sqrt{3}$$

$$\tan 30° = 1/\sqrt{3}$$

GEOMETRY

PLANE FIGURES

Plane figures lie entirely on one plane, i.e. they are two-dimensional. They include polygons, quadrilaterals, triangles, circles and conic sections.

POLYGONS

A polygon is a closed plane figure with three or more straight sides that meet at the same number of vertices and do not intersect other than at those vertices. (A vertex is the point at which two sides of a polygon meet.) Although we tend to think of a polygon as being a many-sided figure, it can have as few sides as three (a triangle).

Some important polygons

triangle	3 sides
quadrilateral	4 sides
pentagon	5 sides
hexagon	6 sides
heptagon	7 sides
octagon	8 sides
nonagon	9 sides
decagon	10 sides
dodecagon	12 sides

Physical properties of polygons

The sum of the interior angles = $(2n - 4) \times 90°$ where n = the number of sides.

Each interior angle of a regular polygon = $\dfrac{((2n - 4) \times 90°)}{n}$

$$\text{or} = 180° - \frac{360°}{n}$$

The sum of the exterior angles of any polygon = 360°, regardless of the number of sides. (An exterior angle of a polygon is the angle between one side extended and the adjacent side.)

The area of any
regular polygon of sides $a = \frac{1}{4} n a^2 \cot \frac{180°}{n}$

Where n = the number of sides; cot = cotangent, a trigonometric function.

QUADRILATERALS

A quadrilateral is a plane figure with four sides. A quadrilateral may be a rectangle, a square, a parallelogram, a rhombus or a trapezium (or trapezoid).

Rectangles

A rectangle is a quadrilateral in which all the angles are right angles, thus the opposite sides are parallel in pairs. A rectangle may be a square (see below). A rectangle that is not a square has two lines of symmetry.

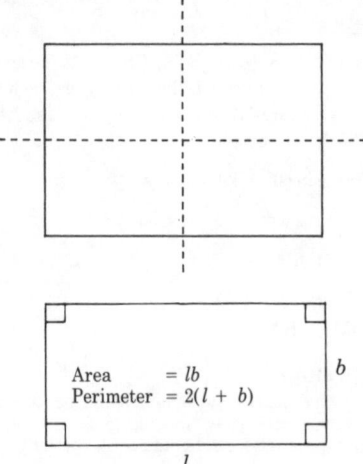

$$\text{Area} = lb$$
$$\text{Perimeter} = 2(l + b)$$

Square

A square is a rectangle whose sides are all equal. It has four lines of symmetry – both diagonals and the two lines joining the middle points of pairs of opposite sides.

$$\text{Area} = l^2$$
$$\text{Perimeter} = 4l$$

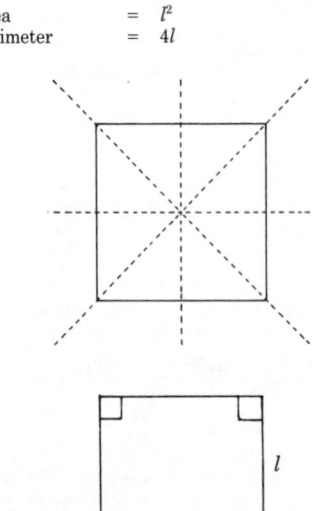

Parallelogram

A parallelogram is a quadrilateral whose opposite sides are equal in length and parallel. It has no lines of symmetry, unless it is also a rectangle, but it does have rotational symmetry about its centre, the point where the diagonals meet.

If one angle of a parallelogram is a right angle, then all the angles are right angles, and it is a rectangle. Any parallelogram can be dissected into a rectangle by cutting a right-angled triangle off one end, and sliding it to the opposite end.

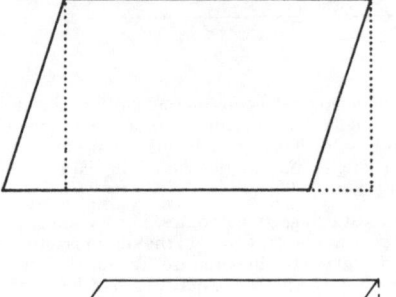

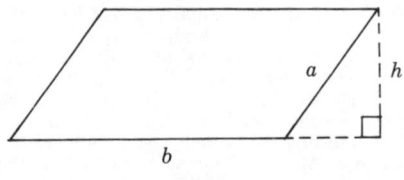

This dissection changes neither the area of the parallelogram nor the length of the sides – the area of any parallelogram is equal to the area of a rectangle with same base and the same height.

$$\text{Area} = bh$$
$$\text{Perimeter} = 2(a + b)$$

Rhombus

A rhombus is a parallelogram whose sides are all equal in length. Its diagonals are both lines of symmetry, and therefore bisect each other at right angles.

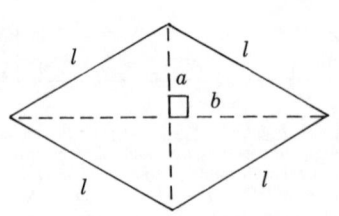

$$\text{Area} = \frac{1}{2}(2a)(2b)$$
$$\text{i.e.} = \frac{1}{2}(\text{product of the diagonals})$$
$$\text{Perimeter} = 4l$$

Trapezium

A trapezium is a quadrilateral with two parallel sides of unequal length. (In North America – where such a plane figure is described as a *trapezoid* – a trapezium is a quadrilateral with no sides parallel.)

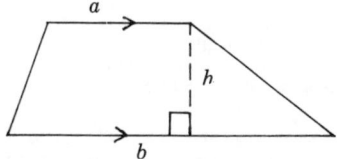

Area   = ½(a + b)h

To find the area three measurements have to taken – the *height* between the pair of parallel sides and the length of both of the parallel sides. The area of a trapezium is equal to the height multiplied by the *average* length of the parallel sides.

i.e.   = ½(the sum of the
                  parallel sides)
                  × the perpendicular
                  distance between
                  them

TRIANGLES

A triangle is a three-sided polygon. A *scalene* triangle has sides of three different lengths, and has no axes of symmetry. If two sides of a triangle are equal in length, the triangle is *isosceles*, and has one axis of symmetry, and a pair of equal angles.

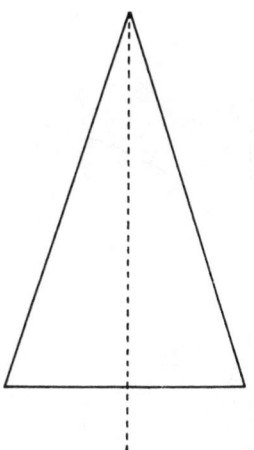

An *equilateral* triangle has all its sides equal, and all its angles are equal to 60°.

Triangles have many curious properties. For example, the three lines that join the vertices of a triangle to the middle points of the opposite sides, meet in a point – they are said to be *concurrent*.

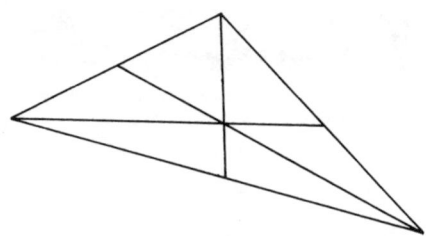

The three lines that bisect the sides of a triangle at right angles also meet. The point at which they meet is the centre of the circle through the vertices of the triangle.

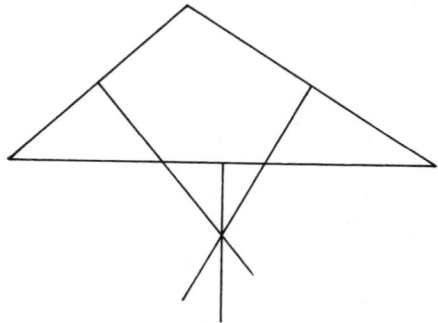

Any triangle can be thought of as one half of a parallelogram that has been divided in two by one of its diagonals (see below).

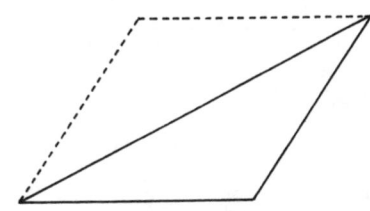

The area of a triangle is one half of the area of a parallelogram with the same base and the same height.

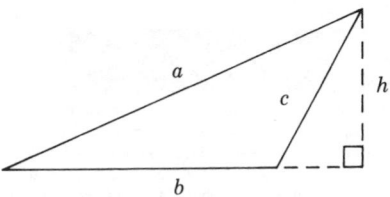

Area   = ½bh

The area of a triangle can also be calculated from the lengths of its sides, using a formula discovered by the Greek mathematician Archimedes:

If half the sum of the sides is s, then,

Area = $\sqrt{\{ s(s - a)(s - b)(s - c)\}}$

The Greek mathematician Pappus (c. AD 300) discovered the earliest theorem in *projective geometry*.

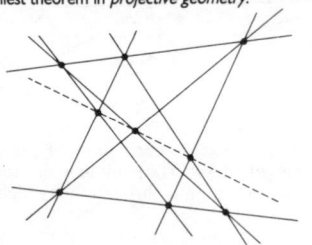

Take three points on each of two lines, and join them as in the figure with three 'X's, so that each point is joined to the points that are not directly opposite to it on the other line. The centres of the 'X's lie on a straight line.

Notice that this theorem involves no measurement at all – it is entirely about lines meeting and points lying on lines.

CIRCLES

A circle is the path of a point that moves at a constant distance – *the radius* – from a fixed point (the centre of the circle).

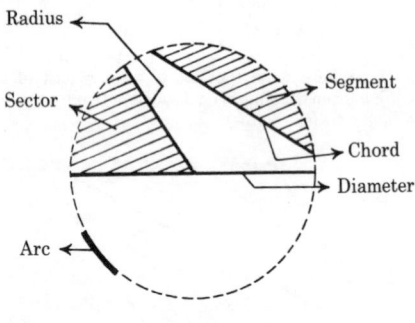

Circumference	=	$2\pi r$
	or	πd
Area	=	πr^2

where r = radius, d = diameter, and π = pi, the ratio of the circumference of a circle to its diameter (approximately 3.141592...).

Visiting the great Indian mathematician Srinivasa Ramanujan in hospital, his friend G.H. Hardy remarked that the number of his taxi had been 1729, surely a dull number. Ramanujan replied, 'No, it is a very interesting number. It is the smallest number expressible as a sum of two cubes in two different ways.'

$1729 = 10^3 + 9^3 = 12^3 + 1^3$

Ramanujan was fascinated by numbers, and it is no surprise that he found some weird approximations for π. You can check the following example easily with an electronic calculator.

π is the fourth root of $9^2 + 19^2/22$

CONIC SECTIONS

Conic sections are curves that are formed by the intersection of a plane and a cone. An ellipse, a parabola, a hyperbola, a rectangular hyperbola and a circle are all conic sections.

Ellipse

An ellipse is a closed conic section with the appearance of a flattened circle. It is formed by an inclined plane that does not intersect the base of the cone. An ellipse can also be thought of as a circle that has been stretched in one direction. The orbital path of each of the planets round the Sun is approximately an ellipse.

There are many ways to draw an ellipse. One of the simplest is to stretch a loop of thread round two pins, and hold it taut with a pencil. The path of the pencil will be an ellipse.

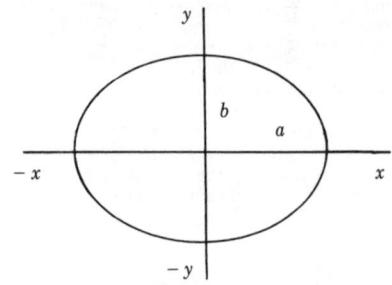

| Area | $= \pi ab$ |

Basic equation (centre at the origin)
$(x^2 / a^2 + y^2 / b^2) = 1$

Parabola

A parabola is a conic section that is formed by the intersection of cone by a plane parallel to its side.

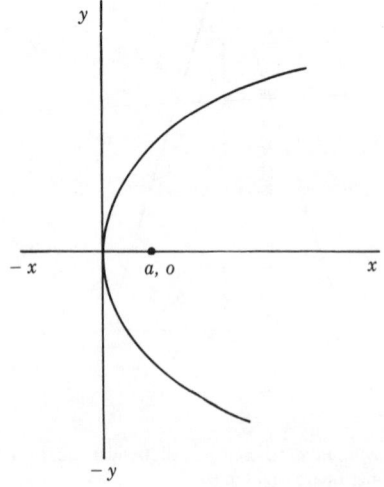

If you throw a ball in the air, then the path of the ball will be approximately a parabola with its axis vertical.

Basic equation (symmetrical about the x-axis with the focus at $a, 0$)
$y^2 = 4ax$

Hyperbola
A hyperbola is a conic section that is formed by a plane that cuts a cone making a larger angle with the base than the angle made by the side of the cone.

Basic equation (centre at the origin)
$(x^2 / a^2 - y^2 / b^2) = 1$

Circle The circle is a special case of an ellipse (see also above).
General equation (centre at $-g, -f$)
$x^2 + y^2 + 2gx + 2fy + c = 0$
Basic equation (centre at the origin)
$x^2 + y^2 = r^2$

PENROSE   TRIANGLE

Roger Penrose is a brilliant mathematician as well as one of the greatest living physicists. Twenty years ago he invented twister theories.

Yet he also discovered, with his father, the Penrose tribar – a triangle that looks real but cannot actually exist.

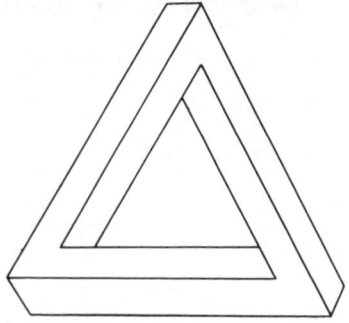

As so often, physical and mathematical ability go together with a subtle visual imagination.

FERMAT NUMBERS

Pierre Fermat made one very famous mistake in his career. He claimed that all the numbers in this sequence, called the Fermat numbers, were prime:

$F_0 = 2^1 + 1 = 3$; $F_1 = 2^2 + 1 = 5$; $F_2 = 2^4 + 1 = 17$; $F_3 = 2^8 + 1 = 257$; $F_4 = 2^{16} + 1 = 65\,537$.....

Unfortunately, only the first five are known to be prime. Euler showed in 1732 that $F_5 = 294\,967\,297 = 641 \times 6\,700\,417$, and every Fermat number tested since then has proved to be composite.

Actually finding the factors of a large number, even when you know that it is not prime, is very difficult. Only in 1990 did Mark Manasse and Arjen Lenstra manage to find the factors of F_9, a number of 155 digits, using a Connection machine, a massive parallel supercomputer at Florida State University. It has three prime factors, of 7, 49, and 99 digits.

PYTHAGORAS' THEOREM

Pythagoras' Theorem is the most-proved theorem in geometry, indeed in the whole of mathemetics. E.S. Loomis published in 1940 a collection of more than 370 different proofs, and more have been discovered since. This proof is by Leonardo da Vinci.

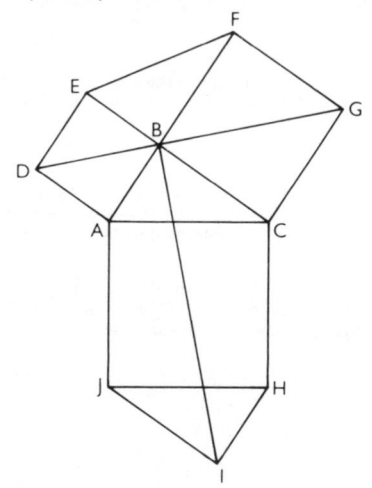

DEFG, DACG, ABIJ and IHCB are all congruent (i.e. identical) shapes. The first two together make up the two smaller squares and the original triangle (ABC) twice. The second two make up the larger square and the triangle twice.

SOLIDS
Solids are three-dimensional figures, i.e. they have length, breadth and depth.

Rectangular block
A rectangular block is a solid figure, all the faces of which are rectangles.

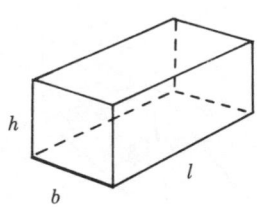

Surface area	=	$2(lb + bh + hl)$
Volume	=	lbh
		(i.e. the area of the base multiplied by the height)

The volume of any solid is always equal to the area of the base × the perpendicular height.

Prism
A prism is a solid figure whose ends are identical polygons and whose sides are parallelograms (which could be rectangles).

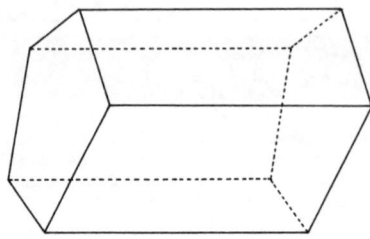

The volume of a prism equals the area of either of the ends, multiplied by the perpendicular distance between the ends.

Pyramid
A pyramid is a solid figure whose base is a polygon, and whose special vertex – the *apex* – is joined to each vertex of the base. Therefore all its faces, apart from the base, are triangles.

Any pyramid can be fitted inside a prism so that the base of the pyramid is one end of the prism, and the apex of the pyramid is on the other end of the prism.

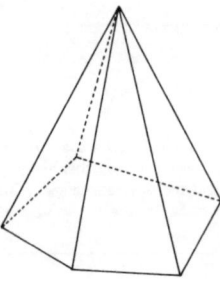

The volume of a pyramid on a rectangular base = ⅓*(lbh)*.

Tetrahedron
A tetrahedron is a pyramid whose base is a triangle. Any of the faces of a tetrahedron can be thought of as its base.

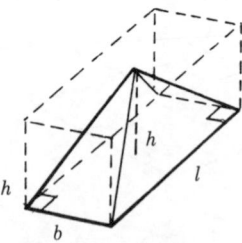

The volume of a tetrahedron = ⅓ (the area of the triangular base × the height)

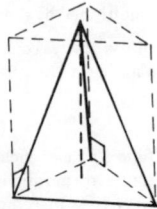

Cylinder
A cylinder is a solid figure with straight sides and a circular section.

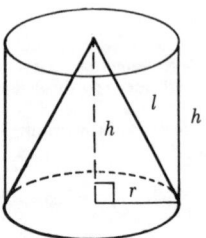

The area of the curved surface of a cylinder = $2\pi rh$. If the circles at both ends are included, then the total surface area = $2\pi rh + 2\pi r^2$.

The volume of a cylinder can be found by thinking of it as a special case of a prism. The volume equals the area of the base, multiplied by the height.
The volume of a cylinder = $\pi r^2 h$

Cone
A cone is a solid figure with a circular plane base, narrowing to a point or apex.

If the slant height of the cone is *l*, the area of the curved surface is πrl.

The volume of a cone can be calculated as if the cone were a special case of a pyramid. The volume is one third the volume of a cylinder with the same base and height.

The volume of a cone = $\frac{1}{3}\pi r^2 h$.

Sphere
A sphere is a solid figure every point of whose surface is equidistant from its centre.

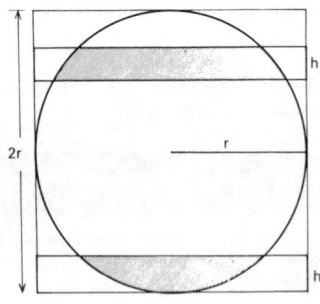

Surface area	=	$4\pi r^2$
Volume	=	$4/3\pi r^3$

POLYHEDRA

A polyhedron is a solid shape with all plane faces. The faces of a regular polyhedron, or regular solid, are all identical regular polygons.

There are just five regular polyhedra – the regular tetrahedron, the cube, the regular octahedron, the regular dodecahedron and the regular icosahedron.

The cube and the octahedron are dual polyhedra. The cube has six faces and eight vertices, while the

POLYHEDRA

	Faces	Type of face	Vertices	Edges
Regular Tetrahedron	4	equilateral triangles	4	6
Cube	6	squares	8	12
Regular Octahedron	8	equilateral triangles	6	12
Regular Dodecahedron	12	regular pentagons	20	30
Regular Icosahedron	20	equilateral triangles	12	30

octahedron has six vertices but eight faces. The regular dodecahedron and regular icosahedron are also dual polyhedra.

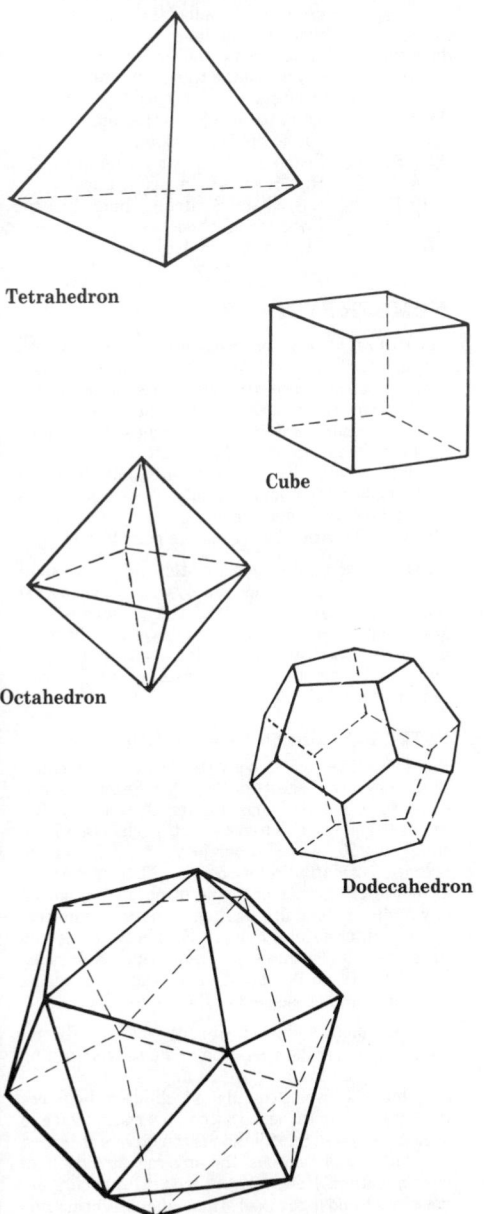

Tetrahedron

Cube

Octahedron

Dodecahedron

Icosahedron

There are many more irregular polyhedra. The simplest to visualize have faces that are mixtures of two kinds of regular polygons. For example, the faces of the cuboctahedron (below) are equilateral triangles and squares.

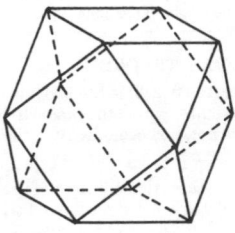

The mathematician Euler made an interesting discovery about the relationship between the number of faces (F), vertices (V) and edges (E) of polyhedra.

The equation $F + V - E = 2$ is true for all 'simple' polyhedra – the regular polyhedra listed in the table below.

The same relationship is true for an area divided into any number of regions (R) by boundaries or arcs (A) that join at nodes (N). Thus, $R + N - A = 2$.

For the area shown below:
$R = 8$ (the surrounding space counts as a region)
$N = 12$
$A = 18$

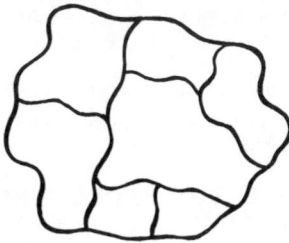

Thus $R + N - A$
$= 8 + 12 - 18$
$= 2$

Note: For such a region, or indeed any map, no more than four colours are necessary so that no two adjoining regions have the same colour.

THE SPHERE

A little-known and interesting fact about the sphere is that the area of any zone of its curved surface lying between two parallel planes is exactly equal to the curved surface of the surrounding cylinder between the same two planes. This fact was discovered by Archimedes, who requested that a sphere inscribed in a cylinder be engraved on his tomb.

This applies to any belt of the sphere, or to a cap or to the whole sphere. It thus makes the calculation of what might appear to be a difficult area quite simple.

Thus, either shaded area of the sphere on p. 238 is equal to the curved surface area of a cylinder of radius r and height h, the height of the zone.

PYTHAGORAS' THEOREM

Pythagoras (see p. 230) is the probable discoverer of the geometrical theorem that came to be named after him. (He did not, however, discover the theorem in its Euclidean form.)

The theorem states that the area of the square drawn on the *hypotenuse* of a right-angled triangle is equal to the sum of the areas of the squares drawn on the other two sides. (It is, however, also true that the area of any shape drawn on the hypotenuse is equal to the sum of the areas of similar shapes drawn on the other two sides.)

In the triangle ABC right-angled at B:
$$AC^2 = AB^2 + BC^2$$

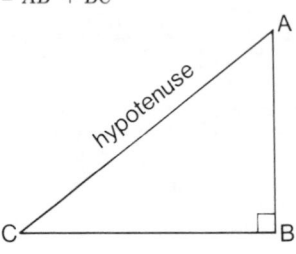

There are an infinite number of right-angled triangles whose sides are integers. Four of the smallest have the sides:

3, 4, 5   5, 12, 13
8, 15, 17   and 7, 24, 25

Such whole-number sets are sometimes called *Pythagorean triples*.

SOME MILESTONES IN ARITHMETIC AND ALGEBRA

c. 1700 BC	Babylonians developed arithmetic in the sexagesimal system (base 60).
330 BC	Euclid's *Elements* represented algebraic results in terms of lengths.
220 BC	Apollonius' *Conica*.
AD 200	Diophantus' *Arithmetica*.
630	Brahmagupta studied indeterminate equations.
1515–45	del Ferro, Tartaglia and Cardano solve the cubic equation.
1614	Napier discovered logarithms.
1637	Fermat's last theorem.
1654	The first slide rule.
1771–72	Vandermonde and Laplace developed determinant theory.
1799	Gauss proved the fundamental theory of algebra.
1801	Gauss developed groups.
1820s	Abel proved the impossibility of solving algebraically the general equation of the fifth degree.
1829	Sturm functions.
1831	Galois applied group theory to equations.
1854	Boole's *Investigation into the Laws of Thought* applied the methods of algebra to logic.
late 19th century	Weierstrasse and Dedekind developed the theory of real numbers.
1880s	Poincaré developed the concept of automorphic function.
1889–94	Peano developed a logic notation.
1906	Hilbert's work on eigenvalues.
1910–13	Russell and Whitehead published *Principia Mathematica*.
1970s	Electronic calculators came into general use.

NUMBER SYSTEMS

The *natural numbers* or *whole numbers* are those we use in counting. We learn these at an early age, perhaps pairing them with our fingers or else learning to chant their names in order: 'one, two, three, four, . . .'. Important features of our number system, these numbers can be used to count sets of objects, and form a naturally ordered progression that has a first member, the number 1, but no last member: no matter how big a number you come up with, I can always reply with a bigger one – simply by adding 1.

However, even quite simple arithmetic, as we shall see, cannot be carried out wholly within the natural numbers. Ordinarily we take the principles that govern such systems for granted, yet merely to be able to subtract and divide, for example, requires other, more complex, number systems, such as fractions and negative numbers.

NATURAL NUMBERS AND ARITHMETIC

If I have 3 sheep and you give me 4 more, I can count that I now have 7 sheep, or I can use the operation of *addition* to get the same answer: $3 + 4 = 7$. If I promise to give 5 children 4 sweets each, again I can count out 20 sweets altogether, or I can use the operation of *multiplication*: $5 \times 4 = 20$. Here, we have examples of another principle of natural numbers: any addition or multiplication of natural numbers gives another natural number. Such a system is said to be *closed* under these operations. (A closed system is one where an operation on two of its elements produces another element of that system.)

If I had 3 sheep and when you gave me your sheep I had 7, I can use the operation of *subtraction* to find how many sheep you gave to me: $7 - 3 = 4$. If I distribute 20 sweets equally to 5 children, I can use the operation of *division* to find how many I gave to each: $20 \div 5 = 4$. Subtraction is the *inverse operation* of addition; division is the inverse operation of multiplication. However, the natural numbers are not closed under the operations of subtraction and division, as we shall see later.

SIMPLE ALGEBRA

In simple algebra, we generalize arithmetic by using letters to stand for unknown numbers whose value is to be discovered, or to stand for numbers in general. Usually letters from the beginning of the alphabet are used in the latter way – for example, to express a general truth about numbers, such as $a + b = b + a$. The letters at the end of the alphabet are generally used to represent unknown numbers. For example, the information about the sheep can be expressed by the *equation*, $3 + x = 7$, where x represents the unknown number of sheep you gave to me. Since the two sides of this equation are equal, they remain equal if we treat them both the same way. If we then subtract 3 from each side we get $x = 7 - 3$, that is $x = 4$. We have *solved the equation*.

SUBTRACTION AND THE INTEGERS

The set of natural numbers is not closed under the operation of subtraction; for example, $3 - 7$ does not give a natural number as an answer. We need a system of numbers that is closed under subtraction. The smallest set of numbers that is closed under subtraction is the set of *integers*, i.e. the set $\{..., -3, -2, -1, 0, 1, 2, 3, ...\}$. Here, the positive integers can be identified with the natural numbers; zero (0) is defined as the result of subtracting any integer from itself; and the negative integers are the result of subtracting the corresponding positive integers from zero (e.g. $-3 = 0 - 3$).

Now, every subtraction has an answer within the number system of integers, that is, the integers are closed under subtraction.

DIVISION AND THE RATIONAL NUMBERS

The integers, however, are still not closed under the operation of division. We can construct a system that is by defining the result of any division, $a \div b$ to be the pair of integers, a and b, written in a notation that clearly distinguishes which divides which. Thus, we write $a \div b$ as the *ratio* or *fraction*, a/b, and we have the system of *rational numbers*.

It is important to note that rational numbers are not identical with their symbols. The same rational number may be represented by many different fractions (in fact, an infinite number of them). For example, 24/8 is the same rational number as 12/4 or 6/2. We adopt the convention of representing them, where possible, by the unique fraction in which there is no *common factor*, that can be cancelled out (thus, 14/21 becomes 2/3, where the factor, 7, has been cancelled out). It should also be noted that decimals are rational numbers, since, for example, $0.5 = 5/10 = 1/2$, and $1.61 = 161/100$.

We do have a problem, however: the rationals cannot be closed under division, because of the integer 0. We cannot give value to $a/0$ for any rational number a. This problem, however, cannot be avoided: we have to be content with the fact that the rationals, excluding the integer 0, are closed under division.

ROOTS AND IRRATIONAL NUMBERS

The figure 6^9, which we read as, '6 to the *power* 9' means 6 multiplied by itself 9 times ($6 \times 6 \times 6 \times 6 \times 6 \times 6 \times 6 \times 6 \times 6$). Generally, a^b, which we read as, 'a to the power b', means a multiplied by itself b times. These are closed operations for the systems of numbers we have so far considered. However, none of these systems guarantees the possibility of the inverse operation, the *extraction of roots*. If $b = a^n$, (where n represents an integer), then a is the nth root

of b, written $a = {}^n\sqrt{b}$. For example, since $3 \times 3 = 9$, the second or *square root* of 9 (written ${}^2\sqrt{9}$ or more usually $\sqrt{9}$) equals 3. To give another example, since $2 \times 2 \times 2 = 8$, the third or *cube root* of 8 (written ${}^3\sqrt{8}$) is 2. But none of the systems we have considered is closed under this operation. For example, $\sqrt{2}$, $\sqrt{3}$, and $\sqrt{5}$ cannot be expressed as fractions or as terminating decimals; they are examples of what are called *irrational numbers*. They have exact meaning – for example, by Pythagoras' theorem (see p. 240), $\sqrt{2}$ is the length of the hypotenuse of a right-angled triangle whose other sides are each length 1; $\sqrt{5}$ is the length of the hypotenuse of a right-angled triangle whose other sides have lengths 1 and 2, etc. Obviously, we need to add the irrationals to our number systems to ensure closure under these calculations.

All the systems we have discussed, the natural numbers, the integers, the rational numbers and the irrationals form together the system of *real numbers*.

IMAGINARY AND COMPLEX NUMBERS

However, now we have admitted the extraction of roots, we have opened up a new gap in our number system: we have not, as yet, defined the square root of a negative number. At first sight, we may wonder why this omission should be of any great importance, but without the development of a system to include such numbers, many valuable applications to engineering and physics would not be possible. Surprisingly, we need only extend the number system by one new number. Since all negative numbers are positive multiples of -1 (for example, -6 is 6×-1, so that $\sqrt{-6} = \sqrt{6} \times \sqrt{-1}$) we are concerned only with the square root of -1. The square root of -1 is denoted by the letter i, so we have $i^2 = -1$.

Real multiples of i, such as $3i$, $2.7i$, $2i/3$, $i\sqrt{2}$, etc., are called *imaginary numbers*. The sum of a real number and an imaginary number, such as $5 + 3i$ is a *complex number*. It can be shown that every complex number can be expressed uniquely as the sum of its real and imaginary parts.

The rules for using complex numbers are the same as those for real numbers. It can be shown, for example, that

$$(a + ib)(a - ib) = a^2 + b^2.$$

The terms in brackets are thus the factors of $a^2 + b^2$. In fact it turns out that in the complex number system any algebraic expression with integer powers has exactly the same number of factors as the highest power in the expression. This result is so important that it is called the *fundamental theorem of algebra*.

OTHER NUMBER NOTATIONS

The usual notation for numbers is a *decimal place-value system*. This means that there are ten distinct digits (0, 1, 2, 3, 4, 5, 6, 7, 8, 9) and that the position of each digit determines what it contributes to the value of the number. Each position gives a value 10 times as great as the position to the right, so, for example, 7234 can be written as four units (4×10^0) on the right, plus 3 tens (3×10^1) plus 2 hundreds (2×10^2) plus 7 thousands (7×10^3). We say that ten is the *base* of the decimal place-value system.

We can easily construct systems with other bases to suit other needs.

BINARY SYSTEM

The binary system uses only the digits 0 and 1; so it

has base 2. This is used in the representation of numbers within computers, since the two numerals correspond to the on and the off positions of an electronic switch. In the binary system we count as follows: $1, 10 (= 2 + 0), 11 (= 2 + 1), 100 (= 4 + 0 + 0), 1001 (= 8 + 0 + 0 + 1)$ etc.

Binary numbers 1–20

Decimal	Binary
1	1
2	10
3	11
4	100
5	101
6	110
7	111
8	1000
9	1001
10	1010
11	1011
12	1100
13	1101
14	1110
15	1111
16	10000
17	10001
18	10010
19	10011
20	10100

This appears difficult at first sight, but is relatively easy to decipher if the following rules are remembered:
–ignore all noughts in calculation;
–count the right columns as 1 (2^0);
–count the second column on the right as 2 (2^1);
–count the third column on the right as 4 (2^2);
–count the fourth column on the right as 8 (2^3);
–count the fifth column on the right as 16 (2^4); and so on.

Thus 1101001 in the binary system would be the equivalent of 105 in the decimal system.

OCTAL ARITHMETIC

Sometimes, especially in computing, it is convenient to use *octal arithmetic* (with base 8) or *hexadecimal arithmetic* (base 16). In base 16, the letters A to F are used as well as the numerals 0 to 9. Obviously it is necessary to know which base is being used, so the base is indicated by a subscript, for example, $31_{10} = 1F_{16} = 37_8 = 11111_2$.

There are many other ways in which number systems vary. The following examples are taken from history.

THE EGYPTIAN NUMBER SYSTEM

The earliest example of a grouping system to represent numbers is that used by the ancient Egyptians who gave hieroglyphic symbols to $1, 10, 10^2, 10^3, 10^4, 10^5$ and 10^6. Each digit was represented by a group of the relevant hieroglyphic symbols arranged from right to left.

THE BABYLONIAN NUMBER SYSTEM

The Babylonians used a sexagesimal system, that is one with base 60. Each number up to and including 60 was represented by a grouping of only two cuneiform symbols incorporating an additional subtractive symbol for higher numbers, thus 48 was represented by 50, the subtractive symbol and two. Large numbers were represented by the grouping of cuneiform symbols for the base followed by the grouping for the remainder – thus, 607 was represented by 10

(i.e. 10 times base 60) plus seven. The system has been compared to the digital representation of time, e.g. 10.17 for 10 hours and 17 minutes.

THE GREEK NUMBER SYSTEM

The Greeks also used a grouping system on their inscriptions, but with a number of refinements. Numbers from one to 10 were represented by the initial letter of their names, thus △ (delta) represented ten ('deka'). Similarly, 100 was represented by H (for 'hekaton'), 1000 by X (for 'chilioi') and 10 000 by M (for 'murioi'). A further refinement was the use of the symbol for five in conjunction with others to represent 50, 500 and so on. Large numbers were compiled by listing the appropriate letters from left to right, beginning with the largest element.

Because the first known description of this system was written by the grammarian Herodianus (in the

NUMERICAL TRADITIONS

Numbers have always been associated with good or bad luck, and with rhymes, folklore, colours and symbols of the zodiac.

1 The Ancient Greeks associated the number 1 with unity and reason. Both they and the Chinese believed that 1 was both an odd and an even number.

2 The Ancient Greeks thought that all even numbers were feminine and all odd numbers masculine. The Chinese held a similar belief. Two, being the first feminine number, was thought to be particularly lucky.

3 The number three is important in religion and in magic. It is significant to Christians because of the Trinity. It was equally important to the Babylonians and Ancient Egyptians because of their trinities of gods, to the Ancient Greeks because of the trinity of the Fates and to many ancient religions because of the traditional threefold division of the world into the underworld, earth and the heavens. The number is associated with good luck in most cultures and throughout Europe oaths and spells were traditionally uttered three times. The Ancient Greeks held three to be particularly important as it was the first masculine number and the symbol of strength.

4 The number four was held to be lucky by most ancient peoples as it symbolized the four elements of earth, fire, water and air. To the Ancient Greeks it symbolized harmony.

5 The number five was held to be unlucky in the Middle Ages because it was thought to represent the five wounds inflicted at the Crucifixion and the five points of a witch's pentacle. The Ancient Greeks believed five to be lucky and held that it represented marriage (being the addition of two and three, the first male and female numbers).

6 The Ancient Greeks and the Romans believed that six was significant as it is the first perfect number (see p. 256).

7 Most ancient civilizations believed that the number seven had magical properties. There were seven days to the week and (then) seven known planets in the sky. The number seven features in the folkore of all European countries; for example, the seventh child of a seventh child was thought to possess special psychic powers.

8 The number eight is traditionally associated with wisdom.

9 The number nine frequently occurs in folklore. To the Ancient Greeks it held special significance because the numbers 1–9 make a 'magic square' (see p. 256).

2nd century BC), Greek numbers are often referred to as Herodianic numerals.

THE ROMAN NUMBER SYSTEM

Of all the early grouping systems, the Roman system is the one that has remained in regular use. It still appears on clock faces, on inscriptions on public buildings, and in some publications to indicate listings or divisions. The system uses seven of the Roman letters of the alphabet, used in isolation or in various combinations to represent numbers.

The Romans incorporated a subtractive system in which a lesser symbol appearing before a greater one altered the value of the latter, thus LX represents 60 while XL represents 40.

Arabic numeral	Roman numeral
1	I
2	II
3	III
4	IV
5	V
6	VI
7	VII
8	VIII
9	IX
10	X
11	XI
12	XII
13	XIII
14	XIV
15	XV
20	XX
25	XXV
30	XXX
40	XL
50	L
60	LX
70	LXX
80	LXXX
90	XC
100	C
200	CC
500	D
1000	M

Thus, 1991 in Roman numerals would be MCMXCI.

THE CHINESE NUMBER SYSTEM

The Chinese number system is an example of multi-plicative grouping systems. In multiplicative systems, specific digits (such as the conventional 1, 2, 3, 4, 5, 6, 7, 8, 9) are combined with basic symbols to avoid the repetition involved in a simple grouping system such as the Roman number system. In the Chinese system the number 4624 would be represented by the character for four followed by the character for one thousand, the character for six followed by one hundred, two followed by 10 and, finally, the character for four. The system – in both traditional and modern Chinese script – employs twelve characters representing 1, 2, 3, 4, 5, 6, 7, 8, 9, 10, 100 and 1000.

The traditional Chinese abacus reflects this number system by using a mixture of base 5 and base 10.

The abacus has been described as a manual calculating machine. It has been used for thousands of years and may still be seen, for example, on shop counters in Russia. It consists of a frame or board containing wires upon which counters or balls are slid. Each wire represents a power of ten. The wires are sometimes divided in half by a vertical barrier to enable decimal numbers to be expressed. The Chinese abacus usually has 11 wires with two beads representing 5s on each wire above a bar, and five beads representing 1s on each wire below the bar.

POSITIONAL NUMBER SYSTEMS

Our modern system is an example of positional number systems in which the place value is predetermined. This removes the need for symbols other than the basic digits, thus – in the conventional system using base 10 – it is understood that the second place from the right represents tens, the third place from the right represents hundreds, the fourth place from the right represents thousands, and so on. The conventional system uses base 10, but it is possible to choose any number as base, e.g. the binary system (see above).

There are many other ways in which number systems can vary. Sometimes one can see vestiges of other systems in the numerical terms of a language. In French, for example, one counts up to 100 in a mixture of base 10 and base 20 – thus *quatre-vingt-dix* ('four times twenty plus ten') equals 90. Even English retains vestiges of base 12 with the words 'eleven' and 'twelve'.

PRIME NUMBERS

A prime number is a natural number that has no *proper factors* – that is, which cannot be divided by any natural numbers other than itself and 1. We can find the primes by taking a sequence of numbers such as

$$1, 2, 3, 4, 5, 6, 7, 8, 9, 10, 11, 12, 13, 14, 15, 16 \ldots$$

and first deleting all the numbers divisible by 2 (excluding 2 itself, which is only divisible by itself and 1), then all those divisible by 3, then (since anything divisible by 4 has already been deleted) all those divisible by 5, and so on.

All non-prime natural numbers must by definition be divisible by other numbers apart from themselves and 1; these other numbers can in turn be repeatedly divided until one is left with a series of prime factors. Hence, all non-prime numbers can be expressed as the product of a series of primes – in fact, for each number, the expression is unique.

Prime numbers from 1 to 1000

2	3	5	7	11	13	17
19	23	29	31	37	41	43
47	53	59	61	67	71	73
79	83	89	97	101	103	107
109	113	127	131	137	139	149
151	157	163	167	173	179	181
191	193	197	199	211	223	227
229	233	239	241	251	257	263
269	271	277	281	283	293	307
311	313	317	331	337	347	349
353	359	367	373	379	383	389
397	401	409	419	421	431	433
439	443	449	457	461	463	467
479	487	491	499	503	509	521
523	541	547	557	563	569	571
577	587	593	599	601	607	613
617	619	631	641	643	647	653
659	661	673	677	683	691	701
709	719	727	733	739	743	751
757	761	769	773	787	797	809
811	821	823	827	829	839	853
857	859	863	877	881	883	887
907	911	919	929	937	941	947
953	967	971	977	983	991	997

The prime numbers have been studied since the days of the ancient Greeks, who knew, for example, that there is no largest prime. Their proof is quite easy to understand: suppose there is a largest prime, so that all the prime numbers can be listed in order of size. Now consider the number we obtain if we multiply all these primes together, and add 1; call this number N. Clearly N cannot be divided by any of the list of primes without leaving a remainder of 1. But since these are (we are assuming) all the primes, any other number is non-prime and so has prime factors (see above). Therefore it cannot divide N unless its prime factors divide N – but no primes can divide N. Thus N must itself be prime. But it is a bigger prime than what we supposed was the biggest prime, so that supposition has led us to a contradiction and must be false. The largest known prime number is $2^{756839} - 1$, which is a number of 227 832 digits. It was discovered on a CRAY-2 supercomputer in February 1992.

On the other hand it is not known whether or not there are infinitely many *twin primes*. These are pairs of successive odd numbers that are both prime, like 5 and 7, 11 and 13, or 29 and 31.

Another famous conjecture about prime numbers is that of Christian Goldbach (1690–1764), who postulated that every even number is the sum of two prime numbers. It is not known whether this is true or false.

Prime numbers have recently become of great interest to cryptographers: certain codes are based on the result of multiplying two very large primes together, and because even the fastest possible computer would take years to factorize this product, the resulting code is virtually unbreakable.

PERFECT NUMBERS

FACTORS

A factor is a number that divides exactly into another number. Six divides exactly into 48 eight times – thus both six and eight are factors of 48. Similarly two divides into 6 three times – thus two and three are factors of 6 – and two divides into 8 four times – thus two and four are factors of 8.

PERFECT NUMBERS ·

Perfect numbers are numbers that are equal to the sum of all their factors, excluding the number itself. The first perfect number is 6 whose factors (excluding 6 itself) are one, two and three. As $1 + 2 + 3 = 6$, 6 is a perfect number.

The next perfect number is 28. The factors of 28 are one, two, four, seven and fourteen, which when added together make 28. Pythagoras knew of these first two perfect numbers in the 6th century BC. In the 3rd century BC Nichomachus of Alexandria discovered the next two perfect numbers – 496 and 8128. The fifth perfect number – 33 550 336 – was not discovered until over 1000 years later. Until the 1950s only seven perfect numbers had been discovered. Today, even with the help of computers, only thirty perfect numbers are known.

ARITHMETIC AND ALGEBRA

NUMBER BASES

Our familiar denary (base 10) system of calculating undoubtedly arose because we have 5 'digits' on each hand. Had we been created with 4 instead, we should have been just as happily working in the *octal scale* (base 8). A denary number may be easily converted to any other base simply by repeated division by the new base, the remainders being recorded at each step, thus:

$$8)543_{10}$$
$$8)67 \text{ r } 7$$
$$8)8 \text{ r } 3$$
$$1 \text{ r } 0$$

Reading from the bottom up, 543_{10} is equivalent to 1037_8 (read 'one nought three seven base eight').

MAGIC SQUARES

Magic squares are sets of figures arranged in a square in which the figures in each vertical, horizontal and diagonal line all add up to the same number. Magic squares have been known in India for over 2000 years and became popular in Europe from the 15th century.

2	9	4
7	5	3
6	1	8

Vertical lines:
$2 + 7 + 6 = 15$
$9 + 5 + 1 = 15$
$4 + 3 + 8 = 15$

Diagonal lines:
$2 + 5 + 8 = 15$
$6 + 5 + 4 = 15$

Horizontal lines:
$2 + 9 + 4 = 15$
$7 + 5 + 3 = 15$
$6 + 1 + 8 = 15$

Superstitious people used to belief that a magic square carved by the door would keep the plague from entering a building. They may also be found engraved on old charms and ornaments.

In a magic square with four digits along each side, the numbers in the smaller squares at each corner of the greater square also add up to the same number.

13	8	12	1
2	11	7	14
3	10	6	15
16	5	9	4

Vertical lines:
$13 + 2 + 3 + 16 = 34$
$8 + 11 + 10 + 5 = 34$
$12 + 7 + 6 + 15 = 34$
$1 + 14 + 15 + 4 = 34$

Horizontal lines:
$13 + 8 + 12 + 1 = 34$
$2 + 11 + 7 + 14 = 34$
$3 + 10 + 6 + 15 = 34$
$16 + 5 + 9 + 4 = 34$

Diagonal lines:
$13 + 11 + 6 + 4 = 34$
$16 + 10 + 7 + 1 = 34$

Corner squares:
$13 + 8 + 11 + 2 = 34$
$12 + 1 + 14 + 7 = 34$
$15 + 4 + 6 + 9 = 34$
$5 + 16 + 3 + 10 = 34$

To convert a number in any other base into base 10, however, each digit must be given its appropriate place-value in the given base.

Thus, 1037_8

$$= (1 \times 8^3) + (0 \times 8^2) + (3 \times 8^1) + (7 \times 8^0)$$
$$= 512 + 0 + 24 + 7$$
$$= 534_{10}$$

Base 2 or the *binary scale* is the most important non-denary base since it uses only the digits 0 and 1 (see pp. 241–42), and these can easily be related to the 'off' and 'on' of an electrical impulse and form the basis for the operation of electronic calculators and computers.

As above, a number may be converted to base 2 by repeated division. Thus, to convert 217_{10}:

2)217
2)108 r 1
 2)54 r 0
 2)27 r 0
 2)13 r 1
 2)6 r 1
 2)3 r 0
  1 r 1
   i.e. $217_{10} = 11011001_2$

The reverse process would be 11011001_2
$$= (1 \times 2^7) + (1 \times 2^6) + (0 \times 2^5) + (1 \times 2^4) + (1 \times 2^3) + (0 \times 2^2) + (0 \times 2^1) + (1 \times 2^0)$$
$$= 128 + 64 + 0 + 16 + 8 + 0 + 0 + 1$$
$$= 217_{10}$$

The denary-binary conversion table on p. 242 reveals some interesting points about binary numbers. Note the repetitive patterns in the columns of the successive numbers. Since odd numbers always end in 1 and even numbers end in 0, a number is doubled simply by adding a 0 (in the same way that a denary number is multiplied by 10 by adding a nought), and divided by 2, where possible, by removing a terminal 0. Denary numbers that are powers of 2 have a binary equivalent consisting of a 1 followed by the same number of zeros as the appropriate power of 2.

The other system that is most relevant to the age of modern technology is the *hexadecimal* (base 16) system. This uses extra symbols – commonly A, B, C, D, E, F to represent 10, 11, 12, 13, 14, 15, so that: $1A5D_{16}$ represents $(1 \times 16^3) + (10 \times 16^2) + (5 \times 16^1) + (13 \times 16^0) = 6749$

PERCENTAGES

A percentage is the proportion or rate per hundred parts of a number or item.

$x\%$ of a number N
 $= (x \text{ divided } 100) \times N$

To find what percentage a quantity A is of a quantity B

 $\% = (A \text{ divided by } B) \times 100$

To find the percentage change – increase or decrease – of a quantity

 $\%$ change $= ($actual change divided by original amount$) \times 100$

The same principle applies to profits and losses.

To find 100% given that $x\% = N$
 $100\% = (N \text{ divided by } x) \times 100$

Percentages may not be added or subtracted unless they are percentages of the same quantity. Thus successive depreciations of 10% and 15% are not equivalent to a single depreciation of 25%.

QUICK MULTIPLICATION

The pocket calculator has made arithmetic easy. But there are times when it is handy to know short cuts in multiplication. There are several well-known short cuts that can be used in multiplying numbers by 5, 25, 50, 125, 250, and 11.

Multiplying by 5
Add one nought to the number and divide the total by two.
Example: 897 x 5 = 8970 ÷ 2 = 4485.

Multiplying by 25
Add two noughts to the number and divide the total by four.
Example: 7738 x 25 = 773 800 ÷ 4 = 193 450.

Multiplying by 50
Add two noughts to the number and divide the total by two.
Example: 6969 x 50 = 696 900 ÷ 2 = 348 450.

Multiplying by 125
Add three noughts to the number and divide the total by eight.
Example: 77 x 125 = 77 000 ÷ 8 = 9625.

Multiplying by 250
Add three noughts to the number and divide the total by four.
Example: 39 x 250 = 39 000 ÷ 4 = 9750.

Multiplying a two-figure number by 11
Separate the digits of the number to be multiplied. Add them together and place the result in the space between the digits.
Example: 72 x 11
 Separate 7 and 2   7 2
 Add 7 and 2   = 9
 Place the total in the space 792
 72 x 11 = 792.
Example: 49 x 11
 Separate 4 and 9   4 9
 Add 4 and 9   = 13
 Place the second digit of the total in the space 439
 Add the 10 to the first digit of the answer 539
 49 x 11 = 539.

NINE

The number nine displays interesting properties in the nine times table. All the digits in every total add up to nine.

1 x 9 = 9	9 + 0 = 9
2 x 9 = 18	1 + 8 = 9
3 x 9 = 27	2 + 7 = 9
4 x 9 = 36	3 + 6 = 9
5 x 9 = 45	4 + 5 = 9
6 x 9 = 54	5 + 4 = 9
7 x 9 = 63	6 + 3 = 9
8 x 9 = 72	7 + 2 = 9
9 x 9 = 81	8 + 1 = 9
238 x 9 = 2142	2 + 1 + 4 + 2 = 9
44349 x 9 = 399141	3 + 9 + 9 + 1 + 4 + 1 = 27
	2 + 7 = 9

RUSSIAN MULTIPLICATION

One of the most puzzling methods of doing long multiplication is said to have been invented centuries ago by Russian peasants. The method involves division and multiplication by two.

Example: 27 x 39.

Method:

Put one of the numbers to be multiplied in one column and the other number in a second column.	27	39
Divide the first column by 2 and ignore any remainders. Multiply the second column by 2.	13	78
Continue dividing the figures in the first column – and doubling the figures in the second column – until 1 is reached in the first column.	6 3 1	156 312 624
List all numbers in the *second* column that are on the same line as an *odd* number in the first column.		39 78 312 624
Add together these numbers.		39 78 312 +624 =1053
		27 x 39 = 1053

NUMBER PATTERNS

Rectangular numbers Rectangular numbers are composite numbers, that is any number that is not prime (see p. 243). Any composite number can be represented in the form of a rectangle of dots. Thus 6 =

$$2 \times 3 = 6$$

Square numbers

Square numbers are numbers with a pair of equal factors, and may therefore be represented as a square. Thus 4 =

$$2 \times 2 = 2^2$$
$$= 4$$

and 9 =

$$3 \times 3 = 3^2$$
$$= 9$$

1, 4, 9, 16, 25, 36, 49, 64, 81, 100, 121, 144, 169 are the squares of the first 13 numbers. They – and all square numbers – are positive.

Triangular numbers

Triangular numbers are numbers that can be formed into a series of equilateral triangles. Triangular numbers – such as 3, 6, 10 and 15 – can be represented by a triangular pattern of dots. Thus 6 =

The differences between successive triangular numbers are the *natural* numbers.

1		3		6		10		15		21		28	
	2		3		4		5		6		7		8

FIBONACCI NUMBERS

Fibonacci numbers were named in the 19th century after Leonardo Fibonacci of Pisa (c. 1175–c. 1250), who introduced the Arabic figures 1 to 9 plus 0 to Europe in his *Liber abaci* in 1202. He earned the title of *Stupor Mundi* (wonder of the world) from the Holy Roman Emperor. In 1225 he published a recursive sequence of his Arabic numbers 1, 1, 2, 3, 5, 8, 13, 21, 34, 55, etc., in which each number is the sum of the two preceding numbers. In the 19th century this sequence was found to occur in nature – in the arrangement of leaf buds on a stem, animal horns, the genealogy of the male bee, and spirals in sunflower heads and pine cones.

PASCAL'S TRIANGLE

Pascal's triangle is one of the most famous and most important of all number patterns.

Although it was known long before Pascal – who died in 1626 – he was the first to make ingenious and wide use of its properties. The numbers in Pascal's triangle appear in the binomial theorem, in problems about the selection of combinations of objects, and therefore in the theory of probability and statistics.

The numbers in each row are formed by adding the numbers above and to each side of it. The numbers in the rows so formed are then the coefficients of the terms in the binomial theorem. Thus the numbers in the 4th row (1 3 3 1) are the coefficients in the expansion of $(a + x)^3$, while those in the 6th row would be the expansion of $(a + x)^5$, i.e. 1 5 10 10 5 1.

```
                1
              1   1
            1   2   1
          1   3   3   1
        1   4   6   4   1
      1   5  10  10   5   1
```

Totals

First line	$1 = 2^0$
Second line	$2 = 2^1$
Third line	$4 = 2^2$
Fourth line	$8 = 2^3$
Fifth line	$16 = 2^4$
Sixth line	$32 = 2^5$

MATRICES

A matrix is an array of numbers, of rectangular shape, which presents information in a concise form. Matrices serve many purposes, and according to the circumstances they may be multiplied or added or subtracted.

Two matrices may be multiplied if there are the same number of *rows* in the second matrix as there are *columns* in the first, but they may only be added or subtracted if they have the same number of rows and columns. A 2×3 matrix is one with 2 rows and 3 columns. Thus a 2×3 matrix may be multiplied by a 3×4 or a 3×2 or a $3 \times n$ matrix where n is any number.

If $A = \begin{pmatrix} a & b \\ c & d \end{pmatrix}$ and $B = \begin{pmatrix} p & q \\ r & s \end{pmatrix}$

Then, $AB = \begin{pmatrix} a & b \\ c & d \end{pmatrix}\begin{pmatrix} p & q \\ r & s \end{pmatrix}$

$$= \begin{pmatrix} ap + br & aq + bs \\ cp + dr & cq + ds \end{pmatrix}$$

$$A + B = \begin{pmatrix} a & b \\ c & d \end{pmatrix} + \begin{pmatrix} p & q \\ r & s \end{pmatrix}$$

$$= \begin{pmatrix} a + p & b + q \\ c + r & d + s \end{pmatrix}$$

Transformation matrices

The transformation matrices change the position or shape of a geometrical figure, and sometimes both. The following are the principal transformation matrices:

(1) Reflection in the x-axis $\begin{pmatrix} 1 & 0 \\ 0 & -1 \end{pmatrix}$

(2) Reflection in the y-axis $\begin{pmatrix} -1 & 0 \\ 0 & 1 \end{pmatrix}$

(3) Reflection in the line $y = x$ $\begin{pmatrix} 0 & 1 \\ 1 & 0 \end{pmatrix}$

(4) Reflection in the line $y = -x$ $\begin{pmatrix} 0 & -1 \\ -1 & 0 \end{pmatrix}$

(5) Rotation through 90° about the origin in a $+ve$ (anticlockwise) direction $\begin{pmatrix} 0 & -1 \\ 1 & 0 \end{pmatrix}$

(6) Rotation through 180° ($+ve$ or $-ve$) $\begin{pmatrix} -1 & 0 \\ 0 & -1 \end{pmatrix}$

(7) $+ve$ rotation about the origin through an angle θ $\begin{pmatrix} \cos & -\sin θ \\ \sin θ & \cos θ \end{pmatrix}$

(8) The *identity matrix* $\begin{pmatrix} 1 & 0 \\ 0 & 1 \end{pmatrix}$ leaves the elements of the multiplied matrix unchanged.

The following matrices change the shape of the figure.

(9) An enlargement, factor E $\begin{pmatrix} E & 0 \\ 0 & E \end{pmatrix}$

(e.g. if $E = 3$ the figure will have its linear dimensions trebled)

(10) A stretch parallel to the x-axis, factor S $\begin{pmatrix} S & 0 \\ 0 & 1 \end{pmatrix}$

(11) A stretch parallel to the y-axis, factor S $\begin{pmatrix} 1 & 0 \\ 0 & S \end{pmatrix}$

(12) A shear parallel to the x-axis $\begin{pmatrix} 1 & S \\ 0 & 1 \end{pmatrix}$

(13) A shear parallel to the y-axis $\begin{pmatrix} 1 & 0 \\ S & 1 \end{pmatrix}$

The inverse of matrix A above (denoted by A^{-1}) is

$$\frac{1}{(ad - bc)} \begin{pmatrix} d & -b \\ -c & a \end{pmatrix}$$

The expression $(ad - bc)$ is called the determinant of the matrix.

The value of the determinant of a matrix represents the ratio by which the area of the original figure has been changed. If the determinant is zero, all the points will be moved to lie on a line, and the matrix is said to be 'singular'.

If a matrix is multiplied by its inverse the result is the identity matrix.

A transformation which does not change either the shape or the size of a figure is called an isometric transformation.

SETS

Sets can be considered simply as collections of objects. However, in the early 20th century, when attempts were made to formalize the properties of sets, contradictions were discovered that have affected mathematical thinking ever since.

A set can be specified either by stipulating some property for an object as a condition of *membership* of the set, or by listing the *members* of the set in any order.

Sets are usually indicated by the use of curly brackets { and }, known as *braces*. Consider, as an example, the Smith family that has a bicycle, a motor cycle, a van, a family car and a sports car. We could represent the vehicles ridden or driven by Mrs Smith as {bicycle, van, family car}. Sets are often shown by drawing a circle around representations of their members.

Union and intersection

We can use circles to represent the relationship between two or more sets. If Mr Smith drives the sports car and the motor cycle but also shares the use of the van with Mrs Smith, the set of vehicles used by him is {motor cycle, van, sports car}. If R is the set of vehicles used by Mr Smith and S is the set of vehicles used by Mrs Smith, R and S can be shown as two intersecting circles.

The set of all the vehicles used by the Smiths is {bicycle, motor cycle, van, family car, sports car}. This is called the *union* of the two sets and is written $R \cup S$ and spoken as 'R union S'.

The two sets have one member in common, the van. The set of members that belong to both sets are known as their *intersection*. In the example given here it is the set whose only member is the van. This is written $R \cap S = \{van\}$. This is a set even though it has only one member, the van. It is written 'van $\in$ {van}', where the symbol $\in$ means 'is a member of'.

Subsets

Formally, a set is a *subset* of another set if all the

members of the first set are members of the other set, that is, one set is contained within the other. Thus, among the Smiths' vehicles {van} is a subset of {bicycle, motor cycle, van, family car, sports car}.

If the larger set is x and the smaller set – the subset – is y, the equation $y \subset x$ means that y is a subset of x. The equation $x \supset y$ means that set x contains subset y.

Universal sets
A *universal set* groups all the items under consideration. Here that would be all the vehicles used by the Smith family.

Complements
In the universal set – the vehicles used by the Smiths – the vehicles not driven by Mrs Smith form what is known as the *relative complement* of the set of the vehicles that she uses. Thus where S is the set of vehicles used by Mrs Smith, the complement set is written $C(S)$ or S'.

Null or empty sets
An *empty* or *null* set is one containing no members. For example, the set of vehicles driven by the Smiths' young child would be a null set. It would be written

{child's vehicles} $\cap$ {Mr Smith's vehicles} $= \varnothing$

This means that set of vehicles driven by both Mr Smith and the child is an empty set.

Disjoint set
Disjoint sets have no members *in common*. Suppose the Smith's young child has a bicycle – obviously a small one that only she can ride. The set of vehicles used by the child – C – is {child's bicycle}, a set of vehicles that does not intersect with the set of vehicles used by her mother. Thus, C and S have no members in common and their intersection is an empty set. This can be expressed by the equation

$C \cap S = \varnothing$

PARADOXES
Although the concept of sets outlined above is applicable for most purposes, various paradoxes came to light when *axioms* for the theory of sets were sought. Frege and Russell independently attempted to prove that all mathematics could be reduced to pure logic. In 1908 Russell discovered his axioms gave rise to important contradictions.

Russell's paradox
Some sets are members of themselves, while other sets are not members of themselves. In the set Q – a set of all sets that are not members of themselves – is Q a member of itself or not? An element of a set must have the property that defines the set – in this case Q is a member of the set of sets that are not members of themselves. Q, therefore, cannot be a member of itself – but that only means that it can't be a member of Q. But the fact that Q is not a member of itself is the property that defines Q, so Q must be a member of Q. It is therefore a member of itself. Either way, there is a contradiction. In the case of any set and any entity, either the thing is in the set or it is not.

NETWORKS
A series of nodes joined by arcs is called a network. A node is odd or even, according to the number of arcs which are drawn from it. The network may represent a road or railway system, an electricity grid and so on. Such a system will be traversable (i.e. can be drawn without covering any arc twice or taking the

pencil off the paper) if there are not more than 2 odd nodes. In such a case the route must begin and end at an odd node. Two simplified networks are shown below – one is traversable and one is not. The latter was used by Euler to solve the famous Konigsberg Bridge problem.

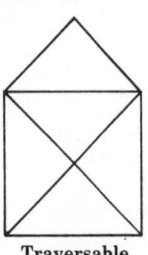

Traversable

HILBERT'S INFINITE HOTEL

The German mathematician David Hilbert dramatized the paradoxical property of infinite sets by an exercise of the imagination.

Imagine a hotel with an infinite number of rooms; then it can be full and still able to accommodate more guests. The manager simply moves the guest in room 1 to room 2, the guest in room 2 into room 3, and so on. Each guest is then in a room with a number higher than before and room 1 remains vacant for a late arrival.

Unfortunately, not one latecomer, but an infinite busload of them arrive. Instead of the moves as before, the manager puts the guest in room 1 into room 2, the guest from room 2 into room 4, the guest from room 3 into room 6, and so on. The infinite number of rooms with odd numbers are now vacant for the infinite number of latecomers.

SOME MILESTONES IN CALCULUS AND MECHANICS

1670s–80s	Leibniz and Newton independently developed calculus.
1687	Newton published his *Principia*.
1728	Bernouilli previewed Fournier series.
1748	Euler published his *Introduction to Infinitesimal Analysis*.
1788	Lagrange published his *Mécanique Analytique*.
early 19th century	Laplace published *Celestial Mechanics*.
1822	Fournier series developed.
1828	Gauss extended differential geometry.
1843	Hamilton's advances in mechanics.
late 19th century	Maxwell's equations.
1902	Lebesque integration.

CALCULUS AND MECHANICS

CALCULUS
Calculus is the branch of mathematics that studies continuous change in terms of the mathematical properties of the functions that represent it, and these results can also be interpreted in geometric

terms relating to the graph of the function.

Calculus was developed independently by Newton and Leibniz in the late 17th century. Because their presentation involved paradoxical references to *infinitesimals* (infinitely small quantities), many scientists rejected their 'infidel mathematics', but at the same time there was considerable dispute about who should have the credit for its discovery.

Functions

Suppose we go out for a cycle run and keep up a speed of 15 km/h. Then our distance from home is determined by how long we have been travelling. For example, after half an hour we will have travelled 7.5 km; after an hour 15 km; after 2 hours 30 km, and so on. We can express this relationship by saying that the distance we travelled is a *function* of the time we have been travelling. Here the two quantities, time and distance, might be represented by the variables t and d, and the mathematical relationship between them means that for any number of units of time, t, we can work out the number of units of distance travelled, d, by multiplying t by 15.

In general the notation for a function is $y = f(x)$, which indicates that the value of y depends upon the value of x; in that case, y is called the *dependent variable*, and x is called the *independent variable*. The variables are thought of as running through a range of values – for example, if our journey takes a total of 3 hours, the range of t is the *interval* (0,3), and the range of d is the interval (0,45).

Coordinates

The real numbers can be represented geometrically by a line (an *axis*) marked off from the origin (0) using some numerical scale. Any point in a *plane*, a two-dimensional area, can similarly be represented by the pair of numbers that correspond to its respective distances from two such axes, as shown here; these numbers are the *coordinates* of the point P. Thus the coordinates of the point P in the accompanying diagram are (1,2):

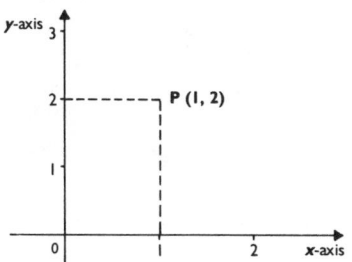

Here the independent and the dependent variables of a function are represented by the two lines at right angles (the x-axis and the y-axis) that cross at the origin. The curve representing the function is then the line that passes through the points whose coordinates satisfy the function. For example, the curve of the function $y = x^2$ is the set of pairs, (x, y), of real numbers for which y is the square of x; thus, for example, (2,4), (−1,1), (−2,4), (√2,2), etc., are all in the graph of the function. The curve corresponding to this function is shown here:

The system of coordinates is named Cartesian coordinates after the French philosopher and mathematician René Descartes.

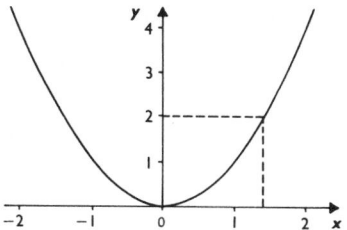

Graphs

Because a function associates elements of one set with those of another, it defines the set of all pairs of elements, (x,y), in which x is a value of the independent variable and y is the value of the function for the argument x. Another way of expressing this is that any point that *satisfies* the function $y = f(x)$ can be represented by the point $(x,f(x))$. Since a function must be a many-one relation, every such pair has a different first element, so the pairs can be listed in a unique order. The function can be thought of as moving through the values of the dependent variable as the value of the independent variable increases. This is what is represented by a graph in the Cartesian coordinate system: if we now draw a line joining the points $(x,f(x))$ as x increases, this line passes through all and only the points whose coordinates satisfy the function. Such a line is usually called a *graph*, although mathematicians prefer to use that term for the set of values of the variables, and call the diagram a *curve*. Since this way of representing change and dependency is equivalent to the function itself, curves provide us with a way of visualizing processes of change.

DIFFERENTIATION

The process of finding the derivative of a function is called *differentiation*, and this branch of mathematics is known as *differential calculus*. This process can also be interpreted geometrically. However, it is not always necessary to work out a derivative by means of a graph. Instead, certain general principles apply. The derivative of a function can itself be differentiated; for example, acceleration is the rate of change of velocity, and the derivative of the velocity function with respect to time can be worked out. This is the *second derivative* of the displacement function.

If y is any function of x, and Δy, Δx are corresponding increments of y and x, then the differential coefficient of y with respect to x

$\left(\text{written } \dfrac{dy}{dx}\right)$ is defined as $\underset{\Delta x \to 0}{\text{Lt}} \dfrac{[f(x + \Delta x) - f(x)]}{\Delta x}$

$\dfrac{dy}{dx}$ gives the gradient of a curve, i.e. it measures the rate of change of one variable with respect to another.

Thus, since velocity is the rate of change of displacement with respect to time, it may be expressed in calculus terms as $\dfrac{ds}{dt}$ where s is the displacement of a body from a fixed point and the equation of motion of the body is of the form $s = f(t)$.

Similarly, since acceleration is the rate of change of *velocity* with time, it may be expressed as $\frac{dv}{dt}$ or as $\frac{d^2s}{dt^2}$, i.e. as the second differential of s with respect to t. Acceleration may also be expressed as $v\frac{dv}{ds}$ i.e. as the velocity multiplied by the rate of change of velocity with distance. In general, if: $y = ax^n$

then $\frac{dy}{dx} = nax^{n-1}$

Since $\frac{dy}{dx}$ gives the gradient of a curve it may be used to find the maximum and minimum values of a function. Thus if $y = f(x)$, then when $\frac{dy}{dx} = 0$, the tangents to the curve will be parallel to the x axis, and will indicate the positions of the critical values (the maximum or minimum) but without distinguishing them. However,

if $\frac{d^2y}{dx^2}$ is +ve   the critical value of x gives a *minimum* value of the function, while

if $\frac{d^2y}{dx^2}$ is −ve   the critical value gives a *maximum* value of the function, and

if $\frac{d^2y}{dx^2} = 0$,   and changes sign as x increases through the point, the curve is passing through a point of inflection

Differential coefficient of a product
If $y = uv$ where u and v are functions of x, then

$$\frac{dy}{dx} = u\frac{dv}{dx} + v\frac{du}{dx}$$

Differential coefficient of a quotient
If $y = \frac{u}{v}$ where u and v are functions of x, then

$$\frac{dy}{dx} = \frac{v\frac{du}{dx} - u\frac{dv}{dx}}{v^2}$$

NEWTON'S LAWS OF MOTION
Newton's Laws of Motions were first published in his *Principia* in 1687. See p. 194.

The basic equations of motion with constant acceleration

$s = \frac{1}{2}t(u + v)$

$v = u + at$

$v^2 = u^2 + 2as$

$s = ut + \frac{1}{2}at^2$

where a = acceleration
s = displacement
t = time
u = initial velocity
v = final velocity

Constant velocity:
distance = velocity x time

RELATIVE VELOCITY

To find the velocity of a body A relative to a body B, combine with the velocity of A a velocity equal and opposite to that of B. The sides of the triangle represent the velocities in magnitude and direction.

Thus to a person on a ship B, the ship A would *appear* to be moving in the direction (and at the speed) represented by the double-arrowed line.

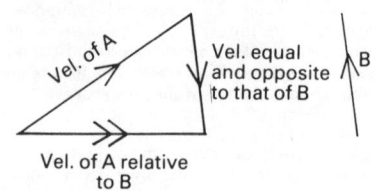

Triangle of velocities
The triangle ABC shows how the track (i.e. the actual direction) and velocity relative to the ground (the ground speed) of an aircraft or boat may be found from the course set and the wind or current.

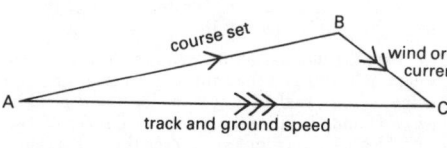

In vector terms, $\overrightarrow{AB} + \overrightarrow{BC} = \overrightarrow{AC}$

PROJECTILES

For simple cases, in which air resistance is neglected and the vertical velocity is subject only to the force of gravity, the following results may be derived from the fundamental equations of motion:

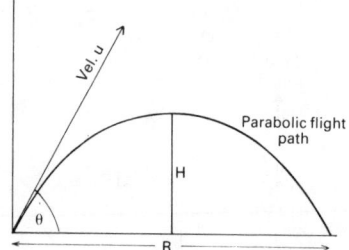

Parabolic flight path

The time of flight
$$T = \frac{2u \sin \theta}{g}$$

The time to the greatest height
$$= \frac{T}{2}$$

$$= \frac{u \sin \theta}{g}$$

The greatest height attained
$$H = \frac{u^2 \sin^2 \theta}{2g}$$

The range on a horizontal plane
$$R = \frac{u^2 \sin 2\theta}{g}$$

For a given velocity of projection u there are, in general, two possible angles of projection to obtain a given horizontal range. These directions will make equal angles with the vertical and horizontal respectively. For maximum range the angle makes 45° with the horizontal.

Note that:
(1) the time taken for a body moving freely under gravity is the same to rise as it is to descend.
(2) the velocity at any point on its upward path is equal to that at the same point on its downward path, and that consequently . . .
(3) its velocity on striking the ground at the same horizontal level is equal to that with which it was projected.

The impact of elastic bodies
If the bodies are smooth (e.g. two billiard balls) and only the forces between the bodies are considered, then the following equations will determine the velocities and directions of the bodies after the impact.

Momentum:
Momentum (i.e. the product of the individual masses and velocities) along the line of centres after impact is equal to momentum *in the same direction* before impact.

The velocity of separation:
The velocity of separation is equal to the velocity of approach (also measured along the line of centres) multiplied by the coefficient of elasticity between the two bodies. If the impact is oblique (and the bodies are smooth) the velocities at right angles to the line of centres are unchanged.

If u_1 and u_2, m_1 and m_2 are the initial velocities and masses of the two spheres, and α and β are the angles these velocities make with the line of centres, and v_1 and v_2 are the components of velocities *along the line of centres* after impact, then the above statements are represented by the following equations:

Momentum:
$$m_1 v_1 + m_2 v_2 = m_1 u_1 \cos \alpha + m_2 u_2 \cos \beta$$

The velocity of separation:
$$v_2 \pm v_1 = e (u_1 \cos \alpha - u_2 \cos \beta)$$

where e is the coefficient of elasticity between the two bodies.

Note that in the second equation v_1 and v_2 will be added or subtracted to get the 'velocity of separation' according to whether the bodies are considered to be going in the opposite or same direction respectively. The conditions of the problem will determine this for the 'velocity of approach'. In the example m_1 is 'catching up' on m_2 and therefore we take the difference in their velocities to obtain the velocity of approach.

CIRCULAR MOTION
If a body is moving in a circle with uniform speed, then its linear velocity v is given by the equation:
$$v = r\omega$$
where r is the radius of the circle, and ω is the angular velocity. The body will nevertheless have an acceleration (since a force is acting on it to make it move in a circle) but this will be directed *towards* the centre.

The acceleration will be: $r\omega^2$

The force will be: $mr\omega^2$
where m is the mass of the body.

If a body is whirled round on the end of a string there

is no tendency for it to move outwards along the *radius* of the circle. If the string breaks, it will instead move straight on along the *tangent* to the circle.

In the case of a train going round a curve the necessary force is provided by the flanges on the wheels, while in the case of a car going round a track it is provided by the friction between the wheels and the ground. By banking the rails or road the weight of the train or car may be made to provide the necessary force.

The required angle to prevent any tendency to skid is given by the equation:

$\tan \theta = v^2$ divided by gr
where θ is the angle made with the horizontal by the banking.

WORK AND ENERGY
The work done by a force F acting on a body as it covers a displacement s is Fs.

The kinetic energy (KE) of a particle of mass m moving with velocity v is $\frac{1}{2}mv^2$.

The potential energy (PE) gained by a mass m as it is raised through a height h is mgh.

When no forces other than weight do any work on a body, then the total energy (KE + PE) remains constant.

SIMPLE HARMONIC MOTION
If a particle moves so that its acceleration is directed towards a fixed point in its path, and is proportional to its distance from that point, it is said to move with simple harmonic motion.

The fundamental equation is $\dfrac{d^2x}{dt^2} = -\omega^2 x$. By integrating the corresponding equation $v\dfrac{dv}{dx} + \omega^2 x = 0$ the velocity at any displacement x is given by

$v = \sqrt{a^2 - x^2}$ where a is the maximum value of x.
By solving the first equation we find that
$x = a \cos \omega t$ (if $t = 0$ when $x = a$) or
$x = a \sin \omega t$ (if $t = 0$ when $x = 0$)

The period of motion is given by $T = \dfrac{2\pi}{\omega}$

STATICS
Statics is the study of forces acting on bodies at rest. It can be compared with *dynamics*, which is the study of bodies in motion.

Some fundamental principles of statics include:
(1) The *moment of a force* about a point is the product of the force and the perpendicular distance of the line of action of the force from the point.
(2) For a body to be at rest under a system of forces in one plane,
  (a) the algebraic sum of the resolved parts of the forces in any two directions which are not parallel must be zero, and
  (b) the algebraic sum of the moments of the forces about any point must be zero (i.e. clockwise moments = anticlockwise moments).

(3) For a system of particles of weights w_1 w_2, w_3 etc. whose distances from a fixed axis are x_1, x_2, x_3 etc.,

the position of the centre of gravity from that axis is given by $\dfrac{\Sigma wx}{\Sigma w}$ where Σwx is the sum of all the weights of the particles. From this, the centres of gravity of irregular shapes, or shapes with portions missing, can be found by the principles that: the Moment of the whole = the sum of the moments of the parts

and the Moment of the remainder = the moment of the whole − the sum of the moments of the parts removed

The positions of the centres of gravity of some important shapes are as follows:

(a) A triangle — at the intersection of the medians (i.e. the lines joining the vertices to the midpoints of the opposite sides) or at one-third of the length of the median from the base.

(b) Square, rectangle, parallelogram, rhombus — at the intersection of the diagonals.

(c) Sector of a circle of angle 2θ radians — at a distance $\tfrac{2}{3}\,\dfrac{r\sin\theta}{\theta}$ from the centre along the line bisecting the sector, where r = the radius.

For a semicircle — $\theta = \dfrac{p}{2}$ and the distance of the centre of gravity from the centre of the circle will $= \dfrac{4r}{3\pi}$

(d) A solid pyramid on any base — at a point one-quarter of the height of the pyramid above the base.

(e) A hollow cone — at a point one-third of the height from the base.

(f) A solid hemisphere — at a point along the axis distant $\dfrac{3r}{8}$ from the centre where r is the radius.

(g) A hollow hemisphere — at a point distant $\dfrac{r}{2}$ along the axis from the centre.

[Note that this is the same as for the centre of gravity of the cylinder which would surround, or contain, the hemisphere.]

(4) If a rigid body is in equilibrium under the action of three forces in a plane, the lines of action of these forces must either all be parallel, or must meet at a common point. The sum of the three forces must be zero, and therefore it must thus always be possible to draw a triangle to represent the forces.

(5) The Laws of Friction.

(a) The direction of the frictional force is opposite to that in which the body tends to move.

(b) The magnitude of the friction is, up to a certain point, exactly equal to the force tending to produce motion.

(c) Only a certain amount of friction can be called into play. This is called 'limiting friction'.

(d) The magnitude of the limiting friction for a given pair of surfaces bears a constant ratio to the normal (i.e. perpendicular) pressure between the surfaces. This ratio is denoted by m and is called the Coefficient of Friction.

(e) The amount of friction is independent of the areas and shape of the surfaces in contact provided the normal pressure remains unaltered.

(f) When motion takes place, the friction still opposes the motion. It is independent of the velocity, and is proportional to the normal pressure, but is less than the limiting friction.

If F is the limiting friction (i.e. the force of friction when motion is about to occur), and R is the normal (perpendicular) force, then

$$F = \mu R \text{ where } \mu \text{ is the coefficient of friction}$$

The resultant of the forces F and R makes an angle (usually denoted by λ) with R, and thus

$$\tan\lambda = \dfrac{F}{R}$$
$$= \mu$$

λ is called the Angle of Friction.

These relationships are illustrated in the following diagrams:

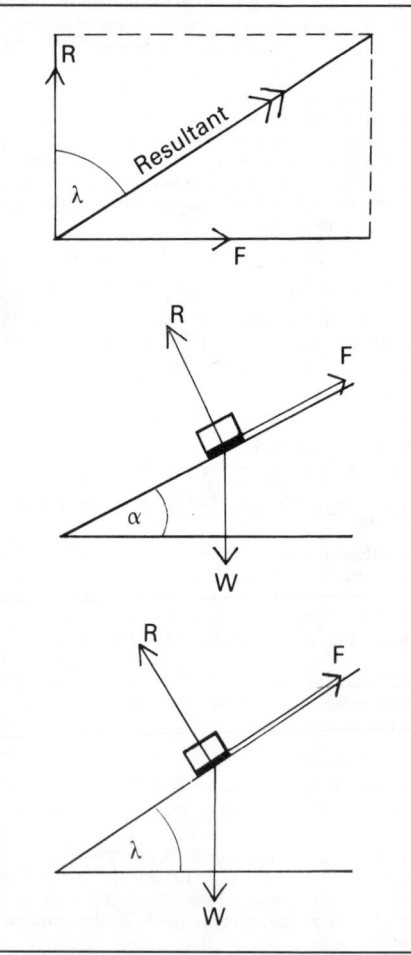

If the angle of the plane (α) is less than the angle of friction, a body on an inclined plane will not slide. If the angle of the plane is equal to λ, the angle of friction, the body will be on the point of sliding – if the angle is greater the body will slide.

COMPUTING

COMPUTERS

Computers are machines that carry out programmed sequences of instructions to manipulate coded data. The more common digital computers – the type described here – use number codes to represent data such as letters of the alphabet, numbers, visible images, sounds and other material. The number system used is the binary system, by which all numbers (and hence number codes) can be represented by sequences of 0s and 1s (binary digits or *bits*), which on a computer can be represented by electric current being turned off and on respectively.

Each particle of data is represented by an 8-digit binary number, a *byte*. The ASCII – American Standard Code for Information Interchange (pronounced 'ass-key') – code is used for letters of the alphabet, digits 0 to 9 and punctuation marks and other signs. Other data can be coded in ways that may be specific to a type of computer or to a program and may not be easily interchangeable. Data size is measured in bytes, kilobytes (K; $1K = 2^{10}$ bytes) and megabytes (Mb; $1Mb = 2^{20}$ bytes).

HARDWARE AND SOFTWARE

The electronic and mechanical components of a computer are called the *hardware*. The hardware of a computer contains the processor, which can carry out actions of arithmetic and comparison on binary digits. The bytes of information are stored in memory, allowing the processor to process them as fast as it can read them and deal with them. Circuits called *ports* deal with the input of new data and the output of processed data (to a screen, printer or disk, for example). All of these processes are carried out under the control of a *program*, which is another set of bytes in code. The program and the data – in other words the procedures required for computer operation – are called the *software* of the system. Computers are classified as:

Microcomputers use a microprocessor, which is formed on one tiny chip of silicon.

Minicomputers are computers (often used for small office networks) that are intermediate in capacity between a microcomputer and a mainframe.

Mainframes are the most powerful general-purpose computers.

Supercomputers are designed specifically for speed.

Minicomputers, large mainframe computers and supercomputers use sets of separate chips.

THE PROCESSOR AND STORAGE

The *processor* must be able to read bytes from the memory in sequence, and the bytes must be available in the correct order. Data is stored inside the computer in memory and externally in *backing stores*. Each unit of memory is a tiny semiconductor switch storing one bit of information. A memory consists of a set of such units, organized into bytes and with each set accessible by using an address number, applied in binary signal form to the chip(s). The two fundamental types of memory are *ROM* and *RAM*.

ROM is Read-Only Memory. Each byte can be read when its address number is supplied (from the microprocessor) but the contents of the memory cannot be changed nor erased.

RAM is Random-Access Memory. RAM can be read or written and is usually volatile – its contents are lost when power is cut off. CMOS (complementary metal-oxide semiconductor) RAM will retain data either with battery back-up or even without any power supply and is used for retaining small amounts of permanent data.

Backing stores are used for long-term retention. Most read-write backing stores use magnetic storage on disk or tape and it is now possible to store 1.44 Mb on a disk whose diameter is about 90 mm (3.5 in). Another form of backing store is the *CD-ROM* type, which stores data in read-only form using an optical disk (like an audio compact disk); read-write versions of this are being developed. Another form is the *WORM* (Write Once Read Many) disk, which can be written by signals of higher-than-normal size and from then on used like the CD-ROM disk.

PROGRAMS

Originally, programmers worked in binary code using sets of switches in place of a keyboard. This *machine-code programming (first-generation language)* is feasible only for very short programs, and has been replaced by *assembly-language programming (second-generation language)*, which uses brief instruction words like ADD. A program called an *assembler* then reads the words and associated numbers and converts them into machine code, but such programming demands that the programmer should have a very detailed knowledge of how the hardware works. The writing of reliable large programs is a major problem. Such programs have to be divided and each programmer writes a section. The problems start when the sections are made to work together. The development of programming has aimed to make cooperation easier and reduce errors. The *operating system* is an important aid. This is a program that attends to all the simple needs of the system, such as controlling the memory, keyboard, disk system, screen and other inputs and outputs. It also provides a set of standard routines that writers of programs can use with confidence. The other main aid is the use of *higher-level programming languages*, including third- or fourth-generation languages.

COMPUTER LANGUAGES

A *third-generation language* uses intelligible commands that allow the program to be read more easily. In addition, good languages are *portable* – the same commands can be used for programming any type of computer. The differences between computers are dealt with by using different versions of the language program. Early third-generation languages (FORTRAN, ALGOL and COBOL) were each developed for specific needs. The popular BASIC language was first developed as a way of learning FORTRAN. More modern third-generation languages include Pascal, C and Prolog. All these languages are procedural, meaning that the programmer must write the sequence of instructions to be used on the data. Object-oriented program languages are adaptations of familiar languages that allow for better organization when work is split among many writers. *Fourth-generation languages* (4GL) can be described as programs that write programs. The programmer writes only descriptions of the types of data and how they are to be manipulated. Most 4GLs are specialized, creating one type of program only. Typical modern 4GLs for small computers include Matrix Layout, DataBoss and SkyMaster.

SPEED AND PERFORMANCE

The 'power' of a computer is measured in terms of its processing speed, memory capacity, and backing store size. Modern microcomputers operate with four-byte units, running the timing clock at around 16 MHz, using 1Mb of memory and a backing store of 32 Mb to 640 Mb. Microcomputers can be connected together into networks to share a common backing store and printer(s). The speed of micros is determined mainly by the speed of moving data to and from the memory and backing stores. This can be improved by using *memory caches* – small pieces of fast-acting memory. Since the same data is often needed several times, it can be reached more quickly from fast memory than from main memory or backing stores. Larger machines can use memory that operates much faster but which requires much more space and also needs cooling. *Supercomputers* are used for fast real-time processing (missile tracking, weather forecasting, analysing fast reactions) and are built in circular or spherical form to minimize the length of connectors between units. The speed of electric current in cables limits such computers, and it seems likely that the use of lasers, fibre optics and light-operated switches will result in even faster machines in the late 1990s.

Recent development has concentrated on desktop and laptop machines. Desktop machines now use faster processes, have larger memory capacity, and use much larger hard disk capacity than before – all at lower prices. Laptop machines are now expected to match the performance of a desktop machine, and use high-resolution LCD screens, some in colour. Laptop machines are still handicapped by the limited performance of existing batteries, particularly rechargeable cells. By 1992, the entry-level PC machine used the 80486 chip, with a specification which was the highest attainable in PC machines only two years earlier. Networked PC machines, or PCs networked to a minicomputer, are now more commonly used than a mainframe.

MILESTONES IN COMPUTING

3000 BC The abacus, using rods and beads for counting, probably developed in the Middle East and was widely used in Mediterranean countries.

1614 The Scot John Napier's logarithms allowed multiplication and division to be carried out by adding and subtracting. A device called 'Napier's bones' led to the invention of the slide rule.

1642 Blaise Pascal invented a mechanical adding machine using 10:1 gearing to represent decimal columns. The computing language Pascal is named after this pioneer of computation.

1666 Gottfried Wilhelm Leibniz proposed the basis of a language that would allow logical statements to be dealt with mathematically. The essence was the use of digits 0 for FALSE and 1 for TRUE. Leibniz went on to develop binary arithmetic.

1673 Leibniz improved Pascal's calculator by adding a method of shifting columns that allowed it to multiply and divide as well as add and subtract.

1804 The French weaver J.M. Jacquard invented a loom in which changes of pattern or material could be programmed by feeding in a set of punched cards.

The Jacquard loom was the first programmable device to be perfected.

1822 Charles Babbage, with support from the British Admiralty, set out to design a *differential engine*, an advanced form of calculator for application to navigation problems. He was helped by Ada, Countess Lovelace (Byron's daughter), who pursued the idea that the analytical engine could be made programmable, and devised some programs. (The programming language ADA was named after her.) Escalating costs prevented Babbage's machine being built, but another version is now being constructed.

1847 The English mathematician George Boole – working on Leibniz's ideas – developed a mathematical system for dealing with logical problems, Boolean algebra – now used for designing control systems and incorporated into computer systems.

1890 Herman Hollerith in the USA combined the ideas of the Jacquard loom and the *differential engine* to construct an analyser, the *tabulator*, which used data in the form of punched cards. The device was commissioned for processing the 1890 census, which was achieved in six weeks rather than the six years it would have taken manually. The Hollerith Tabulator Corporation eventually became International Business Machines (IBM).

1898 The Dane Valdemar Poulsen devised the *telegraphone*, a magnetic recorder using steel wire – the ancestor of all modern magnetic disk devices.

1907 Lee de Forest in the USA devised the *triode thermionic valve* (vacuum tube). This allowed an electric current between two connectors to be controlled by a voltage at a third connector and paved the way for fast computers in the 1950s.

1930 Vannevar Bush, working in the USA at MIT, devised a form of *analogue computer*, a machine in which sizes of quantities are represented by electrical voltage size and actions such as addition and multiplication are represented by alterations of the voltage levels. This machine – *the differential analyser* – used the principles of calculus in electrical form and allowed differential equations such as those governing missiles, flow of liquid in pipes, and flow of air over wings to be solved much more rapidly than by using pencil and paper. The machine was only partly electrical and required mechanical gearing to be changed at frequent intervals.

1936 The mathematician Alan Turing in the UK suggested that many apparently insoluble problems might become soluble if a 'universal computer' could be built which could be completely controlled by program instructions. He also devised the 'Turing test' to determine if a computer could think for itself. This was based on the principle that if a human could communicate with such a device without seeing it and never know that the device was a computer, then the device would have true intelligence.

1941 The German mathematician Konrad Zuse developed a digital computer using binary code to solve problems connected with rocket ballistics. The storage of bits during calculation was by electromagnetic relays, but the machine had no memory.

1943 Howard Aitken working at Harvard, USA, developed the Mark I computer, using relays as bit stores and with switches to input data in binary form. The machine stood 2·5 m (8 ft) high and 15·5 m (51 ft) wide and was used to solve the ballistics problems of large naval guns. Under Turing's guidance, the decoding station at Bletchley Park

(Buckinghamshire, UK) developed the Colossus computer to break the German Enigma codes, which were thought to be unbreakable. In some cases the information that was decoded could not be used for fear of revealing that the code was being cracked. Colossus was the first machine to use electronic devices (*thermionic valves*) in place of mechanical or electromechanical (relay) devices, allowing much faster processing and greater reliability. The sheer size of the machine and number of valves meant that the time between failures was short. Neither Mark I nor Colossus had a memory, so they could not be reprogrammed by using software.

1946 The ENIAC (Electronics Number Indicator and Calculator) machine was completed in the USA. This was the first really large and fast digital computer that used thermionic valves (vacuum tubes) as storage elements. ENIAC was 5·5 m (18 ft) high, 24 m (80 ft) long and weighed 30 tons, but it worked a thousand times faster than the Harvard Mark I. Nowadays even this machine could be outperformed by a modest laptop computer. ENIAC was initially used to carry out the calculations on the feasibility of the hydrogen bomb, although it was not its original purpose. Reprogramming the machine for other purposes had to be done by reconnecting wires, because, at that time, there was no provision for using software to control a digital computer.

1948 Manchester University demonstrated a computer that used thermionic valves and had a small and simple form of memory. This allowed for some software, for easier reprogramming and for more complex calculations in which intermediate results had to be held in the memory. The huge number of valves meant low reliability – one valve had to be replaced for every eight minutes of working time.

1949 Shockley, Brittain and Bardeen, working at Bell Laboratories (USA), invented the *transistor*, and the *switching device*. These were eventually able to replace thermionic valves in computers. The transistor was small, consumed very little electrical power and could be manufactured by automated methods. Initial samples measured 13 mm (0·5 in) long, but by the time transistors could be manufactured in quantity, in 1951, much smaller sizes were achieved. The semiconductor material used was germanium, but by 1956 silicon was being used to make superior devices.

Konrad Zuse constructed and marketed *digital computers* in Germany. These were developments of his Z4 design and used thermionic valves.

Wilkes and Renwick at Cambridge University demonstrated the EDSAC (Electronic Delay Storage Automatic Calculator) machine. This was said to achieve a calculating speed 15 000 times faster than the human brain.

Lyons, the British catering firm, developed LEO (Lyons Electronic Office), the first computer intended for commercial data processing as distinct from scientific and military engineering work. LEO was used for accounting and stock control. A later LEO MARK III was one of the first computers to use transistors in place of valves.

1951 The EDVAC (Electronic Digital Vacuum-tube Analysing Computer) was developed in the USA. Using thermionic valves, it was the first computer to use binary codes and to be programmed to create its own machine code using an assembler program.

1952 A computer was used for the first time in the USA to analyse voting patterns in a national election. It correctly predicted the outcome.

1954 IBM began the mass-production of computers. The IBM 7000 series were the first commercially obtainable computers that used transistors.

1956 The term *artificial intelligence* was coined.

1958 The first computer dating agency was set up.

1959 The *microchip* – or *integrated circuit* (IC) – was developed by Robert Noyce in the USA. A silicon transistor was manufactured on a surface of 6·45 mm^2 (0·1 in^2). It soon became possible to make ten transistors, and the electrical connections between them, in the same space. The microchip allowed circuits to be constructed using vastly greater numbers of transistors. This immensely improved reliability because failures arise mainly from interconnections and the use of chips greatly reduces the need for interconnections.

1965 Digital Equipment Corporation (DEC) – making use of transistor and IC techniques – produced the first widely-marketed minicomputer, leading to the famous PDP11 and VAX machines. By this time several hundred transistors and their connections could be made on a single chip. In Germany, print was typeset by computer for the first time. The PROLOG language was devised to develop programs for artificial intelligence (AI) work. The IBM 360 computers made extensive use of ICs.

1971 The microprocessor, containing several thousand transistors on one chip, was developed by Ted Hoff at Intel. This device, the 4004, worked with 4-bit units and provided all the processing needed for a simple computer in one chip, to which a manufacturer needed only to add memory and input/output ports. A coin-operated Hewlett-Packard computer was installed in a California public library, the first instance of easy access to a computer for the public.

1975 The first kit for constructing a personal computer became available.

1977 Steve Wozniak and Steve Jobs – working from the garage at Jobs' home and with a capital of $1300 – developed the Apple-1 computer, the first home computer. This was soon followed by the much more advanced Apple-2.

Reports began of health problems connected to the intensive use of VDUs, including eyestrain, back and shoulder problems, head and neck strains, and arm, wrist and leg pains.

1978 The first case of computer-related fraud by 'hacking' was reported. A hacker was charged with defrauding a Los Angeles bank of $10·2 million.

1979 Visicalc, the first spreadsheet program, was demonstrated on the Apple-2. This caused the demand for the machine to increase enormously and created a business – rather than academic – market for microcomputers. Loughborough University (UK) published its VDU manual, which has been widely used for its recommendations on the best use of VDUs so as to avoid medical problems.

1980 The UK Post Office telephone service began its Prestel service using large mainframe computers to provide information to subscribers (such as travel agents) over telephone lines. The system later allowed electronic mail messages to be sent between subscribers. New models of microcomputers proliferated worldwide, but most of the machines were incompatible with each other, had a limited range of uses, and were short-lived.

1981 IBM launched the IBM-PC microcomputer. Though the first models were less powerful than other contemporary designs, the use of an advanced form of Intel chip allowed IBM to develop the machine into a powerful unit (the PC-XT) that made the use of microcomputers acceptable for business purposes and imposed some standards on a chaotic industry. Software developed for the PC was aimed at business users rather than at computer enthusiasts, and included the famous Lotus 1-2-3 spreadsheet and Word Perfect word processor. The MS-DOS operating system developed for the IBM PC was made available to users wishing to develop machines that will run IBM software.

Germany introduced regulations on the design and use of VDUs in an attempt to reduce medical problems.

1983 The IBM PC-XT was introduced, standardizing the 5·25 in floppy disk format for years to come. This machine could also be fitted with a hard disk.

1984 IBM introduced the PC-AT, a vastly faster and more advanced machine that could run the same software as their earlier models. This compatibility has been a feature of the IBM machines, allowing users to change machines without the need to scrap all of their software. The PC-AT used the Intel 80286 chip with 1Mb of memory and a 1·2Mb floppy disk drive along with a 20Mb hard disk.

The Apple Macintosh was introduced, using Motorola microprocessor chips (incompatible with other types) and pioneering WIMP (Window, Ikon, Mouse Programming) techniques. These ideas – first developed by Xerox – allowed computers to be used more easily. The *mouse* is a small hand-held device that can be pushed around a desk and which causes an arrow marker to move on the VDU screen. Buttons on the mouse are used to confirm selection of whatever the arrow on-screen is pointing to. Selections of menus appear in separate windows on-screen. The mouse is now available on all microcomputers.

1985 The Transputer – a form of microprocessor that can be linked to other identical units – was developed by Iain Barron in the UK. This allowed *parallel-processing* – in which several actions can be carried out simultaneously – as distinct from *serial* (one item at a time) action of conventional processors. When *conventional processors* appear to be carrying out several tasks at once – *multi-tasking* – they are, in fact, timesharing the tasks by carrying out portions from each task in sequence.

1986 Machines of very similar construction to IBM machines – and able to run the same software – were suddenly reduced in price, particularly after the introduction of the Amstrad PC 1512. The availability of low-cost computers, along with the development of a vast library of software for the PC, led to a huge surge in the use of the PC type of machine. The Data Protection Act was introduced in the UK.

1987 IBM and other manufacturers introduced a machine using the Intel 80386 chip. This allowed older software to be run at very high speeds, and also permitted multi-tasking, so that several programs could seem to be running together. New standards

for VDU construction and use appeared from the BSI (British Standards Institute).

Laser printers, using the principle of the Xerox copier, became available, allowing the rapid printing of very high-quality material. Laser printers are extensively used along with DTP (desktop publishing) software to revolutionize the production of documents. Laptop computers started to appear in large numbers.

1988 Acorn (UK) developed their RISC (Reduced Instruction Set Computer) microprocessor, which operates at a very high speed by using only the most common and simplest instruction steps. This led to the development of the advanced, fast Archimedes computer, which is sold extensively to UK educational institutes.

ICL and Tender Electronic Industries jointly designed an improved laser-read optical-disk system for computers. Wang's Freestyle computer was developed. This can work with handwritten data (using an electronic pen) and with spoken messages. Steve Jobs announced the NEXT computer.

1989 Low-price clones of the fast 80386 computers became easily available, making this type of machine a standard for business. Intel released the 80496 chip, a development of the 80386 that includes some on-chip memory and avoids the need for a set of supporting chips. Intel also produced their first RISC chip, the i860.

British Telecom developed light-operated computer circuits that promise much faster operation and the ability to be linked over large distances by optical fibres.

The Science Museum, London, started a fund-raising campaign to construct Babbage's difference engine (see above).

1990 IBM and others announced computers using the 80686 Intel chip. The price of clone machines – using the older chips – fell sharply, particularly those using 80386 chips. IBM also announced a machine that runs both MS-DOS (for older software) and the UNIX operating system (for software that runs on mainframe and mini computers).

Several firms announced multimedia systems, combining computing and video techniques. NEC announced the first laptop machine with a full-colour screen.

1991 The Windows 3.0 software provided the IBM PC type of machine with the ease of use of the Apple Macintosh, but at lower prices, stimulating a boom in software and faster machines to use it.

High-capacity storage devices using rewritable optical disks became available. Small ink-jet printers became available for portable computers.

1992 Windows 3.1 launched. Its software dominated PC desktop computing, with both desktop and laptop machines requiring larger disk and memory capacity, while newer operating systems were developed. Nickel hydride batteries were being developed to overcome problems with portables. Dye-transfer colour printers became available at comparatively low prices.

Amstrad launched an A4 sized laptop using older technology – useful particularly for its built-in word-processor. Networking became almost universal.

ARTIFICIAL INTELLIGENCE

A computer simply carries out orders and cannot think for itself. In the 1940s and 1950s computer scientists pioneered Artificial Intelligence (AI) with the aim of creating a thinking machine. So far they have failed, but in the process they have taught us much about the way that humans think.

Alan Turing

The British mathematician Alan Turing (1912–54) designed an experiment to test whether a machine shows intelligence. In Turing's experiment a human conducts a dialogue – by means of a computer terminal – with both a machine and another human, hidden behind a screen. Both respondents must answer every question put to them. Turing argued that if the questioner could not decide which of the two respondents was the machine, then the machine would have demonstrated intelligence.

AI researchers have adopted two very different approaches to building intelligent machines. Some have tried to build machines that use the same principles as biological intelligence, while others have chosen examples of intelligent behaviour (such as chess playing or language) and tried to build machines that copy it. Since research began AI scientists have attacked a wide range of problems. These include problem solving, natural language and vision.

The first attempts to tackle problem solving (often used as a measure of intelligence) produced the Logic Theorem program in the 1950s. As its name suggests, it was capable of proving theorems. Later came a more advanced program called the General Problem Solver, which was able to tackle more complex mathematical problems. Since then computer scientists have made great strides in improving the problem-solving abilities of computers, but these are still confined to those problems that lie within the realms of logic.

A major goal of AI research is to enable humans to interact with computers using natural language – language that is written and spoken by humans, as distinct from computer-program languages. To understand and interpret such language, much more knowledge is needed than was once thought. Computers have to be able to work out the context in which a word is uttered in order to interpret what is being said; for example, there is a huge difference between 'close the door' and 'stay close to me'. To this end AI researchers have made use of the ideas of the linguist Noam Chomsky who suggested that language obeys a set of rules that can be expressed in mathematical terms.

Running parallel with this work on natural language, research has been undertaken into speech recognition. Speech-recognition systems use information about the structure and components of speech and are typically 'trained' in on one person's voice. The challenge is to develop a machine that can recognize what any one of a variety of speakers is saying – even if their voice is affected by, for instance, a cold – and distinguish speech from background noise.

Expert systems

The most tangible and practical result of AI research has been in the area of expert systems. These are designed to help humans make decisions, typically in solving problems where it would otherwise be necessary to call in an expert in a particular area. Many early expert systems tackled medical diagnosis, but industry and commerce have now begun to take them seriously. An expert system has three components: a _knowledge base_, in which the knowledge and experience of an expert are summarized in the form of rules; an _inference engine_, which is a program that searches the knowledge base for the best possible answer to a question; and a _user interface_, which allows the user to 'talk' to the system.

Experts often find it difficult to explain to a computer engineer exactly how they reach their decisions, and translating the mechanics of these decisions – which may rely heavily on experience and intuition – into the exact mathematical logic required by a computer is a complex task. In fact expert systems are of no use where intuition or common sense is necessary – they can only be used where the decision-making process follows a simple, well-defined logic path. But such systems are very valuable where experts are scarce, or as a means of preserving knowledge and transferring it to others as individuals retire or change jobs.

Neural computing

The most promising approach to the creation of artificial intelligence has used the structure of the brain as the basis for computer architecture. _neural networks_ are connected microprocessors that mimic the complex network of interlinking neurones in the brain. The idea of neural networks has been around since the 1940s, but only since the early 1980s has interest been rekindled. Neural networks offer big advantages over conventional computers in searching large databases for close matches, or storing and accessing data. They consist of a large number of processors (_nodes_) – the points at which the information is processed – linked by communication channels. Neural computers learn by example; they are not programmed like conventional computers, which means that they are not simply given a series of instructions to carry out. They use the concept of _feedback_ – where part of the output of a node is returned as input for another process, for self-correction – and hence they can interact with their environment. However, they are still a long way from a thinking machine.

Robotics

Another major branch of AI is robotics. While robots are used on the production lines of most car-manufacturing plants – for assembly and simple spot welding – they are very primitive. They inhabit a 'perfect' world, and have no sense of touch or vision to adapt to their environment, such as dealing with misplaced, faulty or missing components. Three-dimensional vision is crucial to developing practical systems. A wide range of techniques is being developed for extracting the salient features of an image; this would allow a robot to recognize and pick up an object from the production line, for example, even if the object were not in its correct position.

The thinking machine

The road to the thinking machine is proving longer and more difficult than the AI pioneers of the 1940s and 1950s believed. There is still much debate in the AI community about whether computers will ever be able to think, or to display the traits normally considered essential for intelligence. While the debate continues, research into AI is bringing a better understanding of brain function and our own intelligence, and an insight into such things as speech disorders and learning problems.

GLOSSARIES

CHEMISTRY GLOSSARY

ablation degradation due to heat.

absolute temperature temperature measured on the absolute scale in kelvins (K), -1 K being equal to $1\,°C$. Zero on the absolute scale is $-273\cdot16\,°C$.

absorptiometer a device used to measure the absorption of light.

acetal a compound derived from an alcohol and an aldehyde or a ketone.

acetate an ester of acetic acid.

acetic acid an old name for ethanoic acid.

acetin an acetate derived from glycerol.

acetylation the introduction of one or more acetyl groups, CH_3CO, into organic compounds.

acid a substance able to form hydrogen ions when in solution, whether in water or in a non-aqueous solvent.

acid-base indicator an indicator that has a markedly different colour in acid and base solutions. The difference in colour is due to the ionized and non-ionized forms of the indicator.

acid rain pollution caused by sulphur and nitrogen oxides released into the environment by burning fuels.

actinides a series of radioactive elements, many of them artificially produced by irradiation. The series comprises actinium, thorium, protactinium, uranium, neptunium, plutonium, americium, curium, berkelium, californium, einsteinium, fermium, mendelevium and nobelium.

acyl a group left after the $-OH$ group has been removed from carboxylic acid.

addition reaction a reaction in which unsaturated carbon bonds are saturated to give single bonds.

adhesive a substance that wets surfaces that are to be stuck together and then solidifies to form the actual joint.

adiabatic process a thermodynamic process by which heat is neither added to nor allowed to leave a system.

adsorbate a substance that is adsorbed on to an adsorbent.

adsorbent a substance that provides an adsorption surface.

adsorption the process by which free atoms or molecules become attached to a surface.

aerosol fine particles of a solid or liquid suspended in air.

BUCKMINSTERFULLERENE

Fullerenes are hollow clusters of carbon atoms that are joined into geometrical shapes. Before the discovery of the fullerenes in the 1990s, elemental carbon was only known in tetrahedral crystals (diamonds) and a hexagonal form (graphite). The most publicized fullerene is *buckminsterfullerene* – C_{60}. Nicknamed 'buckyballs', buckminsterfullerene molecules consist of 60 carbon atoms that are bonded together to resemble a soccer ball.

---

alcohol an organic compound in which hydroxyl– $-OH$ group or groups are attached to carbon atoms.

aldehyde an organic compound in which a $-CHO$ group is attached to a carbon atom.

aliphatic organic compounds with carbon atoms arranged in chains rather than rings.

alkali a substance that gives a pH of greater than 7 in water.

alkanes (formerly known as paraffins) the principal constituents of petroleum. These organic compounds have the general formula C_nH_{2n+2}.

alkenes aliphatic hydrocarbons containing one double $C=C$ bond. They have the general formula C_nH_{2n}.

alkyd resins compounds used extensively in paints and other coatings. They are formed by condensation reactions between polybasic acids and polyhydric alcohols.

alkyls aliphatic hydrocarbons with the final hydrogen atom removed.

allotropy the existence of an element in more than one physical form in the same physical state, e.g. carbon as diamond and graphite.

alloy a combination of two or more metals, or of metallic and non-metallic elements. The physical characteristics of this combination are metallic.

alum potassium alum – $KAl(SO_4)_2.12H_2O$ – a compound used in a variety of industrial processes including dyeing, paper manufacture, and waterproofing.

alumina aluminium oxide, Al_2O_3.

aluminates compounds containing an Al^{3+} ion in anions that are hydroxide or oxide based.

amalgam compounds of a metal and mercury. They can be both liquid and solid.

amides organic compounds derived from carboxylic acids.

amines organic compounds based on ammonia. One or more of the hydrogen atoms in the ammonia molecule is substituted by alkyl groups to give primary, secondary and tertiary amines.

amino acids organic compounds containing the amino group, $-NH_2$, and the carboxyl group, $-COOH$. Proteins are built up from amino acids.

ammonia a pungent gas with a strong alkaline reaction.

ammonium a cation, $(NH_4)^+$, that behaves similarly to the alkali metal cations.

amphoteric having both acid and basic properties.

aniline an important organic chemical used in the dye industry. Based on the benzene ring, its formula is $C_6H_5.NH_2$. Also called phenylamine.

anion a negatively charged ion occurring in crystals, solutions and melts.

anisotropic having different properties in different directions, e.g. an anisotropic crystal has different physical properties along different crystal axes.

annealing a reduction of the stresses within a metal by heating it and then cooling it in a controlled fashion.

anode (in electrolysis) the positive electrode.

aromatic an organic compound based on the benzene ring, C_6H_6. The benzene ring is stable, even though the carbon atoms within it are unsaturated.

It therefore undergoes substitution reactions rather than addition reactions.

aryls an aromatic hydrocarbon with a hydrogen atom removed.

asbestos any of a group of silicate minerals. The SiO_4 groups are linked together into chains, giving the characteristic fibrous texture.

atom the smallest particle of a chemical element.

atomic mass unit one-twelfth of the mass of a carbon-12 atom. It is equivalent to 1.66×10^{-27} kg, approximately the mass of a proton or neutron.

atomic number the number of protons in the nucleus of an atom of an element.

atomic weight the old name for relative atomic mass.

Avogadro's number (symbol L) the number of atoms or molecules in one mole of any pure substance. $L = 6.023 \times 10^{23}$.

azo dyes a group of dyes containing the group $-N=N-$ linking two aromatic groups.

base a compound that acts as a proton acceptor and, on reaction with an acid, gives a salt and water.

benzene (C_6H_6) a colourless flammable liquid used as a solvent and an insecticide. The six carbon atoms are arranged in a ring. The bonds between the carbon atoms have characteristics between single and double bonds; they are said to resonate between the two, and as such are stable.

benzyl the $C_6H_5.CH_2-$ group.

bimolecular reaction a reaction in which only two molecular types react together, e.g.:
$H_2 + I_2 \rightarrow 2HI$.

biuret reaction a test for peptides and proteins, in which the peptide linkage gives a pinkish colour with sodium hydroxide, NaOH, and copper sulphate, $CuSO_4$.

body-centred lattice a crystal structure in which atoms or molecules occur at the corners of each crystal cell and at the centre of the body of the crystal cell.

bond the link that holds atoms together in molecules and that is also the basis of crystal structure. Bonds may be covalent, ionic or hydrogen bonds.

bond energy the amount of energy that must be supplied to break a covalent bond.

borates boric acid (H_3BO_3) salts.

borax a naturally occurring source of boron, $Na_2(B_4O_5(OH)_4 . 8H_2O)$.

Bordeaux mixture copper sulphate, $CuSO_4$, and calcium hydroxide, $Ca(OH)_2$, mixed in water. It is used as a fungicide.

brass an alloy of copper and zinc. Two principal forms of brass are made, one containing less than 30% zinc, the other between 30% and 40% zinc.

brine a solution of sodium chloride, NaCl.

bromates salts with bromium oxy-anions. The term is commonly taken to mean the BrO_3^- oxy-anion, but BrO^- and BrO_2^- oxy-anions are also found.

bromides salts of hydrogen bromide, HBr, based on the bromide ion, Br^-.

bronze a group of alloys of copper and, originally, tin, often with smaller amounts of other elements. The term can now mean copper alloys with no tin, e.g. aluminium bronze.

buffer a mixture of acid, or alkali, and an associ-ated salt, whose pH alters only gradually with the addition of more acid or alkali. The salt acts as a supply of anions or cations that combine with hydrogen or base ions.

butane a member of the alkane series, C_4H_{10}. It is widely used in cylinders and canisters as camping gas.

carboxylic acid an organic acid containing a carboxyl group, $-COOH$.

calcite a form of naturally occurring calcium-carbonate, $CaCO_3$, found as chalk, limestone and marble.

calcium carbonate the most commonly occur-ring salt of calcium, $CaCO_3$. See also calcite.

camphor ($C_{10}H_{16}O$) an extract from the wood of the camphor tree. Also manufactured, it is used in medicines, as insect-repellent and in plastics.

carbohydrates naturally occurring compounds used as energy compounds, energy stores and for structural uses. The general formula for carbo-hydrates is $C_xH_{2y}O_y$.

carbonates salts of carbonic acid, H_2CO_3. The carbonate ion is CO_3^{2-} and forms a number of commercially important salts, including calcium carbonate.

carbon dioxide (CO_2) a product of respiration and a constituent of air. It represents the complete combustion of carbon.

carbon monoxide (CO) a toxic gas formed by the incomplete combustion of carbon.

carotene ($C_{40}H_{56}$) a precursor of vitamin A. It occurs naturally in plants as one of the chief colouring pigments, and is also found in many animal tissues.

catalyst a substance that speeds up the rate of a chemical reaction without being permanently chemically altered by the reaction.

catalytic converter a device containing pla-tinum and rhodium metals fitted to car exhausts to reduce emissions of carbon monoxide, nitrogen oxides and hydrocarbon pollutants.

cathode (in electrolysis) the negative electrode.

cation a positively charged ion, occurring in crystals, solutions and melts.

cellulose ($C_6H_{10}O_5)_n$ the principal structural component of cell walls, formed by the polymeri-zation of glucose.

ceramics hard non-metallic inorganic materials with high melting points, e.g. enamels, pottery, porcelain, abrasives.

CFC abbreviation for chlorofluorocarbons. Used as refrigerants and in aerosols, CFCs are now believed to damage the ozone layer.

chain reaction a process by which the product of one reaction takes part in a further reaction, the products of which take part in yet more reactions, etc.

chalk a naturally occurring form of calcium carbonate, $CaCO_3$.

charcoal a form of carbon produced by the slow burning of wood in conditions in which the supply of air is limited.

chiral a molecule that cannot be superimposed

on its mirror image.

chlorates chlorine oxy-acid salts, formed from the ClO^-, ClO_2^-, ClO_3^- and ClO_4^- ions.

chlorides compounds containing the Cl^- ion.

chlorofluorocarbons see CFCs.

chlorophyll a complex organic chemical colouring matter found in green plants. It is an essential constituent of the photosynthetic process, by which carbohydrates are produced in plants from carbon dioxide and water, using the energy of sunlight.

cholesterol $(C_{27}H_{46}O)$ a complex organic chemical based on the sterol ring structure. It is found in animals, particularly in membranes, and also in some plants, e.g. some vegetable oils, such as coconut oil.

chromates salts based on chromic acid, i.e. containing the CrO_4^{2-} and $Cr_2O_7^{2-}$ ions.

chromatography a technique for separating the components of a mixture by distribution between a mobile phase, e.g. water, and a stationary phase, e.g. paper.

clay naturally occurring aluminosilicates consisting of $AlSiO_4$, together with $Mg(OH)_2$ and $Al(OH)_3$.

coenzymes compounds necessary for the action of enzymes. They may be altered during the course of the reaction, but will be re-formed during later reactions.

colloids small particles, larger than atoms or molecules but too small to be seen by a light microscope, usually found in suspension or solution.

complexion a species formed by coordination of a metal ion to other ions or molecules, e.g. Fe^{3+} and CN^- ions give $Fe(CN)_6^{3-}$.

concentration see molarity.

condensation reaction a reaction in which two molecules react together to give one product molecule plus a simple molecule such as water, H_2O.

conformation the shape taken by a molecule owing to the positioning a group may have in relation to a bond. In complex organic molecules the conformation may affect physical properties.

copolymer a polymer resulting from the combination of two or more monomers.

covalent bond a chemical bond in which two atoms are linked by sharing two electrons – one electron originating from each atom.

crude oil a naturally occurring mixture of hydrocarbons, often mixed with water, sulfur and other inorganic impurities.

crystal a solid particle with a regular geometric shape caused by the regular arrangement of atoms or ions or molecules.

crystallization the process by which crystals of a substance are removed from a solution by increasing the concentration above the saturation point.

cyanates salts formed from the cyanate ion, NCO^-.

cyanides salts formed from the cyanide ion, CN^-.

deliquescence the absorption of water by a solid to give a solution.

detergent a water-soluble surface-active agent that can wet surfaces and help to loosen oil and grease. Detergents invariably consist of a hydrophobic group that allows them to dissolve the oils and grease, and a hydrophilic group that promotes water-solubility.

dextrose see glucose.

dialysis the purification of a colloidal mixture by the diffusion of impurities through a semipermeable membrane.

diamond a naturally occurring crystalline form of carbon.

dicarboxylic acids organic acids containing two carboxyl groups –COOH.

dienes organic chemicals with two carbon–carbon double bonds.

diffusion the movement of a gas or liquid caused by the random movement of its atoms or molecules.

diketones organic compounds with two keto groups – CO.

dimer a polymer consisting of two molecules of a monomer.

distillation the separation of two liquids or a liquid from a solid by evaporation and recondensation.

doping the introduction of impurities into a crystal lattice, giving different electrical or other properties to the crystal.

double bond two atoms sharing two pairs of electrons, i.e. two covalent bonds.

dry ice solid carbon dioxide (CO_2).

EDTA ethylenediaminetetra-acetic acid, an acid that forms complexes with most metal ions.

efflorescence the formation of a powdery solid from crystals (by the loss of water of crystallization) or from liquids (by evaporation).

elastomer a material with elastic properties, e.g. rubber.

electrochemical series a series in which the elements are placed in decreasing order of oxidation potential. An element higher up the series will displace from solution an element lower down the series.

electrolysis the decomposition of a substance in solution by the passage of an electric current.

electrolyte a substance that – in solution – dissociates into ions. It can thus act as an electric conductor.

electronegativity the degree to which an atom in a molecule attracts electrons to itself. In general, values of electronegativity decrease from right to left and from top to bottom of the Periodic Table of elements.

element a substance formed of atoms all with the same atomic number.

emulsion a dispersed colloid of one liquid in another.

enantiomers isomers that are non-superimposable mirror images of each other in the spatial arrangement of their constituent atoms.

endothermic reaction a reaction in which

heat is absorbed.

enthalpy (symbol: *H*) the thermodynamic function of a system equal to the sum of its internal energy and the product of its pressure and volume.

entropy (symbol *S*) a parameter used to describe the disorder or chaos of a system. The greater the disorder of a system, the greater the entropy.

enzyme a protein that catalyses one specific chemical reaction in a living organism.

epimer a type of isomer that differs in the configuration around only one of a number of atoms.

epoxy an oxygen atom joined to two different groups that are also joined to other groups.

equilibrium any state in which the properties do not change with time, e.g. in a reversible reaction it is the stage at which the rate of the forward reaction equals the rate of the reverse reaction.

ester the product of a condensation reaction between an organic acid and an alcohol.

ethane (C_2H_6) a naturally occurring constituent of natural gas; it is also extensively synthesized.

ethanoic acid (CH_3) the modern name for acetic acid. Vinegar is impure dilute ethanoic acid.

ethanol (CH_3CH_2OH) the systematic name for ethyl alcohol or alcohol. Although originally produced as result of fermentation, most ethanol is now synthesized.

ethene ($CH_2=CH_2$) the systematic name for ethylene.

ether ($C_2H_5OC_2H_5$) a volatile flammable liquid used as a solvent or as an anaesthetic. Otherwise known as diethyl ether and ethoxyethane.

ethers compounds with the general formula R^1-O-R^2, where R^1 and R^2 are alkyl or aryl groups.

ethyne the systematic name for acetylene.

eutectic a mixture of two substances having the lowest melting point of any such mixture.

evaporation the conversion of a liquid to a vapour at a temperature below its boiling point.

fats compounds of fatty acids and glycerol.

fatty acids organic acids consisting of an alkyl group attached to a carboxyl group, with the general formula $C_nH_{2n}O_2$.

Fehling's solution a solution of copper sulphate, sodium potassium tartrate and sodium hydroxide, used for testing for reducing sugars.

fermentation the use of microorganisms to break down substances and release, generally, useful products, e.g. the fermentation of sugar by yeasts, yielding alcohol and carbon dioxide.

ferrates oxy-anions of iron, incorporating the FeO_4^{2-} ion.

ferric compounds compounds incorporating Fe(III) iron.

ferrous compounds compounds incorporating Fe(II) iron.

flash point the temperature to which a substance must be heated before it can be ignited.

flocculation the coagulation of a colloid into larger particles.

fluorescein ($C_{20}H_{12}O_5$) a red crystalline substance that fluoresces bright green.

fluorides the salts of hydrogen fluoride, HF.

foam a dispersion of bubbles of gas in a liquid or solid.

fractional crystallization the separation of two or more substances by using changes in solubility with temperature. As the temperature is lowered, one substance will crystallize out first, then another, and so on.

fractional distillation the separation of two or more substances by evaporating the mixture, allowing the vapours to pass up a fractionating column. The various fractions collected are condensed at different points up the column, depending on their volatility.

free radical an atom or group of atoms with unpaired electrons. It is therefore very reactive.

gas a substance that does not resist change of shape. Gases will expand spontaneously to fill a container. The intermolecular attractions are very weak and the constituent atoms or molecules show random movement.

gasification the conversion of a solid or liquid to a gas with lower molecular weight. Gasification is usually applied to the conversion of hydrocarbon solids and liquids to fuel gases.

gasoline a mixture of various hydrocarbons used as motor fuel or aviation fuel.

gel a colloid suspension in which the particles are linked by a form of partial coagulation to form a jelly.

gelatin a protein made by boiling collagen in dilute acid.

glucose ($C_6H_{12}O_6$) the most common hexose sugar; also known as dextrose. Found in plants and animals, it is the constituent monomer of cellulose, starch, glycogen, etc.

glue a colloid mixture of proteins. It is prepared from animal waste containing collagen.

gluten a protein from wheat dough.

glycerides the esters produced from glycerol. Depending on how many of the hydroxyl groups in the glycerol molecule combine with acid radicals, the glycerides are called mono-, di- or tri-glycerides.

glycerol an odourless syrupy liquid that is also known as glycerin or 1,2,3- trihydroxypropane.

gram molecule a mole.

graphite a crystalline form of carbon, occurring naturally. It consists of flat sheets of hexagonal cells, which slip easily over each other, giving graphite its characteristic properties.

group in the Periodic Table of elements, a group is a vertical column of elements. A group will have distinct properties and characteristics in common.

haem a complex three-dimensional molecule with the formula $C_{34}H_{32}FeN_4O_4$. Haem is an important constituent of a number of active biochemicals, including haemoglobin. It has an iron atom at its centre, which can act as an electron carrier, changing from the ferrous to the ferric state and back again.

halogenation the addition or substitution of halogen atoms to a molecule.

halogens the elements making up group VII in the Periodic Table, consisting of fluorine, chlorine, bromine, iodine and astatine.

hard water water containing calcium and magnesium salts. Soft water lacks these salts.

hexanes liquid alkanes. A group of chemicals with the formula C_6H_{14}.

hexose a carbohydrate containing six carbon atoms. Glucose is the most important of the hexoses.

hydration the addition of water to a substance, particularly to ions, e.g.: $H^+ + H_2O \rightarrow H_3O^+$

hydrocarbons compounds of hydrogen and carbon only.

hydrochloric acid an aqueous solution of hydrogen chloride, HCl.

hydrogenation a form of reduction in which hydrogen gas is used to add hydrogen to a compound.

hydrogen bond a weak bond between an electronegative atom, e.g. oxygen, and a hydrogen atom covalently bonded to another electronegative atom.

hydrolysis a reaction in which water combines with a compound.

hydroxylation the introduction of a hydroxyl group, OH^-, into a molecule.

imides organic compounds containing the –CO–NH–CO–group.

imines organic compounds containing the –NH–group. The nitrogen atom is not linked to a carbonyl group or hydrogen atom.

indicator a substance that shows the presence of a particular compound or group of compounds by a characteristic colour. Indicators are used to show when the completion of a titration has occurred.

indole an organic double-ring structure based on the formula C_8H_7N.

inorganic chemistry the chemistry of all elements and molecules other than those containing carbon. Compare organic chemistry.

ion an atom or molecule that has lost or gained one or more electrons, thereby carrying a positive or negative charge. See also anion, cation.

ionic bond a chemical bond due to the electrostatic force of attraction between oppositely charged ions in a crystal lattice.

isocyanates organic compounds containing the group $-N = C = O$.

isomers compounds with the same molecular formula, but having different arrangements of atoms bonded together or existing in different three-dimensional structures due to a differing orientation about certain atoms.

isomorphism the existence of different compounds with the same crystal structure.

isonitriles organic compounds containing the group –N–C. Otherwise known as isocyanides or carbylamines.

isotonic (of two solutions) having the same osmotic pressure.

isotopes atoms of an element having the same number of protons but differing numbers of neutrons.

ketones organic compounds with the general formula R^1-CO-R^2, where R^1 and R^2 are generally alkyl groups.

lactose a disaccharide sugar with the formula $C_{12}H_{22}O_{11}$. It occurs in varying amounts in the milk of all animals.

lanthanides a series of related metallic elements with atomic numbers between 57 and 71. The series comprises lanthanum, cerium, praseodymium, neo-

dymium, promethium, samarium, europium, gadolinium, terbium, dysprosium, holmium, erbium, thulium, ytterbium, lutetium.

lattice the regular three-dimensional arrangement of atoms in a crystal.

lime water a solution of calcium hydroxide, $Ca(OH)_2$.

liquefied petroleum gas hydrocarbon gases produced as a result of refining petroleum and liquefied under pressure. It occurs as butane and propane, although neither is a pure form of the gas.

liquid crystal a phase formed by certain substances that has the mobility of a liquid but a definite ordered structure. It is used in display units, e.g. in pocket calculators.

litmus a colouring obtained from lichens. It is used as an indicator to detect pH changes.

macromolecules large molecules with molecular weight in excess of 10 000.

magnesium alloys a group of very light alloys.

manganates salts containing the ion MnO_4^{2-}.

mercaptans a group of organic compounds containing the – SH group linked to a carbon atom. Mercaptans are otherwise known as thiols.

meta- a prefix denoting the position of groups attached to the benzene ring.

metals elements that are malleable, lustrous, and conduct heat and electricity. They tend to form cations.

methanal (HCHO) the systematic name for formaldehyde.

methane (CH_4) a gas that occurs naturally as a result of the decay of vegetable matter; othewise known as marsh gas.

methanol (CH_3OH) a volatile liquid used as a solvent and as a fuel. It is also known as methyl alcohol.

methylation the addition of a methyl group, $-CH_3$, to an organic compound.

micelle a submicroscopic aggregate of molecules.

miscibility the ability of one substance to mix with another.

molar volume the volume occupied by 1 mole of a substance in the gaseous state.

molarity the strength of a solution, usually measured by the number of moles of a substance dissolved in 1 litre of the solution; otherwise called concentration.

mole (formerly known as a gram molecule) the amount of substance that contains the same number of elementary entities (molecules, ions, atoms, etc.) as there are in 0·012 kg of carbon-12.

molecular weight the ratio of the mass per molecule of a substance to one atomic mass unit (1/12 of the mass of a carbon-12 atom).

molecule the smallest independent particle of a compound that can exist, containing two or more atoms linked by chemical bonds.

monotropy the existence of a substance in only one stable crystalline form.

naphthalene ($C_{10}H_8$) a double benzene ring structure.

natural gas a mixture of over 90% methane with other hydrocarbon gases, as well as nitrogen and carbon dioxide.

ninhydrin ($C_9H_4O_3.H_2O$) an indicator that gives

a blue colour on heating with amino acids and proteins.

nitrates salts of nitric acid, containing the ion NO_3.

nitric acid (HNO_3) a corrosive liquid that has many important industrial uses, including the manufacture of fertilizers.

nitrides compounds of nitrogen and other elements.

nitrites salts of nitrous acid, containing the ion NO_2.

nitro compounds a group of aromatic compounds with the basic formula $R–NO_2$.

noble gases a group of unreactive gases. The group comprises helium, neon, argon, krypton, xenon, and radon. Traces of all these gases are found in the atmosphere.

nylons a group of synthetic plastics and fibres, largely formed by condensation polymerization.

octanes a group of hydrocarbons with eight carbon atoms and the basic formula C_8H_{18}. The group falls in the alkane series, and the constituents are all found in crude oil.

optical activity the ability of certain substances to rotate the polarization plane of polarized light, due to the asymmetry of the molecules.

organic chemistry the chemistry of the almost infinite number of actual or potential compounds containing carbon.

ortho- a prefix denoting the position of groups attached to the benzene ring.

osmotic pressure the excess pressure that must be applied to prevent the flow of solvent through a semipermeable membrane between a solvent and solution.

oxidation the process by which a substance loses electrons, e.g. $Fe^{2+} \rightarrow Fe^{3+} + e$.

oxide a compound containing oxygen and other elements.

oximes a group of organic compounds containing $=N.OH$ linked to a carbon atom.

oxonium a positive ion with the basic formula R_3O^+, where R is hydrogen or an organic group, e.g. the hydroxonium ion H_3O^+.

ozone (O_3) an allotrope of oxygen. A layer of ozone in the upper atmosphere absorbs harmful radiation from the sun.

para- a prefix denoting the position of groups attached to the benzene ring.

patina an oxide layer formed on metals and alloys.

pentanes a group of hydrocarbons with five carbon atoms and the basic formula C_5H_{12}. The constituents are all found in crude oil.

pentose a carbohydrate containing five carbon atoms.

peptides chains of two or more amino acids linked by a peptide linkage, $–CO–NH–$. Peptide chains are arranged in three-dimensional structures to form proteins.

period a period in the Periodic Table of elements is a horizontal series of elements, from an alkali metal to a noble gas. Compare group.

Periodic Table the arrangement of elements in a table in order of increasing atomic number so that similarities between elements are emphasized (see pp. 226–28).

permanganates a group of salts containing the MnO_4^- ion.

peroxides derivatives of hydrogen peroxide, H_2O_2, containing linked pairs of oxygen atoms.

pH the logarithm (base 10) of the reciprocal of the concentration of hydrogen ions in a solution, giving a measure of the acidity or alkalinity of a solution.

phenol ($C_6H_5 \cdot OH$) an aromatic hydroxy compound.

phenolphthalein ($C_{20}H_{14}O_4$) an aromatic compound used as an indicator.

phenyl the aromatic group $C_6H_5–$.

phosphates salts based on the PO_4^{3-} and $P_2O_7^{4-}$ ions.

phosphoric acid an oxy-acid of phosphorus, the best known being H_3PO_4.

phosphors substances that phosphoresce, i.e. absorb radiation and re-emit after removal of radiation source.

phosphorus acid oxy-acids of phosphorus (III), the best known being H_3PO_3.

plastics artificial organic polymers that can be moulded to shape.

polyesters polymers formed by condensation reactions between polybasic acids and polyhydric alcohols.

polymers a compound consisting of long-chain molecules made up of repeating molecular units.

polymorphism a substance existing in more than one crystalline form.

polysaccharides carbohydrates formed by condensation reactions between monosaccharides.

precipitation the production of an insoluble compound in a solution by a chemical reaction.

propane $CH_3.CH_2.CH_3$. A constituent of natural gas. An alkane.

proteins a large group of naturally occurring organic compounds consisting of chains of amino acids folded into complex three-dimensional molecules. Proteins are the basic structural materials of all living organisms.

radical an atom or molecule that has one or more free valencies.

rare earths the lanthanide series of elements.

rectification fractional distillation used to separate an organic liquid into its constituent parts.

redox simultaneous oxidation and reduction occurring in one chemical reaction.

reduction the process by which a substance gains electrons, e.g. $Cu^{2+} + 2e \rightarrow Cu$.

relative atomic mass the average mass of one atom of an element divided by one-twelfth of the mass of one atom of carbon-12.

resin a solid natural or synthetic polymer.

reversible reaction a reaction that can proceed in either direction. Such a reaction usually attains an equilibrium, depending on the concentrations of the reactants and the physical conditions.

ribose a pentose sugar, $C_5H_{10}O_5$, found in the nucleic acids.

rust a coating of impure hydrated iron (III) oxide found on iron.

salt (in popular usage) sodium chloride, $NaCl$; (in chemistry) the product of the reaction between a base and an acid.

sand a mixture of SiO_2 and other minerals, formed by the degradation of rocks.

saponification the hydrolysis of an ester using an alkali.

saturated compound a compound in which there are no double or triple bonds, only single bonds.

silica silicon dioxide, SiO_2, one of the most common constituents of the earth's crust.

silicates compounds containing the $SiO_4{}^{4-}$ ion. However, the term extends to cover a wide range of minerals based on the SiO_4 tetrahedral crystal structure.

silicones organic polymers that contain –Si–O–Si– linkages.

single bond a bond between two atoms involving two electrons in a single bonding orbital.

sintering the fusion of two or more substances by heating powders together under pressure at a temperature below their melting point.

soap the salt of a fatty acid.

solders alloys used to join metals together. The solder melts at a temperature below that of the metals.

solution a single-phase homogeneous mixture of two or more compounds; one of the compounds is often a liquid in which the solute is dissolved.

standard temperature and pressure (abbreviated to STP) a temperature of 273·15 K and a pressure of 101·325 kPa.

starch a naturally occurring polymer of glucose.

strength the ability of an acid or alkali to give hydroxonium ions, H_3O^+.

sublimation the change from a solid to a gaseous state without passing through a liquid state.

substitution a displacement reaction in which one atom or group in a molecule is replaced by another atom or group.

substrate the substance on which an enzyme acts.

sucrose a disaccharide carbohydrate with the formula $C_{12}H_{22}O_{11}$.

sugars carbohydrates generally based on six- or twelve-carbon atoms. They are crystalline, soluble in water and sweet to taste. They include sucrose, glucose (dextrose), lactose, and fructose.

sulfates salts based on the $SO_4{}^{2-}$ ion.

sulfides compounds of elements and sulfur, usually based on the S^{2-} ion.

sulfites salts based on the $SO_3{}^{2-}$ ion.

sulfuric acid a colourless liquid, H_2SO_4.

superconductor a substance that exhibits zero electrical resistance, usually at very low temperature.

superphosphate a mixture of calcium hydrogen phosphate, $Ca(H_2PO_4)_2$, and calcium sulphate, $CaSO_4$. It is used as a fertilizer.

surface active agents mainly organic substances that reduce surface tension when dissolved in water. They are also known as surfactants.

tellurates salts containing oxy-anions of tellurium, i.e. $TeO_6{}^{6-}$ and $TeO_3{}^{2-}$ ions.

terpenes volatile aromatic hydrocarbons with the formula $(C_5H_8)_n$. They are naturally occurring in the essential oils of many plants.

thermoplastics plastics that can be repeatedly softened by heating and hardened by cooling.

thio- containing sulfur.

titration the determination of the amount of one substance needed to react with a fixed amount of another substance. The endpoint is determined by a change in property, e.g. change in colour.

transition elements a series of elements with an incomplete inner shell of electrons. On the Periodic Table (see p. 227) they comprise scandium to zinc, yttrium to cadmium, and lanthanum to mercury.

triple bond a bond formed by three pairs of electrons shared between two atoms.

valency (also known as oxidation state) the difference between the number of electrons attached to an atom of the free element and the number of electrons associated with an atom of the element in a compound.

van der Waals' bonds weak forces between molecules due to electronic coupling.

vapour pressure the pressure of a vapour produced by a solid or liquid. In a closed system a saturated vapour pressure will eventually be established, at which the vapour will be in equilibrium with the solid or liquid.

vinegar a dilute solution of ethanoic acid.

vinyl the $CH_2=CH$ groups, otherwise known as ethenyl.

water oxygen hydride, H_2O.

zeolites aluminosilicates that have a negatively charged framework with cations present in cavities. They are used to separate mixtures, and to soften water, and as catalysts.

COMPUTING GLOSSARY

ADA a language developed for the US Defense Department to allow programming of missile-detection and similar systems with the minimum of flaws (bugs).

addressing selecting memory by using a number unique to a unit memory applied in binary form along address lines.

ALGOL a third-generation language. ALGOL was the first to concentrate on logical as distinct from mathematical processing needs.

ALU abbreviation for arithmetic and logic unit, the central part of any microprocessor.

analogue (analog) computer a computer that deals with data having physical quantity and which is constantly changing. These changes are represented by changes in voltages. The output – which may be graphed instantly by a plotting pen – can in turn drive another device. Analogue computers operate in real-time, as events occur, rather than handling previously stored and coded data as a digital computer does.

archive data stored in a form intended for long-term retention.

artificial intelligence the field of computing science involving the development of computer programs intended to simulate human learning and decision-making abilities. (See also Turing test.)

assembly language a low-level programming language that uses abbreviated commands that can easily be translated, using a program, into machine code.

backing store a storage system that is non-volatile (usually magnetic). This will retain large quantities of data when the computer is switched off.

BASIC acronym for Beginners All-Purpose Symbolic Instruction Code, a language developed originally for teaching FORTRAN but now recognized in its own right. Lack of standardization is the main drawback to use of BASIC.

binary code the representation of symbols or characters by patterns of 0s and 1s, which on a computer can be represented by electric current being turned off and on.

bit (from BInary digiT) the smallest unit of information (a 0 or a 1) that can be recognized by a computer.

bug a fault in a program. This may be minor (requiring a key to be pressed twice) or major (causing a program to 'crash').

bulletin board a computer-linked database for holding messages and information.

byte a unit of measurement for computer memory capacity. A byte usually contains eight bits. Each byte corresponds to one character of data: a single letter, number or symbol.

C a third-generation language of great power and flexibility. An object-orientated version called C++ is also available. Criticized on the grounds of obscurity ('a read-only language'), C is widely used for writing other programs.

CD-ROM a CD-type of disk that can be read by a conventional laser reader. It contains digital data from computers as distinct from digital representation of sound.

character any symbol (including numbers, letters, punctuation marks, mathematical symbols, etc.) capable of being stored and processed by a computer.

chip or **microchip** a small piece of crystal (usually silicon or other semiconductor material) printed and etched in a pattern to form a logical circuit (an integrated circuit).

circuit the complete path of an electrical current.

clock an electronic circuit that provides electrical pulses at regular intervals to produce timing for the microprocessor actions. Clock rates of 16 MHz (16 million pulses per second) are common.

clone a close copy of a machine that will run the same software. Only the PC type of machine has been extensively cloned.

COBOL acronym for Common Business Orientated Language, the first (and main) language intended for writing data-processing programs for business use.

compiler a program that will convert the statements (commands) of a programming language into machine code that can be run in one step.

conductor a substance (such as a metal) that enables the passage of electricity.

crash a total program failure. This may result in the loss of all data held in memory.

cursor a small block or arrow on the computer screen to show the position of where the next keyed instruction will be implemented.

data raw material such as characters or symbols stored in a computer from which 'information' is derived after processing.

database a structured collection of data that can be analysed and interrogated on computer to retrieve items (or combinations of items) that match selected criteria.

digital computer a computer that deals with data in binary-coded number form as distinct from the variable-voltage signals used in analogue computers.

disk a magnetic disk for storing data. See floppy disk, hard disk.

dot-matrix the method of representing characters by a set of dots either on the VDU screen or on paper when a dot-matrix printer is used.

electronic mail information directed to specific users' screens or held in 'computer mailboxes' for access by users who type in codes. Information held on a bulletin board (see above) can be accessed by any user.

fibre optics the use of thin glass fibres to carry light signals. This is now replacing the use of copper cable carrying electronic signals. Digital computers can use any medium that represents on and off signals; light is faster than electric current, and fibre optic cables can carry a far greater density of signals than can the equivalent size of electric cable.

fifth-generation language a computer language that involves the ability to make decisions and to learn. A computer using a fifth-generation language is addressed in normal language rather than in a programming language.

floppy disk a magnetic data-storage disk that is removable from the medium. Early disks were contained in cardboard envelopes and were floppy, but later versions use rigid plastic containers. Floppy disks operate at lower speeds and can handle less data than hard disks.

FORTRAN acronym for Formula Translation, one of the first programming languages for scientific and engineering uses.

fourth-generation language a computer language that requires no description of procedures, only a list of data and what is needed to be processed. The output of a 4GL is generally a set of commands in a third-generation language, usually Pascal or C.

hacker (originally) a skilled mender of faulty programs. The term now refers to a person who gains illegal access to other computers either mischievously or for criminal intent.

hard disk a magnetic data-storage disk that is not removable from the medium (except on mainframe machines). It operates at much higher speeds and with much greater amounts of data than the removable (floppy) disks.

hardware all the electronics and mechanical parts of the computer as distinct from the programs and data (the software).

hard-wired restricted functioning of a computer, limited by soldered connections and not responsive to varying software commands.

ikon a screen picture that represents a standard computer function. A typical example would be an onscreen 'wastebasket' to which a user can point to delete a file.

ink-jet a form of printer mechanism in which ink is squirted from a matrix or tiny jets on to the paper.

integrated circuit see chip.

interface an electronic circuit that converts electronic signals from one form to another or organizes the signals differently. An interface is needed to allow the computer to be connected to any other piece of equipment, including the disk system and the screen.

interpreter a program that allows the statements of a programming language to be run line-by-line.

K symbol for kilobyte.

keying in typing at a computer keyboard.

kilobyte (K) loosely one thousand bytes, although strictly 1 K = 2^{10} = 1024 bytes.

laptop a portable computer that can be battery-operated and is light enough to be used on the lap while travelling.

laser disk a disk – like an audio CD – capable of storing vast quantities of archive files in a minute area. It is prepared by focusing a narrow beam of light on to it. Its main use is archive storage of data (CD-ROM), but it can be used interactively (CDI).

machine-code the most elementary way of programming a computer by using binary codes directly.

mainframe a large computer whose stored data may be accessed by 100 or more terminals.

megabyte (Mb) loosely one million bytes, although strictly 1 Mb = 2^{20}.

memory usually refers to the currently accessible store (RAM). The term is sometimes used to refer to disk storage capabilities.

microchip see chip.

microprocessor a device capable of holding memory and instructions. A microprocessor is a basic unit of a microcomputer.

microcomputer a low-cost, independent computer unit based on the microprocessor. It requires low power and, unless linked to a network, has a limited memory.

minicomputer a small computer whose capabilities in speed, power and data handling are between those of a microcomputer and a mainframe. Minicomputers were developed during the American space research programme to meet the need for a small computer that could be moved on site.

modem a circuit that converts between digital signals and tone signals. It is used when computers need to communicate along telephone lines or radio links.

monitor see screen.

mouse a hand-held device that rolls across a table or board, its position reflecting the position of the cursor on the screen. It is used as an alternative to the computer keyboard to access a screen.

MS-DOS see operating system.

network a system of computers connected to each other through cables, by telephone, data communication technology or even by radio.

OCCAM a language developed specially for programming parallel-processing computers.

operating system a program that attends to all the routine tasks of running a computer, allowing other programs (applications programs) to make use of the disks, screen and keyboard, etc., without needing to write their own code for such operations. PC machines all use the MS-DOS operating system; many minicomputers use a system called UNIX (which requires vast amounts of memory). Mainframe machines normally use operating systems that are provided by the manufacturer.

parallel-processor a microprocessor that can be run in conjunction with another, sharing memory and other parts of a computer system. One common example is the use of a mathematical co-processor along with the main processor in PC machines. A more complex type is the transputer.

PASCAL a programming language originally designed for academic uses by Niklaus Wirth, but now widely used for systems programming, particularly in the form of Turbo-pascal from Borland International.

port a form of interface used to connect a computer to other units such as the keyboard, printer or modem.

portable language any programming language for which a program can be written that will work on all computers for which a compiler or interpreter is available without modification to the program.

processor the central unit of a computer that carries out the actions of arithmetic and comparison. It controls all of the other units under the command of a program.

program a set of instructions that a system follows to carry out tasks.

Prestel the British Telecom videotext information service, designed to be received on home television sets and computers. The communications are carried on public telephone lines.

PROM Programmable Read-Only Memory. A chip that can be written by larger-than-normal signals and then used as a ROM, retaining its data. Data is erased by, for example, exposing the chip to ultra-violet light.

RAM Random Access Memory, memory available for current work. This is lost when the computer is switched off unless work is transferred out of the RAM on to permanent store such as a disk.

register a temporary store used in a processor to hold data while it is being used in arithmetic, logical or comparison actions.

relay switches switches controlled electromagnetically. They are typically used in analogue computers.

resistor a substance impeding the flow of a current.

ROM Read-Only Memory, a non-volatile memory (i.e. a memory that is not erased when the power is switched off) that must be present in any computer in order to make the machine usable. The ROM normally contains the commands that allow the machine to make use of its disk system so that further commands (of an operating system) can be read in.

scanner a device that transforms an image into digitally coded signals that can be stored on computer and redisplayed. Using scanners, printed text can be stored directly on to the disk without having to be keyed in.

screen the display device on a computer – also called a monitor, VDU (visual display unit) or VDT (visual display terminal). Screens basically use cathode-ray tube technology of television to create an image.

semiconductor a material, such as silicon, whose pure form has very low electrical conductivity but whose conductivity is enormously changed when traces of other elements are added – a process called *doping*. The movement of particles within the semiconductor allows its electrical conduction to be controlled by electrical signals, making it an electrically-operated switch.

silicon chip see chip, semiconductor.

software the programs that give instructions to, or run on, a computer, as opposed to the electronics and mechanical parts of a computer (the hardware).

spreadsheet a form of data-analysing program that can be used for a very wide range of applications ranging from word tables to the analysis of complex mathematical relationships. In this latter use, altering one item of data on the screen will result in the recalculation of all the other items that depend on that item. Spreadsheets are widely used for financial data and particularly in forecasting work.

terminal a device linked to a computer, comprising a keyboard or a screen, or both.

thermionic valve a device that uses metal plates to control the flow of electrons in a vacuum inside an evacuated tube. The electrons are emitted from a hot surface – the cathode – and the current between the cathode and the opposite surface – the anode – is controlled by the voltage on an intermediate grid. Thermionic valves were formerly used for electronics circuits before the invention of transistors.

transistor a device that transfers current across a resistor.

transputer a large, fast and powerful chip. When paired with another chip it enables a computer to carry out two tasks simultaneously.

Turing test a test for successful artificial intelligence that depends on a human not knowing that he or she is communicating with a computer. No computer has ever passed the Turing test.

UNIX see operating system.

user-friendly (of computer products) simple and easy-to-use.

vacuum tube the American name for the thermionic valve.

VDT see screen.

VDU see screen.

voice recognition a computer's ability to respond to spoken words.

volatile (of memory) losing all data when the power is disconnected. RAM in computers is generally volatile, making it important to save data to a backing store.

window a portion of a screen that is used as if it were an independent separate screen.

workstation the equipment used by a computer operator and, increasingly, the associated furniture, lighting and working environment.

WORM acronym for Write Once Read Many times – a form of optical disk that can be written as well as read by the computer using it.

PHYSICS GLOSSARY

A symbol for ampere.

Å symbol for Ångström.

Ar symbol for atomic weight.

absolute zero the lowest temperature theoretically possible, at which the random motion of the particles in a system is zero. It is equal to $-273 \cdot 15\,°C$ $= 0\,K = -459 \cdot 67\,°F$.

absorption spectrum a characteristic pattern of dark bands that appears in the spectrum – due to the absorption of light – when light of a continuous frequency passes through a medium into a spectroscope. The medium will absorb the wavelengths that it would normally emit if it were raised to a high enough temperature, i.e. the absorbed radiation excites atoms from the ground state to an excited state.

acceleration the rate of increase of velocity with time.

accelerator a large machine in which an electric field is used to increase the kinetic energy of charged particles such as electrons and protons by accelerating them. The stream of accelerated particles is guided into the desired path by a magnetic field.

acoustics the study and use of sound waves.

alpha (α) particle a helium nucleus that consists of two protons and two neutrons. It carries a positive charge.

alpha rays a stream of alpha particles, emitted by many radioactive substances. The alpha particles can be stopped by a piece of paper, i.e. they have a very low penetrating power.

alternating current an electric current that regularly reverses its direction in a circuit.

ammeter an instrument for measuring electric current.

amp or **ampere** (symbol A) the unit of electric current.

Ångström (symbol Å) 0.1 nanometre (= 10^{-10} m).

anion a negatively charged ion.

anode a positive electrode.

antimatter matter consisting of antiparticles, i.e. those with opposite charge but equal mass to their normal counterparts. For example, the antiparticle of an electron (negatively charged particle) is a positron (a positively charged particle). When a particle meets an antiparticle there is mutual annihilation. Anti-matter has never actually been detected but is theoretically necessary.

Archimedes' principle states that a body floating in a fluid displaces a weight of fluid equal to its own weight.

atom the smallest particle of a pure element that can take part in a chemical reaction.

atomic mass unit (symbol u) one-twelfth of the mass of a carbon-12 atom, which is approximately the mass of a proton or neutron.

atomic number (symbol Z) the number of protons in the nucleus of an atom of an element.

atomic weight (symbol A_r) the average mass of atoms in an element, in atomic mass units.

Avogadro's hypothesis states that equal volumes of all gases measured at the same temperature and pressure contain the same number of molecules.

background radiation low-intensity radiation resulting from bombardment of the earth by cosmic rays and from naturally occurring isotopes in soil, air, buildings, etc.

bar a unit of pressure equal to 10^5 pascals. The millibar (1/1000 bar) is used by meteorologists.

barometer a device for measuring atmospheric pressure.

becquerel (symbol Bq) the unit of radioactivity equal to one disintegration per second.

Becquerel rays alpha, beta and gamma rays emitted by uranium compounds.

beta (β) particle an electron emitted by a radioisotope during beta decay.

beta rays a stream of beta particles, emitted by nuclei of certain radioisotopes. They can penetrate thin metal foil.

betatron an accelerator producing high-energy electrons. They are accelerated by means of magnetic induction.

black body a body that absorbs all radiation falling on it.

boiling point the temperature at which the saturated vapour pressure of a liquid equals the external pressure.

boson a subatomic particle with symmetric wavefunction.

breeder reactor a nuclear reactor in which more fissile material is produced than is used.

Brownian movement the irregular movement of smoke particles, or of very small particles, e.g. pollen, in a liquid. The movement is due to molecular bombardment by moving molecules.

c the velocity of light in a vacuum, equal to 2.99792458×10^8 m s^{-1} (approximately 300 000 km or 186 000 miles per second).

C symbol for capacitance.

calorimeter a device in which thermal measurements can be made.

candela (symbol cf) the unit of luminous intensity.

capacitance (symbol C) the ability of an isolated electrical conductor to store electrical charge.

capacitor a device containing one or more pairs of electrical conductors separated by insulators (the dielectric). It is used to store electrical charge.

capillarity the effect of surface tension on a liquid in a fine tube, causing the liquid to rise or fall in the tube.

cathode a negative electrode.

cathode ray tube a device used in TV sets, VDUs, etc. Electrons from a heated cathode are projected on to a phosphor screen. The intensity and movement of the electron beam can be controlled, and the phosphor screen converts the kinetic energy of the electrons into a bright spot of light.

Celsius scale the official name of the Centigrade temperature scale. The freezing point of water at normal atmospheric pressure is 0 °C, and the boiling point 100 °C (see p. 126).

centrifugal force the inertial force directed radially outwards, in equilibrium with the applied centripetal force.

cf symbol for candela.

centripetal force a lateral force that makes a body move in a circular path. It is directed towards the centre of the circle.

CGS the system of units based on the centimetre, gram and second. It has now been superseded by the more coherent SI system.

charge (symbol Q) the ability of some elementary particles, such as electrons and protons, to exert forces on one another. Like forces repel, unlike forces attract.

Ci symbol for curie.

concave curving inwards. Concave mirrors converge rays of light, concave lenses diverge them.

conductor any substance (such as a metal) that offers a relatively low resistance to an electric current. (See insulator.)

conservation of mass and energy the principle that, in any system, the sum of the mass and energy is always constant.

conservation of momentum the principle that, in any system, the linear or angular momentum remains the same unless there is an external force acting on the system.

convection the transfer of heat in a fluid by movement of the fluid.

convex curving outwards. A convex mirror diverges rays of light, a convex lens converges them.

cosmic rays particle radiation reaching the earth from space.

cryogenics the study and production of very low temperatures.

curie (symbol Ci) the former unit of activity of a radioactive substance. It corresponds to 3.7×10^{10} disintegrations per second, and is about equal to the activity of 1 g of radium.

current (symbol I) the rate of flow of electricity. The unit is the ampere.

cyclotron an accelerator in which the beam of charged particles follows a spiral path.

decay the breakdown of a radioactive nuclide into a daughter product by disintegration.

decibel one-tenth of a bel. (A bel is a logarithmic unit for comparing two amounts of power.) One decibel represents an increase in intensity of about 26 per cent – about the smallest increase that the ear can detect. (The decibel is *not* a measure of loudness, as the sensitivity of the ear varies with frequency.)

densitometer an instrument for measuring the density of a substance.

density (symbol r) the mass per unit volume of a substance, usually measured in kilograms per cubic metre.

dielectric an insulator that has very low electrical conductivity.

diffraction the phenomenon of waves appearing to travel round corners. It occurs when a wavefront meets a narrow slit or obstacle.

diffractometer an instrument used to measure the intensities of diffracted X-rays or neutron beams at different angles to each other.

diffusion the process by which substances – atoms, molecules, or groups of molecules – mix due to the kinetic motions of the particles.

diode an electronic device with only two electrodes.

direct current an electric current that flows in one direction only and is reasonably constant in magnitude.

discharge the passage of electric current through a gas-discharge tube, usually with luminous effects.

disintegration the emission of particles by a nucleus, either after a collision or spontaneously.

dispersion the process by which a beam of white light is spread out to produce spectra.

Döppler effect the apparent change in frequency of a harmonic wave (e.g. light or sound) when there is relative motion along a line between the source and the observer.

dynamo a machine that converts mechanical energy into electrical energy; a generator.

e the charge on an electron.

earth a connection between an electrical circuit and the earth, which has an electronic potential of zero.

efficiency (symbol *h*) the ratio of the useful energy output of a machine to the energy input. A perfect machine would have an efficiency of 1.

Einstein's law ($E = mc^2$) the law of equivalence of mass and energy, whereby the product of a mass *m* and the square of the speed of light *c* has energy *E*, and vice versa.

elasticity the ability of a substance to return to its original size and shape after being deformed.

electric field strength (symbol *E*) the strength of an electric field at a given point, measured in volts per metre.

electric flux (symbol *c*) the quantity of electricity displaced across a given area in a dielectric, measured in coulombs.

electric potential (symbol *V*) the work done in bringing a unit positive charge from infinity to a point. (See also potential difference.)

electrolyte a substance that conducts electricity in solution because of the presence of ions.

electron a negatively charged elementary particle, found spinning around the nuclei of atoms. As free electrons they are responsible for electrical conduction.

electronics the study and use of electricity in semiconductors.

electronvolt (symbol eV) the energy acquired by an electron in falling freely through a potential difference of 1 volt.

elementary particle any particle of matter that cannot be subdivided into smaller particles.

energy (symbol *E*) a measure of the capacity of a system to do work, measured in joules.

enthalpy (symbol *H*) the thermodynamic function of a system equal to the sum of its internal energy and the product of its pressure and volume.

entropy (symbol *S*) the disorder of a system. The greater the disorder of a system, the greater the entropy.

evaporation the conversion of a liquid to a vapour at a temperature below the boiling point.

Fahrenheit scale temperature scale on which the freezing point of water at normal atmospheric pressure is 32 °F, and the boiling point 212 °F (see p. 126).

fallout radioactive material that falls to earth after a nuclear explosion.

farad (symbol F) the unit of capacitance, in which a charge of 1 coulomb is acquired when 1 volt is applied.

fermion a particle with anti-symmetric wave function.

ferromagnetism the phenomenon by which certain solids (e.g. iron, cobalt, nickel) can be magnetized by weak magnetic fields.

fibre optics the study and use of the transmission of light by very fine flexible glass rods.

fission a type of nuclear reaction in which a heavy nucleus is split into two or more fragments, normally accompanied by the emission of neutrons or gamma rays.

fluid a liquid or gas.

fluidics the study and use of jets of fluid in circuits to perform tasks usually carried out by electronic circuits.

fluorescence the emission of light or radiation. When electromagnetic radiation, e.g. X-rays, ultra-violet light, etc., strikes a fluorescent substance, radiation of a longer wavelength, e.g. visible light, is emitted.

flux the strength of a field of force through a specified area.

force (symbol *F*) any action that tends to alter a body's state of rest or uniform motion.

free fall the downward motion in a gravitational field, unimpeded by any buoyancy effects.

freezing point the temperature at which both the solid and liquid phases of a substance can exist in equilibrium, e.g. the temperature at which water freezes and ice melts.

frequency (symbol *v* or *f*) the number of complete cycles or oscillations that occur in a unit of time, normally measured in hertz.

fusion (1) the change of state from liquid to solid at the melting point. (2) **nuclear fusion** type of nuclear reaction in which light atomic nuclei combine to form a heavier atomic nucleus with the release of energy (see fission).

g the symbol for the acceleration due to free fall. On the earth it is approximately $9·81 \text{ m s}^{-2}$.

gain the efficiency of an electronic system.

galvanometer an instrument for measuring or detecting electrical currents.

gamma (γ) rays electromagnetic radiation emitted by certain radioactive substances. Gamma rays can penetrate much greater distances than alpha and beta rays, and form the extreme short-wave end of the electromagnetic spectrum.

Geiger counter a device for detecting ionizing radiation, especially alpha particles. Because a Geiger counter can count the particles it can measure the strength of radioactivity.

gravitation the attraction that all bodies have for one another.

gray the unit for the absorbed dose.

h the symbol for Planck's constant.

hadron a subatomic particle that interacts through the strong force. It is made up of quarks.

half-life the time in which a radioactive substance decays to half its original quantity or half its original activity.

harmonic a simple multiple of a fundamental frequency.

heat the form of energy transferred between bodies as a result of differences in their temperature.

heat pump a device for extracting heat from large quantities of a substance, e.g. water, air, at a low temperature and supplying it at a higher temperature, e.g. to a building.

hertz (symbol Hz) the unit of frequency, equal to 1 cycle or oscillation per second.

holography a laser technique for producing stereoscopic images without cameras.

hydrodynamics the study and use of the motion of fluids.

hysteresis the lagging of an effect behind the cause when the cause varies in amount, e.g. magnetic induction lagging behind an applied cycle of magnetic changes.

Hz symbol for hertz.

I symbol for current.

ice point the temperature at which ice and water are in equilibrium at standard pressure.

induction the process by which electricity is passed from one circuit to another without the need for physical contact between them. When an electrical conductor is moved so that it cuts the flux of a magnetic field, a potential difference is induced between the ends of the conductor. This is the basis of the way dynamos generate electricity.

inertia the tendency for a body to remain at rest or in a state of uniform motion in a straight line.

infrared rays electromagnetic radiation (heat) emitted by hot bodies. It consists of radiation of longer wavelengths than the red end of the visible spectrum.

insulator any substance (such as rubber, plastic, ceramic) that offers a high resistance to electric current. (See conductor).

integrated circuit a complete circuit in a single package, usually in or on a single chip of silicon.

interference the combination of two or more coherent waves from different sources by which areas of minimum and maximum intensity occur where the waves are superimposed on each other.

ion an atom, group of atoms, molecule or group of molecules that is electrically charged by the presence or absence of one or more electrons than normal.

isobar a line joining places with the same atmospheric pressure.

isotopes atoms of an element having the same number of protons but different numbers of neutrons.

joule (symbol J) the unit of energy or work; the work done by a constant force of 1 newton when moving an object 1 metre in the direction of the applied force.

kelvin (symbol K) the unit of thermodynamic temperature, equivalent to 1 °C.

kinetic energy (symbol T) the energy possessed by virtue of a body's motion.

laminar flow a steady flow in which a fluid moves in parallel layers (laminae), although the velocities of the fluid particles in each lamina are not necessarily equal.

laser (abbreviation for Light Amplification by Stimulated Emission of Radiation) a source of intense coherent radiation of a single wavelength in the infrared, visible and ultraviolet regions of the spectrum.

latent heat the quantity of heat released or absorbed when a substance changes phase at a fixed temperature.

lattice a regularly repeated three-dimensional array of points that determines the positions of atoms or molecules in a crystalline structure.

lens a piece of transparent material, bounded by two regularly curved surfaces and designed to focus light to a fixed point (see also concave, convex).

lepton a subatomic particle that interacts through the weak or electromagnetic interaction.

light a narrow section of the electromagnetic spectrum that is visible to the human eye.

longitudinal waves waves in which displacement of the transmitting medium is in the same plane as the direction of travel, e.g. sound waves.

lumen (symbol lm) the unit of luminous flux, i.e. the rate of flow of radiant energy.

lux (symbol lx) the unit of illumination.

machine a device for doing work, in which a small effort is used to overcome a larger force or load.

Mach number (symbol M) the ratio of the relative velocity of a body in a fluid to the velocity of sound in the fluid. Mach 1 thus indicates the speed of sound.

magnetic bottle an arrangement of magnetic fields designed to contain a plasma.

magnetic field a field of force containing magnetic flux.

magnetism attractive and repulsive forces due to the motion of electrons around the atoms in a substance.

magnifying power the ratio of the size of an image produced by an instrument to the size of the image as seen by the naked eye.

maser (abbreviation for Microwave Amplification by Stimulated Emission of Radiation) the microwave equivalent of a laser.

mass the quantity of matter in a body; the reluctance of a body to accelerate when acted on by a force. It is measured in kilograms in the SI system (see p. 197).

mass number (symbol A) the number of nucleons in a nucleus.

mass spectrometer an instrument for measuring atomic masses of elements that can be formed into a beam of ions.

mechanics the study of motion and the equilibrium of bodies.

metrology the study of the accurate measurement of mass, length and time.

microscope an instrument, containing converging lenses, that produces an enlarged image of small objects.

microwaves electromagnetic waves with a wavelength between infrared radiation and radio waves.

mm HG (abbreviation for millimetres of mercury) a unit of pressure measured by the height in mm of a column of mercury supported by the pressure.

mole (symbol mol) the amount of substance that contains the same number of elementary entities (molecules, ions, atoms, etc.) as there are in 0·012 kg of carbon-12.

moment a turning effect, equal to the magnitude of the force and the perpendicular distance from the line of action of the force to the axis.

momentum (symbol p) the product of the mass and the velocity of a body.

monochromatic radiation radiation of one wavelength or of a very narrow band of wavelengths.

motor a machine that converts electrical energy into mechanical energy.

neutrino a lepton with little or no rest mass and zero electric charge.

neutron a constituent of the atomic nucleus, with zero charge and about the same mass as the proton.

neutron number (symbol N) the number of neutrons present in the nucleus of an atom.

neutron star a massive star consisting largely of neutrons.

newton (symbol N) the unit of force that gives a mass of 1 kilogram an acceleration of 1 metre per second per second.

Newton's laws see p. 202.

Newton's rings circular interference fringes formed between a lens and a glass plate with which the lens is in contact.

NTP abbreviation for normal temperature and pressure.

nuclear fusion see fusion.

nuclear isomers nuclei with the same mass number and atomic number but different radioactive properties.

nuclear magnetic resonance an effect observed when radio-frequency radiation is absorbed by matter. It is due to the spin of atomic nuclei developing characteristic magnetic moments. The effect is exploited in, for example, medical imaging devices.

nucleon the collective name for the constituents of the atomic nucleus, i.e. protons and neutrons.

nucleus the most massive part of an atom, consisting of neutrons and protons held together by binding forces.

ohm (symbol Ω) the unit of resistance; the resistance between two points if an applied potential difference of 1 volt produces a current of 1 amp.

optics the study and use of light.

orbit a curved path described, for example, by a planet or comet around the sun or a particle such as an electron in a field of force such as that encountered around an atomic nucleus.

oscillation a vibration (i.e. a movement backwards and forwards between two points) with a regular frequency.

osmosis the use of a semipermeable membrane that allows certain kinds of molecule in a liquid to pass through it but that prevents the passage of other molecules.

parallax the apparent displacement of an object caused by an actual change of point of observation.

parity (symbol P) a physical property characterized by the behaviour of wave functions when reflected. Parity invariance states that no distinction can be made between laws of physics for a right-handed system of coordinates and for a left-handed system of coordinates.

pascal (symbol Pa) the unit of pressure; the pressure resulting from 1 newton acting uniformly over 1 m².

Pascal's principle states that pressure applied at any point to a fluid at rest is transmitted without loss to all other parts of the fluid.

Pauli exclusion principle states that no two fermions can exist in identical quantum states, e.g. no two electrons in an atom can have the same quantum number.

pendulum a mass suspended from a fixed point that oscillates with a known and fixed period.

period (symbol T) the time occupied by one complete vibration or oscillation.

permeability (symbol m) the ratio of magnetic flux density in a body to the external magnetic field strength inducing it.

phase (1) the proportion of a period that has elapsed, taken from a fixed point in the cycle. (2) any of three physical states – solid, liquid, gas – in which a substance can exist.

photoemission the release or emission of electrons due to bombardment of the substance by electromagnetic radiation, e.g. light.

piezoelectric effect the production of an electrical potential difference across a piece of crystal, e.g. quartz, when subjected to pressure.

pitch the frequency of a sound.

Planck's constant a universal constant equal to the energy of any quantum of radiation divided by its frequency: $h = 6.626 \times 10^{-34}$ J s.

Planck's law states that electromagnetic radiation consists of small indivisible packets called photons or quanta whose energy equals hf, where h is Planck's constant and f is the frequency of the radiation.

plasma a gas of positive ions and free electrons with roughly equal positive and negative charges.

polarization the restriction of particle displacement to a single plane. It can only occur in transverse waves, e.g. electromagnetic radiation.

pole a point towards which lines of magnetic flux converge.

positron a positive electron, the antiparticle of the electron.

potential difference the difference in electric potential between two points in an electric field. The potential difference between two points is the work done per coulomb of positive electrical charge taken from one point to the other, measured in volts.

power (symbol P) the work done per second, measured in watts.

pressure (symbol p) the force per unit area, measured in pascals.

prism a refracting substance, such as glass, with two plane intersecting surfaces. It deviates a beam of light and disperses it into its constituent colours.

proton a positively charged elementary particle with about 1836 times the mass of an electron (which is negatively charged) and the same mass as a neutron (which has no charge). With the exception of hydrogen, all atomic nuclei contain protons and neutrons; the hydrogen nucleus consists solely of one proton.

Q symbol for charge.

quantum mechanics a mathematical physical theory based on Planck's quantum theory and the probability of finding an elementary particle at any particular point.

quantum theory the theory based on Planck's idea of discrete quanta of electromagnetic radiation.

quark a fundamental constituent of hadrons.

r symbol for density.

rad the former unit of absorbed radiation, equal to 0.01 joule per kilogram of absorbing material.

radiation any energy propagated as rays, streams of particles or waves.

radioactivity the spontaneous disintegration of the nuclei of some isotopes in certain elements, with the emission of alpha or beta particles, sometimes together with gamma rays.

radiopaque the property of being opaque to radiation, especially gamma rays and X-rays, e.g. bones are radiopaque to X-rays but other body tissues are not.

radio waves electromagnetic radiation of radio frequency.

rectifier an electrical device that allows current to flow in only one direction and thus converts alternating to direct current.

reflection the process by which some of the light or sound striking a surface between two different media is thrown back into the original medium.

refraction the change of direction a ray of light or

sound wave undergoes when it passes from one medium to another.

relativity a theory developed by Einstein, confirming the unification of mass and energy, the former being a 'congealed' form of the latter.

resistance (symbol R) the ratio between the potential difference across a conductor and the current passing through it, measured in ohms.

resistivity (symbol r) the resistance per unit length of unit cross-sectional area of a conductor, measured in ohm-metres.

resonance the maximum response that occurs when a driving frequency applied to a system is equal to the natural frequency of the system.

rheology the study and use of the deformation and flow of matter.

saturated vapour a vapour in dynamic equilibrium with its liquid at a given temperature. Saturated vapour can hold no more substance in the gaseous phase at that temperature.

scalar a quantity – such as speed – that has magnitude but not direction (see vector).

scattering the deflection of radiation by interaction with nuclei or electrons, the deflection of sound waves by a reflecting surface, or the deflection of light waves by fine particles.

Schrödinger wave equation the basic equation of wave mechanics. It shows the behaviour of a particle moving in force field.

scintillation the emission of small flashes of light when radiation strikes certain substances.

second (symbol s) the basic SI unit of time.

semiconductor a substance – such as silicon or germanium – with a resistivity between that of conductors and insulators. Junctions between semiconductors form the basis of the modern electronics industry.

semipermeable membrane a membrane that allows the passage of certain molecules in a fluid while preventing the passage of other molecules (see osmosis).

shell any of various energy states in which electrons move round the atomic nucleus.

simple harmonic motion the periodic motion of a body subjected to a restoring force proportional to the displacement from the centre. The period of oscillation is independent of amplitude and the displacement varies sinusoidally with time.

sinusoidal the condition of having a waveform the same as that of a sine function.

SI (abbreviation for *Système International d'Unités*) an internationally agreed coherent system of units based on the metre, kilogram and second (see p. 197).

Snell's law see Wave Theory.

solenoid a coil of wire with a greater length than diameter. When an electric current is passed through the wire it forms an electromagnet.

specific (when applied to an extensive physical property) a restriction on the meaning of 'per unit mass' of the substance.

spectrometer an instrument for producing, recording or examining a spectrum of radiation.

spectrum a distribution of electromagnetic radiation. It is usually applied to the visible display of colours, but can be applied to any part of the range of electromagnetic radiation.

speed the rate of increase of distance travelled with time.

standard atmosphere (symbol atm) a unit of pressure equal to 101 325 pascals.

standard temperature and pressure a standard condition for the reduction of gas pressures and temperatures. It is equal to 0 °C and 101 325 pascals.

steam point the temperature at which the liquid and vapour phases of water are in equilibrium at standard pressure, i.e. 100 °C.

strain the change of shape and/or volume of a body due to applied forces.

strange particle a subatomic particle with an exceptionally long lifetime.

stress forces in equilibrium acting on a body and tending to produce strain.

superconductivity the property of a substance that has virtually no electrical resistance at a low temperature. When many metals and alloys are cooled to near absolute zero (0 K, –273 °C), their electrical resistance almost vanishes.

supercooling the slow and continuous cooling of liquids to below their normal freezing point.

superfluid a fluid, at a very low temperature, that has very high thermal conductivity and can flow through very fine channels without friction.

telescope an instrument for producing a magnified or intensified image of a distant object. Optical telescopes use lenses or lenses and mirrors; radio telescopes use electronic circuitry to amplify radio signals from distant sources.

temperature (symbol T) the hotness of a body that determines which direction heat flows when the body is in contact with other bodies.

thermodynamics the study and use of the inter-relationships between heat and other forms of energy.

tone the quality of a musical sound, caused by the presence of harmonics.

transducer a device for converting a non-electrical variable into a proportionately variable electrical signal.

transformer a device, consisting of two electrical circuits magnetically coupled together, that either steps up voltage and steps down current, or vice versa.

transistor a semiconductor device in which a small base current or voltage can control or modulate a larger collector current or voltage.

transverse waves waves in which displacement of the transmitting medium is perpendicular to the direction of travel, e.g. electromagnetic waves.

tribology the study of friction, lubrication and wear of surfaces.

triple point the temperature at which, for any substance, the three physical states of the substance can exist at equilibrium. For water this occurs at 0.01 °C and b10Pa.

u symbol for atomic mass unit.

ultrasonics the study and use of frequencies beyond the limits of human hearing, i.e. above about 20 kHz.

ultraviolet radiation electromagnetic radiation lying beyond the violet end of the visible spectrum and before the X-ray region.

unified field theory a theory – yet to be developed – that seeks to link together the properties of gravitational, nuclear and electromagnetic fields.

vacuum a space or vessel devoid of matter or from

which all air has been removed.

valence electrons those electrons in the outermost shell of an atom that are involved in chemical changes.

vapour a substance in gaseous form but below its critical temperature. It can thus be liquefied merely by pressure, without the need for cooling.

vector a quantity – such as velocity – that has direction as well as magnitude (see scalar).

velocity (symbol v) the rate of increase of distance travelled by a body in a particular direction.

viscosity the ability of fluids to offer resistance to flow.

visible spectrum visible electromagnetic radiation between 380 and 780 nm.

volt (symbol V) the potential difference between two points such that 1 joule of work is done by every coulomb of positive charge moved from one point to the other.

watt (symbol W) the unit of power resulting from the dissipation of 1 joule in 1 second.

wave a curve of an alternating quantity plotted against time, giving rise to a disturbance travelling through a medium.

wavelength (symbol l) the distance between one vibrating particle in a wave train and the next particle that is vibrating in the same phase.

wave mechanics a form of quantum mechanics.

weight the pull of gravity on a body, measured in newtons (see mass).

work (symbol w or W) a transfer of energy. Work is carried out when a force moves its point of application. It is measured in joules (1 joule = 1 newton moved through 1 metre).

X-rays electromagnetic radiation lying between ultraviolet radiation and gamma rays.

Z symbol for atomic number.

PHYSICAL EXTREMES

Highest temperature

The highest temperatures are those produced at the centres of thermonuclear fusion explosions, namely of the order of 4000 000 000° C. This temperature was attained in 1990 under controlled experimental conditions in the Tokamak Fusion Test Reactor at the Princetown Plasma Physics Laboratory, New Jersey (USA) by deuterium injection into a deuterium plasma.

Lowest temperature

The absolute zero of temperature, namely 0 K on the Kelvin scale, corresponds to -273.15° C (-459.67° F). The lowest temperature reached is 2×10^{-9}, i.e. two billionths of a degree above absolute zero, achieved at the Low Temperature Laboratory, Helsinki University of Technology (Finland) in a nuclear demagnetization device and announced in October 1989.

Highest pressure

A sustained laboratory pressure of 1.70 megabars (170 GPa / 11 000 tons force/in²), was reported in June 1978 to have been achieved in the giant hydraulic diamond-faced press at the Carnegie Institution's Geophysical Laboratory, Washington DC (USA).

SCIENTIFIC SOCIETIES

Among the principal national scientific academies, the following are particularly notable:

The *Royal Society* – or in full *The Royal Society of London for the Promotion of Natural Knowledge* – was founded in 1660 and incorporated by Charles II in 1660. It has its origins in the 'Invisible College' of London and Oxford that first met in 1645. The Royal Society awards the following medals for scientific achievement – the annual Copley Medal (the premier award, for physical and biological sciences in alternate years), three annual Royal Medals (including one for applied science), the annual Davy Medal (for chemistry), the annual Hughes Medal (for physical sciences), the biennial Rumford Medal (for optics and thermal science), the biennial Darwin Medal (for biology), the biennial Gabor Medal (for life sciences), the triennial Leverhulme Medal (for physical sciences, chemistry and engineering), the triennial Sylvester Medal (for mathematics), and the quinquennial Buchanan Medal (for medicine). In 1993 there were nearly 1150 fellows of the Royal Society.

The Russian *Academy of Sciences* was originally founded in 1724 by Peter the Great to study the development of Siberia. As the Academy of Sciences of the USSR (from 1925 to 1991), it was responsible for all scientific activity in the former Soviet Union. Organized into 17 sections on the basis of subject, the Academy is responsible for the university town of Akademgorodok, in the suburbs of the Siberian city of Novosibirsk, where some 40 institutes – with a total staff of about 12 000, including about one third of the Academy's 330 members – are situated.

The French *Académie des Sciences* was founded in 1666 by Jean-Baptiste Colbert to formalize meetings by French scientists including Pascal and Descartes that had begun in 1662. The Academy was reformed in 1976. It has 130 academicians (plus 80 foreign associates) and 160 correspondents. Its studies are organized into two divisions – mathematical and physical sciences, and chemical and natural sciences. Since 1721 the Academy has awarded a number of prestigious prizes in various fields of science.

The *Royal Swedish Academy of Sciences* – founded in 1739 – awards the Nobel Prizes of chemistry, physics and economic sciences, and the Crafoord Prizes of astronomy, biology, geography, geophysics and mathematics. The Academy has about 300 Swedish members and 150 foreign members.

The American *National Academy of Sciences* was established by the US Congress in Washington DC in 1863 as a nongovernmental scientific organization responsible for advising the US government on all matters scientific and technological. The National Research Council, which was founded by the Academy in 1916, coordinates the scientific activities of American industries, universities and the government. The National Academy of Engineering and the Institute of Medicine are associated organizations.

Germany has several prestigious scientific academies rather than a single national body. These include the (Berlin, formerly Prussian) Academy of Sciences (founded 1700), the Saxon Academy of Sciences of Leipzig (founded 1849), the Academy of Sciences of Göttingen (founded 1751), the Bavarian Academy of Sciences (founded 1759) and the Heidelberg Academy of Sciences (founded 1763).

TECHNOLOGY

TECHNOLOGY AND INDUSTRY

AIRCRAFT

The term 'aircraft' includes every man-made device that flies in the atmosphere. The most important group of aircraft, called *aerodynes*, are not naturally buoyant but heavier than air. Aerodynes obtain their lift in a variety of ways: by jet thrust; by means of rotating blades; or by means of fixed wings, with a separate propulsion system to make the wings move through the air. A smaller group is the *aerostats*, which are naturally buoyant (lighter than air). Those without power are called balloons (gas-filled or hot-air), while those with propulsion and some means of steering are called airships or dirigibles.

THE PRINCIPLE OF FLIGHT

When the *weight* of an aircraft (due to the force of gravity) is exceeded by the *lift* (the upward force created by the wings or by hot air or lighter-than-air gases), the aircraft will rise in the air. In the case of aeroplanes and gliders, lift is produced as a result of the characteristic profile – the *aerofoil section* – of the wing. The wing is rounded and thicker at the front (the *leading edge*), and tapers away to a sharp edge at the back (the *trailing edge*).

Lift is created as the wings move through the air at speed and relies on the fact that air pressure drops as air speed increases. As air passes over the wing, it has to move further, and thus faster, over the more curved upper surface than the lower surface. This causes a considerable reduction in pressure above the wing, especially at the front, where the wing is thickest and the upper surface most sharply curved. Lift can be increased both by increasing the speed of airflow over the wing and by increasing the curvature of the upper wing surface.

Any aircraft with propulsion also experiences *thrust* – the resultant force pulling or pushing it through the air; and *drag* – the equal and opposite force caused by the resistance of the air to the frontal surfaces of the aircraft. Drag is effectively wasted energy, so the aim of aircraft designers is to reduce drag without sacrificing lift.

Gliders, lacking an independent source of propulsion, have to fly downhill from the moment they are cast off after take-off. The pilot thus seeks columns of rising warmer air, called *thermals*. Modern gliders are so efficient that they have climbed to nearly 15 000 m (49 200 ft) and flown 1460 km (907 mi).

AIRCRAFT STABILITY

In the absence of other forces, an aircraft's centre of gravity would have to be at the same point as its centre of lift for the craft to remain in equilibrium. In practice, however, because of thrust and drag, nearly all aeroplanes are designed to be naturally stable in the longitudinal plane, but with the centre of gravity ahead of the centre of lift. This causes a downward movement of the nose, which is counteracted by a constant download on the horizontal tail. Any disturbance tending to tilt the aircraft nose-up or nose-down is countered automatically by the change in the angle of the wings and of the horizontal tail.

Today, thanks to extremely fast computers, fighter planes can be deliberately made naturally unstable. This has two advantages: instead of a download the tailplane imparts an upload, thus helping the wing instead of fighting it; and as the fighter is always trying to depart from straight flight (restrained by computers that apply restoring forces 40 or more times per second), the aircraft can be made exceptionally agile.

AIRCRAFT CONTROLS

Aeroplanes and gliders are controlled in the longitudinal (*pitch*) axis by *elevators* on the tailplane, or by having a fully powered pivoted tailplane. A few modern designs have a foreplane instead of a tailplane, and a very few have both. Directional control is provided by a vertical *rudder*, which is usually located on the tailplane. The rudder is also an important control surface if a multi-engined aircraft should suffer failure of an engine mounted far out on a wing. Lateral (*roll*) control was formerly provided only by *ailerons* – pivoted portions of the trailing edge near the tips of the wings – but today roll control can be effected by asymmetric use of the tailplanes or by asymmetric deflection of *spoilers*. The spoilers are door-like surfaces hinged along the top of the wing. Differentially they control roll, and symmetrically they serve as airbrakes by increasing drag. Spoilers can also be used in *direct lift control* to enable the aircraft trajectory to be varied up or down without changing the attitude of the fuselage. On landing, spoilers act as 'lift dumpers', instantly killing wing lift and thus increasing the weight on the wheels and the effectiveness of the brakes.

All early aircraft used cables in tension or push/pull pivoted rods to convey pilot commands to the control surfaces. From about 1950 powered controls were widely introduced, in which the surfaces were moved by hydraulic actuators, the pilot's controls being provided with some form of artificial 'feel' so that he could sense what was happening. By 1970 *fly by wire* was rapidly becoming common, in which the pilot's controls send out small electrical signals, which are carried through multiple wires to the surface power units. Today *fly by light* is being introduced: pilot signals are conveyed as variable light output along optical fibres, thus offering colossal bandwidth and data-handling capacity.

THE HIGH-LIFT SYSTEM

An aircraft has to work hardest during take-off and landing, when airspeed is at its lowest and yet maximum lift is required. To facilitate these manoeuvres, most aircraft have a *high-lift system*, brought into action for the approach and landing, and usually also for take-off.

Along the leading edge of the wing there may be *slats*, slender portions of the wing moved out and away on parallel arms, or alternatively *Krüger flaps*, which swing down and around from underneath the leading edge. These full-span devices greatly increase the available lift, especially from a thin wing suitable for fast jets.

Along the trailing edge are fitted *flaps*. These again come in many forms, but all swing back and down from the wing. When selected to a take-off setting, such as 15°, they increase lift and slightly increase drag; when fully down, at the landing setting of perhaps 40°, they increase lift even more but also greatly increase drag.

AIRCRAFT PROPULSION

Until 1939 virtually all aeroplanes were powered by piston engines driving a *propeller*, which provides thrust by accelerating air through aerodynamic rotating blades. Almost all modern propellers are of the variable-pitch type – the angle at which the blades attack the air can be altered. The blades are set to fine pitch for take-off to match high engine speed with low aircraft speed, and then automatically adjusted to coarse pitch for cruising flight, to match economical low engine speed to high forward speed. After landing, some propellers can be set to reverse pitch to help brake the aircraft.

During and after World War II, the propeller gave way to the turbojet for most purposes. The turbojet itself was largely eclipsed by the turbofan, which offers better fuel economy and reduced noise levels.

MILESTONES IN AVIATION

1783 First manned balloon flight by the Montgolfier brothers in hot-air balloon in Paris.

1783 First hydrogen-balloon flight by the French physicist Jacques A.C. Charles. He travelled 26 km (16 miles), beginning in Paris.

1797 First parachute jump by André-Jacques Garenerin. He dropped 1981 m (6500 ft) over Paris in a parachute made of white canvas with a basket attached.

1852 Henri Giffard of France manned the first flight of a mechanically-propelled airship – a *dirigible*. It measured 43 m (144 ft) long and 12 m (39 ft) wide.

1891 Otto Lilienthal of Germany began his controlled glider flight experiments.

1900 Count Ferdinand von Zeppelin of Germany flew the first of his rigid-frame airships. With an internal combustion engine and aluminium frame, it reached a speed of 29 kph (18 mph).

1903 The first successful flight by a 'heavier-than-air machine' by Orville and Wilbur Wright near Kitty Hawk, North Carolina, USA. During a later flight that day Wilbur Wright sustained flight for 59 seconds.

1907 Paul Cornu of France manned the first free vertical flight of a twin-rotor helicopter.

1908 The first cross-country flight of a 'heavier-than-air machine' by Henry Farman, from Mourmelons to Reims in France, in a machine using ailerons.

1909 Louis Blériot made the first cross-Channel flight, from Calais to Dover in 37 minutes.

1910 The Zeppelin airship entered commercial service in Germany.

1912 Construction of the monocoque introduced for the Deperdussin racer.

The leading woman aviator of the day, Harriet Quimby, became the first woman to fly across the Channel.

1915 Start of the Zeppelin bomb raids over Great Britain.

The first all-metal cantilever-wing aircraft, the German Junker J1, was built.

1919 Britons John Alcock and Arthur Brown made the first direct non-stop transatlantic crossing in 16 hours 27 minutes.

1923 The Spanish aviator Juan de la Cierva designed and flew the first autogyro.

1927 The American Charles Lindbergh made the first solo transatlantic flight, from New York to Paris.

1930 The jet engine was patented by Frank Whittle in Britain. It used a gas turbine for jet propulsion.

1935 The Douglas DC-3 'Dakota' – conceived as an airliner – made its maiden flight.

1936 The first entirely successful helicopter, Heinrich Focke's Fa-61, made its maiden flight.

1937 The world's largest airship, the *Hindenburg*, burst into flames in New Jersey, USA, ending the age of airship travel.

The first flight of the US Lockheed XC-35, the first fully pressurized aircraft.

1939 The German Heinkel He-178 was the first aircraft to fly solely on the power of a turbojet engine.

Igor Sikorsky designed the prototype modern helicopter, with a single main rotor and a small tail rotor.

1947 The American Bell X-1 exceeded the speed of sound in level flight.

1949 The De Havilland Comet became the first jet airliner. It entered service in 1952.

1954 The first experimental flight of vertical take-off aircraft.

1958 The first US jet airliner – the Boeing 707 – entered commercial service.

1964 First flight by the USAF Lockheed SR-71, reconnaissance aircraft which is the world's fastest jet. (It achieved an airspeed record of 3529.5 km/h – 2193.17 mph – on 28 July 1976.)

1967 Computer guidance systems were fitted into aircraft for the first time. The Autoland blind landing system was introduced into service in Britain.

1968 The first flight of the Soviet supersonic airliner, the Tupolev Tu-144.

1969 The Anglo-French supersonic airliner, Concorde, made its maiden flight.

The first operational V/STOL (vertical/short take-off and landing) aircraft – the Harrier – entered service with the Royal Air Force.

1970 The Boeing 747 became the first wide-bodied 'jumbo' jet to enter service.

1976 The supersonic airliner Concorde entered commercial service.

1977 The American *Gossamer Condor* became the first successful heavier-than-air human-powered aircraft.

1973 The MB-E1, the first electrically propelled aircraft, made its maiden flight.

1979 The first man-powered flight across the Channel is made by *Gossamer Albatross*.

1981 At the average speed of 48 kph (30 mph), Stephen Ptacek flew the *Solar Challenger* across the Channel, powered only by solar cells.

1987 Richard Branson and Per Lindstrand made the first transatlantic hot-air balloon flight.

1989 The Bell-Boeing V-22 Osprey flew for the first time. Its tilt rotor concept combines the advantages of the aeroplane with those of the helicopter.

1991 The Stealth bomber used in the Gulf War. The low flat design of the aircraft has been successful in avoiding detection by radar.

MOTOR VEHICLES

The engine is the power unit of a car, providing the motion that is ultimately transmitted to the driven wheels. However, a series of interconnected mechanisms, including the clutch, the gearbox and the differential, is required to transmit the power of the engine to the wheels in a usable form. At the same time, a number of subsidiary systems, including steering and brakes, are necessary in order to give adequate control over the movement of the car.

Most cars today are fitted with an overhead-valve, four-stroke petrol engine, with four or six cylinders linked to the crankshaft. The crankshaft also drives a camshaft, which opens and closes the valves at the top of each cylinder in the correct sequence. The four cylinders fire in turn so there is a power stroke for every half-revolution of the crankshaft.

Although the primary function of the engine is to spin the flywheel – the first link in the chain that transmits the engine's power to the wheels – the rotary motion of the crankshaft is also used to turn the *alternator*, which generates the current for the car's electrical systems. At the same time, the rotation of the camshaft drives both the oil pump and the distributor.

THE IGNITION SYSTEM

The purpose of the ignition system is to produce a spark of sufficient strength to ignite the petrol–air mixture at the exact moment when each piston in turn is nearly at the top of the compression stroke. The spark is produced as an electric current jumps (arcs) between the two electrodes of a spark plug; however, the voltage supplied by the battery is insufficient for this purpose. The voltage from the battery is first boosted by the *coil* to around 15 000 volts before passing to the *distributor*, in which a spinning rotor (driven by the camshaft) directs the current to each spark plug in turn.

THE FUEL SYSTEM

For efficient and economical combustion within the engine, the precise proportions of petrol and air in the fuel mixture entering the cylinders must be carefully regulated. This is generally achieved by a *carburettor*. Although different types of carburettor exist, nearly all are in the form of a tube into which air is drawn by the downward movement of the pistons on their successive induction strokes. As the air accelerates through the narrowed middle section of the carburettor, its pressure falls, so causing a jet of fuel to be drawn through a nozzle from a reservoir, which is itself fed by a pump from the petrol tank. Within the carburettor, on the engine-side of the fuel jet, a circular flap (known as a butterfly valve) is actuated by the accelerator pedal in such a way as to control the volume of air–fuel mixture drawn into the engine, thus regulating engine speed. In most designs, a similar valve (the *choke*) on the air-intake side of the fuel jet regulates the amount of air entering the carburettor and thus the richness of the fuel mix.

Increasingly, direct *fuel-injection* is being used in place of the carburettor. This is more efficient and economical than the carburettor, since accurately metered and appropriate amounts of fuel can be delivered to each cylinder's combustion chamber. There are several systems – both mechanical and electrical – but the basic principle is that fuel is injected at high pressure into the combustion chamber from a point behind the inlet valve.

Suspension. The *Mac-Pherson strut* is a very common suspension arrangement, consisting of a spring mounted on an arm that runs from the wheel to a secure place on the bodyframe. The arm moves up and down with road irregularities, so compressing the spring and absorbing bumps.

To counteract the compressed spring's tendency to rebound, a *shock absorber* is fitted (within the spring, in the case of the MacPherson strut). This is essentially a fluid-filled piston-and-cylinder assembly. The piston moves in and out to the same extent as the spring, so forcing the thick fluid back and forth through channels in the piston and thus deadening the bounce of the spring.

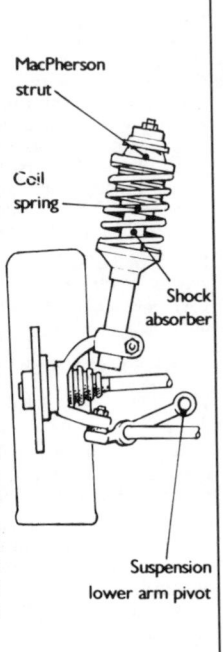

MacPherson strut

Coil spring

Shock absorber

Suspension lower arm pivot

TRANSMISSION

The term 'transmission' embraces all the components that are responsible for transferring the engine's power from the flywheel to the driven wheels. The spinning motion of the flywheel is transmitted to the *gearbox* via the *clutch* (see diagram). When the clutch pedal is depressed, the spinning flywheel is disconnected from the shaft transmitting power to the gearbox, so allowing the car to move off gently and smooth gear-changes to be made.

A gearbox is necessary because – unlike (say) an electric motor – most internal-combustion engines develop their full power and torque (turning effort) within a relatively narrow band of engine speeds (usually between 3000 and 5000 revolutions per minute). By means of the gearbox (and partly by the differential; see below), the engine speed is kept within these limits while allowing the car to operate at widely varying speeds and in a wide range of driving conditions.

For example, a steep hill requires a low gear, because it is only at high engine speeds that the engine is able to deliver enough torque to keep the wheels turning. On the other hand, where little torque is required, as when travelling at speed on a level road, a high gear may be used, thus matching high road speed with (relatively) low engine speed. In this way engine life is prolonged, passenger comfort enhanced and fuel consumption kept to a minimum.

After passing through the gearbox-and-clutch assembly, the drive is transferred to the *differential*. In front-wheel-drive cars, transmission from gearbox to differential is direct; in rear-wheel-drive cars, if

Clutch-and-gearbox assembly. The clutch consists of the flywheel (driven round by the crankshaft), a clutch (or friction) plate and a pressure plate. When the clutch is engaged (i.e. with the pedal released), powerful springs force the clutch plate against the flywheel, thereby linking the flywheel to the shaft transmitting power to the gearbox. When the clutch is disengaged, levers work against the springs to separate the clutch plate from the flywheel, so disconnecting the transmission. The friction linings on the clutch plate allow the plate to slip before becoming fully engaged, so preventing a shuddering jerk on starting.

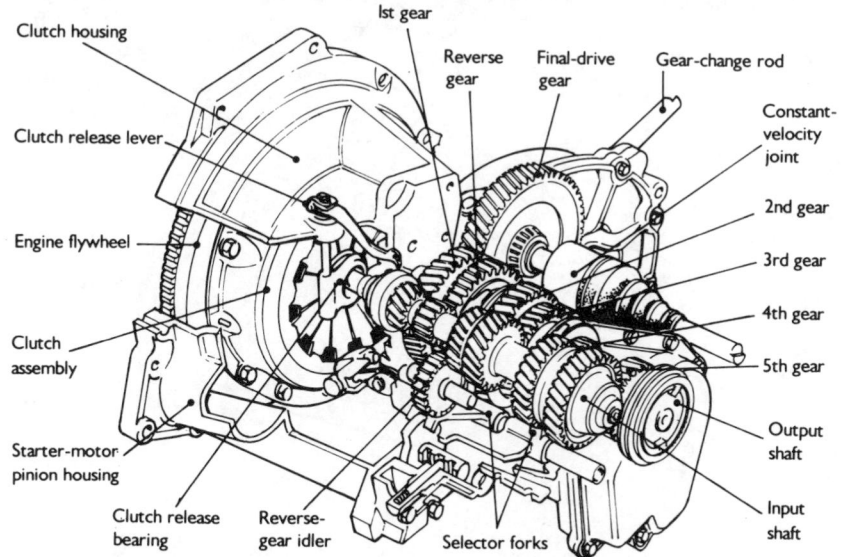

The gearbox allows optimum (i.e. high) engine speed to be matched to a wide variety of driving conditions. By means of selector forks actuated by the gearstick, different-sized gears linked to the input shaft can be engaged with different-sized gears on the shaft transmitting power to the differential. A (relatively) small gear on the input shaft engaged with a large gear on the transmission shaft produces low speed but high power; high speed and low power are achieved by reversing the gear ratios on the input and output shafts. In top gear, no gears are engaged and transmission passes directly through the gearbox to the differential.

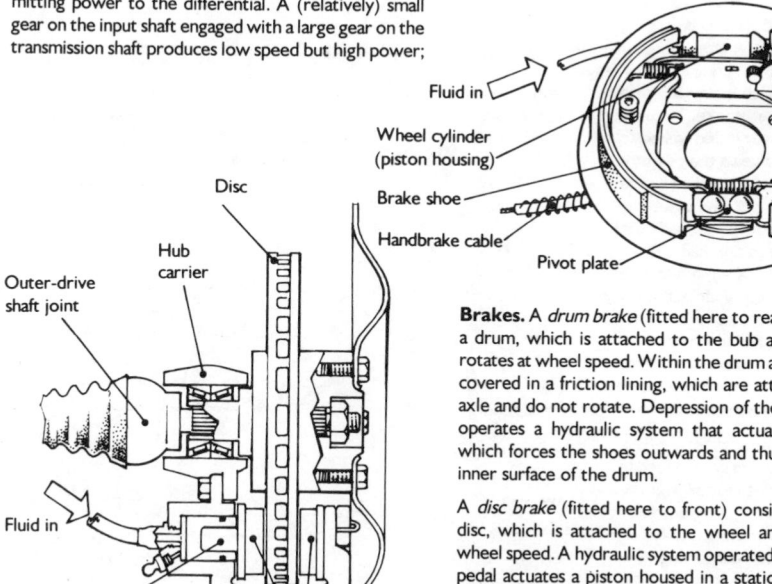

Brakes. A *drum brake* (fitted here to rear) consists of a drum, which is attached to the bub and therefore rotates at wheel speed. Within the drum are two shoes covered in a friction lining, which are attached to the axle and do not rotate. Depression of the brake pedal operates a hydraulic system that actuates a piston, which forces the shoes outwards and thus against the inner surface of the drum.

A *disc brake* (fitted here to front) consists of a steel disc, which is attached to the wheel and rotates at wheel speed. A hydraulic system operated by the brake pedal actuates a piston housed in a stationary calliper that straddles the disc, causing two brake pads to be forced onto each side of the disc. As with the drum brake, the resulting friction causes the car to slow down.

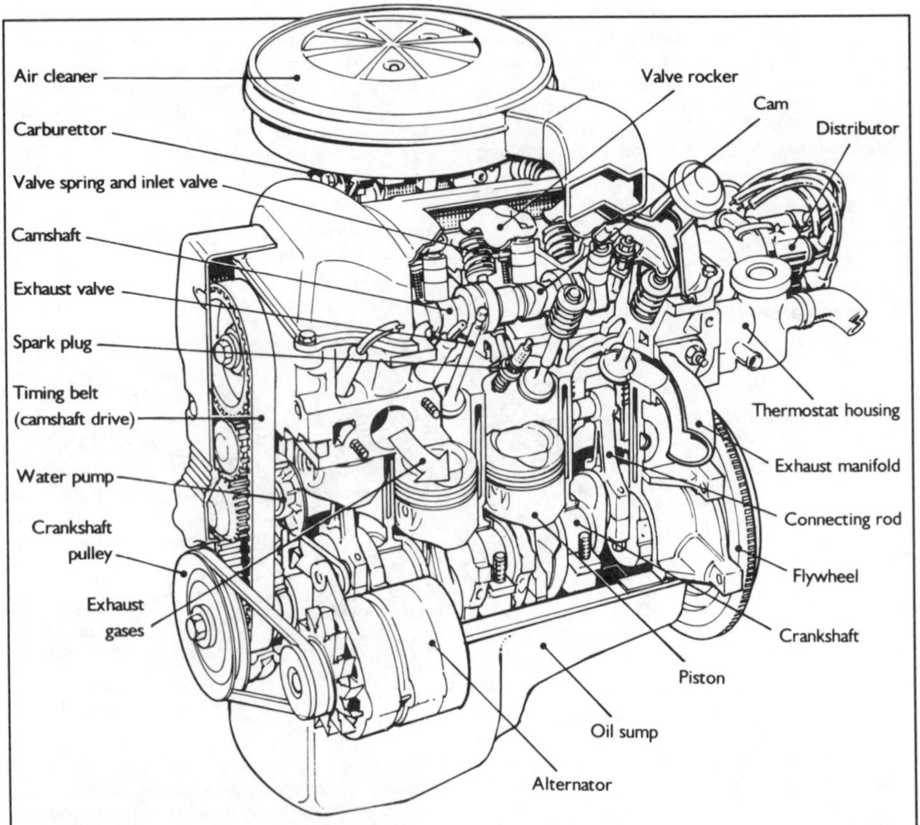

Air cleaner

Carburettor

Valve spring and inlet valve

Camshaft

Exhaust valve

Spark plug

Timing belt (camshaft drive)

Water pump

Crankshaft pulley

Exhaust gases

Valve rocker

Cam

Distributor

Thermostat housing

Exhaust manifold

Connecting rod

Flywheel

Crankshaft

Piston

Oil sump

Alternator

Engine. Four pistons fit tightly in four cylinders bored into the cylinder block. Each piston is driven downwards in a fixed sequence on the power stroke of the four-stroke cycle. A *connecting rod* from each cylinder is attached to a cranked (dog-legged) shaft (*the crankshaft*), which is turned a half-revolution by each successive power stroke. To one end of the crankshaft is bolted a heavy disc called *the flywheel*, which provides the drive to the gearbox via the clutch; at the other end, a belt-and-pulley system causes *the camshaft* to rotate at half the speed of the crankshaft. Pear-shaped lobes (*cams*) along the length of the camshaft act on a series of rocker mechanisms that cause the inlet and exhaust valves on each cylinder to open and close in exact timing with the four strokes of the piston.

Rack-and-pinion steering is a simple and effective system used in many cars. A toothed pinion at the base of the steering column acts on a toothed rack, moving it to left or right and thus converting the rotary motion of the steering wheel into linear motion. At each end of the rack, track rods act on pivoted steering arms, so altering the angle of the front wheels.

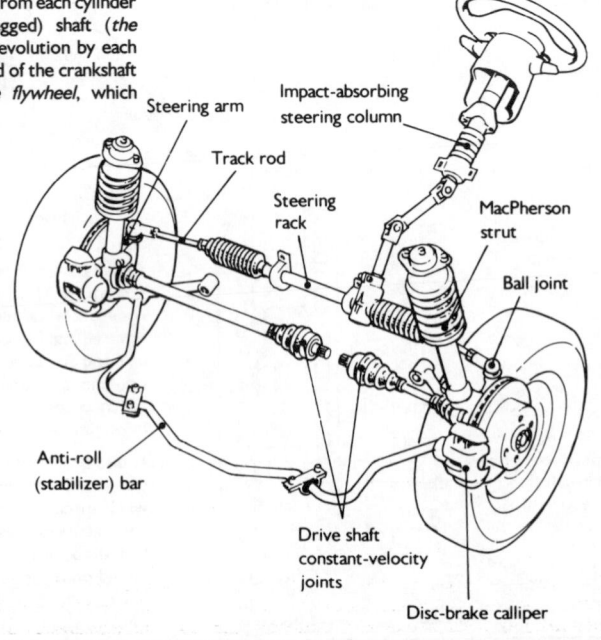

Steering arm

Impact-absorbing steering column

Track rod

Steering rack

MacPherson strut

Ball joint

Anti-roll (stabilizer) bar

Drive shaft constant-velocity joints

Disc-brake calliper

the engine is mounted at the front of the car, the differential is driven by a crown wheel and pinion at the end of a propeller shaft.

The rotation rate of the shaft from the gearbox is further stepped down by the differential (normally to about a quarter of the gearbox speed). However, the differential's distinctive function is to allow power to be divided between the driven wheels in whatever proportion is required. Such a mechanism is necessary when cornering, because the outside driven wheel needs to be turned more rapidly than the inside wheel.

MOTORING MILESTONES

1885 Karl Benz produced the prototype of the automobile using an internal combustion motor.

1885–1886 Gottlieb Daimler patented his gas engine, using it first on a motorcycle and then on a four-wheeled vehicle.

1895 Pneumatic tyres – invented in 1888 – were adapted for use on motor vehicles.

The first motor car race was held, from Paris to Bordeaux and back.

1896 Henry Ford built his first car.

1903 The Ford Motor Company was founded by Henry Ford.

1906 Rolls-Royce began the production of the 'Silver Ghost'. A seven-litre, six-cylinder luxury tourer, it was capable of travelling considerable distances with complete reliability.

1908 The Ford Motor Company introduced the first production-line car – the Model T Ford.

1922 Independent front suspension was introduced in the Lambda, but was not in general use until after 1945.

1920s Mercedes pioneered supercharging.

1934 Citroën made the first car with front-wheel drive and independent front-wheel suspension.

1936 The first diesel-engined production car, the Mercedes-Benz 260D, was launched.

1940 The Jeep, the first vehicle to realize the potential of four-wheel drive, was launched.

1959 Austin Morris launched the Mini Minor, which profoundly influenced the design of all subsequent small cars.

1966 Electronic fuel-injection systems were developed in Britain.

1980 The Audi Quattro, the first mass-produced saloon car with four-wheel drive, was launched.

1980s Many countries introduced legislation to enforce or encourage the use of catalytic converters in cars to detoxify some of the harmful substances in the exhaust gases.

CAR GLOSSARY

air cleaner filter, usually of paper, to remove dust from air and protect engine.

anti-lock braking system of braking which incorporates electronic (or other) means to stop a wheel from locking up and sliding under heavy braking. A major cause of accidents in slippery conditions is due to wheel lock-up.

alternator generates electricity to recharge battery.

anti-roll bar device to limit roll on cornering.

cam eccentric shape on camshaft which operates rockers as the shaft rotates.

camshaft shaft which operates valves through a series of cams along its length.

carburettor device for mixing air and fuel in correct proportions.

catalytic converter device installed in the exhaust system containing a catalyst (benign chemical). Exhaust emissions passing over the catalyst are converted into water, carbon dioxide and nitrogen (see exhaust emissions). Catalytic converters can only work with cars using unleaded fuel.

chassis term used to describe the complete car except the body.

choke device that regulates the amount of air entering the carburettor and thus the richness of the fuel mixture, which allows for easier starting in cold weather.

connecting rod link which transmits force of burning fuel from piston to crankshaft.

constant-velocity joints used on front-wheel-drive cars to provide smooth power when cornering.

crankshaft reciprocal motion of pistons is converted to rotary motion through cranks (dog-legs) on shaft.

differential an assembly of gears within the driving axle which allows one powered wheel to travel at a different speed from the other powered wheel, for example when a car goes around a bend.

distributor device for directing high voltage to spark plugs.

exhaust emissions pollutants released with exhaust gas. The most environmentally damaging are hydrocarbons, carbon monoxide, and oxides of nitrogen.

exhaust manifold tubes which gather exhaust from cylinders and direct it into exhaust pipe.

fan belt belt that drives a cooling fan together with a dynamo or alternator in car engine.

flywheel smooths out uneven operation of engine.

four-wheel drive type of vehicle designed to transmit engine power to the road via all four wheels instead of the more usual two wheels.

front-wheel drive type of vehicle designed to transmit engine power to the road via the front wheels.

fuel-injection efficient method of injecting the fuel mixture into the engine instead of causing it to be drawn in, as with a carburettor.

oil sump reservoir of oil which flows through main bearings.

piston fits tight in cylinder and transmits pressure of burning fuel mixture.

spark plug source of the spark which ignites the fuel mixture inside the cylinder.

thermostat closes off radiator when engine cold, to reduce warming-up time.

timing belt link between crankshaft and camshaft, to ensure valves open at right moment.

valve rocker lever arrangement for transmitting force from camshaft to valves.

valve spring used to close valve through which fuel enters engine, or exhaust gases leave it.

water pump circulates cooling water through radiator and cylinder block.

RAILWAYS

The ancient Babylonians and Greeks laid short lines of grooved stones, while in medieval Europe horse-drawn wagons running on wooden planks were occasionally used in mining. But railways as we know them resulted from the combination of two elements – mechanical traction, provided by the steam engine, and the flanged metal wheel running on metal rails.

Being both a stimulus and a result of the Industrial Revolution, railways have had an enormous social and economic impact over the last 175 years. Although railways have provided a public service for most of their history, it was in fact from old horse-drawn industrial lines used in the British coalfields that the modern railway developed.

STEAM RAILWAYS

In 1812 steam locomotives began regular service in England on the industrial Middleton Railway near Leeds, and in 1814 the English engineer George Stephenson introduced his first steam locomotive at the Killingworth Colliery, near Newcastle-upon-Tyne (see Milestones). Stephenson went on to complete the Stockton & Darlington Railway, the first public steam line, in 1825. In 1830 the first intercity railway, the Liverpool & Manchester, was opened, and in the same year the initial length of the first US public steam line, the Baltimore & Ohio Railroad, was completed.

Many continental European countries built their first railways in the 1830s, often using Stephenson locomotives. Canada built a line in the same decade, but more distant parts of the British Empire waited longer, with Australia's first line opening in 1854, South Africa's in 1860, and New Zealand's in 1863.

In Europe and North America the great period of railway building was the second half of the 19th century. The peak British mileage of 32 908 km (20 449 mi) was reached in 1931, but 90% of that had been built before 1900. The US peak mileage was reached in 1916, at 408 762 km (254 000 mi). In developed countries competition from road transport has since caused many lines to close, but elsewhere in the world new railways are still being built.

TECHNICAL PROGRESS

Nineteenth-century innovations included automatic train brakes controlled from the locomotive and, in passenger service, corridor trains with toilet and dining facilities, steam heating, and electric lighting. Luxury trains, including sleeping cars with a high degree of personal service, have been successfully operated, mainly by the Pullman company in the USA and Wagons-Lits in Europe.

In the 20th century the steam locomotive was gradually replaced by electric and diesel traction. Electrification enabled trains to run more cheaply, more cleanly, and in practice more often, while the greater power of electric locomotives allowed heavier trains and higher speeds. Diesel traction was particularly advantageous on lines where traffic was not heavy enough to justify the cost of electrification.

To keep up with the image created by aircraft and racing cars, railways introduced streamlined trains – or 'streamliners' – in the 1930s, with trains such as the *Silver Jubilee* in England averaging 112 km/h (70 mph) or more. In the USA many of the streamliners were diesel-powered.

In some countries, including Britain, but not the USA, freight traffic has diminished since the 1920s. Freight trains tended to become faster and more specialized. 'Piggyback' (road trailers carried on flat cars) and removeable containers were widely used from the 1950s to combine the long-haul advantage of the train with the door-to-door advantage of the motor vehicle.

In 1964 high-speed trains, running on special track, appeared in Japan. The French TGV service between Paris and Lyon began in 1981, and has running speeds of up to 270 km/h (168 mph). In Britain the 200 km/h (125 mph) High-Speed Train (HST) differs from the Japanese and French examples in that it is diesel, not electric, and runs on existing track. Maglev (magnetic levitation) trains, which dispense with the steel rail and flanged wheel, became technically feasible in the 1970s, but seem unlikely (at least in the short term) to prove economic except for specialized short-haul transit.

GAUGES

The *gauge* of a railway track – the distance between the two rails – is partly a matter of convention but can also be varied to suit particular purposes. The gauge used by Stephenson – 1435 mm (4 ft 8½ in) – became known as *standard gauge*, and has been used for more than half of the railway track ever laid. The advantage of narrow gauge is that it is cheaper to build, especially in hilly terrain, and allows the use of smaller and lighter rolling stock, which is cheaper to operate. Broad gauge, on the other hand, is suitable for larger rolling stock and generally allows higher running speeds, because of greater lateral stability.

The inconvenience of different gauges is exemplified by Australia, where Victoria and South Australia chose 1600 mm (5 ft 3 in), Western Australia and Queensland 1067 mm (3 ft 6 in), and New South Wales standard gauge. These gauges are still in use, but the mainland state capitals now have standard-gauge connections. Sometimes, to accommodate trains of different gauges, a third rail is laid to create *mixed gauge*.

THE IMPACT OF RAILWAYS

Railways revolutionized economic and social life. They enabled industries to be located far from their fuel sources and to enjoy nationwide markets for their products. People could choose from a wider range of commodities and easily travel outside their own district for business and pleasure. The cheap mass movement of people and commodities that was now possible caught the popular imagination and encouraged new enterprise, thus changing static agrarian communities and nations into dynamic industrialized societies.

MILESTONES IN RAILWAYS

1500s Tramways – wooden tracks along which trolleys ran – were used in mines.

1804 Richard Trevithick (1771–1833) successfully operated his steam locomotive in South Wales.

1812 Matthew Murray (1765–1826) brought his steam cog locomotives into service at Middleton Colliery, Yorkshire.

1813 William Hedley (1779–1843) and Timothy Hackworth (1786–1850) built a smooth-wheeled steam locomotive for Wylam Colliery, Northumberland.

1814 George Stephenson (1781–1848) built the *Blücher*, his first locomotive.

1825 George Stephenson opened the Stockton and Darlington Railway, the first public railway to use steam locomotives.

1827 Hackworth's *Royal George* was the first locomotive with six coupled wheels (to increase wheel-to-rail adhesion), and the first with cylinders driving direct to the wheels.

1829 At the Rainhill locomotive trials the *Rocket*, designed by Robert Stephenson (1803–59) and his father George, impressed the Liverpool & Manchester Railway management.

1830 The first intercity railway, the Liverpool and Manchester Line was opened. The first scheduled service in North America began when the South Carolina Railroad opened.

1835 Germany's first steam locomotive, built by Stephenson, went into service.

1836 First Russian locomotive, built by Stephenson, went into service.

1839 Queen Victoria made the first royal railway journey from Slough to London, Paddington.

1848 First railway in South America: Georgetown to Plaisance, Guyana (closed 1972).

1853 First railway in India, Bombay to Thana.

1854 First public railway service in Australia, from Melbourne to Port Melbourne, Victoria.

1856 Train services began on the first railway in Africa: Alexandria to Cairo.

1859 First sleeping car built, desgined by George Pullman.

1863 The world's first underground railway opened in London.

1869 The first US transcontinental, the Union Pacific–Central Pacific Line stretched from Nebraska to California.

1872 First railway in Japan opened, from Yokohama to Shinagawa (to Tokyo later that year).

1879 Werner von Siemens demonstrated the first electric train in Berlin.

1880 First permanent railway in China.

1881 First public electric railway in the world opened near Berlin.

1883 Charles Lartique pioneered the first successful monorail in Ireland.

1887 Canada's first transcontinental service opened, running from Montreal to Vancouver.

1890 The first electric underground railway opened in London.

1897 The German Wilhelm Schmidt (1858–1924) introduced the first successful superheater, enhancing steam locomotive performance.

1900 Electrification of the Paris–Orléans line began.

1901 Opening of the Trans-Siberian Railway: from Moscow to Vladivostock (9336 km / 5801 mi), the longest railway in the world.

1913 The first diesel locomotive was built in Ger-

many. A diesel-electric railcar began running successfully in Sweden.

1915 The Hungarian Kalman Kando built the first electric locomotive using high-frequency current.

1917 Trans-Australian railway opened: its 1693 km (1052 mi) between Kalgoorlie and Port Augusta traversed the Nullarbor Plain for 478 km (297 mi) without a curve, the world's longest straight stretch of railway.

1924 First diesel trains introduced in the USA.

1932 The record-breaking diesel train *Flying Hamburger* began running between Berlin and Hamburg.

1934 The *Burlington Zephyr*, the first diesel-electric streamliner, covered the 1626 km (1010 mi) from Denver to Chicago at an average speed of 125 km/h (77.6 mph).

1938 The British streamlined locomotive *Mallard* won the all-time steam speed record by reaching 203 km/h (126 mph).

1958 A French electric locomotive reached 331 km/h (206 mph).

1960 Regular mainline steam traction ended in the USA. First electronic speed and braking control system introduced on Leningrad (now St Petersburg) subway.

1965 The Japanese Shinkansen high-speed trains entered service.

1968 Regular mainline steam traction ended in Britain.

1973 British Rail's High Speed Train (HST) set a diesel rail speed record of 229 km/h (143 mph).

1977 Testing of Japan's National Railways' maglev (magnetic levitation; see box), reaching speeds of 517 km/h (321 mph).

1981 The French TGV reached 270 km/h (168 mph) in its regular passenger service between Paris and Lyon.

1983 The French TGV cut the scheduled time for the 425 km (264 mi) journey from Paris to Lyon to 2 hours exactly.

FLOATING TRAINS

Conventional trains have a limit to the speeds they can obtain because of the friction between flanged metal wheels and steel tracks. Research into high-speed technology for trains has therefore turned to the application of the principle of magnetic levitation (maglev). With maglev, trains are suspended above the track by magnetic force, thus eliminating friction.

Maglev designs have been of two types. The German Transrapid programme has used a system, in which electromagnets in the wings of the train lie beneath the guideway and are drawn up towards the steel rail as the power is turned on. Meanwhile the Japanese have developed a 'repulsive' maglev, in which superconducting magnets in the guideway create a magnetic field of the same polarity as magnets set in the train itself; the train is thus levitated as the two fields repel one another.

SHIPPING

Over the last 50 years the design of commercial and naval ships has undergone radical changes both as a result of advances in technology and as a response to changing economic pressures and military threats. In all types of ship, automation has helped to reduce crew size and the cost of construction and operation. In spite of competition from the air, ships still carry the great majority of cargoes; and although the great transatlantic liners have disappeared, cruise ships and ferries flourish. In the military field, the need to cope with high-speed missiles – both in attack and defence – has meant that modern warships are now equipped with complex electronic and computer systems.

PASSENGER SHIPPING

The growth of relatively cheap air travel has meant that virtually all long-distance passenger transport is now by air. The few liners that were built after World War II were either scrapped or converted to cruise ships or floating hotels. However, on shorter sea crossings, car and passenger ferries have expanded their activities to cope with the growth of demand for holidays abroad. Partly for economic reasons and partly in order to win customers, ferries have grown in size and speed, with particular attention being paid to on-board amenities and provision for fast boarding and unloading. The roll-on/roll-off design is now common. On some routes, the greater speed of the hovercraft has made it attractive to travellers.

With increasing leisure time, a demand has grown for sea cruises. Initially converted liners were used, but now most ships are specifically designed for the cruising trade. Visits are made to a number of ports where passengers can disembark for excursions to places of interest. Larger cruise liners can carry some 3000 people in relative luxury and with all facilities – such as swimming pools and dance halls – on board.

CARGO SHIPPING

The rapid growth in demand for energy has meant that large volumes of oil need to be shipped around the world. To keep the price per tonne (ton) of oil as low as possible, the size of tankers has grown dramatically. Whereas before 1956 there were no tankers larger than 50 000 tonnes, ships of 100 000 tonnes were built in the 1960s. There are now Very Large Crude Carriers (VLCC) of between 200 000 to 400 000 tonnes and Ultra Large Crude Carriers (ULCC) of more than 400 000 tonnes. To transport natural gas to where it is needed has led to the development of the Liquefied Natural Gas (LNG) carrier.

Whilst the extraction of gas and oil from shallow-water off-shore sites had long been carried out, the need for more oil caused oil companies to look further afield to deeper, more exposed areas, such as the North Sea. In order to remain stationary while drilling, drilling ships with dynamic position control systems were required, as were saturated diving systems, production rigs and supply vessels of specialized design.

Bulk carriage of grain and metal ores was influenced by the need to keep transport as cheap as possible, with minimum manpower and minimum time in port. Bulk carriers therefore grew in the same way as tankers, and like them had machinery and accommo-dation aft with holds or tanks forward. Some large ships are designed to be able to take different cargoes (say oil or ore) on different occasions. Load distribution is then important to ensure that the strength limits of the hull are not exceeded.

WARSHIP DEFENCES

The design of warships is dictated both by the need to carry out certain types of operation and by the need to counter the threat posed by an enemy. During World War II the pace of change accelerated and has continued to do so since. With developments in materials, electronics and computers, the growing complexity of the threats posed has been matched by the sophisticated means used to combat them.

One example is the threat posed by mines. World War II saw the appearance of *influence mines*, which are triggered by the magnetic, acoustic and/or pressure 'signature' of the target. The result of the development of mines and homing weapons (such as missiles and torpedoes which use similar devices) is that great emphasis has been placed on reducing the ship's signatures thus their susceptibility to attack. The radar reflection of modern warships is reduced in a variety of ways: special materials are used, and much attention is paid to shaping and to minimizing the above-water profile. The magnetic signature of a ship can be significantly reduced by *degaussing*, a process in which special equipment is used to produce an opposing magnetic field. The acoustic signature can be reduced by specially designed propulsion units and by isolating noise sources within the ship. Finally, the susceptibility to infrared detection can be decreased by reducing hot spots within the ship.

Ships must be robust enough to withstand some damage and still remain effective fighting units. Various means of reducing vulnerability include protective plating against splinters, duplication of important systems, subdivisions of the ship, and limiting the area of the ship over which a hit can put any particular system out of action.

MILESTONES IN SHIPBUILDING

8th millennium BC　Reed and dugout boats were used.

3rd millennium BC　Sailing boats were used in Egypt.

c. 1200 BC　The Phoenicians developed ocean-going 'roundships'.

5th century BC　The Greek trireme, the fastest of the Mediterranean galleys, was widely used.

8th century AD　The Vikings of Scandinavia developed the longship with a hinged sternpost rudder and mast. It was sturdy enough to enable the Vikings to cross the Atlantic.

15th–16th centuries　The Mediterranean *carrack* – with as many as four masts – became the standard large ship. The smaller version of the carrack, the *caravel*, was widely used by the Spanish and Portuguese for the voyages of discovery.

16th century　The galleon became the standard fighting ship in western Europe.

18th century　The ships of the line evolved from galleons. They had heavier timbers to allow bigger and more numerous guns to be carried.

18th to 19th centuries　Clipper cargo ships

developed. The clipper sacrificed cargo space for a more streamlined design, increasing speed.

1802 The launch of the first commercially successful paddle-steamer, the *Charlotte Dundas*, in Scotland. (A small paddle-steamer had briefly sailed in 1783 in France but had proved impractical.)

1816 A steam-paddle service ran across the English Channel.

1821 The Royal Navy ordered its first paddle steamers for auxiliary missions (such as towing ships of the line over short distances).

The first iron-hulled merchant ship, the *Aaron Manby*, was launched.

1836 The Swedish-American John Ericsson and Englishman Francis Pettit-Smith developed the screw propeller.

1838 The *Great Western* (designed by Brunel) and the *Sirius* crossed the Atlantic, proving that steam power was suitable for long voyages.

1840 The Royal Navy ordered its first screw steamer, HMS *Rattler*. Brunel redesigned the passenger liner SS *Great Britain* for screw propulsion.

1858–1859 Construction began on the first ironclad, the French *Gloire*, a wooden warship covered with armoured plate. However, the British HMS *Warrior*, which had an iron hull and armoured plate, was the first ironclad to be launched (1859).

The *Great Eastern*, five times as large as the largest ship then afloat, was launched. Of revolutionary length (to give it greater speed), the ship was divided into 22 compartments to make it more resistant to damage.

1886 The first custom-built oil tanker, the German ship *Gluckauf*, was launched.

1890s Battleships were designed to an all-metal (steel) construction.

1897 The first turbine-driven steamship, the *Turbinia*, was built by C. Parsons.

1898 The Italian Enrico Forlanini developed the first true hydrofoil.

1902 The first marine diesel engine was installed, on a French canal boat.

1905 The Royal Navy adopted the steam-turbine for the revolutionary battleship HMS *Dreadnought*.

1902–1914 The diesel engine was widely adopted as a cheap propulsion unit for merchant ships and minor naval craft.

1920–39 The heyday of ocean liners. Their ever-increasing size, speed and standards of comfort culminated in the *Queen Mary* and the *Queen Elizabeth*.

1957–58 The first nuclear-powered ship, the Soviet naval icebreaker *Lenin*, was launched. The American merchant ship *Savannah* was the first commercial nuclear-powered ship.

1960s Container ships – carrying standardized containers for transporting cargo – were increasingly used by the world's merchant navies.

Roll-on, roll-off vessels were developed from the design of naval landing-ships for ferry traffic.

1970s Larger oil tankers were launched, such as the Japanese Universe class of 326 000 tonnes (tons) deadweight.

Hydrofoils entered commercial service as passenger ferries.

SHIPPING TONNAGES

Tonnage is the capacity of a ship expressed in terms of tonnes (tons). In the UK, the four tonnage systems are in use. **Gross registered tonnage** (GRT) is used for merchant shipping. It is the sum in cubic feet of all the enclosed spaces divided by 100, i.e. 1 grt = 100 ft^3 of enclosed space. **Net registered tonnage** (NRT) is also used for merchant shipping. It is the gross registered tonnage (see above) less deductions for crew spaces, engine rooms and ballast, which cannot be utilized for paying passengers or cargo. **Deadweight tonnage** (DWT) is used mainly for tramp ships and oil tankers. It is the number of UK long tons (2240 lb; 1.016 tonnes) of cargo, stores, bunkers and passengers that is required to bring down a ship from her height line to her load-water line, i.e. the carrying capacity of a ship. **Displacement tonnage** is used for warships and US merchant shipping. It is the number of tons (tonnes) of sea water displaced by a vessel charged to its load-water line, i.e. the weight of the vessel and its contents in tons.

LARGEST SHIPS

Largest passenger ship
The largest passenger vessel ever launched was the liner *Queen Elizabeth* (UK), which was 314 m (1031 ft) long and had a gross tonnage of 82 998 tons (tonnes). She was retired in 1968 and sold for conversion as a seagoing college, *Seawise University*, which was destroyed by fire in Hong Kong in 1972. The largest active liner is the *Norway*, which was built as the *France* and served on the transatlantic route from 1961 to 1975. In 1979 she was bought by the Norwegian Knut Kloster, renamed *Norway*, and recommissioned as a cruise ship in August 1979. *Norway* is 70 202·19 GRT and 315·66 m (1035 ft 7 in) in length.

Largest battleship
The largest battleships ever commissioned were the Japanese vessels *Yamato* and *Musashi* (both completed and sunk during World War II). Both ships had a full load displacement of 73 977 tonnes, an overall length of 263 m (863 ft), a beam of 38·7 (127 ft) and a full load draught of 10·8 m (35·5 ft). The largest battleship in active service is the USS *Missouri*, which is 270 m (887 ft) long and has a beam of 32·9 m (108 ft) with a full load displacement of 58 000 tonnes. The ship can attain a maximum speed of over 35 knots (64·75 mph). Two other ships of the same class – USS *New Jersey* and USS *Iowa* are now in reserve.

Largest aircraft carriers
The warships with the largest full load displacement are the Nimitz class US Navy aircraft carriers, which includes USS *Abraham Lincoln* and *George Washington*, which displace 102 000 tonnes. They are 332·9 m (1092 ft) long, have 1·82 ha (4½ acres) of flight deck and can reach speeds of well over 30 knots (56 km/h). Their complement is 5986.

Largest oil tanker
The largest ship of any kind is the oil tanker *Jahre Viking* (formerly the *Happy Giant* and *Seawise Giant*), at 564 739 tonnes deadweight. The tanker is 485·45 m (1504 ft) long overall, has a beam of 68·8 m (226 ft) and a draught of 24·61 m (80½ ft). Declared a total loss after being disabled by severe bombardment in 1987–88 during the Iran-Iraq war, the tanker underwent extensive renovation – costing 60 million US dollars – and was relaunched under its new name in November 1991.

IRON AND STEEL

Iron is extracted industrially from naturally occurring ores. The two most important of these are iron oxides – hematite (Fe_2O_3) and magnetite (Fe_3O_4). Mixed with carbon and heated to 1500 °C (2730 °F), iron oxides are reduced to metallic iron, the carbon combining with the oxygen to form carbon dioxide. This process is called *smelting*. In the Middle Ages charcoal was used to provide the carbon, but in 1709 Abraham Darby (1677–1717) of Coalbrookdale in Shropshire, England, succeeded in smelting iron with coke, which could readily be produced from coal. This made possible a huge increase in iron production during the Industrial Revolution.

The first link in the production of iron is the *blast furnace*, in which iron ore is reduced to iron. The biggest modern blast furnaces are huge constructions up to 30 m (100 ft) tall, with walls more than 3 m (10 ft) thick, and capable of making more than 10 000 tonnes (tons) of iron a day. The iron produced in the blast furnace is still contaminated with some residual impurities. Depending on the ore, it usually contains some 3 to 5% carbon, 1% manganese and 3% silicon.

FROM IRON TO STEEL

The iron tapped from a blast furnace is a raw material, not a finished product. To be useful, it must be converted either into cast iron or into steel. *Cast iron* is produced by remelting pig iron (iron that has been cast into moulds and allowed to cool) and carefully adjusting the proportions of carbon, silicon and other alloying elements. Strong and resistant to wear, cast iron can be machined and is easily cast into quite complex shapes. The moulds into which it is cast are made of sand contained in moulding boxes. The shape to be cast is impressed into the sand, and the molten iron poured into it. When solid, the casting is removed.

The great bulk of the iron produced in a blast furnace is converted into steel, by greatly reducing the carbon content. A way of removing carbon economically from pig iron was discovered in 1857 by the English engineer Henry Bessemer (1813–98). In the *Bessemer process*, air blown through the molten iron combined with some of the carbon, carrying it away as carbon monoxide and carbon dioxide. It also oxidized some of the iron, which then combined with the silicon and manganese to form a slag. After just 15 minutes, several hundred tonnes (tons) of iron had been converted into steel. The entire converter rotated on an axle like a cement mixer to pour out the molten steel.

A much slower and more controllable process was invented in the 1860s by a number of engineers – the *open-hearth process*. In this process gas from low-grade coal was used to heat pig iron in a shallow furnace. The chemical changes were the same as in the Bessemer converter, but the process had the advantage that scrap steel could be added to the mixture. The process took up to 12 hours to produce steel, allowing very careful control of the final composition. Both the Bessemer and the open-hearth processes have been superseded in most countries by a process that combines the merits of both. In the *L-D process* (short for Linz-Donawitz), a jet of almost pure oxygen is blown through a lance onto the surface of molten iron. The process is quick and can absorb up to 20% scrap, while producing steel of very high quality. The addition of lime to the oxygen enables iron of higher phosphorus content to be converted,

and in this form the process is known as the *basic oxygen furnace*.

For the more expensive steels, including alloy and stainless steels, *electric-arc furnaces* are used. Heat is provided by three carbon electrodes, which are lowered into a mixture of scrap and alloying additions. Silicon, manganese and phosphorus are removed as slag, and carbon is removed by adding some iron ore, which reacts just as in the blast furnace. The fact that an electric-arc furnace can melt a charge consisting entirely of scrap is a big advantage in developed countries, where recycled steel makes up a large proportion of total production.

TYPES OF STEEL

Steel is sold in the form of cast slabs, or rolled into plates, strips, rods (for nails, screws and wire) or beams (for buildings, bridges and other constructional uses). To make it suitable for a particular use, the characteristics of a steel can be altered by a number of processes, including heat treatment and alloying.

The most important factor in any steel is the carbon content. High-carbon steels are harder and stronger, but they are also more brittle and cannot be welded. For adequate weldability, carbon contents below 0.2% are needed. The precise characteristics of any steel also depend on heat treatment, which determines the microstructure of the steel. Steel can be hardened by heating it to red heat – around 850 °C (1560 °F) – and then quenching it in water, but such a steel is also brittle. The hardness can largely be retained and the brittleness reduced by a second heating to a lower temperature – to around 250 °C (480 °F). The steel is then allowed to cool in air. Such steel is said to be *tempered*.

Alloying steel with other elements in addition to carbon is also important. A steel containing 3% nickel, for example, is immensely tough, and is used for gears and shafts that have to take a lot of strain. Steels containing up to 13% manganese have very hard edges, and are used for items such as rock-breaking machinery. The metal molybdenum is added to alloy steels to reduce brittleness. *Stainless steels*, containing around 14% chromium and sometimes nickel as well, do not rust because of the formation of an impermeable oxide layer on their surface. Such steels are now widely used for cutlery, kitchen sinks and the cladding of buildings.

TYPES OF STEEL

Type of steel	Carbon content (%)	Typical uses
Mild steel	0.08	Car bodies, tin cans
	0.2	Buildings, bridges, ships
Medium-carbon	0.25–0.45	Gun barrels, railway wheels
High-carbon	0.45–1.5	Tools, scissors, cutlery
Cast iron	2.5–4.5	Machine tools, engine blocks, ironmongery

BUILDING CONSTRUCTION

Buildings have many purposes and construction is not confined to providing dwellings: it embraces the provision of shelter for most human activities.

The part of a building above ground level is called the *superstructure*; the part falling below ground level is referred to as the *substructure*. The stability of a building depends on its load-bearing components. There are three kinds of load:

1. *Dead* – resulting from the weight of the building itself;

2. *Live* – the result of furnishing, equipment and bodies;

3. *Lateral* – the result of sideways pressure, typically due to wind.

In a typical house, the load is borne principally by load-bearing walls. Internal dividing walls or partitions may or may not carry loads. Larger buildings may also use columns, arches and domes to support loads. The load-bearing substructure is known as the *foundations*, or *footings*, and for a house this is usually concrete supports for the load-bearing walls. Where the ground is soft, *raft foundations* may be used, which distribute the load evenly over the area occupied by the building. For larger buildings, *piles* may be driven through the ground to connect the substructure with ground of sufficient strength to support the building.

An alternative to load-bearing walls is *skeleton construction*, in which a structural frame carries the load, and the walls (*curtain walls*) are used simply to enclose space. In most buildings, load-bearing walls are not suitable for structures of more than four floors.

THE DEVELOPMENT OF BUILDING CONSTRUCTION

The *post-and-lintel technique*, in which vertical posts support horizontal lintels, has a long history; it is exemplified in its basic form by the ancient stone circle at Stonehenge in England. The method has been used from antiquity for supporting roofs, the posts often taking the form of pillars, as in Egyptian and Greek temples. It is suitable for timber as well as masonry construction.

A way of spanning larger openings is provided by the *arch* (developed by the Romans), but this is not required in smaller, domestic buildings. The *pointed arch*, a feature of Gothic architecture, foreshadowed modern skeleton building in that loads were not transferred from the arch to the walls, but to load-bearing ribs, buttresses, shafts and piers. This enabled walls to be pierced for large openings.

In most countries timber was the favoured material for dwellings. Where wood was plentiful, planks or split trunks could form walls, but elsewhere the spaces between the wooden frame were filled with wattle (intertwined sticks and twigs) covered in clay and, later, with brick or tile. By about 1600 – when good wood was already becoming scarce – most town houses in Europe were *half-timbered*, having a load-bearing oak frame filled in with various materials. The box-like frame was often designed to allow the upper storey to overhang, thereby casting rainwater at a safe distance from the lower storey. Foundations were usually of stone.

The large floor area needed by the factories of the 18th and 19th centuries was provided by the use of timber or cast-iron pillars to support beams and floors. The construction of the Crystal Palace in London in 1851 encouraged the design of buildings with cast-iron frames, which in turn eventually led to steel-framed multistorey buildings and finally to the skyscraper. The latter became possible with the introduction of steel-skeleton construction.

After World War II, skeleton-frame buildings became increasingly popular, especially for offices. Walls could be thin and light, thereby allowing the frames to support a greater weight of floor. The outer face of the building could take many decorative or practical forms, including aluminium or stainless-steel sheeting, enamelled steel, glass and bronze. Sometimes these faces had a fire-resistant backing consisting of a concrete layer, insulation, seal and internal finish, forming a *prefabricated sandwich*.

Domestic dwellings saw fewer changes in the postwar years. Skeleton-frame construction, however, was used in the form of timber-framed housing, in which the timber members carried the loads and were covered by curtain walls on the outside, and by plasterboard or other finishing materials on the inside. In many countries, especially where skilled labour was scarce, *prefabricated* or *industrialized building systems* were introduced, in which the main components were made in factories for easy assembly on site. *Panel systems*, in which the walls were load-bearing, became popular, as did *box systems*, in which prefabricated boxes consisting of wall, roof and floor were designed to be assembled in various configurations.

MATERIALS

Over the long history of building construction, there has been a steady substitution of man-made materials for natural ones. Brick, concrete and steel have largely replaced natural stone, such as granite and sandstone, as the latter require expensive skilled labour both in preparation and in assembly. In the same way, thatch and slate have given way to tile for roofing and cladding. Although wood is still widely used for construction purposes, it too is increasingly being replaced by cheaper composite materials such as plywood (glued layers of wood) and particle board (wood and resin). Concrete and steel are now used for many building purposes, while synthetic materials such as PVC are becoming ever more common in non-structural applications.

NEW TECHNOLOGY

In recent years building innovation has centred around the use of new materials and the potential for saving energy by means of refined insulation and ventilation techniques. The *dome* has also been resurrected as a means of covering the greatest area at the least cost. The stressed-skin dome, in which thin aluminium is stretched over a ribbed framework to form a combined curtain wall and roof, has been successful in specialized uses. In a refined version known as the geodesic dome, the somewhat heavy ribs are replaced by metal tubing in the form of linked hexagons and triangles.

Another trend is towards the development of *tensile structures*, in which the roof is supported by means of cables stretched from pylons. This frees the space beneath the roof from any supporting structure, thereby increasing the usable area. The most notable application is in new sports stadiums, such as the Munich Olympic Stadium.

CIVIL ENGINEERING

Civil engineering embraces the design and building of major structures and systems, usually concerned with transport: roads and railways, bridges, canals and tunnels, harbours and airports.

ROADS

Roman roads were constructed with a deep stone surface for stability and load-bearing. They had straight alignments and therefore were often hilly. The Roman roads remained the main arteries of European transport for many centuries. Roman builders were largely unsurpassed until the resurgence of road-building over 1000 years later.

In the 18th-century, engineers, with horse-drawn coaches in mind, preferred to curve their roads to avoid hills. The road surface was regarded as merely a face to absorb wear, the load-bearing strength being obtained from a properly prepared and well-drained foundation. The Scottish engineer John McAdam (1756–1836) typically used a surface layer of only 5 cm (2 in), composed of crushed stone compacted with a mixture of stone dust and water, and then rolled. McAdam's later roads were surfaced with a layer of *tarmacadam* (or *tarmac*) – hot tar on which a layer of stone chips were laid. Roads of this kind were known as *flexible pavements*.

In the 20th century the ever-increasing use of motor vehicles threatened to break up roads built to 18th- and 19th-century standards, so new techniques were developed. On routes with heavy traffic, flexible pavements were replaced by *rigid pavements*, in which the top layer was concrete, 15 to 30 cm (6 to 12 in) thick, laid on a prepared bed. Nowadays steel bars are laid within the concrete. The demands of heavy traffic led to the concept of high-speed, long-distance roads. The US Bronx River Parkway of 1925 was followed by several variants – Mussolini's autostradas, Hitler's autobahns, and the Pan American Highway. Such roads were the predecessors of today's motorways.

BRIDGES

The development of the *arched bridge* in Roman times marked the beginning of scientific bridge-building. Absorbing the load by compression, arched bridges and viaducts are very strong. They were usually built of stone, but brick and timber were also used. In modern times, metal and concrete arched bridges have been constructed. The first significant metal bridge, built of cast iron in 1779, still stands at Ironbridge (Shropshire, England).

Steel, with its superior strength-to-weight ratio, soon replaced iron in metal bridgework. In the railway age the *truss* (or *girder*) *bridge* became popular. Built of wood or metal, the truss beam consists of upper and lower horizontal booms joined by vertical or inclined members. The truss thus formed is designed to resist the three forces of tension, compression and shear.

The *suspension bridge* has a deck supported by suspenders that drop from one or more overhead cables. It requires strong anchorage at each end to resist the inward tension of the cables, and the deck is strengthened to control distortion by moving loads or high winds. Such bridges are nevertheless light-weight, and therefore the most suitable for very long spans. The Clifton Suspension Bridge, designed by the English engineer Isambard Kingdom Brunel (1806–59), is famous both for its beautiful setting and

for its elegant design. *Cantilever bridges*, such as the 1889 Forth rail bridge in Scotland, exploit the potential of steel construction to produce a wide clearwater space. The spans have a central supporting pier and meet in mid-stream. The downward thrust where the spans meet is countered by firm anchorage of the spans at their other ends. Although the suspension bridge can span a wider gap, the cantilever offers better stability, which was important for 19th-century railway-builders.

In the 20th century, new forms of construction have been facilitated by the use of *prestressed concrete* – concrete surrounding tensioned steel cables that counter the stresses that occur under load. The *box girder* – a massive hollow box-shaped girder, which is both strong and light – has become a key component of concrete bridges.

CANALS

Canals also have a long history, although it was not until the invention of the mitre gate in the 16th century that extensive canal-building was undertaken. The *mitre gate*, formed by two leaves meeting at an angle and pointing upstream, greatly simplified the construction of locks, which are used where canals pass over rising ground. In the 19th century, inland waterways suffered from railway competition, but canals for ocean-going ships remained practicable, and the Suez Canal of 1869 and the Panama Canal of 1914 shortened key shipping routes.

TUNNELS

Tunnel-building was developed in the 18th century to enable canals to penetrate hills, and the same techniques were exploited by the 19th-century railway-builders. Tunnels through hard rock could be unlined, but in soft or moist ground millions of bricks were used as lining.

DAMS

Dams, initially used for flood control and water storage, are of great antiquity. The crescent (horizontally arched) dam, which first appeared in the Byzantine Empire in the 6th century AD, enabled a much greater weight of water to be held than was possible with earlier constructions. Correct judgement of underlying rock strata is as important as good design. Concrete is now the preferred material for dam-construction, but earth, rock, stone and brick have been used.

CIVIL ENGINEERING RECORDS

Longest motorable road The Pan-American Highway from NW Alaska to Santiago, Chile, thence eastward to Buenos Aires, Argentina and ending in Brasilia, Brazil at 24 140 km (15 000 mi).

Longest suspension bridge Humber Estuary Bridge, England (1980) at 1410 m (4626 ft).

Longest cantilever bridge Québec rail bridge, Canada (1918) at 549 m (1800 ft).

Longest rail tunnel Seikan railway tunnel, Japan (1985) at 54 km (33 mi).

Longest tunnel of any kind is the New York City West Delaware water-supply tunnel (built 1937–44), which is 169 km (105 mi) long.

MINING

The Earth's crust, a thin layer that accounts for only about 0.6% of the planet's total volume, provides the fuels, metals and minerals upon which developed societies depend. The quantities of most metals in the crust are small – only iron, aluminium and magnesium are really plentiful. We are able to extract them only because they are not evenly distributed but occur in local concentrations where mining is economically possible. There are far greater concentrations of some metals, such as iron and nickel, in the Earth's mantle and core, but for the moment they are beyond our reach.

MINING METHODS

There are basically two kinds of mine – underground mines and opencast (or surface) mines. In an underground mine, horizontal tunnels several kilometres long are cut to get at a seam containing the desired mineral. Various techniques are then used to remove the mined material from the seam. In *room-and-pillar mining*, a common technique in coal mines in the USA, the coal is broken up by means of explosives and drills, and then removed to form large underground caverns, with the roof supported by pillars of unmined material. *Longwall mining* is more suitable for deeper deposits, such as those generally found in Europe. A working face of 100 m (320 ft) or more is cut by huge machines, and the coal is transported back along roadways by automatic conveyors. Powered roof supports are used to prevent falls of rock at the working face. Some deep mines are very deep indeed: gold is mined in South Africa at depths of more than 3500 m (11 500 ft), where the temperature of the rock may reach 49 °C (120 °F).

In opencast mining, the desired material is first exposed by removing any overlying material (the *overburden*) by means of scrapers, excavators, or draglines (huge buckets pulled along by steel cables). Relatively soft materials, such as coal, may then be removed by draglines, while for harder minerals the rock must first be broken up by blasting. In deep surface mines, such as the copper mines of Chile and Bingham Canyon in the USA, the ore is dug out in a series of terraces, or 'benches', that gradually expand and enlarge the pit. Roadways spiralling to the surface are provided for trucks to carry away the ore.

Alluvial mining, often used to recover tin and gold, makes use of the erosion of ores by water. Carried down by the flow of water, the ores (or native metal in the case of gold) can be recovered from the bottom of lakes and rivers by dredging or suction. The most primitive version of this is the panning technique used by gold prospectors. In Malaysia, huge dredges are used to pick up the tin-bearing gravels from the bottom of lakes.

An unusual method is used for mining sulphur, an element vital to the chemical industry. Developed by the American engineer Herman Frasch (1851–1914) at the end of the 19th century, the system uses three tubes of different diameters, one inside another, that are drilled down into reserves of naturally occurring sulphur. Water under pressure and at a temperature of 160 °C (320 °F) is pumped down the outer pipe, melting the sulphur. Compressed air is then pumped down the centre tube, driving the molten sulphur up through the middle tube. Sulphur obtained in this way is 99% pure. Today a considerable proportion of the world's sulphur is produced as a by-product of the purification of natural gas.

Common salt (sodium chloride) is found as salt deposits and in sea water. The salt deposits can be mined, while salt is recovered from sea water by evaporation in shallow pools. Magnesium chloride is also found in sea water in small but consistent amounts, and is extracted by reacting the sea water with lime, causing the magnesium to be deposited as a precipitate.

TYPES OF MINES

The mining method chosen to extract coal or other minerals depends principally on the depth of the seam or deposit:

Shaft mines are built to reach deep deposits. The mineral is reached by a shaft descending vertically into the ground.

Drift mines are used where seams appear as an outcrop at the surface, usually on the side of a hill. The seam can be entered and mined directly.

Slope mines are used for deposits at moderate depths. The mineral to be hauled up an inclined tunnel in wagons.

Opencast mines are used where a mineral lies close to the surface. Layers of overlying soil and rock are removed to expose the mineral.

DISCOVERING MINERALS

Fortunately for mankind, metals and minerals occur unevenly. Copper, tin, nickel, zinc, lead, mercury, silver and gold – all vital to our industrial society – are in fact extremely rare. Copper makes up only 100 parts per million of the Earth's crust, and lead only 20 parts per million. But the availability of metals does not depend so much on their abundance as on how easy it is to find and exploit their ores.

Sometimes bodies of ore advertise their presence by appearing at the surface, perhaps where erosion has scoured the rocks on a cliff face. Hidden reserves can be found by *magnetic* or *gravimetric* surveys – a mountain rich in iron ore will affect the Earth's magnetic field and the force of gravity in the immediate vicinity. Seismic and satellite surveying and knowledge of the local geology may also indicate the likelihood of a particular ore occurring.

MINE RECORDS

Gold The deepest gold mine – and the deepest mine of any kind in the world – is Western Deep Levels, Carletonville (Rand), South Africa at 3777 m (12 391 ft). The most productive gold mine may be Muruntau, Kyzyl KUm, Uzbekistan with an estimated 80 tonnes per year.

Coal The deepest coal mine is an exploratory shaft 2042 m (6700 ft) deep in the Donbas field in Ukraine.

Quarry The largest quarry in the world is at Bingham Canyon, Utah, USA (see main text). It is 7.21 km² (2.81 sq mi) in area and represents 3355 million tonnes extracted.

Oldest mine The world's oldest known mine is an ochre (clay and hydrated ferric oxide) mine in Belgium dating from 41 250 BC ± 1600.

Iron The largest iron mine, at Lebedinsky, in Kursk region, Russia, has produced 20 300 million tonnes, of which 45-65% is ore.

PRINTING

Three methods of printing are of particular significance. In *letterpress printing*, the method used by Gutenberg (see Milestones), the raised surfaces of the typeset page are covered in ink by rollers, and paper is pressed against it in a press to transfer the image. *Lithography* (or 'litho'), which has now almost entirely taken over from letterpress, was invented in 1796. The technique depends on the fact that water and grease do not mix. The images to be printed are transferred to flexible metal plates photographically, in such a way that the areas to be printed consist of chemicals that attract ink and repel water, while the blank areas attract water and repel ink. First water and then ink is applied to the plate; all the ink congregates in the areas of the image, and can be transferred to paper in a rotary press (see below). A better image is achieved if the cylinder carrying the plate first transfers the image to a rubber-coated cylinder, which in turn transfers it to paper. This rubber 'offset' cylinder gives the method its name – *offset litho*.

A third technique is widely used for printing colour supplements and magazines. In *gravure* (short for 'rotogravure' or 'photogravure') the image is etched on the plate photographically, forming cells whose depth depends on the intensity of the colour. As the plate rotates, it picks up ink, which is wiped off blank areas by a blade. When the paper passes between the cylinders of the press, the deeper cells produce denser images, while the shallower ones produce lighter ones. In a related process, known as *copperplate gravure* or *line intaglio*, the image consists of discrete lines that vary in depth and width. It is the preferred method for printing stamps and banknotes.

Gravure and litho are carried out almost exclusively on some variant of *rotary press*, which achieved great printing speed, particularly important for newspaper production. Rotary presses operate cylinder to cylinder. Letterpress type was formed into a curve by a process known as *stereotyping*, invented in 1727. An impression was taken of the typeset page using papier-mâché, which was then curved into a half circle and used as a mould to cast copies of the typeset page. The curved page was fitted together with another page around a cylinder and locked in place. Rotary presses may be sheet-fed or web-fed; in the latter case a continuous roll (or *web*) of paper passes between the cylinders. Rotary printing allows more rapid production than older flat-bed methods.

Computer technology has revolutionized every stage of printing. Text may be keyed directly into the computer typesetting system, or an author's word-processed disks may be made compatible with a particular system. The text is displayed on screen to be edited or corrected; typesetting commands – specifying the desired typeface, typesize and so on – are also added at this stage. A designer may then assemble the page on screen, juggling pictures and text into the final layout. Next the text is set in type by a laser guided by the computer. The laser scans to and fro across an sheet of film or photographic paper ('bromide'), tracing the shapes of all the characters according to the instructions prepared at the page-layout terminal. After development, the result is a positive or negative film, or a bromide; in the latter, the characters traced by the laser appear black against a white background. The film or bromide can then be used to prepare printing plates.

To print in *colour*, paper must pass successively over a number of printing cylinders, a different colour being transferred to the paper at each stage. The process is made simpler by the fact that any colour can be made by mixing three basic colours in the right proportions. Separate plates are made for printing in cyan (bluish green), magenta (purplish red) and yellow, and the images from each printing are superimposed exactly on top of one another. A fourth printing is then made in black, principally to add definition and contrast, as well as to print the text and captions for the page. The four printing plates are prepared from four separate pieces of film, or *separations*, which – when placed one upon another – re-create the colours of the original illustration. The separation is achieved by means of a *colour scanner*; a computer-guided laser beam moves back and forth across a rotating drum to which the original is attached, measuring the quality and intensity of each of the basic colours at every point of the image.

PRINTING MILESTONES

2nd century AD Chinese invented paper, ink and blocks with pictures or letters cut into them.

c. 1450 Johannes Gutenberg invented printing press and movable type in Germany.

1642 Ludwig van Siegen introduced Mezzotint process of printing in graduated tones.

1719 First three-colour engraving process demonstrated by Jakob Le Bon.

1768 Jean Baptiste Le Prince invented aquatinting method of engraving.

1796 Aloys Senefelder introduced lithography in Germany.

1800 Earl of Stanhope built first all-metal press in England.

1810 The first steam-powered press invented by Friedrich König and Andreas Bauer.

1822 William Church patented typesetting machine.

1837 Godefroy Engelmann patented the chromo-lithography process.

1844 The rotary printing press invented in the USA by William Hoe.

1865 William Bullock built first roll-fed rotary press.

1880 Introduction of half-tone process for reproducing photographs.

1884 Ottmar Mergenthaler invented the Linotype hot-metal setting machine in the USA.

1887 In the USA Tolbert Lanston patented Monotype system of typesetting.

1895 Invention of the rotogravure printing process by Karl Klič.

1904 Ira Rubel built first printing press for offset lithography.

1937 First practical dry photocopier introduced by Chester Carlson in the USA.

1947 Introduction of mechanical phototypesetting.

1949 Introduction of functional typesetting, with Lumitype.

1954 Programmed composition using perforated tape invented.

1960s Magnetic tape replaced perforated tape for phototypesetting. Newspapers began to use Web offset printing machines.

1970 Introduction of computer-controlled systems.

1973 Colour duplication photocopiers introduced.

1976 Laser typesetters introduced by Monotype.

1984 Introduction of image-processing colour scanners.

RUBBER AND PLASTICS

Beyond its curiosity value, raw rubber has relatively few uses. It was known to the Mayas and Aztecs in Pre-Columbian America. They heated the latex – a whitish milky fluid – that flowed from the bark of the rubber tree until it coagulated. From it they made balls with which they played games. The Frenchman Charles de la Condamine (1701–74) brought it Europe in the 18th century.

It was given its name by the chemist Joseph Priestley (chiefly known as the discoverer of oxygen), who observed in 1770 how useful it was for rubbing out pencil marks. In 1823 the Scottish chemist Charles Macintosh (1766–1843) made his name immmortal by inventing the 'mackintosh' – a waterproof raincoat made from a fabric produced by sandwiching a layer of sheet rubber between two pieces of cloth.

It was a Philadelphia hardware merchant, Charles Goodyear (1800–60), who transformed the future of rubber. Looking for a way of preventing it going sticky when hot and hard when cold, he mixed it with sulphur and heated it. The result was a far more stable and useful product – tougher and more consistent in its properties, yet retaining all the resilience of untreated rubber. The name *vulcanization* was given to this process. Vulcanized rubber could be used for a whole new range of applications – conveyor belts, hoses, valves, insulation of electrical cables, and, on the horizon – the biggest use of all – pneumatic tyres for road vehicles. By the end of the 19th century Michelin in France, Dunlop in England and Goodrich in the USA were all producing tyres for the motorcar.

RUBBER PRODUCTION

Although other plants have sometimes been used, most of the world's rubber originates in cultivated plantations of *Hevea brasiliensis*, a tree native to Brazil. Seeds from this tree were brought to England in 1876 and exported to parts of the British Empire where the climate was suitably tropical and humid. Today more than 4 million tonnes (tons) of rubber is produced annually, 90% of it from Southeast Asia, principally from Malaysia.

Latex is still tapped from rubber trees in the traditional manner. At the factory the latex is first caused to coagulate (usually by the addition of chemicals) and then masticated – kneaded and worked between steel rollers rotating in opposite directions – to break it down and make it flexible. Next, the rubber is mixed with various compounding agents to improve its performance. Carbon black may be added to reinforce the rubber, while antioxidants are incorporated to prolong its life. The colour of the rubber may be altered by adding various pigments. The sulphur for vulcanizing is also added at this stage. The rubber is then shaped on a variety of machines into its final form, and only then is it vulcanized, usually by heating it in a metal mould. For tyres, the final shaping and vulcanization are carried out at the same time, by applying heat and pressure in metal moulds.

PLASTICS

Chemically, rubber is a polymer – a compound containing large molecules that are formed by the bonding of many smaller, simpler units, repeated over and over again. The same bonding principle – *polymerization* – underlies the creation of a huge range of plastics by the chemical industry.

Celluloid Celluloid, the first plastic, was developed in the 1860s by John Wesley Hyatt, who had been seeking a substitute for ivory in the manufacture of billiard balls. It was made by dissolving cellulose, a carbohydrate obtained from plants, in a solution of camphor dissolved in ethanol. This new material rapidly found uses in the manufacture of products such as knife handles, detachable collars and cuffs, spectacle frames and photographic film. Without celluloid, the film industry could never have got off the ground. Celluloid can be repeatedly softened and reshaped by heat, and is known as a *thermoplastic*.

Bakelite In 1907 Leo Baekeland (1863–1944), a Belgian chemist working in the USA, invented a different kind of plastic, by causing phenol and formaldehyde to react together. Baekeland called it Bakelite, and it was the first of the *thermosets* – plastics that can be cast and moulded while hot but cannot be softened by heat and reshaped once they have set. Bakelite was a good insulator, and was resistant to water, acids, and moderate heat. With these properties it was soon being used in the manufacture of switches, household items such as knife handles, and electrical components for cars.

Polythene, polypropylene and PVC In the 1930s British chemists discovered that the gas ethylene would polymerize under heat and pressure to form a thermoplastic they called *polythene*. *Polypropylene* followed in the 1950s. Both are used to make bottles, pipes and plastic bags. A small change in the starting material – replacing a hydrogen atom in ethylene with a chlorine atom – produced *PVC* (polyvinyl chloride), a hard, fireproof plastic suitable for drains and gutters. By adding certain chemicals, a soft form of PVC can be produced, suitable as a substitute for rubber in items such as waterproof clothing.

Teflon Closely related to polythene is Teflon or PTFE (polytetrafluoroethylene). It has a very low coefficient of friction, making it ideal for bearings, rollers, and non-stick frying pans.

Polystyrene Developed during the 1930s in Germany, polystyrene is a clear glass-like material, used in food containers, domestic appliances and toys. Expanded polystyrene – a white rigid foam – is widely used in packaging and insulation.

Polyurethanes Also developed in Germany, polyurethanes found uses as adhesives, coatings, and – in the form of rigid foams – as insulation materials.

All these plastics are produced from chemicals derived from crude oil, which contains exactly the same elements – carbon and hydrogen – as many plastics.

MAN-MADE FIBRES

In the 1930s the first of the man-made fibres was created – *nylon*. Its inventor was an American chemist called Wallace Carothers (1896–1937), who found that under the right conditions two chemicals – hexamethylenediamine and adipic acid – would form a polymer that could be pumped out through holes and then stretched to form long glossy threads that could be woven like silk. Its first use was to make parachutes for the US armed forces in World War II. In the postwar years it completely replaced silk in the manufacture of stockings. Many other synthetic fibres joined nylon, including Orlon, Acrilan, and Terylene. Today most garments are made of a blend of natural fibres and man-made fibres that make fabrics easier to look after.

CHEMICALS AND BIOTECHNOLOGY

The chemical industry turns readily available raw materials into thousands of useful products. Principally from coal, oil, natural gas, air, water, limestone, salt and sulphur, the industry manufactures drugs, fertilizers and pesticides, soap and detergents, cosmetics, plastics, acids and alkalis, dyes, solvents, paints, explosives and gases. Biotechnology also produces useful products, but by biological rather than chemical methods. Living organisms – or substances produced from them – are used to make drugs, to improve crops, to brew alcohols, and even to extract minerals. Some of its methods, such as fermentation, are ancient, while others are so new that they are barely out of the research laboratory.

THE CHEMICAL INDUSTRY

The first chemical to be produced on a large scale was *soda* (sodium carbonate), which was needed primarily in glass and soap manufacture. In 1787 the French chemist Nicolas Leblanc (?1742–1806) devised a method of mixing common salt (sodium chloride) with sulphuric acid to produce sodium sulphate, which was then mixed with coal and limestone and roasted. The resultant 'black ash' was dissolved in water and then evaporated to extract the soda. Subsequently the Leblanc process was replaced by a process using salt, carbon dioxide and ammonia. Soda is typical of most products manufactured by the chemical industry in that it requires further processing to make useful products.

Other important landmarks in the growth of the chemical industry were the production of bleaching powder (a bleaching agent and disinfectant) in 1799, and the invention of synthetic dyes, beginning with Perkin's mauve in 1856. The production of artificial fertilizers, which supply plants with nitrogen, potassium and phosphorus, was also significant. The first of these was *superphosphate*, manufactured from 1834 onwards by mixing phosphates with sulphuric acid. The use of electrolysis to extract valuable chemicals by passing electrical currents through salt solutions began in 1894 with the Castner–Kellner process for making pure caustic soda.

The modern chemical industry can be divided for convenience into three categories: the *heavy inorganic sector*, which includes fertilizers and other chemicals produced in large amounts; the *fine chemicals sector*, which includes drugs and dyes; and the *heavy organic sector*, which includes plastics, man-made fibres and paints. The term *'organic'* was originally used to designate any chemical found in living organisms, but today the term refers to any chemical containing carbon. Because of the facility with which carbon atoms link to form molecules, the variety of such compounds is enormous – literally millions of carbon compounds can be synthesized.

In the heavy inorganic sector, *sulphuric acid* is the largest single product. Nearly half is used to produce superphosphate, with the rest going to a variety of chemical processes, including the production of explosives and artificial fibres. In 1908 the German chemist Fritz Haber (1868–1934) developed a catalytic method for combining the nitrogen in air with hydrogen to form *ammonia*, which is chiefly used in the manufacture of explosives and nitrate fertilizers.

In the fine chemicals sector, chemical substances are produced in smaller quantities than is the case with (say) fertilizers, but higher prices are charged. *Dyes* are produced in a huge range of colours, originally from coal but now mostly from crude oil. Many *drugs* are also synthesized using the methods of organic chemistry; some are produced biochemically.

In the heavy organic sector, materials are produced in large quantities, usually as raw materials for further processing into plastics, fibres, films or paints. Typical examples are benzene, phenol, toluene, vinyl chloride and ethylene. The main raw material is crude oil, which contains a range of hydrocarbons – chemicals made up of carbon and hydrogen. From crude oil individual hydrocarbons can be extracted by distillation or catalytic cracking. Hydrocarbons thus obtained are used to build more complex molecules by polymerization.

BIOTECHNOLOGY

The technique of *fermentation*, in which microorganisms such as yeast convert raw materials into useful products, has been known since earliest times. By the middle of the 19th century, industrial alcohol was being produced by fermentation in much the same way as beer or wine. After the price of crude oil went up in the 1970s, alcohol produced in this way has been able to compete under some circumstances with petrol, and large fermentation plants have been built in the USA and Brazil to convert plant material such as maize into fuel.

A number of acids can also be produced by fermentation – vinegar (dilute acetic acid) being an important example. Citric acid, widely used in food and drinks, was originally produced from citrus fruits, but a fermentation process developed by the US Pfizer company in the 1920s soon dominated the market. Pfizer still produces half the 250 000 tonnes (tons) of citric acid used every year. Other chemicals that can be produced by fermentation include glycerol, acetone and propylene glycol. Fermentation has proved equally useful in the drug industry. Following the discovery of the antibiotic penicillin in 1928, large-scale fermentation methods were developed in the 1940s to produce the drug commercially. Today a large number of drugs are produced in this way, as well as other biochemicals such as enzymes (biochemical catalysts), alkaloids, peptides and proteins.

The technique of *genetic engineering* has greatly increased the range of possible products. By altering the genetic blueprint of a microorganism, it can be made to produce a protein quite unlike anything it would produce naturally. For example, if the short length of the genetic material DNA responsible for producing growth hormones in humans is inserted into cells of a certain bacterium, the bacterium will produce the human hormone as it grows. It can then be extracted and used to treat children who would otherwise not grow properly. The same methods can be used to produce insulin for diabetics, while sheep have been genetically engineered so that they produce a human blood-clotting agent in their milk.

The damage done to the environment by the growth of the chemical industry is an issue of widespread concern. The first attempts at controlling pollution by legislation were made in the 19th century, but poisonous discharges into streams still occur, and there is little control of the dumping of toxic wastes. A longer-term hazard is posed by the use of fertilizers, such as nitrates, which can pollute lakes and streams, and by percolating through the soil can reach groundwater. There is also anxiety about the use of genetic engineering techniques. It is possible, for example, that an accident could produce superresistant species of germs or pests.

TELECOMMUNICATIONS

The transfer of information by wire or by radio waves is the basis of telecommunications, which, is now one of the world's biggest and fastest-growing industries. Currently, the most important systems are the telephone, the telegraph, telex, facsimile, and information systems based on the telephone or television.

Today it is possible to send information in different forms – telephone conversations, data and images of documents – around the world in seconds.

MILESTONES IN
TELECOMMUNICATIONS

1820 The Danish physicist Hans Christiaan Oersted discovered that a magnetized needle could be deflected by an electric current flowing in a wire.

1837 Englishmen Sir Charles Wheatstone and William Cooke patented first practical electric telegraph based on Oersted's discovery.

1838 American inventor Samuel Morse and Alfred Vial devised the Morse code in which individual letters of the alphabet and digits are represented by different sequences of dots and dashes.

1844 First morse telegraph line was opened between Baltimore and Washington DC.

1851 First telegraph cable was laid across the English Channel.

1858 First transatlantic cable was laid.

1872 Most of the world's major cities were in contact with one another by telegraph.

1876 Alexander Graham Bell invented the first telephone.

1878 First commercial telephone exchange was opened at New Haven, Connecticut.

1889 The American undertaker Almon Strowger invented first practical automatic exchange system (making the use of operators redundant).

1892 First public automated exchange was set up at La Porte, Indiana.

1900 Introduction of load circuits to reduce signal distortion.

1910 Introduction of multiplexing which allowed more than one call to be sent down the same set of telephone wires at the same time.

1915 A transcontinental telephone circuit was opened in USA. It used triode valve repeaters which amplify signals in order to send them over a long distance.

1926 Short-wave radio was used to transmit transatlantic telephone signals.

1946 High-frequency microwaves were used to transmit telephone signals.

1956 Telex introduced in Canada.

1956 First transatlantic telephone cables with submerged repeaters were laid.

1962 First telecommunications satellite, *Telstar*, demonstrated potential in relaying telephone signals. Commercial satellite relays began in 1963.

1964 Introduction of code teleprinters.

1965 Introduction of first electronic telephone exchange (New Jersey).

1967 Introduction of mobile phones (cordless) in the USA.

1970 Corning Glass, USA produced the first long optical-fibre for telecommunications.

1970s Teletext communication systems on TV (Ceefax and Oracle in the UK) launched.

1976 First optical-fibre cable for telecommunications installed. Each glass fibre in the cable can handle thousands of telephone calls at once.

1980s Introduction of facsimilie (fax) transmissions of documents and diagrams over a telephone network. Growth of Electronic Funds Transfer (EFT), seen most visibly in cash dispensers.

DATA TRANSMISSION

Telephones are not restricted to communication by voice. Increasingly they are being used to send data from computer to computer, and images of documents by facsimile transmission (fax). In many Western countries telephones are widely used to send information for display on a TV set. These services are known generically as *viewdata*. They offer a great range of information, which is stored centrally on a computer database and covers topics as varied as stock-market prices, sports and general news, holiday information, job advertisements, weather forecasts and entertainment guides.

For transmission of computer data, a *modem* – modulator-demodulator – is needed at each end of the line. A modem converts the digital signals from the computer into a form that can be transmitted by telephone and reconverts them at the other end. Provided the telephone lines are good enough, portable computers can now be connected up to the telephone system anywhere in the world, and used to send information elsewhere. Where lines are poor, *telex systems* – the descendants of the telegraph – survive. These send images of documents along the line, letter by letter, to be printed out at the far end.

Facsimile transmission – fax – is one of the fastest growing of the new telephone services. It has been available for many years – particularly in Japan, where the language, with its many symbols, makes telex too complex. Fax has only really begun to grow rapidly, however, with the availability of much cheaper machines. Fax works by scanning a sheet of typed or handwritten material, and turning the result into a digital signal that can be sent over the telephone network to a designated fax machine somewhere else. It is by far the quickest way to transmit images of drawings or typed documents.

The telephone network can also be used to send electronic mail from terminal to terminal, and to replace the use of cash for purchasing goods. *Electronic funds transfer* (EFT) is a system for automatically debiting a customer's bank account and transferring money to that of the store, without handling cash, cheques or credit cards. EFT is still in its infancy, but offers great economies over the existing paper-laden systems and is likely to grow.

RADIO, TELEVISION AND VIDEO

The media used to carry information are radio waves, which lie at the low-frequency end of the electromagnetic spectrum. Radio waves occur naturally in space, emitted by stars and galaxies, but for broadcasting purposes, they are generated by accelerating electrons inside an *aerial* (or *antenna*) – a device used both to emit and receive radio waves. Like all electromagnetic waves, radio waves travel at the speed of light – 300 000 km (186 000 mi) per second in a vacuum.

The idea of using radio waves to carry visual information dates back to the early days of radio, but became practical only in 1926. The basic principle is to break up the image into a series of dots, which are then transmitted and displayed on a screen so rapidly that the human eye perceives them as a complete picture. A TV set is basically a *cathode-ray tube*, in which a 'gun' fires a beam of electrons at a luminescent screen. As they strike it, the screen lights up. To make up the whole picture the beam is scanned to and fro in a series of lines (625 in modern sets), covering the entire screen in $^{1}/_{25}$ of a second.

The principle for recording TV programmes on video (magnetic tape) is the same as that of an audio tape recorder but the technology is more complex. The signals are recorded as magnetic patterns on the tape.

MILESTONES IN RADIO, TELEVISION AND VIDEO

1861 James Clerk Maxwell, Scottish physicist and mathematician, predicted the existence of an invisible form of electromagnetic wave travelling at the speed of light.

1887 Heinrich Hertz, German physicist, demonstrated the reality of Maxwell's waves, by allowing a small spark to jump across an air gap, and detecting the waves at the other side of a room with a similar air gap.

1894 Guglielmo Marconi, a young Italian inventor, made a bell ring in the attic of his parents' house in Bologna by sending a radio message across the room.

1901 Marconi succeeded in sending a radio message in Morse Code across the Atlantic, from Cornwall to Newfoundland.

1906 Music and speech was broadcast for the first time, by the American physicist Reginald Fessenden. The sounds were carried on radio waves by 'modulating' them, superimposing the sound waves on to the radio waves. The amplitude of the radio wave was altered to carry the sound – giving rise to the term *amplitude modulation*, or AM.

1907 Lee De Forest, an American inventor, used a triode valve to amplify radio signals.

1917 Lucien Lévy, in France, and Edwin Armstrong, in the USA, devised 'superheterodyne' circuits that made tuning much easier, reduced power requirements and simplified the construction of receivers.

1921 The first radio station, KDKA, began broadcasting in Pittsburgh, USA. The British Broadcasting Company (BBC) began daily transmissions the following year.

1925 Using a mechanical scanning system, the Scot John Logie Baird transmitted the first recognizable pictures of human faces.

1931 Vladimir Zworykin, a Russian-born inventor living in the USA, demonstrated the first practical electronic television camera.

1933 Edwin Armstrong devised frequency modulation (FM), in which the frequency rather than the amplitude of the carrier wave is modulated by the signal. This reduced the problem of random noise caused by static.

1936 The BBC television service was inaugurated at Alexandra Palace in London. It utilized two systems: Logie Baird's mechanical system, and an electronic system developed by an EMI research team under Isaac Schoenberg.

1945 Arthur C. Clarke, British science-fiction writer, described in *Wireless World* the possible use of a satellite in geostationary orbit for broadcasting radio and TV signals.

1951 Regular television broadcasting in colour was begun by Columbia Broadcasting System in New York.

1952 The first transistor radio, small enough to carry in the pocket, was made by Sony in Japan.

1953 The Federal Communications Commission in the USA adopted the NTSC (National Television Systems Committee) system for colour broadcasting.

1956 Improved colour TV became available using a system called SECAM (*Sequential Couleur à Memoire*) developed in France.

1958 The first video recording device, in which TV signals were recorded on magnetic tape, was installed in a US TV studio by the Ampex Corporation. A key invention, by Alexander Poniatoff of Ampex, was the rotating playback head, which enabled more information to be packed on to the tape.

1962 A third colour TV System PAL (Phase Alternance Line) was developed in Germany. (All three colour systems are incompatible.)

1962 The first transatlantic pictures are carried live, bounced off the communications satellite Telstar.

1963 The first geostationary satellites, the Syncom series built by Hughes Aircraft Corporation, were placed in orbit.

1965 Intelsat-1, Early Bird, went into geostationary orbit. It had the capacity for a single TV channel between Europe and North America.

1967 A colour TV service began in Britain, using the PAL system.

1970s Rival Video Cassette Recorder (VCR) systems emerged from Philips, Sony and JVC. The JVC system, known as VHS (video home system) proved the most successful and by the mid-80s millions of VCRs were installed in homes.

1974 Information systems, using the spare lines on a 625-line TV system, were broadcast in Britain. The BBC version is called Ceefax, the ITV system Oracle.

1974 ATS-6, an experimental direct broadcasting satellite, was launched by NASA and used to broadcast to Indian villages equipped with a receiver dish.

1979 The first regular direct broadcasting system, beaming pictures directly to people's houses (rather than through a ground station), was launched in Canada. The ANIK-B, requiring only a small rooftop dish, was the forerunner of many direct broadcasting systems.

1989 Commercial satellite broadcasting began in Britain with Sky Television, followed in 1990 by British Satellite Broadcasting (now merged).

HI-FI

Three forms of recorded sound now exist: records in which a fine stylus travels along grooves; tapes in which sounds are recorded as magnetic patterns; and digital ('compact') discs and cassettes in which beams of laser light read patterns of binary digits.

Today's record decks use fundamentally the same principles as the original gramophone. Sound vibrations are converted into a groove that runs in a spiral from the edge of the flat disc towards the centre. The sound vibrations are played by side-to-side movements of the needle inside the groove. In the 1920s, the introduction of electrical recording methods improved the quality of recordings. *Microphones* were used to convert sounds into electrical currents, which could then be used to drive cutting machines to create the grooves. In playback, the vibrations picked up by the stylus were used to generate an electrical current, which could be amplified by electronic circuits and played through loudspeakers that converted the electrical signals back into sound.

Long-playing records (LPs), made of vinyl plastic instead of the breakable shellac and rotating at 33 rpm (revolutions per minute) instead of 78 rpm, were first produced in 1946. They required much lighter stylus pressures to avoid grinding away the soft plastic; and because the grooves were narrower, the styluses needed finer points, usually provided by the use of diamond or sapphire.

Stereophonic recordings became widely available after 1958. In making a stereo recording, two microphones are set up at a distance from one another, and each of them records its own set of sound signals. The aim is to simulate the way in which we hear sounds: having two ears, we simultaneously hear two sounds, which are slightly different and come from slightly different directions. Two signals recorded on separate strips along a tape are played back through two speakers.

At the heart of any hi-fi system is the *amplifier*. An amplifier is essentially a set of electronic circuits that boost the signal from the stylus or tape deck to operate the loudspeakers. The circuits are made from transistors, and amplifiers are designed to produce the minimum distortion of the signal. *Loudspeakers* convert the electrical signal from the amplifier back into sound. The current from the amplifier flows around a coil of wire inside the field of a permanent magnet. Interaction between the field produced by the current flowing through the coil and that of the permanent magnet makes the coil vibrate. The coil is attached to a cone of stiff lightweight material that vibrates with it and creates the sounds.

TAPE RECORDING

The *telegraphone*, introduced in 1898, recorded sound by the alternating magnetization of a steel wire, replaced in the 1930s by steel tape. After 1935 strong plastic tape covered with iron-oxide powder made tape recording widely available, and domestic *tape recorders* appeared in the 1950s. Sounds are recorded by passing the tape in front of a recording head that consists of an electromagnet fed by electrical signals from a microphone. A magnetic pattern corresponding to the sounds is created on the tape as iron oxide fragments align themselves with the magnetic field. In playback, the tape passes in front of a second head, inducing an electrical current that is proportional to the magnetization of the tape. The current is then passed through an amplifier to loudspeakers. The most common type of tape is the *compact cassette*.

DIGITAL RECORDING

Sounds are now recorded digitally, as a series of binary digits, or *bits*. In a *digital system*, the sound is 'sampled' 40 000 times a second, and its amplitude and frequency (volume and pitch) are recorded as a binary number. Recordings made in this way can be turned into ordinary discs, but the advantages of low distortion and a good signal-to-noise ratio are better preserved in the form of digital ('compact') discs. *Compact discs*, which were launched commercially in 1982, record the bits as a series of minute pits or blank spaces in the surface of the disc. The pits are 'read' by a laser device that scans the record, picking up a series of signals that are the original binary digits of the recording. The signals are converted to analogue currents that can be amplified and fed to loudspeakers. *Digital compact cassettes* and *recordable compact discs* are being developed.

MILESTONES IN HI-FI

1877 Thomas Edison invented the phonograph, using a cylinder with grooves on the surface, to record and play sound.

1888 The Gramophone demonstrated for the first time by Emile Berliner. It used flat discs made from vulcanized rubber.

1895 Shellac replaced vulcanized rubber in the production of records.

1898 Valdemar Poulsen invented the telegraphone: forerunner of the modern tape recorder.

1901 Black discs with spiral grooves introduced by Emile Berliner.

1925 Introduction of electrical recording, with sounds recorded by microphones, transformed into electric current and converted into mechanical form to cut the master disk.

1933 The British company EMI pioneered stereophonic sound. It recorded two sound tracks within a single groove which were replayed through one stylus in two separate amplifying systems.

1935 The German companies AEG Telefunken and IG Farben introduced Magnetophone, the first commercial tape recorder using new magnetized plastic tape covered with iron-oxide powder.

1946 Columbia Records introduced long-playing 12-inch vinylite disks rotating at 33⅓ rpm.

1949 RCA introduced 7-inch disks rotating at 45 rpm.

1950s Domestic tape recorders on sale.

1958 Introduction of standard system of two-channel stereo for LPs.

1960s Transistors replaced valves in amplifiers.

1963 Philips introduced compact cassettes (more convenient that the open reel tapes).

1967 RM Dolby introduced the Dolby system of sound recording, which eliminates background hiss and improves sound quality.

1971 Introduction of quadrophonic sound systems.

1980 Walkmans – small portable tape recorders – introduced by Sony in Japan.

1982 Development of the compact disc (digital audio discs) by Philips and Sony.

Late 1980s Digital compact cassettes and recordable compact discs were developed.

PHOTOGRAPHY

A *camera* is essentially a box that is lightproof except where the optical component, the *lens*, projects an image onto a sheet of material – *film* – inside the camera. Film is coated with an emulsion whose chemical properties are changed by exposure to light, and which – after appropriate processing – can reproduce the image. The *emulsion* is made of silver halide grains (often silver bromide or iodide), suspended in gelatin. After exposure to light and chemical processing (*development*), the grains become black metallic silver. When the unexposed silver halide in the parts wholly or partially untouched by light is dissolved away, the picture becomes permanent, or *fixed*. It is, however, a reversed, or *negative*, image, with the original light areas reproduced as dark areas, and vice versa. The conversion of the negative to a true, or *positive*, picture was a problem until a negative/positive technique was evolved, which brought the bonus that an unlimited number of positive prints could be produced from a single negative.

MILESTONES IN PHOTOGRAPHY

1725 J. Schulze discovered that in the presence of nitric acid silver was darkened by the action of light, but more discoveries were needed to transform images cast by a lens into records that were positive and permanent.

c. 1800 Thomas Wedgewood was making short-lived silhouette images with silver nitrate.

1826 Joseph Niepce made his first successful picture, with the image projected by a lens on to a metal plate covered with bitumen of judea, which hardens under the influence of light. Washing away the unhardened parts produced a printing plate.

1835 The first successful silver image, on a copper plate, was produced by Louis Daguerre, who discovered that there was a second ('latent') image that could be developed with mercury vapour.

1837 Daguerre made permanent pictures using a salt 'fixer'. Positive and permanent, his 'Daguerreotype' was the first popular photographic system.

1839 John Herschel suggested sodium thiosulphate ('hypo') as a fixing agent. Hippolyte Bayard invented a way of making positive images on paper. Joseph Reade discovered that gallic acid is a powerful developer.

1840 A mathematically calculated portrait lens designed by Josef Petzval, providing a large aperture and therefore shorter exposures, was produced.

1841 William Fox Talbot patented his 'Calotype' process, using a paper-base negative image from which unlimited numbers of positive prints could be made. The use of gallic acid reduced his average exposure time to five minutes.

1847 Niepce made binder for silver iodide from white of egg (albumen). This made fine-detail glass negatives possible. Louis Blanquart-Evrard improved the Calotype process by impregnating rather than coating paper with the light-sensitive mixture.

1851 Gustave le Gray introduced his waxed-paper process, which produced a negative almost as good as a glass plate. Frederick Scott Archer introduced the 'wet-plate' process, using collodion (guncotton and ether) as a binding agent poured on a glass plate, which was then dipped in silver nitrate and exposed in the camera and developed before it was dry. Using this method, exposures for portraits were reduced to ten seconds or less. Fox Talbot took the first high-speed flash photograph, using the spark discharge of a battery.

1854 After Fox Talbot – reluctant to share his knowledge – lost his legal claim to sole rights to the wet-plate process, photography progressed rapidly.

1861 James Clerk Maxwell demonstrated the possibility of producing colour pictures by superimposing red, green and blue negatives of the same subject (the 'additive' process). Each negative was exposed through the corresponding colour filter. Practical application was delayed by the lack of red-sensitive emulsions.

1868 Louis du Hauron suggested that colour pictures could be made with a single plate, through a screen covered with tiny transparent dots or lines of red, blue and yellow.

1871 Richard Maddox, following previous experimenters, devised a method of producing dry plates, with gelatine replacing collodion.

1873 John Burgess introduced commercially viable gelatine dry plates. Hermann Vögel discovered that silver particles dyed orange had greater sensitivity to green light.

1874 Edmond Becquerel's discovery that green dyes increase sensitivity to red made 'panchromatic' (red-sensitive) emulsion possible.

1878 Charles Bennett discovered that prolonged heating during the manufacture of emulsions greatly increases their sensitivity.

1880s Flash powder, a mixture of magnesium powder and potassium chlorate, was introduced.

1888 George Eastman introduced his roll-film box camera, bringing photography to the masses.

1890 Carl Zeiss's 'Protar' lens utilized a wide range of different barium glasses to reduce distortions.

1893 The 'kinetoscope', a peep-box for viewing moving pictures on a 35 mm perforated film strip, was marketed by Thomas Edison.

1895 Auguste and Louis Lumière introduced their cinematograph for moving pictures. This apparatus – which advanced and held the film by a claw device – became the basis of the movie film industry.

1904 The Lumière brothers marketed colourplates, with an outer coating of green, red and blue starch grains. The developed image was re-exposed and redeveloped ('reversed') to produce a positive colour transparency.

1924 The Leica miniature camera, utilizing 35 mm movie film, was introduced.

1925 The first flashbulb was introduced.

1935 Kodachrome, the first successful colour film utilizing three emulsion layers of differing colour response, was introduced for the production of positive transparencies.

1940 The modern electronic, or speed, flash was introduced.

1947 The Polaroid-Land 'instant picture' camera was demonstrated. Processing agents were incorporated in the film and activated within the camera after exposure.

1963 'Instant print' colour films were introduced.

1977 Polaroid introduced an 8 mm colour movie film.

1981 The first commercial video camera, the Sony Mavica, was demonstrated.

1982 Polaroid introduced still transparency films that can be processed rapidly outside the camera.

TEXTILES

The history of textiles is a long one. More than 3000 years before the birth of Christ, Egyptian mummies were laid in thier tombs wrapped in linen, a fabric woven from flax. The Chinese were weaving delicate patterns in silk by about 1000 BC.

The creation of textiles requires two processes: the spinning of yarn, and the weaving of cloth. The basic principles of these two crafts have not changed since the earliest times, although the materials used have been supplemented in the 20th century by man-made fibres.

NATURAL FIBRES

Natural fibres come from a variety of sources: *wool* from sheep, *cotton* from the seed pod of the cotton plant, *flax* from the stem of the flax plant, *silk* from the delicate webs spun by silkworms fattened on the leaves of the mulberry tree. Among the more specialized fibres, the Angora goat produces *mohair*, while *cashmere* comes from the Kashmir goat. Camel hair and the fleece of the vicuña, a relative of the llama, are used in rugs and overcoats. *Jute*, a plant fibre, is used for making sacks and carpet backings, while *hemp*, another plant fibre, is used in sailcloth and canvas.

In their natural state, none of these fibres is very long. Wool fibres may be up to 20 cm (8 in) long, and flax a metre or more, but cotton fibres are rarely more than a few centimetres and are often as short as 3 mm (⅛ in). In order to make a continuous strand or *yarn*, the fibres have to be laid out in parallel lines and twisted together in the process called *spinning*.

SPINNING

Having first been cleaned, the fibres are carded (laid parallel) by rolling them between two surfaces faced with points. Then they are combed to remove short fibres, and rolled in machines that pull out the yarn and give it a twist, which helps to hold the fibres together. Stronger yarns are created by twisting two or more yarns together, and mixtures are made by combining fibres from different sources, such as wool and polyester. Finally the finished yarn is dyed and wound on bobbins (spools) for dispatch. Continuous improvement in mechanization since the 18th century has led to modern machines that are capable of producing thousands of metres of yarn an hour.

Unlike natural fibres, man-made fibres like *nylon* are continous. In principle, therefore, they can be used without spinning to make items such as net curtains, nylon stockings or tights. For more substantial garments, however, several filaments are wound together to make a thicker yarn. Synthetic fibres may also be cut into shorter lengths, and then blended with natural fibres and spun into a combination yarn.

WEAVING

Two techniques are available for turning yarn into fabric: *weaving* and *knitting*. Traditionally knitting has been used for hosiery (including nylon stockings), for sweaters, and for women's dresses. Weaving is used to create bolts (rolls) of cloth, both for clothing and for furnishing fabrics.

The pattern of the weave can be altered to produce different effects. *Satin* gets its glossy appearance because the warp threads are interwoven not with every weft thread, but with every fourth or fifth. In *damask*, the same technique is used, but places where

the warp lies on top are alternated with places where the weft does, producing subtle variations of shading. *Twill weaves* are used to produce gaberdine, serge and whipcord, and *pile weaves* for corduroy, plush, velour and velvet. The pile in such fabrics is created by cutting some of the threads after weaving, so that they stand out vertically from the surface of the fabric.

PRINTED PATTERNS

Not all fabric patterns are produced by weaving. Colour printing, using as many as 16 different colours, can also be used. This method originated in India, and today printing is done on a series of rollers, one for each colour that is to be applied. Each roller, engraved with a part of the pattern, picks up dye from a trough as it rotates. The pattern is transferred to the fabric as it passes between the rollers, care being taken to ensure that the fabric cannot slip – otherwise the pattern would get out of register. After coming off the final roller at speeds of up to 180 m (590 ft) a minute, the fabric is dried in an oven.

KNITTING

In knitting, the yarns are not interwoven with one another but knotted. The range of patterns is more limited, but with modern knitting machines far more ambitious designs can be achieved than had previously been possible. The use of modern combination fabrics in which wool is mixed with man-made fibres has also allowed garments to be knitted that are easier to look after and that keep their shape better.

MILESTONES IN TEXTILES

Paleolithic (c. 30 000 years ago)
Bone awls and later bone needles were used to sew animal skins together.

Neolithic (3200 years ago)
The spindle, used for spinning animal and vegetable fibres into yarn, and the loom, used for weaving cloth, were invented. No textiles from this period have survived.

1000 BC
Elaborate fabrics woven in silk were being produced on hand looms in China.

c. AD 1300
The spinning wheel came into use, doubling the speed at which yarn could be made. Its origins are obscure, some scholars think it originated in India much earlier. The horizontal frame loom, set on legs and with treadles to raise and lower the threads, also came into use at about the same time.

1589
The stocking-frame, a device for increasing the speed of knitting, invented by a Nottinghamshire clergyman, William Lee. For fear of unemployment, its use was discouraged by Queen Elizabeth I.

1733
John Kay, a Lancashire weaver, invented the flying shuttle, a device that could carry the threads through a piece of cloth much wider than the span of a weaver's arms. It doubled the productivity of the loom.

1764
James Hargreaves, a weaver and carpenter, invented

the spinning jenny which allowed several strands of yarn to be spun at once.

1769
Richard Arkwright of Preston, an early industrialist, produced the first truly mechanical spinning machine, the water frame, so called because it was powered by water wheels. This vital invention, requiring power beyond that of a single human being, began the factory system and led to a huge expansion of cotton production in England.

1779
Samuel Crompton of Bolton devised a machine that combined the merits of the jenny and the water frame. Because of its mixed parentage it became known as the spinning mule. It produced a yarn both fine and strong, and finally solved the problems of mechanical spinning.

1785
The power loom was invented by Edmund Cartwright, a Leicestershire clergyman, bringing mechanization to the weaving of cloth. Early designs, made of wood, were not very satisfactory, and only the arrival of cast iron frames in the 19th century solved the problems.

1801
Joseph-Marie Jacquard devised a method for the automatic weaving of the complex silks, using a series of punched cards to control the lifting of the warp threads in the correct sequence. This was the first use of punched cards, later important in computers.

1823
Collier and Magnan, of Paris, introduced heavy duty, wide looms capable of weaving draperies and tarpaulins. Similar machines were produced in England (Sharpe and Roberts, 1830) and in Saxony (Schonherr, 1845).

1824
Charles Mackintosh, a Glasgow chemist, produced the first waterproof garments, using rubber, hence the mackintosh.

1851
Isaac M. Singer, of Boston, Massachusetts, produced the first practical domestic sewing machine.

1856
In Leicester, Matthew Townsend invented the latch needle, which increased the possibilities of knitting machines. In 1864 William Cotton, also of Leicester, produced a powered machine capable of knitting a dozen socks or stockings at once.

1892
The first artificial fibre, rayon, was made from cellulose by the chemists C. F. Cross and E. J. Bevan.

1893
The zip fastener was invented by the American engineer Whitcomb Judson. It finally became a huge success in 1918, after improvements made by the Swedish engineer Gideon Sundback.

1937
The American chemist Wallace Carothers, working for Du Pont, discovered nylon, the product of mixing adipic acid with hexamethylinediamine.

1941
J. T. Dickinson and J. R. Whinfield produced ter-

ylene (dacron in the USA) from terephthalic acid and ethylene glycol.

1948
The Swiss engineer Georges de Mestral invented Velcro, a form of woven nylon that consists of hooks and loops that link together to create a fastener.

1960
Open-end spinning, a faster system capable of producing high-quality yarn, developed in Czechoslovakia.

1970s
Lasers introduced for cutting out cloth into the shapes needed to make clothes.

TEXTILE GLOSSARY

carding the process of teasing out the mass of natural fibres and lining them up for spinning.

cashmere a fine wool from the coat of the Kashmir goat.

chintz fabric printed with patterns rather than woven, originally from the Hindi word 'tchint', meaning mottled.

combing alternative to carding for untangling and straightening fibres before spinning.

damask form of satin weave in which areas where warp threads lie on top are alternated with areas where weft threads do, producing variations of shading.

dry cleaning method of cleaning using solvents rather than water, thereby avoiding shrinkage. The solvent used today is perchlorethylene.

flax plant which produces from its stem the natural fibre flax, used to make linen.

fulling process for thickening woollen cloth, using alkalis like Fuller's Earth.

heddle fine wire with an eyelet through which a warp thread passes. Used for raising and lowering the warp threads to allow passage of the shuttle.

hemp Fibre from hemp plant, used for canvas and sailcloth.

jute plant fibre used for making sacks and carpet backings.

loom framework for holding parallel warp threads through which the weft threads are carried by the shuttle.

mohair luxury fibre produced from the hair of the Angora goat.

satin weave in which the warp threads are interwoven not with every weft thread but with every third or fourth. This means that they lie on top, producing a glossy finish.

shuttle boat-shaped object attached to the weft thread and used to carry it to and fro through the warp threads.

twill form of weave used to produce gaberdine, serge and whipcord.

warp the set of threads running lengthwise along the loom, and hence along the length of the finished cloth.

weft the set of threads running across the loom, weaving in and out of the warp threads.

velvet a pile weave in which some of the threads are cut after weaving so that they stand up to produce a carpet-like effect. Corduroy, plush and velour are also pile weaves.

INVENTIONS

Inventions in the fields of medicine and music are treated in those sections; inventions in science are treated in more detail in the chapter Physical Sciences. Other inventions are dealt with in more detail in this chapter, see pp. 286–308. ⟨Milestones⟩

abacus c. 3000 BC; probably developed in the Middle East.

adding machine 1623; by Wilhelm Schickard (German); Blaise Pascal invented an adding machine using 10:1 gearing to represent decimal columns in 1642. The earliest commercial machine was devised by William Burroughs (US) in St Louis, Missouri (1885).

aeropile c. AD; by Hero of Alexandria (Greek); a toy-like aeropile that may be considered to be the ancestor of the piston steam engine.

aircraft (theory) 1717; by Emmanuel Swedenborg (Swedish) who produced the first 'rational design' for a flying machine.

aircraft (practical) 1890; by Clément Ader (French) whose steam-powered *Eole* made the first hop by a man-carrying aeroplane at Armainvilliers, France. The first controlled and sustained power-driven flight occurred at Kitty Hawk, North Carolina, USA, on 17 December 1903 when Orville and Wilbur Wright (US) flew their chain-driven *Flyer 1* for a distance of 36.5 m (120 ft) at an airspeed of 48 km/h (30 mph).

airship 1852; by Henri Giffard (French) whose steam-powered coal-gas airship made the first airship flight from Paris to Trappes, France.

airship (rigid frame) 1900; by Count Ferdinand von Zeppelin (German).

aquatinting 1768; by Jean Baptiste Le Prince (French).

autogyro 1923; by Juan de la Cierva (Spanish), whose first successful autogyro flew at Girona, Spain, in January 1923.

bakelite 1909; by Leo Baekeland (Belgian-born US).

ball-point pen 1888; by John J. Loud (US); the first practical and low cost writing pens were perfected by Lazlo and Georg Biro (Hungarian) in 1938.

barbed wire 1867; by Lucien B. Smith (US).

barometer 1644; by Evangelista Torricelli (Italian).

battery (electric) 1800; by Alessandro Volta (Italian); the battery was demonstrated to Napoleon I in 1801.

bicycle 1839–40; by Kirkpatrick Macmillan (Scottish), whose invention had pedal-driven cranks.

bicycle (first direct drive) 1861; by Ernest Michaux (French).

bicycle tyres (pneumatic) 1888; by John Boyd Dunlop (Scottish), although the principle was patented but not developed by Robert William Thomson (English) in 1845.

bifocal lens 1780; by Benjamin Franklin (US).

boats 8th millennium BC; reed and dugout boats used.

boats (sailing) 3rd millennium BC; in ancient Egypt.

bridge (metal) 1779; at Ironbridge, Telford, Shropshire, England.

bronze c. 3700 BC; in pre-dynastic Egypt.

Bunsen burner 1855; by Robert Wilhelm von Bunsen (German); Michael Faraday (English) had previously designed an adjustable burner.

burglar alarm 1858; by Edwin T. Holmes (US); the first electric burglar was installed at Boston, Massachusetts, USA.

calculator (advanced) 1822; by Charles Babbage (English), who set out to design a 'differential engine', an advanced form of calculator for application to the problems of navigation.

car (petrol-driven) 1885; by Karl Benz (German); the first successful run was in Mannheim (late 1885); the car was patented in January 1886.

car (pneumatic tyres) 1895; by André and Edouard Michelin (French).

carburettor 1876; by Gottlieb Daimler (German).

carburettor spray 1892; by Charles E. Duryea (US).

carpet sweeper 1876; by Melville R. Bissell (US) at Grand Rapids, Mich., USA.

cash register 1879; by James Ritty (US); built in Dayton, Ohio, USA.

cassette (compact) 1963; by Philips (Dutch).

cellophane 1908; by Dr Jacques Brandenberger (Swiss); machine production did not begin until 1911.

cement (portland) 1824; by Joseph Aspdin (English) at Wakefield, Yorkshire, England.

chronometer 1735; by John Harrison (English), who invented (1772) a prize of £20 000 that had been on offer by the British government since 1714.

clock (mechanical) 725; by I-Hsing and Liang-Tsan (Chinese); earliest escapement.

clock (pendulum) 1656; by Christiaan Huygens (Dutch).

clockwork 80 BC; by the ancient Greeks.

colour printing 1719; by Jakob Le Bon (German), who devised a three-colour engraving process.

compact disc 1978; by Philips (Dutch) and Sony (Japanese); launched commercially in 1982.

computer (programmable electronic) 1943; by Prof. Max Newman (English) and built by T.H. Flowers; this device – the Colossus (see Computing section) was used to break the German code Enigma.

computer (store-programmed) 1948; at Manchester University, England.

computer (integrated circuit) 1952; by W.A. Dummer (US).

computer language 1666; by Gottfried Wilhelm Leibniz, who proposed the basis of a language that would allow logical statements to be dealt with mathematically. The essence was the use of digits 0 for FALSE and 1 for TRUE. Leibniz – who went on to develop binary arithmetic – thus laid the foundations of the first computer language long before the invention of the computer.

dental plate 1817; by Anthony A. Plantson (US).

dental plate (rubber) 1855; by Charles Goodyear (US).

diesel engine 1895; by Rudolph Diesel (German), whose first commercial success with his engine was at Augsburg two years later.

disc brake 1902; by Dr F. Lanchester (English); the brake was first used on aircraft in 1953.

dynamo 1832; by Hyppolite Pixii (French).

dynamo (rotative) 1833; by Joseph Saxton (English).

electric blanket 1883; exhibited in Vienna at the Austria Exhibition.

electric flat iron 1882; by H. W. Seeley (US) in New York City.

electric lamp 1879; by Thomas Alva Edison (US); the first practical demonstration was at Menlo Park, New Jersey, USA.

electric lamp (carbon filament) 1860; pioneer work on carbon filaments by Sir Joseph Swan (English).

electric motor (DC) 1873; by Zénobe Gramme (Belgian).

electric motor (AC) 1888; by Nikola Tesla (Serbian-born, US).

electrolysis 1894; by means of the German Castner-Kellner process.

electromagnet 1824; by William Sturgeon (English).

fountain pen 1884; by Lewis E. Waterman (US), although a fountain pen was patented but not developed by D. Hyde (US) in 1830.

galvanometer 1834; by André-Marie Ampère; the first measurement of the flow of electricity with a free-moving needle.

gas lighting 1792; by William Murdoch (English); a private house in Cornwall was lit by gas in 1792, a factory in Birmingham in 1798 and London streets in 1807.

glass (blowing) c. 50 BC; in Sidon, Lebanon.

glass (stained) *ante* 850; the earliest complete window is at Augsburg, Germany, and dates from c. 1080.

glassware c. 2600 BC; in Mesopotamia (modern Iraq).

glider 1853; by Sir George Cayley (English); a flight took place near Brompton Hall, Yorkshire. Sketches of a glider (dated 1716) were made by Emmanuel Swedenborg (Swedish).

gramophone 1878; by Thomas Alva Edison (US).

gyro-compass 1911; by Elmer A. Sperry (US); tested on USS *Delaware*.

gyroscope 1852; by Jean Foucault (French).

helicopter (theory) c. 1500; by Leonardo da Vinci who proposed the idea of a helicopter-like craft, although it is now known that the French built 'helicopter' toys before this time.

helicopter (operational) 1909; by Igor Sikorsky (Ukrainian-born US) who built an unsuccessful helicopter in Russia. (The first practical helicopter was the German Focke-Achgelis built in 1936.)

hot-air balloon 1709; by Father Bartolomeu de Gusmão (Brazilian-born Portuguese), whose model hot-air balloon – which made an indoor flight at Terreiro do Paço, Portugal – is the earliest known.

hot-air balloon (full-size) 1783; by Jacques and Joseph Montgolfier (French), who achieved both tethered and free flight in the autumn of 1783.

hovercraft 1953; by Sir Christopher Cockerell (English), although the first air-cushion vehicle patent was made in 1877 by J. I. Thornycroft (English).

ink 2nd century AD; in China.

integrated circuit 1952; by Geoffrey Dummer (English); the first practical circuit was perfected by Harwick Johnson (US), at Princeton, New York, in 1953.

internal combustion powered vehicle 1805; by Isaac de Rivaz (Swiss); a primitive vehicle comprising a carriage powered by de Rivaz's 'explosion' engine.

jet engine 1930; by Frank Whittle (English); it was a gas turbine for jet propulsion.

laser 1960; by Dr Charles H. Townes (US) and demonstrated at Hughes Research, Malibu, California.

laser typesetting 1976; by Monotype.

lift 1852; by Elisha G. Otis (US); the first elevator was installed at Yonkers, New York.

lightning conductor 1752; by Benjamin Franklin (US) at Philadelphia, Pennsylvania, USA.

linoleum 1860; by Frederick Walton (English).

lithography 1796; by Aloys Senefelder (German).

loudspeaker 1900; by Horace Short (English); a compressed air 'auxetophone', which was first used on the Eifel Tower, Paris, in the summer of 1900.

loudspeaker (outdoor electric public address system) 1916; by Bell Telephone on Staten Island Island, New York, USA.

machine gun (Gatling gun) 1861; by Richard Gatling (US). An earlier gun that operated on a basic machine gun principle was invented by James Puckle in 1718.

mackintosh 1823; by Charles Macintosh (Scottish), who produced a waterproof coat made from a fabric that sandwiched a layer of rubber between two layers of cloth.

map c. 2250 BC; in Sumeria; clay tablets of the River Euphrates.

map (printed) 1477; in Bologna, Italy.

margarine 1869; by Hippolyte Mège-Mouries (French).

match 1816; by François Devosne (French); a phosphorus (unsafe) match.

match (safety) 1845; by Anton von Schrötter (Austrian).

measure (weight) c. 3800 BC; the *beqaa* – a unit of weight equivalent to between 188.7–211.2 gm (6.65–7.45 oz) – was in use in the Amratian period of the ancient Egyptian civilization.

measure (length) c. 3500 BC; the unit of length now generally referred to as the megalithic yard was used by megalithic tomb builders in NW Europe. It was equivalent to c. 82.9 cm (c. 2.72 ft).

mezzotint process 1642; by Ludwig van Siegen (German) who introduced printing in graduated tones.

microcomputer 1968–70; by Gilbert Hyatt (US) at Micro Computer Inc, who devised a single chip microcomputer.

microphone 1876; by Alexander Graham Bell (US); the name was coined two years later.

microprocessor 1971; by Marcian E. Hoff (US); it was launched by the US company Intel in the same year.

microscope 1590; by Zacharias Janssen (Dutch), whose device had a compound convex-concave lens.

mobile (cordless) telephone 1967; in USA.

motor cycle 1885; by Gottlieb Daimler (German); the motor cycle was first ridden by Paul Daimler on 10 November 1885 at Cannstatt, Germany.

moveable type c. 1450; by Johannes Gutenberg (German).

neon lamp 1910; by Georges Claude (French); the neon lamp was first installed at the 1910 Paris Motor Show.

nuclear power station 1951; the first nuclear power station producing electricity was the EBR-1 in the USA.

nylon 1930s; by Walter Carrothers (US).

paper 2nd century AD; in China, although papyrus was used in ancient Egypt.

parachute 1783; by Louis-Sébastien Lenormand (French) who used a quasi-parachute in a descent in Montpellier, France, although Faustus Verancsis (Hungarian) is reputed to have used a framed canopy for a descent in Hungary in 1617. (The king of Ayutthaya in Siam was reported in 1687 to have been diverted by an ingenious athlete who parachuted with two large umbrellas.)

parking meter 1935; by Carlton C. Magee (US) and first used in Oklahoma City, USA.

photocopier 1937; by Chester Carlson (US), who developed the first practical dry photocopier.

pipeline 1863; at Oil Creek, Pennsylvania, USA, although the pipes were torn up by Luddites.

pocket calculator 1971; by Jack St Clair Kilby (US), James van Tassell (US) and Jerry D. Merryman (US); the 'Pocketronic' which was manufactured by Texas Instruments Inc., Dallas, USA.

polythene 1930s; by British chemists.

porcelain 851; (earliest known) in China.

potter's wheel c. 6500 BC; in Asia Minor.

pressure cooker 1679; by Denis Papin (French).

printing (blocks) 2nd century AD; in China where blocks with pictures or letters cut into them were developed.

printing (linotype) 1884; by Otto Mergenthaler (US).

printing (monotype) 1887; by Tolbert Lanston (US).

printing press c. 1450; by Johannes Gutenberg (German).

printing press (rotary) 1844; by William Hoe (US).

programmable device 1804; by J. M. Jacquard (French), a weaver who invented a loom in which changes of pattern or material could be programmed by feeding in a set of punched cards.

pyramid 2856 BC; by Imhotep (Egyptian); the earliest pyramid was the Djoser step pyramid, at Sakkara, Egypt.

radar (pulse ranging) 1925; by Gregory Breit (US) and Merle A. Tuve (US); measured the height of the ionosphere by bouncing radio pulses off the ionized layer.

radar 1922; by Dr Albert H. Taylor (US) and Leo C. Young (US); radio reflection effect first noted. Radar was first harnessed by Dr Rudolph Kühnold (German) at Kiel, Germany, in 1934.

radio echo device 1904; by Christian Hülsmeyer (German), who developed a primitive radar-like device.

rail transport 1550; at Leberthal, Alsace, France, where wagons ran on wooden rails at a mine.

railway (electric) 1879; by Werner von Siemens (German) whose oval metre gauge demonstration track was shown at the Berlin Trades Exhibition.

railway (steam locomotive) 1803; by Richard Trevithick (English), who built a steam locomotive for a 914 mm (3 ft) gauge iron plateway, although there is no evidence that it ran. His second locomotive drew wagons in which men rode at Penydarren, Glamorgan, Wales, on 22 February 1804.

rayon 1883; by Sir Joseph Swan (English); produced commercially at Courtauld's Ltd, Coventry, England in 1905; the name rayon was not used until 1924.

razor (electric) 1931; by Col. Jacob Schick (US) and first manufactured at Stamford, Connecticut, USA.

razor (safety) 1895; by King C. Gillette (US), who patented the first disposable blades.

record (gramaphone) 1901; by Emile Berliner (German-born US).

record (long-playing) 1948; by Dr Peter Goldmark (US) at the CBS Research laboratories.

refrigerator 1850; by James Harrison (Australian) and Alexander Catlin Twining (US); simultaneous development at Rodey Point, Victoria, Australia, and in Cleveland, Ohio; the first domestic refrigerator was installed at Chicago, Illinois, USA in 1913.

rocket (war) 1042; in China; war rockets propelled by gun-powder (charcoal-saltpetre-sulphur) were described by Zeng Gongliang.

rubber (latex foam) 1928; by Dunlop Rubber Co (UK).

rubber (vulcanized) 1841; by Charles Goodyear (US).

safety pin 1849; by Walter Hunt (US); first manufactured in New York City, USA.

Scotch tape 1930; by Richard Drew (US).

screw propeller 1836; by Sir Francis Pettit Smith (English).

self-starter 1911; by Charles F. Kettering (US) at Dayton, Ohio, USA and sold to Cadillac.

sewing machine 1829; by Barthélemy Thimmonnier (French), although a patent was issued to Thomas Saint (English) in 1793 for a type of sewing machine that was apparently undeveloped.

ship (power-driven) 1801–02; by William Symington (Scottish) whose *Charlotte Dundas* was the first successful power-driven vessel. She was a stern paddle-steamer built for the Forth and Clyde Canal and used a double-acting condensing engine constructed by James Watt.

silk manufacture c. 50 BC; in China where reeling machines were devised. (There were silk mills in Italy c. 1250.)

skyscraper 1882; by William Le Baron Jenny (US) who constructed the Home Insurance Co. Building (Chicago, USA), which had 10 storeys (the top four with steel beams).

slide rule 1621; by William Oughtred (English); the earliest slide between a fixed stock was developed by Robert Bissaker in 1654.

spectacles (convex) c. 1286; in Pisa, Italy.

spectacles (concave) c. 1450; by Nicholas of Cusa (Italian), who developed concave lens for myopia.

spinning frame 1769; by Sir Richard Arkwright (English).

spinning jenny 1764; by James Hargreaves (English).

spinning mule 1779; by Samuel Crompton (English).

steam engine 1698; by Thomas Savery (English).

steam engine (condenser) 1769; by James Watt (Scottish).

steam engine (marine) 1783; by Marquis Jouffroy d'Abbans, who ascended a reach of the River Saône, near Lyon, France in the 180 tonnes paddle steamer *Pyroscaphe.*

steam engine (piston) 1712; by Thomas Newcomen (English).

steam-powered vehicle 1769; by Nicolas-Joseph Cugnot (French); a three-wheeled steam-driven military tractor.

steam-powered vehicle (model) 1668; by Father Ferdinand Verbiest (Belgian).

steam powered vehicle (passenger) 1801; by Richard Trevithick (English); an eight-seater vehicle which operated in Camborne, Cornwall, England.

steel production 1855; by Henry Bessemer (English).

stereophonic sound 1933; pioneer work by the British company EMI.

stocking frame 1589; by William Lee (English).

submarine 1776; by David Bushnell (US), who developed a device with a hand-propelled screw and a one-man crew; the vessel was used in New York.

submersible 1624; by Cornelius Drebbel (Dutch) who demonstrated a 12-man wooden and leather submersible in the River Thames.

tape recorder 1935; by the German companies AEG Telefunken and IG Farben who both introduced commercial tape recorders in 1935. (See also telegraphone.)

tank 1914; by Sir Ernest Swinton (English); a model was designed by William Tritton and tested in 1915.

telegraph (mechanical) 1787; by M. Lammond (French) who demonstrated a working model in Paris.

telegraph code 1837; by Samuel B.P. Morse (US), although a very major part was played by his assistant Alfred Vail who was the first to transmit a code.

telegraphone 1898; by Valdemar Poulsen (Danish), whose pioneer magnetic recorder was the ancestor of the tape recorder.

telephone (theory) 1849; by Antonio Meucci (Italian), who devised and produced an instrument that worked imperfectly by electrical impulses.

telephone (practical) 1876; by Alexander Graham Bell (US); the first telephone exchange was constructed as Boston, Massachusetts, USA in 1878.

telephone (automatic exchange) 1889; by Alfred Strowger (US), a US undertaker who suspected he was losing trade through the transfer of his calls to another undertaker by telephonists.

telescope (refractor) 1608; by Hans Lippershey (Dutch).

telescope (reflecting) 1668–69; by Isaac Newton (English).

television 1925; by John Logie Baird (Scottish), who transmitted the first recognizable pictures.

television camera 1931; by Vladimir Zworykin (Russian-born US), who developed the first practical electronic television camera.

terylene 1941; by J.R. Whinfield (English) at Accrington, Lancashire, England.

thermometer 1593; by Galileo Galilei (Italian) for clinical use.

thermometer (mercury) c. 1615; by Santorio Santorio (Italian).

transistor 1948; by John Bardeen (US), William Shockley (US) and Walter Brattain (US) at Bell Telephone Laboratories, although the first application for a patent was by Dr Julius E. Lilienfeld (Canadian) in 1925.

transistor (junction) 1951; by R.L. Wallace (US), Morgan Sparks (US) and Dr William Bradford Shockley (US).

transistor radio 1952; by Sony (Japan).

turbine (ship) 1894; by Hon. Sir Charles Parsons, whose *Turbinia* was 30 m (100 ft) long and had a displacement of 45.2 tonnes.

turbojet engine 1937; by Dr Hans Pabst von Ohain (Germany); the first flight by an aeroplane powered by a turbojet engine was made by the Heinkel He 178, piloted by Erich Warsitz at Marienehe, Germany in August 1939.

typewriter 1867; by Christopher Sholes (US); manufactured by the gunsmith Philo Remington in 1874.

tyres (rubber) 1846; by Thomas Hancock (English).

vehicle (gas-powered) 1826; by Samuel Brown (English); the first vehicle powered with an internal combustion engine was a gas-powered carriage on Shooter's Hill, Blackheath, SE London.

Walkman 1980; by Sony (Japan) who developed small portable tape recorders, launching them commercially in 1980.

washing machine 1907; by Hurley Machine Co (US); marketed under the name of 'Thor' in Chicago, Illinois, USA.

watch before 1462 when there was the earliest mention of a named watchmaker, Bartholomeo Manfredi (Italian), in a reference to an earlier unnamed watchmaker.

watch (wrist) 1790; by Jacquet-Droz and Leschot of Geneva, Switzerland.

water closet 1589; by Sir John Harington (English) and installed at Kelston, near Bath, England.

weaving (flying shuttle) 1733; by John Kay (English).

welder (electric) 1877; by Elisha Thomson (US).

wheel c. 3580 BC; by the Sumerian civilization, at Uruk (now in modern Iraq). (A pottery cup depicting three four-wheeled wagons – and dating from c. 3500 BC – has been found at Brónócice, Poland.)

windmill c. 600; in Iran for corn grinding.

writing c. 3600 BC; in Sumeria; pictographs.

zip fastener 1891; by Whitcomb L. Judson (US), although the first practical zip fastener was developed by in the USA by Gideon Sundback (Swedish) in 1913.

ENERGY

In the industrialized world, the vast amount of power that we demand is most often provided by means of electricity – the most convenient and flexible medium in which to transfer power from its source to where it is needed. However, in deciding how best to generate electricity in ever-increasing quantities, we are confronted with an unenviable choice. On the one hand, there is the gradual but inevitable damage to the environment caused by burning coal and oil; on the other, the unlikely but potentially catastrophic risks associated with nuclear power. The environmentally friendly and safe sources of energy – wind, solar and geothermal – still account for very little of the world's energy.

Most of the developed world's electricity is generated by burning coal, oil or from nuclear fission. In each case the heat produced by the fuel is used to raise steam, which turns the blades of a steam turbine. The turbine rotor is connected to the shaft of an electrical generator. In most developed countries and increasingly in the Third World, the power output is fed into a national grid system. Most developed countries have extensive and complex supply networks. Power stations are interlinked and centrally controlled, allowing power to be channelled to where it is required and extra stations to be started up to meet peaks in demand.

OIL

Oil and natural gas are hydrocarbons – organic compounds built from just two elements, hydrogen and carbon. Hydrocarbons range from light gases like methane (CH_4) to heavy solids like asphalt. Crude oil is a mixture of hydrocarbons – some light, some heavy – and is often found in conjunction with natural gas (see below). Three types of rock are needed to form an oil reserve: the sedimentary rocks in which the hydrocarbons form; porous rocks that can store the oil and gas like a sponge; and an impervious layer of rock over the top, ideally in the form of a dome, to form a trap.

When a likely area of oil has been identified, exploratory drilling begins. If economic amounts of oil are found, production wells are drilled. From a single derrick, many holes can be drilled, fanning outwards to reach all corners of the reserve. This is done with a tool called the *whipstock*, which forces the flexible drillstring to bend slightly. A large field may be drilled from several different platforms. Each hole is lined with steel casing embedded in concrete, and explosives are used to punch holes through the casing, to allow the oil to get into the hollow casing from the surrounding rock.

Once the well has been drilled, an arrangement of pipework and valves – called a 'christmas tree' because of its shape – is installed at the surface to control the flow. The pressure of the oil may be enough to drive it to the surface, but pumps can also be used. As pressure falls, it may be artificially increased by pumping water down other holes. Even with such techniques no more than 30 to 40% of the oil in place can be recovered.

To turn crude oil into useful products it must be refined. Two basic processes are used. *Fractional distillation* allows lighter fractions to be separated from heavier ones. *Catalytic cracking* uses heat, pressure, and certain catalysts to convert or 'split' some of the heavier fractions obtained by distillation into lighter, more useful ones. Today the most valuable product is petrol (gasoline), used to drive the world's cars, so a growing proportion of each barrel is converted into that. The main producers and consumers of crude petroleum are listed below

PRODUCERS OF CRUDE PETROLEUM

	Production (in tonnes)
Russia	569 000 000
USA	366 000 000
Saudi Arabia	323 000 000
Iran	147 000 000
China	138 000 000
Mexico	133 000 000
Venezuela	118 000 000
United Arab Emirates	102 000 000
Iraq	101 000 000
United Kingdom	88 000 000
Nigeria	87 000 000
Norway	82 000 000
Canada	76 000 000
Indonesia	75 000 000
Libya	65 000 000
Kuwait	61 000 000
Algeria	55 000 000

CONSUMERS OF OIL

	Consumption (in million barrels)
USA	4938
Russia	c. 2200
Japan	1300
China	744
Germany	673
UK	566
Canada	510
France	509
Saudi Arabia	509
Italy	488
Mexico	450
Brazil	433
India	393
Spain	375
Netherlands	346
Venezuela	329
South Korea	296

OIL RESERVES

The following figures relate to proved reserves of petroleum that are generally considered to be recoverable using current technology. The figures for Russia, Iran, Norway and the United Arab Emirates are averages of widely differing estimates by various authorities.

	Estimated reserves (in million barrels)
Saudi Arabia	260 000
Iraq	100 000
Kuwait	98 000
United Arab Emirates	82 000
Iran	77 000
Venezuela	60 000
Russia	56 000
Mexico	51 300
USA	26 300
Libya	22 000

Nigeria	17 300
Norway	12 000
Indonesia	11 000

GAS

Natural gas is often found together with oil, because it is formed in the same way and collects in the same kind of geological formations (see above). The development of long-distance pipelines and ships that carry liquefied natural gas has greatly increased the market for gas, which is both an excellent fuel and a useful raw material for the chemical industry. Gas flows more readily than crude oil, so as much as 80% of the gas in place may be recovered.

The processing of gas involves separating it from any liquids and 'sweetening' it by removing ases such as hydrogen sulphide and carbon dioxide. The end product consists mostly of methane (more than 80%) combined with smaller amounts of ethane, propane and butane. The main producers and consumers of natural gas are listed below.

PRODUCERS OF NATURAL GAS

	Production (in terajoules*)
Russia	21 700 000
USA	17 500 000
Canada	4 100 000
Turkmenistan	2 700 000
Netherlands	2 290 000
United Kingdom	1 840 000
Algeria	1 580 000
Indonesia	1 240 000
Azerbaijan	1 230 000
Romania	1 160 000
Norway	1 120 000
Saudi Arabia	1 070 000

* a terajoule is a measure of energy equivalent to 34.13 tonnes of coal.

CONSUMERS OF NATURAL GAS

	Consumption (in million m³)
Russia	590 000
USA	535 400
Germany	72 380
Canada	68 870
UK	60 330
Japan	46 000
Netherlands	41 200
Italy	41 050
Romania	33 750
France	30 340
Saudi Arabia	26 700
Argentina	25 070
Mexico	22 600
Iran	22 000

NATURAL GAS RESERVES

The following figures relate to proved reserves of natural gas that are generally considered to be recoverable using current technology. The figures for Russia, Turkmenistan, Venezuela, Azerbaijan, the Netherlands, Indonesia, Iraq, Norway and Nigeria are averages of widely differing estimates by various authorities.

	Estimated reserves (in million m³)
Russia	1 250 000 000
Iran	600 000 000

United Arab Emirates	195 000 000
Saudi Arabia	185 000 000
USA	169 300 000
Turkmenistan	165 000 000
Qatar	162 000 000
Algeria	115 000 000
Venezuela	113 000 000
Iraq	102 000 000
Canada	97 000 000
Indonesia	95 000 000
Nigeria	90 000 000
Norway	85 000 000
Azerbaijan	75 000 000
Mexico	72 000 000
Netherlands	65 000 000
Malaysia	55 000 000
Kuwait	53 000 000

COAL

Coal is a carbon-based mineral that formed over many millions of years as a result of the gradual compacting of partially decomposed plant matter. Three basic types of coal are found: lignite, bituminous coal and anthracite. Lignite (brown coal) has the lowest heat value, since it was formed more recently and contains less carbon and more water than the other varieties. About half the coal mined is

ENERGY SOURCES

The respective contributions of fossil fuels (coal, oil, etc), hydroelectric power and nuclear power to the power requirements of selected countries are given as percentages in the following table.

	Fossil fuels	HEP	Nuclear power
Argentina	59.3	29.8	10.9
Australia*	89.7	9.8	---
Belgium	37.8	0.6	61.6
Brazil	6.0	93.2	0.8
Canada	25.7	58.3	16.0
China	81.2	18.8	---
Denmark*	98.0	0.1	---
France	12.7	12.6	74.7
Germany	67.7	3.3	29.0
Iceland*	0.1	93.9	---
India	72.7	24.5	2.8
Italy*	82.0	16.5	---
Japan	64.7	12.2	23.1
Korea, South	49.5	4.5	46.0
Mexico	76.5	19.2	4.3
Netherlands	94.4	0.1	5.5
Nigeria	77.8	22.2	---
Norway	0.4	99.6	---
Pakistan	58.8	41.1	0.1
Poland	97.4	2.6	---
Russia	75.0	13.0	12.0
Saudi Arabia	100.0	---	---
Spain	48.4	13.3	38.3
Sweden	4.1	50.1	45.8
UK	77.1	2.2	20.7
USA	72.6	9.1	18.3

* The remaining contribution to national energy requirements is made by geothermally generated electricity.

used for generating electricity, with another quarter going to the steel industry as coking coal. The remainder is used in other industries or for home heating.

The burning of fossil fuels such as coal in power stations leads to the emission of several by-products that are potentially damaging to the environment. *Fly ash*, which results from burning pulverized coal, is effectively removed by passing the flue (or waste) gases from the furnace through an *electrostatis precipitator* – a series of electrically charged plates that hold back the tiny particles of ash.

However, other by-products pass straight out of the chimney and into the atmosphere, including sulphur dioxide and nitrogen oxides, major causes of acid rain, and carbon dioxide, which contributes to the greenhouse effect. Major coal-fired stations are likely to include desulphurization equipment. The major producers and consumers of coal are listed below.

PRODUCERS OF COAL (bituminous)

	Production (tonnes)
China	1 051 000 000
USA	861 000 000
Russia	415 000 000
India	198 000 000
South Africa	180 000 000
Australia	162 000 000
Ukraine	155 000 000
Poland	148 000 000
Kazakhstan	138 000 000
United Kingdom	93 000 000
Germany	76 000 000
North Korea	55 000 000

CONSUMERS OF COAL

	Consumption (tonnes)
China	1 025 000 000
USA	812 000 000
Germany	499 000 000
Russia	c. 390 000 000
Poland	223 000 000
India	213 000 000
Ukraine	c. 145 000 000
South Africa	132 000 000
Japan	112 000 000
UK	110 000 000
Australia	96 000 000

NUCLEAR ENERGY

In terms of electricity generation, the only difference between nuclear power stations and conventional stations is the means of raising steam to drive the turbines: the coal- or oil-burning furnace is simply replaced by a nuclear reactor. However, this entails a whole industry of its own.

Uranium-235 (U-235) is the form (or *isotope*) of the element uranium used as the fuel in most nuclear reactors. However, it is only present in tiny quantities – less than 1% – in mined uranium. The rest is made up of uranium-238. For many reactors, the proportion of U-235 has to be increased by a complex and very costly process known as *enrichment*. The fuel – enriched or natural uranium as required – is packed into fuel rods, which are placed in the core of a nuclear reactor.

The nuclei of U-235 atoms sometimes break apart when struck by neutrons, in a process known as *nuclear fission*. As the nucleus splits, two or three more neutrons are released. These go on to bombard other nuclei and may cause them to split, thus setting off a chain reaction. The reaction is essentially a controlled version of what happens when an atomic bomb explodes. To increase their chance of fissioning U-235 (rather than being captured without fission by U-238), the neutrons are slowed down using a *moderator* such as graphite. So much energy is released as the fuel is fissioned that a single tonne (ton) of uranium is equivalent of 25 000 tonnes of coal.

The vessel in which the fuel rods are placed is filled with a *coolant*. As nuclei split, energetic fragments fly off and are brought to rest in the surrounding coolant, so causing its temperature to rise. The coolant is constantly circulated through the core, so preventing the core from overheating and at the same time acting as the medium by which heat is channelled away from the core to raise steam. The nuclear reaction can be slowed down or stopped altogether if control rods containing a material that absorbs neutrons, such as boron, are lowered into the reactor core.

TYPES OF NUCLEAR REACTORS

The first commercial nuclear power station, opened in 1956 at Calder Hall in Cumbria, England, was a *magnox reactor*. Magnox reactors are so called because their fuel – natural (unenriched) uranium – is clad in an alloy of magnesium and aluminium called magnox. They are cooled by carbon dioxide gas. In the 1970s a new generation of much bigger gas-cooled reactors was developed in Britain – the *advanced gas-cooled reactors* or AGRs. In an AGR, the heat exchangers are located within the pressure vessel itself. The carbon-dioxide coolant is pressurized and heated up to 600 °C (1112 °F) or more as it is pumped through the core, which is made up of fuel rods filled with enriched uranium dioxide. Meanwhile, the Canadians have developed reactors that use 'heavy water' (deuterium oxide). Because heavy water (unlike ordinary water) absorbs few neutrons itself, reactors using it as moderator and coolant can operate with unenriched (and thus cheaper) fuel. The economy in fuel costs is offset, however, by the additional expenditure involved in producing heavy water.

Today, the most widespread nuclear power plants are *light-water reactors*. The coolant and moderator – ordinary ('light') water – is readily available and cheap, but the uranium fuel has to be highly enriched. In the case of *boiling-water reactors* (BWRs), the water is allowed to boil to make steam, which is less efficient at cooling and moderating the reactor, and so must be prevented from building up in the reactor core. In *pressurized-water reactors* or PWRs, the water must remain at even higher pressure than is required in a BWR, so that it can reach useful temperatures without boiling.

The world's reserves of uranium will not last for ever, but one sort of reactor could make them go a lot further – the *fast breeder reactor* or FBR. The drawback of fast reactors is that they require the reprocessing of spent nuclear fuel both to extract plutonium (its main fuel) in the first place and to recover it from the uranium blanket. Reprocessing is a highly complex and expensive operation – as well as being unpopular with environmentalists. Reservations about fast reactors have led some countries to halt FBR programmes and research.

NUCLEAR SAFETY

The world's worst nuclear accident at Chernobyl in the Ukraine in April 1986 highlighted the potential dangers of nuclear power. As a result of Chernobyl and another costly, though less serious, accident at a PWR on Three Mile Island in the USA many countries have slowed or halted their nuclear programmes.

NUCLEAR ELECTRICITY GENERATION

	Number of reactors	Generation in megawatt-hours
USA	111	99 800
France	56	56 900
Japan	42	32 000
Russia	27[1]	c. 21 000
Germany	16[2]	c. 17 000
Canada	20	14 000
UK	37	11 700

[1] The figure for Russia is an estimate based on the percentage of nuclear capacity of the Russian Federation within the former USSR; some reactors in Russia have closed, although over a dozen are in an advanced state of construction.

[2] The figure for Germany is an estimate that allows for the closure of five reactors in 1990–91.

HYDROELECTRIC POWER

In some countries , *hydroelectric power* (or hydropower) is the most important source of energy. Hydropower provides 8% of Western Europe's energy, and worldwide it provides roughly as much energy as nuclear power.

In a typical hydroelectric power plant, a river is dammed to create a reservoir that can provide a steady and controllable supply of running water. Water from the reservoir is channelled downstream to the power plant, where it causes a turbine to rotate. The turbine, in turn, drives an electric generator. The electricity generated is then stepped up by transformers at a substation to the high voltages suitable for transmission. In areas where there are considerable fluctuations in electricity demand, pumped-storage plants may be installed. The surplus power available at off-peak periods is used to pump water to a separate reservoir. At peak times, the stored water is released to generate extra electrical power.

Major projects can be controversial as they may involve flooding environmentally sensitive areas. However, the latest design of low-head water turbines has reduced the necessary height difference (the *'head'*) between the turbine and the surface of the reservoir, making it possible to build smaller barrages or to place turbines directly into river beds.

WIND POWER

The traditional windmill has tapped the energy of the winds for centuries. Its modern counterpart is far more sophisticated. The biggest ones have blades resembling giant aircraft propellers up to 60 m (200 ft) across, and can generate 3 MW of electricity. Two such machines provide a significant proportion of the electricity of the Orkney Islands, and several large 'wind farms' have been built at coastal sites both in Europe and in the USA. Another approach,

LARGEST HEP PLANTS

The figures relate to the capacity of individual plants in 1991. Planned capacity is shown in italics.

	Dam	Capacity MW
Itaipu	Brazil/	12 600
	Paraguay	*13 320*
Guri (Raul Leoni)	Venezuela	10 300
Grand Coulee	USA	6 495
		10 830
Krasnoyarsk	Russia	6 000
La Grande 2	Canada	5 328
Churchill Falls	Canada	5 225

The Turukhansk (Lower Tunguska) plant, under construction in Russia, will have a capacity of 20 000 MW.

pioneered in Britain, is a wind turbine with blades like a giant letter H, which rotate around a vertical axis. The mechanism tilts the blade tips inwards in high winds, thus regulating the supply.

SOLAR POWER

Direct solar energy is one of the simplest sources of power. Building designs, old and new, take advantage of the Sun for heating and lighting. Today, more active designs are becoming widespread. Each square metre (11¾ sq ft) of a solar collector in northern Europe receives roughly 1000 kilowatt-hours of solar energy in the course of a year, and can use about half of this energy to heat water. A similar collector in California receives twice as much energy as this.

GEOTHERMAL POWER

Just 30 km (19 mi) beneath our feet, the rock has a temperature of around 900 °C (1650 °F). This heat comes primarily from the gradual radioactive decay of elements within the Earth. This source of power is not renewable, but it is immense. There is enough heat in the top 10 km (6 mi) of the Earth's crust, at depths accessible with current drilling techniques, to supply all our energy needs for hundreds of years.

In some parts of the world – for example, Iceland – the amount of geothermal heat reaching the surface is considerably greater than elsewhere, and can be used directly as a means of domestic heating. In other countries, blocks of flats are heated by hot water from wells 2 to 3 km (1 to 2 mi) deep.

The biggest reserves of geothermal heat, however, are to be found deeper still, at 6 km (4 mi) or so. As the rocks at this depth are dry, it is harder and more costly to get the heat out, because it is necessary to pump down water in order to bring the heat up. In an experimental project in Cornwall, England, three boreholes drilled to a depth of 2 km (1¼ mi) have been interconnected with a system of cracks, allowing water to be pumped from one borehole to another. There are plans to drill holes to three times this depth, but even at current depths the water returns to the surface hot enough to produce steam to drive turbines. Some estimates suggest that in Cornwall and other areas where the rocks are hotter at shallower depths, schemes of this kind could ultimately yield energy for Britain equivalent to 10 billion tonnes (tons) of coal.

TRANSPORT

ROADS

All countries, no matter how small, have a road system, although only the states of the developed world have motorways and similar multi-lane highways. In the developing world, the greater part of the road system is not paved.

LONGEST ROAD LENGTHS

	Total road length	
	km	mi
USA	6 228 670	3 870 309
India	2 000 000	1 250 000
Brazil	1 484 705	922 551
Japan	1 110 000	689 700
China	1 014 342	630 282
Russia	854 000	530 300
Canada	844 386	524 676
Australia	810 264	503 474
France	804 450	499 917
Germany	621 267	386 037
Poland	360 629	224 084
UK	356 517	221 529
Turkey	320 611	199 218
Spain	318 022	197 609
Italy	302 403	187 793
Ukraine	247 000	153 400
Mexico	235 431	146 290
Indonesia	219 791	136 572
Argentina	211 369	131 338

SHORTEST ROAD LENGTHS

Sovereign countries only

	Total road length	
	km	mi
Vatican City	>2	<1
Tuvalu	8	5
Nauru	19	12
Monaco	50	31
Andorra	220	137
Micronesia	226	140
San Marino	237	147

PERCENTAGE OF PAVED ROADS

Sovereign countries with the lowest percentage of paved raods.

	Percentage of paved roads
Chad	1
Central African Republic	2
Mongolia	2
Bangladesh	4
Bolivia	4
Guinea	4
Tanzania	4
Congo	5
Kiribati	5
Cameroon	6
Papua New Guinea	6
Rwanda	7
Mali	8
Niger	8
Solomon Islands	8

In Austria, the Czech Republic, Denmark, Israel, Italy, Jordan, Kuwait, Monaco, Nauru, the Vatican City and the UK all roads are classed as 'paved'.

MOTORWAYS

The first dual carriageway was constructed in 1909 near Berlin in Germany. In 1924 the world's first motorway was opened between Milan and Varese in northern Italy. This was the beginning of a 500 km (275 mi) network of motorways constructed in Piedmont and Lombardy between 1925 and 1939. In 1933 the German autobahn network was begun.

The following countries had the greatest length of motorways in 1988 (the latest year for which comparable figures are available).

	Length	
Country	kilometres	miles
USA	83 964	52 142
Australia*	16 100	9 998
Canada	14 796	9 188
Germany†	9 930	6 170
Italy	6 695	4 158
France	6 570	4 080
Japan	4 280	2658

* 1987 figures.
† combined 1987 figures for the former East Germany and West Germany.

CAR OWNERSHIP

	Persons per car	Total no. of cars
USA	1.8	148 081 443
Japan	3.4	36 621 085
Germany	2.3	34 051 299
Italy	2.4	24 307 000
France	2.5	23 010 000
United Kingdom	3.0	19 266 000
Brazil	10.2	14 995 837
Canada	2.1	12 811 318
Spain	3.7	10 787 500
Russia	22.9	9 200 000
Australia	2.3	7 672 300
Mexico	13.2	6 219 104
The Netherlands	2.7	5 509 000
Poland	7.9	4 845 105
Argentina	7.9	4 088 000
Belgium	2.6	3 864 159
Sweden	2.4	3 578 042
South Africa	11.3	3 372 507
Switzerland	2.3	2 916 959
Austria	2.7	2 902 949
Saudi Arabia	6.4	2 300 000
India	381.4	2 284 000
Taiwan	10.4	1 969 291
Finland	2.6	1 896 895
Hungary	5.6	1 848 200
Venezuela	11.1	1 770 000

The figures are for 1990.

INTERNATIONAL VEHICLE REGISTRATION LETTERS

A	Austria
AFG	Afghanistan
AL	Albania
AND	Andorra
AUS	Australia
B	Belgium
BD	Bangladesh
BDS	Barbados
BER*	Belarus
BG	Bulgaria
BH	Belize
BR	Brazil
BRN	Bahrain
BRU	Brunei
BS	Bahamas
BUR	Burma (Myanmar)
C	Cuba
CDN	Canada
CH	Switzerland
CI	Côte d'Ivoire (Ivory Coast)
CL	Sri Lanka
CO	Colombia
CR	Costa Rica
CRO*	Croatia
CS	Czech Republic
CY	Cyprus
D	Germany
DK	Denmark
DOM	Dominican Republic
DY	Benin
DZ	Algeria
E	Spain
EAK	Kenya
EAT	Tanzania
EAU	Uganda
EAZ	Zanzibar (Tanzania)
EC	Ecuador
ES	El Salvador
ET	Egypt
ETH	Ethiopia
EW	Estonia*
F	France and territories
FJI	Fiji
FL	Liechtenstein
FR	Faeroe Islands
GB	United Kingdom
GBA	Alderney
GBG	Guernsey
GBJ	Jersey
GBM	Isle of Man
GBZ	Gibraltar
GCA	Guatemala
GH	Ghana
GR	Greece
GRU*	Georgia
GUY	Guyana
H	Hungary
HK	Hong Kong
HKJ	Jordan
I	Italy
IL	Israel

IND	India
IR	Iran
IRL	Republic of Ireland
IRQ	Iraq
IS	Iceland
J	Japan
JA	Jamaica
K	Cambodia
KWT	Kuwait
L	Luxembourg
LAO	Laos
LAR	Libya
LB	Liberia
LR*	Latvia
LS	Lesotho
LT	Lithuania
M	Malta
MA	Morocco
MAL	Malaysia
MC	Monaco
MEX	Mexico
MOL*	Moldova
MS	Mauritius
MW	Malawi
N	Norway
NA	Netherlands Antilles
NIC	Nicaragua
NL	Netherlands
NZ	New Zealand
P	Portugal
PA	Panama
PAK	Pakistan
PE	Peru
PL	Poland
PNG	Papua New Guinea
PY	Paraguay
RA	Argentina
RB	Botswana
RC	Taiwan
RCA	Central African Republic
RCB	Congo
RCH	Chile
RH	Haiti
RI	Indonesia
RIM	Mauritania
RL	Lebanon
RM	Madagascar
RMM	Mali
RN	Niger
RO*	Russia
RO	Romania
ROK	Korea
ROU	Uruguay
RP	Philippines
RSM	San Marino
RU	Burundi
RWA	Rwanda
S	Sweden
SD	Swaziland
SF	Finland
SGP	Singapore
SLO*	Slovenia
SME	Suriname

SN	Senegal
SQ*	Slovakia
SWA	Namibia
SY	Seychelles
SYR	Syria
T	Thailand
TG	Togo
TN	Tunisia
TR	Turkey
TT	Trinidad and Tobago
UKR*	Ukraine
USA	United States of America
V	Vatican City
VN	Vietnam
WAG	Gambia
WAL	Sierra Leone
WAN	Nigeria
WD	Dominica
WG	Grenada
WL	St Lucia
WS	Western Samoa
WV	St Vincent and the Grenadines
YU	Yugoslavia
YV	Venezuela
Z	Zambia
ZA	South Africa
ZRE	Zaïre
ZW	Zimbabwe

* indicates a registration that is in use but has not been officially accepted.

Other countries either do not have registration letters or use letters that are not internationally recognized.

DRIVING ON THE LEFT

In the majority of sovereign states and dependent territories, it is the custom to drive on the right. In the UK it is believed that left-hand driving is a legacy of passing an approaching horseman or carriage right side to right side to facilitate right-armed defence against sudden attack. On the Continent postillions were mounted on the rearmost left horse in a team and thus preferred to pass left side to left side.

Left-hand driving is practised in the following: Anguilla, Antigua, Australia, Bahamas, Bangladesh, Barbados, Bermuda, Bhutan, Botswana, Brunei, Cook Islands, Cyprus, Dominica, Falkland Islands, Fiji, Grenada, Guyana, Hong Kong, India, Indonesia, Ireland (Republic of), Jamaica, Japan, Kenya, Kiribati, Lesotho, Malaysia, Malawi, Malta, Mauritius, Montserrat, Mozambique, Namibia, Nepal, New Zealand, Norfolk Island, Pakistan, Papua New Guinea, St Christopher-Nevis, St Lucia, St Vincent, Seychelles, Singapore, Solomon Islands, Somalia, South Africa, Sri Lanka, Suriname, Swaziland, Tanzania, Thailand, Tonga, Trinidad and Tobago, Tuvalu, Uganda, UK (including Guernsey, Jersey and the Isle of Man), Virgin Islands (British), Zambia and Zimbabwe.

CAR PRODUCTION

Cars are an essential part of the modern developed world. It has been said that the average American is only prepared to walk 200 years before using a car. Car production worldwide has generally risen year by year (see Production and Consumerism) until 1992–93 when a major slump in production occurred. In 1992 car sales were down by nearly 10% in the USA and the Japanese motor industry suffered its worst slump since World War II.

Nevertheless, the USA and Japan continue to dominate car production as the following table shows.

Company	Country of parent company	Worldwide production (no. of cars)
General Motors	USA	7 000 000
Ford	USA	5 400 000
Toyota	Japan	4 700 000
Volkswagen	Germany	3 100 000
Nissan	Japan	3 100 000
Fiat	Italy	2 500 000
Peugeot-Citroen	France	2 100 000
Honda	Japan	2 000 000
Mitsubishi Motors	Japan	1 900 000
Renault	France	1 800 000
Mazda	Japan	1 600 000
Chrysler	USA	1 500 000

ROAD HAULAGE

In Western Europe and North America, road transport has gradually taken the place of the railways in road haulage. Many 'freight only' branch railway lines have been axed even though the resulting increase in large lorries – popularly known as juggernauts – is widely regarded as an environmental disaster. In many developing countries, railways – where they exist – tend to play a greater role in road haulage.

The following table – based upon 1990–91 data – records the total tonnage of goods transported by road.

Country	Tonnes of goods transported by road pa (million tonnes)
USA	1 125 000
China	337 500
Russia*	c. 300 000
Brazil	260 400
Japan	246 150
Germany	171 500
Italy	157 400
France	143 800
UK	130 200
Spain	124 250
India	81 000
Iran	68 000
Turkey	62 500
Australia	48 100
Canada	42 400
Poland	38 500
Egypt	31 200
Jordan	27 900
Sweden	26 000
Indonesia	25 000
Finland	24 200
Netherlands	22 000

* an estimated 60% of the 1990 Soviet road haulage figure of 491 960 000 000 tonnes of goods carried by road.

PRINCIPAL RAILWAY SYSTEMS OF THE WORLD

Railway system	Year of first railway	Gauge mm	Gauge ft in	Route length km	Route length miles	Ownership
USA	1830*	1435	4 8½	261 124	162 254	private, except Alaska RR
	Class I RRs			202 739	125 976	846 km (526 mi), state-owned
	Class II and III			53 916	33 502	
	Commuter RRs			4469	2777	
Russia	1837	1524†	5 0†	86 300	53 624	state-owned
Canada	1836	1435	4 8½	63 549	39 487	private, except: Canadian National 34 347 km (21 342 mi) British Columbia R 1953 km (1213 mi) owned by BC
India	1853			61 976	38 510	state-owned
		1676	5 6	33 831	21 021	
		1000	3 3⅜	23 898	14 849	
		610 and 762	2 0 and 2 6	4247	2639	
China	1880	1435	4 8½	c. 54 000	c. 33 500	state-owned
Germany	1835			41 039	25 500	state-owned
		1435	4 8½	40 764	25 329	
			narrow	275	171	
Australia	1854			38 803	24 111	owned by separate states except
		1600	5 3	6642	4127	Australian National, 7315 km
		1435	4 8½	16 259	10 103	(4545 mi) of three gauges, owned
		1067	3 6	15 902	9881	by the Commonwealth
France	1832	1435	4 8½	34 680	21 549	state-owned
Argentina	1857			c. 34 500	c. 21 400	to be privatized
		1676	5 6	c. 20 500	c. 12 700	
		1435	4 8½	c. 3000	c. 1860	
		1000	3 3⅜	c. 11 000	c. 6840	
Poland	1845			27 137	16 862	state-owned
		1435	4 8½	24 287	15 091	
			narrow	2357	1465	
		1524	5 0	493	306	
South Africa	1860			23 619	14 676	state-owned
		1065	3 5⅞	23 259	14 452	
		610	2 0	360	224	
Ukraine	1866	1524†	5 0†	22 760	14 142	state-owned
Brazil	1854			22 417	13 929	state-owned
		1600	5 3	1740	1081	
		1000	3 3⅜	20 664	12 840	
		760	2 6	13	8	
Japan	1872			20 984	13 038	all privatized
		1067	3 6	18 950	11 775	
		1435	4 8½	2034	1263	
Mexico	1850			20 306	12 618	state-owned
		1435	4 8½	20 216	12 562	
		914	3 0	90	56	
UK	1825			16 915	10 510	state-owned
British Rail		1435	4 8½	16 583	10 304	
N. Ireland Railways Co Ltd		1600	5 3	332	206	
Italy	1839	1435	4 8½	15 982	9931	state-owned
also in Sicily		950	3 1⅜	71	44	
Kazakhstan	1897	1524†	5 0†	14 550	9041	state-owned
Spain	1848	1668	5 5⅝	12 691	7886	state-owned

MAJOR 'METRO' AND RAPID TRANSIT SYSTEMS

'Metros' systems are partly or wholly underground; rapid transit systems are generally partly or wholly overground.

City	System begun	Total length of route		Number of lines	Number of stations
London (UK)	1863	408 km	254 mi	10	273
New York (USA)	1868	373 km	232 mi	23	466
Paris (France)	1900	307 km	191 mi	18	430
Moscow (Russia)[1]	1935	225 km	140 mi	8	123
Tokyo (Japan)	1927	217 km	135 mi	10	192
Berlin (Germany)[2]	1902	212 km	132 mi	8	134
Chicago (USA)	1892	156 km	97 mi	6	142
Mexico City (Mexico)	1969	141 km	88 mi	9	123
Copenhagen (Denmark)	1934	135 km	84 mi	7	61
Washington DC (USA)[3]	1976	118 km	73 mi	4	64
Seoul (South Korea)[4]	1974	117 km	72 mi	4	102
San Francisco (USA)	1972	115 km	71 mi	1	34
Madrid (Spain)[5]	1919	112 km	70 mi	11	141
Stockholm (Sweden)[6]	1950	108 km	67 mi	3	99
Osaka (Japan)	1933	91 km	57 mi	6	88
Hamburg (Germany)	1912	90 km	56 mi	3	82
St Petersburg (Russia)	1955	83 km	52 mi	3	43
Barcelona (Spain)[7]	1924	71 km	44 mi	4	96
Boston (USA)	1897	70 km	43 mi	3	51
Nagoya (Japan)	1957	69 km	43 mi	4	61
Milan (Italy)	1964	66 km	41 mi	2	66
Montreal (Canada)[8]	1966	64 km	40 mi	4	65
Toronto (Canada)	1954	64 km	40 mi	3	65
Philadelphia (USA)	1907	63 km	39 mi	3	68
Bucharest (Romania)	1979	60 km	38 mi	2	21

[1] an additional 17 km under construction; [2] an additional 8 km under construction; [3] an additional 434 km under construction and projection; [4] an additional 34 km under construction; [5] an additional 4 km under construction; [6] an additional 6 km under construction; [7] an additional 21 km under construction; [8] an additional 13 km under construction.

OTHER 'METRO' AND RAPID TRANSIT SYSTEMS
(with the year in which the first section was opened)
* rapid transport systems that are wholly above ground

Amsterdam, Netherlands (1977); Athens, Greece (1925); Atlanta, USA (1979); Baku, Azerbaijan (1967); Baltimore, USA (1983); Beijing (Peking), China (1971); Brussels, Belgium (1976); Budapest, Hungary (1896); Buenos Aires, Argentina (1913); Buffalo, USA (1992); Cairo, Egypt (1987); Calcutta, India (1984); Caracas, Venezuela (1983); Cleveland, USA (1955); Detroit, USA (1986); Dneipropetrovsk, Ukraine (1984); Dublin*, Ireland (1984); Frankfurt, Germany (1968); Fukuoka, Japan (1981); Glasgow, UK (1896; reopened 1979); Haifa, Israel (1959); Helsinki, Finland (1982); Hong Kong (1979); Jakarta*, Indonesia (1992); Kharkov, Ukraine (1975); Kiev, Ukraine (1960); Kobe, Japan (1977); Kyoto, Japan (1981); Lille, France (1983); Lisbon, Portugal (1959); Los Angeles, USA (1993); Lyon, France (1978); Manchester*, UK (1992); Manila*, Philippines (1984); Marseille, France (1977); Medellín, Colombia (1990); Miami, USA (1984); Minsk, Belarus (1984); Munich, Germany (1971); Naples, Italy (1987); Newcastle-upon-Tyne*, UK (1980); Nizhny Novgorod (formerly Gorky), Russia (1985); Novosibirsk, Russia (1985); Nürnberg, Germany (1972); Oslo, Norway (1966); Prague, Czech Republic (1974); Pusan, South Korea (1984); Pyongyang, North Korea (1973); Rio de Janeiro, Brazil (1979); Rome, Italy (1955); Rotterdam, Netherlands (1968); Samara (formerly Kubyshev), Russia (1986); Santiago, Chile (1975); São Paulo, Brazil (1974); Sapporo, Japan (1971); Sendai, Japan (1985); Singapore (1986); Seville, Spain (1987); Tashkent, Uzbekistan (1977); Tbilisi, Georgia (1966); Tianjin, China (1980); Toulouse*, France (1985); Tunis*, Tunisia (1991); Valencia, Spain (1988); Vancouver, Canada (1985); Vienna, Austria (1976); Wuppertal*, Germany (1902); Yerevan, Armenia (1981); and Yokohama, Japan (1972).

'Metros' or rapid transit systems are under construction and are scheduled to open in the following cities: Bogotá, Colombia (1993); Nottingham*, UK (1993); Sheffield*, UK (1993); Sofia, Bulgaria (1993); Tehran, Iran (1993); Yekaterinburg (formerly Sverdlovsk), Russia (1993); Ankara*, Turkey (1994); Bangkok*, Thailand (1994); Taipei*, Taiwan (1999); Birmingham*, UK (2000). Metros or rapid transit systems are also planned for Baghdad, Iraq; Bilbao, Spain; Edinburgh, UK; Kua;a Lumpur, Malaysia; and Turin, Italy.

MAIN COMMERCIAL AIRCRAFT IN AIRLINE SERVICE

Name of aircraft*	Nationality	Wingspan	Length	Max. cruising speed	Range with max. payload	Max. takeoff weight	Max seating capacity
Boeing 737 (200)	USA	28.35 m (93 ft 0 in)	30.53 m (100 ft 2 in)	927 kph (500 knots)	4262 km (2300 naut miles)	56 472 kg (124 500 lb)	130
Boeing 727 (200)	USA	32.92 m (108 ft 0 in)	46.69 m (153 ft 2 in)	964 kph (520 knots)	3966 km (2140 naut miles)	95 025 kg (209 500 lb)	189
McDonnell Douglas DC-9 (Super 81)	USA	32.87 m (107 ft 10 in)	45.6 m (147 ft 10 in)	902 kph (487 knots)	4925 km[1] (2657 naut miles)	63 500 kg (140 000 lb)	172
McDonnell Douglas MD-80	USA	32.87 m (107 ft 10 in)	45.06 m (147 ft 10 in)	855 kph (478 knots)	2896 kph[2] (1563 naut miles)	63 500 kg (140 000 lb)	172
Boeing 747 (200)	USA	59.46 m (195 ft 8 in)	70.66 m (231 ft 10 in)	964 kph (520 knots)	10 563 km[3] (5700 naut miles)	377 840 kg (833 000 lb)	516
Fokker F27 (Mk 500)	Netherlands	29.00 m (95 ft 2 in)	25.06 m (82 ft 2 in)	480 kph (259 knots)	1741 km (935 naut miles)	20 410 kg (45 000 lb)	60
McDonnell Douglas DC-10 (Srs 40)	USA	50.41 m (165 ft 5 in)	55.50 m (182 ft 1 in)	992 kph (498 knots)	7505 km (4050 naut miles)	259 450 kg (572 000 lb)	380
Boeing 767 (200)	USA	47.57 m (156 ft 1 in)	48.51 m (159 ft 2 in)	914 kph (493 knots)	7040 km (3800 naut miles)	142 900 kg (315 000 lb)	290
McDonnell Douglas DC-8 (Srs 63)	USA	45.23 m (148 ft 5 in)	57.12 m (187 ft 5 in)	965 kph (521 knots)	7240 km (3907 naut miles)	158 000 kg (350 000 lb)	259
Boeing 757	USA	38.05 m (124 ft 10 in)	47.32 m (155 ft 3 in)	914 kph (493 knots)	5150 km[4] (2780 naut miles)	115 670 kg (255 000 lb)	239
Airbus A300B (A300B4-200)	International	44.84 m (147 ft 1 in)	53.62 m (175 ft 11 in)	911 kph (492 knots)	5095 km[5] (2750 naut miles)	165 000 kg (363 760 lb)	336
Boeing 707/720 (707-320)	USA	44.42 m (145 ft 9 in)	46.61 m (152 ft 11 in)	973 kph (525 knots)	9265 km[6] (5000 naut miles)	151 315 kg (333 600 lb)	219
Lockheed L-1011 Tristar (500)	USA	47.34 m (155 ft 4 in)	50.05 m (164 ft 2 in)	973 kph (525 knots)	9653 km (5209 naut miles)	224 980 kg (496 000 lb)	400
BAC One-eleven (Srs 500)	UK	28.50 m (93 ft 6 in)	32.61 m (107 ft 0 in)	871 kph (470 knots)	2744 km (1480 naut miles)	47 400 kg (104 500 lb)	119
BAC Aérospatiale Concorde	International	25.56 m (83 ft 10 in)	62.10 m (203 ft 9 in)	2179 kph (1176 knots)	6230 km (3360 naut miles)	185 065 kg (408 000 lb)	128

*Scheduled and non-circulated services including all-freight. Specifications apply to version in brackets. [1] Range quoted with max. fuel. [2] With 115 passengers. [3] With 442 passengers. [4] With 186 passengers. [5] With 269 passengers. [6] With 147 passengers.

DISTANCE IN KILOMETRES BETWEEN AIRPORTS

	Athens	Bahrain	Bangkok	Bombay	Buenos Aires	Cairo	Chicago	Copenhagen	Frankfurt	Hong Kong	Johannesburg	Karachi	Lagos	Lima	London	Madrid	Manila	Mexico City	Montreal	Moscow	Nairobi	New York	Paris	Peking (Beijing)	Rio de Janeiro	Rome	San Francisco	Singapore	Sydney	Tehran	Tokyo	Vancouver
Athens		2829	7916	5164	11699	1117	8758	2136	1807	8541	7131	4320	4043	11762	2414	2359	9637	11274	7616	2251	4564	7914	2093	7617	9704	1047	10918	9053	15315	2458	9543	9792
Bahrain	2829		5358	2411	13293	1929	11460	4461	4437	6389	6297	1661	5457	14333	5090	5185	7364	13963	12069	3467	3389	10614	4822	6182	11460	3862	12730	6326	12504	1048	8314	11782
Bangkok	7916	5358		3008	16877	7249	13912	8601	8963	1719	8989	3701	10604	19676	9540	10157	2199	15717	13378	7069	7207	13912	9433	3296	16073	8814	13062	1443	7538	5457	4642	11782
Bombay	5164	2411	3008		14935	4339	12934	6849	6564	4298	8109	876	7617	16134	7207	7512	5132	14582	12069	5047	4529	12523	6999	4763	14716	6258	14395	3917	10152	2803	6782	11297
Buenos Aires	11699	13293	16877	14935		11844	9009	12086	11494	18443	8109	14716	3151	11129	10079	11745	12363	7391	9051	13488	10411	8528	11062	19277	1996	11170	10395	15867	11760	13781	18285	11297
Cairo	1117	1929	7249	4339	11844		9866	3197	2922	8123	6258	3556	3927	12435	3531	3349	9162	12363	8722	2913	3540	9009	3204	7530	9893	1320	11994	8255	14395	1955	9588	10835
Chicago	8758	11460	13912	12934	9009	9866		6849	6966	12460	14009	12934	9866	6849	6349	6989	13062	2718	1198	7968	12665	1187	6650	10603	8548	7734	2978	15039	14857	10604	10067	2828
Copenhagen	2136	4461	8601	6849	12086	3197	6849		678	9165	9204	5537	5511	11086	982	2058	9780	9507	5799	1539	6699	6184	1035	7191	9560	1535	9142	10270	16031	3765	8706	7657
Frankfurt	1807	4437	8963	6564	11494	2922	6966	678		9165	8684	5690	4853	10717	654	1420	10290	9545	5851	2021	6312	6185	471	7783	9560	966	9271	10270	16484	3657	9360	8057
Hong Kong	8541	6389	1719	4298	18443	8123	12460	9165	9165		10694	4775	11835	18344	9640	10619	1125	14122	12425	7149	8750	12956	9627	1985	17687	9271	11097	2576	7374	6186	2936	10245
Johannesburg	7131	6297	8989	8109	8109	6258	14009	9204	8684	10694		7041	4522	10901	9068	8097	10975	14588	12962	9164	2910	12822	9068	11699	7146	7718	16966	8649	11019	7283	13513	11938
Karachi	4320	1661	3701	876	14716	3556	12934	5537	5690	4775	7041		7041	16605	6334	6658	5716	14588	11241	4202	4367	11675	6128	4862	13004	5303	12983	4736	11003	1930	6969	11706
Lagos	4043	5457	10604	7617	7939	3927	9866	5511	4853	11835	4522	7041		10834	5209	3827	10975	14588	11455	6251	4685	8440	6128	11455	6022	4018	7255	11160	18812	5850	13506	11938
Lima	11762	14333	19676	16134	3151	12435	6449	11086	10717	18344	10901	16605	10834		10143	9520	17520	4241	6419	12620	12665	5861	10248	16605	3776	10834	7255	18812	12828	14333	15413	8154
London	2414	5090	9540	7207	11129	3531	6349	982	654	9640	9068	6334	5209	10143		1244	10759	8901	5213	2506	6830	5536	365	8148	9245	1460	8610	10873	17008	4411	9585	7574
Madrid	2359	5185	10157	7512	10079	3349	6989	2058	1420	10619	8097	6658	3827	9520	1244		11644	9063	3418	3418	6189	5758	1031	9199	8140	1360	9271	11373	17661	4753	10764	8422
Manila	9637	7364	2199	5132	17520	9162	13062	9780	10290	1125	10975	5716	10975	17520	10759	11644		14218	13686	8273	9401	13686	10752	2873	18107	10390	11221	2373	6258	7247	2993	10556
Mexico City	11274	13963	15717	14582	7391	12363	2718	9507	9545	14122	14588	14588	14588	4241	8901	9063	14218		3712	10683	15446	3366	9195	12363	7661	10052	3027	12978	12978	12427	11247	3940
Montreal	7616	9927	13378	12069	9051	8722	1198	5799	5851	12425	12962	11241	11455	6419	5213	3418	13686	3712		7036	11701	536	5523	10440	8189	6605	4072	15329	16011	10384	10384	3679
Moscow	2251	3467	7069	5047	13488	2913	7968	1539	2021	7149	9164	4202	6251	12620	2506	3418	8273	10683	7036		6366	7477	2479	5802	11526	2397	9219	8443	16002	2486	7502	8180
Nairobi	4564	3389	7207	4529	10411	3540	12665	6699	6312	8750	2910	4367	4685	12665	6830	6189	9401	15446	11701	6366		11828	6475	9219	8937	5380	15446	7456	12128	4374	11296	15446
New York	7914	10614	13912	12523	8528	9009	1187	6184	6185	12956	12822	11675	8440	5861	5536	5758	13686	3366	536	7477	11828		5829	10971	7723	6886	4149	15329	16002	9839	10824	3926
Paris	2093	4822	9433	6999	11062	3204	6650	1035	471	9627	9068	6128	6128	10248	365	1031	10752	9195	5523	2479	6475	5829		8214	9144	1100	8971	10728	16954	4198	9736	7938
Peking (Beijing)	7617	6182	3296	4763	19277	7530	10603	7191	7783	1985	11699	4862	11455	16605	8148	9199	2873	12363	10440	5802	9219	10971	8214		17302	8120	9186	4486	8214	4374	2132	8487
Rio de Janeiro	9704	11460	16073	13503	1996	9893	8548	9560	9560	17687	7146	13004	6022	3776	9245	8140	18107	7661	8189	11526	8937	7723	9144	17302		9186	10633	15738	13516	3396	18519	11206
Rome	1047	3862	8814	6258	11170	1320	7734	1535	966	9271	7718	5303	4018	10834	1460	1360	10390	10052	6605	2397	5380	6886	1100	8120	9186		10052	10010	16302	3396	9880	9007
San Francisco	10918	12730	13062	14395	10395	11994	2978	9142	9271	11097	16966	12983	7255	7255	8610	9271	11221	3027	4072	9219	15446	4149	8971	9186	10633	10052		13579	11941	11829	8222	1286
Singapore	9053	6326	1443	3917	15867	8255	15039	10270	10270	2576	8649	4736	11160	18812	10873	11373	2373	12978	15329	8443	7456	15329	10728	4486	15738	10010	13579		6296	6615	5361	12811
Sydney	15315	12504	7538	10152	11760	14395	14857	16031	16484	7374	11019	11003	18812	12828	17661	17661	6258	12978	16002	6313	12128	16002	16954	8214	13516	16302	11941	6296		12909	7826	12492
Tehran	2458	1048	5457	2803	13781	1955	10604	3765	3657	6186	7283	1930	5850	14333	4411	4753	7247	12427	10384	2486	4374	9839	4198	4374	3396	3396	11829	6615	12909		7713	10556
Tokyo	9543	8314	4642	6782	18285	9588	10067	8706	9360	2936	13513	6969	13506	15413	9585	10764	2993	11247	10384	7502	11296	10824	9736	2132	18519	9880	8222	5361	7826	7713		7500
Vancouver	9792	11782	11782	11297	11297	10835	2828	7657	8057	10245	11938	11706	11938	8154	7574	8422	10556	3940	3679	8180	15446	3926	7938	8487	11206	9007	1286	12811	12492	10556	7500	

WORLD'S MAJOR AIRPORTS

Airport name and location	Terminal passengers (000)	International passengers (000)	Air transport movements (000)	Cargo (000 tonnes)
O'Hare International, Chicago, USA	56 936	4 700*	781.3	748.8
Dallas/Fort Worth Regional, USA	48 515	n.a.	714.0	401.8
Hartsfield International, Atlanta, USA	48 025	n.a.	767.6	431.9
Los Angeles International, USA	45 810	10 000	621.4	1025.0
Heathrow Airport, London, UK	42 647	35 250	367.4	697.8
Tokyo International (Haneda), Japan	40 233	n.a	n.a	484.9
San Francisco International, USA	31 060	4 350	397.5	449.2
John F. Kennedy International, NY, USA	29 787	18 100	280.6	1207.3
Frankfurt International, Germany	28 713	21 860	308.5	1083.5
Stapleton International, Denver, USA	27 433	n.a.	444.0	n.a.
Miami International, USA	25 837	10 100	336.0	907.7
Orly, Paris, France	24 330	9 210	201.7*	254.5*
Osaka International, Japan	23 512	n.a.	n.a.	445.7
Honolulu International, Oahu, USA	23 368	5 100	251.9	332.7
Logan International, Boston, USA	22 936	3 400	399.6	309.9
La Guardia Airport, NY, USA	22 754	1 380	331.4	64.2
Metropolitan, Detroit, USA	22 585	1 500*	334.1*	127.1*
Charles de Gaulle, Paris, France	22 506	20 875	233.0*	617.9
Newark, NY, USA	22 255	3 000*	356.7	449.3
Gatwick, London, UK	21 047	19 650	188.2	216.9
Minneapolis–St Paul International, USA	20 381	n.a.	322.2	n.a.
Lambert International, St Louis, USA	20 066	n.a.	391.5	n.a.
New Tokyo International, Japan	19 257	18 312	115.9	1361.2
Toronto International (Pearson), Canada	19 050	10 250	320.0	320.0
Hong Kong International	18 688	18 688	106.1	801.9
Orlando International, USA	18 398	n.a.	n.a.	n.a.
Kimpo International, Korea Republic	16 821	8 454	113.2	630.5
Philadelphia International, USA	16 290*	690*	351.9*	320.1*
Seattle–Tacoma, USA	16 240*	1 910*	343.9*	245.1*
Barajas, Madrid, Spain	15 869	7 330	158.4	220.9
Fiumicino, Rome, Italy	15 550†	8 052†	165.5†	226.4†
Schiphol, Amsterdam, Netherlands	14 895*	14 800	191.5*	585.0
Arlanda, Stockholm, Sweden	14 822	6 555	252.7	74.6
Bangkok International, Thailand	14 329	10 906	120.2	404.3
Zürich, Switzerland	12 277	11 585	172 .2	255.5

The figures given (for 1990) are the latest available. * Provisional/estimate figures; † 1989 figures

MAJOR WORLD AIRLINES

Airline	Passenger km (000)	Aircraft km (000)	Passengers carried	Total no. of aircraft
Aeroflot, Russia	242 173 800	n.a	137 198 200	103
American Airlines, USA	123 924 492	1 124 897	73 243 658	552
United Airlines, USA	122 219 206	959 399	57 752 906	462
Delta Air Lines, USA	94 918 792	947 634	65 871 280	444
British Airways, UK	66 794 988	385 483	25 172 160	228
Continental Airlines, USA	63 042 012	634 543	35 165 180	386
Northwest Airlines, USA	57 212 200	n.a	60 100 000	321*
USAir, USA	57 211 439	783 243	60 059 269	454
Trans World Airlines (TWA), USA	55 596 484	427 332	24 482 822	206
Japan Airlines, (JAL), Japan	55 195 157	237 125	23 463 918	98
Pan American World Airways, USA	49 985 109	297 959	17 527 380	154
Lufthansa, Germany	41 902 960	375 801	21 612 934	177
Air France, France	36 653 023	274 868	15 693 320	121
All Nippon Airways, (ANA), Japan	33 043 255	153 088	33 069 828	108
Singapore Airlines, Singapore	31 544 000	122 311	7 093 000	40
Quantas Airways, Australia	27 686 631	123 229	4 207 510	45
Eastern Air Lines, USA	26 955 100	n.a	21 510 000	259*
KLM, Netherlands	26 389 622	151 502	6 902 989	57
Air Canada, Canada	24 504 808	219 991	10 324 948	115
Cathay Pacific, Hong Kong	23 604 353	98 915	7 519 628	40
Alitalia, Italy	22 754 174	181 543	18 202 689	119
Iberia, Spain	22 111 812	173 594	16 227 735	93
Canadian Airlines International, Canada	21 623 033	190 493	8 550 373	88

The figures given (for 1990) are the latest available. * 1988 figures

MAJOR SHIP CANALS

The following canals can be used by ocean-going shipping.

Canal	Route	Year opened	Length
St Lawrence Seaway (Canada – USA)	Montreal to Lake Ontario	1959	304 km[1] (189 mi)
Main-Danube Canal (Germany)	Main River (Bamberg) to Danube River Kelheim	1992	171 km (106 mi)
Suez Canal (Egypt)	Mediterranean Sea to Red Sea	1869	162 km (101 mi)
Albert Canal (Belgium)	River Meuse (Maes) to River Scheld	1939	129 km (80 mi)
Kiel Canal (Germany)	North Sea to Baltic Sea	1895	99 km (62 mi)
Alfonso XIII Canal (Spain)	Seville to Gulf of Cadiz	1926	85 km (53 mi)
Panama Canal (Panama)	Pacific Ocean to Caribbean Sea	1914	81 km (50 mi)
Sabine–Neches Waterway (USA)[2]	Beaumont to Gulf of Mexico	1916	72 km (45 mi)
Houston Ship Canal (USA)[2]	Houston to Gulf of Mexico	1914	69 km (43 mi)
Manchester Ship Canal (UK)	Manchester to the Mersey estuary	1894	58 km (36 mi)
Welland Canal (Canada)	Lake Ontario to Lake Erie	1933	44 km (28 mi)
North Sea Canal (Noordzeekanaal) (Netherlands)	Amsterdam to Ijmuiden on the North Sea	1876	27 km (17 mi)
Chesapeake and Delaware Canal[3] (USA)	Chesapeake Bay to Delaware River	1829	22 km (14 mi)

[1] The canalized section of the St Lawrence Seaway that enables shipping to sail 3769 km (2342 mi) from the North Atlantic up the St Lawrence estuary and through the Great Lakes to Duluth, Minnesota.

[2] Part of a series of artificial and natural channels providing a discontinuous navigation, linking the Texan Gulf coast ports with the Mississippi Delta and Florida. Total length: 1770 km (1100 mi).

[3] Part of the Atlantic Intracoastal Waterway, a series of artificial and natural channels providing a discontinuous navigation of 1900 km (3057 mi) between Massachusetts and Florida.

OTHER MAJOR NAVIGATION CANALS

The following canals are suitable for barges rather than for ocean-going shipping.

Canal	Route	Year opened	Length
Volga–Baltic Waterway (Russia)	Astrakhan to Leningrad	1965	2300 km (1850 mi)
Grand Canal (China)	Beijing (Peking) to Harchon	540 BC – AD 1327	1781 km (1107 mi)
Karakumsky Canal (Turkmenistan)	Amu-Dar'ya (Oxus) to Khrebet Kopet Dag	1980	1069 km (664 mi)
New York State Barge Canal (USA)	Hudson River to Lake Erie	1918	837 km (520 mi)
Rajasthan Canal (India)	Bamgarh to Western Haryana	1955	649 km (403 mi)
Trent Canal (Canada)	Lake Huron to Lake Ontario	1833 – 1918	443 km (275 mi)
Irtysh–Karaganda Canal (Kazakhstan))	Karaganda to River Irtysh	1971	451 km (280 mi)

China	1 950
Indonesia	1 880
UK	1 880
Greece	1 810
Liberia	1 680
Italy	1 610
Germany	1 550

† 95% of the merchant fleet of the former Soviet Union.

MAJOR PORTS

The figures in this list of the world's busiest ports are in millions of tonnes of goods handled per year (1990).

Rotterdam (Netherlands)	287.7
Singapore (Singapore)	187.8
Kobe (Japan)	171.5
Shanghai (China)	133.0*
Nagoya (Japan)	128.9
Yokohama (Japan)	123.9
Antwerp (Belgium)	102.0
Osaka (Japan)	97.4
Kitakyushu (Japan)	95.2
Marseille (France)	90.3
Hong Kong (Hong Kong)	89.0
Tokyo (Japan)	79.3
Kaohsiung (Taiwan)	78.0
Long Beach (USA)	74.8
Philadelphia (USA)	68.6
Los Angeles (USA)	67.9

* ranking based on last available figure (1988)

INLAND WATERWAYS

The major shipping canals and barge canals are recorded on p. 325. The following table lists the total length of inland waterways – canals, canalized rivers and lakes – of major countries.

Country	Length of navigable inland waterways	
	km	mi
China	109 040	67 750
Russia	c. 85 000	c. 53 000
USA	41 010	25 480
Brazil	50 000	31 100
Indonesia	21 580	13 400
Vietnam	17 700	11 000
India	16 180	10 050
France	14 930	9 280
Colombia	14 300	8 900

MERCHANT SHIPPING

Merchant shipping may be defined as shipping that is engaged in commerce.

FLAGS OF CONVENIENCE

A large proportion of the world's merchant shipping flies flags of convenience. Ships are registered by their owners in other countries that offer financial, legal or other incentives to fly their flag. The first countries to offer such advantages were Liberia and Panama, which now have the world's largest registered merchant fleets, although almost all of the vessels involved are owned by European and North American companies.

In 1991, the largest merchant fleets in terms of registered tonnage were those of:

Country	Registered tonnage
Liberia	52 400 000
Panama	44 900 000
Japan	26 400 000
Russia†	c. 25 000 000
Norway	23 600 000
Greece	22 800 000
Cyprus	20 300 000
USA*	20 300 000
Bahamas	17 500 000
China	14 300 000

* The US Reserve Fleet is included in the figure.
† 95% of the merchant fleet of the former Soviet Union.

In 1990, the largest merchant fleets in terms of the number of registered vessels over 100 gross tonnes were those of:

Country	Number of vessels
Japan	10 000
Russia†	c. 7 000
USA	6 260
Panama	4 750
Norway	2 550
Spain	2330
South Korea	2 110

LAND-LOCKED STATES

The majority of countries have coastlines, although some have only very short littorals (see p. 69). Although the following sovereign countries are entirely land-locked, some of them have registered merchant fleets – mostly for use on rivers and lakes.

In Europe
Andorra, Austria, Belarus, the Czech Republic, Hungary, Liechtenstein, Luxembourg, Macedonia, (the Former Yugoslav Republic of), Moldova, San Marino, Slovakia, Switzerland, and the Vatican City are land-locked. Of these countries, the following have registered merchant fleets: Austria, the Czech Republic, Hungary, Luxembourg, and Switzerland.

In Africa
Botswana, Burkina Faso, Burundi, the Central African Republic, Chad, Ethiopia, Lesotho, Malawi, Mali, Niger, Rwanda, Swaziland, Uganda, Zambia, and Zimbabwe are land-locked. Of these countries, Burundi, Malawi and Uganda have registered merchant fleets.

In Asia
Afghanistan, Armenia, Azerbaijan, Bhutan, Kazakhstan, Kyrgyzstan, Laos, Mongolia, Nepal, Tajikistan, Turkmenistan, and Uzbekistan are land-locked. Although Azerbaijan, Kazakhstan and Turkmenistan have coasts on the Caspian Sea, and Kazakhstan and Uzbekistan have coasts on the Aral Sea, these 'seas' are, in fact, regarded as lakes and the countries concerned may be said to be land-locked. Of these countries, Azerbaijan, Laos and Turkmenistan have registered merchant fleets.

In South America
Bolivia and Paraguay are land-locked, but both of these countries have registered merchant fleets.

BELIEFS AND IDEAS

PHILOSOPHY

CLASSICAL PHILOSOPHY

The word 'philosophy' is derived from the Greek, meaning 'love of wisdom'. Broadly speaking, 'philosophy' can be taken to mean any questioning of or reflection upon those principles underlying all knowledge and existence.

Philosophy differs from religion since its quest for underlying causes and principles does not depend on dogma and faith; and it differs from science, since it does not depend solely on fact. Its interrelation with both science and religion can be seen in the large number of philosophers who were also either theologians or scientists, and the few, such as Blaise Pascal and Roger Bacon, who were all three. Philosophy developed from religion, but became distinct when thinkers sought truth independent of theological considerations.

Until the 19th century the term 'philosophy' was used to include what we now distinguish as 'science' (from the Latin for 'knowledge'), and this terminology persists in some university courses such as 'natural philosophy' for physics and 'moral sciences' for what we now call philosophy. Eventually all the branches of science, from physics to psychology, broke away – psychology being the last to do so in the 20th century.

ETHICS

Ethics is the study of how we decide how people ought to live and act. Philosophers' opinions about ethics tend to resolve into an opposition between two main schools: the Idealists and the Utilitarians. The *Idealists* consider that the goodness or badness of a course of action must be judged by standards derived from the everyday world: from God, or heaven, or perhaps from a human higher self. The *Utilitarians* hold that the effects that a course of action produces in this world are all that is relevant to its ethical value.

The Idealist school began with the Greek philosopher Plato, who wrote in the 4th century BC. Plato, in a series of dialogues, depicts his former teacher Socrates discussing the problems of philosophy with friends and opponents. In the dialogues, Socrates' procedure is to draw out wisdom from those with whom he is discussing the question. He rarely makes a statement of his own – rather he asks questions which compel others either to discover the truth for themselves or else to appear foolish.

In these dialogues, especially the *Protagoras*, the *Phaedo* and the *Gorgias*, Plato developed a system of ethics that is essentially idealistic. Socrates argues that the good comes from the realm of 'ideas' or 'forms'. This is a perfect world of which the world of ordinary experience is only a pale replica. For Plato, individual conduct is good in so far as it is governed by the form or idea of the good, which is to be discovered only after a thorough philosophical education.

Another important work that has to be classed as Idealist is Aristotle's *Nicomachean Ethics*. Aristotle was a pupil of Plato and he also thought of the good as divine, but his ethics had a more 'practical' bent. He equated happiness with the good and was responsible for the doctrine of the *golden mean*. This stated that every virtue is a middle-point between prodigality and stinginess. The same tendency to give Idealism a practical turn is found in the works of the 18th-century philosopher Immanuel Kant. The most famous part of Kant's ethics is that connected with the phrase 'categorical imperative'. In Kant's own words: 'Act only according to a maxim of which you can at the same time will that it shall become a general law'. In other words, before acting in a certain way, the individual must ask himself: 'Would I be happy if everyone behaved like this?'

The Utilitarians are more directly concerned than the Idealists with earthly welfare. The earliest Western philosopher in this tradition was *Epicurus*, a Greek of the 4th century BC. Instead of deriving ideas of right and wrong from above, Epicurus maintained that 'we call pleasure the beginning and end of the blessed life'. The term *Epicurean* is often used to describe one who indulges in excessive pleasure, but the usage is not just. Epicurus did not condone excesses. On the contrary, he said that pleasure was only good when moderate and calm.

The Utilitarian tradition has on the whole had more adherents than the Idealistic tradition in modern philosophy. Jeremy Bentham, for example, writing in the 18th century, acknowledged his debt to Epicurus in his *Principles of Morals and Legislation*. Bentham agreed that pain and pleasure were the 'sovereign masters' governing man's conduct. He added to this doctrine of *utility*, which argued that 'the greatest happiness of the greatest number is the measure of right and wrong'. *John Stuart Mill* is perhaps the most famous of the Utilitarians. He extended Bentham's doctrines by arguing that 'some kinds of pleasure are more valuable than others'. This doctrine is explained in his essay *Utilitarianism*(1863).

METAPHYSICS

The term 'metaphysics' originated as the title of one of Aristotle's treatises. It probably meant only that he wrote it after his treatise *Physics*, but the term is usually employed to describe speculation as to the ultimate nature of reality.

EPISTEMOLOGY

Epistemology is the study of the nature, grounds and validity of human knowledge – how we come to know; how far we can rely on different kinds of belief; how science can be separated from superstition; and how conflicts between rival scientific theories can be resolved. Those epistemologists who are usually called *Rationalists* assert that knowledge is born in the individual and has only to be drawn forth. The other point of view – *Empiricism* – is that at birth the mind is a passive blank sheet on which knowledge is then imprinted.

Rationalists This school is represented classically by Plato, who discussed various theories of knowledge and discarded those built on the shifting sands of sense perception. The senses are, he thought, too fallible. True knowledge comes from those general notions that are derived from the realm of the ideas which the soul possesses prior to birth.

The 17th-century French philosopher-scientist René Descartes, although not a Platonist, was a rationalist in that he regarded sensory knowledge as a bad foundation for science. Its certainty, he argued, could never equal that of mathematics or of our own knowledge of our thoughts. This inalienable certainty is expressed in his famous statement 'I think; therefore I am': however deep my doubt, I must exist in order to doubt.

Empiricism The classic representative of Empiricism was John Locke, a 17th-century English philosopher. In his *Essay Concerning Human Understanding*, Locke defined an opposite point of view to Plato and Descartes. He regarded the mind at birth as comparable to an empty cabinet. As we live, 'experience' fills it with 'ideas' either of our inner states (*ideas of reflection*) or of external objects (*ideas of sensation*). He argued that human knowledge could never get beyond the limits of such ideas.

MODERN PHILOSOPHY

The classical description of philosophy is in terms of the three fields of metaphysics, ethics and epistemology. The main movements of modern philosophy – Hegelianism, Analytic Philosophy, and Phenomenology – would regard such a division of the subject as outmoded.

Hegelianism At the beginning of the 19th century, Georg Wilhelm Friedrich Hegel criticized all previous conceptions of philosophy as being lifeless, one-sided and unhistorical. Hegel proposed that philosophy must always be rooted in history, but at the same time always striving for a conception of reality as a single developing whole, every part of which is animated by all the others.

Analytical Philosophy This movement was founded at the beginning of the 20th century by Bertrand Russell, building on the work of the mathematician Gottlob Frege. Analytical philosophy – which is no less critical of philosophical tradition – is based on the idea that authentic philosophy is essentially the study of logic, that is to say of formal patterns of reasoning abstracted from their metaphysical, ethical, epistemological or historical contexts.

Phenomenology This movement – which was founded at the same time as analytic philosophy – has come to dominate 20th-century European philosophy just as the analytic school has dominated philosophy in the English-speaking world. This movement claims that philosophers always tend to miss the one fundamental question – why our experience should be framed in terms of a distinction between an objective world and our subjective experience of it. Heidegger and Derrida have developed this line of thought by arguing that, so far from trying to build on past philosophy, we should attempt to 'destroy' or 'deconstruct' it.

PHILOSOPHICAL TERMS

a posteriori knowledge knowledge that comes from experience.

a priori knowledge knowledge that can be derived from pure reasoning, without reference to experience, i.e. by reasoning (as in mathematics and logic).

aesthetics the study of the nature of beauty and taste, especially in art.

analytic truths truths that can be proved by analysing the concepts they involve.

axiom a necessary and self-evident proposition requiring no proof.

causality the relationship between a cause and its effect.

deduction reaching a conclusion by purely *a priori* means.

dialectic literally, debate; by extension, the technique of proceeding from a thesis, through its negation or antithesis, to a synthesis in which both are reconciled on a higher level.

empirical knowledge knowledge derived from experience rather than reason.

epistemology a branch of philosophy that attempts to answer questions about the nature of knowledge and especially the nature of science.

ethics a branch of inquiry that attempts to answer questions about right and wrong, good and evil; and how we decide how human life should be lived.

induction the process of drawing general conclusions from particular instances.

logic the study of the structure or form of valid arguments, disregarding their content.

metaphysics a branch of philosophy concerned with systems of ideas that attempt to explain the nature of reality.

paradox a statement whose truth implies its falsehood, e.g. the Cretan philosopher Epimenides said 'All Cretans are liars'. As he was Cretan himself, is his statement true or false?

sophistry a fallacious argument.

synthesis the outcome of the confrontation of two arguments by which a truth is discovered.

teleology the practice of explaining processes in terms of what they achieve rather than what preceded them.

PHILOSOPHICAL SCHOOLS AND THEORIES

Since the days of the early Greeks, philosophers have been divided into different schools and have advanced opposing theories. Among the many basic outlooks and theories are the following:

altruism the principle of living and acting in the interest of others rather than for oneself.

analytical philosophy (see Modern Philosophy above)

asceticism the belief that withdrawal from the physical world into the inner world of the spirit is the highest good attainable.

atomism the belief that the entire universe is ultimately composed of interchangeable indivisible units.

critical theory a philosophical version of Marxism associated with the *Frankfurt School* (founded 1921).

criticism the theory that the path to knowledge lies midway between dogmatism and scepticism.

determinism the belief that the universe and everything in it (including individual lives) follows a fixed or pre-determined pattern. This belief has often been used to deny free will.

dialectical materialism the theory – often attributed to Marx – that reality is strictly material and is based on an economic struggle between opposing forces, with occasional interludes of harmony.

dogmatism the assertion of a belief without arguments in its support.

dualism the belief that the world consists of two radically independent and absolute elements, e.g. good and evil, or (especially) spirit and matter.

egoism the belief that the serving of one's own interests is the highest end.

empiricism the doctrine that there is no knowledge except that which is derived from experience.

existentialism the doctrine that the human self and human values are fictions, but inevitable ones, and that it is bad faith to deny one's own free will, even in a deterministic universe.

fatalism the doctrine that what will happen will happen and nothing we do will make any difference.

hedonism the doctrine that pleasure is the highest good.

humanism any system that regards human interests and the human mind as paramount in the universe.

idealism any system that regards thought or the idea as the basis either of knowledge or existence.

interactionism the theory that physical events can cause mental events, and vice versa.

materialism the doctrine that asserts the existence of only one substance – matter – thus denying the existence of spirit.

monism a belief in only one ultimate reality, whatever its nature.

naturalism a position that seeks to explain all phenomena by means of strictly natural (as opposed to supernatural) categories.

nominalism the doctrine that general terms are, in effect, nothing more than words. (Compare realism.)

operationalism the doctrine that scientific concepts are tools for prediction rather than descriptions of hidden realities.

pantheism the belief that God is identical with the universe.

personalism the theory that ultimate reality consists of a plurality of spiritual beings or independent persons.

phenomenology (see Modern Philosophy above)

pluralism the belief that there are more than two irreducible kinds of reality.

positivism the doctrine that man can have no knowledge outside science.

pragmatism a philosophical method that makes practical consequences the test of truth.

predestination the doctrine that the events of a human's life are determined beforehand.

rationalism the theory that reason alone, without the aid of experience, can arrive at the basic reality of the universe.

realism the doctrine that general terms have a real existence.

relativism the rejection of the concept of absolute and invariable truths.

scepticism the doctrine that nothing can be known with certainty.

sensationalism the theory that sensations are the ultimate and real components of the world.

stoicism a philosophical school that believed that reason (God) was the basis of the universe and that humanity should live in harmony with nature.

structuralism the doctrine that language is essentially a system of rules; or the extension of this idea to culture as a whole.

theism the belief in a God.

transcendentalism the belief in an ultimate reality that transcends human experience.

voluntarism the theory that will is a determining factor in the universe.

PHILOSOPHERS AND THEIR THEORIES

PRE-SOCRATIC GREEKS

Thales of Miletus (624–550 BC). Thales – an exponent of monism – is regarded as the first Western philosopher.

Anaximander of Miletus (611–547 BC). Anaximander continued Thales' quest for universal substance, but reasoned that universal substance need not resemble any known substances.

Heraclitus of Ephesus (533–475 BC). Heraclitus opposed the concept of a single ultimate reality and held that the only permanent thing is change.

Empedocles of Acragas (c. 495–435 BC). Empedocles believed that there were four irreducible substances (water, fire, earth and air) and two forces (love and hate).

Parmenides of Elea (c. 495 BC). A member of the Eleatic school, Parmenides formulated the basic doctrine of idealism.

Zeno of Elea (c. 495–430 BC). Zeno argued that plurality and change are appearances, not realities.

Protagoras of Abdera (481–411 BC). An early relativist and humanist who doubted human ability to attain absolute truth.

CLASSICAL GREEK PHILOSOPHERS

Socrates (c. 470–399 BC). Socrates developed the Socratic method of enquiry (see Ethics, above). Socrates was the teacher of Plato, through whose writings his idealistic philosophy was disseminated.

Democritus of Abdera (460–370 BC). Democritus began the tradition in Western thought of explaining the universe in mechanistic terms.

Antisthenes (c. 450–c. 360 BC). The chief of the group known as the Cynics, Antisthenes stressed discipline and work as the essential good.

Plato (c. 428–347 BC). The founder of the Academy at Athens, Plato developed the idealism of his teacher Socrates and was the teacher of Aristotle.

Aristotle (384–322 BC). Greek philosopher and scientist, whose works have influenced the whole of Western philosophy. Aristotle taught that there are four factors in causation: form; matter; motive cause, which produces change; and the end, for which a process of change occurs.

HELLENISTIC PERIOD

Pyrrho of Elis (c. 365–275 BC). Pyrrho – who initiated the Sceptical school of philosophy – believed that man could not know anything for certain.

Epicurus (341–270 BC). A proponent of atomism and hedonism, Epicurus taught that the test of truth is in sensation.

Zeno of Citium (c. 335–263 BC). Chief of the Stoics – so called because they met in the _Stoa Poikile_ or Painted Porch at Athens – Zeno taught that man's role is to accept nature and all it offers, good or bad.

Plotinus (AD 205–270). Plotinus was the chief exponent of Neo-Platonism, a combination of the teachings of Plato and Oriental concepts.

Augustine of Hippo (AD 354–430). St Augustine of Hippo was an exponent of optimism. One of the greatest influences on medieval Christian thought, Augustine believed that God transcends human comprehension.

Boethius (c. AD 480–524). Late Roman statesman. In *The Consolations of Philosophy* Boethius proposed that virtue alone is constant.

MEDIEVAL PERIOD

Avicenna (980–1037). Arabic follower of Aristotle and Neo-Platonism. Avicenna's works revived interest in Aristotle in 13th-century Europe.

Anselm (1033–1109). Italian Augustinian and realist. Anselm is famous for his examination of the proof of God's existence.

Peter Abelard (1079–1142). French theologian and philosopher. Abelard's nominalism caused him to be declared a heretic by the Church.

Averroës (1126–98). A great philosopher of Muslim Spain, and a leading commentator on Aristotle. Averroës regarded religion as allegory for the common man and philosophy as the path to truth.

Maimonides (1135–1204). Jewish student of Aristotle. Maimonides sought to combine Aristotelian teaching with that of the Bible.

St Thomas Aquinas (1225–74). Italian scholastic philosopher. Aquinas evolved a compromise between Aristotle and Scripture, based on the belief that faith and reason are in agreement. His philosophical system is known as Thomism.

THE RENAISSANCE

Desiderius Erasmus (1466–1536). Dutch. The greatest of the humanists, Erasmus helped spread the ideas of the Renaissance throughout northern Europe.

Niccolò Machiavelli (1469–1527). Italian. Machiavelli placed the state as the paramount power in human affairs. His book *The Prince* brought him a reputation for amoral cynicism.

TRANSITION TO MODERN THOUGHT

Francis Bacon (1561–1626). English statesman and philosopher of science. In his major work, *Novum Organum*, Bacon sought to revive the inductive system of deductive logic in interpreting nature.

Thomas Hobbes (1588–1679). English materialist. Hobbes believed the natural state of man is war. In *Leviathan* Hobbes outlined a theory of human government whereby the state and man's subordination to it form the sole solution to human selfishness.

René Descartes (1596–1650). French dualist, rationalist and theist. The Cartesian system of Descartes is at the base of all modern philosophy. Descartes evolved a theory of knowledge that underlies modern science and philosophy based on the certainty of the proposition 'I think, therefore I am'.

Blaise Pascal (1623–62). French theist. Pascal held that sense and reason are mutually deceptive, that truth lies between dogmatism and scepticism.

Benedict de Spinoza (1632–77). Dutch rationalist metaphysician. Spinoza developed the ideas of Descartes while rejecting his dualism.

John Locke (1632–1704). English empiricist. Locke's influence in political, religious, educational and philosophical thought was wide and deep. In his great *Essay Concerning Human Understanding* he sought to refute the rationalist view that knowledge derives from first principles.

EIGHTEENTH CENTURY

Gottfried Wilhelm von Leibniz (1646–1716). German idealist and absolutist. Leibniz's optimistic view was ridiculed by Voltaire in *Candide*. Leibniz held that reality consisted of units of force called monads.

George Berkeley (1685–1753). Anglo-Irish idealist and theist. Berkeley taught that things exist only in being perceived and that the very idea of matter is contradictory.

David Hume (1711–76). Scottish empiricist, philosopher and historian. Hume developed the ideas of Locke into a system of scepticism according to which human knowledge is limited to the experience of ideas and sensations whose truth cannot be verified.

Jean-Jacques Rousseau (1712–78). French social and political philosopher. Rousseau advocated a 'return to nature' to counteract the inequality among men brought about by civilized society.

Immanuel Kant (1724–1804). German founder of critical philosophy. At first influenced by Leibniz, then by Hume, Kant sought to find an alternative approach to the rationalism of the former and the scepticism of the latter. In ethics, he formulated the *Categorical Imperative*, which states that what applies to oneself must apply to everyone else unconditionally.

Jeremy Bentham (1748–1832). English utilitarian. Bentham believed, like Kant, that the interests of the individual are at one with those of society. He regarded pleasure and pain rather than basic principle as the motivation for right action.

Johann Gottlieb Fichte (1762–1814). German. Fichte formulated a philosophy of absolute idealism based on Kant's ethical concepts.

NINETEENTH CENTURY

Georg Wilhelm Friedrich Hegel (1770–1831). German. Hegel's metaphysical system was rationalist and absolutist, based on the belief that thought and being are one, and nature is the manifestation of an Absolute Idea.

Arthur Schopenhauer (1788–1860). German idealist. Schopenhauer gave the will a leading place in his metaphysics. The foremost exponent of pessimism, expressed in *The World as Will and Idea*, he rejected absolute idealism as wishful thinking, and taught that the only tenable attitude lay in utter indifference to an irrational world. He held that highest ideal was nothingness.

Auguste Comte (1798–1857). French. Comte was the founder of positivism, a system which denied transcendent metaphysics and stated that the Divinity and man were one, that altruism is man's highest duty, and that scientific principles explain all phenomena.

Ludwig Feuerbach (1804–72). German. Feuerbach argued that religion was no more than a projection of human nature. He was an important influence on Marx.

John Stuart Mill (1806–73). English exponent of utilitarianism. Mill differed from Bentham by recognizing differences in quality as well as quantity in pleasure. His most famous work is *On Liberty* (1859).

Søren Kierkegaard (1813–55). Danish religious existentialist. Kierkegaard's thought is the basis of modern (atheistic) existentialism. He taught that only existence has reality, and the individual has a unique value.

Karl Marx (1818–83). German revolutionary thinker who, with Friedrich Engels, was the founder of modern Communism. Marx was a critical follower of Hegel.

Herbert Spencer (1820–1903). English evolutionist. Spencer's 'synthetic philosophy' interpreted all phenomena according to the principle of evolutionary progress.

Charles S. Peirce (1839–1914). American physicist, mathematician and founder of the philosophical school called pragmatism. Peirce regarded logic as the basis of philosophy and taught that the test of an idea is whether it works.

William James (1842–1910). American psychologist and pragmatist. James held that reality is always in the making and that each man should choose the philosophy best suited to him.

Friedrich Wilhelm Nietzsche (1844–1900). German. Nietzsche held that the 'will to power' is basic in life and that the spontaneous is to be preferred to the orderly. He attacked Christianity as a system that fostered the weak, whereas the function of evolution is to evolve 'supermen'.

TWENTIETH CENTURY

Gottlob Frege (1848–1925). German mathematician. Frege revolutionized formal logic and thus paved the way for analytic philosophy.

Henri Bergson (1859–1941). French evolutionist. Bergson asserted the existence of a 'vital impulse' that carries the universe forward, with no fixed beginning and no fixed end. He believed that the future is determined by the choice of alternatives made in the present.

John Dewey (1859–1952). American pragmatist. Dewey developed a system known as instrumentalism. He saw man as continuous with, but distinct from, nature.

Edmund Husserl (1859–1938). German. Husserl developed a system called phenomenology, which sought to ground knowledge in pure experience without presuppositions.

Alfred North Whitehead (1861–1947). British evolutionist and mathematician. Whitehead held that reality must not be interpreted in atomistic terms, but in terms of events. He held that God is intimately present in the universe, yet distinct from it – a view called pantheism.

Benedetto Croce (1866–1952). Italian. Croce was noted for his role in the revival of historical realism.

Bertrand Russell (1872–1970). British agnostic. Russell adhered to many systems of philosophy before becoming a major expounder of logical positivism – the view that scientific knowledge is the only factual knowledge.

George Edward Moore (1873–1958). British moral philosopher. Moore developed the doctrine of ideal utilitarianism in *Principia Ethica*, 1903.

Martin Heidegger (1889–1976). German student of Husserl. Heidegger furthered the development of phenomenology and greatly influenced atheistic existentialists.

Gabriel Marcel (1889–1973). French. Initially a student of the English-speaking idealists, Marcel was preoccupied with the Cartesian problem of the relation of mind and matter.

Ludwig Wittgenstein (1889–1951). Austrian. The most influential philosopher of the 20th century, Wittgenstein developed two highly original but incompatible systems of philosophy, both dominated by a concern with the relations between language and the world.

Herbert Marcuse (1898–1979). A German-American philosopher who attempted to combine existentialism and psychoanalysis with a libertarian Marxism which was critical of Communism.

Gilbert Ryle (1900–76). British. Ryle studied the nature of philosophy and the concept of mind as well as the nature of meaning and the philosophy of logic.

Sir Karl Popper (1902–90). British critical rationalist. He held that scientific laws can never be proved to be true and that the most that can be claimed is that they have survived attempts to disprove them.

Theodor Adorno (1903–69). A German philosopher who combined Marxism with avant-garde aesthetics.

Jean-Paul Sartre (1905–80). French. An influential philosopher who developed the existentialist thought of Heidegger. An atheistic supporter of a subjective, irrational human existence, he was opposed to an orderly overall reality. His slogan was 'existence before essence'.

Maurice Merleau-Ponty (1907–61). French phenomenologist. Merleau-Ponty was famous for insisting on the role of the human body in our experience of the world.

Simone de Beauvoir (1908–86). French existentialist. The founder of modern feminist philosophy.

Claude Lévi-Strauss (1908–). A French anthropologist and proponent of structuralism. His writings investigate the relationship between culture (exclusively an attribute of humanity) and nature, based on the distinguishing characteristics of man – the ability to communicate in a language.

Willard van Orman Quine (1908–). An American philosopher who combined pragmatism with logical positivism and destroyed many of the dogmas of early analytic philosophy.

Sir Isaiah Berlin (1909–90). British moral and political philosopher and historian. Berlin argued against determinist philosophies of history. He emphasized the importance of moral values, and the necessity of rejecting determinism if the ideas of human responsibility and freedom are to be retained.

Alfred J. Ayer (1910–89). British philosopher. Ayer was the principal advocate of logical positivism, developed from Russell.

Donald Davidson (1917–). American. A leading philosopher of language, and follower of Quine.

Jurgen Habermas (1929–). German. Habermas is a critical Marxist with strong Kantian and liberal affinities.

Jacques Derrida (1930–). French. The founder of deconstruction, a development of Heidegger's technique of interpreting traditional philosophers with great care in order to reveal their constant incoherence.

RELIGION

WHAT IS RELIGION?

Religion is one of the most universal activities known to humankind, being practised across virtually all cultures, and from the very earliest times to the present day. Although various writers have attempted a wide and general definition, none of these definitions has been universally accepted.

Religion appears to have arisen from the human desire to find an ultimate meaning and purpose in life, and this is usually centred around belief in a supernatural being (or beings). In most religions the devotees attempt to honour and/or to influence their god or gods – commonly through such practices as prayer, sacrifice or right behaviour.

MAJOR RELIGIONS OF THE WORLD

It is difficult to obtain figures for the number of practising – rather than nominal – adherents of the world's major religions. In the case of religions practised in China – Daoism, Confucianism and Buddhism – no reliable figures are available and the totals given for these religions should be treated with caution. The following figures are estimates based upon United Nations statistics and figures released by individual religious bodies.

CHRISTIANS 1 780 000 000

This total includes:
Roman Catholics c. 1 000 000 000
Orthodox Christians 170 000 000
Anglicans 74 000 000
Lutherans 55 000 000
Methodists 55 000 000
Calvinists, Reformed Churches and Presbyterians 47 000 000
Baptists 35 000 000
(excluding independent African churches of a Baptist persuasion).

ISLAM c. 950 000 000

This total includes:
Sunnis over 800 000 000
Shiite sects over 80 000 000
Some Islamic authorities estimate that there are over 1 000 000 000 followers of Islam.

HINDUS c. 720 000 000

Some authorities estimate the number of practising adherents of Hinduism as under 500 000 000.

BUDDHISTS c. 310 000 000

The majority of Buddhists are thought to follow the *Mahayana ('Great Vehicle').*

CONFUCIANS 200 000 000–300 000 000

The number of Confucians in China is not known. Many other estimates of the number of practising adherents of Confucianism range between 5 000 000 and 6 000 000.

FOLLOWERS OF ASIAN PRIMAL RELIGIONS c. 180 000 000

FOLLOWERS OF AFRICAN PRIMAL RELIGIONS c. 69 000 000

SHINTOISTS 20 000 000–30 000 000

Estimates of the number of practising adherents of Shinto range between 3 000 000 and 35 000 000. Over 90 000 000 Japanese are said to belong to the Shinto 'community' but have no active allegiance to the religion.

DAOISTS c. 20 000 000

JEWS 18 000 000

The majority of Jews belong to Liberal, Reform and other traditions rather than Orthodox.

SIKHS 18 500 000

BAHA'IS 5 400 000

JAINS 3 700 000

CHRISTIANITY

The Western calendar, shaped and determined by Christianity, sees the birth of Jesus of Nazareth, known as the Christ, as the turning point of history. In dating the modern era from the supposed date of his birth (it seems likely Jesus was actually born c. 4 BC), Christianity was making a profound statement about the significance of Jesus Christ.

Jesus means the Saviour, taken from the Hebrew root *'yasha'*, to save; Christ means the anointed one, from the Greek verb *chrio*, to anoint.

For Christians, the Jewish child born in Bethlehem was no ordinary human. He was and is both human and divine, the Son of God. While it is possible to say that a historical person named Jesus lived between c. 4 BC and c. AD 29, it is only faith that can claim that he was the Christ, the anointed one of God, the long-awaited Messiah of the Jews.

THE NATURE OF GOD

Christians believe that God is the creator of the universe and all life. They believe that Jesus Christ is the only Son of God, who has existed with God the Father from before time began. Jesus was incarnated (given human form), when by the power of the Holy Spirit, his human mother, Mary, gave birth to him. (The subsequent husband of the Virgin Mary – Joseph of Nazareth – was 27 generations descended from King David.) Christians believe that the purpose of Christ's incarnation was to reconcile humanity with God, as human sinfulness had broken the relationship with God. Through the death of Jesus upon the Cross at Calvary, God broke the power of sin and evil, and through the Resurrection (the rising) of Jesus from the dead on the third day God showed the triumph of life over death, and gave the promise of everlasting life to those who believe in Jesus.

In the doctrine of the Trinity, Christians believe that God is one but has three co-equal 'persons' – God the Father, God the Son (Jesus Christ) and the Holy Spirit.

CHRISTIAN TEACHING

The life and teaching of Christ are recorded in the four Gospels and in several quotations and stories found in other books of the New Testament of the Bible. These were all written by Christians who believed Jesus to be in some way both human and divine. Our knowledge of Jesus therefore comes from the pens of believers.

Jesus taught that God is like a father who cares for every person on Earth. He taught that through repentance and forgiveness, God calls all humanity to him in love and seeks every individual to do his will on Earth. Jesus taught that through living as God wishes, the Kingdom of God – justice, love, mercy and peace – could come upon Earth, either in individual lives or possibly to the world as a whole.

THE APOSTLES AND THE CHURCH

The Church holds that through the 12 key disciples of Jesus, the apostles, authority on Earth was given to the Church, which is seen to be the body of Christ on Earth. The Church is therefore held to be essential to salvation – to being freed from sin and to the possibility of everlasting life.

Jesus appointed 12 disciples. The following are common to the lists in the books of Matthew, Mark, Luke and the Acts.

Peter (martyred in Rome c. AD 64). A fisherman from Galilee called to be a disciple by Jesus at the beginning of his ministry, St Peter was recognized in the early Church as the leader of the disciples and is recognized by the Roman Catholic Church as the first of the popes. Peter – originally called Simon – was the brother of Andrew (see below).

Andrew (traditionally said to have been crucified at Patras in Greece c. AD 65). The brother of Peter, St Andrew was a fisherman called by Jesus to be a fisher of men. He was previously a disciple of John the Baptist.

James the son of Zebedee (beheaded in the Holy Land c. AD 44). St James the Great – like his brother John and the apostles Peter and Andrew – was a fisherman, and was one of the first disciples to be called by Jesus.

John the Apostle (fate unknown). St John the Apostle (also known as St John the Divine) was a fisherman and the brother of James (see above). He wrote the Gospel according to St John, the Revelation and three letters in the New Testament.

Philip (fate unknown). St Philip came from Bethsaida and was called at the same time as Nathaniel (see Bartholomew).

Bartholomew (traditionally said to have been martyred by the Babylonians). St Bartholomew is thought to have been called Nathaniel, the disciple whose calling is mentioned in St John, as Bartholomew is a family name – meaning son of Tolmai – rather than a given name.

Thomas (traditionally said to have died in India). Known as 'Doubting Thomas', St Thomas was the apostle who requested physical proof of the Resurrection.

Matthew (fate unknown). St Matthew – who is believed to have been a tax collector – is traditionally said to have been the author of the first Gospel.

James the son of Alphaeus (fate unknown, although traditionally said to have been martyred in Persia). Also known as St James the Less.

Simon the Canaanite (or Simon Zelotes) (fate unknown). St Simon is thought to have been a member of the Jewish nationalist group, the Zealots.

Thaddeus (or Jude) (fate unknown). Called Judas (not Iscariot) in St Luke, Thaddeus in St Mark and St Matthew and referred to as Judas of James in some versions of the Bible, this apostle is (like Simon) believed to have been a Zealot. He is better known as St Jude, patron of the desperate.

Judas Iscariot (traditionally said to have hanged himself after the Crucifixion.) The treasurer of the apostles, Judas betrayed Jesus to the chief priests for 30 pieces of silver. The name Iscariot is thought to derive from the Latin word *sicarius*, meaning murderer. Matthias was elected by the apostles to take the place of Judas.

FORMS OF CHRISTIANITY

Christianity has three major forms: Roman Catholic, with the pope as head of the Church; Orthodox, with the patriarch of Constantinople (Istanbul) as the first amongst equals of the various patriarchs of the different Orthodox Churches, such as the Russian Church; and the Protestant movement, made up of denominations such as the Lutheran, Methodist, Baptist and Anglican Churches, and so on.

ROMAN CATHOLICISM

Rome was the only Western Church founded by an apostle (St Peter). From Ireland to the Carpathians, Christians came to acknowledge the bishop of Rome as pope (from the Vulgar Latin *papa*, 'father'), and used Latin for worship, scripture-reading and theology. Roman Catholics recognize the pope as the lawful successor of St Peter, who was appointed by Christ to be head of the Church.

In the 16th century most of northern Europe broke the link with Rome to form reformed Protestant Churches. This division of Western Christianity led to the terms 'Protestant' for these northern Churches and 'Roman Catholic' (though to its members it was simply 'the Church') for Latin Christianity.

Supreme in southern Europe, Catholic Christianity was extended to the Americas and parts of Asia and Africa. Since the Second Vatican Council (1962–66) Latin has for most purposes given way to local languages.

The Roman Catholic Church claims catholicity inasmuch as it was charged (*de jure*) by Christ to 'teach all nations' and *de facto* since it is by far the largest Christian Church. The Roman Catholic Church claims infallibility in interpreting both the written and unwritten word of God. The pope has delegated certain administrative powers to the Curia, the work of which is done by 11 permanent departments or congregations, but the Church's strong centralized authority is focused on the papacy.

POPES

The pope – otherwise known as the bishop of Rome – is the chief bishop of the Roman Catholic Church and is considered by Catholics to be the Vicar of Christ on Earth and the successor of St Peter, the first bishop of Rome. He is elected by the College of Cardinals in the Vatican, meeting in secret conclave. The College consists of those cardinals aged under 80; in May 1991, 101 of the 141 cardinals were eligible as electors.

There have been over 30 antipopes, rivals to the papacy elected in opposition to the one who has been chosen canonically. In the 11th and 12th centuries the Holy Roman Emperors chose over a dozen antipopes; in the 14th century several antipopes were elected following the Great Schism. Unity was restored at the Council of Constance in 1415.

St Peter c. 33–67
St Linus 67–76
St Cletus (also called Anacletus) 76–88
St Clement I 88–97

St Evaristus 97–105
St Alexander I 105–15
St Sixtus I 115–25
St Telesphorus 125–36
St Hyginus 136–40
St Pius I 140–55
St Anicetus 155–66
St Soterus 166–75
St Eleutherius 175–89
St Victor I 189–99
St Zephyrinus 199–217
St Callistus I 217–22
St Urban I 222–30
St Pontian 230–35
St Anterus 235–36
St Fabian I 236–50
St Cornelius 251–53
St Lucius I 253–54
St Stephen I 254–57
St Sixtus II 257–58
St Dionysius 259–68
St Felix I 269–74
St Eutychianus 275–83
St Caius 283–96
St Marcellinus 296–304
St Marcellus I 308–09
St Eusebius 309–10
St Miltiades 311–14
St Silvester I 314–35
St Mark 336–37
St Julius I 337–52
Liberius 352–66
St Damasus 366–84
St Siricius 384–99
St Anastasius I 399–401
St Innocent I 401–17
St Zosimus 417–18
St Boniface I 418–22
St Celestine I 422–432
St Sixtus III 432-40
St Leo I 440–61
St Hilary 461–68
St Simplicius 468–83
St Felix II 483–92
St Gelasius I 492–96
St Anastasius II 496–98
St Symmachus 498–514
St Hormisdas 514–23
St John I 523–26
St Felix III 526–30
Boniface II 530–32
John II (Mercurius) 533–35
St Agapetus I 535–36
St Silverius 536–37
Vigilius 537–55
Pelagius I 556–61
John III 561–74
Benedict I 575–79
Pelagius II 579–90
St Gregory I 590–604
Sabinianus 604–06
Boniface III 607
St Boniface IV 608–15
St Deusdedit I 615–18
Boniface V 619–25
Honorius I 625–38
Severinus 638–40
John IV 640–42
Theodore I 642–49
St Martin I 649–55
St Eugenius I 654–57
St Vitalian 657–72
Deusdedit II 672–76

Donus 676–78
St Agatho 678–81
St Leo II 681–83
St Benedict II 683–85
John V 685–86
Conon 686–87
St Sergius I 687–701
John VI 701–05
John VII 705–07
Sisinnius 707
Constantine 708–15
St Gregory II 715–31
St Gregory III 731–41
Saint Zacharias 741–52
Stephen 'II' 752 (died before he could be enthroned)
Stephen II or III 752–57
St Paul I 757–67
Stephen III or IV 768–72
Adrian I 772–95
St Leo III 795–816
Stephen IV or V 816–17
St Paschal I 817–24
Eugenius II 824–27
Valentine 827
Gregory IV 827–44
Sergius II 844–47
St Leo IV 847–55
Benedict III 855–58
St Nicholas I 858–67
Adrian II 867–72
John VIII 872–82
Marinus I 882–84
Adrian III 884–85
Stephen V or VI 885–91
Formosus 891–96
Boniface VI 896
Stephen VI or VII 896–97
Romanus 897
Theodore II 897
John IX 898–900
Benedict IV 900–03
Leo V 903
Sergius III 904–11
Anastasius III 911–13
Lando 913–14
John X 914–28
Leo VI 928
Stephen VII or VIII 928–31
John XI 931–35
Leo VII 936–39
Stephen VIII or IX 939–42
Marinus II 942–46
Agapetus II 946–55
John XII 955–64
Leo VIII 963–65
Benedict V 964–65
John XIII 965–72
Benedict VI 973–74
Benedict VII 974–83
John XIV (Pietro Canepanova) 983–84
John XV 985–96
Gregory V (Bruno of Carinthia) 996–99
Silvester II (Gerbert) 999–1003
John XVII (Sicco) 1003
John XVIII (Fasino) 1003–09
Sergius IV (Pietro Buccaporci) 1009–12
Benedict VIII 1012–24
John XIX 1024–32
Benedict IX 1032–44
Silvester III 1045
Benedict IX (restored) 1045
Gregory VI 1045–46

Clement II 1046–47
Benedict IX (restored) 1047–48
Damasus II (Poppo) 1048
St Leo IX 1048–54
Victor II 1055–57
Stephen IX or X 1057–58
Nicholas II 1058–61
Alexander II 1061–73
St Gregory VII (Hildebrand de Soana) 1064–85
Victor III (Desiderius, Prince of Benevento) 1086–87
Urban II (Odon de Lagery) 1088–99
Paschal II (Ranieri) 1099–1118
Gelasius II (Giovanni Gaetani) 1118–19
Callistus II (Gui de Bourgogne) 1119–24
Honorius II (Lamberto Scannabecchi) 1124–30
Innocent II (Gregorio Papareschi) 1130–43
Celestine II (Guido di Castello) 1143–44
Lucius II (Gerardo Caccianemici) 1144–45
Eugenius III (Bernardo Paganelli) 1145–53
Anastasius IV (Corrado) 1153–54
Adrian IV (Nicholas Breakspeare*) 1154–59
Alexander III (Rolando Bandinelli) 1159–81
Lucius III (Ubaldo Allucingoli) 1181–85
Urban III (Uberto Crivelli) 1185–87
Gregory VIII (Alberto di Morra) 1187
Clement III (Paolo Scolari) 1187–91
Celestine III (Giacinto Buboni) 1191–98
Innocent III (Lothario, Count of Segni) 1198–1216
Honorius III (Cencio Savelli) 1216–27
Gregory IX (Ugolino, Count of Segni) 1227–41
Celestine IV (Goffredo Castiglioni) 1241
Innocent IV (Sinibaldo Fieschi) 1243–54
Alexander IV (Rainaldo, Count of Segni) 1254–61
Urban IV (Jacques Pantaléon) 1261–64
Clement IV (Gui Faucois) 1265–68
Gregory X (Theobaldo Visconti) 1271–76
Innocent V (Pierre de Tarentaise) 1276
Adrian V (Ottobono dei Fieschi) 1276
John XXI (Pedro Juliani) 1276–77
Nicholas III (Giovanni Gaetano Orsini) 1277–80
Martin IV (Simon de Brion) 1281–85
Honorius IV (Giacomo Savelli) 1285–87
Nicholas IV (Girolamo Moschi) 1288–92
St Celestine V (Pietro del Morrone) 1294
Boniface VIII (Benedetto Gaetani) 1294–1303
Benedict XI (Nicola Boccasini) 1303–04
Clement V (Bertrand de Got) 1305–14
John XXII (Jacques Duèse) 1316–34
Benedict XII (Jacques Fournier) 1334–42
Clement VI (Pierre Roger) 1342–52
Innocent VI (Etienne Aubert) 1352–62
Urban V (Guillaume Grimoard) 1362–70
Gregory XI (Pierre Roger de Beaufort) 1370–78
Urban VI (Bartolommeo Prignano) 1378–89
Boniface IX (Pietro Tomacelli) 1389–1404
Innocent VII (Cosimo dei Migliorati) 1404–06
Gregory XII (Angelo Corrari) 1406–15
Martin V (Odo Colonna) 1417–31
Eugenius IV (Gabriele Condolmieri) 1431–47
Nicholas V (Tommaso Parentucelli) 1447–55
Callistus III (Alonso Borgia) 1455–58
Pius II (Aeneas Piccolomini) 1458–64
Paul II (Pietro Barbo) 1464–71
Sixtus IV (Francesco della Rovere) 1471–84
Innocent VIII (Giovanni Battista) 1484–92
Alexander VI (Roderigo Borgia) 1492–1503
Pius III (Francesco Todeschini) 1503
Julius II (Giuliano della Rovere) 1503–13
Leo X (Giovanni de Medici) 1513–21
Adrian VI (Adrian Florensz Boeyens**) 1522–23
Clement VII (Giulio de Medici) 1523–34
Paul III (Alessandro Farnese) 1534–49

Julius III (Giovanni Maria Ciocchi del Monte) 1550–55
Marcellus II (Marcello Cervini) 1555
Paul IV (Giovanni Pietro Carafa) 1555–59
Pius IV (Gianangelo de Medici) 1559–65
St Pius V (Antonio Michele Ghislieri) 1566–72
Gregory XIII (Ugo Buoncompagni) 1572–85
Sixtus V (Felice Perretti) 1585–90
Urban VII (Giovanni Battista Castagna) 1590
Gregory XIV (Niccolo Sfondrati) 1590–91
Innocent IX (Giovanni Antonio Facchinetti) 1591
Clement VIII (Ipollito Aldobrandini) 1592–1605
Leo XI (Alessandro Ottaviano de Medici) 1605
Paul V (Camillo Borghese) 1605–21
Gregory XV (Alessandro Ludovisi) 1621–23
Urban VIII (Maffeo Barberini) 1623–44
Innocent X (Giovanni Battista Pamfili) 1644–55
Alexander VII (Fabio Chigi) 1655–67
Clement IX (Giulio Rospigliosi) 1667–69
Clement X (Emilio Altieri) 1670–76
Innocent XI (Benedetto Odescalchi) 1676–89
Alexander VIII (Pietro Ottoboni) 1689–91
Innocent XII (Antonio Pignatelli) 1691–1700
Clement XI (Gianfrancesco Albani) 1700–21
Innocent XIII (Michelangelo de Conti) 1721–24
Benedict XIII (Pietro Francesco Orsini) 1724–30
Clement XII (Lorenzo Corsini) 1730–40
Benedict XIV (Prospero Lambertini) 1740–58
Clement XIII (Carlo della Torre Rezzonico) 1758–69
Clement XIV (Giovanni Vincenzo Antonio Ganganelli) 1769–74
Pius VI (Giovanni Angelo Braschi) 1775–99
Pius VII (Barnabo Chiaramonti) 1800–23
Leo XII (Annibale della Genga) 1823–29
Pius VIII (Francesco Xaverio Castiglioni) 1829–30
Gregory XVI (Bartolomeo Cappellari) 1831–46
Pius IX (Giovanni Maria Mastai-Ferretti) 1846–78
Leo XIII (Vincenzo Gioaccchino Pecci) 1878–1903
St Pius X (Giuseppe Sarto) 1903–14
Benedict XV (Giacomo della Chiesa) 1914–22
Pius XI (Achille Ratti) 1922–39
Pius XII (Eugenio Pacelli) 1939–58
John XXIII (Angelo Giuseppe Roncalli) 1958–63
Paul VI (Giovanni Battista Montini) 1963–78
John Paul I (Albino Luciani) 1978
John Paul II (Karol Wojtyla) 1978–

Key: * Adrian IV was the only English Pope.
** A Dutchman, Adrian VI was the last non-Italian to be elected to the papacy until the Pole, Karol Wojtyla, was elected in 1978.

UNIAT CHURCHES

Some smaller non-Latin Churches owe allegiance to the pope. They are called the Uniat Churches. Although these Churches are in full communion with the Roman Catholic Church, they retain their own organization and liturgies. Apart from the Malankara Orthodox Syrian (Jacobite) Church in southern India – which has 1 600 000 adherents – most of the Uniat Churches are in the Middle East and Eastern Europe. The largest of these Churches – with over 8 000 000 adherents – is the Ukrainian Uniat Church, which until 1990 was illegal in the USSR, but is now Ukraine's biggest Church.

Apart from the Ukrainians, the (Roman) Catholic Christians of the Uniat Churches belong to congregations owing allegiance to:
– the (Armenian rite) patriarch of Cilicia (based in Beirut, Lebanon);

- the (Chaldean rite) patriarch of Babylon (based in Baghdad, Iraq);
- the (Coptic rite) patriarch of Alexandria (based in Cairo, Egypt);
- the (Maronite rite) patriarch of Antioch (based in Bkerke, Lebanon);
- the (Melchite rite) patriarch of Antioch (based in Damascus, Syria);
- the (Syrian rite) patriarch of Antioch (based in Beirut, Lebanon).

PATRON SAINTS

Patron saints of groups and professions – and their feast days according to the Roman calendar – include the following:

academics St Albert the Great, 15 November.

accountants St Matthew, 21 September.

actors St Genesius, 26 August.

advertising executives St Bernardine of Siena, 20 May.

air pilots St Joseph of Copertino, 18 September.

announcers St John Chrysostom, 13 September.

archers St Sebastian, 20 January.

architects St Benedict, 21 March, and St Thomas, 21 December.

artillerymen St Barbara, 4 December.

bakers St Michael, 29 September, and St Honorius of Amiens, 16 May.

bankers St Matthew, 21 September.

basket makers St Paul the Hermit, 25 January.

bellfounders St Agatha, 5 February.

biologists St Albert the Great, 15 November.

blind people St Clair, 2 January.

boatmen St Nicholas, 6 December.

boilermakers St Maurus, 15 January.

bookbinders St Celestine the Fifth, 19 May, and St John of God, 8 March.

booksellers St John of the Latin Gate, 6 May.

business executives St Expeditus, 19 April.

butchers St Nicholas, 6 December.

carpenters St Joseph, 19 March.

cavalrymen St George, 23 April.

charity St Vincent de Paul, 19 July, and St Louise de Marillac, 15 March.

chemists St Albert the Great, 15 November.

children St Nicholas, 6 December.

choirboys St Nicholas, 6 December.

circus performers St Julian the Hospitaller, 29 January.

clockmakers St Eligius, 1 December.

cooks St Martha, 29 July.

coopers St John the Baptist, 24 June, and St Michael, 29 September.

customs officers St Matthew, 21 September.

cutlers St John the Baptist, 24 June.

deaf people St Francis de Sales, 29 January.

delicatessans St Anthony, 17 January.

dentists St Appollonia, 9 February.

diplomats St Gabriel, 24 March.

disabled ex-servicemen St Raphael, 24 October.

disabled people St Giles, 1 September.

doctors St Luke, 18 October, and St Pantaleon, 27 July.

domestic staff St Zita, 5 July.

down-and-outs St Alexis, 17 July, and St Giles, 1 September.

drinkers St Bibiana, 2 December.

drivers St Christopher, 25 July, and St Frances of Rome, 9 March.

dry cleaners/dyers St Maurice, 22 September.

editors St John Bosco, 31 January.

electricians St Lucy, 13 December.

emigrants St Frances Cabrini, 22 December.

engineers St Dominic La Caussade, 12 May.

farmers St Benedict, 21 March.

farm workers St Isidore the Labourer, 15 May.

ferrymen St Julian the Hospitaller, 29 January.

fireman St Lawrence, 10 August.

fishermen St Peter, 29 June.

forestry workers St Hubert, 3 November.

furnishers St Louis of France, 25 August.

gardeners St Fiacre, 30 August, and St Dorothy, 2 February.

glaziers St Luke, 18 October.

glassworkers St Clair, 2 January.

glove makers St Mary Magdalene, 22 July.

gravediggers St Maurus, 15 December.

hairdressers St Louis of France, 25 August.

hatters St James the Less, 1 May.

hermits St Anthony the Hermit, 17 January.

hired hands St Notburga, 13 September.

hospital staff St John of God, 8 March.

housekeepers St Martha, 29 JUly.

hunters St Hubert, 3 November.

immigrants St Frances Cabrini, 22 December.

innkeepers St Julian, 29 January, and St Vincent, 28 January.

insurance agents St Yves, 19 May.

interior decorators St Genevieve, 3 January.

jewellers St Eligius, 1 December.

joiners St Joseph, 19 March.

journalists St Francis de Sales, 29 January, and St Bernardine of Siena, 20 May.

labourers St Isidore the Labourer, 10 May.

lacemakers St Anne, 26 July.

laundry workers St Clare, 12 August.

lawyers St Yves, 19 May, and St Raymund of Penafort, 23 January.

learner drivers St Expeditus, 19 April.

leatherworkers St Bartholomew, 24 August, and St Crispin and St Crispinian, 25 October.

locksmiths St Peter, 29 April.

lost objects St Anthony of Padua, 13 June.

lovers St Valentine, 14 February.

machine workers St Benedict, 21 March.

managers St Thomas, 21 December.

market gardeners St Phocas, 22 September, and St Fiacre, 30 August.

merchants St Nicholas, 6 December.

messengers St Adrian, 8 September.

metalworkers St Stephen, 26 December.

midwives St Raymund Nonnatus, 31 August.

millers St Blaise, 3 February, and St Winnoc, 6 November.

miners St Barbara, 4 December.

missionaries St Teresa of Avila, 3 October, and St Francis Xavier, 3 December.

musicians St Cecilia, 22 November, St Blaise, 3 February, and St Dunstan, 19 May.

naturalists St Albert the Great, 15 November.

navigators St Nicholas of Bari, 7 May, St Cuthbert, 20 March, and St Elmo, 2 June.

needlewomen St Clare, 12 August.

nurses St Camillus, 14 July.

opticians St Clair, 2 January.

orphans St Jerome Emiliani, 8 February.

painters St Luke, 18 October.

parachutists St Michael, 29 September.

pawnbrokers St Nicholas, 6 December.

pedestrians St Martin of Tours, 11 November.

people in desperate straits St Jude, 28 October.

perfumers St Mary Magdalene, 22 July.

pharmacists St James the Great, 25 July.

philosophers St Catherine, 25 July.

photographers St Veronica, 6 August.

physicians St Luke, 18 October, and St Cosmas and St Damian, 27 September.

physicists St Albert the Great, 15 November.

pilgrims St James the Great, 25 July.

plumbers St Eligius, 1 December.

police St Genevieve, 3 January, and St Sebastian, 20 January.

poor people St Lawrence, 10 August.

porters St Christopher, 25 July.

potholers St Benedict, 21 March.

preachers St John Chrysostom, 13 September.

pregnant women St Anne, 26 July.

priests St John Vianney, 4 August.

printers St Augustine, 28 August.

prisoners St Leonard, 6 November.

prison officers St Hippolytus, 13 August.

quarry workers St Rock, 16 August.

race relations St Martin de Porres, 3 November.

radiologists St Michael, 29 September.

radio workers St Gabriel, 24 March.

refugees St Benedict Labre, 16 April.

roofers St Vincent Ferrer, 5 April.

ropemakers St Paul, 29 June.

sacristans St Guy, 12 June.

sailors St Nicholas of Bari, 7 May.

scouts St George, 23 April.

sculptors St Luke, 18 October.

secretaries St John Cassian, 23 July.

servants St Blandina, 2 June.

shepherds St Germaine of Pibrac, 19 January.

shepherdesses St Genevieve, 3 January.

shipwrights St Julian the Hospitaller, 29 January.

shoemakers/repairers St Crispin and St Crispinian, 25 October.

shopkeepers St Francis of Assisi, 4 October.

sick people St Camillus, 14 July.

soldiers St Maurice, 22 September, St Martin of Tours, 11 November, and St George, 23 April.

spokesmen/women St John Chrysostom, 13 September.

students St Catherine, 11 November.

surgeons St Luke, 18 October.

tanners St Bartholomew, 24 August.

tax collectors St Matthew, 21 September.

taxi drivers St Fiacre, 30 August, and St Christopher, 25 July.

teachers St Cassian of Imola, 13 August.

television workers St Gabriel, 24 March, and St Clare, 12 August.

tourists St Christopher, 25 July.

tour operators St Francis Xavier, 3 December.

tradesmen St Francis of Assisi, 4 October.

translators St Jerome, 30 September.

travellers St Julian the Hospitaller, 29 January, and St Christopher, 25 July.

underwriters St Yves, 19 May.

university academics St Thomas Aquinas, 28 July.

upholsterers St Genevieve, 3 January.

virgins St Maria Goretti, 6 July.

weavers St Blaise, 3 February, and St Barnabas, 11 June.

wine growers St Vincent, 22 January, and St John of the Latin Gate, 6 May.

wine merchants St Nicholas, 6 December.

workers St Joseph, 19 March.

writers St Francis de Sales, 29 January.

young people St Casimir, 4 March, and St Louis Gonzaga, 21 July.

NATIONAL PATRONS

Patrons saints of countries include those given below. The lists include the feast day(s) of these saints according to the current Roman Catholic or Orthodox calendars, as appropriate. (*Note: Not all of these saints are recorded in the Anglican calendar and some of those that are recorded appear on different dates.*)

Andorra the Virgin of Meritxell (St Mary), 8 September – the feast of the coronation of Virgin of Meritxell.

Argentina St Faith, 6 October.

Austria St Leopold, 15 November, and St Florian, 14 December.

Belgium St Joseph, 19 March, and St Charles the Good, 2 March.

Brazil St Faith, 6 October.

Bulgaria St Cyril and Methodius, 7 July (Orthodox) or 14 February (Roman Catholic).

Canada St Joseph, 19 March; St Anne, 26 July; and St René Goupil, 18 October.

Central American countries (Costa Rica, El Salvador, Guatemala, Honduras and Nicaragua) St James the Great, 25 July.

Chile St Faith, 6 October.

Colombia St Faith, 6 October.

Croatia Virgin Mary (the Assumption), 15 August; St Nicholas Tavelic, 14 November; and St Leopold Manvic, 12 May.

Cyprus St Barnabas, 11 June.

Czech Republic St Wenceslaus, 28 September, amd St Ludmilla, 16 September.

Denmark St Canute, 19 January and 10 June.

England St George, 23 April.

Finland St Henry of Uppsala, 19 January.

France St Joan of Arc, 30 May; St Martin of Tours, 11 November; and St Michael the Archangel, 29 September.

Germany St Boniface, 5 June.

Hungary St Stephen of Hungary, 2 September, and St Stanislas Kostka, 15 August.

Iceland St Olaf, 29 July.

India St Francis Xavier, 3 December.

Ireland St Patrick, 17 March, and St Brigit, 2 February.

Italy St Catherine of Siena, 24 April, and St Francis of Assisi, 4 October.

Japan St Francis Xavier, 3 December.

Jordan St John the Baptist, 24 June.

Liechtenstein Virgin Mary (the Assumption), 15 August.

Lithuania St Casimir, 4 March.

Luxembourg St Peter of Luxembourg, 5 July, and St Willibrord, 7 November.

Madagascar St Vincent de Paul, 19 July.

Malta St Paul, 29 June.

Mexico Our Lady of Guadalupe, 12 October.

Moldova St Cyril and St Methodius, 7 July.

Monaco St Dévote of Monaco, 27 January.

Nigeria St Patrick, 17 March.

North African countries (Algeria, Egypt, Morocco and Tunisia) St Augustine, 28 August, and St Cyprian, 16 September.

Norway St Olaf, 29 July.

Pakistan St Francis Xavier, 3 December.

Peru St Rose of Lima, 23 August, and St Joseph, 19 March.

Philippines St Rose of Lima, 23 August.

Poland St Casimir, 4 March, and St Stanislas, 7 May.

Portugal St Anthony of Padua, 13 January.

Romania St Cyril and St Methodius, 7 July (Orthodox) and 14 February (Roman Catholic).

Russia St Nicholas, 6 December.

San Marino St Marinus, 4 September.

Scotland St Andrew, 30 November, and St Margaret, 16 June (general) or 20 July (CofE only).

Serbia St Sava, 14 January.

Slovakia St Cyril and St Methodius, 5 or 7 July.

Slovenia St Mary, Mother of God, 25 March.

Spain St James the Great, 25 July, and St Ferdinand, 30 May.

Sweden (Lutheran) St Bridget of Sweden, 8 October; (Roman Catholic) St Eric, 18 May.

Switzerland St Gall, 16 October, and St Nicholas von Flue, 25 September.

Turkey St George, 23 April; St Andrew 30 November; and St John the Evangelist, 27 December.

Ukraine St Vladimir, 15 July.

USA (Roman Catholic) Virgin Mary, 8 December – feast day of the Roman Catholic festival of Mary conceived without sin.

Uruguay St Philip and St James, 1 May.

Venezuela St Faith, 6 October.

Vietnam St Joseph, 19 March.

Wales St David, 1 March.

Europe The co-patrons of Europe are St Benedict (c. 480–c. 550; feast day 11 July) and St Cyril and St Methodius (Roman Catholic feast day 14 February). St Benedict is commemmorated as the founder of Western monaticism; the Greek brothers St Cyril (c. 827–869) and St Methodius (c. 825–884) evangelized the Slavs.

ECUMENICISM

One characteristic of Christianity today is the increased understanding and co-operation both between Christians in different parts of the world and between Christians of different traditions and backgrounds. The word *ecumenical* is used to describe such spirit and action. Though sometimes used in a narrower sense to refer to the movement associated with the World Council of Churches, the word simply means 'world-wide' (from the Greek *oikumene*, 'inhabited world').

The World Council of Churches
The World Council of Churches (founded in 1948) has its headquarters in Geneva, Switzerland. The Council – whose membership includes most of the main Christian Churches, except the Roman Catholic – promotes ecumenical Christian action and study. There are similar organizations in many countries, for example Churches Together in England.

THE ORTHODOX CHURCHES

Most of the Churches called Orthodox derived from the ancient Greek Christianity of the Eastern Mediterranean. The direct link with Churches founded by apostles and the memory of a Christian Roman Empire (the Byzantine Empire) that lasted until 1453 heighten the importance of tradition as a guide of the Church. Tradition includes the scriptures, the first seven Church councils and the writings of the Church fathers (the early medieval writers on Christian doctrine), the liturgy and the veneration of holy pictures (icons).

The Orthodox Church maintains that it is the 'one true Church of Christ which is not and has not been divided' and it regards the Roman Catholic Church as schismatic. The Ecumenical Patriarch of Constantinople (Istanbul) is the senior figure, but each autonomous Church has its own patriarch and is self-governing.

PRINCIPAL ORTHODOX CHURCHES

Russian Orthodox Church over 40 000 000 members
Ethiopian Orthodox Church 22 000 000 members
Romanian Orthodox Church 18 900 000 members
Greek Orthodox Church (in Greece) 9 700 000 members
Serbian Orthodox Church 9 000 000 members
Bulgarian Orthodox Church 7 200 000 members
Ukrainian Autocephalous Orthodox Church (seceded from the Russian Orthodox Church) over 5 000 000 members
Georgian Orthodox Church 5 000 000 members
Greek Orthodox Archdiocese of North and South America 5 000 000 members
Armenian Apostolic Church 4 000 000 members
Macedonian Orthodox Church 1 000 000 members

Polish Autocephalous Orthodox Church 1 000 000 members

PROTESTANTISM

In 16th-century Europe, movements to reform the Church accompanied fresh interpretations of the Bible and the use of everyday language in place of Latin. These movements rejected Roman authority and established reformed national forms of Christianity in the various states of northern Europe, such as Lutheranism in Sweden and parts of Germany, Calvinism in Switzerland and Scotland, and Anglicanism in England. This process is known as the *Reformation*.

The majority Protestant movement aimed to reform the Church within each state while keeping the idea that the Church embraced the whole community. The Radical (or Anabaptist) movement insisted that the Church consisted only of those who made a commitment to Christ, and broke the link with the state. A minority in Europe, this movement produced the dominant Christian forms in North America.

The 18th century saw movements for spiritual reform in Protestant countries – Pietism in Germany and the Evangelical Revival in Britain, North America and elsewhere. These brought the majority and radical streams closer together. European emigration brought all the Protestant traditions to America, Canada and Australia. In the USA they took new life and new shapes in a huge community – largely Christian, but multi-ethnic and with no national Church. Some completely new forms of Christianity also arose, such as Pentacostalism. Today the American scene is characterized by a large number of denominations.

New expressions of Christianity are appearing in the southern continents as Christians there meet situations not encountered in the West. There are some signs that a tradition of Christianity is developing that may be as distinctly African as Catholicism or Protestantism have been Western, in that African Independent Churches reflect African ways of worship and address issues of African life. In India, united Churches of South India and North India have developed, and these replace the denominational Churches of Western origin.

THE ANGLICAN COMMUNION

THE CHURCH OF ENGLAND

Henry VIII renounced the supremacy of the pope in 1534, founding the Church of England with the monarch as its head. Protestant reforms were instituted during the reign of Edward VI (1547–53). After the reign of the Catholic Mary I, the independent Church of England was re-established in 1558. The Church of England retains the episcopal form of government and has preserved many of the Catholic traditions of liturgy. However, it holds most of the basic tenets of the reformed faith of Protestantism. Its doctrine is based upon the Thirty-Nine Articles; its liturgy is based upon *The Book of Common Prayer* (1549 and 1662) and its successors. The 18th-century Evangelical Movement emphasized the Protestant tradition, while the 19th-century Oxford Movement emphasized the Catholic tradition. These two movements continue in the Church of England as the Low Church and the High Church.

The Church in England is divided into two provinces – Canterbury and York – each headed by an archbishop. The archbishop of Canterbury is recognized as first among equals by the leaders of the provinces of the Anglican Communion. (The dioceses of the Anglican Communion in Britain are detailed in the UK chapter.) Each of the Churches of the Anglican Communion is self-governing. Some Churches, including the Church of the Province of Aotearoa, New Zealand and Polynesia, the Anglican Church of Australia, and the Episcopal Church in the USA, ordain women priests and elect women bishops. The Church of Ireland also has women priests, and the Church of England has voted to have women priests.

PRINCIPAL ANGLICAN CHURCHES

Church of England 26 000 000 members (1 590 000 practising)

Church of the Province of Nigeria 10 000 000 members

Church of the Province of Uganda 4 000 000 members

Anglican Church of Australia 3 700 000 members

Episcopal Church in the USA 2 400 000 members

Church of the Province of Southern Africa 2 000 000 members

Church of the Province of Kenya 1 000 000 members

Church of the Province of Aotearoa, New Zealand and Polynesia 900 000 members

Anglican Church of Canada 850 000 members

Other provinces include the Anglican Church of Papua New Guinea, the Anglican Church of the Southern Cone of America, the Church in Wales, the Church of Ireland, the Church of the Province of Burundi, the Church of the Province of Central Africa, the Church of the Province of the Indian Ocean, the Church of the Province of Kenya, the Church of the Province of Melanesia, the Church of the Province of Myanmar, the Church of the Province of Rwanda, the Church of the Province of the Sudan, the Church of the Province of Tanzania, the Church of the Province of West Africa, the Church of the Province of the West Indies, the Church of the Province of Zaïre, the Episcopal Church in Jerusalem and the Middle East, the Episcopal Anglican Church of Brazil, the Holy Catholic Church in Japan, the Philippine Episcopal Church and the Scottish Episcopal Church.

BAPTISTS

Baptist Churches, which take their name from the practice of baptism by immersion of adult believers, developed within the English and American Puritan movements in the 17th century. Individual Baptist churches are self-governing. There are more than 35 000 000 Baptists, the majority of whom live in the USA.

PRINCIPAL BAPTIST CHURCHES

Southern Baptist Convention (USA) 15 000 000 members

National Baptist Convention (USA) 6 300 000 members

American Baptist Churches in the USA 1 500 000 members

Nigerian Baptist Convention 500 000 members

Society of Evangelical Christians – Baptists (Russia) 500 000

Myanmar Baptist Convention 450 000 members

Samavesam of Telegu Baptist Church (India) 425 000 (members from 717 independent Baptist churches).

Conservative Baptist Association of America 250 000 members

General Association of Regular Baptist Churches
(USA) 158 000 members
American Baptist Association 250 000 members
Baptist Union of Great Britain 160 000 members
Canadian Baptist Federation 132 000 members

CONGREGATIONALISTS

The liberal Protestant Congregationalist churches
developed from the Independents in England in the
16th and 17th centuries. Each congregation is
independent in the organization of its own affairs. In
England, Australia, Canada, India and the USA the
majority of Congregationalist churches have joined
United Churches (see below).

CHRISTIAN SCIENTISTS

The Church of Christ, Scientist, is a liberal Protestant denomination founded in the USA by Mary
Baker Eddy in 1879. Christian Scientists – who deny
the deity but not the divinity of Jesus – emphasize the
practice of spiritual healing. Christian Scientists
claim their own sources of knowledge supplementary
to the Scriptures.

DISCIPLES OF CHRIST

The Disciples of Christ were founded during a period
of religious revival on the American frontier in the
first half of the 19th century. They attempted to unite
the divisions of Protestantism through a return to
New Testament practice.

PRINCIPAL CHURCH OF THE DISCIPLES

Christian Church (Disciples of Christ; USA)
1 100 000 disciples

INDEPENDENT AFRICAN CHURCHES

Dissatisfaction with Western forms of worship has
encouraged the emergence of a number of African
Churches. The Kimbanguist Church of Zaïre began
in the 1920s when followers were attracted by the
preaching and miraculous healings of Simon Kimbangui, a Baptist catechist. Various Zion Churches
in South Africa emphasize adult baptism by immersion, divine healing and preparation for a Second
Coming. Aladura ('Owners of Prayer') Churches in
West Africa emphasize prophets and divine healing.
The incorporation of traditional African beliefs and
values is a feature of a number of Churches.

PRINCIPAL AFRICAN CHURCHES

Church of Jesus Christ on Earth through the
Prophet Simon Kimbangui (Zaïre) 5 000 000
members
Zion Christian Church (South Africa) 4 000 000
members
Church of the Lord – Aladura (Nigeria) 1 100 000
members
African Israel Nineveh Church (Kenya) 350 000
members

LUTHERANS

The beliefs of the Lutheran Churches are derived
from the teaching of the German Martin Luther

(1483–1546) and were formulated in the Augsburg
Confession of 1530. Luther taught that redemption
could only be achieved through faith in Christ
(justification by faith), and that Scripture is the sole
rule of faith. Over 55 000 000 people belong to
Lutheran Churches, whose greatest influence is in
Germany and in Scandinavia.

PRINCIPAL LUTHERAN CHURCHES

United Churches (Germany) 13 500 000 members
United Lutheran Protestant Church of Germany
9 400 000 members
Evangelical Lutheran Church in America 5 300 000
members
Evangelical Lutheran Church of Denmark 4 700 000
members
Evangelical Lutheran Church of Finland 4 400 000
members
Lutheran Church – Missouri Synod (USA) 2 600 000
members
United Evangelical Lutheran Churches in India
1 500 000 members
Evangelical Lutheran Church in Southern Africa
620 000 members
Evangelical Church in Hungary 430 000 members
Evangelical Church of the Lutheran Confession in
Brazil 200 000 members

METHODISM

Methodism developed out of the religious revival
within the Church of England led by John Wesley
(1703–91) and his brother Charles (1707–88). The
differences between the early Methodists and contemporary Anglicans were largely of emphasis
rather than doctrine. All Methodist Churches have a
strong central authority, and those of the American
tradition are episcopal. Over 55 000 000 people
belong to Methodist Churches, whose greatest influence is in the USA and Africa.

PRINCIPAL METHODIST CHURCHES

United Methodist Church (USA) 9 000 000 members
African Methodist Episcopal Church (USA)
2 200 000 members
African Methodist Episcopal Zion Church (USA)
1 200 000 members
Korean Methodist Church 1 050 000 members
Methodist Church of Southern Africa 490 000
members
Methodist Church Nigeria 480 000 members
Methodist Church in India 470 000 members
Methodist Church (UK) 430 000 members

OLD CATHOLICS

The Old Catholics comprise congregations that have
separated from the Roman Catholic Church since the
18th century. The Dutch Church of Utrecht was
formed in 1724 in support of Jansenism, a movement
based on the teachings of Cornelius Jansen, who
held that the efficacy of the sacraments depended
upon the state of grace of the recipient. Various
Central European Old Catholic congregations
seceded because of their opposition to the doctrine of
papal infallability. There are 16 000 Old Catholics in
Switzerland, and 28 000 in Germany.

PENTECOSTALISTS

Pentecostalism grew out of the charismatic movement in a number of Protestant Churches in the USA in the last 150 years. Pentecostalists emphasize 'baptism by the Holy Spirit', a post-conversion religious experience, which may be accompanied by divine healing and 'speaking in tongues'. The Pentecostalists' largest Church is the United Pentecostal Church International (USA and Canada), which has 500 000 adherents.

PLYMOUTH BRETHREN

The Plymouth Brethren were founded in 1831 by J.N. Darby in Plymouth (England). They have no clergy and no formal creed, and emphasize biblical prophecy and an imminent Second Coming.

REFORMED CHRISTIANS AND PRESBYTERIANS

The Reformed Churches are Calvinistic rather than Lutheran in doctrine. They trace their origins to the teaching of the French Protestant John Calvin (1509–64), a leader of the Reformation in France and Switzerland. While believing that faith is dependent upon Scripture alone, Calvinists insist that, as man lacks free will, only the elect are predestined to be saved. The Reformed Churches include the Presbyterians, whose name is derived from their form of government by lay leaders – known as presbyters or elders – and by pastors.

THE CHURCH OF SCOTLAND

The established Church of Scotland is Presbyterian in constitution. It is presided over by a Moderator who is chosen annually by the elected General Assembly, at which the British sovereign (as head of the Church) is represented by a Lord High Commissioner. Scotland is divided into 12 synods for administrative purposes.

PRINCIPAL REFORMED AND PRESBYTERIAN CHURCHES

Presbyterian Church (USA) 2 900 000 members
Federation of Swiss Protestant Churches (comprising 18 reformed churches) 2 900 000 members
Netherlands Reformed Church 2 700 000 members
Protestant Church in Indonesia 2 300 000 members
Reformed Church in Hungary 2 000 000 members
Church of Jesus Christ (Madagascar) 2 000 000 members
Presbyterian Church of Korea 1 540 000 members
Dutch Reformed Church (South Africa) 1 470 000 members
United Church of Zambia 1 000 000 members
Church of Scotland 840 000 members
Reformed Churches in the Netherlands 760 000 members
Reformed (Calvinist) Church (Romania – 700 000 members

SEVENTH-DAY ADVENTISTS

Adventist Churches emphasize the imminence of the Second Coming. The Seventh-day Adventist Church was established in the 19th century in the USA, where there are 702 000 members (41 000 in Canada).

SOCIETY OF FRIENDS (QUAKERS)

The Society of Friends was founded in the 17th

century by the English Puritan George Fox. Quakerism emphasizes the immediate application of Christ's teaching to everyday life, while rejecting the need for formalized services, creeds or clergy. Worship is spontaneous. Friends' meetings wait in silence for the 'inward light'. Quakers are pacifists. In the UK there are 18 000 members.

UNITARIANS

Unitarians deny the doctrine of the Trinity. The belief that God is one person was held by some in the early Church (Arianism), but modern Unitarianism dates in Europe from the 16th century, and in the English-speaking world from 1774, when Theophilus Lindsey founded a Unitarian chapel in London.

UNITED CHURCHES

The ecumenical movement among Christian Churches has resulted in the union of a number of Protestant Churches. The pressure for unity has been particularly strong in countries without a Christian tradition where the historic differences between denominations appear meaningless.

PRINCIPAL UNITED CHURCHES

Church of South India 2 200 000 members
(formed 1947 with the union of Anglican, Congregational, Methodist, Presbyterian and Reformed Churches)
United Church of Christ (USA) 1 700 000 members
(formed 1957 from the union of Congregational, Evangelical and Reformed Churches)
Uniting Church in Australia 1 100 000 members
(formed 1977 with the union of Congregational, Methodist and Presbyterian Churches)
Church of North India 1 000 000 members
(formed 1970 with the union of Anglican, Baptist, Congregational, Methodist and Presbyterian Churches)
United Church of Canada 860 000 members
(formed 1925 with the union of Congregational, Methodist and Presbyterian Churches. The Evangelical United Bretheren of Canada joined in 1968)

OTHER CHURCHES

Other denominations include:

Mennonites
A Protestant sect that originated in Friesland, the Netherlands, in the 16th century. They are opposed to child baptism, military service and the taking of oaths. The majority of Mennonites are in North and South America. There are over 300 000 members of a number of Mennonite and allied Churches in the USA including the Amish, a radical pacificist sect that originated in Switzerland in the 16th century. The Amish – who are now most settled in closed communities in Pennsylvania – deny themselves all modern forms of technology.

Moravians
The Moravian Churches originated in 1722 in Saxony (Germany) among migrants from Moravia (in what is now the Czech Republic), who were followers of the Czech reformer Jan Hus (c. 1372–1415). Moravian Christianity follows the literal teaching of the Bible, which they believe is the only source of faith. Moravians are now strongest in the Czech Republic and in the USA (where there are over 60 000 members in three Churches).

TAIZE COMMUNITY

Taizé is an ecumenical community founded in 1940 at the small village of Taizé (in Burgundy, France) by a Swiss, Brother Roger (1915–). The community comprises about 100 brothers from many different Christian denominations (both Catholic and Protestant) and from over 20 countries. It is not a denomination itself but a Christian monastic community that cuts across the divisions of denomination. The community invites the young people of the world to come to Taizé to live with them for a short period. The community is famous for its distinctive chants, now used in many Christian denominations.

MARGINAL GROUPS

Various movements related to Christianity stand apart from the forms mentioned above by not giving ultimate significance to Christ. Western examples include some forms of Unitarianism (which deny Christ's divinity); the Watchtower Movement or Jehovah's Witnesses (who also deny Christ's divinity) and Mormonism (which claims its own supplementary literature to the Scriptures.)

JEHOVAH'S WITNESSES

The Jehovah's Witnesses – or the Watchtower Movement as they are officially known – grew out of the International Bible Studies Association, founded in Pittsburgh, Pennsylvania (USA) by Charles Taze Russell (1872). This movement is known for its literal interpretation of the Bible and its concern with Armageddon, the imminent final battle in which Witnesses will be saved. Although Witnesses deny Christ's divinity, they recognize Jesus as God's agent. They believe that the Theocracy (God's Kingdom) will be established on Earth after Armageddon and the Second Coming. The Witnesses have faced persecution in a number of countries because they refuse to acknowledge many of the claims made on the individual by secular governments. They are renowned for not accepting blood transfusions.

MORMONS

The Mormons – or the Church of Jesus Christ of Latter-Day Saints as they are officially known – are active missionaries. They were founded in the USA in 1830 by Joseph Smith. Smith claimed to have received from an angel the Book of Mormon, which is accepted by the Latter-Day Saints as an addition to Scripture. Mormons hold the belief that God evolved from man and that man himself has the potential to attain deity. Mormonism denies the Trinity in favour of a polytheistic belief in three independent persons. It teaches that after death there is a full resurrection of the body and a reuniting of families. Dead relatives can be baptized or married in the faith to ensure their salvation.

The Mormons were led to their current centre in Salt Lake City, Utah, by Brigham Young. There are over 6 000 000 Mormons, the majority (4.2 million) in North America.

UNIFICATION CHURCH

Sometimes known as 'the Moonies', the Unification Church was founded in the 1950s by a Korean, Sun Myung Moon. It is thought to have over 2 000 000 members, the majority in South Korea and Japan. The Church teaches the 'Divine Principle' which holds that, following humanity's fall from grace, a restoration to perfection can be achieved through the first messiah, Jesus, and the second, the Reverend Moon. Love of creation and family life are of central importance to members.

THE BIBLE

THE HEBREW BIBLE

The 24 books of the Hebrew Bible are grouped into three divisions – *Torah* (The Law), *Nevi'im* (Prophets) and *Ketuvim* (Writings).

The Torah. The Torah was traditionally ascribed to Moses and is known to Christians as the Pentateuch. It has five books – Genesis, Exodus, Leviticus, Numbers and Deuteronomy.

The Nevi'im. The Nevi'im has eight books – Joshua, Judges, Samuel, Kings, Isaiah, Jeremiah, Ezekiel, and the Book of the Twelve (the Minor Prophets).

The Ketuvim. The Ketuvim comprises religious poetry and 'wisdom literature'. It has 11 books – Psalms, Proverbs, Job, the Song of Songs, Ruth, Lamentations, Ecclesiastes, Esther, Daniel, Ezra and Nehemiah, and Chronicles.

THE OLD TESTAMENT

The Christian Church received the Old Testament from Greek-speaking Jews. This version contained additional books, and parts of books, not found in Hebrew. These writings, which later became known as the *Apocrypha*, are regarded as part of Holy Scripture by the Roman Catholic Church, but at the Reformation they were denied this status by Protestants. The Authorized Version of 1611 included these books between the Old and New Testaments.

The Old Testament reorders and divides some of the books of the Hebrew Bible. Samuel, Kings and Chronicles are each divided into two, while Ezra and Nehemiah and each of the 12 Minor Prophets are counted as separate books. The English Authorized Version has 39 Old Testament books, and the Roman Catholic Vulgate (including books regarded by Protestant Churches as Apocryphal) has 46.

BOOKS OF THE OLD TESTAMENT

The 1611 Authorized Version	*The Roman Catholic Vulgate*
Genesis	Genesis
Exodus	Exodus
Leviticus	Leviticus
Numbers	Numbers
Deuteronomy	Deuteronomy
Joshua	Josue
Judges	Judges
Ruth	Ruth
First Book of Samuel	First Book of Kings
Second Book of Samuel	Second Book of Kings
First Book of Kings	Third Book of Kings
Second Book of Kings	Fourth Book of Kings
First Book of Chronicles	First Book of Paralipomenon
Second Book of Chronicles	Second Book of Paralipomenon
Ezra	First Book of Esdras
Nehemiah	Second Book of Esdras

Esther
Job
Psalms
Proverbs
Ecclesiastes
Song of Solomon

Isaiah
Jeremiah
Lamentations

Ezekiel
Daniel
Hosea
Joel
Amos
Obadiah
Jonah
Micah
Nahum
Habakkuk
Zephaniah
Haggai
Zechariah
Malachi

Tobias
Judith
Esther
Job
Psalms
Proverbs
Ecclesiastes
Canticle of
  Canticles
Wisdom of
  Solomon
Sirach
Isaias
Jeremias
Lamentations
Baruch
Ezechiel
Daniel
Osea
Joel
Amos
Abdias
Jonas
Micheas
Nahum
Habacuc
Sophonias
Aggeus
Zacharias
Malachias
First Book of
  Machabees
Second Book of
  Machabees

THE NEW TESTAMENT

Like the Old Testament the New Testament is part of the sacred literature of Christianity. It is called the 'New Testament' because it is believed that its writings represent a new covenant of God with his people, based principally on the person and work of Jesus Christ. The 27 books of the New Testament were written between AD 50 and 100. Covering the period from the birth of Christ to the spread of Christianity through the Roman Empire, these books are grouped into four divisions – the Gospels, the Acts of the Apostles, the Epistles and the Apocalypse.

The Gospels
The Gospels are the four books that describe the life and works of Jesus Christ. They are traditionally attributed to Matthew, Mark, Luke and John the Divine.

The Acts of the Apostles
The Acts of the Apostles is a single book, traditionally ascribed to Luke. It describes the spread of Christianity from Jerusalem to Rome.

The Epistles
The Epistles are 21 books written as letters to early churches and Christian individuals. They are the Letters of Paul to the Romans, Corinthians (1 and 2), Galatians, Ephesians, Philippians, Colossians, Thessalonians (1 and 2), Timothy (1 and 2), Titus and Philemon, the anonymous Letter to the Hebrews, the Letter of James, the two Letters of Peter, the three Letters of John, and the Letter of Jude. The letters teach the meaning and implications of the faith.

The Apocalypse
The Apocalypse is also known as the Book of Revelation. It contains a prophetic description of the end of the world and the return of Christ.

OLDEST TEXTS

The earliest surviving Biblical texts are from two silver amulets found under the Scottish Church, Jerusalem, in 1979 bearing Numbers Ch. 6 v. 22–27 and dated to c. 587 BC. In 1945 various papyrus texts were discovered at Nag Hammodi, Egypt, including gnostic gospels or secret books (apocryphal) ascribed to Thomas, James, John, Peter and Paul. They were buried c. AD 350 but the originals are thought to have been written c. AD 120–150.

ISLAM

Islam is the world's second largest religion. The Arabic term *islam* means 'the act of resignation' to God. It is derived from the root letters *slm*, from which come the noun *salam* (which means 'peace') and the verb *aslama* (which means 'he submitted'). Islam emphasizes an uncompromising monotheism and a strict adherence to religious practices. Muslims believe that Islam is the religion that brings peace to mankind when man commits himself to God and submits himself to His will, and that God's will was made known through the Qur'an (Koran), the book revealed to his messenger, the Prophet Muhammad (570–632).

Muhammad was a member of the Quraysh tribe, which guarded the sacred shrine known as the Kaaba in the Arab trading city of Mecca (Makka). In 610 Muhammad received his first revelations, which commissioned him to preach against the idolatry and polytheism of the Arab tribes. In 622, he led his followers to Medina (al-Madina), where political power was added to his spiritual authority. Before Muhammad died in 632, the whole of Arabia had embraced Islam or entered into a peace treaty with the Prophet.

Muslims believe that – over a period of 20 years – Muhammad received revelations from God (Allah) via the Archangel Gabriel. These revelations form the Qur'an (literally 'The Recitation'), Islam's scripture. Muhammad also accepted the inspiration of the Jewish and Christian scriptures. The collections of Muhammad's sayings and doings – the *Hadith* – are next in importance, for the Prophet is regarded as the best model of obedience to God's will. Muslims teach that Islam was the religion of Adam and the main prophet sent by God to call man back to his path. Muslims revere Abraham, Moses and Jesus amongst other prophets, but Muhammad is the final prophet, because the Qur'an completed and superseded earlier revelations.

THE PILLARS OF FAITH

Certain essential religious duties, described as the 'Five Pillars', are intended to develop the spirit of submission to God. They are:

Profession of the faith The basic belief of Islam is expressed in the *Shahada*, the Muslim confession of faith: 'There is no God but Allah and Muhammad is his Prophet!' From this fundamental belief are derived beliefs in angels (particularly Gabriel), the revealed Books (of the Jewish and Christian faiths in addition to the Qur'an), a series of prophets, and the Last Day, the Day of Judgement.

Prayer The act of worship is performed five times a day – at dawn, midday, mid-afternoon, sunset and before bed. After washing themselves, Muslims face in the direction of Mecca and pray communally at the mosque or individually in any place that is ritually clean, often using a prayer rug. Each prayer consists of a set number of 'bowings', for example two at dawn, four at midday. The 'bowing' is composed of a prescribed succession of movements, in which the worshipper stands, bows, kneels with forehead to the ground, and sits back on the haunches. Recitations in Arabic, mostly words of praise and verses from the Qur'an, accompany each movement. Attendance at the mosque is not compulsory, but men are required to go to the special congregational prayers held every Friday at noon. (The mosque also has an educational role and teaching ranges from advanced theology to religious instruction for children.)

Alsmgiving An offering, known as *zakat*, is given by Muslims with sufficient means as an annual charitable donation.

Fasting Muslims fast from shortly before sunrise until sunset every day during the Islamic month of Ramadan, the month in which they believe the Qur'an was first revealed. The person fasting may not eat, drink or smoke. However, the sick, the elderly and children are exempt from fasting.

Pilgrimage Pilgrimage to Mecca (the *hajj*) is to be undertaken at least once in a lifetime by every Muslim who can afford it. The pilgrimage takes place during the Islamic month of Dhu'l-Hijja. See Holy Places of Islam, below.

Jihad Jihad is sometimes regarded as another pillar of the faith. It means 'striving' and is commonly used to describe the duty of waging 'holy wars' to spread Islam and to defend Islamic lands.

SECTS OF ISLAM

Sunnism and Shiism (or Shiah Islam) are the two main forms of Islam. Although the majority of Muslims are Sunnis, the Shiites are dominant in Iran, which is about 93 per cent Shiite. The main difference between Sunni and Shiah Islam lies in the latter's belief that the charisma of the Prophet was inherited by his descendants, in whom they invest supreme spiritual and political authority. The Sunnis believe that orthodoxy is determined by the consensus of the community. Sunni caliphs exercised political but not spiritual authority – the historic caliphate ceased to exist in 1924 in Turkey.

Shiism has produced a variety of sects, including the Ismailis and Zaidis, though the majority are known as 'Twelvers' (*Ithna 'Ashariyya*). They believe that the 12th Imam or successor to Muhammad in linear descent disappeared and is now the Hidden Imam, who will return as the Mahdi before the end of the world. Senior religious lawyers, known as *mujtahids*, interpret the Hidden Imam and share his infallibility. The Ayatollah (literally 'sign of God') Khomeini was regarded, in Iran, as such a mujtahid. Other Shiites revere living Imams, such as the Aga Khan Khojas, whose leader (the Aga Khan) claims to be a descendant of Muhammad through Ismail, the 7th Imam.

Islam's mystical or Sufi tradition has both Sunni and Shiite adherents. Many of its orders or circles have appointed or hereditary *pirs* (spiritual guides) and venerate their predecessors as saints. Sufi missionaries played an important role in Islam's expansion into Africa and Asia.

Though the sheer variety of races and cultures embraced by Islam has produced differences, all segments of Muslim society are bound by a common faith and a sense of belonging to a single community. With the loss of political power during the period of Western colonialism in the 19th and early 20th centuries, the concept of the Islamic community,

instead of weakening, became stronger. This, in harness with the discovery of immense oil reserves, helped various Muslim peoples in their struggle to gain political freedom and sovereignty in the mid-20th century.

Islam as a total way of life is a missionary religion committed to bringing all men into the Household of Faith (*Dar-al-Islam*). However, it affords special status to followers of its sister faiths, Judaism and Christianity, which have existed as protected minority communities in many Muslim lands.

HOLY PLACES OF ISLAM

Mecca
Mecca is the most holy city of Islam and was the birthplace of the Prophet Muhammad. Every Muslim with sufficient means attempts a pilgrimage (or *hajj*) to Mecca at least once. The main goal of pilgrims is the al-Haram Mosque. In the mosque's central courtyard is the Kaaba, a cube-shaped building that is believed to have been built by Abraham at the place on earth immediately below God's house in heaven. The city is forbidden to non-Muslims.

Medina
In Arabic the city's name is al-Madina or, more fully, Madinat Rasul Allah (meaning City of the Messenger of God). Medina contains many Islamic holy places, including the Prophet's Mosque (within which is the tomb of Muhammad), the Mosque of Quba (the first in Islam), and a number of sites connected with the Prophet's participation in the Battle of Uhud and the Battle of the Ditch. The city is forbidden to non-Muslims.

Jerusalem
Jerusalem is the third most holy city of Islam. In the area of Solomon's Temple is the Dome of the Rock, a golden-domed mosque containing the rock on which it is believed Abraham prepared to sacrifice his son and from which the Prophet Muhammad made his ascent into heaven.

Shiite holy places
While Mecca, Medina and Jerusalem are places of pilgrimage for all Muslims, Shiite Muslims have their own additional holy places.

Najaf (in Iraq) contains the tomb of Ali ibn Abi Talib, the founder of Shiah Islam and cousin and son-in-law to the Prophet Muhammad.

Karbala (in Iraq) is the site of the death in battle of Ali's son Husayn.

Meshhed (in Iran) is the burial place of the eighth Shiite Imam.

MAJOR POPULATIONS OF MUSLIMS

Country	Form of Islam	Muslim pop.
Indonesia	Sunni	143 500 000
Pakistan	Sunni	116 300 000
	Shia	6 300 000
India	Sunni	92 900 000
Bangladesh	Sunni	91 800 000
Iran	Shia	55 900 000
Turkey	Sunni	38 100 000
	Shia	17 500 000
Egypt	Sunni	49 100 000
Nigeria	Sunni	42 500 000

HINDUISM

The word Hindu was first used by Arab invaders in the 8th century AD to describe those who lived beyond the Sind or Indus Valley. The term Hinduism is now used to describe the religion and social institutions of the great majority of the people of India, though strictly speaking it is an English word.

The origins of Hinduism (or *Sanatan-Dharma*, meaning 'ancient way of life') lie in the *Arya-Dharma* (Aryan way of life) of the Indo-Europeans who invaded the Indus Valley from Asia Minor and Iran c. 1500 BC. They wrote the *Vedas* (Rig-Veda, Yajur-Veda, Sama-Veda, Atharva-Veda), which are collections of prayers, hymns and formulas for worship. The Aryans worshipped nature-deities, including *Agni* (fire) and *Surya* (Sun).

The Aryans absorbed some of the traditions of the indigenous inhabitants. This process of assimilation resulted in the great epic poems composed between 200 BC and AD 200, the *Ramayana* and the *Mahabharata*, which includes the famous *Bhagavadagita*.

Three deities dominate these epics: Brahma, Vishnu and Shiva, representing creation, preservation and destruction. There are other gods and demi-gods, and also important *avatars* (incarnations), such as Krishna (a form of Vishnu; see below). Some gods (such as the goddess of smallpox) are renowned for particular activities; others are local deities operating only in a particular area.

Philosophical Hinduism developed in the 5th century BC with a core of 18 *Upanishads* (philosophical scriptures). The laws of Manu (written during the first two centuries AD) contain the concept that God created distinct orders of men; priests (*Brahmans*); soldiers and rulers (*Kshatriyas*); farmers and traders (*Vaisyas*); and artisans and labourers (*Sudras*). The so-called caste system thus developed.

Hinduism tolerates a great variety of beliefs and practices and there is absolute freedom with regard to the choice and mode of one's philosophy. The Brahmans recognize six schools as orthodox. The best known are yoga, sankhya and vedanta, of which the great philosopher Shankara (Sankara; AD 788–820) was an exponent. The Brahmans regard Buddhism and Jainism as heterodox.

The aim of most Hindus is to be reunited with the absolute and thereby to escape the wheel of existence (*Samsara*), which is determined by *Karma* (literally 'deeds' or 'actions'). *Moksa* (release) may be gained through yoga, through *Jnana* (knowledge) or through *Bhakti* (devotion to one's God).

Hinduism traditionally divides life into four ideal periods: *Brahmacharya* (celibate period), *Grihastha* (householder), *Vanaprastha* (retired stage), and *Sannyasa* (renunciation). Hinduism embraces many local as well as national traditions and has numerous pilgrim centres, temples, ashrams (religious retreats) and orders of monks.

A Hindu temple (*mandir*) may be a huge, ornate building dedicated to the worship of a major deity – visited particularly during festivals and pilgrimages – or it may be a small shrine at the roadside at which offerings to a local spirit are made. The concept of the spiritual teacher, or guru, is important, and many contemporary gurus attract European as well as Indian devotees.

HINDU GODS AND GODDESSES

Gods of the Vedas
Indra Thunder god, god of battle.
Varuna Guardian of order; divine overseer.
Agni God of fire.
Surya God associated with the sun.

Major gods of Hinduism
Brahma The creator; linked with the goddess Saraswati.
Vishnu The preserver; with Shiva, one of Hinduism's greatest gods. Vishnu has ten incarnations or avatars, and is married to Lakshmi.
Shiva A great god, associated with destruction. In Hindu mythology, Shiva is married to Parvati and is the father of Ganesh.
Ganesh The elephant-headed god, worshipped as the remover of obstacles and god of good luck.
Hanuman The monkey warrior-god associated with the god Rana.

Vishnu's ten avatars (incarnations)
Matsya The fish.
Kurma The tortoise.
Varaha The boar.
Narasimha The man-lion.
Vamana The dwarf.
Ramachandra or *Rama* The god of the *Ramayana* epic, identified by his bow and quiver of arrows.
Parasurama Rama bearing an axe.
Krishna The important god featured in the *Bhagavadgita*. He is worshipped particularly as a baby and as a flute-playing cowherd.
The Buddha The great teacher from the 6th–5th centuries BC and founder of Buddhism.
Kalki 'The one to come'; a future *avatar*.

Major goddesess of Hinduism
The goddesses are manifestations of the great creative spirit or *Shakti*. The most popular are:
Parvati Wife of Shiva; also known as *Uma*.
Durga All-powerful warrior goddess, also known as *Amba*, and linked with Shiva.
Kali Goddess associated with destruction.
Lakshmi Goddess of beauty, wealth and good fortune; wife of Vishnu.
Sarawati Goddess of learning, arts and music; wife of Brahma.

HARE KRISHNA

The International Society for Krishna Consciousness was started in 1966 in the USA by a *sannyasi* or monk from India, Bhaktivedanta Swami, known to his Western and Indian followers as 'Prabhupada'. It is a neo-Hindu movement based on a philosophy from northern India that focuses on love of the God *Krishna*. Service to God and humanity takes the form of temple worship, chanting and singing God's name, active missionary work through the sale of the movement's publications and distribution of food.

BUDDHISM

Buddhism is based on the teaching of Siddhartha Gautama (c. 563–483 BC) of the Gautama clan of the Sakyas in India. He was later named the Buddha, meaning 'the enlightened one'.

After an early life of pleasure, Gautama became deeply dissatisfied, and he experimented with asceticism and yoga before experiencing *bodhi* or awakening during a long period of meditation under a tree in Gaya. For the rest of his long life, Gautama taught about the impermanence and suffering of human life and the way to escape such suffering.

The Buddha is said to have taught the four noble truths. These are:
(1) All forms of existence are subject to suffering (*dukkha*);
(2) The origin of suffering is craving;
(3) The cure for suffering is the cessation of craving;
(4) There is a 'Way' to end suffering. The 'Way' differs with the type of Buddhism. Zen Buddhists rely upon meditation, while Therevada Buddhists believe that craving ceases by means of the Eight-fold Path of right view, right thought, right speech, right action, right livelihood, right effort, right mindfulness and right concentration. This is represented in the Wheel of Law (*dharma chakra*), which has eight spokes for the eight steps towards enlightenment (*nirvana*).

The Buddha taught that since impermanence (*anicca*) is an unalterable fact of life, we can be truly happy only by becoming detached from the delusive notions of 'me' and 'mine'. This detachment is called the not-self (*anatta*). His teaching made no provision for God or the soul. He taught the law (*dharma*) of cause and effect, and encouraged his disciples to take refuge in the *sangha*, the monastic way of celibacy, non-violence, poverty and vegetarianism.

SCHOOLS OF BUDDHISM

Buddhism, as it developed, separated into three broad schools.

Therevada Buddhism. Therevada Buddhism ('the school of the elders') is practised in Sri Lanka, Burma (Myanmar) and Thailand. It is said to have been the original Buddhism of India. This school remains non-theistic and emphasizes the importance of the celibate life to gain *nirvana*. In 1956, Dr Bhimrao Ramji Ambedkar (1891–1956), the leader of India's untouchables, converted to Buddhism, and approximately four million of his disciples followed his example.

Mahayana Buddhism. Mahayana Buddhism (which refers to itself as the 'Greater Vehicle') is practised in Vietnam, Cambodia, Laos, China and Japan. It has several sub-divisions, including Zen and Pure Land Buddhism. In Mahayana, the concept of the *Bodhisattva* (literally 'one bound for enlightenment who delays entry into nirvana in order to help others') developed to include many such heavenly beings alongside, but subordinate to, the Buddha, who was regarded as having three bodies (*kaya*), the historical body, the bliss body, and the absolute body.

Vajrayana or Tantric Buddhism. Vajrayana (the 'Diamond Vehicle') developed in Tibet. This makes much use of *mantras* (sacred chants) and also of images, which depict the Bodhisattvas as very active in the world, opposing evil. The male quality of compassion is often united with the female quality of wisdom.

In the West, Buddhism in all forms has attracted a significant following. The Friends of the Western Buddhist Order was formed in 1969 and seeks to find forms of expression amenable to the West, which some call *Navayana* (a 'New Vehicle').

CONFUCIANISM

Confucianism is an approach to life and way of thinking based on the teachings of Kongfuzi (Confucius; 551–479 BC). Kongfuzi was not the sole founder of Confucianism, but was rather a member of the founding group of *Ju* or meek ones. He was a scholar-official, a keeper of accounts from the province of Lu in China.

Kongfuzi taught that the main ethic is *jen* (ben-evolence), and that truth involves the knowledge of one's own faults. He believed in altruism and restraint, and insisted on filial piety. He believed that people could be led by example, and encouraged the rulers of his own time to imitate those in former periods whose leadership had brought about prosperity. Kongfuzi hoped for a true king (*wang*) who would rule by moral example rather than constraint. He stressed *li*, the rules of proper conduct in ritual, etiquette and social behaviour. Kongfuzi himself is considered to represent the Confucian 'Ideal Person', a model of sincerity, modesty and right-mindedness. Gradually through diligent training and study ('self-cultivation'), he was able to remould his own character to conform to the Will of Heaven.

Confucianism is better described as a philosophy or code of social behaviour than a religion. It has no church or clergy and is not a formal institution. Kongfuzi's teachings were developed by Mengzi (Mencius; 372–289 BC) and became the basis of Chinese ethics and behaviour, in which there is an emphasis on the preservation of the family and the state, and the performance of proper rites for the ancestors. As its object was to emphasize the development of human nature and the person, Confucianism had a great hold over Chinese education for many years. During the early 19th century a good deal of Confucian teaching remained alongside other aspects of Chinese philosophy and practice. Confucianism has even survived the onslaught of Communist ideology.

PRIMAL RELIGIONS

The word 'primal' is used to convey the idea that these religions came first in human history, and underlie all the major religions of the world. By studying the religious beliefs and customs of primal peoples we can learn much about the religious heritage that we share. It is wrong to think of these religions as primitive. They often contain beliefs and ideas about the world that achieve high levels of sophistication.

The primal religions that survive today are the religions of non-literate, usually tribal societies. Unlike the universal religions such as Christianity, Islam, Hinduism and Buddhism – which have a wealth of written records and scriptures – the primal religions have no written sources. This does not mean, however, that primal religions are without history or are in some way 'fossilized' remnants of a past age. Like the universal religions, they have long and complex histories.

AFRICAN TRADITIONAL RELIGIONS

Christianity and Islam are popular in Africa, but there are also many traditional religions practised there by different tribal groups, such as the Nuer, Dinka, Dogon, Yoruba, Zande and Shona. These religions developed in pre-literate communities and environments that were often independent of one another and far apart.

In African traditional religions – as in most primal religions – there is a conception of a supreme being, sometimes prominent in religious life, sometimes remote and uninterested in human affairs.

The Ashanti of Ghana call their god Nyame, and

other West African peoples have similar names for their deity. The supreme god of the Yoruba people of Nigeria is known as Olorun, 'Owner of the Sky'. He is the creator of all things, the giver of life and breath, and the final judge of all people. In many parts of Africa the supreme being is considered so great and so remote that he is not worshipped. Divinities and ancestors, who act as intermediaries between people and the supreme god, are worshipped instead. Only in times of extreme distress is the god directly approached by the people.

Divinities are powerful named spirits, each with their own specific characteristics. Most African peoples believe in a multitude of divinities other than the supreme god. Common themes in African primal religions include divination, cults of affliction and possession, ancestor veneration, and secret societies.

OTHER MODERN PRIMAL RELIGIONS

In the Americas, Asia and Oceania, there is widespread belief in many deities. As well as powerful divinities and ancestor spirits, most primal peoples believe in numerous minor spirits, who may be good, malevolent or capricious. They may be the souls of the forgotten dead, who haunt the living, or the spirits of places such as rivers, mountains, bridges, rocks or trees. Among Arctic hunting peoples, spirits commonly take animal form.

In Oceania and in some other societies *mana* is a spiritual power or life force that is believed to permeate the universe. Originally a Melanesian word, it is now applied by anthropologists to spiritual power in other primal religions. Mana is not a spirit, and it has no will or purpose – it is impersonal and flows from one thing to another, and can be manipulated to achieve certain ends. Charms, amulets and medicines contain this power for the benefit of the wearer and user.

There is a whole range of religious specialists, including the medicine men of North America and the shamans of Siberia and the Arctic. Shamanism is generally found in hunting and gathering societies among peoples living in scattered, often migratory, groups. It is the dominant religious element among the Inuit (Eskimo) from Greenland to Alaska, and among the reindeer herders and fishers of northeastern Asia.

The shaman is a religious specialist – either a man or a woman – who, in times of trouble, mediates with the spirit world on behalf of his people. The shaman's power lies in his ability to enter an ecstatic trance. During ecstasy he sends out his soul to communicate with the spirit world, to ensure a favourable result for the hunt or to diagnose or cure disease.

MODERN FORMS OF PRIMAL RELIGION

Most primal peoples today are profoundly influenced by contact with more powerful societies and their religions. This has led to the development of new movements within primal religions, and in some cases to new religions. Most of these movements have developed out of interaction with Christianity. In Latin America and the Caribbean, for example, a mixture of African religion and rites involving Latin words and the crucifix has produced new cults such as voodoo, while in Papua New Guinea and Vanuatu primal and Christian elements have combined in movements known as 'cargo cults'.

SHINTO

Shinto ('the way of the gods') is the native religion of Japan. The religion gained the name Shinto during the 6th century AD to distinguish it from Buddhism, which was then reaching Japan from the Chinese mainland. The earliest surviving Shinto texts include semi-mythological genealogies of the emperors, tracing their divine descent from Amaterasu, the sun-goddess.

Early Shinto consisted of ritual practices directed at agriculture rather than philosophical or moral beliefs. The help of the deities (*kami*) was sought for the physical and spiritual needs of the people, and there was great stress laid upon purification by Shinto priests, and upon offerings and prayer. The more important national shrines were dedicated to well-known national figures, but other shrines were set up for the worship of deities of mountain and forest.

In the 19th century, the religion was divided into Shrine Shinto (*jinja*) and Sect Shinto (*kyoha*). A number of denominations were formed and these were dependent on private support for their teaching and organization. Different denominations had very little in common and varied widely in belief and practice. Some adhered to the traditional Shinto deities while others did not. Of the 13 denominations, *Tenrikyo* is the best known.

In 1871, Shinto became the Japanese national religion. State Shinto taught that a citizen's religious duty was obedience to the divine emperor. In 1946 Emperor Hirohito renounced all claims to divinity, and the new postwar constitution safeguards religious freedom and prohibits any association between religion and state. Estimates of the number of practising adherents of Shinto range between 3 400 000 and 35 000 000. Over 90 000 000 Japanese are said to belong to the Shinto 'community' but have no active allegiance to the religion. However, interest in Shinto is increasing and in 1990 Emperor Akihito was enthroned according to Shinto rites.

DAOISM (TAOISM)

Daoism, the Chinese teachings of the Way or Dao, is grounded in the works of Lao Tzu (6th–5th century BC) and Chuang-Tzu (4th century BC). It teaches that the Dao is the source of all things. The Dao works within the world, bringing about harmonious development. It acts as a model for rulers and leaders who allow their people to live spontaneously according to their own conditions and needs. The Dao is symbolized by water and by female rather than male imagery.

The goal of the Way is immortality which can only be achieved by the return to a properly balanced body composed of *yin* (the quiescent, feminine side) and *yang* (the active, male side).

Unlike Confucianism, Daoism advocates spontaneity and naturalness, abandoning oneself to the current of the Dao. Everything, good or bad, is the sublime operation of the Dao and should not be interfered with. Daoists naturally tend to solitude, meditation and simple living. Their techniques of quiet contemplation are similar to Buddhist meditation.

Daoism developed many schools and texts until the 16th century, and continued to have some impact on popular religion after that time in synthesis with other philosophical ideas and religious practices. The aspects of Daoism most well-known in the West are yin and yang, the book of divination — the *I Ching* — and a meditative form of exercise, *T'ai Chi*.

JUDAISM

The biblical account of the origin of the Jewish religion traces its history back to the revolt by Abraham against the idol-worship of his native Mesopotamia (now Iraq), when he smashed his father's idols and fled to Canaan (present-day Israel). Judaism is the oldest monotheistic religion. The word Jew is derived from the Latin *Judaeus*, that in turn is derived from the Hebrew *Yehudhi*, signifying a descendant of Jacob, Abraham's grandson.

The Exodus of the Jews from Egypt is believed to have occurred c. 1290 BC and was the decisive event or watershed in Israel's history. The Exodus resulted in the emergence of Israel as a distinct nation. The observance of the Passover (*Pesach*) makes every believing Jew a participant in the event that delivered their ancestors from bondage and established a special relationship between themselves and the One True God (the God of Abraham, Isaac and Jacob). The special relationship with the One God consists of an undertaking by the Jewish people to keep God's laws faithfully. Although Judaism expects non-Jews to observe certain basic ethical laws, it does not regard Jewish ritual as obligatory and does not seek converts. In fact, God promises the righteous of all people a place in the world to come, and the eventual re-establishment of the royal house of David; the *Messiah* (meaning the 'anointed') will inaugurate an age of universal peace and security.

Jewish scripture comprises the same books as the Christian Old Testament (see above). The *Torah* is the Hebrew name for the Law of Moses (the Pentateuch) which was divinely revealed to Moses on Mount Sinai, soon after the Exodus. The Hebrew scriptures also contain the books of the prophets, the wisdom literature (e.g. Solomon) and the historical writings (e.g. Kings). The *Talmud* contains civic and religious laws and is a collection of originally oral traditions. The two main versions were completed in Jerusalem in the 5th century BC and in Babylon at the end of the 6th century. The *Mishnah* is the oral law dating from between the 1st century BC to the 3rd century AD.

At the beginning of the Christian era, Judaism was divided into several sects, including the Pharisees, the Sadducees and the Essenes. The fall of Jerusalem (AD 70) resulted in the diaspora, which led to Jews settling throughout Europe, Africa and Asia Minor, often under severe discrimination and disabilities. During this period, the Yiddish language evolved in Central Europe from German and Hebrew elements. Jewish philosophy also developed, as did *Cabala* (mysticism), especially in Spain, where under the tolerant Muslim Moors there was much interaction between Jewish, Muslim and Christian scholars.

Jewish emancipation began with the enfranchisement of Jews in France in September 1791. The new climate stimulated the growth of the Reform movement, founded by David Friedlander (1756–1834), which accepted for Judaism the status of a religious sect within the European nations, loyal to their countries of adoption. Orthodox Judaism regards all religious authority as deriving from the Torah, and the beliefs of Orthodox Judaism were codified as the Thirteen Principles of Faith by the Spanish court physician and philosopher Rabbi Moses Maimonides (1135–1204). Conservative Judaism – which is strongest in the USA – stands midway between Orthodoxy and Reformed Judaism. Associated with the name of Solomon Schechter (1830–1915), it teaches that the faith must find its place in the contemporary world. There are also Liberal and Progressive Jews who reject the divinity of the Torah and rabbinic authority, and believe, to varying degrees, that Jewish practice must adapt to changing circumstances. They have introduced changes such as holding services partly in the vernacular (rather than Hebrew).

RITUAL AND WORSHIP

Jewish law lays down a complex set of laws of *kashrut*, which distinguishes permitted (*kosher* or *kasher*) from prohibited (*treifa*) foods. Only mammals that have both cloven hoofs and chew the cud, such as cows and sheep, are permitted as food, and they must be killed by a skilled *shochet* in a way that minimizes pain to the animal and drains as much blood as possible. Fish must have scales and fins (so that eels and sturgeon are forbidden), and shellfish and birds of prey are prohibited. In addition, milk and meat and their derivatives must be strictly separated and must not be cooked or prepared together, nor eaten at the same meal.

The Jewish day starts at sunset, and the week on Sunday, so that the *Shabbat*, the day of rest ordained by the Torah, is observed from dusk on Friday to nightfall on Saturday. This day of rest derives from the account of the creation in the Bible, where God rested on the seventh day. During Shabbat – the Sabbath – productive work and kindling fire are prohibited; other prohibitions include carrying, writing, cooking and travelling (except short distances by foot).

Synagogues were first built to serve as temporary places of worship after the destruction of the Temple in Jerusalem by the Babylonians in 586 BC, but although the Jews did rebuild the Temple, the practice of local houses of prayer continued. However, the second Temple was also destroyed and never rebuilt, and to this day the synagogue service is modelled upon, and refers to, the Temple service. The central role of the synagogue in Jewish religion is attested by its Hebrew name, which translates as 'house of meeting' and 'house of study', as well as 'house of prayer'.

Although there are no requirements for a specially constructed building, many synagogues incorporate such ancient Jewish symbols as the Star of David, the *Menorah* (the seven-branched Temple candlestick), and the two tablets containing the Ten Commandments in their decoration. The congregation usually faces the Ark, a cupboard containing the Torah scrolls, which are handwritten on parchment by a specially trained scribe. Above the Ark, which is usually in the wall facing Jerusalem, a light is kept burning as a sign of God's eternal presence.

Services are held in the evening, morning and afternoon. Each service has as its centre a period of silent prayer. For a formal service to take place, a quorum of ten men – a *minyan* – must be present, otherwise the Torah cannot be read. Any of the minyan can read the Torah or lead prayers. The function of the rabbi is as a teacher and interpreter of the Law.

Judaism as a total way of life revolves around the family as its main institution. Jews cannot surrender their religion. You are a Jew if your mother was Jewish. A boy becomes a man for religious purposes at his bar mitzvah at the age of 13, but is circumcised eight days after birth. Festivals include the Passover, Shavuot (Pentecost), Rosh Hashanah (New Year) and Yom Kippur (Day of Atonement).

The majority of Jews still live in the diaspora, but the state of Israel (although officially secular) is important to most Jews as a symbol of the hope and pride that sustained their faith during centuries of persecution. Israeli Judaism is very cosmopolitan. Different groups from the diaspora preserve their distinctive traditions – including the Sephardim (from Portuguese, Spanish and North African communities), the Ashkenazim (from Central Europe), and most recently the Falasha (from Ethiopia).

SIKHISM

Sikhism originated in the Punjab (India), where it is still the majority religion. It was founded by Guru Nanak (1479–1539), who taught how to lead a good life and seek final union with God. Sikhism is based on the concept of the guru: that God is the true Guru; the Sikh spiritual teachers were called gurus; and the scriptures, the *Granth* are said to be the guru. Sikhs believe in the existence of only one true God and that through worship and meditation the most devoted Sikhs can experience and know him. They believe that each person is trapped in his own failings and weaknesses and the only hope is found in the mercy of the true Guru.

THE TEN GURUS

Sikhism was developed under Nanak and the nine successive Sikh orthodox gurus, each chosen by his predecessor on the basis of his spiritual enlightenment. The succession of gurus is as follows: Nanak 1469–1539; Angad 1504–52; Amar Das 1479–1534; Ram Das 1534–81; Arjan 1563–1606; Har Govind 1595–1644; Har Rai 1630–61; Har Krishan 1656–64; Tegh Bahadur 1621–75; Gobind Singh 1666–1708.

THE FIVE Ks

The first five gurus developed the majority of the Sikh doctrines. The final guru, Gobind Singh, established the Sikh community with its shared symbols and the names 'Singh' and 'Kaur' for men and women respectively. The shared symbols are the so-called *five Ks*: *Kesh* uncut hair worn in a turban and uncut beard; *Kangha* a comb, to keep the hair clean; *Kara* a metal bracelet; *Kaccha* knee-length undershorts; *Kirpan* a dagger.

WORSHIP AND SOCIETY

The holy scripture, the *Guru Granth*, is the central document for all Sikh rituals and ceremonies. It contains the teachings of the first five gurus. The Sikhs worship in temples known as *gurdwara* (the guru's door). The most important temple is the Golden Temple at Amritsar, built in the 16th century. There are no priests to conduct the services – anyone can lead the worship, although some are specially trained to read the *Granth*.

The Sikh community in the Punjab has called for the establishment of a separate Sikh homeland, *Khalistan*, and in the 1980s, a minority of extremist Sikhs began a campaign of terrorism to achieve this aim. Sikhism has spread outside the Punjab during the 20th century to Britain, the USA, Canada and parts of Southern and East Africa. It is an ethnic religion in that it attempts to keep the community intact and does not aim to convert members from outside. It does not deny the existence of other faiths but strives for its members to be devoted to God.

BAHA'ISM

Baha'ism evolved from the teachings of two 19th-century Persian visionaries – Mirza Ali Muhammad (1820–50), who called himself the Bab ('gateway'); and Mirza Husain Ali (1817–92), who called himself Baha'ullah ('Glory of God'). In 1863 Baha'ullah announced that he was the manifestation of God sent to redeem the world, as earlier prophesied by the Bab. He was imprisoned and exiled many times. He developed his teachings into a religion based on a new scripture, the *Kitab Akdas*.

After his death the followers of this faith grew in number until, today, it is present in over 70 countries but predominantly in south-west Asia. About two-thirds of its followers are converts from Islam or their descendants. The remainder are mostly west Europeans and Americans.

Baha'ullah's followers see him as a divine healer, relieving human suffering and uniting mankind. The Baha'i faith does not predict an end to this world, or any intervention by God, but declares that there will be a change within humanity and society by which the world will return to peace and recover from the deterioration of moral values.

Baha'ism is not a minor sect but a universal religion that emphasizes the value of all religion and the spiritual unity of all humanity. The Baha'i faith has been persecuted in Iran since 1979 and all Baha'i institutions were banned in that country in 1983.

JAINISM

Jainism (from Hindi *jaina*, meaning 'saint') is an ancient religion that probably evolved during the first millennium BC. It spread from east to west across India, but with the rise of Hinduism declined and became restricted to two different regions, where it still exists today – Gujarat and Rajasthan in western India, and the Deccan in southern India.

Jainism has its own scriptures passed down orally from Mahavira (born c. 540 BC), one of the religion's great teachers. Jainism holds that the material world is eternal, moving on in a never-ending series of vast cycles. Like all Indian religions, it upholds the universal law of *karma*, which states that all actions, thoughts and words produce results that affect future deeds, forming a chain of cause and effect.

Jains do not believe in God – or gods – but in the perfectibility of the individual soul. In practice, the faith of Jainism seems very pessimistic as it sees the world as full of misery. However, prayer and worship can lead to liberation and salvation (*moksha*), when the individual soul is freed from matter and the suffering it brings. Jains practise non-violence (*ahimsa*), respect for all creatures, and vegetarianism.

ZOROASTRIANISM AND PARSIISM

The origins of Zoroastrianism are attributed to the Persian (Iranian) prophet Zoroaster or Zarathustra (c. 1200 BC). It was the Persian state religion from the 6th century BC to the 6th century AD. Following the expansion of Islam in Iran, the Zoroastrians were persecuted and retreated to the cities of Yazd and Kerman. In the 10th century AD, some fled to India. Bombay has become the centre for these Zoroastrians, known as Parsis.

Zoroastrianism acknowledges the existence of a good god, *Ahura Mazda*, and an evil spirit, *Angra Mainyu*. Ahura Mazda is assisted by angelic beings and it is believed that through their efforts good will finally triumph. The main scripture is the *Avesta*, which stresses the importance of worship based on fire. Zoroastrians are also known for the towers of silence (*daxma*) they use for the disposal of the dead.

Zoroastrianism is a small religion, but its followers are spread throughout the world. Intermarriage and conversion are not encouraged.

OTHER RELIGIONS

Other religions include:

Scientology
The Church of Scientology was founded in 1955 by the American L. Ron Hubbard, a science fiction writer. It derived from *dianetics*, a form of psychotherapy developed by Hubbard. Followers aim to 'clear' or free the mind from past painful experiences or 'engrams'. Scientologists believe in a highly structured spiritual world, the *thetan* (the soul) and reincarnation. The sect has been criticized concerning its claims and because of the financial demands that it makes upon members.

Spiritualism
Spiritualism is a religious belief in the ability of the spirits of the dead to communicate with the living – a belief common to most primitive religions. Modern practices date from the experiences in 1848 of the American Fox sisters who heard strange tapping sounds in their house and devised a similar code to communicate with the (deceased) intelligence that they claimed was making these noises. Spiritualism relies upon *mediums* who use *telepathy* to communicate with the spirit world.

Theosophy
Theosophy is a religious philosophy whose name is derived from the Greek *theos* 'god' and *sophia* 'wisdom'. The term is used in a general sense to imply a particular type of mysticism that is based on knowledge of God through spiritual ecstasy. Modern theosophy derives from the Theosophical Society, which was founded by the Russian Helena Blavatsky and Col. H.S. Olcott in 1875. Modern theosophy – which denies a personal god – teaches an intricate system of psychology and cosmology. Theosophists believe in the transmigration of souls and a brotherhood of all humanity that ignores differences of creed and race. Rudolf Steiner developed *anthroposophy* (see p. 170) from theosophical principles.

Transcendental meditation
Transcendental meditation (TM) was founded in India in 1958 by the Indian Maharishi Mahesh Yogi, whose teachings became very popular among young people in the West in the 1960s. The Maharishi developed a system of meditation that uses a *mantra* – a word or phrase in Sanskrit – which is mentally repeated to bring an individual into a deeper quieter sense of consciousness. Followers are trained, and receive a personal mantra. TM has been criticized concerning the financial demands made upon members. There are over 3 000 000 practitioners worldwide, mainly in India and the USA.

ANCIENT RELIGIONS

ANCIENT GREEK AND ROMAN RELIGION

Written evidence about religion in Europe begins with the Linear B texts of the Mycenaean civilization in Greece (c. 1450 BC). These show the importance of Poseidon the sea god and of 'the Lady' of various locations (presumably a mother goddess). Some other divine names occur, including Zeus and Hera, which later appear in the epic poetry of Homer. Homer's gods lived ageless and immortal on Mount Olympus, but acted like humans – and not the best-behaved humans. They could change shape, intervene in human life, and might respond to gifts and prayers to change human destiny, but they did not change human nature. By the 6th century BC the Olympian gods were part of the official worship of the Greek city-states. But ancient Greek religion had little to do with morality, and the moral, metaphysical and scientific concerns of the Athenian philosophers of the 5th and 4th centuries led to very different ideas of God. These ideas challenged popular religion, and in 399 BC the philosopher Socrates was condemned for atheism and corrupting youth by undermining the gods of the state.

Two forms of religious expression developed in early Rome. Domestic piety recognized household gods (*lares* and *penates*), while the state cult ensured corporate well-being. As Rome encountered Greek culture, the state deities were identified with Olympian equivalents. As the Roman Empire expanded, its armies brought back foreign cults and religious ideas. The most important of these cults – until Christianity became the state religion in the 4th century AD – was Mithraism, a male-only mystery cult based on the worship of Mithras, the Persian god of light, truth and justice.

THE TWELVE OLYMPIAN GODS

Zeus overlord of the Olympian gods; God of the sky and its properties (Roman: Jupiter).

Hera protector of women and marriage, and goddess of the sky; wife of Zeus (Roman: Juno).

Poseidon god of the sea and earthquakes (Roman: Neptune).

Demeter goddess of the harvest (Roman: Ceres).

Apollo god of prophecy, music and medicine (no direct Roman equivalent).

Artemis goddess of chastity, childbirth and the young (Roman: Diana).

Ares god of war (Roman: Mars).

Aphrodite goddess of love and beauty (Roman: Venus).

Hermes God of trade and travellers (Roman: Mercury).

Athene (or Athena) goddess of prudence and wise council; the protectress of Athens (Roman: Minerva).

Hephaestus god of fire and metalcraft (Roman: Vulcan).

Hestia goddess of fire (Roman: Vesta).

OTHER IMPORTANT DEITIES

Adonis god of vegetation and rebirth.

Aeolus god of the winds.

Alphito barley goddess of Argos.

Arethusa goddess of springs and fountains.

Asclepius god of healing.

Atlas a Titan who carries the earth.

Attis god of vegetation.

Boreas god of the northern wind.

Cronus father of the god Zeus.

Cybele goddess of the earth.

Dionysus god of wine and the 'good life' (Roman: Bacchus).

Eos goddess of the dawn (Roman: Aurora).

Erebus god of darkness.

Eros god of love (Roman: Cupid).

Gaia (Gaea) goddess of the earth.

Ganymede beautiful youth who became cup-bearer to Zeus.

Hades see Pluto.

Hebe goddess of youth.

Hecate goddess of witchcraft, magic and the moon.

Helios god of the sun (Roman: Sol).

Hygiea goddess of health (Roman: Salus).

Hypnos god of sleep (Roman: Somnus).

Irene goddess of peace (Roman: Pax).

Iris goddess of the rainbow.

Morpheus god of sleep and dreams.

Nemesis god of retribution.

Nereus god of the sea.

Nike goddess of victory (Roman: Victoria).

Oceanus Titan with divinity of the rivers and seas.

Pan god of flocks and herds (and associated with fertility) (Roman: Sylvanus).

Persephone goddess of the underworld and of corn (Roman: Proserpina).

Pluto (or Hades) god of the underworld.

Prometheus Titan; god of fire and the creation of man.

Rhea Titaness; mother of many gods, wife of Cronus.

Selene goddess of the moon (Roman: Luna).

Thanatos goddess of night and death (Roman: Mors).

Triton a merman sea god.

Uranus sky god responsible for the sun and rain.

ANCIENT EGYPTIAN RELIGION

The pharaohs of ancient Egypt were regarded as divine, and were called 'Horus' or 'Son of Re'. The autocratic rule of the pharaohs was legitimized by the mythology of Re as the Sun god and ruler of the gods; as 'Son of Re' the pharaoh embodied the life-giving power of the sun. Horus was the son of Isis, the Divine Mother, and of Osiris, the god of inundation, vegetation and the dead. As Horus, the pharaoh embodied the periodic renewal of life and fertility borne on the annual flooding of the land by the River Nile. Local deities were often linked with national ones. The most significant was Amun, the god of invisibility, one of the characteristic elements of chaos out of which the Earth emerged. From c. 2000 BC he was combined with Amun to become Amun-Re, whose temple at Thebes was to become the most powerful and wealthiest in Egypt.

GODS AND GODDESSES OF ANCIENT EGYPT

Amun god of Thebes; often represented as a man, sometimes with an erect penis.

Anubis the jackal-headed god of the necropolis; patron of the embalmers.

Aten creator god manifest in the sun disc.

Atum the original sun god of Heliopolis.

Bastet cat goddess.

Bes domestic god, usually depicted as a dwarf.

Edjo cobra goddess who appears as the pharaoh's protector on the royal diadem.

Geb god of the Earth; the physical support of the world.

Hathor often represented as a cow, a cow-headed woman, or a woman with a cow's headdress. Recognized as the suckler of the pharaoh.

Horus falcon god, identified with the pharaoh during his reign. The son of Osiris and Isis, Horus grew up to avenge his father's murder by Seth.

Imhotep architect of the Step Pyramid, chief minister of Djoser (c. 2700 BC). Later venerated as the god of learning and medicine

Isis wife of Osiris and mother of Horus.

Khepri the scarab-beetle god, identified with the sun god Re as creator god.

Maat goddess of truth, justice and order; depicted as a woman with an ostrich feather on her head.

Min god of fertility and harvest; protector of desert travellers and god of the road.

Mut vulture goddess of Thebes; a mighty divine mother.

Nekhbet vulture goddess, who sometimes appears beside Edjo on the royal diadem.

Nephthys sister of Isis.

Nut goddess of the sky.

Osiris god of the dead. Identified with the dead king and depicted as a mummified king. Also god of the inundation of the Nile and of vegetation.

Ptah creator god of Memphis and patron of craftsmen. Represented as a mummified man.

Ptah-Soker-Osiris god combining the principal gods of creation, death and the afterlife. Represented as a mummified king.

Re or Ra the sun god of Heliopolis and the supreme judge. Other gods aspiring to universal recognition would often link their name to his, e.g. Amun-Re.

Re-Harakhti falcon god, incorporating the characteristics of Re and Horus.

Sebek a protector of reptiles and patron of kings.

Sekhmet lion-headed goddess, wife of Ptah, venerated in the area of Memphis. Regarded as the bringer of sickness and destruction to the enemies of Re.

Seth god of violence and storms. Brother and murderer of Osiris, represented as an animal of unidentified type.

Shu god of light and air.

Sobek crocodile god.

Thoueris hippopotamus goddess, the patron of women in childbirth.

Thoth the ibis-headed god of Hermopolis; scribe to the gods and inventor of writing.

GERMANIC (NORSE) RELIGION

The religions of the Germanic peoples survived into the Middle Ages: Denmark, Norway and Iceland did not become Christian until the 10th and 11th centuries, and Sweden not until the 12th century. Germanic religion had many deities. In early times, Odin, Tyr and Thor (see box) in particular were worshipped. There was no supreme deity, only a chaos of divine energy. The worshipper chose the divinity thought most likely to serve him.

PEOPLE AND PLACES IN NORSE RELIGION

Aesir race of gods including Odin and Thor; defeated the Vanir.

Asgard home of the gods.

Balder 'the Beautiful', son of Odin, slain by Loki.

Fenrir 'Great Wolf', son of Loki; bound up by Tyr, but will break free at Ragnarok.

Frey fertility god, one of the Vanir.

Freya Frey's sister, consort of Odin.

Frigg Odin's wife. Her name is preserved in 'Friday'.

Hel kingdom of the dead; also personified as Loki's daughter.

Loki the trickster god of Asgard. Imprisoned in a cave for the murder of Balder, he will break loose at Ragnarok.

Midgard world of men. It is held by a coiled serpent, who will show himself at Ragnarok.

Njord father of Frey and Freya, associated with ships and sailing.

Norns three maidens who rule the fates of men and daily water the world tree Yggdrasil.

Odin[1] chief of the Aesir; god of battle, poetry and death.

Ragnarok[2] 'the twilight of the gods', the coming day of destruction for Asgard and Midgard and their inhabitants in a battle with the forces of evil.

Thor god of thunder.

Tyr[3] a war god who has bound Fenrir.

Valhalla Odin's great hall for warriors.

Valkyries spirit maidens who guide in battle and conduct the chosen slain to Valhalla.

Vanir race of gods associated with fertility; defeated by the Aesir.

Yggdrasil the self-renewing world tree, which forms the centre of the worlds of gods, giants and men.

[1] Old Germanic: Wotan, Anglo-Saxon: Woden.
[2] German: Götterdämmerung. [3] Old Germanic: Tiwaz.

CELTIC RELIGION

Little is known about the Celtic deities owing to a lack of written material. Celtic religious beliefs were centred on the relationship between the divine spirit world with the land and the waters. Hills, rocks, springs, rivers and many other features were thought to be the homes of guardian spirits. Trees were also inhabited by spirits and certain species had a ritualistic role. The druids – the priest-poets of the Celts – took their name from an ancient Indo-European word meaning 'knowing the oak'.

CELTIC GODS AND FESTIVALS

Belenus god of war.

Beltane festival of Bel's fire (May 1); marks the beginning of hunting and wooing.

The Brigits three Irish mother goddesses who presided over poetry, metalwork and healing.

Cernunnos stag-horned Lord of the Animals; appears on many surviving artifacts.

Imbolc festival of springtime (February 1).

Lug sun god; also the patron of music.

Lugnasag festival of harvest and the marriage of Lug.

Macha known in Britain as Rhiannon, Macha was the mare goddess.

Manannan god of the oceans.

Morrígan powerful crow goddess associated with death and battle.

Samain festival of the dead (November 1) and the end of summer.

PRE-COLUMBIAN DEITIES

Aztec gods included:

Centéotl the maize god.

Centzon Totochtin the '400 rabbits' – fertility gods.

Chalchiuhtlicue wife of Quetzacóatl; the freshwater goddess.

Cihuacóatl the snake-woman goddess.

Ehécatl the wind god.

Huehuetéotl the god of fire.

Huixtocihuatl god of the sea.

Nanahuatzin a small ulcer-covered god who sacrificed himself in a sacred fire to become the Sun.

Omecihuatlt Lady of the Duality; one half of the Supreme Couple.

Ometecuhtli Lord of the Duality; one half of the Supreme Couple.

Quetzalcóatl the plumed serpent, he was the god of the morning and evening stars; Quetzalcóatl was patron of the priests. His worship demanded human sacrifice.

Tecciztécatl a bejewelled god who sacrificed himself in a sacred fire to become the Moon.

Teteoinnan goddess of fecundity and mother of all gods.

Tezcatlipoca god of the night sky; protector of warriors.

Tlaloc the god of rain, thunder and lightning.

The Tlaloques the rain gods.

Tlazoltéotl the goddess of love and foregiveness.

Xipe Totec god of spring and plant growth.

Xochipilli the god of flowers.

Xolotl twin of Quetzacóatl; the dog-headed god.

Inca gods included:

Apu Illapu the rain god; god of farmers.

Inti the sun god; he was said to be the divine ancestor of the Sapa Incas.

Mama-Kilya wife of Inti; the moon goddess.

Mama-Qoca Sea Mother.

Paca-Mama Mother Earth.

Viracocha the supreme god; creator of the Incas, of earth, humanity and all living creatures. His many titles included Old Man of the Sky and the Ancient One.

LANGUAGE AND LITERATURE
LANGUAGE

LANGUAGES OF THE WORLD

No one is certain how many living languages there are in the world, but it is likely that the number exceeds 5000. Each language is unique in that it has its own system of sounds, words and structures, and yet almost all are related either closely or distantly to other languages found in the same part of the world.

LANGUAGE FAMILIES

Languages are classed in families containing related tongues. The languages of the largest family — Indo-European – are spoken by about half the world's population. Based in South Asia and Europe, these languages have been taken to many parts of the world by European colonists. The group includes all the languages of Europe (except Finnish, Estonian, Lappish, Magyar and Basque) as well as the Iranian group of languages and the Indic languages, including Gujarati, Marathi, Hindi, Urdu, Bengali, Sindhi, Sinhalese, Rajasthani and Punjabi.

WORLD'S PRINCIPAL LANGUAGES

1. Mandarin (Chinese) (or Putonghua) is standardized Northern Chinese. It was converted to the Pinyin system of phonetic pronunciation in 1958. Spoken in China and by Chinese communities throughout Southeast Asia, including those in Singapore and Malaysia. Language family: Indo-Chinese. 910 000 000 speakers; 820 000 000 as a first language.

2. English English evolved from Anglo-Saxon, and shows strong Norman-French and Latin influences. It is the first language in Australia, Canada, Caribbean Commonwealth countries, Ireland, New Zealand, UK and the USA. English is widely understood in Commonwealth and former Commonwealth nations, including Nigeria, India, South Africa, Kenya, Tanzania, Malaysia, Ghana and Zimbabwe. Language family: Indo-European. 455 000 000 speakers; 315 000 000 as a first language.

3. Hindustani (Hindi) Hindi is the main language of India. Language family: Indo-European. 385 000 000 speakers; 325 000 000 as a first language.

4. Spanish (Castilian) Castilian evolved as a separate language in the 10th century and has been the most widely used language of Spain since the 13th century. It is spoken as the first language in Spain (except the Basque Country, Catalonia and Galicia) and in the Latin American countries except Brazil. Language family: Indo-European. 365 000 000 speakers; 320 000 0000 as a first language.

7. Great Russian Great Russian is the foremost of languages of Russia and is spoken spoken as a second language by over 50% of the population of the former USSR. Language family: Indo-European. 290 000 000 speakers; 170 000 000 as a first language.

6. Arabic Arabic dates from the 6th century, when it originated in the Arabian peninsula. It is spoken throughout North Africa and southwest Asia. Language family: Semitic-Hamitic. 210 000 000 speakers; 180 000 000 as a first language.

7. Bengali Bengali is the official language of Bangladesh and of the Indian state of West Bengal. Language family: Indo-European. 190 000 000 speakers; 180 000 000 as a first language.

8. Portuguese Portuguese became a language distinct from Spanish in the 14th century. It is spoken in Portugal, Brazil and in former Portuguese territories in Africa, including Angola and Mozambique. Language family: Indo-European. 180 000 000 speakers; 165 000 000 as a first language.

9. Malay-Indonesian Malay-Indonesian originated in Sumatra, although the dialect of south West Malaysia is recognized as the standard form of the language. It is spoken in Malaysia, Indonesia (where it is called Bahasa) and south Thailand. Language family: Malayo-Polynesian. 150 000 000 speakers; 50 000 000 as a first language.

9. Japanese The earliest inscription of Japanese (in Chinese characters) dates from the 5th century. It is spoken in Japan with minorities in former Japanese territories. Language family: Japanese is unrelated to any other language. 126 000 000 speakers; 125 000 000 as a first language.

10. French French developed in the 9th century from a mixture of Frankish and Gaulish. It is spoken in France, Belgium, Québec (Canada), Switzerland, Luxembourg, Haiti, French possessions (including Polynesia, Martinique and Guadeloupe) and former French and Belgian colonies in Africa. Language family: Indo-European. 125 000 000 speakers; 71 000 000 as a first language.

11. German German has been known in a written form since the 8th century. It is spoken in Germany, Switzerland and Austria, and by minorities throughout central and southeast Europe. There are considerable variations between spoken dialects. Language family: Indo-European. 120 000 000 speakers; 98 000 000 as a first language.

13. Urdu Urdu, which is related closely to Hindustani, is written in Arabic script. It is the official language of Pakistan and an official languages of India. Language family: Indo-European. 96 000 000 speakers; 30 000 0000 as a first language.

14. Punjabi Punjabi is considered by some linguists to be a variety of Hindustani. One of the 15 official languages of India, Punjabi is spoken in the Indian Punjab and in adjoining parts of Pakistan. Language family: Indo-European. 90 000 000 speakers; 85 000 000 as a first language.

15. Korean Korean became a written language in the 5th century, using Chinese characters In the 15th century it adopted its own alphabet. It is spoken in North and South Korea. Language family: Korean is unrelated to any other tongue. 73 000 000 speakers; 67 000 000 as a first language.

16. Telugu Telugu became a written language in the 11th century. It is spoken in Andhra Pradesh (south India). Language family: Dravidian. 71 000 000 speakers; 70 000 000 as a first language.

17 =. Tamil Tamil – the second oldest written Indian language – has a distinctive script. It is spoken in Tamil Nadu (India), in Sri Lanka and in parts of Malaysia. Language family: Dravidian. 67 000 000 speakers; 65 000 000 as a first language.

17 = . Marathi A written language since the 6th century, Marathi is spoken in Maharashtra (India). Langauge family: Indo-European. 67 000 000 speakers; 66 000 000 as a first language.

19. Cantonese Cantonese is a distinct dialect of Chinese spoken in Guangdong province, China. Language family: Indo-Chinese. 65 000 000 speakers; 64 000 000 as a first language.

20. Wu Wu is a dialect spoken, but not officially encouraged, in the Chiang Jiang delta of China. Language family: Indo-Chinese. 64 000 000 speakers.

21. Italian Italian developed from Latin in the 10th century. It is spoken in Italy and Ticino (Switzerland). Language family: Indo-European. 63 000 000 speakers; 57 000 000 as a first language.

22. Javanese Javanese, which is related to Malay, is spoken by about 50% of the people of Indonesia. Language family: Malayo-Polynesian. 62 000 000 speakers; 60 000 000 as a first language.

ARTIFICIAL LANGUAGES

Over 500 artificial languages have been devised, the majority since the middle of the 19th century. The following are among the best known:

Esperanto Esperanto was devised by Luwik Lejzer Zamenhof, a Polish oculist, in 1887. It is a phonetic language using 28 letters, each letter representing a single sound. The language is written as it sounds and sounds as it is written. There are 16 simple rules of grammar to which there are no exceptions. A vocabulary of over 12 000 words is constructed from 2629 'roots', the majority of which are Romance. Esperanto is spoken by several million people and taught at over 150 universities and other institutes of higher education. Over 160 Esperanto dictionaries and nearly 135 000 books in the language have been published. A world Esperanto congress has been held in most years since 1905 – the most recent conference attracted delegates from over 70 countries.

Ido Ido was devised by the French linguists Louis Couturat and Louis de Beaufront in 1908. It is a simplified version of Esperanto, but is not nearly so widely used or studied as its 'parent' language.

Novial Novial is a simplification of Ido. Devised by the Danish linguist Otto Jespersen in 1924, Novial attempts to balance ease of speech with regularity of grammar.

Volapük Volapük was devised by Johann Martin Schleyer, a German priest, in 1879. It is based on a simplified Germanic vocabulary and has a regular grammar. The language is now almost extinct, but it enjoyed considerable popularity in academic German circles in the 1880s, when up to half a million people were reported to be learning it.

Interlingua Interlingua was devised by Giuseppe Peano, an Italian mathematician, in 1908. Originally known as Latino sine flexione, it is based on a synthesis of Latin, English, French and German vocabulary with a simplified regular grammar derived from Latin. Interlingua enjoyed a brief vogue and there is still an Academia pro Interlingua.

Other artificial languages Other artificial languages that have enjoyed a brief period of popularity included *Sol-Ré-Sol* (patronized by Napoleon III and Victor Hugo), *Anglo-latin* (a 19th-century cross between English and Latin vocabulary and grammar) and *Timiero* (a 'numerical' language).

LITERATURE

LITERARY FORMS AND TERMS

acrostic a number of lines of writing, eg a poem, in which certain letters, especially the first letters of each line, make a word or words.

act a major division of a dramatic work.

alexandrine a line of verse with six iambic feet.

allegory a poem, novel, drama, etc., in which the events and characters symbolize a deeper meaning beyond their apparent literal meaning.

alliteration a figure of speech in which the same consonant or vowel is repeated at the beginning of each or some of the words or stressed syllables in a line of poetry (eg the stuttering rifle's rapid rattle).

anagram a word made from another word by changing the order of the letters (eg god – dog).

anecdote a short amusing story about a person or event.

antonym a word that means the opposite of another word.

aphorism a short statement expressing a general truth in witty fashion (eg necessity is the mother of invention).

assonance the repetition of the same vowel sound in a line of verse.

autobiography an account of a person's life written by himself or herself.

ballad a song or poem that tells a story.

ballade a verse form consisting of three stanzas and an envoi, each ending with the same line.

biography an account of a person's life written by someone else.

blank verse unrhymed verse, often in iambic pentameters.

canto a division of a long poem.

clerihew a comic poem consisting of two couplets each with an irregular meter.

cliché an expression that has lost its force by being used too much (eg time flies).

colloquialism a word or phrase used in everyday informal speech rather than in a formal or literary context.

couplet two successive lines of poetry, usually rhyming and having the same meter.

dialogue speech of the characters in a novel or play.

doggerel comic verse of poor quality, usually with an irregular meter.

drama a work to be performed on stage, radio or television by actors.

dramatis personae (a list of) all the characters in a play or story.

eclogue a short pastoral poem in the form of a conversation or soliloquy.

elegy a serious meditative poem, esp. a lament for the dead.

envoi a brief dedicatory stanza at the end of certain forms of poetry, esp. ballads.

epic a long narrative poem recounting in an elevated style the deeds of a legendary hero.

epigram a short witty statement in verse or prose.

epithet a descriptive word or phrase added to or substituted for a person's name (eg Charles the Bold).

euphemism an inoffensive word or phrase substituted for an unpleasant or hurtful one.

fable a short tale in prose or verse that points a moral.

farce a humorous play characterized by absurd or improbable situations.

fiction literary works invented by the imagination, such as novels and short stories.

foot a metrical division or unit of verse, consisting of two or more syllables, one of which has a strong stress, the other or others a weak stress (eg for mén/may cóme/ and mén/ may gó).

free verse unrhymed verse without a regular rhythm.

heroic couplet two lines of rhyming verse in iambic pentameters.

hyperbole deliberate use of exaggeration for emphasis.

iambic pentameter a line of verse consisting of five feet, each of which consists of a short syllable followed by a long one.

idiom an expression or group of words whose meaning cannot be worked out from the literal meaning of its constituent words.

idyll a work in verse or prose describing an idealized country life.

legend a popular story passed down from earlier times, the truth of which has not been established.

limerick a short humorous poem five lines in length.

litotes ironic understatement, especially the use of a negative to express the contrary (eg *I won't be sorry when it's over* = *I will be extremely glad when it's over*).

lyric poetry verse expressing the personal thoughts and feelings of the writer.

maxim a short phrase or statement expressing a general truth or principle or rule of conduct.

melodrama a dramatic work characterized by exciting and sensational events and usually having a happy ending.

metaphor a figure of speech in which one person or thing is described in terms of another (eg he is a cunning fox).

metonym a word used in metonymy (eg *the bottle* used to stand for alcoholic drink).

metonymy a figure of speech in which the name of an attribute or adjunct is substituted for that of the thing that is being referred to (eg *crown* used to refer to a monarch).

meter the rhythmic arrangement of syllables in poetry, according to the number and type of feet in a line.

monologue a long speech for a single performer in a drama.

myth a story about superhuman beings, regarded by ancient societies as being a true explanation of certain natural phenomena, how the world came into existence, etc.

novel an extended prose narrative recounting the story of fictional characters within a recognizable social context.

novella a short novel.

octave group of eight lines of verse.

ode a lyric poem in which the poet directly addresses the subject, with lines of differing lengths and a complex rhythm.

onomatopoeia formation of words whose sound imitates the sound of the noise or action described (eg *bang, buzz, hiss*).

oxymoron a figure of speech in which apparently contradictory terms are used together to achieve an epigrammatic effect (eg *precious bane*).

paradox a statement that appears to be self-contradictory, but on closer examination can be seen to contain a truth.

parody a literary work which imitates the style of a particular writer in a humorous or satirical way.

plot the story line of a novel or play.

poem a literary work in verse, characterized by concentrated or striking language used for its suggestive power as well as its literal meaning and often making use of rhyme, meter, alliteration, etc.

prose written language as in ordinary usage, as distinct from poetry.

pun the humorous use of a word to suggest different meanings, or of words of the same sound with different meanings; a play on words.

quatrain group of four lines of verse, often with alternate rhymes.

rhyme identity or similarity of sound between the endings of words or lines of verse.

rhyme royal verse form consisting of stanzas of seven lines of iambic pentameters with a complex rhyme scheme.

rondeau verse form consisting of ten or thirteen lines using only two rhymes throughout and repeating the opening words twice as a refrain.

saga a long story recounting heroic deeds, especially a medieval tale of Scandinavian heroes; series of connected books about several generations of a family or other social group.

satire a literary work using ridicule, irony or sarcasm to expose folly or vice.

scene a subdivision of a play, smaller than an act, in which the action is continuous.

sestet a group of six lines of verse.

short story a prose narrative of shorter length than a novel.

soliloquy a speech in a drama in which a character expresses his or her thoughts aloud without addressing a particular person.

sonnet a poem consisting of 14 lines of iambic pentameters with rhymes arranged according to a fixed scheme, and divided into an octave and a sestet (Petrarchan sonnet), or three quatrains and a couplet (Elizabethan sonnet).

stanza a group of lines in a poem, arranged in a particular metrical pattern.

synecdoche figure of speech in which a part is used to indicate a whole, or a whole used to indicate a part.

synonym a word identical or similar in meaning to another one.

tautology the use of words that repeat a meaning that has already been conveyed.

tercet group of three lines of verse.

tragedy a drama in which the protagonist, usually a man of outstanding personal qualities, falls from grace through a combination of personal failing and circumstances that he cannot control; any dramatic or literary work dealing with sad or serious events and ending in disaster.

verse written language with a metrical structure; poetry.

villanelle a verse form usually consisting of five stanzas of three lines (tercets) and one stanza of four lines (quatrain), using only two rhymes throughout according to a fixed scheme.

CLASSICAL LITERATURE

Western literature began with the literature of Greece and Rome, and the literatures of Europe have constantly imitated, adapted, reacted against and returned to this inescapable Classical inheritance. The 1500 years from Homer to the early Middle Ages saw the birth of almost all the major forms of prose and poetry, and the very concept of literature itself as a separate activity first made its appearance. The term 'Classical literature' may give the impression of order and a uniformity of style, but on closer inspection the literatures of Greece and Rome present a more varied scene.

Early Greek literature began with the epics of Homer. The first personal poetry appeared in the middle of the 7th century BC, while philosophical and historical writing in the 6th century BC marked the beginning of Greek literary prose. Tragedy – which is thought to have its roots in primitive rituals – began with the plays of Aeschylus, while comedy first appeared about the same time in the works of Aristophanes. The 4th century BC was an age of prose, but the chief writers of this Hellenistic age – Plato and Aristotle – worked in a genre (philosophy) sometimes now excluded from the category of literature.

From its beginning early Roman literature was heavily influenced by Greek, and it was not until the middle years of the 1st century BC that Latin really began to rival Greek for literary creativity. The greatest period of Roman literature was under the emperor Augustus, when Virgil and Horace flourished. Later genres range from imperial histories and elegant love poems to satire and low comedy.

MAJOR GREEK WRITERS

Homer (?8th century BC), epic poet: *Iliad, Odyssey* (These may not in fact be the work of the same man.)

Hesiod (?8th–7th centuries BC), epic poet: *Theogony*.

Archilochus (mid-7th century BC), soldier-poet.

Alcaeus (7th–6th centuries BC), lyric poet.

Sappho (b. mid-7th century BC), lyric poetess, the pioneer of the brief subjective love poem.

Pindar (c. 520–445 BC), lyric poet: *Epinician Odes*.

Bacchylides (6th–5th centuries BC), lyric poet of choral songs for victorious athletes.

Aeschylus (c. 525–456 BC), tragic poet and dramatist: *Oresteia*, a trilogy of plays.

Sophocles (c. 497–405 BC), dramatist and tragic poet: *Oedipus Rex* (c. 430 BC), *Antigone* (441 BC).

Herodotus (c. 490–c. 425 BC), historian and prose writer, known as the 'father of history'.

Euripides (c. 485–406 BC), tragic dramatist: *Medea* (431).

Thucydides (c. 455–399 BC), Athenian historian.

Aristophanes (c. 445–385 BC), comic dramatist: *Peace* (421 BC) and *Lysistrata* (411 BC).

Isocrates (436–338 BC), orator and speechwriter.

Plato (c. 428–347 BC), philosopher: *The Republic* and *The Laws*.

Aristotle (384–322 BC), philosopher: treatises on logic, metaphysics, politics, biology, etc.

Demosthenes (384–322 BC), orator and statesman.

Menander (342–292 BC), comic dramatist.

Callimachus (c. 310–240 BC), poet and epigrammatist.

Theocritus (c. 3rd century BC), pastoral poet: *Idylls*.

Plutarch (c. AD 46–120), biographer: *Parallel Lives*, a biography of 50 lives of famous Greeks and Romans.

MAJOR ROMAN WRITERS

Plautus (c. 250–184 BC), comic dramatist and writer.

Ennius (239–169 BC), poet: the *Annals*, an historical epic.

Cicero (106–43 BC), orator, statesman and writer.

Lucretius (c. 98–c. 55 BC), poet and philosopher.

Sallust (86–35 BC), historian.

Catullus (c. 84–c. 55 BC), love poet.

Virgil (70–19 BC), poet: *Eclogues, Georgics* and the *Aeneid* (a national epic).

Horace (65–8 BC), poet: *Odes, Satires* and *Epistles*.

Livy (59 BC–AD 17), historian: *History of Rome*.

Propertius (c. 50–after 16 BC), elegiac poet.

Ovid (43 BC–AD 17), poet: *Art of Love*.

Seneca (AD 4–65), philosopher-playwright and essayist.

Petronius (d. AD 65), satirical writer: *Satyricon*, comic novel.

Lucan (AD 39–65), epic poet: *Pharsalia*.

Martial (c. AD 40–104), epigrammatist.

Tacitus (c. AD 56–117), historian.

Juvenal (?AD 60–?140), satirical poet.

Pliny the Younger (AD ?62–c.113), orator and statesman, remembered for his letters.

Apuleius (active AD 155), philosopher and author: *The Golden Ass*, a romance.

ASIAN LITERATURE

The diverse cultures of the Middle East, India, China, and Japan produced bodies of writing which, while relatively unknown in the wider world, nonetheless offer a richness and scope equal to any other.

Literature written in Arabic owes much of its inspiration to the emergence of Islam. Persia possessed a literature more varied in its forms and content than that written in classical Arabic, and was to enrich the Arabic literary tradition with new genres such as the epic poem. Indian literature appeared extensively only in the 16th century when classical Sanskrit literature (c. 200 BC–AD c. 1100) became popular. Key Sanskrit texts include the epic poems *Ramayana* and *Mahabharata* (from the 3rd century BC). Popular prose in all Indian languages appeared in the 19th century and there is now a large literature in English.

China's literary heritage is particularly distinguished by its poetry, which was generally sung to musical accompaniment. The earliest and most famous work to survive is the *Shi jing* (Book of Songs), which includes love songs, folk songs, ritual hymns, and political songs. Chinese literature exerted a major influence on that of Japan, which, despite its briefer history, boasts high achievement in poetry, drama (particularly the *No* plays) and the novel. The *haiku* – a 17-syllable verse usually in lines of seven, five and seven syllables – is the best known of the characteristic forms of Japanese poem.

MAJOR ARABIC WRITERS

Abu Nuwas (c. AD 762–c. 813), major court poet.

Mutanabbi (915–965), a leading classical poet.

Abu Muhammad al-Kasim al-Hariri (1054–1122), writer of tales: *The Assemblies of al-Hariri*.

Masudi (d. 956), historian, geographer and philosopher.

Ghazali (1058–1111), theologian and Islamic philosopher: *Restoration of the Sciences of Religion*.

Ahmad Shawqi (1868–1932), neoclassical poet.

Hafiz Ibrahim (1870–1932), neoclassical poet.

Tawfiq al-Hakim (1898?–1987), novelist and playwright: *The Return of the Spirit* (1933), *People of the Cave* (1933), and *Sheherazade* (1934).

Naguib Mahfouz (1911–), Egyptian novelist and short-story writer: *Midaq Alley* and *Miramar*.

Badr Shakir al-Sayyab (1929–64), free verse poet.

MAJOR PERSIAN WRITERS

Rudaki (d. 940–41), poet.

Firdausi (933–1031), epic poet: *Book of Kings*.

Omar Khayyám (?1048–?1122), poet: *Rubáiyát*, well known in the West through its translation by Edward Fitzgerald.

Nizami (1140–1202), epic poet: *Five Treasures*.

Farid ad-Din Attar (d. c. 1229), mystic poet: *Conference of the Birds*.

Jalal ed-Din Rumi (d. 1273), classical poet.

Sa'di (c. 1213–1291), classical poet: *Gulistan* and *Bustan*.

Hafiz (1325–89), classical poet: *Diwan*.

MAJOR CHINESE WRITERS

Qu Yuan (4th–3rd century BC), allegorical poet.

Du Fu (Tu Fu; 712–770), poet whose works commented on social conditions: *The Army Carts*.

Li Bo (Li Po; 701–762), widely regarded as the greatest Chinese poet.

Wang Shifu (c. 1250–?1337), dramatist: *Romance of the Western Chamber*.

Luo Guan-zhong (active 14th century), novelist: *The Water Margin*.

Cao Zhan (1715–63), novelist: *The Dream of the Red Chamber*.

Lu Xun (1881–1936), essayist and short-story writer.

Mao Dun (1896–1985), short-story writer and novelist: *Zi ye* (*Midnight*, 1933).

Lao She (1899–1966), novelist and playwright.

Ding Ling (1904–86), novelist and short-story writer.

Ba Jin (1904–), novelist, essayist and short-story writer: *Jia* (*Family*, 1931).

MAJOR INDIAN WRITERS

Kālidsa (?c. 4–5th centuries), Sanskrit poet and dramatist: *Meghadūla* and *Sakuntalā and the token of recognition*.

Jayadeva (12th century), poet: *Gitagovinda*.

Bankim Chandra Chatterjee (1838–94), nationalist writer: *Anandamath* (1882).

Rabindranath Tagore (1861–1941), poet, novelist, playwright and essayist: *Gitanjali* (1912).

R.K. Narayan (1906–), novelist writing in English: *The Financial Expert* (1952), *The Vendor of Sweets* (1967), and *Malgudi Days* (1982).

Raja Rao (1909–), novelist writing in English: *Kanthapura* and *The Serpent and the Rope*.

Bhabhani Bhattacharya (1906–), writer of social novels in English.

MAJOR JAPANESE WRITERS

Murasaki Shikibu (973–1014), novelist: *The Tale of Genji*.

Sei Shonagon (966/7–1013), prose writer: *The Pillow Book*.

Matsuo Basho (1644–94), haiku poet: *The Narrow Road to the Deep North* (1694).

Ihara Saikaku (1642–93), novelist: *The Life of an Amorous Man* (1682).

Ueda Akinari (1734–1809), novelist: *Tales of Rain and Moon* (1776).

Kawabata Yasunari (1899–1972), novelist.

Mishima Yukio (1925–70), novelist: *The Temple of the Golden Pavilion* (1956) and *The Sea of Fertility* (1965–70).

MEDIEVAL LITERATURE

Epic and *Romance* are loose terms used to describe the narrative literature of medieval Western Europe, most of which was in the form of long poems about mythical heroes. In epic and romance, national languages replaced the old universal literary language, Latin. This literature retains its vividness and immediacy and continues to spawn new creations in all the arts.

Perhaps the chief glory of medieval European literature lies in its stories, which were composed in poetry or prose for reciting, or in the form of plays for acting. They covered the known world, both its past and its present. Stories were the main source of popular and aristocratic entertainment and education. Since few people outside the Church and the nobility could read and write, the stories that have survived were written down and preserved within religious or noble communities. The most famous European collections of stories are Boccaccio's *Decameron* and Chaucer's *Canterbury Tales*. However, the chief subject of medieval literature was religion, alliterative religious poetry and mystery plays (based on the Christian story from the Creation to the Last Judgement) being among the most prominent genres. In the 15th century dramatized sermons called *moralities* first appeared, and throughout the medieval period *fables* (short tales or poems with a moral) were popular.

CANTERBURY TALES

The English poet Geoffrey Chaucer (?1343-1400) was one of the most outstanding contributors to Medieval literature. His *Canterbury Tales* – which drew on the *Decameron* – was an unfinished collection of 24 stories extending to 17 000 lines of verse and prose. In the *Canterbury Tales*, 30 pilgrims – representing the most diverse trades and social classes – gather at an inn in Southwark and agree to engage in a storytelling contest as they ride to the shrine of St Thomas Beckett in Canterbury. The tales they tell are preceded by a prologue presenting vivid and humorous character sketches of the pilgrims, and are linked together by vigorous exchanges between them.

The *Canterbury Tales* presents a highly varied collection of different types of story: courtly romance (in the classical *Knight's Tale*, a shortened version of Boccaccio's epic, the *Teseida*), allegorical tale, the devotional tale, beast tale and racy fabliau – a short verse tale usually in couplets with lines of eight syllables. Prologue, tales and 'links' combine to present a unified whole – a profound and satisfying portrayal of medieval England – from which Chaucer's genius for characterization and understanding of social relationships shines forth.

MEDIEVAL WRITERS

Geoffrey of Monmouth (d. 1155), Welsh chronicler: *History of the Kings of Britain* and *Vita Merlini*.

Wace (b. c. 1100), Anglo-Norman poet: *Roman de Brut* and *Roman de Rou*.

Chrétien de Troyes (active 1170–90), French poet: *Érec et Énide*, *Cligès* and *Perceval*.

Gottfried von Strassburg (active 1210), German poet: *Tristan and Isolde*.

Wolfram von Eschenbach (?1170–1220), German poet: *Parzival*.

Guillaume de Lorris (d. 1237), French poet: *Roman de la Rose* (the first 4058 lines of the poem).

Jean de Meun (?1250–?1305), French poet: *Roman de la Rose* (the last 17 722 lines; see Guillaume de Lorris).

Dante Alighieri (1265–1321), Italian poet: *Divine Comedy*.

Francesco Petrarch (1304–74), Italian sonnet writer.

Giovanni Boccaccio (1313–75), Italian poet and storyteller: *Decameron*, a collection of a hundred often earthy tales.

John Gower (?1330–1408), English poet: *Confessio Amantis* ('The Lover's Confession').

William Langland (c. 1330–c. 1386), English alliterative poet: *Piers Plowman*.

François Villon (b. 1431), French poet: *Le Lais* and *Le Testament*.

Geoffrey Chaucer (?1343–1400), English poet: *Canterbury Tales* (see box), and *Troilus and Criseyde*.

John Skelton (c. 1460–1529): English colloquial poet.

Sir Thomas Malory (d. 1471), English writer of Arthurian romance in prose: *Morte D'Arthur*.

RENAISSANCE LITERATURE

The Renaissance drama of the 16th century is a secular theatre of human activity rather than the religious drama of the Middle Ages. The stage no longer represents Heaven and Hell, but the world of history and the material present. In the 16th century a flowering of the professional theatre in England produced the plays of Marlowe, Kyd and Shakespeare. Their plays are largely dramatic reworkings of traditional stories. Ben Jonson, however, dealt with bourgeois characters in a contemporary English setting. The late 16th and early 17th centuries were also a 'golden age' for Spanish drama. Lope de Vega and Calderon achieved popularity through their prolific output of dramas. The English Jacobean theatre was dominated by revenge tragedies and court entertainments comprising expensive and elaborate masques.

Renaissance poetry, while less often celebrated than Renaissance painting, sculpture, architecture, or drama, flourished from the late 15th to the mid-17th century throughout Western Europe. The period saw a reawakening of interest in Classical learning that is reflected in the work of poets who showed a deep and imaginative interest in antiquity, its civilizations and especially its literature. Renaissance poetry is richly diverse in form and style and includes romantic epic, narrative verse and varieties of lyric (of which the most celebrated form was the sonnet).

MAJOR RENAISSANCE WRITERS

Lodovico Ariosto (1474–1533), Italian epic poet: *Orlando Furioso*.

Sir David Lindsay (c. 1486–1555), Scottish poet: *Ane Pleasant Satyre of the Thrie Estaitis*.

François Rabelais (c. 1494–c. 1553), French humanist and physician: *Gargantua and Pantagruel*, a comic prose satire.

Hans Sachs (1494–1576), German comic poet and dramatist.

Joachim Du Bellay (?1522–1560), French poet.

Pierre de Ronsard (?1524–1585), French poet: *Sonnets pour Hélène*.

Luis de Camoëns (1524–80), Portuguese poet: *The Lusiads* (1572), an epic of Portuguese exploration.

Guillaume du Bartas (1544–1590), French religious poet: *La Semaine*.

Torquato Tasso (1544–95), major Italian epic poet: *Aminta* (1573) and *Jerusalem Delivered* (1575).

Edmund Spenser (1552–99), English poet: *The Fairie Queene* (1590 and 1596), a moral allegory.

Sir Philip Sidney (1554–86), English pastoral poet: *Arcadia* (1590).

Thomas Kyd (1558–94), English dramatist: *The Spanish Tragedy* (1592), a revenge tragedy.

Felix Lope de Vega (1562–1635), prolific Spanish playwright and poet, who claimed to have written 1500 plays, of which only 500 survive.

William Shakespeare (see box).

Christopher Marlowe (1564–93), English dramatist and poet: *Tamburlaine the Great* (c. 1587), *Dr Faustus* (c. 1588), *The Jew of Malta* (1589), and *Edward II* (c. 1592).

John Donne (1572–1631), English metaphysical poet: *Divine Sonnets*.

Ben Jonson (1572–1637), English dramatist and poet: *Volpone* (1606), *The Alchemist* (1610) and *Bartholomew Fair* (1614).

John Webster (c. 1578–c. 1632), English tragic dramatist: *The White Devil* (1612) and *The Duchess of Malfi* (1613–14).

John Fletcher (1579–1625), English dramatist who wrote romantic tragi-comedies, in collaboration with Beaumont (see below).

Thomas Middleton (1580–1627), English tragic dramatist: *Women Beware Women* (1621) and *The Changeling* (1622; with William Rowley).

Francis Beaumont (1584–1616), English dramatist who wrote romantic tragi-comedies in collabor-

ation with Fletcher (see above).

John Ford (1586–?1639), English dramatist: *'Tis Pity She's a Whore*.

George Herbert (1593–1633), English metaphysical poet: *The Temple*.

John Davies (1596–1626), English poet: *Orchestra* (1596).

Pedro Calderon de la Barca (1600–81), Spanish dramatist: *El Alcalde de Zalamea*.

John Milton (1608–74), English poet: the Christian epics *Paradise Lost* (1667) and *Paradise Regained* (1677).

WILLIAM SHAKESPEARE

The dramatic achievement of William Shakespeare (1564–1616), the elder surviving child of a Stratford-upon-Avon alderman and trader, is without parallel in English literature. No other dramatist has had such success in so many different genres. His 37 plays – written between 1594 and 1611 – include comedies, history plays, tragedies and tragi-comedies.

In comedies such as *Twelfth Night* and *As You Like It*, Shakespeare excelled in a particular type of romantic festive drama depicting the maturing of a romantic hero with the help of an assertive and powerful woman. In his huge cycle of history plays, Shakespeare covers the period of English history from 1399 to 1485. In tragedy, Shakespeare began with melodrama but went on to produce such mature masterpieces as *Hamlet, King Lear* and *Macbeth*. Later in his career, as popular fashion veered towards romantic tragi-comedy, Shakespeare wrote some extraordinary and complex plays, notably *The Tempest* and *The Winter's Tale*, which re-examine, within a framework of romance, the conventions of comedy, history and tragedy.

Although some works were published individually, Shakespeare's plays were not collected together for publication during his lifetime. Thanks to the efforts of Shakespeare's fellow-actors John Heminges and Henry Condell, the majority of the plays appeared in collected form in the First Folio in 1623.

As well as being considered the greatest English dramatist, Shakespeare was also a notable poet – the *Sonnets* (1609), variously addressed to a fair young man and a dark lady, deal with the themes of time, death, love and art.

SHAKESPEARE'S PLAYS	Publication date
Titus Andronicus (early tragedy)	1594
Henry VI Part 2* (early history)	1594
The Taming of the Shrew (see also 1623, First Folio; early comedy)	1594
Henry VI Part 3* (early history)	1595
Romeo and Juliet (early tragedy)	1597
Richard II (history)	1597
Richard III (history)	1597
Henry VI Part 1 (early history)	1598
Love's Labour's Lost (early comedy; revised version; original (?1596) probably lost)	1598
Henry IV Part 2 (history)	1600
A Midsummer Night's Dream (comedy)	1600
The Merchant of Venice (comedy)	1600
Much Ado About Nothing (comedy)	1600
Henry V (history; first 'true' text published 1623 in First Folio) (history; first performed 1599)	1600
Sir John Falstaff and the Merry Wives of Windsor* (comedy; first 'true' text published in 1623 in First Folio) (*Hamlet**	1602 1603)
Hamlet (tragedy; 'according to the true and perfect copy')	1604
King Lear (tragedy)	1608
Pericles, Prince of Tyre (late tragi-comedy or 'romance')	1609
Troilus and Cressida (tragi-comedy)	1609

Posthumously Published

Othello (tragedy)	1622
First Folio – 36 plays in all, including the first publication of *The Taming of the Shrew* (Shakespeare's revised version of the 1594 version)	1623

Henry IV Part 1 (history)
The Two Gentlemen of Verona (early romantic comedy)
The Comedy of Errors (comedy)
King John (history)
As You Like It (comedy)
Julius Caesar (Roman play)
Twelfth Night (comedy)
Measure for Measure (tragi-comedy)
All's Well That Ends Well (tragi-comedy)
Macbeth (tragedy)
Timon of Athens (tragedy)
Antony and Cleopatra (Roman play)
Coriolanus (Roman play)
Cymbeline (late tragi-comedy or 'romance')
The Winter's Tale (late tragi-comedy or 'romance')
The Tempest (late tragi-comedy or 'romance')
Henry VIII (late tragi-comedy or 'romance')

*Bad quartos or unauthorized editions.

SHAKESPEARIAN ROLES

Hamlet is widely considered to be the greatest role in English drama. It is also the longest in the Shakespearian canon. In Shakespeare's plays the following characters present the greatest challenge to actors in terms of the number of lines to learn.

Hamlet (Hamlet)	1569
Richard III (Richard III)	1161
Iago (Othello)	1117
Othello (Othello)	888
Coriolanus (Coriolanus)	886
Timon (Timon of Athens)	863
Antony (Antony and Cleopatra)	820
Lear (King Lear)	770
Richard II (Richard II)	755
Brutus (Julius Caesar)	727
Macbeth (Macbeth)	705
Cleopatra (Antony and Cleopatra)	670
Prospero (The Tempest)	665
Romeo (Romeo and Juliet)	618
Petruchio (Taming of the Shrew)	585
Imogen (Cymbeline)	541

CLASSICISM IN LITERATURE

Knowledge of and interest in the works of ancient Greek and Roman authors was a key aspect of the Renaissance. After that explosive fusion of old and new ideas came a period when *Neoclassical* writers tried to imitate in modern languages what they thought was the spirit and style of the classics. *Neoclassicism* was especially strong in the French theatre during the 17th century and in England from the Restoration of 1660 to the end of the 18th century. In poetry, a taste for natural description and meditation became popular in the 18th century. Pastoral verse began with Pope and achieved perfection with Gray.

MAJOR NEOCLASSICAL WRITERS

Pierre Corneille (1606–84), French classical tragic dramatist: *Le Cid* (1637), *Horace* (1640), *Cinna* (1640), *Polyeucte* (1643) and *Le Menteur* (1643).

Molière (Jean-Baptiste Poquelin; 1622–73), French actor and classical comic dramatist of comedy: *Tartuffe* (1664), *Le Misanthrope* (1666), and *L'Avare* (1668; 'The Miser').

John Dryden (1631–1700), English satirical poet and tragic dramatist: *All for Love* (1677; a reworking of Shakespeare's *Antony and Cleopatra*) and *Absalom and Achitophel*, an allegorical poem.

Nicolas Boileau (1636–1711), French poet and critic: *L'Art Poétique*, a statement of classical aesthetics.

Jean Racine (1639–99), French classical tragic dramatist: *Andromaque* (1667), *Britannicus* (1669), *Bérénice* (1670), *Bajazet* (1672), *Mithridate* (1673) and *Phèdre* (1677).

William Wycherley (1641–1715), English comic dramatist: *The Country Wife* (1675), a Restoration comedy.

Sir John Vanbrugh (1664–1726), English comic dramatist: *The Relapse* (1696) and *The Provoked Wife* (1697), Restoration comedies.

William Congreve (1670–1729), English comic dramatist: *The Way of the World* (1700) and *Love for Love* (1695), Restoration comedies.

George Farquhar (1678–1707), English comic dramatist: *The Beaux' Stratagem* (1707).

Pierre Marivaux (1688–1763), French comic dramatist and novelist: *The Game of Love and Chance* (1730) and *The False Confidences* (1737).

Gotthold Ephraim Lessing (1728–81), German dramatist and critic: *Miss Sara Sampson* (1755), *Minna von Barnhelm* (1767) and *Nathan the Wise* (1779).

Alexander Pope (1688–1744), English satirical poet: *The Rape of the Lock* (1714), *The Dunciad* (1728–43), *Epistle to Arbuthnot* (1735) and *An Essay on Man* (1733–34).

Thomas Gray (1716–71), English poet: *Ode on a Distant Prospect of Eton College* and *Elegy Written in a Country Churchyard* (1751).

Oliver Goldsmith (?1730–74), Irish poet, dramatist and novelist: *The Deserted Village* (1771), a poem, *The Vicar of Wakefield* (1766), a novel, and *She Stoops to Conquer* (1773), a comedy.

Pierre-Augustin Caron de Beaumarchais (1732–99), French comic dramatist: *Le Barbier de Seville* (1775) and *The Marriage of Figaro* (1784).

Richard Sheridan (1751–1816), English dramatist; *The Rivals* (1775) and *School for Scandal* (1777).

THE BEGINNINGS OF THE NOVEL

One of the most dramatic shifts in literary fashion occurred in the early 18th century, when a relatively new form, the *novel* – an extended prose narrative treating in a realistic manner the story of fictional individuals within a recognizable social context – achieved popularity with a wide audience. The novel soon came to be seen as a vehicle for serious literary expression.

Up to the 16th century the dominant literary form had been verse. There had been earlier examples of prose fiction, notably the *Satyricon* of Petronius, and *The Golden Ass* of Apuleius. The Italian *novella* – a type of short story of a humorous nature (found in Boccaccio's *Decameron* – lent its name to the extended prose fictions of Defoe, Richardson and others. A number of important strands can be seen in the early novel. Some novels had a strong emphasis on *realism* – the representation of life as it is. The use of the *first person narrative* was often used to increase the realism. The *epistolary novel* written in the form of letters was also common. The *picaresque novel* – from the Spanish word *picaro*, meaning a wily rogue – enjoyed a vogue in the 17th century and is probably best represented by *Don Quixote*.

MAJOR EARLY NOVELISTS

Miguel de Cervantes (1547–1616), Spanish poet and prose writer: *Don Quixote* (1615), a parody of chivalric literature – regarded by many as the first true novel.

J.J.C. von Grimmelshausen (c. 1621–76), German novelist: *Simplicissimus* (1669), a picaresque novel set during the Thirty Years War.

Madame de la Fayette (Marie-Madeleine, Countess de la Fayette; 1634–93), French novelist: *The Princess of Cleves* (1678).

Daniel Defoe (1660–1731), English novelist: *Robinson Crusoe* (1719) and *Moll Flanders* (1722).

Jonathan Swift (1667–1745), Anglo-Irish satirist: *Gulliver's Travels* (1726), a satirical fantasy.

Pierre Marivaux (1688–1763), French dramatist and novelist (see also Neoclassical writers): *The Life of Marianne* (1731–41) and *The Fortunate Peasant* (1735).

Samuel Richardson (1689–1761), English novelist: *Pamela* (1740–41) and *Clarissa* (1747–48), epistolary novels.

Voltaire (François-Marie Arouet; 1694–1778), French philosopher, dramatist and prose-writer: *Candide* (1759), a philosophical tale.

Antoine-François Prévost (L'Abbé Prévost; 1697–1763), French novelist: *Manon Lescaut* (1731).

Henry Fielding (1707–54), English novelist and dramatist: *Joseph Andrews* (1742), *Shamela* (1741; a parody of Richardson's *Pamela*), *Jonathan Wild* and *Tom Jones* (1749).

Laurence Sterne (1713–68), Irish-born English novelist: *The Life and Opinions of Tristam Shandy* (1759–68).

Tobias Smollett (1721–71), Scottish novelist: *The Expedition of Humphry Clinker* (1741).

Bernardin de Saint Pierre (1737–1814), French novelist: *Paul and Virginie* (1787).

Choderlos de Laclos (1741–1803), French novelist: *Dangerous Liaisons* (1782).

ROMANTICISM

The word 'Romantic' was first used to describe a genre of literature around 1800 by the brothers *Schlegel, August Wilhelm* (1767–1845) and *Friedrich* (1772–1829). These German intellectuals idealized the era of classical antiquity, especially the culture of ancient Greece, and then contrasted it with the literature of the Christian era from the Middle Ages up to their own time. This second era they called modern – as distinct from ancient – and defined as Romantic.

Romanticism in British literature emerged, in the 1780s, in parallel with the revolutionary struggles of the French people. In a reaction against the rigidity of Classicism the Romantics believed in imagination, nature and the free expression of emotion. These traits are evident in the works of the English 'Lake poets' – Wordsworth, Coleridge and Southey.

Whereas in Europe Romanticism tended to seek a home in the novel and the drama, in Britain the movement was largely a poetic one; but it also manifested itself in certain types of prose. Among these were *Gothic novels*, tales of the macabre and the fantastic set in wild landscapes of rugged mountains, and ruined castles.

MAJOR ROMANTIC WRITERS

Horace Walpole (1717–97), English Gothic novelist: *The Castle of Otranto* (1765).

Johann Wolfgang von Goethe (1749–1832), German poet, dramatist, and novelist: the Romantic novella, *Die Leiden des jungen Werthers* (1774), the classical verse dramas *Iphigenia* (1787) and *Torquato Tasso* (1790) and his masterpiece *Faust* (1808).

William Blake (1757–1827), English poet: *Songs of Innocence* (1789) and *Songs of Experience* (1794).

Friedrich Schiller (1759–1805), German dramatist and poet: *The Robbers* (1781), the historical dramas *Wallenstein* (1798–9), and *Maria Stuart* (1800).

Robert Burns (1759–96), Scottish poet: notable for his use of the Scottish dialect: '*Tam o'Shanter*'.

Mrs Ann Radcliffe (1764–1823), English Gothic novelist: *The Mysteries of Udolpho* (1794).

François René de Chateaubriand (1768–1848), French novelist and prose-writer: *Le Génie du Christianisme* (1802), *Atala* (1801) and *René* (1805).

William Wordsworth (1770–1850), English poet: *Lyrical Ballads* (1798; a collection of poems written with Coleridge) and *The Prelude* (1798–1805).

Sir Walter Scott (1771–1832), Scottish novelist and poet: *Minstrelsy of the Scottish Border* (1802–3), a collection of ballads, *Ivanhoe* (1819), and *The Heart of Midlothian* (1818).

Samuel Taylor Coleridge (1772–1834), English poet: *Lyrical Ballads* (see Wordsworth), including *The Rime of the Ancient Mariner* and *Kubla Khan*.

Thomas De Quincey (1785–1859), English essayist: *Confessions of an English Opium Eater* (1821).

Lord Byron (George Gordon Byron; 1788–1824) English poet: *Childe Harold's Pilgrimage* (1812–18), and *Don Juan* (1819–24), a satirical epic.

Alphonse de Lamartine (1790–1869), French poet: *Méditations poétiques* (1820).

Percy Bysshe Shelley (1792–1822), English poet: *Queen Mab*, a poem, *The Cenci* and *Prometheus Unbound*, (1820), verse dramas, *Adonais* (1821), an elegy on the death of Keats, and *The Mask of Anarchy* (1832).

John Keats (1795–1821), English poet: *Odes* (*To a Nightingale*, *On a Grecian Urn*, *To Autumn*).

Heinrich Heine (1797–1856), German poet and essayist: *Reisebilder* (1826) and *Das Buch der Lieder* (1827).

Mary Wollstonecraft Shelley (1797–1851), English Gothic novelist: *Frankenstein* (1818).

Giacomo Leopardi (1798–1837), Italian lyric poet: *I Canti* (1816–36).

Alexander Pushkin (1799–1837), Russian poet and novelist: *Eugene Onegin* (1833), a verse novel.

Victor Hugo (1802–85), French poet, dramatist and novelist: the verse collections *Autumn Leaves* (1831) and *Les Contemplations* (1856), and the novels *The Hunchback of Nôtre Dame* (1831) and *Les Misérables* (1862).

Alexandre Dumas (1802–70), French novelist: *The Three Musketeers* (1844).

George Sand (Amandine Aurore Lucie Dupin; 1804–76), French novelist: *The Haunted Pool* (1841) and *Fanchon the Cricket* (1850).

Elizabeth Barrett Browning (1806–61), English poet: *Sonnets from the Portuguese* (1847) and *Aurora Leigh* (1857).

Alfred, Lord Tennyson (1809–92), English poet: the poems *The Lady of Shalott* (1832) and *The Lotus Eaters* (1833), the collections *In Memorium* (1850) and the *Idylls of the King* (1855).

Alfred de Musset (1810–57), French poet and dramatist: *Les Nuits* (1835–37), a collection of lyric poems, and *Lorenzaccio* (1834), a drama.

Robert Browning (1812–89), English poet: the poems *The Pied Piper of Hamelin* (1842) and *Home Thoughts from Abroad* (1845), the play *Pippa Passes* and *The Ring and the Book* (1868–69), a long poem in the form of a series of dramatic monologues.

Mikhail Lermontov (1814–41), Russian poet and novelist: the poems *The Angel* (1832) and *The Demon* (1841) and the novel *A Hero of Our Time* (1840).

LATER 19TH-CENTURY LITERATURE

The novel became the dominant literary form in 19th-century Britain. At its best it is both popular and literary. The world that most 19th-century British novelists were writing about was one characterized by increasing urbanization and industrialization – a world dominated by the owners of capital.

In the 19th century American literature took on a specifically national character in its treatment of certain themes and ideas. Uncontaminated by history or tradition, the New World presented exciting possibilities for the creative writer. The writing of a native literature was a key factor in this process. Torn apart by the Civil War there was an even deeper need for literature to unite the nation and re-establish a national consciousness.

REALISM

The term Realism is commonly used to describe works of art that appear to represent the world as it is, not as it might or should be. It can be applied to literature from almost any period but is especially associated with those 19th-century novelists and dramatists who claimed to be giving detailed, accurate and objective descriptions of life, in sharp contrast to what they saw as the idealizing of their 18th-century predecessors.

NATURALISM

Towards the end of the 19th century prose fiction assumed a new focus with the appearance of Naturalism, a specialized form of Realism based on the philosophical doctrines of materialism and determinism. For the novelist it amounts to a belief that everything in the world – including human behaviour – has observable physical causes; and that the individual is therefore shaped by society.

MAJOR REALIST AND NATURALIST WRITERS

Honoré de Balzac (1799–1850), French novelist: *La Comédie humaine*, a sequence of 94 novels, including *Old Goriot* (1835) and *Lost Illusions* (1837–43).

Stendhal (Marie Henri Beyle; 1783–1842), French novelist: *Scarlet and Black* (1830) and *The Charterhouse of Parma* (1839).

Nikolai Gogol (1809–52), Russian novelist and dramatist: *Dead Souls* (1842), a novel, and *The Government Inspector* (1836), a comic drama.

Georg Büchner (1813–37), German dramatist: *Danton's Death* (1835) and *Woyzeck* (1837).

Ivan Turgenev (1818–83), Russian novelist, short-story writer and dramatist: *A Month in the Country* (1850), a play, and *Fathers and Sons* (1861), a novel.

Gustave Flaubert (1821–80), French novelist: *Madame Bovary* (1857) and *Sentimental Education* (1869).

Fyodor Dostoevski (1821–81), Russian novelist: *Crime and Punishment* (1866) and *The Brothers Karamazov* (1880).

Henrik Ibsen (1828–1906), Norwegian dramatist: *Ghosts* (1881), *Hedda Gabler* (1890), and *The Master Builder* (1892).

Leo Tolstoy (1828–1910), Russian novelist: *War and Peace* (1869) and *Anna Karenina* (1877).

Émile Zola (1840–1902), French novelist: *The Dram Shop* (1877), *Nana* (1880), the novel cycle *The Rougon-Macquart*, including *Germinal* (1885) and *La Débâcle* (1892), and *J'accuse*, a letter criticizing the accusers of Dreyfus.

August Strindberg (1849–1912), Swedish dramatist: *Miss Julie* (1888) and *The Dance of Death* (1901).

Guy de Maupassant (1850–93), French novelist and short-story writer: *Boule de suif* (1881), a short story, and *Bel-Ami* (1885).

Anton Chekhov (1860–1904), Russian dramatist: *Uncle Vanya* (1899), *The Three Sisters* (1901), and *The Cherry Orchard* (1904).

Maxim Gorki (1868–1936), Russian novelist: *Mother* and an autobiographical trilogy (1913–23).

MAJOR 19TH-CENTURY BRITISH WRITERS

Jane Austen (1775–1817), novelist: *Sense and Sensibility* (1811), *Pride and Prejudice* (1813), *Mansfield Park* (1814), *Emma* (1815), and *Persuasion* (1818).

Benjamin Disraeli (1804–81), novelist and politician: the trilogy *Coningsby* (1844), *Sybil* (1845) and *Tancred* (1847).

Elizabeth Gaskel (1810–65), novelist: *Mary Barton* (1848), *Ruth* (1853), and *Cranford* (1853).

William Makepeace Thackeray (1811–63); novelist: *Vanity Fair* (1846–8) and *Pendennis* (1848–50).

Charles Dickens (1812–70), novelist: *Oliver Twist* (1838), *Nicholas Nickleby* (1839), *The Old Curiosity Shop* (1841), *Barnaby Rudge* (1841), *David Copperfield* (1850), *Bleak House* (1853), *Hard Times* (1854), *Little Dorrit* (1857), *A Tale of Two Cities* (1859), and *Great Expectations* (1861).

Anthony Trollope (1815–82), novelist: *Barsetshire Chronicles* (1857–67), a sequence of six novels, including *The Warden* and *Barchester Towers*.

Charlotte Brontë (1816–55), novelist: *Jane Eyre* (1847), *Shirley* (1849) and *Villette* (1853).

Emily Brontë (1818–48), novelist: *Wuthering Heights* (1847).

Charles Kingsley (1819–75), novelist: *Westward Ho!* (1855) and *The Water Babies* (1863), a children's story.

George Eliot (Mary Ann Evans; 1819–80), novelist: *Adam Bede* (1859), *The Mill on the Floss* (1860), *Silas Marner* (1861) and *Middlemarch* (1871–2).

Anne Brontë (1820–49), novelist: *The Tenant of Wildfell Hall* (1847).

Matthew Arnold (1822–88), English poet, essayist and critic: *The Forsaken Merman*, *Thyrsis*, *Dover Beach*, and *Essays in Criticism*.

William Wilkie Collins (1824–89), novelist: the mystery novels *The Woman in White* (1860) and *The Moonstone* (1868).

William Morris (1834–96), novelist, poet, and artist: *News from Nowhere* (1891).

Thomas Hardy (1840–1928), novelist and poet: *Far from the Madding Crowd* (1874), *The Return of the Native* (1878), *The Mayor of Casterbridge* (1886), *The Woodlanders* (1887), *Tess of the D'Urbervilles* (1891), and *Jude the Obscure* (1895) – all set in Dorset (part of Hardy's fictional 'Wessex').

Robert Louis Stevenson (1850–94), Scottish novelist: *Treasure Island* (1883) and *The Strange Case of Dr Jekyll and Mr Hyde* (1886).

Oscar Wilde (Fingal O'Flahertie Wills; 1854–1900), Irish dramatist, poet and novelist, famous for his witty epigrams: *The Picture of Dorian Gray* (1891), a novel, *The Importance of Being Earnest* (1895), a play, and *Ballad of Reading Goal* (1898), a poem.

George Bernard Shaw (1856–1950), Irish dramatist and critic. *Pygmalion* (1913) and *Saint Joan* (1923).

Joseph Conrad (Teodor Jozef Konrad Korzeniowski; 1857–1924), Polish-born English writer. *Lord Jim* (1900), *Heart of Darkness* (1902), *Nostromo* (1904), and *The Secret Agent* (1907).

Sir Arthur Conan Doyle (1859–1930), detective novelist: *The Memoirs of Sherlock Holmes* (1894) and *The Hound of the Baskervilles* (1902).

Rudyard Kipling (1865–1936), novelist, poet and short-story writer: *Plain Tales from the Hills* (1888), *Kim* (1902), and the children's stories *Jungle Book* (1894), and *Just So Stories* (1902).

H(erbert) G(eorge) Wells (1866–1946), novelist: the science-fiction stories *The Time Machine* (1895) and *War of the Worlds* (1898), *The Invisible Man* (1897), and the humorous novel *Kipps* (1904).

Arnold Bennett (1867–1931), novelist and critic: the trilogy *Clayhanger, Hilda Lessways*, and *These Twain* (1910–15).

J(ohn) M(illington) Synge (1871–1909), Irish dramatist: *Playboy of the Western World* (1907).

MAJOR 19TH-CENTURY AMERICAN WRITERS

Washington Irving (1783–1859), essayist and short-story writer: *Sketch Book of Geoffrey Crayon* (1820), including the stories *Rip Van Winkle* and *The Legend of the Sleepy Hollow*.

James Fenimore Cooper (1789–1851), novelist: *The Spy* (1821), *The Last of the Mohicans* (1826), and *The Pathfinder* (1840).

Ralph Waldo Emerson (1803–82), poet and essayist.

Nathaniel Hawthorne (1804–64), novelist and short-story writer: *The Scarlet Letter* (1850), *The Blithedale Romance* (1852) and *The Marble Faun* (1860).

Edgar Allan Poe (1809–49), poet, critic and short-story writer: *Tales of the Grotesque and Arabesque* (1840), including the macabre tale *The Fall of the House of Usher*.

Henry David Thoreau (1817–62), writer and essayist: *A Life in the Woods* (1854) and the influential essay *Civil Disobedience* (1849).

Herman Melville (1819–91), short-story writer and novelist: *Moby-Dick* (1851) and *Billy Budd* (1924).

Emily Dickinson (1830–86), poet.

Mark Twain (Samuel Langhorne Clemens; 1835–1910), novelist and short-story writer: *The Adventures of Tom Sawyer* (1876), *Life on the Mississippi* (1883), and *The Adventures of Huckleberry Finn* (1884).

Henry James (1843–1916), novelist: *The Wings of the Dove* (1902), *The Ambassadors* (1903), and *The Golden Bowl* (1904).

MODERN LITERATURE

The literary movements of the late 19th- and early 20th century – Symbolism, Aestheticism and Modernism – shared a belief in the absolute value of art, reinforced by various forms of contempt for the everyday world, and especially for people who served its interests. There resulted a rift between writers and the public at large, who were seen as 'bourgeois' in a disparaging sense. Artists lived for their art alone, sometimes flaunting their difference from the rest of society by affected or deliberately shocking behaviour.

Towards the end of the 19th century and in the early years of the 20th, the great Realist consensus on the modern novel began to exhibit signs of strain, and finally broke up altogether. This development did not, of course, happen overnight, though there are signs of its origin in the later writings of Hardy, Conrad, James, Dostoevski, and even in those of the Realist novelist *par excellence*, Tolstoy himself.

Modern drama in Britain and America is distinctive for its concern with issues. These may, amongst other things, relate to politics, morality, racism, and/or religion. Equally, the main concerns of modern theatre may be to do with theatre itself – how it works; what it means; the nature of its conventions, and the kind of language it uses. The ideas explored in modern drama may be those specifically associated with Modernism. Foremost among these are the workings of time and memory; the problems surrounding communication, and a sense that life is meaningless. European theatre of the 20th century witnessed enormous expansion in experiment and innovation. Radical developments fundamentally challenged the basic relationship between performers and spectators established in the 19th century. Movements such as German Expressionism, Epic Theatre, the Theatre of Cruelty and the Theatre of the Absurd were designed to break away from the dominant theatrical convention of Naturalism.

Modern poetry includes both 'difficult' poetry and poetry that is more directly accessible to the reader. The difficult poetry is obscure and highly allusive in the Modernist manner exemplified by T.S. Eliot's *The Waste Land* and Ezra Pound's *Cantos*. The more accessible poetry – though not necessarily easy to understand – belongs to a tradition which does not break so abruptly with previous poetry.

MAJOR MODERN WRITERS

Luigi Pirandello (1867–1936), Italian dramatist: *Six Characters in Search of an Author* (1921).

André Gide (1869–1951), French novelist: *The Immoralist* (1902), *Strait is the Gate* (1909), and *The Vatican Cellars* (1914).

Marcel Proust (1871–1922), French novelist: *Remembrance of Things Past* (1913–27).

W. Somerset Maugham (1874–1965), English novelist and short-story writer: *Of Human Bondage* (1915), *The Moon and Sixpence* (1919), *Cakes and Ale* (1930) and the play *The Circle* (1921).

Thomas Mann (1875–1955), German novelist: *Death in Venice* (1912), a short story, and the novels *Buddenbrooks* (1900), *The Magic Mountain* (1924), and *Doctor Faustus* (1947).

Herman Hesse (1877–1962), German novelist (from 1923 a Swiss citizen): *Siddhartha* (1922) and *Steppenwolf* (1927).

E(dward) M(organ) Forster (1879–1970), English novelist: *A Room with a View* (1908), *Howard's End* (1910) and *A Passage to India* (1924).

P(elham) G(renville) Wodehouse (1881–1975), English comic novelist: the *Psmith* and *Jeeves* novels.

James Joyce (1882–1941), Irish writer: *Dubliners* (1914), a collection of short stories, and the novels

Portrait of the Artist as a Young Man (1914–15), *Ulysses* (1922), and *Finnegan's Wake* (1939).

Virginia Woolf (1882–1941), English novelist: *Mrs Dalloway* (1925) and *To the Lighthouse* (1927).

Franz Kafka (1883–1924), Czech novelist writing in German: *The Trial* (1925) and *The Castle* (1926).

D(avid) H(erbert) Lawrence (1885–1930), English novelist, short-story writer and poet: *Sons and Lovers* (1913), *The Rainbow* (1915), *Women in Love*, and *Lady Chatterley's Lover* (1928).

Eugene O'Neill (1888–1953): American dramatist: *The Iceman Cometh* (1946) and *A Long Day's Journey Into Night* (1956).

Jean Cocteau (1889–1963): French poet, novelist and dramatist: *Les Enfants terribles* (1929) and the play *La Machine Infernale* (1934).

Boris Pasternak (1890–1960), Russian novelist: *Dr Zhivago* (1957).

Aldous Huxley (1894–1963), English novelist: *Brave New World* (1932).

J(ohn) B(oynton) Priestley (1894–1984), English novelist and dramatist: the novel *The Good Companions* (1929) and the play *Laburnum Grove*.

Robert Graves (1895–1985), English poet and novelist: *Goodbye to all that* (1929), his World War I autobiography, and *I, Claudius* (1934), a historical novel.

F. Scott Fitzgerald (1896–1940), American novelist: *The Beautiful and Damned* (1922), *The Great Gatsby* (1925), and *Tender is the Night* (1934).

William Faulkner (1897–1962), American novelist: *The Sound and the Fury* (1929).

Bertolt Brecht (1898–1956), German dramatist: *The Threepenny Opera* (1928), a musical drama, and the plays *Mother Courage* (1941), *The Good Woman of Setzuan* and *The Caucasian Chalk Circle*.

Ernest Hemingway (1899–1961), American novelist: *A Farewell to Arms* (1929) and *For Whom the Bell Tolls* (1940).

Noel Coward (1899–1973), English comic dramatist: *Private Lives* (1930) and *Blithe Spirit* (1941).

Vladimir Nabokov (1899–1977), Russian-born American writer: *Lolita* (1958) and *Pale Fire* (1962).

Jorge Luis Borges (1899–1986), Argentinian poet and short-story writer: *Fictions* (1944).

John Steinbeck (1902–68), American novelist: *Of Mice and Men* (1937) and *Grapes of Wrath* (1939).

Evelyn Waugh (1903–66), English novelist: *Decline and Fall* (1928), *A Handful of Dust* (1934), and *Brideshead Revisited* (1945).

George Orwell (1903–50), English novelist and essayist: *Animal Farm* (1945), a political allegory, and *Nineteen Eighty-Four* (1949), a nightmarish fable of the future.

Christopher Isherwood (1904–86), English novelist and dramatist: *Mr Norris Changes Trains* (1935) and *Goodbye to Berlin* (1939).

Graham Greene (1904–91), English novelist: *Brighton Rock* (1938), *The Power and the Glory* (1940), *The Heart of the Matter* (1948), *Our Man in Havana* (1958) and *The Honorary Consul* (1973).

Jean-Paul Sartre (1905–80), French philosopher, dramatist and novelist: the novel *Nausea* (1937), the philosophical essay *Being and Nothingness* (1943), and the trilogy *Les Chemins de la liberté* (1945–49).

Mikhail Sholokhov (1905–84), Soviet novelist: *And Quiet Flows the Don* (1934).

Samuel Beckett (1906–89), Irish dramatist and novelist: the plays *Waiting for Godot* (1952), *Endgame* (1957) and *Happy Days* (1961), and the novel *Malone Dies* (1951).

Alberto Moravia (Alberto Pincherle; 1907–90), Italian novelist: *The Time of Indifference* (1929) and *The Conformist* (1952).

Christopher Fry (1907–), English dramatist: *The Lady's Not for Burning* (1948), a verse drama.

Tennessee Williams (1911–83), American dramatist: *The Glass Menagerie* (1944), *A Street Car Named Desire* (1947), and *Cat On A Hot Tin Roof* (1955).

William Golding (1911–), English novelist: *Lord of the Flies* (1954), *Pincher Martin* (1956), and *The Spire* (1964).

Eugène Ionesco (1912–), Romanian-born French dramatist: the absurd dramas *The Bald Prima Donna* and *The Rhinoceros*.

Patrick White (1912–1990), Australian novelist: *The Tree of Man* (1955), *Voss* (1957) and *Riders in the Chariot*.

Albert Camus (1913–60), French novelist, dramatist and essayist: the novels *The Outsider* (1942) and *The Plague* (1947), and the essay *The Myth of Sisyphus*.

Arthur Miller (1915–), American dramatist: *Death of a Salesman* (1949) and *The Crucible* (1952).

Saul Bellow (1915–); American novelist: *Henderson the Rain King* (1959) and *Herzog* (1964).

Anthony Burgess (1917–), English novelist and critic: *Clockwork Orange* (1962) and *Earthly Powers* (1980).

Alexander Solzhenitsyn (1918–), Russian novelist: *One Day in the Life of Ivan Denisovitch* (1962), *First Circle* (1964), and *Cancer Ward* (1966).

Doris Lessing (1919–), English novelist: *The Golden Notebook* (1962) and *The Good Terrorist* (1985).

Iris Murdoch (1919–), English novelist: *The Bell* (1958), *A World Child* (1975) and *The Sea, The Sea* (1978).

Alain Robbe-Grillet (1922–), French novelist: *The Voyeur* (1955) and *Jealousy* (1957).

Norman Mailer (1923–), American novelist: *The Naked and the Dead* (1948).

James Baldwin (1924–87), American novelist: *Go Tell It On the Mountain* (1954).

John Fowles (1926–), English novelist: *The Magus* (1966) and *The French Lieutenant's Woman* (1969).

Günter Grass (1927–), German novelist: *The Tin Drum* (1959) and *Dog Years* (1965).

Edward Albee (1928–), American dramatist: *Who's Afraid of Virginia Woolf?* (1962).

Gabriel Garcia Marquez (1928–), Colombian novelist: *One Hundred Years of Solitude* (1967).

John Osborne (1929–), English dramatist: *Look Back in Anger* (1956).

Harold Pinter (1930–), English playwright: *The Birthday Party* (1958) and *The Caretaker* (1960).

John Updike (1932–), American novelist: *Rabbit, Run* and *Couples*.

Joe Orton (1934–67), English dramatist: *Loot* (1965) and *What the Butler Saw* (1969).

Thomas Pynchon (1937–), American novelist: *V*

(1963) and *Gravity's Rainbow* (1973).

Tom Stoppard (1937–), English dramatist: *Rosencrantz and Guildenstern are Dead* (1966) and *The Real Inspector Hound* (1968).

Alan Ayckbourn (1939–), English playwright: *Relatively Speaking* (1967) and *The Norman Conquests* (1974).

Salman Rushdie (1947–), Indian-born British novelist: *Midnight's Children* (1981) and *Satanic Verses* (1988).

MAJOR MODERN POETS

Charles Baudelaire (1821–67), French poet: *Les fleurs du mal* (1857; The Flowers of Evil).

Stéphane Mallarmé (1842–98), French poet: *L'après-midi d'un faune* (1876; The Afternoon of a Faun) and *Vers et Prose*.

Gerard Manley Hopkins (1844–89), English poet: the poems *Pied Beauty* and *The Windhover* (1918).

W(illiam) B(utler) Yeats (1865–1939), Irish poet and dramatist: the poems *Sailing to Byzantium*, *Among School Children*, and *Lapis Lazuli*.

Walter De La Mare (1873–1956), English poet noted for his children's verse: the collection *The Listeners and Other Poems* (1912).

Robert Frost (1874–1963), American poet: *North of Boston* (1914) and *New Hampshire* (1923).

Rainer Maria Rilke (1875–1926), Austrian poet: *Duino Elegies* (1922) and *Sonnets to Orpheus* (1923).

Edward Thomas (1878–1917), English poet: *Collected Poems*, including the poem *Adlestrop*.

Wallace Stevens (1879–1955), American poet: *Harmonium* (1923) and *The Man with the Blue Guitar* (1937).

Ezra Pound (1885–1972), American poet: *Cantos* (1925–69).

Siegfried Sassoon (1886–1967), English war poet.

Rupert Brooke (1887–1915), English war poet: the sonnet *The Soldier* (1915).

Edith Sitwell (1887–1965), English poet: *Façade* (1922).

T(homas) S(tearns) Eliot (1888–1965), English poet, dramatist and critic: *The Waste Land* (1922), *Four Quartets* (1943), and the plays *Murder in the Cathedral* (1935) and *The Cocktail Party* (1950).

Isaac Rosenberg (1890–1918), English war poet: the poem *Dead Man's Dump*.

Hugh MacDiarmid (1892–1978), Scottish poet: *A Drunk Man Looks at the Thistle* (1926).

Wilfred Owen (1893–1918), English war poet: the poems *Anthem for Doomed Youth* and *Strange Meeting*.

John Betjeman (1906–84), English poet: *Collected Poems* (1968).

W(ystan) H(ugh) Auden (1907–73), Anglo-American poet, dramatist and critic: *On the Frontier* (1938), *New Year Letter* (1941), *The Age of Anxiety* (1948), *Nones* (1951), and *About the House* (1965).

Louis MacNeice (1907–63), Irish poet: *Blind Fireworks* (1929) and *Autumn Journal* (1939).

Dylan Thomas (1914–53), Welsh poet: *Deaths and Entrances* (1946), and the play for voices *Under Milk Wood* (1954).

Robert Lowell (1917–77), American poet: *Lord Weary's Castle* (1946) and *For the Union Dead* (1964).

Philip Larkin (1922–85), English poet: *The North Ship* (1945), *The Less Deceived* (1955) and *The Whitsun Weddings* (1964).

Ted Hughes (1930–), English poet: *The Hawk in the Rain* (1975) and *Crow* (1970).

Sylvia Plath (1932–63), American poet: the verse collections *The Colossus* (1960) and *Ariel* (1965), and the novel *The Bell Jar* (1971).

Seamus Heaney (1939–), Irish poet: *North* (1975), *Field Work* (1979), and *Station Island* (1984).

POPULAR MODERN WRITERS

John Buchan (1875–1940), English adventure novelist: *The Thirty-Nine Steps*.

Raymond Chandler (1888–1969), American detective novelist: *The Big Step* (1939) and *The Long Goodbye* (1953).

Agatha Christie (1890–1976), English detective novelist, the creator of the detectives Hercule Poirot and Miss Marple.

J(ohn) R(onald) R(euel) Tolkien (1892–1973), English novelist: *The Hobbit* and *The Lord of the Rings*.

Dorothy L. Sayers (1893–1957), English detective novelist: *The Nine Tailors* (1934) and *Gaudy Night* (1935).

Dashiell Hammett (1894–1961), American detective novelist: *The Maltese Falcon* (1930).

Dennis Wheatley (1897–1977), English horror novelist.

Barbara Cartland (1901–), English writer of romantic fiction.

Georgette Heyer (1902–74), English writer of historical romance.

Georges Simenon (1903–89), Belgian detective novelist, creator of the detective Maigret.

Catherine Cookson (1906–), English writer of romantic fiction.

Victoria Holt (1906–), English writer of historical romances.

Ian Fleming (1908–64), English suspense novelist, creator of James Bond: *Casino Royale* (1953) and *Diamonds are Forever* (1956).

Harold Robbins (1912–), American novelist: *The Carpetbaggers* (1961).

Arthur C. Clarke (1917–), English science fiction novelist: *2001: A Space Odyssey*.

Isaac Asimov (1920–92), American science fiction novelist: *I, Robot* (1950).

Alistair Maclean (1922–87), Scottish adventure novelist: *HMS Ulysses* (1955), *The Guns of Navarone* (1957) and *Where Eagles Dare* (1967).

John Le Carré (1931–), English spy novelist: *The Spy Who Came in from the Cold* (1963) and *Tinker, Tailor, Soldier, Spy* (1974).

Barbara Bradford Taylor (1933–), English novelist: *A Woman of Substance* and *Hold the Dream*.

Frederick Forsyth (1938–), English adventure novelist: *The Day of the Jackal* (1971) and *The Fourth Protocol* (1984).

Stephen King (1946–), American horror novelist: *Carrie* and *Salem's Lot*.

POPULAR CHILDREN'S WRITERS

Johann Rudolph Wyss (1782–1830), Swiss novelist: *Swiss Family Robinson* (1827).

Jakob Grimm (1785–1863), German philologist and, with his brother Wilhelm (see below), collector of German folktales.

Wilhelm Grimm (1786–1859), German philologist and collector of folktales (see Jakob Grimm).

Captain Marryat (Frederick Marryat; 1792–1848), English novelist and children's story writer: *The Children of the New Forest* (1847).

Hans Christian Andersen (1805–75), Danish novelist, dramatist and fairy tale writer: *The Ugly Duckling, The Snow Queen* and *The Little Mermaid*.

Edward Lear (1812–88), English artist, poet and writer of children's verse: *The Book of Nonsense* (1846).

Charles Kingsley (1819–75), English novelist (see also Major 19th-century British Writers): *The Water Babies* (1863).

Thomas Hughes (1822–96), English politician, novelist and children's story writer: *Tom Brown's Schooldays* (1857).

C. Collodi (Carlo Lorenzini; 1826–90), Italian novelist, journalist and writer of children's stories: *Pinocchio* (1880).

Louisa May Alcott (1832–88), American novelist: *Little Women* (1868).

Lewis Carroll (Charles Lutwidge Dodgson; 1832–98), English mathematician and children's story writer: *Alice's Adventures in Wonderland* (1865) and *Through the Looking-Glass* (1872).

Frances Hodgson Burnett (1849–1924), Anglo-American children's story writer: *Little Lord Fauntleroy* (1885) and *The Secret Garden* (1911).

Robert Louis Stevenson (1850–94), Scottish novelist (see also Major 19th-century British Writers): *Treasure Island* (1883).

L. Frank Baum (1856–1919), American novelist and children's story writer: *The Wonderful Wizard of Oz* (1900).

Selma Lagerlöf (1858–1940), Swedish novelist (see also Nobel Prizewinners in Literature): *The Wonderful Adventures of Nils* (1907).

E(dith) Nesbit (1858–1924), English children's story writer: *The Railway Children* (1906).

Kenneth Grahame (1859–1932), Scottish children's story writer: *The Wind in the Willows* (1908).

James Barrie (1860–1937), Scottish novelist, dramatist and children's story writer: *Peter Pan* (1904).

Rudyard Kipling (1865–1936), English novelist, poet and short-story writer (see also Major 19th-century British Writers): *Jungle Book* (1894) and *Just So Stories* (1902).

Beatrix Potter (1866–1943), English illustrator and children's story writer: *The Tale of Peter Rabbit* (1900).

Hilaire Belloc (1870–1955), French-born English poet, essayist, historian and writer of verse for children: *The Bad Child's Book of Beasts* (1896) and *Cautionary Tales* (1907).

Walter De La Mare (1873–1956), English poet (see also Major Modern Poets): *Songs for Childhood* (1902).

A(lan) A(lexander) Milne (1882–1956), English novelist, dramatist and children's story writer: *Winnie-the-Pooh* (1926) and *The House at Pooh Corner* (1928).

Arthur Ransome (1884–1967), English journalist and children's story writer: *Swallows and Amazons* (1931).

Enid Blyton (1892–1968), English children's story writer, the creator of Noddy.

J(ohn) R(onald) R(euel) Tolkien (1892–1973), English novelist (see also Popular Modern Writers): *The Hobbit* (1937).

C(live) S(taples) Lewis (1898–1963), English scholar, science fiction novelist and children's story writer: *The Lion, the Witch and the Wardrobe* (1950) and *The Last Battle* (1956).

Erich Kästner (1899–1974), German novelist, poet and children's story writer: *Emil and the Detectives* (1929).

Antoine de Saint-Exupéry (1900–44), French aviator, novelist and children's story writer: *Le Petit Prince* (1943).

(Georges Rémi) Hergé (1907–83), Belgian illustrator and children's story writer, the creator of Tintin.

Roald Dahl (1916–91), English novelist and children's story writer: *Charlie and the Chocolate Factory* (1964).

Rosemary Sutcliff (1920–92), English novelist and writer of historical novels for children: *Warrior Scarlet* (1958).

René Goscinny (1926–77), French writer of children's stories, the creator of Asterix.

Raymond Briggs (1934–), English illustrator and writer of children's stories: *The Snowman* (1978).

POETS LAUREATE

The title of poet laureate has been bestowed upon a contemporary poet by the British monarch since the reign of Charles II. The laureate writes commemorative verses to celebrate major public occasions.

John Dryden (1631–1700; laureate 1668–88)

Thomas Shadwell (1642?–92; laureate 1688–92)

Nahum Tate (1652–1715; laureate 1692–1715)

Nicholas Rowe (1674–1718); laureate 1715–18)

Laurence Eusden (1688–1730; laureate 1718–30)

Colley Cibber (1671–1757; laureate 1730–57)

William Whitehead (1715–85; laureate 1757–85; appointed after Thomas Gray declined the offer)

Thomas Warton (1728–90; laureate 1785–90)

Henry James Pye (1745–1813; laureate 1790–1813)

Robert Southey (1774–1843; laureate 1813–43)

William Wordsworth (1770–1850; laureate 1843–50)

Alfred, Lord Tennyson (1809–92; laureate 1850–92; appointed after Samuel Rogers declined the offer)

Alfred Austin (1835–1913; laureate 1896–1913)

Robert Bridges (1844–1930; laureate 1913–30)

John Masefield (1878–1967; laureate 1930–67)

Cecil Day-Lewis (1904–72; laureate 1968–72)

Sir John Betjeman (1906–84; laureate 1972–84)

Ted Hughes (b. 1930; laureate 1984–)

NOBEL PRIZEWINNERS IN LITERATURE

ORIGIN OF THE NOBEL PRIZES

The five original Nobel Prizes are awarded for outstanding achievement in the fields of physics, chemistry, medicine, literature and peace. The prizes were established by the chemist and inventor of dynamite, Alfred Nobel (1833–96). Concerned about the destructive uses of dynamite, he left a fortune in trust for the foundation and administration of the prizes which he hoped would encourage international co-operation and world peace. A sixth Nobel prize, the Nobel Memorial Prize in Economic Science, was introduced in 1968 by the Swedish national bank (see relevant chapters for other Nobel prizewinners).

The literature prize was first given in 1901 and is judged by the Swedish Academy.

1901　Sully-Prudhomme, French poet, noted for his later philosophical poetry.
1902　Theodor Mommsen, German historian: *History of Rome* (1854–56, 1885).
1903　Bjornstjerne Bjornsen, Norwegian novelist, poet and dramatist: helped revive Norwegian as a literary language.
1904　Frédéric Mistral, French poet: promoted Provençal as a literary language.
　　　Juan Echegaray, Spanish dramatist: *The World and his Wife* (1881)
1905　Henryk Sienkiewicz, Polish novelist: *Quo Vadis?* (1895).
1906　Giosue Carducci, Italian Classical poet.
1907　Rudyard Kipling, British novelist and poet (see later 19th-century literature).
1908　Rudolf Eucken, German Idealist philosopher.
1909　Selma Lagerlöf, Swedish novelist: well-known for novels based on legends and sagas (see Popular Children's writers).
1910　Paul von Heyse, German poet, novelist and dramatist.
1911　Maurice Maeterlinck, Belgian Symbolist poet and dramatist: *Pelléas et Mélisande* (1892) and *The Blue Bird* (1908)
1912　Gerhart Hauptmann, German dramatist, novelist and poet: introduced Naturalism to German theatre.
1913　R. Tagore, Indian playwright and poet (see Indian literature).
1914　No award
1915　Romain Rolland, French novelist and biographer: the 10-volume *Jean-Christophe* (1904–12).
1916　Verner von Heidenstam, Swedish lyric poet.
1917　Karl Gjellerup, Danish novelist
　　　Henrik Pontoppidan, Danish novelist: *Lucky Peter* (1898–1904).
1918　No award
1919　Carl Spitteler, Swiss poet and novelist: *The Olympic Spring* (1900–05).
1920　Knut Hamsun, Norwegian novelist: *Pan* (1894) and *The Growth of the Soil* (1917).
1921　Anatole France, French novelist; his work is noted for its elegance and scepticism.
1922　Jacinto Benavente y Martinez, Spanish dramatist of social satires.
1923　William Butler Yeats, Irish poet (see Modern poets).
1924　Wladyslaw Stanislaw Reymont, Polish novelist: *The Promised Land* (1895)

and *The Peasants* (1904–05).
1925　George Bernard Shaw, Irish dramatist (see Modern writers).
1926　Grazia Deledda, Italian Naturalist novelist.
1927　Henri Bergson, French dualist philosopher.
1928　Sigrid Undset, Norwegian novelist; her novels are about women and religion.
1929　Thomas Mann, German novelist (see Modern writers).
1930　Sinclair Lewis, American satirical novelist: *Babbitt* (1922).
1931　Erik Axel Karlfeldt, Swedish lyric poet; wrote about love, nature and peasant life.
1932　John Galsworthy, British novelist and dramatist: *The Forsyte Saga* (1906–28).
1933　Ivan Bunin, Russian émigré novelist, best known for his short stories.
1934　Luigi Pirandello, Italian dramatist (see Modern writers).
1935　No award
1936　Eugene O'Neill, American dramatist (see Modern writers).
1937　Roger Martin du Gard, French novelist: the *Les Thibaults* (1922–40).
1938　Pearl Buck, American novelist; famous for her novels about China.
1939　Frans Eemil Sillanpää, Finnish novelist: *Meek Heritage* (1919) and *People of the Summer Night* (1934).
1940–43　No award
1944　Johannes V. Jensen, Danish writer of essays and travel books.
1945　Gabriela Mistral, Chilean lyric poet.
1946　Hermann Hesse, German-born Swiss novelist (see Modern writers).
1947　André Gide, French novelist and essayist (see Modern writers).
1948　T.S. Eliot, American-born English poet (see Modern poets).
1949　William Faulkner, American novelist (see Modern writers).
1950　Bertrand Russell, British philosopher and mathematician: *A History of Western Philosophy* (1945).
1951　Pär Lagerkvist, Swedish novelist whose work was concerned with good and evil and man's search for God.
1952　François Mauriac, French poet, novelist and dramatist, well known for his Catholic novels.
1953　Sir Winston Churchill, British statesman, historian and orator.
1954　Ernest Hemingway, American novelist (see Modern writers).
1955　Halldór Laxness, Icelandic novelist who wrote about Icelandic life in the style of the sagas.
1956　Juan Ramón Jiménez, Spanish lyric poet.
1957　Albert Camus, French novelist and dramatist (see Modern writers).
1958　Boris Pasternak, Russian novelist and poet; declined award (see Modern writers).
1959　Salvatore Quasimodo, Italian poet.
1960　Saint-John Perse, French lyric poet.
1961　Ivo Andrić, Yugoslav novelist; best known for his Bosnian historical trilogy.
1962　John Steinbeck, American novelist (see Modern writers).
1963　George Seferis, Greek poet and essayist; introduced Symbolism to Greek literature.
1964　Jean-Paul Sartre, French philosopher-writer; declined award (see Modern writers).

1965 Mikhail Sholokhov, Russian novelist (see Modern writers).
1966 Shmuel Yosef Agnon, Israeli novelist, considered the leading writer in Hebrew. Nelly Sachs, German-born Swedish Jewish poet; her works concentrate on the persecution of Jews.
1967 Miguel Angel Asturias, Guatemalan novelist and poet, his work ranges from Guatemalan legends to international politics.
1968 Kawabata Yasunari, Japanese novelist (see Japanese writers).
1969 Samuel Beckett, Irish novelist, dramatist (see Modern writers).
1970 Aleksandr Solzhenitsyn, Russian novelist (see Modern writers).
1971 Pablo Neruda, Chilean poet who champions the cause of the working class.
1972 Heinrich Böll, German novelist, critical of Germany's political past.
1973 Patrick White, Australian novelist (see Modern writers).
1974 Eyvind Johnson, Swedish novelist, well known for his 4 autobiographical novels. Harry Martinson, Swedish novelist and poet: the poem *Aniara* (1956) and the novel *The Road* (1948).
1975 Eugenio Montale, Italian poet, well known for his complexity and pessimism.
1976 Saul Bellow, American novelist (see Modern writers).
1977 Vicente Aleixandre, Spanish lyric poet, whose work sympathized with the Republican cause.
1978 Isaac Bashevis Singer, American author who wrote in Yiddish: described Jewish life in Poland.
1979 Odysseus Elytis, Greek poet: distinguished by his joyful and sensuous poetry.
1980 Czeslaw Milosz, Polish-American poet and novelist: *The Captive Mind* (1953).
1981 Elias Canetti, Bulgarian-born German writer: *Auto da fé* (1935) and *Crowds and Power* (1960).
1982 Gabriel García Márquez, Colombian novelist (see Modern writers).
1983 William Golding, British novelist (see Modern writers).
1984 Jaroslav Seifert, Czech poet: *Switch off the Lights* (1938).
1985 Claude Simon, French novelist; exponent of the *nouveau Roman*.
1986 Wole Soyinka, Nigerian playwright and poet whose work merges Nigerian and Western traditions.
1987 Joseph Brodsky, American (Russian émigré) poet and essayist; much of his work deals with loss and exile.
1988 Naguib Mahfouz, Egyptian novelist (see Arabic writers).
1989 Camilo José Cela, Spanish novelist, well known for his brutally realistic novels.
1990 Octavio Paz, Mexican poet, exponent of Magic Realism, noted for his international perspective.
1991 Nadine Gordimer, South African novelist, whose work highlights relations between the races in contemporary South Africa.
1992 Derek Walcott, Saint Lucian poet, whose work reflects a historical vision of the West Indies.

BOOKER PRIZEWINNERS

The Booker McConnell Prize is an annual award for a novel by a citizen of the United Kingdom, a Commonwealth country, the Republic of Ireland or South Africa and first published in Britain. It was established in 1968 by the trading company Booker McConnell in collaboration with the Publishers' Association.

1969 P.H. Newby, *Something to Answer For*
1970 Bernice Rubens, *The Elected Member*
1971 V.S. Naipaul, *In a Free State*
1972 John Berger, *G*
1973 J.G. Farrell, *The Siege of Krishnapur*
1974 (joint prizewinners)
Nadine Gordimer, *The Conservationist*
Stanley Middleton, *Holiday*
1975 Ruth Prawer Jhabvala, *Heat and Dust*
1976 David Storey, *Saville*
1977 Paul Scott, *Staying On*
1978 Iris Murdoch, *The Sea, The Sea*
1979 Penelope Fitzgerald, *Offshore*
1980 William Golding, *Rites of Passage*
1981 Salman Rushdie, *Midnight's Children*
1982 Thomas Keneally, *Schindler's Ark*
1983 J.M. Coetzee, *Life and Times of Michael K.*
1984 Anita Brookner, *Hôtel du Lac*
1985 Keri Hulme, *The Bone People*
1986 Kingsley Amis, *The Old Devils*
1987 Penelope Lively, *Moon Tiger*
1988 Peter Carey, *Oscar and Lucinda*
1989 Kazuo Ishiguro, *The Remains of the Day*
1990 A.S. Byatt, *Possession*
1991 Ben Okri, *The Famished Road*
1992 (joint prizewinners)
Michael Ondaatje, *The English Patient*
Barry Unsworth, *Sacred Hunger*

PULITZER FICTION AWARD-WINNERS

The Pulitzer prizes are annual awards endowed by the American publisher Joseph Pulitzer in 1917. They are given for achievements in American journalism and literature. Awards are made for the best reporting of national news and of international news, the most distinguished editorial, the best local reporting and the best news photograph as well as for achievement in fiction.

1918 Ernest Poole, *His Family*
1919 Booth Tarkington, *The Magnificent Ambersons*
1920 No award
1921 Edith Wharton, *The Age of Innocence*
1922 Booth Tarkington, *Alice Adams*
1923 Willa Cather, *One of Ours*
1924 Margaret Wilson, *The Able McLaughlins*
1925 Edna Ferber, *So Big*
1926 Sinclair Lewis, *Arrowsmith*
1927 Louis Bromfield, *Early Autumn*
1928 Thornton Wilder, *The Bridge at San Luis Rey*
1929 Julia Peterkin, *Scarlet Sister Mary*
1930 Oliver LaFarge, *Laughing Boy*

1931	Margaret Ayer Barnes, *Years of Grace*
1932	Pearl S. Buck, *The Good Earth*
1933	T.S. Stribling, *The Store*
1934	Caroline Miller, *Lamb in His Bosom*
1935	Josephine Winslow Johnson, *Now in November*
1936	Harold L. Davis, *Honey in the Horn*
1937	Margaret Mitchell, *Gone With the Wind*
1938	John Phillips Marquand, *The Late George Apley*
1939	Marjorie Kinnan Rawlings, *The Yearling*
1940	John Steinbeck, *The Grapes of Wrath*
1941	No award
1942	Ellen Glasgow, *In This Our Life*
1943	Upton Sinclair, *Dragon's Teeth*
1944	Martin Flavin, *Journey in the Dark*
1945	John Hersey, *A Bell for Adano*
1946	No award
1947	Robert Penn Warren, *All the King's Men*
1948	James A. Michener, *Tales of the South Pacific*
1949	James Gould Cozzens, *Guard of Honor*
1950	A.B. Guthrie, Jr *The Way West*
1951	Conrad Richter, *The Town*
1952	Herman Wouk, *The Caine Mutiny*
1953	Ernest Hemingway, *The Old Man and the Sea*
1954	No award
1955	William Faulkner, *A Fable*
1956	Mackinley Kantor, *Andersonville*
1957	No award
1958	James Agee, *A Death in the Family*
1959	Robert Lewis Taylor, *The Travels of Jamie McPheeters*
1960	Allen Drury, *Advise and Consent*
1961	Harper Lee, *To Kill a Mockingbird*
1962	Edwin O'Connor, *The Edge of Sadness*
1963	William Faulkner, *The Reivers*
1964	No award
1965	Shirley Ann Grau, *The Keepers of the House*
1966	Katherine Anne Porter, *The Collected Stories of Katherine Anne Porter*
1967	Bernard Malamud, *The Fixer*
1968	William Styron, *The Confessions of Nat Turner*
1969	N. Scott Momaday, *House Made of Dawn*
1970	Jean Stafford, *Collected Stories*
1971	No award
1972	Wallace Stegner, *Angle of Repose*
1973	Eudora Welty, *The Optimist's Daughter*
1974	No award
1975	Michael Shaara, The Killer Angels
1976	Saul Bellow, *Humboldt's Gift*
1977	No award
1978	James Alan McPherson, *Elbow Room*
1979	John Cheever, *The Stories of John Cheever*
1980	Norman Mailer, *The Executioner's Song*
1981	John Kennedy Toole, *A Confederacy of Dunces*
1982	John Updike, *Rabbit is Rich*
1983	Alice Walker, *The Color Purple*
1984	William Kennedy, *Ironweed*
1985	Alison Lurie, *Foreign Affairs*
1986	Larry McMurtry, *Lonesome Dove*
1987	Peter Taylor, *A Summons to Memphis*
1988	Toni Morrison, *Beloved*
1989	Anne Tyler, *Breathing Lessons*
1990	Oscar Hijuelos, *The Mambo Kings Play Songs of Love*
1991	John Updike, *Rabbit at Rest*
1992	Jane Simley, *A Thousand Acres*

OTHER PRIZES

France

The Goncourt Prize – *Prix Goncourt* – is the most prestigious French literary prize. Founded in 1903, it is awarded annually by the Académie Goncourt for the best French novel of the year. The prize money, however, is nominal at 50 F.

Notable winners of the Goncourt Prize include:
1919 Marcel Proust, *A l'ombre des jeunes filles en fleurs*
1933 André Malraux, *La condition humaine*
1948 Maurice Druon, *Les Grandes Familles*
1954 Simone de Beauvoir, *Les Mandarins*
1968 Bernard Clavel, *Les Fruits d'hiver*
1975 Emile Ajar, *La Vie devant soi*

Other notable French literary prizes include the *Prix Femina*, founded in 1904 by the magazine *Vie heureuse*, the forerunner of the magazine *Femina* and the *Prix Interallié*, founded in 1930.

Notable winners of the Femina Prize include:
1931 Antoine de Saint-Exupéry, *Vol de nuit*
1968 Marguerite Yourcenar, *L'OEuvre au noir*
1977 Régis Debray, *La neige brûle*

Germany

Founded in 1927, the Goethe Prize is the most eminent German annual literary prize.

Notable winners of the Goethe Prize include:
1928 Albert Schweitzer
1930 Sigmund Freud
1946 Herman Hesse
1949 Thomas Mann
1976 Ingmar Bergman

Italy

Major literary prizes in Italy include the Bagutta Prize (founded in 1927), the Bancarella Prize (founded in 1952), the Campiello Prize (founded in 1963) and the Antonio Feltrenelli International Prize.

Russia

In 1992 the committee in charge of the Booker Prize established a Russian Booker Prize for a novel in the Russian language. The first prize-winner was Mark Kharitonov for *Lines of Fate*.

United Kingdom

The Whitbread Literary Awards are given annually in six classes: novel, first novel, children's novel, poetry, biography and book of the year.

Notable winners of the Whitbread Literary Award for a novel include:
1974 Iris Murdoch, *The Sacred and Profane Love Machine*
1977 Beryl Bainbridge, *Injury Time*
1978 Paul Theroux, *Picture Palace*
1985 Peter Ackroyd, *Hawksmoor*
1986 Kazuo Ishiguro, *An Artist of the Floating World*
1988 Salman Rushdie, *The Satanic Verses*

MEDIA

AUSTRALIA

Because of the great distances between Australia's five large urban agglomerations, Australian newspapers are almost exclusively regional. There are only two major national dailies: *The Australian* and *The Australian Financial Review*. Some local weekly papers have greater circulation figures than major dailies. There are six main newspaper groups. Principal titles include:

Sun-Herald (weekly), published in Melbourne, 670 000 circulation;
Herald-Sun News Pictorial (daily), published in Melbourne, 650 000 circulation;
Sunday Telegraph (Sunday), published in Sydney, 560 000 circulation;
Sunday Sun (Sunday), published in Brisbane, 380 000 circulation;
Sunday Times (Sunday), published in Perth, 325 000 circulation.
The Sydney Morning Herald (daily), published in Sydney, 265 000 circulation (400 000 Saturday edition);
Sunday Mail (Sunday), published in Adelaide, 280 000 circulation;
The West Australian (daily), published in Perth, 260 000 circulation;
Courier-Mail (daily), published in Brisbane, 250 000 circulation;
The Truth (twice weekly), published in Melbourne, 240 000 circulation;
The Age (daily), published in Melbourne, 235 000 circulation;
Advertiser (daily), published in Adelaide, 215 000 circulation;
The Australian (daily), published in Sydney, 155 000 circulation.

The majority of periodicals are published in Melbourne or Sydney and distributed nationally. The periodicals with the largest circulations are:
The Open Road (6 a year), motoring, 1 500 000 circulation;
Woman's Day (weekly), 930 00 circulation (including New Zealand);
TV Week (weekly), TV listings guide, 700 000 circulation;
Reader's Digest (monthly), 475 000 circulation;
What's On Video and Cinema (monthly), 300 000 circulation;
Cleo (monthly), women's magazine, 270 000 circulation;
People (weekly), general interest, 230 000 circulation;
Australian Post (weekly), general interest, 205 000 circulation;
Cosmopolitan (monthly), women's magazine, 205 000 circulation;
Australian House and Garden (monthly), 120 000 circulation;
Time Australia Magazine (weekly), general interest, 105 000 circulation.

The government-funded Australian Broadcasting Corporation (ABC) operates nationally providing one TV network and five radio networks. Commercial TV and radio operate under licences granted by the Australian Broadcasting Tribunal. There were 45 TV and 149 radio licencees in 1990, many of them having more than one station on the air.

BRAZIL

The size of Brazil – and the rivalry between São Paulo and Rio de Janeiro – militates against the existence of a national press. All local or regional papers are dailies. The only 'weekly' press is represented by the Sunday editions of the dailies. Readership of papers is small in comparison to the size of the population and most people rely upon radio and television for news. There are 288 daily papers. Principal titles include:
O Globo (daily), published in Rio de Janeiro, 350 000 circulation (Sunday edition 520 000);
O Estado de São Paulo (daily), published in São Paulo, circulation 230 000 (Sunday edition 460 000);
Zero Hora (daily), published in Porto Alegre, 225 000 circulation (Sunday edition 250 000);
Fôlha de São Paulo (daily), published in São Paulo, 210 000 circulation (Sunday edition 315 000);
O Dia (daily), published in Rio de Janeiro, 210 000 circulation (Sunday edition 400 000);
Jornal do Brasil (daily), published in Rio de Janeiro, 200 000 circulation (Sunday edition 325 000).

The principal periodicals include:
Veja (weekly), general interest magazine published in São Paulo, 800 000 circulation;
Quatro Rodas (monthly), motoring magazine published in São Paulo, 300 000 circulation;
Manequim (monthly), fashion magazine published in São Paulo, 300 000 circulation;
Carícia (monthly), women's magazine published in Rio de Janeiro, 210 000 circulation.

There are six main TV networks which operate 235 television stations. Most are under governmental control although privatization has begun. There are 2790 radio stations, almost all under state control.

CANADA

Satellite transmission has enabled the Toronto-based *Globe and Mail* and the *Financial Post)* to achieve national circulations but the Canadian press remains regional. Less than one fifth of papers are independently-owned; the rest are owned by nine main newspaper chains, including Southam Inc and Thomson Newspapers Ltd, which between them account for over one half of total daily circulation. There are 108 daily newspapers with those in Québec province published in French. Weekly papers tend to be Sunday or weekend editions of the daily press. Principal titles include:
Toronto Star (daily), 550 000 circulation (Saturday edition 765 000);
The Globe and Mail (daily), published in Toronto, 325 000 circulation;
Le Journal de Montréal (daily), 305 000 (weekend edition 350 000);
Toronto Sun (daily), 290 000 circulation (Sunday edition 455 000);
The Vancouver Sun (daily evening), 220 000 circulation.
La Presse (daily), published in Montréal, 215 000 circulation (325 000 Saturday edition);
The Province (daily), published in Vancouver, 195 000 circulation;
Ottawa Citizen (daily), 185 000 circulation (235 000 Saturday edition);
The Gazette (daily), published in Montréal, 180 000 circulation (245 000 Saturday edition);
Winnipeg Free Press (daily), 170 000 circulation (230 000 Saturday edition);
Edmonton Journal (daily), 170 000 circulation;
Hamilton Spectator (daily evening), 140 000 circulation;

Calgary Herald (daily), 135 000 circulation;
Le Soleil (daily), published in Québec, 110 000 circulation (150 000 Saturday edition).

The only large circulation national magazine is *Maclean's Canada's Weekly Newsmagazine* (weekly), published in Toronto, 610 000 circulation.
Other main periodicals include:
Reader's Digest/Sélection (monthly), general interest, combined circulation of French and English editions, 1 682 000;
TV Guide (weekly), published in Toronto, 820,000 circulation;
WestWorld Magazine (quarterly), general interest magazine, published in Vancouver, 731 000;
Legion Magazine (10 a year), general interest magazine published in Ottawa, 526 000 circulation;
TV Hebdo/TV Plus (weekly), published in Montréal, combined circulation for French and English editions 327 000.
Anglican Journal (monthly), religious magazine published in Toronto, 274 000 circulation;
Western Living (monthly), general interest magazine published in Vancouver, 273 000 circulation.

The Canadian Broadcasting Corporation (CBC) is the national and publicly owned broadcasting service which operates both TV and radio channels. CBC broadcasts in English and French, and (in the north) in Dene and Inuktitut. There are many privately owned TV and radio stations most of which have affiliations with CBC. The four main private networks are CTV, TVA, Quatre Saisons and Global. Satellite and cable TV are well established. US channels are popular.

CHINA

The large circulation figures of the daily press reflect the enormous population of mainland China – indeed, given the size of the population the figures are smaller than might be expected – and the emphasis the Communist government has put on education and literacy. There are 852 newspapers and each province publishes its own daily paper. The press is entirely state-controlled. The principal titles include:
Renmin Ribao (People's Daily), the official organ of the Communist Party of China, published in Beijing, 5 000 000 circulation;
Can Kao Xiao Xi (Reference News), reprints from the foreign press, published in Beijing, 3 600 000 circulation;
Qingdao Ribao (Qingdao Daily), published in Qingdao, 2 600 000 circulation;
Gongren Ribao (Workers' Daily), trade union paper published in Beijing, 2 500 000 circulation;
Wenhui Bao (daily), published in Shanghai, 1 700 000 circulation.

The periodicals with the largest circulations include:
Nongmin Wenzhai ('Peasants' Digest') (weekly), 3 540 000 circulation;
Jiating (Family) (weekly), 1 890 000 circulation;
Shichang Zhoubao (Market Weekly), economic and financial, published in Shenyang, 1 000 000 circulation;

The Ministry for Radio, TV and Films censors all broadcasts. There are 510 local television stations and the China Central Television Station operates three channels nationwide. A cable network is in operation in Shanghai and a similar one is planned for Beijing. There are two national radio stations – Radio Beijing and the Central People's Broadcasting

Station – and nearly 640 local stations, some broadcasting in local languages.

FRANCE

Although 16 daily newspapers are published in Paris, France still has a regional rather than a national press. The 55 provincial daily papers dominate sales outside Paris. There are over 460 other local (mainly weekly) papers. There are only two Sunday papers in Paris – instead weekly news magazines are characteristic of the French press. There are seven large newspaper groups. The main newspaper titles include:
Ouest-France (daily), published in Rennes, 790 000 circulation;
France-Dimanche (Sunday), published in Paris, 710 000 circulation;
Le Figaro (daily), published in Paris, 787 000 circulation;
Le Progrès (daily), published in Lyon, 415 000 circulation (Sunday edition 540 000);
Le Parisien (daily), published in Paris, 400 000 circulation;
La Voix du Nord (daily), published in Lille, 395 000 circulation;
Sud-Ouest (daily), published in Bordeaux, 367 000 circulation;
Le Monde (daily), published in Paris, 365 000 circulation;
L'Humanité-Dimanche (Sunday edition of the organ of the French Communist Party), published in Paris, 360 000 circulation;
France-Soir (daily evening), published in Paris, 305 000 circulation;
L'Equipe (daily sports), published in Paris, 300 000 circulation;
Le Dauphiné Libéré (daily), published in Grenoble, 295 000 circulation;
La Nouvelle République du Centre-Ouest (daily), published in Tours, 270 000 circulation;
L'Est-Républicain (daily), published in Nancy, 265 000 circulation;
Nice-Matin (daily), published in Nice, 265 000 circulation;
La Montagne (daily), published in Clermont-Ferrand, 255 000 circulation;

The periodicals with the largest circulations are television listings magazines. The main periodicals include:
Télé 7 Jours (weekly), TV listings, 3 340 000 circulation;
Télé-Poche (weekly), TV listings, 1 800 000 circulation;
Modes et travaux (monthly), fashion magazine, 1 500 000 circulation;
Sélection du Reader's Digest (monthly), general interest, 1 130 000 circulation;
Femme d'Aujourdhui (weekly), women's magazine, 850 000 circulation;
Nous Deux (monthly), women's illustrated stories, 825 000 circulation;
Paris-Match (weekly), news magazine, 690 000 circulation;
Jours de France (weekly), news and fashion magazine, 675 000 circulation;
L'Express (weekly), news magazine, 670 000 circulation;
Marie-Claire (monthly), women's magazine, 600 000 circulation;
Télérama (weekly), TV listings, 525 000 circulation;
Le Canard Enchaîné (weekly), satirical magazine, 520 000 circulation;

Intimité (weekly), women's illustrated stories, 510 000 circulation;
La Vie Catholique, religious magazine, 400 000 circulation.

Radio France broadcasts seven main channels through 47 local radio stations. There are over 1700 local commercial radio stations and three commercial stations that are almost national in their coverage. The two state-run TV channels (A2 and FR3) compete with the three private TV channels.

GERMANY

Nearly 400 daily newspapers are published in Germany, most of them confined to small regional circulations. For historic reasons there is no national press comparable to Fleet Street although *Frankfurter Allgemeine Zeitung, Berliner Zeitung* and *Süddeutsche Zeitung* enjoy national circulations and prestige. 'Tabloid' papers such as *Bild-Zeitung* and *Super!* are increasing in popularity. There are six principal newspaper groups – three based in Hamburg. Principal papers include:
Bild-Zeitung (daily), published in Hamburg and printed in 15 provincial centres, 4 900 000 circulation;
Bild am Sonntag (Sunday), published in Hamburg, 2 400 000 circulation;
Westdeutsche Allgemeine Zeitung (daily), published in Essen, 1 210 000 circulation;
Freie Presse (daily), published in Chemnitz, 600 000 circulation;
Wochenpost (weekly), published in Berlin, 550 000 circulation;
Sächsische Zeitung (daily), published in Dresden, 500 000 circulation;
Mitteldeutsche Zeitung (daily), published in Halle, 500 000 circulation.
Die Zeit (weekly), published in Hamburg, 490 000 circulation;
Welt am Sonntag (Sunday), published in Hamburg, 430 000 circulation;
Frankfurter Allgemeine Zeitung (daily), published in Frankfurt, 390 000 circulation;
Süddeutsche Zeitung (daily), published in Munich, 390 000 circulation;
Rheinische Post (daily), published in Düsseldorf, 390 000 circulation;
Super! (daily), published in Berlin, 370 000 circulation;
Berliner Zeitung (daily), published in Berlin, 370 000 circulation;
Leipziger Zeitung (daily), published in Leipzig, 360 000 circulation;
Magdeburgische Zeitung (daily), published in Magdeburg, 360 000 circulation;
Nürnberger Nachrichten (daily evening), published in Nürnberg, 350 000 circulation;
Thüringer Allgemeine (daily), published in Erfurt, 330 000 circulation;
Express (daily), published in Cologne, 315 000 circulation;
Hamburger Abendblatt (daily evening), published in Hamburg, 310 000;

The periodicals – by contrast – are mainly national rather than regional. Those with the largest circulations are news magazines and women's magazines, and TV listings guides. They include:
Hörzu (weekly), TV listings guide, 3 900 000;
TV Hören + Sehen (weekly), TV listings guide; 2 690 000 circulation;
burda moden (monthly), fashion and cookery magazine, 2 300 000 circulation;
Funk Uhr (weekly), TV listings guide, 2 000 000 circulation;

Das Beste aus Readers Digest (monthly), general interest, 1 900 000 circulation;
Neue Post (weekly), general interest, 1 750 000 circulation;
Stern (weekly), current affairs and general interest, 1 490 000 circulation;
FF-dabei (weekly), general interest, 1 490 000 circulation;
Der Spiegel (weekly), current affairs, 1 400 000 circulation;
Brigitte (fortnightly), women's magazine, 1 300 000;
Bravo (weekly), young people's magazine, 1 190 000 circulation;
Neue Revue (weekly), general interest, 1 150 000 circulation;
Bild + Funk (weekly), TV listings magazine, 1 040 000 circulation;
Bunte Illustrierte (weekly), family magazine, 1 040 000 circulation;
Gong (weekly), TV listings guide, 1 000 000 circulation.

ARD is the coordinating body for radio and TV networks in Germany. Five radio networks – each broadcasting up to five channels – operate throughout the country. There are 15 regional broadcasting organizations. There are three television channels – one produced by ARD, one controlled by a public corporation and a third educational channel.

INDIA

The size of the country and its many social, religious and linguistic barriers have militated against the development of a national press. However, a small number of English-language newspapers – the *Times of India*, the *Indian Express*, the *Statesman* and *The Hindu* – enjoy wide circulations. These papers have largely metropolitan readerships and cover international issues as well as Indian events. Newspapers published in Indian languages have mainly rural readerships and tend to be more parochial. Most papers publish separate editions in a number of centres within the relevant linguistic region. The papers with the largest circulations include:
Malayala Manorama (Malayalam; daily), published in Kottayam, 665 000 circulation;
Indian Express (English; daily), published in Delhi, Vijayawada, Madras, Bombay etc, 580 000 combined circulation;
Daily Jagran (Hindi; daily), published in Kanpur, 580 000 circulation;
Punjab Kesari (Punjabi; daily), published in Jalandhar, 555 000 circulation (840 000 Sunday edition);
The Times of India (English; daily), published in Delhi, Bombay, Bangalore etc, 515 000 combined circulation;
Gujarat Samachar (Gujarati; daily), published in Ahmedabad, 475 000 circulation;
The Hindu (English; daily), published in Madras, 470 000 circulation;
Mathrubhumi (Malayalam; daily), published in Kozhikode, 470 000 circulation;
Anandabazar Patrika (Bengali; daily), published in Calcutta, 450 000 circulation;
Sandesh (Gujarati; daily), published in Ahmedabad, 360 000 circulation;
Eenadu (Telegu; daily), published in Hyderabad, 345 000 circulation;
Aj (Hindi; daily), published Varanasi, 345 000 combined circulation;
Daily Thanthi (Tamil; daily), published in Madras, 325 000 circulation;
The Hindustan Times (English; daily), published in Delhi, 325 000 circulation;

Jugantar (Bengali; daily), published in Calcutta, 300 000 circulation;
The Tribune (English, Hindi, Punjabi; daily), published in Chandigarh, 275 000 combined circulation for three separate language editions;
Navbharat Times (Hindi; daily), published in Delhi, 265 000 circulation;
Lokasatta (Marathi; daily), published in Bombay, 250 000 circulation.

The magazines with the largest circulations include:
India Today (English, Tamil, Hindi; fortnightly), general interest, 790 000 combined circulation for three separate language editions;
Grih Shobha (Hindi, Marathi, Gujarati; monthly), women's magazine, 420 000 combined circulation for three separate language editions;
Employment News (English, Hindi, Urdu; weekly), official publication, 405 000 combined circulation for three separate language editions;
Competition Success Review (English; monthly), 285 000 circulation;
Sarita (Hindi; fortnightly), family interest, 235 000 circulation.

All India Radio (AIR) runs 104 radio stations, operating in 81 languages. Doordarshan India (Television India) runs 18 TV stations. Both organizations are government-financed and controlled. Satellite TV has recently become both popular and influential.

ITALY

The Italian press is characterized by the small number of daily papers published – only 80 – and by their low circulations compared with other G7 countries. The press is concentrated in Milan and Rome and several other provincial centres produce important daily titles. There is no national press in the British sense but *Corriere della Sera*, *La Repubblica* and *La Stampa* enjoy national circulations and prestige. Each of the major political parties has a paper to reflect its views. Principal titles include:
Corriere della Sera (daily evening), published in Milan, 850 000 circulation;
La Gazetta dello Sport (daily sports), published in Milan, 830 000 circulation;
La Repubblica (daily), published in Rome, 800 000 circulation;
Corriere dello Sport (daily sports), published in Rome with a dozen regional editions, 620 000 circulation;
La Stampa (daily), published in Turin, 570 000 circulation;
Stampa Sera (daily evening), published in Turin, 570 000 circulation;
Il Messaggero (daily), published in Rome, 390 000 circulation;
Il Sole/24 Ore (daily financial), published in Milan, 350 000;
Il Resto del Carlino (daily), published in Bologna, 310 000 circulation;
L'Unità (daily), the organ of the former Communist Party, published in Rome; 250 000 circulation (Sunday edition 800 000);
La Nazione (daily), published in Florence, 270 000 circulation;
Il Giornale (daily), published in Milan, 250 000 circulation;
Il Mattino (daily), published in Naples, 225 000 circulation.

There are over 9000 periodicals – most with small circulations. However, a few women's and general interest magazines (some sensationalist in tone and content) attract circulations that compare with the top magazines in major Western countries and the popularity of motoring magazines confirms the Italian passion for the automobile. Italy also lacks the large circulation TV listings guides that are characteristic of most Western countries. The periodicals with the largest readerships are:
L'Automobile (monthly), motoring magazine, 1 500 000 circulation;
Familia Cristiana (weekly), Catholic, 1 050 000 circulation;
Gente (weekly), political and current affairs, 900 000 circulation;
Oggi (weekly), topical and literary, 700 000 circulation;
Quattroruote (monthly), motoring magazine, 700 000 circulation;
Panorama (weekly), current affairs, 500 000 circulation;
Intimità (weekly), women's magazine, 470 000 circulation;
Mille Idee per la Donna (weekly), women's magazine, 360 000 circulation;
Confidenze (weekly), women's magazine, 360 000 circulation;
Grazia (weekly), women's magazine, 360 000 circulation;
Gioia (weekly), women's magazine, 350 000 circulation;
Visto (weekly), general interest, 350 000 circulation;
Annabella (weekly), women's magazine, 270 000 circulation;
Tempo (weekly), general interest, 230 000 circulation.

Italy has over 450 local commercial TV stations, seven of which are virtually national, as well as RAI (Radiotelevisione Italiana) – the national network which runs three channels – and a Catholic network. RAI broadcasts national radio channels and there are over 1000 local commercial radio stations.

JAPAN

Japanese papers enjoy the highest circulations in the world. There are over 100 principal daily newspapers in Japan where 569 copies of papers are printed for every 1000 people. The press is concentrated in Tokyo, whose papers form a national press. There are also important regional papers in Osaka, Nagoya and other major cities. Most Japanese newspapers publish both morning and evening editions. The principal titles include:
Yomiuri Shimbun (daily), published in Tokyo; circulation – 5 800 000 (morning edition), 3 300 000 (evening edition);
Seikyo Shimbun (daily), organ of the Sakka Gakkai sect, published in Tokyo, 5 500 000 circulation;
Asahi Shimbun (daily), published in Tokyo; circulation – 4 400 000 (morning edition), 2 800 000 (evening edition);
Yomiuri Shimbun (daily), published in Osaka; circulation – 2 370 000 (morning edition), 1 450 000 (evening edition);
Asahi Shimbun (daily), published in Osaka; circulation – 2 300 000 (morning edition), 1 450 000 (evening edition);
Chunichi Shimbun (daily), published in Nagoya; circulation – 2 160 000 (morning edition), 850 000 (evening edition);
Mainichi Shimbun (daily), published in Tokyo; circulation – 1 800 000 (morning edition), 900 000 (evening edition);
Nihon Keizai Shimbun (daily), published in Tokyo; circulation – 1 800 000 (morning edition), 3 000 000 (evening edition);
Mainichi Shimbun (daily), published in Osaka; circulation – 1 400 000 (morning edition), 950 000 (evening edition);

Sankei Shimbun (daily), published in Osaka; circulation – 1 230 000 (morning edition), 750 000 (evening edition);

Yukan Fuji (daily), published in Tokyo, 1 200 000 circulation.

By contrast, periodicals have low circulations and – because of the great number of TV stations – TV listings guides are largely absent. The periodicals with the highest circulations include the following:

Kaisha Shikiho (quarterly), business statistical magazine, 1 300 000 circulation;

Ie-no-Hikari (monthly), countryside magazine, 1 100 000 circulation;

Lettuce Club (fortnightly), cookery, 750 000 circulation;

Bungei-Shunju (monthly), general interest, 670 000 circulation;

Popeye (fortnightly), teenage magazine, 650 000 circulation;

Hot-Dog Press (fortnightly), men's magazine, 650 000 circulation;

Croissant (fortnightly), women's and domestic magazine, 600 000 circulation.

NHK – a non-commercial public corporation – runs two TV and three radio stations. There are nearly 400 commercial radio stations and over 6800 commercial television stations.

RUSSIA

The press in Russia is undergoing drastic restructuring. Lenin recognized the power of the press, saying it was 'the most strong and powerful weapon of the Party'. The purpose of the press in the former USSR was traditionally to disseminate Marxist-Leninism and to provide information on Soviet life. Staid daily newspapers were published by public organizations – *Izvestia* ('News') by the Supreme Soviet, *Pravda* ('Truth') by the Communist Party and *Trud* ('Labour') by the Central Council of Trade Unions. These and other papers are now largely independent and have livelier editorials and content. However, their very high circulation figures have shrunk since Russia gained a free press and there has been a corresponding increase in readership of the innovative weekly paper *Argumenty y Fakty*. Some titles are now published intermittently and several new commercial papers have appeared, including at least one 'tabloid'. The press remains highly centralized in Moscow, although some important national papers are published in cities such as St Petersburg. Major titles (all published in Moscow) include:

Argumenty y Fakty (weekly), 32 000 000 circulation;

Izvestia, 3 800 000 circulation;

Pravda, 900 000 circulation.

Komosolskaya Pravda and *Trud* both had a circulation of over 10 000 000 in the former Soviet Union. Both have lost readership dramatically, but recnt no reliable recent figures are available.

Periodicals used to be published by organizations such as the Leninist Young Communist League, various trade unions and goverment and Communist Party bodies. The vast majority were of an educational and 'improving' nature, and carried propaganda. Their circulation figures were very large. Some of these titles continue to be published – in much smaller numbers – by successor bodies, although they have changed greatly in style. A number of new independent magazines have appeared whose emphasis is on sensationalism amnd mysticism.

Broadcasting is in the hands of the All-Russian State Television Radio Broadcasting Company.

SPAIN

Strong historic regional identities and the lack of a single national language have conspired to prevent the emergence of a national press in Spain. Only *ABC*, *Ya* and *El País* circulate thoughout most of the country. *El País* – published in Madrid, Barcelona, Valencia and Seville is the nearest thing to a national newspaper. Circulation figures for Spain's 120 daily papers are low. Local weekly papers published on a Monday and carrying national and international news – *Hoja del Lunes* – were a feature of the Spanish regional press until recently. The greatest circulations are enjoyed by:

El País (daily), see above, 460 000 combined circulation (1 050 000 Sunday edition);

ABC (daily), published in Madrid and Seville, 360 000 combined circulation (600 000 Sunday edition);

La Vanguardia (daily), published in Barcelona, 195 000 circulation (320 000 Sunday edition);

La Opinión de Murcia (daily), published in Murcia, 180 000 circulation;

Diario 16 (daily evening), published in Madrid, 180 000 circulation (210 000 Sunday edition);

El Periódico (daily), published in Barcelona, 160 000 circulation (380 000 Sunday edition);

El Mundo (daily), published in Madrid, 145 000 circulation (215 000 Sunday edition);

As (daily sports), published in Madrid, 145 000 circulation;

El Correo Español-El Pueblo Vasco (daily), published in Bilbao, 135 000 circulation;

El Observador de la Actualidad (daily), published in Barcelona, 120 000 circulation;

Marca (daily sports), published in Madrid, 115 000 circulation.

Current affairs, women's and general interest magazines and TV listings guides outsell newspapers in Spain. The periodicals with the largest sales are:

TP Teleprogramma (weekly), TV listings guide, 1 400 000 circulation;

Estar Viva (monthly), women's magazine, 1 220 000 circulation;

Tele Indiscreta (weekly), TV listings guide, 950 000 circulation;

Pronto (weekly), general interest, 925 000 circulation;

Hola! (weekly), general interest, 585 000 circulation;

Hogar y Moda (weekly), women's magazine, 550 000 circulation;

Interviú (weekly), general interest, 495 000 circulation;

Panorama Internacional (weekly), general interest, 420 000 circulation;

Diez Minutos (weekly), general interest, 380 000 circulation;

Lecturas (weekly), women's magazine, 345 000;

Semana (weekly), general interest, 340 000;

Super Pop (fortnightly), teenage, 300 000;

Muy Interestante (weekly), general interest, 290 000 circulation;

Entorno de Mujer (monthly), women's magazine, 220 000 circulation;

RTVE is a public corporation that controls and coordinates TV and radio. There are seven regional television companies including those broadcasting in Basque, Catalan and Galician. RNE runs five national channels and there are three regional stations broadcasting in Basque, Catalan and Galician. There are over 300 local radio stations.

UNITED KINGDOM
See UK chapter.

USA
In the USA there are more than 210 daily morning newspapers with an average of over 50 000 copies and over 1600 daily papers in total. American daily papers place great emphasis on local news because of the strong interest in state, as opposed to national, news. The size of the country militates against the existence of a national press, although the *Wall Street Journal* and the *New York Times* (both of which are printed at several locations) and the *Washington Post*, the *Los Angeles Times* and the (Boston) *Christian Science Monitor* enjoy national readerships. There are nine major newspaper groups. Newspaper circulations have fallen significantly in recent years, particularly among young people who tend to rely more and more upon television for news. The papers with the biggest circulations include:
Wall Street Journal (daily), published in New York, 1 800 000 circulation;
USA Today (daily), published in Arlington (Greater Washington DC), 1 420 000 circulation;
Los Angeles Times (daily), 1 180 000 circulation (1 530 000 Sunday edition);
New York Times (daily), 1 115 000 circulation (1 700 000 Sunday edition);
Washington Post (daily), 790 000 circulation (1 140 000 Sunday edition);
Newsday (daily), published in New York, 765 000 circulation (875 000 Sunday edition);
New York Daily News (daily), 760 0000 circulation (915 000 Sunday edition);
Chicago Tribune (daily), 725 000 circulation (1 100 000 Sunday edition);
Atlanta Journal-Constitution (Sunday), 700 000 circulation;
Detroit Free Press (daily), 600 000 circulation (725 000 Sunday edition);
San Francisco Chronicle (daily), 555 000 circulation (705 000 Sunday edition);
New York Post (daily), 550 000 circulation;
Chicago Sun-Times (daily), 535 000 circulation;
Boston Globe (daily), 505 000 circulation (800 000 Sunday edition);
Philadelphia Inquirer (daily), 505 000 circulation (980 000 Sunday edition);
Star-Ledger (daily), published in Newark (Greater New York), 480 000 circulation (700 000 Sunday edition);
Houston Chronicle (daily), 450 000 circulation (530 000 Sunday edition);
Detroit News (daily), 450 000 circulation (1 200 000 Sunday edition);
Cleveland Plain Dealer (daily), 415 000 circulation (545 000 Sunday edition);
Star Tribune (daily), published in Minneapolis, 410 000 circulation (680 000 Sunday edition);
Miami Herald (daily), 400 000 circulation (510 000 Sunday edition);
St Petersburg Times (daily), 400 000 circulation (500 000 Sunday edition)
Baltimore Sun (daily), 400 000 circulation (490 000 Sunday edition);
Dallas Morning News (daily), 395 000 circulation (620 000 Sunday edition);

Denver Rocky Mountain News (daily), 355 000 circulation (425 000 Sunday edition).
St Louis Post-Dispatch (daily), 350 000 circulation (560 000 Sunday edition);
Orange County Register (daily), published in Greater Los Angeles, 350 000 circulation;
Arizona Republic (daily), published in Phoenix, 345 000 circulation (530 000 Sunday circulation);
Milwaukee Journal (daily), 290 000 circulation (520 000 Sunday edition);
San Diego Union (daily), 260 000 circulation (450 000 Sunday edition).
Pittsburgh Press (daily evening), 235 000 circulation (550 000 Sunday edition).

The periodicals enjoying the highest circulations in the USA include;
TV Guide (weekly), 16 330 000 circulation;
Reader's Digest (monthly), 16 250 000 circulation;
National Geographic Magazine (monthly), 10 000 000 circlation;
Better Homes and Gardens (monthly), 8 000 000 circulation;
Family Circle (every three weeks), general interest, 5 900 000 circulation;
Consumer Reports (monthly), 5 300 000 circulation;
Good Housekeeping (monthly), 5 200 000 circulation;
McCall's Magazine (monthly), women's magazine, 5 120 000;
Ladies' Home Journal (monthly), 5 120 000 circulation;
Time (weekly), current affairs, 4 720 000 circulation;
National Enquirer (weekly), general interest, 4 380 000 circulation;
Redbook Magazine (monthly), women's magazine, 4 000 000 circulation;
Star (weekly), general interest, 3 560 000 circulation;
People Magazine (weekly), general interest, 3 240 000 circulation;
Newsweek (weekly), current affairs, 3 200 000 circulation;
Sports Illustrated (weekly), 3 200 000 circulation;
Playboy (monthly), men's magazine, 3 000 000 circulation;
Prevention (monthly), health, 3 000 000 circulation;
Highlights for Children (monthly), 3 000 000 circulation;
Cosmopolitan (monthly), women's magazine, 2 870 000 circulation;
American Legion Magazine (monthly), 2 850 000 circulation;
US News and World Report (weekly), 2 330 000 circulation;
Smithsonian Magazine (monthly), learned, 2 300 000 circulation;
Glamour (monthly), women's magazine, 2 300 000 circulation;
Southern Living (monthly), regional interest, 2 280 000 circlation;
Penthouse (monthly), men's magazine, 2 230 000 circulation;
Motorland (alternate months), 2 090 000.

There are over 1000 commercial TV stations and 325 educational TV stations. There are over 10 000 commercial and educational radio stations.

VISUAL ARTS
PAINTING AND SCULPTURE

ART TECHNIQUES AND MEDIA

DRAWING

Drawing is the process of artistic depiction of objects or abstractions on a two-dimensional surface by linear (and sometimes tonal) means. The result may be a cartoon – a full size preparatory drawing for a painting or a work in another medium – or a finished work.

Drawing tools and media include:

chalk Black chalk (black stone) and red chalk (mineral) were used extensively from the 16th century for preparatory drawings. Chalk is also used for finished works.

charcoal charred wood, used extensively from the 16th century in preparatory drawings.

ink liquids for drawing or painting. Generally the colours are a suspension or are present in a dye. Sometimes, as with Indian ink or white ink, there may be opaque pigments in suspension. Ink may be applied with a pen or a brush for a preparatory drawing or a finished work.

pencil The graphite pencil – developed in the 17th century – replaced the silverpoint in preparing the surface to be painted on. Pencils are manufactured in varying degrees of softness and darkness. The graphite pencil is not only used to produce preliminary sketches but also for finished works.

silverpoint a metal point used mainly in the 15th century on prepared paper to make rough outlines that will be covered over by other media or to achieve a delicate effect through the tiny (and eventually tarnished) particles of silver left behind.

PAINTING

Painting is the visual and aesthetic expression of ideas and emotions primarily in two dimensions, using colour, line, shapes, texture and tones. The great variety of painting techniques reflects the range of surfaces that are painted on; for instance, tempera technique is used for painting on wood panels, and fresco technique for painting on walls.

Painting tools and media include:

airbrush technique a system of spraying colour with an airbrush, an implement that resembles a fountain pen. It has a small container near the nozzle. Air pressure is applied via a mechanical compressor and can be controlled to create fine, delicate lines or a wide sweep.

acrylic an opaque, water-soluble quick-drying paint. It can be applied with heavy knife-laid impasto (see below) or diluted with water to wash-like consistency. Acrylic paint is manufactured from pigment bound in a synthetic resin, normally acrylic or PVA. It is a 20th-century development, initially used in wall painting. The colour, unlike that of oil paint, does not alter with time.

fresco (Italian, 'fresh') a wall-painting technique in which powdered pigments are mixed in water and applied to a wet lime-plaster.

gouache a painting technique, similar to watercolour, in which the binding medium is glue. White pigment is added to give some opacity. Used by French painters since the 18th century, gouache is widely used in commercial illustration.

impasto the laying on of paint so thickly on a canvas that it protrudes from the surface.

oils the most widely used painting technique. Oil paint is based on a mixture of dry pigment and vegetable oil, commonly linseed, poppy or walnut oil. It is slow drying, so the artist is able to make revisions and build up layers of colour. The composition is built up in layers of thicker or thinner paint, and variety in brushwork can have significant visual effect.

pastels sticks of pigment made by mixing powdered pigment with gum or resin binder. Pastels give soft colours which retain their freshness.

pigments colours derived from earths, natural dyes and minerals or chemically synthesized. The earliest pigments, used by prehistoric man, included burnt wood, bone, chalk and earth colours. In addition to these, medieval painters used *verdigris* (copper resinate; green), *ultramarine* (lapis lazuli; blue), *white lead*, *azurite* (copper carbonate; blue), *madder* (red), *lead-tin yellow*, and *vermilion* (cinnabar; red). Later came *Prussian blue* (1705) and *Naples yellow*, but during the 19th century the range of colours expanded to include new chemical colours.

tempera a technique – used for painting on wood panels – based on a mixture of a water-based liquid with an oily or waxy medium. Traditionally egg white and egg yolk are used together with an oil such as linseed oil, but egg (which acts as a binder) may also be used with water alone. Its quick-drying properties and luminosity of colour account for the attraction of tempera.

watercolour painting a technique in which pigment is bound in a gum arabic medium and thinned with water for use. It was used as a paint in Egyptian painting, but most fully exploited by 18th- and 19th-century British landscape artists. Distinguished by its translucent quality, watercolour is extremely versatile. Some watercolours are *monochrome* – painted in only one colour.

SCULPTURE

Sculpture describes the processes of carving, engraving, modelling, casting or assembling so as to produce representations or abstractions of an artistic nature in relief, in intaglio, or in the round. The two main sculpture techniques are *carving* and *modelling*.

Carving The carved image is created by cutting unwanted material away from a block of hard material, usually stone or wood. *Stone carving* can be done from granite, limestone, sandstone, alabaster and a variety of marbles. Other materials that have been commonly carved for small-scale sculpture include ivory, amber and semi-precious stones.

Modelling Modelling involves manipulating some soft and yielding material such as wax, clay or plaster until the desired image is achieved. A three-dimensional shape is built up around an *armature* (framework) in metal or wood. Models are generally turned into a more lasting form, either by heating, as with clay, or by *casting* them in bronze or some other metal. The two principal techniques of casting are the *lost-wax process* and *sand casting*.

Assemblage Assemblage is the term used for all works of art constructed from everyday objects. It refers to works of three-dimensional and planar construction, including collage.

PRINTMAKING

Images were first printed from engraved wooden blocks onto parchment some 3000 to 4000 years ago. In the West, the development of printing coincided with the invention of movable type in the 15th century. Since then, a great variety of different printing techniques have evolved, including *relief techniques, intaglio techniques* (where the image is printed from lines cut into a metal plate) and *planographic techniques* (which are characterized by surface-printing methods). The principal techniques include:

aquatint an intaglio technique used to imitate the effect of watercolours. A copper plate is coated with powdered resin. Repeated immersions in an acid bath produce a tonal effect as small areas of copper between the particles of dust are exposed.

engraving an intaglio technique that originated from the carving of gems and armour. A zinc or copper plate is engraved with a sharp tool. The plate is then inked with a tacky ink and all the uncut surfaces are wiped clean – leaving the ink only in the recessed furrows.

etching an intaglio technique used during the 17th and 18th centuries and revived in the late 19th century by James Whistler (1834–1903). The design is etched onto a copper plate coated in a blackened acid-resistant material, using a steel needle, which exposes the metal. Before being inked and printed – using the same method as for engraving – the plate is immersed in acid, which bites into the exposed lines. To accentuate areas of light and shade, parts of the plate are protected with a varnish, and the plate is then re-immersed in the acid.

linocuts a relief technique using the floor-covering material linoleum, a cheap and easily carved surface. Although it does not allow great subtlety of detail, it was favoured by artists in the 1920s, including Picasso.

lithography a planographic technique depending upon the mutual incompatibility of water and grease. A design is drawn or painted onto a grained alloy plate – originally a thin limestone slab – using a greasy material such as crayon or lithographic ink. A solution of nitric acid and gum arabic is applied to the unmarked areas which repels the lithographic ink wiped onto the plate before printing. The drawn surfaces attract the ink and the moist surfaces repel it. The method was invented by the Bavarian Aloys Senefelder, in 1776.

mezzotint an intaglio technique used for reproductions after oil paintings in the 18th and 19th centuries. A serrated rocker is passed over the plate, leaving a varying number of indentations in which ink will collect and produce tonal effects. The tone engraving is then produced by scraping away for darker tones and burnishing for highlights.

screen printing a 20th-century planographic method where a screen of silk or gauze is tautly stretched over a wooden or metal frame. The design is applied to the screen in the form of a stencil so that areas not to be coloured are blocked out. Ink is wiped across the screen and forced through the mesh onto paper.

woodcuts a relief technique used as early as the 14th century and used extensively by Albrecht Dürer (1471–1528). The design is drawn onto wood and cut away – along the grain – leaving only the raised lines of the image ready to be inked. The woodcut is printed by laying paper onto the inked block.

wood engraving a relief technique – thought to have been invented by Thomas Bewick (1753–1828) – that differs from woodcutting in that normally a hard, fine-grained wood is cut into across the grain. The resulting image is usually much finer than a woodcut. The technique was commonly used for fine book illustrations during the 19th century.

PREHISTORIC ART

The world's most ancient works of art date from 30 000 BC. This is vastly earlier than the first written records and means that the greater part of art history is, in fact, prehistoric. It was during the prehistoric period that virtually all the major artistic media evolved, including drawing, painting, sculpture, ceramics and, arguably, architecture.

PALAEOLITHIC ART FROM 30 000 BC

Figurines Figurines shaped out of clay, bone, stone, wood and ivory have been found scattered over a wide area from Spain to Siberia. They depict both animals and humans. Some, typified by the famous 'Venus' of Willendorf in Austria, portray women with exaggerated breasts and buttocks, and have been linked to a supposed fertility cult. Others, such as the female head from Brassempouy in France, are more elegant and naturalistic.

Cave painting Painting, engraving and relief on the walls of caves began later than figurine sculpture, and flourished soon after 16 000 BC. The hunters who created cave art were inspired by the animals around them, particularly by large mammals such as deer, horses, wild cattle, bison, woolly rhinoceroses and mammoths. The first examples rediscovered were at Chaffaud (Vienne), France, in 1834. The famous Lascaux cave paintings in France were discovered in 1940. Cave art has been found mostly in southern France and northeastern Spain (Altamira), although notable examples have also been discovered in Czechoslovakia, the Urals (USSR), India, Australia – the cave art at Mootwingie dates from c. 1500 BC – and the Sahara, where the earliest cave art dates from *post* 5400 BC.

NEOLITHIC ART

In the Neolithic (New Stone Age) period, farming and settled village life spread across Europe (c. 6500–4000 BC). This encouraged both the use of pottery and the development of architecture. Shaped and decorated vessels were produced almost everywhere, but the most inventive and prolific potters lived in eastern Europe. The Vinca culture produced thousands of fired-clay figurines, including some dramatically stylized heads found at Predionica in Serbia. Related cultures produced pots shaped like human figures, animals or even houses. Neolithic houses, tombs and temples have also produced many examples of prehistoric art. At the Maltese temple complex of Tarxien (c. 3000–2000 BC) there are animal friezes and the surviving half of a monumental sculpture depicting a monumentally corpulent diety.

BRONZE AND IRON AGE ART

During later European prehistory, despite advances in pottery and architecture, the most exciting artistic innovations arose from the development of metalwork. In the 2nd millennium BC in eastern Europe, early cast bronze weapons and jewellery were delicately engraved with curved-line designs. Similar decoration appears on Scandinavian metalwork: a remarkable ritual object found at Trundholm in Denmark consists of a cast bronze horse pulling an engraved gold-covered sun. Duirng the 1st millennium BC many more bronze figures were cast, notably in Scandinavia, central Europe and Sardinia. Engraving remained common, but the beating or embossing of metalwork grew in importance. Embossed friezes on *situlae* (buckets) from northern Italy and Yugoslavia illustrate religious processions. The early Celts decorated weapons, vessels and pieces of jewellery in such a fluid style that it is often impossible to separate the stylized Celtic heads and animals from the surrounding plant-like ornament.

THE ART OF THE ANCIENT NEAR EAST AND EGYPT

Early civilizations flourished along the great river valleys of the Nile in Egypt, and the Tigris and Euphrates from Anatolia (present-day Turkey), through Syria into Mesopotamia (present-day Iraq). The rivers linked these regions in an extensive trade network that also encompassed Persia (present-day Iran) to the east, but variations in climate, geography, natural resources and population resulted in corresponding variations in artistic traditions.

MESOPOTAMIAN ART 6000–3600 BC

Covering the Sumerian, Assyrian and Babylonian epochs, Mesopotamian art is represented by many styles, although most incorporate figures, animals (both real and mythical) and plants. It is now seen mainly in the sculptural works on palaces (e.g. Nineveh) and on tiles.

EGYPTIAN ART 3100–341 BC

Egyptian art is essentially a decorative tomb art, based on the notion of immortality; the deceased were recorded and equipped for the afterlife in writing (hieroglyphs), pictures and material wealth and goods.

GREEK AND ROMAN ART

The arts of Greece and Rome are characterized by a sense of proportion, harmony and balance. Since the Renaissance, Classical decoration, whether ornate or simple, has frequently provided architects with a fruitful source of ideas, and Classical imagery has enriched the work of poets, painters and sculptors. In general, Classical form has exerted a largely civilizing influence over the past two and a half millennia.

GREEK ART 2000–27 BC

Minoan and Mycenaean art (2000–1100 BC) consists mainly of sculptured engravings, decorated pottery and some frescos. The Archaic period (800–500 BC) saw the development of sculpture, especially human figures. This tendency was developed in the Classical period (500–323 BC), where the body was glorified and drapery carved to imitate movement. The Hellenistic period (323–27 BC) was characterized by greater emotional expression, and is notable for its portraits. Throughout the period pottery was decorated with figures and scenes from story and legend.

ROMAN ART 100 BC–AD 400

Roman art excelled in copying Greek sculpture and relief carving to a very high quality. Portrait busts were popular, and Roman painting was mainly executed in fresco in a naturalistic style (e.g. at Pompeii). Mosaic floors were also highly decorative.

The concentration on what has survived, and the elevation of some of it to the first rank of artistic excellence in modern eyes, have tended to obscure the fact that we now possess very little of what ancient Greeks and Romans might have considered to be artistically important. The Greeks and Romans themselves tended rather to appreciate highly wrought works in gold and silver. Since articles of precious metal were the first to be seized or melted down in times of war or hardship, such works have virtually all vanished, but contemporary accounts of shrines and individuals speak of great amounts of sculpture and vases made of gold and silver, and it was in these media that eminent craftsmen preferred to work.

ISLAMIC ART: 7TH–17TH CENTURY

Geographically Islamic art extends from Indonesia in the east to Morocco and Spain in the west. The word 'Islamic' reflects a culture and society united by Islam, but as artistic influences from Arabia (the birthplace of Islam) were minimal, Islam can in some ways also be seen as a catalyst for the development of existing Byzantine, Persian and later Indian styles that prevailed when the conquering Muslim armies arrived.

Originally based on superb Koranic calligraphy, it is a highly decorative art form which reaches its apotheosis in the miniature painting, the ceramic tile, and carpetmaking, in which floral and geometric motives reach a high peak of formal perfection. Although by no means absolute, traditionally there is a ban on the representation of living figures in a religious context, which accounts for the often semi-abstract nature of Islamic ornament and for the virtual absence of sculpture.

SOUTH ASIAN ART

India's earliest civilization flourished in the Indus Valley between 2300–1700 BC, centred on the cities of Harappa and Mohenjo-Daro. Its architecture was utilitarian, but some fine statues in sandstone and slate were produced. Little survives between the time of the Harappa civilization and that of the Mauryas (321–185 BC), during whose rule Persian and Greek influences are apparent, notably in architecture.

Essentially traditional and religious, Buddhist and Hindu works of art are symbols and manifestations of gods. One of the most distinctive Buddhist architectural forms is the *stupa* – an ornate burial mound. The Mauryas popularized man-made caves and initiated a revival in sculpture. Temples for both religions became increasingly ornate and complex. In the 7th century fresco painting and rock sculpture in India had reached a peak and by the 13th century erotic carvings had become popular.

CHINESE AND JAPANESE ART

China is the longest surviving civilization in the world, with an art history stretching back at least

4000 years. Because it was the most advanced country in eastern Asia, China influenced many of its neighbours, and later also the Islamic world and western Europe. The distinctiveness of Chinese art has been complemented by very high technical skills, and for many centuries ceramics, bronzes, jade carvings, silk and lacquer were produced to standards surpassing those of all other cultures.

The advent of Buddhism (1st century AD) encouraged religious art in China, in particular sculptures of Buddha. Landscape painting became popular under the Tang Dynasty (618–907) and Chinese pottery reached perfection under the Sung (960–1279), becoming much more elaborate under the Ming (1368–1644). Japan was heavily influenced by Chinese art, but later indigenous Japanese art forms include *netsuke* (miniature sculptures), painted screens, and *Ukiyo-e* woodblock colour prints.

MAJOR ARTISTS

Gu Kaizhi (Ku K'ai-Chih; c. 345–405), a leading Chinese painter, considered to be the founder of landscape painting.

Hui Zong (1082–1135), an emperor and major painter of the flower-and-bird category of painting.

Huang Gong-Wang (1269–1354), major Chinese landscape painter of his time, celebrated for the introduction of dry ink and slanting brush technique.

Suzuki Harunobu (1725–70), Japanese colour-print artist.

Toshusai Sharaku (d. 1801), Japanese *Ukiyo-e* printer. Unpopular in his day, but his work is now highly prized in the West.

Kitagawa Utamaro (1753–1806), Japanese colour-print artist (*Ukiyo-e* school): *Insects* (1788).

Katsushika Hokusai (1760–1849), Japanese painter, draughtsman and wood engraver (a major *Ukiyo-e* print designer): *Mangwa* (1814–78) and *Views of Mt Fuji*.

Ando Hiroshige (1797–1858), Japanese painter and colour-print artist: *Fifty-three Stages of the Tokaido Highway* (1833).

AUSTRALASIAN AND OCEANIC ART

Pottery and metalwork were unknown in Australasia and Oceania before the arrival of Europeans. However, other art forms were flourishing. Cave paintings – both representational and abstract – and tree bark paintings have been found in Australia. Melanesia boasts highly decorated tools and utensils, bark drawings and 'Uli' statues – statues with huge heads, small bodies, and tiny legs. The art of bark painting, plaiting, weaving, tattooing, wood carving and personal adornment reached a degree of perfection in Polynesia, particularly New Zealand and Samoa. The Easter Island Heads are remarkable statue heads carved from soft volcanic stone, some of them standing 12 m (40 ft) high and weighing up to 50 tonnes (tons). They were erected between AD 1000 and 1600, but their meaning is still not fully understood.

NATIVE AMERICAN ART

The greatest architecture and stone sculpture of the Americas is divided between the ancient civilizations of Mesoamerica and the Central Andes. Before and after the arrival of Europeans, tribal North America excelled in wooden sculpture, textiles and pottery.

The Aztec altars were covered with detailed sculpted stone images of gods and animals. Other notable Aztec art includes worked gold, cut stone, featherwork and intricate weaving. The Olmec and Maya were also sculptors; the latter inscribed their *stelae* (stone columns) with writing and animal motifs, and adorned their temples with carved friezes.

AFRICAN ART

The finest African art, excluding the products of Egypt and the Muslim north, is largely concentrated in the rain forests and savannah woodland of central western Africa. Far to the north and south lies the ancient rock art of the Sahara and southern Africa.

The earliest known sculptural tradition of sub-Saharan Africa emerged c. 500 BC in northern Nigeria. Its products are grouped together as the 'Nok culture', and consist of naturalistic terracottas of animals and more stylized terracottas of human figures; the figures often have simplified bodies, disproportionately large heads and distinctive eyes. It may have influenced the realistic, if idealized, terracottas and bronzes of the Ife Kingdom (11th–16th century). Superb metalworkers, the Benin Kingdom (1500–1700) produced plaques decorated in high and low relief with scenes of warriors, chiefs and Portuguese traders.

African art is probably best known for its carved wooden masks and sculptures. Both masks and figures tend to face forward, are symmetrically arranged around a vertical axis, and are carved from a single piece of wood. Masks often have beads, feathers, hair or fibre as added decoration.

EARLY MEDIEVAL ART

The period between the Classical Age and the Renaissance has sometimes been described dismissively as the 'Dark Ages'. This is both inaccurate and misleading. These centuries formed an essential artistic bridgehead, when new approaches to pictorial form were worked out and deeper spiritual values attached to works of art. The major patron became the Christian Church, and most of the greatest monuments are related to churches and monasteries.

BYZANTINE ART

At first an admixture of Hellenic, Roman, Middle Eastern and Oriental styles, Byzantine art dates from and has its first centre in the establishment of Constantinople as capital of the Roman Empire in the East. The First Golden Age was in the 6th century, when Hagia Sophia (St Sophia) was built in the city. The Second Golden Age occurred between 1051 and 1185, when Western Europe was influenced by the severe, spiritually uplifted style of the Byzantines. These two Ages are dominated by the use of mosaic work, but by the Third Golden Age (1261–1450) this expensive medium was being replaced by fresco painting.

ROMANESQUE ART

A widespread western European style in the 11th and 12th centuries was mainly architectural, distinguished by the use of rounded arches. The sculpture is mainly church work intended to inspire awe of the divine power by depicting scenes of heaven and hell, demons and angels, and the omnipotent deity. Illuminated manuscripts of high quality include the Winchester Bible.

GOTHIC ART

Gothic painting and sculpture flourished alongside architecture. The Romanesque world of fantastic beasts is largely left behind and a new emphasis is placed on nature and humanity's place within its hierarchy. This is shown in a more human relationship between God and the individual, and in the greater expression of human emotions.

Gothic sculpture is narrative and realistic, particularly the friezes. In painting the style evolved more slowly and is seen in manuscript illumination and frescos.

INTERNATIONAL GOTHIC

A later mixture of styles of painting and sculpture in Europe due to the movements of notable peripatetic artists and the increase in trade, travel and court rivalry. The main influences were northern France, the Netherlands and Italy, and its main features are rich and decorative colouring and detail, and flowing line.

MAJOR ARTISTS

Giovanni Pisano (active 1265–1314), Pisan sculptor: the pulpit in S Andrea, Pistoia (1301), particularly the panel of the *Massacre of the Innocents*.

Giotto di Bondone (c. 1267–1337), influential Florentine painter, who introduced a new naturalism: *Ognissanti Madonna* (c. 1310–15).

Cimabue (active 1272–1302), Florentine painter who introduced more realistic painting: *The S. Trinità Madonna*.

Duccio di Buoninsegna (active 1278–1319), Sienese painter; influential in his introduction of two-dimensional decorative surface art in Siena.

Ambrogio and Pietro Lorenzetti (active c. 1319–48), Sienese sculptors and painters: Ambrogio's early realistic landscapes and Pietro's *Descent from the Cross*.

Gentile da Fabriano (c. 1370–1427), Italian painter of the International Gothic style: *Adoration of the Magi* (1423).

Lorenzo Monaco (c. 1370/2–1422/5), Sienese International Gothic painter and miniaturist: *Adoration* (c. 1424).

Claus Sluter (active c. 1380–d. 1405/6), Flemish International Gothic sculptor: monumental figures at Chartreuse de Champmol, Dijon (1390s–1403).

Antonio Pisanello (c. 1395–1455/6), Veronese painter: *St George and the Princess* and *Vision of St Eustace* (1435–38).

Limbourg Brothers (Paul, Jean, Herman; d. c. 1416), Franco-Flemish manuscript illuminators: *Très Riches Heures*.

THE EARLY RENAISSANCE

The term *renaissance* ('rebirth') was first coined in the 19th century to describe a period of intellectual and artistic renewal that lasted from about 1350 to about 1550. The dominant theme of this period is the revival of interest in classical literature and art by 14th- and 15th-century humanists and the rediscovery by artists of their cultural past. Florence was the first centre of such rediscovery, with Padua, Venice and finally Rome rivalling Florence in the pursuit of antiquarian learning and artistic

excellence. After 1500, the movement also spread to northern Europe.

Architecture, painting and sculpture, deriving from Greek and Roman models and using classical motifs, moved into unparalleled prominence. Advances were made in the realistic depiction of figures. Other artistic inventions included perspective and painting with oil. Religious art continued into the 15th century, but painters were also able to decorate private palaces with secular narratives of historical or mythological subjects.

MAJOR ARTISTS

Lorenzo Ghiberti (1378–1455), Florentine sculptor and goldsmith: bronze doors for the Florence Baptistery, the second set, so-called 'Gates of Paradise', includes highly sophisticated representations of space and form.

Donatello (c. 1386–1466), highly influential Florentine sculptor: equestrian statue of *Gattemalata* (1443–47) and the high altar for the church of St Anthony.

Paolo Uccello (c. 1397–1475), Florentine painter: fresco *Deluge* and the panels depicting the *Rout of Romano*, which experiment with perspectives.

Fra Angelico (c. 1399–1455), Florentine religious painter: cycle of frescos in San Marco, Florence.

Masaccio (1401–c. 1428), influential Florentine painter: *Trinity* fresco (1428), in Santa Maria Novella, Florence, and the fresco paintings in the Brancacci Chapel, Florence (c. 1425–28).

Fra Filippo Lippi (c. 1406–69), Florentine painter: fresco paintings of the lives of St Stephen and St John the Baptist, Prato Cathedral (1452–65).

Piero della Francesca (c. 1420–92), Italian painter: *The Flagellation of Christ* (c. 1456) and the cycle *The Story of the True Cross* at the Church of San Francesco, Arezzo (1452–66).

Giovanni Bellini (c. 1430–1516), member of a notable artistic Venetian family: the altarpieces of the Frari (1488), San Zaccaria (c. 1505) and other mythological scenes.

Andrea Mantegna (c. 1431–1506), northern Italian painter, celebrated for his perfectionist work on perspective.

Sandro Botticelli (c. 1445–1510), Florentine painter: *Primavera* ('Spring'; 1477–78) and *Birth of Venus*.

Leonardo da Vinci (1452–1519), one of the greatest Italian painters and sculptors (also architect, musician, engineer, and scientist): the unfinished *Adoration of the Magi*, *Madonna of the Rocks* (two versions: 1483–c. 1486 and 1483–1508), *The Last Supper* (c. 1495–98), and *Mona Lisa* (c. 1503).

EARLY NETHERLANDISH AND GERMAN ART

The Netherlandish and German art of the period from around 1400 to 1570 is often described under the blanket term 'Northern Renaissance'. While this label recognizes the originality and vitality of the northern contemporaries of the Italian Renaissance masters, it obscures the very important divide between the 15th and 16th centuries. In the earlier century the rediscoveries of the Italians aroused little interest north of the Alps, but in the 16th century Netherlandish and German artists became increasingly fascinated by classical antiquity.

As in Italy, Flemish and German painters moved towards more realistic figure work, and their experimentations led to the development of portraiture, nudes, meticulously accurate details, distant landscapes, spatial illusionism and careful depiction of light and shadow. Oil painting was introduced and woodcuts and engravings achieved a new depth of expression.

MAJOR ARTISTS

Rogier van der Weyden (c. 1399–1464), influential Flemish painter: *The Deposition* (pre-1443) and the altarpiece of the *Last Judgement* (c. 1450).

Jan van Eyck (active 1422–41), Flemish painter, celebrated for the realistic detail of his portraits: the Ghent altarpiece (1432; in collaboration with his brother Hubert; d. 1426).

Petrus Christus (active 1444–72/3), Flemish painter: noted for the use of geometric perspective in *Lamentation* (c. 1448) and *St Eligius and Two Lovers* (1449).

Dierick Bouts (active 1448–75), early Flemish painter, distinguished by his calm, reflective and elongated figures.

Quentin Massys (1464/5–1530), Flemish painter: portrait of *Erasmus* (1517).

Hugo van der Goes (active 1467–82), Flemish painter: Portinari altarpiece (c. 1474–76) and Monforte altarpiece (c. 1472).

Martin Schongauer (active 1469–91), early German engraver: celebrated for his subtle description of light and texture.

Albrecht Dürer (1471–1528), German painter, engraver and theoretician: *Knight, Death and the Devil, St Jerome in his Cell*, and *Melancholia*.

Joachim Patenir (c. 1480–1524), Flemish landscape and religious painter: *Flight into Egypt*.

Albrecht Altdorfer (c. 1480–1538), German painter and engraver, distinguished by his development of the landscape genre: *The Battle of Alexander and Darius on the Issus* (1529).

Hieronymous Bosch (active 1480/1–1516), Flemish painter, celebrated for his fantastic and grotesque imagery: *Garden of Earthly Delights* (c. 1505–10).

Hans Baldung Grien (1484/5–1545), German religious and mythological painter: *Death and the Maiden*.

Lucas van Leyden (c. 1489–1533), Dutch painter and engraver of historical and domestic scenes: *Last Judgement* (1526–27).

Hans the Younger Holbein (1497/8–1543), German portrait and religious painter: *Dead Christ* (1521) and *Erasmus* (1517).

Mathias Grünewald (c. 1470–1528), German religious painter: crucifixion of Christ on the Isenheim altarpiece.

Pieter the Elder Bruegel (c. 1525–69), foremost of a Flemish family of painters: *Peasant Wedding Dance* (1566), series of landscape paintings depicting the months of the year such as *Hunters in the Snow* (1565) and the proverb series including *The Blind Leading the Blind* (1568).

THE HIGH RENAISSANCE AND MANNERISM

The focus of artistic activity in Italy shifted during the early 16th century from Florence to Rome. One of the most concentrated groups of artistic genius ever known was gathered in the papal city. The role of the artist changed even more dramatically than in the previous century, and a number of academies were established, confirming the professional status of the artist. At the same time, the artistic innovations of the Italian Renaissance began to spread to northern Europe.

Artistic innovation later led to the superficial elegance of Mannerism. A style that became popular all over Catholic Europe, Mannerism displayed exaggerated sophistication and virtuosity – sometimes combined with a heightened emotionalism and religiosity. However, the Counter-Reformation brought in restrictions on both subject matter and treatment in religious art, and by the end of the 16th century Mannerism had lost much of its vigour.

MAJOR ARTISTS

Michelangelo Buonarroti (1475–1564), foremost Italian sculptor, painter, and architect: the sculpture *David* (1501–4), the ceiling of the Sistine Chapel (1508–12), statues *Moses and the Slaves* (1513–16) and the fresco *Last Judgement* (Sistine Chapel; 1536–41).

Raphael (1483–1520), highly successful Italian painter: wall paintings in the Vatican, including *School of Athens, Triumph of Religion, The Miracle of Bolsena* and *The Deliverance of St Peter*.

Fra Bartolommeo (c. 1474–c. 1517), Florentine High Renaissance painter: *Last Judgement* in the Santa Maria Nuova.

Giorgione (c. 1476/8–1510), Venetian painter who introduced pastoral subjects to paintings.

Andrea del Sarto (1486–1530), Italian High Renaissance painter of frescos and altarpieces: *The Madonna of the Harpies* (1517).

Titian (Tiziano Vecellio; c. 1487/90–1576), Venetian Renaissance painter, notable for his dream-like pastorals, colour, and free handling of paint: *Venus and Adonis* (1554) and the altarpiece of the *Assumption of the Virgin* (Church of Santa Maria Gloriosa dei Frari, Venice).

Jacopo da Pontormo (1494–1556), Florentine painter, one of the creators of Mannerism: *Deposition* (c. 1526).

Giulio Romano (1492–1546), Italian painter, architect, decorator and one of the founders of Mannerism: the decoration of the Palazzo del Tè.

Antonio Correggio (c. 1495–1534), influential Italian High Renaissance painter: *Jupiter and Io*.

Parmigianino (1503–40), Italian Mannerist painter and etcher: *The Vision of St Jerome* and *Madonna of the Long Neck* (c. 1535).

Agnolo Bronzino (1507–72), Florentine Mannerist painter, well known for his portraits: *Venus, Cupid, Folly* and *Time*.

Jacopo Tintoretto (1518–94), Venetian Mannerist painter: *Last Judgement*.

Paolo Veronese (1528–88), Venetian painter: frescos in the Villa Maser near Treviso, a series of religious feast scenes, including *Marriage at Cana* (1562) and *The Feast in the House of Levi* (1573).

Jean Goujon (active 1540–62), French Mannerist sculptor and architect: *Fountain of the Innocents* (1547–49) and the *Tribune of Caryatids*.

Giambologna (1529–1608), Flemish Mannerist sculptor: the influential sculpture *The Rape of the Sabines* (1579–83).

El Greco (Domenikos Theotocopoulos; 1541–1614), Greek Mannerist painter and sculptor (working in Spain): *The Burial of Count Orgaz* (1586) and *Christ Stripped of his Garments* (1577–79).

THE BAROQUE AND CLASSICISM

Classicism and the Baroque were the two dominant trends in the visual arts of the 17th century, particularly in Catholic countries and most importantly in Italy and France. Although frequently divergent and opposed, they both originated in the reaction in Italy against the aridity of Late Mannerism. A return to the naturalism, harmonious equilibrium and compositional coherence of the High Renaissance was combined with a new physical realism, emotional immediacy and dynamic vigour.

The Baroque style combined the dramatic effects of energetic movement, vivid colour and decorative detail with expressive originality and freedom. Classicism deployed more restrained qualities of directness and precision to enliven traditional ideas of balance and decorum.

MAJOR ARTISTS

Annibale Carracci (1560–1609), member of a notable family of Italian painters: decoration of the gallery ceiling in the Farnese Palace, Rome.

Michelangelo Merisis da Caravaggio (1573–1610), early Italian Baroque painter notable for the dramatic use of light and shade: *The Beheading of St John the Baptist*.

Guido Reni (1575–1642), Italian Classical painter: ceiling fresco *Aurora* (1613).

Peter Paul Rubens (1577–1640), foremost Flemish painter, celebrated for the epic grandeur of his work: *The Raising of the Cross* (1610–11) and *Descent from the Cross* (1611–14; Antwerp Cathedral).

Domenichino (1581–1641), Bolognese painter, noted for his landscapes.

Nicolas Poussin (1594–1665), French Classical painter, notable for the mathematical precision of his landscapes: *Landscape with Diogenes*.

Pietro da Cortona (1596–1669), Italian Baroque painter: *Allegory of Divine Providence and Barberini Power* (1633–39), a ceiling fresco.

Gianlorenzo Bernini (1598–1680), Italian High Baroque sculptor and painter: the sculptures *Apollo and Daphne* (1625) and *Ecstasy of Saint Theresa* (1645–52).

Anthony van Dyck (1599–1641), Flemish painter and etcher, known for his elegant portraits.

Diego Velásquez (1599–1660), Spanish painter: *Las Meninas* (1656), *Pope Innocent X* (1650), and *The Surrender of Breda* (1634–35).

Claude Lorraine (1600–82), French Classical landscape painter, notable for his rendering of light and atmosphere in his paintings.

Salvator Rosa (1615–73), Italian Baroque painter and etcher noted for his tempestuous landscapes.

THE DUTCH SCHOOL

In the 17th century a sudden flowering of the art of painting in the Netherlands coincided with the overthrow of Spanish rule and Dutch mercantile success throughout the world. The stubborn tenacity that enabled them to triumph over apparently superior forces at home and abroad was reflected in the solid sobriety with which the Dutch viewed their surroundings. Dutch artists concentrated on the types of painting in which they had long specialized – still life, genre (scenes of everyday life), landscape and portraiture.

MAJOR ARTISTS

Frans Hals (1580/85–1666), genre and portrait painter: *The Merry Drinker*, *The Laughing Cavalier*, *The Governors of the Almshouse*, and *Lady Regents of the Almshouse*.

Hendrick Terbrugghen (1588–1629), painter specializing in genre painting: *The Flute Player* (1621).

Gerard von Honthorst (1590–1656), painter specializing in portraits and genre painting: *The Merry Fiddler* (1623).

Pieter Saenredam (1597–1665), painter of church interiors: *View in the Nieuwe Kert at Haarlem* (1652).

Adriaen Brouwer (1605/6–38), painter specializing in scenes of peasant revelry: *The Smokers* (c. 1637).

Rembrandt van Rijn (1606–69), painter, etcher and draughtsman, particularly celebrated for his portraits: *The Anatomy Lesson* (1632), *The Night Watch* (1642), and his series of self-portraits.

Gerard Terborch (1617–81), portrait and genre painter of genteel interiors: *Parental Admonition* (c. 1654/55).

Willem Kalf (1619–93), still-life painter: *Still Life with a Nautilus Cup* (1642–46).

Aelbert Cuyp (1620–91), landscape painter, noted for his views of rivers and towns in evening and morning light: *View of the Dordrecht*.

Jan Steen (1626–79), prolific genre painter, notable for his scenes of merry-making: *St Nicholas' Feast*.

Jacob van Ruisdael (1628/9–82), landscape painter and etcher, distinguished by his dramatic scenes: *Jewish Cemetery* (c. 1660).

Pieter de Hooch (1629–84), genre painter celebrated for his use of light in garden and courtyard scenes: *Courtyard in Delft* (1658).

Jan Vermeer (1632–75), genre painter noted for his domestic interiors with subtle lighting and geometrical shapes: *Allegory of the Faith* (1669–70), *Allegory of Painting* (c. 1665), and *Girl with a Pearl Earring*.

Meindert Hobbema (1638–1709), landscape painter: *Avenue at Middelharnis* (1689).

ROCOCO AND NEOCLASSICISM

The synthesis in later 17th-century Italy of Classicist idealization and Baroque vigour was taken up in France and spread throughout Europe as the accepted courtly 'Grand Manner'. It was soon diluted by the 18th-century desire for the informal and undemanding, which found its artistic expression in the style known as Rococo. For perhaps the first time the prime function of art was perceived as decorative rather than illustrative or didactic.

Neither the attitude nor the style were fully accepted in England, where Baroque licence had already been challenged early in the new century by the more 'rational' concept of Palladianism. By the 1750s a reaction to the still freer and more exotic forms of the Rococo appeared not only in England but in France, cradle of the style. Archaeological discoveries in Italy and Greece prompted a re-examination of the origins of European civilization. French intellectualism developed this into international Neoclassicism.

MAJOR ARTISTS

Antoine Watteau (1684–1721), French Rococo painter who introduced romantic figures in a park or garden setting to the Rococo style: *Embarkation for Cythera* (1717).

Giambattista Tiepolo (1696–1770), Italian Rococo painter: noted for the ceiling paintings and frescos in the Labia Palace and Palacio Real, Madrid.

Antonio Canaletto (1697–1768), Venetian view painter of the period, noted for the topographical quality in his art.

François Boucher (1703–70), French Rococo painter: *The Rising of the Sun, The Setting of the Sun* (1753), and *Reclining Girl* (1751), a famous female nude.

Francesco Guardi (1712–93), member of a family of notable Venetian painters; celebrated for his view paintings and architectural scenes.

Thomas Gainsborough (1727–88), English portrait and landscape painter: *Mr and Mrs Andrews* (c.1750), *The Blue Boy* (c. 1770), and *The Harvest Wagon* (c. 1770).

Jean-Honoré Fragonard (1732–1806), French Rococo painter: four *Progress of Love* paintings (1771–73) and *The Swing* (1769).

Jacques-Louis David (1748–1825), French Neoclassical painter: *Death of Marat* (1793), *View of the Luxembourg Gardens* (1794), and *Mme de Verninac* (1799).

Antonio Canova (1757–1822), Italian Neoclassical sculptor: *Daedalus and Icarus* (1779).

ROMANTICISM

Romanticism was a movement in art that emerged in the late 18th century, and that flourished until the middle of the 19th. The movement was a reaction both against the aesthetic and ethical values of Classical and Neoclassical art, and against the ugliness and materialism of the Industrial Revolution. The influence of Romantic writers such as Rousseau, Schiller, Goethe, Scott and Byron was particularly important in providing both subject matter and a philosophy for the Romantic painters. The values of the wider Romantic movement (see p.<del>36</del> 357) are central to an understanding of the visual art of the period. Indeed it is the *content* of Romantic painting and the attitude of the artists themselves that give the movement coherence, as in terms of style and technique there are enormous variations.

MAJOR ARTISTS

John Constable (1776–1837), English landscape painter: *The Hay Wain* (1821).

Eugène Delacroix (1798–1863), French painter: *The Massacre at Chios* (1823) and *The Death of Sardanapalus* (1827).

Caspar David Friedrich (1774–1840), German landscape painter, noted for his evocative scenes of mountain peaks and moonlit shores.

Henry Fuseli (1741–1825), Swiss painter living in England, notable for his explorations of the darker side of human nature: *The Nightmare* (1782).

Théodore Géricault (1791–1824), French painter and one of the founders of Romanticism: *Charging Chasseur* and *The Raft of the Medusa* (1819).

Francisco de Goya y Lucientes (1746–1848), Spanish painter and etcher: *Maja Nude* and *Maja Clothed* (1797–1800), *The Third of May* (1814), and

The Disasters of War (etchings, 1810–20).

John Martin (1789–1854), British painter and engraver, noted for his sensationalist apocalyptic scenes: *The Deluge* (1834).

Samuel Palmer (1805–81), English painter and etcher of pastoral scenes.

Joseph Mallord William Turner (1775–1851), foremost English landscape painter: *The Fighting Téméraire* (1838), and *Rain, Steam and Speed* (1844).

REALISM

Realism was a movement that flourished between 1840 and 1880, originating in France, and soon spreading throughout Europe and to America. The Realists reacted against the subjectivity, individualism and historical obsessions of many of the Romantics, adopting instead a naturalistic style of art based on truth to nature. The grand, heroic subject matter of the Romantic movement was replaced by simple views of everyday life, and Romantic emotionalism was abandoned in favour of detached, objective observation. The term 'Realism' applies to both style and subject matter. Usually Realists avoided the vivid, dramatic brushstrokes favoured by Romantic artists, preferring to make their paintings distinct and precise, with straight forward subjects.

THE BARBIZON SCHOOL

During the 1840s, the village of Barbizon, on the outskirts of the Fontainebleau forest, became the centre for a group of French landscape painters. They began the direct study of nature, aiming to create a naturalistic depiction of landscape without the restrictions of academic conventions. Their work encouraged the emergence of Impressionism.

THE PRE-RAPHAELITE BROTHERHOOD

A brotherhood of seven London artists (1848–56) formed to make a return to the style of Italian painting before Raphael (hence the name) as a protest against the frivolity of the prevailing English School of the day. The founders and most important exponents of the movement were William Holman Hunt, John Everett Millais and Dante Gabriel Rossetti. Their subject matter was often drawn from religion and legend, and their style minutely detailed.

THE ARTS AND CRAFTS MOVEMENT c. 1870–1900

Based on the revival of interest in the medieval craft system, and led by William Morris (1834–96), the aims of the movement were to fuse the functional and the decorative, and to restore the worth of handmade crafts in the face of the growing mass-produced wares of the late 19th century.

MAJOR ARTISTS

Eugène Boudin (1824–98), French painter of seascapes and beach scenes: *Women on the Beach at Trouville* (1872).

Ford Madox Brown (1821–93), English painter, whose style was similar to that of the Pre-Raphaelites: his social beliefs were reflected in his famous painting *Work* (1852–65).

Edward Burne-Jones (1833–98), English Symbolist painter, illustrator, and designer. Strongly influenced by the Pre-Raphaelites, he is noted for his ethereal aesthetic and dreamlike style.

Camille Corot (1796–1875), French landscape and figure painter, an important precursor of the Impressionists: *The Studio* (1870), *Ponte de Mantes* (1870), and *Sens Cathedral* (1874).

Gustav Courbet (1819–77), French painter and foremost Realist artist: *The Peasants of Flagey*, *The Stonebreakers* and *A Burial at Ornans*.

Charles-François Daubigny (1817–78), French landscape painter of the Barbizon school.

Honoré Daumier (1808–79), French caricaturist, whose works contain bitter satires on political and social subjects.

Thomas Eakins (1844–1916), American Realist painter: *The Biglen Brothers Racing* (1873) and *The Writing Master* (1881).

William Powell Frith (1819–1909), English narrative painter: *Derby Day* (1858) and *The Railway Station* (1862).

Winslow Homer (1836–1910), American landscape, seascape and genre painter: *The Northeaster*, *Cannon Rock* (1895), and *Saguenay River* (1899).

William Holman Hunt (1827–1910), English painter and one of the founders of the Pre-Raphaelite Brotherhood, noted for the detail and symbolism in his paintings: *The Awakening Conscience* (1853–54).

Sir John Everett Millais (1829–96), English portrait, genre, landscape and history painter and co-founder of the Pre-Raphaelite Brotherhood. Best-known for *Bubbles* (1886), which was subsequently used in a soap advertisement.

Jean-François Millet (1814–75), French Realist painter, celebrated for his dignified depiction of French peasants: *The Gleaners* (1857) and *The Angelus* (1859).

Dante Gabriel Rossetti (1828–82), English painter, poet and co-founder of the Pre-Raphaelite Brotherhood. He later worked in watercolours before returning to oils.

Théodore Rousseau (1812–67), French landscape painter of the Barbizon School: *Descent of the Cattle* (1835).

IMPRESSIONISM AND NEOIMPRESSIONISM

Although often regarded as the first of the modern movements, Impressionism was neither a school nor a movement with a clearly defined programme. Instead it is better regarded as an ill-defined association of artists who joined together for the purpose of mounting independent group exhibitions, rather than compromise their art in order to be included in the Paris Salon, the official state-sponsored exhibition. In all there were eight Impressionist exhibitions, held from 1874 to 1886. While they had no stated aims or manifesto their work shared some techniques and certain subjects. Their approach was naturalistic, and their two main subjects were landscape and modern (often city) life. Often painted in the open air, their paintings show a concern with capturing the fleeting moment, particularly the effects of light, which they attempted to capture with a free handling of paint.

NEOIMPRESSIONISM

At the final Impressionist exhibition, Seurat, Signac and Pissarro all showed canvases using the latest *divisionist* (or *pointillist*) techniques. This involved the use of pure colours applied in such small patches (often dots) that they appeared to fuse to form an intermediary tone when viewed from an appropriate distance. Hence grass might be composed of touches

of blue alongside areas of yellow. These ideas were not new, but had been used in a much less systematic way by the Impressionist painters. However, the static quality of works such as Seurat's *Bathers at Asnières* (1884) and its large format marked a departure from the aims of orthodox Impressionism.

MAJOR ARTISTS

Mary Cassatt (1844–1926), American Impressionist painter, noted for her paintings of mothers and children and her graphics based on Japanese prints.

Edgar Degas (1834–1917), French Impressionist painter and sculptor, whose favourite subjects were dancers and race horses: the bronze *The Little Dancer of Fourteen* (1880–81), *The Rehearsal* (1882), and *Two Laundresses* (1882).

Edouard Manet (1832–83), French painter, considered the father of modern painting: *Déjeuner sur l'herbe* ('Picnic on the grass'; 1863) and *Olympia* (1863).

Claude Monet (1840–1926), French Impressionist painter, particularly of landscapes: *Women in the Garden* (1867) and the series *Waterlilies* (1899–1926).

Berthe Morisot (1841–95), French painter notable for her paintings of women and children.

Camille Pissarro (1831–1903), French Impressionist painter, briefly flirted with pointillism during the 1880s.

Auguste Renoir (1841–1919), French Impressionist painter: *Umbrellas* (1883), *The Bathers* (1884–87), and *The Theatre Box* (1874).

Georges Seurat (1859–91), French painter, founder and leading exponent of Neoimpressionism: *Bathers at Asnières* (1884).

Paul Signac (1863–1935), French Neoimpressionist painter, theoretician of Neoimpressionism.

Alfred Sisley (1839–99), French Impressionist painter born of English parents, well known for his landscapes.

James McNeill Whistler (1834–1903), American painter and graphic artist, who worked in England. Briefly with the Realist school, his later, more Impressionist work became abstract: *Nocturne* series.

POST-IMPRESSIONISM AND FAUVISM

Just as the Impressionists reacted against the established art of their day, a succession of artists later reacted against Impressionism itself. The Post-Impressionists, as they became known, were active mainly in France between about 1880 and 1905. They included artists who painted in a wide variety of styles but who shared a desire to go beyond pure naturalism and to give more emphasis to colour, emotions and imagination. From these individuals the major art movements of the 20th century emerged.

Fauvism (c. 1905–7) was a short-lived but highly influential French movement of artists surrounding Matisse. It is summarized by the daring and spontaneous handling of paint in bold, brilliant, sometimes non-representational colour, in a subjective, joyous response to the visual world.

MAJOR ARTISTS

Pierre Bonnard (1864–1947), French painter, noted for his middle-class interiors and nudes.

Paul Cézanne (1839–1906), French painter, briefly painted with the Impressionist group. Many of his works had a crucial influence on the Cubists.

André Derain (1880–1954), French painter, one of the founders of Fauvism.

Kees van Dongen (1877–1968), Dutch painter. His work developed along Fauvist lines, but his later works were principally of Parisian society.

Raoul Dufy (1877–1953), French painter. Briefly connected with the Fauves but celebrated for his colourful scenes of racecourses and the seaside.

Paul Gauguin (1848–1903), French painter, sculptor and printmaker, celebrated for his brightly coloured, mystical paintings of Brittany and the South Seas: *Where Do We Come From? What Are We? Where Are We Going?* (1897).

Vincent van Gogh (1853–90), Dutch painter, a major influence on 20th-century art: *The Potato Eaters* (1885), *Les Souliers*, *A Cornfield of Cypresses*, *The Yellow Chair* and *Sunflowers* (1888–89).

Albert Marquet (1875–1947), French painter, noted for his bright Fauve colours in his early paintings.

Henri Matisse (1869–1954), influential 20th-century artist and founder of Fauvism: *Dance* and *Music* (1909–10), and the series of *Odalisques*.

George Rouault (1871–1958), French painter, noted for his expressionist religious work.

Henri Rousseau (1844–1910), French painter, noted for his naïve, stylized jungle paintings (1900–10).

Walter Sickert (1860–1942), English painter who concentrated on paintings of lower-class London life: *Ennui* (c. 1913).

Henri de Toulouse-Lautrec (1864–1901), French painter and draughtsman, famous for his lithographs and posters of dance halls and cabarets: *Le Moulin Rouge* (1891).

Maurice de Vlaminck (1876–1958), French Fauvist painter: *The Bridge at Chatou* (1906).

Edouard Vuillard (1868–1940), French painter, noted for his domestic paintings: *Mother and Sister of the Artist* (c. 1893).

SYMBOLISM, SECESSION AND EXPRESSIONISM

The Symbolist movement emerged in the 1880s as a reaction against the naturalist movement (the idea that art was an imitation of nature) and against modern industrialism and materialistic values. The Symbolists sought to escape into the past or into the world of fantasy, including dreams. They believed that art existed alongside, not in direct relation to, the real world, and that it had its own rules. Symbolism foreshadowed Surrealism.

Anti-naturalism was also shared by many of the German and Austrian Secessions of the 1890s – breakaway groups who revolted against the academicism of conventional painting. Similarly, a diverse group of later artists, known as the Expressionists, wished to emphasize – often through unnaturalistic distortion – the importance of emotion and the artist's inner vision. A group of German Expressionist artists, known as *Die Brücke* ('The Bridge'), aimed to integrate art and life by using art as a means of communication. Though to some extent the German equivalent of Fauvism, their work was deliberately rougher and cruder, with broken, unnaturalistic colours and heavily expressive, stylized forms. Another independent German Expressionist group was *Der Blaue Reiter* ('The Blue Rider'). Rather than promoting one particular tendency, its aim was for each artist to achieve an individual style. They did, however, share a use of bold colours and a tendency towards abstraction.

MAJOR ARTISTS

Aubrey Beardsley (1872–98), English Symbolist artist and illustrator, noted for his decadent illustrations.

Max Beckman (1884–1950), German Expressionist painter: *The Night* (1918–19).

Edward Burne-Jones (see Realism); his work became increasingly Symbolist.

James Ensor (1860–1949), Belgian painter, a major influence on Expressionism and Surrealism: *Entry of Christ into Brussels* (1880).

George Grosz (1893–1959), German illustrator, painter and satirical caricaturist.

Erich Heckel (1883–1970), German Expressionist painter, graphic artist and co-founder of *Die Brücke*.

Alexej Jawlensky (1864–1941), Russian painter loosely associated with *Der Blaue Reiter*: *Head of a Young Girl* and *Night* (1933).

Wassily Kandinsky (1866–1944), Russian-born painter, pioneer of abstract art and member of *Der Blaue Reiter*.

Ernst Ludwig Kirchner (1880–1938), German Expressionist painter, graphic artist and co-founder of *Die Brücke*.

Gustave Klimt (1863–1918), Austrian painter, and founder of the Vienna Secession, distinguished by his highly decorative paintings: *The Kiss* (1908).

Oskar Kokoschka (1886–1980), Austrian Expressionist painter: *The Tempest* (1914).

Max Liebermann (1847–1935), German painter and founder of the Berlin Secession.

Auguste Macke (1887–1914), German painter, founder of *Der Blaue Reiter*.

Franz Marc (1880–1916), German Expressionist painter, member of *Der Blaue Reiter*: *The Blue Horse* (1911) and *Fighting Forms* (1913).

Gustave Moreau (1826–98), French painter and one of the leading Symbolists, noted for his *femme fatale* paintings: *The Apparition* (1876) and *Sâlome Dancing* (1876).

Edvard Munch (1863–1944), Norwegian painter, a forerunner of Expressionism: *The Scream* (1893).

Emil Nolde (1867–1956), German Expressionist and member of *Die Brücke*, well known for his landscapes and religious pictures.

Odilon Redon (1840–1916), French Symbolist painter and lithographer: *The Cyclops* (1898).

Egon Schiele (1890–1918), Austrian Expressionist draughtsman and painter, famous for his explicit and angular nudes.

ABSTRACTION

In the first half of the 20th century a revolution occurred in the practice of art. From 1910 artists in different countries began to produce abstract or non-figurative art, sometimes abstracting from a landscape or still life until the subject disappeared.

CUBISM

From around 1907 artists such as Picasso and Braque began to analyse objects, breaking them down into geometrical shapes and restructuring them in order to show each form's many facets in a single image. Continuing into the 1920s, Cubism never became completely abstract.

FUTURISM, VORTICISM AND RAYONISM

Futurism was founded in Italy in 1909 by the poet Filippo Marinetti. He urged artists to turn their backs on the art of the past and to seek inspiration from industrial society and the dynamism of modern life. Futurism aimed to incorporate the thrust of modern technology (particularly the sense of speed) into art. Vorticism in Britain and Rayonism in Russia shared some of the aims of Futurism, and also employed crisp geometrical forms and jagged lines.

DE STIJL, SUPREMATISM AND CONSTRUCTIVISM

These slightly later movements – the first Dutch and the other two Russian – restricted themselves to pure geometrical abstraction. Constructivism was a sculptural movement using man-made materials.

MAJOR ARTISTS

Giacomo Balla (1871–1958), Italian Futurist painter and sculptor: the painting *Dynamism of a Dog on a Leash* (1912).

Umberto Boccioni (1882–1916), Italian Futurist painter and sculptor: the sculpture *Unique Forms of Continuity in Space* (1913).

Constantin Brancusi (1876–1957), highly influential Romanian-French abstract sculptor, famous for his concentration of form and the qualities of his materials: *Endless Column* (1937).

Georges Braque (1882–1963), French painter and co-founder of Cubism: *Grand Nu* ('Great Nude'; 1907–08) and the *Atelier* series (1948 onwards).

Carlo Carra (1881–1966), Italian Futurist painter.

Robert Delaunay (1885–1941), French painter, influenced by Cubism: *Circular Forms* (from 1912).

Jacob Epstein (1880–1959), American-born English sculptor. Early Vorticist works include *The Rock-Drill* (1913–14); later work was more representational.

Naum Gabo (1890–1977), Russian sculptor and co-founder of Constructivism.

Henri Gaudier-Brzeska (1891–1915), influential French Vorticist sculptor.

Natalia Goncharova (1881–1962), Russian Rayonist painter.

Juan Gris (1887–1955), Spanish painter, noted for his development of the Cubist style: *Homage to Picasso* (1911–12).

Barbara Hepworth (1903–75), British abstract sculptress.

Wassily Kandinsky (see Expressionism); his work developed from Expressionism to Abstraction.

Paul Klee (1879–1940), Swiss painter, graphic artist and an influential 20th-century artist. His works range from Symbolist to Abstract.

Fernand Léger (1881–1955), French painter, famous for his distinctive semi-abstract monumental style, often depicting people and machines.

Wyndham Lewis (1882–1957), British painter, writer and leader of the Vorticists: *Workshop* (1914).

Kasimir Malevich (1878–1935), Russian painter, founder of Suprematism: *White on White* series (c. 1918).

Amedeo Modigliani (1884–1920), 20th-century Italian painter and sculptor, famous for his elongated figures and erotic nudes: *Reclining Nude* (c. 1919).

Piet Mondrian (1872–1944), Dutch painter who developed from Symbolism to the pure abstraction of De Stijl: *Composition with Red, Yellow and Blue* (1939–42).

Henry Moore (1898–1986), British sculptor, draughtsman and graphic artist, well known for his rounded forms: *Two Forms* (1934) and *Reclining Figure* (1938).

Ben Nicholson (1894–1982), British abstract painter, some of whose works involve carved relief.

Antoine Pevsner (1886–1962), Russian-born French painter, abstract sculptor and co-founder of Constructivism.

Pablo Picasso (1881–1973), Spanish painter, sculptor, graphic artist, founder of Cubism and most outstanding artist of the 20th century: *The Old Guitarist* (1904), the Cubist *Les Demoiselles d'Avignon* (1907), *Guernica* (1937).

DADA AND SURREALISM

The aftermath of World War I brought a crisis of faith in a society whose intellectual and moral values were held responsible for the appalling destruction of the war. There already existed a growing revolt against traditional values, derived from the writings of Darwin, Marx and Freud. Two art movements that grew out of this climate were Dada and Surrealism. Although they were essentially different in purpose and character, some common ground existed, and a number of Dada artists later joined the Surrealist movement.

Dada, which first emerged in 1916, was an international movement that rejected existing social values and its art. Instead it aimed to be anarchic, anti-aesthetic and anti-rational; simultaneously art and anti-art. Surrealism, founded in 1924, was a French avant-garde movement of literary origin inspired by Dadaism, and greatly influenced by Freud's theories of psychoanalysis. Irrational association, spontaneous techniques and an elimination of premeditation to free the workings of the unconscious mind, as well as an interest in dreams, were the main motivations of its practitioners.

MAJOR ARTISTS

Jean (Hans) Arp (1887–1966), French Dadaist artist, celebrated for his rounded abstract sculptures.

Marc Chagall (1887–1985), Russian-born French painter; although not a Surrealist his work has a dreamlike style with irrational juxtapositions: *I and the Village* (c. 1911).

Giorgio de Chirico (1888–1928), Italian painter and forerunner of the Surrealists, notable for his haunting city-scapes.

Salvador Dali (1904–89), Spanish Surrealist artist, famous for his hallucinatory paintings (and Surrealist film-making): *The Persistence of Memory* (1931).

Marcel Duchamp (1887–1968), highly influential French Dadaist artist: *The Bride Stripped Bare by her Bachelors, Even* (1915–23).

Max Ernst (1891–1976), German Dadaist painter,

sculptor and collagist, initially a Dadaist, then a Surrealist: *Here Everything is Still Floating* (1920).

George Grosz (see Expressionism); member of the Berlin Dada group.

Raoul Hausmann (1886–1971), Austrian Dadaist, well known for his photomontages.

John Heartfield (Helmut Herzfelde; 1891–1968), German artist, notable for his political photomontages: *Hurrah, the butter is finished* (1935).

René Magritte (1898–1967), Belgian Surrealist, famous for his conventional paintings made bizarre by the unexpected juxtaposition of objects: *The Key of Dreams* (1930) and *Time Transfixed* (1938).

André Masson (1896–1987), French Surrealist painter, notable for his spontaneous drawings undertaken while in a trance.

Joan Miró (1893–1983), Spanish Surrealist painter: *Still Life with an Old Shoe* and *Dog Barking at the Moon*.

Paul Nash (1889–1946), British painter, whose visionary landscapes and war paintings show Surrealist influences.

Francis Picabia (1879–1953), French painter of the Dada school: *I see again in memory my dear Udnie* (1914).

Man Ray (1890–1976), American painter, photographer and film-maker, involved both with Dada and Surrealism, and famous for his technical experimentation (see Photography).

Kurt Schwitters (1887–1948), German Dadaist painter and sculptor, famous for his Merz pieces (haphazard combinations of materials).

Graham Sutherland (1903–80), British painter whose early landscapes had a dreamlike Surreal quality; his later works include well-known portraits.

MOVEMENTS IN ART SINCE 1945

The postwar period has been characterized by extremely varied approaches to the problems of art. Although much of the best work has been abstract, some artists have continued to work in more traditional styles.

Abstract Expressionism emerged in New York soon after World War II. It places emphasis on spontaneous personal expression, rejecting contemporary, social and aesthetic values. It was the first movement in the USA to develop independently of and actually influence Europe. Some exponents practised action painting.

Action Painting was a technique used by some of the Abstract Expressionists. It involved spattering the canvas in a semi-random fashion, so recording the action of the painter at the moment of painting as well as his emotional state.

Conceptual Art grew partly out of Minimal Art as artists started to make works of a temporary character utilizing different types of process and system, e.g. inscribing imaginary geometric patterns on the landscape, and working with photographs and texts.

Environmental Art is an art movement in which the artist aims to create not just an object but an entire environment. In order to involve all the senses of the spectator it can include sight and sound effects combined with painted or sculptured work.

Kinetic Art is all art that incorporates movement – real or apparent – generated by motors, artificial light or optical illusion.

Minimal Art emerged in the mid-1960s from the rejection of the aesthetic qualities of art in favour of the physical reality of the art object. The material used is important, as are their strictly geometrical formats and placings within settings.

Neoexpressionism is primarily, although not exclusively, a German movement that became prominent in the 1980s. Paintings are executed with great vigour in styles sometimes reminiscent of German Expressionism. It marks a return to myths, religion and mysterious symbolism as subject matter.

Op Art (optical art) is an abstract art form based on creating optical effects which appear to move on a flat surface. It reached its peak in the 1960s.

Pop Art was an almost simultaneous reaction against Abstract Expressionism in the UK and USA in the late 1950s. It uses the images of mass media, advertising and pop culture, presenting the common, everyday object as art.

Performance Art (also known as **Happenings**) began in the late 1950s, and involves the artist in directing and/or performing an entertainment (intended to be spontaneous) that involves a strong visual element and that may also include theatre, music, film, and the participation of the audience.

Photo-Realism a mainly American movement, beginning in the late 1960s, in which the artist meticulously copies from a photograph.

MAJOR ARTISTS

Francis Bacon (1909–92), British painter (born in Dublin), noted for the disturbing quality of his twisted figures: *Three Studies at the Base of a Crucifixion* (1944) and *Study after Velazquez*, a series of portraits of Pope Innocent X.

Joseph Beuys (1921–86), influential German Performance artist: *Coyote* (1974), a week-long dialogue with a live coyote.

Alexander Calder (1898–1976), American Kinetic sculptor, best known for his metal mobiles.

César (1921–), French sculptor, notable for his use of plastics and used materials: *The Yellow Buick* made from crushed car bodies.

Christo (1935–), Bulgarian-born Belgian artist, who has embarked on such projects as wrapping up sections of the Australian coastline in plastic.

Willem De Kooning (1904–), American Abstract Expressionist: *Woman* series.

Alberto Giacometti (1901–66), Swiss sculptor, well known for his elongated bronze human figures.

Gilbert and George (Gilbert Proesch, 1943– , and George Passmore, 1942–), English avant-garde artists involved in various art forms, including Performance Art; noted for the presentation of themselves as works of art.

Richard Hamilton (1922–), English Pop artist, his work reflects his interest in marketing styles: *$he* (1958–61).

David Hockney (1937–), English painter and draughtsman, initially prominent in Pop Art, but notable for his innovations in many styles: *A Bigger Splash*.

Jasper Johns (1930–), American painter, printmaker and sculptor, best known as the founder of Pop Art: *Target* and *Flags* paintings.

Donald Judd (1928–), American Minimalist sculptor. His work concentrates on rows of geometric units (often boxes).

Anselm Kiefer (1945–), German Neoexpressionist painter, his work concentrates on German history.

Franz Kline (1910–62), American Abstract Expressionist painter, distinguished by his black strokes on white backgrounds.

Sol LeWitt (1928–), American Minimalist sculptor, noted for his displays of white and black cubes.

Roy Lichtenstein (1923–), American Pop artist, best known for his enlarged paintings of comic strip images: *Whaam!* (1963).

Robert Motherwell (1915–), American Abstract Expressionist painter, also notable for his collages.

Barnett Newman (1905–70), American Abstract Expressionist painter, noted for his large, coloured canvases broken by 'zips' (bands) of colour.

Jackson Pollock (1912–56), American Abstract Expressionist painter, a notable exponent of Action Painting.

Robert Rauschenberg (1925–), American artist best known for his combination of Pop Art and Abstract Expressionism: *Combine* paintings and *Monogram* (1959).

Bridget Riley (1931–), foremost British Op artist: *Fall* (1963).

Mark Rothko (1903–70), American Abstract Expressionist, noted for his vast expanses of colour that fill the canvas.

Nicolas de Staël (1914–55), French-Russian abstract painter, whose works are characterized by broad patches of paint: *The Roofs* (1952).

Jean Tinguely (1925–91), Swiss Kinetic artist, celebrated for his machines: *Homage to New York* (1960), a machine from assorted junk materials that blew itself up before an audience.

Victor Vasarély (1908–), French painter (born in Hungary). Considered the pioneer of Op art, he is well known for his grid-like compositions.

Andy Warhol (1928–87), American painter and graphic designer, celebrated as one of the foremost Pop artists: prints of Campbell soup cans, Coca-cola bottles and Marilyn Monroe.

HIGHEST PRICES FOR PAINTINGS

This list shows the highest prices for paintings fetched at auction (to January 1993).

Artist	Painting	Price
Van Gogh	*Docteur Gachet*	£49,100,000
Renoir	*Au Moulin de la Galette*	£46,488,095
Van Gogh	*Irises*	£30,187,623
Picasso	*Self-portrait: Yo Picasso*	£28,825,301
Picasso	*Au Lapin Agile*	£25,710,675
Picasso	*The Mirror*	£16,677,195
Manet	*Rue Mosnier*	£16,600,000
Van Gogh	*Self-portrait*	£15,714,000
Gauguin	*Mata Mua (In Olden Times)*	£14,478,313
Monet	*Dans la prairie*	£14,300,000
Picasso	*Les Tuileries*	£13,750,000
de Kooning	*Interchange*	£13,039,092
Van Gogh	*le Vieil If*	£12,790,000
Kandinsky	*Fugue*	£12,440,476
Picasso	*Mère et Enfant*	£11,813,013
Cézanne	*Pommes et Serviette*	£11,000,000
Renoir	*Jeune fille au char*	£10,803,571

AUSTRALIA
Melbourne *National Gallery of Victoria*: Northern Renaissance; Italian 16th–18th-century (Titian, Canaletto, Tiepolo); French 17th–19th-century; Dutch and Flemish 17th-century (Rubens, van Dyck, Rembrandt); British school.

AUSTRIA
Vienna *Kunsthistorisches Museum*: Italian Renaissance and 17th–18th-century; Netherlandish Renaissance; German 16th–19th-century (Dürer, Holbein); French 16th–19th-century; Dutch and Flemish 17th-century (Rembrandt, Hals, Rubens, van Dyck); Spanish Baroque art; British school. *Österreichisches National Museum*: 18th–19th-century Austrian painting (Secession, Klimt, Schiele, Kokoschka).

CANADA
Ottawa *National Gallery of Canada*: Italian 14th–18th-century; Northern Renaissance; Dutch and Flemish 17th-century (Rubens, van Dyck, Rembrandt, Hals); French 17th–19th-century; Spanish Baroque art; 17th–20th-century British; 20th-century US and international.
Toronto *Art Gallery of Ontario*: Italian 16th–18th-century (Tintoretto, Canaletto); Flemish and Dutch 17th-century (van Dyck, Hals, Rembrandt, Rubens); French 17th- and 19th-century; British school; 19th–20th-century Canadian and American; 20th-century international (Picasso, Matisse).

FRANCE
Paris *Musée du Louvre*: Italian 15th–17th-century Old Masters (Uccello, Leonardo, Caravaggio); French 17th–19th-century (Poussin, Watteau, Delacroix); Northern Renaissance and Baroque (van Eyck, Dürer, Rubens); and Spanish art (Velásquez, Murillo, Goya).
Musée d'Orsay: French 19th-century art; Impressionists (Monet, Degas, Renoir); Post-Impressionists (Cézanne, Gauguin, Van Gogh).

GERMANY
Berlin *Gemälde Galerie (Dahlem)*: Renaissance (Bellini, Raphael, Dürer, van Eyck, Bosch); Dutch and Flemish 17th-century (Rembrandt, Rubens, Vermeer); and Baroque and Rococo art (Velásquez, Watteau).
Bode Museum: Italian Renaissance and Baroque; Northern 15th–17th-century art; German Romantics.
Cologne *Wallraf-Richartz-Museum/Ludwig Museum*: Renaissance and Baroque (Van Dyck, Claude Lorraine, Murillo); 19th-century French (Corot, Monet); 19th-century German art; 20th-century Pop and American Conceptual art.
Frankfurt *Stadelsches*: German and Flemish 14th–19th-century (van Eyck, Dürer); Italian and Spanish (Botticelli, Tiepolo, Velásquez); German Romantic and Expressionist; 19th-century French; and 20th-century art (Picasso, Ernst).
Munich *Alte Pinakothek*: Renaissance (Dürer, Altdorfer, van der Weyden, van Leyden); 17th-century Flemish and Dutch (Rubens, Rembrandt, van Goyen); Italian Renaissance and Baroque (Leonardo, Titian); French Baroque and Rococo (Poussin, Boucher); and Spanish art (El Greco, Goya).
Neue Pinakothek: 18th–19th-century European art (Nazarenes, Romantics, Secessionists).

HUNGARY
Budapest *Museum of Fine Arts*: Italian 14th–16th-century, Baroque and Rococo; Netherlandish Renaissance (Memling, Bruegel); German 16th–19th-century (Dürer, Cranach, Altdorfer); Dutch and Flemish 17th-century (Rembrandt, van Dyck, Rubens); French 17th-and 19th-century; Spanish 16th–18th-century (El Greco, Velásquez, Goya); British school.

ITALY
Florence *Uffizi Gallery*: 13th–14th-century Italian (Cimabue, Duccio, Giotto); Florentine Renaissance (Uccello, Botticelli, Michelangelo); 16th-century Venetian (Titian, Tintoretto); Northern Renaissance and Italian and Northern

MAJOR ART GALLERIES

Baroque art (Caravaggio, Rubens, Claude Claude Lorraine).
Pitti Palace: 16th–17th-century art (Raphael, Van Dyck).
Milan *Brera Gallery:* Italian 15th–19th-century art.
Naples *Capodimonte:* 14th–17th-century Italian (Titian, Caravaggio); Northern Renaissance (Bruegel, Witz); and Neapolitan Baroque art (Caracciolo, Ribera, Solimena).
Rome *Pinacoteca:* Byzantine to 18th-century Italian art (Leonardo, Raphael, Caravaggio).
National Gallery of Rome: 13th–18th-century Italian art.
Borghese Gallery: 16th–18th-century Italian art (Raphael, Titian, Caravaggio).
Venice *Galleria dell'Accademia:* 14th–18th-century Venetian art (Bellini, Titian, Veronese).

NETHERLANDS

Amsterdam *Rijksmuseum:* 15th–16th-century Dutch (van Leyden, Cornelis van Haarlem); 17th-century Dutch (Rembrandt, Hals, Vermeer) and Italian art (Veronese, Tiepolo).
Stedelijk Museum: International art from c. 1860 (Van Gogh, Mondrian, Cobra school, Pop Art, Conceptual Art).
The Hague *Mauritshuis:* Netherlandish and German 15th–16th-century (van der Weyden, Cranach, Holbein); Flemish and Dutch 17th–18th-century (Rembrandt, Vermeer); and Italian 16th–17th-century art (Raphael, Titian).

RUSSIA

Moscow *Pushkin Museum of Fine Arts:* Italian 16th–18th-century (Tiepolo); Northern Renaissance (Bruegel); Dutch and Flemish 17th-century (Rubens, Rembrandt, van Dyck); French 17th–18th-century (Poussin, Claude Lorraine, Watteau, Boucher); Spanish Baroque; 18th–19th-century European art (Constable to Corot); Impressionism (Degas, Renoir, Monet); Post-Impressionism (Cézanne, Gauguin, Toulouse-Lautrec); 20th-century international art (Picasso, Matisse).
St Petersburg *The Hermitage Museum:* Italian 14th–16th-century, Baroque and Mannerism (Leonardo and Venetian Renaissance to Tiepolo); Netherlandish Renaissance and Mannerism (van der Weyden, Bruegel); German 16th–19th-century; Dutch and Flemish 17th-century (Rembrandt, Hals, Rubens, van Dyck); French 17th–19th-century (Le Nain to Post-Impressionism); British school; 20th-century European art (Matisse, Picasso).

SPAIN

Madrid *The Prado:* Spanish (Velásquez, Zurbarán, Goya); Italian Renaissance (Titian, Tintoretto, Veronese); Northern Renaissance and Baroque (Bosch, Bruegel, Rubens); French and British art (Poussin, Gainsborough).
The Escorial: Northern 15th–17th-century (van der Weyden, Dürer, Rubens); Italian 16th-century (Titian, Tintoretto); and Spanish 17th–18th-century art (Velásquez, Goya).

SWEDEN

Stockholm *Nationalmuseum:* Italian and Spanish 16th–17th-century (Bellini, Veronese, El Greco); Northern Renaissance; French 17th–19th-century (Claude Lorraine to Gauguin); Dutch and Flemish 17th-century (Rembrandt, van Dyck, Hals, Vermeer); Scandinavian painting.

SWITZERLAND

Lugano *Thyssen-Bornemisza Collection:* Italian 14th–16th-century (Raphael, Venetian school); Netherlandish Renaissance (van Eyck, Memling); German Renaissance (Altdorfer, Dürer); Italian 17th–18th-century (Caravaggio); Spanish school (El Greco, Goya); French 17th–19th-century; Dutch and Flemish 17th-century (Rembrandt, Hals, van Dyck, Rubens); 20th-century international art.

UNITED KINGDOM

Edinburgh *National Gallery of Scotland:* Italian Renaissance (Titian, Raphael); Baroque (Velásquez); French 17th–18th-century (Poussin, Claude Lorraine, Watteau); Flemish and

Dutch Baroque (Rubens, van Dyck, Vermeer); and British 18th–19th-century art (Gainsborough, Constable).
London *National Gallery:* Italian medieval–18th century (Piero della Francesca to Canaletto); Northern Renaissance; Dutch and Flemish 16th-century (Rubens, Rembrandt); Spanish 17th–18th-century (Velásquez, Goya); and French 17th–20th-century art (Claude Lorraine to Cézanne).
Tate Gallery: British 17th–19th-century (Turner, Hogarth, Reynolds, Blake, Pre-Raphaelites); Modern and 20th-century British (Sickert, Spencer, Sutherland, Hockney), modern and 20th-century European and international art.
Wallace Collection: Dutch and Flemish (Rembrandt, Van Dyck, Rubens); Italian 16th–17th-century (Titian); French 18th–19th-century; British art (Gainsborough, Reynolds).

UNITED STATES OF AMERICA

Boston *Museum of Fine Arts:* Italian Renaissance, Baroque and Rococo (Raphael to Tiepolo); Spanish 16th–18th-century (El Greco, Velásquez, Goya); Dutch and Flemish 17th-century (van Dyck, Rubens, Rembrandt); French 17th–19th-century (Claude Lorraine and Poussin to Gauguin and Van Gogh); British and 20th-century international art.
Isabella Stewart Gardner Museum: Italian 14th–18th-century (Raphael, Titian, Tiepolo); 17th- and 19th–20th century European art (Velásquez and Rubens to manet and Matisse).
Fogg Art Museum (Harvard): Italian 14th–18th-century (Tintoretto, Canaletto); Dutch and Flemish 17th-century (Rembrandt); French 17th–19th-century (Poussin to Symbolism); Spanish school (Murillo, Picasso); British school.
Chicago *Institute of Fine Arts:* Italian Renaissance and Baroque (Correggio, Tiepolo); Northern Renaissance; Spanish 16th–18th-century (El Greco, Goya); Dutch and Flemish 17th-century; French 17th–20th-century (Poussin to van Gogh); British and American schools; American school; 20th-century international art; Modern American art.
Fort Worth–Dallas *Kimbell Art Museum:* Italian 15th–18th-century (Bellini, Tintoretto); Dutch and Flemish 15th–17th-century; Spanish 16th–20th-century (El Greco, Goya, Picasso); French 17th–19th-century; British school.
Los Angeles *John Paul Getty Museum:* Italian 14th–18th-century (Mantegna, Canaletto); Netherlandish Renaissance; Dutch and Flemish 17th-century (Rembrandt, van Dyck); Spanish school (Goya); French 17th–19th-century (Poussin, David, Impressionism, Toulouse-Lautrec).
New York *Metropolitan Museum of Art:* Italian and Spanish Renaissance and 17th–18th century; Netherlandish Renaissance (van Eyck, Brueghel); German Renaissance (Holbein, Dürer); Dutch and Flemish 17th-century (Hals, Rembrandt, Rubens, van Dyck); French 18th–19th-century (Boucher to Post-Impressionism); British and US schools.
Frick Collection: Italian 14th–17th-century; Northern Renaissance (van Eyck, Holbein); Spanish 16th–17th-century (El Greco, Velásquez, Goya); Dutch and Flemish 17th-century (Rembrandt, van Dyck, Hals); French 17th–19th-century; British school (Constable, Gainsborough, Turner).
Museum of Modern Art: 19th-century French (Impressionism and Post-Impressionism); 20th-century international art (Cubism to Pop and Land Art); North American painting (Abstract Expressionism, Conceptual Art); Mexican painting.
Los Angeles *Los Angeles County Museum:* Italian Renaissance and Baroque (Titian, Veronese); German Renaissance (Holbein); Dutch and Flemish 17th-century (Rembrandt, Rubens, van Dyck, Hals); French 17th–19th-century (de la Tour to Monet); British school (Gainsborough, Turner).
Washington *National Gallery of Arts:* Italian 14th–18th-century (Giotto to Tiepolo); Northern Renaissance (van Eyck, Dürer); Dutch and Flemish 17th-century (Rembrandt, Vermeer, Rubens, van Dyck); French 16th–19th-century (Poussin to Post-Impressionism); Spanish 16th–18th-century (El Greco, Velásquez, Goya); British school; 20th-century art (Picasso, Matisse, Modigliani).

PHOTOGRAPHY

When Louis Daguerre announced his discovery of a process for making photographic images (or *daguerreotypes*) in 1839, the French painter Paul Delaroche declared, 'From today painting is dead!' Delaroche voiced the expectations of many: that the camera's ability to capture in an instant every detail of the real world would spell the end of painting and drawing, and that photography was the art form of the future. An equally vocal opposing camp claimed that photography was a science, not an art – a purely mechanical process that could never rival in feeling or expression the sensitive hand of the painter or draughtsman.

Since 1839, photography has assumed a vast range of forms and uses – in science and medicine, geographic exploration, anthropology, journalism and advertising – but its close relationship with art has continued throughout.

NINETEENTH-CENTURY PHOTOGRAPHERS: THE PIONEERS

Many early photographers attempted to gain status and approval by self-consciously adopting the high moral themes – and even copying the forms of – 19th-century painters; others favoured the deep tones and soft focus that suggested the delicate sweep of brushstrokes. Despite this, and with gradual improvements in photographic technology, photographers came to respect the photograph for its unique immediacy, its ability to capture a real sense of life.

Julia Margaret Cameron (1815–79), British photographer; pioneer of portrait photography.

Roger Fenton (1819–69), English pioneer war photographer, noted for his Crimean War pictures.

William Henry Fox Talbot (1800–77), English chemist, linguist and photographer who in 1839 invented the photographic negative.

Eadweard Muybridge (Edward James Muggeridge; 1830–1904), English photographer, famous for his early experiments in capturing motion in photographic images, and for his landscape photographs of the American West.

EARLY MODERNISTS

Photography began to gain new status as an independent medium in the early 20th century. Early modernist photographers advocated 'pure' photograph, with aesthetic value beyond its descriptive or utilitarian function.

Alfred Stieglitz (1864–1946), American photographer, publisher and gallery owner whose work turned from pictorialism to a search for abstract form and a specifically photographic way of seeing.

Paul Strand (1890–1976), American photographer who abandoned pictorialism for a pure, objective photographic approach to his subjects.

Edward Weston (1886–1958), American photographer. His precise photographs of natural and human forms combine a formal beauty with the reality of the object.

DOCUMENTARY PHOTOGRAPHERS

Many photographers now regarded as great masters would never have regarded themselves as artists at all, but they detected surreal qualities in everyday life. They documented the life they saw around them, and so fit into a broad documentary approach that encompasses a vast span of attitudes and subject matter.

Bill Brandt (1904–83), English photographer who mixed grim realism with the surreal, creating an evocative record of the British social scene.

Henri Cartier Bresson (1908–), French photographer; combined an artist's genius for perfect composition with a photojournalist's insistence on capturing the 'decisive moment'.

Walker Evans (1903–75), American photographer; produced a powerful record of the faces, homes and lives of America's 1930s rural poor.

Lewis Hine (1874–1940), American photographer, noted for his campaigning pictures of New York's poor and immigrant population from the turn of the century.

Erich Salomon (1886–1944), German photojournalist. Master of the candid shot, he caught politicians and celebrities off guard for the new magazines of the 1920s.

Eugene Smith (1918–78), American photojournalist, notable for his impassioned documentary photographs from around the world (seen mostly in *Life* magazine in the 1940s and 50s).

THE AVANT-GARDE

Photographers continued to innovate and to find new ground. Photomontage – the technique of combining several photographs into one photograph – became popular, while some photographers experimented with 'new objectivity' and Pop Art.

John Heartfield (1891–1968), German pioneer of the photomontage (see p. 387).

Laszlo Moholy Nagy (1894–1946), Hungarian-born American photographer, celebrated for his constructivist-inspired, semi-abstract images, and his inspiring teaching at the Bauhaus.

Alexander Rodchenko (1891–1956), Soviet photographer and photomontagist; introduced 'New Photography' to post-revolutionary Russia.

August Sander (1876–1964), German photographer; celebrated for his ambitious project *Man of the Twentieth Century*, a picture of a society – the doomed Weimar Republic – through the faces of its people.

Andy Warhol (1928–1987), American Pop artist who used photographic images from the media (see p. 388).

THE SURREAL AND THE EVERYDAY

Since the 1950s photography and art have become more closely aligned. At the same time in the USA, a new, seemingly informal approach to urban or 'street' photography evolved.

Diane Arbus (1923–71), American photographer, well known for her intense portraits of American social outcasts.

Eugene Atget (1857–1927), French photographer, recording the streets and scenes of old Paris; his unusual images of the commonplace inspired the Surrealists.

Brassai (Gyula Halasz; 1899–1984), Hungarian-born French photographer. His pictures of bohemian Paris and his eye for the bizarre and the taboo was much appreciated by the Surrealists.

Andre Kertesz (1894–1985), Hungarian-born American photographer, noted for his pioneering use of the small hand-held camera, the well-observed social scene, the surreal figure study, still life, and later the fashion image.

Man Ray (Emanuel Rabinovitch; 1890–1976), American photographer who produced poetic and bizarre surreal images.

Garry Winogrand (1928–84), American photographer who created a highly influential brand of urban street photography, fusing the 'snapshot' approach with a sense of energy and crowded events in his images.

MAJOR PHOTOGRAPHY FESTIVALS

Arles (France) *Rencontres Internationales de la Photographie.* Biennial, held since 1980; a gala of exhibitions, workshops and audiovisual presentations at a number of locations in and around Arles.

Barcelona (Spain) *Primavera Photografica de Catalunya.* Biennial, held since 1982; a large number of photographic exhibitions, discussions and related events in Barcelona and other Catalan towns.

Cologne (Germany) *Photokina.* Annual, held since 1950; an industrial showcase for camera and photographic equipment manufacturers, with concurrent exhibitions of photographs at other locations in the city.

Houston (USA) *Fotofest* Biennial, held since 1986; the major photographic event in the USA, with scores of exhibitions from around the world, mainly under one roof.

Paris (France) *Mois de la Photo.* Biennial, held since 1978; a month of exhibitions (loosely based on a changing series of themes) and photography-related events in over 100 public spaces, museums and private galleries.

Rotterdam (Netherlands) *Fotografie Bienale.* Biennial, held since 1980; a major international exhibition on a changing theme, with a concurrent conference and exhibitions in public and private galleries.

ARCHITECTURE

Architecture is the art and science of designing and erecting buildings that are both suitable for an intended purpose and aesthetically pleasing. The design of a particular building will depend upon many factors, including the technology and materials available, the cost of those materials, the function of the building, and the taste of the building's architect, its owner and its users.

In ancient times buildings were monumental in scale, constructed to the greater glory of a deity or the dead. Secular architecture developed more slowly with an emphasis upon grandeur and security rather than comfort. Not until the Greeks developed the Classical orders of architecture did ideas of proportion and harmony evolve. Succeeding architectural styles have both reflected and influenced contemporary technology and artistic taste.

EGYPTIAN ARCHITECTURE

The appearance of Egyptian buildings was influenced by climatic features such as fierce heat and

bright sunshine – which meant only small windows were required – and by a plentiful local supply of building stone. At the time of the Third Dynasty – during the Ancient Kingdom (2575–2134 BC) – *mastabas* or tomb houses were built, and from these small, flat-topped buildings with sloping sides the pyramids developed. The 4th-dynasty Great Pyramids at Giza are the largest and best preserved, but the oldest pyramid still in existence, and the world's first large-scale monument in stone, is the Djoser step pyramid at Saqqara, built c. 2620 BC by Imhotep, who is considered to be the first architect in history.

During the Middle Kingdom (2040–1640 BC) monolithic buildings were increasingly replaced by a system of construction consisting of series of stone columns and horizontal beams; e.g. the mortuary temples of Mentuhetep at Deir el-Bahari (11th Dynasty). The most imposing buildings were tombs and temples, reflecting the importance of religion, the priesthood and the afterlife to the Egyptians. Temples, such as the great temple of Amun at Karnak (12th Dynasty), were vast sprawling complexes of courtyards, halls and avenues built of stone. Stone was used only sparingly for secular buildings – even the Pharaohs' palaces were built principally of sun-dried brick.

Notable New Kingdom buildings (1552–1070 BC) include the great Hypostyle Hall – a vast columned hall with 134 columns – built at Karnak by Rameses I, the mortuary temple of Rameses III at Medinet Habu in Thebes, and the funerary temple at Deir el-Bahari for Queen Hatshepsut.

NEAR EASTERN ARCHITECTURE

The use of mud-brick rather than stone and the increasing importance of vast palace complexes characterize Near Eastern architecture. In the 5th millennium BC huge circular buildings occur alongside T-shaped units with elaborately niched and buttressed façades. These temples display a monumentality only paralleled by *ziggurats*, stepped pyramid-shaped temple towers. The largest surviving example is the Ziggurat of Ur (c. 2113–2096 BC) – built to three stories surmounted by a summit temple – with a base of 61 m by 45.7 m (200 by 150 ft). The public buildings of the city of Babylon were of vast dimensions, but only mounds now show where the original city stood because its mud-bricks had little resistance to weathering.

The major buildings of the Assyrian period were the palaces in Nineveh of kings such as Ashurbanipal. These enormous palaces were raised on platforms of mud-bricks and reached by broad stairs and ramps. Planned around inner courtyards, with numerous rooms connected by corridors, they were faced with stone and decorated with bas-reliefs of sculptured monsters, painting on plaster, and coloured glazed bricks. Structurally the buildings were quite sophisticated with some use of arches, vaults and domes.

Persian architecture made greater use of stone and wooden columns and flat roofs. The palace of Persepolis (6th–4th centuries BC) displays some Assyrian features – raised platforms, bas-relief sculptures and coloured glazed bricks – but is distinguished by its halls of tall columns.

GREEK ARCHITECTURE

Buildings of the Early Greek period (before c. 700 BC) are characterized by the distinct appearance of the masonry wall in their construction. There are three types: *cyclopean*, which is constructed of large stone piles, the gaps between which are filled with smaller stones held together by clay; *stone blocks* laid in a regular course with joints that are not always vertical; and *polygonal*, where many-sided blocks are worked together to form a strong structure.

Doric   **Ionic**   **Corinthian**

The architecture of the later (Hellenic) period is distinguished by the use of the column. Columns gave Classical Greek buildings an uncomplicated appearance. The most important buildings were temples, usually located on a prominent site, e.g. the 5th-century Parthenon on the Acropolis in Athens (designed by Praxiteles). The typical temple was a simple rectangle. Its low-pitched roof was supported by a colonnade of columns. The three *orders* of column were Doric (c. 640–c. 300 BC), Ionic (c. 560–c. 200 BC) and Corinthian (c. 420–c. 100 BC). An order is the design of an entire column consisting of base, shaft and capital with an entablature over the top as the horizontal element. The Doric order is the simplest of the three orders, the capital being a simple flattened cushion of stone (e.g. the columns of the Parthenon). The more slender and ornamental columns of the Ionic order are topped by a capital that is ornamented with four spiral motifs called *volutes* (e.g. the temple of Artemis in Ephesus and the Erechtheion in Athens). The Corinthian order is the lightest and least-used of the three Greek orders. The capital displays acanthus-leaf decoration combined with volutes that are smaller and more open than the Ionic (e.g. the Olympeion in Athens).

ROMAN ARCHITECTURE

The character of Roman architecture derives from the fusion of the Etruscan and Greek cultures on the Italian peninsula between the 8th and 6th centuries BC. The Romans adopted the central concept of Greek architecture – the three orders – but changed the manner in which the orders were expressed through adopting arches and vaults, both Etruscan technical innovations not used by the Greeks. The Romans also added two new orders – the rarely used Tuscan (which is similar to the Doric but with a plain entablature) and the Composite (which displays Ionic volutes and Corinthian leaves). The new techniques and orders were applied to an array of new building types and shapes, including circular temples, triumphal arches, baths, aqueducts, basilicas and amphitheatres. Roman architects used a wider variety of building materials than the Greeks. The introduction by the Romans of tufa, limestone, brick and especially concrete allowed structural innovations that were employed most successfully in vast structures such as the Baths of Caracalla (AD 211–17).

The major public buildings of Imperial Rome were characterized by flamboyant luxury, but only the husks of a few great buildings remain. The Pantheon (AD 120–24) in Rome is one of the most impressive survivors. A large circular temple dedicated to all the gods, the Pantheon has a height and a diameter of 43.2 m (142 ft). Its huge hemispherical dome is partly concealed on the outside by the massive walls which rise up in counterthrust to the dome, and an opening at the centre of the dome's apex reduces its weight and allows in natural light.

MAJOR ARCHITECTS

Vitruvius (fl. first century BC), Roman architect, engineer and writer: *De architectura*, 10 books covering building materials, city planning and the design and construction of public and private buildings.

Apollodorus of Damascus (fl. first century AD), Greek engineer and architect: Trajan's Forum in Rome.

BYZANTINE ARCHITECTURE

With the demise of the Roman Empire in the West, the power base shifted to the East, to Constantinople (formerly Byzantium). From the 5th century AD Byzantine emperors provided lavish patronage for architects, who inherited and developed the structural innovations of the Romans, and combined them with a variety of decorative influences from both Greece and Asia. Byzantine architecture is characterized by the construction of domes over square bases. The Romans had always built domes over cylindrical or polygonal bases, but the Byzantines effected the transition of the circular dome to the square base, usually composed of four arches, by inserting *pendentives*. The advantage of a square base over a circular or polygonal base was that vaulted aisles, semi-domed apses and other domes could be easily erected adjacent to a central dome. The most famous example of this type of structure is Hagia Sophia (begun AD 537) in Constantinople (now Istanbul), designed by Anthemius of Tralles and Isidorus of Miletus. A former cathedral – it became a mosque when Constantinople fell to the Ottoman Turks in 1453 – Hagia Sophia is a vast rectangle 76 m (250 ft) by 67 m (220 ft), with a large central dome 33 m (108 ft) in diameter.

Byzantine architecture spread throughout Asia Minor and as far north as the Ukraine and Russia. Russian architects initially followed the Byzantine pattern, but a distinct Russian personality soon emerged in the buildings of Novgorod and Kiev. The wide Byzantine windows were narrowed and roofs steepened to cope with the heavy snow of Russian winters, and in time domes were constructed in the bulbous shape that became a distinguishing feature of Russian architecture. To the west Venice was the only major state in direct contact with the Byzantine Empire. St Mark's in Venice was begun in 1063 and is essentially a Byzantine church.

EARLY MEDIEVAL ARCHITECTURE

In the West, the fall of the Roman Empire in the 5th century brought fragmentation and a power vacuum. Barbarian tribes overran Europe, producing a climate hardly conducive to ambitious building. The products of these (largely nomadic) civilizations were mostly portable and their buildings were in general constructed of wood. Where stone was used many of the features of Roman building persisted, but often in a much simplified or debased form.

ANGLO-SAXON ARCHITECTURE

In England, much of the architecture of the Anglo-Saxons, from the 6th century until the Norman Conquest of 1066, was timber-framed. Surviving stone buildings, such as the 10th- or early 11th-century tower at Earl's Barton, in Northamptonshire, reflect this in the application of long strips of stone, called 'long-and-short work', to wall-surfaces as non-structural decoration. Ecclesiastical and private buildings were generally small in scale, with small spaces or rooms opening into one another through narrow doorways.

CAROLINGIAN ARCHITECTURE

Charlemagne, crowned Holy Roman Emperor in 800, consciously evoked the grandeur of Imperial Rome at his court at Aachen (Germany). For his Palatine Chapel there he closely followed late Roman prototypes and even reused Roman materials. The chapel (792–805) has an octagonal interior, showing the influence of Byzantine domed structures. Its massive sturdy piers are typical of the solidity of all Carolingian architecture.

ROMANESQUE ARCHITECTURE

In the decades following the year 1000 a huge increase in church building took place and all the most important buildings and developments until the 16th century can be traced in church architecture. These new churches swept away the older, smaller structures, and over the years, new building techniques developed, such as the barrel-and-rib vault seen for the first time at Durham Cathedral in northern England.

The typical Romanesque church grew from the simple groundplan of a Roman basilica – the addition of *transepts*, a *chancel* and an *apse* at the east end produced the cross-shaped groundplan followed with innumerable variations throughout the Middle Ages. The *nave* was often of considerable height. The interior elevations of the nave were often divided into two or three storeys with the *clerestory* at the top, *arcades* of columns at the bottom (opening into aisles parallel to but lower than the nave) and a *triforium* in the middle storey opening into the roofspace of the aisles. High towers were often built over the *crossing* of transepts and nave, and at the west end. These innovations were made possible by the development of simple stone vaulting systems. In earlier buildings vaults were usually either barrel vaults or *groin vaults*. Romanesque builders reversed

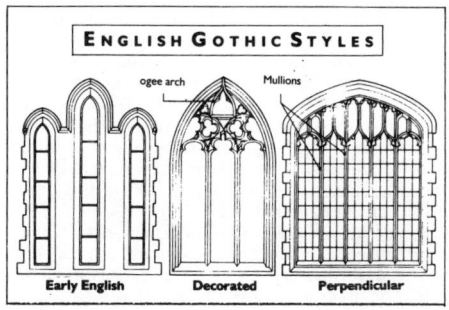

ENGLISH GOTHIC STYLES

ogee arch | Mullions

Early English | Decorated | Perpendicular

previous practice by constructing the vaults before the arches. This meant that the arches could be made much lighter as the stonework between the groins (or ribs) was not load-bearing.

The Romanesque style was disseminated throughout Europe quickly because of the network of related monasteries ruled over by a single great house. The most influential of these was Cluny in Burgundy, whose church was – until it was demolished in the 19th century – the largest Romanesque building. Typically Romanesque architecture is massive and simple. Piers are large and where there are attached columns or mouldings these are large in scale. Local variations – or schools – are most noticeable in building materials and decoration. In Romanesque buildings in England and France special attention was paid to the embellishment of capitals surmounting columns and to doorways – the *tympanum* was usually elaborately carved, often with a figure of Christ in Majesty. Fine surviving Romanesque buildings include Peterborough Cathedral in England (1117–93), St Etienne, Caen (c. 1068–1115), St Sernin, Toulouse (1077–1119 and later), Angouleme Cathedral (c. 1105–28 and later) and Notre Dame la Grande, Poitiers (c. 1130–45), all in France, and Trier Cathedral in Germany (1016–47).

GOTHIC ARCHITECTURE

The Gothic style emerged in the 12th century and survived in some areas of northern Europe until the 16th. In Gothic architecture a transcendental quality is evoked by pointed arches, vaulted ceilings and an emphasis on light through large pointed windows. Although pointed arches and windows are perhaps the most obvious features of Gothic building, what characterizes Gothic architecture is a method of building and a sense of structure and space that pervades the whole building, rather than any specific design feature.

Rib-vaulting was begun by Romanesque builders, but the idea of building 'skeletons of stone' was not fully developed until Gothic buildings were designed. Walls became just infill between supporting piers as by big windows for stained glass, and the thick walls with passages typical of Romanesque were replaced with thin walls.

It is generally accepted that the first Gothic structure is the choir of St Denis in Paris rebuilt by Abbot Suger (1140–44). In the following 80 years Gothic cathedrals were built in the region around Paris; e.g. Laon (1160–1225), Noyon (1145–1228), and Notre Dame de Paris (1168–c. 1250), all of which had four-storey elevations to the nave, with massive round piers at the aisle level. Later examples include Chartres (1194–1260), Reims (1211–90), Amiens (1220–88), and Beauvais (1247–1568). Chartres was the first important example of an emphasis on *tracery*. Tracery gradually became lighter and more complex and decorative, leaving even larger areas of stained glass. The interiors of Gothic cathedrals became increasingly vast, with naves of great height. The interior surfaces are articulated by ribs beginning at the ceiling vaults of the nave and running down the piers of the clerestory, triforium and nave arcades. This vertical thrust emphasizes the great height of the buildings, and as the clusters of ribs become increasingly narrow in diameter the whole interior seems lighter. The divisions between the aisles, nave, transepts, apse and chapels are less emphatic, creating a sense of spaces flowing into one another, quite different from the solid division and massiveness of the Romanesque. Although the walls of great Gothic churches were lighter they still required support and *buttresses* – and sometimes *flying buttresses* – were added to the exterior of the building to carry the structural thrust from the vaults.

Gothic architecture is found, with various regional variations, throughout western and central Europe. The earliest Gothic work in England is probably the choir of Canterbury Cathedral (1174–85), begun by the French architect William of Sens. English Gothic is generally divided into three stylistic periods, characterized by their window styles.

The English style which corresponds to the early Gothic of Laon and Noyon in France is the *Early English* (c. 1190–1250). Typically, Early English buildings – such as the choir (1192–1200) and Angel Choir (1256–80) of Lincoln Cathedral – have simple pointed *lancet* windows, without tracery, and clear horizontal divisions between the internal storey or wall divisions.

The *Decorated* style (c. 1250–1360) is exemplified by the nave of Exeter Cathedral (early 14th century), where the vaults have additional ribs, the main piers are made up of clusters of small columns, and window tracery is used in a variety of flowing patterns. Decorated style is characterized by the *ogee arch* and decorated wall surfaces. During this period the tracery changed from geometric to flowing.

The *Perpendicular* style (c. 1360–c. 1550), as its name implies, emphasized vertical features. Perpendicular tracery is made up of many geometrically arranged narrow stone bars, and arches and vaults are much flatter. Whereas the Decorated style added extra ribs to the vaulting, the Perpendicular was distinguished by many subordinate ribs in the vaults curving round to form a fan shape, often with additional carved decoration (e.g. the south transept and cloisters of Gloucester Cathedral). The primary examples of English Gothic can be seen at Westminster Abbey and the cathedrals of Canterbury, Lincoln, Salisbury, Ely and Wells.

Gothic in Germany and the rest of central Europe seems to have been imported from France, rather than to have developed from the indigenous Romanesque. A particular feature of German Gothic is the *hall church* (e.g. St Elizabeth, Marburg). In Italy the Classical, Romanesque and Byzantine traditions persisted much longer than in northern Europe and Italian Gothic, with the exception of Milan Cathedral (c. 1385–1485) in the north, has none of the structural and spatial daring of northern Gothic. Roofs are often flat or open timber, as at S. Croce, Florence (1294–1442), with an absence of pinnacles and flying buttresses.

RENAISSANCE ARCHITECTURE

The Renaissance was a period of intellectual and artistic renewal that lasted from c. 1350 to c. 1550. The dominant theme of the period was the revival of interest in the arts and literature of Classical Greece and Rome. The Renaissance began in Italy because the physical remains of Classical Rome were more plentiful there than elsewhere in Europe, and also because the Gothic had never taken hold in Italy as it had in northern Europe. The most important figure of the Early Renaissance is the Florentine Filippo Brunelleschi, who studied Roman remains at first hand. Another Florentine, Leon Battista Alberti, was the theorist of the Renaissance style in its early years. In his book *De Re Aedificatoria* (1485) he attempted to define the Renaissance aesthetic. Alberti studied classical geometry as well as architecture and applied this to his buildings whose parts relate to each other and to the whole construction according to mathematical laws.

The Early Renaissance style is found in various forms throughout Italy, but the High Renaissance style, which flourished first in Rome, is found with much less regional variation. High Renaissance buildings are generally bolder than Early Renaissance ones, reflecting the architects' greater familiarity with the Classical precedents, and the variety of uses to which they could put the orders of columns and pilasters.

The Renaissance in France and England developed principally in palaces and large country houses rather than in church architecture. It also differed in character from Italian Renaissance architecture because the Gothic had flourished in northern Europe much longer. In English and French Renaissance architecture, Classical features such as columns, pilasters and pediments were mixed with Gothic features and decoration to form picturesque buildings quite different from those of Brunelleschi and Alberti. France's geographical proximity to Italy meant that Renaissance features first appeared there before the end of the 15th century, but the style dominated from the mid-16th century. The Palais du Louvre (1546–1878) in Paris shows French Renaissance architecture at every stage of its development. Renaissance architecture did not appear in England until the 16th century. Although houses such as Longleat (1567–80), in Wiltshire, and Wollaton Hall (1580–88), in Nottinghamshire, have symmetrical façades and Renaissance details such as pilasters and balustrades, the rooms are frequently distributed asymmetrically throughout the groundplan and the houses retain such medieval features as the great hall. Their rooflines are made lively by the addition of elaborate chimneys and carving, and window bays break forward from the line of the façade, so that the character of the buildings is as much Gothic as Renaissance.

MAJOR ARCHITECTS

Filippo Brunelleschi (1377–1446), Florentine architect and engineer: the dome of Florence Cathedral (1420–36), a double shell of brickwork supported on ribs.

Leon Battista Alberti (1404–72), Florentine architect, writer and principal founder of Renaissance architectural theory.

Donato Bramante (1444–1514), Italian architect: the Tempietto at S. Pietro in Montorio, Rome – one of the finest High Renaissance buildings, although it is only 4.5 m (15 ft) in diameter.

Philibert Delorme (1510–1570), French architect: the châteaux of Anet and Saint-Germain-en-Laye, and the palace at Fontainebleau.

Pierre Lescot (c. 1515–78), French architect: rebuilding of the Louvre.

Jean Bullant (c. 1520–1578), French architect: Petit-Château (Chantilly).

Robert Smythson (c. 1536–1614), English architect: Wollaton Hall (Nottinghamshire) and Longleat House (Wiltshire) with Sir John Thynne.

MANNERISM

Mannerism followed hard on the heels of the High Renaissance in Italy. When Italian architects had thoroughly studied the way Classical architects used the basic elements of columns, pilasters and entablatures, they felt able to use these elements in new ways, for example greatly exaggerating the proportion of one element or adding features such as *consoles* for decoration rather than support. Although such typically Mannerist features are found in buildings elsewhere in Europe, it is a particularly Italian phenomenon and flourished in Italy at a time when other European countries were just beginning to discover the Renaissance.

EARLY PALLADIAN ARCHITECTURE

A different kind of Mannerism was practised by Andrea Palladio, who built many villas and palaces around Vicenza, near Venice. Palladio followed the Mannerist practice of using Classical elements in ways that the Romans would never have done. However, he always followed a strict system of proportional rules, and the effect is always harmonious. The Palladian style became highly influential in England, where Inigo Jones was an early but isolated follower. Jones travelled to Italy and studied Classical remains, as well as Palladio's thesis *The Four Books on Architecture*, which describes both his theories of proportion and his own buildings which exemplified them. Palladianism did not take root in England until the 18th century, although Jones' ideas encouraged a new compactness in the groundplans of 17th-century English country houses.

MAJOR ARCHITECTS

Michelangelo Buonarroti (1475–1564), Italian painter, sculptor, poet and architect (see also Painting): the Biblioteca Laurentiana (1526), Florence, and the Dome of St Peter's in Rome.

Giulio Romano (Giulio Pippi; 1492–1546), Roman architect and principal founder of the Mannerist style: Palazzo del Tè (1525–35) in Mantua.

Giacomo da Vignola (1507–73), Italian architect: church of Il Gèsu (1568–84), in Rome.

Andrea Palladio (1508–80), Italian architect and founder of the Palladian style: the Palazzo Chiericati (1550–c. 1580) and the Villa Capra (Rotonda) (c. 1550–54), Vicenza.

Giorgio Vasari (1511–1574), Florentine painter, writer and court architect: the Uffizi (Florence).

Inigo Jones (1573–1652), English designer and architect: the Queen's House at Greenwich (begun 1616), whose entrance hall is a perfect cube.

BAROQUE AND ROCOCO

The Baroque style – one of the dominant trends in the visual arts in the 17th century – has been described as work that utilized movement, whether actual (e.g. curving walls) or implied (e.g. figures portrayed in vigorous action). It produced striking visual effects in buildings and decoration, although it could occasionally be over-ornate and theatrical. The Baroque style began in Italy, where its leading exponents were Bernini, Borromini and Maderna. In Spain, Germany and Austria, Baroque architecture attained and even exceeded the exuberance of Italian Baroque. The Neumünster-Stiftskirche (façade, 1710–19), at Würzburg (Germany), is truly Baroque with its concave modelling, clustered and variously disposed orders, and vigorous dramatic effect. In England – where the chief proponents of the style were Wren and Vanbrugh – and also in France, Baroque exteriors are much more restrained and traditionally Classical. Only interior decoration attains levels of lively and theatrical exuberance. At the end of the 17th century Baroque reached Russia, where a clearly national variation – Naryshkin Baroque – developed.

ROCOCO

In the 18th century the desire for the informal in architecture found expression in the highly decorative Rococo style. The origins of Rococo can be seen in the later works commissioned by Louis XIV of France, such as the châteaux of Marly and La Ménagerie, and under Louis XV, the Rococo style dominated. Rooms became wholly or partly elliptical and decoration was derived from foliage, grotesques and shells. In Germany and Austria Rococo became more even lavish, and an emphasis on whimsical decoration and oval and circular spaces created a sense of fluidity. Rococo was not fully accepted in England, where Baroque licence had already been challenged by the more 'rational' Palladian style.

MAJOR ARCHITECTS

Carlo Maderna (1556–1629), Italian architect who largely determined the style of early Baroque.

François Mansart (1598–1666), French Baroque architect who replaced the traditional steep pitch roof with the lower-angled form of the *mansard roof.*

Giovanni Lorenzo Bernini (1598–1680), Italian Baroque architect and sculptor: the colonnade of St Peter's in Rome.

Francesco Borromini (1599–1667), Italian Baroque architect: the facade of the church of S. Carlo alle Quattro Fontane (1665–67) in Rome.

Pieter Post (1608–65), Dutch Baroque architect: (with Jacob van Campen) Mauritshuis (the Dutch Parliament) in the Hague.

Louis Le Vau (1612–70), French Baroque architect: the plan of Versailles.

Sir Christopher Wren (1632–1723), English Baroque architect: St Paul's Cathedral (1675–1710) and numerous London churches.

Jules Hardouin-Mansart (1646–1708), French Baroque architect who completed the design of Versailles.

Johann Fischer von Erlach (1656–1723), Austrian Baroque and Rococo architect and influential architectural historian.

Nicholas Hawksmoor (1661–1736), English Baroque architect famous for his London churches.

Sir John Vanbrugh (1664–1726), English architect who developed a particularly personal and English Baroque: Blenheim Palace and Castle Howard.

José de Churriguera (1665–1725), member of a prominent family of architects who developed a distinctly Spanish Baroque.

Germain Boffrand (1667–1754), French Rococo architect.

Johann Lucas von Hildebrandt (1668–1745), Austrian Baroque architect: the Belvedere Palace (Vienna) and the Mirabell Palace (Salzburg).

Nicolas Pineau (1684–1754), French woodcarver, interior designer and architect who was influential in introducing Rococo to St Petersburg (now Leningrad), Russia.

Dominikus Zimmerman (1685–1766), Bavarian architect whose church at Wies (1746–54) in Bavaria is widely considered to be the finest example of German Baroque.

Balthasar Neumann (1687–1753), German Baroque and Rococo architect: The Residenz in Würzburg (Germany).

Johann Michael Fischer (1692–1766), Bavarian architect of late Baroque and Rococo churches.

PALLADIANISM AND NEOCLASSICISM

The influence of Palladio and his English interpreter Inigo Jones was not reflected in British architecture in general until around 1710, when a group of aristocrats 'rediscovered' Palladio, and began to build themselves country mansions and suburban villas, often very closely following Palladio's work. This fascination with Palladio was not reflected elsewhere in Europe: in Spain and Italy the Baroque persisted well into the 18th century. In France a grander classicism, more decorative and 'muscular' than Palladio's, prevailed. Typical is the monumental façade of St Sulpice, Paris (1733–49), composed of superimposed Doric and Ionic screens of columns, flanked by towers, but both in France and in Germany restrained Classical exteriors contrasted with lavish Rococo interiors.

Around the middle of the 18th century British architecture became more consciously 'Antiquarian' or Neoclassical in character. Architects travelled to Italy to study not just Renaissance architecture and Palladio, but also their Classical precedents. There was also a great proliferation of books of Classical, Renaissance and Neoclassical buildings for architects to study. Until 1762 – and the publication of *The Antiquities of Athens* by Nicholas Revett and James Stewart – the term 'Neoclassical' meant 'Neo-Roman', for Greece was, in the 18th century, still a wild and little-known country. Although Stuart and Revett designed several monuments and churches in the Greek style from the 1760s, the Greek Revival reached its height in Britain between 1805 and 1830. It was especially popular with those architects – such as William Wilkins – who favoured simple, bold forms, over the more elegant decorative Roman style.

Although there was not the same Greek Revival in France, the designs of Etienne-Louis Boullée and Claude-Nicolas Ledoux share some of the same fascination with simplified forms. Ledoux designed buildings whose plans reflect their functions, and whose forms are massive and undecorated, presaging both the modern movement and Fascist architecture of the 20th century (see below). Contrasting with the purism of the Greek Revival is the Picturesque movement, which affected all the arts, including architecture. The architect John Nash – whose celebrated works are Neoclassical – was equally at home designing 'picturesque' buildings such as the Royal Pavilion (1815–21) in Brighton, mixing exotic styles such as Indian and Chinese.

MAJOR ARCHITECTS

William Kent (1685–1748), English Palladian architect and the pioneer of the English informal garden: Horse Guards Building, Whitehall, London (1750–58).

Richard Boyle, Earl of Burlington (1694–1753), English architect and patron of Palladian architecture: Chiswick House (begun 1725), west London, (designed with William Kent).

Giovanni Nicolò Servandoni (1695–1766), Italian theatre designer and architect: façade of St Sulpice, Paris.

Jacques-Germain Soufflot (1713–80), French Neoclassical architect: the Panthéon (1757–90).

Giambattista Piranesi (1720–78), Italian architect, artist and draughtsman whose prints of Classical Rome were an important influence on the early Neoclassical movement.

Sir William Chambers (1723–96), pioneer English Neoclassical architect: Somerset House (1776–1856) in London.

Etienne-Louis Boullée (1728–99), French architect, teacher and co-founder of the Revolutionary Neoclassical movement.

Robert Adam (1728–92), Scottish furniture and interior designer and Palladian architect: the south front and interior of Kedleston Hall, Derbyshire.

Claude-Nicolas Ledoux (1736–1806), French architect and co-founder of the Revolutionary Neoclassical movement.

Jean-François-Thérèse Chalgrin (1739–1811), French Neoclassical architect: arc de Triomphe (1806–35).

Giacomo Quarenghi (1744–1817), Italian architect who designed many important Neoclassical and Palladian buildings in Russia.

John Nash (1752–1835), English Neoclassical architect and planner: Regent's Park and Regent Street, London.

Sir John Soane (1753–1837), English Neoclassical architect: the Bank of England (1792–1833) in London.

Benjamin Latrobe (1764–1810), British-born American architect who pioneered Neoclassicism in the USA.

William Wilkins (1778–1839), English Neoclassical architect: Downing College, Cambridge (designed 1804).

Karl Friedrich Schinkel (1781–1841), German Neoclassical pioneer and state architect of Prussia: Altes Museum (1822–30) in Berlin.

Leo von Klenze (1784–1864), German architect: many Greek Revival public buildings, including the Glyptothek (1816–34) in Munich.

William Strickland (1788–1854), American Neoclassical architect and engineer: Second Bank of the United States.

THE AGE OF REVIVALS

Although the Greek Revival remained strong in Scotland and in Germany until the 1850s, it was past its peak in England by about 1830 when the Gothic

Revival began. Architects had used Gothic details in their buildings sporadically throughout the 18th century, usually in the spirit of the Picturesque movement. Features such as fan vaults were used purely for decoration, often in materials such as plaster rather than the stone of the medieval originals. Arbury Hall (1776) in Warwickshire and Fonthill Abbey (1796–1807) are early examples of this style.

As scholars studied medieval buildings and began to classify the different styles within the Gothic, so architects became more serious about building in a consistent and authentic manner. By the time the new Palace of Westminster came to be designed by Barry and Pugin in the 1830s and 1840s, the Gothic had been appropriated as a particularly British style, and thus especially suitable for the British Houses of Parliament. Pugin, along with the art critic John Ruskin, did not see the Gothic as just another style to be adopted and adapted – they believed that the Gothic was the only Christian style (Classical buildings being 'pagan'). From the late 1840s Gothic Revival buildings appeared all over Britain, and to a lesser extent Europe and the English-speaking world, at first favouring the Perpendicular style (e.g. the Houses of Parliament in London) and later a much bolder 12th-century French Gothic style (e.g. St Finbar's Cathedral, Cork).

The Arts and Crafts movement in Britain is often seen as a secular and domestic equivalent to the Gothic Revival. It was begun in the late 1850s by William Morris, who hated the mechanical quality of machine-made goods and wished to revive traditional craftsmanship. Arts and Crafts is reflected in architecture in the revived use of traditional British building techniques and styles such as tile-hung walls, windows with small panes, and half-timbering.

New building materials and new building types were developed during the 19th century. The most important technological advance was the use of iron for construction. Iron could be used with glass to create great new structures such as the Crystal Palace, built by Joseph Paxton for the Great Exhibition of 1851, or with more conventional brick or stone supports for such purposes as roofing railway stations. It also began to be used structurally for buildings which would otherwise have been built only of stone or brick; e.g. the interior of the National Library in Paris (1860–62), by Henri Labrouste, is composed entirely of a framework of iron columns and floors. Later in the century, buildings entirely supported by a steel framework – often concealed within masonry walls – began to be built, (e.g. the Reliance Building, Chicago, by Burnham and Root), but the full potential of this system was not realized until the 20th century.

Outside Britain 19th-century architects used a tremendous variety of architectural styles, although none predominates. At the end of the 19th century Art Nouveau appeared – a style that affected not only architecture but also the decorative and graphic arts. It is characterized by undulating curves and extreme forms of decoration derived from burgeoning vegetation.

MAJOR ARCHITECTS

Horace Walpole (1717–97), English writer: Strawberry Hill at Twickenham near London (1749, with William Robinson), the first Gothic Revival building.

James Wyatt (1746–1813), English architect: the extravagant early Gothic Fonthill Abbey in Wiltshire.

Karl Friedrich von Schinkel (1781–1841), German (see Neoclassical Architects): Werdersche Kirche (1821–30) in Berlin, one of the first Gothic Revival buildings in Europe.

Sir Charles Barry (1795–1860), English architect: Houses of Parliament (1840–60) in London.

Henri Labrouste (1801–75), French architect and pioneer of iron-frame construction.

Sir George Gilbert Scott (1811–78), English Gothic Revival architect: the Albert Memorial (1863–72) in London.

Augustus Welby Northmore Pugin (1812–52), English Gothic Revival church architect.

William Butterfield (1814–1900), English architect of Gothic Revival churches characterized by their horizontal lines and strong use of colour.

Eugène-Emmanuel Viollet-le-Duc (1814–79), the leading French Gothic Revival architect.

James Renwick (1818–95), American Gothic Revival architect: St Patrick's Cathedral, New York.

George Edmund Street (1824–81), English architect of Gothic Revival churches: the Law Courts (begun 1874) in London.

William Burges (1827–81), English Gothic Revival architect: St Finbar's Cathedral, Cork (1863–76).

Richard Norman Shaw (1831–1912), Scottish architect and urban designer: noted for his domestic architecture.

Antonio Gaudi (1852–1926), Spanish (Catalan) architect of extraordinary organic-looking Art Nouveau façades which rise up to an undulating roofline: Casa Batlló, Barcelona (1905–07).

(Baron) Victor Horta (1861–1946), Belgian Art Nouveau architect: town houses including the Hotel Tassel (1892–93) with its sinuous iron that flows down from the ceilings to form the banisters.

Hector Guimard (1867–1942), French architect: Art Nouveau stations on the Paris Metro.

Charles Rennie Mackintosh (1868–1928), Scottish Art Nouveau architect whose designs had a sparseness and economy: Glasgow School of Art (1897–1909).

Sir Edwin Lutyens (1869–1941), English architect and town planner: the plan and principal buildings of New Delhi, India.

20th-CENTURY ARCHITECTURE

INTERNATIONAL MODERNISM

Structural advances such as steel framing, pioneered in the 19th century, have revolutionized architectural design in the 20th century. Buildings supported by a steel frame can be built much higher than those relying upon a traditional load-bearing wall. The steel frame also allows the construction of buildings whose walls are little more than a skin of steel and glass. When concrete came into general use this principle was further extended by the use of cantilevers, where floors can be internally supported by columns, thus making the outer walls a separate structural element. One of the earliest examples of this is the Fagus factory (1914) at Alfeld-an-der-Leine, Germany, by Walter Gropius. Gropius founded the Bauhaus school, where architects and designers were taught to be aware of the needs of modern-day living and to design functionally according to this understanding.

Le Corbusier popularized the use of reinforced concrete (concrete with steel frame set within it for strength), flat roofs and buildings raised on stilts ('pilotis'). He also designed whole cities (e.g. Chandigarh in India), dividing them up logically into areas for living and working, with green spaces and vast blocks of flats. His theories greatly influenced town planning and were much practised in the post-war rebuilding of Europe.

The style of buildings popularized by the Bauhaus, Le Corbusier and others is known as International Modernism, for the simple reason that the simplicity of the designs meant that similar buildings were found throughout the world. It remained the principal style for large-scale projects until the 1960s, when High-Tech architecture appeared. High-tech began as student drawing-board exercises in the 1960s, and is a logical extension of the Modernist thesis that a building's structure should be evident from its appearance. High-Tech buildings such as the Lloyds' Building in London and the Centre Beaubourg (the Pompidou Centre) in Paris express a building's machine-like functionalism by having its heating, electrical and water piping, and aircon-ditioning, on the exterior.

POST-MODERNISM

Post-Modernism literally means any style of architecture that is not Modernist but has been used since the advent of Modernism. It has been particularly associated with architecture that uses such Classical details as columns and pediments in a decorative manner. Michael Graves in his Portland Public Building (1982) in Portland, Oregon, used brightly coloured and simplified columns, pediments and garlands on a grand scale. This use of bright colours, simplified details, plastics, reflective glass and other shiny materials such as chromium is typical of Post-Modernism.

Although International Modernism has been the most influential style in the 20th century, it has not been the only one. Classical buildings continued to be built in different variations and in the 1930s a particularly simplified and monumental Classicism was used in Nazi Germany and Fascist Italy as a way of suggesting to the people that these were régimes comparable in grandeur and durability to the Roman Empire. In the 1970s and 1980s a more traditional form of Classicism developed when, for example, Quinlan Terry and his teacher Raymond Erith built Classical-style houses that were archaeologically correct in their detailing. This style became very popular in the mid-1980s in Britain, partly as a reaction against the all-pervasive concrete of Modernism, and Terry was called upon to build on a larger, more public scale, as at Richmond Riverside (London). This style has won some important patrons, including the Prince of Wales, who proposes to build an entire new village, with Classically arcaded shops and a town square, in Dorset to the designs of the Luxembourg-born American architect Leon Krier.

MAJOR ARCHITECTS

Louis Sullivan (1856–1924), American architect and pioneer of skyscrapers: Wainwright Building, St Louis, Missouri.

Frank Lloyd Wright (1869–1959), American International Modernist architect: Guggenheim Museum, New York (designed 1943).

Max Berg (1870–1947), German Expressionist architect: the Centenary Hall, Breslau (now Wroclaw, in Poland).

Robert Maillart (1872–1941), Swiss architect who experimented with reinforced concrete.

Eliel Saarinen (1873–1950), Finnish architect who had a profound influence upon modern American architecture, in particular skyscrapers and churches: *Chicago Tribune* office tower and the Tabernacle Church of Christ, Columbus, Indiana.

Walter Gropius (1883–1969), German architect, architectural theorist, teacher and founder of the Bauhaus, who aimed to make architecture reflect social needs.

Le Corbusier (Charles-Édouard Jeanneret; 1887–1965), Swiss-born French International Modernist architect and town planner: Notre-Dame-du-Haut (1950–55), Roncamp (France), and Chandigarh (a new administrative town in India). Le Corbusier used pure geometrical forms in an innovative manner and was noted for an imaginative application of technical advances.

Ludwig Mies van der Rohe (1888–1969), German-born American architect who popularized the rectilinear forms of International Modernism.

Pier Luigi Nervi (1891–1979), Italian architect who specialized in large-scale structures built of reinforced concrete: Turin exposition hall.

Richard Buckminster Fuller (1895—1983), American architect and engineer who developed the geodesic dome: US pavilion at Expo 67, Montréal. (Buckminsterfullerene – see Chemistry chapter – was named after his geodesic dome, which it resembles in shape.)

Alvar Aalto (1898–1976), Finnish architect, city planner and furniture designer: Säynätsalo town hall (1950–52).

Arne Jacobsen (1902–71), Danish architect and furniture designer whose designs were characterized by their severe modernity: SAS building, Copenhagen.

Eero Saarinen (1910–61), Finnish-born American architect, son of Eliel. He experimented in various modern styles: Dulles International Airport and the chapel at Massachusetts Institute of Technology.

Oscar Niemeyer (1907–), Brazilian architect who is best known for his work in the new Brazilian capital, Brasilia.

Minoru Yamasaki (1912–), innovative Japanese architect.

Richard Rogers (1933–), English High-Tech architect: the Lloyds' Building (1981–86) in London.

Quinlan Terry (1937–), English Post-Modernist architect of Classical buildings including Brentwood Cathedral, Essex.

Léon Krier (1946–), Luxembourgeois architect who is known for his detailed city centre and housing redevelopments.

GLOSSARY OF TERMS

abacus the flat upper part of the capital of a column.

apse a semicircular termination or recess at the end of a chapel or the chancel of a church.

arcade a set of arches and its supporting columns.

architrave a beam extending across the top of the columns in Classical architecture.

baptistry a building used for baptisms; sometimes merely a bay or chapel reserved for baptisms.

barrel vault a continuous vault, either semicircular or pointed in section; also called tunnel vault.

bay a compartment or unit of division of an interior or of a façade – usually between one window or pillar and the next.

belvedere an open-sided structure designed to offer extensive views, usually in a formal garden.

boss a projection, usually carved, at the intersection of stone ribs of Gothic vaults and ceilings.

buttress a vertical mass of masonry built against a wall to strengthen it and to resist the outward pressure of a vault.

campanile a bell tower.

capital the top of a column, usually carved.

caryatid a sculptured female figure serving as a supporting column.

chancel that part of a church containing the altar, sanctuary and choir.

clerestory a row of windows in the upper part of the wall of a church.

console an ornamental Classical bracket supporting part of a wall.

cornice the projecting upper part of the entablature in Classical architecture; also decorative plasterwork between the wall and ceiling.

cross vault see groin vault.

crossing the intersection of the nave and transepts in a church.

dado the lower part of an interior wall when panelled or painted separately from the main part.

drum the cylindrical lower part of a dome or cupola.

entablature in Classical architecture, the beam-like division above the columns, comprising architrave, frieze and cornice.

flying buttress an arch conveying the thrust of a vault towards an isolated buttress.

frieze the decorated central division of an entablature, between the architrave and the cornice.

groin vault (also called a cross vault) the intersection of two barrel vaults. Where barrel vaults require support along both edges, a groin vault only requires support at its four corners, thus allowing windows to be inserted between the supports.

hall church a church where the aisles are more or less the same height as the nave.

keystone the central, wedge-shaped stone of an arch, so called because the arch cannot stand up until it is in position.

lancet window a window with a single, sharply pointed arch. The style is associated with the Early English period of Gothic architecture.

mezzanine a low storey introduced between two loftier ones, usually the ground and first floors.

nave the main body of a church.

ogee arch a pointed arch with an S-shaped curve on both sides.

order any of several Classical styles of architecture. Each order is distinguished by its design of column. (See Greek Architecture.)

oriel a bay window on an upper floor, supported by projecting stonework.

pediment in Classical architecture, the low-pitched gable above the entablature, usually filled with sculpture.

pendentive a triangular section of vaulting with concave sides supporting a circular dome over a square or polygonal base.

pier the vertical masonry support for a wall arch.

rustication heavy stonework with the surface left rough, or with deeply channelled joints, used principally on Renaissance buildings.

spandrel a triangular space between the curves of two adjacent arches and the horizontal moulding above them.

tracery ornamental stonework dividing Gothic windows up into smaller areas of glass.

triforium an arcade of arches, forming a gallery, above the arches of the nave or chancel of a church.

tunnel vault see barrel vault.

tympanum the triangular space bounded by the mouldings of a pediment; also, the semicircular space, often carved, between the lintel and arch of a Gothic doorway.

vault an arched structure – usually of stone, brick or concrete – forming a roof or ceiling.

THE SEVEN WONDERS OF THE WORLD

In the 2nd century BC the writer Antipater of Sidon described the following seven buildings as the pre-eminent sights of the ancient world:

The Pyramids of Giza the only one of the seven wonders in still existence. (See Egyptian architecture.)

The Hanging Gardens of Babylon a series of landscaped terraces, probably 7th century BC.

The Statue of Zeus at Olympia a large figure of Zeus enthroned, c. 420 BC.

The Temple of Artemis at Ephesus a structure famous for its great size.

The Mausoleum of Halicarnassus the huge tomb of the Anatolian king, Mausolus.

The Colossus of Rhodes a vast bronze statue commemorating the siege of Rhodes (305–04 BC).

The Pharos of Alexandria a huge lighthouse constructed c. 280 BC.

Various modern writers have suggested 20th-century equivalents but there is no agreement upon which structures constitute the 'seven modern wonders of the world'.

WORLD'S TALLEST BUILDING

The tallest office building in the world is the Sears Tower, the national headquarters of Sears, Roebuck and Co. in Wacker Drive, Chicago Illinois, USA.

It has 110 storeys and rises to 443 m (1454 ft). Begun in August 1970, it was 'topped out' on 4 May 1973. The addition of two TV antennae brought the total height to 520.29 m (1707 ft). The building's working population of 16 700 is served by 103 elevators and 18 escalators. It has 16 000 windows.

Britain's tallest building is Canary Wharf Tower in London Docklands. It is 243.5 m (800 ft) high.

THE PERFORMING ARTS
MUSIC

THE ORIGINS OF MUSIC

In its most primitive form, music may evoke the sound of the elements – earth, air, fire, water. Since humans have always been imitative animals, it seems natural that nature itself should have provided the scope for the earliest music and the materials for the earliest musical instruments. Where these materials – sticks, stones, bones, bells, reed pipes or whatever – were not available, the human voice was a more than adequate substitute, relieving loneliness, making contact with other people, reflecting the rhythms of manual labour or simply of walking, celebrating victories, or paying tribute to primitive deities – often in combination with dancing.

The sophisticated evolution of music – even the notes of a simple scale or chord – took place over a period of centuries. There was certainly a rich musical tradition in the years before Christ – for example in India, China, Egypt and Greece, much of it tantalizing because it was passed on orally, not written down. Even today, in Asia particularly, this tradition persists, because music is regarded as improvisatory and contemplative, ceaselessly changing, rather than something perfected and fixed on paper.

In Europe, much of what we today call music emerged through the spread of Christianity and of Judaism, particularly through medieval *plainsong* chants, which were single lines of notated vocal melody in free rhythm (i.e. not divided into bar lengths) sung in churches, and through *Gregorian chant*, named after Pope Gregory I, in whose time (around AD 600) it was systematized. This still forms part of Roman Catholic musical ritual. However, its *modes* (or 'scales') gradually gave way to the modern scale.

THE COMPONENTS OF MUSIC

A musical *note*, therefore, is more than just a 'noise'. It is a single sound of definite pitch and duration, which can be identified in writing. The *pitch* of a note is its height or depth in relation to other notes, or in relation to an absolute pitch. This absolute pitch has internationally been set at A = 440 Hz (hertz); that is, the A above middle C has a frequency of 440 cycles or vibrations per second.

A *scale* is a progression of notes in ascending or descending order, while a *melody* (or tune) assembles a series of notes into a recognizable musical shape. However, to suggest, as some people do, that modern music lacks 'melody' may merely mean that the listener has failed to identify, or come to terms with, the melodies it contains – even Beethoven and Verdi, to some ears, once seemed unmelodic.

A melody usually, though not necessarily, possesses *rhythm*, which listeners often assume to mean *beat*. In fact, the beat of a piece of music is simply its regular pulse, determined by the *bar lines* by which music is metrically divided (two beats in the bar and so forth). Rhythm can be an infinitely more complex arrangement of notes into a mixture of short and long durations within a single bar or across a series of bars. The *time* in which a piece of music (or section of a piece) is written is identified by a *time signature* at the beginning of the piece or section. Thus 3/4 time (three-four time), which is waltz time, represents three crotchets to the bar. This means that the main beat comes every three crotchets: 1 2 3, 1 2 3, etc.; 4/4 time, which is march time, has four crotchets: 1 2 3 4, 1

2 3 4, etc.; 3/8 and 6/8 represent three and six quavers, respectively. There are also many more complex time signatures.

A melody may have *harmony*. This means that it is accompanied by *chords*, which are combinations of notes, simultaneously sounded. It may also have *counterpoint*, whereby another melody, or succession of notes with musical shape, is simultaneously combined with it. 'Rules' of harmony and counterpoint, stating which notes could be acceptably combined and which could not, have been matters of concern to scholars, teachers and pupils in the course of musical history. But as with any other grammar, progressive composers have known when to break or bend the rules to the benefit of their own music.

TONALITY

The old modes, or scales, employed in the Middle Ages gradually gave way in the 17th century to a modern *tonality* – scales laid out in 12 major and minor *keys*, each consisting of a sequence of seven notes, divided into tones and semitones. Each of the 12 major and minor scales starts on one of the 12 semitones into which an octave is divided. Melodies in a specific key use the notes of that scale, and the order in which the notes are used determines the nature of the melody. On a piano the scale of C major consists entirely of white notes, starting on C.

The notes from C to the next C, either above or below, form an *octave*. A note and another note an octave above sound 'the same' because the higher note has double the frequency. For example, the A above middle C is 440 cycles per second, and the A above that is 880 cycles. From C to D (the first 'white' note above) represents an interval of a tone, from C to C sharp (the first 'black' note) an interval of a semitone, so called because it represents half a tone. But from E to F, and from B to C, also forms a semitone (on a piano there is no black note between them). A scale therefore consists of a mixture of tone and semitone intervals.

A *chromatic scale*, on the other hand, employs nothing but semitones, and thus requires all 12 of the white and black notes to be used. The *whole-tone scale* – used, for example, by Debussy – moves entirely in tones. Starting on C, it would consist of the notes C–D–E–F sharp–G sharp–A sharp.

In musical terminology, a sharp indicates a semitone rise in pitch, and a flat a semitone fall. A natural is a note that is neither sharp nor flat, though the indication sign needs only to be used in special circumstances.

The first note of a scale is known as the *tonic*, or 'keynote'. The tonic of the scale of C is therefore note C. All other scales require one or more black notes to be played in order to produce the same sequence of intervals.

It is important to remember that scales are conventions – conventions to which our ears are attuned through familiarity. The modes of ancient Greece and medieval Europe employed different sequences of tones and semitones, and the scales used in Indian music and some modern jazz, for example, may use quarter tones.

The development of tonality was celebrated by Johann Sebastian Bach (1685–1750) in 24 keyboard preludes and fugues, one in each key, known as the *Well-tempered Clavier*. These displayed the advantages of the (at the time) novel system of *equal temperament*, whereby all of the notes of a keyboard instrument were 'tempered' to be precisely a semitone apart. The notes C sharp and D flat thus became identical, which was not (and still is not) the case with other instruments. On a string instrument, where the notes are not pre-set, C sharp and D flat are slightly different from each other – imperceptibly so to the ears of most listeners.

In the course of a piece of music, a composer may often *modulate*, or change key, in order to avoid monotony. In Bach's time, an established and logical change was to the key based on the fifth note of the scale, known as the *dominant*. But modulations to harmonically more 'distant' keys were found to be a source of dramatic effects, as also was the sudden contrast between a minor key and a major, exploited by composers such as Beethoven with increasing freedom. By the time Wagner composed *Tristan and Isolde* (1865), modulation had become so fluid that it was only a step away from *atonality*, or the composition of music in no fixed key at all. Atonality was systematized by Schoenberg in what he described as *dodecaphonic* or 'twelve-note' music. In this method of composition, one of the major influences on 20th-century music, the twelve notes within an octave were employed in such a way that there was no home key and no reliance on modulation in the old sense, though key relationships did often remain implied, even if not specifically stated.

MUSICAL FORMS, STRUCTURES AND TERMS

absolute music music in which no extra-musical (i.e. descriptive) element is intended or should be inferred.

a cappella term to describe a vocal work without instrumental accompaniment.

aleatory music music in which each performance is dictated by chance elements.

anthem a short sacred vocal work.

aria a sung solo in opera or oratorio.

arietta a short aria.

atonal (of music) using all 12 notes of the scale.

aubade or **alborda** a morning song.

barcarolle a piece suggesting the song of a Venetian gondolier.

Baroque a period of music, c. 1650 to the death of Bach (1750).

boléro a Spanish dance in three-time.

bourrée an old French dance in common time (4/4).

cadence musical phrase used for ending phrases, sections or complete works.

cadenza a solo virtuoso piece before the final cadence in an aria, or at appropriate places in a concerto.

canon a work or section in which successive entries of the same melody overlap.

cantata a vocal work – sacred or secular – for one or more voices with instruments, sometimes short and light, sometimes extensive and with large forces, but always in several movements.

capriccio or **caprice** a fanciful work in free style.

cassation a divertimento-like work, probably intended for performance in the street.

catch a witty vocal piece for several voices in which the singers 'catch up' each other's words, often making puns with scatalogical or obscene results.

chaconne a graceful Spanish dance in three-time, its melody varied over a repeated bass phrase. Originally it was always in a major key.

chord a group of notes played simultaneously.

chromatic scale a scale including semitones so that all 12 notes within the octave are sounded.

classical strictly: a musical period of c. 1750 to c. 1800; loosely: 'serious' music as opposed to pop, jazz and light.

clef ('key') an indication of the 'register' in which the piece is to be performed. It takes the form of a medieval letter (C, F, or G) placed upon the relevant line of the stave. C = middle C; G = the fifth above; F = the fifth below. See Music Symbols.

coda ('tail') an ending piece designed to close a composition.

concertino a small concerto; also, the soloists in a concerto grosso.

concerto a work, usually in three movements, for one or more solo instruments with orchestra.

concerto grosso a Baroque form in which several soloists (the concertino) play against an orchestra; *cf* the later symphonie concertante.

concertstück ('concert piece') piece for soloist(s) and orchestra, usually in one movement.

continuo (often preceded by 'basso'), up to c. 1800, a keyboard instrument together with viol/double bass/cello/bassoon/archlute (in various combinations). Both instruments 'continued' the sound, i.e. they 'filled in' any missing harmonies not actually written down by the composer.

contrapuntal using counterpoint.

counterpoint two or more tunes played simultaneously without violating the rules of harmony.

descriptive music see programme music.

development see sonata form.

diatonic relating to the notes of the given key.

divertimento a multi-movement work of a diverting nature.

dodecaphony another term for twelve-note music.

dominant the keynote a fifth above the tonic.

duet a piece for two musicians.

ecossaise a piece in 'Scottish style'.

electronic music music consisting entirely of electronically produced sounds.

elegy a piece of a sad or funereal nature.

ensemble a group of musicians, smaller than an orchestra.

étude or **study** an exercise.

exposition see sonata form.

fantasia a piece whose imaginative course follows no formal rules.

finale the last movement of a multi-movement work; also, the ending of a movement.

fugato in fugal style. See fugue.

fugue a polyphonic composition in which the first statement of a tune is in the tonic; the second statement overlaps the first, and is in the dominant; and so on.

gavotte a lively dance in two-time.

gigue a jig, a sprightly dance in 6/8 or 12/8 time.

glee an 18th-century English piece for three or more voices unaccompanied.

harmony the art of combining notes into chords according to strict rules in a way that is pleasing.

hymn a song of praise to God.

impromptu a form originated by Chopin, supposedly extemporized.

incidental music music for a stage work.

intermezzo ('in the middle') a piece lying between two sections, whether in a piece of music, a play or an opera, etc.

introduction a piece which begins a work, often with material unrelated to the main work.

libretto ('little book') the text of an oratorio or opera. The 'big book' is the musical score.

lied a type of German Romantic song introduced in the late 18th century.

madrigal a secular song for several voices unaccompanied.

mass the Roman Catholic sung service of communion.

minimalism a modern American style of composition involving the extensive repetition of the simplest of melodies or rhythms, sometimes over slowly changing harmonies.

minuet an 18th-century dance in three-time.

modern a musical period from c. 1900 to the present day.

motet a part song, usually sacred in nature and usually unaccompanied.

movement a division of a musical work. The term derives from the various dance movements of the original suite.

musique concrète a French invention in which recorded sounds (usually from everyday life) are manipulated on tape into a composition.

nocturne a night piece.

obligato or **obbligato** ('obligatory' meaning 'indispensable') a vocal or instrumental part which plays an important, but not necessarily solo, role.

occasional music music written for a specific occasion.

opera drama set to music, in which most, or all, of the words are sung.

operetta light opera, often with spoken dialogue.

opus ('work') an individual work or group of works of a composer; each opus is given a number either by the composer or by a subsequent cataloguer. Opus numbers do not always reflect the chronology of composition.

oratorio the religious equivalent of opera but without action, costumes or scenery.

ornaments embellishments of a note or phrase, such as a trill (a rapid alternation of a written note with the one above or below), a gracenote (a subsidiary note appended to a written note), a mordent (a quick touching of the note below during the playing of a written note), etc.

overture the orchestral introduction to an opera or oratorio. A concert overture has no connection with a staged work.

passacaglia ('passing along the street') a form akin to the chaconne, but originally always in a minor key.

pentatonic scale a scale only using five notes (such as the black notes on a piano); often used in folk music.

pitch the precise height or depth of a note, according to its vibrations (cycles) per second. Today, A above middle C = 440 cycles per second.

polka a lively dance of Bohemian or Polish origin in three-time.

polonaise a slow or moderately-paced Polish dance in three-time.

polyphony ('many voiced') a style combining independent but interconnected melodic lines, i.e. using counterpoint.

prelude or **praeludium** an introductory movement.

programme music music which describes a place, event, person, etc. Compare absolute music.

recapitulation see sonata form.

recitative a vocal linking passage in an opera or oratorio imitating speech patterns; often declamatory, and less florid than an aria.

register the compass (lowest to highest notes) of a voice or instrument.

requiem a mass for the dead.

rhapsody a multi-sectioned piece akin to the capriccio, often with a nationalistic content.

ricercare ('research'), a learned piece written in the 16th and 17th centuries to explore obscure avenues of polyphony.

romance a vocal piece which sets a lyric tale to music; also, an instrumental work or movement in a graceful vein with a more agitated central section.

Romantic a period of music, c. 1800–c. 1900.

rondo a work in which the main section alternates with different sections ('episodes').

saltarello an Italian dance, quick, exciting, and involving jumping steps.

sarabande a stately Spanish dance in three-time.

scherzo ('joke') usually a rapid and light-hearted piece.

serenade a work for evening performance.

serial music music in which a sequence of notes are used equally and in strict rotation; the usual form is twelve-note music (see below).

siciliano a graceful dance in three-time, originating in Sicily.

singspiel a play with alternating musical pieces.

solo a work for one musician. In the 18th century solos were often accompanied.

sonata a (usually) multi-movement chamber work for one to four instrumentalists.

sonata form an 18th-century invention in which the first part ('exposition') states the musical material, modulating from tonic to dominant, the second part ('development') develops it (or other material), and the third part ('recapitulation') repeats it often with modifications in the tonic key. There is sometimes a coda.

song a sung melody, with or without accompaniment.

study see étude.

suite a work comprising several separate sections, or 'movements'; each section was originally a different dance.

symphonic poem or **tone** a 19th-century orchestral form, descriptive or evocative in character.

symphonie concertante a showy French invention (often wrongly termed 'sinfonia concertante') in which several soloists play against an orchestra; cf the earlier concerto grosso.

symphony a major orchestral work, usually of four movements.

tempo the pace at which a work is performed.

toccata a fantasia-like piece requiring brilliant execution.

tone poem see symphonic poem.

tonic term relating to the first degree of a minor or major scale.

trio a piece for three musicians. Larger groupings are equally self-explanatory: quartet, quintet, sextet, septet, octet, nonet, dectet.

trio sonata a Baroque and Classical chamber work for two melody instruments and continuo.

twelve-note music system of musical composition devised by Arnold Schoenberg (1874–1951) in which all 12 notes of the scale are used in sequence and in strict rotation.

variations a work which subjects a theme to a series of variations.

MUSICAL DIRECTIONS

accelerando becoming faster.

adagietto the diminutive of adagio, i.e. slightly quicker than adagio.

adagio ('at ease') a slow, comfortable pace.

allegretto the diminutive of allegro, i.e. a little slower than allegro.

allegro ('cheerful' or 'sprightly') a lively but not too fast a pace.

andante ('walking pace') moving along unhurriedly but regularly.

andantino the diminutive of andante. Originally this meant a little slower but today is taken to mean a little faster than andante.

arpeggio notes of a chord played upward or downward in quick succession, in imitation of a harp.

crescendo getting louder.

diminuendo getting quieter.

forte loudly.

fortissimo very loudly.

largo ('spacious') a broad, slow tempo.

lento slow.

mezza voce ('middle voice'), a subdued tone, between piano and forte.

mezzo moderately.

moderato moderate pace. Often used in conjunction with allegro, andante, etc, to moderate that pace.

pianissimo very quietly.

piano quietly.

pizzicato plucking the strings of a bowed instrument.

prestissimo very fast.

presto fast.

ralentando, ritardando or **ritenuto** getting slower.

sotto voce ('under the voice' or 'secretly') between forte and piano but nearer the latter.

vibrato rapid alteration of pitch or intensity of a note intended to impart 'expression'.

vivace lively. In old music, brightly but not too fast.

MUSIC SYMBOLS

CLEFS

Clef symbols denote the register in which a work is to be performed.

Treble: 𝄞   = **G clef.** A representation of a medieval letter G, the focal point of which indicates the line G.

Bass: 𝄢   = **F clef.** A relic of the medieval letter F, centred on the F line.

INDICATIONS OF PITCH

♭   = **Flat.** This sign flattens all the notes of the pitch indicated which follow it in the bar.

♯   = **Sharp.** This sign sharpens all the notes of the pitch indicated which follow it in the bar.

♮   = **Natural.** This sign indicates that a previously flattened or sharpened note is to return to its natural pitch.

REPEAT SIGNS

Repeat (or da capo). Two vertical lines preceded by a colon instruct the player(s) to return to the beginning of the movement or piece, or to the previous repeat sign.

NOTE LENGTHS

Early notation employed four note lengths: double long, long, short ('breve'), and half-short ('semibreve'). Today, the longest note used – the breve – equals the early 'short', but it is uncommon.

Note	Names	Meaning
𝅝	semibreve (whole note)	half-short
𝅗𝅥	minim (half-note)	shortest (i.e. minimum)
𝅘𝅥	crotchet (quarter-note)	hook or crook (from its old appearance)
𝅘𝅥𝅮	quaver (eighth-note)	to trill, or quaver (quiver) in very short notes
𝅘𝅥𝅯	semiquaver (sixteenth-note)	half-quaver
𝅘𝅥𝅰	demisemiquaver (thirty-second-note)	half of half a quaver

The hemidemisemiquaver has one half of the duration or time value of the demisemiquaver. The semihemidemisemiquaver, in turn, has one half of the duration or time value of the hemidemisemiquaver.

American notation In the USA, the semibreve is known as the whole note, the minim as the half note, the crochet as the quarter note, the quaver as the eighth note and so on.

TIME SIGNATURES

Examples of time signatures:

$\frac{3}{4}$ = three quarter-notes (crotchets) to the bar

$\frac{3}{8}$ = three eighth-notes (quavers) to the bar

Other time signature meanings may be inferred from these examples.

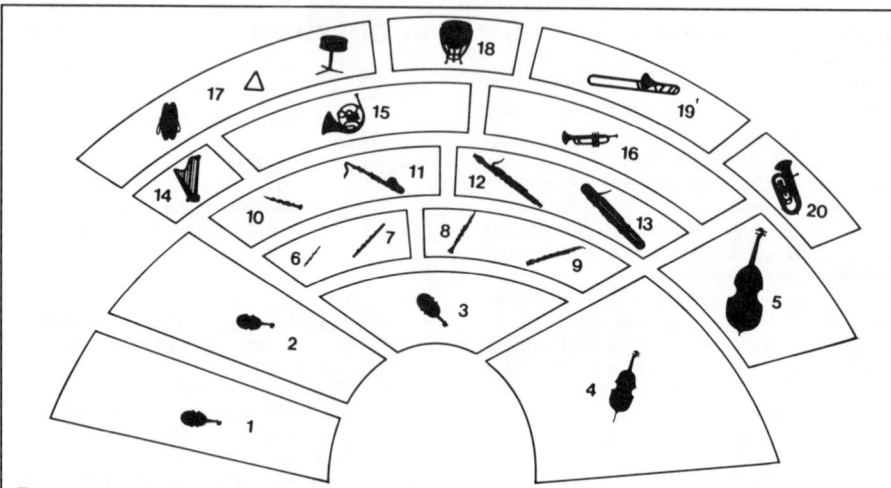

The standard arrangement of a modern symphony orchestra: 1) 1st violins; 2) 2nd violins; 3) violas; 4) cellos; 5) double basses; 6) piccolos; 7) flutes; 8) oboes; 9) cor anglais; 10) clarinets; 11) bass clarinets; 12 bassoons; 13) double bassoons; 14) harps; 15) horns; 16) trumpets; 17/18) percussions; 19) trombones; 20) tubas.

POPULAR INSTRUMENTS

accordion and **concertina** The accordion, invented in Germany in 1822, is box-like, with studs and, sometimes, a keyboard for note selection. The concertina, an English invention of 1829, is hexagonal and never boasts a keyboard.

bongos The bongos are small single-headed paired drums played with the hands. They are popular in Latin American music.

comb and paper Although this impromptu noisemaker is primitive, the membrane and reed principle is widespread and ancient in music. See kazoo.

guitar The guitar is a six-stringed development of the lute, possibly Moorish. It became the dominant instrument in Spanish music as early as the 8th century. The earliest surviving printed music for the guitar dates from 1546, while the first concerto for guitar dates from 1808.

hurdy-gurdy The hurdy-gurdy was a European import from the East in the 9th century. It is roughly violin-shaped. The strings are activated by a resined wheel turned by a crank, and a keyboard stops the strings. The first 'art' use of the instrument was in 1733.

Jew's harp The Jew's harp is a metal frame holding a metal tongue which is plucked with the finger. The resulting vibrations are amplified by the player's mouth cavity. The first concerto was written for the instrument c. 1750, and sophisticated multi-instrument versions appeared later.

kazoo The kazoo is a membrane-vibrating instrument popular with children. The player hums through the instrument, modifying the voice with a hand over the membrane. It was first made in America c. 1850, probably based on ethnic African models.

keyboards 'Keyboards' is a generic term for keyboard instrument(s). The tone is often extensively varied electronically.

mirliton Mirliton is another name for kazoo.

mouth organ or **harmonica** The harmonica was invented in Germany in 1821, but the first concerto

was not written for the instrument until 1951. Different notes are produced according to whether the instrument is blown or sucked; the chromatic version can reach four octaves by the use of a slide.

ocarina The ocarina (Italian 'little goose') is a goose-egg-shaped wind instrument, originally clay but now made from plastic. It originated in Egypt c. 3000 BC.

synthesizer A synthesizer is an electronic sound-generator, created c. 1950 to imitate natural instruments, although it also creates its own tones. It is now common in popular music and commercialized jazz, where it is often attached to a keyboard.

tom tom The tom tom is a Western imitation of African drums, used since the 1920s in dance and jazz bands. The first 'art' use of the instrument was in 1943.

ukelele The ukelele (Hawaiian 'jumping flea') was developed in Hawaii from a version of the Portuguese machada in the 1870s. It is popular in America, and has been widely used in jazz and light music.

zither The zither is a horizontal stringed instrument associated with Central Europe but widespread elsewhere in different varieties. The strings are plucked.

ORCHESTRAL INSTRUMENTS

WOODWIND

piccolo or **octave flute** *Earliest concerto:* c. 1735, by Vivaldi. *Earliest orchestral use:* 1717, Handel's Water Music. *History:* The name 'piccolo' (Italian 'small') dates from 1856, but the instrument goes back to prehistory with the flute and sopranino recorder as its more immediate parents.

flute (transverse or cross-blown). *Earliest concerto:* 1725, A. Scarlatti. *Earliest orchestral use:* 1681, Lully. *History:* Prehistoric (c. 18 000 BC); the modern Boehm flute dates from 1832.

oboe *Earliest concerto:* 1708, Marcheselli. *Earliest orchestral use:* 1657, Lully's *L'amour malade*. *History:* The oboe – the name comes from French *hautbois*, 'high wood' (1511) – originated in the Middle Ages from the schalmey family.

cor anglais *Earliest extant concerto:* 1817, Donizetti. *Earliest orchestral use:* 1722, Volckmar cantata. *History:* Purcell wrote for 'tenor oboe' c. 1690; this may have become the English horn. Alternatively, the name may come from 'angled horn', referring to its crooked shape.

clarinet *Earliest concerto:* c. 1740?, Vivaldi (concerto for two clarinets); c. 1747, Molter (concerto for one clarinet). *Earliest orchestral use:* 1726, Faber's *Mass. History:* The clarinet was developed by J. C. Denner (1655–1707) from the recorder and schalmey families.

bass clarinet *Earliest orchestral use:* 1838, Meyerbeer's *Les Huguenots. History:* The prototype was made in 1772 by Gilles Lot of Paris; the modern Boehm form originated in 1838.

bassoon *Earliest concerto:* c. 1730?, Vivaldi. *Earliest orchestral use:* c. 1619. *History:* The bassoon was introduced in Italy c. 1540 as the lowest of the double-reed group.

double bassoon *Earliest orchestral use:* c. 1730, Handel. *History:* The instrument was 'borrowed' from military bands for elemental effects in opera.

saxophone *Earliest concerto:* 1903, Debussy's *Rhapsody. Earliest orchestral use:* 1844, Kastner's *Last King of Judah. History:* The saxophone was invented by Adolphe Sax, c. 1840.

BRASS

trumpet *Earliest concerto:* before 1700, Torelli; 1796, Haydn (keyed trumpet). *Earliest orchestral use:* c. 1800, keyed; 1835 valved, in Halévy's *La Juive. History:* The natural trumpet is of prehistoric origin: it formed the basis of the earliest orchestras.

horn *Earliest concerto:* 1717–21, Bach or Vivaldi (two horns); before 1721, Telemann (one horn). *Earliest orchestral use:* 1639, Cavalli. *History:* The horn was a prehistoric hunting instrument. The earliest music horns were the German helical horns of the mid-16th century; the rotary valve horn patented in 1832.

trombone *Earliest concerto:* c. 1760, Wagenseil. *Earliest orchestral use:* c. 1600, as part of bass-line. *History:* The Roman *buccina* or slide-trumpet developed into the medieval sackbut, which became the modern trombone c. 1500.

tuba *Earliest concerto:* 1954, Vaughan Williams. *Earliest orchestral use:* 1830, Berlioz's *Symphonie Fantastique. History:* The tuba was patented by W. Wieprecht and Moritz, in Berlin in 1835.

PERCUSSION

anvil *History:* The anvil has been used for musical effect since 1528.

bass drum *Earliest Western use:* 1680, Freschi's opera *Berenice vendicativa. Earliest orchestral use:* 1725, Finger's *Concerto alla Turchesa. History:* The bass drum originated in the ancient Orient.

bells *History:* Bells have been used since ancient Egypt c. 3500 BC, but were first used in 'art' music in a funeral cantata by G. M. Hoffman, c. 1730.

castanets *History:* Castanets were known to the Egyptians by 730 BC. The name comes from the material from which they were made – chestnut wood (Spanish *castaña*).

Chinese blocks or **temple blocks** *Earliest orches-tral use:* 1923, Walton's *Façade. History:* Chinese blocks originated in the ancient Far East and entered European music via jazz bands, c. 1920.

cymbals *Earliest orchestral use:* 1680, Strungk's *Esther. History:* Cymbals originated in Ottoman Turkish military bands.

gong or **tam tam** *Earliest orchestral use:* 1791, Gossec's *Funeral March. History:* The gong originated in Indonesia by or before 300 BC.

marimba *Earliest orchestral use:* before 1914, Grainger's *In a Nutshell. History:* The marimba is an African form of the xylophone.

side or **snare drum** *Earliest orchestral use:* 1749, Handel's *Fireworks Music. History:* The small drums of prehistory were the direct ancestor of the medieval tabor, which developed into its modern form in the 18th century.

tambourine *Earliest orchestral use:* 1820. *History:* The tambourine was used by Arabs in the Middle Ages, but the prototype came from ancient Assyria or Egypt. The word 'tambourine' was first used in 1579.

tenor drum *Earliest orchestral use:* 1842. *History:* The tenor drum was originally developed for military use.

timpani or **kettle drum** *Earliest concerto:* c. 1780, J.C.C. Fischer. *Earliest orchestral use:* in an anonymous intermedia of 1565. *History:* The kettle drum originated in the ancient Orient.

triangle *Earliest orchestral use:* 1774, Glantz's *Turkish Symphony,* but used in opera from 1680. *History:* The triangle was used in Ottoman Turkish military bands.

vibraphone *Earliest orchestral use:* 1932. *History:* The instrument was first used in dance bands in the 1920s.

xylophone *Earliest orchestral use:* 1852, Kastner's *Livre-Partition. History:* The xylophone dates back to ancient times, probably originating in Africa. The earliest known use in Western music was in 1511.

STRINGS

violin *Earliest concerto:* 1698, Torelli. *Earliest orchestral use:* c. 1600. *History:* The violin family is descended from the lyre, although its more direct ancestors were the 6th-century crwth, rebec and fiddle. The first modern instruments, of Lombardic origin, appeared c. 1545. The words violin and fiddle derive ultimately from Latin *vitulari* ('to skip like a calf').

viola *Earliest concerto:* before 1721, Telemann. *Earliest orchestral use:* c. 1600. *History:* See the violin, above.

violoncello or **cello** *Earliest concerto:* 1701, Jacchini. *Earliest orchestral use:* c. 1600. *History:* See the violin, above.

double bass *Earliest extant concerto:* c. 1765, Vanhal. *Earliest orchestral use:* c. 1600. *History:* The double bass developed alongside the violin family, but is a closer relative to the bass viol or violone.

harp *Earliest concerto:* 1738, Handel. *Earliest orchestral use:* c. 1600. *History:* The harp is possibly prehistoric, but it did not attain its modern form until 1792.

KEYBOARD INSTRUMENTS

celesta Instead of strings, as in the piano, the celesta's hammers strike metal plates to give a bell-like effect. The celesta was invented by Mustel in Paris, in 1880; it was first used by an orchestra in Widor's ballet *Der Korrigane*, in the same year. The related **glockenspiel** (German 'bell-play') is sometimes equipped with a keyboard but more usually the plates are struck by hand-held hammers.

clavichord In the clavichord, metal tangents (blades) strike upward to activate the string part-way along its length and to 'stop' (damp) the rest. Therefore, one string may serve for many notes but not simultaneously. The clavichord – which dates from the Middle Ages – has an exceedingly intimate voice, making it ideal for domestic use.

harmonium This portable reed-organ was invented by Grenié in Paris, c. 1835. Usually heard as accompaniment for hymns in church, its first 'art' use was by César Franck about 1858.

harpsichord The harpsichord evolved from the psaltery during the 14th century – the earliest surviving example is dated 1521. It usually has two manuals which control sets of strings that are plucked by plectra. Mainly a domestic instrument, it also supported the bass line in early orchestras. The first solo concerto for harpsichord was written c. 1720, but by c. 1800 it was eclipsed by the pianoforte, although it has been reintroduced since 1903.

organ The organ ultimately derives from the antique panpipes, but subsequent developments have made it the biggest and most powerful of all instruments. The first organ concerto was by Handel, c. 1730, while Saint-Saëns first used it in a symphony in 1886.

pianoforte The first piano was built by Cristofori in Florence before 1700, working on the dulcimer principle of hammers hitting strings, and seeking a keyboard instrument which, unlike the harpsichord, could play both loud and soft (hence, its early name, 'fortepiano'). The earliest printed music for piano was by Giustini (1732); first concerto for piano was probably by J. B. Schmidt in 1763. The instrument attained its current name about 1776 and its modern iron-framed form about 1850.

spinet The spinet is the same shape as a harpsichord but it is smaller. The name may come from the Latin *spina* ('spines' or 'quills' – the plucking agent). It developed early in the 15th century.

virginals A table harpsichord, the virginals are rectangular in shape. The English first printed music for the instrument was *Parthenia*, published in London in 1611.

PLAINSONG AND POLYPHONY

Two of the crucial developments in the early history of Western music were *plainsong* and *polyphony*, both of which came about through the spread of the Christian religion, and whose musical foundations lay partly in Jewish chant, partly in Greece and Rome, and almost anywhere else where Christianity had taken root.

PLAINSONG

Plainsong, consisting of a single line of vocal melody in 'free' rhythm (i.e. not divided into metred bar lengths), gained ground during the early years of Christianity and reached its peak in Gregorian chant, still used in the Roman Catholic Church today. Other parts of Europe produced their own ritual music of similar type. In *antiphons*, two separate bodies of singers performed plainsong chants in response to one another.

MONOPHONY AND POLYPHONY

Plainsong, being confined to a single line of unaccompanied melody, falls into the category of *monophonic* music – Greek for 'single sound', implying absence of harmonic support or other melodies performed simultaneously with the original. *Polyphony*, conversely, means 'many sounds', and indicates the simultaneous sounding of two or more independent melodic lines to produce a coherent musical texture. The melodies in polyphony are described as being in *counterpoint* to each other, and the resulting music as *contrapuntal*. The art of polyphony began to emerge in Europe in the 12th and 13th centuries.

ARS ANTIQUA AND ARS NOVA

The most influential centre of musical activity in the 12th and 13th centuries was the church of Notre Dame in Paris. Here there developed a musical style based on plainsong and *organum*, an early form of polyphony involving the addition of parts to a plainsong melody. Such music was described by writers of the early 14th century as 'Ars Antiqua' (Latin for 'old art') to distinguish it from its successor 'Ars Nova' (Latin for 'new art'). Ars Nova, which flourished in France and Italy in the 14th century, incorporated significant innovations in the areas of rhythm and harmony. The polyphonic setting of poetry to music began in this period in the form of the *ballade*, *rondeau* and *virelai*, collectively known as *chansons*. In France the *troubadours* – itinerant poet-musicians, often of aristocratic birth – were active in Provence in the 11th and 12th centuries. Their German equivalents were the *Minnesinger* (German 'love singers'), whose successors, the guilds of *Meistersinger* ('Mastersingers'), established themselves in some German cities in the 15th and 16th centuries.

MAJOR COMPOSERS

Léonin (active 12th century), French choirmaster of Notre Dame in Paris.

Pérotin (c. 1160–1240), French choirmaster of Notre Dame in Paris.

Walther von der Vogelweide (active late 12th century, early 13th century), the most notable of the German Minnesinger.

Guillaume de Machaut (c. 1300–77), French composer who championed *isorhythms*, whereby rhythm and melody followed strictly repeated patterns that were not in synchronization, and was a pioneer of chansons.

Hans Sachs (1494–1576), the most famous of the Meistersinger. He is the hero of Wagner's opera of that name.

THE RENAISSANCE

Generally, the beginning of the Renaissance in music is reckoned to be found in the increasing secularization of music that took place at the court of Burgundy in the early years of the 15th century. During this period significant developments occurred both in religious and secular musical forms. In the domain of religious music, composers concentrated their efforts on the forms of the mass and the motet. Different types of mass setting developed, especially where the Reformation had established Protestant worship. In Germany the Lutheran chorale (later to exercise a deep influence on the music of J.S. Bach) took root, while in England the anthem (the Protestant equivalent of the Latin motet) took its place in the liturgy of the Church of

England. But as the 16th century progressed, it was Italy that emerged as the crucially important musical centre. The polyphonic mass reached its apogee in the work of three great composers: Palestrina, Victoria and Lassus.

The art of the madrigal – a secular polyphonic composition for several voices, usually based on poems of some literary merit – had its roots in Italy, where early forms of the madrigal first appeared in the 14th century. Early madrigal composers were Flemish composers resident in Italy, and their madrigals were written for three or four voices. A larger number of voices and a more consistently polyphonic style became the norm as the century progressed. Madrigals began to appear in England in the late 16th century. A native English tradition of madrigal composition incorporating features of the secular song as exemplified by Byrd and Gibbons was quickly established by composers such as Morley and Weelkes.

In the Middle Ages instruments were principally used to double voices in vocal polyphony or to provide music for dancing. A burgeoning of instrumental music took place in the 16th century when dance forms such as the stately *pavane* and vigorous *galliard* emerged. Non-dance forms of instrumental music included the *canzona*, the *ricercare* and the *fantasia*. Instrumental music in the 16th century was performed principally on the lute, the organ, the virginal and other stringed keyboard instruments, and by ensembles of viols and other instruments.

MAJOR COMPOSERS

John Dunstable (c. 1385–1453), English composer active in France.

Guillaume Dufay (c. 1400–74), Franco-Flemish composer active at the Burgundian court.

Gilles Binchois (c. 1400–60), Franco-Flemish composer active at the Burgundian court.

Johannes Ockeghem (c. 1425–c. 1495), Flemish composer of sacred and secular music.

Josquin Desprès (1440–1521), Flemish composer of masses, motets and chansons.

Thomas Tallis (c. 1505–85), English composer who introduced the European polyphonic tradition to England: masses, two settings of the Magnificat, and the extraordinary 40-part motet, *Spem in alium*.

Andrea Gabrieli (c. 1510–86), Venetian composer in a flamboyant polychoral (multi-choir) style.

Giovanni Palestrina (c. 1525–84), Italian composer of over 100 masses and 250 motets.

Roland de Lassus (1532–94), Flemish composer of nearly 2000 works.

William Byrd (1543–1623), English composer of sacred music, in particular for the Roman liturgy, and of fantasias for viol consort.

Luis de Victoria (c. 1548–1611), Spanish composer of church music characterized by intense dramatic feeling.

Luca Marenzio (c. 1553–99), Italian composer of madrigals.

Giovanni Gabrieli (1557–1612), Venetian composer of motets featuring a rich instrumental accompaniment. He was the nephew and pupil of Andrea Gabrieli (see above).

Thomas Morley (1557–c. 1602), English organist and composer of madrigals.

Carlo Gesualdo (c. 1560–1613), Italian composer of madrigals.

John Bull (c. 1562–1628), English composer of keyboard music, especially for the virginals.

John Dowland (1563–1626), English composer of songs with lute accompaniment.

Claudio Monteverdi (1567–1643) , Italian composer of three innovative operas and the *Vespro della Beata Vergine* ('Vespers of the Blessed Virgin'; 1610), which runs the entire gamut of contemporary types of sacred music.

Thomas Tomkins (1572–1656), Welsh composer of polyphonic madrigals.

John Wilbye (1574–1638), English composer of madrigals.

Thomas Weelkes (c. 1576–1623), English organist and composer of madrigals.

Gregorio Allegri (1582–1652), Italian composer: *Miserere*.

Girolamo Frescobaldi (1583–1643), Italian organist and composer of toccatas, fugues and capriccios.

Orlando Gibbons (1583–1625), English composer of sacred and secular music, including anthems.

Heinrich Schütz (1585–1672), German composer of choral music whose style was to prove an influence on German composers up until the time of Bach and Handel.

MUSIC OF THE BAROQUE

Baroque, *Classical* and *Romantic* are the categories to which most music performed in the concert hall or opera house are assigned. But the boundaries of each are hazy, and the word Baroque is particularly difficult to define. A word of obscure origin, by the 17th and 18th centuries Baroque had become a term for the ornate, particularly ecclesiastical, architecture of the period. Other than defining a particular period between 1650 and 1750, Baroque has little meaning in application to music, though in its suggestion of ornateness of style it is obviously descriptive of certain types of 17th- and 18th-century composition. A distinction is generally made between composers of the 'early Baroque' (such as Monteverdi, Frescobaldi and Schütz; see above) and those of the 'late Baroque' (most notably Bach and Handel).

The vocabulary and techniques of instrumental and vocal composition underwent a massive expansion in the 17th century. Revolutionary change took place also in the formal organization of music: the medieval modes that had been the basis of polyphonic composition in the 16th century giving way during the 17th century to a system involving the exclusive use of modern scales. In addition, innovations such as the *concertato* style – in which specific instrumental or vocal parts were accompanied by a *basso continuo*, or 'thorough bass' (involving a low-pitched instrument such as a cello or bass viol combined with a harpsichord, organ or lute) – distinguish the Baroque from the Renaissance that preceded it. The development of the two major new instrumental genres of the Baroque – the sonata and the concerto – was largely the work of Italian composers. As well as providing the emerging vocal genres of opera, cantata and oratorio, Italy was the principal source of instrumental ensemble music throughout the 17th century.

In France, as in England and Germany, composers were strongly influenced by Italian models of instrumental music. However, the greatest achievements of the French Baroque were in the domain of harpsichord music and opera. The overtures and dance movements from Lully's operas enjoyed a flourishing life outside the operatic context. So-called French overtures on the Lullian model were used by Handel in some of his operas and oratorios, and became an integral part of the Baroque orchestral suite.

Opera is the Italian word for 'work', but as an abbreviation of _opera in musica_ (a 'musical work'), it began to be used in 17th-century Italy for music dramas in which singers in costume enacted a story with instrumental accompaniment. The first true masterpieces in the form were by the Venetian composer Monteverdi (see above), and many of the most prominent opera composers of the late 17th century and early 18th century came from Naples, giving rise to the term the _Neapolitan School_. The greatest operas of the early 18th century were written in England by Handel.

MAJOR COMPOSERS

Louis Couperin (c. 1626–61), French composer of harpsichord and organ music.

Jean-Baptiste Lully (1632–87), Italian-born French composer who established the form of the French opera, which was to reach its peak in the operas of Rameau.

Marc-Antoine Charpentier (1634–1704), French composer of oratorios and motets: _Te Deum_.

Arcangelo Corelli (1653–1713), Italian pioneer composer of concertos and sonatas: the 12 _Concerti Grossi_ (1714) established the form of the concerto grosso.

Johann Pachelbel (1653–1706), German composer of canons, airs and 78 choral preludes.

Henry Purcell (1659–95), English composer of theatre music, church music, string fantasias and sonatas: the miniature opera _Dido and Aeneas_ (1689), the incidental music for _The Fairy Queen_ (1692) and _Queen Mary's Funeral Music_ (1695).

Alessandro Scarlatti (1660–1725), Neapolitan composer of operas (of which 115 survive). One of Scarlatti's important innovations was the three-movement form of the Italian opera overture or _sinfonia_, regarded by many as being the earliest forerunner of the Classical symphony.

François Couperin ('_Le Grand_'; 1668–1733), French composer – nephew of Louis (see above). He composed in a wider range of genres than his uncle, but is best known for his elegant harpsichord pieces.

Tommaso Albinoni (1671–1750), Italian composer who wrote prodigious amounts of instrumental and vocal music, including 42 operas.

Antonio Vivaldi (1678–1741), Italian priest, violinist and composer: sacred music, 94 operas (of which 50 survive), sonatas, cantatas and more than 460 concertos, including _The Four Seasons_ (1725).

Georg Phillipp Telemann (1681–1767), German composer of concertos and orchestral suites who, in his lifetime, enjoyed a greater reputation than his friends Bach and Handel.

Jean-Philippe Rameau (1683–1764), French composer of operas: _Hippolyte et Aricie_ (1733) and _Castor et Pollux_ (1737).

Domenico Scarlatti (1685–1757), Neapolitan composer – son of Alessandro (see above). His 550 single-movement sonatas for harpsichord considerably extended the technical and musical possibilities of keyboard writing.

George Frideric Handel (1685–1759), German-born British composer, impresario, musical director, virtuoso keyboard player and teacher. In his operas, oratorios, concertos and suites, he created a highly individual style of writing, best seen in: _Water Music_ (1717), _Music for the Royal Fireworks_ (1749), 14 operas, anthems including _Zadok the Priest_ (1727), the _Concerti Grossi_ (1734–40) and numerous oratorios, including _Saul_ and _Israel in Egypt_ (1739), _Messiah_ (1741), _Solomon_ (1748) and _Jephtha_ (1751).

Johann Sebastian Bach (1685–1750), German composer of concertos, sonatas, over 250 cantatas and keyboard music. He is held by many to be the greatest of all Baroque composers: _Brandenburg Concertos_ (1721), a collection of 48 preludes and fugues _The Well-Tempered Clavier_ (1722–44), _St John Passion_ (1723), _St Matthew Passion_ (1729), the _Mass in B minor_ (1733–38), and the _Goldberg Variations_ (1742).

Wilhelm Friedemann Bach (1710–84), German organist and composer – eldest son of Johann Sebastian (see above).

Carl Philipp Emmanuel Bach (1714–88), German composer of over 200 sonatas and symphonies – 3rd son of Johann Sebastian.

Johann Christian Bach ('The English Bach'; 1735–82), German composer of concertos, symphonies, sacred music and 13 operas – 11th son of Johann Sebastian (see above).

THE CLASSICAL PERIOD

If the music of J.S. Bach represents the summit of the Baroque era, that of his sons, particularly Carl Philip Emanuel and Johann Christian (see above), provides a link with the period loosely known as Classical. It was a time of new developments in the art of the symphony and concerto, of the birth of the string quartet and piano sonata, and of the humanizing of opera.

Vienna, the capital of the Austrian Habsburg Empire, now became the centre of musical progress, with Haydn, Mozart, and, before long, Beethoven as its principal representatives. In the next generation Schubert was to sustain Vienna's musical pre-eminence. Both Beethoven and Schubert were to extend the Classical forms and infuse them with a Romantic sensibility. All four composers collectively became known as the First Viennese School. Classicism, in musical terms, has been defined as a style accepting certain basic conventions of form and structure (notably the sonata form; see under Musical Forms, Structures and Terms above), and using these as a natural framework for the expression of ideas. Unlike Romantic music (see below), which developed out of Classicism, it saw no need to break the set boundaries, although in a discreet way its greatest practitioners did so more often than not.

MAJOR COMPOSERS

Giovanni Battista Sammartini (c. 1698–75), Italian composer of about 2000 works in many genres.

Christoph Willibald von Gluck (1714–87), German composer who made opera more genuinely dramatic: the operas _Orpheus and Eurydice_ (1762) and _Alceste_ (1767).

Johann Stamitz (1717–57), German composer of the Mannheim School, whose works are characterized by 'Mannheim rockets' (brilliant scale passages).

Jiří Benda (1722–95), Czech composer who pioneered melodrama: *Ariadne auf Naxos* (1774).

Franz Joseph Haydn (1732–1809), Austrian composer of piano sonatas and trios, concertos, operas, masses, string quartets (a form he established) and 104 symphonies: the *London Symphonies* (Nos. 92–104; 1789–95), and the oratorios *The Creation* (1798) and *The Seasons* (1801).

Karl Stamitz (1745–1801), German composer of the Mannheim School – son of Johann (see above).

Luigi Boccherini (1747–1805), Italian composer of operas, 20 symphonies and 91 string quartets.

Domenico Cimarosa (1749–1801), Italian composer of comic operas and of harpsichord sonatas.

Antonio Salieri (1750–1825), Italian composer of over 40 operas. His hostility to Mozart led to (groundless) rumours that he poisoned Mozart.

Wolfgang Amadeus Mozart (1756–91), Austrian composer of 49 symphonies, over 40 concertos, 26 string quartets, 21 operas, 7 string quintets and sonatas: the operas *Le nozze di Figaro* (The Marriage of Figaro; 1786), *Don Giovanni* (1787), *Così fan tutte* (1790) and *Die Zauberflöte* (The Magic Flute; 1791), the symphonies *Paris* (1778), *Prague* (1786) and *Jupiter* (1790), and the orchestral piece *Eine kleine Nachtmusik* (1787).

Luigi Cherubini (1760–1842), Italian composer of masses and 30 operas: the operas *Médée* (1797) and *les Deux Journées* (adapted in English as The Water Carrier; 1800).

Ludwig van Beethoven (1770–1827), German composer of chamber music, 9 symphonies, 5 piano concertos, violin concerto, triple concerto, 32 piano sonatas, 16 string quartets and over 200 song settings: the opera *Fidelio* (1805), the symphonies *Eroica* (No. 3; 1803–04), *Pastoral* (No. 6; 1807–08) and *Choral* (No. 9; 1817–23), the piano sonatas *Pathétique* (1799), *Moonlight* (1800–01) and *Hammerklavier* (1817–19), the *Emperor* piano concerto (1809), and the *Missa Solemnis* (1818–23). See also the Music of the Romantics, below.

Niccoló Paganini (1782–1840), Italian virtuoso violinist and composer of violin concertos and 24 caprices.

Franz Schubert (1797–1828), Austrian composer of 9 symphonies, string quartets, piano sonatas and 600 *Lieder*: the symphonies *Unfinished* (No. 8; 1822) and *Great* (No. 9; 1825), the piano quintet *Die Forelle* (The Trout; 1819), a string quartet in C major (1828), the piano sonata *Grand Duo* (1824), the song cycles *Die schöne Müllerin* (1823) and *Winterreise* (1827), and the song settings *Erlkönig* (1815) and *Die Forelle* (The Trout; 1817).

MUSIC OF THE ROMANTICS

Romanticism in music was not necessarily born in 1800. But the first year of the 19th century, when Beethoven had just produced the first of his nine symphonies, is as good a time as any by which to commemorate the establishment of composers as individual artists – rather than as servants of rich patrons, which had been the case throughout the Baroque and Classical periods.

Beethoven, in his third symphony, the *Eroica* (1803–4), finally shattered the bounds of Classicism. It was not only the biggest symphony ever written until that time (though Beethoven himself was to surpass it in his ninth), it was also recognized to be a personal testament in music, the first of its kind, symbolizing Beethoven's battle with the growing

deafness that was to destroy his career as a public performer, but which intensified his inspiration as a composer. The crucial role played by Beethoven in the progress of symphonic form, and of the art of the string quartet and piano sonata, was something no later composer could ignore. In his last quartets in particular, Beethoven explored the most profound emotional and spiritual tensions with a musical daring not seen again for another century.

The composer as artist was attracted to representational or *programme music* – music that evokes pictorial scenes or finds some way to tell a story in purely musical terms. Berlioz, Mendelssohn and Liszt were notable proponents of this genre. Liszt coined the term 'symphonic poem' for his descriptive orchestral works. In opera, Wagner expanded and transformed the art of opera into what he preferred to describe as 'music drama'. In Italy, Verdi followed a parallel if more cautious path.

The rise of nationalist feeling all over Europe inspired many composers. Although Liszt's Hungarian Rhapsodies lacked Hungarian authenticity (in that Liszt mistook gypsy music for Hungarian folk music), nationalism in music was becoming a major force. Folk rhythms, folk dances, folk songs, folk legends and folk harmonies served as important sources of inspiration to such composers as Smetana, Dvořák, Grieg and Tchaikovsky.

MAJOR COMPOSERS

Ludwig van Beethoven (1770–1827), see above and The Classical Period.

Niccolo Paganini (1782–1840), see The Classical Period.

Daniel Auber (1782–1871), French composer of 42 operas: *La Muette de Portici* (1828).

Carl Maria von Weber (1786–1826), German composer of operas, symphonies, chamber and piano music: the operas *Der Freischütz* (1821) and *Oberon* (1826).

Gioacchino Rossini (1792–1868), Italian composer of 36 operas: *Tancredi* (1813), *The Barber of Seville* (1816), *La Cenerentola* (Cinderella; 1817), *La gazza ladra* (The Thieving Magpie; 1817) and *William Tell* (1829).

Gaetano Donizetti (1797–1848), Italian composer: the operas *Maria Stuarda* (1834) and *Lucia di Lammermoor* (1835).

Franz Schubert (1797–1828), see The Classical Period.

Vincenzo Bellini (1801–35), Italian composer: the opera *Norma* (1825).

Hector Berlioz (1803–69), French composer: the symphonies *Symphonie Fantastique* (1830) and *Harold in Italy* (1833), the choral symphony *Roméo et Juliette* (1839), the operas *Benvenuto Cellini* (1838) and *Les Troyens* (The Trojans; 1856–59), and the cantata *La Damnation de Faust* (1846).

Johann Strauss the elder (1804–49), Austrian composer of waltz music and *Radetzky March* (1848).

Mikhail Glinka (1804–57), Russian composer: the operas *A Life for the Tsar* (1836) and *Ruslan and Ludmilla* (1842).

Felix Mendelssohn (1809–47), German composer: the overtures *A Midsummer Night's Dream* (1826) and *Hebrides* (or *Fingal's Cave*; 1830), and the oratorios *St Paul* (1836) and *Elijah* (1846).

Frédéric Chopin (1810–49), Polish composer of nocturnes, ballades, mazurkas, polonaises, studies, waltzes and scherzos, all for the piano.

Robert Schumann (1810–56), German composer of songs, piano music and symphonies: the song cycles *Dichterliebe* (Poet's Love; 1840) and *Frauen-liebe und -Leben* (1840).

(Ferencz) Franz Liszt (1811–86), Hungarian composer of a series of 13 descriptive orchestral works ('symphonic poems') and of piano pieces: the symphonies *Faust* (1853–61) and *Dante* (1856), symphonic poem *Les Préludes* (1856), and the piano piece *Liebesträume* (1850).

Giuseppe Verdi (1813–1901), Italian composer of opera: *Nabucco* (1842), *Il Trovatore* (1853), *La Traviata* (1853), *Aida* (1871), *Otello* (1887) and *Falstaff* (1893).

Richard Wagner (1813–83), German composer of opera: *The Flying Dutchman* (1843), *Tannhäuser* (1845), *Lohengrin* (1846–48), *Tristan and Isolde* (1857–59), *The Mastersingers of Nuremberg* (1862–67), *Parsifal* (1877–82) and the opera cycle *The Ring* (*Das Rheingold, Die Walküre, Siegfried* and *Götterdämmerung*; 1852–74).

Charles François Gounod (1818–93), French composer: the opera *Faust* (1859).

Jacques Offenbach (1819–80), French composer of operetta: the opera *The Tales of Hoffmann* (1881).

César Franck (1822–90), Belgian composer: *Symphonic Variations* (1885).

Bedřich Smetana (1824–84), Czech composer of operas, chamber music and symphonic poems: the opera *The Bartered Bride* (1866).

Anton Bruckner (1824–96), Austrian composer: *Te Deum* (1881–84) and nine symphonies.

Johann Strauss the younger (1825–99), Austrian composer: the operetta *Die Fledermaus* (1874), and the waltzes *An der schönen blauen Donau* (Blue Danube) and *Kaiser-Walzer* (Emperor Waltz).

Johannes Brahms (1833–97), German composer of symphonies, choral works and a large canon of chamber music: the choral works *A German Requiem* (1868) and *Alto Rhapsody* (1869).

Camille Saint-Saëns (1835–1921), French composer: the opera *Samson et Dalila* (1877) and the orchestral pieces *Danse macabre* (1874) and *Carnaval des animaux* (1886).

Léo Delibes (1836–91), French composer: the opera *Lakmé* (1883) and the ballet *Coppélia* (1870).

Mily Balakirev (1837–1910), Russian composer who made an important contribution to the national school of Russian music.

Georges Bizet (1838–75), French composer: the opera *Carmen* (1875).

Modest Musorgsky (1839–81), Russian composer: the opera *Boris Godunov* (1868–72) and the piano piece *Pictures at an Exhibition* (1874).

Pyotr Ilyich Tchaikovsky (1840–93), Russian composer: the symphony *Pathétique* (1893), the opera *Eugène Onegin* (1877–78), and the ballets *Swan Lake* (1875–76), *The Sleeping Beauty* (1888–89) and *Nutcracker* (1891–92).

Antonin Dvořák (1841–1904), Czech composer: *Slavonic Dances* (1878–86) and the symphony *From the New World* (No. 9; 1893).

Jules Massenet (1842–1912), French composer: the operas *Manon* (1884) and *Don Quichotte* (1910).

Sir Arthur Sullivan (1842–1900), English composer of operetta and oratorios, the former to libretti by W.S. Gilbert.

Edvard Hagerup Grieg (1843–1907), Norwegian composer: the incidental music for the play *Peer Gynt* (1876).

Nikolay Rimsky-Korsakov (1844–1908), Russian composer of operas including *The Snow Maiden* (1881–82) and *The Golden Cockerel* (1906–07), and of orchestral pieces including *Scheherazade* (1888).

Gabriel Fauré (1845–1924), French composer: the opera *Pénélope* (1913) and the *Requiem* (1884).

Hubert Parry (1848–1918), English composer of songs and choral music: *Songs of Farewell* (1916) and *Jerusalem* (1916).

Vincent D'Indy (1851–1931), French composer: *Symphonie Cévenole* (1886).

Charles Villiers Stanford (1852–1924), Irish composer: *Irish Symphony* (No. 3; 1886) and *Songs of the Sea* (1904).

Leoš Janáček (1854–1928), Czech composer of operas: *Jenufa* (1904), *Katya Kabanova* (1921), *The Cunning Little Vixen* (1924), *The Makropoulos Case* (1926) and *From the House of the Dead* (1930).

Engelbert Humperdinck (1854–1921), German composer: the opera *Hansel und Gretel* (1893).

Ruggero Leoncavallo (1858–1919), Italian composer: the opera *Pagliacci* (1892).

Giacomo Puccini (1858–1924), Italian composer of operas: *La Bohème* (1896), *Madama Butterfly* (1904) and *Tosca* (1904).

Isaac Albéniz (1860–1909), Spanish composer whose works are characterized by traditional Spanish rhythms: *Iberia* (1906–09).

Gustav Mahler (1860–1911), Austrian composer of nine large-scale symphonies: the symphonies *Resurrection* (No. 2; 1884–94) and *Symphony of a Thousand* (No. 8; 1906–07).

Pietro Mascagni (1863–1945), Italian composer: the opera *Cavalleria rusticana* (1890).

Richard Strauss (1864–1949), German composer of operas and symphonic poems: the operas *Salome* (1905), *Elektra* (1909) and *Der Rosenkavalier* (1911).

Enrique Granados (1867–1916), Spanish composer of operas and piano music: *Goyescas* (1914).

MODERNISTS AND NEW MUSIC

The years around 1900 marked the beginnings of Modernism. Wagner's *Tristan and Isolde* (1865) – see above – was the German figurehead, with Debussy's *Pelléas and Mélisande* (1902) as its French counterpart. From these two operas, the major trends in 20th-century music all flowed.

Modernism in music – as in the visual arts and literature – involved a radical break with existing conventions. It also involved what often appears as a greater distancing between the composer and the audience – audiences have tended to find Modernist works 'difficult'. However, although Modernism has been in the intellectual forefront of music in the 20th century, many composers have followed more accessible paths.

Music since 1945 has evolved in many different ways. for many composers – especially in the 1950s – the once revolutionary twelve-note technique of Schoenberg became the new orthodoxy, while the avant-garde of the 1960s and 1970s enthusiastically embraced the novel sound possibilities offered by the development of electronic music.

MAJOR COMPOSERS

Edward Elgar (1857–1934), English composer:

Enigma Variations (1898–99) and the oratorio *The Dream of Gerontius* (1899–1900).

Hugo Wolf (1860–1903), Austrian composer, notably of songs: *Italian Serenade* (1892).

Frederick Delius (1862–1934), English composer: the orchestral piece *On hearing the first cuckoo in spring*.

Claude Debussy (1862–1918), French composer whose works are characterized by a 'dream-like' quality sometimes called 'musical impressionism': numerous works for piano, the orchestral pieces *Prélude à l'après-midi d'une faune* (1892–4), *Nocturnes* (1893–99) and *La Mer* (1903–05), and the opera *Pelléas et Mélisande* (1902).

Carl Nielsen (1865–1931), Danish composer whose work is characterized by 'progressive tonality': six symphonies including *The Inextinguishable* (No. 4; 1915–16).

Jean Sibelius (1865–1951), Finnish composer: seven symphonies, the symphonic poems *Kullervo* (1892) and *Finlandia* (1899), and the suite *Karelia* (1893).

Alexander Glazunov (1865–1936), Russian composer: the ballet *The Seasons* (1901).

Ferruccio Busoni (1866–1924), Italian composer: the piano piece *Fantasia contrappuntistica* (1910–12).

Erik Satie (1866–1925), French composer for piano: the ballet *Parade* (1917), and the piano pieces *Trois Gymnopédies* (1888) and *Trois morceaux en forme de poire* (1903).

Franz Lehár (1870–1948), Hungarian composer of operetta: *The Merry Widow* (1905).

Alexander Skryabin (1872–1915), Russian composer of symphonies and piano sonatas: the symphony *Prometheus* (No. 5; 1909–10).

Ralph Vaughan Williams (1872–1958), English composer: *Sea Symphony* (1906–09), the opera *The Pilgrim's Progress* (1951) and songs based upon folk-songs.

Sergey Rakhmaninov (1873–1943), Russian composer whose works – notably for piano – are characterized by Romantic nostalgia.

Gustav Holst (1874–1934), English composer: the suite *The Planets* (1914–16) and *Egdon Heath* (1927).

Charles Ives (1874–1954), American composer of highly individualistic works: the orchestral set *Three Places in New England* (1903–14).

Arnold Schoenberg (1874–1951), Austrian composer whose later works are characterized by atonality, particularly the twelve-note system which he devised: the string sextet *Verklarte Nacht* (1899), the orchestral piece for soprano and five instruments *Pierrot Lunaire*, and the unfinished opera *Moses und Aron* (1932–51).

Maurice Ravel (1875–1937), French composer: the orchestral pieces *Rapsodie espagnole* (1907), *Pavane pour une infante défunte* (1910) and *La Valse* (1919–20), and the ballet score *Boléro* (1928).

Manuel de Falla (1876–1946), Spanish composer whose works echo Andalusian folk music: the ballet *The Three-Cornered Hat* (1917–19).

Ottorino Respighi (1879–1936), Italian composer: the ballet *The Fantastic Toyshop* (1919) and the orchestral suites *Fountains of Rome* (1914–16), *Old Airs and Dances for Lute* (1917) and *Pines of Rome* (1924).

John Ireland (1879–1962), English composer of chamber music and songs.

Ernst Bloch (1880–1959), Swiss composer who became a naturalized American citizen: *Israel Symphony* (1912–16).

Béla Bartók (1881–1945), Hungarian composer of fiercely modernist music based on folk music: *Music for Strings, Percussion and Celesta* (1936) and *Concerto for Orchestra* (1943).

Karol Szymanowski (1882–1937), Polish composer: the ballet *Harnasie* (1926).

Igor Stravinsky (1882–1971), Russian-born composer: the ballets *The Firebird* (1910), *Petrushka* (1911) and *The Rite of Spring* (1913).

Zoltán Kodály (1882–1967), Hungarian composer whose works are characterized by a strong national flavour: the opera *Háry János* (1925–27).

Percy Grainger (1882–1961), Australian composer who became a naturalized American citizen: folk songs and lighter works often based upon traditional tunes.

Edgard Varèse (1883–1965), French-born American composer, who made early experiments in electronic music.

Anton Webern (1883–1945), Austrian composer whose works are characterized by serialism: chamber symphony (1924) and chamber concerto (1934).

Alban Berg (1885–1935), Austrian composer: the operas *Wozzeck* (1914–20) and *Lulu* (1928–35), and the *Lyric Suite* (1928).

Heitor Villa-Lobos (1887–1959), Brazilian composer: the orchestral works *Bachianas Brasileiras* (1930–44).

Frank Martin (1890–1974), Swiss composer: *Petite Symphonie Concertante* (1946).

Sergey Prokofiev (1891–1953), Russian composer: the ballet *Romeo and Juliet* (1935), the operas *The Love for Three Oranges* (1921) and *War and Peace* (1941–52), and the piece for orchestra and narrator *Peter and the Wolf* (1936).

Arthur Honegger (1892–1955), Swiss composer: the orchestral piece *Pacific 231* and the oratario *Jeanne d'Arc au bûcher*.

Darius Milhaud (1892–1974), French composer whose works are characterized by polytonality.

Paul Hindemith (1895–1963), German composer who is associated with the term 'utility music': the opera *Mathis der Maler* (1938).

Carl Orff (1895–1982), German composer: the oratorio *Carmina Burana* (1935–36).

Henry Cowell (1897–1965), American composer of 20 symphonies.

Ernst Křenek (1900–91), Austrian composer who became a naturalized American citizen: the opera *Jonny spielt auf* (1925–26).

Kurt Weill (1900–50), German composer: *Die Dreigroschenoper* (The Threepenny Opera; 1927).

Aaron Copland (1900–90), American composer of works based on American folk idioms: the ballets *Billy the Kid* (1938) and *Appalachian Spring* (1944).

William Walton (1902–83), English composer: *Façade* (1921) and the cantata *Belshazzar's Feast* (1931).

Joaquin Rodrigo (1902–), Spanish composer of music for guitar and orchestra in a traditional Spanish style: *Aranquez Concerto* (1940).

Luigi Dallapiccola (1902–75), Italian composer whose works were the first in Italy to use the twelve-note method.

Aram Khachaturian (1903–1978), Armenian composer: the ballet *Spartacus* (1956).

Michael Tippett (1905–), English composer: the operas *The Midsummer Marriage* (1955), *The Knot*

Garden (1970) and *New Year* (1989).

Dmitri Shostakovitch (1906–75), Russian composer of 15 symphonies and string quartets: the opera *The Lady Macbeth of the Mtsensk District.*

Olivier Messiaen (1908–92), French composer of organ, piano and religious works: the piano work *Catalogue d'oiseaux.*

Elliott Carter (1908–), American composer: *Symphony of Three Orchestras* (1977).

Samuel Barber (1910–81), American composer: *Adagio for Strings* (1938), the opera *Vanessa* (1958).

John Cage (1912–92), American composer: the percussion and electronic pieces *Imaginary Landscapes* (1939–62).

Benjamin Britten (1913–76), English composer: operas *Peter Grimes* (1945), *Billy Budd* (1951), *The Turn of the Screw* (1954) and *Death in Venice* (1973).

Witold Lutoslawski (1913–), Polish composer of works incorporating modern techniques: *String Quartet* (1964).

Iannis Xenakis (1922–), Romanian-born Greek composer of works scored for conventional instruments but often written with the aid of a computer.

Gyorgy Ligeti (1923–), Hungarian composer: *Requiem* (1965) and the opera *Le Grand Macabre* (1975).

Luigi Nono (1924–90), Italian composer of works characterized by their uncompromising severity: the opera *Intolleranza* (1960).

Luciano Berio (1925–), Italian composer of electronic and other modern music.

Pierre Boulez (1925–), French composer of works using the twelve-note technique: *Le Marteau sans maître* (1953–55) and *Pli selon pli* (1957–62).

Hans Werner Henze (1926–), German composer: the oratorio *The Raft of Medusa* (1968) and the war opera *We Come to the River* (1976).

Karlheinz Stockhausen (1928–), German composer: the seven-part opera cycle *Licht* (1984–), the piece for three orchestras *Gruppen* (1957), and *Hymnen* (1967), *Prozession* (1967), *Stimmung* (1968) and *Jubilaeum* (1977).

Edison Denisov (1929–), Russian composer of highly original music which draws upon electronic techniques and folk music.

Krzysztof Penderecki (1933–), Polish composer of works characterized by the use of sensational effects: *Threnody for the Victims of Hiroshima* (1960) and the opera *The Devils of Loudon* (1969).

Henryk Górecki (1933–), Polish composer: *Symphony No. 3* (1976) and the choral work *Beatus Vir.*

Harrison Birtwhistle (1934–), English composer: the opera *Punch and Judy* (1966–67).

Peter Maxwell Davies (1934–), English composer: the opera *Taverner* (1970), the theatre pieces *Vesalii Icones* (1969) and *Eight Songs for a Mad King* (1969).

Alfred Shnitke (1934–), Russian composer of works that often include a humorous element, for example a 'silent' cadenza' in which the performer goes through the motions of playing.

Terry Riley (1935–), American composer of minimalist music characterized by the extensive repetition of simple melodies in changing harmonies.

Arvo Pärt (1935–), Estonian composer: *Meie Ard* (1959) and *St John Passion* (1981).

Philip Glass (1937–), American minimalist composer of avant-garde operas.

MAJOR ORCHESTRAS

Australia
Australian Chamber Orchestra, founded 1975.
Sydney Symphony Orchestra (present name dates from 1946).
Australian Broadcasting Corporation Orchestra.

Austria
Concentus Musicus Wein, founded 1953. Performs Baroque music on period instruments.

Canada
Montreal Symphony Orchestra (title dates from 1963). Principal conductor: Charles Dutoit.
Toronto Symphony Orchestra, founded 1926. Principal conductor: Günther Herbig.

Czech Republic
Czech Philharmonic Orchestra (Prague), founded 1901. Chief conductor: Jiří Bělohlávek.

Denmark
Danish National Radio Symphony Orchestra, founded 1925. Conductor: Leif Seegarstam.

France
French Philharmonic Orchestra (Radio France), founded 1976. Principal conductor: Maris Janowski.
Orchestre de Paris, founded 1967. Conductor: Semyon Bychkov.
Orchestre National de France (Paris), founded 1934.

Finland
Helsinki Philharmonic Orchestra, founded 1882. Conductor: Sergiu Comissiona.

Germany
Bavarian Radio Symphony Orchestra (Munich), founded 1949. Conductor: Colin Davis.
Berlin Philharmonic Orchestra, founded 1882. Principal conductor: Claudio Abbado.
Dresden State Orchestra (Dresdner Staatskapelle), origins traced to 1548. Principal conductor: Giuseppe Sinopoli.
Gewandhaus Orchestra of Leipzig, founded 1781. Conductor: Kurt Masur.
Stuttgart Chamber Orchestra, founded 1945. Director: Karl Münchinger.
Südwestfunk Orchestra (Baden-Baden), founded 1946. Principal conductor: Michael Gielen.

Italy
Santa Cecilia Orchestra (Rome), founded 1907.

Israel
Israel Philharmonic Orchestra (Tel Aviv), founded 1936. Music director: Zubin Mehta.

Japan
Tokyo Philharmonic Orchestra, founded 1940 (as the Central Symphony Orchestra).
Yumiuri Nippon Symphony Orchestra, founded 1962. Music director: Heinz Rogner.

Mexico
Mexico City Symphony Orchestra. Conductor: Enrico Batiz.

Netherlands
Royal Concertgebouw Orchestra (Amsterdam), founded 1888. Principal conductor: Riccardo Chailly.

Norway
Gothenburg Symphony Orchestra. Conductor: Neeme Järvi.
Oslo Philharmonic Orchestra, founded 1871. Chief conductor: Mariss Jansons.

Russia
Moscow Philharmonic Orchestra. Principal conductor: Vassili Sinaiski.

Moscow Radio Symphony Orchestra, founded 1931. Principal conductor: Vladimir Fedoseyev.

Moscow Virtuosi, founded 1979. Director: Vladimir Spivakov.

St Petersburg Philharmonic Orchestra (formerly Leningrad PO), founded 1921. Principal conductor: Mariss Jansons.

Ministry of Culture Orchestra, founded 1982. Principal conductor: Gennadi Rozdestvensky.

State Symphony Orchestra, founded 1936.

Spain

National Orchestra of Spain (Madrid), founded 1940. Director: Jesús López Cobos.

Sweden

Stockholm Philharmonic Orchestra, founded 1902. Principal conductor: Yuri Ahranovitch.

Switzerland

Orchestre de la Suisse Romande (Geneva), founded 1918. Principal conductor: Armin Jordan.

United Kingdom

Academy of Ancient Music, plays on period instruments. Director: Christopher Hogwood.

Academy of St Martin-in-the-Fields. Director: Sir Neville Marriner.

BBC Philharmonic Orchestra. Conductor: Yan Pascal Tortelier.

BBC Scottish Symphony Orchestra. Chief conductor: Jerzy Maksymiuk.

BBC Symphony Orchestra. Chief conductor: Andrew Davis.

BBC Welsh Symphony Orchestra. Principal conductor: Tadaaki Otaka.

Bournemouth Symphony Orchestra. Principal conductor: Andrew Litton.

Chamber Orchestra of Europe. Artistic advisor: Claudio Abbado.

City of Birmingham Symphony Orchestra. Music director: Simon Rattle.

English Chamber Orchestra. Principal conductor: Jeffrey Tate.

The English Concert plays on period instruments. Music director: Trevor Pinnock.

Hallé Orchestra (Manchester), founded 1858. Principal conductor: Stanislaw Skrowaczewski.

London Philharmonic Orchestra, founded 1932. Music director: Franz Welser-Möst.

London Symphony Orchestra, founded 1904. Principal conductor: Michael Tilson Thomas.

The Philharmonia (London), founded 1945. Music director: Giuseppe Sinopoli.

Royal Liverpool Philharmonic Orchestra, founded 1840s. Music director: Libor Pešek.

Royal Philharmonic Orchestra, founded 1946. Music director: Vladimir Ashkenazy.

Royal Scottish Orchestra (Glasgow), founded 1891. Music director/principal conductor: Walter Weller.

Ulster Orchestra (Belfast), founded 1966. Principal conductor/artistic director: Yan Pascal Tortelier.

USA

Boston Symphony Orchestra, founded 1881. Music director: Seji Ozawa.

Chicago Symphony Orchestra, founded 1891. Music director: Daniel Barenboim.

The Cleveland Orchestra, founded 1918. Conductor: Christoph von Dohnanyi.

The Detroit Symphony Orchestra, founded 1914. Principal conductor: Günther Herbig.

Houston Symphony Orchestra, founded 1913. Principal conductor: Christoph Eschenbach.

Los Angeles Philharmonic Orchestra, founded 1919. Principal conductor: Esa-Pekka Salonen.

New York Philharmonic Orchestra, founded 1842. Principal conductor: Kurt Masur.

Philadelphia Orchestra, founded 1900. Music director: Wolfgang Sawallisch.

Pittsburgh Symphony Orchestra, founded 1895. Principal conductor: Lorin Maazel.

Saint Louis Symphony Orchestra, founded 1880. Music director: Leonard Slatkin.

San Francisco Symphony Orchestra, founded 1911. Principal conductor: Herbert Blomstedt.

MAJOR OPERA COMPANIES

Argentina *Buenos Aires*: Teatro Colón.

Australia *Sydney*: Australian Opera Company.

Austria *Salzburg*: Festival Opera (Grosses Festspielhaus). *Vienna*: Staatsoper, Volksoper.

Belgium *Brussels*: Opéra Nationale Théâtre de la Monnaie.

Bulgaria *Sofia*: National State Opera.

China *Beijing*: Peking Opera (stages 'Chinese opera', a ritualised combination of singing, acting and physical theatre).

Czech Republic *Prague*: National Theatre, State Opera.

France *Lyon*: Opéra. *Paris*: Opéra, Salle Garnier and L'Opéra Comique, Opéra de Bastille. *Strasbourg*: Opéra du Rhin. *Toulouse*: Opéra, Théâtre du Capitolet.

Germany *Bayreuth*: Festival Opera. *Berlin*: Deutsche Oper, Deutsche Staatsoper, Komische Oper. *Cologne*: Oper der Stadt. *Dresden*: Saxon State Opera, Semper Oper. *Düsseldorf*: Deutsche Oper am Rhein. *Frankfurt*: Oper Frankfurt. *Hamburg*: Hamburgische Staatsoper. *Leipzig*: Opera House. *Munich*: Bayerische Staatsoper. *Stuttgart*: Wurttemburgische Staatsoper.

Hungary *Budapest*: Hungarian State Theatre.

Italy *Bologna*: Teatro Communale. *Milan*: Teatro alla Scala. *Palermo*: Teatro Massimo. *Venice*: Teatro la Fenice.

Mexico *Mexico City*: Opera Nacional.

Netherlands *Amsterdam*: Netherlands Opera.

Russia *Moscow*: Bolshoi Theatre. *St Petersburg*: Maryinsky Theatre (formerly Kirov Opera), National Opera Company (Maly Theatre).

Slovakia *Bratislava*: Slovak National Theatre.

Spain *Barcelona*: Gran Teatre del Liceu. *Madrid*: Compania Lirica del Teatro de la Zarzuela.

Sweden *Stockholm*: Drottningholm Court Theatre, a unique 18th-century theatre in the palace grounds, presenting repertoire of the 18th and early 19th centuries.

Switzerland *Geneva*: Grand Theatre. *Zürich*: Opera House.

UK *Cardiff*: Welsh National Opera. *Glasgow*: Scottish Opera. *Lewes*: Glyndebourne Festival Opera. *London*: English National Opera (ENO; international opera in English), Royal Opera (Royal Opera House).

USA *Chicago*: Lyric Opera. *Dallas*: Opera. *Houston*: Grand Opera. *Los Angeles*: Music Center Opera. *New York*: City Opera (Lincoln Center), Metropolitan Opera (Lincoln Center). *San Francisco*: Opera. *St Louis*: Opera Theatre.

NOTABLE OPERA SINGERS

Adreana Basile (c. 1580–c. 1640), Italian contralto
Luigi Lablanche (1794–1858), Italian bass
Henriette Sontag (1806–54), German soprano
Osip Petrov (1806–78), Russian bass
Maria Malibran (1808–36), Spanish mezzo-soprano
Jenny Lind (1820–87), Swedish soprano, the 'Swedish nightingale'
Pauline Viardot Garcia (1821–1910), French mezzo-soprano
Teresa Stolz (1834–1902), Bohemian soprano
Christine Nilsson (1843–1921), Swedish soprano
Victor Maurel (1848–1923), French baritone
Dame Nellie Melba (Helen Porter Mitchell; 1861–1931), Australian soprano
Enrico Caruso (1873–1921), Italian tenor
Feodor Chaliapin (1873–1938), Russian bass
Amelita Galli-Curci (1882–1963), Italian soprano
Giovanni Martinelli (1885–1969), Italian tenor
Maggie Teyte (Maggie Tate; 1886–1976), English soprano
Beniamino Gigli (1890–1957), Italian tenor
Toti dal Monte (1893–1975), Italian soprano
Kirsten Flagstad (1895–1962), Norwegian soprano
Rosa Ponselle (1897–1981), American soprano
Marian Anderson (1902–93), American contralto
Sir Peter Pears (1910–86), English tenor
Jussi Bjorling (1911–60), Swedish tenor
Kathleen Ferrier (1912–53), English contralto
Licia Albanese (1913–), Italian-born American soprano
Mario del Monaco (1915–82), Italian tenor
Elisabeth Schwarzkopf (1915–), German soprano
Tito Gobbi (1915–84), Italian baritone
Boris Christoff (1918–), Bulgarian bass
Birgit Nilsson (1918–), Swedish soprano
Nicola Rossi-Lemeni (1920–), Italian bass
Franco Corelli (1921–), Italian tenor
Giuseppe di Stefano (1921–), Italian tenor
Renata Tebaldi (1922–), Italian soprano
Maria Callas (1923–77), Greek soprano
Victoria de los Angeles (1923–), Spanish soprano
Carlo Bergonzi (1924–), Italian tenor
Dietrich Fischer-Dieskau (1925–), German baritone
Nicolai Gedda (1925–), Swedish tenor
Dame Joan Sutherland (1926–), Australian soprano
Leontyne Price (1927–), American soprano
Dame Janet Baker (1933–), English mezzo-soprano
Montserrat Caballé (1933–), Spanish soprano
Teresa Berganza (1935–), Spanish mezzo-soprano
Luciano Pavarotti (1935–), Italian tenor
Placido Domingo (1941–), Spanish tenor
Dame Kiri te Kanawa (1944–), New Zealand soprano
Frederica von Stade (1945–), American mezzo-soprano
José Carreras (1946–), Spanish tenor

JAZZ

The roots of jazz lie in the music that began to develop in the Black communities of the Southern States of the USA towards the end of the 19th century. Particularly in New Orleans, the fusion of Black and European cultures enabled jazz to formulate and gain its own identity, at first in saloon bars and brothels but also in the street parades that were part of New Orleans life. Street bands playing slow marches for funeral processions, and fast ones for celebrating the memory of the deceased as the mourners returned home, were thus one of the original elements of jazz.

Ragtime – an early form of jazz – was characterized by witty syncopation of simple tunes. Ragtime was particularly associated with solo piano performance. In the early days the form and harmony of jazz were simple; the complexity came from the way the performers improvised collectively upon the simple melodies, and from their command of syncopation. Jazz music inevitably soon swept northwards to Chicago and other cities, before spreading abroad.

The improvisation on the harmonic sequence of tunes rather than the melodies themselves was a development of immense importance. By the 1940s some jazz performances never stated the original melody, which was merely implied by its underlying harmonies.

Though jazz in the early days was predominantly the music of Black Americans, White musicians proved that it was not exclusively a Black preserve. As the popularity of jazz began to spread, so the bands, which had tended to comprise five, six or seven players, began to grow larger. During what became known as the 'swing' era, which dominated jazz just before World War II, bands consisting of brass and reed sections blowing against each other over a solid beat, grew fashionable.

The major jazz watershed occurred, significantly, in 1945, at the end of World War II, when 'traditional' jazz, with its simple harmonies, gave way to the complexity, tension, abrasiveness and virtuosity of 'modern' jazz. Whether identified as 'cool' jazz, or as 'bop', 'bebop' or 'rebop', modern jazz gains much of its intensity of expression from the contrast between a steady beat and a convoluted, often apparently agonized, solo line.

JAZZ SINGERS AND PERFORMERS

William Christopher Handy (1873–1958), American blues musician and songwriter: the song *St Louis Blues*.

Buddy Bolden (Charles Bolden; 1878–1931), American jazz cornetist.

'Jelly Roll' Morton (Ferdinand la Menthe Morton; 1885–1941), American jazz pianist, singer and songwriter.

Joe 'King' Oliver (1885–1938), American jazz cornetist.

Sidney Bechet (1897–1959), American jazz clarinetist and soprano saxophonist.

Bessie Smith (1898–1937), American blues singer.

Duke Ellington (Edward Kennedy Ellington; 1899–1974), American jazz composer, bandleader and pianist: the song *Mood Indigo* was one of over 900 compositions. His band – which remained together for some 30 years – was one of the most influential in the development of jazz.

Louis 'Satchmo' Armstrong (1900–71), American jazz trumpeter, bandleader and singer, who was known for his remarkable ability to improvise.

Bix Beiderbecke (Leon Beiderbecke; 1903–31), American jazz cornetist, pianist and composer: the piano piece *In a Mist*.

Glenn Miller (1904–44), American jazz trombonist, composer and bandleader: the songs *Moonlight Serenade* and *In the Mood*.

Count Basie (William Basie; 1904–84), American jazz pianist and bandleader who was famous for his 'big band' style.

Jimmy Dorsey (James Dorsey; 1904–57), American jazz alto saxophonist, clarinetist and bandleader.

Earl Hines (1905–83), American jazz pianist, composer and bandleader.

Tommy Dorsey (Thomas Dorsey; 1905–56), American jazz trombonist and bandleader.

Stéphane Grappelli (1908–), French jazz violinist and pianist.

Benny Goodman (Benjamin David Goodman; 1909–86), American jazz clarinetist and bandleader, known as the 'King of Swing'. His style began a new era in jazz.

Art Tatum (Arthur Tatum; 1910–56), American jazz pianist.

Django Reinhardt (1910–53), Belgian jazz guitarist.

Artie Shaw (Arthus Arshewsky; 1910–), American jazz clarinetist and bandleader.

Gil Evans (1912–88), American jazz pianist and composer.

Woody Herman (Woodrow Herman; 1913–87), American clarinetist and bandleader.

Nat King Cole (Nathanial Coles; 1919–65), American jazz pianist and singer.

Billie Holiday (1915–59), American blues singer.

Theolonius Monk (1917–82), American jazz pianist.

Dizzy Gillespie (John Birks Gillespie; 1917–93), American jazz trumpeter.

Ella Fitzgerald (1918–), American jazz singer.

Dave Brubeck (1920–), American jazz pianist.

Charles Brown (1920–), American jazz guitarist.

Charlie 'Bird' Parker (Christopher Parker; 1920–55), American jazz saxophonist who became a leader of the 'bebop' movement.

Erroll Garner (1923–), American jazz pianist.

Sarah Vaughan (1924–90), American jazz singer.

Oscar Peterson (1925–), American jazz pianist.

Max Roach (1925–), American jazz drummer.

John Coltrane (1926–67), American jazz saxophonist.

Miles Davis (1926–91), American jazz composer and trumpeter.

Fats Domino (Antoine Domino; 1928–), American jazz and blues pianist, singer and composer: the song *Blueberry Hill*.

Carl Perkins (1928–58), American jazz pianist.

Ray Charles (1932–), American jazz singer, pianist and composer.

Ornette Coleman (1930–), American jazz alto saxophonist.

Wayne Shorter (1933–), American tenor saxophonist.

POPULAR MUSIC

Jazz has exerted a powerful influence on more obviously popular music. 'Rhythm and blues', an offshoot of the blues, featured an ensemble rather than a solo voice, and produced its own Negro-spiritual-inspired offshoot known as 'soul music'. 'Reggae', an Afro-Jamaican hybrid, originated in the 1960s and employs topical lyrics. 'Country and western' is America's modern equivalent of the European country dances of previous centuries. But above all jazz has inspired rock, a hybrid of American popular forms, both Black and White: blues, rhythm and blues, gospel, and country-and-western music. Since the advent of 'rock 'n' roll' in the 1950s, rock music – usually performed by groups using electronically amplified instruments – has established itself as the major force of present-day popular music.

In the 1950s Black artists such as the guitarist Chuck Berry (1926–) vied for popularity with Whites such as Buddy Holly (1936–59) and most notably Elvis Presley (1935–77), whose blend of physicality and tremulous baritone delivery in such numbers as 'Heartbreak Hotel' inspired an almost religious devotion in his millions of fans.

The most significant developments in rock music in the 1960s took place in Britain, where the Beatles introduced more sophisticated lyricism to the genre, and the Rolling Stones brought an overt sexuality to their vigorous and pungent dance numbers. The 'Mersey Sound', associated with the Beatles in the 1960s, was not only a skilful brew of British and American trends of the period, but also combined genuine melodic flair with words (the best of them by John Lennon, 1940–80) of real literary merit. Nor did the talents of the Beatles suffer from the short-windedness of some pop music. Their LP album, *Sergeant Pepper's Lonely Hearts Club Band* (1967), was the pop equivalent of an integrated classical song cycle, a milestone in the progress of popular music. A similar literary distinction has stamped the songs of the American Bob Dylan (1941–), who achieved a synthesis of elements of rock and roll and folk in his songs of protest.

Other 1960s rock trends were the drug-influenced *acid rock* of such performers as the American guitarist Jimi Hendrix (1942–70), and the highly amplified, rhythmic style of rock and roll, known as *hard rock*, practised by such bands as The Who. A significant development in the late 1960s was the use of rock music in stage works or 'rock operas', such as *Hair, Jesus Christ Superstar* and The Who's *Tommy*.

In the early 1970s the *progressive rock* of British bands such as Pink Floyd and Genesis involved longer tracks, more advanced harmonies, and more complicated instrumental solo passages. It was partly in response to what some perceived as the artistic pretensions and pompous self-indulgence of such music that *punk rock* exploded onto the scene in Britain in the mid-1970s. In common with certain songs of the Rolling Stones, notably 'Street Fighting Man', punk rock gave vivid and sometimes anarchic expression to working-class discontent, most notably in the abrasive and nihilistic anthems of its most notorious practitioners, the Sex Pistols.

The 1980s and early 1990s saw an increasing divergence of styles and a growing use of electronic equipment. Production teams have played an increasingly influential role in the creation of rock music.

TOP BRITISH SINGLES 1955–92

The top single for each year is determined by the number of weeks the single stayed at number 1, 2 and 3 in the charts.

1955	*Rock Around the Clock*	Bill Haley and his Comets
1956	*Just Walkin' in the Rain*	Johnnie Ray
1957	*Diana*	Paul Anka
1958	*Magic Moments*	Perry Como
1959	*Living Doll*	Cliff Richards and the Shadows
1960	*It's Now or Never*	Elvis Presley
1961	*Wooden Heart*	Elvis Presley
1962	*Wonderful Land*	Shadows
1963	*From Me to You*	Beatles
1964	*You're My World*	Cilla Black
1965	*Tears*	Ken Dodd
1966	*Distant Drums*	Jim Reeves
1967	*Release Me*	Engelbert Humperdinck
1968	*Those Were the Days*	Mary Hopkin
1969	*Sugar Sugar*	Archies
1970	*In the Summertime*	Mungo Jerry
1971	*Hot Love*	TRex
1972	*Without Love*	Nilsson
1973	*Blockbuster*	Sweet
1974	*She*	Charles Aznavour
1975	*Bye Bye Baby*	Bay City Rollers
1976	*Save Your Kisses for Me*	Brotherhood of Man
1977	*Knowing Me Knowing You*	Abba
1978	*You're the One that I Want*	John Travolta and Olivia Newton-John
1979	*Bright Eyes*	Art Garfunkel
1980	*Don't Stand So Close to Me*	Police
1981	*Stand and Deliver*	Adam and the Ants
1982	*Come On Eileen*	Dexys Midnight Runners
1983	*Karma Chameleon*	Culture Club
1984	*Two Tribes*	Frankie Goes to Hollywood
1985	*The Power of Love*	Jennifer Rush
1986	*Don't Leave me this Way*	Communards with Sarah Jane Morris
1987	*Never Gonna give you up*	Rick Astley
1988	*I Should Be So Lucky*	Kylie Minogue
1989	*Ride on Time*	Black Box
1990	*Sacrifice/Healing*	Elton John
1991	*Everything I do (I do it for You)*	Bryan Adams
1992	*Stay*	Shakespears Sister

TOP AMERICAN SINGLES 1955–91

1955	*Rock Around the Clock*	Bill Haley and his Comets
1956	*Don't be Cruel*	Elvis Presley
1957	*All Shook up*	Elvis Presley
1958	*At the Hop*	Danny and the Juniors
1959	*Mack the Knife*	Bobby Darin
1960	*The Theme from 'A Summer Place'*	Percy Faith
1961	*Tossin' and Turnin'*	Bobby Lewis
1962	*I Can't Stop Loving You*	Ray Charles
1963	*Sugar Shack*	Jimmy Gilmer and the Fireballs
1964	*I Want to hold your Hand*	Beatles
1965	*(I Can't get no) Satisfaction*	Rolling Stones
1966	*I'm a Believer*	The Monkees
1967	*To Sir with Love*	Lulu
1968	*Hey Jude*	Beatles
1969	*Aquarius/Let the Sunshine in*	5th Dimension
1970	*Bridge over Troubled Waters*	Simon and Garfunkel
1971	*Joy to the World*	Three Dog Night
1972	*The First Time Ever I saw your Face*	Roberta Flack
1973	*Killing me Softly with his Song*	Roberta Flack
1974	*The Way We Were*	Barbra Streisand
1975	*Love will Keep us Together*	Captain and Tennille
1976	*Tonight's the Night (Gonna Be Alright)*	Rod Stewart
1977	*You Light up my Life*	Debby Boone
1978	*Night Fever*	Bee Gees
1979	*My Sharona*	The Knack
1980	*Lady*	Kenny Rogers
1981	*Physical*	Olivia Newton-John
1982	*I Love Rock 'n' Roll*	Joan Jett and the Blackhearts
1983	*Every Breath you Take*	Police
1984	*Like a Virgin*	Madonna
1985	*Say You, Say Me*	Lionel Richie
1986	*That's What Friends Are For*	Dionne and Friends
1987	*Faith*	George Michael
1988	*Roll With It*	Steve Winwood
1989	*Another Day in Paradise*	Phil Collins
1990	*Vision of Love*	Mariah Carey
1991	*(Everything I do) I do it for you*	Bryan Adams

GRAMMY AWARDS

The principal awards for popular music are the Grammy Awards presented by the (American) National Academy of Recording Arts and Sciences. Recent winners of Record of the Year have been:

1983	*Beat It* Michael Jackson
1984	*What's Love Got to Do With It* Tina Turner
1985	*We Are the World* USA for Africa
1986	*Higher Love* Steve Winwood
1987	*Graceland* Paul Simon
1988	*Don't Worry, Be Happy* Bobby McFerrin
1989	*Wind Beneath My Wings* Bette Midler
1990	*Another Day in Paradise* Phil Collins
1991	*Unforgettable* Natalie Cole, with Nat'King'Cole
1992	*Tears in Heaven* Eric Clapton

DANCE

Forms of dance vary from those that employ the whole body in free and open movement to those in which movement is restricted to certain parts – just to the eyes in the case of one Samoan courtship dance. Dance is usually rhythmic, often with an element of repetition, and forms a pattern in both time and space. Dance can be a simple expression of pleasure in movement of the body or an art form of complex patterns and significant gestures.

Folk dances, the traditional dances of particular areas, are dances that have evolved rather than have been invented. They often retain features that once had magical and ritual significance. Emphasis is usually on the group, although pairs or individuals may be featured or encouraged to give bravura displays. More modern social dances developed from courtship dances and, although some may involve unison dancing by the group, the emphasis is usually placed on couples.

HISTORY OF DANCE

PREHISTORY AND ANCIENT TIMES
In prehistory, unorganized or loosely organized dances took place for warlike or communal purposes – courtship, harvest, rain or religion. The origins of theatrical dance in Greece date from c. 500 BC. Folk dances in Europe gradually became divorced from magic and ritual, but their origins are often still clear to see (e.g. the *horn dance* performed annually at Abbot's Bromley in England, the *hora* of eastern Europe, and the *sardanas* of Catalonia).

THE MIDDLE AGES
In the 12th century, court dancing began to develop, particularly in Provence. Processional or winding chain dances began to give way to couples dancing together. By the 14th century two main forms of dance had emerged. The basic medieval dance – the *basse danse* – used small gliding steps, the feet scarcely losing contact with the floor. The *haute danse* was a high leaping dance, mainly for men. Popular dances in the Middle Ages included:

pavane a stately processional dance, derived from instrumental music in Padua, and possibly the first stylized dance.

galliard a sprightly jigging dance from Italy. Its name implies 'gaiety'.

THE 15th CENTURY
In 1416, Domenico de Piacenza published the first European dance manual *De Arte Saltandi et Choreas Ducendi* (On the Art of Dancing and Directing Choruses). The first true ballet, with settings by Leonardo da Vinci, was danced at Tortona, in Piedmont, Italy, in 1489. Ballet was introduced to the court of Henry VIII of England as masque. Popular dances in the 15th century included:

branle an English clog dance with circular figures.

allemande (French 'from Germany') a stately processional dance.

courante (Italian 'current', that is 'running'), a stately Italian dance which included the elegant bending of the knees.

volta (Italian 'vault') a twirling dance in which the woman is lifted from the floor and bounced upon the man's knees.

THE 16th CENTURY
The first printed account of a ballet – dated 15 October 1581 – described the dance held to celebrate the marriage of the duc de Joyeuse and Marguerite de Lorraine. During the 16th century, brighter social dances appeared with faster livelier steps. Popular dances in the 16th century included:

morisca (Spanish 'Moorish') a Spanish dance derived from dances of Moorish Spain and first recorded in 1446 in Burgos.

sarabande a slow and graceful dance, involving advances and retreats and couples passing between rows of dancers. It was introduced to Spain probably from Morocco c. 1588.

THE 17th CENTURY
In 1661 the French king, Louis XIV, established a group of dancing instructors, the *Académie Royale de Danse*, to codify court dances. Its director, Charles Louis Beauchamp (1636–1705), is credited with inventing the 'five positions'. After the founding of the *Académie Royale de Musique et de Danse* under the composer Lully in 1672 there was a permanent demand for professional dancers. Ballet masques, often with hideous and elaborate masks, became popular.

In Britain lively longways (facing rows) and circle dances became very popular. They involved simple walks, runs, and skipping and hopping steps, often with couples changing positions within a set. In 1651 John Playford's *English Dancing Master*, a collection of tunes and steps, was published.

The first waltz was developed from the minuet and the Ländler in 1660, but the dance did not gain popularity until considerably later. Popular dances in the 17th century included:

mazurka a Polish round dance for eight couples with the second beat accentuated.

gigue a lively dance based on the traditional English jig.

bourée a lively dance starting on the upbeat.

chaconne a graceful dance introduced into Spain from Peru c. 1580 and then spread through western Europe.

gavotte (Provençal dialect *gavoto*, 'a native of the Alps') a lively dance in which each couple had the chance to dance on their own. It reached its greatest popularity at the court of the French king Louis XIV.

minuet (from the French *pas menu*, 'small steps') a favourite at the French court, this delicate dance was often followed by the boisterous gavotte as a contrast. It was recorded by Lully in 1663.

passacaglia a popular Italian dance, resembling the chaconne, but in a minor key.

rigaudon a lively French dance, known in England as the rigadoon.

Ländler (German 'small country') a traditional Austrian dance in which the partners turned in each other's arms with a hop and a step.

matelot a Dutch sailor's clog dance.

contredanse a dance for opposing groups. A mistranslation of 'country dance', contredanse developed in France and was reintroduced into England.

cotillion (French 'petticoat') a dance for two groups of four pairs each. The quadrille developed from the cotillion in the 19th century.

THE 18th CENTURY

The movement towards dance as a form of artistic expression is often said to have begun with the publication of Jean-Georges Noverre's *Lettres sur la danse er sur les ballets* (1760). In ballet, Gaetano Vestris perfected the *grand jeté* at the Paris Opera. Pirouettes and leaps pushed forward the physical frontiers of ballet, and Vestris's abandonment of the customary masks in *Medée et Jason* (1770) opened ballet to the possibility of showing emotion through movement.

In social dance the waltz developed in Austria – the first recorded use of the word 'waltz' was in 1754. The gavotte and the minuet continued to be popular.

THE 19th CENTURY

By the 19th century court dances had been superseded by professional dancers. *La Sylphide* (1832) – choreographed by Filippo Taglione – is said to have ushered in the era of true European ballet, abandoning the more rigid portrayal of Greek myths. Sometime after 1800 ballerinas began to dance 'on point' (on the tips of the toes), stiffening the ends of their dancing slippers to give more support. Pointwork became a key feature of choreography for women.

In social dance improvisation was allowed by the two most popular dances of the age, the waltz and the polka. In these dances contact was made in the embrace that dancers used for much of the 20th century. Dance styles were also developed for the popular theatre, including the cancan, a high-kicking exhibitionist female dance that originated on the Paris stage c. 1835. Popular dances in the 19th century included:

waltz an Austrian dance that developed from the Ländler – see above.

quadrille a French derivation of the 17th-century contredanse. It comprises a series of five 'figure' dances for four couples.

polka a bouncing dance which was introduced to Paris in 1843. It developed from a Bohemian courtship dance.

cakewalk a graceful walking dance which takes its name from the cakes offered as prizes for competitive performances held in the southern states of the USA from c. 1872. It was introduced into ballrooms from c. 1900.

Paul Jones a group dance in which partners are exchanged.

the lancers a quadrille for eight or 16 couples.

THE 20th CENTURY

In ballet, the *Ballets Russes* was established in Paris by Diaghilev in 1909. His dazzling dancers and stunning stagings attracted wild enthusiasm, and brought Russian ballet to the West. Offshoots from the *Ballets Russes* established companies in the Russian classical tradition in the USA, UK, Australia and other countries. New free dance forms emerged as dancers such as Isadora Duncan and Ruth St Denis incorporated elements from other cultures – particularly Greek and Far Eastern – into abstract dance. Rudolf Laban and his disciples greatly extended the range of dance movement, while

Emile Jacques-Dalcroze developed a system of musical rhythm in movement. Later in the century younger choreographers such as Twyla Tharp and Alvin Ailey incorporated rock, African, West Indian and jazz music into their work.

In social dance, most of the new dances of the 20th century originated in the Americas, and had their origins in the offbeat syncopated rhythms originally brought by black slaves from Africa. Other influences included the jigs and clog dances of Irish immigrants and the mixing of African, Spanish and Portuguese styles in Latin American dance. Other dances have been invented for particular shows or films, or to promote sheet music or record sales. The ballroom dance craze, which began in the 1920s, involved mostly couples dancing to the music of small instrumental groups. From 1939, dancing became increasingly energetic as jazz and pseudo-jazz groups provided the musical accompaniment. The modern discothèque style – that is the use of recorded music for dancing – originated in Paris c. 1951.

Popular 20th-century dances include:

samba a lively Latin American dance in double time. It originated in Brazil c. 1885 and was introduced to ballrooms c. 1920 as the maxixe. The name 'samba' was resumed c. 1940.

quickstep a dance in rapid quadruple time. It was invented in the USA in 1900 and reached a peak of popularity in the 1920s.

tango a lively syncopated Latin American dance characterized by gliding steps and dramatic pauses. It was introduced to the USA from Argentina, but its origins may have been the Cuban *habañera*.

barn dance a traditional American form of dancing associated with festivities held on the completion of a new barn.

one-step an early 20th-century dance characterized by long quick steps. It was a precursor of the foxtrot.

Boston a slow dance derived from the waltz.

turkey trot a ragtime variation of the one-step. It gained considerable popularity during World War I.

foxtrot a dance in quadruple time, alternating long and short steps. There are both slow and quick variations. It was introduced in 1912 in the USA and was, allegedly, named after Harry Fox. The slow foxtrot evolved c. 1927 into the 'blues dance'.

Charleston one of the most popular dances of the 1920s, named after a Mack and Johnson song of 1923 about the town Charleston, South Carolina. The dance is characterized by a side kick from the knee.

pasodoble a Spanish-style two-step.

rumba a Cuban dance popularized in 1923.

black bottom a type of jerky athletic foxtrot first mentioned in the *New York Times* in December 1926.

conga a single-file dance developed in 1935 from the rumba and African dances.

jitterbug a fast American dance to jazz accompaniment. It gained great popularity during World War II.

jive a jerky improvised variation of the jitterbug.

mambo an off-beat rumba of Cuban origin. It was introduced into the USA in 1948.

rock'n'roll an energetic free dance, in part evolved from the jive and in part improvised. Characterized by a heavy beat and simple melody, it was introduced by Bill Haley and his Comets in 1953.

cha cha cha a variation of the mambo in which couples dance with lightly linked hands. It was introduced in 1954.

twist a lively dance – characterized by body torsion and knee-flexing – in which partners rarely touch. It was introduced in 1961.

bossa nova a variation of the samba, originating in Brazil.

go-go a repetitious dance of verve, usually exhibitionist. It dates from 1965.

reggae a dance introduced from Jamaica in 1969. It is characterized by the strong accentuation of the upbeat.

pogo a dance invented by punk rockers in 1976. Dancers jump vertically from the ground in imitation of a pogo stick.

disco dancing a flamboyant freestyle modern dance accompanied by exaggerated hand movement. It was popularized by the film *Saturday Night Fever* (1977).

break dancing a modern style of dance in which dancers perform acrobatic feats. It was introduced c. 1980.

robotics a style of dance in which dancers imitate clockwork dolls with rigid limb movements.

BALLET

Ballet is a theatrical form of dance based upon a set of positions, steps and expressive gestures that demand considerable skill and training. Ballet may tell a story or offer abstract patterns of movement. Though generally aiming at an appearance of effortless grace, it can also be highly dramatic. Balletic entertainments were first developed in the French court in the 16th century, but ballet companies in many countries have created their own distinctive national styles.

There are several ways in which ballet differs from other forms of dance. Most obvious is the 90° 'turned-out' position of the feet, which permits a remarkable degree of balance in all positions. Ballet also requires a tension and arching of the foot and Achilles tendon to provide a powerful jump and to cushion landing. Dancers begin training at an early age to achieve the positions required, and must continue to exercise every day.

The history of ballet is summarized in the History of Dance (above).

BALLET TERMS

à terre steps which do not entail high jumps. They include the *glissade*, *pas ballone* and *pas brise*.

battement ballet exercises.

batterie or battu a jump during which a dancer beats the calves sharply together.

corps de ballet a group of dancers supporting the principal dancers.

divertissement a self-contained dance within a ballet, designed purely as an entertainment or to show off a dancer's technique.

elevation any high jump in ballet. Elevations include the *entrechat*, *rivoltade*, *pas de chat*, and *cabriole*.

enchaînement a sequence of steps linked to make a harmonious whole.

entrechat a vertical jump during which the dancer changes the position of the legs after beating the calves together.

fouetté a spectacular pirouette in which the dancer throws his raised leg to the front and side in order to achieve momentum for another turn.

jeté a jump from one leg to the other, basic to many ballet steps. These include the *grand jeté en avant*, in which the dancer leaps forward as if clearing an obstacle, and the *jeté fouetté* where the dancer performs a complete turn in mid-air.

pas a basic ballet step in which weight is transferred from one leg to another. The term is also used in combination to indicate the number of performers in a dance; a *pas seul* is a solo and a *pas de deux* a dance for two dancers.

pirouette a complete turn on one leg, performed either on the ball of the foot or on the toes.

plié bending the legs from a standing position. *Demi-plié* involves bending the knees as far as possible while keeping the heels on the floor.

relevé bending the body from the waist to one side or the other during a turn or a pirouette.

rivoltade or revoltade a step in which a dancer raises one leg in front, jumps from the other and turns in the air, landing in the original position but facing the other way.

saut a plain jump in the air without embellishment.

soutenu a movement executed at a slower tempo than usual.

sur les pointes on the toes.

variation a solo by a male dancer in a *pas de deux*.

MAJOR CHOREOGRAPHERS

Pierre Beauchamps (1636–?1705), French choreographer and theorist who is credited with inventing the 'five positions'.

John Weaver (1673–1760), English choreographer of 'pantomime-ballets'.

Marie Sallé (1707–56), French choreographer who placed emphasis on plot and interpretation.

Jean-Georges Noverre (1727–1810), French choreographer: the inventor of the 'ballet d'action'.

Charles-Louis Didelot (1767–1837), Swedish choreographer and ballet master at St Petersburg.

Salvatore Vigagno (1769–1821), Neapolitan classical choreographer.

Filippo Taglioni (1777–1871), Italian Romantic choreographer.

Auguste Bournonville (1805–79), Danish Romantic choreographer who developed a free, more lyrical technique.

Jules Perot (1810–92), French Romantic choreographer.

François Delsarte (1811–71), French ballet theorist and choreographer who influenced Dalcroze and Shawn.

Christian Johansson (1817–1903), Danish teacher who was influential in the flowering of Russian ballet in the second half of the 19th century.

Marius Petipa (1818–1910), French choreographer and ballet master at St Petersburg: the founder of the Russian classical style.

Arthur Sainte-Leon (1821–70), French Romantic choreographer: *Coppelia*.

Lev Ivanov (1834–1901), Russian classical choreographer who worked with Petipa: *Nutcracker*.

Emile Jacques-Dalcroze (Jacob Dalkes; 1865–1950), Austrian ballet theorist who trained Rambert and Wigman.

Rudolph von Laban (1879–1958), Polish ballet theorist and notator.

Michel Fokine (1880–1942), Russian classical choreographer.

Adolph Bolm (1884–1951), Russian classical choreographer.

Fyodor Lopokov (1886–1973), Russian classical choreographer.

Mary Wigman (1886–1973), German modern choreographer.

Oskar Schlemmer (1888–1943), German choreographer who pioneered the Bauhaus style.

Bronislav Nijinska (1891–1972), Russian choreographer for Diaghilev's *Ballets Russes*.

Hanya Holm (1893–), German ballet teacher of modern dance.

*Martha Graham (1894–91), American founder of a distinctive style of modern dance.

Doris Humphrey (1895–1958), American modern choreographer.

Leonide Massine (1895–1979), Russian classical choreographer.

*Kurt Joos (1901–79), German classical and modern choreographer.

Frederick Ashton (1904–88), English classical choreographer.

George Balanchine (1904–83), Russian classical choreographer: founder-choreographer of the New York City Ballet.

Leonid Lavrovsky (1905–67), Russian classical choreographer.

Serge Lifar (1905–67), Russian classical choreographer.

Birgit Cullberg (1908–), Swedish classical amd modern choreographer.

*José Limon (1908–72), Mexican modern choreographer.

Anthony Tudor (1908–87), English modern choreographer.

Agnes de Mille (1909–), American classical and modern choreographer.

*Alwin Nikolais (1912–), American modern choreographer.

Anna Sokolow (1915–), American pioneer of modern dance.

Jerome Robbins (1918–), American classical and contemporary choreography.

*Merce Cunningham (1919–), American post-modern pioneer.

Roland Petit (1924–), French dramatic classical choreographer.

Robert Cohan (1925–), American contemporary choreographer.

Glen Tetley (1926–), American modern choreographer.

Yuri Grigorovich (1927–), Soviet classical choreographer whose work is characterized by its spectacular quality.

*Maurice Bejart (1927–), French choreographer of dance theatre.

John Cranko (1927–73), South African classical choreographer.

Erik Bruhn (1928–), Danish classical choreographer.

Kenneth MacMillan (1929–), Scottish classical and modern choreographer.

*Paul Taylor (1930–), American contemporary choreographer.

*Alvin Ailey (1931–), American modern and contemporary choreographer.

*Twyla Tharp (1941–), American choreographer in a variety of genres.

John Neumeier (1942–), American classical choreographer.

Jiri Kylian (1947–), Czech classical choreographer.

*Mark Morris (1956–), American classical and post-modern choreographer.

David Bintley (1957–), English classical choreographer.

[*Choreographers with their own companies, often bearing their names.]

MAJOR DANCERS

Marie Sallé (1707–56), see Major Choreographers.

Marie Camargo (Marie-Anne de Cupis; 1710–70), Belgian dancer – *La Camargo* – acclaimed for her jumps, especially the entrechat.

Auguste Vestris (1760–1842), French dancer who developed the execution of ballet technique.

Marie Taglioni (1804–84), Italian dancer whose dancing typified the early Romantic ballet.

Fanny Cerrito (1817–1909), Neapolitan dancer.

Fanny Esler (1818–84), Austrian dancer.

Carlotta Grisi (1819–99), Italian dancer.

Virginia Zucchi (1849–1930), Italian dancer who performed mainly in Russia.

Isadora Duncan (1877–1927), American pioneer of modern dance.

Adeline Genee (Anita Jensen; 1878–1970), Danish dancer who was influential in maintaining standards of British dancing.

Anna Pavlova (1881–1931), Russian classical dancer who was a member of Diaghilev's *Ballets Russes*: She created the chief role of *Les Sylphides*.

Tamara Karsavina (1885–1978), Russian classical dancer.

Vaslav Nijinsky (?1888–1950), Russian classical dancer who was a member of Diaghilev's *Ballets Russes*. The ballets *Petrushka* and *Scheherazade* were created for him.

Olga Spessivtseva (1895–1991), Russian classical dancer.

Alexandra Danilova (1903–), Russian classical dancer and teacher.

Anton Dolin (Sydney Healey-Kay; 1904–83), English classical dancer who danced with the *Ballets Russes*.

Robert Helpmann (1909–1986), Australian classical and modern dancer and actor.

Alicia Markova (Lilian Alicia Marks; 1910–), English classical dancer.

Galina Ulanova (1910–), Russian classical dancer.

Margot Fonteyn (Margaret Hookham; 1918–91), English classical dancer who is widely recognized as the greatest British dancer.

Rosella Hightower (1920–), American classical dancer.

Maya Plisetskaya (1925–), Russian classical dancer who gained acclaim for her ability to integrate acting and dancing.

Maria Tallchief (1925–), American classical dancer.

Margorie Tallchief (1927–), American classical dancer – sister of Maria.

Rudolph Nureyev (1938–93), Russian classical dancer acclaimed for the power and athleticism of his dancing.

Lynn Seymour (1939–), Canadian classical dancer.

Antoinette Sibley (1939–), English classical dancer.

Natalia Makarova (1940–), Russian classical dancer.

Suzanne Farrell (1945–), American classical dancer.

Peter Martins (1946–), Danish classical dancer.

Mikhail Baryshnikov (1948–), Latvian-born classical dancer based in North America.

Wayne Sleep (1948–), English classical, modern and show dancer.

Peter Schaufuss (1949–), Danish classical dancer.

Gelsey Kirkland (1952–), American classical dancer.

Patrick Dupond (1959–), French classical and modern dancer (and pop singer).

Michael Clark (1962–), English innovative contemporary dancer.

Sylvie Guillem (1966–), French classical dancer.

MAJOR DANCE COMPANIES

Australia
Australian Ballet, Victoria, formed in 1962 by Peggy van Praagh. Robert Helpmann became co-director in 1965.

Canada
National Ballet of Canada, Toronto, formed in 1951 by Celia France.

Cuba
Ballet Nacional de Cuba, Havana, formed in 1948 as the Ballet Alicia Alonso.

Denmark
Royal Danish Ballet, Copenhagen. One of the oldest companies in the world, it is also in the first flight of international companies.

France
Ballets de l'Opéra, Paris, Palais Garnier and Opéra Bastille, formed in 1669 by Louis XIV.

Germany
Stuttgart Ballet, Wurttemberg State Theatre Ballet, formed in 1759. It rose to prominence when the influential choreographer John Cranko became director in 1961.

Tanztheater Wuppertal, led by the noted choreographer Pina Bausch.

Netherlands
Netherlands Dance Theatre, The Hague, formed in 1959. It is noted for both classical and modern work.

Russia
Bolshoi Ballet, Moscow, formed in 1776 by Michael Maddox and Prince Urusov.

Maryinsky Ballet, formerly Kirov, St Petersburg. It was formed in 1738 as the St Petersburg School of Ballet by Jean Baptiste Landé and Empress Anna Ivanova. It was known as the Kirov Ballet from 1918 to 1991. The impresario Diaghilev used dancers from this company to start his Ballets Russes.

Switzerland
Rudra Béjart Lausanne, a new small company founded by Europe's foremost dance theatre choreographer.

UK
Birmingham Royal Ballet, formed in London in 1946 as the Sadlers Wells Opera Ballet (it gained its present name upomn moving to Birmingham in 1990). Director: Peter Wright.

English National Ballet. A London-based touring company, founded in 1950 as the Festival Ballet. Artistic director: Ivan Nagy.

London Contemporary Dance Theatre. A touring company formed in 1967 as the Contemporary Dance Group with Robert Cohan. Director: Nancy Duncan.

Royal Ballet, based at the Royal Opera House, London. It was formed in 1931 as the Vic-Wells Ballet by Ninette de Valois. Director: Anthony Dowell.

Scottish Ballet. Based at the Theatre Royal, Glasgow, it was formed in 1969 by Peter Darrell from the Western Theatre Ballet. Artistic director: Galina Samsova.

USA
American Ballet Theatre, New York. Formed in 1940 as the Ballet Theatre, it is a leading classical company.

Dance Theatre of Harlem, New York. Formed in 1969 by Arthur Mitchell, it was originally a classical company for black dancers.

Joffrey Ballet, New York and Los Angeles. Formed in 1956 by Robert Joffrey, it is noted for its modern and experimental work.

Mark Morris Dance Group. A classical post-modern company formed by Mark Morris.

Martha Graham Dance Company, New York. Founded in 1929 by Martha Graham, one of the most important originators of modern dance.

Merce Cunningham Dance Company, New York. Formed in 1953 by contemporary dance pioneer Merce Cunningham.

New York City Ballet, formed in 1948 from the Ballet Society. It is dominated by the work and vision of its founding choreographer George Balanchine.

San Francisco Ballet. Formed in 1933 by Adolf Bolm as the San Francisco Opera Ballet.

CINEMA

THE SILENT CINEMA

Long before the invention of the kinematograph – or cinema as it is now called – the *camera obscura* and the magic lantern had been used to project images upon a screen. Although lantern slides sometimes had mechanical parts that made the image move, 'films' make use of the phenomenon known as 'persistence of vision' to give an optical simulation of movement, and their development only became possible with the invention of photographic films.

There are several claims to the invention of cinema. The American Thomas Edison (1847–1931) was the first to market a successful film machine, but it was in Europe that the potential of cinema was first recognized. Then came World War I and the American film industry, uninterrupted by the conflict that held back development in Europe, began its long dominance.

The early American cinemas, known as 'nickelodeons', attracted only the working classes, who paid 5 cents to see a 20-minute programme of short films. A little later, French films of successful plays running an hour or more, featuring stage actors, brought in patrons who would pay a dollar a ticket. For a time Italy took the lead in film-making with a series of spectacular productions of historical subjects including *The Last Days of Pompeii, Quo Vadis!* (1913) and the two-hour long *Cabiria* (1914), about the Punic Wars. In the years after World War I the European cinema could not compete with Hollywood commercially but led in terms of experiment.

Early feature films were often tinted with a colour appropriate to the scene, or even with several colours applied by stencil for parts of a major film. *Kinemacolor*, invented in Britain in 1906, used two colour filters in the camera and projector, and two reels of film exposed alternately. It was the first 'natural' colour. *Technicolor*, developed in the USA about 1915, at first used a prism to split colour to two film reels. It was replaced by a variety of different processes until, in 1941, a three-colour system on a single film was introduced. *Eastmancolor* – a negative three-colour movie – was introduced in 1951.

In silent films, dialogue or any information that could not be presented as part of the action had to be conveyed by text inserted between the pictures. Additional atmosphere was supplied by live music, usually a honkytonk piano. Separate sound recordings were used with film in Berlin as early as 1896, and a sound-on-movie process was patented by Lauste in 1906 (see below). In 1926 Warner Brothers presented a synchronized music track on disc to accompany their film *Don Juan*. This was followed by *The Jazz Singer* (1927), which included songs and a snatch of dialogue and is generally accepted as the first 'talkie'.

PIONEERS OF THE CINEMA

Etienne Marey (1830–1904), French physiologist who invented a photographic 'gun' (1882) that took a sequence of pictures on a revolving photographic plate.

Thomas Edison (1847–1931), American inventor – see above. His first film *Fred Ott's Sneeze*, showed a laboratory assistant sneezing and was less than a minute long. His later films featured vaudeville and circus acts, but made no attempt to tell a story.

George Eastman (1854–1932), American inventor of flexible film.

William Friese-Greene (1855–1921), British inventor who outlined designs for a camera and projector.

Eugene Lauste (1856–1935), French inventor who patented a sound-on-movie process in 1906, though it was not at first effective for speech.

W.K.L. Dickson (1860–1935), American inventor of a camera (the *Kinetograph*, patented 1891) and a viewer (the *Kinetoscope*). This system was launched commercially in 1894 as a slot machine for solo viewing.

Georges Méliès (1861–1938), French impresario who turned his theatre into a cinema and developed trick photography through the use of stop action and double exposure: the fantasy film *Voyage to the Moon* (1902).

August Lumière (1862–1954), with his brother Louis (see below), French inventor of a *cinematographe*, a camera and projector in one. It was first demonstrated in public in Paris on 28 December 1895. The portable camera developed by the Lumière brothers enabled them to film real life and not to be restricted by their equipment to filming in a studio.

Louis Lumière (1864–1948), French inventor – see August Lumière above.

Thomas Armat (1866–1948), American inventor of the *Vitascope* projector.

Edwin Porter (1869–1941), American film maker: the 12-minute *The Great Train Robbery* (1903), which was shot on outside locations.

Adolphe Zukor (1873–1976), Hungarian-born American film maker and founder of the Famous Players-Paramount studios for which Edwin Porter directed *The Count of Monte Cristo* and *The Prisoner of Zenda*.

Cecil Hepworth (1874–1956), English film maker: *Rescued by Rover* (1905), shot on outside location.

D.W. Griffith (1875–1948), American pioneer film maker who experimented with lighting, long-shots and close-ups, takes of different lengths, and different camera set-ups and angles within a scene. He built up a team of actors including Mary Pickford, Dorothy and Lilian Gish, and Lionel Barrymore. Griffith was probably the first American director to make a film lasting more than one reel (12 minutes) and, in 1910, one of the earliest to take his crew to California. Griffith's epic *The Birth of a Nation* (1915) was a landmark in early cinema.

Robert Weine (1881–1938), German film director: *Cabinet of Dr Cagliari* (1919), a film using expressionist settings.

Jack Warner (1882–1978), American film producer who founded – with his brothers Harry (1881–1958), Albert (1884–1967), and Samuel (1888–1927) – the Warner Brothers studios.

Mack Sennett (1884–1960), American director of slapstick comedy films: the cleverly edited and speeded-up antics of the Keystone Cops, and films featuring such actors as Roscoe 'Fatty' Arbuckle, Charlie Chaplin and Buster Keaton.

Georg Pabst (1887–1967), German film director: *Pandora's Box* (1928).

F.W. Murnau (1888–1931), German film maker: *Nosferatu* (1921), an early Dracula film.

Jean Cocteau (1889–1963), French writer, critic and film director who experimented with film as a serious art form: *Blood of a Poet* (1930).

Fritz Lang (1890–1976), Austrian film director: *Metropolis* (1931).

René Clair (1898–1981), French film director: early comedies including *An Italian Straw Hat* (1927), films experimenting with sound including *Sous les toits de Paris* (1930) and notable later films including *Les Belles de Nuit* (1952).

Sergei Eisenstein (1898–1948), Russian director who used symbols to reinforce ideas and edited shots to make a 'collision' of images: *Battleship Potemkin* (1925).

Abel Gance (1899–1981), French film director: the epic *Napoléon* (1927), which used a wide screen with three overlapping images.

Luis Buñuel (1900–83), Spanish film director who collaborated with Salvador Dali in the first surreal films: *Un Chien Andalou* (1928), and notable later films including *Belle de jour* (1966) and *The Discreet Charm of the Bourgeoisie* (1972).

HOLLYWOOD

Hollywood is not so much a place as a whole style of films and film-making. Within a year of the Nestor Studio opening in this suburb of Los Angeles, California, in 1911 there were 15 other studios close by, and Hollywood rapidly became the centre of the industry and the film community. For 40 years, the 'majors' – the handful of big production companies – dominated world cinema.

In the early years of cinema, films were made all over the USA, but three factors led to the development of Hollywood as a film centre. The first was the weather – sunshine almost throughout the year allowed virtually unrestricted outside shooting. The second was the great variety of scenic location. The third was the Motion Picture Patents Company (established 1909) which tried to restrict film-making in America to its nine member companies.

Hollywood became an efficient production machine. Top directors were capable of turning out as many as six productions a year.

MAJOR HOLLYWOOD DIRECTORS

Cecil B. De Mille (1881–1959), American film producer and director: *The Ten Commandments* (1923), *King of Kings* (1927) and *The Greatest Show on Earth* (1952).

Ernst Lubitsch (1892–1947), German-born American director of comedies: *Heaven Can Wait* (1943).

King Vidor (1894–1982), American film director and producer who directed films for 66 years: *The Big Parade* (1925), *Hallelujah!* (1929) and *The Citadel* (1938).

Josef von Sternberg (1894–1969), Austrian-born American film director: *Blue Angel* (1930).

Busby Berkeley (William Berkeley Enos; 1895–1976), American film director whose films were characterized by spectacular dancing sequences: *Gold Diggers of 1933* (1933).

John Ford (Sean O'Feeney; 1895–1973), American film director: *The Grapes of Wrath* (1940), *How Green Was My Valley* (1941), *The Quiet Man* (1952), and Western films including *Stagecoach* (1939).

Frank Capra (1897–91), American film director of gently satirical comedy films: *It Happened One Night* (1934), *Mr Deeds Goes To Town* (1936) and *You Can't Take It with You* (1938).

Alfred Hitchcock (1899–1980), English film director who worked in Hollywood from 1939: *Rebecca* (1940), *Psycho* (1960) and *The Birds* (1963).

George Cukor (1899–83), American film director: *Little Women* (1933), *A Star Is Born* (1954) and *My Fair Lady* (1964).

Walt Disney (1901–66), American film producer and director who created the cartoon characters Mickey Mouse and Donald Duck.

William Wyler (1902–81), American film director: *The Best Years of Our Lives* (1946).

Elia Kazan (Elia Kazanjoglou; 1909–), Greek-born American film director: *A Streetcar Named Desire* (1951) and *On the Waterfront* (1954).

Billy Wilder (Samuel Wilder; 1906–), Austrian-born American film director: *Double Indemnity* (1944) and *Sunset Boulevard* (1950).

Otto Preminger (1906–86), Austrian-born American film director: *Exodus* (1961).

John Huston (1906–87), American film director: *The Maltese Falcon* (1941), *The African Queen* (1951) and *The Night of the Iguana* (1964).

Fred Zinneman (1907–), Austrian-born American film director: *High Noon* (1952), *A Man For All Seasons* (1966) and *The Day of the Jackal* (1973).

Edward Dmytryk (1908–), American film director: *Crossfire* (1947).

Joseph Losey (1909–84), American film director who worked mainly in Britain: *The Servant* (1963) and *The Go-Between* (1971).

Jules Dassin (1911–), American film director: *Never on Sunday* (1959).

Orson Welles (1915–85), American film director: *Citizen Kane* (1940).

Bob Fosse (1925–88), American film director: *All That Jazz* (1979).

Sam Peckinpah (1926–84), American director of Western films: *The Wild Bunch* (1969).

Stanley Kubrick (1928–), American film director and writer: *Paths of Glory* (1957), *Lolita* (1962), *2001: A Space Odyssey* (1968) and *A Clockwork Orange* (1971).

Woody Allen (1935–), see also Notable Film Actors. As a director his films include: *Annie Hall* (1977) and *Hannah and her Sisters* (1986).

Francis Ford Coppola (1939–), American film director: *Patton* (1969), *The Godfather* (1972) and *Apocalypse Now* (1979).

Steven Spielberg (1947–), American film director and producer: *E.T.* (1982) and *The Color Purple* (1986).

WORLD CINEMA

Despite Hollywood's long dominance in world cinema, the country producing the highest number of films per annum has long been India, apart from a period in the 1950s when there was a boom in production in Japan. Hong Kong also produces large numbers of films and even France often exceeds the USA in the number made each year.

MAJOR DIRECTORS

Jean Cocteau (1889–1963), French writer, critic and film director: *Beauty and the Beast* (1946) – see also Pioneers of the Cinema.

Jean Renoir (1894–1979), French film director: *La Grande Illusion* (1937) and *La Règle du Jeu* (1939).

Alfred Hitchcock (1899–1980), British film director who worked in Hollywood from 1939 – see above.

Luis Buñuel (1900–83), Spanish film director – see Pioneers of the Cinema.

Vittorio De Sica (1902–74), Italian director: *Bicycle Thieves* (1948).

Leni Riefenstahl (1902–), German film director: the propagandist films *Triumph of the Will* (1934) and *Olympia* (1938).

Grigori Kozintsev (1905–73), Soviet film director: *Hamlet* (1964).

Luchino Visconti (1906–76), Italian film director: *Ossessione* (1942) and *Death in Venice* (1970).

Roberto Rossellini (1906–77), Italian film director: *Rome, Open City* (1945).

Carol Reed (1906–76), English film director: *The Third Man* (1949).

Robert Bresson (1907–), French film director: *Les Anges du péché* (1943) and *Un condamné à mort s'est echappé* (1956).

Laurence Olivier (1907–89), English actor and director: *Henry V* (1944).

Jacques Tati (1908–82), French actor and director of comedy films: *Monsieur Hulot's Holiday* (1951).

David Lean (1908–91), English film director: *Oliver Twist* (1948), *The Bridge on the River Kwai* (1957) and *Lawrence of Arabia* (1962).

Marcel Carné (1909–), French film director: *Le Jour se Lève* (1939) and *Les Enfants du Paradis* (1945).

Akira Kurosawa (1910–), Japanese film director: *Seven Samurai* (1954) and *Rann* (1986).

Masaki Kobayashi (1916–), Japanese film director: *The Human Condition* (1959–61).

Ingmar Bergman (1918–), Swedish film writer, producer and director: *The Seventh Seal* (1957), *Through a Glass Darkly* (1961) and *Cries and Whispers* (1972).

Federico Fellini (1920–), Italian film director: *La Dolce Vita* (1959) and *8½* (1963).

Sergei Bondarchuk (1920–), Russian film director: *Boris Godunov* (1986).

Satyajit Ray (1921–92), Indian film director: *Pather Panchali* (1955).

Grigori Chukrai (1921–), Soviet film director: *The Forty-First* (1956).

Michael Cacoyannis (1922–), Greek film director: *Stella* (1955) and *Electra* (1961).

Pier Paolo Pasolini (1922–75), Italian film director: *Gospel According to St Matthew* (1963).

Alain Resnais (1922–), French film director: *Hiroshima Mon Amour* (1959).

Richard Attenborough (1923–), English actor, producer and director: *Gandhi* (1982).

Lindsay Anderson (1923–), English film director: *This Sporting Life* (1963).

Franco Zeffirelli (Franco Zeffirelli Corsi; 1923–), Italian film director: *Romeo and Juliet* (1968).

Andrzej Wajda (1926–), Polish film director: *Ashes and Diamonds* (1958).

Karel Reisz (1926–), Czech-born British film director: *Saturday Night and Sunday Morning* (1960) and *The French Lieutenant's Woman* (1984).

John Schlesinger (1926–), British director: *Midnight Cowboy* (1969).

Ken Russell (1927–), English film director: *Women in Love* (1969) and *Tommy* (1975).

Nicholas Roeg (1928–), British director: *Performance* (1970) and *Bad Timing* (1980).

Claud Chabrol (1930–), French film director: *Le Boucher* (1969).

Jean-Luc Godard (1930–), French film director: *A Bout de Souffle* (1960).

Louis Malle (1932–), French film director: *Les Amants* (1958) and *Au revoir les enfants* (1987).

Andrei Tarkovsky (1932–88), Soviet film director: *Andrei Rublev* (1966) and *Solaris* (1971).

Milos Forman (1932–), Czech film director: *The Fireman's Ball* (1967).

François Truffaut (1932–84), French film director: *Les Quatre-cent Coups* (1959) and *Day for Night* (1973).

Ken Loach (1936–), English film director: *Kes* (1970).

Yilmaz Güney (1937–84), Turkish film director: *Yol* (1981).

Werner Hertzog (1942–), German film director: *Aguirre, Wrath of God* (1973) and *Fitzcarraldo* (1982).

Bernardo Bertolucci (1940–), Italian film director: *Last Tango in Paris* (1972) and *The Last Emperor* (1988).

Peter Weir (1944–), Australian film director: *Picnic at Hanging Rock* (1975) and *Green Card* (1991).

Rainer Werner Fassbinder (1946–82), German film director: *Despair* (1977).

Bill Forsyth (1947–), Scottish film director: *Gregory's Girl* (1980) and *Local Hero* (1983).

Claude Berri (1954–), French film director: *Jean de Florette* and *Manon des Sources* (1986).

MOTION PICTURE ACADEMY AWARDS (OSCARS)

1928
Actor: Emil Jannings, *The Way of All Flesh*.
Actress: Janet Gaynor, *Seventh Heaven*.
Director: Frank Borzage, *Seventh Heaven*; Lewis Milestone, *Two Arabian Knights*.
Picture: *Wings*, Paramount.

1929
Actor: Warner Baxter, *In Old Arizona*.
Actress: Mary Pickford, *Coquette*.
Director: Frank Lloyd, *The Divine Lady*.
Picture: *Broadway Melody*, MGM.

1930
Actor: George Arliss, *Disraeli*.
Actress: Norma Shearer, *The Divorcee*.
Director: Lewis Milestone, *All Quiet on the Western Front*.
Picture: *All Quiet on the Western Front*, Universal.

1931
Actor: Lionel Barrymore, *Free Soul*
Actress: Marie Dressler, *Min and Bill*
Director: Norman Taurog, *Skippy*
Picture: *Cimarron*, RKO.

1932
Actor: Fredric March, *Dr Jekyll and Mr Hyde*; Wallace Beery, *The Champ* (tie).
Actress: Helen Hayes, *Sin of Madelon Claudet*.
Director: Frank Borzage, *Bad Girl*.
Picture: *Grand Hotel*, MGM.
Special: Walt Disney, *Mickey Mouse*.

1933
Actor: Charles Laughton, *Private Life of Henry VIII*.
Actress: Katharine Hepburn, *Morning Glory*.
Director: Frank Lloyd, *Cavalcade*.
Picture: *Cavalcade*, Fox.

1934
Actor: Clark Gable, *It Happened One Night*.
Actress: Claudette Colbert, *It Happened One Night*.
Director: Frank Capra, *It Happened One Night*.
Picture: *It Happened One Night*, Columbia.

1935
Actor: Victor McLaglen, *The Informer*.
Actress: Bette Davis, *Dangerous*.
Director: John Ford, *The Informer*.
Picture: *Mutiny on the Bounty*, MGM.

1936
Actor: Paul Muni, *Story of Louis Pasteur*.
Actress: Luise Rainer, *The Great Ziegfeld*.
Sup. Actor: Walter Brennan, *Come and Get It*.
Sup. Actress: Gale Sondergaard, *Anthony Adverse*.
Director: Frank Capra, *Mr Deeds Goes to Town*.
Picture: *The Great Ziegfeld*, MGM.

1937
Actor: Spencer Tracy, *Captains Courageous*.
Actress: Luise Rainer, *The Good Earth*.
Sup. Actor: Joseph Schildkraut, *Life of Emile Zola*
Sup. Actress: Alice Brady, *In Old Chicago*.
Director: Leo McCarey, *The Awful Truth*.
Picture: *Life of Emile Zola*, Warner Bros.

1938
Actor: Spencer Tracy, *Boys Town*.
Actress: Bette Davis, *Jezebel*.
Sup. Actor: Walter Brennan, *Kentucky*.
Sup. Actress: Fay Bainter, *Jezebel*.
Director: Frank Capra, *You Can't Take It With You*.
Picture: *You Can't Take It With You*. Columbia.

1939
Actor: Robert Donat, *Goodbye, Mr Chips*.
Actress: Vivien Leigh, *Gone With the Wind*.
Sup. Actor: Thomas Mitchell, *Stage Coach*.
Sup. Actress: Hattie McDaniel, *Gone With the Wind*.
Director: Victor Fleming, *Gone With the Wind*.
Picture: *Gone With the Wind*, Selznick International, MGM.

1940
Actor: James Stewart, *The Philadelphia Story*.
Actress: Ginger Rogers, *Kitty Foyle*.
Sup. Actor: Walter Brennan, *The Westerner*.
Sup. Actress: Jane Darwell, *The Grapes of Wrath*.
Director: John Ford, *The Grapes of Wrath*.
Picture: *Rebecca*, Selznick International, UA.

1941
Actor: Gary Cooper, *Sergeant York*.
Actress: Joan Fontaine, *Suspicion*.
Sup. Actor: Donald Crisp, *How Green Was My Valley*.
Sup. Actress: Mary Astor, *The Great Lie*.
Director: John Ford, *How Green Was My Valley*.
Picture: *How Green Was My Valley*, 20th Century Fox.

1942
Actor: James Cagney, *Yankee Doodle Dandy*.
Actress: Greer Garson, *Mrs Miniver*.
Sup. Actor: Van Heflin, *Johnny Eager*.
Sup. Actress: Teresa Wright, *Mrs Miniver*.
Director: William Wyler, *Mrs Miniver*.
Picture: *Mrs Miniver*, MGM.

1943
Actor: Paul Lukas, *Watch on the Rhine*.
Actress: Jennifer Jones, *The Song of Bernadette*.
Sup. Actor: Charles Coburn, *The More the Merrier*.
Sup. Actress: Katina Paxinou, *For Whom the Bell Tolls*.
Director: Michael Curtiz, *Casablanca*.
Picture: *Casablanca*, Warner.

1944
Actor: Bing Crosby, *Going My Way*.
Actress: Ingrid Bergman, *Gaslight*.
Sup. Actor: Barry Fitzgerald, *Going My Way*.
Sup. Actress: Ethel Barrymore, *None But the Lonely Heart*.
Director: Leo McCarey, *Going My Way*.
Picture: *Going My Way*, Paramount.

1945
Actor: Ray Milland: *The Lost Weekend*.
Actress: Joan Crawford, *Mildred Pierce*.
Sup. Actor: James Dunn, *A Tree Grows in Brooklyn*.
Sup. Actress: Anne Revere, *National Velvet*.
Director: Billy Wilder, *The Lost Weekend*.
Picture: *The Lost Weekend*, Paramount.

1946
Actor: Frederic March, *The Best Years of Our Lives*.
Actress: Olivia de Havilland, *To Each His Own*.
Sup. Actor: Harold Russell, *The Best Years of Our Lives*.
Sup. Actress: Anne Baxter, *The Razor's Edge*.
Director: William Wyler, *The Best Years of Our Lives*.
Picture: *The Best Years of Our Lives*, Goldwyn, RKO.

1947
Actor: Ronald Colman, *A Double Life*.
Actress: Loretta Young, *The Farmer's Daughter*.
Sup. Actor: Edmund Gwenn, *Miracle on 34th Street*.
Sup. Actress: Celeste Holm, *Gentleman's Agreement*.
Director: Elia Kazan, *Gentleman's Agreement*.
Picture: *Gentleman's Agreement*, 20th Century Fox.

1948
Actor: Laurence Olivier, *Hamlet*.
Actress: Jane Wyman, *Johnny Belinda*.
Sup. Actor: Walter Huston, *Treasure of Sierra Madre*.
Sup. Actress: Claire Trevor, *Key Largo*.
Director: John Huston, *Treasure of Sierra Madre*.
Picture: *Hamlet*, Two Cities Film, Universal International.

1949
Actor: Broderick Crawford, *All the King's Men*.
Actress: Olivia de Havilland, *The Heiress*.
Sup. Actor: Dean Jagger, *Twelve O'Clock High*.
Sup. Actress: Mercedes McCambridge, *All the King's Men*.
Director: Joseph L. Mankiewicz, *Letter to Three Wives*.
Picture: *All the King's Men*. Columbia.

1950
Actor: Jose Ferrer, *Cyrano de Bergerac*.
Actress: Judy Holliday, *Born Yesterday*.
Sup. Actor: George Sanders, *All About Eve*.

Sup. Actress: Josephine Hull, *Harvey*.
Director: Joseph L. Mankiewicz, *All About Eve*.
Picture: *All About Eve,* 20th Century Fox.

1951
Actor: Humphrey Bogart, *The African Queen*.
Actress: Vivien Leigh, *A Streetcar Named Desire*.
Sup. Actor: Karl Malden, *A Streetcar Named Desire*.
Sup. Actress: Kim Hunter, *A Streetcar Named Desire*.
Director: George Stevens, *A Place in the Sun*.
Picture: *An American in Paris,* MGM.

1952
Actor: Gary Cooper, *High Noon*.
Actress: Shirley Booth, *Come Back, Little Sheba*.
Sup. Actor: Anthony Quinn, *Viva Zapata!*
Sup. Actress: Gloria Grahame, *The Bad and the
   Beautiful*.
Director: John Ford, *The Quiet Man*.
Picture: *Greatest Show on Earth,* C.B. DeMille,
   Paramount.

1953
Actor: William Holden, *Stalag 17*.
Actress: Audrey Hepburn, *Roman Holiday*.
Sup. Actor: Frank Sinatra, *From Here to Eternity*.
Sup. Actress: Donna Reed, *From Here to Eternity*.
Director: Fred Zinnemann, *From Here to Eternity*.
Picture: *From Here to Eternity,* Columbia.

1954
Actor: Marlon Brando, *On the Waterfront*.
Actress: Grace Kelly, *The Country Girl*.
Sup. Actor: Edmond O'Brien, *The Barefoot Contessa*.
Sup. Actress: Eve Marie Saint, *On the Waterfront*.
Director: Elia Kazan, *On the Waterfront*.
Picture: *On the Waterfront,* Horizon-American,
   Columbia.

1955
Actor: Ernest Borgnine, *Marty*.
Actress: Anna Magnani, *The Rose Tattoo*.
Sup. Actor: Jack Lemmon, *Mister Roberts*.
Sup. Actress: Jo Van Fleet, *East of Eden*.
Director: Delbert Mann, *Marty*.
Picture: *Marty,* Hecht and Lancaster's Steven
   Prods., UA.

1956
Actor: Yul Brynner, *The King and I*.
Actress: Ingrid Bergman, *Anastasia*.
Sup. Actor: Anthony Quinn, *Lust for Life*.
Sup. Actress: Dorothy Malone, *Written on the Wind*.
Director: George Stevens, *Giant*
Picture: *Around the World in 80 Days,* Michael Todd,
   UA.

1957
Actor: Alec Guinness, *The Bridge on the River Kwai*.
Actress: Joanne Woodward, *The Three Faces of Eve*.
Sup. Actor: Red Buttons, *Sayonara*.
Sup. Actress: Miyoshi Umeki, *Sayonara*.
Director: David Lean, *The Bridge on the River Kwai*.
Picture: *The Bridge on the River Kwai,* Columbia.

1958
Actor: David Niven, *Separate Tables*.
Actress: Susan Hayward, *I Want to Live*.
Sup. Actor: Burl Ives, *The Big Country*.
Sup. Actress: Wendy Hiller, *Separate Tables*.
Director: Vincente Minnelli, *Gigi*.
Picture: *Gigi,* Arthur Freed Production, MGM.

1959
Actor: Charlton Heston, *Ben Hur*.
Actress: Simone Signoret, *Room at the Top*.
Sup. Actor: Hugh Griffith, *Ben Hur*.
Sup. Actress: Shelley Winters, *Diary of Anne Frank*.

Director: William Wyler, *Ben Hur*.
Picture: *Ben Hur,* MGM.

1960
Actor: Burt Lancaster, *Elmer Gantry*.
Actress: Elizabeth Taylor, *Butterfield 8*.
Sup. Actor: Peter Ustinov, *Spartacus*.
Sup. Actress: Shirley Jones, *Elmer Gantry*.
Director: Billy Wilder, *The Apartment*.
Picture: *The Apartment,* Mirisch Co.,
   UA.

1961
Actor: Maximilian Schell, *Judgement at Nuremberg*.
Actress: Sophia Loren, *Two Women*.
Sup. Actor: George Chakiris, *West Side Story*.
Sup. Actress: Rita Moreno, *West Side Story*.
Director: Jerome Robbins, Robert Wise, *West Side
   Story*.
Picture: *West Side Story,* UA.

1962
Actor: Gregory Peck, *To Kill a Mockingbird*.
Actress: Anne Bancroft, *The Miracle Worker*.
Sup. Actor: Ed Begley, *Sweet Bird of Youth*.
Sup. Actress: Patty Duke, *The Miracle Worker*.
Director: David Lean, *Lawrence of Arabia*.
Picture: *Lawrence of Arabia,* Columbia.

1963
Actor: Sidney Poitier, *Lilies of the Field*.
Actress: Patricia Neal, *Hud*.
Sup. Actor: Melvyn Douglas, *Hud*.
Sup. Actress: Margaret Rutherford, *The VIPs*.
Director: Tony Richardson, *Tom Jones*.
Picture: *Tom Jones,* Woodfall Prod., UA-Lopert
   Pictures.

1964
Actor: Rex Harrison, *My Fair Lady*.
Actress: Julie Andrews, *Mary Poppins*.
Sup. Actor: Peter Ustinov, *Topkapi*.
Sup. Actress: Lila Kedrova, *Zorba the Greek*.
Director: George Cukor, *My Fair Lady*.
Picture: *My Fair Lady,* Warner Bros.

1965
Actor: Lee Marvin, *Cat Ballou*.
Actress: Julie Christie, *Darling*.
Sup. Actor: Martin Balsam, *A Thousand Clowns*.
Sup. Actress: Shelley Winters, *A Patch of Blue*.
Director: Robert Wise, *The Sound of Music*.
Picture: *The Sound of Music,* 20th Century Fox.

1966
Actor: Paul Scofield, *A Man for All Seasons*.
Actress: Elizabeth Taylor, *Who's Afraid of Virginia
   Woolf?*
Sup. Actor: Walter Matthau, *The Fortune Cookie*.
Sup. Actress: Sandy Dennis, *Who's Afraid of
   Virginia Woolf?*
Director: Fred Zinnemann, *A Man for All Seasons*.
Picture: *A Man for All Seasons,* Columbia.

1967
Actor: Rod Steiger, *In the Heat of the Night*.
Actress: Katharine Hepburn, *Guess Who's Coming to
   Dinner*
Sup. Actor: George Kennedy, *Cool Hand Luke*.
Sup Actress: Estelle Parsons, *Bonnie and Clyde*.
Director: Mike Nichols, *The Graduate*.
Picture: *In the Heat of the Night,* Mirisch Co., UA.

1968
Actor: Cliff Robertson, *Charly*.
Actress: Katharine Hepburn, *The Lion in Winter*;
   Barbra Streisand, *Funny Girl* (tie).

Sup. Actor: Jack Albertson, *The Subject Was Roses*.
Sup. Actress: Ruth Gordon, *Rosemary's Baby*.
Director: Sir Carol Reed, *Oliver!*
Picture: *Oliver!* Romulus, Columbia.

1969
Actor: John Wayne, *True Grit*.
Actress: Maggie Smith, *The Prime of Miss Jean Brodie*.
Sup. Actor: Gig Young, *They Shoot Horses Don't They?*
Sup. Actress: Goldie Hawn, *Cactus Flower*.
Director: John Schlesinger, *Midnight Cowboy*.
Picture: *Midnight Cowboy*, Hellman-Schlesinger, UA.

1970
Actor: George C. Scott, *Patton*. (refused)
Actress: Glenda Jackson, *Women in Love*.
Sup. Actor: John Mills, *Ryan's Daughter*.
Sup. Actress: Helen Hayes, *Airport*.
Director: Franklin Schaffner, *Patton*.
Picture: *Patton*, 20th Century Fox.

1971
Actor: Gene Hackman, *The French Connection*.
Actress: Jane Fonda, *Klute*.
Sup. Actor: Ben Johnson, *The Last Picture Show*.
Sup. Actress: Cloris Leachman, *The Last Picture Show*.
Director: William Friedkin, *The French Connection*.
Picture: *The French Connection*, D'Antoni-Schine-Moore 20th Century Fox.

1972
Actor: Marlon Brando, *The Godfather*.
Actress: Liza Minnelli, *Cabaret*.
Sup. Actor: Joel Grey, *Cabaret*.
Sup. Actress: Eileen Heckart, *Butterflies Are Free*.
Director: Bob Fosse, *Cabaret*.
Picture: *The Godfather*, Ruddy, Paramount.

1973
Actor: Jack Lemmon, *Save the Tiger*.
Actress: Glenda Jackson, *A Touch of Class*.
Sup. Actor: John Houseman, *The Paper Chase*.
Sup. Actress: Tatum O'Neal, *Paper Moon*.
Director: George Roy Hill, *The Sting*.
Picture: *The Sting*, Bill/Phillips-Hill, Zanuck/Brown, Universal.

1974
Actor: Art Carney, *Harry and Tonto*.
Actress: Ellen Burstyn, *Alice Doesn't Live Here Anymore*.
Sup. Actor: Robert DeNiro, *The Godfather, Part II*
Sup. Actress: Ingrid Bergman, *Murder on the Orient Express*.
Director: Francis Ford Coppola, *The Godfather, Part II*
Picture: *The Godfather, Part II*, Coppola Co., Paramount.

1975
Actor: Jack Nicholson, *One Flew Over the Cuckoo's Nest*.
Actress: Louise Fletcher, *One Flew Over the Cuckoo's Nest*.
Sup. Actor: George Burns, *The Sunshine Boys*.
Sup. Actress; Lee Grant, *Shampoo*.
Director: Milos Forman, *One Flew Over the Cuckoo's Nest*.
Picture: *One Flew Over the Cuckoo's Nest*, Fantasy Films, UA.

1976
Actor: Peter Finch, *Network*.

Actress: Faye Dunaway, *Network*.
Sup. Actor: Jason Robards, *All the President's Men*.
Sup. Actress: Beatrice Straight, *Network*.
Director: John G Avildsen, *Rocky*.
Picture: *Rocky*, Chartoff-Winkler, UA.

1977
Actor: Richard Dreyfuss, *The Goodbye Girl*.
Actress: Diane Keaton, *Annie Hall*.
Sup. Actor: Jason Robards, *Julia*.
Sup. Actress: Vanessa Redgrave, *Julia*.
Director: Woody Allen, *Annie Hall*.
Picture: *Annie Hall*, Rollins-Joffe, UA.

1978
Actor: John Voight, *Coming Home*.
Actress: Jane Fonda, *Coming Home*.
Sup. Actor: Christopher Walken, *The Deer Hunter*.
Sup. Actress: Maggie Smith, *California Suite*.
Director: Michael Cimino, *The Deer Hunter*.
Picture: *The Deer Hunter*, EMI Films/Cimino, Universal.

1979
Actor: Dustin Hoffman, *Kramer vs Kramer*.
Actress: Sally Field, *Norma Rae*.
Sup. Actor: Melvyn Douglas, *Being There*.
Sup. Actress: Meryl Streep, *Kramer vs Kramer*.
Director: Robert Benton, *Kramer vs Kramer*.
Picture: *Kramer vs Kramer*, Joffe, Columbia.

1980
Actor: Robert DeNiro, *Raging Bull*.
Actress: Sissy Spacek, *Coal Miner's Daughter*.
Sup. Actor: Timothy Hutton, *Ordinary People*.
Sup. Actress: Mary Steenburgen, *Melvin and Howard*.
Director: Robert Redford, *Ordinary People*.
Picture: *Ordinary People*, Wildwood, Paramount.

1981
Actor: Henry Fonda, *On Golden Pond*.
Actress: Katharine Hepburn, *On Golden Pond*.
Sup. Actor: John Gielgud, *Arthur*.
Sup. Actress: Maureen Stapleton, *Reds*.
Director: Warren Beatty, *Reds*.
Picture: *Chariots of Fire*, Enigma, The Ladd Co., Warner Bros.

1982
Actor: Ben Kingsley, *Gandhi*.
Actress: Meryl Streep, *Sophie's Choice*.
Sup. Actor: Louis Gossett, Jr, *An Officer and a Gentleman*.
Sup. Actress: Jessica Lange, *Tootsie*.
Director: Richard Attenborough, *Gandhi*.
Picture: *Gandhi*, Indo-British Films, Columbia.

1983
Actor: Robert Duvall, *Tender Mercies*.
Actress: Shirley MacLaine, *Terms of Endearment*.
Sup. Actor: Jack Nicholson, *Terms of Endearment*.
Sup. Actress: Linda Hunt, *The Year of Living Dangerously*.
Director: James L. Brooks, *Terms of Endearment*.
Picture: *Terms of Endearment*, Brooks, Paramount.

1984
Actor: F. Murray Abraham, *Amadeus*.
Actress: Sally Field, *Places in the Heart*.
Sup. Actor: Haing S Ngor, *The Killing Fields*.
Sup. Actress: Peggy Ashcroft, *A Passage to India*.
Director: Milos Forman, *Amadeus*.
Picture: *Amadeus*, Zaintz, Orion.

1985
Actor: William Hurt, *Kiss of the Spider Woman*.

Actress: Geraldine Page, *The Trip to Bountiful.*
Sup. Actor: Don Ameche, *Cocoon.*
Sup. Actress: Anjelica Huston, *Prizzi's Honor.*
Director: Sydney Pollack, *Out of Africa.*
Picture: *Out of Africa,* Universal.

1986
Actor: Paul Newman, *The Color of Money.*
Actress: Marlee Matlin, *Children of a Lesser God.*
Sup. Actor: Michael Caine, *Hannah and Her Sisters.*
Sup. Actress: Dianne West, *Hannah and Her Sisters.*
Director: Oliver Stone, *Platoon.*
Picture: *Platoon,* Herndale, Orion.

1987
Actor: Michael Douglas, *Wall Street.*
Actress: Cher, *Moonstruck.*
Sup. Actor: Sean Connery, *The Untouchables.*
Sup. Actress: Olympia Dukakais, *Moonstruck.*
Director: Bernardo Bertolucci, *The Last Emperor.*
Picture: *The Last Emperor,* Herndale, Columbia.

1988
Actor: Dustin Hoffman, *Rain Man.*
Actress: Jodie Foster, *The Accused.*
Sup. Actor: Kevin Kline, *A Fish Called Wanda.*
Sup. Actress: Geena Davis, *The Accidental Tourist.*
Director: Barry Levinson, *Rain Man.*
Picture: *Rain Man,* Guber-Peters, UA.

1989
Actor: Daniel Day Lewis, *My Left Foot.*
Actress: Jessica Tandy, *Driving Miss Daisy.*
Sup. Actor: Denzel Washington, *Glory.*
Sup. Actress: Brenda Fricker, *My Left Foot.*
Director: Oliver Stone, *Born on the Fourth of July.*
Picture: *Driving Miss Daisy,* Zanuck Co., Warner
Bros.

1990
Actor: Jeremy Irons, *Reversal of Fortune.*
Actress: Kathy Bates, *Misery.*
Sup. Actor: Joe Pesci, *Goodfellas.*
Sup. Actress: Whoopi Goldberg, *Ghosts.*
Director: Kevin Costner, *Dances with Wolves.*
Picture: *Dances with Wolves,* Majestic Films.

1991
Actor: Anthony Hopkins, *The Silence of the Lambs.*
Actress: Jodie Foster, *The Silence of the Lambs.*
Sup. Actor: Jack Palance, *City Slickers.*
Sup. Actress: Mercedes Ruehl, *The Fisher King.*
Director: Jonathan Demme, *The Silence of the Lambs.*
Picture: *The Silence of the Lambs.*

1992
Actor: Al Pacino, *Scent of a Woman.*
Actress: Emma Thompson, *Howard's End.*
Sup. Actor: Gene Hackman, *Unforgiven.*
Sup. Actress: Marisa Tomei, *My Cousin Vinny.*
Director: Clint Eastwood, *Unforgiven.*
Picture: *Unforgiven.*

OSCAR LOSERS

Among the above list of Oscar winners, some names are notably absent. Peter O'Toole has been nominated seven times but has never won an Oscar. Richard Burton was also nominated seven times without winning, while Deborah Kerr was nominated six times without winning.

Alfred Hitchcock never won an Oscar and the following actors have won Oscars for directing but not for acting: Richard Attenborough, Warren Beatty, Kevin Costner, Clint Eastwood and Robert Redford.

Famous films that did not win an Oscar include: *The Maltese Falcon, High Society* and *Double Indemnity.*

NOTABLE FILM ACTORS

Woody Allen (Allen Stewart Konigsberg; 1935–), American: *What's New Pussycat* (1965), *Annie Hall* (1977; **AA**), *Hannah and Her Sisters* (1986), *Crimes and Misdemeanours* (1990)

Julie Andrews (Julia Wells; 1934–), English: *Mary Poppins* (1964; **AA**), *The Sound of Music* (1965)

Lauren Bacall (Betty Jean Perske; 1924–), American: *To Have and Have Not* (1944), *The Big Sleep* (1946), *Key Largo* (1948)

Anne Bancroft (Anna Maria Italiano; 1931–), American: *The Miracle Worker* (1962; **AA**)

Brigitte Bardot (Camille Javal; 1933–), French: *And God Created Woman* (1956), *En Cas de Malheur* (1957), *Babette Goes to War* (1959), *Vie Privée* (1961), *Viva Maria* (1965), *The Novices* (1970)

Ingrid Bergman (1915–1982), Swedish: *Intermezzo* (1936), *Casablanca* (1943), *For Whom the Bell Tolls* (1943), *Gaslight* (1944; **AA**), *Spellbound* (1945), *Joan of Arc* (1948), *Anastasia* (1956; **AA**), *The Inn of the Sixth Happiness* (1958)

Dirk Bogarde (Derek Van Den Bogaerd; 1921–), English: *Doctor in the House* (1953), *A Tale of Two Cities* (1958), *The Servant* (1963), *The Damned* (1969), *Death in Venice* (1970)

Humphrey Bogart (1899–1957), American: *A Devil With Women* (1930), *The Maltese Falcon* (1941), *Casablanca* (1942), *To Have and Have Not* (1943), *The Big Sleep* (1946), *Key Largo* (1948), *The African Queen* (1952; **AA**), *The Caine Mutiny* (1954)

Ernest Borgnine (1917–), American: *Marty* (1955; **AA**)

Clara Bow (1905–1965), American: *Mantrap* (1926), *It* (1927), *Wings* (1927)

Marlon Brando (1924–), American: *A Streetcar Named Desire* (1951), *The Wild One* (1953), *On the Waterfront* (1954; **AA**), *The Teahouse of the August Moon* (1956), *The Young Lions* (1958), *The Godfather* (1972; **AA**), *Last Tango in Paris* (1972)

Yul Brynner (Youl Bryner; 1915–1985), Russian-born: *The King and I* (1956; **AA**), *The Brothers Karamazov* (1958), *The Magnificent Seven* (1960), *Invitation to a Gunfighter* (1964)

Richard Burton (Richard Jenkins; 1925–1984), Welsh: *Look Back in Anger* (1959), *Cleopatra* (1962), *The VIPs* (1963), *Becket* (1964), *The Night of the Iguana* (1964), *Who's Afraid of Virginia Woolf?* (1966), *Anne of a Thousand Days* (1970)

James Cagney (1899–1986), American: *The Public Enemy* (1931), *Angels With Dirty Faces* (1938), *Yankee Doodle Dandy* (1942; **AA**)

Michael Caine (Maurice Micklewhite; 1933–), English: *Zulu* (1963), *Ipcress File* (1965), *Educating Rita* (1983), *Hannah and Her Sisters* (1985)

Lon Chaney (Alonzo Chaney; 1883–1930), American: *The Hunchback of Notre Dame* (1923), *The Phantom of the Opera* (1925)

Sir Charles Chaplin (1889–1977), English: *The Tramp* (1915), *The Kid* (1920), *The Gold Rush* (1924), *The Circus* (1928; **AA**), *City Lights* (1931), *Modern Times* (1936), *The Great Dictator* (1940), *Limelight* (1952)

Maurice Chevalier (1888–1972), French: *Love Me Tonight* (1932), *Gigi* (1958), *Fanny* (1961)

Julie Christie (1940–), English: *Darling* (1965; AA), *Doctor Zhivago* (1965), *The Go-Between* (1971), *Heat and Dust* (1983)

Montgomery Clift (1920–66), American: *Red River* (1948), *A Place in the Sun* (1951), *From Here to Eternity* (1953), *The Misfits* (1960) *Freud* (1963)

Claudette Colbert (Lily Claudette Chauchoin; 1905–), French: *It Happened One Night* (1934; AA), *I Met Him in Paris* (1937), *Three Came Home* (1950)

Ronald Colman (1891–1958), English: *Raffles* (1930), *A Tale of Two Cities* (1935), *The Prisoner of Zenda* (1937), *Random Harvest* (1942), *A Double Life* (1948; AA)

Sean Connery (Thomas Connery; 1929–), Scottish: *Doctor No* (1962), *From Russia With Love* (1963), *Goldfinger* (1964), *The Untouchables*(1987; AA)

Gary Cooper (Frank J. Cooper; 1901–61), American: *Mr Deeds Goes to Town* (1936), *Sergeant York* (1941; AA), *For Whom the Bell Tolls* (1943), *High Noon* (1952; AA), *Vera Cruz* (1954)

Kevin Costner (1955–), American: *Dances with Wolves* (1990).

Sir Noel Coward (1899–1973), English: *In Which We Serve* (1941; AA) *Our Man in Havana* (1959)

Joan Crawford (Lucille le Sueur; 1906–77), American: *Grand Hotel* (1932), *The Women* (1939), *Mildred Pierce* (1945; AA), *Whatever Happened to Baby Jane?* (1962)

Bing Crosby (Harry Lillis Crosby; 1901–77), American: *Road to Singapore* (1940), *Going My Way* (1944; AA), *The Bells of St Mary's* (1945), *White Christmas* (1954)

Tom Cruise (1962–), American: *Top Gun* (1985), *Rain Man* (1988), *Born on the Fourth of July* (1989)

Tony Curtis (Bernard Schwarz; 1925–), American: *Some Like it Hot* (1959), *Spartacus* (1960)

Bette Davis (Ruth Elizabeth Davis; 1908–89), American: *Dangerous* (1935; AA), *The Private Lives of Elizabeth and Essex* (1939), *The Little Foxes* (1941), *All About Eve* (1950), *Whatever Happened to Baby Jane?* (1962)

Doris Day (Doris Kappelhoff; 1924–), American: *Calamity Jane* (1953), *The Pyjama Game* (1957), *Pillow Talk* (1959)

Olivia de Havilland (1916–), American: *Gone With the Wind* (1939), *To Each His Own* (1946; AA), *The Heiress* (1949; AA)

Robert De Niro (1943–), American: *The Godfather Part Two* (1974; AA), *The Deer Hunter* (1978), *Raging Bull* (1980; AA), *The Mission* (1986)

James Dean (1931–55), American: *East of Eden*(1955), *Rebel Without a Cause* (1955)

Catherine Deneuve (Catherine Dorleac; 1943–), French: *Les Parapluies de Cherbourg* (1964), *Belle de Jour* (1967), *Mayerling* (1968)

Gerard Depardieu (1948–), French: *Le Dernier Metro* (1980), *Jean de Florette* (1985), *Trop Belle Pour Toi* (1989), *Cyrano de Bergerac* (1991)

Marlene Dietrich (Maria Magdalena von Losch; 1901–92), German: *The Blue Angel* (1930), *Shanghai Express* (1932), *Destry Rides Again* (1939), *A Foreign Affair* (1948)

Robert Donat (1905–58), English: *The Thirty-Nine Steps* (1935), *The Citadel* (1938), *Goodbye Mr Chips* (1939; AA), *The Winslow Boy* (1948)

Kirk Douglas (Issur Danielovitch Demsky; 1916–), American: *Gunfight at the OK Corral* (1957),

Paths of Glory (1957), *Spartacus* (1960), *Lonely Are the Brave* (1962)

Michael Douglas (1944–), son of Kirk, American: *Wall Street* (1987; AA)

Faye Dunaway (1941–), American: *Bonnie and Clyde* (1967), *Network* (1976; AA)

Clint Eastwood (1930–), American: *A Fistful of Dollars* (1964), *For a Few Dollars More* (1965), *The Good The Bad and the Ugly* (1966), *Dirty Harry* (1971), *Every Which Way But Loose* (1978)

Douglas Fairbanks (Douglas Ullman; 1883–1939), American: *The Mark of Zorro* (1920), *The Three Musketeers* (1921), *Robin Hood* (1921), *The Thief of Baghdad* (1923), *Don Q Son of Zorro* (1925)

W.C. Fields (Claude Dukinfield; 1879–1946), American: *David Copperfield* (1934), *My Little Chickadee* (1940), *The Bank Dick* (1940)

Peter Finch (William Mitchell; 1916–77), English: *A Town Like Alice* (1956), *The Trials of Oscar Wilde* (1960), *Sunday Bloody Sunday* (1971), *Network* (1976; AA)

Errol Flynn (1909–59), Irish-born American: *Captain Blood* (1935), *The Adventures of Robin Hood* (1938), *The Sea Hawk* (1940), *They Died With Their Boots On* (1941), *Too Much Too Soon* (1958)

Henry Fonda (1905–82), American: *Young Mr Lincoln* (1939), *The Grapes of Wrath* (1940), *Twelve Angry Men* (1957), *On Golden Pond* (1981; AA)

Jane Fonda (1937–), daughter of Henry, American: *They Shoot Horses Don't They?* (1969), *Klute* (1971; AA), *Coming Home* (1978; AA), *On Golden Pond* (1981)

Harrison Ford (1942–), American: *Star Wars* (1977), *Raiders of the Lost Ark* (1981), *Indiana Jones and the Temple of Doom* (1984), *The Witness* (1985)

Jean Gabin (Alexis Moncourge; 1904–76), French: *Pepe le Moko* (1937), *La Grande Illusion* (1937), *La Bete Humaine* (1938), *Le Jour se Leve* (1939), *Le Chat* (1972)

Clark Gable (1901–60), American: *It Happened One Night* (1934; AA), *Mutiny On the Bounty* (1935), *Gone With the Wind* (1939), *The Misfits* (1961)

Greta Garbo (Greta Gustafson; 1905–90), Swedish: *Grand Hotel* (1932), *Queen Christina* (1933), *Anna Karenina* (1935), *Camille* (1936), *Ninotchka* (1939)

Ava Gardner (1922–90), American: *Show Boat* (1951), *The Barefoot Contessa* (1954), *The Night of the Iguana* (1964)

Judy Garland (Frances Gumm; 1922–69), American: *The Wizard of Oz* (1939), *Meet Me in St Louis* (1944), *A Star is Born* (1954)

Richard Gere (1949–), American: *Yanks* (1979), *An Officer and a Gentleman* (1982), *Pretty Woman* (1990)

Mel Gibson (1956–), American-born Australian: *Mad Max Beyond the Thunderdome* (1985), *Lethal Weapon* (1987)

Lillian Gish (Lillian de Guiche; 1896–93), American: *Birth of a Nation* (1914), *Intolerance* (1916), *The Wind* (1928), *A Wedding* (1978), *The Whales of August* (1987)

Paulette Goddard (Marion Levee; 1905–90), American: *Modern Times* (1936), *The Great Dictator* (1940)

Cary Grant (Archibald Leach; 1904–86), English-born American: *She Done Him Wrong* (1933), *Bringing Up Baby* (1938), *The Philadelphia Story* (1940), *Arsenic and Old Lace* (1944), *North by Northwest* (1959), *Charade* (1963)

Sir Alec Guinness (1914–), English: *Oliver Twist* (1948), *Kind Hearts and Coronets* (1949), *The Lavender Hill Mob* (1951), *The Bridge on the River Kwai* (1957; **AA**), *Tunes of Glory* (1960), *Lawrence of Arabia* (1962)

Gene Hackman (1930–), American: *Bonnie and Clyde* (1967), *The French Connection* (1971; **AA**), *Mississippi Burning*(1989)

Oliver Hardy (1892–1957), American, and **Stan Laurel** (Arthur Stanley Jefferson; 1890–1965), English-born: *The Music Box* (1932; **AA**), *Sons of the Desert* (1933), *Way Out West* (1936), *A Chump at Oxford* (1940)

Jean Harlow (Harlean Carpentier; 1911–37), American: *Hell's Angels* (1930)

Rex Harrison (Reginald Carey; 1908–90), English: *Blithe Spirit* (1945), *My Fair Lady* (1964; **AA**), *The Yellow Rolls-Royce* (1964), *Doctor Dolittle* (1967)

Helen Hayes (Helen Brown; 1900–93), American: *Sin of Madelon Claudet* (1932; **AA**), *Airport* (1970; **AA**)

Rita Hayworth (Margarita Carmen Cansino; 1918–87), American: *The Strawberry Blonde* (1941), *Cover Girl* (1944), *Miss Sadie Thompson* (1953), *Pal Joey* (1957)

Audrey Hepburn (Audrey Hepburn-Ruston; 1929–93), Belgian-born American: *Roman Holiday* (1953; **AA**), *The Nun's Story* (1959), *Breakfast at Tiffany's* (1961), *Charade* (1963)

Katharine Hepburn (1907–), American: *Morning Glory* (1932; **AA**), *Little Women* (1933), *The Philadelphia Story* (1940), *The African Queen* (1951), *Guess Who's Coming to Dinner?* (1967; **AA**), *The Lion in Winter* (1968; **AA**), *On Golden Pond* (1981; **AA**)

Charlton Heston (John Charlton Carter; 1924–), American: *The Ten Commandments* (1956), *Ben Hur* (1959; **AA**), *El Cid* (1961), *55 Days at Peking* (1963), *The Agony and the Ecstasy* (1965), *Khartoum* (1966)

Dustin Hoffman (1937–), American: *The Graduate* (1967), *Midnight Cowboy* (1969), *All the President's Men* (1976), *Kramer vs Kramer* (1980; **AA**), *Tootsie* (1983), *Rain Man* (1988; **AA**)

William Holden (1918–81): *Sunset Boulevard* (1950), *Stalag 17* (1953; **AA**), *The Bridge on the River Kwai* (1957), *The Wild Bunch* (1969)

Bob Hope (Leslie Townes Hope; 1903–), English-born American: *Thanks For the Memory* (1938), *Road to Singapore* (1940), *Road to Morocco* (1942)

Anthony Hopkins (1937–), Welsh: *The Silence of the Lambs* (1991; **AA**)

Leslie Howard (Leslie Stainer; 1890–1943), English: *The Scarlet Pimpernel* (1935), *Pygmalion* (1938), *Gone With the Wind* (1939)

Trevor Howard (1916–88), English: *Brief Encounter* (1946), *The Third Man* (1949), *Mutiny on the Bounty* (1962), *The Charge of the Light Brigade* (1968)

Rock Hudson (1925–85), American: *Magnificent Obsession* (1954), *Pillow Talk* (1959)

Glenda Jackson (1937–), English: *Women in Love* (1969; **AA**), *Sunday Bloody Sunday* (1971), *A Touch of Class* (1972; **AA**)

Al Jolson (Asa Yoelson; 1886–1950), Lithuanian-born American: *The Jazz Singer* (1927), *The Singing Fool* (1928), *Sonny Boy* (1929)

Boris Karloff (William Henry Pratt; 1887–1969), English: *Frankenstein* (1931), *The Mask of Fu Manchu* (1932)

Danny Kaye (David Daniel Kaminsky; 1913–87), American: *The Secret Life of Walter Mitty* (1947), *Hans Christian Andersen* (1952)

Buster Keaton (1895–1966), American: *The Butcher Boy* (1917), *The Paleface* (1922).

Gene Kelly (Eugene Curran Kelly; 1912–), American: *For Me and My Gal* (1942), *An American in Paris* (1951), *Singin' in the Rain* (1952), *Invitation to the Dance* (1956)

Grace Kelly (from 1956 HSH Princess Grace of Monaco; USA 1928–82), American: *The Country Girl* (1954; **AA**), *High Society* (1956)

Deborah Kerr (Deborah Kerr-Trimmer; 1921–), Scottish: *Love on the Dole* (1941), *From Here to Eternity* (1953), *The King and I* (1956), *The Sundowners* (1960)

Alan Ladd (1913–64), American: *This Gun For Hire* (1942), *The Great Gatsby* (1949), *Shane* (1953)

Dorothy Lamour (Dorothy Kaumeyer; 1914–), American: *Road to Singapore* (1940), *Road to Morocco* (1942)

Burt Lancaster (1913–), American: *Elmer Gantry* (1960; **AA**), *Birdman of Alcatraz* (1962)

Charles Laughton (1899–1962), English: *The Private Life of Henry VIII* (1933; **AA**), *Mutiny on the Bounty* (1935), *The Hunchback of Notre Dame* (1939), *Hobson's Choice* (1954)

Cloris Leachman (1926–), American: *The Last Picture Show* (1971; **AA**)

Vivien Leigh (Vivien Hartley; 1913–67), English: *Gone With The Wind* (1939; **AA**), *Lady Hamilton* (1941), *A Streetcar Named Desire* (1951; **AA**)

Jack Lemmon (1925–), American: *Mister Roberts* (1955; **AA**), *Some Like it Hot* (1959), *Irma La Douce* (1963), *The Odd Couple* (1968), *Save the Tiger* (1973; **AA**)

Gina Lollobrigida (1927–), Italian: *Belles de Nuit* (1952), *Solomon and Sheba* (1959)

Sophia Loren (Sophia Scicoloni; 1934–), Italian: *Boy on a Dolphin* (1957), *Two Women* (1961; **AA**), *The Millionairess* (1961)

Myrna Loy (Myrna Williams; 1905–), American: *The Jazz Singer* (1927), *The Mask of Fu Manchu* (1932), *The Rains Came* (1939), *The Best Years of our Lives* (1946)

Shirley Maclaine (Shirley Maclean Beaty; 1934–), American: *Irma La Douce* (1963), *Sweet Charity* (1968), *Terms of Endearment* (1983; **AA**)

Steve McQueen (1930–80), American: *The Magnificent Seven* (1956), *The Great Escape* (1963), *The Cincinnati Kid* (1965), *Bullitt* (1968)

Lee Marvin (1924–87), American: *Cat Ballou* (1965; **AA**)

James Mason (1909–84), English: *The Wicked Lady* (1946), *The Desert Fox* (1951), *A Star is Born* (1954), *The Shooting Party* (1984)

Marcello Mastroianni (1923–), Italian: *La Dolce Vita* (1959), *Divorce Italian Style* (1962)

Walter Matthau (Walther Matasschanskayasky; 1920–), American: *The Fortune Cookie* (1966; **AA**), *The Odd Couple* (1968), *Hello Dolly* (1969), *The Sunshine Boys* (1975)

Sir John Mills (1908–), English: *Waterloo Road* (1944), *Great Expectations* (1946), *Hobson's Choice* (1954), *Tunes of Glory* (1960), *Ryan's Daughter* (1971; **AA**)

Ray Milland (Reginald Truscott-Jones; 1905–86), American: *The Lost Weekend* (1945; **AA**)

Liza Minnelli (1946–), American: *Cabaret* (1972; **AA**)

Robert Mitchum (1917–), American: *Night of the Hunter* (1955), *The Sundowners* (1960), *Ryan's Daughter* (1971)

Marilyn Monroe (Norma Jean Baker; 1926–62), American: *All About Eve* (1950), *Gentlemen Prefer Blondes* (1953), *The Seven Year Itch* (1955), *Some Like it Hot* (1959), *The Misfits* (1961)

Jeanne Moreau (1928–), French: *The Lovers* (1959), *Jules et Jim* (1961), *Diary of a Chambermaid* (1964)

Anna Neagle (Marjorie Robertson; 1904–86), English: *Nell Gwyn* (1934), *Victoria the Great* (1937), *Nurse Edith Cavell* (1939)

Paul Newman (1925–), American: *The Hustler* (1961), *Butch Cassidy and the Sundance Kid* (1969)

Jack Nicholson (1937–), American: *Easy Rider* (1969), *Five Easy Pieces* (1970), *One Flew Over the Cuckoo's Nest* (1976; **AA**), *Terms of Endearment* (1983; **AA**), *Prizzi's Honor* (1985)

David Niven (1909–83), Scottish: *Raffles* (1940), *Around the World in Eighty Days* (1956), *Separate Tables* (1958; **AA**)

Merle Oberon (Estelle O'Brien Merle Thompson; 1911–79), English: *The Scarlet Pimpernel* (1934), *Wuthering Heights* (1939)

Laurence Olivier (Lord Olivier; 1907–89), English: *Wuthering Heights* (1939), *Pride and Prejudice* (1940), *Henry V* (1944; **special AA**), *Hamlet* (1948; **AA**), *Richard III* (1956), *The Entertainer* (1960)

Peter O'Toole (1932–), Irish: *Lawrence of Arabia* (1962), *Becket* (1964), *The Lion in Winter* (1968), *Goodbye Mr Chips* (1969)

Al Pacino (Alfredo Pacino; 1939–), American: *The Godfather* (1972)

Gregory Peck (1916–), American: *The Gunfighter* (1950), *The Big Country* (1958), *Beloved Infidel* (1959), *To Kill a Mockingbird* (1963; **AA**)

Mary Pickford (Gladys Smith; 1893–1979), Canadian: *Pollyanna* (1919), *Little Lord Fauntleroy* (1921), *Coquette* (1929; **AA**)

Walter Pidgeon (1897–1984), Canadian: *How Green Was My Valley* (1941), *Mrs Miniver* (1942)

Sidney Poitier (1924–), American: *The Blackboard Jungle* (1955), *Porgy and Bess* (1959), *Lilies of the Field* (1963; **AA**), *In the Heat of the Night* (1967), *Guess Who's Coming to Dinner?* (1967)

Anthony Quinn (1915–), American: *Viva Zapata* (1952; **AA**), *Lust for Life* (1956; **AA**), *Zorba the Greek* (1964)

Robert Redford (1936–), American: *Butch Cassidy and the Sundance Kid* (1969), *The Candidate* (1972), *The Sting* (1973), *All the President's Men* (1976)

Vanessa Redgrave (1937–), English: *Camelot* (1967), *Isadora* (1968), *Julia* (1977; **AA**), *The Ballad of the Sad Cafe* (1991)

Edward G. Robinson (Emanuel Goldenberg; 1893–1973), Romanian-born American: *Little Caesar* (1930), *Double Indemnity* (1944), *Key Largo* (1948)

Ginger Rogers (Virginia McMath; 1911–), American: *Flying Down to Rio* (1933), *Top Hat* (1935), *Follow the Fleet* (1936), *Kitty Foyle* (1940; **AA**)

Mickey Rooney (Joe Yule Jnr; 1920–), American: *Boys' Town* (1938; **special AA**), *Babes in Arms* (1939), *The Bold and the Brave* (1956)

Jane Russell (1921–), American: *The Paleface* (1948), *Gentlemen Prefer Blondes* (1953)

George Sanders (1906–72), American: *The Moon and Sixpence* (1942), *The Picture of Dorian Gray* (1944), *All About Eve* (1952; **AA**)

George Segal (1934–), American: *The Owl and the Pussycat* (1970), *A Touch of Class* (1973)

Peter Sellers (1925–80), English: *I'm All Right Jack* (1959), *Only Two Can Play* (1962), *The Pink Panther* (1963), *Dr Strangelove* (1963), *Being There* (1979)

Simone Signoret ((1921–85), French: *Room at the Top* (1959; **AA**)

Jean Simmons (1929–), English: *Great Expectations* (1946), *Black Narcissus* (1946), *Elmer Gantry* (1960)

Frank Sinatra (1915–), American: *From Here to Eternity* (1953; **AA**), *The Man With the Golden Arm* (1956), *High Society* (1956), *Pal Joey* (1957), *The Manchurian Candidate* (1962)

Maggie Smith (1934–), English: *The VIPs* (1963), *The Prime of Miss Jean Brodie* (1969; **AA**), *California Suite* (1978; **AA**)

Sylvester Stallone (1946–), American: *Rocky* (1976), *Rambo* (1985)

Barbara Stanwyck (1907–90), American: *Stella Dallas* (1937), *The Lady Eve* (1941), *Double Indemnity* (1944).

Rod Steiger (1925–), American: *On the Waterfront* (1954), *Al Capone* (1958), *In the Heat of the Night* (1967; **AA**)

James Stewart (1908–), American: *Mr Smith Goes to Washington* (1939), *Destry Rides Again* (1939), *The Philadelphia Story* (1940; **AA**), *It's a Wonderful Life* (1946), *Harvey* (1950)

Meryl Streep (Mary Louise Streep; 1951–), American: *Kramer vs Kramer* (1979; **AA**), *The French Lieutenant's Woman* (1981), *Sophie's Choice* (1982; **AA**), *Silkwood* (1983), *Out of Africa* (1986)

Barbra Streisand (1942–), American: *Funny Girl* (1968; **AA**), *Hello Dolly* (1969), *Funny Lady* (1975), *A Star is Born* (1976)

Donald Sutherland (1935–), Canadian: *M*A*S*H* (1970), *Kelly's Heroes* (1970), *Klute* (1971).

Gloria Swanson (G. Svensson; 1897–1983), American: *Sadie Thompson* (1928), *Queen Kelly* (1928), *Sunset Boulevard* (1950)

Elizabeth Taylor (1932–), English: *National Velvet* (1944), *Cat on a Hot Tin Roof* (1958), *Butterfield 8* (1960; **AA**), *Cleopatra* (1962), *Who's Afraid of Virginia Woolf?* (1967; **AA**)

Shirley Temple (1928–), American: *Bright Eyes* (1934; **AA**)

Spencer Tracy (1900–67), American: *The Power and the Glory* (1933), *Captains Courageous* (1937; **AA**), *Northwest Passage* (1940), *Pat and Mike* (1952), *Guess Who's Coming to Dinner?* (1967)

Rudolph Valentino (Rodolpho d'Antonguolla; 1895–1926), Italian-born: *The Four Horsemen of the Apocalypse* (1921), *The Sheik* (1921), *Blood and Sand* (1922), *Son of the Sheik* (1926)

Orson Welles (1915–85), American: *Citizen Kane* (1941), *The Third Man* (1949), *The Trial* (1962)

Natalie Wood (Natasha Gurdin; 1938–81): *Rebel Without a Cause* (1955), *West Side Story* (1961), *Bob and Carol and Ted and Alice* (1969)

THEATRE

THE ORIGINS OF THEATRE

The origins of drama were in the rituals that hunters enacted to ensure success or to placate the spirit of their prey and in the ceremonies through which farmers sought to ensure the renewal of the seasons. The religious rituals in which the Egyptian pharaohs re-enacted the murder and resurrection of the god Osiris may have been one of the first 'plays'.

GREEK AND ROMAN THEATRE

Western drama had its first flowering in ancient Greece in the festival that honoured Dionysus, the god of fertility and wine. From the orgiastic cele-brations of his cult developed a form of choral performance – the *dithyramb* – in which a tale of gods and heroes was recounted in song and dance. To this, in the 6th century BC, Thespis, a priest, is credited with adding a solo performer who engaged in dia-logue with the leader of the chorus, resulting in the first Greek play.

These early plays were known as *tragedies*, a word originally meaning 'goat-song', perhaps because the song was offered at the same time that a goat was sacrificed. Thespis is believed to have taken a troupe of actors around Greece performing plays, and modern actors are sometimes referred to as *thespians* after him.

Within a century, serious tragedies had been joined by bawdy *satyrs* – the satyrs were horse-tailed goat-eared men who were supposed to be Dionysus's followers. These plays often made fun of the scanda-lous love-life of the gods.

The actors – all male – increased in number from a single speaker (the first actor) to three men. In a single play, the three actors might each play several roles, each character clearly identified by its costume and face mask, but no more than three characters could appear in any one scene.

Touring troupes may have performed in market places, but most Hellenic cities had a hillside theatre where people could stand or sit on a semicircle of wooden or stone benches to watch the actors perform on a flattened circle called the *orchestra* ('threshing floor'). Later a row of buildings across the back of the orchestra provided a narrow raised platform which the actors could sometimes use, although eventually all of the action took place upon this stage. Large theatres, such as the one at Epidavros, could hold up to 14 000 spectators, and performances could last all day.

Roman theatre followed the style of the Greek in staging and performance, although Roman theatre buildings were considerably more elaborate than their Hellenic counterparts. However, a preference for scabrous plots drew the disapproval of the Christian Church with the result that the Byzantine Emperor Justinian I ordered the closure of all theatres in the 6th century AD.

Greek and Roman dramatists and their works are summarized under Classical Literature.

MEDIEVAL AND RENAISSANCE THEATRE

Travelling entertainers probably preserved the elements of theatre, but it was in the Church itself that formal drama reappeared as parts of Christian teaching and liturgy began to be given dramatic form. The performance of plays retelling Bible stories – *miracle* or *mystery plays* – developed, to be followed by moral secular tales. These were staged in a variety of ways. Sometimes there were settings – or *mansions* – side by side on a wide outdoor stage; sometimes the plays were performed within a ring of platforms. In Britain and Iberia, each scene was often acted on a separate cart – or *pageant* – which was pulled through the streets for the play to be performed at a number of locations.

Medieval actors – again all male – were usually members of various craft guilds, the 'mysteries' being not those of religion but of trades and professions. Individual craft guilds became responsible for the performance of an appropriate play.

With the renewed interest in classical ideas during the Renaissance, schools and universities began to perform Roman plays in Latin texts. Some attempts were even made to re-create theatres like those of ancient Rome, for example, the Teatro Olimpico (1585) in Vincenza, Italy, which unlike ancient Roman theatres was roofed over.

The flowering of drama in Elizabethan England was accompanied by the construction of the first modern public theatres in northern Europe. London's first public playhouse opened in 1576. It was built in the fields to the north of the city walls because the city fathers had forbidden the performance of plays within 'the Square Mile'. It was soon followed by a group of theatres south of the River Thames – again outside the City of London – and these included the Rose, the Swan and the Globe. Their circular, galler-ied design was based upon the courtyards of inns. The stage jutted out into the centre of the yard which was open to the sky. Although some scenic elements were used, and there were colourful costumes and effects, most of the scene-setting was built into the text.

This was the type of theatre for which Shakespeare wrote. It allowed for rapidly moving dramas in which one scene followed straight on from another. The actors were in close contact with the audience, members of which either stood in the yard or sat in the galleries and even on the stage itself. Even in the largest London Elizabethan theatre – which could accommodate up to 3000 spectators – no one was more than about 10 m (30 ft) from the stage.

Indoor performances were largely restricted to court *masques*, an entertainment that emphasized music, dance and elaborate effects. Masques – which ori-ginated at the French and Italian courts – were enacted by nobles and were not intended for viewing by a wider public. Masques were, however, the direct ancestor of both ballet and opera.

Renaissance dramatists and their works are summar-ized under Renaissance Literature and Shakes-peare (see Language and Literature).

THEATRE IN THE 17th AND 18th CENTURIES

In the middle of the 16th century, some Italian court masques were performed behind a frame separating the stage from the spectators. Originally scenic elements had been arranged around the performance space, but the retreat behind this frame (originally a temporary structure) marked the birth of the *prosce-nium* and the beginning of the modern theatre. Although these temporary proscenium arches did support curtains they were erected to provide atmosphere and spectacle rather than to hide changes of scene. The first permanent proscenium to be installed in a theatre was at the Teatro Farnese in Parma, Italy (1618–19), but scenery was not usually changed behind curtains until the 18th century.

European theatres in the 17th century were almost invariably roofed, and English open courtyard theatres did not survive the ban on stage plays during the Civil War and Commonwealth (1642–60).

During the 18th century, important changes in stage design were introduced by the Bibiena family of Bologna in Italy. Previously stage sets were based upon one-point perspective using a single vanishing point. Ferdinando Bibiena developed angle perspective, that is perspective with two vanishing points. The Bibienas created sets that gave the impression of great size. Late in the 18th century new styles of scenery appeared. Classical ruins became popular and stage designers strove to create a 'mood', emphasizing light and dark.

In France the Italian designer Giacomo Torelli mystified audiences by changing scenery while the opera or ballet continued rather than at the end of scenes. To celebrate the wedding of Louis XIV in 1660, Gaspare Vigarani built the Salle des Machines, a large theatre equipped with many machines and special effects, including a platform that could 'fly' the French royal family on to the stage. The Comédie Française, by contrast, made its home in a stark converted tennis court, although the Opéra enjoyed a lavish Baroque building well equipped with scenery and machines.

Italian models were used for most theatrical and stage designs in Europe in the 18th century. The stage was enlarged and, initially, the forestage – the area in front of the proscenium – was fairly deep with doors opening on to it for the entrances and exits of performers, and some members of the public sat in 'boxes' on either side. By the end of the 18th century the standing pit had been abolished and the audience was all seated. However, permanent theatres were uncommon. Most plays were staged by travelling troupes who had many plays in their repertoire. This prevented sufficient rehearsals and discouraged the development of acting skills.

Neoclassical and Romantic dramatists and their works are summarized in the Literature section.

THEATRE IN THE 19th and 20th CENTURIES

Many theatres retained close proximity between actors and audience well into the 19th century, but as stronger lighting was developed, eventually using gas and electricity, it became possible to light up both actors and scenery more brilliantly, even well upstage. The proscenium advanced further and further until it became a 'picture frame' for the whole action of the play.

In the 19th century, theatres increased in number and different types of theatre evolved for different genres – plays, opera, ballet, music hall and so on. There were also major innovations in acting and staging. The design of theatres with improved acoustics encouraged players to forsake the traditional declamatory style of acting in favour of a more natural manner. Scenery, however, remained elaborate. Wagner's opera house at Bayreuth (opened in 1876) introduced the orchestra pit, and he is thought to be the first person to darken the house lights during a performance. A bigger long-term impact was made by the Meiningen troupe founded and directed by the German prince Georg II of Saxe-Meiningen, who emphasized the importance of research and rehearsal, and introduced the split stage, historical accuracy in scenery and the concept that scenery, lighting, costumes, properties, actors, text and actions formed an interwoven whole, every part of which must fit.

From c. 1850 to c. 1945 the picture-frame stage was the kind of theatre most people expected. Improved lighting techniques allowed the side walls of a 'room' to be constructed and the ceiling to be lowered above the stage so that the audience appeared to be looking into a room with one wall removed – the 'fourth wall', as the division between the actors and audience came to be known. This box proved the ideal setting for the theatrical revival at the end of the 19th century in Europe, which has been seen as the final flowering of Realism. Plays emphasized the lives and concerns of ordinary people. Scenes became shorter and sometimes abrupt, while settings became more intimate and less monumental and spectacular.

At the end of the 19th century André Antoine revolutionized staging by removing the 'fourth wall' and establishing the concept that every play requires its own distinct setting. Realism in acting triumphed while scenery and settings became simpler, often stark. Settings often became a shorthand indication of locale or mood. Skeleton tracery, primitive masonry, sometimes cloth, paper or even light rather than structures have all enjoyed favour as settings for performances. This revolution reached its climax in Jerzy Grotowski's Lab Theatre in Poland, in which every performance is seen as an independent entity requiring a unique playing space and arrangement of the audience and actors.

Theatres with picture frame prosceniums and tiered seating are still in the majority, but all kinds of arrangements are now used, including the projecting apron stage and 'theatre in the round'. Many performance settings can be arranged to suit a particular production, sometimes with no seats and no stage as such, but with the action moving from place to place among the audience, as for example in street theatre.

Dramatists of the 19th and 20th centuries, and their works, are summarized in the Literature chapter.

NOTABLE STAGE ACTORS AND DIRECTORS

Lope de Rueda (?1509–65), Spanish actor-manager.

Andre Calmo (1509/10–71), Venetian actor-dramatist.

Richard Tarlton (d. 1588), English clown.

Will Kempe (c. 1550–c. 1607), English actor-clown.

Edward Alleyn (1566–1626), English actor who played leading roles in Marlowe's plays.

Richard Burbage (1567–1619), English actor who played leading roles in many first performances of Shakespeare's plays.

Molière (Jean-Baptiste Poquelin; 1622–73), French actor-dramatist – see Literature (p. 336).

Thomas Betterton (c. 1635–1710), English actor who played leading roles in many Restoration and Shakespearean plays.

Nell Gwyn (Eleanor Gwyn; ?1642–87), English actress.

Michel Baron (Michel Boyron; 1653–1729), French actor (created many of Racine's roles).

Colley Cibber (1671–1757), English actor-manager, dramatist and Poet Laureate.

Adrienne Lecouvreur (1692–1730), French actress who was noted for her natural style.

James Quin (1692–1766), English actor.

Charles Macklin (1699–1797), Irish actor and dramatist.

David Garrick (1717–79), English Shakespearean actor and manager.

Konrad Ekhof (1720–78), German actor.

Friedrich Ludwig Schröder (1744–1816), German actor-manager and dramatist who introduced Shakespeare to the German stage.

Sarah Siddons (1755–1831), English tragic actress (famous for her Lady Macbeth).

John Philip Kemble (1757–1823), English tragic actor-manager – brother of Sarah Siddons.

François Joseph Talma (1763–1826), French actor-manager who developed realism in acting.

Edmund Kean (1787–1833), English Shakespearean actor.

Mikhail Semyonovich Shchepkin (1788–1863), Russian actor.

William Macready (1793–1873), English actor who developed the techniques of acting.

Frédérick Lemaître (1800–76), French actor.

Johann Nepomuck Nestroy (1801–62), Austrian dramatist and character actor.

Edwin Forrest (1806–72), American actor.

Ira Aldridge (1807–67), Afro-American tragic actor who worked mainly in Europe.

Charles Kean (1811–68), English actor-manager who revived the Shakespearean canon.

Charlotte Cushman (1816–76), the first American actress to achieve an international reputation.

Rachel (Elisa Félix; 1820–58), Swiss-born French tragic actress.

Adelaide Ristori (1922–06), Italian tragic actress.

Tommasso Salvini (1829–1915), Italian actor.

Joseph Jefferson (1829–1905), American actor.

Edwin Booth (1833–93), American tragic actor. He was the brother of the assassin of President Lincoln.

Henry Irving (John Henry Brodribb; 1838–1905), English director and Shakespearean actor.

Helena Modjeska (1840–1909), Polish-born American actress who achieved great success in English-speaking roles despite her poor English.

Jean-Mounet Sully (1841–1916), French actor.

Constant-Benoît Coquelin (1841–1909), French actor.

Sarah Bernhardt (1844–1923), French actress who gained international acclaim for her tragic roles in *Phèdre*, *La Dame aux camélias* and *L'Aiglon*.

James O'Neill (1846–1920), Irish-born American actor.

Ellen Terry (1847–1928), English actress – leading lady in many of Irving's productions.

Herbert Beerbohm Tree (1853–1917), English actor-manager.

Réjane (Gabrielle Réju; 1856–1920), French actress.

Eleanora Duse (1858–1924), Italian actress.

André Antoine (1858–1943), French actor, director, critic and film producer.

Vladimir Nemirovich-Danchenko (1858–1943), Russian director, drama teacher and co-founder of the Moscow Art Theatre.

Annie Horniman (1860–1937), English theatre manager who started the repertory theatre movement in the UK.

Constantin Stanislavsky (1863–1938), Russian actor and director who developed the Stanislavsky method of acting, better known as 'the method'.

Mrs Patrick Campbell (Beatrice Stella Tanner; 1865–1940), English actress.

Olga Knipper (1868–1959), Russian actress who gained great acclaim in leading roles in the plays of her husband, Chekhov.

Max Reinhardt (Max Goldman; 1873–1943), Austrian director who was instrumental in the foundation of the Salzburg Festival.

Lillian Baylis (1874–1937), English theatre manager who founded the Old Vic.

Vsevolod Emilievich Meyerhold (1874–1940), Russian actor, director and producer who experimented in 'nonrealistic' theatre.

Ivan Mikhailovich Moskvin (1874–1946), Russian actor.

Harley Granville Barker (1877–1946), English-born director and producer who worked mainly in France.

Lionel Barrymore (1878–1954), American character actor and director.

Jacques Copeau (1878–1949), French actor-director.

Ethel Barrymore (Ethel Blythe; 1878–1959), American stage and film actress.

Sybil Thorndyke (1882–1976), English Shakespearean actress who created the title role in Shaw's *Saint Joan*.

John Barrymore (1882–1942), American actor who played romantic leading men and Shakespearean roles.

Laurette Taylor (Loretta Cooney; 1884–1946), American actress.

Charles Dullin (1885–1949), French actor-director.

Lyn Fontanne (Lillie Louise Fontanne; 1887–1983), English-born American actress who usually played opposite her husband Alfred Lunt.

Louis Jouvet (1887–1951), French actor, director and designer who had a great influence on 20th-century French theatre.

Edith Evans (1888–1976), English actress who won acclaim in a wide variety of dramatic roles.

Alfred Lunt (1892–1977), American actor-director who was particularly associated with the plays of Noel Coward – see also Lyn Fontanne, above.

Margaret Rutherford (1892–1972), English stage and film actress.

Erwin Piscator (1893–1966), German producer and director, who, with Brecht, developed 'epic theatre'.

Antonin Artaud (1896–1949), French actor and director.

Ruth Gordon (1896–1985), American actress.

Michel Saint-Denis (1897–1971), American director.

Frederic Marsh (1897–1975), American actor.

Judith Anderson (1898–), Australian-born actress.

Bertolt Brecht (1898–1956), German director and dramatist.

Paul Robeson (1898–1976), American actor and singer.

Micheál macLiammóir (1898–1978), Irish actor-director.

Noel Coward see Notable Film Actors.

Charles Laughton see Notable Film Actors.

Helen Hayes see Notable Film Actors.

Katina Paxinou (1900–74), Greek actress.

Tyrone Guthrie (1900–71), Anglo-Irish director.

Helen Weigel (1900–72), German actress.

Florence Eldridge (1901–88), American actress.

Flora Robson (1902–84), English actress.

Ralph Richardson (1902–83), English actor.

Donald Wolfit (1902–68), English actor-manager.

John Gielgud (1904–), English actor.

Henry Fonda see Notable Film Actors.

Emlyn Williams (1905–87), Welsh actor-dramatist.

Peggy Ashcroft (1907–91), English actress.

Roger Blin (1907–84), French actor.

Laurence Olivier see Notable Film Actors.

Anna Magnani (1908–73), Italian actress.

John Mills see Notable Film Actors.

Michael Redgrave (1908–85), English actor.

Cyril Cusack (1910–), Irish actor, dramatist and director.

George Devine (1910–66), English director.

Lee J. Cobb (1911–76), American actor.

Hume Cronyn (1911–), American actor.

Jean Vilar (1912–71), French actor-director.

Vivian Leigh see Notable Film Actors.

Alec Guinness see Notable Film Actors.

Joan Littlewood (1914–), English director.

Orson Welles see Notable Film Actors.

Irene Worth (1916–), American actress.

Vittorio Gassman (1922–), Italian actor-director.

Paul Scofield (1922–), English Shakespearean actor.

Franco Zeffirelli (Franco Zeffirelli Corsi; 1923–), Italian stage and film director and designer.

Marlon Brando see Notable Film Actors.

Geraldine Page (1924–87), American stage actress.

Julian Beck (1925–85), American producer, director and actor.

Peter Brook (1925–), English director, noted for innovative productions of international theatre.

Richard Burton see Notable Film Actors.

John Dexter (1925–90), English director.

John Neville (1925–), English actor and director, who has been particularly associated with the Stratford Festival in Ontario, Canada.

Dario Fo (1926–), Italian actor, writer and director of popular political theatre.

Judith Malina (1926–), German-born American producer and director.

George C. Scott (1927–), American stage and film actor and director.

Eric Porter (1928–), English actor.

William Gaskill (1930–), English director.

Peter Hall (1930–), English director. Founder of the Royal Shakespeare Company.

Anne Bancroft see Notable Film Actors.

Dorothy Tutin (1931–), English stage and film actress.

Ian Holm (1931–), English actor.

Mike Nichols (1931–), American director.

Roger Planchon (1931–), French director of the Theatre National Populaire since 1972.

Jerzy Grotowski (1933–), Polish director of the innovative Lab Theatre.

Alan Bates (1934–), English actor.

Jonathan Miller (1934–), English director of plays for stage and television, and of opera.

Ariane Mnouchkine (1934–), French director.

Joseph Chaikin (1935–), American director.

Judi Dench (Judith Dench; 1935–), English actress.

Albert Finney (1936–), English actor.

Nuria Espert (1936–), Spanish actress.

Glenda Jackson see Notable Film Actors.

Carmelo Bene (1937–), Italian actor, director and dramatist.

Dustin Hoffman see Notable Film Actors.

Anthony Hopkins see Notable Film Actors.

Alan Howard (1937–), English actor.

Vanessa Redgrave , daughter of Michael Redgrave; see Notable Film Actors.

Peter Stein (1937–), German director.

Derek Jacobi (1938–), English actor.

Nicol Williamson (1938–), Scottish actor.

Ian McKellan (1939–), English actor.

Michael Gambon (1940–), English actor.

Trevor Nunn (1940–), English director – particularly associated with the Royal Shakespeare Company.

Robert Wilson (1941–), American director.

Patrice Chereau (1944–), French director.

Helen Mirren (1946–), English actress.

Kevin Kline (1947–), American stage and film actor.

Glen Close (1947–), American stage and film actress.

Anthony Sher (1949–), South African-born British actor.

John Malkovich (1953–), American actor-director.

Emma Thompson (1959–), English stage and film actress; wife of Kenneth Branagh.

Kenneth Branagh (1961–), Irish-born British actor-director.

HISTORY
KINGS, RULERS AND STATESMEN

The following tables list heads of state and/or recent heads of government for selected countries. Further information on the recent history and present constitution of these and other states will be found in the Countries of the World section.

ARGENTINA

PRESIDENTS (since 1946)
Gen. Juan Domingo Perón *Peronist* 1946–55
Gen. Eduardo Lonardi *military* 1955
Gen. Pedro Eugenio Aramburu *military* 1955–58
Arturo Frondizi *Radical* 1958–62
Dr José Maria Guido *np* 1962–63
Dr Arturo Umberto Illia *Radical* 1963–66
Gen. Juan Carlos Ongania *military* 1966–70
Gen. Roberto Levingston *military* 1970–71
Gen. Alejandro Agustin Lanusse *military* 1971–73
Héctor Cámpora *Peronist* 1973
Raúl Lastiri *Coalition* 1973
Gen. Juan Domingo Perón *Peronist* 1973–74
Maria Estela Martinez de Perón *Peronist* 1974–76 (the first woman president in the world)
Gen. Jorge Rafael Videla *military* 1976–81
Gen. Roberto Viola *military* 1981
Gen. Leopoldo Fortunato Galtieri *military* 1981–82
Gen. Reynaldo Bignone *military* 1982–83
Dr Raúl Alfonsin *Radical* 1983–88
Carlos Saul Menem *Peronist* 1988–

Key: *np* = non-party

AUSTRIA

EMPERORS (before 1804, see Holy Roman Empire)
Franz I 1804–35
Ferdinand I 1835–48
Franz Joseph I 1848–1916
Karl I 1916–18

PRESIDENTS
Dr Karl Seitz 1918–20
Dr Michael Hainisch 1920–28
Dr Wilhelm Miklas 1928–1938 when Austria was included within the German Reich
Dr Karl Renner 1945–50
Dr Theodor Körner 1951–57
Dr Adolf Schärf 1957–65
Dr Franz Jonas 1965–74
Dr Rudolf Kirchschläger 1974–86
Dr Kurt Waldheim 1986–92
Thomas Klestil 1992–

CHANCELLORS (since 1945)
Dr Karl Renner *Coalition* 1945
Dr Leopold Figl *PP* 1945–53
Dr Julius Raab *PP* 1953–61
Dr Alfons Gorbach *PP* 1961–74
Dr Josef Klaus *PP* 1974–70
Dr Bruno Kreisky *Soc* 1970–83
Dr Fred Sinowatz *Soc-PP* 1983–86
Dr Franz Vranitzky *Soc-PP* 1986–

Key: *PP* = People's Party (conservative)
Soc = Social Democrat

AUSTRALIA

PRIME MINISTERS
Sir Edmund Barton *Coalition* 1901–03
Alfred Deakin *Lib-Lab* 1903–04
John Christian Watson *Lab* 1904
Sir George Houston Reid *Coalition* 1904–05
Alfred Deakin *Lib-Lab* 1905–08
Andrew Fisher *Lab* 1908–09
Alfred Deakin *Lib-Con* 1909–10
Andrew Fisher *Lab* 1910–13
Sir Joseph Cook *Lib* 1913–14
Andrew Fisher *Lab* 1914–15
William Morris Hughes *Lab-Nat* 1915–23
Stanley Melbourne Bruce *Nat-Co* 1923–29
James Henry Scullin *Lab* 1929–32
Joseph Aloysius Lyons *UA* 1932–39
Sir Earle Christmas Grafton Page *Co-UA* 1939
Sir Robert Gordon Menzies *UA-Co* 1939–41
Sir Arthur William Fadden *Co-UA* 1941
John Joseph Curtin *Lab* 1941–45
Francis Michael Forde *Lab* 1945
Joseph Benedict Chifley *Lab* 1945–49
Sir Robert Gordon Menzies *Lib-Co* 1949–66
Harold Edward Holt *Lib-Co* 1966–67
Sir John McEwen *Lib-Co* 1967–68
John Grey Gorton *Lib-Co* 1968–71
William McMahon *Lib-Co* 1971–72
Edward Gough Whitlam *Lab* 1972–75
John Malcolm Fraser *Lib-Co* 1975–83
Robert (Bob) James Lee Hawke *Lab* 1983–91
Paul Keating *Lab* 1991–

Key: *Co* = Country Party (now National Party)
Lab = Labor Party
Lib = Liberal Party
Nat = Nationalist (after 1931, United Australia Party)
UA = United Australia Party (after 1944, Liberal Party)

BELGIUM

KINGS
Léopold I 1831–65
Léopold II 1865–1909
Albert I 1909–34
Léopold III 1934–51
Baudouin I 1951–

PRIME MINISTERS (since 1958)
Gaston Eyskens *SC* 1958–61
Théo Lefèvre *SC* 1961–65
Pierre Harmel *SC* 1965–66
Paul vanden Boeynants *SC* 1966–68
Gaston Eyskens *SC* 1968–72
Edmond Leburton *Soc* 1972–74
Léo Tindemans *SC* 1974–78
Paul vanden Boeynants *SC* 1978–79
Wilfried Martens *SC* 1979–81
Mark Eyskens *SC* 1981
Wilfried Martens *SC* 1981–92
Jean-Luc Dehaene *SC* 1992–

Key: *SC* = Social Christian (conservative)
Soc = Socialist

BRAZIL

PRESIDENTS (since 1930)
Dr Getúlio Dornelles Vargas *New State* 1930–45
Chief Justice Dr José Linhares *caretaker* 1945–46
Marshal Eurico Gaspar Dutra *military* 1946–51
Dr Getúlio Dornelles Vargas *PTB* 1951–54
Dr João Café Filho *PTB* 1954–55
Carlos Coimbra de Luz *caretaker* 1955

Nereu de Oliveira Ramos *caretaker* 1955–56
Juscelino Kubitschek de Oliveira *Coalition* 1956–61
Jânio de Silva Quadros *np-UDN* 1961
Pascoal Ranieri Mazzilli *caretaker* 1961
João Belchior Goulart *PTB* 1961–64
Pascoal Ranieri Mazzilli *caretaker* 1964
Marshal Humberto de Alencar Castelo *military* 1964–67
Marshal Artur da Costa e Silva *military* 1967–69
Gen. Emilio Garrastazu Medici *military* 1969–74
Gen. Ernesto Geisel *military* 1974–79
Gen. João Baptista de Oliveira Figueiredo *military* 1979–85
Tancredo Neves *PFL* 1985
José Sarney *PFL* 1985–90
Fernando Collor de Mellor *PRN* 1990–92
Itamar Franco *PRN* 1992–

Key: *np* = non-party
PFL = Liberal Front
PRN = National Reconstruction Party
PTB = Brazilian Labour Party
UDN = National Democratic Union

BULGARIA

PRINCES
Alexander I 1879–86
Ferdinand I 1886–1908 when he became king

KINGS
Ferdinand I 1908–1918
Boris III 1918–43
Simeon II 1943–46

PRESIDENTS
Vassil Kolarov *Comm* 1946–47
Mintso Neitsev *Comm* 1947–50
Georgi Damyanov *Comm* 1950–58
Dimiter Ganev *Comm* 1958–64
Georgi Traikov *Comm* 1964–71
Todor Zhivkov *Comm* 1971–89
Petar Mladenov *Comm* 1989–90
Zhelo Zhelev *UDF* 1990–

Key: *Comm* = Communist
UDF = Union of Democratic Forces

CANADA

PRIME MINISTERS
Sir John Alexander MacDonald *Lib-Con* 1867–73
Alexander MacKenzie *Lib* 1873–78
Sir John Alexander MacDonald *Lib-Con* 1878–91
Sir John Joseph Caldwell Abbott *Lib-Con* 1891–92
Sir John Sparrow David Thompson *Lib-Con* 1892–94
Sir Mackenzie Bowell *Lib-Con* 1894–96
Sir Charles Tupper *Lib-Con* 1896
Sir Wilfred Laurier *Lib* 1896–1911
Sir Robert Laird Borden *Con* 1911–20
Arthur Meighen *Con* 1920–21
William Lyon MacKenzie King *Lib* 1921–26
Arthur Meighen *Con* 1926
William Lyon MacKenzie King *Lib* 1926–30
Richard Bedford Bennett *Con* 1930–35
William Lyon Mackenzie King *Lib* 1935–48
Louis Stephen St Laurent *Lib* 1948–57
John George Diefenbaker *PCon* 1957–63
Lester Bowles Pearson *Lib* 1963–68
Pierre Elliott Trudeau *Lib* 1968–79
Charles Joseph Clark *PCon* 1979–80
Pierre Elliot Trudeau *Lib* 1980–84
John Napier Turner *Lib* 1984
Brian Mulroney *PCon* 1984–

Key: *Con* = Conservative (succeeded by Progressive Conservative Party in 1942)
Lib = Liberal
PCon = Progressive Conservative

HOLY ROMAN EMPERORS

Karl I (*Charlemagne*) 800–814
Ludwig I (*Louis I*) 814–840
Lothar I 840–855
Ludwig II (*Louis II*) 855–875
Karl II (*Charles II*) 875–877
Karl III (*Charles III*) 877–887
Arnulf 887–898
Ludwig III* (*Louis III*) 899–911
Konrad I* 911–918
Heinrich I* (*Henry I*) 919–936
Otto I 936–973
Otto II 973–983
Otto III 983–1002
Heinrich II (*Henry II*) 1002–24
Konrad II 1024–39
Heinrich III (*Henry III*) 1039–56
Heinrich IV (*Henry IV*) 1056–1105
Heinrich V (*Henry V*) 1105–25
Lothar II 1125–37
Konrad III* 1138–52
Friedrich I (*Frederick Barbarossa*) 1152–90
Heinrich VI (*Henry VI*) 1190–97
Philipp* 1198–1208
Otto IV 1198–1215
Friedrich II (*Frederick II*) 1215–50
Konrad IV* 1250–54
Konrad V 1254 (claimant)
Richard* 1257
Alfons* 1267
Rudolf I* 1273–91
Adolf* 1292–98
Albrecht I (*Albert I*) 1298–1308
Heinrich VII (*Henry VII*) 1308–13
Ludwig IV (*Louis IV*) 1314–47
Karl IV (*Charles IV*) 1347–78
Wenzel 1378–1400
Rupprecht Klem* 1400–10
Sigismund 1410–37
Albrecht II* (*Albert II*) 1438–39
Friedrich III (*Frederick III*) 1440–93
Maximilian I 1493–1519
Karl V (*Charles V*) 1519–55
Ferdinand I 1556–64
Maximilian II 1564–76
Rudolf II 1576–1612
Matthias 1612–19
Ferdinand II 1619–37
Ferdinand III 1637–57
Leopold I 1658–1705
Joseph I 1705–11
Karl VI (*Charles*) 1711–40
Karl III (*Charles*) 1742–45
Franz I Stephan (*Francis I*) 1745–65
Joseph II 1765–90
Leopold II 1790–92
Franz II (*Francis II*) 1792–1806 when he abdicated and abolished the Holy Roman Empire; see Austria

Key: * = emperor-elect. Frederick III was the last emperor to go to Rome for coronation; all succeeding emperors assumed the imperial title upon election.

CHILE

PRESIDENTS (since 1946)
Juan Antonio Rios *Radical* 1942–46
Alfredo Duhalde *interim* 1946
Admiral Vicente Merino Bielech *interim* 1946
Gabriel González Videla *Radical* 1946–52
Carlos Ibáñez del Campo *Coalition* 1952–58
Jorge Alessandri *Con-Lib* 1958–64
Eduardo Frei *Christian Democrat* 1964–70
Salvador Allende *Marxist* 1970–73 (killed)
Gen. Augusto Pinochet *military* 1973–90
Patricio Aylwin *Christian Democrat* 1990–

CHINA

MANCHU EMPERORS
Shun-Chih 1644–61
Kangxi 1661–1722
Yangzheng 1722–35
Qian-long 1735–96
Jiajiang 1796–1820
Daoguang 1821–50
Xian Feng 1851–61
Tongzhi 1862–75
Guangxu 1875–1908
Xuan Zong (personal name *Puyi*) 1908–12

PRESIDENTS (Republic of China)
In all there were 15 presidents or claimants to the
presidency of China between 1912 and 1949; the more
notable included:
Sun Yixian (*Sun Yat-sen*) 1912, 1917–25
Gen. Yuan Shikai 1912–16
Jiang Jie Shi (*Chiang Kai-shek*) 1928–31, 1943–49

PRESIDENTS (People's Republic)
Mao Zedong 1949–58
Marshal Zhu De 1958–59
Liu Shaoqui 1959–68
Dung Pi Wu 1968–75
(No president 1975–83)
Li Xiannian* 1983–88
Yang Shangkun 1988–93
Jiang Zemin 1993–

PRIME MINISTERS (since 1949)
Zhou Enlai 1949–76
Hua Guofeng* 1976–80
Zhao Ziyang 1980–87
Li Peng 1987–

LEADERS OF THE COMMUNIST PARTY
Mao Zedong 1949–76
Hua Guofeng* 1976–81
Hu Yaobang 1981–87
Zhao Ziyang 1987–89
Jiang Zemin 1989–

Key: * Since 1977 Deng Xiaoping has been the
effective ruler of China although he has not held any
of the three major offices of state.

CHINA, REPUBLIC OF (TAIWAN)

PRESIDENTS
Gen. Li Tsung-jen *KMT* 1949–50
Chiang Kai-shek (*Jiang Jie Shi*) *KMT* 1950–75
Dr Yen Chia-kan *KMT* 1975–78
Chiang Ching-kuo *KMT*1978–88
Lee Teng-hui *KMT* 1988–
Key: *KMT* = Kuomintang

CZECH REPUBLIC

PRESIDENTS (of Czechoslovakia)
Tomás Garrigue Masaryk 1918–35
Edvard Beneš 1935–38
Gen. Jan Sirovy 1938
Dr Emil Hacha 1938–39 when Czechoslovakia was
overrun by German forces
(German occupation 1939–45)
Edvard Beneš *np* 1940–45 (in exile); 1945–48
Klemens Gottwald *Comm* 1945–53
Antonín Zapotocky *Comm* 1953–57
Antonín Novotny *Comm* 1957–68
Gen. Ludvik Svoboda *Comm* 1968–75
Dr Gustáv Husák *Comm* 1975–89
Vaclav Havel *CF* 1989–92

PRIME MINISTERS* (1946–92)
Klemens Gottwald *Comm* 1946–48
Antonín Zapotocky *Comm* 1948–53
Viliam Siroky *Comm* 1953–63
Josef Lenart *Comm* 1963–68
Oldrich Cernik *Comm* 1968–70
Lubomir Strougal *Comm* 1970–88
Ladislav Adamec *Comm* 1988–89
Marian Calfa *CF-PAV coalition* 1989–92
Vaclav Klaus *CDU* 1992

PRESIDENT OF THE CZECH REPUBLIC
Vaclav Havel 1993–

PRIME MINISTER OF THE CZECH REPUBLIC
Vaclav Klaus *CDU* 1993–

Key: *CDU* = Civic Democratic Union
CF = Civic Forum
Comm = Communist
np = non-party
PAV = Public Against Violence
* From 1948 to 1989 the effective ruler of Czechoslo-
vakia was the leader of the Communist Party; the
more notable included: Rudolf Slánský 1948–52;
Antonín Novotny 1953–68; Alexander Dubček
1968–69; Gustáv Husák 1969–87

DENMARK

PRIME MINISTERS (since 1945)
Vilhelm Buhl *Coalition* 1945
Knud Kristensen *Lib* 1945–47
Hans Hedtoft *Soc Dem* 1947–50
Erik Eriksen *Lib-Con* 1950–53
Hans Hedtoft *Soc Dem* 1953–55
Hans Christian Hansen *Soc Dem* 1955–60
Viggo Kampmann *Soc Dem* 1960
Jens Otto Krag *Soc Dem* 1960–68
Hilmar Baunsgaard *Radical* 1968–71
Jens Otto Krag *Soc Dem* 1971–72
Anker Jorgensen *Soc Dem* 1972–73
Poul Hartling *Lib* 1973–75
Anker Jorgensen *Soc Dem* 1975–82
Poul Schlüter *Lib-Con* 1982–93
Poul Nyrup Rasmussen *Soc Dem* 1993–

Key: *Con* = Conservative
Lib = Liberal
Soc Dem = Social Democrat

EGYPT (Modern)

KINGS
Fuad I 1922–36
Faruq 1936–1952
Fuad II 1952–53

PRESIDENTS

Gen. Muhammad Neguib *military* 1952–54
Col. Gamal Abdel Nasser *military* 1954–70
Anwar Sadat *NDP* 1970–81 (assassinated)
Gen. Muhammad Hosni Mubarak *NDP* 1981–
Key: *NDP* = National Democratic Party

FINLAND

PRESIDENTS

Dr Kaarlo Juho Stahlberg *NPP* 1919–25
Lauri Relander *AP* 1925–31
Dr Pehr Svinhufvud *Coalition* 1931–37
Kyösti Kallio *Coalition* 1937–40
Risto Ryti *Coalition* 1940–44
Marshal Carl Gustav Mannerheim *Coalition* 1944–46
Juhi Kusti Paasikiva *Coalition* 1946–56
Dr Urho Kaleva Kekkonen *AP* 1956–82
Mauno Henrik Koïvisto *Soc Dem* 1982–
Key: *AP* = Rural Party
NPP = National Progressive Party
Soc Dem = Social Democrat

FRANCE

KINGS (since 987)

Hugues 987–996
Robert II 996–1031
Henri I 1031–60
Philippe I 1060–1108
Louis VI 1108–37
Louis VII 1137–80
Philippe II 1180–1223
Louis VIII 1223–26
Louis IX (St Louis) 1226–70
Philippe III 1270–85
Philippe IV 1285–1314
Louis X 1314–16
Jean I 1316
Philippe V 1316–22
Charles IV 1322–28
Philippe VI 1328–50
Jean II 1350–64
Charles V 1364–80
Charles VI 1380–1422
Charles VII 1422–61
Louis XI 1461–83
Charles VIII 1483–98
Louis XII 1498–1515
François I 1515–47
Henri II 1547–59
François II 1559–60
Charles IX 1560–74
Henri III 1574–89
Henri IV 1589–1610
Louis XIII 1610–43
Louis XIV 1643–1715
Louis XV 1715–74
Louis XVI 1774–92
(Louis XVII nominally 1793–95)

FIRST REPUBLIC

The Convention 1792–1795
Directorate 1795–99
Consulate (three consuls) 1799–1804

EMPEROR (First Empire)

Napoleon I (Bonaparte) 1804–14

KING

Louis XVIII 1814–15

EMPERORS (First Empire)

Napoleon I (restored) 1815
(Napoleon II nominally 1815, for 16 days)

KINGS

Louis XVIII (restored) 1815–24
Charles X 1824–30
(Louis XIX nominally 1830, for 1 day)
(Henri V nominally 1830, for 8 days)
Louis-Philippe 1830–48

PRESIDENT OF SECOND REPUBLIC

Louis-Napoleon Bonaparte 1848–52

EMPEROR (Second Empire)

Napoleon III (Louis-Napoleon Bonaparte) 1852–70

PRESIDENTS OF THIRD REPUBLIC

Adolphe Thiers 1871–73
Patrice Mac-Mahon, duc de Magenta 1873–79
Jules Grévy 1879–87
Sadi Carnot 1887–94 (assassinated)
Jean Casimir-Périer 1894–95
Félix Faure 1895–99
Émile Loubet 1899–1906
Armand Fallières 1906–13
Raymond Poincaré 1913–20
Paul Deschanel 1920
Alexandre Millerand 1920–24
Gaston Doumergue 1924–31
Paul Doumer 1931–32 (assassinated)
Albert Lebrun 1932–40

FRENCH STATE (at Vichy)

Philippe Pétain 1940–44

HEADS OF PROVISIONAL GOVERNMENT

General Charles de Gaulle 1944–46
Félix Gouin 1946
Georges Bidault 1946
Vincent Auriol 1946
Léon Blum 1946–47

PRESIDENTS OF FOURTH REPUBLIC

Vincent Auriol 1947–54
René Coty 1954–58

PRESIDENTS OF FIFTH REPUBLIC

General Charles de Gaulle 1959–69
Georges Pompidou 1969–74
Valéry Giscard d'Estaing 1974–81
François Mitterand 1981–

PRIME MINISTERS OF THIRD REPUBLIC

In all there were 88 PMs of the Third Republic; the
more notable included:
Léon Gambetta 1881–82
Georges Clemenceau 1906–09, 1917–20
Aristide Briand 1909–11, 1913, 1915–17, 1921–22,
1925–26, 1929
Raymond Poincaré 1912–13, 1922–24, 1926–29
Édouard Herriot 1924–25, 1926, 1932
Pierre Laval 1931–32, 1935–36
Édouard Daladier 1933, 1934, 1938–40
Léon Blum 1936–37, 1938

HEADS OF GOVERNMENT OF FRENCH STATE

The head of the Vichy government was the Vice
President of the Council; occupants of the post
included:
Pierre Laval 1940; 1942–44

PRIME MINISTERS OF FOURTH REPUBLIC

In all there were 24 PMs of the Fourth Republic; the
more notable included:

Robert Schuman 1947–1948; 1948
Pierre Mendès-France 1954–55
General Charles de Gaulle 1958–59

PRIME MINISTERS OF FIFTH REPUBLIC
Michel Debré *Gaullist* 1959–62
Georges Pompidou *Gaullist* 1962–68
Maurice Couve de Murville *Gaullist* 1968–69
Jacques Chaban-Delmas *Gaullist* 1969–72
Pierre Messmer *Gaullist* 1972–74
Jacques Chirac *Gaullist* 1974–76
Raymond Barre *np* 1976–81
Pierre Mauroy *Soc* 1981–84
Laurent Fabius *Soc* 1984–86
Jacques Chirac *Gaullist* 1986–88
Michel Rocard *Soc* 1988–91
Edith Cresson *Soc* 1991–92
Pierre Beregovoy *Soc* 1992–93
Edouard Balladur *Gaullist* 1993–
Key: *np* = non-party
Soc = Socialist

GERMANY

KINGS OF PRUSSIA
Friedrich I 1701–13
Friedrich Wilhelm I 1713–40
Friedrich II (*Frederick the Great*) 1740–86
Friedrich Wilhelm II 1786–97
Friedrich Wilhelm III 1797–1840
Friedrich Wilhelm IV 1840–61
Wilhelm I 1861–71 when he also became Emperor
of Germany

EMPERORS OF GERMANY
Wilhelm I 1871–88
Friedrich III 1888
Wilhelm II 1888–1918

PROVISIONAL GOVERNMENT
Six-man ruling council 1918–19

PRESIDENTS
Friedrich Ebert 1919–25
Marshal Paul von Beneckendorff und von
Hindenburg 1925–34

LEADERS OF THE THIRD GERMAN REICH
Adolf Hitler 1934–45
Admiral Karl Dönitz 1945 (6 days)

ALLIED OCCUPATION
1945–49

PRESIDENTS OF FEDERAL REPUBLIC
Prof. Theodor Heuss 1949–59
Dr Heinrich Lübke 1959–69
Dr Gustav Heinemann 1969–74
Walter Scheel 1974–79
Karl Carstens 1979–84
Richard von Weizsaecker 1984–

CHANCELLORS OF THE GERMAN EMPIRE
Otto, Prince von Bismarck-Schönhausen 1871–90
Count Leo von Caprivi 1890–94
Prince Chlodwig von Hohenlohe-Schillingsfürst
1894–1900
Prince Bernhard von Bülow 1900–09
Theobald von Bethmann-Hollweg 1909–17
Dr George Michaelis 1917
Count Georg von Hertling 1917

Prince Maximilian of Baden 1918
Friedrich Ebert 1918

CHANCELLORS OF THE REPUBLIC
Six man ruling council 1918–19
Philipp Scheidemann *SPD* 1919
Gustav Bauer *SPD* 1919–20
Hermann Müller *SPD* 1920
Konstantin Fehrenbach *Centre-Cath* 1920–21
Dr Joseph Wirth *Centre* 1921–22
Dr Wilhelm Cuno *np* 1922–23
Dr Gustav Stresemann *DVolk* 1923
Dr Wilhelm Marx *Centre* 1923–25
Dr Hans Luther *np* 1925–26
Dr Wilhelm Marx *Centre* 1926–28
Hermann Müller *SPD* 1928–30
Dr Heinrich Brüning *Centre* 1930–32
Franz von Papen *Nat* 1932
General Curt von Schleider *np* 1932–33
Adolf Hitler *Nazi* 1933–34

THE THIRD GERMAN REICH
1934–45 (see above)

ALLIED OCCUPATION
1945–49 (see above)

FEDERAL GERMAN CHANCELLORS
Konrad Adenauer *CDU* 1949–63
Prof Ludwig Erhard *CDU* 1963–1966
Dr Kurt Georg Kiesinger *CDU* 1966–1969
Dr Willy Brandt *SPD* 1969–1974
Walter Scheel *FDP* 1974
Helmut Schmidt *SPD* 1974–82
Helmut Kohl *CDU* 1982–
Key: *Cath* = Catholic
CDU = Christian Democrat (conservative)
DVolk = German People's Party
Nat = National Party
np = non-party
SPD = Social Democrat
FDP = Free Democratic Party

EAST GERMANY
The German Democratic Republic (East Germany),
which was established in the Soviet zone of occupa-
tion in 1949, united with the Federal Republic of
Germany in October 1990. Effective power was held
by the leader of the Socialist Unity Party (the
Communist Party); the more notable included:
Walter Ulbricht 1950–71
Erich Honecker 1971–89

GREECE

KINGS
Othon 1832–62
Giorgios I 1863–1913
Konstantinos I 1913–17
Alexandros 1917–20
Konstantinos I (restored) 1920–22
Giorgios II 1922–24

PRESIDENTS OF THE HELLENIC REPUBLIC
Admiral Pavlos Kondoriotis 1924–26
Gen. Theodoros Pangalos 1926
Admiral Pavlos Kondoriotis 1926–29
Alexandros Zaimis 1929–35

KINGS
Giorgios II (restored) 1935–47
Pavlos 1947–64
Konstantinos II 1964–73

PRESIDENTS OF THE HELLENIC REPUBLIC

Giorgios Papadopoulos 1973
Gen Phaedon Gizikis 1973–74
Mikael Stassinopoulos 1974–75
Konstantinos Tsatos 1975–85
Christos Sartzetakis 1985–90
Konstantinos Karamanlis 1990–

PRIME MINISTERS OF GREECE (since 1967)

Giorgios Papadopoulos *military* 1967–73
Spyros Markezinis *military* 1973
Adamantios Androutsopoulos *military* 1973–74
Konstantinos Karamanlis *NDP* 1974–80
Giorgios Rallis *NDP* 1980–84
Andreas Papandreou *PASOK* 1984–89
Tzannis Tzannetakis *caretaker* 1989
Yannis Grivas *caretaker* 1989–90
Xenefon Zolotas *caretaker* 1990
Konstantinos Mitsotakis *NDP* 1990–

Key: *NDP* = New Democracy Party (conservative)
PASOK = Panhellic Socialist Movement

HUNGARY

PRESIDENTS

Zoltan Tildy *SP* 1946–48
Arpad Szakasits *Comm* 1948–50
Sándor Rónai *Comm* 1950–52
István Dobi *Comm* 1952–67
Pál Losonczi *Comm* 1967–87
Károly Németh *Comm* 1987–88
Bruno Straub *Comm* 1988–89
Mátyás Szuros *caretaker* 1989–90
Arpad Goncz *AFD* 1990–

PRIME MINISTERS* (since 1948)

István Dobi *Comm* 1948–52
Mátyás Rákosi *Comm* 1952–53
Imre Nagy *Comm* 1953–55
Andras Hegedus *Comm* 1955–56
Imre Nagy *Comm* 1956
Janos Kadar *Comm* 1956–58
Dr Ferenc Münnich *Comm* 1958–61
Janos Kadar *Comm* 1961–65
Gyula Kallai *Comm* 1965–67
Jenö Fock *Comm* 1967–75
György Lázár *Comm* 1975–87
Károly Grocz *Comm* 1987–88
Miklos Németh *Comm* 1988–90
Joszef Antall *DF* 1990–

Key: *AFD* = Alliance of Free Democrats (liberal)
Comm = Communist
DF = Democratic Forum (conservative)
SP = Smallholders' Party
* From 1948 to 1989 the effective ruler of Hungary was the leader of Socialist Workers' (Communist) Party; the more notable included: Mátyás Rákosi 1949–53 and 1953–56; Janos Kadar 1956–88

INDIA

PRESIDENTS

Dr Rajendra Prasad 1949–62
Dr Sarvapalli Radhakrishnan 1962–67
Dr Zahir Hussain 1967–69
Varahgiri Venkata Giri 1969–74
Fakhruddin Ali Ahmed 1974–77
Basappa Danappa Jatti 1977
Neelam Sanjiva Reddy 1977–82
Giani Zail Singh 1982–87
Ramaswamy Venkataraman 1987–

PRIME MINISTERS

Jawaharlal Nehru *Congress* 1949–64
Gulzarilal Nanda *Congress* 1964
Lal Bahadur Shastri *Congress* 1964–66
Gulzarilal Nanda *Congress* 1966
Indira Gandhi *Congress (I)* 1966–77
Morarji Desai *Janata* 1977–79
Charan Singh *Janata* 1979–80
Indira Gandhi *Congress (I)* 1980–84 (assassinated)
Rajiv Gandhi *Congress (I)* 1984–89
Vishwanath Pratap Singh *Coalition* 1989–90
Chandra Shekhar *Coalition* 1990–91
P.V. Narasimha Rao *Congress (I)* 1991–

INDONESIA

PRESIDENTS

Dr Muhammad Achmed Sukarno *np* 1949–67
Gen. T.N.I. Suharto *Golkar* 1967–

Key: *np* = non-party

IRAN

SHAHS (from 1796)

Agha Muhammad Khan 1796–97 (assassinated)
Fath 'Ali Shah 1797–1834
Muhammad Shah 1834–48
Naser od-Din Shah 1848–96 (assassinated)
Mozaffar od-Din Shah 1896–1907
Muhammad 'Ali Shah 1907–09
Ahmed Mirza Shah 1909–25
Reza Shah Pahlavi 1925–41
Muhammad Reza Shah Pahlavi 1941–79

PRESIDENTS

Islamic Council 1979–80
Abdolhasan Bani–Sadr 1980
Presidential Council 1980–81
Muhammad Ali Rajai 1981
Ali Khamenei 1981–89
Hashemi Rafsanjani 1989–

THE REPUBLIC OF IRELAND

PRESIDENTS

Dr Douglas Hyde 1938–45
Sean Thomas O'Kelly 1945–59
Eamon de Valera 1959–73
Erskine Childers 1973–74
Cearbhall O'Dalaigh 1974–76
Dr Patrick Hillery 1976–90
Mary Robinson 1990–

HEAD OF GOVERNMENT (before 1937 Executive President; since 1937 Taoiseach)

Arthur Griffith *Rep* 1922
Michael Collins *Rep* 1922
William Thomas Cosgrave *FG* 1922–32
Eamon de Valera *FF* 1932–48
John Costello *FG* 1948–51
Eamon de Valera *FF* 1951–54
John Costello *FG* 1954–57
Eamon de Valera *FF* 1957–59
Sean Lemass *FF* 1959–66
John Mary (Jack) Lynch *FF* 1966–73
Liam Cosgrave *FG-Lab* 1973–77
John Mary (Jack) Lynch *FF* 1977–79
Charles Haughey *FF* 1979–81
Garret Fitzgerald *FG-Lab* 1981–82
Charles Haughey *FF* 1982

Garret Fitzgerald *FG-Lab* 1982–87
Charles Haughey *FF* 1987–92
Albert Reynolds *FF-Lab* 1992–
Key: *FF* = Fianna Fail
FG = Fine Gael
Lab = Labour
Rep = Republican

ISRAEL

PRIME MINISTERS
David Ben Gurion *Mapai* 1948–53
Moshe Sharett *Mapai* 1953–55
David Ben Gurion *Mapai* 1955–63
Levi Eshkol *Mapai* 1963–69
Gen. Yigal Allon *Lab* 1969
Golda Meir *Lab* 1969–74
Itzhak Rabin *Lab* 1974–77
Menahem Begin *Likud* 1977–83
Itzhak Shamir *Likud* 1983–84
Shimon Peres *Coalition* 1984–86
Itzhak Shamir *Coalition** 1986–92
Itzhak Rabin *Lab* 1992–
Key: *Lab* = Labour (formed from Mapai in 1968)
* from 1990 *Likud*

ITALY

KINGS
Vittorio Emanuele II 1861–78
Umberto I 1878–1900 (assassinated)
Vittorio Emanuele III 1900–46
Umberto II 1946

PRESIDENTS
Alcide de Gasperi 1946
Enrico de Nicola 1946–48
Luigi Einaudi 1948–55
Giovanni Gronchi 1955–62
Antonio Segni 1962–64
Giuseppe Saragat 1964–71
Giovanni Leone 1971–78
Amintore Fanfani (acting) 1978
Alessandro Pertini 1978–85
Francesco Cossiga 1985–92
Oscar Luigi Scalfaro 1992–

PRIME MINISTERS OF THE KINGDOM OF ITALY
In all there were 42 PMs of the Kingdom of Italy; the more notable included:
Camillo Benso, Count Cavour 1861
Francesco Crispi 1879–81, 1893–96
Giovanni Giolitti 1892–93, 1903–05, 1911–14, 1920–21
Francesco Nitti 1919–20
Benito Mussolini 1922–43
Marshal Pietro Badoglio 1943–44
Alcide de Gasperi 1945–46

PRIME MINISTERS OF THE REPUBLIC
Alcide de Gasperi *CD Coalition* 1946–53
Giuseppe Pella *CD Coalition* 1953–54
Amintore Fanfani *CD Coalition* 1954
Mario Scelba *CD Coalition* 1954–55
Antonio Segni *CD Coalition* 1955–57
Adone Zoli *CD Coalition* 1957–58
Amintore Fanfani *CD Coalition* 1958–59
Antonio Segni *CD Coalition* 1959–60
Fernando Tambroni *CD Coalition* 1960
Amintore Fanfani *CD Coalition* 1960–63
Giovanni Leone *CD Coalition* 1963
Aldo Moro *CD Coalition* 1963–68
Giovanni Leone *CD Coalition* 1968
Mariano Rumor *CD Coalition* 1968–70

Emilio Colombo *CD Coalition* 1970–72
Giulio Andreotti *CD Coalition* 1972–73
Mariano Rumor *CD Coalition* 1973–74
Aldo Moro *CD Coalition* 1974–76
Giulio Andreotti *CD Coalition* 1976–79
Ugo La Malfa *Rep Coalition* 1979
Giulio Andreotti *CD Coalition* 1979
Francesco Cossiga *CD Coalition* 1979–80
Arnaldo Forlani *CD Coalition* 1980–81
Giovanni Spadolini *Coalition* 1981–82
Amintore Fanfani *CD Coalition* 1982–83
Bettino Craxi *Soc Coalition* 1983–87
Amintore Fanfani *CD Coalition* 1987
Giovanni Goria *CD Coalition* 1987–88
Ciriaco De Mita *CD Coalition* 1988–90
Giulio Andreotti *CD Coalition* 1990–92
Giuliano Amato *Soc Coalition* 1992–93
Carlo Azeglio Ciampi *non-party* 1993–
Key: *CD* = Christian Democrat
Coalition = some of the periods indicated as government by coalition included more than one coalition
Rep = Republican
Soc = Socialist

JAPAN

EMPERORS (since 1763)
Gosakuramachi 1763–71
Gomomozono 1771–79
Kokaku 1779–1817
Ninko 1817–46
Komei (*personal name* Osahito) 1846–66
Meiji (*personal name* Mutsuhito) 1867–1912
Taisho (*personal name* Yoshihito) 1912–26
Showa (*personal name* Hirohito) 1926–89
Heisei (*personal name* Akihito) 1989–

PRIME MINISTERS OF JAPAN (since 1945)
Kijuro Shidehara *np* 1945–46
Ichiro Hatayma *Lib* 1946
Shigeru Yoshida *np* 1946–47
Tetsu Katayama *Soc* 1947–48
Hitoshi Ashida *Coalition* 1948
Shigeru Yoshida *Lib* 1948–55
Ichiro Hatoyama *Lib-Dem* 1955–56
Tanzan Ishibashi *Lib-Dem* 1956–1957
Nobusuke Kishi *Lib-Dem* 1957–60
Hayeto Ikeda *Lib-Dem* 1960–64
Eisaku Sato *Lib-Dem* 1964–72
Kakeui Tanaka *Lib-Dem* 1972–74
Takeo Miki *Lib-Dem* 1974–76
Takeo Fukuda *Lib-Dem* 1976–78
Masayoshi Ohira *Lib-Dem* 1978–80
Zenko Suzuki *Lib-Dem* 1980–82
Yasuhiro Nakasone *Lib-Dem* 1982–87
Noboru Takeshita *Lib-Dem* 1987–89
Sosuke Uno *Lib-Dem* 1989
Toshiki Kaifu *Lib-Dem* 1989–91
Kiichi Miyazawa *Lib-Dem* 1991–
Key: *Lib* = Liberal
Lib-Dem = Liberal Democrat
np = non-party
Soc = Socialist

KOREA

PRESIDENTS OF SOUTH KOREA
Dr Syngman Rhee *Lib* 1948–60
Huh Chung *acting* 1960
Yun Po Sun *Dem* 1960–62
Gen. Park Chung Hi *military-DRP* 1962–1980
  (assassinated)
Choi Kyu Hah *DRP* 1980

Gen. Chun Doo Hwan *military-DJP* 1980–87
Roh Tae Woo *DJP/DLP* 1987–93
Kim Young Sam *DLP* 1993–

Key: *Lib* = Liberal
DJP = Democratic Justice Party
DLP = Democratic Liberal Party
DRP = Democratic Reunification Party
Dem = Democrat

MEXICO

PRESIDENTS

There have been over 80 presidents of Mexico; the more notable before 1924 included:
Gen. Antonio López de Santa Anna 1833–35, 1839, 1842, 1843, 1844
Gen. Benito Juárez 1858, 1859–61, 1867–72
Gen. Porfirio Diáz 1877–80, 1884–1911

Presidents since 1924
Gen. Plutarco Elías Calles *PRI* 1924–28
Emilio Portes Gil *PRI* 1928–30
Pascual Ortiz Rubio *PRI* 1930–32
Gen. Abelardo Rodríguez *PRI* 1932–34
Gen. Lázardo Cárdenas *PRI* 1934–40
Gen. Manuel Ávila Camacho *PRI* 1940–46
Miguel Alemán Valdès *PRI* 1946–52
Adolfo Ruiz Cortines *PRI* 1952–58
Adolfo López Mateos *PRI* 1958–64
Dr Gustavo Díaz Ordaz *PRI* 1964–70
Luis Echeverría Alvárez *PRI* 1970–76
José López Portillo *PRI* 1976–82
Miguel de la Madrid Hurtado *PRI* 1982–88
Carlos Salinas de Gortari *PRI* 1988–

Key: *PRI* = Institutional Revolutionary Party (so-named since 1929)

NETHERLANDS

KINGS AND QUEENS

Willem I 1815–40
Willem II 1840–49
Willem III 1849–90
Wilhelmina 1890–1948
Juliana 1948–80
Beatrix 1980–

MOGUL EMPERORS

Babur 1526–30
Humayan 1530–39
(Interregnum – usurpers 1539–55)
Humayan (restored) 1555–56
Akbar 1556–1605
Jahangir 1605–27
Dawar Bakhsh 1627–28
Shah Jahan 1628–58
Aurangzeb Alamgir I 1658–1707
Bahadur Shah I (*also known as Shah Alam I*) 1707–12
Farrukhsiyar 1713–19 (assassinated)
Rafi-ud-Daulat 1719
Shah Jahan II 1719 (assassinated)
Nikusiyar 1719 (assassinated)
Muhammad Shah 1719–20
Muhammad Ibrahim 1720
Muhammad Shah (restored) 1720–48
Ahmad Shah 1748–54
Alamgir II 1754–59 (assassinated)
Shah Jahan III 1759–60
Shah Alam II 1759–1802 when he became King of Delhi

PRIME MINISTERS (since 1945)
Prof. Willem Schermerhorn *Lab-Cath* 1945–46
Dr Louis Beel *Cath-Lab* 1946–48
Dr Willem Drees *Lab-Cath* 1948–58
Dr Louis Beel *Cath-led coalition* 1958–59
Prof. Jan de Quay *Cath-led coalition* 1959
Dr Louis Beel *Cath-led coalition* 1959
Prof. Jan de Quay *Cath-led coalition* 1959–63
Dr Victor Marijnen *Cath-led coalition* 1963–65
Dr Joseph Cals *Cath-led coalition* 1965–66
Prof. Jelle Zijstra *Cath-led coalition* 1966–67
Petrus de Jong *Cath-led coalition* 1967–71
Barend Biesheuvel *Cath-led coalition* 1971–73
Dr Johannes den Uyl *Lab-led coalition* 1973–77
Andreas van Agt *CDA-led coalition* 1977–82
Rudolph Lubbers *CDA-led coalition* 1982–

Key: *Cath* = Catholic (merged with another confessional party to form Christian Democratic Appeal in 1980)
CD = Christian Democratic Appeal
Lab = Labour

NEW ZEALAND

PRIME MINISTERS OF THE DOMINION

Sir Joseph Ward *Lib* 1907–12
William Fergusson Massey *Ref* 1912–25
Sir Francis Bell *Ref* 1925
Joseph Gordon Coates *Ref* 1925–28
Sir Joseph Ward *UP* 1928–30
George Forbes *Ref-UP* 1930–35
Michael Joseph Savage *Lab* 1935–40
Peter Fraser *Lab* 1940–49
Sir Sidney George Holland *Nat* 1949–57
Sir Keith Jacka Holyoake *Nat* 1957
Sir Walter Nash *Lab* 1957–60
Sir Keith Jacka Holyoake *Lab* 1960–72
Sir John Ross Marshall *Nat* 1972
Norman Eric Kirk *Lab* 1972–74
Hugh Watt (acting PM) *Lab* 1974
Wallace Rowling *Lab* 1974–75
Sir Robert David Muldoon *Nat* 1975–84
David Lange *Lab* 1984–89
Geoffrey Palmer *Lab* 1989–90
Michael Moore *Lab* 1990
Jim Bolger *Nat* 1990–

Key: *Lab* = Labour
Lib = Liberal (succeeded by the United Party in 1927)
Nat = National Party (formed from a merger of the Reform Party and the United Party in 1936)
Ref = Reform Party
UP = United Party

NIGERIA

PRESIDENTS

Dr Nnamdi Azikiwe *NCNC* 1963–66
Dr Nwafor Orizu *caretaker* 1966
Gen Johnson Aguiyi-Ironsi* *military* 1966 (assassinated)
Gen Yakubu Gowon* *military* 1966–75
Brig Murtala Ramat Muhammad* *military* 1975–76 (assassinated)
Lieut-Gen Olusegun Obasanjo* *military* 1976–79
Alhaji Shehu Shagari *NPN* 1979–83
Gen Muhammadu Buhari *military* 1983–85
Gen Ibrahim Babangida *military* 1985–

Key: *NCNC* = National Council for Nigeria and the Cameroons
NPN = National Party of Nigeria
*Heads of state who did not assume the presidency.

NORWAY

KINGS (since independence restored)
Haakon VII 1905–51
Olav V 1951–91
Harald V 1991–

PRIME MINISTERS (since 1945)
Einar Gerhardsen *Lab* 1945–51
Oscar Torp *Lab* 1951–55
Einar Gerhardsen *Lab* 1955–63
Johan Lyng *Lib-CP-CPP* 1963
Einar Gerhardsen *Lab* 1963–65
Per Borten *CP-led coalition* 1965–71
Trygve Bratteli *Lab* 1971–72
Lars Korvald *Coalition* 1972–73
Trygve Bratteli *Lab* 1973–76
Odvar Nordli *Lab* 1976–81
Gro Harlem Bruntland *Lab* 1981
Kare Willoch *Con (from 1983 coalition)* 1981–86
Gro Harlem Bruntland *Lab* 1986–89
Jan Syse *Con-led coalition* 1989–90
Gro Harlem Brundtland *Lab* 1990–

Key: *CP* = Centre Party
CPP = Christian People's Party
Lab = Labour
Lib = Liberal

PAKISTAN

PRESIDENTS
Maj. Gen. Iskander Mirza 1956–58
Gen. Muhammad Ayub Khan 1958–69
Gen. Agha Muhammad Yahya Khan 1969–71
Zulfiqar Ali Bhutto 1971–73
Fazal Elahi Chaudhri 1973–78
Gen. Muhammad Zia ul-Haq 1978–88
Ghulam Ishaq Khan 1988–

PRIME MINISTERS
Liaquat Ali Khan *ML* 1947–51
Khwaja Nazimuddin *ML* 1951–53
Mohammed Ali *ML* 1953–55
Chaudhri Muhammad Ali *ML* 1955–56
Hussein Shaheed Suhrawardy *AL* 1956–57
Ismael Ibrahim Chundrigar *AL* 1957
Malik Firoz Khan Noon *AL* 1957–58
Gen. Muhammad Ayub Khan *military* 1958–69
Gen. Agha Muhammad Yahya Khan *milit.* 1969–71
Nural Amin *caretaker* 1971
Zulfiqar Ali Bhutto *PPP* 1971–77
Gen. Muhammad Zia ul-Haq *military* 1977–85
Muhammad Khan Junejo *ML* 1985–88
Gen. Muhammad Zia ul-Haq *military* 1988
(Period without a PM 1988)
Benazir Bhutto *PPP* 1988–90
Ghulam Mustafa Jatoi *IDA* 1990
Nawaz Sharif *IDA* 1990–93
Balkh Sher Mazari *caretaker* 1993
Nawaz Sharif *IDA* 1993–

Key: *AL* = Awami League
IDA = Islamic Democratic Alliance
ML = Muslim League
PPP = Pakistan People's Party

PHILIPPINES

PRESIDENTS
Manuel Roxas *Lib* 1946–48
Elphino Quirino *Lib* 1948–53
Rámon Magsaysay *Nat* 1953–57
Carlos Polestico Garcia *Nat* 1957–61
Diosdado Macapagal *Lib* 1961–65
Ferdinand Marcos *Nat* 1965–86
Corazón Aquino *UNIDO* 1986–92

Gen. Fidel Ramos *PPP* 1992–
Key: *Lib* = Liberal
Nat = Nacionalista
PPP = People Power Party

POLAND

PRESIDENTS†
Marshal Jósef Pilsudski* *PPS* 1918–22
Gabriel Narutowicz *caretaker* 1922
Stanislaw Wojciechowski *np* 1922–26
Prof Ignacy Móscicki *np* 1926–39
(Poland under German occupation 1939–44)
Boleslaw Bierut *Comm* 1944–52
Aleksander Zawadski *Comm* 1952–64
Edward Ochab *Comm* 1964–68
Marshal Marian Spychalski *Comm* 1968–70
Józef Cyrankiewicz *Comm* 1970–72
Prof Henryk Jablonski *Comm* 1972–85
Gen. Wojciech Jaruzelski *Comm* 1985–1990
Lech Walesa *Solidarity* 1990–

PRIME MINISTERS (since 1949)
Józef Cyrankiewicz *Comm* 1949–52
Boleslaw Bierut *Comm* 1952–54
Józef Cyrankiewicz *Comm* 1954–70
Piotr Jaroszewicz *Comm* 1970–80
Edward Babiuch *Comm* 1980
Józef Pinkowski *Comm* 1980–81
Gen. Wojciech Jaruzelski *Comm* 1981–85
Prof. Zbigniew Messner *Comm* 1985–88
Dr Mieczyslaw Rakowski *Comm* 1988–89
Tadeusz Mazowiecki *Solidarity* 1989–91
Jan Krzysztof Bielecki *Solidarity* 1991
Jan Olszewski *Centre Alliance* 1991–92
Waldemar Pawlak *PPP* 1992
Hannah Suchocka *Dem U* 1992–

Key: *Comm* = Communist
Dem U = Democratic Union
np = non-party
PPP = Polish Peasant Party
PPS = Polish Socialist Party
* Pilsudski was military dictator of Poland 1926–35
† From 1945 to 1989 the effective ruler of Poland was the leader of the Communist Party; the more notable included: Boleslaw Bierut 1945–56; Wladyslaw Gomulka 1956–70; Edward Gierek 1970–89

PORTUGAL

PRESIDENTS
Dr Téofilo Braga 1910–11
Dr Manuel da Arriaga 1911–15
Dr Téofilo Braga 1915
Dr Bernardino Luis Machado 1915–17
Major Cardoso da Silva Pais 1917–18
Admiral João da Canto e Castro 1918–19
Dr Antonio José de Almeida 1919–23
Manoel Teixeira Gomes 1923–25
Dr Bernardino Luis Machado 1925–26
Commander José Mendes Cabecadas 1926
Gen. Manoel Gomes de Costa 1926
Gen. Oscar de Carmona 1926–51
Marshal Francisco Craveiro Lopes 1951–58
Admiral Américo Tomás 1958–74
Gen. Antonio de Spinola 1974
Gen. Francisco da Costa Gomes 1974–76
Gen. Antonio Ramalho Eanes 1976–86
Dr Mário Lopés Soares 1986–

PRIME MINISTERS (since 1932)
Dr Antonio de Oliveira Salazar *NU* 1932–68
Prof. Marcelo Caetano *NU* 1968–74
Gen. Antônio de Spinola *MFA* 1974
Prof. Adelino da Palma Carlos *MFA-Soc-Comm* 1974

Col. Vasco dos Santos Goncalves   *Soc-Comm* 1974–75
Admiral José Pinheiro de Azevedo   *Soc-Comm* 1975–1976
Commander Vasco Almeida e Costa   *Coalition* 1976
Dr Mário Lopés Soares   *Soc* 1976–78
Prof. Carlos Mota Pinto   *Coalition* 1978–79
Dr Maria de Lourdes Pintasilgo   *caretaker* 1979–80
Dr Francisco sá Carneiro   *AD* 1980
Dr Francisco Pinto Balsemão   *AD* 1980–82
Prof. Diogo Freitas do Amaral   *Coalition* 1982–83
Dr Mário Lopés Soares   *Soc* 1983–85
Anibal Cavaco Silva   *PSD* 1985–

Key: *AD* = Democratic Alliance
Comm = Communist
MFA = Armed Forces Movement
NU = National Union
PSD = Social Democrat
Soc = Socialist

ROMANIA

KINGS

Carol I 1881–1914
Ferdinand I 1914–27
Mihai I 1927–30
Carol II 1930–40
Mihai I (restored) 1940–47

PRESIDENTS

Prof. Constantin Parhon   *Comm* 1948–52
Dr Petru Groza   *Comm* 1952–58
Ion Gheorghe Maurer   *Comm* 1958–61
Gheorghe Gheorghiu-Dej   *Comm* 1961–65
Chivu Stoica   *Comm* 1965–67
Nicolae Ceausescu   *Comm* 1967–89
Ion Iliescu   *NSF* 1989–

Key: *Comm* = Communist
NSF = National Salvation Front

RUSSIA

TSARS (from 1533; after 1721 the tsar was officially styled emperor)
Ivan IV (*Ivan the Terrible*) 1533–84
Fyodor I (*Theodore I*) 1584–98
Boris (*Boris Godunov*) 1598–1605
Fyodor II (*Theodore II*) 1605
Dmitri 1605–06
Vasily IV 1606–10
Mikhail (*Michael*) 1613–45
Aleksey (*Alexei*) 1645–76
Fyodor III (*Theodore III*) 1676–82
Ivan V (co-Tsar) 1682–96
Piotr I (*Peter I; the Great*) 1682–1725
Ekaterina I (*Catherine I*) 1725–27
Piotr II (*Peter II*) 1727–30
Anna 1730–40
Ivan VI 1740–41
Elisaveta (*Elizabeth*) 1741–62
Piotr III (*Peter III*) 1762
Ekaterina II (*Catherine II; the Great*) 1762–96
Pavel (*Paul*) 1796–1801
Aleksandr I (*Alexander I*) 1801–25
Nikolai I (*Nicholas I*) 1825–55
Aleksandr II (*Alexander II*) 1855–81
Aleksandr III (*Alexander III*) 1881–94
Nikolai II (*Nicholas II*) 1894–1917

PRESIDENTS OF THE RUSSIAN FEDERATION

Yakov Sverdlov 1917–19
Mikhail Kalinin 1919–22

PRESIDENTS OF THE USSR

Mikhail Kalinin 1922–46
Nikolai Shvernik 1946–53

Marshal Kliment Voroshilov 1953–60
Leonid Ilich Brezhnev 1960–64
Anastas Mikoyan 1964–65
Nikolai Podgorny 1965–77
Leonid Ilich Brezhnev 1977–82
Vassili Kuznetsov (acting President) 1982–83
Yuri Andropov 1983–84
Konstantin Chernenko 1984–85
Andrei Gromyko 1985–88
Mikhail Gorbachov 1988–91

PRIME MINISTERS (1917–92)
Vladymir Ilich Lenin (*b. Ulyanov*) 1917–24
Aleksey Rykov 1924–30
Genrikh Yagoda 1930–31
Vyacheslav Molotov 1931–41
Marshal Josif Djugashvili Stalin 1941–53
Georgy Malenkov 1953–55
Marshal Nikolai Bulganin 1955–58
Nikita Khruschev 1958–64
Alexei Kosygin 1964–80
Nikolai Tikhonov 1980–85
Nikolai Ryzhkov 1985–1990
Valentin Pavlov 1990–91

USSR COMMUNIST PARTY LEADERS

Marshal Josif Djugashvili Stalin 1922–53
Nikita Khruschev 1953–64
Leonid Brezhnev 1964–82
Yuri Andropov 1982–84
Konstantin Chernenko 1984–85
Mikhail Gorbachov 1985–91

WOMEN PRESIDENTS AND PREMIERS

Sirimavo Bandaranaike PM of Sri Lanka 1960–65, 1970–77
Indhira Gandhi PM of India 1966–77, 1980–84
Golda Meir PM of Israel 1969–74
Isabel Perón president of Argentina 1974–75
Elisabeth Domitien PM of Central African Republic 1975–76
Soong Ching-ling acting head of state of China 1976–78
Margaret Thatcher PM of the United Kingdom 1979–90
Maria de Lourdes Pintassilgo PM of Portugal 1979–80
Lidia Gueiler Tejada president of Bolivia 1979–80
Vigdis Finnbogadottir president of Iceland 1980–
Eugenia Charles PM of Dominica 1980–
Gro Harlem Bruntland PM of Norway 1981, 1986–89, 1990–
Agatha Barbara president of Malta 1982–87
Milka Planinc PM of Yugoslavia 1982–86
Corazon Aquino president of the Philippines 1986–92
Benazir Bhutto PM of Pakistan 1988–90
Violetta Chamorro president of Nicaragua 1990–
Ertha Pascal-Trouillot president of Haiti 1990–91
Kazimiera Prunskiene PM of Lithuania 1990–91 (before Lithuania's independence was internationally recognized)
Mary Robinson president of Ireland 1990–
Edith Cresson PM of France 1991–92
Khalida Zia PM of Bangladesh 1991–
Hannah Suchocka PM of Poland 1992–

PRESIDENTS OF THE RUSSIAN FEDERATION
Boris Yeltsin 1991–

PREMIERS OF THE RUSSIAN FEDERATION
Ygor Gaidar (acting PM) 1992
Victor Chernomyrdin 1992–

SAUDI ARABIA

KINGS
Abdul Aziz (better known as *ibn Saud*) 1932–53
Saud 1953–64
Faisal 1964–75 (assassinated)
Khaled 1975–82
Fahd 1982–

SOUTH AFRICA

PRESIDENTS
Charles Robberts Swart *Nat* 1961–67
Jozua François Naudé *Nat* 1967–68
Jacobus Johannes Fouché *Nat* 1968–75
Dr Nicolaas Diederich *Nat* 1975–78
Balthazar John Vorster *Nat* 1978–79
Marais Viljoen *Nat* 1979–84
Pieter Willem Botha *Nat* 1984–89
Frederick Willem de Klerk *Nat* 1989–

PRIME MINISTERS (the post of Prime Minister was abolished in 1984)
Gen Louis Botha *SA* 1910–19
Field Marshal Jan Christiaan Smuts *SA* 1919–24
Gen James Barry Munnik Hertzog *Nat* 1924–39
Field Marshal Jan Christiaan Smuts *UP* 1939–48
Daniel François Malan *Nat* 1948–54
Johannes Gerhardhus Strijdom *Nat* 1954–58
Charles Robberts Swart *Nat* 1958
Hendrik Verwoerd *Nat* 1958–66 (assassinated)
Balthazar John Vorster *Nat* 1966–78
Pieter Willem Botha *Nat* 1978–84
Key: *Nat* = Nationalist Party
SA = South African Party
UP = United Party

SPAIN

KINGS*
Fernando V (*Ferdinand V*) 1474–1516
Isabel I (*Isabella I*) 1474–1504
Juana 1504–55
Felipe I (*Philip I*) 1504–06
Carlos I (*Emperor Charles V*) 1516–56
Felipe II (*Philip II*) 1556–98
Felipe III (*Philip III*) 1598–1621
Felipe IV (*Philip IV*) 1621–65
Carlos II (*Charles II*) 1665–1700
Felipe V (*Philip V*) 1700–24
Luis 1724
Felipe V (restored) 1724–46
Fernando VI (*Ferdinand VI*) 1746–59
Carlos III (*Charles III*) 1759–88
Carlos IV (*Charles IV*) 1788–1808
Fernando VII (*Ferdinand VII*) 1808
Carlos IV (restored) 1808
José (*Joseph Bonaparte*) 1808–13
Fernando VII (restored) 1813–33
Isabel II (*Isabella II*) 1833–68
(Regency 1868–70)
Amadeo 1870–73

PRESIDENTS OF THE FIRST REPUBLIC
Estanislao Figueras y Moragas 1873
Francisco José Pi y Margall 1873
Nicolás Salmerón 1873

Emilio Castelar y Ripoli 1873–74
Marshal Francisco Serrano y Domínguez 1874

KINGS
Alfonso XII 1874–85
Maria Cristina 1885–86
Alfonso XIII 1886–1931

PRESIDENTS OF THE SECOND REPUBLIC
Niceto Alcalá Zamora y Torres 1931–36
Manuel Azaña y Diaz 1936

LEADER (Caudillo) OF THE SPANISH STATE
Gen. Francisco Franco y Bahamonde 1936–75

KING
Juan Carlos I 1975–

PRIME MINISTERS(since 1936)
Gen. Francisco Franco y Bahamonde (Head of government) *Falange* 1936–73
Admiral Luis Carrero Blanco *Falange* 1973
Carlos Arias Navarro *np* 1973–75
Adolfo Suárez González *UCD* 1975–81
Leopoldo Calvo Sotelo *UCD* 1981–82
Felipe González *PSOE* 1982–
Key: *np* = non-party
PSOE = Socialist Workers' Party
UCD = Centre Democrat
* (including joint sovereigns)

SWEDEN

KINGS(since 1523)
Gustaf I Adolf 1523–60
Eric XIV 1560–68
Johan III 1568–92
Sigismund 1592–99
Carl IX 1599–1611
Gustaf II Adolf (*Gustavus Adolphus*) 1611–32
Christina 1632–54
Carl X Gustaf 1654–60
Carl XI 1660–97
Carl XII 1697–1718
Ulrika Eleonora 1718–26
Fredrik 1726–51
Adolf Fredrik 1751–71
Gustaf III 1771–92 (assassinated)
Gusfav IV Adolf 1792–1809
Carl XIII 1809–18
Carl XIV Johan 1818–44
Oscar I 1844–59
Carl XV 1859–72
Oscar II 1872–1907
Gustaf V 1907–50
Gustaf VI Adolf 1950–73
Carl XVI Gustaf 1973–

PRIME MINISTERS(since 1932)
Per Albin Hansson *Soc Dem* 1932–46
Tage Erlander *Soc Dem* 1946–69
Olof Palme *Soc Dem* 1969–76
Nils Olof Thorbjörn Fälldin *Centre* 1976–78
Ola Ullsten *Lib* 1978–79
Nils Olof Thorbjörn Fälldin *Centre* 1979–82
Olof Palme *Soc Dem* 1982–86 (assassinated)
Ingvar Carlsson *Soc Dem* 1986–91
Carl Bildt *Mod* 1991–
Key: *Lib* = Liberal
Soc Dem = Social Democrat
Mod = Moderate Party

THAILAND

KINGS (since 1782)
Rama I 1782–1809
Rama II 1809–24

Rama III (*Nang Klao*) 1824–51
Mongkut (*Rama IV*) 1851–68
Chulalongkorn (*Rama V*) 1868–1910
Vijiravudh (*Rama VI*) 1910–25
Prajadhipok (*Rama VII*) 1925–35
Ananda Mahidol (*Rama VIII*) 1935–46
Bhumipol (*Rama IX*) 1946–

PRIME MINISTERS (since 1958)
Field Marshal Sarit Thanarat *military* 1958–63
Gen Thanom Kittikachorn *military* 1963–73
Dr Sanya Thammasak *interim* 1973–75
Seni Pramoj *Democratic Party* 1975
Kukrit Pramoj *Social Action* 1975–76
Seni Pramoj *Democratic Party* 1976
Admiral Sa'ngad Chaloryoo *military* 1976
Thanin Kraivichien *interim* 1976–77
Gen. Kriangsak Chomanan *military* 1977–80
Gen. Prem Tinsulanonda *military/Social Action* 1980–88
Gen. Chatichai Choonhavan *Coalition* 1988–91
Anand Panyarachun *interim* 1991–92
Narong Wongwan *Coalition* 1992
Gen. Suchinda Kraprayoon *military* 1992
Anand Panyarachun *Coalition* 1992–

TURKEY
PRESIDENTS
Kemal Atatürk (*b. Mustafa Kemal*) *RPP* 1923–38
Gen Ismet Inönü *RPP* 1938–50
Gen Celal Bayer *DP* 1950–60
Gen Cemal Gürsel *military* 1960–66
Gen Cevdet Sunay *np* 1966–73
Admiral Fahri Korutürk *np* 1973–80
Gen Kenan Evren *military* 1980–89
Turgat Özal *MP* 1989–93
Hussmettin Cindoruk (acting) 1993
Suleyman Demirel *True Path* 1993–
Key: *DP* = Democrat
MP = Motherland Party
np = non-party
RPP = Republican People's Party

UNITED KINGDOM
See UK Chapter

UNITED STATES OF AMERICA
PRESIDENTS
George Washington *Fed* 1789–97
John Adams *Fed* 1797–1801
Thomas Jefferson *Dem Rep* 1801–09
James Madison *Dem Rep* 1809–17
James Monroe *Dem Rep* 1817–25
John Quincy Adams *Dem Rep* 1825–29
Andrew Jackson *Dem Rep* 1829–37
Martin Van Buren *Dem* 1837–41
William H. Harrison *Whig* 1841
John Tyler *Whig* 1841–45
James K. Polk *Dem* 1845–49
Zachary Taylor *Whig* 1849–50
Millard Fillmore *Whig* 1850–53
Franklin Pierce *Dem* 1853–57
James Buchanan *Dem* 1857–61
Abraham Lincoln *Rep* 1861–65 (assassinated)
Andrew Johnson *Dem U* 1865–69
Ulysses Simpson Grant (*b. Hiram Grant*) *Rep* 1869–77
John Tyler *Whig* 1841–45
James K. Polk *Dem* 1845–49
Zachary Taylor *Whig* 1849–50
Millard Fillmore *Whig* 1850–53
Franklin Pierce *Dem* 1853–57

James Buchanan *Dem* 1857–61
Abraham Lincoln *Rep* 1861–65 (assassinated)
Andrew Johnson *Dem U* 1865–69
Ulysses S. Grant (*b. Hiram Grant*) *Rep* 1869–77
Rutherford B. Hayes *Rep* 1877–81
James A. Garfield *Rep* 1881 (assassinated)
Chester A. Arthur *Rep* 1881–85
Grover Cleveland *Dem* 1885–89
Benjamin Harrison *Rep* 1889–93
Grover Cleveland *Dem* 1893–97
William McKinley *Rep* 1897–1901 (assassinated)
Theodore Roosevelt *Rep* 1901–09
William H. Taft *Rep* 1909–13

POLITICAL ASSASSINATIONS OF THE 20TH CENTURY

William McKinley (1843–1901). Republican president of the USA. Shot by an anarchist in Buffalo.
Alexander Obrenović, King of Serbia (1876–1903). His murder ended the Obrenović dynasty.
Carlos I, King of Portugal (1863–1908). Assassinated in Lisbon with his elder son Luis.
Archduke Franz Ferdinand (1863–1914), Archduke of Austria and heir to the Austrian throne. His assassiation in Sarajevo on 28 June 1914 by a Serbian nationalist precipitated the outbreak of World War I.
Engelbert Dollfuss (1892–1934), Austrian chancellor, assassinated by the Nazis.
Alexander I, King of Yugoslavia (1888–1934), assassinated by an agent of Croatian separatists while on a state visit to France.
Leon Trotsky (Lev Davidovich Bronstein; 1879–1940). Russian revolutionary murdered by one of Stalin's agents while in exile in Mexico.
Mohandas Karamchand (Mahatma) Gandhi (1869–1948). Indian religious and political leader assassinated by a Hindu extremist.
Abdullah, King of Jordan (1882–1951). Assassinated by a Palestinian nationalist.
Liaquat Ali Khan (1895–1951). Pakistani prime minister.
Feisal II, King of Iraq (1935–58). Assassinated with his uncle when an army revolt established a republic.
John Kennedy (1917–1963). Democrat president of the USA. Shot in Dallas by Lee Harvey Oswald, who was in turn shot dead by Jack Ruby.
Hendrik Frensch Verwoerd (1901–66). South African prime minister, assassinated in parliament.
Martin Luther King Jr (1929–68). Black American civil rights leader. He was shot by James Earl Ray in Memphis, Tennessee.
Robert Kennedy (1925–68). American statesman, assassinated by Sirhan Bissara Sirhan, a Jordanian Arab.
King Faisal of Saudi Arabia (1905–75). Assassinated by his nephew.
Anwar Sadat (1918–81). Egyptian president shot by four militant Islamic fundamentalists.
Indira Gandhi (1917–84). Indian prime minister, assassinated by a Sikh extremist.
Olof Palme (1927–86). Swedish prime minister, assassinated by an unknown assailant in Stockholm.
Rajiv Gandhi (1944–92). Indian statesman, killed by Tamil terrorists in a bomb explosion.

Woodrow Wilson *Dem* 1913–21
Warren Gamaliel Harding *Rep* 1921–23
Calvin Coolidge *Rep* 1923–29
Herbert C. Hoover *Rep* 1929–33
Franklin Delano Roosevelt *Dem* 1933–45
Harry S. Truman *Dem* 1945–53
Dwight D. Eisenhower *Rep* 1953–61
John Fitzgerald Kennedy *Dem* 1961–63
(assassinated)
Lyndon B. Johnson *Dem* 1963–69
Richard M. Nixon *Rep* 1969–74
Gerald R. Ford (*b. Leslie Lynch King*) *Rep* 1974–77
Jimmy Carter *Dem* 1977–81
Ronald Reagan *Rep* 1981–89
George Bush *Rep* 1989–93

William J. (Bill) Clinton *Dem* 1993–
Key: *Dem* = Democrat
Dem Rep = Democratic Republican
Dem U = Democrat (Union)
Fed = Federalist
Rep = Republican

VIETNAM
PRESIDENTS (of North Vietnam 1945–76; of united Vietnam since 1976)

Ho Chi Minh 1945–69
Ton Duc Thang 1969–80
Troung Chinh 1981–87
Vo Chi Cong 1987–

ROMAN EMPERORS

Claudian Emperors
Augustus (Octavianus) 27 BC–AD 14
Tiberius AD 14–37
Gaius Caesar (*better known as Caligula*) 37–41 (assassinated)
Claudius I 41–54
Nero 54–68
Later Claudian Emperors
Galba 68–69 (assassinated)
Otho 69
Vitellius 69 (assassinated)
Flavian Emperors
Vespasianus 69–79
Titus 79–81
Domitianus 81–96 (assassinated)
Antonine Emperors
Nerva 96–98
Trajanus 98–117
Hadrianus 117–38
Antoninus Pius 138–61
Lucius Verus 161–69
Marcus Aurelius 169–180
Commodus 180–192 (assassinated)
Emperors of African and Asian origin
(including co-emperors)
Pertinax 193 (assassinated)
Didius Julianus 193 (assassinated)
Septimius Severus 193–211
Marcus Aurelius Antoninus I (*better known as Caracalla*) 211–217 (assassinated)
Geta 209–12 (assassinated)
Macrinus 217–19 (assassinated)
Marcus Aurelius Antoninus II (*better known as Elagabalus*) 218–22 (assassinated)
Severus Alexander 222–35 (assassinated)
Maximinus 235–38 (assassinated)
Gordianus I 238
Gordianus II 238 (assassinated)
Pupienus Maximus 238 (assassinated)
Balbinus 238 (assassinated)
Gordianus III 238–44 (assassinated)
Philippus 244–49 (assassinated)
Decius 249–51 (assassinated)
Gallius 251–53 (assassinated)
Hostilianus 251
Aemilianus 253 (assassinated)
Valerianus 253–60
Gallienus 260–68 (assassinated)
Illyrian Emperors
Claudius II 268–70
Quintillus 270
Aurelianus 270–75 (assassinated)
Ulpia Severina (Empress) 275
Tacitus 275–76 (assassinated)
Florianus 276 (assassinated)

Probus 276–82 (assassinated)
Carus 282–83
Carinus 283–85
Numerianus 283–84 (assassinated)
Collegiate Emperors
(More than one emperor ruled at a time in a 'collegiate' system.)
Diocletianus 284–305
Maximianus 286–305
Constantius I (*better known as Chlorus*) 305–06
Galerius 305–11
Severus 306–07
Maximianus (restored) 307–08
Maximinus Daia 308–13
Constantinus I (*Constantine the Great*) 312–37
Maxentius 306–12 (assassinated)
Licinius 308–24
Constantinus II 337–40
Constans I 337–50 (assassinated)
Constantius II 337–61
Magnus Magnentius 350–53
Julianus (*Julian the Apostate*) 361–63
Jovianus 363–64
Collegiate Emperors
(ruling part of the Roman Empire)
Valentinianus I 364–75 (Emperor in the West)
Gratianus 367–83 (Emperor in the West; assassinated).
Valens 364–78 (Emperor in the East)
Procopius 365–66 (Emperor in the East)
Valentinianus II 375–85 (Emperor in the West)
Magnus Maximus 383–88 (Emperor in the West)
Flavius Victor 386–88 (Emperor in the West)
Theodosius I 379–95 (Emperor in the East 379–88; in the East and in the West 388–95)
Valentinianus II (restored) 388–92 (Emperor in the West)
Eugenius 392–94 (Emperor in the West)
Honorius 393–95 (Emperor in the West; in 395 he became emperor of the Western Roman Empire)
Emperors of the Western Empire
Honorius 395–423
Constantius III 421
Valentinianus III 425–55 (assassinated)
Petronius Maximus 455 (assassinated)
Avitus 455–56
Majorianus 457–61
Libius Severus 461–65
Anthemius 467–72
Olybrius 472
Glycerius 473–74
Julius Nepos 474–75
Romulus Augustus 475–76 when he was expelled from Rome by the Vandals

TIME CHARTS

PREHISTORY TO 3000 BC

c. 70 million   First primates appear.

c. 6–4 million   *Australopithecus* genus appears in southern and eastern Africa with perfect erect posture.

c. 2·5 million   Probable appearance of *Homo habilis* and first tools in Africa.

c. 1·7 million   First structured habitat is built by *Homo habilis* in southern and eastern Africa.

c. 1.6 million   Emergence of *Homo erectus* in eastern Africa.

c. 1·5 million   More sophisticated Acheulian bifacial tools are in use in Africa.

c. 1 million   Beginning of lower Palaeolithic Culture in Europe and the Near East. *Homo erectus* controls fire.

c. 700 000   Acheulian bifacial tools are used in Europe.

c. 300 000   *Homo erectus* develops strategies for hunting large mammals.

c. 250 000   Development of the Levalloisian method of cutting stone; flakes of a predetermined form are produced.

c. 200 000   Emergence of *Homo sapiens*.

c. 100 000   Rise of stone flake industries; beginning of Middle Palaeolithic Culture in Europe and the Near East.

c. 130 000   *Homo sapiens* splits into two lines, *Homo sapiens neanderthalensis* and *Homo sapiens sapiens* (modern humans) in Africa and possibly the Near East.

c. 80 000   Appearance of *Homo sapiens sapiens* in western Asia and Near East. First burials and religious thought.

c. 40 000   Probable arrival of *Homo sapiens sapiens* (modern humans) in Australia.

c. 35 000   *Homo sapiens sapiens* (modern man) in Europe.

c. 30 000   Beginning of Upper Palaeolithic Age. Appearance of figurative art. Neanderthals extinct.

c. 23 000   Modern humans probably arrive in America.

c. 18 000   Development of arrowhead industry influenced by Eastern cultures. Height of Palaeolithic art.

c. 15 500–10 000   Development of cave art and more sophisticated mural art.

c. 15 000   Cave wall paintings at Lascaux. Cave art begins in South America.

c. 14 000–11 000   Free standing round cabins are built for the first time.

c. 11 000   First permanent settlements in Middle East. Systematic gathering, storing of wild cereal and hunting.

c. 9 000–4 000   Beginning of the Neolithic period.

c. 8 500–8 000   Wheat and barley – the first cereals – grown in Jordan.

c. 8 000   First systematic harvesting of pulses in France.

c. 8 000–7 000   Beginning of art in northern Europe.

c. 7 600   First agriculture in southwest Asia.

c. 7 500–7 000   The domestication of goats and sheep in Near East.

c. 6 000   The first farming communities of southeast Europe appear.

c. 5 000   Domestication of llamas in South America and some agricultural development in Mexico.

c. 4 500   Megalithic menhirs in Brittany and Portugal.

c. 4 000   Rice cultivation in China.

c. 4 000–3 000   Development of the world's first known cities in Mesopotamia.

c. 3 000–2 500   Gradual progression to Bronze Age in central-western Asia, Europe, Egypt and China.

THE ANCIENT WORLD

Europe

c. 3000 BC Development of the Minoan civilization in Crete: foundation of Knossos and Phaestus.

c. 2500–2400 Simple henges erected in England.

c. 2200–1450 Middle Minoan Age: control of the sea ensures Minoan prosperity.

c. 2000 Stone circles of Carnac (Brittany) erected.

c. 1700 Bronze Age in Western Europe.

c. 1600 Linear B script in use in Minoan civilization.

1500–1150 Mycenaean civilization begins its domination in mainland Greece.

c. 1500 Beginning of Urnfield cultures in Hungary and Romania.

c. 1450 The Minoan city of Knossos falls to invaders (possibly Mycenaeans).

c. 1300 First Celts appear in the Upper Danube area.

c. 1200 Sack of Troy (possibly by Mycenaeans).

1200–1100 Dorians overthrow the Mycenaean civilization and usher in period of Greek 'Dark Ages'.

1000 A village settlement existed on the site of Rome.

900–500 Celtic Hallstatt culture (iron-using) supersedes Urnfield cultures.

850 Foundation of Carthage by Phoenicians from Tyre.

c. 800 Emergence of polis – Greek city-states.

753 Traditional date of foundation of Rome.

750 Greeks settle southern Italy.

c. 750–600 Increase in the number of city-states; the political rights of the citizen restricts the power of the aristocracy.

594 Solon introduces reforms in Athens.

509 Last Roman king expelled; establishment of Republic.

499–479 Greek–Persian Wars: Greek city-states revolt against Persian rule; Persians eventually routed and Athens and Sparta emerge as the dominant forces in Greece.

c. 450 Celtic La Tène culture: Celtic, Greek and Etruscan civilizations come into contact; culture characterized by abstract and figurative patterned art and ironwork with Greek influences.

Egypt

c. 3100–2700 BC Menes conquers the Delta, unites Upper and Lower Egypt and becomes pharaoh of the first unified dynasty; foundation of Memphis.

c. 3000 Hieroglyphic and Elamite pictographic scripts in use.

c. 2575–2134 Old Kingdom. Building of Great Pyramids at Giza.

c. 2134–2040 First Intermediate Period: era of anarchy and political fragmentation.

c. 2040 Unity of Egypt is restored under Mentuhotep of Thebes: start of the Middle Kingdom: administrative reforms, co-regencies and the conquest of Nubia.

c. 1640–1550 Hyksos invade and rule Egypt; Thebans remain independent; Hebrews enter Egypt.

c. 1550 Ahmose, Prince of Thebes, expels Hyksos and reunites Egypt.

1540–1479 Tutmosis begins period of Egyptian expansion: foundation of empire in Palestine and Syria extending to the Euphrates.

1360 Amenhotep IV (Akhenaton) rejects all gods except Aton, the Sun disc; imperial neglect leads to loss of Asian empire.

c. 1300 Oppression of Jews under Rameses II; Jewish exodus from Egypt.

1200–1100 Attempts by the Sea People to invade Egypt thwarted by Rameses III.

1070–1000 Egypt divided: priesthood of Amun rule in Thebes, while pharaohs rule in Tanis.

814 Traditional date of the foundation of Carthage.

750 Nubians conquer Egypt.

525 Egyptian attempt to regain independence fails; Persians take control.

332 Egypt conquered by Alexander the Great; on his death (305) Ptolemy (Alexander's general) founds the Hellenistic Kingdom of Egypt.

Near East

c. 3000 BC Beginnings of the Sumerian civilization; foundation of city states Uruk, Eridu and Ur.

c. 2334–2279 Sargon the Great founds Akkad and Akkadian Empire; conquers all Mesopotamia.

c. 2200 Guti tribesmen from Iran destroy Akkadian Empire.

c. 2113 Third dynasty of Ur founded by Ur-Nammu; a period of prosperity follows.

c. 2006 Sack of Ur by Elamites (a people of ancient Iran).

c. 1792–1750 Hammurabi of Babylon reunites Mesopotamia.

c. 1650 Foundation of Hittite Old Kingdom by King Mursilis.

c. 1500 Migration of Phrygians into Asia Minor: establishment of Phrygia.

1380–1350 Hittite Empire reaches greatest extent under Suppiluliumas I.

1313–1283 Unsuccessful Hittite invasions of Egypt.

c. 1230 Jews occupy Israel.

c. 1200 Overthrow of Hittite Empire by Phrygians and allied tribes.

1200–1100 'Sea People' raid Syria and Palestine.

c. 1100 Assyrian Empire set up in Mesopotamia.

c. 1000 Israelite Kingdom founded by Saul and David.

911–824 Period of Assyrian expansion.

c. 935 Israelite Kingdom divided into Israel and Judah.

c. 850 Chaldea (now Armenia) attacked by Assyrians.

722 Palestine annexed by Assyrians; many Jews exiled to Babylon.

670 Assyrians destroy Memphis and Thebes but fail to hold Egypt.

626 Nabopolassar establishes the Chaldean dynasty of Babylon.

612 Medes, Babylonians and Scythians bring down Assyrian Empire.

600 Assyrian Empire divided amongst its conquerors.

605–562 Nebuchadnezzar II of Babylon extends the empire to include Syria and Palestine; extensive building programme (including the Hanging Gardens).

539 Cyrus the Great conquers Babylonian Empire and founds Achaemenid Persian Empire that dominates the Middle East.

536 Return of Jews from Babylon to Judah.

Southern and Eastern Asia

2850 BC Legendary Golden Age of China begins.

c. 2300 Indus Valley civilization: development of the cities of Harappa and Mohenjo-daro.

c. 2000 Neolithic farming spread to southern India.

c. 1500 Aryan invasion of India: fall of Indus Civilization; intermingling of Aryan and indigenous Dravidian cultures produces Hinduism. Rice farming established in Indochina.

c. 1500–1050 Shang dynasty in China; Bronze Age in China; first evidence of Chinese script.

1500–400 Ganges civilization in India.

1122–256 Zhou dynasty in China.

c. 800 Hindu Iron Age culture established in the Ganges basin.

c. 800–700 Growth of Chinese cities and merchant class; iron industry develops; flourishing of literature and philosophy: Kongfuzi (Confucius), Mengzi (Mencius) and Taoism.

771 Nomad attacks on China cause removal of capital to Luoyang: start of Later Zhou period: imperial power diminished.

c. 500 Emergence of Buddhist and Jain religions. Indian agriculturalists colonize Sir Lanka.

c. 481–221 'Warring States' in China – a period of anarchy during which power devolved to smaller states.

326 Alexander the Great conquers the Indus Valley.

c. 300 Sir Lanka converted to Buddhism.

CLASSICAL WORLD (to fall of Rome)

Hellenic World

499 BC Ionian Greeks revolt against Persian rule: beginning of the Greek-Persian wars.

490 Battle of Marathon: defeat of the Persians by the Greeks.

480 Battle of Salamis: Greeks defeat Persian fleet.

479 Greek army defeat Persians at Plataca and Mycale and liberate Greece.

478 Athenian empire; Athens assumes leadership of the Delian League.

462–429 Pericles dominates Athens as the city-state's leading politician.

431 Outbreak of Peloponnesian War between Athens and Sparta.

413 Athenian fleet destroyed.

404 Athenian surrender to Sparta: beginning of Spartan domination of Greece.

399 Execution of Socrates.

378–7 Athens founds the Aegean Confederacy.

371 Thebans defeat Spartans and begin Theban hegemony in Greece.

338 Philip II of Macedon conquers Greek city-states (at Battle of Chaeronea).

336 Philip II assassinated: accession of Alexander (the Great).

334–326 Alexander's invasion and conquer of the Persian Empire: Granikos (334), Issos (333), Gaugamela (332) and Hydaspes (326).

326–323 Spread of Greek Civilization: Alexander occupies Egypt, Syria and invades the Punjab.

323 Alexander the Great dies at Babylon: the Hellenistic Age in Middle East and Eastern Mediterranean begins.

323–301 Power-struggle between Alexander's generals for control of the empire. By 301 BC Ptolemy gains Egypt, Seleucus most of the Asiatic provinces (the Seleucid Empire).

c. 240 Greece dominated by two federations of city-states: Aetolia and Achaea.

238 Foundation of kingdom of Pergamon.

c. 211–167 Macedonian Wars: Rome finally defeats Macedonia which becomes a Roman province.

148–146 Rome annexes Greece.

133 Attalos III of Pergamon bequeaths his kingdom to Rome.

64 Seleucid Empire falls to Rome.

AD 324–37 Constantine I (the Great) reunited Roman Empire but moved the capital to Constantinople (formerly Byzantium).

395 Division of Roman Empire into East (Byzantine Empire) and West.

Roman World

509 BC Foundation of Roman republic.

390 Rome sacked by Celts.

290 End of Third Samnite War; Rome dominates central Italy.

275 Rome completes conquest of peninsular Italy after the defeat of Pyrrhus and southern Italian Greek cities.

264–241 First Punic War between Rome and Carthage: Sicily becomes first Roman province.

218–202 Second Punic War: Hannibal initially inflicts crushing blows on Roman forces but is finally defeated at Zama. Rome gains Carthaginian provinces in Spain.

149–146 Third Punic War: Carthage destroyed and Africa becomes a Roman province.

133–96 Expansion of Roman Empire to include Asia (W. Turkey; 133), southern Gaul (121), Cilicia (101) and Cyrenaica (96).

91 Social War: Italian cities revolt against Rome. Roman franchise granted to most Italians.

73 Spartacus leads Third Servile War (suppressed 71).

60 First Triumvirate: Pompey, Caesar and Crassus.

58 Caesar begins his conquest of Gaul.

49 Caesar at war with Pompey and Senate.

48 Caesar takes Rome and becomes dictator.

44 Caesar assassinated by Brutus and Cassius.

43–42 Second Triumvirate: Antony and Octavian effectively divide Roman Empire.

31 Octavian defeats Antony and Cleopatra at Actium, annexes Egypt and becomes dictator of Rome.

27 Octavian is proclaimed emperor – 'Augustus'.

AD 43 Roman invasion of Britain.

66 First Jewish revolt.

68–69 Anarchy following death of Nero; order restored by Vespasian.

70 Titus destroys Jerusalem.

98–180 Period of peace and prosperity under Antonine emperors.

122–26 Construction of Hadrian's Wall.

193–197 Civil war in Rome; order restored by Severus.

212 All free inhabitants of Empire gain Roman citizenship.

260 Persians overrun Syria and capture Emperor Valerian.

284–305 Diocletian reforms Roman Empire; establishes 'college' of emperors.

313 Edict of Milan: Christianity tolerated in Roman Empire.

395 Empire divided into East and West.

410 Visigoths sack Rome; Romans withdraw from Britain.

476 Final Western Roman Empire overthrown: fall of the Roman Empire.

AFRICA (c. 900 to the Colonial Age)

Northern and Eastern Africa

973–1171 Fatimid dynasty in Egypt.

1050–1140 Almoravid Empire flourishes in Morocco.

1147–1269 Almohad Empire controls coast of North Africa from western Sahara to Egyptian border.

1171–1250 Ayyubid dynasty in Egypt.

c. 1200 Christian kingdoms in the Sudan fall to Muslim invaders.

1250–1517 Mamelukes rule Egypt.

1448 First European fort on African coast established by the Portuguese at Arguin (Mauritania).

c. 1450 Sultanate of Agadès (in modern Niger) becomes powerful in southern Sahara.

1498–c. 1600 Portuguese active on Kenyan coast.

1516 Corsair (pirate) cities of North African coast accept authority of Ottoman Empire.

1517 Egypt comes under Ottoman rule.

1553 Beginning of Sharifian dynasties in Morocco.

1591 Songhay Empire (modern Mali) destroyed by Morocco.

c. 1600–c. 1800 Kingdom of Gondar flourishes in Ethiopia.

1798–1801 French invasion of Egypt.

1805–40 Reign of Mehemet Ali in Egypt.

1820 Mehemet Ali takes northern Sudan.

1830 French invasion of Algeria.

1841 Egypt achieves virtual independence from Ottoman Empire.

1850–68 Emperor Theodore consolidates independent Ethiopia.

1861 Zanzibar becomes independent from Oman.

1862 France acquires Djibouti.

1867 British expedition to Ethiopia.

1869 Suez Canal opens.

1881 France establishes a protectorate over Tunisia.

1882 Britain occupies Egypt.

1885 The Mahdists take Khartoum, kill General Gordon and create a theocratic state in the Sudan.

1890 Germany colonizes modern Rwanda, Burundi and mainland Tanzania. Zanzibar becomes a British protectorate.

1894 British protectorate established in Uganda.

1896 Ethiopia successfully counters attempted invasion by Italian forces.

1899 Joint Anglo-Egyptian rule established in the Sudan. Southern Somalia becomes an Italian colony.

1904 French and Spanish rule established in Morocco.

1905–06 First Moroccan Crisis: French interests in Morocco disputed by Germany.

Southern and Western Africa

c. 800–1000 Takrur state controls modern Senegal.

c. 1000 Rise of the Kanem Empire (northern Nigeria).

c. 1200–1400 Great Zimbabwe Empire.

c. 1400 Kanem-Borno Empire powerful in northern Nigeria and Chad.

c. 1400 Rise to power of Mossi states in modern Burkina Faso.

1441 Portuguese arrive in Guinea-Bissau.

1482 Portuguese establish trading base on Gold Coast (Ghana).

c. 1450–1550 Powerful Kongo and Ndongo kingdoms in Angola and Zaïre.

c. 1500 Portuguese slaving bases established along West coast of Africa.

1531 Portuguese establish trading posts in Mozambique.

1638 The Dutch take Mauritius. France establishes fort of Saint-Louis in Senegal.

1652 Cape settlement established by Dutch East India Company.

c. 1700–1830 Kingdom of Dahomey (modern Benin) flourishes as one of the principal slave trading states.

c. 1700 Rise of Asante kingdom to power in modern Ghana.

1713 Britain becomes dominant in Nigerian slave trade.

1798 Britain occupies the Cape.

1813 British missionaries become active in Bechuanaland (modern Botswana).

1821–22 American Colonization Society establishes Liberia for freed slaves.

1835–37 The Great Trek: Boers leave the Cape to found the republics of the Transvaal and Orange Free State.

1843 Britain annexes the Gambia and Natal.

1847 Liberia becomes independent.

1850 Britain ousts Danes from Gold Coast (Ghana).

1861 Britain acquires Lagos (Nigeria).

1880s Brazza establishes French protectorate over the Congo.

1884 German protectorates of Kamerun (Cameroon) and South West Africa (Namibia) proclaimed.

1885 Congo Free State (Zaïre) becomes a personal possession of King Léopold II of the Belgians. British colonization of Nigeria.

1889–90 French rule in Central Africa and Chad begins.

1890s French take Mossi kingdom (modern Burkina Faso). British South Africa Company establishes control in modern Zambia and Zimbabwe.

1896 French take Madagascar, overthrowing the Merina monarchy.

1899 Beginning of Boer War in South Africa.

THE EARLY MIDDLE AGES

Britain and Northern Europe

400–500 Saxons, Jutes and Angles (Germanic tribes) invade and settle in Britain.

519 Kingdom of Wessex founded.

c. 595 Kingdom of Mercia founded.

407 Withdrawal of the last Roman troops from Britain.

654 Kingdom of Northumbria formed.

787 Viking raids on Britain begin: pillage of Lindisfarne.

757–796 Construction of Offa's Dyke separates England and Wales during the reign of Offa of Mercia.

795 Norwegians settle in Ireland.

800s Viking settlements made in Ireland.

844 Kenneth MacAlpin becomes king of Picts and Scots: forms Kingdom of Alban, unifying Scotland.

866 Danes conquer Northumbria, East Anglia and Mercia.

874 Danes and Norwegians settle Iceland.

937 Battle of Brunanburh: Athelstan of Wessex defeats north Welsh, Scots and Norse.

954 England united by Wessex.

991 Renewed Viking raids on England.

1013 The Dane Swegn overthrows King Aethelred and becomes King of England.

1016 Cnut, son of Swegn, becomes king of England after succession dispute with Aethelred.

1027 Cnut becomes king of Norway.

1035 Death of Cnut: division of the Danish Empire (Denmark, England and Norway).

1042 Edward the Confessor succeeds Cnut's son Harthacnut to the English throne.

1066 Harold, Earl of Wessex succeeds Edward; William of Normandy challenges succession and defeats Harold at the Battle of Hastings.

1070 Rebellion in northern England crushed by William the Conqueror.

Byzantine Empire

527 Accession of Justinian I to Byzantine throne: beginning of military expansion and administrative reform.

534 Byzantines under General Belisarius conquer Vandal kingdom in North Africa.

551 Belisarius recovers Italy from Ostrogoths.

c. 650 Byzantine empire overrun by Persians, Slavs, Bulgars and Arabs: Constantinople besieged by Arabs in 673–77 and 718.

726 Emperor Leo III introduces Iconoclastic Decree banning use of religious images: leads to religious disunity.

c. 750 The Byzantine Empire retains only Greece and Asia Minor.

751 Foundation of Carolingian dynasty ends Byzantine power in the west.

811 Bulgars defeat Byzantines.

843 Restoration of images as an aid to worship; end of period of religious disunity.

867–86 Revival of Byzantine Empire under Basil I.

961 Byzantines recover Crete.

965 Byzantines recover Cyprus.

971 Eastern Bulgaria conquered by Byzantines.

976–1025 Basil II's reign over Byzantine Empire.

1018 Byzantines finally conquer the Bulgarians under Basil II ('the Bulgar-Slayer').

1048 Seljuk Turks begin expansion into Byzantine Empire and attack Armenia.

1055 Seljuk Turks take Baghdad.

1060 Normans invade and annex Sicily.

c. 1070 Byzantines lose southern Italy to the Normans.

1071 Byzantine army destroyed by Seljuk Turks at Manzikert: Turks overrun Anatolia (present-day Asian Turkey).

1081 Revival of Byzantine power under Alexius I Comnenus.

Western Europe

c. 486 Clovis defeats last Roman governor in Western Europe and founds the Frankish kingdom and the Merovingian dynasty.

c. 496 Franks acquire Rhineland.

c. 500 Franks conquer Visigoths and extend their empire to the Pyrenees.

638 Death of King Dagobert I: power passes to 'mayors of the palace'.

711 Successful Muslim invasion of Spain.

718 Foundation of Christian kingdom of Asturias in northern Spain.

732 Battle of Poitiers: Arabs defeated by Franks under Charles Martel.

751 Pepin I founds Carolingian dynasty after usurping the Merovingian throne.

771 Charlemagne (Carolingian king) begins military campaign of conquest: Saxony (772), Lombard Kingdom (773), Bavaria (788), Avar Kingdom (795–6).

792–793 Revolts in Benevento and Saxony against Carolingian rule; attacks by Muslims; famine.

800 Charlemagne crowned Emperor of what became known as Holy Roman Empire.

c. 840 Viking raids on Carolingian Empire begin.

843 Treaty of Verdun divides Carolingian Empire.

845 Viking attack on Paris.

846 Arabs attack Rome.

884–887 Temporary reunion of Carolingian Empire under Charles the Fat.

885–886 Viking siege of Paris.

929 Umayyad caliphatē established in Córdoba, Spain.

955 Battle of Lechfeld: Germans halt westward expansion of Magyars.

962 Coronation of Emperor Otto: Holy Roman Empire becomes largely German.

987 Hugh Capet, King of France, founds Capetian dynasty.

1031 Fragmentation of Muslim Spain: northern Spain dominates Iberian Peninsula.

1032 Kingdom of Burgundy becomes part of German Empire.

1092 Almoravids dominate most of Muslim Spain.

1094 Christian soldier, El Cid, takes Valencia.

The Church

563 Foundation of Iona monastery by St Columba: Celtic Christianity established in northern Britain.

590 Gregory the Great becomes pope.

597 St Augustine of Canterbury travels to Kent to convert English to Christianity; becomes first Archbishop of Canterbury. Conversion of King Ethelbert.

653 Lombards convert to Christianity.

663 Synod of Whitby establishes the domination of Roman Christianity over Celtic Christianity.

726 Beginning of the Iconoclast Movement (the abolition of the veneration of icons).

754 Pope gains temporal powers in central Italy.

c. 750 Boniface evangelized Germany.

843 Restoration of the veneration of icons in the Eastern Christian Church.

864–5 Bulgars and Serbs converted to Orthodox Christianity.

910 Abbey of Cluny founded in France: spreads monastic reforms.

955 Magyars accept Christianity.

965–966 Danish and Polish sovereigns accept Christianity.

970s Christianity spread to Bohemia.

988 Orthodox Christianity established in Kiev Rus.

1053 Pope defeated and captured by the Normans at Melfi.

1054 East-West Schism: Eastern (Orthodox) Church and Western (Roman) Church finally split.

1059 Pope Nicholas II decrees that only cardinals have the right to elect the pope.

1073 Gregory VII becomes pope and enforces papal authority and Church discipline.

1099 Godfrey of Bouillon leads First Crusade: takes Jerusalem.

THE LATER MIDDLE AGES

British Isles

1100 William Rufus killed in New Forest.

1135 Stephen of Blois seizes English throne.

1138–46 Civil war between adherents of Stephen and Matilda.

1141 Matilda becomes 'Lady of England' for 7 months.

1144 Geoffrey Plantagenet, Count of Anjou, conquers Normandy.

1152 Henry Plantagenet, Duke of Normandy and Count of Anjou, marries Eleanor, Duchess of Aquitaine: gains half of France.

1154 Henry Plantagenet inherits English throne and establishes Plantagenet empire in England and France.

1169 Beginning of the Anglo-Norman invasion of Ireland.

1171 Henry II invades Ireland and claims sovereignty.

1179 Grand Assize: judicial reform.

1204 King John loses Normandy to France.

1215 King John forced to concede Magna Carta (charter of rights for Clergy, Barons and Commoners).

1258 Simon de Montfort forces reforms on Henry III.

1277–83 Conquest of Wales by Edward I.

1290 Scottish throne disputed by 13 claimants. Jews expelled from England.

1296 Annexation of Scotland by Edward I.

1298 Scottish hero, William Wallace, defeated by Edward I.

1298 Robert Bruce continues struggle for Scottish independence.

1306 Robert Bruce crowned King Robert I of Scotland.

1314 Battle of Bannockburn: Edward II of England disastrously defeated by Robert the Bruce and his army: ensures Scottish independence.

1337 Beginning of the Hundred Years War: series of Anglo-French conflicts originating from English claims on the French throne.

1340 Battle of Sluys: English gain control of the English Channel in the Hundred Years War.

1346 English victory at Battle of Crécy. Scottish King captured at Battle of Neville's Cross.

Northern and Eastern Europe

1081–1118 Revival of Byzantine power under Alexius Comnenus.

1138 Beginning of Hohenstaufen dynasty (Holy Roman Emperors). Poland fragments into independent principalities.

1139 Division of Russian state into independent principalities.

1174 Coast of Finland settled by Swedes.

1176 Byzantine Emperor suffers major defeat by the Seljuk Turks: end of Byzantine revival.

1177 Peace of Venice between Pope and Emperor.

1198 Bohemia becomes a kingdom.

1223 Byzantines recover Salonika.

1227 Danes defeated by Germans: cede Holstein to German Empire.

1237 Volga Bulgars conquered by Mongols.

1238 Mongols conquer principality of Vladimir, the Georgians and the Cumans.

1240 Kiev falls to Mongols.

1241 Mongols invade Poland and Hungary but withdraw shortly after.

1261 Restoration of the Byzantine Empire in Constantinople.

1291 The Swiss cantons of Uri, Schwyz and Unterwalden declare themselves independent of the Habsburgs.

1300 Foundation of the Islamic Ottoman Empire in northern Anatolia by Osman I.

1316–41 Creation of the Lithuanian Empire by Gediminas.

1320 Golden Horde (Mongols) lose Kiev to Lithuanians.

1336 Ottomans take Bergama.

1346 Estonia is sold to Teutonic Knights by Danes. The Black Death enters Europe and spreads to western and southern Europe.

THE LATER MIDDLE AGES

Western and Southern Europe

1110 Saragossa (last independent emirate of Muslim Spain) taken over by the Almoravid Berber dynasty.

1118 King of Aragon captures Saragossa.

1137 Union of Catalonia and Aragon through marriage.

1138–39 Foundation of the Kingdom of Portugal.

1144 Alfonso of Portugal annexes Lisbon.

c. 1150–1200 Rise of the early Italian city-states.

1155 Frederick Barbarossa, a bitter rival of Pope Alexander III, becomes Emperor.

1158 Imperial authority in northern Italy is restored by Frederick Barbarossa.

1160 Henry the Lion, Duke of Saxony and Bavaria, conquers the Wends of the Lower Elbe.

1180 Frederick Barbarossa banishes Henry the Lion.

1191 Richard I of England captures Cyprus.

after 1204 Great expansion of Venetian territory and commerce in the eastern Mediterranean.

1209–28 Simon de Montfort leads crusades against the Albigensian sect (European followers of the Cathar heresy).

1212 Christian kings defeat Almohades in southern Spain.

1218 Frederick II succeeds Otto IV and becomes master of the Empire and Kingdom of Sicily.

1229 Albigensian heretics crushed; territory ceded to France and Inquisition established in Toulouse.

1248 Moors lose Seville to Ferdinand III of Castile.

1249 Moors expelled from Portugal.

1250 Death of Emperor Frederick II.

1256–73 Interregnum in Holy Roman Empire: period of political anarchy in Germany.

1266 Angevin French gain control of Sicily.

1266–68 Charles of Anjou takes Sicilian crown and defeats Conradin of the Hohenstaufen.

1282 'Sicilian Vespers': rule of Charles of Anjou overthrown in successful Sicilian rebellion.

1302 Matins of Bruges, popular revolt in Flanders.

1306 Jews expelled from France.

1328 Extinction of Capetian dynasty in France; Philip VI (Valois) challenged by Edward III of England.

1330 Moors reconquer Gibraltar.

1347 Calais is taken by Edward III. Popular revolt in Rome led by Cola di Rienzi.

The Church

1100 Foundation of the Latin Kingdom of Jerusalem: becomes a Crusader state along with Antioch and Edessa.

1109 Capture of Tripoli by Crusaders: becomes fourth Crusader state.

1122 Concordat of Worms: reaffirms papal spiritual, and imperial temporal, power over bishops.

1147 Second Crusade: prompted by the fall of Edessa.

1170 Murder of Thomas Becket, Archbishop of Canterbury: later canonized by Pope.

1184 Creation of the Inquisition.

1189–92 Third Crusade prompted by Saladin's capture of Jerusalem: led by Richard Lionheart, Frederick Barbarossa and Philip Augustus of France; only Acre retained.

1199 Foundation of the Order of Teutonic Knights by Emperor Frederick II to overcome and convert pagans in the north-east of Europe.

1202–4 Fourth Crusade: sack of Constantinople.

1209 St Francis of Assisi founds Franciscan Order.

1215 Fourth Lateran Council – major pastoral reforms; foundation of the Dominican friars.

1217–21 Fifth Crusade: Damietta, Egypt taken.

1221 Crusades surrender Damietta on assurances of safe conduct from Egypt.

1228 Crusade of Frederick II: by negotiation adds Jerusalem to the Kingdom of Acre.

1229 Teutonic Knights begin conversions in Prussia.

1244 Jerusalem falls to band of fugitive Turks.

1248 Seventh Crusade led by Louis IX of France takes Damietta, Egypt.

1270 Eighth Crusade; Louis IX dies on Crusade against Tunis.

1274 Death of Thomas Aquinas.

1291 Fall of Acre: end of Crusades in Holy Land.

1307–14 Destruction of the Order of Knights Templar.

1309 Teutonic Knights take Danzig. Papal court moves to Avignon and is dominated by French interests.

THE LATER MIDDLE AGES

British Isles

1360 Treaty of Brétigny temporarily halted the Hundred Years War: England renounces claim to French throne and gains Aquitaine, Calais and Ponthieu.

1369 Renewal of Hundred Years War.

1375 Truce in Hundred Years War.

1381 Peasants' Revolt against the Poll Tax led by Wat Tyler and John Ball.

1399 Richard II deposed in England; the House of Lancaster usurps the throne.

1400–1408 National Welsh rebellion led by Owen Glendower fails.

1406 Prince James of Scotland captured by the English.

1415 Henry V again claims the French throne; invades France and wins battle of Agincourt.

1420 Henry V marries daughter of Charles VI and becomes heir to French throne.

1424 James I of Scotland finally released by English.

1455 Beginning of War of the Roses (civil war): House of York (white rose), and House of Lancaster (red rose) go to war over the succession to the throne.

1460 Yorkist victory in Battle of Northampton, but Richard of York is later killed at Wakefield.

1461 Yorkists defeated at Battle of St Albans, but son of Richard of York crowned Edward IV.

1469 Orkney and Shetland incorporated into Scotland.

1470 Lancastrian invasion restores Henry VI to throne.

1471 Edward regains throne after Battles of Barnet and Tewkesbury.

1485 Henry Tudor finally defeats Richard III at Bosworth field; his marriage to Edward IV's eldest daughter ends war: beginning of Tudor dynasty.

Northern and Eastern Europe

1354 Ottomans take Ankara.

1356 Ottoman Turks enter Europe.

1361 Ottomans capture of Adrianople, which becomes their European capital.

1363 Ottomans defeat Bosnians, Serbs and Hungarians.

1380 Supremacy of Ottoman Sultan recognized by Byzantine Emperor John Palaeologus. Union of Norway and Denmark.

1386 Union of the crowns of Poland and Lithuania.

1389–93 Ottoman annexation of Serbia, the Turkish emirates in Anatolia and Bulgaria.

1393 Ottoman annexation of Bulgaria and last emirate of Anatolia.

1395 Tamerlane defeats the Golden Horde.

1397 Norway, Sweden and Denmark come under one sovereign: Eric of Pomerania.

1399 Lithuanians defeated by Golden Horde.

By 1400 All territories surrounding Constantinople have been conquered by the Ottoman Turks.

1404 Four sons of Beyazit, Ottoman Sultan, fight for the succession to the Ottoman Empire.

1417 Followers of John Huss begin Hussite movement in Bohemia.

1410 Battle of Tannenberg – the Teutonic Order is defeated by the Poles and Lithuanians.

1419 Hussites reject Emperor Sigismund's claim to Bohemian crown: beginning of Hussite War (till 1436).

1439 End of Scandinavian Union.

1453 Constantinople falls to Ottoman Turks; end of Byzantine Empire.

1460 The Ottoman Turks capture Morea (the Peloponnese).

1466 Restoration of western Prussia to Poland by Teutonic Knights.

1475–77 War between Swiss and Charles the Bold of Burgundy: Charles defeated and killed at Nancy.

1477 Habsburg Emperor Frederick III driven out of Austria by King of Hungary.

1478 Hungary gains Lusatia, Moravia and Silesia through treaty with the Bohemians.

1480 Ivan III of Moscow defeats the Mongols.

THE LATER MIDDLE AGES

Western and Southern Europe

1356 Black Prince of England captures French King John at Poitiers.

1358 Jacquerie French peasant uprising: ends with the massacre of peasants at Meaux.

1366–67 War in Castile: the Black Prince invades and restores King Pedro to the throne.

1369 Renewal of Hundred Years War.

1383 Establishment of the House of Avis in Portugal.

1384 Philip of Burgundy gains Flanders through marriage: beginning of Burgundian Empire.

1385 Portuguese defeat of Castile ensures Portuguese independence.

1396 Peace of Paris: 28-year truce in the Hundred Years War.

The Church

1377 Papacy returns to Rome.

1378 Death of Pope Gregory XI: The Great Schism: two Popes elected; Pope Urban VI in Rome recognized by England, Italy and Germany, and Clement VII in Avignon recognized by France, Scotland, Spain and Sicily; the split reflects the political split of the Hundred Years War.

1387 Lithuania accepts Christianity.

late 14th century Lollard heresy in England.

1410 France weakened by Civil War between Burgundy and Orléans.

1411 Sigismund of Hungary is elected German Emperor.

1417 Normandy falls to Henry V.

1419 Anglo-Burgundian alliance.

1422 Death of Henry V and Charles VI: France divided between English Duke of Bedford and French Charles VII.

1428 English lay siege to Orléans.

1429 French inspired to retake Orléans by Joan of Arc: Charles VII crowned King of France.

1430 Joan of Arc captured by Burgundians and burnt at stake (1431).

1434 Cosimo di Medici dominates Florence and begins Medici dynasty.

1435 Burgundians abandon alliance with England and ally with Charles VII (who recaptures Paris in 1436).

1442 All of southern Italy comes under Spanish rule.

1409 Attempt by General Council of Pisa to end Schism fails.

1412 John Huss excommunicated for speaking out against sale of indulgences.

1414–17 Council of Constance finally ends Great Schism; election of new Pope, Martin V. John Huss burnt at stake.

1454 Peace of Lodi ends Italian wars.

1450–53 France regains Normandy (1450), Guienne (1451) and Bordeaux (1453) from English.

1453 England ceases attempts to conquer France (retains only Calais): end of Hundred Years War.

1469 Marriage of Ferdinand II (king of Aragon after 1479) to Isabella I (queen of Castile after 1474) led to the unification of Spain.

1477 Burgundy is annexed by French crown.

1492 Granada, the last Muslim state in Spain, falls to Ferdinand and Isabella.

1494–95 French invasion of Italy.

1478 Establishment of the Spanish Inquisition.
1492 Jews expelled from Spain.

RENAISSANCE AND THE REFORMATION

Spanish possessions

1492 Granada, the last Muslim emirate in Iberia, falls to Spain. Jews are expelled from Spain.
1494 Treaty of Tordesillas: Spain and Portugal agree to divide the New World.

1516 Charles I of Spain (Emperor Charles V) succeeds.
1518–23 Revolt in Spain by comunero movement.

1550 Duke of Alba sent to restore order in rebellious Spanish Netherlands.

1556 Charles V abdicates: hands Spain, Netherlands and Naples to his son, Philip II.

1567 Protestant Dutch revolt against Spanish Habsburg rule begins.
1576 Sack of Antwerp by Spanish soldiers.
1579 Dutch northern provinces form Union of Utrecht.

1580 Philip II of Spain takes throne of Portugal.
1581 United Provinces – the northern Protestant Netherlands – proclaim independence from Spain.
By 1600 The Spanish Empire comprises the Iberian Peninsula, most of Latin America, parts of Italy and the Netherlands and the East Indies.

Britain and Ireland

1494 Irish Parliament made subservient to English Parliament (Poynings' Laws).

1513 Battle of Flodden: English defeat Scots and kill James IV.
1514 Anglo-French alliance.
1515 Thomas Wolsey becomes a cardinal and Lord Chancellor of England.

1533 Henry VIII divorces Catherine of Aragon and breaks with Rome to become Supreme Head of the English Church: beginning of the English Reformation.
1535 Sir Thomas More and John Fisher executed for refusing to accept Succession Oath.
1536–39 Dissolution of the monasteries by Henry VIII.
1536 Union of England and Wales.

1552 Cranmer's Prayer Book: Protestant in character.
1553 England becomes Catholic again under Queen Mary: persecution of Protestants.
1558 Elizabeth I comes to the throne.
1559–63 Protestantism re-established in England by Acts of Supremacy and Uniformity, and the 39 Articles.

1560s Beginning of Anglo-Spanish maritime feud.
1567 Mary Queen of Scots forced to abdicate.
1568 Flight of Mary Queen of Scots to England, where she is imprisoned by Elizabeth I.

1587 Execution of Mary Queen of Scots after implication in plot to assassinate Elizabeth I.
1588 Defeat of Spanish Armada by English fleet.
1594 Irish rebellion against English rule led by Earl of Tyrone.

France

1491 Charles VIII of France acquires Brittany through marriage.
1494 Charles VIII invades Italy to claim the crown of Naples: start of Franco-Italian wars.

1513 France invaded by English forces under Henry VIII.
1515 Francis I invades Italy and defeats the Swiss and Milanese.
1520 Abortive Anglo-French alliance: Field of the Cloth of Gold.

1529 Peace of Cambrai between France and Spain temporarily halts the Habsburg-Valois Wars.
1536 Emperor Charles V invades Provence.

1552 Annexation of Metz, Toul and Verdun by King Henry II of France.
1558 France gains Calais, England's last possession in France.
1559 Treaty of Cateau: Cambrésis ends Franco-Italian wars.
1559–98 French Wars of Religion between Huguenots (Protestants) and the Catholic League.

1560–74 Regency of Catherine de Medici.
1572 Massacre of St Bartholomew: slaughter of Huguenots.

1589 Henry, King of Navarre, becomes Henry IV of France and converts to Catholicism.
1598 Edict of Nantes guarantees freedom of worship for Protestants; end of French Wars of Religion.

RENAISSANCE AND THE REFORMATION

The Empire and Eastern Europe

1496 Philip of Habsburg marries Joan (the Mad), heiress to Castile and Aragon.

1504 Philip of Habsburg becomes King of Castile, as Philip I.

1519 Charles I of Spain inherits Austrian Habsburg lands; elected Holy Roman Emperor as Charles V.

1522 Charles V divides his dominions between Austrian and Spanish Habsburgs: his brother Ferdinand I succeeds to Austria.

1524–25 Peasants' War in Germany.

1526 Ferdinand I gains Hungarian and Bohemian crowns through marriage. Hungary defeated by Ottoman Turks at Battle of Mohács.

1547 Ivan the Terrible becomes Tsar.

1555 Peace of Augsburg: every prince of the Empire allowed to choose the faith of his territory.

1556 Charles V abdicates: his brother Ferdinand I becomes emperor.

1564 Ivan the Terrible embarks on reign of terror.

1571 Battle of Lepanto between Ottoman Turks and Holy League (forces of Venice, Spain, Genoa and Papacy): Ottomans defeated.

1584 Death of Ivan the Terrible: his successor, Theodore I, is challenged by the aristocratic boyar families.

Italy

1494 French forces drive the Medici out of Florence and invade Rome.

1495 French retreat from Italy.

1501 France and Spain agree to divide the Kingdom of Naples between them.

1503 Ferdinand V of Spain becomes King of Naples.

1512 France expelled from Italy by joint Venetian, Spanish and Papal forces.

1527 Italy falls under the control of Charles V. Expulsion of the Medici.

1530 The Medici family return to Florence.

1531 Alessandro de Medici becomes duke of Tuscany.

1535 Death of the last Sforza ruler of Milan.

1540 Milan becomes Spanish.

1545 Beginning of Farnese dynasty in Parma.

1556 Charles V abdicates: Naples in favour of his son, Philip II as successor.

1580 Carlo Emmanuele I begins territorial expansion of duchy of Savoy.

1597 Death of last Este duke of Ferrara.

The Church

1478 Establishment of Spanish Inquisition.

1492 Rodrigo Borgia becomes Pope Alexander VI.

1517 Martin Luther nails his 95 Theses criticizing the Church to the Wittenberg Church door: beginning of the Reformation.

1519 Luther renounces papal supremacy.

1520 Luther declared a heretic: accepts the protection of the Elector of Saxony.

1523 Ulrich Zwingli presents his Theses in Zurich: precipitates the spread of Protestantism in Switzerland.

1525–27 Spread of Lutheranism: Teutonic Knights (1525), Sweden (1527) and parts of Switzerland.

1529 Luther and Zwingli divided on the nature of the Eucharist.

1533–5 The English Reformation begins.

1536 Denmark becomes Lutheran.

1541–63 Council of Trent: the Roman Catholic Church reforms in a response to the Reformation: Counter-Reformation.

1551–2 Council of Trent rejects Lutheran and Zwinglian beliefs.

1559 Church of England re-established on the basis of the 39 Articles.

1562–63 Council of Trent ends any hope of reconciliation with the Protestants.

1582 Pope Gregory XIII introduces Gregorian Calendar.

1596 Catholic influence in Poland and the Ukraine extended by the Union of Brest-Litovsk.

1598 Edict of Nantes recognizes the rights of Protestant Huguenots in France.

ASIA: 500 BC TO THE COLONIAL AGE

China

1122–256 BC Zhou dynasty.

800–300 China beset by warring states.

481–221 'Warring states' in China.

551–479 Development of Confucian social thought.

221 The State of Qin unites China: abolition of feudalism and the building of the Great Wall.

202 BC–AD 220 Han dynasty assumes power: conquest of Korea (107 BC), invention of paper and the introduction of Buddhism.

220–280 North China succumbs to warlordism and invasions from non-Chinese people.

265–316 Jin dynasty.

589–618 Sui dynasty: reunites China and undertakes major government reforms. Expensive military ventures contribute to the Empire's collapse.

618–907 Tang dynasty: empire extended; invention of printing and gunpowder and increase in international trade.

755 Abortive rebellion of An Lushan: nomad invasions and revolts further weaken the empire.

907 Last Tang emperor abdicates: China fragments; period of military dictators and warfare.

960 Sung dynasty reunites much of northern China and restores peace.

1127 Northern invasion by Jin horsemen forces the removal of the Sung dynasty to the south.

1279 Mongols conquer all of China: beginning of harsh Mongol rule under Kublai Khan.

1275–1292/5 Marco Polo enters the service of Kublai Khan and travels widely within the empire.

1368 Overthrow of the Mongols in China by the native Ming dynasty.

1403–24 Emperor Yongle extends empire, moves capital to Beijing and encourages Confucianism.

1424 Death of Yongle; expansionist policies abandoned; 150 years of relative peace.

1517 European traders and missionaries given limited access to the empire.

1592 Unsuccessful Japanese incursions into China.

1644 Ming dynasty collapses after rebellions and attacks by the Manchus; foundation of Qing dynasty.

1662–1722 Enlargement of the Chinese Empire into Central Asia and Tibet under Emperor Kangxi.

1683 Taiwan is incorporated into China.

1693 Kangxi leads invasion of Mongolia.

1692 Catholic missionaries are allowed to make conversions.

1715 Christianity banned.

1735–95 Expansion of Empire into Turkistan, Annam (Vietnam), Burma and Nepal.

1757 Foreign traders are restricted to Guangzhou.

1793 British delegations denied diplomatic relations.

c. 1800–1900 Western involvement in China increases; imperial power diminished.

Japan

c. 400 BC Rice farming reaches Japan from Korea.

2nd century AD Civil war in Japan.

c. 400 The Yamamoto clan dominate their rivals and unite Japan, establishing imperial rule.

594–622 Under Prince Shotoku Taishi the study of Buddhism and Chinese writing is encouraged; the Chinese administrative system and calendar is copied.

710–84 Chinese-style imperial court established at Nara.

c. 800–900 Imperial power is undermined by the Fujiwara family. Decline in Chinese influence.

c. 1000–1100 The Fujiwara effectively hold power. Development of a military class – the Samurai – in the provinces.

1100–1192 Civil war between military rivals.

1192 Samurai Minamoto Yoritomo conquers rivals; establishes first shogunate (military government), usurping the power of the emperor.

1192–1333 Under the Kamakura Shogunate Zen Buddhism becomes popular. Feudalism is introduced.

1333 Takanju Ashikaya defeats the Hojos (regents), overthrows the emperor and installs Koyo on throne.

1339 Emperor Koyo appoints Ashikaya as Shogun.

1339–1400 Fighting between daimyo (feudal lords) and their Samurai armies leads to political chaos.

1542 Portuguese introduce muskets into Japan.

1573 The Japanese warrior Oda Nobunaga ousts the Shogun from Kyoto and establishes firm rule.

1582 Oda Nobunaga is assassinated; his successor, Hideyoshi, continues to unify country.

1591 Hideyoshi breaks power of daimyo and disarms peasants.

1592 Invasion of Korea; Seoul is captured, but the Chinese armies force a retreat.

1598 Hideyoshi dies. Establishment of Tokugawa shogunate; further curbs on the freedom of daimyo.

1630s Christianity and travel abroad is proscribed and foreigners discouraged: Japan becomes isolated from the rest of the world.

1650–1800 Period of economic growth: emergence of merchant class and rising educational standards.

c. 1750 Tokyo becomes world's largest city.

1853–4 US commodore Perry enters two Japanese ports and forces Japan to trade: end of Japanese isolation.

1868 Popular support for the Tokugawa shogunate declines and imperial power (Meiji restoration) is restored. Beginning of Japanese industrialization.

ASIA: 500 BC TO THE COLONIAL AGE

India

c. 500–400 BC Emergence of Buddhism and Jainism: leads to a succession of Hindu and later Buddhist dynasties.

362 Alexander the Great conquers the Indus Valley.

321–185 BC The Maurya dynasty becomes the first all India Hindu empire (excluding the southern tip).

185 BC–AD 320 Disintegration of Maurya dynasty: India dissolves into small kingdoms with local power struggles.

AD 320–540 Northern India is reunited by the Gupta dynasty.

606–647 Harsha dynasty: Buddhist empire in the north.

c. 700–800 First Muslim invasion of India; Sind (southern Pakistan) is made a province of the Caliphate.

c. 900 Tamils from southern India begin to settle in Sri Lanka.

1000–1200 Beginning of the main Muslim invasions from Afghanistan; collapse of Hindu kingdoms.

14th century Muslim conquest of northern India complete.

1526 Mogul invasions; Mogul Empire established by Babur.

1530 Hamayun succeeds Babur as Mogul Emperor.

1540 Unable to assert his authority Hamayun is exiled to Persia.

1554–5 Hamayun recovers the throne: Persian culture influences the administration, architecture and court language.

1555 Akbar, the greatest Mogul ruler, succeeds. Military conquest of Rajasthan, Gujarat, Bengal, Kashmir and North Deccan; introduction of centralized administration and religious tolerance.

1605–27 Encouragement of the arts under the rule of Jahangir.

1628–56 Reign of Shah Jahan: building of the Taj Mahal.

1657 Shah Jahan falls ill; struggle for succession by his four sons; Aurangzeb kills his brothers, imprisons his father and becomes emperor.

1659–1707 Aurangzeb continues expansionist policies and by 1700 covers all of India except the far south. He ends religious tolerance (discriminates against Hindus) which increases opposition to Mogul rule.

1674 Sivaji defeats Moguls; Maratha kingdom established in west central India.

c. 1700 British East India Company secures the important ports in India.

1707–61 Aurangzeb dies: regional dynasties assert their independence, leading to a power vaccum.

1761 Battle of Panipat: Maratha defeated in their attempt to dominate all India.

c. 1760s British East India Company has become the dominant force in India.

Southeast Asia

c. AD 400–500 The Mon Kingdom in Burma established.

c. 800 Arrival of the Burmans from China; hostilities break out with indigenous people.

c. 800 Jayavarman II expels Javanese invaders from Khmer (Cambodia), re-unites country and founds Khmer Kingdom: introduction of cult of god-king and foundation of Angkor.

c. 800–900 Migration of people from southern China: foundation of Lao people.

c. 849–1287 Burma unified by the people of Pagan; revolts by Mon and Shan people; spread of Buddhism.

c. 900–1000 People of southern and western China migrate to and settle Siam (Thailand).

939 Annamese (of central Vietnam) overthrow Chinese and set up independent kingdom.

1220–96 Overthrow of Khmer control in Siam: the kingdoms of Sukhothai and Chiangmai dominate.

1287–1301 Pagan falls to Mongols.

late 13th century Islam arrives in northern Sumatra and begins to spread throughout the East Indies.

1350–1400 The Ayuthia succeeds the Sukhothai kingdom; Siamese devastate declining Khmer kingdom and unite Siam.

1354 Foundation of kingdom of Lanxang in Laos.

1431 Khmer rulers abandon Angkor for Phnom Penh: decline of Khmer empire.

1471 Annamese conquer the Champa (part of Vietnam) and found Kingdom.

1539 Burma reunited under the Toungoo.

1550–1700 Siamese–Burmese Wars.

1558 Rebellion in Annam (Vietnam): kingdom divides into two.

1620–1802 Division of Vietnam into rival states.

1701 Kingdom of Lanxang divides into two.

1752 Toungoo dynasty falls in Burma.

1757 The Burmese dynasty of Konbaung is established; series of wars with Siam begins.

1767 Burma overthrows Ayuthia Kingdom and occupies Siam.

1770 Burma repels a Chinese invasion.

1777 Burmese expelled from Siam under leadership of General Taksin.

1784 Burma conquers kingdom of Arakan, bringing Burmese territory to the border of British India.

c. 1800–50 Laos fragments into several states.

1802 Reunion of Vietnam under Nguyen Anh (with French assistance).

1824–51 General Chakri of Siam (later Rana I) founds new dynasty; Bangkok becomes new capital and Thai empire extended into Laos and northern Malaya.

1864 Cambodia becomes a French protectorate.

THE AMERICAS TO THE COLONIAL AGE

Caribbean and North America

10 000 BC Temporary landbridge during Ice Age connects Asia and Alaska: a few Siberian families reach North America. Population spreads from Alaska over North America; their descendants become American Indian hunters.

c. 8000 BC Ciboney (hunter-gatherer-fishing people) of South America reach Hispaniola.

c. 5000 BC First centres of population in Mexico.

5000–4000 BC Arrival of Inuit (Eskimo) in North America.

c. 1500–400 BC Olmec culture in Mesoamerica (Mexico and Northern Central America).

c. 100 BC Development of first true city, Teotihuacán; dominates central Mexico for 600 years.

AD 200–1000 Migration of Arawak Indians from NE South America to Caribbean.

AD 300 Rise of Maya civilization in Central America (Mexico, Guatemala and Yucatán peninsula).

AD 500 Beginning of maize cultivation in North America.

AD 500–1600 American Indians in the Mississippi Basin, become farmers with small settlements.

c. 900 Toltecs establish a military state in Tula, Northern Mexico, and by 985 control Mexico.

c. 1000 Arawak culture in the Caribbean destroyed by migrating Caribs from South America.

c. 1180 Toltec state overrun by nomadic tribes.

c. 1200–1250 Migration of Aztec people into North Mexico; foundation of Aztec Empire.

c. 1200–1450 Mayapán becomes a powerful city.

1400–1500 Expansion of Aztec Empire to cover most of modern Mexico.

1441 Sack of Mayapán by rival cities; several smaller Maya states are formed.

1519 The Spaniard Cortés reaches the Aztec Empire; Montezuma welcomes him believing him to be a demi-god.

1520 Aztec revolt; Montezuma is killed.

1521 Aztec Empire defeated by Spaniards.

Andean America

9000 BC South America settled from Central America.

2500 BC Development of agriculture in Indian communities.

1000–200 BC Chavin culture flourishes on Peruvian coast; improved agriculture (maize) and metallurgy.

AD 600–1000 Rise of Ayamará Indians in Bolivia.

AD 1000 Chimú state formed on north coast of Peru.

c. 1200 Foundation of Inca dynasty by Manco Capac; foundation of capital, Cuzco.

1438 Emperor Pachacuti rebuilds Cuzco and embarks on period of expansion.

1471–74 Emperor Topa Inca extends empire (Tahuantinsuyu) into southern Peru; begins road-building programme.

1476 Chimú state (Ecuador) conquered by Topa Inca.

1480 Bolivia succumbs to Inca rule.

1484 North and central Chile and north-west Argentina conquered by Incas.

1493 Huayna Capac becomes Inca emperor; founds second capital, Quito.

1498 Inca territory extends to Colombia.

1525 Disputed Inca succession leads to civil war: empire partitioned between the brothers Huascar and Atahuallpa.

1532 Spaniards, under Pizarro reach the coast and Atahuallpa is taken prisoner.

1533 Spanish execute Atahuallpa and taken Cuzco.

1535 Inca Empire completely dominated by the Spanish.

COLONIAL AMERICA TO 1850

North America

1497 Cabot discovers Newfoundland.

1605 French settle Nova Scotia.

1607 Jamestown, Virginia, is founded by the English.

1620 English Pilgrim Fathers settle Plymouth, Massachusetts.

1650s Colonization of Canada by the French.

1664 English gain New York, from the Dutch.

1670 Foundation of Hudson's Bay Company.

1699–1702 French colonization of Louisiana.

1744–54 Britain and France go to war over control of North America.

1763 France ousted from Canada by British.

1765 British impose the Stamp Act on American colonies.

1773 Boston Tea Party.

1774 Continental Congress issues Declaration of Rights.

1775 War of American Independence breaks out at Lexington.

1776 US Declaration of Independence.

1778 France, Holland and Spain (1779) join war against Britain.

1781 British surrender at Yorktown; American loyalists emigrate to Canada.

1787 US Constitution.

1803 Louisiana Purchase: Mississippi Valley sold to US by France.

1819 USA gains Florida from Spain.

1837 Papineau and McKenzie Rebellions in Canada.

Caribbean

1492 Columbus discovers Bahamas, Cuba and Hispaniola.

1493 Hispaniola settled by Spanish. Columbus discovers Jamaica and Puerto Rico.

1498 Columbus discovers Trinidad.

1505 Discovery of Bermuda by Juan Bermudez. First black slaves brought to Hispaniola. Puerto Rico conquered by Spanish.

1536–1609 Beginning of French and British penetration into Spanish Caribbean.

1612 English colonization of Bermuda.

1630–1640 First English and French claims to West Indian islands.

1655 English capture Jamaica from Spanish and begin colonization.

1697 Spain loses Haiti (half of Hispaniola) to the French.

1761 British dominate the West Indies.

1763 Britain gains Grenada from France.

1791 Toussaint L'Ouverture leads successful Black slave revolt in Haiti.

1796 British capture Guyana.

1801 Haiti becomes a republic.

1833–1880 Abolition of slavery in colonies by Britain 1833; France 1848; Holland 1863; Spain (Puerto Rico) 1873, (Cuba) 1880.

Latin America

1494 Spain and Portugal agree to divide New World colonies.

1498 Third journey by Columbus; discovers Venezuela.

1500 Pedro Alvares Cabral lands in Brazil and claims territory for Portugal.

1501 Portuguese exploration of Brazil.

1502 Columbus explores Central American coastline.

1519 Cortez begins expedition to Mexico.

1520 Last emperor of Aztecs surrenders to Cortez; foundation of Spanish Mexico.

c. 1520 Missionaries arrive in Spanish colonies: forced conversions begin.

1523–35 Spanish conquest of Central America.

1532 Portuguese begin to settle Brazil.

1532–33 Pizarro conquers Incas in Peru.

c. 1549 Silver found in Peru and Mexico: wealth sent to Spain.

1717 Spanish reorganization of South American colonies.

1780–81 Peruvian Indians revolt against Spanish rule.

1808–20 Nationalist uprisings in Spanish colonies; Simon Bolívar emerges as nationalist leader.

1811–30 Full independence in South American colonies: Paraguay and Venezuela (1811), Argentina (1816), Chile (1818), Colombia (1819), Mexico, Central America and Peru (1821), Brazil (1822), Uruguay (1828).

THE 17TH CENTURY

Britain and Ireland

1600 Irish Rebellion ends when Earl Tyrone surrenders to English Governor.

1603 James VI of Scotland succeeds to English throne as James I, uniting the two crowns.

1605 Failure of Catholic Gunpowder Plot to blow up Parliament; conspirators executed (1606).

1629 Charles I begins personal rule.

1638–39 First Bishops' War: Charles unsuccessfully attempts to impose Anglicanism on Scots.

1640 Second Bishops' War: Charles defeated by Scots; forced to call Long Parliament.

1642 Outbreak of Civil War between supporters of the King (Cavaliers) and Parliamentarians (Roundheads); King flees London.

1644 Battle of Marston Moor: a decisive victory for the Roundheads and Scots.

1645 Formation of the Roundhead New Model Army; Oliver Cromwell becomes second in Command; victory in Battle of Naseby.

1646–47 Scots sell Charles to Parliament.

1649 Charles executed; England becomes a Commonwealth.

1649–50 Irish and Scottish rebels defeated by Cromwell.

1653 Cromwell becomes Lord Protector and effective dictator.

1658 Death of Cromwell; succeeded by son Richard.

1660 Richard Cromwell loses political control and retires; Restoration of Charles II (after agreeing to an amnesty and religious toleration).

1665 Great Plague of London; 60 000 killed.

1666 Great Fire of London.

1677 Mary, daughter of Duke of York and eventual heir to the throne, marries the Dutch William III of Orange.

1678 'Popish Plot': wave of anti-Catholicism.

1679 Exclusion Crisis: Parliament attempts to prevent the succession of Catholic James, Duke of York.

1685 Death of Charles II; Catholic James II succeeds; countrywide revolts.

1688 'Glorious Revolution': William III of Orange arrives in England to take throne (with Parliamentary backing); James II flees to France.

1689 William III and Mary become joint sovereigns; Bill of Rights establishes a constitutional monarchy.

1690 Battle of the Boyne (in Ireland): William III defeats James and retains crown.

1694 Death of Queen Mary: William III becomes sole sovereign.

France

1610 Marie de Medici becomes Regent for the child Louis XIII.

1627–8 La Rochelle, a Huguenot port, is attacked and besieged by Chief Minister Richelieu; Huguenots surrender and lose political power.

1635 France declares war on Spain entering the Thirty Years War.

1643 French defeat Spanish at Rocroi. Louis XIV 'The Sun King' succeeds to French throne.

1648 Fronde (a period of civil disorder) begins with riots in Paris.

1652 France paralysed by Fronde; Dunkirk falls to Spain.

1658 Battle of the Dunes: French and British defeat Spanish; England regains Dunkirk.

1659 Treaty of Pyrenees ends Franco-Spanish War; France replaces Spain as major western European power.

1661 Louis XIV takes control of government.

1662 Charles II sells Dunkirk to Louis XIV.

1665 Colbert becomes Controller-General of Finance: heralds period of economic prosperity.

1669 Protestant worship further restricted.

1672 France declares war on Dutch who are joined by the Holy Roman Empire, Brandenburg and finally Spain and Lorraine. Third Anglo-Dutch War (1672–74).

1678 Treaty of Nijmegen ends war between France and the Netherlands (and Spain); Peace of Nijmegen (1679) ends war between France and Empire.

1683 Death of Colbert: end of economic prosperity.

1685 Edict of Nantes revoked: Protestantism banned; thousands of Huguenots flee France.

1688 France invades Rhineland; precipitates Nine Years War (or War of the Grand Alliance).

1689 Formation of the Grand Alliance of England, the United Provinces, Austria, Spain and Savoy against France.

1697 France finally defeated by Grand Alliance: Peace of Ryswick.

Spain

1604 General Spinola of Spain captures Ostend.

1607 Spanish fleet defeated by Dutch.

1609 Spain agrees to a nine-year truce in the war with the Netherlands.

1621–48 Spain wages an unsuccessful war against the United Provinces.

1635 Spain at war with France, entering the Thirty Years War.

1640 Catalans and Portuguese rebel against Spanish rule.

1643 Spain defeated by French at Rocroi.

1659 Treaty of Pyrenees ends Franco-Spanish War; Spain loses its place as principal western European power to France.

1665 Spanish defeated by British and Portuguese forces: Portugal regains independence.

1668 Spain recognizes independence of Portugal in Treaty of Lisbon.

1692 Spanish crown declares bankruptcy.

1698 Spanish Empire partitioned. Charles II of Spain leaves territories to Infant Elector Prince of Bavaria in his will.

1699 Death of Infant Elector Prince of Bavaria; re-opens question of Spanish Succession.

1700 Philip of Anjou, grandson of Louis XII becomes heir.

Rest of Europe

1600 Failure of coup against Geneva by Carlo Emmanuele I (of Savoy).

1613 Beginning of Romanov Dynasty in Russia.

1618 Protestant Bohemian revolt against future Habsburg Emperor Ferdinand II sparks off Thirty Years War.

1625 Protestant Danes renew war against the Catholic Habsburg Emperor, Ferdinand II.

1629 Danes suffer a series of defeats and withdraw from war; Swedes – led by Gustavus Adolphus – declare war on Habsburg Emperor.

1632 Gustavus Adolphus defeats Habsburgs at Lützen but is killed in battle.

1635 France goes to war with Habsburgs in alliance with Sweden and United Provinces.

1648 Treaty of Westphalia settles most of the issues of the Thirty Years War except the Franco-Spanish War; full Dutch independence.

1649 Establishment of serfdom in Russia.

1652–54 Anglo-Dutch sea war; Dutch finally recognize English Navigation Acts.

1654 Abdication of Queen Christina of Sweden.

1658 Danes finally expelled from southern Sweden: Peace of Roskilde.

1665–67 Second Anglo-Dutch Naval War.

1667 Truce of Andrusovo ends 13-year war between Russia and Poland; Kiev ceded to Russia.

1671 Turks declare war on Poland.

1672 Poland invaded by Turks and Cossacks; Poles surrender Podolia and Ukraine.

1673 Battle of Khorzim: Turks defeated by Poles led by Jan Sobieski.

1674 Jan Sobieski elected King of Poland.

1681 Treaty of Radzin: Russia gains most of Ukraine from Turkey.

1682 Accession of Peter the Great in Russia.

1683 Sobieski expels Turks from Vienna.

THE 18TH CENTURY

Britain

1701 Act of Settlement excludes Roman Catholic Stuarts from throne and recognizes the Hanoverian claim.

1707 Act of Union unites Scotland and England.

1712 Last execution for witchcraft in Britain.

1714 George the Elector of Hanover becomes George I.

1715 First Jacobite uprising in Scotland defeated.

1720 South Sea Bubble: failure of South Sea Company causes financial panic.

1721 Walpole becomes first Prime Minister.

1730 Methodists founded by John and Charles Wesley. Introduction of four-year crop rotation by Lord Townshend.

1736 Porteous riots in Edinburgh.

1742 Fall of Walpole.

1745–46 Last Jacobite rebellion in Britain fails.

c. 1750 Development of manufacturing industry; beginning of the Industrial Revolution.

1750 Britain joins Austro-Russian alliance against Prussia.

1755 Joint French and Indian War against Britain in North America.

1756 Outbreak of the Seven Years War.

Western and Southern Europe

1701 War of the Spanish Succession begins.

1704 British defeat French at Blenheim; British fleet captures Gibraltar from Spain.

1713 Treaty of Utrecht: end of War of Spanish Succession.

1715 Death of Louis XIV.

1719 France declares war on Spain.

1720 'Mississippi Bubble' in France. Treaty of Hague ends hostilities between Spain and Quadruple Alliance (Britain, France, Holy Roman Empire and the Netherlands).

1725 Treaty of Vienna: alliance between Spanish Bourbons and Austrian Habsburgs.

1727–29 War between Britain and Spain and France: Spain besieges Gibraltar (until 1728).

1739 Britain and Spain at war over British trade with South American colonies; merges with War of the Austrian Succession in 1740.

1740 War of the Austrian Succession: Maria Theresa succeeds to the thrones of Austria, Bohemia and Hungary: Frederick the Great seizes Silesia for Prussia.

1744–48 Britain and France at war over the colonies in North America.

1748 End of the War of the Austrian Succession.

1753 France faces national bankruptcy.

1755 Lisbon destroyed by earthquake.

1756 Diplomatic revolution: alliance between Britain and Prussia and alliance between France and Austria. Beginning of Seven Years War sparked off by British and French colonial rivalry and European struggle between Prussia and Austria.

Northern and Eastern Europe

1700 Great Northern War breaks out between Sweden and Russia, Denmark and Poland over supremacy in the Baltic.

1701 Charles XII of Sweden invades Poland.

1703–12 Hungarian revolt against Austria.

1706 Sweden imposes Stanislaus on the Polish throne.

1708 Sweden invades Russia.

1709 Peter (the Great) of Russia defeats Charles XII of Sweden at Battle of Poltava.

1711 Turkey declares war on Russia.

1720 Treaty of Nystadt ends Great Northern War: Sweden loses an empire and Russia becomes a major Baltic power.

1725 Death of Peter the Great.

1733–35 War of the Polish Succession: France and Spain fight Austria and Russia.

1734–35 War between Turkey and Persia.

c. 1740s Danubian principalities (Moldavia and Walachia) increasingly independent under Greek 'princes'.

1756 Outbreak of the Seven Years War.

1757 Sweden joins Seven Years War against Britain and Prussia.

Britain

1760 Enclosure Act changes farming practice: beginning of the Agricultural Revolution.

1762 Britain declares war on Spain.

1763 End of Seven Years War. MP and journalist John Wilkes is imprisoned for attacking the government in his paper.

1764 Wilkes is expelled from the House of Commons.

1765 Stamp Act imposes a tax on the American colonies: anti-British feeling increases campaign for independence.

1771 Richard Arkwright establishes first factory system for cotton spinning.

1775 War of American Independence breaks out at Lexington.

1776 American Declaration of Independence.

1780 Anti-Catholic riots in London.

1781 British troops surrender in America: end of War of Independence.

1782 Irish Parliament made independent of British parliament.

1791 Birmingham riots: fear of the spread of revolution in France leads to repressive rule.

1793 Britain joins continental powers against Revolutionary France.

Western and Southern Europe

1761 Influenza epidemic spreads across Europe.

1763 Peace of Paris: end of Seven Years War.

1770 Smallpox epidemic in Europe.

1778 Holland and France join American colonies in War of Independence.

1779–83 Spain enters War of Independence against Britain and lays siege to Gibraltar.

1781 Joseph I of Austria introduces religious toleration and abolishes serfdom.

1789 French Revolution: overthrow of Bourbon monarchy; abolition of feudal rights and privileges.

1792 France declares war on Austria and Prussia; beginning of Revolutionary Wars; National Convention formed to rule France; France becomes a Republic.

1793 Louis XVI executed; Reign of Terror begins under Robespierre.

1794 Robespierre executed: end of Reign of Terror.

1795 Napoleon leads army into renewed Revolutionary Wars.

1799 Napoleon seizes power in France.

Northern and Eastern Europe

1762 Accession of Catherine II (the Great); Russia changes sides in Seven Years War and allies with Prussia against Austria. Russian noblemen gain economic and social rights that free them from service obligations.

1766 Catherine II grants freedom of worship in Russia.

1772 First partition of Poland between Russia, Prussia and Austria.

1773–74 The Cossack leader Pugachev leads popular revolt against rule of Catherine II: uprising crushed.

1775 Reforms of provincial government carried out by Catherine II.

1784 Convention of Constantinople: Turkey accepts Russian annexation of Crimea.

1787 Russia and Turkey at war.

1788 Famine in Hungary.

1793 Second partition of Poland.

1795 Third partition of Poland.

THE 19TH CENTURY

Britain and Ireland

1801 Act of Union joins Britain and Ireland, abolishing Irish Parliament.

1805 British fleet defeats the French and Spanish at Battle of Trafalgar; Nelson mortally wounded.

1807 Slave trade abolished in British Empire.

1810 Durham miners strike.

1811 Prince of Wales becomes regent (future George IV), owing to insanity of George III.

1812 Assassination of PM Spencer Percival. Anglo-American War (until 1814).

1815 Britain gains the Cape, Mauritius, Ascension Island, Heligoland, Ceylon, Trinidad, Tobago, St Lucia in postwar settlement.

1819 Peterloo Massacre of peaceful radical demonstrators in Manchester.

1820 Cato Street conspiracy: plot to assassinate Cabinet uncovered.

1828 Nonconformists allowed to hold office.

1829 Catholic Emancipation Act: Catholics can hold office.

1832 First Reform Bill extends vote.

1833 Slavery abolished in British Empire.

1834 Tamworth Manifesto.

1836 Chartist Movement begins.

1838 Foundation of the Anti-Corn Law League.

1839 First Chartist Petition.

Western Europe

1802 Peace of Amiens ends war between Britain and France.

1803 Britain declares war on France in renewal of Napoleonic Wars.

1804 Napoleon becomes Emperor; Code Napoleon adopted in France.

1805 Nelson defeats the French and Spanish fleets at Trafalgar. Napoleon defeats Austro-Russian forces at Austerlitz.

1806 Napoleon abolishes Holy Roman Empire; creation of the Confederation of the Rhine; beginning of economic warfare between France and Britain.

1810 Napoleon marries Marie Louise of Austria.

1813 Napoleon defeated at Battle of Leipzig.

1814 Napoleon abdicates and is exiled to Elba; Congress of Vienna.

1815 Napoleon's 100 Days end in defeat at Waterloo; Congress of Vienna resumes; Confederation of Germany formed.

1822 End of Congress System of diplomatic alliances. Civil war in Spain.

1823 Spanish Liberals defeated in civil war with help of French troops.

1830 July Revolution in France – Bourbons overthrown and Liberal Orleans monarchy established. Revolution in Belgium leads to independence.

1830–31 Successful Belgian revolt against Dutch rule.

Southern and Eastern Europe

1801 France defeats Turks at Heliopolis, Egypt. Assassination of Tsar Paul of Russia; accession of Alexander I.

1804 Persia and Russia at war over Russian annexation of Georgia.

1804–13 Serbian revolt against Turkish Ottoman rule.

1805 Napoleon crowns himself king of Italy.

1807 Peninsular War sparked off by Napoleon's invasion of Portugal.

1811 French finally driven out of Portugal.

1812 Napoleon invades Russia and defeats Russian forces at Battle of Borodino, but retreats from Moscow in the severest winter conditions.

1813 Battle of Vittoria: French driven from Spain by Wellington's forces: ends Peninsular War.

1815 Kingdom of Poland re-established (under Russian rule). UK gains the Ionian Islands at Congress of Vienna.

1817 Revolt of Greeks against Turkish rule.

1820–32 Greek war of independence against Turks.

1825 Decembrist uprising in Russia leads to repressive rule by Tsar Nicholas I.

1826 Russia and Persia at war.

1827 Russians win war and annex Armenia.

1830 Polish uprising against Russia. Revolution in northern Italy against Austrian occupation.

1831 Italian nationalist movement founded by Mazzini.

1832 Poland becomes a Russian province.

The Americas

1803 USA makes 'Louisiana Purchase' from France.

1804 Haiti proclaims its independence from France.

1807 Colombian independence movement begins.

1808 Uprisings in Spain's South American colonies.

1810 Simon Bolívar becomes popular nationalist leader in South America.

1812–14 Anglo-American War.

1810–20 Independence for Paraguay and Venezuela (1811), Argentina (1816), Chile (1818), Colombia (1819).

1813 USA seizes West Florida from Spain.

1817 Independent government of Venezuela formed by Bolívar.

1819 Spain cedes Florida to USA.

1820 Missouri Compromise: slave-owning states allowed to join union.

1820–30 Independence for Mexico and Peru (1821), Brazil (1822), Uruguay (1828).

1823 Monroe Doctrine warns European powers against further New World colonization.

1830 Large-scale removal of Indians to reservations begins. Ecuador becomes independent of Colombia.

1836 Battles of the Alamo and San Jacinto; Texas gains independence from Mexico.

1837 Papineau and Mackenzie Rebellions in Canada.

1838 Foundation of Central American republics.

Africa and Middle East

1801 Third Xhosa War between the Xhosa people and colonial forces.

1805 Mehemet Ali becomes Pasha of Egypt and begins to modernize Egypt.

1806 Britain seizes Cape Colony from Dutch.

1807 Sierra Leone and Gambia become British colonies.

1809 Ecuador becomes part of Colombia.

1810 Mauritius and Seychelles annexed by Britain.

1811 Fourth Xhosa War (see 1801).

1815 UK gains the Cape at Congress of Vienna.

1818 Zulu Kingdom formed by Shaka.

1818–19 Fifth Xhosa War (see 1801).

1820 Gold Coast becomes a British colony.

1821–22 Foundation of Liberia.

1824–31 First Ashanti War in the Gold Coast.

1830 Algeria becomes a French colony.

1834–35 Sixth Xhosa War: Chief Hintsa shot while in British custody (see 1801).

1836 Great Trek begins: Boers settle Orange Free State and Transvaal.

1838 Massacre of Zulus at Battle of Blood River.

Asia and Australasia

1803–5 First Maratha War in India.

1804 Castle Hill Rising of convicts in New South Wales.

1806 Sepoy mutiny against British at Vellore, India.

1808 Overthrow of Governor Bligh in Rum Rebellion, Australia.

1811 British occupy Java; restored to Dutch in 1819. Russians fail to force Japan to open trade with West.

1814 Missionary work in New Zealand.

1815 UK gains Ceylon; revolt against British rule (1817) repressed.

1819 Singapore is founded as British colony.

1824 Britain gains Assam. First Anglo-Burmese War (until 1826).

1825–30 Java War: Dutch defeat Javanese anti-colonial forces.

1828 Western Australia founded.

1834 South Australia founded.

1837 Colonization of New Zealand begins.

1838–42 First Anglo-Afghan War.

1839 First Opium War between Britain and China.

THE 19TH CENTURY

Britain and Ireland

1843 Agitation in Ireland for repeal of Act of Union.

1846 Repeal of Corn Laws. Potato famine in Ireland.

1847 Young Ireland Movement founded.

1850 Palmerston intervenes in Don Pacifico Affair.

1851 Great Exhibition of London.

1853 Gladstone's first Budget.

1867 Second major Reform Act doubles the electorate. Trade Unions declared illegal.

1868 First Trades Union Congress. Disraeli becomes PM.

1869 Disestablishment of Church of Ireland.

1870 Gladstone's Irish Land Act.

1871 Trade Unions declared legal.

1872 Ballot Act introduces secret ballot in elections.

1877 Parnell leads Irish Nationalist MPs in policy of obstruction in House of Commons.

1881–82 Parnell imprisoned.

1882 Phoenix Park Murders spark off Anglo-Irish Crisis.

1884 Third Reform Act.

1886 First Irish Home Rule Bill fails.

1890 Divorce scandal ends Parnell's political career.

1891 Keir Hardie becomes first Independent Labour Party MP.

1893 Second Irish Home Rule Bill fails.

Western Europe

1848 Revolutions in Paris and Berlin suppressed by 1849; universal suffrage introduced in France.

1848 Second French Republic established; Louis Philippe abdicates.

1850 France abolishes universal suffrage.

1851 Fall of Second Republic in France; Louis Napoleon becomes Emperor Napoleon III.

1862 Bismarck becomes Chancellor of Prussia. Prussia gains Schleswig Holstein after war with Denmark (1864).

1866 Austro-Prussian War. Prussia defeats Austria at Könninggrätz and ends Austrian influence in Germany; Prussia annexes Hanover, Nassau and Hesse-Cassel.

1867 Formation of North German Confederation. Austro-Hungarian 'Dual Monarchy' founded.

1871 France defeated in Franco-Prussian War: Alsace ceded to Germany; German unification under Kaiser Wilhelm I: Bismarck becomes Chancellor of Germany. Paris Commune is crushed.

1882 Italy, Germany and Austria form the Triple Alliance.

1884 Berlin Conference intensifies 'Scramble for Africa' – race by European powers for African colonies.

1890 Fall of Bismarck. Anglo-German agreement over colonies.

1894 Dreyfus Affair begins in France; splits nation.

1897 First Zionist Congress meets in Basel, Switzerland.

Southern and Eastern Europe

1841 Straits Convention closes the Dardanelles to non-Ottoman warships.

1848 Revolution against Austrian Empire in Italian states, Prague and Budapest suppressed by 1849.

1854 Crimean War starts: France, Britain, Austria and Turkey against Russia.

1856 End of Crimean War: Treaty of Paris guarantees Turkey's integrity.

1861 Italian unification led by Garibaldi and Cavour. Emancipation of Russian serfs.

1863 Polish and Lithuanian revolt against Russian rule.

1868 Liberal uprising in Spain: Isabella II deposed.

1869 Carlist uprising in Spain crushed.

1870 Italy annexes Rome.

1873 First Spanish Republic.

1877 Massacre of Bulgarians by Turks: Russo–Turkish War.

1878 End of Russo–Turkish War; Romania, Serbia and Montenegro independent.

1887 Renewal of Russo-German Reinsurance Treaty and Triple Alliance.

1891 Launch of the Young Turk Movement.

1894 and **1896** Massacres of Armenians by Turks.

The Americas

1840 Act of Union joins Upper and Lower Canada.

1845 US–Mexican War starts.

1847 Mormons settle Salt Lake City.

1848 End of US–Mexican War. USA gains California and New Mexico. Californian gold rush.

1850 Compromise over slavery in new US states.

1850–90 Indian wars on the western US plains.

1860–1 Southern US states secede to form Confederacy.

1861 American Civil War begins.

1863 Emancipation of slaves in USA.

1865 Confederacy surrenders; Lincoln assassinated.

1866 Civil Rights Bill for US Blacks passed.

1867 USA purchases Alaska from Russia.

1876 Battle of Little Big Horn Custer's US cavalry wiped out by Sioux.

1879 War of the Pacific: Chile defeats Peru and Bolivia; Bolivia loses Pacific coast.

1889 Panama Canal Scandal. Brazil becomes a republic. North and South Dakota, Washington, Montana join USA.

1890 Battle of Wounded Knee: final defeat of Sioux.

1893 USA overthrows Hawaiian government.

1898 Spanish-American War: Spain cedes Puerto Rico, Guam, Philippines and Cuba to USA.

Africa and Middle East

1841 Mehemet Ali recognized as hereditary ruler of Egypt.

1846–53 Xhosa War: Xhosa resist expansion of Dutch and British colonists in Cape Colony.

1851 British occupy Lagos. End of slave trade.

1854 Livingstone begins exploration of central Africa.

1866 Livingstone's third expedition in Africa.

1868 Britain annexes Basutoland.

1869 Opening of Suez Canal.

1873 Second Ashanti War.

1875–1900 The 'Scramble for Africa' – intensifies after the 1884 Berlin Conference.

1877 Britain annexes the Transvaal.

1879 Britain and France gain control of Egypt. Zulu Wars.

1881 First Boer War. Nationalist revolt in Egypt.

1883 Kruger becomes President of the Transvaal.

1885 Khartoum falls to Mahdi: death of General Gordon.

1890 Establishment of Rhodesia by Cecil Rhodes.

1895 Rhodes resigns after Jameson Raid.

1896 Italy fails to take Ethiopia.

1898 Fashoda Incident.

1899 Second Boer War starts.

Asia and Australasia

1840 New Zealand becomes a British colony.

1841 Britain occupies Hong Kong.

1842 Massacre in Khyber Pass as British retreat from Afghanistan.

1845 Maori rising against British in New Zealand.

1845–49 Sikh Wars: British annexation of the Punjab.

1850 Taiping Rebellion starts in China.

1856–60 Second Opium War.

1857–58 Indian Mutiny suppressed; Crown government of India begins.

1859 Cambodia becomes a French protectorate.

c. 1860s Gold rushes in New Zealand.

1860 Second Maori War in New Zealand. Chinese ports forced to trade with West.

1864 Qing Dynasty finally crushes Taiping Rebellion; 20 million dead.

1867 End of transportation of convicts to Australia.

1867–69 Tokugawa shogunate toppled in Japan; Meiji reforms begin.

1877 Queen Victoria becomes Empress of India.

1878 Second Anglo–Afghan War.

1882 French capture Hanoi. Chinese assert suzerainty over Annam.

1885 Indian National Congress meets for first time. Britain and Germany annex New Guinea.

1894 War between China and Japan begins.

1895 End of war between China and Japan: Japan gains Formosa (Taiwan) and Korea.

THE 20TH CENTURY TO 1939

Britain and Ireland

1900 Labour Representative Committee formed.

1901 Death of Queen Victoria.

1902 End of Boer War.

1906 British Labour Party founded after election.

1909 Lloyd George's 'People's Budget' introduces social security measures: leads to constitutional crisis (1910–11).

1911 Parliament Act reduces powers of House of Lords.

1913 House of Lords rejects Third Irish Home Rule Bill. Militant suffragette demonstrations held in London.

1914 Britain declares war on Germany: outbreak of World War I.

1915 Coalition government formed.

1916 Easter Rising in Ireland suppressed.

1918 Civil war in Ireland.

1921 Irish Free State established in Southern Ireland: civil war continues (until 1923).

1924 First Labour Government.

1926 General Strike.

1929 Hunger march from Glasgow to London.

1931 Dominion states gain full independence. National government formed after fall of Labour government.

1932 Great Hunger March.

1936 Abdication of Edward VIII.

1937 PM Chamberlain adopts policy of appeasement of Germany.

1939 Britain declares war on Germany: outbreak of World War II.

Western Europe

1904 Entente Cordiale between Britain and France established.

1905 Norway becomes independent from Sweden.

1906 End of Dreyfus affair.

1907 Germany opposes arms limitations at the Hague Peace Conference. Triple Entente of France, Britain and Russia formed.

1908 Austria annexes Bosnia and Herzegovina.

1914 Austrian heir Archduke Franz Ferdinand assassinated: Austria declares war on Serbia; Germany declares war on Russia and France: outbreak of WWI.

1914 Beginning of trench warfare on Western Front.

1916 One million dead at Battle of the Somme.

1918 Austria–Hungary and Germany surrender.

1919 Treaty of Versailles; Spartacist Rising in Berlin crushed.

1920 Weimar Republic established in Germany.

1923 Kapp Putsch fails: Hitler arrested.

1923–25 Franco-Belgian occupation of Ruhr when Germany defaults on reparations.

1927 German economy collapses on Black Friday.

1930 107 Nazis are elected to Reichstag.

1933 Hitler becomes Chancellor of Germany.

1935 Anti-semitism is legalized in Germany by Nuremberg laws.

1936 Rome-Berlin Axis formed.

1936 Germany and Japan sign Anti-Comintern Pact.

1938 German annexation of Austria – *Anschluss* – and Czech Sudetenland.

1939 Germany signs non-aggression pact with USSR; invades Czechoslovakia and Poland: outbreak of WWII.

Southern and Eastern Europe

1900 Assassination of Umberto I, King of Italy.

1903 Formation of Bolshevik Party in Russia.

1905 'Bloody Sunday' Revolution in Russia: Duma (Parliament) set up with limited powers.

1908 Assassination of Carlos, King of Portugal.

1910 Portugal becomes a republic.

1915 Italy joins Allies and Bulgaria joins Central Powers.

1916 Portugal and Romania join war against Germany.

1917 October Revolution: Bolsheviks take control.

1918 Russia withdraws from war; Russian Civil War.

1919 End of Habsburg Empire: independence for Czechoslovakia, Poland, Yugoslavia and Hungary.

1921 Greece and Turkey at war.

1921 End of Russian Civil War.

1922 Fascists march on Rome: Mussolini becomes PM.

1924 Death of Lenin: Stalin emerges as successor.

1925 Mussolini establishes dictatorship.

1929 Lateran Treaties recognize sovereignty of Vatican City.

1930 Beginning of the extermination of Kulaks (wealthy peasants) in USSR.

1933 Stalinist purges begin.

1935 Soviet 'Show Trials' of ex-Party members.

1936 Outbreak of Spanish Civil War.

1937 Italy joins Anti-Comintern Pact.

1939 Nationalists win Spanish Civil War. German-Soviet pact assigns Baltic States to USSR. USSR invades Finland.

THE 20TH CENTURY TO 1939

The Americas

1901 US President McKinley assassinated: T. Roosevelt succeeds him.

1902 Cuba becomes fully independent.

1903 USA gains control of Panama Canal zone. Panama seceeds from Colombia.

1910 Mexican Civil War begins.

1914 Canada enters war against Central Powers.

1915 *Lusitania* sunk by German U-boat.

1916 US troops occupy Dominican Republic.

1917 USA declares war on Germany.

1919 US President Wilson instrumental in the establishment of the League of Nations.

1920 USA enters period of isolation after Senate votes against membership of the League of Nations. Beginning of Prohibition in USA.

1921 US women are given the vote.

1928 Outbreak of Chaco War between Paraguay and Bolivia.

1929 Wall St Crash precipitates Great Depression worldwide.

1930 Vargas comes to power in Brazil.

1930s Order restored in Mexico by Institutional Revolutionary Party – redistribution of land (1934–39).

1933 President F.D. Roosevelt launches New Deal policy to counter effects of Depression. End of Prohibition.

1935–39 US Neutrality Acts prevent US involvement in non-American wars.

Africa and Middle East

1900 North and South Nigeria become British protectorates.

1902 End of Boer War.

1904 Massacres of Herero rebels by Germans in South West Africa.

1906 Revolution in Iran forces the establishment of a constitution.

1907 Belgian government takes over control of Congo from Léopold III following atrocities.

1910 South Africa becomes independent dominion.

1911 Agadir Crisis: Germany sends gunboat to Morocco to force territorial concessions from France.

1914 South Africa enters the war against the Central Powers.

1917 Britain supports idea of Jewish state in Palestine in Balfour Declaration.

1919 Ottoman Empire dismantled: Britain gains mandate over Palestine and Iraq; France gains mandate over Syria.

1920 Kenya becomes a British colony.

1921 Reza Khan seizes power in Iran (becomes Shah in 1925).

1922 British protectorate over Egypt ends.

1923 Turkish republic formed with Mustapha Kemal as president.

1929 Arab–Jewish clashes and anti-British riots in Palestine.

1930 Haile Selassie crowned emperor of Ethiopia.

1930s Growth of Afrikaner nationalism in South Africa.

1932 Saudi Arabia established.

1935–36 Italians invade and occupy Ethiopia.

Asia and Australia

1900 Anti-Western Boxer Rebellion in China ends after foreign intervention.

1901 Australian Commonwealth established.

1904 Russo–Japanese War.

1907 New Zealand becomes an independent dominion.

1911–12 Revolution in China ends imperial rule: republic established.

1914 Australia and New Zealand enter the war against the Central Powers; German territories in the Pacific occupied – Western Samoa by New Zealand, Nauru by Australia, Micronesia and the Marshall Islands by Japan.

1919 Punjab riots; Amritsar Massacre by British troops fuels Indian nationalist sentiment.

1921 Gandhi begins civil disobedience campaign in India. Chinese Communist Party formed.

1923 Sun Yat-sen establishes Nationalist Chinese government.

1927–28 Civil War in China: Nationalists defeat Communists and form government.

1931 Mukden Incident: Japan seizes Manchuria.

1932 Indian Congress is declared illegal: Gandhi is arrested.

1934–35 'Long March' by defeated Chinese Communists.

1935 Burma separated from India.

1937 Japan invades China.

1938 Japan gains effective control over China.

THE 20TH CENTURY SINCE 1939

Britain and Ireland

1940 National government formed under Churchill following Dunkirk evacuation. Battle of Britain.

1940–41 London Blitz.

1945 Labour government comes to power: establishment of welfare state.

1948 British Citizenship Act: all Commonwealth citizens qualify for British passports.

1949 Irish Republic leaves Commonwealth.

1956 Suez Crisis leads to resignation of PM Eden.

1958 Race riots in London and Nottingham.

1963 France vetoes Britain's application to join EEC.

1968 Britain withdraws from East of Suez. Immigration control introduced.

1969 Troops sent to Northern Ireland to restore order.

1972 Direct rule introduced in Northern Ireland.

1973 Britain and Ireland join EC.

1974 Power-sharing experiment in Northern Ireland abandoned.

1979 Winter of industrial action. Right-wing Conservative premiership of Margaret Thatcher begins.

1982 Falklands War.

1984–85 Year-long miners' strike.

1985 Anglo-Irish Accord on Northern Ireland.

1987 Third Thatcher government formed.

1990 Thatcher resigns; John Major becomes PM.

1992 Conservatives win fourth consecutive term of office.

Western Europe

1940 Germany invades France.

1941 First extermination camps set up in Germany.

1944 D–Day Allied landings.

1945 Germany surrenders; Germany and Austria occupied; United Nations founded.

1945–46 Nuremburg Trials.

1948 Communists blockade Berlin: Allied Berlin Airlift.

1949 NATO is formed. Germany is divided into East and West Germany.

1952 End of Allied occupation of West Germany.

1957 Treaty of Rome establishes the European Economic Community (EEC; later EC).

1958 Fifth Republic of France established under Charles De Gaulle.

1959 EFTA founded.

1961 Berlin Wall is built.

1968 Anti-government student demonstrations and strikes in France.

1969 Beginning of Ostpolitik in West Germany. French president De Gaulle resigns.

1971 Women gain the vote in Switzerland.

1973 East and West Germany establish diplomatic relations.

1973 Denmark joins EC.

1981 Miterrand, first socialist president of French Fifth Republic.

1986 Spain and Portugal join EC.

1989 Berlin Wall opened.

1990 German reunification.

1992 Single European market established.

Southern and Eastern Europe

1940 Italy joins war against Allies.

1941 Germany invades Yugoslavia, Greece and USSR.

1941 Bulgaria and Romania join the Axis Powers.

1943 Invasion of Sicily by Allies; Italy surrenders.

1944 Soviet offensive in East.

1945–48 Communist takeover in eastern Europe.

1946 Civil War in Greece.

1952–57 Campaign by Greek Cypriots to end British rule.

1953 Death of Stalin; Khrushchev comes to power.

1955 Warsaw Pact formed.

1956 De-Stalinization in Eastern Europe; Soviet troops crush anti-Soviet uprising in Hungary.

1964 Clashes between Greeks and Turks break out in Cyprus.

1964 Brezhnev comes to power, insists USSR has right to intervene in the affairs of Communist states.

1967 Military coup in Greece.

1968 'Prague Spring' in Czechoslovakia; reform ended when Soviet troops invade.

1970 Unrest in Poland; riots in Gdansk.

1974 Overthrow of Portuguese dictatorship. Turkish invasion of Cyprus leads to partition. Democracy restored in Greece.

1975 Death of Franco: restoration of democracy in Spain.

1981 Greece joins EC.

1985 Gorbachov comes to power: begins policy of reform.

1989–90 Fall of Communist regimes in Eastern Europe: free elections.

1990 German reunification.

1991 Break up of USSR into 15 independent republics; Gorbachov resigns.

1992 Civil war leds to break up of Yugoslavia.

THE 20TH CENTURY SINCE 1939

The Americas

1941 Lend Lease Act passed. USA enters war on Allied side.

1942 US troops arrive in Europe, North Africa and the Pacific.

1946–55 Juan Perón in power in Argentina.

1947 Truman Doctrine: containment of Communism.

1948 Marshall Plan adopted to provide US aid to Europe.

1949 Escalation of Cold War between USA and USSR after explosion of first Soviet atomic bomb.

1950–54 McCarthy witch-hunt of suspected Communists in USA.

1956–58 Cuban Civil War: Fidel Castro comes to power.

1957 US Civil Rights Act passed; race riots in southern states.

1960 Bay of Pigs: attempt by US-backed exiles to invade Cuba fails.

1961 Cuban Missile Crisis.

1963 President Kennedy is assassinated; Martin Luther King leds Civil Rights Campaign.

1967 Race riots in the USA.

1968 Martin Luther King and Robert Kennedy assassinated. Growing opposition to US role in Vietnam.

1972 Civil War breaks out in El Salvador.

1973 Peace of Paris: US troops withdraw from Vietnam. Left-wing Allende government overthrown in Chile by General Pinochet with indirect US help.

1974 Watergate scandal forces Nixon to resign.

1979 Somoza overthrown by Sandinistas in Nicaragua.

1980 Cold War heats up following invasion of Afghanistan.

1986 'Iran-gate' scandal.

1987 INF Treaty signed by USA and USSR.

1990 Chile and Brazil hold free elections: return to civilian government.

Africa and Middle East

1941 War extends to North Africa.

1942 Montgomery defeats German-Italian forces at El Alamein.

1943 Germans and Italians withdraw from North Africa.

1948 State of Israel established; first Arab-Israeli War.

1948 Nationalists in power in South Africa: policy of apartheid begins.

1952 Moroccan uprising against French; Mau Mau rebellion starts in Kenya.

1954 Nasser takes full control of Egypt. Beginning of Algerian War of Independence.

1956 Suez Crisis. Independence for Morocco, Sudan and Tunisia.

1957–75 Decolonization in Black Africa.

1962 Algeria achieves independence after bitter struggle.

1965 White Rhodesian government unilaterally declares independence: guerrilla fighting follows.

1967 Six Day Arab-Israeli War; Israel defeats Arabs and captures Sinai, the West Bank, Gaza and Golan: PLO formed.

1970 Jordanian civil war; Palestinians expelled.

1973 Third Arab-Israeli War; Arab oil embargo on the West.

1974–5 Portuguese African colonies gain independence.

1975 Lebanese civil war begins.

1977 Crackdown on anti-apartheid activity in South Africa.

1979 Islamic Revolution in Iran.

1980 Rhodesia becomes independent; renamed Zimbabwe.

1980–88 Iran-Iraq War.

1982 Israel invades Lebanon.

1986 Palestinians intensify violent anti-Israeli campaign.

1990 South Africa begins to dismantle apartheid: Nelson Mandela is set free. Iraq invades Kuwait.

1991 Gulf War: US led coalition defeats Iraq.

Asia and Australasia

1941 Japan bombs Pearl Harbor: Britain and USA declare war on Japan.

1940–42 Japan invades Indochina (1940), the Philippines (1941), Malaya, Singapore, East Indies and Burma (1942).

1945 US atomic bombs dropped on Hiroshima and Nagasaki; Japan surrenders.

1946–49 Nationalists defeated in Chinese Civil War: Mao Zedong and Communists come to power.

1947 India gains independence; Pakistan becomes separate state.

1948 Gandhi assassinated.

1950–53 Korean War.

1950–51 Chinese invasion of Tibet.

1954 Vietnam gains independence form French; divided into Communist North and Western-backed South Vietnam.

1959 Uprising in Tibet crushed by China.

1962 A US military command is set up in South Vietnam.

1965 US marines sent to Vietnam. Chinese Cultural Revolution begins.

1968 Tet Offensive by North Vietnamese forces.

1969 USA begins talks with North Vietnamese.

1971 Bangladesh becomes an independent state.

1973 US troops leave Vietnam.

1975 South Vietnam surrenders: end of Vietnam War.

1976 Mao Zedong dies: end of era in Chinese history.

1979 Soviet forces back coup in Afghanistan: civil war breaks out. Vietnam invades Cambodia.

1986 Overthrow of President Marcos of the Philippines.

1988 Vietnamese forces withdraw from Cambodia.

1989 Soviet troops are gradually withdrawn from Afghanistan. Peaceful pro-democracy demonstrations are violently crushed in Tiananmen Square, China.

BATTLES

100 MAJOR BATTLES

The following list outlines 100 battles that were either important turning points in the history of the world or have otherwise achieved lasting fame.

Marathon 490 BC Greco-Persian Wars: Under Miltiades and Callimachus, the Athenians defeated a Persian sea-borne invasion of Attica (central Greece). Pheidippides ran to bring news of the victory to Athens, giving the name 'marathon' to the long-distance race.

Thermopylae 480 BC Greco-Persian Wars: the Greek advance guard – consisting of 300 Spartans under Leonidas, Helots (semi-slaves) and others – defended the pass against Xerxes' invading army. Even when surrounded, cut off and facing certain death, the Greek advance guard fought on in an act of epic heroism.

Salamis 480 BC Greco-Persian Wars: following Themistocles' strategy, the Greeks were able to out-manoeuvre and defeat the Persian fleet. The Persians were forced to abandon the Peloponnese (southern Greece), checking their conquest of Greece.

Plataea 479 BC Greco-Persian Wars: victory of the Greek infantry forces led by Pausanias the Spartan, over the Persian forces of Xerxes I, at Plataea. The battle forced the Persians to abandon their attempt to conquer Greece and ended the Greco-Persian Wars.

Aegosopotami 405 BC Peloponnesian War (Athens against Sparta): the Athenian fleet was taken by surprise and destroyed by the Spartans under Lysander. The siege and surrender of Athens followed, making Sparta the dominant power in Greece.

Leuctra 371 BC Epaminondas led the Thebans to victory over the Spartans, making Thebes the dominant power in Greece.

Chaeronea 338 BC Philip II of Macedon defeated the Greek allies (mainly Thebans and Athenians) ensuring Macedonian domination of Greece.

Issus 333 BC Conquests of Alexander the Great: Alexander lead the Macedonian army to victory against the Persians under King Darius. The conquest added Syria and Egypt to his sphere of domination.

Gaugamela 331 BC Conquests of Alexander the Great: despite being outnumbered, Alexander lead the Macedonian army to victory against the Persians under King Darius. He conquered Mesopotamia (modern Iraq) and Persia (modern Iran), ending the Persian empire.

Hydaspes 326 BC Conquests of Alexander the Great: Alexander and the Macedonian army defeated the forces of King Porus, but the troops demanded a return home.

Cannae 216 BC Second Punic War (Rome against Carthage): at Cannae in southern Italy, Rome suffered its worst military defeat when Hannibal's Carthaginian army surrounded and annihilated the Roman forces, with estimates of Roman losses from c. 50 000 to 70 000 men. However, Hannibal was unable to follow up his victory.

Metaurus 207 BC Second Punic War: Hasdrubal led a Carthaginian force to bring reinforcements to his brother Hannibal, but was defeated and destroyed by the Romans at Metaurus in northern Italy. The defeat helped force Hannibal to withdraw from Italy.

Zama 202 BC Second Punic War: Hannibal was defeated at Zama (in modern Tunisia) by Scipio Africanus in northern Africa, forcing Carthage to concede defeat and ending the Second Punic War. Rome became the dominant power in the western Mediterranean.

Pydna 168 BC Rome against Macedon: the Romans showed the superiority of their tactics when they defeated the Macedonian phalanx led by King Perseus. The victory at Pydna (central Greece) gave Rome effective control of Greece.

Carrhae 53 BC Crassus' expedition against the Parthians: Crassus' Roman army was defeated by the Parthian horse-archers and heavy cavalry when they attempted to capture Ctesiphon, the capital of the Parthian Empire. The defeat checked Roman eastward expansion.

Actium 31 BC Mark Antony and Cleopatra's Egyptian fleet was defeated by Octavian, the nephew of Julius Caesar, at Actium (western Greece). It brought to an end the civil wars that had plagued the Roman world for the last 50 years. Octavian became the first emperor (Augustus).

Teutoburger Wald AD 9 In their attempt to conquer Germany, three Roman legions led by Quintilius Varus were defeated and killed by the Germans under Arminius. The defeat fixed the Roman frontier at the Rhine.

Milvian Bridge AD 312 In the power struggle following the breakdown of the Tetrarchy system for running the Roman Empire, Constantine defeated his rival Maxentius. Having had a dream in which he saw the 'Chi-rho' symbol and words 'In hoc signo vinces' ('in this sign you will conquer'), Constantine became a Christian and the first Christian emperor.

Adrianople AD 378 In an attempt to escape the Huns, the Goths settled in the Roman Empire. However, they were treated so badly that they rebelled, and defeated the Romans, killing the Emperor Valens. They went on to sack Rome in AD 410, eventually establishing a kingdom in Spain.

Catalaunian Fields AD 451 Attila and the Huns were defeated by a combined force of Romans and Visigoths under Aetius and Theodoric. Attila retreated into central Europe.

Yarmuk AD 636 Arab conquests: at Yarmuk in Palestine the Arabs defeated the forces of the Byzantine emperor and conquered Syria and Egypt (including the Holy Places). It allowed them to go on to conquer Egypt and North Africa.

Quadisiya AD 636 Arab conquests: the Arabs defeated the Persians and conquered Iraq. The defeat enabled them to go on and conquer Persia the following year.

Poitiers AD 732 Arab conquests: the Franks, led by Charles Martel, defeated an Arab invasion of France, limiting the Arab conquests in Europe to Spain and Portugal.

Ethandune AD 878 Viking battles: Alfred of Wessex defeated the 'Great Army' of Danish Vikings, and forced them to make peace at Wedmore. The defeat prevented the total conquest of England by Vikings, and allowed Alfred's successors to reconquer and unite the country.

Lechfeld AD 955 Magyar (Hungarian) conquests: at Lechfeld in southern Germany, the Emperor Otto I inflicted a crushing and fatal defeat on the Hungarians, who then adopted Christianity and settled down as a bulwark against attacks on Europe from the East during the rest of the Middle Ages.

Hastings 1066 Norman Conquest: an army of Norman and French soldiers led by Duke William of Normandy defeated the Saxon army of King Harold (who died in battle). William was subsequently crowned king of England.

Manzikert 1071 At Manzikert (in modern Turkey), the Seljuk Turks under their sultan Alp Arslan defeated a large Byzantine army led by Emperor Romanus Diogenes (who was captured). The Byzantine Empire was severely weakened by the permanent loss of control of the interior of Asia Minor.

Hattin 1187 The Crusades: Saladin led the Arab forces in victory against the army of the Latin (Christian) kingdom of Jerusalem, and were able to conquer almost all of Palestine.

Las Navas de Tolosa 1212 La Reconquista: The Christian Spaniards defeated the Muslim Almoravids of North Africa at Hattin in Palestine, recovering the impetus in their reconquest of Spain from the Muslims. The success of the Reconquista was now assured.

Muret 1213 Albigensian Crusade: Northern French forces under Simon de Montfort defeated the forces of Count Raymond of Toulouse and King Peter of Aragon. Most of Languedoc fell under de Montfort's control, marking the beginning of the end of both Languedoc's independence and the Cathar heresy.

Ain Jalut 1260 Mongol conquests: at Ain Jalut in Palestine, the Egyptian Mamluks led by Sultan Qutuz defeated the Mongols and repelled their invasion of Syria. The Mamluks became the chief power in the eastern Mediterranean.

Courtrai 1302 The communal militias of Flanders showed that infantry, if determined enough, could repel armoured knights. They defeated the army of the king of France when the French knights embarked on a rash charge.

Bannockburn 1314 Anglo-Scottish Wars: Robert the Bruce's Scottish forces defeated the English under Edward II who had employed poor tactics. The victory helped secure Scottish independence.

Morgarten 1315 Swiss Wars of Independence: the Swiss combined missile and halberd attacks with an ambush to defeat a superior Austrian army, ensuring the eventual independence of the Swiss Confederation.

Crécy 1346 Hundred Years War: a smaller English army, led by Edward III, used its archers to shoot to pieces the ill-coordinated assaults of the poorly led French.

Poitiers 1356 Hundred Years War: the French, led by John II, dismounted most of their fully armoured men, to avoid a repetition of Crecy, but were outmanoeuvred and defeated by the Black Prince (son of Edward III of England). King John and most of the great nobles were captured.

Kosovo 1389 Ottoman conquests: Turkish forces destroyed the Serbian army, gaining control over much of the western Balkans, as the Serbian Empire collapsed.

Nicopolis 1396 Ottoman conquests: a Crusading force, intending to bring help to Byzantium, was outmanoeuvred at Nicopolis (in modern Bulgaria) and forced to surrender by the Turks under Sultan Bayezit. Subsequent Turkish conquests continued unchecked.

Agincourt 1415 Hundred Years War: after a long period of French dominance, Henry V of England invaded France and, although outnumbered three to one, defeated the over-confident French. Much of France subsequently fell under English control.

Orléans 1429 Hundred Years War: inspired by Joan of Arc, the French defeated the English and raised the siege of Orleans. The defeat led to the eventual expulsion of the English from France.

Castillon 1454 Hundred Years War: the English attempt to recover lost territory in France came to an end with their defeat at the hands of a reorganized French army. Cannon played a part in the French victory.

Nancy 1477 Swiss-Burgundian War: Swiss pikemen defeated the army of Charles the Bold, Duke of Burgundy, whose dreams of creating a powerful state between France and Germany died with him on the battlefield. Swiss mercenaries became the most sought-after troops in Europe.

Bosworth 1485 Wars of the Roses: Henry Tudor's Lancastrian army defeated the army of King Richard III (the Yorkist claimant). Richard was killed, and Henry became King Henry VII, founding the Tudor dynasty.

Marignano 1515 Italian Wars: French and Venetian forces under King Francis I defeated the forces of the Holy Roman Empire (Swiss mercenaries), shattering the myth of Swiss invincibility.

Pavia 1525 Italian Wars: Francis I of France was defeated and captured by the forces of the Holy Roman Empire, who recaptured control of Italy from the French.

Panipat 1526 An Indian (Hindu) army was defeated and destroyed by the Muslim forces of Zahir-ud-din (Babur) at Panipat in northern India. He went on to found the Mogul Empire, which later dominated most of India.

Mohács 1526 Turkish forces led by Suleiman 'the Magnificent' defeated the Hungarians. Hungary was incorporated into the Ottoman Empire, and the Turks went on to besiege Vienna (1529), but failed to take it.

Malta 1565 Turkish forces led by Dragut and Piali attacked Malta, which was defended by the Knights of St John under Grand Master La Valette. The Turkish failure to capture the island put a limit on their westward expansion.

Lepanto 1571 In a major sea battle off the coast of central Greece, the Ottoman fleet was destroyed by the fleet of the Holy League organized by Pope Pius V and led by Don John of Austria. It was the first major Turkish defeat by the Christian powers.

Gravelines 1588 The Spanish Armada fleet sent by Philip II of Spain to conquer England was attacked at anchor and defeated by the English fleet led by Lord Howard of Effingham. Invasion plans were abandoned and the fleet suffered severe losses on the way home round the north and west of the British Isles.

Ivry 1590 French Wars of Religion: Huguenot (French Protestant) forces under Henry of Navarre (later Henry IV of France) defeated the forces of the Catholic League. The wars came to an end when Henry became a Catholic and introduced religious toleration.

White Mountain 1620 Thirty Years War: the army of the Catholic League, commanded by Tilly, defeated the Bohemian rebels near Prague, and the authority of the Habsburg family was restored in

Bohemia. However, the campaign against Frederick of the Palatinate, who had been named as king by the rebels, led to the spread of war throughout the Holy Roman Empire and the involvement of many countries.

Breitenfeld 1631 Thirty Years War: the Swedes under King Gustavus Adolphus defeated the army of the Catholic League, commanded by Tilly, in southern Germany. This checked Habsburg attempts to increase their control over the Holy Roman Empire and strengthen Catholicism.

Lützen 1632 Thirty Years War: the Swedes again defeated the Habsburg forces under Wallenstein, and achieved a dominant position in Germany. However, Gustavus Adolphus was killed in this battle in southern Germany.

Nordlingen 1634 Thirty Years War: the combined forces of the Austrian and Spanish Habsburgs inflicted a severe defeat on the Swedes at Nordlingen in Bavaria. This led France (Sweden's ally) to take a direct part in the war, which prevented the Peace of Prague (1635) from taking effect.

Rocroi 1643 Thirty Years War: the French under Prince de Condé defeated the Spanish, shattering the myth of Spanish invincibility, and beginning an era of French military superiority.

Marston Moor 1644 English Civil War: Parliamentary forces under the command of Sir Thomas Fairfax, David Leslie and Oliver Cromwell, defeated the Royalist forces led by Prince Rupert of the Rhine, nephew of King Charles I. The king lost control of virtually all of the north of England.

Naseby 1645 English Civil War: the reorganized forces of Parliament – the New Model Army – under Oliver Cromwell inflicted a crushing defeat on the army of King Charles I. The battle decided the outcome of the war and the king surrendered to the Scots in 1646.

Boyne 1690 War of the English Succession: north of Dublin, the army of William of Orange (King William III) defeated the Irish and French forces of King James II, who abandoned the struggle to regain his throne and returned to France.

Zenta 1697 War of the Holy League: the Turks had been in retreat since the failure of the siege of Vienna, and this defeat by the Austrians forced them to make peace at Carlowitz, and cede the whole of Hungary to Austria. This marked the beginning of decline of the Ottoman Empire.

Blenheim 1704 War of the Spanish Succession: English and Dutch troops under John Churchill, later Duke of Marlborough, marched across Germany to defeat a Franco-Bavarian force at Blenheim in Bavaria and save Vienna. This prevented France from gaining a major advantage in the first years of the war, and marked England's re-emergence as a military power.

Ramillies 1706 War of the Spanish Succession: the Anglo-Dutch army under Marlborough defeated the French. However, they were unable to break through the French ring of fortresses that defended the north-eastern frontier.

Oudenarde 1708 War of the Spanish Succession: Marlborough's army again defeated the French, but without any conclusive result.

Poltava 1709 Great Northern War: Charles XII of Sweden turned his forces on his Russian enemy, Peter 'the Great' of Russia. However, his invasion failed when he was surrounded during an extremely hard winter and defeated at Poltava (in modern Ukraine). Although the war contined until 1721, Sweden never really recovered and her days of empire were over.

Peterwardein 1716 Austro-Turkish War: Eugene of Savoy, the colleague of Marlborough, led the Austrian forces to its greatest victory over the Turks. By the Peace of Passarowitz the Turks handed Serbia to Austria.

Dettingen 1744 War of the Austrian Succession: Allied forces – British, Dutch and German – under George II of England defeated the French. This was the last time a British sovereign commanded his troops in battle.

Culloden 1746 Jacobite Rebellions: the British army under the Duke of Cumberland defeated the Scottish Highland clans – led by Prince Charles Edward (Bonnie Prince Charlie) – who were supporting the Stuart claim to the throne. It marked the end of Jacobite Rebellions.

Plassey 1757 Seven Years War: the forces of the British East India Company under Robert Clive defeated a much larger army under the Rajah of Bengal, partly by bribing an ally of the Rajah. The victory – at Plassey, north of Calcutta – allowed the company (and therefore Britain) to begin its control over India.

Heights of Abraham 1759 Seven Years War: British forces led by General Wolfe captured Québec when they defeated French forces under Montcalm. Canada fell under British control as a result.

Wandewash 1760 Seven Years War: the French under Lally Tollendal were defeated by British forces led by Sir Eyre Coote at Wandewash, south of Madras. This ended any French challenge to British dominance in India.

Bunker Hill 1775 American War of Independence: the British redcoats defeated the American rebels, despite their stiff resistance, in the first major battle of the war, but at the cost of 1000 British casualties.

Saratoga 1777 American War of Independence: a British attack, led by 'Gentleman Johnny' Burgoyne, on New England through the Hudson Valley ended in failure when he was surrounded and forced to surrender at Saratoga.

Yorktown 1781 American War of Independence: the British under Cornwallis were penned into a corner by the Americans, led by George Washington, and the French fleet. The British were forced to surrender and accept American independence.

Valmy 1792 French Revolutionary Wars: an Austro-Prussian army under the Duke of Brunswick, which had invaded France to restore the monarchy, was defeated by the French. This safeguarded the Revolution.

Trafalgar 1805 Napoleonic Wars: after a failed attempt to invade England, the combined fleets of France and Spain were defeated by the British fleet under Horatio Nelson. The victory – off the southern coast of Spain – heralded the era of total British command of the sea, despite Nelson's death.

Austerlitz 1805 Napoleonic Wars: abandoning his invasion of England, Napoleon turned on his continental enemies and – at Austerlitz, near Brno – defeated the Austrians and Russians, who both soon made peace.

Jena 1806 Napoleonic Wars: the Prussians challenged Napoleon and were routed at Jena in five weeks. It left Napoleon supreme in Europe, and led to massive reforms in Prussia which enabled her to become dominant in Germany later.

Leipzig 1813 Napoleonic Wars: following his disastrous Russian campaign, Napoleon was attacked by a large coalition of Austrian, Prussian, Russian and Swedish forces under Schwarzenberg and Blücher. Napoleon was defeated and had to abandon Germany to his enemies. The defeat contributed to the collapse of the Napoleonic empire (Napoleon abdicated in 1814).

Waterloo 1815 Napoleonic Wars: escaping from exile in Elba, Napoleon returned to France, only to be defeated by the British army under Arthur Wellesley, the Duke of Wellington. He returned to exile in St Helena, and Europe enjoyed a long period of peace.

Gettysburg 1863 American Civil War: the Confederate (Southern) invasion of the North under Lee failed with heavy losses. The repeating rifles of the Union army inflicted massive casualties on the attackers.

Königgratz (Sadowa) 1866 Austro-Prussian War: Moltke's Prussian forces defeated the Austro-Hungarian army under Benedek at Sadowa (in the modern Czech Republic). Austria was forced to accept Prussian dominance in Germany.

Sedan 1870 Franco-Prussian War: the French forces under Marshal MacMahon and Emperor Napoleon III were defeated by the Prussians under Moltke and forced to surrender. It led ultimately to the overthrow of the Second Empire and the unification of Germany.

Ondurman 1898 Second Sudanese Campaign: the British and Egyptian forces under Kitchener defeated the Sudanese thanks to their repeating rifles. It was the first battle in which a fully automatic machine-gun (the Maxim gun) was used.

Tsushima 1905 Russo-Japanese War: the Russian Baltic fleet had been sent to support the Russian campaign in Korea, but was completely defeated by the Japanese, who went on to win the war. Japan emerged as a major power and Russia experienced an unsuccessful revolution.

Marne 1914 World War I: the German invasion of France via Belgium was stopped by French counter-attacks on the line of the River Marne. The Germans fell back to the River Aisne and 'dug in', setting the pattern of trench warfare.

Tannenberg 1914 World War I: two Russian armies advancing towards Königsberg (modern Kaliningrad, Russia) were respectively defeated and forced to retreat by Generals von Hindenburg and Ludendorff. Russia never again entered Germany during the war.

Verdun 1916 World War I: in an attempt to inflict massive casualties on the French, the German commander Falkenhayn attacked the symbolic fortress of Verdun with massive firepower. The French, commanded by Pétain, held the fort, but at a cost of 700 000 lives on each side.

Somme 1916 World War I: the British Army under Haig attacked in their first major offensive of the war. Allied casualties were high, 600 000 men, and the gains, a few kilometres of mud, very limited.

Jutland 1916 World War I: in the war's only major sea battle, the Germans inflicted more damage to the British fleet than they suffered, but the Germans retired into harbour for the rest of the war, leaving Britain's vital control of the sea secure.

Passchendaele 1917 World War I: a British offensive under Haig to relieve the pressure on the mutinous French army and capture German submarine bases on the Belgian coast failed as a result of atrocious conditions. The sea of mud made advance impossible, but 300 000 British casualties were suffered after persistent frontal assaults.

Cambrai 1917 World War I: the first use of tanks on a large scale (381 British tanks) made a serious gap in the German defences. Unfortunately, the initial success was not exploited.

Meggido 1918 World War I: the Battle of Meggido, fought on the traditional site of Armageddon (Palestine), saw the British under Allenby defeat the Turks and go on to occupy Damascus and the rest of Syria, effectively ending the Ottoman Empire.

Battle of Britain 1940 World War II: during the first air battle the German Air Force (Luftwaffe) attempted to gain control of the air to neutralize the British Navy and allow an invasion of Britain. After early successes, the switch to attacking London gave the hard-pressed RAF time to recover as German losses mounted. Soon the Germans abandoned day bombing attacks, and postponed the invasion plans. The use of radar for the first time made a significant contribution to the British effort.

El Alamein 1942 World War II: the British 8th Army under Montgomery defeated the German and Italian forces under Rommel, removing the threat to Egypt and the Suez Canal and beginning a continuous advance that cleared North Africa by 1943. It is often seen as the turning point in British fortunes in the war.

Stalingrad 1942 World War II: following a successful offensive in the second year of the Russian campaign, the German Sixth Army was surrounded and cut off by the Russians in Stalingrad (now Volgograd). Hitler refused to allow them to retreat, and 100 000 German troops were captured.

Coral Sea 1942 World War II: Japanese and American carrier-borne aircraft clashed and although losses were about even, the Japanese plans for an attack on New Guinea were stopped.

Midway 1942 World War II: in a naval battle dominated by carrier-borne aircraft, the Japanese attack on the Hawaiian Islands was defeated. This marked the end of the Japanese advance in the Pacific.

Philippine Sea 1944 World War II: the biggest carrier battle of all time was a crushing American victory. Japanese losses of carriers and planes were so heavy that the Japanese Navy lost its capability to launch air-borne operations.

Leyte Gulf 1944 World War II: in the last major naval battle of the war, the Japanese fleet lost three battleships, four carriers, ten cruisers and eleven destroyers in clashes with American forces at Leyte Gulf in the Philippines.

Imphal/Kohima 1944 World War II: after the Japanese conquest of Malaya and Burma, their attempted invasion of India was checked by General Slim's 14th Army at Imphal and Kohima. Supported by the American-led Chinese in the northeast, the British and Commonwealth forces began an offensive that liberated al of Burma (Myanmar) by summer 1945.

Dien Bien Phu 1954 The French attempt to keep control of their former colony Vietnam ended when their fortified base at Dien Bien Phu was overrun by the Vietminh guerrillas led by General Giap. It led to the establishment of the Communist state of North Vietnam and the non-Communist state of South Vietnam.

ECONOMY AND SOCIETY

ECONOMICS

ECONOMIC SCARCITY

Economics is concerned with the problem of using the available resources of a country as efficiently as possible to achieve the maximum fulfilment of society's unlimited demands for goods and services. The ultimate purpose of economic endeavour is to satisfy human wants for products. The problem is that although wants are virtually without limit, the resources – natural resources, labour and capital – available to produce goods and services are limited in supply. Since resources are scarce – relative to the demands they are called upon to satisfy – mechanisms are required in order to allocate resources between individual end uses (see microeconomics, below) and to ensure that all the available resources are fully employed (see macroeconomics, below).

ECONOMIC SYSTEMS

An economy can be 'organized' in a number of ways.

Market economies
In a *private enterprise* or *market economy* the means of production are privately held by individuals and businesses. Economic decision-making is highly decentralized, and resources are allocated through a large number of individual markets for goods and services. The *market* brings together buyers and producers. By establishing prices for products and suitable profit rewards for suppliers, the market will determine how much of a product will be produced and sold. Proponents of enterprise systems highlight the inefficiencies and rigidities usually associated with state bureaucracies (see Command economies, below), and suggest that competition, far from being wasteful, acts as an important spur to efficiency and encourages enterprise, leading to lower prices and better goods and services.

Command economies
In a *command, centrally planned* or *state economy*, economic decision-making is centralized in the hands of the state. The means of production – except labour – are under collective ownership. The state bureaucracy decides which products – and how many of each – are to be produced in accordance with some centralized national plan. Resources are allocated between producing units by quotas. Advocates of this system emphasize the benefits of synchronizing and coordinating the allocation of resources as a unified whole, avoiding the 'wastes' of duplication inherent in competition.

Mixed economies
In a *mixed economy* the state provides some goods and services (for example, electricity, postal services, medical care, education, etc), while others are provided by private enterprise. The precise 'mix' of private enterprise and state activities to be found in particular countries varies substantially and is very much influenced by the political philosophies of the government concerned.

The formation of the European Community, programmes of 'privatization' in Britain, France and a number of Latin American countries, and the collapse of the command economies of the countries of eastern and central Europe bear testimony to the current ascendancy of the 'free' market economies.

MICROECONOMICS

THE PRICE SYSTEM

Microeconomics is concerned with how resources that are scarce are allocated to produce a multitude of goods and services to meet the demands of consumers for these products. In a market economy, the *price system* operates to synchronize the actions of buyers and sellers of products, and so determining the underlying pattern of resource allocation. The following simple example explains how the price system 'works' to this end.

Let us assume two products, coffee and tea, and that initially prices are such as to equate supply and demand for these products in their respective markets. If there is a change in consumer demand away from tea and towards coffee, the increased demand for coffee – coupled with an unchanged coffee supply in the short-run – results in an *excess demand* for coffee at the prevailing price. This extra demand causes the price of coffee to rise. By the same token, the fall in demand for tea – coupled with an unchanged tea supply in the short-run – results initially in an *excess supply* of tea at the prevailing price and a fall in the price of tea as suppliers seek to clear unsold stocks.

These changes in prices will affect the profits of coffee and tea suppliers. The rising price of coffee will increase the profitability of supplying coffee and the falling price of tea will decrease the profitability of supplying tea. Over the longer term, existing coffee producers will expand production and new producers will enter the market, causing the price of coffee to fall until a new *equilibrium price* – at which supply will again equal demand – is reached. Similarly, the falling price of tea will drive less efficient suppliers out of the market, while other suppliers will curtail their output. The resulting decline in tea supply will continue until tea supply adjusts to the lower level of demand and prices stabilize, restoring the equality of supply and demand.

Changes in product markets will have repercussions in the resource markets. In order to expand coffee supply, extra labour and capital resources must be drawn into coffee production and this can only be achieved by offering them a higher return than they receive elsewhere. By contrast, the tea industry will release resources as firms leave the market, and the remaining resources will earn lower returns. The 'price' of a product acts as a resource 'signaller', serving to reallocate resources away from products where the demand is falling (as reflected in lower prices) to be redeployed in the production of products where demand is increasing (as reflected in higher prices).

However, the response of supply within the price system to changes in consumer demand may be very slow and painful, because less efficient firms are not eliminated quickly but linger on making low profits or losses. Also, resources cannot always be easily 'switched' from one activity to another. For example, in the case of labour, a significant amount of retraining may be required or workers may be required to move from one area of the country to another. Thus, occupational and geographical immobilities may inhibit effective resource redeployment.

The market may also be distorted by monopolies. Monopoly suppliers of products may deliberately restrict supply in order to force up prices; similarly, powerful labour unions may force up wage rates.

MICROECONOMIC POLICY

Because of the problems noted above, governments often attempt to improve the allocation of resources by using a variety of industrial, competition, regional and labour policies. _Industrial policy_, for example, can be used to reorganize industries beset by excess capacity, by compensating firms for leaving the industry or encouraging firms to merge and close down redundant plant. Industrial policy can also be used to foster innovation by providing grants and tax benefits to firms investing in research and development and to provide retraining facilities to improve occupational mobility. _Competition policy_ can be used to prevent dominant firms from profiteering at the expense of consumers and to outlaw price-fixing agreements between firms. Similarly, competition policy can be used to prevent mergers and takeovers likely to have anti-competitive consequences. _Regional policies_ can be used alongside macroeconomic policies to stimulate employment opportunities by encouraging new firms and industries to invest in areas of high unemployment to replace declining industries. Finally, it is possible for a government to improve the functioning of resource markets by adopting _labour policies_ – for example, attacking restrictive labour practices and reducing the monopoly power of trade unions.

MACROECONOMICS AND THE MARKET ECONOMY

Macroeconomics is concerned with how the economy as a whole 'works'. It seeks to identify determinants of the levels of national income, output and spending, employment and prices, and the balance of payments.

The premise of macroeconomics – and the rationale for governments 'managing the economy' – is that there are certain 'forces' at work in the economy that transcend individual markets. The level of spending in the economy affects all markets to a greater or lesser degree as well as affecting the overall levels of employment and prices in the economy. Thus, if total spending (i.e. _aggregate demand_) is too low relative to the output potential of the economy (i.e. _aggregate supply_) the result is likely to be rising unemployment. If total spending is too high, causing the economy to 'overheat', the result may be inflation and/or rising levels of imports, leading to balance-of-payments problems.

THE CIRCULAR FLOW OF NATIONAL INCOME AND EXPENDITURE

'Households' purchase goods and services from 'businesses', using income received from supplying economic resources (their labour and/or capital) to businesses. Businesses produce goods and services using resources supplied to them by households.

This basic model can be developed to incorporate a number of 'injections' to and 'withdrawals' from the income flow. For example, not all of the income received by households is spent – some is saved. Saving is a withdrawal from the income flow. Businesses not only produce _consumer goods_, they also produce _investment_ or _capital goods_ (factories, machines, etc). Investment injects funds back into the income flow. Part of the income received by households is taxed by the government and serves to reduce the amount of income consumers have available to spend. Taxation is a withdrawal from the income flow. However, when governments spend their taxation receipts by providing public goods (schools, roads, etc.) and benefits such as old-age pensions and unemployment benefit, they inject income back into the 'flow'. Households spend some of their income on goods and services produced abroad. Imports are a withdrawal from the income flow. On the other hand, some output is sold to overseas customers. Exports represent spending by foreigners on domestically produced goods and services and so constitute an injection into the income flow.

MACROECONOMIC POLICY

Governments attempt to 'manage' or control income and spending flows in the economy in order to ensure that they are consistent with their overall economic objectives. Typically, governments are concerned to secure four main macroeconomic objectives: _full employment_ (unemployment is to be avoided because it results in 'lost' output to the economy); _price stability_ (inflation is to be avoided because it produces harmful effects, for example people on fixed incomes – such as pensioners – suffer a fall in their standard of living); _economic growth_ (growth is desirable because it enables the economy to produce more goods and services over time, serving to increase living standards); and a _balance of payments equilibrium_ (a persistent excess of imports over exports is to be avoided since this is likely to lower domestic incomes and lead to job losses).

Governments use four main methods – _fiscal policy, monetary policy, prices and incomes policies_ and _management of the exchange rate_ – to control the level and distribution of spending in the economy.

Fiscal policy involves the use of various taxation measures to control spending. If spending needs to be reduced, the authorities can, for example, increase 'direct taxes' on individuals (raising income tax rates) and companies (raising corporation tax rates). Spending can also be reduced by increasing 'indirect taxes' – an increase in value-added taxes (VAT0 on products in general, or an increase in excise duties on particular products such as petrol and beer, will, by increasing their prices, lead to a reduction in purchasing power. Alternatively, the government can use changes in its own expenditure to affect spending levels; a cut in current purchases of products or capital investment by the government, for example, will reduce total spending in the economy.

Taxation and government expenditure are linked together in terms of the government's overall fiscal or budget position. A _budget surplus_ (with government taxation and other receipts exceeding expenditure) serves to decrease total spending, while a _budget deficit_ (where expenditure is greater than taxation receipts) serves to increase total spending in the economy.

Monetary policy involves the regulation of the money supply (notes and coins, bank deposits, etc.), and of credit and interest rates in the economy. If, for example, the authorities wish to reduce the level of spending they can seek to reduce the money supply by an _open market operation_ such as selling government securities to the general public. Buyers pay for these securities by running down their bank deposits – an important component of the money supply. This forces the banks in turn to reduce the amount of bank loans to personal and business customers.

The authorities can also seek to reduce spending by making borrowing more expensive, i.e. by increasing interest rates on loans used to buy cars, televisions, houses, etc. This is done by direct government intervention in the money markets to reduce the availability of monetary assets relative to the demand for them, and so forcing up base lending rates. Occasionally, the authorities use more direct methods to limit credit by, for example, 'instructing' the banks to limit or reduce the amount of loans they make available.

Prices and incomes policies are statutory controls on costs and prices.

The management of the exchange rate influences the country's external trade and payments position.

NOBEL PRIZEWINNERS IN ECONOMICS

Established in 1969.

1969 Ragnar Frisch, Norwegian, and Jan Tinbergen, Dutch: for work in econometrics.
1970 Paul A. Samuelson, USA: for scientific analysis of economic theory.
1971 Simon Kuznets, USA (naturalized citizen): for research on the economic growth of nations.
1972 Sir John Hicks, English, and Kenneth J. Arrow, USA: for contributions to the general economic equilibrium theory.
1973 Wassily Leontief, USA (naturalized citizen): for work on input analysis.
1974 Gunnar Myrdal, Swedish, and Friedrich von Hayek, British: for analysis of the interdependence of economic, social and institutional phenomena.
1975 Leonid V. Kantorovich, Russian, and Tjalling C. Koopmans, USA (naturalized citizen): for contributions to the theory of optimum allocation of resources.
1976 Milton Friedman, USA: for consumption analysis, monetary theory and economic stabilization.
1977 Bertil Ohlin, Swedish, and James Meade, English: for contributions to theory of international trade.
1978 Herbert A. Simon, USA: for decision-making processes in economic organization.
1979 W. Arthur Lewis, English, and Theodore W. Schultz, USA: for analysis of economic processes in developing nations.
1980 Lawrence R. Klein, USA: for development and analysis of empirical models of business fluctuations.
1981 James Tobin, USA: for empirical macro-economic theories.
1982 George Stigler, USA: for work on the economic effects of governmental regulation.
1983 Gerard Debrau, USA: for mathematical proof of supply and demand theory.
1984 Sir Richard Stone, English: for the development of a national income accounting system.
1985 Franco Modigliani, USA: for analysis of household savings and financial markets.
1986 James McGill Buchanan, USA: for political theories advocating limited government role in the economy.
1987 Robert M. Solow, USA: for contributions to the theory of economic growth.

1988 Maurice Allais, French: for contributions to the theory of markets and efficient use of resources.
1989 Trygve Haavelmo, Norwegian: for testing fundamental econometric theories.
1990 Harry Markowitz, Merton Miller and William Sharpe, USA: for pioneering theories on managing investment portfolios and corporate finances.
1991 Ronald H. Coase, British-born economist working in the USA: honoured for his work on the value and social problems of companies.
1992 Gary S. Becker, USA: for his work linking economic theory to aspects of human behaviour, drawing on other social sciences.

THE ERM

The ERM (the Exchange Rate Mechanism) is an agreement originally between 10 of the 12 members of the EC to limit movement in the value of their currencies (the Greek drachma is not a member and Sterling was withdrawn from the ERM in 1992; see below). The ERM is not a totally fixed system. ERM members agree a set of exchange rates against each other's currencies and a margin on either side of these *central rates* to allow for some daily movement in the markets.

The pivot of the system is the German mark, against which all other ERM currencies have an agreed central rate.

In September 1992 Britain suspended its membership of the ERM after sterling fell below the permitted lowest level against the mark.

UNEMPLOYMENT

The average rate of unemployment as a percentage of the total workforce during 1991 for the G7 countries was as follows:

Canada	10.2%
Italy	9.9%
France	9.5%
UK	8.7%
USA	6.6%
Germany	4.3%
Japan	2.1%

THE ECU

The ecu is a unit of account, based upon a basket of European currencies, used as a reserve asset in the *European Monetary System*, the system that enables member states of the EC to coordinate their exchange rates through the Exchange Rate Mechanism (ERM). ECU is an abbreviation for European Currency Unit; the *écu* was also a late medieval French coin.

The ERM is the first stage of the plan for monetary union within the EC. The ecu is widely envisaged as the eventual European currency, and a limited issue of ecu coins has already been made in Belgium, where they are legal tender. Commemorative ecu coins have been issued in France, Ireland and Spain.

ECONOMIC TERMS

accelerator the impetus to increase new investment in an economy as rising demand puts pressure on existing supply capacities.

advertising the use of the media (commercial, television, newspapers, posters) to promote the sales of products and services.

aggregate demand the total amount of spending on goods and services in an economy.

aggregate supply the total amount of goods and services produced by an economy. (See gross national product.)

agricultural policy a policy aimed at improving the efficiency of the farm sector and protecting farmers' incomes by the use of grants and price and income support.

appreciation an increase in the price of an asset, or value (exchange rate) of a country's currency that makes imports cheaper and exports more expensive. (See depreciation, and floating exchange rate.)

arbitrage the buying and selling of products, etc., between separate markets (e.g. two countries) in order to take advantage of any price differences in these markets.

asset an item of property (a house, shares, etc.) that has a money value.

balance of payments the balance of a country's imports and exports; a financial statement of a country's transactions with other countries in goods and services ('the current account') and capital flows (investment, loans, etc.).

balance of trade a financial statement of a country's transactions with other countries in *goods*.

balance sheet a financial statement of a firm's assets and liabilities on the last day of a trading period.

bank a financial institution that accepts deposits from persons and businesses, and provides them with various facilities (money transmission via cheques, loans and overdrafts, etc.).

bank deposit a sum of money held on deposit with a bank either as a 'current account' (withdrawable on demand) or a 'deposit account' (from which withdrawals can be made, subject to notice being given).

barriers to entry obstacles in the way of new firms attempting to enter a market, such as customer brand loyalty to established firm's products.

barter the exchange of one product for another product. (See money.)

base rate the lowest or 'floor' interest rate charged by the banks on loans and overdrafts. This usually applies only to their most credit-worthy customers, others being charged higher rates.

bill of exchange a financial security representing an amount of credit extended by one firm to another, usually for three months.

black economy economic activities that go 'unrecorded', in particular, work performed by people who wish to avoid disclosing their income to the tax authorities.

black market an 'unofficial' market in a product which is either prohibited by law (e.g. narcotics) or which is in short supply.

bond a financial security issued by a company or the government as a means of raising long-term loan finance.

budget (government) a financial statement of a government's receipts (from taxes, etc.) and expenditures (social security, etc.).

budget deficit an excess of expenditure over receipts in a government's budget.

budget surplus an excess of receipts over expenditures in a government's budget.

building society a financial institution that accepts deposits from persons and businesses and makes mortgages available for house purchase (and limited banking facilities).

business cycle the tendency for industrial production to swing upwards ('recovery' to 'boom') and downwards ('recession' to 'slump') as demand in the economy rises and falls.

capital physical assets, such as factories used to produce products, and financial assets, such as shares used to finance physical investment.

capital formation additions to the capital stock of an economy.

capital goods products such as machinery and equipment that are purchased by businesses as opposed to consumers. (See consumer.)

capital stock a country's accumulated stock of productive assets such as factories, machinery and equipment.

cartel a group of producers (e.g. the OPEC oil cartel) who act together to fix uniform prices, limit production, etc.

central bank: the premier bank of a country (usually owned by the state). It is responsible for regulating the state's internal and external monetary affairs. (See monetary policy, and exchange rate.)

centrally planned economy an economy in which all or most of the country's productive assets are owned by the state as opposed to individuals and firms. (See nationalization.)

cheque a written order drawn upon a bank. It is a means of purchasing products or withdrawing cash from a bank deposit.

collusion a market situation where suppliers act together to suppress competition. (See cartel.)

commodity market a market that is engaged in the buying and selling of commodities such as tin, copper, wheat, cattle, etc., and the determination of market prices for these products.

common market a group of countries that have entered a formal agreement to provide for the free movement of products, capital and labour across national boundaries.

comparative advantage the advantage possessed by a country engaged in international trade if it can produce a given good at a lower resource cost than other countries.

competition a market situation where suppliers compete against one another in terms of price, quality, advertising, etc.

competition policy a policy aimed at improving market efficiency and protecting consumers by controlling monopolies, mergers, cartels and anti-competitive practices such as refusals to supply, exclusive dealing, etc.

concentration a measure of the extent to which the supply of a particular product is controlled by the leading suppliers.

consumer goods products such as toys, bread, etc., which are purchased by consumers as opposed to businesses. (See capital goods.)

consumption the proportion of current income that is used to purchase goods and services. (See savings.)

convertibility the ability to exchange one foreign currency (e.g. the UK £) for another currency (e.g. the US $).

corporation tax a levy by the government on the income (profits) earned by businesses.

cost the payment (wages, materials, etc.) incurred by a firm in producing its products.

cost of living the general level of prices in an economy as measured by a price index. (See retail price index.)

credit an amount of money made available in the form of a loan, overdraft, mortgage, etc., to persons or businesses.

currency bank notes and coins issued by the monetary authorities of a country. They form part of a country's money supply.

debt an amount of money owing to a person or business that has advanced credit in the form of a loan, overdraft, or mortgage.

deflation a reduction in the level of demand and a fall in the rate of growth of the general price level (disinflation). (See inflation.)

deindustrialization a relative decline in the industrial sector of the economy compared to other sectors, particularly services.

demand the want, need or desire for a product backed by the money to purchase it.

demand curve a line depicting the total amount of a product buyers are prepared to purchase over a range of prices. (See equilibrium market price.)

depreciation a fall in the value of an asset due to wear and tear, or in the value (exchange rate) of a country's currency; the latter makes imports more expensive and exports cheaper. (See appreciation and floating exchange rate.)

devaluation an administered reduction in the value (exchange rate) of a country's currency under a fixed exchange rate system; this makes imports more expensive and exports cheaper. (See revaluation.)

discount market a market engaged in the buying and selling of bills of exchange and Treasury bills.

disposable income the income remaining to households after the payment of all taxes on income.

diversification the combination in one firm of a number of unrelated productive activities, e.g. brewing and publishing.

dividend income received from the ownership of shares.

dumping the sale of a product in an export market at a price that is *lower* than its domestic price.

economic growth an increase in the amount of goods and services produced in an economy over time.

economics the study of the allocation of *limited* resources of capital, labour, etc., to meet the (*unlimited*) demands of society for goods and services.

economies of scale a fall in the average cost of producing a product as the volume of output is increased.

elasticity of demand the extent to which the demand for a product is affected by changes in its *own* price, consumer's income and the prices of *other* products.

embargo a ban on international trade with a particular country or in particular products.

equilibrium market price the price at which the total demand for a product is exactly equal to the total quantity supplied so that the market price 'stabilizes' for the present. (See excess demand, and excess supply.)

eurocurrency a currency that is used to finance trade and investment outside its country of origin, in Western Europe.

European Community (EC) an alliance of 12 countries that seeks to establish free trade between members (the 'Common Market').

European Currency Unit (ECU) the monetary asset used by the European Community to settle payments imbalances between members and to value intra-EC government transactions.

European Monetary System (EMS) the mechanism that co-ordinates the exchange rates of member countries of the European Community and facilitates the settlement of payments imbalances. (See European Currency Unit and fixed exchange rates)

excess demand demand for a product that is greater than supply at the prevailing price which causes the price to rise. (See equilibrium market price.)

excess supply supply of a product that is greater than demand at the prevailing price. Excess supply causes the price to fall. (See equilibrium market price.)

exchange rate the price of one foreign currency expressed in terms of another. Exchange rates between currencies may be left to 'float' upwards or downwards day-by-day according to market forces, or the authorities may intervene to stabilize or 'fix' the exchange rate at a particular value. (For the exchange rates of all currencies against the US$, see currencies listing)

export a product (or asset) that is sold in an overseas market. (See balance of payments.)

factors of production natural resources (tin, wheat, etc.), labour and capital that are used as inputs in the production of goods and services.

fiscal policy the manipulation by the government of taxes, tax rates and government expenditure as a means of controlling the level of spending in the economy.

fixed exchange rate an exchange rate for a currency that is 'pegged' at a particular value by the authorities as opposed to being allowed to 'float' according to market forces.

floating exchange rate an exchange rate for a currency that is free to fluctuate according to market forces as opposed to being 'fixed' by the authorities.

foreign exchange market a market that is engaged in the buying and selling of foreign currencies and the determination of exchange rates between currencies.

free trade international trade that takes place without barriers such as tariffs being placed on the free movement of products between countries. (See common market.)

futures market a market in which financial securities and commodities are transacted for delivery at some specified future date. (See spot market.)

General Agreement on Tariffs and Trade (GATT) a negotiating forum for the removal of tariffs and other obstacles to free trade.

gross domestic product (GDP) the money value of the total amount of goods and services produced by an economy over a one-year period.

gross national product (GNP) GDP plus net property income (profits, interest, dividends) from abroad.

hedging the buying and selling of commodities and financial securities on the futures market in order to counteract price fluctuations.

horizontal integration the specialization by a firm in a *particular* line (or 'stage') of production.

import a product (or asset) that is bought from an overseas supplier. (See balance of payments.)

income wages, profits, interest, rents, etc., that are received for performing work, or supplying an asset.

income tax a levy by the government on the income received by individuals.

index-linking the linking of incomes (wages, pensions, etc.) and assets to the general price level so that their values are not eroded by inflation.

industrial policy a policy aimed at improving market efficiency by supporting innovation and promoting rationalization schemes to remove excess capacity.

inflation a persistent tendency for the general price level of goods to rise over a period of time.

insurance company a financial institution that specializes in collecting premiums from policy holders, to provide them with cover against various risks, including loss of life, fire and theft.

interest income received from lending out money in the form of loans, mortgages, etc.

interest rate the (percentage) rate at which charges are made for borrowing money in the form of loans, overdrafts, mortgages, etc.

International Monetary Fund (IMF) an institution that oversees the exchange-rate policies of member countries and provides financial support for countries in balance-of-payments difficulties.

international trade the import and export of goods and services between countries. (See free trade, and comparative advantage.)

investment the creation of *physical* assets such as factories and the acquisition of *financial* assets such as stocks and shares.

investment trust company a financial institution that issues shares and uses its capital to invest in other companies' stocks and shares.

invisible trade imports and exports of *services*, transfers of interest, profit etc. as opposed to goods. (See visible trade, and balance of payments.)

legal tender that part of the money supply which is issued by the government (typically, notes and coins).

loan a sum of money advanced by a lender (creditor) to a borrower (debtor). (See interest rate.)

M0 a UK money supply definition comprising bank notes and coins plus banks' till money and operational balances at the Bank of England.

M3 a UK money supply definition comprising M0

(see above) plus private sector bank deposits and public sector sterling deposits.

market an exchange mechanism that brings together the buyers and sellers of a product, thereby establishing product prices. (See equilibrium market price.)

merger a combination of two or more firms by the mutual agreement of the firm's management and shareholders. (See takeover.)

mixed economy an economy in which a country's productive resources are owned both by the state (the public sector) and by individuals and firms (the private sector). (See private enterprise economy, and centrally planned economy.)

monetarism an economic doctrine that emphasizes the influence of money on the functioning of the economy, in particular its role in causing inflation.

monetary policy the manipulation by the government of the money supply, credit and interest rates as a means of controlling the level of spending in the economy.

money a financial asset such as notes and coins issued by the government, which is generally acceptable as a 'medium of exchange' and can be used to pay for goods and services.

money market a market dealing in the short-run lending and borrowing of money to finance bills of exchange and Treasury bills.

money supply the total amount of money (principally, notes, coins, and bank deposits) in an economy that can be used to finance the purchase of goods, services and assets.

Monopolies and Mergers Commission a UK body that investigates monopolies, mergers and takeovers to determine whether or not they are in 'the public interest'.

monopoly a market situation where one producer controls the entire supply of a good or service.

mortgage a sum of money advanced by a lender (e.g. a building society) to a borrower, usually as a means of financing the purchase of an asset (a house, or a factory).

multinational company a business that owns productive assets (factories, offices, etc.) in a number of countries.

multiplier the process whereby some initial increase in income in an economy leads to further increases in income as that income is spent and re-spent.

national debt the money owed by the government to domestic and overseas lenders arising from accumulated budget deficits.

national income the total money value of the income resulting from a country's economic activities over a one-year period.

nationalization the taking into public ownership of a business or resource previously in the private sector.

Office of Fair Trading the UK body charged with administering British competition policy.

oligopoly a market situation where the supply of a product is controlled by a few large producers.

OPEC a group of major oil-producing countries. OPEC acts as a cartel in regulating oil prices.

option the right to sell or buy a commodity or financial asset at an agreed price on the futures market.

overdraft a facility provided by a bank, etc., that enables a customer to take out more money than they have deposited with the bank up to a specified limit.

pension fund a financial institution that specializes in collecting superannuation contributions from members during their working lives, and providing them with a pension income when they retire.

price the money value of a product or asset.

price level the general level of prices in an economy as measured by a price index. (See retail price index.)

prices and incomes policy the control of prices and incomes (particularly wages) in order to stop or slow inflation in an economy.

price system an allocative mechanism in which the interaction of buyers and sellers in markets establishes product prices and determines which and how many products are required.

private enterprise economy an economy in which all or most of a country's productive assets are owned by individuals and firms as opposed to the state.

privatization the sale of a nationalized (publicly owned) business, etc., to the private sector by issuing share capital.

productivity a measure of the efficiency of a given resource input (labour, capital) in producing output.

profit the income received from selling a product or asset at a price higher than it cost to produce or buy.

protectionism the erection of barriers to trade, such as tariffs, to protect domestic producers from the competition of low-priced imports.

public sector borrowing requirement (PSBR) the money borrowed by the government to cover a budget deficit.

quantity theory of money the proposition that inflation is caused by an 'excessive' increase in the money supply.

quota a limitation on the production of, or trade in, a product. Quotas are imposed by suppliers or by the government.

regional policy a policy aimed at removing regional imbalances in income and unemployment levels by e.g. providing financial support to firms located in 'depressed' areas.

rent income received from the ownership of property.

Restrictive Practices Court a UK body that investigates trade practices such as price-fixing agreements between firms to determine whether they are in 'the public interest'.

retail price index (RPI) a measure of the average prices of a 'basket' of goods and services bought by consumers over time. (See inflation.)

revaluation an administered increase in the value of an asset, or value (exchange rate) of a country's currency under a fixed exchange-rate system.

savings that proportion of current income that is not immediately spent, but is invested and used to finance future consumption.

share a financial security issued by a joint-stock company as a means of raising capital, which in the case of an ordinary share carries voting and dividend rights.

specialization a form of division of labour whereby each individual or business concentrates their productive efforts on a single or limited number of activities.

speculation the buying and selling of a commodity or financial asset in order to make a capital gain.

spot market a market in which financial securities, commodities, etc., are transacted for *immediate* delivery. (See futures market.)

standard of living the general level of economic prosperity in an economy.

stock a fixed-interest financial security issued by a company or the government as a means of raising capital.

stock exchange or **capital market** a market engaged in the buying and selling of existing stocks and shares and in raising capital by the issue of new securities.

supply the amount of a product offered for sale by suppliers.

supply curve a line depicting the total amount of a product that producers are prepared to supply over a range of prices. (See equilibrium market price.)

takeover the acquisition by one firm of another firm by purchasing its share capital. (See merger.)

tariff a tax levied by the government on imported goods, often as a means of protecting domestic producers from foreign competition.

tax a levy by the government on the income of individuals and businesses (e.g. income tax and corporation tax), spending (e.g. value added tax), wealth (e.g. inheritance tax), imported goods (e.g. customs duty), etc.

terms of trade an index of the relative prices of a country's imports and exports, indicating that if export prices go up faster than import prices the country is better off.

Treasury bill a British financial security (with a life of three months) issued by the government as a means of borrowing money.

unemployment rate the percentage of the available labour force in an economy currently out of work.

unit trust a financial institution that sells 'units' to savers, using the moneys received to invest in stocks and shares, etc.

value added tax (VAT) a levy by the government on the value added to a good or service at each separate 'stage' in its production.

vertical integration the combination in one firm of a number of sequentially linked activities in the production of a good or service, e.g. oil extraction, refining and petrol retailing.

visible trade imports and exports of *goods* that are recorded by the customs authorities as they enter or leave a country. (See invisible trade, and balance of payments.)

wage income received by persons for undertaking employment.

wealth the stock of assets owned by an individual or a country.

wealth tax a tax (called an inheritance tax in the UK) levied on a person's assets when those assets are transferred to others.

World Bank an institution that provides economic and financial assistance to less developed countries.

NATIONAL ECONOMIES

The gross national product (GNP) and the gross national product per head of the population are given for each sovereign state. Figures (in US $) are also given for total imports and total exports. For the currency of each state see the following section.

The figures given in this section are mainly for 1990; however, for most major countries 1992 estimates are given.

NB:: The figures given for former Soviet republics are 1992 estimates and are much lower than the official figures published during the last years of the former USSR. These lower figures represent a more realistic assessment of the economies of these countries and reflect both a steep decline in economic output and a dramatic fall in the exchange rate of the former Soviet currency in terms of the US $.

Afghanistan *GNP ($ million):* 3100 (1988); *per head:* $220. *Imports ($ million):* 930 (1990). *Exports ($ million):* 235 (1990). *Main imports:* machinery and transport equipment 37.7% (1989/90), basic manufacture 18.3% (1989/90). *Main exports:* dried fruit and nuts 42.7% (1990), carpets and rugs 16.5% (1990). *Principal trading partners:* Iran, Russia.

Albania *GNP ($ million):* 3800 (1988); *per head:* $200. *Imports ($ million):* 446.5 (1990). *Exports ($ million):* 267.4 (1990). *Main imports:* machinery and transport equipment 28.2% (1989), fuels, minerals and metals 26.0% (1989). *Main exports:* crude minerals and metalliferous ores 41.3% (1989), food and food preparations 17.2% (1989). *Principal trading partners:* Italy, Germany, Czech Republic.

Algeria *GNP ($ million):* 47 200 (1992 est); *per head:* $1696. *Imports ($ million):* 7396 (1988). *Exports ($ million):* 8164 (1988). *Main imports:* industrial equipment 39.0% (1990), food and beverages 22.5% (1990). *Main exports:* minerals, fuels and lubricants 96.3% (1990). *Principal trading partners:* France, Italy, USA, Germany.

Andorra *GNP ($ million):* 892 (1992 est); *per head:* $16 600. *Imports ($ million):* 700.4 (1987). *Exports ($ million):* 24.6 (1987). *Main imports:* wearing apparel 52.1% (1990), food and live animals 25.1% (1990). *Main exports:* machinery and transport equipment 26.8% (1990), food and live animals 25.0% (1990). *Principal trading partners:* France, Spain.

Angola *GNP ($ million):* 6010 (1989); *per head:* $620. *Imports ($ million):* 443 (1987). *Exports ($ million):* 2147 (1987). *Main imports:* raw materials 59.2% (1990). *Main exports:* mineral fuels 93.4% (1990), diamonds 6.2% (1990). *Principal trading partners:* USA, Brazil, UK.

Antigua and Barbuda *GNP ($ million):* 363 (1990); *per head:* $4600. *Imports ($ million):* 225 (1988). *Exports ($ million):* 22 (1988). *Main imports:* basic manufacture 27.0% (1987), machinery and transport equipment 26.8% (1987). *Main exports:* reexports 57.5% (1987), domestic exports 42.5% (1987). *Principal trading partners:* Dominica, UK, Canada.

Argentina *GNP ($ million):* 273 000 (1992 est); *per head:* $8142. *Imports ($ million):* 4076 (1990). *Exports ($ million):* 12 353 (1990). *Main imports:* electrical machinery 11.5% (1987), minerals, fuels and oils, and bituminous substances 11.4% (1987). *Main exports:* animal fodder 13.8% (1987), cereals 11.7% (1987). *Principal trading partners:* USA, Netherlands, Brazil, Germany.

Armenia *GNP ($ million):* c. 2500 (1992 est); *per head:* c. $720 ($2150 in 1991; see note above). *Imports ($ million):* n/a. *Exports ($ million):* n/a. *Main imports:* food products; coal and natural gas. *Main exports:* processed food, chemicals. *Principal trading partners:* Georgia, Russia.

Australia *GNP ($ million):* 308 700 (1992 est); *per head:* $17 320. *Imports ($ million):* 38 542 (1991). *Exports ($ million):* 41 793 (1991). *Main imports:* machinery 30.4% (1989/90), basic manufacturers 16.0% (1989). *Main exports:* crude materials 27.2% (1989/90), food and live animals 20.8% (1989/90). *Principal trading partners:* Japan, USA, New Zealand, Germany, UK.

Austria *GNP ($ million):* 190 000 (1992 est); *per head:* $23 800. *Imports ($ million):* 50 740 (1991). *Exports ($ million):* 41 086 (1991). *Main imports:* machinery and transport equipment (1989) 37.1%, chemicals and related products 10.1% (1989). *Main exports:* machinery and transport equipment 34.4% (1989), chemicals 9.3% (1989). *Principal trading partners:* Germany, Italy, Switzerland, France.

Azerbaijan *GNP ($ million):* c. 4000 (1992 est); *per head:* c. $560 ($1670 in 1991; see note above). *Imports ($ million):* n/a. *Exports ($ million):* n/a. *Main imports:* food and live animals. *Main exports:* petroleum and petroleum products. *Principal trading partners:* Russia, Turkey.

Bahamas *GNP ($ million):* 2913 (1990); *per head:* $11 510. *Imports ($ million):* 3001 (1989). *Exports ($ million):* 2786 (1989). *Main imports:* crude petroleum 51.9% (1989), petroleum products 12.0% (1989). *Main exports:* crude petroleum 66.0% (1989), chemicals 17.9% (1989). *Principal trading partner:* USA, UK, Nigeria.

Bahrain *GNP ($ million):* 3120 (1989); *per head:* $6380. *Imports ($ million):* 3711 (1990). *Exports ($ million):* 3758 (1990). *Total imports:* crude-petroleum products 54.3% (1990), non-petroleum products 45.7% (1990). *Total exports:* petroleum products 79.0% (1990), aluminium products 5.6% (1990). *Principal trading partners:* USA, United Arab Emirates, Saudi Arabia.

Bangladesh *GNP ($ million):* 22 579 (1990); *per head:* $200. *Imports ($ million):* 3405 (1990). *Exports ($ million):* 1690 (1991). *Main imports:* machinery and transport equipment 11.5% (1989/90), textile, yarn, fabrics and made-up articles 10.6% (1989/90). *Main exports:* ready-made garments 39.8% (1989/90), hides, skins and leather 11.2% (1989/90). *Principal trading partners:* Japan, USA, Singapore, India.

Barbados *GNP ($ million):* 1680 (1990); *per head:* $6540. *Imports ($ million):* 695 (1991). *Exports ($ million):* 202 (1991). *Main imports:* machinery 17.5% (1990), food and beverages 14.9% (1990). *Main exports:* mineral fuels 28.3% (1990), sugar 13.0% (1990). *Principal trading partners:* UK, USA, Trinidad.

Belarus *GNP ($ million):* c. 10 640 (1992 est); *per head:* c. $1040 ($3110 in 1991). *Imports ($ million):* n/a. *Exports ($ million):* n/a. *Main imports:* food transport equipment and vehicles, industrial raw materials. *Main exports:* food and live animals, vehicles. *Principal trading partners:* Russia, Ukraine, Germany.

Belgium *GNP ($ million):* 225 000 (1992 est); *per head:* $22 600. *Imports ($ million):* 119 756 (1990). *Exports ($ million):* 117 989 (1990). *Main imports:* machinery and transport equipment 24.3% (1989), chemicals and chemical products 11.6% (1990). *Main exports:* chemicals and chemical products 13.7% (1989), cars 10.1% (1989). *Principal trading partners:* France, Germany, Netherlands, UK, Italy.

Belize *GNP ($ million):* 373 (1990); *per head:* $1970. *Imports ($ million):* 211 (1990). *Exports ($ million):* 129 (1990). *Main imports:* manufactured goods 29.3% (1987), food 22.1% (1987). *Main exports:* sugar 32.9% (1990), orange concentrate 13.3% (1990). *Principal trading partners:* USA, UK, Mexico.

Benin *GNP ($ million):* 1716 (1990); *per head:* $360. *Imports ($ million):* 288 (1984). *Exports ($ million):* 167 (1984). *Main imports:* cereals 17.1% (1987), machinery and transport equipment 13.5% (1987). *Main exports:* raw cotton 55.6% (1987), fuels 27.5% (1987). *Principal trading partners:* France, Thailand, Portugal, USA, Netherlands.

Bhutan *GNP ($ million):* 273 (1990); *per head:* $190. *Imports ($ million):* 48 (1986). *Exports ($ million):* 22 (1986). *Main imports:* road vehicles 14.4% (1987), iron and steel 10.9% (1987). *Main exports:* electricity 39.3% (1987), wood and wood manufactures 17.7% (1987). *Principal trading partner:* India.

Bolivia *GNP ($ million):* 4526 (1990); *per head:* $620. *Imports ($ million):* 942 (1991). *Exports ($ million):* 858 (1991). *Main imports:* raw materials for industry 32.0% (1989), capital goods for industry 24.0% (1989). *Main exports:* natural gas 26.0% (1989), zinc 16.1% (1989). *Principal trading partners:* Argentina, Brazil, USA, UK.

Bosnia-Herzegovina No figures available.

Botswana *GNP ($ million):* 2561 (1990); *per head:* $2040. *Imports ($ million):* 1780 (1990). *Exports ($ million):* 1779 (1990). *Main imports:* transport equipment 19.2% (1990), machinery and electrical goods 18.5% (1990). *Main exports:* diamonds 80.1% (1990); copper-nickel matte 7.8% (1990). *Principal trading partners:* South Africa, Switzerland, UK.

Brazil *GNP ($ million):* 393 000 (1992 est); *per head:* $2466. *Imports ($ million):* 21 004 (1991). *Exports ($ million):* 31 622 (1991). *Main imports:* machinery and electrical equipment 26.5% (1989), minerals 20.5% (1989). *Main exports:* soya products 9.1% (1990), boiler equipment 7.9% (1990). *Principal trading partners:* USA, Germany, Netherlands, Japan, Argentina.

Brunei *GNP ($ million):* 3302 (1989); *per head:* $13 290. *Imports ($ million):* 883 (1989). *Exports ($ million):* 1894 (1989). *Main imports:* machinery and transport equipment 38.0% (1986), manufactured goods 21.1% (1986). *Main exports:* natural gas 52.9% (1986), crude oil 40.6% (1986). *Principal trading partners:* Japan, Thailand, South Korea.

Bulgaria *GNP ($ million):* 8800 (1992 est); *per head:* $1021. *Imports ($ million):* 12 893 (1990). *Exports ($ million):* 13 347 (1990). *Main imports:* machinery and equipment 46.7% (1990), fuels, minerals, raw materials and metals 33.4% (1990). *Main exports:* machinery and equipment 59.0% (1990), beverages and food 12.1% (1990). *Principal trading partners:* Russia, Germany, Poland.

Burkina Faso *GNP ($ million):* 2955 (1990); *per head:* $330. *Imports ($ million):* 322 (1989). *Exports ($ million):* 95 (1989). *Main imports:* manufactured goods 26.8% (1988), chemicals 11.8% (1988). *Main exports:* raw cotton 45.3% (1988), manufactured goods 33.7% (1988). *Principal trading partners:* France, Ivory Coast, Taiwan.

Burundi *GNP ($ million):* 1151 (1990); *per head:* $210. *Imports ($ million):* 236 (1990). *Exports ($ million):* 75 (1990). *Main imports:* machinery and transport equipment 35.4% (1990); mineral oil 13.1% (1990). *Main exports:* coffee 74.8% (1990), tea 10.4% (1990). *Principal trading partners:* Belgium, Germany, France.

Cambodia *GNP ($ million):* 4000 (1989 est); *per head:* $450. *Imports ($ million):* 118 (1985 est). *Exports ($ million):* 12 (1985 est). *Main imports:* machinery and transport equipment 36.9% (1985), petroleum and petroleum products 30.2% (1985). *Main exports:* rubber 82.9% (1985), basic manufactures 5.1% (1985). *Principal trading partner:* Thailand, Singapore.

Cameroon *GNP ($ million):* 11 233 (1990); *per head:* $940. *Imports ($ million):* 1271 (1988). *Exports ($ million):* 924 (1988). *Main imports:* machinery and transport equipment 35.6% (1987). *Main exports:* crude petroleum 44.1% (1987), cacao 16.5% (1987). *Principal trading partners:* Netherlands, France, Germany, Japan.

Canada *GNP ($ million):* 588 000 (1992 est); *per head:* $21 710. *Imports ($ million):* 118 119 (1991). *Exports ($ million):* 126 883 (1991). *Main imports:* road motor vehicles and parts 19.2% (1989), chemicals 5.6% (1989). *Main exports:* road motor vehicles and parts 22.1% (1989), crude materials 11.7% (1989). *Principal trading partners:* USA, Japan, UK, Germany, France.

Cape Verde *GNP ($ million):* 331 (1990); *per head:* $890. *Imports ($ million):* 112 (1991). *Exports ($ million):* 7 (1989). *Main imports:* foodstuffs and beverages 27.2% (1988), machinery 16.0% (1988). *Main exports:* bananas 36.7% (1988), frozen tuna 30.5% (1988). *Principal trading partners:* Portugal, Netherlands, Japan.

Central African Republic *GNP ($ million):* 1194 (1990); *per head:* $390. *Imports ($ million):* 145 (1991). *Exports ($ million):* 74 (1991). *Main imports:* food 20.5% (1988/89), chemicals and plastics 15.6% (1988/89). *Main exports:* coffee 47.9% (1988/89), diamonds 25.2% (1988/89). *Principal trading partners:* France, Germany, Belgium.

Chad *GNP ($ million):* 1074 (1990); *per head:* $190. *Imports ($ million):* 419 (1988). *Exports ($ million):* 141 (1988). *Total imports:* petroleum products 16.8% (1983), cereal products 16.8% (1983). *Total exports:* raw cotton 91.1% (1983), live cattle and frozen meat 1.8% (1983). *Principal trading partners:* France, Cameroon, USA, Nigeria.

Chile *GNP ($ million):* 46 000 (1992 est); *per head:* $3074. *Imports ($ million):* 7424 (1990). *Exports ($ million):* 8924 (1991). *Total imports:* intermediate goods 52.4% (1989), capital goods 27.1% (1989). *Total exports:* mining 59.1% (1989), industrial products 30.5% (1989). *Principal trading partners:* USA, Japan, Germany, Brazil.

China *GNP ($ million):* 475 900 (1992 est); *per head:* $399. *Imports ($ million):* 63 791 (1991). *Exports ($ million):* 71 910 (1991). *Main imports:* machinery and transport equipment 30.8% (1989), products of textile industries, rubber and metal products 20.9% (1989). *Main exports:* basic manufactures 22.1% (1988), light industrial products 15.9% (1988). *Principal trading partners:* Hong Kong, Japan, USA, Germany, Singapore.

China (Taiwan) *GNP ($ million):* 241 000 (1992 est); *per head:* $11 500. *Imports ($ million):* 54 716 (1990). *Exports ($ million):* 67 020 (1990). *Main imports:* machinery and transport equipment 30.8% (1989), products of textile industries, rubber and metal products 20.9% (1989). *Main exports:* basic manufactures 22.1% (1988), light industrial products 15.9% (1988). *Principal trading partners:* Japan, USA, Hong Kong, Germany.

Colombia *GNP ($ million):* 40 805 (1988); *per head:* $1240. *Imports ($ million):* 5590 (1990). *Exports ($ million):* 6745 (1990). *Main imports:* machinery 26.2%

(1990), chemicals 9.4% (1990). *Main exports*: petroleum and products 36.8% (1990), coffee 21.0% (1990). *Principal trading partners*: USA, Germany, Japan, Venezuela, Netherlands.

Comoros *GNP ($ million):* 227 (1990); *per head:* $480. *Imports ($ million):* 43 (1989). *Exports ($ million):* 18 (1989). *Main imports*: rice 20.4% (1989), petroleum products 5.8% (1989). *Main exports*: vanilla 63.0% (1989), ylang-ylang 11.0% (1989). *Principal trading partners*: France, USA, Madagascar.

Congo *GNP ($ million):* 2296 (1990); *per head:* $1010. *Imports ($ million):* 600 (1990). *Exports ($ million):* 976 (1990). *Main imports*: machinery 22.4% (1988), food, beverages and tobacco 21.3% (1988). *Main exports*: petroleum and products 76.7% (1988), wood and wood products 15.6% (1988). *Principal trading partners*: USA, France, Spain.

Costa Rica *GNP ($ million):* 5342 (1990); *per head:* $1910. *Imports ($ million):* 1853 (1991). *Exports ($ million):* 1543 (1991). *Main imports*: basic manufactures for industry 44.0% (1989), non-durable consumer goods 15.9% (1989). *Main exports*: coffee 20.4% (1989), bananas 19.3% (1989). *Principal trading partners*: USA, Germany, Japan.

Côte d'Ivoire (Ivory Coast) *GNP ($ million):* 8920 (1990); *per head:* $730. *Imports ($ million):* 2185 (1989). *Exports ($ million):* 2931 (1989). *Main imports*: machinery and transport vehicles 20.9% (1988), petroleum products 13.9 % (1988). *Main exports*: cocoa and cocoa products 29.6% (1988), coffee and coffee products 17.6% (1988). *Principal trading partner*: France, Netherlands, Nigeria.

Croatia *GNP ($ million):* 14 000 (1990 est); *per head:* $2941. *Imports ($ million):* 4430 (1990). *Exports ($ million):* 2910 (1990). *Main imports*: petroleum and petroleum products, food. *Main exports*: aluminium products, food and live animals. *Principal trading partners*: Italy, Germany.

Cuba *GNP ($ million):* 20 900 (1989); *per head:* $2000. *Imports ($ million):* 7579 (1988). *Exports ($ million):* 5518 (1989). *Main imports*: minerals, fuels and lubricants 32.4% (1989), machinery and transport equipment 31.2% (1989). *Main exports*: sugar 73.2% (1989), minerals and concentrates 9.2% (1989). *Principal trading partner*: Russia, Germany, China.

Cyprus *GNP ($ million):* 5633 (1990); *per head:* $8040. *Imports ($ million):* 2621 (1991). *Exports ($ million):* 960 (1991). *Main imports*: consumer goods 14.9% (1990), transport equipment 12.6% (1990). *Main exports*: clothing 16.1% (1990), potatoes 6.7% (1990). *Principal trading partners*: UK, Italy, Germany, Japan.

Czech Republic *GNP ($ million):* 26 600 (1992 est); *per head:* $2562. *Imports ($ million):* 6970 (1990 est). *Exports ($ million):* 7600 (1990 est). *Main imports*: machinery and transport equipment, minerals, fuels and lubricants. *Main exports*: machinery and transport equipment, basic manufactures. *Principal trading partners*: Germany, Austria, Slovakia, UK, Russia.

Denmark *GNP ($ million):* 145 000 (1992 est); *per head:* $28 200. *Imports ($ million):* 32 257 (1991). *Exports ($ million):* 35 812 (1991). *Main imports*: consumer goods 23.3% (1989), machinery and capital equipment 10.5% (1989). *Main exports*: machinery and instruments 24.1% (1989), agricultural products of animal origin 11.7% (1989). *Principal trading partners*: Germany, Sweden, UK, USA, Netherlands.

Djibouti *GNP ($ million):* 407 (1988); *per head:* $600. *Imports ($ million):* 215 (1990). *Exports ($*

million): 25 (1990). *Main imports*: food and beverages 27.0% (1990), textiles and footwear 11.8% (1990). *Main exports*: live animals 36.1% (1989), food and food products 5.9% (1989). *Principal trading partner*: France, Ethiopia, Japan.

Dominica *GNP ($ million):* 160 (1990); *per head:* $1940. *Imports ($ million):* 118 (1990). *Exports ($ million):* 55 (1990). *Main imports*: basic manufactures 25.5% (1988), machinery and transport equipment 20.7% (1988). *Main exports ($ million)*: bananas 55.5% (1989), coconut-based soaps 18.8% (1988). *Principal trading partners*: UK, USA, Jamaica.

Dominican Republic *GNP ($ million):* 5847 (1990); *per head:* $820. *Imports ($ million):* 1788 (1990). *Exports ($ million):* 734 (1990). *Main imports*: crude petroleum and petroleum products 18.8% (1986), machinery 16.1% (1986). *Main exports*: ferronickel 33.9% (1990), raw sugar 19.4% (1990). *Principal trading partners*: USA, Netherlands, Venezuela, Japan, Mexico.

Ecuador *GNP ($ million):* 10 112 (1990); *per head:* $960. *Imports ($ million):* 2399 (1991). *Exports ($ million):* 2851 (1991). *Main imports*: industrial raw materials 40.6% (1990), industrial capital goods 20.2% (1990). *Main exports*: crude petroleum 46.5% (1990), bananas 17.2% (1990). *Principal trading partner*: USA, Japan, Germany, Brazil.

Egypt *GNP ($ million):* 42 700 (1992 est); *per head:* $751. *Imports ($ million):* 9202 (1990). *Exports ($ million):* 2582 (1990). *Main imports*: machinery and transport equipment 22.6% (1989/90), foodstuffs 21.8% (1989/90). *Main exports*: cotton yarn, textiles and fabrics 26.1% (1989/90), petroleum and petroleum products 23.6% (1989/90). *Principal trading partners*: USA, Germany, France, Italy.

El Salvador *GNP ($ million):* 5767 (1990); *per head:* $1100. *Imports ($ million):* 902 (1990). *Exports ($ million):* 412 (1990). *Main imports*: chemical products 14.5% (1990), crude petroleum 9.7% (1990). *Main exports*: coffee 45.3% (1990), pharmaceuticals 3.6% (1990). *Principal trading partners*: USA, Guatemala, Germany, Mexico.

Equatorial Guinea *GNP ($ million):* 136 (1990); *per head:* $330. *Imports ($ million):* 39 (1987). *Exports ($ million):* 41 (1989). *Main imports*: machinery and transport equipment 25.4% (1984), fuels and lubricants 20.1% (1984). *Main exports*: cocoa 42.4% (1989), fuels and lubricants 19.5% (1989). *Principal trading partners*: Spain, France.

Estonia *GNP ($ million):* c. 2020 (1992 est); *per head:* c. $1280 ($3830 in 1991). *Imports ($ million):* n/a. *Exports ($ million):* n/a. *Main imports*: food and live animals, coal. *Main exports*: agricultural products. *Principal trading partners*: Russia, Finland, Sweden.

Ethiopia *GNP ($ million):* 6041 (1990); *per head:* $120. *Imports ($ million):* 1076 (1990). *Exports ($ million):* 294 (1990). *Main imports*: road transport machinery 16.5% (1988/89), equipment 13.9% (1988/89). *Main exports*: coffee 69.4% (1988/89), animal hides 13.7% (1988/89). *Principal trading partners*: Italy, Germany, USA.

Fiji *GNP ($ million):* 1326 (1990); *per head:* $1770. *Imports ($ million):* 652 (1991). *Exports ($ million):* 451 (1991). *Main imports*: machinery and transport equipment 31.1% (1990), durable manufactures 22.4% (1990). *Main exports*: sugar 37.0% (1990), gold 10.4% (1990). *Principal trading partners*: UK, Australia, New Zealand, Japan.

Finland *GNP ($ million):* 105 000 (1992 est); *per head:* $24 400. *Imports ($ million):* 21 711 (1991).

Exports ($ million): 23 111 (1991). *Main imports:* raw materials and produced goods 53.8% (1990), consumer goods 23.2% (1990). *Main exports:* metal products and machinery 35.0% (1990), paper, paper products and graphic arts 31.3% (1990). *Principal trading partners:* Germany, Sweden, UK, Russia, France.

France *GNP ($ million):* 1 360 000 (1992 est); *per head:* $23 900. *Imports ($ million):* 230 786 (1991). *Exports ($ million):* 213 299 (1991). *Main imports:* machinery 23.9% (1990), agricultural products 10.9% (1990). *Main exports:* machinery 26.2% (1990), agricultural products 16.2% (1990). *Principal trading partners:* Germany, Italy, Belgium, UK, Netherlands, USA.

Gabon *GNP ($ million):* 3654 (1990); *per head:* $3220. *Imports ($ million):* 767 (1989). *Exports ($ million):* 1288 (1987). *Main imports:* machinery and mechanical equipment 29.2% (1989), food and agricultural products 14.6% (1989). *Main exports:* crude petroleum and petroleum products 70.8% (1989), manganese ore and concentrate 11.6% (1989). *Principal trading partners:* France, USA, Germany, Spain.

Gambia *GNP ($ million):* 229 (1990); *per head:* $260. *Imports ($ million):* 200 (1990). *Exports ($ million):* 41 (1990). *Main imports:* food (1990) 33.2%, basic manufactures (1990) 19.7%. *Main exports:* fish and fish preparations 13.1% (1990), peanut meal 2.4% (1990). *Principal trading partners:* France, UK, Switzerland.

Georgia *GNP ($ million):* c. 3000 (1992 est); *per head:* c. $550 ($1640 in 1991). *Imports ($ million):* n/a. *Exports ($ million):* n/a. *Main imports:* food and live animals. *Main exports:* food and live animals. *Principal trading partners:* Russia, Azerbaijan.

Germany *GNP ($ million):* 1 950 000 (1992 est); *per head:* $24 120. *Imports ($ million):* 382 050 (1991). *Exports ($ million):* 391 295 (1991). *Main imports:* machinery and transport equipment 32.3% (1990), chemicals and chemical products 9.0% (1990). *Main exports:* transport 16.8% (1990), chemicals and chemical products 12.7% (1990). *Principal trading partners:* France, Italy, Netherlands, UK, Belgium, USA.

Ghana *GNP ($ million):* 5824 (1990); *per head:* $390. *Imports ($ million):* 1275 (1991). *Exports ($ million):* 1024 (1991). *Main imports:* mineral fuels and lubricants 29.1% (1985), machinery and transport equipment 26.4% (1985). *Main exports:* cocoa 59.4% (1985), gold 15.0% (1985). *Principal trading partners:* UK, USA, Germany, Nigeria, Netherlands.

Greece *GNP ($ million):* 80 000 (1992 est); *per head:* $7600. *Imports ($ million):* 21 582 (1991). *Exports ($ million):* 8653 (1991). *Main imports:* machinery and transport equipment 31.0% (1990), food, beverages and tobacco 14.4% (1990). *Main exports:* food, beverages and tobacco 25.8% (1990), textiles and footwear 21.6% (1990). *Principal trading partners:* Germany, Italy, France, Netherlands, Japan.

Grenada *GNP ($ million):* 199 (1990); *per head:* $2120. *Imports ($ million):* 92 (1988). *Exports ($ million):* 32 (1987). *Main imports:* machinery and transport equipment 22.6% (1989), food 24.0% (1988). *Main exports:* nutmeg 31.9% (1989), bananas 14.3% (1989). *Principal trading partners:* USA, UK, Trinidad and Tobago, Netherlands.

Guatemala *GNP ($ million):* 8309 (1990); *per head:* $900. *Imports ($ million):* 1674 (1991). *Exports ($ million):* 1033 (1991). *Main imports:* primary and intermediate materials for industry 41.5% (1989), capital goods 21.3% (1989). *Main exports:* coffee 33.7% (1989), sugar 7.8% (1989). *Principal trading partners:* USA, Germany, Mexico, Japan.

Guinea *GNP ($ million):* 2756 (1990); *per head:* $480. *Imports ($ million):* 491 (1988). *Exports ($ million):* 548 (1988). *Main imports:* intermediate goods 33.7% (1988), capital goods 13.1% (1988). *Main exports:* bauxite and alumina 73.0% (1990), diamonds 6.8% (1990). *Principal trading partners:* France, Belgium.

Guinea-Bissau *GNP ($ million):* 176 (1990); *per head:* $180. *Imports ($ million):* 39 (1984). *Exports ($ million):* 19 (1984). *Main imports:* transport equipment 28.7% (1988), building materials 17.9% (1988). *Main exports:* cashews 52.8% (1988), peanuts 11.3% (1988). *Principal trading partners:* Portugal, France, Germany.

Guyana *GNP ($ million):* 293 (1990); *per head:* $370. *Imports ($ million):* 512 (1990). *Exports ($ million):* 255 (1990). *Main imports:* capital goods 44.9% (1990), fuels and lubricants 22.7% (1990). *Main exports:* bauxite 31.4% (1990), sugar 30.7% (1990). *Principal trading partners:* UK, USA, Venezuela, Trinidad.

Haiti *GNP ($ million):* 2400 (1990); *per head:* $370. *Imports ($ million):* 374 (1991). *Exports ($ million):* 103 (1991). *Main imports:* mineral fuels 26.0% (1989/90), food and live animals 21.0% (1989/90). *Main exports:* local manufactures 68.4% (1989/90), coffee 11.1% (1989/90). *Principal trading partners:* USA, France, Japan, Canada, Italy.

Honduras *GNP ($ million):* 3023 (1990); *per head:* $590. *Imports ($ million):* 981 (1990). *Exports ($ million):* 912 (1990). *Main imports:* machinery and transport equipment 25.3% (1989), chemical products 21.3 (1989). *Main exports:* bananas 35.0 (1989), coffee 19.5% (1989). *Principal trading partners:* USA, Japan, Mexico, Germany.

Hungary *GNP ($ million):* 40 200 (1992 est); *per head:* $3896. *Imports ($ million):* 11 532 (1991). *Exports ($ million):* Main imports: semi-finished products 50.6% (1990), raw and basic materials 18.1% (1990). *Total exports:* semi-finished products, raw and basic materials 36.4% (1990), machinery and transport equipment 24.0% (1990). *Principal trading partners:* Germany, Austria, Italy, Czech Republic, Russia.

Iceland *GNP ($ million):* 5456 (1990); *per head:* $22 580. *Imports ($ million):* 1720 (1991). *Exports ($ million):* 1554 (1991). *Main imports:* consumer goods 19.2% (1990), capital goods 17.9% (1990). *Main exports:* frozen fish 33.7% (1990), salted fish 14.5% (1990). *Principal trading partners:* Germany, UK, USA, Netherlands.

India *GNP ($ million):* 236 000 (1992 est); *per head:* $269. *Imports ($ million):* 23 267 (1990). *Exports ($ million):* 17 663 (1990). *Main imports:* mineral fuels and lubricants 15.5% (1988/89), pearls and stones 11.3% (1988/89). *Main exports:* pearls, stones and jewellery 21.7% (1988/89), transport equipment and metal manufactures 11.4% (1988/89). *Principal trading partners:* USA, Japan, Germany, UK, Belgium, Saudi Arabia.

Indonesia *GNP ($ million):* 140 000 (1992 est); *per head:* $740. *Imports ($ million):* 21 931 (1990). *Exports ($ million):* 25 675 (1990). *Main imports:* machinery and transport equipment 41.7% (1990), chemicals 17.2% (1990). *Main exports:* crude petroleum 25.7% (1990), natural gas 12.5% (1990). *Principal trading partners:* Japan, USA, Singapore, Germany.

Iran *GNP ($ million):* 60 300 (1992 est); *per head:*

$957. *Imports ($ million):* 11 989 (1990). *Exports ($ million):* 13 200 (1986). *Main imports*: machinery and transport equipment 32.5% (1985/86), iron and steel 14.7% (1985/86). *Main exports*: petroleum and products 92.6% (1989), carpets, nuts, fruits and hides 7.4% (1989). *Principal trading partners*: Germany, Japan, Turkey, UK, United Arab Emirates.

Iraq *GNP ($ million):* 20 800 (1992 est); *per head:* $1000. *Imports ($ million):* 4834 (1990). *Exports ($ million):* 392 (1990). *Main imports*: machinery and transport equipment 39.8% (1987), manufactured goods 27.1% (1987). *Main exports*: fuels and other energy 99.5% (1989), food and agricultural raw materials 0.5% (1989). (The export of petroleum and petroleum products virtually in 1990 under the terms of UN sanctions.) *Principal trading partners*: Turkey, Germany.

Ireland *GNP ($ million):* 50 000 (1992 est); *per head:* $14 700. *Imports ($ million):* 20 761 (1990). *Exports ($ million):* 24 232 (1990). *Main imports*: machinery and transport equipment 35.9% (1990), chemicals 12.4% (1990). *Main exports*: machinery and transport equipment 31.3% (1990), food 19.9% (1990). *Principal trading partners*: UK, Germany, USA, France, Netherlands.

Israel *GNP ($ million):* 71 000 (1992 est); *per head:* $12 241. *Imports ($ million):* 16 906 (1990). *Exports ($ million):* 11 889 (1990). *Main imports*: diamonds 19.2% (1990), investment goods 14.8% (1990). *Main exports*: machinery 28.8% (1990), diamonds 26.4% (1990). *Principal trading partners*: USA, UK, Germany, Belgium, Japan.

Italy *GNP ($ million):* 1 170 000 (1992 est); *per head:* $20 200. *Imports ($ million):* 182 554 (1991). *Exports ($ million):* 169 399 (1991). *Main imports*: machinery and transport equipment 30.5% (1989), chemicals and chemical products 15.4% (1989). *Main exports*: non-transport machinery 29.8% (1989), chemicals and chemical products 15.4% (1989). *Principal trading partners*: Germany, France, USA, UK, Switzerland, Netherlands.

Jamaica *GNP ($ million):* 3606 (1990); *per head:* $1510. *Imports ($ million):* 1864 (1990). *Exports ($ million):* 1116 (1990). *Main imports*: fuels 21.7% (1990), machinery and apparatus 16.8% (1990). *Main exports*: aluminium 55.8% (1990), bauxite 9.2% (1990). *Principal trading partners*: USA, UK, Canada.

Japan *GNP ($ million):* 4 000 000 (1992 est); *per head:* $32 018. *Imports ($ million):* 236 744 (1991). *Exports ($ million):* 314 525 (1991). *Main imports*: petroleum and petroleum products 17.6% (1990), machinery and transport equipment 17.4% (1990). *Main exports*: motor vehicles 17.8% (1990), office machinery 7.2% (1990). *Principal trading partners*: USA, South Korea, Germany, Taiwan, China, Australia.

Jordan *GNP ($ million):* 3408 (1990); *per head:* $1076. *Imports ($ million):* 2512 (1991). *Exports ($ million):* 902 (1991). *Main imports*: machinery and transport equipment 22.9% (1988), basic manufactures 17.3% (1988). *Main exports*: chemicals 28.2% (1988), phosphate fertilizers 23.5% (1988). *Principal trading partners*: Saudi Arabia, Germany, UK, Iraq.

Kazakhstan *GNP ($ million):* c. 14 000 (1992 est); *per head:* c. $830 ($2470 in 1991). *Imports ($ million):* n/a. *Exports ($ million):* n/a. *Main imports*: food and live animals. *Main exports*: natural gas, food and live animals. *Principal trading partners*: Russia, Uzbekistan.

Kenya *GNP ($ million):* 8100 (1992); *per head:* $320.

Imports ($ million): 2226 (1990). *Exports ($ million):* 1052 (1990). *Main imports*: machinery and transport equipment 38.9% (1989), crude petroleum 13.4% (1989). *Main exports*: tea 26.7% (1989), coffee 20.0% (1989). *Principal trading partners*: UK, Germany, United Arab Emirates, Japan.

Kiribati *GNP ($ million):* 54 (1990); *per head:* $760. *Imports ($ million):* 27 (1990). *Exports ($ million):* 3 (1990). *Main imports*: food 26.6% (1990), machinery and transport equipment 19.1% (1990). *Main exports*: copra 27.8% (1990), fish and fish preparations 27.1% (1990). *Principal trading partners*: Fiji, Australia, Japan.

Korea (North) *GNP ($ million):* 28 000 (1990); *per head:* $1240. *Imports ($ million):* 2900 (1989). *Exports ($ million):* 1800 (1989). *Principal trading partners*: Russia, Japan, China.

Korea (South) *GNP ($ million):* 354 000 (1992 est); *per head:* $8040. *Imports ($ million):* 81 557 (1991). *Exports ($ million):* 71 898 (1991). *Main imports*: machinery and transport equipment 32.7% (1989), manufactured goods 15.7% (1989). *Main exports*: machinery and transport equipment 37.7% (1989), manufactured goods 22.0% (1989). *Principal trading partners*: USA, Japan, Germany, Australia, Canada, Singapore.

Kuwait *GNP ($ million):* 33 089 (1989); *per head:* $16 160. *Imports ($ million):* 6303 (1989). *Exports ($ million):* 11 476 (1989). *Main imports*: transport equipment 31.1% (1987), miscellaneous manufactured articles 24.7% (1987). *Main exports*: petroleum and products 92.2% (1989). *Principal trading partners*: Japan, Netherlands, USA, Germany.

Kyrgyzstan *GNP ($ million):* c. 2320 (1992 est); *per head:* c. $520 ($1550 in 1990). *Imports ($ million):* n/a. *Exports ($ million):* n/a. *Main imports*: food, coal. *Main exports*: food and live animals. *Principal trading partners*: Russia, Kazakhstan.

Laos *GNP ($ million):* 848 (1990); *per head:* $200. *Imports ($ million):* 162 (1988). *Exports ($ million):* 81 (1988). *Main imports*: machinery and transport equipment. *Main exports*: wood 47.6 (1988), electricity 17.5 (1988). *Principal trading partners*: Thailand, Japan, China.

Latvia *GNP ($ million):* c. 3100 (1992 est); *per head:* c. $1140 ($3410 in 1991). *Imports ($ million):* n/a. *Exports ($ million):* n/a. *Main imports*: fuel and raw materials. *Main exports*: food and live animals. *Principal trading partners*: Russia, Belarus.

Lebanon *GNP ($ million):* 1800 (1990); *per head:* $690. *Imports ($ million):* 2580 (1989). *Exports ($ million):* 570 (1989). *Main imports*: consumer goods 40.0% (1982), machinery and transport equipment 35.0% (1982). *Main exports*: jewellery 10.2% (1985), clothing 5.2% (1985). *Principal trading partners*: Saudi Arabia, Italy, France.

Lesotho *GNP ($ million):* 832 (1990); *per head:* $470. *Imports ($ million):* 587 (1988). *Exports ($ million):* 64 (1988). *Main imports*: manufactured goods 44.1% (1985), food and live animals 18.2% (1985). *Main exports*: miscellaneous manufactured goods 57.3% (1988/89), crude materials 18.7% (1988/89). *Principal trading partners*: South Africa, Switzerland, UK.

Liberia *GNP ($ million):* 1030 (1987); *per head:* $440. *Imports ($ million):* 272 (1988). *Exports ($ million):* 382 (1987). *Main imports*: machinery and transport equipment 31.1% (1988), petroleum and products 22.7% (1988). *Main exports*: iron ore 55.1% (1988), rubber 28.0% (1988). *Principal trading partners*: Germany, USA, Italy, Netherlands.

Libya *GNP ($ million):* 23 333 (1989); *per head:* $5310. *Imports ($ million):* 4723 (1987). *Exports ($ million):* 8766 (1987). *Main imports:* foodstuffs 42.3% (1989), agricultural goods 18.5% (1989). *Main exports:* crude petroleum 96.8% (1989). *Principal trading partners:* Italy, Germany, Spain, France.

Liechtenstein *GNP ($ million):* 610 (1992 est); *per head:* $21 020. *Imports ($ million):* 535 (1989). *Exports ($ million):* 989 (1989). *Main imports:* machinery and transport equipment 31.2% (1989), metal products 13.6% (1989). *Main exports:* machinery and transport equipment 48.4% (1989), metal products 20.4% (1989). *Principal trading partners:* Switzerland, Austria.

Lithuania *GNP ($ million):* c. 3375 (1992); *per head:* c. $1125 ($2710 in 1991). *Imports ($ million):* n/a. *Exports ($ million):* n/a. *Main imports:* coal, fuel and petroleum products. *Main exports:* food and food products. *Principal trading partners:* Russia, Poland.

Luxembourg *GNP ($ million):* 11 225 (1992 est); *per head:* $31 080. *Imports ($ million):* 6193 (1990). *Exports ($ million):* 5402 (1989). *Main imports:* metal products, machinery and transport equipment 45.2% (1990), mineral products 12.7% (1990). *Main exports:* metal products, machinery and transport equipment 56.0% (1990), plastic materials and rubber manufactures 12.9% (1990). *Principal trading partners:* Germany, France, Belgium.

Macedonia (Former Yugoslav Republic of) *GNP, Imports* and *Exports:* no available figures. *Main imports:* fuel, machinery and transport equipment. *Main exports:* agricultural products. *Principal trading partner:* Bulgaria. Before the imposition of UN sanctions in May 1992, over 60% of Macedonia's trade was with Yugoslavia (Serbia and Montenegro.)

Madagascar *GNP ($ million):* 2710 (1990); *per head:* $230. *Imports ($ million):* 426 (1991). *Exports ($ million):* 306 (1991). *Main imports:* machinery 13.6% (1989), vehicles and parts 10.4% (1989). *Main exports:* coffee 25.2% (1989), vanilla 13.4% (1989). *Principal trading partners:* France, USA, Japan, Germany.

Malawi *GNP ($ million):* 1662 (1990); *per head:* $200. *Imports ($ million):* 705 (1991). *Exports ($ million):* 473 (1991). *Main imports:* basic manufactures 42.5% (1988), machinery and equipment 15.5% (1988). *Main exports:* tobacco 63.1% (1990), tea 13.3% (1990). *Principal trading partners:* UK, South Africa, Germany, Japan.

Malaysia *GNP ($ million):* 66 000 (1990); *per head:* $3468. *Imports ($ million):* 36 699 (1991). *Exports ($ million):* 34 375 (1991). *Main imports:* machinery and transport equipment 47.9% (1989), manufactured goods 16.4% (1989). *Main exports:* thermionic valves and tubes 15.0% (1989), crude petroleum 11.6% (1989). *Principal trading partners:* Japan, Singapore, USA, UK, Germany.

Maldives *GNP ($ million):* 96 (1990); *per head:* $440. *Imports ($ million):* 129 (1990). *Exports ($ million):* 52 (1990). *Main imports:* food, beverages and tobacco 28.9% (1990), basic manufactures 24.5% (1990). *Main exports:* apparel and clothing 27.6% (1990), frozen skipjack tuna 26.3% (1990). *Principal trading partners:* Thailand, Japan, Sri Lanka.

Mali *GNP ($ million):* 2292 (1990); *per head:* $270. *Imports ($ million):* 500 (1990). *Exports ($ million):* 271 (1989). *Main imports:* machinery, appliances and transport equipment 22.1% (1987), food products 16.3% (1987). *Main exports:* raw cotton and cotton products 38.3% (1988), live animals 29.5% (1988). *Principal trading partners:* France, Ivory Coast, Senegal.

Malta *GNP ($ million):* 2342 (1990); *per head:* $6630. *Imports ($ million):* 1953 (1990). *Exports ($ million):* 1126 (1990). *Main imports:* machinery and transport equipment 40.4% (1989), semi-manufactured goods 22.2% (1989). *Main exports:* machinery and transport equipment 46.6% (1989), semi-manufactured goods 9.5% (1989). *Principal trading partners:* Italy, Germany, France, UK.

Marshall Islands *GNP ($ million):* 63 (1989); *per head:* $1500. *Imports ($ million):* 34 (1988). *Exports ($ million):* 2 (1988). *Main imports:* food, agricultural raw materials, mineral ores, and concentrates 45.5% (1988), fuels and other energies 10.7% (1988). *Main exports:* food and agricultural raw materials 100% (1988). *Principal trading partner:* USA.

Mauritania *GNP ($ million):* 987 (1990); *per head:* $500. *Imports ($ million):* 351 (1989). *Exports ($ million):* 451 (1989). *Main imports:* food 30.6% (1988). *Main exports:* fish 58.6% (1989), iron ore 31.3% (1989). *Principal trading partner:* France, Japan, Spain.

Mauritius *GNP ($ million):* 2422 (1990); *per head:* $2250. *Imports ($ million):* 1619 (1990). *Exports ($ million):* 1193 (1990). *Main imports:* manufactured goods – material 38.9% (1989/90), machinery and transport equipment (1989/90) 21.1%. *Main exports:* clothing and textiles 51.5% (1989/90), sugar 29.2% (1989/90). *Principal trading partners:* UK, France, USA, Germany.

Mexico *GNP ($ million):* 382 000 (1992 est); *per head:* $4186. *Imports ($ million):* 29 993 (1990). *Exports ($ million):* 26 524 (1990). *Main imports:* metallic products, machinery and equipment 41.0% (1990), food, beverages and tobacco 8.6% (1990). *Main exports:* crude petroleum 33.0 (1990), metallic products, machinery and equipment 18.0% (1990). *Principal trading partners:* USA, Japan, Germany, Spain, Canada.

Micronesia *GNP ($ million):* 99 (1989); *per head:* $980. *Imports ($ million):* 68 (1988). *Exports ($ million):* 2 (1988). *Main imports:* food, beverages and tobacco 41.4% (1988), manufactured goods 28.1% (1988). *Main exports:* copra 25.6% (1988), manufactured goods 12.8% (1988). *Principal trading partners:* Japan, USA.

Moldova *GNP ($ million):* c. 3200 (1992 est); *per head:* c. $720 ($2170 in 1991). *Imports ($ million):* n/a. *Exports ($ million):* n/a. *Main imports:* coal, natural gas. *Main exports:* food and agricultural products. *Principal trading partners:* Ukraine, Romania.

Monaco *GNP ($ million):* 375 (1992 est); *per head:* $12 609. *Imports ($ million):* n/a. *Exports ($ million):* n/a. *Principal trading partners:* France, Italy. No separate figures are available for Monaco whose imports and exports are included in the French total.

Mongolia *GNP ($ million):* 1161 (1988); *per head:* $473. *Imports ($ million):* 2030 (1988). *Exports ($ million):* 812 (1988). *Main imports:* fuels, minerals and metals 33.5% (1988), machinery and transport equipment 30.2% (1988). *Main exports:* raw materials and food products 41.7% (1988), minerals and metals 39.0% (1988). *Principal trading partners:* Japan, China, Russia.

Morocco *GNP ($ million):* 23 788 (1990); *per head:* $950. *Imports ($ million):* 6919 (1990). *Exports ($ million):* 4229 (1990). *Main imports:* capital goods 26.8% (1990), crude oil 14.3% (1990). *Main exports:* food 24.8% (1990), phosphates 9.7% (1990). *Principal trading partners:* France, Spain, USA, Germany, Italy.

Mozambique *GNP ($ million):* 1208 (1990); *per*

head: $80. *Imports ($ million):* 715 (1989). *Exports ($ million):* 101 (1989). *Main imports:* foodstuffs 22.1% (1989), capital equipment 18.8% (1989). *Main exports:* shrimps 34.3% (1990), cashew nuts 11.3% (1990). *Principal trading partners:* Spain, USA, Japan, South Africa.

Myanmar (Burma) *GNP ($ million):* 16 330 (1989–90); *per head:* $400. *Imports ($ million):* 616 (1991). *Exports ($ million):* 412 (1991). *Main imports:* machinery and equipment 51.4% (1989), raw materials for industry 31.4% (1989). *Main exports:* agricultural products 31.5% (1989), forest products 23.8% (1989). *Principal trading partners:* Japan, India, Germany, China.

Namibia *GNP ($ million):* 1600 (1988); *per head:* $1300. *Imports ($ million):* 861 (1988). *Exports ($ million):* 940 (1988). *Main imports:* food and other consumer goods 33.5% (1983), fuel 27.5% (1983). *Main exports:* minerals 75.9% (1989) , agricultural products 11.0% (1989). *Principal trading partner:* South Africa.

Nauru *GNP ($ million):* 90 (1989); *per head:* $10 000. *Imports ($ million):* 14 (1988). *Exports ($ million):* 74 (1988). *Main exports:* phosphates 99%. *Principal trading partners:* Australia, New Zealand.

Nepal *GNP ($ million):* 3289 (1990); *per head:* $170. *Imports ($ million):* 790 (1991). *Exports ($ million):* 273 (1991). *Main imports:* machinery and transport equipment 31.1% (1987/88), basic manufactured goods 29.6% (1987/88). *Main exports:* basic manufactures 66.0% (1987/88), food and live animals 18.2% (1987/88). *Principal trading partners:* India, China, Bangladesh.

Netherlands *GNP ($ million):* 330 000 (1992 est); *per head:* $21 400. *Imports ($ million):* 125 906 (1990). *Exports ($ million):* 133 554 (1991). *Main imports:* machinery and transport equipment 30.9% (1990), chemicals and chemical products 10.5% (1990). *Total exports ($ million):* machinery and transport equipment 23.5% (1990), foodstuffs, beverages and tobacco 17.1% (1990). *Principal trading partners:* Germany, Belgium, France, UK, USA, Italy.

New Zealand *GNP ($ million):* 43 185 (1990); *per head:* $12 680. *Imports ($ million):* 8522 (1991). *Exports ($ million):* 9720 (1991). *Main imports:* machinery 26.8% (1990/91), minerals, chemicals and plastics 25.0% (1990/91). *Main exports:* food and live animals 46.9% (1990/91), basic manufactures 22.7% (1990/91). *Principal trading partners:* Australia, Japan, USA, UK, South Korea.

Nicaragua *GNP ($ million):* 2911 (1987); *per head:* $830. *Imports ($ million):* 923 (1987). *Exports ($ million):* 300 (1987). *Main imports:* primary and intermediate goods for industry 20.1% (1988), crude petroleum and products 15.0% (1988). *Main exports:* coffee 35.9% (1988), cotton 22.5% (1988). *Principal trading partners:* Germany, Japan, Mexico.

Niger *GNP ($ million):* 2365 (1990); *per head:* $310. *Imports ($ million):* 345 (1985). *Exports ($ million):* 209 (1985). *Main imports:* raw materials and machinery 42.5% (1989), consumer goods 36.6% (1989). *Main exports:* uranium 71.5% (1989), live animals 10.5% (1989). *Principal trading partners:* France, Nigeria, USA.

Nigeria *GNP ($ million):* 27 800 (1992 est); *per head:* $301. *Imports ($ million):* 3419 (1989). *Exports ($ million):* 13 649 (1990). *Main imports:* machinery and transport equipment 42.8% (1989), chemicals 21.6% (1989). *Main exports:* crude petroleum 94.9% (1989), palm kernels 0.9% (1989). *Principal trading partners:* USA, Germany, France, UK, Italy.

Norway *GNP ($ million):* 120 000 (1992 est); *per head:* $28 200. *Imports ($ million):* 25 244 (1991). *Exports ($ million):* 34 034 (1990). *Main imports:* machinery and transport equipment 35.5% (1990), metals and metal products 8.9% (1990). *Main exports:* crude petroleum 35.2% (1990), metals and metal products 12.8% (1990). *Principal trading partners:* UK, Sweden, Germany, France, Denmark.

Oman *GNP ($ million):* 7756 (1989); *per head:* $4770. *Imports ($ million):* 2681 (1990). *Exports ($ million):* 5215 (1990). *Main imports:* machinery and transport equipment 36.1% (1990), manufactured goods 18.4% (1990). *Main exports:* petroleum 91.7% (1990). *Principal trading partners:* Japan, South Korea, United Arab Emirates, USA.

Pakistan *GNP ($ million):* 53 000 (1992 est); *per head:* $430. *Imports ($ million):* 8427 (1991). *Exports ($ million):* 6471 (1991). *Main imports:* non-electric machinery and electrical goods 21.7% (1989/90), mineral oils 17.1% (1989/90). *Main exports:* cotton yarn 16.5% (1989/90), cotton fabrics 11.3% (1989/90) . *Principal trading partners:* USA, Japan, Germany, UK, Saudi Arabia.

Panama *GNP ($ million):* 4414 (1990); *per head:* $1830. *Imports ($ million):* 1695 (1991). *Exports ($ million):* 342 (1991). *Main imports:* mineral fuels 16.9% (1989), chemicals and chemical products 15.9% (1989). *Main exports:* bananas 27.8% (1989), shrimps 21.1% (1989). *Principal trading partner:* USA, Japan, Germany, Ecuador.

Papua New Guinea *GNP ($ million):* 3372 (1990); *per head:* $860. *Imports ($ million):* 1403 (1991). *Exports ($ million):* 1283 (1991). *Main imports:* machinery and transport equipment 37.5% (1988), basic manufactures 18.1% (1988). *Main exports:* copper ore and concentrates (1990) 35.4%, gold (1990) 35.3%. *Principal trading partners:* Japan, Australia, Germany, USA.

Paraguay *GNP ($ million):* 4796 (1990); *per head:* $1110. *Imports ($ million):* 695 (1989). *Exports ($ million):* 1163 (1989). *Main imports:* machinery and transport equipment 48.1% (1990), fuels and lubricants 12.3% (1990). *Main exports:* cotton fibres 34.7% (1990), soya beans 27.9% (1990). *Principal trading partners:* Brazil, Argentina, USA, Netherlands, Japan.

Peru *GNP ($ million):* 25 149 (1990); *per head:* $1160. *Imports ($ million):* 2885 (1990). *Exports ($ million):* 3276 (1990). *Main imports:* raw and intermediate materials 50.4% (1989). *Main exports:* copper 23.5 % (1989). *Principal trading partners:* USA, Germany, Japan, Brazil, Argentina.

Philippines *GNP ($ million):* 54 000 (1992 est); *per head:* $823. *Imports ($ million):* 13 042 (1990). *Exports ($ million):* 8186 (1990). *Main imports:* petroleum and products 12.6% (1989), iron and steel 7.1% (1989). *Main exports:* electrical machinery and parts 7.9% (1989), clothing 7.3% (1989). *Principal trading partners:* USA, Japan, Taiwan, Germany.

Poland *GNP ($ million):* 63 700 (1992 est); *per head:* $1660. *Imports ($ million):* 14 261 (1991). *Exports ($ million):* 14 460 (1991). *Main imports:* machinery and transport equipment 37.0% (1989), chemicals 15.0% (1989). *Main exports:* machinery and transport equipment 38.4% (1989), chemicals 10.5% (1989). *Principal trading partners:* Germany, Russia, UK, Austria, Switzerland.

Portugal *GNP ($ million):* 80 000 (1992); *per head:* $7600. *Imports ($ million):* 26 113 (1991). *Exports ($ million):* 16 281 (1991). *Main imports:* machinery and transport equipment 30.2% (1990), chemicals and chemical products 8.5% (1990). *Main exports*: textiles and clothing 28.9% (1990), machinery and transport equipment 17.0% (1990). *Principal trading partners*: Germany, Spain, France, UK, Italy.

Qatar *GNP ($ million):* 6962 (1990); *per head:* $15 860. *Imports ($ million):* 1326 (1989). *Exports ($ million):* 2687 (1989). *Main imports*: machinery and transport equipment 37.0% (1989), manufactured goods 23.9% (1989). *Main exports*: crude petroleum and products 82.0% (1989), liquefied gas chemicals 12.4% (1989). *Principal trading partners*: Japan, UK, Germany.

Romania *GNP ($ million):* 15 800 (1992 est); *per head:* $680. *Imports ($ million):* 5600 (1991). *Exports ($ million):* 4124 (1991). *Main imports*: mineral fuels 41.1% (1989), machinery and transport equipment 40.4% (1989). *Main exports*: machinery and transport equipment 56.7% (1989), fuels 11.0% (1989). *Principal trading partners*: Russia, Germany, Italy, Ukraine.

Russia *GNP ($ million):* c. 137 800 (1992); *per head:* c $950. *Imports ($ million):* n/a. *Exports ($ million):* n/a. *Main imports*: Food and food products. *Main exports*: Food, cola, natural gas. *Principal trading partners*: Germany, Ukraine, Kazakhstan, Poland, Bulgaria.

Rwanda *GNP ($ million):* 2214 (1990); *per head:* $310. *Imports ($ million):* 369 (1988). *Exports ($ million):* 101 (1988). *Main imports*: machinery and transport equipment 21.7% (1989), mineral fuels and lubricants 14.4% (1989). *Main exports*: coffee 61.2% (1989), tea 23.4% (1989). *Principal trading partners*: Belgium, Germany, Kenya, Japan.

St Christopher and Nevis *GNP ($ million):* 133 (1990); *per head:* $3330. *Imports ($ million):* 79 (1987). *Exports ($ million):* 28 (1987). *Main imports*: machinery and transport equipment 29.6% (1987), basic manufactures 19.5% (1987). *Main exports*: sugar 41.1% (1989), electrical components 30.0% (1989). *Principal trading partners*: USA, UK, Trinidad.

St Lucia *GNP ($ million):* 286 (1990); *per head:* $1900. *Imports ($ million):* 221 (1988). *Exports ($ million):* 119 (1988). *Main imports*: machinery and transport equipment 25.0% (1989), food and live animals 18.2% (1989). *Main exports*: bananas 55.3% (1989), clothing 14.3% (1989). *Principal trading partner*: UK, USA, Trinidad.

St Vincent and the Grenadines *GNP ($ million):* 184 (1990); *per head:* $1610. *Imports ($ million):* 98 (1987). *Exports ($ million):* 52 (1987). *Main imports*: basic manufactures 24.8% (1989), food products 23.0% (1989). *Main exports*: bananas 44.0% (1989), tennis rackets. *Principal trading partners*: USA, UK, Trinidad.

San Marino *GNP ($ million):* 205 (1992 est); *per head:* $8590. *Imports ($ million):* n/a. *Exports ($ million):* n/a. No other figures are available. *Principal trading partner*: Italy.

São Tomé e Princípe *GNP ($ million):* 47 (1990); *per head:* $380. *Imports ($ million):* 13 (1987). *Exports ($ million):* 7 (1987). *Main imports*: food and other agricultural products 35.2% (1988), capital goods 30.5% (1988). *Main exports*: cocoa 95.4% (1988), copra 4.0% (1988). *Principal trading partners*: Portugal, Germany, Netherlands.

Saudi Arabia *GNP ($ million):* 122 000 (1992 est); *per head:* $7463. *Imports ($ million):* 24 069 (1990). *Exports ($ million):* 44 417 (1990). *Main imports*:

transport equipment 18.5% (1989), machinery and appliances 18.4% (1989). *Main exports*: crude petroleum 54.0% (1989), refined petroleum 18.9% (1989). *Principal trading partners*: USA, Japan, UK, France, Netherlands.

Senegal *GNP ($ million):* 5260 (1990); *per head:* $710. *Imports ($ million):* 1023 (1987). *Exports ($ million):* 606 (1987). *Main imports*: crude petroleum and products 17.9% (1988), agricultural and industrial equipment 13.4% (1988). *Main exports*: peanut oil 12.4% (1988), crustaceans, molluscs and shellfish 10.6% (1988). *Principal trading partner*: France, Italy, Spain, Ivory Coast.

Seychelles *GNP ($ million):* 318 (1990); *per head:* $4670. *Imports ($ million):* 173 (1991). *Exports ($ million):* 48 (1991). *Main imports*: machinery and transport equipment 26.2% (1989), food, beverages and tobacco 18.4% (1989). *Main exports*: petroleum products (reexports) 52.7% (1989), canned tuna 24.7% (1989). *Principal trading partners*: France, Kuwait, UK, South Africa.

Sierra Leone *GNP ($ million):* 981 (1990); *per head:* $240. *Imports ($ million):* 164 (1990). *Exports ($ million):* 143 (1990). *Main imports*: machinery and transport equipment 33.5% (1989), food and live animals 27.1% (1989). *Main exports*: rutile 47.0% (1989), bauxite 18.2% (1989). *Principal trading partners*: USA, UK, Netherlands, China, Germany.

Singapore *GNP ($ million):* 52 000 (1992 est); *per head:* $18 143. *Imports ($ million):* 66 108 (1991). *Exports ($ million):* 59 046 (1991). *Main imports*: crude petroleum 11.4% (1990), office machines 7.2% (1990). *Main exports*: office machines 17.5% (1990), petroleum products 15.1% (1990). *Principal trading partners*: USA, Japan, Malaysia, Thailand, Hong Kong.

Slovakia *GNP ($ million):* 10 000 (1992 est); *per head:* $1898. *Imports ($ million):* 2990 (1990 est). *Exports ($ million):* 3260 (1990 est). *Main imports*: petroleum and petroleum products, natural gas. *Main exports*: metals and finished engineering products. *main trading partners*: Czech Republic, Ukraine, Poland, Germany.

Slovenia *GNP ($ million):* 14 000 (1990 est); *per head:* $7132. *Imports ($ million):* n/a. *Exports ($ million):* n/a. *Main imports*: mineral fuels, raw materials. *Main exports*: textiles, metal goods. *Principal trading partners*: Italy, Austria, Croatia, Germany.

Solomon Islands *GNP ($ million):* 187 (1990); *per head:* $580. *Imports ($ million):* 92 (1990). *Exports ($ million):* 70 (1990). *Main imports*: machinery and transport equipment 24.8% (1990), manufactured goods 24.5% (1990). *Main exports*: timber products 34.1% (1990), fish products 29.9% (1990). *Principal trading partners*: Australia, Japan, UK.

Somalia *GNP ($ million):* 946 (1990); *per head:* $150. *Imports ($ million):* 132 (1987). *Exports ($ million):* 104 (1987). *Main imports*: petroleum 33.1% (1988), agricultural inputs 20.9% (1988). *Main exports*: live animals 56.7% (1991), bananas 26.7% (1991). *Principal trading partners*: Italy, Saudi Arabia, Yemen.

South Africa *GNP ($ million):* 123 000 (1992 est); *per head:* $3312. *Imports ($ million):* 17 506 (1991). *Exports ($ million):* 17 052 (1990). *Main imports*: machinery and transport equipment 42.9% (1990), chemicals 10.8% (1990). *Main exports*: gold 29.6% (1990), metals and products 15.0% (1990). *Principal trading partners*: Germany, UK, Japan, USA, Netherlands.

Spain *GNP ($ million):* 540 000 (1992 est); *per head:* $13 600. *Imports ($ million):* 93 314 (1991). *Exports ($ million):* 60 182 (1991). *Main imports:* machinery 14.0% (1990), energy products 11.6% (1990). *Main exports:* transport equipment 18.1% (1990), agricultural products 13.9% (1990). *Principal trading partners:* France, Germany, Italy, UK, USA, Netherlands.

Sri Lanka *GNP ($ million):* 7971 (1990); *per head:* $470. *Imports ($ million):* 3083 (1991). *Exports ($ million):* 1965 (1990). *Main imports:* machinery and transport equipment 15.4% (1990), petroleum products 13.3% (1990). *Main exports:* tea 24.9% (1990), rubber 3.9% (1990). *Principal trading partner:* USA, Japan, UK, Iran.

Sudan *GNP ($ million):* 28 906 (1990); *per head:* $390. *Imports ($ million):* 1060 (1988). *Exports ($ million):* 672 (1989). *Main imports:* machinery and transport equipment 30.0% (1989), manufactured goods 21.9% (1989). *Main exports:* cotton 44.6% (1989), sesame seeds 11.0% (1989). *Principal trading partners:* UK, USA, Japan, Germany.

Suriname *GNP ($ million):* 1365 (1990); *per head:* $3050. *Imports ($ million):* 294 (1987). *Exports ($ million):* 306 (1987). *Main imports:* machinery and transport equipment 23.6% (1988), fuels and lubricants 14.4% (1988). *Main exports:* aluminium 71.9% (1987), rice 9.6% (1988). *Principal trading partners:* Netherlands, USA, Norway.

Swaziland *GNP ($ million):* 645 (1990); *per head:* $820. *Imports ($ million):* 590 (1989). *Exports ($ million):* 468 (1989). *Main imports:* machinery and transport equipment 23.0% (1988), minerals, fuels and lubricants 13.5% (1988). *Main exports:* sugar 31.8% (1988), wood and products 17.6% (1988). *Principal trading partners:* South Africa, UK.

Sweden *GNP ($ million):* 260 000 (1992 est); *per head:* $29 600. *Imports ($ million):* 49 751 (1991). *Exports ($ million):* 55 129 (1990). *Main imports:* machinery and transport equipment 38.5% (1990), chemicals 9.5% (1990). *Main exports:* machinery and transport equipment 43.3% (1990), paper products 11.0% (1990). *Principal trading partners:* Germany, UK, USA, Norway, Denmark.

Switzerland *GNP ($ million):* 240 000 (1992); *per head:* $35 500. *Imports ($ million):* 66 517 (1991). *Exports ($ million):* 61 537 (1991). *Main imports:* machinery and electronics 20.2% (1989), chemical products 11.3% (1989). *Main exports:* industrial machinery 19.9% (1989), pharmaceuticals 8.7% (1989). *Principal trading partners:* Germany, France, Italy, USA, UK.

Syria *GNP ($ million):* 12 404 (1990); *per head:* $990. *Imports ($ million):* 3151 (1991). *Exports ($ million):* 3143 (1991). *Main imports:* machinery and equipment 25.7% (1988), foods, beverages and tobacco 17.5% (1989). *Main exports:* crude petroleum and products 43.9% (1989), textiles, wearing apparel and leather 15.9% (1989). *Principal trading partners:* France, Italy, Germany, Saudi Arabia.

Tajikistan *GNP ($ million):* c. 1800 (1992); *per head:* c. $350 ($1050 in 1991). *Imports ($ million):* n/a. *Exports ($ million):* n/a. *Main imports:* food and food products. *Main export:* food products, electricity. *Principal trading partners:* Uzbekistan, Russia.

Tanzania *GNP ($ million):* 2779 (1990); *per head:* $120. *Imports ($ million):* 1495 (1988). *Exports ($ million):* 337 (1988). *Main imports:* machinery 25.6% (1987), transport equipment 17.0% (1987). *Main exports:* coffee 25.9% (1988), cotton 23.6% (1988). *Principal trading partners:* Germany, UK, Japan, Italy.

Thailand *GNP ($ million):* 117 000 (1992 est); *per head:* $1605. *Imports ($ million):* 33 379 (1990). *Exports ($ million):* 23 068 (1990). *Main imports:* electrical power equipment and machinery 31.2% (1990), transport equipment 10.2% (1990). *Main exports:* electrical power equipment and machinery 21.1% (1990), textiles and apparel 12.1% (1990). *Principal trading partners:* USA, Japan, Singapore, Germany.

Togo *GNP ($ million):* 1474 (1990); *per head:* $410. *Imports ($ million):* 487 (1988). *Exports ($ million):* 242 (1988). *Main imports:* machinery and transport equipment 27.2% (1987), food products 14.4% (1987). *Main exports:* calcium phosphates 45.8% (1987), coffee 12.6% (1987). *Principal trading partners:* France, Netherlands, Germany, UK.

Tonga *GNP ($ million):* 100 (1990); *per head:* $1010. *Imports ($ million):* 65 (1990). *Exports ($ million):* 13 (1990). *Main imports:* food and live animals 26.3% (1990), machinery and transport equipment 18.4% (1990). *Main exports:* squash 31.6% (1990), vanilla beans 18.1% (1990). *Principal trading partners:* Japan, USA, New Zealand, Australia.

Trinidad and Tobago *GNP ($ million):* 4458 (1990); *per head:* $3470. *Imports ($ million):* 1222 (1990). *Exports ($ million):* 2049 (1990). *Main imports:* machinery 16.5% (1990), food 14.3% (1990). *Main exports:* crude petroleum and petroleum products 67.1% (1990), chemicals and chemical products 14.1% (1990). *Principal trading partner:* USA, UK, Jamaica, Barbados.

Tunisia *GNP ($ million):* 11 592 (1990); *per head:* $1420. *Imports ($ million):* 5189 (1991). *Exports ($ million):* 3713 (1991). *Main imports:* textiles 8.4% (1989), wheat 4.9% (1989). *Main exports:* clothing and accessories 26.0% (1989), petroleum and products 20.0% (1989). *Principal trading partners:* France, Italy, Germany, Belgium.

Turkey *GNP ($ million):* 130 000 (1992 est); *per head:* $2170. *Imports ($ million):* 20 019 (1991). *Exports ($ million):* 13 603 (1990). *Main imports:* fuels 17.1% (1990), machinery and transport equipment 16.8% (1990). *Main exports:* textiles 31.3% (1990), agricultural products 18.8% (1990). *Principal trading partners:* Germany, USA, Italy, Saudi Arabia, France.

Turkmenistan *GNP ($ million):* c. 2180 (1992 est); *per head:* c. $560 ($1700 in 1991). *Imports ($ million):* n/a. *Exports ($ million):* n/a. *Main imports:* food and food products. *Main exports:* natural gas, food products. *Main trading partners:* Russia, Uzbekistan, Iran.

Tuvalu *GNP ($ million):* 4.6 (1990); *per head:* $530. *Imports ($ million):* 4 (1989). *Exports ($ million):* 0.06 (1989). *Main imports* : food and live animals 29.5% (1986), manufactured goods 25.2% (1986). *Main exports:* copra 86.4% (1986). *Principal trading partners:* Fiji, Australia, New Zealand.

Uganda *GNP ($ million):* 3814 (1990); *per head:* $220. *Imports ($ million):* 544 (1988). *Exports ($ million):* 152 (1990). *Main imports:* sugar 16.0% (1984), motor vehicles 10.8% (1984). *Main exports:* unroasted coffee 79.6% (1990), cotton 3.3% (1990). *Principal trading partners:* Kenya, UK, Germany, USA.

Ukraine *GNP ($ million):* c. 40 600 (1992 est); *per head:* c. $800 ($2340 in 1991). *Imports ($ million):* n/a. *Exports ($ million):* n/a. *Main imports:* food products, natural gas and petroleum. *Main exports:* food products, coal. *Main trading partners:* Russia, Poland, Germany, Iran.

United Arab Emirates *GNP ($ million):* 31 613 (1990); *per head:* $19 680. *Imports ($ million):* 11 199

(1990). *Exports ($ million):* 15 837 (1990). *Main imports*: machinery and transport equipment 31.0% (1986), basic manufactures 21.1% (1986). *Main exports*: crude petroleum 65.6% (1989). *Principal trading partners*: Japan, UK, USA, France.

UK *GNP ($ million):* 1 000 000 (1992 est); *per head:* $17 300. *Imports ($ million):* 210 019 (1991). *Exports ($ million):* 185 212 (1991). *Main imports*: machinery and transport equipment 37.5% (1990), chemicals and chemical products 8.6% (1990). *Main exports*: machinery and transport equipment 40.6% (1990), chemicals and chemical products 12.7% (1990). *Principal trading partners*: Germany, USA, France, Netherlands, Italy, Belgium, Ireland.

USA *GNP ($ million):* 5 670 000 (1992 est); *per head:* $22 520. *Imports ($ million):* 509 320 (1991). *Exports ($ million):* 421 850 (1991). *Main imports*: machinery transport equipment 42.0% (1990), basic and miscellaneous manufactures 28.6% (1990). *Main exports*: machinery and transport 43.8% (1990), chemicals and related products 9.9% (1990). *Principal trading partners*: Canada, Japan, Mexico, Germany, UK, Taiwan.

Uruguay *GNP ($ million):* 7929 (1990); *per head:* $2560. *Imports ($ million):* 1619 (1991). *Exports ($ million):* 1590 (1991). *Main imports*: machinery and appliances 18.9% (1990), mineral products 16.7% (1990). *Main exports*: textiles and products 28.8 (1990), live animals and animal products 24.9% (1990). *Principal trading partners*: Brazil, USA, Germany, Argentina.

Uzbekistan *GNP ($ million):* c. 9600 (1992 est); *per head:* c. $450 ($1350 in 1991). *Imports ($ million):* n/a. *Exports ($ million):* n/a. *Main imports*: food and food products. *Main exports*: food products, natural gas. *Principal trading partners*: Russia, Kazakhstan, Turkmenistan.

Vanuatu *GNP ($ million):* 167 (1990); *per head:* $1060. *Imports ($ million):* 97 (1990). *Exports ($ million):* 19 (1990). *Main imports*: machinery and transport equipment 35.3% (1990), basic and miscellaneous manufactures 31.1% (1990). *Main exports*: copra 27.2% (1990), beef and veal 16.7% (1990). *Principal trading partners*: Netherlands, Japan, Australia, New Zealand.

Vatican City no figures available. The Holy See does not have an 'economy' in the accepted sense of the term.

Venezuela *GNP ($ million):* 66 000 (1992 est); *per head:* $3110. *Imports ($ million):* 9963 (1991). *Exports ($ million):* 17 586 (1991). *Main imports*: machinery and transport equipment 43.2% (1989), chemicals 14.2% (1989). *Main exports*: crude petroleum and products 73.4% (1989), iron ore 2.1% (1989). *Principal trading partners*: USA, Germany, Japan, Italy, Colombia.

Vietnam *GNP ($ million):* 14 200 (1989); *per head:* $210. *Imports ($ million):* 3050 (1989). *Exports ($ million):* 1502 (1989). *Main imports*: fuel and raw materials 44.7% (1985), machinery 23.2% (1985). *Main exports*: raw materials 46.0% (1985), handicrafts 24.1% (1985). *Principal trading partners*: Singapore, Japan, Hong Kong, France.

Western Samoa *GNP ($ million):* 121 (1990); *per head:* $730. *Imports ($ million):* 76 (1988). *Exports ($ million):* 15 (1988). *Main imports*: food 21.3% (1983), machinery 21.0% (1983). *Main exports*: coconut oil 37.2% (1988), taro 16.6% (1988). *Principal trading partners*: New Zealand, Australia, Japan, USA.

Yemen *GNP ($ million):* 7203 (1989); *per head:* $640. *Imports ($ million):* 1378 (1987). *Exports ($ million):* 101 (1987. *Main imports*: food and live animals 31.6% (1987), basic manufactured goods 28.6% (1987). *Main exports*: coffee 16.6 (1987), cigarettes 15.6% (1987). *Principal trading partner*: USA, Saudi Arabia, Italy, France.

Yugoslavia (Serbia and Montenegro) *GNP ($ million):* 28 400 (1990); *per head:* $2729; inflation

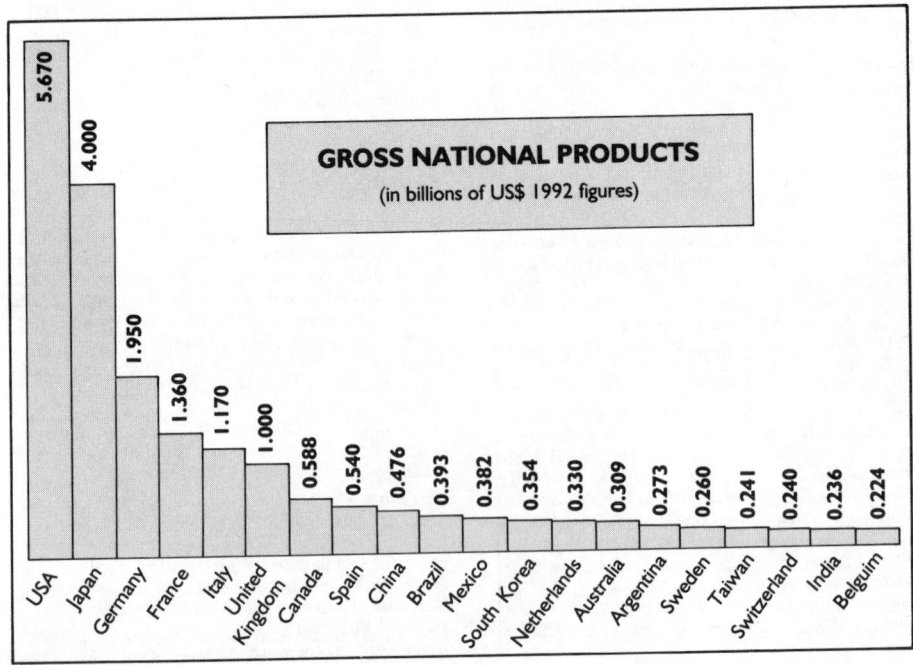

GROSS NATIONAL PRODUCTS

(in billions of US$ 1992 figures)

USA	5.670
Japan	4.000
Germany	1.950
France	1.360
Italy	1.170
United Kingdom	1.000
Canada	0.588
Spain	0.540
China	0.476
Brazil	0.393
Mexico	0.382
South Korea	0.354
Netherlands	0.330
Australia	0.309
Argentina	0.273
Sweden	0.260
Taiwan	0.241
Switzerland	0.240
India	0.236
Belgium	0.224

topping 9000% has greatly reduced this figure. *Imports ($ million):* n/a. *Exports ($ million):* n/a. *Main imports:* machinery and transport equipment 23.7% (1990), basic manufactures 15.6% (1990). *Main exports:* basic manufactures 25.8% (1990), machinery and transport equipment 25.7% (1990). *Principal trading partners:* Russia, Italy, Germany. **NB** UN sanctions in May 1992 interrupted trade except for foodstuffs and medicines.

Zaïre *GNP ($ million):* 8117 (1990); *per head:* $230. *Imports ($ million):* 886 (1990). *Exports ($ million):* 999 (1990). *Main imports:* mining equipment 32.0% (1987), food, beverages and tobacco 14.6% (1987). *Main exports:* copper 51.5% (1987), coffee 16.0% (1987). *Principal trading partners:* Belgium, USA, France, Germany, Japan.

Zambia *GNP ($ million):* 3391 (1990); *per head:* $420. *Imports ($ million):* 1243 (1990). *Exports ($ million):* 899 (1990). *Main imports:* machinery and transport equipment 38.3% (1988), basic manufactures 19.8% (1988). *Main exports:* copper 85.2% (1988), cobalt 6.1% (1988). *Principal trading partner:* Japan, UK, USA, South Africa.

Zimbabwe *GNP ($ million):* 4100 (1992 est); *per head:* $412. *Imports ($ million):* 1850 (1990). *Exports ($ million):* 1723 (1990). *Main imports:* machinery and transport equipment 34.7% (1987), chemicals 17.8% (1987). *Main exports:* tobacco 19.0% (1987), gold 18.9% (1987). *Principal trading partners:* South Africa, UK, Germany, USA, Japan.

HIGHEST GNP PER HEAD

The countries with the highest GNP per head (1990–92 est) are as follows:

Country	GNP per head (US $)
Switzerland	35 500
Japan	32 018
Luxembourg	31 080
Sweden	29 600
Denmark	28 200
Norway	28 200
Finland	24 400
Belgium	22 600
Iceland	22 580
USA	22 520
Canada	21 170
Netherlands	21 400
Liechtenstein	21 020
Italy	20 200
United Arab Emirates	19 680
Singapore	18 143
Australia	17 320
UK	17 300

LOWEST GNP PER HEAD

The countries with the highest GNP per head (1990–92 est) are as follows:

Country	GNP per head (US $)
Mozambique	80
Ethiopia	120
Tanzania	120
Somalia	150
Nepal	170
Guinea-Bissau	180
Bhutan	190
Chad	190

CURRENCIES OF THE WORLD
At 19 April 1993
On the financial markets, currencies are most commonly quoted in US dollars, as given here.

Afghanistan 1 afghani = 100 puls (puli); 1$US = Af 64.4689.

Albania 1 new lek = 100 qindarka (qintars); 1$US = 109.25 leks.

Algeria 1 dinar = 100 centimes; 1$US = DA 22.2734.

Andorra uses French and Spanish currency (qqv).

Angola 1 new kwanza = 100 lwei; 1$US = Kz 6751.09. Angola is experiencing rampant inflation and the value of its currency is rapidly diminishing.

Antigua and Barbuda 1 East Caribbean dollar[1] = 100 cents; 1$US = EC$ 2.6761.

Argentina 1 peso = 100 centavos; 1$US = $A 0.9949.

Armenia uses Russian currency (qv); to be replaced by the dram.

Australia 1 Australian dollar = 100 cents; A$ 1.39.

Austria 1 Schilling = 100 Groschen; 1$US = S 11.2601.

Azerbaijan uses Russian currency (qv); to be replaced by the manat.

Bahamas 1 Bahamian dollar = 100 cents; 1$US = US$ 1.

Bahrain 1 Bahrain dinar = 1000 fils; 1$US = BD 0.3739.

Bangladesh 1 taka = 100 poisha; 1$US = Tk 38.7216.

Barbados 1 Barbados dollar = 100 cents; 1$US = BD$ 1.9975.

Belarus 1 Belarussian rouble = 100 kopeks (on a par with the Russian rouble, qv); to be replaced by 1 taler = 100 grosches.

Belgium 1 Belgian franc (frank) = 100 centimes (centiemen); 1$US = BF 32.9327.

Belize 1 Belizean dollar = 100 cents; 1$US = BZ$ 1.9863.

Benin 1 CFA franc[2] = 100 centimes; 1$US = CFAF 270.14.

Bhutan 1 ngultrum = 100 chetrums; 1$US = Nu 31.0555. The ngultrum is fixed at a par with the Indian rupee which is also legal tender in Bhutan.

Bolivia 1 boliviano = 100 centavos; 1$US = Bs 4.1614.

Bosnia-Herzegovina Croatian and Serbian/Yugoslav currency in use (qqv).

Botswana 1 pula = 100 thebe; 1$US = P 2.3329.

Brazil 1 cruzeiro = 100 centavos; 1$US = C$ 28 937.6. Brazil is experiencing a high rate of inflation and the value of its currency is diminishing.

Brunei 1 Brunei dollar = 100 cents; 1$US = B$ 1.6141.

Bulgaria 1 lev = 100 stotinki (stotinka); 1$US = 24.6053.

Burkina Faso 1 CFA franc[2] = 100 centimes; 1$US = CFAF 270.14.

Burundi 1 Burundi franc = 100 centimes; 1$US = FBu 228.548.

Cambodia 1 new riel = 100 sen; 1$US = 3774.08

riels. Cambodia is experiencing a high rate of inflation and the value of its currency is diminishing.

Cameroon 1 CFA franc^2 = 100 centimes; 1$US = CFAF 270.14.

Canada 1 Canadian dollar = 100 cents; 1$US = Can$ 1.2543.

Cape Verde 1 Cape Verde escudo = 100 centavos; 1$US = CV Esc 73.6927.

Central African Republic 1 CFA franc^2 = 100 centimes; 1$US = CFAF 270.14.

Chad 1 CFA franc^2 = 100 centimes; 1$US = CFAF 270.14.

Chile 1 Chilean peso = 100 centavos; 1$US = Ch$ 412.576.

China, People's Republic 1 yuan (or renminbiao) = 10 jiao (chiao) = 100 fen; 1$US = Y 5.6397.

China (Taiwan) 1 new Taiwan dollar = 100 cents; 1$US = NT$ 25.9012.

Colombia 1 Colombian peso = 100 centavos; 1$US = Col$ 835.31.

Comoros 1 CFA franc^2 = 100 centimes; 1$US = CFAF 270.14.

Congo 1 CFA franc^2 = 100 centimes; 1$US = CFAF 270.14.

Costa Rica 1 Costa Rican colón = 100 céntimos; 1$US = ¢ 137.246.

Croatia 1 Croatian dinar = 100 para; 1$US = CD 1693.64. Croatia is experiencing a high rate of inflation and the value of its currency is diminishing.

Cuba 1 Cuban peso = 100 centavos; 1$US = 0.7529 pesos.

Cyprus 1 Cyprus pound = 100 cents; 1$US = £C 0.4772. Turkish currency (qv) is used in northern Cyprus.

Czech Republic 1 koruna = 100 haléřu (haléř); 1$US = Kčs 28.4085.

Denmark 1 Danish krone = 100 øre; 1$US = Dkr 6.1302. Danish currency is also used in the Faeroe Islands and Greenland.

Djibouti 1 Djibouti franc = 100 centimes; 1$US = DF 175.382.

Dominica 1 East Caribbean dollar^1 = 100 cents; 1$US = EC$ 2.6761

Dominican Republic 1 Dominican peso = 100 centavos; 1$US = RD$ 12.9113.

Ecuador 1 sucre = 100 centavos; 1$US = 1 S 1864.18 centavos.

Egypt 1 Egyptian pound = 100 piastres = 1000 millièmes; 1$US = LE 3.3127.

El Salvador 1 Salvadorian colón = 100 centavos; 1$US = ¢ 8.6902.

Equatorial Guinea 1 CFA franc^2 = 100 centimes; 1$US = CFAF 270.14.

Estonia 1 Kroon = 100 cents; 1$US = 12.8405.

Ethiopia 1 birr = 100 cents; 1$US = Br 4.9195.

Fiji 1 Fiji dollar = 100 cents; 1$US = F$ 1.5024.

Finland 1 markka (Finnmark) = 100 penniä (penni); 1$US = Fmk 5.5053.

France 1 French franc = 100 centimes; 1$US = F 5.4027.
French currency is also used in overseas départements and collectivités territoriales – Guadeloupe, Guyane, Martinique, Réunion, Mayotte, and St

Pierre et Miquelon. The French overseas territories of French Polynesia, New Caledonia, and the Wallis and Futuna Islands use the CFP franc. 1 CFP franc = 100 centimes; 1$US = CFPF 97.4342.

Gabon 1 CFA franc^2 = 100 centimes; 1$US = CFAF 270.14.

Gambia 1 dalasi = 100 butut; 1$US = D 8.442.

Georgia uses Russian currency (qv); to be replaced by the Lary.

Germany 1 Deutschmark = 100 Pfennige; 1$US = DM 1.5995.

Ghana 1 new cedi = 100 pesewas; 1$US = 591.101 cedis.

Greece 1 drachma = 100 leptae (lepta); 1$US = Dr 218.626.

Grenada 1 East Caribbean dollar^1 = 100 cents; 1$US = EC$ 2.6761.

Guatemala 1 quetzal = 100 centavos; 1$US = Q 5.4326.

Guinea 1 franc guineén = 100 centimes; 1$US = GF 806.749.

Guinea-Bissau 1 Guinea peso = 100 centavos; 1$US = PG 4965.9.

Guyana 1 Guyanese dollar = 100 cents; 1$US = G$ 124.147.

Haiti 1 gourde = 100 centimes; 1$US = G 11.9181.

Honduras 1 lempira = 100 centavos; 1$US = L 5.8995.

Hungary 1 forint = 100 fillér; 1$US = Ft 87.2685.

Iceland 1 new Icelandic króna = 100 aurar (eyrir); 1$US = ISK 63.1763.

India 1 Indian rupee = 100 paisa (paise); 1$US = Rs 31.0555.

Indonesia 1 rupiah = 100 sen; 1$US = Rp 2058.04.

Iran 1 Iranian rial = 100 dinars; 1$US = Rls 1640.47. Iran is experiencing a high rate of inflation and the value of its currency is diminishing.

Iraq 1 Iraqi dinar = 5 riyals = 20 dirhams = 1000 fils; 1$US = ID 0.3855.

Ireland 1 Irish pound (punt) = 100 pence; 1$US = I£ 0.6547.

Israel 1 new Israel shekel = 100 agorot (agora); 1$US = NIS 2.7216.

Italy 1 Italian lira (lire) = 100 centesimi; 1$US = 1526.96 lire.

Ivory Coast 1 CFA franc^2 = 100 centimes; 1$US = CFAF 270.14.

Jamaica 1 Jamaican dollar = 100 cents; 1$US = J$ 21.9162.

Japan 1 yen = 100 sen; 1$US = Y 111.075.

Jordan 1 Jordanian dinar = 1000 fils; 1$US = JD 0.6822.

Kazakhstan uses Russian currency (qv); to be replaced by the tan'ga.

Kenya 1 Kenya shilling = 100 cents; 1$US = K Sh 45.4173.

Kiribati uses Australian currency (qv).

Korea, Democratic People's Republic (North Korea) 1 won = 100 chon (jun); 1$US = 2.1353 won.

Korea, Republic of (South Korea) 1 won = 10 hwan = 100 chun (jeon); 1$US = W 789.737.

Kuwait 1 Kuwaiti dinar = 1000 fils; 1$US = KD 0.3002.

Kyrgyzstan Uses Russian currency (qv).

Laos 1 new kip = 100 at; 1$US = KN 715.089.

Latvia 1 Latvian rouble = 100 cents (on a par with the Russian rouble, qv); to be replaced by the lat.

Lebanon 1 Lebanese pound = 100 piastres; 1$US = LL 1747.66.

Lesotho 1 loti (maloti) = 100 lisente; 1$US = M 3.1685. The Lesothan loti is kept on a par with the South African rand.

Liberia 1 Liberian dollar = 100 cents; 1$US = L$ 1. The Liberian dollar is fixed on a par with the US dollar which is also legal tender in Liberia.

Libya 1 Libyan dinar = 1000 dirhams; 1$US = LD 0.2935.

Liechtenstein uses Swiss currency (qv).

Lithuania 1 Lithuanian 'rouble coupon' = 100 kopeks (on a par with the Russian rouble, qv); to be replaced by the litas.

Luxembourg 1 Luxembourg franc = 100 centimes; 1$US = Lux F 32.9327. The Luxembourg franc is fixed on a par with the Belgian franc which is also legal tender in Luxembourg.

Macedonia (Former Yugoslav Republic of) 1 Macedonian dinar = 100 para. This currency was not quoted on the international markets in April 1993.

Madagascar 1 Malagasy franc (franc malgache) = 100 centimes; 1$US = FMG 1787.72.

Malawi 1 Malawi kwacha = 100 tambala; 1$US = MK 4.2423.

Malaysia 1 ringgit or Malaysian dollar = 100 sen; 1$US = M$ 2.567.

Maldives 1 rufiyaa (Maldivian rupee) = 100 laaris (larees); 1$US = Rf 11.8928.

Mali 1 CFA franc[2] = 100 centimes; 1$US = CFAF 270.14.

Malta 1 Maltese lira (Maltese pound) = 100 cents = 1000 mils; 1$US = Lm 0.369.

Marshall Islands uses US currency (qv).

Mauritania 1 ouguiya = 5 khoums; 1$US = UM 113.03.

Mauritius 1 Mauritian rupee = 100 cents; 1$US = Mau Rs 16.6937.

Mexico 1 Mexican peso = 100 centavos; 1$US = Mex$ 3.0818.

Micronesia uses US currency (qv).

Moldova uses Russian currency (qv).

Monaco uses French currency (qv).

Mongolia 1 tugrik = 100 möngös; 1$US = 148.977 tugriks. Mongolia is experiencing a very high rate of inflation and the value of its currency is diminishing.

Morocco 1 dirham = 100 francs (centimes); 1$US = DH 8.6897.

Mozambique 1 metical (meticais) = 100 centavos; 1$US = Mt 2746.14.

Myanmar (Burma) 1 kyat = 100 pyas; 1$US = K 6.1545.

Namibia uses South African currency (qv).

Nauru uses Australian currency (qv).

Nepal 1 Nepalese rupee = 100 paisa; 1$US = NRs 46.1304.

Netherlands 1 Netherlands gulden (guilder) or florin = 100 cents; 1$US = F 1.7876.
The Netherlands overseas dependencies have their own currencies. In Aruba, 1 Aruban florin = 100 cents; 1$US = AF 1.7777. In the Netherlands Antilles, 1 Antillean guilder = 100 cents; 1$US = NA F 1.7921.

New Zealand 1 New Zealand dollar = 100 cents; 1$US = $NZ 1.8447.

Nicaragua 1 Córdoba oro = 100 centavos; 1$US = Córdobas oro 6.0352.

Niger 1 CFA franc[2] = 100 centimes; 1$US = CFAF 270.14.

Nigeria 1 naira = 100 kobo; 1$US = N 29.7953. Nigeria is experiencing inflation and the value of its currency is diminishing.

Norway 1 Norwegian krone (kroner) = 100 ore; 1$US = NKr 6.783.

Oman 1 rial Omani = 1000 baiza; 1$US = RO 0.3822.

Pakistan 1 Pakistani rupee = 100 paisa; 1$US = PRs 26.3603.

Panama 1 balboa = 100 centésimos; 1$US = B 1. The Panamanian balboa is kept on a par with the US dollar which is also legal tender in Panama. The only notes circulating in Panama are in US denominations; Panamanian currency circulates in coins.

Papua New Guinea 1 Kina = 100 toea; 1$US = K 0.9612.

Paraguay 1 guaraní = 100 céntimos; 1$US = G 1700.82.

Peru 1 new sol = 100 céntimos; 1$US = NS 1.9097.

Philippines 1 Philippine peso = 100 centavos; 1$US = P 25.3329.

Poland 1 zloty = 100 groszy; 1$US = Zl 16 577.5.

Portugal 1 Portuguese escudo = 100 centavos; 1$US = Esc 147.775.
The Portuguese overseas territory of Macau has its own currency, the pataca. 1 pataca = 100 avos; 1$US = 7.9321 patacas.

Qatar 1 Qatar riyal = 100 dirhams; 1$US = QR 3.621.

Romania 1 leu (lei) = 100 bani; 1$US = 601.968 lei. Romania is experiencing a high rate of inflation and the value of its currency is diminishing.

Russia 1 rouble = 100 kopeks; 1$US = 782.39 roubles. Russia is experiencing near rampant inflation and the value of its currency is rapidly diminishing.

Rwanda 1 Rwanda franc (Franc rwandais) = 100 centimes; 1$US = RF 138.422.

St Christopher and Nevis 1 East Caribbean dollar[1] = 100 cents; 1$US = EC$ 2.6761.

St Lucia 1 East Caribbean dollar[1] = 100 cents; 1$US = EC$ 2.6761.

St Vincent and the Grenadines 1 East Caribbean dollar[1] = 100 cents; 1$US = EC$ 2.6761.

San Marino uses Italian currency (qv).

São Tomé e Príncipe 1 dobra = 100 cêntimes; 1$US = Db 1700.82. São Tomé is experiencing rampant inflation and the value of its currency is rapidly diminishing.

Saudi Arabia 1 Saudi riyal = 100 halalah; 1$US = SRls 3.7361.

Senegal 1 CFA franc[2] = 100 centimes; 1$US = CFAF 270.14.

Seychelles 1 Seychelles rupee = 100 cents; 1$US = SR 5.0535.

Sierra Leone 1 leone = 100 cents; 1$US = Le 536.317.

Singapore 1 Singapore dollar = 100 cents; 1$US = S$ 1.6141.

Slovakia 1 koruna = 100 haléřu (haléř); 1$US = Kčs 28.4085.

Slovenia 1 tolar = 100 cents; 1$US = 104.717 tolars.

Solomon Islands 1 Solomon Islands dollar = 100 cents; 1$US = SI$ 3.1451.

Somalia 1 Somali shilling = 100 cents; 1$US = Soh Sh 2602.13.

South Africa 1 rand = 100 cents; 1$US = R 3.1685.

Spain 1 Spanish peseta = 100 céntimos; 1$US = Ptas 115.557.

Sri Lanka 1 Sri Lanka rupee = 100 cents; 1$US = SL Rs 47.0737.

Sudan 1 Sudanese dinar = 100 piastres; 1$US = SD 12.9113.

Suriname 1 Suriname gulden (guilder) or florin = 100 cents; 1$US = Sf 1.7727.

Swaziland 1 lilangeni (emalangeni) = 100 cents; South African (qv); 1$US = E 3.1685. The Swazi lilangeni is kept on a par with the South African rand.

Sweden 1 Swedish krona (kronor) = 100 öre; 1$US = SKr 7.3871.

Switzerland 1 Swiss franc (Schweizer Franken) = 100 Rappen (centimes); 1$US = Sw F 1.468.

Syria 1 Syrian pound = 100 piastres; 1$US = LS 20.8567.

Tajikistan Uses Russian currency (qv).

Tanzania 1 Tanzanian shilling = 100 cents; 1$US = T Sh 341.156.

Thailand 1 baht = 100 satangs; 1$US = B 25.0211.

Togo 1 CFA franc[2] = 100 centimes; 1$US = CFAF 270.14.

Tonga 1 pa'anga = 100 seniti; 1$US = T$ 1.39. The Tongan pa'angal is kept on a par with the Australian dollar.

Trinidad and Tobago 1 Trinidad and Tobago dollar = 100 cents; 1$US = TT$ 4.25.

Tunisia 1 Tunisian dinar = 1000 millimes; 1$US = D 0.9725.

Turkey 1 Turkish lira = 100 kurus; 1$US = LT 9629.78.

Turkmenistan uses Russian currency (qv); to be replaced by the manat.

Tuvalu uses Australian currency (qv).

Uganda 1 Uganda new shilling = 100 cents; 1$US = U Sh 1211.48.

Ukraine Karbovanets (no subdivisions), which is on a par with the Russian rouble (qv); to be replaced by 1 hryvnia = 100 kopeks.

United Arab Emirates 1 UAE dirham = 100 fils; 1$US = Dh 3.6589.

United Kingdom 1 pound sterling = 100 new pence (pennies); 1$US = £ 0.6495.

The Channel Islands, Gibraltar and the Isle of Man use British currency. A number of other British dependencies and overseas territories have their own currencies.

Anguilla and Montserrat use the East Caribbean dollar.

Bermuda, the Cayman Islands and Hong Kong have their own dollars. The Bermuda dollar is kept on a par with the US dollar. In the Cayman Islands, 1$US = 0.8441 Caymanian $. In Hong Kong, 1$US = HK$ 7.703.

The pound sterling and the US dollar are legal tender in the British Indian Ocean Territory.

The US dollar is legal tender in the British Virgin Islands and the Turks and Caicos Islands.

The Falkland Islands £ and the St Helena £ are kept on a par with the pound sterling.

USA 1 US dollar = 100 cents. US currency is also used in American Samoa, Guam, North Mariana Islands, Palau (Belau), Puerto Rico, and the US Virgin Islands. (See also Liberia, Marshall Islands, Micronesia and Panama.)

Uruguay 1 Uruguayan new peso = 100 centésimos; 1$US = NUr$ 3.6925.

Uzbekistan Uses Russian currency (qv); to be replaced by the soum.

Vanuatu vatu; 1$US = VT 118.454.

Vatican City uses Italian currency (qv).

Venezuela 1 bolívar = 100 céntimos; 1$US = Bs 84.7677.

Vietnam 1 dông = 10 hào = 100 xu; 1$US = D 10 458.2.

Western Samoa 1 tala = 100 sene; 1$US = WS$ 2.5407.

Yemen 1 Yemeni riyal = 100 fils; 1$US = YRls 16.3819. The dinar – the currency of the former People's Democratic Republic of Yemen (South Yemen) – is also is circulation. 1$US = YD0.4617.

Yugoslavia (Serbia and Montenegro) 1 new dinar = 100 para; 1$US = Din 50 843.8. Yugoslavia is experiencing hyper-inflation and the value of its currency is diminishing dramatically.

Zaïre 1 Zaïre = 100 makuta (likuta) = 10 000 sengi; 1$US = Z 2 514 128. Zaïre is experiencing hyper-inflation and the value of its currency is diminishing dramatically.

Zambia 1 Zambian kwacha = 100 ngwee; 1$US = K 501.552. Zambia is experiencing a high rate of inflation and the value of its currency is diminishing.

Zimbabwe 1 Zimbabwe dollar = 100 cents; 1$US = Z$ 6.3189.

[1] The East Caribbean dollar is the common currency of Anguilla, Antigua and Barbuda, Dominica, Grenada, Montserrat, St Christopher and Nevis, St Lucia, and St Vincent and the Grenadines.

[2] The CFA Franc is the common currency of Benin, Burkina Faso, Cameroon, Central African Republic, Chad, Congo, Equatorial Guinea, Gabon, Ivory Coast, Mali, Niger, Senegal, and Togo.

STOCK EXCHANGES

The world's principal stock exchanges are those listed below.

Canada Toronto.
France Paris.
Germany Frankfurt.
Hong Kong Hong Kong.
Italy Milan.
Japan Tokyo.
Netherlands Amsterdam.
Singapore Singapore.
Spain Madrid.
United Kingdom London.
USA New York (Wall Street).

PRODUCTION AND CONSUMER FIGURES

Most of the annual production figures given below are for 1990. In some cases the latest comparable figures were for 1989, which are indicated with an *.

MAJOR MINERAL ORES

BAUXITE*

Country	Production (in tonnes)
Australia	35 600 000 p.a
Guinea	17 500 000 p.a
Jamaica	9 400 000 p.a
Brazil	7 900 000 p.a
Russia	5 800 000 p.a
India	4 300 000 p.a
China	3 700 000 p.a.
Suriname	3 500 000 p.a.

COAL (bituminous)
See p. 315

COPPER ORE*

Country	Production (in tonnes)
Chile	1 610 000 p.a.
USA	1 500 000 p.a.
Canada	730 000 p.a
Russia	550 000 p.a
Zambia	500 000 p.a
Zaïre	440 000 p.a
Kazakhstan	400 000 p.a

CRUDE PETROLEUM
See p. 313

DIAMONDS

Country	Production (in carats)
Australia	36 000 000 p.a
Zaïre	24 000 000 p.a
Botswana	17 300 000 p.a
Russia	15 000 000 p.a
South Africa	8 500 000 p.a
Angola	1 300 000 p.a

GOLD

Country	Production (in tonnes)
South Africa	610 p.a
USA	295 p.a
Russia	280 p.a
Australia	241 p.a
Canada	165 p.a
China	80 p.a
Brazil	75 p.a.

IRON ORE

Country	Production (in tonnes)
Brazil	104 500 000 p.a
China	84 700 000 p.a
Australia	70 300 000 p.a
Ukraine	66 300 000 p.a
Russia	60 500 000 p.a
USA	34 900 000 p.a
India	34 000 000 p.a
Canada	21 700 000 p.a.
South Africa	19 900 000 p.a.

NATURAL GAS
See p. 314

SILVER

Country	Production (in tonnes)
Mexico	2300 p.a.
USA	2000 p.a.
Peru	1840 p.a
Russia	1500 p.a
Canada	1300 p.a
Poland	1080 p.a

TIN ORE*

Country	Production (in tonnes)
Brazil	50 200 p.a
China	33 000 p.a
Malaysia	32 000 p.a
Indonesia	31 300 p.a
Bolivia	15 800 p.a
Thailand	14 700 p.a

URANIUM

Country	Production (in tonnes)
Russia	31 200 p.a
Canada	8 700 p.a
Australia	3 500 p.a
USA	3 500 p.a
Namibia	3 200 p.a
Germany	3 000 p.a
France	2 800 p.a.
Niger	2 800 p.a.

ZINC ORE*

Country	Production (in tonnes)
Canada	1 215 000 p.a
Russia	940 000 p.a
Australia	800 000 p.a
China	620 000 p.a
Peru	600 000 p.a
Mexico	285 000 p.a

MAJOR CROPS

BARLEY

Country	Production (in tonnes)
Russia	28 000 000 p.a
Ukraine	14 000 000 p.a
Germany	13 300 000 p.a
Canada	13 200 000 p.a
France	10 000 000 p.a
Spain	9 300 000 p.a
USA	9 100 000 p.a.
UK	8 000 000 p.a.

MAIZE (CORN)

Country	Production (in tonnes)
USA	201 500 000 p.a
China	82 300 000 p.a

Brazil 21 400 000 p.a
Mexico 12 000 000 p.a
South Africa 9 200 000 p.a
Romania 9 200 000 p.a

RICE

Country	Production (in tonnes)
China	188 400 000 p.a
India	112 500 000 p.a
Indonesia	44 500 000 p.a
Bangladesh	29 400 000 p.a
Vietnam	19 200 000 p.a
Thailand	18 500 000 p.a
Burma (Myanmar)	13 600 000 p.a.
Japan	12 500 000 p.a.

COCOA BEANS

Country	Production (in tonnes)
Ivory Coast	740 000 p.a
Brazil	372 000 p.a
Ghana	299 000 p.a
Malaysia	250 000 p.a
Nigeria	170 000 p.a
Cameroon	109 000 p.a

COFFEE

Country	Production (in tonnes)
Brazil	1 440 000 p.a
Colombia	780 000 p.a
Indonesia	390 000 p.a
Mexico	309 000 p.a
Guatemala	240 000 p.a
Côte d'Ivoire	220 000 p.a
(Ivory Coast)	

COTTON LINT

Country	Production (in tonnes)
China	4 400 000 p.a
USA	3 200 000 p.a
Uzbekistan	2 600 000 p.a
Pakistan	1 500 000 p.a
India	1 500 000 p.a
Brazil	660 000 p.a

JUTE

Country	Production (in tonnes)
India	1 920 000 p.a
Bangladesh	850 000 p.a
China	590 000 p.a

POTATOES

Country	Production (in tonnes)
Russia	38 000 000 p.a
Poland	36 300 000 p.a
China	28 000 000 p.a
USA	17 800 000 p.a
Germany	17 500 000 p.a
Ukraine	16 700 000 p.a

RUBBER

Country	Production (in tonnes)
Malaysia	1 420 000 p.a
Indonesia	1 300 000 p.a
Thailand	930 000 p.a
India	290 000 p.a
China	250 000 p.a
Philippines	180 000 p.a

SUGAR BEET

Country	Production (in tonnes)
Ukraine	44 000 000 p.a
Russia	33 900 000 p.a
France	29 900 000 p.a
Germany	28 900 000 p.a
USA	25 000 000 p.a
Poland	15 200 000 p.a

SUGAR CANE

Country	Production (in tonnes)
Brazil	272 500 000 p.a
India	210 000 000 p.a
Cuba	85 900 000 p.a
China	61 800 000 p.a
Pakistan	38 000 000 p.a
Mexico	34 900 000 p.a

TEA*

Country	Production (in tonnes)
India	735 000 p.a
China	521 000 p.a
Sri Lanka	225 000 p.a
Kenya	193 000 p.a
Indonesia	165 000 p.a
Turkey	140 000 p.a

TOBACCO

Country	Production (in tonnes)
China	2 710 000 p.a
USA	680 000 p.a
India	490 000 p.a
Brazil	470 000 p.a
Turkey	210 000 p.a
Italy	200 000 p.a

WHEAT

Country	Production (in tonnes)
China	96 000 000 p.a.
USA	74 000 000 p.a.
India	49 600 000 p.a.
Russia	47 500 000 p.a.
France	33 360 000 p.a.
Canada	31 800 000 p.a.
Ukraine	27 000 000 p.a.
Germany	15 800 000 p.a.
Australia	15 700 000 p.a.

LIVESTOCK

CATTLE

Country	Number
India	197 300 000
Brazil	140 000 000
USA	99 300 000
China	77 000 000
Russia	60 000 000
Argentina	50 600 000
Ethiopia	30 000 000
Mexico	28 200 000

SHEEP

Country	Number
Australia	167 800 000
China	113 500 000
Russia	62 000 000

New Zealand	58 300 000
India	54 800 000
Iran	34 000 000
South Africa	32 600 000
Turkey	31 500 000

PIGS

Country	Number
China	360 600 000
USA	53 900 000
Russia	39 200 000
Germany	34 200 000
Brazil	33 200 000
Poland	19 800 000

AGRICULTURAL FORESTRY AND FISHING PRODUCTS

BEEF AND VEAL*

Country	Production (in tonnes)
USA	10 700 000 p.a
Russia	5 000 000 p.a
Argentina	2 600 000 p.a
Brazil	2 500 000 p.a
Germany	2 000 000 p.a
Mexico	1 800 000 p.a

BEER

Country	Production (hectolitres; 1987)
USA	230 000 000 p.a
Germany	111 000 000 p.a
UK	60 000 000 p.a
Japan	54 000 000 p.a
China	54 000 000 p.a
Russia	40 000 000 p.a

BUTTER (AND GHEE)*

Country	Production (in tonnes)
Russia	900 000 p.a
India	840 000 p.a
Germany	690 000 p.a
USA	570 000 p.a
France	540 000 p.a
Pakistan	330 000 p.a

COW'S MILK*

Country	Production (in tonnes)
USA	65 400 000 p.a
Russia	52 800 000 p.a
Germany	33 500 000 p.a
France	27 300 000 p.a
Ukraine	24 500 000 p.a
India	23 000 000 p.a

EGGS

Country	Production (in tonnes)
China	7 700 000 p.a
USA	4 000 000 p.a
Russia	2 800 000 p.a
Japan	2 400 000 p.a
Brazil	1 300 000 p.a
India	1 100 000 p.a

FISHING CATCH
(Maritime and Freshwater)

Country	Catch (in tonnes; 1988)
Japan	11 900 000 p.a
China	10 400 000 p.a
Russia	10 000 000 p.a
Peru	6 600 000 p.a
USA	6 000 000 p.a
Chile	5 200 000 p.a
India	3 150 000 p.a.
South Korea	2 720 000 p.a.

PAPER

Country	Production (in tonnes; 1988)
USA	69 500 000 p.a
Japan	24 600 000 p.a
Canada	16 600 000 p.a
China	14 100 000 p.a
Germany	11 900 000 p.a
Finland	8 700 000 p.a

ROUNDWOOD – CONIFEROUS

Country	Production (in cubic metres; 1988)
USA	345 000 000 p.a
Russia	300 000 000 p.a
Canada	164 000 000 p.a
China	134 000 000 p.a
Sweden	44 200 000 p.a
Brazil	41 800 000 p.a

ROUNDWOOD – NON-CONIFEROUS

Country	Production (in cubic metres; 1988)
India	243 000 000 p.a
USA	185 000 000 p.a
Indonesia	172 000 000 p.a
Brazil	170 000 000 p.a
China	142 000 000 p.a
Nigeria	96 200 000 p.a

SHEEP MEAT*

Country	Production (in tonnes)
New Zealand	570 000 p.a
Australia	540 000 p.a
China	420 000 p.a
Russia	420 000 p.a
UK	350 000 p.a
Turkey	300 000 p.a

SUGAR*

Country	Production (in tonnes)
India	10 200 000 p.a
Cuba	8 200 000 p.a
Brazil	7 400 000 p.a
USA	6 500 000 p.a
China	5 600 000 p.a
Ukraine	4 700 000 p.a

WINE*

Country	Production (in tonnes)
Italy	6 000 000 p.a
France	5 900 000 p.a
Spain	3 000 000 p.a
Argentina	2 000 000 p.a

USA	1 800 000 p.a
Germany	1 200 000 p.a

WOOL

Country	Production (in tonnes)
Australia	1 100 000 p.a
New Zealand	320 000 p.a
China	240 000 p.a
Russia	210 000 p.a
Argentina	160 000 p.a
Kazakhstan	110 000 p.a

MANUFACTURED GOODS

ALUMINIUM*

Country	Production (in tonnes)
USA	6 100 000 p.a
Russia	2 400 000 p.a
Canada	1 700 000 p.a
Germany	1 300 000 p.a
Australia	1 300 000 p.a
Japan	1 100 000 p.a

CARS

Country	Production (thousands)
Japan	9 950 000
USA	6 050 000
Germany	4 620 000
France	3 210 000
Italy	1 970 000
Spain	1 700 000
United Kingdom	1 300 000
Belgium	1 120 000
Canada	940 000

NB: See also p. 319 for production by company.

CEMENT

Country	Production (in tonnes)
China	204 000 000 p.a
Russia	84 500 000 p.a
Japan	84 400 000 p.a
USA	70 900 000 p.a
India	43 200 000 p.a
Germany	40 000 000 p.a
Italy	40 000 000 p.a.

COMMERCIAL VEHICLES

Country	Number
USA	3 720 000 p.a
Japan	3 550 000 p.a
Canada	810 000 p.a
Brazil	670 000 p.a
France	530 000 p.a
UK	270 000 p.a

CRUDE STEEL

Country	Production (tonnes)
Japan	110 330 000
Russia	94 000 000
USA	87 000 000
China	64 600 000
Ukraine	57 000 000
Germany	45 600 000
Italy	25 000 000
South Korea	24 500 000
Brazil	20 600 000
UK	18 000 000

RADIO RECEIVERS

Country	Production
Singapore	19 900 000 p.a
China	17 600 000 p.a
Taiwan	11 600 000 p.a
Japan	10 500 000 p.a
Brazil	8 700 000 p.a

SHIPPING (MERCHANT)

Country	Launched (tonnes)
Japan	6 500 000 p.a
South Korea	3 300 000 p.a
Germany	860 000 p.a
China	450 000 p.a
Denmark	400 000 p.a
Spain	380 000 p.a

TELEVISION SETS

Country	Production (1988)
Japan	17 700 000 p.a
China	16 700 000 p.a
USA	13 700 000 p.a
South Korea	7 800 000 p.a
Russia	6 000 000 p.a
Germany	4 400 000 p.a

CONSUMPTION

Possession of a car, a telephone and a television set are indicators of a high standard of living.

CAR OWNERSHIP

See p. 317

TELEPHONE OWNERSHIP

Country	Persons per receiver (1990)
Liechtenstein	0.7
Sweden	1.1
Switzerland	1.1
Denmark	1.2
France	1.2
Canada	1.3
USA	1.3
New Zealand	1.4
Netherlands	1.5
San Marino	1.5
Finland	1.6
Monaco	1.6
Norway	1.6

TELEVISION OWNERSHIP

Country	Persons per receiver (1990)
USA	1.2
Canada	1.7
Monaco	1.7
Japan	2.8
Denmark	2.0
Finland	2.0
France	2.0
Spain	2.0
Germany	2.1
Sweden	2.3
Cyprus	2.4
Kuwait	2.4
Belgium	2.5
Hungary	2.5

HOUSING

The number of persons per room in domestic accommodation is a reasonable guide to standards of living. The less crowded, in general, the higher the standard of living. Domestic piped water, electricity supplies and indoor WCs are taken for granted as an everyday part of modern life. The following tables record those countries with the highest percentages of these amenities.

Country	Persons per room in domestic accommodation
Monaco	0.4
Norway	0.4
Belgium	0.5
Canada	0.5
Denmark	0.5
Germany	0.5
Luxembourg	0.5
New Zealand	0.5
USA	0.5
Australia	0.6
Austria	0.6
France	0.6
Switzerland	0.6
UK	0.6

DOMESTIC ELECTRICITY

The following countries have the highest percentage of domestic dwellings with an electricity supply.

Country	Percentage of dwellings with electricity
Belgium	100.0%
Canada	100.0%
Czech Republic	100.0%
Denmark	100.0%
Monaco	100.0%
San Marino	100.0%
Bulgaria	99.8%

INDOOR SANITATION

The following countries have the highest percentage of domestic accommodation with an indoor WC.

Country	Percentage of dwellings with an indoor WC
Netherlands	100.0%
Canada	99.4%
Denmark	99.2%
UK	99.0%
Israel	98.8%
Malta	98.8%
Germany	98.3%
San Marino	98.2%
USA	98.2%

PIPED WATER

The following countries have the highest percentage of domestic accommodation with piped water.

Country	Percentage of dwellings with piped water
Denmark	100.0%
Germany	100.0%
Monaco	100.0%
Netherlands	100.0%
Sweden	100.0%
Switzerland	100.0%
Canada	99.8%
San Marino	99.8%
France	99.6%
Luxembourg	99.4%
Iceland	99.1%

POPULATION AND SOCIAL TRENDS

WORLD POPULATION

Somewhere between 24 June and 11 July 1987, the human population of the planet Earth reached 5 billion. Yet, two hundred years before that, when the world's population was barely more than one billion, political economists such as Thomas Malthus and David Ricardo were already predicting that the human species would breed itself into starvation. Nevertheless, despite their predictions, the human population keeps increasing – but so too does the food supply.

Two contending views have emerged concerning the extent to which burgeoning populations affect food supply. The first is that population must be controlled if persistent malnutrition and starvation are not to become the inevitable lot for a substantial portion of the globe. The second is that, even with a projected global population of 10 billion by the year 2070, there is sufficient food to feed everyone.

POPULATION INCREASE

In 1992, every day, the population of the world increased by an estimated 220 000 people – that is nearly an additional 80 000 000 people in one year. The rate of increase varies from an average of 0.75% per annum in Europe to 3.05% in Africa (see below).

LIFE EXPECTANCY

HIGHEST

Japan	79
Iceland	78
Sweden	78
Switzerland	78
Australia	77
Canada	77
France	77
Italy	77
Netherlands	77
Norway	77
San Marino	77

LOWEST

Guinea-Bissau	39
Afghanistan	42
Sierra Leone	42
Guinea	43
Gambia	44
Niger	45
Angola	46
Malawi	46
Burundi	47
Chad	47
Equatorial Guinea	47
Mauritania	47
Mozambique	47
Senegal	47
Uganda	47

Figures are the average life expectancy for 1990.

POPULATION OF MAJOR WORLD REGIONS (millions)

	1900	1950	1990	2025	2100
World	**1 622**	**2 518**	**5 292**	**8 504**	**11 186**
Asia*	1 070	1 558	3 402	5 265	6 385
Africa	110	222	642	1 597	2 931
Latin America	64	166	448	757	1 075
North America	81	166	276	332	314
Europe†	290	393	498	515	440
Oceania	7	13	26	38	41

* includes the populations of the states of the former USSR.
† excludes the populations of the states of the former USSR.

POPULATION GROWTH: SELECTED COUNTRIES

	1900	1950	1990	2025
China	453 000 000	554 000 000	1 123 815 000	1 475 159 000
India	240 000 000	357 561 000	827 152 000	1 228 829 000
USA	*76 000 000*	*152 271 000*	*248 429 000*	*311 936 000*
Indonesia	38 000 000	79 538 000	181 539 000	272 744 000
Brazil	18 000 000	53 444 000	150 368 000	245 809 000
Japan	*45 000 000*	*83 625 000*	*123 865 000*	*132 082 000*
Bangladesh	29 000 000	42 484 000	115 244 000	219 383 000
Nigeria	13 600 000	32 935 000	113 343 000	338 105 000
Pakistan	16 000 000	40 031 000	112 226 000	209 976 000
Mexico	13 500 000	27 376 000	89 012 000	154 085 000
Vietnam	11 500 000	29 954 000	66 153 000	108 462 000
Canada	*5 250 000*	*13 737 000*	*26 746 000*	*33 261 000*
Germany	*43 000 000*	*68 376 000*	*77 221 000*	*71 060 000*
Italy	*47 000 000*	*46 789 000*	*57 563 000*	*57 178 000*
United Kingdom	*38 325 000*	*50 616 000*	*56 190 000*	*55 919 000*
France	*41 000 000*	*41 736 000*	*55 475 000*	*58 431 000*

Russia had a population of 148 543 000 in 1990–91; projections for the country are not available.
G7 countries are shown in italics.

Population growth

Period	World population
Neolithic period	under 10 000 000
4000 BC	c. 50 000 000
AD 500	c. 100 000 000
AD 800	c. 200 000 000
c. 1550	c. 500 000 000
1805	1 000 000 000
1926	2 000 000 000
1960	3 000 000 000
1974	4 000 000 000
1987	5 000 000 000
1998 (projected)	6 000 000 000
2010 (projected)	7 000 000 000
2023 (projected)	8 000 000 000
2040 (projected)	9 000 000 000
2070 (projected)	10 000 000 000

FERTILITY

In the following tables the crude birth rate measures the number of births per year per thousand. In the table listing territories with the highest crude birth rates, the figures given refer to the period 1985–90 (except for Mali and Malawi where earlier estimates are given).

Territories with the highest crude live birth rates

Country or territory	Births per thousand
Uganda	52.2
Rwanda	51.2
Zambia	51.1
Guinea	51.0
Tanzania	50.5
Somalia	50.1
Ivory Coast	49.9
Benin	49.2
Mali	48.7
Ethiopia	48.6
Botswana	48.5
Nigeria	48.5
Malawi	48.3
Sierra Leone	48.2

Territories with the lowest crude live birth rates

Country or territory*	Births per thousand
Falkland Islands	7.5 (1988)
Italy	9.7 (1989)
Japan	9.9 (1990)
Norfolk Island	10.0 (1981)
Greece	10.1 (1989)
San Marino	10.1 (1989)
Spain	10.7 (1988)
Austria	11.6 (1990)
Hungary	11.6 (1990)
Hong Kong	11.7 (1990)
Portugal	11.9 (1988)
Germany	11.4 (1989)
Belgium	12.0 (1988)
Isle of Man	12.1 (1989)
Andorra	12.2 (1990)

* non-sovereign territories are indicated in italics

POPULATION DENSITY

The least densely populated territories are to be found in high latitudes (e.g. Greenland and the Falkland Islands), in the major desert areas (e.g. Mongolia, Western Sahara, Mauritania and Namibia), or in parts of the world where tropical rain forests still remain the dominant vegetation type. The most densely-populated territories are mostly very small states or former colonial trading outposts with the character of city-states, or relatively small islands with diverse economies. Among the most populous states in the table is one low income country that is heavily dependent on the productivity of its rich soils (Bangladesh), one middle income country now rapidly industrializing (South Korea), and one major high-income country (The Netherlands).

Territories with the greatest density of population

Country or territory*	Population per km² (1990)
Macau	29 962
Monaco	28 500
Hong Kong	5551
Gibraltar	5083
Singapore	4859
Vatican City	1705
Gaza Strip	1698
Bermuda	1144
Malta	1120
Bangladesh	803
Guernsey	760
Bahrain	742
Maldives	722
Jersey	714
Barbados	594
Mauritius	531
Nauru	457
South Korea	432
Puerto Rico	405
San Marino	385
Tuvalu	373
The Netherlands	366

* non-sovereign territories are indicated in italics

Territories with the least density of population

Country or territory*	Population per km² (1990)
Greenland	0.03
Falkland Islands	0.16
Guyane (French Guiana)	1.10
Mongolia	1.40
Western Sahara	1.50
Mauritania	1.97
Namibia	2.16
Australia	2.22
Botswana	2.22
Iceland	2.48
Libya	2.58
Suriname	2.58
Canada	2.66
Guyana	3.70
Gabon	4.38
Chad	4.42
Central African Republic	4.88

* non-sovereign territories are indicated in italics

POPULATION BY AGE

Third World countries with high birth rates tend to have young populations; developed countries with low birth rates tend to have more elderly populations.

Territories with the youngest population

Country	% of population under 25
Kenya	50
Uganda	50
Yemen	50
Botswana	49
Malawi	49
Rwanda	49
Tanzania	49
Zambia	49
Côte d'Ivoire	48
Niger	48
Nigeria	48
Comoros	47
Mali	47
Somalia	47
Swaziland	47
Zaïre	47

Territories with the oldest population

Country	% of population over 60
Sweden	23
Belgium	21
Norway	21
UK	21
Austria	20
Denmark	20
Greece	20
Italy	20
Switzerland	20
Bulgaria	19
France	19
Hungary	19
Luxembourg	19

URBANIZATION

Urbanization – the increased migration of rural dwellers into cities – has been a particular feature of the second half of the 20th century. In 1950 under 30% of the population of the world lived in urban regions, but by 1990 almost 44% lived in cities, towns or their suburbs. The greatest proportion of urban dwellers is to be found in countries of the developed world. Some 97% of the population of Belgium, for example, is urban.

THE WORLD'S LARGEST CITIES

In early 1993, there were 290 cities with a population of over 1 000 000 – 130 in Asia, 55 in North America, 48 in Europe, 27 in South America, 25 in Africa and 5 in Oceania. The growth of the largest cities in the world has been impressive, especially those in the Third World.

By contrast, it is interesting to note that in 1900 only 16 cities (including suburbs) had over 1 000 000 inhabitants. They were: London (England, UK) 6 400 000, New York (USA) 4 200 000, Paris (France) 3 900 000, Berlin (Germany) 2 400 000, Chicago (USA) 1 700 000, Vienna (Austria) 1 600 000, Tokyo (Japan) 1 400 000, St Petersburg (Russia) 1 400 000, Philadelphia (USA) 1 400 000, Manchester (England, UK) 1 200 000, Birmingham (England, UK) 1 200 000, Moscow (Russia) 1 200 000, Peking (China) 1 100 000, Calcutta (India) 1 000 000, Boston (USA) 1 000 000 and Glasgow (Scotland, UK) 1 000 000.

The population figures given below relate to the agglomeration or urban area; that is the city, its suburbs and surrounding built-up area rather than for local government districts. By using this definitions for the urban area of every city listed a more accurate comparison of size has been possible.

City	Country	Population	Date of census/ estimate	Details
Mexico City	Mexico	20 200 000	1990 census	*8 237 000 within city limits; 13 636 000 in 'Greater Mexico City'*
Tokyo	Japan	18 200 000	1990 estimate	*11 855 000 within city limits; 3 220 000 in Yokohama*
New York	USA	18 087 000	1990 census	*7 323 000 within city limits*
São Paulo	Brazil	16 832 000	1991 estimate	*9 700 000 within city limits*
Los Angeles	USA	14 532 000	1990 census	*3 485 000 within city limits*
Shanghai	China	13 342 000	1990 census	*municipal province*
Buenos Aires	Argentina	12 582 000	1991 census	*2 961 000 within city limits*
Bombay	India	12 572 000	1991 census	*9 910 000 within city limits*
Cairo	Egypt	12 287 000	1990 estimate	
Rio de Janeiro	Brazil	11 141 000	1991 estimate	*5 487 000 within city limits*
Calcutta	India	10 916 000	1991 census	*4 388 000 within city limits*
Beijing (Peking)	China	10 819 000	1990 census	*municipal province*
Seoul	South Korea	10 726 000	1990 census	
Paris	France	9 063 000	1990 census	*2 175 000 within city limits*
Moscow	Russia	8 967 000	1989 estimate	
Tianjin (Tientsin)	China	8 785 000	1990 census	*municipal province*
Osaka	Japan	8 500 000	1990 estimate	*2 624 000 within city limits 1 477 000 in Kobe*
Delhi	India	8 375 000	1991 census	*7 175 000 within city limits*
Chicago	USA	8 066 000	1990 census	*2 784 000 within city limits*
Manila	Philippines	7 832 000	1990 census	*1 599 000 within city limits*
Jakarta	Indonesia	7 829 000	1985 estimate	
London	UK	7 825 000	1991 estimate	*6 803 000 in Greater London*
Karachi	Pakistan	6 771 000	1992 estimate	
Istanbul	Turkey	6 620 000	1990 census	
Lima	Peru	6 405 000	1990 estimate	*5 494 000 within city limits*
San Francisco	USA	6 253 000	1990 census	*724 000 within city limits*
Dhaka	Bangladesh	6 105 000	1991 census	
Tehran	Iran	6 022 000	1986 census	
Philadelphia	USA	5 899 000	1990 census	*1 586 000 within city limits*
Bangkok	Thailand	5 876 000	1990 census	
Lagos	Nigeria	5 686 000	1991 census	*1 347 000 within city limits*
Hong Kong	Hong Kong	5 674 000	1991 census	
Madras	India	5 361 000	1991 census	*3 795 000 within city limits*
Baghdad	Iraq	5 348 000	1985 estimate	
Santiago	Chile	5 343 000	1991 estimate	
St Petersburg	Russia	5 020 000	1989 estimate	
Bogota	Colombia	4 921 000	1990 estimate	*now officially known as Santa Fé de Bogota, DE*
Madrid	Spain	4 846 000	1991 census	*3 121 000 within city limits*
Essen(-Ruhr)	Germany	4 700 000	1990 estimate	*621 000 within Essen city limits; 589 000 in Dortmund 530 000 in Duisburg*
Detroit	USA	4 665 000	1990 census	*1 028 000 within city limits*
Shenyang	China	4 500 000	1990 census	
Hyderabad	India	4 280 000	1991 census	*3 005 000 within city limits*
Boston	USA	4 172 000	1990 census	*574 000 within city limits*
Bangalore	India	4 087 000	1991 census	*2 651 000 within city limits*
Ho Chi Minh City	Vietnam	4 076 000	1992 estimate	

URBAN POPULATION

The definitions of 'urban' vary from country to country, often quite markedly, and these variations influence the positions of countries within the tables. Rapid urbanization is characteristic of the Third World. Conversely, in developed countries there is little scope for further growth in the level of urbanization. Indeed, in developed states the pattern of net population movement from country to town has been succeeded by a net movement from town to country ('counterurbanization').

Territories with the highest % of urban population

Country or territory*	Births per thousand
Gaza Strip	100.0
Macau	100.0
Monaco	100.0
Singapore	100.0
Vatican City	100.0
Belgium	97.0
Kuwait	96.0
Andorra	94.8
Hong Kong	93.1
Iceland	90.4
San Marino	90.4
Israel	89.9
UK	89.0
Uruguay	88.8
Netherlands	88.6

* non-sovereign territories are indicated in italics

Territories with the lowest % of urban population

Country or territory	Births per thousand
Bhutan	5.0
Burundi	5.0
Rwanda	8.0
Burkina Faso	9.0
Nepal	10.0
Ethiopia	12.1
Malawi	14.6
Bangladesh	16.0
Afghanistan	17.7
Vanuatu	18.4
Papua New Guinea	18.9
Lesotho	20.0
Niger	20.0

MARRIAGE RATES
(selected countries)

	Marriages per 1000 population	Year
Bangladesh	11.3	1988
Brazil	6.6	1988
Canada	7.2	1988
France	5.0	1989
Germany	6.4	1989
Iceland	4.7	1989
Indonesia	7.4	1986
Italy	5.4	1989
Jamaica	4.7	1989
Japan	5.8	1988
Sweden	4.7	1990
UK	6.8	1989
USA	9.7	1989

DIVORCE RATES
(selected countries)

	Divorces per 1000 population	Year
Brazil	0.2	1988
Cuba	3.6	1989
Italy	0.4	1988
France	1.9	1988
Russia	3.4	1989
Sri Lanka	0.2	1988
Sweden	2.2	1900
UK	2.9	1989
USA	4.7	1990

MALE-FEMALE RATIO

The countries with the highest percentage of male inhabitants are territories that attract a male labour force from abroad. The country with the greatest percentage of males is the Vatican City where the overwhelming majority of the resident population is male, but no precise figures are available. The countries with the highest percentage of females tend to be territories from which migrant male workers are drawn. The figures for Russia and Austria reflect the much higher percentages of elderly women than elderly men as a result of fatalities among service personnel during World War II.

The countries with the highest percentage of males are as follows:

Country	% of males
Qatar	67.2%
United Arab Emirates	64.9%
Bahrain	58.4%
Kuwait	56.9%
Christmas Island	55.1%
Pitcairn	54.7%
Greenland	54.1%
Libya	53.6%
Brunei	53.4%
Palau	53.3%
Saudi Arabia	53.2%
Andorra	53.1%

The countries with the highest percentage of females are as follows:

Country	% of females
Monaco	53.4%
Botswana	52.9%
Gabon	52.9%
Grenada	52.9%
St Lucia	52.8%
Swaziland	52.8%
Russia	52.7%
Yemen	52.7%
Antigua	52.6%
Austria	52.6%
Tuvalu	52.6%

Non-sovereign territories are shown in italics.

THE INTERNATIONAL WORLD

INTERNATIONAL ORGANIZATIONS

THE UNITED NATIONS

'A general international organization...for the maintenance of international peace and security'. The signatories were Anthony Eden, Cordell Hull (USA), Vyacheslav M. Skryabin Molotov (USSR) and Ambassador Foo Ping-Sheung (China).

Proposals to found such an organization were agreed between the four powers at Dumbarton Oaks, Washington DC, USA, between 21 August and 7 October 1944. On the final day of the United Nations Conference at San Francisco (beginning on 25 April 1945) delegates of 50 participating states signed the Charter, which came into force on 24 October 1945. The first UN General Assembly had 51 members – the 50 original signatories plus Poland, which signed on 15 October 1945.

In June 1993 there were 183 members of the United Nations. The following sovereign states are not members of the UN:
Andorra,
China (Republic of – Taiwan) – a member of the UN from 1945 to 1971,
Kiribati,
Nauru,
Switzerland,
Tonga,
Tuvalu
Vatican City (the Holy See).

However, Switzerland and the Vatican City have observer status at the UN, with the right to be present at sessions of the General Assembly but without the privilege of being able to participate.

MEMBERS OF THE UNITED NATIONS

Original members: (October 1945)
Argentina, Australia, Belgium, Bolivia, Brazil, Belarus[1], Canada, Chile, China[2], Colombia, Costa Rica, Cuba, Czechoslovakia[3], Denmark, the Dominican Republic, Ecuador, Egypt, El Salvador, Ethiopia, France, Greece, Guatemala, Haiti, Honduras, India[4], Iran, Iraq, Lebanon, Liberia, Luxembourg, Mexico, the Netherlands, New Zealand, Nicaragua, Norway, Panama, Paraguay, Peru, the Philippines, Poland, Saudi Arabia, South Africa, Syria, Turkey, Ukraine[1], USSR[5], UK, USA, Uruguay, Venezuela and Yugoslavia (suspended 1992).

[1] Belarus and Ukraine became independent countries in 1991. Despite their status as Union republics of the USSR before 1991 they had separate membership of the UN. Belarus joined the UN as Byelorussia.
[2] From 1945 until 1971 the seat for China at the UN was occupied by the Republic of China (Taiwan). In 1971 the UN withdrew recognition of the Republic of China in favour of the People's Republic of China.
[3] Since 1993 this seat has been held by the Czech Republic.
[4] Although India did not gain independence until 1947, an Indian delegation signed the UN Charter in 1945.
[5] Since 1992 this seat has been held by Russia.

Members elected in 1946: Afghanistan, Iceland, Sweden, Thailand.

Members elected in 1947: Pakistan, Yemen. (From 1962 Yemen was officially known as the Yemen Arab Republic and popularly known as North Yemen. In 1990 North Yemen merged with the People's Democratic Republic of Yemen – popularly known as South Yemen – which had been a UN member since 1967.)

Member elected in 1948: Burma (since 1989 officially known as Myanmar).

Member elected in 1949: Israel.

Member elected in 1950: Indonesia.

Members elected in 1955: Albania, Austria, Bulgaria, Cambodia, Finland, Hungary, Ireland, Italy, Jordan, Laos, Libya, Nepal, Portugal, Romania, Spain, Sri Lanka[1].
[1] Elected as Ceylon.

Members elected in 1956: Japan, Morocco, Sudan, Tunisia.

Members elected in 1957: Ghana, Malaysia (elected as Malaya).

Member elected in 1958: Guinea.

Members elected in 1960 Benin[1], Burkina Faso[2], Cameroon, Central African Republic, Chad, Congo, Cyprus, Gabon, Ivory Coast, Madagascar, Mali, Niger, Nigeria, Senegal, Somalia, Togo, Zaïre[3].
[1] Elected as Dahomey.
[2] Elected as Upper Volta.
[3] Elected as the Republic of the Congo.

Members elected in 1961: Mauritania, Mongolia, Sierra Leone, Tanzania[1].
[1] Tanganyika and Zanzibar – a UN member since 1963 – merged to form Tanzania in 1964.

Members elected in 1962: Algeria, Burundi, Jamaica, Rwanda, Trinidad and Tobago, Uganda.

Members elected in 1963: Kenya, Kuwait.

Members elected in 1964: Malawi, Malta, Zambia.

Members elected in 1965: The Gambia, the Maldives, Singapore.

Members elected in 1966: Barbados, Botswana, Guyana, Lesotho.

Members elected in 1968: Equatorial Guinea, Mauritius, Swaziland.

Member elected in 1970: Fiji.

Members elected in 1971: Bahrain, Bhutan, Oman, Qatar, United Arab Emirates.

Members elected in 1973: The Bahamas, Germany[1].
[1] From 1973 to 1990 both the German Democratic Republic – East Germany – and the Federal Republic of Germany – West Germany – were members of the UN.

Members elected in 1974: Bangladesh, Grenada, Guinea-Bissau.

Members elected in 1975: Cape Verde, the Comoros, Mozambique, São Tomé e Principe, Papua New Guinea, Suriname.

Members elected in 1976: Angola, Seychelles, Western Samoa.

Members elected in 1977: Djibouti, Vietnam.

Members elected in 1978: Dominica, Solomon Islands.

Member elected in 1979: St Lucia.

Members elected in 1980: St Vincent and the Grenadines, Zimbabwe.

Members elected in 1981: Antigua and Barbuda, Belize, Vanuatu.

Member elected in 1983: St Christopher and Nevis.

Member elected in 1984: Brunei.

Members elected in 1990: Liechtenstein, Namibia.

Members elected in 1991: Estonia, Korea (People's Democratic Republic – North Korea), Korea (Republic of – South Korea), Latvia, Lithuania, Marshall Islands, Micronesia.

Members elected in 1992: Armenia, Azerbaijan, Bosnia-Herzegovina, Croatia, Georgia, Kazakhstan, Kyrgyzstan, Moldova, San Marino, Slovenia, Tajikistan, Turkmenistan, Uzbekistan.

Members elected in 1993: Macedonia (Former Yugoslav Republic of), Monaco, Slovakia. (Eritrea is expected to be elected to membership in 1993.)

THE ORGANIZATION OF THE UN

The UN has six principal organs (see below). All are based in New York, with the exception of the International Court of Justice, which is based in The Hague (Netherlands).

THE GENERAL ASSEMBLY

The Assembly is composed of all member states and can discuss anything within the scope of the Charter. Each member state has up to five delegates but only one vote. The annual session of the General Assembly begins on the third Tuesday of September. The Charter also has provision for special sessions. A President is elected by the General Assembly each September for a single term.

Decisions of the General Assembly are made by a qualified majority of those present (two thirds) on 'important' questions, and by a simple majority on other issues.

THE SECURITY COUNCIL

The Charter of the UN identifies the Security Council as the main organ for maintaining international peace and security. It has five permanent members – China, France, Russia (from 1945 to 1991 this seat was held by the USSR), the UK and the USA (the 'great powers' at the end of World War II) – and 10 other members who are elected by the General Assembly for a term of two years. (From 1945 to 1971, China was represented by the Republic of China – Taiwan. Since 1971, China has been represented by the People's Republic of China.)

Decisions of the Security Council are reached by a majority vote of at least nine of the 15 members. However, any one of the permanent members of the Security Council can exercise its right of veto.

In 1993 Japan and Germany advocated claims to permanent membership of the Security Council for their countries.

THE ECONOMIC AND SOCIAL COUNCIL

The Economic and Social Council acts as a coordinating body for the numerous specialized agencies created by the UN. The Council – which has 54 members elected for a term of three years – aims to promote international cooperation in the economic, social and related fields.

THE TRUSTEESHIP COUNCIL

The Trusteeship Council has effectively been wound up as all of the territories – mostly former German and Japanese colonies – placed under its supervision have achieved independence, except for Palau (Belau).

THE INTERNATIONAL COURT OF JUSTICE

The International Court of Justice (the 'World Court') is available to offer legal rulings on any case brought before it by UN members. (All member states plus Switzerland are parties to the Statute of the Court.) In the event of a party failing to adhere to a judgement of the Court, the other party may have recourse to the Security Council.

The World Court comprises 15 judges elected by the Security Council and the General Assembly for a term of nine years.

THE SECRETARIAT

The Secretariat performs the role of a civil service for the UN. Its head is the Secretary General, who combines the tasks of chief administrative officer of the organization with that of international mediator.

Secretaries-General of the UN
Trygve Lie (Norway)   1946–53
Dag Hammarskjöld (Sweden)   1953–61
U Thant (Burma)   1961–72
Kurt Waldheim (Austria)   1972–81
Javier Perez de Cuellar (Peru)   1981–91
Boutros Boutros Ghali (Egypt)   1992–

SPECIALIZED AGENCIES OF THE UN

FAO (Food and Agricultural Organization) 169 members. *Aim:* to fight malnutrition and hunger and to coordinate development programmes. *Headquarters:* Rome, Italy.

GATT (General Agreement on Tariffs and Trade) 104 contracting countries. *Aim:* to lay down a common code of practice in international trade. *Headquarters:* Geneva, Switzerland.

IAEA (International Atomic Energy Agency) 116 members. *Aim:* to encourage the use of atomic energy for peaceful means. *Headquarters:* Vienna, Austria.

IBRD (International Bank for Reconstruction and Development) or World Bank 159 members. *Aim:* to encourage development through capital investment (in particular, investment in poorer member nations). *Headquarters:* Washington DC, USA.

ICAO (International Civil Aviation Organization) 167 members. *Aim:* to encourage safety measures and coordinate facilities for international flight. *Headquarters:* Montréal, Canada.

IDA (International Development Organization) 140 members. *Aim:* to assist less developed countries by providing credits on special terms. *Headquarters:* an affiliate of the World Bank, see above.

IFAD (International Fund for Agricultural Development) 148 members. *Aim:* to generate grants or loans to increase food production in developing countries. *Headquarters:* Rome, Italy.

IFC (International Finance Corporation) 143 members. *Aim:* to promote the flow of private capital internationally and to stimulate the capital markets. *Headquarters:* an affiliate of the World Bank, see below.

ILO (International Labour Organization) 152 members. *Aim:* to establish international labour standards and to improve social and economic well-being. *Headquarters:* Geneva, Switzerland.

IMF (International Monetary Fund) 159 members. *Aim:* to promote international monetary cooperation. **Headquarters:** Washington DC, USA

IMO (International Maritime Organization) 135 members. *Aim:* to coordinate safety at sea. *Headquarters:* London, UK.

UN FINANCE

The UN budget is mainly financed by contributions from member states. However, in the early 1990s the organization experienced a financial crisis because a substantial number of members were seriously behind with their contributions. The depth of this crisis was increased by the high cost of the large number of operations in which the UN was involved.

The following UN members are assessed to make the lowest contributions to the expenses of the organization – each pays only 0.01% contributions to the UN budget: Afghanistan, Albania, Angola, Antigua and Barbuda, Bangladesh, Barbados, Belize, Benin, Bhutan, Bolivia, Botswana, Burkina Faso, Burundi, Cambodia, Cameroon, Cape Verde, Central African Republic, Chad, Comoros, Congo, Djibouti, Dominica, El Salvador, Equatorial Guinea, Ethiopia, Fiji, Gambia, Ghana, Grenada, Guinea, Guinea-Bissau, Guyana, Haiti, Honduras, Jordan, Kenya, Laos, Lesotho, Liberia, Liechtenstein, Madagascar, Malawi, Maldives, Mali, Malta, Marshall Islands, Mauritania, Mauritius, Micronesia, Mongolia, Mozambique, Myanmar (Burma), Namibia, Nepal, Nicaragua, Niger, Papua New Guinea, Rwanda, St Christopher and Nevis, St Lucia, St Vincent and the Grenadines, San Marino, São Tomé and Principe, Senegal, Seychelles, Sierra Leone, Solomon Islands, Somalia, Sri Lanka, Sudan, Suriname, Swaziland, Tanzania, Togo, Uganda, Vanuatu, Vietnam, Western Samoa, Yemen, Zaïre and Zambia.

The major contributors to UN finances are:

Country	% of contribution
USA	25.00%
Japan	11.38%
Russia	9.99%
Germany	9.36%
France	6.25%
UK	4.86%
Italy	3.99%
Canada	3.09%
Spain	1.96%
Netherlands	1.65%
Australia	1.57%
Brazil	1.45%
Ukraine	1.25%
Sweden	1.21%

ITU (International Telecommunications Union) 179 members. *Aim:* to allocate telecommunications frequencies and to standardize telecommunication procedures. *Headquarters:* Geneva, Switzerland.

MIGA (Multilateral Investment Guarantee Agency) 58 members. *Aim:* to encourage the flow of investments among member countries. *Headquarters:* an affiliate of the World Bank, see above.

UNESCO (UN Educational, Scientific and Cultural Organization) 169 members. *Aim:* to stimulate popular education and the spread of culture. *Headquarters:* Paris, France.

UNIDO (UN Industrial Development Organization) 156 members. *Aim:* to promote industrialization in developing countries. *Headquarters:* Vienna, Austria.

UPU (Universal Postal Union) 183 members. *Aim:* to unite members in a single postal territory. *Headquarters:* Berne, Switzerland.

WHO (World Health Organization) 183 members. *Aim:* to promote the attainment by all peoples of the highest possible standards of health. *Headquarters:* Geneva, Switzerland.

WIPO (World Intellectual Property Organization) 129 members. *Aim:* to promote protection of intellectual property (inventions, copyright, etc.). *Headquarters:* Geneva, Switzerland.

WMO (World Meteorological Organization) 172 members. *Aim:* to standardize meteorological observations and apply the information to the greatest international benefit, for shipping, agriculture, etc. *Headquarters:* Geneva, Switzerland.

World Bank see IBRD.

SUBSIDIARY ORGANS OF THE UN
Subsidiary organs of the UN include:

UNHCR (United Nations High Commissioner for Refugees) *Aim:* to provide international protection for refugees. *Headquarters:* Geneva, Switzerland.

UNICEF (United Nations International Children's Emergency Fund) *Aim:* to meet the needs of children, particularly those in developing countries. *Headquarters:* New York, USA.

UNRWA (United Nations Relief and Works Agency) *Aim:* to provide relief and welfare services for Palestinian refugees. *Headquarters:* Vienna, Austria.

UN PEACEKEEPING

In the event of an armed dispute between member states of the UN, the Security Council, or, in special circumstances, the General Assembly, may offer to mediate or negotiate a ceasefire. If requested, armed forces may be provided, under the control of the Secretary General, to supervise the ceasefire or monitor the disengagement. These peacekeeping units – drawn from member states who volunteer their services and are acceptable to the states in conflict – have only limited powers.

Only once, during the Korean War (1950–53), did the UN provide forces to fight, although during the Congo (Zaïre) troubles (1960–64) UN forces were used to intervene to put down an illegal revolt. Except in these two cases, UN forces have been entrusted only with a peacekeeping – as opposed to a peacemaking –

role. They cannot do more than defend themselves in the event of fighting breaking out and must be withdrawn if requested to do so by the host country.

The US-led multinational force dispatched to the Gulf after August 1990 to evict Iraqi trops from occupied Kuwait acted in response to a UN resolution but was not a UN force.

Some recent UN forces have been empowered to assume other duties including administration (in Cambodia) and humanitarian relief (in Bosnia and Somalia).

In 1993 UN forces were involved in more theatres than at any other time in the organization's history. However, the cost of maintaining so many operations, particularly the extensive interventions in Cambodia, Somalia, Mozambique and the former Yugoslavia, has put pressure on the UN to seek urgent solutions to other long-running problems that have led to involvements in, for example, Cyprus and Palestine. In April 1993, UN forces were involved in:

Angola a humanitarian and observational role, although the civil war between MPLA and UNITA forces has resumed. UN personnel: under 900.

Cambodia the UN's biggest involvement currently. The UN has a peacekeeping role and is participating in the administration of the country until multi-party elections can be held. UN personnel: 18 000.

Cyprus a peacekeeping role, maintaining the 'Attila Line' between the Greek and Turkish sectors of the island. UN personnel: over 2000.

El Salvador a peacekeeping and monitoring role after the civil war. UN personnel: over 1100.

Golan Heights a peacekeeping and monitoring role between the Israeli and Syrian front lines. UN personnel: 1300.

Jerusalem a monitoring role. UN personnel: 300.

Kashmir a monitoring role along the ceasefire line between Indian and Pakistani forces. UN personnel: under 50.

Kuwait a peacekeeping role along the border with Iraq. UN personnel: 500.

Lebanon a peacekeeping role between the Israeli and Lebanese front lines. UN personnel: under 6000.

Mozambique a major peacekeeping and humanitarian role following the negotiated end of the civil war. UN personnel: substantial but not yet deployed.

Somalia initially a humanitarian role, which became a peacekeeping operation. The UN is involved in negotiations for an end to the civil wars and is likely to participate in the administration of the country (as in Cambodia). UN personnel: over 1000 (rising).

Western Sahara a monitoring and peacekeeping role prior to the holding of a referendum on the disputed territory's future. UN personnel: under 400.

(Former) Yugoslavia a humanitarian role in Croatia and Bosnia–Herzegovina. UN involvement steadily increased in 1993 and possible military involvement was debated. UN personnel: 15 000 early in 1993, but rising as humanitarian relief projects increased. The principal contributors – in humanitarian and/or monitoring operations – were France, Egypt, Ukraine, Spain, Canada, UK and the Scandinavian countries.

THE EUROPEAN COMMUNITY

In 1950 the governments of Belgium, France, the Federal Republic of Germany, Italy, Luxembourg and the Netherlands began negotiations to integrate their interests in specific fields. The result was the Treaty of Paris (1951) under which the European Coal and Steel Community was created. Attempts to establish a community concerned with cooperation in foreign affairs and defence proved abortive, but in 1957 the European Economic Community (the EEC) and the European Atomic Energy Community (Euratom) – with memberships identical to the European Coal and Steel Community – came into being under the terms of the Treaty of Rome.

The three Communities were distinct entities until 1967, when they merged their executives and decision-making bodies into a single European Community (the EC). The Community has been enlarged through the accession of Denmark, Greece, Ireland, Portugal, Spain and the UK.

EC plans for economic and monetary union have been discussed (see below), and there has been increased coordination in foreign policies and research and development. Since 1975 the EC has had its own revenue independent of national contributions.

EC INSTITUTIONS

The Commission of the EC
The Commission consists of 17 members appointed by their national governments for a term of four years. The Commissioners elect from their number a President and six Vice Presidents. The Commission – which acts independently of national governments – makes proposals to the Council of Ministers and executes the decisions of the Council.
Composition of the European Commission: Belgium is represented by 1 Commissioner, Denmark 1, France 2, Germany 2, Greece 1, Ireland 1, Italy 2, Luxembourg 1, Netherlands 1, Portugal 1, Spain 2, and the UK 2.
President: Jacques Delors (France)

The Council of Ministers
The Council is the main decision-making body of the EC. The Council consists of the foreign ministers of

MEMBERS OF THE EC		
	Date of joining	Next period as President of the Council of Ministers
Belgium	1950	Jul–Dec 93
Denmark	1973	Jul–Dec 98
France	1950	Jan–Jun 95
Germany	1950	Jul–Dec 94
Greece	1981	Jan–Jun 94
Ireland	1973	Jul–Dec 96
Italy	1950	Jan–Jun 96
Luxembourg	1950	Jul–Dec 97
The Netherlands	1950	Jan–Jun 97
Portugal	1986	Jul–Dec 98
Spain	1986	Jul–Dec 95
United Kingdom	1973	Jan–Jun 98

each of the member states. Specialist councils – for example, of the 12 ministers of agriculture – also meet, while heads of government meet three times a year as the *European Council*.

Ministers represent national interests. The decisions of the Council are normally unanimous although there is provision for majority voting in certain areas. The Presidency of the Council of Ministers rotates, with each member state taking the chair for a period of six months (see the table below).

The European Parliament
The Parliament consists of 567 members directly elected for five years by universal adult suffrage according to the local practice of each member state. Members (MEPs) have the right to be consulted on legislative proposals submitted by the Council of Ministers or the Commission and the power to reject or amend the budget of the EC. The Parliament meets in Strasbourg (France), its committees meet in Brussels (Belgium), and its Secretariat is based in Luxembourg.
Composition of the European Parliament: Belgium returns 25 MEPs, Denmark 16, France 87, Germany 99, Greece 25, Ireland 15, Italy 87, Luxembourg 6, Netherlands 31, Portugal 25, Spain 64, and the UK 87.

The European Court of Justice
The Court consists of 13 judges and six advocates-general appointed for six years by the governments of member states acting in concert. At least one representative is appointed from each member state. The Court is responsible for deciding upon the legality of the decisions of the Council of Ministers and the Commission and for adjudicating between states in the event of disputes.

A WIDENING COMMUNITY

The Single European Market
In 1992 the EC achieved a Single European Market in which all duties, tariffs and quotas have been removed on trade between member states and many obstacles to the free movement of people, money and goods have been abolished within the Community. In theory a citizen of any EC member state may live, work and bank where he or she chooses. There are no restrictions on the purchase of property and educational qualifications are granted recognition throughout the EC. The majority of EC countries have already implemented open borders – alcohol and cigarettes may now, for example, be taken from one EC country to another 'in reasonable quantities' without attracting customs duties. However, the UK and Denmark have insisted upon the right to maintain entry checks on individuals at ports and airports to guard against terrorism.

Subsidiarity
The transfer of certain economic and social responsibilities to the Community implies a loss of sovereignty by national parliaments. This lack of accountability is referred to as the 'democratic deficit'. Remedies to cure the deficit range from the preferred solution of the Danes – which would involve empowering their national parliament with a veto over all EC matters – to the adoption of a federal system. It is claimed that national rights are protected by the doctrine of *subsidiarity*, which says that decisions should only be taken at the higher (supranational or federalist) level if the matter cannot be as easily dealt with at the local (national) level. The majority of EC gøvernments and the Commission are committed to this idea.

The Maastricht Agreement
In 1991 at Maastricht in the Netherlands, EC heads of government agreed a new European treaty that disappointed federalists. Under the agreement, cooperation in certain fields is to be channelled through new inter-governmental bodies rather than through existing institutions of the EC. A *European Union* was defined resting upon three 'pillars'. The 'first pillar' is the EC, which would assume additional monetary responsibilities. The 'second pillar' – concerned with foreign and security matters – and the 'third pillar' – concerned with cooperation in a wide variety of areas such as immigration, asylum and law enforcement – were defined as inter-governmental bodies representing the 12 member states. The Maastricht summit thus agreed a considerable widening of cooperation between the EC states without adding substantially to the powers of the EC. The Commission did, however, gain the right to propose initiatives in certain areas of education and cultural affairs, health, industrial policy and consumer protection, as well as a statutory role in discussions on foreign policy.

Eleven of the 12 delegations at Maastricht also agreed to a wider EC common policy on social issues. The British government objected to this *Social Charter*, arguing that the proposed legislation on working conditions would increase the costs of production. The Community is to introduce the Charter, but its terms will not be binding upon the UK without the agreement of the British government.

All 12 member states agreed to the establishment of a *European Monetary Institute* (EMI) in 1994 to harmonize national monetary policies. In 1998 the EMI is scheduled to become the European central bank and by 1999 the Ecu (see p. 484) is meant to become the common currency. The UK secured the right not to adopt the Ecu without the agreement of Parliament. The other 11 states pledged to join the system if their currencies achieved the necessary 'convergence'. However, strong public reaction in Germany in favour of retaining the Deutschmark and devaluation of some currencies within, and the withdrawal of the UK from, the ERM (see p. 484) have combined to make the achievement of these targets unlikely.

By April 1993, the parliaments of Belgium, Germany, Greece, Italy, Luxembourg, the Netherlands, Portugal and Spain had approved the Maastricht agreement, and those of France and Ireland had also done so following referenda. The Danish electorate rejected the agreement in a referendum in 1992 and is scheduled to vote again on the matter during 1993. Britain will not ratify the treaty until Denmark has done so.

The Common Agricultural Policy (CAP)
The CAP is the largest single item on the Community's budget. The CAP protects the domestic market in each state by variable tariffs that raise domestic market prices substantially above those on the world market. The long-established aim of the CAP is to provide better incomes for farmers and the level of state support for agriculture is important throughout the community. The CAP includes *'set aside'* payments to farmers to take land out of use and quotas to reduce overproduction.

The CAP is likely to change as intense international pressure demands a substantial reduction in agricultural protectionism. There is likely to be a significant shift from the present EC price-support policies to a more integrated approach to the problems of rural areas that will be more discriminatory in providing assistance to farmers and regions.

Candidates for EC membership

Austria, Finland, Norway and Sweden are expected to begin negotiations for membership in 1993 and to become members by 1995. Turkey, Cyprus and Malta are also applicants. Switzerland, which has also considered membership, has rejected joining the EEA (see below) and is therefore unlikely to pursue any application for EC membership. The Czech Republic, Hungary, Poland and Slovakia have indicated that EC membership is a long-term aim.

CONFERENCE ON SECURITY AND COOPERATION IN EUROPE (CSCE)

The CSCE was established in 1975 under the Final Act of a security conference held in Helsinki, Finland. The aims of CSCE were formulated in the Charter of Paris, which was signed by the original 34 member nations on 21 November 1990. Members affirmed a 'commitment to settle disputes by peaceful means' and a 'common adherence to democratic values and to human rights and fundamental freedoms'.

The Charter – which was described as formally ending the Cold War – envisaged a CSCE parliamentary assembly with members of parliament drawn from all member states. It was agreed that CSCE foreign ministers should meet at least once a year. The Charter established the following CSCE institutions:

CSCE Secretariat A small secretariat has been established in Prague, the Czech Republic.

CSCE Conflict Prevention Centre The Centre has been charged with reducing the risk of conflict in Europe. It is based in Vienna, Austria.

CSCE Office of Free Elections The Office was established to monitor the conduct of elections throughout Europe. It is based in Warsaw, Poland.

Membership: Albania, Armenia, Austria, Azerbaijan, Belarus, Belgium, Bosnia-Herzegovina, Bulgaria, Canada, Croatia, Cyprus, Czech Republic, Denmark, Estonia, Finland, France, Georgia, Germany, Greece, Hungary, Iceland, Ireland, Italy, Kazakhstan, Kyrgyzstan, Latvia, Liechtenstein, Lithuania, Luxembourg, Malta, Moldova, Monaco, Netherlands, Norway, Poland, Portugal, Romania, San Marino, Slovakia, Slovenia, Spain, Sweden, Switzerland, Tajikistan, Turkey, Turkmenistan, Ukraine, UK, USA, Russia, Uzbekistan, Vatican City and Yugoslavia (suspended 1992).

CEFTA

The Central European Free Trade Agreement was signed in December 1992 by Poland, the Czech Republic, Slovakia and Hungary. Under the terms of the agreement member states intend to set up a free trade area between them by the year 2001.

COUNCIL OF EUROPE

The Council of Europe was founded in 1949. It aims to achieve a greater unity between its members to safeguard their common European heritage and to facilitate their economic and social progress. Membership is restricted to European democracies,

that is those states which 'accept the principles of the rule of law and of the enjoyment by all persons within their jurisdiction of human rights and fundamental freedoms'.

The Council of Ministers, consisting of the foreign minister of each member state, meets twice each year. Agreements by the Council members are either formalized as European Conventions or recommendations to individual governments. The Parliamentary Assembly of the Council meets three times a year to debate reports on social, economic, political and other matters. The Council has achieved some 140 conventions and other agreements, including the European Convention for the Protection of Human Rights in 1950.

Headquarters: Strasbourg, France.

Membership: Austria (which joined the Council in 1956) has 6 Assembly members, Belgium (1949) 7, Bulgaria (1992) 12, Cyprus (1961) 3, Czech Republic (joined as Czechoslovakia in 1991) 7, Denmark (1949) 5, Finland (1989) 5, France (1949) 18, Germany (1951) 18, Greece (1949; withdrew 1969–74) 7, Hungary (1990) 6, Iceland (1950) 3, Ireland (1949) 4, Italy (1949) 18, Liechtenstein (1978) 2, Luxembourg (1949) 3, Malta (1965) 3, Netherlands (1949) 7, Norway (1949) 5, Poland (1992) 12, Portugal (1976) 7, San Marino (1988) 2, Spain (1977) 12, Sweden (1949) 6, Switzerland (1963) 6, Turkey (1949) 12, UK (1949) 18.

Estonia, Lithuania and Slovenia joined in 1993.

EUROPEAN ECONOMIC AREA

EEA is an open market area for the free movement of people, goods and money agreed between the EC and EFTA (qv). It was originally scheduled to come into existence in 1992, but Swiss rejection of participation has postponed its establishment. When operational the European Economic Area will comprise Austria, Belgium, Denmark, Finland, France, Germany, Greece, Iceland, Ireland, Italy, Liechtenstein, Luxembourg, the Netherlands, Norway, Portugal, Spain and the UK.

EUROPEAN FREE TRADE ASSOCIATION

The European Free Trade Association (EFTA) aims to achieve free trade in industrial goods between member states, to help create a single West European market and to encourage an expansion in world trade. The first aim was met in December 1966 when nearly all internal tariffs on industrial goods were abolished. Considerable progress was made towards the second aim in April 1984 when trade agreements with the EC abolished tariffs on industrial goods between EFTA and EC countries. The EC and EFTA are creating a single European trading area (see European Economic Area, above), which would not, however, replace either of the two existing trade groupings, although most EFTA members have applied or are considering an application to join the EC.

EFTA was founded in 1960 with Austria, Denmark, Norway, Portugal, Sweden, Switzerland and the UK as original members. Iceland joined EFTA in 1970. Denmark and the UK withdrew from EFTA in 1972 and Portugal withdrew in 1986 to become members of the EC. Finland, an associate member of EFTA since 1961, became a full member in 1986. Liechtenstein, formerly an associate member, became a full member of EFTA in 1991.

Each full member state maintains a permanent delegation in Geneva, the heads of which meet once a fortnight. Ministers of EFTA governments meet twice a year.

Headquarters: Geneva, Switzerland.

Current membership: Austria, Finland, Iceland, Liechtenstein, Norway, Sweden and Switzerland.

WEST EUROPEAN UNION

The WEU was founded 1948 with the original intention of collaborating 'in economic, social and cultural matters and for collective self-defence'. These functions have been gradually transferred to the EC, the Council of Europe and NATO. However, in 1984 the WEU was reactivated to improve military cooperation between members and to strengthen NATO.

Headquarters: London, UK.

Membership: Belgium, France, Germany, Italy, Luxembourg, Netherlands, Portugal, Spain, UK.

Denmark, Greece, Ireland and Turkey are associate or observer members.

REGIONAL ORGANIZATIONS

ANDEAN PACT

The Andean Pact was established in 1992 to create a free-trade area – with a common external tariff – in northern and eastern South America.
Headquarters: Lima, Peru.
Members: Bolivia, Colombia, Ecuador, Peru, Venezuela.

ALADI (LATIN AMERICAN INTEGRATION ASSOCIATION)

ALADI (Asociación Latinoamericana de Integración) was established on 31 December 1980 as a replacement for the Latin American Free Trade Area, which was formed in 1961. It aims to encourage trade and to remove tariffs between member states.
Headquarters: Montevideo, Uruguay.
Secretary General: Jorge Luis Ordonez (Colombia).
Members: Argentina, Bolivia, Brazil, Chile, Colombia, Ecuador, Mexico, Paraguay, Peru, Uruguay, and Venezuela.

Costa Rica, Cuba, Dominican Republic, El Salvador, Guatemala, Honduras, Italy, Nicaragua, Panama, Portugal and Spain have observer membership.

ASSOCIATION OF SOUTH EAST ASIAN NATIONS (ASEAN)

ASEAN was founded in Bangkok, Thailand in 1967. It aims to accelerate the economic, social and cultural development of member states, to maintain stability in South East Asia, and to encourage cooperation between members.
Headquarters: Djakarta, Indonesia.
Secretary General: Rusli Noor (Indonesia).
Members: Brunei, Indonesia, Malaysia, Philippines, Singapore, and Thailand.

BLACK SEA ECONOMIC COOPERATION ZONE

Founded in 1992, the Black Sea Economic Cooperation Zone aims to promote trade and economic cooperation between member states and to control pollution.
Members: Armenia, Azerbaijan, Bulgaria, Georgia, Moldova, Romania, Russia, Turkey, Ukraine.

CARIBBEAN COMMUNITY AND COMMON MARKET (CARICOM)

CARICOM was founded 1973 at Chaguaramas, Trinidad. The aims of the Caribbean Community are to promote cooperation in cultural, educational, health, scientific and technological matters, and to co-ordinate foreign policy. The associated Caribbean Common Market aims to promote economic cooperation.
Headquarters: Georgetown, Guyana.
Secretary General: Roderick Rainford (Jamaica).
Members: Antigua and Barbuda, Bahamas (Community only), Barbados, Belize, Dominica, Dominican Republic, Grenada, Guyana, Haiti, Jamaica, St Christopher and Nevis, St Lucia, St Vincent and the Grenadines, Trinidad and Tobago. Suriname and Venezuela are associate members. Non-sovereign territories in membership: Montserrat, British Virgin Islands, Turks and Caicos Islands.

CENTRAL AMERICAN COMMON MARKET (CACM)

CACM was founded in 1960 but lapsed in 1969. The organization was revived (1992–93) and is scheduled to establish a free-trade area in Central America by 1994.
Headquarters: Guatemala City, Guatemala.
Secretary General: Rafael Rodriguez Loucel (Guatemala).
Members: Costa Rica, El Salvador, Guatemala, Honduras, and Nicaragua.

COLOMBO PLAN

The Colombo Plan for Cooperative Economic and Social Development in Asia and the Pacific was founded in 1950 to promote economic and social development within the region and to encourage training programmes, capital aid and technical cooperation.
Headquarters: Colombo, Sri Lanka.
Members: Afghanistan, Australia, Bangladesh, Bhutan, Cambodia, Canada, Fiji, India, Indonesia, Iran, Japan, Korea (South), Laos, Malaysia, Maldives, Myanmar (Burma), Nepal, New Zealand, Pakistan, Papua New Guinea, Philippines, Singapore, Sri Lanka, Thailand, UK, and USA

CIS (COMMONWEALTH OF INDEPENDENT STATES)

Following the dissolution of the USSR in December 1991, most of the former Soviet republics formed the CIS. It maintains some elements of the economic, military and political coordination that existed within the former USSR. Azerbaijan withdrew in 1992.
Members: Armenia, Belarus, Kazakhstan, Kyrgyzstan, Moldova, Russia, Tajikistan, Turkmenistan, Ukraine, Uzbekistan.

COOPERATION COUNCIL FOR THE ARAB STATES OF THE GULF

The Council was established in 1981 to promote economic, cultural and social cooperation between the Arab states of the Gulf. It has since also taken on a security role, notably during the Second Gulf War (January to February 1991). In March 1991 member states concluded economic and defence agreements with Egypt and Syria, although the latter two states are not members of the Council.
Headquarters: Riyadh, Saudi Arabia.
Members: Bahrain, Kuwait, Oman, Qatar, Saudi Arabia, UAE.

ECONOMIC COMMUNITY OF WEST AFRICAN STATES (ECOWAS)

ECOWAS was founded in Lagos, Nigeria, in May 1975. It aims to promote trade and cooperation between member states and to increase self-reliance within West Africa. An ECOWAS force intervened in an attempt to stop the civil war in Liberia in 1990. The Assembly of heads of state and heads of government meets once a year and is chaired by each country in turn.
Headquarters: Abuja, Nigeria.
Members: Benin, Burkina Faso, Cape Verde, The Gambia, Ghana, Guinea, Guinea-Bissau, Ivory Coast, Liberia, Mali, Mauritania, Niger, Nigeria, Senegal, Sierra Leone, and Togo.

ECONOMIC COOPERATION ORGANIZATION

The ECO was founded in 1965 to promote trade in southwest Asia. The organization lapsed but was revived and expanded in 1992 to aid the development of Central Asia.
Members: Azerbaijan, Iran, Kyrgyzstan, Pakistan, Tajikistan, Turkmenistan, Turkey, Uzbekistan.

LEAGUE OF ARAB STATES

The League of Arab States, which is popularly known as the *Arab League*, was founded in Cairo, Egypt, on 22 March 1945. It aims to protect the independence and sovereignty of member states, to strengthen ties between them, and to encourage coordination of their social, economic, political, cultural and legal policies. The League comprises a Council (on which each state has one vote), special committees, over 20 specialized agencies and a Secretariat.
Headquarters: Cairo, Egypt.
Secretary-General: Dr Ahmad al-Meguid (Egypt).
Members: Algeria, Bahrain, Djibouti, Egypt, Iraq, Jordan, Kuwait, Lebanon, Libya, Mauritania, Morocco, Oman, Palestine Liberaton Organization, Qatar, Saudi Arabia, Somalia, Sudan, Syria, Tunisia, United Arab Emirates, and Yemen.

MERCOSUR

Originating in a free-trade pact between Argentina and Brazil in 1988, Mercosur (Mercado del Sur – the market of the South) is scheduled to become a free market in goods, services and labour in 1994.
Members: Argentina, Brazil, Paraguay, Uruguay.

NORDIC COUNCIL

The Nordic Council was founded in 1950 to promote cooperation between the governments and parliaments of the Nordic nations.
Headquarters: Stockhom, Sweden.
Members: Denmark, Finland, Iceland, Norway and Sweden. The Faeroe Islands and Greenland have separate representation within the Danish delegation, and the Aland Islands have separate representation within the Finnish delegation.

NORTH AMERICAN FREE TRADE AGREEMENT (NAFTA)

NAFTA was founded in 1992 to eliminate tariffs, quotas and import licences between member states. NAFTA and the EC are the two largest free trade areas in the world. NAFTA has not, as yet, set up any administrative bodies.
Members: Canada, Mexico, USA.

ORGANIZATION OF AFRICAN UNITY (OAU)

The OAU was founded on 25 May 1963 in Addis Ababa, Ethiopia. It aims to promote African unity and collaboration in economic, social, cultural, political, defence, scientific, health and other matters, and to eliminate colonialism and apartheid from Africa. The Assembly of heads of state and heads of government meets annually and is presided over by a chairman elected for a one year term by the Assembly. The main administrative body is the Secretariat.
Headquarters: Addis Ababa, Ethiopia.
Secretary General: Salim Ahmed Salim (Tanzania).
Members: Algeria, Angola, Benin, Botswana, Burkina Faso, Burundi, Cameroon, Cape Verde, Central African Republic, Chad, Comoros, Congo, Djibouti, Egypt, Equatorial Guinea, Ethiopia, Gabon, The Gambia, Ghana, Guinea, Guinea-Bissau, Ivory Coast, Kenya, Lesotho, Liberia, Libya, Madagascar, Malawi, Mali, Mauritania, Mauritius, Mozambique, Namibia, Niger, Nigeria, Rwanda, São Tomé e Principe, Senegal, Seychelles, Sierra Leone, Somalia, Sudan, Swaziland, Tanzania, Togo, Tunisia, Uganda, Zaïre, Zambia, and Zimbabwe. In 1982 the Sahrawi Arab Democratic Republic (Western Sahara) was admitted to membership; Morocco, which claims the Western Sahara, withdrew from the OAU in protest.

ORGANIZATION OF ARAB PETROLEUM EXPORTING COUNTRIES

OAPEC was founded in 1968 to encourage cooperation in economic activities, to ensure the flow of oil to consumer markets, and to promote a favourable climate for the investment of capital and expertise. The oil ministers of member countries form the Ministerial Council, which meets twice a year. The General Secretariat is the executive organ of OAPEC.
Headquarters: Cairo, Egypt.
Members: Algeria, Bahrain, Egypt, Iraq, Kuwait, Libya, Qatar, Saudi Arabia, Syria, and the United Arab Emirates.

ORGANIZATION OF AMERICAN STATES (OAS)

OAS was founded in Bogota, Colombia in 1948 as a successor to the International Union of American Republics (later the Pan American Union) founded 1890. Its aims are to maintain the independence and territorial integrity of member states, to achieve peace and justice on the continent, and to encourage collaboration and inter-American solidarity.
Headquarters: Washington DC, USA
Secretary-General: João Clemente Baena Soares (Brazil).
Members: Antigua and Barbuda, Argentina, Bahamas, Barbados, Belize, Bolivia, Brazil, Canada, Chile, Colombia, Costa Rica, Cuba (suspended since 1962), Dominica, Dominican Republic, Ecuador, El Salvador, Grenada, Guatemala, Guyana, Haiti, Honduras, Jamaica, Mexico, Nicaragua, Panama, Paraguay, Peru, St Christopher and Nevis, St Lucia, St Vincent and the Grenadines, Suriname, Trinidad and Tobago, USA, Uruguay, and Venezuela.

ORGANIZATION OF THE ISLAMIC CONFERENCE

OIC was established in Rabat, Morocco, in May 1971 to promote Islamic solidarity, to consolidate economic, social and cultural cooperation between member states, and to safeguard the Holy Places of Islam and the independence of Muslim peoples.
Headquarters: Jeddah, Saudi Arabia.
Members: Afghanistan, Algeria, Bahrain, Bangladesh, Benin, Brunei, Burkina Faso, Cameroon, Chad, Comoros, Djibouti, Egypt, Gabon, The Gambia, Guinea, Guinea-Bissau, Indonesia, Iran, Iraq, Jordan, Kuwait, Lebanon, Libya, Malaysia, Maldives, Mali, Mauritania, Morocco, Niger, Oman, Pakistan, Palestine Liberation Organization, Qatar, Saudi Arabia, Senegal, Sierra Leone, Somalia, Sudan, Syria, Tunisia, Turkey, Uganda, UAE, and Yemen. Mozambique is an associate member.

SOUTH ASIAN ASSOCIATION FOR ECONOMIC CO-OPERATION

SAARC was founded in December 1985. It aims to encourage trade and economic development in South Asia.
Headquarters: Delhi, India.
Members: Bangladesh, Bhutan, India, Maldives, Nepal, Pakistan, and Sri Lanka.

SOUTHERN AFRICAN DEVELOPMENT COORDINATION CONFERENCE

SADCC was founded in Arusha, Tanzania, in July 1979. It aims to harmonize the development plans of member states and reduce their dependence on South Africa. An annual summit meeting is held.
Headquarters: Gaborone, Botswana.
Members: Angola, Botswana, Lesotho, Malawi, Mozambique, Namibia, Swaziland, Tanzania, Zambia, and Zimbabwe.

SOUTH PACIFIC FORUM

The Forum was founded in 1971 in Wellington, New Zealand. It has no formal constitution but exists to further cooperation in a wide range of issues of mutual interest. The membership and the organization of the Forum is common with the South Pacific Bureau for Economic Co-operation (SPEC), established in 1973 to encourage trade, economic and transport matters.
Headquarters: Suva, Fiji.
Secretary-General: Ieremia Tabai (Kiribati).
Members: Australia, Cook Islands (a self-governing New Zealand territory), Fiji, Kiribati, Marshall Islands, Micronesia, Nauru, New Zealand, Niue (a self-governing New Zealand territory), Papua New Guinea, Solomon Islands, Tonga, Tuvalu, Vanuatu, and Western Samoa.

WORLD ORGANIZATIONS

THE COMMONWEALTH

The Comonwealth may be said to have its foundations in the 1926 Imperial Conference which defined the position of the dominions as 'freely associated...members of the British Commonwealth of Nations'. The modern Commonwealth dates from 1949 when India became a republic but remained a member of the British Commonwealth recognizing 'the King as the symbol of the free association of...independent member nations'.

The majority of Commonwealth members are republics and some have their own sovereign, but all recognize the British sovereign as Head of the Commonwealth.

The Commonwealth is an informal grouping of the UK and the majority of its former dependencies. It has no written constitution. It aims to encourage international, scientific and technical, educational and economic cooperation between members.

Commonwealth heads of government meet every two years, and other ministers meet at irregular intervals. The Commonwealth Secretariat was established in 1965 as the main agency for multilateral communications between the governments of members.
Secretary-General: Chief Emeka Anyaoku (Nigeria).
Headquarters: London, UK.
Members: Antigua and Barbuda*, Australia*, Bahamas*, Bangladesh‡, Barbados*, Belize*, Botswana‡, Brunei†, Canada*, Cyprus‡, Dominica‡, The Gambia‡, Ghana‡, Grenada*, Guyana‡, India‡, Jamaica*, Kenya‡, Kiribati‡, Lesotho†, Malawi‡, Malaysia†, Maldives‡, Malta‡, Mauritius‡, Namibia‡, Nauru‡ (special member), New Zealand*, Nigeria‡, Pakistan‡, Papua New Guinea*, St Christopher and Nevis*, St Lucia*, St Vincent and the Grenadines*, Seychelles‡, Sierra Leone‡, Singapore‡, Solomon Islands*, Sri Lanka‡, Swaziland†, Tanzania‡, Tonga†, Trinidad and Tobago‡, Tuvalu* (special member), Uganda‡, UK*, Vanuatu‡, Western Samoa†, Zambia‡, and Zimbabwe‡. (Special members do not participate in ministerial meetings.)

* = countries of which the British sovereign is head of state.
† = countries with their own sovereigns or with a head of state analogous to a constitutional monarch.
‡ = republics (the Solomon Islands is to become a republic during the 1990s, but no date for the assumption of a republican constitution has been set.)

GROUP OF SEVEN – G7

G7 is an informal grouping of the leading Western economic powers. Since 1975 the heads of government of these states have met for regular summits concerning major economic, monetary and political problems. G7 has no agency or secretariat.
Members: Canada, France, Germany, Italy, Japan, UK, and USA. The EC has observer status.

INTERNATIONAL CRIMINAL POLICE ORGANIZATION (INTERPOL)

INTERPOL was established in 1923 as the International Criminal Police Commission and was restructured and renamed in 1956. It aims to promote mutual assistance between criminal police authorities. The policy-making body of the Organization is the General Assembly, which meets annually.
Headquarters: Lyon, France.
Members: 155 member states.

INTERNATIONAL ENERGY AGENCY

IEA, an autonomous agency of OECD (see below), was founded in 1974. It aims to improve energy supplies and to develop alternative sources of energy.
Headquarters: Paris, France.
Membership: Australia, Austria, Belgium, Canada, Denmark, Germany, Greece, Ireland, Italy, Japan, Luxembourg, the Netherlands, New Zealand,

Norway, Portugal, Spain, Sweden, Switzerland, Turkey, UK, and USA.

INTERNATIONAL OLYMPIC COMMITTEE
The Committee was founded in 1894 to ensure the holding of the Olympic Games – see also Sports chapter. The ICO is a non-governmental body whose members are delegates of the Olympic committees in their respective countries rather than representatives of the governments of those countries. An Executive Board – chaired by a President – conducts the IOC's affairs.
Headquarters: Lausanne, Switzerland.
President: Juan Antonio Samaranch (Brazil).
Members: There are 185 recognized National Olympic Committees; the ICO has 94 members who are the representatives of these Committees.

INTERNATIONAL RED CROSS AND RED CRESCENT
(The Red Crescent is the equivalent of the Red Cross in Islamic countries.) The International Red Cross and Red Crescent movement is a neutral non-governmental organization founded to negotiate armed conflict, to develop the activities of individual societies, to protect prisoners of war (through the terms of the *Geneva Convention*) and to coordinate relief for the victims of natural and other disasters. The Conference of the International Red Cross and Red Crescent meets every four years.
Headquarters: Geneva, Switzerland.
Members: the Red Cross or Red Crescent Societies of over 160 countries.

NON-ALIGNED MOVEMENT
The non-aligned movement is not a formal organization but a conference that meets every three years. The aims of the movement are to promote world peace, to reject the system of world power blocs and to help bring about a more even distribution of the world's wealth. Over 100 countries attended the last two conferences of the non-aligned movement, membership of which varies from one conference to another.

ORGANIZATION OF THE PETROLEUM EXPORTING COUNTRIES (OPEC)
OPEC was founded in Baghdad, Iraq, in 1960. It aims to coordinate the petroleum-producing and exporting policies of its member states.
Headquarters: Vienna, Austria.
Members: Algeria, Gabon, Indonesia, Iran, Iraq, Kuwait, Libya, Nigeria, Qatar, Saudi Arabia, United Arab Emirates, and Venezuela. (Ecuador withdrew in 1992.)

ORGANIZATION FOR ECONOMIC COOPERATION AND DEVELOPMENT (OECD)
OECD was founded in September 1961 to replace the Organization for European Economic Cooperation which had been established in connection with the Marshall Aid Plan in 1948. It aims to encourage economic and social welfare in member states and to stimulate aid to developing countries.
Headquarters: Paris, France.
Members: Australia, Austria, Belgium, Canada, Denmark, Finland, France, Germany, Greece, Iceland, Ireland, Italy, Japan, Luxembourg, the Netherlands, Norway, Portugal, Spain, Sweden, Switzerland, Turkey, UK, and USA. Yugoslavia (an observer) was suspended in 1992.

DEFENCE

The existence of nuclear weapons of proven capability has deterred direct conflict between the major powers since the end of World War II. The collapse of Communism in Eastern Europe has effectively ended the confrontation between East and West. The signature of the Charter of Paris in November 1990 formally ended the Cold War, but large nuclear stockpiles remain. However, fear of superpower imbalance has been replaced by fear of 'proliferation' – the spread of nuclear capability to powers outside the major blocs.

Until 1989–90 the greatest danger of conflict seemed to lie in Europe. Soviet forces withdrew from Hungary and the former Czechoslovakia in 1991, and are being removed from Poland and the former East Germany. A number of US bases in western Europe have also closed. Local or regional conflicts in other parts of the world are now seen as a greater threat, for example the Iraqi invasion of Kuwait in August 1990 although the civil wars in former Yugoslavia greatly increased tension in Europe in 1992–93.

NATO
The North Atlantic Treaty Organization came into existence in April 1949 and into force in August 1949. NATO is a collective defence organization whose member countries agree to treat an armed attack on any one of them as an attack against all. The North Atlantic Council is the highest authority of the alliance. It comprises 16 permanent representatives – one from each member state – and is chaired by the Secretary General of NATO. The foreign ministers of the member states meet at least twice a year. The defence of the NATO area is the responsibility of the Defence Planning Committee. France is not a member of the DPC, which meets regularly at ambassadorial level and twice a year at ministerial level.
Headquarters: Brussels, Belgium.
Secretary-General: Manfred Wörner (Germany).
Members: Belgium (founder member), Canada (founder member), Denmark (founder member), France (founder member), Germany (West Germany admitted on 5 May 1955; the former East Germany was included as part of reunified Germany on 3 Oct 1990), Greece (admitted 18 February 1952), Iceland (founder member), Italy (founder member), Luxembourg (founder member), Netherlands (founder member), Norway (founder member), Portugal (founder member), Spain (admitted on 30 May 1982), Turkey (admitted on 18 February 1952), United Kingdom (founder member), and USA (founder member).

OTHER DEFENCE ORGANIZATIONS
Other organizations that have a role to play in defence, particularly on a regional basis, include:
ANZUS was set up in 1951 as a collective defence policy for the preservation of peace in the Pacific. Its members are Australia, New Zealand and the USA.
The Arab League (see p. 519).
The CIS (see p. 518).
The Cooperation Council for the Arab States of the Gulf (see p. 518).
ECOWAS (see p. 519).
The West European Union (see p. 518).

MAJOR ARMED FORCES

The strength of major armed forces is most commonly compared in terms of nuclear capacity or total manpower. Other important factors include the numbers of combat aircraft and the size of navies. In the following lists, the armed forces of major countries are compared in terms of these four categories. In each list the first eight states in each category are given.

Manpower

Country	Total excluding reserves
China	3 030 000
Russia	2 720 000
USA	1 910 000
India	1 270 000
North Korea	1 130 000
Vietnam	860 000
South Korea	630 000
Pakistan	580 000

Navies

Country	Vessels including submarines
Russia	1730
China	1301
USA	579
North Korea	569
Taiwan	197
Germany	172
UK	161
Japan	159

Combat aircraft

Country	Number of combat aircraft
China	4970
USA	3864
Russia	3700
Ukraine	1100
France	808
North Korea	732
India	674
Israel	662

Nuclear warheads The US and Russian totals given below are subject to the START agreements and are in the process of being reduced. In addition to the eight countries listed below there are other countries with nuclear stockpiles, but their existence is not proven. They are thought to include Israel, India and North Korea. In 1993 South Africa admitted that it had had a nuclear capability but had destroyed its weapons. Both Iran and Iraq have ambitions to acquire nuclear weapons.

Country	Number of nuclear warheads
USA	5921
Russia	2968
France	426
Ukraine*	176
UK	144
Kazakhstan*	104
China	80
Belarus*	54

* = the warheads indicated for these countries are under the control of the Commonwealth of Independent States (CIS; see p. 518) and are unlikely to be used unilaterally.

WARS IN THE 1990s

The conflicts listed below (chronologically) started or continued in the 1990s.

Ethiopia (1961–1991): Rebel forces in Eritrea and Tigray fought government forces for independence. Eritrea effectively seceded in 1991 and was scheduled to assume full sovereignty in May 1993; spasmodic fighting continues in Ethiopia, especially in Tigray and Oromo districts.

Chad (1965–): Civil wars between the Muslim Arab North and the Christian and animist Black African South – Idriss Deby successfully led rebel forces against the government (1989). Unrest continues in the north.

Northern Ireland (1969–): Sectarian conflict between Protestant extremists intent on remaining part of the UK and Catholic extremists intent on reuniting Ireland. British troops – initially deployed in a peacekeeping role – are opposed by paramilitary groups such as the Ulster Defence Association (UDA) and the Provisional Irish Republican Army (IRA).

Lebanon (1975–): Civil war between Christian and Muslim forces reduced Lebanon to ungovernable chaos. Syria and Israel intervened and a Syrian-backed government imposed a semblance of order (1991), but spasmodic fighting in the South between Hizbollah fundamentalists and Israeli-backed forces continues.

Mozambique (1975–): Mozambique virtually disintegrated in civil war between the Front for Liberation of Mozambique (FRELIMO) government and the Mozambique National Resistance Organization (RENAMO). Peace moves have been made, but fighting continues.

Sri Lanka (1975–): Indian intervention (1987–90) led to a bitter counter-insurgency operation of the civil war between the ruling Sinhalese and the ethnic-Indian Tamils (particularly the Tamil Tigers), who are fighting for an independent Tamil state.

Angola (1976–): UNITA (National Union for the Total Independence of Angola) forces – initially aided by South Africa – fought the left-wing MPLA (People's Movement for the Liberation of Angola) government. The MPLA won the civil war of 1975–76, but continued to be opposed by UNITA rebels. A UN-supervised ceasefire (1991) was breached and the civil war resumed in 1992 when UNITA refused to accept the result of multi-party elections.

Afghanistan (1979–): Civil war was triggered by the Soviet invasion (1979). Mujahaddin guerrillas (Muslim fundamentalists) fought government forces even after the Soviet withdrawal (1989). In 1992 fundamentalists took Kabul and formed a provisional government, but factional – largely ethnic – fighting continues.

Cambodia (1979–1991): The 1991 ceasefire ended civil war between the Vietnamese-backed government and Pol Pot's Khmer Rouge. A UN Transitional Authority was established but spasmodic fighting continues as the Khmer Rouge has effectively withdrawn from the peace process.

El Salvador (1980–91): A UN-supervised peace agreement ended civil war between the government and left-wing Farabundo Marti National Liberation Front (FMLN) guerrillas.

Peru (1980–): Revolutionary activities of the

Maoist Sendero Luminoso ('Shining Path') group triggered a counter-insurgency campaign by the government. Guerrilla activity has decreased since the capture of the Sendero Luminoso leader.

Sudan (1983–): Civil war continues between Islamic government forces and the Christian and pagan guerrillas of the Sudan People's Liberation Army (SPLA). The latter is subject to violent internal fighting. Western humanitarian aid has been disrupted.

Palestinian Intifada (1987–): The Palestinian uprising in the West Bank and Gaza Strip against Israeli occupying forces has been characterized by riots and shootings. Unrest continues despite ongoing peace negotiations in the Middle East.

Myanmar (Burma; 1988–): Military rule since 1988 has been opposed by a variety of political and nationalist groups. Non-Burman minorities have joined forces to fight against the military.

Somalia (1988–): An Ethiopian-backed uprising in N Somalia (1988) began armed opposition to President Barre, who fled (1991) after guerrillas attacked the capital, Mogadishu. The rebels have since fought among themselves and Somalia has descended into chaos. US Marines intervened (1992) to deliver humanitarian aid.

Liberia (1989–): ECOWAS deployed a peacekeeping force (1990) to end a civil war initially between the National Patriotic Front of Liberia (NLFL) and government forces, but fighting flared up between NLFL and rival rebel groups (1992) and is still continuing.

Kuwait (1990–91): Iraqi troops invaded Kuwait in 1990. A US-led multi-national force – under the auspices of the UN – used air attacks on Iraq and a 100-hour ground campaign to liberate Kuwait in 1991. Since then, the UN has monitored the border and the USA has initiated air strikes to deter Iraqi aggression.

Iraq (1991–): After the Gulf War (see Kuwait), Saddam Hussein faced uprisings by Shi'ite Muslims in the south and Kurds in the north. Allied 'no-fly zones' in these areas (and threats of intervention) have restrained Iraq, but small-scale attacks on the Shi'ites continue.

Georgia (1991–): Civil war between supporters and opponents of President Gamsakhurdia (1992), was followed by continuing secessionist wars as Muslims in Abkhazia and South Ossetia press for independence.

Croatia (1991–): War between Croats and ethnic Serbs in Krajina and parts of Slavonia following the break-up of Yugoslavia. A ceasefire was negotiated in early 1992 and a UN force deployed, but fighting resumed in 1993.

Bosnia-Herzegovina (1991–): Bosnian Serbs fought against Croats and Muslims (although the latter also fought each other) for control of what was central Yugoslavia. A UN force was deployed in 1992 to supervise the delivery of humanitarian aid. Peace negotiations were attempted, but fighting continues.

Armenia-Azerbaijan (1992–): Azeri and Armenian forces are fighting for control of Nagorno Karabakh, an enclave of Orthodox Christian Armenians surrounded by the Shi'ite Muslim Azeris.

Tajikistan (1992–): The ex-Communist rulers of this former Soviet republic have effectively defeated Islamic fundamentalists in the north.

WINNERS OF THE NOBEL PEACE PRIZE

1901 Jean Henri Dunant, Swiss philanthropist: founder of the Red Cross.
Frédéric Passy, French economist: advocate of international arbitration and peace.

1902 Elie Ducommun, Swiss writer, and Charles Albert Gobat, Swiss: for their work for peace within the International Peace Bureau.

1903 Sir William Cremer, English trade unionist; an advocate of international arbitration.

1904 Institute of International Law (fd. 1873).

1905 Bertha von Suttner, Austrian novelist: for her influential peace novels.

1906 Theodore Roosevelt, US President: for mediation at the end of Russo-Japanese War (1904).

1907 Ernesto Teodoro Moneta, Italian journalist: founder of the International League for Peace, president of the International Peace Conference (1906).
Louis Renault, French jurist: for his international arbitration.

1908 Klas Pontus Arnoldson, Swedish politician: for mediating the dissolution of the Norwegian-Swedish Union.
Fredrik Bajer, Danish politician: for his work for female emancipation and the peace movement.

1909 Baron d'Estournelles de Constant, French diplomat.
Auguste Beernaert, Belgian politician: for work at the Hague Peace Conferences.

1910 International Peace Bureau (fd. 1891).

1911 Tobias Asser, Dutch jurist: for his part in forming the Permanent Court of Justice (1899 Hague Peace Conference).
Alfred Fried, Austrian pacifist: co-founder of the German peace movement.

1912 Elihu Root, US politician: for his international arbitration.

1913 Henri Lafontaine, Belgian lawyer: president of International Peace Bureau.

1914–1916 No award.

1917 International Red Cross Committee (see p. 521).

1918 No award.

1919 Woodrow Wilson, US president.

1920 Léon Bourgeois, French politician: advocate of the League of Nations and international cooperation.

1921 Karl Branting, Swedish politician: for his conciliatory international diplomacy.
Christian Lous Lange, Norwegian peace advocate: for his work as secretary general of the Inter-Parliamentary Union.

1922 Fridtjof Nansen, Norwegian explorer and statesman: for relief work after World War I.

1923–24 No award.

1925 Sir Austen Chamberlain, English politician: for work on the Locarno Pact (1925).
Charles G. Dawes, US politician: for reorganization of German reparation payments.

1926 Aristide Briand, French politician.
Gustav Stresemann, German politician: for his work for European reconciliation.

1927 Ferdinand Buisson, French educationalist: co-founder of League of Human Rights (1898).
Ludwig Quidde, German historian and politician: for his work for peace in Germany.

1928 No award.
1929 Frank B. Kellogg, US politician: for the Kellogg-Briand Pact (1928).
1930 Nathan Söderblom. Swedish Lutheran archbishop: for his efforts for peace through church unity.
1931 Jane Addams, US social reformer and pacifist: for her social work, support of women's suffrage, and peace, and Nicholas Murray Butler, US educationalist: for his work in forming the Carnegie Endowment for International Peace.
1932 No award.
1933 Sir Norman Angell, English economist: for his work on the economic futility of war.
1934 Arthur Henderson, English politician: for his work for disarmament.
1935 Carl von Ossietzky, German journalist who spoke out against Nazi rearmament.
1936 Carlos Saavedra Lamas, Argentinian jurist: for his efforts to end the Chaco War (1932–35).
1937 Viscount Cecil of Chelwood, English politician: drafting the League of Nations Covenant 1919.
1938 Nansen International Office for Refugees.
1939–1943 No awards.
1944 International Red Cross Committee.
1945 Cordell Hull, US politician: for his part in organizing the United Nations.
1946 Emily Greene Balch, US sociologist and political scientist: leader of the women's movement for peace.
John R. Mott, US Methodist evangelist: for work in international missionary movements.
1947 American Friends Service Committee, a US Quaker organization that promotes peace through programmes of social service and Friends Service Council, its British counterpart.
1948 No award.
1949 Lord Boyd-Orr, Scottish scientist: for his work on nutritional requirements.
1950 Ralph Bunche, US diplomat: for negotiating the Arab–Israeli truce in 1949.
1951 Léon Jouhaux, French trade unionist: cofounder of the International Confederation of Free Trade Unions.
1952 Albert Schweitzer, German missionary, doctor and philosopher: for his medical and other work in Africa.
1953 George C. Marshall, US politician: for the Marshall (European recovery) Plan.
1954 Office of the United Nations High Commissioner for Refugees (see United Nations).
1955–1956 No award.
1957 Lester B. Pearson, Canadian politician: for his efforts to solve the Suez Crisis (1956).
1958 Dominique Georges Pire, Belgian cleric and educationalist: for his aid to displaced Europeans after World War II.
1959 Philip Noel-Baker, English politician: an advocate of world disarmament.
1960 Albert Lutuli, South African: for his nonviolent struggle against apartheid.
1961 Dag Hammarskjöld, Swedish Secretary General of the UN (posthumously awarded).
1962 Linus Pauling, US chemist: for his campaigns for the control of nuclear weapons and nuclear testing.

1963 International Red Cross Committee.
League of Red Cross Societies: for their relief work after natural disasters.
1964 Martin Luther King, Jr., US Black civil rights leader.
1965 United Nations Children's Fund (see UN).
1966–67 No award.
1968 René Cassin, French jurist: principal author of the UN Declaration of Human Rights.
1969 International Labour Organization (see UN).
1970 Norman E. Borlaug, US agricultural scientist: for agricultural technology.
1971 Willy Brandt, German politician: for reconciliation between West and East Germany.
1972 No award.
1973 Henry Kissinger, US politician, and Le Duc Tho, North Vietnamese politician: for the peace settlement of the Vietnam War. (Le Duc Tho declined the award.)
1974 Eisaku Satō, prime minister of Japan: for his anti-nuclear policies.
Sean MacBride, Irish statesman: for his campaign for human rights.
1975 Andrei D. Sakharov, Russian nuclear physicist: for his advocacy of human rights and disarmament.
1976 Mairead Corrigan, Northern Irish, and Betty Williams, Northern Irish: for campaigning to end sectarian strife in Northern Ireland.
1977 Amnesty International: for work to secure the release of political prisoners.
1978 Menachem Begin, Israeli prime minister, and Anwar el-Sadat, president of Egypt: for the Israel–Egypt peace treaty (1979).
1979 Mother Teresa of Calcutta, Macedonian-born Indian charity worker: for her help with the destitute in India.
1980 Adolfo Pérez Esquivel, Argentinian sculptor and architect: for work for human rights in Latin America.
1981 United Nations High Commissioner for Refugees (see UN).
1982 Alva Myrdal, Swedish diplomat: for advocacy of nuclear disarmament and Alfonso García Robles, Mexican diplomat: for advocacy of nuclear disarmament.
1983 Lech Walesa, Polish politician and trade unionist: for the Solidarity movement.
1984 Desmond Tutu, Anglican Archbishop of Johannesburg: for peaceful anti-apartheid work.
1985 International Physicians for the Prevention of Nuclear War.
1986 Elie Wiesel, French writer and human rights activist.
1987 Oscar Arias Sánchez, president of Costa Rica: for promoting a peace in Central America.
1988 United Nations Peacekeeping Forces.
1989 The Dalai Lama, spiritual and exiled temporal leader of Tibet.
1990 Mikhail Gorbachev, Soviet president: for promoting greater openness in the Soviet Union, and helping to end the Cold War.
1991 Aung San Suu Kyi, Burmese politician: for her non-violent campaign for democracy.
1992 Rigoberta Menchu, Guatemalan Indian spokeswoman: for her campaign for indigenous people.

COUNTRIES OF THE WORLD

This section describes the sovereign states of the world, that is the independent states that, in theory, exercise unrestricted power over their own destinies. However, in some ways the concept of sovereignty is of limited value in the closing years of the 20th century. It could be argued that there is no such thing as a truly independent state. The overwhelming majority of sovereign states are members of one or more of the various economic and military alliances described on pp. 512–21. Most states have come to recognize that the demands of security and trade bring agreed limits upon the freedom of action of individual countries. Countries rely upon their neighbours and other states, at least economically, and are therefore restricted in their independence.

Individual entries in this chapter detail:
Official name: Each sovereign state's official name in its principal language(s).
Member of: Its membership of major international organizations (see pp. 512–21).
Area: Its *de facto* area in square kilometres (and in square miles). Where a country's area may be disputed or not defined, or where a country may lay claim to part of a neighbouring territory, more than one figure is given.
Population: Its population according to figures given in the latest census or official estimate. Where there is no recent or reliable official estimate, an estimate of the national population from UN sources is given.
Capital and major cities: In many cases the names of cities in their local languages are given in brackets. Except where noted, the population figure given for a city relates to the agglomeration or urban area: that is the city, its suburbs and surrounding built-up areas rather than for local government districts.
Languages: Principal languages only are indicated.
Religion: The principal religions only are indicated. As most censuses do not question respondents concerning their religious affiliation, the percentages given are an approximation.
Government: The constitutional provisions of each state are summarized. In some cases, the provisions recorded may not in practice be adhered to owing to dictatorship, the role of the military, etc. The names of the main political parties and the heads of state and of government are given.
Federal states: The area, population and capital of each state, province or other unit within all federal and similar systems are given.
Education: The literacy rate, the years in which schooling is compulsory and the number of universities and/or equivalent institutions are given.
Defence: The total armed strength and details of the length and nature of military service are given.
Geography: The main geographical features are described, including the principal rivers, highest point and a summary of the climate.
Economy: The most important economic activities, resources and trends are summarized. Details of each country's international trade are given on pp. 489–98 and details of its currency are given on pp. 499–502.
Recent history: Summaries of the principal events of each country's 19th- and 20th-century history are given. (See also the History chapter; p. 436.)
Dependent Territories: The area, population, capital and largest city of each country's dependent territories are given.

AFGHANISTAN

Official name: Jamhuria Afghanistan (Republic of Afghanistan).
Member of: UN.
Area: 652 225 km² (251 773 sq mi).
Population: 18 052 000 (1992 est). Almost 3 500 000 Afghan refugees (1990 est) have returned from Pakistan and Iran.
Capital and major cities: Kabul 1 425 000 (including suburbs), Kandahar (Qandahar) 226 000, Herat 177 000, Mazar-i-Sharif 131 000, Qonduz 108 000, Charikar 100 000 (1988 est).
Languages: Pushto (52%), Dari (Persian; 30%) – both official.
Religions: Sunni Islam (74%), Shia Islam (25%).
Education: *Literacy rate:* 29.4% (1990 est). *Years of compulsory schooling:* (in theory) 7–15. *Universities:* 4.
Defence: *Total armed strength:* 40 000 (1991 est). *Military service:* 4 years.

GOVERNMENT

The constitution provides for a two-chamber National Assembly, elected by universal adult suffrage. The Loya Jirgha (the supreme state body) consists of the National Assembly and the Cabinet, and provincial, legal and tribal representatives. The Loya Jirgha elects the President, who appoints a Prime Minster, who, in turn, appoints the Council of Ministers. A provisional government was formed in 1992. Various political groupings are active, but political parties do not currently operate within a recognizable constitutional framework.
President: Burhanuddin Rabbani.
Prime Minister: Gulbuddin Hekmatyar.

GEOGRAPHY

The central highlands, dominated by the Hindu

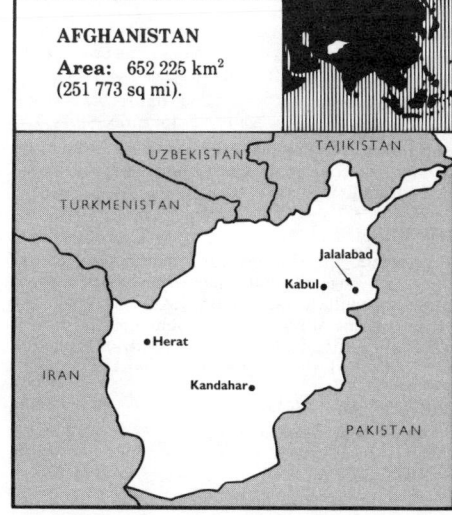

AFGHANISTAN
Area: 652 225 km²
(251 773 sq mi).

UZBEKISTAN
TAJIKISTAN
TURKMENISTAN
Jalalabad
Kabul
Herat
IRAN
Kandahar
PAKISTAN

Kush, cover over 75% of the country and contain several peaks over 6400 m (21 000 ft). North of the highlands are plains, an important agricultural region, while the southwest is desert and semidesert. *Principal rivers:* Helmand, Amu Darya (Oxus). *Highest point:* Noshaq 7499 m (24 581 ft).

Climate: The central highlands have very cold winters and short cool summers, while the desert regions have cold winters and hot summers. Except in parts of the highlands, it is dry.

ECONOMY

Farmers and herdsmen account for over 60% of the labour force. Most of the usable land is pasture, mainly for sheep, but cereal crops, particularly wheat and maize, are also important. Principal exports include fresh and dried fruit, wool and cotton. Natural gas is also exported. Economic development has been held back by civil war, and much of the basic infrastructure of the country has been damaged.

RECENT HISTORY

Afghanistan secured its independence in 1921 after three wars with the British. A period of unrest followed until a more stable monarchy was established in 1933. A coup in 1973 overthrew the monarchy. A close relationship with the USSR resulted from the 1978 Saur Revolution, but the Soviet invasion (1979) led to civil war. In 1989 the Soviets withdrew, leaving the cities in the hands of the government and Muslim fundamentalist guerrillas controlling the countryside. In 1992 fundamentalists took Kabul and formed a provisional government but factional – largely ethnic – fighting continues.

ALBANIA

Official name: Republika e Shqipërisë (Republic of Albania).

Member of: UN, CSCE.

Area: 28 748 km² (11 100 sq mi).

Population: 3 303 000 (1991 est).

Capital and major cities: Tirana (Tiranë) 238 000, Durrës 83 000, Elbasan 81 000, Shkodër 80 000, Vlorë 72 000 (1989 est).

Languages: Albanian (Gheg and Tosk dialects). Tosk is the official language.

Religions: Sunni Islam (20%), small Greek Orthodox and Roman Catholic minorities – the practice of religion was banned from 1967 to 1990.

Education: *Literacy rate:* no figure available. *Years of compulsory schooling:* 7–15. *Universities:* 1.

Defence: *Total armed strength:* 48 000 (1991 est). *Military service:* 2 years army; 3 years navy, air force and paramilitary units.

GOVERNMENT

A President and a 140-member Assembly are elected under a system of proportional representation by universal adult suffrage for four years. The Assembly elects a Prime Minister and a Council of Ministers. The main political parties are the (centre) Democratic Party and the (former Communist) Socialist Party.
President: Sali Berisha.
Prime Minister: Aleksandr Meksi.

GEOGRAPHY

Coastal lowlands support most of the country's

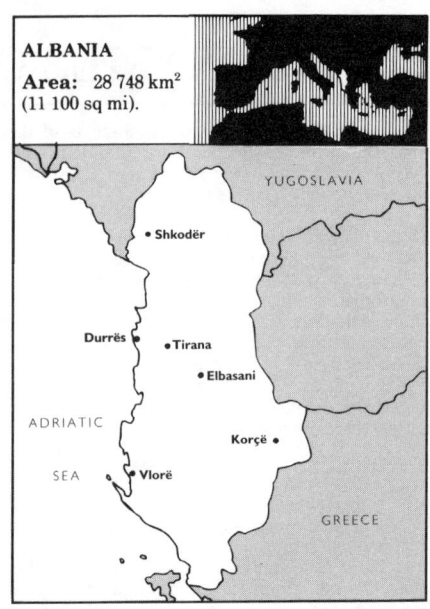

ALBANIA
Area: 28 748 km² (11 100 sq mi).

agriculture. Mountain ranges cover the greater part of Albania. *Principal rivers:* Semani, Drini. *Highest point:* Mount Korab 2751 m (9025 ft).

Climate: Hot, dry summers with mild, wet winters along the coast; equally hot summers but with very cold winters in the mountains.

ECONOMY

Albania is poor by European standards. The economy, which is still largely state-owned, relies on agriculture and the export of chromium. In 1990 Albania ended its self-imposed economic isolation and sought foreign financial, technical and humanitarian assistance. Nevertheless, the country has experienced famine, emigration and the collapse of much of its industrial infrastructure.

RECENT HISTORY

Independence from the Ottoman (Turkish) Empire was declared in 1912. The country was occupied in both the Balkan Wars and World War I, and the formation of a stable government within recognized frontiers did not occur until the 1920s. Interwar Albania was dominated by Ahmed Zogu (1895–1961), who made himself king (as Zog I) in 1928. He developed his impoverished country using Italian loans but fled when Mussolini invaded in 1939. Communist-led partisans took power when the Germans withdrew (1944). Under Enver Hoxha (1908–85), the regime pursued rapid modernization on Stalinist lines, allied, in turn, to Yugoslavia, the USSR and China, before opting (in 1978) for self-sufficiency and isolation. In 1990, a power struggle within the ruling Communist Party was won by the more liberal wing led by President Alia, who instituted a programme of economic, political and social reforms. The Communist Party retained a majority in multi-party elections in 1991 but (as the Socialist Party) was defeated in 1992.

ALGERIA

Official name: El Djemhouria El Djazaïria Demokratia Echaabia (the Democratic and Popular Republic of Algeria).

Member of: UN, OAU, Arab League, OPEC.

Area: 2 381 741 km² (919 595 sq mi).

Population: 25 888 000 (1991 est).

Capital and major cities: Algiers (El Djazaïr or Alger) 1 722 000, Oran (Ouahran) 664 000, Constantine (Qacentina) 449 000, Annaba 348 000, Blida (el-Boulaïda) 191 000, Sétif (Stif) 187 000 (all including suburbs; 1989 est).

Languages: Arabic (official), French, Berber.

Religion: Sunni Islam (official).

Education: *Literacy rate*: 58.4% (1990 est). *Years of compulsory schooling*: 6–15. *Universities*: 10, plus 5 institutes of university status.

Defence: *Total armed strength*: 125 500 (1991 est). *Military service*: 18 months.

GOVERNMENT

The constitution provides for the election of a President, who is executive head of state, and a 296-member National Assembly by universal adult suffrage every five years. In 1992 the constitution was suspended and a military council – whose chairman is President – was appointed. The main political parties are the (banned fundamentalist) Islamic Salvation Front (FIS), the (socialist) National Liberation Front (FLN) and the (largely Berber) Socialist Forces Front (FFS).
President: Ali Kafi.
Prime Minister: Belaid Abdelsalam.

GEOGRAPHY

Over 85% of Algeria is covered by the Sahara Desert. To the north lie the Atlas Mountains, which enclose a dry plateau. In the southeast are the Hoggar mountains. Along the Mediterranean coast are plains and lower mountain ranges. *Principal river*: Chéliff. *Highest point*: Mont Tahat 2918 m (9573 ft).

Climate: There is a Mediterranean climate along the coastline with hot summers, mild winters and adequate rainfall. In the Sahara, it is hot and arid.

ECONOMY

Petroleum and natural gas are the main exports and the basis of important industries. The country faces

severe economic problems including high unemployment. Farmers and farm workers account for nearly 25% of the labour force, but lack of rain and suitable land means that Algeria has to import two thirds of its food. The small amount of arable land mainly produces wheat, barley, fruit and vegetables, while arid pasturelands support sheep, goats and cattle. Tourism has become an important source of foreign currency.

RECENT HISTORY

France gradually colonized Algeria between 1830 and 1860. Nationalist riots against French colonial rule were ruthlessly suppressed in 1945, and in 1954 the FLN initiated a revolt that became a bitter war. A rising by French settlers, in favour of the integration of Algeria with France, led to the crisis that returned de Gaulle to power in France (1958). Despite two further risings by the settlers, and the activities of the colonists' terrorist organization, the OAS, Algeria gained independence in 1962. The first president, Ahmed Ben Bella (1916–), was overthrown in 1965 by Colonel Houari Boumédienne (1932–78), who aimed to re-establish the principles of the 1963 socialist constitution. His successor, Colonel Benjedid Chadli (1929–), began to steer Algeria towards democracy in the late 1980s. In 1992 the second round of national multi-party elections was cancelled when the fundamentalist FIS gained a large lead in the first round. The military took power and suspended political activity. Tension increased when military-appointed President Boudiaf was assassinated.

ANDORRA

Official name: Les Valls d'Andorrà (The Valleys of Andorra).

Member of: Andorra is not a member of any major international organizations but intends to join to the Council of Europe.

Area: 467 km² (180 sq mi).

Population: 55 400 (1991 est).

Capital: Andorra la Vella 33 400 (town 20 400; Les Escaldes 13 000; 1990 est).

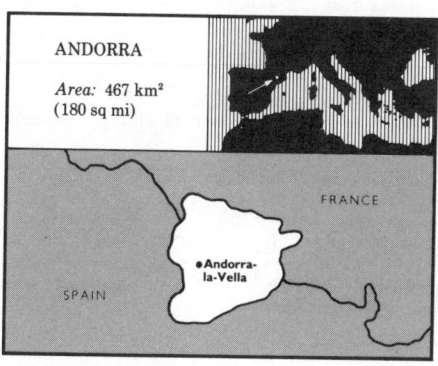

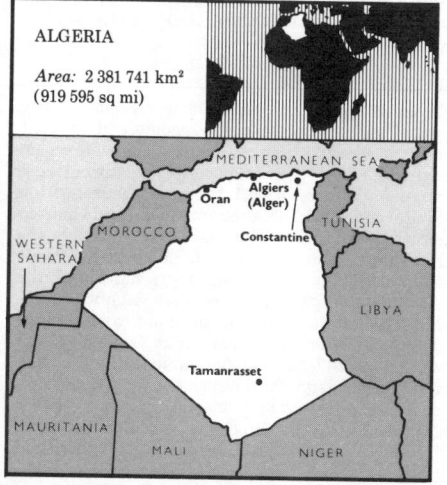

Languages: Catalan (30%; official), Spanish (59%), French (6%).

Religion: Roman Catholic.

Education: *Literacy rate*: 95% (1990 est). *Years of compulsory schooling*: 6–14. *Universities*: none.

Defence: *Total armed strength*: there are no armed forces. (Andorra has no defence budget.)

GOVERNMENT

Andorra has joint heads of state (co-princes) – the president of France and the Spanish bishop of Urgel – who delegate their powers to permanent representatives who will retain certain rights of veto under the new constitution approved by a referendum in 1993. A new legislative body will replace the traditional 28-member General Council – four councillors from each parish – which was elected for four years by universal adult suffrage, and (since 1981) chose an Executive Council (government). The referendum also approved the establishment of political parties.
Head of government (President of the Executive Council): Oscar Ribas Reig.

GEOGRAPHY

Situated in the eastern Pyrenees, Andorra is surrounded by mountains. *Principal river*: Valira. *Highest point*: Pla del'Estany 3011 m (9678 ft).

Climate: Andorra is mild in spring and summer, but cold for six months, with snow in the winter.

ECONOMY

The economy used to be based mainly on sheep and timber. Tourism has been encouraged by the development of ski resorts and by the duty-free status of consumer goods.

RECENT HISTORY

The country's joint allegiance to the French head of state and to the Spanish bishop of Urgel has made difficulties for Andorra in obtaining international recognition. However, reforms in 1993 included a proposed new constitution and independent diplomatic representation.

ANGOLA

Official name: A República de Angola (The Republic of Angola).

Member of: UN, OAU, SADCC.

Area: 1 246 700 km² (481 354 sq mi).

Population: 10 284 000 (1991 est).

Capital and major cities: Luanda 1 200 000 (1988; including suburbs), Huambo 203 000, Benguela 155 000, Lobito 150 000 (1982–3 est).

Languages: Portuguese (official), Kimbundu (27%), Umbundu (38%), Lunda (13%), Kikongo (11%).

Religions: Roman Catholic (over 60%), animist (20%).

Education: *Literacy rate*: 41.7% (1990 est). *Years of compulsory schooling*: (in theory) 7–15. *Universities*: 1.

Defence: *Total armed strength*: 96 000 (1991 est). *Military service*: selective.

GOVERNMENT

The constitution provides for the election by universal adult suffrage of a 318-member Assembly for three years and a President for five years. The President appoints a Prime Minister and a Council of Ministers. The main political movements are the (former Marxist-Leninist) MPLA (People's Liberation Movement of Angola) and (pro-Western) UNITA (the National Union for the Total Independence of Angola).

President: José Eduardo dos Santos.
Prime Minister: Fernando Van Dunem.

GEOGRAPHY

Plateaux, over 1000 m (3300 ft), cover 90% of Angola. In the west is a narrow coastal plain and in the southwest is desert. *Principal rivers*: Cunene (Kunene), Cuanza (Kwanza), Congo (Zaïre), Cuando (Kwando), Zambezi. *Highest point*: Serra Mòco 2610 m (8563 ft).

Climate: Angola is tropical, with slightly lower temperatures in the uplands. October to May is the rainy season, but the southwest is dry all year.

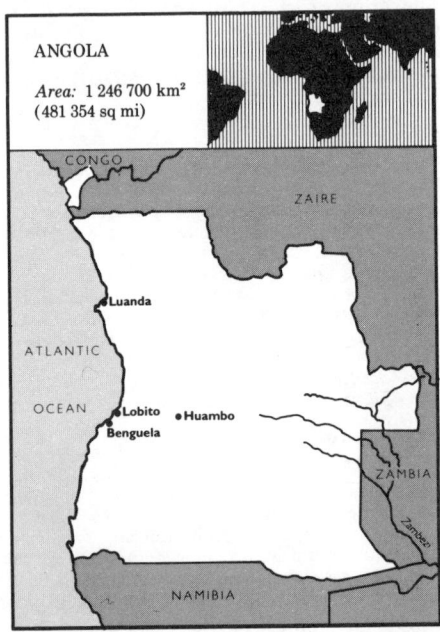

ANGOLA

Area: 1 246 700 km²
(481 354 sq mi)

ECONOMY

The development of Angola has been hampered by war. The country is, however, rich in minerals, particularly diamonds, iron ore and petroleum. Although less than 5% of the land is arable, over half the adult population is engaged in agriculture, mainly producing food crops. The main export crop is coffee.

RECENT HISTORY

In the 20th century, forced labour, heavy taxation and discrimination from Portuguese colonial settlers helped to stimulate nationalism. Portugal's repression of all political protest led to the outbreak of guerrilla wars in 1961. When independence was finally conceded (1975), three rival guerrilla movements fought for control of the country. With Soviet and Cuban support, the MPLA, under Dr Agostinho Neto (1922–79), gained the upper hand and also managed to repulse an invasion from South Africa. In the 1980s, Cuban troops continued to support the MPLA government against Jonas Savimbi's South African-aided UNITA movement in the South. Foreign involvement in the civil war ended in 1990 and a ceasefire was negotiated in 1991. Fighting between MPLA and UNITA forces resumed after the latter refused to accept the results of multi-party elections in 1992.

ANTIGUA AND BARBUDA

Member of: UN, Commonwealth, CARICOM, OAS.

Area: 442 km² (170.5 sq mi).

Population: 81 600 (1991 est).

Capital: St John's 36 000 (1986 est).

Language: English.

Religions: Anglican (44%), Moravian.

Education: *Literacy rate*: 90%. *Years of compulsory schooling*: 5–16. *Universities*: 1 university college (part of the University of the West Indies).

Defence: *Total armed strength*: almost 100 (1992). *Military service*: none.

GOVERNMENT

The 17-member House of Representatives is elected by universal adult suffrage for up to five years. The Senate, which also has 17 members, is appointed. Government is by a Cabinet of Ministers. A Prime Minister, commanding a majority in the lower house, is appointed by the Governor General, the representative of the British Queen as sovereign of Antigua. The main political party is the Antigua Labour Party.
Prime Minister: Vere C. Bird.

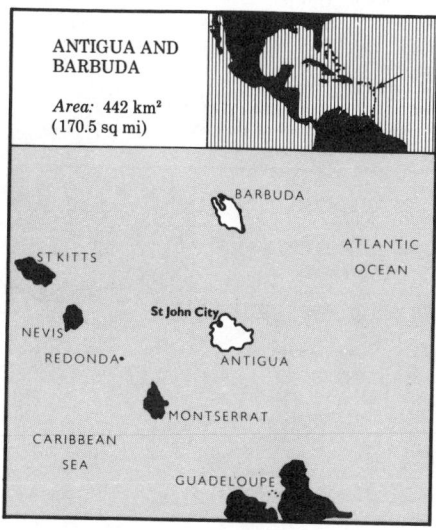

ANTIGUA AND BARBUDA

Area: 442 km² (170.5 sq mi)

GEOGRAPHY

Antigua is a low limestone island, rising in the west. Barbuda – 45 km / 25 mi to the north – is a flat wooded coral island. Redonda is a rocky outcrop. There are no significant rivers. *Highest point*: Boggy Peak 402 m (1319 ft).

Climate: The tropical climate is moderated by sea breezes. Rainfall is low for the West Indies, and Antigua island suffers from drought.

ECONOMY

Tourism is the mainstay of the country. In an attempt to diversify the economy, the government has encouraged agriculture, but the lack of water on Antigua island is a problem.

RECENT HISTORY

The British colonies of Antigua and Barbuda were united in 1860. Britain granted Antigua complete internal self-government in 1967 and independence in 1981.

ARGENTINA

Official name: República Argentina (the Argentine Republic).

Member of: UN, OAS, ALADI, Mercosur.

Area: 2 766 889 km² (1 068 302 sq mi), excluding territories claimed by Argentina: the Falkland Islands (Islas Malvinas), South Georgia, South Sandwich Islands, and parts of the Antarctic.

Population: 33 070 000 (1992 est).

Capital and major cities: Buenos Aires 12 582 000 (city 2 961 000), Córdoba 1 179 000, Rosario 1 096 000, Mendoza 729 000, La Plata 644 000, San Miguel de Tucumán 626 000, Mar del Plata 523 000, San Juan 358 000 (all including suburbs; 1991 census).

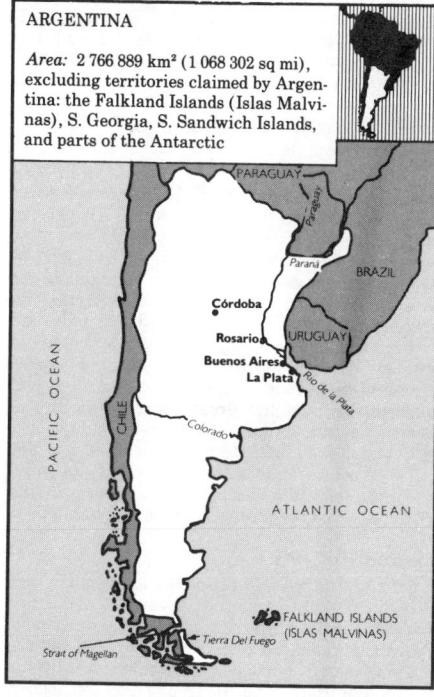

ARGENTINA

Area: 2 766 889 km² (1 068 302 sq mi), excluding territories claimed by Argentina: the Falkland Islands (Islas Malvinas), S. Georgia, S. Sandwich Islands, and parts of the Antarctic

Languages: Spanish (95%; official), Guarani (3%).

Religion: Roman Catholic (nearly 93%).

Education: *Literacy rate*: 95.3% (1990 est). *Years of compulsory schooling*: 6–14. *Universities*: 28 state and 20 private universities.

Defence: *Total armed strength*: 83 000 (1991). *Military service*: 6–12 months army; 12 months air force; 14 months navy.

GOVERNMENT

The President and Vice-President are elected for a six-year term of office by an electoral college of 600

members who are chosen by universal adult suffrage. The lower house of Congress (the Chamber of Deputies) has 254 members elected by universal suffrage for four years, with one half of its members retiring every two years. The 46 members of the upper house (the Senate) are chosen by provincial legislatures to serve for nine years, with 18 members retiring every three years. The main political parties are the Radical Civil Union (UCR), the Partido Justicialista (Peronist), and the Union of the Democratic Centre.
President: Carlos Saul Menem.

GEOGRAPHY

The Andes extend as a rugged barrier along the border with Chile. South of the Colorado River is Patagonia, an important pastureland – although much of it is semidesert. Over three-quarters of the population live in the pampas, whose prairies form one of the world's most productive agricultural regions. The subtropical plains of northeast Argentina contain part of the Gran Chaco prairie and rain forests. *Principal rivers*: Paraná, Colorado, Negro, Salado, Chubut. *Highest point*: Cerro Aconcagua 6960 m (22 834 ft).

Climate: Most of Argentina has a mild temperate climate, although the south is cooler and the northeast is subtropical. The higher parts of the Andes have a subpolar climate. Rainfall is heavy in the Andes and the far northeast, but generally decreases towards the dry south and southwest.

ECONOMY

Argentina is one of the world's leading producers of beef, wool, mutton, wheat and wine. The pampas produce cereals, while fruit and vines are important in the northwest. Pasturelands cover over 50% of Argentina – for beef cattle in the pampas and for sheep in Patagonia. However, manufacturing (including chemicals, steel, cement, paper, pulp and textiles) now makes the greatest contribution to the economy. The country is rich in natural resources, including petroleum, natural gas, iron ore and precious metals, and has great potential for hydroelectric power. Argentina is remarkably self-sufficient, although its status as an economic power has declined owing to political instability and massive inflation. However, financial reforms in the 1990s improved the prospects of the economy.

RECENT HISTORY

From 1880, large-scale European immigration and British investment helped Argentina, a former Spanish colony, to develop a flourishing economy. Prosperity was ended by the Depression, and, in 1930, the long period of constitutional rule was interrupted by a military coup. In 1946, a populist leader, Juan Perón (1895–1974), came to power with the support of the unions. His wife Eva was a powerful and popular figure, and after her death (1952), Perón was deposed (1955) because of his unsuccessful economic policies and his anticlericalism. Succeeding civilian governments were unable to conquer rampant inflation, and the military took power again (1966–73). An unstable period of civilian rule (1973–76) included Perón's brief second presidency. In the early 1970s, urban terrorism grew and the economic crisis deepened, prompting another coup. The military junta that seized control in 1976 received international condemnation when thousands of opponents of the regime were arrested or disappeared. In April 1982, President Galtieri ordered the

invasion of the Falkland Islands and its dependencies, which had long been claimed by Argentina. A British task force recaptured the islands in June 1982, and Galtieri resigned. Constitutional rule was restored in 1983 under President Raul Alfonsin.

ARMENIA

Official name: Haikakan (Armenia).
Member of: UN, CIS, CSCE.
Area: 29 800 km^2 (11 500 sq mi).
Population: 3 376 000 (1989 census).
Capital and major cities: Yerevan 1 215 000, Kumayri (Gyumri; formerly Leninakan) 228 000, Karaklis 169 000 (1989 census).
Languages: Armenian (official; 93%), Azeri (3%), Kurdish (2%).
Religion: Armenian Apostolic (Orthodox) majority.
Education: *Literacy rate:* no figure available. *Years of compulsory schooling:* 5–15. *Universities:* 1 university and 1 polytechnic.
Defence: *Total armed strength:* No figures available. *Military service:* 2 years.

GOVERNMENT

A 259-member Assembly and an executive President are elected by universal adult suffrage for four years. A new constitution is to be drafted. The main political parties are the Armenian National Movement, the (ultra-nationalist) Union for National Self-Determination and the Armenian Revolutionary Federation.
President: Levon Ter-Petrosyan.
Prime Minister: Grant Bagratyan.

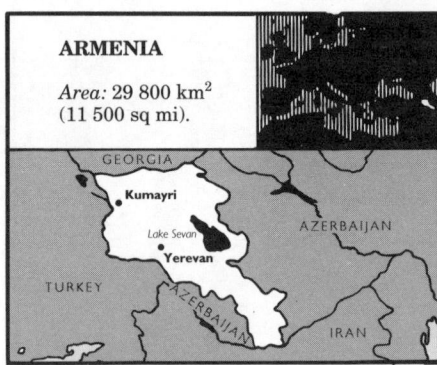

ARMENIA

Area: 29 800 km^2 (11 500 sq mi).

GEOGRAPHY

All of Armenia is mountainous – only 10% of the country is under 1000 m (3300 ft). *Principal rivers:* Araks, Zanga. *Highest point:* Mt Aragats 4090 m (13 418 ft).

Climate Armenia has a dry continental climate with considerable local variations owing to altitude and aspect.

ECONOMY

The diverse industrial sector includes chemicals, metallurgy, textiles, precision goods and food processing. Major projects have provided hydroelectric power as well as irrigation water for agriculture. Steps have been taken to introduce a market economy, but an effective blockade by Azerbaijan has devastated the economy.

RECENT HISTORY

Russia took eastern Armenia between 1813 and 1828. The western Armenians under Ottoman rule suffered persecution and, in 1896 and again in 1915, large-scale massacres. During World War I Turkey deported nearly 2 000 000 Armenians (suspected of pro-Russian sympathies) to Syria and Mesopotamia. The survivors contributed to an Armenian diaspora in Europe and the USA. Following the collapse of Tsarist Russia, an independent Armenian state emerged briefly (1918–22), but faced territorial wars with all its neighbours. Armenia became part of the Transcaucasian Soviet Republic in 1922 and a separate Union Republic within the USSR in 1936. After the abortive coup by Communist hardliners in Moscow (September 1991), Armenia declared independence and received international recognition when the USSR was dissolved (December 1991). Since 1990 Azeri and Armenian forces have been involved in a violent dispute concerning the status of Nagorno Karabakh, an enclave of Orthodox Christian Armenians surrounded by the Shiite Muslim Azeris.

AUSTRALIA

Official name: The Commonwealth of Australia.
Member of: UN, Commonwealth, ANZUS, OECD, South Pacific Forum.
Area: 7 682 300 km² (2 966 150 sq mi).
Population: 17 562 000 (1992 est).
Capital and major cities: Canberra 310 000, Sydney 3 699 000, Melbourne 3 154 000, Brisbane 1 327 000, Perth 1 193 000, Adelaide 1 050 000, Newcastle 433 000, Gold Coast 274 000, Wollongong 240 000, Hobart 184 000, Geelong 151 000, Townsville 114 000, Launceston 89 000, Cairns 76 000, Ballarat 75 000, Darwin 73 000, Bendigo 62 000, Rockhampton 61 000 (including suburbs; 1991 census).

Language: English.
Religions: Anglican (26%), Roman Catholic (26%), Uniting Church in Australia (8%), Orthodox.
Education: Literacy rate: over 95%. Years of compulsory schooling: 6–15. Universities: 38.
Defence: Total armed strength: 68 300 (1991). Military service: none.

GOVERNMENT

The Federal Parliament consists of two chambers elected by compulsory universal adult suffrage. The Senate has 76 members elected by proportional representation – 12 senators elected from each state for six years, 2 from both territories elected for three years. The House of Representatives has 148 members elected for three years. A Prime Minister, who commands a majority in the House of Representatives, is appointed by the Governor General, who is the representative of the British Queen as sovereign of Australia. The Prime Minister chairs the Federal Executive Council (or Cabinet), which is responsible to Parliament. Each state has its own government. The main political parties are the Australian Labor Party, the Australian Democrats (liberal), the Liberal Party of Australia (conservative), and the National Party of Australia (conservative).
Prime Minister: Paul Keating.

STATES AND TERRITORIES

State populations are 1992 estimates.
New South Wales Area: 801 600 km² (309 500 sq mi). Population: 5 962 000. Capital: Sydney.
Queensland Area: 1 727 200 km² (666 875 sq mi). Population: 3 022 000. Capital: Brisbane.
South Australia Area: 984 000 km² (379 925 sq mi). Population: 1 458 000. Capital: Adelaide.

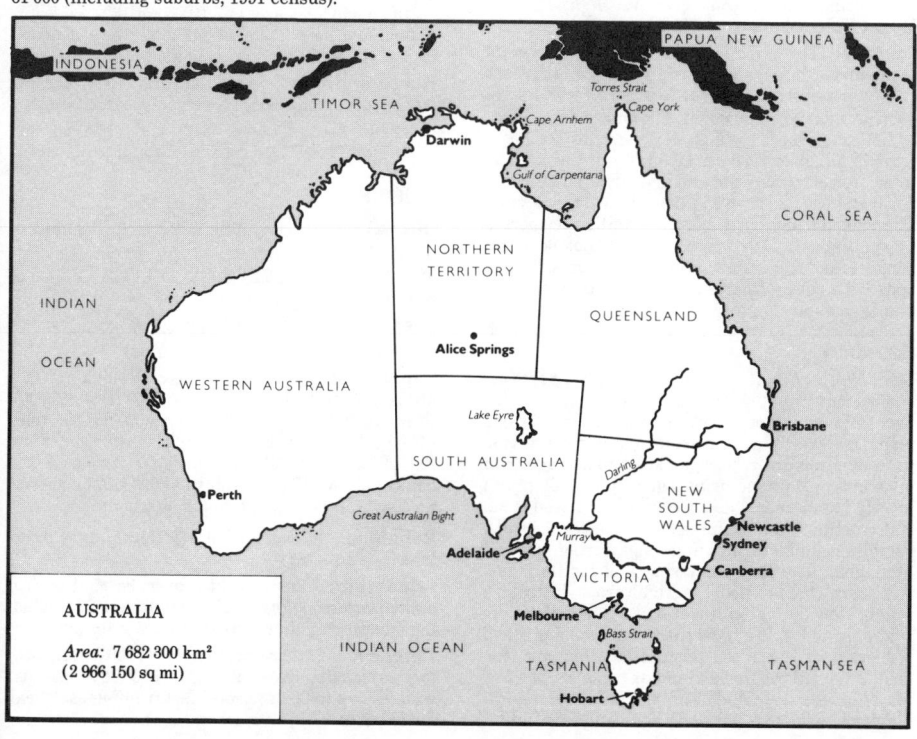

AUSTRALIA

Area: 7 682 300 km²
(2 966 150 sq mi)

Tasmania *Area*: 67 800 km² (26 175 sq mi). *Population*: 470 000. *Capital*: Hobart.

Victoria *Area*: 227 600 km² (87 875 sq mi). *Population*: 4 452 000. *Capital*: Melbourne.

Western Australia *Area*: 2 525 500 km² (975 100 sq mi). *Population*: 1 658 000. *Capital*: Perth.

Australian Capital Territory *Area*: 2400 km² (925 sq mi). *Population*: 296 000. *Capital*: Canberra. (The population given for Canberra above includes suburbs in New South Wales.)

Northern Territory *Area*: 1 346 200 km² (519 750 sq mi). *Population*: 169 000. *Capital*: Darwin.

GEOGRAPHY

Vast areas of desert cover most of the land in central and western Australia, a region of plateaux between 400 and 600 m (1300–2000 ft) with occasional higher regions, such as the Kimberley Plateau. In contrast to this arid, scarcely populated area – which covers more than 50% of the country – are the narrow coastal plains of the fertile, well-watered east coast where the majority of Australians live. Behind the plains – which range from temperate forest in the south, through subtropical woodland to tropical rain forest in Queensland – rise the Eastern Uplands, or Great Dividing Range. This is a line of ridges and plateaux, interrupted by basins, stretching from Cape York Peninsula in the north to the island of Tasmania. West of the uplands is the Great Artesian Basin extending from the Gulf of Carpentaria to the Murray River and Eyre Basins. Landforms in the basin include rolling plains, plateaux, salt lakes and river valleys. Between the Murray River and Eyre Basins are the Flinders and Mount Lofty Ranges. Many of Australia's rivers flow intermittently. *Principal rivers*: Murray, Darling, Lachlan, Flinders, Diamentina, Ashburton, Fitzroy. *Highest point*: Mount Kosciusko 2230 m (7316 ft).

Climate: The north is tropical with wet summers (January to March) and dry winters. The north coast of Western Australia and the Northern Territory are subject to summer monsoons. The Queensland coast, which experiences tropical cyclones, has the heaviest rainfall, over 2500 mm (100 in) near Cairns. The interior is extremely hot and dry – over one third of Australia has less than 255 mm (10 in) of rain a year. The coastal fringes in the south are either temperate or subtropical, with winter rainfall, hot or warm summers and moderate winter temperatures. Winter snowfall is common in the highlands of the southeast and Tasmania.

ECONOMY

Since World War II, Australia's economy has been dominated by mining, and minerals now account for over 30% of the country's exports. Australia has major reserves of coal, petroleum and natural gas, uranium, iron ore, copper, nickel, bauxite, gold and diamonds. Manufacturing and processing are largely based upon these resources: iron and steel, construction, oil refining and petrochemicals, vehicle manufacturing and engineering are all prominent. The food-processing and textile industries are based upon agriculture. Australia's reliance on the agricultural sector has fallen considerably and in the 1990s there has been a planned reduction in the sheep population. However, the country is still the world's leading producer of wool. Major interests include sheep, cattle, cereals (in particular wheat), sugar (in Queensland) and fruit. A strong commercial sector, with banks and finance houses, adds to the diversity of the economy.

RECENT HISTORY

In 1901, the Commonwealth of Australia was founded when the six British colonies of New South Wales, Queensland, South Australia, Tasmania, Victoria, and Western Australia came together in a federation. Australia made an important contribution in World War I – one fifth of its servicemen were killed in action. The heroic landing at Gallipoli in the Dardenelles is commemorated with a day of remembrance in Australia. The Depression hit the country badly, but the interwar years did see international recognition of Australia's independence. World War II, during which the north was threatened by Japan, strengthened links with America. Australian troops fought in Vietnam and important trading partnerships have been formed with Asian countries. Since 1945, migrants from all over Europe have gained assisted passage to Australia, further diluting the British connection. Australia now has a close relationship with the USA and is a regional power in the South Pacific region.

AUSTRALIAN EXTERNAL TERRITORIES

Ashmore and Cartier Islands *Area:* 5 km² (2 sq mi). *Population:* uninhabited.

Australian Antarctic Territory see Other Territories following this chapter.

Christmas Island *Area:* 135 km² (52 sq mi). *Population:* 1770 (1991 est). *Capital:* Flying Fish Cove.

Cocos (Keeling) Islands *Area:* 14 km² (5.5 sq mi). *Population:* 600 (1990 census). *Capital:* Bantam Village (on Home Island).

Coral Sea Islands Territory *Area:* 8 km² (5 sq mi) of land in a sea area of 780 000 km² (300 000 sq mi). *Population:* no permanent inhabitants. A meteorological station is staffed by 3 officers.

Heard and MacDonald Islands *Area:* 292 km² (113 sq mi). *Population:* no permanent inhabitants.

Norfolk Island *Area:* 34.5 km² (13.3 sq mi). *Population:* 1980 (1986 census). *Capital:* Kingston.

AUSTRIA

Official name: Republik Österreich (Republic of Austria)

Member of: UN, EFTA, OECD, CSCE, Council of Europe.

Area: 83 855 km² (32 367 sq mi).

Population: 7 812 000 (1991 census).

Capital and major cities: Vienna (Wien) 2 045 000 (city 1 533 000), Linz 434 000 (city 203 000), Graz 395 000 (city 232 000), Salzburg 267 000 (city 144 000), Innsbruck 235 000 (city 115 000), Klagenfurt 135 000 (city 90 000), Villach 55 000, Wels 53 000, Sankt Pölten 50 000, Dornbirn 41 000 (1991 census).

Language: German (official; 96%).

Religions: Roman Catholic (84%); various Protestant Churches (6%).

Education: *Literacy rate*: over 98%. *Years of compulsory schooling*: 6–15. *Universities*: 18, including 6 institutes of university status.

Defence: *Total armed strength*: 44 000 (1991). *Military service*: 6 months training; up to 60 days reservist training; up to 90 days specialist training each year for 15 years.

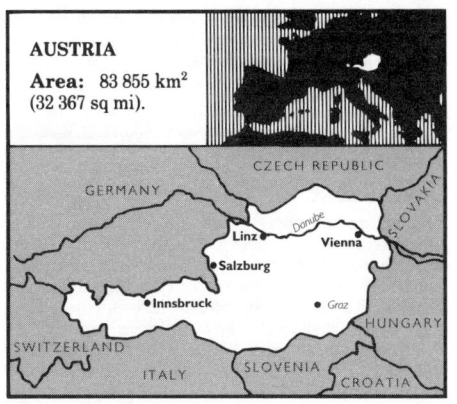

AUSTRIA

Area: 83 855 km² (32 367 sq mi).

GOVERNMENT

Executive power is shared by the Federal President – who is elected by universal adult suffrage for a six-year term – and the Council of Ministers (Cabinet), led by the Federal Chancellor. The President appoints a Chancellor who commands a majority in the Federal Assembly's lower chamber, the Nationalrat, whose 183 members are elected by universal adult suffrage according to proportional representation for a term of four years. The 63 members of the upper chamber – the Bundesrat – are elected by the assemblies of the nine provinces of the Federal Republic. The main political parties are the (socialist) Social Democrat Party (SPO), the (conservative) People's Party, the (right-wing) Freedom Party (FPO) and the Greens (VGO).
Federal President: Thomas Klestil.
Federal Chancellor: Franz Vranitzky.

AUSTRIAN STATES (Länder)

State populations are from the 1991 census.
Burgenland *Area*: 3966 km² (1531 sq mi). *Population*: 274 000. *Capital*: Eisenstadt.
Carinthia (Kärnten) *Area*: 9533 km² (3681 sq mi). *Population*: 552 000. *Capital*: Klagenfurt.
Lower Austria (Niederösterreich) *Area*: 19 171 km² (7402 sq mi). *Population*: 1 481 000. *Capital*: Sankt Pölten.
Salzburg *Area*: 7154 km² (2762 sq mi). *Population*: 484 000. *Capital*: Salzburg.
Styria (Steiermark) *Area*: 16 387 km² (6327 sq mi). *Population*: 1 185 000. *Capital*: Graz.
Tirol *Area*: 12 647 km² (4883 sq mi). *Population*: 630 000. *Capital*: Innsbruck.
Upper Austria (Oberösterreich) *Area*: 11 979 km² (4625 sq mi). *Population*: 1 340 000. *Capital*: Linz.
Vienna (Wien) *Area*: 415 km² (160 sq mi). *Population*: 1 533 000. *Capital*: Vienna.
Vorarlberg *Area*: 2601 km² (1004 sq mi). *Population*: 333 000. *Capital*: Bregenz.

GEOGRAPHY

The Alps – much of which are covered by pastures and forests – occupy nearly two thirds of Austria. Lowland Austria – in the east – consists of low hills, the Vienna Basin and a flat marshy area beside the Neusiedler See on the Hungarian border. Along the Czech border is a forested massif rising to 1200 m (4000 ft). *Principal rivers*: Danube (Donau), Inn, Mur. *Highest point*: Grossglockner 3798 m (12 462 ft).

Climate: There are many local variations in climate owing to altitude and aspect. The east is drier than the west, and is, in general, colder than the Alpine region in the winter and hotter, but more humid, in the summer. Areas over 3000 m (10 000 ft) are snow-covered all year.

ECONOMY

Although Austria produces about 90% of its own food requirements, agriculture employs only 8% of the labour force. The arable land in the east has fertile soils producing good yields of cereals, as well as grapes for wine. Dairy produce is an important export from the pasturelands in the east and in the Alps. The mainstay of the economy is manufacturing industry, including machinery and transport equipment, iron and steel products, refined petroleum products, cement and paper. Natural resources include magnesite and iron ore, as well as hydroelectric power potential and the most considerable forests in central Europe. The Alps attract both winter and summer visitors, making tourism a major earner of foreign currency. Austria retains economic links with countries in central Europe that were once part of the Habsburg empire.

RECENT HISTORY

In 1918–19, the Austro-Hungarian Habsburg empire was dismembered. An Austrian republic was established as a separate state, despite considerable support for union with Germany. Unstable throughout the 1920s and 1930s, Austria was annexed by Germany in 1938 (the Anschluss). Austria was liberated in 1945, but Allied occupation forces remained until 1955 when the independence of a neutral republican Austria was recognized. The upheavals in central Europe in 1989–90 encouraged Austria to renew traditional links with Hungary, the Czech Republic, Slovenia, Croatia and Slovakia – all once part of the Habsburg Empire. Austria is a candidate for membership of the EC.

AZERBAIJAN

Official name: Azarbaijchan (Azerbaijan).
Member of: UN, CSCE.
Area: 86 600 km² (33 400 sq mi).
Population: 7 137 000 (1989 census).
Capital and major cities: Baku 1 757 000, Gyanzha (Gäncä; formerly Kirovabad) 270 000, Sumgait (Sumqayit) 234 000 (1989 census).
Languages: Azeri (83%), Russian (6%), Armenian (2%).
Religion: Shia Islam majority.

AZERBAIJAN

Area: 86 600 km² (33 400 sq mi).

Education: *Literacy rate:* over 99% (1970). *Years of compulsory schooling:* 5–15. *Universities:* 2.
Defence: *Total armed strength:* No figures available. *Military service:* 2 years.

GOVERNMENT
An executive President and a 350-member Parliament are elected by universal adult suffrage for four years. A new constitution is to be drafted. Party politics are at an early stage and there are many small Azeri parties and political groupings. The main parties are the Popular Front of Azerbaijan and the Social Democratic Group.
President: Albulfaz Elchibey.
Prime Minister: Rakhim Guseynov.

GEOGRAPHY
Azerbaijan comprises lowlands beside the Caspian Sea, part of the Caucasus Mountains in the N and the Little Caucasus in the SW. The republic includes the Nakhichevan enclave to the W of Armenia. *Principal rivers:* Kura, Araks. *Highest point:* Bazar-Dyuzi 4480 m (14 694 ft).
Climate: A wide climatic range includes dry and humid subtropical conditions beside the Caspian Sea and continental conditions in the mountains.

ECONOMY
Important reserves of oil and natural gas are the mainstay of the economy and the basis of heavy industries. Although industry dominates the economy, agriculture contributes a variety of exports including cotton and tobacco. Sturgeon are caught in the Caspian Sea for the important caviar industry. Initial steps have been taken to introduce a market economy, and trade agreements have been concluded with Turkey.

RECENT HISTORY
Russia conquered northern Azerbaijan early in the 19th century, but the greater part of the land of the Azeris remained under Persian rule. During World War I, a nationalist Azeri movement became allied with the Turks. An independent Azeri state was founded with Turkish assistance (1918), but was invaded by the Soviet Red Army in 1920. Azerbaijan was part of the Transcaucasian Soviet Republic from 1922 until 1936 when it became a separate Union Republic within the USSR. Independence was declared following the abortive coup in Moscow by Communist hardliners (September 1991) and was internationally recognized when the USSR was dissolved (December 1991). Since 1990 Azeri and Armenian forces have been involved in a violent dispute concerning the status of Nagorno Karabakh, an enclave of Orthodox Christian Armenians surrounded by the Shiite Muslim Azeris. Azerbaijan withdrew from the CIS in 1992 and established close links with Turkey.

BAHAMAS

Official name: The Commonwealth of the Bahamas.
Member of: UN, Commonwealth, OAS, CARICOM (Community only).
Area: 13 939 km² (5382 sq mi).
Population: 255 000 (1990 census).
Capital: Nassau 169 000, Freeport 25 000 (1990 census).
Language: English.

Religions: Baptist (29%), Anglican (21%), Roman Catholic (26%).
Education: *Literacy rate:* 96%. *Years of compulsory schooling:* 5–14. *Universities:* 1 university college.
Defence: *Total armed strength:* 850 (1991). *Military service:* none.

GOVERNMENT
The Senate (the upper house of Parliament) has 16 appointed members. The House of Assembly (the lower house) has 49 members elected by universal adult suffrage for five years. A Prime Minister, who commands a majority in the House, is appointed by the Governor General, who is the representative of the British Queen as sovereign of the Bahamas. The Prime Minister chairs the Cabinet, which is responsible to the House. The main political parties are the Progressive Liberal Party and the Free National Movement.
Prime Minister: Hubert A. Ingraham.

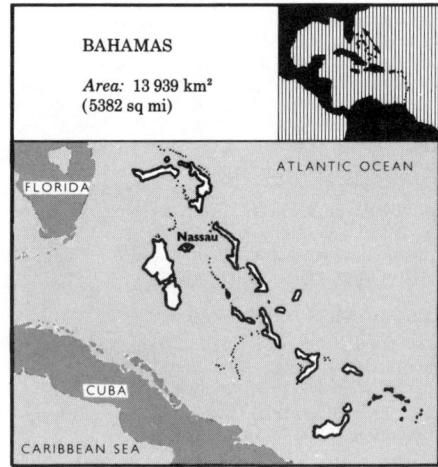

BAHAMAS

Area: 13 939 km²
(5382 sq mi)

ATLANTIC OCEAN

FLORIDA

Nassau

CUBA

CARIBBEAN SEA

GEOGRAPHY
The Bahamas comprises some 700 long, flat, narrow islands, and over 2000 barren rocky islets. There are no significant rivers. *Highest point:* Mount Alvernia, Cat Island 63 m (206 ft).
Climate: The climate is mild and subtropical, with no great seasonal variation in temperature. Rainfall averages just over 1000 mm (39 in). The islands are liable to hurricanes.

ECONOMY
Tourism – mainly from the USA – is the major source of income, and, with related industries, it employs the majority of the labour force. The islands have become a tax haven and financial centre.

RECENT HISTORY
Britain granted internal self-government to the Bahamas in 1964. Since independence in 1973, the Bahamas have developed close ties with the USA, although the relationship has been strained at times owing to an illegal drug trade through the islands.

BAHRAIN

Official name: Daulat al-Bahrain (The State of Bahrain).

Member of: UN, Arab League, OPEC, GCC.

Area: 691 km² (267 sq mi).

Population: 516 000 (1991 est).

Capital: Manama 152 000, al-Muharraq 78 000 (1988 est).

Language: Arabic.

Religions: Sunni Islam (33%), Shia Islam (60%).

Education: *Literacy rate*: 77.4% (1990). *Years of compulsory schooling*: schooling is not compulsory. *Universities*: 2.

Defence: *Total armed strength*: 7450 (1991). *Military service*: none.

GOVERNMENT

Bahrain is ruled directly by an Amir (a hereditary monarch), who appoints a Prime Minister and a Cabinet of Ministers. The 1973 Constitution provides for a National Assembly consisting of Cabinet plus 30 other members elected by popular vote. However, the Assembly was dissolved in 1975 and has not been reconvened. The Amir appoints an advisory Council.
Amir: HH Shaikh Isa II bin Sulman Al-Khalifa (succeeded upon the death of his father, 2 November 1961).
Prime Minister: HH Shaikh Khalifa bin Sulman Al-Khalifa.

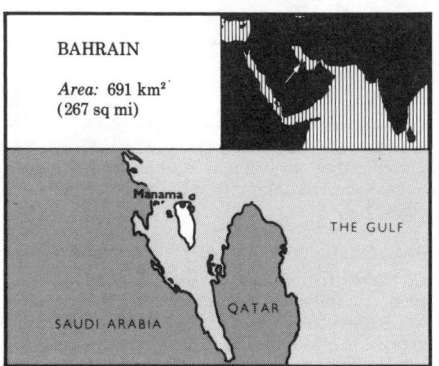

GEOGRAPHY

Bahrain Island, the largest of the 35 small islands in the archipelago, consists mainly of sandy plains and salt marshes, and is linked to Saudi Arabia by causeway. There are no rivers. *Highest point:* Jabal al-Dukhan 134 m (440 ft).

Climate: The climate is very hot. The annual average rainfall is 75 mm (3 in).

ECONOMY

The wealth of Bahrain is due to its petroleum and natural gas resources, and the oil-refining industry. As reserves began to wane in the 1970s, the government encouraged diversification. As a result, Bahrain is now one of the Gulf's major banking and communication centres.

RECENT HISTORY

Bahrain – a British protectorate from the end of the 19th century – was the first state in the region to develop its petroleum industry. Since independence in 1971, there has been tension between the Sunni and Shiite communities. Responding to threats from revolutionary Shiite Iran, Bahrain entered defence agreements with Saudi Arabia and other Gulf states, and joined the coalition forces against Iraq after the invasion of Kuwait (August 1990).

BANGLADESH

Official name: Gana Praja Tantri Bangla Desh (People's Republic of Bangladesh).

Member of: UN, Commonwealth, SAARC.

Area: 143 998 km² (55 598 sq mi).

Population: 110 602 000 (1992 est).

Capital and major cities: Dhaka 6 105 000, Chittagong 2 133 000, Khulna 1 029 000, Rajshahi 427 000, Mymensingh 191 000, Comilla 185 000, Sylhet 169 000, Barisal 159 000 (1991 census).

Languages: Bengali (official; 97%), tribal dialects.

Religion: Sunni Islam (over 85%); Hindu (12%).

Education: *Literacy rate*: 35% (1990). *Years of compulsory schooling*: (as from 1992) 5–10. *Universities*: 6.

Defence: *Total armed strength*: 106 500 (1991). *Military service*: none.

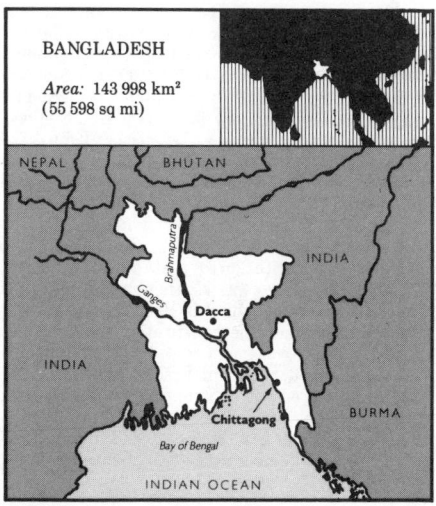

GOVERNMENT

The Parliament (Jatiya Sangsad) comprises 300 members elected for five years by universal adult suffrage and 30 women chosen by the elected members. Parliament elects a President – who serves for five years – and a Prime Minister who appoints a Council of Minister. The main political parties include the Jatiya Party, the Awami League, Jamit-i-Islami and the BNP (Bangladesh Nationalist Party).
President: Abdur Rahman Biswas.
Prime Minister: Begum Khaleda Zia.

GEOGRAPHY

Most of Bangladesh comprises alluvial plains in the deltas of the rivers Ganges and Brahmaputra, which combine as the Padma. The swampy plains – generally less than 9 m (30 ft) above sea level – are dissected by rivers dividing into numerous distributaries with raised banks. The south and southeast coastal regions contain mangrove forests (the Sundarbans). The only uplands are the Sylhet Hills in the northeast and the Chittagong hill country in the east. *Principal rivers*: Ganges, Brahmaputra. *Highest point*: Keokradong 1230 m (4034 ft).

Climate: The climate is tropical with the highest temperatures between April and September. Most of the country's rainfall comes during the annual monsoon (June to October) when intense storms accompanied by high winds bring serious flooding. Rainfall totals range from 1000 mm (40 in) in the west to 5000 mm (200 in) in the Sylhet Hills.

ECONOMY

With a rapidly increasing population, Bangladesh is among the world's poorest countries and is heavily dependent on foreign aid. Agriculture involves over 70% of the population. Rice is produced on over 75% of the cultivated land, but although the land is fertile, crops are often destroyed by floods and cyclones. A major Flood Action Plan, started in 1992, will alter the course of rivers and raise embankments. The main cash crops are jute and tea. Industries include those processing agricultural products – jute, cotton and sugar. Mineral resources are few, but there are reserves of natural gas.

RECENT HISTORY

On the partition of British India in 1947, as the majority of its inhabitants were Muslim, the area became the eastern province of an independent Pakistan. Separated by 1600 km (1000 mi) from the Urdu-speaking, politically dominant western province, East Pakistan saw itself as a victim of economic and ethnic injustice. Resentment led to civil war in 1971 when Indian aid to Bengali irregulars gave birth to an independent People's Republic of Bangladesh ('Free Bengal') under Sheik Mujib-ur-Rahman. The Sheik's assassination in 1975 led eventually to a takeover by General Zia-ur-Rahman, who amended the constitution to create an 'Islamic state'. The General in turn was assassinated in 1981, and General Ershad took power in 1982. Martial law was lifted in 1986 when the constitution was amended and a civilian government took office. Following a period of unrest, President Ershad was deposed in 1990 and charged with corruption. In March 1991, the BNP, led by Zia's widow, won multi-party elections. Bangladesh has since switched from a presidential to a parliamentary system of government.

BARBADOS

Member of: UN, Commonwealth, CARICOM, OAS.

Area: 430 km² (166 sq mi).

Population: 257 000 (1990 census).

Capital: Bridgetown 102 000 (city 7500; 1990 census).

Language: English.

Religions: Anglican (40%), Pentecostalist (8%), Methodist (7%).

Education: *Literacy rate*: 98% (1985). *Years of compulsory schooling*: 5–16. *Universities*: 1 university college (part of the University of the West Indies).

Defence: *Total armed strength*: 154 plus volunteers and reservists. *Military service*: none.

GOVERNMENT

The 21 members of the Senate are appointed; the 27 members of the House of Assembly are elected by universal adult suffrage for five years. The Governor General, the representative of the British Queen as sovereign of Barbados, appoints a Prime Minister who commands a majority in the House. The PM appoints a Cabinet responsible to the House. The main political parties are the Democratic Labour Party and the Barbados Labour Party.
Prime Minister: L. Erskine Sandiford.

GEOGRAPHY

Barbados is generally flat and low, except in the north. There are no significant rivers. *Highest point*: Mount Hillaby (340 m/1115 ft).

Climate: Barbados has a tropical climate. Rainfall is heavy, with totals everywhere above 1000 mm (40 in). The island is subject to hurricanes.

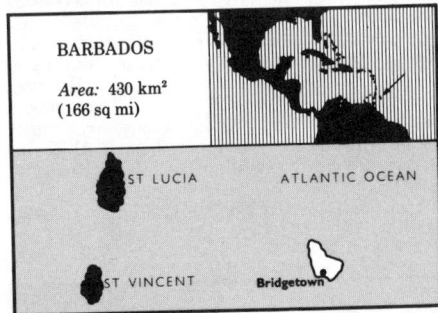

BARBADOS

Area: 430 km² (166 sq mi)

ST LUCIA   ATLANTIC OCEAN

ST VINCENT   Bridgetown

ECONOMY

Tourism – which employs about one third of the labour force – is the main source of income. The government has encouraged diversification, and there has been a growth in banking and insurance. Sugar – once the mainstay of Barbados – remains the main crop.

RECENT HISTORY

In the British colony of Barbados in the 1930s, economic and social conditions for black Barbadians were miserable. Riots in 1937 led to reforms and also greatly increased black political consciousness. As a result, Barbadians, such as Grantley Adams and Errol Barrow, became prominent in Caribbean politics. Barbados gained independence in 1966 and has become an important influence among the smaller islands of the Lesser Antilles.

BELARUS (BYELORUSSIA)

Official name: Belarus. Formerly known as Byelorussia.

Member of: UN, CIS, CSCE.

Area: 207 600 km² (80 200 sq mi).

Population: 10 260 000 (1989 census).

Capital and major cities: Minsk (Mensk) 1 589 000, Gomel (Homyel) 500 000, Mogilev (Mahilyow) 359 000, Vitebsk (Vitsyebsk) 347 000, Grodno (Hrodna) 263 000, Brest 238 000 (1989 census).

Languages: Belarussian (also known as Belorussian) (79%), Russian (13%), Polish (4%).

Religions: Russian Orthodox majority, Roman Catholic minority.

Education: *Literacy rate:* over 95% (1992 est). *Years of compulsory schooling:* 5-15. *Universities:* 3 universities and 4 polytechnics.

Defence: *Total armed strength:* no figures available. Military service: 2 years.

GOVERNMENT

A 360-member legislature and a President – who appoints a Premier and a Council of Ministers – are elected by universal adult suffrage for four years. A new constitution is to be drafted. Many small political parties and groups are active – the largest is the Belarussian Popular Front (BNF).
President: Stanislav Shushkevich.
Prime Minister: Vyacheslav Kebich.

GEOGRAPHY

Belarus comprises lowlands covered with glacial debris in the N, fertile well-drained tablelands and ridges in the centre, and the low-lying Pripet Marshes in the S and E. Much of the country is flat.
Principal rivers: Dnepr, Pripyat, Dvina, Neman.
Highest point: Dzyarzhynskaya Mountain 346 m (1135 ft).

Climate: The continental climate is moderated by the proximity of the Baltic Sea. Belarussian winters are considerably milder than those experienced in European Russia to the E.

ECONOMY

Although Belarus has few natural resources, its economy is overwhelmingly industrial. Major heavy engineering, chemical, fertilizer, oil refining and synthetic fibre industries were established as part of the centrally-planned Soviet economy. Belarus is dependent upon trade with other former Soviet republics from which it imports the raw materials for its industries and upon which it relies as a market for its industrial goods. Little progress towards establishing a market economy has been made and Belarus faces severe economic problems. Agriculture is dominated by raising fodder crops for beef cattle, pigs and poultry. Flax is grown for export and the local linen industry. Extensive forests supply important woodworking and paper industries.

RECENT HISTORY

The region – part of Russia since the end of the 18th century – suffered some of the fiercest fighting between Russia and Germany during World War I. Following the Russian Revolution, a Byelorussian Soviet republic was proclaimed (1919). The republic was invaded by the Poles in the same year and divided between Poland and the USSR in 1921.

Byelorussia was devastated during World War II. In 1945 the Belarussians were reunited in a single Soviet republic. A perceived lack of Soviet concern for the republic at the time of the accident at the Chernobyl nuclear power station (just over the Ukrainian border) strengthened a reawakening Belarussian national identity. Contamination from Chernobyl affected about 20% of the republic, causing some areas to be sealed off and necessitating the eventual resettlement of up to 2 000 000 people. Byelorussia declared independence following the abortive coup by Communist hardliners in Moscow (September 1991) and – as Belarus – received international recognition when the USSR was dissolved (December 1991).

BELGIUM

Official name: Royaume de Belgique or Koninkrijk België (Kingdom of Belgium).

Member of: UN, NATO, EC, CSCE, WEU, Council of Europe, OECD.

Area: 30 519 km² (11 783 sq mi).

Population: 9 849 000 (1991 census).

Capital and major cities: Brussels (Bruxelles or Brussel) 960 000, Antwerp (Antwerpen or Anvers) 920 000 (city 468 000), Liège (Luik) 590 000 (city 185 000), Ghent (Gent or Gand) 485 000 (city 230 000), Charleroi 429 000 (city 207 000), Malines (Mechelen) 293 000 (city 75 000), Courtrai (Kortrijk) 275 000 (city 76 000), Namur (Namen) 264 000 (city 104 000), Bruges (Brugge) 260 000 (city 117 000), Mons (Bergen) 92 000, Ostend (Oostende or Ostende) 69 000 (1990 est).

Languages: Flemish (a dialect of Dutch; 59%), French (42%) – 10% of the population is officially bilingual.

Religion: Roman Catholic (86%).

Education: *Literacy*: 98%. *Years of compulsory schooling*: 6–16. *Universities*: 18 (including 11 institutes of university status).

Defence: *Total armed strength*: 85 450 (1991). *Military service*: 10 months or 1 year.

GOVERNMENT

Belgium is a constitutional monarchy. The Chamber of Deputies (the lower house of Parliament) comprises 212 members elected by universal adult suffrage for four years under a system of proportional representation. The Senate (the upper house) has 182 members: 106 directly elected, 50 chosen by provincial councils, 25 co-opted, plus the heir to the throne. The King appoints a Prime Minister, who commands a majority in the Chamber, and, upon the PM's advice, other members of the Cabinet. The main political parties are the (Flemish) CVP (Christelijke Volkspartei) and its French-speaking equivalent the Parti social chrétien (PSC), the two Socialist parties – Socialistische Partei (SP) and the Parti socialiste belge (FS), two liberal parties – the (Flemish) Liberal Freedom and Progress Party (PVV) and the (French-speaking) Liberal Reform Party (PRL), and Flemish and Walloon regional parties such as the (Flemish) Vlaams Blok and Volksunie. The directly elected regional councils of Flanders, Wallonia and Brussels have very considerable powers.
King: HM Baudouin I, King of the Belgians (succeeded 15 July 1951 upon the abdication of his father).
Prime Minister: Jean-Luc Dehaene.

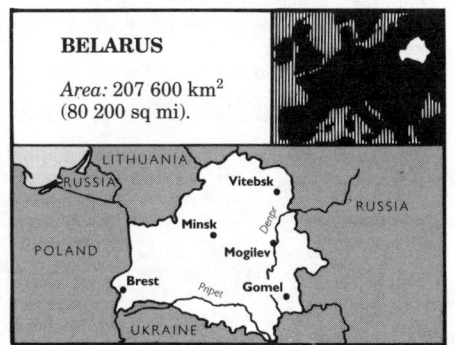

BELARUS

Area: 207 600 km² (80 200 sq mi).

LITHUANIA
RUSSIA
Vitebsk
RUSSIA
Minsk
Dnepr
POLAND
Mogilev
Brest
Pripet
Gomel
UKRAINE

REGIONS

Population figures are from the 1991 census.

Brussels (Bruxelles/Brussel) *Area:* 162 km^2 (63 sq mi). *Population:* 960 000. *Administrative centre:* Brussels.

Flanders (Vlaanderen) *Area:* 13 512 km^2 (5217 sq mi). *Population:* 5 725 000. *Administrative centre:* Ghent.

Wallonia (Wallonie) *Area:* 16 844 km^2 (6503 sq mi). *Population:* 3 165 000. *Administrative centre:* Namur.

GEOGRAPHY

The forested Ardennes plateau occupies the southeast of the country. The plains of central Belgium, an important agricultural region, are covered in fertile loess. The north, which is flat and low-lying, contains the sandy Kempenland plateau in the east and the plain of Flanders in the west. Enclosed by dykes behind coastal sand dunes are polders – former marshes and lagoons reclaimed from the sea. *Principal rivers*: Scheldt (Schelde or Escaut), Meuse (Maes), Sambre. *Highest point*: Botrange 694 m (2272 ft).

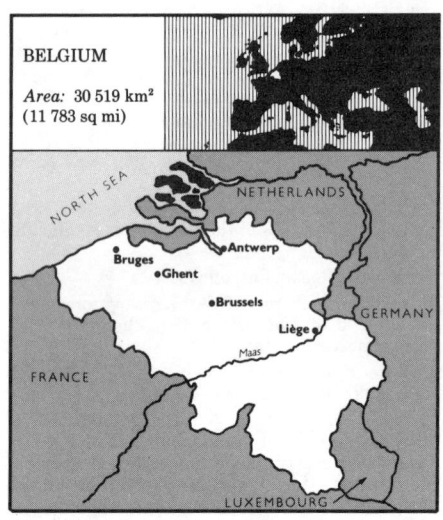

Climate: Belgium experiences relatively cool summers and mild winters, with ample rainfall throughout the year. Summers are hotter and winters colder inland.

ECONOMY

Belgium is a small, densely populated industrial country with few natural resources. In the centre and the north, soils are generally fertile and the climate encourages high yields of wheat, sugar beet, grass and fodder crops. Metalworking – originally based on small mineral deposits in the Ardennes – is the most important industry. Textiles, chemicals, ceramics, glass and rubber are also important, but, apart from coal, almost all the raw materials required by industry now have to be imported. Economic problems since the 1970s have mirrored Belgium's linguistic divide, with high unemployment largely confined to the French-speaking (Walloon) south, while the industries of the Flemish

north have prospered. Banking, commerce and, in particular, administration employ increasing numbers, and Brussels has benefited from its role as the unofficial EC 'capital'.

RECENT HISTORY

Belgium's neutrality was broken by the German invasion in 1914 (which led to Britain's declaration of war against Germany). The brave resistance of King Albert in 1914–18 earned international admiration; the capitulation of Leopold III when Belgium was again occupied by Germany (1940–45) was severely criticized. The Belgian Congo (Zaïre), acquired as a personal possession by Leopold II (1879), was relinquished amidst scenes of chaos in 1960. Belgium is now the main centre of administration of the EC and of NATO, but the country is troubled by the acute rivalry between its Flemish and French speakers and a federal system based on linguistic regions has gradually evolved.

BELIZE

Member of: UN, Commonwealth, CARICOM, OAS.

Area: 22 965 km^2 (8867 sq mi).

Population: 191 000 (1991 est).

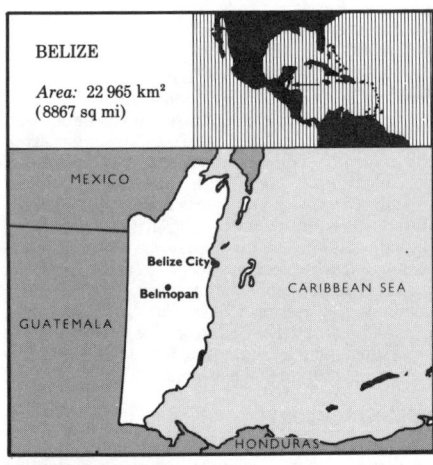

Capital and major cities: Belmopan 4000, Belize City 50 000, Orange Walk 10 500, Corozal 8500, Dangriga 8000 (1989 est).

Languages: English (majority; official), Creole (33%), Spanish (32%), Garifuna (7%).

Religions: Roman Catholic (62%), various Protestant Churches (28% – mainly Anglican and Methodist).

Education: *Literacy rate*: 90% (1988 est). *Years of compulsory schooling*: 6–14. *Universities*: 1 university college plus 1 department of University of West Indies.

Defence: *Total armed strength*: 660 (1991). *Military service*: none.

GOVERNMENT

The eight members of the Senate (the upper house of the National Assembly) are appointed by the Governor General, the representative of the British Queen as sovereign of Belize. The 28 members of the House of Representatives (the lower house) are elected by

universal adult suffrage for five years. The Governor General appoints a Prime Minister, who commands a majority in the House, and – on the PM's advice – a Cabinet, which is responsible to the House. The main political parties are the People's United Party and the United Democratic Party.
Prime Minister: George Price.

GEOGRAPHY

Tropical jungle covers much of Belize. The south contains the Maya Mountains. The north is mainly swampy lowlands. *Principal rivers*: Hondo, Belize, New River. *Highest point*: Victoria Peak 1122 m (3681 ft).

Climate: The subtropical climate is tempered by trade winds. Rainfall is heavy, but there is a dry season between February and May.

ECONOMY

The production of sugar, bananas and citrus fruit for export dominates the economy.

RECENT HISTORY

The colony of British Honduras was renamed Belize in 1973 and gained independence in 1981. Following a severe hurricane in 1961, the capital was moved inland from Belize City to a purpose-built new town, Belmopan. Guatemala continued to claim Belize as part of her territory until 1991.

BENIN

Official name: La République du Bénin (the Republic of Benin).
Member of: UN, OAU, ECOWAS.
Area: 112 622 km² (43 484 sq mi).
Population: 4 776 000 (1991 est).
Capital and major cities: Porto-Novo 208 000, Cotonou 487 000, Parakou 66 000 (1983 est).
Languages: French (official), Fon (47%), Adja (12%).
Religions: Animist (61%), Sunni Islam (16%), various Christian Churches (22% – mainly Roman Catholic).

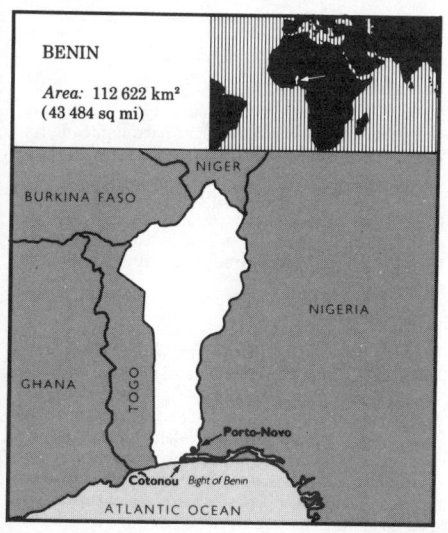

BENIN

Area: 112 622 km²
(43 484 sq mi)

Education *Literacy rate*: 23.4% (1990). *Years of compulsory schooling*: (in theory) 6–13. *Universities*: 1.

Defence *Total armed strength*: 12 000. *Military service*: selective.

GOVERNMENT

An executive President and an 80-member National Assembly are elected by universal adult suffrage for four years. Multi-party elections in 1991 were contested by 34 political parties.
President: Nicephore Soglo.

GEOGRAPHY

In the northwest lies the Atacora Massif; in the northeast, plains slope down to the Niger Valley. The plateaux of central Benin fall in the south to a low fertile region. A narrow coastal plain is backed by lagoons. *Principal rivers*: Ouémé, Niger. *Highest point*: Atacora Massif 635 m (2083 ft).
Climate: The north is tropical; the south is equatorial.

ECONOMY

The economy is based on agriculture, which occupies the majority of the labour force. The main food crops are cassava (manioc), yams and maize; the principal cash crop is palm oil. In the late 1980s, central planning was abandoned in favour of a market economy.

RECENT HISTORY

Benin was known as Dahomey until 1975. Political turmoil followed independence from France in 1960, and five army coups took place between 1963 and 1972. The regime established by Colonel Kérékou in 1972 brought some stability, and after 1987, experiments with state socialism were moderated. In 1989 President Kérékou disavowed Marxist-Leninism, and appointed a civilian administration to guide Benin towards becoming a market economy. Kérékou was defeated in multi-party elections in 1991. Benin has since sought Western assistance.

BHUTAN

Official name: Druk-yul (Realm of the Dragon).
Member of: UN, SAARC.
Area: 46 500 km² (17 954 sq mi).
Population: 1 442 000 (1990 UN est; a 1992 Bhutanese government estimate gives a population of over 700 000).
Capital: Thimphu 60 000 (1987 est).
Languages: Dzongkha (Tibetan; official; 70%); Nepali (30%).
Religions: Buddhist (70%), Hindu (30%).
Education: *Literacy rate*: 15% (1988). *Years of compulsory education*: education is free but not compulsory. *Universities*: 1 university and 1 polytechnic.
Defence: *Total armed strength*: 5000 (1991). *Military service*: part-time militia training (selective).

GOVERNMENT

Bhutan is a hereditary monarchy without a written constitution. The King shares power with a Council of Ministers, the National Assembly and the head of Bhutan's 5000 Buddhist monks. Of the 150 members of the National Assembly, 100 are directly elected by universal adult suffrage for a three-year term; the remainder include the Royal Advisory Council, the Ministers and 10 religious representatives. There are no political parties.

King: HM the *Druk Gyalpo* Jigme Singhye Wangchuk, King of Bhutan (succeeded 24 July 1972 on the death of his father).

GEOGRAPHY

The Himalaya make up most of the country. The valleys of central Bhutan are wide and fertile. The narrow Duars Plain – a subtropical jungle – lies along the Indian border. *Principal rivers*: Amo-chu, Wang-chu, Machu. *Highest point*: Khula Kangri 7554 m (24 784 ft).

Climate: Hot and very wet in the Duars Plain, temperatures get progressively lower with altitude resulting in glaciers and permanent snow cover in the north. Precipitation is heavy.

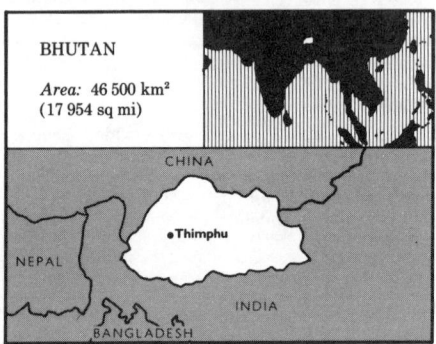

BHUTAN

Area: 46 500 km²
(17 954 sq mi)

ECONOMY

Bhutan is one of the poorest and least developed countries in the world. Farm workers producing food crops account for about 90% of the labour force.

RECENT HISTORY

In 1907 the governor of Tongsa became the first king of Bhutan. In 1949 India returned to Bhutan territory that had been annexed by British India in 1865, but India also assumed influence over Bhutan's external affairs. Bhutan remains largely closed to outside influences and measures taken in the 1990s discriminate against the Nepali minority in favour of the Bhutanese.

BOLIVIA

Official name: República de Bolivia (Republic of Bolivia).

Member of: UN, OAS, ALADI, Andean Pact.

Area: 1 098 581 km² (424 164 sq mi).

Population: 7 530 000 (1991 est).

Capital and major cities: La Paz (administrative capital) 1 050 000, Sucre (legal capital) 96 000, Santa Cruz 615 000, Cochabamba 377 000, Oruro 195 000, Potosí 114 000, Tarija 69 000 (1988 est).

Languages: Spanish (official; 55%), Quéchua (5%), Aymara (22%).

Religion: Roman Catholic (official; 95%).

Education: *Literacy rate*: 77.5% (1990). *Years of compulsory schooling*: 6–13. *Universities*: 8 state and 2 private universities.

Defence: *Total armed strength*: 31 000 (1991). *Military service*: 1 year selective.

GOVERNMENT

The President (who appoints a Cabinet), the 27-member Senate and the 130-member Chamber of Deputies are elected for four-year terms by universal adult suffrage. The main political parties are the Movimiento Nacionalista Revolucionario and Acción Democrática Nacionalista.

President: Jaime Paz Zamora.

GEOGRAPHY

The Andes divide into two parallel chains between which is an extensive undulating depression (the Altiplano), containing Lake Titicaca, the highest navigable lake in the world. In the east and north-east, a vast lowland includes tropical rain forests (the Llanos), subtropical plains and semiarid grasslands (the Chaco). *Principal rivers*: Beni, Mamoré, Pilcomayo, Paraguay. *Highest point*: Sajama 6542 m (21 463 ft).

Climate: Rainfall is negligible in the southwest, and heavy in the northeast. Temperature varies with altitude from the cold Andean summits and cool, windy Altiplano to the tropical northeast.

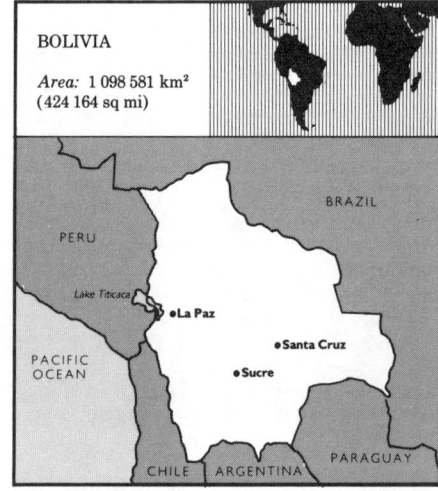

BOLIVIA

Area: 1 098 581 km²
(424 164 sq mi)

ECONOMY

Bolivia is a relatively poor country, despite being rich in natural resources such as petroleum and tin. Lack of investment, political instability and the high cost of extraction have retarded development. Agriculture, which is labour intensive, produces domestic foodstuffs (potatoes and maize), as well as export crops (sugar cane and cotton). The cultivation of coca (the source of cocaine) is causing concern.

RECENT HISTORY

In three devastating wars – the War of the Pacific (1879–83), alongside Peru against Chile, and the Chaco Wars (1928–30 and 1933–35) against Paraguay – Bolivia sustained great human and territorial losses. For most of its independent history Bolivia has been characterized by political instability with a succession of military and civilian governments. Since 1982, however, Bolivia has had democratically elected governments.

BOSNIA-HERZEGOVINA

Official name: Bosna i Hercegovina (Bosnia-Herzegovina).

Member of: UN, CSCE.

Area: 51 129 km² (19 741 sq mi).

Population: 4 365 000 (1991 census); c. 2 000 000–2 500 000 (late 1992 est; up to 2 000 000 refugees left Bosnia in 1992 and over 150 000 people have been killed in the war).

Capital and major cities: Sarajevo 526 000 (city 416 000; by 1993 the population of Sarajevo was c. 200 000–250 000), Tuzla 130 000 (by 1993 the population of Tuzla had increased to over 230 000), Banja Luka 143 000, Mostar 110 000 (1991 census).

Language: Serbo-Croat – a single language with two written forms.

Religions: (pre-1991 figures) Sunni Islam (44%), Serbian Orthodox (33%), Roman Catholic (17%).

Education: *Literacy rate:* 92.7% (1990 est). *Years of compulsory schooling:* 7–15. *Universities:* 4.

Defence: *Total armed strength:* 90 000 Bosnian government forces (1993 est).

GOVERNMENT

There is constitutional provision for an Assembly and a President – who appoints a Prime Minister and a Cabinet of Ministers – to be directly elected by universal adult suffrage for four years. In early 1993 the government's authority was restricted to about 10% of central Bosnia.
President: Alija Izetbegovic.

GEOGRAPHY

Ridges of the Dinaric Mountains, rising to over 1800 m (6000 ft), occupy the greater part of the country and in places form arid karst limestone plateaux. The N comprises restricted lowlands in the valley of the River Sava. The combined length of two tiny coastlines on the Adriatic is less than 20 km (13 mi). *Principal rivers:* Sava, Drina, Bosna. *Highest point:* Maglic 2387 m (9118 ft).

Climate: Bosnia (the N) has cold winters and warm summers; Herzegovina (the S) enjoys milder winters and warmer summers.

ECONOMY

The economy was devastated by war in 1992–93. Central and E Bosnia is forested. Agriculture has traditionally been a major employer with sheep, maize, olives, grapes and citrous fruit as the most important interests. Bosnia has little industrybut possesses natural resources including including coal, lignite, copper and asphalt.

RECENT HISTORY

A major Bosnian revolt (1875–6) attracted international concern, but the great powers overrode Bosnia's pan-Slavic aspirations at the Congress of Berlin (1877–8) and assigned Bosnia-Herzegovina to Habsburg Austro-Hungarian rule. In Sarajevo in 1914, Gavrilo Princip, a Bosnian Serb student, assassinated Archduke Franz Ferdinand, the heir to the Austro-Hungarian Empire – an event that helped precipitate World War I. In 1918, Bosnia became part of the new Kingdom of Serbs, Croats and Slovenes, which was renamed Yugoslavia in 1929. Following the German invasion (1941), Bosnia was included in the Axis-controlled puppet state of Croatia. In 1945, when Yugoslavia was reorganized by Marshal Tito on Soviet lines, Bosnia-Herzegovina became a republic within the Communist federation. After the secession of Slovenia and Croatia and the beginning of the Yugoslav civil war (1991), tension grew between Serbs and Croats in Bosnia. The Muslim Bosnians reasserted their separate identity. In 1992, a referendum – which was boycotted by the Serbs – gave a majority in favour of Bosnian independence. International recognition of Bosnia-Herzegovina was gained in April 1992 but Bosnian Serbs, encouraged by Serbia, seized 70% of the country, killing or expelling Muslims and Croats in a campaign of 'ethnic cleansing'. International peace and humanitarian efforts were attempted and in an attempt to contain the Bosnian Serbs strict UN sanctions were imposed on Serbia and Montenegro (Yugoslavia).

BOTSWANA

Official name: The Republic of Botswana.

Member of: UN, OAU, Commonwealth, SADCC.

Area: 582 000 km² (224 711 sq mi).

Population: 1 320 000 (1991 est).

Capital and major cities: Gaborone 130 000 (1991 est), Francistown 56 000, Selibi-Pikwe 53 500 (1990 est).

Languages: English (official), Setswana (national).

Religions: Animist (over 50%), various Christian Churches – mainly Congregational, Anglican, Roman Catholic.

Education: *Literacy rate:* 86.7% (1990). *Years of compulsory schooling:* schooling is not compulsory. *Universities:* 1.

Defence: *Total armed strength:* 115 000 (1991) (plus 80 000 paramilitary). *Military service:* 1–2 years.

GOVERNMENT

Thirty-four of the 40 members of the National Assembly are elected by universal adult suffrage for five years. Of the remainder, four are nominated by the President and specially elected; the Speaker and Attorney General are non-voting members. The President, who chairs and appoints a Cabinet, is elected for five years by the Assembly. (There is also a 15-member House of Chiefs whose sole brief is to deal with tribal, constitutional and chieftancy matters.) The main political parties are the Botswana Democratic Party and the Botswana National Front. *President:* Dr Quett Masire.

BOSNIA-HERZEGOVINA

Area: 51 129 km² (19 741 sq mi).

CROATIA

Banja Luka

Sarajevo

Mostar

YUGOSLAVIA

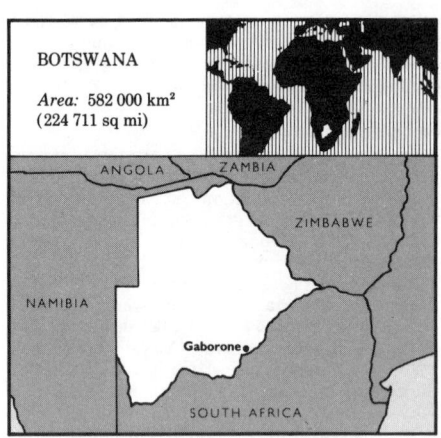

BOTSWANA

Area: 582 000 km²
(224 711 sq mi)

ANGOLA   ZAMBIA

ZIMBABWE

NAMIBIA

Gaborone

SOUTH AFRICA

GEOGRAPHY

A central plateau divides a flat near-desert in the east of Botswana from the Kalahari Desert and Okavango Swamps in the west. *Principal rivers*: Chobe, Shashi. *Highest point*: Tsodilo Hill 1375 m (4511 ft).

Climate: The climate is subtropical with extremes of heat and occasionally temperatures below freezing. Most of Botswana is periodically subject to drought.

ECONOMY

Nomadic cattle herding and the cultivation of subsistence crops occupies the majority of the labour force. The mainstay of the economy is mining for diamonds, copper-nickel and coal.

RECENT HISTORY

The area became the British protectorate of Bechuanaland in 1885. Development was slow, and many Africans had to seek work in South Africa. Nationalism was late to develop, and independence – as Botswana – was granted without a struggle in 1966. Under the first president, Sir Seretse Khama, and his successor, Botswana has succeeded in remaining a democracy.

BRAZIL

Official name: A República Federativa do Brasil (the Federative Republic of Brazil).

Member of: UN, OAS, ALADI, Mercosur.

Area: 8 511 965 km² (3 286 488 sq mi).

Population: 153 322 000 (1991 est).

Capital and major cities: Brasília 1 864 000 (city 1 841 000), São Paulo 16 832 000 (city 9 700 000), Rio de Janeiro 11 141 000 (city 5 487 000), Belo Horizonte 3 446 000 (city 2 103 000), Recife 2 945 000 (city 1 336 000), Pôrto Alegre 2 924 000 (city 1 255 000), Salvador 2 362 000 (city 2 075 000), Fortaleza 2 169 000 (city 1 709 000), Curitiba 1 926 000 (city 1 248 000), Nova Iguaçu (part of Rio de Janeiro agglomeration) 1 325 000, Belém 1 296 000 (city 1 236 000), Goiânia 998 000, Manaus 997 000 (1991 est).

Language: Portuguese (official).

Religions: Roman Catholic (89%), various Protestant Churches (7%), Candomble.

Education: *Literacy rate*: 81.2% (1989). *Years of compulsory schooling*: 7–14. *Universities*: 74.

Defence: *Total armed strength*: 296 700 (1991). *Military service*: 1 year.

GOVERNMENT

The President – who appoints and chairs a Cabinet – is elected for a five-year term by universal adult suffrage. The lower house of the National Congress (the Chamber of Deputies) has 503 members elected for four years by compulsory universal adult suffrage. The 91-member upper house (the Federal Senate) is elected directly for an eight-year term – one third and two thirds of the senators retiring alternately every four years. Each of the 26 states and the Federal District of Brasília has its own legislature. The principal political parties are the (moderate) PMDB (Brazilian Democratic Movement), the (moderate) PFL (Liberal Front), the (conservative) National Reconstruction Party, the (socialist) PT (Worker's Party) and the Democratic Labour Party. A referendum in 1993 rejected the options of either a parliamentary system or a restoration of the monarchy in favour of the present presidential system.
President: Itamar Franco.

GUYANA
VENEZUELA   SURINAME
                FRENCH GUIANA
COLUMBIA
          Amazon
PERU
                    Brasília   Salvador
                                 (Bahía)
ECUADOR   BOLIVIA
PARAGUAY
                              Rio de Janeiro
                              São Paulo
CHILE
ARGENTINA
                    URUGUAY   OCEAN

BRAZIL

Area: 8 511 965 km²
(3 286 488 sq mi)

ATLANTIC

BRAZILIAN STATES AND TERRITORIES

Population figures are 1991 estimates.

Acre *Area*: 152 589 km² (58 915 sq mi). *Population*: 428 000. *Capital*: Rio Branco.

Alagoas *Area*: 27 731 km² (10 707 sq mi). *Population*: 2 459 000. *Capital*: Maceió.

Amazonas *Area*: 1 564 445 km² (604 032 sq mi). *Population*: 2 055 000. *Capital*: Manaus.

Bahia *Area*: 561 026 km² (216 612 sq mi). *Population*: 11 953 000. *Capital*: Salvador.

Ceará *Area*: 150 630 km² (58 158 sq mi). *Population*: 6 587 000. *Capital*: Fortaleza.

Espirito Santo *Area*: 45 597 km² (17 605 sq mi). *Population*: 2 571 000. *Capital*: Vitória.

Goiás *Area*: 364 770 km² (140 838 sq mi). *Population*: 4 036 000. *Capital*: Goiânia.

Maranhão *Area*: 328 663 km² (126 897 sq mi). *Population*: 5 287 000. *Capital*: São Luis.

Mato Grosso *Area*: 881 001 km² (340 154 sq mi). *Population*: 1 776 000. *Capital*: Cuiaba.

Mato Grosso do Sul *Area*: 350 548 km² (135 347 sq mi). *Population*: 1 838 000. *Capital*: Campo Grande.

Minas Gerais *Area*: 587 172 km² (226 707 sq mi). *Population*: 16 071 000. *Capital*: Belo Horizonte.

Pará *Area*: 1 250 722 km² (482 904 sq mi). *Population*: 5 142 000. *Capital*: Belém.

Paraíba *Area*: 56 372 km² (21 765 sq mi). *Population*: 3 294 000. *Capital*: João Pessoa.

Paraná *Area*: 199 554 km² (77 048 sq mi). *Population*: 9 340 000. *Capital*: Curitiba.

Pernambuco *Area*: 98 281 km² (37 946 sq mi). *Population*: 7 482 000. *Capital*: Recife.

Piauí *Area*: 250 934 km² (96 886 sq mi). *Population*: 2 715 000. *Capital*: Teresina.

Rio de Janeiro *Area*: 44 268 km² (17 092 sq mi). *Population*: 14 420 000. *Capital*: Rio de Janeiro.

Rio Grande do Norte *Area*: 53 015 km² (20 469 sq mi). *Population*: 2 360 000. *Capital*: Natal.

Rio Grande do Sul *Area*: 282 184 km² (108 951 sq mi). *Population*: 9 298 000. *Capital*: Pôrto Alegre.

Rondônia *Area*: 243 044 km² (93 839 sq mi). *Population*: 1 135 000. *Capital*: Pôrto Velho.

Santa Catarina *Area*: 95 985 km² (37 060 sq mi). *Population*: 4 536 000. *Capital*: Florianópolis.

São Paulo *Area*: 247 898 km² (95 714 sq mi). *Population*: 33 777 000. *Capital*: São Paulo.

Sergipe *Area*: 21 994 km² (84 919 sq mi). *Population*: 1 440 000. *Capital*: Aracaju.

Tocantins *Area:* 277 322 km² (107 075 sq mi). *Population:* 1 009 000. *Capital*: Palmas.

Amapá (territory) *Area*: 140 276 km² (54 161 sq mi). *Population:* 264 000. *Capital*: Macapá.

Federal District (Distrito Federal) *Area*: 5814 km² (2245 sq mi). *Population:* 1 925 000. *Capital*: Brasília.

Fernando de Noronha (territory) *Area*: 26 km² (10 sq mi). *Population*: 1300. The island territory is administered from the mainland.

Roraima (territory) *Area*: 230 104 km² (88 843 sq mi). *Population:* 124 000. *Capital*: Boa Vista.

GEOGRAPHY

Nearly one half of Brazil is drained by the world's largest river system, the Amazon, whose wide, low-lying basin is still largely covered by tropical rain forest, although pressure on land has led to extensive deforestation. North of the Amazon Basin, the Guiana Highlands contain Brazil's highest peak. A central plateau of savannah grasslands lies south of the Basin. The east and south of the country contain the Brazilian Highlands – a vast plateau divided by fertile valleys and mountain ranges. A densely populated narrow coastal plain lies at the foot of the Highlands. *Principal rivers*: Amazon, Paraná, São Francisco, Madeira, Juruá, Purus. *Highest point*: Pico da Neblina 3014 m (9888 ft).

Climate: The Amazon Basin and the southeast coast are tropical with heavy rainfall. The rest of Brazil is either subtropical or temperate (in the savannah). Only the northeast has inadequate rainfall.

ECONOMY

Agriculture employs about one quarter of the labour force. The principal agricultural exports include coffee, sugar cane, soyabeans, oranges, beef cattle and cocoa. Timber was important, but environmental concern is restricting its trade. Rapid industrialization since 1945 has made Brazil a major manufacturing country. While textiles, clothing and food processing are still the biggest industries, the iron and steel, chemical, petroleum-refining, cement, electrical, motor-vehicle and fertilizer industries have all attained international stature. Brazil has enormous – and, in part, unexploited – natural resources, including iron ore, phosphates, uranium, copper, manganese, bauxite, coal and vast hydroelectric-power potential. In the last two decades, rampant inflation has hindered development.

RECENT HISTORY

In 1889 a coup ended the long reign of the liberal Emperor Pedro II and established a republic. The republic was initially stable, but social unrest mounted and, in 1930, Getúlio Vargas seized power. Vargas attempted to model Brazil on Mussolini's Italy, but was overthrown by the military in 1945. In 1950, Vargas was elected president again, but he committed suicide rather than face impeachment (1954). Short-lived civilian governments preceded a further period of military rule (1964–85), during which the economy expanded rapidly, but political and social rights were restricted. Brazil returned to civilian rule in 1985 and in 1990 Brazilians were able to vote for a president for the first time in 29 years. The country faces problems concerning the development of the Amazon Basin and in balancing the needs of developers and landless peasants on the one hand and the advice of conservationists and the interests of tribal peoples on the other.

BRUNEI

Official name: Negara Brunei Darussalam (Sultanate of Brunei).

Member of: UN, Commonwealth, ASEAN.

Area: 5765 km² (2226 sq mi).

Population: 264 000 (1991 est).

Capital: Bandar Seri Begawan 52 000 (1988 est).

Languages: Malay (official; over 50%), Chinese (26%), English.

Religions: Sunni Islam (official; over 50%), Buddhist (12%), various Christian Churches (9%).

Education: *Literacy rate*: 86.8% (1990). *Years of compulsory schooling*: schooling is not compulsory. *Universities*: 1.

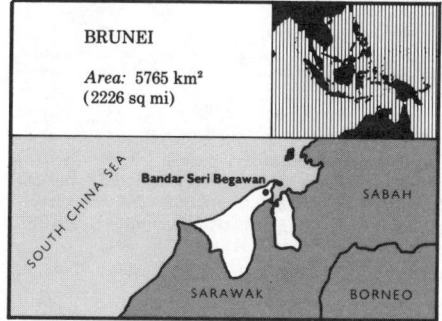

BRUNEI

Area: 5765 km² (2226 sq mi)

Defence: *Total armed strength*: 4250 (1991). *Military service*: none.

GOVERNMENT

The Sultan, a hereditary monarch, rules by decree, assisted by a Council of Ministers whom he appoints. There are no political parties.
Sultan: HM Haji Hassanal Bolkiah, Sultan of Brunei (succeeded upon the abdication of his father, 5 October 1967).

GEOGRAPHY

Brunei consists of two coastal enclaves. The (larger) western part is hilly; the eastern enclave is more mountainous and forested. *Principal river*: Brunei River. *Highest point*: Bukit Pagon (on the border with Malaysia) 1850 m (6070 ft).

Climate: Brunei has a tropical monsoon climate with rainfall totals in excess of 2500 mm (100 in).

ECONOMY

Exploitation of substantial deposits of petroleum and natural gas has given Brunei one of the world's highest per capita incomes. Most of the country's food has to be imported.

RECENT HISTORY

In the 19th century the sultans of Brunei ruled a fraction of their former territory. The British restored order to what had become a pirates' paradise and established a protectorate from 1888 to 1971. Oil was discovered in 1929. Full independence was restored in 1984 under the absolute rule of Sultan Hassanal Bolkiah, allegedly the world's richest man.

BULGARIA

Official name: Republika Bulgariya (Republic of Bulgaria).

Member of: UN, CSCE, Council of Europe.

BULGARIA

Area: 110 912 km² (42 823 sq mi).

ROMANIA

YUGOSLAVIA

Danube ● Ruse

Varna

● Sofia

BLACK SEA

● Plovdiv

TURKEY

GREECE

Area: 110 912 km² (42 823 sq mi).

Population: 9 005 000 (1991 est).

Capital and major cities: Sofia (Sofiya) 1 221 000, Plovdiv 379 000, Varna 315 000, Burgas 205 000, Ruse 192 000, Stara Zagora 165 000, Pleven 138 000, Dobrich (formerly Tolbukhin) 116 000, Sliven 112 000, Shumen 111 000 (1990 est).

Languages: Bulgarian (official; 89%), Turkish (11%).

Religions: Orthodox (80%), Sunni Islam (8%).

Education: *Literacy rate*: no figure available. *Years of compulsory schooling*: 6–16. *Universities*: 18 including 8 institutes of university status.

Defence: *Total armed strength*: 107 000 (1991 est). *Military service*: 18 months.

GOVERNMENT

The 240-member National Assembly is elected every five years by universal adult suffrage under a system of proportional representation. The President – who is directly elected for five years – appoints a Prime Minister and a Council of Ministers that enjoy a majority in the Assembly. The main political parties are the (centre) Union of Democratic Forces, the (former Communist) Socialist Party and the (Turkish) Movement for Rights and Freedom.
President: Zhelo Zhelev.
Prime Minister: Lyuben Berov.

GEOGRAPHY

The Balkan Mountains run from east to west across central Bulgaria. To the north, low-lying hills slope down to the River Danube. To the south, a belt of lowland separates the Balkan Mountains from a high, rugged massif, which includes Bulgaria's highest peak. *Principal rivers*: Danube, Iskur, Maritsa, Tundzha. *Highest point*: Musala 2925 m (9596 ft).

Climate: The continental north has warm summers and cold winters, while the southeast has a more Mediterranean climate.

ECONOMY

With fertile soils, and few other natural resources, Bulgaria has a strong agricultural base. Production is centred on large-scale, mechanized cooperatives. The principal crops include: cereals (wheat, maize, barley), fruit (grapes) and, increasingly, tobacco. Agricultural products are the basis of the food-processing, wine and tobacco industries. Eastern bloc grants helped develop industry including engineering, fertilizers and chemicals. Trade patterns were disrupted in Eastern Europe after 1990 following the social, economic and political upheavals that had swept the region. Bulgaria – whose trade links with the USSR had been particularly close – suffered more than most East European countries, with severe shortages of many commodities including oil. Industrial production declined but progress has been made towards the privatization of industry and agriculture.

RECENT HISTORY

Russian intervention in the Ottoman (Turkish) Empire in the Balkans at the end of the 19th century produced an autonomous Bulgarian state (1878). Bulgaria was a principality until 1908, and an independent kingdom until 1946. However, the boundaries, established at the Congress of Berlin (1878), failed to satisfy the Bulgarians, who waged five wars to win the lands they had been promised in the earlier Treaty of San Stefano (1877). Victorious in the first two wars (1885 and 1912), Bulgaria was on the losing side in the final Balkan War (1913) and in World Wars I and II (1915–1918 and 1941–1944), and forfeited territory. After the Red Army invaded (1944), a Communist regime, tied closely to the USSR, was established and the king was exiled (1946). Following popular demonstrations in 1989, the hardline leader Todor Zhivkov (1911–) was replaced by reformers who promised free elections and renounced the leading role of the Communist

Party. Free elections were held in June 1990, when the Bulgarian Socialist Party (BSP) – formerly the Bulgarian Communist Party – was returned to power. Faced by severe economic problems, the BSP was unable to govern alone and a coalition government with a non-party premier took office in 1991. Short-lived coalitions involving various combinations of the three main parties have followed.

BURKINA FASO

Official name: Burkina Faso or République de Burkina (previously Upper Volta).

Member of: UN, OAS, ECOWAS.

Area: 274 200 km² (105 869 sq mi).

Population: 9 261 000 (1991 est).

Capital and major cities: Ouagadougou 442 000, Bobo-Dioulasso 229 000, Koudougou 52 000, Ouahigouya 39 000, Banfora 36 000 (1985 est).

Languages: French (official), Mossi (48%), Fulani (10%).

Religions: Animist (49%), Sunni Islam (40%), various Christian Churches (11% - mainly Roman Catholic).

Education: *Literacy rate*: 18.2% (1990). *Years of compulsory schooling*: (in theory) 7–14. *Universities*: 1.

Defence: *Total armed strength*: 8700 (1991). *Military service*: none.

GOVERNMENT

The constitution provides for the election by universal adult suffrage of a 77-member Assembly for four years and a President for seven years. The Chamber of Representatives (the upper house) is indirectly elected. The main political party is the (coalition) Popular Front (FP).
Head of state: Capt Blaise Campoare.
Prime Minister: Youssouf Ouedraogo.

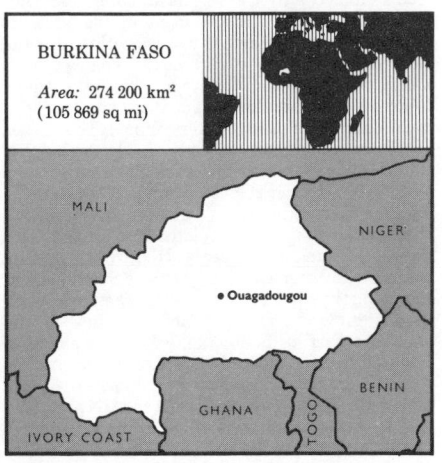

BURKINA FASO

Area: 274 200 km² (105 869 sq mi)

MALI

NIGER

● Ouagadougou

BENIN

GHANA

IVORY COAST

TOGO

GEOGRAPHY

The country consists of plateaux about 500 m (1640 ft) high. *Principal rivers*: Mouhoun (Black Volta), Nakambe (White Volta), Nazinon (Red Volta). *Highest point*: Mt Tema 749 m (2457 ft).

Climate: The country is hot and dry, with adequate rainfall – 1000 mm (40 in) – only in the savannah of the south. The north is semidesert.

ECONOMY

Burkina Faso, one of the world's poorest states, has been severely stricken by drought in the last two decades. Nomadic herdsmen and subsistence farmers – producing mainly sorghum, sugar cane and millet – form the bulk of the population. Cotton, manganese and zinc are exported.

RECENT HISTORY

Burkina Faso was the French colony of Upper Volta. During the colonial era, the country acted as a labour reservoir for more developed colonies to the south. Since independence in 1960, the country – which changed its name to Burkina Faso in 1984 – has had a turbulent political history, with a succession of military coups. After pressure for liberalization (1990–91), a new constitution was introduced in 1991 and a multi-party system restored in 1992.

BURUNDI

Official name: La République du Burundi or Republika y'Uburundi (The Republic of Burundi).

Member of: UN, OAU.

Area: 27 834 km² (10 747 sq mi).

Population: 5 611 000 (1991 est).

Capital and major city: Bujumbura 227 000, Gitega 95 000 (1990 est).

Languages: Kirundi (majority) and French – both official, Kiswahili.

Religion: Roman Catholic (65%).

Education: *Literacy rate*: 50% (1990). *Years of compulsory schooling*: (in theory) 7–12. *Universities*: 1.

Defence: *Total armed strength*: 7200 (1991). *Military service*: none.

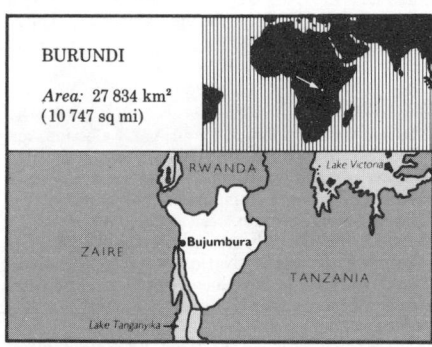

BURUNDI

Area: 27 834 km² (10 747 sq mi)

RWANDA

Lake Victoria

ZAIRE

●Bujumbura

TANZANIA

Lake Tanganyika

GOVERNMENT

Power is held by a 31-member military committee, whose Chairman is President. The Committee has appointed a civilian Council of Ministers. A multi-party system was reintroduced in 1993 and free elections were held.
President: Maj. Pierre Buyoya.
Prime Minister: Adrien Sibomana.

GEOGRAPHY

Burundi is a high plateau, rising from Lake Tanganyika in the west. *Principal rivers*: Kagera, Ruzizi. *Highest point*: Mt Hela 2685 m (8809 ft).

Climate: The lowlands are hot and humid. Temperatures are cooler in the mountains.

ECONOMY

Farmers and farm labourers account for over 92% of the labour force. Agriculture produces both subsistence crops and crops for export, such as coffee.

RECENT HISTORY

Burundi was a semi-feudal kingdom in which the minority Tutsi tribe of pastoralists dominated the Hutu majority of agriculturalists. Colonized by Germany in 1890, it was taken over by Belgium after World War I under a League of Nations mandate. Independence came in 1962, after much conflict throughout the country. Following a military coup in 1966, a republic was established. The killing of the deposed king in 1972 led to a massacre of the Hutu. There have since been further coups. Serious ethnic unrest in 1988 led to an exodus of Hutu refugees to Rwanda.

CAMBODIA

Official name: Roat Kampuchea (The State of Cambodia) – previously known as the Khmer Republic and Kampuchea.

Member of: UN.

Area: 181 035 km² (69 898 sq mi).

Population: 8 780 000 (1991 est).

Capital and major cities: Phnom-Penh 900 000 (1991 est), Battambang 45 000, Kampong Chan 32 000 (1987 est).

Languages: Khmer (official), French.

Religion: Buddhist (official; majority).

Education: *Literacy rate*: 87.5% (1991 est). *Years of compulsory schooling*: (in theory) 5–14. *Universities*: 1.

Defence: *Total armed strength*: 112 000 (1991 est) plus KPNLF c. 12 000 and Prince Sihanouk's National Army of Independent Cambodia c. 17 000. *Military service*: 5 years.

GOVERNMENT

Internationally supervised multi-party elections are scheduled to be held in 1993 for a 123-member National Assembly, which will draft a new constitution. Government remains in the hands of the existing administration, assisted by the UN. Sovereignty is temporarily vested in the hands of a 12-member Supreme National Council (whose membership has been reduced to 10 since the withdrawal of the Khmer Rouge). The main political parties are the (monarchist) FUNCINPEC, the (left-wing) Khmer People's National Liberation Front (KPNLF), the (former Communist) Cambodian People's Party and the (Khmer Rouge) Party of Democratic Kampuchea.

Head of state: Heng Samrin.
Head of the Supreme National Council: HRH Prince Norodom Sihanouk.
Prime Minister: Hun Sen.

GEOGRAPHY

Central Cambodia consists of fertile plains in the Mekong River valley and surrounding the Tonle Sap (Great Lake). To the north and east are plateaux covered by forests and savannah. The southern Phnom Kravanh mountains run parallel to the coast. *Principal river*: Mekong. *Highest point*: Phnum Aoral 1813 m (5947 ft).

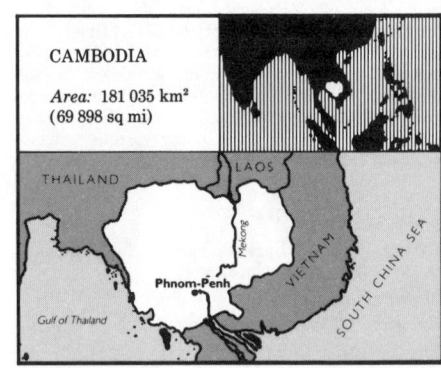

CAMBODIA

Area: 181 035 km²
(69 898 sq mi)

THAILAND · LAOS · VIETNAM · SOUTH CHINA SEA · Mekong · Phnom-Penh · Gulf of Thailand

Climate: Cambodia is tropical and humid. The monsoon season (June–November) brings heavy rain to the whole country, with annual totals as high as 5000 mm (200 in) in the mountains.

ECONOMY

Invasion, civil wars, massacres of the civilian population (1976–79) and the (temporary) abolition of currency (in 1978) all but destroyed the economy. Aided by the Vietnamese since 1979, agriculture and – to a lesser extent – industry have been slowly rebuilt, but Cambodia remains one of the world's poorest nations. Rice yields – formerly exported – still fall short of Cambodia's own basic needs.

HISTORY

A French protectorate was established in 1863 and continued, apart from Japanese occupation during World War II, until independence was regained in 1953. Throughout the colonial period, Cambodia's monarchy remained in nominal control. In 1955, King (now Prince) Norodom Sihanouk abdicated to lead a broad coalition government, but he could not prevent Cambodia's involvement in the Vietnam War or allay US fears of his sympathies for the Communists. In 1970 he was overthrown in a pro-US military coup. The military regime was attacked by Communist Khmer Rouge guerrillas, who sought to create a self-sufficient workers' utopia. The Khmer Rouge were finally victorious in 1975. Under Pol Pot, they forcibly evacuated the towns and massacred up to 2 000 000 of their compatriots. In 1978 Vietnam – Cambodia's traditional foe – invaded, overthrowing the Khmer Rouge. After Vietnamese troops withdrew in 1989, resistance forces of the exiled tripartite coalition government – led by Prince Sihanouk and including the Khmer Rouge – became active in much of western and southern Cambodia. In 1991 the country's warring factions agreed a peace plan that included free elections and UN supervision, and the reduction of all Cambodian forces. A large UN peace keeping force was deployed (1992) and UN participation in the administration of Cambodia was agreed. However, violence resumed when the Khmer Rouge effectively withdrew from the peace plan.

CAMEROON

Official name: La République unie du Cameroun (The United Republic of Cameroon).

Member of: UN, OAU.

Area: 475 442 km² (183 569 sq mi).

Population: 12 239 000 (1991 est).

Capital and major cities: Yaoundé 712 000, Douala 1 117 000, Nkongsamba 112 000, Maroua 106 000, Bafoussam 99 000 (1987 est).

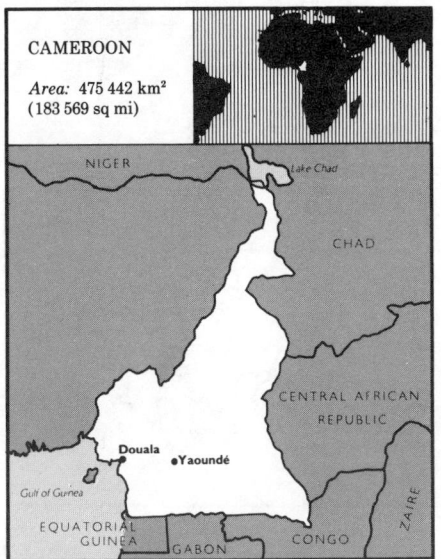

CAMEROON

Area: 475 442 km² (183 569 sq mi)

Languages: French and English (both official), Fulani, Sao, Bamileke.

Religions: Animist (40%), Sunni Islam (20%), Roman Catholic (20%).

Education: *Literacy rate*: 54.1% (1985 est). *Years of compulsory schooling*: (in theory) 6–12 (East Cameroon; 6–13 in West Cameroon but not compulsory). *Universities*: 1 plus 5 university colleges.

Defence: *Total armed strength*: 7700 (1991) plus 4 000 paramilitary. *Military service*: none.

GOVERNMENT

The 180 members of the National Assembly are elected for a five-year term by universal adult suffrage. The President – who is also directly elected for a five-year term – appoints a Council of Ministers and a Prime Minister. The main political parties are the (former monopoly) Cameroon People's Democratic Movement (RDPC), the Cameroon People's Union (UPC) and the Democratic Movement for the Defence of the Republic (RDDR).
President: Paul Biya.
Prime Minister: Simon Achidi Achu.

GEOGRAPHY

In the west, a chain of highlands rises to the volcanic Mont Cameroun. In the north, savannah plains dip towards Lake Chad. The coastal plains and plateaux in the south and the centre are covered with tropical forest. *Principal rivers*: Sanaga, Nyong. *Highest point*: Mont Cameroun 4069 m (13 353 ft).

Climate: Cameroon is tropical, with hot, rainy conditions on the coast, but drier inland.

ECONOMY

Cameroon is a major producer of cocoa, and other export crops include bananas, coffee, cotton, rubber and palm oil. The diversity of Cameroon's agriculture, and the rapid development of the petroleum industry, have given the country one of the highest standards of living in tropical Africa.

RECENT HISTORY

Germany declared a protectorate over Kamerun in 1884. After World War I, Cameroon was divided between the UK and France. The French Cameroons became independent in 1960. Following a plebiscite (1961), the north of the British Cameroons merged with Nigeria; the south federated with the former French territory. A unitary state replaced the federation in 1972. A number of arrests followed attempts to establish an opposition political party in 1990. Political pluralism returned in 1992 when multiparty elections were held.

CANADA

Member of: UN, Commonwealth, OAS, NATO, CSCE, G7, NAFTA.

Area: 9 970 610 km² (3 849 674 sq mi).

Population: 27 737 000 (1992 est).

Capital and major cities: Ottawa 921 000 (city 301 000), Toronto 3 893 000 (city 612 000), Montréal 3 127 000 (city 1 015 000), Vancouver 1 603 000 (city 431 000), Edmonton 840 000 (city 574 000), Calgary 754 000 (city 636 000), Winnipeg 652 000 (city 595 000), Québec 646 000 (city 165 000), Hamilton 600 000 (city 307 000), London 382 000 (city 269 000), St Catharine's–Niagara 365 000 (St Catharine's city 123 000), Kitchener 356 000 (city 151 000), Halifax 321 000 (city 114 000), Victoria 288 000 (city 66 000), Windsor 262 000 (city 193 000), Oshawa 240 000 (city 124 000), Saskatoon 210 000 (city 178 000), Regina 192 000 (city 175 000), St John's 172 000 (city 69 000) (1991 census; city populations from the 1986 census).

Languages: English (62% as a first language; official), French (25% as a first language; official), bilingual English-French (10%).

Religions: Roman Catholic (45%), United Church of Canada (15%), Anglican (10%).

Education: *Literacy rate*: over 97% (est). *Years of compulsory schooling*: varies from province to province, generally 5–16. *Universities*: 66.

Defence: *Total armed strength*: 86 000 (1991). *Military service*: none.

GOVERNMENT

The Canadian Federal Parliament has two houses – a 118-member Senate appointed by the Governor General to represent the provinces, and the House of Commons, whose 295 members are elected for five years by universal adult suffrage. A Prime Minister, commanding a majority in the House of Commons, is appointed by the Governor General, who is the representative of the British Queen as sovereign of Canada. The PM, in turn, appoints a Cabinet of Ministers which is responsible to the House. Each province has its own government and legislature. The main political parties are the Liberal Party, the Progressive Conservative Party, the (socialist) New Democratic Party, the (radical) Reform Party and the (nationalist) Parti Québecois.
Prime Minister: Brian Mulroney (who is scheduled to resign during the summer of 1993).

CANADIAN PROVINCES AND TERRITORIES

Population figures are from the 1991 census.

Alberta *Area*: 661 199 km² (255 285 sq mi). *Population*: 2 546 000. *Capital*: Edmonton.

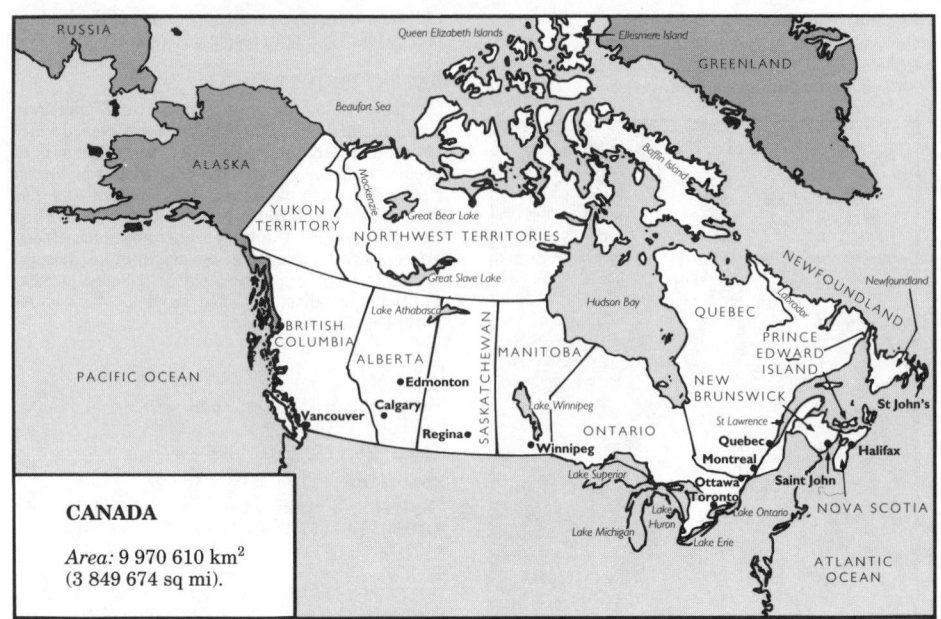

CANADA

Area: 9 970 610 km²
(3 849 674 sq mi).

British Columbia *Area*: 948 596 km² (366 255 sq mi). *Population*: 3 282 000. *Capital*: Victoria.

Manitoba *Area*: 650 087 km² (251 000 sq mi). *Population*: 1 092 000. *Capital*: Winnipeg.

New Brunswick *Area*: 73 437 km² (28 354 sq mi). *Population*: 724 000. *Capital*: Fredericton.

Newfoundland and Labrador *Area*: 404 517 km² (156 185 sq mi). *Population*: 569 000. *Capital*: St John's.

Nova Scotia *Area*: 55 490 km² (21 425 sq mi). *Population*: 900 000. *Capital*: Halifax.

Ontario *Area*: 1 068 582 km² (412 582 sq mi). *Population*: 10 085 000. *Capital*: Toronto.

Prince Edward Island *Area*: 5657 km² (2184 sq mi). *Population*: 130 000. *Capital*: Charlottetown.

Québec *Area*: 1 540 680 km² (594 860 sq mi). *Population*: 6 896 000. *Capital*: Québec.

Saskatchewan *Area*: 651 900 km² (251 700 sq mi). *Population*: 989 000. *Capital*: Regina.

Northwest Territories *Area*: 1 178 000 km² (454 900 sq mi). *Population*: 36 000. *Capital*: Yellowknife. (The Northwest Territories were divided in 1993 when Nunavut was created.)

Nunavut *Area:* 2 201 400 km² (850 000 sq mi). *Population:* 22 000. *Capital:* Iqaluit (formerly Frobisher Bay).

Yukon Territory *Area*: 482 515 km² (186 299 sq mi). *Population*: 28 000. *Capital*: Whitehorse.

GEOGRAPHY

Nearly one half of Canada is covered by the Laurentian (or Canadian) Shield, a relatively flat region of hard rocks stretching round Hudson's Bay and penetrating deep into the interior. Inland, the Shield ends in a scarp that is pronounced in the east, beside the lowlands around the St Lawrence River and the Great Lakes. To the west, a line of major lakes (including Lake Winnipeg) marks the boundary with the interior plains, the Prairies. A broad belt of mountains – over 800 km (500 mi) wide – lies west of the plains. This western cordillera comprises the Rocky, Mackenzie, Coast and St Elias Mountains – which include Canada's highest point. A lower, more discontinuous, chain of highlands borders the east of Canada, running from Baffin Island, through Labrador and into New Brunswick and Nova Scotia. *Principal rivers*: Mackenzie, Slave, Peace, St Lawrence, Yukon, Nisutlin, Nelson, Saskatchewan. *Highest point*: Mount Logan 5951 m (19 524 ft).

Climate: Much of Canada experiences extreme temperatures, with mild summers and long, cold winters. The climate in the far north is polar. Average winter temperatures only remain above freezing point on the Pacific coast. In most of British Columbia precipitation is heavy. In the rest of the country, rainfall totals are moderate or light. Nearly all of Canada experiences heavy winter snowfalls.

ECONOMY

Canada enjoys one of the highest standards of living in the world, due, in part, to great mineral resources. There are substantial deposits of zinc, nickel, gold, silver, iron ore, uranium, copper, cobalt and lead, as well as major reserves of petroleum and natural gas, and enormous hydroelectric-power potential. These resources are the basis of such industries as petroleum refining, motor vehicles, metal refining, chemicals, and iron and steel. Canada is one of the world's leading exporters of cereals – in particular, wheat from the Prairie provinces. Other agricultural interests include fruit (mainly apples), beef cattle and potatoes. Vast coniferous forests have given rise to large lumber, wood-pulp and paper industries. Rich Atlantic and Pacific fishing grounds have made Canada the world's leading exporter of fish and seafood. The country has an important banking and insurance sector, and the economy is closely linked with that of the USA within NAFTA.

RECENT HISTORY

Britain, anxious to be rid of responsibility for

Canada, encouraged confederation, and in 1867 Ontario, Québec, New Brunswick and Nova Scotia formed the Dominion of Canada. Other provinces joined between 1870 and 1905, but Newfoundland did not become part of Canada until 1949. The late 19th century saw important mineral finds, such as the Klondike gold rush, and the western provinces developed rapidly. The nation was linked by the Canadian Pacific Railway. In World War I, Canadian forces distinguished themselves at Vimy Ridge, and Canada won itself a place as a separate nation at the peace conferences after the war. The Statute of Westminster (1931) recognized Canadian independence. The Depression of the 1930s had a severe impact on Canada – Newfoundland, for example, went bankrupt. Canada played an important role in World War II and the Korean War, and was a founder member of NATO. Throughout the 1970s and 1980s, there was friction over the use and status of the French language, and separatism became an issue in Québec. The Canadian constitution was redefined in 1982, but Québec refused to ratify it. A series of constitutional amendments – the Meech Lake Accord – was formulated to persuade Québec to adhere to the constitution, but a number of English-speaking provinces would not agree to Québec being declared 'a distinct society' with additional powers. The failure of the Accord (1990) encouraged the nationalist party in Québec (the Parti Québecois) to call for 'sovereignty association' (a politically independent Québec in economic association with Canada).

CAPE VERDE

Official name: A República de Cabo Verde (The Republic of Cape Verde).

Member of: UN, OAU, ECOWAS.

Area: 4033 km² (1557 sq mi).

Population: 341 000 (1991 est).

Capital: Praia 62 000, Mindelo 47 000 (1990 est).

Languages: Portuguese (official), Crioulu (Creole; majority).

Religion: Roman Catholic (over 92%).

Education: *Literacy rate*: 66.5%. *Years of compulsory schooling*: 7–13. *Universities*: none.

Defence: *Total armed strength*: 1290 (1991). *Military service*: selective.

GOVERNMENT

The 83 members of the National People's Assembly are elected for five years by universal adult suffrage. The Assembly elects a President – also for five years – who appoints a Council of Ministers and a Prime Minister. The main political parties are the (centre) Movement for Democracy (MPD) and the (socialist) PAICV party.
President: Antonio Mascarenhas.
Prime Minister: Carlos Veiga.

GEOGRAPHY

Cape Verde consists of ten volcanic, semi-arid islands. There are no significant rivers. *Highest point*: Monte Fogo 2829 m (9281 ft).

Climate: Cooled by northeast winds, temperatures seldom exceed 27 °C (80 °F). Rainfall is low.

ECONOMY

Lack of surface water hinders agriculture, and over 90% of Cape Verde's food has to be imported. Money

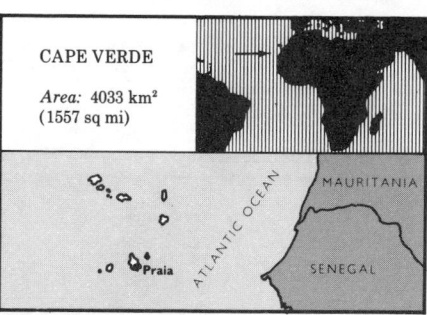

CAPE VERDE

Area: 4033 km²
(1557 sq mi)

ATLANTIC OCEAN

MAURITANIA

SENEGAL

Praia

sent back by over 600 000 Cape Verdeans living abroad is vital to the economy.

RECENT HISTORY

Cape Verde – a former Portuguese colony – was linked with Guinea-Bissau in the struggle against colonial rule, but gained independence separately in 1975. The monopoly PAICV party offended Catholics by decriminalizing abortion and unrest grew in 1987–88. Social and political reforms were agreed in 1990, and in 1991 the PAICV was overwhelmingly defeated in elections by a newly legalized opposition group – the Movement for Democracy. Since then a free market economy has been introduced.

CENTRAL AFRICAN REPUBLIC

Official name: La République Centrafricaine (The Central African Republic).

Member of: UN, OAU.

Area: 622 984 km² (240 535 sq mi).

Population: 2 937 000 (1991 est).

Capital and major cities: Bangui 598 000 (1988 est), Bambari 52 000, Bouar 50 000 (1987 est).

Languages: French (official), Sangho (national).

Religions: Various Protestant Churches (48%), Roman Catholic (32%), animist (20%).

Education: *Literacy rate*: 37.7 (1990 est). *Years of compulsory schooling*: (in theory) 6–14. *Universities*: 1.

Defence: *Total armed strength*: 3800 (1991) plus 2700 paramilitary. *Military service*: selective.

GOVERNMENT

The President – who appoints a Council of Ministers – is elected for a six-year term by universal adult suffrage. The Congress consists of a 52-member National Assembly (elected directly for a five-year term) and an Economic and Regional Council (half of whose members are elected by the Assembly; the remainder are appointed by the President). The main political parties are the (former monopoly) Rassemblement démocratique centrafricain (RDC) and the Mouvement pour la libération du peuple centrafricain (MLPC).
President: Gen. André-Dieudonné Kolingba.
Prime Minister: Edouard Franck.

GEOGRAPHY

The country is a low plateau, rising along the border with Sudan to the Bongos Mountains and in the west to the Monts Karre. *Principal rivers*: Oubangui, Zaïre, Chari. *Highest point*: Mt Gaou 1420 m (4659 ft).

Climate: The north is savannah, with little rain between November and March. The south is equatorial with high temperatures and heavy rainfall.

ECONOMY

Subsistence farming dominates, although cotton and coffee are produced for export. Diamonds contribute over 25% of the country's foreign earnings. The country is one of the poorest in the world, and – largely owing to mismanagement during Bokassa's rule – its economy has declined since independence.

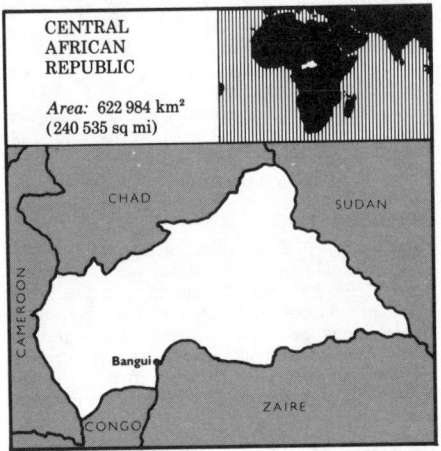

CENTRAL
AFRICAN
REPUBLIC

Area: 622 984 km²
(240 535 sq mi)

RECENT HISTORY

French influence began in 1889, and in 1903 the region became the French colony of Oubangi-Chari, which suffered greatly from the activities of companies that were granted exclusive rights to large areas of the colony. Independence – as the Central African Republic – was gained in 1960. Jean-Bédel Bokassa took power in a coup in 1965. In 1976 he declared himself emperor and was crowned in an extravagantly expensive ceremony. Revolts by students and schoolchildren helped to end his murderous regime in 1979. A multi-party system has been permitted since 1991.

CHAD

Official name: La République du Tchad (The Republic of Chad).

Member of: UN, OAU.

Area: 1 284 000 (495 750 sq mi).

Population: 5 823 000 (1991 est.)

Capital and major cities: N'Djamena 594 000, Sarh 113 000, Moundou 102 000 (1988 est).

Languages: French and Arabic (both official), plus over 100 local languages.

Religions: Sunni Islam (50%), animist (25%), various Christian Churches – mainly Roman Catholic.

Education: *Literacy rate:* 29.8% (1990 est). *Years of compulsory schooling:* (in theory) 6–14. *Universities:* 1.

Defence: *Total armed strength:* 25 000 (reduced from 47 000 in late 1991). *Military service:* selective.

GOVERNMENT

The constitution provides for a 123-member National Assembly and a President to be elected by universal adult suffrage for five years. Following a military coup in 1991, these provisions have been suspended but multi-party elections have been agreed in principle. Legislative power is currently exercised by a 31-member Consultative Provisional Republican Council.

President: Idriss Deby.
Prime Minister: Fidèle Moungar.

GEOGRAPHY

Deserts in the north include the Tibesti Mountains, the highest part of the country. Savannah and semidesert in the centre slope down to Lake Chad. The Oubangui Plateau in the south is covered by tropical rain forest. *Principal river:* Chari. *Highest point:* Emi Koussi 3415 m (11 204 ft).

Climate: Chad is hot and dry in the north, and tropical in the south.

ECONOMY

Chad – one of the poorest countries in the world – has been wracked by civil war and drought. With few natural resources, it relies on subsistence farming, exports of cotton and on foreign aid.

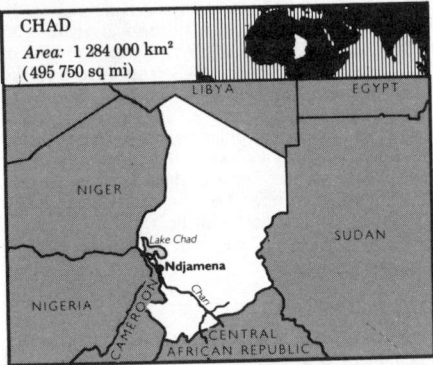

CHAD
Area: 1 284 000 km²
(495 750 sq mi)

RECENT HISTORY

The area around Lake Chad became French in the late 19th century. The French conquest of the north was not completed until 1916. Since independence in 1960, Chad has been torn apart by a bitter civil war between the Muslim Arab north and the Christian and animist Black African south. Libya and France intervened forcefully on several occasions, but neither was able to achieve its aims. In October 1988, the civil war was formally ended. However, from March 1989 the former Chadian army chief, Idriss Deby, led a rebel force from bases in Sudan against the government in N'Djamena and took control of the whole country late in 1990. Unrest continues in the north.

CHILE

Official name: República de Chile (The Republic of Chile).

Member of: UN, OAS, ALADI.

Area: 756 945 km² (292 258 sq mi).

Population: 13 385 000 (1991 est.)

Capital and major cities: Santiago (capital) 5 343 000, Valparaiso (legislative capital) 277 000, Concepción 307 000, Viña del Mar 281 000, Talcahuano 247 000, Antofagasta 219 000, Temuco 212 000 (1991 est).

Languages: Spanish (official; over 96%), Araucanian (5%).

Religions: Roman Catholic (79%), various Protestant Churches.

Education: *Literacy rate:* 93.4%. *Years of compulsory schooling:* 6 or 7–14. *Universities:* 27 including 3 institutes of university status.

Defence: *Total armed strength*: 92 000 (1991) plus 27 000 paramilitary. *Military service*: 2 years.

GOVERNMENT

Executive power is held by the President, who appoints a Cabinet of Ministers. The President is elected by universal adult suffrage for a single eight-year term. The National Congress has an upper chamber – of 38 senators directly elected for eight years and 10 senators appointed by the President – and a lower chamber of 120 deputies elected for a four-year term by universal adult suffrage. Since 1990 the National Congress has met in Valparaiso. The main political parties include the (conservative) Christian Democrat Party, the (centrist) National Renovation Party, the Socialist Party, and the (right-wing) Independent Democratic Union.
President: Patricio Aylwin.

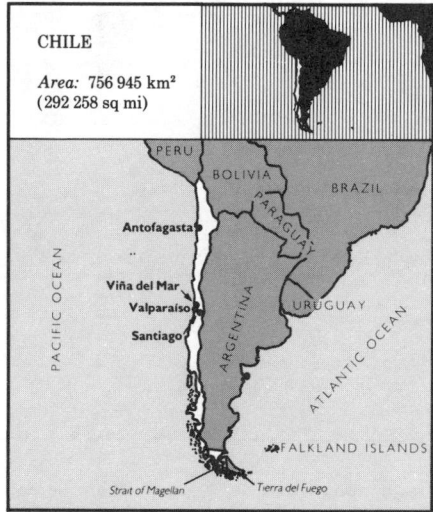

CHILE

Area: 756 945 km²
(292 258 sq mi)

GEOGRAPHY

For almost 4000 km (2500 mi), the Andes form the eastern boundary of Chile. Parallel to the Andes is a depression, in which lies the Atacama Desert in the north and fertile plains in the centre. A mountain chain runs between the depression and the coast, and, in the south, forms a string of islands. *Principal rivers*: Loa, Maule, Bio-Bio. *Highest point*: Ojos del Salado 6895 m (22 588 ft).

Climate: The temperate climate is influenced by the cool Humboldt Current. Rainfall ranges from being negligible in the Atacama Desert in the north to heavy – over 2300 mm (90 in) – in the south.

ECONOMY

The main agricultural region is the central plains, where cereals (mainly wheat and maize) and fruit (in particular grapes) are important. Excellent fishing grounds yield one of the world's largest catches of fish. There are considerable mineral resources and great hydroelectric-power potential. Chile is a leading exporter of copper, and has major reserves of iron ore, coal, petroleum, and natural gas.

RECENT HISTORY

During the century following independence (1821), conservative landowners held power and Chile gained territory in two wars against Peru and Bolivia. Between the late 1920s and the 1940s, Chile was governed by liberal and radical regimes, but social and economic change was slow. The election of the Christian Democrats (1964) brought some reforms, but not until Salvador Allende's Marxist government was elected in 1970 were major changes – including land reform – realized. Chile was polarized between right and left, and political chaos resulted in an American-backed military coup led by General Augusto Pinochet in 1973. Tens of thousands of leftists were killed, imprisoned or exiled by the junta. Pinochet reversed Allende's reforms, restructuring the economy in favour of landowners and exporters. Pressure on the dictatorship from within Chile and abroad encouraged the junta to return the country to democratic rule in 1990.

CHILEAN EXTERNAL TERRITORY

Chilean Antarctic Territory see Other Territories following this chapter.

CHINA

Official name: Zhonghua Renmin Gongheguo (The People's Republic of China).

Member of: UN.

Area 9 571 300 km² (3 695 500 sq mi).

Population: 1 150 000 000 (1991 est).

Capital and major cities: Beijing (Peking) 10 819 000, Shanghai 13 342 000, Tianjin 8 785 000, Shenyang 4 500 000, Wuhan 3 710 000, Guangzhou (Canton) 3 540 000, Chongquin 2 960 000, Harbin 2 800 000, Chengdu 2 780 000, Xian 2 710 000, Nanjing (Nanking) 2 470 000, Zibo 2 430 000, Dalian (Darien) 2 370 000, Jinan 2 290 000, Changchun 2 070 000, Qingdao (Tsingtao) 2 040 000, Shenzhen 2 000 000, Taiyuan 1 900 000, Zhengzhou 1 660 000, Kunming 1 500 000, Guiyang (Kweiyang) 1 490 000, Tangshan 1 490 000, Lanzhou (Lanchow) 1 480 000, Anshan 1 370 000, Qiqihar (Tsitsihar) 1 370 000, Fushun 1 330 000, Hangzhou 1 330 000, Nanchang 1 330 000, Changsha 1 300 000, Shijiazhuang (Shihkiachwang) 1 300 000, Fushu (Foochow) 1 270 000, Jilin (Kirin) 1 250 000, Baotou (Paotow) 1 180 000, Huainan 1 170 000, Luoyang 1 160 000, Ürümqi 1 110 000, Datong 1 090 000, Handan 1 090 000, Ningbo 1 070 000, Nanning 1 050 000 (1990 census). Twenty-one other municipalities – with overwhelmingly rural populations – have over 1 000 000 inhabitants; these municipalities are Lupanshui, Zhaozhuang, Linyi, Pingxiang, Xintao, Yancheng, Yulin, Chao'an, Dongguang, Xiaogan, Suining, Xintai, Puyang, Bozhou, Zhongshan, Laiwu, Leshan, Heze, Linhai, Macheng, and Changshu.

Languages: Chinese ('Mandarin' dialect in the majority, with local dialects in south and southeast, e.g. Cantonese, Wu), with small Mongol, Tibetan and other minorites.

Religions: Officially atheist but those religions and philosophies practised include Confucianism and Daoism (over 20% together), Buddhism (c. 15%).

Education: *Literacy rate*: 73.3% (1990 est). *Years of compulsory schooling*: education is not compulsory but is available from 7–17; there are plans to introduce 9 years of compulsory schooling by 1995. *Universities*: 79 state universities, 1 private university plus 45 institutes of university status.

Defence: *Total armed strength*: 3 030 000 (1991 est). *Military service*: selective – 3 years for the army and marines, 4 years air force and navy.

1 ANHUI 2 BEIJING 3 FUJIAN 4 GANSU 5 GUANGDONG
6 GUANGXI ZHUANG 7 GUIZHOU 8 HAINAN 9 HEBE
10 HEILONGJIANG 11 HENAN 12 HUBEI 12 HUNAN
14 JIANGSU 15 JIANGX 16 JILIN 17 LAONING 18 NEI MONGGOL
19 NINGXIA HUI 20 QINGHAI 21 SHAANXI 22 SHANDONG
23 SHANGHAI 24 SHANXI 25 SICHUAN 26 TIANJIN
27 XINJIANG UYGUR 28 XIZANG (Tibet) 29 YUNNAN
30 ZHEJIANG

CHINA

Area 9 571 300
km² (3 695 500 sq mi).

GOVERNMENT

The 2978 deputies of the National People's Congress
are elected for a five-year term by the People's
Congresses of the 22 provinces, five autonomous
provinces and three municipal provinces, and by the
People's Liberation Army. The Congress elects a
Standing Committee, a President (for a five-year
term), a Prime Minister and a State Council (or
Cabinet) – all of whom are responsible to the Con-
gress. The only legal party is the Chinese Communist
Party, which holds a Congress every five years. The
Party Congress elects a Central Committee, which in
turn elects a Politburo, and it is these two bodies that
hold effective power.
President: Jiang Zemin.
Prime Minister: Li Peng.
General Secretary of the Communist Party: Jiang
Zemin.

CHINESE PROVINCES

Populations are from the 1990 census.

Anhui *Area*: 139 900 km² (54 020 sq mi). *Population*:
56 180 000. *Capital*: Hefei.

Beijing (Peking) (municipal province) *Area*:
17 800 km² (6870 sq mi). *Population*: 10 819 000. *Capital*: Beijing.

Fujian *Area*: 123 100 km² (47 530 sq mi). *Population*: 30 048 000. *Capital*: Fushu.

Gansu *Area*: 530 000 km² (204 600 sq mi). *Population*: 22 371 000. *Capital*: Lanzhou.

Guangdong *Area*: 197 900 km² (76 400 sq mi).
Population: 62 829 000. *Capital*: Guangzhou
(Canton).

Guangxi Zhuang (autonomous province) *Area*:
220 400 km² (85 100 sq mi). *Population*: 42 246 000.
Capital: Nanning.

Guizhou *Area*: 174 000 km² (67 200 sq mi). *Population*: 32 391 000. *Capital*: Guiyang.

Hainan *Area*: 33 570 km² (12 960 sq mi). *Population*: 6 557 000. *Capital*: Haikou.

Hebei *Area*: 202 700 km² (78 260 sq mi). *Population*:
61 082 000. *Capital*: Shijiazhuang (Shihkiachwang).

Heilongjiang *Area*: 463 600 km² (179 000 sq mi).
Population: 35 215 000. *Capital*: Harbin.

Henan *Area*: 167 000 km² (64 480 sq mi). *Population*: 85 510 000. *Capital*: Zhengzhou.

Hubei *Area*: 187 500 km² (72 400 sq mi). *Population*:
53 969 000. *Capital*: Wuhan.

Hunan *Area*: 210 500 km² (81 270 sq mi). *Population*: 60 660 000. *Capital*: Changsha.

Jiangsu *Area*: 102 200 km² (39 460 sq mi). *Population*: 67 057 000. *Capital*: Nanjing (Nanking).

Jiangxi *Area*: 164 800 km² (63 630 sq mi). *Population*: 37 710 000. *Capital*: Nanchang.

Jilin *Area*: 187 000 km² (72 200 sq mi). *Population*:
24 659 000. *Capital*: Changchun.

Liaoning *Area*: 151 000 km² (58 300 sq mi).
Population: 39 460 000. *Capital*: Shenyang.

Nei Monggol (Inner Mongolia; autonomous province) *Area*: 450 000 km² (173 700 sq mi). *Population*: 21 457 000. *Capital*: Hohhot (Huhehot).

Ningxia Hui (autonomous province) *Area*: 170 000 km² (65 600 sq mi). *Population*: 4 655 000. *Capital*: Yinchuan 410 000.

Qinghai *Area*: 721 000 km² (278 400 sq mi). *Population*: 4 457 000. *Capital*: Xining.

Shaanxi *Area*: 195 800 km² (75 600). *Population*: 32 882 000. *Capital*: Xian.

Shandong *Area*: 153 300 km² (59 190 sq mi). *Population*: 84 393 000. *Capital*: Jinan.

Shanghai (municipal province) *Area*: 5800 km² (2240 sq mi). *Population*: 13 342 000. *Capital*: Shanghai.

Shanxi *Area*: 157 100 km² (60 660 sq mi). *Population*: 28 759 000. *Capital*: Taiyuan.

Sichuan *Area*: 569 000 km² (219 700 sq mi). *Population*: 107 218 000. *Capital*: Chengdu.

Tianjin (municipal province) *Area*: 4000 km² (1540 sq mi). *Population*: 8 785 000. *Capital*: Tianjin.

Xinjiang Uygur (Sinkiang) (autonomous province) *Area*: 1 646 900 km² (635 870 sq mi). *Population*: 15 156 000. *Capital*: Urümqi.

Xizang (Tibet) (autonomous province) *Area*: 1 221 600 km² (471 660 sq mi). *Population*: 2 196 000. *Capital*: Lhasa.

Yunnan *Area*: 436 200 km² (168 420 sq mi). *Population*: 36 973 000. *Capital*: Kunming.

Zhejiang *Area*: 101 800 km² (39 300 sq mi). *Population*: 41 446 000. *Capital*: Hangzhou.

GEOGRAPHY

China is the third largest country in the world in area and the largest in population. Almost half of China comprises mountain chains, mainly in the west, including the Altaï and Tien Shan Mountains in Xinjiang Uygur, and the Kun Lun Mountains to the north of Tibet. The Tibetan Plateau – at an altitude of 3000 m (10 000 ft) – is arid. In the south of Tibet is the Himalaya, containing 40 peaks over 7000 m (23 000 ft). In the far south, the Yunnan Plateau rises to nearly 3700 m (12 000 ft), while in the far northeast, ranges of hills and mountains almost enclose the Northeast Plain, more usually known as Manchuria. Crossing central China – and separating the basins of the Yellow (Huang He) and Yangtze (Chang Jiang) rivers – is the Nan Ling Range of hills and mountains. In east and central China, three great lowlands support intensive agriculture and dense populations – the plains of central China, the Sichuan Basin and the flat North China Plain. A vast loess plateau, deeply dissected by ravines, lies between the Mongolian Plateau – which contains the Gobi Desert – and the deserts of the Tarim and Dzungarian Basins in the northwest. *Principal rivers*: Yangtze (Chang Jiang), Huang He (Yellow River), Xijiang (Sikiang or Pearl River), Heilongjiang (Amur). *Highest point*: Mount Everest 8863 m (29 078 ft).

Climate: In general, temperatures increase from north to south, and rainfall increases from northwest to southeast. Northeast China has a continental climate with warm and humid summers, long cold winters, and rainfall of less than 750 mm (30 in). The central lowlands contain the hottest areas of China, and have 750 to 1100 mm (30 to 40 in) of rainfall. The south is wetter, while the extreme subtropical south experiences the monsoon. The continental loess plateau is cold in the winter, warm in summer and has under 500 mm (20 in) of rain. The northwest is arid, continental and experiences cold winters. The west – Tibet, Xinjiang Uygur, Gansu and Nei Monggol – experiences an extreme climate owing to its altitude and distance from the sea; rainfall is low and most of Tibet has less than two months free of frost.

ECONOMY

Agriculture occupies three quarters of the labour force. All large-scale production is on collective farms, but traditional and inefficient practices remain. Nearly two thirds of the arable land is irrigated, and China is the world's largest producer of rice. Other major crops include wheat, maize, sweet potatoes, sugar cane and soyabeans. Livestock, fruit, vegetables and fishing are also important, but China is still unable to supply all its own food. The country's mineral and fuel resources are considerable and, for the most part, underdeveloped. They include coal, petroleum, natural gas, iron ore, bauxite, tin, antimony and manganese in major reserves, as well as huge hydroelectric power potential. The economy is centrally planned, with all industrial plant owned by the state. Petrochemical products account for nearly one quarter of China's exports. Other major industries include iron and steel, cement, vehicles, fertilizers, food processing, clothing and textiles. The most recent five-year plans have promoted modernization and reform, including an 'open-door' policy under which joint ventures with other countries and foreign loans have been encouraged, together with a degree of small-scale private enterprise. Most of this investment went into light industry and textiles. Special Economic Zones and 'open cities' were designated in the south and central coastal areas to encourage industrial links with the west. Although progress was halted when foreign investment diminished after the 1989 pro-democracy movement was suppressed, sustained economic growth has been achieved in southern China, in particular Guangdong where the new city of Shenzhen (near Hong Kong) is the centre of industrial development.

RECENT HISTORY

At the beginning of the 20th century China was in turmoil. The authority of the emperor had been weakened in the 19th century by outside powers greedy for trade and by huge rebellions which had left large areas of the country beyond the control of the central government. In 1911 a revolution, led by the Guomintang (Kuomintang or Nationalists) under Sun Zhong Shan (Sun Yat-sen; 1866–1925), overthrew the last of the Manchu emperors. Strong in the south (where Sun had established a republic in 1916), the Nationalists faced problems in the north, which was ruled by independent warlords. Sun's successor, Jiang Jie Shi (Chiang Kai-shek; 1887–1975), made some inroads in the north, only to be undermined by the emergent Communist Party.

After a series of disastrous urban risings, the Communist Mao Zedong (Mao Tse-tung; 1893–1976) concentrated on rural areas. After being forced to retreat from Jiangxi in 1934, Mao led his followers for 12 months on a 9000 km (5600 mi) trek, the 'Long March', to the remote province of Shaanxi. In 1931 the Japanese seized Manchuria and established a puppet regime. After the Japanese occupied Beijing (Peking) and most of coastal China in 1937, Jiang and Mao combined against the invaders but were able to achieve little against superior forces. After

World War II, the Soviets tried to ensure that Mao's Communists took over China. In 1946 Mao marched into Manchuria, beginning a civil war that lasted until 1949 when Mao declared a People's Republic in Beijing and Jiang fled to the offshore island of Taiwan, where a Nationalist government was set up (see below).

In 1950 Chinese forces invaded Tibet – an independent state since 1916. Repressive Communist rule alienated the Tibetans, who, loyal to their religious leader the Dalai Lama, unsuccessfully rose in revolt in 1959. Chinese 'volunteers' were active in the Korean War on behalf of the Communist North Koreans (1950–53). China has been involved in a number of border disputes and conflicts, including clashes with the USSR in the late 1950s, with India in 1962 and with Vietnam in 1979. Relations with the USSR deteriorated in the 1950s, triggered by ideological clashes over the true nature of Communism. The Sino-Soviet rift led to the acceleration of Chinese research into atomic weapons – the first Chinese bomb was tested in 1964 – and a rapprochement with the USA in the early 1970s.

The 'Great Leap Forward', an ambitious programme of radicalization in the 1950s, largely failed. In the 1960s Mao tried again to spread more radical revolutionary ideas in the so-called Cultural Revolution. Militant students formed groups of 'Red Guards' to attack the existing hierarchy. Thousands died as the students went out of control, and the army had to restore order. Since Mao's death (1976), China has effectively been under the leadership of Deng Xiaoping (1904–), although he holds none of the major state or party offices. A more careful path has been followed both at home and abroad; a rapprochement with the USSR was achieved in 1989, and agreement has been reached with the UK for the return of Hong Kong to Chinese rule in 1997. China was opened to foreign technology and investment, together with a degree of free enterprise, but this led to internal pressures for political change, culminating in massive pro-democracy demonstrations by students and workers early in 1989. These were brutally suppressed in the massacre of students in Tiananmen Square (June 1989) and hardline leaders gained in influence.

Economic progress has been a priority in the 1990s. Living standards have improved drastically, and the southern provinces and Shanghai have experienced very high economic growth rates. However, an ageing political leadership continued to deny many basic human rights. Relations with the UK became strained when Britain proposed to widen the suffrage in the British colony of Hong Kong, which is due to revert to China in 1997.

CHINA, REPUBLIC OF (TAIWAN)

Official name: Chung-hua Min Kuo (The Republic of China).

Member of: Taiwan is not a member of any major international organization.

Area: 35 981 km² (13 893 sq mi).

Population: 20 489 000 (1991 est.).

Capital and major cities: Taipei 2 720 000, Kaohsiung 1 393 000, Taichung 762 000, Tainan 683 000, Panchiao 539 000 (1990 est.).

Language: Chinese (northern or Amoy dialect).

Religions: Buddhist (24%), Daoist (14%), Roman Catholic (14%).

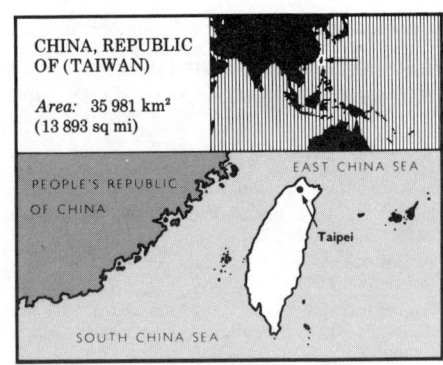

CHINA, REPUBLIC OF (TAIWAN)

Area: 35 981 km² (13 893 sq mi)

PEOPLE'S REPUBLIC OF CHINA

EAST CHINA SEA

Taipei

SOUTH CHINA SEA

Education: *Literacy rate:* 94% (1988). *Years of compulsory schooling:* 6–15. *Universities:* 18 including 1 institute of university status.

Defence: *Total armed strength:* 370 000 (1991). *Military service:* 2 years.

GOVERNMENT

Under the terms of a new constitution (1991), the National Assembly comprises 325 members elected by universal adult suffrage for six years. The Assembly elects a President for a six-year term. The President appoints a Prime Minister and a Council of Ministers. The main political parties are the (Nationalist) Guomintang (Kuomintang) and the (Taiwanese) National Democratic Progressive Party. *President:* Lee Teng-hui. *Prime Minister:* Lien Chan.

GEOGRAPHY

Taiwan is an island 160 km (100 mi) off the southeast coast of mainland China with a mountainous interior. Most of the inhabitants live on the coastal plain in the west. The Republic of China also includes the small islands of Quemoy and Matsu close to the Chinese mainland. *Principal rivers:* Hsia-tan-shui Chi, Chosui Chi. *Highest point:* Yu Shan 3997 m (13 113 ft).

Climate: Taiwan – which is subtropical in the north, and tropical in the south – has rainy summers and mild winters. Tropical cyclones (typhoons) may occur between July and September.

ECONOMY

Despite Taiwan's diplomatic isolation, the island is a major international trading nation, exporting machinery, electronics, and textiles. Taiwan has achieved high economic growth rates over the past four decades. Mineral resources include coal, marble, gold, petroleum and natural gas. Despite the fertility of the soil, agriculture has declined in relative importance.

RECENT HISTORY

In 1895, the Chinese province of Taiwan – which used to be called Formosa – was taken by the Japanese, who began the modernization of agriculture, transport and education. In 1949, the Nationalist forces of Jiang Jie Shi (Chiang Kai-shek) were driven onto Taiwan by the Communist victory on the mainland (see China above). Under US protection, the resulting authoritarian regime on Taiwan declared itself the Republic of China, and claimed to be the legitimate government of all China. America's rapprochement with the mainland People's Republic of

China lost Taiwan its UN seat in 1971 and US recognition in 1978. By the late 1980s Taiwan was moving cautiously towards democracy, although its international status remained problematic. In 1988 a native Taiwanese became president and in 1990 an agreement was reached to speed up the retirement of Guomintang 'life members' from Taiwan's political bodies. A new constitution in 1991 marked the transition to a more Taiwanese, less Chinese, identity. In 1993 Taiwan and China entered into 'non-official' level discussions about trade and communications.

COLOMBIA

Official name: La República de Colombia (The Republic of Colombia).

Member of: UN, OAS, ALADI, Andean Pact.

Area: 1 141 748 km² (440 831 sq mi).

Population: 33 613 000 (1991 est).

Capital and major cities: Bogotá (officially known as Santa Fé de Bogotá DE; DE stands for Distrito Especial – Special District) 4 921 000, Medellín 2 121 000, Cali 1 637 000, Barranquilla 1 029 000, Cartagena 688 000, Cúcuta 407 000, Bucaramanga 364 000, Manizales 310 000, Ibagué 306 000 (all including suburbs; 1990 est).

Languages: Spanish, over 150 Indian languages.

Religion: Roman Catholic (official; over 95%).

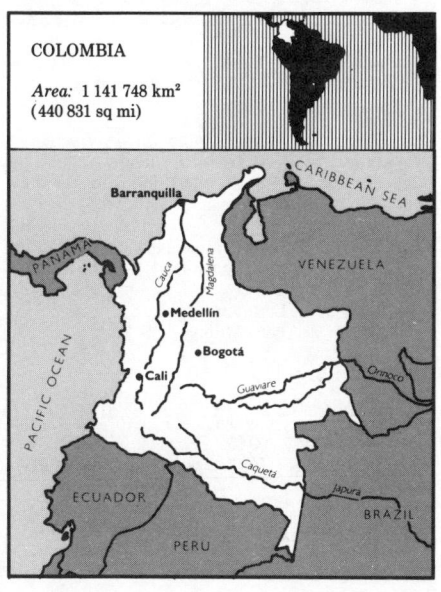

COLOMBIA

Area: 1 141 748 km²
(440 831 sq mi)

Education: *Literacy rate:* 86.7% (1990). *Years of compulsory schooling:* 6–12. *Universities:* 25 state and 24 private.

Defence: *Total armed strength:* 115 000 (1991) (plus 80 000 paramilitary). *Military service:* 1–2 years.

GOVERNMENT

A President (who appoints a Cabinet of 13 members), a Senate of 102 members and a House of Representatives of 161 members are elected for a four-year term by universal adult suffrage. The main political parties are the Liberal Party, the Social Conservative Party, the (leftist) M-19 (April 19th Movement) and the (leftist) UP (Patriotic Union). *President:* Cesar Gaviria.

GEOGRAPHY

The Andes run north to south through Colombia with the greater part of the country lying to the east of the mountains in the mainly treeless grassland plains of the Llanos and the tropical Amazonian rain forest. A coastal plain lies to the west of the Andes. *Principal rivers:* Magdalena, Cauca, Amazon (Amazonas). *Highest point:* Pico Cristóbal Colón 5775 m (18 947 ft).

Climate: The lower Andes are temperate; the mountains over 4000 m (13 100 ft) experience perpetual snow. The rest of the country is tropical. The coasts and the Amazonian Basin are hot and humid, with heavy rainfall. The Llanos have a savannah climate.

ECONOMY

Colombian coffee is the backbone of the country's exports; other cash crops include bananas, sugar cane, flowers and tobacco. However, profits from the illegal cultivation and export of marijuana and cocaine probably produce the greatest revenue. Mineral resources include iron ore, silver and platinum as well as coal, petroleum and natural gas. The main industries are food processing, petroleum refining, fertilizers, cement, textiles and clothing, and iron and steel.

RECENT HISTORY

The struggle for independence from Spain (1809–1819) was fierce and bloody. Almost from Colombia's inception, the centralizing pro-clerical Conservatives and the federalizing anti-clerical Liberals have struggled for control, leading to civil wars (1899–1902 and 1948–1957) in which 400 000 people died. Since 1957 there have been agreements between the Liberals and Conservatives to protect a fragile democracy threatened by left-wing guerrillas, right-wing death squads and powerful drug-trafficking cartels. The 1990 presidential and legislative elections were disrupted by the assassination of several candidates, but the uncomprising stand taken against the drug cartels by President Virgilio Barco and his successor Cesar Gaviria has paid some dividends. Violence decreased and a number of leading drug-traffickers were arrested. In a separate development, left-wing former guerrillas – such as M-19 – abandoned their armed struggle in favour of legitimate political activity.

COMOROS

Official name: La République fédérale islamique des Comores (The Federal Islamic Republic of the Comoros).

Member of: UN, OAU.

Area: 1862 km² (719 sq mi; excluding Mayotte which is administered by France).

Population: 479 000 (1991 est; excluding Mayotte).

Capital and main towns: Moroni 60 000 (city 22 000), Mutsamudu 14 000 (1987 est).

Languages: French and Arabic – both official; Comoran (a blend of Swahili and Arabic).

Religion: Sunni Islam (official; 99%).

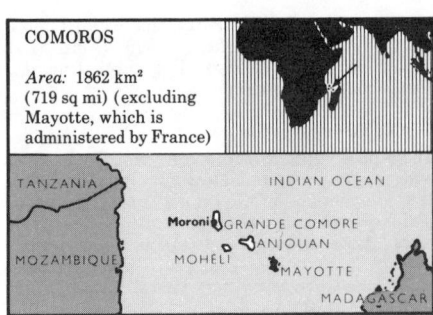

COMOROS

Area: 1862 km²
(719 sq mi) (excluding
Mayotte, which is
administered by France)

TANZANIA

INDIAN OCEAN

MOZAMBIQUE

Moroni GRANDE COMORE
ANJOUAN
MOHÉLI
MAYOTTE

MADAGASCAR

Education: *Literacy rate*: 15% (1985 est). *Years of compulsory schooling*: (in theory) 7–15. *Universities*: none.

Defence: *Total armed strength*: 800 (1990). *Military service*: none.

GOVERNMENT

The President – who is elected for a six-year term by universal adult suffrage – appoints a Council of Ministers. The 42 members of the Federal Assembly are directly elected for five years. The main political parties are the (former monopoly) Udzima party and Rachade (a breakaway group).
President: Siad Mohamed Djohar.
Prime Minister: to be appointed.

GEOGRAPHY

Ngazidja (Grande Comore) – the largest island – is dry and rocky, rising to an active volcano. Ndzouani (Anjouan) is a heavily eroded volcanic massif. Moili (Mohéli) is a forested plateau with fertile valleys. There are no significant rivers. *Highest point*: Mont Kartala (active volcano; 2361 m/7746 ft).

Climate: The tropical climate of the Comoros is dry from May to October, but with heavy rain for the rest of the year.

ECONOMY

Poor and eroded soils, overpopulation and few resources combine to make these underdeveloped islands one of the world's poorest countries. Subsistence farming occupies the majority of the population, although vanilla, cloves and ylang-ylang are produced for export.

RECENT HISTORY

The four Comoran islands became a French colony in 1912. In a referendum in 1974, three islands voted to become independent, which they declared themselves without French agreement. The fourth island, Mayotte, voted against independence, and remains under French rule. Following a coup in 1978, an Islamic republic was proclaimed, and a single-party state established. In 1989, the third attempted coup in a decade resulted in the assassination of the president and a brief period of rule by European mercenaries. Multi-party rule was restored in 1990 although Udzima retains all the seats in the Assembly.

CONGO

Official name: La République du Congo (The Republic of the Congo).
Member of: UN, OAU.
Area: 342 000 km² (132 047 sq mi).

Population: 2 692 000 (1991 est).
Capital and major cities: Brazzaville 940 000, Pointe-Noire 576 000, Loubomo 84 000 (1992 est).
Languages: French (official), Lingala patois (50%), Monokutuba patois (over 40%), Kongo (45%), Teke (20%).
Religions: Roman Catholic (53%), various Protestant Churches (22%), animist (25%).
Education: *Literacy rate*: 56.6% (1990). *Years of compulsory schooling*: (in theory) 6–16. *Universities*: 1.

CONGO

Area: 342 000 km²
(132 047 sq mi)

CAMEROON
CENTRAL
AFRICAN
REPUBLIC

EQUATORIAL
GUINEA

Oubangui

Zaïre

GABON

ZAIRE

Brazzaville
Pointe-Noire
CABINDA

Defence: *Total armed strength*: 11 000 (1991) (plus 6100 paramilitary). *Military service*: none.

GOVERNMENT

The 153-member Assembly and the President are elected for a five-year term by universal adult suffrage. The President appoints a Prime Minister and a Council of Ministers. The main political parties are the Pan-African Union for Social Democracy (UPADS), the Congolese Movement for Democracy (MDD) and the (former Communist) Congolese Party of Labour (PCT).
President: Pascal Lissouba.
Prime Minister: André Milongo.

GEOGRAPHY

Behind a narrow coastal plain, the plateaux of the interior are covered by tropical rain forests and rise to over 700 m (2300 ft). *Principal rivers*: Zaïre (Congo), Oubangui. *Highest point*: Mont de la Lékéti 1040 m (3412 ft).

Climate: Congo's tropical climate is hot and humid. Rainfall exceeds 1200 mm (47 in) a year.

ECONOMY

Until 1991, Congo had a centrally-planned economy. Privatization has begun but the country is crippled by the highest per capita external debt in Africa. Petroleum and timber are the main exports. Subsistence agriculture – chiefly for cassava – occupies over a third of the labour force.

RECENT HISTORY

In the 1880s, the explorer Brazza placed the kingdom of the Teke people under French protection, and in 1905 the region became the colony of Moyen-Congo. Independence was gained in 1960. In 1963, following industrial unrest, a Marxist-Leninist state was established. Since then, ethnic tensions have led to political unrest and military coups. A multi-party system was restored in 1991.

COSTA RICA

Official name: República de Costa Rica (The Republic of Costa Rica).

Member of: UN, OAS, CACM.

Area: 51 100 km² (19 730 sq mi).

Population: 3 088 000 (1991 est).

Capital and major cities: San José 1 040 000 (city 294 000), Alajuela 158 000, Cartago 109 000, Puntarenas 92 000, Limón 68 000 (all including suburbs; 1990 est).

Language: Spanish (official).

Religion: Roman Catholic (official).

Education: *Literacy rate*: 92.8% (1990) – the highest in Central America. *Years of compulsory schooling*: 6–13. *Universities*: 4.

Defence: *Total armed strength*: none, although there are 750 civil guards.

GOVERNMENT

Executive power is vested in the President, who is assisted by two Vice-Presidents and by a Cabinet of Ministers that he appoints. The President, Vice-Presidents and the 57-member Legislative Assembly are elected for four-year terms by compulsory universal adult suffrage. The main political parties are the PUSC (Social Christian Unity Party) and the PLN (National Liberation Party).
President: Rafael Angel Calderón Fournier.

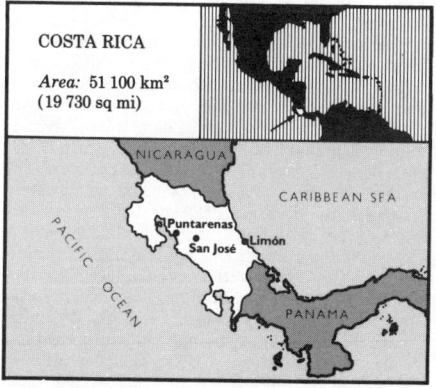

COSTA RICA

Area: 51 100 km²
(19 730 sq mi)

GEOGRAPHY

Between a narrow plain on the Pacific coast and a wider plain along the Caribbean coast rise a central plateau and mountain ranges. *Principal river*: Rio Grande. *Highest point*: Chirripó Grande 3820 m (12 533 ft).

Climate: Rainfall is heavy along the Caribbean coast, but the Pacific coast is drier. Temperatures are warm in the lowlands, cooler in the highlands.

ECONOMY

Coffee is Costa Rica's major export. Bananas, sugar cane, beef cattle, cocoa and timber are also important.

RECENT HISTORY

In the 19th century, Costa Rica developed largely in isolation from its neighbours. Dominated by small farms, Costa Rica prospered, attracted European immigrants, and developed a stable democracy. Following a brief civil war in 1948, the army was disbanded. Costa Rica has since adopted the role of peacemaker in Central America.

CÔTE D'IVOIRE

Official name: La République de la Côte d'Ivoire (The Republic of the Ivory Coast). Since 1986 Côte d'Ivoire has been the only official name.

Member of: UN, OAU, ECOWAS.

Area: 322 462 km² (124 503 sq mi).

Population: 12 464 000 (1991 est).

Capital and major cities: Yamoussoukro (de jure and administrative capital) 120 000, Abidjan (de facto and legislative capital) 1 850 000, Bouaké 220 000 (1987 est).

Languages: French (official), Bete (20%), Senufo (14%), Baoulé (12%).

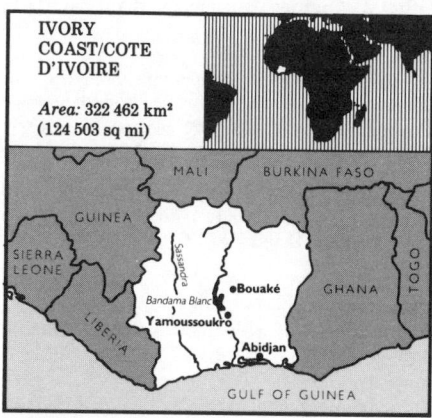

IVORY COAST/CÔTE D'IVOIRE

Area: 322 462 km²
(124 503 sq mi)

Religions: Animist (60%), Christian, mainly Roman Catholic (20%), Sunni Islam (20%).

Education: *Literacy rate*: 53.8% (1990). *Years of compulsory schooling*: (in theory) 7–13. *Universities*: 1.

Defence: *Total armed strength*: 7100 (1990) (plus 7800 paramilitary). *Military service*: none.

GOVERNMENT

The President – who is elected for a five-year term by universal adult suffrage – appoints a Premier and a Council of Ministers who are responsible to him. The 175-member National Assembly is also directly elected for five years. The main political parties are the (former monopoly) Democratic Party, the Ivorian Popular Front, the Workers' Party, the Socialist Party and the Social Democratic Party.
President: Felix Houphouët-Boigny.
Prime Minister: Alassane Ouattara.

GEOGRAPHY

The north is a savannah-covered plateau. In the south, tropical rain forest – increasingly cleared for plantations – ends at the narrow coastal plain. *Principal rivers:* Sassandra, Bandama, Komoé. *Highest point:* Mont Nimba 1752 m (5748 ft).

Climate: The south is equatorial with high temperatures and heavy rainfall; the north has similar temperatures but is drier.

ECONOMY
The country depends on exports of cocoa, coffee and timber, and suffered in the 1980s when prices for these commodities fell. Natural resources include petroleum, natural gas and iron ore. Political stability has helped economic growth.

RECENT HISTORY
Colonized by France in the 19th century, the Ivory Coast became a relatively prosperous part of French West Africa. Independence was achieved in 1960 under the presidency of Félix Houphouët-Boigny (1905–), who has kept close links with France in return for aid and military assistance, and is Africa's longest-serving president. Multi-party elections were held in 1990, but the opposition parties made claims of electoral fraud.

CROATIA
Official name: Republika Hrvatska (The Republic of Croatia).
Member of: UN, CSCE.
Area: 56 538 km² (21 829 sq mi) including the area (about one third) that is controlled by Serb forces.
Population: 4 760 000 (1991 census). Since early 1992 Croatia has received over 400 000 refugees from Bosnia.
Capital and major cities: Zagreb 1 175 000 (city 704 000), Split 236 000 (city 189 000), Rijeka 193 000 (city 168 000), Osijek 159 000 (city 105 000) (1991 census).
Languages: Croat (75%) – the form of Serbo-Croat written in the Latin alphabet, Serb (24%) – the form of Serbo-Croat written in the Cyrillic alphabet.
Religions: Roman Catholic majority, Orthodox minority.
Education: *Literacy rate:* 92.7% (1990 est). *Years of compulsory schooling:* 6–15. *Universities:* 4.

CROATIA
Area: 56 538 km² (21 829 sq mi) including the area (one third) controlled by Serb forces

AUSTRIA
HUNGARY
ITALY
SLOVENIA
Zagreb
Drava
Osijek
Rijeka
Sava
BOSNIA-
HERZEGOVINA
ADRIATIC
SEA
Split
Dubrovnik

Defence: *Total armed strength:* over 100 000 (1993 est).

GOVERNMENT
The 356-member Parliament and an executive President are directly elected. A Prime Minister and Cabinet are appointed by the President. The main political parties include the (nationalist) Croatian Democratic Union, the (former Communist) Social Democratic Party-Party of Democratic Reform, the Croatian Democratic Party and the Croatian Peasants Party.
President: Franjo Tudjman.
Prime Minister: Nikica Valentic.

GEOGRAPHY
Croatia comprises plains in the east (Slavonia), hills around Zagreb, and barren limestone ranges running parallel to the Dalmatian coast. Dubrovnik is detached from the rest of Croatia. *Principal rivers:* Sava, Danube, Drava. *Highest point:* Troglav 1913 m (6275 ft).
Climate: The interior is colder and drier than the Mediterranean coast.

ECONOMY
Manufacturing (aluminium, textiles and chemicals), mining (bauxite) and oil dominate the economy. Slavonia grows cereals, potatoes and sugar beet. In 1991–3 the economy was damaged by the Yugoslav civil war, and the lucrative Dalmatian tourist industry collapsed.

RECENT HISTORY
At the start of the 20th century a Croat national revival looked increasingly to independent Serbia to create a South ('Yugo') Slav state. After World War I when the Habsburg Empire was dissolved (1918), the Croats joined the Serbs, Slovenes and Montenegrins in the state that was to become Yugoslavia in 1929. However, the Croats soon resented the highly centralized Serb-dominated kingdom. Following the German invasion (1941), the occupying Axis powers set up an 'independent' Croat puppet state that adopted anti-Serb policies. In 1945 Croatia was reintegrated into a federal Communist Yugoslav state by Marshal Tito, but after Tito's death (1980), the Yugoslav experiment faltered in economic and nationalist crises. Separatists came to power in Croatia in free elections (1990) and declared independence (June 1991). Serb insurgents, backed by the Yugoslav federal army, occupied one third of Croatia including those areas with an ethnic Serb majority – Krajina and parts of Slavonia. The fierce Serbo-Croat war came to an uneasy halt in 1992 after Croatian independence had gained widespread diplomatic recognition and a UN peace-keeping force was agreed. By mid-1993 Croats controlled about 20% of Bosnia-Herzegovina where an embryo Croat state was effectively established.

CUBA
Official name: La República de Cuba (The Republic of Cuba).
Member of: UN, OAS (suspended), ALADI (observer).
Area: 110 860 km² (42 803 sq mi).
Population: 10 700 000 (1991 est).
Capital and major cities: Havana (La Habana) 2 096 000, Santiago de Cuba 405 000, Camagüey 283 000, Holguín 228 000, Guantánamo 200 000, Santa

Clara 194 000 (all including suburbs; 1990 est).
Language: Spanish.
Religion: Roman Catholic (39%).
Education: *Literacy rate*: 94% (1990). *Years of compulsory schooling*: 6–12. *Universities*: 5 (including 1 university college).
Defence: *Total armed strength*: 180 500 (1991), reservists 135 000 (plus 119 000 paramilitary forces). *Military service*: 3 years (conscripts also work on the land).

GOVERNMENT
The Communist Party is the only legal political party. A constitutional amendment in 1993 replaced the indirectly-elected parliamentary system with a directly-elected 589-member National Assembly. The Assembly elects 31 of its members to form the Council of State, whose President – as head of state and government – appoints a Council of Ministers.
President: Fidel Castro Ruz.

GEOGRAPHY
Three ranges of hills and mountains run east to west across Cuba. *Principal river*: Cauto. *Highest point*: Pico Turquino 1971 m (6467 ft).
Climate: The climate is semitropical. Temperatures average 26 °C (78 °F), and rainfall is heavy. The island is subject to hurricanes.

ECONOMY
Sugar (the leading export), tobacco and coffee are the main crops. State-controlled farms occupy most of the land but are unable to meet Cuba's food needs. Rationing is in force. Production of nickel – Cuba's second most important export – is increasing. The disruption of trading patterns that has followed the adoption of market economies in Eastern Europe and the end of Soviet subsidies have severely damaged the Cuban economy, which is on the verge of collapse.

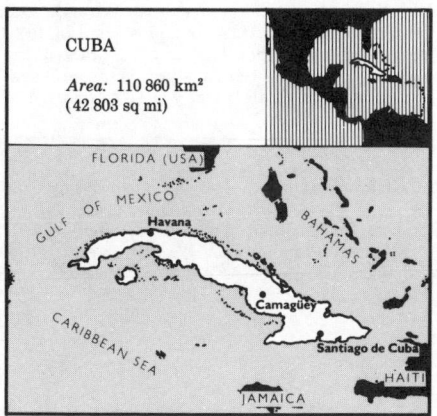

CUBA

Area: 110 860 km² (42 803 sq mi)

FLORIDA (USA)
GULF OF MEXICO
Havana
BAHAMAS
CARIBBEAN SEA
Camagüey
Santiago de Cuba
HAITI
JAMAICA

RECENT HISTORY
The first war for independence from Spain (1868–78) was unsuccessful. The USA intervened in a second uprising (1895–98), forcing Spain to relinquish the island, but independence was not confirmed until after two periods of American administration (1899–1901 and 1906–09). Under a succession of corrupt governments, the majority of Cubans suffered abject poverty. In 1959, the dictatorship of Fulgencio Batista was overthrown by the guerrilla leader Fidel

Castro (1926–), whose revolutionary movement merged with the Communist Party to remodel Cuba on Soviet lines. In 1961, US-backed Cuban exiles attempted to invade at the Bay of Pigs, and relations with America deteriorated further in 1962 when the installation of Soviet missiles on Cuba almost led to world war. Castro has encouraged revolutionary movements throughout Latin America, and his troops have bolstered Marxist governments in Ethiopia and Angola. Despite being a close ally of the USSR, Cuba became a leading Third World power, but the upheavals in the USSR and Eastern Europe in 1989–90 left the Cuban government increasingly isolated as a hardline Marxist state.

CYPRUS
Official name: Kypriaki Dimokratia (in Greek) or Kibris Cumhuriyeti (in Turkish) (The Republic of Cyprus).
Member of: UN, Commonwealth, CSCE, Council of Europe.
Area: 9251 km² (3572 sq mi) – of which 3355 km² (1295 sq mi) are occupied by the Turkish-controlled zone.
Population: 748 000 (1991 est) – of whom 167 000 are in the Turkish-controlled zone.
Capital and major cities: Nicosia 338 000 (including 39 000 in Lefkosa, the Turkish-controlled zone), Limassol 135 000, Larnaca 63 000, Famagusta/Gazi Magusa 40 000 (all including suburbs; 1990 est).
Languages: Greek (80%), Turkish (19%).
Religions: Orthodox (80%), Sunni Islam (19%).
Education: *Literacy rate*: no figure available. *Years of compulsory schooling*: 5½–12; (7–15 in the Turkish-controlled zone). *Universities*: 1.
Defence: *Total armed strength*: 10 000 (1991) (plus 1300 seconded Greek Army officers), reservists 108 000 (plus 3700 paramilitary police). *Military service*: 26 months.

GOVERNMENT
A 56-member House of Representatives is elected by universal adult suffrage in the Greek Cypriot community for five years – an additional 24 seats for the Turkish Cypriot community remain unfilled. The President – who appoints a Council of Ministers – is elected from the Greek Cypriot community by universal adult suffrage for a five-year term. There is provision in the constitution for a Vice President to be similarly elected from the Turkish Cypriot community. In 1975, the administration of the Turkish Cypriot community unilaterally established the 'Turkish Republic of Northern Cyprus', which is unrecognized internationally except by Turkey. The main Greek Cypriot political parties are the Democratic Rally (DISY), the Liberal Party, the (Communist) AKEL party and the Democratic Party. The main Turkish Cypriot political parties are the National Union Party, the New Dawn Party and the Free Democratic Party.
President: Glafcos Clerides.

GEOGRAPHY
The south of the island is covered by the Troodos Mountains. Running east to west across the centre of Cyprus is a fertile plain, north of which are the Kyrenian Mountains and the Karpas Peninsula. *Principal rivers*: Seranhis, Pedieas. *Highest point*: Mount Olympus 1951 m (6399 ft).

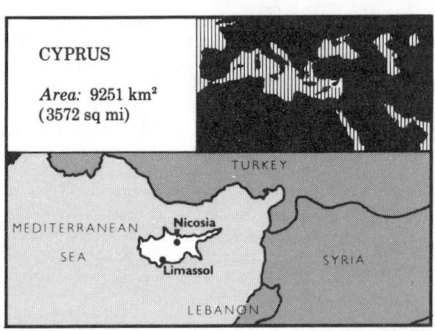

CYPRUS

Area: 9251 km²
(3572 sq mi)

Climate: Cyprus has a Mediterranean climate with hot dry summers and mild, variable winters, during which snow falls in the Troodos Mountains.

ECONOMY

Potatoes, fruit, wine, clothing and textiles are exported from the Greek Cypriot area, in which ports, resorts and an international airport have been constructed to replace facilities lost since partition. The Turkish-controlled zone – which exports fruit, potatoes and tobacco – relies heavily on aid from Turkey. Tourism is important in both areas.

RECENT HISTORY

British administration in Cyprus – formerly an Ottoman (Turkish) possession – was established in 1878. During the 1950s, Greek Cypriots – led by Archbishop (later President) Makarios III (1913–77) – campaigned for Enosis (union with Greece). The Turkish Cypriots advocated partition, but following a terrorist campaign by the Greek Cypriot EOKA movement, a compromise was agreed. In 1960, Cyprus became an independent republic. Power was shared by the two communities, but the agreement broke down in 1963, and UN forces intervened to stop intercommunal fighting. The Turkish Cypriots set up their own administration. When pro-Enosis officers staged a coup in 1974, Turkey invaded the north. Cyprus was effectively partitioned. Over 200 000 Greek Cypriots were displaced from the north, into which settlers arrived from Turkey. Since then, UN forces have manned the 'Attila Line' between the Greek south and Turkish north, but attempts to reunite Cyprus as a federal state have been unsuccessful.

CZECH REPUBLIC

Official name: Ceská Republika (Czech Republic).

Member of: UN, CSCE, Council of Europe.

Area: 78 880 km² (30 456 sq mi).

Population: 10 299 000 (1991 census).

Capital and major cities: Prague (Praha) 1 212 000, Brno 388 000, Ostrava 328 000, Olomouc 224 000, Zlin 197 000, Plzen 174 000, Ceské Budejovice 173 000, Hradec Kralové 163 000, Pardubice 162 000, Liberec 160 000 (all including suburbs; 1991 census).

Languages: Czech, with a small Slovak minority .

Religions: Roman Catholic (39%), various Protestant Churches including Hussite (8%).

Education: *Literacy rate:* 99%. *Years of compulsory schooling:* 6–16. *Universities:* 14.

Defence: *Total armed strength:* 90 000 (1993 est).

Military service: 18 months (to be reduced to 1 year during 1993).

GOVERNMENT

The 200-member Assembly is elected by universal adult suffrage for five years. The Assembly elects a President, who appoints a Prime Minister and Cabinet responsible to the Assembly. The main political parties are the (conservative) Civic Democratic Party, the (conservative) Civic Democratic Alliance, the Social Democratic Party, the (Moravian and Silesian nationalist) MAD-SMS, the Christian Democratic Party and the Communist Party.
President: Václav Havel.
Prime Minister: Václav Klaus.

GEOGRAPHY

In the west (Bohemia), the Elbe basin is ringed on three sides by uplands. The Moravian plain lies to the east of Bohemia. *Principal rivers:* Elbe (Labe), Vltava (Moldau), Morava. *Highest point:* Snezka 1603 m (5259 ft).

Climate: The climate is continental with cold winters and warm summers.

ECONOMY

Apart from coal, there are few mineral resources, but the country is heavily industrialized. Some areas have suffered heavy pollution. Manufactures include industrial machinery, motor vehicles and consumer goods. The country is switching from a centrally planned to a free-market economy. The majority of businesses have been privatized. The Czech Republic has attracted considerable foreign investment (over 80% German) and its economy is increasingly linked to that of Germany. The timber industry is important. The main crops include wheat, maize, potatoes, barley and sugar beet.

RECENT HISTORY

On the collapse of the Habsburg Empire, the Czechs and Slovaks united in an independent state (1918) – largely due to the efforts of Thomas Masaryk, who became Czechoslovakia's first president. In 1938, Hitler demanded that Germany be granted the Sudetenland, where Germans predominated. Lacking allies, Czechoslovakia was dismembered –

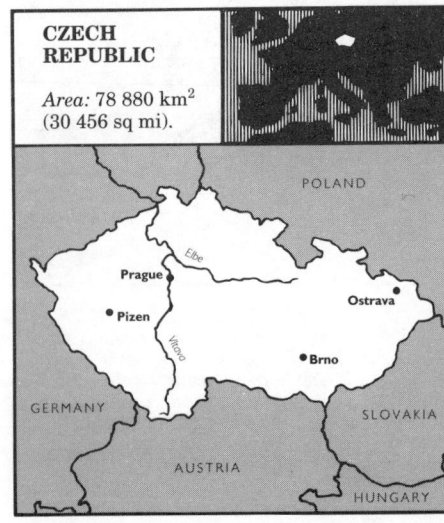

CZECH
REPUBLIC

Area: 78 880 km²
(30 456 sq mi).

Bohemia and Moravia became German 'protectorates'. The Nazi occupation included the massacre of the inhabitants of Lidice (1942). Following liberation (1945), a coalition government was formed, but the Communists staged a takeover in 1948. In 1968, moves by Party Secretary Alexander Dubček to introduce political reforms met with Soviet disapproval, and invasion by Czechoslovakia's Warsaw Pact allies. The conservative wing of the Communist party regained control until 1989, when student demonstrations developed into a peaceful revolution led by the Civic Forum movement. Faced by overwhelming public opposition, the Communist Party renounced its leading role and hardline leaders were replaced by reformers. A new government, in which Communists were in a minority, was appointed and Civic Forum's leader – the playwright Vaclav Havel – was elected president. In 1990 free multi-party elections were held, Soviet troops were withdrawn and the foundations of a market economy were laid. Increased Slovak separatism led to the division of the country in 1993, when the secession of poorer, more rural Slovakia left the more developed Czech Republic as a likely future EC member.

DENMARK

Official name: Kongeriget Danmark (Kingdom of Denmark).

Member of: UN, EC, NATO, Council of Europe, CSCE, OECD, WEU (associate).

Area: 43 092 km² (16 638 sq mi) – 'metropolitan' Denmark, excluding dependencies.

Population: 5 194 000 (including the Faeroe Islands; 1991 census).

Capital and major cities: Copenhagen (København) 1 337 000 (city 465 000), Aarhus (Århus) 264 000, Odense 178 000, Aalborg (Ålborg) 156 000, Esbjerg 82 000, Randers 61 000, Kolding 58 000, Helsingor 57 000, Horsens 55 000 (all including suburbs; 1991 census).

Language: Danish.

Religion: Lutheran (91%).

Education: *Literacy rate:* nearly 100%. *Years of compulsory schooling:* 7–16. *Universities:* 8, (including the open university), plus 2 university colleges (1

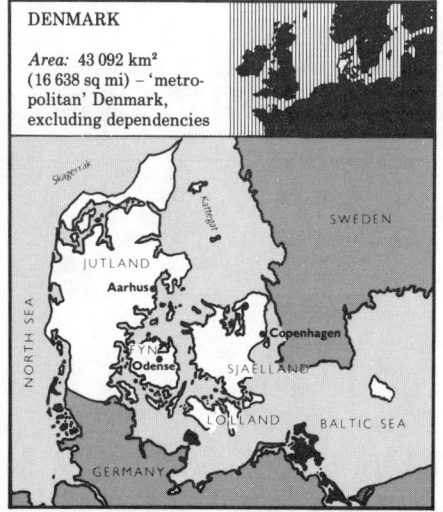

DENMARK

Area: 43 092 km²
(16 638 sq mi) – 'metropolitan' Denmark,
excluding dependencies

SKAGERRAK
KATTEGAT
SWEDEN
JUTLAND
Aarhus
NORTH SEA
Copenhagen
FYN
Odense
SJÆLLAND
LOLLAND
BALTIC SEA
GERMANY

in the Faeroe Islands).

Defence *Total armed strength:* 29 400 (1991) (plus 72 700 reservists) and the Volunteer Home Guard 70 000. *Military service:* 9–12 months.

GOVERNMENT
Denmark is a constitutional monarchy. The 179 members of Parliament (the Folketing) are elected by universal adult suffrage under a system of proportional representation for a four-year term. Two members are elected from both of the autonomous dependencies. The Monarch appoints a Prime Minister, who commands a majority in the Folketing. The PM, in turn, appoints a State Council (Cabinet), which is responsible to the Folketing. The main political parties are the Liberal Party, the Conservative People's Party, the Social Democratic Party, the Socialist People's Party, the Progress Party, the Centre Democrats, the Christian People's Party and the Radical Liberals.
Queen: HM Queen Margrethe II (succeeded upon the death of her father, 14 January 1972).
Prime Minister: Poul Nyrup Rasmussen.

GEOGRAPHY
Denmark is a lowland of glacial moraine – only Bornholm, in the Baltic, has ancient hard surface rocks. The islands to the east of Jutland make up nearly one third of the country. *Principal river:* Gudená. *Highest point:* Yding Skovhøj 173 m (568 ft).
Climate: The climate is temperate and moist, with mild summers and cold winters. Bornholm – to the east – is more extreme.

ECONOMY
Denmark has a high standard of living, but few natural resources. Danish agriculture is organized on a cooperative basis, and produces cheese and other dairy products, bacon and beef – all mainly for export. About one fifth of the labour force is involved in manufacturing, with iron and metal working, food processing and brewing, engineering and chemicals as the most important industries. The high cost of imported fuel has been a problem for the economy, but this has been partly alleviated by petroleum and natural gas from the North Sea.

RECENT HISTORY
In the 1860s, the Danish duchies of Schleswig and Holstein became the subject of a complicated dispute with Prussia. After a short war with Prussia and Austria (1864), Denmark surrendered the duchies, but northern Schleswig was returned to Denmark in 1920. In the 20th century, Denmark's last colonial possessions were either sold (Virgin Islands) or given independence (Iceland) or autonomy (Greenland and the Faeroe Islands). The country was occupied by Nazi Germany (1940–45), and has since been a member of the Western Alliance. From the 1960s, Denmark's economic and political ties have increasingly been with Germany, the UK and the Netherlands, rather than the traditional links with the Nordic countries (Norway and Sweden). Thus, in 1973 Denmark joined the EC, but the political consequence of joining the Common Market has been a further fragmentation of the country's political parties, which has made the formation of coalition and minority governments a protracted and difficult process. The failure of the Danish electorate to approve the EC Maastricht Treaty (1992) raised doubts about moves towards European integration.

DANISH AUTONOMOUS DEPENDENCIES

Faeroe Islands (Faeroerne) *Area*: 1399 km² (540 sq mi). *Population*: 48 400 (1990 est). *Capital*: Tórshavn 16 200 (1990 est).

Greenland (Gronland or **Kalaallit)** *Area*: 2 175 600 km² (840 000 sq mi). *Population*: 55 500 (1991 est). *Capital*: Nuuk (formerly Godthab) 12 200 (1991 est).

DJIBOUTI

Official name: Jumhuriya Jibuti (The Republic of Djibouti).

Member of: UN, OAU, Arab League.

Area: 23 200 km² (8950 sq mi).

Population: 541 000 (1991 est).

Capital: Djibouti 290 000 (1988 est).

Languages: Arabic and French – both official; Somali (Issa; 37%).

Religion: Sunni Islam.

Education: *Literacy rate:* no figure available. *Years of compulsory schooling:* education is available from 7 to 13 but is not compulsory. *Universities:* none.

Defence *Total armed strength:* 2770 (1991) plus 600 paramilitary police, 1200 National Security force and 4000 French troops. *Military service:* none.

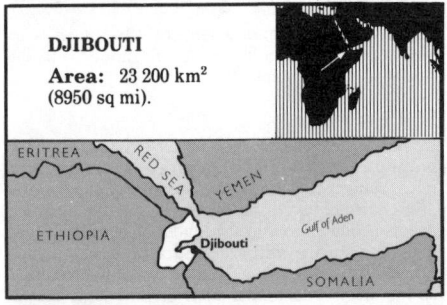

DJIBOUTI
Area: 23 200 km²
(8950 sq mi).

GOVERNMENT

Every five years the 65-member Chamber of Deputies is elected by universal adult suffrage. The President – who is directly elected every six years – appoints a Prime Minister and a Council of Ministers who are responsible to him. The main political party is the (former monopoly) Rassemblement populaire pour le progrès.
President: Hassan Gouled Aptidon.
Prime Minister: Barkat Gourad Hamadou.

GEOGRAPHY

Djibouti is a low-lying desert – below sea level in two basins, but rising to mountains in the north. There are no significant rivers. *Highest point:* Musa Ali Terara 2062 m (6768 ft).

Climate: Djibouti is extremely hot and dry, with rainfall under 125 mm (5 in) on the coast.

ECONOMY

Lack of water largely restricts agriculture to grazing sheep and goats. The economy depends on the expanding seaport and railway, which both serve Ethiopia.

RECENT HISTORY

France acquired a port in 1862 and established the colony of French Somaliland in 1888. In the 1950s and 1970s, the Afar tribe and Europeans voted to remain French, while the Issas (Somalis) opted for independence. In 1977, the territory became the Republic of Djibouti, but the new state has suffered ethnic unrest and drought.

DOMINICA

Official name: Commonwealth of Dominica.

Member of: UN, Commonwealth, CARICOM, OAS.

Area: 751 km² (290 sq mi).

Population: 83 400 (1991 est).

Capital: Roseau 22 000 (city 8300), Portsmouth 5000 (town 2200) (1991 est).

Languages: English (official), French patois.

Religion: Roman Catholic (80%).

Education: *Literacy rate*: 94.4% (1986). *Years of compulsory schooling*: 5–15. *Universities*: 1 university college (part of the University of the West Indies).

Defence *Total armed strength*: there are no armed forces.

GOVERNMENT

Every five years, 21 members of the House of Assembly are elected by universal adult suffrage and nine are appointed by the President, who is elected for a five-year term by the House. The President appoints a Prime Minister and Cabinet. The main political parties are the (conservative) Dominica Freedom Party, the United Workers' Party, and the Dominica Labour Party.
President: Clarence Seignoret.
Prime Minister: Eugenia Charles.

GEOGRAPHY

Dominica is surrounded by steep cliffs with a forested mountainous interior. *Principal river*: Layou. *Highest point*: Morne Diablotin 1447 m (4747 ft).

Climate: Dominica has a tropical climate with little seasonal variation and very heavy rainfall. The island is subject to hurricanes.

ECONOMY

Dominica is a poor island. It produces bananas, timber and coconuts, and exports water to drier neighbours. Tourism is increasing in importance.

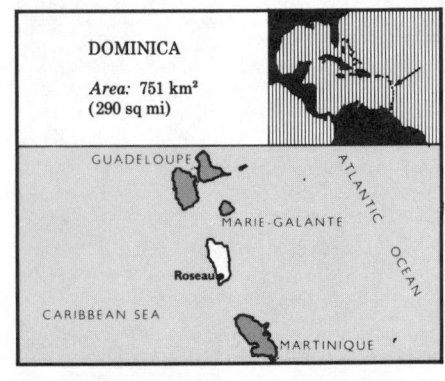

DOMINICA

Area: 751 km²
(290 sq mi)

RECENT HISTORY

A former British colony, Dominica was a member of the West Indies Federation (1958–62), gained autonomy in 1967 and independence in 1978.

DOMINICAN REPUBLIC

Official name: República Dominicana (The Dominican Republic).

Member of: UN, OAS, ALADI (observer), CARICOM.

Area: 48 422 km² (18 696 sq mi).

Population: 7 471 000 (1992 est).

Capital and major cities: Santo Domingo 2 200 000, Santiago 467 000, La Vega 189 000, San Pedro 137 000 (all including suburbs; 1989 est).

Language: Spanish.

Religion: Roman Catholic (official; over 90%).

Education: *Literacy rate:* 83.3% (1990 est). *Years of compulsory schooling:* 7–14. *Universities:* 8.

Defence: *Total armed strength:* 23 200 (1991). *Military service:* none.

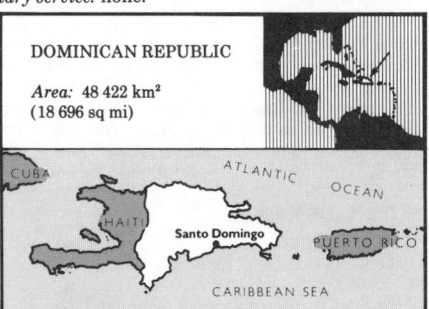

DOMINICAN REPUBLIC

Area: 48 422 km²
(18 696 sq mi)

CUBA   ATLANTIC OCEAN   HAITI   Santo Domingo   PUERTO RICO   CARIBBEAN SEA

GOVERNMENT

The President and the National Congress – a 30-member Senate and a 120-member Chamber of Deputies – are elected for four years by universal adult suffrage. The President appoints a Cabinet. The main political parties are the (conservative) PR (Partido Reformista), the (left-wing) PRD (Partido Revolucionario Dominicano) and the (left-wing) PLD (Partido de la Liberación Dominicano).
President: Joaquin Balaguer.

GEOGRAPHY

The republic consists of the eastern two thirds of the island of Hispaniola. The fertile Cibao Valley in the north is an important agricultural region. Most of the rest of the country is mountainous. *Principal river:* Yaque del Norte. *Highest point:* Pico Duarte 3175 m (10 417 ft).

Climate: The climate is largely subtropical, but it is cooler in the mountains. Rainfall is heavy, but the west and southwest are arid. Hurricanes are a hazard.

ECONOMY

Sugar is the traditional mainstay of the economy, but nickel and iron ore have become the principal exports. Tourism is now the greatest foreign-currency earner.

RECENT HISTORY

The 19th century witnessed a succession of tyrants, and by 1900 the republic was bankrupt and in chaos.

The USA intervened (1916–24). Rafael Trujillo (1891–1961) became president in 1930 and ruthlessly suppressed opposition. He was assassinated in 1961. Civil war in 1965 ended after intervention by US and Latin American troops. Since then, an infant democracy has survived violent elections. The country faces grave economic problems.

ECUADOR

Official name: República del Ecuador (The Republic of Ecuador).

Member of: UN, OAS, ALADI, Andean Pact.

Area: 270 670 km² (104 506 sq mi).

Population: 10 782 000 (1990 census).

Capital and major cities: Quito 1 388 000 (city 1 101 000), Guayaquil 1 764 000 (city 1 531 000), Cuenca 272 000 (city 195 000), Ambato 229 000 (city 124 000), Portoviejo 201 000 (city 133 000), Esmeraldas 173 000, Riobamba 160 000 (all including suburbs; 1990 census).

Languages: Spanish (official; 93%), Quéchua.

Religion: Roman Catholic (93%).

Education: *Literacy rate:* 85.8% (1990). *Years of compulsory schooling:* Schooling is compulsory for 6 years; pupils may start at age 6, 7 or 8. *Universities:* 18 (including technical universities) and 3 polytechnics of university status.

Defence: *Total armed strength:* 57 800 (1991). *Military service:* 1 year (selective).

GOVERNMENT

The President is elected by compulsory universal adult suffrage for a single term of 4 years. The 72-member Chamber of Representatives is also directly elected; 12 members are elected for four years on a national basis and 60 members for a single term of two years on a provincial basis. The President appoints a Cabinet of Ministers. The main political parties include the (conservative coalition) FRN (National Reconstruction Front), the (left-wing coalition) Front of Democratic Progress, and the Christian Democrat coalition.
President: Sixto Duran Ballo.

GEOGRAPHY

The Andes divide the Pacific coastal plain in the west from the Amazonian tropical rain forest in the east. *Principal rivers:* Napo, Pastaza, Curaray, Daule. *Highest point:* Chimborazo 6267 m (20 561 ft).

Climate: The Amazonian Basin has a wet tropical climate. The tropical coastal plain is humid in the north, arid in the south. The highland valleys are mild, but the highest peaks have permanent snow.

ECONOMY

Agriculture is the largest single employer, and major export crops include cocoa, coffee and, in particular, bananas. Petroleum is the major foreign-currency earner. High inflation and foreign debt are severe problems.

RECENT HISTORY

Throughout the 19th century there were struggles between liberals and conservatives. Since 1895 there have been long periods of military rule, but democratically elected governments have been in power since 1978. Relations with neighbouring Peru have long

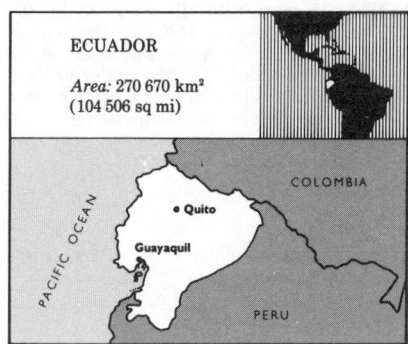

ECUADOR

Area: 270 670 km²
(104 506 sq mi)

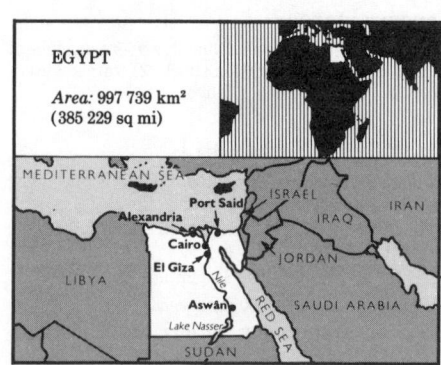

EGYPT

Area: 997 739 km²
(385 229 sq mi)

been tense – war broke out in 1941, when Ecuador lost most of its Amazonian territory, and there were border skirmishes in 1981. Emergency economic measures in 1988 led to a wave of strikes and unrest.

EGYPT

Official name: Jumhuriyat Misr al-'Arabiya (Arab Republic of Egypt).

Member of: UN, OAU, Arab League.

Area: 997 739 km² (385 229 sq mi).

Population: 54 609 000 (1991 est).

Capital and major cities: Cairo (El-Qahira) 12 287 000 (including suburbs), Alexandria (El-Iskandariyah) 3 170 000, El-Giza 2 156 000 and Shubrâ El-Kheima 811 000 are both part of the Cairo agglomeration, Port Said (Bur Sa'id) 461 000, Suez (El Suweis) 392 000 (1990 est).

Language: Arabic (official).

Religions: Sunni Islam (90%), Coptic Christian (7%).

Education: *Literacy rate:* 48.4% (1990). *Years of compulsory schooling:* 6–15. *Universities:* 13.

Defence: *Total armed strength:* 420 000 (1991) (plus 604 000 reservists). *Military service:* 3 years (selective).

GOVERNMENT

Every five years, 454 members are elected by universal adult suffrage to the Majlis ash-Sha'ab (People's Assembly); 10 additional members are appointed by the President, who is nominated by the Assembly and confirmed by referendum for a six-year term. The President appoints a Prime Minister, Ministers and Vice-President(s). The main political parties include the (socialist) National Democratic Party, the (traditional) New Wafd Party, the Socialist Labour Party and the Progressive Unionist Rally.
President: Mohammed Hosni Mubarak.
Prime Minister: Atef Sedki.

GEOGRAPHY

Desert covers more than 90% of Egypt. The Western Desert – which stretches into Libya and Sudan – is low-lying. The Eastern Desert is divided by wadis and ends in the southeast in mountains beside the Red Sea. Most Egyptians live in the Nile River valley and delta, intensively cultivated lands that rely on irrigation by the annual flood of the Nile. East of the Suez Canal is the Sinai Peninsula. *Principal river:* Nile. *Highest point:* Mount Catherine (Jabal Katrina) 2642 m (8668 ft).

Climate: Egyptian winters are mild and summers are hot and arid. Alexandria has the highest rainfall total – 200 mm/8 in – while the area beside the Red Sea receives virtually no rain.

ECONOMY

Over a third of the labour force is involved in agriculture, producing maize, wheat, rice and vegetables for the domestic market, and cotton and dates mainly for export. Petroleum reserves (small by Middle Eastern standards), canal tolls and tourism are major foreign-currency earners. The economy is held back by rapid population growth and by the demands of a large public sector and food subsidies.

RECENT HISTORY

In the 19th century, Egypt was nominally part of the Ottoman (Turkish) Empire, although it was effectively ruled by a local dynasty. The construction of the Suez Canal bankrupted Egypt, and the UK – a major creditor – occupied Egypt (1882) and established a protectorate (1914–22). The corrupt regime of King Farouk was toppled in a military coup (1952) and a republic was established (1953). The radical Gamal Abdel Nasser (1918–70) became president in 1954. He nationalized the Suez Canal and made Egypt the leader of Arab nationalism. Nasser was twice defeated by Israel in Middle East wars (1967 and 1973), but his successor, President Anwar Sadat, made peace with Israel (1979) and was ostracized by the Arab world. Since Sadat's assassination (1981), Egypt has regained its place in the Arab fold, and the prominent role played by Egypt in the coalition against Saddam Hussein's Iraq (1991) confirmed Egypt as one of the leaders of the Arab world. The country is faced by severe economic problems, and there is a growth in Islamic fundamentalism.

EL SALVADOR

Official name: La República de El Salvador (The Republic of El Salvador).

Member of: UN, OAS, CACM.

Area: 21 393 km² (8260 sq mi).

Population: 5 392 000 (1991 est).

Capital and major cities: San Salvador 1 151 000 (city 477 000), Santa Ana 224 000 (city 145 000), San Miguel 176 000 (city 93 000), Mejicanos 107 000 (city 96 000) (1987 est).

Language: Spanish (official).

Religion: Roman Catholic (over 90%).

Education: *Literacy rate:* 73% (1990). *Years of compulsory schooling:* 7–16. *Universities:* 6.

Defence: *Total armed strength:* 43 600 (1992). *Military service:* abolished in 1992.

GOVERNMENT

The President – who appoints a Cabinet of Ministers – is elected by universal adult suffrage for a single five-year term. Every three years, direct elections are also held for the 60-member National Assembly. The main political parties include (right-wing) ARENA (the Nationalist Republican Alliance), the PCN (National Reconstruction Party), the (left-wing) Democratic Convergence, and the PDC (Christian Democratic Party).
President: Alfredo Cristiani.

GEOGRAPHY

The country is mountainous, with ranges along the border with Honduras and a higher volcanic chain in the south. *Principal rivers:* Lempa, San Miguel. *Highest point:* Volcán de Santa Ana 2381 m (7812 ft).

Climate: The tropical coast is hot and humid, while the interior is temperate.

ECONOMY

Agricultural products – in particular coffee and sugar cane – account for nearly two thirds of the country's exports. The economy has declined since the 1970s owing to the state of near civil war.

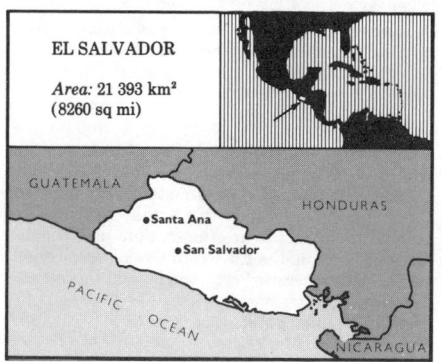

EL SALVADOR

Area: 21 393 km² (8260 sq mi)

GUATEMALA
HONDURAS
Santa Ana
San Salvador
PACIFIC OCEAN
NICARAGUA

RECENT HISTORY

El Salvador was liberated from Spanish rule in 1821, but remained in the Central American Federation until 1838. The country has suffered frequent coups and political violence. In 1932 a peasant uprising – led by Agustín Farabundo Martí – was harshly suppressed. El Salvador's overpopulation has been partially relieved by migration to neighbouring countries. Following a football match between El Salvador and Honduras in 1969, war broke out because of illegal immigration by Salvadoreans into Honduras. Political and economic power is concentrated into the hands of a few families, and this has led to social tension. The country was in a state of virtual civil war from the late 1970s to 1992 with the US-backed military, assisted by extreme right-wing death squads, combating left-wing guerrillas – the FMLN-FDR (Farabundo Martí National Liberation Movement and Democratic Revolutionary Front). A peace agreement between these forces was reached in 1992 and constitutional multi-party rule was restored.

EQUATORIAL GUINEA

Official name: La República de Guinea Ecuatorial (The Republic of Equatorial Guinea).

Member of: UN, OAU.

Area: 28 051 km² (10 831 sq mi).

Population: 358 000 (1991 est).

Capital and major cities: Malabo 37 000, Bata 24 000 (1988 est).

Languages: Spanish (official), Fang, Bubi, Portuguese patois on Pagalu.

Religion: Roman Catholic majority.

Education: *Literacy rate:* 62% (1983). *Years of compulsory schooling:* (in theory) 6–14. *Universities:* none.

Defence: *Total armed strength:* 1300 (1991) plus 2000 paramilitary forces. *Military service:* none.

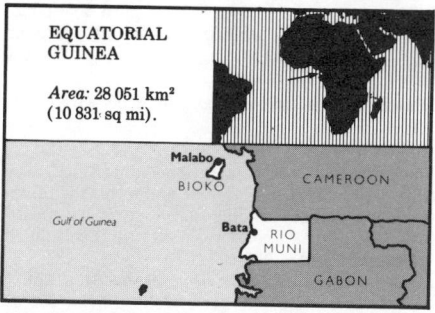

EQUATORIAL GUINEA

Area: 28 051 km² (10 831 sq mi).

Malabo
BIOKO
CAMEROON
Gulf of Guinea
Bata
RIO MUNI
GABON

GOVERNMENT

The constitution provides for the election of a President for a seven-year term. However, effective power is in the hands of the Supreme Military Council, whose President is head of state and of government. A 41-member House of Representatives is directly elected for a five-year term. All candidates for election are nominated by the President and since 1987 all are members of the single party of government, the PDGE (Partido Democratico de Guinea Ecuatorial). In 1992 the restoration of a multi-party system was approved.
President: Brig. Gen. Teodoro Obiang.

GEOGRAPHY

The republic consists of the fertile island of Bioko (formerly Fernando Póo), the much smaller islands of Pagalu (formerly Annobón) and the Corisco Group, and the district of Mbini (formerly Río Muni) on the African mainland. *Principal rivers:* Campo, Benito, Muni. *Highest point:* Pico de Moca (Moka) 2850 m (9350 ft).

Climate: The tropical climate is hot and humid with heavy rainfall.

ECONOMY

Mbini exports coffee and timber, but cocoa production on Bioko slumped after the departure of Nigerian workers (1976). The economy relies heavily upon foreign aid.

RECENT HISTORY

The colony of Spanish Guinea was created in 1856. The harsh plantation system practised during the colonial era attracted much international criticism. Independence in 1968 began under the dictatorship of Francisco Nguema, who was overthrown by his nephew Teodoro Obiang in a military coup in 1979. One-party rule has been in force since 1987, but coups were attempted in 1981, 1983, 1986 and 1988. The return of political pluralism is expected.

ERITREA

Official name: Eritrea.

Area: 117 400 km² (45 300 sq mi).

Population: 3 323 000 (1991 est).

Capital: Asmara (Asmera) 344 000, Missawa (Mitsiwa) 40 000 (1991 est).

Languages: Tigrinya (majority), Tigre, Arabic, Afar, Saho.

Religions: Sunni Islam (majority), Coptic Christian (minority).

Education: *Literacy rate:* no figure available. *Years of compulsory schooling:* schooling is free for up to 12 years from the age of six, but it is not compulsory. *Universities:* 1.

Defence: *Total armed strength:* 60 000 (1991).

GOVERNMENT

The Eritrean People's Liberation Front (EPLF) took control of Eritrea in May 1991 and forms the provisional government pending the adoption of a constitution. Multi-party constitutional rule is scheduled to be introduced by 1995.
Head of provisional government: Issaias Afewerki.

GEOGRAPHY

Eritrea is physically an extension of the Ethiopian high plateau, although there are low coastal plains. *Principal river:* Barka (seasonal). *Highest point:* Ramlo 2130 m (6986 ft).

ECONOMY

A 30-year secessionist war has shattered the economy. The labour force is largely agricultural, growing sorghum and keeping livestock for hides (the major export). However, scarce and unreliable rainfall is a hazard. The main natural resource is salt.

RECENT HISTORY

The Italian colony of Eritrea was created out of coastal districts of Ethiopia and areas claimed by the (Turkish) Ottoman Empire in 1890. Used as the base for Italy's conquest of Ethiopia (1935–36), Eritrea came under British rule in 1941 when Italy was removed from East Africa. In 1952 the territory was federated as an autonomous state with Ethiopia but its incorporation as an Ethiopian province in 1962 sparked a rebellion against Ethiopia that lasted until 1991. In 1977 Eritrean guerrillas almost completely cleared the territory of Ethiopian forces, but the Marxist Ethiopian government of Col. Mengistu fought back with Soviet arms to reverse the position in the following year. The EPLF (see above) – with the Ethiopian Tigrayan Liberation Front – was finally instrumental in toppling Mengistu in 1991, when Eritrea effectively seceded from Ethiopia. A referendum in Eritrea in April 1993 produced an overwhelming majority in favour of independence and the territory is scheduled to assume complete sovereignty on 24 May 1993.

ESTONIA

Official name: Eesti Vabariik (Republic of Estonia).

Member of: UN, CSCE, Council of Europe.

Area: 45 100 km² (17 413 sq mi).

Population: 1 589 000 (1991 est).

Capital and major cities: Tallinn 505 000, Tartu 115 000, Narva 82 000, Kohtla-Järve 77 000, Parnu 54 000 (1991 est).

Languages: Estonian (over 62%), Russian (30%).

Religions: Lutheran (30%), Orthodox (10%).

Education: *Literacy rate:* almost 100%. *Years of compulsory schooling:* 7–17. *Universities:* 2.

Defence: *Total armed strength:* an Estonian army is being established on the basis of conscription. (Some 40 000 Russian armed personnel were still based in Estonia in 1992.)

GOVERNMENT

A 106-member Assembly and a President are elected by universal adult suffrage for four years. The President appoints a Prime Minister and a Council of Ministers who are responsible to the Assembly. The main political parties are the (nationalist) Popular Front of Estonia, the Christian Democratic Union, the Social Democratic Party, the Liberal Democratic Party and the Communist Party.
President: Lennart Meri.
Prime Minister: Mart Laar.

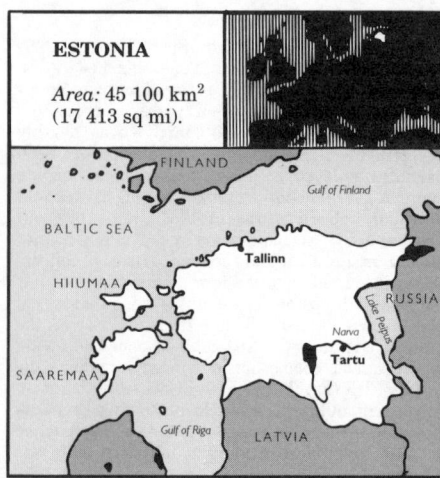

ESTONIA

Area: 45 100 km² (17 413 sq mi).

ERITREA

Area: 117 400 km² (45 300 sq mi).

GEOGRAPHY

Estonia comprises a low-lying mainland – rising in the SE to 318 m (1042 ft) – and two main islands.

Climate The moist temperate climate is characterized by mild summers and cold winters.

ECONOMY

Major industries include engineering and food processing. Gas for heating and industry is extracted from bituminous shale. The important agricultural sector is dominated by dairying. Since 1991 severe economic difficulties have resulted from Estonia's heavy dependency upon trade with Russia. The economy is still largely state-run, but some progress towards privatization has been made.

RECENT HISTORY

When the Communists took power in Russia (1917), Estonia seceded, but a German occupation and two Russian invasions delayed independence until 1919. Estonia's fragile democracy was replaced by a dictatorship in 1934. The Non-Aggression Pact (1939) between Hitler and Stalin assigned Estonia to the USSR, which invaded and annexed the republic (1940). Estonia was occupied by Nazi Germany (1941–44). When Soviet rule was reimposed (1945), large-scale Russian settlement replaced over 120 000 Estonians who had been killed or deported to Siberia. In 1988, reforms in the USSR allowed Estonian nationalists to operate openly. Nationalists won a majority in the republic's parliament, gradually assumed greater autonomy and seceded following the failed coup by Communist hardliners in Moscow (August 1991). The USSR recognized Estonia's independence in September 1991. In 1992 the introduction of strict Estonian citizenship laws that denied full rights to most Russian-speakers increased tension with Russia, which halted the withdrawal of troops from Estonia.

ETHIOPIA

Official name: Ityopia (Ethiopia). Previously known as Abyssinia.

Member of: UN, OAU.

Area: 1 106 200 km² (427 135 sq mi) excluding Eritrea.

Population: 48 294 000 (1991 est) excluding Eritrea.

Capital and major cities: Addis Ababa 1 739 000, Dire Dawa 122 000, Gondar 88 000, Dese (Dessie) 78 000 (1991 est).

Languages: Amharic (official), Arabic, Oromo (43%).

Religions: Sunni Islam (45%), Ethiopian Orthodox (40%).

Education: *Literacy rate:* 71% (1987 est). *Years of compulsory schooling:* education is free from 6 to 19 but is not compulsory. *Universities:* 2.

Defence: *Total armed strength:* over 65 000 (1991). *Military service:* 12–18 months.

GOVERNMENT

The constitution provides for elections every five years by universal adult suffrage for the 835-member National Assembly (Shengo), which elects the President and appoints the Cabinet. The main political movements include the Tigrayan People's Liberation

Front, the Ethiopian People's Democratic Organization and the Oromo People's Democratic Organization. In 1992 a plan for a federal system of 14 autonomous regions (including Eritrea) was announced. Eritrea (*qv*) has *de facto* been an independent state since 1991 and is scheduled to attain sovereignty on 24 May 1993.
President: Meles Zenawi.
Prime Minister: Tamirat Layne.

GEOGRAPHY

The Western Highlands – including the Tigré Plateau and the Semien Mountains – are separated from the lower Eastern Highlands by a wide rift valley. *Principal rivers:* Blue Nile (Abay Wenz), Tekeze, Awash, Omo, Sagan. *Highest point:* Ras Dashen 4620 m (15 158 ft).

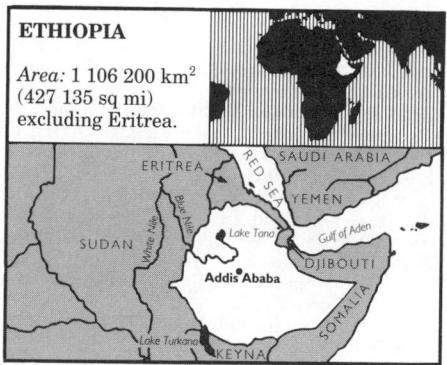

ETHIOPIA

Area: 1 106 200 km² (427 135 sq mi) excluding Eritrea.

Climate: Very hot and dry in the north and east, with a temperate climate in the highlands.

ECONOMY

Secessionist wars have damaged an impoverished, underdeveloped economy. Most Ethiopians are involved in subsistence farming, but drought and overgrazing have led to desertification. Coffee is the main foreign-currency earner. The economy is in serious difficulties owing to the end of aid from the former Eastern bloc.

RECENT HISTORY

Under Emperor Menelik II, Ethiopia survived the European scramble for empire and defeated an Italian invasion (1896). However, the Italians occupied Ethiopia from 1936 to 1941. Emperor Haile Selassie (1892–1975) played a prominent part in African affairs, but – failing to modernize Ethiopia or overcome its extreme poverty – he was overthrown in 1974. Allied to the USSR, a left-wing military regime instituted revolutionary change, but, even with Cuban help, it was unable to overcome secessionist guerrilla movements in Eritrea and Tigray. Drought, soil erosion and civil war brought severe famine in the 1980s. President Mengistu – who ruled a one-party Marxist-Leninist state from 1979 to 1991 – was toppled by an alliance of Tigrayan, Eritrean, Oromo and other forces in 1991. Multi-party rule was restored and new constitutional arrangements to accommodate various regional secessionist movement are to be implemented. However, Eritrea effectively seceded in 1991 and – following a referendum in favour of independence (April 1993) – is scheduled to assume sovereignty on 24 May 1993.

FIJI

Official name: Matanitu Ko Viti (Republic of Fiji).
Member of: UN, South Pacific Forum.
Area: 18 376 km² (7095 sq mi).
Population: 738 000 (1991 est).
Capital: Suva 141 000 (city 70 000), Lautoka 29 000 (1988 census).
Languages: English, Fijian (48%), Hindi (46%).
Religions: Methodist (45%), Hindu (over 40%).
Education: *Literacy rate:* 87% (1986). *Years of compulsory schooling:* schooling is not compulsory. *Universities:* 1.
Defence: *Total armed strength:* 5000 (1991). *Military service:* none.

GOVERNMENT

The 70-seat House of Representatives is elected for five years by universal adult suffrage – 37 members by Fijians (Melanesians), 27 by Indians, 1 by Rotumans, 5 by others. The 34-seat Senate comprises 24 members chosen by the traditional Council of Chiefs, 1 to represent Rotuma, and 9 appointed by the President. The Council appoints the President who, in turn, appoints a PM who commands a majority in the House. Political parties include the Fijian Nationalist Party, the Fijian Political Party, the National Federation Party, the (right-wing) Taukei Solidarity Movement, the Fiji Labour Party and the (liberal) Western United Front.
President: Penaia Ganilau.
Prime Minister: Sitiveni Rabuka.

GEOGRAPHY

The mountainous larger islands are volcanic in origin. The smaller islands are mainly coral reefs.
Principal rivers: Rewa, Sigatoka, Navva, Nodi, Ba.
Highest point: Tomaniivi (Mount Victoria) 1323 m (4341 ft).
Climate: Fiji experiences high temperatures and heavy rainfall with local variations.

ECONOMY

Fiji's economy depends on agriculture, with sugar cane as the main cash crop. Copra, ginger, fish and timber are also exported. Tourism is increasing in importance.

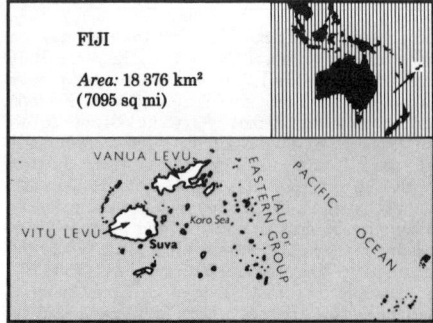

FIJI

Area: 18 376 km²
(7095 sq mi)

VANUA LEVU

VITU LEVU · Koro Sea · Suva · LAU OR EASTERN GROUP · PACIFIC OCEAN

RECENT HISTORY

During a period of great unrest, outside interests supported rival factions until Chief Cakobau, who controlled the W, requested British assistance and ceded Fiji to Britain (1874). Indian labourers arrived to work on sugar plantations, reducing the Fijians, who retained ownership of most of the land, to a minority. Since independence (1970), racial tension and land disputes have brought instability. A military takeover in 1987 overthrew an Indian-led government and established a Fijian-dominated republic outside the Commonwealth. Fiji returned to civilian rule in January 1990, with the resignation of the military officers from the cabinet. The new constitution guarantees political power for the native Melanese (Fijian) population.

FINLAND

Official name: Suomen Tasavalta (Republic of Finland).
Member of: UN, EFTA, CSCE, Council of Europe, OECD.
Area: 338 145 km² (130 557 sq mi).
Population: 4 999 000 (1990 census).
Capital and major cities: Helsinki (Helsingfors) 994 000 (city 492 000), Turku (Åbo) 265 000 (city 159 000), Tampere (Tammerfors) 261 000 (city 173 000), Espoo (Esbo) 173 000 and Vantaa (Vanda) 155 000 are both part of the Helsinki agglomeration, Oulu (Uleaborg) 101 000, Lahti 93 000, Kuopio 81 000, Pori (Björneborg) 76 000 (all including suburbs; 1990 census).
Languages: Finnish (94%), Swedish (6%).
Religion: Lutheran (88%).
Education: *Literacy rate:* almost 100% (1988). *Years of compulsory schooling:* 7–16. *Universities:* 13 plus 6 institutes of university status.
Defence: *Total armed strength:* 31 800 (1991) (plus 700 000 reserves and 4400 frontier guards). *Military service:* 11 months (residents of the Åland Islands are exempt).

GOVERNMENT

The 200-member Parliament (Eduskunta) is elected for four years under a system of proportional representation by universal adult suffrage. Executive power is vested in a President elected for six years by direct popular vote. The President appoints a Council of State (Cabinet) – headed by a Prime Minister – responsible to the Parliament. The main political parties include the Centre Party, the (conservative) National Coalition Party, the Social Democratic Party, the Left-Wing Alliance, the Green Union, the Swedish People's Party, the Liberal People's Party, the Rural Party, and the Communist Party. The Åland Islands have a considerable degree of self-government.
President: Mauno Koivisto.
Prime Minister: Esko Aho.

FINNISH AUTONOMOUS COUNTY

Åland Islands (Ahvenanmaa) *Area*: 1527 km² (590 sq mi). *Population*: 24 600 (1990 census). *Capital*: Mariehamn.

GEOGRAPHY

Nearly one third of Finland lies north of the Arctic Circle and one tenth of the country is covered by lakes, some 50 000 in all. Saimaa – the largest lake – has an area of over 4400 km² (1700 sq mi). During the winter months the Gulfs of Bothnia (to the west) and of Finland (to the south) freeze, and ports have to be kept open by icebreakers. The land has been heavily glaciated, and except for mountains in the northwest most of the country is lowland. *Principal rivers:* Paatsjoki, Torniojoki, Kemijoki, Kokemäenjoki. *Highest point:* Haltiatunturi 1342 m (4344 ft).

Climate: Summers are warm, but winters are long and extremely cold, particularly in the north.

FINLAND

Area: 338 145 km²
(130 557 sq mi).

ECONOMY

Forests cover about two thirds of the country and wood products provide over one third of Finland's foreign earnings. Metalworking and engineering – in particular shipbuilding – are among the most important of Finland's industries, which have a reputation for quality and good design. Finland enjoys a high standard of living, although – apart from forests, copper and rivers suitable for hydro-electric power – the country has few natural resources. There is a large fishing industry, and the agricultural sector produces enough cereals and dairy products for export. The collapse of trade with Russia – traditionally a major trading partner – brought severe economic difficulties to Finland in 1992–93.

RECENT HISTORY

Throughout the 19th century Finland was a grand duchy ruled by Russia. Tension grew as Russia sought to strengthen its political and cultural leverage. In 1906 Finland was allowed to call its own Duma (Parliament), but repression followed again in 1910. After the Russian Revolution of 1917, civil war broke out in Finland. The pro-Russian party was defeated and an independent republican constitution (still in force today) was established (1919). Finland's territorial integrity lasted until the Soviet invasion in 1939, after which land was ceded to the USSR. The failure of a brief alliance with Germany led to further cession of territory to the Soviet Union in 1944. Finland has, since 1945, retained its neutrality and independence. Finland has achieved some influence through the careful exercise of its neutrality, for example, hosting the initial sessions of CSCE (the 'Helsinki accords'). Government in Finland is characterized by multi-party coalitions, and since 1987 parties of the left have lost favour. Economically, Finland is integrated into Western Europe through membership of EFTA and OECD, and is a candidate for EC membership.

FRANCE

Official name: La République française (The French Republic).

Member of: UN, EC, NATO, WEU, G7, OECD, CSCE, Council of Europe.

Area: 543 965 km² (210 026 sq mi) – 'metropolitan' France, excluding overseas départements and collectivités territoriales.

Population: 56 614 000 (1990 census) – 'metropolitan' France.

Capital and major cities: Paris 9 063 000 (city 2 175 000), Lyon 1 262 000 (city 422 000), Marseille 1 087 000 (city 808 000), Lille 950 000 (city 178 000), Bordeaux 686 000 (city 213 000), Toulouse 608 000 (city 366 000), Nantes 492 000 (252 000), Nice 476 000 (city 346 000), Toulon 438 000 (170·000), Grenoble 400 000 (city 154 000), Strasbourg 388 000 (city 256 000), Rouen 380 000 (city 105 000), Valenciennes 336 000 (town 39 000), Cannes 336 000 (city 69 000), Lens 323 000 (town 35 000), Saint-Etienne 313 000 (city 202 000), Nancy 311 000 (city 102 000), Tours 272 000 (city 133 000), Béthune 260 000 (town 26 000), Clermont-Ferrand 254 000 (city 140 000), Le Havre 254 000 (city 197 000), Rennes 245 000 (city 204 000), Orléans 243 000 (city 108 000), Montpellier 235 000 (city 211 000), Dijon 226 000 (city 152 000), Mulhouse 224 000 (city 110 000), Reims 206 000 (city 185 000), Angers 206 000 (city 146 000), Brest 201 000 (city 153 000), Douai 200 000 (city 44 000), Dunkerque 193 000 (town 71 000), Metz 193 000 (city 124 000), Le Mans 189 000 (city 148 000), Caen 189 000 (city 116 000), Mantes-la-Jolie 189 000 (town 45 000), Avignon 181 000 (city 89 000), Limoges 170 000 (city 136 000) (all including suburbs; 1990 census).

Languages: French, with Breton and Basque minorities.

Religions: Roman Catholic (74%), Sunni Islam (4%).

Education: *Literacy rate:* nearly 100%. *Years of compulsory schooling:* 6–16. *Universities:* 70, plus 3 national polytechnics with university status.

Defence: *Total armed strength:* 453 100 (1991) (plus 89 300 paramilitary police and 419 000 reservists). *Military service:* 10 months.

GOVERNMENT

Executive power is vested in the President, who is elected for a 7-year term by universal adult suffrage. The President appoints a Prime Minister and a Council of Ministers – both responsible to Parliament – but it is the President, rather than the PM, who presides over the Council of Ministers. Parliament has two chambers. The Senate (the upper house) comprises 321 members – 296 of whom represent individual départements and 13 of whom represent overseas départements and territories – elected by members of municipal, local and regional councils. The remaining 12 senators are elected by French citizens resident abroad. Senators serve for nine years, with one third of the Senate retiring every three years. The National Assembly (the lower house) comprises 577 deputies – including 22 for overseas départements and territories – elected for a five-year term by universal adult suffrage from single-member constituencies, with a second ballot for the leading candidates if no candidate obtains an absolute majority in the first round. The main political parties include the (conservative Gaullist) RPR (Rally for the Republic), the (centrist) UDF (Union for French Democracy), the PS (Socialist

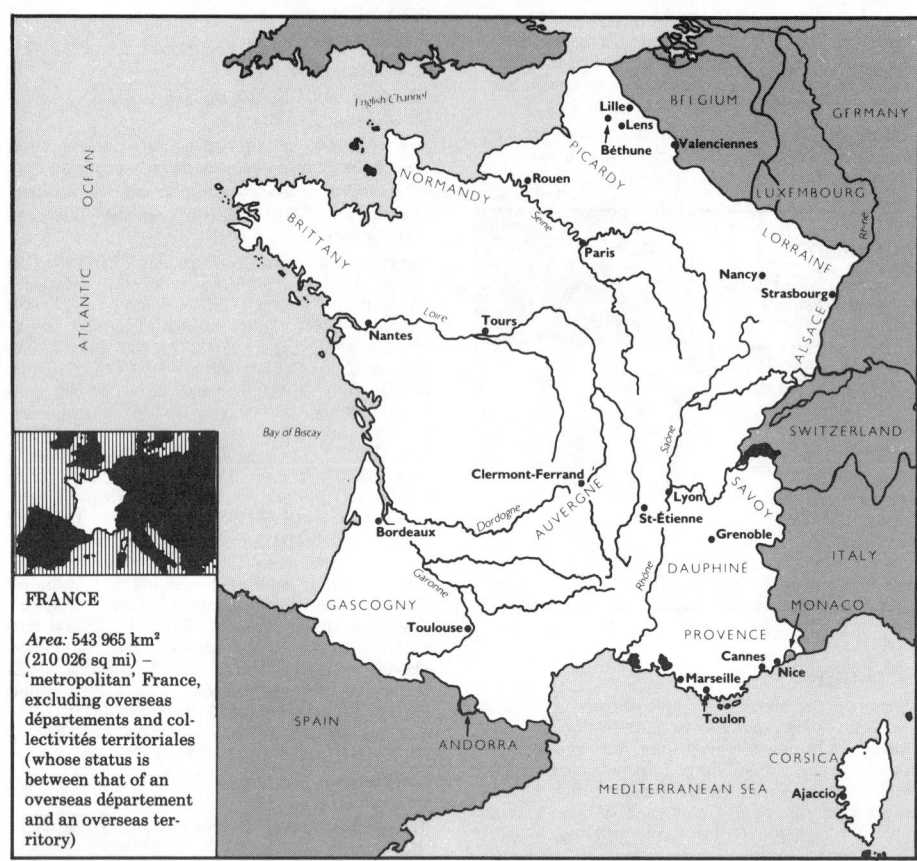

FRANCE

Area: 543 965 km²
(210 026 sq mi) –
'metropolitan' France,
excluding overseas
départements and col-
lectivités territoriales
(whose status is
between that of an
overseas département
and an overseas ter-
ritory)

Party), the Centre Union, the PC (Communist Party),
and the (right-wing) FN (National Front). Since
1982, the 96 metropolitan French départements have
been grouped into 22 regions which have increased
powers of local government.
President: François Mitterrand.
Prime Minister: Edouard Balladur.

FRENCH REGIONS

Population figures are from the 1990 census.

Alsace *Area:* 8280 km² (3197 sq mi). *Population:*
1 624 000. *Administrative centre:* Strasbourg.

Aquitaine *Area:* 41 308 km² (15 949 sq mi).
Population: 2 796 000. *Administrative centre:*
Bordeaux.

Auvergne *Area:* 26 013 km² (10 044 sq mi).
Population: 1 321 000. *Administrative centre:*
Clermont-Ferrand.

Brittany (Bretagne) *Area:* 27 208 km² (10 505 sq
mi). *Population:* 2 796 000. *Administrative centre:*
Rennes.

Burgundy (Bourgogne) *Area:* 31 582 km² (12 194
sq mi). *Population:* 1 609 000. *Administrative centre:*
Dijon.

Centre *Area:* 39 151 km² (15 116 sq mi). *Population:*
2 371 000. *Administrative centre:* Orléans.

Champagne-Ardenne *Area:* 25 606 km² (9886 sq
mi). *Population:* 1 348 000. *Administrative centre:*
Reims.

Corsica (Corse) *Area:* 8680 km² (3351 sq mi).
Population: 250 000. *Administrative centre:* Ajaccio.

Franche-Comté *Area:* 16 202 km² (6256 sq mi).
Population: 1 097 000. *Administrative centre:*
Besançon.

Ile-de-France *Area:* 12 012 km² (4638 sq mi).
Population: 10 660 000. *Administrative centre:* Paris.

Languedoc-Roussillon *Area:* 27 376 km² (10 570
sq mi). *Population:* 2 115 000. *Administrative centre:*
Montpellier.

Limousin *Area:* 16 942 km² (6541 sq mi).
Population: 723 000. *Administrative centre:* Limoges.

Lorraine *Area:* 23 547 km² (9091 sq mi).
Population: 2 306 000. *Administrative centre:* Nancy.

Lower Normandy (Basse-Normandie) *Area:*
17 589 km² (6791 sq mi). *Population:* 1 391 000.
Administrative centre: Caen.

Midi-Pyrénées *Area:* 45 348 km² (17 509 sq mi).
Population: 2 431 000. *Administrative centre:* Toulouse.

Nord-Pas-de-Calais *Area:* 12 414 km² (4793 sq
mi). *Population:* 3 965 000. *Administrative centre:*
Lille.

Pays de la Loire *Area:* 32 082 km² (12 387 sq mi).
Population: 3 059 000. *Administrative centre:* Nantes.

Picardy (Picardie) *Area:* 19 399 km² (7490 sq mi).
Population: 1 811 000. *Administrative centre:* Amiens.

Poitou-Charentes *Area:* 25 810 km² (9965 sq mi).
Population: 1 595 000. *Administrative centre:* Poitiers.

Provence-Côte d'Azur *Area*: 31 400 km² (12 124 sq mi). *Population*: 4 258 000. *Administrative centre*: Marseille.

Rhône-Alpes *Area*: 43 698 km² (16 872 sq mi). *Population*: 5 351 000. *Administrative centre*: Lyon.

Upper Normandy (Haute-Normandie) *Area*: 12 317 km² (4756 sq mi). *Population*: 1 737 000. *Administrative centre*: Rouen.

GEOGRAPHY

The Massif Central – a plateau of old hard rocks, rising to almost 2000 m (6500 ft) – occupies the middle of France. The Massif is surrounded by four major lowlands, which together make up almost two thirds of the total area of the country. The Paris Basin – the largest of these lowlands – is divided by low ridges and fertile plains and plateaux, but is united by the river system of the Seine and its tributaries. To the east of the Massif Central is the long narrow Rhône-Saône Valley, while to the west the Loire Valley stretches to the Atlantic. Southwest of the Massif Central lies the Aquitaine Basin, a large fertile region drained by the River Garonne and its tributaries. A discontinuous ring of highlands surrounds France. In the northwest the Armorican Massif (Brittany) rises to 411 m (1350 ft). In the southwest the Pyrenees form a high natural boundary with Spain. The Alps in the southeast divide France from Italy and contain the highest peak in Europe (outside the Caucasus). The lower Jura – in the east – form a barrier between France and Switzerland, while the Vosges Mountains separate the Paris Basin from the Rhine Valley. In the northeast, the Ardennes extend into France from Belgium. The Mediterranean island of Corsica is an ancient massif rising to 2710 m (8891 ft). *Principal rivers:* Rhine (Rhin), Loire, Rhône, Seine, Garonne, Saône. *Highest point:* Mont Blanc 4807 m (15 771 ft).

Climate: The south is Mediterranean with warm summers and mild winters. The rest of France has a temperate climate, although the more continental east experiences warmer summers and colder winters. Rainfall is moderate, with highest falls in the mountains and lowest falls in the Paris Basin.

ECONOMY

Nearly two thirds of France is farmed. The principal products include cereals (wheat, maize, barley and even rice), meat and dairy products, sugar beet, and grapes for wine. France is remarkably self-sufficient in agriculture, with tropical fruit and animal feeds being the only major imports. However, the small size of land holdings remains a problem, despite consolidation and the efforts of cooperatives. Reafforestation is helping to safeguard the future of the important timber industry. Natural resources include coal, iron ore, copper, bauxite and tungsten, as well as petroleum and natural gas, and plentiful sites for hydroelectric power plants. The major French industries include: textiles, chemicals, steel, food processing, motor vehicles, aircraft, and mechanical and electrical engineering. Traditionally French firms have been small, but mergers have resulted in larger corporations able to compete internationally. France is world's fourth industrial power after the USA, Japan and Germany. During the later 1980s many of the state-owned corporations were privatized. Over one half of the labour force is involved in service industries, in particular administration, banking, finance, and tourism.

RECENT HISTORY

The Second Empire (1852–70) of Napoleon III (nephew of Napoleon I) was brought to an end by defeat in the Franco-Prussian war of 1870–1. After this defeat, the Third Republic (1871–1940) was established, and immediately faced the revolt of the Paris Commune, when radical republicans and socialists set up a self-governing commune in the capital. It was bloodily suppressed by French troops in May 1871, and 20 000 communards were killed or excuted. Continuing controversy over the role of religion in the state – particularly the question of religious-based or secular education – did not end until Church and state were finally separated in 1905. At the end of the 19th century the French colonial empire reached its greatest extent, in particular in Africa, SE Asia and the Pacific. The Third Republic also saw continuing conflict over France's own boundaries – Alsace-Lorraine was lost in 1870 but recovered in 1918 at the end of World War I (1914–18), during which trench warfare in northern France claimed countless lives. Georges Clemenceau (1841–1929) – who had led France as prime minister during the war – lost power in 1919 when the French electorate perceived the harsh peace terms as being too lenient to Germany.

Between 1919 and 1939 French government was characterized by instablity and frequent changes of administration. In 1936 Léon Blum (1872–1950) led a Popular Front (Socialist-Communist-Radical) coalition to power and instituted many important social reforms. In World War II (1939–45), Germany rapidly defeated the French in 1940 and completely occupied the country in 1942. Marshal Philippe Pétain (1856–1951) led a collaborationist regime in the city of Vichy, while General Charles de Gaulle (1890–1970) headed the Free French in exile in London from 1940. France was liberated following the Allied landings in Normandy in 1944. After the war, the Fourth Republic (1946–58) was marked by instability and the Suez Crisis of 1956 – when France and the UK sought to prevent Egypt's nationalization of the canal. The end of the colonial era was marked by nationalist revolts in some of the colonies, notably Vietnam – where the Communists defeated French colonial forces at Dien Bien Phu in 1954 – and Algeria. The troubles in Algeria – including the revolt of the French colonists and the campaign of their terrorist organization, the OAS – led to the end of the Fourth Republic and to the accession to power of General de Gaulle in 1959.

As first president of the Fifth Republic, de Gaulle granted Algerian independence in 1962. While the French colonial empire – with a few minor exceptions – was being disbanded, France's position within Western Europe was being strengthened, especially by vigorous participation in the European Community. At the same time, de Gaulle sought to pursue a foreign policy independent of the USA, building up France's nuclear capability and withdrawing French forces from NATO's integrated command structure. Although restoring political and economic stability to France, domestic dissatisfaction – including the student revolt of May 1968 – led de Gaulle to resign in 1969. De Gaulle's policies were broadly pursued by his successors as president, Georges Pompidou (in office 1969–74) and Valéry Giscard d'Estaing (1974–81). The modernization of France continued apace under the country's first Socialist president, François Mitterand (1916–), who was elected in 1981, although the Socialist Party was heavily defeated in the general election in 1993.

FRENCH OVERSEAS DEPARTEMENTS

The overseas départements are integral parts of the French Republic.

Guadeloupe (a group of islands in the Caribbean including Guadeloupe, the immediate dependencies of La Désirade, Les Saintes, Marie-Galante, and the more distant islands of Saint-Barthélemy and Saint-Martin). *Area*: 1780 km² (687 sq mi) – Guadeloupe and immediate dependencies 1706 km² (659 sq mi), Saint-Barthélemy 21 km² (8 sq mi), Saint-Martin 53 km² (20.5 sq mi). *Population*: 387 000 (1990 census). *Capital*: Basse-Terre 38 000 (town 14 000). (The capital of Saint-Barthélemy is Gustavia; the capital of Saint-Martin is Marigot.) *Largest town*: Pointe-à-Pitre 122 000 (town 26 000) (1990 census).

Guyane (French Guiana) (a territory situated between Brazil and Suriname) *Area*: 90 000 km² (34 750 sq mi). *Population*: 115 000 (1990 census). *Capital*: Cayenne 42 000 (1990 census).

Martinique (an island in the Caribbean) *Area*: 1100 km² (425 sq mi). *Population*: 360 000 (1990 census). *Capital*: Fort-de-France 102 000 (1990 census).

Réunion (an island in the southern Indian Ocean) *Area*: 2512 km² (970 sq mi). *Population*: 597 000 (1990 census). *Capital*: Saint-Denis 122 000 (1990 census).

FRENCH COLLECTIVITES TERRITORIALES

The collectivités territoriales – a status between that of an overseas département and an overseas territory – are integral parts of the French Republic.

Mayotte (an island in the Comoros group) *Area*: 376 km² (145 sq mi). *Population*: 94 400 (1990 census). *Capital*: Dzaoudzi 5900. *Largest town:* Mamoudzou 12 000 (1990 census).

Saint-Pierre-et-Miquelon (two main islands and six small islets south of the Newfoundland coast) *Area*: 242 km² (93 sq mi). *Population*: 6400 (1990 census). *Capital*: Saint-Pierre 5700 (1990 census).

FRENCH OVERSEAS TERRITORIES

French Polynesia (five archipelagos in the Pacific Ocean including the Australes, Marquises and Gambier islands). *Area*: 4200 km² (1622 sq mi). *Population*: 199 000 (1991 est.) *Capital*: Papeete (on Tahiti) 23 500 (1991 est.).

New Caledonia (New Caledonia and its dependencies – the Loyalty Islands, Ile des Pins and the Bélep archipelago – are situated in the south Pacific Ocean.) *Area*: 19 103 km² (7376 sq mi). *Population*: 168 000 (1990 est.) *Capital*: Nouméa 65 000 (1989 est.).

Southern and Antarctic Territories (Southern Territories only – two archipelagos and two small islands situated in the extreme south of the Indian Ocean.) *Area*: Kerguelen Archipelago 18 130 km² (7000 sq mi); Crozet Archipelago 1295 km² (500 sq mi), Amsterdam Island 155 km² (60 sq mi), St Paul Island 18 km² (7 sq mi). *Population*: there is a fluctuating population of scientific missions of c. 140. *Principal settlement*: Port-aux-Français (on Kerguelen) 100. (Information regarding the Antarctic Territories is the section Other Territories following this chapter.)

Wallis and Futuna Islands (two small archipelagos in the Pacific Ocean) *Area*: 274 km² (106 sq mi) – kingdom of Uvéa 159 km² (61 sq mi), kingdom of Sigave 64 km² (25 sq mi), kingdom of Alo 51 km² (20 sq mi). *Population*: 13 700 (1990 est.) – Uvéa 7600, Sigave 3000, Alo 3000. *Capital*: Mata-Utu (in Uvéa) 810 (1990 est.).

GABON

Official name: La République gabonaise (The Gabonese Republic).

Member of: UN, OAU, OPEC.

Area: 267 667 km² (103 347 sq mi).

Population: 1 133 000 (1990 est.).

Capital and major cities: Libreville 352 000, Port-Gentil 164 000, Masuku (formerly Franceville) 75 000 (1987 est.).

Languages: French (official), 40 local languages including Fang (30%).

Religions: Roman Catholic (71%), animist (29%).

Education: *Literacy rate:* 60.7% (1990). *Years of compulsory schooling:* 6–16. *Universities:* 2.

Defence: *Total armed strength:* 4750 (1991) (plus 2800 paramilitary and 2000 gendarmes). *Military service:* none.

GOVERNMENT

The President – who is elected by compulsory universal adult suffrage for a seven-year term – appoints a Council of Ministers (over which he presides) and a Prime Minister. The National Assembly has 120 members directly elected for five years. The main political parties include the (former monopoly) Gabonese Democratic Party (PDG), the African Forum for Reconstruction (FAR) and the Woodcutters' Union (RB).
President: Omar Bongo.
Prime Minister: Casimir Oye Mba.

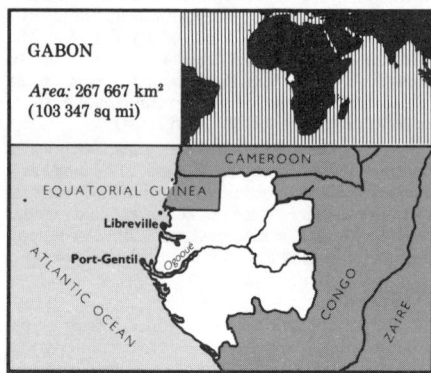

GABON

Area: 267 667 km²
(103 347 sq mi)

GEOGRAPHY

Apart from the narrow coastal plain, low plateaux make up most of the country. *Principal river:* Ogooué. *Highest point:* Mont Iboundji 1580 m (5185 ft).

Climate: The equatorial climate is hot and humid with little seasonal variation.

ECONOMY

Petroleum, natural gas, manganese, uranium and iron ore – and a relatively small population – make Gabon the richest Black African country, although most Gabonese are subsistence farmers.

RECENT HISTORY

Gabon was colonized by the French in the late 19th century. Pro-French Léon M'Ba (1902–67) led the country to independence in 1960. Deposed in a coup (1964), he was restored to power by French troops. Under his successor, Omar Bongo, Gabon has continued its pro-Western policies. Pro-democracy demonstrations and strikes, followed by anti-government riots in 1990, prompted France to dispatch troops to Gabon to restore order. President Bongo appointed a transitional government and permitted the establishment of a multi-party system.

GAMBIA

Official name: The Republic of the Gambia.

Member of: UN, OAU, ECOWAS, Commonwealth.

Area: 11 295 km² (4361 sq mi).

Population: 883 000 (1991 est).

Capital and major cities: Banjul 147 000 (city 44 000), Brikama 24 000 (1986 est).

Language: English (official), local languages.

Religions: Sunni Islam (90%), various Protestant Churches (9%) – mainly Anglican.

Education: *Literacy rate:* 27.2% (1990). *Years of compulsory schooling:* schooling is not compulsory. *Universities* none.

Defence: *Total armed strength:* 900 (1991) (including an armed police force of over 600). *Military service:* normally voluntary, but compulsory in certain circumstances.

GOVERNMENT

The President and 36 of the 50 members of the House of Representatives are elected by universal adult suffrage every five years. The remaining members of the House are appointed. The President appoints a Vice-President – to lead the government in the House – and a Cabinet of Ministers. The main political parties are the People's Progressive Party and the National Convention Party.
President: Sir Dawda Kairaba Jawara.

GEOGRAPHY

The Gambia is a narrow low-lying country on either bank of the River Gambia. *Principal river:* Gambia. *Highest point:* an unnamed point on the Senegalese border 43 m (141 ft).

Climate: The climate is tropical, with a dry season from November to May.

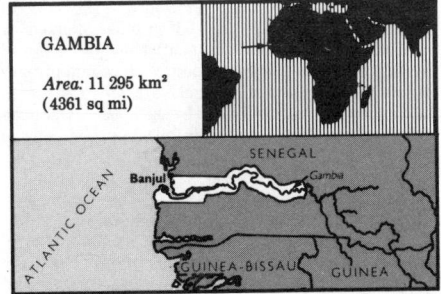

GAMBIA

Area: 11 295 km² (4361 sq mi)

ECONOMY

Until recent years the economy was largely based on the cultivation of groundnuts. Tourism is now the major foreign-currency earner.

RECENT HISTORY

A British colony was established in 1843. The Gambia achieved independence in 1965 under Sir Dawda K. Jawara. In 1981 an attempted coup against

his rule encouraged efforts to merge with the neighbouring French-speaking country of Senegal, but the confederation was dissolved in 1989. The Gambia remains a democracy.

GEORGIA

Official name: Sakartvelo (Georgia) or Sakartvelos Respublica (The Republic of Georgia).

Member of: UN, CSCE.

Area: 69 700 km² (26 900 sq mi).

Population: 5 464 000 (1991 est).

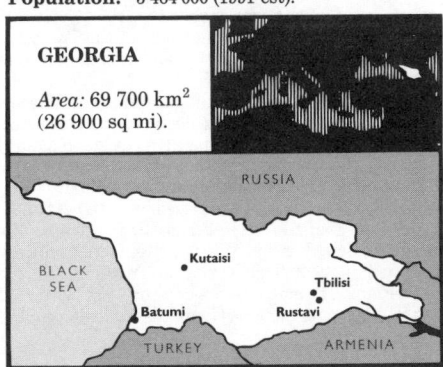

GEORGIA

Area: 69 700 km² (26 900 sq mi).

Capital and major cities: Tbilisi 1 264 000, Kutaisi 235 000, Rustavi 159 000, Batumi 136 000, Sukhumi 121 000 (1991 est).

Languages: Georgian (70%), Armenian (8%), Russian (6%), Azeri (3%), Ossetian (2%), Greek (2%), Abkhazian (2%).

Religions: Georgian Orthodox majority.

Education: *Literacy rate:* No figure available. *Years of compulsory schooling:* 7–17. *Universities:* 3 universities and 1 polytechnic.

Defence: *Total armed strength:* no figure available.

GOVERNMENT

The constitution provides for the election for four years by universal adult suffrage of a 234-member legislature and a President – who appoints a Council of Ministers. A new constitution is to be drafted. The main political parties – out of 23 in parliament – include the (coalition nationalist) Round Table-Free Georgia, the National Democratic Party and the Social Democratic Party.
President: Eduard Shevardnadze.
Prime Minister: Tamaz Nodarishvili.

GEOGRAPHY

The spine of the Caucasus Mountains forms the N border of Georgia. A lower range, the Little Caucasus, occupies S Georgia. Central Georgia comprises the Kolkhida lowlands. *Principal rivers:* Kura, Rioni. *Highest point:* Elbrus (on the Russian border) 5642 m (18 510 ft).

Climate: Coastal and central Georgia has a moist Mediterranean climate. The rest of the country is drier but the climate varies considerably with altitude and aspect.

ECONOMY

Despite a shortage of cultivable land, Georgia has a diversified agricultural sector including tea, citrus fruit, tobacco, cereals, vines, livestock and vegetables. Natural resources include coal, manganese and plentiful hydroelectric power. Machine building, food processing and chemicals are major industries. The private sector is probably more highly developed than in any other former Soviet republic, but the economy was damaged by civil war (1991–92).

RECENT HISTORY

Russia annexed Georgia by degrees early in the 19th century. Following the Russian Revolution (1918), a Georgian republic, allied to Germany, was proclaimed. A British occupation (1918–20) in favour of the Tsarist White Russians failed to win local support, and Georgia was invaded by the Soviet Red Army (1921). Georgia became part of the Transcaucasian Soviet Republic in 1921 and a separate Union Republic within the USSR in 1936. Following the abortive coup by Communist hardliners in Moscow (September 1991), Georgia declared independence. Locked into a fierce civil war, Georgia remained outside the Commonwealth of Independent States (the defence and economic community founded when the USSR was dissolved in December 1991). A temporary state council – led by Eduard Shevardnadze, the former Soviet Foreign Minister – replaced a military council in 1992. The Abkhazian Muslims and the Ossetians attempted secession in 1992 and civil unrest continues among Georgia's minority peoples.

GERMANY

Official name: Bundesrepublik Deutschland (The Federal Republic of Germany).

Member of: UN, EC, NATO, CSCE, WEU, G7, OECD, Council of Europe.

Area: 357 050 km² (137 857 sq mi).

Population: 79 096 000 (1991 est).

Capital and major cities: Berlin (capital in name only; the lower house of parliament is scheduled to move to Berlin in 1995) 3 410 000, Bonn (capital *de facto*) 284 000, Essen 4 700 000 (Essen/ Ruhr; city 621 000), Hamburg 1 626 000, Munich (München) 1 218 000, Cologne (Köln) 940 000, Frankfurt 629 000, Dortmund (part of the Essen/ Ruhr agglomeration) 589 000, Düsseldorf 570 000, Stuttgart 556 000, Bremen 546 000, Leipzig 539 000, Duisburg (part of the Essen/Ruhr agglomeration) 530 000, Dresden 516 000, Hannover 502 000, Nuremberg (Nürnberg) 482 000, Bochum (part of the Essen/ Ruhr agglomeration) 390 000, Wuppertal 372 000, Bielefeld 313 000, Chemnitz 310 000, Mannheim 303 000, Magdeburg 290 000, Gelsenkirchen (part of the Essen/Ruhr agglomeration) 288 000, Karlsruhe 267 000, Wiesbaden 255 000, Rostock 255 000, Brunswick (Braunschweig) 254 000, Mönchengladbach 254 000, Münster 250 000, Augsburg 248 000, Kiel 241 000, Krefeld 237 000, Halle 235 000, Aachen 234 000, Oberhausen (part of the Essen/Ruhr agglomeration) 221 000, Erfurt 220 000, Lübeck 211 000, Hagen 210 000, Kassel 190 000, Saarbrücken 189 000, Freiburg 185 000, Mülheim 176 000, Hamm 175 000, Herne (part of the Essen/Ruhr agglomeration) 175 000, Mainz 175 000, Solingen 162 000, Ludwigshafen 159 000, Leverkusen 158 000, Osnabrück 157 000 (1990 est).

Language: German, small Sorb minority.

Religions: Various Protestant Churches (34% – mainly Lutheran), Roman Catholic (35%), Sunni Islam (2%).

Education: *Literacy rate:* almost 100%. *Years of*

compulsory schooling: 6–18. *Universities:* 78 (including the open university and institutes of university status).

Defence: *Total armed strength:* 476 300 (1991). *Military service:* 12 months.

GERMANY
Area: 357 050 km² (137 857 sq mi).

GOVERNMENT

Each of the 16 states (Länder; singular Länd) is represented in the 79-member upper house of Parliament – the Federal Council (Bundesrat) – by three, four or six members of the state government (depending on population). These members are appointed for a limited period. The lower house – the Federal Assembly (Bundestag) – has 662 members elected for four years by universal adult suffrage under a mixed system of single-member constituencies and proportional representation. Executive power rests with the Federal Government, led by the Federal Chancellor – who is elected by the Bundestag. The Federal President is elected for a five-year term by a combined sitting of the Bundesrat and an equal number of representatives of the states. The Parliament, Government, ministries and the Federal Chancellor and President are based in Bonn, although Berlin was named as capital in August 1990. The main political parties include the (socialist) SPD (Social Democratic Party), the (conservative) CDU (Christian Democratic Union) and CSU (Christian Social Union, its Bavarian equivalent), the (liberal) FDP (Free Democratic Party), Die Grünen (the Green Party), and the PDS (Party of Democratic Socialism; the former East German Communist Party). Each state has its own Parliament and Government.

Federal President: Dr Richard von Weizsäcker.
Federal Chancellor: Dr Helmut Kohl.

GERMAN LÄNDER

Population figures are 1990 estimates.

Baden-Württemberg *Area*: 35 752 km² (13 803 sq mi). *Population*: 9 619 000. *Capital*: Stuttgart.

Bavaria (Bayern) *Area*: 70 546 km² (27 238 sq mi). *Population*: 11 221 000. *Capital*: Munich (München).

Berlin *Area*: 883 km² (341 sq mi). *Population*: 3 410 000. *Capital*: Berlin.

Brandenburg *Area*: 28 016 km² (10 817 sq mi). *Population*: 2 641 000. *Capital*: Potsdam.

Bremen *Area*: 404 km² (156 sq mi). *Population*: 674 000. *Capital*: Bremen.

Hamburg *Area*: 755 km² (292 sq mi). *Population*: 1 626 000. *Capital*: Hamburg.

Hesse (Hessen) *Area*: 21 114 km² (8152 sq mi). *Population*: 5 661 000. *Capital*: Wiesbaden.

Lower Saxony (Niedersachsen) *Area*: 47 431 km² (18 313 sq mi). *Population*: 7 284 000. *Capital*: Hannover.

Mecklenburg-West Pomerania (Mecklenburg-Vorpommern) *Area*: 26 694 km² (10 307 sq mi). *Population*: 1 964 000. *Capital*: Schwerin.

North Rhine-Westphalia (Nordrhein-Westfalen) *Area*: 34 066 km² (13 153 sq mi). *Population*: 17 104 000. *Capital*: Düsseldorf.

Rhineland-Palatinate (Rheinland-Pfalz) *Area*: 19 848 km² (7663 sq mi). *Population*: 3 702 000. *Capital*: Mainz.

Saarland *Area*: 2571 km² (993 sq mi). *Population*: 1 065 000. *Capital*: Saarbrücken.

Saxony (Sachsen) *Area*: 17 713 km² (6839 sq mi). *Population*: 4 901 000. *Capital*: Dresden.

Saxony-Anhalt (Sachsen-Anhalt) *Area*: 20 297 km² (7837 sq mi). *Population*: 2 965 000. *Capital*: Magdeburg.

Schleswig-Holstein *Area*: 15 720 km² (6069 sq mi). *Population*: 2 595 000. *Capital*: Kiel.

Thüringen (Thuringia) *Area*: 15 209 km² (5872 sq mi). *Population*: 2 684 000. *Capital*: Erfurt.

GEOGRAPHY

The North German Plain – a region of fertile farmlands and sandy heaths – is drained by the Rivers Elbe and Weser and their tributaries. In the west, the plain merges with the North Rhine lowlands which contain the Ruhr coalfield and almost one quarter of the country's population. A belt of plateaux, formed of old hard rocks, crosses the country from east to west and includes the Hunsrück and Eifel highlands in the Rhineland, the Taunus and Westerwald uplands in Hesse, and extends into the Harz and Erz Mountains in Thuringia. The Rhine cuts through these central plateaux in a deep gorge. In southern Germany, the Black Forest (Schwarzwald) separates the Rhine valley from the fertile valleys and scarplands of Swabia. The forested edge of the Bohemian uplands marks the Czech border, while the Bavarian Alps form the frontier with Austria. *Principal rivers:* Rhine (Rhein), Elbe, Danube (Donau), Oder, Moselle (Mosel), Neckar, Havel, Leine, Weser. *Highest point:* Zugspitze 2963 m (9721 ft).

Climate: The climate is temperate, but with considerable variations between the generally mild north coastal plain and the Bavarian Alps in the south, which have cool summers and cold winters. The eastern part of the country has warm summers and cold winters.

ECONOMY

Germany is the world's third industrial power after the USA and Japan. The country's recovery after World War II has been called the 'German economic miracle'. The principal industries include mechanical and electrical engineering, chemicals, textiles, food processing and vehicles, with heavy industry and engineering concentrated in the Ruhr, chemicals in cities on the Rhine, and motor vehicles in large provincial centres such as Stuttgart. From the 1980s, there has been a spectacular growth in high-technology industries. Apart from coal and brown coal, and relatively small deposits of iron ore, bauxite, copper ore, nickel, tin, silver, potash and salt, Germany has relatively few natural resources, and the country relies heavily upon imports. Labour has also been in short supply, and large numbers of 'guest workers' (Gastarbeiter) – particularly from Turkey and the former Yugoslavia – have been recruited. Since 1990 the labour shortage in the western part of the country has also been met by migration from the east, the former German Democratic Republic. Service industries employ almost twice as many people as manufacturing industry. Banking and finance are major foreign-currency earners, and Frankfurt is one of the world's leading financial and business centres.

The unification of Germany in October 1990 presented a major problem for the German economy. The GDR's economy had previously been the most successful in CMEA (Comecon), but, compared with West Germany, it lagged in terms of production, quality, design, profitability and standards of living. A trust – the Treuhandanstalt – was established to oversee the privatization of the 8000 state-run firms in eastern Germany. The main industries of the former GDR include machinery and transportation equipment, steel, cement, chemicals, fertilizers and plastics, but many of these have been unable to compete with their western counterparts. The Trabant and Wartburg car firms, for example, ceased production in 1991, and, bought by West German firms, began production of western models. However, many other East German firms have gone bankrupt, and by late 1992 unemployment in the former GDR stood at nearly 20%.

The main German agricultural products include hops (for beer), grapes (for wine), sugar beet, wheat, barley, and dairy products. The collectivized farms of the former GDR – which provided that country's basic food needs – were privatized in 1990–91. Forests cover almost one third of the country and support a flourishing timber industry.

RECENT HISTORY

In 1871, a German Empire – of four kingdoms, six grand duchies, five duchies and seven principalities – was proclaimed with the King of Prussia as Emperor of Germany (Kaiser). From 1871 to 1918, an expansionist unified Germany attempted to extend its influence throughout Europe, engaged in naval and commercial rivalry with Britain, and built a colonial empire. Under the mercurial Kaiser Wilhelm (reigned 1888–1918), Germany was a destabilizing force in world politics.

In June 1914, the heir to the throne of Austria-Hungary was assassinated in Sarajevo. The Austrians – supported by the Germans, who feared for the disintegration of their ally – blamed Serbia and threatened to attack. The Serbs in turn appealed for aid from their fellow Slavs in Russia, who began to mobilize their vast army. Fearing attack, Germany put into action a strategy known as the Schlieffen Plan, and declared war on both Russia and France. The plan was designed to knock out France (Russia's ally) before the Russians completed mobilization. As German troops crossed into neutral Belgium, as a preliminary to attacking France, the UK – as a guarantor of Belgium's independence – declared war on Germany. The war lasted from 1914 to 1918, with Germany, Austria and Turkey ranged against a worldwide alliance. The Western Front quickly became bogged down in trench warfare, and the balance of power between the two sides only shifted in favour of the Allies when the USA entered the war against Germany in 1917. On the Eastern Front Russia dissolved into revolutionary chaos (1917) and the Germans took the opportunity to attack with decisive results. By August 1918, Austrian and Turkish power was broken and the Germans were isolated. With public confidence at home evaporating, Germany surrendered in November 1918.

Defeat in World War I led to the loss of much territory in Europe and the colonies overseas, the end of the German monarchies, the imposition of a substantial sum for reparations, and the occupation of the Rhineland by Allied forces until 1930. The liberal Weimar republic (1919–33) could not bring economic or political stability. In the early 1930s the National Socialist German Workers', or Nazi, Party increased in popularity, urging the establishment of a strong centralized government, an aggressive foreign policy, 'Germanic character' and the overturn of the postwar settlement. In 1933, the Nazi leader, Adolf Hitler (1889–1945) became Chancellor and in 1934 President. His Third Reich (empire) annexed Austria (1938), dismembered Czechoslovakia (1939), and embarked on the extermination of the Jews and others that the Nazis regarded as 'inferior'. In furtherance of territorial claims in Poland, Hitler concluded the Nazi-Soviet Non-Aggression Pact (24 August), which allowed the USSR to annex Estonia, Latvia and Lithuania and agreed to divide Poland between the Soviets and the Nazis. Invading Poland on the 1 September 1939, Hitler launched Germany into war.

Britain and France declared war on Germany two days later but could do nothing to help the Poles. After a pause known as the 'Phoney War', Hitler turned towards the west (1940) and invaded Denmark, Norway, Belgium, the Netherlands, Luxembourg and France. After Italy entered the war against the UK and France (1941), the Balkan Front opened up, when Italy invaded Albania and Greece. The German invasion of the USSR (1941) opened the Eastern Front. Also in 1941 Japan joined the Axis powers (Germany and Italy) by attacking the US naval base at Pearl Harbor, Hawaii. At the height of Axis power in 1942, Germany controlled – directly or through allies – virtually the whole of Europe except the British Isles, and neutral Switzerland, Sweden, Spain and Portugal. The tide against the Axis states turned in North Africa late in 1942. In 1943, Italy surrendered, and Soviet forces started to push back the Germans. In 1944 the Allied landings in Normandy began the liberation of Western Europe, and advances into the Balkans cleared the Germans from Soviet territory. After massive Allied bombing attacks, the end came swiftly for Germany. Hitler committed suicide in April 1945 and Berlin fell to the Soviets early in May.

In 1945, Germany lost substantial territories to Poland, and was divided – as was its capital, Berlin – into four zones of occupation by the Allies (Britain, France, the USA and the USSR). Their intention was a united, disarmed Germany, but cooperation between the Allies rapidly broke down, and in 1948–49 the USSR blockaded West Berlin. The western zones of Germany were merged economically in 1948. After the merger of the western zones to form the Federal Republic of Germany, the German Democratic Republic was proclaimed in the Soviet zone (October 1949). The GDR's economic progress suffered by comparison with that of the Federal Republic. Food shortages and repressive Communist rule led to an uprising in 1953. West Germany gained sovereignty – as a member of the Western alliance – in 1955.

The division of Germany was only grudgingly accepted in West Germany. Chancellor Konrad Adenauer (1876–1967) refused to recognize East Germany as a separate state and relations with the Soviet Union remained uncertain. Major problems with the Eastern bloc included the undefined status of the areas taken over by Poland in 1945 and the difficult position of West Berlin – a part of the Federal Republic isolated within Communist East Germany. Relations between the two Germanies were soured as large numbers of East Germans fled to the West, and this outflow was stemmed only when Walter Ulbricht (East German Communist Party leader 1950–71) ordered the building of the Berlin Wall (1961). Adenauer strove to gain the acceptance of West Germany back into Western Europe through reconciliation with France and participation in the European Community. The economic revival of Germany begun by Adenauer continued under his Christian Democrat (conservative) successors as Chancellor – Ludwig Erhard (1963–66) and Georg Kiesinger (1966–69). Under the Social Democrat Chancellors – Willy Brandt (1969–74) and Helmut Schmidt (1974–82) – treaties were signed with the USSR (1970) and Poland (recognizing the Oder-Neisse line as Poland's western frontier), and relations with the GDR were normalized (1972). Under Helmut Kohl – Christian Democrat Chancellor from 1982 – West Germany continued its impressive economic development and enthusiastic membership of the EC.

In the late 1980s, West Germany acted as an economic and cultural magnet for much of Eastern Europe. The root causes of the GDR's problems remained, however, and resurfaced in the late 1980s. The ageing Communist leadership led by Erich Honecker proved unresponsive to the mood of greater freedom emanating from Gorbachov's USSR. In 1989 fresh floods of East Germans left the GDR for the West by way of Poland, Czechoslovakia and Hungary. Massive public demonstrations in favour of reform – led by the New Forum opposition movement – resulted in the appointment of a new leader. The Berlin Wall was reopened (November 1989) allowing free movement between the two Germanies, but demonstrations in favour of more radical change continued, prompting a further change of leadership. A non-Communist president, a new Prime Minister and a government including members of opposition groups were appointed. Free elections were held in East Germany in March 1990 when the Communist Party was reduced to a minority. When the East German economy collapsed, West German Chancellor Helmut Kohl proposed the monetary union of the two Germanies. The call for German reunification became unstoppable. Despite the initial opposition of the USSR, the reunification of Germany as a full EC and NATO member was agreed. German reunification took place on 3 October 1990 and all-German elections took place in December 1990. Soviet troops are scheduled to withdraw from the former GDR by 1994. Reunited Germany is the greatest economic power in Europe, and, after Russia, the most populous state.

GHANA

Official name: The Republic of Ghana.
Member of: UN, OAU, ECOWAS, Commonwealth.
Area: 238 537 km² (92 099 sq mi).
Population: 15 509 000 (1991 est).
Capital and major cities: Accra 1 580 000, Kumasi 490 000, Tema (part of the Accra agglomeration) 190 000, Sekondi-Takoradi 175 000, Tamale 170 000 (1988 est).
Languages: English (official), Asante, Ewe, Ga.
Religions: Various Protestant Churches (30%), Sunni Islam (20%), Roman Catholic (over 25%), animist (17%).
Education: *Literacy rate:* 60.3% (1990). *Years of compulsory schooling:* (in theory) 6–15. *Universities:* 3.
Defence: *Total armed strength:* 11 900 (1991) (plus paramilitary 5000). *Military service:* voluntary.

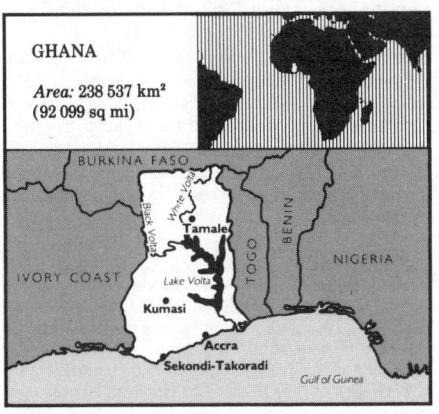

GHANA
Area: 238 537 km²
(92 099 sq mi)

BURKINA FASO
Black Volta
White Volta
Tamale
BENIN
TOGO
NIGERIA
IVORY COAST
Lake Volta
Kumasi
Accra
Sekondi-Takoradi
Gulf of Guinea

GOVERNMENT

Under a new constitution (1992), a 140-member Assembly and a President are elected for four years by universal adult suffrage. The main political parties include the National Democratic Convention (NDC), the (Nkrumahist left-wing) People's National Convention Party and the New Patriotic Party.
President: Flight. Lt. Jerry Rawlings.

GEOGRAPHY

Most of the country comprises low-lying plains and plateaux. In the centre, the Volta Basin – which ends in steep escarpments – contains the large Lake Volta reservoir. *Principal river:* Volta. *Highest point:* Afadjato 872 m (2860 ft).
Climate: The climate is tropical with 2000 mm (80 in) of rainfall on the coast, decreasing markedly inland. The north is subject to the hot, dry Harmattan wind from the Sahara.

ECONOMY

Political instability and mismanagement have damaged the economy of Ghana. Agriculture occupies nearly 50% of the labour force, with cocoa being the main cash crop. Forestry and mining for bauxite, gold and manganese are also important activities.

RECENT HISTORY

Britain ousted the Danes (1850) and the Dutch (1872) to establish the Gold Coast colony in 1874. The great inland kingdom of Ashanti was not finally conquered until 1898. After World War II, the prosperity of the cocoa industry, increasing literacy and the dynamism of Dr Kwame Nkrumah (1909–72) helped the Gold Coast set the pace for decolonization in Black Africa. After independence in 1957 – as Ghana – Nkrumah's grandiose policies and increasingly dictatorial rule led to his overthrow in a military coup in 1966. Ghana has since struggled to overcome its economic and political problems. There were six coups in 20 years, including two by Flight Lieutenant Jerry Rawlings (1979 and 1982). A multi-party system was restored in 1992.

GREECE

Official name: Ellenikí Dimokrátia (Hellenic Republic) or Ellás (Greece).
Member of: UN, EC, NATO, Council of Europe, CSCE, OECD, WEU (associate).
Area: 131 957 km² (50 949 sq mi).
Population: 10 269 000 (1991 census).
Capital and major cities: Athens (Athínai) 3 097 000, Thessaloníki (formerly known as Salonika) 706 000, Piraeus (Piraiévs; part of the Athens agglomeration) 196 000, Patras (Pátrai) 155 000, Volos 107 000, Lárisa 102 000, Heraklion (Iráklion, formerly known as Candia) 102 000, Kavalla 57 000, Canea (Khania) 48 000 (all including suburbs; 1991 census).
Language: Greek (official).
Religion: Orthodox (98%; official).
Education: *Literacy rate:* 93.2% (1990). *Years of compulsory schooling:* 6–15. *Universities:* 10 plus 6 institutes of university status.
Defence: *Total armed strength:* 158 500 (1991) plus 26 500 paramilitary police and 120 000 National Guard. *Military service:* 20–24 months.

GOVERNMENT

The 300-member Parliament is elected for four years by universal adult suffrage under a system of proportional representation. The President – who is elected for a five-year term by Parliament – appoints a Prime Minister (who commands a majority in Parliament) and other Ministers. The main political parties include the (conservative) NDP (New Democracy Party), PASOK (the Pan-Hellenic Socialist Party), the (centre) Democratic Renewal Party, and the (Communist-led) Left Alliance.
President: Konstantinos Karamanlis.
Prime Minister: Konstantinos Mitsotakis.

GREEK SELF-GOVERNING COMMUNITY

Mount Athos (Ayion Oros) (an autonomous monks' republic). *Area:* 336 km² (130 sq mi). *Population:* 1400 (1990 est). *Capital:* Karyai.

GEOGRAPHY

Over 80% of Greece is mountainous. The mainland is

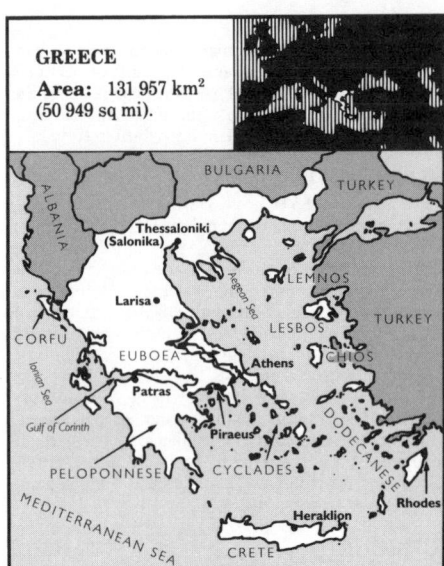

GREECE

Area: 131 957 km²
(50 949 sq mi).

dominated by the Pindus Mountains, which extend from Albania south into the Peloponnese Peninsula. The Rhodope Mountains lie along the Bulgarian border. Greece has some 2000 islands, of which only 154 are inhabited. *Principal rivers:* Aliákmon, Piniós, Akhelóös. *Highest point:* Mount Olympus 2911 m (9550 ft).

Climate: Greece has a Mediterranean climate with hot dry summers and mild wet winters. The north and the mountains are colder.

ECONOMY

Agriculture involves over one quarter of the labour force. Much of the land is marginal – in particular the extensive sheep pastures. Greece is largely self-sufficient in wheat, barley, maize, sugar beet, fruit, vegetables and cheese, and produces enough wine, olives (and olive oil) and tobacco for export. The industrial sector is expanding rapidly and includes the processing of natural resources such as petroleum and natural gas, lignite, uranium and bauxite. Tourism, the large merchant fleet, and money sent back by Greeks working abroad are all important foreign-currency earners. Greece receives special economic assistance from the EC.

RECENT HISTORY

The outbreak of revolution against Turkish rule in 1821 attracted support throughout Europe. The leaders of the Greek state established in 1830 brought Western European constitutional institutions to Greece, but the monarchy established under a Bavarian prince in 1832 was swept away by revolution in 1862. Under a Danish prince – who became King George I in 1863 – Greece gained extra territory in 1863, 1881 and 1913, as Turkish power declined. The 20th century has been marked by great instability. Eleuthérios Venizélos (1864–1936) dominated Greek politics from 1910 to 1935, a period of rivalry between republicans and royalists. An attempt by his rival King Constantine I to seize Anatolia from Turkey (1921–22) ended in military defeat and the establishment of a republic in 1924. The monarchy was restored in 1935, but it depended upon a military leader, General Ioannis Metaxas

(1871–1941), who, claiming the threat from Communism as justification, ruled as virtual dictator. The nation was deeply divided.

The German invasion of 1941 was met by rival resistance groups of Communists and monarchists, and the subsequent civil war between these factions lasted from 1945 to 1949, when, with British and US aid, the monarchists emerged victorious. Continued instability in the 1960s led to a military coup in 1967. King Constantine II, who had not initially opposed the coup, unsuccessfully appealed for the overthrow of the junta and went into exile. The dictatorship of the colonels ended in 1974 when their encouragement of a Greek Cypriot coup brought Greece to the verge of war with Turkey. Civilian government was restored, and a new republican constitution was adopted in 1975. Greece has since forged closer links with Western Europe, in particular through membership of the EC (1981). Greek opposition prevented recognition of the former Yugoslav republic of Macedonia by the EC in 1992.

GRENADA

Official name: The State of Grenada.

Member of: UN, OAS, Commonwealth, CARICOM.

Area: 344 km² (133 sq mi).

Population: 96 000 (1991 est).

Capital: St George's 36 000 (city 7500) (1989 est).

Language: English (official); French-African patois.

Religions: Roman Catholic (over 60%), Anglican.

Education: *Literacy rate:* almost 100%. *Years of compulsory schooling:* 6–14 (in urban areas). *Universities:* 1 university college plus a department of the University of the West Indies.

Defence: *Total armed strength:* none except for the small paramilitary Special Service Unit. *Military service:* none.

GOVERNMENT

The Governor General – the representative of the British Queen as sovereign of Grenada – appoints a Prime Minister (who commands a majority in the House of Representatives), other members of the Cabinet and the 13-member Senate (the upper house of Parliament). The 15-member House of Representatives is elected for five years by universal adult suffrage. The main political parties include the National Democratic Congress, the National Party, the United Labour Party and the New National Party.
Prime Minister: Nicholas Braithwaite.

GEOGRAPHY

A forested mountain ridge covers much of this well-watered island. The island of Carriacou forms part of Grenada. *Principal rivers:* there are no significant rivers. *Highest point:* Mount St Catherine 840 m (2706 ft).

Climate: Grenada has a tropical maritime climate with a dry season from January to May.

ECONOMY

The production of spices, in particular nutmeg, is the mainstay of a largely agricultural economy. Tourism is increasing in importance.

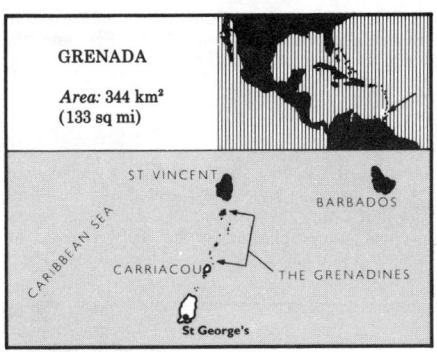

GRENADA

Area: 344 km²
(133 sq mi)

ST VINCENT

BARBADOS

CARIBBEAN SEA

CARRIACOU

THE GRENADINES

St George's

RECENT HISTORY

Grenada was became British in 1783. Independence was gained in 1974. The left-wing New Jewel Movement seized power in a coup in 1979. In 1983 the PM Maurice Bishop was killed in a further coup in which more extreme members of the government seized power. Acting upon a request from East Caribbean islands to intervene, US and Caribbean forces landed in Grenada. After several days' fighting, the coup leaders were detained. Constitutional rule was restored in 1984.

GUATEMALA

Official name: República de Guatemala (Republic of Guatemala).

Member of: UN, OAS, CACM.

Area: 108 889 km² (42 042 sq mi).

Population: 9 442 000 (1992 est).

Capital and major cities: Guatemala City 2 074 000 (city 1 114 000), Mixco 369 000 and Villa Nueva 134 000 are part of the Guatemala City agglomeration, Quezaltenango 88 000 (1992 est).

Languages: Spanish (official), Mayan languages (45%).

Religions: Roman Catholic (official; 70%), various Protestant evangelical Churches (30%).

Education: *Literacy rate:* 55.1% (1990). *Years of compulsory schooling:* 7–14 (in urban areas). *Universities:* 5.

Defence: *Total armed strength:* 39 600 (1991) (plus 10 000 paramilitary). *Military service:* 2 years or more.

GOVERNMENT

A President – who appoints a Cabinet – and a Vice President are elected for a five-year term by universal adult suffrage. The 100-member National Congress is also directly elected for five years – 75 members are directly elected; the remaining 25 members are returned under a system of proportional representation. The main political parties include the (right-wing) Christian Democratic Party (PDGC), the (centre) Union of National Centre (UCN), the (cntre-right) Movement for Action and Solidarity (MAS), and the (coalition left-wing) Platform NO-Venta. Constitutional rule is suspended. *President (acting):* Gustavo Espina.

GEOGRAPHY

Pacific and Atlantic coastal lowlands are separated by a mountain chain containing over 30 volcanoes. *Principal rivers:* Usumacinta, Montagua. *Highest point:* Tajumulco 4220 m (13 881 ft)

Climate: The coastal plains have a tropical climate; the mountains are more temperate.

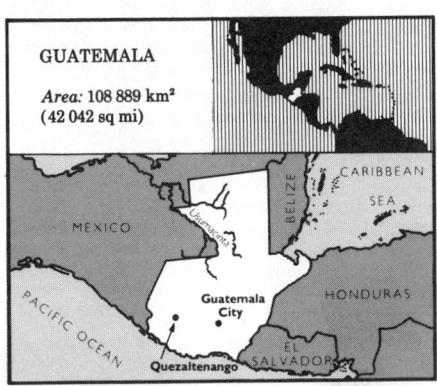

GUATEMALA

Area: 108 889 km²
(42 042 sq mi)

CARIBBEAN SEA

BELIZE

MEXICO

Chixand...

Guatemala City

HONDURAS

PACIFIC OCEAN

Quezaltenango

EL SALVADOR

ECONOMY

More than one half of the labour force is involved in agriculture. Coffee is the major export, while the other main crops include sugar cane and bananas.

RECENT HISTORY

Guatemala was the administrative centre of Spanish Central America. Independence was proclaimed in 1821, but the country was part of Mexico (1821–23) and the Central American Federation (1823–39). Guatemala has a history of being ruled by dictators allied to landowners. However, in the 1950s President Jacobo Arbenz expropriated large estates, dividing them among the peasantry. Accused of being a Communist, he was deposed by the army with US military aid (1954). For over 30 years, the left was suppressed, leading to the emergence of guerrilla armies. Thousands of dissidents were killed or disappeared. Civilian government was restored in 1986, but after mounting unrest the military took over in 1993.

GUINEA

Official name: La République de Guinée (The Republic of Guinea).

Member of: UN, OAU, ECOWAS.

Area: 245 857 km² (94 926 sq mi).

Population: 7 052 000 (1991 est).

Capital and major cities: Conakry 705 000, Kankan 89 000, Kindia 56 000 (1983 est).

Languages: French (official), Soussou (11%), Fulani (40%).

Religions: Sunni Islam (85%), Roman Catholic and animist minorities.

Education: *Literacy rate:* 24% (1990). *Years of compulsory schooling:* (in theory) 7–13. *Universities:* 2.

Defence: *Total armed strength:* 9700 (1991), plus 9600 paramilitary. *Military service:* 2 years.

GOVERNMENT

Power is exercised by the Military Committee for National Recovery, whose President is head of state and of government. Political pluralism is permitted but no date has been set for multi-party elections for a new unicameral parliament.
President: Gen. Lansana Conte.

GEOGRAPHY

Tropical rain forests cover the coastal plain. The interior highlands and plains are covered by grass and scrubland. There are mountains in the south-west. *Principal river:* Niger, Bafing, Konkouré, Kogon. *Highest point:* Mont Nimba 1752 m (5748 ft).

Climate: The climate is tropical with heavy rainfall. Temperatures are cooler in the highlands.

ECONOMY

Bauxite accounts for nearly 80% of Guinea's exports. However, agriculture involves over 75% of the labour force, producing bananas, oil palm and citrus fruits for export, and maize, rice and cassava as subsistence crops. Despite mineral wealth, Guinea is one of the world's poorest countries and relies heavily on aid.

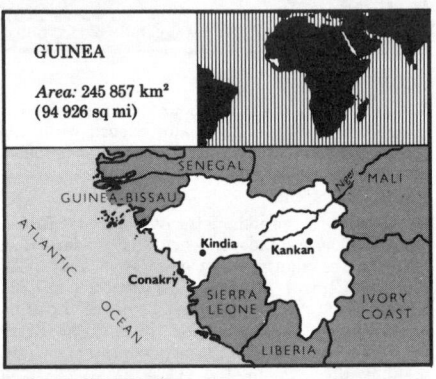

RECENT HISTORY

Increasing French influence in the 19th century led to the establishment of the colony of French Guinea (1890). Unlike the rest of French Africa, Guinea voted for a complete separation from France in 1958, suffering severe French reprisals as a result. The authoritarian radical leader Sékou Touré (1922–84) isolated Guinea, but he became reconciled with France in 1978. The leaders of a military coup (1984) have achieved some economic reforms.

GUINEA-BISSAU

Official name: Republica da Guiné-Bissau (Republic of Guinea-Bissau).

Member of: UN, OAU, ECOWAS.

Area: 36 125 km² (13 948 sq mi).

Population: 994 000 (1991 est.).

Capital and major towns: Bissau 125 000 (1988 est), Bafatá 13 500 (1980 est).

Languages: Portuguese (official), Crioulo.

Religions: Animist (55%), Sunni Islam (40%), Roman Catholic (5%).

Education: *Literacy rate:* 36.5% (1990). *Years of compulsory schooling:* (in theory) 7–12. *Universities:* none.

Defence: *Total armed strength:* 9200 (1991) (plus 2000 paramilitary police). *Military service:* none.

GOVERNMENT

The 150-member National Assembly is elected for five years by universal adult suffrage. The Assembly elects a President, who appoints Ministers. The main political parties are the (former monopoly) PAIGC,

the Guinea-Bissau Resistance-Bafata Movement (RGB-MB), the Democratic Front (FD) and the Social Democratic Front (FDS).
President: Brig. Gen. João Bernardo Vieira.
Prime Minister: Carlos Correia.

GEOGRAPHY

Most of the country is low-lying, with swampy coastal lowlands and a flat forested interior plain. The northeast is mountainous. *Principal rivers:* Cacheu, Mansôa, Géba, Corubel. *Highest point:* an unnamed point in the Fouta Djallon plateau 180 m (591 ft).

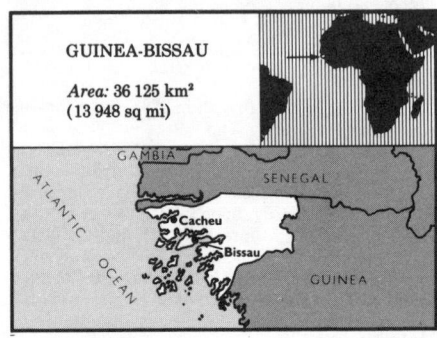

Climate: The climate is tropical with a dry season from December to May.

ECONOMY

The country has one of the lowest standards of living in the world. Its subsistence economy is based mainly on rice. Timber is exported.

RECENT HISTORY

The colony of Portuguese Guinea was created in 1879. Failing to secure reform by peaceful means, the PAIGC movement mounted a liberation war (1961–1974). Independence was proclaimed in 1973 and recognized by Portugal in 1974. Following a military coup in 1980, the aim of union with Cape Verde was dropped. A multi-party system was introduced in 1991.

GUYANA

Official name: The Cooperative Republic of Guyana.

Member of: UN, Commonwealth, OAS, CARICOM.

Area: 214 969 km² (83 000 sq mi).

Population: 760 000 (1991 est.).

Capital: Georgetown 187 000, Linden 35 000 (all including suburbs; 1986 est).

Languages: English (official), Hindu, Urdu.

Religions: Hinduism (34%), various Protestant Churches (34%) – mainly Anglican, Sunni Islam (9%), Roman Catholic (18%).

Education: *Literacy rate:* 96.4% (1990). *Years of compulsory schooling:* 6–14. *Universities:* 1.

Defence: *Total armed strength:* 1900 (1991) (plus 3500 paramilitary). *Military service:* selective service in the paramilitary.

GOVERNMENT

The 65-member National Assembly is elected for five

years under a system of proportional representation by universal adult suffrage. The President – the leader of the majority in the Assembly – appoints a Cabinet led by the First Vice-President. The main political parties are the (left-wing) People's National Congress, the (left-wing) People's Progressive Party, the (conservative) United Force, and the (left-wing) Working People's Alliance.
President: Cheddi Jagan.
First Vice-President and Prime Minister: Samuel Hinds.

GEOGRAPHY
A coastal plain is protected from the sea by dykes. Tropical rain forest covers much of the interior. *Principal rivers:* Essequibo, Courantyne, Mazaruni, Demarara. *Highest point:* Mt Roraima 2772 m (9094 ft).
Climate: The interior is tropical, while the coastal plain is more moderate.

ECONOMY
Guyana depends on mining bauxite and growing sugar cane and rice. Nationalization and emigration have caused economic problems.

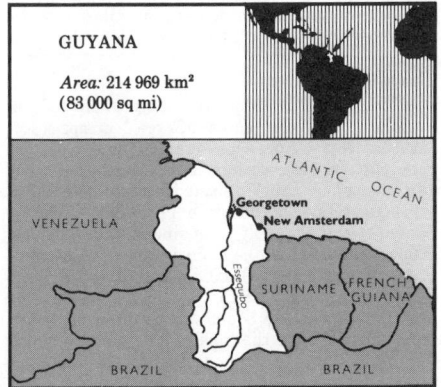

GUYANA
Area: 214 969 km²
(83 000 sq mi)

RECENT HISTORY
Guyana is the former colony of British Guiana. From the 1840s large numbers of Indian and Chinese labourers were imported from Asia to work on sugar plantations. Racial tension between their descendants – now the majority – and the black community (descended from imported African slaves) led to violence in 1964 and 1978. Guyana has been independent since 1966. After 1987–88 President Hoyte introduced economic reforms, but austerity measures have been in force since the end of 1988.

HAITI
Official name: La République d'Haïti (Republic of Haiti).
Member of: UN, OAS, CARICOM.
Area: 27 750 km² (10 714 sq mi).
Population: 6 764 000 (1992 est).
Capital and major cities: Port-au-Prince 1 256 000, Jacmel 217 000, Les Cayes 215 000, Jérémie 152 000 (all including suburbs; 1988 est).
Languages: Creole (90%) and French – both official.
Religions: Voodoo (majority), Roman Catholic (official).

Education: *Literacy rate:* 53% (1990). *Years of compulsory schooling:* (in theory) 6–12. *Universities:* 2.

Defence: *Total armed strength:* 5400 (1991 est). *Military service:* none.

GOVERNMENT
The constitution provides for elections by universal adult suffrage of a 27-member Chamber of Deputies and a President, all to serve a five-year term. A large number of new political parties were formed during the period 1987–90, but constitutional rule was overturned by a military coup in 1991.
Acting President and Prime Minister: Marc Bazin.

GEOGRAPHY
Haiti is the western part of the island of Hispaniola. Mountain ranges run from east to west, alternating with densely populated valleys and plains. *Principal river:* Artibonite. *Highest point:* Pic La Selle (2680 m/8793 ft).
Climate: Haiti's tropical climate is moderated by altitude and by the sea.

ECONOMY
Agriculture involves some two thirds of the labour force, mainly growing crops for domestic consumption. Coffee is the principal cash crop. With few resources, overpopulated Haiti is the poorest country in the western hemisphere.

RECENT HISTORY
Independence from France was proclaimed in 1804 during a revolt led by Jean-Jacques Dessalines and Henri Christophe, both of whom reigned as monarchs of Haiti. A united republic was achieved in 1820. Coups, instability and tension between blacks and mulattos wracked Haiti until the US intervened (1915–35). President François Duvalier ('Papa Doc'; in office 1956–71) and his son Jean-Claude ('Baby

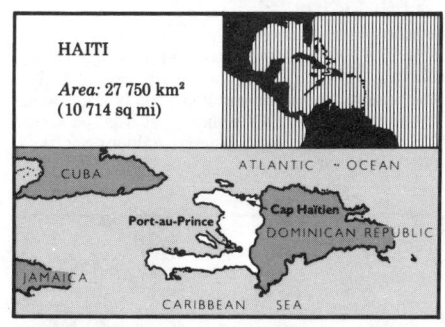

HAITI
Area: 27 750 km²
(10 714 sq mi)

Doc'; 1971–86) cowed the country into submission by means of their infamous private militia, the Tontons Macoutes. The military took control after the younger Duvalier fled during a period of violent popular unrest. A period of unrest preceded Haiti's only democratic multi-party elections in 1991. However, the victor – a radical priest, Fr. Aristide – was toppled by the military within seven months. Violence and intimidation by the Tontons Macoutes remain endemic. Many thousands of Haitians attempt to enter the USA illegally every year.

HONDURAS

Official name: La República de Honduras (Republic of Honduras).

Member of: UN, OAS, CACM.

Area: 112 088 km² (43 277 sq mi).

Population: 4 708 000 (1991 est).

Capital and major cities: Tegucigalpa 648 000, San Pedro Sula 301 000, La Ceiba 72 000 (all including suburbs; 1988 census).

Language: Spanish (official).

Religions: Roman Catholic (85%), various Protestant evangelical Churches (15%).

Education: *Literacy rate:* 73.1% (1990). *Years of compulsory schooling:* 7–13. *Universities:* 2.

Defence: *Total armed strength:* 17 500 (1991) plus 5000 paramilitary. *Military service:* 8 months.

GOVERNMENT

The President and the 134-member National Assembly are elected by universal adult suffrage for four years. The main political parties are the PLH (Liberal Party of Honduras), the (right-wing) PN (National Party) and PINU-SD (Party of Innovation and Unity).
President: Rafael Callejas.

GEOGRAPHY

Mountains occupy about three quarters of Honduras; the remainder comprises small coastal plains. *Principal rivers:* Patuca, Ulúa. *Highest point:* Cerio las Minas 2849 m (9347 ft).

Climate: The tropical lowlands experience high rainfall (1500–2000 mm / 60–80 in). The more temperate highlands are drier.

ECONOMY

The majority of Hondurans work in agriculture, but despite agrarian reform, living standards remain low. Bananas and coffee are the leading exports, although meat is increasingly important. There are few natural resources.

RECENT HISTORY

Between independence from Spain (1821) and the early 20th century, Honduras experienced constant political upheaval and wars with neighbouring countries. US influence was immense, largely owing to the substantial investments of the powerful United Fruit Company in banana production. After a short civil war in 1925, a succession of military

HONDURAS

Area: 112 088 km²
(43 277 sq mi)

BELIZE

CARIBBEAN SEA

GUATEMALA

San Pedro Sula

PACIFIC OCEAN

EL SALVADOR

•Tegucigalpa

NICARAGUA

dictators governed Honduras until 1980. Since then the country has had democratically elected pro-US centre-right civilian governments.

HUNGARY

Official name: Magyarország (Hungary) or Magyar Köztársásag (The Hungarian Republic)

Member of: UN, CSCE, Council of Europe.

Area: 93 036 km² (35 921 sq mi).

Population: 10 375 000 (1990 census).

Capital and major cities: Budapest 2 018 000, Debrecen 214 000, Miskolc 194 000, Szeged 176 000, Pécs 170 000, Györ 130 000, Nyíregyháza 115 000, Székesfehérvár 109 000, Kecskemét 104 000 (1990 census).

Language: Magyar (Hungarian; 97%), German (2%), Slovak (1%).

Religions: Roman Catholic (56%), Calvinist and Lutheran (22%).

Education: *Literacy rate:* nearly 100%. *Years of compulsory schooling:* 6–14. *Universities:* 19, plus 6 institutes of university status.

Defence: *Total armed strength:* 86 500 (1991 est). *Military service:* 12 months (with an alternative to military service for conscientious objectors).

GOVERNMENT

The 386-member National Assembly is elected for five years by universal adult suffrage. It comprises 58 members elected from a national list under a system of proportional representation, 152 members elected on a county basis and 176 elected from single-member constituencies. An executive President – who is elected by the Assembly – appoints a Cabinet and a Prime Minister from the majority in the Assembly. The main political parties include the (centre right) Democratic Forum (MDF), the (liberal) Alliance of Free Democrats, the Socialist Party (formerly the Communist Party), the Smallholders' Party (ISP), the Federation of Young Democrats and the Christian Democratic People's Party (KDNP).
President: Arpad Goncz.
Prime Minister: Jozsef Antall.

GEOGRAPHY

Hungary west of the River Danube is an undulating lowland. There are thickly wooded highlands in the northeast. The southeast is a great expanse of flat plain. *Principal rivers:* Danube (Duna), Tisza, Drava. *Highest point:* Kékes 1015 m (3330 ft).

Climate: The climate is continental, with long, hot, dry summers, and cold winters.

ECONOMY

Nearly one fifth of the labour force is involved in agriculture. Major crops include cereals (maize, wheat and barley), sugar beet, fruit, and grapes for wine. Despite considerable reserves of coal, Hungary imports more than half of its energy needs. The steel, chemical fertilizer, pharmaceutical, machinery and vehicle industries are important. Since the early 1980s, private enterprise and foreign investment have been encouraged, and between 1989 and 1991 most of the large state enterprises were privatized.

RECENT HISTORY

In the 19th century Hungarian resentment against Austrian rule grew. Lajos Kossuth (1802–94) led a

HUNGARY

Area: 93 036 km²
(35 921 sq mi).

nationalist revolt against Austrian rule (1848–49), but fled when Austria regained control with Russian aid. Austria granted Hungary considerable autonomy in the Dual Monarchy (1867) – the Austro-Hungarian Empire. Defeat in World War I led to a brief period of Communist rule under Béla Kun (1919), then occupation by Romania. In the postwar settlement, Hungary lost two thirds of its territory. The Regent, Admiral Miklás Horthy (1868–1957), cooperated with Hitler during World War II in an attempt to regain territory, but defeat in 1945 resulted in occupation by the Red Army, and a Communist People's Republic was established in 1949. The Hungarian Uprising in 1956 was a heroic attempt to overthrow Communist rule, but was quickly suppressed by Soviet forces, and its leader, Imre Nagy, was executed. János Kadar – Party Secretary 1956–88 – tried to win support with economic progress. However, in the late 1980s reformers in the Communist Party gained the upper hand, and talks with opposition groups led to agreement on a transition to a fully democratic, multi-party state. The (Communist) Hungarian Socialist Workers' Party transformed itself into the Socialist Party but was heavily defeated in the first free elections in 1990 when conservative and liberal parties won most seats. Soviet troops left Hungary in 1990, and the country has taken rapid steps to join Western European organizations and establish a free-market economy. The status of over 3 000 000 Hungarians who are citizens of Slovakia, Romania and the former Yugoslavia has become an issue.

ICELAND

Official name: Lýdveldid Island (The Republic of Iceland).

Member of: UN, NATO, EFTA, Council of Europe, CSCE, OECD.

Area: 103 001 km² (39 769 sq mi).

Population: 258 000 (1991 est).

Capital and major cities: Reykjavik 146 000 (city 98 000), Kópavogur 16 000 and Hafnarfjördhur 15 000 are part of the Reykjavik agglomeration, Akureyri 14 000, Keflavik 7500 (1990 est).

Language: Icelandic (official).

Religion: Evangelical Lutheran (93%).

Education: *Literacy rate:* 100%. *Years of compulsory schooling:* 7–16. *Universities:* 1.

Defence: *Total armed strength:* There are no armed forces except for a small coastal defence force.

GOVERNMENT

The 63-member Althing (Parliament) is elected under a system of proportional representation by universal adult suffrage for a four-year term. The Althing elects 20 of its members to sit as the Upper House and the remaining 43 members to sit as the Lower House. The President – who is also directly elected for four years – appoints a Prime Minister and a Cabinet who are responsible to the Althing. The main political parties include the (conservative) Independence Party, the Progressive Party, the (socialist) People's Alliance, the Social Democratic Party, and the Women's Alliance.
President: Vigdis Finnbogadottir.
Prime Minister: David Oddsson.

GEOGRAPHY

The greater part of Iceland has a volcanic landscape with hot springs, geysers and some 200 volcanoes – some of them active. Much of the country is tundra. The south and centre are covered by glacial icefields. *Principal rivers:* Thjórsá, Skjalfanda Fljót. *Highest point:* Hvannadalshnúkur 2119 m (6952 ft).

Climate: The cool temperate climate is warmed by the Gulf Stream, which keeps Iceland milder than most places at the same latitude.

ECONOMY

The fishing industry provides the majority of Iceland's exports. Hydroelectric power is used in the aluminium-smelting industry, while geothermal power warms extensive greenhouses. Ample grazing land makes the country self-sufficient in meat and dairy products. Economic problems include high inflation and over dependence upon a single industry.

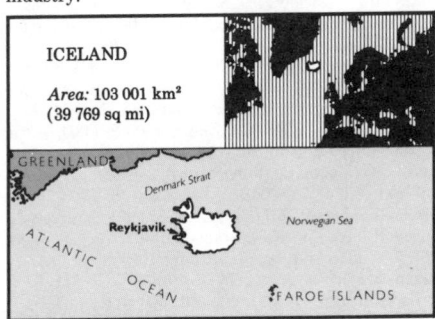

ICELAND

Area: 103 001 km²
(39 769 sq mi)

RECENT HISTORY

Icelandic nationalism grew in the 19th century, and in 1918 Iceland gained independence from Denmark. However, the two countries remained linked by their shared monarchy. In World War II the Danish link was severed and a republic was declared (1944). Disputes over fishing rights in Icelandic territorial waters led to clashes with British naval vessels in the 1950s and 1970s.

INDIA

Official name: Bharat (Republic of India).

Member of: UN, Commonwealth, SAARC.

Area: 3 287 263 km² (1 269 212 sq mi) – including the Indian-held part of Jammu and Kashmir.

Population: 844 324 000 (1991 census) – including the Indian-held part of Jammu and Kashmir.

Capital and major cities: Delhi 8 375 000 (city 7 175 000; New Delhi 294 000), Bombay 12 572 000

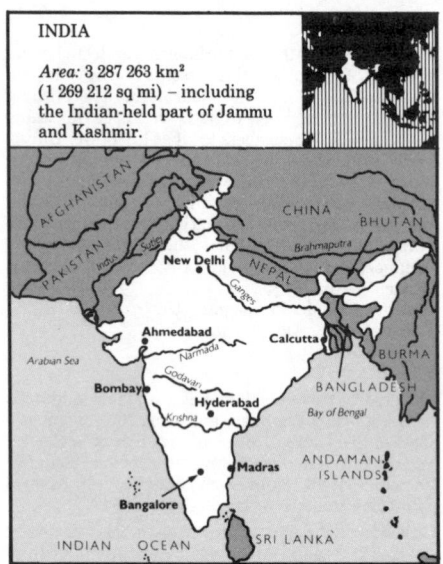

INDIA

Area: 3 287 263 km²
(1 269 212 sq mi) – including
the Indian-held part of Jammu
and Kashmir.

(city 9 910 000), Calcutta 10 916 000 (city 4 388 000),
Madras 5 361 000 (city 3 795 000), Hyderabad
4 280 000 (city 3 005 000), Bangalore 4 087 000 (city
2 651 000), Ahmedabad 3 298 000 (city 2 873 000), Pune
(formerly Poona) 2 485 000 (city 1 560 000), Kanpur
2 111 000 (city 1 958 000), Nagpur 1 661 000 (city
1 622 000), Lucknow 1 642 000 (city 1 592 000), Surat
1 517 000 (city 1 497 000), Jaipur 1 514 000 (city
1 455 000), Kochi (formerly Cochin) 1 140 000 (city
564 000), Coimbatore 1 136 000 (city 853 000),
Vadodara (formerly Baroda) 1 115 000 (city
1 021 000), Indore 1 104 000 (city 1 087 000), Patna
1 099 000 (city 917 000), Madurai 1 094 000 (city
952 000), Bhopal 1 064 000, Visakhapatnam 1 052 000
(city 750 000), Varanasi (formerly Banaras and
Benares) 1 026 000, Kalyan (part of the Bombay
agglomeration) 1 014 000, Ludhiana 1 012 000, Agra
956 000 (city 899 000), Hoara (formerly Howrah; part
of the Calcutta agglomeration) 946 000, Jabalpur
887 000 (city 740 000), Allahabad 858 000 (city
806 000), Meerut 847 000 (city 752 000), Vijaywada
845 000 (city 701 000), Jamshedpur 835 000 (city
461 000), Thiruvananthapuram (formerly Trivandrum) 826 000 (city 524 000), Dhanbad 818 000, Kozhikode (formerly Calicut) 801 000 (city 420 000),
Thane (formerly Thana; part of the Bombay agglomeration) 797 000 (1991 census).

Languages: Hindi (30%; official), English
(official), Bengali (8%), Telugu (8%), Marathi (8%),
Tamil (7%), Urdu (5%), Gujarati (5%), with over 1600
other languages.

Religions: Hindu (83%), Sunni Islam (11%),
Christian (mainly Roman Catholic) (nearly 3%).

Education: *Literacy rate:* 52.1% (1991). *Years of
compulsory schooling:* (in theory) 6–14, except in
Nagaland and Himachal Pradesh. *Universities:* 157
including the open university and institutes of university status.

Defence: *Total armed strength:* 1 270 000 (1992
est). *Military service:* none, but it is the legal duty of
every citizen to perform national service if called
upon.

GOVERNMENT

India is a federal republic in which each of the 25

states has its own legislature. The upper house of the
federal parliament – the 250-member Council of
States (Rajya Sabha) – consists of 12 members
nominated by the President and 238 members elected
by the assemblies of individual states. One third of
the Council retires every two years. The lower house
– the House of the People (Lok Sabha) – consists of
542 members elected for a five-year term by universal
adult suffrage, plus two nominated members. The
President – who serves for five years – is chosen by an
electoral college consisting of the federal parliament
and the state assemblies. The President appoints a
Prime Minister – who commands a majority in the
House – and a Council of Ministers, who are responsible to the House. The main political parties include
the Congress (I) Party, the Janata Dal (People's
Party), the (right-wing Hindu) Bharatiya Janata
Party (Indian People's Party), the Communist Party
of India – Marxist, the Communist Party of India,
and a number of regional groupings.
President: Ramaswamy Venkataraman.
Prime Minister: P.V. Narasimha Rao.

INDIAN STATES

The population figures are from the 1991 census.

Andhra Pradesh *Area:* 276 814 km² (106 878 sq
mi). *Population:* 66 355 000. *Capital:* Hyderabad.

Arunachal Pradesh *Area:* 83 587 km² (32 269 sq
mi). *Population:* 858 000. *Capital:* Itanagar.

Assam *Area:* 78 523 km² (30 310 sq mi). *Population:*
22 295 000. *Capital:* Gauhati.

Bihar *Area:* 173 876 km² (67 134 sq mi). *Population:*
86 339 000. *Capital:* Patna.

Goa *Area:* 3701 km² (1429 sq mi). *Population:*
1 169 000. *Capital:* Panaji.

Gujarat *Area:* 195 984 km² (75 669 sq mi).
Population: 41 174 000. *Capital:* Gandhinagar.

Haryana *Area:* 44 222 km² (17 074 sq mi).
Population: 16 318 000. *Capital:* Chandigarh (a separate Union territory, see below) 450 000.

Himachal Pradesh *Area:* 55 673 km² (21 495 sq
mi). *Population:* 5 111 000. *Capital:* Simla.

Jammu and Kashmir *Area:* 101 283 km² (39 105
sq mi) – the Indian-held part of the state only.
Population: 7 719 000. *Capital (summer only):* Srina-
gar. *Capital (winter only):* Jammu.

Karnataka *Area:* 191 773 km² (74 044 sq mi).
Population: 44 806 000. *Capital:* Bangalore.

Kerala *Area:* 38 864 km² (15 005 sq mi). *Population:*
29 033 000. *Capital:* Thiruvananthapuram (formerly
Trivandrum).

Madhya Pradesh *Area:* 442 841 km² (170 981 sq
mi). *Population:* 66 136 000. *Capital:* Bhopal.

Maharashtra *Area:* 307 762 km² (118 827 sq mi).
Population: 78 748 000. *Capital:* Bombay.

Manipur *Area:* 22 356 km² (8632 sq mi). *Population:*
1 847 000. *Capital:* Imphal.

Meghalaya *Area:* 22 429 km² (8660 sq mi).
Population: 1 761 000. *Capital:* Shillong.

Mizoram *Area:* 21 090 km² (8143 sq mi).
Population: 686 000. *Capital:* Aizawl.

Nagaland *Area:* 16 527 km² (6381 sq mi).
Population: 1 216 000. *Capital:* Kohima.

Orissa *Area:* 155 707 km² (60 118 sq mi).
Population: 31 512 000. *Capital:* Bhubaneshwar.

Punjab *Area:* 50 376 km² (19 450 sq mi). *Population:*
20 191 000. *Capital:* Chandigarh (a separate Union
territory, see below).

Rajasthan *Area*: 342 239 km² (132 138 sq mi). *Population*: 43 881 000. *Capital*: Jaipur.

Sikkim *Area*: 7298 km² (2818 sq mi). *Population*: 406 000. *Capital*: Gangtok.

Tamil Nadu *Area*: 130 357 km² (50 331 sq mi). *Population*: 55 638 000. *Capital*: Madras.

Tripura *Area*: 10 477 km² (4045 sq mi). *Population*: 2 745 000. *Capital*: Agartala.

Uttar Pradesh *Area*: 294 413 km² (113 673 sq mi). *Population*: 139 031 000. *Capital*: Lucknow.

West Bengal *Area*: 87 853 km² (33 920 sq mi). *Population*: 67 983 000. *Capital*: Calcutta.

INDIAN UNION TERRITORIES

Andaman and Nicobar Islands (territory) *Area*: 8293 km² (3202 sq mi). *Population*: 279 000. *Capital*: Port Blair.

Chandigarh *Area*: 114 km² (44 sq mi). *Population*: 641 000. *Capital*: Chandigarh.

Dadra and Nagar Haveli *Area*: 491 km² (190 sq mi). *Population*: 138 000. *Capital*: Silvassa.

Daman and Diu *Area*: 112 km² (43 sq mi). *Population*: 101 000. *Capital*: Daman.

Delhi *Area*: 1485 km² (573 sq mi). *Population*: 9 370 000. *Capital*: Delhi.

Lakshadweep *Area*: 32 km² (12 sq mi). *Population*: 52 000. *Capital*: Kavaratti.

Pondicherry *Area*: 492 km² (190 sq mi). *Population*: 807 000. *Capital*: Pondicherry.

GEOGRAPHY

The Himalaya cut the Indian subcontinent off from the rest of Asia. Several Himalayan peaks in India rise to over 7000 m (23 000 ft). South of the Himalaya, the basins of the Rivers Ganges and Brahmaputra and their tributaries are intensively farmed and densely populated. The Thar Desert stretches along the border with Pakistan. In south India, the Deccan – a large plateau of hard rocks – is bordered in the east and west by the Ghats, discontinuous ranges of hills descending in steps to coastal plains. Natural vegetation ranges from tropical rain forest on the W coast and monsoon forest in the northeast and far south, through dry tropical scrub and thorn forest in much of the Deccan to Alpine and temperate vegetation in the Himalaya. *Principal rivers:* Ganges (Ganga), Brahmaputra, Sutlej, Yamuna, Tapti, Godavari, Krishna. *Highest point:* Kangchenjunga 8598 m (28 208 ft).

Climate: India has three distinct seasons: the hot season from March to June, the wet season – when the southwest monsoon brings heavy rain – from June to October, and a cooler drier season from November to March. Temperatures range from the cool of the Himalaya to the tropical heat of the southern states.

ECONOMY

Two thirds of the labour force are involved in subsistence farming, with rice and wheat as the principal crops. Cash crops tend to come from large plantations and include tea, cotton, jute and sugar cane – all grown for export. The monsoon rains and irrigation make cultivation possible in many areas, but drought and floods are common. India is one of the 20 largest industrial powers in the world. Major coal reserves provide the power base for industry. Other mineral deposits include diamonds, bauxite, and titanium, copper and iron ore, as well as substan-

tial reserves of natural gas and petroleum. The textile, vehicle, iron and steel, pharmaceutical and electrical industries make important contributions to the economy, but India has balance-of-payment difficulties and relies upon foreign aid for development. Privatization of some state enterprises began in the early 1990s. Over one third of the population is below the official poverty line.

RECENT HISTORY

The British Indian Empire included present-day Pakistan and Bangladesh, and comprised the Crown Territories of British India and over 620 Indian protected states. The Indian states covered about 40% of India, and enjoyed varying degrees of autonomy under the rule of their traditional princes. From the middle of the 19th century the British cautiously encouraged Indian participation in the administration of British India. British institutions, the railways and the English language – all imposed upon India by a modernizing imperial power – fostered the growth of an Indian sense of identity beyond the divisions of caste and language. However, ultimately the divisions of religion proved stronger. The Indian National Congress – the forerunner of the Congress Party – was first convened in 1885, and the Muslim League first met in 1906. Political and nationalist demands grew after British troops fired without warning on a nationalist protest meeting – the Amritsar Massacre (1919). The India Acts (1919 and 1935) granted limited autonomy and created an Indian federation, but the pace of reform did not satisfy Indian expectations. In 1920 Congress – led by Mohandas (Mahatma) Karamchand Gandhi (1869–1948) – began a campaign of non-violence and non-cooperation with the British authorities. However relations between Hindus and Muslims steadily deteriorated, and by 1940 the Muslim League was demanding a separate sovereign state.

By 1945, war-weary Britain had accepted the inevitability of Indian independence. However, religious discord forced the partition of the subcontinent in 1947 into predominantly Hindu India – under Jawaharlal (Pandit) Nehru (1889–1964) of the Congress Party – and Muslim Pakistan (including what is now Bangladesh) – under Mohammed Ali Jinnah (1876–1948) of the Muslim League. Over 70 million Hindus and Muslims became refugees and crossed the new boundaries, and thousands were killed in communal violence. The frontiers remained disputed. India and Pakistan fought border wars in 1947–49, 1965 (over Kashmir) and again in 1971 – when Bangladesh gained independence from Pakistan with Indian assistance. Kashmir is still divided along a cease-fire line. There were also border clashes with China in 1962.

Under Nehru (PM 1947–64) India became one of the leaders of the nonaligned movement of Third World states. Under the premiership (1966–77 and 1980–84) of his daughter Indira Gandhi (1917–84) India continued to assert itself as the dominant regional power. Although India remained the world's largest democracy – despite Mrs Gandhi's brief imposition of emergency rule (1975–77) – local separatism and communal unrest have threatened unity. The Sikhs have conducted an often violent campaign for an independent homeland – Khalistan – in the Punjab. In 1984 Mrs Gandhi ordered the storming of the Golden Temple of Amritsar, a Sikh holy place that extremists had turned into an arsenal. In the same year Mrs Gandhi was assassinated by her Sikh bodyguard and was succeeded as PM by her son Rajiv

Gandhi (PM 1984–89), who was assassinated during the 1991 election campaign. Tension and violence between Hindus and Muslims has increased since a campaign to build a Hindu temple on the site of a mosque in the holy city of Ayodhya. The destruction of the mosque by Hindu fundamentalists (1992) led to widespread disorders.

INDONESIA

Official name: Republik Indonesia (Republic of Indonesia).

Member of: UN, OPEC, ASEAN.

Area: 1 919 443 km² (741 101 sq mi) – including East Timor which has an area of 14 874 km² (5743 sq mi).

Population: 179 322 000 (1990 census) – including East Timor which had a population of 748 000.

Capital and major cities: Jakarta 7 829 000, Surabaya 2 345 000, Medan 2 110 000, Bandung 1 613 000, Semarang 1 208 000, Palembang 874 000, Ujung Pandang (Makassar) 842 000 (all including suburbs; 1985 est).

Languages: Bahasa Indonesia (official), Javanese (34%), Madurese (6%), Sundanese (14%) and about 25 other main languages.

Religions: Sunni Islam (80%), Roman Catholic (3%), other Christians (7%), Hindu (2%).

Education: *Literacy rate:* 77% (1990). *Years of compulsory schooling:* 7–13. *Universities:* 35 state and 26 private.

Defence: *Total armed strength:* 278 000 (1991) plus 180 000 paramilitary police and 1 500 000 trainees in the KAMRA (People's Security). *Military service:* 2 years selective.

GOVERNMENT

Every five years elections are held by universal adult suffrage for 400 members of the House of Representatives; the remaining 100 members are chosen by the President. The People's Consultative Assembly – which consists of the members of the House plus 500 representatives of provincial governments, occupational and special interests – meets once every five years to oversee broad principles of state policy and to elect the President, who appoints a Cabinet. The main political parties are (the government alliance) Golkar, the (Islamic) United Development Group, and the (Christian and nationalist) Indonesian Democratic Party. Of the country's 27 provinces, two are autonomous (see below).
President: Gen. T.N.I. Suharto.

AUTONOMOUS PROVINCES

Population figures are from the 1990 census.

Aceh *Area:*55 392 km² (21 387 sq mi). *Population:* 3 416 000. *Capital:* Banda Aceh.

Yogyakarta *Area:* 3169 km² (1224 sq mi). *Population:* 2 913 000. *Capital:* Yogyakarta.

GEOGRAPHY

Indonesia consists of nearly 3700 islands, of which about 3000 are inhabited. The southern chain of mountainous, volcanic islands comprises Sumatra, Java with Madura, Bali, and the Lesser Sunda Islands (including Lombok, Flores and Timor). Java and its smaller neighbour Madura are fertile and densely populated, containing nearly two thirds of Indonesia's people. The northern chain comprises Kalimantan (the Indonesian sector of Borneo), the irregular mountainous island of Sulawesi (Celebes),

INDONESIA

Area: 1 919 443 km² (741 101 sq mi) – including East Timor

the Moluccas group, and Irian Jaya (the western half of New Guinea). Over two thirds of the country is covered by tropical rain forests. *Principal rivers:* Kapuas, Digul, Barito. *Highest point:* Ngga Pulu (Carstenz Pyramid) 5030 m (16 503 ft) (on Irian Jaya).

Climate: The climate is tropical with heavy rainfall throughout the year.

ECONOMY

Indonesia has great mineral wealth – petroleum, natural gas, tin, nickel, coal, bauxite and copper – but is relatively poor because of its great population. Over 50% of Indonesians are subsistence farmers with rice being the major crop, but both estate and peasant farmers produce important quantities of rubber, tea, coffee, tobacco and spices for export. Industry is largely concerned with processing mineral and agricultural products. Indonesia achieved high economic growth rates throughout the 1980s and early 1990s.

RECENT HISTORY

From the 17th century, the East Indies became the major and most profitable part of the Dutch Empire. Except for a brief period of British occupation (1811–14) and occasional local risings, the Netherlands retained control until 1942 when the Japanese invaded and were welcomed by most Indonesians as liberators from colonial rule. Upon Japan's surrender in 1945, Achmed Sukarno (1901–70) – the founder of the nationalist party in 1927 – declared the Dutch East Indies to be the independent republic of Indonesia. Under international pressure, the Dutch accepted Indonesian independence (1949) after four years of intermittent but brutal fighting. Sukarno's rule became increasingly authoritarian and the country sank into economic chaos. In 1962 he seized Netherlands New Guinea, which was formally annexed as Irian Jaya in 1969, although a separatist movement persists. Between 1963 and 1966 Sukarno tried to destabilize the newly-created Federation of Malaysia by armed incursions into north Borneo.

General T.N.I. Suharto's suppression of a Communist uprising in 1965–66 enabled him to reverse Sukarno's anti-Americanism and eventually to displace him with both student and army support. Around 80 000 members of the Communist Party were killed in this period. The annexation of Portuguese East Timor by Indonesia in 1976 is unrecognized by the international community, and guerrilla action by local nationalists continues. International protests followed the killing of unarmed Timorese demonstrators by Indonesian troops in 1991. An ambitious programme of resettlement has been attempted to relieve overcrowded Java, but the

Javanese settlers have been resented in the outlying, underdeveloped islands.

IRAN

Official name: Jomhori-e-Islami-e-Irân (Islamic Republic of Iran). Until 1935 Iran was known as Persia.

Member of: UN, OPEC.

Area: 1 648 000 km² (636 296 sq mi).

Population: 57 050 000 (1991 est).

Capital and major cities: Tehran 6 022 000, Mashad 1 464 000, Isfahan 987 000, Tabriz 971 000, Shiraz 848 000, Ahvaz 580 000, Bakhtaran 561 000, Qom 543 000 (all including suburbs; 1986 census).

Languages: Farsi or Persian (official; 45%), Azeri (26%), Kurdish, Luri, Baluchi and Arabic minorities.

Religion: Shia Islam (official; 98%).

Education: *Literacy rate:* 52% (1986). *Years of compulsory schooling:* 6–10. *Universities:* 29.

Defence: *Total armed strength:* 528 000 (1991) (plus 350 000 reserves). *Military service:* 24 months.

GOVERNMENT

A Council of Experts – 83 Shiite clerics – is elected by universal adult suffrage to appoint the Wali Faqih (religious leader), who exercises supreme authority over the executive, legislature, judiciary and military. There is no fixed term for the Wali Faqih, whose role may be taken by a joint leadership of three or five persons. The 270-member Islamic Consultative Assembly (Majlis) and the President are directly elected for four years. The President appoints a Cabinet which is responsible to the Majlis. Iran is effectively a non-party state although the Liberation Movement of Iran is allowed to operate.
Supreme Religious Leader (Wali Faqih): Ayatollah Ali Khamenei.
President: Hashemi Rafsanjani.

GEOGRAPHY

Apart from restricted lowlands along the Gulf, the Caspian Sea and the Iraqi border, Iran is a high plateau, surrounded by mountains. The Elburz Mountains lie in the north; the Zagros Mountains form a barrier running parallel to the Gulf. In the east, lower areas of the plateau are covered by salt deserts. *Principal rivers:* Kàrùn, Safid, Atrak, Karkheh. *Highest point:* Demavend 5604 m (18 386 ft).

IRAN
Area: 1 648 000 km²
(636 296 sq mi).

Climate: Iran has an extreme climate ranging from very hot on the Gulf to sub-zero temperatures in winter in the northwest. The Caspian Sea coast has a subtropical climate with rainfall totals around 1000 mm (40 in) a year. Most of Iran, however, has little rain.

ECONOMY

Petroleum is Iran's main source of foreign currency. The principal industries are petrochemicals, carpet-weaving, textiles, vehicles and cement, but the war with Iraq and the country's international isolation have severely interrupted trade. Over a quarter of the labour force is involved in agriculture, mainly producing cereals (wheat, maize and barley) and keeping livestock, but lack of water, land ownership problems and manpower shortages have restricted yields.

RECENT HISTORY

In the 19th century, Russia and Britain became rivals for influence in the region. In 1921 an Iranian Cossack officer, Reza Khan Pahlavi (1877–1944), took power. Deposing the Qajar dynasty in 1925, he became Shah (emperor) himself as Reza I and modernized and secularized Iran. However, because of his pro-German sentiments, he was forced to abdicate by Britain and the USSR (1941) and was replaced by his son Mohammed Reza (1919–80). The radical nationalist prime minister Muhammad Mussadiq briefly toppled the monarchy (1953). On regaining his throne, the Shah tightened his grip through oppression and sought popularity through land reform and rapid development with US backing.

However, the policy of Westernization offended the clergy, and a combination of students, the bourgeoisie and religious leaders eventually combined against him, overthrowing the monarchy in 1979 and replacing it with a fundamentalist Islamic Republic inspired · by the Ayatollah Ruhollah Khomeini (1900–89). The Western-educated classes fled Iran as the clergy tightened control. Radical anti-Western students seized the US embassy and held 66 American hostages (1979–81). In 1980 Iraq invaded Iran, beginning the bitter First Gulf War, which lasted until 1988 and resulted in great losses of manpower for Iran. Following the death of Khomeini in 1989, economic necessity brought about a less militant phase of the Islamic revolution. The new president, Rafsanjani, emphasized pragmatic rather than radical policies and attempted to heal the diplomatic rift with Western powers. After the collapse of the USSR (1991), Iran began to look for closer ties with Islamic former Soviet republics of Central Asia.

IRAQ

Official name: Al-Jumhuriya al-'Iraqiya (The Republic of Iraq).

Member of: UN, Arab League, OPEC.

Area: 441 839 km² (170 595 sq mi).

Population: 17 754 000 (1990 est).

Capital and major cities: Baghdad 5 348 000 (including suburbs), Basrah (Al Basrah) 617 000, Mosul (Al Mawsil) 571 000, Irbil 334 000, As Sulaymaniyah 279 000, An Najaf 243 000 (1985 est).

Languages: Arabic (official; 80%), Kurdish (19%).

Religions: Sunni Islam (41%), Shia Islam (51%), with a small Christian minority.

IRAQ
Area: 441 839 km²
(170 595 sq mi).

Caspian Sea

TURKEY

SYRIA

IRAN

LEBANON

Baghdad

Tigris

Euphrates

ISRAEL

JORDAN

Shatt al Arab

SAUDI ARABIA

Basra

KUWAIT

THE GULF

Education: *Literacy rate:* no figure available. *Years of compulsory schooling:* 6–12. *Universities:* 8. **Defence:** *Total armed strength:* 382 500 (1991 est). *Military service:* 21–24 months.

GOVERNMENT
The 250-member National Assembly is elected for a four-year term by universal adult suffrage. The non-elected Revolutionary Command Council appoints the President, who – in turn – appoints the Council of Ministers. The only effective legal party is the Arab Ba'ath Socialist Party, which is part of the National Progressive Front coalition.
President: Saddam Hussein.
Prime Minister: Muhammad Hamza al-Zubaydi.

GEOGRAPHY
The basins of the Rivers Tigris and Euphrates contain most of the arable land and most of the population. Desert in the southwest occupies nearly one half of Iraq. *Principal rivers:* Tigris (Dijlah), Euphrates (al Furat). *Highest point:* Rawanduz 3658 m (12 001 ft).
Climate: Summers are hot and dry with temperatures over 40 °C (104 °F). Most of the rainfall – ranging from 100 mm (4 in) in the desert to 1000 mm (40 in) in the mountains – comes in winter.

ECONOMY
Agriculture involves one third of the labour force. Irrigated land in the Tigris and Euphrates basins produces cereals, fruit and vegetables for domestic consumption, and dates for export. Iraq traditionally depends upon its substantial reserves of petroleum, but exports were halted by international sanctions (1990). The Iraqi economy was badly damaged during the First Gulf War against Iran, and devastated by the Second Gulf War.

RECENT HISTORY
Iraq was absorbed by the Turkish Ottoman Empire in the 16th century. In World War I the British occupied the area, but Iraqi nationalists were disappointed when Iraq became a British mandate with virtual colonial status (1920). In 1921 the Amir Faisal ibn Husain became King and in 1932 Iraq became fully independent. Following a military coup that brought pro-German officers to power in 1941, the British occupied Iraq until 1945. The royal family and the premier were murdered in the 'Free Officers' coup in 1958. Differences in the leadership led to a further coup in 1963 and a reign of terror against the left. In 1968 Ba'athist (pan-Arab nationalist) officers carried out another coup. Embittered by the Arabs' humiliation in the 1967 war and by US support for the Israelis, the regime turned to the Soviets.

In 1980 President Saddam Hussein attacked a weakened Iran, responding to Iran's threat to export Islamic revolution. What had been intended as a quick victory became the costly First Gulf War (1980–88), resulting in many casualties and the virtual bankruptcy of the country. In an attempt to restore Iraq's economic fortunes, Saddam Hussein invaded oil-rich Kuwait (1990). UN sanctions against Iraq were imposed. Forces from the USA, the UK and over 20 other countries (including Egypt and Syria) were dispatched to the Gulf to prevent an Iraqi invasion of Saudi Arabia. Following Saddam Hussein's failure to respond to repeated UN demands to withdraw from Kuwait, the Second Gulf War began (January 1991). Coalition forces routed the Iraqi army which sustained heavy casualties. Iraq accepted all the UN resolutions regarding Kuwait and agreed to a ceasefire after a campaign that lasted only 100 hours. During March and April Saddam Hussein suppressed revolts by Shiites in the south and Kurds in the north. International efforts were made to feed and protect over 1 000 000 Shiite and Kurdish refugees who had fled. Despite being forced to accept UN inspection of Iraq's chemical and biological weapons and the country's nuclear capacity, Saddam continued to defy UN demands concerning disarmament and recognition of the Kuwaiti border.

IRELAND
Official name: Poblacht na h'Éireann (Republic of Ireland).
Member of: UN, EC, CSCE, Council of Europe, OECD, WEU (associate).
Area: 70 282 km² (27 136 sq mi).
Population: 3 523 000 (1991 census)
Capital and major cities: Dublin 921 000 (city 478 000), Cork 174 000 (city 127 000), Limerick 77 000 (city 52 000), Dún Laoghaire (part of the Dublin agglomeration) 55 000, Galway 51 000, Waterford 41 000 (city 40 000) (1986 census).
Languages: Irish (official), English.
Religion: Roman Catholic (95%).
Education: *Literacy rate:* 99%. *Years of compulsory schooling:* 6–15. *Universities:* 7 universities and university colleges (plus 4 institutes offering university level courses).
Defence: *Total armed strength:* 12 900 (1991) (plus 16 100 reservists). *Military service:* none.

GOVERNMENT
The Seanad (Senate) comprises 60 members – 11 nominated by the Taoiseach (Prime Minister), six elected by the universities and 43 indirectly elected for a five-year term to represent vocational and special interests. The Dáil (House) comprises 166 members elected for five years by universal adult suffrage under a system of proportional representation. The President is directly elected for a seven-year term. The Taoiseach and a Cabinet of Ministers are appointed by the President upon the nomination of the Dáil, to whom they are responsible. The main

political parties include (centre-right) Fianna Fáil (Soldiers of Destiny), (centre-right) Fine Gael (United Ireland Party), the (left-wing) Labour Party, the (centre-right) Progressive Democrats and the Worker's Party.
President: Mary Robinson.
Prime Minister: Albert Reynolds.

GEOGRAPHY

Central Ireland is a lowland crossed by slight ridges and broad valleys, bogs and large lakes, including Loughs Derg and Ree. Except on the east coast north of Dublin, the lowland is surrounded by coastal hills and mountains including the Wicklow Mountains (south of Dublin), the Comeragh Mountains (Co. Waterford) and the Ox Mountains and the hills of Connemara and Donegal in the west. The highest uplands are the Macgillicuddy's Reeks in the southwest. The rugged Atlantic Coast is highly indented.
Principal rivers: Shannon, Suir, Boyne, Barrow, Erne. *Highest point:* Carrauntuohill 1041 m (3414 ft).
Climate: Ireland has a mild temperate climate. Rainfall is high, ranging from over 2500 mm (100 in) in the west and southwest to 750 mm (30 in) in the east.

ECONOMY

Manufactured goods – in particular machinery, metals and engineering, electronics and chemical products – now accounts for over 80% of Ireland's exports. Agriculture – which was the traditional mainstay of the economy – concentrates upon the production of livestock, meat and dairy products. Food processing and brewing are major industries. Natural resources include lead-zinc, offshore petroleum and natural gas, and hydroelectric power sites. Ireland suffers high rates of unemployment and emigration.

RECENT HISTORY

In 1798 the failure of a nationalist revolt against British rule was followed by the amalgamation of the

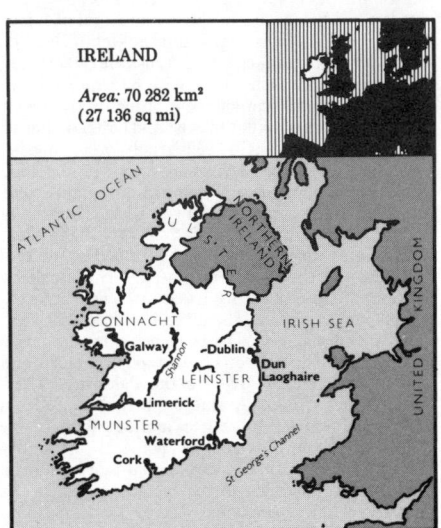

IRELAND

Area: 70 282 km²
(27 136 sq mi)

ATLANTIC OCEAN
ULSTER
NORTHERN IRELAND
UNITED KINGDOM
IRISH SEA
CONNACHT
Galway
Dublin
Dun Laoghaire
LEINSTER
Limerick
MUNSTER
Waterford
Cork
St George's Channel

British and Irish parliaments and the establishment of the United Kingdom of Great Britain and Ireland (1801). In the 1840s thousands died in the Irish potato

famine, and many more were evicted by Anglo-Irish landowners and joined a mass emigration, especially to the USA. The result was that between 1845 and 1851 the population of Ireland declined by almost three million. Daniel O'Connell (1775–1847) led a movement seeking to repeal the Union, and to gain land and civil rights for the Roman Catholic majority. His campaign helped lead to Catholic Emancipation (1829), after which Irish Catholics were able to become MPs in the British Parliament at Westminster. However, relations between the Protestant and Catholic communities deteriorated, in part owing to the increasingly violent actions of the nationalist Fenians, whose goal was Irish independence. British policy on Ireland vacillated between conciliation and coercion – Gladstone, recognizing the need for reform, disestablished the (Anglican) Church of Ireland and granted greater security of tenure to peasant farmers. In the 1880s Charles Stewart Parnell (1846–91) led a sizeable bloc of Irish MPs in a campaign to secure Irish Home Rule (i.e. self-government). Home Rule Bills were introduced in 1883 and 1893, but after their rejection by Parliament, more revolutionary nationalist groups gained support in Ireland.

Fearing Catholic domination, Protestant Unionists in Ulster strongly opposed the Third Home Rule Bill in 1912. Nationalists declared an independent Irish state in the Dublin Easter Rising of 1916, which was put down by the British. After World War I, Irish nationalist MPs formed a provisional government in Dublin led by Eamon de Valera (later PM and President; 1882–1975). Except in the northeast, British administration in Ireland crumbled and most of the Irish police resigned to be replaced by British officers – the 'Black and Tans'. Fighting broke out between nationalists and British troops and police, and by 1919 Ireland had collapsed into violence. The British response in 1920 was to offer Ireland two Parliaments – one in Protestant Ulster, another in the Catholic south. Partition was initially rejected by the south, but by the Anglo-Irish Treaty (1921) dominion status was granted, although six (mainly Protestant) counties in Ulster – Northern Ireland – opted to remain British. The Irish Free State was proclaimed in 1922 but de Valera and the Republicans refused to accept it. Civil war broke out between the provisional government – led by Arthur Griffith and Michael Collins – and the Republicans. Although fighting ended in 1923, de Valera's campaign for a republic continued and in 1937 the Irish Free State became the Republic of Eire. The country remained neutral in World War II and left the Commonwealth – as the Republic of Ireland – in 1949. Relations between south and north – and between the Republic and the UK – have often been tense during the 'troubles' in Northern Ireland (1968–). However, the Anglo-Irish Agreement (1985) provided for the participation of the Republic in political, legal and security matters in Northern Ireland. Irish political life has been characterized by the alternation of the two main parties – Fine Gael and Fianna Fail – in government.

ISRAEL

Official name: Medinat Israel (The State of Israel).

Member of: UN.

Area: 21 946 km² (8473 sq mi), including East Jerusalem but excluding Golan, Gaza and the West Bank.

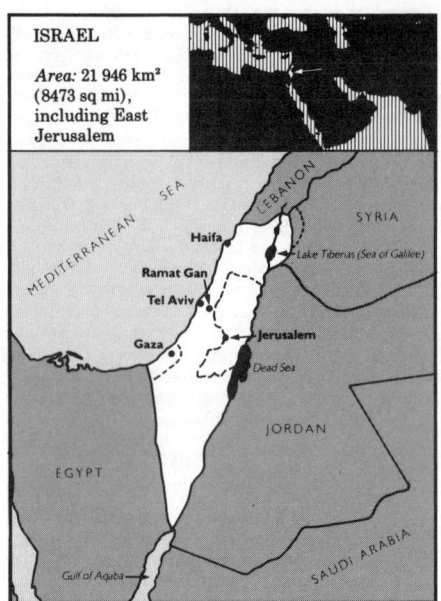

ISRAEL

Area: 21 946 km²
(8473 sq mi),
including East
Jerusalem

Population: 4 821 000 (1991 est) – including East
Jerusalem but excluding Golan, Gaza and the West
Bank.

Capital and major cities: Jerusalem (not recognized internationally as capital) 525 000, Tel-Aviv
1 157 000 (city 339 000), Haifa 395 000 (city 246 000),
Netanya 132 000, Beersheba (Be'er Sheva) 122 000.
Holon 157 000, Petach-Tikva 144 000, Bat-Yam
141 000 and Rishon LeZiyyon 140 000 are all part of
the Tel-Aviv agglomeration (1990 est).

Languages: Hebrew (official; 85%), Arabic (15%).
Religions: Judaism (official; 85%), Sunni Islam
(13%), various Christian denominations.

Education: *Literacy rate:* 88% Jews; 70% Arabs.
Years of compulsory schooling: 5–15. *Universities:* 8
including the open university and 2 institutes of
university status.

Defence: *Total armed strength:* 141 000 (1991) (plus
504 000 reserves). *Military service:* 36 and 24 months
for men and women respectively; military service is
voluntary for Christians and Arabs.

GOVERNMENT

The 120-member Knesset (Assembly) is elected by
proportional representation for four years by universal adult suffrage. A Prime Minister and Cabinet
take office after receiving a vote of confidence from
the Knesset. The President is elected for a five-year
term by the Knesset. Over ten political parties are
represented in the Knesset – the largest are the (right
wing) Likud Party and the (centre-left) Labour
Alignment.
President: Ezer Weizman.
Prime Minister: Yitzhak Rabin.

GEOGRAPHY

Israel – within the boundaries established by the
1949 cease-fire line – consists of a fertile thin coastal
plain beside the Mediterranean, parts of the arid
mountains of Judaea in the centre, the Negev Desert
in the south, and part of the Jordan Valley in the
northeast. *Principal rivers:* Jordan (Yarden),

Qishon. *Highest point:* Har Meron (Mt Atzmon) 1208
m (3963 ft).

Climate: Israel's climate is Mediterranean with
hot, dry summers and mild, wetter winters. The
greater part of Israel receives less than 200 mm (8 in)
of rain a year.

ECONOMY

Severe economic problems stem, in part, from Israel's
large defence budget and political circumstances,
which prevent trade with neighbouring countries.
Israel is a major producer and exporter of citrus
fruit. Much land is irrigated and over 75% of Israel's
arable land is farmed by collectives (kibbutzim) and
cooperatives. Mineral resources are few, but processing imported diamonds is a major source of
foreign currency. Tourism – to biblical sites – is
important.

RECENT HISTORY

The Turkish Ottoman Empire ruled the area from the
early 16th century until 1917–18, when Palestine was
captured by British forces. The Zionists had hoped to
establish a Jewish state, and this hope was intensified following the Balfour Declaration by the British
foreign secretary in favour of a homeland (1917).
However, Palestine came under British administration and it was not until 1948–9 – after the murder of
some 6 million Jews in concentration camps by the
Nazis – that an explicitly Jewish state emerged. The
establishment of a Jewish state met with hostility
from Israel's neighbours and indigenous Palestinians (many of whom left the country), leading to a
series of Arab-Israeli wars. In 1956, while the UK and
France were in conflict with Egypt over the Suez
Canal, Israel attacked Gaza – from which the Palestinians had raided Israel – and overran Sinai, but
withdrew following UN condemnation. After an
uneasy peace, the UN emergency force between
Israel and Egypt was expelled in 1967. Egypt imposed
a sea blockade on Israel, which responded by invading Sinai. In six days, an Arab coalition of Egypt,
Jordan and Syria was defeated, and Israel occupied
Sinai, Gaza, the West Bank and the Golan Heights.
In 1973, Egypt attacked Israel across the Suez Canal,
but a ceasefire was arranged within three weeks. In
1979 Israel and Egypt signed a peace treaty; Egypt
recognized Israel's right to exist and Israel withdrew
from Sinai in stages. In 1982 Israeli forces invaded
Lebanon, intent on destroying bases of the PLO
(Palestinian Liberation Organization), and became
involved in the complex civil war there. Eventually
Israeli forces withdrew in 1985. In 1987 the intifada
(Palestinian uprising) against continued Israeli rule
in Gaza and the West Bank began. The harsh reaction of Israeli security forces attracted international condemnation. The intifada continued sporadically and was given extra impetus by the large-
scale influx of Soviet Jews into Israel (from 1990) and
the encouragement given to the Palestinians and
their leader Yasser Arafat by President Saddam
Hussein of Iraq. Israeli politics in the 1980s and early
1990s was characterized by political instability
owing to the system of proportional representation
and the large number of very small parties. In the
1990s Israel has come under increased international
pressure to achieve an Middle East settlement.

Information concerning the occupied territories –
Golan, Gaza and the West Bank (Judaea and Sama-
ria) – can be found on in the section following this
chapter.

ITALY

Official name: Italia (Italy) or Repubblica Italiana (Republic of Italy).

Member of: UN, EC, NATO, WEU, G7, Council of Europe, OECD, CSCE.

Area: 301 277 km² (116 324 sq mi).

Population: 57 104 000 (1991 census).

Capital and major cities: Rome (Roma) 2 985 000 (city 2 791 000), Milan (Milano) 3 670 000 (city 1 432 000), Naples (Napoli) 2 905 000 (city 1 206 000), Turin (Torino) 992 000, Palermo 734 000, Genoa (Genova) 701 000, Bologna 412 000, Florence (Firenze) 408 000, Catania 364 000, Bari 353 000, Venice (Venezia) 317 000, Messina 275 000, Verona 257 000, Taranto 244 000, Trieste 230 000, Padua (Padova) 217 000, Caligari 212 000, Brescia 196 000, Reggio di Calabria 179 000, Modena 177 000, Parma 173 000, Livorno 170 000, Prato 166 000, Foggia 159 000, Salerno 151 000, Perugia 150 000 (1991 census).

Languages: Italian (official), with small minorities speaking German, French and Albanian.

Religion: Roman Catholic (over 90%).

Education: *Literacy rate:* 97% (1985 est). *Years of compulsory schooling:* 6–14. *Universities:* 59 including the open university plus two polytechnics of university status.

Defence: *Total armed strength:* 361 400 (1991). *Military service:* 1 year.

GOVERNMENT

Until 1993 the two houses of Parliament were elected for a five-year term under a system of proportional representation. Scheduled reforms include elections to the Senate by first-past-the-post for the majority of seats with a minority still elected by proportional representation. A similar sytem is proposed for the Chamber of Deputies. The Senate has 315 members elected by citizens aged 25 and over to represent the regions, plus two former Presidents and five life senators, chosen by the President. The Chamber of Deputies has 630 members elected by citizens aged 18 and over. The President is elected for a seven-year term by an electoral college consisting of Parliament and 58 regional representatives. The President appoints a Prime Minister – who commands a majority in Parliament – and a Council of Ministers (Cabinet) who are responsible to Parliament. The main political parties include the (conservative) Popular Party (formerly the Christian Democrat Party), the Democratic Party of the Left (formerly the Communist Party) – which divided in May 1993, the PSI (Socialist Party), the (separatist) Northern League (including the Lombard League), the (southern-based anti-Mafia) La Rete, the RPI (Republican Party), the Radical Party, the Liberal Party, the Social Democratic Party, the (reformist) Democratic Alliance and the (right-wing) MSI-DN. The 20 regions of Italy have their own regional governments.

President: Oscar Luigi Scalfaro.
Prime Minister: Carlo Azeglio Ciampi.

ITALIAN REGIONS

Population figures are from the 1991 census.

Abruzzi *Area:* 10 794 km² (4168 sq mi). *Population:* 1 249 000. *Capital:* L'Aquila. (Pescara shares some of the functions of capital with L'Aquila.).

Basilicata *Area:* 9992 km² (3858 sq mi). *Population:* 592 000. *Capital:* Potenza.

ITALY
Area: 301 277 km² (116 324 sq mi).

Calabria *Area:* 15 080 km² (5822 sq mi). *Population:* 2 010 000. *Capital:* Catanzaro.

Campania *Area:* 13 595 km² (5249 sq mi). *Population:* 5 626 000. *Capital:* Naples (Napoli).

Emilia Romagna *Area:* 22 123 km² (8542 sq mi). *Population:* 3 984 000. *Capital:* Bologna.

Fruili-Venezia Giulia *Area:* 7846 km² (3029 sq mi). *Population:* 1 216 000. *Capital:* Trieste.

Lazio *Area:* 17 203 km² (6642 sq mi). *Population:* 5 146 000. *Capital:* Rome (Roma).

Liguria *Area:* 5413 km² (2090 sq mi). *Population:* 1 702 000. *Capital:* Genoa (Genova).

Lombardy (Lombardia) *Area:* 23 834 km² (9202 sq mi). *Population:* 8 941 000. *Capital:* Milan (Milano).

Marche *Area:* 9692 km² (3742 sq mi). *Population:* 1 447 000. *Capital:* Ancona.

Molise *Area:* 4438 km² (1714 sq mi). *Population:* 321 000. *Capital:* Campobasso.

Piedmont (Piemonte) *Area:* 25 399 km² (9807 sq mi). *Population:* 4 338 000. *Capital:* Turin (Torino).

Puglia *Area:* 19 347 km² (7470 sq mi). *Population:* 3 970 000. *Capital:* Bari.

Sardinia (Sardegna) *Area:* 24 090 km² (9301 sq mi). *Population:* 1 645 000. *Capital:* Cagliari.

Sicily (Sicilia) *Area:* 25 708 km² (9926 sq mi). *Population:* 4 990 000. *Capital:* Palermo.

Trentino-Alto Adige *Area:* 13 613 km² (5256 sq mi). *Population:* 935 000. *Joint capitals:* Trento (Trent) and Bolzano (Bozen).

Tuscany (Toscana) *Area:* 22 992 km² (8877 sq mi). *Population:* 3 599 000. *Capital:* Florence (Firenze).

Umbria *Area:* 8456 km² (3265 sq mi). *Population:* 823 000. *Capital:* Perugia.

Valle d'Aosta *Area:* 3262 km² (1259 sq mi). *Population:* 117 000. *Capital:* Aosta.

Veneto *Area:* 18 368 km² (7092 sq mi). *Population:* 4 453 000. *Capital:* Venice (Venezia).

GEOGRAPHY

The Alps form a natural boundary between Italy and

its western and northern neighbours. A string of lakes – where the mountains meet the foothills – include Lakes Maggiore, Lugano and Como. The fertile Po Valley – the great lowland of northern Italy – lies between the Alpine foothills in the north, the foothills of the Apennine Mountains in the south, the Alps in the W and the Adriatic Sea in the east. The narrow ridge of the Ligurian Alps joins the Maritime Alps to the Apennines, which form a backbone down the entire length of the Italian peninsula. Coastal lowlands are few and relatively restricted but include the Arno Basin in Tuscany, the Tiber Basin around Rome, the Campania lowlands around Naples, and plains beside the Gulf of Taranto and in Puglia (the 'heel' of Italy). The two major islands of Italy – Sardinia and Sicily – are both largely mountainous. Much of Italy is geologically unstable and liable to earthquakes. The country has four active volcanoes, including Etna on Sicily and Vesuvius near Naples. *Principal rivers:* Po, Tiber (Tevere), Arno, Volturno, Garigliano. *Highest point:* a point just below the summit of Monte Bianco (Mont Blanc) 4760 m (15 616 ft).

Climate: Italy enjoys a Mediterranean climate with warm, dry summers and mild winters. Sicily and Sardinia tend to be warmer and drier than the mainland. The Alps and the Po Valley experience colder, wetter winters.

ECONOMY
Northern Italy, with its easy access to the rest of Europe, is the main centre of Italian industry. The south, in contrast, remains mainly agricultural, producing grapes, sugar beet, wheat, maize, tomatoes and soya beans. The majority of farms are small – and many farmers in the south are resistant to change – thus incomes in southern Italy (the 'Mezzogiorno') are on average substantially lower than in the north. Agriculture in the north is more mechanized and major crops include wheat, maize, rice, grapes (for the important wine industry), fruit and fodder crops for dairy herds. Industrialization in the south is being actively promoted. The industries of the north are well-developed and include electrical and electronic goods, motor vehicles and bicycles, textiles, clothing, leather goods, cement, glass, china and ceramics. The north is also an important financial and banking area, and Milan is the commercial capital of Italy. Apart from stone – in particular marble – and Alpine rivers that have been harnessed for hydroelectric power, Italy has few natural resources. Tourism and money sent back by Italians living abroad are important sources of foreign currency. Recession and a crippling public deficit have added to Italy's growing economic problems.

RECENT HISTORY
The kingdom of Italy – uniting most of the peninsula – was proclaimed in March 1861. Venetia (1866) and Rome (1870) were subsequently included. Political development after unification was unsteady. Overseas ventures – such as the attempt to annex parts of Ethiopia (1895–96) – were often frustrated. Parliament was held in low esteem and the end of the 19th century saw a series of assassinations – including King Umberto I in 1900. Italy entered World War I on the Allied side in the expectation of territorial gains from Austria. However, Italy won far less territory than anticipated in the peace treaties after the war, when fear of Communist revolution led to an upsurge of Fascism. The Fascist Benito Mussolini (1883–1945), became Prime Minister in 1922 with a pro-

gramme of extensive domestic modernization and an aggressive foreign policy. In 1936 Italy allied with Germany in the Rome-Berlin Axis, and declared war on Britain and France in 1940. When Italy was invaded by Allied troops in 1943, Mussolini was dismissed by the king and Italy joined the Allies. In 1946 a republic was proclaimed. Communist influence increased, both at local and national level – in 1976, for example, the Communists controlled the local administration in Rome, Naples, Florence and Bologna. However, the dominance of the (conservative) Christian Democrat Party has kept the Communists out of the succeeding coalitions that have ruled Italy. Particularly in the 1970s, terrorist movements – of both the left and the right – have been active, kidnapping and assassinating senior political and industrial figures, including the former PM Aldo Moro in 1978. Considerable attempts have been made to effect a true unification of the country by encouraging the economic development of the S. However, the political structure of Italy remains unstable and coalitions have often been short-lived – for example, between 1945 and 1993 over 50 governments came to and fell from power. In the 1990s, public disillusion with state institutions grew and Italy was weakened by corruption, the activities of the Mafia and the growth of separatism in the north. In 1993 a non-political interim government was formed to effect constitutional changes.

JAMAICA
Member of: UN, Commonwealth, CARICOM, OAS.

Area: 10 991 km² (4244 sq mi).

Population: 2 420 000 (1991 est).

Capital and major cities: Kingston 662 000 (1990 est), Spanish Town 89 000, Montego Bay 70 000 (1985 est).

Language: English.

Religions: Church of God (17%), Anglican (10%), Baptist, Roman Catholic.

Education *Literacy rate:* 85%. *Years of compulsory schooling:* 6–12 (not compulsory in all districts of the island). *Universities:* 1.

Defence: *Total armed strength:* 3350 (1991) (plus 870 reserves). *Military service:* none.

GOVERNMENT
The 60-member House of Representatives (the lower house of Parliament) is elected for five years by universal adult suffrage. The 21-member Senate is appointed on the advice of the Prime Minister and the Leader of the Opposition. The Governor General – the representative of the British Queen as sovereign of Jamaica – appoints a Prime Minister who commands a majority in the House. The PM, in turn, appoints a Cabinet of Ministers who are responsible to the House. The main political parties are the (radical) People's National Party and the (centre) Jamaican Labour Party.
Prime Minister: P.J. Patterson.

GEOGRAPHY
Coastal lowlands surround the interior limestone plateaux (the 'Cockpit Country') and mountains. *Principal river:* Black River. *Highest point:* Blue Mountain Peak 2256 m (7402 ft).

Climate: The lowlands are tropical and rainy; the highlands are cooler and wetter. Jamaica is subject to hurricanes.

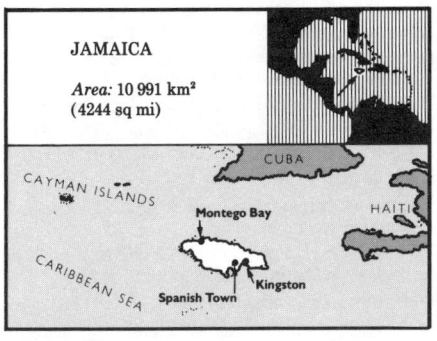

JAMAICA
Area: 10 991 km²
(4244 sq mi)

ECONOMY

Agriculture is the mainstay of the economy, with sugar cane and bananas as the main crops. Jamaica is one of the world's leading exporters of bauxite. Tourism is a major foreign-currency earner.

RECENT HISTORY

Jamaica became a British colony in the 17th century. By the 1930s, severe social and economic problems led to rioting and the birth of political awareness. Since independence in 1962, power has alternated between the radical People's National Party – led by Michael Manley – and the more conservative Jamaican Labour Party – whose leaders have included Sir Alexander Bustamente and Edward Seaga.

JAPAN

Official name: Nippon or Nihon ('The Land of the Rising Sun').

Member of: UN, G7, OECD.

Area: 377 815 km² (145 874 sq mi).

Population: 123 612 000 (1990 census).

Capital and major cities: Tokyo 18 200 000 (city 11 855 000), Osaka 8 500 000 (city 2 624 000), Yokohama (part of the Tokyo agglomeration) 3 220 000, Nagoya 2 155 000, Sapporo 1 672 000, Kobe (part of the Osaka agglomeration) 1 477 000, Kyoto 1 461 000, Fukuoka 1 237 000, Kawasaki (part of the Tokyo agglomeration) 1 174 000, Hiroshima 1 086 000, Kitakyushu 1 026 000, Sendai 889 000, Chiba (part of the Tokyo agglomeration) 816 000, Sakai (part of the Osaka agglomeration) 803 000 (1990 est).

Language: Japanese.

Religions: Shintoism (86%) overlaps with Buddhism (74%), various Christian denominations (under 1%).

Education: *Literacy rate:* almost 100%. *Years of compulsory schooling:* 6–15. *Universities:* 79 state (including the open university) plus 69 private universities.

Defence: *Total armed strength:* 246 400 (1991). *Military service:* none.

GOVERNMENT

The head of state is the Emperor who has no executive power. The 252-member House of Councillors – the upper house of the Diet (Parliament) – is elected for six years by universal adult suffrage. One half of the councillors retire every three years. A system of proportional representation is used to elect 100 of the councillors. The 512-member House of Representatives is elected for four years, also by universal adult suffrage. The Diet chooses a Prime Minister who commands a majority in the lower house. The PM in turn appoints a Cabinet of Ministers who are responsible to the Diet. The main political parties are the Liberal Democratic Party, the Socialist Party, Komeito (Clean Government Party), the Communist Party, the Democratic Socialist Party and the Social Democratic Federation.

Emperor: HIM the Heisei Emperor – known outside Japan as Emperor Akihito (who succeeded upon the death of his father, 7 January 1989).

Prime Minister: Kiichi Miyazawa.

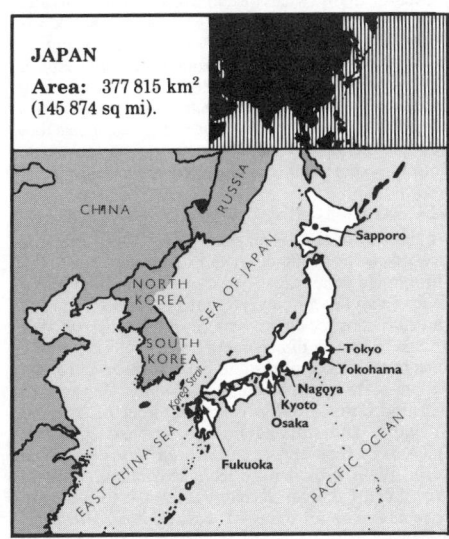

JAPAN
Area: 377 815 km²
(145 874 sq mi).

GEOGRAPHY

Japan consists of over 3900 islands, of which Hokkaido in the north occupies 22% of the total land area, and Shikoku and Kyushu in the south respectively occupy 5% and 11% of the area. The central island of Honshu occupies 61% of the total land area and contains 80% of the population. To the south of the four main islands, the Ryukyu Islands – including Okinawa – stretch almost to Taiwan. Nearly three quarters of Japan is mountainous. Coastal plains – where the population is concentrated – are limited. The principal lowlands are Kanto (around Tokyo), Nobi (around Nagoya) and the Sendai Plain in the north of Honshu. There are also over 60 active volcanoes in Japan, and the country is prone to severe earthquakes. *Principal rivers:* Tone, Ishikarai, Shinano, Kitakami. *Highest point:* Fujiyama (Mount Fuji) 3776 m (12 388 ft).

Climate: Japan experiences great variations in climate. Although the whole country is temperate, the north has long cold snowy winters, while the south has hot summers and mild winters. Rainfall totals are generally high, with heavy rain and typhoons being common in the summer months.

ECONOMY

Despite the generally crowded living conditions in the cities, the Japanese enjoy a high standard of living. The country has the second largest industrial economy in the world, despite having very few natural resources. Japanese industry is heavily dependent on imported raw materials – about 90% of the country's energy requirements come from abroad and petroleum is the single largest import. There is, therefore, considerable interest in offshore petroleum exploration, particularly in the Korean Straits. Japan's economic success is based on manufacturing industry, which – with construction – employs nearly one third of the labour force. Japan is the world's leading manufacturer of motor vehicles, and one of the major producers of ships, steel, synthetic fibres, chemicals, cement, electrical goods and electronic equipment. Rapid advances in Japanese research and technology have helped the expanding export-led economy. The banking and financial sectors have prospered in line with the manufacturing sector, and Tokyo is one of the world's principal stock exchanges and commercial centres. Agriculture is labour intensive. Although Japan is self-sufficient in rice, agriculture is not a priority and 30% of its food requirements – particularly cereals and fodder crops – have to be imported. The traditional Japanese diet is sea-based and the fishing industry is a large one, both for export and for domestic consumption.

RECENT HISTORY

At the end of the 19th century, the Meiji Emperor overthrew the last shogun and restored power to the throne. He encouraged Western institutions and a Western-style economy, so that by the beginning of the 20th century Japan was rapidly industrializing and on the brink of becoming a world power. By the time of the death of the Meiji Emperor in 1912, the Japanese had established an empire. Japan had defeated China (1894–95) – taking Port Arthur and Taiwan – and startled Europe by beating Russia (1904–5) by land and at sea. Korea was annexed in 1910. Allied with Britain from 1902, Japan entered World War I against Germany in 1914, in part to gain acceptance as an imperial world power. However, Japan gained little except some of the German island territories in the Pacific and became disillusioned that the country did not seem to be treated as an equal by the Great Powers. The rise of militarism and collapse of world trade in the 1930s led to the rise of totalitarianism and a phase of aggressive Japanese expansion. In 1931 the Japanese army seized Chinese Manchuria, and in 1937 mounted an all-out attack on China itself, occupying large areas. Japan became allied to Nazi Germany and in 1941 Japanese aircraft struck Pearl Harbor in Hawaii, bringing the USA into World War II. An initial rapid Japanese military expansion across SE Asia and the Pacific was halted, and the war ended for Japan in disastrous defeat and the horrors of atomic warfare.

Emperor Hirohito (reigned 1926–89) surrendered in September 1945. Shintoism – which had come to be identified with aggressive nationalism – ceased to be the state religion, and in 1946 the emperor renounced his divinity. The Allied occupation (1945–52) both democratized politics and began an astonishing economic recovery based on an aggressive export policy. The economy was jolted by major rises in petroleum prices in 1973 and 1979, but Japan nevertheless maintained its advance to become a technological front-runner. By 1988 Japan surpassed the USA as the world's largest aid-donor. The Japanese political world is dominated by the Liberal Democrats, who have held office since 1955 despite a number of financial scandals.

JORDAN

Official name: Al-Mamlaka al-Urduniya al-Hashemiyah (The Hashemite Kingdom of Jordan).

Member of: UN, Arab League.

Area: 89 206 km² (34 443 sq mi) – East Bank only (Jordan cut all legal and administrative ties with the Israeli-occupied West Bank in July 1988).

Population: 3 285 000 (1991 est) – East Bank only.

Capital and major cities: Amman 1 160 000, Zarqa 318 000, Irbid 168 000, Salt 134 000 (1986 est).

Language: Arabic (official).

Religion: Sunni Islam (over 80%), Shia Islam and various Christian minorities.

Education: *Literacy rate:* 71% (1988 est). *Years of compulsory schooling:* 5–14. *Universities:* 5.

Defence: *Total armed strength:* 101 300 (1991) (plus 35 000 reserves and 231 000 paramilitary). *Military service:* none.

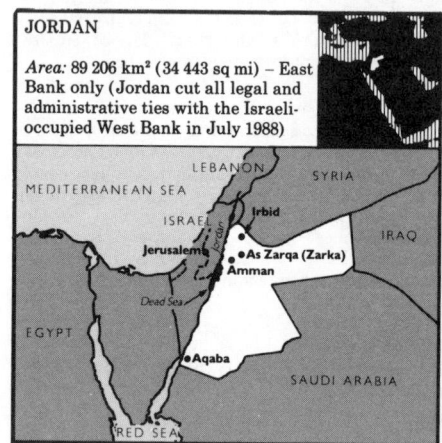

JORDAN

Area: 89 206 km² (34 443 sq mi) – East Bank only (Jordan cut all legal and administrative ties with the Israeli-occupied West Bank in July 1988)

GOVERNMENT

Jordan is a constitutional monarchy. The King appoints the 30 members of the Senate – the upper house of the National Assembly – and names a Prime Minister and Cabinet. The senators serve an eight-year term, with one half of their number retiring every four years. The 80 members of the House of Representatives are elected every four years by universal adult suffrage. The main political party is the Muslim Brotherhood.

King: HM King Hussein I (succeeded upon the deposition of his father, on grounds of illness, 11 August 1952).

Prime Minister: Sharif Zeid bin-Shaker.

GEOGRAPHY

The steep escarpment of the East Bank Uplands borders the Jordan Valley and the Dead Sea. Deserts cover over 80% of the country. *Principal river:* Jordan (Urdun). *Highest point:* Jabal Ramm 1754 m (5755 ft).

Climate: The summers are hot and dry; the winters are cooler and wetter, although much of Jordan experiences very low rainfall.

ECONOMY

Apart from potash – the principal export – Jordan has few resources. Arable land accounts for only about 5% of the total area. Foreign aid and money sent back by Jordanians working abroad are major sources of foreign currency.

RECENT HISTORY

The area was conquered by the (Turkish) Ottoman Empire in the 16th century. In World War I the British aided an Arab revolt against Ottoman rule. The League of Nations awarded the area east of the River Jordan – Transjordan – to Britain as part of Palestine (1920), but in 1923 Transjordan became a separate emirate. In 1946 the country gained complete independence as the Kingdom of Jordan with Amir Abdullah (1880–1951) as its sovereign.

The Jordanian army fought with distinction in the 1948 Arab-Israeli War, and occupied the West Bank territories which were formally incorporated into Jordan in April 1950. In 1951 Abdullah was assassinated. His grandson King Hussein (reigned 1952–) was initially threatened by radicals encouraged by Egypt's President Nasser. In the 1967 Arab-Israeli War, Jordan lost the West Bank, including Arab Jerusalem, to the Israelis. In the 1970s the power of the Palestinian guerrillas in Jordan challenged the very existence of the Jordanian state. After a short but bloody civil war in September 1979 the Palestinian leadership fled abroad. King Hussein renounced all responsibility for the West Bank in 1988. The Palestinians – who form the majority of the Jordanian population – supported Iraq in the Gulf Crisis of 1990–91, although King Hussein adopted a position of neutrality.

KAZAKHSTAN

Official name: Kazakhstan.

Member of: UN, CSCE, CIS.

Area: 2 717 300 km² (1 049 200 sq mi).

Population: 16 793 000 (1991 est.)

Capital and major cities: Alma-Ata (Almaty) 1 151 000, Karaganda (Qaraghandy) 615 000, Chimkent (Shymkent) 389 000, Pavlodar 331 000, Semipalatinsk (Semey) 330 000 (1989 census).

Languages: Kazakh (40%), Russian (38%), German (6%), Ukrainian (5%).

Religions: Sunni Islam majority, Russian Orthodox minority.

GOVERNMENT

A 510-member legislature and a President are elected for four years by universal adult suffrage. The President appoints a Prime Minister and a Cabinet of Ministers. A new constitution is to be drafted. The main political parties are the (former Communist) Socialist Party and the (coalition) Popular Congress of Kazakhstan.

President: Nursultan Nazarbayev.

Prime Minister: Sergei Tereshchenko.

Education: *Literacy rate:* no figures available. *Years of compulsory education:* 7-17. *Universities:* 3 universities and 2 polytechnics.

Defence: *Total armed strength:* no figures available. The majority of troops based on Kazakh soil are part of the joint CIS armed forces.

GEOGRAPHY

Kazakhstan comprises a vast expanse of low tablelands (steppes) in the middle of Central Asia. In the W, plains descend below sea level beside the Caspian Sea. Uplands include ranges of hills in the N and mountain chains, including the Tien Shan, in the S and E, where Khan Tengri, at 6398 m (20 991 ft), is the highest point. Kazakhstan has several salt lakes, including the Aral Sea, which is shrinking because of excessive extraction of irrigation water from its tributaries. Deserts include the Kyzylkum in the S, the Kara Kum in the centre, and the Barsuki in the N. *Principal river:* Syrdarya 3019 km (1876 mi).

Climate: The Kazkah climate is characterized by bitterly cold winters and hot summers. Rainfall is low, ranging between 200 mm (8 in) in the N to 500 mm (20 in) or more in the SE, and precipitation is negligible in the deserts.

ECONOMY

Kazakhstan is a major supplier of food and raw materials for industry to other former Soviet republics, particularly Russia. The transition to a market economy has hardly begun. Agriculture employs almost one half of the labour force. Large collective farms on the steppes in the N contributed one third of the cereal crop of the former USSR. Other major farming interests include sheep, fodder crops, fruit, vegetables and rice. Kazakhstan is rich in natural resources including coal, tin, copper, lead, zinc, gold, chromite, oil and nickel. Industry is represented by iron and steel (in the Karaganda coalfield), pharmaceuticals, food processing and cement.

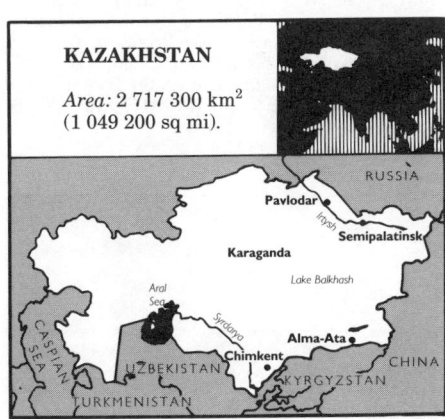

KAZAKHSTAN

Area: 2 717 300 km² (1 049 200 sq mi).

RECENT HISTORY

Russia completed conquest of the Kazakh lands in 1822 and 1848. During the Tsarist period there was large-scale Russian peasant settlement on the steppes, but Russian rule was resented and there was a major Kazakh revolt during World War I. After the Russian revolution, Kazakh nationalists formed a local government and demanded autonomy (1917). The Soviet Red Army invaded in 1920 and established an Autonomous Soviet Republic. Kazakhstan did not become a full Union Republic within the USSR until 1936. Widespread immigration from other parts of the USSR became a flood in 1954-6 when the 'Virgin Lands' of N Kazakhstan were opened up for farming. By the time Kazakhstan declared independence – following the abortive coup by Communist hardliners in Moscow (September 1991) – the Kazakhs formed a minority within their own republic. When the USSR was dissolved (December 1991), Kazakhstan was internationally recognized as an independent republic. The vast new Kazakh state – in theory, a nuclear power because of former Soviet nuclear weapons on its territory – occupies a pivotal position within Central Asia.

KENYA

Official name: Jamhuri ya Kenya (Republic of Kenya).

Member of: UN, OAU, Commonwealth.

Area: 580 367 km² (224 081 sq mi).

Population: 25 905 000 (1991 est).

Capital and major cities: Nairobi 1 505 000 (including suburbs), Mombasa 426 000, Kisumu 167 000, Nakuru 102 000 (1985 est).

Languages: Swahili (official), English, Kikuyu (21%), Luhya (14%), Luo (11%), Kamba (11%).

Religions: Roman Catholic (27%), Independent African Churches (27%), various Protestant Churches (19%), animist (19%), Sunni Islam (6%).

Education: *Literacy rate:* 69%. *Years of compulsory schooling:* education is available at all levels but schooling is not compulsory. *Universities:* 4 plus 1 university college.

Defence: *Total armed strength:* 23 600 (1991) (plus 4000 paramilitary police). *Military service:* none.

GOVERNMENT

The President and 188 members of the 202-member National Assembly are elected by universal adult suffrage every five years. The remaining 14 Assembly members, the Vice President and the Cabinet of Ministers are appointed by the President. The main political parties are (the former monopoly) KANU (Kenya African National Union), the Forum for the Restoration of Democracy (FORD-Kenya), FORD-Asili and the Democratic Party.
President: Daniel arap Moi.

KENYA
Area: 580 367 km²
(224 081 sq mi)

GEOGRAPHY

The steep-sided Rift Valley divides the highlands that run from north to south through central Kenya. Plateaux extend in the west to Lake Victoria and in the east to coastal lowlands. *Principal rivers:* Tana, Umba, Athi, Mathioya. *Highest point:* Mount Kenya 5199 m (17 058 ft).

Climate: The coastal areas have a hot and humid equatorial climate. The highlands – which are cooler – experience high rainfall. The north is very hot and arid.

ECONOMY

Agriculture involves occupies over 75% of the labour force. The main crops include wheat and maize for domestic consumption, and tea, coffee,

sisal, sugar cane and cotton for export. Large numbers of beef cattle are reared, and Kenya is one of the few states in black Africa to have a major dairy industry. Tourism is an important source of foreign currency.

RECENT HISTORY

The peoples of the area were forcibly brought under British rule in 1895 in the East African Protectorate, which became the colony of Kenya in 1920. White settlement in the highlands was bitterly resented by the Africans – particularly the Kikuyu – whose land was taken. Racial discrimination and attacks on African customs also created discontent. Black protest movements emerged in the 1920s, and after World War II these had developed into nationalism. From the 1920s, black protest was led by Jomo Kenyatta (c. 1893–1978), who in 1947 became the first president of the Kenya African Union. When the violent Mau Mau rising – which involved mainly Kikuyu people – broke out (1952–56), Kenyatta was held responsible and was imprisoned on doubtful evidence (1953–61). After the British had crushed the Mau Mau revolt in a bloody campaign, they negotiated with Kenyatta and the other African nationalists. Independence, under Kenyatta's KANU party, followed in 1963. His moderate leadership and pro-capitalist policies earned him British support and the gratitude of the remaining whites. His policies were continued by his successor, Daniel arap Moi, but considerable restrictions on political activity followed an attempted military coup in 1982. A campaign to end the one-party state included violent demonstrations in 1990. Multi-party elections were held in 1993.

KIRIBATI

Official name: Republic of Kiribati.

Member of: Commonwealth, South Pacific Forum.

Area: 717 km² (277 sq mi).

Population: 73 000 (1991 est).

Capital: Bairiki (on Tarawa) 25 000 (1990 census).

Languages: English (official), I-Kiribati.

Religions: Roman Catholic (over 50%), Kiribati Protestant (Congregational; over 40%).

Education: *Literacy rate:* over 90%. *Years of compulsory schooling:* 6–14. *Universities:* none, but there is a college teaching degree level courses.

Defence: *Total armed strength:* Kiribati has no armed forces.

GOVERNMENT

The President and 39 members of the Assembly are elected by universal adult suffrage every four years. An additional member for Banaba is appointed to the Assembly, whose members nominate three or four of their number as presidential candidates. The President appoints a Cabinet of Ministers, which is responsible to the Assembly. All the members of the Assembly are independents, although a political party has been formed in opposition.
President: Teateo Teannaki.

GEOGRAPHY

With the exception of the island of Banaba – which is composed of phosphate rock – Kiribati comprises three groups of small coral atolls. There are no

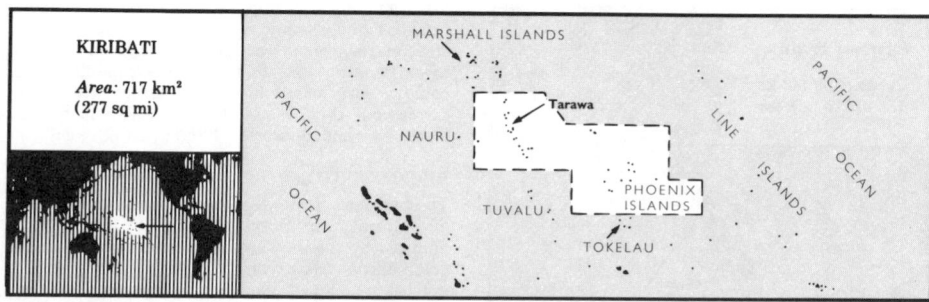

KIRIBATI

Area: 717 km²
(277 sq mi)

significant rivers. *Highest point:* 81 m (265 ft) on Banaba.

Climate: Kiribati has a maritime equatorial climate with high rainfall.

ECONOMY

Most islanders are involved in subsistence farming and fishing. The only significant export is copra.

RECENT HISTORY

In the 18th century, the atolls were discovered by British sea captains, including Thomas Gilbert. The Gilbert Islands – which became British in 1892 – were occupied by Japan (1942–43). British nuclear weapons were tested on Christmas Island (1957–64). In 1979 the islands gained independence as Kiribati (pronounced Kiri-Bass).

KOREA, DEMOCRATIC PEOPLE'S REPUBLIC OF

Official name: Chosun Minchu-chui Inmin Konghwa-guk (Democratic People's Republic of Korea). Popularly known as North Korea.

Member of: UN.

Area: 120 538 km² (46 540 sq mi).

Population: 21 815 000 (1991 est).

Capital and major cities: Pyongyang 2 640 000, Hamhung 775 000, Chongjin 755 000, Chinnamp'o 690 000, Sinuiju 500 000 (1986 est).

Language: Korean.

Religions: Daoism and Confucianism (14%), Chondism (14%), Buddhism (2%).

Education: *Literacy rate:* no figure is available. *Years of compulsory schooling:* 5–16. *Universities:* 5 including colleges of university status.

Defence: *Total armed strength:* 1 130 000 (1993 est) (plus 200 000 security and border troops and a workers and peasants militia (the Red Guards) 3 800 000). *Military service:* selective.

GOVERNMENT

The Party Congress of the (Communist) Korean Worker's Party elects a Central Committee, which in turn elects a Politburo, the seat of effective power. Citizens aged 17 and over vote in unopposed elections every four years for the 615-member Supreme People's Assembly. The Assembly elects the President, Prime Minister and Central People's Committee, which nominates Ministers.
President: Kim Il-Sung.
Prime Minister: Yon Hyong Muk.

GEOGRAPHY

Over three quarters of the country consists of moun-

tains. *Principal rivers:* Imjin, Ch'ongch'ŏn, Yalu. *Highest point:* Paek-tu 2744 m (9003 ft).

Climate: The country has long cold dry winters and hot wet summers.

ECONOMY

Over one third of the labour force works on cooperative farms, mainly growing rice. Natural resources include coal, zinc, magnetite, iron ore and lead. Great emphasis has been placed on industrial development, with the metallurgical, machine-building, chemical and cement industries being the most important. The end of barter deals with the former USSR (1990–91) brought a sharp economic decline.

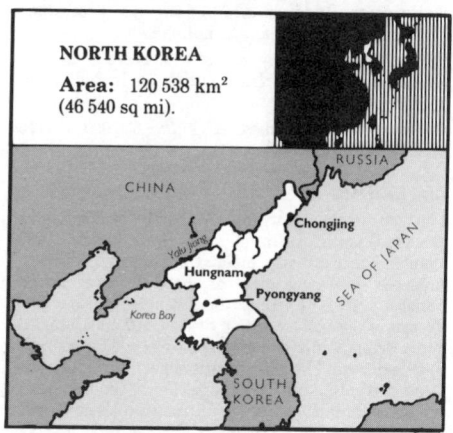

NORTH KOREA

Area: 120 538 km²
(46 540 sq mi).

RECENT HISTORY

Korea – a Japanese possession from 1910 to 1945 – was divided into zones of occupation in 1945. The USSR established a Communist republic in their zone N of the 38th parallel (1948). North Korea launched a surprise attack on the South in June 1950, hoping to achieve reunification by force. The Korean War devastated the peninsula. At the ceasefire in 1953 the frontier was re-established close to the 38th parallel. North Korea has the world's first Communist dynasty, whose personality cult has surpassed even that of Stalin. President Kim Il-Sung (1912–) and his son and anticipated successor, Kim Jong-Il, have rejected political reforms. Since the collapse of Communism in the former USSR and Eastern Europe, North Korea has become increasingly isolated.

KOREA, REPUBLIC OF

Official name: Daehan-Minkuk (Republic of Korea). Popularly known as South Korea.

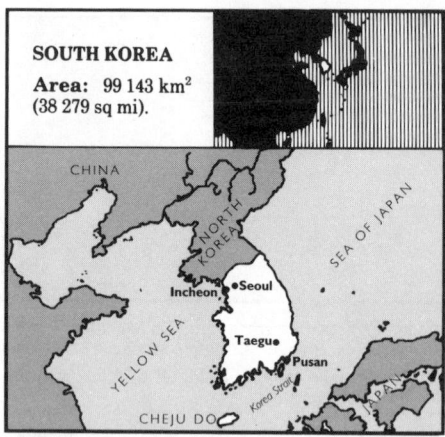

SOUTH KOREA
Area: 99 143 km²
(38 279 sq mi).

Member of: UN.

Area: 99 143 km² (38 279 sq mi).

Population: 43 520 000 (1990 census).

Capital and major cities: Seoul (Soul) 10 726 000, Pusan 3 825 000, Taegu 2 248 000, Inchon 1 682 000, Kwangju 1 206 000, Taejon 1 062 000, Ulsan 683 000, Sowon 645 000 (1990 census).

Language: Korean (official).

Religions: Buddhist (24%), various Protestant Churches (16%), Roman Catholic (5%).

Education: *Literacy rate: 96.3%. Years of compulsory schooling: 6–12. Universities:* 39 including an open university.

Defence: *Total armed strength:* 630 000 (1992). *Military service:* 30–36 months.

GOVERNMENT

The 299-member National Assembly is elected by universal adult suffrage every four years – 237 members are directly elected to represent constituencies; the remaining 62 members are chosen under a system of proportional representation. The President – who appoints a State Council (Cabinet) and a Prime Minister – is directly elected for a single five-year term. The main political parties include the Democratic Liberal Party (a merger of the Democratic Justice Party, the Reunification Democratic Party and the New Democratic Republican Party), the Democratic Party and the Party for National Unification.
President: Kim Young Sam.
Prime Minister: Soont Jong Hyan.

GEOGRAPHY

Apart from restricted coastal lowlands and the densely-populated river basins, most of the country is mountainous. *Principal rivers:* Han, Kum, Naktong, Somjin, Yongsan. *Highest point:* Halla-san 1950 m (6398 ft) on Cheju Island.

Climate: Korea experiences cold dry winters and hot summers during which the monsoon brings heavy rainfall.

ECONOMY

Agriculture involves about 20% of the labour force. The principal crops are rice, wheat and barley. A flourishing manufacturing sector is dominated by a small number of large family conglomerates. The important textile industry was the original manufacturing base, but South Korea is now the world's leading producer of ships and footwear, and a major producer of electronic equipment, electrical goods, steel, petrochemicals, motor vehicles (Hyundai) and toys. Banking and finance are expanding. The country experienced high economic growth rates throughout the 1980s and early 1990s and South Korea now has the world's 12th largest economy.

RECENT HISTORY

The Yi dynasty (1392–1910) gave Korea a long period of cultural continuity, but in 1910 Korea was annexed by the Japanese, who instituted a harsh colonial rule. After World War II, the peninsula was divided into Soviet and US zones of occupation. In 1948 the Republic of Korea was established in the American (southern) zone. The surprise invasion of the South by the Communist North precipitated the Korean War (1950–53). The war cost a million lives and ended in stalemate with the division of Korea confirmed. Closely allied to the USA, an astonishing economic transformation took place in South Korea. However, the country has experienced long periods of authoritarian rule including the presidencies of Syngman Rhee and Park Chung-Hee, but the election of ex-General Roh Tae Woo – amid political unrest in 1987 – introduced a more open regime. Much prestige was gained through the successful Seoul Olympic Games, and trading and diplomatic contacts have been established with the USSR and all the former Communist countries of Eastern Europe. This has left North Korea increasingly isolated. In 1990 North and South Korea tentatively began talks at prime ministerial level.

KUWAIT

Official name: Daulat al-Kuwait (State of Kuwait).

Member of: UN, Arab League, OPEC, GCC.

Area: 17 818 km² (6880 sq mi).

Population: 1 100 000 (1992) (The population of Kuwait in 1990 prior to the Iraqi invasion was estimated to be 2 014 000.)

Capital: Kuwait City 750 000 (including agglomeration; 1992 unofficial est).

Language: Arabic (official).

Religions: Sunni Islam (official; about 70%), Shia Islam (30%).

Education: *Literacy rate:* 73% (1990). *Years of compulsory schooling:* 6–14. *Universities:* 1.

Defence: *Total armed strength:* 8 200 (1991) (plus a paramilitary national guard). *Military service:* 2 years (1 year for university students).

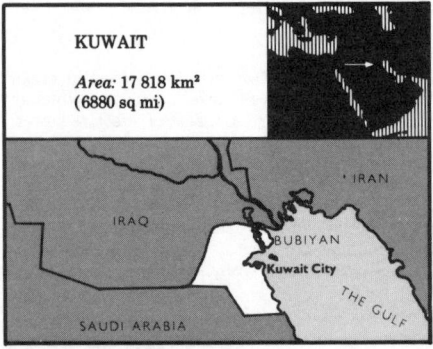

KUWAIT
Area: 17 818 km²
(6880 sq mi)

GOVERNMENT

Kuwait is a monarchy ruled by an Amir, who is chosen from and by the adult male members of the ruling dynasty. The Amir appoints a Prime Minister and a Council of Ministers. A 50-member National Assembly is elected for four years by literate adult male Kuwaiti nationals whose families fulfil stringent residence qualifications. There are no political parties but unofficial groupings exist within the Assembly.

Amir: HH Shaikh Jabir III bin Ahmad as-Sabah (succeeded upon the death of his cousin, 31 December 1977).

Prime Minister: HH Shaikh Saad al-Abdullah as-Sabah, Crown Prince of Kuwait.

GEOGRAPHY

Most of the country is desert, relatively flat and low lying. There are no permanent rivers. *Highest point:* 289 m (951 ft) at Ash Shaqaya.

Climate: Kuwait experiences extremely high temperatures in summer. Almost all the annual rainfall of 100 mm (4 in) comes during the cooler winter.

ECONOMY

The Kuwaiti economy was devastated by the Iraqi invasion and the Second Gulf War, but reconstruction followed rapidly. Large reserves of petroleum and natural gas are the mainstay of Kuwait's economy. Owing to lack of water, little agriculture is possible.

RECENT HISTORY

In 1760 the Sabah family created the emirate that has lasted to today, although from 1899 to 1961 Kuwait was a British-protected state. Oil was discovered in 1938 and was produced commercially from 1946. Iraq attempted to take over Kuwait in 1961, but the dispatch of British troops to the Gulf discouraged an Iraqi invasion. In August 1990 – despite having recognized the emirate's sovereignty in 1963 – Iraq invaded and annexed Kuwait. Iraq refused to withdraw despite repeated UN demands and in January 1991 the war to remove Iraqi forces from Kuwait – the Second Gulf War – began. In February, coalition forces entered the emirate to liberate Kuwait from Iraqi rule. The emirate was freed within 100 hours in a campaign during which the Iraqi forces were routed. The country was found to have been devastated by the occupying Iraqi forces. Following the liberation of Kuwait, pressure for constitutional reform grew and the constitution, which had been suspended in 1968, was restored in 1992. Large numbers of Palestinians – who were perceived to have favoured Iraq – were expelled from Kuwait in 1991–92.

KYRGYZSTAN

Official name: Kyrgyzstan. Formerly known as Kirghizia.

Member of: UN, CSCE, CIS.

Area: 198 500 km² (76 600 sq mi).

Population: 4 422 000 (1991 est).

Capital and major cities: Bishkek (formerly Frunze) 626 000, Osh 213 000, Przhevalsk 56 000 (1989 census).

Languages: Kyrgyz (53%), Russian (21%), Uzbek (13%), Ukrainian (3%).

Religions: Sunni Islam majority, Russian Orthodox.

KYRGYZSTAN

Area: 198 500 km² (76 600 sq mi).

Education: *Literacy rate:* no figures available. *Years of compulsory schooling:* 7–17. *Universities:* 1 university and 1 polytechnic.

Defence: *Total armed strength:* no figures available. Most of the forces based in Kyrgyzstan are currently part of the joint CIS armed forces.

GOVERNMENT

A 250-member legislature and a President are elected for four years by universal adult suffrage. A new constitution is to be drafted. The main political parties are the Kyrgyzstan Democratic Movement, the Kyrgyz Democratic Wing, and National Unity. *President and Prime Minister:* Askar Akayev.

GEOGRAPHY

Most of Kyrgyzstan lies within the Tien Shan mountains. Restricted lowlands – including the Chu valley and part of the Fergana valley – contain most of the population. *Principal rivers:* Sarydzhaz, Naryn, Kyzylsu. *Highest point:* Pik Pobedy 7439 m (24 406 ft)

Climate: The country's altitude and position deep within the interior of Asia combine to produce an extreme continental climate. Precipitation is low in many areas.

ECONOMY

Agriculture is dominated by large collectivized farms that specialize in growing fodder crops for sheep and goats, and cotton under irrigation. Natural resources include coal, lead, zinc and considerable hydroelectric-power potential. Food processing and light industry are expanding but the economy remains centrally planned.

RECENT HISTORY

The Kyrgyz – a Turkic people – retained their independence until after 1850 when the area was annexed by Russia. Opposition to the Russians – who were given most of the best land – found expression in a major revolt in 1916 and continuing guerrilla activity after the Russian Revolution. A Kirghiz Soviet Republic was founded in 1926 and became a full Union Republic within the USSR in 1936. After the abortive coup by Communist hardliners (September 1991), Kirghizia declared independence and – under its new name, Kyrgyzstan – received international recognition when the Soviet Union was dissolved (December 1991).

LAOS

Official name: Saathiaranagroat Prachhathippatay Prachhachhon Lao (The Lao People's Democratic Republic).

Member of: UN.

Area: 236 800 km² (91 400 sq mi).

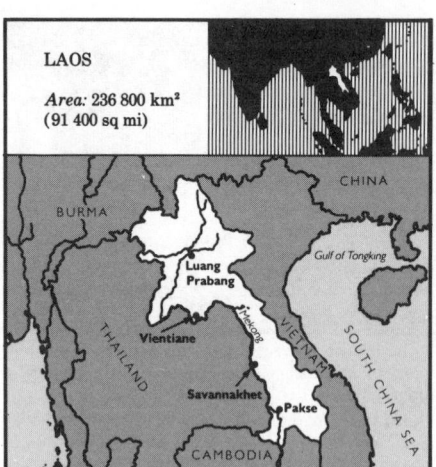

LAOS

Area: 236 800 km²
(91 400 sq mi)

Population: 4 290 000 (1991 est.).

Capital: Vientiane (Viengchane) 377 000, Savannakhet 97 000, Luang Prabang (Louangphrabang) 68 000, Pakse 47 000 (1985 est).

Language: Lao (official).

Religions: Buddhism (57%), various traditional local religions (over 30%).

Education: *Literacy rate:* 83.9% (1985). *Years of compulsory schooling:* 7–15. *Universities:* 1 (plus 8 other institutions that offer degree level courses).

Defence: *Total armed strength:* 52 600 (1991 est) (plus paramilitary forces). *Military service:* 18 months.

GOVERNMENT

Effective power is exercised by the Central Committee of the (Communist) Lao People's Revolutionary Party. Pending the implementation of a new constitution, representatives of directly elected local authorities have met as the National Congress to appoint the President, the Prime Minister and the Council of Ministers. There is constitutional provision for a 79-member Supreme People's Assembly to be elected for five years by universal adult suffrage.
President: Nouhak Phoumsavan.
Prime Minister: Khamtai Siphandon.

GEOGRAPHY

Except for the Plain of Jars in the north and the Mekong Valley and low plateaux in the south, Laos is largely mountainous. *Principal river:* Mekong. *Highest point:* Phou Bia 2820 m (9252 ft).

Climate: Laos has a tropical climate with heavy monsoon rains between May and October.

ECONOMY

War, floods and drought have retarded the development of Laos, one of the poorest countries in the world. The majority of Laotians work on collective farms, mainly growing rice. Since 1990, the Laotian government has attempted to encourage Western investment.

RECENT HISTORY

A French protectorate was established in 1893. Japanese occupation in World War II led to a declaration of independence, which the French finally accepted in 1954. However, the kingdom was wracked by civil war, with royalist forces fighting the Communist Pathet Lao. The Viet Cong used Laos as a supply route in the Vietnam War, and US withdrawal from Vietnam allowed the Pathet Lao to take over Laos (1975). Since 1990, the government has begun to introduce reforms, but there is no suggestion that a multi-party system will be tolerated.

LATVIA

Official name: Latvija (Latvia).

Member of: UN, CSCE.

Area: 64 589 km² (24 938 sq mi).

Population: 2 686 000 (1991 est).

Capital and major cities: Riga 917 000, Dagauvpils 128 000, Liepaja 115 000, Jelgava 75 000 (1990 est).

Languages: Lettish (over 52%), Russian (33%).

Religions: Lutheran (22%), Roman Catholic (7%), small Russian Orthodox minority.

Education: *Literacy rate:* nearly 100% (est). *Years of compulsory schooling:* 7–17. *Universities:* 2.

Defence: *Total armed strength:* 1000 border guards; 10 000 home guards; 400 Supreme Council security guards; 15 000 Internal Affairs security force (1992). *Military service:* yes.

GOVERNMENT

A President – who appoints a Prime Minister and a Cabinet (Supreme Council) – and a 100-member Assembly are elected by universal adult suffrage for three years. The main political parties are the Popular Front of Latvia (LTF), the Latvian National Independence Movement (LNNK), the Social Democratic Workers' Party (LSDSP) and the Green Party (LZP).
President: Anatolijs Gorbunovs.
Prime Minister: Ivars Godmanis.

GEOGRAPHY

Latvia comprises an undulating plain, lower in the W (Courland) than in the E (Livonia). *Principal river:* Daugava. *Highest point:* Osveyskoye 311 m (1020 ft).

Climate: Latvia has a moist, temperate climate with mild summers and cold winters.

ECONOMY

Engineering dominates a heavily industrialized

LATVIA

Area: 64 589 km²
(24 938 sq mi).

economy. Latvia has relied on Russian trade and faces severe difficulties as it begins to introduce a free market. Agriculture specializes in dairying and meat production.

RECENT HISTORY

Latvia was annexed by Russia in the 18th century. Latvian national consciousness grew throughout the 19th century. Following the Communist takeover in Russia (1917), Latvian nationalists declared independence (1918). A democratic system lasted until 1936 when General Ulmanis established a dictatorship. The Non-Aggression Pact (1939) between Hitler and Stalin assigned Latvia to the USSR, which invaded and annexed the republic (1940). After occupation by Nazi Germany (1941–44), Soviet rule was reimposed. Large-scale Russian settlement replaced over 200 000 Latvians who were killed or deported to Siberia. In 1988, reforms in the USSR allowed Latvian nationalists to operate openly. Nationalists won a majority in Latvia's parliament and seceded following the failed coup by Communist hardliners in Moscow (1991). The USSR recognized Latvia's independence in September 1991. Tension remains over the large Russian minority in Latvia.

LEBANON

Official name: Al-Lubnan (The Lebanon).

Member of: UN, Arab League.

Area: 10 452 km² (4036 sq mi).

Population: 2 745 000 (1991 est).

Capital and major cities: Beirut (Bayrūt 1 100 000), Tripoli (Tarabulus) 240 000, Zahleh 200 000, Sidon (Saida) 100 000 (all including suburbs; 1990 est).

Languages: Arabic (official).

Religions: Shia Islam (31%), Sunni Islam (27%), Druze minority; Maronite Christian (22%), other Christian Churches (16% – mainly Armenian, Greek Orthodox, Syrian and various Roman Catholic Uniat Churches).

Education: *Literacy rate:* 80.1% (1990). *Years of compulsory schooling:* education is free 5–17 but not compulsory. *Universities:* 5.

Defence: *Total armed strength:* 18 800 (1991) (plus

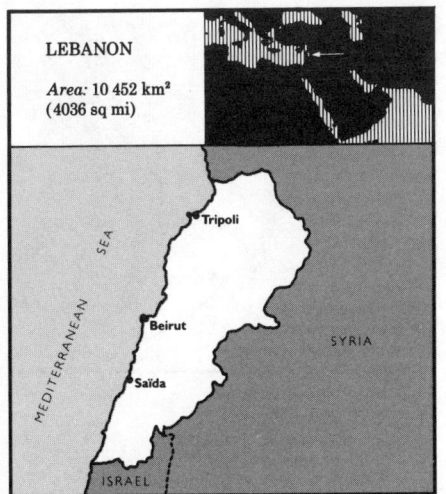

about 9000 paramilitary, 30 000 Syrian troops. The Israeli-supported 'South Lebanon Army' has 2500 men and there are several thousand Palestinian guerrillas). *Military service:* none.

GOVERNMENT

The constitution was amended in 1990 to provide for the election by universal adult suffrage of a 108-member National Assembly (comprising 54 members elected by Muslims and 54 deputies elected by Christians). The Assembly elects a (Maronite) President, who appoints a (Sunni Muslim) Prime Minister, who, in turn, appoints a Council of Ministers (six Christians and five Muslims). The main political parties include (Islamic fundamentalist) Hizbollah (Party of God), the (Maronite) Phalangist Party, the (pro-Syrian) Amal Party, and the (mainly Druze) Progressive Socialist Party.
President: Elias Hrawi.
Prime Minister: Rafik al-Hariri.

GEOGRAPHY

A narrow coastal plain is separated from the fertile Beka'a Valley by the mountains of Lebanon. To the east are the Anti-Lebanese range and Hermon Mountains. *Principal river:* Nahr al-Litāni. *Highest point:* Qurnat as-Sawdā 3088 m (10 131 ft).

Climate: The lowlands have a Mediterranean climate. The cooler highlands experience heavy snowfall in winter.

ECONOMY

Reconstruction of an economy devastated by civil war began in 1991. The principal agricultural crops are citrus fruit (grown mainly for export), wheat, barley and olives. The illegal cultivation of opium poppies is economically important. The textile and chemical industries and the financial sector are important.

RECENT HISTORY

Intercommunal friction was never far from the surface when the Ottoman Turks ruled Lebanon. A massacre of thousands of Maronites by the Druzes (1860) brought French intervention. After World War I, France received Syria as a League of Nations mandate, and created a separate Lebanese territory to protect Christian interests. The constitution under which Lebanon became independent in 1943 enshrined power-sharing between Christians and Muslims. The relative toleration between the various religious groups in Lebanon began to break down in the late 1950s when Muslim numerical superiority failed to be matched by corresponding constitutional changes. Radical Muslim supporters of the union of Syria and Egypt in 1958 clashed with the pro-Western party of Camille Chamoun (President 1952–58). Civil war ensued, and US marines landed in Beirut to restore order. The 1967 Arab-Israeli war and the exile of the Palestinian leadership to Beirut (1970–71) destabilized Lebanon. Civil war broke out in 1975, with subsequent Syrian and Israeli interventions. The war continued, plunging the country into ungovernable chaos, with Maronites, various Sunni and Shia Lebanese groups (including Iranian-backed fundamentalists), Syrian troops, Druze militia and UN peace-keeping forces all occupying zones of the fragmented country. In 1990, the Christian militia of Michel Aoun was crushed by the Syrians and the Lebanese government was able to reassert its authority over the whole of Beirut. However, Israeli sponsored forces continue to occupy the south and the (Islamic fundamentalist) Hizbollah forces control the Beka'a Valley. A new constitution (1990) – which enshrines Muslim-Christian equality in government – and the continuing presence of Syrian troops have allowed a reconstruction of the Lebanese state.

LESOTHO

Official name: The Kingdom of Lesotho.

Member of: UN, Commonwealth, OAU, SADCC.

Area: 30 355 km² (11 720 sq mi).

Population: 1 806 000 (1991 est).

Capital: Maseru 110 000, Maputsoe (1988 est).

Languages: Sesotho and English (official).

Religions: Roman Catholic (44%), various Protestant Churches (49% – mainly Lesotho Evangelical and Anglican).

Education: *Literacy rate:* 74% (1985 est). *Years of compulsory schooling:* (in theory) 6–13. *Universities:* 1.

Defence: *Total armed strength:* 2000 (1991). *Military service:* none.

GOVERNMENT

Lesotho is a constitutional monarchy in which elections are held by universal adult suffrage for a 65-member National Assembly to serve for five years. A Prime Minister and a Cabinet of Ministers are responsible to the Assembly. The main political parties are the Basotho Congress Party and the Basotho National Party.
King: HM King Letsie III (succeeded upon the exile and deposition of his father, 12 November 1990).
Prime Minister: Ntsu Mokhehle.

GEOGRAPHY

Most of Lesotho is mountainous. *Principal rivers:* Orange, Caledon. *Highest point:* Thabana Ntlenyana 3482 m (11 425 ft).

Climate: Lesotho has a mild subtropical climate with lower temperatures in the highlands.

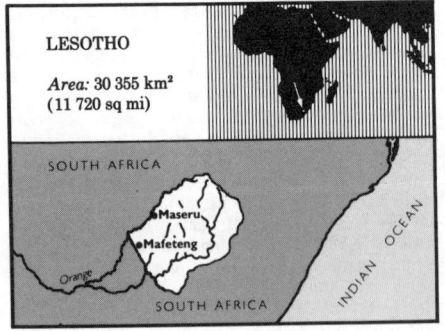

LESOTHO
Area: 30 355 km² (11 720 sq mi)

ECONOMY

Livestock – cattle, sheep and goats (for mohair) – are the mainstay of the economy. Natural resources include diamonds and abundant water, which is exported to South Africa.

RECENT HISTORY

Lesotho was founded in the 1820s by the Sotho leader, Moshoeshoe I (c. 1790–1870). The kingdom escaped incorporation into South Africa by becoming a British protectorate (known as Basutoland) in 1868. Although independence was achieved in 1966, the land-locked state remained dependent on South Africa. Chief Jonathan (Prime Minister 1966–86) – who curbed the monarchy's powers and attempted to limit South African influence – was deposed in a military coup. In 1990, the Military Council exiled King Moshoeshoe II and placed his son on the throne. Multi-party constitutional rule was restored in 1993.

LIBERIA

Official name: The Republic of Liberia.

Member of: UN, OAU, ECOWAS.

Area: 111 369 km² (43 000 sq mi).

Population: 2 607 000 (1990 est); in 1992 there were up to 700 000 Liberian refugees in neighbouring countries.

Capital: Monrovia 465 000, Buchanan 25 000 (1987 est).

Language: English (official).

Religions: Animist (50%), Sunni Islam (26%), various Christian Churches (24% – mainly Methodist, Baptist and Episcopalian).

Education: *Literacy rate:* 35% (1985 est). *Years of compulsory schooling:* (in theory) 6–16. *Universities:* 1.

Defence: *Total armed strength:* as a result of the civil wars, the armed forces of Liberia have ceased to exist. The interim government is supported by an ECOWAS force of about 8000. The combined strength of two rebel forces is about 11 000. *Military service:* none.

GOVERNMENT

The constitution provides for a President, Vice President, 26-member Senate and 64-member House of Representatives to be elected for six years by universal adult suffrage. The President appoints a Cabinet of Ministers. The Liberian political system broke down in 1990 owing to civil war.
Head of state (acting president): Amos Sawyer.

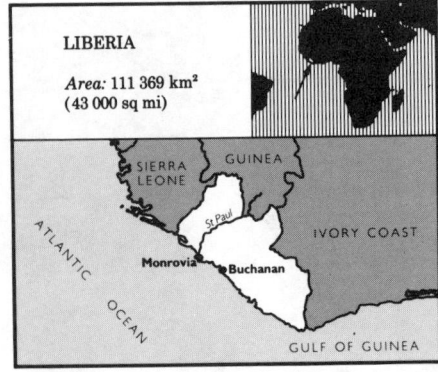

LIBERIA
Area: 111 369 km² (43 000 sq mi)

GEOGRAPHY

A low swampy coastal belt borders a higher zone of tropical forest. *Principal rivers:* St Paul, St John, Cess. *Highest point:* Mount Nimba 1380 m (4540 ft).

Climate: Liberia has a tropical climate with a wet season in the summer and a dry season in winter.

ECONOMY

Agriculture involves over 70% of the labour force. Cassava and rice are grown as subsistence crops, and rubber, coffee and cocoa for export. Liberia is a major exporter of iron ore, but the economy has been shattered by civil war.

RECENT HISTORY

Founded by the American Colonization Society in 1821–22 as a settlement for freed slaves, Liberia was declared a republic in 1847. Black American settlers dominated the local Africans and extended their control inland. From 1878 to 1980 power was held by presidents from the True Whig Party, including William Tubman (President 1944–71). His successor, William Tolbert, was assassinated during a military coup led by Samuel Doe, the first Liberian of local ancestry to rule. Doe was overthrown in a coup in 1990. Troops from several West African countries were dispatched by ECOWAS to restore order but civil war, initially involving two rebel forces, has continued despite a ceasefire in 1991.

LIBYA

Official name: Daulat Libiya al-'Arabiya al-Ishtrakiya al-Jumhuriya (The Great Socialist People's Libyan Arab Jamahiriya).

Member of: UN, Arab League, OPEC.

Area: 1 759 540 km² (679 363 sq mi).

Population: 4 325 000 (1991 est).

Capital and major cities: Tripoli (Tarabulus) 991 000, Benghazi (Banghazi) 485 000, Misurata (Misratah) 178 000 (1984). In 1988 government functions were decentralized to Sirte (Surt) and Al Jofrah as well as Tripoli and Benghazi.

Language: Arabic (official).

Religion: Sunni Islam (over 97%).

Education: *Literacy rate:* 63.8% (1985 est). *Years of compulsory schooling:* 6–15. *Universities:* 5.

Defence: *Total armed strength:* 85 000 (1991) (including 2500 in the 'Islamic pan-African legion' recruited by Libya). *Military service:* 3 years army, 4 years navy and air force.

GOVERNMENT

Over 1110 delegates from directly elected local Basic People's Congresses, trade unions, 'popular committees' and professional organizations meet as the Great People's Congress, which chooses a Revolutionary Leader – the head of state – and the 22-member General People's Committee (which is equivalent to a Council of Ministers). The appointed General Secretariat assists the Congress. There are effectvely no political parties.
Head of state: Moamar al Gaddafi.
Head of government (Secretary-General of the General People's Committee): Abdal Raziq al-Sawsa.

GEOGRAPHY

The Sahara Desert covers most of Libya. In the northwest – Tripolitania – coastal oases and a low plain form the country's main agricultural region. In the northeast (Cyrenaica) a coastal plain and mountain ranges support Mediterranean vegetation. *Principal river:* Wādi al-Fārigh. *Highest point:* Pico Bette 2286 m (7500 ft).

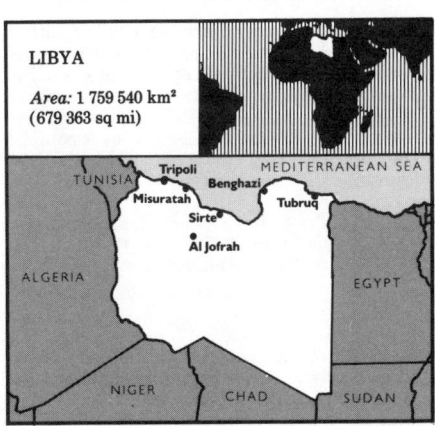

LIBYA

Area: 1 759 540 km²
(679 363 sq mi)

Climate: Libya is hot and dry, with lower temperatures and higher rainfall near the coast.

ECONOMY

Libya is one of the world's largest producers of petroleum. Liquefied gas is also exported. Coastal oases produce wheat, barley, nuts, dates and grapes.

RECENT HISTORY

In 1911 the Italians took Libya, which had been under Ottoman (Turkish) rule since the 16th century. The British Eighth Army defeated the Italians in the Libyan Desert (1942), and after World War II the country was divided between British and French administrations. Libya gained independence in 1951 under King Idris, formerly Amir of Cyrenaica. Although oil revenues made Libya prosperous, the pro-Western monarchy became increasingly unpopular. In 1969 junior army officers led by Col. Moamar al Gaddafi (1942–) took power. Gaddafi nationalized the oil industry, but his various attempts to federate with other Arab countries proved abortive. In the 1970s he began a cultural revolution, dismantled formal government, collectivized economic activity, limited personal wealth and suppressed opposition. Libya's alleged support of international terrorism provoked US air raids on Tripoli and Benghazi in 1986, since when Gaddafi has kept a lower international profile. However, alleged Libyan involvement in the bombing of a US airliner led to the imposition of UN sanctions in 1992.

LIECHTENSTEIN

Official name: Fürstentum Liechtenstein (The Principality of Liechtenstein).

Member of: UN, Council of Europe, CSCE, EFTA.

Area: 160 km² (62 sq mi).

Population: 29 000 (1991 est).

Capital and major settlements: Vaduz 4800, Schaan 4900 (1990 est).

Language: German (official).

Religions: Roman Catholic (87%), Lutheran (9%).

Education: *Literacy rate:* 100%. *Years of compulsory schooling:* 7–16. *Universities:* none.

Defence: *Total armed strength:* none.

GOVERNMENT

The country is a constitutional monarchy ruled by a

Prince. The 25-member Landstag (Parliament) is elected under a system of proportional representation by universal adult suffrage for four years. The Landstag elects a 5-member National Committee (Cabinet) including a Prime Minister, who is formally appointed by the Prince. The main political parties are the VU (Fatherland Union), the FBP (Progressive Citizens' Party) and the (Green) Free List.
Prince: HSH Prince Hans Adam II (succeeded upon the death of his father, 13 November 1989).
Prime Minister: Markus Buechel.

GEOGRAPHY
The Alps stand in the east of the principality. The west comprises the floodplain of the River Rhine.
Principal rivers: Rhine (Rhein), Samina. *Highest point:* Grauspitze 2599 m (8326 ft).
Climate: The country has a mild Alpine climate.

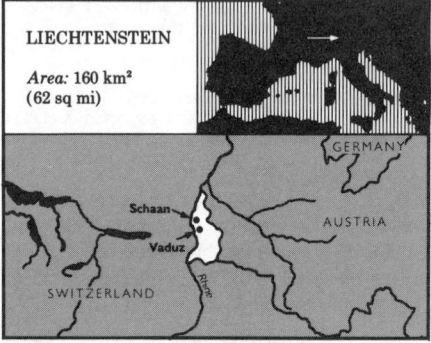

LIECHTENSTEIN
Area: 160 km² (62 sq mi)

ECONOMY
Liechtenstein has one of the highest standards of living in the world. Tourism, banking and manufacturing (precision goods) are all important.

RECENT HISTORY
Separated from Germany by Austrian territory, Liechtenstein was the only German principality not to join the German Empire in 1871. Since 1924 the country has enjoyed a customs and monetary union with Switzerland, although since 1989 the country has taken a more active role internationally, for instance joining the UN and EFTA.

LITHUANIA
Official name: Lietuva (Lithuania).
Member of: UN, CSCE, Council of Europe.
Area: 62 500 km² (25 174 sq mi).
Population: 3 739 000 (1991 est).
Capital and major cities: Vilnius 593 000, Kaunas 430 000, Klaipeda 206 000, Siauliai 148 000, Panevezys 129 000 (all including suburbs; 1990 est).
Languages: Lithuanian (80%), Russian (9%), Polish (7%), Belarussian (2%).
Religions: Roman Catholic (80%), Lutheran minority.
Education: *Literacy rate:* nearly 100% (est). *Years of compulsory schooling:* 6–15. *Universities:* 4.
Defence: *Total armed strength:* no figures available; a small national defence force is being formed.

GOVERNMENT
The 141-member Parliament and a President are

LITHUANIA
Area: 62 500 km² (25 174 sq mi).

elected by universal adult suffrage for five years. The President appoints a Prime Minister, who, in turn, appoints a Cabinet of Ministers. The main political parties are the (former Communist) Democratic Labour Party, the (nationalist) Sajudis Movement, the Christian Democratic Party, and the Green Party.
President: Mykolas Brazauskas.
Prime Minister: Bronislovas Lubya.

GEOGRAPHY
Lithuania comprises a low-lying plain dotted with lakes and crossed by ridges of glacial moraine.
Principal rivers: Nemunas (Neman), Vilnya. *Highest point:* Juozapine 294 m (964 ft).
Climate: Lithuania has a transitional climate between the milder temperate areas to the W and the more extreme continental areas to the E.

ECONOMY
One fifth of the labour force is engaged in agriculture, principally cattle rearing and dairying. Much of the country is heavily forested. The engineering, timber, cement and food-processing industries are important. Lithuania – whose economy is weaker than that of the other two Baltic republics – faces an uncertain future as it dismantles state control and breaks away from the former Soviet trade system.

RECENT HISTORY
Lithuania was annexed by Russia in 1795. Lithuanian national consciousness increased throughout the 19th century and Lithuanians rose with the Poles against Russian rule in 1830–31 and 1863. German forces invaded in 1915 and encouraged the establishment of a Lithuanian state. After World War I, the new republic faced invasions by the Red Army from the E and the Polish army from the W (1919–20). Internationally recognized boundaries were not established until 1923. The dictatorship of Augustinas Voldemaras (1926–29) was followed by that of Antonas Smetona (1929–40). The Non-Aggression Pact (1939) between Hitler and Stalin assigned Lithuania to the USSR, which invaded and annexed the republic (1940). Lithuania was occupied by Nazi Germany (1941–44). When Soviet rule was reimposed (1945), large-scale Russian settlement replaced over 250 000 Lithuanians who had been

killed or deported to Siberia. In 1988, reforms in the USSR allowed Lithuanian nationalists to operate openly. Nationalists won a majority in the republic's parliament, but their declaration of independence (1990) brought a crackdown by Soviet forces in Lithuania. Following the failed coup by Communist hardliners in Moscow (August 1991), the USSR recognized Lithuania's independence. Following the econoimic collapse of Lithuania (1992–93), Sajudis lost elections to the former Communists who slowed the pace of reforms.

LUXEMBOURG

Official name: Grand-Duché de Luxembourg (Grand Duchy of Luxembourg).

Member of: UN, EC, NATO, WEU, CSCE, OECD, Council of Europe.

Area: 2586 km² (999 sq mi).

Population: 385 000 (1991 census).

Capital: Luxembourg 117 000 (city 78 000), Esch-sur-Alzette 24 000, Differdange 16 000, Dudelange 14 000, Pétange 12 000, Sanem 12 000 (1991 census).

Languages: Letzeburgish (national), French and German – both official.

Religions: Roman Catholic (95%).

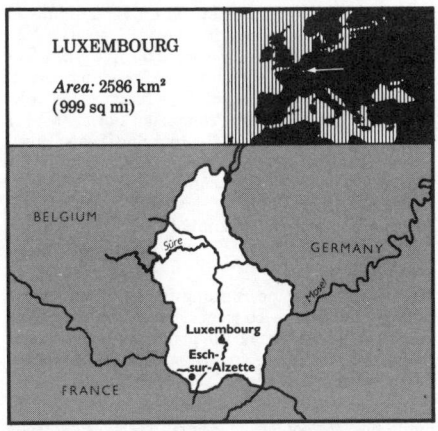

LUXEMBOURG

Area: 2586 km²
(999 sq mi)

Education: *Literacy rate:* 100%. *Years of compulsory schooling:* 6–15. *Universities:* 1.

Defence: *Total armed strength:* (1991) 800, plus 560 gendarmes. *Military service:* none.

GOVERNMENT

Luxembourg is a constitutional monarchy with a Grand Duke or Duchess as sovereign. The 60-member Chamber of Deputies is elected under a system of proportional representation by universal adult suffrage for five years. A Council of Ministers and a President of the Council (Premier) – commanding a majority in the Chamber – are appointed by the sovereign. The main political parties are the (centre-right) Social Christian Party, the Socialist Party, the (liberal) Democratic Party, Green Alternative and Green Ecologists.

Grand Duke: HRH Grand Duke Jean I (succeeded upon the abdication of his mother, 12 November 1964).

Prime Minister: Jacques Santer.

GEOGRAPHY

The Oesling is a wooded plateau in the north. The Gutland in the south is a lowland region of valleys and ridges. *Principal rivers:* Moselle, Sûre, Our, Alzette. *Highest point:* Huldange 550 m (1833 ft).

Climate: Luxembourg has cool summers and mild winters.

ECONOMY

The iron and steel industry – originally based on local ore – is important. Luxembourg has become a major banking centre. The north grows potatoes and fodder crops; the south produces wheat and fruit, including grapes.

RECENT HISTORY

In 1815 Luxembourg became a Grand Duchy with the Dutch king as sovereign, but in 1890 it was inherited by a junior branch of the House of Orange. Occupied by the Germans during both World Wars, Luxembourg concluded an economic union with Belgium in 1922 and has enthusiastically supported European unity.

MACEDONIA (FORMER YUGOSLAV REPUBLIC)

Official name: (*internal*) Republika Makedonija (Republic of Macedonia); (*international*) The Former Yugoslav Republic of Macedonia.

Member of: UN.

Area: 25 713 km² (9928 sq mi).

Population: 2 034 000 (1991 census).

Capital and major cities: Skopje (Skoplje) 563 000, Tetovo 181 000, Kumanovo 136 000, Bitola (Bitolj) 122 000 (1991 census).

Languages: Macedonian (67%), Albanian (20%), Turkish (4%).

Religions: Macedonian Orthodox (over 60%), Sunni Islam (nearly 25%).

Education: *Literacy rate:* no figures available. *Years of compulsory schooling:* 7–15. *Universities:* 2.

Defence: *Total armed forces:* no figures available. *Military service:* 12 months.

GOVERNMENT

The 120-member Assembly and a President – who appoints a Cabinet and a Prime Minister – are directly elected for four years by universal adult suffrage. The main political parties include the (former Communist) Democratic Alliance of Macedonia, the Internal Macedonian Revolutionary Organization (IMRO), the Party of Democratic Prosperity and the Alliance of Reform Forces.

President: Kiro Gligorov.

Prime Minister: Branko Crvenkovski.

GEOGRAPHY

Macedonia is a plateau about 760 m (2500 ft) high, bordered by mountains including the Sar range. The central Vardar valley is the only major lowland. *Principal rivers:* Vardar, Strumica. *Highest point:* Korab 2753 m (9032 ft).

Climate: The climate tends towards continental with cold, snowy winters and warm summers.

ECONOMY

Macedonia was one of the least developed regions of Yugoslavia. The republic is largely agricultural, raising sheep and cattle and growing cereals and tobacco. Steel, chemical and textile industries rely, in part, upon local resources that include iron ore,

MACEDONIA
(FORMER YUGOSLAV
REPUBLIC)
Area: 25 713 km² (9928 sq mi).

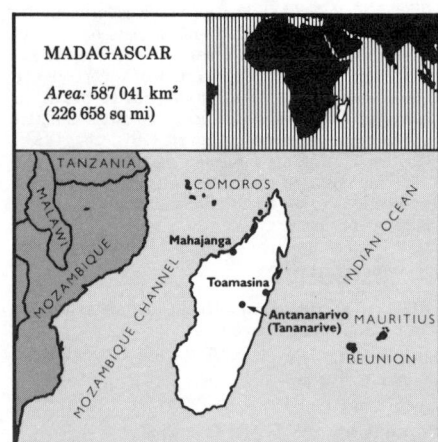

MADAGASCAR

Area: 587 041 km²
(226 658 sq mi)

lead and zinc. The economy has been severely damaged by a Greek economic blockade.

RECENT HISTORY

After centuries of rule by the (Turkish) Ottoman Empire, Macedonia was partitioned following the First Balkan War (1912). Those areas with a Greek-speaking majority – the site of the ancient kingdom of Macedon – were assigned to Greece and the remainder was partitioned between Bulgaria and Serbia, the latter gaining the area comprising the present republic. Bulgaria continued to claim all Macedonia and occupied the region during World War I. In 1918 Serbian Macedonia was incorporated within the new kingdom of Serbs, Croats and Slovenes, which was renamed Yugoslavia in 1929. When Yugoslavia was reorganized on Soviet lines by Marshal Tito in 1945 a separate Macedonian republic was formed within the Communist federation. After Tito's death (1980), the Yugoslav experiment faltered and local nationalist movements arose. Following the secession of Slovenia and Croatia and the outbreak of the Yugoslav civil war (1991), Macedonia declared its own sovereignty. Greece – which denied the existence of a 'Macedonian' people and objected to the use of the name 'Macedonia' – prevented the EC from recognizing the republic which remained in diplomatic limbo until it was admitted to the UN in 1993 under the temporary name of The Former Yugoslav Republic of Macedonia.

MADAGASCAR

Official name: Repoblika Demokratika n'i Madagaskar (The Democratic Republic of Madagascar).

Member of: UN, OAU.

Area: 587 041 km² (226 658 sq mi).

Population: 11 197 000 (1990 est).

Capital and major cities: Antananarivo (Tananarive) 802 000, Toamasina 145 000, Fianarantsoa 125 000, Mahajanga 122 000 (1990 est).

Languages: Malagasy and French (both official).

Religions: Animist (47%), Roman Catholic (28%), Protestant Church of Jesus Christ in Madagascar (22%).

Education: *Literacy rate:* 80.2% (1990). *Years of compulsory schooling:* (in theory) 6–13. *Universities:* 6.

Defence: *Total armed strength:* 21 000 (1991) (plus 7500 paramilitary gendarmes). *Military service:* none.

GOVERNMENT

The President is elected by universal adult suffrage for a seven-year term. He and the Supreme Revolutionary Council together appoint a Prime Minister and a Council of Ministers. The 137-member National Assembly is directly elected for five years. The main political parties include the (former monopoly) AREMA (Advanced Guard of the Malagasy Revolution), the Movement for Proletarian Power (MFM), the (centrist) VONJY (the Popular Spirit of National Unity), and the (radical) National Movement for the Independence of Madagascar.

President: Albert Zafy.

Prime Minister: to be appointed.

GEOGRAPHY

Massifs form a spine running from north to south through the island. To the east is a narrow coastal plain; to the west are fertile plains. *Principal rivers:* Ikopa, Mania, Mangoky. *Highest point:* Maromokotro Tsaratanana Massif 2885 m (9465 ft).

Climate: The climate is tropical, although the highlands are cooler. The north receives monsoon rains, but the south is dry.

ECONOMY

Agriculture employs three quarters of the labour force. The main crops are coffee and vanilla for export, and rice and cassava for domestic consumption. The island is an important producer of chromite. Drought and fluctuations in the prices of primary products have added to Madagascar's severe economic problems.

RECENT HISTORY

In the early 19th century, the island was united by the Merina kingdom. The Merina sovereigns attempted to modernize Madagascar but the island was annexed by France in 1896, although resistance continued until 1904. Strong nationalist feeling found expression in a major rising (1947–48) that was only suppressed with heavy loss of life. Independence was finally achieved in 1960, but the pro-Western rule of President Philibert Tsirana became increasingly unpopular. After a military coup in 1972, Madagascar had left-wing governments until multi-party presidential elections in 1993 resulted in a change of power.

MALAWI

Official name: The Republic of Malawi.

Member of: UN, Commonwealth, OAU, SADCC.

Area: 118 484 km² (45 747 sq mi).

Population: 9 152 000 (1991 est).

Capital and major cities: Lilongwe 220 000, Blantyre 403 000, Mzuzu 115 000 (1987 census).

Languages: English (official), Chichewa (over 50%; official).

Religions: Animist (67%), Roman Catholic (17%), Sunni Islam (6%), Presbyterian (6%).

Education: *Literacy rate:* 41.2% (1985) *Years of compulsory schooling:* education is available but not compulsory. *Universities:* 1.

Defence: *Total armed strength:* 7250 (1991) (plus 500 paramilitary and a national police force). *Military service:* none.

GOVERNMENT

Under the constitution the President is directly elected, but in 1971 Dr Hastings Kamuzu Banda was declared President for life. Elections are held by universal adult suffrage every five years for 112 members of the National Assembly. The President appoints additional members as well as a Cabinet of Ministers. The Malawi Congress Party is the only legal party but a referendum on whether or not the country should keep to one-party rule is scheduled to be held in June 1993.
President: Dr Hastings Kamuzu Banda.

GEOGRAPHY

Plateaux cover the north and centre. The Rift Valley contains Lake Malawi and the Shire Valley. The Shire Highlands lie on the Mozambique border. *Principal river:* Shire. *Highest point:* Mount Sapitawa 3002 m (9849 ft).

Climate: Malawi has an equatorial climate with heavy rainfall from November to April.

ECONOMY

Agriculture is the mainstay of the economy, providing most of Malawi's exports. Tobacco, maize, tea and sugar cane are the main crops.

RECENT HISTORY

David Livingstone and other British missionaries became active in the area from the 1860s. A British protectorate, later called Nyasaland, was declared in 1891. In 1915 the Rev. John Chilembwe led a violent rising in the fertile south where Africans had lost much land to white settlers. Dr Hastings Kamuzu Banda (c. 1902–) led the country's opposition to the resented union with the white-dominated Central African Federation (1953–63). Since independence as Malawi in 1964, Banda has provided strong rule and – despite criticism – maintained close relations with South Africa. In 1992–93, pressure for political reforms grew.

MALAYSIA

Official name: Persekutuan Tanah Melaysiu (The Federation of Malaysia).

Member of: UN, Commonwealth, ASEAN.

Area: 329 758 km² (127 320 sq mi).

Population: 17 556 000 (1991 census).

Capital and major cities: Kuala Lumpur 1 233 000 (including suburbs; 1991 census), Ipoh 390 000, George Town 325 000, Johor Baharu 325 000, Petaling Jaya 270 000, Kelang (Klang) 250 000, Kuala Trengganu (Kuala Terengganu) 235 000, Kota Baharu 220 000, Taiping 190 000, Seramban 175 000, Kuantan 170 000, Kota Kinabalu 140 000, Malacca (Melaka) 115 000 (1990 est).

Languages: Bahasa Malaysia (Malay; official; over 58%), English, Chinese (32%), Tamil.

Religions: Sunni Islam (official; over 55%), with Buddhist, Daoist and various Christian minorities.

Education: *Literacy rate:* 78.4% (1990). *Years of compulsory schooling:* education is free but not compulsory. *Universities:* 7.

Defence: *Total armed strength:* 127 000 (1991) (plus paramilitary forces: 18 000 Police Field Force and 180 000 Peoples Volunteer Corps). *Military service:* none.

GOVERNMENT

The Yang di-Pertuan Agong (the King of Malaysia) holds office for five years. He is elected – from their own number – by the hereditary sultans who reign in 9 of the 13 states. The 70-member Senate (upper house) comprises 40 members appointed by the King and two members elected by each of the state and territorial assemblies for a three-year term. The 180-member House of Representatives is elected by universal adult suffrage for five years. The King appoints a Prime Minister and a Cabinet commanding a majority in the House, to which they are responsible. The main political parties include the National Front (a coalition of parties including UMNO – the United Malays National Organization), the (democratic socialist) Democratic Action Party, and the (coalition) Muslim Unity Movement (APU; including the Spirit of '46 Party). Each state has its own parliament and government.
King of Malaysia: HM Azlan Shah (ibni Sultan Yusof Izzudin), Raja of Perak, Yang di-Pertuan Agong, inaugurated 26 April 1989.
Prime Minister: Mohamad Mahathir.

MALAYSIAN STATES AND TERRITORIES

Population figures are from the 1991 census.

Johore (Johor) (sultanate) *Area:* 18 985 km² (7330 sq mi). *Population:* 2 107 000. *Capital:* Johor Baharu.

Kedah (sultanate) *Area:* 9425 km² (3639 sq mi). *Population:* 1 413 000. *Capital:* Alor Star (Alur Setar).

Kelantan (sultanate) *Area:* 14 931 km² (5765 sq mi). *Population:* 1 220 000. *Capital:* Kota Baharu.

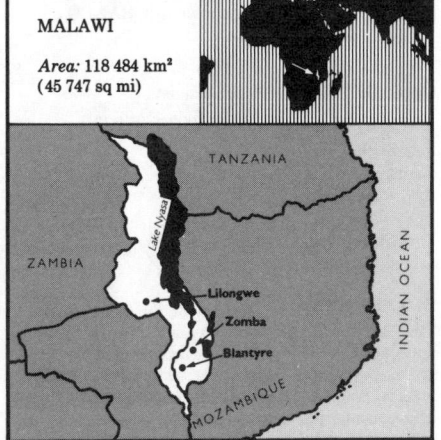

MALAWI

Area: 118 484 km²
(45 747 sq mi)

TANZANIA

ZAMBIA

Lake Nyasa

Lilongwe

Zomba

Blantyre

MOZAMBIQUE

INDIAN OCEAN

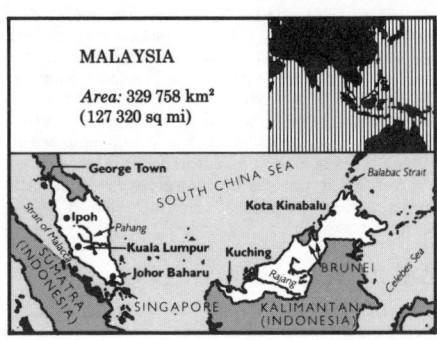

MALAYSIA
Area: 329 758 km²
(127 320 sq mi)

Malacca *Area*: 1650 km² (637 sq mi). *Population*: 584 000. *Capital*: Malacca.

Negeri Sembilan (sultanate) *Area*: 6643 km² (2565 sq mi). *Population*: 724 000. *Capital*: Seremban.

Pahang (sultanate) *Area*: 35 965 km² (13 886 sq mi). *Population*: 1 055 000. *Capital*: Kuantan.

Penang (Pinang) *Area*: 1033 km² (399 sq mi). *Population*: 1 142 000. *Capital*: George Town.

Perak (sultanate) *Area*: 21 005 km² (8110 sq mi). *Population*: 2 220 000. *Capital*: Ipoh.

Perlis (sultanate) *Area*: 795 km² (307 sq mi). *Population*: 188 000. *Capital*: Kangar.

Sabah *Area*: 80 429 km² (29 353 sq mi). *Population*: 1 470 000. *Capital*: Kota Kinabalu.

Sarawak *Area*: 121 449 km² (48 250 sq mi). *Population*: 1 669 000. *Capital*: Kuching.

Selangor (sultanate) *Area*: 7962 km² (3074 sq mi). *Population*: 1 978 000. *Capital*: Shah Alam.

Trengganu (Terengganu) (sultanate) *Area*: 12 955 km² (5002 sq mi). *Population*: 752 000. *Capital*: Kuala Trengganu.

Federal Territory *Area*: 243 km² (94 sq mi). *Population*: 1 233 000. *Capital*: Kuala Lumpur.

Labuan (territory) *Area*: 91 km² (35 sq mi). *Population*: 26 000. *Capital*: Victoria.

GEOGRAPHY

Western (peninsular) Malaysia consists of mountain ranges – including the Trengganu Highlands and Cameron Highlands – running north to south and bordered by densely populated coastal lowlands. Tropical rainforest covers the hills and mountains of Eastern Malaysia – Sabah and Sarawak, the northern part of the island of Borneo. *Principal rivers:* Pahang, Kelantan. *Highest point:* Kinabalu (in Sabah) 4101 m (13 455 ft).

Climate: Malaysia has a tropical climate with heavy rainfall (up to 2500 mm / 100 in in the west). There is more seasonal variation in precipitation than temperature, with the northeast monsoon (from October to February) and the southwest monsoon (from May to September) bringing increased rainfall, particularly to peninsular Malaysia.

ECONOMY

Rubber, petroleum and tin are the traditional mainstays of the Malaysian economy, but all three suffered drops in price on the world market in the 1980s. Pepper (mainly from Sarawak), cocoa and timber are also important. Over one quarter of the labour force is involved in agriculture, with large numbers of Malays growing rice as a subsistence crop. Manufac-

turing industry is now the largest exporter; major industries include rubber, tin, timber, textiles, machinery and cement. The government has greatly encouraged industrialization, investment and a more active role for the ethnic Malay population in industry, which – along with commerce and finance – has been largely the preserve of Chinese Malaysians. Malaysia has experienced high economic growth rates since the early 1980s. A growing tourist industry is being very actively promoted.

RECENT HISTORY

Malaysia's ethnic diversity reflects its complex history and the lure of its natural wealth and prime trading position. The British established themselves on the island of Penang in 1786, founded Singapore in 1819, and in 1867 established an administration for the Straits Settlements – Malacca, Penang and Singapore. Ignoring Thai claims to overlordship in the peninsula, the British took over the small sultanates as protected states. The British suppressed piracy, developed tin mining with Chinese labour and rubber plantations with Indian workers. Sarawak became a separate state under Sir James Brooke – the 'White Raja' – and his family from 1841, and was ceded to the British Crown in 1946. Sabah became British – as British North Borneo – from 1881. The Japanese occupied the whole of Malaysia during World War II. A Federation of Malaya – the peninsula – was established in 1948, but was threatened by Communist insurgency until 1960.

Malaya became independent in 1957 with a constitution protecting the interests of the Malays, who were fearful of the energy and acumen of the Chinese. Sabah, Sarawak and Singapore joined the Federation – renamed Malaysia – in 1963. Singapore left in 1965, but the unity of the Federation was maintained, with British armed support, in the face of an Indonesian 'confrontation' in Borneo (1965–66). Tension between Chinese and Malays led to riots and the suspension of parliamentary government (1969–71), but scarcely hindered the rapid development of a resource-rich economy. During the 1980s and early 1990s, the growth of Islamic fundamentalism led to a defensive re-assertion of Islamic values and practices among the Muslim Malay ruling elite.

THE MALDIVES

Official name: Dhivehi Jumhuriya (Republic of Maldives).

Member of: UN, Commonwealth, SAARC.

Area: 298 km² (115 sq mi).

Population: 213 000 (1990 census).

Capital: Malé 55 000 (1990 census).

Language: Dhivehi (Maldivian; official).

Religion: Sunni Islam (official).

Education: *Literacy rate:* 98.2% (1991). *Years of compulsory schooling:* schooling is not compulsory. *Universities:* none.

Defence: *Total armed strength:* there are no armed forces.

GOVERNMENT

The Majilis (Assembly) consists of 8 members appointed by the President, and 40 elected by universal adult suffrage for five years. The President – who is directly elected for five years – appoints a Cabinet. There are no political parties.
President: Abdul Maumoon Gayoom.

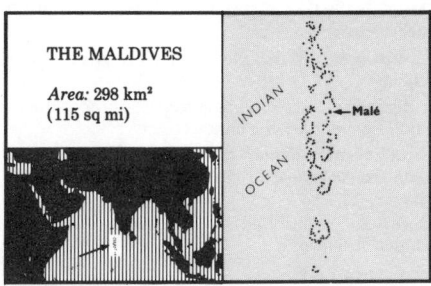

THE MALDIVES

Area: 298 km²
(115 sq mi)

Malé

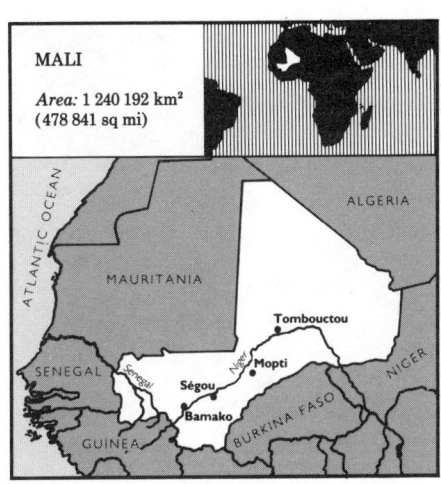

MALI

Area: 1 240 192 km²
(478 841 sq mi)

GEOGRAPHY

The country is a chain of over 1190 small low-lying coral islands, of which 203 are inhabited. There are no significant rivers. *Highest point:* 3 m (10 ft).

Climate: The Maldives have a tropical climate with heavy rainfall brought by the monsoon between May and August.

ECONOMY

The growing tourist industry has displaced fishing as the mainstay of the economy. However, most Maldivians subsist on fish and coconuts.

RECENT HISTORY

From 1887 until independence in 1965 the Maldives were a British protectorate, but the ad-Din sultanate, established in the 14th century, was only abolished in 1968.

MALI

Official name: La République du Mali (The Republic of Mali).

Member of: UN, OAU, ECOWAS.

Area: 1 240 192 km² (478 841 sq mi).

Population: 8 299 000 (1991 est).

Capital: Bamako 650 000, Ségou 89 000, Mopti 74 000 (1987 census).

Languages: French (official), Bambara (60%), Soninké, Fulani.

Religions: Sunni Islam (90%), animist (9%).

Education: *Literacy rate:* 32% (1990). *Years of compulsory schooling:* (in theory) 8–15. *Universities:* none.

Defence: *Total armed strength:* about 7300 (1991) (plus 7800 paramilitary). *Military service:* selective.

GOVERNMENT

The constitution provides for the election by universal adult suffrage of 116 deputies of a 129-member National Assembly (to serve for three years) and a President (to serve for six years). The remaining 13 members of the Assembly are elected by Malians living abroad. The President appoints a Premier and a Council of Ministers. The main political parties are the Alliance for Democracy in Mali (ADEMA), the Union for Democracy and Development (UDD) and the Sudanese Union (US-RDA).
President: Alpha Oumar Konari.
Prime Minister: Younoussi Touré.

GEOGRAPHY

Mali comprises low-lying plains but rises in the Adrar des Iforas range in the northeast. The south is savannah; the Sahara Desert is in the north. *Principal rivers:* Niger, Sénégal, Falémé. *Highest point:* Hombori Tondo 1155 m (3789 ft).

Climate: Mali is hot and largely dry, although the south has a wet season from June to October.

ECONOMY

Drought in the 1970s and 1980s devastated Mali's livestock herds. Only one fifth of Mali can be cultivated, producing mainly rice, millet and cassava for domestic use, and cotton for export.

RECENT HISTORY

Conquered by France (1880–95), Mali became the territory of French Sudan. Mali became independent in 1960. A radical socialist government was toppled in 1968 by the military regime of General Moussa Traore, whose government faced severe economic problems. A single-party state operated from 1979 to 1992 when a multi-party system was restored.

MALTA

Official name: Repubblika Ta'Malta (Republic of Malta).

Member of: UN, Commonwealth, CSCE, Council of Europe.

Area: 316 km² (122 sq mi).

Population: 357 000 (1991 est).

Capital and principal towns: Valletta 204 000 (city 9200). Birkirkara 21 000, Qormi 19 000, Hamrun 14 000 and Sliema 14 000 are part of the Valletta agglomeration (1991 est).

Languages: Maltese and English (official).

Religion: Roman Catholic (official; 98%).

Education: *Literacy rate:* 87.9% (1986). *Years of compulsory schooling:* 5–16. *Universities:* 1.

Defence: *Total armed strength:* 1650 (1991). *Military service:* none.

GOVERNMENT

The 65-member House of Representatives is elected by universal adult suffrage under a system of proportional representation for five years. The President – who is elected for five years by the House – appoints a Prime Minister and a Cabinet who command a majority in the House. The main political parties are the (conservative) National Party, the Malta Labour Party and the Democratic Alternative.
President: Vincent Tabone.
Prime Minister: Eddie Fenech Adami.

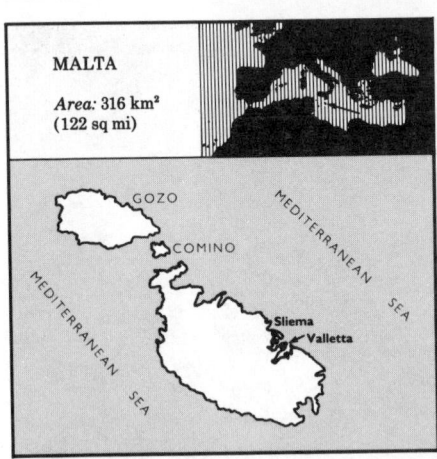

MALTA

Area: 316 km²
(122 sq mi)

GOZO

COMINO

MEDITERRANEAN SEA

MEDITERRANEAN SEA

Sliema
Valletta

GEOGRAPHY

The three inhabited islands of Malta, Gozo and Comino consist of low limestone plateaux with little surface water. There are no significant rivers. *Highest point:* an unnamed point, 249 m (816 ft).

Climate: The climate is Mediterranean with hot dry summers, and cooler wetter winters.

ECONOMY

The main industries are footwear and clothing, food processing and beverages, and ship repairing. Tourism is the main foreign-currency earner. Malta is virtually self-sufficient in agricultural products.

RECENT HISTORY

The French held Malta from 1798 to 1800, provoking the Maltese to request British protection (1802). As a British colony (from 1814), Malta became a vital naval base, and the island received the George Cross for its valour in World War II. Malta gained independence in 1964. Maltese political life has been polarized between the National Party and the Maltese Labour Party, the latter led by Dom Mintoff. As PM (1971–84), Mintoff developed close links with Communist and Arab states, notably Libya. Malta has an association agreement with the EC and has applied for full membership of the Community.

MARSHALL ISLANDS

Official name: The Republic of the Marshall Islands.

Member of: UN, South Pacific Forum.

Area: 181 km² (70 sq mi).

Population: 49 000 (1991 est).

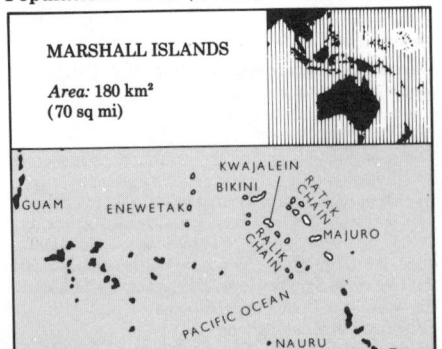

MARSHALL ISLANDS

Area: 180 km²
(70 sq mi)

GUAM

ENEWETAK

KWAJALEIN

BIKINI

RATAK CHAIN

RALIK CHAIN

MAJURO

PACIFIC OCEAN

NAURU

Capital: Dalap-Uliga-Darrit (on Majuro) 20 000 (1990 census).

Languages: Marshallese and English (both official).

Religions: Various Protestant Churches (over 50%), Roman Catholic minority.

Education: *Literacy rate:* over 95% (1989 est). *Years of compulsory schooling:* 6–14. *Universities:* none.

Defence: The United States is responsible for the islands' defence.

GOVERNMENT

The 33-member Nitijela (Parliament) and the President are elected by universal adult suffrage for four years. The traditional Council of Chiefs is a consultative body. There are, in effect, no political parties in government, although an opposition group has been formed.
President: Amata Kabua.

GEOGRAPHY

The Marshall Islands comprise two chains of small coral atolls and islands, with over 1150 islands in total. There are no significant rivers. *Highest point:* unnamed, 6 m (20 ft).

Climate: The climate is tropical with heavy rainfall.

ECONOMY

The islands have practically no resources and depend upon subsistence agriculture, tourism and US grants.

RECENT HISTORY

The Marshall Islands were under Spanish (1875–85), German (1885–1914), and Japanese administration (1914–1945) before becoming part of the US Pacific Islands Trust Territory. They became internally self-governing in 1979. In 1986 US administration in the islands was formally terminated and the Marshall Islands became a sovereign republic, able to conduct its own foreign affairs, although under a Compact of Free Association the USA retains complete responsibility for the republic's defence and security until 2001. The UN did not recognize this new status of the Marshall Islands until December 1990, when the trusteeship was finally dissolved.

MAURITANIA

Official name: Jumhuriyat Muritaniya al-Islamiya (Islamic Republic of Mauritania).

Member of: UN, OAU, Arab League, ECOWAS.

Area: 1 030 700 km² (397 950 sq mi).

Population: 2 053 000 (1991 est).

Capital: Nouakchott 600 000 (city 330 000), Nouadhibou (Port Etienne) 59 000, Kaédi 31 000 (1988 census).

Languages: Arabic (official; 81%), French.

Religion: Sunni Islam (official; 99%).

Education: *Literacy rate:* 34% (1990). *Years of compulsory schooling:* schooling is not compulsory. *Universities:* 1.

Defence: *Total armed strength:* 11 100 (1990) (plus 5 700 paramilitary). *Military service:* none.

GOVERNMENT

A President and a 77-member National Assembly are elected by universal adult suffrage for six years. A Senate (upper house) is indirectly elected. The Presi-

MAURITANIA

Area: 1 030 700 km²
(397 950 sq mi)

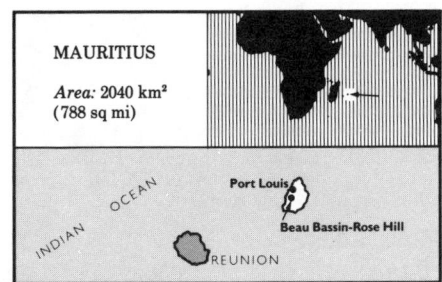

MAURITIUS

Area: 2040 km²
(788 sq mi)

dent appoints a Prime Minister and a Council of Ministers. The main political parties are the (former monopoly) Democratic and Social Republican Party, the Mauritanian Party for Renewal, and the Rally for Democracy and National Unity.
President: Col. Maaouiya Ould Taya.

GEOGRAPHY

Isolated peaks rise above the plateaux of the Sahara Desert that cover most of Mauritania. *Principal river:* Sénégal. *Highest point:* Kediet Ijill 915 m (3050 ft).

Climate: The climate is hot and dry, with adequate rainfall only in the south.

ECONOMY

Persistant drought has devastated the nomads' herds of cattle and sheep. Fish from the Atlantic and iron ore are virtually the only exports.

RECENT HISTORY

The French arrived on the coast in the 17th century, but did not annex the Arab emirates inland until 1903. Mauritania became independent in 1960. When Spain withdrew from the Western Sahara in 1976, Morocco and Mauritania divided the territory between them, but Mauritania could not defeat the Polisario guerrillas fighting for West Saharan independence and gave up its claim (1979). Tension between the dominant Arab north and Black African south led to violence in 1989. The country was ruled by military governments after 1976 and became a one-party state in 1979. Multi-party elections were held in 1992.

MAURITIUS

Official name: Republic of Mauritius.

Member of: OAU, Commonwealth.

Area: 2040 km² (788 sq mi).

Population: 1 087 000 (1991 est.).

Capital: Port Louis 142 000, Beau Bassin/Rose Hill 94 000, Curepipe 67 000, Quatre Bornes 66 000 (1990 est.).

Languages: English (official), Creole (French; nearly 30%), Hindi (over 20%), Bhojpuri.

Religions: Hindu (51%), Roman Catholic (25%), Sunni Islam (17%), with Protestant minorities.

Education: *Literacy rate:* 83% (1985 est.) *Years of compulsory schooling:* schooling is free but not compulsory. *Universities:* 1.

Defence: *Total armed strength:* none; internal security is handled by a special police mobile unit. *Military service:* none.

GOVERNMENT

Elections are held by universal adult suffrage every five years for 62 members of the Assembly; up to 8 additional members may be appointed. The President – who is elected by the Assembly – appoints a Prime Minister who commands a majority in the Assembly. The PM, in turn, appoints a Cabinet responsible to the Assembly. The main political parties are the Mouvement Socialiste Militant, the Labour Party, the Parti Mauricien Social Democrate, the Mouvement Militant Mauricien and the Mouvement Travailliste Démocrate.
President: Cassam Uteem.
Prime Minister: Aneerood Jugnauth.

GEOGRAPHY

The central plateau of Mauritius is surrounded by mountains. Other islands in the group include Rodrigues and the Agalega Islands. *Principal rivers:* Grand River South East, Grand River North West. *Highest point:* Piton de la Rivière Noire (826 m/2711 ft).

Climate: The climate is subtropical, although it can be very hot from December to April. Rainfall is high in the uplands.

ECONOMY

The export of sugar cane dominates the economy. Diversification is being encouraged, and light industry – in particular clothing – and tourism are of increasing importance.

RECENT HISTORY

Mauritius was French from 1715 until 1814, when it became British. Black slaves were imported, followed in the 19th century by Indian labourers whose descendants are the majority community. Independence was gained in 1968.

MEXICO

Official name: Estados Unidos Mexicanos (United Mexican States).

Member of: UN, OAS, NAFTA, ALADI.

Area: 1 958 201 km² (756 066 sq mi).

Population: 83 151 000 (1991 est.).

Capital and major cities: Mexico City 20 200 000 (city 8 237 000; Greater Mexico City 13 636 000), Guadalajara 3 187 000 (city 2 847 000), Monterrey 2 859 000 (city 2 522 000), Puebla 1 707 000 (city 1 055 000), Nezahualcoyotl (part of the Mexico City agglomeration) 1 260 000, León 1 081 000 (city 872 000), Ciudad Juárez 798 000, Tijuana 743 000, Mexicali 602 000 (all including suburbs; 1990 census).

Languages: Spanish (92%; official), various Indian languages.

Religion: Roman Catholic (91%).

Education: *Literacy rate:* 87.3% (1990). *Years of compulsory schooling:* 6–12. *Universities:* 54 including 2 institutes of university status.

Defence: *Total armed strength:* 175 000 (1991) (plus rural defence militia 14 000). *Military service:* part-time, compulsory.

GOVERNMENT

The 64-member Senate and the President – who may serve only once – are elected by universal adult suffrage for six years. The 500-member Chamber of Deputies is directly elected for three years – 200 of the members are elected under a system of proportional representation; the remaining 300 represent single-member constituencies. The President appoints a Cabinet. The main political parties are the PRI (Institutional Revolutionary Party), the PAN (National Action Party), the PRD (Democratic Revolutionary Party), the (Marxist) Cardenista Front of National Reconstruction (PFCRN), and the Authentic Party of the Mexican Revolution. Each of the 31 states has its own Chamber of Deputies.

President: Carlos Salinas de Gortari.

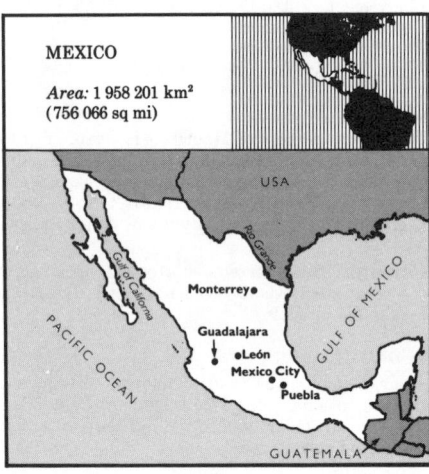

MEXICO

Area: 1 958 201 km²
(756 066 sq mi)

MEXICAN STATES

Population figures are from the 1990 census.

Aguascalientes *Area:* 5471 km² (2112 sq mi). *Population:* 720 000. *Capital:* Aguascalientes.

Baja California *Area:* 69 921 km² (26 996 sq mi). *Population:* 1 658 000. *Capital:* Mexicali.

Baja California Sur *Area:* 73 475 km² (28 369 sq mi). *Population:* 317 000. *Capital:* La Paz.

Campeche *Area:* 50 812 km² (19 619 sq mi). *Population:* 529 000. *Capital:* Campeche.

Chiapas *Area:* 74 211 km² (28 653 sq mi). *Population:* 3 204 000. *Capital:* Tuxtla Gutiérrez.

Chihuahua *Area:* 244 938 km² (94 571 sq mi). *Population:* 2 440 000. *Capital:* Ciudad Juárez.

Coahuila *Area:* 149 982 km² (57 908 sq mi). *Population:* 1 971 000. *Capital:* Saltillo.

Colima *Area:* 5191 km² (2004 sq mi). *Population:* 425 000. *Capital:* Colima.

Durango *Area:* 123 181 km² (47 560 sq mi).

Population: 1 352 000. *Capital:* (Victoria de) Durango.

Guanajuato *Area:* 30 491 km² (11 773 sq mi). *Population:* 3 980 000. *Capital:* Guanajuato.

Guerrero *Area:* 64 281 km² (24 819 sq mi). *Population:* 2 622 000. *Capital:* Chilpancingo.

Hidalgo *Area:* 20 813 km² (8036 sq mi). *Population:* 1 881 000. *Capital:* Pachuca de Soto.

Jalisco *Area:* 80 836 km² (31 211 sq mi). *Population:* 5 279 000. *Capital:* Guadalajara.

México *Area:* 21 355 km² (8245 sq mi). *Population:* 9 816 000. *Capital:* Toluca de Lerdo.

Michoacán *Area:* 59 928 km² (23 138 sq mi). *Population:* 3 534 000. *Capital:* Morelia.

Morelos *Area:* 4950 km² (1911 sq mi). *Population:* 1 195 000. *Capital:* Cuernavaca.

Nayarit *Area:* 26 979 km² (10 417 sq mi). *Population:* 816 000. *Capital:* Tepic.

Nuevo León *Area:* 64 924 km² (25 067 sq mi). *Population:* 3 086 000. *Capital:* Monterrey.

Oaxaca *Area:* 93 952 km² (36 275 sq mi). *Population:* 3 022 000. *Capital:* Oaxaca.

Puebla *Area:* 33 902 km² (11 493 sq mi). *Population:* 4 118 000. *Capital:* Puebla.

Querétaro *Area:* 11 449 km² (4420 sq mi). *Population:* 1 044 000. *Capital:* Querétaro.

Quintana Roo *Area:* 50 212 km² (19 387 sq mi). *Population:* 494 000. *Capital:* Chetumal.

San Luis Potosí *Area:* 63 068 km² (24 351 sq mi). *Population:* 2 002 000. *Capital:* San Luis Potosí.

Sinaloa *Area:* 58 328 km² (22 520 sq mi). *Population:* 2 211 000. *Capital:* Culiacán Rosales.

Sonora *Area:* 182 052 km² (70 290 sq mi). *Population:* 1 822 000. *Capital:* Hermosillo.

Tabasco *Area:* 25 267 km² (9756 sq mi). *Population:* 1 501 000. *Capital:* Villahermosa.

Tamaulipas *Area:* 79 304 km² (30 619 sq mi). *Population:* 2 244 000. *Capital:* Ciudad Victoria.

Tlaxcala *Area:* 4016 km² (1551 sq mi). *Population:* 764 000. *Capital:* Apizaco.

Veracruz *Area:* 71 699 km² (27 683 sq mi). *Population:* 6 215 000. *Capital:* Jalapa Enrique.

Yucatán *Area:* 38 402 km² (14 827 sq mi). *Population:* 1 364 000. *Capital:* Mérida.

Zacatecas *Area:* 73 252 km² (28 283 sq mi). *Population:* 1 278 000. *Capital:* Zacatecas.

Federal District *Area:* 1479 km² (570 sq mi). *Population:* 8 237 000. *Capital:* Mexico City.

GEOGRAPHY

Between the Sierra Madre Oriental mountains in the east and the Sierra Madre Occidental in the west is a large high central plateau with several volcanoes. The coastal plains are generally narrow in the west, but wider in the east. The Yucatán Peninsula in the southeast is a broad limestone lowland; Baja California in the northwest is a long narrow mountainous peninsula. Mexico is prone to earthquakes. *Principal rivers:* Río Bravo de Norte (Rio Grande), Balsas, Grijalva, Pánuco. *Highest point:* Volcán Citlaltepetl (Pico de Orizaba) 5610 m (18 405 ft).

Climate: There is considerable climatic variation, in part reflecting the complexity of the relief. In general, the south and the coastal lowlands are tropical, while the central plateau and the mountains are cooler and drier.

ECONOMY

One quarter of the labour force is involved in agriculture and many Mexicans are still subsistence farmers growing maize, wheat, kidney beans and rice. Coffee, cotton, fruit and vegetables are the most important export crops. Mexico is the world's leading producer of silver. The exploitation of large reserves of natural gas and petroleum enabled the country's spectacular economic development in the 1970s and 1980s. An expanding industrial base includes important petrochemical, textile, motor-vehicle and food-processing industries. In the early 1990s major US companies were encouraged by a combination of government policy, the new NAFTA trade agreement and low labour costs to set up factories in Mexico. The result has been a spectacular growth in the Mexican economy which is now the 11th largest in the world. Economic problems remain, and high unemployment has stimulated immigration – often illegal – to the USA.

RECENT HISTORY

The first revolt against Spanish rule broke out in 1810, but Mexican independence was not gained until 1821 after a guerrilla war led by Vicente Guerrero. Initially an empire – under Agustín Itúrbide – Mexico became a republic in 1823, but conflict between federalists and centralists erupted, developing into civil war. In 1836 Texas rebelled against Mexico, declaring independence. When the USA annexed Texas in 1845, war broke out, resulting in the loss of half Mexico's territory – Texas, New Mexico and California. A period of reform began in 1857, with a new liberal constitution. A civil war (1858–61) between reformists and conservatives was won by the reformists under Benito Juárez (1806–72), but the economy was shattered. After Mexico failed to repay debts, Spain, Britain and France invaded in 1863. Although Spain and Britain soon withdrew, France remained, appointing Archduke Maximilian of Austria (1832–67) as Emperor (1864). Under US pressure and Mexican resistance, the French withdrew in 1867. Maximilian remained in Mexico City and was captured and executed. Juárez re-established the republic.

The authoritarian rule of General Porfirio Díaz (President 1876–80 and 1888–1910) brought peace, but wealth was concentrated into a few hands. Revolution against the power of the landowners erupted in 1910. The reformist policies of President Francisco Madero (1873–1913) were supported by the outlaw Pancho Villa (1877–1923), but revolutionary violence continued, and in 1916–17 a US expeditionary force was sent against Villa. From 1924 the revolution became anticlerical and the Church was persecuted. Order was restored when the Institutional Revolutionary Party came to power in 1929. In the 1930s the large estates were divided and much of the economy was nationalized. Political opposition has been tolerated, although the ruling party is virtually guaranteed perpetual power. In 1989, the first non-PRI state governor was elected, but opposition claims of electoral fraud have continued. A more liberal economic and political climate has emerged since 1990.

MICRONESIA

Official name: The Federated States of Micronesia.

Member of: UN, South Pacific Forum.

Area: 702 km² (271 sq mi).

Population: 111 000 (1991 est).

Capital: Palikir (on Pohnpei) 2000, Wenn (formerly Moen) 10 400, Tol 6700, Kolonia (the former capital) 6300 (1990 est).

Languages: English, Trukese, Ponapean, Yapese, Kosraean.

Religions: Various Protestant Churches (mainly Assembly of God, Jehovah's Witnesses and Seventh-day Adventists), Roman Catholic minority.

Education: *Literacy rate:* over 95% (1989 est). *Years of compulsory schooling:* 6–14. *Universities:* none.

Defence: *Total armed strength:* none; the USA is responsible for the islands' defence.

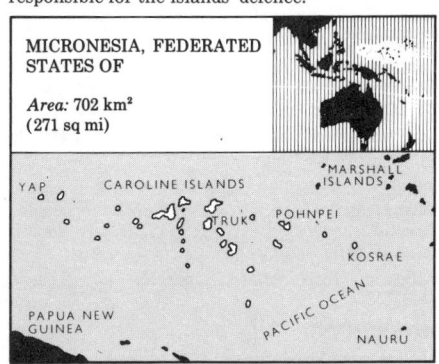

MICRONESIA, FEDERATED STATES OF

Area: 702 km² (271 sq mi)

GOVERNMENT

The President (who serves for four years) and the 14-member National Congress are elected by universal adult suffrage. The Congress comprises one senator elected from each of the four states for four years, and ten senators representing constituencies elected for two years.
President: Bailey Olter.

MICRONESIAN STATES

Population figures are 1990 estimates.

Chuuk (formerly Truk) *Area:* 116 km² (45 sq mi). *Population:* 53 700. *Capital:* Wenn (formerly Moen).

Kosrae *Area:* 109 km² (42 sq mi). *Population:* 7200. *Capital:* Kosrae.

Pohnpei (formerly Ponape) *Area:* 373 km² (144 sq mi). *Population:* 33 100. *Capital:* Kolonia.

Yap *Area:* 101 km² (39 sq mi). *Population:* 13 900. *Capital:* Colonia.

GEOGRAPHY

The Micronesian islands comprise over 600 islands in two main groups. The majority of the islands are low coral atolls, but Kosrae and Pohnpei are mountainous. *Highest point:* Mt Totolom 791 m (2595 ft).

Climate: The climate is tropical with heavy rainfall.

ECONOMY

Apart from phosphate, the islands have practically no resources and depend upon subsistence agriculture, fishing, US grants and (increasingly) tourism.

RECENT HISTORY

Previously known as the Caroline Islands, the islands were under Spanish (1874–99), German (1899–1914), and Japanese administration (1914–45) before becoming part of the US Pacific Islands Trust Territory. They became internally self-governing in 1979.

In 1986 US administration in the islands was formally terminated and the Federated States became a sovereign republic, able to conduct its own foreign affairs, although under a Compact of Free Association the USA retains complete responsibility for the republic's defence and security until 2001. The UN did not recognize this new status of the Federated States until December 1990, when the trusteeship was finally dissolved.

MOLDOVA

Official name: Republica Moldoveneasca (Republic of Moldova). Formerly known as Moldavia.

Member of: UN, CSCE, CIS.

Area: 33 702 km² (13 012 sq mi).

Population: 4 367 000 (1991 est).

Capital and major cities: Chisinau (formerly Kishinev) 720 000, Tiraspol 182 000, Beltsy (Balti) 159 000, Bendery (Bender) 130 000 (1989 census).

Languages: Romanian (64%), Ukrainian (14%), Russian (13%), Gagauz (4%).

Religion: Romanian Orthodox majority.

Education: *Literacy rate:* no figures available. *Years of compulsory schooling:* 7–17. *Universities:* 1 university and 1 polytechnic.

Defence: *Total armed strength:* no figures available.

GOVERNMENT

A 350-member legislature and a President are elected for four years by universal adult suffrage. A new constitution is to be drafted. The main political party is the (coalition) National Alliance. There are several ethnic political groups.
President: Mircea Snegur.
Prime Minister: Andrei Sangheli.

GEOGRAPHY

Moldova comprises a hilly plain between the River Prut and the Dnestr valley. *Principal rivers:* Dnestr, Prut. *Highest point:* Balaneshty 430 m (1409 ft).

Climate: The country experiences a mild, slightly continental climate.

ECONOMY

Large collective farms produce fruit (particularly grapes for wine), vegetables, wheat, maize, tobacco and sunflower seed. Food processing and machine building are the main industries. Little progress has been made to privatize agriculture and industry.

RECENT HISTORY

Known as Bessarabia, the area was part of the Romanian principality of Moldavia – within the (Turkish) Ottoman Empire – before being ceded to the Russians in 1812. Briefly restored to Moldavia (1856–78), Bessarabia remained Russian until World War I. An autonomous Bessarabian republic was proclaimed in 1917, but was suppressed by a Russian Bolshevik invasion (1918). The Russians were removed by Romanian forces and Bessarabia was declared, in turn, an independent Moldavian republic and a part of the kingdom of Romania (1918). When Romania entered World War II as a German ally, the USSR reoccupied Bessarabia, which was reorganized as the Moldavian Soviet Republic in 1944. Following the abortive coup by Communist hardliners in Moscow (September 1991), Moldavia declared independence but affirmed its intention of eventual reunion with Romania. As Moldova, the republic received international recognition when

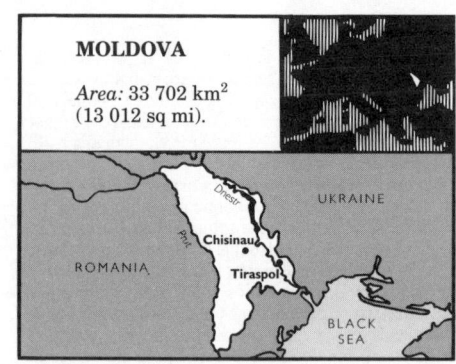

MOLDOVA
Area: 33 702 km² (13 012 sq mi).

the Soviet Union was dissolved (December 1991). Civil war broke out in 1992 when Russian and Ukrainian minorities – fearing an eventual reunion of Moldova with Romania – proclaimed the republic of Trans-Dnestr and attempted to secede. The intervention of CIS forces brought an uneasy peace.

MONACO

Official name: Principauté de Monaco (Principality of Monaco).

Member of: CSCE, UN.

Area: 2.21 km² (0.85 sq mi).

Population: 29 900 (1990 est).

Capital and major cities: Monaco 1200, Monte-Carlo 13 200 (1990 est).

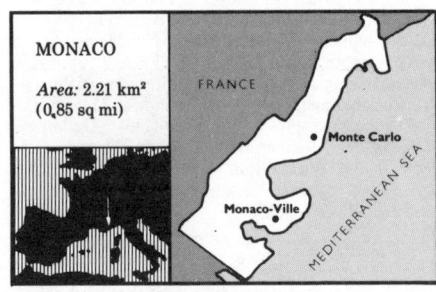

MONACO
Area: 2.21 km² (0.85 sq mi)

Languages: French (official), Monegasque.

Religion: Roman Catholic (90%).

Education: *Literacy rate:* 99%. *Years of compulsory schooling:* 6–16. *Universities:* none.

Defence: *Total armed strength:* there are no armed forces except for a small palace guard.

GOVERNMENT

Monaco is a constitutional monarchy. Legislative power is jointly held by the Prince and the 18-member National Council, which is elected by universal adult suffrage for five years. Executive power is held by the Prince, who appoints a four-member Council of Government headed by the Minister of State, a French civil servant chosen by the sovereign. There are no formal political parties, but political groupings include the (majority) National and Democratic Union and the (Marxist) Democratic Union Movement.
Prince: HSH Prince Rainier III (succeeded upon the death of his grandfather, 9 May 1949).
Minister of State: Jacques Dupont.

GEOGRAPHY

Monaco consists of a rocky peninsula and a narrow stretch of coast. Since 1958 the area of the principality has increased by one fifth through reclamation of land from the sea. *Principal river:* Vésubie. *Highest point:* on Chemin de Révoirés 162 m (533 ft).

Climate: Monaco has a Mediterranean climate.

ECONOMY

Monaco depends upon real estate, banking, insurance, light industry and tourism.

RECENT HISTORY

Monaco was annexed by France in 1793 but restored in 1814, under the protection of the king of Sardinia. The greater part of the principality was lost – and eventually annexed by France – in 1848. Since 1861 Monaco has been under French protection. Prince Rainier III granted a liberal constitution in 1962.

MONGOLIA

Official name: Mongol Uls (Mongolian Republic).

Member of: UN.

Area: 1 565 000 (604 250 sq mi).

Population: 2 156 000 (1992 est).

Capital: Ulan Bator (Ulaan Baatar) 575 000, Darhan 90 000, Erdenet 58 000 (1991 est).

Languages: Khalkh Mongolian (official; 78%), Kazakh (6%).

Religion: Religion was suppressed from 1924 to 1990; there has been a recent revival of Buddhism.

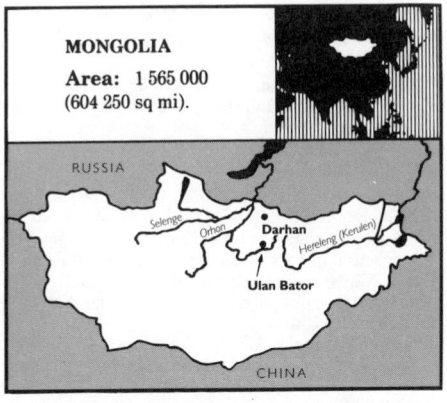

MONGOLIA
Area: 1 565 000 (604 250 sq mi).
RUSSIA
Selenge Orhon Darhan Hereleng (Kerulen)
Ulan Bator
CHINA

Education: *Literacy rate:* 80% (est). *Years of compulsory schooling:* 6–16. *Universities:* 4.

Defence: *Total armed strength:* 14 500 (1991) (plus 10 000 paramilitary). *Military service:* 2 years.

GOVERNMENT

Under the 1992 constitution, a 76-member Great Hural (Assembly) and a President are elected by universal adult suffrage for four years. The President appoints a Prime Minister and a Council of Ministers. The main political parties are the Mongolian People's Revolutionary (Communist) Party and the Mongolian Democratic Party.

President: Punsalmaagiyn Ochirbat.

Prime Minister: Dashin Byambasuren.

GEOGRAPHY

Mongolia comprises mountains in the north, a series of basins in the centre, and the Gobi Desert and Altai Mountains in the south. *Principal rivers:* Selenge, Orhon, Hereleng. *Highest point:* Mönh Hayrhan Uul 4362 m (14 311 ft).

Climate: Mongolia has a dry climate with generally mild summers and severely cold winters.

ECONOMY

Mongolia depends on collectivized animal herding (cattle, sheep, goats and camels). Cereals (including fodder crops) are grown on a large scale on state farms. The industrial sector is dominated by food processing, hides and wool. Copper is a major export. The collapse of trade with the former Soviet Union has created severe economic difficulties and Mongolia is increasingly looking to Japan and China for trade and economic assistance.

RECENT HISTORY

In 1921, Outer Mongolia broke away from China with Soviet assistance, and in 1924 the Mongolian People's Republic was established. Pro-democracy demonstrations early in 1990 led to a liberalization of the regime. The first multi-party elections were held in July 1990 when the Communists were returned to power.

MOROCCO

Official name: Al-Mamlaka al-Maghribiya (The Kingdom of Morocco).

Member of: UN, Arab League.

Area: 458 730 km² (177 115 sq mi) excluding the disputed Western Sahara; 710 850 km² (274 461 sq mi) including the Western Sahara.

Population: 25 208 000 (1990 est) excluding the Western Sahara, which had an estimated population of 185 000 in 1987.

Capital and major cities: Rabat (incl. Salé) 1 472 000, Casablanca (Dar el Beida) 3 210 000, Marrakech 1 517 000, Fez (Fès) 1 012 000, Oujda 962 000, Kénitra 905 000, Tetouan (with Larache) 856 000 (all including suburbs; 1990 est).

Languages: Arabic (official; 75%), Berber, French.

Religions: Sunni Islam (official; 98%), Roman Catholic (2%).

Education: *Literacy rate:* 49.5% (1990). *Years of compulsory schooling:* (in theory) 7–13. *Universities:* 7.

Defence: *Total armed strength:* 195 500 (1991) (plus paramilitary 'gendarmerie royale' 10 000 and paramilitary 'force auxiliaire' 30 000). *Military service:* 18 months.

GOVERNMENT

Morocco is a constitutional monarchy. The 306-member Chamber of Representatives consists of 206 members elected by universal adult suffrage for six years and 100 members chosen by an electoral college representing municipal authorities and professional bodies. The King appoints a Prime Minister and Cabinet and may also dissolve the Chamber. The main political parties include the Union Constitutionnelle, the Rassemblement National des Indépendents, the Mouvement Populaire, Istiqlal, the Union Socialiste des Forces Populaires and the Parti National Démocrate.

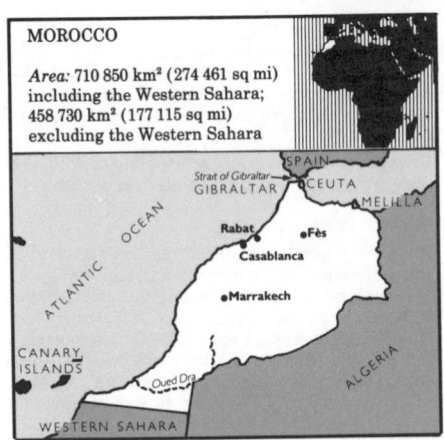

MOROCCO

Area: 710 850 km² (274 461 sq mi)
including the Western Sahara;
458 730 km² (177 115 sq mi)
excluding the Western Sahara

King: HM King Hassan II (succeeded upon the death of his father, 26 February 1961).
Prime Minister: Mohammad Karim Lamrami.

GEOGRAPHY

Over one third of Morocco is mountainous. The principal uplands are the Grand, Middle and Anti Atlas Mountains in the west and north and a plateau in the east. Much of the country – including the disputed Western Sahara territory – is desert. *Principal rivers:* Oued Dra, Oued Moulouya, Sebov. *Highest point:* Jebel Toubkal 4165 m (13 665 ft).

Climate: The north has a Mediterranean climate with hot dry summers and warm wetter winters. The south and much of the interior have semiarid and tropical desert climates.

ECONOMY

Agriculture employs over 40% of the labour force. The main crops include citrus fruits, grapes (for wine) and vegetables for export, and wheat and barley for domestic consumption. Morocco is the world's leading exporter of phosphates. Other resources include iron ore, lead and zinc. Since independence many important industries and services have come into state ownership. Tourism is growing.

RECENT HISTORY

In the 19th century Spain confirmed control of several long-claimed coastal settlements. In the 'Moroccan Crises' (1905–6 and 1911), French interests in Morocco were disputed by Germany. Under the Treaty of Fez in 1912 France established a protectorate over Morocco, although the Spanish enclaves remained. The 1925 Rif rebellion stirred nationalist feelings, but independence was not gained until 1956. King Hassan II (reigned 1961–) has survived left-wing challenges through strong rule and vigorous nationalism – as in his 1975 'Green March' of unarmed peasants into the then-Spanish (Western) Sahara. Morocco continues to hold the Western Sahara despite international pressure and the activities of the Algerian-backed Polisario guerrillas fighting for the territory's independence. A ceasefire was agreed in 1991. Discussions concerning a UN-sponsored referendum in the disputed territory are continuing.

For informaton on the disputed Western Sahara, see Other Territories, following this chapter.

MOZAMBIQUE

Official name: A República de Moçambique (Republic of Mozambique).
Member of: UN, OAU, SADCC.
Area: 799 380 km² (308 641 sq mi).
Population: 15 656 000 (1990 est).
Capital and main cities: Maputo 1 070 000, Beira 292 000, Nampula 197 000 (1989 est).

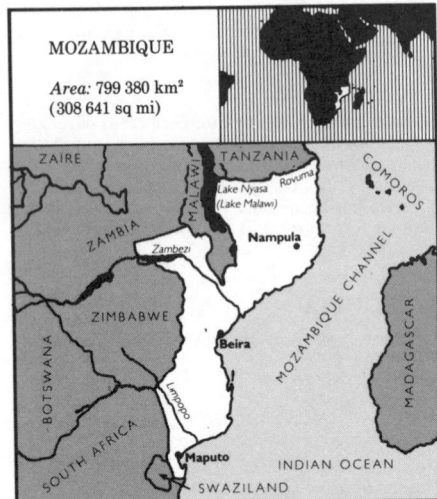

MOZAMBIQUE

Area: 799 380 km²
(308 641 sq mi)

Languages: Portuguese (official), Makua-Lomwe (52%), Malawi (12%).
Religions: Animist (60%), Sunni Islam (15%), Roman Catholic (15%).
Education: *Literacy rate:* 32.9% (1990). *Years of compulsory schooling:* (in theory) 7–14. *Universities:* 1.
Defence: *Total armed strength:* 72 000 (1990) (including 5000 paramilitary). *Military service:* (men and women) 2 years.

GOVERNMENT

A new constitution provides for a 250-member Assembly of the Republic and a President to be elected by universal adult suffrage for five years. The President appoints a Council of Ministers and a Prime Minister. The main legal political parties are the (former monopoly) Frelimo and the National Mozambican Union.
President: Joaquim Alberto Chissano.
Prime Minister: Mario da Gracia Machungo.

GEOGRAPHY

The Zambezi River separates high plateaux in northern Mozambique from lowlands in the south. *Principal rivers:* Limpopo, Zambezi, Shire. *Highest point:* Mount Bingo 2436 m (7992 ft).

Climate: Mozambique has a tropical climate, with maximum rainfall and temperatures from November to March.

ECONOMY

Farming involves over 80% of the labour force, mainly growing cassava and maize as subsistence crops. Fishing is a major employer – prawns and shrimps make up nearly one half of Mozambique's exports. The economy has been devastated by civil war and drought, and Mozambique is usually stated to be the poorest country in the world (in terms of GDP per head).

RECENT HISTORY

By the end of the 19th century the Portuguese gained control over the whole country. Forced labour and minimal development helped to fuel nationalist feelings, and in 1964 the Frelimo movement launched a guerrilla war against Portuguese rule. Independence was achieved in 1975, and a Marxist-Leninist state was established. The pressures of poverty and the destabilization of the country by South Africa – through support for the Renamo guerrilla movement – led to renewed ties with the West, and Marxism was abandoned by Frelimo in 1989. At the beginning of 1991, the country faced severe famine. A ceasefire – and a UN presence in Mozambique – were agreed in 1992.

MYANMAR (BURMA)

Official name: Myanmar Naingngandaw (The Union of Myanmar). The name Burma was officially dropped in May 1989.

Member of: UN.

Area: 676 552 km² (261 218 sq mi).

Population: 42 561 000 (1991 est).

Capital and major cities: Rangoon (Yangon) 2 513 000, Mandalay 533 000, Moulmein 220 000, Pegu (Bago) 151 000, Bassein (Pathein) 144 000, Taunggyi 108 000 (1983 census).

Languages: Burmese (official; 80%), Karen, Mon, Shan, Kachin.

Religion: Buddhist (68%).

Education: *Literacy rate:* 80.6% (1990). *Years of compulsory schooling:* (in theory) 5–10. *Universities:* 3.

Defence: *Total armed strength:* 280 000 (1991) (plus 50 000 paramilitary People's Police Force and 35 000 People's Militia). *Military service:* none.

GOVERNMENT

Power is held by a 19-member State Law-and-Order Restoration Council whose Chairman is head of state. There is constitutional provision for a 489-member Assembly which is empowered to elect a Council of Ministers and a Council of State, whose Chairman will be head of state and plans for a constitutional conference were announced in April 1992. Multi-party elections were held in May 1990 but

the Military State Law-and-Order Restoration Council refused to transfer power to the majority National League for Democracy. The other main political party is the (military-backed) National Unity Party.

President and head of government: Gen. Than Shwe.

GEOGRAPHY

The north and west of Burma are mountainous. In the east is the Shan Plateau along the Thai border. Central and south Burma consists of tropical lowlands. *Principal rivers:* Irrawaddy, Sittang, Mekong. *Highest point:* Hkakado Razi 5881 m (19 296 ft).

Climate: Burma is tropical, experiencing monsoon rains – up to 5000 mm (200 in) in the S – from May to October.

ECONOMY

Burma is rich in agriculture, timber, and minerals, but because of poor communications, lack of development and serious rebellions by a number of ethnic minorities, the country has been unable to realize its potential. Subsistence farming involves about 80% of the labour force.

RECENT HISTORY

Separated from British India in 1937, Burma became a battleground for British and Japanese forces in World War II. In 1948, Burma left the Commonwealth as an independent republic, keeping outside contacts to a minimum, particularly following the coup of General Ne Win in 1962. Continuing armed attempts to gain autonomy by non-Burman minorities have strengthened the army's role. In 1988–89, demonstrations for democracy appeared to threaten military rule, but were repressed. The military retained power following multi-party elections in 1990, and detained or restricted the principal members of the National League for Democracy, including the party leader, Aung San Suu Kyi. The military successfully increased their activities against separatists in the 1990s.

NAMIBIA

Official name: The Republic of Namibia or Republiek van Namibie.

Member of: UN, Commonwealth, SADCC, OAU.

Area: 823 168 km² (317 827 sq mi) excluding the South African enclave of Walvis Bay.

Population: 1 334 000 (1991 est).

Capital and major cities: Windhoek 115 000, Swakopmund 16 000 (1988 est).

Languages: Afrikaans and English (both official), German, local languages.

Religions: Lutheran (30%), Roman Catholic (20%), other Christian Churches (30%).

Education: *Literacy rate:* 72.5% (1985). *Years of compulsory schooling:* 7–16. *Universities:* 1.

Defence: *Total armed strength:* no figures available.

GOVERNMENT

A 72-member Assembly is elected by universal adult suffrage every five years. The President – who appoints the Prime Minister – is also directly elected for a term of five years and can nominate up to six non-voting members of the National Assembly. The main political parties include the (left wing) SWAPO (South West African People's Organization), the

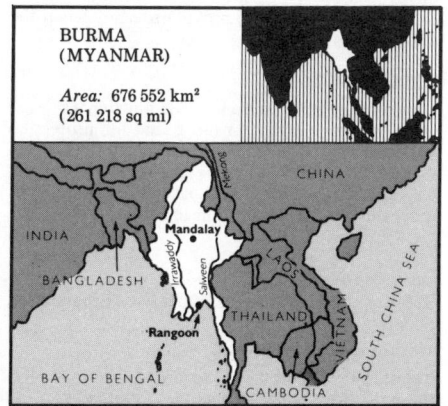

BURMA
(MYANMAR)

Area: 676 552 km²
(261 218 sq mi)

CHINA

INDIA

Mandalay

BANGLADESH

LAOS

THAILAND

VIETNAM

SOUTH CHINA SEA

Rangoon

BAY OF BENGAL

CAMBODIA

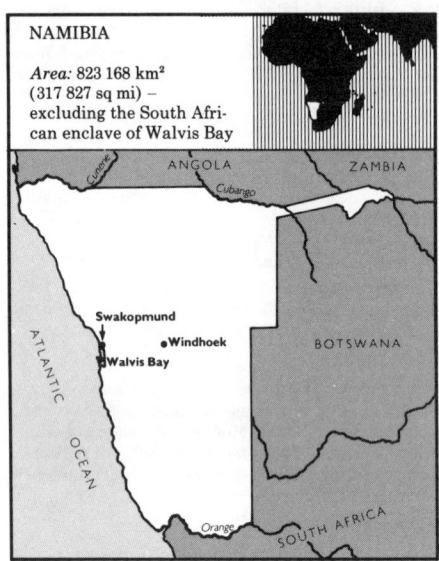

NAMIBIA

Area: 823 168 km²
(317 827 sq mi) –
excluding the South Afri-
can enclave of Walvis Bay

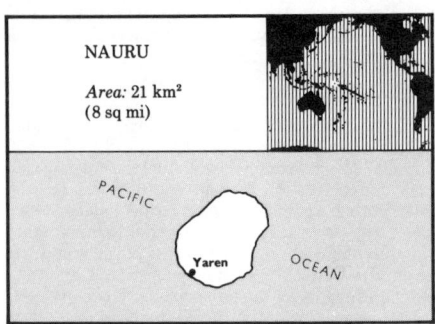

NAURU

Area: 21 km²
(8 sq mi)

South Pacific Forum.
Area: 21 km² (8 sq mi).
Population: 9400 (1990 est).
Capital: No official capital. Yaren – which is the largest settlement – is capital *de facto*. Domaneab is the other main settlement, but no population figure for either place is available.
Languages: Nauruan (official), English.
Religions: Nauruan Protestant Church (majority), Roman Catholic (minority).
Education: *Literacy rate:* 99%. *Years of compulsory schooling:* 6–16. *Universities:* there is a university extension centre of the (Fijian-based) University of the South Pacific.
Defence: *Total armed strength:* none; Australia is responsible for Nauru's defence.

GOVERNMENT
The 18-member Parliament is elected by universal adult suffrage for three years. Parliament elects the President, who in turn appoints a Cabinet of Ministers. There is only one formal political party, the (opposition) Democratic Party of Nauru.
President: Bernard Dowiyogo.

GEOGRAPHY
Nauru is a low-lying coral atoll. There are no rivers. *Highest point:* 68 m (225 ft) on the central plateau.
Climate: Nauru has a tropical climate with heavy rainfall, particularly between November and February.

ECONOMY
Nauru depends almost entirely upon the export of phosphate rock, stocks of which are expected to run out by 1995. Shipping and air services and 'tax haven' facilities are planned to provide revenue when the phosphate is exhausted.

RECENT HISTORY
Germany annexed Nauru in 1888 following a request from German settlers on the island for protection during unrest between Nauru's 12 clans. Australia captured Nauru in 1914 and administered it – except for a period of Japanese occupation (1942–45) – until independence was granted in 1968.

NEPAL
Official name: Nepal Adhirajya (Kingdom of Nepal).
Member of: UN, SAARC.
Area: 147 181 km² (56 827 sq mi).
Population: 19 379 000 (1991 est).

(centre) Democratic Turnhalle Alliance, and Action Christian National.
President: Sam Nujoma.
Prime Minister: Hage Geingob.
GEOGRAPHY
The coastal Namib Desert stretches up to 160 km (100 mi) inland. Beyond the Central Plateau, the Kalahari Desert occupies the eastern part of the country. *Principal river:* Orange. *Highest point:* Brandberg 2579 m (8461 ft).
Climate: Namibia has a hot dry tropical climate. Rainfall on the coast averages under 100 mm (4 in).

ECONOMY
Agriculture involves over 60% of the labour force, mainly raising cattle and sheep. The economy depends upon exports of diamonds and uranium, and is closely tied to South Africa.

RECENT HISTORY
A German protectorate of South West Africa – excluding Walvis Bay, which had been British since 1878 – was declared in 1884. Seeking land for white settlement, the Germans established their rule only after great bloodshed – over three quarters of the Herero people were killed in 1903–4. South Africa conquered the territory during World War I, and (after 1919) administered it as a League of Nations mandate. In 1966, the UN cancelled the mandate, but South Africa – which had refused to grant the territory independence – ignored the ruling. The main nationalist movement, SWAPO, began guerrilla warfare to free Namibia, the name adopted by the UN for the country. South Africa unsuccessfully attempted to exclude SWAPO's influence. After a cease-fire agreement in 1989, UN-supervised elections were held for a constituent assembly. Independence – under the presidency of SWAPO leader Sam Nujoma – was achieved in March 1990.

NAURU
Official name: The Republic of Nauru.
Member of: Commonwealth (special member),

Capital: Kathmandu 420 000 (city 235 000), Birat-nagar 120 000, Lalitpur 100 000 (1987 est).

Languages: Nepali (official; 53%), Bihari (19%), Maithir (12%).

Religions: Hindu (official; 90%), Buddhist (5%), Sunni Islam (3%).

Education: *Literacy rate:* 25·6% (1990). *Years of compulsory schooling:* 6–11. *Universities:* 2.

Defence: *Total armed strength:* 35 000 (1991). *Military service:* none.

GOVERNMENT

Nepal is a constitutional monarchy. Since 1990, Nepal has had a two-chamber Parliament. The Lower House consists of 205 members elected for five years by universal adult suffrage. The Upper House consists of 60 appointed and indirectly elected members, including six members appointed by the King. The main political parties are the Nepali Congress Party and the Communist Party-United Leninist Party Alliance.

King: HM King Birendra (succeeded upon the death of his father, 31 January 1972).

Prime Minister: Girija Prasad Koirala.

GEOGRAPHY

In the south are densely populated subtropical lowlands. A hilly central belt is divided by fertile valleys. The Himalaya dominate the north. *Principal rivers:* Karnali, Naryani, Kosi. *Highest point:* Mount Everest 8863 m (29 078 ft).

Climate: The climate varies between the subtropical south and the glacial Himalayan peaks. All of Nepal experiences the monsoon.

ECONOMY

Nepal is one of the least developed countries in the world, with most of the labour force involved in subsistence farming, mainly growing rice, beans and maize. Forestry is important, but increased farming has led to serious deforestation.

RECENT HISTORY

In 1768 the ruler of the principality of Gurkha in the west conquered the Kathmandu valley, and began a phase of expansion that ended in defeat by the Chinese in Tibet (1792) and the British in India (1816). From 1846 to 1950 the Rana family held sway as hereditary chief ministers of a powerless monarchy. Their isolationist policy preserved Nepal's independence at the expense of its development. A brief experiment with democracy was followed by a re-assertion of royal autocracy (1960) by King Mahendra (reigned 1952–72). Mass unrest and violent pro-democracy demonstrations in 1990 forced the King to concede a democratic constitution.

THE NETHERLANDS

Official name: Koninkrijk der Nederlanden (The Kingdom of the Netherlands).

Member of: UN, EC, NATO, CSCE, WEU, Council of Europe, OECD.

Area: 41 785 km² (16 140 sq mi).

Population: 15 065 000 (1991 est).

Capital and major cities: Amsterdam – capital in name only – 1 062 000 (city 702 000), The Hague ('s Gravenhage) – capital *de facto*; the seat of government and administration – 690 000 (city 444 000), Rotterdam 1 051 000 (city 582 000), Utrecht 535 000 (city 231 000), Eindhoven 386 000 (city 193 000), Arnhem 303 000 (city 132 000), Heerlen-Kerkrade 268 000 (Heerlen city 94 000), Enschede 252 000 (city 146 000), Nijmegen 244 000 (city 146 000), Tilburg 232 000 (city 159 000), Haarlem 214 000 (city 149 000), Groningen 208 000 (city 169 000), Dordrecht 208 000 (city 110 000), 's Hertogenbosch 198 000 (city 89 000), Leiden 189 000 (city 112 000), Geleen-Sittard 182 000 (Sittard town 43 000), Maastricht 163 000 (city 117 000), Breda 161 000 (city 125 000) (1991 est).

Language: Dutch (official).

Religions: Roman Catholic (under 30%), Netherlands Reformed Church (17%), Reformed Churches (Calvinistic; 8%).

Education: *Literacy rate:* 99%. *Years of compulsory schooling:* 5–16. *Universities:* 22 (15 universities including an open university plus 7 institutes of university status).

Defence: *Total armed strength:* 101 400 (1991) (plus a small Civil Defence Corps). *Military service:* 12–15 months.

THE NETHERLANDS

Area: 41 785 km² (16 140 sq mi), or 33 937 km² (13 103 sq mi) excluding fresh-water

GOVERNMENT

The Netherlands is a constitutional monarchy. The 75-member First Chamber of the States-General is elected for a six-year term by the 12 provincial councils – with one half of the members retiring every three years. The 150-member Second Chamber is elected for a four-year term by universal adult suffrage under a system of proportional representation. The monarch appoints a Prime Minister who commands a majority in the States-General. The PM, in turn, appoints a Council of Ministers (Cabinet) who are responsible to the States-General. The main

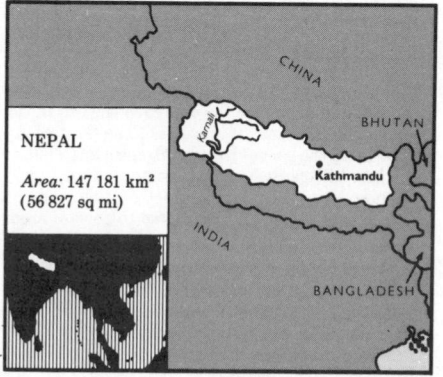

NEPAL

Area: 147 181 km² (56 827 sq mi)

political parties include the (conservative) CDA (Christian Democratic Appeal Party), PvdA (the Labour Party), the (liberal) VVD (People's Party for Freedom and Democracy), D66 (Democracy 66), the (Calvinist) SGP (Political Reformed Party), and the PPR (Political Party of Reformed Democrats).
Queen: HM Queen Beatrix (succeeded on the abdication of her mother, 30 April 1980).
Prime Minister: Ruud Lubbers.

GEOGRAPHY

Over one quarter of the Netherlands – one of the world's most densely populated countries – lies below sea level. A network of canals and canalized rivers cross the west of the country where sand dunes and man-made dykes protect low-lying areas and polders (land reclaimed from the sea). The coast has been straightened by sea walls protecting Zeeland in the southwest and enclosing a freshwater lake, the IJsselmeer, in the north. The east comprises low sandy plains. *Principal rivers:* Rhine (Rijn) – dividing into branches including the Lek, Waal and Oude Rijn, Maas (Meuse). *Highest point:* Vaalserberg 321 m (1053 ft).
Climate: The country has a maritime temperate climate, with cool summers and mild winters.

ECONOMY

Despite having few natural resources – except natural gas – the Netherlands has a high standard of living. Agriculture and horticulture are highly mechanized with a concentration on dairying and glasshouse crops, particularly flowers. Food processing is a major industry, and the country is a leading exporter of cheese. Manufacturing includes chemical, machinery, petroleum refining, metallurgical and electrical engineering industries. Raw materials are imported through Rotterdam, which is the largest port in the world and serves much of Western Europe. Banking and finance are well developed.

RECENT HISTORY

The Congress of Vienna (1815) united all three Low Countries in the Kingdom of the Netherlands under the House of Orange, but Belgium broke away in 1830 and Luxembourg in 1890. The Dutch were neutral in World War I, but suffered occupation by the Germans 1940 to 1945. Following a bitter colonial war, the Dutch accepted that they could not reassert control over Indonesia after World War II. The Netherlands has shown enthusiasm for European unity, and, with the other Low Countries, founded Benelux, the core of the EC. Dutch politics has been characterized by a large number of small parties, some of a confessional nature, and a system of proportional representation has prevented any of these parties attaining a parliamentary majority. The formation of a new coalition government after each general election has been difficult and time-consuming.

DUTCH EXTERNAL TERRITORIES

Aruba (an island off the coast of Venezuela) *Area:* 193 km² (75 sq mi). *Population:* 66 000 (1991 est). *Capital:* Oranjestad 20 000 (1986 est).

Netherlands Antilles also called **The Antilles of the Five** (Curaçao and Bonaire are off the coast of Venezuela; the other three islands are in the Leeward Islands in the eastern Caribbean.) *Area:* 800 km² (309 sq mi) – Curaçao 444 km² (171 sq mi), Bonaire 288 km² (111 sq mi), St Maarten 34 km² (13 sq mi), St

Eustatius – popularly known as Statia – 21 km² (8 sq mi), Saba 13 km² (5 sq mi). *Population:* 191 000 (1990 est) – Curaçao 147 000, Bonaire 8800, St Maarten 13 200, St Eustatius 1400, Saba 1000 (all 1981). *Capital:* Willemstad 125 000 (including suburbs; 1985 est). (Kralendijk is the capital of Bonaire, Philipsburg of St Maarten, Oranjestad of St Eustatius, and Bottom of Saba.)

NEW ZEALAND

Official name: Dominion of New Zealand.
Member of: UN, Commonwealth, ANZUS, South Pacific Forum, OECD.
Area: 269 057 km² (103 883 sq mi).
Population: 3 435 000 (1991 census).
Capital and major cities: Wellington 325 000 (city 150 000), Auckland 885 000 (city 316 000), Christchurch 307 000 (city 293 000), Manakau 227 000 and North Shore 151 000 are both part of the Auckland agglomeration, Hamilton 149 000 (city 101 000), Napier with Hastings 110 000 (Napier city 52 000), Dunedin 109 000, Palmerston North 71 000, Rotorua 54 000, Invercargill 52 000, New Plymouth 49 000, Nelson 47 000, Whangarei 44 000, Wanganui 41 000 (all including suburbs; 1991 census).
Languages: English (official), Maori.
Religions: Anglican (24%), Presbyterian (18%), Roman Catholic (15%), Methodist (5%).
Education: *Literacy rate:* almost 100%. *Years of compulsory schooling:* 6–15. *Universities:* 7.
Defence: *Total armed strength:* 11 300 (1991). *Military service:* none.

GOVERNMENT

The 97-member House of Representatives is elected by universal adult suffrage for three years to represent single-member constituencies, four of which have a Maori electorate and representative. A system of proportional representation is to be adopted. The Governor General – the representative of the British Queen as sovereign of New Zealand – appoints a Prime Minister who commands a majority in the House. The PM, in turn, appoints a Cabinet, which is responsible to the House. The main political parties are the Labour Party, the (conservative) National Party and the New Labour Party. Tokelau is an autonomous island territory.
Prime Minister: Jim Bolger.

ISLAND TERRITORY

Tokelau *Area:* 13 km² (5 sq mi). *Population:* 1700 (1986 census). *Capital:* there is no capital; each atoll has its own administrative centre.

GEOGRAPHY

On South Island, the Southern Alps run from north to south, and in the southwest reach the sea in the deeply indented coast of Fjordland. The Canterbury Plains lie to the east of the mountains. North Island is mainly hilly with isolated mountains, including volcanoes – two of which are active. Lowlands on North Island are largely restricted to coastal areas and the Waikato Valley. *Principal rivers:* Waikato, Clutha, Waihou, Rangitaiki, Mokau, Wanganui, Manawatu. *Highest point:* Mount Cook 3754 m (12 315 ft) – before a major rock slide reduced the height of the mountain in December 1991, Mount Cook stood at 3764 m (12 349 ft).
Climate: The climate is temperate, although the

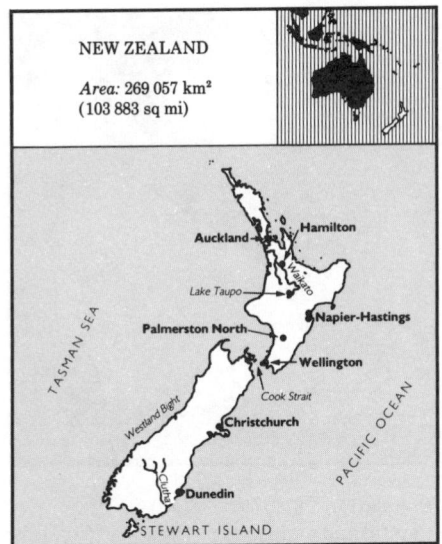

NEW ZEALAND

Area: 269 057 km²
(103 883 sq mi)

north is warmer. Rainfall is abundant almost everywhere, but totals vary considerably with altitude and aspect, rising to over 6350 mm (250 in) on the west coast of South Island.

ECONOMY

The majority of New Zealand's export earnings come from agriculture, in particular meat, wool and dairy products. Forestry is expanding and supports an important pulp and paper industry. Apart from coal, lignite, natural gas and gold, the country has few natural resources, although its considerable hydro-electric-power potential has been exploited to produce plentiful cheap electricity – an important basis of New Zealand's manufacturing industry. Natural gas – from the Kapuni Field on North Island and the Maui Field off the Taranaki coast – is converted to liquid fuel. Despite having only a small domestic market and being remote from the world's major industrial powers, New Zealand has a high standard of living.

RECENT HISTORY

North Island was ceded to the British Crown by Maori chiefs under the Treaty of Waitangi (1840), while South Island was claimed by right of discovery. New Zealand was governed as a part of New South Wales until a separate colonial government was established in 1841. The 1840s were marked by fierce armed resistance to British settlement by the Maoris, the majority of whom live in North Island. Relations between the Maoris and the white settlers deteriorated further during the 1850s as the colonists sought more land and Maori chiefs increasingly refused to sell it. When troops were used to evict Maoris from disputed lands in Waitara, war broke out (1860). Fighting continued for most of the decade in North Island, and guerrilla action in the King Country – the centre of North Island – was not suppressed until 1870. The Maori Wars retarded the European settlement of North Island, while – in the last quarter of the 19th century – the discovery of gold and the introduction of refrigerated ships to export meat and dairy products greatly stimulated the colonization and economy of South Island. However, by the beginning of the 20th century, North

Island was dominant again, and by 1911 migrants from Britain had boosted the country's population to one million. Subsequent immigration has remained overwhelmingly British, although there are sizeable communities of Samoans, Cook Islanders, Yugoslavs and Dutch.

Liberal governments (1891–1912) pioneered many reforms and social measures, including votes for women (1893) and the world's first old-age pensions (1898). Dominion status was granted in 1907, although the country did not formally acknowledge its independent status until 1947. In World War I, New Zealand fought as a British ally in Europe, achieving distinction in the disastrous Allied expedition to the Gallipoli peninsula during the campaign against Turkey (1915). When Japan entered World War II in 1941, New Zealand's more immediate security was threatened. The major role played by the USA in the Pacific War led to New Zealand's postwar alliance with Australia and America in the ANZUS pact, and the country sent troops to support the Americans in Vietnam.

The entry of Britain into the EC in 1973 restricted the access of New Zealand's agricultural products to what had been their principal market. Since then New Zealand has been forced to seek new markets, particularly in the Far and Middle East. Under Labour governments (1972–75 and 1984–90), the country adopted an independent foreign and defence policy. A ban on vessels powered by nuclear energy or carrying nuclear weapons in New Zealand's waters placed a question mark over the country's role as a full ANZUS member.

NEW ZEALAND'S DEPENDENT TERRITORIES

Ross Dependency   See Other Territories, following this chapter.

NEW ZEALAND'S ASSOCIATED TERRITORIES

Cook Islands (a group of 15 islands in the southern Pacific Ocean). *Area:* 234 km² (90 sq mi). *Population:* 19 000 (1991 est). *Capital:* Avarua 5000 (1985 est).

Niue (an island in the southern Pacific Ocean). *Area:* 259 km² (100 sq mi). *Population:* 2300 (1989 census). *Capital:* Alofi 1000 (1989 est).

NICARAGUA

Official name: República de Nicaragua (Republic of Nicaragua).

Member of: UN, OAS, CACM.

Area: 120 254 km² (46 430 sq mi).

Population: 4 000 000 (1991 est).

Capital and main cities: Managua 979 000 (city 682 000), León 101 000, Granada 89 000 (1988 est).

Languages: Spanish (official), Amerindian languages (including Miskito, 4%).

Religion: Roman Catholic (90%).

Education: *Literacy rate:* 88% (est). *Years of compulsory schooling:* 7–13. *Universities:* 4.

Defence: *Total armed strength:* 21 000 (1992 est). *Military service:* none (since 1990).

GOVERNMENT

The 92-member National Assembly is elected by proportional representation for six years by universal adult suffrage. The President – who appoints a Cabinet – is also directly elected for a six-year term.

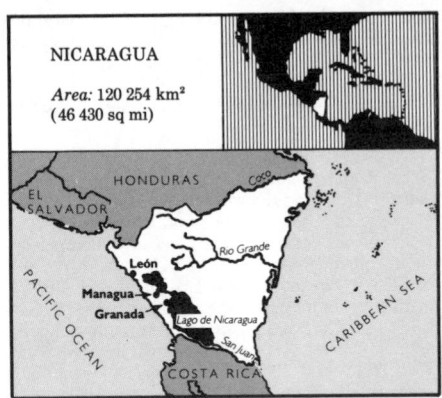

NICARAGUA

Area: 120 254 km²
(46 430 sq mi)

The main political parties include the (14-party coalition) UNO (National Opposition Union) and the (left-wing) FSLN (Sandinista National Liberation Front).
President: Violetta Chamorro.

GEOGRAPHY

A fertile plain on the Pacific coast contains the majority of the population. Mountain ranges rise in the centre of the country. Tropical jungle covers the Atlantic coastal plain. *Principal rivers:* Coco, Rio Grande, San Juan, Escondido. *Highest point:* Pico Mogotón 2107 m (6913 ft).

Climate: The climate is tropical and humid with a rainy season from May to October.

ECONOMY

A largely agricultural economy was damaged in the 1980s by guerrilla warfare, a US trade embargo and hurricanes. Privatization and strict austerity programmes have been implemented. Coffee, cotton and sugar cane are the main export crops.

RECENT HISTORY

Nicaragua remained a Spanish possession until independence was gained in 1821. Independent Nicaragua witnessed strife between conservatives and liberals. Early in the 20th century, the political situation deteriorated, provoking American intervention – US marines were based in Nicaragua from 1912 to 1925, and again from 1927 until 1933. General Anastasio Somoza became president in 1937. Employing dictatorial methods, members of the Somoza family, or their supporters, remained in power until overthrown by a popular uprising led by the Sandinista guerrilla army in 1979. Accusing the Sandinistas of introducing Communism, the USA imposed a trade embargo on Nicaragua, making it increasingly dependent on Cuba and the USSR. Right-wing Contra guerrillas, financed by the USA, fought the Sandinistas from bases in Honduras. A ceasefire between the Contras and Sandinistas was agreed in 1989. In free presidential elections in February 1990, the Sandinista incumbent Daniel Ortega was defeated by Violetta Chamorro of the opposition coalition.

NIGER

Official name: La République du Niger (The Republic of Niger).
Member of: UN, OAU, ECOWAS.
Area: 1 267 000 km² (489 191 sq mi).

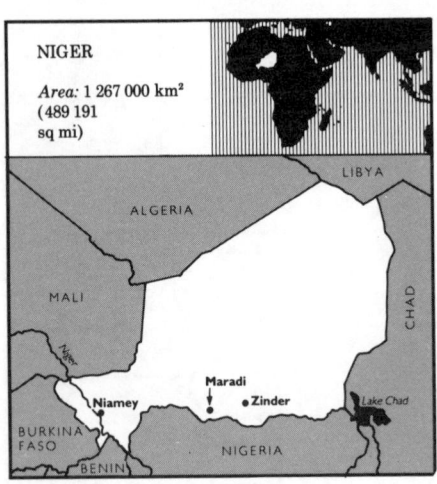

NIGER

Area: 1 267 000 km²
(489 191 sq mi)

Population: 8 024 000 (1991 est).
Capital and main cities: Niamey 398 000, Zinder 121 000, Maradi 113 000 (1988 census).
Languages: French (official), Hausa (85%).
Religion: Sunni Islam (85%).
Education: *Literacy rate:* 28·4% (1990). *Years of compulsory schooling:* (in theory) 7–15. *Universities:* 2.
Defence: *Total armed strength:* 3200 (1991) (plus 1300 paramilitary). *Military service:* 2 years (selective).

GOVERNMENT

A 93-member National Assembly and a President are elected by universal adult suffrage. A multi-party system was restored in 1992–93.
President: Mahamane Ouamane.
Prime Minister: to be appointed.

GEOGRAPHY

Most of Niger lies in the Sahara Desert; the south and the Niger Valley are savannah. The central Aïr Mountains rise to just over 2000 m (6562 ft). *Principal rivers:* Niger, Dillia. *Highest point:* Mont Gréboun 2022 m (6634 ft).

Climate: Niger is dry and hot. The south has a rainy season from June to October.

ECONOMY

Livestock herds and harvests of subsistence crops – millet, sorghum, cassava and rice – have been reduced by desertification. Uranium is mined.

RECENT HISTORY

The French territory of Niger was proclaimed in 1901, but much of the country was not brought under French control until 1920. Independence was achieved in 1960 under President Hamani Diori. After the economy was wracked by a prolonged drought, Diori was overthrown in a military coup (1974). Political pluralism was permitted in 1992 and free elections for a constituent assembly were held in 1993.

NIGERIA

Official name: The Federal Republic of Nigeria.
Member of: UN, OAU, Commonwealth, OPEC, ECOWAS.

Area: 923 768 km² (356 669 sq mi).

Population: 88 514 000 (1991 census) – previous World Bank and UN estimates of Nigeria's population are 20 000 000 higher than the figure recorded in the 1991 census.

Capital and major cities: Abuja (new federal capital) 379 000, Lagos 5 686 000 (city 1 347 0000), Ibadan 1 295 000, Kano 700 000, Ogbomosho 661 000, Oshogbo 442 000, Ilorin 431 000 (1991 census).

Languages: English (official), with over 150 local languages, of which Hausa, Yoruba and Ibo are the most widely spoken.

Religions: Sunni Islam (48%), various Protestant Churches (17% – mainly Anglican, Methodist, Lutheran, Baptist and Presbyterian), Roman Catholic (17%).

Education: *Literacy rate:* 50·7% (1990). *Years of compulsory schooling:* (in theory) 6–12. *Universities:* 30 universities (including an open university) and 24 polytechnics.

Defence: *Total armed strength:* 94 500 (1991). *Military service:* none.

GOVERNMENT

Since 1983 Nigeria has been ruled by the Armed Forces Ruling Council whose President is head of state and of government. Elections by universal adult suffrage are scheduled in 1993–94 for the 30 state administrations, a 450-member Federal Assembly and a President to serve a six-year term. Two political parties – the Social Democratic Party and the National Republican Convention – were legalized in 1989.
President: Gen. Ibrahim Babangida.

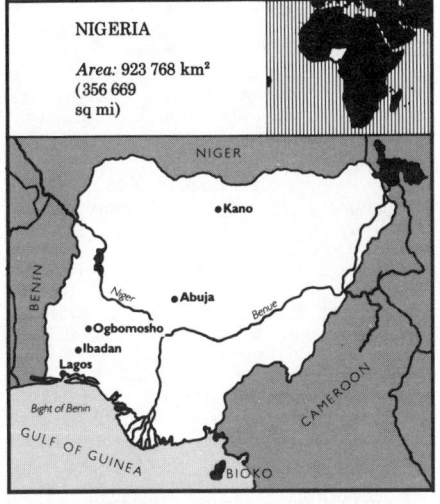

NIGERIA

Area: 923 768 km²
(356 669
sq mi)

NIGERIAN STATES

In 1991 the number of states was increased from 21 to 30 by redrawing the boundaries of most of the existing states. As the exact limits of these new states have not been delineated, the area of these units cannot be given. Population figures are from the 1991 census.

Abia *Population:* 2 298 000. *Capital:* Umuahia.

Adamawa *Population:* 2 124 000. *Capital:* Yola.

Akwa Ibom *Population:* 2 360 000. *Capital:* Uyo.

Anambra *Population:* 2 768 000. *Capital:* Akwa.

Bauchi *Population:* 4 294 000. *Capital:* Bauchi.

Benue *Population:* 2 780 000. *Capital:* Makurdi.

Borno *Population:* 2 597 000. *Capital:* Maiduguri.

Cross River *Population:* 1 866 000. *Capital:* Calabar.

Delta *Population:* 2 570 000. *Capital:* Asaba.

Edo *Population:* 2 160 000. *Capital:* Benin City.

Enugu *Population:* 3 161 000. *Capital:* Enugu.

Imo *Population:* 2 486 000. *Capital:* Owerri.

Jigawa *Population:* 2 830 000. *Capital:* Dutse.

Kaduna *Population:* 3 969 000. *Capital:* Kaduna.

Kano *Population:* 5 632 000. *Capital:* Kano.

Katsina *Population:* 3 878 000. *Capital:* Katsina.

Kebbi *Population:* 2 062 000. *Capital:* Birnin Kebbi.

Kogi *Population:* 1 566 000. *Capital:* Ilorin.

Kwara *Population:* 2 099 000. *Capital:* Lokoja.

Lagos *Population:* 5 686 000. *Capital:* Ikeja.

Niger *Population:* 2 482 000. *Capital:* Minna.

Ogun *Population:* 2 339 000. *Capital:* Abeokuta.

Ondo *Population:* 3 884 000. *Capital:* Akure.

Osun *Population:* 2 203 000. *Capital:* Oshogbo.

Oyo *Population:* 3 489 000. *Capital:* Ibadan.

Plateau *Population:* 3 284 000. *Capital:* Jos.

Rivers *Population:* 3 984 000. *Capital:* Port Harcourt.

Sokoto *Population:* 4 392 000. *Capital:* Sokoto.

Taraba *Population:* 1 481 000. *Capital:* Jalingo.

Yobe *Population:* 1 411 000. *Capital:* Damaturu.

Federal Capital Territory *Population:* 379 000. *Capital:* Abuja.

GEOGRAPHY

Inland from the swampy forest and tropical jungles of the coastal plains, Nigeria comprises a series of plateaux covered – for the most part – by open woodland or savannah. The far north is semi-desert. Isolated ranges of hills rise above the plateaux, the highest of which are the central Jos Plateau and the Biu Plateau in the northeast. *Principal rivers:* Niger, Benue, Cross River, Yobe, Osse. *Highest point:* Vogel Peak (Dimlany) 2042 m (6700 ft).

Climate: The coastal areas are very humid and hot, with an average temperature of 32 ° C (90 ° F). Rainfall is heavy on the coast but decreases gradually inland – although there is a rainy season from April to October. The dry far north experiences the Harmattan, a hot wind blowing out of the Sahara.

ECONOMY

Nigeria is the major economic power in West Africa. The country depends upon revenue from petroleum exports, but a combination of falling petroleum prices and OPEC quotas has resulted in major economic problems, although it has also encouraged diversification. Natural gas is to be exported in liquid form to Europe. Major industries include petrochemicals, textiles and food processing. Over one half of the labour force is involved in agriculture, mainly producing maize, sorghum, cassava, yams and rice as subsistence crops. Cocoa is an important export.

RECENT HISTORY

In 1861, Britain acquired Lagos, and in 1885 a British

protectorate was established on the coast. In the scramble for empire, the commercial Royal Niger Company colonized the interior from 1886, and in 1900 its territories were surrendered to the British Crown as the protectorate of Northern Nigeria. In 1914 the coast and the interior were united to form Britain's largest African colony. An unwieldy federal structure introduced in 1954 was unable to contain regional rivalries after independence (1960). In 1966, the first Prime Minister, Sir Abubakar Tafawa Balewa (1912–66), and other prominent politicians were assassinated in a military coup. After a counter-coup brought General Yakubu Gowon to power, a bitter civil war took place (1967–70) when the Eastern Region – the homeland of the Ibo – attempted to secede as Biafra. Although the East was quickly re-integrated once Biafra was defeated, Nigeria remained politically unstable. The number of states was gradually increased from 3 to 21 (and in 1991 to 30) in an attempt to prevent any one region becoming dominant. A military coup overthrew Gowon in 1975, and an attempt at civilian rule (1979–83) also ended in a coup. Another coup brought General Ibrahim Babangida to power in 1985. The reintroducion of civilian rule is planned during 1993–94.

NORWAY

Official name: Kongeriket Norge (Kingdom of Norway).

Member of: UN, EFTA, NATO, CSCE, Council of Europe, OECD.

Area: 323 878 km^2 (125 050 sq mi) or 386 958 km^2 (149 469 sq mi) including the Arctic island territories of Svalbard (formerly known as Spitsbergen) and Jan Mayen. Svalbard – including Bear Island (Bjornoya) – has an area of 62 924 km^2 (24 295 sq mi); Jan Mayen has an area of 380 km^2 (147 sq mi).

Population: 4 259 000 (1991 est) plus 3700 in Svalbard. Jan Mayen has no permanent population.

Capital and major cities: Oslo 462 000, Bergen 213 000, Trondheim 138 000, Stavanger 98 000, Kristiansand 66 000, Drammen 52 000, Tromso 51 000 (1991 est).

Languages: Two official forms of Norwegian – Bokmaal (80%), Nynorsk (or Landsmaal; 20%); Lappish.

Religion: Lutheran (official; nearly 90%).

Education: *Literacy rate:* virtually 100%. *Years of compulsory schooling:* 7–16. *Universities:* 4, plus 10 institutions of university status (including 4 university colleges).

Defence: *Total armed strength:* 32 700 (1991) (plus 285 000 reserves). *Military service:* 12 months army, 15 months navy and air force. Conscripts are liable to recall.

GOVERNMENT

Norway is a constitutional monarchy. The 165-member Parliament (Storting) is elected under a system of proportional representation by universal adult suffrage for a four-year term. In order to legislate, the Storting divides itself into two houses – the Lagting (containing one quarter of the members) and the Odelsting (containing the remaining three quarters of the members). The King appoints a Prime Minister who commands a majority in the Storting. The PM, in turn, appoints a Council of Ministers who are responsible to the Storting. The main political parties include the Labour Party, the Con-

NORWAY

Area: 323 878 km^2 (125 050 sq mi) or 386 958 km^2 (149 469 sq mi) including the Arctic island territories of Svalbard and Jan Mayen.

servative Party, the Christian Democratic Party, the Centre Party, the Socialist Left Party, the Progress Party and the Liberal Party.

King: HM King Harald V (succeeded upon the death of his father, 17 January 1991).

Prime Minister: Gro Harlem Bruntland.

GEOGRAPHY

Norway's coastline is characterized by fjords, a series of long, deep, narrow inlets formed by glacial action. The greater part of Norway comprises highlands of hard rock. The principal lowlands are along the Skagerrak coast and around Oslofjord and Trondheimsfjord. Svalbard (Spitsbergen) is a bleak archipelago in the Arctic. Jan Mayen is a volcanic island between Norway and Greenland. *Principal rivers:* Glomma (Glama), Lågen, Tanaelv. *Highest point:* Galdhøpiggen 2469 m (8098 ft).

Climate: Norway's temperate climate is the result of the warming Gulf Stream. Summers are remarkably mild for the latitude, while winters are long and very cold. Precipitation is heavy – over 2000 mm (80 in) in the west, with marked rain shadows inland.

ECONOMY

Norway enjoys a high standard of living. Only a small proportion of the land can be cultivated, and agriculture – which is heavily subsidized – is chiefly concerned with dairying and fodder crops. Timber is a major export of Norway, over one half of which is forested. The fishing industry is an important foreign-currency earner, and fish farming – which has been encouraged by government development schemes – is taking the place of whaling and deep-sea fishing. Manufacturing – which has traditionally been concerned with processing fish, timber and iron ore – is now dominated by petrochemicals and allied industries, based upon large reserves of petroleum and natural gas in Norway's sector of the North Sea. Petroleum and natural gas supply over one third of the country's export earnings. The development of industries such as electrical engineering has been helped by cheap hydroelectric power.

RECENT HISTORY

Danish kings ruled Norway as a part of their own realm from the 14th century until 1814. At the end of the Napoleonic Wars, Norway attempted to regain autonomy, but the country came under the rule of the kings of Sweden, although a separate Norwegian Parliament was allowed a considerable degree of independence. Growing nationalism in Norway placed great strains upon the union with Sweden, and in 1905 – following a vote by the Norwegians to repeal the union – King Oscar II of Sweden gave up his claims to the Norwegian crown to allow a peaceful separation of the two countries. After a Swedish prince declined the Norwegian throne, Prince Carl of Denmark was confirmed as King of Norway – as Haakon VII – by a plebiscite. Norway was neutral in World War I, and declared neutrality in World War II, but was occupied by German forces (1940) who set up a puppet government under Vidkun Quisling. After the war, Norway joined NATO and agreed in 1972 to enter the EC, but a national referendum rejected membership. In 1992 a Norwegian reapplication for EC membership became a serious option.

NORWEGIAN EXTERNAL TERRITORIES

Norwegian Antarctic Territories (Bouvet Island, Peter I Island, Queen Maud Land): see Other Territories, followimng this chapter.

OMAN

Official name: Sultanat 'Uman (Sultanate of Oman).

Member of: UN, Arab League, GCC.

Area: 300 000 km² (120 000 sq mi).

Population: 1 502 000 (1990 est).

Capital: Muscat 380 000 (city 85 000), Sohar 92 000 (1990 est).

Languages: Arabic (official), Baluchi.

Religions: Ibadi Islam (75%), Sunni Islam (25%).

Education: *Literacy rate:* 20% (1988). *Years of compulsory schooling*: schooling is not compulsory. *Universities:* 1.

Defence: *Total armed strength:* 30 400 (1991). *Military service:* none.

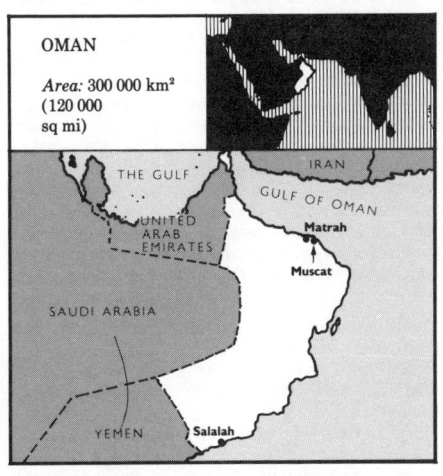

GOVERNMENT

Oman is an absolute monarchy in which the Sultan – who rules by decree – is advised by an appointed Cabinet. The Sultan appoints the 52 members of the State Consultative Council. In 1990 it was announced that an elected consultative assembly would be established eventually. There are no political parties.

Sultan: HM Qaboos bin Said (succeeded upon the deposition of his father, 23 July 1970).

GEOGRAPHY

A barren range of hills rises sharply behind a narrow coastal plain. Desert extends inland into the Rub' al Khali ('The Empty Quarter'). A small detached portion of Oman lies north of the United Arab Emirates. There are no significant rivers. *Highest point:* Jabal ash Sham 3170 m (10 400 ft).

Climate: Oman is very hot in the summer, but milder in the winter and the mountains. The country is extremely arid with an average annual rainfall of 50 to 100 mm (2 to 4 in).

ECONOMY

Oman depends almost entirely upon exports of petroleum and natural gas. Owing to aridity, less than 1% of Oman is cultivated.

RECENT HISTORY

Ahmad ibn Sa'id, who became Imam in 1749, founded the dynasty that still rules Oman. His successors built an empire including the Kenyan coast and Zanzibar, but in 1861 Zanzibar and Oman separated. A British presence was established in the 19th century and Oman did not regain complete independence until 1951. Sultan Qaboos – who came to power in a palace coup in 1970 – has modernized and developed Oman. In the 1970s South Yemen supported left-wing separatist guerrillas in the southern province of Dhofar, but the revolt was suppressed with military assistance from the UK.

PAKISTAN

Official name: Islami Jamhuria-e-Pakistan (Islamic Republic of Pakistan).

Member of: UN, Commonwealth, SAARC.

Area: 803 943 km² (310 403 sq mi) or 888 102 km² (333 897 sq mi) including the Pakistani-held areas of Kashmir (known as Azad Kashmir) and the disputed Northern Areas (Gilgit, Baltistan and Diamir).

Population: 126 406 000 (1991 est; including the Pakistani-held areas of Kasmir – Azad Kashmir – and the disputed Northern Areas – Gilgit, Baltistan and Diamir).

Capital and major cities: Islamabad 266 000, Karachi 6 771 000, Lahore 3 850 000, Faisalabad 1 435 000, Rawalpindi 1 100 000, Hyderabad 1 041 000, Multan 999 000, Gujranwala 912 000, Peshawar 770 000, Sialkot 418 000 (all including suburbs; 1992 est).

Languages: Urdu (national; 20%), Punjabi (60%), Sindhi (12%), English, Pushto, Baluchi.

Religions: Sunni Islam (official; 92%), Shia Islam (5%), with small Ismaili Muslim and Ahmadi minorities.

Education: *Literacy rate:* 34.8% (1990). *Years of compulsory schooling:* schooling is not compulsory. *Universities:* 22, including an open university.

Defence: *Total armed strength:* 580 000 (1992 est) (plus 238 000 paramilitary). *Military service:* none.

GOVERNMENT

The 87-member Senate (the upper house of the Federal Legislature) comprises 19 senators elected for six years by each of the four provinces, plus 8 senators elected from the federally administered Tribal Areas and 3 senators chosen to represent the federal capital. The 237-member National Assembly comprises 207 members elected by universal adult

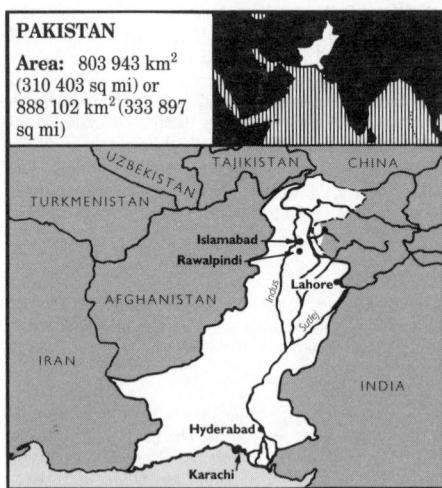

PAKISTAN

Area: 803 943 km^2 (310 403 sq mi) or 888 102 km^2 (333 897 sq mi)

suffrage for five years, 20 seats reserved for women, and 10 members representing non-Islamic minorities. The President – who is chosen by the Federal Legislature – appoints a Prime Minister who commands a majority in the National Assembly. The PM, in turn, appoints a Cabinet of Ministers, responsible to the Assembly. The President has the power to dismiss the current government and dissolve the national and provincial assemblies. The main political parties include the PPP (Pakistan People's Party) and the (coalition) Islamic Democratic Alliance. The four provinces, Azad Kashmir and the Northern Areas have their own legislatures.
President: Ghulam Ishaq Khan.
Prime Minister: Nawaz Sharif.

PAKISTANI PROVINCES AND TERRITORIES

Population figures are 1990 estimates.

Baluchistan *Area*: 347 188 km^2 (134 050 sq mi). *Population*: 5 670 000. *Capital*: Quetta.

North-West Frontier *Area*: 74 522 km^2 (28 773 sq mi). *Population*: 14 340 000. *Capital*: Peshawar.

Punjab *Area*: 205 345 km^2 (79 284 sq mi). *Population*: 62 060 000. *Capital*: Lahore.

Sind *Area*: 140 913 km^2 (54 407 sq mi). *Population*: 24 980 000. *Capital*: Karachi.

Federal Capital Territory *Area*: 907 km^2 (350 sq mi). *Population*: 266 000. *Capital*: Islamabad.

DISPUTED TERITORIES

Population figures are 1990 estimates.

Azad Kashmir (that part of the state of Jammu and Kashmir held by Pakistan) *Area*: 11 639 km^2 (4494 sq mi). *Population:* 2 580 000. *Capital:* Muzaffarabad.

Northern Areas (Baltistan, Diamir and Gilgit) (administered by Pakistan but disputed by India.) *Combined area*: 72 520 km^2 (28 000 sq mi). *Combined population*: 730 000. *Capitals:* (of Baltistan) Skardu, (of Diamir) Chilas, (of Gilgit) Gilgit.

GEOGRAPHY

The Indus Valley divides Pakistan into a highland region in the west and a lowland region in the east. In Baluchistan – in the south – the highlands consist of ridges of hills and low mountains running northeast to southwest. In the north – in the North-West Frontier Province and the disputed territories – the mountain chains rise to over 7000 m (21 300 ft) and include the Karakoram, and parts of the Himalaya and Hindu Kush. The Indus Valley – and the valleys of its tributaries – form a major agricultural region and contain the majority of Pakistan's population. A continuation of the Indian Thar Desert occupies the east. *Principal rivers:* Indus, Sutlej, Chenab, Ravi, Jhelum. *Highest point:* K2 (Mount Godwin Austen) 8607 m (28 238 ft).

Climate: The north and west of Pakistan are arid; the south and much of the east experience a form of the tropical monsoon. Temperatures vary dramatically by season and with altitude, from the hot tropical coast to the cold mountains of the far north.

ECONOMY

Nearly one half of the labour force is involved in subsistence farming, with wheat and rice as the main crops. Cotton is the main foreign-currency earner. The government is encouraging irrigation schemes, but over one half of the cultivated land is subject to either waterlogging or salinity. Although there is a wide range of mineral reserves – including coal, gold, graphite, copper and manganese – these resources have not been extensively developed. Manufacturing is dominated by food processing, textiles and consumer goods. Unemployment and underemployment are major problems, and the country relies heavily upon foreign aid and money sent back by Pakistanis working abroad.

RECENT HISTORY

From the 18th century the region came under British rule. Pakistan as a nation was born in August 1947 when British India was partitioned as a result of demands by the Muslim League for an Islamic state in which Hindus would not be in a majority. Large numbers of Muslims moved to the new state and up to 1 000 000 people died in the bloodshed that accompanied partition. Pakistan had two 'wings' – West Pakistan (the present country) and East Pakistan (now Bangladesh) – separated by 1600 km (1000 mi) of Indian territory. A number of areas were disputed with India. Kashmir – the principal bone of contention – was effectively partitioned between the two nations, and in 1947–49 and 1965 tension over Kashmir led to war between India and Pakistan. The problem of Kashmir remains unsolved, with fighting continuing intermittently along parts of the cease-fire line.

The Muslim League leader Muhammad Ali Jinnah (1876–1949) was the first Governor General, but Jinnah, who was regarded as 'father of the nation', died soon after independence. Pakistan – which became a republic in 1956 – suffered political instability and periods of military rule, including the administrations of General Muhammad Ayub Khan (from 1958 to 1969) and General Muhammad Yahya Khan (from 1969 to 1971). Although East Pakistan contained the majority of the population, from the beginning West Pakistan held political and military dominance. In elections in 1970, Shaikh Mujibur Rahman's Awami League won an overwhelming majority in East Pakistan, while the Pakistan People's Party (PPP) won most of the seats in West Pakistan. Mujibur Rahman seemed less interested in leading a new Pakistani government than in winning autonomy for the East. In March 1971, after abortive negotiations, the Pakistani army was sent from the West to East Pakistan, which promptly declared its independence as Bangladesh. Civil war broke out and India supported the new state, forcing the Pakistani army to surrender by the end of the year.

The leader of the PPP, Zulfiqar Ali Bhutto (PM 1972–77), was deposed in a military coup led by the Army Chief of Staff, Muhammad Zia al-Haq. Bhutto was imprisoned (1977) for allegedly ordering the murder of the father of a former political opponent, sentenced to death (1978) and, despite international protests, hanged (1979). In 1985 Zia lifted martial law and began to return Pakistan to civilian life. In 1988 Zia was killed in a plane crash. In elections a few months later the PPP – led by Bhutto's daughter, Benazir – became the largest party, and Benazir Bhutto became the first woman prime minister of an Islamic state. In 1990, she was accused of nepotism and corruption by the president and dismissed. The following elections were won by the Islamic Democratic Alliance (IDA). In 1993 the IDA's leader, Nawaz Sharif, was also dismissed as premier but was reinstated by the Supreme Court.

PANAMA

Official name: La República de Panamá (The Republic of Panama).

Member of: UN, OAS.

Area: 77 082 km² (29 762 sq mi) including the former Canal Zone.

Population: 2 329 000 (1990 census).

Capital: Panama City 828 000 (city 585 000), San Miguelito (part of the Panama City agglomeration) 243 000, Colón 141 000, David 103 000 (all including suburbs; 1990 census).

Language: Spanish (official).

Religions: Roman Catholic (85%), various Evangelical Protestant Churches (5%), Sunni Islam (5%).

Education: *Literacy rate:* 88.1%. *Years of compulsory schooling:* 6–15. *Universities:* 2.

Defence: *Total armed strength:* 11 650 (1991). *Military service:* none.

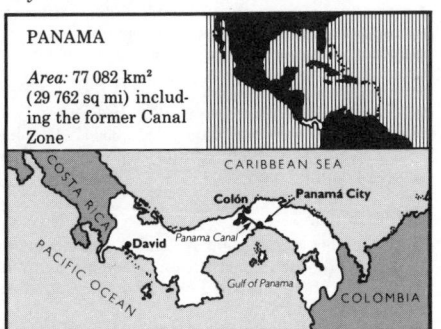

PANAMA

Area: 77 082 km²
(29 762 sq mi) including the former Canal Zone

CARIBBEAN SEA

COSTA RICA

Colón • Panamá City

David • Panama Canal

PACIFIC OCEAN

Gulf of Panama

COLOMBIA

GOVERNMENT

The constitution provides for the election by compulsory universal adult suffrage of a 67-member Legislative Assembly, a President and two Vice Presidents for five years. The President appoints a Cabinet of Ministers. The main political parties include the Authentic Liberal Party, the Christian Democratic Party and the Nationalist Republican Liberation Movement (who cooperated in the 1989 elections as the Democratic Alliance), the Authentic Panamen-ista Party, and the (coalition) Colina.
President: Guillermo Endara.

GEOGRAPHY

Panama is a heavily forested mountainous isthmus joining Central America to South America. *Principal rivers:* Tuira (with Chucunaque), Bayano, Santa Maria. *Highest point:* Baru 3475 m (11 467 ft).

Climate: Panama has a tropical climate with little seasonal change in temperature.

ECONOMY

Income from the Panama Canal is a major foreign-currency earner. Panama has a higher standard of living than its neighbours, although the political crisis of 1989 damaged the economy. Major exports include bananas, shrimps and mahogany.

RECENT HISTORY

Panama was part of Spanish New Granada (Colombia). In the 1880s a French attempt to construct a canal through Panama linking the Atlantic and Pacific Oceans proved unsuccessful. After Colombia rejected US proposals for completing the canal, Panama became independent (1903), sponsored by the USA. The canal eventually opened in 1914. The USA was given land extending 8 km (5 mi) on either side of the canal – the Canal Zone – complete control of which will be handed to Panama in 2000. From 1983 to 1989 effective power was in the hands of General Manuel Noriega, who was deposed by a US invasion and taken to stand trial in the USA, where he was found guilty of criminal activities.

PAPUA NEW GUINEA

Official name: The Independent State of Papua New Guinea.

Member of: UN, Commonwealth, South Pacific Forum.

Area: 462 840 km² (178 704 sq mi).

Population: 3 790 000 (1990 census).

Capital and main cities: Port Moresby 193 000 (city 174 000), Lae 81 000, Madang 27 000, Wewak 23 000 (1990 census).

Languages: English (official), Pidgin English, Motu, and over 700 other local languages.

Religions: Roman Catholic (33%), various Protestant Churches (over 60%).

Education: *Literacy rate:* 52% (1990). *Years of compulsory schooling:* schooling is not compulsory. *Universities:* 2.

Defence: *Total armed strength:* 3840 (1991) (plus 4600 paramilitary border police). *Military service:* none.

GOVERNMENT

A 109-member Parliament is elected for five years by universal adult suffrage. The Governor General – the representative of the British Queen as sovereign of Papua New Guinea – appoints a Prime Minister who commands a majority in Parliament. The PM, in turn, appoints a Cabinet, which is responsible to Parliament. The main political parties are the People's Democratic Movement, the Pangu Party, the National Party, and the United Party. Each of the 20 provinces has its own government.
Prime Minister: Wiwa Koriwi.

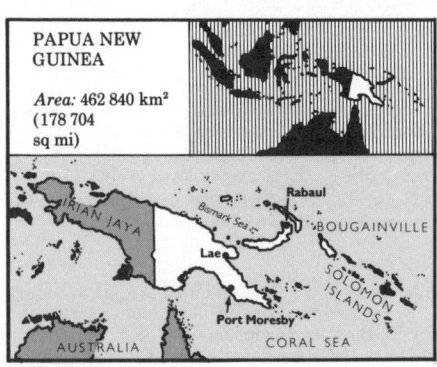

PAPUA NEW
GUINEA

Area: 462 840 km²
(178 704
sq mi)

PROVINCES

Population figures are 1990 estimates.

Central Province *Area:* 29 500 km² (11 400 sq mi). *Population:* 134 000. *Capital:* Port Moresby (i.e. outside the province; see below).

Eastern Highlands *Area:* 11 200 km² (4300 sq mi). *Population:* 333 000. *Capital:* Goroka.

East New Britain *Area:* 15 500 km² (6000 sq mi). *Population:* 151 000. *Capital:* Rabaul.

East Sepik *Area:* 42 800 km² (16 550 sq mi). *Population:* 276 000. *Capital:* Wewak.

Enga *Area:* 12 800 km² (4950 sq mi). *Population:* 194 000. *Capital:* Wabag.

Gulf *Area:* 34 500 km² (13 300 sq mi). *Population:* 74 000. *Capital:* Kerema.

Madang *Area:* 29 000 km² (11 200 sq mi). *Population:* 262 000. *Capital:* Madang.

Manus *Area:* 2100 km² (800 sqmi). *Population:* 30 000. *Capital:* Lorengau.

Milne Bay *Area:* 14 000 km² (5400 sq mi). *Population:* 155 000. *Capital:* Alotau (Samara).

Morobe *Area:* 34 500 km² (13 300 sq mi). *Population:* 404 000. *Capital:* Lae.

New Ireland *Area:* 9600 km² (3700 sq mi). *Population:* 80 000. *Capital:* Kavieng.

North Solomons (formerly **Bougainville**) *Area:* 9300 km² (3600 sq mi). *Population:* 160 000. *Capital:* Arawa (Buka).

Oro (formerly **Northern Province**) *Area:* 22 800 km² (8800 sq mi). *Population:* 96 000. *Capital:* Popondetta.

Sandaun (formerly **West Sepik**) *Area:* 36 300 km² (14 000 sq mi). *Population:* 131 000. *Capital:* Vanimo.

Simbu (formerly **Chimbu**) *Area:* 6100 km² (2350 sq mi). *Population:* 193 000. *Capital:* Kundiawa.

Southern Highlands *Area:* 23 800 km² (9200 sq mi). *Population:* 278 000. *Capital:* Mendi.

Western Province *Area:* 99 300 km² (38 350 sq mi). *Population:* 100 000. *Capital:* Daru.

Western Highlands *Area:* 8500 km² (3300 sq mi). *Population:* 330 000. *Capital:* Mount Hagen.

West New Britain *Area:* 21 000 km² (8100 sq mi). *Population:* 118 000. *Capital:* Kimbe.

National Capital District *Area:* 240 km² (100 sq mi). *Population:* 174 000. *Capital:* Port Moresby.

GEOGRAPHY

Broad swampy plains surround New Guinea's mountainous forested interior. In the east, the country includes the Bismarck archipelago (New Britain,

New Ireland and the Admiralty Islands) and the northern Solomon Islands (including Bougainville). *Principal rivers:* Fly (with Strickland), Sepik. *Highest point:* Mount Wilhelm 4509 m (14 493 ft).

Climate: The country experiences a tropical climate with high temperatures and heavy monsoonal rainfall.

ECONOMY

Agriculture occupies over 80% of the labour force. Most Papuans are subsistence farmers, although agricultural exports include palm oil, copra and cocoa. The mainstay of the economy is minerals, including large reserves of copper, gold, silver and petroleum.

RECENT HISTORY

European colonization was not attempted until 1828 when the Dutch claimed western New Guinea. A British protectorate, established in the SE in 1884, was transferred to Australia (1906) and renamed Papua. NE New Guinea came under German administration in 1884, but was occupied by Australian forces in 1914. From 1942 to 1945 Japanese forces occupied New Guinea and part of Papua. In 1949 Australia combined the administration of the territories, which achieved independence as Papua New Guinea in 1975. Bougainville island – a major source of copper – attempted to secede (1990–92). Fighting on the island diminished in 1992 and peace talks began.

PARAGUAY

Official name: La República del Paraguay (The Republic of Paraguay).

Member of: UN, OAS, Mercosur, ALADI.

Area: 406 752 km² (157 048 sq mi).

Population: 4 157 000 (1989 est).

Capital and major cities: Asunción 732 000 (city 608 000), San Lorenzo (part of the Asunción agglomeration) 124 000, Ciudad del Este 110 000, Pedro Juan Caballero 80 000, Concepción 63 000, Encarnación 44 000 (1990 est).

Languages: Spanish (official; 7%), Guaraní (40%), bilingual Spanish-Guaraní (48%).

Religion: Roman Catholic (97%).

Education: *Literacy rate:* 90.1% (1990). *Years of compulsory schooling:* 7–13. *Universities:* 2.

Defence: *Total armed strength:* 17 000 (1991) (plus 8000 paramilitary police). *Military service:* 18 months army, 24 months navy.

GOVERNMENT

A 198-member Constituent Assembly was elected in 1992 to draft a new constitution. The main political parties are the Colorado Party and the Authentic Radical Liberal Party.
President: Juan Carlos Wosmosy.

GEOGRAPHY

The country west of the Paraguay River – the Chaco – is a flat semiarid plain. The region east of the river is a partly forested undulating plateau. *Principal rivers:* Paraguay, Paraná, Pilcomayo. *Highest point:* Cerro Tatug 700 m (2297 ft).

Climate: The climate is subtropical, with considerable variation in rainfall between the wet southeast and the dry west.

ECONOMY

Agriculture – the main economic activity – is dominated by cattle ranching, cotton and soyabeans. Cheap hydroelectric power installations on the Paraná River have greatly stimulated industry.

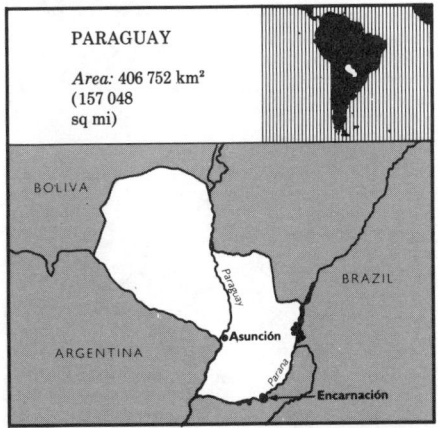

PARAGUAY

Area: 406 752 km² (157 048 sq mi)

BOLIVA

BRAZIL

ARGENTINA

Asunción

Paraguay

Paraná

Encarnación

RECENT HISTORY

The Jesuits controlled the country from 1609 until 1767, when they were expelled. Since independence from Spain in 1811, Paraguay has suffered many dictators, including General José Francia, who totally isolated Paraguay (1814–40). War against Argentina, Brazil and Uruguay (1865–70) cost Paraguay over one half of its people and much territory. The Chaco Wars with Bolivia (1929–35) further weakened Paraguay. General Alfredo Stroessner gained power in 1954, ruling with increasing disregard for human rights until his overthrow in a military coup in 1989. Free multi-party elections were held in 1993.

PERU

Official name: República del Perú (Republic of Peru).

Member of: UN, OAS, ALADI, Andean Pact.

Area: 1 285 216 km¹ (496 225 sq mi).

Population: 22 881 000 (1991 est).

Capital and major cities: Lima 6 405 000 (city 5 494 000), Arequipa 612 000, Callao (part of the Lima agglomeration) 515 000, Trujillo 513 000, Chiclayo 410 000, Piura 310 000 (1990 est).

Languages: Spanish (68%), Quechua (27%), Aymara (3%) – all official.

Religion: Roman Catholic (official; 91%).

Education: *Literacy rate:* 85.1% (1990). *Years of compulsory schooling:* 6–15. *Universities:* 25 national and 10 private (2 of which are Catholic).

Defence: *Total armed strength:* 105 000 (1991) (plus 70 000 paramilitary police). *Military service:* 2 years selective.

GOVERNMENT

The President and the National Congress – comprising a 60-member Senate and a 180-member Chamber of Deputies – are elected by universal adult suffrage for five years. The President appoints a Council of Ministers headed by a Prime Minister. The main political parties include the (left-wing) APRA (Amer-ican Popular Revolutionary Alliance), the (centre-right) Democratic Front (FREDEMO), the IU (Izquierda Unida – Unified Left), Izquierda Socialista, and Cambio 90.

President: Alberto Fujimori.

Prime Minister: Oscar Puente Ramgada.

GEOGRAPHY

The coastal plain is narrow and arid. The Andes – which are prone to earthquakes – run in three high parallel ridges from north to south. Nearly two thirds of Peru is tropical forest (the Selva) in the Amazon Basin. *Principal rivers:* Amazon, Ucayali, Napo, Marañón. *Highest point:* Huascarán 6768 m (22 205 ft).

Climate: A wide climatic variety includes semitropical desert – cooled by the Humboldt Current – on the coast, the very cold Alpine High Andes, and the tropical Selva with heavy rainfall.

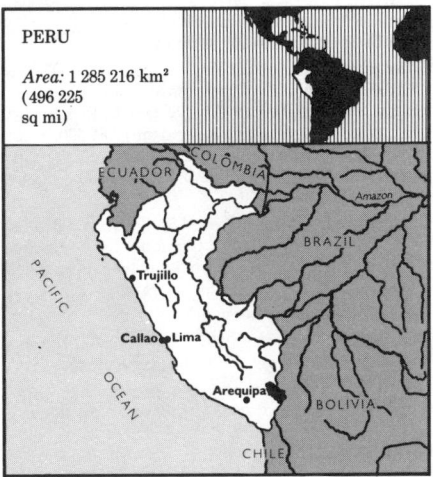

PERU

Area: 1 285 216 km² (496 225 sq mi)

COLOMBIA

ECUADOR

Amazon

BRAZIL

PACIFIC

Trujillo

Callao Lima

OCEAN

Arequipa

BOLIVIA

CHILE

ECONOMY

About one third of the labour force is involved in agriculture. Subsistence farming dominates in the interior; crops for export are more important near the coast. Major crops include coffee, sugar cane, cotton and potatoes, as well as coca for cocaine. Sheep, llamas, vicuñas and alpacas are kept for wool. Rich natural resources include silver, copper, coal, gold, iron ore, petroleum and phosphates. The fishing industry – once the world's largest – has declined since 1971. A combination of natural disasters, a very high birth rate, guerrilla warfare and the declining value of exports have severely damaged the economy.

RECENT HISTORY

Much of South America was governed from Lima as the Spanish Viceroyalty of Peru. Independence was proclaimed in 1821 after the Argentine San Martín took Lima, but Spanish forces did not leave until 1824. Independent Peru saw political domination by large landowners. Progress was made under General Ramon Castilla (1844–62) and civilian constitutional governments at the beginning of the 20th century, but instability and military coups have been common. War (1879–83) in alliance with Bolivia against Chile resulted in the loss of nitrate deposits in the S, while victory against Ecuador (1941) added Amazonian territory. From 1968 a reformist military government instituted a programme of land reform, attempting to benefit workers and the Indians, but faced with mounting economic problems the military swung to the right in 1975. After 1980 elections were held regularly, but owing to the economic crisis and the growth of an extreme left-wing guerrilla movement – the Sendero Luminoso ('Shining Path') – Peru's democracy remained fragile. In 1992, the president effected a coup, suspending the constitution and detaining opposition leaders. Subsequent elections were boycotted by the principal opposition parties. Guerrilla activity lessened after the capture of Abimael Guzman, the leader of the Sendero Luminoso in 1992.

THE PHILIPPINES

Official name: República ñg Pilipinas (Republic of the Philippines).

Member of: UN, ASEAN.

Area: 300 000 km² (115 831 sq mi).

Population: 62 354 000 (1991 est).

Capital and major cities: Manila 7 832 000 (city 1 599 000), Quezon City (part of the Manila agglomeration) 1 667 000, Davao City 850 000, Caloocan City (part of the Manila agglomeration) 761 000, Cebu City 610 000, Zamboango City 442 000, Pasay City (part of the Manila agglomeration) 367 000, Bacolod City 364 000 (1990 census).

Languages: Pilipino (based on Tagalog; national; 55%), Tagalog (over 20%), Cebuano (24%), Ilocano (11%), English, Spanish, with many local languages.

Religions: Roman Catholic (84%), Aglipayan Church (4%), Sunni Islam (5%).

Education: *Literacy rate:* 89.7% (1980). *Years of compulsory schooling:* 7–13. *Universities:* 55.

Defence: *Total armed strength:* 106 500 (1991) (plus 45 000 paramilitary). *Military service:* none.

GOVERNMENT

The President and the 24-member Senate – the upper House of Congress – are elected by universal adult suffrage for six years. The House of Representatives – the lower House of Congress – comprises 200 directly elected members and no more than 50 members appointed by the President from minority groups. The President appoints a Cabinet. The main political parties include the Liberal Party, PDP-Laban (Pilipino Democratic Party–People's Power Movement), the Labor Party, and the Grand Alliance for Democracy. Part of Mindanao island and the Sulu Archipelago form an autonomous region (see below).
President: Fidel Ramos.

AUTONOMOUS REGION

Muslim Mindanao *Area:*13 122 km² (5698 sq mi). *Population:* 1 830 000 (1990 est). *Capital:* Cotabato City.

GEOGRAPHY

Some 2770 of the Philippines' 7000 islands are named. The two largest islands, Luzon and Mindanao, make up over two thirds of the country's area. Most of the archipelago is mountainous with restricted coastal plains, although Luzon has a large, densely populated central plain. Earthquakes are common. *Principal rivers:* Cagayan, Pampanga, Abra, Agusan, Magat, Laoang, Agno. *Highest point:* Mount Apo 2954 m (9692 ft).

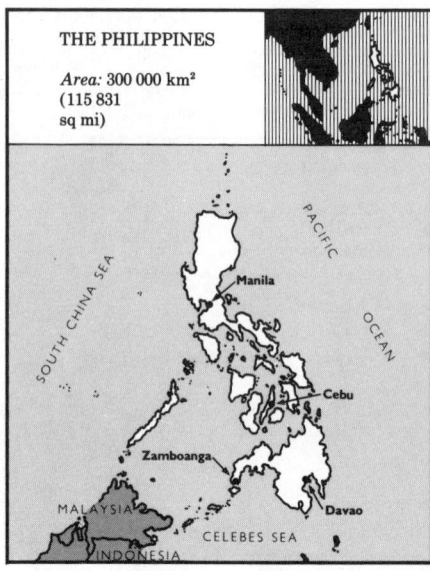

THE PHILIPPINES

Area: 300 000 km² (115 831 sq mi)

Climate: The climate is tropical maritime with high humidity, high temperatures and heavy rainfall. Typhoons are frequent.

ECONOMY

Almost one half of the labour force is involved in agriculture. Rice and maize are the principal subsistence crops, while coconuts, sugar cane, pineapples and bananas are grown for export. The timber industry is important, but deforestation is a problem as land is cleared for cultivation. Major industries include textiles, food processing, chemicals and electrical engineering. Mineral resources include copper (a major export), gold, petroleum and nickel. Money sent back by Filipinos working abroad is an important source of foreign currency.

RECENT HISTORY

A combination of rising nationalism and resentment at economic injustice led to an unsuccessful revolt (1896) against Spanish rule. The islands were ceded to the USA after the Spanish-American War (1898), but American rule had to be imposed by force and resistance continued until 1906. A powerful American presence had a profound effect on Filipino society, which bears the triple imprint of Asian culture, Spanish Catholicism and American capitalism. US policy in the Philippines wavered between accelerating and delaying Filipino self-rule. In 1935 the nationalist leader Manuel Quezon became president of the semi-independent 'Commonwealth' of the Philippines. The surprise Japanese invasion of 1941 traumatized the islands' American and Filipino defenders. Japan set up a puppet 'Philippine Republic', but, after the American recapture of the archipelago, a fully independent Republic of the Philippines was established in 1946.

Between 1953 and 1957 the charismatic President Ramon Magsaysay crushed and conciliated Communist-dominated Hukbalahap guerrillas, but his death ended a programme of land reforms. Coming to power in 1965, Ferdinand Marcos (1917–89) inaugurated flamboyant development projects, but his administration presided over corruption on an unprecedented scale. Marcos used the continuing guerrilla activity as a justification for his increasingly repressive rule. When he attempted to rig the result of presidential elections in 1986, Marcos was overthrown in a popular revolution in favour of Corazon Aquino, the widow of a leading opposition politician who had allegedly been murdered on Marcos' orders. Her government faced several attempted military coups but she was succeeded by the democratically-elected President Ramos in 1992. Insurgency by groups including the (Islamic) Moro National Liberation Front and the (Communist) New People's Army remains a problem.

POLAND

Official name: Polska Rzecpospolita (Republic of Poland).

Member of: UN, CSCE, Council of Europe.

Area: 312 683 km² (120 727 sq mi).

Population: 38 273 000 (1991 est).

Capital and major cities: Warsaw (Warszawa) 1 656 000, Katowice 1 409 000 (city 367 000), Lódź 848 000, Kraków 751 000, Wroclaw 643 000, Poznań 590 000, Gdańsk 465 000, Szczecin 413 000, Bydgoszcz 382 000, Lublin 351 000, Bialystok 271 000, Sosnowiec (part of the Katowice agglomeration) 260 000, Czestochowa 258 000, Gdynia 252 000 (1990 est).

Languages: Polish (97%), with German, Ukrainian, Lithuanian and Belarussian minorities.

Religion: Roman Catholic (94%).

Education: *Literacy rate*: 98%. *Years of compulsory schooling*: 7–14. *Universities*: 25 (including 14 polytechnics of university status), plus 9 other institutes of university status.

Defence: *Total armed strength*: 305 000 (1991). *Military service*: 18 months (plus 15 000 border guards and 18 000 citizens militia).

GOVERNMENT

The 100-member Senate – the upper house – and the 460-member Sejm – the lower house – are elected for four years by universal adult suffrage. The President – who is directly elected – appoints a Prime Minister who commands a majority in the Sejm. The PM, in turn, appoints a Council of Ministers. The main political parties are the Democratic Union, the Alliance of the Democratic Left, Catholic Action, the Peasant Party, the Confederation for an Independent Poland, the Congress of Liberals, Rural Solidarity, and Trade Union Solidarity.
President: Lech Walesa.
Prime Minister: Hannah Suchocka.

GEOGRAPHY

Most of Poland consists of lowlands. In the north are the Baltic lowlands and the Pomeranian and Mazurian lake districts. Central Poland is a region of plains. In the south are the hills of Little Poland and the Tatra Mountains, part of the Carpathian chain. *Principal rivers:* Vistula (Wisa), Oder (Odra), Narew. *Highest point:* Rysy 2499 m (8199 ft).

Climate: Poland's climate tends towards continental with short warm summers and longer cold winters.

ECONOMY

Polish agriculture remains predominantly small-scale and privately owned. Over one quarter of the labour force is still involved in agriculture, growing

POLAND
Area: 312 683 km² (120 727 sq mi).

potatoes, wheat, barley, sugar beet and a range of fodder crops. The industrial sector is large-scale and, until the switch to a free-market economy began in 1990, centrally planned. Poland has major deposits of coal, as well as reserves of natural gas, copper and silver. Engineering, food processing, and the chemical, metallurgical and paper industries are important, but the economic situation has steadily deteriorated since the 1960s. To add to inflation and a rampant black market, Poland has crippling foreign debts. Privatization has been accelerated since 1991 but living standards have decreased.

RECENT HISTORY

In the 19th century the greater part of Poland was within Imperial Russia, against which the Poles revolted unsuccessfully in 1830, 1848 and 1863. National feeling also grew in the areas ruled by Austria and Prussia. After World War I, Poland was restored to statehood (1919), but the country was unstable. Marshal Józef Pilsudski (1867–1935) staged a coup in 1926, and became a virtual dictator. During the 1930s relations with Hitler's Germany – which made territorial claims on parts of Poland – became strained. An alliance with Britain was not enough to deter Hitler from attacking Poland, and thus precipitating World War II (1939). Poland was partitioned once again, this time between Nazi Germany and the USSR. Occupied Poland lost one sixth of its population, including almost all the Jews, and casualties were high after the ill-fated Warsaw Rising (1944). Poland was liberated by the Red Army (1945), and a Communist state was established. The new Poland lost almost one half its territory in the E to the USSR, but was compensated in the N and W at the expense of Germany.

A political crisis in 1956 led to the emergence of a Communist leader who enjoyed a measure of popular support, Wladyslaw Gomulka. In 1980, following the downfall of Gomulka's successor, Edward Gierek, a period of unrest led to the birth of the independent trade union Solidarity (Solidarność), led by Lech Walesa (1943–). Martial law was declared by General Wojciech Jaruzelski in 1981 in an attempt to restore Communist authority. Solidarity was banned and its leaders were detained, but public unrest and economic difficulties continued. In 1989 Solidarity was legalized and agreement was reached on political reform. Solidarity won free elections to the new Senate, and with the support of former allies of the

Communists won enough seats to gain a majority in the Sejm, and Tadeusz Mazowiecki of Solidarity became PM. Disagreements concerning the speed at which market reforms were advancing and personality clashes during the presidential election split Solidarity in 1990. Walesa became president in 1990. Since multi-party elections in 1991, several short-lived coalition governments have held office.

PORTUGAL

Official name: A República Portuguesa (The Portuguese Republic).

Member of: UN, EC, NATO, Council of Europe, CSCE, WEU, OECD.

Area: 92 072 km² (33 549 sq mi) including Madeira and the Azores.

Population: 10 421 000 (1991 est) including Madeira and the Azores.

Capital and major cities: Lisbon (Lisboa) 2 131 000 (city 950 000), Oporto (Porto) 1 695 000 (city 450 000), Amadora (part of the Lisbon agglomeration) 100 000, Setúbal 80 000, Coímbra 75 000, Braga 67 000, Vila Nova de Gaia (part of the Oporto agglomeration) 65 000, Barreiro (part of the Lisbon agglomeration) 55 000, Funchal 47 000 (all including suburbs; 1990 est).

Language: Portuguese (official).

Religion: Roman Catholic (nearly 90%).

Education: *Literacy rate:* 86% (1988). *Years of compulsory schooling:* 6–15. *Universities:* 15.

Defence: *Total armed strength:* 61 800 (1991) (plus 43 500 paramilitary). *Military service:* up to 18 months (to be reduced to 4 months by 1993–94).

GOVERNMENT

An executive President is elected for a five-year term by universal adult suffrage. The 250-member Assembly is directly elected for four years. The President appoints a Prime Minister who commands a majority in the Assembly. The PM, in turn, appoints a Council of Ministers (Cabinet), responsible to the Assembly. The main political parties include PSD (the Social Democratic Party), PS (the Socialist Party), the (centre-left) PRD (Democratic Party), and the Communist Alliance. Madeira and the Azores have their own autonomous governments.
President: Mario Alberto Soares.
Prime Minister: Annibal Cavaco Silva.

PORTUGUESE AUTONOMOUS REGIONS

Population figures are 1991 estimates.

Azores (Açores) *Area*: 2247 km² (868 sq mi). *Population*: 253 000. *Capital*: Ponta Delgada.

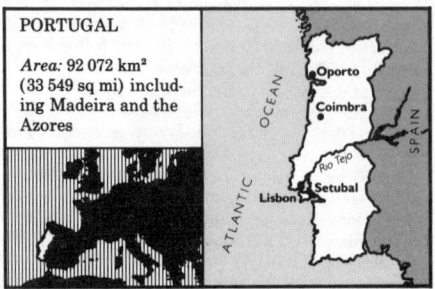

PORTUGAL

Area: 92 072 km² (33 549 sq mi) including Madeira and the Azores

Madeira (includes Porto Santo) *Area*: 794 km² (306 sq mi). *Population*: 273 000. *Capital*: Funchal.

GEOGRAPHY

Behind a coastal plain, Portugal north of the River Tagus is a highland region, at the centre of which is the country's principal mountain range, the Serra da Estrela. A wide plateau in the northeast is a continuation of the Spanish Meseta. Portugal south of the Tagus is mainly an undulating lowland. The Atlantic islands of Madeira and the Azores are respectively nearly 1000 km (620 mi) and 1200 km (745 mi) SW of the mainland. *Principal rivers:* Tagus (Rio Tejo), Douro, Guadiana. *Highest point:* Pico 2315 m (7713 ft) in the Azores. Malhao de Estrela, at 1993 m (6537 ft), is the highest point on the mainland.

Climate: Portugal has a mild and temperate climate which is wetter and more Atlantic in the north, and drier, hotter and more Mediterranean inland and in the south.

ECONOMY

Agriculture involves about 20% of the labour force, but lacks investment following land reforms in the 1970s, since when production has fallen. The principal crops include wheat and maize, as well as grapes (for wines such as port and Madeira), tomatoes, potatoes and cork trees. The country lacks natural resources. Manufacturing industry includes textiles and clothing (major exports), footwear, food processing, cork products, and, increasingly, electrical appliances and petrochemicals. Tourism and money sent back by Portuguese working abroad are major foreign-currency earners. Despite recent impressive economic development – following severe disruption during and immediately after the 1974 revolution – Portugal remains Western Europe's poorest country.

RECENT HISTORY

Portugal experienced political instability for much of the 19th century. Portugal's African empire was confirmed, although the country lacked the power to gain more territory in the scramble for Africa. The monarchy was violently overthrown in 1910, but the Portuguese republic proved unstable and the military took power in 1926. From 1932 to 1968, under the dictatorship of Premier Antonio Salazar (1889–1970), stability was achieved but at great cost. Portugal became a one-party state, and expensive colonial wars dragged on as Portugal attempted to check independence movements in Angola and Mozambique. In 1974 there was a left-wing military coup whose leaders granted independence to the African colonies (1974–75), and initially attempted to impose a Marxist system on the country. However, elections in 1976 decisively rejected the far left. Civilian rule was restored as Portugal effected a transition from dictatorship to democracy, and simultaneously – through the loss of empire and membership of the EC (from 1986) – became more closely integrated with the rest of Europe.

PORTUGUESE OVERSEAS TERRITORY

Macau (an enclave on the southern Chinese coast) *Area*: 17 km² (6.5 sq mi). *Population*: 402 000 (1991 census). *Capital*: Macau 402 000.

QATAR

Official name: Dawlat Qatar (State of Qatar).

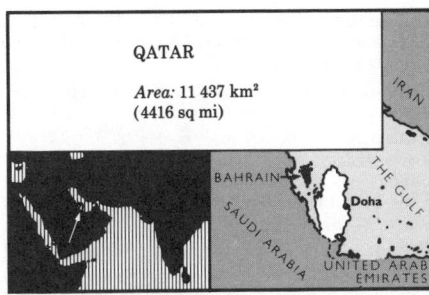

QATAR

Area: 11 437 km²
(4416 sq mi)

Member of: UN, Arab League, OPEC, GCC.

Area: 11 437 km² (4416 sq mi).

Population: 456 000 (1991 est).

Capital and major cities: Doha 272 000 (city 217 000), ar-Rayyani 42 000 and al-Wakrah 13 000 are part of the Doha agglomeration, Umm Sa'id 6000 (1986 est).

Language: Arabic.

Religion: Wahhabi Sunni Islam (official; 98%).

Education: *Literacy rate:* 75.7% (1986). *Years of compulsory schooling:* schooling is not compulsory. *Universities:* 1.

Defence: *Total armed strength:* 7500 (1991). *Military service:* none.

GOVERNMENT

Qatar is an absolute monarchy. The Amir – who is head of state and of government – appoints a Council of Ministers. There are neither formal political institutions nor parties.
Amir and head of government: HH Shaikh Khalifa bin Hamad Al-Thani (succeeded upon the deposition of his cousin, 22 February 1972).

GEOGRAPHY

Qatar is a low barren peninsula projecting into the Gulf. There are no rivers. *Highest point:* 73 m (240 ft) in the Dukhan Heights.

Climate: Qatar is very hot in summer, but milder in winter. Rainfall averages between 50 and 75 mm (2 to 3 in).

ECONOMY

Qatar's high standard of living is due almost entirely to the export of petroleum and natural gas. The steel and cement industries have been developed in an attempt to diversify.

RECENT HISTORY

In the 1860s Britain intervened in a dispute between Qatar and its Bahraini rulers, installing a member of the Qatari Al-Thani family as sheik. Qatar was part of the Ottoman Empire from 1872 until 1914. Its ruler signed protection treaties with Britain in 1916 and 1934, and did not regain complete independence until 1971. Qatar joined the coalition forces against Saddam Hussein's Iraq in the Second Gulf War (1991).

ROMANIA

Official name: Rômania.

Member of: UN, CSCE, Council of Europe (guest).

Area: 237 500 km² (91 699 sq mi).

Population: 22 749 000 (1992 census).

Capital and major cities: Bucharest (Bucuresti) 2 325 000, Brasov 352 000, Constanta 351 000, Iasi 343 000, Timisoara 334 000, Cluj-Napoca 328 000, Galati 305 000, Craiova 298 000, Ploiesti 249 000 (1992 census).

Languages: Romanian (official; 89%), Hungarian (10%), German (1%).

Religions: Orthodox (70%), Uniat (Greek Catholic) Church (3%), Roman Catholic (5%), Calvinist (2%).

Education: *Literacy rate:* 98%. *Years of compulsory schooling:* 6–16. *Universities:* 15 including 3 institutes of university status.

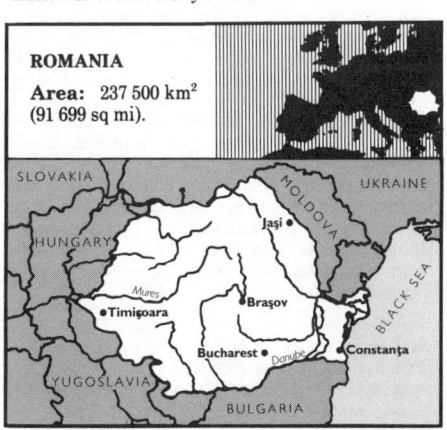

ROMANIA

Area: 237 500 km²
(91 699 sq mi).

Defence: *Total armed strength:* 200 800 (1991 est) (plus 18 400 border guards and 34 800 paramilitary gendarmes). *Military service:* 12 months army and air force, 18 months navy.

GOVERNMENT

The President is directly elected by universal adult suffrage for a 30-month term. A 396-seat National Assembly and 119-seat Senate also serve 30-month terms of office, and are elected on a modified system of proportional representation. The main political parties include the National Salvation Front, the Magyar Democratic Union of Romania, the National Liberal Party, and the National Peasants' Party.
President: Ion Iliescu.
Prime Minister: Nicolae Vacaroiou.

GEOGRAPHY

The Carpathian Mountains run through the north, east and centre of Romania. To the west of the Carpathians is the tableland of Transylvania and the Banat lowland. In the south the Danube Plain ends in a delta on the Black Sea. *Principal rivers:* Danube (Dunäria), Mures, Prut. *Highest point:* Moldoveanu 2544 m (8346 ft).

Climate: Romania experiences cold snowy winters and hot summers. Rainfall is moderate in the lowlands but heavier in the Carpathians.

ECONOMY

State-owned industry – which employs nearly 40% of the labour force – includes mining, metallurgy, mechanical engineering and chemicals. Natural resources include petroleum and natural gas. Considerable forests support a timber and furniture industry. Major crops include maize, sugar beet, wheat, potatoes and grapes for wine, but agriculture has been neglected, and – because of exports – food supplies have fallen short of the country's needs. Economic mismanagement under Ceausescu decreased already low living standards. Romania has sought to obtain Western aid and investment to overcome severe social and economic problems.

RECENT HISTORY

Romania's independence from the (Turkish) Ottoman Empire was internationally recognized in 1878. When both the Russian and Austro-Hungarian Empires collapsed at the end of World War I, Romania won additional territory with substantial Romanian populations from both. 'Greater Romania' was beset with deep social and ethnic divisions, which found expression in the rise of the Fascist Iron Guard in the 1930s. King Carol II suppressed the Guard and substituted his own dictatorship, but he was forced by Germany to cede lands back to Hungary (1940), while the USSR retook considerable territories, including the present Moldavian Soviet Republic. Carol fled and Romania – under Marshal Ion Antonescu – joined the Axis powers (1941), fighting the USSR to regain lost territories. King Michael dismissed Antonescu and declared war on Germany as the Red Army invaded (1944), and a Soviet-dominated government was installed (1945). The monarchy was abolished in 1947.

From 1952, under Gheorghe Gheorghiu-Dej (1901–65) and then under Nicolae Ceausescu (1918–89), Romania distanced itself from Soviet foreign policy while maintaining strict Communist orthodoxy at home. Ceausescu – and his wife Elena – impoverished Romania by their harsh, corrupt and nepotistic rule. When the secret police – the Securitate – put down demonstrations in Timisoara (1989), a national revolt (backed by the army) broke out. A National Salvation Front (NSF) was formed (22 December 1989) and a military tribunal executed Nicolae and Elena Ceausescu on charges of genocide and corruption (25 December 1989). The Communist Party was dissolved and much of Ceausescu's oppressive social and economic legislation was annulled. However, opposition groups expressed doubts concerning the NSF's commitment to democracy and were unable to gain access to the media. In May 1990, Ion Ilescu was elected president, and the National Salvation Front, of which he was leader, was confirmed in power by a huge majority. An international team of monitors judged Romania's first post-war multi-party elections to be 'flawed' but not fraudulent. The NSF has been returned to power in subsequent elections.

RUSSIA

Official name: Rossiyskaya Federativnaya Respublika (Republic of the Russian Federation) or Rossiya (Russia)

Member of: UN, CIS, CSCE.

Area: 17 075 400 km² (6 592 800 sq mi).

Population: 149 469 000 (1991 est.).

Capital and major cities: Moscow (Moskva) 8 967 000, St. Petersburg (Sankt-Peterburg; formerly Leningrad) 5 020 000, Nizhny Novgorod (formerly Gorky) 1 438 000, Novosibirsk 1 436 000, Yekaterinburg (formerly Sverdlovsk 1 367 000, Samara (formerly Kuybyshev) 1 257 000, Omsk 1 148 000, Chelyabinsk 1 143 000, Kazan 1 094 000, Ufa 1 083 000, Rostov 1 020 000, Volgograd 999 000, Krasnoyarsk 912 000, Saratov 905 000, Voronezh 887 000, Vladivostok 648 000, Izhevsk (formerly Ustinov) 635 000, Yaroslavl 633 000 (1989 est.).

Languages: Russian (83%), Tatar (4%), Ukrainian (3%), Chuvash (1%), plus more than 100 other languages.

Religions: Orthodox (27%), with Sunni Islam, Jewish, Baptist and other minorities.

Education: *Literacy rate:* nearly 100% (1992 est.). *Years of compulsory schooling:* 7–15. *Universities:* 42 universities, 32 polytechnics of university status (plus over 100 other institutes offering courses of degree level).

Defence: *Total armed strength:* 2 720 000 (some of whom are part of the joint CIS armed forces, which include an additional 1 200 000 personnel). *Military service:* 2 years army and air force; 2–3 years navy and border force.

GOVERNMENT

Constitutional reform is expected in 1993. Under the proposed constitution, Russia would have a parliament of two houses elected for four years by universal suffrage – a lower house comprising representatives elected on a system of proportional representation and a smaller upper house comprising representatives of each of the 88 provinces, republics and autonomous regions. The existing Congress of People's Deputies was elected under the former Soviet system – of its present membership, about two fifths were elected by universal adult suffrage from constituencies, about one fifth directly elected to represent regions and republics, and the remaining members were elected by 32 official organizations including the (now disbanded) Communist Party. An executive State President – who appoints a Prime Minister and a Council of Ministers – is elected by universal adult suffrage for five years. The principal political groupings include (pro-Yeltsin) Democratic Russia, (hardline) Civic Union and the (conservative) People's Party of Russia. Under the terms of a new Russian Federal Treaty (1992), varying degrees of self-government are exercised by the autonomous republics and autonomous regions listed below. (Tatarstan and Chechenya have not yet signed the Treaty.)
President: Boris Yeltsin.
Prime Minister: Viktor Chernomyrdin.

REPUBLICS AND AUTONOMOUS REGIONS

Population figures are 1991 estimates.

Adygea (formerly **Adygei**) *Area:* 7600 km² (2934 sq mi). *Population:* 437 000. *Capital:* Maikop.

Agin-Buryat (autonomous region) *Area:* 19 000 km² (7300 sq mi). *Population:* 78 000. *Capital:* Aginskoye.

Bashkortostan (formerly **Bashkiria**) *Area:* 143 600 km² (55 430 sq mi). *Population:* 3 984 000. *Capital:* Ufa.

Buryatia *Area:* 351 500 km² (135 630 sq mi). *Population:* 1 049 000. *Capital:* Ulan-Ude.

Chechenya *Area:* 10 300 km² (5000 sq mi). *Population:* 700 000. *Capital:* Grozny.

Chuckchi *Area:* 737 700 km² (284 800 sq mi). *Population:* 154 000. *Capital:* Anadyr.

Chuvashia *Area:* 18 300 km² (7064 sq mi). *Population:* 1 346 000. *Capital:* Cheboksary.

Dagestan *Area:* 50 300 km² (19 416 sq mi). *Population:* 1 854 000. *Capital:* Makhachkala.

Evenki (autonomous region) *Area:* 767 000 km² (296 400 sq mi). *Population:* 25 000. *Capital:* Tura.

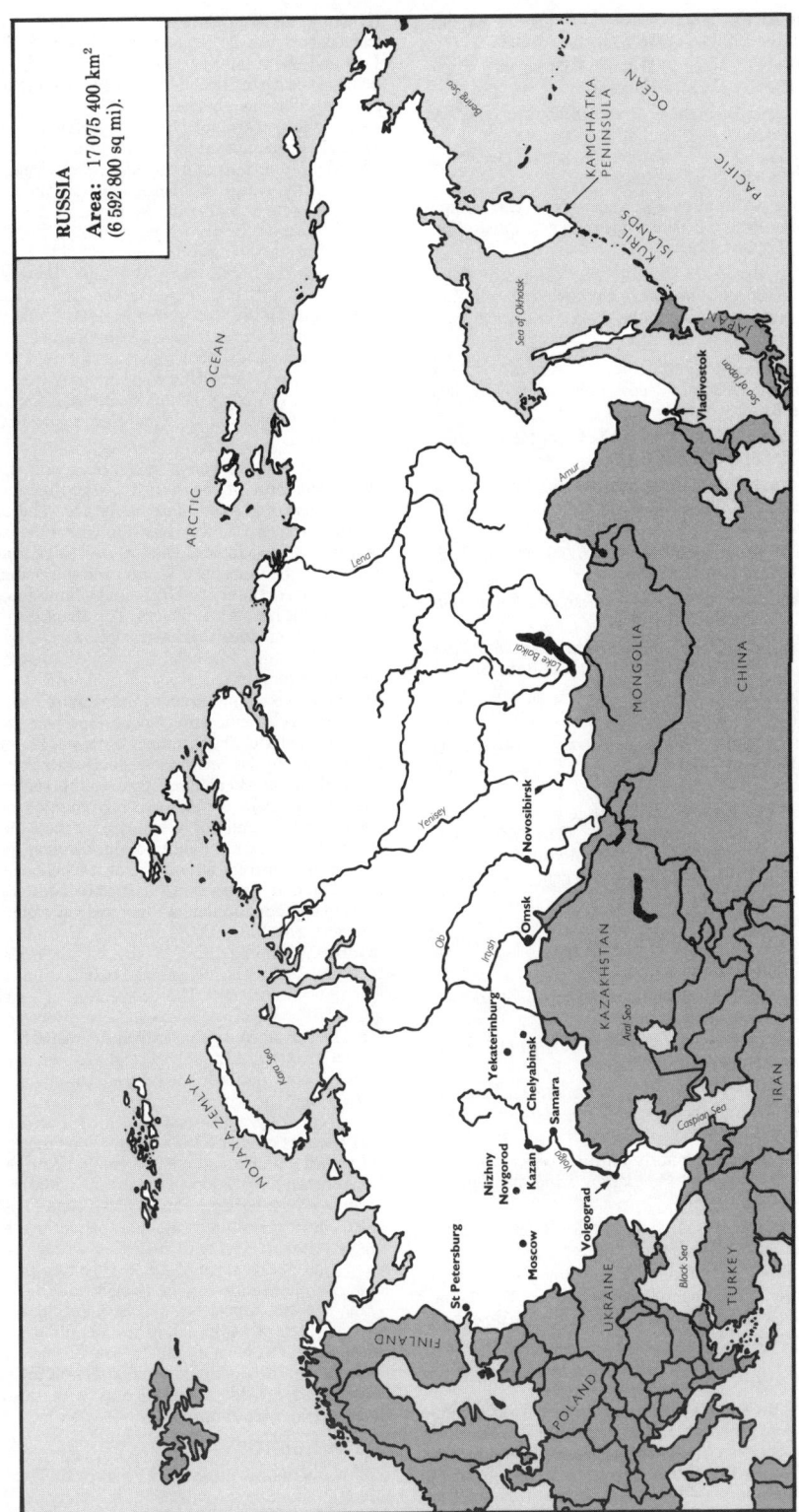

RUSSIA

Area: 17 075 400 km²
(6 592 800 sq mi).

Gorno-Altay *Area:* 92 600 km² (35 740 sq mi). *Population:* 197 000. *Capital:* Gorno-Altaisk.

Ingushetia *Area:* 9000 km² (3500 sq mi). *Population:* 500 000. *Capital:* Nazran.

Kabardino-Balkaria *Area:* 12 500 km² (4825 sq mi). *Population:* 768 000. *Capital:* Nalchik.

Kalmykia *Area:* 75 900 km² (29 300 sq mi). *Population:* 329 000. *Capital:* Elista.

Karachay-Cherkessia (formerly Karachevo-Cherkess) *Area:* 14 100 km² (5442 sq mi). *Population:* 427 000. *Capital:* Cherkessk.

Karelia *Area:* 172 400 km² (83 730 sq mi). *Population:* 799 000. *Capital:* Petrozavodsk.

Khakassia *Area:* 61 900 km² (23 900 sq mi). *Population:* 577 000. *Capital:* Abakan.

Khanty-Mansi (autonomous region) *Area:* 523 100 km² (202 000 sq mi). *Population:* 1 314 000. *Capital:* Khanty-Mansiysk.

Komi *Area:* 415 900 km² (160 540 sq mi). *Population:* 1 265 000. *Capital:* Syktyvkar.

Komi-Permyak (autonomous region) *Area:* 32 900 km² (12 700 sq mi). *Population:* 161 000. *Capital:* Kudymkar.

Koryak *Area:* 301 500 km² (116 400 sq mi). *Population:* 40 000. *Capital:* Palana.

Mari El *Area:* 23 200 km² (8955 sq mi). *Population:* 758 000. *Capital:* Yoshkar-Ola.

Mordvinia (formerly **Mordovia**) *Area:* 26 200 km² (10 110 sq mi). *Population:* 964 000. *Capital:* Saransk.

Nenets *Area:* 176 400 km² (68 100 sq mi). *Population:* 55 000. *Capital:* Naryan-Mar.

North Ossetia (Severo Ossetiya) *Area:* 8000 km² (3088 sq mi). *Population:* 643 000. *Capital:* Vladikavkaz.

Russia (i.e. Russia as a component of the Russian Federation) *Area:* 7 969 100 km² (3 077 100 sq mi). *Population:* 122 368 000. *Capital:* Moscow.

Tatarstan *Area:* 68 100 km² (26 650 sq mi). *Population:* 3 679 000. *Capital:* Kazan.

Taymyr or **Dolgano-Nenets** (autonomous region) *Area:* 862 100 km² (332 900 sq mi). *Population:* 54 000. *Capital:* Dudinka.

Tuva *Area:* 170 500 km² (65 810 sq mi). *Population:* 307 000. *Capital:* Kyzyl-Orda.

Udmurtia *Area:* 42 100 km² (16 250 sq mi). *Population:* 1 628 000. *Capital:* Izhevsk.

Ust-Ordynsky Buryat (autonomous region) *Area:* 22 400 km² (8600 sq mi). *Population:* 138 000. *Capital:* Ust-Ordynsky.

Yakut-Sakha (formerly **Yakutia**) *Area:* 3 103 200 km² (1 197 760 sq mi). *Population:* 1 109 000. *Capital:* Yakutsk.

Yamalo-Nenets *Area:* 750 300 km² (289 700 sq mi). *Population:* 493 000. *Capital:* Salekhard.

Yevreysk Republic or **Yereyskayaya (Jewish Republic)** (autonomous region) *Area:* 36 000 km² (13 895 sq mi). *Population:* 220 000. *Capital:* Birobijan (Birobidzhan).

GEOGRAPHY

Russia is the largest country in the world and covers over 10% of the total land area of the globe. Much of the area between the Baltic and the Ural Mountains is covered by the North European Plain, south of which the relatively low-lying Central Russian Uplands stretch from the Ukrainian border to north of Moscow. The Urals run north-south for 2000 km (1250 mi), dividing European Russia from Asia. To the east of the Urals is the vast West Siberian Lowland, the greater part of which is occupied by the basin of the River Ob and its tributaries. The Central Siberian Plateau – between the Rivers Yenisey and Lena – rises to around 1700 m (5500 ft). Beyond the Lena are the mountains of east Siberia, including the Chersky Mountains and the Kamchatka Peninsula. Much of the south of Siberia is mountainous. The Yablonovy and Stanovoy Mountains rise inland from the Amur Basin, which drains to the Pacific coast. The Altai Mountains lie south of Lake Baikal and along the border with Mongolia. Between the Caspian and Black Seas are the high Caucasus Mountains on the Georgian and Azeri borders. The Kaliningrad enclave between Poland and Lithuania on the Baltic is a detached part of Russia. *Principal rivers:* Yenisey, Ob (with Irytsh), Amur (with Argun), Lena, Volga, Angara, Dvina, Pechora, Kama. *Highest point:* Elbrus (on the Georgian border) 5642 m (18 510 ft).

Climate: Russia has a wide range of climatic types, but most of the country is continental and experiences extremes of temperature. The Arctic north is a severe tundra region in which the subsoil is nearly always frozen. The forested taiga zone – to the south – has long hard winters and short summers. The steppes of the central Russian Uplands have cold winters but hot, dry summers. The Black Sea coast has a Mediterranean climate.

ECONOMY

Russia is one of the largest producers of coal, iron ore, steel, petroleum and cement. However, its economy is in crisis. The economic reforms (1985–91) of Mikhail Gorbachov introduced decentralization to a centrally-planned economy. Since 1991, reform has been accelerated through the introduction of free market prices and the encouragement of private enterprise. However, lack of motivation in the labour force affects all sectors of the economy and poor distribution has resulted in shortages of many basic goods. Production has declined and inflation is rampant, reaching 2200% in 1992. Manufacturing involves over one third of the labour force and includes the steel, chemical, textile and heavy machinery industries. The production of consumer goods is not highly developed. Agriculture is large scale and organized either into state-owned farms or collective farms, although the right to own and farm land privately has been introduced. Despite mechanization and the world's largest fertilizer industry, Russia cannot produce enough grain for its needs, in part because of poor harvests, and poor storage and transport facilities. Imports from Ukraine and Kazakhstan have assumed importance. Major crops include wheat, barley, oats, potatoes, sugar beet and fruit. Natural resources include the world's largest coal reserves, nearly one third of the world's natural gas reserves, one third of the world's forests, major deposits of manganese, gold, potash, bauxite, nickel, lead, zinc and copper, as well as plentiful sites for hydroelectric power installations. Machinery, petroleum and petroleum products are Russia's major exports and the republic is self sufficient in energy. Russia has a large trade surplus with the other former Soviet republics.

RECENT HISTORY

Following the revolution of February 1917 – largely brought about by the catastrophic conduct of World War I – Tsar Nicholas II abdicated and a provisional government was established. On 7 November 1917 the Bolsheviks (Communists) – led by Vladymir Ilich Lenin (1870–1924) – overthrew the provisional government in a bloodless coup. Russia withdrew from the war, ceded Poland to Germany and Austria, and recognized the independence of Estonia, Finland, Georgia, Latvia, Lithuania and the Ukraine. Other parts of the former empire soon declared independence, including Armenia, Azerbaijan and Central Asia. A civil war between the supporters of Joseph and the White Russians (led by former Tsarists) lasted until 1922. The Communists gradually reconquered most of the former Russian empire and in December 1922 formed the Union of Soviet Socialist Republics. The economy was reorganized under central control, but shortages and famine were soon experienced. After Lenin's death (1924), a power struggle took place between the supporters of Joseph Stalin (1879–1953) and Leon Trotsky (1879–1940). Stalin expelled Trotsky's supporters from the Communist Party and exiled him. The rapid industrialization of the country began. In 1929–30 Stalin liquidated the kulaks (richer peasants). Severe repression continued until his death – opponents were subjected to 'show trials' and summary execution, and millions died as a result of starvation or political execution.

In World War II – in which up to 20 million Soviet citizens may have died – the USSR at first concluded a pact with Hitler (1939), and invaded Poland, Finland, Romania and the Baltic states, annexing considerable territory. However, in 1941 the Germans invaded the USSR, precipitating the Soviet Union's entry into the war on the Allied side. In victory the Soviet Union was confirmed as a world power, controlling a cordon of satellite states in Eastern Europe and challenging the West in the Cold War. However, the economy stagnated and the country was drained by the burdens of an impoverished and overstretched empire. Leonid Brezhnev (leader 1964–82) reversed the brief thaw that had been experienced under Nikita Khruschev (leader 1956–64), and far-reaching reform had to await the policies of Mikhail Gorbachov (1931–) after 1985.

Faced with severe economic reforms, Gorbachov attempted to introduce reconstruction (*perestroika*) and greater openness (*glasnost*) by implementing social, economic and industrial reforms. The state of the economy also influenced the desire to reduce military spending by reaching agreements on arms reduction with the West. Dissent was tolerated, a major reform of the constitution led to more open elections, and the Communist Party gave up its leading role. Many hardliners in the Communist Party were defeated by reformers (many of them non-Communists) in elections in 1989. The abandonment of the Brezhnev Doctrine – the right of the USSR to intervene in the affairs of Warsaw Pact countries (as it had done militarily in Hungary in 1956 and Czechoslovakia in 1968) – prompted rapid change in Eastern Europe, where one after another the satellite states renounced Communism and began to implement multi-party rule. From 1989 there were increased nationalistic stirrings within the USSR, particularly in the Baltic republics and the Caucasus.

In August 1991, an attempt by a group of Communist hardliners to depose Gorbachov was defeated by the resistance of Russian President Boris Yeltsin (1931–) and by the refusal of the army to take action against unarmed civilian protestors. The opposition of Yeltsin and the Russian parliament to the coup greatly enhanced the status and powers of Russia and the 14 other Union Republics. Fourteen of the 15 republics declared independence and the secession of the three Baltic republics was recognized internationally. The remaining republics began to renegotiate their relationship. Gorbachov suspended the Communist Party and – with Yeltsin – initiated far-reaching political and economic reforms. However, it was too late to save the Soviet Union, whose fate was sealed by the refusal of Ukraine, the second most important of the republics, to participate in the new looser Union proposed by Gorbachov.

By the end of 1991 the initiative had passed from Gorbachov to Yeltsin, who was instrumental in establishing the Commonwealth of Independent States (CIS), a military and economic grouping of sovereign states that included the majority of the former Union republics. After Gorbachov resigned and the Soviet Union was dissolved (December 1991), Russia took over the international responsibilities of the USSR, including its seat on the UN Security Council. Externally, Russia faces disputes concerning the future of CIS forces and potential territorial claims on other former Soviet republics. Internally, Russia faces a severe economic crisis as the command economy is replaced by a market economy. These changes have been impeded by the activities of former Communist hardliners in the Congress of People's Deputies, who have also held up constitutional reform.

RWANDA

Official name: La République rwandaise (French) or Republika y'u Rwanda (Kinyarwanda) (Republic of Rwanda).

Member of: UN, OAU.

Area: 26 338 km² (10 169 sq mi).

Population: 7 347 000 (1992 est.).

Capital and main cities: Kigali 233 000, Ruhengeri 30 000, Butare 29 000 (1991 census).

Languages: French and Kinyarwanda (both official).

Religions: Roman Catholic (63%), animist (21%), Sunni Islam (8%), various Protestant Churches (8%).

Education: *Literacy rate:* 50.2% (1990). *Years of compulsory schooling:* (in theory) 7–15. *Universities:* 1.

Defence: *Total armed strength:* 5200 (1991) (plus 1200 paramilitary). *Military service:* none.

GOVERNMENT

The President (who appoints a Council of Ministers) and the 70-member National Development Council are elected for five years by compulsory universal adult suffrage. The (former monopoly) MRND party (Mouvement Révolutionnaire National pour le Développement) is the main political party.
President: Maj. Gen. Juvenal Habyarimana.

GEOGRAPHY

Rwanda is a mountainous country. Most of the western boundary is formed by Lake Kivu. *Principal river:* Luvironza. *Highest point:* Mont Karisimbi 4507 m (14 787 ft).

Climate: The climate is tropical with cooler temperatures in the mountains.

ECONOMY

Subsistence farming dominates Rwanda's economy. Coffee and tin are the main exports. There are major (largely unexploited) reserves of natural gas under Lake Kivu.

RECENT HISTORY

The feudal kingdom of Rwanda was a German possession from 1890 until it was taken over by Belgium after World War I. The monarchy – of the dominant minority Tutsi people – was overthrown by the majority Hutu population shortly before independence in 1962. Tribal violence followed an unsuccessful Tutsi attempt to regain power in 1963, and strife between the Hutu and Tutsi has continued

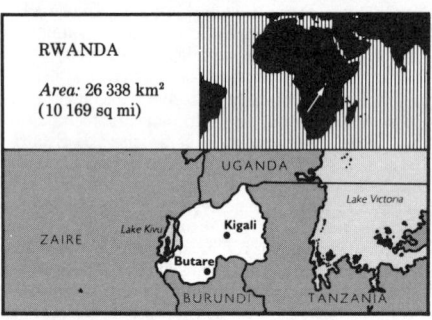

RWANDA

Area: 26 338 km² (10 169 sq mi)

intermittently. In 1990–91 an army of Tutsi refugees invaded Rwanda, occupying much of the north. In February 1991, in an attempt to solve the problem, Rwanda's neighbours agreed to grant citizenship to Tutsi refugees, and Rwanda conceded the principle of multi-party elections.

SAINT CHRISTOPHER AND NEVIS

Official name: The Federation of Saint Christopher and Nevis. St Christopher is popularly known as St Kitts.

Member of: UN, Commonwealth, CARICOM, OAS.

Area: 262 km² (101 sq mi).

Population: 43 000 (1992 est).

Capital and major towns: Basseterre 18 500, Charlestown 1700 (1986 est).

Language: English (official).

Religion: Anglican (36%), Methodist (32%), Roman Catholic (11%).

Education: *Literacy rate:* 91.5% (1980). *Years of compulsory schooling:* 5–17. *Universities:* an extramural department of the University of the West Indies.

Defence: *Total armed strength:* there are no armed forces.

GOVERNMENT

The National Assembly consists of 11 members elected by universal adult suffrage for five years and 3 or 4 appointed members. The Governor General – the representative of the British Queen as sovereign of St Kitts – appoints a Prime Minister who commands a majority in the Assembly. The PM appoints a Cabinet responsible to the Assembly. The main political parties are the People's Action Movement, the Labour Party, the Nevis Reformation Party and the Concerned Citizens Movement. Nevis has its own legislature.

Prime Minister: Kennedy Simmonds.

AUTONOMOUS ISLAND

Nevis *Area:* 93 km² (36 sq mi). *Population:* 10 100 (1989 est). *Capital:* Charlestown.

GEOGRAPHY

St Kitts and Nevis are two well-watered mountainous islands, set 3 km (2 mi) apart. There are no significant rivers. *Highest point:* Nevis Peak 985 m (3232 ft).

Climate: The moist tropical climate is cooled by sea breezes.

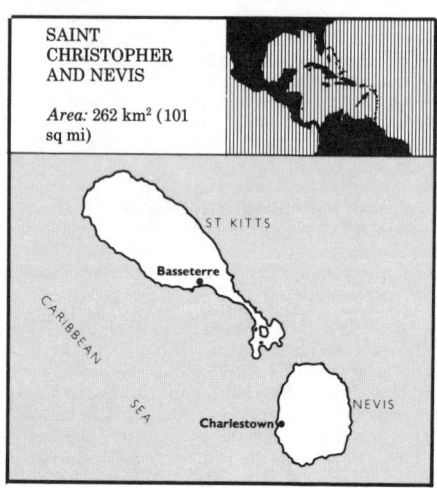

SAINT CHRISTOPHER AND NEVIS

Area: 262 km² (101 sq mi)

ECONOMY

The economy is based on agriculture (mainly sugar cane) and tourism.

RECENT HISTORY

St Kitts was united with Nevis and the more distant small island of Anguilla in a single British colony, which gained internal self-government in 1967. When Anguilla – a reluctant partner – proclaimed independence in 1967, the British intervened, eventually restoring Anguilla to colonial rule while St Kitts-Nevis progressed to independence in 1983.

SAINT LUCIA

Member of: UN, Commonwealth, CARICOM, OAS.

Area: 616 km² (238 sq mi).

Population: 150 000 (1990 census).

Capital and main towns: Castries 57 000, Vieux Fort 23 000 (1990 census).

Languages: English (official), French patois (majority).

Religion: Roman Catholic (over 80%).

Education: *Literacy rate:* 78%. *Years of compulsory schooling:* 5–15. *Universities:* 1 (extra-mural branch of the University of the West Indies).

Defence: *Total armed strength:* there are no armed forces.

GOVERNMENT

The 11-member Senate is appointed. The 17-member House of Assembly is elected by universal adult suffrage for five years. The Governor General – as representative of the British Queen as sovereign of St Lucia – appoints a Prime Minister who commands a majority in the House. The PM, in turn, appoints a Cabinet which is responsible to the House. The main political parties are the United Workers' Party, the Labour Party, and the Progressive Labour Party. *Prime Minister*: John Compton.

GEOGRAPHY

St Lucia is a forested mountainous island. There are no significant rivers. *Highest point:* Mount Gimie 959 m (3145 ft).

Climate: St Lucia has a wet tropical climate. There is a dry season from January to April.

ECONOMY

The economy depends on agriculture, with bananas and coconuts as the main crops. Tourism is increasingly important.

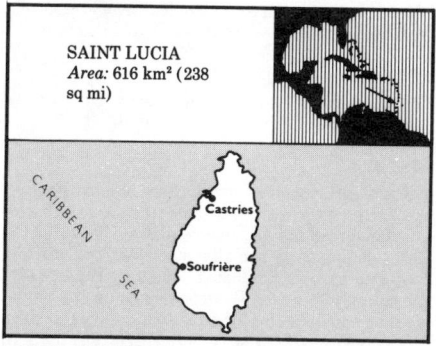

SAINT LUCIA
Area: 616 km² (238 sq mi)

RECENT HISTORY

After being disputed by England and France, St Lucia finally became a British colony in 1814. Internal self-government was achieved in 1967 and independence in 1979.

SAINT VINCENT AND THE GRENADINES

Member of: UN, OAS, CARICOM, Commonwealth.

Area: 389 km² (150 sq mi).

Population: 108 000 (1991 census).

Capital: Kingstown 34 000 (city 19 000; 1989 est).

Language: English (official).

Religions: Anglican (42%), Methodist (21%), Roman Catholic (12%).

Education: *Literacy rate:* 85% (1983). *Years of compulsory schooling:* schooling is not compulsory. *Universities:* none.

Defence: *Total armed strength:* there are no armed forces.

GOVERNMENT

The single-chamber House of Assembly consists of 6 nominated senators and 15 representatives elected for five years by universal adult suffrage. The Governor General – who is the representative of the British Queen as sovereign of St Vincent – appoints a Prime Minister who commands a majority of the representatives. The PM in turn appoints a Cabinet responsible to the House. The main political parties are the New Democratic Party and the Labour Party. *Prime Minister*: David Jack.

GEOGRAPHY

St Vincent is a mountainous wooded island. The Grenadines – which include Bequia and Mustique – are a chain of small islands to the south of St Vincent. There are no significant rivers. *Highest point:* Mount Soufrière, an active volcano, 1234 m (4048 ft).

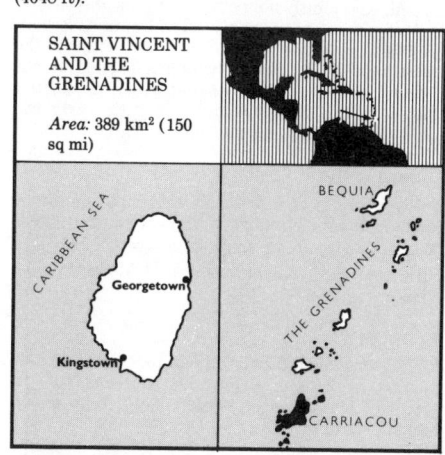

SAINT VINCENT AND THE GRENADINES

Area: 389 km² (150 sq mi)

Climate: The country experiences a tropical climate with very heavy rainfall in the mountains.

ECONOMY

Bananas and arrowroot are the main crops of a largely agricultural economy.

RECENT HISTORY

The island became a British colony in 1763, gained internal self-government in 1969, and achieved independence in 1979.

SAN MARINO

Official name: Serenissima Repubblica di San Marino (Most Serene Republic of San Marino).

Member of: CSCE, Council of Europe, UN, CSCE.

Area: km² (23 sq mi).

Population: 23 700 (1991 est).

Capital and main towns: San Marino 9000 (city 4200), Seravalle 7300, Borgo Maggiore (part of the San Marino city built-up area) 4200 (1991 est).

Language: Italian.

Religion: Roman Catholic (official; 95%).

Education: *Literacy rate:* 99% (1990). *Years of compulsory schooling:* 6–14. *Universities:* none.

Defence: *Total armed strength:* a small voluntary force. *Military service:* citizens may be enlisted in times of national emergency.

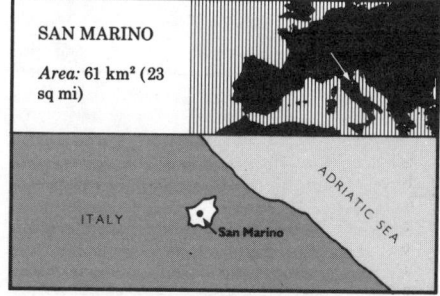

SAN MARINO

Area: 61 km² (23 sq mi)

GOVERNMENT

The 60-member Great and General Council is elected by universal adult suffrage for five years. The Council elects two of its members to be Captains-Regent, who jointly hold office as heads of state and of government for six months. The Captains-Regent preside over a 10-member Congress of State – the equivalent of a Cabinet – which is elected by the Council for five years. The main political parties are the (conservative) Christian Democratic Party, the Socialist Party, and the Communist Party.

GEOGRAPHY

The country is dominated by the triple limestone peaks of Monte Titano, the highest point at 739 m (2424 ft). There are no significant rivers.

Climate: San Marino has a mild Mediterranean climate.

ECONOMY

Manufacturing and tourism – in particular visitors on day excursions – are the mainstays of the economy. Out-of-season conferences are an important source of revenue.

RECENT HISTORY

San Marino has retained its autonomy because of its isolation and by playing off powerful neighbours against each other. Its independence was recognized by Napoleon (1797), the Congress of Vienna (1815) and the new Kingdom of Italy (1862). In 1957 a bloodless 'revolution' replaced the Communist-Socialist administration that had been in power since 1945.

SÃO TOMÉ E PRÍNCIPE

Official name: A República Democrática de São Tomé e Príncipe (The Democratic Republic of São Tomé and Príncipe).

Member of: UN, OAU.

Area: 964 km² (372 sq mi).

Population: 123 000 (1991 est).

Capital: São Tomé 35 000 (1989 est).

Language: Portuguese (official), Fang (90%).

Religion: Roman Catholic (50%).

Education: *Literacy rate:* 57.4% (1981). *Years of compulsory schooling:* (in theory) 3 years in total between the ages of 6 and 14. *Universities:* none.

Defence: *Total armed strength:* 900 (1991 est). *Military service:* none.

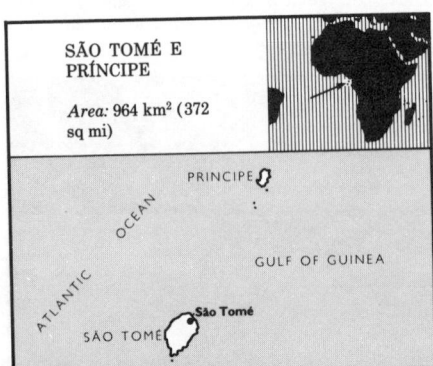

SÃO TOMÉ E
PRÍNCIPE

Area: 964 km² (372 sq mi)

PRÍNCIPE

OCEAN

GULF OF GUINEA

ATLANTIC

São Tomé

SÃO TOMÉ

GOVERNMENT

The 55-member National People's Assembly is elected by universal adult suffrage for five years. The President – who appoints a Prime Minister and Council of Ministers – is also directly elected. Political parties include the (left-wing former monopoly) MLSTP (Movimento de Libertação de São Tomé e Príncipe) and the (moderate) PCD (Democratic Convergence Party).
President: Miguel Trovoada.
Prime Minister: Norberto Jose Costa Alegre.

GEOGRAPHY

The republic consists of two mountainous islands about 144 km (90 mi) apart. There are no significant rivers. *Highest point:* Pico Gago Coutinho (Pico de São Tomé) 2024 m (6640 ft).

Climate: The climate is tropical. A wet season – with heavy rainfall – lasts from October to May.

ECONOMY

Cocoa is the mainstay of a largely agricultural economy. Most of the land is nationalized.

HISTORY

The islands are former Portuguese colonies. Early in the 20th century, the islands' plantations were notorious for forced labour. Independence was gained in 1975 as a one-party socialist state. An invasion and coup attempt failed in 1988. Economic difficulties led the country to lessen its dependence on the Soviet bloc, and in 1990 the MLSTP abandoned Marxism. The opposition PCD won multi-party elections in 1991.

SAUDI ARABIA

Official name: Al-Mamlaka al-'Arabiya as-Sa'udiya (The Kingdom of Saudi Arabia).

Member of: UN, Arab League, OPEC, GCC.

Area: 2 240 000 km² (864 869 sq mi).

Population: 15 267 000 (1992 est).

Capital and major cities: Riyadh (Ar Riyad) – the royal capital – 2 000 000, Jeddah (Jiddah) – the administrative capital – 1 400 000, Mecca (Makkah) 620 000, Medina (Al-Madinah) 500 000, Taif 205 000, Buraida 185 000, Abha 155 000 (all including suburbs; 1986 est).

Language: Arabic (official).

Religion: Islam (official) – Sunni (92%; mainly Wahhabi), Shia (8%).

Education: *Literacy rate:* 62.4% (1980 est). *Years of compulsory schooling:* schooling is available free of charge but not compulsory. *Universities:* 7.

Defence: *Total armed strength:* 76 500 (1991) (plus National Guard 35 000 and 20 000 tribal levies). *Military service:* none.

GOVERNMENT

Saudi Arabia is an absolute monarchy with neither formal political institutions nor parties. The King – whose official title in Saudi Arabia is 'Custodian of the Two Holy Mosques' – appoints a Council of Ministers. In 1991 it was announced that an 80-member consultative body would eventually be appointed.
King: HM King Fahd ibn Abdul Aziz Al Saud (succeeded upon the death of his brother, 13 May 1982).

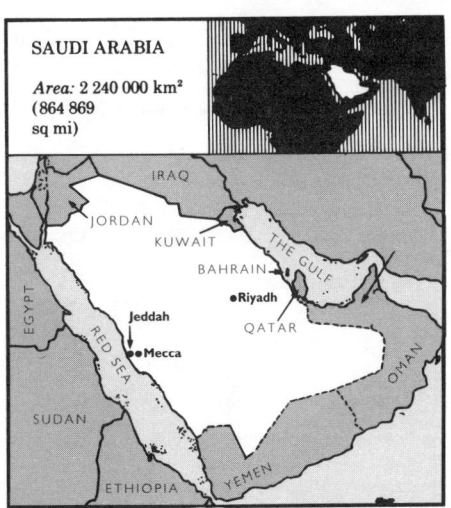

SAUDI ARABIA

Area: 2 240 000 km² (864 869 sq mi)

GEOGRAPHY

Over 95% of the country is desert, including the Rub 'al-Khali ('The Empty Quarter') – the largest expanse of sand in the world. The Arabian plateau ends in the west in a steep escarpment overlooking a coastal plain beside the Red Sea. There are no permanent streams. *Highest point:* Jebel Razikh 3658 m (12 002 ft).

Climate: The country is very hot – with temperatures up to 54 °C (129 °F). The average rainfall is 100 mm (4 in), but many areas receive far less and may not experience any precipitation for years.

ECONOMY

Saudi Arabia's spectacular development and present prosperity are based almost entirely upon exploiting vast reserves of petroleum and natural gas. Industries include petroleum refining, petrochemicals and fertilizers. The country has developed major banking and commercial interests. Less than 1% of the land can be cultivated.

RECENT HISTORY

In the 20th century the Wahhabis – a Sunni Islamic sect – united most of Arabia under Ibn Saud (1882–1953). In 1902 Ibn Saud took Riyadh and in 1906 defeated his rivals to control central Arabia (Nejd). Between 1912 and 1927 he added the east, the southwest (Asir) and the area around Mecca (Hejaz). In 1932 these lands became the kingdom of Saudi Arabia. Although the country has been pro-Western, after the 1973 Arab-Israeli War, Saudi Arabia put pressure on the USA to encourage Israel to withdraw from the occupied territories by cutting oil production. Saudi Arabia has not escaped problems caused by religious fundamentalism and the rivalry between Sunni and Shia Islam. In 1980 Saudi Arabia found itself bound to support Iraq in its war with Shiite Iran. Influenced by the Iranian revolution and the First Gulf War, Saudi Arabia formed the defensive Gulf Cooperation Council (GCC) with its neighbouring emirates. Saudi Arabia was threatened by Iraq following the invasion of Kuwait (August 1990), and played a major role in the coalition against Saddam Hussein in the Second Gulf War (1991).

SENEGAL

Official name: La République du Sénégal (The Republic of Senegal).

Member of: UN, OAU, ECOWAS.

Area: 196 722 km² (75 954 sq mi).

Population: 7 691 000 (1992 est).

Capital: Dakar 1 730 000, Thies 201 000, Kaolack 180 000, Ziguinchor 149 000, St Louis 126 000 (1992 est).

Languages: French (official), Wolof (36%), Serer (19%), Fulani (13%).

Religions: Sunni Islam (94%), Roman Catholic.

Education: *Literacy rate*: 38.3% (1990). *Years of compulsory schooling*: (in theory) 7–13. *Universities*: 3.

Defence: *Total armed strength*: 9700 (1991). *Military service*: 2 years (selective).

GOVERNMENT

Every five years the 120-member National Assembly is elected by universal adult suffrage. Sixty deputies are elected by a system of proportional representation on a national basis; the remainder represent single-member constituencies. The President – who is directly elected for seven years – appoints and leads a Cabinet. The number of political parties is constitutionally limited to three – the PS (Parti Socialiste), the (liberal) PDS, and the (Marxist) PAI. *President*: Abdou Diouf. *Prime Minister:* Habib Thiam.

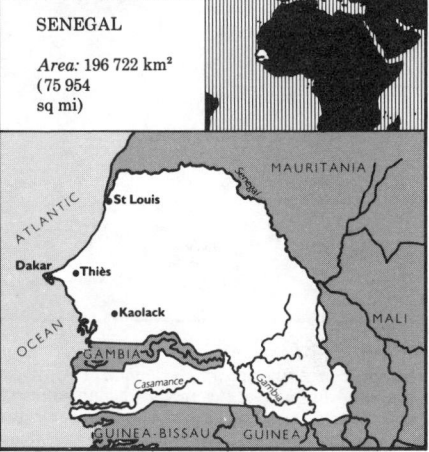

SENEGAL

Area: 196 722 km² (75 954 sq mi)

GEOGRAPHY

Senegal is mostly low-lying and covered by savannah. The Fouta Djalon mountains are in the south. *Principal rivers*: Sénégal, Gambia, Casamance. *Highest point*: Mont Gounou 1515 m (4970 ft).

Climate: Senegal has a tropical climate with a dry season from October to June.

ECONOMY

Agriculture involves over three quarters of the labour force. Groundnuts and cotton are grown as cash crops, and rice, maize, millet and sorghum as subsistence crops. The manufacturing sector is one of the largest in West Africa, but unemployment is high.

RECENT HISTORY

Senegal gradually came under French control from

the 17th century. A national political awareness developed early in the 20th century, and the country contributed substantially to the nationalist awakening throughout French Africa. After independence in 1960, under the poet, Léopold Sedar Senghor (1906–   ), Senegal maintained close relations with France, and received substantial aid. Attempted federations with Mali (1959–60) and Gambia (1981–89) were unsuccessful. Senghor retired in 1980, having re-introduced party politics.

SEYCHELLES

Official name: The Republic of Seychelles.

Member of: UN, OAU, Commonwealth.

Area: 454 km² (173 sq mi).

Population: 71 000 (1992 est).

Capital: Victoria 24 000 (1987 est).

Languages: Creole (95%), English and French – all official.

Religion: Roman Catholic (92%), Anglican (6%).

Education: *Literacy rate:* 75% (1990). *Years of compulsory schooling:* 6–15. *Universities:* none, but there is a polytechnic.

Defence: *Total armed strength:* 1300 (plus 800 paramilitaries) (1991). *Military service:* 2 years.

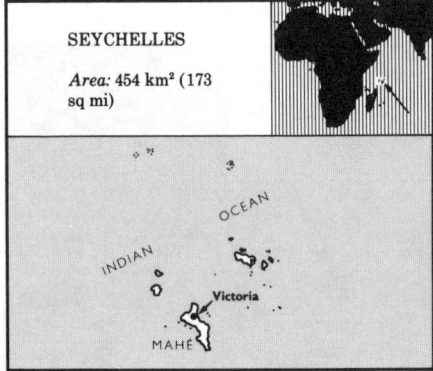

GOVERNMENT

The President – who appoints a Council of Ministers – is elected for five years by universal adult suffrage. The National Assembly comprises 23 directly elected members and 2 members appointed by the President. The (former monopoly) Seychelles People's Progressive Front is the main political party.
President: France Albert René.

GEOGRAPHY

The Seychelles consist of 40 mountainous granitic islands and just over 50 smaller coral islands. There are no significant rivers. *Highest point:* Morne Seychellois 906 m (2972 ft) on the island of Mahé.

Climate: The islands have a pleasant tropical maritime climate with heavy rainfall.

ECONOMY

The economy depends heavily on tourism, which employs about one third of the labour force.

RECENT HISTORY

The islands became a French colony in the middle of the 18th century, were ceded to Britain in 1814 and gained independence in 1976. The Prime Minister –

Albert René – led a coup against President James Mancham in 1977, and established a one-party socialist state seeking nonalignment. Attempts to overthrow René, including one involving South African mercenaries (1981), were unsuccessful. Multi-party elections were held in 1992.

SIERRA LEONE

Official name: The Republic of Sierra Leone.

Member of: UN, OAU, ECOWAS, Commonwealth.

Area: 71 740 sq mi).

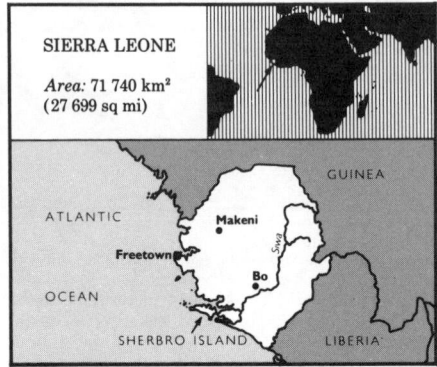

Population: 4 260 000 (1991 est).

Capital and main cities: Freetown 550 000 (city 470 000), Koidu (part of the Freetown agglomeration) 80 000, Bo 26 000 (1985 census).

Languages: English (official), Krio (Creole), Mende (34%), Temne (31%).

Religions: Animist (52%), Sunni Islam (39%), Anglican (6%).

Education: *Literacy rate:* 20.7% (1990 est). *Years of compulsory schooling:* schooling is not compulsory. *Universities:* 1.

Defence: *Total armed strength:* 3150 (1991). *Military service:* none.

GOVERNMENT

There is constitutional provision for a President – who appoints a Cabinet – to be elected for seven years by universal adult suffrage, and for a 124-member House of Representatives to be elected for five years. Power is currently exercised by a military council, but a return to multi-party rule has been agreed.
Head of state (Chairman of the National Provisional Ruling Council): Capt. Valentine Strasser.

GEOGRAPHY

The savannah interior comprises plateaux and mountain ranges. The swampy coastal plain is forested. *Principal rivers:* Siwa, Jong, Rokel. *Highest point:* Bintimani Peak 1948 m (6390 ft).

Climate: The climate is tropical with a dry season from November to June.

ECONOMY

Subsistence farming – mainly rice – involves the majority of the labour force. The decline of diamond mining has added to economic problems.

RECENT HISTORY

Freetown was founded by British philanthropists

(1787) as a settlement for former slaves, and became a British colony in 1808. The interior was added in 1896. Independence was gained in 1961. A disputed election led to army intervention (1967), and Dr Siaka Stevens – who came to power in a coup in 1968 – introduced a one-party state. An army junta seized power in 1992.

SINGAPORE

Official name: Hsing-chia p'o Kung-ho Kuo (Chinese) or Republik Singapura (Malay) or Republic of Singapore.

Member of: UN, ASEAN, Commonwealth.

Area: 623 km^2 (240 sq mi).

Population: 2 792 000 (1992 est).

Capital: Singapore 2 792 000 (1992 est).

Languages: Chinese (77%), Malay (14%), Tamil (5%) and English – all official.

Religions: Buddhist and Daoist (54%), Sunni Islam (15%), various Christian Churches (13%), Hindu (4%).

Education: *Literacy rate:* 87.2% (1988). *Years of compulsory schooling:* education is not compulsory. *Universities:* 5 (2 plus 3 institutes of university status).

DEFENCE

Total armed strength: 55 500 (1991 est) plus 11 600 paramilitary police and 100 000 civil defence force). *Military service:* 30 months enlisted men, 24 months officers.

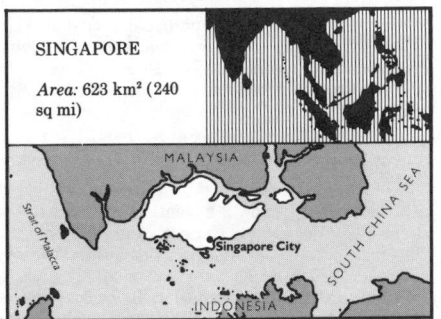

SINGAPORE

Area: 623 km^2 (240 sq mi)

MALAYSIA

Strait of Malacca

Singapore City

SOUTH CHINA SEA

INDONESIA

GOVERNMENT

The 81 members of Parliament are elected from single- and multi-member constituencies by universal adult suffrage for five years. There is constitutional provision for a small number of 'non-constituency' seats for non-elected members of the opposition. The President – who is elected by Parliament for four years – appoints a Prime Minister who commands a parliamentary majority. The PM, in turn, appoints a Cabinet which is responsible to Parliament. The constitution is to revised to create an executive presidency in 1993. The main political is the People's Action Party; other parties include the Singapore Democratic Party and the Workers' Party.
President: Wee Kim Wee.
Prime Minister: Goh Chok Tong.

GEOGRAPHY

Singapore is a low-lying island – with 56 islets – joined to the Malay peninsula by causeway. *Principal river:* Sungei Seletar. *Highest point:* Bukit Timah 177 m (581 ft).

Climate: The climate is tropical with monsoon rains from December to March.

ECONOMY

Singapore relies on imports for its flourishing manufacturing industries and entrepôt trade. Finance and tourism are important. Singapore has the second highest standard of living in Asia, after Japan.

RECENT HISTORY

Singapore was revived by Sir Stamford Raffles for the British East India Company (1819), and developed rapidly as a port for shipping Malaya's tin and rubber. It acquired a cosmopolitan population and became a strategic British base. Occupied by the Japanese (1942–45), it achieved self-government (1959), and joined (1963) and left (1965) the Federation of Malaysia. Since independence it has become wealthy under the strong rule of Prime Minister Lee Kuan Yew (1923– ; PM 1965–91).

SLOVAKIA

Official name: Republika Slovenská (Slovak Republic).

Member of: UN, CSCE.

Area: 49 025 km^2 (18 929 sq mi).

Population: 5 269 000 (1991 census).

Capital and major cities: Bratislava 442 000, Kosice 235 000, Nitra 212 000, Zilina 183 000 (all including suburbs; 1991 census).

Languages: Slovak (87%), Hungarian (12%).

Religions: Roman Catholic (60%), Evangelical Churches (6%).

Education: *Literacy rate:* no figures available. *Years of compulsory schooling:* 6–16. *Universities:* 6.

Defence: *Total armed strength:* c. 70 000 (1993 est). *Military service:* 2 years army; 3 years air force.

GOVERNMENT

The 150-member Assembly is elected by universal adult suffrage for five years. The Assembly elects a President who appoints a Prime Minister and a Council of Ministers, responisble to the Assembly. The main political parties are the (socialist) Movement for a Democratic Slovakia, the (centre) Christian Democratic Movement, the (former Communist) Party of the Democratic Left and the Slovak National Party.

SLOVAKIA

Area: 49 025 km^2 (18 929 sq mi).

POLAND

CZECH REPUBLIC

Kôsice

UKRAINE

AUSTRIA

Nitra

Bratislava

HUNGARY

ROMANIA

President: Michal Kovac.
Prime Minister: Vladimir Meciar.

GEOGRAPHY
Slovakia mainly comprises mountain ranges including the Tatra Mountains on the Polish border. The only significant lowlands are in the South adjoining the River Danube. *Principal rivers:* Danube, Vah, Hron. *Highest Point:* Gerlachovka 2655 m (8737 ft).

ECONOMY
Slovakia has a mainly agricultural economy into which heavy industry – particularly steel and chemicals – was introduced when the country was part of Communist Czechoslovakia. Wheat, maize, potatoes, barley and sheep are important. Varied natural resources include iron ore and brown coal. Slovakia has slowed the privatization of its uncompetitive out-ofdate factories.

RECENT HISTORY
On the collapse of the Habsburg Empire (1918), the Slovaks joined the Czechs to form Czechoslovakia. When Hitler's Germany dismembered Czechoslovakia in 1938, Slovakia became an Axis puppet state. A popular revolt against German rule (the Slovak Uprising) took place in 1944. Following liberation (1945) Czechoslovakia was re-established. After the Communist takeover in 1948, heavy industry was introduced into rural Slovakia. In 1968, moves by Party Secretary Alexander Dubček (a Slovak) to introduce political reforms met with Soviet disapproval, and invasion by Czechoslovakia's Warsaw Pact allies. The conservative wing of the Communist party regained control until 1989, when student demonstrations developed into a peaceful revolution. The Communist Party renounced its leading role. A new government, in which Communists were in a minority, was appointed. In 1990 free multi-party elections were held, Soviet troops were withdrawn and the foundations of a market economy were laid, but the pace of economic reform brought distress to Slovakia, whose old-fashioned industries were ill-equipped to face competition. Increased Slovak separatism led to the division of the country in 1993. Independent Slovakia faces possible tension concerning the large Hungarian minority.

SLOVENIA
Official name: Republika Slovenija (The Republic of Slovenia)
Member of: UN, CSCE, Council of Europe.
Area: 20 251 km² (7819 sq mi)
Population: 1 963 000 (1991 census)
Capital and major cities: Ljubljana 338 000 (city 286 000), Maribor 186 000 (city 105 000) (1991 census)
Languages: Slovene (91%), Serbo-Croat (5%)
Religion: Roman Catholic (over 90%)
Life expectancy:
Labour force:
Education *Literacy rate:* no figures available. *Years of compulsory schooling:* 7–15. *Universities:* 3.
Defence *Total armed strength:* 60 000 (1992 est). *Military service:* 12 months.

GOVERNMENT
The 240-member Assembly and a President – who appoints a Prime Minister and Cabinet – are directly

SLOVENIA

Area: 20 251 km²
(7819 sq mi).

elected by universal adult suffrage for four years. A new constitution is under consideration. The main political parties are the Liberal Democratis Party, the Christian Democrats and the (former Communist) Party of Democratic Renewal.
President: Milan Kucan.
Prime Minister: Janez Drnovsek.

GEOGRAPHY
Most of Slovenia comprises mountains including the Karawanken Alps and Julian Alps. In the E, hill country adjoins the Drava valley; in the W, Slovenia has a very short Adriatic coastline. *Principal rivers:* Drava, Sava, Mura. *Highest point:* Triglav at 2864 m (9396 ft).

Climate: The S and W have a Mediterranean climate; the N and E are more continental.

ECONOMY
With a standard of living approaching that of West European countries, Slovenia was the most industrialized and economically developed part of Yugoslavia. Industries include iron and steel, textiles and coal mining. Agriculture specializes in livestock and fodder crops.

RECENT HISTORY
The Slovenes arrived in the W Balkans in the 6th and 7th centuries. In the 9th century, the area was divided between several German rulers and only the Slovenes in the S (Carniola) resisted Germanization. Carniola became a Habsburg (Austrian) province in 1335 and, although it remained under Habsburg rule almost continuously until 1918, the Slovenes managed to preserve their national identity. Official encouragement of the Slovene language under Napoleonic French rule (1809–14) gave impetus to a Slovene national revival in the 19th century. When the Habsburg Empire collapsed (1918), the Slovenes joined the Serbs, Croats and Montenegrins in the new state that was renamed Yugoslavia in 1929. When Yugoslavia became a Communist federal state in 1945, the Slovene lands were reorganized as the republic of Slovenia. After the death of Yugoslav President Tito (1980), the federation faltered in nationalist crises. Slovenia, the wealthiest part of Yugoslavia, edged towards democracy. In free elections in 1990, nationalists gained a majority in the Slovene Assembly, which declared independence in June 1991. Following reverses in a short campaign, Yugoslav federal forces were withdrawn from Slovenia, whose independence gained widespread diplomatic recognition in 1992.

SOLOMON ISLANDS
Member of: UN, Commonwealth, South Pacific Forum.

Area: 27 556 km² (10 639 sq mi).

Population: 328 000 (1991 est).

Capital and main cities: Honiara 37 000, Gizo 3700 (1991 est).

Languages: English (official), Pidgin English, over 85 local (mainly Melanesian) languages (85%).

Religions: Anglican (34%), Roman Catholic (19%), other Christian Churches.

Education: *Literacy rate:* 60% (1985). *Years of compulsory schooling:* schooling is not compulsory. *Universities:* part of the University of the South Pacific.

Defence: *Total armed strength:* there are no armed forces.

GOVERNMENT

The 38-member National Parliament – which is elected by universal adult suffrage for four years – elects a Prime Minister who appoints a Cabinet. A Governor General is the representative of the British Queen as sovereign of the islands. The main political parties are the Solomon Islands United Party and the People's Alliance Party. It is expected that a federal republican system will be introduced during the 1990s.

Prime Minister: Solomon Mamaloni.

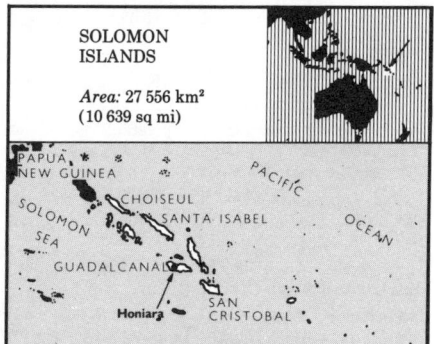

SOLOMON
ISLANDS

Area: 27 556 km²
(10 639 sq mi)

PAPUA
NEW GUINEA

PACIFIC

SOLOMON SEA

CHOISEUL

SANTA·ISABEL

OCEAN

GUADALCANAL

Honiara

SAN
CRISTOBAL

PROVINCES

Population figures are 1991 estimates.

Central Islands *Area:* 1286 km² (497 sq mi). *Population:* 21 000. *Capital:* Tulagi.

Guadalcanal *Area:* 5336 km² (2060 sq mi). *Population:* 61 000. *Capital:* Honiara (i.e. outside the province, see below).

Isabel *Area:* 4136 km² (1597 sq mi). *Population:* 16 500. *Capital:* Buala.

Makira *Area:* 3188 km² (1231 sq mi). *Population:* 25 000. *Capital:* Kira Kira.

Malaita *Area:* 4225 km² (1631 sq mi). *Population:* 87 000. *Capital:* Auki.

Temotu *Area:* 865 km² (334 sq mi). *Population:* 16 500. *Capital:* Santa Cruz.

Western Province *Area:* 9312 km² (3595 sq mi). *Population:* 65 000. *Capital:* Gizo.

Capital Territory *Area:* 22 km² (8 sq mi). *Population:* 37 000. *Capital:* Honiara.

GEOGRAPHY

The mountainous volcanic Solomons comprise six main islands and several hundred small islands. There are no significant rivers. *Highest point:* Mount Makarakomburu 2447 m (8028 ft).

Climate: The climate is tropical, with temperature and rainfall maximums from November to April.

ECONOMY

One third of the labour force is involved in subsistence farming, although copra, cocoa and coconuts are exported. Lumbering is the main industry.

RECENT HISTORY

The Solomon islanders were exploited as a workforce for plantations in other Pacific islands before Britain established a protectorate in 1893. Occupied by the Japanese (1942–45), the Solomons were the scene of fierce fighting, including a major battle for Guadalcanal. Independence was gained in 1978.

SOMALIA

Official name: Jamhuuriyadda Dimuqraadiga Soomaaliya (Somali Democratic Republic).

Member of: UN, Arab League, OAU.

Area: 637 657 km² (246 201 sq mi).

Population: 7 691 000 (1991 est).

Capital: Mogadishu 1 000 000, Hargeisa 400 000, Baidoa 300 000, Burao 300 000 (1986 est).

Languages: Somali (national), Arabic (official).

Religion: Sunni Islam (official).

Education: *Literacy rate:* 24.1% (1990 est). *Years of compulsory schooling:* (in theory) 6–14. *Universities:* 1.

Defence: Since 1991 there has been no national armed force.

GOVERNMENT

The constitution provides for an Assembly comprising 171 members – 165 elected by universal adult suffrage for five years and 6 appointed by the President who is elected by direct universal suffrage for a seven-year term. Since 1991 there has been no effective government.

GEOGRAPHY

Somalia occupies the 'Horn of Africa'. Low-lying plains cover most of the south, while semi-arid mountains rise in the north. *Principal rivers:* Juba, Shebelle. *Highest point:* Surud Ad 2408 m (7900 ft).

Climate: Somalia is hot and largely dry with rainfall totals in the north as low as 330 mm (13 in).

ECONOMY

Nearly two thirds of the labour force are nomadic herdsmen or subsistence farmers. Bananas are grown for export in the south, but much of the country suffers from drought. As a result of the civil war since 1991, much of the economic infrastructure of the country has been destroyed and famine is widespread.

RECENT HISTORY

In 1886 Britain established a protectorate in the north of the region, while the Italians took the south. In World War II the Italians briefly occupied British Somaliland. In 1960 the British and Italian territories were united as an independent Somalia. In 1969 the president was assassinated and the army – under Major-General Muhammad Siad Barre – seized control. Barre's socialist Islamic Somalia became an ally of the USSR. In 1977 Somali guerrillas – with Somali military support – drove the

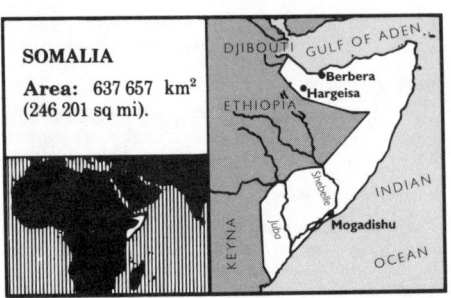

SOMALIA

Area: 637 657 km²
(246 201 sq mi).

Ethiopians out of the largely Somali-inhabited Ogaden. Somalia's Soviet alliance was ended when the USSR supported Ethiopia to regain the Ogaden. In the late 1980s dissident groups within Somalia challenged Barre. In January 1991 they overran the capital and deposed Barre, but rival groups seized districts in the north and south. The infrastructure of Somalia collapsed in bitter civil war. In 1992 a US-led force intervened to relieve famine victims.

SOUTH AFRICA

Official name: Republic of South Africa or Republiek van Suid-Afrika.

Member of: UN.

Area: 2 347 661 km² (906 437 sq mi) including Walvis Bay – 1124 km² (434 sq mi) – and the 'independent homelands' – 1 125 500 km² (434 558 sq mi).

Population: 33 140 000 (1991 est) including Walvis Bay – 21 000 (1985 census) – and the 'independent' homelands – 5 954 000 (1985 est).

Capital and major cities: Pretoria (administrative capital) 823 000 (city 443 000), Cape Town (Kaapstadt) (legislative capital) 1 912 000 (city 777 000), Bloemfontein (judicial capital) 233 000 (city 104 000), Johannesburg 4 000 000 (city proper 632 000; Greater Johannesburg 1 609 000), Durban 982 000 (city 634 000), Soweto (part of the Johannesburg agglomeration) 915 000, Port Elizabeth 652 000 (city 273 000), Sasolburg 540 000 and Vereeniging 540 000 are part of the Johannesburg agglomeration, East London 194 000 (city 85 000) (all including suburbs; 1985 census).

Languages: Afrikaans and English (both official), Xhosa (21%), Zulu (16%), Sesotho.

Religions: Dutch Reformed Church, independent African Churches, with Anglican, Methodist, Roman Catholic, Hindu and Sunni Islam minorities.

Education: *Literacy rate:* (1984) whites 93%, Asians 71%, coloureds 62%, blacks 32%. *Years of compulsory schooling:* 7–16 (7–11 for black children). *Universities:* 20 including 3 in 'independent homelands' and an open university.

Defence: *Total armed strength:* 124 000 (1991) (plus reserves and approximately 97 000 paramilitary). *Military service:* 1 year (whites).

GOVERNMENT

A new power-sharing transitional government, including a collective presidency, and a multi-racial constituent assembly are under discussion. Parliament consists of three chambers elected for five years – the House of Assembly elected by adult white suffrage, the House of Representatives elected by coloured (mixed race) voters, and the House of Delegates elected by Indian voters. The State President – who appoints a Cabinet – is chosen by an electoral college in which members of the (white) House of Assembly form a majority. Blacks have no parliamentary vote, but elect the Legislative Assemblies of the ten homelands. Four homelands – Bophuthatswana, Ciskei, Transkei and Venda – were granted 'independence' by South Africa, but this status was unrecognized internationally and – during 1993 – these homelands were effectively reabsorbed into South Africa. The main political parties are the (mainly Xhosa) African National Congress, the (mainly Zulu) Inkatha movement, the (mainly white conservative) National Party, the (white and mixed race) Democratic Party and the (white right-wing) Conservative Party.
President: Frederik Willem De Klerk.

SOUTH AFRICAN PROVINCES

Population figures are from the 1991 census.

Cape (Kaap) (includes Walvis Bay) *Area:* 641 379 km² (247 638 sq mi). *Population:* 5 514 000. *Capital:* Cape Town (Kaapstadt).

Natal *Area:* 55 281 km² (21 344 sq mi). *Population:* 2 074 000. *Capital:* Pietermaritzburg.

Orange Free State (Oranje Vrystaat) *Area:* 127 338 km² (49 166 sq mi). *Population:* 1 929 000. *Capital:* Bloemfontein.

Transvaal *Area:* 227 034 km² (87 658 sq mi). *Population:* 8 630 000. *Capital:* Pretoria.

HOMELANDS

Population figures are from the 1991 census – except for the 'independent homelands'.

Bophuthatswana (an 'independent' homeland) *Area:* 44 000 km² (16 988 sq mi). *Population:* 3 200 000 (1989 est). *Capital:* Mmabatho.

Ciskei (an 'independent' homeland) *Area:* 8500 km² (3280 sq mi). *Population:* 2 000 000 (1987 est). *Capital:* Bisho.

Gazankulu *Area:* 6565 km² (2535 sq mi). *Population:* 689 000. *Capital:* Giyani.

KaNgwane *Area:* 3823 km² (1476 sq mi). *Population:* 446 000. *Capital:* Louieville.

KwaNdebele *Area:* 3244 km² (1253 sq mi). *Population:* 297 000. *Capital:* Siyabuswa.

Kwazulu *Area:* 36 074 km² (13 928 sq mi). *Population:* 4 507 000. *Capital:* Ulundi.

Lebowa *Area:* 21 833 km² (8430 sq mi). *Population:* 2 102 000. *Capital:* Lebowakgomo.

Qwaqwa *Area:* 655 km² (253 sq mi). *Population:* 314 000. *Capital:* Phuthadithaba.

Transkei (an 'independent' homeland) *Area:* 41 002 km² (15 831 sq mi). *Population:* 2 876 000 (1985 est). *Capital:* Umtata.

Venda (an 'independent' homeland) *Area:* 6677 km² (2578 sq mi). *Population:* 460 000 (1985 est). *Capital:* Thohoyandou.

GEOGRAPHY

The Great Escarpment rises behind a discontinuous coastal plain and includes the Drakensberg Mountains. A vast plateau occupies the interior, undulating in the west and rising to over 2400 m (about 8000 ft) in the east. Much of the west is semi-desert, while the east is predominantly savannah grassland (veld). Walvis Bay is an enclave on the Namibian coast. *Principal rivers:* Orange (Oranje), Limpopo, Vaal. *Highest point:* Injasuti 3408 m (11 182 ft).

Climate: South Africa has a subtropical climate

with considerable regional variations. The hottest period is between December and February. Rainfall is highest on the east coast, but much of the country is dry.

ECONOMY

The country is the world's leading exporter of gold – which normally forms about 40% of South African exports – and a major producer of uranium, diamonds, chromite, antimony, platinum and coal (which meets three quarters of the country's energy needs). Industry includes chemicals, food processing, textiles, motor vehicles and electrical engineering. Agriculture supplies one third of South Africa's exports, including fruit, wine, wool and maize. The highest standard of living in Africa is very unevenly distributed between whites and non-whites. The withdrawal of some foreign investors has increased the drive towards self-sufficiency.

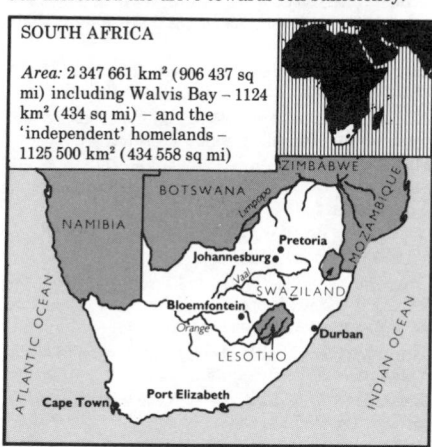

SOUTH AFRICA

Area: 2 347 661 km² (906 437 sq mi) including Walvis Bay – 1124 km² (434 sq mi) – and the 'independent' homelands – 1125 500 km² (434 558 sq mi)

RECENT HISTORY

Black African peoples were long established in what is now South Africa when white settlement began in the Dutch colony of Cape Town (1652). The conquest of the local African societies was only completed late in the 19th century. Britain acquired the Cape (1814), abolished slavery (1833), and annexed Natal (1843). The Boers (or Afrikaners) – of Dutch and French Huguenot descent – moved inland on the Great Trek (1835–37) to found the republics of the Transvaal and Orange Free State. After the discovery of diamonds (1867) and gold (1886), the Boers (Afrikaners) – led by Paul Kruger (1825–1904), president of the Transvaal – resisted British attempts to annex their republics, in which British settlers were denied political rights. This culminated in the Boer War (1899–1902). Although they lost the war, the Afrikaners were politically dominant when the Union of South Africa was formed (1910).

The creation of the African National Congress (ANC) in 1912 was a protest against white supremacy, and by the 1920s black industrial protest was widespread. South Africa entered World War I as a British ally, taking German South West Africa (Namibia) after a short campaign (1914–15); after the war, the territory came under South African administration. Despite strong Afrikaner opposition, South Africa – under General Jan Christiaan Smuts (1870–1950; PM 1919–24 and 1939–48) – joined the Allied cause in World War II. After the Afrikaner National Party came to power (1948), racial segregation was increased by the policy of apartheid ('separate development'), which deprived blacks of civil rights, segregated facilities and areas of residence by race, and confined black political rights to restricted homelands ('Bantustans'). Black opposition was crushed following a massacre of demonstrators at Sharpeville, and the ANC was banned (1960) by the government of Hendrik Verwoerd (1901–66; PM from 1958 to 1966, when he was assassinated). International pressure against apartheid increased. In 1961 South Africa left the Commonwealth, the majority of whose members continue to press for economic sanctions against South Africa. In 1966 the UN cancelled South Africa's trusteeship of South West Africa (Namibia), but South Africa continued to block the territory's progress to independence.

Black opposition revived in the 1970s and 1980s and found expression in strikes, the Soweto uprising of 1976, sabotage and the rise of the black consciousness movement. South African troops intervened in the Angolan civil war against the Marxist-Leninist government (1981) and were active in Namibia against SWAPO black nationalist guerrillas. P.W. Botha (1916– ; PM 1978–1984 and president 1984–89) granted political rights to the coloured and Indian communities, and implemented minor reforms for blacks. However, in 1986 – in the face of continuing unrest – Botha introduced a state of emergency, under which the press was strictly censored, the meetings of many organizations were banned and the number of political detainees – including children – rose sharply. His successor F.W. de Klerk released some ANC prisoners, and agreed to UN-supervised elections in Namibia leading to independence for that territory. In 1990 de Klerk lifted the ban on the ANC and released its imprisoned leader Nelson Mandela (1918–). In 1990–91, negotiations between the government and black leaders led to the dismantling of the legal structures of apartheid. Fighting between ANC and Inkatha supporters in black townships has caused concern. Negotiations concerning a new multi-racial constitution have continued intermittently but there has been a growing white right-wing movement against power sharing.

SPAIN

Official name: España (Spain).

Member of: UN, NATO, EC, WEU, CSCE, Council of Europe, OECD.

Area: 504 782 km² (194 897 sq mi) including the Canary Islands, Ceuta and Melilla.

Population: 39 952 000 (1991 census) including the Canary Islands, Ceuta and Melilla.

Capital and major cities: Madrid 4 846 000 (city 3 121 000), Barcelona 3 400 000 (city 1 707 000), Valencia 777 000, Seville (Sevilla) 754 000 (city 684 000), Zaragoza 614 000, Málaga 525 000, Bilbao 477 000 (city 372 000), Las Palmas de Gran Canaria 348 000, Valladolid 345 000, Murcia 329 000, Córdoba 309 000, Palma de Mallorca 309 000, Granada 287 000, Vigo 277 000, Alicante 271 000, L'Hospitalet (part of the Barcelona agglomeration) 269 000, Gijón 260 000, La Coruña 251 000, Cádiz 240 000 (city 157 000), Vitoria 209 000, Badalona (part of the Barcelona agglomeration) 206 000, Oviedo 203 000, Santander 194 000, Móstoles (part of the Madrid agglomeration) 193 000, Santa Cruz de Tenerife 192 000, Pamplona 191 000, Salamanca 186 000, Sabadell (part of the Barcelona agglomeration) 184 000, Jérez de la Frontera 184 000, Elche 181 000, Donostia-San Sebastián 174 000, Leganés (part of the Madrid agglomeration) 168 000,

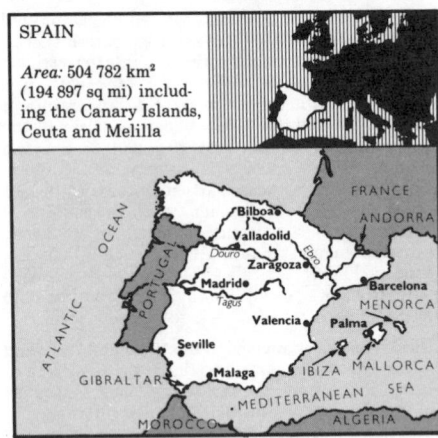

SPAIN

Area: 504 782 km²
(194 897 sq mi) including the Canary Islands, Ceuta and Melilla

Cartagena 172 000, Burgos 169 000 (all including suburbs; 1991 census).

Languages: Spanish or Castilian (official; as a first language over 70%), Catalan (as a first language over 20%), Basque (3%), Galician (4%).

Religion: Roman Catholic (98%); Sunni Islam (1%).

Education: *Literacy rate:* 97% (1985). *Years of compulsory schooling:* 6–16. *Universities:* 37 including an open university and 3 polytechnics of university status.

Defence: *Total armed strength:* 257 400 (1991) (plus 63 000 paramilitary Guardia Civil). *Military service:* 9 months.

GOVERNMENT

Spain is a constitutional monarchy. The Cortes (Parliament) comprises a Senate (Upper House) and a Chamber of Deputies (Lower House). The Senate consists of 208 senators – 4 from each province, 5 from the Balearic Islands, 6 from the Canary Islands and 2 each from Ceuta and Melilla – elected by universal adult suffrage for four years, plus 46 senators indirectly elected by the autonomous communities. The Congress of Deputies has 350 members directly elected for four years under a system of proportional representation. The King appoints a Prime Minister (President of the Council) who commands a majority in the Cortes. The PM, in turn, appoints a Council of Ministers (Cabinet) responsible to the Chamber of Deputies. The main political parties include the PSOE (Socialist Workers' Party), the (conservative) AP (Popular Alliance), the (left-wing coalition) Izquierda Unida (United Left, which includes the Communist Party), the (centre) CDS (Democratic and Social Centre), the (Catalan) Convergencia i Unio, and the (Basque) Herri Batasuna. Each of the 17 autonomous communities (regions) has its own legislature.
King: HM King Juan Carlos I (succeeded upon the restoration of the monarchy, 22 November 1975).
Prime Minister: Felipe Gonzalez Marquez.

SPANISH AUTONOMOUS COMMUNITIES

Population figures are from the 1991 census.
Andalusia (Andalucia) *Area:* 87 268 km² (33 694 sq mi). *Population:* 6 860 000. *Capital:* Sevilla (Seville).
Aragón *Area:* 47 669 km² (18 405 sq mi). *Population:* 1 179 000. *Capital:* Zaragoza.

Asturias *Area:* 10 565 km² (4079 sq mi). *Population:* 1 091 000. *Capital:* Oviedo.
Balearic Islands (Islas Baleares) *Area:* 5014 km² (1936 sq mi). *Population:* 703 000. *Capital:* Palma de Mallorca.
Basque Country (Euzkadi or Pais Vasco) *Area:* 7 261 km² (2803 sq mi). *Population:* 2 093 000. *Capital:* Vitoria.
Canary Islands (Islas Canarias) *Area:* 7273 km² (2808 sq mi). *Population:* 1 456 000. *Equal and alternative capitals:* Las Palmas and Santa Cruz de Tenerife.
Cantabria *Area:* 5289 km² (2042 sq mi). *Population:* 524 000. *Capital:* Santander.
Castile–La Mancha (Castilla–La Mancha) *Area:* 79 226 km² (30 589 sq mi). *Population:* 1 650 000. *Capital:* Toledo.
Castile–Leon (Castilla–León) *Area:* 94 147 km² (36 350 sq mi). *Population:* 2 538 000. *Capital:* Valladolid.
Catalonia (Catalunya) *Area:* 31 930 km² (12 328 sq mi). *Population:* 5 960 000. *Capital:* Barcelona.
Extremadura *Area:* 41 602 km² (16 063 sq mi). *Population:* 1 050 000. *Capital:* Mérida.
Galicia (Galiza) *Area:* 29 434 km² (11 364 sq mi). *Population:* 2 710 000. *Capital:* Santiago de Compostela.
Madrid *Area:* 7995 km² (3087 sq mi). *Population:* 4 846 000. *Capital:* Madrid.
Murcia *Area:* 11 317 km² (4369 sq mi). *Population:* 1 032 000. *Capital:* Murcia (although the regional parliament meets at Cartagena).
Navarre (Navarra) *Area:* 10 421 km² (4024 sq mi). *Population:* 516 000. *Capital:* Pamplona.
La Rioja *Area:* 5034 km² (1853 sq mi). *Population:* 262 000. *Capital:* Logroño.
Valencia *Area:* 23 305 km² (8998 sq mi). *Population:* 3 831 000. *Capital:* Valencia.

SPANISH ENCLAVES IN NORTH AFRICA

Ceuta and Melilla *Area:* Ceuta – 19 km² (7 sq mi); Melilla – 14 km² (5.5 sq mi). *Population:* 125 000. *Capitals:* Ceuta and Melilla.

GEOGRAPHY

In the north of Spain a mountainous region stretches from the Pyrenees – dividing Spain from France – through the Cantabrian mountains to Galicia on the Atlantic coast. Much of the country is occupied by the central plateau, the Meseta. This is around 600 m (2000 ft) high, but rises to the higher Sistema Central in Castile, and ends in the south at the Sierra Morena. The Sierra Nevada range in Andalusia in the south contains Mulhacén, mainland Spain's highest peak at 3478 m (11 411 ft). The principal lowlands include the Ebro Valley in the northeast, a coastal plain around Valencia in the east, and the valley of the Guadalquivir River in the south. The Balearic Islands in the Mediterranean comprise four main islands – Mallorca (Majorca), Menorca (Minorca), Ibiza and Formentera – with seven much smaller islands. The Canary Islands, off the coast of Morocco and the Western Sahara, comprise five large islands – Tenerife, Fuerteventura, Gran Canaria, Lanzarote and La Palma – plus two smaller islands and six islets. The cities of Ceuta and Melilla are enclaves on the north coast of Morocco. *Principal rivers:* Tagus (Tajo), Ebro, Douro (Duero),

Guadiana, Guadalquivir. *Highest point:* Pico del Tiede 3716 m (12 192 ft) in the Canaries.

Climate: The southeast has a Mediterranean climate with hot summers and mild winters. The dry interior has a continental climate with warm summers and cold winters. The high Pyrenees have a cold Alpine climate, while the northeast (Galicia) has a wet Atlantic climate with cool summers.

ECONOMY

Over 15% of the labour force is involved in agriculture. The principal crops include barley, wheat, sugar beet, potatoes, citrus fruit and grapes (for wine). Pastures for livestock occupy some 20% of the land. Manufacturing developed rapidly from the 1960s, and there are now major motor-vehicle, textile, plastics, metallurgical, shipbuilding, chemical and engineering industries, as well as growing interests in telecommunications and electronics. Foreign investors have been encouraged to promote new industry, but unemployment remains high. Banking and commerce are important, and tourism is a major foreign-currency earner with around 50 000 000 foreign visitors a year, mainly staying at beach resorts on the Mediterranean, Balearic Islands and the Canaries. After the G7 countries, Spain has the largest GNP in the world.

RECENT HISTORY

During the first half of the 19th century, Spain saw a series of struggles between liberal and monarchist elements, with radical republicans poised to intervene from the left and army officers from the right. In the Carlist Wars (1833–39, 1849 and 1872–76) the supporters of Queen Isabella II (1830 – 1904) – Ferdinand VII's daughter – countered the rival claims of her uncle Don Carlos and his descendants. Isabella was deposed in the revolution of 1868, which was followed by a short-lived liberal monarchy under an Italian prince (1870–73) and a brief republican experiment in 1873–4. In the last decades of the 19th century, the political situation became increasingly unstable, with anarchist violence, the turmoil of labour disturbances, pressure for provincial independence, and growing anti-clericalism. As a result of the Spanish-American War of 1898 the last significant colonial possessions – Cuba, the Philippines, Guam and Puerto Rico – were lost. The end of Spain's empire inflicted a severe wound to Spanish pride and led to doubts as to whether the constitutional monarchy of Alfonso XIII (1886–1941) was capable of delivering the dynamic leadership that Spain was thought to require.

Spain remained neutral in World War I, during which social tensions increased. A growing disillusionment with parliamentary government and political parties led to a military coup in 1923 led by General Miguel Primo de Rivera (1870–1930). Primo was initially supported by Alfonso XIII, but in 1930 the King withdrew that support. However, the range of forces arrayed against the monarchy and the threat of civil war led Alfonso to abdicate (1931). The peace of the succeeding republic was short-lived. Neither of the political extremes – left nor right – was prepared to tolerate the perceived inefficiency and lack of authority of the Second Spanish Republic. In 1936, nationalist army generals rose against a newly elected republican government. Led by General Francisco Franco (1892–1975) and supported by Germany and Italy, the nationalists fought the republicans in the bitter Spanish Civil War. Franco triumphed in 1939 to become ruler – Caudillo – of the

neo-Fascist Spanish State. Political expression was restricted, and from 1942 to 1967 the Cortes (Parliament) was not directly elected. Spain remained neutral in World War II, although it was beholden to Germany. After 1945, Franco emphasized Spain's anti-Communism – a policy that brought his regime some international acceptance from the West during the Cold War.

In 1969, Franco named Alfonso XIII's grandson Juan Carlos (1938–) as his successor. The monarchy was restored on Franco's death (1975) and the King eased the transition to democracy through the establishment of a new liberal constitution in 1978. In 1981 Juan Carlos played an important role in putting down an attempted army coup. In 1982 Spain joined NATO and elected a socialist government, and since 1986 the country has been a member of the EC. Despite the granting of some regional autonomy since 1978, Spain continues to be troubled by campaigns for provincial independence – for example in Catalonia – and by the violence of the Basque separatist movement ETA.

SRI LANKA

Official name: Sri Lanka Prajatantrika Samajawadi Janarajaya (Democratic Socialist Republic of Sri Lanka). Known as Ceylon until 1970.

Member of: UN, Commonwealth, SAARC.

Area: 65 610 km² (25 332 sq mi).

Population: 17 464 000 (1992 est).

Capital and major cities: Colombo (current capital) 1 459 000 (city 615 000), Sri Jayawardenepura Kotte (legislative capital and capital designate) 109 000 and Dehiwala-Lavinia 191 000 and Moratuwa 170 000 are all part of the Colombo agglomeration, Jaffna 143 000, Kandy 102 000, Galle 82 000 (1989 est).

Languages: Sinhala (official; 72%), Tamil (official; 21%), English (official).

Religions: Buddhist (69%), Hindu (15%), with Roman Catholic and Sunni Islam minorities.

Education: *Literacy rate:* 88.4% (1990). *Years of compulsory schooling:* 5–15. *Universities:* 9 including an open university.

Defence: *Total armed strength:* 88 500 (1991). *Military service:* none.

GOVERNMENT

The 225-member Parliament is elected for six years under a system of proportional representation by

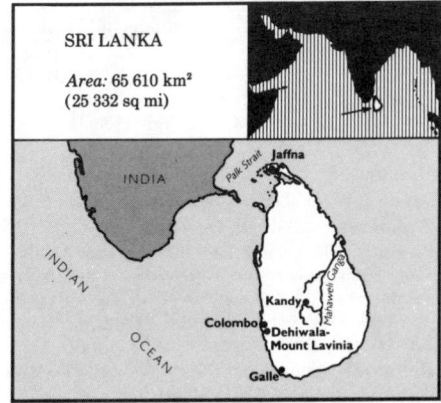

SRI LANKA

Area: 65 610 km²
(25 332 sq mi)

universal adult suffrage. The President – who is also directly elected for six years – appoints a Cabinet and a Prime Minister who are responsible to Parliament. The main political parties are the UNP (United National Party), the SLFP (Sri Lanka Freedom Party), the LSSP (Lanka Sama Samaja Party), the Communist Party, and several Tamil parties.
President: Dingiri Banda Wijetunga.
Prime Minister: Ranil Wickremasinghe.

GEOGRAPHY

Central Sri Lanka is occupied by highlands. Most of the rest of the island consists of forested lowlands, which in the north are flat and fertile. *Principal rivers:* Mahaweli Ganga, Kelani Ganga. *Highest point:* Pidurutalagala 2527 m (8292 ft).

Climate: The island has a tropical climate modified by the monsoon. Rainfall totals vary between 5000 mm (20 in) in the southwest and 1000 mm (40 in) in the northeast.

ECONOMY

About one half of the labour force is involved in agriculture, growing rice for domestic consumption, and rubber, tea and coconuts for export. Major irrigation and hydroelectric installations on the Mahaweli Ganga river are being constructed. Industries include food processing, cement, textiles and petroleum refining. Tourism is increasingly important.

RECENT HISTORY

From 1796 British rule replaced the Dutch in Ceylon, uniting the entire island for the first time. Nationalist feeling grew from the beginning of the 20th century, leading to independence in 1948, and a republican constitution in 1972. The country has been bedevilled by Tamil-Sinhalese ethnic rivalry, which led to major disorders in 1958, 1961 and since 1977. In 1971 a Marxist rebellion was crushed after heavy fighting. Sri Lanka elected the world's first woman Prime Minister, Sirimavo Bandaranaike (1916–   ; PM 1960–65 and 1970–77). In the 1980s separatist Tamil guerrillas fought for an independent homeland (Eelam). Fighting between rival Tamil guerrilla groups, Sinhalese extremists and government forces reduced the northeast to near civil war. An Indian 'peace-keeping' force intervened (1987), but this aggravated an already complex situation. Indian forces were completely withdrawn in 1990. The Tamils are scheduled to achieve a degree of autonomy. The Tamil Tigers guerrillas registered as a political party in 1989 but Tamil guerrilla activity continues in the northeast. Tension increased in 1993 following the assassination of President Premasada.

SUDAN

Official name: Al Jumhuriyat al-Sudan (The Republic of Sudan).

Member of: UN, Arab League, OAU.

Area: 2 505 813 km² (967 500 sq mi).

Population: 29 129 000 (1991 est).

Capital: Khartoum 1 334 000 (comprising Omdurman 526 000, Khartoum 476 000, Khartoum North 341 000), Port Sudan (Bur Sudan) 207 000, Wadi Medani 141 000, El Obeid 140 000 (1983 census).

Language: Arabic (over 50%; official).

Religions: Sunni Islam (70%), animist (22%), with various Christian Churches (8%).

Education: *Literacy rate:* 27.1% (1990). *Years of compulsory schooling:* schooling is free but not compulsory. *Universities:* 7 plus a polytechnic.

Defence: *Total armed strength:* 71 500 (1991) (plus 3000 paramilitary). *Military service:* compulsory (effective only in the north).

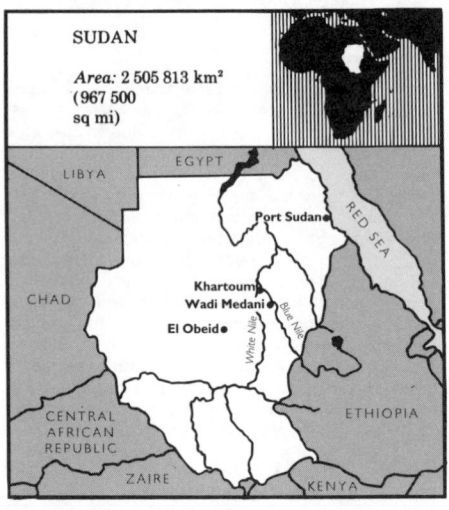

SUDAN
Area: 2 505 813 km² (967 500 sq mi)

GOVERNMENT

Since the military coup in June 1989, the country has been ruled by the 15-member Command Council of the Revolution of National Salvation, whose chairman is head of state and of government. Political activity has been suspended, although in 1991 a federal system comprising nine regions was instituted and a 300-member Transitional National Assembly has been appointed. In future, the Assembly will comprise representatives from the nine provinces, whose councils will consist of delegates from directly-elected popular committees.
Head of state and government: Lt. Gen. Omar Hassan Ahmed al-Bashir.

SUDANESE REGIONS

Population figures are from the 1983 census.

Bahr el Ghazal *Area*: 200 894 km² (77 566 sq mi). *Population*: 2 266 000. *Capital*: Wau (Waw).

Central Region (al-Wasta) *Area*: 139 017 km² (53 675 sq mi). *Population*: 4 013 000. *Capital*: Wadi Medani.

Dafur *Area*: 508 684 km² (196 404 sq mi). *Population*: 3 094 000. *Capital*: El Fasher.

Eastern Region (ash-Sharqiyah) *Area*: 334 074 km² (129 086 sq mi). *Population*: 2 208 000. *Capital*: Kassala.

Equatoria (al-Istiwaiyah) *Area*: 197 969 km² (76 436 sq mi). *Population*: 1 406 000. *Capital*: Juba.

Khartoum *Area*: 28 165 km² (10 875 sq mi). *Population*: 1 803 000. *Capital*: Khartoum.

Kurdufan *Area*: 380 255 km² (146 817 sq mi). *Population*: 3 093 000. *Capital*: El Obeid.

Northern Region (ash-Shamiliyah) *Area*: 476 040 km² (183 941 sq mi). *Population*: 1 083 000. *Capital*: ad-Damir.

Upper Nile (A'ali an-Nil) *Area*: 238 792 km² (92 198 sq mi). *Population*: 1 600 000. *Capital*: Malakal.

GEOGRAPHY

The Sahara Desert covers much of the north and west, but is crossed by the fertile Nile Valley. The southern plains are swampy. Highlands are confined to hill country beside the Red Sea and mountains on the Ugandan border. *Principal rivers:* Nile (Nil), Nil el Azraq (Blue Nile), Nil el Abyad (White Nile). *Highest point:* Kinyeti 3187 m (10 456 ft).

Climate: The south is equatorial, but the north is dry with some areas receiving negligible rainfall.

ECONOMY

Agriculture involves almost two thirds of the labour force, growing cotton for export, and sorghum, cassava and millet for domestic consumption. Since the early 1980s Sudan has been severely affected by drought and famine.

RECENT HISTORY

In 1820–21 Sudan was conquered by the Egyptians, who were challenged in the 1880s by an Islamic leader who claimed to be the Mahdi. The Mahdists took Khartoum, killed Sudan's Egyptian-appointed governor, General Charles George Gordon (1885), and created a theocratic state. Britain intervened, and from 1899 Sudan was administered jointly by Britain and Egypt. Nationalism developed strongly after World War I, but independence was only achieved in 1956. Sudan remains politically unstable, alternating between civilian and military regimes, the most recent gaining power in a coup in June 1989. The civil war between the Muslim north and the animist–Christian south that began in 1955 has intensified under the current Islamic fundamentalist government. Sudan is increasingly isolated internationally owing to its backing for Iraq and Libya.

SURINAME

Official name: Republiek Suriname (Republic of Suriname).

Member of: UN, OAS.

Area: 163 265 km² (63 037 sq mi).

Population: 417 000 (1991 est).

Capital: Paramaribo 246 000 (city 68 000), Nieuw Amsterdam 6000 (1988 est).

Languages: Dutch (official; 30%), Sranang Togo (Creole; 31%), Hindi (30%), Javanese (15%), Chinese, English, Spanish (official – designate).

Religions: Hinduism (28%), Roman Catholic (22%), Sunni Islam (20%), Moravian (15%).

Education: *Literacy rate*: 94.9% (1990). *Years of compulsory schooling*: 6–12. *Universities*: 1.

Defence: *Total armed strength*: 2200 (1991). *Military service*: none (abolished 1993–93).

GOVERNMENT

A 51-member National Assembly is elected for five years by universal adult suffrage. A President and a Vice-President – who is also the Prime Minister – are elected by the Assembly, and a Cabinet is appointed by the President. The main political parties are the New Front Coalition, the New Democratic Party and the (coalition) Democratic Alliance.
President: Ronald Venetiaan.
Prime Minister: Jules Ajodhia.

GEOGRAPHY

Suriname comprises a swampy coastal plain, a for-

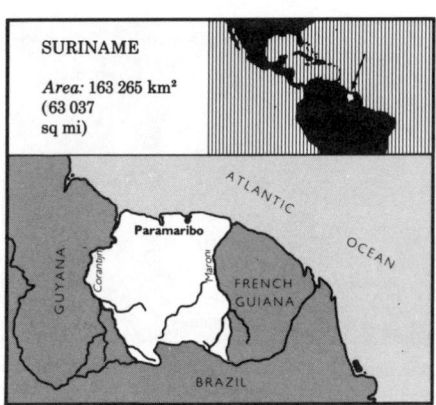

SURINAME

Area: 163 265 km² (63 037 sq mi)

Paramaribo

ATLANTIC OCEAN

GUYANA   Corantijn   FRENCH GUIANA   Maroni

BRAZIL

ested central plateau, and southern mountains. *Principal rivers*: Corantijn, Nickerie, Coppename, Saramacca, Suriname, Commewijne, Maroni. *Highest point*: Julianatop 1286 m (4218 ft).

Climate: Suriname has a tropical climate with heavy rainfall.

ECONOMY

The extraction and refining of bauxite is the mainstay of the economy. Other exports include shrimps, sugar and oranges. Economic development is hampered by political instability and emigration.

RECENT HISTORY

Dutch settlement began in 1602 and the area was confirmed as a Dutch colony in 1667. Suriname has a mixed population, including American Indians, and the descendants of African slaves and of Javanese, Chinese and Indian plantation workers. Since independence in 1975, racial tension has contributed to instability, and there have been several coups in which Col. Desi Bouterse played an important role. Constitutional rule was restored in 1991.

SWAZILAND

Official name: Umbuso Weswatini (The Kingdom of Swaziland).

Member of: UN, Commonwealth, OAU, SADCC.

Area: 17 363 km² (6704 sq mi).

Population: 798 000 (1991 est).

Capital and major cities: Mbabane – administrative capital – 39 000, Lobamba – legislative and royal capital – 6000, Manzini 52 000 (1986 census).

Languages: siSwati and English (both official).

Religions: Animist (majority), various Christian Churches (18%).

Education: *Literacy rate:* 67.9% (1985). *Years of compulsory schooling:* schooling is not compulsory. *Universities:* 1, plus 1 university centre.

Defence: *Total armed strength:* 2657 (1983) (plus paramilitary police). *Military service:* 2 years.

GOVERNMENT

Swaziland is a monarchy in which the King appoints a Prime Minister and Cabinet. The King is advised by the 20-member Senate and the 50-member House of Assembly, and appoints 10 members to both. Each of the 40 traditional tribal communities elects 2 members to the Electoral College, which in turn elects 10 members of the Senate and 40 members of the House

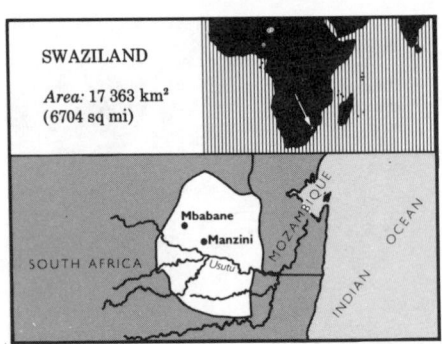

SWAZILAND

Area: 17 363 km²
(6704 sq mi)

Mbabane
•Manzini

SOUTH AFRICA

Usutu

MOZAMBIQUE

INDIAN OCEAN

of Assembly. No political parties are permitted.
King: HM King Mswati III (succeeded upon the
resignation of his mother as Queen Regent, 25 April
1986).
Prime Minister: Obed Dlamini.

GEOGRAPHY

From the mountains of the west, Swaziland descends
in steps of savannah (veld) towards hill country in
the east. *Principal rivers:* Usutu, Komati, Umbuluzi,
Ingwavuma. *Highest point:* Emlembe 1863 m (6113
ft).

Climate: The veld is subtropical, while the highlands are temperate.

ECONOMY

The majority of Swazis are subsistence farmers. Cash
crops include sugar cane (the main export).

RECENT HISTORY

The Swazi kingdom came under British rule in 1904.
The country resisted annexation by the Boers in the
1890s and by South Africa during the colonial period.
Following independence (1968), King Sobhuza II
suspended the constitution in 1973 and restored
much of the traditional royal authority. A bitter
power struggle after his death (1982) lasted until
King Mswati III was invested in 1986.

SWEDEN

Official name: Konungariket Sverige (Kingdom
of Sweden).

Member of: UN, EFTA, CSCE, Council of
Europe, OECD.

Area: 449 964 km² (173 732 sq mi).

Population: 8 586 000 (1990 census).

Capital and major cities: Stockholm 1 471 000
(city 679 000), Göteborg (Gothenburg) 720 000 (city
432 000), Malmö 466 000 (city 235 000), Uppsala
171 000 (city 168 000), Linköping 124 000, Orebro
122 000, Norrköping 121 000, Västeras 120 000, Jön-
köping 112 000, Helsingborg 110 000, Boras 102 000,
Sundsvall 94 000, Umea 93 000, Lund (part of the
Malmo agglomeration) 90 000 (all including suburbs;
1990 census).

Languages: Swedish (official), small Lappish
minority.

Religions: Evangelical Lutheran Church of
Sweden (over 90%), Roman Catholic (2%).

Education: *Literacy rate*: 100%. *Years of compulsory schooling*: 7–16. *Universities*: 13 plus 21 institutes of university status (including 7 university
colleges).

Defence: *Total armed strength*: 63 000 (1991) (plus
volunteer defence reservists 709 000). *Military service*: 7½–15 months army and navy, 8–12 months air
force.

GOVERNMENT

Sweden is a constitutional monarchy in which the
King is ceremonial and representative head of state
without any executive role. The 349-member Riksdag
(Parliament) is elected for three years by universal
adult suffrage under a system of proportional repre-
sentation. The Speaker of the Riksdag nominates a
Prime Minister who commands a parliamentary
majority. The PM, in turn, appoints a Cabinet of
Ministers who are responsible to the Riksdag. The
main political parties are the Social Democratic
Labour Party, the (conservative) Moderate Party,
the Liberal Party, the Centre Party, the (right-wing)
New Democracy Party, and the (former Communist)
Left Party.
King: HM King Carl XVI Gustaf (succeeded upon the
death of his grandfather, 15 September 1973).
Prime Minister: Carl Bildt.

GEOGRAPHY

The mountains of Norrland – along the border with
Norway and in the north of Sweden – cover two
thirds of the country. Svealand – in the centre – is
characterized by a large number of lakes. In the
south are the low Smaland Highlands and the fertile
lowland of Skane. *Principal rivers*: Ume, Torne,
Angerman, Klar, Dal. *Highest point*: Kebnekaise
2123 m (6965 ft).

Climate: Sweden experiences long cold winters
and warm summers, although the north – where
snow remains on the mountains for eight months – is
more severe than the south, where Skane has a
relatively mild winter.

ECONOMY

Sweden's high standard of living has been based
upon its neutrality in the two World Wars, its cheap
and plentiful hydroelectric power, and its mineral
riches. The country has about 15% of the world's
uranium deposits, and large reserves of iron ore that
provide the basis of domestic heavy industry and
important exports to Western Europe. Agriculture –
like the bulk of the population – is concentrated in
the south. The principal products include dairy
produce, meat (including reindeer), barley, sugar
beet and potatoes. Vast coniferous forests are the
basis of the paper, board and furniture industries,
and large exports of timber. Heavy industries include
motor vehicles (Saab and Volvo), aerospace and
machinery, although the shipbuilding industry – in
the 1970s the world's second largest – has ceased to
exist.

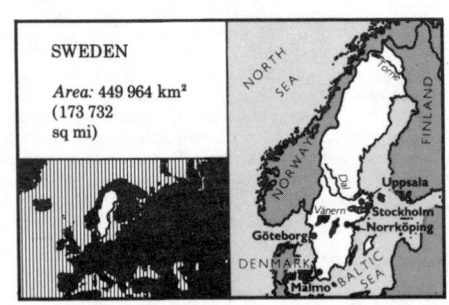

SWEDEN

Area: 449 964 km²
(173 732
sq mi)

NORTH SEA

NORWAY

FINLAND

Uppsala
Stockholm
Göteborg   Norrköping
Vänern

DENMARK

BALTIC SEA

Malmö

RECENT HISTORY

The founder of the present Swedish dynasty, the French marshal Jean-Baptiste Bernadotte, was elected crown prince to the childless king (1810), and succeeded in 1818. In 1814 Sweden lost Finland and the last possessions S of the Baltic, but gained Norway from Denmark in compensation. The union of Norway and Sweden was dissolved in 1905 when King Oscar II (reigned 1872–1907) gave up the Norwegian throne upon Norway's vote for separation. In the 20th century neutral Sweden has developed a comprehensive welfare state under social democratic governments. The country assumed a moral leadership on world issues but was jolted by the (unclaimed) assassination of PM Olof Palme (1986). In the 1990s economic necessity has obliged Sweden to dismantle aspects of the welfare system. The country has become a candidate for EC membership.

SWITZERLAND

Official name: Schweizerische Eidgenossenschaft (German) or Confédération suisse (French) or Confederazione Svizzera (Italian) or Confederaziun Helvetica (Romansch); (Swiss Confederation).

Member of: EFTA, CSCE, OECD, Council of Europe, UN (observer).

Area; 41 293 km² (15 943 sq mi).

Population: 6 820 000 (1991 est).

Capital and major cities: Berne (Bern) 299 000 (city 134 000), Zürich 839 000 (city 343 000), Geneva (Genève) 389 000 (city 165 000), Basel 359 000 (city 170 000), Lausanne 263 000 (city 123 000), Lucerne (Luzern) 161 000 (city 59 000), St Gallen 126 000 (city 73 000), Winterthur 108 000 (city 86 000), Biel/Bienne 83 000 (city 53 000), Thun 78 000 (city 38 000), Lugano 69 000 (city 25 000), Neuchâtel 66 000 (city 33 000), Fribourg (Freiburg) 57 000 (city 34 000), Schaffhausen 54 000 (city 34 000), Zug 52 000 (all including suburbs; 1990 est).

Languages: German (65% as a first language), French (18% as a first language), Italian (10% as a first language), Romansch (under 1%) – all official.

Religions: Roman Catholic (48%), various Protestant Churches (44%).

Education: *Literacy rate*: 99%. *Years of compulsory schooling*: 7–16. *Universities*: 10 including 2 polytechnics and 1 institute of university status.

Defence: *Total armed strength*: 1 100 000 (when mobilized; there is no standing army). *Military service*: 1 year between ages 20–50, with recall for training.

GOVERNMENT

Switzerland is a federal republic in which each of the 20 cantons and 6 half cantons has its own government with very considerable powers. Federal matters are entrusted to the Federal Assembly comprising the 46-member Council of States and the 200-member National Council. The Council of States is directly elected for three or four years with two members from each canton and one from each half canton. The National Council is elected for four years by universal adult suffrage under a system of proportional representation. The Federal Assembly elects a seven-member Federal Council – the equivalent of a Cabinet – for four years. The Federal Council appoints one of its members to be President for one year. All federal and cantonal constitutional amendments must be approved by a referendum. The main

political parties include the (liberal) Radical Democratic Party, the Social Democratic Party, the (conservative) Christian Democratic Party, the (centre) People's Party, and the Liberal Party.
President: Adolf Ogi (President for 1993).

SWISS CANTONS

Population figures are 1990 estimates.

Aargau (Argovie) *Area*: 1404 km² (542 sq mi). *Population*: 490 000. *Capital*: Aarau.

Appenzell: Ausser Rhoden (a half canton). *Area*: 243 km² (94 sq mi). *Population*: 51 000. *Capital*: Herisau.

Appenzell: Inner Rhoden (a half canton). *Area*: 172 km² (66 sq mi). *Population*: 14 000. *Capital*: Appenzell.

Basel-Land (a half canton). *Area*: 428 km² (165 sq mi). *Population*: 229 000. *Capital*: Liestal.

Basel-Stadt (a half canton). *Area*: 37 km² (14 sq mi). *Population*: 190 000. *Capital*: Basel.

Berne (Bern) *Area*: 6049 km² (2336 sq mi). *Population*: 937 000. *Capital*: Berne (Bern).

Fribourg (Freiburg) *Area*: 1670 km² (645 sq mi). *Population*: 204 000. *Capital*: Fribourg (Freiburg).

Geneva (Genève) *Area*: 282 km² (109 sq mi). *Population*: 373 000. *Capital*: Geneva (Genève).

Glarus *Area*: 684 km² (264 sq mi). *Population*: 37 000. *Capital*: Glarus.

Graubünden (Grisons). *Area*: 7109 km² (2745 sq mi). *Population*: 169 000. *Capital*: Chur.

Jura *Area*: 838 km² (324 sq mi). *Population*: 65 000. *Capital*: Delémont.

Lucerne (Luzern) *Area*: 1494 km² (577 sq mi). *Population*: 315 000. *Capital*: Lucerne (Luzern).

Neuchâtel *Area*: 797 km² (308 sq mi). *Population*: 159 000. *Capital*: Neuchâtel 66 000.

St Gallen *Area*: 2016 km² (778 sq mi). *Population*: 415 000. *Capital*: St Gallen.

Schaffhausen *Area*: 298 km² (115 sq mi). *Population*: 71 000. *Capital*: Schaffhausen.

Schwyz *Area*: 908 km² (351 sq mi). *Population*: 108 000. *Capital*: Schwyz.

Solothurn *Area*: 791 km² (305 sq mi). *Population*: 224 000. *Capital*: Solothurn.

Thurgau (Thurgovie) *Area*: 1006 km² (388 sq mi). *Population*: 202 000. *Capital*: Frauenfeld.

Ticino (Tessin) *Area*: 2811 km² (1085 sq mi). *Population*: 283 000. *Capital*: Bellinzona.

Unterwalden–Nidwalden (a half canton). *Area*: 274 km² (106 sq mi). *Population*: 32 000. *Capital*: Stans.

Unterwalden–Obwalden (a half canton). *Area*: 492 km² (190 sq mi). *Population*: 28 000. *Capital*: Sarnen.

Uri *Area*: 1075 km² (415 sq mi). *Population*: 34 000. *Capital*: Altdorf.

Valais (Wallis) *Area*: 5231 km² (2020 sq mi). *Population*: 244 000. *Capital*: Sion.

Vaud *Area*: 3211 km² (1240 sq mi). *Population*: 572 000. *Capital*: Lausanne.

Zug *Area*: 239 km² (92 sq mi). *Population*: 84 000. *Capital*: Zug.

Zürich *Area*: 1729 km² (668 sq mi). *Population*: 1 145 000. *Capital*: Zürich.

GEOGRAPHY

The parallel ridges of the Jura Mountains lie in the

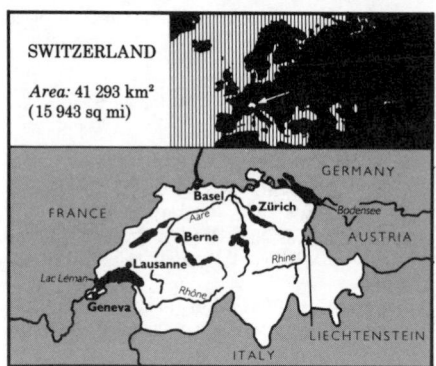

SWITZERLAND

Area: 41 293 km²
(15 943 sq mi)

northwest on the French border. The south of the country is occupied by the Alps. Between the two mountain ranges is a central plateau that contains the greater part of Switzerland's population, agriculture and industry. *Principal rivers*: Rhine (Rhein), Rhône, Aare, Inn, Ticino. *Highest point*: Dufourspitze (Monte Rosa) 4634 m (15 203 ft).

Climate: Altitude and aspect modify Switzerland's temperate climate. Considerable differences in temperature and rainfall are experienced over relatively short distances; for instance, the cold Alpine climate around the St Gotthard Pass is only 50 km (just over 30 miles) from the Mediterranean climate of Lugano.

ECONOMY

Nearly two centuries of neutrality have allowed Switzerland to build a reputation as a secure financial centre. Zürich is one of the world's leading banking and commercial cities. The country enjoys one of the highest standards of living in the world. Industry – in part based upon cheap hydroelectric power – includes engineering (from turbines to watches), textiles, food processing (including cheese and chocolate), pharmaceuticals and chemicals. Dairying, grapes (for wine) and fodder crops are important in the agricultural sector, and there is a significant timber industry. Tourism and the international organizations based in Switzerland are major foreign-currency earners. Foreign workers – in particular Italians – help alleviate the country's labour shortage.

RECENT HISTORY

Switzerland occupies a strategic position, but the Swiss have used their remarkable position to withdraw from, rather than participate in, European power politics. The French Revolutionary Wars saw the creation of a Helvetian Republic in 1798, but in 1803 Napoleon dismantled this unitary state and returned the country to a confederation. At the Congress of Vienna (1815) Swiss neutrality was recognized and the country gained its present boundaries. Continuing tensions in the early 19th century saw attempts by some cantons to secede and set up a new federation, but the compromises of a new constitution in 1848 – which is still the basis of Swiss government – balanced cantonal and central power. As a neutral country Switzerland proved the ideal base for the Red Cross (1863), the League of Nations (1920) and other world organizations, but Switzerland itself avoids membership of any body it considers might compromise its neutrality – referenda in 1986 and 1992 respectively confirmed that

Switzerland should not seek membership of the United Nations or of the EEA.

SYRIA

Official name: Al-Jumhuriya al-'Arabiya as-Suriya (The Syrian Arab Republic).

Member of: UN, Arab League.

Area: 185 180 km² (71 498 sq mi) – including the Israeli-occupied Golan Heights.

Population: 12 958 000 (1992 est).

Capital and major cities: Damascus (Dimashq) 1 451 000, Halab (formerly Aleppo) 1 445 000, Homs 518 000, Latakia 284 000, Hama 254 000 (1992 est).

Languages: Arabic (89%; official), Kurdish (6%), Armenian (3%).

Religions: Islam (official; Sunni 90%, Shia and Druze minorities), with various Orthodox and Roman Catholic minorities.

Education: *Literacy rate*: 64.5% (1990). *Years of compulsory schooling*: 6–12. *Universities*: 4.

Defence: *Total armed strength*: 404 000 (1991) (plus 400 000 reserves and 8000 paramilitary gendarmes) (30 000 of these troops were in the Lebanon mid-1991). *Military service*: 30 months.

GOVERNMENT

The 250-member National People's Assembly is elected by universal adult suffrage for four years. The President – who is directly elected for seven years – appoints a Prime Minister (to assist him in government) and a Council of Ministers. The National Progressive Front – including the ruling Ba'ath Arab Socialist Party, the Arab Socialist Union Party, the Syrian Arab Socialist Party, the Arab Socialist Party and the Communist Party – has a leading role.
President: Hafez al-Assad.
Prime Minister: Mahmoud Zubi.

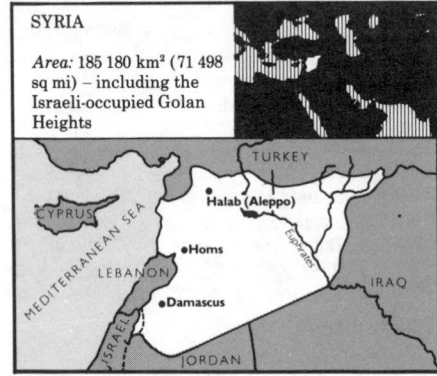

SYRIA

Area: 185 180 km² (71 498 sq mi) – including the Israeli-occupied Golan Heights

GEOGRAPHY

Behind a well-watered coastal plain, mountains run from north to south. Inland, much of the country is occupied by the Syrian Desert. *Principal river*: Euphrates (Al Furat), Asi (Orontes). *Highest point*: Jabal ash Shaik (Mount Hermon) 2814 m (9232 ft).

Climate: The coast has a Mediterranean climate. The arid interior has hot summers and cool winters.

ECONOMY

Petroleum is the main export although Syria's petroleum reserves are small by Middle Eastern standards. Agriculture involves nearly one quarter of the labour force, with cultivation concentrated in the coastal plain and irrigated land in the Euphrates Valley. Major crops include cotton, wheat and barley.

RECENT HISTORY

Ottoman rule in Syria lasted from 1516 until 1917, when a combined British-Arab army was led into Damascus by Prince Faisal ibn Husain. In 1920 independence was declared with Faisal as king, but the victors of World War I handed Syria to France (1920) as a trust territory. Since independence in 1946 Syria has suffered political instability. The pan-Arab, secular, socialist Ba'ath Party engineered Syria's unsuccessful union with Egypt (1958–61). Syria fought wars with Israel in 1948–49, 1967 and 1973, and in the 1967 Arab-Israeli War Israel captured the strategic Golan Heights from Syria. A pragmatic Ba'athist leader Hafiz al-Assad came to power in 1970 and allied Syria to the USSR. Assad's popularity has been challenged by Syria's increasing involvement in Lebanese affairs since 1976 and by Shiite fundamentalism. In 1990 Syria defeated the Lebanese Christian militia of Michel Aoun and restored the authority of the Lebanase government to the whole of Beirut. Since 1989–90, economic pressures lessened Syria's dependence upon the USSR. Syria's participation in the coalition against its old rival Iraq in 1990–1 gained greater international acceptance for Syria, which had attracted criticism for its sponsorship of terrorism.

TAJIKISTAN

Official name: Respublika i Tojikiston (Republic of Tajikistan).

Member of: UN, CIS, CSCE.

Area: 143 100 km² (55 300 sq mi).

Population: 5 358 000 (1991 est).

Capital and major cities: Dushanbe 604 000, Khodzhent (Khujand; formerly Leninabad) 157 000 (1989 census).

Language: Tajik (59%), Uzbek (23%), Russian (10%).

Religion: Sunni Islam majority.

Education: *Literacy rate:* No figures available. *Years of compulsory schooling:* 7–17. *Universities:* 1 university and 1 polytechnic.

Defence: *Total armed strength:* no figures available.

GOVERNMENT

A 230-member legislature and a President are elected for four years by universal adult suffrage. A new constitution is to be drafted. The main political parties are the Comunist Party, the Democratic Party and Islamic Renaissance.
President (acting): Imomali Rakhmonov.

GEOGRAPHY

The mountainous republic of Tajikistan lies within the Tien Shan range and part of the Pamirs.The most important lowland is the Fergana valley. *Principal rivers: Highest point:* Mount Garmo 7495 m (24 590 ft) – Mount Garmo was known as Pik Kommunizma (Communism Peak) when it was the highest mountain in the USSR.

Climate: High altitude and the country's position deep in the interior of Asia combine to give most of Tajikistan a harsh continental climate. The Fergana valley has a subtropical climate.

ECONOMY

Cotton is the mainstay of the economy. Other agricultural interests include fruit, vegetables and raising cattle. Major natural resources include coal, natural gas, iron ore, oil, lead, zinc and hydroelectric-power potential. Industries include textiles and carpet-making. The economy remains centrally planned and largely state-owned.

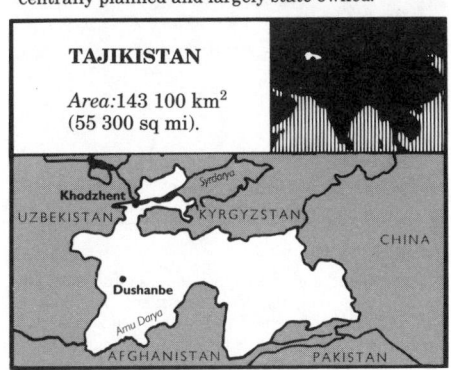

TAJIKISTAN

*Area:*143 100 km² (55 300 sq mi).

RECENT HISTORY

The Tajiks, who are an Iranian people, were included in the Persian Empire until the 8th century AD when the Arabs extended their influence over the area. In the 13th century the Tajiks were overrun by the Mongols and became part of the empire of Tamerlane (Timur) and his dynasty. A period of Uzbek rule was ended when the Afghans invaded in the 18th century. In the 19th century most of the Tajiks owed allegiance to the (Uzbek) khan of Bukhara. The area was annexed by Tsarist Russia (1860–68). After the Russian Revolution (see p. 438), the area was reoccupied by the Soviet Red Army (1920), but Tajik revolts simmered from 1922 to 1931. Tajikistan became a Union Republic within the USSR in 1929, declared independence after the abortive coup by Communist hardliners in Moscow (September 1991), and was internationally recognized when the Soviet Union was dissolved (December 1991). Since independence the country has been wracked by civil war between former Communists and Islamic fundamentalists.

TANZANIA

Official name: Jamhuri ya Muungano wa Tanzănia (Swahili) or The United Republic of Tanzania.

Member of: UN, Commonwealth, OAU.

Area: 945 087 km² (364 900 sq mi).

Population: 25 096 000 (1991 est).

Capital and major cities: Dodoma (legislative and de jure capital) 204 000, Dar es Salaam (administrative capital) 1 361 000, Mwanza 223 000, Tanga 188 000, Zanzibar 158 000 (1988 census).

Languages: English, Swahili (90%; 9% as a first language) – both official.

Religions: Sunni Islam (33%), animist (40%), Roman Catholic (20%), Hindu, Anglican.

Education: *Literacy rate:* 90.4% (1986). *Years of compulsory schooling:* 7–14. *Universities:* 2.

Defence: *Total armed strength:* 46 800, plus 1400 paramilitary Police Field Force and 110 000 citizens militia (1991). *Military service:* 2 years.

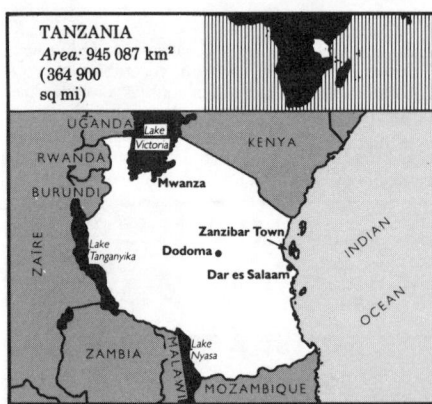

TANZANIA
Area: 945 087 km²
(364 900
sq mi)

UGANDA
RWANDA
BURUNDI
ZAIRE
KENYA
Lake Victoria
Mwanza
Zanzibar Town
Dodoma
Dar es Salaam
INDIAN
OCEAN
Lake Tanganyika
ZAMBIA
Lake Nyasa
MALAWI
MOZAMBIQUE

GOVERNMENT

The President is elected by universal adult suffrage for a five-year term. The President appoints a Cabinet of Ministers and two Vice-Presidents – one President of Zanzibar, the other concurrently Prime Minister. The 244-member National Assembly comprises 119 members elected from the mainland, 50 members directly elected from Zanzibar, plus appointed and indirectly elected members. Zanzibar has its own legislature. The main political party is the CCM (Chama Cha Mapinduzi – the Revolutionary Party).
President: Ali Hassan Mwinyi.
Prime Minister: John Malecela.

AUTONOMOUS STATE

Zanzibar *Area:* 1660 km² (641 sq mi). *Population:* 376 000 (1988 census). *Capital:* Zanzibar.

GEOGRAPHY

Zanzibar comprises three small islands. The mainland – formerly Tanganyika – comprises savannah plateaux divided by rift valleys and a north–south mountain chain. *Principal rivers:* Pangani (Ruvu), Rufiji, Rovuma. *Highest point:* Kilimanjaro 5894 m (19 340 ft), the highest point in Africa.

Climate: Tanzania has a tropical climate, although the mountains are cooler.

ECONOMY

Subsistence agriculture involves over 70% of the labour force. Cash crops include coffee, tea, cotton and tobacco. Mineral resources include diamonds and gold. Tanzania had a centrally planned economy, but more pragmatic policies have been implemented since 1985–87.

RECENT HISTORY

In 1964 Tanganyika and Zanzibar united to form Tanzania. Zanzibar – formerly an Omani possession – became an independent sultanate in 1856 and then a British protectorate (1890–1963). After independence in 1963 the sultan of Zanzibar was deposed in a radical left-wing coup. The mainland became the colony of German East Africa in 1884, the British trust territory of Tanganyika in 1919 and an independent state in 1961. President Julius Nyerere's policies of self-reliance and egalitarian socialism were widely admired, but proved difficult to implement and were largely abandoned by the time he retired as President in 1985. In 1992 amendments to the constitution to legalize a multi-party political system were presented to the National Assembly.

THAILAND

Official name: Prathet Thai (Kingdom of Thailand).
Member of: UN, ASEAN.
Area: 513 115 km² (198 115 sq mi).
Population: 57 150 000 (1991 est).
Capital and major cities: Bangkok 5 876 000, Nakhon Ratchasima (Khorat) 207 000, Songkhla 173 000, Chiang Mai 150 000, Chon Buri 164 000 (all including suburbs; 1990 census).
Language: Thai (official).
Religions: Buddhism (95%), Sunni Islam (4%).
Education: *Literacy rate:* 93% (1990). *Years of compulsory schooling:* between the ages of 7 and 15, 6 years schooling is compulsory. *Universities:* 19 including an open university and institutes of university status.
Defence: *Total armed strength:* 283 000 (1991). *Military service:* 2 years.

GOVERNMENT

Thailand is a constitutional monarchy. The constitution provides for a National Assembly, which comprises a non-political Senate – whose 270 members are appointed by the (military) National Peacekeeping Council – and a 360-member House of Representatives elected by universal adult suffrage for four years. The King appoints a Prime Minister who commands a majority in the House. The PM in turn appoints a Cabinet of Ministers responsible to the House. The main political parties include the (conservative) Samakkhi Tham, (right-wing) Chart Thai, the New Aspiration Party, the (liberal) Democrat Party, Palang Dharma (Righteous) Party, and (conservative) Social Action.
King: HM King Bhumibol Adulyadej (Rama IX) (succeeded upon the death of his brother, 9 June 1946).
Prime Minister: Anand Panyarachun.

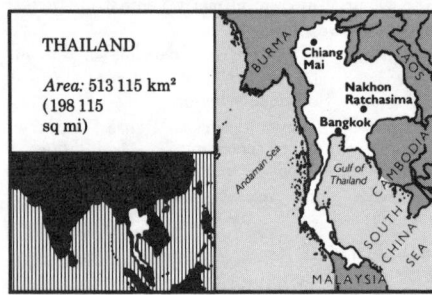

THAILAND

Area: 513 115 km²
(198 115
sq mi)

BURMA
Chiang Mai
LAOS
Nakhon Ratchasima
Bangkok
Andaman Sea
Gulf of Thailand
CAMBODIA
SOUTH CHINA SEA
MALAYSIA

GEOGRAPHY

Central Thailand is a densely populated fertile plain. The north is mountainous. The infertile Khorat Plateau occupies the northeast, while the mountainous Isthmus of Kra joins southern Thailand to Malaysia. *Principal rivers:* Mekong, Chao Pyha, Mae Nam Mun. *Highest point:* Doi Inthanon 2595 m (8514 ft).

Climate: Thailand has a subtropical climate with heavy monsoon rains from June to October, a cool season from October to March, and a hot season from March to June.

ECONOMY

Agriculture occupies two thirds of the labour force, mainly growing rice – Thailand is the world's largest exporter of rice. Other important crops include tapioca and rubber. Tin and natural gas are the main natural resources. Manufacturing – based on cheap labour – is expanding and includes textiles, clothes, electrical and electronic engineering, and food processing. Thailand achieved high economic growth rates throughout the 1980s and early 1990s. Tourism has become a major foreign-currency earner.

RECENT HISTORY

Thailand was known as Siam before 1939. Rama I (reigned 1782–1809), founder of the present Chakkri dynasty, moved the capital to Bangkok. His successors were forced to cede their claims over neighbouring lands to Britain and France. A constitutional monarchy was established by a bloodless coup (1932), whose Westernized leaders – Pibul Songgram and Pridi Phanomyang – struggled for political dominance for the next quarter of a century. During World War II Thailand was forced into an alliance with Japan. Since then Thailand has made a decisive commitment to the US political camp, which has brought major benefits in military and technical aid. Despite continuing army interventions in politics – in February 1991 the military took over the government for the 17th time in 50 years – Thailand has prospered. However, the stability of the country was compromised by the wars in Vietnam and by the continuing Cambodian conflict (until 1991). Constitutional rule was restored in 1992.

TOGO

Official name: La République togolaise (The Togolese Republic).

Member of: UN, OAU, ECOWAS.

Area: 56 785 km² (21 925 sq mi).

Population: 3 531 000 (1990 est).

Capital: Lomé 366 000, Sokodé 33 500, Kpalimé 25 500 (1983 est).

Languages: French, Ewe (47%), Kabre (22%) – all official.

Religions: Animist (50%), Roman Catholic (26%), Sunni Islam (15%), various Protestant Churches (6%).

Education: *Literacy rate*: 43.3% (1990). *Years of compulsory schooling*: (in theory) 6–12. *Universities*: 1.

Defence: *Total armed strength*: 5150 (1991) (plus 750 paramilitary gendarmes). *Military service*: 2 years (selective).

GOVERNMENT

The President – who appoints a Council of Ministers – is elected by universal adult suffrage for seven years. The 79-member National Assembly is elected for five years. The main political parties are the (former monopoly) Rassemblement du peuple togolais, the Coalition for Democratic Opposition (COD) and the Union of the Forces for Change (UFC).
President: Gen. Gnassingbe Eyadema.
Prime Minister: Joseph Kokou Koffigoh.

GEOGRAPHY

Inland from a narrow coastal plain is a series of plateaux rising in the north to the Chaine du Togo. *Principal rivers*: Moni, Oti. *Highest point*: Pic Baumann 983 m (3225 ft).

Climate: Togo has a hot and humid tropical climate, although the north is drier.

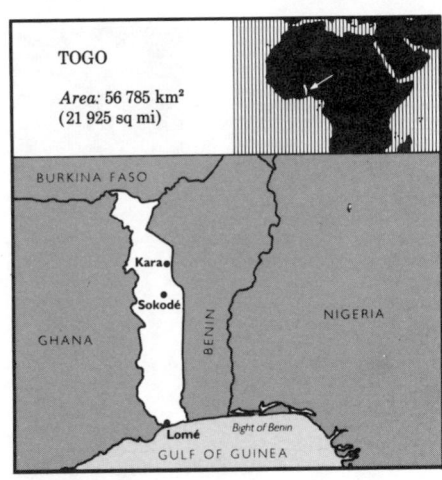

TOGO
Area: 56 785 km² (21 925 sq mi)

BURKINA FASO
Kara
Sokodé
GHANA
BENIN
NIGERIA
Lomé   *Bight of Benin*
GULF OF GUINEA

ECONOMY

The majority of the labour force is involved in subsistence farming, with yams and millet as the principal crops. Phosphates are the main export.

RECENT HISTORY

Colonized by Germany in 1884, Togoland was occupied by Franco-British forces in World War I, after which it was divided between them as trust territories. British Togoland became part of Ghana; the French section gained independence as Togo in 1960. Togo has experienced great political instability and several coups. Following anti-government protests, a multi-party system was restored in 1991.

TONGA

Official name: Pule'anga Fakatu'i'o Tonga (The Kingdom of Tonga).

Member of: Commonwealth, South Pacific Forum.

Area: 748 km² (289 sq mi).

Population: 97 000 (1991 est).

Capital and major towns: Nuku'alofa 28 900, Mu'a 4000 (1986 est).

Languages: Tongan, English.

Religions: Methodist (40%; official), Roman Catholic.

Education: *Literacy rate*: 90–95% (1985). *Years of compulsory schooling*: 5–14. *Universities*: none.

Defence: *Total armed strength*: a small land and marine force is maintained. *Military service*: none.

GOVERNMENT

Tonga is a constitutional monarchy. The King appoints a Prime Minister and other Ministers to the Privy Council, which acts as a Cabinet. The 31-member Legislative Assembly comprises the King, the Privy Council, 9 hereditary nobles (chosen by their peers) and 9 representatives of the people elected for three years by universal adult suffrage. There are no political parties.
King: King Taufa'ahau Tupou IV (succeeded upon the death of his mother, 15 December 1965).
Prime Minister: Baron Vea.

GEOGRAPHY

The 172 Tongan islands – 36 of which are inhabited –

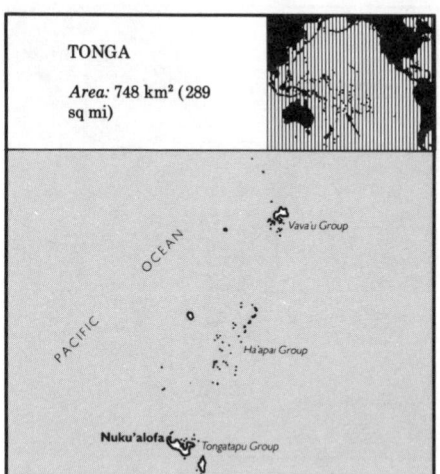

TONGA

Area: 748 km² (289 sq mi)

comprise a low limestone chain in the east and a higher volcanic chain in the west. There are no significant rivers. *Highest point:* Kao 1030 m (3380 ft).

Climate: The climate is warm with heavy rainfall.

ECONOMY

Agriculture involves most Tongans, with yams, cassava and taro being grown as subsistence crops. Coconut products are the main exports.

RECENT HISTORY

Civil war in the first half of the 19th century was ended by King George Tupou I (reigned 1845–93), who reunited Tonga, preserved its independence and gave it a modern constitution. From 1900 to 1970 Tonga was a British protectorate. Since 1987 pressure for constitutional reform has increased.

TRINIDAD AND TOBAGO

Official name: Republic of Trinidad and Tobago.

Member of: UN, Commonwealth, CARICOM, OAS.

Area: 5130 km² (1981 sq mi).

Population: 1 234 000 (1990 census).

Capital: Port of Spain 51 000, San Fernando 30 000, Arima 29 000 (1990 census).

Languages: English (official), Hindi (25%).

Religions: Roman Catholic (34%), Hinduism (25%), Anglican (15%), Sunni Islam (6%).

Education: *Literacy rate:* 96.1% (1985). *Years of compulsory schooling:* 5–11. *Universities:* 1.

Defence: *Total armed strength:* 2650 (1991) (plus 4000 paramilitary police). *Military service:* none.

GOVERNMENT

The 31-member Senate – the Upper House of Parliament – is appointed by the President, who is elected by a joint sitting of Parliament. The 36-member House of Representatives is elected for five years by universal adult suffrage. The President appoints a Prime Minister who commands a majority in the House. The PM, in turn, appoints a Cabinet, which is responsible to the House. The main political parties include the (socialist coalition) National Alliance for Reconstruction, the (centre) People's National Movement, and the (socialist) United National Congress. Tobago has full internal self-government.

President: Noor Mohammed Hassanali.
Prime Minister: Patrick Manning.

AUTONOMOUS ISLAND

Tobago *Area:* 301 km² (116 sq mi). *Population:* 50 000 (1990 census). *Capital:* Scarborough.

GEOGRAPHY

Trinidad is generally undulating. Tobago is more mountainous. *Principal rivers:* Caroni, Orotoire, Oropuche. *Highest point:* Cerro Aripo 940 m (3085 ft) in Trinidad.

Climate: Trinidad has a humid tropical climate, with a dry season from January to May.

ECONOMY

Petroleum and petrochemicals are the mainstay of the economy. Trinidad also has important reserves of natural gas and asphalt. Tourism is a major foreign-currency earner.

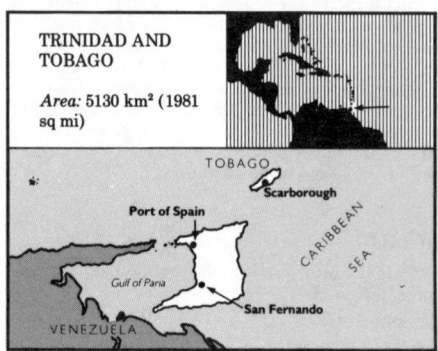

TRINIDAD AND TOBAGO

Area: 5130 km² (1981 sq mi)

RECENT HISTORY

Trinidad became British in 1797; Tobago was ceded to Britain in 1802. African slaves were imported to work sugar plantations, but after the abolition of slavery in the 1830s, labourers came from India. The islands merged as a single colony in 1899 and gained independence in 1962 under Dr Eric Williams. His moderate policies brought economic benefits but provoked a Black Power revolt and an army mutiny in 1970. The country has been a republic since 1976. In July 1990, a small group of Islamic fundamentalists held the PM and several government ministers and parliamentarians hostage during an attempted coup.

TUNISIA

Official name: Al-Jumhuriya at-Tunisiya (Republic of Tunisia).

Member of: UN, Arab League, OAU.

Area: 163 610 km² (63 170 sq mi).

Population: 8 413 000 (1992 est).

Capital and major cities: Tunis 1 420 000 (city 620 000), Sfax (Safaqis) 222 000, Aryanah 131 000 and Ettadhamen 112 000 are both part of the Tunis agglomeration, Sousse (Susah) 102 000 (all including suburbs; 1989 est).

Languages: Arabic (official), Berber minority.

Religion: Sunni Islam (official; 99%).

Education: *Literacy rate:* 65.3% (1990). *Years of compulsory schooling:* schooling is not compulsory. *Universities:* 5.

Defence: *Total armed strength:* 35 000 (1991) (plus

3500 paramilitaries Public Order Brigade and 10 000 National Guard).

GOVERNMENT

The President and the 141-member National Assembly are elected by universal adult suffrage for a five-year term. The President appoints a Cabinet, headed by a Prime Minister. The main political parties are the (socialist) RCD (Democratic Constitutional Rally), the MDS (Movement of Democratic Socialists), and independents standing for the (banned Islamic) Renaissance Party.
President: Zine el-Abidine Ben Ali.
Prime Minister: Hamed Karoui.

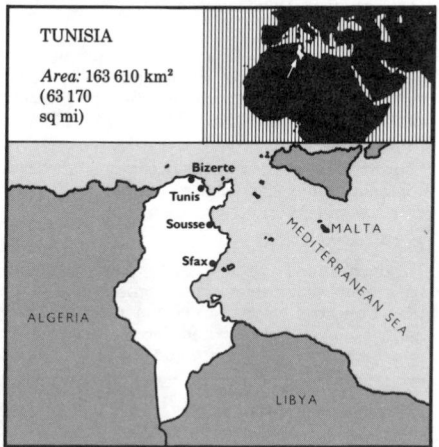

TUNISIA

Area: 163 610 km²
(63 170 sq mi)

Bizerte
Tunis
Sousse
Sfax
MEDITERRANEAN SEA
MALTA
ALGERIA
LIBYA

GEOGRAPHY

The north is occupied by the Northern Tell and High Tell mountains. Wide plateaux cover central Tunisia. The Sahara Desert lies south of a zone of shallow salt lakes. *Principal river*: Medjerda. *Highest point*: Jabal ash-Shanabi 1544 m (5066 ft).

Climate: The north has a Mediterranean climate with adequate rainfall. The south has a hot dry climate.

ECONOMY

Phosphates and petroleum are the mainstay of the economy, normally providing over 40% of Tunisia's exports. The principal crops are wheat, barley and vegetables, as well as olives and citrus fruit for export. Tourism is a major foreign-currency earner.

RECENT HISTORY

In 1881 France established a protectorate, although the key (monarch) remained the nominal ruler. Nationalist sentiments grew in the 20th century. Tunisia was occupied by the Germans from 1942 to 1943, but French rule was restored until 1956, when independence was gained under Habib Bourguiba (1903–). In 1957 the monarchy was abolished. In the late 1980s the regime became increasingly unpopular and intolerant of opposition. Since Bourguiba was deposed by his PM (1988) – because of 'incapacity' – multi-party politics have been permitted.

TURKEY

Official name: Türkiye Cumhuriyeti (Republic of Turkey).

Member of: UN, NATO, OECD, CSCE, Council of Europe, WEU (associate).

Area 779 452 km² (300 948 sq mi).

Population: 58 376 000 (1991 est).

Capital and major cities: Ankara 2 560 000, Istanbul 6 620 000, Izmir 1 757 000, Adana 916 000, Bursa 835 000, Gaziantep 603 000, Konya 513 000, Mersin (Icel) 422 000, Kayseri 421 000, Eskisehir 413 000, Diyarbakir 381 000, Antalya 378 000, Samsun 304 000 (all including suburbs; 1990 census).

Languages: Turkish (official); Kurdish (20%).

Religion: Sunni Islam (67%), Shia Islam (30%), various Christian Churches (3%).

Education: *Literacy rate*: 80.7% (1989). *Years of compulsory schooling*: Between the ages of 6–14, 5 years schooling is compulsory. *Universities*: 29.

Defence: *Total armed strength*: 579 200 (1991) (plus 120 000 gendarmes). *Military service*: 18 months (army only).

GOVERNMENT

The 450-member National Assembly is elected by universal adult suffrage for five years. The President – who is elected by the Assembly for seven years – appoints a Prime Minister and a Cabinet commanding a majority in the Assembly. The main political parties are the (conservative) Motherland Party, the Social Democratic Populist Party, the True Path Party, the Prosperity Party, and the Democratic Left.
President: Suleyman Demirel.
Prime Minister (interim): Erdal Inonu.

GEOGRAPHY

Turkey west of the Dardenelles – 5% of the total area – is part of Europe. Asiatic Turkey consists of the central Anatolian Plateau and its basins, bordered to the north by the Pontic Mountains, to the south by the Taurus Mountains, and to the east in high ranges bordering the Caucasus. *Principal rivers:* Euphrates (Firat), Tigris (Dicle), Kizilirmak (Halys), Sakarya. *Highest point*: Büyük Ağridaği (Mount Ararat) 5185 m (17 011 ft).

Climate: The coastal regions have a Mediterranean climate. The interior is continental with hot, dry summers and cold, snowy winters.

ECONOMY

Agriculture involves just under one half of the labour force. Major crops include wheat, rice, tobacco, and cotton. Both tobacco and cotton have given rise to important processing industries, and textiles account for one quarter of Turkey's exports. Manufacturing – in particular the chemical and steel industries – has grown rapidly. Natural resources include copper, coal and chromium. Unemployment is severe. Money sent back by the large number of Turks working in Western Europe is a major source of foreign currency. Tourism is increasingly important.

RECENT HISTORY

At the beginning of the 19th century, the (Turkish) Ottoman Empire extended from the Danube to Aden, and from the Euphrates to Algiers. The empire was, however, suffering a long decline in military and political might and in extent. The Ottoman Empire came to be regarded as 'the sick man of Europe', and the future of the empire and its Balkan territories troubled the 19th century as 'the Eastern Question'. In 1908 the Young Turks revolt attempted to stop the decline, but defeat in the Balkan Wars (1912–13) virtually expelled Turkey from Europe.

Alliance with Germany in World War I ended in defeat and the loss of all non-Turkish areas. The future of Turkey in Asia itself seemed in doubt when Greece took the area around Izmir and the Allies defined zones of influence. General Mustafa Kemal (1881–1938) – later known as Atatürk ('father of the Turks') – led forces of resistance in a civil war and went on to defeat Greece. Turkey's present boundaries were established in 1923 by the Treaty of Lausanne. With the abolition of the sultanate (1922) Turkey became a republic, which Atatürk transformed into a secular Westernized state. Islam was disestablished, Arabic script was replaced by the Latin alphabet, the Turkish language was revived, and women's veils were banned.

Soviet claims on Turkish territory in 1945 encouraged a pro-Western outlook, and in 1952 Turkey

TURKEY

Area 779 452 km²
(300 948 sq mi).

joined NATO. PM Adnan Menderes was overthrown by a military coup in 1960 and hanged on charges of corruption and unconstitutional rule. Civilian government was restored in 1961, but a pattern of violence and ineffective government led to a further army takeover in 1980. In 1974, after President Makarios was overthrown in Cyprus by a Greek-sponsored coup, Turkey invaded the island and set up a Turkish administration in the N (1975). Differences with Greece over Cyprus have damaged the country's attempts to join the EC, as has the country's record on human rights.

In 1983 civilian rule replaced the military government. Since then Turkey has drawn as close as possible to Western Europe, although the emergence of Islamic fundamentalism in the late 1980s has raised doubts concerning Turkey's European identity. Since the dissolution of the USSR (1991), Turkey has forged economic and cultural links with the former Soviet republics of Central Asia, most of which are Turkic in language and tradition. Unrest among Turley's ethnic Kurds – in the southeast – has increased.

TURKMENISTAN

Official name: Tiurkmenostan (Turkmenistan).

Member of: UN, CIS, CSCE, ECO.

Area: 488 100 km² (188 500 sq mi).

Population: 3 714 000 (1991 est).

Capital and major cities: Ashkabad (Ashgabat) 411 000, Chardzhou (Charjew) 166 000 (1989 census).

Languages: Turkmen (72%), Russian (9%), Uzbek (9%), Kazakh (3%).

Religion: Sunni Islam majority.

Education: *Literacy rate:* no figures available. *Years of compulsory schooling:* 7–15. *Universities:* 1 university and 1 polytechnic.

Defence: *Total armed strength:* no figures available. *Military service:* 18 months.

GOVERNMENT

A 50-member (Majlis) legislature and a President are elected by universal adult suffrage for four years. A new constitution is to be drafted. The main political parties are the (former Communist) Democratic Party, Agzybirlik, and the Party of Islamic Renaissance. The Democratic Party has a leading role.
President: Saparmuryad Niyazov.
Prime Minister: Khan Akhmedov.

GEOGRAPHY

The sandy Kara-Kum Desert occupies the centre of the republic, over 90% of which is desert. The Kopet Dag mountains form the border with Iran. *Principal rivers:* Amu Darya, Murgah. *Highest point:* Firyuza 2942 m (9652 ft).

Climate: Turkmenistan has a continental climate characterized by hot summers, freezing winters and very low precipitation.

ECONOMY

Turkmenistan is rich in oil and natural gas. Industries include engineering, metal processing and textiles. Collective farms grow cotton under irrigation and raise sheep, camels and horses. The economy remains largely state-owned and centrally planned.

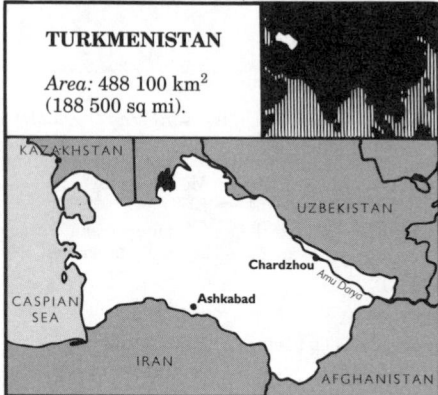

TURKMENISTAN

Area: 488 100 km²
(188 500 sq mi).

RECENT HISTORY

The Turkmens are a nomadic Turkic people who were nominally subject to Persia, or to the khans of Khiva and Bukhara (now both in Uzbekistan), before coming under Russian rule between 1869 and 1881. The Turkmens fiercely resisted the Russians and rose in revolt in 1916. An autonomous Transcaspian government was formed after the Russian Revolution (see p. 438), and the area was not brought under Soviet control until the Red Army invaded in 1919. The Turkmen territories were reorganized as the Republic of Turkmenistan in 1924 and admitted to the USSR as a full Union Republic in 1925. Independence was declared following the abortive coup by Communist hardliners in Moscow (September 1991), and the republic received international recognition when the USSR was dissolved (December 1991).

TUVALU

Member of: Commonwealth (special member), South Pacific Forum.

Area: 26 km² (10 sq mi).

Population: 9300 (1991 est).

Capital: Fongafale (on Funafuti) 2800 (1985 est).

Languages: Tuvaluan and English.

Religion: Protestant Church of Tuvalu (98%).

Education: *Literacy rate*: 45%. *Years of compulsory schooling*: 6–12. *Universities*: 1 extension centre of the (Fijian-based) University of the South Pacific.

Defence: *Total armed strength*: there are no armed forces.

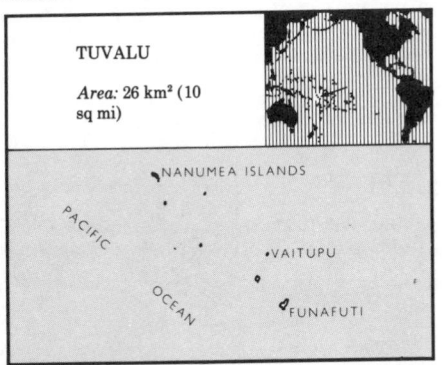

GOVERNMENT

The 12-member Parliament – which is elected by universal adult suffrage for four years – chooses a Prime Minister who appoints other Ministers. A Governor General represents the British Queen as sovereign of Tuvalu. There are no political parties. *Prime Minister*: Bikenibeu Paeniu.

GEOGRAPHY

Tuvalu comprises nine small islands. There are no rivers. *Highest point*: an unnamed point, 6 m (20 ft).

Climate: Tuvalu experiences high temperatures and heavy rainfall of 3000–4000 mm (120–160 in) per year.

ECONOMY

Subsistence farming – based on coconuts, pigs and poultry – involves the majority of the population. The only export is copra from coconuts.

RECENT HISTORY

Tuvalu was claimed for Britain in 1892 as the Ellice Islands, which became linked administratively with the Gilbert Islands. A referendum in 1974 showed a majority of Polynesians in the Ellice Islands in favour of separation from the Micronesians of the Gilbert Islands (Kiribati). Independence was achieved as Tuvalu in 1978.

UGANDA

Official name: The Republic of Uganda.

Member of: UN, Commonwealth, OAU.

Area: 241 139 km² (93 104 sq mi).

Population: 16 583 000 (1991 census).

Capital: Kampala 773 000, Jinja 61 000, Mbale 54 000, Masaka 49 000, Entebbe 42 000 (1991 census).

Languages: English and Swahili (both official), with local languages including Luganda.

Religions: Roman Catholic (45%), various Protestant Churches (17%), animist (32%), Sunni Islam (6%).

Education: *Literacy rate*: 52% (1985). *Years of compulsory schooling*: schooling is not compulsory. *Universities*: 1.

Defence: *Total armed strength*: 70 000 (1991) (plus 16 890 police). *Military service*: none.

GOVERNMENT

The commander of the National Resistance Army – which took power in 1986 – is President. He appoints a Prime Minister and other Ministers. The advisory 278-member National Resistance Council comprises 210 indirectly elected members and 68 members appointed by the President. Political activity has been suspended.

President: Yoweri Museveni.

Prime Minister: George Adyebo.

GEOGRAPHY

Most of Uganda is a plateau that ends in the west at the Great Rift Valley and the Ruwenzori Mountains. Lake Victoria covers southeast Uganda. *Principal rivers*: Nile, Semliki. *Highest point*: Ngaliema 5118 m (16 763 ft).

Climate: Uganda's tropical climate is moderated by its altitude.

ECONOMY

Agriculture involves over three quarters of the labour force. Coffee normally accounts for 90% of Uganda's exports. Subsistence crops include plantains, cassava and sweet potatoes.

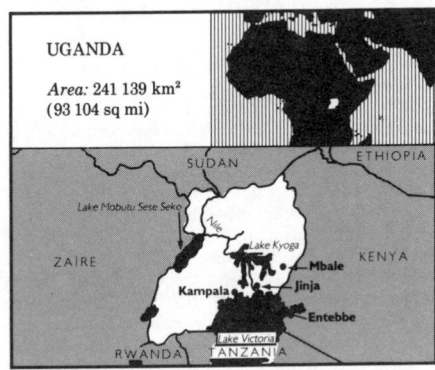

RECENT HISTORY

The British protectorate of Uganda – established in 1894 – was built around the powerful African kingdom of Buganda, whose continuing special status contributed to the disunity that has plagued the country since independence in 1962. Dr Milton Obote, who suppressed the Buganda monarchy in 1966, was overthrown in a coup by General Idi Amin in 1971. Amin earned international criticism when political and human rights were curtailed, opponents of the regime were murdered and the Asian population was expelled. The army took over in 1979, supported by Tanzanian troops. Obote was restored but was ousted in a military coup in 1985, since when instability and guerrilla action have continued.

UKRAINE

Official name: Ukraina (The Ukraine).

Member of: UN, CIS, CSCE.

Area: 603 700 km² (233 100 sq mi).

Population: 51 944 000 (1991 est).

Capital and major cities: Kiev (Kyiv) 2 587 000, Kharkov (Kharkiv) 1 611 000, Dnepropetrovsk (Dnipropetrovske) 1 179 000, Odessa 1 141 000, Donetsk (Donetske) 1 110 000, Zaporozhye (Zaporizhia) 875 000, Lvov (Lviv) 767 000, Krivoy Rog (Kryvyi Rih) 698 000 (1989 census).

Languages: Ukrainian (73%), Russian (22%), Belarussian (2%).

Religions: Ukrainian Uniat (Roman Catholic), Orthodox (Ukrainian Autocephalous and Russian)

Education: *Literacy rate:* (1990 est) nearly 100%. *Years of compulsory schooling:* 7–15. *Universities:* 10 universities and 8 polytechnics.

Defence: *Total military strength:* 230 000. *Military service:* 18 months.

GOVERNMENT

A 450-member legislature and a President – who appoints a Council of Ministers – are elected for four years by universal adult suffrage. A new constitution is to be drafted. The main political parties include (centre left) New Ukraine, the (nationalist) People's Movement of Ukraine (Rukh), the (conservative) Congress of National Democratic Forces and the Communist Party (which was allowed to reform in 1993). Crimea is an autonomous republic.
President: Leonid Kravchuk.
Prime Minister: Leonid Kuchma.

AUTONOMOUS REPUBLIC

Crimea *Area:* 27 000 km² (10 400 sq mi). *Population:* 2550 000 (1991 est). *Capital:* Simferopol.

GEOGRAPHY

Most of Ukraine – after Russia, the largest country in Europe – comprises plains (steppes), interrupted by low plateaux and basins. The N includes part of the Pripet Marshes; the S is a coastal lowland beside the Black Sea and the Sea of Azov. Central Ukraine comprises the Dnepr Lowland and the Dnepr Plateau, the most extensive upland in the republic. Eastern Ukraine comprises the Don Valley and part of the Central Russian Upland. The most diverse scenery is in the W where an extensive lowland extends into Hungary and the Carpathian Mountains rise to over 2000 m (6700 ft). The Crimean Peninsula consists of parallel mountain ridges and fertile valleys. *Principal rivers:* Don, Dnepr, Dnestr, Donets, Bug. *Highest point:* Mount Hoverla 2061 m (6762 ft).

Climate: The Crimean Peninsula has a Mediterranean climate. The rest of Ukraine is temperate. Winters are milder and summers are cooler in the W. Snowfall is heaviest in the N and the Carpathians. Rainfall is moderate, usually with a summer maximum.

ECONOMY

Ukraine was known as the bread basket of the USSR. Large collectivized farms on the steppes grow cereals, fodder crops and vegetables. Potatoes and flax are important in the N; fruit farming (including grapes and market gardening) is widespread, particularly in the Crimea. Natural resources include iron ore, oil, manganese and rock salt, but the vast Donets coalfield is the principal base of Ukraine's industries. The Ukrainian iron and steel industry is almost as large as that of Russia. Other major industries include consumer goods, heavy engineering (railway locomotives, shipbuilding, generators), food processing, and chemicals and chemical equipment. Within the USSR, Ukraine had surpluses of electricity, cereals and many industrial goods. The first steps in privatization have been taken but the economy faces serious difficulties including rampant inflation and declining industries.

RECENT HISTORY

In 1648–51 the Cossacks – Slavic warrior-peasants in Ukraine who formed mercenary cavalry forces – rebelled against Polish rule and requested assistance from the Russian tsar. Two Russo-Polish wars followed and in 1660 Ukraine was partitioned between Poland and Russia. The Ottoman Turks occupied Polish Ukraine from 1672 to 1699. Tsarist Russia suppressed the autonomy of the Cossacks in 1775 and reunited most of Ukraine under Russian rule (1793) in the second partition of Poland. In 1876 Russia banned the use of the Ukrainian language in schools and in print. However, the Ukrainian nationalist

UKRAINE

Area: 603 700 km² (233 100 sq mi).

movement continued in the more liberal atmosphere of Galicia in the W, which had been annexed by Austria in the first partition of Poland (1772).

The Ukrainians in Russia took the opportunity afforded by World War I and the Russian Revolution to proclaim independence (January 1918), but a Ukrainian Soviet government was established in Kharkov. Ukraine united with Galicia when the Austro-Hungarian Empire collapsed (November 1918). The new state was invaded by Poland in pursuit of territorial claims and by the Soviet Red Army in support of the Kharkov Soviet. The Red Army prevailed and in 1922 Ukraine became one of the founding republics of the USSR, but the Lvov district of Galicia remained in Polish hands.

From 1928, Soviet leader Joseph Stalin instituted purges in Ukraine and a new programme of Russification. After World War II – when Ukraine was occupied by Nazi Germany – Soviet Ukraine was enlarged by the addition of Lvov (from Poland), Bukovina (from Romania), and Ruthenia (from Czechoslovakia), and, finally, Crimea (from Russia) in 1954. Ukrainian nationalism was spurred by the perceived Soviet indifference to Ukraine at the time of the nuclear accident at Chernobyl, N of Kiev, in 1986. Ukrainian politicians responded to the restructuring of the USSR in the late 1980s by seeking increased autonomy. The decision of the republic to declare independence following the abortive coup by Communist hardliners (September 1991) hastened the demise of the USSR. Ukraine gained international recognition in December 1991 when the Soviet Union was dissolved, but tension remained between Moscow and Kiev concerning the allegiance of

Soviet forces in Ukraine, and the status of Crimea and the Black Sea fleet.

UNITED ARAB EMIRATES

Official name: Al-Imarat Al'Arabiya Al-Muttahida (The United Arab Emirates).

Member of: UN, Arab League, OPEC, GCC.

Area: 77 700 km² (30 000 sq mi).

Population: 1 945 000 (1991 est).

Capital and major cities: Abu Dhabi 243 000, Dubai 266 000, Sharjah 125 000, al'Ayn 102 000 (1985 census).

Languages: Arabic (official); English (commercial).

Religion: Sunni Islam (official).

Education: *Literacy rate*: 53.5% (1975). *Years of compulsory schooling*: 6–12. *Universities*: 1.

Defence: *Total armed strength*: 44 000 (1991). *Military service*: voluntary.

GOVERNMENT

The hereditary rulers of the seven emirates – who are absolute monarchs – form the Supreme Council of Rulers, which elects one of its members as President. The Prime Minister and Council of Ministers are appointed by the President. The Supreme Council appoints a 40-member advisory Federal National Council for 2 year terms of office. There are no political parties.
President: HH Shaikh Zayid bin Sultan Al Nihayyan.
Prime Minister: HH Shaikh Maktum bin Rashid Al Maktum.

EMIRATES

Population figures are from the 1985 census.

Abu Dhabi *Area*: 67 350 km² (26 000 sq mi). *Population*: 670 000. *Capital*: Abu Dhabi.

Ajman *Area*: 250 km² (100 sq mi). *Population*: 64 000. *Capital*: Ajman.

Dubai *Area*: 3900 km² (1510 sq mi). *Population*: 419 000. *Capital*: Dubai.

Fujairah *Area*: 1150 km² (440 sq mi). *Population*: 54 000. *Capital*: Fujairah.

Ras al-Khaimah *Area*: 1700 km² (660 sq mi). *Population*: 116 000. *Capital*: Ras al-Khaimah.

Sharjah *Area*: 2600 km² (1000 sq mi). *Population*: 269 000. *Capital*: Sharjah.

Umm al-Qaiwain *Area*: 750 km² (290 sq mi). *Population*: 29 000. *Capital*: Umm al-Qaiwain.

GEOGRAPHY

The country is a low-lying desert except in the Jajar Mountains in the east. There are no permanent streams. *Highest point*: Al-Hajar 1189 m (3901 ft).

Climate: Summer temperatures may rise to over 40° C (104° F); winter temperatures are milder. Rainfall totals are very low.

ECONOMY

Based upon the export of offshore and onshore reserves of petroleum and natural gas, the country has one of the highest standards of living in the world. Dry docks, fertilizer factories, commercial banking interests, international airports and an entrepôt trade have been developed. Immigrants from the Indian subcontinent and Iran form the majority of the labour force. Agriculture is confined

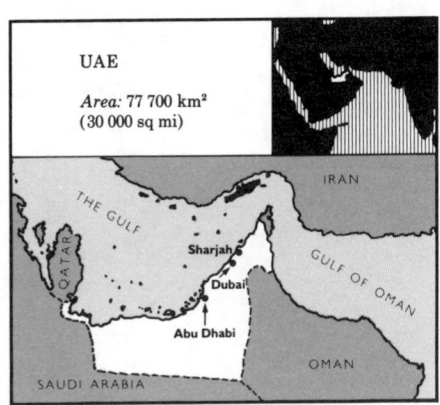

UAE

Area: 77 700 km² (30 000 sq mi)

to oases and a few coastal sites irrigated by desalinated water.

RECENT HISTORY

A political vacuum in the mid-18th century was filled by the British, who saw the region as a link in the trade route to India. Treaties ('truces') were signed with local rulers during the 19th century, bringing the Trucial States under British protection. In 1958 oil was discovered in Abu Dhabi. In 1968 the Trucial States, Bahrain and Qatar laid the foundations of a federation, but when the British withdrew in 1971 only six states formed the United Arab Emirates. Bahrain and Qatar gained separate independent statehood, while Ras al-Khaimah joined the federation in 1972. The UAE – as members of the GCC – joined the coalition against Saddam Hussein's Iraq (1990–91).

UNITED KINGDOM

Official name: The United Kingdom of Great Britain and Northern Ireland.

Member of: UN, EC, NATO, Commonwealth, G7, OECD, CSCE, Council of Europe.

Area: 244 103 km² (94 249 sq mi).

Population: 57 561 000 (1992 est).

Capital and major cities: London 7 825 000 (London Urban Area – Greater London 6 803 100), Birmingham 2 326 000 (West Midlands Urban Area; city 994 500), Manchester 2 281 000 (Greater Manchester Urban Area; city 432 600), Glasgow 1 648 000 (Central Clydeside Urban Area; city 687 600), Leeds-Bradford 1 543 000 (West Yorkshire Urban Area; Leeds city 706 300, Bradford city 468 700), Newcastle-upon-Tyne 761 000 (Tyneside Urban Area; city 273 300), Liverpool 663 000 (Urban Area; city 474 500), Sheffield 644 000 (Urban Area; city 520 300), Nottingham 612 000 (Urban Area; city 276 000), Bristol 547 000 (Urban Area; city 392 600), Edinburgh 527 000 (Urban Area; city 438 800), Brighton 482 000 (Brighton-Worthing Urban Area; borough 153 800), Portsmouth 461 000 (Urban Area; city 185 200), Belfast 433 000 (Urban Area; city 287 100), Leicester 406 000 (Urban Area; city 280 500), Stoke-on-Trent 377 000 (The Potteries Urban Area; city 249 700), Middlesbrough 372 000 (Teesside Urban Area; borough 144 400), Bournemouth 364 000 (Urban Area; borough 159 100), Coventry 338 000 (Coventry-Bedworth Urban Area; city 306 300), Cardiff 320 000 (Urban Area; city 290 000), Preston 317 000 (Urban Area; borough 129 900), Hull 317 000 (Kingston-upon-Hull Urban Area; city 262 900), Southampton 311 000

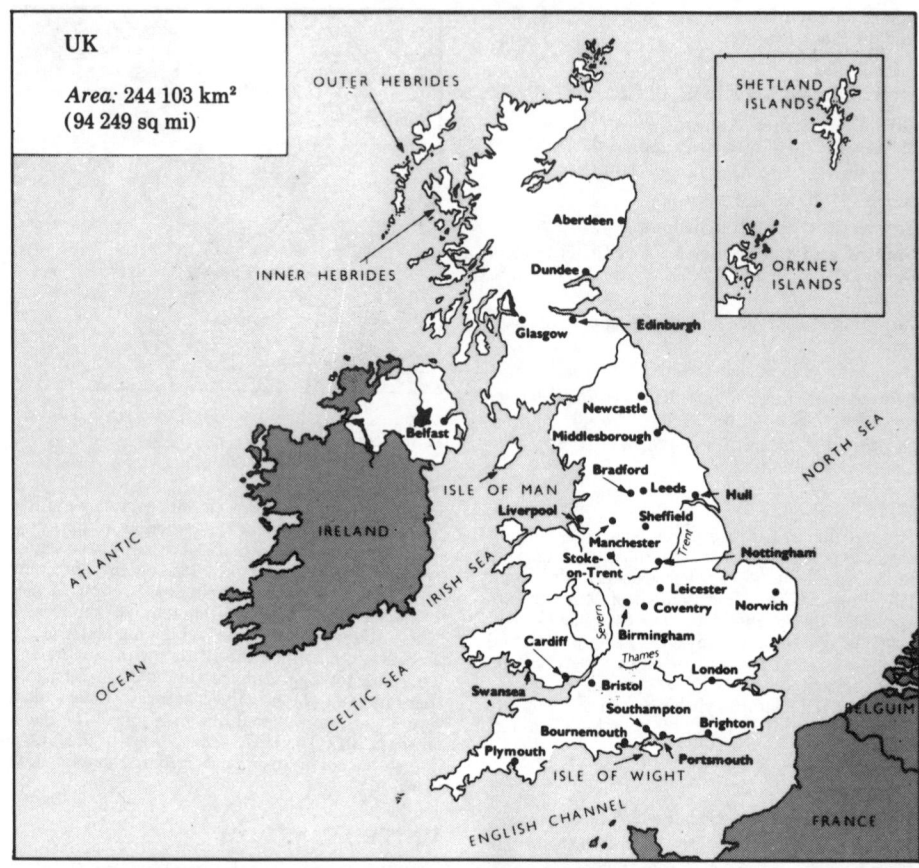

UK

Area: 244 103 km²
(94 249 sq mi)

OUTER HEBRIDES

SHETLAND ISLANDS

INNER HEBRIDES

Aberdeen

Dundee

ORKNEY ISLANDS

Glasgow

Edinburgh

Newcastle

Middlesborough

Belfast

Bradford

Leeds

Hull

NORTH SEA

ISLE OF MAN

Liverpool

Sheffield

IRELAND

Manchester

Stoke-on-Trent

Trent

Nottingham

ATLANTIC

IRISH SEA

Leicester

Coventry

Norwich

Cardiff

Severn

Birmingham

OCEAN

Thames

London

CELTIC SEA

Bristol

Swansea

Southampton

Brighton

BELGUIM

Bournemouth

Plymouth

Portsmouth

ISLE OF WIGHT

FRANCE

ENGLISH CHANNEL

(Southampton-Eastleigh Urban Area; city 204 500), Southend 292 000 (Urban Area; borough 162 900), Blackpool 292 000 (Urban Area; borough 151 100), Swansea 287 0000 (Urban Area; city 187 600), Birkenhead 279 000 (Urban Area; former borough 93 000), Plymouth 255 000 (Urban Area; city 254 400), Rochester 243 000 (Medway Towns Urban Area; city 147 100), Aldershot 242 000 (Urban Area; Aldershot with Farnborough 86 000), Luton 223 000 (Luton-Dunstable Urban Area; borough 174 600), Derby 223 000 (Urban Area; city 222 500), Aberdeen 219 000 (Urban Area; city 213 900), Reading 212 000 (Urban Area; borough 134 600), Sunderland 202 000 (Urban Area; the city has a population of 296 400 and covers a wider area than the Urban Area), Norwich 192 000 (Urban Area; city 125 300), Northampton 185 000 (Urban Area; borough 184 400), Milton Keynes 179 000 (Urban Area and borough). (The population figures for the Urban Areas – the cities and their agglomerations; 1991 est. based on the 1991 census).

Languages: English, Welsh (21% of the population of Wales, though only 1% of the population of Wales speak Welsh as their first language), Gaelic (under 1% of the population of Scotland).

Religions: Anglican (55% nominal, 4% practising), Roman Catholic (9%), Presbyterian (3%, including Church of Scotland), Methodist (2%), various other Christian Churches (4%), Sunni Islam (2%), Judaism (under 1%).

Education: *Literacy rate:* nearly 100% (1992 est).

Years of compulsory schooling: 5–16. *Universities:* 92 (including the university colleges of the University of Wales) plus 8 other colleges of degree-awarding status.

Defence: *Total armed strength:* 300 100 (1991) (of which 18 100 were the women's services and 9100 enlisted outside Britain). *Military service:* none.

GOVERNMENT

The UK is a constitutional monarchy without a written constitution. The House of Lords – the Upper (non-elected) House of Parliament – comprises over 750 hereditary peers and peeresses, over 20 Lords of Appeal (non-hereditary peers), over 370 life peers, and 2 archbishops and 24 bishops of the Church of England. The House of Commons consists of 651 members elected for five years by universal adult suffrage. The sovereign appoints a Prime Minister who commands a majority in the Commons. The main political parties include the Conservative Party, the Labour Party, the Liberal Democrats and regional parties including the Scottish National Party, the (Welsh Nationalist) Plaid Cymru, the Ulster Unionists, the Democratic Unionist Party and the (Northern Ireland) Social Democratic and Labour Party. The UK comprises four countries – England, Scotland, Wales and Northern Ireland; there is constitutional provision for devolved government for the latter.

Queen: HM Queen Elizabeth II (succeeded upon the death of her father, 6 February 1952).

Prime Minister: John Major.

COUNTRIES OF THE UNITED KINGDOM

England *Area*: 130 441 km² (50 363 sq mi). *Population*: 47 837 300. *Capital*: London.

Northern Ireland *Area*: 14 120 km² (5452 sq mi). *Population*: 1 589 400. *Capital*: Belfast.

Scotland *Area*: 78 775 km² (30 415 sq mi). *Population*: 5 102 400. *Capital*: Edinburgh.

Wales *Area*: 20 768 km² (8019 sq mi). *Population*: 2 881 000. *Capital*: Cardiff.

CROWN DEPENDENCIES

The Crown Dependencies are associated with but not part of the UK.

Guernsey (includes Alderney, Sark and smaller dependencies) *Area*: 75 km² (29 sq mi). Guernsey (island) has an area of 63.3 km² (24.5 sq mi). Alderney has an area of 7.9 km² (3.07 sq mi); Sark has an area of 5.1 km² (1.99 sq mi). *Population*: 57 000 (Guernsey island; 1989 est). Alderney has a population of 2000 (1986 est) and Sark has a population of 600 (1986 est). *Capital*: St Peter Port 18 000 (1986 est). The capital of Alderney is St Anne's. There are no towns or villages on Sark, on which settlement is scattered.

Isle of Man *Area*: 572 km² (221 sq mi). *Population*: 70 000 (1991 census). *Capital*: Douglas 22 000 (1991 census).

Jersey *Area*: 116.2 km² (44.8 sq mi). *Population*: 83 000 (1989 est). *Capital*: St Helier 30 000 (1986 est).

GEOGRAPHY

The UK comprises the island of Great Britain, the northeast part of Ireland plus over 4000 other islands. Lowland Britain occupies the south, east and centre of England. Clay valleys and river basins – including those of the Thames and the Trent – separate relatively low ridges of hills, including the limestone Cotswolds and Cleveland Hills, and the chalk North and South Downs and the Yorkshire and Lincolnshire Wolds. In the east, low-lying Fenland is largely reclaimed marshland. The flat landscape of East Anglia is covered by glacial soils. The northwest coastal plain of Lancashire and Cheshire is the only other major lowland in England. A peninsula in the southwest – Devon and Cornwall – contains granitic uplands, including Dartmoor and Exmoor. The limestone Pennines form a moorland backbone running through northern England. The Lake District (Cumbria) is an isolated mountainous dome rising to Scafell Pike, the highest point in England at 978 m (3210 ft).

Wales is a highland block, formed by a series of plateaux above which rise the Brecon Beacons in the south, Cader Idris and the Berwyn range in the centre, and Snowdonia in the north, where Snowdon reaches 1085 m (3560 ft).

In Scotland, the Highlands in the north and the Southern Uplands are separated by the rift valley of the Central Lowlands, where the majority of Scotland's population, agriculture and industry are to be found. The Highlands are divided by the Great Glen in which lies Loch Ness. Although Ben Nevis is the highest point, the most prominent range of the Highlands is the Cairngorm Mountains. The Southern Uplands lie below 853 m (2800 ft). Other Scottish lowlands include Buchan in the northeast, Caithness in the north, and a coastal plain around the Moray Firth. To the west of Scotland are the many islands of the Inner and Outer Hebrides, while to the north are the Orkney and Shetland Islands.

Northern Ireland includes several hilly areas, including the Sperrin Mountains in the northwest, the uplands in County Antrim, and the Mourne Mountains rising to Slieve Donard at 852 m (2796 ft). Lough Neagh – at the centre of Northern Ireland – is the UK's largest lake.

Principal rivers: Severn, Thames (with Churn), Trent-Humber, Aire (with Ouse), (Great or Bedford) Ouse, Wye, Tay (with Tummel), Nene, Clyde. *Highest point*: Ben Nevis 1392 m (4406 ft).

Climate: The temperate climate of the UK is warmed by the North Atlantic Drift. There is considerable local variety, particularly in rainfall totals, which range from just over 500 mm (20 in) in the southeast to 5000 mm (200 in) in northwest Scotland.

ECONOMY

Over one fifth of the British labour force is involved in manufacturing. The principal industries include iron and steel, motor vehicles, electronics and electrical engineering, textiles and clothing, aircraft, and consumer goods. British industry relies heavily upon imports of raw materials. The country is self-sufficient in petroleum (from the North Sea) and has important reserves of natural gas and coal – although the coal industry is declining as seams in traditional mining areas become uneconomic. As Britain is a major trading nation, London is one of the world's leading banking, financial and insurance centres, and the 'invisible earnings' from these services make an important contribution to exports. Tourism is another major foreign-currency earner. Agriculture (with forestry) involves about 2% of the labour force and is principally concerned with raising sheep and cattle. Arable farming is widespread in the E, where the main crops are barley, wheat, potatoes and sugar beet. Since the 1970s the UK has not experienced the same rate of economic growth as most other West European countries. Economic problems have included repeated crises of confidence in the value of the pound, credit squeezes and high (regional) rates of unemployment. Since 1980 most major nationalized industries have been privatized.

RECENT HISTORY

The United Kingdom – formed in 1801 through the union of Great Britain and Ireland – fought almost continuous wars against Revolutionary and Napoleonic France (1789–1815), and emerged from the wars with colonial gains. The reign of Queen Victoria (1837–1901) witnessed the height of British power. Britain – the first country to undergo an industrial revolution – dominated world trade. British statesmen – including PMs Sir Robert Peel (1788–1850), Lord Palmerston (1784–1865), William Ewart Gladstone (1809–98) and Benjamin Disraeli (1804–81) – dominated the world stage. The British Empire included much of Africa, the Indian subcontinent, Canada and Australasia. Parliamentary democracy increased with the gradual extension of the right to vote, starting with the Reform Act of 1832. Representative government was granted to distant colonies, beginning with Canada and Australia, but was denied to Ireland, where nationalist sentiment was stirring. By the end of the 19th century Britain's economic dominance was beginning to be challenged by the USA and, more particularly, by Germany. Rivalry with Imperial Germany was but one factor contributing to the causes of World War I. PM Herbert Asquith (1852–1928) led a reforming Liberal Government from 1908 to 1916 but

– after criticism of his conduct of the war – he was replaced by David Lloyd George (1863–1945), who as Chancellor of the Exchequer had introduced health and unemployment insurance.

The 'old dominions' – Canada, Australia, New Zealand and South Africa – emerged from the war as autonomous countries, and their independent status was confirmed by the Statute of Westminster (1931). The Easter Rising in Ireland (1916) led to the partition of the island in 1922. Only Northern Ireland – the area with a Protestant majority – stayed within the United Kingdom, but in the 1970s and 1980s bitter conflict resurfaced in the province as Roman Catholic republicans – seeking unity with the Republic of Ireland – clashed with Protestant Loyalists intent upon preserving the link with Britain. British troops were stationed in Northern Ireland to keep order and to defeat the terrorist violence of the IRA.

In World War II Britain – led by PM Sir Winston Churchill (1874–1965), who had strenuously opposed appeasement in the 1930s – played a major role in the defeat of the Axis powers, and from 1940 to 1941 the UK stood alone against an apparently invincible Germany. Following the war, the Labour government of Clement Attlee (1883–1967) established the 'welfare state'. At the same time, the British Empire began its transformation into a Commonwealth of some 50 independent states, starting with the independence of India in 1947. By the late 1980s decolonization was practically complete and Britain was no longer a world power, although a British nuclear deterrent was retained. By the 1970s the United Kingdom was involved in restructuring its domestic economy and, consequently, its welfare state – from 1979 to 1990 under the Conservative premiership of Margaret Thatcher (1925–). The country has also joined (1973) and has attempted to come to terms with the European Community. Since 1990, under the premiership of John Major (1943–), the UK participated in the coalition against Iraq in the Second Gulf War (1991) and has suffered a deep economic recession.

UK DEPENDENCIES

Anguilla (a small island in the Leeward Islands in the eastern Caribbean. The colony includes Sombrero, 48 km (30 mi) north of Anguilla.) *Area*: 96 km² (37 sq mi) – Anguilla 91 km² (35 sq mi); Sombrero 5 km² (2 sq mi). *Population*: 6900 (1989 est); Sombrero has no permanent population. *Capital*: The Valley 500 (1988 est).

Bermuda (a group of 100 small islands in the western Atlantic) *Area*: 54 km² (21 sq mi). *Population*: 60 000 (1990 est). *Capital*: Hamilton 6000 (1990 est).

British Antarctic Territory see Other Territories following this chapter.

British Indian Ocean Territory (the Chagos archipelago in the Indian Ocean) *Area*: 60 km² (23 sq mi). *Population*: 2900 military personnel; the islands are used as US and British defence bases. There is no permanent civilian population.

British Virgin Islands (the eastern part of the Virgin Islands group in the Caribbean) *Area*: 153 km² (59 sq mi). *Population*: 16 600 (1991 census). *Capital*: Road Town 2500 (1991 census).

Cayman Islands (a group of three islands 290 km (180 mi) west of Jamaica) *Area*: 259 km² (100 sq mi). *Population*: 25 500 (1989 census). *Capital*: George Town 12 900 (1989 census).

Falkland Islands (a group of two main and over 100 small islands in the southern Atlantic, about 770 km (480 mi) northeast of Cape Horn) *Area*: 12 170 km² (4698 sq mi). *Population*: 2100 (1991 census). *Capital*: Port Stanley 1300 (1991 census).

Gibraltar (a small peninsula on the south coast of Spain, commanding the north side of the Atlantic entrance to the Mediterranean Sea) *Area*: 6.5 km² (2.5 sq mi). *Population*: 31 000 (1990 est). *Capital*: Gibraltar 31 000 (1991 est).

Hong Kong (Kowloon peninsula on the coast of the Chinese province of Guangdong, Hong Kong Island, some 235 other small islands and the New Territories, adjoining the Kowloon peninsula. China will recover sovereignty over Hong Kong and the New Territories on 1 July 1997.) *Area*: 1045 km² (403 sq mi) – Hong Kong Island 79 km² (30.4 sq mi), Kowloon peninsula 42 km² (16.3 sq mi), New Territories 924 km² (356.6 sq mi). *Population*: 5 674 000 (1991 census). *Capital*: Victoria, part of the Hong Kong agglomeration.

Montserrat (a small island north of Guadeloupe in the Caribbean) *Area*: 98 km² (38 sq mi). *Population*: 12 400 (1989 est). *Capital*: Plymouth 1500 (1989 est).

Pitcairn Islands (four islands in the South Pacific about 4800 km (3000 mi) east of New Zealand) *Area*: 48 km² (18.5 sq mi) – Pitcairn 4.5 km² (1.75 sq mi), Henderson, Ducie and Oeno 43.5 km² (16.75 sq mi). *Population*: 52 (all on Pitcairn; 1990 est). *Capital*: Adamstown 52 (1990 est).

St Helena and Dependencies (St Helena is an island in the South Atlantic, 1930 km (1200 mi) west of Africa. The dependencies are Ascension, an island 1130 km (700 mi) to the northwest of St Helena, and Tristan da Cunha, a group of six islands 2120 km (1320 mi) southwest of St Helena.) *Area*: 419 km² (162 sq mi) – St Helena 122 km² (47.3 sq mi), Ascension 88 km² (34 sq mi), Tristan da Cunha group 200 km² (78 sq mi). (Tristan da Cunha has an area of 98 km² (38 sq mi), Gough 90 km² (35 sq mi), Inaccessible 10 km² (4 sq mi) and the Nightingale Islands 2 km² (0.75 sq mi). *Population*: 7100 (1991 est) – St Helena 5600 (1991 est), Ascension 1100 (1991 census), Tristan da Cunha 300 (1990 census; Gough, Inaccessible and the Nightingale Islands are uninhabited). *Capital*: Jamestown (on St Helena) 1400 (1987 est) – the capital of Ascension is Georgetown; the capital of Tristan da Cunha is Edinburgh.

South Georgia and South Sandwich Islands (South Georgia is an island 1290 km (800 km) east of the Falkland Islands. The South Sandwich Islands are 760 km (470 mi) southeast of South Georgia.) *Area*: 4091 km² (1580 sq mi) – South Georgia 3755 km² (1450 sq mi), South Sandwich Islands 336 km² (130 sq mi). *Population*: there is no permanent population, although a scientific settlement is maintained at Grytviken on South Georgia.

Turks and Caicos Islands (two groups of islands – 30 in all – southeast of the Bahamas) *Area*: 430 km² (166 sq mi). *Population*: 12 400 (1990 census). *Capital*: Cockburn Town 2500 (1990 census) on Grand Turk.

UNITED STATES OF AMERICA

Member of: UN, NATO, OAS, CSCE, G7, NAFTA, ANZUS.

Area: 9 372 614 km² (3 618 770 sq mi).

Population: 256 600 000 (1993 est).

Capital and major cities: Washington D.C. 3 924 000 (city 598 000), New York 18 087 000 (city

7 323 000, Newark 275 000), Los Angeles 14 532 000 (city 3 485 000, Long Beach 429 000, Anaheim 266 000), Chicago 8 066 000 (city 2 784 000), San Francisco 6 253 000, (city 724 000, San Jose 782 000, Oakland 372 000), Philadelphia 5 899 000 (city 1 586 000), Detroit 4 665 000 (city 1 028 000), Boston 4 172 000 (city 574 000), Dallas 3 885 000 (city 1 007 000; Fort Worth 478 000), Houston 3 711 000 (city 1 631 000), Miami 3 193 000 (city 359 000), Atlanta 2 834 000 (city 394 000), Cleveland 2 760 000 (city 506 000), Seattle 2 559 000 (city 516 000), San Diego 2 498 000 (city 1 111 000), Minneapolis – St Paul 2 464 000 (city 368 000; St Paul 272 000), St Louis 2 444 000 (city 397 000), Baltimore 2 382 000 (city 736 000), Pittsburgh 2 243 000 (city 370 000), Phoenix 2 122 000 (city 983 000), Tampa 2 068 000 (city 280 000), Denver 1 848 000 (city 468 000), Cincinnati 1 744 000 (city 364 000), Milwaukee 1 607 000 (city 628 000), Kansas City 1 566 000 (city 435 000), Sacramento 1 481 000 (city 369 000), Portland 1 478 000 (city 437 000), Norfolk 1 396 000 (city 261 000), Columbus 1 377 000 (city 633 000), San Antonio 1 302 000 (city 936 000), Indianapolis 1 250 000 (city 742 000), New Orleans 1 239 000 (city 497 000), Buffalo 1 189 000 (city 328 000), Charlotte 1 162 000 (city 396 000), Providence 1 142 000 (city 161 000), Hartford 1 086 000 (city 140 000), Orlando 1 073 000 (city 165 000), Salt Lake City 1 072 000 (city 160 000), Rochester 1 002 000 (city 232 000), Nashville 985 000 (city 511 000), Memphis 982 000 (city 610 000), Oklahoma City 959 000 (city 445 000), Louisville 953 000 (city 269 000), Dayton 951 000 (city 182 000), Greensboro 942 000 (city 184 000), Birmingham 908 000 (city 266 000), Jacksonville 907 000 (city 673 000), Albany 874 000 (city 101 000), Richmond 866 000 (city 203 000), West Palm Beach 864 000 (city 365 000), Honolulu 836 000 (city 365 000), Austin 782 000 (city 466 000), Las Vegas 741 000 (city 258 000), Raleigh 735 000 (city 208 000), Scranton 734 000 (city 82 000), Tulsa 709 000 (city 367 000) (all including suburbs; 1990 census).

Languages: English (official), Spanish (6%, as a first language).

Religions: Roman Catholic (23%), Baptist (10%), Methodist (5%), Lutheran (3%), Judaism (2%), Orthodox (2%), Presbyterian (2%), Mormons (2%).

Education: *Literacy rate:* 97%. *Years of compulsory schooling:* 7–16 (most states). *Universities:* 658 universities and 980 other colleges of university status.

Defence: *Total armed strength:* 1 910 600 plus 1 721 700 reservists (1993). *Military service:* none, although there is a selective call-up in time of war.

GOVERNMENT

Congress comprises the Senate (the Upper House) and the House of Representatives (the Lower House). The Senate has 100 members – two from each state – elected by universal adult suffrage for six years, with one third of the senators retiring every two years. The 435-member House of Representatives is directly elected for a two-year term from single-member constituencies. Additional non-voting members of the House are returned by the District of Columbia, Guam, Puerto Rico, United States Virgin Islands and American Samoa. Executive federal power is vested in the President, who serves a maximum of two four-year terms. Presidential candidates submit to a series of 'state primary' elections to enable individual parties to select a preferred candidate. The President and Vice President are elected by an electoral college of delegates pledged to support individual presidential candidates – the college itself

is elected by universal adult suffrage. Upon the approval of the Senate, the President appoints a Cabinet of Secretaries. Each of the 50 states has a separate constitution and legislature with wide-ranging powers. Executive power in each state is held by a Governor who is elected by direct popular vote. The main political parties are the Democratic Party and the Republican Party.
President: William Jefferson Clinton.

AMERICAN STATES

Population figures for the states are 1991 estimates.

Alabama *Area:* 133 915 km^2 (51 705 sq mi). *Population:* 4 089 000. *Capital:* Montgomery.

Alaska *Area:* 1 530 693 km^2 (591 004 sq mi). *Population:* 570 000. *Capital:* Juneau.

Arizona *Area:* 295 259 km^2 (114 000 sq mi). *Population:* 3 750 000. *Capital:* Phoenix.

Arkansas *Area:* 137 754 km^2 (53 187 sq mi). *Population:* 2 372 000. *Capital:* Little Rock.

California *Area:* 411 047 km^2 (158 706 sq mi). *Population:* 30 380 000. *Capital:* Sacramento.

Colorado *Area:* 269 594 km^2 (104 091 sq mi). *Population:* 3 377 000. *Capital:* Denver.

Connecticut *Area:* 12 997 km^2 (5018 sq mi). *Population:* 3 291 000. *Capital:* Hartford.

Delaware *Area:* 5292 km^2 (2044 sq mi). *Population:* 680 000. *Capital:* Dover.

Florida *Area:* 151 939 km^2 (58 664 sq mi). *Population:* 13 277 000. *Capital:* Tallahassee.

Georgia *Area:* 152 576 km^2 (58 910 sq mi). *Population:* 6 623 000. *Capital:* Atlanta.

Hawaii *Area:* 16 760 km^2 (6471 sq mi). *Population:* 1 135 000. *Capital:* Honolulu.

Idaho *Area:* 216 430 km^2 (83 564 sq mi). *Population:* 1 039 000. *Capital:* Boise City.

Illinois *Area:* 149 885 km^2 (57 871 sq mi). *Population:* 11 543 000. *Capital:* Springfield.

Indiana *Area:* 94 309 km^2 (36 413 sq mi). *Population:* 5 610 000. *Capital:* Indianapolis.

Iowa *Area:* 145 752 km^2 (56 275 sq mi). *Population:* 2 795 000. *Capital:* Des Moines.

Kansas *Area:* 213 096 km^2 (82 277 sq mi). *Population:* 2 495 000. *Capital:* Topeka.

Kentucky *Area:* 104 659 km^2 (40 409 sq mi). *Population:* 3 713 000. *Capital:* Frankfort.

Louisiana *Area:* 123 677 km^2 (47 752 sq mi). *Population:* 4 252 000. *Capital:* Baton Rouge.

Maine *Area:* 86 156 km^2 (33 265 sq mi). *Population:* 1 235 000. *Capital:* Augusta.

Maryland *Area:* 27 091 km^2 (10 460 sq mi). *Population:* 4 860 000. *Capital:* Annapolis.

Massachusetts *Area:* 21 455 km^2 (8284 sq mi). *Population:* 5 996 000. *Capital:* Boston.

Michigan *Area:* 251 493 km^2 (97 102 sq mi). *Population:* 9 368 000. *Capital:* Lansing.

Minnesota *Area:* 224 329 km^2 (86 614 sq mi). *Population:* 4 432 000. *Capital:* St Paul.

Mississippi *Area:* 123 514 km^2 (47 689 sq mi). *Population:* 2 592 000. *Capital:* Jackson.

Missouri *Area:* 180 514 km^2 (69 697 sq mi). *Population:* 5 158 000. *Capital:* Jefferson City.

Montana *Area:* 380 847 km^2 (147 046 sq mi). *Population:* 808 000. *Capital:* Helena.

Nebraska *Area:* 200 349 km^2 (77 355 sq mi). *Population:* 1 593 000. *Capital:* Lincoln.

Nevada *Area:* 286 352 km² (110 561 sq mi). *Population:* 1 284 000. *Capital:* Carson City.

New Hampshire *Area:* 24 023 km² (9279 sq mi). *Population:* 1 105 000. *Capital:* Concord.

New Jersey *Area:* 20 168 km² (7787 sq mi). *Population:* 7 760 000. *Capital:* Trenton.

New Mexico *Area:* 314 924 km² (121 593 sq mi). *Population:* 1 548 000. *Capital:* Santa Fe.

New York *Area:* 136 583 km² (52 735 sq mi). *Population:* 18 058 000. *Capital:* Albany.

North Carolina *Area:* 136 412 km² (52 669 sq mi). *Population:* 6 737 000. *Capital:* Raleigh.

North Dakota *Area:* 183 117 km² (70 702 sq mi). *Population:* 635 000. *Capital:* Bismarck.

Ohio *Area:* 115 998 km² (44 787 sq mi). *Population:* 10 939 000. *Capital:* Columbus.

Oklahoma *Area:* 181 185 km² (69 956 sq mi). *Population:* 3 175 000. *Capital:* Oklahoma City.

Oregon *Area:* 251 418 km² (97 073 sq mi). *Population:* 2 922 000. *Capital:* Salem.

Pennsylvania *Area:* 119 251 km² (46 043 sq mi). *Population:* 11 961 000. *Capital:* Harrisburg.

Rhode Island *Area:* 3139 km² (1212 sq mi). *Population:* 1 004 000. *Capital:* Providence.

South Carolina *Area:* 80 582 km² (31 113 sq mi). *Population:* 3 560 000. *Capital:* Columbia.

South Dakota *Area:* 199 730 km² (77 116 sq mi). *Population:* 703 000. *Capital:* Pierre.

Tennessee *Area:* 109 152 km² (42 144 sq mi). *Population:* 4 953 000. *Capital:* Nashville.

Texas *Area:* 691 027 km² (266 807 sq mi). *Population:* 17 349 000. *Capital:* Austin.

Utah *Area:* 219 887 km² (84 899 sq mi). *Population:* 1 770 000. *Capital:* Salt Lake City.

Vermont *Area:* 24 900 km² (9614 sq mi). *Population:* 567 000. *Capital:* Montpelier.

Virginia *Area:* 105 586 km² (40 767 sq mi). *Population:* 6 286 000. *Capital:* Richmond.

Washington *Area:* 176 479 km² (68 139 sq mi). *Population:* 5 018 000. *Capital:* Olympia.

West Virginia *Area:* 62 758 km² (24 231 sq mi). *Population:* 1 801 000. *Capital:* Charleston.

Wisconsin *Area:* 171 496 km² (66 215 sq mi). *Population:* 4 955 000. *Capital:* Madison.

Wyoming *Area:* 253 324 km² (97 809 sq mi). *Population:* 460 000. *Capital:* Cheyenne.

FEDERAL DISTRICT District of Columbia *Area:* 179 km² (69 sq mi). *Population:* 598 000. *Capital*: Washington.

GEOGRAPHY

The Atlantic coastal plain stretches along the entire east coast, including the lowland peninsula of Florida, and along the coast of the Gulf of Mexico, where it reaches up to 800 km (500 mi) inland. The Blue Ridge escarpment rises sharply to the west of the plain. This is the most easterly part of the forested Appalachian Mountains, which stretch north – south for some 2400 km (1500 mi) and reach 2037 m (6684 ft) at Mount Mitchell. The largest physical region of the USA is a vast interior plain drained by the Mississippi and major tributaries, including the Missouri, Arkansas, Nebraska, Ohio and Red River. This lowland stretches from the Great Lakes in the north to the coastal plain in the south, and from the Rocky Mountains in the west to the Appalachians in the east. The Central Lowlands –

the eastern part of the lowland – comprise the Cotton Belt in the south and the Corn (maize) Belt in the north. The Great Plains – the drier western part of the lowland – begin some 480 km (300 mi) west of the Mississippi. The west of the USA is the country's highest region and includes the Rocky Mountains in the east and the Cascades, the Sierra Nevada and the Coastal Ranges in the west. The mountains continue north through Canada into Alaska. The western mountainous belt is prone to earthquakes, in particular along the line of the San Andreas Fault in California. Within the mountains are deserts – including the Mojave and the Arizona Deserts – and the large Intermontane Plateau containing the Great Basin, an area of internal drainage around the Great Salt Lake. The 20 islands of Hawaii – in the Pacific – are volcanic in origin and contain active volcanoes. The USA's natural vegetation ranges from tundra in Alaska to the tropical vegetation of Hawaii, and includes coniferous forest in the northwest, Mediterranean scrub in southern California, steppe and desert in the Intermontane Plateau, and prairie grasslands on the Great Plains. *Principal rivers:* Mississippi (with Missouri and Red Rock), Rio Grande, Yukon (with Nisutlin), Arkansas, Colorado, Ohio (with Allegheny), Red River, Columbia. *Highest point*: Mount McKinley 6194 m (20 320 ft) in Alaska.

Climate: Within the USA there are great regional differences in climate. The mountains behind the Pacific northwest coast are the wettest region of the USA. Coastal California has a warm Mediterranean climate. Desert or semidesert conditions prevail in mountain basins. The continental Great Plains receive 250–750 mm (10–30 in) of rain a year, while the Central Lowlands to the east are generally wetter. Extremes of temperature are experienced in the north of the continental interior. The east is generally temperate. The Appalachians and the eastern coastal plain are humid, with temperatures rising in the south where Florida is subtropical. Coastal Alaska has a cold maritime climate while the north and interior is polar. Hawaii has a Pacific climate with high temperatures and little seasonal variation.

ECONOMY

The position of the USA as the world's leading economic power is threatened by Japan. The USA is self-sufficient in most products apart from petroleum, chemicals, certain metals and manufactured machinery, and newsprint. Agriculture is heavily mechanized and produces considerable surpluses for export. The main crops include maize, wheat, soyabeans, sugar cane, barley, cotton, potatoes and a wide variety of fruit (including citrus fruit in Florida and California). More than one quarter of the USA is pastureland, and cattle and sheep are important in the Great Plains. Forests cover over 30% of the country and are the basis of the world's second largest timber industry. The USA has great natural resources, including coal (mainly in the Appalachians), iron ore, petroleum and natural gas (mainly in Texas, Alaska and California), copper, bauxite, lead, silver, zinc, molybdenum, tungsten, mercury and phosphates, and major rivers that have proved suitable for hydroelectric power plants. The industrial base of the USA is diverse. Principal industries include iron and steel, motor vehicles, electrical and electronic engineering, food processing, chemicals, cement, aluminium, aerospace industries, telecommunications, textiles and clothing, and a wide range of consumer goods. Tourism is a major

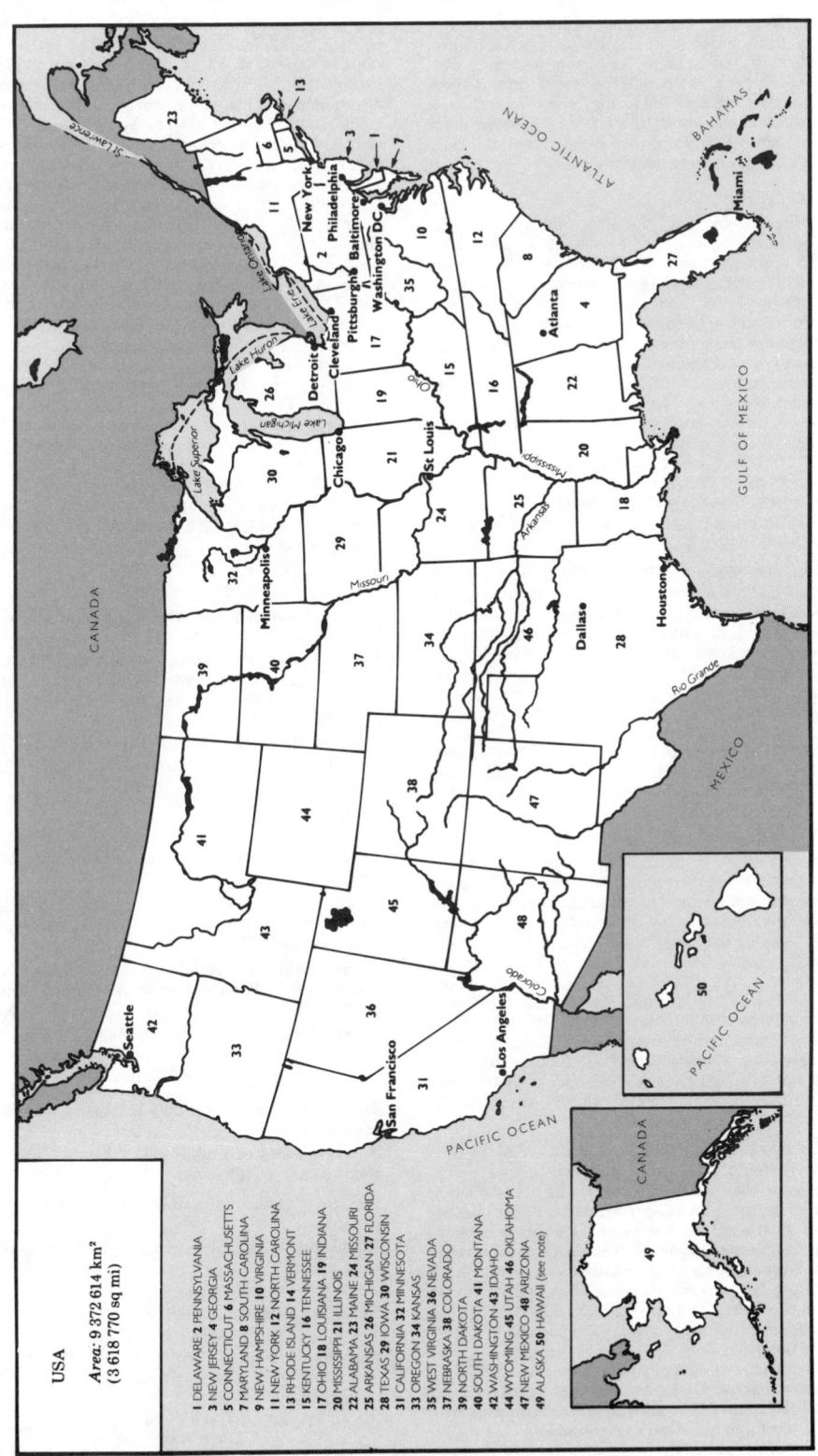

USA

Area: 9 372 614 km²
(3 618 770 sq mi)

1 DELAWARE 2 PENNSYLVANIA
3 NEW JERSEY 4 GEORGIA
5 CONNECTICUT 6 MASSACHUSETTS
7 MARYLAND 8 SOUTH CAROLINA
9 NEW HAMPSHIRE 10 VIRGINIA
11 NEW YORK 12 NORTH CAROLINA
13 RHODE ISLAND 14 VERMONT
15 KENTUCKY 16 TENNESSEE
17 OHIO 18 LOUISIANA 19 INDIANA
20 MISSISSIPPI 21 ILLINOIS
22 ALABAMA 23 MAINE 24 MISSOURI
25 ARKANSAS 26 MICHIGAN 27 FLORIDA
28 TEXAS 29 IOWA 30 WISCONSIN
31 CALIFORNIA 32 MINNESOTA
33 OREGON 34 KANSAS
35 WEST VIRGINIA 36 NEVADA
37 NEBRASKA 38 COLORADO
39 NORTH DAKOTA
40 SOUTH DAKOTA 41 MONTANA
42 WASHINGTON 43 IDAHO
44 WYOMING 45 UTAH 46 OKLAHOMA
47 NEW MEXICO 48 ARIZONA
49 ALASKA 50 HAWAII (see note)

foreign-currency earner. Service industries involve over three quarters of the labour force. Finance, insurance and banking are important, and Wall Street (New York) is one the world's major stock exchanges. US economic policy exerts an influence throughout the world; thus a revival of pressure for trade protectionism in the late 1980s and the early 1990s caused international concern.

RECENT HISTORY

At the beginning of the 19th century, the USA doubled in size with the Louisiana Purchase (1803). This acquisition took the US frontier deep into the Central Lowlands. The expansion of the USA to the west was part of the transformation of the country from an underdeveloped rural nation into a world power stretching from the Atlantic to the Pacific. As a result of wars against Mexico in the 1840s vast new territories were added to the Union – Texas, California, Arizona and New Mexico. Strains appeared between the increasingly industrial North and the plantation South over the issue of slavery. This led to the Civil War under the presidency of Abraham Lincoln (1809–65). The North was victorious, but after federal troops were withdrawn from the South in 1877 racial segregation returned to the South until after World War II.

Between 1880 and 1900 the USA emerged as an industrial giant. At the same time, the population increased dramatically, as immigrants flocked to the New World, in particular from Germany, Eastern Europe and Russia. Interest in world trade increased American involvement abroad. The Cuban revolt against Spanish rule led the USA into a war against Spain (1898) and brought US rule to the Philippines, Puerto Rico and Guam. American participation in World War I from 1917 hastened the Allied victory, but the idealistic principles favoured by President Woodrow Wilson (1856–1924) were compromised in the post-war settlement.

After the war the USA retreated into isolationism and protectionism in trade. The imposition of Prohibition (1919–33) increased smuggling and the activities of criminal gangs, but the 1920s were prosperous until the Depression began in 1929 with the collapse of the stock market. Federal investment and intervention brought relief through the New Deal programme of President Franklin Roosevelt (1882–1945). The Japanese attack on Pearl Harbor brought the USA into World War II (1941). American involvement in the European and Pacific theatres of war was decisive and committed the USA to a world role as a superpower in 1945. US assistance was instrumental in rebuilding Europe (through the Marshall Plan) and Japan.

From the late 1940s to the end of the 1980s, the USA confronted the Soviet Union's perceived global threat in the Cold War. As the leader of the Western alliance, the USA established bases in Europe, the Far East and the Indian and Pacific Oceans, so encircling the Soviet bloc. The USA was involved in the Korean War (1950–53) against Chinese and North Korean forces, and in direct military intervention in Guatemala (1954), Lebanon (1958 and 1983–85), the Dominican Republic (1965), Panama (1968 and 1989) and Grenada (1983). The greatest commitment, however, was in Vietnam, where from 1964 to 1973 US forces attempted to hold back a Communist takeover of Indochina, but a growing disenchantment with the war forced an American withdrawal.

From the 1950s the civil rights movement – led by Martin Luther King (1929–68) – campaigned for full political rights for blacks and for desegregation of schools, hospitals, buses, etc. In the early 1960s President John F. Kennedy (1917–63) made racial discrimination illegal. Kennedy supported the unsuccessful invasion of Cuba by right-wing exiles (1961), successfully pressured the USSR to withdraw its missiles from Cuba (1962), and was assassinated in 1963. Growing economic problems in the 1970s led to the election of a monetarist President, Ronald Reagan (1911–   ), in 1981. The USA continued to support movements and governments perceived as being in the Western interest – for example, backing Israel in the Middle East and providing weapons to the UNITA guerrillas in Angola and the Contra guerrillas in Nicaragua. However, the increasing economic challenge from Japan, and the collapse of Soviet power in Eastern Europe in 1989, raised questions about the USA's future world role. Early in 1990 President George Bush (1924–   ) announced plans to close certain overseas bases, but later in the same year he organized the international coalition against Iraq after the invasion of Kuwait (1990). American forces played a major role in the massive but short air and ground war (1991) that liberated Kuwait. In 1992 American forces led relief efforts in Somalia.

US DEPENDENCIES

Commonwealth Territories in Association with the USA

North Mariana Islands   *Area*: 471 km² (184 sq mi). *Population*: 43 300 (1990 census). *Capital*: Chalan Kanoa (on Saipan). (Saipan had a population of 17 200 in 1985.)

Puerto Rico   *Area*: 9104 km² (3515 sq mi). *Population*: 3 522 000 (199o census). *Capital*: San Juan 1 836 000 (city 438 000; 1990 census).

US External Territories

American Samoa   *Area*: 197 km² (76 sq mi). *Population*: 47 000 (1990 est). *Capital*: Pago Pago 3100 (1990 est).

Guam   *Area*: 541 km² (209 sq mi). *Population*: 133 000 (1990 census). *Capital*: Agaña 43 000 (city 1100; 1990 est).

Palau (Belau)   *Area*: 497 km² (192 sq mi). *Population*: 15 100 (1990 census). *Capital*: Koror 10 500 (1990 census).

Virgin Islands of the United States   *Area*: 352 km² (136 sq mi). *Population*: 102 000 (1990 census). *Capital*: Charlotte Amalie 12 300 (1990 census).

Territory administered by US Fish and Wildlife Service

Howland, Baker and Jarvis Islands   *Area:* 5 km² (2 sq mi). Uninhabited.

Territories administered by US Department of Defense

Johnston Atoll   *Area*: under 1 km² (0.5 sq mi). *Population*: 330 service personnel (1990 est). No permanent population.

Kingman Reef   *Area*: 0.03 km² (0.01 sq mi). Uninhabited.

Midway Islands   *Area*: 5 km² (2 sq mi). *Population*: 450 service personnel (1990 est). No permanent population.

Wake Island   *Area*: 8 km² (3 sq mi). *Population*: 300 service personnel (1990 est). No permanent population.

URUGUAY

Official name: La República Oriental del Uruguay (The Eastern Republic of Uruguay).

Member of: UN, OAS, ALADI, Mercosur.

Area: 176 215 km² (68 037 sq mi).

Population: 3 112 000 (1991 est).

Capital and major cities: Montevideo 1 312 000 (including suburbs), Salto 80 000, Paysandú 76 000, Las Piedras (part of the Montevideo agglomeration) 58 000, Rivera 57 000 (1985 census).

Language: Spanish (official).

Religions: Roman Catholic (58%), various Protestant Churches.

Education: *Literacy rate:* 96.2% (1990). *Years of compulsory schooling:* Between the ages of 6 and 14, 6 years of schooling are compulsory. *Universities:* 2.

Defence: *Total armed strength:* 22 900 (1991) (plus 3150 paramilitaries). *Military service:* none.

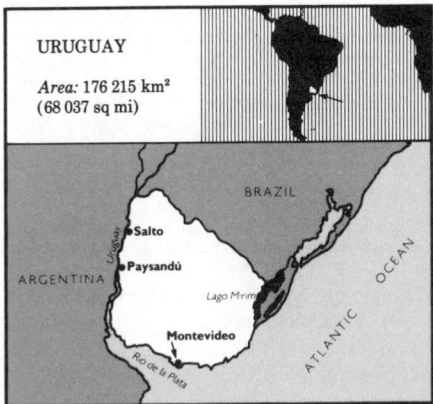

URUGUAY

Area: 176 215 km²
(68 037 sq mi)

GOVERNMENT

The President and Congress – consisting of a 31-member Senate and a 99-member Chamber of Deputies – are elected for four years by universal adult suffrage. The President appoints a Council of Ministers. The main political parties are the (conservative) National Blanco Party, the (centre) Colorado Party, and the (left-wing coalition) Broad Front.
President: Luis Alberto Lacalle.

GEOGRAPHY

Uruguay consists mainly of low undulating plains and plateaux. The only significant ranges of hills are in the southeast. *Principal rivers:* Río Negro, Uruguay, Yi. *Highest point:* Cerro de las Animas 500 m (1643 ft).

Climate: Uruguay has a temperate climate with warm summers and mild winters. Rainfall averages around 900 mm (35 in).

ECONOMY

Pastureland – for sheep and beef cattle – covers about 80% of the land. Meat, wool and hides are the leading exports. Despite a lack of natural resources, Uruguay has a high standard of living. However, the country faces economic difficulties as a result of high inflation and the financial demands of a large public sector and social security system.

RECENT HISTORY

In 1808 independence was declared from Spain, but Uruguay had to repulse successive Brazilian and Argentinian armies (1811–27) before independence was achieved (1828). Until 1903 Uruguay was ruled by dictators and wracked by civil war. However, prosperity from cattle and wool, and the presidencies of the reformer José Battle (1903–7 and 1911–15), turned Uruguay into a democracy and an advanced welfare state. A military dictatorship held power during the Depression. By the late 1960s severe economic problems had ushered in a period of social and political turmoil, and urban guerrillas became active. In 1973 a coup installed a military dictatorship that made Uruguay notorious for abuses of human rights. In 1985 the country returned to democratic rule.

UZBEKISTAN

Official name: Ozbekiston (Uzbekistan).

Member of: UN, CIS, CSCE.

Area: 447 400 km² (172 700 sq mi).

Population: 20 708 000 (1991 est).

Capital and major cities: Tashkent 2 079 000, Samarkand (Samarqand) 388 000, Namangan 291 000, Andizhan 288 000 (1989 census).

Languages: Uzbek (71%), Russian (8%), Tajik (4%).

Religion: Sunni Islam majority.

Education: *Literacy rate:* 80% (1990). *Years of compulsory schooling:* 7–15. *Universities:* 3 universities and 2 polytechnics.

Defence: *Total armed strength:* 15 000 (1992). *Military service:* 18 months.

GOVERNMENT

A 500-member legislature and a President are elected for four years by universal adult suffrage. A new constitution is to be drafted. The main political parties are the (former Communist) People's Democratic Party, Birlik (Unity) and Erk (Freedom).
President: Islam A. Karimov.
Prime Minister: Adbulhashim Mutalov.

GEOGRAPHY

Western Uzbekistan is flat and mainly desert. The mountainous E includes ridges of the Tien Shan and part of the Fergana valley. *Principal rivers:* Amu Darya, Kara Darya. *Highest point:* Bannovka 4488 m (14 724 ft).

Climate: Uzbekistan has a warm continental climate characterized by hot summers and low rainfall. Only the mountains receive over 500 mm (20 in) of rain a year.

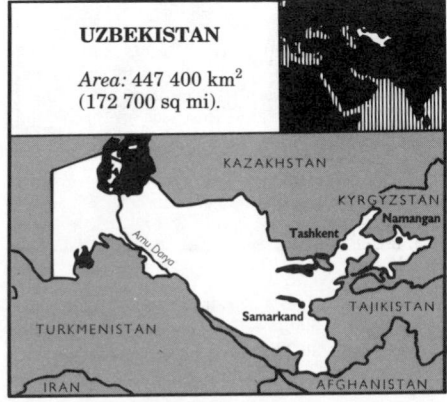

UZBEKISTAN

Area: 447 400 km²
(172 700 sq mi)

ECONOMY

Uzbekistan is one of the world's leading producers of cotton, but the extraction of irrigation from the Amu Darya and its tributaries has contributed to the gradual shrinkage of the Aral Sea. The republic has important reserves of natural gas and major machine and heavy engineering industries. The economy is still mainly state-owned and centrally planned.

RECENT HISTORY

The Uzbeks did not finally come under Russian rule until the khans of Bukhara and Khiva became vassals of the Tsar (1868–73). After the Russian Revolution (see p. 438), the Basmachi revolt (1918–22) resisted Soviet rule, but the khans were eventually deposed (1920) and Soviet republics established (1923–4). Uzbekistan was created in 1924 when the boundaries of Soviet Central Asia were reorganized. Independence was declared after the abortive coup in Moscow by Communist hardliners (September 1991) and international recognition was achieved when the USSR was dissolved (December 1991).

VANUATU

Official name: The Republic of Vanuatu or La République de Vanuatu.

Member of: UN, Commonwealth, South Pacific Forum.

Area: 12 189 km² (4706 sq mi).

Population: 150 000 (1991 est).

Capital and major cities: Port-Vila 19 000, Luganville 7000 (1991 est).

Languages: English (official; 60%), French (official; 40%), Bislama (national; 82% as a first language), and 130 other local dialects.

Religions: Presbyterian (33%), Anglican (30%), animist (20%), Roman Catholic (17%).

Education: *Literacy rate:* 10–20%. *Years of compulsory schooling:* schooling is not compulsory. *Universities:* none.

Defence: *Total armed strength:* There are no armed forces.

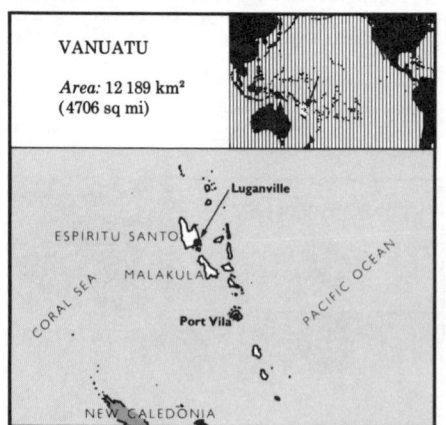

VANUATU

Area: 12 189 km²
(4706 sq mi)

Luganville
ESPIRITU SANTO
MALAKULA
Port Vila
CORAL SEA
PACIFIC OCEAN
NEW CALEDONIA

GOVERNMENT

The 46-member Parliament is elected for four years by universal adult suffrage. It elects a Prime Minister who appoints a Council of Ministers. The President is elected for five years by Parliament and the Presidents of Regional Councils. The main politi-cal parties include the (socialist) Vanuaaku Pati, the Union of Moderate Parties, the Melanesian Progressive Party and a number of regional parties.
President: Fred Timakata.
Prime Minister: Maxim Carlot.

GEOGRAPHY

Vanuatu comprises over 75 islands, some of which are mountainous and include active volcanoes. There are no significant rivers. *Highest point:* Mt Tabwebesana 1888 m (6195 ft).

Climate: Vanuatu's tropical climate is moderated by southeast trade winds from May to October.

ECONOMY

Subsistence farming occupies the majority of the labour force. The main exports include copra, fish and cocoa. Tourism is increasingly important.

RECENT HISTORY

British and French commercial interests in the 19th century resulted in joint control over the islands – then known as the New Hebrides – and the establishment of a condominium in 1906. The islands gained independence as Vanuatu in 1980, but have been troubled by attempted secession and political unrest.

VATICAN CITY

Official name: Stato della Cittá del Vaticano (State of the Vatican City). Also known as the Holy See.

Membership of: CSCE, UN (observer).

Area: 0.44 km² (0.17 sq mi).

Population: 750 (1989 est).

Languages: Italian and Latin (both official).

Religion: The Vatican is the headquarters of the Roman Catholic Church.

Education: *Universities:* 5 pontifical universities.

Defence: *Total armed strength:* ceremonial Swiss Guard.

GOVERNMENT

The Pope is elected Bishop of Rome and head of the Roman Catholic Church for life by the Sacred College of Cardinals. The administration of the Vatican City is in the hands of a Pontifical Commission appointed by the Pope.
Pope: HH (His Holiness) Pope John Paul II (elected 16 October 1978).

GEOGRAPHY

The state consists of the Vatican City, a walled enclave on the west bank of the River Tiber in Rome, plus a number of churches in Rome (including the cathedral of St John Lateran) and the papal villa at Castelgandolfo.

RECENT HISTORY

The tiny Vatican City state is all that remains of the once extensive Papal States. During the Revolutionary and Napoleonic Wars, the Papal States were variously annexed to countries created by Napoleon and absorbed into the French Empire (1798–1815). The Papal States were restored in 1815, but all except Rome and Latium were lost during Italian unification (1859–60). When the French troops protecting the Pope were withdrawn in 1870, Italian forces

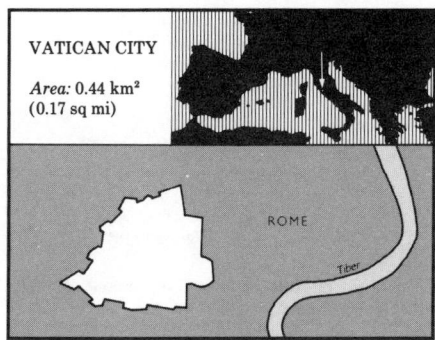

VATICAN CITY

Area: 0.44 km² (0.17 sq mi)

ROME

Tiber

VENEZUELA

Area: 912 050 km² (352 144 sq mi)

CARIBBEAN SEA

TRINIDAD AND TOBAGO

Valencia • Caracas

Maracaibo

Orinoco

COLOMBIA

GUYANA

BRAZIL

entered Rome, which became the capital of the new kingdom of Italy. Pope Pius IX (reigned 1846–78) protested at the loss of his temporal power and retreated into the Vatican, from which no Pope emerged until 1929, when the Lateran Treaties provided for Italian recognition of the Vatican City as an independent state. Since the 1960s the Papacy has again played an important role in international diplomacy, particularly under Popes Paul VI (reigned 1963–78) and John Paul II (1978–).

VENEZUELA

Official name: La República de Venezuela (Republic of Venezuela).

Member of: UN, OAS, ALADI, Andean Pact.

Area: 912 050 km² (352 144 sq mi).

Population: 20 226 000 (1991 est.).

Capital and major cities: Caracas 3 436 000 (city 1 290 000), Maracaibo 1 401 000 (1 207 000), Valencia 1 274 000 (city 955 000), Maracay 957 000 (city 538 000), Barquisimeto 787 000 (city 724 000), Cuidad Guayana 543 000 (1990 census).

Languages: Spanish (official; 98%), various Amerindian languages.

Religion: Roman Catholic (92%).

Education: *Literacy rate:* 88.1% (1990). *Years of compulsory schooling:* 5–14. *Universities:* 22 including 2 polytechnics of university status.

Defence: *Total armed strength:* 75 000 (1991) (including a National Guard of 23 000). *Military service:* 2 years (selective).

GOVERNMENT

The President and both Houses of the National Congress are elected for five years by universal adult suffrage. The Senate – the upper House – comprises 49 elected senators, plus former Presidents. The Chamber of the Deputies has 200 directly elected members. The President appoints a Council of Ministers. The main political parties are AD (Democratic Action), COPEI (the Social Christian Party), and the (left-wing) Radical Cause Party. Each of the 20 states has its own governments. *President:* Carlos Perez.

VENEZUELAN STATES

Population figures are from the 1990 census.

Anzoátegui *Area:* 43 300 km² (16 700 sq mi). *Population:* 924 000. *Capital:* Barcelona.

Apure *Area:* 76 500 km² (29 500 sq mi). *Population:* 305 000. *Capital:* San Fernando de Apure.

Aragua *Area:* 7014 km² (2700 sq mi). *Population:* 1 195 000 *Capital:* Maracay.

Barinas *Area:* 35 200 km² (13 600 sq mi). *Population:* 456 000. *Capital:* Barinas.

Bolivar *Area:* 238 000 km² (91 900 sq mi). *Population:* 969 000. *Capital:* Ciudad Bolivar.

Caraboto *Area:* 4650 km² (1795 sq mi). *Population:* 1 559 000. *Capital:* Valencia.

Cojedes *Area:* 14 800 km² (5700 sq mi). *Population:* 197 000. *Capital:* San Carlos.

Falcón *Area:* 24 800 km² (9600 sq mi). *Population:* 633 000. *Capital:* Coro.

Guárico *Area:* 64 985 km² (25 090 sq mi). *Population:* 526 000. *Capital:* San Juan de Los Morros.

Lara *Area:* 19 800 km² (7600 sq mi). *Population:* 1 270 000. *Capital:* Barquisimeto.

Mérida *Area:* 11 300 km² (4400 sq mi). *Population:* 615 000. *Capital:* Mérida.

Miranda *Area:* 7950 km² (3070 sq mi). *Population:* 2 026 000. *Capital:* Los Teques.

Monagas *Area:* 28 900 km² (11 200 sq mi). *Population:* 503 000. *Capital:* Maturin.

Nueva Esparta *Area:* 1150 km² (440 sq mi). *Population:* 281 000. *Capital:* La Asunción.

Portuguesa *Area:* 15 200 km² (5900 sq mi). *Population:* 626 000. *Capital:* Guanare.

Sucre *Area:* 11 800 km² (4600 sq mi). *Population:* 723 000. *Capital:* Cumaná.

Táchira *Area:* 11 100 km² (4300 sq mi). *Population:* 860 000. *Capital:* San Cristóbal.

Trujillo *Area:* 7400 km² (2900 sq mi). *Population:* 520 000. *Capital:* Trujillo.

Yaracuy *Area:* 7100 km² (2700 sq mi). *Population:* 412 000. *Capital:* San Felipe.

Zulia *Area:* 63 100 km² (24 400 sq mi). *Population:* 2 387 000. *Capital:* Maracaibo.

Amazonas (territory) *Area:* 175 750 km² (67 900 sq mi). *Population:* 60 000. *Capital:* Puerto Ayacucho.

Delta Amacuro (territory) *Area:* 40 200 km² (15 500 sq mi). *Population:* 91 000. *Capital:* Tucupita.

Federal Dependencies (Dependencias Federales) (the islands of San Andres and Providencia) *Area:* 120 km² (50 sq mi). *Population:* 2 200. *Capital:* no capital; the islands are administered by the federal government.

Federal District (Distrito Federal) *Area:* 1930 km² (745 sq mi). *Population:* 2 266 000. *Capital:* Caracas.

GEOGRAPHY
Mountains in the north include the north-south Eastern Andes and the Maritime Andes, which run parallel to the Caribbean coast. Central Venezuela comprises low-lying grassland plains (the Llanos). The Guiana Highlands in the southeast include many high steep-sided plateaux. *Principal river:* Orinoco, Rio Meta, Coroni, Apure. *Highest point:* Pico Bolivar 5007 m (16 423 ft).

Climate: The tropical coast is arid. The cooler mountains and the tropical Llanos are wet, although the latter has a dry season from December to March.

ECONOMY
Petroleum and natural gas normally account for over 80% of export earnings. Agriculture is mainly concerned with raising beef cattle, and growing sugar cane and coffee for export; bananas, maize and rice are grown as subsistence crops.

RECENT HISTORY
Spain began to develop Venezuela in the 17th century. In 1806 Francisco Miranda (1752–1816) led a war of independence that was successfully concluded by Simon Bolívar (1783–1830) in 1823. Initially united with Colombia and Ecuador, Venezuela seceded in 1830. Independence was followed by a series of military coups, revolts and dictators, including Juan Vicente Gómez, whose harsh rule lasted from 1909 to 1935. Since General Marcos Peréz Jiménez was overthrown in 1958, Venezuela has been a civilian democracy. There have, however, been two abortive coup attempts in the 1990s, partly as a result of economic uncertainty and austerity.

VIETNAM
Official name: Công hoa xâ hôi chu nghia Viêt (The Socialist Republic of Vietnam).

Member of: UN.

Area: 329 566 km² (127 246 sq mi).

Population: 69 052 000 (1992 est).

Capital and major cities: Hanoi 2 095 000, Ho Chi Minh City (formerly Saigon) 4 076 000, Haiphong 1 517 000, Da Nang 371 000, Long Xuyen 217 000 (1991–92 est).

Language: Vietnamese (official; 84%), Tay, Khmer, Thai, Muong.

Religions: Buddhist (55%), Roman Catholic (7%), Cao Dai (3%), Daoist.

Education: *Literacy rate:* 87.6% (1990). *Years of compulsory schooling:* 6–11. *Universities:* 6.

Defence: *Total armed strength:* 860 000 (1993 est) (plus paramilitary People's Regional Force 500 000 and local forces estimated at 2.6 million). *Military service:* 3 years.

GOVERNMENT
Under the 1992 constitution, the 496-member National Assembly is elected by universal adult suffrage for five years. The Assembly elects, from its own members, a Council of State – whose Chairman is President – and a Council of Ministers, headed by a Prime Minister. Effective power is the hands of the Communict Party, which is constitutionally the only legal party.
President: Vo Chi Cong.
Prime Minister: Do Muoi.

GEOGRAPHY
Plateaux, hill country and chains of mountains in Annam (central Vietnam) lie between the Mekong River delta in the south and the Red River (Hongha) delta in the north. *Principal rivers:* Mekong, Songkoi, Songbo, Ma, Hongha. *Highest point:* Fan si Pan 3142 m (10 308 ft).

Climate: Vietnam has a hot humid climate, although winters are cool in the north. Heavy rainfall comes mainly during the monsoon season from April to October.

ECONOMY
Agriculture involves over three quarters of the labour force, mainly cultivating rice. Other crops include cassava, maize and sweet potatoes for domestic consumption, and rubber, tea and coffee for export. Natural resources include coal, phosphates and tin, which are the basis of industries in the north. The wars in Vietnam, involvement in Cambodia and the loss of skilled workers through emigration have all had a serious effect on the economy. Vietnam received aid from the USSR and East European countries in the 1980s. Nevertheless, Viet-

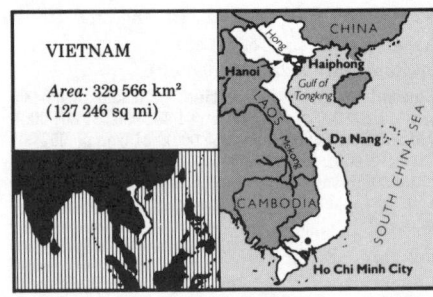

nam remains underdeveloped, and lacks the investment to overcome basic problems such as food shortages. The virtual end of aid from former Communist countries in the 1990s has added to Vietnam's economic problems, and attempts have been made to encourage Western investment.

RECENT HISTORY
In 1802 Nguyen Anh united Tonkin (the north), Annam (the centre) and Cochin-China (the south), and made himself emperor of Vietnam. The French intervened in the area from the 1860s, established a protectorate in Vietnam in 1883 and formed the Union of Indochina – including Cambodia and Laos – in 1887. Revolts against colonial rule in the 1930s marked the start of a period of war and occupation that lasted for over 40 years. The Japanese occupied Vietnam in 1940 and eventually set up a puppet government under the Emperor Bao Dai. In 1941 the Communist leader Ho Chi Minh established the Viet Minh as a nationalist guerrilla army to fight the Japanese. In the closing months of the war, the Viet Minh received US aid, and – after the Japanese surrender – a Democratic Republic of Vietnam was established in Hanoi with Ho as president. French rule was not re-established until 1946, with Ho's republic initially recognized as a 'free state' within

French Indochina. After clashes between the Hanoi government and the French, Ho left Hanoi and began a guerrilla war against the colonial authorities and the restored Emperor Bao Dai.

The Viet Minh gradually gained all of Tonkin and in 1954 forced the French to surrender at Dien Bien Phu after a siege of 55 days. The Geneva Peace Agreement (July 1954) partitioned Vietnam between a Communist zone in the north and a zone ruled by Boa Dai in the south. Elections for the entire country were scheduled for 1956, but the north refused to participate. In 1955 Bao Din was deposed and Ngo Dinh Diem proclaimed a republic in South Vietnam. Diem's oppressive regime encouraged Communist guerrilla activity in the south and in 1960 the (Communist) Viet Cong was formed in South Vietnam with the aim of overthrowing the pro-Western government.

In 1961 US President John F. Kennedy sent American military advisers to help South Vietnam. By 1964 the 'advisers' had grown into an army of regular US troops. After the North Vietnamese allegedly attacked US naval patrols (1964), the Americans began regular aerial bombardment of the north. By the end of 1964 nearly 200 000 US combat troops were in action in Vietnam. The 1968 (Communist) Tet offensive was withstood but the weakness of South Vietnam became evident. Opposition to the war increased in the USA. Peace talks began in 1969 but in 1970 US forces were active against the Viet Cong in both Laos and Cambodia. The war was formally ended by the Paris Peace Agreements (1973), but continued after the withdrawal of US troops. Since the Communist takeover of the south (1975) and the reunification of Vietnam, reconstruction has been hindered by a border war with China (1979) and the occupation of Cambodia (1979–89) by Vietnamese forces. Lack of Western aid and investment has hindered economic development, and this, combined with political repression, has led to large numbers of refugees (the 'Boat People') fleeing the country. Since 1989–90 more pragmatic policies have been adopted in an attempt to attract Western capital.

WESTERN SAMOA

Official name: The Independent State of Western Samoa.

Member of: UN, Commonwealth, South Pacific Forum.

Area: 2831 km² (1093 sq mi).

Population: 160 000 (1991 census).

Capital: Apia 33 000 (1991 census).

Languages: English and Samoan (official).

Religions: Congregational (47%), Roman Catholic (22%), Methodist (15%).

Education: *Literacy rate:* 97% (1990). *Years of compulsory schooling:* 6–15. *Universities:* 1.

Defence: *Total armed strength:* there are no armed forces. Defence remains the responsibility of New Zealand.

GOVERNMENT

The Legislative Assembly comprises 45 members elected for three years by universal adult suffrage and 2 members directly elected by non-Samoan citizens. The current head of state is analogous to a constitutional monarch, but future heads of state will be elected for a five-year term by the Assembly. The head of state appoints a Prime Minister who commands a majority in the Assembly. The PM, in turn, appoints a Council of Ministers, who are responsible to the Assembly. The main political parties include the Human Rights Protection Party and the Samoan National Development Party.
Head of state: Malietoa Tanumafili II.
Prime Minister: Eti Tofilau.

GEOGRAPHY

The country consists of seven small islands and two larger and higher volcanic islands. There are no significant rivers. *Highest point:* Mauga Silisli 1857 m (6094 ft).
Climate: The islands have a tropical climate with high temperatures and very heavy rainfall.

ECONOMY

The majority of Samoans are involved in subsistence agriculture. Copra (from coconuts), cocoa and bananas are the main exports. The country – which is one of the poorest in the world – has suffered through fluctuations in the prices of its main exports. Large numbers of Samoans migrate to New Zealand to work.

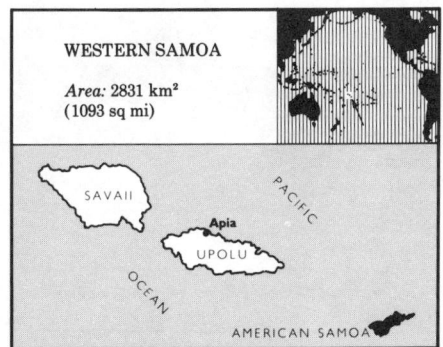

WESTERN SAMOA

Area: 2831 km² (1093 sq mi)

SAVAII

PACIFIC

Apia

UPOLU

OCEAN

AMERICAN SAMOA

RECENT HISTORY

From the 1870s the USA, Britain and Germany became active in Samoa, and in 1899 the three rival powers divided the group, giving the nine western islands to Germany. New Zealand occupied the German islands in 1914, and administered Western Samoa until independence was granted in 1962.

YEMEN

Official name: Al-Jamhuriya al-Yamaniya (The Republic of Yemen).

Member of: UN, Arab League.

Area: 531 870 km² (205 360 sq mi).

Population: 11 843 000 (1991 est).

Capital: Sana'a 427 000, Aden 318 000, Taiz 178 000, Hodeida 155 000, Mukalla 154 000 (1986 est).

Language: Arabic (official).

Religions: Sunni Islam (54%), Zaidist Shia Islam (46%).

Education: *Literacy rate:* 38.8% (1990). *Years of compulsory schooling:* schooling is not compulsory in the former North Yemen, but was, in theory, compulsory in the former South Yemen from 7 to 15. *Universities:* 2.

Defence: *Total armed strength:* 65 000 (1991 est) (plus 20 000 paramilitary). *Military service:* 3 years in the former North Yemen, 2 years in the former South Yemen.

GOVERNMENT

The first elections by universal adult suffrage for a new 301-member House of Representatives for a united Yemen were held in April 1993. This replaced a transitional House formed by merging the former North Yemeni Consultative Council and the former South Yemeni Supreme People's Council. Pending presidential elections, the President of former North Yemen remains President. A Prime Minister and a Council of Ministers are appointed by the President. The main political parties include the General People's Congress, the Yemen Socialist Party, the (liberal) Yemeni Unionist Party and the (Islamic) Yemen Reform Group.
President: Col. Ali Abdullah Saleh.
Prime Minister: Hayder Abu Bakr al-Attas.

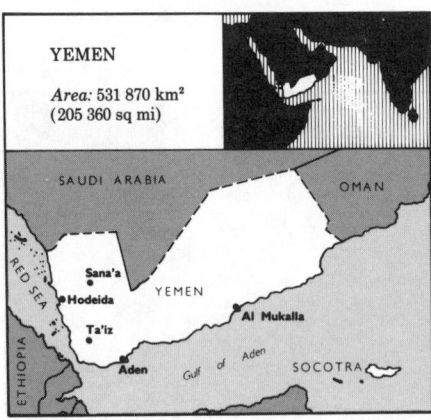

GEOGRAPHY

In the west, the Yemen Highlands rise from a narrow coastal plain. In the south, an arid plateau – 3200 m (10 500 ft) high – extends from the coastal plain into the Arabian Desert that occupies most of the north and east. *Principal river:* Bana (almost the only significant permanent river). *Highest point:* Jebel Hadhar 3760 m (12 336 ft).

Climate: Most of the highlands in the north and west have a temperate climate. The rest of the country is very hot and dry, although the mountains are cooler in winter.

ECONOMY

Cereal crops, coffee and citrus fruit are grown under irrigation in the fertile highlands in the north and west. In the south, subsistence agriculture and fishing occupy the majority of the labour force. Petroleum is becoming a major export, although the reserves are small by Middle Eastern standards. Money sent back by Yemenis working in Saudi Arabia is an important source of revenue.

RECENT HISTORY

The Ottoman Turks first occupied the north and west in the 16th century and were not finally expelled until 1911, when Imam Yahya secured (North)

Yemen's independence. In the south, Britain took Aden as a staging post to India (1839) and gradually established a protectorate over the 20 sultanates inland. Tension grew in the Aden Protectorate in 1959 when Britain created a federation of the feudal sultanates and the city of Aden. In 1963 an armed rebellion began against British rule. After much bloodshed – and a civil war between two rival liberation movements – independence was gained in 1967 as South Yemen. In (North) Yemen, a republican revolution broke out in 1962, and from 1963 until 1970 a bloody civil war was fought, with President Nasser's Egypt supporting the victorious republicans and Saudi Arabia supporting the royalists. Marxist South Yemen became an ally of the USSR and was frequently in conflict with North Yemen, although eventual union of the two Yemens was the objective of both states. The collapse of the Communist regimes in Eastern Europe and the end of considerable Soviet aid (1989–90) hastened the collapse of South Yemen's weak economy, and the two countries merged in May 1990.

YUGOSLAVIA (SERBIA AND MONTENEGRO)

Official name: Federativna Republika Jugoslavija (The Federal Republic of Yugoslavia).

Member of: UN (suspended), CSCE (suspended).

Area: 102 173 km² (39 449 sq mi).

Population: 10 407 000 (1991 census).

Capital and major cities: Belgrade (Beograd) 1 555 000 (city 1 500 000), Novi Sad 260 000 (city 179 000), Niš 230 000 (city 176 000), Pristina 210 000, Subotica 155 000 (city 100 000), Podgorica (formerly Titograd) 130 000 (city 118 000) (1991 census).

Languages: Serb – the version of Serbo-Croat written in the Cyrillic alphabet – (including Montenegrin; 80%), Albanian (13%), Hungarian (4%).

Religions: Orthodox (over 75%), Sunni Islam (over 12%), small Roman Catholic minority.

Education: *Literacy rate:* no figures available. *Years of compulsory schooling:* 7–15. *Universities:* 7 (1 of which is effectively closed).

Defence: *Total armed strength:* 135 000 (1992 est). *Military service:* 12 months.

GOVERNMENT

Under the terms of a new federal constitution (April 1992), Yugoslavia consists of two equal republics — Serbia and Montenegro. A Federal Assembly and a Federal President are elected by universal adult suffrage. The President appoints a Prime Minister and a Council of Ministers. The republics have their own legislatures with considerable powers – the Serbian presidency has assumed virtual sovereign powers and both republics act as virtually independent countries. The main political parties include the (former Communist) Socialist Party of Serbia, the (former Communist Montenegrin) Democratic Party of Socialists, the Alliance of Reform Forces for Montenegro, the (right-wing) Serbian Renaissance Movement, and the (Serbian) National Peasants' Party.
President: to be appointed.
Prime Minister: Radoje Kontic.
President of Serbia: Slobodan Milosevic.
President of Montenegro: Momir Bulatovic.

YUGOSLAV REPUBLICS

Population figures are from the 1991 census.

Montenegro (Cran Gora) *Area:* 13 812 km² (5333 sq mi). *Population:* 615 000. *Capital:* Podgorica (formerly Titograd).

Serbia (Srbija) *Area:* 88 361 km² (34 116 sq mi) including the formerly autonomous provinces of Kosovo (10 817 km² or 4203 sq mi) and Vojvodina (21 508 km² or 8304 sq mi). *Population:* 9 791 000 including the formerly autonomous provinces of Kosovo (1 955 000) and Vojvodina (2 013 000). *Capital:* Belgrade; the capitals of Kosovo and Vojvodina are Pristina and Novi Sad respectively.

GEOGRAPHY

Ridges of mountains occupy the south and centre of the country. The north (Vojvodina) is occupied by plains drained by the rivers Danube and Tisa. Since the secession of Croatia and Slovenia, the Yugoslav coastline is confined to a short stretch on the Adriatic in Montenegro. *Principal rivers:* Danube (Dunav), Tisa, Morava, Drina. *Highest point:* Titov Vrh 2747 m (9012 ft).

Climate: Coastal Montenegro has a Mediterranean climate; the rest of Yugoslavia has a moderate continental climate.

YUGOSLAVIA

Area: 127 346 km² (49 377 sq mi).

ECONOMY

Agriculture involves over one quarter of the labour force. Most of the land is privately owned. Major crops include maize, wheat, sugar beet, potatoes, citrus fruit and fodder crops for sheep. Industry – which is mainly concentrated around Belgrade – includes food processing, textiles, metallurgy, motor vehicles and consumer goods. The country's economy was severely damaged by the civil wars that began in 1991, by rampant inflation – over 20 000% in 1992 – and by international trade sanctions imposed on Serbia and Montenegro.

RECENT HISTORY

Both Serbia and Montenegro were recognized as independent in 1878. By the beginning of the 19th century the Slavs within the Austro-Hungarian Habsburg Empire looked increasingly to Serbia to create a South ('Yugo') Slav state. After Serbia gained Macedonia in the Balkan Wars (1912–13), Austria grew wary of Serb ambitions. The assassination of the Habsburg heir (1914) by a Bosnian Serb student provided Austria with an excuse to quash

Serbian independence. This led directly to World War I and the dissolution of the Habsburg Empire, whose South Slav peoples united with Serbia and Montenegro in 1918. The interwar Kingdom of Serbs, Croats and Slovenes – renamed Yugoslavia in 1929 – was run as a highly centralized 'Greater Serbia'. The country was wracked by nationalist tensions, and Croat separatists murdered King Alexander in 1934.

Yugoslavia was attacked and dismembered by Hitler in 1941, and Yugoslavs fought the Nazis and each other. The Communist-led partisans of Josip Broz Tito (1892–1980) emerged victorious in 1945, and re-formed Yugoslavia on Soviet lines. Expelled by Stalin from the Soviet bloc in 1948 on account of their indiscipline, the Yugoslav Communists rejected the Soviet model, and pursued policies of decentralization, workers' self-management and non-alignment. However, after Tito's death in 1980, the Yugoslav experiment faltered in economic and nationalist crises. The wealthier northern republics of Slovenia and Croatia adopted multi-party democracy while Serbia forcefully resisted the separatist aspirations of Albanian nationalists in Kosovo province.

In 1990 free elections were held throughout Yugoslavia. In June 1991 Slovenia and Croatia declared independence. Following reverses in a short campaign, federal forces were withdrawn from Slovenia, but Serb insurgents, backed by Yugoslav federal forces, occupied one third of Croatia including those areas with an ethnic Serb majority. In 1992 the fierce Serbo-Croat war came to an uneasy halt and a UN peace-keeping force was agreed. Croatia and Slovenia gained widespread diplomatic recognition of their independence. After Bosnia-Herzegovina gained similar recognition, Yugoslavia was reduced to a small Serb-dominated state. Macedonia also declared sovereignty (1991), but was denied international recognition until 1993, although it had effectively seceded from the federation. The Serb leadership, however, continued to promote the idea of a Greater Serbia that would join the rump Yugoslavia to Serb areas of Croatia (Krajina) and Bosnia-Herzegovina.

In 1992 the Bosnian Serbs, encouraged and supplied by Serbia, seized 70% of Bosnia-Herzegovina, killing or expelling Muslims and Croats in a campaign of 'ethnic cleansing'. International peace and humanitarian efforts to end the Bosnian war were attempted. Serbia was widely blamed for the continuation of the conflict and – with Montenegro – was subjected to international trade sanctions. After the Bosnian Serbs rejected the Owen-Vance peace plan for Bosnia (1993), international pressure upon Serbia to exert influence upon the Bosnian Serbs increased. Sanctions upon Yugoslavia were tightened, effectively isolating the country. Serbia, in turn, promised sanctions against the Bosnian Serbs.

ZAÏRE

Official name: La République du Zaïre (Republic of Zaïre).

Member of: UN, OAU.

Area: 2 344 885 km² (905 365 sq mi).

Population: 41 151 000 (1992 est.)

Capital and major cities: Kinshasa 3 804 000, Lubumbashi 740 000, Mbuji-Mayi 613 000, Kisangani 373 000, Kananga 372 000 (1991 est.)

Languages: French (official); four national languages – Kiswahili, Tshiluba, Kikongo and Lingala, with over 400 local languages.

Religions: Roman Catholic (48%), various Protestant churches (28%), Kimbanguists (17%), animist (6%).

Education: *Literacy rate*: 71.8 (1990). *Years of compulsory schooling*: (in theory) 6–12. *Universities*: 3.

Defence: *Total armed strength*: 25 700 (1991), (plus 25 000 paramilitary gendarmes and 10 000 Civil Guard). *Military service*: compulsory; length varies.

GOVERNMENT

The 222-member National Legislative Council is elected by compulsory universal suffrage for five years. The President – who is directly elected for seven years – appoints the National Executive Council of Commissioners (Ministers). The one-party state was abolished in 1991 when a national conference was convened to bring democracy to Zaïre. Some 160 political groups, including the (former monopoly) Mouvement populaire de la révolution, are active. Multi-party elections have yet to be held.
President: Marshal Mobutu Sese Seko.
Prime Minister: (recognized by the national conference) Etienne Tshisekedi.
Prime Minister: (appointed by President Mobutu) Faustin Birindwa.

ZAÏRE
Area: 2 344 885 km²
(905 365 sq mi)

GEOGRAPHY

Over 60% of the country comprises a basin of tropical rain forest, drained by the River Zaïre (Congo) and its tributaries. Plateaux and mountain ranges surrounding the basin include the Ruwenzori Massif in the east. *Principal rivers*: Zaïre, Lualaba, Lomami, Oubangui, Uganbi, Kasai. *Highest point*: Mont Ngaliema 5109 m (16 763 ft).

Climate: Zaïre has a humid, tropical climate with little seasonal variation, although the north is drier from December to February.

ECONOMY

Agriculture occupies over two thirds of the labour force. Although subsistence farming predominates, coffee, tea, cocoa, rubber and palm products are exported. Minerals are the mainstay of the economy, with copper, cobalt, zinc and diamonds normally

accounting for about 60% of Zaïre's exports. Zaïre suffers rampant inflation and one of the lowest standards of living in Africa.

RECENT HISTORY

The region – now Zaïre – was ravaged by the slave trade, and in 1885 became the personal possession of King Leopold II of the Belgians. However, international outrage at the brutality of the regime in the Congo Free State forced the king to grant the region to Belgium as a colony in 1908. As the Belgian Congo, the colony became a major exporter of minerals. The provision of social services, especially primary education, was relatively advanced, but the administration curbed almost all African political activity. As a result, the country was inadequately prepared when Belgium suddenly decolonized the Congo in 1960. Within days of independence, the army mutinied and the richest region – Katanga, under Moïse Tshombe – attempted to secede. The Congo invited the United Nations to intervene, but the UN force was only partly successful in overcoming continuing civil wars. Colonel Mobutu twice intervened and in 1965 made himself head of state. Pursuing 'authenticity', he renamed the country Zaïre and himself Mobuto Sése Séko. He gradually restored the authority of the central government and introduced a one-party state (1967). Mobutu's strong rule has attracted international criticism, but he has maintained the support of Western countries that value Zaïre as a source of strategic minerals. In 1990, popular discontent won some reforms and – following the legal abolition of the one-party state – a national conference was summoned to bring democracy to Zaïre (1991). In 1992–93 conflicts developed between the national conference and the prime minister on one side and President Mobutu on the other. Sections of the armed forces became disaffected and law-and-order has broken down in parts of the country.

ZAMBIA

Official name: The Republic of Zambia.
Member of: UN, Commonwealth, OAU, SADCC.
Area: 752 614 km² (290 586 sq mi).
Population: 7 818 000 (1990 census).
Capital and major cities: Lusaka 982 000, Ndola 376 000, Kitwe 338 000, Mufulira 153 000 (1990 census).
Languages: English (official), with local languages including Nyanja, Bemba (34%), and Tonga (16%).
Religions: Various Protestant Churches (50%), Roman Catholic (20%), animist.
Education: *Literacy rate:* 72.8% (1990). *Years of compulsory schooling:* (in theory) 7–14. *Universities:* 2.
Defence: *Total armed strength:* 18 000 (1991) (plus 1200 paramilitary). *Military service:* none.

GOVERNMENT

The 150-member National Assembly is elected by universal adult suffrage for five years. The President – who is directly elected for five years – appoints a Cabinet. The 27-member House of Chiefs has advisory powers. The main political parties are the Movement for Multiparty Democracy (MMD) and the (former monopoly) United National Independence Party.
President: Frederick Chiluba.

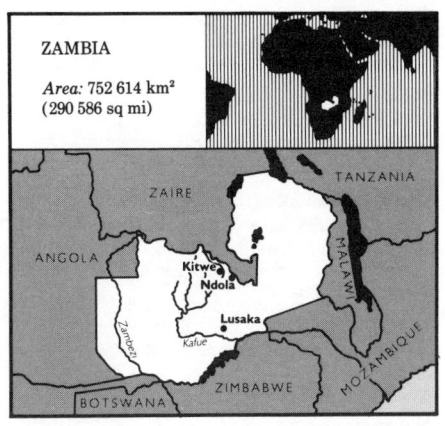

ZAMBIA

Area: 752 614 km²
(290 586 sq mi)

GEOGRAPHY

Zambia comprises plateaux some 1000 to 1500 m (3300 to 5000 ft) high, above which rise the Muchinga Mountains and the Mufinga Hills. *Principal rivers:* Zambezi, Kafue, Luapula. *Highest point:* an unnamed peak in the Muchinga Mountains, 2164 m (7100 ft).

Climate: Zambia has a tropical climate with a wet season from November to April.

ECONOMY

Zambia's economy depends upon the mining and processing of copper, lead, zinc and cobalt. Agriculture is underdeveloped and many basic foodstuffs have to be imported. Maize, groundnuts and tobacco are the main crops.

RECENT HISTORY

The area was brought under the control of the British South Africa Company of Cecil Rhodes in the 1890s. In 1924 Britain took over the administration from the Company, but development of the colony (known as Northern Rhodesia) was initially slow. Skilled mining jobs were reserved for white immigrants, and, fearing increased discrimination, Africans unsuccessfully opposed inclusion in the Central African Federation – with Nyasaland (Malawi) and Southern Rhodesia (Zimbabwe) – in 1953. Against strong opposition from white settlers, Kenneth Kaunda (1924–) led Northern Rhodesia, renamed Zambia, to independence in 1964. A one-party state was introduced in 1972–73. Popular discontent at the lack of a democratic alternative erupted in mid-1990 and free elections were held in October 1991 when Kuanda was defeated in the first democratic change of government in English-speaking Black Africa.

ZIMBABWE

Official name: The Republic of Zimbabwe.

Member of: UN, Commonwealth, OAU, SADCC.

Area: 390 759 km² (150 873 sq mi).

Population: 9 619 000 (1991 est).

Capital and major cities: Harare (formerly Salisbury) 863 000, Bulawayo 495 000, Chitungwiza 229 000, Gweru 79 000, Mutare (Umtali) 70 000 (1989 est).

Languages: English (official), Chishona, Sindebele.

Religions: Animist (42%), Anglican (30%), Roman Catholic (15%), Presbyterian.

Education: *Literacy rate:* 66.9% (1990). *Years of compulsory schooling:* (in theory) 7–14. *Universities:* 1.

Defence: *Total armed strength:* 54 600 (1991). *Military service:* 1 year.

GOVERNMENT

The 150–member House of Assembly comprises 120 members directly elected by universal adult suffrage for six years, 12 nominated members, 10 traditional chiefs and 8 appointed provincial governors. The House elects a President for a six-year term of office. The ZANU-PF (Zimbabwe African National Union) party has a leading role, although other parties – including ZUM (Zimbabwe Unity Movement) are permitted.
President: Robert Mugabe.

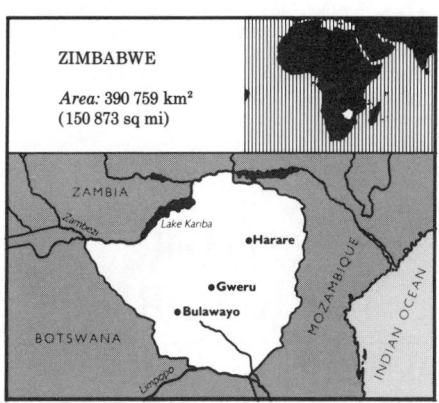

ZIMBABWE

Area: 390 759 km²
(150 873 sq mi)

GEOGRAPHY

Central Zimbabwe comprises the ridge of the Highveld, rising to between 1200 and 1500 m (about 4000 to 5000 ft). The Highveld is bounded on the southwest and northeast by the Middle Veld and the Lowveld plateaux. *Principal rivers:* Zambezi, Limpopo, Sabi. *Highest point:* Mount Inyangani 2592 m (8504 ft).

Climate: The climate is tropical in the lowlands and subtropical at altitude. There is a pronounced dry season from June to September.

ECONOMY

Agriculture involves about two thirds of the labour force. Tobacco, sugar cane, cotton, wheat and maize are exported as well as being the basis of processing industries. Natural resources include coal, gold, asbestos and nickel.

RECENT HISTORY

The area was gradually penetrated by British and Boer hunters, missionaries and prospectors from the 1830s, and was occupied by the British South Africa Company of Cecil Rhodes in the 1890s. The highlands of what became Southern Rhodesia were settled by white farmers, who deprived Africans of land and reduced them to a cheap labour force. Britain took over the administration from the Company in 1923 and granted self-government to the white colonists. Immigration from Britain and South Africa increased after World War II, but the whites remained outnumbered by the Africans by more than

20 to 1. Racial discrimination stimulated African nationalism, initially led by Joshua Nkomo (1917–). Southern Rhodesia – with Northern Rhodesia (Zambia) and Nyasaland (Malawi) – formed the Central African Federation in 1953. When the Federation was dissolved (1963), Britain refused the white Southern Rhodesian administration independence without progress to majority rule. The white government led by Ian Smith (1919–) unilaterally declared independence in 1965, renaming the country Rhodesia. Internal opposition was crushed and international economic sanctions were overcome, but guerrilla wars, mounted by African nationalists during the 1970s, became increasingly effective. In 1979 Smith had to accept majority rule, but the constitution he introduced was unacceptable either to the Zimbabwe African People's Union (ZAPU) of Joshua Nkomo or to the Zimbabwe African National Union (ZANU) of Robert Mugabe (1928–). All parties agreed to the brief reimposition of British rule to achieve a settlement. ZANU under Mugabe took the country to independence in 1980. In 1987 ZANU and ZAPU finally agreed to unite, effectively introducing a one-party state, although proposals for an official one-party system have been shelved.

OTHER TERRITORIES

ANTARCTICA

All territorial claims south of latitude 60° S are in abeyance under the terms of the Antarctic Treaty (signed in 1959), which came into force in 1961. Territorial claims in Antarctica have been made by Argentina, Australia, Chile, France, New Zealand, Norway, and the UK. The Argentinian, Chilean and British claims overlap, while that part of the continent between 90° W and 150° W is not claimed by any country. Neither the USA nor Russia recognize any territorial claim in Antarctica.

Area: 14 245 000 km² (5 500 000 sq mi).

Population: no permanent population, but over 40 scientific stations are maintained.

ADELIE LAND

France claims that part of Antarctica between 136° E and 142° E, extending to the South Pole.

Area: 432 000 km² (166 800 sq mi). Adélie Land is part of the French Southern and Antarctic Territories (Terres Australes et Antarctiques Françaises).

ARGENTINIAN ANTARCTIC TERRITORY

Argentina claims that part of Antarctica between 74° W and 25° W, extending to the South Pole, a claim that overlaps with the British territorial claim.

AUSTRALIAN ANTARCTIC TERRITORY

Australia claims that part of Antarctica between 160° E and 45° E, except for Adélie Land.

Area: 6 120 000 km² (2 320 000 sq mi).

BOUVET ISLAND

A Norwegian Antarctic territory (54° 25 S and 3° 21 E).

Area: 50 km² (19 sq mi). As Bouvet Island is north of 60° S, the Antarctic Treaty does not apply and Norway's claim to the island is uncontested.

BRITISH ANTARCTIC TERRITORY

The UK claims that part of Antarctica between 20° W and 80° W, extending to the South Pole.

Area: 1 810 000 km² (700 000 sq mi).

CHILEAN ANTARCTIC TERRITORY

Chile claims that part of Antarctica between 90° W and and 53° W, extending to the South Pole, a claim that overlaps with the British and Argentinian territorial claims.

PETER I ISLAND

Norway claims the island, which is 68° 48 S and 90° 35 W.

Area: 180 km² (69 sq mi).

QUEEN MAUD LAND

Norway claims that part of Antarctica between 20° W and 45° E.

Area: as no inland limit has been made to the Norwegian claim, no estimate of the area of the territory can be made.

ROSS DEPENDENCY

New Zealand claims that part of Antarctica between 160° E and 150° W, extending to the South Pole.

Area: 450 000 km² (175 000 sq mi).

EAST TIMOR

See Indonesia

GAZA, THE WEST BANK AND GOLAN

Area: 7433 km² (2870 sq mi) – Gaza 378 km² (146 sq mi); the West Bank 5879 km² (2270 sq mi); Golan 1176 km² (454 sq mi).

Population: 1 623 000 (1990 est) – Gaza 642 000 (1990 est); West Bank 955 000 (1990 est); Golan 26 000 (1990 est).

Main cities: Gaza (Ghazzah) 175 000, Nablus (Nabulus) 106 000, Hebron (Al-Khalil) 87 000 (1989 est).

Languages: Arabic.

Religions: Sunni Islam majority, Christian and small Jewish minorities.

GOVERNMENT

Gaza, the West Bank and Golan are under Israeli occupation. Golan was formally annexed by Israel in 1981, an action that has not received general international recognition.

GEOGRAPHY

The Gaza Strip is a small lowland area, between Israel and Egypt, beside the Mediterranean. The West Bank is a mountainous arid area between the Israeli border in the west and the River Jordan and the Dead Sea in the east. Golan is a mountainous region on the Syrian border. *Principal river* (West Bank): Jordan. *Highest point*: unnamed, south of Khan Yunis (Gaza), 110 m (361 ft); unnamed, north of Hebron (West Bank), 1013 m (3323 ft); Mt Hermon (Golan) 2814 m (9232 ft).

ECONOMY

The overpopulated Gaza Strip has little industry and a little agriculture. Only the Jordan Valley in the

West Bank can support arable farming. Both areas rely heavily upon foreign (largely Arab) aid and money sent back by Palestinians working abroad. The *intifada* (see below) has retarded recent development. Golan has been settled by Israeli farmers who have established kibbutzim.

RECENT HISTORY

The Gaza Strip, formerly under Egyptian rule, and the West Bank, formerly under Jordanian administration, were occupied by Israeli forces in June 1967. At the same time, Golan – legally part of Syria – was also occupied by Israeli forces. Golan was annexed by Israel in 1981. In 1988, Jordan severed all legal ties with the West Bank. Beginning in 1988, an uprising (*intifada*) by Palestinians living in Gaza and the West Bank increased tension in these areas. On 15 November 1988, the Palestinian Liberation Organization issued a declaration of Palestinian independence in Gaza and the West Bank. This declaration has received recognition by over 30 countries.

SOVEREIGN MILITARY ORDER OF MALTA

Area: 1.2 ha (3 acres), comprising the Villa del Priorato di Malta (on the Aventine Hill in Rome) and 68 via Condotti (in the same city).

GOVERNMENT

The Knights of Justice of this charitable, monastic Roman Catholic order live as a religious community in two buildings in Rome. They elect for life one of their number to be Prince and Grand Master, who is recognized as a sovereign by over 40 countries. The military order, which issues its own passports, has many of the trappings of a state and is frequently said to be the 'smallest country in the world'.
Head of State: HEH (His Eminent Highness) Fra' (Brother) Andrew Bartie, Prince and Grand Master (elected on 8 April 1988).

RECENT HISTORY

The 'Knights of Malta' ruled Rhodes until 1523, and then Malta until expelled by Napoleon I (1798). Since the 1830s, their sovereignty has been confined to their properties in Rome.

WESTERN SAHARA

Area: 266 000 km² (102 676 sq mi).
Population: 185 000 (1987 est) – including many Moroccan settlers in El-Aaiun (Laayoune).
Capital: El-Aaiun (Laayoune) 97 000 (1982).
Language: Arabic.
Religion: Sunni Islam.

GOVERNMENT

Most of the Western Sahara is under Moroccan administration. In 27 February 1976 Sahrawi exiles in Algeria proclaimed the Saharan Arab Democratic Republic, which has been recognized by over 70 countries and admitted to membership of the OAU.
President: Mohammed Abdulaziz.

GEOGRAPHY

Western Sahara is a low flat desert region with no permanent streams.

ECONOMY

All trade is controlled by the Moroccan government.

The territory has few resources except for phosphate deposits.

RECENT HISTORY

Spain, Morocco and Mauritania reached an agreement to end Spanish rule (1975) and to divide Western Sahara between Morocco and Mauritania (1976). Morocco absorbed the Mauritanian sector when Mauritania withdrew (1979). The Polisario liberation movement – which had been fighting Spanish rule since 1973 – declared the territory independent. They control the eastern part of Western Sahara and continued guerrilla activity against the Moroccans until informal UN talks between the Sahrawis (the indigenous population) and Morocco began (1988–89). Agreement for a ceasefire and a referendum on the future of the territory was reached (1991), but no date has been agreed to hold the referendum.

FORMER NAMES

Since World War II a number of countries have changed their names, mainly substituting a traditional or local language name for a colonial name.

Former name	Present name
Basutoland	Lesotho
Bechuanaland	Botswana
Belgian Congo	Zaïre
British Guiana	Guyana
British Honduras	Belize
Burma	Myanmar
Byelorussia	Belarus
Caroline Islands	Micronesia
Ceylon	Sri Lanka
Congo, The	Zaïre
Dahomey	Benin
Dutch East Indies	Indonesia
Dutch Guiana	Suriname
Ellice Islands	Tuvalu
French Soudan	Mali
Gilbert Islands	Kiribati
Gold Coast	Ghana
Ivory Coast	Côte d'Ivoire
Kampuchea	Cambodia
Khirgizia	Kyrgyzstan
Khmer Republic	Cambodia
Moldavia	Moldova
Muscat and Oman	Oman
New Hebrides	Vanuatu
Northern Rhodesia	Zambia
Nyasaland	Malawi
Oubangui-Chari	Central Africa Republic
Persia	Iran
Portuguese Guinea	Guinea-Bissau
Portuguese Timor	East Timor
Rhodesia	Zimbabwe
Siam	Thailand
Southern Rhodesia	Zimbabwe
South West Africa	Namibia
Spanish Guinea	Equatorial Guinea
Spanish Sahara	Western Sahara
Tanganyika	Tanzania
Transjordan	Jordan
Trucial States	United Arab Emirates
Upper Volta	Burkina Faso
Urundi	Burundi

SPORT

A – Z OF SPORTS

Lists of British sporting champions and record holders are to be found in the United Kingdom chapter.

AMERICAN FOOTBALL

American football evolved in American universities in the second half of the 19th century as a descendant from soccer and rugby in Britain. The first professional game was played in 1895 at Latrobe, Pennsylvania. The American Professional Football Association was formed in 1920 and twelve teams contested the first league season. The association became the National Football League (NFL) in 1922. The American Football League (AFL) was formed in 1960. The two leagues merged in 1970, and under the NFL were reorganized into the National Football Conference (NFC) and the American Football Conference (AFC).

The major trophy is the Super Bowl, held annually since 1967 as a competition between firstly champions of the NFL and AFL, and since 1970 between the champions of the NFC and AFC.

The game is 11-a-side (12-a-side in Canada) with substitutes freely used. Pitch dimensions (NFL): 109.7×47.8 m (360×160 ft). Ball length 280–286 mm ($11–11\frac{1}{4}$ in), weighing 397–425 g (14–15 oz).

Super Bowl winners

1967–8	Green Bay Packers
1969	New York Jets
1970	Kansas City Chiefs
1971	Baltimore Colts
1972	Dallas Cowboys
1973–4	Miami Dolphins
1975–6	Pittsburgh Steelers
1977	Oakland Raiders
1978	Dallas Cowboys
1979–80	Pittsburgh Steelers
1981	Oakland Raiders
1982	San Francisco 49ers
1983	Washington Redskins
1984	Los Angeles Raiders
1985	San Francisco 49ers
1986	Chicago Bears
1987	New York Giants
1988	Washington Redskins
1989–90	San Francisco 49ers
1991	New York Giants
1992	Washington Redskins
1993	Dallas Cowboys

ARCHERY

Although developed as an organized sport from the 3rd century AD, archery is portrayed much earlier as a skill in Mesolithic cave paintings. Archery became firmly established as an international sport in 1931 with the founding of the governing body, *Federation Internationale de Tir à l'Arc* (FITA). The most popular form of archery is termed target archery. Other forms are field archery, shooting at animal figures, and flight shooting, which has the sole object of achieving distance.

The World Target Championships were first held in Poland in 1931 and have been biennial since 1957. The sport was included in the Olympic Games from 1900 to 1908, then again in 1920 (the Belgian style of shooting) and was re-introduced in 1972. In 1992 a new format was introduced for the Olympic competition with archers initially tackling a FITA round of 36 arrows each at 90 m, 70 m, 50 m and 30 m for men; and at 70 m, 60 m, 50 m and 30 m for women. The top 32 then met in a head-to-head knock-out competition to determine the medals.

The 1992 Olympic champions were: (men) *individual* Sébastien Flute (France), *team* Spain; (women) *individual* Cho Youn-jeong (South Korea), *team* South Korea.

ATHLETICS (TRACK AND FIELD)

There is evidence that competitive running was involved in early Egyptian rituals at Memphis c. 3800 BC, but organized athletics is usually dated to the ancient Olympic Games c. 1370 BC. The earliest known Olympiad was in July 776 BC, when Coroibos of Elis is recorded as winning the foot race over a distance of about 180–185 m (164–169 yd).

The sport is administered internationally by the International Amateur Athletic Federation (IAAF), formed in 1912, initially with 17 members. It ratified the first list of world records in 1914. The IAAF now has 203 nations affiliated to it, more than any other international organization, sporting or otherwise. The major championships are the quadrennial Olympic Games and the World Championships. The modern Olympics were revived in 1896 and separate World Championships were introduced in 1983, when they were held in Helsinki, Finland. Subsequent championships was held in Rome, Italy in 1987 and in Tokyo, Japan in 1991. From the 1993 Championships in Stuttgart, Germany they are being staged biennially.

Marathon events, held since 1896, commemorate the legendary run of an unknown Greek courier, possibly Pheidippides, who in 490 BC ran some 38·6 km (24 miles) from the Plain of Marathon to Athens with news of a Greek victory over the numerically superior Persian army. Delivering his message – 'Rejoice! We have won' – he collapsed and died. Since 1908 the distance has been standardized as 42 195 m (26 miles 385 yd).

Dimensions in field events:

Shot (men) – weight 7·26 kg (16 lb), diameter 110–130 mm (4·33–5·12 in)
Shot (women) – weight 4 kg (8 lb 13 oz), diameter 95–110 mm (3·74–4·33 in)
Discus (men) – weight 2 kg (4·409 lb), diameter 219–221 mm (8·622–8·701 in)
Discus (women) – weight 1 kg (2·204 lb), diameter 180–182 mm (7·086–7·165 in)
Hammer – weight 7·26 kg (16 lb), length 117·5–121·5 cm (46·259–47·835 in), diameter of head 110–130 mm (4·33–5·12 in)
Javelin (men) – weight 800 g (28·219 oz), length 260–270 cm (102·362–106·299 in)
Javelin (women) – weight 600 g (21·164 oz), length 220–230 cm (86·61–90·55 in).

TRACK & FIELD ATHLETICS WORLD RECORDS

Men

	min:sec	
100 m	9·86	Carl Lewis (USA) 1991
200 m	19·72	Pietro Mennea (Italy) 1979
400 m	43·29	Butch Reynolds (USA) 1988
800 m	1:41·73	Sebastian Coe (UK) 1981
1000 m	2:12·18	Sebastian Coe (UK) 1981
1500 m	3:28·82	Noureddine Morceli (Morocco) 1992

1 mile	3:46·32	Steve Cram (UK) 1985
2000 m	4:50·81	Saïd Aouita (Morocco) 1987
3000 m	7:28·96	Moses Kiptanui (Kenya) 1992
5000 m	12:58·39	Saïd Aouita (Morocco) 1987
10 000 m	27:08·23	Arturo Barrios (Mexico) 1989
20 km	56:55·60	Arturo Barrios (Mexico) 1991
1 hour	21 101 m	Arturo Barrios (Mexico) 1991
25 000 m	1hr 13:55·80	Toshihiko Seko (Japan) 1981
30 000 m	1hr 29:18·80	Toshihiko Seko (Japan) 1981
Marathon	2hr 06:50·00	Belayneh Dinsamo (Ethiopia) 1988
3000 m steeple	8:02·08	Moses Kiptanui (Kenya) 1992
110 m hurdles	12·92	Roger Kingdom (USA) 1989
400 m hurdles	46·78	Kevin Young (USA) 1992
4 × 100 m relay	37·40	USA 1992
4 × 400 m relay	2:55·74	USA 1992

	metres	
High jump	2·44	Javier Sotomayor (Cuba) 1989
Pole vault	6·13	Sergey Bubka (USSR) 1992
Long jump	8·95	Mike Powell (USA) 1991
Triple jump	17·97	Willie Banks (USA) 1985
Shot	23·12	Randy Barnes (USA) 1990
Discus	74·08	Jürgen Schult (GDR) 1986
Hammer	86·74	Yuriy Sedykh (USSR) 1986
Javelin	95·54	Jan Zelezný (Czech Republic) 1993
Decathlon	8891 pts	Dan O'Brien (USA) 1992

Track walking

	min:sec	
20 km	1hr 35·20	Stefan Johannsson (Sweden) 1992
50 km	3hr 41:38·40	Raúl González (Mexico) 1979

Road walking – fastest recorded times

20 km	1hr 18:13·00	Pavol Blazek (Czechoslovakia) 1990
50 km	3hr 37:41·00	Andrey Perlov (USSR) 1989

* Ben Johnson's 9·83 in 1987 was nullified as a record following his admission of drug taking

Women

	min:sec	
100 m	10·49	Florence Griffith-Joyner (USA) 1988
200 m	21·34	Florence Griffith-Joyner (USA) 1988
400 m	47·60	Marita Koch (GDR) 1985
800 m	1:53·28	Jarmila Kratochvilová (Czechoslovakia) 1983
1000 m	2:30·67	Christine Wachtel (GDR) 1990
1500 m	3:52·47	Tatyana Kazankina (USSR) 1980
1 mile	4:15·61	Paula Ivan (Romania) 1989
2000 m	5:28·69	Maricica Puica (Romania) 1986
3000 m	8:22·62	Tatyana Kazankina (USSR) 1984
5000 m	14:37·33	Ingrid Kristiansen (Norway) 1986
10 000 m	30:13·74	Ingrid Kristiansen (Norway) 1986
Marathon	2hr 21:06	Ingrid Kristiansen (Norway) 1985
100 m hurdles	12·21	Yordanka Donkova (Bulgaria) 1988
400 m hurdles	52·94	Marina Stepanova (USSR) 1986
4 × 100 m	41·37	GDR 1985
4 × 400 m	3:15·17	USSR 1988
	metres	

High jump	2·09	Stefka Kostadinova (Bulgaria) 1986
Long jump	7·52	Galina Chistyakova (USSR) 1988
Triple Jump	14·95	Inessa Kravets (USSR) 1991
Shot	22·63	Natalya Lisovskaya (USSR) 1987
Discus	76·80	Gabrielle Reinsch (GDR) 1988
Javelin	80·00	Petra Felke (GDR) 1988
Heptathlon	7291 pts	Jackie Joyner-Kersee (USA) 1988

Track walking

	min:sec	
5000 m	20:07·52	Beate Anders (GDR) 1990
10 km	41:56·23	Nadezhda Ryashkina (USSR) 1990

Road walking – fastest recorded time

10 km	41:30	Kerry Saxby (Australia) 1988

1992 OLYMPIC CHAMPIONS

Men

	min:sec	
100 m	9·96	Linford Christie (UK)
200 m	20·01	Michael Marsh (USA)
400 m	43·50	Quincy Watts (USA)
800 m	1:43·66	William Tanui (Kenya)
1500 m	3:40·12	Fermin Cacho (Spain)
5000 m	13:12·52	Dieter Baumann (Germany)
10 000 m	27:46·70	Khalid Skah (Morocco)
Marathon	2hr 13:23	Hwang Young-cho (S Korea)
3000 m steeple	8:08·94	Matthew Birir (Kenya)
110 m hurdles	13·12	Mark McKoy (Canada)
400 m hurdles	46·78	Kevin Young (USA)
4 × 100 m	37·40	USA
4 × 400 m	2:55·74	USA
20 km walk	1hr 21:45	Daniel Plaza (Spain)
50 km walk	3hr 50:13	Andrey Perlov (Russia)
	metres	
High jump	2·34	Javier Sotomayor (Cuba)
Pole vault	5·80	Maksim Tarasov (Russia)
Long jump	8·67	Carl Lewis (USA)
Triple jump	18·17w	Mike Conley (USA)
Shot	21·70	Mike Stulce (USA)
Discus	65·12	Romas Ubartas (Lithuania)
Hammer	82·54	Andrey Abduvaliyev (Tajikistan)
Javelin	89·66	Jan Zelezný (Czechoslovakia)
Decathlon	8611 pts	Robert Zmelík (Czechoslovakia)

Women

	min:sec	
100 m	10·82	Gail Devers (USA)
200 m	21·81	Gwen Torrence (USA)
400 m	48·83	Marie-José Pérec (France)
800 m	1:55·54	Ellen van Langen (Netherlands)
1500 m	3:55·30	Hassiba Boulmerka (Algeria)
3000 m	8:46·04	Yelena romanova (Russia)
10 000 m	31:06·02	Derartu Tulu (Ethiopia)
Marathon	2hr 32:41	Valentina Yegorova (Russia)
100 m hurdles	12·64	Paraskevi Patoulidou (Greece)
400 m hurdles	53·23	Sally Gunnell (UK)
4 × 100 m	42·11	USA
4 × 400 m	3:20·20	*United team
	metres	
High jump	2·02	Heike Henkel (Germany)
Long jump	7·14	Heike Drechsler (Germany)
Shot	21·06	Svetlana Krivelyova (Russia)

Discus	70·06	Maritza Martén (Cuba)
Javelin	68·34	Silke Renk (Germany)
Heptathlon	7044 pts	Jackie Joyner-Kersee (USA)

* a combined team representing 12 of the 15 former Soviet republics.

EUROPEAN CHAMPIONSHIPS

European Championships are held every four years. They were first staged in Turin in 1934 for men only. Women's championships were held separately in 1938, but men's and women's events were combined at one venue from 1946.

1990 EUROPEAN CHAMPIONS

Men

	min:sec	
100 m	10·00	Linford Christie (UK)
200 m	20·11	John Regis (UK)
400 m	45·08	Roger Black (UK)
800 m	1:44·76	Tom McKean (UK)
1500 m	3:38·25	Jens-Peter Herold (GDR)
5000 m	13:22·00	Salvatore Antibo (Italy)
10 000 m	27:41·27	Salvatore Antibo (Italy)
Marathon	2:14·02	Gelindo Bordin (Italy)
3000 m steeple	8:12·66	Francesco Panetta (Italy)
110 m hurdles	13·18	Colin Jackson (UK)
400 m hurdles	47·92	Kriss Akabusi (UK)
4 x 100 m	37·79	France
4 x 400 m	2:58·22	United Kingdom
20 km walk	1:22:05	Pavol Blazek (Czechoslovakia)
50 km walk	3:54:36	Andrey Perlov (USSR)
	metres	
High jump	2·34	Dragutin Topic (Yugoslavia)
Pole vault	5·85	Rodion Gataullin (USSR)
Long jump	8·25	Dietmar Haaf (West Germany)
Triple Jump	17·74	Leonid Voloshin (USSR)
Shot	21·32	Ulf Timmermann (GDR)
Discus	64·58	Jürgen Schult (GDR)
Hammer	84·14	Igor Astapkovich (USSR)
Javelin	87·30	Steve Backley (UK)
Decathlon	8574 pts	Christian Plaziat (France)

Women

	min:sec	
100 m	10·89	Katrin Krabbe (GDR)
200 m	21·95	Katrin Krabbe (GDR)
400 m	49·50	Grit Breuer (GDR)
800 m	1:55·87	Sigrun Wodars (GDR)
1500 m	4:08·12	Snezana Pajkic (Yugoslavia)
3000 m	8:43·06	Yvonne Murray (UK)
10 000 m	31:46·83	Yelena Romanova (USSR)
Marathon	2:31:27	Rosa Mota (Portugal)
100 m hurdles	12·79	Monique Ewanje-Épée (France)
400 m hurdles	53·62	Tatyana Ledovskaya (USSR)
4 x 100 m	41·68	GDR
4 x 400 m	3:21·02	GDR
10 km walk	44:00	Anna Rita Sidoti (Italy)
	metres	
High jump	1·99	Heike Henkel (West Germany)
Long jump	7·30	Heike Drechsler (GDR)
Shot	20·38	Astrid Kumbernuss (GDR)
Discus	68·46	Ilke Wyludda (GDR)
Javelin	67·68	Päivi Alafranti (Finland)
Heptathlon	6688 pts	Sabine Braun (West Germany)

See also the United Kingdom chapter

AUSTRALIAN FOOTBALL

Originally a hybrid of soccer, Gaelic football and rugby, Australian football laws were codified in 1866 in Melbourne, with the oval (rather than round) ball in use by 1867. In 1877 the Victorian Football Association was founded, from which eight clubs broke away to form the Victorian Football League (VFL). Four more teams had been admitted by 1925, and in 1987 teams from Queensland and Western Australia joined the league to now make it the Australian Football League. The AFL (formerly the VFL) Grand Final is played annually at the Melbourne Cricket Ground.

Teams are 18-a-side. Pitch dimensions are: width 110–155 m (120–170 yd), length 135–185 m (150–200 yd), encompassing an oval boundary line. The oval ball measures 736 mm (29½ in) in length, 572 mm (22¾ in) in diameter and weighs 452–482 g (16–17 oz).

BADMINTON

The modern game is believed to have evolved from Badminton Hall, Avon, England, c. 1870, or from a game played in India at about the same time. Modern rules were first codified in Poona, India, in 1876. A similar game was played in China 2000 years earlier.

The International Badminton Federation was founded in 1934, and membership reached 110 member nations in 1992. The main centres of the sport are Canada, China, Denmark, India, Indonesia, Japan, Malaysia, New Zealand, South Africa, USA, and the UK.

The World Championships were instituted in 1977 and initially held every three years, but are now staged biennially, as are the international team competitions – the Thomas Cup (for men; first held 1949) and the Uber Cup (for women; first held 1957). China won both competitions in 1986, 1988 and 1990. In 1992 Malaysia won the Thomas Cup and China and the Uber Cup. The major tournament prior to the introduction of World Championships was the annual All England Championships, initially held in 1899. Court dimensions: 13·41 × 6·1 m (44 × 20 ft; singles game 3ft narrower). The net is 1·5 m (5 ft) high at the centre; two or four players.

Badminton was played as a demonstration sport at the Olympic Games in 1972 and 1988, and it became a medal sport in 1992, when the winners were:

Men's singles: Alan Budi Kusuma (Indonesia)
Women's singles: Susi Susanti (Indonesia)
Men's doubles: Kim Moon-soo and Park Joo-bong (S Korea)
Women's doubles: Hwant Hye-young and Chung So-young (S Korea)

BASEBALL

The modern, or Cartwright, rules, were introduced in New Jersey on 19 June 1846, although a game of the same name had been played in England prior to 1700. Baseball is mainly played in America, where there are two leagues, the National (NL) and the American (AL), founded in 1876 and 1901 respectively. It is also very popular in Japan. The winners of each US league meet annually in a best of seven series of games – the World Series – established permanently in 1905.

Baseball was added to the Olympic programme in 1992, when the gold medal was won by Cuba.

Recent World Series winners

1980 Philadelphia Phillies (NL)
1981 Los Angeles Dodgers (NL)
1982 St Louis Cardinals (NL)
1983 Baltimore Orioles (AL)
1984 Detroit Tigers (AL)
1985 Kansas City Royals (AL)
1986 New York Mets (NL)
1987 Minnesota Twins (AL)
1988 Los Angeles Dodgers (NL)
1989 Oakland Athletics (AL)
1990 Cincinnati Reds (NL)
1991 Minnesota Twins (AL)
1992 Toronto Blue Jays (AL)

The game is 9-a-side. A standard ball weighs 148 g
(5–5¼ oz) and is 23 cm (9–9½ in) in circumference.
Bats are up to 7 cm (2¾ in) in diameter and up to 1·07
m (42 in) in length.

BASKETBALL

A game not dissimilar to basketball was played by
the Olmecs in Mexico in the 10th century BC, but the
modern game was devised by (Canadian-born) Dr
James Naismith in Massachusetts, in December
1891.

The governing body is the *Fédération Internationale
de Basketball Amateur* (FIBA), formed in 1932. The
game is played worldwide and by 1989, 178 national
federations were members of FIBA. An Olympic
sport for men since 1936, and for women since 1976,
the 1988 titles were won by the USSR (men) and USA
(women). The World championships, first held for
men in 1950 and for women in 1953, are staged every
four years.

Teams are 5-a-side, with seven substitutes allowed.
The rectangular court is 26·0 m (85 ft) in length, and
14·0 m (46 ft) wide, and the ball is 75–78 cm (30 in) in
circumference and weighs 600–650 g (21–23 oz).

Olympic champions
Men
USA: 1936, 1948, 1952, 1956, 1960, 1964, 1968, 1976,
  1984, 1992
USSR: 1972, 1988
Yugoslavia: 1980

Women
USSR: 1976, 1980
USA: 1984, 1988
**Unified team:* 1992
* a combined team representing 12 of the 15 former
Soviet republics.

World champions
Men
Argentina: 1950
USA: 1954, 1986
Brazil: 1959, 1963
USSR: 1967, 1974, 1982
Yugoslavia: 1970, 1978, 1990

Women
USA: 1953, 1957, 1979, 1986, 1990
USSR: 1959, 1964, 1967, 1971, 1975, 1983

BIATHLON

A combination of cross-country skiing and rifle
shooting, in which competitors ski over prepared
courses carrying a small-bore rifle, the biathlon has
been an Olympic event for men since 1960. Women's
events were introduced in 1992. Men compete individually over 10 km or 20 km distances. There are two
shooting competitions at a target 50 metres away
over the 10 km distance and four – both prone and
standing – over the 20 km distance. The relay event is
four by 7·5 km, each member shooting once prone and
once standing. Penalties are imposed for missing the
target. The women's equivalent distances are 7·5 km,
15 km and 3 by 7.5 km relay.

The sport's governing body is *L'Union Internationale
de Pentathlon Moderne et Biatholon* (UIPMB), which
took on the administration of biathlon in 1957, and
staged the first World Championships in 1958.

BILLIARDS

Probably deriving from the old French word *billiard*
(a stick with a curved end), a reference as early as
1429 suggests the game was originally played on
grass. Louis XI of France (1461–83) is believed to be
the first to have played billiards on a table. Rubber
cushions were introduced in 1835, and slate beds in
1836.

The World Professional and Amateur Championships have been held since 1870 and 1926
respectively.

Dimensions of table: 3·66 × 1·87 m (12 × 6 ft).

BOARDSAILING (WINDSURFING)

Following a High Court decision, Peter Chilvers has
been credited with devising the prototype boardsail
in 1958. As a sport, it was pioneered by Henry Hoyle
Schweitzer and Jim Drake in California in 1968. The
World Championships were first held in 1973 and
boardsailing was added to the Olympic Games in
1984.

BOBSLEIGH AND TOBOGGANING

Although the first known sledge dates back to c. 6500
BC in Heinola, Finland, organized bobsleighing
began in Davos, Switzerland, in 1889.

The International Federation of Bobsleigh and
Tobogganing was formed in 1923, followed by the
International Bobsleigh Federation in 1957.

The World and Olympic Championships began in
1924, and competition is for crews of two or four. The
driver steers while the rear man operates brakes and
corrects skidding. With the four-man, the middle two
riders alter weight transference for cornering.

The oldest tobogganing club is the St Moritz in
Switzerland, founded in 1887, and home of the Cresta
Run, which dates from 1884. The course is 1212·25 m
(3977 ft) long with a drop of 157 m (514 ft). Solo speeds
reach 145 km/h (90 mph). In lugeing, the rider sits or
lies back, as opposed to lying face down in
tobogganing.

BOWLING (TEN-PIN)

The ancient German game of nine-pins was banned
in Connecticut in 1847, and subsequently in other US
states. Ten-pin bowling was introduced to beat the
ban. Rules were first standardized by the American
Bowling Congress (ABC), formed in September 1895.

Concentrated in the USA, the game is also very
popular in Japan and Europe. The World Championships were introduced for men in 1954 and
women in 1963, under the *Fédération Internationale*

des Quilleurs (FIQ), which governs a number of bowling games.

The ten pins are placed in a triangle at the end of a lane of total length 19·16 m (62 ft 10¾ in) and width 1·06 m (42 in).

BOWLS

The known history of outdoor bowls goes back as far as the 13th century in England, but it was forbidden by Edward III because its popularity threatened the practice of archery. The modern rules were not framed until 1848–9 in Scotland by William Mitchell. There are two types of greens, the crown and the level, the former being played almost exclusively in northern England and the Midland counties.

Lawn bowls is played mostly in the UK and Commonwealth countries. The International Bowling Board was formed in July 1905. The Men's and Women's World Championships are held every four years, with singles, pairs, triples and fours events. The World Championships for Indoor Bowls were introduced in 1979 and are staged annually.

BOXING

Competitively, boxing began in ancient Greece as one of the first Olympic sports. Boxing with gloves was first depicted on a fresco from the isle of Thera, c. 1520 BC. Prize-fighting rules were formed in England in 1743 by Jack Broughton, but modern day boxing was regularized in 1867 when the 8th Marquess of Queensberry gave his name to the new rules. Boxing only became a legal sport in 1901.

Professional boxing has several world governing bodies, the two oldest being the World Boxing Council (WBC) and the World Boxing Association (WBA), based in Mexico City and Manila respectively. Neither body has been able to agree on fight regulations, and the situation has been further complicated by the formation of the International Boxing Federation (IBF) in the USA in 1983 and the World Boxing Organization (WBO) in 1988. Recognized weight categories are:

Limit in lb (kg)	Weight category
105 (48)	strawweight (WBC), mini-flyweight (WBA, IBF, WBO)
108 (49)	light-flyweight (WBC), junior flyweight (WBA, IBF, WBO)
112 (51)	flyweight
115 (52)	super-flyweight (WBC), junior bantamweight (WBA, IBF, WBO)
118 (54)	bantamweight
122 (55)	super bantamweight (WBC), junior featherweight (WBA, IBF, WBO)
126 (57)	featherweight
130 (59)	super featherweight (WBC) junior lightweight (WBA, IBF, WBO)
135 (61)	lightweight
140 (64)	super lightweight (WBC), junior welterweight (WBA, IBF, WBO)
147 (67)	welterweight
154 (70)	super lightweight (WBC), junior middleweight (WBA, IBF, WBO)
160 (73)	middleweight
168 (76)	super middleweight
175 (79)	light heavyweight
190 (86)	junior heavyweight (WBO), cruiser-weight (WBC, WBA, IBF)
190 (86) +	heavyweight

Weight categories in amateur boxing are:

Limit in kg (lb)	Weight category
48 (106)	light flyweight
51 (112)	flyweight
54 (119)	bantamweight
57 (126)	featherweight
60 (132)	lightweight
63.5 (140)	light welterweight
67 (148)	welterweight
71 (157)	light middleweight
75 (165)	middleweight
81 (179)	light heavyweight
91 (201)	heavyweight
91 (201) +	super heavyweight

CANOEING

Modern canoes and kayaks originated among the Indians and Inuit (Eskimos) of North America, but canoeing as a sport is attributed to an English barrister, James MacGregor, who founded the Royal Canoe Club in 1866.

With a kayak, the paddler sits in a forward-facing position and uses a double-bladed paddle, whereas in a canoe the paddler kneels in a forward-facing position and propels with a single-bladed paddle. An Olympic sport since 1936, competitions for Olympic titles are now held at flat water in nine events for men at 500 m and 1000 m, and three for women each at 500 m. In 1992 slalom events were reintroduced with three men's events and one women's event.

CHESS

Derived from the Persian word *Shah*, meaning a king or ruler, the game itself originated in India under the name *Caturanga*, a military game (literally 'four corps'). The earliest surviving chessmen are an ivory set found in Russia and dated c. AD 200. By the 10th century, chess was played in most European countries and there are today some 40 million enthusiasts in Russia and the former Soviet republics. The governing body, founded in 1922, is the *Fédération Internationale des Echecs* (FIDE), which has been responsible for the World Chess Championship competitions since 1946, although official champions date from 1886 and there were unofficial champions before then.

Players are graded by FIDE according to competitive results on the ELO scoring system, with results issued twice yearly. Grandmaster level is 2500, a rating currently attained by about 100 players. The highest rating ever achieved is 2805 by the current world champion Gary Kasparov, reached in December 1992, having surpassed Bobby Fishcher's previous best of 2785 (January 1991). The highest rated woman player is Judit Polgar (Hungary) at 2595. She became the youngest ever Grandmaster at 15 on 20 December 1991.

World champions

1851–8 Adolf Anderssen (Germany)
1858–62 Paul Morphy (USA)
1862–6 Adolf Anderssen (Germany)
1866–94 Wilhelm Steinitz (Austria)
1894–1921 Emanuel Lasker (Germany)
1921–7 José Capablanca (Cuba)
1927–35 Alexandre Alekhine (France)
1935–7 Max Euwe (Netherlands)
1937–46 Alexandre Alekhine* (France)

1948–57 Mikhail Botvinnik (USSR)
1957–8 Vasiliy Smyslov (USSR)
1958–60 Mikhail Botvinnik (USSR)
1960–1 Mikhail Tal (USSR)
1961–3 Mikhail Botvinnik (USSR)
1963–9 Tigran Petrosian (USSR)
1969–72 Boris Spassky (USSR)
1972–5 Bobby Fischer (USA)
1975–85 Anatoliy Karpov (USSR)
1985– Gary Kasparov (USSR/Russia)

Women's world champions
1927–44 Vera Menchik* (UK)

1950–3 Lyudmila Rudenko (USSR)
1953–6 Yelizaveta Bykova (USSR)
1956–8 Olga Rubtsova (USSR)
1958–62 Yelizaveta Bykova (USSR)
1962–78 Nona Gaprindashvili (USSR)
1978–91 Maya Chiburdanidze (USSR)
1991– Xie Jun (China)

* The reorganization of the sport after 1946, and the death of Alekhine in 1946 and Menchik in 1944 left the sport without a world or women's champion in 1947 and 1945–49 respectively.

CRICKET

SUMMARY OF TEST MATCH RESULTS
(as at 1 June 1993)
The first figure is the number of wins by the team on the left, over the team in that column, the second figure is the number of draws. Thus in England v Australia Tests, England have won 88, Australia 104, with 82 Tests left drawn.

	A	E	I	NZ	P	SA	SL	WI	Z	Wins	Tests
Australia	–	104/82	24/17*	10/10	12/13	29/13	4/3	30/20*	–	213	522
England	88/82	–	31/36	33/35	14/31	46/38	3/1	24/37	–	239	690
India	8/17*	14/36	–	12/13	4/33	0/3	3/4	6/30	1/1	44	282
New Zealand	7/10	4/35	6/13	–	3/16	2/6	4/6	4/12	1/1	31	217
Pakistan	9/13	7/31	7/33	14/16	–	–	6/5	7/11	–	50	210
South Africa	11/13	18/38	1/3	9/6	–	–	–	0/0	–	39	177
Sri Lanka	0/3	1/1	1/4	1/6	1/3	–	–	–	–	4	43
West Indies	26/20*	43/37	26/30	8/12	12/12	1/0	–	–	–	116	299
Zimbabwe	–	–	0/1	0/1	–	–	–	–	–	0	4

* plus one tie. There have been two tied Tests: Australia v West Indies 1960 and Australia v India 1986

A drawing dated c. 1250 shows a bat and ball game reseLmbling cricket, although the formal origins are early 18th century. The formation of the MCC (Marylebone Cricket Club) in 1787 resulted in codified laws by 1835.

The International (Imperial until 1965) Cricket Conference (ICC), was formed by representatives of England, Australia and South Africa in 1909. India, New Zealnd and West Indies were elected members in 1926, Pakistan in 1953 and Sri Lanka in 1981. South Africa ceased to be a member in 1961, but was readmitted to Test cricket in 1992, and later that year Zimbabwe became the ninth Test cricketing nation. Other, non-Test playing nations have been admitted: 19 as associate members and five as affiliated members.

The World Cup, the international one-day tournament, is held every four years, with the Test-playing countries plus the winner of the ICC Trophy, which is competed for by non-Test playing countries.

World Cup winners
1975 West Indies
1979 West Indies
1983 India
1987 Australia
1991 Pakistan

The first Women's World Cup was held in 1973. *Winners:* 1973 England, 1978 Australia, 1982 Australia, 1988 Australia.

Dimensions: Ball circumference 20·79–22·8 cm (8³⁄₁₆–9 in), weight 155–163 g (5½–5¾ oz); pitch 20·11 m (22 yd) from stump to stump.

In the UK, the first-class counties – now numbering 18 – have competed in the county championship, or in its preceding inter-county matches, since 1864. See the United Kingdom chapter.

In Australia, the annual first-class inter-state competition has been contested for the Sheffield Shield from 1891–92. Sheffield Shield winners (up to an including 1992) have been New South Wales (40 times), Victoria (25), South Australia (12) and Western Australia (11). Queensland and Tasmania have never won the Shield. Recent winners have been:
1982 South Australia
1983 New South Wales
1984 Western Australia
1985 New South Wales
1986 New South Wales
1987 Western Australia
1988 Western Australia
1989 Western Australia
1990 New South Wales
1991 Victoria
1992 Western Australia

In India, the annual first-class inter-state championship is the Ranji Trophy, instituted in 1934. Bombay has won the Trophy on no fewer than 30 occasions. Recent winners have been:
1983 Karnataka
1984 Bombay
1985 Bombay
1986 Delhi
1987 Hyderabad
1988 Tamil Nadu
1989 Delhi

1990 Bengal
1991 Haryana
1992 Delhi

In New Zealand, the annual first-class competition was the Plunkett Shield from 1906 to 1974–75. Since 1974–75, the six first-class sides have competed in the Shell series. Recent winners have been:

1983 Wellington
1984 Canterbury
1985 Wellington
1986 Otago
1987 Central Districts
1988 Otago
1989 Auckland
1990 Wellington
1991 Auckland
1992 Central Districts and
     Northern Districts

In Pakistan, the premier first-class competition is the Quaid-e-Azam Trophy which has been contested since 1954. Karachi has won the competition eight times. Recent winners have been:

1983 United Bank
1984 National Bank
1985 United Bank
1986 Karachi
1987 National Bank
1988 Habib Bank
1989 ADBP
1990 PIA
1991 Karachi
1992 Karachi

In South Africa, the annual first-class competition for the Currie Cup has been held since 1889–90. Transvaal has won the competition outright no fewer than 28 times and shared the championship four times; Natal has won 21 times and shared the title three times. Recent winners have been:

1983 Transvaal
1984 Transvaal
1985 Transvaal
1986 Western Province
1987 Transvaal
1988 Transvaal
1989 Eastern Province
1990 Eastern Province
1991 Western Province
1992 Eastern Province

In the West Indies, the annual first-class competition is the Red Stripe Cup (which was preceded by the Shell Shield from 1966 to 1987). Barbados has won the championship no fewer than 13 times. Recent winners have been:

1983 Guyana
1984 Barbados
1985 Trinidad and Tobago
1986 Barbados
1987 Guyana
1988 Jamaica
1989 Jamaica
1990 Leeward Islands
1991 Barbados
1992 Jamaica

CURLING

Similar to bowls on ice, curling dates from the 15th century, although organized administration of the sport only began in 1838 with the Grand (later Royal) Caledonian Curling Club in Edinburgh. The sport is traditionally popular in Scotland and Canada. The International Curling Federation was formed in 1966, and curling was included in the 1988 and 1992 Olympic Games as a demonstration sport, as it had been in 1924, 1932, 1964.

CYCLING

The first known cycling race was held over 2 km (1·2 mi) in Paris on 31 May 1868. The Road Record Association in Britain was formed in 1888, and F. T. Bidlake devised the time trial (1890) as a means of avoiding traffic congestion caused by ordinary mass road racing.

Competitive racing, popular worldwide, is now conducted both on road and track. The Tour de France (founded in 1903) is the longest-lasting non-motorized sporting event in the world, taking 21 days to stage annually. The yellow jersey, to distinguish the leading rider, was introduced in 1919. The World Championships were first held in 1893 at two events, the sprint and motor-paced over 100 km. A range of road and track events are now contested annually for amateur and professional men and for women.

Tour de France winners (from 1947)

1947 Jean Robic (France)
1948 Gino Bartali (Italy)
1949 Fausto Coppi (Italy)
1950 Ferdinand Kübler (Switzerland)
1951 Hugo Koblet (Switzerland)
1952 Fausto Coppi (Italy)
1953–5 Louison Bobet (France)
1956 Roger Walkowiak (France)
1957 Jacques Anquetil (France)
1958 Charly Gaul (Luxembourg)
1959 Frederico Bahamontès (Spain)
1960 Gastone Nencini (Italy)
1961–4 Jacques Anquetil (France)
1965 Felice Gimondi (Italy)
1966 Lucien Aimar (France)
1967 Roger Pingeon (France)
1968 Jan Janssen (Netherlands)
1969–72 Eddy Merckx (Belgium)
1973 Luis Ocana (Spain)
1974 Eddy Merckx (Belgium)
1975 Bernard Thevenet (France)
1976 Lucien van Impe (Belgium)
1977 Bernard Thevenet (France)
1978–9 Bernard Hinault (France)
1980 Joop Zoetemelk (Netherlands)
1981–2 Bernard Hinault (France)
1983–4 Laurent Fignon (France)
1985 Bernard Hinault (France)
1986 Greg LeMond (USA)
1987 Stephen Roche (Ireland)
1988 Pedro Delgado (Spain)
1989–90 Greg LeMond (USA)
1991–92 Miguel Induráin (Spain)

Cycling has been included in the modern Olympic Games since 1896. There are currently seven men's and two women's events on the Olympic programme.

1992 Olympic champions
Men
Sprint: Jens Fiedler (Germany)
1000 m time trial: José Moreno (Spain) 1:03·342
4000 m individual pursuit: Chris Boardman (UK)
50 km points race: Giovanni Lombardi (Italy)
Road race: Fabio Casartelli (Italy)
Team time trial: Germany
Team pursuit: Germany

Women
Sprint: Erika Salumyae (Estonia)
Road race: Kathryn Watt (Australia)
3000 m individual pursuit: Petra Rossner (Germany).

World Championships were first held in 1893 at two events, the sprint and the motor-paced over 100 km. A range of road and track events are now contested annually for amateur and professional men and for women.

DARTS

Brian Gamlin of Bury, Lancashire, is credited with devising the present numbering system on the darts board, although in non-sporting form darts began with the heavily weighted throwing arrows used in Roman and Greek warfare. Immensely popular in the UK – there are today some 6 000 000 players – the sport is rapidly spreading in America and parts of Europe. The World championships were first held in 1978. Winners have been:

1978	Leighton Rees (Wales)
1979	John Lowe (England)
1980–1	Eric Bristow (England)
1982	Jocky Wilson (Scotland)
1983	Keith Deller (England)
1984–6	Eric Bristow (England)
1987	John Lowe (England)
1988	Bob Anderson (England)
1989	Jocky Wilson (Scotland)
1990	Phil Taylor (England)
1991	Dennis Priestley (England)
1992	Phil Taylor (England)
1993	John Lowe (England)

EQUESTRIANISM

Horse riding is some 5000 years old, but schools of horsemanship, or equitation, were not established until the 16th century, primarily in Italy and then in France. The earliest known jumping competition was in Islington, London in 1869.

An Olympic event since 1912, events are held in dressage, show jumping and three-day event, with team and individual titles for each. Dressage (the French term for the training of horses) is a test of a rider's ability to control a horse through various manoeuvres within an area of 60 × 20 m (66× 22 yd). In show jumping, riders jump a set course of fences, incurring four faults for knocking a fence down or landing (one or more feet) in the water, three faults for a first refusal, six faults then elimination for 2nd and 3rd, and eight faults for a fall. The three-day event encompasses dressage, cross country and jumping. The governing body is the *Fédération Equestre Internationale*, founded in May 1921.

1992 Olympic champions
Individual:
Show jumping: Ludger Beerbaum (Germany) on Classic Touch.
Three-day event: Matthew Kyan (Australia) on Kibah Tic Toc.
Dressage: Nicole Uphof (Germany) on Rembrandt.
Team:
Show jumping: Netherlands.
Three-day event: Australia.
Dressage: Germany.

FENCING

Fencing (fighting with single sticks) was practised as a sport, or as part of a religious ceremony, in Egypt as early as 1360 BC. The modern sport developed directly from the duelling of the Middle Ages.

There are three types of sword used today. With the foil (introduced in the 17th century), only the trunk of the body is acceptable as a target. The épée (a mid-19th century introduction) is marginally heavier and more rigid, and the whole body is a valid target. The sabre (a late 19th-century introduction) has cutting edges on both sides of the blade, and scores on the whole body from the waist upwards. Only with the sabre can points be scored with the edge of the blade rather than the tip.

Women compete in foil only at the Olympic Games, but the women's épée was added to the annual World Championships from 1989. For men, there are individual and team events for each type of sword in the Olympics. The world governing body is the *Fédération Internationale d'Escrime*, founded in 1913.

1992 Olympic champions
Men

	Individual	*Team*
Foil	Philippe Omnès (France)	Germany
Epée	Eric Srecki (France)	Germany
Sabre	Bence Szabó (Hungary)	*Unified Team

* a combined team representing 12 of the 15 former Soviet republics.

Women

Foil	Giovanna Trillini (Italy)	Italy

FIVES

Eton Fives originate from a handball game first recorded as being played against the buttress of Eton College Chapel in 1825. The rules were codified in 1877, and last amended in 1981.

Rugby Fives, a variation, dates from c. 1850. Both are more or less confined to the UK.

FOOTBALL (Association)

A game resembling football, *Tsu-Chu-Tsu*, meaning 'to kick the ball with feet' (*chu* meaning 'leather') – was played in China around 400 BC. Calcio, closer to the modern game, existed in Italy in 1410. Official references to football date to Edward II's reign in England – he banned the game in London in 1314; later monarchs issued similar edicts. The first soccer rules were formulated at Cambridge University in 1846; previously football was brutal and lawless. The Football Association (FA) was founded in England on 26 October 1863. Eleven per side became standard in 1870.

The governing body, *the Fédération Internationale de Football Association* (FIFA), was founded in Paris on 21 May 1904 and football is now played throughout the world.

Internationally, the World Cup has been held every four years since 1930 (except in 1942 and 1946). The European Championship, instituted in 1958 as the Nations Cup, is held every four years. The European Champions Club Cup, instituted in 1955 as the European Cup, is contested annually by the League Champions of the member countries of the Union of European Football Associations (UEFA). The European Cup Winners Cup was instituted in 1960 for national cup winners (or runners-up if the winners are in the European Cup). The UEFA Cup was instituted in 1955 as the Inter-City Fairs Cup, and has been held annually since 1960. The European Super Cup (instituted in 1972) is played between the winners of the European Champions Club Cup and the Cup Winners Cup; and the World Club Championship (instituted in 1960) is a contest between the winners of the European Cup and the Copa Libertadores (the South American championship).

Football is an 11-a-side game; the ball's circumference is 68–71 cm (27–28 in) and weight 396–453 g (14–16 oz). Pitch length 91–120 m (100–130 yd), width 45–91 m (50–100 yd).

THE WORLD CUP

Year	Winner	Venue
1930	Uruguay	Uruguay
1934	Italy	Italy
1938	Italy	France
1950	Uruguay	Brazil
1954	Germany (W)	Switzerland
1958	Brazil	Sweden
1962	Brazil	Chile
1966	England	England
1970	Brazil	Mexico
1974	Germany (W)	Germany (W)
1978	Argentina	Argentina
1982	Italy	Spain
1986	Argentina	Mexico
1990	Germany (W)	Italy

Lists of English and Scottish champions and cup-winners are to be found in the United Kingdom chapter.

The major football leagues are in Western Europe and Latin America. They include the following.

The Brazilian National Championship was founded as late as 1971 – previously soccer was played at state championship level. Up to and including 1992, Corinthians (Sao Paulo) has won the title five times, Flamengo (Rio de Janeiro) four times and Santos four times. Recent winners have been:
1983 Flamengo (Rio de Janeiro)
1984 Fluminense (Rio de Janeiro)
1985 Coritiba FC (Curitiba)
1986 Sao Paulo FC
1987 Flamengo (Rio de Janeiro)
1988 EC Bahia (Salvador)
1989 Vasco da Gama (Rio de Janeiro)
1990 Corinthians (Sao Paulo)
1991 Sao Paulo FC
1992 Flamengo (Rio de Janeiro)

The French League was founded in 1933. Up to and including 1992, AS Saint-Etienne has won the championship ten times, Olympique Marseille eight times and FC Nantes six times. Recent winners have been:
1983 FC Nantes
1984 Girondins Bordeaux
1985 Girondins Bordeaux
1986 Paris Saint-Germain
1987 Girondins Bordeaux
1988 AS Monaco
1989 Olympique Marseille
1990 Olympique Marseille
1991 Olympique Marseille
1992 Olympique Marseille

The German League was founded in 1903. Up to and including 1992, Bayern München has won the championship 12 times, I. FC. Nürnberg nine times and Hamburger SV six times. Recent winners have been:

1983 Hamburger SV
1984 VfB Stuttgart
1985 Bayern München
1986 Bayern München
1987 Bayern München
1988 Werder Bremen
1989 Bayern München
1990 Bayern München
1991 I.FC. Kaiserslautern
1992 VfB Stuttgart.

The Italian League was founded in 1898. Up to and including 1992, Juventus has won the championship 22 times, Internazionale Milano 14 times, AC Milano 12 times and Genova nine times. Recent winners have been:
1983 Roma
1984 Juventus
1985 Hellas-Verona
1986 Juventus
1987 Napoli
1988 AC Milano
1989 Internazionale Milano
1990 Napoli
1991 Sampdoria (Genova)
1992 AC Milano

The Spanish League was founded in 1926. Up to and including 1992, Real Madrid has won the championship 25 times, Barcelona 12 times, Atlético Madrid eight times and Athletic Bilbao eight times. Recent winners have been:
1983 Athletic Bilbao
1984 Athletic Bilbao
1985 Barcelona
1986 Real Madrid
1987 Real Madrid
1988 Real Madrid
1989 Real Madrid
1990 Real Madrid
1991 Barcelona
1992 Barcelona

EUROPEAN CHAMPION CLUBS CUP

1956–60	Real Madrid
1961–2	Benfica (Lisbon)
1963	AC Milan
1964–5	Internazionale Milan
1966	Real Madrid
1967	Glasgow Celtic
1968	Manchester United
1969	AC Milan
1970	Feyenoord (Rotterdam)
1971–3	Ajax Amsterdam
1974–6	Bayern Munich
1977–8	Liverpool
1979–80	Nottingham Forest
1981	Liverpool
1982	Aston Villa
1983	SV Hamburg
1984	Liverpool
1985	Juventus (Turin)
1986	Steaua Bucharest
1987	FC Porto
1988	PSV Eindhoven
1989–90	AC Milan
1991	Red Star Belgrade
1992	Barcelona
1993	Marseille

EUROPEAN CUP WINNER'S CUP

1961	Fiorentina
1962	Atletico Madrid
1963	Tottenham Hotspur
1964	Sporting Lisbon
1965	West Ham United
1966	Borussia Dortmund
1967	Bayern Munich
1968	AC Milan
1969	Slovan Bratislava
1970	Manchester City
1971	Chelsea
1972	Glasgow Rangers
1973	AC Milan
1974	FC Magdeburg
1975	Dynamo Kiev
1976	Anderlecht
1977	SV Hamburg
1978	Anderlecht
1979	Barcelona
1980	Valencia
1981	Dynamo Tbilisi
1982	Barcelona
1983	Aberdeen
1984	Juventus (Turin)
1985	Everton
1986	Dynamo Kiev
1987	Ajax Amsterdam
1988	Mechelen
1989	Barcelona
1990	Sampdoria (Genoa)
1991	Manchester United
1992	Werder Bremen
1993	Parma

UEFA CUP

1958	Barcelona
1960	Barcelona
1961	AS Roma
1962–3	Valencia
1964	Real Zaragoza
1965	Ferencvaros (Budapest)
1966	Barcelona
1967	Dynamo Zagreb
1968	Leeds United
1969	Newcastle United
1970	Arsenal
1971	Leeds United
1972	Tottenham Hotspur
1973	Liverpool
1974	Feyenoord (Rotterdam)
1975	Borussia Mönchengladbach
1976	Liverpool
1977	Juventus (Turin)
1978	PSV Eindhoven
1979	Borussia Mönchengladbach
1980	Eintracht Frankfurt
1981	Ipswich Town
1982	IFK Göteborg
1983	Anderlecht
1984	Tottenham Hotspur
1985–6	Real Madrid
1987	IFK Göteborg
1988	Bayer Leverkusen
1989	Napoli
1990	Juventus (Turin)
1991	Internazionale Milan
1992	Ajax
1993	Juventus (Turin)

EUROPEAN CHAMPIONSHIPS

1960	USSR
1964	Spain
1968	Italy
1972	Germany (W)
1976	Czechoslovakia
1980	Germany (W)
1984	France
1988	Netherlands
1992	Denmark

GAELIC FOOTBALL

Gaelic football developed from a traditional inter-parish 'football free for all' with no time limit, no defined playing area nor specific rules. The Gaelic Athletic Association established the game in its present form in 1884; teams are 15-a-side. Played throughout Ireland, the All-Ireland Championship, first held in 1887, is contested annually by Irish counties; the final is played at Croke Park, Dublin, each September.

GLIDING

Around AD 1500 Leonardo da Vinci defined the difference between gliding and powered flight in some drawings. However, the first authenticated man-carrying glider was designed by Sir George Cayley in 1853.

In competitive terms, gliders contest various events – pure distance, distance to a declared goal, to a declared goal and back, height gain and absolute altitude. The World Championships were first held in 1937 and have been biennial since 1948.

Hang gliding has flourished in recent years, boosted by the invention of the flexible 'wing' by Professor Francis Rogallo in the early 1960s. The first official World Championships were held in 1976.

GOLF

A prohibiting law passed by the Scottish Parliament in 1457 declared 'goff be utterly cryit doune and not usit'. This is the earliest mention of golf, although games of similar principle date as far back as AD 400. Golf is played worldwide today.

Competition is either 'match play', contested by individuals or pairs and decided by the number of holes won, or 'stroke play', decided by the total number of strokes for a round. The modern golf course measures an average total distance of between 5500 and 6400 metres, and is divided into 18 holes of varying lengths. Clubs are currently limited to a maximum of 14, comprising 'irons' Nos. 1–10 (with the face of the club at increasingly acute angles), and 'woods' for driving. Golf balls in the UK and North America have the minimum diameter of 42·62 mm (1·68 in).

Professionally, the four major tournaments are the British Open, the US Open, the US Masters and the US Professional Golfers' Association (USPGA).

The Ryder Cup has been contested every two years from 1927 (apart from during the War). The USA have been opposed by Great Britain 1927–91, Great Britain and Ireland 1973–77, and Europe from 1979.

The current format is for four foursomes and four fourball matches on each of the first two days, and 12 singles on the third and final day. The USA have 22 wins to 5 (with two draws) to date, with Europe successful in 1985 and 1987, the 1989 match drawn, and the USA winning in 1991.

The Walker Cup has been contested every two years from 1927 (apart from during the War) between amateur teams from the USA and Great Britain (Great Britain and Ireland from 1981). The USA have 29 wins to 3 (with one draw) to date, with Great Britain winning in 1938, 1971 and 1989.

The Curtis Cup is a biennial team competition between women's team from the USA and Great Britain and Ireland, first held at Wentworth in 1932 and named after the American sisters Margaret and Harriot Curtis. The USA have 20 wins to 5 (with two draws) to date, with Great Britain and Ireland winning in 1952, 1956, 1986, 1988 and 1992.

THE BRITISH OPEN GOLF CHAMPIONSHIP

The oldest open championship in the world, 'The Open', was first held on 17 October 1860 at the Prestwick Club, Ayrshire, Scotland. It was then over 36 holes; since 1892 it has been over 72 holes of stroke play. Since 1920, the Royal and Ancient Golf Club has managed the event.

Winners	*Score*
(UK unless specified)	
1860 Willie Park, Sr	174
1861 Tom Morris, Sr	163
1862 Tom Morris, Sr	163
1863 Willie Park, Sr	168
1864 Tom Morris, Sr	167
1865 Andrew Strath	162
1866 Willie Park, Sr	169
1867 Tom Morris, Sr	170
1868 Tom Morris, Jr	170
1869 Tom Morris, Jr	154
1870 Tom Morris, Jr	149
1871 Not held	
1872 Tom Morris, Jr	166
1873 Tom Kidd	179
1874 Mungo Park	159
1875 Willie Park, Sr	166
1876 Robert Martin	176
1877 Jamie Anderson	160
1878 Jamie Anderson	170
1879 Jamie Anderson	170
1880 Robert Ferguson	162
1881 Robert Ferguson	170
1882 Robert Ferguson	171
1883 Willie Fernie	159
1884 Jack Simpson	160
1885 Bob Martin	171
1886 David Brown	157
1887 Willie Park, Jr	161
1888 Jack Burns	171
1889 Willie Park, Jr	155
1890 John Ball	164
1891 Hugh Kirkcaldy	169
1892 Harold Hilton	305
1893 William Auchterlonie	322
1894 John Taylor	326
1895 John Taylor	322
1896 Harry Vardon	316
1897 Harry Hilton	314
1898 Harry Vardon	307
1899 Harry Vardon	310
1900 John Taylor	309
1901 James Braid	309
1902 Alexander Herd	307
1903 Harry Vardon	300
1904 Jack White	296
1905 James Braid	318
1906 James Braid	300
1907 Arnaud Massy (France)	312
1908 James Braid	291
1909 John Taylor	295
1910 James Braid	299
1911 Harry Vardon	303
1912 Edward (Ted) Ray	295
1913 John Taylor	304
1914 Harry Vardon	306
1920 George Duncan	303
1921 Jock Hutchinson (USA)	296
1922 Walter Hagen (USA)	300
1923 Arthur Havers	295
1924 Walter Hagen (USA)	301
1925 James Barnes (USA)	300
1926 Robert T. Jones, Jr (USA)	291
1927 Robert T. Jones, Jr (USA)	285
1928 Walter Hagen (USA)	292
1929 Walter Hagen (USA)	292
1930 Robert T. Jones, Jr (USA)	291
1931 Tommy Armour (USA)	296
1932 Gene Sarazen (USA)	283
1933 Denny Shute (USA)	292
1934 Henry Cotton	283
1935 Alfred Perry	283
1936 Alfred Padgham	287
1937 Henry Cotton	283
1938 Reg Whitcombe	295
1939 Richard Burton	290
1946 Sam Snead (USA)	290
1947 Fred Daly	293
1948 Henry Cotton	284
1949 Bobby Locke (S Africa)	283
1950 Bobby Locke (S Africa)	279
1951 Max Faulkner	285
1952 Bobby Locke (S Africa)	287
1953 Ben Hogan (USA)	282
1954 Peter Thomson (Australia)	283
1955 Peter Thomson (Australia)	281
1956 Peter Thomson (Australia)	286
1957 Bobby Locke (S Africa)	279
1958 Peter Thomson (Australia)	278
1959 Gary Player (S Africa)	284
1960 Kel Nagle (Australia)	278
1961 Arnold Palmer (USA)	284
1962 Arnold Palmer (USA)	276
1963 Bob Charles (New Zealand)	277
1964 Tony Lema (USA)	279
1965 Peter Thomson (Australia)	285
1966 Jack Nicklaus (USA)	282
1967 Robert de Vicenzo (Argentina)	278
1968 Gary Player (S Africa)	299
1969 Tony Jacklin	280
1970 Jack Nicklaus (USA)	283
1971 Lee Trevino (USA)	278
1972 Lee Trevino (USA)	278
1973 Tom Weiskopf (USA)	276
1974 Gary Player (S Africa)	282
1975 Tom Watson (USA)	279
1976 Johnny Miller (USA)	279
1977 Tom Watson (USA)	268
1978 Jack Nicklaus (USA)	281
1979 Severiano Ballesteros (Spain)	283
1980 Tom Watson (USA)	271
1981 Bill Rogers (USA)	276
1982 Tom Watson (USA)	284
1983 Tom Watson (USA)	275
1984 Severiano Ballesteros (Spain)	276
1985 Sandy Lyle	282
1986 Greg Norman (Australia)	280

1987	Nick Faldo	279
1988	Severiano Ballesteros (Spain)	273
1989	Mark Calcavecchia (USA)	275
1990	Nick Faldo	270
1991	Ian Baker-Finch (Australia)	272
1992	Nick Faldo	272

US OPEN

First played on a 9-hole course at Newport, Rhode Island, on 4 October 1895, and annually – over 72 holes of stroke play – at a variety of venues from 1898.

Winners	*Score*

(since 1946; US unless specified)

1946	Lloyd Mangrum	284
1947	Lew Worsham	282
1948	Ben Hogan	287
1949	Cary Middlecoff	286
1950	Ben Hogan	287
1951	Ben Hogan	287
1952	Julius Boros	281
1953	Ben Hogan	283
1954	Ed Furgol	284
1955	Jack Fleck	287
1956	Cary Middlecoff	281
1957	Dick Mayer	282
1958	Tommy Bolt	283
1959	Billy Casper	282
1960	Arnold Palmer	280
1961	Gene Littler	281
1962	Jack Nicklaus	283
1963	Julius Boros	293
1964	Ken Venturi	278
1965	Gary Player (S Africa)	282
1966	Billy Casper	278
1967	Jack Nicklaus	275
1968	Lee Trevino	275
1969	Orville Moody	281
1970	Tony Jacklin (UK)	281
1971	Lee Trevino	280
1972	Jack Nicklaus	290
1973	Johnny Miller	279
1974	Hale Irwin	287
1975	Lou Graham	287
1976	Jerry Pate	277
1977	Hubert Green	278
1978	Andy North	285
1979	Hale Irwin	284
1980	Jack Nicklaus	272
1981	David Graham (Australia)	273
1982	Tom Watson	282
1983	Larry Nelson	280
1984	Fuzzy Zoeller	276
1985	Andy North	279
1986	Raymond Floyd	279
1987	Scott Simpson	277
1988	Curtis Strange	278
1989	Curtis Strange	278
1990	Hale Irwin	280
1991	Payne Stewart	283
1992	Tom Kite	285

US MASTERS

Held annually at the Augusta National course in Georgia, the Masters was introduced in 1934. Both the course and the tournament were the idea of the legendary golfer Bobby Jones. Entry to the Masters is by invitation only and the eventual winner is presented with the coveted green jacket. It is contested over 72 holes of stroke play.

Winners	*Score*

(since 1946; US unless specified)

1946	Herman Keiser	282
1947	Jimmy Demaret	281
1948	Claude Harmon	279
1949	Sam Snead	282
1950	Jimmy Demaret	283
1951	Ben Hogan	280
1952	Sam Snead	286
1953	Ben Hogan	274
1954	Sam Snead	289
1955	Cary Middlecoff	279
1956	Jack Burke, Jr	289
1957	Doug Ford	282
1958	Arnold Palmer	284
1959	Art Wall, Jr	284
1960	Arnold Palmer	282
1961	Gary Player (S Africa)	280
1962	Arnold Palmer	280
1963	Jack Nicklaus	286
1964	Arnold Palmer	276
1965	Jack Nicklaus	271
1966	Jack Nicklaus	288
1967	Gay Brewer	280
1968	Bob Goalby	277
1969	George Archer	281
1970	Billy Casper	279
1971	Charles Coody	279
1972	Jack Nicklaus	286
1973	Tommy Aaron	283
1974	Gary Player (S Africa)	278
1975	Jack Nicklaus	276
1976	Raymond Floyd	271
1977	Tom Watson	276
1978	Gary Player (S Africa)	277
1979	Fuzzy Zoeller	280
1980	Severiano Ballesteros (Spain)	275
1981	Tom Watson	280
1982	Craig Stadler	284
1983	Severiano Ballesteros (Spain)	280
1984	Ben Crenshaw	277
1985	Bernhard Langer (Germany)	282
1986	Jack Nicklaus	279
1987	Larry Mize	285
1988	Sandy Lyle (UK)	281
1989	Nick Faldo (UK)	283
1990	Nick Faldo (UK)	278
1991	Ian Woosnam (UK)	277
1992	Fred Couples	275

GREYHOUND RACING

Greyhounds were first used in sport at coursing – chasing of hares by pairs of dogs – and brought to England by the Normans in 1067. The use of mechanical devices was first practised in England, but the sport was popularized in the USA. The first regular track was opened at Emeryville, California, in 1919.

Races are usually conducted over distances of between 210 m (230 yd) for the sprint and 1096 m (1200 yd) for the marathon. The Derby, the major race in Britain, was instituted in 1927.

GYMNASTICS

Tumbling and similar exercises were performed c. 2600 BC as religious rituals in China, but it was the ancient Greeks who coined the word gymnastics, which encompassed various athletic contests including boxing, weightlifting and wrestling. A primitive form was practised in the ancient Olympic Games, but the foundations of the modern sport were laid by the German Johann Friedrich Simon in 1776, and the first national federation was formed in Germany in 1860.

The International Gymnastics Federation was founded in Belgium in 1881, and gymnastics was included in the first modern Olympic Games in 1896. Current events for men are: floor exercises, horse vaults, rings, pommel horse, parallel bars and horizontal bar. The events for women are: floor exercises, horse vault, asymmetrical bars and balance beam. Rhythmic gymnastics for women was introduced for the first time at the 1984 Los Angeles Games. Russia, Belarus, Ukraine, USA, Romania, China and Japan are now the strongest nations.

At the 1992 Olympics the Unified team – representing 12 of the 15 former Soviet republics – won both men's and women's team competitions. The men's all-round champion was Vitaliy Shcherbo of Belarus who won six gold medals in all (four individual golds and a team gold). He became the most bemedalled Olympian in 1992 at any sport. The women's all-round champion was Tatyana Gutsu (Ukraine).

1992 Individual Olympic champions
Men
Overall Vitaly Shcherbo (Belarus)
Floor exercises Li Xiaosahuang (China)
Parallel bars Vitaly Shcherbo (Belarus)
Pommel horse Vitaly Shcherbo (Belarus) and Pae Gil-su (N Korea)
Rings Vitaly Shcherbo (Belarus)
Horizontal bars Trent Dimas (USA)
Horse vault Vitaly Shcherbo (Belarus)

Women
Overall Tatyana Gutsu (Ukraine)
Asymmetrical bars Li Lu (China)
Balance beam Tatyana Lysenko (Ukraine)
Floor exercises Lavinia Milosovici (Romania)
Horse vault Lavinia Milosovici (Romania) and Henrietta Onodi (Hungary)
Rhythic gymnastics Alexandra Timoschenko (Ukraine)

HANDBALL

Handball, similar to soccer only using the hands rather than the feet, was first played at the end of the 19th century. It is a growing sport; by 1992 there were 102 countries affiliated to the International Handball Federation.

Handball was introduced into the Olympic Games at Berlin in 1936 as an 11-a-side outdoor game, but on its reintroduction in 1972, it was an indoor 7-a-side sport (the standard size of the team was reduced to its present level in 1952, although in Britain handball is often played with teams of five).

At the 1992 Olympics the winners were the *Unified Team (men) and South Korea (women).
* a combined team representing 12 of the 15 former Soviet republics.

HARNESS RACING

Trotting races were held in Valkenburg, in the Netherlands, in 1554, but harness racing was developed, and is most popular in North America. The sulky, the lightweight vehicle, first appeared in 1829. Horses may trot, moving their legs in diagonal pairs, or pace, moving fore and hind legs on one side simultaneously.

HOCKEY

Early Greek wall carvings c. 500 BC show hockey-like games, while curved-stick games appear on

Egyptian tomb paintings c. 2050 BC. Hockey in its modern form, however, developed in England in the second half of the 19th century, with Teddington HC (formed 1871) standardizing the rules. The English Hockey Association was founded in 1886. The governing body the Fédération Internationale de Hockey (FIH) was formed in 1924.

Hockey was included in the 1908 and 1920 Olympic Games, with England the winners on both occasions. It has been held at every Games from 1928 and the tournaments were dominated for many years by India, winners at all six Games 1928–1956, and also in 1964 and 1980, and by Pakistan, winners in 1960, 1968 and 1984. However their supremacy has been successfully challenged by nations from Europe and Australasia in recent years. Women's hockey was introduced to the Olympics in 1980. The 1992 Olympic champions were Germany (men) and Spain (women).

Dimensions: ball circumference 223–224 cm (8⅛–9½ in) and weight 155–163 g (5½–5¾ oz); pitch length 91·44 m (100 yd); width 50–55 m (55–60 yd).

FIH (IHF) World Cup
First contested in 1971 for men and 1974 for women. Winners:

Men

Pakistan	1971, 1978, 1982
Netherlands	1973, 1990
India	1975
Australia	1986

Women

Netherlands	1974, 1978, 1983, 1986, 1990
Germany (W)	1976, 1981

HORSE RACING

Early organized racing appears to have been confined to chariots – Roman riders had a foot on each of two horses. The first horse-back races were staged by the Greeks in the 33rd Ancient Olympiad in 648 BC. The first recognizable modern race meeting was held at Smithfield, London, in 1174, while the first known prize money was a purse of gold presented by the English king Richard I in 1195.

Winners of the major British horse races are to be found in the United Kingdom chapter.

Prix de l'Arc de Triomphe
Europe's most prestigious race was first run in 1920. It is run over 2400 metres (c. 1 mile 4 furlongs) at Longchamp on the first Sunday in October. Recent winners have been:

1980 Detroit (Pat Eddery)
1981 Gold River (Gary Moore)
1982 Akiyda (Yves Saint-Martin)
1983 All Along (Walter Swinburn)
1984 Sagace (Yves Saint-Martin)
1985 Rainbow Quest (Pat Eddery)
1986 Dancing Brave (Pat Eddery)
1987 Trempolino (Pat Eddery)
1988 Tony Bin (John Reid)
1989 Carroll House (Michael Kinane)
1990 Saumarez (Gerald Mossé)
1991 Suave Dancer (Cash Asmussen)
1992 Subotica (Thierry Jarnet)

HURLING

Hurling is an ancient game that has been played in Ireland since pre-Christian times, but has been standardized only since the founding of the Gaelic

Athletic Association in 1884. The hurl, or stick, is similar to a hockey stick only flat on both sides. The All-Ireland Championship, first held in 1887, is contested annually by Irish counties; the final is played at Croke Park, Dublin, each September.

ICE HOCKEY

A game similar to hockey on ice was played in Holland in the early 16th century, but the birth of modern ice hockey took place in Canada, probably at Kingston, Ontario, in 1855. Rules were first formulated by students of McGill University in Montreal, who formed a club in 1880.

The International Ice Hockey Federation was formed in 1908, and the World and Olympic Championships inaugurated in 1920. The USSR and the *Unified team have won eight of the last nine Olympic titles. The major professional competition is the National Hockey League (NHL) in North America, founded in 1917, whose teams contest the Stanley Cup.

Teams are 6-a-side; the ideal rink size is 61 m (200 ft) long and 26 m (85 ft) wide.
* a combined team representing 12 of the 15 former Soviet republics.

ICE AND SAND YACHTING

Ice, sand and land yachting require, in basic form, a wheeled chassis beneath a sailing dinghy. Dutch ice yachts are thought to date back to 1768, but ice yachting today is mainly confined to North America. Land and sand yachts of Dutch construction go back even further to 1595. The sports are governed by the International Federation of Sand and Land Yacht which recognizes speed records. International championships were first staged in 1914.

ICE SKATING

Second-century Scandinavian literature refers to ice skating, although archaeological evidence points to origins ten centuries earlier. The first English account of the sport is dated 1180, while the first British club, the Edinburgh Skating Club, was formed around 1742. Steel blades, allowing precision skating, were invented in America in 1850. The International Skating Union was founded in the Netherlands in 1892.

Ice skating competition is divided into figure skating, speed skating and ice dancing. Figure skating has been an Olympic event since the Winter Games were first organized in 1924, but there were also events at the 1908 and 1920 Games. Ice dancing was not included until 1976.

The first international speed skating competition was in Hamburg, Germany, in 1885, with World Championships officially dated from 1893. Speed skating for men was first included in the 1924 Olympics; women's events were included in 1960.

Recent Olympic figure skating champions

Singles

	Men	Women
1980	Robin Cousins (UK)	Anett Pötzsch (GDR)
1984	Scott Hamilton (USA)	Katarina Witt (GDR)
1988	Brian Boitano (USA)	Katarina Witt (GDR)
1992	Viktor Petrenko (Ukraine)	Kristi Yamaguchi (USA)

Pairs
1980 Irina Rodnina and Aleksandr Zaitsev (USSR)
1984 Yelena Valova and Oleg Vasilyev (USSR)
1988 Yekaterina Gordeyeva and Sergey Grinkov (USSR)
1992 Natalya Mishkutienok and Artur Dmitriyev (*Unified Team)

Ice Dance
1980 Natalya Linichuk and Gennadiy Karponosov (USSR)
1984 Jayne Torvill and Christopher Dean (UK)
1988 Natalya Bestemianova and Andrey Bukin (USSR)
1992 Marina Klimova and Sergey Ponomarenko (*Unified Team)
* a combined team representing 12 of the 15 former Soviet republics.

JUDO

Judo developed from a mixture of pre-Christian Japanese fighting arts, the most popular of which was ju-jitsu – thought to be of ancient Chinese origin. 'Ju' means 'soft', i.e. the reliance on speed and skill as opposed to 'hard' brute force. Judo as a modern combat sport was devised in 1882 by Dr Jigoro Kano. Points are scored by throws, locks on joints, certain pressures on the neck, and immobilizations. Today, students are graded by belt colours from white to black, the 'master' belts. Grades of black belts are 'Dans', the highest attainable being Tenth Dan.

The International Judo Federation was founded in 1951 and the World Championships were first held in Tokyo in 1956, with women competing from 1980. Judo has been included in the Olympics since 1964 (except 1968), and there are currently eight weight divisions. Women's judo became an Olympic sport in 1992.

1992 Olympic champions

Men

Weight	Winner
Over 95 kg	David Kakkaleichvili (Georgia)
95 kg	Antal Kovács (Hungary)
86 kg	Waldemar Legien (Poland)
78 kg	Hidehiko Yoshida (Japan)
71 kg	Toshihiko Koga (Japan)
65 kg	Rogeno Sampalo (Brazil)
60 kg	Nazim Gusseinov (Azerbaijan)

Women

Weight	Winner
Over 75 kg	Zhuang Xiaoyan (China)
Up to 72 kg	Kim Mi-jung (S Korea)
66 kg	Odalis Reve (Cuba)
61 kg	Catherine Fleury (France)
56 kg	Miríam Blasco (Spain)
52 kg	Almudena Munoz (Spain)
48 kg	Cécile Nowak (France)

KARATE

Literally meaning 'empty hand' fighting, karate is based on techniques devised from the 6th-century Chinese art of Shaolin boxing (*Kempo*), and was developed by an unarmed populace in Okinawa as a weapon against Japanese forces c. 1500. Transmitted to Japan in the 1920s by Funakoshi Gichin, the sport was refined and organized with competitive rules.

There are five major styles in Japan: shotokan, wado-ryu, goju-ryu, shito-ryu and kyokushinkai, each placing different emphases on speed and power. The military form of taekwondo is the Korean martial art. Wu shu is a comprehensive term embracing all Chinese martial arts. Kung fu is one aspect of these arts popularized by the cinema. Many forms of the martial arts have gained devotees in Europe and the Americas.

LACROSSE

North American Indians played the ancestor of the sport *baggataway*, and a French clergyman, likening the curved stick to a bishop's crozier, called it *la crosse*. The French may also have named it after their game *Chouler à la crosse*, known in 1381. Certainly in its recognizable form the game had reached Europe by the 1830s, and was introduced into Britain in 1867.

The International Federation of Amateur Lacrosse (IFAL) was founded in 1928. The men's World Championships were held in 1967 and every four years from 1974, with the USA winning on each occasion to 1990, except against Canada in 1978. Lacrosse was played in the 1904 and 1908 Olympic Games, and as a demonstration sport in 1928, 1932 and 1948. The women's World Championships were held in 1969, 1974 and 1978, and a World Cup in 1982, 1986 and 1989, when the winners were the USA.

The game is 10-a-side (12-a-side for women at international level). Pitch dimensions: 100 × 64 m (100 × 70 yd). Ball weight in England 142 g (5 oz), circumference 184–203·2 mm (7¼–8 in), colour yellow; in USA weight 142–149 g (5–5¼ oz), circumference 196·9–203·2 mm (7¾–8 in), colour orange or white.

MODERN PENTATHLON AND BIATHLON

In the ancient Olympic Games, the pentathlon was the most prestigious event. It then consisted of discus, javelin, running, jumping and wrestling. The modern pentathlon, introduced into the Olympics in 1912, consists of riding (an 800 m course with 15 fences; riders do not choose their mounts); fencing (épée), shooting, swimming (300 m freestyle) and finally a cross-country run of 4000 m. Each event is held on a different day, with scaled points awarded for each activity.

The sport's governing body is *L'Union Internationale de Pentathlon Moderne et Biathlon*, the UIPMB. It was founded in 1948 as the UIPM, taking on the administration of biathlon in 1957 (see Biathlon). Poland won the 1992 Olympic team title and provided the individual champion in Arkadiusz Skvzypaszrek. The World Championships have been held annually for men from 1949 and for women from 1981.

MOTORCYCLE RACING

The earliest motorcycle race – which also included motorcars – was held at Sheen House, Richmond, Surrey, UK, in 1897 over a 1·6 km (1 mile) oval course. The first international race for motorcycles only was held in 1905. The *Fédération Internationale des Clubs Motocyclystes* (FICM) organized the 1905 event, but it has since been succeeded as the governing body by the *Fédération Internationale Motocycliste* (FIM).

The World Championships were started in 1949 by the FIM and competitors gain points from a series of grand prix races. Races are currently held for the following classes of bike: 50 cc, 125 cc, 250 cc, 500 cc and sidecars.

In road racing the Isle of Man TT races (Auto-Cycle Union Tourist Trophy), first held in 1907, are the most important series. The 60·72 km (37·73 miles) 'Mountain' course, with 264 corners and curves, has been in use since 1911.

In moto-cross, or scrambling, competitors race over rough country including steep climbs and drops, sharp turns, sand, mud and water.

MOTOR RACING

The first known race between automobiles was over 323 km (201 miles) in Wisconsin (USA) in 1878, but it is generally accepted that the first 'real' race was the Paris–Bordeaux–Paris run of 1178 km (732 miles) in 1895. Emile Levassor (Fra), the winner, averaged 24·15 kph (15·01 mph). The first closed circuit race was in Rhode Island (USA), 1896, while the oldest grand prix is the French, inaugurated in 1906.

Competition at the highest level, the Formula One, is over the series of grand prix races (each usually about 656 km/200 miles in length) held worldwide, points scored according to placing. The first World Championships were held in 1950, with the Manufacturers' Championships starting in 1958. Formula Two and Three Championships are held for cars with lesser cubic capacities.

Other forms of competition include the Le Mans circuit, a 24-hour race for touring cars; 'rallying' over public roads through several thousands miles; and drag racing, a test of sheer acceleration, most firmly established in the USA.

Indy Car racing and the Indianapolis 500 are major motor racing competitions in the USA.

WORLD DRIVER CHAMPIONS

1950 Giuseppe Farina (Italy)
1951 Juan Manuel Fangio (Argentina)
1952 Alberto Ascari (Italy)
1953 Alberto Ascari (Italy)
1954 Juan Manuel Fangio (Argentina)
1955 Juan Manuel Fangio (Argentina)
1956 Juan Manuel Fangio (Argentina)
1957 Juan Manuel Fangio (Argentina)
1958 Mike Hawthorn (UK)
1959 Jack Brabham (Australia)
1960 Jack Brabham (Australia)
1961 Phil Hill (USA)
1962 Graham Hill (UK)
1963 Jim Clark (UK)
1964 John Surtees (UK)
1965 Jim Clark (UK)
1966 Jack Brabham (Australia)
1967 Denny Hulme (New Zealand)
1968 Graham Hill (UK)
1969 Jackie Stewart (UK)
1970 Jochen Rindt (Austria)
1971 Jackie Stewart (UK)
1972 Emerson Fittipaldi (Brazil)
1973 Jackie Stewart (UK)
1974 Emerson Fittipaldi (Brazil)
1975 Niki Lauda (Austria)
1976 James Hunt (UK)
1977 Niki Lauda (Austria)
1978 Mario Andretti (USA)
1979 Jody Scheckter (S Africa)
1980 Alan Jones (Australia)
1981 Nelson Piquet (Brazil)
1982 Keke Rosberg (Finland)
1983 Nelson Piquet (Brazil)
1984 Niki Lauda (Austria)

1985 Alain Prost (France)
1986 Alain Prost (France)
1987 Nelson Piquet (Brazil)
1988 Ayrton Senna (Brazil)
1989 Alain Prost (France)
1990 Ayrton Senna (Brazil)
1991 Ayrton Senna (Brazil)
1992 Nigel Mansell (UK)

NETBALL

Modern netball – which grew out of basketball – was invented in the USA in 1891. The use of rings instead of baskets dates from 1897, and the term netball was coined in 1901 in England, where the sport was introduced in 1895. National Associations date from 1924 and 1926 in New Zealand and England, but the International Federation was not formed until 1960. The World Championships have been held every four years, since 1963, with the most recent winners being Australia in 1983 and 1991, and New Zealand in 1987.

Netball is a no-contact, 7-a-side sport played almost exclusively by females. The court measures 30·48 × 15·24 m (100 × 50 ft); ball circumference 68–71 cm (27–28 in), weight 397–454 g (14–16 oz).

ORIENTEERING

'Orienteering' was first used to describe an event held in Oslo (Norway) in 1900, based on military exercises, but the founding of the modern sport is credited to a Swede Major Ernst Killander in 1918.

Basically a combination of cross-country running and map-reading, the sport is very popular in Scandinavia and has a keen band of followers in Britain. The International Orienteering Federation was founded in 1961, and the World Championships have been held since 1966, largely dominated by Sweden and Norway.

PELOTA VASCA (Jaï Alaï)

The sport, which originated in Italy as *longue paume,* was introduced into France in the 13th century. Said to be the fastest of all ball games, various forms of pelota are played according to national character or local custom throughout the world. 'Gloves' and 'chisteras' (curved frames attached to a glove) are of varying sizes, and courts can be open or enclosed with wide differences in dimensions and detail. The *Federacion Internacional de Pelota Vasca* has staged the World Championships every four years since 1952. Pelota was a demonstration sport at the 1992 Olympics.

PÉTANQUE

Pétanque, or *boules,* originated in France from its parent game *jeu provencal.* Its origins go back over 2000 years, but it was not until 1945 that the *Fédération Française de Pétanque et Jeu Provençal* was formed, and subsequently the *Fédération Internationale* (FIPJP).

POLO

The game, played by teams of four on horseback, has its origins in Manipur state, India, c. 3100 BC, when it was played as *Sagol Kangjei.* It is also claimed to be of Persian origin, having been played as *Pulu* c. 525 BC. Polo was introduced to England from India in 1869, and now has a keen following in the USA and Argentina. Polo is played on the largest pitch of any

game, with maximum length of 274 m (300 yds) and width of 182 m (200 yds) without boards, or 146 m (160 yds) with boards. Polo games are often contested on a handicap basis, each player being awarded a handicap measured in goals up to a maximum of ten, attained by the world's best players.

POWERBOAT RACING

Steamboat races date from 1827, petrol engines from 1865, but powerboat racing started in about 1900. International racing was largely established by the presentation of a Challenge Trophy in 1903, by Sir Alfred Harmsworth, which has been won most often by the USA. Races are also held for 'circuit' or shorter course competition, and offshore events began in 1958. Speed records are recognized in various categories by the various governing bodies.

RACKETBALL

Two versions of the game exist: (American) racquetball and (British) racketball. The original game was invented in 1949 by the American Joe Sobek when he sawed half the handle off a tennis racquet. In the USA the International Racquetball Association – founded in 1968 – changed its name in 1980 to the American Amateur Racquetball Association (AARA). The sport now has more than ten million players in the USA. The international governing body is the International Racquetball Federation (IRF). British racketball – introduced in 1976 – uses squash courts 9.75 m by 6.4 m (32 ft by 21 ft) and a less bouncy ball than that used in the larger American courts.

RACKETS

Rackets is a racket and ball game for two or four players, derived – as other forms of handball – from games played in the Middle Ages. In England it was often played against walls of buildings, especially those of the Fleet Prison, London, in the 18th century. An inmate, Robert Mackay, claimed the first world title in 1920. The World Championship has been held since 1988 by James Male (GB), and is now determined on a challenge basis.

REAL TENNIS

Real tennis evolved from the game *jeu de paume* ('game of the palm') played in French monasteries in the 11th century, in which the hand, rather than a racket, was used. The long-handled racket was not invented until about 1500. The World Championship at real tennis is the oldest world championship of any sport, dating to approximately 1740. Today, real tennis is only played in five countries – England, Scotland, USA, France and Australia and the total number of courts in use throughout the world has dwindled to approximately 30. Wayne Davies of Australia has been the men's world champion since 1987 and Penny Lumley (née Fellows) (UK) won the women's world title in 1989 and 1991.

ROLLER SKATING

The first roller skate was devised by Jean-Joseph Merlin of Belgium in 1760, but proved disastrous in demonstration. The present four-wheeled type was patented by New Yorker James L. Plimpton in 1863. Competition is along similar lines to ice skating – speed, figure and dance.

ROWING

A literary reference to rowing is made by the Roman poet Virgil in the *Aeneid* (published after his death in 19 BC). Regattas were held in Venice c. AD 300. The earliest established sculling race is the Doggett's Coat and Badge, first rowed in August 1716 from London Bridge to Chelsea on the River Thames, and still contested annually.

The governing body, the *Fédération Internationale de Sociétés d'Aviron*, was founded in 1892, and the first major international meeting, the European Championships, was held a year later.

Olympic Championships were first held in 1900 for men and in 1976 for women. Current events are held for: (men) single, double and coxless quadruple sculls, coxless and coxed pairs, coxless and coxed fours and eights; (women) single and double sculls, coxless pairs, coxless quadruple sculls, coxless fours and eights. With sculling, the sculler has a smaller oar in each hand rather than pulling one oar with both hands.

The Oxford-Cambridge Boat Race was first held in 1829, from Hambledon Lock to Henley Bridge, and won by Oxford. The current course, used continuously since 1864, is from Putney to Mortlake and measures 6·779 km (4 miles 374 yd). In the 139 races to 1993 Cambridge have won 70 times, Oxford 68 and a dead heat was declared in 1877.

RUGBY LEAGUE

The game originated as a breakaway from rugby union on 29 August 1895, on account of the English governing body forbidding northern rugby clubs paying players, who thus lost Saturday wages. Three years later full professionalism came into being. In 1906 the major change from 15-a-side to 13 was made, and the title 'rugby league' was adopted in 1922.

Rugby league is played principally in Great Britain, Australia, New Zealand, France and Papua New Guinea. Australia won the World Cup in 1988 and 1992.

British Rugby League champions are to be found in the United Kingdom chapter.

Dimensions: Pitch length maximum 100·58 m (110 yd), width maximum 68·58 m (75 yd). Ball length 27·3–29·2 cm (10¾–11½ in), circumference at widest point 584–610 mm (23–24 in).

RUGBY UNION

Rugby union was developed at Rugby School, England. A traditional yarn tells of William Webb Ellis illegally picking up the ball and running with it during a football game, although this may be apocryphal. Certainly the game was known to have been played at Cambridge University by 1839. The Rugby Football Union was formed on 27 January 1871.

Rugby World Cup. The first World Cup was contested by 16 national teams in Australia and New Zealand in 1987. In the final New Zealand beat France 29–9. The second World Cup was played in Britain and France in 1991, with Australia beating France 12–6 in the final at Twickenham.

The game is 15-a-side. Dimensions: pitch of maximum 68·58 m (75 yd) width, and 91·44 m (100 yd) between goal lines. Ball length 27·9–28·5 cm (10¾– 11½ in) and weight 382–439 g (13½–15½ oz).

For details of the league and cup-winners of competitions in England, Wales and Scotland, see the United Kingdom chapter.

In New Zealand, the Ranfurly Shield, an inter-provincial championship, was first held in 1904. It is not a knock-out competition, but one in which the champion province puts its title up for a challenge. The title last changed hands in 1985 when Auckland defeated Canterbury. A national league championship began in 1976. Recent winners have been:

1983 Canterbury
1984 Auckland
1985 Auckland
1986 Wellington
1987 Auckland
1988 Auckland
1989 Auckland
1990 Auckland
1991 Otago
1992 Waikato

In South Africa, the inter-provincial tournament is the Currie Cup, first held in 1889. The Cup has most often been won by Western Province (29 times) and Northern Transvaal (18 times). Recent winners have been:

1983 Western Province
1984 Western Province
1985 Western Province
1986 Western Province
1987 Northern Transvaal
1988 Northern Transvaal
1989 Northern Transvaal and
      Western Province
1990 Natal
1991 Northern Transvaal
1992 Natal

In Australia, the game is played chiefly in New South Wales and Queensland. The principal competition is the Sydney First Grade Premiership in which the most successful club is Randwick.

SHINTY

Shinty (from the Gaelic *sinteag*, a bound) goes back some 2000 years in Celtic history and legend, to the ancient game of *camanachd*, the sport of the curved stick. Having been introduced by the invading Irish Gaels it kept close associations with hurling but is essentially native to Scotland. The governing body, the Camanachd Association, was set up in 1893.

SHOOTING

The first recorded club for gun enthusiasts was the Lucerne Shooting Guild in Switzerland, dating from c. 1466, and the first known shooting match took place in Zürich in 1472. The National Rifle Association in Britain was founded in 1860. The Clay Pigeon Shooting Association developed from trap shooting in the USA. Skeet shooting is a form of clay pigeon designed to simulate a range of bird game and was invented in the USA in 1915. Pistol events, like air rifle, are judged by accuracy in scoring on a fixed target, from various distances and positions.

Shooting events for men were held in the first modern Olympic Games in 1896, but the 1984 Games included two mixed events (men and women) for the first time. Only two other Olympic sports have mixed competition, equestrianism and yachting.

At the 1992 Olympics there were seven men's, four women's and two mixed events.

SKIING

A well-preserved ski found in Sweden is thought to be 4500 years old, and various other evidence from Russia and Scandinavia chronicles primitive skiing, but the modern sport did not develop until 1843 with a competition in Tromsø, Norway. The first modern slalom was held at Murren, Switzerland, in 1922 and the International Ski Federation (FIS) was founded in 1924.

Alpine skiing is racing on prepared slopes, against the clock, whereas Nordic skiing is either cross-country or ski jumping. The Alpine World Championships date from 1931, and Alpine skiing has been included in the Olympics since 1936 as a combination event. Events are now split into downhill, slalom, giant slalom, super giant slalom and Alpine combination (slalom and downhill). Nordic events were included in the Olympic Games from 1924 and comprise cross-country, ski jumping, and the combination of the two disciplines.

The world's best skiers contest a series of events each winter for the World Cups in Alpine skiing and the Nordic events of cross-country and ski jumping.

Overall Alpine World Cup champions

Men

1967 Jean-Claude Killy (France)
1968 Jean-Claude Killy (France)
1969 Karl Schranz (Austria)
1970 Karl Schranz (Austria)
1971 Gustavo Thoeni (Italy)
1972 Gustavo Thoeni (Italy)
1973 Gustavo Thoeni (Italy)
1974 Piero Gros (Italy)
1975 Gustavo Thoeni (Italy)
1976 Ingemar Stenmark (Sweden)
1977 Ingemar Stenmark (Sweden)
1978 Imgemar Stenmark (Sweden)
1979 Peter Lüscher (Switzerland)
1980 Andreas Wenzel (Liechtenstein)
1981 Phil Mahre (USA)
1982 Phil Mahre (USA)
1983 Phil Mahre (USA)
1984 Pirmin Zurbriggen (Switzerland)
1985 Marc Girardelli (Luxembourg)
1986 Marc Girardelli (Luxembourg)
1987 Pirmin Zurbriggen (Switzerland)
1988 Pirmin Zurbriggen (Switzerland)
1989 Marc Girardelli (Luxembourg)
1990 Pirmin Zurbriggen (Switzerland)
1991 Marc Girardelli (Luxembourg)
1992 Paul Accola (Switzerland)
1993 Marc Girardelli (Luxembourg)

Women

1967 Nancy Greene (Canada)
1968 Nancy Greene (Canada)
1969 Gertrud Gabi (Austria)
1970 Michèle Jacot (France)
1971 Annemarie Moser-Pröll (Austria)
1972 Annemarie Moser-Pröll (Austria)
1973 Annemarie Moser-Pröll (Austria)
1974 Annemarie Moser-Pröll (Austria)
1975 Annemarie Moser-Pröll (Austria)
1976 Rosi Mittermaier (Germany)
1977 Lise-Marie Morerod (Switzerland)
1978 Hanni Wenzel (Liechtenstein)
1979 Annemarie Moser-Pröll (Austria)
1980 Hanni Wenzel (Liechtenstein)
1981 Marie-Thérèse Nadig (Switzerland)
1982 Erika Hess (Switzerland)
1983 Tamara McKinney (USA)
1984 Erika Hess (Switzerland)
1985 Michela Figini (Switzerland)
1986 Maria Walliser (Switzerland)
1987 Maria Walliser (Switzerland)
1988 Michela Figini (Switzerland)
1989 Vreni Schneider (Switzerland)
1990 Petra Kronberger (Austria)
1991 Petra Kronberger (Austria)
1992 Petra Kronberger (Austria)
1993 Anita Wachter (Austria)

SNOOKER

Colonel Sir Neville Chamberlain concocted the game of snooker as a cross between 'black pool', 'pyramids' and billiards, in 1875 at Madras, India. The term 'snooker' came from the nickname given to first-year cadets at the Royal Military Academy, Woolwich. The game reached England in 1885, when the world billiards champion, John Roberts, who had been introduced to snooker in India, demonstrated the new sport.

Rules were codified in 1919, and the World Professional Championship was instituted in 1927. Since 1970 the professional game has been controlled by the World Professional Billiards and Snooker Association.

A full size table measures 3.66×1.87 m (12×6 ft); ball values are: red (1), yellow (2), green (3), brown (4), blue (5), pink (6) and black (7).

Recent world champions:

1970 Ray Reardon (Wales)
1971 John Spencer (England)
1972 Alex Higgins (Northern Ireland)
1973 Ray Reardon (Wales)
1974 Ray Reardon (Wales)
1975 Ray Reardon (Wales)
1976 Ray Reardon (Wales)
1977 John Spencer (England)
1978 Ray Reardon (Wales)
1979 Terry Griffiths (Wales)
1980 Cliff Thorburn (Canada)
1981 Steve Davis (England)
1982 Alex Higgins (Northern Ireland)
1983 Steve Davis (England)
1984 Steve Davis (England)
1985 Dennis Taylor (Northern Ireland)
1986 Joe Johnson (England)
1987 Steve Davis (England)
1988 Steve Davis (England)
1989 Steve Davis (England)
1990 Stephen Hendry (Scotland)
1991 John Parrott (England)
1992 Stephen Hendry (Scotland)
1993 Stephen Hendry (Scotland)

SOFTBALL

Softball, the indoor derivative of baseball, was invented by George Hancock in Chicago, USA, in 1887, and rules were first codified in Minnesota in 1895. The name softball was not adopted until 1930. A 9-a-side game (except in the USA), softball is played in Canada, Japan, the Philippines, most of Latin America, New Zealand and Australia. The ball is as hard as a baseball, but as distinct from baseball must be pitched underarm and released below hip level. The pitching distance is 14 m (45 ft 11 in) for men, 11·11 m (36 ft 5½ in) for women and 18·3 m (60 ft) in between bases for both. 'Slow pitch' softball is a modern variation.

SPEEDWAY

Motorcycle racing on dust track surfaces has been traced back to 1902 in the USA, but the first 'short track' races were in Australia in 1923. Evolving in Britain in the 1920s, the National League was instituted in 1932. The first World Championships, for individual riders, was held at Wembley, London in 1936. The team competition was introduced in 1960, and the Pairs in 1970. The Long Track championship was inaugurated in 1971. Ice Speedway world championships were instituted in 1966 with an individual competition; a team competition was added in 1979.

SQUASH

Squash developed at Harrow School, England, in 1817 from a game used for practising rackets but with a softer, 'squashy' ball. The first national championship was held in the USA in 1907. The British Open Championships, for women and men were first contested in 1922 and 1930 respectively. The International Squash Rackets Federation (ISRF) was founded in 1967 and the Women's International Squash Rackets Federation in 1976. In 1992 the ISRF abandoned the name of rackets and reconstituted as the World Squash Federation (WSF).

Court dimensions: 9·75 m (31 ft 11¾ in) long and 6·40 m (21 ft) wide, with front wall height 4·75 m (15 ft 7 in) up to the boundary line. The 'tin' runs along the bottom of the front wall, above which the ball must be hit.

SURFING

Originating in Polynesia, the first reference to surfing on a board dates from 1779 in an account written in Hawaii. Revived in the early 20th century in Australia, hollow boards were introduced in 1929. The World Amateur Championships began in 1964.

SWIMMING

Competitive swimming dates from 36 BC in Japan, which was the first country to seriously adopt the sport – Emperor Goyozei decreed its introduction in schools. In Britain, organized competitive swimming was only introduced in 1837 when the National Swimming Society was formed. Australia led modern developments with an unofficial world 100 yd championship in 1858 at Melbourne.

The first widely used technique (possibly excepting the 'doggy paddle') was the breaststroke. From this developed the side-stroke, a similar action performed sideways, last used by an Olympic champion, Emil Rausch (of Germany), to win the 1904 one-mile event. A style resembling the front crawl had been seen in various parts of the world by travellers in the mid-19th century. Backstroke developed as inverted breaststroke, which modified towards inverted crawl. Butterfly began as an exploitation of a loophole in the rules for breaststroke allowing the recovery of arms from the water, and was recognized as a separate stroke in 1952. The medley event, using all four strokes in turn, originated in the USA in the 1930s.

The world-governing body for swimming, diving, water polo and synchronized swimming is the *Fédération Internationale de Natation Amateur* (FINA), founded in 1908. The World Championships in swim-

ming were first held in 1973, and are now held quadrennially.

Swimming has been an integral part of the Olympics since 1896, the first modern Olympic Games, with 100 m, 400 m, 1500 m and 100 m freestyle events for men. Women first competed in 1912. Diving was introduced in 1904 (1912 for women), and water polo in 1900.

Synchronized swimming, a form of water ballet, was first recognized internationally in 1952 and was included in the first World Championships in 1973. It appeared in the Olympics for the first time in 1984.

SWIMMING WORLD RECORDS

Men
50 m freestyle: 21·81 Tom Jager (USA) 1990
100 m freestyle: 48·42 Matt Biondi (USA) 1988
200 m freestyle: 1:46·69 Giorgio Lamberti (Italy) 1989
400 m freestyle: 3:45·00 Yevgeniy Sadoviy (Russia) 1992
800 m freestyle: 7:46·60 Kieren Perkins (Australia) 1992
1500 m freestyle: 14:43·48 Kieren Perkins (Australia) 1992
4 × 100 m freestyle: 3:16·53 USA 1988
  (Chris Jacobs, Troy Dalbey, Tom Jager, Matt Biondi)
4 × 200 m freestyle: 7:11·95 (*Unified team) 1992
  (Dmitriy Lepikov, Vladimir Pychnenko, Venyamin Tayanovich, Yevgeniy Sadoviy)
100 m backstroke: 53·86 Jeff Rouse (USA) 1992
200 m backstroke: 1:57·30 Martin Lopez-Zubero (Spain) 1991
100 m breaststroke: 1:01·29 Norbert Rósza (Hungary) 1991
200 m breaststroke: 2:10·16 Mike Barrowman (USA) 1992
100 m butterfly: 52·84 Pablo Morales (USA) 1986
200 m butterfly: 1:55·69 Melvin Stewart (USA) 1991
200 m individual medley: 1:59·36 Tamás Darnyi (Hungary) 1991
400 m individual medley: 4:12·36 Tamás Darnyi (Hungary) 1991
4 × 100 m medley: 3:36·93 USA 1988
  (David Berkoff, Richard Schroeder, Matt Biondi, Chris Jacobs)

Women
50 m freestyle: 24·79 Yang Wenyi (China) 1992
100 m freestyle: 54·48 Jenny Thompson (USA) 1992
200 m freestyle: 1:57·55 Heike Friedrich (GDR) 1986
400 m freestyle: 4:03·85 Janet Evans (USA) 1988
800 m freestyle: 8:16·22 Janet Evans (USA) 1989
1500 m freestyle: 15:52·10 Janet Evans (USA) 1988
4 × 100 m freestyle: 3:39·46 USA 1992
  (Nicole Haislett, Dara Torres, Angel Martino, Jenny Thompson)
4 × 200 m freestyle: 7:55·47 GDR 1987
  (Manuela Stellmach, Astrid Strauss, Anke Möhring, Heike Friedrich)
100 m backstroke: 1:00·31 Krizstina Egerszegi (Hungary) 1991
200 m backstroke: 2:06·62 Krizstina Egerszegi (Hungary) 1991
100 m breaststroke: 1:07·91 Silke Hörner (GDR) 1987
200 m breaststroke: 2:25·35 Anita Nall (USA) 1992
100 m butterfly: 57·93 Mary T. Meagher (USA) 1981
200 m butterfly: 2:05·96 Mary T. Meagher (USA) 1981
200 m individual medley: 2:11·65 Li Lin (China) 1992
400 m individual medley: 4:36·10 Petra Schneider (GDR) 1982
4 × 100 m medley: 4:02·54 USA (1992)

(Lea Loveless, Anita Nall, Chrissy Ahmann-Leighton, Janet Thompson)
* a combined team representing 12 of the 15 former Soviet republics.

1992 OLYMPIC SWIMMING CHAMPIONS

Men
50 m freestyle: 21·90 Aleksandr Popov (Russia)
100 m freestyle: 49·02 Aleksandr Popov (Russia)
200 m freestyle: 1:46·70 Yergeniy Sadovyi (Russia)
400 m freestyle: 3:45·00 Yergeniy Sadovyi (Russia)
1500 m freestyle: 14:43·48 Keiren Perkins (Australia)
4 × 100 m freestyle: 3:16·74 (USA)
4 × 200 m freestyle: 7:11·95 (*Unified Team)
100 m backstroke: 53·98 Mark Tewksbury (Canada)
200 m backstroke: 1:58·47 Martin Lopez-Zubero (Spain)
100 m breaststroke: 1:01·50 Nelson Diebel (USA)
200 m breaststroke: 2:10·16 Mike Barrowman (USA)
100 m butterfly: 53·32 Pablo Morales (USA)
200 m butterfly: 1:56·26 Melvin Stewart (USA)
200 m individual medley: 2:00·76 Tamás Darnyi (Hungary)
400 m individual medley: 4:14·23 Tamás Darnyi (Hungary)
4 × 100 m medley: 3:36·93 (USA)
Springboard diving: Mark Lenzi (USA)
Highboard diving: Sun Shuwei (China)
* a combined team representing 12 of the 15 former Soviet republics.

Women
50 m freestyle: 24·79 Yang Wenyi (China)
100 m freestyle: 54·64 Zhuang Yong (China)
200 m freestyle: 1:57·65 Nicole Haislett (USA)
400 m freestyle: 4:07·18 Dagmar Hase (Germany)
800 m freestyle: 8:25·52 Janet Evans (USA)
4 × 100 m freestyle: 3:39·46 (USA)
100 m backstroke: 1:00·68 Krisztina Egerszegi (Hungary)
200 m backstroke: 2:07·06 Krisztina Egerszegi (Hungary)
100 m breaststroke: 1:08·00 Yelena Rudkovskaya (Belarus)
200 m breaststroke: 2:26·65 Kyoko Iwasaki (Japan)
100 m butterfly: 58·62 Qian Hong (China)
200 m butterfly: 2:08·67 Summer Sanders (USA)
200 m individual medley: 2:11·65 Li Lin (China)
400 m individual medley: 4:36·54 Krisztina Egerszegi (Hungary)
4 × 100 m medley: 4:02·54 (USA)
Springboard diving: Gao Min (China)
Highboard diving: Fu Mingxia (China)
Synchronized (solo): Kristen Babb-Sprague (USA)
Synchronized (duet): Karen and Sarah Josephson (USA)

EUROPEAN CHAMPIONSHIPS
First held in Budapest in 1926, and subsequently in 1927, 1931, 1934, 1938, 1947, at four-yearly intervals 1950–74, in 1977, and biennially from 1981.

1991 winners
50 m freestyle: Nils Rudolph (Germany) 22·73
100 m freestyle: Aleksandr Popov (USSR) 49·18
200 m freestyle: Artur Wojdat (Poland) 1:48·10
400 m freestyle: Yevgeniy Sadovyi (USSR) 3:49·02
1500 m freestyle: Jörg Hoffmann (GDR) 15:02·57
4 × 100 m freestyle: USSR 3:17·11
4 × 200 m freestyle: USSR 7:15·96
100 m backstroke: Martin López-Zubero (Spain) 55·30
200 m backstroke: Martin López-Zubero (Spain) 1:58·66
100 m breaststroke: Norbert Rózsa (Hungary) 1:01·49

200 m breaststroke: Nick Gillingham (UK) 2:12·55
100 m butterfly: Vladislav Kulikov (USSR) 54·22
200 m butterfly: Franck Esposito (France) 1:59·59
200 m individual medley: Lars Sorensen (Denmark) 2:02·63
400 m individual medley: Luca Sacchi (Italy) 4:17·81
4 × 100 m medley relay: USSR 3:40·68
Springboard diving: Albin Killat (Germany)
1 m springboard diving Andrey Semeniyk (USSR)
Highboard diving Vladimir Tomoshinin (USSR)

Women
50 m freestyle: Simone Osygus (Germany) 25·80
100 m freestyle: Catherine Plewinski (France) 56·20
200 m freestyle: Mette Jacobsen (Denmark) 2:00·29
400 m freestyle: Irene Dalby (Norway) 4:11·63
800 m freestyle: Irene Dalby (Norway) 8:32·08
4 × 100 m freestyle relay: Netherlands 3:45·36
4 × 200 m freestyle relay: Denmark 8:05·90
100 m backstroke: Krisztina Egerszegi (Hungary) 1:00·31
200 m backstroke: Krisztina Egerszegi (Hungary) 2:06·62
100 m breaststroke: Yelena Rudkovskaya (USSR) 1:09·05
200 m breaststroke: Yelena Rudkovskaya (USSR) 2:29·50
100 m butterfly: Catherine Plewinski (France) 1:00.32
200 m butterfly: Mette Jacobsen (Denmark) 2:12·87
200 m individual medley: Daniela Hunger (GDR) 2:15·53
400 m individual medley: Krisztina Egerszegi (Hungary) 4:39·78
4 × 100 m medley relay: USSR 4:08·55
Springboard diving: Irina Lashko (USSR)
1 m springboard diving: Brita Baldus (Germany)
Highboard diving: Yelena Miroshina (USSR)
Synchronized (solo): Olga Sedakova (USSR)
Synchronized (duet): Anna Kozlova and Olga Sedakova (USSR)
Synchronized (team): USSR

TAEKWONDO

Taekwondo is a martial art developed over 20 centuries in Korea. All its activities are based on a defensive spirit and it was officially recognized as part of Korean tradition and culture in 1955. The sport has spread internationally and there are now an estimated 22 million practitioners in the 137 countries that are members of the World Taekwondo Federation. Taekwondo was a demonstration sport at the Olympic Games in 1988 and 1992.

TABLE TENNIS

The earliest evidence of a game resembling table tennis goes back to London sports goods manufacturers in the 1880s. Known as *gossima*, it was the introduction of the celluloid ball and the noise it made when hit that brought the name 'ping pong' and the Ping Pong Association in 1902. Interest declined until the use of attached rubber mats to the wooden bats (allowing spin) in the early 1920s. The International Table Tennis Association was founded in 1926, and the World Championships have been held since 1927. The Swaythling and Corbillon Cups are held as world team championships, instituted in 1927 and 1934 for men and women respectively. China won the Swaythling Cup on four successive occasions from 1981, but Sweden won in 1989 and 1991, and China dominated the Corbillon Cup with eight successive wins to 1989 before the combined Korean team won in 1991.

Dimensions: ball diameter 37·2–38·2 mm (1·46–1·5 in), weight 2·4– 2·53 g (0·08 oz), table length 2·74 m (9 ft), 1·525 m (5 ft) wide.

TENNIS

Lawn tennis evolved from the indoor game of real tennis (see above) and 'field tennis' is mentioned in a 1793 magazine. Major Harry Gem founded the first club in Leamington Spa, Warwickshire (UK), in 1872. The All England Croquet Club added Lawn Tennis to their title in 1877 when they held their first Championships. The United States Lawn Tennis Association (now USLTA) was founded in 1881, the English association was founded in 1888. The International (Lawn) Tennis Federation was formed in Paris in March 1913.

The Wimbledon, or All England, Championships have been regarded since 1877 as the most important in the world, alongside the US, French and Australian Opens. Together these four make up the 'Grand Slam', the elusive distinction of holding all four titles at once. The US Open (instituted 1881) is now held at Flushing Meadows, New York, and the French at Roland Garros, Paris. The Australian Championships, now held at Flinders Park, Melbourne, were instituted in 1905.

Men and women today compete in various 'circuits' in the second richest sport in the world to golf. 'Grand prix' tournaments are scaled according to a standard, with points accumulated to decide world rankings. The international team competition for men is the Davis Cup, won most times by the USA (31), Australia (Australasia 1907–19; 26), and Great Britain (9).

DAVIS CUP WINNERS

(since 1973)
1973	Australia
1974	South Africa
1975	Sweden
1976	Italy
1977	Australia
1978	USA
1979	USA
1980	Czechoslovakia
1981	USA
1982	USA
1983	Australia
1984	Sweden
1985	Sweden
1986	Australia
1987	Sweden
1988	Germany (W)
1989	Germany (W)
1990	USA
1991	France
1992	USA

The women's international team competition for the Federation Cup has been held annually since 1963. The USA have a record 14 wins, including 1986 and 1989–90, with Australia achieving seven wins and the former Czechoslovakia five, including 1983–5 and 1988. Spain won in 1991 and Germany in 1992. The Wightman Cup was an annual USA–GB women's contest. Begun in 1923 the USA has won on 51 occasions to Great Britain's 10 (the last time being 1978). However, with the decline of British tennis standards, the decision was taken to abandon the event.

Lawn Tennis was included in the Olympic Games from 1896 to 1924 and as a demonstration sport in 1968 before being re-introduced as a medal sport in 1988. The 1992 Olympic winners were: men's singles, Marc Rosset (Switzerland); men's doubles, Boris Becker and Michael Stich (Germany); women's singles, Jennifer Capriati (USA); women's doubles, Gigi Fernandez and Mary Joe Fernandez (USA).

THE WIMBLEDON CHAMPIONSHIPS

Wimbledon, 'The All England Championships', dates back to 1877 when it comprised just one event, the men's singles. Women's singles and men's doubles were introduced in 1884, with women's doubles and mixed doubles becoming full Championship events in 1913.

Men's Singles (since 1946)
1946	Yvon Petra (France)
1947	Jack Kramer (USA)
1948	Bob Falkenburg (USA)
1949	Ted Schroeder (USA)
1950	Budge Patty (USA)
1951	Dick Savitt (USA)
1952	Frank Sedgman (Australia)
1953	Vic Seixas (USA)
1954	Jaroslav Drobny (Czechoslovakia)
1955	Tony Trabert (USA)
1956	Lew Hoad (Australia)
1957	Lew Hoad (Australia)
1958	Ashley Cooper (Australia)
1959	Alex Olmedo (USA)
1960	Neale Fraser (Australia)
1961	Rod Laver (Australia)
1962	Rod Laver (Australia)
1963	Chuck McKinley (USA)
1964	Roy Emerson (Australia)
1965	Roy Emerson (Australia)
1966	Manuel Santana (Spain)
1967	John Newcombe (Australia)
1968	Rod Laver (Australia)
1969	Rod Laver (Australia)
1970	John Newcombe (Australia)
1971	John Newcombe (Australia)
1972	Stan Smith (USA)
1973	Jan Kodes (Czechoslovakia)
1974	Jimmy Connors (USA)
1975	Arthur Ashe (USA)
1976	Bjorn Borg (Sweden)
1977	Bjorn Borg (Sweden)
1978	Bjorn Borg (Sweden)
1979	Bjorn Borg (Sweden)
1980	Bjorn Borg (Sweden)
1981	John McEnroe (USA)
1982	Jimmy Connors (USA)
1983–84	John McEnroe (USA)
1985	Boris Becker (Germany)
1986	Boris Becker (Germany)
1987	Pat Cash (Australia)
1988	Stefan Edberg (Sweden)
1989	Boris Becker (Germany)
1990	Stefan Edberg (Sweden)
1991	Michael Stich (Germany)
1992	Andre Agassi (USA)

Women's Singles (since 1946)
1946	Pauline Betz (USA)
1947	Margaret Osborne (USA)
1948	Louise Brough (USA)
1949	Louise Brough (USA)
1950	Louise Brough (USA)
1951	Doris Hart (USA)
1952	Maureen Connolly (USA)
1953	Maureen Connolly (USA)

1954 Maureen Connolly (USA)
1955 Louise Brough (USA)
1956 Shirley Fry (USA)
1957 Althea Gibson (USA)
1958 Althea Gibson (USA)
1959 Maria Bueno (Brazil)
1960 Maria Bueno (Brazil)
1961 Angela Mortimer (UK)
1962 Karen Susman (USA)
1963 Margaret Smith (Australia)
1964 Maria Bueno (Brazil)
1965 Margaret Smith (Australia)
1966 Billie Jean King née Moffitt (USA)
1967 Billie Jean King (USA)
1968 Billie Jean King (USA)
1969 Ann Jones (UK)
1970 Margaret Smith-Court (Australia)
1971 Evonne Goolagong (Australia)
1972 Billie Jean King (USA)
1973 Billie Jean King (USA)
1974 Chris Evert (USA)
1975 Billie Jean King (USA)
1976 Christ Evert (USA)
1977 Virginia Wade (UK)
1978 Martina Navratilova (Czechoslovakia)
1979 Martina Navratilova (Czechoslovakia)
1980 Evonne Goolagong-Cawley (Australia)
1981 Chris Evert-Lloyd (USA)
1982 Martina Navratilova (USA; formerly of Czechoslovakia)
1983 Martina Navratilova (USA)
1984 Martina Navratilova (USA)
1985 Martina Navratilova (USA)
1986 Martina Navratilova (USA)
1987 Martina Navratilova (USA)
1988 Steffi Graf (Germany)
1989 Steffi Graf (Germany)
1990 Martina Navratilova (USA)
1991 Steffi Graf (Germany)
1991–2 Steffi Graf (Germany)

Women's Doubles
1946 Louise Brough & Margaret Osborne (USA)
1947 Pat Todd & Doris Hart (USA)
1948–50 Louise Brough & Margaret Osborne-du Pont (USA)
1951–3 Doris Hart & Shirley Fry (USA)
1954 Louise Brough & Margaret Osborne-du Pont (USA)
1955 Angela Mortimer & Anne Shilcock (UK)
1956 Angela Buxton (UK) & Althea Gibson (USA)
1957 Althea Gibson & Darlene Hard (USA)
1958 Maria Bueno (Brazil) & Althea Gibson (USA)
1959 Jean Arth & Darlene Hard (USA)
1960 Maria Bueno (Brazil) & Darlene Hard (USA)
1961 Karen Hantze & Billie Jean Moffitt (USA)
1962 Karen Hantze-Susman & Billie Jean Moffitt (USA)
1963 Maria Bueno (Brazil) & Darlene Hard (USA)
1964 Margaret Smith & Lesley Turner (Australia)
1965 Maria Bueno (Brazil) & Billie Jean Moffitt (USA)
1966 Maria Bueno (Brazil) & Nancy Richey (USA)
1967 Rosemary Casals & Billie Jean King née Moffitt (USA)
1968 Billie Jean King & Rosemary Casals (USA)
1969 Margaret Smith-Court & Judy Tegart (Australia)
1970 Billie Jean King & Rosemary Casals (USA)
1972 Billie Jean King & Rosemary Casals (USA)
1972 Billie Jean King (USA) & Betty Stove (Netherlands)
1973 Billie Jean King & Rosemary Casals (USA)

1974 Evonne Goolagong (Australia) & Peggy Michel (USA)
1975 Ann Kiyomura (USA) & Kazuko Sawamatsu (Japan)
1976 Chris Evert (USA) & Martina Navratilova (Czechoslovakia)
1977 Helen Cawley (Australia) & Joanne Russell (USA)
1978 Kerry Reid & Wendy Turnbull (Australia)
1979 Billie Jean King (USA) & Martina Navratilova (Czechoslovakia)
1980 Kathy Jordan & Anne Smith (USA)
1981–4 Martina Navratilova (Czechoslovakia) & Pam Shriver (USA)
1985 Kathy Jordan (USA) & Liz Smylie (Australia)
1986 Martina Navratilova & Pam Shriver (USA)
1987 Claudia Kohde-Kilsch (Germany) & Helena Sukova (Czechoslovakia)
1988 Steffi Graf (Germany) & Gabriella Sabatini (Argentina)
1989–90 Jana Novotná and Helena Suková (Czechoslovakia)
1991 Larisa Savchenko and Natalya Zvereva (USSR)
1992 Gigi Fernandez (USA) & Natalya Zvereva (Belarus)

Men's Doubles
1946 Tom Brown & Jack Kramer (USA)
1947 Bob Falkenburg & Jack Kramer (USA)
1948 John Bromwich & Frank Sedgman (Australia)
1949 Ricardo Gonzales & Frank Parker (USA)
1950 John Bromwich & Adrian Quist (Australia)
1951–2 Ken McGregor & Frank Sedgman (Australia)
1953 Lew Hoad & Ken Rosewall (Australia)
1954 Rex Hartwig & Mervyn Rose (Australia)
1955 Rex Hartwig & Lew Hoad (Australia)
1956 Lew Hoad & Ken Rosewall (Australia)
1957 Budge Patty & Gardnar Mulloy (USA)
1958 Sven Davidson & Ulf Schmidt (Sweden)
1959 Roy Emerson & Neale Fraser (Australia)
1960 Rafael Osuna (Mexico) & Dennis Ralston (USA)
1961 Roy Emerson & Neale Fraser (Australia)
1962 Bob Hewitt & Fred Stolle (Australia)
1963 Rafael Osuna & Antonio Palafox (Mexico)
1964 Bob Hewitt & Fred Stolle (Australia)
1965 John Newcombe & Tony Roche (Australia)
1966 Ken Fletcher & John Newcombe (Australia)
1967 Bob Hewitt & Frew McMillan (S Africa)
1968–70 John Newcombe & Tony Roche (Australia)
1971 Roy Emerson & Rod Laver (Australia)
1972 Bob Hewitt & Frew McMillan (S Africa)
1973 Jimmy Connors (USA) & Ilie Nastase (Romania)
1974 John Newcombe & Tony Roche (Australia)
1975 Vitas Gerulaitis & Sandy Mayer (USA)
1976 Brian Gottfried (USA) & Raul Ramirez (Mexico)
1977 Ross Case & Geoff Masters (Australia)
1978 Bob Hewitt & Frew McMillan (S Africa)
1979 John McEnroe & Peter Fleming (USA)
1980 Peter McNamara & Paul McNamee (Australia)
1981 John McEnroe & Peter Fleming (USA)
1982 Peter McNamara & Paul McNamee (Australia)
1983–4 John McEnroe & Peter Fleming (USA)
1985 Balazs Taroczy (Hungary) & Heinz Gunthardt (Switzerland)
1986 Joachim Nystrom & Mats Wilander (Sweden)
1987–8 Ken Flach & Robert Seguso (USA)
1989 John Fitzgerald (Australia) and Anders Järryd (Sweden)
1990 Rick Leach and Jim Pugh (USA)

1991 John Fitzgerald (Australia) and Anders Järryd (Sweden)
1992 John McEnroe (USA) and Michael Stich (Germany)

Mixed Doubles
1946 Tom Brown & Louise Brough (USA)
1947–8 Louise Brough (USA) & John Bromwich (Australia)
1949 Sheila Summers & Eric Sturgess (S Africa)
1950 Louise Brough (USA) & Eric Sturgess (S Africa)
1951–2 Doris Hart (USA) & Frank Sedgman (Australia)
1953–5 Doris Hart & Vic Seixas (USA)
1956 Shirley Fry & Vic Seixas (USA)
1957 Darlene Hard (USA) & Mervyn Rose (Australia)
1958 Lorraine Coghlan & Bob Howe (Australia)
1959–60 Darlene Hard (USA) & Rod Laver (Australia)
1961 Lesley Turner & Fred Stolle (Australia)
1962 Margaret Osborne-du Pont (USA) & Neale Fraser (Australia)
1963 Margaret Smith & Ken Fletcher (Australia)
1964 Lesley Turner & Fred Stolle (Australia)
1965–6 Margaret Smith & Ken Fletcher (Australia)
1967 Billie Jean King (USA) & Owen Davidson (Australia)
1968 Margaret Smith-Court & Ken Fletcher (Australia)
1969 Ann Jones (UK) & Fred Stolle (Australia)
1970 Rosemary Casals (USA) & Ilie Nastase (Romania)
1971 Billie Jean King (USA) & Owen Davidson (Australia)
1972 Rosemary Casals (USA) & Ilie Nastase (Romania)
1973–4 Billie Jean King (USA) & Owen Davidson (Australia)
1975 Margaret Smith-Court (Australia) & Marty Riessen (USA)
1976 Françoise Durr (France) & Tony Roche (Australia)
1977 Greer Stevens & Bob Hewitt (S Africa)
1978 Betty Stove (Netherlands) & Frew McMillan (S Africa)
1979 Greer Stevens & Bob Hewitt (S Africa)
1980 Tracey Austin & John Austin (USA)
1981 Betty Stove (Netherlands) & Frew McMillan (S Africa)
1982 Anne Smith (USA) & Kevin Curren (S Africa)
1983–4 Wendy Turnbull (Australia) & John Lloyd (UK)
1985 Martina Navratilova (USA) & Paul McNamee (Australia)
1986 Kathy Jordan & Ken Flach (USA)
1987 Jo Durie & Jeremy Bates (UK)
1988 Zina Garrison & Sherwood Stewart (USA)
1989 Jana Novotná (Czechoslovakia) & Jim Pugh (USA)
1990 Zina Garrison & Rick Leach (USA)
1991 John Fitzgerald and Elizabeth Smylie (Australia)
1992 Cyril Suk (Czechoslovakia) & Larisa Savchenko (Latvia)

RECENT WINNERS OF THE US OPEN

Men's singles (US unless specified)
1979–81 John McEnroe
1982–3 Jimmy Connors
1984 John McEnroe
1985–7 Ivan Lendl (Czechoslovakia)
1988 Mats Wilander (Sweden)

1989 Boris Becker (Germany)
1990 Pete Sampras
1991–2 Stefan Edberg (Sweden)

Women's singles (US unless specified)
1980 Chris Evert-Lloyd
1981 Tracy Austin
1982 Chris Evert-Lloyd
1983–4 Martina Navratilova
1985 Hanna Mandlikova (Czechoslovakia)
1986–7 Martina Navratilova
1988–9 Steffi Graf (Germany)
1990 Gabriela Sabatini (Argentina)
1991–2 Monica Seles (Yugoslavia)

RECENT WINNERS OF THE FRENCH OPEN

Men's singles
1978–81 Bjorn Borg (Sweden)
1982 Mats Wilander (Sweden)
1983 Yannick Noah (France)
1984 Ivan Llendl (Czechoslovakia)
1985 Mats Wilander (Sweden)
1986–7 Ivan Lendl (Czechoslovakia)
1988 Mats Wilander (Sweden)
1989 Michael Chang (USA)
1990 Andrés Gómez (Ecuador)
1991–2 Jim Courier (USA)

Women's singles
1979–80 Chris Evert-Lloyd (USA)
1981 Hanna Mandlikova (Czechoslovakia)
1982 Martina Navratilova (USA)
1983 Chris Evert-Lloyd (USA)
1984 Martina Navratilova (USA)
1985–6 Chris Evert-Lloyd (USA)
1987–8 Steffi Graf (Germany)
1989 Arantxa Sánchez (Spain)
1990–2 Monica Seles (Yugoslavia)

RECENT WINNERS OF THE AUSTRALIAN OPEN

Men's singles
1980 Brian Teacher (USA)
1981–2 Johan Kriek (S Africa)
1983–4 Mats Wilander (Sweden)
1985 Stefan Edberg (Sweden)
1986 No championship was held.
1987 Stefan Edberg (Sweden)
1988 Mats Wilander (Sweden)
1989–90 Ivan Llendl (Czechoslovakia)
1991 Boris Becker (Germany)
1992 Jim Courier (USA)

Women's singles
1980 Hanna Mandlikova (Czechoslovakia)
1981 Martina Navratilova (USA)
1982 Chris Evert-Lloyd (USA)
1983 Martina Navratilova (USA)
1984 Chris Evert-Lloyd (USA)
1985 Martina Navratilova (USA)
1987 Hanna Mandlikova (Czechoslovakia)
1988–90 Steffi Graf (Germany)
1991–2 Monica Seles (Yugoslavia)

TRAMPOLINING

Equipment similar to today's trampoline was used by a show business group, 'The Walloons', just prior to World War I. The word originates from the Spanish *trampolin*, a springboard, and indeed springboards date to circus acrobats of the Middle Ages. The birth of the sport follows the invention of the prototype 'T' trampoline by the American George Nissen in 1936.

The World Championships, administered by the International Trampolining Association, were instituted in 1964 and held biennially since 1968.

VOLLEYBALL

Although an Italian game *pallone*, similar to volleyball, was played in the 16th century, the modern game was invented as *minnonette* in 1895 by William Morgan at Massachusetts, USA, as a game for those who found basketball too strenuous. The name volleyball came a year later. The game spread rapidly worldwide and reached Britain in 1914. The first international tournament was the inaugural European Championship in 1948, the year after the founding of the International Volleyball Federation. Although proposed for the 1924 Games by the USA, volleyball was not included in the Olympics until 1964. The 1992 Olympic titles were won by Brazil (men) and Cuba (women). World Champions in 1990 were Italy (men) and USSR (women).

Court dimensions are 18 × 9 m (89 ft × 29 ft 6⅜ in); ball circumference 65–67 cm (25½–26½ in), 250–260 g (8·85–9·9 oz) in weight. Net height is 2·43 m (7 ft 11¾ in) for men and 2·24 m (7 ft 4¼ in) for women.

WALKING

Walking races have been included in the Olympic events since 1906 but walking matches have been known since 1859. Walking as a sport is defined as 'progression by steps so that unbroken contact with the ground is maintained'. Road walking has become more prevalent than track walking, and the Olympic distances are currently 20 km and 50 km for men and 10 km for women.

WATER SKIING

Water skiing as we now know it was pioneered by Ralph Samuelson (USA) on Lake Pepin, Minnesota, in 1922. Having tried and failed with snow skis, he gave exhibitions with pine board skis culminating in the first jump, off a greased ramp, in 1925. The *Union Internationale de S i Na ti e* was set up in July 1946 and the British Water Ski Federation was formed in 1954.

Competitively, the sport is divided into trick skiing, slalom and ski jumping. (Trick skiing, performed at lower speeds, involves gymnastic feats rewarded according to difficulty.) The World Championships, begun in 1947 and held biennially, include an overall title, which was won by the USA at all 17 championships 1957–89, but by Canada in 1991.

Skiing barefoot brought a new element to the sport and competitions are held for straight speed records.

WEIGHTLIFTING

In China during the Zhou dynasty, which ended in 256 BC, weightlifting became a compulsory military test. Competitions for lifting weights of stone were held in the ancient Olympic Games. The amateur sport, however, is of modern vintage with competitions dating from c. 1850, and the first championships termed 'world' from 1891. The International Weightlifting Federation was established in 1920 in Estonia. Weightlifting was included in the first modern Olympics in 1896, and then from 1920. There are now ten weight divisions, from up to 52 kg (115 lbs) to over 110 kg (243 lbs). Competition is decided by the aggregate of two forms of lifting, the snatch and the clean and jerk. A third form, the press, was dropped in 1976 because of the difficulty in judging it. Eastern European countries, especially Russia and Bulgaria, have dominated the sport in which world records have, in recent years, been broken more frequently than in any other. Women's world championships were held in 1987.

o erli tin involves different techniques which perhaps have greater emphasis on sheer strength rather than technique. The three basic lifts are the squat (or deep knee bend), bench press and dead lift. The International Powerlifting Federation was founded in 1972, with the USA generally dominant in the majority of the men's and women's weight categories.

WRESTLING

One of the oldest sports in the world, organized wrestling may date to c. 2750–2600 BC. It was the most popular sport in the ancient Olympic Games, and victors were recorded from 708 BC. Wrestling developed in varying forms in different countries, with the classical Greco-Roman style popular in Europe, and free style more to the liking of countries in the East and the Americas. The main distinction is that in Greco-Roman the wrestler cannot seize his opponent below the hips nor grip with the legs. The International Amateur Wrestling Federation (FILA) also recognizes sambo wrestling, akin to judo and popular in the former USSR. FILA was founded in 1912, although the sport was in the first modern Olympics in 1896. There are currently ten weight divisions in both free style and Greco-Roman events at the Games. *S mo re tlin* is a traditional form in Japan dating to 23 BC. Conducted with ceremony and mysticism, weight and bulk are vital since the object is to force the opponent out of the circular ring, using any hold.

YACHTING

Yachting dates to the race for a 100 wager between Charles II and his brother James, Duke of York, on the Thames in 1661 from Greenwich to Gravesend and back. The first recorded regatta was held in 1720 by the Cork Harbour Water Club (later Royal Cork Yacht Club), the oldest yacht club, but the sport did not prosper until the seas became safe after the Napoleonic Wars in 1815. That year the Yacht Club (later the Royal Yacht Squadron) was formed and organized races at Cowes, Isle of Wight, the beginning of modern yacht racing. The International Yacht Racing Union (IYRU) was established in 1907.

There were seven classes of boat at the 1992 Olympic Games, one of which, the 470, had separate competitions for men and women. Other major competitions include the Admiral's Cup – a biennial inter-nation, Channel and inshore race from Cowes to Fastnet Rock, Ireland, and back to Plymouth – and the quadrennial Whitbread Round the World Race, instituted in 1973. The America's Cup was first won as an outright prize by the schooner *meri a* on 22 August 1851 at Cowes and later offered by the New York Yacht Club as a challenge trophy. Since 1870 the Cup has been challenged by the UK in 16 contests, by Canada in two, Australia eight and New Zealand and Italy one each, but the USA were undefeated until 1983, when *tralia II* defeated the American boat *i ert*. However Denis Conner in *Star Stripe* regained the Cup over *oo a rra III* (Australia) in 1987 and defended it against New Zealand in 1988. In 1992 Bill Koch successfully defended the Cup for the USA against Italy.

THE OLYMPIC GAMES

The ancient Olympic Games were staged every four years at Olympia, 120 miles west of Athens. The earliest celebration of which there is a certain record is that of July 776 BC, from which all subsequent Games are dated. However, earlier Games were certainly held, perhaps dating back to 1370 BC. The early Games had considerable religious significance.

The Games grew in size and importance to the height of their fame in the 5th and 4th centuries BC. Events

Celebration of the Modern Olympic Games

	Year	Venue	Date	Countries	Competitors Male	Competitors Female
I	1896	Athens, Greece	6–15 Apr	13	311	–
II	1900	Paris, France	20 May–28 Oct	22	1319	11
III	1904	St Louis, USA	1 July–23 Nov	13[1]	617	8
*	1906	Athens, Greece	22 Apr–2 May	20	877	7
IV	1908	London, England	27 Apr–31 Oct	22	2013	43
V	1912	Stockholm, Sweden	5 May–22 July	28	2491	55
VI	1916	Berlin, Germany	Not held due to war	–	–	–
VII	1920	Antwerp, Belgium	20 Apr–12 Sept	29	2618	74
VIII	1924	Paris, France	4 May–27 July	44	2956	136
IX	1928	Amsterdam, Netherlands	17 May–12 Aug	46	2724	290
X	1932	Los Angeles, USA	30 July–14 Aug	37	1281	127
XI	1936	Berlin, Germany	1–16 Aug	49	3738	328
XII	1940	Tokyo, then Helsinki	Not held due to war	–	–	–
XIII	1944	London, England	Not held due to war	–	–	–
XIV	1948	London, England	29 July–14 Aug	59	3714	385
XV	1952	Helsinki, Finland	19 July–3 Aug	69	4407	518
XVI	1956[2]	Melbourne, Australia	22 Nov–8 Dec	67	2958	384
XVII	1960	Rome, Italy	25 Aug–11 Sept	83	4738	610
XVIII	1964	Tokyo, Japan	10–24 Oct	93	4457	683
XIX	1968	Mexico City, Mexico	12–27 Oct	112	4749	781
XX	1972	Munich, Germany	26 Aug–10 Sept	122	6086	1070
XXI	1976	Montreal, Canada	17 July–1 Aug	92	4834	1251
XXII	1980	Moscow, USSR	19 July–3 Aug	81	4238	1088
XXIII	1984	Los Angeles, USA	28 July–12 Aug	140	5458	1620
XXIV	1988	Seoul, South Korea	20 Sept–5 Oct	159	6279	2186
XXV	1992	Barcelona, Spain	25 July–8 Aug	169	6659	2710
XXVI	1996	Atlanta, USA	20 July–4 Aug			

* This celebration to mark the tenth anniversary of the Modern Games was officially intercalated but is not numbered.
[1] Including newly discovered French national.
[2] The equestrian events were held in Stockholm, Sweden, 10–17 June with 158 competitors from 29 countries.

Celebrations of the Winter Games

	Year	Venue	Date	Countries	Competitors Male	Competitors Female
I*	1924	Chamonix, France	25 Jan–4 Feb	16	281	13
II	1928	St Moritz, Switzerland	11–19 Feb	25	468	27
III	1932	Lake Placid, USA	4–15 Feb	17	274	32
IV	1936	Garmisch-Partenkirchen, Germ.	6–16 Feb	28	675	80
V	1948	St Moritz, Switzerland	30 Jan–8 Feb	28	636	77
VI	1952	Oslo, Norway	14–25 Feb	22	623	109
VII	1956	Cortina d'Ampezzo, Italy	26 Jan–5 Feb	32	687	132
VIII	1960	Squaw Valley, USA	18–28 Feb	30	521	144
IX	1964	Innsbruck, Austria	29 Jan–9 Feb	36	893	200
X	1968	Grenoble, France	6–18 Feb	37	1065	228
XI	1972	Sapporo, Japan	3–13 Feb	35	1015	217
XII	1976	Innsbruck, Austria	4–15 Feb	37	900	228
XIII	1980	Lake Placid, USA	13–24 Feb	37	833	234
XIV	1984	Sarajevo, Yugoslavia†	7–19 Feb	49	1287	223
XV	1988	Calgary, Canada	23 Feb–6 Mar	57	1113	315
XVI	1992	Albertville, France	8–23 Feb	64	1269	460
XVII	1994	Lillehammer, Norway				
XVIII	1998	Nagano, Japan				

* There were Winter Games events included in the Summer Games of 1908 (London) and 1920 (Antwerp) which attracted six countries, 14 males and seven females for the first, and 10 countries, 73 males and 12 females for the latter.
† now in Bosnia-Herzegovina.

included running, jumping, wrestling, throwing the discus, boxing and chariot racing. As well as being sporting contests, the Olympics were great artistic festivals upholding the Greek ideal of perfection of mind and body. Winners were awarded a branch of wild olive, the Greeks' sacred tree.

The final Olympic Games of the ancient era were held in AD 393 before the Roman Emperor, Theodosius I, decreed the prohibition of the Games, which were not favoured by the early Christians and which were then long past their great days.

The first modern Games, in Athens in 1896, were at the instigation of Pierre de Fredi, Baron de Coubertin (1863–1937). A far cry from today's huge organization, just 311 competitors (from 13 countries) took part, of whom 230 were from Greece and others were foreign tourists. By contrast, 169 countries were represented by 9369 participating sports men and women at the 1992 Games in Barcelona, Spain.

Table of Olympic medal winners – Summer Games, 1896–1992*

		Gold	Silver	Bronze	Total
1	USA	789	603	518	1910
2	USSR/Unified team[6]	442	361	333	1136
3	Germany[1]	186	227	236	649
4	United Kingdom	177	224	218	619
5	France	161	175	191	527
6	Sweden	133	149	171	453
7	GDR[2]	154	131	126	411
8	Italy	153	126	131	410
9	Hungary	136	124	144	404
10	Finland	98	77	112	287
11	Japan	90	83	93	266
12	Australia	78	76	98	252
13	Romania	59	70	90	219
14	Poland	43	62	105	210
15	Canada	45	67	80	192
16	Netherlands	45	52	72	169
17	Switzerland	42	63	58	163
18	Bulgaria	38	69	55	162
19	Czechoslovakia	49	50	49	148
20	Denmark	26	51	53	130
21	Belgium	35	47	44	126
22	Norway	43	37	34	114
23	China	36	41	37	114
24	Greece	24	40	39	103
25	South Korea	31	27	41	99
26	Yugoslavia	26	30	30	86
27	Cuba	36	25	23	84
28	Austria	19	29	33	81
29	New Zealand	27	10	28	65
30	Turkey	26	15	12	53
31	South Africa[3]	16	17	20	53
32	Argentina	13	19	15	47
	(Russia[6]	17	16	12	47)
33	Spain	17	19	10	46
34	Mexico	9	13	18	40
35	Brazil	9	10	21	40
36	Kenya	13	13	13	39
37	Iran	4	12	17	33
38	Jamaica	4	13	9	26
39	Estonia[4]	7	6	10	23
40	North Korea[5]	6	5	10	21
	(Ukraine[6]	4	11	4	19)
41	Egypt	6	6	6	18
	(Belarus[6]	9	4	2	15)·
42	Ireland	5	5	5	15
43	India	8	3	3	14
=44	Ethiopia	6	1	6	13
=44	Portugal	2	4	7	13
=44	Mongolia	0	5	8	13
45	Pakistan	3	3	4	10
=46	Morocco	4	2	3	9
=46	Uruguay	2	1	6	9
=47	Venezuela	1	2	5	8
=47	Chile	0	6	2	8
=47	Nigeria	0	4	4	8
=47	Philippines	0	1	7	8
48	Trinidad	1	2	4	7
=49	Indonesia	2	3	1	6
=49	Latvia[4]	0	4	2	6
=49	Colombia	0	2	4	6
	(Georgia[6]	3	0	2	5)
=50	Uganda	1	3	1	5
=50	Tunisia	1	2	2	5
=50	Puerto Rico	0	1	4	5
	(Armenia[6]	3	1	0	4)
=51	Peru	1	3	0	4
=51	Algeria	1	0	3	4
=51	Lebanon	0	2	2	4
=51	Taipei (Taiwan)	0	2	2	4
=51	Ghana	0	1	3	4
=51	Thailand	0	1	3	4
	(Moldova[6]	1	1	1	3)
=52	Bahamas	1	0	2	3
=52	Croatia	0	1	2	3
=53	Luxembourg	1	1	0	2
=53	Lithuania	1	0	1	2
=53	Suriname	1	0	1	2
	(Azerbaijan[6]	1	0	1	2)
=53	Namibia	0	2	0	2
=53	Tanzania	0	2	0	2
	(Uzbekistan[6]	0	2	0	2)
=53	Cameroun	0	1	1	2
=53	Haiti	0	1	1	2
=53	Iceland	0	1	1	2
=53	Israel	0	1	1	2
=53	Panama	0	0	2	2
=53	Slovenia	0	0	2	2
	(Kazakhstan[6]	0	0	2	2)
	(Tajikistan[6]	1	0	0	1)
=54	Zimbabwe	1	0	0	1
=54	Côte d'Ivoire	0	1	0	1
=54	Singapore	0	1	0	1
=54	Sri Lanka	0	1	0	1
=54	Syria	0	1	0	1
=54	Costa Rica	0	1	0	1
=54	Netherlands Antilles	0	1	0	1
=54	Senegal	0	1	0	1
=54	Virgin Islands	0	1	0	1
=54	Barbados	0	0	1	1
=54	Bermuda	0	0	1	1
=54	Dominican Rep	0	0	1	1
=54	Guyana	0	0	1	1
=54	Iraq	0	0	1	1
=54	Niger	0	0	1	1
=54	Zambia	0	0	1	1
=54	Qatar	0	0	1	1
=54	Djibouti	0	0	1	1

* including 1909
[1] Germany 1896–1952 and 1992, Federal Republic of Germany (West) 1956–88 Medals won by the combined German teams of 1956, 1960 and 1964 have been allocated to FDR and the GDR according to the athlete's origins
[2] GDR, East Germany, 1956–88
[3] South Africa, up to 1960 and from 1992
[4] Estonia and Latvia, up to 1936 and from 1992
[5] North Korea, from 1964
[6] the Unified Team was a combined team that took part in the 1992 Games representing 12 of the 15 former Soviet republics; in individual events medals athletes represented their individual republics which are shown above in brackets.

COMMONWEALTH GAMES

The Commonwealth Games are multi-sport competitions held every four years and contested by representatives of the nations of the Commonwealth. They were first staged as the British Empire Games in 1930, when 11 nations competed. The Games became the British Empire and Commonwealth Games in 1954 and the British Commonwealth Games in 1970, although the word 'British' has been dropped from the title. England, Northern Ireland, Scotland, Wales, the Isle of Man, Jersey and Guernsey are represented separately in the Games.

1930 Hamilton, Canada
1934 London, England
1938 Sydney, Australia
1950 Auckland, New Zealand
1954 Vancouver, Canada
1958 Cardiff, Wales
1962 Perth, Australia
1966 Kingston, Jamaica
1970 Edinburgh, Scotland
1974 Christchurch, New Zealand
1978 Edmonton, Canada
1982 Brisbane, Australia
1986 Edinburgh, Scotland
1990 Auckland, New Zealand
1994 Victoria, Canada

Table of Olympic medal winners – Winter Games, 1924–92

		Gold	Silver	Bronze	Total
1	USSR/Unified team[2]	88	63	67	218
2	Norway	63	66	59	188
3	USA	47	50	37	134
4	Austria	34	45	40	119
5	Finland	36	44	37	117
6	GDR*	39	36	35	110
7	Germany*	36	36	29	101
8	Sweden	37	25	34	96
9	Switzerland	24	25	75	76
10	Canada	16	15	20	51
11	France	16	15	17	48
12	Italy	18	16	13	47
13	Netherlands	14	18	14	46
14	Czechoslovakia	2	8	16	26
15	United Kingdom	7	4	10	21
16	Japan	2	6	6	14
17	Liechtenstein	2	2	5	9
18	Hungary	0	2	4	6
=19	South Korea	2	1	1	4
=19	Poland	1	1	2	4
=19	Belgium	1	1	2	4
=19	Yugoslavia	0	3	1	4
20	China	0	3	0	3
=21	Spain	1	0	1	2
=21	Luxembourg	0	2	0	2
=21	North Korea[1]	0	1	1	2
=22	New Zealand	0	1	0	1
=22	Romania	0	0	1	1
=22	Bulgaria	0	0	1	1

Totals include all first, second and third places, including those events not on the current schedule
*Germany to 1952 and 1992, Federal Republic of Germany 1956–88 Medals won by the combined German teams of 1956, 1960 and 1964 have been allocated to the FRG and GDR according to the athlete's origin
[1] From 1964
[2] The Unified Team was a combined team that took part in the 1992 Games representing 12 of the 15 former Soviet republics.

PAN-AMERICAN GAMES

The Pan-American Games are multi-sport competitions open to athletes from North, Central and South American and Caribbean nations. They have been held every four years since 1951.

1951 Buenos Aires, Argentina
1955 Mexico City, Mexico
1959 Chicago, USA
1963 São Paulo, Brazil
1967 Winnipeg, Canada
1971 Cali, Colombia
1975 Mexico City, Mexico
1979 San Juan, Puerto Rico
1983 Caracas, Venezuela
1987 Indianapolis, USA
1991 Havana, Cuba
1995 Mar del Plata, Argentina

WORLD STUDENT GAMES

The World Student Games were first held in 1924 at Warsaw, Poland. Between 1951 and 1963 rival celebrations were held when the Communist-inspired World Youth Games were also celebrated. The cities most recently awarded the Games are:

1977 Sofia, Bulgaria
1979 Mexico City, Mexico
1981 Bucharest, Romania
1983 Edmonton, Canada
1985 Kobe, Japan
1987 Zagreb, Yugoslavia (now Croatia)
1989 Duisburg, Germany
1991 Sheffield, UK
1993 Buffalo, USA
1995 Fukuoka, Japan

ASIAN GAMES

First held in 1951, the Asian Games are multi-sport competitions open to athletes from Asian nations. Since 1954 the Games have been held every four years.

1951 New Delhi, India
1954 Manila, Philippines
1958 Tokyo, Japan
1962 Djakarta, Indonesia
1966 Bangkok, Thailand
1970 Bangkok, Thailand
1974 Tehran, Iran
1978 Bangkok, Thailand
1982 New Delhi, India
1986 Seoul, South Korea
1990 Beijing (Peking), China
1994 Hiroshima, Japan

ALL AFRICAN GAMES

The All African games are multi-sport competitions open to athletes from African nations. The Games were held at irregular intervals between 1965 and 1987. Since 1987 they have been held every four years.

1965 Brazzaville, Congo
1973 Lagos, Nigeria
1978 Algiers, Algeria
1987 Nairobi, Kenya
1991 Cairo, Egypt
1995 Harare, Zimbabwe

THE UNITED KINGDOM

COUNTRIES OF THE UK

The United Kingdom (UK) comprises the island of Great Britain – England, Wales and Scotland – and Northern Ireland.
Area: 244 103 km² (94 249 sq mi).
Population: 57 561 600 (1992 est).

Various names are used for the islands geographically known as the British Isles. Geographical, political, legal and popular usages differ.

The British Isles is a convenient but purely geographical term to describe the group of islands lying off the north west coast of Europe that comprises the United Kingdom, the Republic of Ireland and the Crown dependencies of the Isle of Man and the Channel Islands.
Area: 314 798 km² (121 544 sq mi).

Great Britain is the geographical and political name of the main or principal island of the British Isles group. In a strict geographical sense, off-shore islands, for example the Isle of Wight, Anglesey or Shetland, are not part of Great Britain. The name Great Britain – for the union of England and Wales with Scotland – came into popular (but unofficial) use when James VI of Scotland succeeded Queen Elizabeth I of England in 1603. With the Union of the parliaments of England and Scotland, on 1 May 1707, the style 'Great Britain' was formally adopted.
Area: (of the island of Great Britain) 218 041 km² (84 186 sq mi); (of the union of England and Wales with Scotland) 229 984 km² (88 797 sq mi).

England is geographically the southern and larger part of the island of Great Britain. The islands off the English coast, such as the Isle of Wight and the Isles of Scilly, are administratively part of England. Politically and geographically England is that part of Great Britain governed by English law (which also pertains in Wales).
Area: 130 441 km² (50 363 sq mi).
Population: 47 837 300 (1991 est).
Capital: London.

Wales was incorporated into England by Act of Parliament in 1536. The county boundaries between England and Wales expressly cannot be altered by the ordinary processes of local government reorganization.
Area: 20 768 km² (8019 sq mi).
Population: 2 881 000 (1991 est).
Capital: Cardiff.

Scotland consists of the northern and smaller part of the island of Great Britain. The Kingdom of Scotland effectively lost much of its independence in 1603 when King James VI of Scotland became King James I of England. From 1603 to 1707 Scotland remained (for part of the time only nominally) an independent nation. Scotland and England continued to have separate parliaments until the Union of the Parliaments at Westminster on 1 May 1707. Scotland continues to have its own distinctive legal system.
Area: 78 775 km² (30 415 sq mi).
Population: 5 102 400 (1991 est).
Capital: Belfast.

Northern Ireland consists of six of the nine counties of the ancient Irish province of Ulster in the north-eastern corner of the island. From 1921 until 1973 Northern Ireland had a federal relationship with Westminster. The Northern Ireland Parliament – popularly known as Stormont – enjoyed autonomy. Stormont was abolished in 1973, although some legislative functions were transferred to the new Northern Ireland Assembly and Executive. However, after the collapse of the Executive in 1974, the British Secretary of State for Northern Ireland became responsible for the government of Northern Ireland. This measure was intended to be temporary but direct rule has continued.
Area: 14 120 km² (5452 sq mi).
Population: 1 589 400 (1991 est).
Capital: Belfast.

CROWN DEPENDENCIES

The Crown dependencies are territories associated with but not part of the UK. The islands are not part of the EC, but enjoy a special relationship with it.

THE ISLE OF MAN

Area: 572 km² (221 sq mi). *Population:* 70 000 (1991 census). *Capital:* Douglas 22 000 (1991 census). *Government:* Man is governed by a Council of Ministers who enjoy the confidence of the local parliament, the Tynwald, which comprises two houses – the Legislative Council (the upper house) and the House of Keys (the lower house). The Legislative Council comprises the Bishop of Sodor and Man, the non-voting Attorney-General and members chosen by the lower house. The House of Keys comprises 24 members elected by universal adult suffrage. *Chief Minister:* Miles Walker.

THE CHANNEL ISLANDS

The Channel Islands comprise the Bailiwicks of Jersey and Guernsey – the latter bailiwick includes the dependencies of Alderney and Sark, and the small islands of Herm, Brechou, Jethou and Lihou. *Government:* The States – the parliaments of Jersey and Guernsey – both elect committees that are responsible for the government of the islands.

JERSEY *Area:* 116.2 km² (44.8 sq mi). *Population* 83 000 (1989 est). *Capital:* St Helier 30 000 (1986 est). *Government:* The Assembly of the States of Jersey comprises 12 senators (elected by universal adult suffrage for six years), 12 connétables (constables; three years), 29 deputies (three years) and the non-voting Lieutenant-General, the Dean of Jersey, Attorney-General and Solicitor-General.

GUERNSEY *Area:* (Bailiwick) 75 km² (29 sq mi), (island) 63.3 km² (24.5 sq mi). *Population:* (island) 57 000 (1989 est). *Capital:* St Peter Port 18 800 (1986 est). *Government:* The Assembly of the States of Guernsey comprises 12 jurats, 12 conseillers, 33 people's representatives and 10 douzaine (parish) representatives (all elected by universal adult suffrage), plus two representatives from Alderney and the non-voting Lieutenant-Governor, Procureur (Attorney-General) and Comptrolleur (Solicitor-General).

Alderney *Area:* 7.9 km² (3.07 sq mi). *Population:* 2000 (1986 est). *Capital:* St Anne's. *Government:* Guernsey is responsible for Alderney's aviation, health and police services. Alderney also has its own parliament comprising a President and 12 elected members. *President:* J. Kay-Mouat.

Sark *Area:* 5.1 km² (1.99 sq mi). *Population:* 600 (1986). *Capital:* None as settlement is scattered. *Government:* Sark's parliament (the Chief Pleas) comprises 40 tenants and 12 elected deputies. The hereditary Seigneur of Sark retains certain rights of veto and appoints the president of the Chief Pleas, the Seneschal. *Seigneur:* Michael Beaumont.

PHYSICAL GEOGRAPHY

HIGHEST PEAKS IN THE UK

Scotland's ten highest peaks

	m	ft
1. Ben Nevis, Highland	1392	4406
2. Ben Macdhui, Grampian	1310	4300
3. Braeriach, Grampian-Highland border	1294	4248
North Top (Ben Macdhui)	*1293*	*4244*
4. Cairn Toul, Grampian	1292	4241
South Plateau (Braeriach)	*1264*	*4149*
Sgor an Lochan Uaine (Cairn Toul)	*1254*	*4116*
Coire Sputan Dearg (Ben Macdhui)	*1248*	*4095*
5. Cairngorm, Grampian–Highland border	1244	4084
6. Aonach Beag, Highland	1237	4060
Coire an Lochain (Braeriach)	*1230*	*4036*
7. Càrn Mor Dearg, Highland	1222	4012
8. Aonach Mor, Highland	1218	3999
Carn Dearg (Ben Nevis)	*1216*	*3990*
Coire an t'Saighdeir (Cairn Toul)	*1215*	*3989*
9. Ben Lawers, Tayside	1214	3984
Cairn Lochan (Cairngorm)	*1214*	*3983*
10. Beinn a'Bhùird (North Top), Grampian	1196	3924

Northern Ireland's ten highest peaks

	m	ft
1. Slieve Donard, Down	852	2796
2. Slieve Commedagh, Down	767	2516
3. Slieve Bearnagh, Down	730	2395
4. Slieve Mael Beg, Down	704	2310
5. Slieve Lamagan, Down	703	2306
6. Slieve Binnian, Down	685	2247
7. Slieve Mael Mor, Down	682	2238
8. Sawel Mountain, Tyrone	678	2224
9. Shan Slieve, Down	671	2201
10. Slieve Muck, Down	668	2192

Wales' ten highest peaks (all in Gwynedd)

	m	ft
1. Snowdon (Yr Wyddfa)	1085	3560
Garnedd Ugain or Crib Y Ddisg (Yr Wyddfa)	*1065*	*3493*
2. Carnedd Llewelyn	1062	3484
3. Carnedd Dafydd	1044	3426
4. Glyder Fawr	999	3279
5. Glyder Fâch	994	3262
Pen Yr Oleu-wen (Carnedd Dafydd)	*978*	*3210*
Foel Grach (Carnedd Llewelyn)	*974*	*3195*
Yr Elen (Carnedd Llewelyn)	*960*	*3151*
6. Y Garn	946	3104
7. Foel Fras	942	3091
8. Elidir Fawr	923	3029
Crib Goch (Yr Wyddfa)	*921*	*3023*
9. Tryfan	917	3010
10. Aran Fawddwy	905	2970

England's ten highest peaks (all in Cumbria)

	m	ft
1. Scafell Pike	978	3210
2. Sca Fell	963	3162
3. Helvellyn	950	3116
Broad Crag (Scafell Pikes)	*930*	*3054*
4. Skiddaw	930	3053
Lower Man (Helvellyn)	*922*	*3033*
Ill Crags (Scafell Pikes)	*922*	*3025*
Great End (Scafell Pikes)	*909*	*2984*
5. Bow Fell	902	2960
6. Great Gable	898	2949
7. Cross Fell	893	2930
8. Pillar Fell	892	2927
Catstye Cam (Helvellyn)	*889*	*2917*
9. Esk Pike	884	2903
Raise (Helvellyn)	*880*	*2889*
10. Fairfield	872	2863

LARGEST ISLANDS IN UK

Largest islands in England

	km²	sq mi
Isle of Wight	380·99	*147·09*
*Sheppey (Kent)	94·04	*36·31*
*Hayling (Hampshire)	26·84	*10·36*
*Foulness (Essex)	26·14	*10·09*
*Portsea (Hampshire)	24·25	*9·36*
*Canvey (Essex)	18·45	*7·12*
*Mersea (Essex)	18·04	*6·96*
*Walney (Cumbria)	12·99	*5·01*
*Isle of Grain (Kent)	12·85	*4·96*
*Wallasea (Essex)	10·65	*4·11*
St Mary's, Isles of Scilly	6·29	*2·43*
*Thorney (West Sussex)	4·96	*1·91*

Largest islands in Scotland

	km²	sq mi
Lewis with Harris (Wn. Isles)	2225·30	*859·19*
Skye (Highland)	1666·08	*643·28*
Mainland, Shetland	967·00	*373·36*
Mull (Strathclyde)	899·25	*347·21*
Islay (Strathclyde)	614·52	*246·64*
Mainland, Orkney	536·10	*206·99*
Arran (Strathclyde)	435·32	*168·08*
Jura (Strathclyde)	370·35	*142·99*
North Uist (Western Isles)	351·49	*135·71*
South Uist (Western Isles)	332·45	*128·36*
Yell, Shetland	214·16	*82·69*
Hoy, Orkney	136·85	*52·84*

Largest islands in Wales

	km²	sq mi
*Anglesey (*Ynys Mon*; Gwynedd)	713·80	*275·60*
Holy I (Gwynedd)	39·44	*15·22*
Skomer (Dyfed)	2·90	*1·12*
Ramsey (Dyfed)	2·58	*0·99*
Caldey (Dyfed)	2·79	*0·84*
Bardsey (Gwynedd)	1·99	*0·76*
Skokholm (Dyfed)	1·06	*0·41*
Flat Holm (South Glamorgan)	0·33	*0·13*
*Llanddwyn I (Gwynedd)	0·31	*0·12*
Puffin Island (Gwynedd)	0·28	*0·11*
The Skerries (Gwynedd)	0·15	*0·06*
Cardigan Island (Dyfed)	0·15	*0·06*

* Bridged or linked by causeway to the mainland

LONGEST RIVERS IN THE UNITED KINGDOM

Specially compiled maps issued by the Ordnance Survey in the second half of the last century are still the authority for the length of the rivers of the United Kingdom. It should, however, be noted that these measurements are strictly for the course of a river bearing the one name; thus, for example, where the principal headstream has a different name its additional length is ignored – unless otherwise indicated.

Name of watercourse	Length (km/mi)	Remotest source	Mouth	Basin area (km²/mi²)*
Severn (for 254 km)	354 (220)	Lake on E side of Plinlimmon, Powys	Bristol Channel	11 421 (4409.7)
Thames (for 178 km) – Isis (69 km) – Churn	346 (215)	Severn Springs, Gloucestershire	North Sea (The Nore)	9 948 (3841.6)
Trent (for 236 km) – Humber (61 km)	297 (185)	Biddulph Moor, Staffs	North Sea (as Humber)	10 436 (4029.2)
Aire (for 126 km) – (Yorkshire) Ouse (72 km) and Humber (61 km)	259 (161)	NW of North Yorks	North Sea (as Humber)	11 366 (4388.4)
Ouse (Great or Bedford)	230 (143)	nr Brackley, Northamptonshire	The Wash	8 582 (3313.6)
Wye (or Gwy)	215 (135)	Plinlimmon, Powys	Into Severn S of Chepstow, Gwent	4 184 (1615.3)
Tay (for 150 km) – Tummel	188 (117)	(Tay) Beinn Oss, Tayside	North Sea	5 080 (1961.6)
Nene	161 (100)	nr Naseby, Northants	The Wash	2 369 (914.5)
Clyde (incl. Daer Water)	158 (98.5)	nr Earncraig Hill, Strathclyde	Firth of Clyde (measured to Port Glasgow)	3 040 (1173.8)
Spey	157.5 (98.0)	Loch Spey, Highland	North Sea	2 988 (1153.5)
Tweed	155.3 (96.5)	Tweed's Well, Borders	North Sea	5 160 (1992.3)
Dee (Aberdeenshire)	137.1 (85.2)	W of Cairn Toul, Grampian	North Sea	2 116 (817.2)
Avon (Warwickshire or Upper)	136.7 (85)	nr Naseby, Northants	Into Severn at Tewkesbury	(part of Severn basin)
Don (Aberdeenshire)	129.5 (80.5)	Carn Cuilchathaidh, Grampian	North Sea	1 336 (515.7)
Tees	127 (79)	Cross Fell, Cumbria	North Sea	2 237 (863.6)
Bann (Upper Bann – Lough Neagh – Lower Bann)	122 (76)	Mountains of Mourne, SW Down	Atlantic Ocean	–
Tyne (for 55 km) – North Tyne (63 km)	118.5 (73)	Cheviots between Peel Fell and Carter Fell	North Sea	2 917 (1126.4)
Dee (Cheshire)	112.5 (70)	Bala Lake, Gwynedd	Irish Sea	2 119 (818.1)
Eden (Cumberland)	111 (69)	Pennines, SE of Kirby Stephen	Solway Firth, Irish Sea	2 400 (926.7)
Usk	104.5 (65)	Talsarn Mt. Powys	Bristol Channel	1 740 (672.0)
Wear	104.5 (65)	W of Wearhead, Northumberland	North Sea	1 198 (462.6)
Wharfe	104.5 (65)	12 km S of Hawes,	Into York Ouse, nr Cawood, North Yorks	(part of Ouse basin)
Forth	103.5 (64.5)	Duchray Water, Ben Lomond	Firth of Forth, North Sea	1 626 (627.9)

* This column gives the hydrometric area of the whole river system as per *The Surface Water Survey*.

MAJOR LOCHS AND LAKES

Name	Area km² (sq mi)		Maximum Length km (mi)		Maximum Breadth km (mi)		Maximum Depth m (ft)	
Northern Ireland								
Lough Neagh, Antrim, Down	381.7	*(147.39)*	28	*(18)*	17	*(11)*	31	*(102)*
Armagh, Tyrone, Londonderry								
Lower Lough Erne, Fermanagh	105	*(40.57)*	28	*(18)*	8.8	*(5.5)*	68	*(226)*
Scotland								
Loch Lomond, Strathclyde-	71.2	*(27.5)*	36.4	*(22.64)*	8	*(5)*	189	*(623)*
Central								
Loch Ness, Highland	56.6	*(21.87)*	36.6	*(22.75)*	3.2	*(2)*	228	*(751)*
Loch Awe, Strathclyde	38.7	*(14.95)*	41	*(25.5)*	3.2	*(2)*	93	*(307)*
Loch Maree, Highland	28.4	*(11)*	21.7	*(13.5)*	3.2	*(2)*	111	*(367)*
Loch Morar, Highland	26.6	*(10.3)*	18.5	*(11.5)*	2.4	*(1.5)*	309	*(1017)*
Loch Tay, Tayside	26.3	*(10.19)*	23.4	*(14.55)*	1.7	*(1.07)*	154	*(508)*
Loch Shin, Highland	22.5	*(8.70)*	27.7	*(17.35)*	1.6	*(1.0)*	49	*(162)*
Loch Shiel, Highland	19.5	*(7.56)*	28.1	*(17.5)*	1.4	*(0.9)*	128	*(420)*
England								
Windermere, Cumbria	14.7	*(5.69)*	16.8	*(10.50)*	1.47	*(0.9)*	66	*(219)*
Ullswater, Cumbria	8.9	*(3.44)*	11.8	*(7.35)*	1.0	*(0.6)*	62	*(205)*
Bassenthwaite Water, Cumbria	5.3	*(2.06)*	6.1	*(3.83)*	1.18	*(0.7)*	21	*(70)*
Derwentwater, Cumbria	5.3	*(2.06)*	4.6	*(2.87)*	1.94	*(1.2)*	21	*(72)*
Wales								
Lake Vyrnwy (dammed), Powys	8.2	*(3.18)*	7.5	*(4.7)*	00.6	*(0.6)*	36	*(120)*
Bala Lake (Llyn Tegid), Gwynedd	4.3	*(1.69)*	6.1	*(3.8)*	0.53	*(0.5)*	38	*(125)*

MAJOR RESERVOIRS

Name	Area km²	Area sq mi	Capacity megalitres
England			
Rutland Water, Leicestershire	12.60	4.86	124 000
Kielder Water, Northumberland	11.00	4.25	199 175
Pitsford Water, Northants	7.39	2.85	17 500
Grafham Water, Cambridgeshire	7.38	2.85	56 000
Chew Valley, Avon	4.86	1.88	20 457
Derwent, Derbyshire-South Yorkshire	4.05	1.56	9478
Wales			
Trawsfynydd, Gwynedd	4.78	1.84	32 550
Llyn Brenig, Clywd	3.72	1.44	60 008
Alaw, Anglesey, Gwynedd	3.14	1.21	7456
Scotland			
Carron Valley, Central-Strathclyde	3.9	1.51	19 400
Megget, Borders	2.59	1.00	61 400
Loch Bradan, Strathclyde	2.09	0.81	20 700
Northern Ireland			
Lough Island Reavy, Down	1.05	0.41	7683
Silent Valley, Down	0.97	0.38	12 913

WATERFALLS

The highest British waterfalls are:

Waterfall	Location	Height m (ft)
Eas A'Chùal Aluinn	Highland, Scotland	200 (658)
Falls of Glomach	Highland, Scotland	112 (370)
Pistyll-y-Llyn	Powys/Dyfed, Wales	c.73 (c.230)
Pistyll Rkhaiadr	Clwyd, Wales	73 (240)
Foyers	Highland, Scotland	62 (205)
Falls of Clyde	Strathclyde, Scotland	62* (204)
Falls of Bruar	Tayside, Scotland	60 (200)
Cauldron Snout	Cumbria, England	60 (200)

CAVES

Large or deep caves are few in the United Kingdom. The deepest British cave is Ogof Ffynnon Ddu (308 m / 1010 ft deep) in Powys, Wales.

The largest system is the Ease Gill system with 66 km (41 mi) of surveyed passages.

England's deepest cave is Giant's Hole, Oxlow Caverns, Derbyshire, which descends 214 m (702 ft). Scotland's deepest cave is Cnoc nan Uamh which is 76 m (249 ft) deep. Northern Ireland's deepest cave is Reyfad Pot, Co. Fermanagh, which is 179 m (587 ft) deep.

DESIGNATED AREAS

There has been a gradual awakening to the need to protect and preserve the UK's resources of flora, fauna and wild land in all its diversity, and to conserve environments and historic buildings. To these ends, protection is afforded by legislation, by statutory and voluntary bodies, and through the designation of areas such as national parks, areas of outstanding natural beauty, nature reserves and sites of special scientific interest.

NATIONAL PARKS

Under the 1949 National Park and Access to the Countryside Act, ten large areas in England and Wales have been designated as national parks. Legislation protects these areas of notable scenic and environmental importance. The Peak District and the Lake District are run by financially independent authorities with responsibility for detailed planning in their areas. In 1992 it was announced that similar bodies were to be established in the remaining parks to replace the national park authorities, which are committees of the relevant county councils.

The status of national parks is often misunderstood. The public has no right of access to the large areas of privately owned land within the parks, but access to public footpaths and certain areas of open land is encouraged. Information and study centres have been established within the parks to enhance the enjoyment of these areas by the public.

The Broads and the New Forest enjoy a status equivalent to – and are sometimes referred to as – national parks. They have the legal protection afforded by the National Parks Act without the standard administrative machinery. There are no national parks in Scotland or Northern Ireland, although the designation of certain areas in Scotland is under discussion. The National Parks are (with designation date, area, location and major features):

Brecon Beacons 1957; 1344 km² (519 sq mi); Powys, Dyfed, Gwent and Mid Glamorgan. The park includes the Brecon Beacons, the Black Mountains and the Usk valley.

Dartmoor 1951; 945 km² (365 sq mi); Devon. Dartmoor, a moorland with granite tors (outcrops), bogs and oak woods, is known for its ponies and historic remains.

Exmoor 1954; 686 km² (265 sq mi); Somerset and Devon. Exmoor – a moorland plateau supporting wild ponies and red deer – includes many ancient remains.

Lake District 1951; 2280 km² (880 sq mi); Cumbria. The park includes many lakes and England's highest mountains: Scafell Pike, Helvellyn and Skiddaw.

Northumberland 1956; 1031 km² (398 sq mi); Northumberland. The park is an area of hill country between Hadrian's Wall and the Cheviot Hills.

North York Moors 1952; 1433 km² (553 sq mi); North Yorkshire and Cleveland. The park comprises woods and moorland, including coastal headlands and the Hambleton Hills.

Peak District 1951; 1404 km² (542 sq mi); Derbyshire and small areas of adjoining counties. The park includes limestone dales and caves, woodlands and gritstone moors.

Pembrokeshire Coast 1952; 583 km² (225 sq mi); Dyfed. This discontinuous park – which includes cliffs, beaches, open moorland and Skomer Island –

has many historic buildings and is renowned for its sea birds.

Snowdonia 1951; 2171 km² (838 sq mi); Gwynedd. Snowdonia is a rugged mountain region including lakes, passes, forests and Snowdon, the highest peak in Wales.

Yorkshire Dales 1954; 1762 km² (680 sq mi); North Yorkshire and Cumbria. The park comprises a limestone and gritstone upland containing the summits of Ingleborough, Pen-y-Ghent and Whernside.

The Broads 1989; 287 km² (111 sq mi); Norfolk and Suffolk. The Broads – an area of shallow lakes and marshland – are administered by the Broads Board, local and river authorities.

New Forest 1992; 336 km² (130 sq mi); Hampshire. The New Forest – an area of woodland and heath, noted for its ponies – is administered by the New Forest Board, the Forestry Commission, the ancient Court of Verderers and New Forest District Council.

AREAS OF OUTSTANDING NATURAL BEAUTY AND NATIONAL SCENIC AREAS

The 1949 legislation that designated national parks also provided for the protection and conservation of areas of outstanding natural beauty (AONBs). AONBs are administered by county and district councils. There is no provision for public access to these areas. The Countryside Act of 1968 further defined the role of AONBs, giving emphasis to the needs of agriculture and forestry.

The legislation under which AONBs have been designated does not apply to Scotland. However, a number of national scenic areas (NSAs) – which in some respects enjoy a status similar to AONBs – are recognized by Scottish Natural Heritage. NSAs are administered by the local authorities in consultation with the SNH.

AONBs in England and Wales Anglesey, Arnside and Silverdale, Blackdown Hills, Cannock Chase, Chichester Harbour, Chilterns, Clwydian Range, Cornwall (areas in), Cotswolds, Cranborne Chase and West Wiltshire Downs, Dedham Vale, East Devon, East Hampshire, Dorset (coastal areas), Forest of Bowland, Gower Peninsula, High Weald, Howardian Hills, Isles of Scilly, Isle of Wight, Kent Downs, Lincolnshire Wolds, Lleyn, Malvern Hills, Mendip Hills, Norfolk Coast, North Devon, North Pennines, North Wessex Downs, Northumberland Coast, Quantock Hills, Shropshire Hills, Solway Coast, South Devon, South Hampshire Coast, Suffolk Coast and Heaths, Surrey Hills, Sussex Downs, Wye Valley.

AONBs in Northern Ireland Antrim Coast and Glens, Causeway Coast, Lagan Valley, Lecale Coast, Mourne, North Derry, Ring of Gullion, Sperrin, Strangford Lough.

Scottish NSAs Assynt-Coigach, Ben Nevis and Glen Coe, Cairngorm Mountains, Cuillin Hills, Deeside and Lochnagar, Dornoch Firth, East Stewartry Coast, Eildon and Leaderfoot, Fleet Valley, Glen Affric, Glen Strathfarrar, Hoy and West Mainland, Jura, Kintail, Knapdale, Knoydart, Kyle of Tongue, Kyles of Bute, Loch Lomond, Loch na Keal, Loch Rannoch and Glen Lyon, Loch Shiel, Loch Tummel, Lynn of Lorn, Morar, Moidart and Ardnamurchan, Nith Estuary, North-west Sutherland, River Earn, River Tay, St Kilda, Shetland, Scarba, Lunga and the Garvellachs, the Small Isles, South Lewis, Harris and North Uist, South Uist Machair, the Trossachs, Trotternish, Upper Tweeddale, Wester Ross.

The Traditional Counties of the United Kingdom

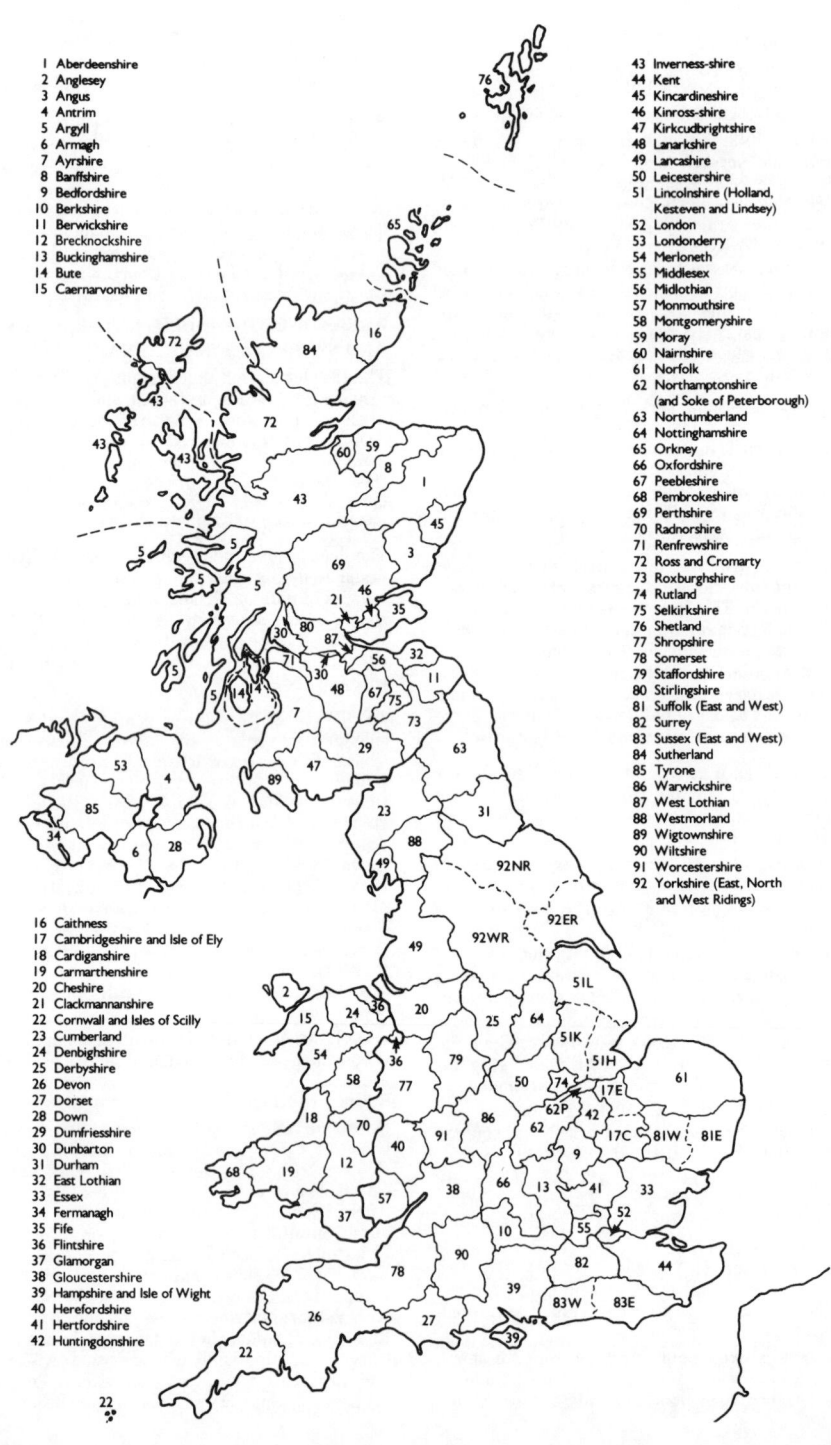

1 Aberdeenshire
2 Anglesey
3 Angus
4 Antrim
5 Argyll
6 Armagh
7 Ayrshire
8 Banffshire
9 Bedfordshire
10 Berkshire
11 Berwickshire
12 Brecknockshire
13 Buckinghamshire
14 Bute
15 Caernarvonshire

16 Caithness
17 Cambridgeshire and Isle of Ely
18 Cardiganshire
19 Carmarthenshire
20 Cheshire
21 Clackmannanshire
22 Cornwall and Isles of Scilly
23 Cumberland
24 Denbighshire
25 Derbyshire
26 Devon
27 Dorset
28 Down
29 Dumfriesshire
30 Dunbarton
31 Durham
32 East Lothian
33 Essex
34 Fermanagh
35 Fife
36 Flintshire
37 Glamorgan
38 Gloucestershire
39 Hampshire and Isle of Wight
40 Herefordshire
41 Hertfordshire
42 Huntingdonshire

43 Inverness-shire
44 Kent
45 Kincardineshire
46 Kinross-shire
47 Kirkcudbrightshire
48 Lanarkshire
49 Lancashire
50 Leicestershire
51 Lincolnshire (Holland,
    Kesteven and Lindsey)
52 London
53 Londonderry
54 Merloneth
55 Middlesex
56 Midlothian
57 Monmouthshire
58 Montgomeryshire
59 Moray
60 Nairnshire
61 Norfolk
62 Northamptonshire
    (and Soke of Peterborough)
63 Northumberland
64 Nottinghamshire
65 Orkney
66 Oxfordshire
67 Peebleshire
68 Pembrokeshire
69 Perthshire
70 Radnorshire
71 Renfrewshire
72 Ross and Cromarty
73 Roxburghshire
74 Rutland
75 Selkirkshire
76 Shetland
77 Shropshire
78 Somerset
79 Staffordshire
80 Stirlingshire
81 Suffolk (East and West)
82 Surrey
83 Sussex (East and West)
84 Sutherland
85 Tyrone
86 Warwickshire
87 West Lothian
88 Westmorland
89 Wigtownshire
90 Wiltshire
91 Worcestershire
92 Yorkshire (East, North
    and West Ridings)

TRADITIONAL COUNTIES

The boundaries of the UK's traditional counties were redrawn in 1974 and 1975 *for administrative purposes only*. The map opposite shows the names and the boundaries of the traditional counties; a map of the administrative areas is on p. 716. The 'new counties' are regarded as artificial by many people and the traditional names continue to be widely used. Moreover, the 1974 Act stated 'The new county councils are solely for the purpose of defining areas of first-level government of the future; they are administration areas and will not alter the traditional boundaries.'

In 1992 a review of local government areas began. The first proposals indicate that a single-tier system is likely, based in part upon existing administrative counties and in part upon district councils. The traditional counties are likely to return for all other purposes.

The traditional counties are listed below. Their areas and county towns – which in many cases were not the administrative centre – are given.

COUNTIES OF ENGLAND

Bedfordshire *Bedford*; 1226 km² (473 sq mi).
Berkshire *Reading*; 1877 km² (725 sq mi).
Buckinghamshire *Aylesbury*; 1940 km² (749 sq mi).
Cambridgeshire *Cambridge*; 2246 km² (867); including the Isle of Ely (*March*).
Cheshire *Chester*; 2629 km² (1015 sq mi).
Cornwall *Bodmin*; 3514 km² (1357 sq mi).
Cumberland *Carlisle*; 3938 km² (1521 sq mi).
Derbyshire *Derby*; 2604 km² (1006 sq mi).
Devon *Exeter*; 6765 km² (2611 sq mi).
Dorset *Dorchester*; 2524 km² (975 sq mi).
Durham *Durham*; 2628 km² (1015 sq mi).
Essex *Chelmsford*; 3958 km² (1528 sq mi).
Gloucestershire *Gloucester*; 3257 km² (1528 sq mi).
Hampshire *Winchester*; 4275 km² (1650 sq mi); including the Isle of Wight (*Newport*).
Herefordshire *Hereford*; 2181 km² (842 sq mi).
Hertfordshire *Hertford*; 1637 km² (632 sq mi).
Huntingdonshire *Huntingdon*; 947 km² (366 sq mi).
Kent *Maidstone*; 3949 km² (1525 sq mi).
Lancashire *Lancaster*; 4864 km² (1878 sq mi).
Leicestershire *Leicester*; 2155 km² (832 sq mi).
Lincolnshire *Lincoln*; 6897 km² (2663 sq mi); comprising the Parts of Holland (*Boston*), Kesteven (*Sleaford*) and Lindsey (*Lincoln*).
London *London*; 303 km² (117 sq mi).
Middlesex *Brentford*; 602 km² (232 sq mi).
Norfolk *Norwich*; 5319 km² (2054 sq mi).
Northamptonshire *Northampton*; 2584 km² (998 sq mi); including the Soke of Peterborough (*Peterborough*).
Northumberland *Newcastle*; 5228 km² (2019 sq mi).
Nottinghamshire *Nottingham*; 2185 km² (844 sq mi).
Oxfordshire *Oxford*; 1939 km² (749 sq mi).
Rutland *Oakham*; 394 km² (152 sq mi).
Shropshire *Shrewsbury*; 3488 km² (1347 sq mi).
Somerset *Taunton*; 4178 km² (1613 sq mi).
Staffordshire *Stafford*; 2988 km² (1154 sq mi).
Suffolk *Ipswich*; 3838 km² (1482 sq mi); comprising East Suffolk (*Ipswich*) and West Suffolk (*Bury St Edmunds*).
Surrey *Guildford*; 1869 km² (722 sq mi).
Sussex *Lewes*; 3774 km² (1457 sq mi); comprising East Sussex (*Lewes*) and West Sussex (*Chichester*).
Warwickshire *Warwick*; 2545 km² (983 sq mi).
Westmorland *Appleby*; 2043 km² (789 sq mi).
Wiltshire *Salisbury*; 3483 km² (1345 sq mi).
Worcestershire *Worcester*; 1813 km² (700 sq mi).
Yorkshire *York*; 15 774 km² (6091 sq mi); comprising the East Riding (*Beverley*), North Riding (*Northallerton*) and West Riding (*Wakefield*).

COUNTIES OF WALES

Anglesey *Beaumaris*; 715 km² (276 sq mi).
Brecknockshire *Brecon*; 1899 km² (733 sq mi).
Caernarvonshire *Caernarfon*; 1473 km² (569 sq mi).
Cardiganshire *Cardigan*; 1794 km² (692 sq mi).
Carmarthenshire *Carmarthen*; 2381 km² (919 sq mi).
Denbighshire *Denbigh*; 1732 km² (669 sq mi).
Flintshire *Flint*; 663 km² (256 sq mi).
Glamorgan *Cardiff*; 2118 km² (818 sq mi).
Merioneth Dolgellau; 1709 km² (660 sq mi).
Monmouthshire *Monmouth*; 1403 km² (542 sq mi).
Montgomeryshire *Montgomery*; 2064 km² (797 sq mi).
Pembrokeshire *Pembroke*; 1590 km² (614 sq mi).
Radnorshire *Presteign*; 1219 km² (471 sq mi).

COUNTIES OF SCOTLAND

Aberdeenshire *Aberdeen*; 5068 km² (1957 sq mi).
Angus *Forfar*; 2213 km² (854 sq mi).
Argyll *Inveraray*; 8055 km² (3110 sq mi).
Ayrshire *Ayr*; 2931 km² (1132 sq mi).
Banffshire *Banff*; 1631 km² (630 sq mi).
Berwickshire *Duns*; 1184 km² (457 sq mi).
Buteshire *Rothesay*; 565 km² (218 sq mi).
Caithness *Wick*; 1776 km² (686 sq mi).
Clackmannanshire *Clackmannan*; 141 km² (55 sq mi).
Dumfries-shire *Dumfries*; 2785 km² (1075 sq mi).
Dunbartonshire *Dumbarton*; 625 km² (241 sq mi).
East Lothian *Haddington*; 692 km² (267 sq mi).
Fife *Cupar*; 1307 km² (505 sq mi).
Inverness-shire *Inverness*; 10 907 km² (4211 sq mi).
Kincardineshire *Stonehaven*; 981 km² (379 sq mi).
Kinross-shire *Kinross*; 212 km² (82 sq mi).
Kirkcudbrightshire *Kirkcudbright*; 2323 km² (897 sq mi).
Lanarkshire *Lanark*; 2169 km² (837 sq mi).
Midlothian *Edinburgh*; 814 km² (314 sq mi).
Moray *Elgin*; 1234 km² (476 sq mi).
Nairnshire *Nairn*; 422 km² (163 sq mi).
Orkney *Kirkwall*; 975 km² (376 sq mi).
Peebles-shire *Peebles*; 899 km² (347 sq mi).
Perthshire *Perth*; 6458 km² (2493 sq mi).
Renfrewshire *Renfrew*; 582 km² (225 sq mi).
Ross and Cromarty *Dingwall*; 8002 km² (3089 sq mi).
Roxburghshire *Jedburgh*; 1722 km² (665 sq mi).
Selkirkshire *Selkirk*; 693 km² (268 sq mi).
Shetland *Lerwick*; 1426 km² (551 sq mi).
Stirlingshire *Stirling*; 1,167 km² (451 sq mi).
Sutherland *Dornoch*; 5252 km² (2028 sq mi).
West Lothian *Linlithgow*; 311 km² (120 sq mi).
Wigtownshire *Wigtown*; 1263 km² (487 sq mi).

COUNTIES OF NORTHERN IRELAND

Antrim *Antrim*; 3046 km² (1176 sq mi).
Armagh *Armagh*; 1326 km² (512 sq mi).
Down *Downpatrick*; 2466 km² (952 sq mi).
Fermanagh *Enniskillen*; 1851 km² (715 sq mi).
Londonderry *Londonderry*; 2075 km² (801 sq mi).
Tyrone *Omagh*; 3400 km² (1313 sq mi).

The Administrative Counties and Regions of the United Kingdom

Shetland

North Atlantic Ocean

Orkney

Western Isles

Scotland

Highland

Grampian

North Sea

Tayside

Strathclyde

Central

Fife

Lothian

Northern Ireland

Strathclyde

Borders

Dumfries and Galloway

Northumberland

North Channel

Cumbria

Tyne and Wear

Durham

Cleveland

North Yorkshire

Humberside

Lancashire

West Yorkshire

Irish Sea

G.Manch.

South Yorks.

England

Merseyside

Cheshire

Derby—shire

Lincolnshire

Clwyd

Notts.

Gwyn.

Staffs.

Wales

Shrop—shire

W. Mid.

Leicester—shire

Norfolk

Powys

Hereford and Worcester

War.

Northants.

Cambs.

Dyfed

Beds.

Suffolk

Glos.

Herts.

Essex

W. Glam.

Mid Glam.

Gwent

Oxford—shire

Bucks.

S. Glam.

Avon

Wiltshire

Berkshire

Greater London

Bristol Channel

Somerset

Hampshire

Surrey

Kent

West Sussex

East Sussex

Strait of Dover

Devon

Dorset

Cornwall

Isle of Wight

English Channel

Isles of Scilly

1 Belfast
2 Newtownabbey
3 Carrickfergus
4 Castlereagh
5 North Down
6 Ards
7 Down
8 Newry& Mourne
9 Banbridge
10 Lisburn
11 Craigavon
12 Armagh
13 Dungannon
14 Fermanagh
15 Omagh
16 Cookstown
17 Magherafelt
18 Strabane
19 Derry
20 Limavady
21 Coleraine
22 Ballymoney
23 Moyle
24 Ballymena
25 Larne
26 Antrim

0   50   100   150 km

LOCAL GOVERNMENT AUTHORITIES

The boundaries of the UK's traditional counties were redrawn in 1974 and 1975 for administrative purposes only. The map on p. 714 shows the names and the boundaries of the traditional counties; a map of the administrative areas is opposite.

In England there are 39 administrative counties, plus 36 metropolitan district councils, 296 district councils and 32 Greater London boroughs. In Scotland there are nine regions, three island authorities and 53 district councils. In Wales there are eight administrative counties and 37 district councils. In Northern Ireland the 6 traditional counties were replaced as administrative units by 26 districts.

In 1992 a review of local government areas began. The first proposals indicate that a single-tier system is likely to emerge, based in part upon the existing administrative councils and in part upon the larger district councils. The traditional counties are likely to return for all other purposes.

Population figures the figures given are mid-1991 estimates.

Metropolitan Counties The councils of the metropolitan counties were abolished on 31 March 1986. The names of the former metropolitan counties are marked by an asterisk.

ADMINISTRATIVE COUNTIES OF ENGLAND

AVON

Area 1345 km^2 (519 miles^2)

Population 962 000. *Density* 715 per km^2 (1854 per mile^2).

Administrative HQ Avon House, The Haymarket, Bristol.

Highest point above sea level Nett Wood, East Harptree 251 m (825 ft).

Districts Bath (city) 84 600; Bristol (city) 392 600; Kingswood 90 600; Northavon (HQ: Thornbury) 132 900; Wansdyke (HQ: Keynsham) 80 800; Woodspring (HQ: Weston-super-Mare) 180 500.

BEDFORDSHIRE

Area 1235 km^2 (477 miles^2).

Population 534 300. *Density* 433 per km^2 (1120 per mile^2).

Administrative HQ County Hall, Cauldwell St, Bedford.

Highest point above sea level Dunstable Downs 243 m (798 ft).

Districts Luton 174 600; Mid Bedfordshire (HQ: Ampthill) 113 300; North Bedfordshire (HQ: Bedford) 136 400; South Bedfordshire (HQ: Leighton Buzzard) 110 000.

BERKSHIRE

Area 1256 km^2 (485 miles^2).

Population 752 500. *Density* 599 per km^2 (1552 per mile^2).

Administrative HQ Shire Hall, Shinfield Park, Reading.

Highest point above sea level Walbury Hill 297 m (974 ft).

Districts Bracknell Forest (HQ: Bracknell) 98 500; Newbury 139 900; Reading 134 600; Slough 102 400; Windsor and Maidenhead (HQ: Maidenhead) 135 200; Wokingham 141 800.

BUCKINGHAMSHIRE

Area 1883 km^2 (727 miles^2).

Population 640 200. *Density* 340 per km^2 (881 per mile^2).

Administrative HQ County Hall, Aylesbury.

Highest point above sea level Nr. Aston Hill 267 m (876 ft).

Districts Aylesbury Vale (HQ: Aylesbury) 148 300; Chiltern (HQ: Amersham) 89 800; Milton Keynes 178 900; South Bucks (HQ: Slough, i.e. outside the district) 62 600; Wycombe (HQ: High Wycombe) 160 500.

CAMBRIDGESHIRE

Area 3409 km^2 (1316 miles^2).

Population 669 900. *Density* 197 per km^2 (509 per mile^2).

Administrative HQ Shire Hall, Castle Hill, Cambridge.

Highest point above sea level 275 m (300 yd) south of the Hall, Great Chishill, 145 m (478 ft).

Districts Cambridge (city) 105 700; East Cambridgeshire (HQ: Ely) 61 300; Fenland (HQ: Wisbech) 75 600; Huntingdonshire (HQ: Huntingdon) 149 600; Peterborough (city) 155 200; South Cambridgeshire (HQ: Cambridge, i.e. outside the district) 122 500.

CHESHIRE

Area 2328 km^2 (899 miles^2).

Population 966 500. *Density* 415 per km^2 (1075 per mile^2).

Administrative HQ County Hall, Chester.

Highest point above sea level Shining Tor 559 m (1834 ft)

Districts Chester (city) 118 300; Congleton (HQ: Sandbach) 85 400; Crewe and Nantwich (HQ: Crewe) 105 300; Ellesmere Port and Neston (HQ: Ellesmere Port) 81 500; Halton (HQ: Widnes) 124 700; Macclesfield 151 400; Vale Royal (HQ: Frodsham) 114 700; Warrington 185 100.

CLEVELAND

Area 590 km^2 (228 miles^2).

Population 557 500. *Density* 945 per km^2 (2445 per mile^2).

Administrative HQ Municipal Buildings, Middlesbrough.

Highest point above sea level Hob on the Hill 328 m (1078 ft).

Districts Hartlepool 91 400; Langbaurgh-on-Tees (HQ: South Bank) 146 400; Middlesbrough 144 400; Stockton-on-Tees 175 300.

Cleveland was one of the first areas for which proposals for local government reform have been made. These proposals recommend the abolition of the administrative county and the reversion of those areas north of the River Tees to County Durham for all purposes except administration and a similar reversion to Yorkshire of those areas south of the River Tees. It was recommended that the four district councils become all-purpose administrative authorities.

CORNWALL (and the Isles of Scilly)

Area 3548 km^2 (1370 miles^2).

Population 475 200. *Density* 134 per km^2 (347 per mile^2).

Administrative HQ County Hall, Truro.

Highest point above sea level Brown Willy 419 m (1375 ft).

Districts Caradon (HQ: Liskeard) 77 500; Carrick (HQ: Truro) 84 000; Kerrier (HQ: Camborne) 89 400; North Cornwall (HQ: Bodmin) 74 400; Penwith (HQ: Penzance) 59 900; Restormel (HQ: St Austell) 87 900.

Isles of Scilly The Isles of Scilly are administered by the Council of the Isles of Scilly. This unique local-government body – which was set up by an Order made under the Local Government Act (1974) – combines the powers of an English county council and district council. For some purposes the Isles are included with Cornwall, whose county council provides services on an agency basis. *Area:* 16·35 km^2 (6·31 sq mi). *Population:* 2000 (1991 estimate). *Centre of administration:* Hugh Town (St Mary's).

CUMBRIA

Area 6810 km^2 (2629 miles^2).

Population 489 700. *Density* 72 per km^2 (186 per mile^2).

Administrative HQ The Courts, Carlisle.

Highest point above sea level Scafell Pike 978 m (3210 ft).

Districts Allerdale (HQs: Wigton and Workington) 96 700; Barrow-in-Furness 73 700; Carlisle (city) 102 000; Copeland (HQ: Whitehaven) 72 000; Eden (HQ: Penrith) 46 000; South Lakeland (HQ: Kendal) 99 300.

DERBYSHIRE

Area 2631 km^2 (1016 miles^2).

Population 939 800. *Density* 357 per km^2 (925 per mile^2).

Administrative HQ County Offices, Matlock.

Highest point above sea level Kinder Scout 636 m (2088 ft).

Districts Amber Valley (HQ: Ripley) 112 800; Bolsover (HQ: Chesterfield, i.e. outside the district) 71 300; Chesterfield 100 300; Derby (city) 222 500; Derbyshire Dales (HQ: Matlock) 67 900; Erewash (HQ: Ilkeston) 107 400; High Peak (HQ: Chapel-en-le-Frith) 86 100; North East Derbyshire (HQ: Chesterfield, i.e. outside the district) 98 700; South Derbyshire (HQ: Burton upon Trent, i.e. outside the district) 72 900.

Derbyshire was one of the first areas for which proposals for local government reform have been made. These proposals recommend the establishment of two all-purpose councils – one for the City of Derby; the other for the rest of the county – or three such councils (with the addition of separate council for Chestefield and its area, based on Chesterfield, Bolsover and North East Derbyshire).

DEVON

Area 6711 km^2 (2590 miles^2).

Population 1 040 000. *Density* 155 per km^2 (402 per mile^2).

Administrative HQ County Hall, Exeter.

Highest point above sea level High Willhays 621 m (2038 ft).

Districts East Devon (HQ: Sidmouth) 118 700; Exeter (city) 104 800; Mid Devon (HQ: Tiverton) 65 200; North Devon (HQ: Barnstaple) 85 800; Plymouth (city) 254 400; South Hams (HQ: Totnes) 78 700; Teignbridge (HQ: Newton Abbot) 110 200; Torbay (HQ: Torquay) 122 800; Torridge (HQ: Bideford) 53 100; West Devon (HQ: Tavistock) 46 300.

DORSET

Area 2654 km^2 (1024 miles^2).

Population 662 900. *Density* 250 per km^2 (647 per mile^2).

Administrative HQ County Hall, Dorchester.

Highest point above sea level Lewesdon Hill 279 m (915 ft).

Districts Bournemouth 159 100; Christchurch 41 300; East Dorset (HQ: Wimborne) 79 300; North Dorset (HQ: Blandford Forum) 54 100; Poole 135 400; Purbeck (HQ: Wareham) 43 400; West Dorset (HQ: Dorchester) 87 400; Weymouth and Portland (HQ: Weymouth) 62 800.

DURHAM

Area 2436 km^2 (940 miles^2).

Population 604 300. *Density* 248 per km^2 (643 per mile^2).

Administrative HQ County Hall, Durham.

Highest point above sea level Mickle Fell 798 m (2591 ft).

Districts Chester-le-Street 53 200; Darlington 99 900; Derwentside (HQ: Consett) 87 000; Durham (city) 86 000; Easington (HQ: Peterlee) 98 900; Sedgefield (HQ: Spennymoor) 91 500; Teesdale (HQ: Barnard Castle) 24 500; Wear Valley (HQ: Crook) 63 300.

Durham was one of the first areas for which proposals for local government reform have been made. These proposals recommend the establishment of two all-purpose councils – one for Darlington; the other for the rest of the county. It was also recommended that the traditional boundaries of County Durham – that is including the city of Sunderland, the metropolitan boroughs of Gateshead and South Tyneside, and the districts of Hartlepool and Stockton-on-Tees – be restored for other purposes.

EAST SUSSEX

Area 1795 km^2 (693 miles^2).

Population 716 500. *Density* 399 per km^2 (1034 per mile^2).

Administrative HQ Pelham House, St Andrew's Lane, Lewes.

Highest point above sea level Ditchling Beacon, 248 m (813 ft).

Districts Brighton 153 800; Eastbourne 85 200; Hastings 83 700; Hove 90 000; Lewes 88 700; Rother (HQ: Bexhill) 83 200; Wealden (HQs: Crowborough and Hailsham) 131 900.

ESSEX
Area 3672 km² (1417 miles²).
Population 1 548 800. *Density* 422 per km² (1093 per mile²).
Administrative HQ County Hall, Chelmsford.
Highest point above sea level In High Wood, Langley 146 m (480 ft).
Districts Basildon 162 400; Braintree 119 900; Brentwood 70 900; Castle Point (HQ: South Benfleet) 87 200; Chelmsford 154 300; Colchester 146 600; Epping Forest (HQ: Epping) 117 200; Harlow 75 500; Maldon 53 000; Rochford 75 900; Southend-on-Sea 162 900; Tendring (HQ: Clacton) 127 200; Thurrock (HQ: Grays Thurrock) 129 600; Uttlesford (HQ: Saffron Walden) 66 300.

GLOUCESTERSHIRE
Area 2643 km² (1020 miles²).
Population 538 800. *Density* 204 per km² (528 per mile²).
Administrative HQ Shire Hall, Gloucester.
Highest point above sea level Cleeve Cloud 330 m (1083 ft).
Districts Cheltenham 107 700; Cotswold (HQ: Cirencester) 75 200; Forest of Dean (HQ: Coleford) 76 200; Gloucester (city) 103 600; Stroud 104 600; Tewkesbury 71 500.

GREATER LONDON*
Area 1580 km² (610 miles²).
Population 6 803 100. *Density* 4306 per km² (11 153 per mile²).
Administrative HQ No central authority. Functions rest with individual Boroughs and the City of London.
Highest point above sea level 246 m (809 ft); 30 m (33 yd) southeast of Westerham Heights (a house) on the Kent-Greater London boundary.
London boroughs Barking and Dagenham (HQ: Dagenham) 145 200; Barnet (HQ: Hendon) 298 100; Bexley (HQ: Bexleyheath) 218 100; Brent (HQ: Wembley) 247 200; Bromley 293 000; Camden 177 800; Croydon 317 200; Ealing 280 000; Enfield 261 500; Greenwich (HQ: Woolwich) 212 000; Hackney 183 600; Hammersmith and Fulham (HQ: Hammersmith) 152 000; Haringey (HQ: Wood Green) 206 800; Harrow 202 900; Havering (HQ: Romford) 231 200; Hillingdon (HQ: Uxbridge) 235 200; Hounslow 207 700; Islington 169 600; Kensington and Chelsea (HQ: Kensington) 141 400; Kingston-upon-Thames 136 800; Lambeth (HQ: Brixton) 249 900; Lewisham (HQ: Catford) 235 700; Merton (HQ: Morden) 170 700; Newham (HQ: East Ham) 217 000; Redbridge (HQ: Ilford) 229 800; Richmond-upon-Thames (HQ: Twickenham) 163 400; Southwark (HQ: Camberwell) 222 200; Sutton 170 300; Tower Hamlets (HQ: Bethnal Green) 165 000; Waltham Forest (HQ: Walthamstow) 216 200; Wandsworth 258 700; Westminster (city) 182 500.

The City of London – population 4100 – is not a London borough. The local government of the historic 'square mile' is the responsibility of the Corporation of the City of London whose boundaries, powers and customs were unaffected by the reform of local government in the 1960s and 1970s.

GREATER MANCHESTER*
Area 1286 km² (496 miles²).

Population 2 561 600. *Density* 1992 per km² (5165 per mile²).
Administrative HQ No central authority. Functions rest with individual districts.
Highest point above sea level Featherbed Moss 540 m (1774 ft).
Districts Bolton 262 900; Bury 179 100; Manchester (city) 432 600; Oldham 219 600; Rochdale 205 200; Salford (city) 227 400; Stockport 288 100; Tameside (HQ: Ashton-under-Lyne) 220 100; Trafford (HQ: Stretford) 216 000; Wigan 310 500.

HAMPSHIRE
Area 3777 km² (1458 miles²).
Population 1 578 700. *Density* 418 per km² (1083 per mile²).
Administrative HQ The Castle, Winchester.
Highest point above sea level Pilot Hill 285 m (937 ft).
Districts Basingstoke and Deane (HQ: Basingstoke) 146 300; East Hampshire (HQ: Petersfield) 104 700; Eastleigh 107 100; Fareham 100 500; Gosport 77 300; Hart (HQ: Fleet) 81 700; Havant 120 500; New Forest (HQ: Lyndhurst) 162 200; Portsmouth (city) 185 200; Rushmoor (HQ: Farnborough) 86 000; Southampton (city) 204 500; Test Valley (HQ: Andover) 103 400; Winchester (city) 99 200.

HEREFORD AND WORCESTER
Area 3927 km² (1516 miles²).
Population 686 000. *Density* 175 per km² (453 per mile²).
Administrative HQ County Hall, Worcester.
Highest point above sea level In the Black Mountains 702 m (2306 ft).
Districts Bromsgrove 92 300; Hereford (city) 51 200; Leominster 40 000; Malvern Hills (HQ: Malvern) 89 200; Redditch 78 900; South Herefordshire (HQ: Hereford, i.e. outside the district) 52 400; Worcester (city) 83 900; Wychavon (HQ: Pershore) 102 400; Wyre Forest (HQ: Stourport-on-Severn) 95 700.

HERTFORDSHIRE
Area 1634 km² (631 miles²).
Population 989 500. *Density* 606 per km (1568 per mile²).
Administrative HQ County Hall, Hertford.
Highest point above sea level Hastoe 244 m (802 ft).
Districts Broxbourne (HQ: Cheshunt) 82 400; Dacorum (HQ: Hemel Hempstead) 133 900; East Hertfordshire (HQ: Hertford and Bishop's Stortford) 117 900; Hertsmere (HQ: Borehamwood) 88 800; North Hertfordshire (HQ: Letchworth) 113 200; St Albans (city) 126 900; Stevenage 76 000; Three Rivers (HQ: Rickmansworth) 79 600; Watford 75 800; Welwyn Hatfield (HQ: Welwyn Garden City) 94 900.

HUMBERSIDE
Area 3512 km² (1356 miles²).
Population 874 400. *Density* 249 per km² (645 per mile²).
Administrative HQ County Hall, Beverley, North Humberside.
Highest point above sea level Cot Nab 246 m (808 ft).

Districts East Yorkshire Borough of Beverley (HQ: Beverley) 113 600; Boothferry (HQ: Goole) 64 800; Cleethorpes 69 800; East Yorkshire (HQ: Bridlington) 85 400; Glanford (HQ: Brigg) 72 400; Great Grimsby (HQ: Grimsby) 91 800; Holderness (HQ: Skirlaugh) 51 400; Kingston-upon-Hull (city; HQ: Hull) 262 900; Scunthorpe 62 400.

In 1990 a report of the Local Government Commission recommended that the districts of Humberside south of the Humber should be transferred back to Lincolnshire. The awaited proposals on the reform of local government for Humberside and North Yorkshire are expected to repeat this recommendation as well as the reversion of those districts north of the Humber to Yorkshire.

ISLE OF WIGHT

Area 381 km² (147 miles²).

Population 126 600. *Density* 332 per km² (861 per mile²).

Administrative HQ County Hall, Newport.

Highest point above sea level St Boniface Down 240 m (787 ft).

Districts Medina (HQ: Newport) 72 100; South Wight (HQs: Newport, i.e. outside the district, and Sandown and Ventnor) 54 500.

The Isle of Wight was one of the first areas for which proposals for local government reform have been made. These proposals recommend the abolition of the administrative county and the two district councils in favour of a single all-purpose administrative authority.

KENT

Area 3732 km² (1441 miles²).

Population 1 538 800. *Density* 412 per km² (1068 per mile²).

Administrative HQ County Hall, Maidstone.

Highest point above sea level Betsom's Hill, Westerham 251 m (824 ft).

Districts Ashford 93 700; Canterbury (city) 130 800; Dartford 81 000; Dover 105 600; Gillingham 96 600; Gravesham (HQ: Gravesend) 93 800; Maidstone 137 700; Rochester upon Medway (city; HQ: Strood) 147 100; Sevenoaks 109 600; Shepway (HQ: Folkestone) 93 800; Swale (HQ: Sittingbourne) 116 900; Thanet (HQ: Margate) 127 200; Tonbridge and Malling (HQ: West Malling) 102 700; Tunbridge Wells 102 200.

LANCASHIRE

Area 3069 km² (1185 miles²).

Population 1 408 300. *Density* 459 per km² (1188 per mile²).

Administrative HQ County Hall, Preston.

Highest point above sea level Gragareth 627 m (2058 ft).

Districts Blackburn 137 800; Blackpool 150 100; Burnley 92 200; Chorley 97 100; Fylde (HQ: St Annes) 72 600; Hyndburn (HQ: Accrington) 79 000; Lancaster (city) 130 300; Pendle (HQ: Nelson) 85 800; Preston 129 900; Ribble Valley (HQ: Clitheroe) 52 100; Rossendale (HQ: Rawtenstall) 66 100; South Ribble (HQ: Leyland) 102 900; West Lancashire (HQ: Ormskirk) 109 100; Wyre (HQ: Poulton-le-Fylde) 103 300.

LEICESTERSHIRE

Area 2553 km² (985 miles²).

Population 890 800. *Density* 349 per km² (904 per mile²).

Administrative HQ County Hall, Glenfield, Leicester.

Highest point above sea level Bardon Hill 277 m (912 ft).

Districts Blaby (HQ: Narborough) 83 500; Charnwood (HQ: Loughborough) 147 900; Harborough (HQ: Market Harborough) 68 200; Hinckley and Bosworth (HQ: Hinckley) 97 200; Leicester (city) 280 500; Melton (HQ: Melton Mowbray) 45 600; North West Leicestershire (HQ: Coalville) 81 400; Oadby and Wigston (HQ: Wigston) 53 100; Rutland (HQ: Oakham) 33 400.

LINCOLNSHIRE

Area 5918 km² (2285 miles²).

Population 592 600. *Density* 100 per km² (259 per mile²).

Administrative HQ County Offices, Lincoln.

Highest point above sea level Normanby-le-Wold 167 m (548 ft).

Districts Boston 53 700; East Lindsey (HQ: Louth) 118 800; Lincoln (city) 83 700; North Kesteven (HQ: Sleaford) 81 400; South Holland (HQ: Spalding) 67 900; South Kesteven (HQ: Grantham) 110 200; West Lindsey (HQ: Gainsborough) 77 000.

In 1990 a report of the Local Government Commission recommended that the districts of Cleethorpes, Glanford, Great Grimsby and Scunthorpe should be transferred from Humberside to Lincolnshire. The awaited proposals on local government reform are expected to repeat this recommendation.

MERSEYSIDE*

Area 652 km² (252 miles²).

Population 1 441 100. *Density* 2210 per km² (5719 per mile²).

Administrative HQ No central authority. Functions rest with individual districts.

Highest point above sea level Billinge Hill 179 m (588 ft).

Districts Knowsley (HQ: Kirkby) 154 500; Liverpool (city) 474 500; St Helens 180 800; Sefton (HQ: Bootle) 295 100; Wirral (HQ: Wallasey) 336 100.

NORFOLK

Area 5369 km² (2072 miles²).

Population 759 400. *Density* 141 per km² (367 per mile²).

Administrative HQ County Hall, Martineau Lane, Norwich.

Highest point above sea level Roman Bank 105 m (346 ft).

Districts Breckland (HQ: Attleborough) 108 600; Broadland (HQ: Norwich, i.e. outside the district) 107 400; Great Yarmouth 89 100; King's Lynn and West Norfolk (HQ: King's Lynn) 132 300; North Norfolk (HQ: Cromer) 92 600; Norwich (city) 125 300; South Norfolk (HQ: Long Stratton) 104 100.

NORTHAMPTONSHIRE

Area 2367 km² (914 miles²).

Population 587 100. *Density* 248 per km² (642 per mile²).

Administrative HQ County Hall, Northampton.
Highest point above sea level Arbury Hill 223 m (734 ft).
Districts Corby 53 500; Daventry 63 100; East Northamptonshire (HQ: Thrapston) 69 000; Kettering 77 000; Northampton 184 400; South Northamptonshire (HQ: Towcester) 71 500; Wellingborough 68 500.

NORTHUMBERLAND
Area 5032 km^2 (1943 miles^2).
Population 307 100. *Density* 61 per km^2 (158 per mile^2).
Administrative HQ County Hall, Morpeth.
Highest point above sea level The Cheviot 815 m (2676 ft).
Districts Alnwick 30 600; Berwick-upon-Tweed 26 900; Blyth Valley (HQ: Seaton Delaval) 80 300; Castle Morpeth (HQ: Morpeth) 50 400; Tynedale (HQ: Hexham) 57 500; Wansbeck (HQ: Ashington) 61 600.

NORTH YORKSHIRE
Area 8312 km^2 (3209 miles^2).
Population 720 900. *Density* 87 per km^2 (225 per mile^2).
Administrative HQ County Hall, Northallerton.
Highest point above sea level Whernside 737 m (2419 ft).
Districts Craven (HQ: Skipton) 50 700; Hambleton (HQ: Northallerton) 80 200; Harrogate 146 200; Richmondshire (HQ: Richmond) 46 300; Ryedale (HQ: Malton) 92 000; Scarborough 109 500; Selby 92 500; York (city) 103 300.

NOTTINGHAMSHIRE
Area 2164 km^2 (835 miles^2).
Population 1 015 500. *Density* 469 per km^2 (1216 per mile^2).
Administrative HQ County Hall, West Bridgford.
Highest point above sea level Herrod's Hill 198 m (652 ft).
Districts Ashfield (HQ: Kirkby-in-Ashfield) 109 700; Bassetlaw (HQ: Worksop) 105 300; Broxtowe (HQ: Beeston) 108 800; Gedling (HQ: Arnold) 111 100; Mansfield 101 600; Newark and Sherwood (HQ: Kelham) 103 700; Nottingham (city) 276 000; Rushcliffe (HQ: West Bridgford) 99 200.

OXFORDSHIRE
Area 2608 km^2 (1007 miles^2).
Population 579 700. *Density* 222 per km^2 (576 per mile^2).
Administrative HQ County Hall, New Road, Oxford.
Highest point above sea level White Horse Hill 260 m (856 ft).
Districts Cherwell (HQ: Bodicote) 125 600; Oxford (city) 127 700; South Oxfordshire (HQ: Crowmarsh Gifford) 120 800; Vale of White Horse (HQ: Abingdon) 113 100; West Oxfordshire (HQ: Witney) 92 400.

SHROPSHIRE
Area 3490 km^2 (1347 miles^2).
Population 412 500. *Density* 118 per km^2 (306 per mile^2).

Administrative HQ Shirehall, Abbey Foregate, Shrewsbury.
Highest point above sea level Brown Clee Hill 545 m (1790 ft).
Districts Bridgnorth 50 700; North Shropshire (HQ: Wem) 54 000; Oswestry 34 600; Shrewsbury and Atcham (HQ: Shrewsbury) 92 800; South Shropshire (HQ: Ludlow) 38 600; The Wrekin (HQ: Telford) 141 700.

SOMERSET
Area 3451 km^2 (1332 miles^2).
Population 469 400. *Density* 136 per km^2 (352 per mile^2).
Administrative HQ County Hall, Taunton.
Highest point above sea level Dunkery Beacon 519 m (170 ft).
Districts Mendip (HQ: Shepton Mallet) 97 900; Sedgemoor (HQ: Bridgwater) 99 400; South Somerset (HQ: Yeovil) 144 000; Taunton Deane (HQ: Taunton) 95 900; West Somerset (HQ: Williton) 32 200.

SOUTH YORKSHIRE*
Area 1560 km^2 (602 miles^2).
Population 1 292 700. *Density* 829 per km^2 (2147 per mile^2).
Administrative HQ No central authority. Functions rest with individual boroughs.
Highest point above sea level Margery Hill 546 m (1793 ft).
Districts Barnsley 224 200; Doncaster 293 600; Rotherham 254 700; Sheffield (city) 520 300.

STAFFORDSHIRE
Area 2716 km^2 (1048 miles^2).
Population 1 047 400. *Density* 386 per km^2 (999 per mile^2).
Administrative HQ County Buildings, Stafford.
Highest point above sea-level Oliver Hill, near Flash 513 m (1684 ft).
Districts Cannock Chase (HQ: Cannock) 90 000; East Staffordshire (HQ: Burton-upon-Trent) 98 500; Lichfield 93 500; Newcastle-under-Lyme 122 100; South Staffordshire (HQ: Codsall) 106 4100; Stafford 120 300; Staffordshire Moorlands (HQ: Leek) 96 000; Stoke-on-Trent (city) 249 700; Tamworth 70 900.

SUFFOLK
Area 3797 km^2 (1466 miles^2).
Population 661 900. *Density* 174 per km^2 (452 per mile^2).
Administrative HQ County Hall, Ipswich.
Highest point above sea level Rede 128 m (420 ft).
Districts Babergh (HQ: Hadleigh) 80 500; Forest Heath (HQ: Mildenhall) 65 300; Ipswich 118 800; Mid Suffolk (HQ: Needham Market) 79 600; St Edmundsbury (Bury St Edmunds) 93 100; Suffolk Coastal (HQ: Woodbridge) 116 000; Waveney (HQ: Lowestoft) 108 500.

SURREY
Area 1679 km^2 (648 miles^2).
Population 1 035 500. *Density* 617 per km^2 (1598 per mile^2).
Administrative HQ County Hall, Kingston-

upon-Thames (i.e. outside the county). The traditional county town is Guildford.

Highest point above sea level Leith Hill 294 m (965 ft).

Districts Elmbridge (HQ: Walton-on-Thames) 114 600; Epsom and Ewell (HQ: Epsom) 68 000; Guildford 126 900; Mole Valley (HQ: Dorking) 79 800; Reigate and Banstead (HQ: Reigate) 118 900; Runnymede (HQ: Addlestone) 74 900; Spelthorne (HQ: Staines) 91 400; Surrey Heath (HQ: Camberley) 80 100; Tandridge (HQ: Oxted) 77 600; Waverley (HQ: Godalming) 116 100; Woking 87 200.

TYNE AND WEAR*

Area 540 km^2 (208 miles^2).

Population 1 125 600. *Density* 2084 per km^2 (5412 per mile^2).

Administrative HQ No central authority. Functions rest with individual boroughs.

Highest point above sea level Leadgate near Chopwell 259 m (851 ft).

Districts Gateshead 203 200; Newcastle upon Tyne (city) 273 300; North Tyneside (HQ: North Shields) 195 400; South Tyneside (HQ: South Shields) 157 300; Sunderland (city) 296 400.

WARWICKSHIRE

Area 1981 km^2 (765 miles^2).

Population 489 900. *Density* 247 per km^2 (640 per mile^2).

Administrative HQ Shire Hall, Warwick.

Highest point above sea level Ilmington Downs 260 m (854 ft).

Districts North Warwickshire (HQ: Atherstone) 61 300; Nuneaton and Bedworth (HQ: Nuneaton) 118 200; Rugby 86 000; Stratford-on-Avon 106 200; Warwick (HQ: Leamington Spa) 118 200.

WEST MIDLANDS*

Area 899 km^2 (347 miles^2).

Population 2 619 200. *Density* 2913 per km^2 (7548 per mile^2).

Administrative HQ No central authority. Functions rest with individual boroughs.

Highest point above sea level Turner's Hill 267 m (876 ft).

Districts Birmingham (city) 994 500; Coventry (city) 306 300; Dudley 309 200; Sandwell (HQ: Oldbury) 295 200; Solihull 201 400; Walsall 263 400; Wolverhampton 249 100.

WEST SUSSEX

Area 1989 km^2 (768 miles^2).

Population 713 600. *Density* 359 per km^2 (929 per mile^2).

Administrative HQ County Hall, West Street, Chichester.

Highest point above sea level Blackdown Hill 280 m (919 ft).

Districts Adur (HQ: Shoreham) 58 900; Arun (HQ: Littlehampton) 131 500; Chichester 103 100; Crawley 88 600; Horsham 110 500; Mid Sussex (HQ: Haywards Heath) 122 700; Worthing 98 200.

WEST YORKSHIRE*

Area 2039 km^2 (787 miles^2).

Population 2 066 200. *Density* 1013 per km^2 (2625 per mile^2).

Administrative HQ No central authority. Functions rest with individual boroughs.

Highest point above sea level Black Hill 581 m (1908 ft).

Districts Bradford (city) 468 700; Calderdale (HQ: Halifax) 194 100; Kirklees (HQ: Huddersfield) 381 200; Leeds (city) 706 300; Wakefield (city) 315 800.

WILTSHIRE

Area 3481 km^2 (1344 miles^2).

Population 575 100. *Density* 165 per km^2 (428 per mile^2).

Administrative HQ County Hall, Trowbridge.

Highest point above sea level Milk Hill and Tan Hill (or St Anne's Hill) 293 m (964 ft).

Districts Kennet (HQ: Devizes) 70 400; North Wiltshire (HQ: Chippenham) 114 600; Salisbury 107 800; Thamesdown (HQ: Swindon) 173 000; West Wiltshire (HQ: Trowbridge) 109 200.

REGIONS AND ISLAND AUTHORITIES OF SCOTLAND

A consultation document on local government reform in Scotland has been published but it gives little indication of the future structure except that it should be single-tier. The existing structure is described below.

BORDERS

Area 4705 km^2 (1817 miles^2).

Population 104 100. *Density* 22 per km^2 (57 per mile^2).

Administrative HQ Regional Headquarters, Newtown St Boswells.

Highest point above sea level Broad Law (southern summit) 840 m (2756 ft).

Districts Berwickshire (HQ: Duns) 19 120; Ettrick and Lauderdale (HQ: Galashiels) 34 350; Roxburgh (HQ: Hawick) 35 350; Tweeddale (HQ: Peebles) 15 280.

CENTRAL

Area 2637 km^2 (1018 miles^2).

Population 272 800. *Density* 103 per km^2 (268 per mile^2).

Administrative HQ Central Regional Council, Viewforth, Stirling.

Highest point above sea level Ben More 1174 m (3852 ft).

Districts Clackmannan (HQ: Alloa) 48 430; Falkirk 143 090; Stirling 81 280.

DUMFRIES AND GALLOWAY

Area 6364 km^2 (2456 miles^2).

Population 147 800. *Density* 23 per km^2 (60 per mile^2).

Administrative HQ Regional Council Offices, Dumfries.

Highest point above sea level Merrick 844 m (2770 ft).

Districts Annandale and Eskdale (HQ: Annan) 37 140; Nithsdale (HQ: Dumfries) 57 140; Stewartry (HQ: Kirkcudbright) 23 550; Wigtown (HQ: Stranraer) 29 970.

FIFE

Area 1308 km² (505 miles²).

Population 346 500. *Density* 265 per km² (686 per mile²).

Administrative HQ Fife House, North Street, Glenrothes.

Highest point above sea level West Lomond 522 m (1713 ft).

Districts Dunfermline 128 330; Kirkcaldy 148 240, North East Fife (HQ: Cupar) 69 930.

GRAMPIAN

Area 8704 km² (3359 miles²).

Population 514 400. *Density* 59 per km² (153 per mile²).

Administrative HQ Woodhill House, Westburn Road, Aberdeen.

Highest point above sea level Ben Macdhui 1310 m (4300 ft).

Districts Aberdeen (city) 213 910 Banff and Buchan (HQ: Banff) 85 640; Gordon (HQ: Inverurie) 77 130; Kincardine and Deeside (HQ: Stonehaven) 53 710; Moray (HQ: Elgin) 84 010.

HIGHLAND

Area 25 391 km² (9 800 miles²).

Population 204 200. *Density* 8 per km² (21 per mile²).

Administrative HQ Regional Buildings, Glenurquhart Road, Inverness. The Regional Council meets at County Buildings, Dingwall.

Highest point above sea level Ben Nevis 1342 m (4406 ft).

Districts Badenoch and Strathspey (HQ: Kingussie) 10 990; Caithness (HQ: Wick) 26 710; Inverness 62 490; Lochaber (HQ: Fort William) 19 320; Nairn 10 630; Ross and Cromarty (HQ: Dingwall) 49 140; Skye and Lochalsh (HQ: Portree) 11 750; Sutherland (HQ: Golspie) 13 170.

LOTHIAN

Area 1755 km² (677 miles²).

Population 750 500. *Density* 428 per km² (1109 per mile²).

Administrative HQ Regional Headquarters, George IV Bridge, Edinburgh.

Highest point above sea level Blackhope Scar 651 m (2137 ft).

Districts East Lothian (HQ: Haddington) 85 300; Edinburgh (city) 438 780; Midlothian (HQ: Edinburgh, i.e. outside the district) 79 990; West Lothian (HQ: Linlithgow) 146 430.

ORKNEY

Area 975 km² (376 miles²).

Population 19 580. *Density* 20 per km² (52 per mile²).

Administrative HQ Council Offices, Kirkwall.

Highest point above sea level Ward Hill, Hoy 478 m (1570 ft).

SHETLAND

Area 1408 km² (543 miles²).

Population 22 500. *Density* 16 per km² (41 per mile²).

Administrative HQ Town Hall, Lerwick.

Highest point above sea level Ronas Hill, Mainland 450 m (1477 ft).

STRATHCLYDE

Area 13 857 km² (5348 mile²).

Population 2 296 300. *Density* 166 per km² (429 per mile²)

Administrative HQ Strathclyde House, 20 India Street, Glasgow G2 4PF.

Highest point above sea level Bidean nam Bian 1147 m (3766 ft).

Districts Argyll and Bute (HQ: Lochgilphead) 65 090; Bearsden and Milngavie (HQ: Milngavie) 41 040; Clydebank 46 380; Clydesdale (HQ: Lanark) 58 110; Cumbernauld and Kilsyth (HQ: Cumbernauld) 63 470; Cumnock and Doon Valey (HQ: Cumnock) 42 950; Cunninghame (HQ: Irvine) 139 100; Dumbarton 78 580; East Kilbride 84 200; Eastwood (HQ: Paisley, i.e. outside the district) 60 580; Glasgow (city) 687 590; Hamilton 106 780; Inverclyde (HQ: Greenock) 91 600; Kilmarnock and Loudon (HQ: Kolmarnock) 81 350; Kyle and Carrick (HQ: Ayr) 113 400; Monklands (HQ: Coatbridge) 103 990; Motherwell 144 750; Renfrew (HQ: Paisley) 200 930; Strathkelvin (HQ: Kirkintilloch) 86 410.

TAYSIDE

Area 7503 km² (2896 miles²).

Population 391 900. *Density* 52 per km² (135 per mile²).

Administrative HQ Tayside House, Dundee.

Highest point above sea level Ben Lawers 1214 m (3984 ft).

Districts Angus (HQ: Forfar) 94 820; Dundee (city) 172 120; Perth and Kinross (HQ: Perth) 124 960.

WESTERN ISLES

Area 2901 km² (1120 miles²).

Population 29 420. *Density* 10 per km² (26 per mile²).

Administrative HQ Council Offices, Stornoway, Isle of Lewis.

Highest point above sea level Clisham, Harris 799 m (2622 ft).

WELSH ADMINISTRATIVE COUNTIES

CLWYD

Area 2428 km² (937 miles²).

Population 413 800. *Density* 170 per km² (442 per mile²).

Administrative HQ Shire Hall, Mold.

Highest point above sea level Moel Sych 826 m (2713 ft).

Districts Alyn and Deeside (HQ: Hawarden) 74 400; Colwyn (HQ: Colwyn Bay) 56 500; Delyn (HQ: Flint) 68 300; Glyndwr (HQ: Ruthin) 42 400; Rhuddlan (HQ: Rhyl) 55 400; Wrexham Maelor (HQ: Wrexham) 116 700.

DYFED

Area 5773 km² (2228 miles²).

Population 350 900. *Density* 61 per km² (158 per mile²).

Administrative HQ County Hall, Carmarthen.

Highest point above sea level Carmarthen Fan Foel 762 m (2500 ft).

Districts Carmarthen 56 100; Ceredigion (HQ: Aberystwyth) 66 700; Dinefwr (HQ: Llandeilo) 39 000;

Llanelli 75 300; Preseli Pembrokeshire (HQ: Haver-fordwest) 71 300; South Pembrokeshire (HQ: Pembroke) 42 300.

GWENT
Area 1374 km² (530 miles²).
Population 446 900. *Density* 325 per km² (843 per mile²).
Administrative HQ County Hall, Cwmbran.
Highest point above sea level Chwarel-y-Fan 679 m (2228 ft).
Districts Blaenau Gwent (HQ: Ebbw Vale) 76 900; Islwyn (HQ: Pontllanfraith) 66 900; Monmouth (HQ: Pontypool, i.e. outside the district) 76 600; Newport 135 400; Torfaen (HQ: Pontypool) 91 200.

WELSH LOCAL GOVERNMENT REFORM

A reform of local government in Wales was proposed in 1993 when a government White Paper envisaged the abolition of the present system of county councils and district councils and the establishment of 21 single-tier authorities.

The new units – outlined below – will come into being on 1 April 1995.
Aberconwy and Colwyn *Area:* 1159 km² (447 sq mi). *Population:* 110 400. *HQ: (probable)* Llandudno.
Anglesey *Area:* 715 km² (276 sq mi). *Population:* 69 800. *HQ:* Llangefni.
Bridgend *Area:* 285 km² (110 sq mi). *Population:* 133 500. *HQ:* Bridgend.
Caernarfon and Meirionnydd *Area:* 2548 km² (984 sq mi). *Population:* 116 400. *HQ (probable):* Bangor.
Caerphilly *Area:* 187 km² (72 sq mi). *Population:* 119 000. *HQ (probable):* Pontllanfraith.
Cardiff *Area:* 120 km² (46 sq mi). *Population:* 290 000. *HQ:* Cardiff.
Cardiganshire *Area:* 1793 km² (692 sq mi). *Population:* 66 700. *HQ:* Aberystwyth.
Carmarthenshire *Area:* 2998 km² (1158 sq mi). *Population:* 170 400. *HQ:* Carmarthen.
Denbighshire *Area:* 1075 km² (415 sq mi). *Population:* 97 800. *HQ (probable):* Ruthin.
Flintshire *Area:* 432 km² (167 sq mi). *Population:* 142 700. *HQ:* Mold.
Glamorgan Valleys *Area:* 446 km² (172 sq mi). *Population:* 243 500. *HQ (probable):* Pentre or Pontypridd.
Heads of the Valleys *Area:* 327 km² 126 sq mi). *Population:* 189 000. *HQ (probable):* Merthyr Tydfil.
Monmouthshire *Area:* 824 km² (318 sq mi). *Population:* 76 600. *HQ (probable):* Cwmbran (i.e. outside the district).
Newport *Area:* 201 km² (78 sq mi). *Population:* 135 400. *HQ:* Newport.
Pembrokeshire *Area:* 2740 km² (1058 sq mi). *Population:* 113 600. *HQ:* Haverfordwest.
Powys *Area:* 5077 km² (1960 sq mi). *Population:* 118 700. *HQ:* Llandrindod Wells.
Swansea *Area:* 459 km² (177 sq mi). *Population:* 251 300. *HQ:* Swansea.
Torfaen *Area:* 126 km² (49 sq mi). *Population:* 91 200. *HQ:* Pontypool.
Vale of Glamorgan *Area:* 296 km² (114 sq mi). *Population:* 115 800. *HQ:* Barry.
West Glamorgan *Area:* 357 km² (138 sq mi). 117 300. *HQ (probable):* Neath.
Wrexham *Area:* 366 km² (141 sq mi). *Population* 116 700. *HQ:* Wrexham.

GWYNEDD
Area 3865 km² (1493 miles²).
Population 240 100. *Density* 62 per km² (161 per mile²).
Administrative HQ County Offices, Caernarfon.
Highest point above sea level Snowdon 1085 m (3560 ft).
Districts Aberconwy (HQ: Llandudno) 53 900; Arfon (HQ: Bangor) 56 100; Dwyfor (HQ: Pwllheli) 27 200; Meirionnydd (HQ: Dolgellau) 33 100; Ynys Môn-Isle of Anglesey (HQ: Llangefni) 69 800.

MID-GLAMORGAN
Area 1019 km² (393 miles²).
Population 541 600. *Density* 532 per km² (1378 per mile²).
Administrative HQ County Hall, Cathays Park, Cardiff (i.e. outside the county).
Highest point above sea level Near Craig-y-Llyn 585 m (1919 ft).
Districts Cynon Valley (HQ: Aberdare) 65 800; Merthyr Tydfil 59 900; Ogwr (HQ: Bridgend) 133 500; Rhondda (HQ: Pentre) 79 300; Rhymney Valley (HQ: Ystrad Mynach) 104 600; Taff-Ely (HQ: Pontypridd) 98 400.

POWYS
Area 5077 km² (1960 miles²).
Population 118 700. *Density* 23 per km² (61 per mile²).
Administrative HQ County Hall, Llandrindod Wells.
Highest point above sea level Pen-y-Fan (Cadet Arthur) 886 m (2906 ft).
Districts Brecknock (HQ: Brecon) 41 600; Montgomeryshire (HQ: Welshpool) 53 200; Radnorshire (HQ: Llandrindod Wells) 23 900.

SOUTH GLAMORGAN
Area 416 km² (161 miles²).
Population 405 900. *Density* 976 per km² (2521 per mile²).
Administrative HQ County Hall, Atlantic Wharf, Cardiff.
Highest point above sea level near Lisvane 264 m (866 ft).
Districts Cardiff (city) 290 000; Vale of Glamorgan (HQ: Barry) 115 800.

WEST GLAMORGAN
Area 818 km² (316 miles²).
Population 368 700. *Density* 451 per km² (1167 per mile²).
Administrative HQ County Hall, Swansea.
Highest point above sea level Cefnffordd 600 m (1969 ft).
Districts Lliw Valley (HQ: Penllergaer) 63 700; Neath 66 000; Port Talbot 51 300; Swansea (city) 187 600.

NORTHERN IRELAND
Area 14 120 km² (5450 miles²).
Population 1 594 400 (1991 estimate). *Density* 113 per km² (293 per mile²).
Administrative HQ Belfast.
Districts For local government purposes the province is now divided into 26 districts, whose councils have responsibility for a wide range of local

services including leisure, environmental, regulatory, etc. The six geographical counties no longer exist as administrative units.

Northern Ireland is also divided into five education and library areas and four health and social services areas. (Other functions such as police, planning, roads, water, housing, fire services, etc., are run centrally from Stormont). The area boards are not directly elected: about a third of their members are district councillors while the rest are persons appointed by the appropriate United Kingdom minister.

DISTRICTS OF NORTHERN IRELAND

Antrim Population: 45 400.

Ards (HQ: Newtownards) Population: 65 000.

Armagh Population: 51 800.

Ballymena Population: 56 600.

Ballymoney Population: 24 200.

Banbridge Population: 33 500.

Belfast (city) Population: 287 100.

Carrickfergus Population: 33 100.

Castlereagh (HQ: Belfast, i.e. outside the district) Population: 61 500.

Coleraine Population: 51 200.

Cookstown Population: 30 900.

Craigavon (HQ: Portadown) 75 400.

Derry (HQ: Londonderry/Derry) Population: 97 100.

Down (HQ: Downpatrick) Population: 58 800.

Dungannon Population: 45 300.

Fermanagh (HQ: Enniskillen) Population: 54 400.

Larne Population: 29 500.

Limavady Population: 29 700.

Lisburn Population: 101 100.

Magherafelt Population: 36 100.

Moyle (HQ: Ballycastle) Population: 14 700.

Newry and Mourne (HQ: Newry) Population: 83 100.

Newtownabbey (HQ: Ballyclare) Population: 74 500.

North Down (HQ: Bangor) Population: 72 900.

Omagh Population: 46 000.

Strabane Population: 35 500.

PARISH COUNCILS

In England, the majority of districts, that is those that do not comprise a single large town or built-up area, contain parish councils. Over 7000 parish councils have responsibilities concerning recreation facilities, community halls, parks, allotments, and footpaths. All parishes in England with a population of over 200 electors have a council; smaller parishes hold biannual meetings. Some parishes have *town* status and their chairman is called the 'town mayor'. In Wales, the equivalent of the English parish council is the community council. Some 770 community councils currently operate in the Principality. The 1350 community councils in Scotland are sometimes cited as the equivalent of English parish councils, but they are not, in fact, local authorities. These councils – which have no powers – are elected to represent the views of local communities. The current proposals for local government reform do not enviasge any changes in the powers or status of town and parish councils, or of community councils.

CITIES AND URBAN AREAS

UK CITIES

The title 'city' is used in the UK by 59 towns of varying local government status by virtue of their importance as either Anglican sees or former sees, or as commercial or industrial centres. The title has been acquired by:

– traditional usage (*trad* in the table below), for example, the Domesday Book describes Coventry, Exeter and Norwich as *civitas*;
– by statute;
– by royal prerogative, and in more recent times solely by royal charter and letters patent; for example, Swansea (1969), Derby (1977) and Sunderland (1992).

St David's (Dyfed), Armagh and several other towns are cities only by repute; although they have a cathedral they do not have the right to be called a 'city'.

Name of City	First recorded charter	City status	Title of civic head
Aberdeen	1179	*trad*	Lord Provost
Bangor (Gwynedd)	1883	1834	Mayor
Bath	1590	1850	Mayor
Belfast	1613	1888	Lord Mayor*
Birmingham	1838	1889	Lord Mayor
Bradford	1847	1897	Lord Mayor
Bristol	1188	1540	Lord Mayor
Cambridge,	1207	1951	Mayor
Canterbury	1448	*trad*	Lord Mayor
Cardiff	1608	1905	Lord Mayor
Carlisle	1158	1158	Mayor
Chester	1506	*trad*	Mayor
Chichester	1135–54	*trad*	Mayor
Coventry	1345	*trad*	Lord Mayor
Derby	1154	1977	Mayor
Dundee	c. 1179	*trad*	Lord Provost
Durham	1602	*trad*	Mayor
Edinburgh	c. 1124	*trad*	Lord Provost
Elgin	1234	*trad*	Lord Provost
Ely	none	*trad*	Mayor
Exeter	1156	*trad*	Mayor
Glasgow	1690	*trad*	Lord Provost*
Gloucester	1483	*trad*	Mayor
Hereford	1189	*trad*	Mayor
Hull (Kingston upon)	1440	1897	Lord Mayor
Lancaster	1193	1937	Mayor
Leeds	1626	1893	Lord Mayor
Leicester	1589	1919	Lord Mayor
Lichfield	1549	*trad*	Mayor
Lincoln	1154	*trad*	Mayor
Liverpool	1207	1880	Lord Mayor
London	1066–87	*trad*	Lord Mayor*
Londonderry	1604	1604	Mayor
Manchester	1838	1847	Lord Mayor
Newcastle upon Tyne	1157	1882	Lord Mayor
Norwich	1194	*trad*	Lord Mayor
Nottingham	1155	1897	Lord Mayor
Oxford	1154–87	1546	Lord Mayor

Perth	1210	*trad*	Lord Provost
Peterborough	1874	1894	Mayor
Plymouth	1439	1928	Lord Mayor
Portsmouth	1194	1926	Lord Mayor
Ripon	886	1836	Mayor
Rochester	1189	*trad*	Mayor
St Albans	1553	1887	Mayor
Salford	1835	1926	Mayor
Salisbury	1227	*trad*	Mayor
Sheffield	1843	1893	Lord Mayor
Southampton	1447	1964	Mayor
Stoke-on-Trent,	1874	1910	Lord Mayor
Swansea	1169	1969	Mayor
Sunderland	1634	1992	Mayor
Truro	1589	1877	Mayor
Wakefield	1848	1888	Mayor
Wells	1201	*trad*	Mayor
Westminster	1256	1965	Lord Mayor
Winchester	1155	*trad*	Mayor
Worcester	1189	*trad*	Mayor
York	1396	*trad*	Lord Mayor*

* Is styled 'Rt Hon.'.

NEW TOWNS

New towns are defined as towns founded as completely new settlements established with government sponsorship. The first wave of the New Towns, begun immediately after World War II to help meet the urgent post-war housing needs in London, were:

Town	County	Founded
Stevenage	Hertfordshire	1946
Crawley	West Sussex	1947
Hemel Hempstead	Hertfordshire	1947
Harlow	Essex	1947
Welwyn Garden City	Hertfordshire	1948
Hatfield	Hertfordshire	1948
Basildon	Essex	1949
Bracknell	Berkshire	1949

Three other New Towns were founded during the same period to aid other specific developments.

Town	County	Founded
Aycliffe	Durham	1947
Peterlee	Durham	1948
Corby	Northamptonshire	1950

The second wave of New Towns (1962–64) was intended to relieve urban congestion in major conurbations such as Liverpool, Newcastle and Birmingham. These towns were:

Town	County	Founded
Skelmersdale	Lancashire	1962
Telford	Shropshire	1963
Runcorn	Cheshire	1964
Redditch	Hereford/Worcester	1964
Washington	Tyne and Wear	1964

The third wave of English New Towns – designated since 1967 – was planned when the country's population was expected to increase considerably.

Town	County	Founded
Milton Keynes	Buckinghamshire	1967
Northampton	Northamptonshire	1968
Peterborough	Cambridgeshire	1968
Warrington	Cheshire	1968
Central Lancashire	Lancashire	1970

In Scotland, East Kilbride and Cumbernauld were set up to house overspill population from Glasgow. Livingston was established to receive overspill and to generate industrial growth, while Irvine and Glenrothes were set up to house overspill population and to help revive areas of industrial decline.

Town	Region	Founded
East Kilbride	Strathclyde	1947
Glenrothes	Fife	1948
Livingston	Lothian	1962
Cumbernauld	Strathclyde	1966
Irvine	Strathclyde	1966

The first Welsh New Town, Cwmbran, was established in an area of industrial decay, while Newtown was intended as a focus for development in rural central Wales.

Town	County	Founded
Cwmbran	Gwent	1949
Newtown	Powys	1967

Only one New Town has been established in Northern Ireland. Craigavon (founded in 1965) was set up to house overspill population from Belfast.

DEVELOPMENT CORPORATIONS

Government-funded Development Corporations (DCs) were established under the Local Government Planning and Land Act (1980) to promote the revival of old urban industrial areas by encouraging restoration and new developments. The only statutory duty of DCs is planning, although they can buy and sell land and buildings. The DCs, with designation date, area and major projects, are:

Merseyside DC 1981; 9.59 km^2 (3.71 sq mi); International Garden Festival, Albert Dock scheme (including Tate Gallery), and Brunswick Business Park.

London Docklands DC 1981; 22.02 km^2 (8.5 sq mi); Canary Wharf, Surrey Quays, Wapping and Poplar schemes, Docklands Light Railway, and the Royal Docks redevelopment including London City Airport.

Teesside DC 1987; 48.56 km^2 (18.75 sq mi); Hartlepool Marina, Preston Farm Industrial Estate, Tees Weir, Middlehaven, Teesside Park, and the Tees Barrage.

Trafford Park DC (Manchester) 1987; 12.14 km^2 (4.69 sq mi); an industrial park and the 'Village' scheme.

Black Country DC 1987; 6.07 km^2 (2.34 sq mi); Black Country spine road, Light Rapid Transit System (rail), Black Country Quays development, restoration of the canal network, and the Sandwell 2000 complex.

Cardiff Bay DC 1987; 10.93 km^2 (4.22 sq mi); Cardiff Bay barrage, Mount Stuart-Butetown redevelopment, Penarth Marina, and Pengam Park.

Tyne and Wear DC 1987; 24.28 km^2 (9.38 sq mi); East Quayside and Royal Quays schemes on Tyneside, and Enterprise Park and St Peter's Riverside in Sunderland.

Leeds DC 1988; 5.42 km^2 (2.09 sq mi); Kirkstall Valley industrial scheme, and business and industrial developments in south central Leeds.

Central Manchester DC 1988; 1.9 km^2 (0.73 sq mi); office, retail, leisure and housing schemes, Castle Quay, and restoration of 13 km (8 mi) of rivers and canals.

Sheffield DC 1988; 8.09 km^2 (3.13 sq mi); Canal Basin retail and leisure development, Atlas North industrial site, and Mayfield Business Park.

Bristol DC 1989; 3.64 km^2 (1.41 sq mi); Temple Meads, and housing, commercial and leisure schemes.

Laganside DC (Belfast) 1989; 1.21 km^2 (0.47 sq mi); sites for commercial, leisure and industrial schemes.

URBAN AREAS

Recognizing the difficulty of defining the population of towns, the Office of Population Censuses and Surveys has defined a number of conurbations and urban areas. Many district councils in urban areas do not meet the ordinary concepts of a town, e.g. Kirklees and Wirral. In some cases, e.g. Newcastle and Nottingham, the local government boundary has been drawn so close to the city centre that most of the suburbs have been excluded from the total. In yet other cases, the figures given for boroughs include large areas of countryside, e.g. Doncaster. The urban areas listed here give a more accurate impression of the size of the major centres in the United Kingdom. The figures given for local government districts are 1990 estimates.

Name of place	Name of urban area	Major local government areas	Population
London	Greater London	Greater London (county) 6 803 100	7 825 000
Birmingham	West Midlands	Birmingham (city) 994 500	2 326 000
Manchester	Greater Manchester	Manchester (city) 432 600	2 281 000
Glasgow	Central Clydesdale	Glasgow (city) 687 590	1 648 000
Leeds	West Yorkshire	Leeds (city) 706 300, Bradford (city) 468 700	1 543 000
Newcastle-upon-Tyne	Tyneside	Newcastle-upon-Tyne (city) 273 300	761 000
Liverpool	Liverpool	Liverpool (city) 474 500	663 000
Sheffield	Sheffield	Sheffield (city) 520 300	644 000
Nottingham	Nottingham	Nottingham (city) 276 000	612 000
Bristol	Bristol	Bristol (city) 392 600	547 000
Edinburgh	Edinburgh	Edinburgh (city) 438 780	527 000
Brighton	Brighton–Worthing–Littlehampton	Brighton (borough) 153 800	482 000
Portsmouth	Portsmouth	Portsmouth (city) 185 200	461 000
Belfast	Belfast	Belfast (city) 287 100	433 000
Leicester	Leicester	Leicester (city) 280 500	406 000
Stoke-on-Trent	The Potteries	Stoke-on-Trent (city) 249 700	377 000
Middlesbrough	Teesside	Middlesbrough (borough) 144 400	372 000
Bournemouth	Bournemouth	Bournemouth (borough) 159 100	364 000
Coventry	Coventry–Bedworth	Coventry (city) 306 300	338 000
Cardiff	Cardiff	Cardiff (city) 290 000	320 000
Preston	Preston	Preston (borough) 129 900	317 000
Hull	Kingston-upon-Hull	Kingston-upon-Hull (city) 262 900	317 000
Southampton	Southampton–Eastleigh	Southampton (city) 204 500	311 000
Southend	Southend-on-Sea	Southend (borough) 162 900	292 000
Blackpool	Blackpool	Blackpool (borough) 150 100	292 000
Swansea	Swansea	Swansea (city) 187 600	287 000
Birkenhead	Birkenhead	Birkenhead (former borough, part of Wirral district) 93 000	279 000
Plymouth	Plymouth	Plymouth (city) 254 400	255 000
Rochester	The Medway Towns	Rochester-upon-Medway (city) 147 100	243 000
Aldershot	Aldershot	Aldershot with Farnborough (Rushmoor Borough) 86 000	242 000
Derby	Derby	Derby (city) 222 500	223 000
Luton	Luton–Dunstable	Luton (borough) 174 600	223 000
Aberdeen	Aberdeen	Aberdeen (city) 213 600	219 000
Reading	Reading	Reading (borough) 134 600	212 000
Sunderland	Sunderland–Whitburn	part of Sunderland (city) 296 400	202 000
Norwich	Norwich	Norwich (city) 125 300	192 000
Northampton	Northampton	Northampton (borough) 184 400	185 000
Milton Keynes	Milton Keynes	Milton Keynes (borough) 178 900	179 000

GOVERNMENT

The UK is a constitutional monarchy without a written constitution. Parliament comprises two houses – the House of Lords (the upper house) and the House of Commons (the lower house). The Lords is made up of over 750 hereditary peers and peeresses, over 20 Lords of Appeal (the Law Lords; non-hereditary peers), over 370 life peers, and 2 archbishops and 24 bishops of the Church of England. All members of the Lords are non-elected. The House of Commons consists of 651 members elected for five years by universal adult suffrage.

THE EVOLUTION OF PARLIAMENT
Unlike most modern parliaments, the British parliament has no written constitution, but has evolved from a feudal relationship between monarch and subjects.

The term 'House of Lords' was not in use until the 16th century. However, from the Middle Ages the great magnates and prelates had a feudal obligation to attend the sovereign's Great Council to judge pleas and to advise the monarch on matters of state. The Commons emerged in the 13th century when the financial support of the shires and boroughs was needed by the king and the nobility for assistance in their disputes with each other and with the Scots, Welsh and French. Originally there was no intention that the Commons should play any part in the deliberation of policy, but gradual changes over centuries in the concepts of law and representation, gave the Commons a clear corporate identity. A change in the relative economic strength of king, Lords and Commons – and civil wars – helped confirm the clear constitutional concept (defined in 1869) that sovereignty lay with the monarch in Parliament of Lords *and* Commons.

THE ROLE OF THE MONARCH
The monarch's power has been largely eroded by convention and statute, and most of the functions she carries out, or prerogatives she possesses, are exercised on the advice of the Prime Minister. Nonetheless, she retains an important formal role within Parliament. Public measures are proposed and enacted in the name of her government, and it is her assent that converts bills passed by both Houses into statutes. The Royal Prerogative, which enables action to be taken without the formal consent of Parliament, is seldom used but is a potential force within the system. Some of these powers, such as the dissolution of Parliament before the end of its statutory maximum of five years, the appointment of the Prime Minister, the creation of peers, and the distribution of honours, facilitate the smooth operation of the wider political system, although they are mostly taken 'on advice' from the prime minister. Other powers, such as the power to make an Order in Council, enables the government to take swift executive action. The monarch also provides informal advice for her Prime Minister.

THE ROLE OF THE HOUSE OF LORDS
The House of Lords has also seen its power gradually diminish over the past two centuries. Since 1911 the Lords have had no right to amend bills concerning taxation, and subsequently, their right to delay bills passed by the Commons has been reduced from two to

one year. Nevertheless, the Lords carries out significant functions. The House retains one of its original roles as the supreme civil and criminal court in the UK. It scrutinizes bills passed by the House of Commons, and proposes amendments. It provides a means of introducing minor public bills, allows additional opportunities for the debate of private member's bills, bears the burden of debate concerning powers under delegated legislation, and debates private bills.

The composition and procedures of the House of Lords give a different emphasis from that of the Commons. Scrutiny is usually less detailed, but procedures more flexible, and the debate less partisan than in the Commons.

THE HOUSE OF COMMONS
The House of Commons is, undoubtedly, the dominant element within Parliament today. Its 651 Members of Parliament are the basis of British parliamentary democracy. Finance remains at the centre of the Commons' power. The House has the sole right to deliberate issues of taxation without which government would be impossible.

THE PRIME MINISTER
The post of Prime Minister was not officially recognized until this century, but it had long been accepted that the monarch's treasurer had to be able to command a majority in the Commons. The power of the premier is still ill-defined, but ultimately it depends upon maintaining a majority in the Commons. The Prime Minister can exercise the prerogative powers of the monarch, and choose, transfer and dismiss Cabinet ministers and junior members of the government. The Prime Minister is also the First Lord of the Treasury, the political head of the Civil Service. He chairs the Cabinet, and the major Cabinet committees.

THE CABINET
The Cabinet is the major policy-making body of the government. Members of the Cabinet are chosen by the Prime Minister from the Commons or Lords – in modern times overwhelmingly from the Commons. They attend Cabinet meetings either as heads of government departments or 'without portfolio' (without the responsibility of a department). Because modern governments have such a great workload, the Cabinet increasingly works through a system of committees. Some are permanent committees dealing with tasks such as managing the economy, while others are formed to deal with particular problems. The Cabinet are collectively responsible to Parliament for the actions of the government, and if defeated in a motion of confidence must either resign or seek a dissolution of Parliament and a renewed mandate from the electorate.

The Cabinet works under the convention of collective responsibility. This means that even if not all Cabinet ministers agree on a subject, the Cabinet must act unanimously.

THE PRIVY COUNCIL
The main purpose of the Privy Council is to advise the sovereign on the approval of Orders in Council and on the issue of royal proclamations. All cabinet ministers must be Privy counsellors and are sworn in on first assuming office. Membership is for life and is awarded by the monarch, on the recommendation of

the Prime Minister. It is awarded to eminent citizens of the UK and of Commonwealth countries with independent monarchs.

THE SPEAKER AND LEADER OF THE HOUSE

The Speaker, the Leader of the House and the party whips do much to ensure that matters on the floor of the House of Commons proceed smoothly. The Speaker's function as spokesperson for the House remains important, but his or her duties to regulate debate, decide points of order and interpret the rules of the House, are vital day-to-day functions that require tact and the confidence of all parties in the selection of one of their number as Speaker. Once selected, the Speaker is extremely careful to betray no hint of his or her former party allegiance.

The working of the Commons is also facilitated by the work of the Leader of the House, who is chosen by the Prime Minister to organize government business going through the Commons. This entails working with the chief whips of the major parties to ensure that adequate scrutiny is given to measures, whilst preserving the government's legislative timetable.

THE OPPOSITION

The Commons has adapted itself over centuries to the changing conditions within which scrutiny of government must take place. The Opposition is now formalized under a Leader of the Opposition, who since 1937 has been paid by the Crown. The Leader of the Opposition – the leader of the second biggest party in the House – creates a 'Shadow Cabinet', so the actions of all ministers can be effectively examined.

COMMITTEES

Perhaps the most effective scrutiny takes place not on the floor of the House but in committees. There are many types of committee. Select Committees usually report on specific matters, such as Public Accounts, Privileges and Members' Interests. In 1978 the select-committee system was reorganized to provide a committee to examine each of the government departments. All bills before Parliament, many statutory instruments and EC documents, must pass through a Standing, or Legislative Committee, appointed to examine their clauses in detail. Similar committees exist in the House of Lords, and on some issues Joint Committees of both Houses are held.

THE ELECTORAL SYSTEM

The UK uses a 'first-past-the-post' system for electing Members of Parliament. Each constituency elects one MP, the person gaining the most votes being elected. In a contest between four parties, it would be possible for an MP to be elected with less than a third of the total vote. At a national level, it is possible for the party that obtains the largest number of votes not to win the election. The British system tends to produce majority governments that do not have to rely on coalition partners to govern.

LOCAL GOVERNMENT

Much of the work of governing Britain is done by local government. Local authorities are responsible for services such as education, social services, policing, local authority housing, and the fire brigade. There has been some loss of responsibility by local government in the 1980s and their role is still a matter of political debate. (For more information on local government see pp. 717–25.)

MINISTRIES AND DEPARTMENTS

The Cabinet Office includes the Secretariat (which supports Cabinet ministers collectively), the Prime Minister's Office, and the Office of the Minister for the Civil Service (the Prime Minister).

The Ministry of Agriculture, Fisheries and Food is responsible for matters concerning agriculture, horticulture, fishing, and food production, safety and standards. The minister is also responsible for the interests of these industries abroad, in particular for negotiating the EC Common Agricultural Policy.

The Ministry of Defence has overall responsibility for the Royal Navy, the Army, the Royal Air Force, defence research, and the Meteorological Office.

The Duchy of Lancaster is responsible for the estates of the Duchy of Lancaster (which are attached to the Crown).

The Department of Education is responsible for education from schools to higher education (including HM Inspectorate of Schools), and the recruitment and training of teachers.

The Department of Employment is responsible for matters concerning the promotion of employment and self-employment, and the reduction of unemployment. The Department also has responsibilities concerning industrial relations, training and enterprise programmes, and safety at work. Its agencies include the Arbitration and Conciliation Service (ACAS), the Health and Safety Commission, the Employment Service, and the Training, Enterprise and Education Directorate.

The Department of the Environment is responsible not only for environmental protection, conservation and rural issues but also for local government, planning, housing, construction, new towns, the inner cities, the royal parks and government property holdings, and the upkeep of ancient monuments.

The Foreign and Commonwealth Office is responsible for maintaining good relations with international organizations (such as the UN) and with the governments of other countries. It notifies the British government about developments overseas and protects British interests and citizens abroad. The Overseas Development Administration, which deals with technical and capital assistance to developing countries, is a subsidiary.

The Department of Health is responsible for the administration of the National Health Service (in England), for personal social services (for example, for the young, the elderly or the handicapped), for the provision of ambulance services, and for food hygiene.

The Home Office administers justice and criminal law, the prison and probation service, the police, immigration and nationality matters, community relations, and public safety. The Office is also responsible for a wide range of matters in England and Wales that are not covered by the other departments.

The Lord Advocate's Department is the office of the Solicitor-General for Scotland. It is responsible for drawing up Scottish legislation and advising other departments on matters relating to Scottish law.

The Lord Chancellor's Department is responsible for civil law and civil courts, and the administration of the Court of Appeal and High Court, and the crown courts and legal aid in England and Wales. The Lord Chancellor advises on the appointment of judges and appoints registrars, district judges, and magistrates.

The Department of National Heritage has responsibility for heritage, the arts, broadcasting, film, tourism and sport.

The Northern Ireland Office has overall responsibility for the government of the province and is directly accountable for law and order, security, and constitutional and electoral matters. A number of subsidiary departments deal with specific areas including agriculture, the Northern Ireland Civil Service, economic development, education, the environment, finance, and health and social services.

The Privy Council Office – the office of the Leader of the House of Commons – has formal responsibilities concerning Royal Proclamations, grants of charters and the appointment of certain officials, for example High Sheriffs.

The Office of Public Service and Science has responsibility for all aspects of the promotion of science and technology, for example the research councils. It is also responsible for the implementation of the Citizen's Charter.

The Scottish Office has responsibility for those statutory functions covered by the Scottish departments of Agriculture and Fisheries, Education, Development, Home and Health, and Industry. The Secretary of State for Scotland also has certain responsibilities concerning courts administration and the work of a number of UK statutory bodies in Scotland.

The Department of Social Security is responsible for social security services in England, Wales and Scotland.

The Department of Trade and Industry is responsible for promoting international trade (particularly UK exports), domestic industry and commerce, competition policy, consumer protection, research, and the administration of company legislation. The Department is also responsible for government policies concerning all energy sources. Related bodies include the Office of Fair Trading.

The Department of Transport has overall responsibility for matters relating to transport policy and safety, the construction and maintenance of motorways and trunk roads, international and domestic aviation policy, railways, shipping and ports.

The Treasury – the office of the Chancellor of the Exchequer – has overall responsibility for monetary policy and the control of public expenditure, Inland Revenue duties and taxes, and a variety of financial matters including the financial system (banks, etc.), Customs and Excise, international finance, privatization policy, and HMSO.

The Welsh Office has responsibility in Wales for health and social services, and certain aspects of education, local government, the arts, agriculture, fisheries, forestry, regional development, and conservation.

THE GOVERNMENT

The membership of the Government at 1 June 1993. Cabinet posts are indicated in bold.

Prime Minister, First Lord of the Treasury and Minister for the Civil Service: John Major.

Agriculture, Fisheries and Food
Minister of Agriculture: Gillian Shephard.
Minister of State: Michael Jack.
Plus two Under Secretaries – The Earl Howe, Nicholas Soames.

Defence
Secretary of State: Malcolm Rifkind.
Ministers of State: (*Defence Procurement*) Jonathan Aitken; (*Armed Forces*) Jeremy Hanley.
Plus an Under Secretary – Viscount Cranborne.

Education
Secretary of State: John Patten.
Minister of State: Baroness Blatch.
Plus three Under Secretaries – Nigel Forman, Eric Forth, Robin Squire.

Employment
Secretary of State: David Hunt.
Minister of State: Michael Forsyth.
Plus two Under Secretaries – Viscount Ullswater, Ann Widdecombe.

Environment
Secretary of State: John Selwyn Gummer.
Ministers of State: (*Environment and Countryside*) Timothy Yeo, (*Local Government and Inner Cities*) David Curry, (*Housing and Planning*) Sir George Young.
Plus two Under Secretaries – Anthony Baldry, The Lord Strathclyde.

Foreign and Commonwealth Affairs
Foreign Secretary: Douglas Hurd.
Ministers of State: (*Overseas Development*) Baroness Chalker of Wallasey, (*Europe*) David Heathcoat-Amory, (*Foreign Affairs*) Douglas Hogg, Alistair Goodlad.
Plus an Under Secretary – Mark Lennox-Boyd.

Health
Secretary of State: Virginia Bottomly.
Minister of State: (*Health*) Dr Brian Mawhinney.
Plus three Under Secretaries – John Bowis, Baroness Cumberledge, Hon. Thomas Sackville.

Home Office
Home Secretary: Michael Howard.
Ministers of State: The Earl Ferrers, Peter Lloyd, David Maclean.
Plus an Under Secretary – Charles Wardle.

National Heritage
Secretary of State: Peter Brooke.
Plus an Under Secretary – Iain Sproat.

Northern Ireland
Secretary of State: Sir Patrick Mayhew.
Ministers of State: Robert Atkins, Michael Mates.
Plus two Under Secretaries – Michael Ancram, The Earl of Arran.

Public Service and Science
Minister of Public Service and Science: William Waldegrave (also Chancellor of the Duchy of Lancaster).
Plus an Under Secretary – David Davis.

Scottish Office
Secretary of State: Ian Lang.
Minister of State: Lord Fraser of Carmyllie.
Plus three Under Secretaries – Lord James Douglas-Hamilton, Sir Hector Monro, Allan Stewart.

Social Security
Secretary of State: Peter Lilley.
Minister of State: (Social Security and Disabled People) Nicholas Scott.
Plus three Under Secretaries – Alistair Burt, William Hague, The Lord Henley.

Trade and Industry
Secretary of State and President of the Board of Trade: Michael Heseltine.
Ministers of State: (Energy) Tim Eggar, *(Trade)* Richard Needham, *(Industry)* Timothy Sainsbury.
Plus three Under Secretaries – *(Consumer Affairs and Small Firms)* Baroness Denton of Wakefield, *(Corporate Affairs)* Neil Hamilton, *(Technology)* Patrick McLoughlin.

Transport
Secretary of State: John MacGregor.
Ministers of State: (Aviation and Shipping) The Earl of Caithness, *(Public Transport)* Roger Freeman.
Plus two Under Secretaries – *(Minister for Roads and Traffic)* Robert Key, *(Minister for Transport in London)* Steven Norris.

Treasury
Chancellor of the Exchequer: Kenneth Clarke.
Chief Secretary to the Treasury: Michael Portillo.
Ministers of State: (Paymaster-General) Sir John Cope, *(Financial Secretary)* Stephen Dorrell, *(Economic Secretary)* Anthony Nelson.

Welsh Office
Secretary of State: John Redwood.
Minister of State: Sir Wyn Roberts.
Plus an Under Secretary – Gwilym Jones.

Duchy of Lancaster
Chancellor of the Duchy of Lancaster: William Waldegrave (see above).

Law Officers
Lord (High) Chancellor: Lord Mackay of Clashfern.
Attorney-General: Sir Nicholas Lyell.
Lord Advocate: Lord Rodger of Earlsferry.
Solicitor-General: Sir Derek Spencer.
Solicitor-General for Scotland: Thomas Dawson.
Plus an Under Secretary – John Taylor.

Privy Council Office
Lord President of the Council: Antony Newton (Leader of the House of Commons).
Lord Privy Seal: Lord Wakeham (Leader of the House of Lords).

THE RESULTS OF THE GENERAL ELECTIONS since 1945

Election and Date	Total Seats	Conservatives	Result (and % share of Poll) Labour	Liberals	Others	% Turn-out of Electorate
5 July 1945	640	213 (39.8)	**393** (47.8)	12 (9.0)	22 (2.8)	72.7 of 33 240 391
23 Feb 1950	625	298 (43.5)	**315** (46.4)	9 (9.1)	3 (1.3)	84.0 of 33 269 770
25 Oct 1951	625	**321** (48.0)	295 (48.7)	6 (2.5)	3 (0.7)	82.5 of 34 465 573
25 May 1955	630	**344** (49.8)	277 (46.3)	6 (2.7)	3 (1.2)	76.7 of 34 858 263
8 Oct 1959	630	**365** (49.4)	258 (43.8)	6 (5.9)	1 (0.9)	78.8 of 35 397 080
15 Oct 1964	630	303 (43.4)	**317** (44.2)	9 (11.1)	1 (1.3)	77.1 of 35 894 307
31 Mar 1966	630	253 (41.9)	**363** (47.9)	12 (8.5)	2 (1.7)	75.9 of 35 965 127
18 June 1970	630	**330** (46.4)	288 (43.0)	6 (7.5)	6 (3.1)	72.0 of 39 247 683
28 Feb 1974	635	297 (38.2)	**301** (37.2)	14 (19.3)	23 (5.3)	78.8 of 39 752 317
10 Oct 1974	635	277 (35.8)	**319** (39.3)	13 (18.3)	26 (6.6)	72.8 of 40 083 286
3 May 1979	635	**339** (43.9)	268 (36.9)	11 (13.8)	17 (5.4)	75.9 of 41 093 262
9 June 1983	650	**397** (42.4)	209 (27.6)	17 (25.4) (Alliance)	21 (4.6)	72.7 of 42 197 344
11 June 1987	650	**375** (42.3)	229 (30.8)	17 (12.8) (Lib. Dem)	24 (3.4)	75.4 of 43 181 321
9 April 1992	651	**336** (41.9)	271 (34.4)	20 (17.8)	24 (5.8)	78 of 43 803 880

On 1 June 1993, the strength of the parties was: Conservatives 334 (reduced from the General Election total of 336 by the deaths of the Members for Newbury and Christchurch); Labour 270 (reduced from the General Election total of 271 by the election of the Member for West Bromwich West as Speaker – see box); Liberal Democrats 21 (increased from the General Election total of 20 by the by-election at Newbury); Plaid Cymru 4, the Scottish National Party 3, Ulster Unionist Party 8, Social Democratic and Labour Party 4, Democratic Unionist Party 1, the Ulster Popular Unionists Party 1, and 1 vacant seat (Christchurch).

THE SPEAKER

The Speaker of the House of Commons: Betty Boothroyd, MP for West Bromwich West, elected in 1992.

She is assisted by:
Chairman of Ways and Means: Michael Morris, MP.
The First Deputy Chairmen of Ways and Means: Geoffrey Lofthouse, MP.
The Second Deputy Chairmen of Ways and Means: Dame Janet Fookes, MP.

PRIME MINISTERS OF GREAT BRITAIN AND THE UNITED KINGDOM

The biographical detail for each of 52 prime ministers of Great Britain and the United Kingdom includes:
– final style as prime minister (with earlier or later styles);
– dates of birth and death;
– party affiliation and date or dates as prime minister;
– membership of Parliament with the constituency and dates.

1. The Rt Hon., Sir Robert **WALPOLE**, KG (1726), 1st Earl of Orford (of the 2nd creation); b. 1676, d. 1745; Whig; ministries 3 Apr 1721–8 Feb 1742, (Walpole's absolute control of the Cabinet can only be said to have dated from 15 May 1730); MP (Whig) for Castle Rising (1701–2); King's Lynn (1702–42) (expelled from the House for a short period 1712–13).

2. The Rt Hon., the Hon. Sir Spencer Compton, 1st and last Earl of **WILMINGTON**, KG (1733), KB (1725, resigned 1733), (PC 1716), cr. Baron Wilmington 1728; cr. Earl 1730; b. 1673, d. 1743; Whig; ministry 16 Feb 1742–2 Jul 1743; MP for Eye (1698–1710; originally Tory until about 1704); East Grinstead (1713–15); Sussex (Whig) (1715–28); Speaker 1715–27.

3. The Rt Hon., the Hon. Henry **PELHAM** (PC 1725); b. c. 1695, d. in office; Whig; ministry 27 Aug 1743–6 Mar 1754 (with an interval 10–12 Feb 1746); MP Seaford (1717–22); Sussex (1722–54).

4. The Rt Hon. Sir William Pulteney, 1st and last Earl of **BATH** (cr. 1742) PC (1716) (struck off 1731); b. 1684, d. 1764; Whig; kissed hands 10 Feb 1746, resigned 13 Feb (unable to form a ministry); MP Hedon (or Heydon) 1705–34; Middlesex 1734–42.

5. His Grace the 1st Duke of **NEWCASTLE** upon Tyne and 1st Duke of Newcastle-under-Lyme (The Rt Hon., the Hon. Sir Thomas Pelham-Holles), Bt, KG (1718), (PC 1717); known as Lord Pelham of Laughton (1711–14); Earl of Claire (1714–15); cr. Duke of Newcastle upon Tyne 1715 and cr. Duke of Newcastle-under-Lyme 1756; b. 1698, d. 1768; ministries (a) 16 Mar 1754–26 Oct 1756, (b) 2 Jul 1757–25 Oct 1760, (c) 25 Oct 1760–25 May 1762.

6. His Grace the 4th Duke of **DEVONSHIRE** (Sir William Cavendish), KG (1756), (PC 1751, but struck off roll 1762); known as Lord Cavendish of Hardwick until 1729 and Marquess of Hartington until 1755; b. 1720, d. 1764; Whig; ministry 16 Nov 1756–May 1757; MP (Whig) for Derbyshire (1741–51). Summoned to Lords (1751).

7. The Rt Hon. James **WALDEGRAVE**, 2nd Earl of Waldegrave from 1741, PC (1752), KG (1757); b. 1715, d. 1763; Tory; ministry, kissed hands 8 Jun 1757, resigned 12 Jun (unable to form a ministry); took seat in House of Lords in 1741.

8. The 3rd Earl of **BUTE** (The Rt Hon., the Hon. Sir John Stuart, KG (1762), KT (1738, resigned 1762), (PC 1760)); until 1723 was The Hon. John Stuart; b. 1713, d. 1792; Tory; ministry 26 May 1762–8 Apr 1763.

9. The Rt Hon., the Hon. George **GRENVILLE** (PC 1754); prior to 1749 was G. Grenville Esq; b. 1712, d. 1770; Whig; ministry 16 Apr 1763–10 Jul 1765; MP for Buckingham (1741–70).

10. The Most Hon. The 2nd Marquess of **ROCKINGHAM** (The Rt Hon. Lord Charles Watson-Wentworth), KG (1760), (PC 1765); known as Hon. Charles Watson-Wentworth until 1739; Viscount Higham (1739–46); Earl of Malton (1746–50); succeeded to Marquessate 1750; b. 1730, d. in office; Whig; ministries (a) 13 Jul 1765–Jul 1766, (b) 27 Mar–1 Jul 1782 (died in office). Took his seat in House of Lords 21 May 1751.

11. The 1st Earl of **CHATHAM** (The Rt Hon. William Pitt (PC 1746)); cr. Earl 4 Aug 1766; b. 1708, d. 1788; Whig; ministry 30 Jul 1766–14 Oct 1768 (his health in 1767 prevented his being PM in other than name); MP (Whig) Old Sarum (1735–47); Seaford (1747–54); Aldborough (1754–6); Okehampton (1756–7) (also Buckingham (1756), Bath (1757–66)).

12. His Grace the 3rd Duke of **GRAFTON** (The Rt Hon. Sir Augustus Henry FitzRoy) KG (1769), (PC 1765); prior to 1747 known as the Hon. Augustus H. FitzRoy; 1747–57 as Earl of Euston; succeeded to dukedom in 1757; b. 1735, d. 1811; Whig; ministry 14 Oct 1768–28 Jan 1770 (he was virtually PM in 1767 when Lord Chatham's ministry broke down); MP (Whig) Bury St Edmunds (1756–7).

13. Lord **NORTH** (The Rt Hon., the Hon. Sir Frederick North), KG (1772), (PC 1766); succ. (1790) as 2nd Earl of Guildford; b. 1732, d. 1792; Tory; ministry 28 Jan 1770–20 Mar 1782; MP (Tory) for Banbury (1754–90) (can be regarded as a Whig from 1783). Took his seat in the House of Lords 25 Nov 1790.

14. The 2nd Earl of **SHELBURNE** (Rt Hon., the Hon. Sir William Petty, KG (1782) (PC 1763); formerly, until 1751, William Fitz-Maurice; Viscount Fitz-Maurice (1753–61); succeeded to Earldom 1761; cr. the 1st Marquess of Lansdowne (1784); b. 1737, d. 1805; Whig; ministry 4 Jul 1782–24 Feb 1783; MP Chipping Wycombe (1760–1). Took seat in House of Lords (as Baron Wycombe) 3 Nov 1761.

15. His Grace the 3rd Duke of **PORTLAND** The Most Noble Sir William Henry Cavendish Bentinck, KG (1794) (PC 1765); assumed additional name of Bentinck in 1775; Marquess of Titchfield from birth until he succeeded to the dukedom 1762; b. 1738, d. 1809; Tory; ministries (a) 2 Apr–Dec 1783 (coalition), (b) 31 Mar 1807–Oct 1809 (Tory); MP (Whig) Weobley, Herefordshire (1761–2).

16. The Rt Hon., the Hon. William **PITT** (PC 1782) prior to 1766 was William Pitt, Esq.; b. 1759, d. in office; Tory; ministry (a) 19 Dec 1783–14 Mar 1801, (b) 10 May 1804–23 Jan 1806 (died in office); MP (Tory) Appleby 1781–1806.

17. The Rt Hon. Henry **ADDINGTON** (PC 1789); cr. 1st Viscount Sidmouth 1805; b. 1757, d. 1844; Tory; ministry 17 Mar 1801–30 Apr 1804; MP Devizes (1783–1805). Speaker 1789–1801. As a peer he supported the Whigs in 1807 and 1812 administration.

18. The Rt Hon. the 1st Baron **GRENVILLE** of Wotton-under-Bernewood (William Wyndham Grenville (PC(I) 1782; PC 1783)); cr. Baron 1790; b. 1759, d. 1834; Whig; ministry 10 Feb 1806–Mar 1807; MP Buckingham (1782–4), Buckinghamshire (1784–90). Speaker Jan–Jun 1789.

19. The Rt Hon., the Hon. Spencer **PERCEVAL** (PC 1807), KC (1796); b. 1762, d. in office; Tory; ministry 4 Oct 1809–11 May 1812 (murdered in the lobby of the House); MP (Tory) Northampton (1796–7).

20. The Rt Hon. the 2nd Earl of **LIVERPOOL** (Sir Robert Banks Jenkinson, KG (1814) (PC 1799)); R.B. Jenkinson, Esq. until 1786; from 1786–96 The Hon. R. B. Jenkinson; from 1796–1808 (when he succeeded to the earldom) Lord Hawkesbury; b. 1770, d. 1828; Tory; ministries (a) 8 Jun 1812–29 Jan 1820, (b) 29 Jan 1820–17 Feb 1827; summoned to House of Lords 1803; elected MP (Tory) for Appleby in 1790 but did not sit as he was under age; Rye (1796–1803).

21. The Rt Hon. George **CANNING** (PC 1800); b. 1770, d. in office; Tory; ministry 10 Apr–8 Aug 1827 (d. in office); MP (Tory) Newtown, I.o.W. (1793–6), Wendover (1796–1802), Tralee (1802–6), Newton (1806–7), Hastings (1807–12), Liverpool (1812–23), Harwich (1823–6), Newport (1826–7), and Seaford (1827).

22. The Viscount **GODERICH** (Rt Hon., the Hon. Frederick John Robinson (PC 1812, PC (I) c. 1833); cr. Earl of Ripon 1833; b. 1782, d. 1859; Tory; ministry 31 Aug 1827–8 Jan 28; MP Carlow (1806–7); Ripon (1807–27).

23. His Grace The 1st Duke of **WELLINGTON** (The Most Noble, The Hon. Sir Arthur Wellesley, KG (1813), GCB (1815), GCH (1816), (PC 1807, PC (I) 1807)); known as The Hon. Arthur Wesley until 1804; then as The Hon. Sir Arthur Wellesley, KB, until 1809 when cr. the Viscount Wellington; cr. Earl of Wellington February 1812; Marquess of Wellington October 1812 and Duke May 1814; Field Marshal (1813); b. 1769, d. 1852; Tory; ministries (a) 22 Jan 1828–26 Jun 30, (b) 26 Jun–21 Nov 1830, (c) 17 Nov–9 Dec 1834; MP Rye (1806); St Michael (1807); Newport, IoW (1807–9). Took seat in House of Lords 1814.

24. The 2nd Earl **GREY** (The Rt Hon., the Hon. Sir Charles Grey, Bt (1808), KG (1831), (PC 1806)); styled Viscount Howick 1806–7 and previously The Hon. Charles Grey; b. 1764, d. 1845; Whig; ministry 22 Nov 1830–Jul 1834; MP (Whig) Northumberland (17 86–1807); Appleby (1807); Tavistock (1807).

25. The 3rd Viscount **MELBOURNE** (The Rt Hon., The Hon. Sir William Lamb, Bt (PC (UK & I) 1827)); b. 1779, d. 1848; Whig; ministries (a) 17 Jul–Nov 1834, (b) 18 Apr 1835–20 Jun 1837, (c) 20 Jun 1837–Aug 1841; MP (Whig) Leominster (1806); Haddington Borough (1806–7); Portarlington (1807–12); Peterborough (1816–19); Hertfordshire (1819–26); Newport, IoW (1827); Bletchingley (1827–28). Took his seat in House of Lords 1 Feb 1829.

26. The Rt Hon. Sir Robert **PEEL**, Bt (PC 1812); until 1830 he was Robert Peel, Esq., MP, when he succeeded as 2nd Baronet; b. 1788, d. 1850; Conservative; ministries (a) 10 Dec 1834–8 Apr 1835, (b) 30 Aug 1841–29 Jun 1846; MP (Tory) Cashel (Tipperary) (1809–12); Chippenham (1812– 17); Univ. of Oxford (1817–29); Westbury (1829–30); Tamworth (1830–50).

27. The Rt Hon. Lord John **RUSSELL** (PC 1830), and after 30 July 1861 1st Earl **RUSSELL**, KG (1862), GCMG (1869); b. 1792, d. 1878; Liberal; ministries (a) 30 Jun 1846–Feb 1852 (Whig), (b) 29 Oct 1865–Jun 1866

(Liberal); MP (Whig) Tavistock (1813–17, 1818–20 and 1830–1); Hunts (1820–6); Bandon (1826–30); Devon (1831–2); S. Devon (1832–5); Stroud (1835–41); City of London (1841–61). Took seat in the House of Lords on 30 July 1861.

28. The 14th Earl of **DERBY**, Rt Hon. Sir Edward Geoffrey Smith-Stanley, Bt, KG (1859), GCMG (1869), PC 1830, PC (I) (1831); until 1834 known as the Hon. E. G. Stanley, MP; 1834–44 known as Lord Stanley MP; b. 1799, d. 1869; Tory; ministries (a) 23 Feb–18 Dec 1852, (b) 20 Feb 1858–11 Jun 1859, (c) 28 Jun 1866–26 Feb 1868; MP (Whig) Stockbridge (1822–6); Preston (1826–30); Windsor (1831–2); North Lancs (1832–44). Summoned 1844 to House of Lords as Lord Stanley (of Bickerstaffe); succeeded to Earldom 1851; became a Tory in 1835.

29. The Rt Hon. Sir George Hamilton Gordon, Bt, 4th Earl of **ABERDEEN**, KG (1855), KT (1808), (PC 1814); until 1791 known as the Hon. G. Gordon; known as Lord Haddo 1791–1801; assumed additional name of Hamilton November 1818; b. 1784, d. 1860; Peelite; ministry 19 Dec 1852–5 Feb 1855. Took seat in House of Lords 1814.

30. The Rt Hon. Sir Henry John Temple, 3rd and last Viscount **PALMERSTON** (a non-representative peer of Ireland), KG (1856), CGB (1832), (PC 1809); known as the Hon. H. J. Temple 1784–1802; b. 1784, d. 1865; Liberal; ministries (a) 6 Feb 1855–19 Feb 1858, (b) 12 Jun 1859–18 Oct 1865; MP (Tory) Newport, IoW (1807–11); Cambridge Univ. (1811–31); Bletchingley (1831–2); S. Hampshire (1832–4); Tiverton (1835–65); from 1829 a Whig and latterly a Liberal.

31. The Rt Hon. Benjamin **DISRAELI**, 1st and last Earl of **BEACONSFIELD**, KG (1878), (PC 1852); prior to 12 Aug 1876 Benjamin Disraeli; b. 1804, d. 1881; Conservative; ministries (a) 27 Feb–Nov 1868, (b) 20 Feb 1874–Apr 1880; MP (Con.) Maidstone (1837–41); Shrewsbury (1841–7); Buckinghamshire (1847–76), when he became a peer.

32. The Rt Hon. William Ewart **GLADSTONE** (PC 1841); b. 1809, d. 1898; Liberal; ministries (a) 3 Dec 1868–Feb 1874, (b) 23 Apr 1880–12 Jun 1885, (c) 1 Feb–20 Jul 1886, (d) 15 Aug 1892–3 Mar 1894; MP Tory, Newark (1832–45); Univ. of Oxford (1847–65) (Peelite to 1859, thereafter a Liberal); S. Lancashire (1865–8); Greenwich (1868–80); Midlothian (1880–95).

33. The Rt Hon. Robert Arthur Talbot Gascoyne-Cecil, the 3rd Marquess of **SALISBURY**, KG (1878), GCVO (1902), (PC 1866); known as Lord Robert Cecil till 1865; and as Viscount Cranbourne, MP, 1865–68; b. 1830, d. 1903; Conservative; ministries (a) 23 Jun 1885–28 Jan 1886, (b) 25 Jul 1886–Aug 1892, (c) 25 Jun 1895–22 Jan 1901, (d) 23 Jan 1901–11 Jul 1902; MP (Con.) for Stamford (1853–68).

34. The Rt Hon. Sir Archibald Philip Primrose, Bt, 5th Earl of **ROSEBERY**, KG (1892), KT (1895), VD (PC 1881); b. the Hon. A. P. Primrose; known as Lord Dalmeny 1851–68; Earl of Midlothian from 1911 although he did not adopt the style; b. 1847, d. 1929; Liberal; ministry 5 Mar 1894–21 Jun 1895.

35. The Rt Hon. Arthur James **BALFOUR** (PC 1885, PC (I) 1887; KG (1922), later (1922) the 1st Earl of Balfour, OM (1916); b. 1848, d. 1930; Conservative; ministry 12 Jul 1902–4 Dec 1905; MP (Con.) Hertford (1874–85); E. Manchester (1885–1906); City of London (1906–22).

36. The Rt Hon. Sir Henry **CAMPBELL-BANNERMAN**, GCB (1895), (PC 1884); known as Henry Campbell until 1872; b. 1836, d. 1908; Liberal; ministry 5 Dec 1905–5 Apr 1908; MP (Lib.) Stirling District (1868–1908).

37. The Rt Hon. Herbert Henry **ASQUITH** (PC 1892, PC (I) 1916); later (1925) 1st Earl of **OXFORD AND ASQUITH**, KG (1925); b. 1852, d. 1928; Liberal; ministries (a) 7 Apr 1908–7 May 1910, (b) 8 May 1910–5 Dec 16 (coalition from 25 May 1915); MP (Lib.) East Fife (1886–1918); Paisley (1920–4).

38. The Rt Hon. David **LLOYD GEORGE**, OM (1919), (PC 1905); later (1945) 1st Earl Lloyd-George of Dwyfor; b. 1863, d. 1945; Liberal; ministry 7 Dec 1916–19 Oct 1922 (Coalition); MP Caernarvon Boroughs (1890–1945) (Lib. 1890–1931 and 1935–45; Ind. Lib. 1931– 5).

39. The Rt Hon. (Andrew) Bonar **LAW** (PC 1911); b. 1858 (in Canada), d. 1923; Conservative; ministry 23 Oct 1922–20 May 1923; MP Bootle Div. of Lancashire (1911–18); Central Div. of Glasgow (1918–23).

40. The Rt Hon. Stanley **BALDWIN** (PC 1920, PC (Can.) 1927); later (1937) 1st Earl Baldwin of Bewdley, KG (1937); b. 1867, d. 1947; Conservative; ministries (a) 22 May 1923–22 Jan 1924 (Conservative), (b) 4 Nov 1924–4 Jun 1929 (Conservative), (c) 7 Jun 1935–20 Jan 1936 (Nat. Government), (d) 21 Jan–11 Dec 1936 (Nat. Government), (e) 12 Dec 1936–28 May 1937 (Nat. Government); MP (Con.) Bewdley Div. of Worcestershire (1908–37).

41. The Rt Hon. (James) Ramsay **MACDONALD** (PC 1924, PC (Can.) (1929); b. 1866, d. 1937; Labour; ministries (a) 22 Jan–4 Nov 1924, (b) 5 Jun 1929–7 Jun 1935 (from 1931 National Coalition); MP (Lab.) Leicester (1906–18); (Lab.) Aberavon (1922–9); (Lab.) Seaham Div. Co. Durham (1929–31); (Nat. Lab.) (1931–5); MP for Scottish Univs. (1936–7).

42. The Rt Hon. (Arthur) Neville **CHAMBERLAIN** (PC 1922); b. 1869, d. 1940; Conservative; ministry 28 May 1937–10 May 1940 (National Government); MP (Con.) Ladywood Div. of Birmingham (1918–29); Edgbaston Div. of Birmingham (1929–40).

43. The Rt Hon. Sir Winston (Leonard Spencer) **CHURCHILL**, KG (1953), OM (1946), CH (1922), TD (PC 1907); b. 1874, d. 1965; Conservative; ministries (a) 10 May 1940–26 Jul 1945 (Coalition but from 23 May 1945 Con.), (b) 26 Oct 1951–6 Feb 1952 (Con.), (c) 7 Feb 1952–5 Apr 1955 (Con.); MP (Con. until 1904, then Lib.) Oldham (1900–6); (Lib.) N.-W. Manchester (1906–8); Dundee (1908–18 as Lib. until 1922 as Coalition Lib.); Epping Div. of Essex (1924–45); Woodford Div. of Essex (1945–64).

44. The Rt Hon. Clement (Richard) **ATTLEE** CH (1945), (PC 1935); cr. 1955 1st Earl Attlee, KG (1956), OM (1951); b. 1883, d. 1967; Labour; ministry 26 Jul 1945–26 Oct 1951; MP Limehouse Div. of Stepney (1922–50); West Walthamstow (1950–5).

45. The Rt Hon. Sir (Robert) Anthony **EDEN**, KG (1954), MC (1917), (PC 1934); cr. 1961 1st Earl of Avon; b. 1897, d. 1977; Conservative; ministry 6 Apr 1955–9 Jan 1957; MP Warwick and Leamington (1923–57).

46. The Rt Hon. (Maurice) Harold **MACMILLAN**, OM (1976) (PC 1942); cr. 1984 1st Earl of Stockton; b. 1894, d. 1986; Conservative; ministry 10 Jan 1957–18 Oct 1963; MP Stockton-on-Tees (1924–9 and 1931–45); Bromley (1945–64).

47. The Rt Hon. Sir Alexander (Frederick) **DOUGLAS-HOME**, KT (1962) (PC 1951); known until 1918 as the Hon. A. F. Douglas-Home; thence until 11 July 1951 as Lord Dunglas; thence until his disclaimer of 23 Oct 1963 as the (14th) Earl of Home, Lord Home of the Hirsel; cr. 1974 Baron Home of the Hirsel (Life Peer); b. 1903; Conservative; ministry 19 Oct 1963–16 Oct 1964; MP South Lanark (1931–45); Lanark (1950–1); Kinross and West Perthshire (1963–74).

48. The Rt Hon. Sir (James) Harold **WILSON**, KG (1976), OBE (civ.) (1945), (PC 1947); cr. 1983 Baron Wilson of Rievaulx (Life Peer); b. 1916; Labour; ministries (a) 16 Oct 1964–30 Mar 1966, (b) 31 Mar 1966–17 Jun 1970, (c) 4 Mar–10 Oct 1974, (d) 10 Oct 1974–5 Apr 1976; Labour; MP Ormskirk (1945–50); Huyton (1950–83).

49. The Rt Hon. Sir Edward (Richard George) **HEATH**, KG (1992), MBE (mil.) (1946), (PC 1955); b. 1916; Conservative; ministry 18 Jun 1970–3 Mar 1974; MP Bexley (1950–74); Old Bexley-Sidcup (1974–).

50. The Rt Hon. Sir (Leonard) James **CALLAGHAN** KG (1987), (PC 1964); cr. 1987 Baron Callaghan of Cardiff (Life Peer); b. 1912; Labour; ministry 5 Apr 1976–4 May 1979; MP South Cardiff (1945–50); Southeast Cardiff (1950–83), Cardiff South and Penarth (1983–87).

51. The Rt Hon. Mrs Margaret (Hilda) **THATCHER** OM *née* Roberts (from Nov 1990 Lady Thatcher although she did not use the style); cr. 1992 Baroness Thatcher of Kesteven (Life Peeress) (PC 1970); b. 1925; Conservative; ministries (a) 4 May 1979–9 Jun 83, (b) 10 Jun 1983–4 May 1987, (c) 12 Jun 1987–28 Nov 90; MP Finchley (1959–74); Barnet, Finchley (1974–92).

52. The Rt Hon. John **MAJOR** (PC 1987); b. 1943; Conservative; ministries (a) 28 Nov 1990–9 Apr 1992, (b) 11 Apr 1992–to date; MP for Huntingdon (1983–).

POLITICAL PARTIES

The following political parties are either represented in Parliament, or contested either the majority of seats in Northern Ireland, Wales or Scotland or a considerable number of seats in England in 1992.

Alliance Party
88 University Street, Belfast BT7 1HE. Membership: 12 000. Leader: Dr John Alderdice.

Conservative Party
32 Smith Square, London SW1P 3HH. Membership: about 1 500 000. Parliamentary Leader: John Major.

Co-operative Party
158 Buckingham Palace Road, London SW1W 9UB. Membership: 12 000. Secretary: David Wise. (By agreement with the Labour Party, the Co-operative Party sponsors Labour and Co-operative election candidates.)

Democratic Unionist Party
296 Albertbridge Road, Belfast BT5 4GX. Membership: not published. Parliamentary Leader: Rev Ian Paisley.

Green Party
10 Station Parade, Balham High Road, London SW12
9AZ. Membership: 17 000. Chair: John Norris.

Labour Party
144-152 Walworth Road, London SE17 1JT. Membership: 288 000 (5 564 000 affiliated members). Parliamentary Leader: John Smith.

Liberal Democrats
(officially Social and Liberal Democrats) 4 Cowley
Street, London SW1P 3NB. Membership: 83 000.
Parliamentary Leader: Paddy Ashdown.

Liberal Party
22 Gayfere Street, London SW1, 3HP. Membership:
not published. Chair: David Morrish.

Natural Law Party
Mentmore Towers, Mentmore, Leighton Buzzard,
Bedfordshire. Membership: figures unavailable.
Leader: Dr Geoffrey Clements.

Plaid Cymru (Welsh Nationalist Party)
51 Cathedral Road, Cardiff CF1 9HD. Membership:
10 000. Parliamentary Leader: Dafydd Wigley.

Scottish National Party
6 North Charlotte Street, Edinburgh EH2 4JH.
Membership: not published. Parliamentary leader:
Margaret Ewing. Leader: Alex Salmond.

Sinn Fein
Falls Road, Belfast, Northern Ireland. Membership:
unavailable. Leader: Gerry Adams.

Social Democratic and Labour Party
24 Mount Charles, Belfast BT7 1NZ. Membership:
not published. Parliamentary Leader: John Hume.

Ulster Popular Unionist Party
Eastonville, Donaghadee Road, Millisle, New-
townards, Co Down, Northern Ireland, BT22 2BZ.
Membership: not published. Parliamentary Leader:
James Kilfedder.

Ulster Unionist Party
3 Glengall Street, Belfast BT12 5AE. Membership:
not published. Parliamentary Leader: James Moly-
neaux.

PARTY LEADERS
(since 1945)

Conservative Party
1940–55 Sir Winston Churchill
1955–57 Sir Anthony Eden
1957–63 Harold Macmillan
1963–65 Sir Alexander Douglas-Hume
1965–75 Edward Heath
1975–90 Margaret Thatcher
1990– John Major

Labour Party
1935–55 Clement Atlee
1955–63 Hugh Gaitskell
1963–76 Harold Wilson
1976–80 James Callaghan
1980–83 Michael Foot
1983–92 Neil Kinnock
1992– John Smith

Liberal Party (from 1988 Liberal Democrats)
1945–56 Clement Davies
1956–67 Joe Grimond
1967–76 Jeremy Thorpe
1976–88 David Steel
1988– J.J.D. (Paddy) Ashdown

THE ROYAL FAMILY

KINGS OF ALL ENGLAND

The West Saxon King Egbert (802–39), grandfather
of King Alfred, is often quoted as the first king of all
England from AD 829, although he never conquered the kingdom of Northumbria ruled by
Eanred (808 or 810 to 840 or 841).

Athelstan eldest son of the eldest son of King
Alfred of the West Saxons, acceded 924 or 925. The
first to establish rule over all England (excluding
Cumbria) in 927; d. 27 Oct 939 aged over 40 years.

Edmund younger half-brother of Athelstan;
acceded 939 but did not regain control of all England
until 944–45. Murdered 26 May 946 by Leofa at
Pucklechurch, near Bristol (Avon).

Edred younger brother of Edmund; acceded May
946. Effectively king of all England 946–48, and from
954 to his death on 23 Nov 955. Also intermittently
during the intervening period.

Edwy son of Edmund, b. c. 941; acceded November
955 (crowned at Kingston, Greater London); lost
control of the Mercians and Northumbrians in 957; d.
1 Oct 959, aged about 18.

Edgar son of Edmund, b. 943; acceded October 959
as king of all England (crowned at Bath, 11 May 973);
d. 8 July 975, aged c. 32.

Edward the Martyr son of Edgar by Aethelflaed,
b. c. 962; acceded 975; d. 18 Mar 978 or 979, aged 16 or
17.

Ethelred the Unready (*unraed*, i.e. ill-
counselled), second son of Edgar by Aelfthryth, b.
?968–69; acceded 978 or 979 (crowned at Kingston, 14
Apr 978 or 4 May 979); dispossessed by the Danish
king, Swegn Forkbeard, 1013–14; d. 23 Apr 1016, aged
c. 47 or 48.

Swegn Forkbeard king of Denmark 987–1014,
acknowledged as king of all England from about
September 1013 to his death on 3 Feb 1014.

Edmund Ironside probably the third son of
Ethelred, b. c. 992; chosen as king in London, April
1016. In the summer of 1016 he made an agreement
with Cnut whereby he retained dominion only over
Wessex; d. 30 Nov 1016.

Cnut younger son of King Swegn Forkbeard of
Denmark, b. c. 995. Secured Mercia and Danelaw in
the summer 1016; assumed dominion over all
England December 1016; king of Denmark 1019–35;
king of Norway 1028–1035; overlord of the king of the
Scots and probably ruler of the Norse-Irish kingdom
of Dublin; d. 12 Nov 1035, aged c. 40 years.

Harold Harefoot natural son of Cnut by Aelfgifu
of Northampton, b. ?c. 1016–17; chosen as regent for
his half-brother, Harthacnut, late 1035 or early 1036;
sole King 1037; d. 17 Mar 1040, aged c. 23 or 24 years.

Harthacnut son of Cnut by Emma, widow of King
Ethelred (d. 1016) b. ?c. 1018; titular king of Denmark
from 1028; effectively king of England from June
1040; d. 8 June 1042, aged c. 24 years.

Edward the Confessor elder half-brother of
Harthacnut and son of King Ethelred and Emma, b.
1002–5; acceded 1042; crowned 3 Apr 1043; d. 5 Jan
1066, aged between 60 and 64. Declared a saint by the
Church.

Harold Godwinson brother-in-law of Edward the Confessor and brother of his Queen Edith, son of Godwin, Earl of Wessex, b. ?c. 1020; acceded 6 Jan 1066; killed 14 Oct 1066.

Edgar Etheling grandson of Edmund Ironside; chosen by Londoners as king after the Battle of Hastings, October 1066, but apparently not crowned; he submitted to William I before 25 Dec 1066; believed to be still living c. 1125.

KINGS AND QUEENS OF ENGLAND, OF GREAT BRITAIN (after 1707) AND OF THE UNITED KINGDOM (after 1801)

William I (the Conqueror) illegitimate son of Robert I, 6th Duke of Normandy, and Herleva, d. of Fulbert the Tanner; m. 1050 or 1051 Matilda (d. 1083), dau of Baldwin V, Count of Flanders, issue 4s 5d; b. 1027/28; acceded 25 Dec 1066; d. 9 Sept 1087, aged 59 or 60, of an abdominal injury from his saddle pommel. He succeeded by right of conquest by winning the Battle of Hastings 1066.

William II third son of William I; b. between 1056 and 1060; unm.; acceded 26 Sept 1087; d. 2 Aug 1100 (according to tradition) of impalement by a stray arrow while hunting, aged 40–44.

Henry I fourth son of William I; b. 1068; m. (1) 1100 Eadgyth (known as Matilda; d. 1118), dau of Malcolm III, King of Scots, issue 1s 1d and a child who d. young; m. (2) 1121 Adela (d. 1151), dau of Godfrey VII, Count of Louvain, no issue; acceded 5 Aug 1100; d. 1 Dec 1135 aged 67.

Stephen third son of Stephen (sometimes called Henry), Count of Blois, and Adela, dau of William I; b. between 1096 and 1100; m. 1125 Matilda (d. 1151), dau of Eustace II, Count of Boulogne, issue 3s 2d; acceded 22 Dec 1135; d. 25 Oct 1154 aged 54–58. He usurped the throne from Henry's only surviving legitimate child, Matilda.

Matilda only surviving legitimate child of Henry I; b. Feb 1102; m. (1) 1114 Henry V, Holy Roman Emperor (b. 1086; d. 1125), no issue; m. (2) 1130 Geoffrey V, Count of Anjou (b. 1113; d. 1151), issue 3s; reigned April–November 1141; d. 10 Sept 1167 aged 65.

Henry II eldest son of Geoffrey V, Count of Anjou (surnamed Plantagenet), and Matilda (see above); b. 5 Mar 1133; m. 1152 Eleanor (b. c.1122; d. 1204), dau of William X, Duke of Aquitaine, issue 5s 3d; acceded 19 Dec 1154; d. 6 July 1189 aged 56.

Richard I (the Lionheart) third son of Henry II; b. 8 Sept 1157; m. 1191 Berengaria (d. after 1230), dau of Sancho VI, King of Navarre, no issue; acceded 3 Sept 1189; d. 6 Apr 1199 from a mortal arrow wound, aged 41.

John fifth son of Henry II; b. 24 Dec 1167; m. (1) 1189 Isabel (also known as Avisa; d. 1217), dau of William, Earl of Gloucester, dissolved, no issue; m. (2) 1200 Isabella (d. 1246), dau of Aimir, Count of Angouleme, issue 2s 3d; acceded 27 May 1199; d. 18–19 Oct 1216 aged 48. John usurped the throne from his nephew, Arthur, the only son of Geoffrey, Duke of Brittany (second son of Henry II), and from his niece, Eleanor.

Henry III elder son of John and Isabella; b. 1 Oct 1207; m. 1236 Eleanor (d. 1291), dau of Raymond Berengar IV, Count of Provence, issue 2s 3d and at least 4 other children who d. in infancy; acceded 28 Oct 1216; d. 16 Nov 1272, aged 65.

Edward I eldest surviving son of Henry III; b. 17/18 June 1239; m. (1) 1254 Eleanor (d. 1290), dau of Ferdinand III, King of Castile, issue 4s 7d; m (2) 1299 Margaret (b. 1282; d. 1317), dau of Philip III, King of France, issue 2s 1d; acceded 20 Nov 1272; d. 7 July 1307, aged 68.

Edward II fourth and only surviving son of Edward I and Eleanor; b. 25 Apr 1284; m. 1308 Isabella (b. 1292; d. 1358), dau of Philip IV, King of France, issue 2s 2d; acceded 8 July 1307 (deposed 20 Jan 1327); murdered 21 Sept 1327, aged 43 (traditionally by disembowelling with red-hot iron). Edward II was deposed by Parliament, having been imprisoned on 16 Nov 1326.

Edward III elder son of Edward II; b. 13 Nov 1312; m. 1328 Philippa (b. c1314; d. 1369), dau of William I, Count of Holland; acceded 25 Jan 1327; d. 21 June 1377, aged 64.

Richard II eldest surviving son of Edward, the Black Prince (eldest son of Edward III); b. 6 Jan 1367; m. (1) 1382 Anne (b. 1366; d. 1394), dau of Charles IV, Holy Roman Emperor, no issue; m. (2) 1396 Isabelle (b. 1389; d. 1409), dau of Charles VI, King of France, no issue; acceded 22 June 1377 (deposed 30 Sept 1399); d. 14 Feb 1400, possibly murdered, aged 33. Richard's throne was usurped by Henry, Duke of Lancaster (later Henry IV), who had him imprisoned from 19 Aug 1399 until his death.

Henry IV eldest son of John of Gaunt (4th son of Edward III), and Blanche (great-great-grand-dau of Henry III); b. probably April 1366; m. (1) c.1380/81 Lady Mary de Bohun (b. c.1368/70; d. 1394), dau of Humphrey, Earl of Hereford, issue 5s 2d; m. (2) 1403 Joan (b. c.1370; d. 1437), dau of Charles II, King of Navarre, no issue; acceded 30 Sept 1399; d. 20 Mar 1413 aged 46 (probably). He usurped the throne of Richard II.

Henry V eldest surviving son of Henry IV and Mary; b. probably 16 Sept 1387; m. 1420 Catherine (b. 1401; d. 1437), dau of Charles VI, King of France, issue 1s; acceded 21 Mar 1413; d. 31 Aug/Sept 1422 aged 34.

Henry VI only son of Henry V; b. 6 Dec 1421; m. 1445 Margaret (b. 1430; d. 1482), dau of René, Duke of Anjou, issue 1s; acceded 1 Sept 1422; deposed by his third cousin Edward IV 4 March 1461; regained the throne 6 Oct 1470–11 Apr 1471, when he was again deposed by Edward IV; murdered by stabbing 21 May 1471 at the Tower of London, aged 49.

Edward IV eldest son of Richard, 3rd Duke of York (who was descended from two sons of Edward III); b. 28 Apr 1442; m. 1464 Elizabeth (b. c.1437; d. 1492), dau of Sir Richard Woodville, issue 3s 7d; acceded 4 Mar 1461; deposed in favour of Henry VI 6 Oct 1470; restored 11 Apr 1471; d. 9 Apr 1483 aged 40.

Edward V eldest son of Edward IV; b. 2 Nov 1470; unm.; acceded 9 Apr 1483 (deposed 25 June 1483); (traditionally) murdered, possibly in 1483 or in 1486, at the Tower of London. Edward was deposed when the throne was usurped by his uncle, Richard III (the only surviving brother of Edward IV).

Richard III only surviving brother of Edward IV (see above); b. 2 Oct 1452; m. 1472 Anne (b. 1456; d. 1485), dau of Richard Nevill, Earl of Warwick, issue 1s; acceded 26 June 1483; killed 22 Aug 1485 at the Battle of Bosworth Field, aged 32.

Henry VII only child of Edmund Tudor, 1st Earl of

Richmond, and Margaret Beaufort, great-great-grand-daughter of Edward III; b. 27 Jan 1457; m. 1486 Elizabeth (b. 1466; d. 1503), dau of Edward IV, issue 3s 4d; acceded 22 Aug 1485; d. 21 Apr 1509 aged 52.

Henry VIII only surviving son of Henry VII; b. 28 June 1491; m. (1) 1509 Catherine (b. 1485; d. 1536), dau of Ferdinand II, King of Aragon and widow of Henry's elder brother Arthur, divorced, 2s 2d; m. (2) 1533 Anne (b. 1507; beheaded 1536), dau of Sir Thomas Boleyn, issue 1d; m. (3) 1536 Jane (d. 1537), dau of Sir John Seymour, issue 1s; m. (4) 1540 Anne (b. 1515; d. 1557), dau of John, Duke of Cleves, divorced, no issue; m. (5) 1540 Catherine (beheaded 1542), dau of Lord Edmund Howard, no issue; m. (6) 1543 Catherine (b. c1512; d. 1548), dau of Sir Thomas Parr, no issue; acceded 22 Apr 1509; d. 28 Jan 1547 aged 55.

Edward VI only surviving son of Henry VIII, by Jane Seymour; b. 12 Oct 1537; unm.; acceded 28 Jan 1547; d. 6 July 1553 aged 15.

Jane eldest daughter of Henry Grey, 3rd Marquess of Dorset, and Frances (dau of Mary Tudor, sister of Henry VIII); b. Oct 1537; m. 1553 Lord Guilford Dudley, son of John Dudley, Duke of Northumberland, no issue; acceded 6 July (proclaimed 10 July) 1553 (deposed 19 July); beheaded 12 Feb 1554 in the Tower of London, aged 16.

Mary I only surviving child of Henry VIII and Catherine of Aragon; b. 18 Feb 1516; m. 1554 Philip II, King of Spain (b. 1527; d. 1598), no issue; acceded 19 July 1553; d. 17 Nov 1558 aged 42. Mary's husband Philip was styled, but not crowned, king.

Elizabeth I daughter of Henry VIII and Anne Boleyn; b. 7 Sept 1533; unm.; acceded 17 Nov 1558; d. 24 Mar 1603 aged 69.

James I only son of Henry Stuart, Lord Darnley, and Mary, Queen of Scots (dau of James V of Scotland, son of Margaret Tudor, sister of Henry VIII); b. 19 June 1566; m. 1589 Anne (b. 1574; d. 1619), dau of Frederick II, King of Denmark, issue 3s 4d; acceded (to English throne) 26 Mar 1603 (to Scottish throne 24 July 1567); d. 27 Mar 1625 aged 58.

Charles I only surviving son of James I; b. 19 Nov 1600; m. 1625 Henrietta Maria (b. 1609; d. 1669), dau of Henry IV, King of France, issue 4s 5d; acceded 27 Mar 1625; beheaded 30 Jan 1649, aged 48. The kingship was *de facto* declared abolished 17 Mar 1649 with the victory of Parliamentarians in the English Civil War.

Charles II eldest surviving son of Charles I; b. 29 May 1630; m. 1662 Catherine (b. 1638; d. 1705), dau of John, Duke of Braganza, no issue; acceded 29 May 1660 (but *de jure* 30 Jan 1649); d. 6 Feb 1685 aged 54.

James II only surviving son of Charles I; b. 14 Oct 1633; m. (1) 1660 Anne (b. 1637; d. 1671), dau of Edward Hyde, issue 4s 4d; m. (2) Mary d'Este (b. 1658; d. 1718), dau of Alfonso IV, Duke of Modena, issue 2s 5d; acceded 6 Feb 1685 (his reign ended 11 Dec 1688 when he was deemed by legal fiction to have ended his reign by flight); d. 6 Sept 1701 aged 67.

William III only son of William II, Prince of Orange, and Mary (Stuart), daughter of Charles I; b. 4 Nov 1650; m. Mary II (see below); acceded 13 Feb 1689 (with Mary II); d. 8 Mar 1702 following a fracture of right collarbone, aged 51.
Mary II elder surviving dau of James II and Anne Hyde; b. 30 Apr 1662; m. 1677 WilliaM III (see above), no issue; acceded 13 Feb 1689 (with William II); d. 28 Dec 1694 aged 32.

Anne only surviving dau of James II and Anne

Hyde; b. 6 Feb 1665; m. 1683 George (b. 1653; d. 1708), son of Frederick III, King of Denmark, 2s 3d – all d. young (and 12 other confinements); acceded 8 Mar 1702; d. 1 Aug 1714 aged 49.

George I eldest son of Ernest Augustus, Duke of Brunswick-Lüneburg and Elector of Hanover, and Princes Sophia, 5th and youngest dau of Elizabeth, Queen of Bohemia, eldest dau of James I; b. 28 May 1660; m. 1682 Sophia (b. 1666; d. 1726), dau of George William, Duke of Lüneburg-Celle, divorced, issue 1s 1d; acceded 1 Aug 1714; d. 11 June 1727 aged 67. George succeeded in the terms of the Act of Settlement (which excluded all Roman Catholics and their spouses).

George II only son of Geroge I; b. 30 Oct 1683; m. 1705 Caroline (b. 1683; d. 1737), dau of John Frederick, Margrave of Brandenburg-Ansbach, issue 3s 5d; acceded 11 June 1727; d. 25 Oct 1760 aged 76.

George III eldest son of Frederick Lewis, Prince of Wales, and grandson of George II; b. 24 May (O.S.) 1738; m. 1761 Charlotte (b. 1744; d. 1818), dau of Charles Louis Frederick, Duke of Mecklenburg-Strelitz, issue 9s 6d; acceded 25 Oct 1760; d. 29 Jan 1820, aged 81. George III's eldest son became Regent 5 Feb 1811 owing to his insanity.

George IV eldest son of George III; b. 12 Aug 1762; m. (1) 1785 (in a ceremony not recognized under English law) Maria Fitzherbert; m. (2) 1795 Caroline (b. 1768; d. 1821), dau of Charles, Duke of Brunswick-Wolfenbüttel, issue 1d; acceded 29 Jan 1820; d. 26 June 1830 aged 67.

William IV oldest surviving son of George III; b. 21 Aug 1765; m. 1818 Adelaide (b. 1792; d. 1849), dau of George, Duke of Saxe-Meiningen, issue 2 d (d. young); acceded 26 June 1830; d. 20 June 1837 aged 71.

Victoria only child of Edward, Duke of Kent and Strathearn, 4th son of George III; b. 24 May 1819; m. 1840 Albert (b. 1819; d. 1861), son of Ernest I, Duke of Saxe-Coburg-Gotha, issue 4s 5d; acceded 20 June 1837; d. 22 Jan 1901, aged 81.

Edward VII elder surviving son of Victoria; b. 9 Nov 1841; m. 1863 Alexandra (b. 1844; d. 1925), dau of Christian IX, King of Denmark, issue 3s 3d; acceded 22 Jan 1901; d. 6 May 1910 aged 68.

George V only surviving son of Edward VII; b. 3 June 1865; m. 1893 Mary (b. 1867; d. 1953), dau of Francis, Duke of Teck, issue 5s 1d; acceded 6 May 1910; d. 20 Jan 1936 aged 70.

Edward VIII eldest son of George V; b. 23 June 1894; m. 1937 Wallis Simpson (nee Warfield), no issue; acceded 20 Jan 1936 (abdicated 11 Dec 1936); d. 28 May 1972 aged 77. Edward VIII abdicated for himself and his heirs in order to marry Wallis Simpson, an American divorcee.

George VI second son of George V; b. 14 Dec 1895; m. 1923 Lady Elizabeth Bowes-Lyon (b. 1900), dau of the 14th Earl of Strathmore, issue 2d; acceded 11 Dec 1936; d. 6 Feb 1952 aged 56.

Elizabeth II elder daughter of George VI; b. 21 Apr 1926; m. 1947 Philip (b. 1921), son of Prince Andrew of Greece and Denmark, acceded 6 Feb 1952.

KINGS OF SCOTLAND

The formation of Scotland began in 843 when Kenneth I (MacAlpin), King of Dalriada (the kingdom of the Scots), became King of Caledonia (the kingdom of the Picts).

From the 6th to the 9th centuries, Scotland was divided into a number of smaller kingdoms whose names and boundaries were constantly changing. About the year 950 four kingdoms existed.

KINGS OF ALBA

Kenneth I (MacAlpin; 843–858/9), King of Dalriada from 841.

Donald I (858/9–862/3), brother of Kenneth I.

Constantine I (862/3–877), son of Kenneth I. Killed in battle by the Danes.

Aedh (877–78), son of Kenneth I. Murdered by King Giric of Strathclyde.

Eochaid (878–89), nephew of Aedh. Deposed by Donald II.

Donald II (889–900), son of Constantine I.

Constantine II (900–42), son of Aedh. Abdicated to become Abbot of St Andrews; d. 952.

Malcolm I (942–54), son of Donald II. Murdered.

Indulf (954–62), son of Constantine II. Killed by the Vikings.

Dubh (962–966/7), son of Malcolm I. Murdered.

Culen (966/7–971), son of Indulf. Murdered.

KINGS OF SCOTS

Kenneth II (971–95), son of Malcolm I. Took the title King of Scots – Alba was from this time known as Scotland. Received Lothian from King Edgar of England.

Constantine III (995–97), son of Culen. Killed by Kenneth III.

Kenneth III (997–1005), son of Dubh. Killed by Malcolm II.

Malcolm II (1005–34), b. c. 954; d. 25 Nov 1034, aged c. 80 years. Consolidated the kingdom of Scotland by annexing Strathclyde, c. 1016.

Duncan I (1034–40), son of Malcolm II's daughter, Bethoc.

Macbeth (1040–57), probably son of Malcolm II's daughter, Donada; d. aged c. 52 years.

Lulach (1057–8), stepson of Macbeth; d. aged c. 26.

Malcolm III (Canmore; 1058–93), son of Duncan I; d. aged c. 62.

Donald Bane (1093–4 and 1094–7), son of Duncan I, twice deposed.

Duncan II (May–Oct 1094), son of Malcolm III; d. aged c. 34.

Edgar (1097–1107), son of Malcolm III, half-brother of Duncan II; d. aged c. 33.

Alexander I (1107–24), son of Malcolm III and brother of Edgar; d. aged c. 47.

David I (1124–53), son of Malcolm III and brother of Edgar; d. aged c. 68.

Malcolm IV (1153–65), son of Henry, Earl of Northumberland, and grandson of David I; d. aged c. 24.

William I (the Lion; 1165–1214), brother of Malcolm IV; d. aged c. 72 (from 1174 to 1189 the king of England was acknowledged as overlord of Scotland).

Alexander II (1214–49), son of William I; d. aged 48.

Alexander III (1249–86), son of Alexander II; d. aged 44.

Margaret (Maid of Norway; 1286–90), dau of Margaret (dau of Alexander III) by King Eric II of Norway. Queen Margaret never visited her realm; d. aged 7.

First Interregnum 1290–2.

John (Balliol; 1292–96), son of Dervorguilla, a great-great-granddau of David I. He was awarded the throne from 13 contestants by the adjudication of King Edward I of England. He was overthrown by an English invasion and abdicated; d. in 1313 aged 63.

Second Interregnum 1296–1306.

Robert I (the Bruce; 1306–29), grandson of Robert de Bruce (one of the 13 claimants to the Scottish throne in 1291) and a descendant of David I; d. aged c. 55.

David II (1329–71; deposed September–December 1332 and not in effective control of most of Scotland 1333–56), son of Robert I; d. aged 46.

Edward (1332 and 1333–56), son of John; he acknowledged Edward III of England as his overlord in 1333 and surrendered all claims to the Scottish crown to him in 1356; d. 1364 aged over 60.

Robert II (1371–90), founder of the Stewart dynasty, son of Walter the Steward and Marjorie Bruce (dau of Robert I); d. aged 74.

Robert III (1390–1406), legitimated natural son of Robert II; d. aged c. 69.

James I (1406–37), son of Robert III, captured by the English 13 days before his accession and kept prisoner in England till March 1424; d. aged 42.

James II (1437–60), son of James I; d. aged 29.

James III (1460–88), son of James II; d. aged 36.

James IV (1488–1513), son of James III and Margaret of Denmark, married Margaret Tudor; d. aged 40.

James V (1513–42), son of James IV and Margaret Tudor; d. aged 30.

Mary (*Queen of Scots*; 1542–67), daughter of James V and Mary of Lorraine, acceded aged 6 or 7 days, abdicated 24 July 1567 and was succeeded by her son, James VI (by her second husband, Henry Stuart, Lord Darnley). She was executed 8 Feb 1587, aged 44.

James VI (1567–1625), son of Mary and Lord Darnley (see above), succeeded to the English throne as James I on 24 Mar 1603, so effecting a personal union of the two realms; d. aged 58.

THE ORDER OF SUCCESSION

The order of succession is determined according to ancient common-law rules, but these may be upset by an enactment of the Crown in Parliament under powers taken in the Succession to the Crown Act of 1707, provided always (since 1931) that the parliaments of all the members of the Commonwealth assent. The Crown descends lineally to the legitimate issue of the sovereign, males being preferred to females, in their respective orders of age. In the event of failure of such issue (e.g. King Edward VIII in 1936) the Crown passes to the nearest collateral being an heir at law. In the event of two or more sisters being next in succession the eldest alone (e.g. The Princess Elizabeth from 1936 to 1952) shall be the heiress. The male issue by a second or subsequent marriage takes precedence over half sisters (e.g. King Edward VI, son of King Henry VIII's third wife, took precedence over Queen Mary I, daughter of his first marriage, and Queen Elizabeth I, daughter of his second marriage). The following is the Order of Succession to the Crown.

1 The heir apparent is HRH The Prince CHARLES, KG, KT, The Prince of Wales, The Duke of Cornwall, The Duke of Rothesay, The Earl of Carrick, and The Baron Renfrew, Lord of the Isles and Great Steward of Scotland, b. 14 Nov 1948. (He m. 29 Jul 1981 (separated 1992), Lady DIANA Spencer – HRH The Princess of Wales – who was b. 1 Jul 1961.)

2 HRH Prince WILLIAM of Wales, b. 21 June 1982 – elder son of The Prince Charles.

3 HRH Prince HENRY of Wales, b. 15 Sept 1984 – younger son of The Prince Charles.

4 HRH The Prince ANDREW, The Duke of York, The Earl of Inverness, and The Baron Killyleagh, b. 19 Feb 1960 – second son of HM Queen Elizabeth II. (He m. 23 Jul 1986 (separated 1992), Miss SARAH Ferguson – HRH The Duchess of York – who was b. 15 Oct 1959.)

5 HRH Princess BEATRICE of York, b. 8 Aug 1988 – elder dau of The Prince Andrew.

6 HRH Princess EUGENIE of York, b. 23 Mar 1990 – younger dau of The Prince Andrew.

7 HRH The Prince EDWARD, b. 10 Mar 1964 – youngest son of HM Queen Elizabeth II.

8 HRH The Princess ANNE, The Princess Royal, b. 15 Aug 1950 – only dau of HM Queen Elizabeth II. (She m. (1) 14 Nov 1973 Captain MARK Anthony Peter Phillips, divorced 1992; m. (2) 12 Dec 1992 Commander Timothy Laurence.)

9 PETER Phillips, b. 15 Nov 1977 – son of The Princess Anne.

10 ZARA Phillips, b. 15 May 1981 – dau of The Princess Anne.

11 HRH The Princess MARGARET Rose, The Countess of Snowdon, b. 21 Aug 1930 – younger dau of HM King George VI. (She m. 6 May 1960 ANTHONY Armstrong-Jones, created Earl of Snowdon; divorced 1978.)

12 DAVID Armstrong-Jones, Viscount Linley, b. 3 Nov 1961 – son of The Princess Margaret. (He m. 1993 Hon Serena Stanhope.)

13 The Lady SARAH Armstrong-Jones, b. 1 May 1964 – dau of The Princess Margaret.

14 HRH Prince RICHARD, the (2nd) Duke of Gloucester, b. 26 Aug 1944 – surviving son of HRH The Prince Henry, Duke of Gloucester, who was the third son of HM King George V. (He m. 8 Jul 1972 BIRGITTE Eva van Deurs – HRH The Duchess of Gloucester.)

15 ALEXANDER, Earl of Ulster, b. 24 Oct 1974 – son of HRH The Duke of Gloucester.

16 The Lady DAVINA Windsor, b. 19 Nov 1977 – elder dau of HRH The Duke of Gloucester.

17 The Lady ROSE Windsor, b. 1 Mar 1980 – younger dau of HRH The Duke of Gloucester.

18 HRH Prince EDWARD, the (2nd) Duke of Kent, the Earl of St Andrews and the Baron Downpatrick, b. 9 Oct 1935 – elder son of HRH The Prince George, Duke of Kent, who was the fourth son of HM King George V. (He m. 8 Jun 1961 KATHARINE Worsley – HRH The Duchess of Kent.)

(GEORGE, Earl of St Andrews, b. 26 Jun 1962 – elder son of HRH The Duke of Kent – forfeited his claim to the throne by his marriage, on 16 Jan 1988, to a Roman Catholic, SYLVANA Tomaselli – the Countess of St Andrews.)

19 EDWARD, Baron Downpatrick, b. 10 Dec 1988 – son of George, Earl of St Andrews.

20 Lord NICHOLAS Windsor, b. 25 July 1970 – younger son of HRH The Duke of Kent.

21 The Lady HELEN Taylor (nee Windsor), b. 28 Apr 1964 – dau of HRH The Duke of Kent. (She m. 18 Jul 1992 Timothy Taylor.)

(HRH Prince MICHAEL of Kent, b. 4 Jul 1942 – younger son of HRH The Prince George, Duke of Kent – forfeited his claim to the throne by his marriage, on 30 Jun 1978, to a Roman Catholic, Baroness MARIE-CHRISTINE von Reibnitz – HRH Princess Michael of Kent.)

22 Lord FREDERICK Windsor, b. 6 Apr 1979 – son of HRH Prince Michael of Kent.

23 The Lady GABRIELA Windsor, b. 23 Apr 1981 – dau of HRH Prince Michael of Kent.

24 HRH Princess ALEXANDRA of Kent, the Lady Ogilvy, b. 25 Dec 1936 – dau of HRH The Prince George, Duke of Kent. (She m. 24 Apr 1963 Hon. – now Sir – Angus Ogilvy.)

25 JAMES Ogilvy, b. 29 Feb 1964 – son of HRH Princess Alexandra of Kent. (He m. 30 Jul 1988 JULIA Rawlinson.)

26 MARINA Mowatt (nee Ogilvy), b. 31 Jul 1966 – dau of HRH Princess Alexandra of Kent. (She m. 2 Feb 1990 Paul Mowatt.)

27 ZENOUSKA Mowatt, b. 26 May 1990 – dau of Marina Mowatt.

28 GEORGE, 7th Earl of Harewood, b. 7 Feb 1923 – elder son of HRH The Princess Mary, only dau of HM King George V. The Earl of Harewood is followed by his descendants and, in turn, by his brother, Hon. Gerald Lascelles, and his descendants.

THE PEERAGE

There are five ranks in the British temporal peerage. In ascending order they are: baron or baroness; viscount or viscountess; earl or countess; marquess (sometimes 'marquis') or marchioness; duke or duchess. The British spiritual peerage comprises the two CofE archbishops and 24 of the bishops (always including the Bishops of London, Durham and Winchester and excluding the Bishop of Sodor and Man), based on their seniority of appointment.

A few women hold peerages in their own right and since the Peerage Act, 1963, have become peers of Parliament. The remaining category of membership of the House of Lords is life peers – both Lords of Appeal in Ordinary, appointed by virtue of the Appellate Jurisdiction Act, 1876, and life peers created under the Life Peerages Act, 1958, by which both men and women may be appointed for life membership of the House of Lords.

Courtesy titles The holder of a courtesy title is a commoner. For example, the Duke of Marlborough's son is known by courtesy as Marquess of Blandford – note the omission of the definite article 'the' because the Duke of Marlborough is also *the* Marquess of Blandford and his secondary peerage style is merely *lent* to this son.

THE ECONOMY

The three basic sectors of an economy are the primary goods sector (raw materials and farming), the industrial goods or secondary sector (manufactures, construction, gas, electricity, etc.) and the service or tertiary sector (retailing, banking, tourism, etc.). The relative importance of each of these sectors tends to change as the economy grows and matures. Most advanced countries such as the UK have been characterized by a relative decline in their industrial goods sector and a corresponding increase in the importance of the service sector. Factors affecting a country's industrial structure include the level and pattern of demand, relative supply costs and prices, technological advance, governmental policies, and exposure to foreign competition. This latter factor has become more important in recent years as the UK's entry into the EC in 1973 served to heighten the competitive pressures facing British firms. These pressures will be hopefully lessened somewhat by the single European market which came into being in 1993.

GOVERNMENT EXPENDITURE

£ billion

Function	1981	1982	1983	1984	1985	1986	1987	1988	1989	1990	1991
Defence	12.6	14.6	15.9	17.0	18.3	19.1	18.9	19.8	21.0	22.9	27.3
Public order and safety	4.3	4.8	5.3	5.9	6.1	6.8	7.5	8.4	9.5	11.0	12.8
Education	14.3	15.2	16.2	17.0	17.5	19.3	20.7	22.4	24.4	26.8	29.5
Health	13.4	14.0	15.9	16.8	17.8	19.2	20.9	22.9	25.3	27.7	30.9
Social Security	31.1	36.2	39.3	42.4	45.9	49.9	52.1	54.2	57.3	62.8	73.9
Housing & community amenities	7.1	6.5	7.3	7.2	6.8	8.1	9.0	8.2	7.7	7.9	9.1
Recreation and cultural affairs	1.6	1.7	1.9	2.0	2.3	2.4	2.6	2.8	3.1	3.6	3.8
Fuel and energy	0.3	1.1	0.8	1.4	1.6	−1.2	−3.5	−3.1	−2.0	−3.8	−5.0
Agriculture, forestry and fishing	1.7	2.0	2.5	2.2	2.8	2.1	2.3	2.5	2.1	2.6	2.4
Mining, manufacturing, mineral resources and construction	3.6	2.8	2.7	2.5	2.4	1.9	1.3	0.9	1.7	1.3	1.6
Transport and communication	4.2	4.9	4.9	3.4	4.1	3.7	4.0	4.5	7.2	9.2	6.7
General public services	4.6	5.6	5.9	6.2	7.9	6.3	6.6	7.6	9.1	10.9	9.2
Other economic affairs and services	2.9	2.7	3.2	3.8	3.8	4.1	3.7	3.9	5.3	6.4	5.5
Other expenditure	15.4	16.3	16.7	18.2	20.0	20.5	22.5	22.7	24.5	25.0	19.7

BALANCE OF PAYMENTS (£ million)

The balance of payments is a measure of Britain's trading position in relation to the rest of the world. Exports and imports ('visible' trade) in addition to 'invisibles' (including tourism, banking and insurance) are taken into account in determining the balance of payments. This balance illustrates whether the UK has a surplus of income over expenditure.

Year	Visible Exports	Visible Imports	Visible Balance	Invisible Balance	Current Balance (− deficit/+ surplus)
1965	4 848	5 071	− 223	+ 198	− 27
1970	8 121	8 163	− 42	+ 818	+ 776
1975	19 463	22 699	− 3 236	+ 1 615	− 1 621
1980	47 389	46 211	+ 1 178	+ 2 028	+ 3 206
1981	50 977	47 325	+ 3 652	+ 3 620	+ 7 272
1982	55 565	53 181	+ 2 384	+ 3 167	+ 5 551
1983	60 658	61 158	− 500	+ 2 549	+ 2 049
1984	70 367	74 751	− 4 384	+ 5 858	+ 1 474
1985	78 111	80 289	− 2 178	+ 5 097	+ 2 919
1986	72 843	81 306	− 8 463	+ 7 483	− 980
1987	79 421	90 350	− 10 929	+ 7 106	− 3 822
1988	80 602	101 428	− 20 826	+ 6 154	− 14 762
1989	92 526	115 638	− 23 112	+ 2 261	− 20 851
1990	102 038	120 713	− 18 675	+ 4 295	− 14 380
1991	103 804	113 770	− 9 966	+ 4 187	− 5 779
1992	106 775	120 546	− 13 771	n.a	n.a

INFLATION: CONSUMER PRICE INDEX (1985 = 100)

	1980	1981	1982	1983	1984	1985	1986	1987	1988	1989	1990	1991	1992
UK	70.7	79.1	85.9	89.8	94.3	100.0	103.4	107.7	113.0	121.8	133.4	141.2	148.4
Germany*	82.7	87.9	92.5	95.6	97.9	100.0	99.9	100.1	101.4	104.2	107.0	110.7	115.1
France	63.3	71.8	80.3	88.0	94.6	100.0	102.5	105.9	108.8	112.6	116.4	120.0	123.0
Italy	51.8	61.9	72.1	82.6	91.6	100.0	105.8	110.8	116.5	123.8	131.7	140.1	147.4
Japan	87.3	91.6	94.1	95.8	98.0	100.0	100.6	100.7	101.4	103.7	106.9	110.4	112.3
USA	76.6	84.5	89.7	92.6	96.6	100.0	101.9	105.7	109.9	115.2	121.4	126.6	130.5

* Figures are for West Germany only.

VALUE OF UK EXPORTS

Category	£ millions	% of total
Food and live animals (chiefly for food)	5 291.1	4.9
Beverages and tobacco	3 417.3	3.1
Beverages	*2 447.6*	*2.3*
Crude materials, inedible (except fuels)	1 879.4	1.7
Mineral fuels, lubricants and related materials	6 929.1	6.4
Petroleum and related products	*6 625.7*	*6.1*
Animal and vegetable oils, fats and waxes	86.0	0.1
Chemicals and related products	14 974.1	13.8
Manufactured goods (classified chiefly by material)†	15 481.9	14.3
Machinery and transport equipment	44 243.0	40.8
Road vehicles	*8 890.2*	*8.2*
Miscellaneous manufactured articles‡	13 963.1	12.9
Others	2 024.9	1.9
Total	**108 290.0**	

1992 figures; † including textiles, metals, iron and steel, leather and paper; ‡ including clothing, furniture, scientific and photographic instruments

VALUE OF UK IMPORTS

Category	£ millions	% of total
Food and live animals (chiefly for food)	11 401.9	9.1
Beverages and tobacco	2 025.5	1.6
Beverages	*1 565.0*	*1.2*
Crude materials, inedible (except fuels)	4668.7	3.7
Mineral fuels, lubricants and related materials	6 988.0	5.5
Petroleum and related products	*5 302.7*	*4.2*
Animal and vegetable oils, fats and waxes	422.8	0.3
Chemicals and related products	11 618.5	9.2
Manufactured goods (classified chiefly by material)†	20 666.6	16.4
Machinery and transport equipment	47 320.5	37.6
Road vehicles	*12 118.6*	*9.6*
Miscellaneous manufactured articles‡	19 109.0	15.2
Others	1 622.5	1.3
Total	**125 843.9**	

1992 figures; † including textiles, metals, iron and steel, leather and paper; ‡ including clothing, furniture, scientific and photographic instrumemts.

WORKFORCE

Agriculture, forestry and fishing	264 000
Production industries	
Coal, oil and natural gas	128 000
Electricity, gas and water supply	267 000
Manufacturing industries	4 516 000
Construction	826 000
Service industries	
Wholesale distribution and repairs	1 173 000
Retail distribution	2 105 000
Hotels and catering	1 215 000
Transport	916 000
Post and telecommunications	389 000
Banking, finance and insurance	2 604 000
Public administration	1 917 000
Education	1 737 000
Medical and other health services, veterinary services	1 506 000
Other services	1 676 000
Total no. of men in employment	*10 992 000*
Total no. of women in employment	*10 225 000*

figures for Great Britain only (1992).

UNEMPLOYMENT
(seasonally adjusted)

Year	Total	% rate
1965	338 200	1.4
1970	602 000	2.6
1975	929 000	3.6
1980	1 667 600	6.3
1981	2 520 400	10.4
1982	2 916 900	12.1
1983	3 104 700	12.9
1984	3 159 800	13.1
1985	3 027 900	10.9
1986	3 097 900	11.1
1987	2 806 500	10.0
1988	2 274 900	8.1
1989	1 784 400	6.3
1990	1 661 700	5.8
1991	2 368 100	8.3
1992	2 767 300	9.8

Unemployment figures for 1981–85 are annual averages. All figures relate to claimants over 18 years old.

UK EXPORTS: BY COUNTRY

Country	£ millions	% of total
Germany	15 060.1	13.9
USA	12 225.9	11.3
France	11 486.7	10.6
Netherlands	8 484.0	7.8
Italy	6 146.7	5.7
Ireland	5 739.6	5.3
Belgium and Luxembourg	5 714.2	5.3
Spain	4 405.3	4.1
Sweden	2 439.0	2.2
Japan	2 227.0	2.0
Saudi Arabia	1 967.6	1.8
Switzerland	1 844.6	1.7
Hong Kong	1 612.9	1.5
Canada	1 582.1	1.5
Denmark	1 560.6	1.4
Norway	1 419.6	1.3
Australia	1 376.7	1.3
Portugal	1 164.1	1.1
Singapore	1 145.1	1.0
South Africa	1 078.7	1.0
Others	19 609.5	18.1
Total	**108 290.0**	

1992 figures

UK IMPORTS: BY COUNTRY

Country	£ millions	% of total
Germany	19 034.6	15.1
USA	13 711.3	10.9
France	12 215.9	9.7
Netherlands	9 908.8	7.9
Japan	7 443.7	6.0
Italy	6 769.2	5.4
Belgium and Luxembourg	5 741.4	4.6
Ireland	5 070.1	4.0
Switzerland	3 918.9	3.1
Norway	3 861.8	3.0
Sweden	3 283.7	2.6
Spain	2 938.7	2.3
Hong Kong	2 397.4	1.9
Denmark	2 385.0	1.9
Canada	1 897.1	1.5
Finland	1 676.6	1.3
Taiwan	1 393.7	1.1
Singapore	1 192.8	0.9
Portugal	1 170.8	0.9
Malaysia	1 103.8	0.9
Others	18 723.6	14.9
Total	**125 843.9**	

1992 figures

OWNERSHIP OF DURABLE GOODS: BY SOCIO-ECONOMIC GROUP (%)

Socio-economic categories by head of household

	Professional	Employers and managers	Other non-manual	Skilled manual	Unskilled manual	Economically inactive	All house-holds
Deep freezers*	89	92	86	88	79	70	81
Washing machine	95	96	91	93	88	77	87
Tumble drier	65	67	53	54	44	28	46
Microwave oven	68	69	57	63	50	29	50
Dishwasher	36	33	14	10	4	4	13
Telephone	98	98	92	86	71	84	88
Television	98	99	98	99	99	98	99
Colour	*93*	*98*	*94*	*96*	*94*	*91*	*94*
Black & white	*5*	*1*	*4*	*3*	*6*	*8*	*5*
Video	81	86	76	82	70	36	64
Home computer	45	35	30	24	12	5	20
CD player	35	34	29	25	18	8	21

Figures for Great Britain 1990–91; * includes fridge-freezers

AVERAGE WEEKLY INCOME: 1960–1991 (in £)

	1960	1965	1970	1975	1980	1985	1988	1989	1990	1991
Average gross household income	18.01	24.64	35.40	72.87	147.18	216.86	283.86	303.84	335.67	362.65
Average disposable household income	16.10	20.19	29.54	58.15	121.50	175.30	233.20	251.62	276.29	299.63

THE CBI

The CBI - the **Confederation of British Industries** – was established in 1965 as an independent non-party voice to articulate the needs and problems of business to government. It is now recognized as the spokesperson of industry in the UK. Directly and indirectly, it represents over 250 000 companies. The CBI – which is financed by commerce and industry – is organized into 13 regional councils and a 400–member national council, which is chaired by a president. Expert standing commitees advise the CBI in over two dozen areas of interest.

BANKING AND FINANCE

'THE CITY'

London is one of the world's leading financial centres. On a world scale, it is challenged only by New York and Tokyo. The term 'the City' is used to describe the concentration of financial institutions in and just beyond the boundaries of 'the square mile' (the City of London).

The greatest concentration of banks in the world is found in the City, which is responsible for just under 25% of bank lending worldwide. Many of these institutions are *merchant banks*, which used to be primarily concerned with accepting foreign bills and underwriting new issues of securities. In recent years merchant banks have diversified their activities and now provide financial services to British industry.

The City contains one of the world's major stock exchanges (see below) and is an important centre for trade in commodities. It is also the world's most important insurance centre, accounting for around 20% of the international market. The City makes an important contribution to UK trade – business and financial services are well in credit in Britain's balance of imports and exports.

THE STOCK EXCHANGE

The Stock Exchange is a market where securities (stocks and shares) are bought and sold, and capital is raised for new investment through the issue of new shares. Members of the Stock Exchange trade securities on behalf of the public and institutions such as pension funds and insurance companies.

The London Stock Exchange was founded in 1773. The International Stock Exchange of the United Kingdom and the Republic of Ireland was formed from the merger of the British and Irish stock exchanges in 1973. London is the headquarters of the Stock Exchange and there are smaller (British) exchanges at Aberdeen, Belfast, Birmingham, Bradford, Bristol, Cardiff, Glasgow, Manchester and Newcastle.

The increasing threat of foreign competition – in Europe from Frankfurt and Paris – and the advent of high technology led in October 1986 to the deregulation of the Stock Exchange, an event known as the *Big Bang*. The results have included a great increase in the importance of London as an international financial centre, the virtual replacement of small partnerships by major financial institutions as Members of the Stock Exchange. Securities are now quoted on the Stock Exchange Automated Quotations (SEAQ) system and displayed on VDUs, and most deals in stocks and shares are conducted by telephone.

THE BANK OF ENGLAND

The Bank of England was established by Act of Parliament in 1694, and nationalized in 1946. The Bank's main responsibilities are:
– to execute the monetary policy of the government;
– to act as banker to the government and to arrange government borrowing and other financial operations;
– to manage the Exchange Equalization Account (EEA), comprising the UK's gold reserves, foreign exchange, ECUs (European Currency Units) and Special Drawing Rights (SDRs), and to intervene in foreign exchange markets to regulate fluctuations in the value of sterling;
– to exercise supervision over the UK's banking system;
– to provide banking facilities for the British banking system;
– and to issue notes of domestic currency. (The Royal Mint has responsibility for issuing coins.)

Notes issued by the Bank of England are backed by government and other securities rather than by gold. In England and Wales, the Bank has exclusive responsibility for issuing notes.

In Scotland, the Bank of Scotland, the Royal Bank of Scotland and the Clydesdale Bank may issue their own notes within certain strict limitations.

In Northern Ireland, the Allied Irish banks (AIB) and the Bank of Ireland (both of which have their headquarters in the Republic of Ireland), and the Northern Bank and the Ulster Bank exercise a similar right.

BANKS

The term 'clearing banks' is no longer employed in the City, although it continues to enjoy widespread popular usage. Since 1985 there have been three separate clearing companies under the umbrella of the Asociation of Payment Clearing Systems (APACS). These are:
– Cheque and Clearing Companies Ltd., which operates the high-volume paper clearings;
– CHAPS (Clearing House Automated Payment System) and Town Clearing Company, which operates the high-value same day clearings; and
– BACS (Bankers Automated Clearing Services) Ltd., which operates bulk electronic clearing.

APACS itself is responsible for currency clearings, cheque card and Eurocheque systems.

Banks and certain building societies (see below) provide banking services – current account operations, deposit and cash withdrawal facilities, and loans – to individual members of the general public and to small businesses. There are approaching 600 banks, authorized to offer these services. The banks and building societies in membership of one or more of the clearing companies (see above) are:

Abbey National, Bank of England, Bank of Scotland, Barclays Bank, Bradford and Bingley Building Society, Citibank, Clydesdale Bank, Co-operative Bank, Coutts & Co, Girobank, Halifax Building Society, Lloyds Bank, Midland Bank, National and Provincial Building Society, National Westminster Bank, Nationwide Anglia Building Society, Northern Bank, The Royal Bank of Scotland Group, Standard Chartered Bank, TSB Group, and Yorkshire Bank.

TRADE UNIONS

Founded in 1868, the Trades Union Congress (TUC) is a voluntary association of 73 affiliated trade unions. It monitors all industrial movements and legislation affecting labour and trade unions, promotes common action on general issues, and assists all trade unions in their organization. Systematic contact between the TUC and the government, the Confederation of British Industry and other bodies is maintained through the General Council and its standing committees.

PRINCIPAL UK TRADE UNIONS
(affiliated to the TUC)

Amalgamated Engineering and Electrical Union (AEEU) founded 1992 from the merger of the Amalgamated Engineering Union and the Electrical, Electronic, Telecommunication and Plumbing Union; 944 000 members.

(The former AEU was a TUC member but the EETPU was not – the new union is in membership of the TUC.)

Associated Society of Locomotive Engineers and Firemen (ASLEF), founded 1880; 19 000 members

Association of University Teachers founded 1919; 31 000 members.

Bakers, Food and Allied Workers' Union founded 1861; 34 000 members.

Banking, Insurance and Finance Union founded 1918; 162 100 members.

British Actors' Equity Association (popularly known as **Equity**); founded 1929; 45 000 members.

Broadcasting, Entertainment and Cinematograph Technicians' Union (BECTU) founded 1990 by the amalgamation of the Association of Cinematograph, Television and Allied Technicians with the Broadcasting and Entertainments Trade Alliance; 60 000 members.

Ceramic and Allied Trades Union founded 1825; 25 900 members.

Civil and Public Services Association founded 1919; 124 600 members.

Confederation of Health Service Employees (COHSE), see UNISON.

Educational Institute of Scotland founded 1851; 46 000 members.

Engineers' and Managers' Association founded 1913; 39 700 members.

Fire Brigades Union founded 1918; 48 200 members.

Furniture, Timber and Allied Trades Union founded 1971; 38 300 members.

GMB (formerly General, Municipal, Boilermakers and Allied Trades Union), founded 1982; 860 000 members.

Graphical, Paper and Media Union (GPMU) founded 1991 from the merger of the Society of Graphical and Allied Trades and the National Graphical Association; 275 000 members.

Inland Revenue Staff Federation founded 1892; 57 000 members.

Institution of Professional Civil Servants founded 1919; 90 400 members.

Iron and Steel Trades Confederation founded 1917 (the Wire Workers Union became a section of the Confederation in 1991); 39 200 members.

Manufacturing, Science and Finance Union founded 1968 (the Health Visitors' Association became a section of the union in 1990); 653 000 members.

Musicians' Union founded 1921; 37 500 members.

National and Local Government Officers' Association (NALGO), see UNISON.

National Association of Schoolmasters/ Union of Women Teachers (NAS/UWT), founded 1919, merged with UWT in 1976; 121 100 members.

National Association of Teachers in Further and Higher Education founded 1976; 80 000 members.

National Communications Union founded 1985, 154 800 members.

National Union of Civil and Public Servants founded 1988; 112 800 members.

National Union of Journalists (NUJ), founded 1907; 30 000 members.

National Union of Knitwear, Footwear and Apparel Trades founded 1991 by the amalgamation of the National Union of Hosiery and Knitwear Workers and the National Union of Footwear, Leather and Allied Trades; 64 600 members.

National Union of Mineworkers (NUM), founded 1945; 44 400 members.

National Union of Public Employees (NUPE), see UNISON.

National Union of Rail, Maritime and Transport Workers founded 1990 from the merger of the National Union of Railwaymen and National Union of Seamen; 110 000 members.

National Union of Teachers (NUT), founded 1870; 214 700 members.

Prison Officers' Association founded 1939; 27 700 members.

Society of Telecom Executives founded 1972; 27 200 members.

Transport and General Workers' Union (TGWU), founded 1897; 1 126 600 members.

Transport Salaried Staffs' Association founded 1897; 40 000 members.

UNISON , founded 1993 from a merger of the Confederation of Health Service Employees (COHSE; founded 1910), the National and Local Government Officers' Association (NALGO; founded 1905) and the National Union of Public Employees (NUPE; founded 1888); 1 400 000 members.

Union of Communication Workers founded 1920; 202 500 members.

Union of Construction, Allied Trades and Technicians (UCATT), founded 1921; 207 000 members.

Union of Shop, Distributive and Allied Workers (USDAW), founded 1947; 341 300 members.

(non-affiliated to the TUC)

Union of Democratic Mineworkers founded 1986 after breaking away from the National Union of Mineworkers; 21 500 members.

UK DEFENCE

The Sovereign, as the head of state, is technically in charge of all the Armed Forces. In reality Parliament is the decision-making body for defence. The Cabinet, and in particular the Secretary of State for Defence, is responsible to Parliament for these matters. The day-to-day running of the Armed Forces – in both peacetime and wartime – is the responsibility of the Defence Council, which is made up of members of Ministry of Defence and the Armed Forces.

PRINCIPAL SERVICE BASES, UK

Army The Army is based at the following places in the UK: Aldermaston, Aldershot, Andover, Arborfield, Ballymena, Belfast, Benbecula, Blandford, Bordon, Beaconsfield, Ballykinler, Blackdown, Bulford, Camberley, Catterick, Chatham, Chattenden, Chichester, Chilwell, Chester, Colchester, Devizes, Donnington, Deepcut, Edinburgh, Exeter, Glasgow, Hereford, Inverness (Fort George), Kirton, Kneller Hall, Larkhill, Lisburn, Lichfield, Liverpool, London, Londonderry, Lulworth, Lurgan, Middle Wallop, Ouston (Newcastle), Pirbright, Preston, Ripon, Royston, Shrewsbury, Shrivenham, South Cerney, Stirling, Strensall (York), Tern Hill, Thorney Island, Tidworth, Warminster, Woolwich, Worthy Down, Winchester, York. Bases are also maintained abroad, mainly in Germany, the Falkland Islands and Cyprus.

Royal Navy/Royal Marines The Royal Navy and the Royal Marines are based at the following places in the UK: Coulport, Devonport, Dartmouth, Deal (RM), Faslane, Greenock, Greenwich, Gosport, Lympstone (RM), Portsmouth, Portland, Poole (RM), Rosyth, South Queensferry, Weymouth.

Royal Air Force The Royal Air Force is based at the following places in the UK: Abingdon, Aberporth, Aldergrove, Benson, Bentley Priory, Boddington, Binbrook, Bracknell, Brawdy, Buchan, Brize Norton, Cranwell, Cardington, Church Fenton, Coltishall, Coningsby, Cosford, Cottesmore, Culdrose, Digby, Dishforth, Fairford, Farnborough, Finningley, Fylingdales, Hendon, Halton, High Wycombe, Honington, Leeming, Lossiemouth, Llanbedr, Linton, Lyneham, Kemble, Kinloss, Manston, Marham, Netheravon, Nocton Hall, Northolt, Newton (Notts), Odiham, Stanmore Park, Scampton, Swinderby, St. Mawgan, Waddington, Wattisham, Woodvale, West Drayton, Wittering, Valley, Yeovilton. Bases are also maintained abroad, mainly in Germany, the Falkland Islands and Cyprus.

COMPOSITION OF THE BRITISH ARMY

The recommendations of the White Paper *Options for Change* will be implemented over the next five years extensively changing the make-up of the regular units of the Army. The following list includes all the principal regular units in May 1993.

Household Cavalry
The Life Guards
The Blues and Royals (Royal Horse Guards and 1st Dragoons)

Royal Armoured Corps
1st The Queen's Dragoon Guards

The Royal Scots Dragoon Guards (Carabiniers and Greys)
The Royal Dragoon Guards
The Queen's Royal Hussars
9th/12th Royal Lancers (Prince of Wales's)
The King's Royal Hussars
The Light Dragoons
The Queen's Royal Lancers
Royal Tank Regiment (2 regiments)

Royal Regiment of Artillery
Royal Horse Artillery

Corps of Royal Engineers

Royal Corps of Signals

The Guards Division
Grenadier Guards (2 battalions)
Coldstream Guards (2 battalions)
Scots Guards (2 battalions)
Irish Guards
Welsh Guards

The Scottish Division
The Royal Scots
The Royal Highland Fusiliers
The King's Own Scottish Borderers
The Black Watch
Queen's Own Highlanders
The Gordon Highlanders
The Argyll and Sutherland Highlanders

The Queen's Division
The Princess of Wales's Own Royal Regiment (2 battalions)
The Royal Regiment of Fusiliers (2 battalions)
The Royal Anglian Regiment (2 battalions)

The King's Division
The King's Own Royal Border Regiment
The King's Regiment
The Prince of Wales' Own Regiment of Yorkshire
The Green Howards
The Royal Irish Regiment (1 general service and 9 ex-UDR battalions)
The Queen's Lancashire Regiment
The Duke of Wellington's Regiment

The Prince of Wales' Division
The Devonshire and Dorset Regiment
The Cheshire Regiment
The Royal Welsh Fusiliers
The Royal Regiment of Wales
The Gloucestershire Regiment
The Worcestershire and Sherwood Foresters
The Staffordshire Regiment
The Duke of Edinburgh's Royal Regiment

The Light Division
The Light Infantry (2 battalions)
The Royal Green Jackets (2 battalions)

The Brigade of Gurkhas
2nd King Edward VII's Own Gurkha (Goorkha) Rifles
6th Queen Elizabeth's Own Gurkha Rifles (2 battalions)
7th Duke of Edinburgh's Own Gurkha Rifles
10th Princess Mary's Own Gurkha Rifles
The Queen's Gurkha Engineers
The Queen's Gurkha Signals
Gurkha Transport Regiment

Others

Artillery, Engineers and Signals
The Parachute Regiment (3 battalions)
The Special Air Service Regiment
The Army Air Corps

The Services

Adjutant General's Corps
(incorporating the Royal Army Pay Corps,
Women's Royal Army Corps, Royal Military
Police, Military Provost Staff Corps, Royal Army
Educational Corps and Army Legal Corps)
Royal Army Chaplain's Department
Royal Corps of Transport
Royal Army Medical Corps
Royal Army Ordnance Corps
Corps of Royal Electrical and Mechanical Engineers
Royal Engineers Postal and Courier Service
Royal Army Veterinary Corps
Small Arms School Corps
Royal Army Dental Corps
Royal Pioneer Corps
Intelligence Corps
Army Physical Training Corps
Army Catering Corps
Queen Alexandra's Royal Army Nursing Corps
The Gibraltar Regiment
The Royal Military Academy Sandhurst
The Royal Military School of Music

HM FORCES PERSONNEL 1993

Total, all Services	
Regular	293 500
Reserve	350 000
Regulars	
Royal Navy male	50 500
Royal Navy female	4 000
Royal Marines	7 600
Army male	137 600
Army female	7 800
RAF male	78 700
RAF female	7 300
Regular Reserves	
Royal Navy	27 500
Royal Marines	2 700
Army	188 600
RAF	44 800
Volunteer Reserves/Auxiliary Forces	
Royal Navy	5 800
Royal Marines	1 200
Territorial Army	71 300
Royal Irish Regiment (part time)	3 000
Home Service Force	2 900
RAF	2 200

SHIPS OF THE LINE

The following is a list of the ships of the line with
their type, number, function and name (with year of
commission). There are also 27 patrol and coastal
combatants, 32 mine-countermeasure vessels, and 32
other (mainly support, reserve and auxiliary)
vessels.

SUBMARINES

Polaris Trident SSBNs 4; nuclear-powered ballistic missile carriers; *Resolution* (1967), *Repulse*
(1968), *Renown* (1968), *Vanguard* (1992).

Fleet 13; nuclear-powered, attack roles;
Courageous (1971), *Sceptre* (1978), *Spartan* (1979),
Splendid (1981), *Sovereign* (1974), *Superb* (1976),
Swiftsure (1973), *Tireless* (1985), *Torbay* (1987), *Tra-
falgar* (1983), *Trenchant* (1989), *Turbulent* (1984),
Valiant (1966).

Type 2400 3; conventional power, patrol subma-
rines; *Upholder* (1989), *Ursula* (1991), *Unicorn* (1992).

Oberon Class 3; Diesel-electric power, patrol sub-
marines; *Ocelot* (1964), *Onyx* (1967), *Opossum* (1964).

GUIDED MISSILE DESTROYERS

Type 42 12; area air defence ships; *Birmingham*
(1976), *Newcastle* (1978), *Glasgow* (1977), *Exeter*
(1980), *Southampton* (1981), *Nottingham* (1983),
Liverpool (1982), *Manchester* (1982), *Gloucester*
(1985), *Edinburgh* (1985), *York* (1985), *Cardiff* (1979).

FRIGATES

Type 23 4; general purpose/anti-submarine warfare; *Norfolk* (1989), *Marlborough*, *Argyll*, *Lancaster*.

Type 22 14; anti-submarine warfare; *Battleaxe*
(1980), *Beaver* (1984), *Boxer* (1983), *Brave* (1986),
Brazen (1982), *Brilliant* (1981), *Broadsword* (1979),
Campbeltown (1989), *Chatham* (1989), *Cornwall*
(1988), *Coventry* (1988), *Cumberland* (1988), *London*
(1987), *Sheffield* (1988).

Type 21 6; anti-submarine warfare; *Active* (1977),
Alacrity (1977), *Amazon* (1974), *Ambuscade* (1975),
Arrow (1976), *Avenger* (1978).

Leander 5; anti-submarine warfare; *Ariadne*
(1973), *Charybdis* (1969), *Hermione* (1969), *Jupiter*
(1969), *Scylla* (1970).

ASW CARRIERS AND ASSAULT SHIPS

Carriers 3; anti-submarine warfare vessels; *Ark
Royal* (1985), *Invincible* (1980), *Illustrious* (1982).

Assault ships 1; landing forces; *Fearless* (1965).

COMPARATIVE TABLE OF RANKS, HM FORCES

Royal Navy	Army	Royal Air Force
Admiral of the Fleet	Field Marshal	Marshal of the RAF
Admiral	General	Air Chief Marshal
Vice Admiral	Lieutenant-General	Air Marshal
Rear Admiral	Major-General	Air Vice Marshal
Commodore	Brigadier	Air Commodore
Captain	Colonel	Group Captain
Commander	Lieutenant-Colonel	Wing Commander
Lieutenant-Commander	Major	Squadron Leader
Lieutenant	Captain	Flight Lieutenant
Sub-Lieutenant	Lieutenant	Flying Officer
Acting Sub-Lieutenant	Second Lieutenant	Pilot Officer

NB Royal Marine ranks are the same as those of the Army, but progress as far as Lieutenant-General only.

LAW AND LAW ENFORCEMENT

THE LAW IN ENGLAND AND WALES

The law of England and Wales is divided into two distinct areas; civil law – disputes between individuals – and criminal law – acts harmful to the community. The law and structure of the judicial procedure is arranged along these two lines. The judicial system of Northern Ireland is very similar to that in England and Wales – it differs only in some of the laws enacted.

CIVIL LAW

Civil law governs rights and duties between citizens. As it includes the law of contract civil law deals with important business matters such as trade, credit and insurance, but also governs more commonplace agreements. In civil cases the person injured – known in England and Wales as 'the plaintiff' – will use the law to bring an action against the defendant in a civil court, probably seeking damages (financial compensation). Another civil remedy is an injunction. In such cases the plaintiff does not seek compensation but a court order to stop the offending behaviour.

CRIMINAL LAW

Criminal law governs those situations where the accused person is said to have broken a law that has caused an injury not just to another individual, but also to the state. This law covers offences that range from murder, manslaughter, assault and sexual crimes, to offences against property such as theft, burglary and criminal damage. The purpose of the criminal law is quite different from that of civil law; the state prosecutes accused persons in a criminal court not to obtain compensation, but to punish them for what they have done.

Serious criminal cases are tried on indictment by a judge and jury, but most cases – summary offences – can be decided by magistrates, or justices of the peace, who are not lawyers and are usually unpaid. With the exception of some libel cases, a jury is never used in a civil case in Britain. In England and Wales a jury is composed of 12 impartial people, aged between 18 and 70. At the end of the case they decide if the accused is guilty or not guilty and a majority verdict, with up to two dissenters, is allowed. If the jury cannot agree, there may be a retrial.

THE COURTS

Most minor civil cases are dealt with in the County Courts. Such cases include those where the sum in dispute is less than £5000, cases where the two parties consent to County Court jurisdiction, uncontested divorces, and some bankruptcy proceedings (outside London). Civil cases pertaining to the family are dealt with in a Magistrates' Court.

The High Court of Justice is the superior civil court and is divided into three Divisions: the Chancery Division, the Queen's Bench, and the Family Division. The Chancery Division deals mainly with equity, bankruptcy and contentious probate business; the Queen's Bench is concerned with commercial and maritime law, civil cases not assigned to other courts, and appeals from the lower courts; and

the Family Division deals with family law. High Court judges sit alone to hear cases at first instance. Appeals from lower courts are heard by two or three judges, or by a single judge of the appropriate division. Further appeals for civil cases can be made to the Courts of Appeal (Civil Division) presided over by the Master of the Rolls, and may go on to the House of Lords.

Most minor criminal offences are dealt with in a Magistrates' Court, which usually consists of three lay magistrates (Justices of the Peace) sitting without a jury and advised by a legally qualified clerk of the justices. A full-time legally qualified and magistrate presides over the busier courts. These courts also deal with the preliminary proceedings of some serious cases in order to decide whether or not evidence justifies a Crown Court trial. For cases involving people under 17 there are separate juvenile courts composed of specially qualified justices.

The Crown Court deals with serious criminal offences, the sentencing of offenders from a Magistrates' Court in cases where its sentencing powers are inadequate, and appeals from the lower courts. Appeals upon a point of law, however, are made to the High Court, and may go on to the House of Lords. They are presided over by a High Court or Circuit judge, always sitting with a 12-member jury. Further appeals from the Crown Court, either against sentence or conviction, are made to the Court of Appeal (Criminal Division), presided over by the Lord Chief Justice. The next level of appeal is to the House of Lords if a point of law of general public importance is considered to be involved.

The House of Lords is the supreme judicial court for the United Kingdom. It is the ultimate court of appeal from all courts, except the Scottish criminal courts. Leave to appeal to it is not as of right and is usually reserved for important points of law. The work is executed by the Lord High Chancellor and nine Lords of Appeal. Only one case in 40 000 ever reaches them.

CROWN COURTS (England and Wales)

The Crown Courts in England and Wales are organized into six circuits and three tiers.

First tier courts are served by both High Court and Circuit judges, and are able to hear civil and criminal cases.

Second tier courts are also served by both High Court and Circuit judges but hear only criminal cases.

Third tier courts are served by Circuit judges and hear criminal cases.

The six circuits are:

Midland and Oxford Circuit
First tier courts Birmingham, Lincoln, Nottingham, Oxford, Stafford, Warwick.
Second tier courts Leicester, Northampton, Shrewsbury, Worcester.
Third tier courts Coventry, Derby, Grimsby, Hereford, Peterborough, Stoke-on-Trent, Wolverhampton.

North Eastern Circuit
First tier courts Leeds, Newcastle-upon-Tyne, Sheffield, Teesside (Middlesbrough).
Second tier court York.
Third tier courts Beverley, Doncaster, Durham, Huddersfield, Wakefield.

Police Force Areas of the United Kingdom

Police area	Headquarters
1 Avon and Somerset	Bristol
2 Bedfordshire	Bedford
3 Cambridgeshire	Huntingdon
4 Central Scotland	Stirling
5 Cheshire	Chester
6 Cleveland	Middlesbrough
7 Cumbria	Penrith
8 Derbyshire	Ripley
9 Devon and Cornwall	Exeter
10 Dorset	Dorchester
11 Dumfries and Galloway	Dumfries
12 Durham	Durham
13 Dyfed-Powys	Carmarthen
14 Essex	Chelmsford

Police area	Headquarters
15 Fife	Kirkcaldy
16 Gloucestershire	Cheltenham
17 Grampian	Aberdeen
18 Gwent	Cwmbran
19 Hampshire	Winchester
20 Hertfordshire	Welwyn Garden City
21 Humberside	Hull
22 Kent	Maidstone
23 Lancashire	Preston
24 Leicestershire	Leicester
25 Lincolnshire	Lincoln
26 Lothian and Borders	Edinburgh
27 Greater Manchester	Manchester
28 Merseyside	Liverpool
29 Metropolitan Police	London
30 Norfolk	Norwich
31 Northamptonshire	Northampton
32 Northern Scotland	Inverness
33 Northumbria	Newcastle
34 North Wales	Colwyn Bay
35 Nottinghamshire	Nottingham
36 South Wales	Bridgend
37 Staffordshire	Stafford
38 Strathclyde	Glasgow
39 Suffolk	Ipswich
40 Surrey	Guildford
41 Sussex	Lewes
42 Tayside	Dundee
43 Thames Valley	Oxford
44 Royal Ulster Constabulary	Belfast
45 Warwickshire	Warwick
46 West Mercia	Worcester
47 West Midlands	Birmingham
48 Wiltshire	Devizes
49 North Yorkshire	Northallerton
50 South Yorkshire	Sheffield
51 West Yorkshire	Wakefield

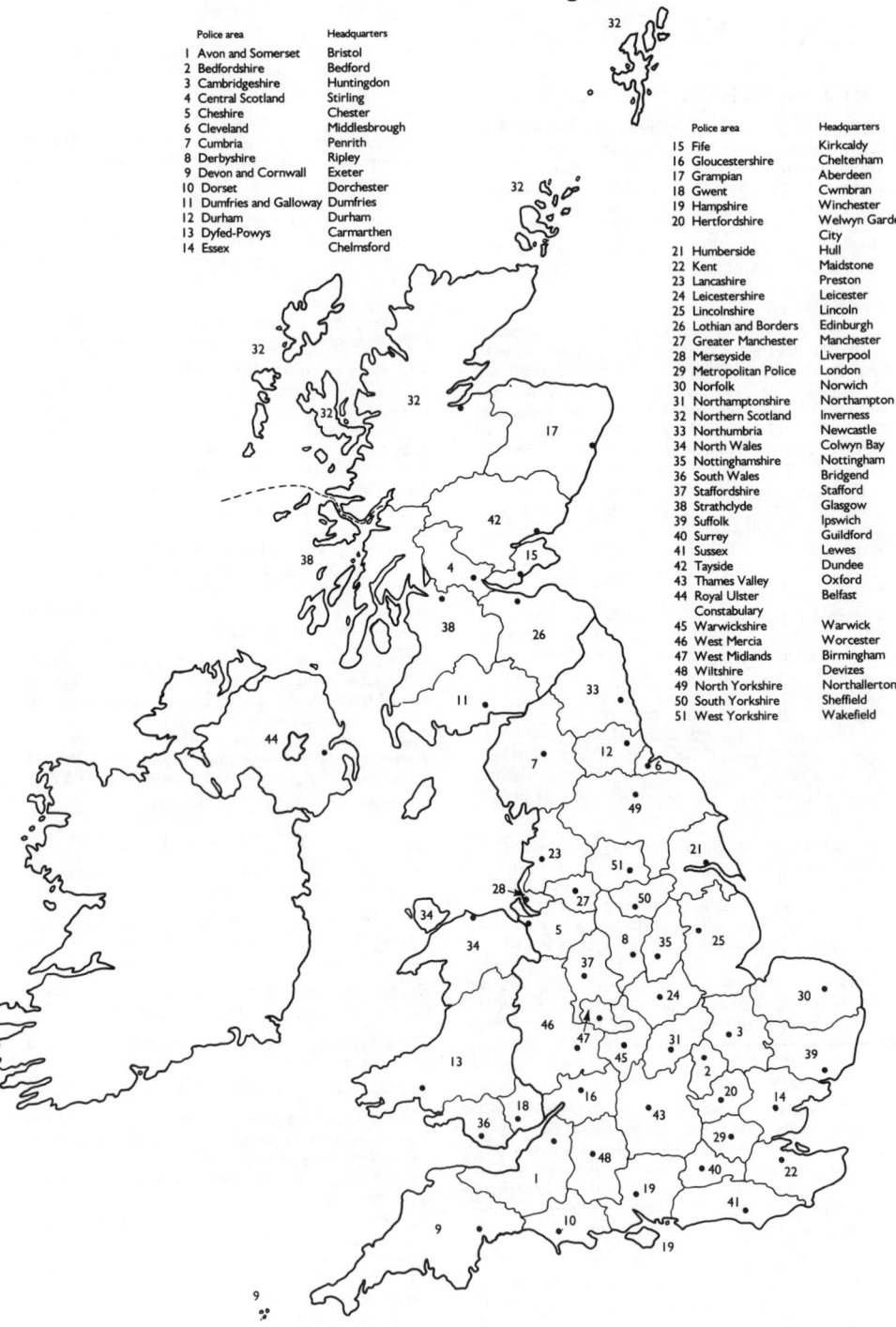

Northern Circuit
First tier courts Carlisle, Liverpool, Manchester, Preston.
Second tier courts none.
Third tier courts Barrow-in-Furness, Bolton, Burnley, Lancaster.

South Eastern Circuit
First tier courts Chelmsford, Lewes, London (Royal Courts of Justice – High Court), Norwich.
Second tier courts Ipswich, London (Central Criminal Court), Maidstone, Reading, St Albans.
Third tier courts Aylesbury, Bury St Edmunds, Cambridge, Canterbury, Chichester, Guildford, King's Lynn, London (Croydon, Harrow, Inner London, Isleworth, Kingston-upon-Thames, Knightsbridge, Middlesex Guildhall, Snaresbrook, Southwark, Wood Green), Southend.

Wales and Chester Circuit
First tier courts Caernarfon, Cardiff, Chester, Mold, Swansea.
Second tier courts Carmarthen, Merthyr Tydfil, Newport, Welshpool.
Third tier courts Dolgellau, Haverfordwest, Knutsford, Warrington.

Western Circuit
First tier courts Bristol, Exeter, Truro, Winchester.
Second tier courts Dorchester, Gloucester, Plymouth.
Third tier courts Barnstaple, Bournemouth, Devizes, Newport (Isle of Wight), Portsmouth, Salisbury, Southampton, Swindon, Taunton.

SCOTTISH LAW

Scotland's judicial system and laws are quite different from those in England and Wales. It is characterized by the system of public prosecution – independent of the police – and headed by the Lord Advocate. The Lord Advocate – through the Crown Office – is responsible for bringing prosecutions in the High Court, sheriff courts and district courts.

The High Court of Justiciary is the senior court for criminal cases, and tries all serious crimes such as murder, rape, treason, etc. It is also the final appeal court for any indictment trial. Prosecutions are conducted in court by a law officer or an advocate-depute. No appeal from the High Court of Justiciary can be made to the House of Lords.

District courts deal with minor summary offences and are administered by local government authorities. Prosecution is carried out by procurators-fiscals – lawyers and full-time civil servants – and presided over by lay justices (in Glasgow by stipendiary magistrates).

Most civil cases are tried in the sheriff courts. Sheriffs principals head the six sheriffdoms of Scotland, which are divided into sheriff court districts and administered by sheriffs. Sheriffs principals and sheriffs have equal powers in criminal cases, and in serious cases they sit with a 15-member jury, who may return a third verdict of 'not proven'. An appeal from the decision of a sheriff court can be made to the Court of Session.

The Court of Session in Edinburgh is divided into two Houses, the Inner House and the Outer House. The Outer House hears more serious civil cases in the first instance. The Inner House is divided into two, and hears appeals from both the sheriff courts and the Outer House. Further appeals from the Inner House can be made to the House of Lords.

SCOTTISH SHERIFFDOMS

Grampian, Highland and Islands
Court districts Aberdeen and Stonehaven; Banff and Peterhead; Elgin; Fort William; Inverness, Lochmaddy, Portree, Stornoway, Dingwall, Tain, Wick and Dornoch; Kirkwall and Lerwick.

Lothian and Borders
Court districts Edinburgh; Haddington; Jedburgh and Duns; Linlithgow; Peebles; Selkirk.

North Strathclyde
Court districts Dumbarton; Dunoon; Greenock; Kilmarnock; Oban and Campbeltown; Paisley.

Glasgow and Strathkelvin
Court district Glasgow.

South Strathclyde, Dumfries and Galloway
Court districts Airdrie; Ayr; Dumfries; Hamilton; Lanark; Stranraer and Kirkcudbright.

Tayside, Central and Fife
Court districts Arbroath and Forfar; Dundee; Perth; Falkirk; Stirling; Alloa; Cupar; Dunfermline; Kirkcaldy.

THE POLICE

The 52 police forces of the UK have responsibility for law enforcement in their own area. These areas are usually individual English or Welsh administrative counties, or Scottish regions, or groups of counties (see map opposite). The Metropolitan Police Force and the City of London Police are responsible for London's law enforcement. The Royal Ulster Constabulary is responsible for law enforcement in Northern Ireland.

Each force is maintained by a police authority, which in England and Wales is currently composed of a committee of local councillors and magistrates. (Changes in this system are proposed.) In Scotland regional and island councils are the authorities. However, the Home Secretary has responsibility for the Metropolitan Force, while the authority for the Royal Ulster Constabulary is the Secretary of State for Northern Ireland.

Police Hierachy (from the highest rank downwards)
Chief Constable
Deputy Chief Constable
Asssistant Chief Constable
Chief Superintendent
Superintendent
Chief Inspector
Inspector
Sergeant
Constable

Metropolitan Police
Metropolitan Commissioner
Deputy Commissioner
Assistant Commissioner
Deputy Assistant Commissioner
Commander
Chief Superintendent
Superintendent
Chief Inspector
Inspector
Sergeant
Constable

TRANSPORT

PASSENGER TRANSPORT 1961–90
(thousand million passenger km)

	1961	1971	1981	1990*
Air	0.9	1.9	3.0	5.0
Rail	38.9	36.0	34.0	41.0
Road	219.0	339.1	456.1	614.0
buses and coaches	66.9	51.0	42.0	41.0
cars, taxis and				
motorcycles	141.9	284.0	410.0	568.0
bicycles	10.0	4.0	4.0	5.0

* provisional figures

NUMBER OF LICENSED VEHICLES
(thousands)

	1986	1987	1988	1990
Private motor cars	16 981	17 421	18 432	21 952
Motor cycles, scooters/mopeds	1 065	978	912	750
Goods vehicles	593	609	647	795
Public passenger vehicles	125	129	132	109

GOODS TRANSPORT (1990)

Tonne kilometres (thousand millions)	
Road	136.2
Rail (British Rail only)	15.8
Water (coastwise oil products)*	32.3
Water (other)*	20.2
Pipelines (excluding gases)	11.0
Total	215.5

Tonnes (million tonnes)	
Road	1749
Rail (British Rail only)	141
Water (coastwise oil products)*	44
Water (other coastwise products)*	105
Pipelines (excluding gases)	121
Total	2160

* coastwise includes all sea traffic within the British Isles. 'Other' means coastwise traffic plus inland waterways and one-port traffic.

MAJOR BRITISH AIRPORTS

Airport	Terminal passengers handled per annum (1991)
London Heathrow	40 250 000
London Gatwick	18 690 000
Manchester	10 101 000
Glasgow	4 150 000
Birmingham	3 250 000
Edinburgh	2 340 000
Belfast (Aldergrove)	2 170 000
Luton	1 960 000
Aberdeen	1 960 000
London Stansted	1 680 000
Jersey	1 640 000
Newcastle	1 530 000
East Midlands	1 140 000
Bristol	780 000
Guernsey	750 000

The following airports are also served by scheduled passenger flights and have been designated as Customs airports:

Blackpool, Bournemouth (Hurn), Bristol, Cambridge, Cardiff, Coventry, Exeter, Humberside, Kent International (Manston), Liverpool, London City (available only to aircraft with short landing and take-off characteristics), Norwich, Plymouth (Roborough), Prestwick, Ronaldsway (Isle of Man), Southampton (Eastleigh), Southend, Sumburgh (Shetland), Teesside.

Customs facilities are also available at Alderney, Biggin Hill, Lydd and Shoreham.

ROAD ACCIDENTS 1965–90

Year	Killed	Injured
1965	7952	389 985
1970	7499	355 869
1975	6366	318 584
1980	6010	323 000
1985	5165	312 359
1990	5217	335 924

ROAD LENGTHS IN APRIL 1991

Road	England	Wales	Scotland	N.Ireland	UK
Public roads	274 856 km	33 359 km	51 816 km	24 157 km	384 188 km
Trunk roads (incl. motorways)	10 544 km	1 696 km	3 146 km	2 213 km	17 599 km
Motorways*	2 721 km	119 km	257 km	111 km	3 210 km

* Additionally there are 48 miles (77 km) of local-authority motorway in England and 15 miles (24 km) in Scotland

AIR TRAFFIC BETWEEN THE UK AND ABROAD

Flights (thousands)

	1980	1982	1984	1986	1988	1990
UK airlines scheduled services	166.1	143.5	151.3	177.5	216.9	271.0
UK airlines non-scheduled services	153.9	176.3	214.0	198.8	225.5	207.9
Overseas airlines scheduled services	157.8	154.3	160.9	195.8	249.8	294.8
Overseas airlines non-scheduled services	29.1	37.3	40.2	43.6	43.0	45.5
Total	**506.9**	**511.4**	**566.3**	**615.8**	**735.2**	**819.2**

Passengers carried (thousands)

UK airlines scheduled services	13 901.0	12 214.7	13 174.2	15 082.9	19 237.6	25 316.8
UK airlines non-scheduled services	11 195.3	13 216.6	16 643.7	12 929.7	23 062.1	19 679.1
Overseas airlines scheduled services	14 900.9	15 520.5	17 623.0	19 409.5	25 029.3	28 224.4
Overseas airlines non-scheduled services	2 647.4	3 180.1	3 713.9	4 186.0	4 086.5	4 187.9
Total	**42 644.6**	**44 131.9**	**51 154.8**	**51 608.1**	**71 415.5**	**77 408.2**

RAILWAYS

British Rail The British Railways Board – which came into being in 1963 – is currently responsible for providing railway services in Great Britain. In the late 1980s and early 1990s, British Rail was divided into six distinct business sectors: InterCity, Network SouthEast, Regional Railways (comprising all other passenger services), Railfreight Distribution (which is responsible for heavy haulage), Trainload (which is responsible for other freight), and European Passenger Services Ltd., which will be responsible for rail services through the Channel Tunnel.

Between 1958 and 1968 the rail system was reduced under the Beeching Plan, which cut the number of stations from just under 5000 to about 2500. However, over the past decade rail travel has been experiencing a modest but steady growth. Between 1981 and 1993 over 180 stations have been opened: some have been relocated, but most are either former stations that have been reopened or entirely new stations. This expansion has been made possible, in part, by the initiative of local authorities, but also by a 1981 amendment to the Transport Act that allows BR to open stations on an experimental basis and close them at short notice if not commercially viable. Since 1981 only one new or reopened station (Corby in Northamptonshire) has had to be closed in this manner. All the other new stations have either been profitable ventures in new centres of population (for example Milton Keynes) or else are run in partnership with local authorities to help stimulate rail travel and to relieve road congestion. Examples of this are the Robin Hood Line in Nottinghamshire, the Aberdare and Mountain Ash line and the Maesteg line in South Wales, and the Bicester line in Oxfordshire.

Rail statistics British Rail now has 2472 passenger stations (2615 stations in all including freight stations). BR maintains a total route length of 16 583 km (10 304 mi) – of which 4546 km (2825 mi) are electrified – and a total track length of 37 809 km (23 494 mi). BR maintains 1752 diesel trains, 278 electric trains and 197 High Speed trains. In 1990 762.4 million passenger journeys were made.

In Northern Ireland, the Northern Ireland Railways Company – a private company –is responsible for passenger and freight services. The company maintains 332 km (206 mi) of route and 553 km (343 mi) of track, with a total of 57 stations. In 1990, 5.2 million passenger journeys were made.

Privatization A programme of rail privatization was announced in 1992. While the lines and maintenance are to be the responsibility of a track authority, services and groups of services are to be offered up for franchise to private companies. The first seven services to be offered for privatization are:
– the InterCity East Coast line;
– the InterCity Great Western main line;
– the InterCity Gatwick express;
– the Isle of Wight line;
– the southwestern division of Network SouthEast;
– the London-Tilbury-Southend line;
– ScotRail.
A second group of services was added to the list in 1993:
– the InterCity West Coast main line;
– the InterCity Midland main line;
– InterCity Anglia;
– InterCity Cross Country;
– Thames Line;
– Chiltern Line;
– Northampton and North London Lines;
– West Anglia and Great Northern;
– Great Eastern;
– Thameslink;
– Kent Services;
– South London and Sussex Coast;
– North East Region;
– Merseyside Electric Services;
– Central Region;
– South Wales and West region;
– Cardiff Valleys Lines.

Channel Tunnel The private-sector Franco-British consortium Eurotunnel has been awarded the concession to operate (until 2042) a cross-Channel rail link. Building work on the tunnel was completed by TransManche Ltd. in spring 1993. At the time of writing, the construction of the track and infrastructure had not been completed. The project comprises three tunnels: two tunnels for high-speed trains and a third tunnel between them for ventilation and maintenance. The main terminals will be St Pancras and, initially, Waterloo (London) and Gare du Nord (Paris) and Gare Centrale (Brussels). Through passenger services are expected to begin in mid-1994.

EDUCATION

NUMBER OF PUBLIC-SECTOR EDUCATIONAL ESTABLISHMENTS

	United Kingdom	England	Wales	Scotland	N. Ireland
Nursery	1 364	566	54	659	85
Primary	24 135	19 047	1 717	2 372	999
Secondary	4 790	3 897	230	424	239
Non-maintained	2 508	2 289	71	131	17
Special	1 824	1 380	61	337	46
Universities**	92	‡71	*7	12	2
Other major establishments†	644	416	37	165	26

* including the university colleges of the University of Wales; ‡ including the Open University; ** the former polytechnics and a number of other institutions became universities in 1992–93; † including maintained, assisted and grant-aided instititions. Statistics for schools are for 1991; statistics for universities and other major establishments are for 1993.

NUMBER OF PUPILS AND TEACHERS 1991

	Pupils	Teachers	Pupils per teacher
Nursery	60 400	2 800	22
Primary	4 812 300	219 200	22
Secondary	3 473 300	229 100	15
Special schools	112 500	19 400	6
Total	9 062 300	526 800	17

THE NATIONAL CURRICULUM

A key element of the 1988 Education Act is the *national curriculum*, which should be fully implemented by 1996. The national curriculum defines three *core subjects* – English (or Welsh), mathematics and science – and seven *foundation subjects* – history, geography, music, art, technology, a modern language (at secondary level) and PE – to be studied by all pupils. State schools must follow the national curriculum. Independent schools need not do so, but many are choosing to follow it fairly closely.

The original intention was that national curriculum subjects should occupy 70% of the timetable, and the Department of Education and Science (DES) laid down percentages of the school timetable to be spent on each subject. Wider educational topics such as social education, political and economic awareness, and careers education were also to be studied. Religious education was to be compulsory and schools were to be free to offer additional subjects.

After protests the DES agreed the necessity for flexibility and asked schools to tailor courses according to pupils' needs. More room was also found for additional subjects including extra languages, business studies, classics and home economics. But making more timetable space for other subjects meant changing the original intention that all core and foundation subjects must be compulsory until the age of 16. Pupils will now study either art or music, and either history or geography, from the age of 14, while technology (a compulsory subject until the age of 16) need not be studied to GCSE standard.

Education under the national curriculum divides a pupil's time into four key stages: 5–7 years old, 8–11, 12–14 and 15–16. Each key stage has standard assessment tasks and attainment targets, defining the knowledge and skills pupils should achieve at the end of each stage.

HIGHER EDUCATION

The 1992 Further and Higher Education Act brought fundamental changes to the delivery and structure of higher education in the UK. Under the Act, the so-called 'binary line' separating universities and polytechnics disappeared, and polytechnics were empowered to award their own degrees (a right previously reserved for universities), and have the right to call themselves universities. During 1992 and 1993 all of the polytechnics and several of the Scottish entral institutions had changed their titles to universities (see listing). There are now two major sectors of education provision – the universities and the colleges and institutes of higher education (CHEs and IHEs). The Council for National Academic Awards (CNAA), which used to validate and accredit the courses of CHEs and IHEs, has been abolished. Its accrediting function has been taken over by the universities including the Open University.

DEGREE-AWARDING INSTITUTIONS

The following alphabetical list of universities details each institution's year of foundation (as a university), location, and full-time student population as at 1992:

UNIVERSITIES

University of Aberdeen (1495), Aberdeen, Scotland AB9 1FX. Student nos: 6580.

Anglia Polytechnic University (1992), Victoria Road South, Chelmsford, Essex, CM1 1LL. Student nos: 4230. There are campuses at Chelmsford, Cambridge and Brentwood.

Aston University (1966), Aston Triangle, Birmingham, B4 7ET. Student nos: 3930.

University of Bath (1966), Claverton Down, Bath, BA2 7AY. Student nos: 4420.

The Queen's University of Belfast (1908), University Road, Belfast, Northern Ireland, BT7 1NN. Student nos: 9520.

University of Birmingham (1900), PO Box 363, Birmingham B15 2TT. Student nos: 10 420.
Associate Colleges: Newman College (Birmingham), Westhill College (Birmingham).

University of Central England in Birmingham (1992), Perry Barr, Birmingham, B42 2SU. Student nos: 8750.

Bournemouth University (1992), Poole House, Fern Barrow, Poole, Dorset, BH12 5BB. Student nos: 6680.

University of Bradford (1966), Richmond Road, Bradford, West Yorkshire, BD7 1DP. Student nos: 5370.
Associate College: Bradford and Bingley Community College.

University of Brighton (1992), Lewes Road, Brighton, BN2 4AT. Student nos: 7260. There are campuses in Brighton and Eastbourne.

University of Bristol (1909), Senate House, Bristol, BS8 1TH. Student nos: 9270.

University of the West of England, Bristol (1992), Coldharbour Lane, Frenchay, Bristol, BS16 1QY. Student nos: 8960.

Brunel, the University of West London (1966), Uxbridge, Middlesex, UB8 3PH. Student nos: 3880. There are two main sites – one at Uxbridge, the other at Runnymede.

University of Buckingham (1976), Buckingham, MK18 1EG. Student nos: 823. (Independent of state finance. Degree courses last two, rather than three, years.)

University of Cambridge (1284 – date of foundation of Peterhouse), Cambridge CB2 1QJ. Student nos: 14 000.
Colleges, Halls and Societies: Peterhouse (1284), Clare (1326), Pembroke (1347), Gonville and Caius (1348), Trinity Hall (1350), Corpus Christi (1352), King's (1441), Queens' (1448), St Catharine's (1473), Jesus (1496), Christ's (1505), St John's (1511), Magdalene (1542), Trinity (1546), Emmanuel (1584), Sidney Sussex (1596), Downing (1800), Fitzwilliam (1869), Girton (1869), Newnham (1871), Selwyn (1882), Hughes Hall (1885), Homerton (1894), St Edmund's

(1896), New Hall (1954), Churchill (1959), Wolfson (1965), Lucy Cavendish (1965), Robinson (1977).

City University (1966), Northampton Square, London, EC1V 0HB. Student nos: 3920.

Coventry University (1992), Priory Street, Coventry, CV1 5FB. Student nos: 5340.

Cranfield Institute of Technology (1969), Cranfield, Bedford, MK43 1EG. Student nos: 2300.
Colleges of the Institute: Silsoe College (Bedford) and the Royal Military College of Science, Shrivenham (Wiltshire).

De Montfort University (1992), PO Box 143, Leicester, LE1 9BH. Student nos: 10 160. There are campuses at Leicester and Milton Keynes.

University of Derby (1992), Keddleston Road, Derby DE3 1GB. Student nos: 3800.

University of Dundee (1967), Dundee, Scotland, DD1 4HN. Student nos: 5600.

University of Durham (1832), Old Shire Hall, Durham DH1 3HP. Student nos: 6090.
Colleges and Schools (in order of foundation): University, Hatfield, Grey, St Chad's, St John's, St Mary's, St Aidan's, St Hild and St Bede, Neville's Cross, St Cuthbert's Society, Van Mildert, Trevelyan, Collingwood, Ushaw, Graduate Society, Joint University College of Teesside (maintained with the University of Teesside).

University of East Anglia (1963), Norwich, NR4 7TJ. Student nos: 5130.

University of East London (1992), Romford Road, London, E15 4LZ. Student nos: 7110. There are three main sites at Barking, Dagenham and Newham.

University of Edinburgh (1583), Old College, Edinburgh, Scotland EH8 9YL. Student nos: 12 510.

University of Essex (1964), Wivenhoe Park, Colchester, Essex, CO4 3SQ. Student nos: 4070.

University of Exeter (1955), The Queen's Drive, Exeter, EX4 4QJ. Student nos: 4020.
Associate Colleges: St Loye's School of Occupational Therapy (Exeter), the College of St Mark and St John (Plymouth).

University of Glamorgan (1992), Pontypridd, Mid Glamorgan, CF37 1DL. Student nos: 5780.

Glasgow Caledonian University (1992), 70 Cowcaddens Road, Glasgow G4 OBA. Student nos: 10 500.

University of Glasgow (1451), Glasgow, Scotland G12 8QQ. Student nos: 12 780.

University of Greenwich (1993), Wellington Street, Woolwich, London, SE18 6PF. Student nos: 8390. There are six main sites including campuses at Greenwich, Avery Hill and Dartford.

Heriot-Watt University (1966), Riccarton, Edinburgh, Scotland, EH14 4AS. Student nos: 7790.
Associate colleges: Moray House College, Edinburgh College of Art and Scottish College of Textiles in Galashiels.

University of Hertfordshire (1992), College Lane, Hatfield, Hertfordshire, AL10 9AB. Student nos: 9260. There are campuses at Hatfield, Watford and Hertford.

University of Huddersfield (1992), Queensgate, Huddersfield, HD1 3DH. Student nos: 6880.

University of Hull (1954), Hull, HU6 7RX. Student nos: 6670.
Associate College: Bishop Grosseteste College (in Lincoln).

University of Humberside (1992), Cottingham Road, Hull, HU6 7RT. Student nos: 7440. There are campuses in Hull and Grimsby.

University of Keele (1962), Keele, Staffordshire, ST5 5BG. Student nos: 4370.

University of Kent at Canterbury (1965), Canterbury, Kent, CT2 7NZ. Student nos: 5310.

Kingston University (1992), Penrhyn Road, Kingston upon Thames, Surrey, KT1 2EE. Student nos: 7930.

University of Central Lancashire (1992), Preston, Lancashire, PR1 2TQ. Student nos: 7990.

University of Lancaster (1964), University House, Lancaster, LA1 4YW. Student nos: 5750.
Associate Colleges: Charlotte Mason College of Education (in Ambleside), Edge Hill College of Higher Education (in Ormskirk), S. Martin's College, Lancaster.

University of Leeds (1904), Leeds, LS2 9JT. Student nos: 13 610.
Associate Colleges: Bretton Hall (near Wakefield), Doncaster College, North Riding College (in Scarborough), Pinderfields College of Physiotherapy (Wakefield), the College of Ripon and York St John, Trinity and All Saints' College (in Horsforth).

Leeds Metropolitan University (1992), Calverley Street, Leeds, LS1 3HE. Student nos: 9310.

University of Leicester (1957), University Road, Leicester, LE1 7RH. Student nos: 6890.

University of Liverpool (1903), PO Box 147, Liverpool, L69 3BX. Student nos: 10 420.
Associate Colleges: Chester College, Liverpool Institute of Higher Education.

Liverpool John Moores University (1992), 70 Mount Pleasant, Liverpool, L3 5UX. Student nos: 11 020.

University of London (1836), Senate House, Malet Street, London WC1E 7HU. Student nos: 51 400.
Colleges and Schools: Birkbeck College; Heythrop College; Goldsmith's College; Imperial College of Science, Technology and Medicine; King's College; London School of Economics and Political Science; Queen Mary and Westfield College; Royal Academy of Music; Royal College of Music; Royal Holloway; Royal Veterinary College; School of Oriental and African Studies; School of Pharmacy; School of Slavonic and East European Studies; Trinity College of Music; University College; Wye College (based at a campus at Ashford, Kent).
Medical Schools: Charing Cross and Westminster Medical School, King's College of Medicine and Dentistry, London Hospital Medical School, Royal Free Hospital School of Medicine, St Bartholomew's Hospital Medical College, St George's Hospital Medical School, St Mary's Hospital Medical School, United Medical and Dental Schools of Guy's and St Thomas's Hospitals, University College and Middlesex School of Medicine.
Institutes: Courtauld Institute of Art, Institute of Commonwealth Studies, Institute of Education, Institute of Germanic Studies, Institute of United States Studies, Warburg Institute.

London Guildhall University (1993), 117–119 Hounsditch, London EC3a 7BU. Student nos: 5500.

Loughborough University of Technology (1966), Loughborough, Leicestershire, LE11 3TU. Student nos: 6970.

University of Manchester (1851), Manchester M13 9PL. Student nos: 13 100.

University of Manchester Institute of Science and Technology (UMIST; 1824), PO Box 88, Manchester M60 1QD. Student nos: 5230.

Manchester Metropolitan University (1992), All Saints, Manchester, M15 6BH. Student nos: 18 120. There are campuses in Manchester, Crewe and Alsager.

Middlesex University (1992), Bramley Road, Oakwood, Middlesex, N14 4XS. Student nos: 9260. There are five main sites with campuses at Barnet, Hendon, Enfield and Trent Park.

Napier University (1992), 219 Colinton Road, Edinburgh EH14 1DJ. Student nos: 5420.

University of Newcastle upon Tyne (1852), Kensington Terrace, Newcastle upon Tyne, NE1 7RU. Student nos: 9730.

University of North London (1992), Holloway Road, London, N7 8DB. Student nos: 6080.

University of Northumbria at Newcastle (1992), Ellison Road, Newcastle upon Tyne, NE1 8ST. Student nos: 9640. There is also a site in Carlisle.

University of Nottingham (1948), University Park, Nottingham, NG7 2RD. Student nos: 9520. There is one campus and a smaller site at Sutton Bonington.

Nottingham Trent University (1992), Burton Street, Nottingham, NG1 4BU. Student nos: 10 980.

The Open University (1969), Walton Hall, Milton Keynes, Buckinghamshire, MK7 6AA. Student nos: 72 600. (The university is non-residential. Tuition is by correspondence and special radio, TV and video programmes, short residential schools and locally-based tutors.)

University of Oxford (1249 – date of foundation of University College), Oxford OX1 2JD. Student nos: 14 450.
Colleges, Halls and Societies: University (1249), Balliol (1263), Merton (1264), St Edmund Hall (1278), Exeter (1314), Oriel (1326), Queen's (1341), New College (1379), Lincoln (1427), Magdalen (1428), All Souls (1438), Brasenose (1509), Corpus Christi (1517), Christ Church (1546), Trinity (1554), St John's (1555), Jesus (1571), Wadham (1610), Pembroke (1624), Worcester (1714), Hertford (1740), Manchester (1786), Regent's Park (1810), Keble (1870), Lady Margaret Hall (1878), Somerville (1879), Mansfield (1886), St Hugh's (1886), St Hilda's (1893), St Anne's (1893), Campion (1896), St Benet's (1897), Greyfriars (1910), St Peter's (1929), St Antony's (1953), Nuffield (1958), St Catherine's (1962), Linacre House (1962), St Cross (1965), Wolfson (1965), Green (1979), Rewley House (1990).

Oxford Brookes University (1992), Headington, Oxford, OX3 0BP. Student nos: 7610.

University of Paisley (1992), High Street, Paisley, Renfrewshire PA1 2BE. Student nos: 3890.

University of Plymouth (1992), Drake Circus, Plymouth, PL4 8AA. Student nos: 9030. There are four main sites with campuses at Plymouth, Exmouth, Exeter and Newton Abbot.

University of Portsmouth (1992), University House, Winston Churchill Avenue, Portsmouth, PO1 2UP. Student nos: 8650.

University of Reading (1926), PO Box 217, Reading, Berkshire, RG6 2AH. Student nos: 8240.

The Robert Gordon University (1992), Schoolhill, Aberdeen AB9 1FR. Student nos: 4600.

University of St Andrews (1411), College Gate, St Andrews, Scotland KY16 9AJ. Student nos: 4200. *Colleges*: United College of St Salvator and St Leonard, College of St Mary.

University of Salford (1967), Salford, M5 3WT. Student nos: 4920.

University of Sheffield (1905), Western Bank, Sheffield, S10 2TN. Student nos: 10 730.

Sheffield Hallam University (1992), Pond Street, Sheffield, S1 1WB. Student nos: 12 140.

South Bank University (1992), Borough Road, London SE1 0AA. Student nos: 8800.

University of Southampton (1952), Highfield, Southampton, SO9 5NH. Student nos: 7900. *Associate Colleges*: La Sainte Union College of Higher Education (Souhampton), West Sussex Institute of Higher Education (in Bognor Regis and Chichester).

Staffordshire University (1992), College Road, Stoke-on-Trent, ST4 2DE. Student nos: 7330. There are campuses at Stoke and Stafford.

University of Stirling (1967), Stirling, Scotland, FK9 4LA. Student nos: 3800.

University of Strathclyde (1964), 16 Richmond Street, Glasgow, Scotland, G1 1XQ. Student nos: 8500.

University of Sunderland (1992), Edinburgh Building, Chester Road, Sunderland SR1 3SD. Student nos: 7160.

University of Surrey (1966), Guildford, Surrey, GU2 5XH. Student nos: 4200. *Associate Colleges*: Roehampton Institute of Higher Education, St Mary's College (Twickenham).

University of Sussex (1961), Sussex House, Falmer, Brighton, BN1 9RH. Student nos: 5680.

University of Teesside (1992), Borough Road, Middlesbrough, Cleveland, TS1 3BA. Student nos: 5410. (The University also maintains the Joint University College on Teesside at Stockton with the University of Durham.)

Thames Valley University (1992), St Mary's Road, London W5. Student nos: 15 000. There are four main sites at Ealing, Slough, Queen Charlotte's Hospital in Chiswick and the London College of Music in Westminster.

University of Ulster (1965), Coleraine, County Londonderry, Northern Ireland, BT52 1SA. Student nos: 10 050. There are two main sites – one at Coleraine, the other at Jordanstown, near Belfast.

University of Wales (1893), Cathays Park, Cardiff, CF1 3NS. Student nos: 23 340. *Colleges*:
University College, Aberystwyth (1872), King's Street, Aberystwyth SY23 2AX.
University College of North Wales (1884), Bangor, Gwynedd LL57 2DG.
University of Wales College of Cardiff (1883), POB 68, Cardiff, CF1 3XA.

St David's University College (1822), Lampeter, Dyfed SA48 7ED.
University College of Swansea (1920), Singleton Park, Swansea, SA2 8PP.
University of Wales College of Medicine (1931), Heath Park, Cardiff CF4 4XN.

University of Warwick (1965), Coventry, CV4 7AL. Student nos: 7300.

University of Westminster (1992), 309 Regent Street, London, W1R 8AL. Student nos: 7800. There are three main sites including a campus in Harrow.

University of Wolverhampton (1992), Wulfrana Street, Wolverhampton, WV1 1SB. Student nos: 8820. There are five main sites including campuses in Wolverhampton, Dudley and Walsall.

University of York (1963), Heslington, York, YO1 5DD. Student nos: 4630.

OTHER DEGREE-AWARDING INSTITUTIONS
The following also have degree-awarding status:

Bath College of Higher Education, Newton Park, Bath, BA2 9BN. Student nos: 1450.

Bolton Institute of Higher Education, Deane Road, Bolton, BL3 5YL. Student nos: 2200.

Cheltenham and Gloucester College of Higher Education, The Park, Cheltenham, Gloucestershire, GL50 2RN. Student nos: 3000.

Dundee Institute of Technology, Bell Street, Dundee, DD1 IHG. Student nos: 1920.

Luton College of Higher Education, Park Square, Luton LU1 3JU. Student nos: 1000.

Royal College of Art, Kensington Gore, London SW7 2EU. Student nos: 700.

Queen Margaret College, Clerwood Terrace, Edinburgh EH12 8TS. Student nos: 1700.

West Surrey College of Art and Design, Falkner Road, The Hart, Farnham, Surrey GU9 7DS. Student

---

VOCATIONAL QUALIFICATIONS

The providers of vocational qualifications include:
Business and Technology Education Council (BTEC) BTEC offers courses that cover a wide range of career-related subjects from agriculture or business to medical laboratory science or performing arts. Generally recognized comparisons equate a BTEC/SCOTVEC national diploma to A levels/Highers.
Scottish Vocational Education Council (SCOTVEC) SCOTVEC is the equivalent of BTEC in Scotland.
City and Guilds of London Institute (C&G) C&G qualifications exist in over 400 subjects including hairdressing, community care, construction and catering. C&G traditionally offered craft-level qualifications to apprentices, but some courses at higher levels are now available.
The Royal Society of Arts (RSA) The RSA offers schemes – the term they use rather than courses – mainly in the business and secretarial areas, including accounts, book keeping, clerical and office skills, typing, computing and office technology.
Pitman The Pitman colleges are important providers of courses in secretarial subjects.
London Chamber of Commerce and Industry (LCCI) A range of secretarial and allied subjects is covered by the examinations of the LCCI.

RELIGION

The doctrines and histories of the major religions are described in the Beliefs and Ideas chapter.

THE ANGLICAN COMMUNION

About 55% of the population of the UK nominally belongs to the Churches of the Anglican Communion (the Church of England, the Church in Wales, the Episcopal Church in Scotland and the Church of Ireland). However, only 4% of the population are practising Anglicans. The Archbishop of Canterbury is Primate of All England.

Archbishops of Canterbury
(since the Reformation)
Thomas Cranmer (1532–1555)
Reginald Pole (under whom allegiance to Rome was briefly restored; 1555–1558)
Matthew Parker (1559–1575)
Edmund Grindal (1575–1583)
John Whitgift (1583–1604)
Richard Bancroft (1604–1610)
George Abbot (1611–1633)
William Laud (1633–1645)
Interregnum (1645–1660)
William Juxon (1660–1663)
Gilbert Sheldon (1663–1677)
William Sancroft (1677–1690)
John Tillotson (1691–1694)
Thomas Tenison (1694–1715)
William Wake (1715–1737)
John Potter (1737–1747)
Thomas Herring (1747–1757)
Matthew Hutton (1757–1758)
Thomas Secker (1758–1768)
Frederick Cornwallis (1768–1783)
John Moore (1783–1805)
Charles Manners Sutton (1805–1828)
William Howley (1828–1848)
John Bird Sumner (1848–1862)
Charles Thomas Longley (1862–1868)
Archibald Campbell Tait (1868–1882)
Edward White Benson (1883–1896)
Frederick Temple (1896–1902)
Randall Thomas Davidson (1903–1928)
Cosmo Gordon Lang (1928–1942)
William Temple (1942–1944)
Geoffrey Francis Fisher (1945–1961)
Arthur Michael Ramsay (1961–1974)
Frederick Donald Coggan (1974–1980)
Robert Alexander Kennedy Runcie (1980–1991)
George Leonard Carey (1991–)

The Church in Wales elects one of its six diocesan bishops to be Archbishop of Wales. In future, the Bishop of Llandaff will concurrently be Archbishop of Wales. The Episcopal Church of Scotland elects one of its seven diocesan bishops to be Primus.

THE ROMAN CATHOLIC CHURCH

About 9% of the population of the UK belongs to the Roman Catholic Church. The head of the Church in England and Wales is the Archbishop of Westminster, and in Scotland, the Archbishop of St Andrews and Edinburgh.

Archbishops of Westminster
Cardinal Nicholas Wiseman 1850–65
Cardinal Henry Edward Manning 1865–92
Cardinal Herbert Vaughan 1892–1903

Cardinal Francis Bourne 1903–35
Cardinal Arthur Hinsley 1935–43
Cardinal Bernard William Griffin 1943–56
Cardinal William Godfrey 1956–63
Cardinal John Carmel Heenan 1963–76
Cardinal (George) Basil Hume 1976–

PRESBYTERIAN CHURCHES

Some 3% of the population belongs to the Presbyterian Churches including the Church of Scotland (see below). Other major Presbyterian Churches in the UK include the Presbyterian Church of Wales (the only Church of Welsh origin), and the Presbyterian Church in Ireland.

The Church of Scotland – the Established Church in Scotland – is governed by kirk sessions, presbyteries, 12 synods and the General Assembly. A kirk session consists of the minister and the elected elders of each of the 1700 churches. Churches are grouped into 46 presbyteries, which in turn are grouped into the 12 regional synods. The annual General Assembly is presided over by the Moderator, who holds office for one year.

METHODIST CHURCHES

Some 2% of the population belongs to Methodist Churches. Most Methodist congregations in the UK belong to the Methodist Church in Great Britain, which was formed in 1932 from the union of the Wesleyan Methodist Church, the Primitive Methodist Church and the United Methodist Church. It is governed by the annual Conference, by district synods, and by local circuit meetings. Other Methodist Churches include the Independent Methodist Church (which is Congregationalist in character) and the Wesleyan Reform Union (which is Methodist in doctrine, Congregationalist in its organization).

OTHER GROUPS

Other major Christian organizations combined in the UK account for about 4% of the population. They include:
The Baptist Union of Great Britain. There are also separate Baptist Unions in Scotland, Ireland and Wales.
The Congregational Federation, which includes those congregations in England and Wales that did not join the United Reformed Church in 1972.
The Salvation Army – founded by William Booth in 1865 – is characterized by a military-style organization. It is administered locally by colonels and over larger areas by commissioners and territorial commissioners who elect the world leader of the Army, the General.
The United Reformed Church was formed by the union of the Congregational Church in England and Wales and the Presbyterian Church of England. It is divided into 12 provinces.

ISLAM

About 2% of the population follows Islam, overwhelmingly Sunni Islam.

JUDAISM

Less than 1% of the population practises Judaism. The representative body of British Judaism is the Board of Deputies of British Jews, established in 1760, and the leader is the Chief Rabbi. The Court of Judgement (the *Beth Din*) is a rabbinic body that arbitrates and gives religious judgements, e.g. in matters of marriage and dietary laws.

Anglican Dioceses in the United Kingdom

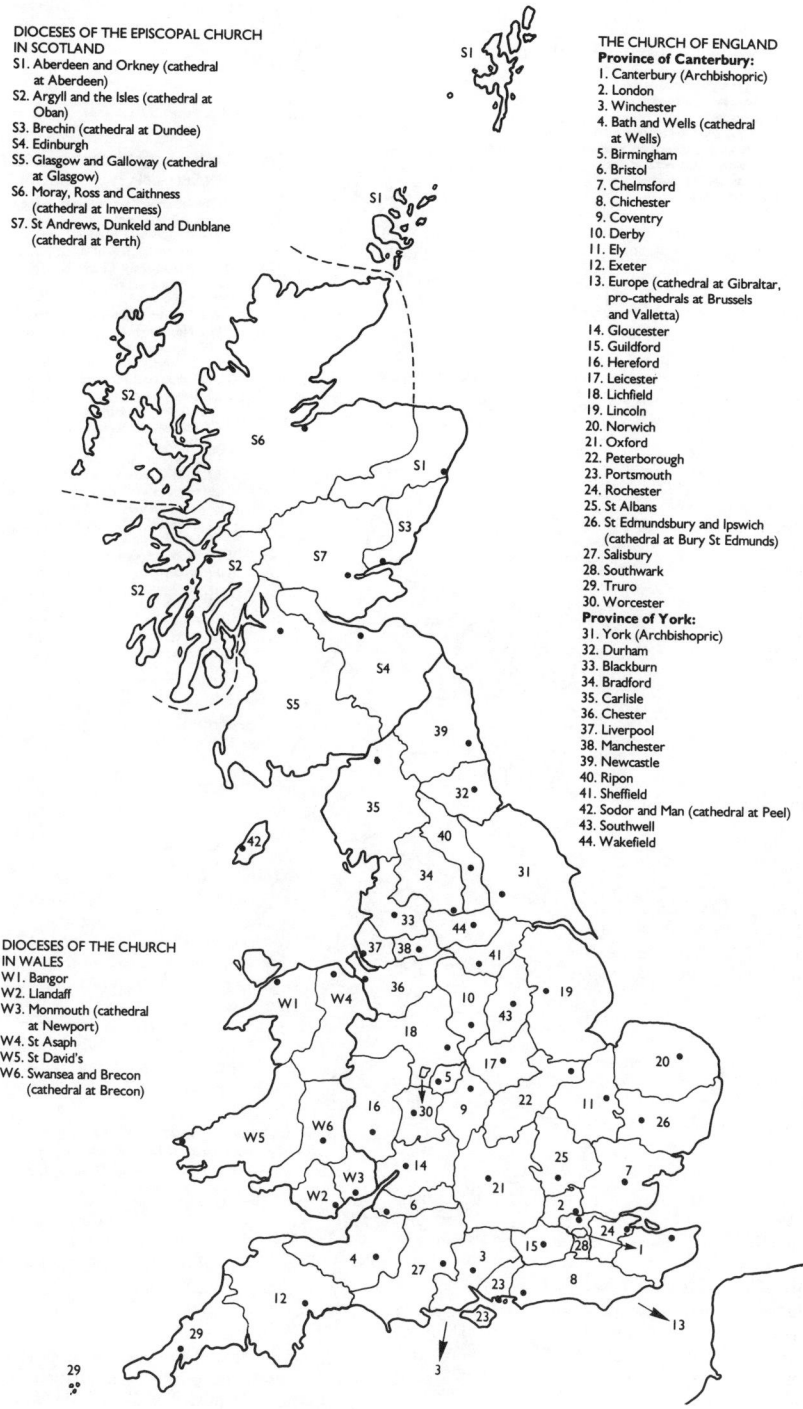

DIOCESES OF THE EPISCOPAL CHURCH IN SCOTLAND

S1. Aberdeen and Orkney (cathedral at Aberdeen)
S2. Argyll and the Isles (cathedral at Oban)
S3. Brechin (cathedral at Dundee)
S4. Edinburgh
S5. Glasgow and Galloway (cathedral at Glasgow)
S6. Moray, Ross and Caithness (cathedral at Inverness)
S7. St Andrews, Dunkeld and Dunblane (cathedral at Perth)

THE CHURCH OF ENGLAND
Province of Canterbury:

1. Canterbury (Archbishopric)
2. London
3. Winchester
4. Bath and Wells (cathedral at Wells)
5. Birmingham
6. Bristol
7. Chelmsford
8. Chichester
9. Coventry
10. Derby
11. Ely
12. Exeter
13. Europe (cathedral at Gibraltar, pro-cathedrals at Brussels and Valletta)
14. Gloucester
15. Guildford
16. Hereford
17. Leicester
18. Lichfield
19. Lincoln
20. Norwich
21. Oxford
22. Peterborough
23. Portsmouth
24. Rochester
25. St Albans
26. St Edmundsbury and Ipswich (cathedral at Bury St Edmunds)
27. Salisbury
28. Southwark
29. Truro
30. Worcester

Province of York:

31. York (Archbishopric)
32. Durham
33. Blackburn
34. Bradford
35. Carlisle
36. Chester
37. Liverpool
38. Manchester
39. Newcastle
40. Ripon
41. Sheffield
42. Sodor and Man (cathedral at Peel)
43. Southwell
44. Wakefield

DIOCESES OF THE CHURCH IN WALES

W1. Bangor
W2. Llandaff
W3. Monmouth (cathedral at Newport)
W4. St Asaph
W5. St David's
W6. Swansea and Brecon (cathedral at Brecon)

Roman Catholic Dioceses in the United Kingdom

E1. St Andrews and Edinburgh (Archbishopric;
     the Archbishop of St Andrews and
     Edinburgh is head of the Church in
     Scotland; cathedral at Edinburgh)
E2. Aberdeen
E3. Argyll and the Isles (cathedral at Oban)
E4. Dunkeld (cathedral at Dundee)
E5. Galloway (cathedral at Ayr)
G1. Glasgow (Archbishopric)
G2. Motherwell
G3. Paisley

ROMAN CATHOLIC DIOCESES
IN BRITAIN

(The letters and figures refer to the
accompanying map)
W1. Westminster (Archbishopric;
     the Archbishop of Westminster
     is head of the Church in
     England and Wales)
W2. Brentwood
W3. East Anglia (cathedral at Norwich)
W4. Northampton
W5. Nottingham
B1. Birmingham (Archbishopric)
B2. Clifton (cathedral at Bristol)
B3. Shrewsbury
C1. Cardiff (Archbishopric)
C2. Menevia (cathedral at Swansea)
C3. Wrexham
L1. Liverpool (Archbishopric)
L2. Hallam (cathedral at Sheffield)
L3. Hexham and Newcastle (cathedral
     at Newcastle)
L4. Lancaster
L5. Leeds
L6. Middlesbrough
L7. Salford
S1. Southwark (Archbishopric)
S2. Arundel and Brighton (cathedral at
     Arundel)
S3. Portsmouth
S4. Plymouth

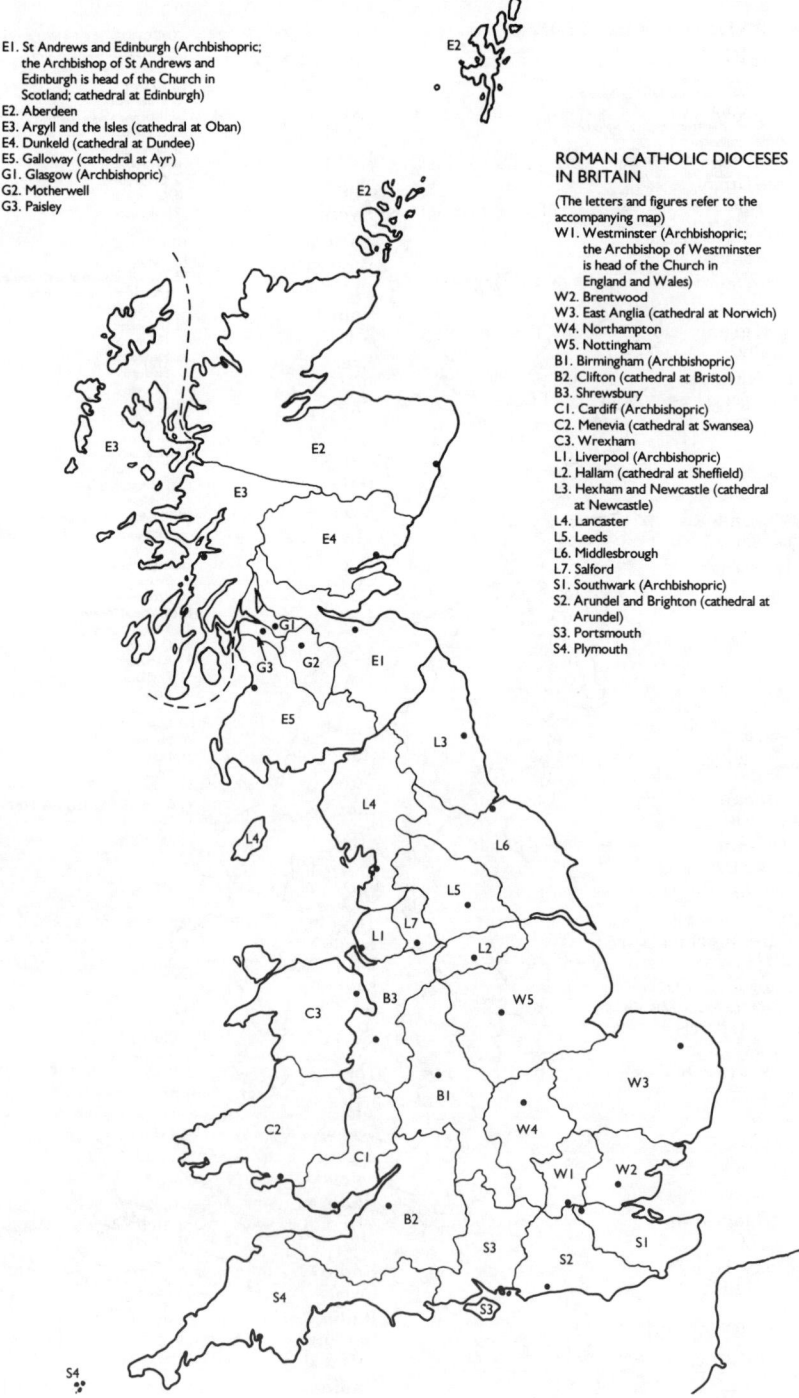

MEDIA

PRINCIPAL DAILY NATIONAL NEWSPAPERS

Circulation figures are for 1993.

Daily Express circ. 1 507 000; part of United Newspapers.

Daily Mail circ. 1 757 000; part of Associated Newspapers Group (Holdings) PLC.

Daily Mirror circ. 2 722 000; part of Mirror Group Newspapers Ltd.

Daily Sport circ. 300 000.

Daily Star circ. 788 000; part of United Newspapers.

Daily Telegraph circ. 1 037 000; part of Daily Telegraph PLC.

Evening Standard circ. 499 000; part of Associated Newspapers Groups (Holdings) PLC.

Financial Times circ. 289 000; part of Pearson PLC.

The Guardian circ. 420 000; part of Guardian Newspapers Ltd.

The Independent circ. 362 000; part of Newspaper Publishing PLC.

Morning Star circ. 25 000.

The Sun circ. 3 546 000; part of News International PLC.

The Times circ. 376 000; part of News International PLC.

Today circ. 538 000; part of News International PLC.

NATIONAL WEEKLY NEWSPAPERS

The European circ. 266 000; published Thursday; owned by the Barclay Brothers.

The Independent on Sunday circ. 407 000; part of Newspaper Publishing PLC.

The Mail on Sunday circ. 2 070 000; part of Associated Newspapers Group (Holdings) PLC.

News of the World circ. 4 692 000; Sunday newspaper; part of News International PLC.

The Observer circ. 537 000; Sunday newspaper; controlled by Lonhro International until bought by Guardian Newspapers Ltd. in 1993.

The People circ. 2 056 000; Sunday newspaper; part of Mirror Group Newspapers Ltd.

Sunday Express circ. 1 727 000; part United Newspapers.

Sunday Mirror circ. 2 671 000; part of Mirror Group Newspapers Ltd.

Sunday Sport circ. 284 000.

Sunday Telegraph circ. 583 000; part of Daily Telegraph PLC.

The Sunday Times circ. 1 202 000; part of News International PLC.

MAJOR REGIONAL DAILIES

The following had a circulation of over 85 000 in early 1993.

Birmingham Evening Mail circ. 203 000.

Evening Post (Bristol) circ. 105 000.

Northern Echo (evening; Darlington) circ. 86 000.

Hull Daily Mail (evening) circ. 97 000.

Yorkshire Evening Post (Leeds) circ. 130 000.

Yorkshire Post (morning; Leeds) circ. 86 000.

Leicester Mercury (evening) circ. 129 000.

Liverpool Echo (evening) circ. 184 000.

Manchester Evening News circ. 328 000.

Evening Chronicle (Newcastle-upon-Tyne) circ. 132 000.

Evening Post (Nottingham) circ. 120 000.

The Star (evening; Sheffield) circ. 119 000.

Evening Sentinel (Stoke-on-Trent) circ. 98 000.

Shropshire Star (evening; Telford) circ. 96 000.

Wolverhampton Express and Star (evening) circ. 218 000.

South Wales Echo (evening; Cardiff) circ. 85 000.

Press and Journal (morning; Aberdeen) circ. 107 000.

Courier and Advertiser (morning; Dundee), circ. 114 000.

Evening News (Edinburgh) circ. 100 000.

Daily Record (morning; Glasgow), circ. 756 000.

Evening Times (Glasgow) circ. 156 000.

The Herald (morning; Glasgow), circ. 119 000.

The Scotsman (morning; Edinburgh), circ. 86 000.

The Telegraph (Belfast) circ. 130 000.

MAJOR REGIONAL SUNDAY PAPERS

The following had a circulation of over 85 000 in early 1993.

Sunday Mercury (Birmingham) circ. 152 000.

Sunday Sun (Newcastle-upon-Tyne) circ. 128 000.

Sunday Mail (Glasgow) circ. 881 000.

Sunday Post (Dundee) circ. 1 140 000.

BROADCASTING

BBC

The British Broadcasting Corporation (BBC) was founded in 1922 under a Royal charter. It is financed by licence fees and a governmental grant (for external services).

RADIO BROADCASTING

There are five national BBC radio services for the UK, plus national regional services in Wales, Scotland and Northern Ireland. BBC local radio services extend over England and the Channel Islands. There are over 50 BBC regional and local stations. The five national BBC stations are:

Radio 1 Pop and rock network; frequencies: VHF-FM 97.6–99.8 MHz and MW 1053 kHz and 1089 kHz.

Radio 2 Light music, entertainment and sport; frequencies VHF-FM 88–90.2 MHz.

Radio 3 Classical music, drama and documentaries, poetry and cricket in season; frequencies VHF-FM 90.2–92.4 MHz and MW 1215 kHz.

Radio 4 News, documentaries, drama and entertainment; frequencies VHF-FM 92.4–94.6 MHz and LW 198 kHz.

Radio 5 Educational and children's programmes, and sport; frequencies MW 693, 909.

INDEPENDENT NATIONAL RADIO STATIONS

The Broacasting Act of 1990 made provision for three national independent radio stations.

Classic FM Classical music; frequency 99.9–101.9 FM. Gained a licence in 1991.

Virgin Radio Pop and rock music; frequency 1215 AM. gained a licence in 1993.

The third franchise has not been allocated.

Local radio is also served by 80 independent radio stations. This figure includes some two dozen community stations that serve communities of interest or offer a service for particular ethnic groups or cover a very small area.

THE RADIO AUTHORITY

The Radio Authority was established 1 January 1991, replacing the former Independent Broadcasting Authority's in its regulating role over radio. The purpose of the Authority is to assign frequencies, to grant licences to provide independent radio services, and to regulate the output of services to ensure they meet programming, advertising and sponsorship standards. The Authority has the right to impose fines on radio stations if complaints are upheld.

TELEVISION

There are four national television stations:

BBC 1 part of the British Broadcasting Corporation; founded in 1929 (with high-definition TV in 1936; see below). Colour service began in 1969; breakfast-time service began 1983.

BBC 2 part of the British Broadcasting Corporation. Colour service began in 1967.

ITV (Channel 3) an independent station made up of (regional) programme contractors picked by the IBA. The service was founded in 1954 and is financed by advertising.

Channel 4 an independent station set up by the IBA and financed by advertising. It was founded in 1982.

S4C Welsh Fourth Channel available only in Wales (instead of Channel Four), broadcasting in Welsh and financed by advertising.

INDEPENDENT TELEVISION COMMISSION

The Independent Television Commission was established at the end of 1990, replacing the Independent Broadcasting Authority (IBA; formerly known as the Independent Television Authority). The ITC is responsible for licensing and regulating all commercially funded UK television services.

INDEPENDENT PROGRAMME CONTRACTORS

Anglia Television Ltd serves eastern England.

Border Television PLC serves the Borders, Cumbria and the Isle of Man.

Carlton Communications serves the London region from 9.00 am on Monday to 5.15 pm on Friday.

Central Independent Television PLC serves the East and West Midlands.

Channel Television serves the Channel Islands.

Grampian Television PLC serves the north of Scotland.

GMTV provides a nationwide breakfast-time service.

Granada Television Ltd serves northwest England.

HTV Ltd serves Wales and the west of England.

London Weekend Television Ltd serves the London region (5.15 pm Friday to closedown on Monday morning).

Meridian Broadcasting serves south and south-east England.

Scottish Television PLC serves central Scotland.

Westcountry TV serves south-west England.

Tyne Tees Television Ltd. serves northeast England.

Ulster Television PLC serves Northern Ireland.

Yorkshire Television Ltd. serves Yorkshire.

Independent Television News (ITN) a non-profit-making organization owned by the ITV companies. It supplies news information to Channel Four and ITV.

SATELLITE BROADCASTING

British Sky Broadcasting PLC founded in 1990 from the merger of British Satellite Broadcasting (BSB) and Sky TV PLC. It offers sport, film, music and news channels.

MAGAZINES

The number of magazines published in the UK continues to increase. Growth areas in the past decade included sports (particularly winter sports and fitness), foreign holidays, computing and, above all, TV listings magazines. Leisure and women's interest magazines attract large readerships. One outstanding success has been the rise of the adult humour magazine *Viz*, while the most notable casualty was probably *Punch*.

In recent years British magazines have faced considerable competition from overseas publishers. In 1986 German publishers Grüner and Jahr launched *Prima* and later *Best*, and in 1987 H. Bauer issued *Bella*. All these magazines were an immediate success and in many ways set the agenda for later magazines for women, with more practical housekeeping plus puzzles and competitions.

The following magazines recorded circulation figures of 500 000 or over early in 1993.

Satellite Times, circ. 2 900 000.
TV Weekly, circ. 2 719 000.
TV First, circ. 2 098 000.
TV Quick, circ. 2 000 000.
Radio Times, circ. 1 592 000.
Reader's Digest, circ. 1 540 000.
What's On TV, circ. 1 401 000.
Take A Break, circ. 1 300 000.
Bella, circ. 1 200 000.
TV Times, circ. 1 113 000.
Viz, circ. 868 000.
Woman's Weekly, circ. 864 000.
Which?, circ. 800 000.
Prima, circ. 739 000.
Woman's Own, circ. 731 000.
Woman, circ. 716 000.
Best, circ. 630 000.
Legion, circ. 630 000.
BBC Good Food Magazine, circ. 543 000.
Chat, circ. 516 000.
Me, circ. 511 000.
Screen, circ. 520 000.
The Economist, circ. 510 000.
Saga Magazine, circ. 503 000.
The Motorist, circ. 500 000.

SPORT

Information on international sport is given in the previous chapter, beginning on p. 682.

ATHLETICS

NATIONAL ATHLETICS RECORDS

UK national records (at 25 April 1992) that are also World, Commonwealth, or European records have been noted: *w* = World record; *c* = Commonwealth record; *e* = European record.

Track events – men

	min:sec	
100 m	9.92	Linford Christie 1991 *c, e*
200 m	20.09	Linford Christie 1988
	20.09	John Regis 1992
400 m	44.47	David Grindley 1992
800 m	1:41.73	Sebastian Coe 1981 *w, c, e*
1000 m	2:12.18	Sebastian Coe 1981 *w, c, e*
1500 m	3:29.67	Steve Cram 1985 *c, e*
1 mile	3:46.32	Steve Cram 1985 *c, e*
2000 m	4:51.39	Steve Cram 1985 *c, e*
3000 m	7:32.79	David Moorcroft 1982
5000 m	13:00.41	David Moorcroft 1982 *c, e*
10 000 m	27:23.06	Eamonn Martin 1988
20 000 m	57:28.7	Carl Thackery 1990 *c*
25 000 m	1 hr 15:22.6	Ronald Hill 1965 *c*
30 000 m	1 hr 31:30.4	James Alder 1970 *c, e*
1 hour	20 855 m	Carl Thackeray 1990 *c*
110 m hurdles	13.04	Colin Jackson 1992 *c, e*
400 m hurdles	47.82	Kriss Akabusi 1991
3000 m steeplechase	8:07.96	Mark Rowland 1988
4 x 100 m	37.98	National Team: D. Braithwaite, J. Regis, M. Adam, L. Christie 1990
4 x 200 m	1:21.29	National Team: M. Adam, A. Mafe, L. Christie, J. Regis 1989
4 x 400 m	2:57.53	National Team: R. Black, D. Redmond, J. Regis, K. Akabusi 1991 *c, e*
4 x 800 m	7:03.89	National Team: P. Elliot, G. Cook, S. Cram, S. Coe 1982 *w, c, e*
4 x 1500 m	14:56.8	National Team: A. Mottershead, G. M. Cooper, S. Emson, R. Wood 1979

Field events – men

	metres	
High jump	2.37	Stephen Smith 1992 *c*
Pole Vault	5.65	Keith Stock 1981
Long Jump	8.23	Lynn Davies 1968
Triple jump	*17.57	Keith Connor 1982 *c*
Shot	21.68	Geoffrey Capes 1980 *c*
Discus	†64.32	William Tancred 1974
Hammer	77.54	Martin Girvan 1984 *c*
Javelin	91.46	Stephen Backley 1992 *c*
Decathlon	8847 pts	Daley Thompson 1984 *c, e*

* set at high altitude; record at low altitude 17.41 m by John Herbert (1985)

† Willam Tancred threw 64.94 m in 1974 and Richard Slaney threw 65.16 m in 1985 but neither of these throws were ratified.

Track events – women

	min:sec	
100 m	11.10	Kathryn Smallwood (now Cook) 1981
200 m	22.10	Kathryn Cook (*née* Smallwood) 1984
400 m	49.43	Kathryn Cook 1984 *c*
800 m	1:57.42	Kirsty McDermott (now Wade) 1985 *c*
1000 m	2:33.70	Kirsty McDermott 1985 *c*
1500 m	3:59.96	Zola Budd (now Pieterse) 1985 *c*
1 mile	4:17.57	Zola Budd (now Pieterse) 1985 *c*
2000 m	5:29.58	Yvonne Murray 1986 *c*
3000 m	8:28.83	Zola Budd (now Pieterse) 1985 *c*
5000 m	14:48.07	Zola Budd (now pieterse) 1985 *c*
10 000 m	30:57.07	Elizabeth McColgan (*née* Lynch) 1991 *c*
100 m hurdles	12.82	Sally Gunnell 1988
400 m hurdles	53.16	Sally Gunnell 1991 *c*
4 x 100 m	42.43	National Team: H. Hunte (now Oakes), K. Smallwood (now Cook), B. Goddard (now Callender), S. Lannaman 1980 *c*
4 x 200 m	1:31.57	National Team: D. Hartley (*née* Murray), V. Elder (*née* Bernard), S. Colyear (now Danville), S. Lannaman 1977 *c*
4 x 400 m	3:22.01	National Team: Phyllis Smith (*née* Watt), L. Hanson, L. Keough, S. Gunnell 1991
4 x 800 m	8:19.90	National Team: A. Williams, P. Fryer, Y. Murray, D. Edwards

Field events – women

	metres	
High jump	1.95	Diana Elliot 1982
Long jump	6.90	Beverly Kinch 1983 *c*
Triple jump	13.56	Mary Berkeley 1992 *c*
Shot	19.36	Judith Oakes 1988
Discus	67.48	Margaret Ritchie 1981 *c*
Javelin	77.44	Fatima Whitbread 1986 *c*
Heptathlon	6623 pts	Judy Simpson (*née* Livermore) 1986

ASSOCIATION FOOTBALL

Domestic competitions in England are dominated by the professional Premier League and the Football League championships. The Football League was formed in 1888 with 12 teams and now has 71 teams divided between three divisions. The 22-team Premier League was formed from the former First Division of the Football League for the season 1992–93. Winners of the Football League since 1888/89–1991/92 were:

1988/9	Preston North End
1989/90	Preston North End
1890/1	Everton
1891/2	Sunderland
1892/3	Sunderland
1893/4	Aston Villa
1894/5	Sunderland
1895/6	Aston Villa
1896/7	Aston Villa
1897/8	Sheffield United
1898/9	Aston Villa
1899/1900	Aston Villa
1900/1	Liverpool
1901/2	Sunderland
1902/3	Sheffield Wednesday
1903/4	Sheffield Wednesday
1904/5	Newcastle United
1905/6	Liverpool
1906/7	Newcastle United
1907/8	Manchester United
1908/9	Newcastle United
1909/10	Aston Villa
1910/1	Manchester United
1911/2	Blackburn Rovers
1912/3	Sunderland
1913/4	Blackburn Rovers
1914/5	Everton
1919/20	West Bromwich Albion
1920/1	Burnley
1921/2	Liverpool
1922/3	Liverpool
1923/4	Huddersfield Town
1924/5	Huddersfield Town
1925/6	Huddersfield Town
1926/7	Newcastle United
1927/8	Everton
1928/9	Sheffield Wednesday
1929/30	Sheffield Wednesday
1930/1	Arsenal
1931/2	Everton
1932/3	Arsenal
1933/4	Arsenal
1934/5	Arsenal
1935/6	Sunderland
1936/7	Manchester City
1937/8	Arsenal
1938/9	Everton
1946/7	Liverpool
1947/8	Arsenal
1948/9	Portsmouth
1949/50	Portsmouth
1950/1	Tottenham Hotspur
1951/2	Manchester United
1952/3	Arsenal
1953/4	Wolverhampton Wanderers
1954/5	Chelsea
1955/6	Manchester United
1956/7	Manchester United
1957/8	Wolverhampton Wanderers
1958/9	Wolverhampton Wanderers
1959/60	Burnley
1960/1	Tottenham Hotspur
1961/2	Ipswich Town
1962/3	Everton
1963/4	Liverpool
1964/5	Manchester United
1965/6	Liverpool
1966/7	Manchester United
1967/8	Manchester City
1968/9	Leeds United
1969/70	Everton
1970/1	Arsenal
1971/2	Derby County

1972/3	Liverpool
1973/4	Leeds United
1974/5	Derby County
1975/6	Liverpool
1976/7	Liverpool
1977/8	Nottingham Forest
1978/9	Liverpool
1979/80	Liverpool
1980/1	Aston Villa
1981/2	Liverpool
1982/3	Liverpool
1983/4	Liverpool
1984/5	Everton
1985/6	Liverpool
1986/7	Everton
1987/8	Liverpool
1988/9	Arsenal
1989/90	Liverpool
1990/1	Arsenal
1991/2	Leeds United

Winners of the Premier League:

1992/3	Manchester United.

'Non-League' or semi-professional football is also widespread in England and Wales with the semi-professional GM Vauxhall Conference as the major competition. Promotion and relegation operate between the Premier League and the Football League, between the Football League and the GM Vauxhall Conference, and between the GM Vauxhall Conference and three regional leagues – the Beazer Homes League (in the south and west of England, Wales and the Midlands), the Diadora League (in the south of England) and the HFS Loans League (in the north of England).

The FA Challenge Cup – which is open to all senior clubs in England and Wales – was introduced in 1871, 17 years before the birth of the Football League. The final has been played at Wembley Stadium since 1923. Winners are listed below.

1872–3	Wanderers
1874	Oxford University
1875	Royal Engineers
1876–8	Wanderers
1879	Old Etonians
1880	Clapham Rovers
1881	Old Carthusians
1882	Old Etonians
1883	Blackburn Olympic
1884–6	Blackburn Rovers
1887	Aston Villa
1888	West Bromwich Albion
1889	Preston North End
1890–1	Blackburn Rovers
1892	West Bromwich Albion
1893	Wolverhampton Wanderers
1894	Notts County
1895	Aston Villa
1896	Sheffield Wednesday
1897	Aston Villa
1898	Nottingham Forest
1899	Sheffield United
1900	Bury
1901	Tottenham Hotspur
1902	Sheffield United
1903	Bury
1904	Manchester City
1905	Aston Villa
1906	Everton
1907	Sheffield Wednesday
1908	Wolverhampton Wanderers
1909	Manchester United
1910	Newcastle United

1911	Bradford City
1912	Barnsley
1913	Aston Villa
1914	Burnley
1915	Sheffield United
1920	Aston Villa
1921	Tottenham Hotspur
1922	Huddersfield Town
1923	Bolton Wanderers
1924	Newcastle United
1925	Sheffield United
1926	Bolton Wanderers
1927	Cardiff City
1928	Blackburn Rovers
1929	Bolton Wanderers
1930	Arsenal
1931	West Bromwich Albion
1932	Newcastle United
1933	Everton
1934	Manchester City
1935	Sheffield Wednesday
1936	Arsenal
1937	Sunderland
1938	Preston North End
1939	Portsmouth
1946	Derby County
1947	Charlton Athletic
1948	Manchester United
1949	Wolverhampton Wanderers
1950	Arsenal
1951–2	Newcastle United
1953	Blackpool
1954	West Bromwich Albion
1955	Newcastle United
1956	Manchester City
1957	Aston Villa
1958	Bolton Wanderers
1959	Nottingham Forest
1960	Wolverhampton Wanderers
1961–2	Tottenham Hotspur
1963	Manchester United
1964	West Ham United
1965	Liverpool
1966	Everton
1967	Tottenham Hotspur
1968	West Bromwich Albiont
1969	Manchester City
1970	Chelsea
1971	Arsenal
1972	Leeds United
1973	Sunderland
1974	Liverpool
1975	West Ham United
1976	Southampton
1977	Manchester United
1978	Ipswich Town
1979	Arsenal
1980	West Ham United
1981–2	Tottenham Hotspur
1983	Manchester United
1984	Everton
1985	Manchester United
1986	Liverpool
1987	Coventry City
1988	Wimbledon
1989	Liverpool
1990	Manchester United
1991	Tottenham Hotspur
1992	Liverpool
1993	Arsenal

The Coca Cola (previously League, Milk, Little-

SCOTTISH LEAGUE CHAMPIONS

Champions of the First Division (1890/1–1974/5) and the Premier Division (since 1975/6) have been:

Aberdeen 1954/5, 1979/80, 1983/4, 1984/5
Dumbarton 1890/1 (shared), 1891/2
Celtic 1892/3, 1893/4, 1895/6, 1897/8, 1904/5, 1905/6, 1906/7, 1907/8, 1908/9, 1909/10, 1913/4, 1914/5, 1915/6, 1916/7, 1918/9, 1921/2, 1925/6, 1935/6, 1937/8, 1953/4, 1965/6, 1966/7, 1967/8, 1968/9, 1969/70, 1970/1, 1971/2, 1972/3, 1973/4, 1976/7, 1978/9, 1980/1, 1981/2, 1985/6, 1987/8
Dundee 1961/2
Dundee United 1982/3
Hearts 1894/5, 1896/7, 1957/8, 1959/60
Hibernian 1902/3, 1947/8, 1950/1, 1951/2
Kilmarnock 1964/5
Motherwell 1931/2
Rangers 1890/1 (shared), 1898/9, 1899/1900, 1900/1, 1901/2, 1910/1, 1911/2, 1912/3, 1917/8, 1919/20, 1920/1, 1922/3, 1923/4, 1924/5, 1926/7, 1927/8, 1928/9, 1929/30, 1930/1, 1932/3, 1933/4, 1934/5, 1936/7, 1938/9, 1946/7, 1948/9, 1949/50, 1952/3, 1955/6, 1956/7, 1958/9, 1960/1, 1962/3, 1963/4, 1974/5, 1975/6, 1977/8, 1986/7, 1988/9, 1989/90, 1990/1, 1991/2, 1992/3
Third Lanark 1903/4

SCOTTISH FA CUP WINNERS

Winners of the Scottish FA Cup since 1874 have been:

Aberdeen 1947, 1970, 1982, 1983, 1984, 1986, 1990
Airdrieonians 1924
Dumbarton 1883
Celtic 1892, 1899, 1900, 1904, 1907, 1908, 1909, 1911, 1912, 1914, 1923, 1925, 1927, 1931, 1933, 1937, 1951, 1954, 1955, 1965, 1967, 1969, 1971, 1972, 1974, 1975, 1977, 1980, 1985, 1988, 1989
Clyde 1939, 1958
Dundee 1910
Dunfermline Athletic 1961, 1968
East Fife 1938
Falkirk 1913, 1957
Hearts 1891, 1896, 1901, 1906, 1956
Hibernian 1887, 1902
Kilmarnock 1920, 1929
Morton 1922
Motherwell 1952, 1991
Partick Thistle 1921
Queen's Park 1874, 1875, 1876, 1880, 1881, 1882, 1884, 1886, 1890, 1893
Rangers 1894, 1897, 1898, 1903, 1928, 1930, 1932, 1934, 1935, 1936, 1948, 1949, 1950, 1953, 1960, 1962, 1963, 1964, 1966, 1973, 1976, 1978, 1979, 1981, 1992, 1993
Renton 1885, 1888
St Bernard's 1895
St Mirren 1926, 1959, 1987
Third Lanark 1889, 1905
Vale of Leven 1877, 1878, 1879

members of the Premier and Football leagues – was instituted in 1960. Winners since 1980 have been:

1980	Wolverhampton Wanderers
1981	Liverpool
1982	Liverpool
1983	Liverpool
1984	Liverpool
1985	Norwich City
1986	Oxford United
1987	Arsenal
1988	Luton Town
1989	Nottingham Forest
1990	Nottingham Forest
1991	Sheffield Wednesday
1992	Manchester United
1993	Arsenal.

The FA Trophy is competed for by the semi-professional clubs in England and Wales. The FA Vase is open to other non-League clubs.

The Scottish League – now comprising 38 teams in three divisions – was founded in 1890. Entrance to the Scottish League is by election rather than promotion. From the 1993/4 season, the Scottish League will comprise 40 clubs in four divisions. Winners of the First Division (to 1974/5) and of the Premier Division (since that date) are listed in the accompanying box.

The Scottish Cup was started in 1873. The final has been held at Hampden Park since World War I (except for 1921 when it was played at Celtic Park and 1924 when it was played at Ibrox Park). Winners are listed in the accompanying box.

In Northern Ireland the premier competition is the 16-member League of Ireland.

CRICKET

There are four English domestic competitions. The County Championship, a league of the 18 first-class counties with matches over four days (from 1993); the one-day knockouts of the Nat. West (previously Gillette) Trophy of 60-over matches and the Benson & Hedges of 55; and the one-day Sunday League. Formerly sponsored by John Player (1969–86) and Refuge Assurance (1987–91). Under a new sponsor Axa Equity and Law games were increased from 40 to 50 overs per innings in 1993. Winners of these competitions are listed in the accompanying boxes.

Records in first-class cricket held by British cricketers include:
Most runs: Sir John Berry 'Jack' Hobbs with 61 237 runs between 1905 and 1934.
Most centuries: Sir Jack Hobbs (see above) with 197 centuries from 1905 to 1934.
Most wickets: Wilfred Rhodes took 4187 wickets between 1898 and 1930.

Matches involving Oxford and Cambridge Universities are also considered to be first class.

The Minor Counties Championship is competed for by 20 teams in two divisions of ten sides – Bedfordshire, Berkshire, Buckinghamshire, Cambridgeshire, Cheshire, Cornwall, Cumberland, Devon, Dorset, Herefordshire, Hertfordshire, Lincolnshire, Norfolk, Northumberland, Oxfordshire, Shropshire, Staffordshire, Suffolk, Wales Minor Counties, and Wiltshire. Championship games last two days. Winners since 1980 have been:
1980 Durham
1981 Durham
1982 Oxfordshire
1983 Hertfordshire

COUNTY CHAMPIONS

From 1864, when eight counties took part in inter-county matches, to 1889, champion counties were proclaimed, principally on the basis of fewest points lost. It was not until 1890 that the county championship was officially recognized and a points system introduced.

Winners
Derbyshire 1936
Durham none
Essex 1979, 1983, 1984, 1986, 1991, 1992
Glamorgan 1948, 1969
Gloucestershire 1873 =, 1874, 1876, 1877
Hampshire 1961, 1973
Kent 1906, 1909, 1910, 1913, 1970, 1977 =, 1978
Lancashire 1879 =, 1881, 1882 =, 1889 =, 1897, 1904, 1926, 1927, 1928, 1930, 1934, 1950 =
Leicestershire 1975
Middlesex 1866, 1903, 1920, 1921, 1947, 1949 =, 1976, 1977 =, 1980, 1982, 1985, 1990
Northamptonshire none
Nottinghamshire 1865, 1868, 1869 =, 1871, 1872, 1873 =, 1875, 1879 =, 1880, 1882 =, 1883, 1884, 1885, 1886, 1889 =, 1907, 1929, 1981, 1987
Somerset none
Surrey 1864, 1887, 1888, 1889 =, 1890, 1891, 1892, 1894, 1895, 1899, 1914, 1950 =, 1952, 1953, 1954, 1955, 1956, 1957, 1958, 1971
Sussex none
Warwickshire 1911, 1951, 1972
Worcestershire 1964, 1965, 1974, 1988, 1989
Yorkshire 1867, 1869 =, 1870, 1893, 1896, 1898, 1900, 1901, 1902, 1905, 1908, 1912, 1919, 1922, 1923, 1924, 1925, 1931, 1932, 1933, 1935, 1937, 1938, 1939, 1946, 1949 =, 1959, 1960, 1962, 1963, 1966, 1967, 1968

GILLETTE/NATWEST CUP WINNERS

Winners
Derbyshire 1981
Durham none
Essex 1985
Glamorgan none
Gloucestershire 1973
Hampshire 1991
Kent 1967, 1974
Lancashire 1970, 1971, 1972, 1975, 1990
Leicestershire none
Middlesex 1977, 1980, 1984, 1988
Northamptonshire 1976, 1992
Nottinghamshire 1987
Somerset 1979, 1983
Surrey 1982
Sussex 1963, 1964, 1978, 1986
Warwickshire 1966, 1968, 1989
Worcestershire none
Yorkshire 1965, 1969

1984 Durham
1985 Cheshire
1986 Cumberland
1987 Buckinghamshire
1988 Cheshire
1989 Oxfordshire
1990 Hertfordshire
1991 Staffordshire
1992 Staffordshire

SUNDAY LEAGUE WINNERS

Winners
Derbyshire 1990
Durham none
Essex 1981, 1984, 1985
Glamorgan none
Gloucestershire none
Hampshire 1975, 1978, 1986
Kent 1972, 1973, 1976
Lancashire 1969, 1970, 1989
Leicestershire 1974, 1977
Middlesex 1992
Northamptonshire none
Nottinghamshire 1991
Somerset 1979
Surrey none
Sussex 1982
Warwickshire 1980
Worcestershire none
Yorkshire 1983

BENSON & HEDGES CUP WINNERS

Winners
Combined Universities none
Derbyshire none
Durham none
Essex 1979
Glamorgan none
Gloucestershire 1977
Hampshire 1988, 1992
Kent 1973, 1976, 1978
Lancashire 1984, 1990
Leicestershire 1972, 1975, 1985
Middlesex 1983, 1986, 1992
Minor Counties none
Northamptonshire 1980
Nottinghamshire 1989
Scotland none
Somerset 1981, 1982
Surrey 1974
Sussex none
Warwickshire none
Worcestershire 1991
Yorkshire 1987

GOLF

For a list of the winners of the British Open see the chapter on international sport beginning on p. 682.

HORSE RACING

In Britain the Jockey Club is now the governing body of flat racing, steeplechasing and hurdle racing, having merged with the National Hunt Committee in 1968. The flat racing season in Britain takes place between late March and early November. Thoroughbreds may not run until they are two years old. The five classic races are the Two Thousand Guineas and the One Thousand Guineas (held at Newmarket over 1600 m / 1 mile), the Derby and the Oaks (held at Epsom over 2400 m / 1½ miles) and the St Leger (held at Doncaster over 2800 m / 1¾ miles).

Steeplechase and hurdle races are run over distances of 2 or more miles, with at least one ditch and six birch fences for every mile. The UK National Hunt season can last from early August to 1st June, and the two most important steeplechases are the Grand National, first run in 1839, at Aintree over a course of 7220 m (4 miles 856 yd) with 30 jumps, and the Gold Cup run over 5·2 km (3¼ miles) at Cheltenham.

The premier British hurdle race is the Champion Hurdle, held annually over 3·2 km (2 miles) at Cheltenham. Recent winners of major races are listed below.)

THE DERBY (winners since 1980)

1980 Henbit (Jockey – Willie Carson)
1981 Shergar (Walter Swinburn)
1982 Golden Fleece (Pat Eddery)
1983 Teenoso (Lester Piggott)
1984 Secreto (Christy Roche)
1985 Slip Anchor (Steve Cauthen)
1986 Shahrastani (Walter Swinburn)
1987 Reference Point (Steve Cauthen)
1988 Kahyasi (Ray Cochrane)
1989 Nashwan (Willie Carson)
1990 Quest for Fame (Pat Eddery)
1991 Generous (Alan Munro)
1992 Dr Devious (John Reid)
1993 Commander in Chief (M. J. Kinane)

GRAND NATIONAL (winners since 1980)

1980 Ben Nevis (Charlie Fenwick)
1981 Aldaniti (Bob Champion)
1982 Grittar (Dick Saunders)
1983 Corbiere (Ben De Haan)
1984 Hallo Dandy (Neale Doughty)
1985 Last Suspect (Hywel Davies)
1986 West Tip (Richard Dunwoody)
1987 Maori Venture (Steve Knight)
1988 Rhyme N'Reason (Brendan Powell)
1989 Little Polveir (Jimmy Frost)
1990 Mr Frisk (Marcus Armytage)
1991 Seagram (Nigel Hawke)
1992 Party Politics (Carl Llewellyn)
1993 race void

CHELTENHAM GOLD CUP (winners since 1980)

1980 Master Smudge (Richard Hoare)
1981 Little Owl (Jim Wilson)
1982 Silver Buck (Robert Earnshaw)
1983 Bregawn (Graham Bradley)
1984 Burrough Hill Lad (Phil Tuck)
1985 Forgive 'N' Forget (Martin Dwyer)
1986 Dawn Run (Jonjo O'Neill)
1987 The Thinker (Ridley Lamb)
1988 Charter Party (Richard Dunwoody)
1989 Desert Orchid (Simon Sherwood)
1990 Norton's Coin (Graham McCourt)
1991 Garrison Savannah (Mark Pitman)
1992 Cool Ground (Adrian Maguire)
1993 Shuil Ar Aghaidh (Charlie Swan)

RUGBY LEAGUE

The major domestic rugby league trophies are the Challenge Cup (instituted 1897), the League Championship (instituted 1907), the Premiership Trophy (instituted 1975) and the Regal Trophy (formerly John Player Trophy; instituted 1972).

CHALLENGE CUP WINNERS (from 1980)
1980 Hull Kingston Rovers
1981 Widnes
1982 Hull
1983 Featherstone Rovers
1984 Widnes
1985 Wigan
1986 Castleford
1987 Halifax
1988–93 Wigan

Rugby League champions are listed in the accompanying box.

RUGBY LEAGUE CHAMPIONS

Batley 1923/4
Bradford Northern 1979/80, 1980/1
Dewsbury 1972/3
Featherstone Rovers 1976/7
Halifax 1906/7, 1964/5, 1985/6
Huddersfield 1911/2, 1912/3, 1914/5, 1928/9, 1929/30, 1948/9, 1961/2
Hull 1919/20, 1920/1, 1935/6, 1955/6, 1957/8, 1982/3
Hull Kingston Rovers 1922/3, 1924/5, 1978/9, 1983/4, 1984/5
Hunslet 1907/8, 1937/8
Leeds 1960/1, 1968/9, 1971/2
Leigh 1905/6, 1981/2
Oldham 1909/10, 1910/1, 1956/7
St Helens 1931/2, 1952/3, 1958/9, 1965/6, 1969/70, 1970/1, 1974/5
Salford 1913/4, 1932/3, 1936/7, 1938/9, 1973/4, 1975/6
Wakefield Trinity 1966/7, 1967/8
Warrington 1947/8, 1953/4, 1954/5
Widnes 1987/8, 1988/9
Wigan 1908/9, 1921/2, 1925/6, 1933/4, 1945/6, 1946/7, 1949/50, 1951/2, 1959/60, 1986/7, 1987/8, 1989/90, 1990/1, 1991/2, 1992/3
Workington Town 1950/1

RUGBY UNION

The International Rugby Football Board was formed in 1890. Teams representing the British Isles have toured Australia, New Zealand and South Africa since 1888, although they were not composed of players from all the Home Countries until 1924, when the term 'British Lions' was first coined.

The International Championship – between England, Ireland, Scotland, and Wales – was first held in 1884, with France included from 1910. Now also known as the Five Nations tournament, the 'Grand Slam' – winning all four matches – is prized. The 'Triple Crown' is achieved when a Home Country side defeats the other three.

INTERNATIONAL CHAMPIONSHIP
Winners (outright/shared wins)

Wales (21/11)	1893, 1900, 1902, 1905, 1906*, 1908–9, 1911, 1920*, 1922, 1931, 1932*, 1936, 1939*, 1947*, 1950, 1952, 1954*–5*, 1956, 1964*, 1965–6, 1969, 1970*, 1971, 1973*, 1975–6, 1978–9, 1988*
England (20/9)	1883–4, 1886*, 1890*, 1892, 1910, 1912*, 1913–4, 1921, 1923–4, 1928, 1930, 1932*, 1934, 1937, 1939*, 1947*, 1953, 1954*, 1957–8, 1960*, 1963, 1973*, 1980, 1991–2
Scotland (13/8)	1886*, 1887, 1890*, 1891, 1895, 1901, 1903–4, 1907, 1920*, 1925, 1926*–7*, 1929, 1933, 1938, 1964*, 1973*, 1984, 1986*, 1990
Ireland (10/8)	1894, 1896, 1899, 1906*, 1912*, 1926*–7*, 1932*, 1935, 1939*, 1948–9, 1951, 1973*, 1974, 1982, 1983*, 1985
France (10/8)	1954*, 1955*, 1959*, 1960*, 1961–2, 1967–8, 1970*, 1973*, 1977, 1981, 1983*, 1986*, 1987, 1988*, 1989, 1993

* denotes shared win (there was a quintuple tie in 1973)

The championships of 1885, 1888–9, 1897–8 and 1972 were not completed for various reasons.

Grand Slam
A Five Nations country has defeated the other four countries during one season as follows:

England (10)	1913–14, 1921, 1923–4, 1928, 1957, 1980, 1991–2
Wales (8)	1908–9†, 1911, 1950, 1952, 1971, 1976, 1978
France (4)	1968, 1977, 1981, 1987
Scotland (3)	1925, 1984, 1990
Ireland (1)	1948

†not including France at that time

The majority of English clubs participate in the Courage Leagues, comprising five national leagues of 10 clubs, two regional leagues, and a pyramid of divisional and county leagues. Courage League champions have been:
1985/6 Gloucester
1986/7 Bath
1987/8 Leicester
1988/9 Bath
1989/90 Wasps
1990/1 Bath
1991/2 Bath
1992/3 Bath

Since 1971/2 the major clubs and winners of county cup competitions have competed in the RFU Knockout Competition (known from 1971 to 1988 as the John Player Special Cup and since 1988 as the Pilkington Cup). Winners have been:
1971/2 Gloucester
1972/3 Coventry
1973/4 Coventry
1974/5 Bedford
1975/6 Newcastle Gosforth
1976/7 Newcastle Gosforth
1977/8 Gloucester
1978/9 Leicester
1979/80 Leicester
1980/1 Leicester
1981/2 Gloucester and Moseley (shared)
1982/3 Bristol
1983/4 Bath
1984/5 Bath

1985/6 Bath
1986/7 Bath
1987/8 Harlequins
1988/9 Bath
1989/90 Bath
1990/1 Harlequins
1991/2 Bath
1992/3 Leicester

The premier competition in Scotland is the McEwans League which began in 1973/4. the eight divisions of the league stand at the top of a pyramid of local competitions. Winners have been:

1973/4 Hawick
1974/5 Hawick
1975/6 Hawick
1976/7 Hawick
1977/8 Hawick
1978/9 Heriot's Former Pupils
1979/80 Gala
1980/1 Gala
1981/2 Hawick
1982/3 Gala
1983/4 Hawick
1984/5 Hawick
1985/6 Hawick
1986/7 Hawick
1987/8 Kelso
1988/9 Kelso
1989/90 Melrose
1990/1 Boroughmuir
1991/2 Melrose
1992/3 Melrose

The (knockout) Welsh Rugby Union Challenge Cup (the Schweppes Cup) was first competed in 1971/2. Winners have been;

1971/2 Neath
1972/3 Llanelli
1973/4 Llanelli
1974/5 Llanelli
1975/6 Llanelli
1976/7 Newport
1977/8 Swansea
1978/9 Bridgend
1979/80 Bridgend
1980/1 Cardiff
1981/2 Cardiff
1982/3 Pontypool
1983/4 Cardiff
1984/5 Llanelli
1985/6 Cardiff
1986/7 Cardiff
1987/8 Llanelli
1988/9 Neath
1989/90 Neath
1990/1 Llanelli
1991/2 Llanelli
1992/3 Llanelli

Since 1990/1 there has also been a league system in Wales with various local competitions feeding the national league. Champions have been:

1990/1 Neath
1991/2 Swansea
1992/3 Llanelli

TENNIS

For a list of Wimbledon champions see the chapter on international sport beginning on p. 682.

BRITISH NATIONAL SWIMMING RECORDS

MEN

Freestyle
50 metres; 22·43 sec; Mark Foster on 24 May 1992
100 metres; 50·24 sec; Michael Wenham Fibbens on 22 May 1992
200 metres; 1 min 48·92 sec; Paul Palmer on 26 Jul 1992
400 metres; 3 min 50·01 sec; Kevin Thomas Boyd on 23 Sep 1988
800 metres; 8 min 00·63 sec; Ian Wilson on 25 Aug 1991
1500 metres; 15 min 03·72 sec; Ian Wilson on 25 Aug 1991
4 × 100 metres; 3 min 21·41 sec; GB team (Michael Wenham Fibbens, Mark Andrew Foster, Paul Howe, Roland Lee) on 29 Jul 1992
4 × 200 metres; 7 min 22·57 sec; GB team (Paul Palmer, Steven Mellor, Stephen Akers, Paul Howe) on 27 Jul 1992
Breaststroke
100 metres; 1 min 01·03 sec; Nicholas Gillingham on 21 May 1992
200 metres; 2 min 11·29 sec; Nicholas Gillingham on 29 Jul 1992
Butterfly
100 metres; 53·30 sec; Andrew David Jameson on 21 Sep 1988
200 metres; 2 min 00·21 sec; Philip Hubble on 11 Sep 1981
Backstroke
100 metres; 57·08 sec; Martin Harris on 12 Jan 1991
200 metres; 2 min 02·58 sec; Matthew O'Connor on 22 May 1992
Medley
200 metres; 2 min 03·20 sec; Neil Cochran on 25 Mar 1988
400 metres; 4 min 24·20 sec; John Philip Davey on 1 Aug 1987
4 × 100 metres; 3 min 42·01 sec; GB team (Neil Cochran, Adrian David Moorhouse, Andrew David Jameson, Roland Lee) on 23 Aug 1987

WOMEN

Freestyle
50 metres; 26·01 sec; Caroline Woodcock on 20 Aug 1989
100 metres; 56·11 sec; Karen Pickering on 14 Jun 1992
200 metres; 1 min 59·74 sec; June Alexandra Croft on 4 Oct 1982
400 metres; 4 min 07·68 sec; Sarah Hardcastle on 27 Jul 1986
800 metres; 8 min 24·77 sec; Sarah Hardcastle on 29 Jul 1986
1500 metres; 16 min 43·95 sec; Sarah Hardcastle on 18 Apr 1985
4 × 100 metres; 3 min 48·87 sec; GB team (Karen Pickering, Sharron Davies, Caroline Woodcock, Joanne Coull) on 17 Aug 1989
4 × 200 metres; 8 min 03·70 sec; England team (Annabelle Cripps, Sarah Hardcastle, Karen Marie Mellor, Zara Letitia Long) on 25 Jul 1986
Breaststroke
100 metres; 1 min 10·39 sec; Susannah 'Suki' Brownsdon on 21 Aug 1987
200 metres; 2 min 31·51 sec; Jean Cameron Hill on 19 Aug 1987
Butterfly
100 metres; 1 min 01·33 sec; Madeleine Scarborough on 28 Jan 1990
200 metres; 2 min 11·97 sec; Samantha Purvis on 4 Aug 1984
Backstroke
100 metres; 1 min 03·49 sec; Katherine Read on 14 Jun 1992
200 metres; 2 min 13·91 sec; Katherine Read on 24 May 1992
Medley
200 metres; 2 min 17·21 sec; Jean Cameron Hill on 21 Jul 1986
400 metres; 4 min 46·83 sec; Sharron Davies on 26 Jul 1980
4 × 100 metres; 4 min 11·88 sec; England team (Joanne Deakins, Susannah 'Suki' Brownsdon, Madeleine Scarborough, Karen Pickering) on 29 Jan 1990

INDEX

Emboldened figures indicate a
main entry.

A
Aalto, Alvar 398
Aargau (Argovie) 653
abacus 255, 309
Abelard, Peter 330
Aberdeen 727
Aberdeen Angus 145
Aberdeen, Earl of 733
Aberdeenshire 715
Abidjan 557
Abruzzi 135, 591
absolute magnitude 14
absolute zero 207
Abstract Expressionism 387
Abstraction 385–86
Abu Dhabi 663
Abuja 623
abyssal plaines 69
abyssal volcanoes 78
acceleration 202, 205
accidental death 169
accordion 404
Accra 577
accumulators 216
ace-inhibitors 153
Aceh 586
acid precipitation (rain) 112, 238
acid rock 415
acids 235
acidulants 174
Acoelomata 137
acoustics 210–11
Acre 542
actinides 228
Action painting 387
Actium, battle of 478
active volcanoes 78
actors, notable film 428–31
actors and directors (stage) 433–35
Acts of the Apostles 343
acupuncture 170
Adam, Robert 396
Adams Ring 26
adding machine 309
Addington, Henry 732
Addis Ababa 567
addition 252
additives 174
Adelaide 533
Adélie Land 680
adiabatic system 208
Adlerian psychology 163
Adorno, Theodor 331
Adrastea 23
adrenal glands 151
Adrianople, battle of 478
advance gas-cooled reactors 315
Advent Sunday 54
Adygea 634
Aedh, King 738
Aegosopotami, battle of 478
aepyornis 144
aerial (antenna) 304
aerobic bacteria 127
aerodynes 286
aerofoil section 286
aeropile 309
aerostats 286
Aeschylus 356
affective disorder 165
Afghanistan 50, 489, 499, 522, **525–26**
Africa 61, 75, 326
　history of 453, 471, 473, 475, 477
　major national parks in 135
African art 379

African churches 340
African religions 332, 346–47
agate 67
aggregate demand 483
aggregate supply 483
Agin-Buryat 634
Agincourt, battle of 479
Agnatha (Cyclostomata) 140
Agni 345
agricultural crops 134
Agriculture, Minister of 730
Aguascalientes 612
ahimsa 349
Ahmedabad 584
Ahura Mazda 350
AIDS 154–55
ailerons 286
Ailey, Alvin 420
Ain Jalut, battle of 479
air, constituents of 100
air pollution 111–12
air temperature 101
air traffic (UK and abroad) 751
airbrush technique 376
aircraft 286–87, 309
　combat 522
　commercial 322
aircraft controls 286
aircraft stability 286
airlines, world's major 324
airports
　distances in km between 323
　major British 750
　world's major 324
airship 309
Ajman 663
Akinari, Ueda 357
Alabama 667
Alagoas 542
Aland Islands 568
Alaska 667
Alba, kings of 738
Albanese, Licia 414
Albania 50, 489, 499, **526**
Albee, Edward 364
Albéniz, Isaac 410
Alberta 547
Alberti, Leon Battista 394
Albinoni, Tommaso 408
Alcaeus 356
Alcott, Louisa May 366
Alder, Alfred 164
Alderney 709
Aldershot 727
Aldridge, Ira 434
Alexander I, king 738
Alexander II, king 738
Alexander III, king 738
Alexander technique 171
Alexandra of Kent, Princess 739
Alexandria 563
algebra 252, 253, **256–60**
Algeria 50, 489, 499, **526–27**
Algiers 527
alienation 165
alimentary (digestive) system 150
Alismatidae 131
alkali metals 228
alkalis 235
All African Games 708
All Saints' Day 54
All Souls' Day 54
Allegri, Gregorio 407
allemande 417
Allen, Woody 423, 428
allergies 161
Alleyn, Edward 433
Alliance Party (UK) 734

allotropes 234
Allum cepa 133
alluvial mining 299
Alma-Ata 595
almsgiving (Islam) 344
Alpha (α) decay 213
alpha particles 312
Alsace 570
Altdorfer, Albrecht 381
alternating current (AC) 217
alternative medicine 170
alternators 217, 288
altocumulus 101
altostratus 101
aluminium, annual production of 506
Amalthea (moon) 23
Amapa (territory) 542
Amastigomycota 128
Amazonas 542, 673
Amazonia National Park 136
amber 67
Americas, history of 464, 465, 471, 473,
　475, 477
American football 682
American native art 379
American notation (music) 403
American Samoa 670
amethyst 67
amino acids 127, 239
Amman 594
ammonia 237, 302
amoebic dysentery 155
ampere 196
Amphibia 140
amplifiers 305
amplitude 95, 204
amplitude modulation (AM) 204–05
Amsterdam 615
anaesthetics 162
analytical philosophy 328
analytical psychology 163
Ananke 23
anatomy **150–51**, 162
anatta 346
Anaximander of Miletus 329
Ancient Greek calendar 45
Ancient World, history of 450–51
Andalusia 648
Andaman and Nicobar Islands 585
Andean Pact 518
Andersen, Hans Christian 366
Anderson, Judith 435
Anderson, Lindsay 424
Anderson, Maria 414
andesite 62, 65
Andhra Pradesh 584
Andorra 50, 489, 499, **527–28**
Andorra la Vella 527
Andrew (apostle) 333
Andrew, Prince, Duke of York 739
Andrews, Julie 428
Andromeda nebula 9, 11
Angeles, Victoria de los 414
Angelico, Fra 380
Angkor National Park 135
angle of incidence 211
Anglesey 715
Anglican Communion 332, 339, 756
Anglican dioceses (UK) 757
Anglo-Latin language 354
Anglo-Saxon architecture 393
Angola 50, 489, 499, 522, **528**
Angra Mainyu 350
Anguilla 666
angular acceleration 205
angular momentum 205
Angus 715
Anhui 552